Cellular Immunology

AN INTERNATIONAL JOURNAL

EDITOR-IN-CHIEF: H. Sherwood Lawrence

Volume 63, 1981

ACADEMIC PRESS
A Subsidiary of Harcourt Brace Jovanovich, Publishers
New York London Toronto Sydney San Francisco

MADE IN THE UNITED STATES OF AMERICA

Contents of Volume 63

Number 1, September 1, 1981

Charles H. Evans. The Role of Lymphotoxin in Natural Cell-Mediated Cytotoxicity 1
Edward L. Morgan, Marilyn L. Thoman, and William O. Weigle. The Immune Response in Aged C57BL/6 Mice. I. Assessment of Lesions in the B-Cell and T-Cell Compartments of Aged Mice Utilizing the Fc Fragment-Mediated Polyclonal Antibody Response 16
Rajiv K. Saxena, William H. Adler, and Albert A. Nordin. Modulation of Natural Cytotoxicity by Alloantibodies. IV. A Comparative Study of the Activation of Mouse Spleen Cell Cytotoxicity by Anti H-2 Antisera, Interferon, and Mitogens 28
Arthur H. Hale, Donald L. Evans, and Maria P. McGee. H-2 Antigens Incorporated into Phospholipid Vesicles Interact Specifically with Allogeneic Cytotoxic T Lymphocytes 42
Patrick G. Holt, Louise A. Warner, and Graham Mayrhofer. Macrophages as Effectors of T Suppression: T-Lymphocyte-Dependent Macrophage-Mediated Suppression of Mitogen-Induced Blastogenesis in the Rat 57
John R. Neefe, G. Richard Curl, and James N. Woody. Absolute Requirement for Adherent Cells in the Production of Human Interleukin 2 (IL2) 71
Laure Thuillier, Florianne Garreau, and Pierre Cartier. Inability of Immunocompetent Thymocytes to Produce T-Cell Growth Factor under Adenosine Deaminase Deficiency Conditions 81
Lindsey M. Hutt-Fletcher and Colleen J. Gilbert. Cytotoxic Cells Induced *in Vitro* by Epstein–Barr Virus Antigens 91
Jeremiah J. Twomey and Nicola M. Kouttab. The Null Cell Compartment of the Mouse Spleen 106
Teresa Y. Basham, Satoshi Toyoshima, Fred Finkelman, and M. J. Waxdal. A Series of Murine Interleukin Molecules Which Stimulate both Murine and Human Lymphocytes. I. Production by *Phytolacca Americana* (Pokeweed) Lectin 2 (Pa-2)-Stimulated Thymus and Thymus-Derived Cells 118
Lanny J. Rosenwasser and Charles A. Dinarello. Ability of Human Leukocytic Pyrogen to Enhance Phytohemagglutinin Induced Murine Thymocyte Proliferation 134
Ronald Palacios and Göran Möller. HLA-DR Antigens Render Resting T Cells Sensitive to Interleukin-2 and Induce Production of the Growth Factor in the Autologous Mixed Lymphocyte Reaction 143
William L. Cleveland, Irene Wood, Ian N. Jacobs, and Bernard F. Erlanger. A General Method for Studying the Secretion of Macromolecules by Single Cells. II. A Simplified Procedure with Enhanced Sensitivity 154
Marcelo B. Sztein, Stefanie N. Vogel, Jean D. Sipe, Patrick A. Murphy, Steven B. Mizel, Joost J. Oppenheim, and David L. Rosenstreich. The Role of Macrophages in the Acute-Phase Response: SAA Inducer Is Closely Related to Lymphocyte Activating Factor and Endogenous Pyrogen 164
Victoria Fraser and Helen Braley-Mullen. Characterization of Suppressor T Cells Induced with the Thymus-Independent Antigen Polyvinylpyrrolidone Coupled to Syngeneic Cells 177

Short Communications

H. C. J. Ertl. Adoptive Transfer of Delayed-Type Hypersensitivity to Sendai Virus. II. Different Modes of Antigen Presentation Determine *K,D*-Region or *I*-Region Restriction of T Cells Mediating Delayed-Type Hypersensitivity to Sendai Virus 188
J. Chutná, V. Holáň, and M. Hašek. Heterogeneity of Tolerance to Xenogeneic Cells in Mice Inoculated at Birth with Rat Cells 193
Daniel Bout, Alice L. Kühner, Volker Klimetzek, Heinz G. Remold, and John R. David. Fractionation of Murine Macrophage Inhibitory Factor into Two Distinct Species 198
Dianne E. Jackson, Edward T. Lally, Mary C. Nakamura, and Paul C. Montgomery. Migration of IgA-Bearing Lymphocytes into Salivary Glands 203
John M. Mansfield, Rita F. Levine, Walla L. Dempsey, Sam R. Wellhausen, and Carl T. Hansen. Lymphocyte Function in Experimental African Trypanosomiasis. IV. Immunosuppression and Suppressor Cells in the Athymic *nu/nu* Mouse 210

ANNOUNCEMENT 216

PAPERS TO APPEAR IN FORTHCOMING ISSUES 217

NUMBER 2, SEPTEMBER 15, 1981

P. HUTCHINGS AND A. COOKE. Analysis of the Cellular Interactions Involved in the Regulation of Induced Erythrocyte Autoantibodies 221

BERENICE KINDRED. A Comparison of H-2 Restriction of Helper Function Using T Cells from Radiation Chimeras and Nude Mice Bearing Thymus Grafts 228

MANUEL PATARROYO, PETER BIBERFELD, EVA KLEIN, AND GEORGE KLEIN. 12-*O*-Tetradecanoylphorbol-13-acetate (TPA) Treatment Elevates the Natural Killer (NK) Sensitivity of Certain Human Lymphoid Lines 237

S. BERRIH, J. LONDON, AND B. BONAVIDA. Murine Spleen Lymphocytes Bearing Receptors for Peanut Agglutinin. VII. Separation and Functional Characterization 249

EMILIA MIA SORDILLO, SUSUMU IKEHARA, ROBERT A. GOOD, AND PAUL P. TROTTA. Immunosuppression by 2′-Deoxycoformycin: Studies on the Mode of Administration 259

NEAL W. ROEHM, YOUNAN A. SIDKY, AND ROBERT AUERBACH. Lyt Phenotype Analysis of the Effector Cells Responsible for Evoking Lymphocyte-Induced Angiogenesis (LIA) 272

L. VARESIO, H. T. HOLDEN, AND D. TARAMELLI. Suppression of Lymphokine Production. II. Macrophage-Dependent Inhibition of Production of Macrophage Activating Factor 279

MARVIN A. CUCHENS, KENNETH L. BOST, MARIE L. HOOVER, AND GERRIE A. LESLIE. Anti-IgD Enhancement of Primary Antibody Responses in Rats 293

JOEL PICUS, RONALD N. GERMAIN, IRA J. FOX, MARK I. GREENE, BARUJ BENACERRAF, AND NORMAN L. LETVIN. Immunologic Effects of Whole-Body Ultraviolet (uv) Irradiation. III. Defective Splenic Adherent Cell Function in Alloantigen-Stimulated T-Cell Proliferation 300

R. L. DUNCAN, JR., AND W. P. MCARTHUR. Lactoferrin-Mediated Modulation of Mononuclear Cell Activities. I. Suppression of the Murine *in Vitro* Primary Antibody Response 308

DAVID R. WEBB AND IRENE NOWOWIEJSKI. Control of Suppressor Cell Activation via Endogenous Prostaglandin Synthesis: The Role of T Cells and Macrophages 321

ADRIANA DEL REY, HUGO O. BESEDOVSKY, ERNST SORKIN, MOSÉ DA PRADA, AND STEFAN ARRENBRECHT. Immunoregulation Mediated by the Sympathetic Nervous System, II 329

THIERRY REME, ARNAUD DUPUY D'ANGEAC, MICHELE RADAL, AND BERNARD SERROU. Stimulatory Cells in the Generation of T-Cell-Mediated Cytotoxicity: Potent Stimulating Activity of a Small Radioresistant Spleen Cell Population (RSCs) 335

JEAN-LUC TEILLAUD, CHANTAL RABOURDIN-COMBE, MARC STANISLAWSKI, CATHERINE NEAUPORT-SAUTES, AND WOLF HERMAN FRIDMAN. FcγR Expressed on T-Cell Hybrids: Specificity, Behavior and Relationship with Ia Antigens 349

ROSELYNN A. DYNESIUS-TRENTHAM, DONNA ROWLAND, ELIZABETH LAROCHE, AND DAVID E. TRENTHAM. Rat Leukocyte Inhibitory Factor (LIF): Similarities to Human LIF and Generation by Cells from Rats with Collagen-Induced Arthritis 362

JOSEPH H. KORN. Modulation of Lymphocyte Mitogen Responses by Cocultured Fibroblasts 374

B. L. PIKE, J. E. LAYTON, N. R. ROSE, AND G. J. V. NOSSAL. Surface Immunoglobulin Isotype, Activation, and Tolerance Susceptibility of B Lymphocytes of New Zealand Black Mice 385

H. J. RADZUN, M. R. PARWARESCH, AND J. W. WITTKE. Polymorphism and Antigenic Specificity of Monocytic Acid Esterase (EC 3.1.1.6) 400

SHORT COMMUNICATIONS

WILLIAM D. LYMAN, ANNA S. KADISH, AND CEDRIC S. RAINE. Experimental Allergic Encephalomyelitis in the Guinea Pig: Variation in Peripheral Blood Lymphocyte Responsiveness to Myelin Basic Protein during Disease Development 409

D. C. HOOPER AND R. A. MURGITA. Regulation of Murine T-Cell Responses to Autologous Antigens by α-Fetoprotein 417

ANNOUNCEMENTS 426

PAPERS TO APPEAR IN FORTHCOMING ISSUES 427

AUTHOR INDEX FOR VOLUME 63 430

The Subject Index for Volume 63 will appear in the December 1981 issue as a part of a cumulative index for the year 1981.

CELLULAR IMMUNOLOGY **63,** 1-15 (1981)

The Role of Lymphotoxin in Natural Cell-Mediated Cytotoxicity

CHARLES H. EVANS

Laboratory of Biology, Division of Cancer Cause and Prevention, National Cancer Institute, Bethesda, Maryland 20205

Received December 17, 1980, accepted April 29, 1981

The contribution of lymphotoxin to guinea pig leukocyte natural cytotoxicity was evaluated with [^{3}H]TdR release and colony-inhibition assays of 104C1 benzo(a)pyrene *in vitro*-transformed and tumorigenic, tumor-specific transplantation antigen-negative, syngeneic strain 2/N fibroblasts. Cytolethal ^{3}H-release activities of mitogen (PHA)[1]-stimulated nonimmune and ovalbumin (OA) immune as well as OA-stimulated OA immune unfractionated, adherent (macrophage-enriched) and nonadherent peritoneal leukocytes are qualitatively similar. ^{3}H release is maximal by 48 hr, increases with antigen or mitogen concentration, is greatest with unfractionated leukocytes, and is least with adherent macrophages. Lymphotoxin produced by peritoneal leukocytes, alone or in combination with the leukocytes does not *or* only minimally induces ^{3}H release even after 6 days of incubation with guinea pig target cells although guinea pig lymphotoxin possesses cytolytic activity as indicated by ^{3}H release from αL929 mouse tumor cells. In contrast to the absent or very weak cytolytic activity of guinea pig lymphotoxin for the guinea pig target cells nonimmune macrophages, nonadherent leukocytes, and lymphotoxin all exhibit readily detectable colony-inhibitory (CI) activity for the syngeneic tumor cells. Macrophage and lymphotoxin CI, moreover, are additive, whereas nonadherent leukocyte and lymphotoxin CI are synergistic. The latter may be due to additional lymphotoxin induced by target cell antigens or other mechanisms of target cell stimulation of effector lymphoid cells and result from very high local levels of lymphotoxin released by the effector cells. Lymphotoxin CI, furthermore, can be cytostatic or cytolethal as indicated by resumption of 104C1 but not αL929 colony growth following removal of lymphotoxin, indicating that natural cell-mediated cytotoxicity consists of lymphotoxin-dependent and -independent cytostatic and cytolethal effector mechanisms.

INTRODUCTION

Natural or spontaneous lymphiod cell-mediated cytotoxicity (1-3), the ability of normal, not specifically immunized, leukocytes to destroy the integrity of, or to inhibit the growth of tumor and other mammalian cells, has been described for human (4, 5) and for a variety of animal species (6). The extent to which natural lymphoid cell cytotoxicity is mediated by direct cellular interaction or by lymphokines and other cytokines remains unsettled (7). Among the effector mechanisms are natural killer (8, 9) and antibody-dependent (10) lymphocytes, macrophages (11-14), the lymphokines lymphotoxin (15, 16) and interferon (17, 18), and macrophage cytokines (19, 20).

Often natural leukocyte cytotoxicity is preferentially toxic or specifically toxic

[1] Abbreviations used: PHA, phytohemagglutinin; OA, ovalbumin; CI, colony inhibitory.

0008-8749/81/130001-15$02.00/0

for tumorigenic in contrast to nontumorigenic cells (21–23) although the reverse has been observed (24, 25). The preferential cytotoxicity of peripheral blood and peritoneal leukocytes from nonimmune guinea pigs for syngeneic guinea pig tumorigenic cells has been demonstrated by leukocyte-induced ^3H release from [^3H]TdR-labeled tumor cells (26). It also has been shown by inhibition of tumorigenic cell colony formation in the presence of the leukocytes, colony-inhibitory activity being due in part to lymphokines (21). The purpose of the present investigation is to further define the mechanisms of natural lymphoid cell-mediated cytotoxicity by evaluating the contributions of guinea pig lymphoid cells and the lymphokine lymphotoxin in the normal immunocytotoxicity reaction assessed by radionuclide release and colony inhibition.

MATERIALS AND METHODS

Target Cells

The target cells for these studies were a benzo(a)pyrene *in vitro*-transformed tumorigenic strain 2/N guinea pig diploid fibroblast, 104 clone 1 (104C1) (27). This cloned cell was selected as it is sensitive to the growth-inhibitory activity of guinea pig lymphotoxin (28) and possesses no detectable individually distinct transplantation rejection (29) or other unique neoantigens (C. H. Evans, unpublished observations) that might contribute to the immunobiologic interactions being studied. The 104C1 cells were evaluated during passages 25–30 and were maintained in exponential growth in RPMI 1640 medium–10% fetal bovine serum as previously described (21).

Effector Lymphoid Cells

Peritoneal leukocytes were collected by lavage with RPMI 1640 medium at room temperature from 6- to 12-month-old male strain 2/N guinea pigs following 48–72 hr intraperitoneal exposure to mineral oil as previously described (21). Cells were obtained from nonimmune or from ovalbumin immunized animals (28). The peritoneal cells were sedimented at 180*g* for 10 min at room temperature, resuspended in serum-free RPMI 1640 medium at 37°C, and resedimented at 400*g* for 5 min at room temperature. The washed peritioneal cells were again resuspended in serum-free RPMI 1640 medium and the nucleated cells enumerated in a hemocytometer. An average of 3.3×10^8 (range $1.8–3.7 \times 10^8$) leukocytes consisting of approximately 60% monocytes–macrophages, 20% polymorphonuclear leukocytes, and 20% lymphocytes was obtained from each animal. The preparations contained less than 1% erythrocytes.

Freshly isolated peritoneal leukocytes were used for lymphokine production or for evaluation of cell-mediated cellular cytotoxicity as described below. Macrophages were obtained by incubation of the pertioneal leukocytes for a short period to obtain adherent cells. Ten million peritoneal leukocytes in 5 ml RPMI 1640–10% fetal bovine serum were added to each 100-mm tissue culture dish and incubated in a 5% CO_2 in air water-saturated atmosphere at 37°C for 30 min. At that time the dishes were washed twice with 1640–10% fetal bovine serum and scraped with a rubber policeman, and the adherent leukocytes pooled, centrifuged at 250*g* for 5 min, enumerated, and adjusted to 8×10^4 cells/ml RPMI 1640–10%

fetal bovine serum. The adherent cells were 90% monocytes/macrophages by morphological criteria upon cytological examination. The isolated macrophages were seeded in 2 ml medium at concentrations of 10^4, 10^5, and 2×10^5 cells/60-mm tissue culture dish. The dishes were incubated for 30 min, washed twice with medium, and refed with 2 ml RPMI 1640 medium–10% fetal bovine serum for subsequent use. Spleen leukocytes were obtained from minced spleen tissue filtered through surgical gauze and resuspended in RPMI 1640 medium–10% fetal bovine serum.

Lymphotoxin Production

Antigen-induced lymphotoxin was obtained as previously described (28). Peritoneal cells from ovalbumin immune guinea pigs were collected as described above and diluted to 1×10^6 leukocytes/ml in 37°C serum-free RPMI 1640 medium containing 10 μg ovalbumin/ml unless otherwise specified. Ten milliliters of the leukocyte–antigen mixture was added to a 100-mm tissue culture dish and incubated in a 5% CO_2 in air water-saturated atmosphere. After 24 hr the cell culture medium was poured off the dishes and centrifuged at 1000*g* for 10 min at room temperature to remove cells. The lymphokines in the medium were concentrated 100-fold by vacuum dialysis using standard dialysis tubing (31) and dialyzed verus 0.01 *M* phosphate-buffered saline, pH 7.4, and aliquots were stored at −35°C.

Assay for Lymphotoxin Activity

The units of lymphotoxin in the concentrated lymphokine preparation were determined using a radionuclide assay in which 1 unit of lymphotoxin during 3 days incubation results in the release of 50% of the counts per minute from 1×10^4 [^{3}H]TdR labeled mouse αL929 tumor cells. These tumor cells are sensitive to lymphotoxin from a variety of species (30). The L cells were labeled with [^{3}H]TdR and the radionuclide release assay performed as described by Zwilling *et al.* (26) with dilutions of lymphokine preparation replacing mitogen and effector cells. The ^{3}H-release method has a standard error of the mean of less than 1% and a sensitivity comparable to the cytoloysis assay of Spofford *et al.* (32) in which the number of mitomycin C-treated cells 48 hr after addition of lymphotoxin is measured using a Coulter counter (See Fig. 1). Interferon activity was assayed by inhibition of bovine vesicular stomatitis virus cytopathic effect in 104C1 cells as reported elsewhere (25). Activity was compared to interferon activity induced in 2/N guinea pig spleen leukocytes by 24-hr culture with 125 μg polyadenyl–uridylic acid/ml medium using the same conditions employed for producing the lymphotoxin. No interferon activity was detectable in the lymphotoxin preparation utilized in this investigation.

Assessment of Natural Cell-Mediated Cytotoxic Activity

(a) Release of ^{3}H from [^{3}H]TdR-labeled target cells. The cytotoxicity of leukocytes and of lymphotoxin produced by the leukocytes from nonimmune and from ovalbumin immune guinea pigs was measured by the release of ^{3}H from [^{3}H]TdR labeled 104C1 syngeneic target cells as previously described (26). The assay included 10^4 target cells preincubated with 0.5 μCi [^{3}H]methylthymidine (sp act 2

Ci/mmol) for 24 hr, followed by trypsinization, 4–6 hr of incubation in 16-mm tissue culture wells, followed by the addition of effector cells or lymphotoxin in a final volume of 1 ml RPMI 1640 medium–10% fetal bovine serum for 48 hr or as otherwise indicated for individual experiments under Results. Effector cells at effector-to-target cell ratios from 500:1 to 10:1 included freshly isolated and unfractioned spleen or peritoneal leukocytes, or the adherent (macrophage enriched) or nonadherent 24- to 72-hr cultured peritoneal leukocytes, cultured in RPMI 1640–10% fetal bovine serum with and without mitogen or antigen as described for individual experiments under Results. Cytotoxicity was determined by measuring the counts per minute ^{3}H released into the medium. Cell-free aliquots of 0.2 ml were added to vials containing 1.8 ml Biofluor (New England Nuclear, Boston, Mass.) scintillation fluid and the counts per minute measured in a Packard liquid scintillation spectrophotometer with the standard preset ^{3}H window. Total counts per minute initially present in the target cells were estimated by measuring the supernate counts per minute from target cells incubated with 0.25% sodium dodecyl sulfate in water in place of the culture medium. Specific cytotoxicity was determined by subtracting the counts per minute in the control medium (spontaneous release) from the counts per minute obtained after incubation of target cells with nonstimulated or with antigen- or mitogen-stimulated lymphoid cells or other effectors such as lymphokines. The spontaneous release was less than 5% and rarely exceeded 1–2%. Specific ^{3}H release was calculated by expressing the specific cytotoxicity value as the percentage of total counts per minute present in the sodium dodecyl sulfate digest of the target cells. The assays were performed in triplicate and the standard error of the mean was less than 5%. For some experiments, as identified under Results, the assays were performed with equivalent results in 60-mm tissue culture dishes containing 5×10^4 104C1 target cells with an effector-to-target cell ration of 100:1 in a final volume of 5 ml RPMI 1640–10% fetal bovine serum.

(b) Inhibition of target cell colony formation. The colony-inhibitory activities of the lymphoid effector cell populations and lymphotoxin preparations were assayed using 104C1 target cells with an assay reproducibility of $\pm 5\%$ as previously described (21). One hundred trypsinized 104C1 cells obtained from an exponentially growing monolayer culture were seeded into each 60-mm tissue culture dish together with effector lymphoid cells or with lymphotoxin in a final volume of 4 ml RPMI 1640 medium-10% fetal bovine serum. After 7 days incubation, the medium was removed, the colonies were washed with Dulbecco's phosphate-buffered saline, fixed in methanol, stained with 10% aqueous Giemsa (Fisher Scientific, Fairlawn, N.J.), and colonies greater than 0.2 mm in diameter counted.

RESULTS

The cytotoxic activity of guinea pig lymphotoxin is demonstrable by radionuclide release as well as by inhibition of cell colony growth when assessed with αL929 mouse tumor cells as illustrated in Fig. 1. The radionuclide release assay is nearly equivalent (within 10%) to the commonly used enumeration of surviving adherent mitomycin C-treated target cells; both the radionuclide release and cell count assays, however, are more than 40 times as sensitive as the colony-inhibition assay in αL929 cells when compared after adjustment of the results to an equivalent

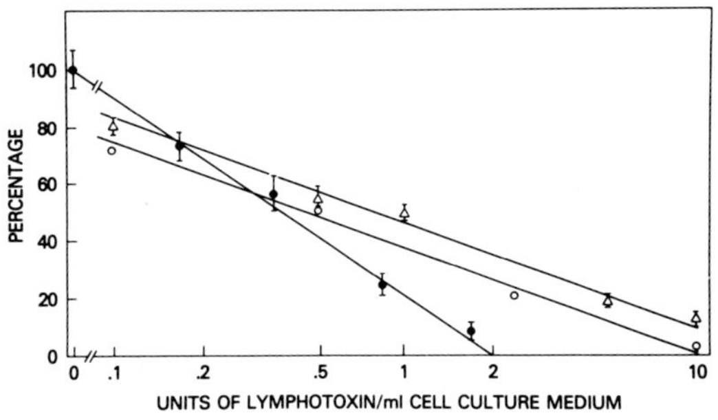

FIG. 1. The cytotoxicity of guinea pig lymphotoxin for mouse αL929 tumor cells. Colony formation (●) by 100 cells after 7 days, intracellular [^{3}H]TdR (△) remaining in 10^4 cells after 3 days, and the percentage (○) of 10^4 adherent mitomycin C-treated cells measured by a Coulter counter after 2 days of incubation of the cells with increasing concentrations of lymphotoxin are shown ±1 SEM.

number of target cells/ml. For example, 1 unit of lymphotoxin induces the release of 50% of the counts per minute ^{3}H from 10^4 αL929 cells compared to 0.4 units lymphotoxin/ml inducing a 50% inhibition of colony formation by 10^2 104C1 cells, or following adjustment—40 units of lymphotoxin/10^4 cells.

In contrast to results with αL929 cells guinea pig lymphtoxin while able to inhibit the colony formation of 104C1 guinea pig cells is unable at the same concentrations to induce the release of ^{3}H from [^{3}H]TdR-labeled 104C1 cells (Fig. 2). The 104C1 cells are susceptible, however, to cytolytic natural immunobiologic attack. This is shown by ^{3}H release in the presence of nonstimulated nonsensitized peritoneal leukocytes in Fig. 2 and by ^{3}H release from 104C1 cells in the presence of nonstimulated and mitogen stimulated peritoneal and spleen leukocytes from nonimmune syngeneic animals at effector-to-target cell ratios of 10 to 500:1 as shown in Table 1. Lymphotoxin, however, does not directly contribute to this cell-mediated cytolysis. Guinea pig lymphotoxin at a concentration inducing 100% lysis of αL929 but no lysis of 104C1 cells when added in combination with macrophages, nonadherent peritoneal, or spleen leukocytes is unable to increase the cell-mediated release of ^{3}H from [^{3}H]TdR-labeled 104C1 cells (Table 1). This is because the cytotoxic activity of guinea pig lymphotoxin for 104C1 cells is primarily cytostatic rather than cytolytic as illustrated in Fig. 3. When the target cells are treated with lymphotoxin and the medium containing lymphotoxin is subsequently replaced with medium free of lymphotoxin, 104C1 cell colony growth resumes indicating a condition of lymphotoxin-induced target cell cytostasis. Furthermore, if 104C1 cell colonies are exposed to lymphotoxin during the last 24 or 48 hr of growth when the colonies have grown to >0.2 mm in diameter there is no resulting diminution of colony formation to <0.2 mm indicating the inability of guinea pig lymphotoxin to directly mediate either lysis or to cause the detachment of 104C1 cells from the culture vessel surface. In contrast to 104C1 cells, colony formation of αL929 cells does not resume when the medium is changed. The number of αL929 cells, furthermore, decreases in the presence of lymphotoxin with time as visualized by microscopic examination of living cultures and of stained colonies (data not shown) in agreement with the totally cytolytic activity of this same concentration of lymphotoxin for αL929 cells demonstrated by the ^{3}H-release results. Colony inhibition of guinea pig 104C1 cells induced by guinea pig lymphotoxin is due, therefore,

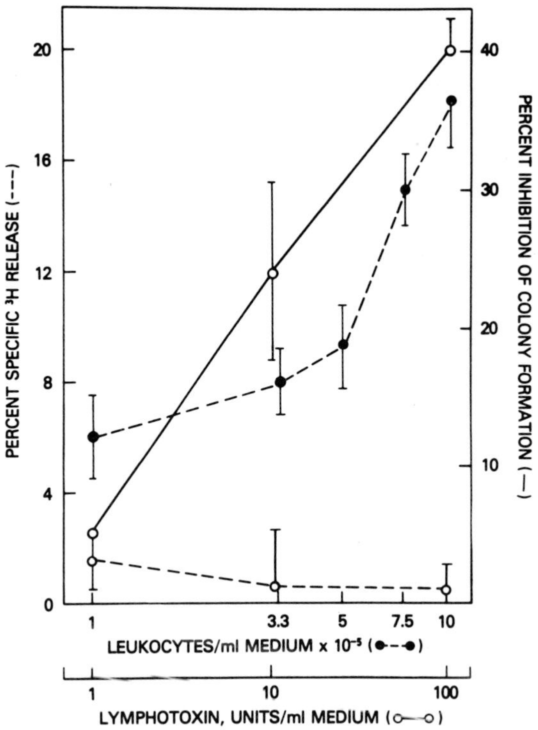

FIG. 2. The cytotoxicity of guinea pig lymphotoxin (○) and nonstimulated nonadherent nonimmune peritoneal leukocytes (●) for syngeneic 104C1 tumorigenic cells ±1 SEM. 104C1 cells, 10^2 and 10^4, were plated in the colony formation and the radionuclide release assays, respectively.

primarily to a nonlytic and reversible cytostatic mechanism. This may be a general property of guinea pig tumorigenic cells. As many as 100 units of lymphotoxin/ml culture fail during 72 hr of incubation to induce the release of >15% of the ^{3}H from [^{3}H]TdR-labeled 107C3, HM2C1, and HM4C1 syngeneic guinea pig tumorigenic cells (C. H. Evans, unpublished observations), with each of the tumorigenic cell populations being susceptible like 104C1 cells to the colony inhibitory activity of the guinea pig lymphotoxin (31).

The cytolytic activity of nonstimulated leukocytes from guinea pigs previously immunized to ovalbumin is similar to the activity of nonimmune leukocytes and increases upon incubation of the immune leukocytes with antigen or mitogen as indicated in Fig. 4. Mitogen stimulation produces greater cytotoxicity than antigen stimulation; both cytotoxic responses are qualitatively similar and unfractionated and nonadherent leukocytes also possess qualitatively and quantitatively similar cytotoxic activity. Macrophages exhibit quantitatively less but qualitatively similar activity. Leukocyte cytolytic activity is maximal by 48 hr incubation (Fig. 5) and lymphotoxin neither enhances the leukocyte induced ^{3}H release (Table 1) nor by itself at 100 units/ml induces ^{3}H release even following 6 days incubation with the target cells (Fig. 5). At higher concentrations lymphotoxin alone may be slightly cytolytic (4% lysis) and augment leukocyte cytolysis (a 6% increase) at high effector-to-target cell ratios (Table 1).

Whereas nonstimulated leukocytes at a 100:1 effector-to-target cell ratio in either

TABLE 1

Lymphotoxin Stimulation of Natural Cytotoxicity

Effector	Effector/target cell ratio	Percentage specific ^{3}H release from [^{3}H]TdR-labeled 104C1 target cells: medium alone	+ lymphotoxin 200 units/ml	+ phytohemagglutinin 50 μg/ml	+ lymphotoxin and phytohemagglutinin
None	—	0	4[a]	2	5[b]
Peritoneal macrophages	10:1	1	3	6	11
	50:1	4	7	21	21
	100:1	16	23[c]	69	66
	200:1	23	28[c]	98	89
	500:1	35	42	113	113
Nonadherent peritoneal leukocytes	10:1	0	4	9	13
	50:1	0	4[c]	23	27
	100:1	11	15[c]	71	72
	200:1	24	30[c]	80	86
	500:1	48	58[d]	106	96
Spleen leukocytes	10:1	7	11	11	18[e]
	50:1	12	16	21	27[e]
	100:1	21	26[c]	49	48
	200:1	32	30	58	59
	500:1	46	41	67	65

[a] $P < 0.05$ by Students' t distribution compared to medium alone.

[b] $P < 0.05$ compared to phytohemagglutinin alone.

[c] $P < 0.05$ compared to medium alone at the same effector/target cell ratio, $P > 0.05$ when lymphotoxin release in the absence of effector cell is subtracted.

[d] $P < 0.05$ compared to medium alone after subtraction of lymphotoxin release in the absence of effector cells.

[e] $P < 0.05$ compared to phytohemagglutinin alone at the same effector/target cell ratio, $P > 0.05$ when lymphotoxin release in the absence of the effector cells is subtracted.

1 ml (Figs. 2 and 4) or 5 ml (Fig. 5) incubation volumes induce 5–18% ^{3}H release from 104C1 cells, an effector-to-target cell ratio of greater than 100:1 is required for inhibition of cell proliferation in the colony inhibition assay (Fig. 6). The colony-inhibitory activity of nonimmune leukocytes is also independent of the leukocyte cell number within the range of 2.5–10 × 10^4 leukocytes/5 ml medium (effector-to-target cell ratios of 250–1000:1) without mitogen stimulation but varies directly with leukocyte number at the 500 and 1000:1 ratios in the presence of mitogen. At the highest ratio of 1000:1 with 200 μg mitogen/ml nearly 80% of the colony formation is inhibited by the leukocytes (Fig. 6). This is similar to the percentage ^{3}H released from [^{3}H]TdR-labeled 104C1 cells incubated at a 1000:1 effector to target cell ratio in the presence of 50 μg mitogen/ml (Fig. 4).

If the leukocytes are incubated for 1, 2, or 3 days with mitogen before being added to the target cells, the leukocytes themselves no longer possess colony-inhibitory activity as shown in Table 2. The colony-inhibitory activity is found in the leukocyte culture medium. The leukocyte culture medium or lymphokine medium, furthermore, in combination with the inactive cultured leukocytes exerts a greater

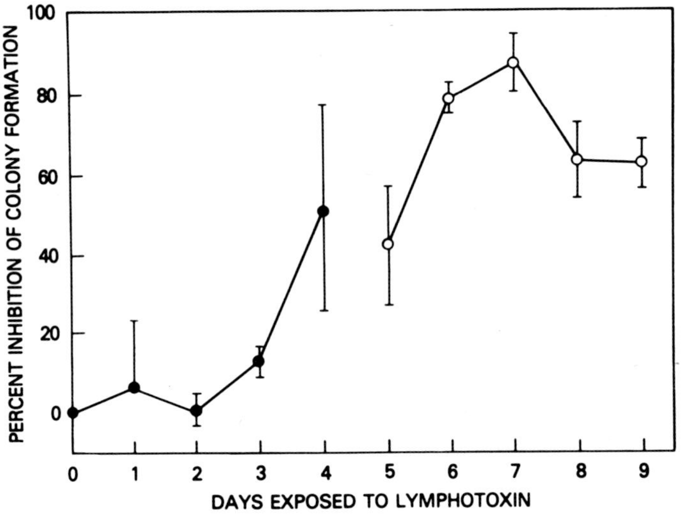

FIG. 3. Colony formation of 104C1 cells exposed to guinea pig lymphotoxin for varying periods of time. All target cells were allowed to grow for 9 days. For 1–4 days of exposure (●), lymphotoxin was added on Days 8,7,6 and 5, respectively, after seeding of the cells. For 5–9 days of exposure (○), lymphotoxin was added at the time of seeding, and the medium removed and replaced with fresh medium without lymphotoxin on Days 5,6,7.8. and 9 as shown with ±1 SEM.

activity than the lymphokines in the culture medium alone. Activation of the leukocytes could occur due to mitogen remaining in the culture medium, by lymphokines in the culture medium, by target cell stimulation of the effector leukocytes in combination with the lymphokines in the medium, or by a combination of these mechanisms.

Activation due to mitogen remaining in the lymphokine medium seems unlikely as no difference in the 1-, 2-, or 3-day preparations was observed. Activation of the effector cells by lymphokine or by the target cells, or target cell induction of additional lymphotoxin is possible if the target cells serve as an antigenic or mitogenic stimulus. Evidence supporting the latter is illustrated in Fig. 7. The colony-inhibitory activity of the lymphokine medium produced by incubation of leukocytes from strain 2/N guinea pigs with increasing numbers of leukocytes from allogeneic Hartley guinea pigs in serum-free medium is similar to the lymphotoxin activity obtained following incubation of leukocytes from ovalbumin immune animals with increasing concentrations of ovalbumin. Similar results are obtained following admixture of the tumorigenic 104C1 cells with syngeneic peritoneal leukocytes (J. H. Ransom and C. H. Evans, unpublished observations). Since tumor cells frequently have neoantigens which may be altered histocompatibility or other altered normal antigens, the target cells may stimulate or activate "nonimmune" leukocyte direct and/or indirect cytotoxic mechanisms thus accounting for the apparent synergistic effect of lymphotoxin on cultured nonadherent leukocytes. This synergism appears to reside in leukocytes other than macrophages as the colony-inhibitory activities of macrophages and of lymphotoxin are additive not synergistic as illustrated in Fig. 8.

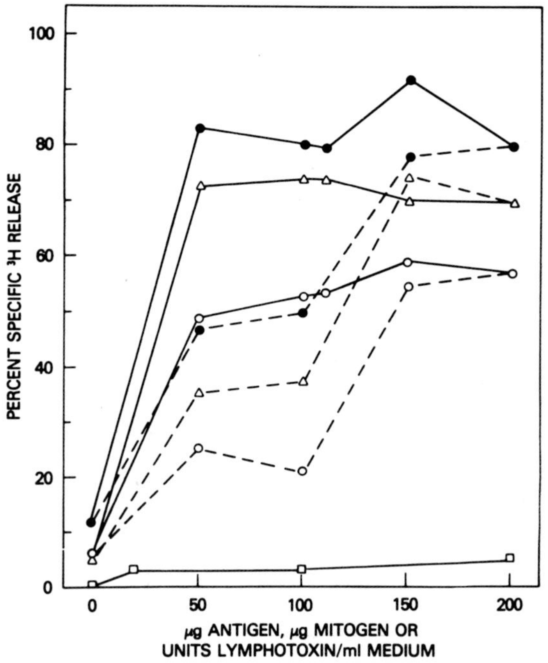

FIG. 4. Comparison of the ^{3}H release from 104C1 cells 48 hr after incubation with ovalbumin immune unfractionated peritoneal leukocytes (●, □), nonadherent peritoneal leukocytes (△) and peritoneal macrophages (○) at various antigen, mitogen, or lymphotoxin concentrations. The assay was performed in 60-mm-diameter tissue culture dishes at a 100:1 effector-to-target cell ratio. The ^{3}H release obtained following mitogen and antigen stimulation is shown by the solid lines; cells were simultaneously stimulated at the concentrations indicated on the abscissa respectively with 50 μg PHA, 100 μg PHA, 100 μg PHA + 10 μg OA, 100 μg PHA + 50 μg OA, and 100 μg PHA + 100 μg OA/ml medium. The results obtained by antigen and mitogen stimulation are shown by the dashed lines; cells were simultaneously stimulated with 50 μg OA, 100 μg OA, 100 μg OA + 50 μg PHA and 100 μg OA + 100 μg PHA/ml medium respectively. The response to the addition of lymphotoxin is shown by (□ —— □).

DISCUSSION

Guinea pig lymphotoxin directly inhibits the growth of syngeneic tumorigenic cells primarily through cytostatic rather than through cytolytic mechanisms. This is revealed by guinea pig lymphotoxin inhibition of target cell colony growth *in vitro* and the inability or very weak ability of lymphotoxin to induce the release of ^{3}H from the same [^{3}H]TdR-labeled tumorigenic cells. Human and rat lymphotoxin also have been observed to have cytostatic and cytolytic activities for human and mouse tumor cells (15, 33). Like the cytostatic effect of guinea pig lymphotoxin for guinea pig tumor cells, human lyphotoxin is also primarily cytostatic rather than cytolytic for human tumor cells (C. H. Evans, unpublished observations). Guinea pig cytolytic natural lymphoid cell cytotoxicity for tumorigenic guinea pig 104C1 cells is primarily a nonlymphotoxin activity resident both in nonadherent leukocyte and in macrophage populations. Other laboratories have also observed that nonstimulated (34) and antigen-stimulated (35) guinea pig macrophages fail to directly induce radionuclide release from cultured syngeneic tumor cells different

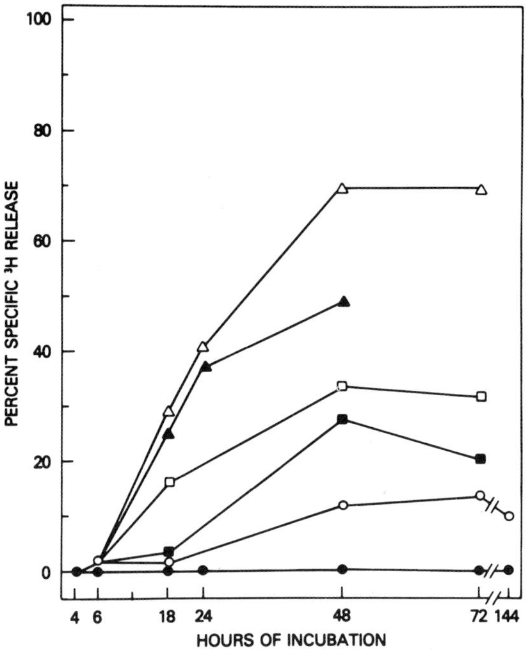

FIG. 5. Kinetics of ^3H release from 104C1 cells incubated with 100 units lymphotoxin/ml (●) or with nonadherent nonimmune peritoneal leukocytes and 0 (○), 12.5 (■), 25 (□), 50 (▲), or 100 (△) μg phytohemagglutinin per milliliter at a 100:1 effector-to-target cell ratio in 60-mm tissue culture dishes.

from those studied in the present investigation although macrophages may be activated by lymphokines (13, 34) to a cytolytic cytotoxic state and can produce their own cytolytic monokine (19, 20). These divergent observations illustrate the complexities of natural cytotoxicity resident in the effector mechanisms, the target cells, and the cytotoxicity assays.

Lymphokines have been observed to amplify lymphoid cell natural cytotoxicity of human (4), mouse (36, 37), and rat (38) cells as shown primarily by radionuclide release. The degree of stimulation has varied from slight to several-fold and has been postulated to be mediated directly or indirectly by interferon (1, 18, 30, 39, 40) and by lymphotoxin (41) or unidentified lymphokines (17). No or at best only minimal lymphotoxin enhancement of macrophage, nonadherent peritoneal leukocyte, or spleen leukocyte natural cytotoxicity as measured by target cell radionuclide release was observed in the present investigation in which no interferon was detectable in the lymphotoxin preparation. Lymphotoxin, however, does amplify the natural colony-inhibitory cytotoxicity of nonadherent peritoneal leukocytes. This augmentation of leukocyte cytotoxicity could be due to lymphokine activation of the effector cells as well as lymphokine sensitization of the target cells to the effector cells. Supporting evidence for the latter mechanism is the recent demonstration that lymphotoxin enhances natural killer cell (glass- and nylon-wool-nonadherent spleen lymphocytes) destruction of syngeneic guinea pig cells during chemical and ultraviolet carcinogenesis by increasing the susceptibility of the carcinogen-treated cells to natural killer cytolysis (J. H. Ransom and C. H. Evans, unpublished observations). Enhanced leukocyte natural cytotoxicity may also occur due to stim-

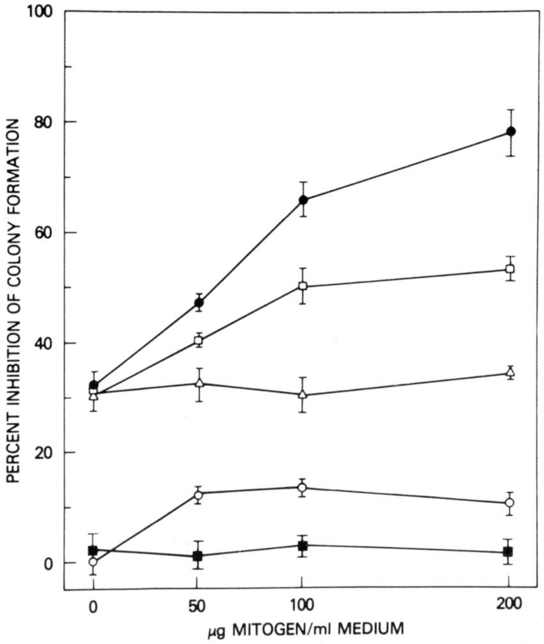

FIG. 6. Inhibition of 104C1 7-day colony growth by unfractionated nonimmune peritoneal leukocytes with varying concentrations of phytohemagglutinin. The assay was performed in 60-mm tissue culture dishes containing 10^2 104C1 cells with 0 (■), 10^4 (○), 2.5×10^4 (△), 5×10^4 (□), or 10^5 (●) leukocytes per dish. Results are shown ±1 SEM.

ulation of the effector cells by other nonlymphokine means such as by the target cells themselves. Augmented cytotoxicity also may be a measure of further and possibly particularly high local concentrations of cytotoxic lymphokine activity produced by the target-cell-stimulated effector lymphoid cells. The heterogeneity

TABLE 2

Colony Inhibitory Activity of Nonimmune Cultured Peritoneal Leukocytes

	Percentage inhibition of colony formation		
Effector	24 hr	48 hr	72 hr
24- to 72-hr cultured nonadherent leukocytes and their culture medium (RPMI 1640 + 10% FBS and 100 μg phytohemagglutinin/ml)	57 ± 0.3	66 ± 1.1	64 ± 1.1
Medium from 24- to 72-hr cultured leukocytes	32 ± 0.4	44 ± 1.7	35 ± 1.8
Nonadherent 24- to 72-hr cultured leukocytes alone	−3 ± 1.1	1 ± 2.3	−3 ± 2.6

Note. 0.4 ml of the medium from the 24- to 72-hr cultured leukocytes or 0.4 ml of that medium or fresh medium containing 5.5×10^4 cultured leukocytes was added to 10^2 syngeneic 104C1 cells in 3.6 ml medium/60-mm dish and incubated for 7 days. Values are ±1 SEM.

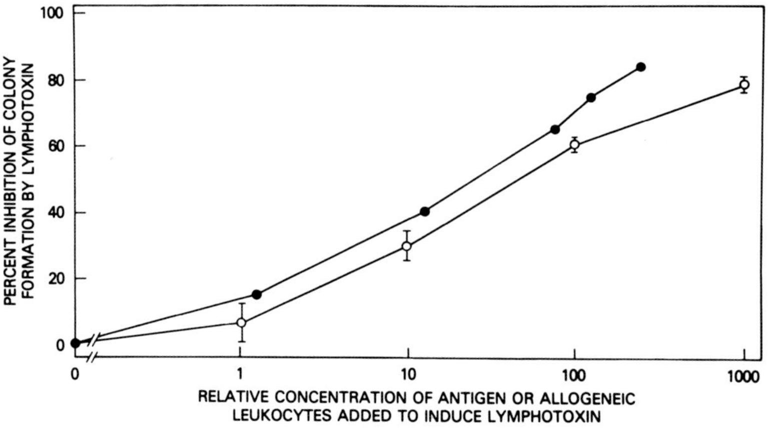

FIG. 7. Colony-inhibitory activity of lymphokine medium produced by nonimmune peritoneal strain 2/N leukocytes incubated in primary culture with increasing concentrations of allogeneic leukocytes from Hartley guinea pigs (○) compared with lymphotoxin generated by ovalbumin stimulation of strain 2/N peritoneal leukocytes from ovalbumin immune animals (●). Both lymphokine preparations were obtained from 10^7 strain 2/N leukocytes stimulated for 24 hr either with 1.25, 12.5, 50, 125, or 250 μg ovalbumin/ml or 10^4, 10^5, 10^6, or 10^7 Hartley leukocytes in 10 ml serum-free RPMI 1640 medium. The cell-free lymphokine colony-inhibitory activity was subsequently assessed by addition of the freshly prepared nonconcentrated lymphokines at 10% v/v to 104C1 cells in the colony-forming assay. The cell-free medium obtained from 24-hr cultures of 10^7 or 2×10^7 strain 2/N or Hartley peritoneal leukocytes exhibited no colony-inhibitory activity. Results are shown with ± 1 SEM.

of these mechanisms for enhancing natural leukocyte cytotoxicity illustrates the continuing difficulty of establishing the direct and/or indirect contributions of specific lymphokine and cellular components in natural cytotoxicity.

The presence of fetal bovine serum has also been implicated in the generation of cytolytic natural cytotoxicity although not demonstrable until 2–4 days after culture of the effector leukocytes (42, 43). Serum would not appear to contribute extensively to the generation of cytolytic natural cytoxicity of the leukocytes in the present investigation since maximal radionuclide release from the target cells was present by 2 days and was markedly enhanced by phytohemagglutinin as early as 18 hr after culture. The leukocyte-mediated natural cytotoxicity displayed in the 7-day colony inhibition assay could be due in part to fetal bovine serum-induced activation of the leukocytes. Antigen and mitogen stimulation, however, are stronger inducers of leukocyte-mediated radionuclide release when the leukocytes are cocultivated with the target cells during the first 24 hr of culture. Leukocytes cultured for 1–3 days in the presence of serum and mitogen in the absence of target cells were devoid of natural cytotoxicity. However, when the cultured leukocytes were subsequently cultured with the target cells in the presence of serum and lymphokine medium, cytotoxicity was partially restored. The natural cytotoxicity of human peripheral blood leukocytes lost during culture can be regained following mitogen stimulation (44). Other investigators have concluded that stimulation or sensitization by the target cells is more important than serum stimulation (45) and that sensitization can be increased by mitogen stimulation (46), findings consistent with those in the present investigation. The difficulty remains, however, of establishing

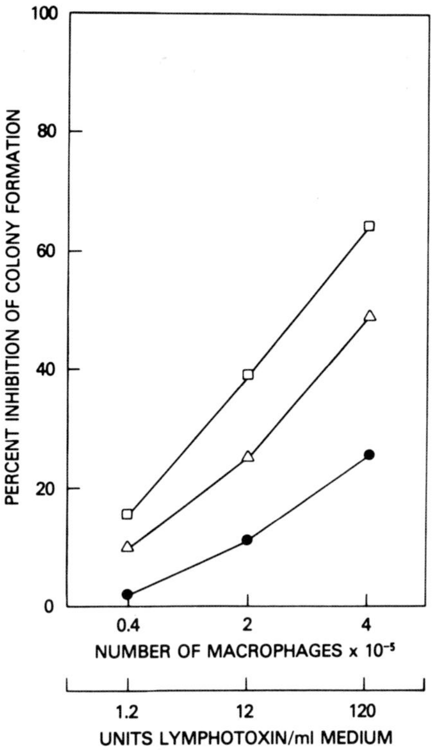

FIG. 8. Macrophage inhibition of 104C1 colony formation. One hundred 104C1 cells were added to 24-hr cultured macrophages (●), to dishes with lymphotoxin (△) or to dishes with macrophages and lymphotoxin (□) and incubated for 7 days.

whatever the mechanism of induction, whether the cytotoxicity is mediated directly by the leukocytes, by cytotoxic lymphokines such as lymphotoxin, or by both.

Target cells can induce lymphoid cells to produce lymphotoxin (41, 47) and natural cytotoxicity can be induced by allogeneic (48, 49) or syngeneic cells (50) and increased by the addition of lymphokines generated in mixed lymphocyte cultures (48). The results of the current investigation suggest that several of these mechanisms may occur concurrently and interdependently in selected assays for natural cytotoxicity. Target cell stimuli resulting from altered normal antigens on autologous or syngeneic tumor cells (51–53) from the presence of heterologous serum components, and from other cell surface alterations potentially can induce and also maintain lymphoid cell natural cytotoxicity. This may be manifest in both cytolytic and cytostatic growth inhibition depending upon the effector and target cells in question and the assay employed to measure cytotoxicity. Natural cytotoxicity, furthermore, includes a variety of effector mechanisms some of which such as lymphotoxin cytotoxicity may enhance or otherwise directly or indirectly modulate the activity of different leukocyte populations. The present investigation suggests that guinea pig lymphotoxin is primarily cytostatic to 104C1 guinea pig cells and has minimal direct contributions to natural leukocyte cytotoxicity at the effector cell. Lymphotoxin may, however, through its direct cytostatic action increase the susceptibility of the target cell to natural leukocyte cytotoxic destruction and in that manner indirectly enhance natural leukocyte cytotoxicity. The varying susceptibilities of different target cells to cytostatic and cytolytic natural cytotoxicity indicate the importance of evaluating a wider selection of target cells then heretofore studied to more fully understand the physiologic role and interrelationships of effector cells and lymphokines in the phenomenon referred to as natural or spontaneous lymphoid cell-mediated cytotoxicity.

ACKNOWLEDGMENTS

I wish to thank Mssrs. Mark D. Feldman, Edward J. Fudman, and Jeffrey A. Heinbaugh for their technical assistance during this investigation.

REFERENCES

1. Herberman, R. B., Nunn, M. E., Holden, and Lavrin, D. H., *Int. J. Cancer* **16,** 230, 1975.
2. Kiessling, R., Klein, E., Pross, H. F., and Wigzell, H., *Eur. J. Immunol.* **5,** 117, 1975.
3. Peter, H., Parie-Fisher, J., Fridman, W. H., Aubert, C., Cesarini, J., Roubin, R., and Kourilsky, F. M., *J. Immunol.* **115,** 539, 1975.
4. deVries, J. E., Mendelsohn, J., and Bont, W. S., *Nature (London)* **283,** 574, 1980.
5. Rosenberg, E. B., McCoy, J. L., Green, S. S., Donnelly, F. C., Siwarski, D. F., Levine, P. H., and Herberman R. B., *J. Nat. Cancer Inst.* **52,** 345, 1974.
6. Herberman, R. B., and Holden, H. T. *Advan. Cancer Res.* **27,** 305, 1978.
7. Ballas, Z. K., and Henney, C. S., *In* "The Biology of The Lymphokines" (S. Cohen, E. Pick, and J. J. Oppenheim, Eds.), pp. 165–180, Academic Press, New York, 1979.
8. Herberman, R. B., Djeu, J. Y., Kay, H. D., Ortaldo, R. R., Riccardi, C., Bonnard, G., Holden, H. T., Fagnani, R., Santoni, A., and Puccetti, P., *Immunol. Rev.* **44,** 43, 1979.
9. Altman, A., and Rapp, H. J., *J. Immunol.* **121,** 2244, 1978.
10. Arnaud-Battandier, F., Bundy, B. M., and Nelson, D. L., *Eur. J. Immunol.* **8,** 400, 1978.
11. Keller, R., *J. Nat. Cancer. Inst.* **56,** 369, 1976.
12. Meltzer, M. S., *Cell. Immunol.* **22,** 176, 1976.
13. Tagliabue, A., Mantovani, A., Kilgallen, M., Herberman, R. B., and McCoy. J. L., *J. Immunol.* **122,** 2363, 1979.
14. Weinberg, D. S., Fishman, M., and Veit, B. C., *Cell. Immunol.* **38,** 94, 1980.
15. Granger, G. A., Hiserodt, J. C., and Ware, C. F., *In* "The Biology of the Lymphokines" (S. Cohen, E. Pick, and J. J. Oppenheim Eds.), pp. 141–164, Academic Press, New York, 1979.
16. Jeffes, E. W. B., and Granger G. A., *J. Immunol,* **117,** 174, 1976.
17. Mantovani, A., Dean, J. H., Jerrells, T. R., and Herberman, R. B., *Int. J. Cancer.* **25,** 691, 1980.
18. Silva, A., Bonavida, B., and Targan, S., *J. Immunol.* **125,** 479, 1980.
19. Sharma, S., D., Piessens, W. F., and Middlebrook, G. *Cell. Immunol.* **49,** 379, 1980.
20. Adams, D. O., Kao, K.-J., Farb, R., and Pizzo, S. U., *J. Immunol.* **124,** 293, 1980.
21. Evans, C. H., Cooney, A. M., and DiPaolo, J. A., *Cancer Res.* **35,** 1045, 1975.
22. Holtermann, O. A., Klein, E., and Casale, G. P., *Cell. Immunol.* **9,** 339, 1973.
23. Jondal, M., Spina, C., and Targan, S., *Nature (London)* **272,** 62, 1978.
24. Brouty-Boye', D., Gresser, I., and Baldwin, C., *Int. J. Cancer* **24,** 261, 1979.
25. Rundell, J. O., and Evans, C. H., *Immunopharmacology* **3,** 9, 1981.
26. Zwilling, B. S., Meltzer, M. S., and Evans, C. H., *J. Nat. Cancer Inst.* **54,** 743, 1975.
27. Evans, C. H., and DiPaolo, J. A., *Cancer Res.* **35,** 1035, 1975.
28. Rundell, J. O., and Evans, C. H., *Immunopharmacology* **2,** 19, 1979.
29. Zbar, B., Ribi, E., Kelly, M., Granger, D., Evans, C., and Rapp, H. J., *Cancer Immunol. Immunother.* **1,** 127, 1976.
30. Ross, M. W., Tiangco, G. J., Horn, P.., Hiserodt, J. C., and Granger, G. A., *J. Immunol.* **123,** 325, 1979.
31. Evans, C. H., Rabin, E. S., and DiPaolo, J. A., *Cancer Res.* **37,** 898, 1977.
32. Spofford, B. T., Daynes, R. A., and Granger, G. A., *J. Immunol.* **112,** 2111, 1974.
33. Namba, Y., and Waksman, B. H., *J. Immunol.* **115,** 1018, 1975.

34. Churchill, W. H., Piessens, W. F., Sulis, C. A., and David, J. R., *J. Immunol.* **115,** 781, 1975.
35. Zwilling, B. S., Leonard, E. J., Bast, R. C., Jr., and Zbar, B., *J. Nat. Cancer Inst.* **53,** 541, 1974.
36. Meltzer, M. S., and Bartlett, G. L., *J. Nat. Cancer Inst.* **49,** 1439, 1972.
37. Okada, M., and Henney, C. S., *J. Immunol.* **125,** 300, 1980.
38. Shellam, G. R., Winterbourn, V., and Dawkins, H. J. S., *Int. J. Cancer.* **25,** 331, 1980.
39. Trinchieri, G., and Santoli, D., *J. Exp. Med.* **147,** 1314, 1978.
40. Vanky, F. T., Argov, S. A., Einhorn, S. A., an Klein, E., *J. Exp. Med.* **151,** 1151, 1980.
41. Peter, H. H., Eife, R. F., and Kalden, J. R., *J. Immunol.* **116,** 342, 1976.
42. Ortaldo, J. R., Bonnard, G. D., and Herberman, R. B., *J. Immunol.* **119,** 1351, 1977.
43. Zielske, J. V., and Golub, S. H., *Cancer Res.* **36,** 3842, 1976.
44. Callewarert, D. M., Lightbody, J. J., Kaplan, J., Jarosewski, J., Peterson, W. D., Jr., and Rosenberg, J. C., *J. Immunol.* **121,** 81, 1978.
45. Koide, Y., and M. Takasugi M., *J. Immunol.* **121,** 872, 1978.
46. Holm, G., and Perlmann, P., *Nature (London)* **207,** 818, 1965.
47. Hiserodt, J. C., Tiangco, G. J., and Granger, G. A., *J. Immunol.* **123,** 311, 1979.
48. Masucci, G., Poros, A., Seeley, J. K., and Klein, E., *Cell. Immunol.* **52,** 247, 1980.
49. Zarling, J. M., Robins, H. I., Raich, P. C., Bach, F. H., and Bach, M. L. *Nature (London)* **274,** 269, 1978.
50. Glaser, M., Bonnard, G. D., and Herberman, R. B., *J. Immunol.* **116,** 430, 1976.
51. Invernizzi, G., and Parmiani, G., *Nature (London)* **254,** 713, 1975.
52. Law, L. W., *Int. J. Cancer* **25,** 251, 1980.
53. Perry, L. L., and Greene, M. I., *J. Immunol.* **125,** 738, 1980.

CELLULAR IMMUNOLOGY 63, 16–27 (1981)

The Immune Response in Aged C57BL/6 Mice

I. Assessment of Lesions in the B-Cell and T-Cell Compartments of Aged Mice Utilizing the Fc Fragment-Mediated Polyclonal Antibody Response[1]

EDWARD L. MORGAN,[2,3] MARILYN L. THOMAN,[4] AND WILLIAM O. WEIGLE

Department of Immunopathology, Scripps Clinic and Research Foundation, La Jolla, California 92037

Received January 20, 1981; accepted April 30, 1981

The Fc fragment-mediated polyclonal antibody response was utilized to assess B-cell, T-cell, and macrophage reactivity in aged C57BL/6 mice. Spleen cells from aged (28–30 months) mice were found to be deficient in their capacity to proliferate and produce polyclonal antibody in response to Fc fragments when compared to adult (2–3 months) controls. Since T cells are required for the Fc-induced polyclonal antibody response, T cells from aged mice were assessed for their ability to restore the polyclonal antibody response in T-cell-depleted adult spleen cell populations. Aged T cells were not as effective as adult T cells in restoring the antibody response. The T-cell requirement in the Fc-induced polyclonal response has been shown to be replaceable by the Fc-stimulated T-cell replacing factor (Fc)TRF. T cells derived from aged mice were unable to produce (Fc)TRF to the level of adult cells. In addition to a defect in the T-cell compartment a lesion exists in the B-cell compartment of aged mice as well. Adult T cells were not capable of restoring the polyclonal antibody response of aged B cells any higher than aged T cells indicating a B-cell defect. Moreover, when a direct B-cell activator, Fc subfragment, was employed, the aged B cells were not stimulated to the level of adult controls. To test the ability of aged macrophages to function as accessory cells in the polyclonal response, macrophage-depleted adult spleen cells were mixed with aged or adult macrophages and the response measured. The results indicate that aged macrophages restore the polyclonal antibody response as efficiently as their adult counterpart.

INTRODUCTION

The study of immune potential during senescence has been the focus of numerous investigations in which it has been established that the magnitude of various parameters of the immune responses declines with age. This decline is manifested by impaired capacity to develop both cell-mediated (1–3) and humoral immunity (4–14). Changes in both the thymus-derived (T) cell and bone-marrow-derived (B)

[1] This is Publication No. 2304 from the Department of Immunopathology, Scripps Clinic and Research Foundation, La Jolla, Calif. This work was supported in part by United States Public Health Service Grants AI07007, AI15761 and AG00783, and Biomedical Research Support Program Grant RRO-5514.

[2] Recipient of United States Public Health Postdoctoral Fellowship AI05813.

[3] To whom all correspondence should be directed.

[4] Recipient of United States Public Health Service Postdoctoral Fellowship AI06085.

0008-8749/81/130016-12$02.00/0

cell compartments have been associated with the reduced ability of aged mice to respond to antigenic stimulation. Despite this general decay of immune function, increased age is also associated with the development of autoimmune disease states in both man (15) and the mouse (16). Thus, it is not surprising that decreased suppressor-T-cell activity has been reported to accompany the aging process (16). Little information is available on the parameters of the immune regulatory circuits, and few studies have been made using one system to simultaneously evaluate the effects of aging on different events involved in lymphocyte activation. As the result of recent studies on B-cell activation with Fc fragments of human immunoglobulin (Ig),[5] it became obvious that this model would lend itself to such an approach, since Fc fragment-induced B-cell activation requires the complex interaction of multiple cell types. The Fc portion of Ig has the capacity to induce murine B cells to proliferate (17–19) and produce polyclonal antibody (20). The cellular and molecular requirements have been extensively investigated and it has been established that both macrophage (18–20) and T cells (20) are required to drive B cells to polyclonal antibody production, whereas only macrophages are required for Fc fragment-mediated B-cell proliferation. Moreover, Fc fragments have been shown to possess adjuvant properties (21, 22). Fc fragments are able to potentiate both humoral (21–23) and cell-mediated (24) immune responses. Taken together these results indicate that the Fc fragment is a potent *in vivo* and *in vitro* immune regulator involving B cells, T cells, and macrophages. The purpose of this study was to evaluate the cellular parameters of Fc fragment-mediated activation in aged mice.

MATERIALS AND METHODS

Animals. Male mice of the inbred C57BL/6 strain age 2–3 months were obtained from Jackson Laboratories (Bar Harbor, Maine) and Charles River (Willmington, Mass.). Aged male C57BL/6 mice (28–30 months) were obtained from Charles River. All experiments were performed with adult mice from both sources with comparable results.

Preparation of Fc fragments. A human IgG_1 myeloma protein (Fi) was a gift from Dr. Hans L. Spiegelberg, Scripps Clinic and Research Foundation. The IgG_1 was purified by ammonium sulfate fractionation followed by DEAE cellulose chromatography with 0.01 *M* phosphate buffer, pH 8, used as the eluent. Fc fragments were obtained by digestion of IgG_1 with papain (Sigma Chemical Co., St. Louis, Mo.) in the presence of L-cysteine (Sigma) and ethylenediaminetetraacetic acid (EDTA) (J. T. Baker Chemical Co., Phillipsburg, N.J.) for 5 hr (25). Following digestion the material was chromatographed on Sephadex G-100 (Pharmacia Fine Chemicals, Piscataway, N.J.) to remove any undigested IgG. The Fc and Fab fragments were then separated from each other by DEAE chromatography (26).

Preparation of Fc subfragments. Stimulatory adherent cell supernate was prepared as previously described (19). A single-cell suspension was prepared by teasing apart the spleens into cold phosphate-buffered saline (PBS). The suspension was allowed to stand for 5 min in ice to allow clumps to settle out. The cells were

[5] Abbreviations used: FCS, fetal calf serum; Ig, immunoglobulin; PFC, plaque-forming cells; SRBC, sheep red blood cells; TNP, trinitrophenyl; TRF, T-cell replacing factor; PBS, phosphate-buffered saline; LPS, lipopolysaccharide; S-III, pneumococcal polysaccharide type III.

washed twice and resuspended to a concentration of 2×10^7/ml in RPMI 1640 (Flow Laboratories, Rockville, Md.), supplemented with 2 m*M* L-glutamine, 1% BME vitamins (Grand Island Biological Co., Grand Island, N.Y.), 100 units penicillin and 100 μg streptomycin (Microbiological Associates, Bethesda, Md.), 5×10^{-5} *M* 2-mercaptoethanol (2-ME), and 5% fetal calf serum (FCS) (Gibco). One-milliliter samples were allowed to adhere to tissue culture dishes (3001, Falcon Plastics, Oxnard, Calif.) for 1 hr in an atmosphere of 5% CO_2 at 37°C. The cells were washed extensively with RPMI 1640 to remove nonadherent cells prior to the addition of Fc fragments. One milligram of Fc in 2 ml RPMI 1640, supplemented with 2 m*M* L-glutamine, 1% vitamins, 100 units penicillin, 100 μg streptomycin, 5×10^{-5} *M* 2-ME, and 0.5% fresh normal mouse serum, was added to the adherent cell layer. The supernatant material was collected after a 1-hr incubation period and centrifuged at 1500 *g* for 10 min in a refrigerated centrifuge and sterilized by filtration through at 0.22-μm filter prior to chromatographic separation. The adherent cell supernate was chromatographed on a Sephadex G-50 superfine (Pharmacia, Piscataway, N.J.) column (1.2 × 30 cm) with a bed volume of 20 ml. The material was eluted with PBS at a flow rate of 30 ml/hr and 0.5-ml samples were collected. The column was calibrated with the following standards, blue dextran (50,000 MW) (Pharmacia), deoxyribonuclease (31,000 MW) (Sigma), and lysozome (14,300 MW) (Calbiochem-Behring Corp., La Jolla, Calif.). The molecular weight of the mitogenic material was calculated from a plot of the elution volumes versus the logarithm of the molecular weights of the standards. Mitogenic activity was found to have a molecular weight of approximately 14,000 (19). The column-purified material was then affinity purified on an anti-Fc affinity column (19) prior to use. Fc subfragment directly induces B cells to proliferate in the absence of accessory macrophages or T cells.

Isolation of macrophages. Splenic macrophages were isolated as previously described (18, 19). Spleen cell preparations were subjected to 2000 R of irradiation from a Gamma Cell 40 small animal irradiator (Atomic Energy of Canada Ltd., Ottawa, Canada) delivered at 107 R/min prior to adherence. The irradiated spleen cells were adjusted to 6×10^5 cells/0.5 ml RPMI 1640 + 10% FCS and 0.5 ml was allowed to adhere to the wells of microtiter plates (3040 Microtest II, Falcon) for 30 min in an atmosphere of 5% CO_2 at 37°C. The wells were washed extensively with RPMI 1640 to remove any nonadherent cells. These cells were used as a source of macrophages in restoration of the polyclonal response in macrophage-depleted cultures.

Depletion of macrophages by Sephadex G-10 filtration. Spleen cells were filtered through columns of Sephadex G-10 (Pharmacia) by the method of Ly and Mishell (27). Briefly, 5×10^7 spleen cells in 2 ml RPMI 1640 supplemented with 5% FCS were filtered through a column containing 9 ml of Sephadex G-10 which was previously equilibrated with RPMI 1640. The number of residual macrophages present was monitored by esterase straining (28). Sephadex G-10 passage reduced the esterase-positive cells from approximately 7–10% to <0.1%.

Depletion of T lymphocytes. T-Cell-depleted spleen cell populations were prepared as previously described (17). Rabbit anti-thymocyte serum (Microbiological Associates) was absorbed with a myeloma cell line (XS-63). Spleen cells were incubated at a concentration of 5×10^7/ml in PBS with a 1:40 dilution of guinea pig complement (Pel-Freez, Inc., Rogers, Ark.) and incubated for 30 min at 37°C.

The complement was preabsorbed for 30 min at 4°C with 1:5 packed volume of red blood cells and then with a mixture of thymocytes and spleen cells from C3H mice.

Enrichment of T lymphocytes. The spleen cell population was enriched for T lymphocytes by filtration through nylon wool columns (Fenwal Laboratories, Deerfield, Ill.) (29).

Production of Fc fragment-induced T-cell replacing factors. Spleen cells were incubated 24 hr in 0.2 ml RPMI 1640 supplemented with 2 m*M* L-glutamine, 100 units penicillin, 100 μg streptomycin, 5×10^{-5} *M* 2-mercaptoethanol, 5% fetal calf serum (FCS) (Grand Island Biological), and 50 μg/ml Fc fragments. Culture supernatants were collected and tested (10–20 μl/well) for T-cell replacing activity in the Fc-induced polyclonal response. The culture supernatants were then subjected to Sephadex G-100 separation as described previously (30). Active fractions were pooled and stored at −20°C prior to use.

Polyclonal antibody response assay. For the generation of the polyclonal plaque-forming-cell (PFC) response spleen cells were suspended to a concentration of 6×10^6/ml in RPMI 1640 supplemented with 2 m*M* glutamine, vitamins, 100 units penicillin, 100 μg streptomycin, 7.5% FCS, and 0.5% fresh normal mouse serum. Duplicate cultures of 6×10^5 cells/0.3 ml were incubated in microtiter plates (3040 Microtest II, Falcon) at 37°C in 5% CO_2. Duplicate cultures were harvested on Day 3 and assayed for a response to 2,4,6-trinitrophenyl (TNP) by the slide modification of the Jerne and Nordin plaque assay (31). Heavily TNP-conjugated sheep red blood cells (TNP-SRBC) were prepared according to the method of Kettman and Dutton (32) and were used as the indicator RBC. Guinea pig serum (Pel-Freez) was the source of complement to develop the direct or IgM plaques. Results of the plaque forming assay are expressed as the mean PFC/10^6 original cells of duplicate pools ± SE. Each experiment was performed a minimum of three times and the experiments shown are representative of all the data.

Proliferative response assay. The Fc fragment-mediated proliferative response was performed as previously described (17–19).

RESULTS

Fc Fragment-Induced Activation of Aged B Cells

To determine whether splenic B cells from aged (28–30 months) mice could be activated by the Fc portion of human Ig, they were compared to normal adult (3 months) B cells. The results in Fig. 1 demonstrated that Fc fragment-induced B-cell proliferation is greater in adult than aged spleen cell cultures. The low response of aged cells was not due to an increased stimulation threshold because the responses obtained with 50 and 100 μg were not significantly different. The optimal concentration of Fc for the adult proliferative response was found to be 100 μg/culture as described previously (18).

Since B-cell proliferation is an integral part of Fc fragment-mediated polyclonal antibody production (20), it was important to determine whether aged spleen cell cultures also showed a reduced polyclonal antibody response. The results in Fig. 2 indicate that adult spleen cells produce a significantly greater polyclonal antibody response compared to aged spleen cells. As observed with the proliferative response, the optimal concentration of Fc needed for the polyclonal antibody response was

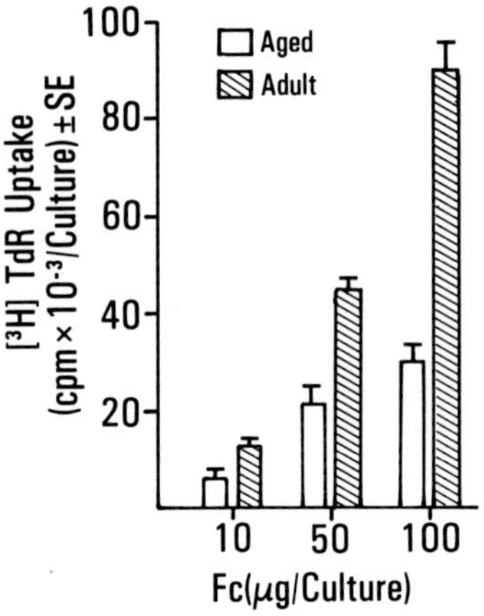

FIG. 1. Comparison of the ability of aged and adult spleen cells to proliferate in response to Fc fragments. The response was measured on Day 3 of culture.

100 μg/culture. The inability of aged spleen cells to produce polyclonal antibody to the level of adult controls was not due to a shift in the response kinetics because the low but significant antibody response produced by aged spleen cells peaked on Day 3 of culture (Fig. 3) as did the much larger response of the adult cells.

Analysis of T- and B-Cell Reactivity in Aged Mice

Since T cells are essential in the Fc fragment-induced polyclonal antibody response (20), it was important to ascertain whether the T cell was a defective component in aged mice. T cells from both aged and adult mice were assessed for their ability to restore the polyclonal antibody response in T-cell-depleted adult spleen cell populations. The results in Fig. 4 show that aged T cells were not as effective as adult T cells in restoring the polyclonal antibody response. This ob-

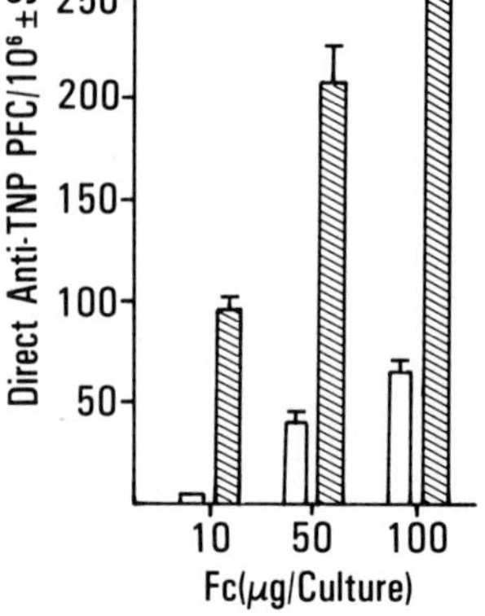

FIG. 2. Comparison of the ability of aged and adult spleen cells to produce polyclonal antibody in response to Fc fragments. The response was measured on Day 3 of culture.

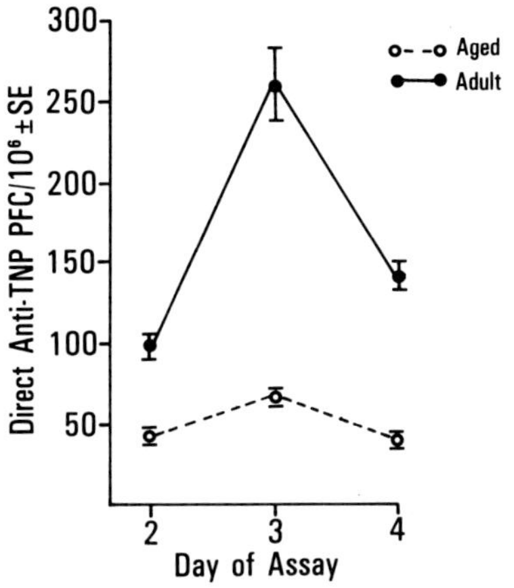

FIG. 3. Kinetic profile of the Fc fragment-induced polyclonal antibody response. 100 μg Fc/culture was used.

servation was found to be true over a wide range of B:T cell ratios. With both aged and adult T cells the optimal response was obtained with approximately equal numbers of T cells and B cells. The response obtained was comparable to that seen with untreated adult spleen cell preparations.

The T-cell requirement in the polyclonal antibody response has recently been shown to be replaceable by supernatant material derived from T cells cultured with Fc fragments (30). This T-cell replacing factor (Fc)TRF, was found, in conjunction with Fc fragments, to stimulate T-cell-depleted cultures to make polyclonal antibody. T cells derived from aged mice were unable to produce (Fc)TRF to the level of adult cells (Fig. 5). The maximal amount of (Fc)TRF was generated at a cell

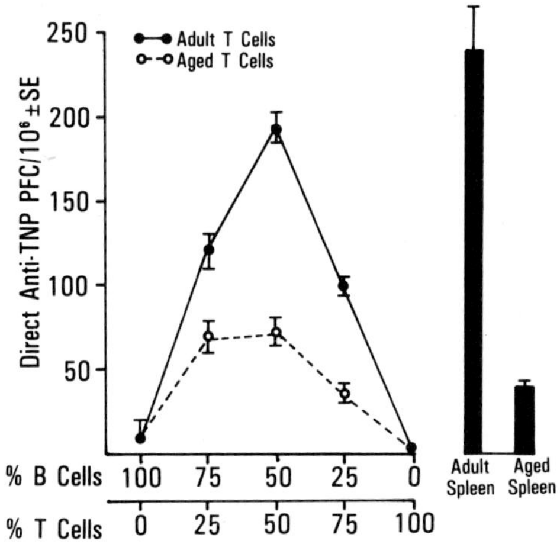

FIG. 4. Comparison of the ability of aged and adult T cells to restore the Fc-mediated polyclonal antibody response in T-cell-depleted adult spleen cell cultures. Varying numbers of B and T cells were added together such that the final cell concentration was held constant at 6×10^5 cells/culture. 100 μg Fc/culture was used and the response measured on Day 3.

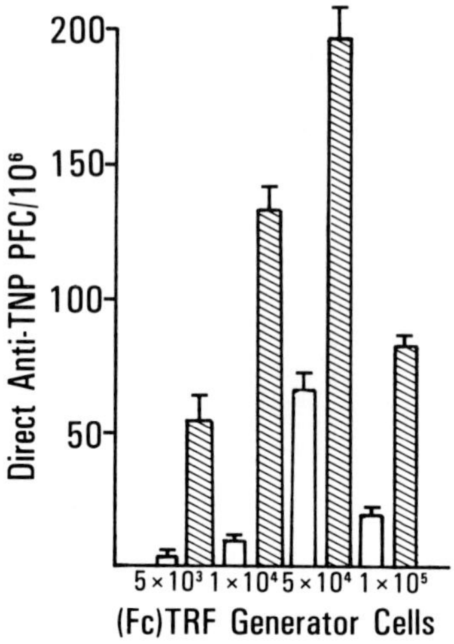

FIG. 5. Comparison of the ability of aged (□) and adult (▨) spleen cells to produce (Fc)TRF. Increasing numbers of spleen cells were incubated with Fc fragments (50 μg/ml) for 24 hr and the supernatants harvested. The supernatant material was subjected to G-100 chromatography prior to use. 20 μl/well of (Fc)TRF was added to T-cell-depleted adult spleen cell cultures along with 100 μg Fc/culture and the polyclonal antibody response measured on Day 3.

density of 5×10^4/0.2 ml for both adult and aged cultures. Taken together these results indicate that T cells from aged mice are not as efficient as adult T cells in supporting Fc fragment-induced polyclonal antibody production.

To assess whether a lesion existed in the B-cell compartment of aged mice, T cells from adult and aged mice were added to T-cell-depleted aged spleen cell populations and the Fc-mediated response was measured. The data expressed in Fig. 6 indicate that aged B cells as well as T cells are defective in the Fc polyclonal

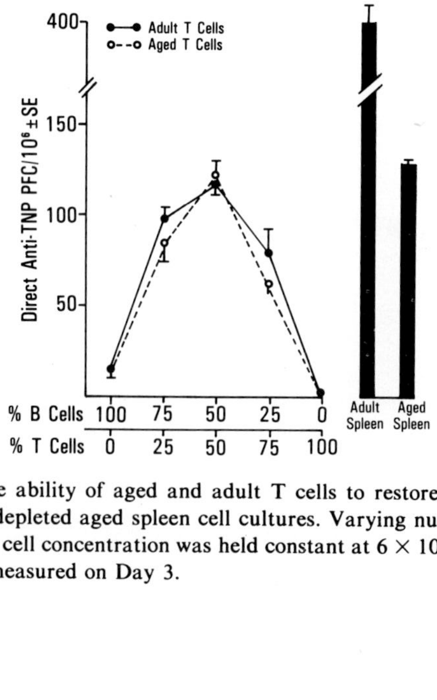

FIG. 6. Comparison of the ability of aged and adult T cells to restore the Fc-mediated polyclonal antibody response of T-cell-depleted aged spleen cell cultures. Varying numbers of B and T cells were added together such that the cell concentration was held constant at 6×10^5/culture. 100 μg Fc/culture was used and the response measured on Day 3.

TABLE 1

Comparison of the Ability of Fc Subfragments to Induce Aged and Adult Spleen Cells to Proliferate

Spleen cells[a]	Fc subfragment[b]	[^{3}H]TdR uptake culture ± SE[c]
Aged	−	2,085 ± 706
	+	7,765 ± 1,127
Adult	−	1,587 ± 378
	+	34,387 ± 3,361

[a] Spleen cells were filtered through Sephadex G-10 columns prior to stimulation with Fc subfragment.
[b] 1.25 μg/culture.
[c] The response was measured on Day 3 of culture.

response. Adult T cells were not capable of restoring the polyclonal antibody response any higher than aged T cells indicating that aged B cells were incapable of being stimulated to the level of adult B cells. Moreover, a shift in the optimal B:T cell ratio had not occurred since approximately equal numbers of B and T cells still produced the maximum response. To further evaluate the aged B cell, advantage was taken of the fact that Fc subfragments, derived from macrophage processing of Fc fragments, directly stimulate B-cell proliferation in the absence of accessory cells (19). When Fc subfragments were added to aged and adult spleen cell cultures, it was found that adult cells proliferated to a greater extent than aged spleen cells directly indicating a lesion in the B-cell compartment of aged mice (Table 1).

Analysis of Macrophage Reactivity in Aged Mice

To test the ability of aged macrophages to function as accessory cells in the Fc-induced polyclonal antibody response, macrophage-depleted adult spleen cells were added to irradiated adherent cell monolayers from aged and adult mice and the response was measured. The results in Fig. 7 reveal that aged macrophages restore the polyclonal antibody response as well as adult splenic macrophages. These results indicate that splenic macrophages from aged mice are as effective as adult macrophages in processing Fc fragments into mitogenic Fc subfragments, the previously reported function of macrophages in this polyclonal response.

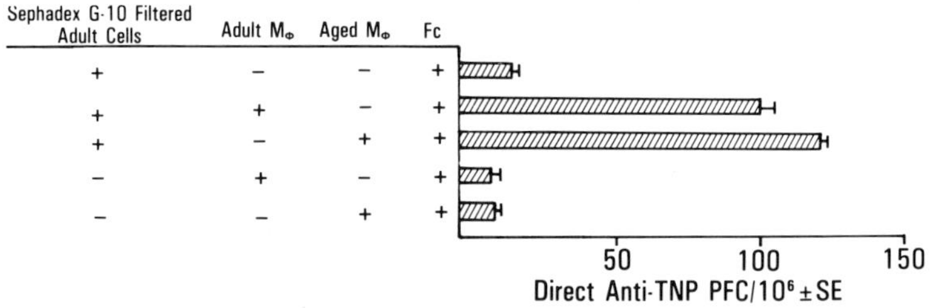

FIG. 7. Comparison of the ability of aged and adult splenic macrophages to restore the Fc-mediated polyclonal antibody response in macrophage depleted adult spleen cell cultures. 6 × 10^5 Sephadex G-10 filtered spleen cells were added to microwells containing either adult or aged macrophages. 100 μg Fc/culture was used and the response measured on Day 3 of culture.

TABLE 2

Inability of Aged T Cells to Suppress the Fc Fragment-Mediated Polyclonal Antibody Response by Adult Spleen Cells

Adult spleen cells	Aged[a] T cells	Fc fragments[b]	Direct anti-TNP PFC/10^6 ± SE[c]
6×10^5	—	−	33 ± 1
	—	+	295 ± 35
	1×10^4	−	16 ± 3
		+	300 ± 27
	1×10^5	−	22 ± 1
		+	304 ± 10
	2×10^5	−	29 ± 4
		+	308 ± 5

[a] Nylon-wool-nonadherent spleen cells.

[b] 100 μg Fc/culture.

[c] The response was measured on Day 3 of culture. The polyclonal antibody response of untreated aged spleen cells was 96 ± 7 PFC/10^6.

Analysis of Suppressor-T-Cell Activity in Aged Mice

To assess whether T cells derived from aged mice had the ability to suppress the Fc fragment-mediated polyclonal antibody response, increasing numbers of aged T cells were added to adult spleen cells and the response was measured. The results in Table 2 reveal that the aged T cells were unable to suppress the Fc-mediated polyclonal antibody response. Moreover, when adult T cells were substituted for the aged T cells, similar results were observed (data not shown). Untreated spleen cells from the aged mice were defective in their response to Fc when compared to adult controls (97 PFC vs 295 PFC). These results indicate that the inability of spleen cells from aged mice to respond to the levels of adult controls was not due to suppressor T cells.

DISCUSSION

The Fc portion of immunoglobulin serves as an ideal activator in the evaluation of lymphocyte and accessory cell reactivity in an aging model because both T cells (20, 30) and macrophages (20) are required to generate the polyclonal antibody response and macrophages are required for B-cell proliferation (18, 19). Both the proliferative and polyclonal antibody responses to Fc fragments were reduced during the process of aging. Spleen cells from individual aged (28–30 months old) mice proliferated and produced polyclonal antibody at a significantly lower level compared to spleen cells from adult (3-month-old) control mice. Spleen cell preparations from aged mice were not pooled due to the observation that a large degree of variability exists in the magnitude of antibody responses from aged mice (33). Moreover, adult control spleen cell populations were not pooled for purposes of consistency. All experiments were performed with adults from both Charles River and Jackson with no observable differences. The data shown were obtained with adult mice from Charles River. Collectively, we have assessed the polyclonal antibody responses of approximately 25 aged mice and all were significantly lower (average five-fold lower) than the adult control values. The reduced responsiveness was not due to a shift in the dose–response or kinetic profiles of the aged mice since the maximum responses obtained with aged spleen cells coincided with maximum responses of adult controls. Callard *et al.* (6) employing bacterial lipopolysaccharide (LPS) and pneumococcal polysaccharide type III (S-III) also observed that the reduced level of polyclonal B-cell activity could not be explained in terms of alterations in the kinetics of the responding cells as the optimal dose and the time of the peak response for both LPS and S-III were similar for aged and adult cells. Moreover, these authors (6) showed that the defect was not due to a decrease in the number of B cells present because an increase rather than a decrease in B cells was found in spleen from aged mice.

Although macrophages are required for the generation of both proliferation and polyclonal antibody production, they appear not to be affected in these capacities by the aging process. Splenic macrophages derived from aged mice are as efficient as adult macrophages in supporting the Fc fragment-induced polyclonal antibody response. It has previously been shown that the role of the macrophage in Fc-induced B-cell activation is the generation of mitogenic 14,000 MW Fc subfragments which then directly induce B cells to proliferate (18, 20). The addition of aged macrophages to macrophage-depleted adult spleen cells was found to restore the polyclonal antibody response. This observation is reminiscent of the work of Heidrick and Makinodan (8) who found that adherent cells from aged mice cultured with adult nonadherent cells responded fully to SRBC, whereas aged nonadherent cells combined with adult adherent cells gave a depressed response comparable to unseparated aged spleen cells. In contrast Nordin and Buchholz (9) demonstrated that peritoneally derived macrophages from aged mice were not as effective as adult macrophages in restoring the antibody response to the thymus-independent antigen dinitrophenyl-β-adanylglycylglycyl (DHGG)–Ficoll. A possible reason for these differences could be that in the work of Heidrick and Makinodan (8) and ourselves T cells as well as macrophages are required whereas that of Nordin and Buchholz (9) is T cell independent, therefore different cellular interactions may be required in generating these responses.

T cells obtained from aged mice are defective as accessory cells in the Fc fragment-induced polyclonal antibody response (200 PFC vs 75 PFC). That T cells from aged mice show reduced reactivity was indicated by their inability to substitute for adult T cells in the polyclonal antibody response. A reduced number of T cells in aged spleen does not appear to be responsible since the optimal response was obtained with the same B:T cell ratio as observed with adult T cells. Moreover, the low level of T-cell replacing factor (Fc)TRF production, in response to Fc fragments, is indicative of a T-cell lesion. Thoman *et al.* (30) have recently reported that the T-cell signal required in the Fc fragment-induced polyclonal antibody response could be replaced by a soluble factor (Fc)TRF, produced by T cells when incubated with Fc fragments. This soluble T-cell factor exerts its effects directly at the level of the responding B-cell population. Adult T cells were found to be approximately threefold more efficient in generating (Fc)TRF than aged T cells. The existence of a lesion in the T-cell compartment of aged mice in generating cell-mediated and humoral immune responses has been extensively reported (3, 5, 11–14, 34–36). This T-cell defect has been characterized as a reduction in T-cell activity (34, 36) and/or an increase in suppressor T-cell function (3, 11, 12, 32). The role of aged T cells as suppressors in the system described here is unknown and must await further investigation.

The inability of aged T cells to support the Fc fragment-induced polyclonal antibody response does not preclude the possibility that a defect exists in the B compartment as well. Aged splenic B cells were found to be defective in their ability to proliferate and produce polyclonal antibody in the presence of Fc fragments. Fc subfragments, derived from macrophage-processing of Fc fragments (19), which directly induce B cells to proliferate in the absence of accessory cells (19), produced only a minimal B-cell proliferation in aged spleen cell populations indicating a B-cell lesion. Moreover, adult T cells were unable to restore the T-cell-depleted aged B-cell polyclonal response to levels greater than those obtained with aged T cells. This finding suggests that although adult T cells are capable of providing a greater amount of help than aged T cells, the aged B cells are incapable of being activated to the level of adult B cells. In addition, aged T cells were found to be unable to suppress the Fc-mediated polyclonal antibody response of adult spleen cells. These results rule out the possibility of suppressor T cells being responsible for the low responses of aged mice. Other investigators have described lesions in the B-cell activity of aged mice as well (6, 13, 14, 35, 36). In addition, spleen cells from aged mice show reduced ability to respond to the adjuvant properties of Fc fragments (Morgan and Weigle, manuscript in preparation). Experimentation is currently in progress to define the cellular lesions for the inability of Fc to augment the humoral immune response of aged mice. In summary, we have shown that in an immune model where the cellular functions are known, lesions in both the B-cell and T-cell compartments exist in the aged C57BL/6 mouse.

ACKNOWLEDGMENTS

The authors wish to thank Nancy Kantor for excellent technical assistance and Janet Kuhns for secretarial expertise.

REFERENCES

1. Waldorf, D. S. Wilkens, R. F., and Decker, J. L., *JAMA* **203,** 111, 1968.
2. Friedman, D., Kerser, V., and Globerson, A., *Nature (London)* **251,** 545, 1974.
3. Callard, R., and Basten, A., *Cell. Immunol.* **31,** 13, 1977.
4. DeLima, G., Wilkinson, M. J., Smith, G. S., and Walford, R. L., *J. Gerontol.* **29,** 261, 1974.
5. Segre, M., and Segre, D., *J. Immunol.* **116,** 731, 1976.
6. Callard, R. E., Basten, A., and Waters, L. K., *Cell. Immunol.* **31,** 26, 1977.
7. Nordin, A. A., and Adler, W. H., *In* "Developmental Immunobiology" (G. Siskind, S. Litwin and M. Weksler, Eds.), p. 215. Grune & Stratton, New York, 1979.
8. Heidrick, M. L., and Makinodan, T., *J. Immunol.* **111,** 1502, 1973.
9. Nordin, A. A., and Buchholz, M. A., *In* "Techniques in Aging—Immunobiology Research" (W. H. Adler and A. A. Nordin, Eds.). CRC Press, New York, 1981, in press.
10. Callard, R. E., and Basten, A., *Cell Immunol.* **31,** 13, 1977.
11. Goidl, E. A., Innes, J. B., and Weksler, M. E. *J. Exp. Med.* **144,** 1037, 1976.
12. Weksler, M. E., Innes, J. B., and Goldstein, G., *J. Exp. Med.* **148,** 996, 1978.
13. DeKruyff, R. H., Kim, Y. T., Siskind, G. W., and Weksler, M. E., *J. Immunol.* **125,** 143, 1980.
14. Szewczuk, M. R., and Campbell, R. J., *Nature (London)* **286,** 164, 1980.
15. Hallgren, H. M., Buckley, C. E., Gilbertsen, U.A., and Yunis, E. J., *J. Immunol.* **111,** 1101, 1975.
16. Talal, N., *In* "Autoimmunity" (N. Talal, Ed.), p. 184. Academic Press, New York, 1977.
17. Berman, M. A., and Weigle, W. O., *J. Exp. Med.* **146,** 241, 1977.

18. Morgan, E. L., and Weigle, W. O., *J. Exp. Med.* **150,** 256, 1979.
19. Morgan, E. L., and Weigle, W. O., *J. Exp. Med.* **151,** 1, 1980.
20. Morgan, E. L., and Weigle, W. O., *J. Immunol.* **124,** 1330, 1980.
21. Morgan, E. L., Walker, S. M., Thoman, M. L., and Weigle, W. O., *J. Exp. Med.* **152,** 113, 1980.
22. Morgan, E. L., Thoman, M. L., Walker, S. M., and Weigle, W. O., *J. Immunol.* **125,** 1275, 1980.
23. Morgan, E. L., and Weigle, W. O., *J. Exp. Med.*, in press, 1981.
24. Morgan, E. L., Thoman, M. L., and Weigle, W. O., *J. Exp. Med.* **153,** 1161, 1981.
25. Porter, R. R., *Biochem. J.* **73,** 119, 1959.
26. Spiegelberg, H. L., *In* "Textbook of Immunopathology" (P. A. Miescher and H. J. Müeller-Eberhard), P. 1101. Grune & Stratton, New York, 1976.
27. Ly, I. A., and Mishell, R. I., *J. Immunol. Methods* **5,** 239, 1974.
28. Mueller, J., Brun del Re, G., Buerki, H., Keller, H. U., Hess, M. W., and Cottier, H., *Eur. J. Immunol.* **5,** 270, 1975.
29. Julius, M. H., Simpson, E., and Herzenberg, L. A., *Eur. J. Immunol.* **3,** 645, 1973.
30. Thoman, M. L., Morgan, E. L., and Weigle, W. O., *J. Immunol.*, in press, 1981.
31. Jerne, N. K., and Nordin, A. A., *Science* **140,** 405, 1963.
32. Kettman, J., and Dutton, R. W., *J. Immunol.* **104,** 1558, 1970.
33. Nordin, A. A., and Adler, W. H., *In* "Proceedings of the Fifth Irwin Strasburger Memorial Symposium on Immunology." Grune & Stratton, New York, 1981, in press.
34. Price, G. B., and Makinodan, T., *J. Immunol.* **108,** 403, 1972.
35. Friedman, D., Keiser, V., and Globerson, A., *Nature (London)* **251,** 545, 1974.
36. Doria, G., D'Agostaro, G., and Gararini, M., *Cell Immunol.* **53,** 195, 1980.

CELLULAR IMMUNOLOGY **63**, 28–41 (1981)

Modulation of Natural Cytotoxicity by Alloantibodies

IV. A Comparative Study of the Activation of Mouse Spleen Cell Cytotoxicity by Anti H-2 Antisera, Interferon, and Mitogens

RAJIV K. SAXENA, WILLIAM H. ADLER, AND ALBERT A. NORDIN

Clinical Immunology Section, Gerontology Research Center, Baltimore City Hospitals, Baltimore, Maryland 21224

Received December 15, 1980; accepted May 11, 1981

Comparisons were made between the characteristics of cytotoxicity activation in mouse spleen cells, induced by specific anti-H-2 antiserum, interferon (IF), interferon inducer (poly (I:C)), and mitogens (concanavalin A (Con A), pokeweed mitogen (PWM)). Important differences were found in the cytotoxicity activation associated with these agents: (a) The cytotoxic enhancing effect of anti-H-2 antiserum was comparatively rapid and was more pronounced in the first 4 hr of the assay, whereas, IF, poly (I:C), and the mitogens were most effective at 20 hr. (b) Anti-IF antiserum could neutrilize the stimulatory effects of IF and poly (I:C) on the cytotoxic activity of mouse spleen cells but had no influence on the stimulatory effects of anti-H-2 antiserum, PWM, and succinyl Con A. (c) The stimulatory effect of anti-H-2 antiserum was target specific and was observed when the K562 cell line was used as the target but not when YAC, P815, or WFu/G1 target cell lines were used. Stimulatory effects of all the other agents were nonspecific and did not depend on the target cells employed. (c) Cellular fractionation studies suggested that the alloantisera and interferon directly activated the natural killer (NK) cells without any participation of T-cells, B-cells, or macrophages. Both T-cells and NK cells, however, contributed to the mitogen-enhanced cytotoxicity of mouse spleen cells. These results indicated that the mechanism by which anti-H-2 antisera induce NK augmentation in mouse spleen cells is distinct from that of interferon and mitogens.

INTRODUCTION

Spleen cells derived from unimmunized mice can lyse a variety of tumor cells *in vitro* (1–3). This cytotoxic activity has been attributed to natural killer (NK)[1] cells which are believed to be distinct from conventional T cells, B cells, and macrophages (1–3). Previous studies from our laboratory have shown that the treatment with specific anti-H-2 antiserum enhanced the NK activity of mouse spleen cells against a human leukemia cell line, K562 (4, 5). Participation of T cells, B cells, or macrophages was not required and the alloantibodies seem to exert their effect directly by binding to NK cells (4, 5). A survey of literature indicates that several other agents also augment the cytotoxicity of mouse spleen cells *in vitro*. Interferon (IF) is a potent stimulator of NK activity (6, 7). Some other agents like poly (I:C)

[1] Abbreviations used: C, complement; Con A, concanavalin A; ELA index, early lysing ability index; E:T, effector:target ratio; IF, interferon; NK, natural killer; nu/nu, nude mice; Poly (I:C), polyinosinic:polycytidylic acid; PWM, pokeweed mitogen; SCA, succinyl Con A.

0008-8749/81/130028-14$02.00/0

and LPS may induce the generation of IF and thereby cause an augmentation in cytotoxic activity (6). The possibility existed that the NK enhancing effect of alloantibodies may also be mediated by IF. A second possibility is that the alloantibodies may mimic the action of certain mitogenic plant lectins which can nonspecifically bind to the cell membrane and also induce cytotoxicity in mouse spleen cells (8–10). Alternatively, the mechanisms of action of alloantibodies may be entirely different from those of interferon inducers or mitogens.

In the present paper, we have attempted to clarify these issues by comparing many parameters of cytotoxicity activation by alloantisera, IF, poly (I:C), and two mitogens (Con A, PWM). Cell fractionation studies were also included to help identify the cell types involved in the activation and effector phase of induction of augmented cytotoxic activity in mouse spleen cells by different test agents. Our results suggest that the NK augmentation by alloantisera is not mediated by IF and unlike mitogens does not represent a nonspecific activation of cytotoxic cells. Unlike all other agents tested, the enhanced NK activity of alloantiserum-treated spleen cells was found to be restricted to certain target cells only. It appears therefore that the alloantibodies may in some way act by modulating the effector–target interaction leading to an enhanced target lysis by alloantibody-coated NK cells.

MATERIALS AND METHODS

Animals. Six- to sixteen-week-old female Balb/c and C57BL/6J mice were obtained from Jackson Laboratories, Bar Harbor, Maine. Eight- to sixteen-week-old female nude mice on a Balb/c background were obtained from NIH.

Chemicals and antisera. Poly (I:C) (polyinosinic:polycytidylic acid) sodium salt was obtained from P-L Biochemicals, Milwaukee, Wisconsin. Con A (concanavalin A) was prepared from jack bean meal as described by Agrawal and Goldstein (11) SCA (succinyl Con A) was prepared as described by Gunther *et al.* (12). Mouse fibroblast interferon (56,000 Units/mg protein) was a product of Calbiochem-Behring Corp., San Diego, California. Pokeweed mitogen was obtained from Sigma Chemical Company, St. Louis, Missouri.

Anti-H-2 antisera were raised as described (4). Rabbit Anti-L (NDV) interferon antiserum was a kind gift from Dr. Kurt Paucker, Medical College of Pennsylvania. The antiserum had a neutralizing titer per milliliter of 1:100,000 against 8 reference units of interferon. Low-tox rabbit complement was a product of Cedarlane Laboratories, Ltd, Toronto, Canada, and was purchased from Accurate Chemical and Scientific Corp., Hicksville, N.Y. The anti-thy-1 IgM type antibody-producing hybridoma H013-4 was propagated in RPMI 1640 + 10% FCS and the pooled culture supernatant was used as a source of monoclonal anti-thy-1 antibody. Production of this hybridoma and characterization of monoclonal anti-thy-1 antibodies have been described (13).

Cellular fractionation. Macrophages were depleted from mouse spleen cells by treatment with carbonyl iron and magnet as described before (4). Depletion of B cells was attained by passing the spleen cells through nylon wool columns by the method of Julius *et al.* (14).

T cells were removed by treatment with anti-thy-1 monoclonal and antibody and complement treatment. For this purpose mouse spleen cells suspended in RPMI 1640 + 10% FCS (10×10^6/ml) were treated with a 1/100 dilution of hybridoma

H013-4 culture supernatant for 1 hr at 4°C. Cells were washed once and resuspended in an equal volume of 1/10 diluted rabbit complement and incubated at 37°C for another hour followed by three washings with fresh medium. With this protocol, 1 μl of culture supernatant was sufficient to lyse 10×10^6 C57BL/6J thymocytes. However, 10 μl of supernatant was routinely used for each 10×10^6 spleen cells to ensure an excess of antibody.

Target cells and ^{51}Cr-release assay. The human myeloid leukemia cell line, K562, the mouse tumor lines P815, YAC, and RL♂1, and the rat cell line WFu/G1 were initially obtained from NCI, NIH (Courtesy of Drs. R. B. Herberman and H. T. Holden) and maintained in tissue culture with RPMI 1640 medium supplemented with 10% heat-inactivated fetal calf serum. Target cells were labeled with ^{51}Cr (sodium chromate, 50–100 Ci/mg chromium) as described (4).

For the assay of cytotoxic activity of spleen cell preparations, variable numbers of effector spleen cells along with 10^4 ^{51}Cr-labeled target cells were placed in the round-bottom wells of microtiter plates (Falcon Products, Oxnard, Calif.). Total volume of the incubation mixture (RPMI 1640 + 10% FCS) was 0.2 ml which included the test dose of any agent. Plates were centrifuged at 400*g* for 3 min and incubated at 37°C. After incubation, 0.1 ml of supernatant was removed from each well without disturbing the cell pellet and the released radioactivity was determined in a Nuclear Chicago gamma counter. Base line release of ^{51}Cr was determined by incubating equal volume of medium with labeled target cells. For estimating the maximum release of ^{51}Cr, 10^4 labeled target cells were suspended in 2 ml of water and incubated with assay microtiter plates and the radioactivity in 1 ml of supernatant was determined. Percentage specific lysis of target cells was calculated by the formula:

$$\% \text{ lysis} = \frac{\text{cpm in supernatants of the test wells} - \text{cpm of base line release}}{\text{cpm released by water} - \text{cpm of base line release}} \times 100.$$

In different experiments, the upper limit of spontaneous release of ^{51}Cr in a 4-hr cytotoxicity assay was 8% for K562, 10% for YAC, RL♂1, and WFu/G1 and 15% for P815. In a 20-hr cytotoxicity assay, 15 to 20% of ^{51}Cr was spontaneously released by K562 cell line. In some experiments, data were transformed into lytic units. One lytic unit was defined as the number of effector cells needed to induce 10% specific target lysis. For this purpose, actual target lysis was obtained from the linear part of E:T vs lysis curves.

Composite 4- and 20-hr assay and early lysing ability (ELA) index. Assays were initiated with ^{51}Cr-labeled K562 target cells as described above. Samples (50 μl) of supernatants were removed from each well at 4 hr and again at 20 hr. Percentage lysis of target cells at 4 and 20 hr could be computed from the counts per minute obtained in these 4- and 20-hr aliquots. The ELA index for any effector cell preparation was calculated by the formula:

$$\text{ELA index} = \frac{\% \text{ specific lysis observed at 4 hr}}{\% \text{ lysis observed at 20 hr} - \% \text{ specific lysis observed at 4 hr}}.$$

The ELA index is a measure of the ability of a given effector cell preparation to lyse target cells in the earlier assay period (0 to 4 hr) as compared to the lytic ability of the same cell preparation at the later part of cytotoxicity assay (4 to 20 hr).

RESULTS

Dose and Time Dependence of Stimulation of Mouse Spleen Cell Cytotoxic Activity of Alloantiserum, Interferon, Poly (I:C), and Mitogens

In previous studies a 4-hr ^{51}Cr-release assay was utilized to demonstrate alloantisera augmentation of NK activity of mouse spleen cells against K562 target cells (4, 5). Many of the activating agents used in the present study showed no significant effect on lytic activity in a 4-hr assay. For this reason, the effects of all test agents were also studied in a cytotoxicity assay of longer (20 hr) duration. Results of a typical experiment showing the dose–response curves for the effects of anti-H-2 alloantiserum, interferon, poly (I/C), Con A, SCA, and PWM on cytotoxic activity of C57BL/6J spleen cells against K562 target cells in a 4- and 20-hr cytotoxicity assay are given in Fig. 1. All the above agents enhanced the cytotoxicity of spleen cells against K562 target cells in a 20-hr assay. The extent of augmentation depended upon the agent and its dose. Higher doses of most agents showed less of a stimulatory effect and Con A inhibited the spleen cell cytotoxic activity at high dose levels.

Differences in the time necessary for obtaining the effects of various stimulatory agents could be appreciated by compairing the ELA indices (early lysing ability index, see Materials and Methods). The ELA index is a relative measure of the lytic efficiency of a spleen cell preparation in the early period of the cytotoxic assay cultures, compared to the lytic efficiency in the later time period. Cytotoxic activities of eight different spleen cell preparations against K562 targets were studied in a 4- and 20-hr assay with different effector agents used at optimal doses. Mean values of percentage target lysis at 4 and 20 hr and the ELA indexes are shown in Table 1. The mean ELA index for control cell preparations was 0.77. This was increased to 1.75 ($P < 0.001$) in the presence of a 1/200 dilution of anti H-2^b antiserum. The addition of IF, poly (I:C) PWM amd SCA, however, markedly depressed the ELA indexes (0.26 to 0.38, $P < 0.001$ in all cases). These results indicated that the alloantiserum increased the lytic activity of spleen cells early in the cytotoxic reaction. All the other agents were comparatively slow in increasing the lytic activity and therefore the cytotoxic activity of spleen cells treated with these agents was seen to be greater in the 20-hr assay period of the cytotoxic reaction. In this respect the augmenting effect of alloantiserum differs from other activating agents.

Effect of Anti-IF Antiserum on the Augmentation of Cytotoxicity of Mouse Spleen Cell by Various Activating Agents

The stimulatory effect of poly (I:C) on NK activity is thought to be mediated through interferon (6). To test for the possibility of interferon mediation as the mechanism of cytotoxic activation by other agents, the effect of anti-IF antiserum on the cytotoxicity activation phenomenon was studied. Various activator agents were used to stimulate the cytotoxic activity of mouse spleen cells in the presence of different concentrations of anti-IF antiserum added to the cultures. Since al-

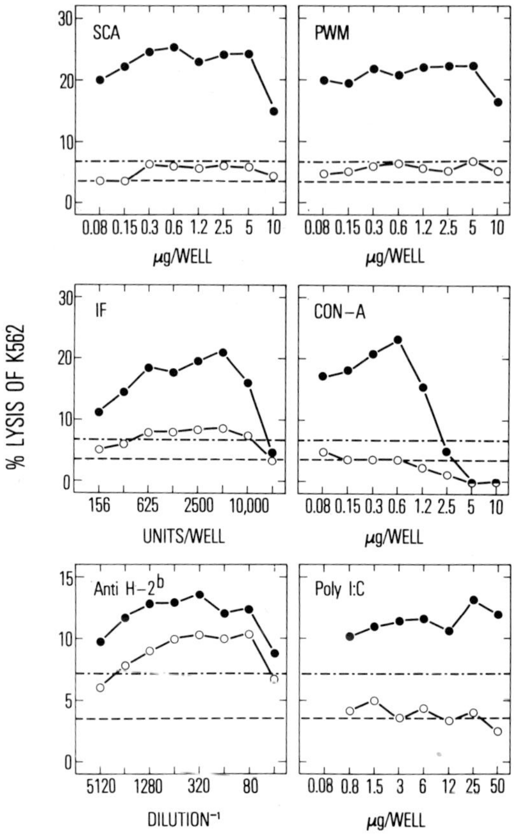

FIG. 1. Dose–response curves for the action of various activating agents on the NK activity of mouse spleen cells. NK activity of pooled C57BL/6J mouse spleen cells was tested against K562 cell line at an E:T ratio of 50:1, in a composite 4- and 20-hr ^{51}Cr-release assay (see Materials and Methods). Six different activating agents were added to the cytotoxicity incubation medium at various given concentrations. Cytotoxicity of control spleen cells at 4 hr (– – –) and 20 hr (------) as well as cytotoxicity generated in the presence of various concentrations of the activating agents at 4 hr (○) and 20 hr (●) are given in the figure. Each value of lysis is a mean of three replicate observations.

loantiserum shows a greater effect in a 4-hr assay and the other activator agents are more effective in a 20-hr assay, the modulating effects of anti-interferon antiserum were studied accordingly in the appropriate (4- or 20-hr) assay of cytotoxic activity. Results of a representative experiment are shown in Fig. 2. In the cultures augmented by the presence of IF it was found that as the concentration of anti-IF antiserum was increased the stimulatory effect of IF decreased until no effect was seen. The augmentation of NK activity, induced by anti-H-2^b antiserum, was not abolished by anti-IF antiserum even at the highest concentration used (Fig. 2A). The augmenting effect of poly (I:C) decreased in the presence of anti-IF antiserum whereas the augmenting effects of SCA and PWM were not influenced by the antiserum (Fig. 2B). Cytotoxic activation induced by Con A was also not influenced by anti-IF antiserum (results not shown). These results indicate that the stimulatory effects of alloantiserum and mitogens may not involve the participation of interferon.

TABLE 1

Effect of Various Stimulatory Agents on the Mouse Spleen Cell NK Activity at Two Time Periods[a]

	Mean percentage lysis of K562 target cells[b]					
Assay duration (hr)	Control	Anti-H-2^b + antiserum	+ IF	+ Poly (I:C)	+ PWM	+ SCA
4	4.7 (3.2– 8.0)[c]	15.8 (9.8–20.2)	9.4 (6.4–15.5)	6.6 (4.1–10.3)	11.2 (6.7–15.7)	7.5 (5.8–11.9)
20	10.8 (6.2–16.6)	25.6 (16.9–31.6)	35.6 (27.1–47.8)	29.0 (20.9–39.8)	45.7 (36.1–59.4)	36.2 (29.4–46.3)
Mean ELA index	0.77	1.75[d]	0.38[e]	0.31[e]	0.33[e]	0.26[e]

[a] Spleen cells were derived from female C57BL/6 mice, 6 weeks to 16 weeks of age.

[b] Cytotoxic activity of mouse spleen cells was studied in a composite 4- and 20-hr ^{51}Cr-release assay as described under Materials and Methods. The various stimulatory agents were added to the assay at the following concentrations: Anti-H-2^b antiserum, 1:200 dilution; IF, 10^3 units/well; poly (I:C), 20 μg/well; PWM, 2 μg/well, and SCA, 1 μg/well. An E:T ratio of 100:1 was used in all experiments. Each value of percentage lysis and ELA index is a mean of eight experiments.

[c] Values in parentheses denote the range of values obtained in eight experiments.

[d] Significant increase over control value ($P < 0.001$) as determined by paired t test.

[e] Significant decrease over control value ($P < 0.001$) as determined by paired t test.

Target Specificity of Spleen Cell NK Activity Augmented by Various Agents

To determine if there was any target specificity for the augmenting effect of the agents on NK activity, three murine cell lines (P815, YAC, RL♂1) and a rat cell line (WFu/G1) were also used as targets in addition to human leukemia cell line K562. Results in Table 2 show that the stimulatory effect of alloantiserum on NK activity could be obtained when K562 target cells were used but not when YAC, P815, or WFu/G1 tumor cells were employed as targets. Though NK activity of mouse spleen cells against RL♂1 cells was slightly higher in the presence of alloantiserum, the increase was considerably less than that observed with K562 target cells. In contrast to anti H-2 antisera, interferon augmented the NK activity of spleen cells regardless of the target cells used (Tables 2 and 3).

As indicated above, mitogens and poly (I:C) augment the cytotoxic activity of mouse spleen cells in a 20-hr assay rather than in a 4-hr assay. To test target specificity of these augmenting agents a 20-hr assay had to be utilized. However, due to high spontaneous release of ^{51}Cr from many target cell lines it was not possible to use a 20-hr cytotoxicity assay. To circumvent this problem, we cultured spleen cells with or without mitogens, interferon, or poly (I:C) for 20 hr, then washed the cells and studied their cytotoxic activity against the various cell lines in a 4-hr ^{51}Cr-release assay. Target-specific NK activation by alloantiserum (as obtained in a 4-hr assay) could be demonstrated by using this experimental protocol also (Table 3B). Pretreatment with various other agents resulted in the activation of cytotoxicity of mouse spleen cells against all target tumor cell lines used (Table 3A). Presence of the activating agent during the cytotoxicity assay was therefore not necessary to demonstrate the activation. These results along with the results

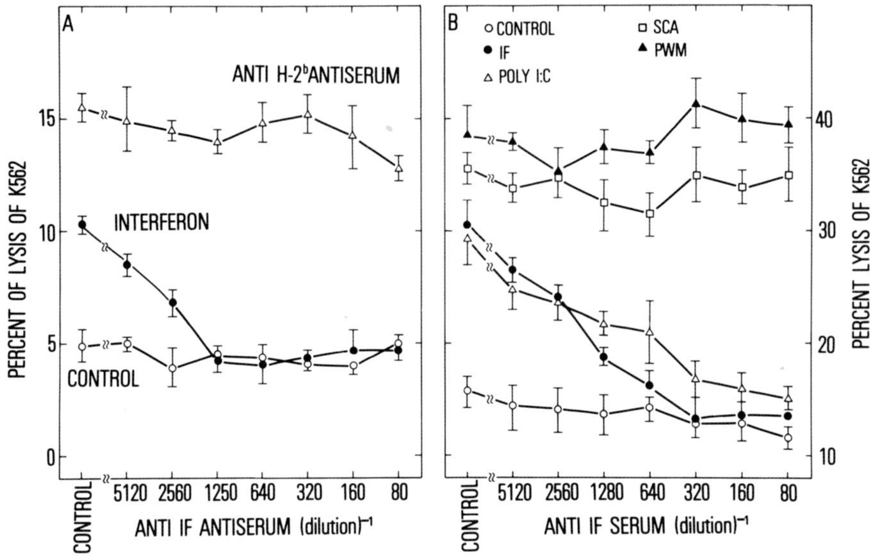

FIG. 2. Effect of anti-interferon antiserum on the stimulatory influence of some activity agents on the NK activity of mouse spleen cells. Natural cytotoxicity of pooled C57BL/6J mouse spleen cells against ^{51}Cr-labeled target cells was studied in a 4 (A) or 20-hr (B) assay at an E:T ratio of 100:1. Various activating agents were used at the following concentrations: Anti H-2^b antiserum, 1/200 dilution; interferon, 1000 units/well; PWM, 2 μg/well; SCA, 1 μg/well; and poly (I:C), 10 μg/well. Anti-interferon antiserum, at various given dilutions, was included in the assay medium. Each value of percentage lysis is a mean of three replicate observations ±SD.

in Table 2 indicate that while most NK activating agents increased the cytotoxic activity nonspecifically against all target cell lines, the stimulating effect of alloantiserum could only be observed against the K562 (and to some extent against RL♂1) target cell line.

We have previously shown that the augmentation of mouse spleen cell cytotoxicity in response to anti-H-2 antisera does not require participation of T cells, B cells, or macrophages and the alloantibodies seem to exert their effect directly by binding to NK cells (4, 5). In order to understand possible roles of different cell types on the cytotoxicity enhancement by various other agents, cellular fractionation studies were carried out.

Role of B Cells and Macrophages

In order to identify the role of B cells and macrophages in mitogen- and (Poly I:C)-augmented cytotoxic activity, spleen cells were subjected to carbonyl iron and magnet treatment or were passed through nylon wool columns, prior to studying their responsiveness to activating agents. Results of three such experiments are given in Table 4. Carbonyl iron and magnet treatment would deplete most phagocytic cells from spleen cell preparations and nylon wool columns remove most B cells and adherent cells. Both procedures failed to have a significant effect on the responses to the stimulatory action of IF, poly (I:C) and mitogens, indicating that B cells and macrophages do not play a significant role in the activation process resulting in a high level of induced cytotoxic activity. Similarly, depletion of B cells

TABLE 2

Effects of Alloantiserum and Interferon on the Cytotoxic Activity of C57BL/6J Mouse Spleen Cells against Different Cell Line Targets

Target cells	Experiment	Percentage lysis of target[a] Control	+ Anti-H-2 antiserum	+ Interferons
K562	1	3.3 ± 0.3	20.7 ± 0.6	8.1 ± 0.3
	2	1.8 ± 0.1	13.1 ± 0.8	4.4 ± 0.5
	3	8.7 ± 0.8	25.4 ± 1.2	14.2 ± 0.6
	4	3.0 ± 0.8	15.4 ± 0.9	9.2 ± 0.2
WFu/G1	1	1.8 ± 0.5	1.5 ± 0.1 (NS)	6.5 ± 1.1
	2	0.8 ± 0.4	1.2 ± 0.5 (NS)	3.1 ± 0.7
YAC	1	30.4 ± 1.2	27.6 ± 1.0 (NS)	40.0 ± 2.1
	2	32.7 ± 1.8	34.0 ± 1.6 (NS)	40.3 ± 2.7
	3	15.5 ± 1.3	18.1 ± 2.5 (NS)	30.0 ± 2.2
	4	15.9 ± 1.8	15.9 ± 1.5 (NS)	23.9 ± 0.7
RL♂1	1	10.6 ± 0.6	14.8 ± 1.5	22.3 ± 0.5
	2	12.7 ± 1.2	16.1 ± 0.8	23.5 ± 1.4
P815	1	0.8 ± 0.4	0.9 ± 0.3 (NS)	2.7 ± 0.5
	2	2.8 ± 1.6	3.2 ± 1.4 (NS)	5.4 ± 0.3

[a] Spleen effector cells were derived from C57BL/6J mice, 8 to 20 weeks of age. NK activity was tested against the target cells in a 4-hr ^{51}Cr-release assay at an E:T ratio of 100:1. Anti-H-2^b antiserum was added at a final dilution of 1/200 and mouse fibroblast interferon was added at a concentration of 1000 units/well. Each value of percentage lysis is a mean of four replicate observations ±SD. NS, no significant effect.

and macrophages after the spleen cells were treated with various test agents did not have any significant effect on the augmented cytotoxic activity of these cell preparations (results not shown). Effector cells responsible for induced cytotoxic activity in activated mouse spleen cells therefore do not appear to be B cells or macrophages.

Role of T Cells in the Activation Process

In order to understand the role of T cells in the process of stimulation of cytotoxic activity by different test agents, we depleted thy-1-bearing cells from spleen cells before or after the spleen cell preparations were treated with various agents. Selection of anti-thy-1 antiserum/antibody preparation to be used for the depletion of T cells was crucial to this study, since many such preparations have previously been shown to react with NK cells also (15, 16). Monoclonal anti-thy-1 antibodies secreted by hybridoma H013-4 were used for T-cell depletion since we have previously shown that treatment with this anti-thy-1 + C had no effect on NK activity but resulted in a complete depletion of T cells as assessed by (a) complete lysis of C57BL/6J thymocytes in parallel treatments and (b) by total abrogation of immune T-cell reactivity in spleen cells derived from alloimmunized mice (16).

The effect of various activating agents was studied in T-cell-depleted spleen cell

TABLE 3

Cytotoxic Activity of Control and Stimulated Spleen Cells against Different Target Cell Lines[a]

Expt	Activating agent	Percentage target lysis[b] K562	YAC	RLδ1	P815	WFu/G-1
A	None	2.3 ± 0.5	17.5 ± 1.1	17.6 ± 1.0	0.8 ± 0.6	2.4 ± 0.5
	IF	9.7 ± 0.8	43.7 ± 0.5	45.0 ± 4.8	3.5 ± 0.7	8.0 ± 0.8
	Poly (I:C)	10.3 ± 0.9	47.4 ± 1.5	63.8 ± 1.2	3.9 ± 0.7	10.3 ± 1.3
	Con A	20.6 ± 0.6	60.7 ± 1.1	78.9 ± 0.6	7.6 ± 0.7	14.2 ± 2.1
	PWM	20.6 ± 0.2	54.4 ± 0.6	72.9 ± 3.4	24.5 ± 1.7	19.7 ± 1.2
B	None	3.9 ± 0.4	9.5 ± 0.2	—	—	—
	Anti-H-2^b antiserum	10.1 ± 0.2	8.1 ± 1.0	—	—	—

[a] Pooled C57BL/6J spleen cells (10×10^6/ml) were cultured for 20 hr in round-bottom microtiter plates (0.2-ml cell suspension/well) at 37°C. The individual agents were present in the cultured medium at the following concentrations. IF, 1000 U/well; poly (I:C), 20 μg/well; Con A, 0.5 μg/well; PWM, 2 μg/well; anti-H-2^b antiserum, 1:200 dilution.

[b] Cytotoxicity of control or activated cells was studied in a 4-hr (expt. A) or 20-hr (expt. B) ^{51}Cr-release assay using various target cell lines, at an E:T ratio of 100:1. Each value of percentage lysis is a mean of three replicate observations ±SD.

preparations from C57BL/6J or nude mice. Results of representative experiments given in Table 5 indicate that the lack of thy-1 bearing cells did not prevent the augmentation of cytotoxic activity by anti-H-2 antisera, IF, and poly (I:C). However, there was no augmentation of cytotoxic activity by Con A or PWM in these

TABLE 4

Effect of B-Cells and Macrophage Depletion on the Activation of Cytotoxicity of Mouse Spleen Cells by Various Activating Agents

Expt	Source of effector cells	Treatment[a]	E:T	Percentage lysis of K562 target cells[b] Control	+ IF	+ Poly (I:C)	+ Con A	+ PWM
1	C57BL/6J	None	100:1	7.0 ± 0.9	12.4 ± 0.4	16.9 ± 0.7	21.3 ± 0.8	34.4 ± 1.3
		CO-Fe, magnet	100:1	6.3 ± 0.4	11.2 ± 0.4	15.2 ± 0.9	22.5 ± 0.7	42.5 ± 0.3
		Nylon wool column	100:1	11.9 ± 0.6	20.6 ± 0.9	24.8 ± 1.5	45.8 ± 1.2	66.8 ± 1.6
2	C57BL/6J	None	100:1	9.5 ± 1.0	15.5 ± 1.3	24.8 ± 1.3	29.6 ± 1.5	43.5 ± 0.4
		CO-Fe, magnet	100:1	6.5 ± 0.8	13.1 ± 1.0	19.0 ± 1.3	29.2 ± 0.9	48.8 ± 1.5
		Nylon wool column	100:1	12.0 ± 0.6	22.7 ± 1.5	22.5 ± 1.5	43.3 ± 4.3	64.9 ± 0.9
3	Balb/c	None	50:1	4.1 ± 1.0	16.9 ± 1.1	16.3 ± 1.0	14.7 ± 1.1	14.5 ± 1.3
		Nylon wool column	25:1	2.2 ± 0.9	15.5 ± 0.6	10.9 ± 1.1	18.4 ± 1.1	13.9 ± 0.5

[a] Effector spleen cells were subjected to carbonyl iron and magnet treatment (CO-Fe), or passed through a nylon wool column as described in the text, prior to the initiation of the cytotoxicity assay.

[b] Cytotoxic activity of spleen cells was studied in a 20-hr ^{51}Cr-release assay using K562 target cells. Test agents were present in the assay medium at the following concentrations. IF, 1000 U/well; poly (I:C), 20 μg/well; Con A, 0.5 μg/well; PWM, 2 μg/well. Each value of percentage lysis is a mean of four replicate observations ±SD.

TABLE 5

Augmentation of Cytotoxic Activity of T-Cell-Depleted Mouse Spleen Cells

Expt	Source of effector cells[a]	Percentage lysis of K562 target cells[b]					
		None	Anti-H-2 + antisera	+ IF	+ Poly (I:C)	+ Con A	+ PWM
1	C57BL/6J	1.8 ± 0.3	13.3 ± 0.8	11.5 ± 1.3	10.4 ± 2.2	0.4 ± 0.6	2.5 ± 0.5
2	C57BL/6J	1.4 ± 0.6	12.1 ± 0.9	11.4 ± 0.4	12.9 ± 0.5	−0.3 ± 0.5	1.8 ± 0.8
3	C57BL/6J	1.5 ± 0.3	9.8 ± 0.7	8.5 ± 0.6	9.2 ± 2.0	0.3 ± 0.4	0.6 ± 0.5
4	nu/nu	5.4 ± 0.4	9.1 ± 0.6	24.6 ± 2.3	23.6 ± 2.3	5.7 ± 0.7	7.8 ± 1.1
5	nu/nu	5.9 ± 1.1	9.8 ± 1.5	22.8 ± 0.7	21.2 ± 2.2	4.0 ± 0.3	6.1 ± 1.1

[a] Spleen cells derived from C57BL/6J or nu/nu mice were treated with anti-thy-1 monoclonal antibody and complement before use in the assay.

[b] Cytotoxicity of effector cell preparations was tested against K562 target cells in a 20-hr ^{51}Cr-release assay. Test agents were included in the assay medium at the following concentrations. Anti-H-2 antisera, 1/200 dilution; IF, 1000 units/well; poly (I:C), 20 μg/well; Con A, 0.5 μg/well; PWM, 2.0 μ/well. Anti-H-2^b antiserum was used with C57BL/6 spleen cells and anti-H-2^d antiserum was used with spleen cells derived from nu/nu mice (Balb/c background). Each value of percentage lysis is a mean of three replicate observations ±SD.

T-cell-depleted preparations. These results indicate that the presence of thy-1 bearing cells is necessary for the stimulatory effect of Con A and PWM on cytotoxic activity of spleen cells but is not necessary for the other agents to exert their effects.

In the second set of experiments, the effect of depleting thy-1-bearing cells on the cytotoxic levels of activated spleen cells was studied. Spleen cells were treated for 20 hr with IF, PWM, or Con A, washed and subjected to anti-thy-1 and C treatment. Cytotoxic activity of these control or thy-1-depleted spleen cells was studied against YAC cells in a 4-hr ^{51}Cr-release assay. The results (Table 6) show that the augmentation of cytotoxic activity induced by IF, PWM, and Con A was resistant to anti-thy-1 + C treatment and was not abolished completely even when activated spleen cell preparations were subjected to two sequential anti-thy-1 + C treatments. From these results it appears that besides T cells, other cell types may also contribute to the elevated cytotoxic activity level in mitogen-activated spleen cell preparations. Since the lack of involvement of B cells and macrophages in the activation and effector phase of activation process has already been shown, the thy-1-negative cells partially responsible for the mitogen-induced cytotoxic activity could be NK cells.

DISCUSSION

The present investigations were primarily aimed at gaining insights into the mechanism of NK enhancement by anti-H-2 antisera, a phenomenon which we have previously described (4, 5). Specific questions raised were, (a) does interferon mediate the action of an alloantiserum and (b) is the effect of alloantibody similar to the cytotoxicity enhancing effects of certain plant lectins which like alloantibodies, also bind to the cell membrane? A summary of results in Table 7 clearly shows that there are several important differences in the characteristics of cytotoxicity activation induced by various agents.

TABLE 6

Sensitivity of the Cytotoxic Activity of Stimulated C57BL/6J Spleen Cells to Anti-thy-1 + C Treatment

Expt	Spleen cells[a]	Treatment to spleen cells after stimulation[b]	Percentage lysis of YAC target cells stimulated with[c] None	IF	PWM	Con A
1	C57BL/6J	Complement (C)	8.8 ± 0.7	28.9 ± 0.8	46.1 ± 1.6	21.8 ± 0.8
		Anti-thy-1 + C	10.4 ± 0.5	27.1 ± 1.2	25.7 ± 0.2	15.3 ± 0.2
2	C57BL/6J	Complement (×2)[d]	19.3 ± 1.1	39.1 ± 1.6	59.9 ± 0.2	30.5 ± 0.7
		Anti-thy-1 + C	14.8 ± 0.1	36.0 ± 0.8	26.0 ± 0.2	19.1 ± 0.4
3	C57BL/6J	Complement	19.2 ± 0.7 (2.48)[e]	54.2 ± 1.7 (7.34)	77.6 ± 1.2 (13.02)	74.7 ± 0.4 (12.40)
		Anti-thy-1 + C	19.1 ± 1.2 (2.44)	48.4 ± 2.0 (6.56)	64.8 ± 0.8 (10.52)	65.5 ± 1.5 (10.40)

[a] Spleen cells (10×10^6/ml) were cultured in round-bottom microtiter plates (0.2-ml cell suspension/well) for 20 hr at 37°C. Stimulating agents were present in the culture medium at the following concentration: IF, 1000 U/well; PWM, 2 μg/well; Con A, 0.5 μg/well.

[b] Control or stimulated spleen cells were washed and treated either with anti-thy-1 and complement or with complement alone, as described in the text.

[c] Cytotoxic activity of control or activated spleen cells, treated either with anti-thy-1 + C or with C alone was studied in a 4-hr ^{51}Cr-release assay using YAC target cells at an E:T ratio of 100:1.

[d] Two sequential treatments with anti-thy-1 + C (or complement alone) were given.

[e] Lytic units per 10^6 spleen cells.

Alloantisera are the only agents which increased the early level of spleen cell cytotoxic activity indicating that the effect is rapid and does not require a long induction phase. Anti-IF antiserum did not block the cytotoxicity activation induced by alloantiserum or mitogens, suggesting that the effect of these agents may not be mediated by IF. These results do not rule out the possibility that alloantisera

TABLE 7

Comparison between the Parameters of Activation in response to Various Test Agents

Activation parameter	Anti-H-2 alloantisera	IF, Poly (I:C)	PWM, Con A
1. ELA index	Increases	Decreases	Decreases
2. Effect of anti-IF antiserum	No effect	Blocked	No effect
3. Target specificity	Yes	No	No
4. Requirement during activation phase			
B cells, macrophages	No	No	No
T cells	No	No	Yes
5. Requirement during effector phase			
B cells, macrophages	No	No	No
T cells	No	No	Yes (partially)
NK cells	Yes	Yes	Yes (partially)

or mitogens induced a different type of IF which was not neutralized by anti-IF antiserum utilized for this purpose. This possibility, however, does not appear very likely in view of major differences in other activation characteristics associated with alloantisera, IF/poly (I:C), and mitogens (Table 7).

The most intriguing and distinguishing feature of alloantiserum-induced NK augmentation in this study was that the effect was observed only when certain target cells were utilized. Thus anti-H-2 antiserum could augment the anti-K562 cytotoxic activity but not the anti-YAC, anti-P815, or anti-WFu/G1 cytotoxic activities of mouse spleen cells. K562 target cells were not unique in this regard since augmentation levels comparable to that obtained with K562 target cells have previously been demonstrated using five different human lymphoblastoid cell lines (5). In contrast to the effect of alloantiserum, cytotoxic activities generated in mouse spleen cells in response to IF/poly (I:C) and mitogens were not restricted to any particular target cell which favors a nonspecific activation of cytotoxic cells by these agents.

Spleen cell preparations pretreated with alloantiserum had augmented anti-K562 cytotoxic activity (4, 5). Moreover a given alloantiserum augmented the anti-K562 cytotoxicity only if it recognized H-2 antigens on the effector cells (4, 5). These observations clearly indicated that the reaction of alloantisera with effector cells was responsible for the NK augmenting effect. Our previous studies have also shown that the participation of T cells, B cells, or macrophages was not required for the effect of alloantisera on anti-K562 NK activity and the alloantibodies acted directly on NK cells (4, 5). In the present investigation, depletion of T cells, B cells, or macrophages, before or after treating the spleen cell preparations with IF or poly (I:C) did not abolish the cytotoxicity activation. A direct activation of NK cells by IF is therefore likely. These results are in agreement with previous reports (6, 7). Poly (I:C) can induce IF synthesis although the identity of cell(s) responsible for IF synthesis is not clear from our studies. Djeu *et al.* (6) have suggested that macrophages produce IF in response to poly (I:C) and IF inturn activated NK cells. On this point there seems to be a discrepancy between their study and our results since we could not abolish the augmenting effects of poly (I:C) by depleting macrophages from the mouse spleen cell population. A reason for this discrepancy may lie in the use of different strains of mice in the two studies (CBA/J and NIH Swiss by Djeu *et al.* (6) and C57BL/6J by us). Secondly, our method of macrophage depletion (carbonyl iron and magnet) was different from the one used by Djeu *et al.* (rayon wool column). It is possible that a small contamination by residual macrophages was responsible for the action of poly (I:C) in our studies. In view of these points the role of macrophages in poly (I:C)-induced activation of NK cells requires further clarification. It should, however, be noted that cells expressing the same antigenic specificity as NK cells have recently been shown to be capable of producing interferon (17).

A characteristic feature of the action of mitogens is an absolute requirement of T cells during the activation phase. This could either mean that (a) T cells are activated by these mitogens to become nonspecific cytotoxic cells or (b) other cell types are activated in the presence of mitogens, and T cells are required for this activation. Postactivation depletion of T cells reduced the cytotoxic activity of spleen cells activated with PWM and Con A, but a residual activation resistent to anti-thy-1 and complement treatment could invariably be demonstrated. Lack of complete abrogation of mitogen-induced cytotoxic activity by anti-thy-1 + C treatment was not due to insufficiency of anti-thy-1 antibodies used for this purpose since this concentration was about 10-fold higher than what would have completely abrogated immune T-cell reactivity under similar conditions (16). These results imply that the effector cytotoxic cells generated in response to mitogens were not entirely cytotoxic T cells. Depletion of B cells or macrophages prior to or after the mitogen-induced activation also did not influence the cytotoxic activity of the activated spleen cells. It therefore appears that besides T cells, NK cells may also partially contribute to the enhanced cytotoxic activity induced by mitogens.

A comparison of cytotoxicity activation characteristics of alloantiserum with IF/poly (I:C) and mitogens, as discussed above, clearly indicates that the NK augmentation in alloantiserum-treated spleen cells was neither due to an induction of IF synthesis nor was it a simulation of lectins by alloantibodies. Generalized activation of NK cells by anti-H-2 antiserum is also unlikely in view of the target specificity of its action. Since NK cells as a class do not become more cytotoxic as a result of treatment with alloantiserum, it appears likely that the alloantibodies may act by modifying the quality of interaction between effector and target cells. How the alloantibody-coated NK cells acquire higher cytotoxic activity selectively against certain target cells is not clear. Our previous work has shown that antisera reacting with any antigen(s) within H-2 region (including anti-Ia antisera) can augment the anti-K562 NK activity of mouse spleen cells. This indicates that no particular H-2 subregion is more relevant in the NK augmentation phenomenon. Recently we have found that anti-NK-1 antiserum, which reacts with a non-H-2 antigen on NK cells, also augments the anti-K562 cytotoxicity of mouse NK cells, suggesting that the interaction with H-2 antigens per se may also not be a necessary condition for NK augmentation.[2] It is likely that the target specificity of alloantiserum augmentation of NK activity may result from certain properties of target cells which may render them more susceptible to lysis by alloantibody-coated NK cells. Our further work in this direction has indicated that the presence of Fc receptors on target cells may be a necessary though not a sufficient factor in this regard.

ACKNOWLEDGMENTS

We wish to thank Ms. Eleanor Wielechowski for her secretarial assistance and Ms. Charlotte Adler for preparing the illustrations.

Note added in proof. We have recently observed that the normal C57BL/6 but not Balb/c nude spleen cells incubated with Con-A release some factor(s) in culture supernatant which can markedly enhance the NK activity of Balb/c nude mouse spleen cells, indicating that Con-A induces the production of some NK-stimulating factor(s) by T cells. A recent report by Kuribayashi *et al.* (*J. Immunol.* **126,** 2321, 1981) showing that interleukin-2 (a lymphokine released by mouse spleen cells in response to Con-A) is a potent stimulator of NK activity has also been confirmed by us. These results suggest that the Con-A-induced NK enhancement may be mediated by interleukin.

[2] R. K. Saxena, Q. B. Saxena, and W. H. Adler. Modulation of natural cytotoxicity by alloantibodies. V. The mechanism of a selective augmenting effect of anti H-2 antisera on the natural killer activity of mouse spleen cells. Submitted for publication.

REFERENCES

1. Herberman, R. B., Nunn, M. E., and Lavrin, D. H., *Int. J. Cancer* **16,** 216, 1975.
2. Kiessling, R., Klein, E., and Wigzall, H., *Eur. J. Immunol.* **5,** 112, 1975.
3. Herberman, R. B., and Holden, H. T., *Advan. Cancer Res.* **27,** 305, 1978.
4. Saxena, R. K., and Adler, W. H., *J. Immunol.* **123,** 846, 1979.
5. Saxena, R. K., Saxena, Q. B., and Adler, W. H., *Cell. Immunol.* **56,** 89, 1980.
6. Djeu, J. Y., Heinbaugh, J. A., Holden, H. T., and Herberman, R. B., *J. Immunol.* **122,** 175, 1979.
7. Senik, A., Gresser, I., Maury, C., Gidlund, M., Orn, A., and Wigzell, H., *Cell. Immunol.* **44,** 186, 1979.
8. Asherson, G. L., Ferluga, J., and Janossy, G., *Clin. Exp. Immunol.* **15,** 573, 1973.
9. Stavy, L., Trevis, A. J., and Feldman, M., *Cell. Immunol.* **3,** 623, 1972.
10. Perlman, P., and Holm, C., *Advan. Immunol.* **11,** 117, 1969.
11. Agrawal, B. B. L., and Goldstein, L. J., *Biochim. Biophys. Acta* **133,** 376, 1967.
12. Gunther, G. R., Wang, J. L., Yahara, I., Cunningham, B. A., and Edelman, G. M., *Proc. Nat. Acad. Sci. USA* **70,** 1012, 1973.
13. Marshak-Rothstein, A., Fink, P., Gridley, T., Raulet, D. H., Brown, M. J., and Gefter, M. L., *J. Immunol.* **122,** 2491, 1979.
14. Julius, M. H., Simpson, E., and Herzenberg, L. A., *Eur. J. Immunol.* **3,** 645, 1973.
15. Mattes, J. M., Sharrow, S. O., Herberman, R. B., and Holden, H. T., *J. Immunol.* **123,** 2851, 1979.
16. Saxena, R. K., Adler, W. H., and Nordin, A. A., *Immunol. Commun.* **9,** 371, 1980.
17. Minato, N., Reid, L., Cantor, H., Langyel, P., and Bloom, B. R., *J. Exp. Med.* **152,** 124, 1980.

CELLULAR IMMUNOLOGY 63, 42–56 (1981)

H-2 Antigens Incorporated into Phospholipid Vesicles Interact Specifically with Allogeneic Cytotoxic T Lymphocytes

ARTHUR H. HALE, DONALD L. EVANS, AND MARIA P. MCGEE

Department of Microbiology and Immunology, Bowman Gray School of Medicine, Wake Forest University, Winston-Salem, North Carolina 27103

Received December 19, 1980; accepted May 5, 1981

Subcellular fractions containing different H-2 antigens were tested for their ability to inhibit specific T cell–target cell conjugate formation. H-2-containing membrane vesicles, lentil-lectin-purified H-2 antigens solubilized with detergent (referred to in the text as high-density fraction) or incorporated into lipid vesicles, inhibited T cell–target cell conjugate formation effectively and specifically. However, two- to threefold more protein was required to inhibit T cell–target cell conjugate formation when detergent-solubilized lentil-lectin-purified H-2 antigens were tested. This suggests that a lipid matrix is advantageous for interaction with anti-H-2 T-cell receptors. Experiments were also undertaken to demonstrate specific binding of liposomes containing ^{125}I-labeled H-2 antigen to anti-H-2-specific cytotoxic T lymphocytes (CTLs). The binding of the ^{125}I-labeled H-2-containing liposomes was saturable and was specifically inhibited by unlabeled H-2 antigens. Monospecific anti-H-2 sera specifically inhibited the binding of liposomes containing H-2 antigen to the CTLs. The results suggest that a specific interaction can occur between serologically defined H-2 antigens and the receptor of anti-H-2 CTLs.

INTRODUCTION

The major histocompatibility antigens (H-2 in mice and HLA in humans) have been implicated as both stimulators and targets for syngeneic and allogeneic cytotoxic T lymphocytes (CTLs).[1] More specifically, the H-2K and/or H-2D ends of the major histocompatibility complex (MHC) in mice are responsible for the recognition process which occurs between thymus-derived cells (T cells) and stimulator or target cells (1). The evidence to date is compelling that the H-2 antigens recognized by alloantisera are closely associated to those recognized by T cells (2–8). In contrast, there is not conclusive evidence as to the identity of the H-2 antigens recognized by T cells (9–14). In addition, the remaining questions concerning the molecular requirements for interaction of T cells with the antigenic determinants require for their solution the capacity to analyze the specific association of isolated target antigen with the T-cell receptor.

Recently a number of laboratories have shown that detergent-solubilized H-2 antigens and reconstituted membrane vesicles are capable of specific elicitation of secondary CTL responses (6, 15–20). These experiments are consistent with the

[1] Abbreviations used: Con A, concanavalin A; C, complement; CTL, cytotoxic T lymphocytes; DOC, deoxycholate; E:T ratio, effector:target ratio; MHC, major histocompatibility complex; PBS, phosphate-buffered saline (0.15 *M* NaCl, 0.01 *M* potassium phosphate, pH 7.4).

0008-8749/81/130042-15$02.00/0

interpretation that the H-2 molecules recognized by T cells are the same as those defined serologically. However, the method used was indirect and did not prove specific and direct antigen recognition by the CTL receptor.

Previous attempts to inhibit the cytolytic activity of T cells have not been very successful (26). One probable reason is that most cytolytic assays require long incubation periods with CTLs mixed with target cells. Because CTLs can lyse multiple target cells within this period, the ability of any inhibitor to specifically reduce lysis is decreased. In this report we have used inhibition of T cell–target cell conjugate formation as a specific assay for the ability of subcellular fractions to interact with T cells. Berke *et al.* (21) described the formation of T cell–target cell conjugate using lymphocyte populations which were enriched for CTLs (20–35%). By using a population of lymphocytes obtained from the peritoneum of mice immunized with an allogeneic H-2 haplotype which induces responses highly enriched for CTLs (>70%), we have analyzed the ability of subcellular fractions to specifically inhibit T cell–target cell conjugate formation. The results indicated that specific inhibition of T cell–target cell conjugates by H-2 antigen-containing fractions does occur. The incorporation of these antigens into a lipid matrix facilitated their ability to specifically inhibit T cell–target cell conjugate formation. Also, from our results, it was clear that serologically defined antigens were responsible for the inhibition of T cell–target cell conjugate formation. In addition we have demonstrated direct specific binding of the H-2 antigens onto anti-H-2 Lyt 2+ cells. The results indicated that a specific interaction can occur between H-2-containing liposomes and receptors found on anti-H-2 CTL.

MATERIALS AND METHODS

Mice. Male and female mice of the following strains were used: BALB/c AnN (d,d), and BALB·B (b,b). These were produced in our own breeding colony from breeding stock obtained from Herman Eisen (Massachusetts Institute of Technology). Letters in parentheses indicate the H-2K and H-2D alleles.

Alloantiserum. Anti-H-2^d serum was raised by multiple intraperitoneal (ip) injections of 2.0×10^7 B10·D2 spleen cells into B10 mice. Anti-H-2^b alloantiserum was raised by multiple ip injections of 2.0×10^7 B10 spleen cells into B10·D2 mice. Antisera were exhaustively absorbed with a variety of tumor, fibroblast, and spleen cells. After absorption, with cells, no antibodies were found which were specific for a glycoprotein (determined by immunoprecipitation) with a molecular weight of approximately 70,000 daltons by immunoprecipitation with anti-H-2. Antibodies within these sera only precipitated proteins of approximately 45,000 and 12,000 daltons. This would suggest that these antisera are primarily directed against the H-2K and/or H-2D gene products.

Anti-thy 1.2 serum and guinea pig complement was purchased from Litton Bionetics (Kensington, Md.). Anti-Lyt 1 or anti-Lyt 2 antisera were obtained from Cedarlane Laboratories, Ontario, Canada.

Medium. RPMI 1640 (90 ml) was supplemented with L-glutamine, penicillin, streptomycin, 2-mercaptoethanol, and heat-inactivated fetal calf serum (56°C, 45 min, Flow Laboratories, Cockeyesville, Md.) as described previously (20).

Tumors. P815 (H-2^d) and EL-4 (H-2^b) were maintained by weekly ip transfers of 1.0×10^6 ascites cells in mice of the strain of origin, DBA/2 and C57/BL6, respectively.

Production of CTLs. Anti-H-2^d effector T cells primed 4 weeks earlier with 2.0×10^7 BALB/c spleen cells were elicited *in vivo* in BALB·B mice by injecting ip 1.0×10^7 irradiated (10,000 R, X-ray, Picker) MOPC-167 tumor cells (H-2^d). Anti-H-2^b peritoneal cells were elicited by injecting 1.0×10^7 irradiated (2000 R, X-ray, Picker) EL-4 cells ip into a BALB/c mouse primed 4 weeks earlier with BALB·B spleen cells (2.0×10^7). The peritoneal cells were harvested 7 to 8 days later.

T cells were purified by incubating the peritoneal cells in supplemental RPMI on plastic tissue culture plates (100 mm, Falcon) for 1 hr. The nonadherent population was further fractionated by passing the cells over nylon wool columns (27). The resultant nonadherent population was again passed through a fresh nylon wool column. After this procedure, the cell preparation contained greater than 95% T cells as determined by their susceptibility to lysis with anti-theta serum plus C. Before use in T cell–target cell conjugate assays, these T cells were then treated with anti-Lyt 1 plus C (Cedarlane Laboratories). Approximately 70% of the T cells were killed by this treatment, with only 25% loss of cytolytic activity. This population will be referred to as Lyt 2^+ T cells since this T-cell population was completely (>95%) lysed by treatment with anti-Lyt 2 plus C (Cedarlane Laboratories).

Target cells. BALB/c and BALB·B spleen cells were stimulated with concanavalin A (Con A) by incubating 5.0×10^7 spleen cells with 2.0 μg of Con A (Sigma, St. Louis, Mo.) in 5 ml of supplemented RPMI 1640 (37°C, 6% CO_2–94% air). After 2–3 days of incubation, cells were harvested and counted and viability was determined by trypan blue exclusion. For experiments requiring ^{51}Cr-labeled cells, Con A-stimulated cells were incubated with 200 μCi of $Na_2{}^{51}CrO_4$ (New England Nuclear, Boston, Mass.) in 0.5 ml of supplemented RPMI 1640 for 1.5 hr at 37°C in an atmosphere of 6% CO_2–94% air (13).

Cytotoxic assays. Cytotoxic cell-mediated assays: ^{51}Cr-labeled target cells (1.0×10^4) are mixed with serial dilutions of effector spleen cells in a total volume of 200 μl of supplemented RPMI 1640. This mixture was incubated 4–6 hr at 37°C in an atmosphere of 6% CO_2 and 94% air. The assay was stopped by diluting with cold phosphate-buffered saline and the amount of radioactivity in the supernatant and pellet was determined (13). Percentage specific release (spec. rel.) was calculated as 100 (E-C/1-C) where E is the fraction ^{51}Cr released by antigen-stimulated effector cells and C is the fraction of ^{51}Cr released by a mock-stimulated responder population.

Antibody-mediated cytotoxic assays were carried out essentially as previously described (13). Inhibition of anti-H-2 antibody plus complement mediated lysis by cells or subcellular fractions was performed as described previously (13).

Partial purification of H-2 antigens. Partial purification of H-2 antigens was done as described previously (20). Briefly, purified plasma membranes from P815 and EL-4 tumor cells were obtained as described by Esko *et. al.* (23). Antigens were solubilized by incubating the plasma membranes at room temperature for 10 min with sodium deoxycholate (DOC) (Sigma) in phosphate-buffered saline (PBS, 13). The detergent extracts were then centrifuged for 30 min at 100,000*g*. Sodium deoxycholate solubilized H-2 antigens were further purified by passing the resulting

100,000*g* supernatant over a *Lens culinaris*-conjugated Sepharose 4B column equilibrated in 0.2% deoxycholate in PBS. A final purification of the H-2 antigens of between 120- and 160-fold was obtained by these procedures (20).

Reconstitution of H-2 antigens into liposomes. Egg lecithin and cholesterol were purchased from Calbiochem (San Diego, Calif.). In a typical preparation, 200 μg of egg lecithin plus cholesterol (30% wt/wt) dissolved in chloroform was dried in the form of a film under N_2. This film was then dissolved into a solution containing partially purified H-2 antigens (0.2% DOC) at a lipid-to-protein ratio of 1:1. This solution was then dialyzed for 36–48 hr against PBS at room temperature. The dialysate was recovered as a opalescent solution with ≥80% of the protein associated with the vesicles. Characterization and isolation of liposomes was done as previously described (20). Partially purified H-2 antigens, and liposomes containing partially purified H-2 antigens, were analyzed by flotation isopycnic centrifugation (5–40% wt/wt sucrose density gradients). H-2 antigen-containing fractions were mixed with 60% (wt/wt) sucrose in PBS to give a final sucrose concentration of 40% (wt/wt). A linear density gradient of sucrose (5–40%) was layered on top of this sample. After 14 hr of centrifugation at 200,000*g* (4°C), fractions were collected and analyzed for the presence of H-2 antigens (assayed by inhibition of anti-H-2 plus complement mediated lysis), and for protein content (Lowry *et al.* (22)). Detergent-solubilized H-2 antigens are referred to as high-density H-2 antigens, because after dialysis against PBS, this protein fraction has a density greater than 1:14 g/cm^3. Liposomes (density between 1.11–1.06 g/cm^3) containing H-2 antigens were defined by the presence of lipid [^{14}C]phosphatidylcholine, protein (presence of [^{3}H]leucine or by direct measurement of protein (21)), and H-2 antigen content.

Removal of serologically defined H-2 specificities. To evaluate the relationship between serologically defined H-2 specificities and H-2 antigens which were responsible for inhibition of T cell–target cell conjugate formation we preincubated detergent-solubilized lentil-lectin-purified H-2 antigens with either normal mouse serum, or anti-H-2, serum at a final dilution of 1:50 or 1:25 at 4°C for 30 min. One tenth of a milliliter of the solubilized H-2 antigen fraction plus serum was incubated with 0.1 ml (packed volume) of *Staphylococcus* protein A conjugated to Sepharose 4B beads (Pharmacia, Piscataway, N.J.) for 10 min. The Sepharose 4B beads were removed by centrifugation (500*g*, 5 min) and the supernatant was mixed with egg lecithin plus cholesterol to form lipid vesicles as described above. Supernatants from this first incubation were tested for incomplete removal of the antigenic determinants by the different antisera. This was done by incubating each supernatant with fresh antisera (identical to the first antiserum used) and *Staphylococcus* protein A–Sepharose 4B beads. After removal of the beads by centrifugation, the resultant supernatant was incorporated into liposomes. The ability of the supernatants to inhibit T cell–target cell conjugate formation or bind to anti-H-2-activated T cells was compared to that of the unfractionated material. In all experiments described in this paper the supernatant material from the first incubation with antisera did not differ from the supernatant from the second incubation with respect to its ability to inhibit T cell–target cell conjugate formation or bind to anti-H-2-activated T cells.

T cell–target cell conjugate formation. T cell–target cell conjugates were made essentially as described by Gilmer *et al.*(24) Briefly, target cells (P815 and EL-4) were loaded with fluorescein diacetate by incubating 1.0×10^7 cells in a solution of 0.001% fluorescein diacetate in PBS at 37°C for 10 min.

Effector (Lyt 2^+) and target cells (with fluorescein diacetate) were mixed at ratios of 2:1 for both BALB·B anti-MOPC-167 and BALB/c anti-EL-4. In a total volume of 100 μl (RPMI 1640), purified T cells (25 μl), target cells (prelabeled with fluorescein diacetate, 25 μl), and 50 μl of a serial dilution of the H-2 antigen-containing preparation were added. The tubes were spun at 250*g* for 5 min in the cold and left on ice until conjugates were counted on an Olympus fluorescence microscope. The conjugates were easily observed because the T cells are small and not fluorescent, while the target cells are large and fluoresce strongly.

By our estimates from T cell–target cell conjugate formation assays, this population of Lyt 2^+ T-cells contained greater than 80% specific CTLs. Lyt 2^+ T cells were mixed with target cells at effector to target ratios of 1:1, 1:2, 1:4, etc. After formation of the conjugates on ice the cell mixtures were warmed to 37°C for 5 min and diluted (1:2) with supplemented RPMI 1640 containing 0.4% agar and 0.25% trypan blue. After 5 min the cells were examined under a phase microscope. The results indicate that >85% of the conjugates formed contained target cells incorporating trypan blue. These data suggest that most of the conjugates formed are between CTLs and target cells. Target cells or Lyt 2^+ T cells incubated alone did not incorporate trypan blue under the conditions used.

Iodination. Tumor cells were iodinated with ^{125}I (New England Nuclear) in the presence of lactoperoxidase and H_2O_2 (20).

RESULTS

Cytolytic Activity of the T-Cell Preparations

The preparations of Lyt 2^+ T cells used in this study were cytolytic and specific (Fig. 1). This cytolysis was T-cell mediated as indicated by the susceptibility of

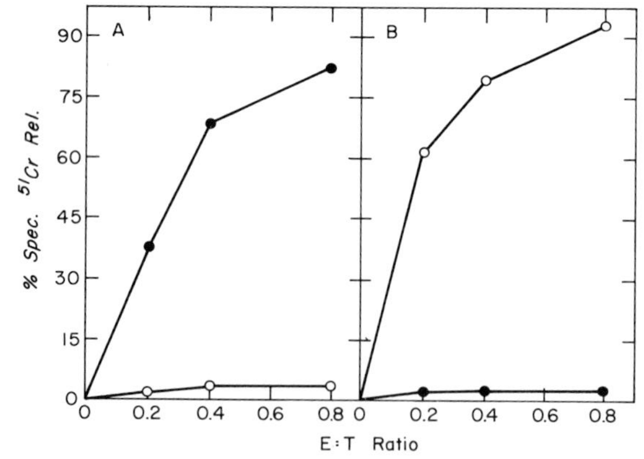

FIG. 1. Cytolytic activity of BALB/c anti-EL-4 (A) and BALB·B anti-MOPC-167(B) Lyt 2^+ T-cells were tested on ^{51}Cr-labeled concanavalin A-stimulated BALB/c (●) or BALB·B (○) spleen cells. The percentage spontaneous ^{51}Cr release was 18.2 and 15.7 for BALB·B and BALB/c target cells, respectively. (E:T ratio is effector-to-target ratio.)

this activity to anti-Thy 1.2 plus C. In addition greater than 80% of the cytolytic activity was mediated by cells which were Lyt 2^+ (Table 1).

Inhibition of T Cell–Target Cell Conjugates by Partially Purified H-2 Antigens

In order to evaluate the CTLs specific for the H-2K and H-2D ends of the MHC more closely, we have assayed for the ability of detergent-solubilized H-2 antigens and H-2 antigen-containing liposomes to inhibit T cell–target cell conjugate formation. From Table 2 it is clear that BALB/c anti-EL-4 T cell–target cell conjugate formation is specifically inhibited by H-2^b plasma membranes, detergent-solubilized H-2^b antigens, and H-2^b antigens incorporated into liposomes. In Table 3 essentially identical results are shown for BALB·B anti-MOPC-167 T cell–target cell conjugates. That is H-2^d containing fractions were able to specifically inhibit T cell–target cell conjugate formation. Subcellular fractions containing the inappropriate H-2 haplotype were not effective inhibitors of T cell–target cell conjugate formations. Consistently for both systems, the data suggest that H-2 liposomes and

TABLE 1

Surface Markers of Anti-H-2 CTLs[a]

Effector	Treatment	Percentage Spec. ^{51}Cr rel.[b] (E:T ratio, 1:1)
BALB/c anti-EL-4	NMS	67.7
	NMS + C	60.7
	Anti-thy 1.2	62.8
	Anti-thy 1.2 + C	6.3
	Anti-ly 1^+	60.4
	Anti-ly 1 $^+$ +C′	54.8
	Anti-ly^2	63.2
	Anti-ly2^+ + C	3.4
BALB·B anti-MOPC-167	NMS	52.8
	NMS + C	50.7
	Anti-thy 1.2	40.9
	Anti-thy 1.2 + C	4.1
	Anti-ly 1^+	50.1
	Anti-ly 1^+ + C	50.8
	Anti-ly 2^+	49.7
	Anti-ly 2^+ + C	3.8

[a] Ly 2^+ were treated with anti-thy 1.2, anti-Ly 1, or anti-Ly2 antiserum in the presence of complement (C; Cedarlane Laboratories). Effector cells (1×10^6) were incubated with a predetermined optimal concentration of each antiserum. After 30 min of incubation at room temperature, the cells were washed by centrifugation (500*g*) and rabbit C was added at a predetermined dilution. These (BALB/c anti-EL-4 or BALB·B anti-MOPC-167) cells were incubated for 20 min at 37°C, washed by centrifugation, and tested for cytolytic activity against Con A-stimualted BALB·B or BALB/c target cells, respectively. The Con A-stimulated BALB/c or BALB·B cells had a spontaneous 13.8 or 14.7% release of ^{51}Cr, respectively. NMS = normal mouse serum. All antisera tested here have been shown to be effective in removing the appropriate T-cell subpopulation (A. H. Hale, unpublished results).

[b] Each number represents the average of six determinations with a standard deviation for all measurements of not greater than 3.1%.

TABLE 2

Inhibition of BALB/c Anti-EL-4 T Cell–Target Cell Conjugate Formation by Detergent-Solubilized H-2 Antigens and H-2 Liposomes

Inhibitor[a]	Percentage target cells binding effector cells[b–d] 100[e]	50	25	12.5	6.25	0
Detergent-solubilized H-2^b antigens (high-density fractions)	7 ± 5	14 ± 6	36 ± 6	40 ± 6	50 ± 8	47 ± 6
H-2^b-EL-4 plasma membranes	6 ± 6	12 ± 4	18 ± 6	26 ± 9	38 ± 8	42 ± 5
H-2^b liposomes	6 ± 6	13 ± 7	22 ± 3	32 ± 6	44 ± 7	48 ± 4
Detergent-solubilized H-2^d antigens (high-density fractions)	38 ± 5	46 ± 8	40 ± 4	38 ± 6	35 ± 6	44 ± 6
H-2^d lipsomes	48 ± 9	46 ± 7	40 ± 8	49 ± 8	47 ± 6	43 ± 8

[a] All H-2 antigen preparations were partially purified from lentil lectin columns.

[b] BALB/c anti-EL-4 T-cells were mixed as described under Materials and Methods with EL-4 cells labeled with fluorescein diacetate with or without the presence of H-2 antigen-containing fractions at an effector:target ratio of 2:1.

[c] BALB/c anti-EL-4 T-cells formed T cell–target conjugates with MOPC-167 (H-2^d) cells at a level of 6 ± 2% (effector:target ratio 2:1).

[d] Each experiment was done in quadruplicate with approximately 200 target cells counted for each determination. Standard deviations for each measurement are also given.

[e] μg of H-2 protein per assay.

purified plasma membranes are better inhibitors of T cell–target cell conjugate formation than the detergent-solubilized H-2 antigens (high-density fraction). The experiments described in Tables 3 and 4 were done at the same time with the same subcellular fractions. In Table 4 a summary of five experiments indicates the amount of protein required to inhibit T cell–target cell conjugate formation by 50%. The results clearly indicate that H-2 antigens incorporated into a lipid matrix are more effective inhibitors of conjugate formation.

In order to further establish the identity of the molecules responsible for the inhibition of T cell–target cell conjugate formation, we removed the serologically defined H-2 antigens by incubating the detergent-solubilized lentil lectin fraction with anti-H-2 serum in the presence of *Staphlococcus* protein A–Sepharose 4B beads as described under Materials and Methods. The results (Table 5) indicate that anti-H-2 antisera were capable of complexing and specifically removing the serologically defined H-2 antigens responsible for inhibition of T cell–target cell conjugate formation. Sequential addition of more anti-H-2 serum, followed by removal with *Staphylococcus* protein A–Sepharose 4B beads did not alter the results shown in Table 5 (data now shown).

Binding of H-2 Containing Liposomes to Anti-H-2 Lyt 2^+ T Cells

BALB·B anti-MOPC-167 Lyt 2^+ T cells bind H-2^d containing liposomes specifically (Fig. 2). This binding is dependent upon the amount of protein added per assay and became saturated at approximately 10 μg of protein per assay (Fig. 2). Addition of more than 24.0 μg of protein per assay, however, resulted in greater binding. This increase in binding (observed when greater than 22–26 μg of protein is added per assay) is probably due to nonspecific absorption of the liposomes onto

TABLE 3

Inhibition of BALB·B Anti-MOPC-167 T Cell–Target Cell Conjugate Formation by Detergent-Solubilized H-2 Antigens and H-2 Liposomes

Inhibitor[a]	Percentage target cells binding effector cells[b–d]					
	100[e]	50	25	12.5	6.25	0
Detergent-solubilized $H\text{-}2^d$ antigens						
(high-density fractions)	10 ± 6	21 ± 7	30 ± 7	39 ± 8	37 ± 6	40 ± 6
$H\text{-}2^d$-P815 plasma membranes	9 ± 6	10 ± 5	15 ± 8	24 ± 7	39 ± 4	38 ± 4
$H\text{-}2^d$ lipsosomes	9 ± 4	14 ± 8	13 ± 4	21 ± 8	43 ± 8	40 ± 8
Detergent-solubilized $H\text{-}2^b$ antigens						
(high-density fractions)	42 ± 2	39 ± 2	41 ± 4	42 ± 6	45 ± 6	38 ± 4
$H\text{-}2^b$ lipsomes	40 ± 6	48 ± 7	46 ± 3	47 ± 12	41 ± 6	37 ± 6

[a] All H-2 antigen preparations were partially purified from lentil lectin columns.

[b] BALB·B anti-MOPC T-cells were mixed as described under Materials and Methods with MOPC-167 ($H\text{-}2^d$) cells labeled with fluorescein diacetate with or without the presence of H-2 antigen-containing fractions at an effector target ratio of 2:1.

[c] BALB·B anti-MOPC-167 T-cells formed T cell–target conjugates with EL-4 cells at a level of 11 ± 7% (effector:target ratio of 2:1).

[d] Each experiment was done in duplicate with approximately 200 target cells counted for each determination. Standard deviations for each measurement are also given.

[e] μg of H-2 protein per assay.

TABLE 4

Amount of Protein Needed to Inhibit T Cell–Target Cell Conjugate Formation by 50%[a]

Effector	Inhibitor	Amount of protein[b] (μg)
BALB/c anti-EL-4	Detergent-solubilized $H\text{-}2^b$ antigens (high-density fraction)	33.8 ± 2.8
	$H\text{-}2^b$ plasma membranes	9.7 ± 3.2
	$H\text{-}2^b$ liposomes	13.8 ± 3.8
	Detergent-solubilized $H\text{-}2^d$ antigens (high-density fraction)	⩾150.0
	$H\text{-}2^d$ liposomes	⩾150.0
BALB·B anti-MOPC-167	Detergent-solubilized H-2 antigens (high-density fraction)	40.7 ± 4.2
	$H\text{-}2^d$ plasma membranes	13.8 ± 4.1
	$H\text{-}2^d$ liposomes	16.7 ± 2.9
	Detergent-solubilized $H\text{-}2^b$ antigens (high-density fraction)	⩾150.0
	$H\text{-}2^b$ liposomes	⩾150.0

[a] The T-cell-target cell conjugate (at an effector:target ratio of 2:1) was mixed as described under Materials and Methods. The 50% level was obtained from a linear plot of the amount of protein plotted against the percentage target cell binding.

[b] These values represent the mean of five experiments with the standard error given.

TABLE 5

Serological Specificity Required to Inhibit T Cell–Target Cell Conjugates[a–d]

Effector system	Inhibition H-2 antigen liposomes (μg)	Serum	Percentage target cell binding effector cells (E:T ratio, 2:1)
BALB/c anti-EL-4	None	None	61.7 ± 3.8
	H-2^d (100)	None	60.1 ± 8.8
	H-2^b (5)	None	41.7 ± 6.2
	H-2^b (5)	Anti-H-2^b	40.7 ± 3.2
	H-2^b (5)	Anti-H-2^b	58.7 ± 6.8
	H-2^b (15)	None	21.7 ± 10.8
	H-2^b (15)	Anti-H-^{d}	20.7 ± 6.3
	H-2^b (15)	Anti-H-2^b	55.7 ± 8.2
BALB·B anti-MOPC-167	None	None	52.8 ± 2.7
	H-2^b (100)	None	50.7 ± 6.0
	H-2^d (5)	None	36.7 ± 4.3
	H-2^d (5)	Anti-H-2^b	35.8 ± 5.7
	H-2^d (5)	Anti-H-2^d	47.8 ± 6.1
	H-2^d (15)	None	15.6 ± 5.3
	H-2^d (15)	Anti-H-^{2}	15.8 ± 8.1
	14.2^d (15)	Anti-H-2^d	47.8 ± 4.1

[a] Each experiment was done in quadruplicate with approximately 200 target cells counted for each determination. Standard deviations for each measurement are also given.

[b] Removal of the serologically defined H2 antigens was done as described under Materials and Methods. Lentil-lectin-purified H-2 antigen was incubated with the appropriate antisera, followed by the addition of *Staphlococcus* protein A bound to Sepharose 4b beads. The beads were removed by centrifugation (450*g*, 5 min) and the supernatant was incorporated into liposomes and tested for its ability to inhibit T cell–target cell conjugate formation.

[c] The microgram quantities in parentheses indicate the amount of protein tested for inhibition of T cell–target cell conjugate formation.

[d] T cell–target cell formation is as described under Materials and Methods and in Tables 1 and 2.

the cells. This interpretation is based upon the observation that H-2^d-containing liposomes did not bind to BALB/c anti-EL-4 Lyt 2$^+$ T cells effectively until greater than 22 μg of protein was added per assay; nor did the binding in this experiment ever reach a clear plateau (Fig. 2). H-2^b-containing liposomes also did not bind effectively to BALB·B anti-MOPC-167 Lyt 2$^+$ T cells (Fig. 2); however, effective binding was observed when BALB/c anti-EL-4 Lyt 2$^+$ cells were studied (Fig. 3). These data shown in Figs. 2 and 3 were done with the same reagents at the same time.

Complete binding of the H-2-containing liposomes occurred within 15 min of the addition of the lipid vesicles with the Lyt 2$^+$ T cells (data not shown). Incubation periods longer than 2.0 hr resulted in decreases in binding (data not shown). All assays were completed within 15 min in this study.

To evaluate more fully the nonspecific binding observed between the Lyt 2+ cells and liposomes either containing large amounts of protein or associated with the inappropriate H-2, we incubated H-2^d-containing liposomes with a predetermined excess of BALB·B anti-MOPC-167 Lyt 2$^+$ T cells (Fig. 4). This mixture was

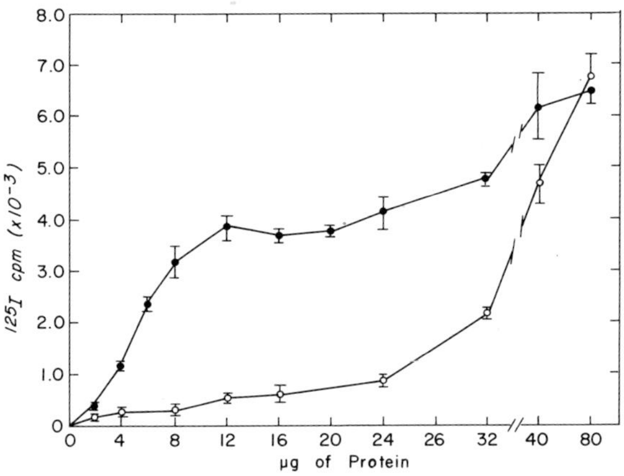

FIG. 2. Serial amounts of ^{125}I-labeled H-2[d]-containing liposomes were incubated with 1.0×10^5 BALB·B anti-MOPC-167 (●) or BALB/c anti-EL-4 (○) Lyt 2^+ T cells. The cells and liposomes were mixed, incubated for 30 min at room temperature, and centrifuged (450*g*, 10 min) and the pellet was counted as described under Materials and Methods. The determinations represent the mean of quadruplicate measurement with the standard deviations.

centrifuged and the supernatant tested for ability to bind to BALB·B anti-MOPC-167 Lyt 2^+ T cells. The results indicate that the supernatant did not bind onto BALB·B anti-MOPC-167 Lyt 2^+ T cells effectively at the lower protein amounts. However, at increasing levels of protein per assay an increase in binding did occur (Fig. 4). This binding did not plateau at any of the doses of protein tested (Fig. 4). The radioactivity found within the supernatant after adsorption represented approximately 20% of the total. This result suggests that 20% of the H-2-containing liposomes are not capable of specific binding to T-cell receptors. The results also suggest that the binding curves observed using large amounts of protein per assay

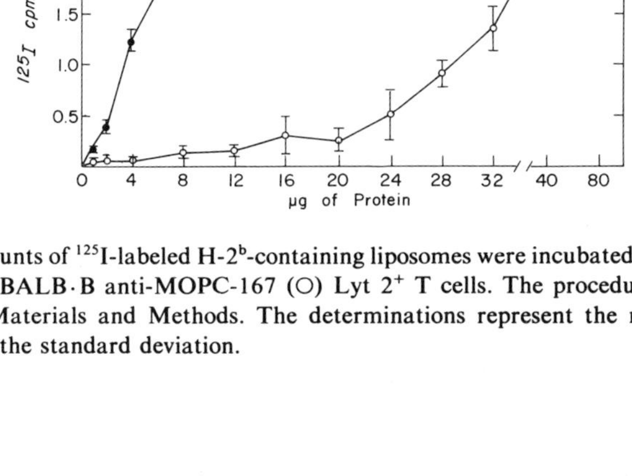

FIG. 3. Serial amounts of ^{125}I-labeled H-2[b]-containing liposomes were incubated with 1.0×10^5 BALB/c anti-EL-4 (●) or BALB·B anti-MOPC-167 (○) Lyt 2^+ T cells. The procedure was as described in Fig. 1 and under Materials and Methods. The determinations represent the mean of quadruplicate measurements with the standard deviation.

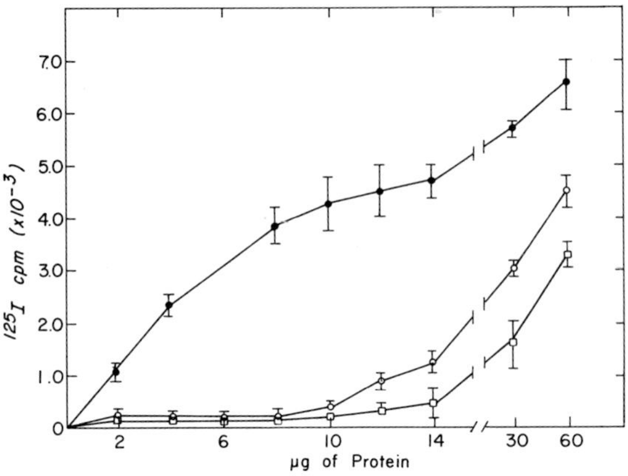

FIG. 4. Serial amounts of ^{125}I-labeled H-2^d-containing liposomes were incubated with 1.0 × 10^5 BALB/c anti-EL-4 (○) and BALB·B anti-MOPC-167 (●) Lyt 2$^+$ T cells. In addition 100 μg of H-2^d-containing liposomes preincubated with 1.0 × 10^7 BALB·B anti-MOPC-167 Lyt 2$^+$ T cells were tested for ability to bind to 1.0 × 10^5 BALB·B anti-MOPC-167 Lyt 2$^+$ T cells (□). The determinations represent the mean of quadruplicate measurement with the standard deviation.

or liposomes containing the H-2 antigens and Lyt 2$^+$ T-cell mixtures are due to nonspecific associations. Similar results were observed when H-2-^{b}-containing liposomes were absorbed onto BALB/c anti-EL-4 Lyt 2$^+$ T cells (data not shown).

In an effort to more precisely define the specificity of binding, we have done competitive inhibition experiments between radioactive-labeled H-2^d-containing liposomes and nonradioactive H-2-containing liposomes (Fig. 5). The results indicate that an indirect proportionality exists between the amount of radioactivity bound to cells and the amount of nonradioactive H-2-containing liposomes in the assay mixture. Similar results were also obtained for binding of H-2^b-containing liposomes (data not shown). In summary the results suggest that a specific association between the H-2 antigen-containing liposomes and anti-H-2-activated T cells can occur.

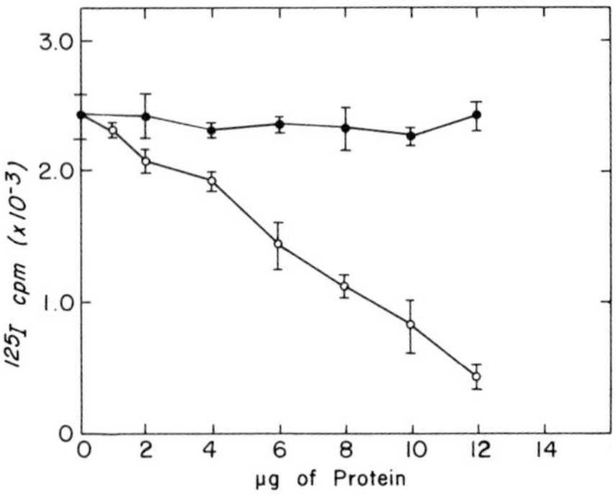

FIG. 5. 6 μg of ^{125}I-labeled H-2^d-containing liposomes were incubated with BALB·B anti-MOPC-167 T cells and serial amounts of nonradioactive H-2^d (○)- and H-2^b (●)-containing liposomes. The determinations represent the mean of quadruplicate measurement with the standard deviation.

Requirement for Serologically Defined H-2 Antigens for Binding

An important consideration was the characterization of the molecules within the lentil lectin fraction which was responsible for the specific binding of H-2-containing liposomes. In order to identify these molecules, we incubated the detergent-solubilized H-2-containing fraction with anti-H-2 serum in the presence of *Staphylococcus* protein A conjugated to Sepharose 4B beads (Table 6). The material not bound by the anti-H-2 antibodies–*Staphylococcus* protein A–Sepharose 4B complex was then incorporated into lipid vesicles and tested for binding to anti-H-2 CTLs. The results indicated that saturating amounts of these vesicles, even at amounts which were saturating in experiments using H-2-containing liposomes, exhibited binding to a level similar to that observed for nonspecific binding. This result suggests that for optimal binding, specific interactions have to occur between the serologically defined H-2 antigens and the antigen-specific receptors associated with the Lyt 2^+ T cells.

Cation Requirement for Binding of H-2 Liposomes to Anti-H-2 Lyt 2^+ T Cells

Several reports have indicated that Mg^{2+} is required for binding of CTL to target cells; however, Ca^{2+} is not as effective for promoting T cell–target cell binding (29). Because of this requirement we investigated if Mg^{2+} was also required for binding of the H-2^d-containing liposomes to BALB·B anti-MOPC-167 Lyt 2^+ T cells. The results indicated that H-2^d-containing liposomes bind effectively in the presence of Mg^{2+}, however, if Mg^{2+} was absent from the medium or if EDTA was added to the liposome–cell mixture, no significant binding was observed (Fig. 6). We tested the Ca^{2+} requirements for binding of H-2-containing liposomes with T cells. The results indicate that Ca^{2+} was not able to augment binding (Fig. 6). These results suggest that the same cation requirements needed for CTL–target

TABLE 6

Requirement of Serologically Defined H-2 Gene Products for Binding[a]

Lyt 2^+ T cells	H-2 liposomes	Antisera	^{125}I cpm ($\times10^3$)
BALB·B anti-MOPC-167	H-2^d	NMS	1.5 ± 0.2
		Anti-H-2^b	1.1 ± 0.4
		Anti-H-2^d	0.2 ± 0.3
	H-2^b	NMS	0.3 ± 0.1
BALB/c anti-EL-4	H-2^b	NMS	1.1 ± 0.3
		Anti-H-2^b	0.2 ± 0.3
		Anti-H-2^d	1.2 ± 0.4
	H-2^d	NMS	0.1 ± 0.1

[a] Lentil-lectin-purified ^{125}I-labeled H-2 antigens were incubated with normal mouse serum (undiluted), anti-H-2^b, or anti-H-2^d serum (undiluted) for 30 min at 4°C. The immunoglobulin was removed with *Staphylococcus* protein A conjugated to Sepharose 4B beads and the remaining supernatant was incorporated into lipid vesicles and tested for binding to the Lyt 2^+ T cells. The amount of protein in all assays was 11.7 μg. The determinations represent the mean of quadruplicate measurements with the standard deviation.

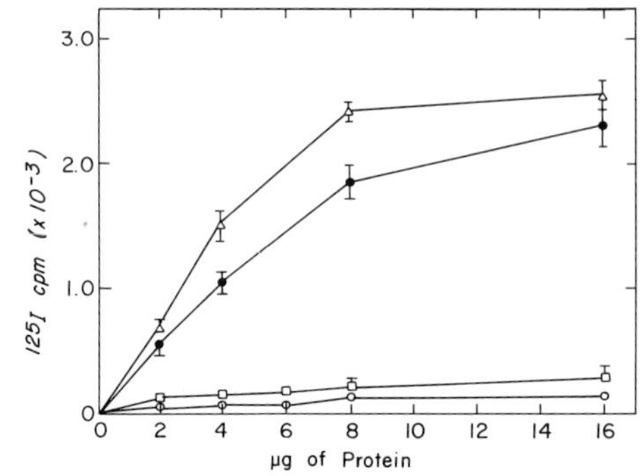

FIG. 6. Serial amounts of ^{125}I-labeled H-2^d-containing liposomes were incubated with 1.0×10^5 BALB·B anti-MOPC-167 Lyt 2^+ T cells in the presence of 1.0 m*M* Ca^{2+} and 1.0 m*M* Mg^{2+} (△), 1.0 m*M* Ca^{2+} (○), 1.0 m*M* Mg^{2+} (●), or in the presence of 1.0 m*M* Ca^{2+}, 1.0 m*M* Mg^{2+}, and 2.5 m*M* EDTA (ph 7.5) (□). The determinations represent the mean of triplicate measurements with the standard deviation never exceeding 5.0×10^2.

cell interaction also exist for binding of H-2-containing liposome to anti-H-2 Lyt 2^+ T cells. Similar cation requirements were observed for H-2^b containing liposomes binding to BALB/c anti-EL-4 Lyt 2^+ T cells.

DISCUSSION

Identification of target antigens recognized by CTLs and analysis of T cell receptor–antigen interaction are areas of research receiving considerable attention. We have investigated the ability of partially purified H-2 antigens incorporated into vesicles or a high-density fraction of H-2 antigens for their ability to inhibit T cell–target cell conjugate formation. Other workers in this area (24, 25, 28) have used enriched anti-H-2 T cell populations which contained 25–30% CTLs. We have come one step further, by analyzing anti-H-2 T cells which were >80% CTLs. With the Lyt 2^+ T-cell population we have demonstrated specific inhibition with H-2 antigen-containing fractions. Incorporation of the H-2 antigens into liposomes enhanced the relative ability (decreased the relative amount of protein needed to give 50% inhibition) of the H-2 antigen preparation to inhibit T cell–target cell conjugate formation. The incorporation of the H-2 antigens into the phospholipid vesicles could allow presentation of the glycoproteins in a more effective orientation, stoichiometry or density. We have no data to evaluate these possibilities. The decreased inhibition obtained by removal of serologically defined H-2 antigens with anti-H-2 serum suggests that indeed those molecules recognized by anti-H-2 sera are responsible for the inhibition of the T cell–target cell conjugate formation.

This system we feel has important implications concerning the identity of the antigens recognized by CTLs and the molecular requirements for T cell receptor–antigen interaction. In contrast with the efficient inhibition of cell interaction reported here and by others (24, 25, 28), experimental inhibition of CTL-mediated cytolysis has not been reproducible (26). The reason for the contradictory findings has not been determined. It may be, as suggested in the Introduction, a kinetic problem in that multiple T cell receptor–antigen interactions may occur within the length of a normal ^{51}Cr assay and/or that molecular interactions between the subcellular components and the T cell receptor are not stable. The latter interpretation would suggest that the fragmentation procedures used have resulted in denaturation of either the antigen or other surface components needed for a stable association between the T-cell and antigen preparation. The ability to elicit CTLs with subcellular H-2-containing fractions (15–20) and the ability to specifically inhibit T cell–target cell conjugates (24, 25, 28) clearly indicate that these fractions are active.

These results also indicate that partially purified H-2 antigens incorporated into lipid vesicles are capable of specific binding to enriched anti-H-2 Lyt 2^+ T cells. This binding was specifically inhibited by nonradioactive H-2-containing liposomes. In addition, binding was highly dependent upon the presence of Mg^{2+}. Since a requirement for Mg^{2+} has been observed for CTL–target cell binding, the requirement of Mg^{2+} for binding of H-2 antigens to anti-H-2 T cells is suggestive that this binding is comparable to the formation of T cell–target cell conjugates. We interpret these results to indicate that this model system can be studied to evaluate the interaction of antigens with anti-H-2 T-cell receptors.

Liposomes prepared with solubilized membrane products treated with specific anti-H-2 sera prevented binding of the H-2 liposomes onto the anti-H-2 Lyt 2^+ T cells. The result suggests that serologically defined H-2 gene products are required for effective interaction of lentil-lectin-purified glycoproteins and anti-H-2 Lyt 2^+ T cells. By immunoprecipitation no detectable anti-Ia or anti-GP-69/70 (after appropriate adsorptions) was detected in this serum (data not shown). However, antibodies were detected (immunoprecipitation) that bound specifically to a glycoprotein of 45,000 and 12,000 daltons. These molecular weights are consistent with those ascribed to the H-2K and/or H-2D gene products by others (6). Therefore, our results indicate that specific removal of the H-2K and/or H-2D gene products prevents lentil-lectin-purified glycoproteins incorporated into liposomes from specifically binding to anti-H-2 Lyt 2^+ T cells. This result is consistent and complements the specific inhibition of T cell–target cell conjugate formation by H-2K and/or H-2D gene products.

This communication described two approaches to study antigen recognization by CTLs. Both approaches were effective in the study of specific interactions between H-2 antigens and cytotoxic lymphocytes. In addition, the results from these studies demonstrated that recognition of subcellular fractions by T cells takes place by specific binding of molecules the antigenic determinants of which are, at least in part, identical to the serologically determined H-2-K and H-2-D antigens.

ACKNOWLEDGMENTS

This work was supported by a research grant from the Forsyth Cancer Service; a grant to the Bowman Gray School of Medicine Cancer Center Support (Core) Grant (2-P30-CA 12197-08), and HL 16769 from the National Institutes of Health. A research grant from the American Cancer Society (MV-41) also supported this work. Arthur H. Hale is the recipient of a Research Career Development Award. The author also would like to thank Ms. Jean Hooker and Brenda Caprani for their excellent secretarial assistance.

REFERENCES

1. Bach, F. H., Bach, M. L., and Sondel, P. M., *Nature (London)* **259,** 173, 1976.
2. Nabholz, M., Young, H., Meo, T., Miggiano, V., Rijnbeck, A., and Schreffler, D. C., *Immunogenetics* **1,** 456, 1975.
3. Forman, J., and Klein, J., *Immunogenetics* **1,** 409, 1975.
4. Forman, J., and Klein, J., *J. Immunol.* **115,** 711, 1975.
5. Brown, J. L., and Nathenson, S. G., *J. Immunol.* **118,** 98, 1977.
6. Lemonnier, F., Burakoff, S. J., Mescher, M., Dorf, M. E., and Benacerraf, B., *J. Immunol.* **120,** 1717, 1978.
7. Bevan, M. J., and Hyman, R., *Immunogenetics* **4,** 7, 1977.
8. Nabholz, M., Vives, J., Young, H. H., Meo, T., Miggiano, V., Rijnbeck, A., and Schreffler, D., *Eur. J. Immunol.* **4,** 378, 1974.
9. Hansen, T. H., Cullen, S. E., Melvold, R., Kohn, H. I., and Flaherty, L., *J. Exp. Med.* **145,** 1550, 1977.
10. Hansen, T. H., Cullen, S. E., and Sachs, D. H., *J. Exp. Med.* **145,** 438, 1977.
11. Neauport, S. C., Morello, D., Freed, J., Nathenson, S. G., and Démant, P., *Eur. J. Immunol.* **8,** 511, 1977.
12. Matzinger, P., and Bevan, M., *Cell. Immunol.* **29,** 1, 1977.
13. Russell, J. R., Hale, A. H., Ginns, L. C., and Eisen, H. N. *Proc. Nat. Acad. Sci. USA* **75,** 441, 1978.
14. Russell, J. H., Hale, A. H., Inbar, D., and Eisen, H. N., *Eur. J. Immunol.* **8,** 640, 1978.
15. Mescher, M., Sherman, L., Lemonnier, F., and Burakoff, S. *J. Exp. Med.* **147,** 946, 1978.
16. Fast, L. D., and Fan, D. P., *J. Immunol.* **120,** 1092, 1978.
17. Engers, H. D., Thomas, K., Cerottini, J. C., and Brunner, K. T., *J. Immunol.* **115,** 356, 1975.
18. Littman, D. R., Cullen, S. E., and Schwartz, B. D., *Proc. Nat. Acad. Sci. USA* **76,** 902, 1979.
19. Engelhard, V. H., Strominger, J. L., Mescher, M., and Burakoff, S., *Proc. Nat. Acad. Sci. USA* **75,** 5688, 1978.
20. Hale, A. H., *Cell. Immunol.* **55,** 236, 1980.
21. Berke, G., Gabison, H., and Feldmann, *Eur. J. Immunol.* **5,** 813, 1975.
22. Lowry, O. H., Rosebrought, N. J., Farr, A. L., and Randall, R. J., *J. Biol. Chem.* **193,** 265, 1951.
23. Esko, J. D., Gilmore, J. R., and Glaser, M., *Biochemistry* **16,** 1881, 1977.
24. Gilmer, P. J., McDevitt, O., and McConnell, H. M., *J. Immunol.* **120,** 774, 1978.
25. Whisnant, C. C., Singer, K. H., and Amos, D. B., *J. Immunol.* **121,** 2253, 1978.
26. Todd, R. F., III, Stulting, R. D., and Amos, D. B., *Cell. Immunol.* **18,** 304, 1975.
27. Julius, M. H., Simpson, E., and Herzanberg, L. A., *Eur. J. Immunol.* **3,** 645, 1973.
28. Roder, J. C., and Rarre, K., *Immunogenetics* **4,** 343, 1980.
29. Berke, G., *Prog. Allergy* **27,** 69, 1980.

CELLULAR IMMUNOLOGY **63,** 57–70 (1981)

Macrophages as Effectors of T Suppression: T-Lymphocyte-Dependent Macrophage-Mediated Suppression of Mitogen-Induced Blastogenesis in the Rat

PATRICK G. HOLT, LOUISE A. WARNER, AND GRAHAM MAYRHOFER

Clinical Immunology Research Unit, Princess Margaret Children's Medical Research Foundation, Princess Margaret Hospital, Subiaco, 6008, Western Australia, Australia

Received December 31, 1980; accepted April 30, 1981

Small numbers of appropriately stimulated (but not resident) peritoneal macrophages in the rat are shown to inhibit mitogen induced lymphocyte proliferation. A variety of *in vivo* and *in vitro* cell selection/fractionation procedures applied to the indicator (lymphocyte) population indicates that the cytostatic potential of the macrophages is not expressed spontaneously *in vitro*, but is dependent upon the activity of a second "regulator" cell from the lymphocyte population. The latter cell is shown to be large, long lived, and recirculating, highly sensitive to anti-thymocyte serum and cyclophosphamide, insensitive to irradiation, indomethacin, and mitomycin C, adherent to glass wool, and to survive poorly in culture—it is most active *in vivo* in the early neonatal period, contributing significantly to the lack of demonstrable PHA-responsiveness in splenocyte cultures from new born rats. A similar cell (nominal suppressor T cell) is shown to appear in lymph nodes during primary immune responses to soluble antigen.

INTRODUCTION

The general concept that regulation of immunological responses proceeds via a "network" of complex cellular interactions (1) is supported by a growing body of evidence. One of the clearest examples of such a network is the interplay between macrophages and T cells associated with T-cell activation. On the one hand, T-cell activation by both mitogens and antigens exhibits absolute macrophage dependency (e.g. (2–5)). In contrast, macrophage suppression of T-cell activation is also readily demonstrable (6–9), especially with "stimulated" macrophages (10, 11).

The mechanism(s) by which macrophages effect suppression of T-cell activation is not clear, and may involve soluble factors (6, 7), cell-to-cell contact, or both (reviewed in (12)). Their role in T-cell activation is better understood, and appears to involve both antigen "presentation" by Ia^+ macrophages (reviewed in (13)), and the provision of a second activation signal in the form of a diffusible molecule (possibly Lymphocyte Activating Factor (14)). This immunogenic activity of macrophages has recently been shown to be under the strict control of a subpopulation of cortisone-resistant thymocytes (15), removal of which (by thymectomy) severely compromises the capacity of macrophages to activate T cells *in vivo* and *in vitro* (16, 17).

0008-8749/81/130057-14$02.00/0

There is also evidence, albeit less direct than that cited above, which establishes a link between the expression of "suppressor" T-cell (Ts) activity and macrophages. Suggested examples include nonspecific suppression of anti-hapten responses by T-cells (18, 19), Ts-dependent inhibition of adoptive transfer of contact sensitivity (20, 21), suppression (via a soluble factor) of the generation of antibody responses by Con A-activated Ts (22), nonspecific immunosuppression accompanying fungal infection (23), and the activity of nonspecific murine Ts in cultures of mitogen-activated proliferating splenocytes (24–26). In virtually all these studies, the establishment of overall T-cell dependency of suppression represented the primary aim, with the demonstration of macrophage involvement in the efferent arm of the phenomenon being a secondary consideration, often relying on largely negative evidence.

The studies reported herein approach the question of macrophage involvement in the expression of suppressor T-cell activity from a different standpoint. Rather than starting with a known Ts-dependent phenomenon and attempting to define the role of macrophages therein, we have instead examined an activity of macrophages—the expression of cytostatic activity in cultures of proliferating splenocytes—and have demonstrated that the expression of the macrophages' potential for cytostasis relies upon the presence of a subset of "regulator" cells in the indicator (replicating) population. A number of independent lines of evidence, including chronic T-cell depletion *in vivo* and the use of anti-thymocyte antiserum *in vitro*, attest to the thymus dependency of this latter regulator cell.

MATERIALS AND METHODS

Animals. Rats of both sexes from the following strains were employed: WAG, Wistar/Furth, Lou/M, DA, and Sprague–Dawley. As no significant strain differences were detected during this study, they are not distinguished in the text.

Materials. Microtest tissue culture plates (FB) were from Nunc (Denmark). Medium RPMI 1640 was from Gibco and fetal calf serum (FCS) for the cultures was obtained from Commonwealth Serum Laboratories, Australia. Indomethacin, mitomycin C, and ovalbumin (OA; Grade V) were from Sigma and Cyclophosphamide (Endoxan) was obtained from Bristol Laboratories, Australia. PHA-P (Difco) was used for mitogenic stimulation, each vial being reconstituted to 10.0 ml before use, rather than the 5.0 ml recommended by the manufacturer.

Lymphoid cell preparation. Excised spleens were finely minced, suspended in chilled phosphate-buffered saline (PBS), and sieved through cotton wool. Viable spleen cell/(SPC) counts were performed by trypan blue exclusion. Lymph node cells (LNC) were prepared in a similar fashion except that minced preparations were first stirred through stainless-steel sieves; inguinal nodes were used from rats immunized subcutaneously (in the base of the tail) 10 days earlier with 100 μg OA in Freund's adjuvant. Thoracic duct lymphocytes (TDL) were collected over varying periods up to 7 days into chilled medium (Dulbecco's A plus B containing 20 U heparin/ml) via an indwelling catheter. In experiments involving SPC from adult thymectomized (ATx) rats, thymectomy had been performed at least 6 months previously.

Macrophage preparation. Alveolar macrophages, (AM), peritoneal exudate cells (PEC), and resident peritoneal macrophages (PM) were prepared by lavage as detailed previously (27). Peritoneal exudates were routinely elicited employing 5.0 ml of 10% peptone given 4 days before cell harvest. As in earlier studies involving the suppressive activity of AM populations (11, 33), preliminary experiments compared the suppressive activity of adherance-purified peritoneal exudate macrophages and unfractionated PEC (containing on average 75% phagocytic cells). As no significant differences were observed, PEC were employed in the bulk of this study.

Column separations. SPC were fractionated on glass wool columns employing a modification of the method of Raff and Hinrichs (25). Briefly, 10-ml syringes were tightly packed with 0.9 g washed glass wool, and autoclaved. Prior to use, they were washed with 30 ml warm PBS, followed by a similar volume of RPMI containing 10% FCS; the columns were then preincubated with the latter for 1 hr at 37°C. Following preincubation, the columns were emptied under gravity, and SPC (up to 1.5×10^8) in 1.0 ml of the same medium run in. Thirty minutes later, nonadherent SPC were eluted by the dropwise addition of prewarmed FCS-supplemented RPMI to the column. Adherent SPC were collected by teasing out the glass wool in medium. Enrichment of T cells on nylon wool columns was performed as described previously (11).

Velocity sedimentation. The method of Miller and Phillips (28) employing the STA/PUT apparatus (Johns Scientific, Canada) was used as previously described (11).

Drug and X-ray treatments. Cyclophosphamide (CY) was administered ip to rats 24 hr prior to removal of spleens, employing a dosage of 50 mg/kg body weight. Preliminary experiments indicated that dosages below this level gave equivocal results.

In other experiments aimed at modifying susceptibility to macrophage suppression, single-cell suspensions of splenocytes in chilled serum-supplemented RPMI, were subjected to graded doses of X-irradiation (1–400 rad) prior to culture. Indomethacin was also employed in this context; in some experiments, PEC were preincubated with the drug (10^{-6} *M* for 1 hr at 37°C (29)) prior to addition to SPC cultures—alternatively, 1–10 μg/ml Indomethacin was included in PEC/SPC cocultures (30). In studies involving mitomycin C, cells were preincubated in serum-supplemented RPMI with 40 μg/ml mitomycin C for 30 min at 37°C; four washings in medium were performed prior to subsequent culture.

Antiserum. Rabbit anti-rat thymocyte serum (RARTS) was prepared as described by Raff and Hinrichs (25). It was used at a final concentration of 1:6 in conjunction with nontoxic rabbit complement. The RARTS preparation employed here was found in preliminary experiments to abolish the capacity of SPC to respond to the T-Cell mitogens PHA and Con A, but did not reduce responsiveness to the B-cell mitogen LPS. It was also without effect upon the capacity of macrophage suspensions to exclude trypan blue.

Cultures. Lymphoid cells (2×10^5) were dispensed into wells of flat-bottomed microtest plates in 200 μl RPMI containing 10% FCS. The RPMI had been adjusted to rat osmolarity (310 mOsm/kg). Macrophages were introduced in 10 μl PBS via a Hamilton syringe. PHA was added where specified; data reported below refer to a single mitogen dose (10 μl/culture).

After 24 hr of incubation at 37°C in 5% CO_2 in air, each well received 0.5 μCi [^{3}H]thymidine. Sixteen hours later, plates were processed employing a Skatron

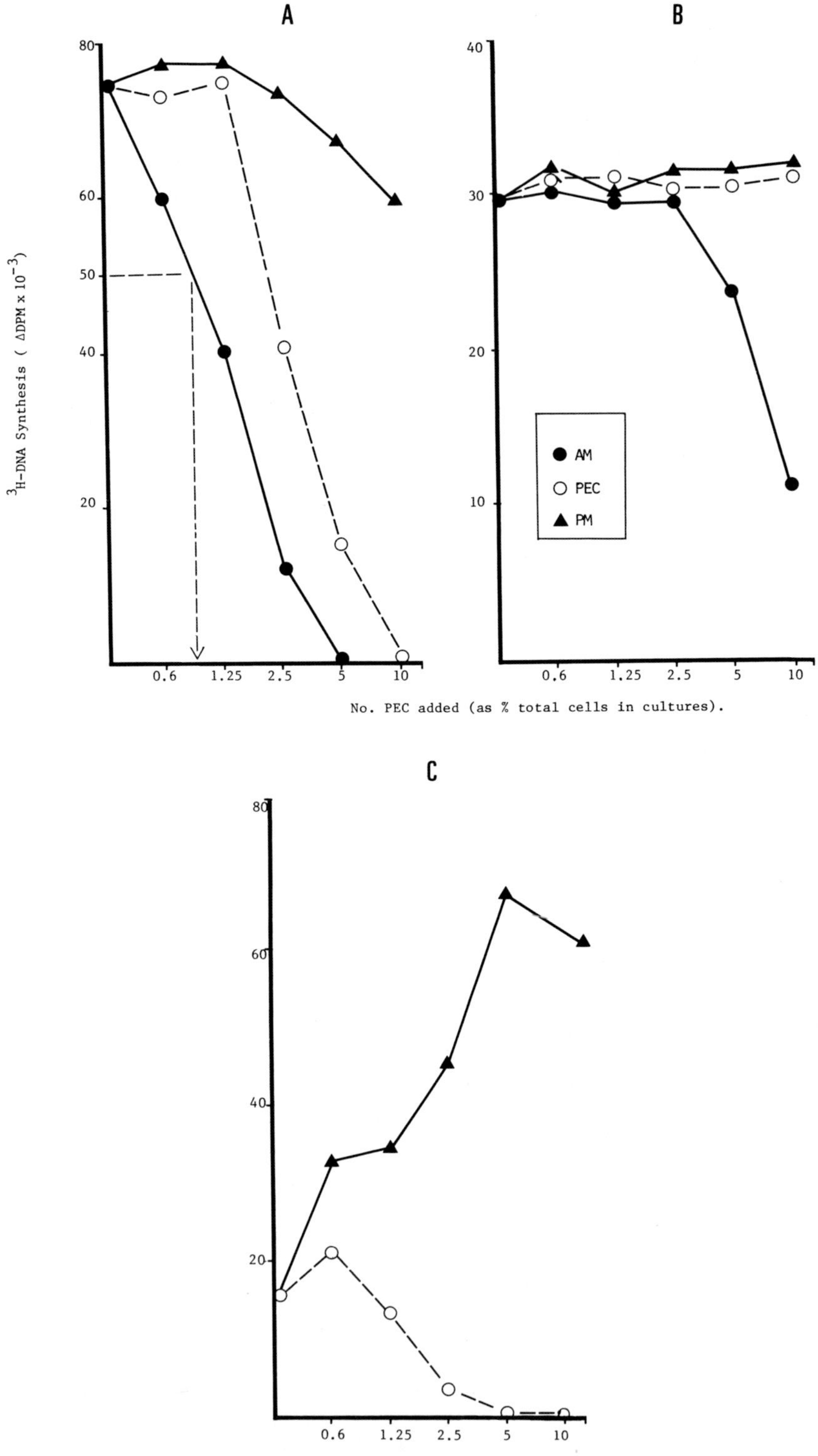

FIG. 1. Suppressive activity of different macrophage populations from the rat. Two preparations of SPC and one of TDL were cocultured with varying numbers of AM, PEC, or resident PM, in the presence and absence of PHA, and [^{3}H]DNA synthesis (shown as ΔDPM per culture) was determined after 48 hr.

TABLE 1

Significance of age of SPC Donor in Relation to Susceptibility to Macrophage-Mediated Suppression of Blastogenesis

Cultures	Age of SPC donors (weeks)					
	<2		3–7		48–72	
2.0×10^5 SPC	<0[a]	741	25,796	81,736	65,419	75,233
$+1.25 \times 10^3$ PEC	<0	732	17,174	79,983	66,317	75,219
$+2.5 \times 10^3$ PEC	<0	1079	11,038	86,719	64,113	79,116
$+5 \times 10^3$ PEC	<0	558	4,712	81,121	65,799	81,206
$+1 \times 10^4$ PEC	<0	326	609	63,827	66,127	76,223
$+2 \times 10^4$ PEC	<0	309	317	42,735	48,126	76,117

Note. SPC were cultured in the presence of increasing numbers of PEC, in the presence and absence of 10 μl PHA, and [^{3}H]DNA synthesis was determined 48 hr later. As in the other tables and figures, data shown are median Δdpm from triplicate cultures, the latter calculated after subtraction of dpm from control cultures (not stimulated with PHA). The examples shown indicate the extremes of the range observed within each age group.

[a] "Negative" PHA responses, indicating that the addition of PHA *lowered* [^{3}H]DNA synthesis to below control (unstimulated) levels.

harvester (Lierbyen, Norway). [^{3}H]DNA synthesis was expressed as median change disintegrations per minute of triplicates, determined after subtraction of disintegrations per minute from control (unstimulated) cultures; replication between cultures was such that standard deviations were within 10% of mean values.

Suppression of blastogenesis resulting from the addition of macrophages was determined by reference to control cultures containing lymphoid cells alone.

In experiments demonstrating antigen-driven blastogenesis, 4×10^5 LNC from OA-immune donors were stimulated with 200 μg/ml OA. The RPMI in these experiments was supplemented with 5% syngeneic rat serum and 5×10^{-5} *M* 2-mercaptoethanol; an incubation period of 96 hr was employed, as opposed to 48 hr as per PHA-induced blastogenesis.

RESULTS

Suppression of T-Cell Blastogenesis by Macrophage

Figure 1 illustrates three experiments which demonstrate the suppressive activity of different rat macrophage populations, employing cultures of mitogen-stimulated lymphocytes as indicator cells. Experiments A & B feature PHA-stimulated splenocytes from animals aged 4 and 26 weeks, which exhibit high and low susceptibility, respectively, to suppression by macrophages (see below). When compared in parallel in this fashion, AM invariably appear more inhibitory than macrophages from PEC, and little or no inhibition is seen with resident PM. These differences in macrophage cytostatic activity have been reported previously by us (11). Experiment C indicates that macrophage density per se is not an important determinant of suppression in this system. The TDL cells used here constitute a natural source of "macrophage-depleted" (<1% phagocytic) lymphocytes, which exhibit only weak blastogenic responses, which are readily boostable by the inclusion of small numbers of unstimulated macrophages, a finding consistent with current

TABLE 2

Fractionation of SPC by Velocity Sedimentation and Glass Wool Adherence: Effects on Susceptibility to Macrophage Suppression

SPC in cultures	No. PEC added (% cells in culture) 0	0.6	1.2	2.5	5	10
Unfractionated SPC	88,527	92,067	88,185	91,300	89,972	64,054
Fraction I (Sed. Veloc. ≥ 6.47 mm/hr)	<0	<0	<0	<0	<0	<0
Nonadherent	54,335	62,512	67,924	70,627	72,936	72,987
Adherent	<0	<0	<0	<0	<0	<0
Fraction II (Sed. Veloc. 4.47–5.80 mm/hr)	27,530	24,249	24,671	19,488	14,775	7,476
Nonadherent	111,391	109,918	11,312	111,609	138,107	114,029
Adherent	<0	<0	<0	<0	<0	<0
Fraction III (Sed. Veloc. 2.47–3.80 mm/hr)	163,318	148,944	150,031	158,604	129,769	124,731
Fraction IV (Sed. Veloc. ≤ 1.13 mm/hr)	42,122	46,209	40,827	45,864	38,839	44,331

Note. SPC were separated via velocity sedimentation at unit gravity employing the STA-PUT apparatus. Adjacent fractions were pooled to yield four cell populations as shown. Fractions I and II were then further divided into adherent and nonadherent cells via the Raff and Hinrichs method (25); adherent:nonadherent yields were in the ratio of 2:1 and 1:4 for Fractions I and II, respectively (preliminary studies with III and IV indicated that ≥95% were nonadherent, and no consistent effects attributable to column passage were detected in subsequent cultures). The various SPC subpopulations were finally cocultured with PEC and stimulated with PHA, [^{3}H]DNA synthesis (shown as Δdpm per culture) being determined 48 hr later.

thoughts on the absolute macrophage dependency of T-cell blastogenesis (2–4). Despite the stimulatory effect of PM in these cultures, appropriately activated macrophages in the PEC population express strong suppressive activity under identical circumstances.

The nature of the stimulant employed to raise peritoneal exudates was found not to be critical here, as PEC produced via Freunds complete & incomplete adjuvant, heat-killed *Bordetella pertussis* and thioglycollate were similarly inhibitory *in vitro*. PEC raised in B rats (thymectomized, irradiated, and reconstituted with T-depleted bone marrow) exhibited comparable activity.

Age of the SPC Donor as a Determinant of Susceptibility to Suppression

Table 1 reflects the spectrum of results obtained from well over 100 separate experiments of this nature. Considerable variation in susceptibility to PEC-mediated suppression of PHA-induced blastogenesis was observed within the age groups, and the extremes for each group are shown. At one end of the scale, SPC from old rats (48–72 weeks) were essentially refractory to suppression, a situation in marked contrast to that observed with 3- to 7-week-old animals, the majority of which were highly susceptible to suppression by macrophages. SPC from rats 7–48 weeks old (not shown) were extremely variable in this regard, and could be placed anywhere in the range encompassed by the 3- to 72-week-old rats. Preweanling (suckling) rats (<2 weeks) yielded SPC which were totally refractory to

TABLE 3

Effects of Preculture on Susceptibility of SPC Blastogenic Responses to Macrophage Suppression

SPC donor:	Adult		Weanling	
Time of PHA addition (hr):	t_0	t_{24}	t_0	t_{24}
2 × 10^5 SPC	69,130	86,004	0	68,499
+2.5 × 10^3 PEC	66,192	74,816	0	145,791
+5.0 × 10^3 PEC	60,342	70,573	0	85,929
+1.0 × 10^4 PEC	74,008	95,201	0	75,057
+2.0 × 10^4 PEC	52,010	83,587	0	87,511
+4.0 × 10^4 PEC	1,156	63,194	0	7,212

Note. SPC from adult and weanling (3–4 weeks) rats were set up in culture with PEC and PHA immediately following preparation (t_0), or after 24 hr preculture in serum-supplemented medium (t_{24}). Data shown reflect [^{3}H]DNA synthesis (Δdpm per culture) 48 hr after PHA stimulation (t_{48} and t_{72}, respectively).

PHA stimulation, and consequently the effects of exogenous macrophages could not be directly tested.

Variation in Susceptibility to (Macrophage) Suppression via Manipulation of Indicator (Spleen) Cells

(i) Fractionation of SPC by velocity sedimentation at unit gravity and adherance to glass wool. The separation of spleen cells on the basis of cell size (the principal determinant of sedimentation velocity) reproducibly yields cell populations of graded susceptibility to macrophage suppression. The example shown (Table 5) indicates that small SPC (sedimentation velocity ≤ 3.80 mm/hr) respond vigorously to PHA, and their PHA reactivity is not suppressed by the addition of PEC. In contrast, large SPC (Fraction II; sedimentation velocity, 4.47–5.50 mm/hr) are susceptible to PEC-mediated suppression. This susceptibility may be abolished by removal of a minor population of glass-wool-adherent cells from Fraction II, which

TABLE 4

Effect of Cyclophosphamide Pretreatment on SPC Susceptibility to Macrophage Suppression

Cultures	Normal SPC	SPC from CY-treated rats
2.0 × 10^5 SPC	50,559	17,792
+1.25 × 10^3 PEC	53,389	14,808
+2.5 × 10^3 PEC	54,031	16,749
+5 × 10^3 PEC	41,239	20,675
+1 × 10^4 PEC	25,748	19,299
+2 × 10^4 PEC	6,729	16,957

Note. SPC were cocultured with PEC in the presence and absence of PHA, and [^{3}H]DNA synthesis (Δdpm per culture) determined at 48 hr. Results are shown for SPC from normal young adult rats, and age/sex-matched cagemates inoculated intraperitoneally 24 hr previously with cyclophosphamide (CY) at a dose of 50 mg/kg body wt.

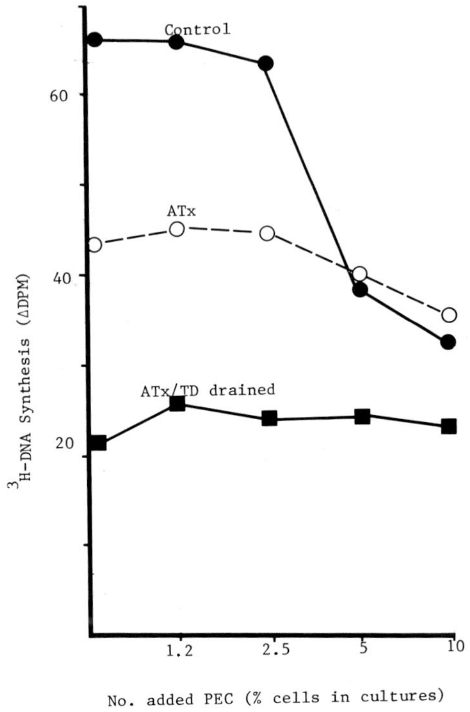

FIG. 2. Effect of T-cell depletion *in vivo* on the susceptibility of SPC to macrophage-mediated suppression of PHA-induced blastogenesis. PEC were titrated into cultures of SPC from intact (●) or ATx rats aged 1 year (○), or ATx rats which had been thoracic duct drained for 7 days prior to sacrifice (■). The cultures were stimulated with PHA, and levels of [^{3}H]DNA synthesis (shown as median ΔDPM from triplicate cultures) determined 48 hr later.

themselves do not respond to PHA. It is also noteworthy that removal of adherent cells from both Fractions I and II results in a massive increase in PHA-induced blastogenesis in the control cultures—this is particularly evident in Fraction I, which does not respond to PHA at all unless first depleted of glass-wool-adherent cells.

(ii) Twenty-four hour preincubation of SPC. Earlier work by Gowans and Uhr (31) indicates that "large" rat lymphocytes survive poorly in overnight culture. Given the evidence of Table 2 linking SPC susceptibility to macrophage suppression with the presence of a "large" adherent cell, we set out to test the possibility that prolonged preincubation of the SPC might effect selective depletion of this latter population.

Two typical experiments are shown in Table 3. Employing adult SPC stimulated with PHA on the day of preparation (t_0), macrophage-mediated suppression of blastogenesis was readily demonstrable. However, if these SPC were first preincubated overnight before the addition of PEC and PHA (i.e., at t_{24}), their responsiveness to PHA was increased, and their susceptibility to PEC-mediated suppression abrogated. Similarly, if weanling SPC were used which were completely refractory to PHA stimulation when tested fresh from the donor (t_0), 24 hr preincubation unmasked strong PHA reactivity—these latter cells were sometimes still suppressible by macrophages, albeit with high numbers only (Table 3).

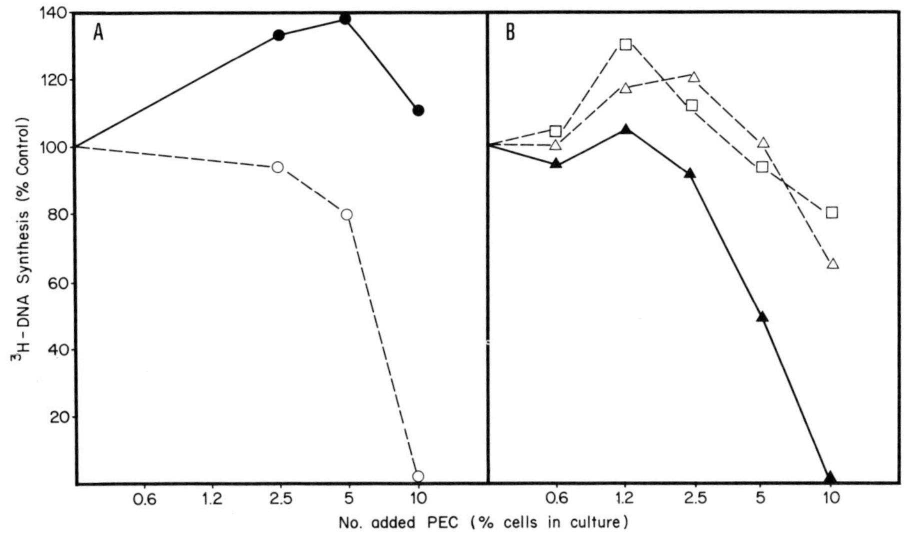

FIG. 3. Effect of pretreatment with RARTS on the susceptibility of SPC to macrophage-mediated suppression of blastogenesis. (A) Unfractionated SPC were preincubated with RARTS plus complement (●) or complement alone (○) prior to coculture with PEC in the presence and absence of PHA. Data shown are [^{3}H]DNA synthesis expressed as a percentage of control (without macrophage) cultures. (B) SPC were fractionated via unit gravity sedimentation, and Fractions I and II further divided into adherent/nonadherent populations as shown in Table 3. 2.0×10^5 nonadherent cells from Fraction II were cultured with PEC alone (△), or in the presence of equal numbers of adherent Fraction I cells (▲). Parallel cultures containing Fraction II cells plus PEC received 2.0×10^5 adherent Fraction I cells preincubated with RARTS plus complement (□). The cultures were stimulated with PHA, and [^{3}H]DNA synthesis was determined at 48 hr. Data shown are percentage control (no added macrophages) responses.

(iii) Pretreatment of spleen cell donors with cyclophosphamide. Representative data from these experiments appear in Table 4. It can be seen that splenocytes from pretreated rats not only exhibit depressed mitogen responsiveness, but also a complete loss of susceptibility to macrophage suppression.

Thymus Dependency of Macrophage-Mediated Suppression

(i) Adult thymectomy and chronic thoracic duct drainage. Figure 2 illustrates experiments which examined the susceptibility of SPC PHA responsiveness to suppression by macrophages, in normal and T-cell-depleted rats. The rats employed were from a single batch of age-matched females, 12 months old at the time of sacrifice. They comprised normal controls, a group which had been thymectomized (ATx) 6 months previously, and a third group similarly thymectomized but also drained via the thoracic duct for 7 days prior to sacrifice. The maximum degree of macrophage-mediated suppression of blastogenesis demonstrable in these groups was 52, 24, and 0%, respectively. These results bear out earlier experiments (11), and suggest that removal of the thymus depletes (but does not completely remove) a subpopulation of cells which confers macrophage susceptibility on the overall SPC population; the data also indicate that chronic thoracic duct cannulation of these thymectomized rats effects a further reduction in susceptibility to macrophage-mediated suppression. We infer from these data that the expression of cytostatic activity by macrophages in cultures of PHA-stimulated SPC is controlled

TABLE 5

Effect of Anti-Thymocyte Serum on the Capacity of Adherent Cells from Suckling Rats to Transfer Susceptibility to Macrophage Suppression

No. PEC added per culture	Unfractionated SPC	Nonadherent SPC	Nonadherent SPC + Adherent SPC	Nonadherent SPC + RARTS-treated adherent SPC
0	4520	17,079	6125	15,100
1.25×10^3	4120	20,089	6929	16,914
2.5×10^3	3679	18,173	5522	16,477
5.0×10^3	3600	17,623	1908	16,404
1×10^4	1048	18,129	0	19,091

Note. SPC from suckling rats were fractionated into adherent and nonadherent fractions on glass wool. Part of the adherent fraction was preincubated with anti-thymocyte serum (RARTS) plus complement. Various combinations of SPC fractions were then cocultured with PEC as shown and stimulated with PHA, and [^{3}H]DNA synthesis was determined at 48 hr. The cultures shown contained 2.0×10^5 unfractionated SPC or 2.0×10^5 nonadherent SPC; cultures containing the latter also received the same number of untreated or RARTS-treated adherent cells.

by a thymus dependent regulator (suppressor) lymphocyte which appears long lived, and which may recirculate.

(ii) Susceptibility of the Suppressor Lymphocyte to RARTS. A variety of experiments have examined the susceptibility of this suppressor cell to anti-thymocyte (RARTS) serum. The first approach employed was to compare the RARTS sensitivity of the putative suppressor T cell to that of the major PHA-responsive SPC

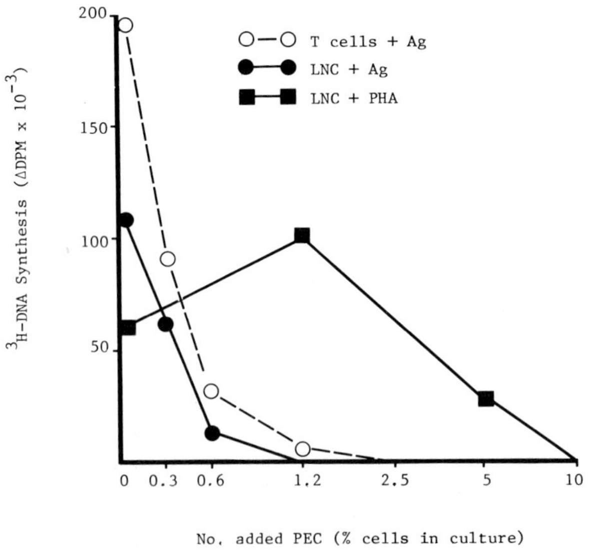

FIG. 4. Suppression of antigen versus mitogen-induced blastogenesis in LNC from immunized rats. LNC were prepared from the inguinal nodes of rats immunized 10 days previously in the base of the tail with 100 μg OA in FCA. Part of the LNC preparation was passed through a nylon wool column to concentrate T cells. These preparations were stimulated in culture with PHA or OA (200 μg/ml), in the presence and absence of PEC, and [^{3}H]DNA synthesis (shown as ΔDPM per culture) ascertained after 4 days.

population. This was achieved by first incubating freshly prepared SPC with low levels of RARTS (at a concentration which decreased the overall PHA response by 50–60%), and then comparing the susceptibility of the surviving T cells to macrophage-mediated cytostasis in relation to non-RARTS-treated controls. As depicted in Fig. 3A, brief exposure to RARTS plus complement renders SPC unresponsive to suppression by macrophages in this blastogenesis assay.

Figure 3B employs the SPC separation system shown in Table 2. In these experiments, non adherent cells from Fraction II of SPC, which are only weakly responsive to macrophage-mediated suppression, are rendered highly susceptible to suppression by the addition of adherent cells from Fraction I (the largest cells from the profile). Pretreatment of these latter adherent cells with RARTS abolishes their capacity to transfer susceptibility to macrophage-mediated suppression of blastogenesis. Comparable data are also shown in Table 5, which indicates that a RARTS-sensitive cell is (at least in part) responsible for the low PHA-responsiveness of SPC from suckling rats.

Lack of Sensitivity of the Suppressor to X-Rays, Indomethacin, and Mitomycin C

The dosages of these agents are detailed under Materials and Methods; they were tested as per RARTS in Fig. 3B and Table 5, and were found to be ineffective in modifying the capacity of adherent cells to transfer susceptibility to macrophage suppression.

Macrophage-Mediated Suppression of Antigen-Driven Blastogenesis

The experiments described above collectively suggest the presence in rat spleen of a mitogen-responsive suppressor cell, which acts to inhibit lymphocyte proliferation via macrophages. The possibility that similar cells are generated during a primary immune response to specfic antigen is examined in the experiments shown in Fig. 4. In this study, cells from lymph nodes draining the site of immunization with OA in FCA were stimulated in culture with the antigen OA or the mitogen PHA, in the presence of increasing numbers of PEC. Macrophage-mediated suppression of blastogenesis was examined in both mitogen and antigen-stimulated cultures, and comparable results were obtained in a large number of experiments. The antigen-driven process invariably displayed greater sensitivity to suppression, as in the example shown.

DISCUSSION

Earlier studies from these laboratories examining the *in vitro* activity of AM from a number of species (32), in particular the rat (33, 34), have demonstrated marked cytostatic activity on the part of this macrophage population. More recent experiments provided evidence for T-cell control of the expression of suppressive activity by AM (11), and the present report extends this observation to "activated" peritoneal macrophages, and provides more substantial evidence for the T-cell dependence of the process.

The general findings of the present study are as follows. First, "activated" macrophages present in the PEC population of rats are capable of markedly suppressing PHA-induced blastogenesis in cultures of SPC. Second, the suppressive activity of macrophages in this system is not expressed spontaneously, but requires the presence of a RARTS-sensitive member of the SPC population. From the data presented above the following properties may be ascribed to this latter cell: large size (Table 2), long life, recirculation, and thymus dependence *in vivo* (Fig. 2), high susceptibility to anti-thymocyte antiserum *in vitro* (Fig. 3A), glass-wool adherence (Fig. 2, Table 5), cyclophosphamide sensitivity *in vivo* (Table 4), poor survival *in vitro* (Table 3), and age-dependent decline in activity *in vivo* (Table 1). Relevant to the mechanism of suppression, we have shown earlier that the crucial events occur within a few hours of culture initiation (33), that the process does not show MHC-restriction (33) and is not susceptible to indomethacin, mitomycin C, or X-irradiation.

These findings are consistent with the activity of a large recirculating T cell (possibly a blast), which does not proliferate upon contact with mitogen, but elaborates a "suppressor" signal which is translated by adjacent activated macrophages into lymphocytostasis. This cell may be termed a macrophage-dependent nonspecific suppressor T cell (T_s^{ns}), to distinguish it from the antigen-reactive suppressor population (T_s^{Ag}) observed in the lymph node experiments of Fig. 4. This suggestion is compatible with earlier models for nonspecific suppressor cell activity in rat spleens suggested by Waksman (26) and Raff and Hinrichs (25), and offers substantial clarification of a number of the controversial aspects of these latter system.

A number of questions relevant to the mechanism of suppression have not yet been addressed directly, and will be the subject of future experiments. In particular, we propose to examine the relative importance of cell-to-cell contact versus soluble factor(s) in the two sets of cellular interactions (viz., T_s/macrophage and macrophage/target cell) proposed here. Macrophage-mediated suppression via T_s-derived soluble factors has been convincingly demonstrated by Tadakuma and Pierce (22, 35) employing PFC systems, and the possibility that a similar process occurs in the system described above will be tested subsequently in diffusion chamber experiments. In this context, recent observations on the role of macrophages in T_s-dependent suppression of contact hypersensitivity (20, 21, 36) which stress the importance of macrophage surface receptors in the transmission of suppressor signals provide other potential avenues for these investgations.

The relationship between T_s^{ns} and T_s^{Ag} in this model also requires clarification. While both clearly exert their suppressive activity via macrophages (Fig. 4), preliminary sedimentation velocity cell separation studies (not shown) suggest considerable heterogeneity within the T_s^{Ag} pool. These observations suggest intrinsic differences between the two populations, and justify more detailed studies of the properties of the T_s^{Ag} per se. The possibilities that the T_s^{ns} may be the immediate precursor of T_s^{Ag} (specificity being conferred via appropriate antigen contact), or alternatively a product thereof (e.g., a cell entering the T_s^{Ag} memory pool, but still susceptible to polyclonal stimuli), will both be considered in future studies.

The most interesting theoretical implication of this model is the potential for amplification of suppressor signals afforded by appropriate prestimulation of the macrophages which serve as effector cells in this system. It is noteworthy that the most active macrophages here are AM, activated *in vivo* during maturation in the environment of the lower lung (33)—in all cases tested, AM were more suppressive than PEC, regardless of the nature of the inflammatory stimulant employed to raise the peritoneal exudate. The high suppressive activity of macrophages activated during normal *in vivo* maturation may also underline the failure of Fraction I splenocytes to respond to PHA, even in the absence of exogenous macrophages (Table 2). The data here indicate that this fraction contains the majority of the splenic T_s^{ns} population, but this observation cannot in itself account for the restoration of normal PHA responsiveness by deletion of adherent cells, unless it is assumed that such procedures also remove endogenous "activated" splenic macrophages. Examination of cells from Fraction I after incubation with colloidal gold indeed reveals the presence of ≥5% phagocytic cells (data not shown), and these latter cells may be the ultimate cause of depressed PHA responsiveness here. Experiments to test this possibility are in progress.

The scheme for macrophage-dependent T suppression proposed above represents only a broad framework for further research, and will undoubtedly require substantial modification in the light of future experiments. Nevertheless, it provides fresh avenues for exploration of the multicellular aspects of T_s activity, and by highlighting the role of the macrophage as the ultimate "effector" in this process opens up new opportunities for modulation of suppressor signals in a number of the available T_s systems.

In conclusion, these results should not be interpreted as indirect evidence for T-cell participation in other manifestations of suppressive activity by "activated" macrophages. The failure of prostaglandin inhibitors to block macrophage suppressive activity in this and other Ts-dependent models (37) clearly distinguishes this mode of suppression from the T-independent cytostatic activity of BCG-treated macrophages (cited in (37)) and related "nonspecific" suppressor macrophages activated via microbial stimulation (29).

ACKNOWLEDGMENTS

This work was supported by the Princess Margaret Children's Medical Research Foundation. The authors thank Mr. J. Flexman for provision of the B rats employed in this study. This is Publication No. 109 from the Princess Margaret CMRF Clinical Immunology Research Unit.

REFERENCES.

1. Jerne, N. K., *In* "Ontogeny of Acquired Immunity" (R. Porter and J. Knight, Eds.), p. 1. Elsevier, Amsterdam, 1972.
2. Rosenstreich, D. L., Farr, J. J., and Dougherty, S. S. *J. Immunol.* **116,** 131, 1976.
3. Seeger, R. C., and Oppenheim, J. J., *J. Exp. Med.* **132,** 44, 1970.
4. Mookerjee, B. K., *Transplantation* **23,** 22, 1977.
5. Thomas, D. W., and Shevach, E. M., *J. Exp. Med.* **144,** 1263, 1976.
6. Nelson, D. S., *Nature (London)* **246,** 306, 1973.
7. Calderon, J., and Unanue, E. R., *Nature New Biol.* **253,** 359, 1976.
8. Keller, R., *Cell. Immunol.* **17,** 542, 1975.
9. Baird, L. G., and Kaplan, A. M., *Cell. Immunol.* **28,** 22, 1977.
10. Wing, E. J., and Remington, J. S., *Cell. Immunol.,* **30,** 108, 1977.
11. Warner, L. A., Holt, P. G., and Mayrhofer, G., *Immunology* **42,** 137, 1981.
12. Nelson, D. S. In "Immunobiology of the Macrophage" (D. S. Nelson, Ed.), pp. 235–257, Academic Press, New York, 1976.
13. Niederhuber, J. E., *In* "Macrophage Regulation of Immunity" (E. R. Unanue and A. S. Rosenthal, Eds.), pp. 197–211, Academic Press, New York, 1980.
14. Rosenstreich, D. C., and Oppenheim, J. J., *In* "Immunobiology of the Macrophage" (D. S. Nelson, Ed.), pp. 162–201, Academic Press, New York, 1976.
15. Segal, S., Tzehoval, E., and Feldman, M., *Proc. Nat. Acad. Sci. USA* **76,** 4056, 1979.
16. Segal, S., Tzehoval, E., DeBaetselier, P., and Feldman, M., *In* "Macrophage Regulation of Immunity" (E. R. Unanue and A. S. Rosenthal, Eds.) pp. 477–490, Academic Press, New York, 1980.

17. Schon-Hegrad, M. A., and Holt, P. G., in press.
18. Basten, A., Miller, J. F. A. P., and Johnson, P. *Transplant. Rev.* **26,** 130, 1975.
19. Taylor, R. B., and Basten, A., *Brit. Med. Bull.* **32,** 152, 1976.
20. Zembala, M., and Asherson, G. L., *Eur. J. Immunol.* **4,** 799, 1974.
21. Ptak, W., Zembala, M., and Gershon, R. K., *J. Exp. Med.* **148,** 424, 1978.
22. Tadakuma, T., and Pierce, C. W., *J. Immunol.* **120,** 481, 1978.
23. Stobo, J. D., *J. Immunol.* **119,** 918, 1977.
24. Bash, J. A., Singer, A. M., and Waksman, B. H., *J. Immunol.* **116,** 1350, 1976.
25. Raff, H. V., and Hinrichs, D. J., *Cell. Immunol.* **29,** 118, 1977.
26. Waksman, B. H., *Clin. Exp. Immunol.* **28,** 363, 1977.
27. Holt, P. G., *J. Immunol. Methods* **27,** 189, 1979.
28. Miller, R. G., and Phillips, R. A., *J. Cell. Physiol.* **73,** 191, 1969.
29. Mattingly, J. A., Eardley, D. D., Kemp, J. D., and Gershon, R. K., *J. Immunol.* **122,** 787, 1979.
30. Ansfield, M. J., Kaltreider, H. B., Caldwell, J. L., and Herscowitz, F. N., *J. Immunol.* **122,** 542, 1979.
31. Gowans, J. L., and Uhr, J., *J. Exp. Med.* **124,** 1017, 1966.
32. Holt, P. G., and Batty, J., *Cell. Immunol.* **50,** 210, 1980.
33. Holt, P. G., *Immunology* **37,** 429, 1979.
34. Holt, P. G., *Immunology* **37,** 437, 1979.
35. Tadakuma, T., and Pierce, C. W., *J. Immunol.* **117,** 967, 1976.
36. Asherson, G. L., and Zembala, M., *Eur. J. Immunol.* **4,** 804, 1974.
37. Gershon, R. K., Naidorf, K. F., and Ptak, W., *In* "Macrophage Regulation of Immunity" (E. R. Unanue and A. S. Rosenthal, Eds.), pp. 431–438. Academic Press, New York, 1980.

CELLULAR IMMUNOLOGY 63, 71–80 (1981)

Absolute Requirement for Adherent Cells in the Production of Human Interleukin 2 (IL2)

JOHN R. NEEFE, G. RICHARD CURL, AND JAMES N. WOODY

Divisions of Immunologic Oncology and Medical Oncology, Lombardi Cancer Research Center, Georgetown University, Washington, D.C. 20007

Received January 27, 1981; accepted April 29, 1981

Activated T lymphocytes appear to require a growth factor, interleukin 2 (IL2), for continued proliferation. It has been hypothesized that T lymphocytes serving an amplifier function produce IL2 in response to an activating signal such as antigen or mitogen; in addition, the producer lymphocytes receive a second signal from macrophages. The present experiments demonstrated that human IL2 production in culture is totally depleted by exhaustive removal of adherent cells and can be completely restored by replacement of the adherent cells.

INTRODUCTION

T-Cell growth factor or interleukin 2 (IL2) is a potent biological material believed to be necessary for the proliferation of activated T lymphocytes. Generation of human culture fluids containing activities attributed to this material was first reported by Morgan *et al.* (1). Subsequent reports defined conditions for optimal production (2–4) and expanded the concept that activated T lymphocytes require IL2 for continued proliferation (5, 6). More recently, it has become clear that complex circuits of cellular interaction are involved in the generation of IL2. Ruscetti *et al.* (7) have suggested the following model. Mitogen or antigen stimulates a subset of T lymphocytes and macrophages. Macrophages elaborate lymphocyte activating factor or interleukin I, which, in cooperation with the stimulating signal, leads a second T-cell subset to produce IL2. The IL2 allows continued growth of the antigen- or mitogen-activated cell. It is obvious that this amplifier circuit could control the extent and duration of proliferation of activated T lymphocytes. Evidence has been presented that kinetics of responses of T lymphocytes to various activating signals *in vitro* are precisely correlated with the amount of IL2 present in the culture fluid (8–10).

A prediction of the above model is that IL2 production should be absolutely macrophage dependent. It has been shown that macrophage depletion techniques reduce the generation of IL2 in mitogen-stimulated human cultures, but complete abrogation of the response has not been achieved (7, 11). This result leaves the possibilities that IL2 production is not macrophage dependent, that different pathways for IL2 exist and at least one is not macrophage dependent, or that exhaustive depletion is required to reduce the macrophage concentration below a very low threshold level. We present evidence that the third alternative is correct.

0008-8749/81/130071-10$02.00/0

MATERIALS AND METHODS

Preparation of human peripheral blood mononuclear cells (PBM). Peripheral blood was obtained from healthy young adult volunteers by venipuncture; the anticoagulant was preservative-free heparin, 5 units/ml. Peripheral blood was centrifuged at 1400*g* for 3 min at 23°C and the buffy coat was collected. Platelets were removed from the supernatant plasma by centrifugation at 1500*g* for 30 min at 23°C. Buffy coat was washed in Hanks' balanced salt solution (HBSS), pH 7.4, and centrifuged once at 80*g* for 15 min at 23°C. The pellet of up to 150 ml blood was suspended in 30 ml HBSS and 8 ml Ficoll–Hypaque (sodium diatrizoate, Winthrop, New York, N.Y.), lymphocyte separation medium was layered under the cell suspension with an 18-gauge spinal needle. The gradient was centrifuged at 400*g* for 20 min at 23°C with the use of a rate controller for slow acceleration and deceleration between 0 and 80*g*. Lymphocytes at the interface were harvested and washed twice with HBSS.

Production of IL2. PBM at 10^6/ml were cultured in McCoy's modified 5A medium (Gibco, Grand Island, N.Y.) supplemented with 200 m*M* glutamine and penicillin/streptomycin mixture; 2% fresh autologous plasma and 0.08% PHA-P (phytohemagglutinin P, Difco, Detroit, Mich.) were also added. Cells were cultured in tightly capped flasks (Corning 25110, Corning, N.Y.) at 37°C for 24–72 hr. Supernatant was harvested after centrifugation of the cell pellet at 850*g* for 20 min, filtered, and frozen at −20°C.

Preparation of nylon-nonadherent lymphocytes. Scrubbed nylon fibers (Fenwal Laboratories 4C2906, Deerfield, Ill.) were washed for several hours in 0.2 *N* HCl, rinsed in several changes of distilled water, dried completely, and teased to remove knots. 1.2 g were packed to the 5-ml level in 5-ml disposable syringes and autoclaved. Prior to use the nylon column was incubated in HBSS with 10% heat-inactivated fetal calf serum (HBSS/FCS) at 37°C for 30 min. Lymphocytes (1–2 × 10^8) were suspended in 1–2 ml HBSS/FCS and injected into the top of the nylon. The cells were washed into the nylon with a further 2 ml HBSS/FCS and the column was incubated upright at 37°C for 45 min. Cells were collected by dropwise addition of 2–4 ml warmed HBSS/FCS. This procedure removes 70–95% of cells capable of ingesting latex particles.

Phagocytic cells. Phagocytic mononuclear cells were enumerated after latex ingestion. A suspension of 10^6 lymphocytes in 50 μl HBSS with 50% fresh autologous serum was incubated with 10 μl of a 1% suspension of uniform latex particles 1.091 μm in diameter (Dow Diagnostics 47807, Indianapolis, Ind.) for 60 min at 37°C. The cells were then washed three times in HBSS and the percentage of cells ingesting beads was determined by counting 200 to 2000 cells in a hemocytometer.

Twice-rosetted lymphocytes. Mononuclear cells were enriched for lymphocytes rosetting with SRBC by gradient centrifugation after rosetting. A suspension of 50 × 10^6 peripheral blood lymphocytes in 5 ml HBSS was mixed with 5 ml 50% neuraminidase-treated SRBC at 37°C for 15 min, centrifuged at 200*g* for 5 min, and incubated for 30 min on ice. The suspension was then mixed gently and 8 ml chilled Ficoll–Hypaque was underlaid with a spinal needle and syringe. The gradient was centrifuged at 400*g* for 30 min at 4°C. The rosetted cells and red cells in the pellet were collected; the incubations, centrifugations, and gradient separation were repeated once to produce twice-rosetted cells. The pellet was then mixed with

10 ml chilled ACK red-cell-lysing buffer (Microbiological Associates, Walkersville, Md.) for 10 min on ice and washed three times with HBSS.

Passage of PBM over Sephadex G-10. Sephadex G-10 (Pharmacia, Piscataway, N.J.) was swollen in saline, settled to a volume of 10–15 ml in a 50-ml syringe barrel over a cushion of nylon wool, and autoclaved. The column was preincubated with 50 ml RPMI 1640 and 20% FCS at 37°C for 1 hr. PBM from 200 ml whole blood were suspended in 2–3 ml RPMI 1640 plus 20% FCS and run into the column. After incubation at 37° for 30–60 min additional medium was added, the elution rate was controlled by attachment of a 20-gauge needle to the outflow, and the first 10–20 ml of effluent was collected.

Production of IL2-dependent assay cells. Lymphocytes dependent on IL2 for growth were used for assay of supernatants containing IL2 (CM). Peripheral blood mononuclear cells were cultured for 7 days with 0.08% PHA-P. They were then cut back to 1.5×10^5 cells/ml in RPMI 1640 medium with added glutamine, antibiotics, 10% FCS, and with 25% CM of known potency. Cultures were split at 5- to 7-day intervals until they grew in the presence of CM but not in the presence of PHA alone. Then the cells were frozen in aliquots for later use. Other assay cells were initially exposed in culture to an allogeneic stimulus. The primed cells were then plated at limiting dilution. All the progeny of a single culture were grown to a total increase in cell number of 2×10^8 and frozen in aliquots; 85–95% of assay cells rosetted with SRBC.

Cell freezing. Lymphocytes were suspended at $10\text{–}40 \times 10^6$ cells/ml in cold RPMI 1640 with antibiotics and 10% fetal calf serum. Freezing medium consisted of cold RPMI 1640 with antibiotics, 40% fetal calf serum, and 20% dimethyl sulfoxide and was added in equal volume to the cell suspension which was aliquoted in sterile vials, capped, frozen in a programmed cell freezer (Cryoson), and stored in the vapor phase of liquid nitrogen.

Growth factor assay. Assay cells were thawed rapidly in a 37°C water bath and diluted by dropwise addition over 10 min of culture medium at room temperature. Cells were washed twice and suspended at an appropriate concentration in RPMI 1640 with added glutamine, antibiotics, and 10% FCS. Cells (100 μl) were plated in quadruplicate with 100 μl of dilutions of CM to be assayed. Controls of medium alone, PHA-P in various concentrations, and CM of known potency were always plated. Cultures were incubated for 24–72 hr at 37°C in humidified 5% CO_2 in air and pulsed for the last 4 hr with 1 μCi of tritiated thymidine (sp act, 2 mCi/mmol, New England Nuclear NET027A, Boston Mass.) Cultures were harvested onto paper strips with a MASH II (Microbiological Associates 23-902). The strips were dried overnight in a 50°C oven and the samples were distributed into BioVials (Beckman 566353, Somerset, N.J.) to which 1 ml of Betafluor (National Diagnostics LS151, Somerville, N.J.) was added. Samples were counted for 2 min in a scintillation counter (Beckman LS7000), and results are given as mean counts per minute.

Anti-PHA column passage. A rabbit was immunized with PHA-P in complete Freund's adjuvant and boosted multiple times. Serum was collected and a bleed which agglutinated sheep erythrocytes coated with a subagglutinating dose of PHA was used. Sepharose 4B coupled to protein A (Pharmacia) was swollen, washed, incubated overnight at 4°C in antiserum with mixing, and washed extensively. Supernatants were incubated overnight at 4°C with 1/20 vol of the serum-coupled

Sepharose and the gel was removed by centrifugation. This procedure removed greater than 90% of radiolabeled purified PHA leukoagglutinating and hemagglutinating components (kindly provided by Dr. R. Felsted). Greater than 97% of hemagglutinating and mitogenic activity was removed by the column.

Data analysis. Data were analyzed with the aid of Wang 2200 computer programs written by Dr. Stephen J. Shaw and Mrs. Elizabeth Phillips. In order to facilitate automatic data processing, a statistical method of eliminating obviously inaccurate data points such as those from empty wells was employed. When the standard error of the mean of a set of replicates was greater than 25% of the mean the program eliminated the data point farthest from the mean and recalculated the mean and standard error. Seven percent of all the data points displayed in this paper were recalculated in this way. The ratio of standard error of the mean to the mean ranged from 0.02 to 0.23 for the data in this paper, and in the majority of cases was less than 0.10. For clarity of visual impact, the error bars are omitted from the figures. Units of IL2 activity were estimated graphically according to the method employed by Gillis *et al.* (8). In order to compare activities statistically, two- or three-way analysis of variance was performed on the titration curves leading to the activity estimates. The Wang System 2200 Analysis of Variance Package was employed. Values of P given in the figure legends correspond to the F values generated by this program.

RESULTS

Conditions for Production of IL2

Optimal conditions for production of IL2 from PHA-stimulated peripheral blood mononuclear cells were determined in earlier experiments. Peak production was a function of time and cell density. A convenient cell density proved to be 10^6/ml. This density was used throughout, and peak concentration of IL2 in the culture supernatant was usually seen at 48 hr. Maximal concentrations of IL2 were induced by optimally mitogenic concentrations of PHA-P in the presence of 2% autologous plasma. These conditions are similar to those previously reported by others (2–4).

Under these conditions normal volunteers were screened and good producers were identified for further studies. Additional measures of enhancing IL2 production such as irradiation of the producing cells (12), addition of lymphoblastoid cell lines (12, 13), or pooling cells were less useful than prescreening donors.

IL2 Production after Depletion of Phagocytic Cells

An initial attempt at macrophage depletion proved to enhance IL2 production in most cases. The peripheral blood mononuclear cells of 14 consecutive donors were tested for IL2 production with or without passage over nylon wool to remove adherent cells. Only 1 of the 14 donors had a mild decrease in IL2 concentration in the 48-hr supernatant of the nylon-passed cells as compared with the unpassed cells. The cells of the remaining donors were unchanged or enhanced in their ability to generate IL2.

Further depletion procedures were performed on selected donors. In preliminary experiments, nylon-wool-passed cells were incubated with carbonyl iron and passed over a magnet; or cells rosetting with sheep red blood cells were positively selected on a Ficoll–Hypaque gradient. Further diminishment of cells capable of ingesting latex was observed; however, at most, a partial decrease in IL2 concentration in the supernatant was seen. Habu and Raff reported that a three-stage depletion procedure could eliminate the mitogen responsiveness of mouse lymphocytes (14). This procedure included an overnight incubation in a tissue culture plastic flask; it was suggested that this 12- to 16-hr incubation period permitted maturing macrophages to adhere to the plastic.

Figure 1 shows the most detailed of three similar experiments in which PBM were carried through a three-stage depletion. The effluent cells from a Sephadex G-10 column (abbreviated G10) were rosetted with sheep red blood cells and the rosetted cells were collected on a Ficoll–Hypaque gradient. This procedure was repeated once. These cells (now abbreviated G10R) were then incubated overnight at 37°C in a tissue culture flask, and the nonadherent cells (G10RI) were gently removed. The frequency of latex-ingesting cells was 20% in the peripheral blood mononuclear cells, 0.2% in the G10 population, 0.1% in the G10R population, and 0.8% in the G10RI population. Each of these populations was cultured for 24, 48, or 72 hr with PHA-P for production of IL2, and the supernatants were collected and assayed. Assayable IL2 was almost totally depleted by the three-stage depletion procedure in this experiment and in each of the others.

Il2 Activity of PHA-Free Supernatants

All supernatants contained PHA. In previous experiments, it had been observed that PHA could act synergistically with low concentrations of IL2 to stimulate the

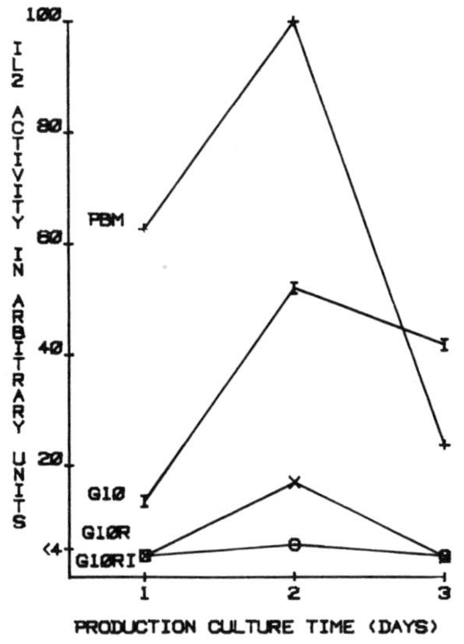

FIG. 1. Depletion of IL2 production by removal of adherent cells. IL2 activity was determined from the titration of culture supernatants against IL2-dependent assay cells. 100 units was the activity present in a standard supernatant. Supernatants to be assayed were harvested from IL2 production cultures at 24, 48, and 72 hr. Four cell populations were tested: peripheral blood mononuclear cells (PBM); PBM passed over Sephadex G-10 (G10); G10 twice rosetted with sheep erythrocytes and separated from nonrosetting cells (G10R); G10R incubated overnight in tissue culture plastic and separated from the plastic-adherent cells (G10RI). For PBM vs G10 and G10 vs G10R, $P < 0.005$. For G10R vs G10RI, $P < 0.1$, but the interaction of cell source with time gave $P < 0.005$; this is because G10R and G10RI are different only at 48 hr.

growth factor assay cells used in the experiments above. Figure 2A shows that supernatants passed over an anti-PHA column were reduced in apparent activity and this activity was restored by replacing the PHA. Passage of concentrated supernatant over the anti-PHA column increased its activity (Fig. 2B). This implies that high concentrations of PHA were inhibitory and provides further evidence that the column did not deplete IL2 from the supernatant. The supernatants from the macrophage-depleted population (G10RI) were reduced to background activity when passed over the PHA column (Fig. 2C). This indicates that no assayable IL2 was present in the supernatant generated from mononuclear cells exhaustively depleted of adherent cells.

Restoration of IL2 Production by Replacement of Adherent Cells

A population of adherent cells was prepared by incubating peripheral blood mononuclear cells overnight in a tissue culture flask and removing nonadherent

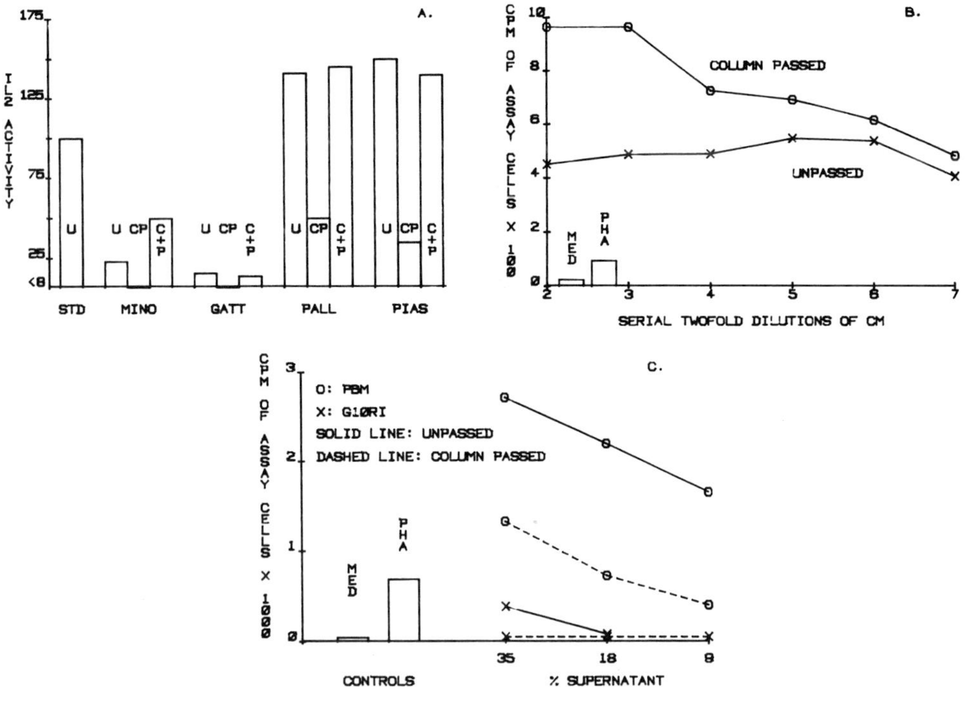

FIG. 2. Passage of adherent-cell depleted supernatant over anti-PHA column. (A). IL2 activity of supernatants from four normal donors (MINO, GATT, PALL, PIAS) was calculated from a titration against IL2-dependent assay cells and compared to a standard (STD) supernatant. (U) Untreated supernatants; (CP) effluent from an anti-PHA column, (C + P) column-passed supernatant with an optimally mitogenic concentration of PHA added back. For U vs CP of all donors, $P \ll 0.001$. For U vs C + P, $P > 0.1$. (B) Titration curve of the 10-fold concentrated standard supernatant before and after passage over an anti-PHA column. Uptake of radiolabeled thymidine by IL2-dependent assay cells is shown on the ordinate. (MED) Activity of assay cells cultured in medium alone, (PHA) activity of assay cells cultured with optimally mitogenic concentration of PHA. (C) Titration of IL2 production culture supernatants. (PBM) peripheral blood mononuclear cells of a normal donor, (G10RI) PBM exhaustively depleted of adherent cells as described in text, (% supernatant) concentration of supernatant in IL2 assay culture. cpm of assay cells, MED, and PHA, as in B. (Unpassed) crude supernatants from IL2 production culture; (Column Passed) supernatant passed over anti-PHA column.

cells by several washes with medium. This population produced some assayable IL2, as shown in Fig. 3. When the population maximally depleted of adherent cells (G10RI) was added back to a flask containing the adherent cells, the IL2 activity of the untreated population was regained. This result indicates that maximal IL2 activity arises from cooperation of the adherent and nonadherent population and provides evidence against the possibility that the extensive depletion procedures led to irreversible inactivation of the IL2-producing cells.

Proliferative Activity of the TCGF Producing Cells

The populations of cells depleted of adherent cells were tested for proliferation in the IL2 production culture by pulsing each culture vessel with [^{3}H]thymidine for 4 hr at the time of harvest of the supernatant (Fig. 4). The PHA response was partially conserved, even in the population which generated no assayable IL2.

DISCUSSION

Human IL2 as prepared by Gillis *et al.* (15), appears to be a single molecular species of molecular weight 15,000–17,000 and isoelectric pH of 6.0 to 6.5. Molecules with these properties obtained after gel exclusion chromatography and flat-bed immunoelectrophoresis have the following functional characteristics. (i) They are required for the growth of IL2-dependent established T-lymphocyte-cell lines. (ii) They permit proliferation of thymocytes in response to mitogen under conditions when no proliferation occurs in the absence of exogenous IL2. (iii) They permit the generation of cytotoxic T lymphocytes from thymocytes or nude mouse sple-

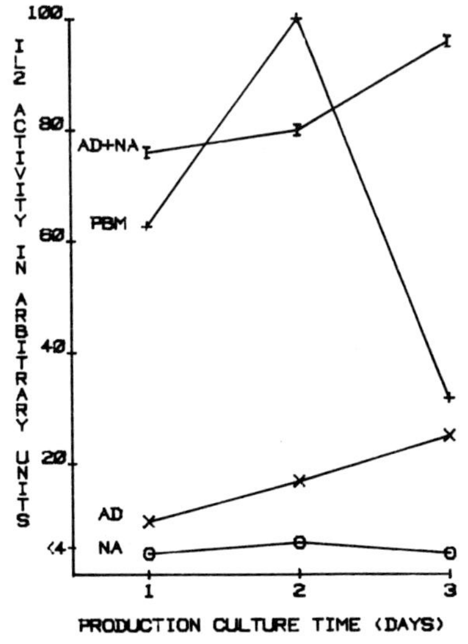

FIG. 3. Restoration of IL2 production to mononuclear populations depleted of adherent cells by replacement of adherent cells. IL2 activity, Production Culture Time, as in Fig. 1. (PBM) Peripheral blood mononuclear cells; (NA) PBM exhaustively depleted of adherent cells as described in text (G10RI); (AD) adherent cells recovered after incubation of PBM on plastic and removal of nonadherent cells; (AD + NA) NA added to the flask containing AD. For NA vs AD + NA and AD vs AD + NA, $P \ll 0.001$.

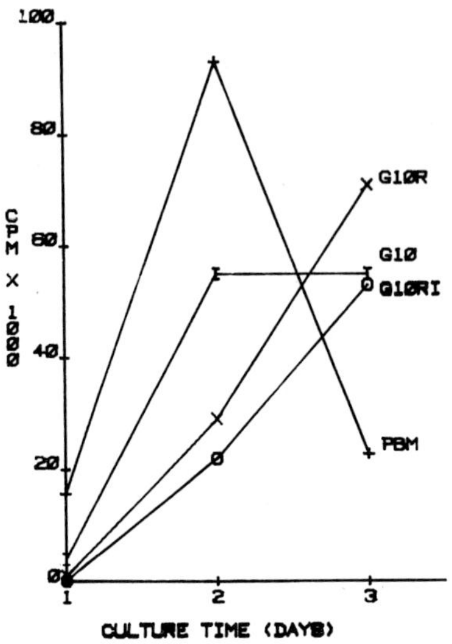

FIG. 4. Mononuclear cell proliferation in IL2 production cultures. At the time of supernatant harvest, an aliquot of the producing cells was removed and pulsed with radiolabeled thymidine for 4 hr. Culture time is the duration of the IL2 production culture at the time of pulsing of cells. PBM, G10, G10R, G10RI, as in text.

nocytes under conditions which do not lead to the generation of cytotoxicity in the absence of exogenous IL2. (iv) They permit the induction of antibody responses to heterologous erythrocytes in nude mouse spleen cells. The fourth, T-cell replacing activity, can also be provided by molecules present in the crude IL2-containing supernatants but possessing a lower isoelectric pH. Gallo and co-workers (7) found material with the first activity to be of molecular weight 23,000 and to be somewhat more heterogeneous in its isoelectric pH than Gillis *et al.* (15). On the whole, the factor permitting T-cell growth appears to be a single molecular species, although there is evidence of heterogeneity of the T-cell replacing activity.

In the murine system it has been shown that mitogen-induced IL2 production requires the cooperation of Thy-1^+ Ly1^+ lymphocytes with Thy-1^- Ia^+ cells (11). Depletion of adherent or phagocytic cells reduced but did not eliminate IL2 production (16), and the adherent cells could be replaced by interleukin I (16). Ruscetti and Gallo demonstrated 60–70% reduction of IL2 production by human peripheral blood mononuclear cells positively selected for lymphocytes rosetting with sheep red blood cells (7).

The T-lymphocyte response to mitogen has been shown to require macrophages, but extensive depletion procedures were required to demonstrate an absolute requirement (14). The present data show an absolute dependence of IL2 production upon the presence of adherent cells. The overnight incubation appeared to be important in reducing the IL2 production to zero after the preliminary depletion procedures. The proportion of phagocytic cells was actually greater after overnight incubation in two of the three experiments. This suggests that some activation or maturation of phagocytic cells may occur under the short-term culture conditions, and partial depletion of these activated or matured cells is necessary to abrogate IL2 production. The depleted population can be restored by adding back adherent cells. There is no formal proof that the cell required in the adherent population is the macrophage, as other cell populations are reduced to some extent by the depletion procedures. Habu and Raff showed that the cell in the adherent population required to restore mitogen responsiveness in the mouse was Thy-1^- Ia^+ and was present in nude mice (14).

The supernatants collected in these experiments are known to be a complex mixture, only partially characterized. Some of the activities which could be present in any given supernatant in addition to IL2 are interleukin I, PHA, and other lymphokines and monokines. Although some residual PHA was left in each of the crude supernatants, and although the growth factor assay cells responded to a limited extent to PHA, the influence of PHA was eliminated by passing some of the supernatants over an anti-PHA column capable of removing more than 90% of the PHA. Further purification of the multiple supernatants tested in the experiments was not performed, and this leaves the theoretical possibility that some of the activities being measured might be attributed to molecules other than IL2. However, other experiments employing these assay cells and various CM showed a clear correlation between the proliferate activity as measured in a short-term thymidine uptake assay and actual cell growth in long-term culture. The other activities are not known to permit growth of T-cell lines (10, 15).

In these experiments, we have not formally demonstrated a requirement for T lymphocytes in IL2 production. The data displayed in Fig. 3 show a synergistic interaction of the adherent-cell-depleted (and T-lymphocyte-enriched) population with the adherent population. From the experiments of Ruscetti and Gallo (7), Smith *et al.* (16), and Wagner and Rollinghoff (17), it is clear that a T-cell subpopulation is required. That the T-lymphocyte subpopulation is the population which produces IL2 was demonstrated by replacing the required adherent cell population with a soluble mediator, IL1 (16). Accordingly, we presume, in our experiments, that the T lymphocytes produce IL2 but have a requirement for accessory adherent cells.

Although human peripheral blood mononuclear cells exhaustively depleted of adherent cells produced no assayable IL2, a delayed and reduced but nevertheless substantial proliferate response to PHA was seen in the production culture. Habu and Raff were able to deplete concanavalin A responsiveness but not PHA responsiveness by their similar depletion procedure (14). The simplest explanation is that a few cycles of cell division can occur with PHA in the absence of macrophages and in the absence of IL2. Alternatively, the minimum requirement for IL2 and macrophages in the PHA response is below the threshold of sensitivity of our assay systems.

In summary, our data demonstrate an absolute requirement for adherent cells for the production of IL2 by human T lymphocytes stimulated by PHA. This observation supports the model that the IL2-producing T lymphocyte must cooperate with or receive a signal from an adherent cell, presumably a macrophage.

REFERENCES

1. Morgan, D. A., Ruscetti, F. W., and Gallo, R., *Science* **193,** 1007, 1976.
2. Ruscetti, F. W., Morgan, D. A., and Gallo, R., *J. Immunol.* **119,** 131, 1977.
3. Strausser, J. L., and Rosenberg, S. A., *J. Immunol.* **121,** 1491, 1978.
4. Alvarez, J. M., Silva, A., and de Landazuri, M. O., *J. Immunol.* **123,** 977, 1979.

5. Bonnard, G. D., Yasaka, K., and Jacobson, D., *J. Immunol.* **123,** 2704, 1979.
6. Baker, P. E., Gillis, S., Ferm, M. M., and Smith, K. A., *J. Immunol.* **121,** 2168, 1978.
7. Ruscetti, F. W., and Gallo, R. C., *Blood* **57,** 379, 1981.
8. Gillis, S., Ferm, M. M., Ou, W., and Smith, K. A., *J. Immunol.* **120,** 2027, 1978.
9. Coutinho, A., Larsson, E. L., Gronvik, K. O., and Anderson, J., *Eur. J. Immunol.* **9,** 587, 1979.
10. Watson, J., Gillis, S., Marbrook, J., Mochizuki, D., and Smith K. A., *J. Exp. Med.* **150,** 849, 1979.
11. Andersson, J., Gronvik, K. O., Larsson, E. L., and Coutinho, A., *Eur. J. Immunol.* **9,** 581, 1979.
12. Inouye, H., Hank, J. A., Alter, B. J., and Bach, F. H., *Scand. J. Immunol.* **12,** 149, 1980.
13. Bonnard, G. D., Yasaka, K., Schendel, D. J., Pappas, F., Maca, R. D., Strong, D. M., Lang, N. P., Fagnani, R., Navarro, N., and Pandolfi, F., *In* "Proceedings of the 13th Leukocyte Culture Conference." (J. G. Kaplan, Ed.), p. 239. Elsevier/North-Holland, Amsterdam, 1979.
14. Habu, S., and Raff, M. C., *Eur. J. Immunol.* **7,** 451, 1977.
15. Gillis, S., Smith, K. A., and Watson, J., *J. Immunol.* **124,** 1954, 1980.
16. Smith, K. A., Lachman, L. B., Oppenheim, J. J., and Favata, M. F., *J. Exp. Med.* **151,** 1551, 1980.
17. Wagner, H., and Rollinghoff, M., *J. Exp. Med.* **148,** 1523, 1978.

CELLULAR IMMUNOLOGY 63, 81–90 (1981)

Inability of Immunocompetent Thymocytes to Produce T-Cell Growth Factor under Adenosine Deaminase Deficiency Conditions

LAURE THUILLIER,[1] FLORIANNE GARREAU, AND PIERRE CARTIER

Département de Biochimie, Faculté de Médecine Necker-Enfants Malades and Unité 75 INSERM, 156 rue de Vaugirard, 75730 Paris, Cedex 15, France.

Received February 18, 1981; accepted May 12, 1981

Five density-defined subpopulations of rat thymocytes were separated by isopycnic centrifugation on a discontinuous density Ficoll gradient and compared with respect to their response to Con A stimulation under normal and adenosine deaminase (ADA) deficiency conditions. This study shows that (a) immunocompetent (low-density) thymocytes and splenic T lymphocytes produce T-cell growth factor (TCGF) in response to mitogenic stimulation in normal culture conditions, but are unable to synthesize effective TCGF in the presence of an adenosine deaminase inhibitor and excess substrate (ADA deficiency conditions), and (b) high-density immunoincompetent thymocytes proliferate and differentiate into mature T cells in response to Con A if effective exogenous TCGF is added to the culture medium but are unable to do so under ADA deficiency conditions.

INTRODUCTION

Congenital deficiency of adenosine deaminase (ADA)[2] (EC 3.5.4.4) is associated with a severe form of immunodeficiency. Clinical observations of predominantly T-cell impairment and thymic hypoplasia (1–3) indicate that ADA deficiency preferentially affects T-lymphocyte differentiation (4) and proliferation (5–7).

On the assumption that the overall cause of the immunoincompetence resides in the toxicity of the accumulated purine substrates of ADA (adenosine: Ado and 2′-deoxyadenosine: dAdo) to lymphoid cells, a number of models have been proposed for the underlying biochemical mechanism of lymphotoxicity. Among these proposals, the one which was thought to be the most plausible involves the high deoxyribonucleotide kinase activity of T lymphocytes, by which dATP is formed from the unmetabolized dAdo. The dATP, in turn, acts as an allosteric inhibitor of diphosphoribonucleotide reductase thus interfering with DNA synthesis and inhibiting T-lymphocyte blastogenesis (8).

However, in light of recent data from our laboratory this simple scheme may need to be modified. We simulated ADA deficiency conditions *in vitro* using a chemical ADA inhibitor (2-deoxycoformycin, dCf) and excess exogenous dAdo and

[1] To whom reprint requests and correspondence should be addressed.

[2] Abbreviations used: TCGF, T-cell growth factor; ADA, adenosine deaminase; dAdo, 2′-deoxyadenosine; Ado, adenosine; dATP, 2′-deoxyadenosine-5′-triphosphate; dCf, deoxycoformycin; [^{3}H]dThd, tritiated thymidine.

0008-8749/81/130081-10$02.00/0

showed that the sensitivity of the metabolic activity of rat thymocytes to the toxic effects of dAdo (as measured by the inhibition of the mitogenic response to Con A) was essentially dependent on the activation state of the cells. When ADA deficiency conditions (ADA inhibition and excess substrate in the culture medium) were imposed simultaneously with Con A, metabolic inhibition was definitive and blastogenesis was abolished. However, when thymocytes were stimulated with Con A 12 hr prior to incubation under ADA deficiency conditions, inhibition of metabolic activity was transitory at best; ultimately blastogenesis was unchanged or even enhanced.

This observation prompted us to suggest an alternative explanation for dAdo toxicity. dAdo or Ado could act on thymocyte proliferation at some earlier stage before the initiation of DNA synthesis, perhaps by interfering with events in the "mitogen recognition phase."

The concurrent findings of Smith, Gillis, and co-workers (9–11) and of Chen and Di Sabato (12) demonstrate that T-cell growth factor (TCGF) is produced by mature T cells derived from the spleen or from the thymic medulla. Release of this lymphokine occurs during the first hours of T-cell stimulation by mitogens or specific antigen, and only in the presence of macrophages. However, such a factor may act as a "second signal" in the induction of T-cell-mediated immunity following membrane binding of lectin or antigen (10).

Combined experimental results over the last few years indicate that partially purified TCGF may be endowed with several immunological properties: (a) it allows exponential proliferation of specific cytotoxic T-cell clones, (b) it enhances the responses of activated T cells (and only *activated* T cells) to mitogens, and (c) it promotes the maturation of prethymocytes such as bone marrow cells or nude prethymocytes to mature effector T cells; nude prethymocytes acquire the ability to respond to lectin stimulation and the capacity to mediate cytotoxic and helper-T-cell functions in the presence of exogenous TCGF.

As has been previously described (13), whole thymocyte populations may be divided into physically and biologically distinct subpopulations by isopycnic centrifugation on discontinuous density Ficoll gradients. The larger, lower-density thymocytes (fractions 1 and 2 on our gradient) tend to be corticoresistant, metabolically active, and more responsive to mitogens or histocompatibility antigens. The smaller, higher-density thymocytes (fractions 3, 4, and 5) on the other hand may be characterized as less active, corticosensitive immunoincompetent cells.

Studies on the membrane antigen patterns of thymocytes have shown that the great majority of mature thymocytes populate the thymic medulla, while the immature thymocytes are those found in the cortex (14, 15).

The present study was undertaken (a) to measure the effects of ADA deficiency on the production of TCGF in mature thymocytes and (b) to compare the five density-defined subpopulations of rat thymocytes with respect to their response to TCGF under normal and ADA deficiency conditions.

MATERIALS AND METHODS

Materials

Chemicals used. Ficoll 400 (Pharmacia, Uppsala, Sweden); concanavalin A, grade IV (Sigma, St. Louis, Mo.); Dulbecco's minimum essential medium (Gibco,

Grand Island, N.Y.); fetal calf serum (Flow Labs., Rockville, Md.); Unisolve (Kock-Light, England); PPO and POPOP (Packard) were used. [6-^{3}H]Thymidine was purchased from the Commissariat à l'Energie Atomique (Saclay, France). All other chemicals were from commercial sources and of the highest grade available.

Medium A. Medium A consisted of Dulbecco's MEM supplemented with Hepes (33 m*M*), 5% fetal calf serum, penicillin (100 U/ml), streptomycin (100 μg/ml).

Medium B. Dulbecco's MEM modified according to Cerottini *et al.* (16), supplemented with Hepes (33 m*M*), penicillin (100 U/ml), streptomycin (100 μg/ml) and 10% fetal calf serum dialyzed for 3 days against 0.9% NaCl and changed daily, constituted medium B.

Methods

Preparation of thymocytes. Thymus glands were removed aseptically from 6-week-old rats (Sprague–Dawley) of either sex and were placed into cold medium A. The glands were cleared from adherent connective tissues, cut into small pieces with scissors and dissociated in 5 ml ice-cold medium A. The aggregates were allowed to sediment and the cells were washed three times by centrifugation 10 min at 150*g* in medium A. Cells were tested for viability by the trypan blue method: cells were incubated with 0.04% trypan blue for 5 min and scored for their ability to exclude dye. Cell preparations with less than 98% viable cells were discarded.

Thymocyte separation on Ficoll gradient. Ficoll gradients were prepared according to Tak Yan Yu *et al.* (17) modified by Incefy *et al.* (18) using Ficoll 400 (Pharmacia) at the following concentrations (w/w): 10, 14.6, 16.1, 17.7, 19.2 and 23% prepared in 0.1 *M* sodium phosphate buffer, pH 7.4. Layer 1 was defined as the interface between 10 and 14.6% Ficoll suspensions with subsequent interphases numbered sequentially. Cells (2×10^9) in 2 ml medium A were layered on top of the gradient and centrifuged at 21,500*g* for 45 min at 4°C. Thymocytes from each of the five layers of the gradient were washed three times in medium A and tested for their viability. From 80 to 90% of the cells layered initially on top of the gradient were recovered in the five layers combined and their viability was 96–98%. Cell numbers were determined with a ZBI Coulter counter.

Preparations of TCGF. The supernates of Con A-stimulated rat thymocyte and spleen cell cultures under normal and ADA deficiency conditions were used as a source of TCGF. Rat spleen cells or immunocompetent thymocytes (low-density thymocytes recovered from gradient fraction 1) were incubated for 30 to 36 hr at 37°C with Con A in medium B supplemented with 25 μ*M* 2-mercaptoethanol to promote T cell–macrophage cooperation (19). The proportion of macrophages in the low-density thymocyte fraction (10%) was appropriate for TCGF production (20). The Con A concentration used was 5 μg/ml in spleen cell cultures and 2 μg/ml in thymocyte cultures. TCGF was first recovered in the culture supernate by removing the cells by centrifugation at 2000*g* for 10 min then filtering on a 0.45-μM Whatman micropore filter. The TCGF could then be stored at −20°C for 4 weeks without loss of activity. The residual Con A was not removed since the same mitogen was used again in all experiments with TCGF prepared in this way.

TCGF activity was assayed by its ability to enhance the response of immunocompetent thymocytes to mitogenic stimulation. Thymocytes (10^5) were suspended either in medium B (controls) or in a mixture of equal parts medium B and TCGF, then incubated for 0, 24, 48, or 72 hr with 2 μg/ml Con A in humidified air containing 5% CO_2. Following the incubation period, [^{3}H] dThd uptake was measured over 15 hr.

Induction of thymocyte mitogenic responses to Con A in normal and ADA deficiency conditions. Following gradient separation of the thymocyte subpopulations, the cells recovered at the various interfaces were resuspended in medium B or in an equal-parts mixture of TCGF and medium B. The cells were incubated in normal or ADA deficiency conditions for 96 hr in humidified air containing 5% CO_2 in the absence (control cultures) or in the presence of 2 μg/ml Con A. The concentration of thymocytes in culture varied for the different gradient fractions; fraction 1: 10^5 cells/ml; fraction 2: 5×10^5 cells/ml; fractions 3, 4, and 5: 10^6 cells/ml.

ADA deficiency conditions were reproduced *in vitro* for the purpose of these experiments by inhibition of ADA activity using 1×10^{-5} *M* deoxycoformycin (dCf) and by simulated accumulation of purine ADA substrates using 1×10^{-5} *M* deoxyadenosine (dAdo). These reagents were added together to cell suspensions 20 min before the addition of Con A. ADA deficient control cultures received no lectin but the same concentrations of dCf and dAdo. In order to check the efficacity of ADA inhibition, aliquots containing 10^6 cells in medium with or without dCf and dAdo were tested for ADA activity in both the cells and the medium (containing fetal calf serum) according to the method of Cartier and Hamet (21). We checked 98% inhibition of ADA activity in "deficient" cultures with respect to control cultures throughout the incubation period.

Blastogenesis was assayed after 0, 24, 48, 72, and 96 hr of incubations with Con A by measurement of DNA synthesis. Aliquots of 0.2 ml of each cell culture were incubated for 15 hr in triplicate in Falcon 3040 microtest plates II with [^{3}H]dThd (1μCi), at 37°C in a humidified atmosphere of 5% CO_2 in air. At the end of the incubation period, incorporated radioactivity into acid-insoluble material was measured acording to the technique of Mans and Novelli (22).

Mitogenic effects are expressed as stimulation index (SI):

$$SI = \frac{\text{cpm incorporation in stimulated cells} - \text{cpm incorporation in control cells}}{\text{cpm incorporation in control cells}}.$$

Evaluation of blastogenic transformation and cell viability. Aliquots (1 ml) were removed from each cell culture, centrifuged at 2000*g* for 10 min, resuspended in one ml isotonic saline solution containing 0.04% trypan blue, and then left to stand 5 min at 25°C. Two hundred to three hundred cells were counted using a Lietz Orthoplan microscope. The criterium for viable cells was the ability to exclude trypan blue; the criterium for blast cell transformation was the determination of cell diameter by means of micrometer microscopy equipment. The mean ± SEM ($n = 50$) nonstimulated immunocompetent thymocyte diameter is 7.92 ± 0.23 μm, the mean ± SEM ($n = 50$) blast cell diameter is 13.2 ± 0.5 μm.

RESULTS

Using gradient-separated rat thymocyte subpopulations as targets for TCGF activity, our experiments demonstrate that mature thymocytes as well as splenic T cells produce TCGF, and that this factor mediates a second signal required for blastogenic transformation.

TABLE 1

Stimulation of the Five Subpopulations of Thymocytes by Con A and Thymocyte-TCGF

Subpopulation of thymocytes	Culture additive	Mean ($\pm$SD) cpm incorporated/hr/10^7 cells				
		0 hr	24 hr	48 hr	72 hr	96 hr
1	a	120,900 ± 5,650	33,180 ± 1,250	29,350 ± 1,240	28,000 ± 1,150	21,060 ± 800
	b	129,650 ± 4,560	88,400 ± 4,750	423,050 ± 15,500	1 038,800 ± 50,750	340,400 ± 10,120
	c	169,400 ± 8,710	312,200 ± 12,120	831,600 ± 30,650	2,243,800 ± 70,450	431,200 ± 20,300
2	a	36,950 ± 1,200	14,250 ± 540	12,650 ± 400	12,600 ± 420	11,060 ± 410
	b	48,050 ± 1,540	33,750 ± 1,120	36,550 ± 1,100	533,950 ± 20,400	202,050 ± 7,060
	c	66,520 ± 2,200	372,400 ± 10,500	1,035,300 ± 30,640	2,031,800 ± 51,700	962,220 ± 40,650
3	a	7,000 ± 350	2,050 ± 280	2,150 ± 260	2,030 ± 280	1,800 ± 150
	b	8,940 ± 460	3,250 ± 370	3,200 ± 350	2,230 ± 210	1,750 ± 170
	c	9,520 ± 510	79,990 ± 4,250	369,900 ± 10,250	933,250 ± 50,720	202,550 ± 6,700
4	a	4,090 ± 420	2,400 ± 200	2,370 ± 250	1,600 ± 150	1,500 ± 150
	b	4,580 ± 550	2,500 ± 230	2,350 ± 240	1,700 ± 240	1,500 ± 180
	c	7,850 ± 880	67,900 ± 7,680	200,760 ± 10,800	549,950 ± 40,720	95,200 ± 8,740
5	a	2,500 ± 210	2,100 ± 180	1,400 ± 180	1,100 ± 120	1,100 ± 140
	b	2,750 ± 240	2,250 ± 240	1,450 ± 170	1,000 ± 180	850 ± 150
	c	3,800 ± 480	30,890 ± 350	99,200 ± 8,760	431,200 ± 20,780	85,400 ± 7,600

Note. The incorporation of [^{3}H]dThd in the acid-insoluble material of the five subpopulations of thymocytes was determined in culture control (a) and stimulated cultures in the presence of Con A (2 μg/ml) alone (b) or in the presence of Con A (2 μg/ml) and thymocyte TCGF (c). At 0, 24, 48, 72, and 96 hr of culture, 0.2-ml aliquots of each cell suspension were incubated in triplicate with 1 μCi of [^{3}H]dThd (1 Ci/mmol) for 15 hr in Falcon 3040 microtest plates II, at 37°C in a humid atmosphere of 5% CO_2 in air. Results are the mean ($\pm$SD) cpm incorporated/hr/10^7 cells of triplicate determinations of the same experiment (similar results were obtained in three other experiments).

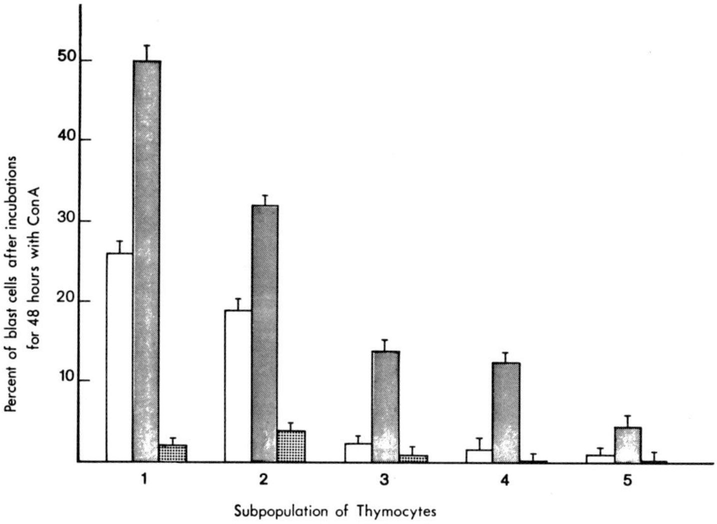

FIG. 1. Percentage blast cells recovered from thymocyte subpopulation cultures after 48 hr of Con A stimulation under different conditions. (□) Con A alone; (▨) thymocyte-TCGF and Con A; (▩) thymocyte-TCGF and Con A under ADA deficiency conditions. The determination of the blast cells was obtained as described under Materials and Methods. The bars represent the standard error for triplicate determinations of a single experiment (similar results were obtained in four additional experiments).

Evidence of TCGF production by immunocompetent rat thymocytes (gradient fraction 1) in response to Con A stimulation is presented in Table 1 and in Fig. 1. First, when the immunocompetent fractions 1 and 2 are stimulated with Con A in the presence of exogenous thymocyte TCGF, the proliferative response is enhanced with respect to control cultures incubated with Con A alone. Second, with TCGF present in the culture medium, the high-density thymocyte fractions 3–5 could be incited to respond to Con. A. The thymocytes found in these gradient fractions are otherwise insensitive to Con A, even after treatment with neuraminidase (results submitted for publication).

On the other hand, our results illustrate the effects of ADA deficiency on the ability of immunocompetent thymocytes or spleen cells to produce efficient TCGF. The supernate from gradient fraction 1—thymocyte cultures or spleen cell cultures after 30 hr of incubation with Con A under ADA deficiency conditions (10 μM 2′-deoxycoformycin and 10 μM deoxyadenosine added to the culture medium fails to enhance the proliferative response of gradient fraction 1 and 2 thymocytes to Con A; for gradient fractions 3, 4, and 5, no proliferative response whatsoever was demonstrable as shown in Tables 2 and 3. Furthermore, when any of the five thymocyte subpopulations are stimulated with Con A under ADA deficiency conditions proven exogenous thymocyte-derived TCGF failed to completely restore the response to Con A (Table 2).

DISCUSSION

Our results concur with those of Smith, Gillis, and co-workers (9–11) and with those of Chen and Di Sabato (12) and demonstrate the existence of a growth factor

TABLE 2

Effects of Thymocyte-TCGF Produced under Normal or ADA Deficiency Conditions on the Stimulation Index for [^{3}H]dThd Uptake in Acid-Insoluble Material of the Five Subpopulations of Thymocytes Maintained 96 hr in the Presence of Con A under Normal or ADA Deficiency Conditions

Subpopulation of thymocytes	Culture additive	Stimulation index				
		0 hr	24 hr	48 hr	72 hr	96 hr
1	a	0.40	8.40	27.33	79.13	19.53
	b	−0.64	1.40	0.94	1	0.82
	c	−0.60	5.30	12.30	32	15.40
	d	−0.08	1.60	0.44	0	−0.06
2	a	0.80	25.13	80.84	160.25	86
	b	−0.66	4	8.6	6.5	11.3
	c	−0.57	9.2	35	135	58
	d	−0.04	3.5	2.55	1.81	−0.54
3	a	0.36	38	171.04	458.73	111.52
	b	−0.48	4.9	1.8	2.06	0.24
	c	−0.75	9.1	25	54	50
	d	−0.35	4.9	−0.09	0	0
4	a	0.92	27.30	83.71	342.72	62.46
	b	−0.43	0.9	0.12	0	0.38
	c	−0.54	6.3	9.10	16.10	18.50
	d	−0.25	0.5	−0.53	−0.07	0.23
5	a	0.52	13.70	68.85	391	76.63
	b	−0.41	0.20	0.40	0	−0.37
	c	−0.70	3.20	9.50	10.30	8.60
	d	−0.18	0.20	0	−0.27	0.30

Note. Stimulation index calculated for the incorporation of [^{3}H]dThd in the acid-insoluble material of the five subpopulations of thymocytes stimulated in the presence of Con A (2 μg/ml) and exogenous thymocyte-TCGF produced under normal or ADA deficiency conditions as described under Materials and Methods. The conditions of incubation are the same as for Table 1. (a) Thymocytes stimulated under normal conditions in the presence of Con A (2 μg/ml) and thymocyte-TCGF produced under normal conditions; (b) thymocytes stimulated under normal conditions in the presence of Con A (2 μg/ml) and thymocytes-TCGF produced under ADA deficiency conditions; (c) thymocytes stimulated under ADA deficiency conditions in the presence of Con A (2 μg/ml) and thymocyte-TCGF produced under normal conditions; (d) thymocytes stimulated under ADA deficiency conditions in the presence of Con A (2 μg/ml) and thymocyte-TCGF produced under ADA deficiency conditions. The means ($\pm$SD) cpm incorporated/1 hr/10^7 cells of triplicate determinations of the same experiment for subpopulation 1 at 72 hr of stimulation with Con A (2 μg/ml) alone are: 1,038,800 $\pm$ 50,750; (a) 2,243,800 $\pm$ 70,450; (b) 56,400 $\pm$ 1,700; (c) 924,000 $\pm$ 45,000; (d) 27,960 $\pm$ 1,500.

in the supernate of Con A-stimulated cultures of mature thymocytes. This substance enhances the blastogenic response of immunocompetent thymocytes and promotes the maturation of immunoincompetent thymocytes, in as much as maturation may be assessed by the capacity to respond to Con A.

The fact that this factor may be produced by mature thymocytes implies that TCGF serves an important regulatory function in T-cell-mediated immunity. The quantity of TCGF produced following antigenic stimulation of specific T cell clones and the capacity to respond to this TCGF might dictate the extent of proliferation and differentiation into immune effector cells.

TABLE 3

Effects of spleen TCGF Produced under Normal or ADA Deficiency Conditions on the Stimulation Index for [^{3}H]dThd Uptake in the Acid-Insoluble Material of the Five Subpopulations of Thymocytes Maintained 96 hr in the Presence of Con A under Normal or ADA Deficiency Conditions

Subpopulation of thymocytes	Culture additive	Stimulation index 0 hr	24 hr	48 hr	72 hr	96 hr
1	a	0.78	4.40	6.90	8.43	14.10
	b	−0.05	1.66	0.55	0	0.12
2	a	1.01	11.40	33.30	125.60	261.50
	b	0.13	4.33	1.88	1.85	−0.17
3	a	0.74	18	29.6	32.5	87
	b	0.18	4	−0.03	0	−0.02
4	a	0.41	4	0.62	0	0.04
	b	0.	0.50	−0.02	−0.11	0
5	a	0.60	2.9	0	0	0.13
	b	−0.25	−0.20	0	0.11	−0.26

Note. Stimulation index calculated for the incorporation of [^{3}H]dThd in the acid-insoluble material of the five subpopulations of thymocytes stimulated in the presence of Con A (2 μg/ml) and exogenous spleen-TCGF produced under normal or ADA deficiency conditions as described under Materials and Methods. The conditions of incubation are the same as for Table 1. (a) Thymocytes incubated under normal conditions in the presence of Con A (2 μg/ml) and spleen-TCGF produced in normal conditions; (b) thymocytes incubated under ADA deficiency conditions in the presence of Con A (2 μg/ml) and spleen-TCGF produced under ADA deficiency conditions. The means (±SD) of cpm incorporated/1 hr/10^7 cells of triplicate determinations of the same experiment for subpopulation 2 at 72 hr of stimulation with Con A (2 μg/ml) alone are: 533,950 ± 20,400; (a) 1,595,160 ± 48,600; (b) 35,910 ± 1,500. Spleen cell cultures under ADA deficiency conditions produced no effective TCGF under normal assay conditions (data not shown).

Further experiments show that mature thymocytes fail to produce effective TCGF when incubated with Con A under ADA deficiency conditions. This profound incapacity may be understood in the light of the devastating effects of accumulated purine substrates of ADA on thymocyte metabolism in the presence of an ADA inhibitor. As we reported earlier, protein synthesis and blastogenesis in immunocompetent thymocytes are severely inhibited when these cells are incubated with exogenous dAdo and dCf during the first 12 hr of Con A stimulation. TCGF has been characterized as a "protein-like" factor and is synthetized mainly during the first 12 hr of mitogenic stimulation (11). Perhaps dAdo interferes with the production of TCGF and it is the lack of this second signal which prevents blastogenic transformation. We also showed that if ADA deficiency conditions are imposed after the first 12 hr of mitogenic stimulation (that is after the peak of TCGF production), the resulting metabolic block was not definitive; inhibition of the pathways studied was only transitory and ultimately blastogenesis resumed.

The second effect of ADA deficiency is illustrated by the inability of immunoincompetent cells to reach maturity under such conditions.

Recent investigations (23–25) into the ontogeny of thymocytes have revealed that the great majority of immunocompetent thymocytes remains within the medulla while post-thymic peripheral T cells are derived from the immature cortical thymocytes. It is conceivable that one physiological role of medullary thymocytes (which constitute the majority of our gradient fraction 1 thymocytes) might be to produce TCGF in response to stimulation by specific antigen which then promotes the differentiation of the immature cortical thymocytes into full-fledged circulating T cells. In ADA-deficient patients, the failure of medullary thymocytes to produce effective TCGF (either by lack of cooperation with macrophages or by lack of protein synthesis) could account for the T lymphopenia and thymic hypoplasia observed (26–28). The failure of maturation of pre-T cells derived from human tonsils observed by Ballet *et al.* (4) could be ascribed to the same phenomenon. Our results are also in good agreement with those of Barton and Goldschneider (29) who reconstituted irradiated rat thymic with bone marrow cells. According to Rubinstein, *et al.* (30) when thymocyte destruction by toxicity of dAdo and Ado reaches the point of complete thymic hypoplasia, the interactions between the thymocytes and the cells of the thymic epithelium necessary for thymosin secretion can no longer take place. The structural integrity of thymic epithelium must still be intact, since transplantation of compatible bone marrow cells has been shown to restore T-cell function in ADA-deficient patients. If suitable transplant material is not available, thymosin transfusions are indicated to complete the effect of enzyme replacement therapy (transfusions of normal irradiated red cells containing the missing enzyme). In the same way, administration of exogenous TCGF to ADA-deficient patients with no matched sibling could prove useful in association with irradiated red cell transfusions.

ACKNOWLEDGMENT

We wish to thank Mrs. A. M. Houllier for her highly competent technical assistance.

REFERENCES

1. Giblett, E. R., Anderson, J. E., Cohen, F., Pollara, B. and Meuwissen, H. J., *Lancet* **2,** 1067, 1972.
2. Pickering, R. J., Pollara, B., and Meuwissen, H. J., *Clin. Immunol. Immunopathol.* **3,** 301, 1974.
3. Hirschhorn, R., *In* "Enzyme Defects and Immune Dysfunction" (Ciba Foundation Symposium 68, Eds.), pp. 35–49. Excerpta Medica, Amsterdam, 1979.
4. Ballet, J. J., Insel, R., Merler, E., and Rosen, F. S., *J. Exp. Med.* **143,** 1271, 1976.
5. Mitchell, B. S., Mejias, E., Daddona, P. E., and Kelley, W. N., *Proc. Nat. Acad. Sci. USA,* **75,** 5011, 1978.
6. Wortmann, R. L., Mitchell, B. S., Edwards, M. L., and Fox, J. H., *Proc. Nat. Acad. Sci. USA,* **76,** 2434, 1979.
7. Gelfand, E. W., Lee, J. J., and Dosch, H. M., *Proc. Nat. Acad. Sci. USA,* **76,** 1998, 1979.
8. Cohen, A., Hirschhorn, R., Horowitz, S. D., Rubinstein, A., Polmar, S. H., Hong, R., and Martin, D. W., Jr., *Proc. Nat. Sci. USA,* **75,** 472, 1978.
9. Smith, K. A., Gillis, S., Baker, P. E., McKenzie, D. and Ruscetti, F. W., *In* "T-Cell Growth Factor-Mediated T-Cell Proliferation" pp. 423–432. Annals New York Academy of Sciences/Academic Press, New York, 1979.
10. Gillis, S., Union, N. A., Baker, P. E., and Smith, K. A., *J. Exp. Med.* **149,** 1460, 1979.
11. Watson, J., Gillis, S., Marbrook, J., Mochizuki, D., and Smith, K. A., *J. Exp. Med.* **150,** 849, 1979.
12. Chen, D. M., and Di Sabato, G., *Cell. Immunol.* **22,** 211, 1976.
13. Papiernik, M., Laroche, L., and Bach, J. F., *Eur. J. Immunol.* **7,** 796. 1977.
14. Schlesinger, M., Gottesfeld, S., and Korash, Z., *Cell Immunol.* **6,** 49, 1973.
15. Konda, S., Stockert, E., and Smith, R. T.,*Cell. Immunol.* **7,** 275, 1973.
16. Cerottini, J. C., Engers, H. D., MacDonald, H. R., and Brunner, K. T., *J. Exp. Med.* **140,** 703, 1974.

17. Tak Yan Yu, D., Peter, J. R., Paulus, H. E., and Machleder, H. I., *J. Immunol.* **110,** 1615, 1973.
18. Incefy, G. S., L'Espérance, P., and Good, R. A., *Clin. Exp. Immunol.* **19,** 475, 1975.
19. Rosenstreich, D. L., Farrar, J. J., and Dougherty, S., *J. Immunol.* **116,** 131, 1976.
20. Nabarra, B., and Papiernik, M., *Cell. Immunol.* **51,** 72, 1980.
21. Cartier, P., and Hamet, M., *Clin. Chim. Acta* **71,** 429, 1976.
22. Mans, R. J., and Novelli, G. D., *Arch. Biochem. Biophys.* **94,** 48, 1961.
23. Weissman, I. L., Masuda, T., Olive, C., and Friedberg, S. H., *Isr. J. Med. Sci.* **11,** 267, 1975.
24. Shortman, R., and Jackson, H., *Cell. Immunol.* **12,** 230, 1974.
25. Goldschneider, I., *Cell. Immunol.* **24,** 289, 1976.
26. Hirschhorn, R., Martiniuk, F., and Rosen, F. S., *Clin. Immunol. Immunopathol.* **9,** 287, 1978.
27. Hirschhorn, R., Vawter, G. F., Kirkpatrick, J. A., Jr., and Rosen, F. S., *Clin. Immunol. Immunopathol.* **14,** 107, 1979.
28. Ziegler, J. B., Lee, C. H., van der Weyden, M. B., Bagnara, A. S., and Beveridge, J., *Arch. Dis. Child.* **55,** 452, 1980.
29. Barton, R. W., and Goldschneider, I., *Mole. Cell. Biochem.* **28,** 135, 1979.
30. Rubinstein, A., Hirschhorn, R., Sicklick, M., and Murphy, R. A., *N. Engl. J. Med.* **300,** 387, 1979.

CELLULAR IMMUNOLOGY **63,** 91–105 (1981)

Cytotoxic Cells Induced *in Vitro* by Epstein–Barr Virus Antigens

LINDSEY M. HUTT-FLETCHER AND COLLEEN J. GILBERT

Cancer Research Center and Department of Bacteriology and Immunology, School of Medicine, University of North Carolina, Chapel Hill, North Carolina 27514

Received February 18, 1981; accepted May 26, 1981

Lymphocyte blastogenesis and cytotoxicity for lymphoid cells lines (LCL) were induced in cells from immune donors by stimulation *in vitro* with irradiated Epstein–Barr Virus (EBV). Velocity sedimentation of blastogenic populations indicated that much of the killing was associated with large E-rosetting cells; it was reduced by [^{3}H]thymidine suicide immediately prior to sedimentation. Target cells were killed irrespective of EBV content or sensitivity to natural killer (NK cells), though the pattern of lysis varied with repeated use of individual donors. Up to 9% of the normal resting lymphocytes became blastogenic though fewer than 30% of the dividing cells at termination of culture had undergone more than one division. It is suggested that EBV antigens induce a polyclonal activation of cytotoxic T cells. The possible significance of this response is discussed with particular reference to the origin of non-EBV-specific cytotoxic blast cells in infectious mononucleosis.

INTRODUCTION

Infectious mononucleosis (IM) is a lymphoproliferative syndrome characterized by an atypical lymphocytosis. Most cases are caused by the Epstein–Barr virus (EBV), however, a smaller proportion results from infection with cytomegalovirus (CMV) and mononucleosis can be induced, albeit rarely, by adenovirus, rubella, and Toxoplasma gondii (1).

The pathogenesis of the disease caused by EBV has received the most study. EBV infects the B cell (2) but the atypical lymphocytosis includes a large T-cell component which is capable of killing lymphoid cell lines (LCL) of B-cell origin (3–5). Most LCL contain EBV and evidence has been presented that the cytotoxicity is generated by an EBV-associated lymphocyte-detected membrane antigen, LYDMA (5, 6). The function of the cytotoxic cells is then seen as recognition and elimination of infected B cells bearing LYDMA.

Two observations complicate this scenario for the origin of cytotoxic atypical lymphocytes. First, we find that the generation of cells which are toxic for EBV-containing lines is not confined to EBV-induced disease but can also occur in mononucleosis caused by CMV (7); the degree of cytotoxicity closely parallels the content of atypical lymphocytes in the effector population and cannot be explained in terms of an EBV-specific response. Second, even in EBV-IM there is cytotoxicity associated with atypical blast cells which will destroy cells lacking EBV (L. M. Hutt-Fletcher; unpublished data).

In vitro stimulations with autologous EBV-transformed lines have been shown

0008-8749/81/130091-15$02.00/0

to generate cytotoxicity which is not EBV-specific (8–10) but little attention has been paid to the cellular immune response generated by EBV virion antigens. Previous work has demonstrated that EBV antigens can induce blast transformation *in vitro* in cells from immune donors (11, 12) but the blast cells have not been extensively characterized. In this paper we describe the cytotoxic functions of blastogenic lymphocytes induced by EBV virion antigens in cells from normal immune donors.

MATERIALS AND METHODS

Cell lines. Four human LCL, Raji (13), P3HR-1 (14), BJAB (15), BJAB-GC (16), and one cell line derived from a myelogenous leukemia, K562 (17), were used. All were grown at 37°C in RPMI (Gibco, Grand Island, N.Y.) supplemented with 10% heat-inactivated fetal calf serum (FCS), 100 iu/ml penicillin and 100 μg/ml streptomycin. Cells were diluted biweekly with fresh medium. The RPMI medium used throughout these experiments was supplemented with the above concentrations of antibiotics.

Antibody titrations. Sera were titrated for antibodies to EBV early antigen (EA) and virus capsid antigen (VCA) by indirect immunofluorescence as previously described (3). All seropositive donors had anti-VCA titers in the range of 1/20–1/80.

Superinfection of Raji cells. Ten million Raji cells were superinfected with the P3HR-1 strain of EBV by incubating cells for 2 hr at 37°C in 1 ml of virus prepared as described below. After this time the cells were washed three times in RPMI 1640 containing 2% FCS, resuspended at a concentration of 10^6 cells/ml, and reincubated. Twenty-four hours later they were washed three times with phosphate-buffered saline (PBS) and acetone-fixed smears of the washed cells were examined by indirect immunofluorescence for induction of EBV EA.

Antigens. Virus antigens were prepared from spent medium of virus-producing P3HR-1 cells which had been kept at 32°C for 2 weeks without addition of fresh medium. The medium was clarified by centrifugation at 400*g* to remove cells and the virus subsequently pelleted by centrifugation at 20,000*g* for 90 min. Pellets were resuspended in 1/100 original volume RPMI 1640, centrifuged at 400*g* to remove any residual cells, and filtered through an 0.45-μ Millipore filter (Millipore Corp., Bedford, Mass.). The preparation (P3HR-S) was uv-irradiated in 1-ml volumes in 60-mm-diameter petri dishes for 30 min at 20 cm from a G15TB germicidal lamp (General Electric). Before irradiation the virus induced EA in 35% of Raji cells superinfected by the procedure described above. After incubation no EA was induced.

Control antigen was prepared, in an identical manner, from the spent medium of BJAB cells which contain no detectable EBV DNA (BJAB-S). Both antigen preparations were stored in small volumes at −70°C.

Leukocyte stimulation. Fifty to one hundred milliliters peripheral blood from normal healthy donors was collected by venipuncture into 5 units/ml preservative-free heparin (Fisher Scientific Co., Pittsburgh, Pa.) and the mononuclear fraction was obtained by Ficoll/Hypaque density gradient centrifugation (18). Twenty million washed mononuclear cells were then incubated with 1 ml of a predetermined optimal dilution of virus or control antigen preparation for 2 hr at 37°C in humidified air containing 5% CO_2. After 2 hr the cells were pelleted and the antigen was removed and replaced with 10 ml of RPMI 1640 supplemented with 5% heat-inactivated human plasma from an EBV-seronegative donor. The cell suspensions were aliquoted in 1-ml volumes in 12 × 75-mm plastic culture tubes (Falcon 2040, Falcon Plastics, Oxnard, Calif.) and reincubated at 37°C. Optimal stimulation was predetermined to occur on Day 6 when duplicate tubes were pulsed for 8 hr with 1 μCi tritiated thymidine ([^{3}H]TdR; sp act 1.9 Ci/mmol, Schwarz/Mann, Orangeburg, N.Y.). Incorporation of radioactivity into trichloroacetic acid-insoluble material was measured in a liquid scintillation counter. A stimulation index (SI) was calculated from this as:

$$\frac{\text{cpm incorporated into cultures stimulated with P3HR1-S}}{\text{cpm incorporated into cultures stimulated with BJAB-S}}.$$

Cells in the remaining tubes were pooled for further analysis. At this point all cultures had a viability of greater than 97% as judged by trypan blue exclusion and contained less than 1% cells capable of latex uptake.

Separation of lymphocytes by velocity sedimentation. The pooled, cultured lymphocytes were fractionated according to size on a linear gradient consisting of 500 ml of 15–30% FCS in PBS (19). Twenty milliliters PBS containing 5% FCS and 1–4 × 10^6 lymphocytes/ml were loaded into an 11-cm-diameter sedimentation chamber (Johns Scientific Co., Montreal) below 30 ml PBS and above the gradient. After sedimentation for 3 hr at room temperature, 1 × 50-ml and 11 × 30-ml fractions were collected from the base of the chamber. The cells in each fraction were pelleted, washed once, resuspended in 1 ml RPMI 1640 containing 10% FCS, and counted. The average diameters of lymphocytes after fixing and staining were 17 μm for cells in the first two fractions and 5 μm for those in fractions 9, 10, and 11 where the majority of the cell population sedimented. If fractions were run through a Cytograf model 6300 A (Biophysics Systems, Inc., Mahopac, N.Y.) the values obtained by reference to a particle of known size were 10 and 3 μm, respectively. In some experiments lymphocytes were pulsed for 1 hr prior to sedimentation with 1 μCi/ml of high-specific-activity [^{3}H]TdR (sp act 55–60 Ci/mmol; Schwarz/Mann). This short pulse had no effect on any subsequent functional assays.

Cytotoxic assays. Cytotoxicity was measured by a modification of previously described methods (3). Target cells were washed in RPMI 1640 and 10^6 cells were incubated for 4 hr at 37°C with 200 μCi sodium [^{51}Cr]chromate (sp act 100–300 mCi/mg Cr; Amersham/Searle, Arlington Heights, Ill.) in RPMI 1640 containing 10% FCS. The labeled cells were washed four times, resuspended at a concentration of 2 × 10^4 cells/ml, and dispensed in 0.05-ml volumes in round-bottomed microtiter plates (Microbiological Associates, Bethesda, Md.). An equal volume of medium, cultured lymphocytes, or cultured lymphocytes fractionated by velocity sedimentation was added to the targets and the plates were centrifuged for 5 min at 250*g*. After 20 hr incubation at 37°C the plates were centrifuged and 0.05-ml samples of supernatant from each well were assayed in a gamma counter. Cytotoxicity was calculated as:

$$\frac{\text{counts released in presence of lymphocytes} - \text{counts released in medium}}{\text{total counts incorporated by target cells}} \times 100.$$

Cytotoxicity assays done with unfractionated lymphocytes are reported at lymphocyte:target ratios of 50:1. Assays with fractionated cells are reported at ratios of 5:1, although killing was seen at ratios as low as 2:1 and was linear to ratios of 10 or 20:1. All assays were done in quadruplicate.

E-rosettes. Fractionated lymphocytes were rosetted with sheep red blood cells (E) by a modification of the method of Jondal and co-workers (20). The lymphocytes were pelleted, resuspended in 100% FCS, and mixed with an equal volume of E in 100% FCS adjusted to give a ratio of E:lymphocytes of 100:1. The mixtures were incubated for 5 min at 37°C, centrifuged at 400*g* for 5 min, and kept at 10°C for 2 hr. Any cell to which two or more E adhered was considered to be positive for sheep cell receptors.

Fc receptors. Fc receptors for IgG were detected by a modification of published methods (21). Ox red blood cells (ORBC) were coated with maximal subagglutinating titers of IgG anti-ORBC for 30 min at 37°C. The cells were then washed, resuspended in RPMI 1640 with 10% FCS, and mixed with an equal volume of washed lymphocytes adjusted to give a ratio of ORBC:lymphocytes of 100:1. The mixtures were incubated at 37°C for 10 min, centrifuged at 400*g* for 5 min, and kept at 4°C for 1 hr. Any cell to which 2 or more ORBC adhered was considered to be positive for Fc receptors for IgG ($Fc\gamma^+$). Cells bearing Fc receptors for IgM ($Fc\mu^+$) were detected by a similar procedure substituting IgM anti-ORBC for IgG.

Autoradiography. Autoradiography was done on fractionated lymphocytes which had been pulsed with high-specific-activity [^{3}H]TdR before sedimentation. The cells were air dried on glass slides and fixed for 3 min with methanol. The slides were dipped in emulsion (Kodak Nuclear Track Emulsion NTB-2, Eastman Kodak, Rochester, N.Y.) at 43°C, air dried, and developed after 48 hr with D19 developer (Eastman Kodak). Developed slides were stained for 30 sec with McNeal's Tretrachrome Blood Stain (Harleco, Gibbstown, N.J.) and examined by light microscopy. Rosettes made with ox or sheep red blood cells were preserved by this procedure.

Analysis of replicative history of blast cells. The number of divisions undergone by a metaphase cell in a 6-day culture was analyzed by the bromodeoxyuridine (BudR) incorporation system for analysis of cellular kinetics (BISACK) of Tice and co-workers (22). Briefly, noninhibitory concentrations of BudR (0.001–0.005 μM depending on the donor) were added to cultures on Day 0. After 6 days incubation 0.1 μg/ml colcemid was added for 1 hr and the cells were washed, resuspended in 0.75 *M* KCl for 20 min and in methanol:acetic acid (3:1) for 2 min on ice, and air dried onto glass slides. The slides were rinsed with water, stained for 5 min in 0.125 μg/ml acridine orange in 0.2 *M* phosphate buffer (pH 7.4 (23)), rinsed in water, incubated for a further 10 min in buffer, and examined by fluorescence microscopy. Cells which had undergone 1, 2, or 3 or more divisions in BudR were distinguished according to the degree of quenching of fluorescence on the chromosomes.

RESULTS

Stimulation with P3HR1-S and BJAB-S

Peripheral blood leukocytes from EBV-seropositive and -seronegative donors were cultured for 6 days after exposure to P3HR1-S, which contained EBV antigens, or BJAB-S, a control antigen pool with no viral determinants. Incorporation of [^{3}H]TdR by the cells was determined for the last 8 hr of culture and was greatest in cells exposed to P3HR1-S and taken from seropositive donors (Fig. 1A). The ratio of counts incorporated after exposure to P3HR1-S to the counts incorporated after exposure to BJAB-S was expressed as a stimulation index. Stimulation indices greater than 2.0 were found only in cultures derived from seropositive donors (Fig. 1B). Repeat experiments with seronegative donors failed to elicit stimulation indices higher than those shown.

Cytotoxicity of Unseparated Cultures

The cytotoxicity of cells from seropositive donors with stimulation indices of 2.0 or greater was assayed against Raji cells which contain EBV DNA but express only one serologically defined EBV nuclear antigen, EBNA. In each experiment the cultures which had been exposed to P3HR1-S were more cytotoxic than those

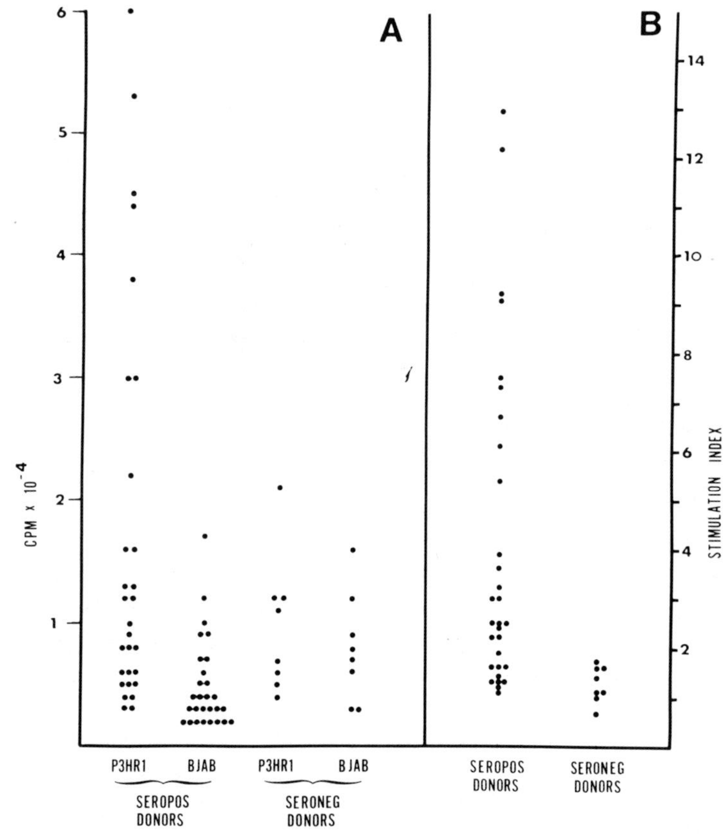

FIG. 1. Stimulation with P3HR1-S or BJAB-S of blood leukocytes from seropositive and seronegative donors. (A) Actual cpm incorporated into cultures stimulated with P3HR1-S or BJAB-S. (B) Stimulation indices (SI) calculated as:

$$\frac{\text{cpm incorporated into cultures stimulated with P3HR1-S}}{\text{cpm incorporated into cultures stimulated with BJAB-S}}.$$

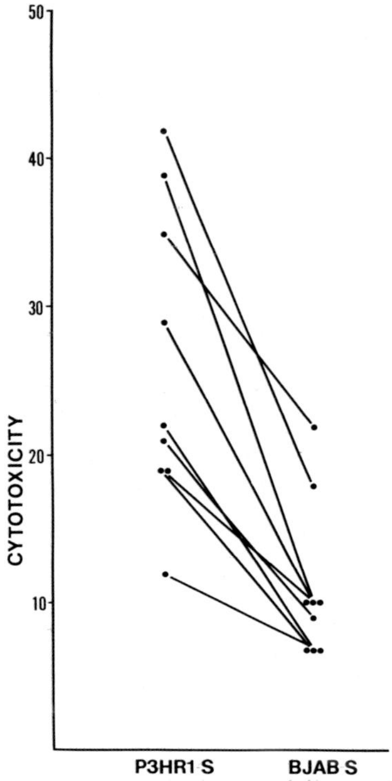

FIG. 2. Cytotoxicity for Raji cells of lymphocytes from seropositive donors 6 days after exposure to P3HR1-S or BJAB-S.

exposed to BJAB-S (Fig. 2). Soluble cytotoxic factors released into the spent culture medium were probably not responsible for cytotoxicity; if on Day 6 the cultured cells were washed and cytotoxicity measured in spent culture medium or in fresh RPMI, those cells to which fresh medium had been added were the most cytotoxic.

Cytotoxicity for Raji Cells of Cultured Lymphocytes after Separation by Sedimentation

We were particularly interested in the cytotoxic functions of the blastogenic cells. Cultures from seropositive and seronegative donors were therefore separated according to size by velocity sedimentation (Fig. 3). Most killing of Raji cells by the seropositive donor lymphocytes exposed to P3HR1-S was seen in fractions enriched for the larger, faster-sedimenting cells. Cytotoxicity was lower in all fractions from the cultures exposed to BJAB-S and also in fractions of unstimulated fresh lymphocytes which had been depleted of adherent cells by adsorption to plastic. It was also low in fractions from the seronegative donor lymphocytes whether they were exposed to P3HR1-S or BJAB-S. The stimulation index for the seropositive donor used in this experiment was 3.3; the stimulation index for the seronegative donor was 1.4. Cytotoxicity patterns similar to that of the seronegative donor were obtained with cells from seropositive donors that gave stimulation indices of less than 2.0 (data not shown).

A series of six stimulations with P3HR1-S and BJAB-S done with the same

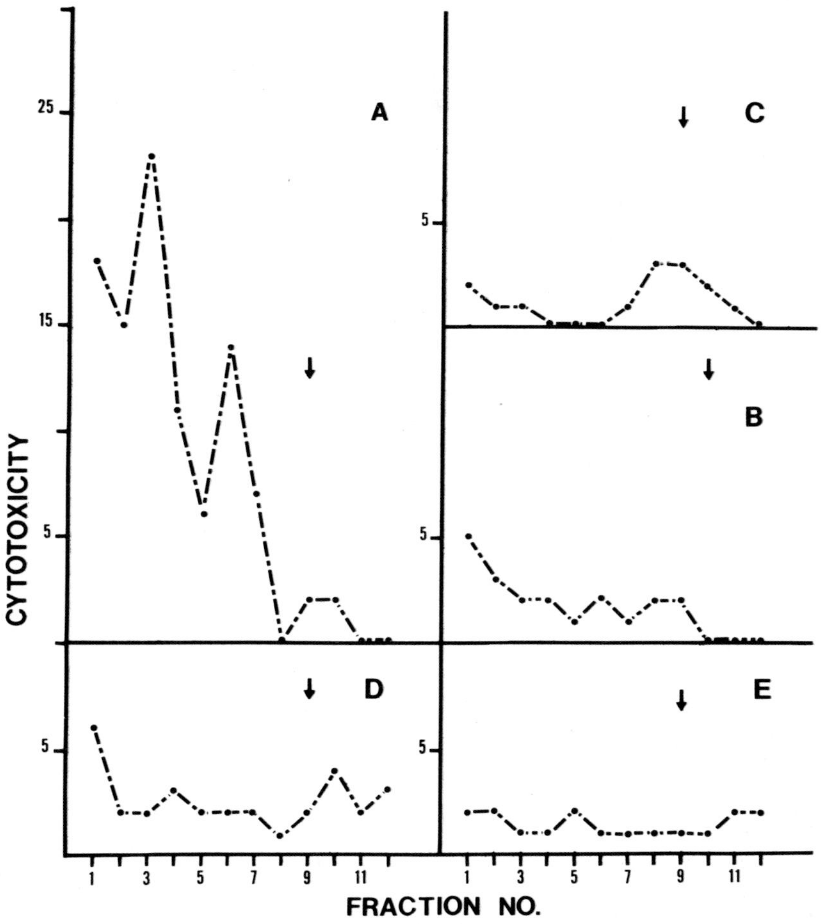

FIG. 3. Cytotoxicity for Raji cells of stimulated lymphocytes after separation by velocity sedimentation: (A) seropositive donor cells stimulated with P3HR1-S; (B) the same seropositive donor cells cultured with BJAB-S; (C) fresh unstimulated seropositive donor lymphocytes depleted of adherent cells; (D) seronegative donor cells stimulated with P3HR1-S; (E) the same seronegative donor cells stimulated with BJAB-S. Stimulation index for the seropositive donor cells used in A (P3HR1-S) and B (BJAB-S) was 3.3; the index for the seronegative donor cells used in D (P3HR1-S) and E (BJAB-S) was 1.4. No index was obtained for cells in C which were not stimulated with either antigen preparation. Cells always sediment from right to left; arrows indicate fractions containing the majority of the sedimented cells.

seropositive donor over a period of several weeks is depicted in Fig. 4. The cells stimulated with P3HR1-S were pooled, pulsed for 1 hr with high-specific-activity [^{3}H]TdR, fractionated, and assayed for cytotoxicity against Raji cells. The number of cells taking up [^{3}H]TdR was determined by autoradiography of samples from each fraction; for simplicity these cells are referred to as activated or "atypical" cells although it is recognized that only a fraction of blast cells are labeled in this 1-hr pulse. The stimulation indices varied from experiment to experiment and there was no apparent correlation between the percentage of the whole population, which was "atypical," the stimulation indices, or the amount of cytotoxicity. However,

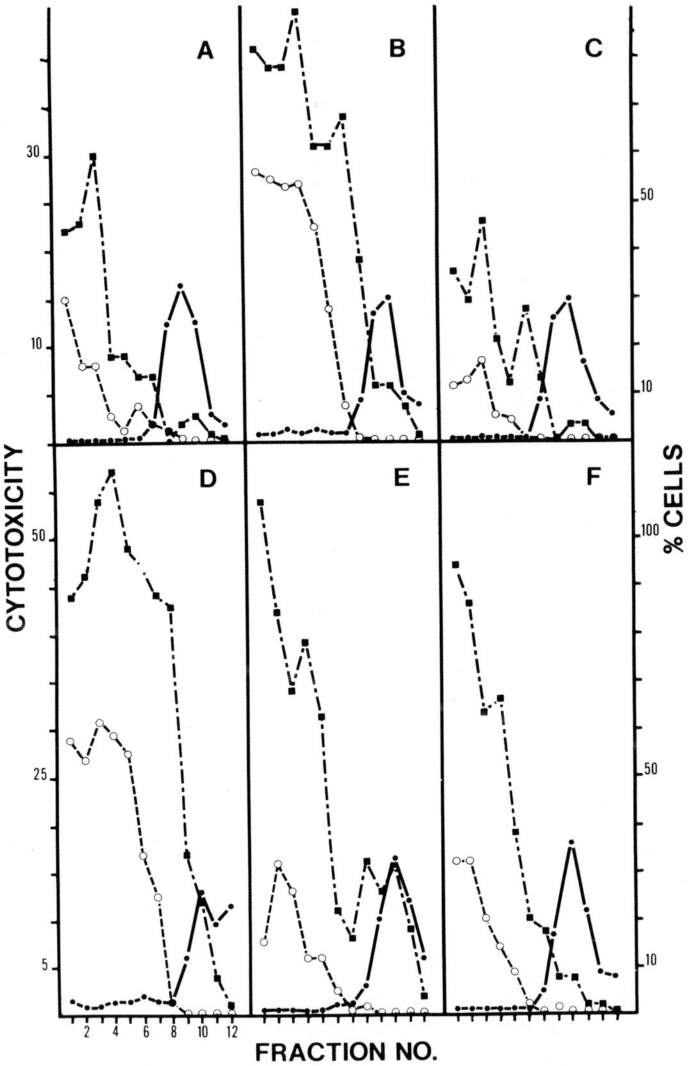

FIG. 4. Cytotoxicity for Raji cells of lymphocytes from one seropositive donor stimulated on six occasions (A-F) with P3HR1-S and separated by velocity sedimentation; ■----■, cytotoxicity; ●——●, total cells; ○ - - - ○, atypical cells. Atypical cells as a percentage of total lymphocytes in each experiment were: (A) 1.8; (B) 7.1; (C) 0.5; (D) 9.2; (E) 0.6; (F) 1.1. The SI values were (B) 3.5; (C) 3.3; (D) 9.2; (E) 2.0; (F) 3.2; no value was obtained for A.

most of the killing was always seen in the fractions which contained the largest cells and the greatest percentage of atypical cells. This is emphasized by an analysis of 14 experiments with different seropositive donors in which the percentage of the total cytotoxicity which appeared in the first four, the second four, and the third four fractions was calculated and compared with the percentage of atypical cells in the same fractions (Fig. 5). Most killing was always found in the first four fractions which contained the largest cells and the greatest number of atypical cells.

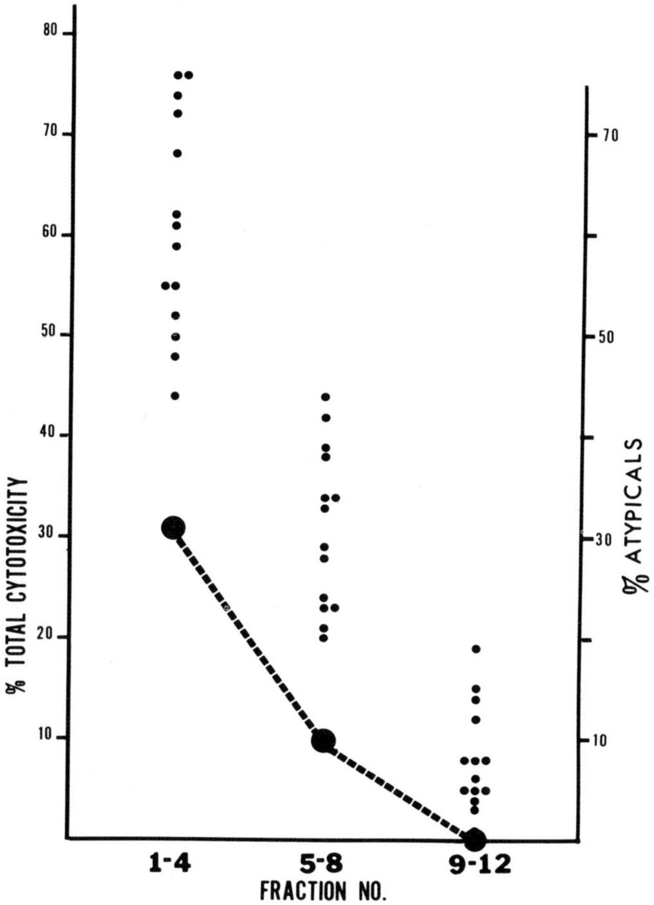

FIG. 5. The percentage of total cytotoxicity for Raji cells found in fractions 1–4, 5–8, and 9–12 of 14 velocity sedimentation separations of lymphocytes from seropositive donors stimulated with P3HR1-S; ● - - - ●, percentage of atypical cells.

To determine whether the atypical cells were actually responsible for any of the killing, stimulated cultures were pulsed with suicidal amounts of [^{3}H]TdR (50 μCi/ml; sp act 55 Ci/mmol) for 8 hr prior to fractionation. Control cultures were stimulated and pulsed with the same amount of [^{3}H]TdR together with 2 μg/ml unlabeled thymidine. The numbers of cells taking up thymidine during the 8-hr pulse were determined in the control cultures by autoradiography. Cytotoxicity in the fractions containing cells which incorporated [^{3}H]TdR was markedly reduced by thymidine suicide (Fig. 6).

Cytotoxicity of Separated Lymphocytes for Other Targets

To determine whether the EBV content of the Raji cell target was a requirement for susceptibility to lysis, two experiments were done with two seropositive donors. On both occasions donor leukocytes were exposed to P3HR1-S, fractionated by size after 6 days, and tested for cytotoxicity against Raji, BJAB, which contains

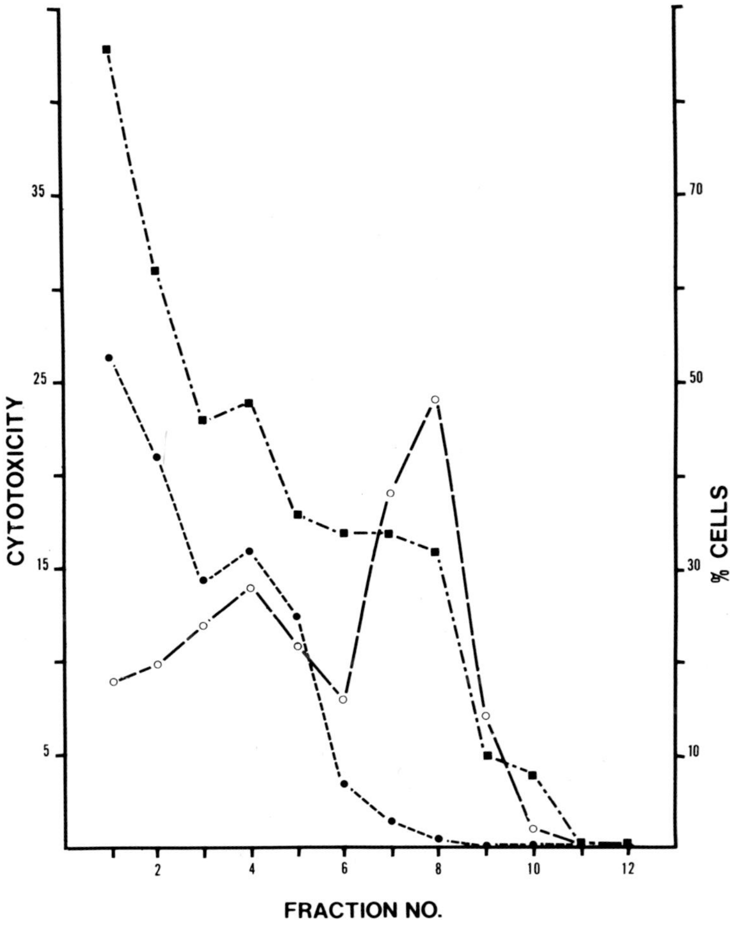

FIG. 6. Cytotoxicity for Raji cells of lymphocytes from a seropositive donor stimulated with P3HR1-S and separated by velocity sedimentation. O——O, cytotoxicity of lymphocytes after incubation with suicidal amounts of [^{3}H]TdR; ■----■, cytotoxicity of lymphocytes after incubation with suicidal amounts of [^{3}H]TdR but protected with unlabeled thymidine; ● - - - ●, distribution of cells taking up [^{3}H]TdR.

no EBV, and BJAB-GC, an EBV-containing subline of BJAB. Although the relative sensitivity of the different targets varied from experiment to experiment even with the same donor, all three targets were sensitive to lysis and maximal killing was always mediated by cells in the first four fractions of the sedimentation gradient (Fig. 7). U698-M, another EBV-negative line, was also susceptible to lysis by lymphocytes exposed to P3HR1-S (data not shown).

Natural killer or NK-cell activity of human blood lymphocytes can be enhanced by a number of *in vitro* manipulations (24). To determine whether NK-like activity was being induced by P3HR1-S, cultures from 14 separate stimulations were fractionated and cytotoxicity was measured for two targets, Raji, which is relatively resistant to NK and K562 which is very sensitive to NK activity (25). Most killing of both Raji and K562 was associated with the larger cells in fractions 1–4 (Fig. 8). The relative sensitivity of the two targets did, however, differ. Raji was more

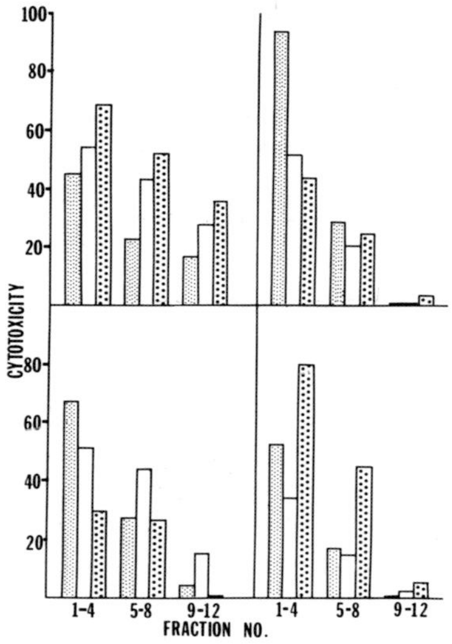

FIG. 7. Total cytotoxicity in fractions 1–4, 5–8, and 9–12 of lymphocytes from two seropositive donors stimulated on two occasions with P3HR1-S and separated by velocity sedimentation; cytotoxicity measured against Raji (▨); BJAB (□); BJAB-GC (⊡). The first two stimulations are represented in the left-hand diagrams.

sensitive than K562 to killing by cells in fractions 1–4; K562 was more sensitive than Raji to killing by cells in the remaining fractions.

Surface Markers of Blast Cells

Analysis of surface markers in the above experiments showed that most of the donor lymphocytes which took up [^{3}H]TdR in a 1-hr pulse on Day 6 formed E

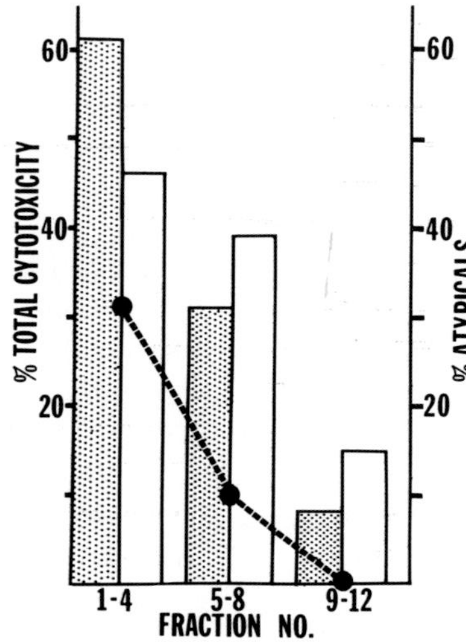

FIG. 8. The percentage of the total cytotoxicity found in fractions 1–4, 5–8, and 9–12 of 14 velocity sedimentation separations of lymphocytes from seropositive donors stimulated with P3HR1-S: comparison of cytotoxicity for Raji cells (▨) and K562 (□); ● - - - ●, percentage of atypical cells.

rosettes (mean 84%; range 63–100%); a variable percentage was also $Fc\gamma^+$ (mean 34%; range 12–67%). In the two experiments in which percentages of labeled cells bearing $Fc\gamma$ and $Fc\mu$ were measured, the values added up to 100%. There was no distinctive sedimentation pattern of the total labeled and unlabeled cells which formed E rosettes or bore Fc receptors. There was no correlation between the percentage of $Fc\gamma^+$ cells and the amount of cytotoxicity.

Replicative History of Blast Cells

Since as many as 9% of the total lymphocyte population in culture on Day 6 might incorporate [^{3}H]TdR in a 1-hr pulse, we were curious as to how many divisions such cells might have undergone in culture. To determine this, donor leukocytes were exposed to P3HR1-S for 2 hr as usual and then cultured in the presence of noninhibitory amounts of BudR for BISACK analysis. In two such experiments the percentages of cells in metaphase on Day 6 that had undergone one, two, or three or more divisions in culture were 68 and 69, 15 and 11, and 17 and 20, respectively.

DISCUSSION

Lymphocyte blastogenesis can be stimulated by EBV virion antigens in cells taken from EBV-seropositive donors (11, 12). In this paper we show that such blastogenic cultures are cytotoxic for lymphoid cell lines. Little cytotoxicity developed in 6-day leukocyte cultures unless they were derived from seropositive donors, were exposed to inactivated EBV, and responded by an increase in [^{3}H]TdR relative to controls.

The EBV antigen pool, P3HR1-S, obviously contains antigenic material in addition to EBV virions; some fetal calf serum and cellular antigens are concentrated along with the virus. However, it seems unlikely that these components make a significant contribution to induction of cytotoxicity. They are presumably common to the BJAB-S control pool which induced little blastogenesis and low cytotoxicity against Raji or even the homologous BJAB target; use of concentrated spent medium from Raji cells as a control pool also failed to induce killing of homologous Raji targets (unpublished data). It is conceivable that P3HR1-S contains more cellular debris than BJAB-S since it is derived from a lytic virus-producing culture; however, the failure to generate blastogenesis or cytotoxicity in seronegative donors implies that the EBV content of the pool is critical. Not all seropositive donors responded to P3HR1-S but the donor pool consisted of normal individuals exposed to different antigenic loads of EBV at indeterminate times over the last 20–30 years and similar variations have been reported for seropositive donors in response to EBV (26, 12) and to other antigens (27).

Size separation of cultures 6 days after exposure to P3HR1-S revealed that fractions enriched for large cells were the most cytotoxic for Raji targets on a per cell basis. These fractions also contained the highest percentages of "atypical" cells that could be labeled with [^{3}H]TdR in a 1-hr pulse immediately prior to separation. Thymidine suicide significantly reduced killing by lymphocytes in fractions that contained the atypical cells and reduced it principally in those fractions that contained the highest percentages. Atypical lymphocytes, a majority of which formed

E rosettes, were then at least required for full expression of cytotoxicity and possibly mediated it.

Despite the apparent immune specificity of induction of cytotoxicity by EBV antigens, there was no obvious specificity in its effect. Sensitivity to lysis was not restricted either to cells expressing EBV virion antigens or to those containing EBV DNA. Such seemingly nonspecific lymphocyte-mediated cytotoxicity has been described as generated *in vitro* under a variety of circumstances and most authors have attributed the killing to activation in culture of natural killer (NK) or NK-like cells.

Spontaneous NK activity in peripheral blood leukocytes disappears if the cells are cultured alone (28) but exposure to mitogens (29), antigens (30–32), fetal calf serum (33), allogeneic lymphocytes (34–39), or allogeneic or autologous lymphoid cell lines (40, 41) has been reported to induce cytotoxic cells with some similar characteristics. Cytotoxicity generated under these circumstances is usually thought to be NK like because it shows no specificity for stimulating antigens, it is mediated by $Fc\gamma^+$, E-rosetting cells and it lyses known NK-sensitive targets such as K562. There are, however, differences between spontaneous NK and NK-like activity induced *in vitro*: cytotoxic populations induced *in vitro* include a higher proportion of cells that adhere to nylon wool, a lower proportion of $Fc\gamma^+$ cells, and they can lyse cells which are relatively resistant to spontaneous NK in short-term assays (39). Masucci and co-workers prefer to use the term "activated lymphocyte killing" or ALK for the *in vitro* phenomenon since it occurs only if culture conditions involve activation (39, 42). A correlation has been demonstrated between [^{3}H]TdR incorporation and ALK (34, 39) although elimination of proliferating cells by BudR and light at the end of a mixed lymphocyte culture (MLC) eliminates only specific alloreactive cytotoxicity and does not influence expression of nonspecific killing (34, 36). Conditions which generate ALK also induce interferon production which acts as an endogenous trigger for cytotoxicity (43, 44).

The cytotoxicity generated by EBV antigens *in vitro* bears some resemblance to ALK; notably, it is associated with blast transformation and affects both K562 cells which are NK-sensitive targets and Raji cells which are relatively resistant to spontaneous NK in a short-term assay (25). Separation of cytotoxic populations by velocity sedimentation does, however, reveal some interesting differences. The fast-sedimenting populations include cells which incorporate [^{3}H]TdR, form E rosettes, and sometimes bear Fc receptors. On a per cell basis these populations kill Raji cells slightly better than K562 cells, but the cytotoxicity is sensitive to elimination of proliferating cells by thymidine suicide immediately prior to sedimentation. The populations which sediment a little slower and contain smaller cells, few of which incorporate [^{3}H]TdR, kill K562 targets slightly better than Raji on a per cell basis. The cytotoxicity in these populations is not reduced by thymidine suicide immediately prior to sedimentation and may possibly be enhanced.

Klein and co-workers (42) have suggested that cytotoxicity is a function of T cells in a certain stage of differentiation or activation. Perhaps then the blast cells generated by EBV virion antigens are cytotoxic by virtue of their "activated" state. It follows that their elimination by thymidine suicide would deplete killing in populations of which they were a significant part. This might be true of any population high in blast cells whether it were artificially enriched for such cells as in our velocity sedimentation experiments or whether it naturally contained a high percentage of specifically identifiable cells as in an MLC. In addition, however, the EBV-induced blast cells might produce interferon to act as an endogenous trigger for cytotoxicity mediated by the smaller cells, activated to kill, but not to divide, and hence not sensitive to thymidine suicide.

Butterworth (30) has suggested that "nonspecific" cytotoxicity induced by antigen stimulation is amplified by recruitment via blast cell production of mitogenic factors (45). Such recruitment may take place in our cultures since we find that as many as 9% of the lymphocytes in 6-day cultures may incorporate [^{3}H]TdR and almost 70% of the blast cells are dividing for the first time. If EBV-induced blast cells recruit bystander lymphocytes to become cytotoxic by virtue of activation, then the cytotoxic potential of the overall population will presumably depend on the cells that happen to be recruited. In our experiments, the amount of Raji killing associated with blast cells was variable in repeat experiments using the same donor, and did not correlate well with the actual numbers of blast cells induced. Additionally, cytotoxicity for other targets varied from experiment to experiment implying that cells with different "specificities" were induced by the same antigen preparation in the same donor at different times. Perhaps this reflects changes in availability of different clones of lymphocytes for recruitment. The repertoire of clones in the peripheral blood is presumably influenced by the current antigenic environment of the donor and would vary in repeated samples taken at different times.

Our original intent in this work was to understand the two observations described in the introduction which we made with cells from patients with acute IM. The observations implied that the cytotoxicity associated with atypical lymphocytes in this disease was not exclusively specific for the putative EBV-determined antigen LYDMA and that cells of a similar type could be found in an infection induced by EBV or CMV. Atypical lymphocytes in peripheral blood are indistinguishable by morphological, histochemical, and metabolic criteria from antigen- or mitogen-induced lymphoblasts and their surface markers are consistent with identification as activated T cells (46). Since we have shown that EBV virion antigens can generate ALK-like phenomena *in vitro* we would then support the concept of Klein and co-workers (42) that the cytotoxicity of cells in acute phase IM is at least in part a consequence of T-cell activation and generation of an ALK-like effect; in this case, the inducing agents, EBV or CMV, would be irrelevant to the effect generated. Such a hypothesis might be tested by application to acute-phase IM lymphocytes of new single-cell assays for identification of individual cytotoxic cells.

ACKNOWLEDGMENTS

This work was supported by United States Public Health Grant RO1-CA22093.

REFERENCES

1. Evans, A. S., *Amer. J. Med. Sci.* **276,** 325, 1978.
2. Pattengale, P. K., Smith, R. W., and Gerber, P., *Lancet* **2,** 93, 1973.
3. Hutt, L. M., Huang, Y.-T., Dascomb, H. E., and Pagano, J. S., *J. Immunol.* **115,** 243, 1975.
4. Royston, I., Sullivan, J. L., Penman, P. O., and Perlin, E., *N. Engl. J. Med.* **293,** 1159, 1975.
5. Svedmyr, E., and Jondal, M., *Proc. Nat. Acad. Sci. USA* **72,** 1622, 1975.
6. Bakacs, T., Svedmyr, E., Klein, E., Rambo, L., and Weiland, D., *Cancer Lett.* **4,** 185, 1978.
7. Lemon, S. M., Hutt, L. M., and Huang, Y.-T., *Clin. Immunol. Immunopathol.* **8,** 513, 1977.

8. Svedmyr, E. A., Deinhardt, F., and Klein, G., *Int. J. Cancer* **13,** 891, 1974.
9. Viallat, J., Svedmyr, E., Steinitz, M., and Klein, G. *Cell. Immunol.* **38,** 65, 1978.
10. Biron, C. A., Hutt-Fletcher, L. M., Wertz, G., and Pagano, J. S., *Int. J. Cancer* **27,** 185, 1981.
11. Gerber, P., and Lucas, S. J., *Cell Immunol.* **5,** 318, 1972.
12. Nikoskelainen, J., Albashi, D. V., Isenberg, R. A., Neel, E. B., Miller, R. G., and Stevens, D. A., *J. Immunol.* **121,** 1239, 1978.
13. Nonoyama, M., and Pagano, J. S., *Nature New Biol.* **233,** 103, 1971.
14. Hinuma, Y., Korn, M., Yamayuchi, J., Wudarski, D. J., Blakeslee, J. R., Grace, J. T., *J. Virol.* **1,** 1045, 1967.
15. Klein, G., Lindahl, T., Jondal, M., Leibold, W., Menezes, J., Nilsson, K., and Sundstrom, C., *Proc. Nat. Acad. Sci. USA* **71,** 3283, 1974.
16. Clements, G. B., Klein, G., and Povey, S., *Int. J. Cancer* **16,** 125, 1975.
17. Lozzio, C. B., and Lozzio, B. B., *Blood* **45,** 321, 1975.
18. Boyum, A., *Scand. J. Clin. Lab. Invest.* **21,** (Suppl. 97), 77, 1968.
19. Miller, R. G., and Phillips, R. A., *J. Cell Physiol.* **73,** 191, 1969.
20. Jondal, M., Holm, G., and Wigzell, H., *J. Exp. Med.* **136,** 207, 1972.
21. Kall, M. A., and Koren, H. S., *Cell Immunol.* **40,** 58, 1978.
22. Tice, R., Thorne, P., and Schneider, E. L. *Cell Tissue Kinet.* **12,** 1, 1979.
23. Schneider, E. L., Tice, R. R., and Kram, D. *In* "Methods in Cell Biology" (D. M. Prescott, Ed.), Vol. 20, pp. 379–409. Academic Press, New York, 1978.
24. Herberman, R. B., Djen, J. Y., Kay, H. D., Ortaldo, J. R., Riccardi, C., Bonnard, G. D., Holden, H. T., Fagnani, R., Santori, A., and Pucetti, P., *Immunol. Rev.* **44,** 43, 1979.
25. Jondal, M., Spina, C., and Targan, S., *Nature (London)* **272,** 62, 1978.
26. Gergely, P., Ernberg, I., Klein, G., and Steinitz, M., *Clin. Exp. Immunol.* **30,** 347, 1977.
27. Wilson, C. B., Desmonts, G., Convreur, J., and Remington, J. S., *New Engl. J. Med.* **302,** 785, 1980.
28. Poros, A., and Klein, E., *Cell. Immunol.* **41,** 240, 1978.
29. Stejskal, V., Lindberg, S., Holm, G., and Perlman, P., *Cell Immunol.* **8,** 82, 1973.
30. Butterworth, A. E., *Cell. Immunol.* **7,** 357, 1973.
31. Stejskal, V., Holm, G., and Perlman, P., *Cell Immunol.* **8,** 71, 1973.
32. Tartof, D., Check, I. J., Matutis, A., Hunter, R. L., and Fitch, F. W., *J. Immunol.* **125,** 2790, 1980.
33. Zielske, J. V., and Golub, S. H., *Cancer Res.* **36,** 3842, 1976.
34. Seeley, J. K., and Golub, S. H., *J. Immunol.* **120,** 1415, 1978.
35. Callewaert, D. M., Lightbody, J. L., Kaplan, J., Jaroszewski, J., Peterson, W. D., Jr., Rosenberg, J. C., *J. Immunol.* **121,** 81, 1978.
36. Zarling, J. M., Bach, F. H., and Kung, P. C., *J. Immunol.* **126,** 375, 1981.
37. Ortaldo, J. R., and Bonnard, G. D., *Fed. Proc.* **36,** 1325, 1977.
38. Seeley, J. K., Masucci, G., Poros, A., Klein, E., Golub, S. H., *J. Immunol.* **123,** 1303, 1979.
39. Masucci, M. G., Klein, E., and Argov, S., *J. Immunol.* **124,** 2458, 1980.
40. Svedmyr, E. A., Wigzell, H., and Jondal, M., *Scand. J. Immunol.* **3,** 499, 1974.
41. Jondal, M., and Targan, S., *J. Exp. Med.* **148,** 1621, 1978.
42. Klein, E., Masucci, M. G., Berthold, W., and Blazar, B. A., *In* "The Cold Spring Harbor Conference on Cell Proliferation" (M. Essex, G. Todaro, H. zurHausen, Eds.), Vol. 7, pp. 1187–1197. Cold Spring Harbor Laboratory, Cold Spring Harbor, N. Y., 1980.
43. Saksela, E., Timonen, T., and Cantell, K., *Scand. J. Immunol.* **10,** 257, 1979.
44. Santoli, D., and Koprowski, H., *Immunol. Rev.* **44,** 125, 1979.
45. Rocklin, R. E., *Clin. Immunobiol.* **3,** 195, 1976.
46. Hutt-Fletcher, L. M., *In* "The Handbook of Cancer Immunology" (H. Waters, Ed.), Vol. 6, pp. 128–143. Garland STPM Press, New York, 1980.

CELLULAR IMMUNOLOGY **63**, 106–117 (1981)

The Null Cell Compartment of the Mouse Spleen

JEREMIAH J. TWOMEY AND NICOLA M. KOUTTAB

The Houston Veterans Administration Medical Center, and Baylor College of Medicine, Houston, Texas 77211

Received February 21, 1981; accepted April 29, 1981

Null lymphocytes were defined as lymphocytes without detectable T- or B-cell markers using a battery of techniques. The null cell compartment was divided into pre-T cells, pre-B cells, and other null cells based upon their acquisition of membrane markers when incubated with ubiquitin. The null cell subpopulations were remarkably consistent in spleen cell suspensions from young adult mice of various strains. Commitment to T- or B-cell differentiation took place at the null cell stage and did not require thymic input. Pre-T cells, but not pre-B cells, were steroid sensitive. Pre-T cells accumulate with congenital thymic deficiency. This differed from senescent thymodeprivation where the outstanding finding was an accumulation of uninducible null cells. Neonatal mouse spleens were deficient in pre-T and pre-B cells but had an accumulation of uninducible cells.

INTRODUCTION

Mature lymphocytes are derived from a pool of precursor cells. Some precursors may be committed to the T- or B-lymphocyte series before the onset of recognizable differentiation (1). Subpopulations of lymphocytes acquire surface markers and functions during maturation (2–5). the overall process of lymphocyte differentiation involves a complex series of events that are modulated to a greater or lesser degree by a number of inducing agents (6, 7).

Lymphoid cells that lack detectable surface markers are arbitrarily termed null lymphocytes (8). These null cells include committed precursors of T or B lymphocytes and other, probably heterogeneous, cells. In the mouse, null cells comprise about 50% of bone marrow lymphocytes (9), 3–13% of splenic lymphocytes (8,10) and 0–5% of lymph node lymphocytes (8, 10). There has been no systematic evaluation of this null cell compartment apart from the recognition of some lymphocytes that have undergone partial B-cell differentiation; these are identified by the presence of small amounts of cytoplasmic (but not surface) μ chains (11).

The composition of the null cell compartment could be altered through a number of mechanisms. It could fail to sustain itself through lowered input from primitive precursors or impaired null cell replication. Alternatively, accelerated differentiation of null cells could outstrip regenerative reserves and thereby deplete the null cell pool. The null cell compartment could be expanded by increased input from primitive precursors, accelerated null cell mitosis, or reduced differentiation toward more mature cells. The latter could result from intrinsic unresponsiveness by null cells to inductive stimuli, a lack of inductive stimuli, or an unfavorable microen-

0008-8749/81/130106-12$02.00/0

vironment for differentiation to take place. Abnormalities could be limited to one or more subpopulations within the null cell compartment. Disorders of more mature lymphocytes may have their origins within the null cell compartment, as exemplified in man by severe combined immunodeficiency (12).

This paper introduces an approach that recognized three subpopulations within the null cell compartment of the mouse spleen. These subpopulations include null cells that acquire T- or B-cell surface markers when optimally induced with ubiquitin and other null cells that are unresponsive to ubiquitin. Ubiquitin is a tissue peptide which, at the concentration employed, stimulates both T- and B-cell differentiation via β-adrenergic receptors (13, 14). We found that the composition of the null cell compartment is remarkably consistent in healthy young adult mice of different strains but is altered during the neonatal period and with advanced age. The latter cannot be ascribed to thymic involution since a different pattern was observed in congenitally athymic mice.

MATERIALS AND METHODS

Mice and cell preparations. Studies were performed on C3H/He and DBA/2 mice purchased from TIMCO Breeding Laboratories, Houston, Texas, C57BL/1, CBA/T6 AKR/J, and Balb/c mice purchased from Jackson Laboratories, Bar Harbor, Maine, and our colony of germ-free nude athymic mice bred on a C3H/He background. Neonatal mice were studied 3–5 days after birth.

Mice were sacrificed by cervical dislocation, their spleens removed aseptically and weighed, and cells freed by gentle teasing. Since our interest was in overall spleen cell composition, no attempts were made at cell fractionation. Fresh smears were prepared and stained with α-naphthyl acetate esterase (Sigma Chemical Co., St. Louis, Mo.) (15) or Wright–Giemsa stains. Percentages of macrophages, hematopoietic cells, granulocytes, and lymphoid cells were determined from counts of 300 cells.

Reagents. Thymopoietin, a thymic peptide of known amino acid sequence (16), and ubiquitin were purified using published techniques (13, 14, 16, 17). Antiserum to Thy 1.2 antigen was raised by immunizing AKR/J mice with C3H/He thymocytes (18). Fluorescein-labeled monoclonal IgM antibody to Thy 1.2 was purchased from New England Nuclear, Boston, Massachusetts. Adsorbed, fluorescein-conjugated antiserum to C3H/He mouse brain raised in rabbits was purchased from Litton Bionetics, Kensington, Maryland. Fluorescein-conjugated goat antisera to mouse μ, γ, or α chains were obtained from Meloy Laboratories, Springfield, Virginia. Fluorescein-conjugated rabbit immunoglobulin (Ig)G containing antibodies to mouse κ chains, unconjugated rabbit IgG containing antibodies to mouse λ chains and fluourescein-conjugated goat antiserum to rabbit IgG were purchased from Litton Bionetics or procured from Dr. E. Vitetta. Affinity-purified rabbit antiserum to mouse Ig was prepared as described by Ligler *et al.* (19). Rhodamine-conjugated goat antiserum to mouse μ chains was obtained from Cappel Laboratories, Cochranville, Pennsylvania. Fresh frozen guinea pig serum that was absorbed with C3H/He mouse thymocytes was used as complement source. All reagents were used at optimal dilutions.

Cell identification. T lymphocytes were identified using a number of different methods. In the cytotoxicity test, 2×10^5 spleen cells in 0.05 ml medium 199 (Gibco,

Grand Island, N.Y.) enriched with 5 g% BSA (Sigma) plus 0.025 ml antiserum to Thy 1.2 antigen were incubated in duplicate with 0.025 ml complement or heat-inactivated complement. Incubations were for 90 min at 37°C in a humidified atmosphere of 5% CO_2 and air and for an additional 30 min after adding 0.625 mg pronase (grade B, Sigma) in 0.125 ml saline. Then 12 ml cetrimide (Eastman Kodak Co., Rochester, N.Y.) was added and cell counts performed using a Coulter counter. Injured cells were solubilized while incubated with pronase (20). This was reflected in lower cell counts in incubations containing complement compared to paired incubations that lacked complement activity. This antibody-specific cytotoxicity test was preferred to dye exclusion or membrane-bound isotope release because it is more sensitive to lesser degrees of cell injury (21).

Thy 1.2 antigen was also identified using both direct and indirect immunofluorescence. For direct immunofluorescene, 1×10^6 spleen cells and optimal concentrations of conjugated monoclonal IgM antibody to Thy 1.2 antigen were kept at 4°C for 30 min, washed, and examined for membrane flourescence using a Leitz Ploem optics uv microscope. For indirect immunofluorescence, 5×10^5 spleen cells, suspended in BSA-enriched medium 199 were incubated with 0.025 ml unconjugated antiserum to Thy 1.2 antigen for 1 hr at 37°C. After washing twice, the cells were treated with 0.025 ml each of fluorescein-conjugated antiserum to mouse Ig heavy chains and 0.025 ml PBS at 4°C for a second hour, washed twice, and examined for membrane immunofluorescence. This procedure identified both T and B cells. Thus, to enumerate T cells, it was necessary to identify B cells concomitantly and subtract these from combined T- plus B-cell values. Cell suspensions were also reacted with fluoresceinated antiserum to mouse brain for 1 hr at 4°C, washed twice, and examined directly for membrane immunofluorescence.

Conjugated antisera to μ, γ, and α chains were mixed at optimal dilutions to demonstrate heavy-chain determinants on B-cell membranes. Spleen cells (5×10^5), suspended in 0.05 ml BSA-enriched medium 199, 0.025 ml of the conjugate mixture and 0.025 ml PBS were kept at 4°C for 1 hr, washed twice, and examined directly for membrane immunofluorescence. There was minimal binding of conjugate by Fc receptors as was evidenced by there being negligible numbers of fluorescing cells after depleting B lymphocytes and macrophages by incubation with nylon wool. When testing for light-chain determinants on cell membranes, κ chains were identified by direct immunofluorescence and λ chains by indirect immunofluorescence using procedures outlined above. The prescence of membrane C_3 receptors was demonstrated using the EAC procedure described by Mendes *et al.* (22).

Cell sorting was done using a series 50-H cytofluorograf (Ortho, Westwood, Mass.). Excitation was done with 400 W of laser power at 488 nm. The photomultiplier tube voltage was set at 435 for direct fluorescence and at 594 for indirect fluorescence. Cells in channels 46–511 were scored positively. Gating on live cells was done using a logarithmic amplifier.

The double immunofluorescence method of Raff *et al.* (23) was used to identify lymphoid cells with Ig limited to their cytoplasm. Cell membrane Ig was first reacted directly with mixed heavy-chain conjugates as described. The cells were then washed twice, fixed at 4°C with 5% acetic acid and 95% ethanol, stained for cytoplasmic Ig by a 1-hr incubation period at 37°C with a rhodamine conjugate to μ-chain determinants, washed, and examined for immunofluorescence.

Induction incubations. After allowing clumps to sediment, spleen cells were washed twice and suspended at 5×10^6 cells/ml in medium 199 plus 5 g% BSA. Incubations were set up in duplicate in 12×75-mm polystyrene tubes containing 0.1 ml cell suspension and 0.1 ml medium plus 20 ng/ml ubiquitin, 1 μg/ml thymopoietin, or medium alone. Preliminary experiments indicated that these represented optimal inductive concentrations of ubiquitin and thymopoietin in this incubation system. Incubations were for 18 hr at 37°C in a humidified 5% CO_2 and air atmosphere. Kinetic studies showed that most induction took place during the first 2 hr of incubation but maximum induction was achieved most consistently when incubation was extended overnight (24). At the end of 18 hr of incubation, T and B cells were identified by surface markers.

Expression of data. All cell populations, except those of the null cell compartment, were identified on fresh spleen cells. First, the total number of cells freed from each spleen was determined for subsequent use in calculating absolute values. Then, percentages of granulocytes, hematopoietic cells, macrophages, and lymphocytes were determined from Wright–Giemsa- and esterase-stained smears. T-cell and B-cell percentages were detected using various procedures outlined above. Pre-T and pre-B cells were defined as null lymphocytes that acquired T- or B-cell membrane markers after overnight incubation with ubiquitin. Pre-T-cell percentages were calculated from the difference in T-cell percentages in overnight incubations with and without ubiquitin. Pre-B-cell percentages were enumerated in a similar fashion. Null lymphoid cells that could not be induced to express detectable T- or B-cell markers were arbitrarily termed other null cells.

Grouped values were expressed as means ± SEMs. The statistical significance of values on the same cell preparations that were treated differently was determined using Student's paired t test. The Wilcoxon rank sum test was used when comparing the same test results performed on different cell preparations.

RESULTS

The Null Cell Compartment in 3-Month-Old C3H/He Mice

By morphologic and histochemical criteria, fresh spleen cell suspensions included 78 ± 1.4% lymphoid cells, 10 ± 0.1% granulocytes, 6 ± 0.3% macrophages, and 6 ± 1.3% hematopoietic cells. About 25% of all spleen cells were T lymphocytes whether detected using Thy 1.2 or mouse brain antiserum (Table 1). Similar values were obtained using cytotoxicity or with direct or indirect immunofluorescence tests. Likewise, similar values were obtained using uv microscopy or a cell sorter. When enumerating B lymphocytes, 40 ± 0.8% fresh spleen cells reacted with antisera to Ig heavy chains by uv microscopy and 38% using a cell sorter. When conjugates and uv microscopy were used, 43 ± 0.5% demonstrated membrane light chains. Receptors for C_3 were identified on 38 ± 1.1% of fresh spleen cells. After 18 hr of unstimulated incubation, 20 ± 1.5% spleen cells bore Thy 1.2 antigen and 42 ± 0.4% bore Ig heavy-chain determinants.

The difference in T-cell percentages after overnight incubation with or without ubiquitin averaged 7% ($P < 0.05$) irrespective of whether Thy 1.2 or mouse brain antisera was used (Table 1). Similar values for pre-T cells were obtained using cytotoxicity, direct, or indirect immunofluorescence tests and when surface fluorescence was demonstrated by uv microscopy or using a cell sorter. The presence of ubiquitin in overnight incubations also increased the number of spleen cells with

TABLE 1

Comparison of Different Methods Used to Identify Lymphocytes

Surface marker	Method for identification	T lymphocytes (%)	Pre-T lymphocytes (%)
Thy 1.2 antigen	Cytotoxicity	25 ± 1.5	7 ± 0.7
	Indirect IF[a]	25 ± 1.2	6 ± 0.4
	Direct IF	25	7[b]
	Direct IF, cytofluorograf	27	7[b]
Brain antigen	Direct IF	25 ± 0.9	7 ± 1.0
μ, γ, α chains	Direct IF	40 ± 0.8	7 ± 0.9
	Direct IF, cytofluorograf	38	7
κ, λ chains	κ, direct, λ, indirect IF	43 ± 0.5	8 ± 0.6
C_3 receptors	EAC rosettes	38 ± 1.1	6 ± 1.1

[a] IF, immunofluorescence.
[b] Mean of two experiments.

membrane Ig heavy or light chains or receptors for C_3 by 5–9% ($P < 0.05$). Again, similar values for pre-B cells were registered using uv microscopy or a cell sorter. Figure 1 shows quantitative differences in T and B cells and the ranges of fluorescence-registering membrane Thy 1.2 antigen or Ig heavy chains on spleen cells after incubation with and without ubiquitin. In all subsequent experiments, T cells were identified using Thy 1.2 antiserum in a complement-dependent cytotoxicity test system and B cells by the presence of Ig heavy chains using direct fluorescence microscopy.

Small quantities of cytoplasmic μ chains, without detectable membrane Ig, are thought to identify a stage in the ontogeny of B-cell differentiation (11). These comprised 4 ± 0.3% of bone marrow cells from 3-month-old mice. While ubiquitin induction significantly increased the number of spleen cells bearing surface Ig, no cytoplasmic μ-chain-positive and membrane Ig-negative cells were observed in fresh spleen cell preparations or after incubation with or without ubiquitin.

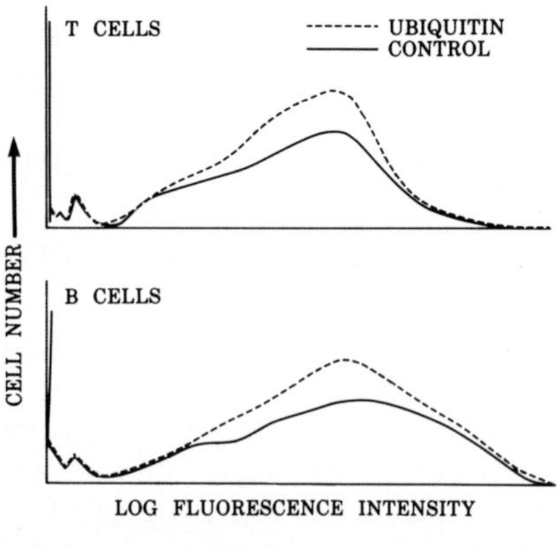

FIG. 1. A representative cytofluorograf analysis of T and B cells in a spleen cell suspension after overnight incubation with and without ubiquitin. T cells were identified using a monoclonal conjugate for Thy 1.2 antigen and B cells using conjugates for μ, γ, and α-chain determinants.

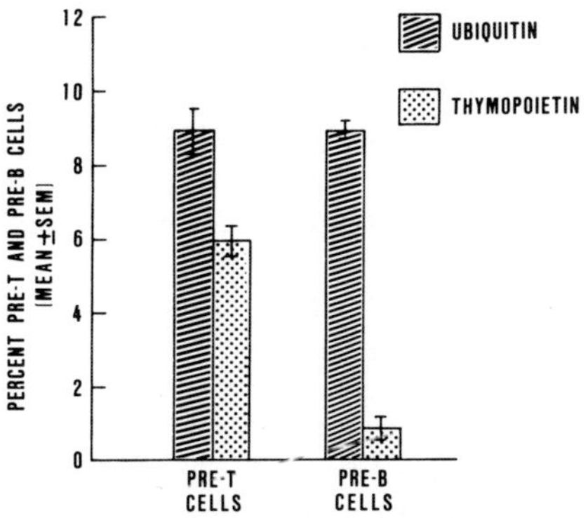

FIG. 2. T- and B-cell induction of spleen cell suspensions with ubiquitin or thymopoietin. T cells were identified by Thy 1.2 antigen in a cytotoxicity system and B cells by heavy-chain conjugates and uv microscopy.

Specificity of Null Cell Induction

Spleen cell suspensions were stimulated with 20 ng/ml ubiquitin or 1 μg/ml thymopoietin. T-Cell induction was 9 ± 0.4% with ubiquitin and 6 ± 0.4% with thymopoietin ($P < 0.05$) (Fig. 2). Ubiquitin induced 9 ± 0.2% B-cell differentiation while thymopoietin did not induce significant B-cell differentiation ($P < 0.001$). Thus, ubiquitin is a potent inducer of both T and B cells; thymopoietin is less potent and only induces T-cell differentiation (13, 24).

After a single 18-hr incubation period, thymopoietin alone induced T-cell but not B-cell differentiation while ubiquitin induced both T- and B-cell differentiation (Table 2). After two consecutive 18-hr incubation periods with thymopoietin, T-cell differentiation increased to a level that was comparable to that achieved with a single 18-hr incubation period with ubiquitin; there was still no B-cell induction. Consecutive incubations were done first with thymopoietin and then with ubiquitin. The initial stimulus with thymopoietin did not remove null cells capable of B-cell differentiation during the second incubation with ubiquitin. This representative experiment provides additional evidence that cells become committed to the T- or B-cell series during the null cell stage of differentiation.

TABLE 2

Differential and Combined T- and B-Cell Induction with Thymopoietin and/or Ubiquitin

	Pre-T (%)	Pre-B (%)
Thymopoietin, 1 μg/ml for 18 hr	7	1
Ubiquitin, 20 ng/ml for 18 hr	9	9
Thymopoietin, 1 μg/ml for 18 hr followed by thymopoietin, 1 μg/ml for 18 hr	9	1
Thymopoietin, 1 μg/ml for 18 hr followed by ubiquitin, 20 ng/ml for 18 hr	11	10

Note. T cells were identified by Thy 1.2 antiserum in a complement-dependent cytotoxicity test and B cells by the presence of Ig heavy chains using immunofluorescence.

Null Cell Compartment in Different Strains of Mice

Spleen cells from 3-month-old C3H/He, DBA/2, CBA/T6, Balb/c, and C57BL/1 mice were incubated with and without ubiquitin and induction of membrane Thy 1.2 antigen and Ig heavy chains was determined. The numbers of pre-T and pre-B cells were remarkably consistent among these different strains ($P > 0.05$) (Fig. 3).

Age and the Null Cell Compartment

The absolute and relative cell compositions of spleens from neonatal, 3-, 8-, and 24-month-old C3H/He mice were compared. Spleens from neonatal mice weighed < 10% of spleens from young adult mice which was reflected in low absolute cell counts (Table 3). However, percentages of various cell populations differed significantly in spleens from neonatal and 3-month-old mice ($P < .01$). The neonates had elevated percentages of hematopoietic cells (49 ± 6.7 vs 6 ± 1.5%), presumably reflecting a residue from splenic hematopoiesis during intrauterine life. Percentages of both T cells (6 ± 0.2 vs 24 ± 1.1%) and B cells (9 ± 0.4 vs 35 ± 0.8%) were greatly reduced in neonatal spleens. However, no significant differences were observed in total null cell percentages.

At age 24 months, absolute numbers of splenic hematopoietic cells, granulocytes, macrophages, T cells, and B cells were not significantly different from values recorded at age 3 months (Table 3). However, the total null cell content of the spleen was elevated at age 24 months ($P < 0.05$).

The relationship of age to the composition of the null cell compartment was evaluated. Spleens from neonatal mice contained few T-cell precursors, reduced percentages of B-cell precursors, and greatly elevated percentages of ubiquitin-unresponsive null cells when compared with spleens from 3-month-old mice ($P < 0.01$) (Fig. 4). At age 24 months, percentages of pre-T cells were reduced ($P < 0.01$), pre-B cells were comparable and ubiquitin-unresponsive null cells were threefold higher than in spleens from 3-month-old mice ($P < 0.01$). This age-related increase in ubiquitin-unresponsive null cells appeared to commence at about 8 months of age.

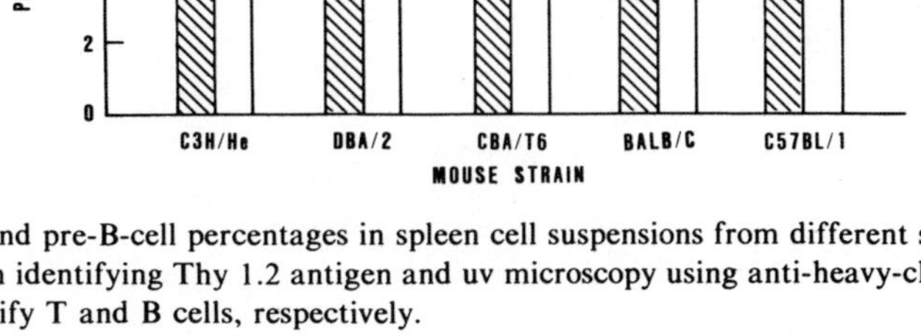

FIG. 3. Pre-T- and pre-B-cell percentages in spleen cell suspensions from different strains of mice. A cytotoxicity system identifying Thy 1.2 antigen and uv microscopy using anti-heavy-chain determinants were used to identify T and B cells, respectively.

TABLE 3

Absolute Numbers of Cell Populations in Mouse Spleens at Different Ages

	Cells per spleen					
Age of mice (months)	Hematopoietic cells	Granulocytes	Macrophages	T cells	B cells	Null cells
Neonates	9.8 ± 2.9	2.7 ± 0.9	0.3 ± 0.1	0.5 ± 0.1	0.8 ± 0.1	1.9 ± 0.2
3	6.4 ± 1.7	8.0 ± 0.8	3.6 ± 0.5	15.7 ± 0.8	22.5 ± 1.7	12.4 ± 1.3
8	4.9 ± 0.8	8.3 ± 0.6	2.3 ± 0.5	15.0 ± 0.9	24.1 ± 1.4	15.9 ± 1.7
24	5.7 ± 0.8	10.6 ± 0.9	2.5 ± 0.4	20.0 ± 1.8	25.1 ± 2.6	28.5 ± 2.2

Note. T cells were identified by membrane Thy 1.2 antigen in a cytotoxicity test and B cells by membrane heavy chains using direct immunofluorescence.

Null Cell Compartment in Athymic Mice

The composition of the null cell compartment was studied at age 3 months on congenitally athymic mice, five of whom were germ free and five others were housed conventionally. These spleens lacked detectable T cells but had a normal B-cell content. Spleen cells from germ-free mice included 18 ± 1.3% pre-T cells which was significantly higher than the 9 ± 0.4% recorded on athymic mice that had been exposed to common environmental stresses ($P < 0.01$) (Fig. 5). The latter were not significantly different from age-matched C3H/He mice. The splenic content of B-cell precursors and ubiquitin-unresponsive null cells was not altered by the athymic state.

Null Cell Compartment and Steroid Sensitivity

We injected 5 mg of hydrocortisone acetate into the thighs of 3-month-old C3H/He mice and studied the null cell compartment 3 days later. Inducible T-cell precursors were reduced to 0.3 ± 0.3% ($P < 0.01$) while B-cell precursors were unaltered after steroid injection.

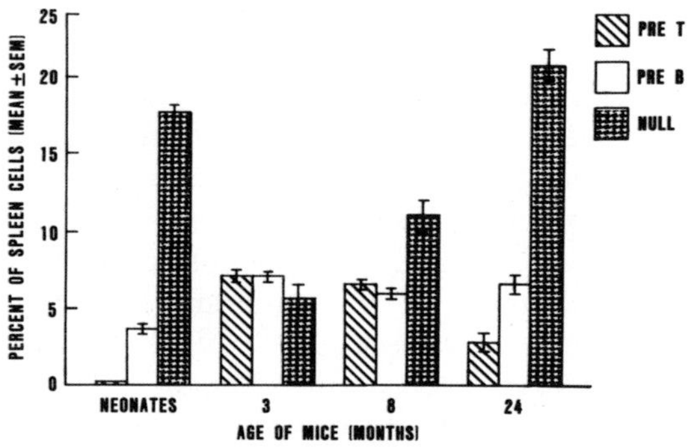

FIG. 4. The composition of the spleen null cell compartment at different ages. Pre-T cells were identified by acquisition of Thy 1.2 antigen in a cytotoxicity system and pre-B cells by acquisition of membrane Ig heavy chains using direct immunofluorescence.

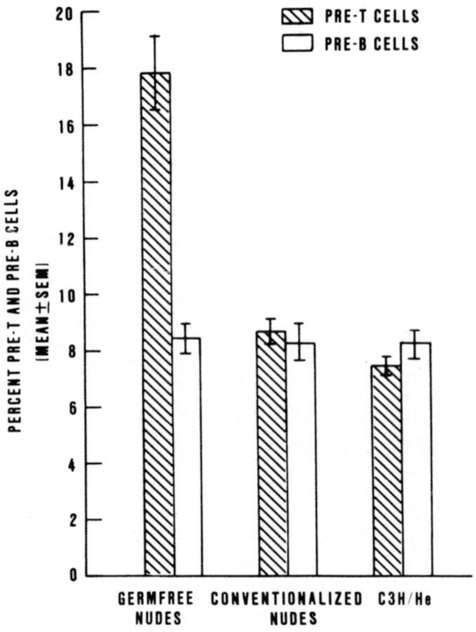

FIG. 5. The effect of congenital thymic deficiency and a germ-free environment upon the spleen null cell compartment. Pre-T cells were enumerated using antiserum to Thy 1.2 antigen and complement-dependent cytotoxicity and pre-B cells using anti-heavy-chain conjugates and direct immunofluorescence.

DISCUSSION

This study indicates that the null cell compartment of the mouse spleen can be divided into three supopulations by differentiation responses to ubiquitin. Similar values were obtained with a number of cell surface markers and techniques. The number of null cells that acquired T- or B-cell membrane markers was about comparable. These inducible null cells are termed pre-T and pre-B lymphocytes. Our use of differential induction with ubiquitin and thymopoietin and an earlier study using flotation (1) suggest that commitment toward T- or B-lymphocyte differentiation takes place in the null cell compartment. A minority of normal null cells were unresponsive to ubiquitin. These could be (a) mature non-T, non-B lymphocytes (25), (b) precursors that respond to a limited number of inductive signals that do not include ubiquitin, (c) null cells whose differentiation potential does not exceed the threshold needed for identification, or (d) nonlymphoid cells such as hematopoietic precursors. There was remarkable consistency in the composition of the null cell compartment of spleens from different strains of mice.

The techniques used in this study identified somewhat fewer T cells but comparable numbers of B cells to published experience in spleen cell suspensions (8, 10, 26). Some null lymphocytes bear small quantities of surface markers (27, 28); even T lymphocytes have low levels of membrane Ig (29) that are not detected using conventional techniques. Thus, cells identified in the present study as null lymphocytes may not be completely devoid of surface markers. The objective was to identify a stage of lymphocyte differentiation under standardized conditions. The null cell compartment was examined in the context of the total cell composition of the spleen.

The null cell compartment comprised about 20% of crude spleen cell suspensions in this study. In similar studies, Raff reported 18% (26), Roelants *et al.* 10% (10), and Stobo *et al.* about 7% (8) of spleen cells were null lymphocytes. Splenic null cells can differentiate *in vivo* as well as *in vitro* (30). It is not known why some null cells, although intrinsically capable of differentiation, do not do so while resident in the spleen. There may be a feedback or other mechanism that regulates the entry of precursor cells into more mature lymphocyte pools. The local splenic environment may be unfavorable for lymphocyte differentiation. Biologic initiators of lymphocyte differentiation are usually of low molecular weight (6, 14, 17) and should be distributed evenly throughout the body unless catabolism is accelerated in the spleen. The triggering of T-cell differentiation by inducing peptides takes less than 10 min (1) and expression of membrane markers is almost complete within 2 hr (24). Thus, it is unlikely that the presence of null cells reflects an obligatory pause in lymphocyte differentiation.

It has been suggested that the appearance of μ chains in the cytoplasm represents a stage in B-cell differentiation. Cells with this primitive Ig chain distribution are not found in spleens from young adult mice (11). In addition, such cells were not induced with ubiquitin in the present study. Different inducing agents induce distinct subpopulations of B cells only some of which pass through a stage where Ig chains are limited to the cytoplasm (31). Perhaps, ubiquitin only induces B-cell precursors that bypass this stage of differentiation. In that case, other B-cell precursors that respond to different inducing agents and pass through a cytoplasmic Ig stage may contribute to the subpopulation of null cells that does not respond to ubiquitin.

Situations were observed where the composition of the null cell compartment was altered. It is apparent that nonthymic T-cell-inducing agents are incapable of significant T-cell differentiation *in vivo* with congenital thymic deficiency (32). Null cells that are committed to T-cell differentiation accumulate in spleens from unstressed congenitally athymic mice. Obviously, the commitment of null cells to T-cell differentiation is a thymic-independent event. Null cells that undergo T- or B-cell differentiation in response to ubiquitin differ in that T-cell precursors are sensitive to stress and adrenocortiocosteroids. This suggests that steroid sensitivity includes null T-cell precursors as well as relatively immature T cells (33). Conversely, the steroid resistance of our B-cell precursors suggests they may be quite primitive cells.

When young adult mice are thymectomized, various T-cell functions eventually decline (34). The decline in T-cell functions with advanced age (35) is also associated with prolonged thymodeprivation due to thymic involution (36). Yet, the distribution of lymphocyte subpopulations in spleens from normal-aged or younger congenitally athymic mice differed significantly. Aged mice maintained a normal number of T lymphocytes despite a significant deficiency of ubiquitin-responsive T-cell precursors. With congenital thymic deficiency, T-cell precursors accumulated but did not sustain a detectable T-cell compartment. The B-lymphocyte series, including ubiquitin-responsive precursors, was normal with both congenital and senescent thymic deficiency. There was a gradual accumulation of ubiquitin-unresponsive null lymphocytes after age 8 months which, because of their normal numbers in spleens from 3-month-old nude mice, cannot be ascribed directly to prolonged thymodeprivation. Thus, splenic T cells of aged mice sustain themselves despite an apparent reduced input from null cell precursors. A gradual accumulation of ubiquitin-unresponsive null cells is a feature of aging within the null cell compartment. Their actual identity and potential to differentiate in response to other stimuli remains to be ascertained.

Some studies suggest that spleen (37) or bone marrow (38) cells from aged mice are capable of normal immunologic reconstitution. The present study and the *in vivo* study of Tyan (39) suggest that T-cell differentiation becomes defective with advanced age. Perhaps, this defect is limited to early T-cell precursors and T-cell homeostasis in aged mice is derived from replication of more differentiated cells. The potential for functional heterogeneity is likely to diminish with cell maturity. Functional restriction, due to T cells being largely derived from relatively mature precursors, could contribute to the overall waning of T-cell vigor with advanced age.

The composition of lymphocyte populations was also altered in neonatal mice. T-cell, B-cell, pre-T-cell, and pre-B-cell percentages were reduced. While the total null cell compartment was not expanded, there were increased numbers of null cells that were unresponsive to ubiquitin induction. In this situation, where thymic influences are optimal, likely explanations include (a) incomplete migration of lymphoid cells to the spleen (40), (b) lymphoid precursors that are unresponsive to inductive stimuli because of immaturity, (c) immaturity of the splenic microenvironment, and (d) suppression exercising effects upon lymphocyte differentiation as well as upon lymphocyte function.

This study introduces a new way to investigate lymphocyte precursors. The changes observed suggest that this approach may help determine the approximate stage of differentiation at which lymphocyte disorders originate and, thereby, may have clinical application. Although multiple myeloma is expressed as a neoplasm of terminal B-cell differentiation, it also involves B lymphocytes (41). The accumulation of null lymphocytes in blood from patients with lymphoblastic leukemia (42) and systemic lupus erythematosus (43) suggests that abnormalities may exist within the null cell compartment with these diseases as well. These, and perhaps other disorders, would be better understood if the stage of differentiation at which abnormalities appear could be identified.

ACKNOWLEDGMENTS

This research was supported by NIH Grants CA 15333 and RO1 NS 16325 and also by a grant from Ellem Laboratories, Milano, Italy. We are grateful to Gideon Goldstein, M. D., Ph. D., Executive Director, Immunosciences, Ortho Pharmaceutical Corporation, for providing us with ubiquitin and thymopoietin; Ellen Vitetta, Ph.D., Prof. Microbiol. University of Texas Southwestern Medical School, Dallas, for reagents used for cell sorting; and David Dennison, Ph. D., Baylor College of Medicine, Houston, for his valuable assistance with use of the cytofluorograf.

REFERENCES

1. Scheid, M. P., Goldstein, G., and Boyse, E. A., *J. Exp. Med.* **147,** 1727, 1978.
2. Komuro, K., and Boyse, E. A., *Lancet* **1,** 740, 1973.
3. Bash, R. S., and Goldstein, G., *Cell. Immunol.* **20,** 218, 1975.
4. Yang, W. C., Miller, S. C., and Osmond, D. G., *J. Exp. Med.* **148,** 1251, 1978.
5. Gathings, W. E., Cooper, M. D., Lawton, A. R., and Alford, C. A., *Fed. Proc.* **35,** 393, 1976.
6. Scheid, M. P., Hoffman, M. D., Komuro, K., Hammerling, U., Abbott, J., Boyse, E. A., Cohen, G. H., Hooper, J. A., Shulof, R. S., and Goldstein, A. L., *J. Exp. Med.* **138,** 1027, 1973.
7. Rotter, V., and Trainin, N., *J. Immunol.* **122,** 414, 1979.
8. Stobo, J. D., Rosenthal, A. S., and Paul, W. E., *J. Exp. Med.* **138,** 71, 1973.
9. Ryser, J. E., and Vassalli, P., *J. Immunol.* **113,** 719, 1974.

10. Roelants, G. E., Loor, F., vonBoehmer, H., Sprent, J., Hagg, L. B., Mayor, K. S., and Ryden, A., *Eur. J. Immunol.* **5,** 127, 1975.
11. Raff, M. C., Magson, M., Owen, J. J. T., and Cooper, M. D., *Nature (London)* **247,** 11, 1974.
12. Keightley, R. G., Lawton, A. R., Cooper, M. D., and Yunis, E. J., *Lancet* **2,** 850, 1975.
13. Goldstein, G., Scheid, M., Hammerling, U., Boyse, E. A., Schlesinger, D. H., and Niall, H. D., *Proc. Nat. Acad. Sci. USA* **72,** 11, 1975.
14. Schlesinger, D. H., Goldstein, G., and Niall, H. D., *Biochemistry* **11,** 2214, 1975.
15. Yam, L. T., Li, C. Y., and Crosby, W. H., *Amer. J. Clin. Pathol.* **55,** 283, 1971.
16. Schlesinger, D. H., and Goldstein, G., *Cell* **5,** 361, 1975.
17. Goldstein, G., *Nature (London)* **247,** 11, 1974.
18. Reif, A. E., and Allen, J. M. V., *J. Exp. Med.* **120,** 413, 1964.
19. Ligler, F. S., Vitetta, E. S., and Uhr, J. W., *J. Immunol.* **119,** 1545, 1977.
20. Stewart, C. C., and Ingram, M., *Blood* **29,** 628, 1967.
21. Twomey, J. J., Rossen, R. D., Lewis, V. M., Morgan, A. C., and McCormick K. J., *Cancer* **41,** 1307, 1978.
22. Mendes, N. F., Tolnai, M. E. A., Silviera, P. A., Gilbertsen, R. B., and Metzgar, R. S., *J. Immunol.* **111,** 860, 1973.
23. Raff, M. C., Magson, M., Owen, J. J. T., and Cooper, M. D., *Nature (London)* **259,** 224, 1976.
24. Twomey, J. J., Goldstein, G., Lewis, V. M., Bealmear, P. M., and Good, R. A., *Proc. Natl. Acad. Sci. USA* **74,** 2541, 1977.
25. Froland, S. S., and Natvig, J. B., *Transplant. Rev.* **16,** 114, 1973.
26. Raff, M. C., *Transplant Rev.* **6,** 52, 1971.
27. Sato, V. L., Waksal, S. D., and Herzenberg, L. A., *Cell. Immunol.* **24,** 173, 1976.
28. Warr, G. W., Lee, J. C., and Marchalonis, J. J., *J. Immunol.* **121,** 1767, 1978.
29. Nossal, G. J. V., Warner, N. L., Lewis, H., and Sprent, J., *J. Exp. Med.* **135,** 405, 1972.
30. Papiernik, M., and Bach, J. F., *J. Immunol.* **123,** 2311, 1979.
31. Muraguchi, A., Kishimoto, T., Kuritani, T., Watanabe, T., and Yamamura, Y., *J. Immunol.* **125,** 564, 1980.
32. Lischner, H. W., and Huff, D. S., *Birth Defects: Original Article Series* **11,** 16, 1975.
33. Katz, D. H., "Lymphocyte Differentiation, Recognition and Regulation." Academic Press, New York, 1977.
34. Kappler, J. W., Hunter, P. C., Jacobs, D., and Lord, E., *J. Immunol.* **113,** 27, 1974.
35. Kay, M. M. B., *Fed. Proc.* **37,** 1241, 1978.
36. Lewis, V. M., Twomey, J. J., Bealmear, P., Goldstein, G., and Good, R. A., *J. Clin. Endocrin. Metabol.* **47,** 145, 1978.
37. Harrison, D. E., and Doubleday, J. W., *J. Immunol.* **114,** 1314, 1975.
38. Micklem, H. S., Ogden, D. A., and Payne, A. C., *Ciba Found. Symp.* **13,** 285, 1973.
39. Tyan, M. L., *J. Immunol.* **118,** 846, 1977.
40. Mosier, D. E., and Cohen, P. L., *Fed. Proc.* **34,** 137, 1975.
41. Abdou, N. E., and Abdou, N. L., *Ann. Intern. Med.* **83,** 42, 1975.
42. Pasino, M., Tonini, G. P., Rosanda, C., and Massimo, L., *Lancet* **1,** 608, 1977.
43. Scheinberg, M. A., Cathcart, E. S., and Goldstein, A. L., *Lancet* **1,** 424, 1975.

CELLULAR IMMUNOLOGY 63, 118–133 (1981)

A Series of Murine Interleukin Molecules Which Stimulate both Murine and Human Lymphocytes[1]

I. Production by *Phytolacca Americana* (Pokeweed) Lectin 2 (Pa-2)-Stimulated Thymus and Thymus-Derived Cells

TERESA Y. BASHAM,[2] SATOSHI TOYOSHIMA,[3] FRED FINKELMAN,[4] AND M. J. WAXDAL[5]

Laboratory of Immunology, National Institute of Allergy and Infectious Diseases, National Institutes of Health, Bethesda, Maryland 20205

Received March 5, 1981; accepted April 30, 1981

Cell-free supernatant fluid, from cultures of *Phytolacca americana* (pokeweed) lectin 2 (Pa-2)-pulsed murine spleen or thymus cells, contains factors which induce cultured lymphocytes to differentiate into IgM-secreting cells (assayed by a reverse plaque technique) and to proliferate (measured by the incorporation of tritiated thymidine) without the addition of mitogen. The factors in this supernatant fluid responsible for these activities have been designated as lymphocyte stimulating factors (LSF). LSF showed no genetic restrictions related to the major histocompatability complex; LSF made in one strain of mice worked in other strains. Indeed, LSF is not restricted by species barriers; human peripheral blood mononuclear cells were also stimulated by murine LSF to proliferate and differentiate into immunoglobulin-secreting cells without further addition of antigen or mitogen. Maximum production of LSF was achieved within 12 hr of culture and was independent of cell division. In contrast to TRF, no further production of LSF was detectable after 24 hr of culture. Unlike T-cell growth factor, this material stimulated increased mitosis of thymic, T, and B lymphocytes without the addition of mitogen or antigen. LSF also stimulated polyclonal B-cell differentiation into IgM-secreting cells. Maximal numbers of immunoglobulin-secreting cells were generated when LSF was added at the initiation of the culture. Indeed, unlike TRF, LSF needed to be present only during the first 6 hr of culture to achieve maximum stimulation, and did not require the presence of antigen. The production of LSF by a T-cell population in the spleen was shown by two independent methods. Spleen cells treated with anti-Thy 1 plus complement failed to produce detectable levels of LSF. On the other hand, purified populations of surface immunoglobulin-negative spleen cells produced LSF. Furthermore, the subset of thymocytes responsible for LSF production was the small population (approximately 10%) of cells in the thymus, which are not agglutinated by peanut agglutinin.

[1] This work was done in partial fulfillment of requirements for a Ph.D. degree, George Washington University, Washington, D.C.

[2] Current address: Department of Medicine, Stanford University Medical School, Palo Alto, Calif. 94305.

[3] Current address: Faculty of Pharmaceutical Sciences, University of Tokyo, Bunko-ku, Tokyo 113, Japan.

[4] Department of Medicine, USUHS, Bethesda, Md. 20014.

[5] To whom correspondence should be addressed.

0008-8749/81/130118-16$02.00/0

INTRODUCTION

It has been known for several years that the T-cell mitogen, concanavalin A (Con A),[6] can stimulate subpopulations of regulatory lymphocytes that enhance or suppress the immune response of murine spleen cells to heterologous erythrocytes (1–3). The amount of Con A added and the time of addition are critically important in the induction of the enhancing effect (2). Another mitogen, PWM (a mixture of several lectins from pokeweed), has been used to stimulate the differentiation and maturation of murine and human B cells into immunoglobulin-secreting cells. PWM has also been used to prepare soluble helper factors from human T-cell cultures (4). Five mitogens have been isolated from pokeweed (5). One of these, Pa-1, stimulates murine B cells in the absence of T cells. Another of these lectins, Pa-2, stimulates murine T cells over a wide concentration range, but has no mitogenic or immunoglobulin synthesis stimulating activity for spleen cells from athymic (nu/nu) mice, except when presented in a crosslinked or aggregated form at high concentrations (6, 7).

We now wish to report that the cell-free supernatant fluid from cultures of murine spleen and thymus cells pulsed with Pa-2 induces cultured lymphocytes from normal or nude mouse spleens to differentiate into IgM-secreting cells (IgM ISC, assayed by a reverse plaque technique), and to proliferate (measured by the incorporation of [^{3}H]thymidine). We have tentatively designated the materials responsible for these activities as lymphocyte stimulating factors (LSF).

MATERIALS AND METHODS

Mice

Female BALB/c mice were obtained from Microbiological Associates, Bethesda, Maryland. Athymic nude mice (nu/nu on a BALB/c background), female C57Bl/6N, and AKR/N mice were obtained from the National Institutes of Health. Experiments were performed with 4- to 12-week-old animals.

Mitogens

The pokeweed mitogens, Pa-1 and Pa-2, were isolated by the method of Waxdal (5) with the following modification. The dialyzed root extracts were chromatographed on DEAE cellulose (DE-52, Whatman; 10 m*M* phosphate buffer, pH 8) instead of hydroxyapatite. The major portion of the dissolved material was not retained on the column. After the effluent absorbance at 280 nm had returned to baseline, a major fraction was eluted with a phosphate buffer (pH 5.3) and KCl gradient (0.1 *M* KP_i to 0.2 *M* KP_i, 0.5 *M* KCl). The eluted material, which con-

[6] Abbreviations used: Con A, concanavalin A; Pa-1, lectin 1 from *Phytolacca americana* (pokeweed); Pa-2, lectin 2 from *P. americana*; PWM, unfractionated lectin preparation from *P. americana*; PNA, peanut agglutinin; LSF, lymphocyte stimulating factor; TCGF, T-cell growth factor; TRF, T-cell replacing factor; BSA, bovine serum albumin; FCS, fetal calf serum; ISC, immunoglobulin-secreting cells; Ig, immunoglobulin; RaMIg, rabbit anti-murine immunoglobulin; RaHIg, rabbit anti-human immunoglobulin; RaMu, rabbit anti-murine μ chain; RaHu, rabbit anti-human μ chain; HBSS, Hanks' balanced salt solution; Hepes, *N*-2-hydroxyethylpiperazine-*N*'-2-ethanesulfonic acid; MHC, major histocompatability complex.

tained the mitogenic activity, was lyophilized and chromatographed on Sephadex G-75 (Pharmacia) in 1 *M* propionic acid as previously described.

Preparation of Cells for Culture and LSF Production

Mice were sacrificed by cervical dislocation and spleens and thymii removed sterily. These organs were teased separately into Hanks' balanced salt solution (HBSS). The clumps of cells were allowed to settle and the supernatant fluid, containing single cells, was transferred to a sterile plastic centrifuge tube. These cells were washed three times with HBSS and the cell number was determined with a Model B Coulter Counter. The cell concentrations were adjusted to 4 $\times 10^6$/ml in RPMI 1640 (Gibco) containing 1% fetal calf serum (Gibco), 1% added glutamine, 0.1 mg/ml streptomycin, and 100 units/ml penicillin (hereafter referred to as complete medium).

For LSF production, 4×10^6 cells/ml in HBSS were pulsed with 5–50 μg/ml Pa-2 (10 μg was used routinely) for 10 min at ambient temperature. The cells were then washed twice with HBSS and cultured at 4×10^6/ml in complete medium in 15 ml polystyrene Falcon culture tubes (2 ml/tube) at 37°C under 5% CO_2. Cell-free supernatants were collected by centrifugation after 12–24 hr of culture and sterilized by passage through a 0.45-μm Swinnex filter. In some cases, the supernatants were then concentrated by ultrafiltration (Amicon, XP-10). The supernatants were found to lose activity after repeated freezing and thawing; therefore separate aliquots of each preparation were stored at −70°C.

Cell Culture and Assay for Mitosis

Murine lymphocytes were cultured in round-bottom microculture plates (Cooke Engineering) at 4×10^5 cells/200 ul/well at 37°C in 5% CO_2. Purified human mononuclear cell suspensions were obtained by Ficoll–Hypaque (Pharmacia) density centrifugation of heparinized venous blood. The cells were cultured in triplicate in RPMI 1640 containing 1% trypticase soy broth, 0.02 *M* glutamine, 100 units/ml penicillin, 100 μg/ml streptomycin, and 10% fetal calf serum. One million cells were cultured in 1 ml of medium in individual 5-ml round-bottomed Falcon polystyrene tubes for up to 6 days on a rocking platform at 37°C in 5% CO_2. DNA synthesis was measured by the incorporation of [^{3}H]thymidine (1 μCi/well, 1.9 mCi/μmol, New England Nuclear) for 18 hr. The cultures (in triplicate) were harvested and washed by filtration. The incorporation of [^{3}H]thymidine was measured by liquid scintillation spectrophotometry.

Blockage of Cell Division with Mitomycin C

Lymphocytes ($4\text{–}8 \times 10^6$/ml) were incubated for 1 hr at 37° in RPMI 1640 containing 40 ug/ml Mitomycin C (Sigma). The cells were then washed 3 times with HBSS. Mitomycin C treated cells were assayed for blockage of cell division by measuring the incorporation of ^{3}H-thymidine after stimulation with Pa-2 as described above.

Reverse Plaque Assay for IgM

The number of immunoglobulin-secreting cells (IgM ISC) in these cultures was determined with a reverse plaque assay. The procedure of Ginsberg *et al.* (8) was followed, using either antisera specific for human immunoglobulin or for murine immunoglobulin. Pa-1-stimulated spleen cells were routinely used as a positive control in all murine IgM ISC assays and Pa-2-stimulated cells were used in all human IgM ISC assays.

A. Preparation of antibodies. The preparation of affinity-purified polyvalent rabbit antibody against murine and human immunoglobulin (RaMIg and RaHIg) and isotype-specific rabbit antisera against the heavy chain of murine or human IgM (RaMu or RaHu) have been previously described (8, 9). RaMu or RaHu was absorbed with packed washed sheep RBC and diluted 1:100 to 1:200 for use as a developing antiserum.

B. Preparation of indicator cells. One milliliter of packed sheep RBC, washed three times with saline, was reacted with 1 ml of RaMIg or RaHIg (1 mg/ml) and 1 ml of 0.1% $CrCl_3$ (pH 5.3) for 7 min. This preparation was then washed three times with saline and diluted to 10 ml. These RaIg-coated SRBC were stable for up to 2 weeks at 5°C.

C. Murine or human lymphocytes. Lymphocytes cultured for 72–96 hr as described above were transferred into small glass tubes, washed with HBSS by centrifugation, and resuspended in RPMI 1640 at 2×10^5/ml. Each plaque assay was performed using 10^4 cells.

Preparation of Murine Peritoneal Exudate Macrophages

Mice were injected intraperitoneally (ip) with 1 ml of a 10% solution of Brewer's thioglycollate medium (Difco). After 5 days, the mice were sacrificed by cervical dislocation. Spinner's medium (7 ml, Gibco) containing 5 to 10 m*M* heparin was injected ip. When aspirated, this fluid contained a cell population of approximately 95% macrophages and 5% lymphocytes. The macrophages were isolated by adherance (10^7 cells/ml in RPMI 1640 containing 2 m*M* Hepes and 10% fetal calf serum) to sterile Corning 100-mm polystyrene tissue culture plates. After incubation for 30 min at 37°C, the nonadherent cells were washed away with warm medium and the adherent cells (macrophages) were removed from the plate with ice-cold medium and the aid of a rubber policeman.

Preparation of Murine B and T Lymphocytes

A. Preparation of complement. One milliliter of reconstituted guinea pig complement (Flow Laboratories) was absorbed on ice with the spleen and thymus cells of one BALB/c mouse for 30 min. This complement was then diluted 1:4 with RPMI 1640 containing 2 m*M* Hepes (Gibco), sterilized by passage through a 0.45-μm Swinnex filter and assayed for nonspecific killing.

B. Treatment of spleen cells with anti-Thy 1.2 and complement. Six million washed spleen cells were suspended in 3 ml of a 1:4 dilution of mouse ascites anti-Thy 1.2 (Bionetics, Lot 231-72-6) in HBSS and incubated for 30 min at 4°C. After washing three times with cold HBSS, the anti-Thy 1.2-coated cells were suspended in 6 ml of the diluted absorbed complement and incubated 30 min at 37°C. After washing, the viability of the cells was determined by trypan blue exclusion. Anti-Thy 1.2-treated cells were tested for residual T-cell contamination by determining $[^3H]$thymidine incorporation after Pa-2 stimulation. Only cell populations which did not respond to Pa-2 were considered to be depleted of T cells.

C. Treatment of cells with anti-Ig and complement. Ten million spleen cells were incubated for 30 min at 37°C in 1 ml of RPMI 1640 containing 2 m*M* Hepes, 0.02% NaN_3, and 100μg of affinity-purified RaMIg. These cells were then washed with the RPMI/Hepes/NaN_3 buffer, suspended in 1 ml of a 1:4 dilution of the absorbed guinea pig complement, further incubated for 30 min at 37°C, washed, and tested for viability by trypan blue exclusion. Anti-Ig-treated cells were tested for residual B lymphocyte contamination by determining [^{3}H]thymidine incorporation after LPS stimulation. Only cell populations which did not respond to LPS were considered to be depleted of B cells.

D. Preparation of murine B and T cells by fluorescence activated cell sorting. BALB/c (female, 5-6 weeks old) spleen cell suspensions were prepared as described above. The cells were centrifuged and 8 ml of ACK-lysing buffer was added to the pellet to lyse the red cells. The lysing buffer was immediately diluted with 30 ml of HBSS, containing 10% fetal calf serum. The cells were centrifuged and rediluted in HBSS (0.6 ml) without phenol red, containing 10% fetal calf serum. Sterile fluorescein-labeled goat anti-murine Ig (gift of Dr. I. Scher) was added and the cells were incubated (30 min, 4°C) and washed three times with HBSS containing 6% FCS. The cells were then separated into Ig-positive and Ig-negative populations under sterile conditions by flow microfluorimetry using a FACS II (Becton–Dickenson) fluorescence-activated cell sorter as previously described (10–12). The separated cells were checked for purity by reanalysis on the FACS II and for viability by trypan blue exclusion. The cells were also tested for cross contamination by mitogen activation assays.

Thymocyte Fractionation with Peanut Agglutinin

Washed thymocytes were resuspended in HBSS (6–8 $\times$ 10^8/ml) containing 0.1% BSA and an equal volume of peanut agglutinin (PNA, 1 mg/ml) in HBSS was added. After incubation for 10 min at ambient temperature, the cell suspension was layered on 30 ml of 20% FCS (in HBSS containing 0.1% BSA) and allowed to settle for 45 min. The agglutinated cells settled to the bottom, leaving the top layer containing mostly single cells (13). Both top and bottom fractions were washed by centrifugation with HBSS containing 0.1% BSA and the recovered cells were resuspended in 0.25 *M* galactose or lactose (at 37°C, containing 0.1% BSA and adjusted to between 305 and 310 mOsm with 10X HBSS) for 10 min at 37°C to remove bound PNA and disperse the aggregated cells. The cells were then washed three times with HBSS.

RESULTS

Production of Murine LSF

In an initial series of experiments, the supernatant fluids from Pa-2-pulsed thymus and spleen cell cultures were harvested at various times and assayed for their ability to stimulate the differentiation of splenic B lymphocytes into IgM-secreting cells (IgM ISC) as detected by a reverse plaque assay.

Supernatants from Pa-2-pulsed spleen and thymus cells stimulated the generation of several-fold more IgM ISC than did supernatants from cells not pulsed with Pa-2. The addition of supernatants from unpulsed cells routinely gave a small increase in IgM ISC and these were used as unstimulated background values. The data presented in Table 1 represent the mean values of the results from three experiments. Maximal amounts of IgM ISC stimulating activity were produced during the first 12 hr of culture. After 24 hr of culture, little further production of IgM ISC stimulating activity was observed.

The rapid appearance of LSF in the culture supernatant suggested that cell division may not be required for its production. To test this hypothesis, 12-hr supernatants were prepared from Pa-2-pulsed spleen cells that had been precultured for 1 hr at 37°C with or without mitomycin C. The mitomycin C-treated cells failed to show enhanced incorporation of [^{3}H]thymidine in response to Pa-2 stimulation. The supernatants from Pa-2-pulsed mitomycin C-treated and untreated cells were tested for LSF activity. As shown in Table 2, blocking cell division with mitomycin C did not abbrogate the production of LSF.

Biological Activities of LSF

Initial studies on the biological activities of the LSF in these supernatants revealed that a mitogenic factor was present in addition to the polyclonal activator which stimulated the differentiation of B cells into antibody-secreting cells (IgM ISC). These two effects are described separately below.

A. Mitogenic activity of LSF. The time course of the mitogenic response of murine spleen cells was assayed by the incorporation of an 18-hr pulse of [^{3}H]thymidine and is presented in Fig. 1A. The pokeweed mitogens, Pa-1 (50 μg/ml), Pa-2 (10 μg/ml), or an optimum concentration of LSF produced by either spleen or thymus, were added at the initiation of spleen cell culture. Little enhanced

TABLE 1

The Time Course of Factor Production in Thymus or Spleen Cell Cultures Stimulated by Pa-2

	IgM ISC/10^6 spleen cells[c]	
Cell control:[a]	400 ± 200	
Pa-1:[b]	12,130 ± 902	
Supernatant fluid from	Thymus	Spleen
Unstimulated control (hr)		
0–24	770 ± 57	630 ± 288
Pa-2 stimulated (hr)		
0–1	1250 ± 530	1570 ± 746
0–6	2470 ± 283	1230 ± 353
0–12	4300 ± 458	3950 ± 1153
12–24	2030 ± 486	3030 ± 856
0–24	3600 ± 283	3850 ± 353
24–48	1170 ± 416	650 ± 404
0–48	3800 ± 424	3570 ± 1414
0–72	4200 ± 200	3700 ± 570
0–96	3650 ± 553	3330 ± 440

[a] No supernatant fluid added.
[b] 50 μg/ml.
[c] The values are means ± SD.

TABLE 2

Mitomycin C Does Not Abrogate Factor Production in Thymus or Spleen Cell Cultures Stimulated by Pa-2

	IgM ISC/10^6 spleen cells[c]	
Cell control:[a]	290 ± 130	
Pa-1:[b]	13,700 ± 1,100	
Supernatant fluid from	Normal cells	Mitomycin C-treated cells
Spleen-unstimulated control (μl)		
25	700 ± 100	670 ± 54
Spleen factor (μl)		
10	1200 ± 57	1300 ± 183
25	3000 ± 583	3200 ± 400
Thymus-unstimulated control (μl)		
25	400 ± 100	300 ± 100
Thymus factor (μl)		
10	3700 ± 230	3400 ± 437
25	2800 ± 266	2900 ± 23

[a] No supernatant fluid added.
[b] 50 μg/ml.
[c] The values are means ± SD.

DNA synthesis was detected at 24 hr after activation by any of these stimulants. While the Pa-1- and Pa-2-stimulated spleen cultures showed maximum incorporation of [^{3}H]thymidine at 48 and 72 hr, cultures stimulated with LSF from either thymus or spleen cells showed maximum incorporation of [^{3}H]thymidine at 72 hr of culture.

In like manner, the time course of the mitogenic response of thymocytes to LSF is presented in Fig. 1B. These data show that Pa-1 and Pa-2 stimulate maximum DNA synthesis at about 72 hr. On the other hand, LSF from both spleen and thymus cultures appeared to stimulate greater DNA synthesis near the end of the culture period.

The Pa-2-stimulated culture supernatants were next tested on spleen cells from athymic nude mice (nu/nu on a BALB/c background). Like the responses elicited in normal spleen cells (Fig. 1A), the time course of mitogenic activation by both spleen and thymus LSF paralleled that of Pa-1, but in this case, the response to all stimulants reached a maximum at 48 hr (Fig. 1C). Pa-2 does not stimulate DNA synthesis by nude spleen cells and therefore was not included in this figure.

B. Murine B-cell differentiation stimulated by LSF. The time course of the polyclonal stimulation of splenic B cells into IgM ISC in response to thymus and spleen LSF are presented in Fig. 2A. Both Pa-1 and LSF from thymocytes stimulated maximum numbers of IgM ISC at 72 hr. LSF from spleen cells was equally effective as a stimulant from 48 to 96 hr. While Pa-1 was clearly the more potent activator in these experiments, preparations of both spleen and thymus LSF were almost equally effective in stimulating the differentiation of B cells into IgM ISC. The time course of the IgM ISC response by nude spleen cells (Fig. 2B) differed from that of normal spleen (Fig. 2A). Maximum stimulation by Pa-1 occurred 1

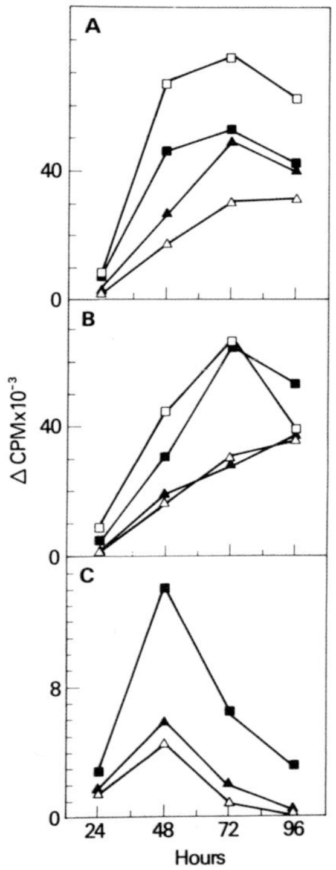

FIG. 1. The time course of the mitogenic response of BALB/c lymphoid cells to lymphocyte-stimulating factors produced by syngeneic spleen or thymus cell cultures. The results, which are the incorporation of an 18-hr pulse of radiolabeled thymidine, are presented as the change in counts per minute. These are the mean values of several experiments, each performed in triplicate, stimulated with optimum concentrations of mitogen and minimal effective concentrations of factor, minus the value of the appropriate control. Pa-2 (10 μg/ml, open squares); Pa-1 (50 μg/ml, solid squares); spleen LSF (20 μl, open triangles); and thymus LSF (15 μl, solid triangles). (A). Spleen cells, three experiments. The standard deviations were 10–15%. Unstimulated control values were 6000 cpm at 24 hr and declined to 3000 cpm at 96 hr. (B) Thymus cells. Six experiments. The standard deviations were 10–15%. Unstimulated control values were 1000 cpm at 24 hr and declined to 350 cpm at 96 hr. (C) Nude spleen cells, two experiments. The standard deviations were 10–12%. Unstimulated control values were 10,000 cpm at 24 hr and declined to 900 cpm at 96 hr.

day earlier than with normal spleen cells. Spleen and thymus LSF stimulated a maximum IgM ISC response in nude spleen cells much earlier than in normal spleen cells with maximum stimulation at 24 hr. The magnitude of the response to LSF was quite similar to the response in normal cells. The Pa-1 response, however, was only approximately one half of the response by normal spleen cell cultures.

The next two series of experiments were to determine the time of addition of LSF and the duration of its presence in the culture to achieve maximum stimulation. Several triplicate cultures were initiated and thymus or spleen LSF was added at various times. The results (Fig. 3) show that LSF must be added at the beginning of culture to achieve maximum stimulation of B-cell differentiation into IgM ISC. It was then determined how long LSF must be present in the culture to achieve maximum stimulation. After the initiation of culture in the presence of LSF, the cells were washed at various times, recultured in the absence of LSF, and harvested at 72 hr. The data (Fig. 4) show that LSF need only be present for 6 hr to achieve maximum stimulation.

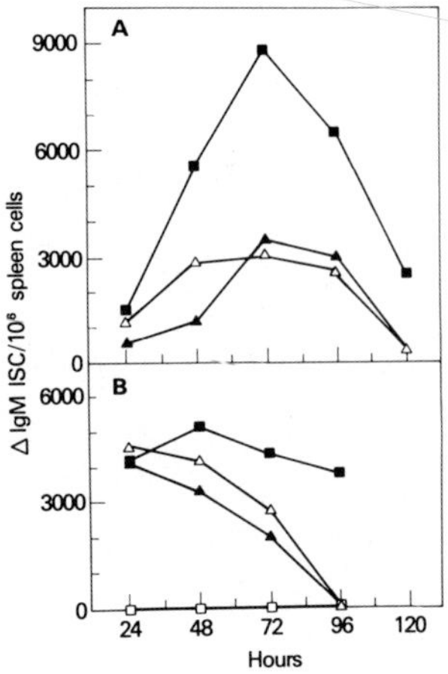

FIG. 2. The time course of the activation of IgM-secreting cells in murine spleen cell cultures. IgM-secreting cells were detected by the reverse plaque assay with rabbit anti-μ chain as the developing antiserum. The results are expressed as the change in IgM plaque-forming cells per million spleen cells. Spleen cells were cultured in triplicate with Pa-1 (50 μg/ml, solid squares); spleen LSF (20 μl, open triangles); and thymus LSF (15 μl, solid triangles). These results are the mean values of three experiments, each performed in triplicate, minus the appropriate controls. (A) Normal BALB/c spleen cells. The standard deviations were 10–20%. Unstimulated control values were 600 ISC at 24 hr and declined to 200 ISC at 120 hr. (B) Nude BALB/c spleen cells. The standard deviations were 10–15%. Unstimulated control values were 5000 ISC at 24 hr and declined to 3700 ISC at 96 hr.

Identification of Cell Types Producing LSF

We next sought to characterize the cells which produce LSF in response to Pa-2 stimulation. To determine if macrophages produced LSF, we attempted to remove

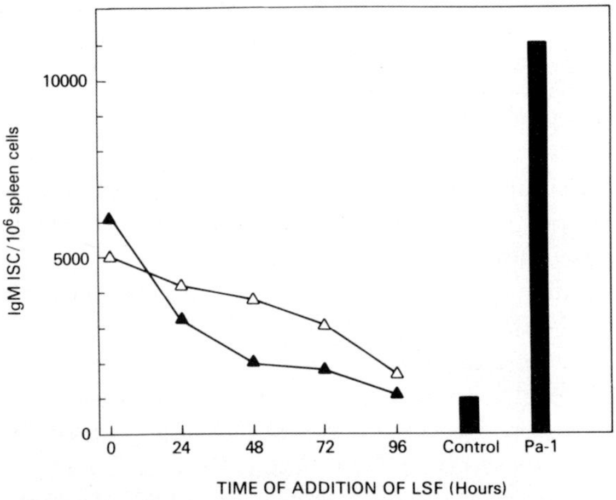

FIG. 3. Lymphocyte-stimulating-factors stimulate maximum IgM-secreting cells when added at the initiation of culture. LSF from spleen or thymus cells was added at the initiation of culture or at 24-hr intervals thereafter. IgM-secreting cells were detected by the reverse plaque assay after 96 hr of culture. The cell control and Pa-1 (50 μg/ml) are depicted by solid bars; spleen LSF (20 μl, open triangles); and thymus LSF (15 μl, solid triangles). The results are the average of three experiments each performed in triplicate. The standard deviations were 15–20%.

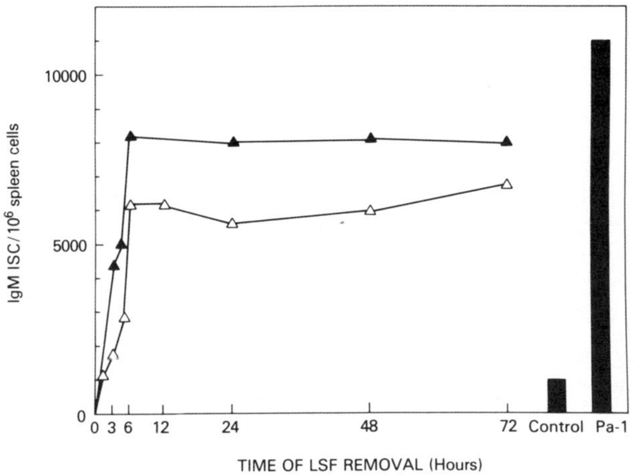

FIG. 4. Lymphocyte-stimulating factors need only be present for the first 6 hr of culture to stimulate maximum numbers of IgM-secreting cells. BALB/c spleen cells (2 million/ml) were cultured in 5-ml round-bottomed plastic culture tubes and a 1:10 dilution of LSF from spleen or thymus was added at the initiation of the culture. Control cultures, without LSF, were performed for each time point. At various time points, cells from the individual tubes were washed and recultured in fresh medium in microculture trays for the duration of the 72 hr culture period. IgM-secreting cells were detected by the reverse plaque assay. The mean values of the cell controls and Pa-1 (50 μg/ml) are depicted by the solid bars; spleen LSF (open triangles); and thymus LSF (solid triangles). These results are the means of three experiments each performed in triplicate. The standard deviations were 15–20%.

these cell from the spleen and thymus cell populations by preferential adherence to polystyrene Corning culture dishes. Although no loss of LSF production was observed (data not shown), it was difficult to evaluate these experiments due to the difficulty of removing all macrophages. Another approach was to enrich for macrophages and assay these cells for the production of LSF after Pa-2 stimulation. Peritoneal exudate cells from BALB/c mice were separated by adherence to Corning culture dishes and the macrophages were recovered as described above. Supernatants from these Pa-2-pulsed adherent macrophages had no ability to stimulate the generation of IgM ISC (Table 3).

We next assayed the abilities of T- and B-cell-depleted spleen cells to generate LSF when pulsed with Pa-2. Depletion of B cells by treatment with rabbit anti-mouse immunoglobulin plus complement did not decrease the production of LSF in response to Pa-2 (Table 3). Indeed, these supernatants appeared to be somewhat enriched in LSF compared to supernatants of the untreated spleen cells. However, the treatment of spleen cells with anti-Thy 1.2 and complement eliminated their ability to generate LSF (Table 3).

The production of LSF by splenic T cells was confirmed by experiments which separated spleen cells into surface Ig-positive and Ig-negative cell pools using a fluorescence-activated cell sorter. It was expected that the B lymphocytes would be labeled with the fluorescent anti-Ig stain and would be sorted into one pool. Reanalysis of the sorted cells showed that this method was effective in attaining an Ig-negative pool (99.9% pure). However, the Ig-positive pool was somewhat less pure (95%). All sorted cells were also assayed for purity by their mitogenic responses to Pa-2 and LPS. There was no mitogenic response to LPS in the Ig-negative pool while there was a residual response to Pa-2 (20% of normal) in the Ig-positive pool.

TABLE 3

Lymphocyte Stimulating Factor Production by Various Murine Lymphoid Cell Populations

	IgM ISC/10^6 spleen cells[c]
Cell control:[a]	206 ± 57
Pa-1:[b]	9,985 ± 1,418
Supernatant fluid from	
Unstimulated peritoneal exudate cells	460 ± 823
Stimulated peritoneal exudate cells	3,760 ± 1,040
Stimulated peritoneal exudate macrophages	233 ± 152
Unstimulated spleen cells	300 ± 100
Stimulated spleen cells	5,350 ± 777
Stimulated anti-Ig + C′-treated spleen cells	7,150 ± 1,909
Stimulated anti-Thy 1.2 + C′-treated spleen cells	433 ± 208
Unstimulated spleen cells	300 ± 133
Stimulated spleen cells	7,836 ± 2,000
Stimulated FACS Ig-positive spleen cells	1,984 ± 694
Stimulated FACS Ig-negative spleen cells	10,416 ± 1,736
Unstimulated nude spleen cells	500 ± 153
Stimulated nude spleen cells	700 ± 231

[a] No supernatant fluid added.
[b] 50 μg/ml.
[c] The values are means ± SD.

The data in Table 3 indicate that 25-μl aliquots of supernatants from surface Ig negative (T) cells stimulated the differentiation of splenic lymphocytes into IgM ISC more effectively than did supernatants from unfractionated spleen cells. On the other hand, 25- to 75-μl aliquots of supernatants from the Pa-2-pulsed surface Ig-positive cells were much less active, although there was not total elimination of LSF production. These results are consistent with our observations using spleen cells from nude mice, which contain macrophages and B cells, but which do not produce LSF (Table 3). The composite data in Table 3 show that T cells, but not B cells, are required for the production of LSF in the spleen.

The population of thymocytes capable of secreting LSF was also investigated. Thymocytes were fractionated into two populations, based upon their ability to be agglutinated by peanut agglutinin (PNA). After separation of the agglutinated and nonagglutinated cells by sedimentation through FCS, the lectin was removed with the specific inhibiting sugars galactose or lactose. The recovered cells were pulsed with Pa-2 and assayed for their ability to produce LSF. The data presented in Table 4 indicate that the PNA-nonagglutinated subpopulation of thymocytes, representing 10% of the total thymus, is responsible for the production of LSF.

Action of LSF is not H-2 Restricted

In order to determine whether LSF activity was restricted to cells bearing the H-2 phenotype of the producing strain, LSF from BALB/c mice (H-2 d) were also tested on C57Bl/6 mice (H-2 b) and vice versa. The data presented in Table 5

TABLE 4

The Small Subset of Thymus Cells Which Produces the Lymphocyte Stimulating Factors Can Be Separated by Agglutination of the Remaining Thymocytes with the Lectin, Peanut Agglutinin

	IgM ISC/10^6 spleen cells[c]
cell control:[a]	430 ± 208
Pa-1:[b]	9650 ± 1202
Supernatant fluid from	
Unstimulated thymus	1330 ± 150
Stimulated thymus	7300 ± 840
Unstimulated PNA nonagglutinated thymus	4300 ± 280
Stimulated PNA nonagglutinated thymus	8300 ± 650
Unstimulated PNA agglutinated thymus	650 ± 350
Stimulated PNA agglutinated thymus	1460 ± 290

[a] No supernatant fluid added.
[b] 50 μg/ml.
[c] The values are means ± SD.

clearly show that the mitogenic and polyclonal activating properties of LSF are not restricted to the H-2 phenotype of the producing strain. Similar results have been obtained using AKR (H-2 k) mice.

Action of LSF Is Not Species Restricted

In order to determine whether LSF activity could also function across species barriers, mouse LSF was assayed for the ability to activate human immunoglobulin-secreting cells *in vitro*. Human PBM are stimulated by Pa-2 at much lower concentrations compared to mouse lymphocytes. Janossy *et al.* (14) demonstrated that human cells could be stimulated by low doses of Pa-2 to produce immunoglobulin.

TABLE 5

Lymphocyte Stimulating Factors Are Not Restricted by Strain Differences Associated with the Major Histocompatibility Locus

	IgM ISC/10^6 responding spleen cells[c]	
	BALB/c (H-2^d)	C57Bl/6N (H-2^b)
Cell control:[a]	2,900 ± 400	800 ± 264
Pa-1:[b]	12,600 ± 1,820	14,700 ± 872
Supernatant fluid from		
BALB/c		
Unstimulated thymus	3,066 ± 230	800 ± 264
Stimulated thymus	9,833 ± 2,003	4,700 ± 384
C57Bl/6N		
Unstimulated thymus	2,233 ± 550	1,300 ± 254
Stimulated thymus	8,133 ± 1,040	3,700 ± 353

[a] No supernatant fluid added.
[b] 50 μg/ml.
[c] The values are means ± SD.

Therefore, a dose–response curve of human PBM to Pa-2 was determined by the reverse plaque technique. The data indicate that human PBM immunoglobulin-secreting cells (ISC) are stimulated by Pa-2 at concentrations as low as 0.01 μg/ml and maximum activity was found at 0.1 μg/ml (130 ISC/10^4 cells). On the other hand, Pa-1 stimulated many more IgM ISC both at 1 μg/ml and at 10 μg/ml (304 ISC/10^4 cells). Studies with ^{125}I-labeled Pa-2-pulsed murine spleen cells indicate that up to 0.025 μg/ml of Pa-2 may be present in the supernatant fluid from these cells after 12 hr of culture. This amount of Pa-2 in the LSF preparations means that there would be from 2.5 to 11.3 ng/ml in the human PBM cultures.

The data in Fig. 5 show the dose–response curves of human PBM to murine spleen and thymus LSF, as assayed by the reverse plaque technique. The results from the control supernatant fluids indicate that mouse antigens are not stimulating the human response. The activation of ISC by both spleen and thymus LSF are greatly enhanced over that of direct Pa-2 stimulation and are comparable to the stimulation observed with Pa-1. This would indicate that murine LSF is indeed active in other species.

DISCUSSION

Pa-2 stimulated both thymus cells and splenic T cells to release soluble factors which stimulated the immune response and replaced the requirement for T cells. These factors stimulated both DNA synthesis, as measured by the incorporation

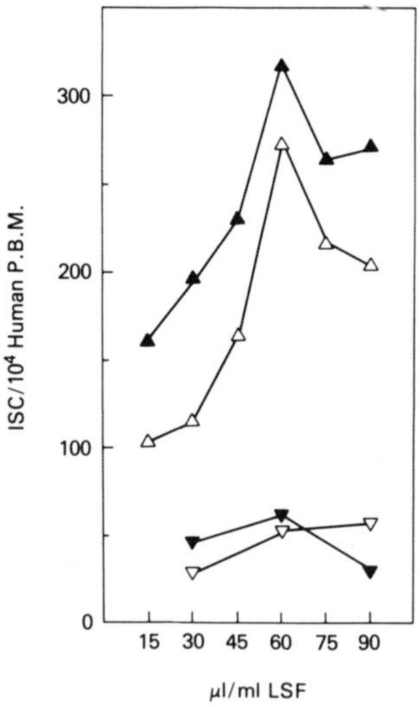

FIG. 5. The immunoglobulin-secreting cell dose–response curves of human peripheral blood mononuclear cells to lymphocyte-stimulating factors produced by murine spleen or thymus cell cultures. Human PBM (10 million/ml) were cultured in individual 5-ml plastic culture tubes for 6 days with various concentrations of unstimulated or Pa-2 stimulated supernatant fluid from BALB/c spleen or thymus cell cultures. Immunoglobulin-secreting cells were detected by the reverse plaque assay using rabbit anti-human Fab as the developing antiserum. Unstimulated spleen cell supernatant fluid (inverted open triangles); Pa-2-stimulated spleen cell supernatant fluid (open triangles); unstimulated thymus cell supernatant fluid (inverted solid triangles). Pa-2-stimulated thymus cell supernatant fluid (solid triangles). The standard deviations were 10–15%.

of [^{3}H]thymidine, and the polyclonal production of immunoglobulins, as measured by a reverse plaque assay. These factors functioned in athymic nude spleen cultures as well as in normal spleen cultures (Figs. 1A and C, 2A and B). The magnitudes of these responses were similar, but there was variation in the time course of these responses. This may indicate further modulation of the B-cell response in the normal spleen where other T-cell functions were also present. These factors also stimulated DNA synthesis in murine thymocytes without the addition of mitogen (Fig. 1B). Because these factors appeared to be able to activate T cells and well as B cells, they have been collectively designated lymphocyte stimulating factor(s) or LSF.

The biological activities of LSF are not due to contaminating Pa-2. Experiments stimulating LSF production with ^{125}I-labeled Pa-2 showed that a maximum of 0.025 μg/ml was shed from the stimulated cells and carried over into the LSF preparations (15). This amount of Pa-2 is far less than that required to stimulate DNA synthesis by murine thymus and spleen cells, or to affect immunoglobulin production (5, 6, 16). This does not rule out the possibilities that LSF is enhanced by minute amounts of Pa-2 or that all or part of the Pa-2 molecule may be incorporated into LSF (see below).

Maximum production of spleen and thymus LSF was achieved within 12 hr of culture and, as would be predicted, was independent of cell division (Tables 1 and 2). Little further production was detectable after 24 hr of culture and the occasional loss of activity from supernatant fluid cultured up to 96 hr appeared to be sporadic and not due to the later activation of a suppressor subset of lymphocytes. Concentrations of Pa-2 from 5 to 50 μg/ml gave similar results in LSF production.

The subset of thymus cells which produce LSF was approached by differential agglutination with PNA and results in the enrichment of an Lyt 2+ population in the PNA-agglutinated cells and an Lyt 2− population in the PNA-nonagglutinated cells (18). This PNA-nonagglutinated population comprises approximately 10% of the thymus. LSF appears to be produced by this small population of thymus cells. Even without stimulation with Pa-2, these PNA-nonagglutinated thymocytes produce substantial amounts of LSF or material which shares some of the biological activities of LSF (Table 4). There are several possible explanations for the high production of LSF by these cells, among them: (i) PNA may stimulate the production of LSF, (ii) subset of thymocytes which normally may supress the production of LSF has been removed, and (iii) the enrichment of these effector cells by the PNA fractionation may have resulted in markedly raising the concentration of LSF normally produced. Preliminary evidence indicates that a similar fractionation of thymus cells can be achieved using Pa-2 in place of PNA. This fractionation obviates the need to remove the agglutinating lectin from the nonagglutinated cells and directly yields the fractionated and stimulated subset of thymocytes which will produce LSF.

LSF from either spleen or thymus increased both cell division and the number of IgM-secreting cells in murine spleen cell cultures. To determine the requirement for T cells in its action, LSF was tested on spleen cells from athymic nude mice. In this case maximum enhanced DNA synthesis occurred at 48 hr and maximum enhanced IgM ISC were found at 24 hr. This temporal discrepency may suggest that both Pa-1 and LSF directly activate murine B cells to IgM ISC and DNA synthesis, but in normal spleen cell cultures, there may be a considerable further modulation of the B-cell response by T cells, which also are stimulated by Pa-1 and LSF. The appearance of most IgM ISC prior to the major DNA synthesis further substantiates the observation that most lectin- or anti-IgM-induced B-cell DNA synthesis can be unrelated to the induced Ig secretion (19, 20).

LSF was not genetically restricted in function by MHC barriers. LSF made in one strain of mice worked equally well in another strain (Table 5). Likewise, neither TRF (21) nor the PWM-induced factor from human lymphocytes (4) appeared to be MHC restricted. In addition, LSF was not functionally restricted across species barriers. Human PBM were stimulated to produce immunoglobulin-secreting cells without the further addition of antigen or mitogen (Fig. 5).

Human lymphocytes were stimulated with 0.01 to 0.1 μg/ml of Pa-2 to produce immunoglobulin. The LSF preparations were calculated to contain approximately 0.025 μg of Pa-2/ml. Therefore, even though these LSF preparations were concentrated before use, the final amount of Pa-2 in the assay culture was between 0.0024 and 0.0112 μg/ml. When tested on human cells, this amount, or any amount of Pa-2, did not stimulate nearly as many ISC as did LSF.

Many of the biological properties of LSF are similar to those of TRF and TCGF. Hence, it may be possible that LSF is a mixture of previously described soluble T-cell factors. However, other properties are different. All three are produced by mature T cells, while LSF is also copiously produced by thymocytes. But, these cells release only 1–2% of TCGF as compared to splenic cells (22, 23). The use of polystyrene culture dishes or nylon wool columns to deplete adherent cells did not significantly decrease the ability of splenic T or thymus cells to produce LSF. However, the removal of adherent cells markedly reduced TCGF production (24). LSF is produced only during the first 24 hr of culture, while TRF is produced mostly after 24 hr (17). Thus, it appears that the conditions for the production of LSF differ from those of both TCGF and TRF.

In terms of their activities, in contrast to TCGF, LSF causes the proliferation of normal, unprimed thymocytes and spleen cells. Prestimulation, or priming, with submitogenic or limited mitogenic amounts of Pa-2 or Con A does not augment this proliferation by murine spleen and thymus cells, or by human peripheral lymphocytes, when stimulated with LSF or several of is partially purified components (Wantyghem *et al.*, manuscript in preparation). In contrast to TRF, LSF does not require the presence of an antigen, such as SRBC, to stimulate IgM production (nor anti-SRBC, T. Y. Basham, unpublished data). LSF is most effective in stimulating B cells to produce Ig if added at the beginning of culture, and need be present for only 6 hr to achieve maximum effect. On the other hand, TRF is most effective when added (or still present) later (24–60 hr) in culture and requires the presence of antigen (17, 25, 26).

While the observed biological activities of LSF appear to be different from TCGF or TRF, it is possible that these factors may be present in preparations of LSF. Indeed, we have fractionated LSF into several distinct biologically active components, most of which do not contain any detectible Pa-2 (15). The final proof that LSF contains previously undescribed molecules awaits the completion of our current studies on the chemical and biological properties of these LSF components.

ACKNOWLEDGMENTS

The authors would like to express their gratitude to Dr. Irwin Scher, Naval Medical Research Institute, for fractionating lymphocytes with the FACS II, and to James DelPriore, CSL/DCRT/NIH, for software maintainance of the laboratory computer.

REFERENCES

1. Dutton, R. W., *J. Exp. Med.* **136,** 1455, 1972.
2. Rich, R. R., and Pierce, C. W., *J. Exp. Med.* **137,** 649, 1972.
3. Sjoberg, O., Moller, G., and Andersson, G., *Clin. Exp. Immunol.* **13,** 213, 1973.
4. Hirano, T., Kuritani, T., Kishimoto, T., and Yamamura, Y., *J. Immunol.* **119,** 1235, 1977.
5. Waxdal, M. J., *Biochemistry* **13,** 3671, 1974.
6. Basham, T. Y., and Waxdal, M. J., *J. Immunol.* **114,** 715, 1975.
7. Waxdal, M. J., and Basham, T. Y., *Nature New Biol.* **251,** 163, 1975.
8. Ginsburg, W. W., Finkelman, F. D., and Lipsky, P. E., *J. Immunol.* **120,** 33, 1978.
9. Hunter, K. W., Finkelman, F. D., Strickland, G. T., Sayles, P. C., and Scher, I., *J. Immunol.* **123,** 133, 1979.
10. Finkelman, F. D., and Scher, I., *J. Immunol.* **122,** 1757, 1979.
11. Loken, M. R., and Herzenberg, L. A., *Ann. N.Y. Acad. Sci.* **254,** 163, 1975.
12. Horan, P. K., and Wheeless, L. L., *Science* **198,** 149, 1977.
13. Reisner, Y., Linker-Israeli, M., and Sharon, N., *Cell. Immunol.* **25,** 129, 1976.
14. Janossy, G., Gomez de la Concha, E., Waxdal, M. J., and Platts-Mills, T., *Clin. Exp. Immunol.* **26,** 108, 1976.
15. Toyoshima, S., Basham, T. T., Findelman, F. D., and Waxdal, M. J., submitted for publication.
16. Basham, T. Y., and Waxdal, M. J., *J. Immunol.* **118,** 863, 1977.
17. Schimpl, A., and Wecker, E., *Transplant. Rev.* **23,** 176, 1975.
18. Betel, I., Mathieson, B. J., and Sharrow, S. O., *In* "Protides of the Biological Fluids, Colloquium 27" (H. Peeters, Ed.), pp. 529–535. Pergamon Press, Oxford, 1979.
19. Waxdal, M. J., *In* "Immune Recognition" (A. S. Rosenthal, Ed), pp. 85–101. Academic Press, New York, 1975.
20. Sieckman, D. G., *Immunol. Rev.* **52,** 1, 1980.
21. Schimpl, A., and Wecker, E., *J. Exp. Med.* **137,** 547, 1973.
22. Smith, K. A., Gillis, S., and Baker, P. E., *In* "The Molecular Basis of Immune Cell Function" (J. G. Kaplan, Ed.), p. 223. Amsterdam, Elsevier/North-Holland Press, 1979.
23. Gillis, S., Baker, P. E., Union, N. A., and Smith, K. A., *J. Exp. Med.* **149,** 1460, 1979.
24. Smith, K. A., *Immunol. Rev.* **51,** 337, 1980.
25. Dutton, R. W., *In* "Mitogens in Immunobiology" (J. J. Oppenheim and D. L. Rosenstreich, Eds.), p. 237. Academic Press, New York, 1980.
26. Hoffman, M. K., and Watson, J., *J. Immunol.* **122,** 1371, 1979.

CELLULAR IMMUNOLOGY 63, 134–142 (1981)

Ability of Human Leukocytic Pyrogen to Enhance Phytohemagglutinin Induced Murine Thymocyte Proliferation[1]

LANNY J. ROSENWASSER AND CHARLES A. DINARELLO

Divisions of Allergy and Experimental Medicine, Department of Medicine, Tufts University School of Medicine, Boston, Massachusetts 02111

Received March 13, 1981; accepted April 30, 1981

Human leukocytic pyrogen, a monokine produced by stimulated human mononuclear phagocytes, will enhance the murine thymocyte proliferation response to phytohemagglutinin (lymphocyte activating factor (LAF) activity). During all steps of purification of human LP, pyrogenicity and LAF activity are coincidental suggesting a single identity for the two monokines. The LAF assay for human LP is highly sensitive and can detect human LP at a concentration of 10^{-12} *M*. Further experiments suggests that human LP and LAF activities could be destroyed by heating to 70°C. Furthermore, while *in vivo* pyrogenicity of human LP can be blocked by ibuprofen, the *in vitro* LAF activity of the same molecule is unaffected by ibuprofen. Immune rabbit serum directed against human LP could also block *in vitro* LAF activity either by preincubation with LP or by blocking during culture.

INTRODUCTION

Mononuclear phagocytes (MØ)[2] have been shown to subserve critical and varied functions in the induction and expression of immune responses (1). Monokines or soluble products of monocytes–macrophages have also been noted to be of great importance in the modulation of various *in vitro* immune phenomena (2). The activity called lymphocyte activating factor (LAF), first described by Gery and coworkers (3, 4), is a monokine that is involved in augmenting thymus-derived (T) lymphocyte proliferative responses to mitogen. Characterization of LAF has led many workers to the conclusion that other partially characterized monokines such as B-cell differentiation factor (BDF) (5), B-cell activating factor (BAF) (6), helper peak-1 (HP-1) (7), T-cell replacing factor derived from macrophages ($TRF_{MØ}$) (8), and mitogenic protein (MP) (9) all share enough biochemical characteristics to be classified as related molecules under the term interleukin-1 (IL-1) (10). As yet none of these *in vitro* activities has been translated into an *in vivo* phenomenon.

Another monokine, however, leukocytic pyrogen (LP), a small polypeptide synthesized by phagocytic cells, has been shown to have a precise *in vivo* activity,

[1] Supported by the Ziskind and Posner Funds, Tufts New England Medical Center, and NIH Grant AI-15614.

[2] Abbreviations used: IL-1, interleukin 1; IRS, immune rabbit serum; LAF, lymphocyte activating factor; LP, leukocytic pyrogen; MØ, macrophage; NRS, normal rabbit serum; PHA, phytohemagglutinin; PG, prostaglandin; RPD, rabbit pyrogen dose.

0008-8749/81/130134-09$02.00/0

namely the mediation of a febrile response (11). Human LP has been purified and confident assessment of its physicochemical and biological characteristics can be made (12–14). The possibility that LP could play an immunoregulatory role was first suggested by experiments carried out in our laboratory whereby purified human LP augmented the antigen-induced proliferative response of murine T cells in a manner consistent with macrophage culture supernatant fluids containing a LAF-like activity (15). Indeed, we speculated that on the basis of biochemical similarities and functional characteristics that LP and LAF were closely related (15, 16). Recent work with LP derived from rabbit MØ confirmed our initial observation that LP has LAF activity (17, 18).

In the present report, we have extended our initial finding to examine in a standard LAF assay (i.e., enhancement of phytohemagglutinin (PHA)-induced murine thymocyte blastogenesis), sequential copurification of LAF and pyrogen activities through four steps of purification, including use of a specific immunoabsorbent. In light of the ability of antipyretics to reduce LP-mediated fever, the role of prostaglandin (PG) synthesis in LP/LAF activity for *in vitro* thymocyte blastogenesis is examined using inhibitors of the cyclooxygenase pathway of arachidonic acid metabolism. Finally, the ability of rabbit antisera raised to human LP was investigated for the ability to block *in vitro* LAF activity.

MATERIALS AND METHODS

Animals. Female C57Bl6/J (B6) mice, 6 weeks old, were used as thymocyte donors and were purchased from Jackson Laboratories, Bar Harbor, Maine. New Zealand-derived white rabbits, weighing 2.5 to 3.0 kg, were purchased from Associated Rabbit Industries, Avon, Massachusetts, and were used in the pyrogen fever assay.

Pyrogen testing. The rabbit pyrogen test was used to quantitate the amount of biologically active human LP in samples added to lymphocyte cultures. A two-point dose response was carried out on all samples. A rabbit pyrogen dose (RPD) is defined as the amount of pyrogen needed to cause peak elevation in rectal temperature between 0.6 and 0.9°C (13).

Production of human LP. Plateletpheresis by-products were obtained from the Northeast Branch of the American Red Cross and separated on Ficoll–Hypaque gradients. Mononuclear cells were washed and resuspended in Hanks' balance salt solution (HBSS) (Grand Island Biological Co., Gibco, Grand Island, N.Y.) at 20×10^6 cell/ml in 5% human AB serum. These cells were stimulated with heat-killed *Staphylococcus albus* at a bacteria:leukocyte ratio of 10:1 for 1 hr, washed, and resuspended in HBSS at 5×10^6 cells/ml. They were allowed to adhere onto flat glass surfaces at a concentration of 1×10^6 cells/cm for 1 hr. Thereafter, non-adherent cells were poured off and fresh HBSS was replaced. After 24 hr at 37°C, 5% CO_2, the supernatant medium was centrifuged at 25,000 *g* and stored at 4°C.

Purification of human LP. Crude supernates containing LP were concentrated in autoclaved dialysis tubing in front of a high-speed fan. Volumes were reduced 1/20 and dialyzed against PBS with 0.02% sodium azide. Concentrated LP was passed over an immunoadsorbent rabbit anti-human LP antibody attached to cyanogen bromide-activated Sepharose (Pharmacia Fine Chemicals, Div. of Pharmacia, Inc. Piscataway, N.J.) (12, 14). LP was eluted from this material in citric acid buffer, pH 3.2 (12, 14), neutralized with 0.1 *M* NaOH, and stored in 0.02% sodium azide. LP eluted from the anti-LP immunoadsorbent was concentrated and chromatographed over Sephadex G-50 (Pharmacia) (fine); 165 × 5.6 cm) at 4°C in PBS with 0.02% sodium, azide. The 15.000-MW LP peak was isolated, dialyzed against H_2O and lyophilized: this material gave a single staining band on 7.5% sodium dodecyl sulfate polyacrylamide gels (14). This material was used at the source of human LP described in the experiments in Tables 1 through 5.

Further purification of human LP was carried out using ^{125}I-labeled LP. Approximately 25% of the LP eluting from both the immunoadsorbent and gel filtration was labeled with ^{125}I (14). After this, LP was chromatographed over Sephadex G-15 (28 × 1.0 cm) in 0.01 *M* Tris, pH 8.1. Further purification of the LP isolated from Sephadex G-15 was carried out using ion-exchange chromatography on DEAE-cellulose in 0.01 *M* Tris, pH 8.1, at 4°C. Labeled LP eluted early during a linear salt gradient at from 0 to 0.2 *M* NaCl.

LAF assay. LAF activity was determined by the enhancement of B6 murine thymocyte mitogenic response to PHA (Burroughs Wellcome Co., Research Triangle Park, N.C.) as described previously (19). Briefly the thymus glands from 6-week-old B6 mice were aseptically removed and teased apart between the frosted ends of two sterile glass slides in HBSS. Cells were washed vigorously and suspended in medium RPMI 1640 supplemented by 100 U/ml penicillin, 10 μg/ml streptomycin, and 0.3 mg/ml fresh L-glutamine (all from Gibco), 5×10^{-5} *M* 2-mercaptoethanol (Eastman Kodak, Rochester, N.Y.), 10 m*M* Hepes buffer (Microbiological Associates, Bethesda, Md.), and 5% fetal calf serum (FCS) (Sterile Systems, Inc. Logan, Utah). Thymocyte density was appropriately adjusted and 5×10^5 thymocytes were aliquoted into each well of a flat-bottom microtiter plate (Linbro Co., Hamden, Conn.), PHA (final concn 1.0 μg/ml) and an accessory addition to culture (media, LP) were added to obtain a final volume of 200 μl of cells and media per well. These cultures were then incubated for 72 hr at 37°C, and in an humidified atmosphere of 5% CO_2 and 95% air. The plates were pulsed with 1 μCi of HTdR (6.7 Ci/mmol, New England Nuclear, Boston, Mass.) for the final 18 hr of culture. The plates were then harvested using a semiautomated MASH harvester and [^{3}H]TdR incorporation was measured using liquid scintillation spectrometry. The results were reported as mean counts per minute (cpm) for triplicate determinations or as Δcpm (counts above control).

Rabbit antiserum to human LP. Immune rabbit serum against human LP has been well characterized with regard to production, purification, and specificity and details have been previously published (12, 14). This immune rabbit serum (IRS) and normal rabbit serum (NRS) controls were used in the inhibition studies described in Tables 4, 5. The rabbit antisera were raised to semipurified preparations of human LP (15,000 daltons, 1000 RPD/mg) following initial intradermal immunization with LP complete Freund's adjuvant, and six monthly intramuscular booster injections with LP in incomplete Freund's adjuvant. These antisera were tested for neutralization of human LP and in the LAF assay as described in Tables 4 and 5.

Prostaglandin inhibitors. Ibuprofen, obtained from the Upjohn Company, Kalamazoo, Michigan, was dissolved in a small volume (20 μl) of ethanol and diluted with FCS containing completed medium for the experiments described in Table 3.

RESULTS

Sequential Copurification of Pyrogenic and Lymphocyte Activating Factor Properties of Human LP

Crude human monocyte supernatants were concentrated and applied to Sephadex G-50 gel filtration columns. Two peaks of pyrogenic activities eluted (40,000 and 15,000 daltons) and these were isolated, dialyzed, and lyophilized. Following reconstitution, these fractions were assayed in the rabbit pyrogen assay and in the LAF assay. In addition unfractionated concentrated LP was first applied to a rabbit anti-human LP Sepharose 4B immunoabsorbent and the LP eluted with citric acid, concentrated, and chromatographed over the same G-50 column. Table 1 illustrates the activities of these three preparations of human LP at various levels of purification and molecular size.

It is clear from the data in Table 1 that preparations of 15,000-dalton human LP in the vicinity of 10^{-4} to 10^{-5} RPD/well will enhance thymocyte PHA response regardless of the level of purification. These data indicate that the LAF or murine thymocyte proliferation assay is highly sensitive and can detect low subpyrogenic concentrations of LP.

The above experiments in Table 1 suggested that the LP molecule is responsible for LAF activity. However, because of the low specific activity of human LP (approximately 10–15 ng or lower required for a rabbit pyrogen dose) other proteins in these preparations may be responsible for PHA enhancement activity. Therefore, it was necessary to carry out further purification methods. Concentrations of LP which do not stain with Coomassie blue on polyacrylamide gels necessitated the use of radiolabeling as a marker. Using ^{125}I-Bolton–Hunter reagent (14), ^{125}I was enzymatically bound to the 15,000-dalton LP after having been purified using

TABLE 1

Enhancement of PHA-Induced Thymocyte Proliferation by Human LP

	[^{3}H]TdR incorporation[b] (Δcpm) $\times 10^{-3}$		
	Gel filtration[c]		Gel filtration[d] and immunoabsorbent
RPD/well[a]	40,000 MW	15,00 MW	(15,000 MW)
1	N.D.[e]	140	N.D.
10^{-1}	115	120	N.D.
10^{-2}	27	35	21
10^{-3}	15	26	17
10^{-4}	6.1	20	15
10^{-5}	N.D.	14	11
10^{-6}	N.D.	N.D.	6.5

[a] LP purified as outlined under Materials and Methods. Baseline (Δcpm) $\times 10^{-3}$ = 4.2 (thymocyte blastogenesis at 1 μg/ml PHA).

[b] Thymocyte blastogenesis, 2.5×10^5 thymocytes/well in flat-bottom microtiter plate for 72 hr. Δcpm = experimental (1 μg/ml PHA) − baseline (no PHA). Mean Δcpm $\times 10^{-3}$ for three experiments.

[c] Sephadex G-50 filtration of monocyte supernatant.

[d] Crude LP applied to immunoadsorbent, eluted, and 15,000-dalton fraction of G-50 column is used.

[e] Not done.

immunoadsorption and gel filtration. The following scheme illustrates the purification sequence:

Crude LP → anti-LP → G-50 → (15,000) → ^{125}I → G-15 → DEAE.

LP (15,000 daltons) purified over anti-LP followed by gel filtration over Sephadex G-50 appears as a single staining band on SDS–polyacrylamide gel electrophoresis, and as shown in Table 1, these preparations enhance thymocyte responses to PHA. However, following labeling with ^{125}I, chromatography over G-15 reveals that other proteins are present. In order to test these and subsequent fractions for LAF activity, we purified 500 RPD and labeled approximately 10%. This labeled material was added back to the remaining unlabeled LP and gel filtration over Sephadex G-15 and ion exchange over DEAE were carried out according to the scheme above.

As shown in Fig. 1, gel filtration of LP chromatographed over Sephadex G-15 reveals several radioactive peaks but only the excluded proteins contained pyrogen activity which again coincide with enhancement of thymocyte PHA response. The peak fractions (8 to 11) from G-15 were pooled and applied directly to DEAE. As shown in Fig. 2, the material from the G-15 peak contained several proteins which were separable during a salt gradient on DEAE. As can be seen within Fig. 2, pyrogenicity and LAF activity once again are coincidental in the third peak of ^{125}I-labeled protein eluted off ion-exchange chromatography (pool of fractions 19 to 21). Thus, through a 4-stage sequence of purification for human LP including two gel filtrations, a specific immunoabsorbant and ion-exchange chromatography, LAF activity and pyrogenicity were coincident.

Effect of Heat and Prostaglandin Synthesis Inhibition of the LAF Activity of Human LP

The data presented in Table 2 suggest that heating human LP in a 56°C waterbath for 60 min has no effect on LAF activity while heating LP to 70°C for 60 min will destroy LAF activity. In addition, temperatures of 70 and 56°C destroy and reduce the fever inducing properties for these preparations. However, this

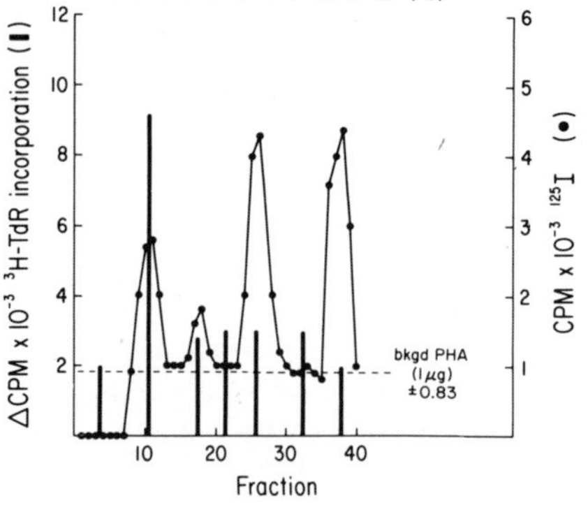

FIG. 1. Gel filtration of human LP over Sephadex G-15 (28 × 1.0 cm) in 0.01 *M* Tris, pH 8.1, 4°C.

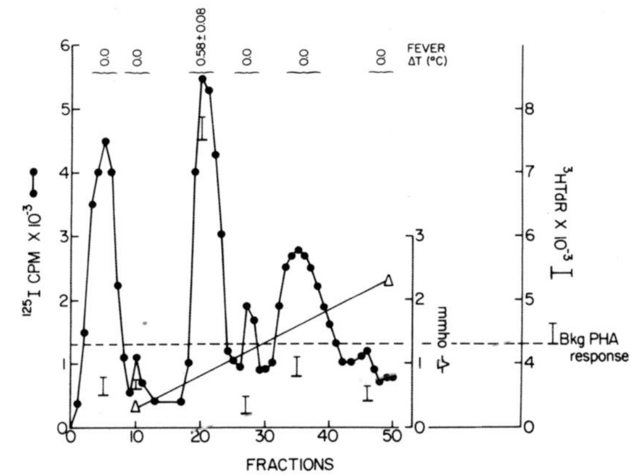

FIG. 2. Ion exchange over DEAE in 0.01 *M* Tris, pH 8.1, 4°C, 2.0 × 1.5 cm, Fractions 8–11 from Fig. 1 were applied to DEAE and a salt gradient begun after the 10th fraction. The salt gradient was 100 fractions and the first 50 fractions are shown. Conductivity is indicated in millimhos. Each fraction was collected in 0.1% final volume HSA (HSA heated at 60°C for 10 hr). Fractions were dialyzed against RPMI and 5% FCS and assayed for LAF and pyrogenicity.

descrepancy may be due to the considerable sensitivity of the LAF assay as opposed to the rabbit fever assay.

The data put forth in Table 3 demonstrate that 5×10^{-5} *M* ibuprofen will not block the LAF activity of human LP. This finding is consistent over a wide range of ibuprofen concentration (10^{-3}–10^{-6} *M*). In addition, ibuprofen and ethanol controls alone were neither suppressive nor stimulatory to the thymocytes.

Inhibition of LAF Activity in Vitro by Immune Rabbit Serum Directed to Human LP

Using two different approaches (Tables 4 and 5), we have demonstrated that a rabbit antiserum to human LP will block LAF activity *in vitro*. For the experiments summarized in Table 4 1% IRS and NRS were preincubated for 18 hr at

TABLE 2

Effect of Heat on LAF-Like Activity of Human LP

Addition to culture[a]	PHA response ([^{3}H]TdR incorporation, Δcpm ± SEM) of thymocytes[b]	Δt, °C[c]
Medium	3,490 ± 120	0.0
LP—10^{-3} RPD/well	16,284 ± 1,943	0.74 ± 0.06
LP—10^{-3} RPD/well after 56°C, 60 min	19,032 ± 1,837	0.28 ± 0.08
LP—10^{-3} RPD/well after 70°C, 60 min	4,576 ± 708	0.0

[a] LP purified by immunoadsorbent and gel filtration.

[b] Usual thymocyte blastogenesis as in Table 1. Δcpm = experimental (1 μg/ml PHA) − baseline (no PHA). Mean Δcpm ± SEM for two experiments. Baseline or spontaneous mean incorporation values of [^{3}H]TdR by thymocytes without PHA all were less than 250 cpm average per triplicate.

[c] Mean (±SEM) peak fever in three rabbits used to assay each experiment.

TABLE 3

Effect of Ibuprofen on LAF Activity of Human LP

Addition to culture[a]	PHA response ([^{3}H]TdR incorporation, Δcpm ± SEM) of thymocytes[b]
Medium	3,231 ± 157
LP—10^{-4} RPD/well	14,352 ± 2,479
Ibuprofen (5 × 10^{-5} *M*)	3,633 ± 293
Ethanol	3,904 ± 373
LP + ibuprofen (5 × 10^{-5} *M*)	13,701 ± 373

[a] LP purified by immunoadsorbent and gel filtration.

[b] Usual thymocyte blastogenesis as in Table 1 and under Materials and Methods. Δcpm = experimental (1 μg/ml PHA − baseline (no PHA). Mean Δcpm ± SEM for four experiments. Baseline or spontaneous mean incorporation of [^{3}H]TdR by thymocytes without PHA all were less than 500 cpm average per triplicate.

4°C with the LP containing accessory addition to culture. Preincubation with IRS completely abrogated LAF activity while preincubation with NRS did not significantly affect LAF activity.

Using a different approach shown in the experiments summarized in Table 5, 1% NRS and IRS are added to the thymocyte cultures directly at the initiation of the culture period. As can be observed in Table 5, 1% IRS effectively "blocked" significant LAF activity in these thymocyte cultures. Additionally 1% NRS in these cultures yields no significant reduction in LAF activity, once again highlighting the specificity of the IRS effects as noted in Tables 4 and 5.

DISCUSSION

The data in this report demonstrate the copurification of LP and LAF activity through four major stages of purification of crude monocyte supernatants. Biochemical analysis included a specific immunoadsorbent, two stages of gel filtration, and ion-exchange chromatography. At the end of this scheme of analysis LP/LAF

TABLE 4

Effect of Preincubation of Human LP with Immune Rabbit Serum on LAF/LP Activity

Accessory additon to culture[a]	PHA response ([^{3}H]TdR incorporation, Δcpm ± SEM) of thymocytes[b]
Medium	5,069 ± 386
LP—10^{-3} RPD/well	13,165 ± 1,584
LP—10^{-3} RPD/well after preincubation with normal rabbit serum (NRS)	11,278 ± 414
LP—10^{-3} RPD/well after preincubation with immune rabbit serum (IRS)	4,128 ± 598

[a] LP purified by immunoadsorbent and gel filtration; 1% NRS and 1% IRS incubated with LP for 18 hr at 4°C prior to additon to thymocyte cultures.

[b] Usual assay and parameters. Mean Δcpm ± SEM for two experiments.

TABLE 5

Effect of Continuous Incubation of Human LP with Immune Rabbit Serum on LAF/LP Activity in Thymocyte Cultures

Accessory addition to culture[a]	PHA response ([^{3}H]TdR incorporation, Δcpm ± SEM) of thymocytes[b]
Medium	2,911 ± 306
LP—10^{-4} RPD/well	9,654 ± 2,601
LP—10^{-4} RPD/well plus 1% NRS	8,362 ± 1,822
LP—10^{-4} RPD/well plus 1% IRS	2,325 ± 281

[a] Purified by immunoadsorbent and gel filtration; 1% NRS and 1% IRS added to each well at initiation of thymocyte cultures.
[b] Usual assay and parameters. Mean Δcpm ± SEM for two experiments.

is at apparent homogeneity and pyrogenic activity and LAF properties are coincident. While microheterogeneity of structure and function is still possible, it is likely that LAF and LP are identical. These data confirm and extend our original hypothesis that LAF and LP may be the same (15, 16). Needless to say, we feel that LP, in addition to being either identical or closely related may also mediate the *in vitro* phenomena associated with IL-1, i.e., MP, HP-1, $TRF_{M\phi}$, BAF, BDF, etc., as well as mediating the production of acute phase proteins such as serum amyloid A protein, i.e., LP/LAF has the same function as the monokine SAA stimulating factor (20).

Also of note is the extraordinary sensitivity of the LAF assay for detecting LP. For example, a value of 10^{-5} RPD, undetectable in the rabbit fever assay, can still cause significant enhancement of murine thymocyte proliferation, and is roughly equal to 10^{-12} to 10^{-13} *M*, putting the biological activity of LP/LAF on thymocytes at a hormone level. Indeed, the sensitivity of the LAF assay for LP is comparable to that of a radioimmunoassay (14), and highlights the potential usefulness of this assay in detecting small amounts of biologically active LP/LAF from the blood or body fluids of febrile individuals. We are presently exploring these possibilities using the LAF assay and the rabbit anti-LP immunoadsorbent.

It has also been demonstrated as shown in Table 2 that heating of LP/LAF to 70°C for 60 min obliterates both activities. On the other hand, while pretreatment of rabbits with the cyclooxygenase pathway inhibitor, ibuprofen, blocks fever, culture of murine thymocytes with LP/LAF and ibuprofen *in vitro* has no effect on LAF properties (Table 3). This finding is in accord with prior studies involving LP/LAF and neutrophils in which LP/LAF-induced neutrophil-specific granule release was not sensitive to inhibitors of PG synthesis such as indomethacin (21). We are pursuing the idea that LP/LAF may exert its influence on thymocyte blastogenesis by affecting another pathway of arachidonic acid metabolism.

Finally, we have shown with two different approaches that rabbit antiserum to LP/LAF blocks LAF activity *in vitro* (Tables 4 and 5). Prior work has shown that this specific rabbit antiserum is capable of blocking fever *in vivo* in the rabbit assay and removing LP activity from monocyte supernatants (12, 14). Hence, these data once again support the notion that LAF and LP are the same or closely related molecules. It is necessary to point out that there may be macrophage/monocyte-derived soluble factors that have LAF-like or thymocyte mitogenic properties and no pyrogenic activity. This may explain the recent observation of Chedid and colleagues that some analogs of muramyl dipeptide will induce monocytes to produce LAF activities without pyrogenic activities (22). However, for the 15,000-dalton material referred to as LAF or IL-1, we feel it is most likely that this molecule is identical or closely related to LP.

Thus, we have shown that LP/LAF is most likely a single molecule whose activity for murine thymocytes is detectable at hormone-like concentrations (10^{-12} *M*). It is likely that LP/LAF represents either a single or restricted class of inflammatory hormone(s) whose activity can affect immunocytes (T and B cells) and macrophages, but whose activity also affects nonimmune cells such as neutrophils, hepatocytes, and brain tissue (23). The biological consequences of such nonimmune activity include specific granule release and inflammation (21), acute phase protein synthesis (20) and, of course, fever (11). Further work on these complex biological properties of purified LP/LAF should provide a remarkable insight into the complicated interactions of inflammation and immunity.

ACKNOWLEDGMENTS

The authors would like to express their gratitude to Dr. Sheldon M. Wolff for his continuing support. The authors wish to thank Dr. Ross Rocklin for his critical reading of the manuscript. In addition, special thanks to Tom Brown and Gail LoPreste for their skillful and enthusiastic technical assistance and to Mrs. Joanne Quigley for her patience while typing the manuscript.

REFERENCES

1. Van Furth, R., "Mononuclear Phagocyte: Functional Aspects." Martinus Nijhoff, The Hague, 1980.
2. Rocklin, R. E., Bendtzen, K., and Greineder, D. K., *In* "Advances in Immunology" (H. G., Kunkel, and F. J. Dixon, Eds.), Vol. 29, p. 56, Academic Press, New York, 1980.
3. Gery, I., Gershon, R. K., and Waksman, B. H., *J. Exp. Med.* **136,** 128, 1972.
4. Gery, I., and Waksman, B. H., *J. Exp. Med.* **136,** 143, 1972.
5. Hoffman, M., Koenig, S., Mittler, R. S., Oettgen, H. F., Ralph, P., Galanos, C., and Hämmerling, U., *J. Immunol.* **122,** 1371, 1979.
6. Wood, D. D., *J. Immunol.* **123,** 2395, 1979.
7. Koopman, W. J., Farrar, J. J., Fuller-Bonar, J., *Cell. Immunol.* **35,** 92, 1978.
8. Hoffman, M. K., and Watson, J., *J. Immunol.* **122,** 1371, 1979.
9. Calderon, J., Kiely, J. M., Lefko, J., and Unanue, E. R., *J. Exp. Med.* **142,** 151, 1975.
10. Aarden, L. *et al., J. Immunol.* **123,** 2928, 1979.
11. Dinarello, C. A., Goldin, N. P., and Wolff, S. M., *J. Exp. Med.* **129,** 1369, 1974.
12. Dinarello, C. A., Renfer, L., and Wolff, S. M., *J. Clin. Invest.* **60,** 465, 1977.
13. Dinarello, C. A., and Wolff, S. M., *Inflammation* **2,** 179, 1977.
14. Dinarello, C. A., Renfer, L., and Wolff, S. M., *Proc. Nat. Acad. Sci. USA* **74,** 4624, 1977.
15. Rosenwasser, L. J., Dinarello, C. A., and Rosenthal, A. S., *J. Exp. Med.* **150,** 709, 1979.
16. Dinarello, C. A. and Rosenwasser, L. J., *In* "Advances in Immunopharmacology" (J. W. Hadden, L. Chedid, P. Mullen, and F. Spreafico, Eds.), pp. 419–425, Pergamon Press, Oxford, 1981.
17. Murphy, P. A., Simon, P. L., and Willoughby, W. F., *J. Immunol.* **124,** 2498, 1980.
18. Kampschmidt, R. F. in *Microbiology* (D. Schlesinger, Ed.), 1981, in press.
19. Oppenheim, J. J., Shneyour, A., and Kook, A. I., *J. Immunol.* **116,** 1466, 1976.
20. McAdam, K. P. W. J., and Dinarello, C. A., *In* "Bacterial Endotoxins and Host Response" (M. K. Agarwal, Ed.), pp. 167–178, Elsevier/North-Holland, Amsterdam, 1980.
21. Klempner, M. S., Dinarello, C. A., and Gallin, J. I., *J. Clin. Invest.* **61,** 1330, 1978.
22. Damais, C., Riveau, G., Parant, M., Gerota, I., and Chedid, L., personal communication.
23. Dinarello, C. A., and Bernheim, H. A., *J. Neurochem.*, in press, 1981.

CELLULAR IMMUNOLOGY 63, 143–153 (1981)

HLA-DR Antigens Render Resting T Cells Sensitive to Interleukin-2 and Induce Production of the Growth Factor in the Autologous Mixed Lymphocyte Reaction[1]

RONALD PALACIOS AND GÖRAN MÖLLER

Department of Immunobiology, Wallenberglaboratory, Karolinska Institute, Lilla Frescati, S-104 05, Stockholm 50, Sweden

Received March 26, 1981; accepted April 30, 1981

Monoclonal anti-HLA-DR (anti-Ia) antibodies inhibited autologous mixed lymphocyte reactions (AMLR) when added from the initiation of the cultures, but not 72 hr later. The suppressive principle was removed by the stimulator non-T cells, but not by the responding T cells. Antibody-treated non-T cells lost their ability to activate T cells, whereas antibody-treated T cells could still respond to untreated non-T cells. The anti-DR antibodies prevented T cells from acquiring responsiveness to Interleukin-2 (IL-2). However, T cells previously activated by AMLR responded to IL-2 even in the presence of the anti-DR antibodies. $OKT4^+$ lymphocytes synthesized IL-2 in the AMLR while $OKT8^+$ cells did not. Anti-DR antibodies caused $OKT4^+$ cells to become unresponsive to Interleukin-1 stimulation and inhibited the production of IL-2. Interleukin-1 (IL-1) promoted the synthesis of IL-2 in non-anti-DR-treated AMLR cultures. Since resting T cells are unresponsive to IL-2 and resting $OKT4^+$ lymphocytes are unable to produce IL-2 even in the presence of IL-1, it is concluded that HLA-DR antigens render resting T cells sensitive to IL-2 and enable $OKT4^+$ lymphocytes to respond to IL-1 and subsequently, to produce Interleukin-2.

INTRODUCTION

Resting T cells require the presence of accessory DR-positive cells to proliferate after stimulation with antigens or mitogens (1–2), which by themselves cannot activate T cells (1–4). Continuous proliferation of T cells in response to antigens or mitogens is maintained by growth factors (Interleukin-2), released by activated T cells rather than by antigens or mitogens themselves (5–7). Interleukin-2 (IL-2) supports the growth of active but not of resting T cells (6–9).

In the autologous mixed lymphocyte reaction (AMLR), purified T lymphocytes proliferate when cocultured with autologous non-T cells (10). In the AMLR, the responding cells are $OKT3,^+$ $4,^+$ 8^+ cells that can bind autologous erythrocytes forming rosettes ((11) and R. Palacios, submitted for publication). The stimulator cells are B cells and/or macrophages (12–14). In this reaction, immunological specificity as well as generation of memory (15), helper (16), suppressor (17), and cytotoxic (18) T-cell functions has been described. The AMLR has been reported

[1] This work was supported by grants from The Swedish Medical Research Council and The Swedish Cancer Society.

0008-8749/81/130143-11$02.00/0

in several species (19–21) and abnormal AMLR has been reported in a variety of diseases (22–25), suggesting that it may possibly have an immunoregulatory role *in vivo.*

This study was initiated to clarify the mechanism of activation of the responding T cells in the AMLR. We found that the HLA-DR antigens of stimulator cells were essential and participated actively in triggering the responding T cells. Thus, DR antigens rendered resting T lymphocytes sensitive to Interleukin-2 and enabled $OKT4^{+}$ lymphocytes to respond to Interleukin-1 and to produce IL-2. Interleukin-1 promoted the synthesis of IL-2 by Interleukin-1-sensitive $OKT4^{+}$ cells.

MATERIALS AND METHODS

Cell Separation

Peripheral blood mononuclear cells (MNC) from adult subjects were obtained by centrifugation over Ficoll–Hypaque gradients as described previously (11, 22). T cells and non-T cells were isolated by rosetting MNC with sheep red cells as described elsewhere (11, 26). After osmotic lysis of the erythrocytes, T cells and non-T cells were washed and resuspended in RPMI 1640 medium (Gibco) supplemented with 10% heat-inactivated human AB serum, 20 μg/ml of gentamicin, glutamine, 0.25% sodium bicarbonate solution, and 1% Hepes buffer solution (Gibco) all of which will be referred to as complete culture medium (CCM).

Monoclonal Antibodies

Anti-HLA-DR Antibody. A monoclonal antibody (7S IgG) to HLA-DR antigens produced by somatic cell hybridization was used (NEI 011, New England Nuclear, West Germany). This antibody is directed against the complex of both chains of DR antigens and it binds to B cells and macrophages, but not to normal T cells. The capacity of this antibody to inhibit the proliferative response in the AMLR (detailed below) was studied by adding four different concentrations (from 20 to 60 μg/ml) to the cultures at the initiation of the cultures or at various times thereafter. As a control, we used the 3A1 monoclonal antibody (IgG) that defines human T-cell subsets (kindly provided by Dr. Anthony S. Fauci)(30).

Anti-human T-Cell subsets antibodies (OKT). Anti-human lymphocyte antibodies OKT4 (defines inducer T cells) and OKT8 (reactive against suppressor/cytotoxic T cells) were purchased from Ortho Pharmaceutical, Inc. (Raritan, N.J.).

Anti-OKT Antiserum Treatment

A purified population of T cells, obtained as described before, was enriched in either OKT4 or OKT8 T lymphocytes. Thereafter, 0.8-ml portions of SRBC-rosetting lymphocytes (2.5×10^{6}) cells/ml in RPMI containing 5% fetal calf serum) were mixed with 100 μl of either OKT4 or OKT8 antibody (final concentration 1 μg/ml). After a preincubation of 10 min at 37°C, 100 μl of fresh rabbit serum (as a source of complement) was added, and the cells were incubated for another 45 min at 37°C. After two washings in CCM, the cells were layered on Ficoll–Hypaque cushions and centrifuged, and viable cells were recovered from the interface. Treatment of total T cells by OKT4 antibody and C resulted in a cell population containing more than 90% OKT8-positive cells and less than 2% of OKT4$^+$ lymphocytes (as determined by indirect immunofluorescence microscopy). This population will therefore be referred to as OKT8$^+$ cells. Treatment of total T cells with OKT8 plus C gave a cell preparation containing more than 89% of OKT4-positive cells and less than 3% of OKT8 cells. These cells will be referred to as OKT4$^+$ lymphocytes.

Autologous Mixed Lymphocyte Cultures (AMLR)

AMLR cultures were carried out essentially as described previously (11, 22). Briefly, 10^5 T cells and 10^5 stimulator irradiated (2500 rad) autologous non-T cells were placed in each well of flat-bottom microtiter plates (Nunclon, Delta, A/S Nunc, Denmark) in a final volume of 0.2 ml of CCM. Cultures in triplicate were incubated at 37°C in a humidified atmosphere of 5% CO_2 in air for 7 days. Proliferation was determined by the incorporation of [^{3}H]-thymidine (0.5 μCi/well, act 5 Ci/mmol, Radiochemical Centre, Amersham England) during the last 12 hr of the culture period. The cells were harvested with a multisample collector and the filter papers were dried, placed in scintillation fluid, and counted in a liquid scintillation counter.

Interleukin-1 Preparation(IL-1)

IL-1 was obtained as described by Lachman *et al* (27). Briefly, 0.5 × 10^6 MNC and 20 μg of *Escherichia coli* lipopolysaccharide (LPS, 3129 Difco Labs. Detroit, Mich) per milliliter of RPMI medium were cultured in sterile plastic petri dishes (100 ml/150 × 25-mm dish, A/S Nunc) and incubated at 37°C in a humidified atmosphere of 5% CO_2 for 24 hr. Cultures that contained either no cells or no LPS were prepared as controls. The conditioned medium containing IL-1 was obtained by removal of cells by centrifugation at 2500 rpm for 15 min. Interleukin-1 activity was determined by the dose-dependent augmentation of phytohemagglutinin (PHA)-initiated thymocyte proliferation as described by Lachman *et al* (27). All IL-1 preparations were screened for IL-2 activity using the IL-2 microassay (see below) and were found to be negative.

Interleukin-2 Synthesis in AMLR

The capacity of both OKT4$^+$ and OKT8$^+$ cells to produce IL-2 in the AMLR was studied. OKT4$^+$ or OKT8$^+$ lymphocytes (5 × 10^6) were cocultured with 5 × 10^6 irradiated autologous non-T cells suspended in 1.5 ml of CCM in 17 × 100-mm round-bottom plastic tubes (Falcon plastics) and incubated at 37°C for 48 hr. The tubes were centrifuged at 2500 rpm for 15 min, the supernatants collected and filtered through 0.45-μm filters (Millipore, S.A.), and the IL-2 activity of each supernatant was tested in a microassay as detailed below. In those experiments in which the capacity of the anti-DR antibody to inhibit the synthesis of IL-2 in AMLR was studied, three different concentrations of this antibody (40, 50, and 60 μg/ml) or of the 3A1 monoclonal antibody (control) were added to cultures established as described above.

Assay for IL-2 Activity

The IL-2 activity of each AMLR culture performed in the presence or absence of the monoclonal anti-DR and 3A1 antibodies was tested by adding two different concentrations (final dilutions 1:2 and 1:4) to 10^4 cells of the following groups: resting T cells, T cells from AMLR cultures performed in the presence of the anti-DR or the 3A1 antibodies or medium, and a PHA-induced T-cell line which has been maintained in culture for 8 weeks with conditioned medium containing IL-2. The microtitre plates were incubated at 37°C for 48 hr and the incorporation of [^{3}H]thymidine (0.5 μCi/well) during the last 12 hr of the culture period was measured as described earlier.

Those supernatant media which only induced proliferation of activated T cells, but not of resting T cells, were considered to possess IL-2 activity. The experiments carried out to determine whether the monoclonal anti-DR antibody inhibits proliferation of previously activated T cells to IL-2 stimulation were carried out as follows: 10^4 T cells activated by AMLR were placed in flat-bottom microtiter plates. Three different dilutions of AMLR supernatants with proved IL-2 activity were added together with 50 μg/ml of the monoclonal anti-DR antibody or medium to each well. Cultures in triplicate were incubated at 37°C for 48 hr and proliferation was determined by [^{3}H]thymidine uptake during the last 12 hr of the culture period as described before.

RESULTS

Inhibition of the AMLR Response by Monoclonal Anti-DR Antibody

Addition of 20 μg/ml or more of the monoclonal anti-DR antibody at the initiation of the cultures strongly inhibited the proliferative response in AMLR, while cultures treated with the 3A1 antibody (control) did not show any modification in the proliferative response (Table 1). These results are in agreement with those previously reported by other authors. (14, 19).

Kinetic studies revealed that the anti-DR antiserum caused detectable suppres-

TABLE 1

Effect of the Anti-DR Antibody on AMLR Response

Responding cells[a]	Anti-DR antibody (μg/ml)	3A1 antibody (final dilution)	[^{3}H]Thymidine uptake (S.I.[b] ± SEM)
T	—	—	12.6 ± 2.0
T	20	—	7.5 ± 1.1
T	30	—	4.7 ± 2.0
T	—	1:500	13.1 ± 2.9
T	50	—	3.3 ± 1.4
T	—	1:200	12.2 ± 1.6
T	60	—	2.4 ± 1.0
T	—	1:100	11.9 ± 2.3
T (preincub. with 50 μg/ml anti-DR)		—	11.7 ± 1.5

[a] AMLR cultures established by culturing 10^5 T cells with 10^5 irradiated autologous non-T cells were treated with different concentrations of either the anti-DR antibody or the 3A1 antibody (control) or medium alone. Cultures in triplicate were incubated at 37°C for 7 days and proliferation was determined by the [^{3}H]thymidine uptake during the last 12 hr of the culture period.

[b] S.I. = stimulation index (ratio between the mean counts per minute in stimulated cultures and the mean counts per minute in unstimulated cultures). Mean ± SEM of six separate experiments.

sion of the AMLR as early as 48 hr after initiation of the reactions (Fig. 1a) and was maintained throughout the culture period. Nevertheless, the addition of the anti-DR antibody 72 hr after initiation of the cultures no longer inhibited the proliferative response (Fig. 1b). Taken together these results indicated that the anti-DR antibody inhibits the AMLR proliferation by interfering with very early events of the process of activation of T lymphocytes.

Absorption of the Inhibitory Activity of the Anti-DR Antibody by Stimulator Non-T Cells

In order to test whether the inhibitory activity of the anti-DR antibody was due to specific blocking effects on DR antigens, we carried out experiments in which

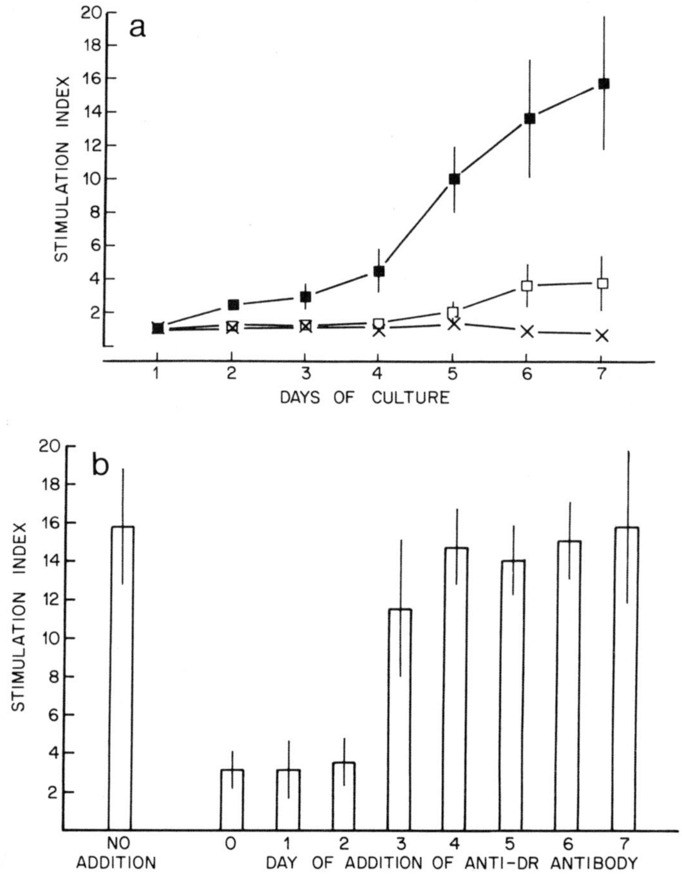

FIG. 1. Kinetics of the inhibitory activity of the anti-DR antibody on the AMLR response. (a) AMLR cultures were carried out as described in (b). Cultures treated (□) or untreated (■) with the monoclonal anti-DR antibody (50 μg/ml) were incubated at 37°C. Every 24 hr for 7 days, the proliferative response was determined by the incorporation of [^{3}H]thymidine. The proliferation of T cells cultured alone (×) is also shown. (b) AMLR between 1×10^5 T cells and 1×10^5 irradiated autologous non-T cells were performed in a final volume of 0.2 ml of complete culture medium. The monoclonal anti-DR antibody (50 μg/ml) was added to the cultures at the initiation of the AMLR and at various times thereafter. Cultures in triplicate were incubated at 37°C for 7 days. Proliferation was measured by the incorporation of [^{3}H]thymidine during the last 12 hr of the culture period. The results are expressed as stimulation index, Mean ± SEM of three separate experiments.

the monoclonal anti-DR antibody (50 μg/ml) was incubated with either T cells or non-T cells (5×10^6 cells) at 37°C for 2 hr. After this, the supernatants were collected and their inhibitory activity on the AMLR response was tested. When the anti-DR antibody was incubated with autologous non-T cells the serum was no longer able to abrogate the proliferative response (Table 2). In contrast, incubation of the same antiserum with T cells did not modify the inhibitory activity of the anti-DR antibody on the AMLR response (Table 2). The stimulator non-T cells, which were employed for the absorption experiments, lost their capacity to induce proliferation of the responding cells. Conversely, T cells used in the same type of experiments showed proliferative activity similar to that of the non-anti-DR-treated T cells (Table 2). These results indicated that the inhibition caused by the anti-DR antibody on the AMLR response was exerted by a specific direct blocking effect of the DR antigens present on stimulator non-T cells and that the antiserum did not have any effect on the responding T cells.

Anti-DR Antibody Reduces T-Cell Responses to IL-2

Since proliferation of T cells mainly depends on the presence of IL-2 (5–9), we investigated whether the anti-DR antibody exerted its effects by preventing the responding T cells from acquiring sensitivity to IL-2 or by inhibiting the production of the growth factor in the AMLR. T cells from AMLR cultures performed in the presence of the 3A1 monoclonal antibody (control) or medium alone proliferated when stimulated by IL-2. In contrast, T cells from cultures treated with the anti-DR serum showed a significantly decreased proliferation to IL-2 stimulation (Table 3). These results suggested that the anti-DR antibody prevented the responding T cells from acquiring sensitivity to IL-2. Therefore, it could be concluded that one mechanism by which the antiserum inhibited the AMLR response was by interfering with the responsiveness of T cells to IL-2.

TABLE 2

Absorption of the Inhibitory Activity of the Monoclonal Anti-DR Antibody by the Stimulator Cells in the AMLR

Cell assay	S.I. ± SD[a]
T	1.0 ± 0.2
T + non-T	14.6 ± 1.8
T + non-T + anti-DR (preincubated with non-T)[b]	13.9 ± 2.4
T + non-T + anti-DR (preincubated with T)[a]	3.5 ± 1.1
T + non-T (preincubated with Anti-DR)	3.0 ± 1.6
T (preincubated with anti-DR) + non-T	14.2 ± 2.0

[a] Mean ± SD of four independent experiments.

[b] Autologous non-T cells or T cells were incubated with the monoclonal anti-DR antibody (50 μg/ml) at 37°C for 2 hr. The supernatants resulting from this procedure were added to AMLR cultures and their inhibitory activity on the proliferative response was tested. The non-T cells and the T cells used in the absorption experiments were also employed as stimulators or responding cells respectively, in the AMLR.

TABLE 3

Response to Interleukin-2 of T Cells from AMLR Cultures Performed in the Presence or Absence of the Anti-DR or 3A1 Antibodies

Cells	Dilutions of IL-2 added to the cultures[a]	
	1:2	1:4
Resting T	1.1 ± 0.1[b]	1.0 ± 0.3
T (AMLR)	7.5 ± 1.1	6.1 ± 0.5
T (AMLR + 30 μg/ml anti-DR)	2.6 ± 0.3	1.9 ± 0.2
T (AMLR + 3A1 antibody, final dilution 1:200)	7.9 ± 1.0	5.8 ± 1.0
T (AMLR + 50 μg/ml anti-DR)	1.8 ± 0.1	1.5 ± 0.4
T (AMLR + 3A1 antibody, final dilution 1:100)	7.1 ± 0.6	6.3 ± 0.9

[a] 10^4 cells of the following groups: resting T cells; T cells from cultures treated with 30 and 50 μg/ml of the anti-DR antibody (T(AMLR + 30 or 50 μg/ml anti-DR)); T cells from cultures treated with the monoclonal 3A1 antibody (control); and T cells from cultures performed in the absence of the antibodies (T(AMLR)) were supplemented with two different dilutions of IL-2. Cultures in triplicate were incubated at 37°C, proliferation was determined by the [^{3}H]thymidine uptake during the last 12 hr of a 2-day culture period.

[b] Stimulation index, mean ± SEM of seven independent experiments.

Already Activated IL-2 Reactive T Cells Are Not Suppressed by the Anti-DR Serum

To determine whether the anti-DR antibody caused T cells to become unresponsive to IL-2 before or after these cells become sensitive to the growth factor, we carried out experiments in which previously activated IL-2 reactive T cells were stimulated with IL-2 in the presence of the anti-DR antibody (50 μg/ml). The results depicted in Table 4, show that proliferation induced by IL-2 on these cells was not inhibited by the anti-DR antibody. Therefore, it can be concluded that the unresponsivenes to IL-2 caused by the anti-DR antibody on T cells occurred at an early stage of the AMLR response, before the responding cells acquired sensitivity to IL-2. Once this has occurred, the capacity to proliferate under the stimulus of the growth factor was no longer inhibited by the anti-DR antibody.

TABLE 4

Effect of Anti-DR Antibody on Proliferation of Activated T Cells in Response to Interleukin-2

Cells	Dilutions of IL-2 added to the cultures		
	1:2	1:4	1:8
T (AMLR)[a]	11.4 ± 1.4[b]	5.3 ± 0.8	4.1 ± 1.0
T (AMLR) + 30 μg/ml anti-DR	10.7 ± 1.2	5.1 ± 1.5	4.4 ± 1.3
T (AMLR) + 50 μg/ml anti-DR	11.0 ± 0.7	4.9 ± 1.2	4.0 ± 1.1

[a] 10^4 T cells activated in AMLR were incubated with three different dilutions of Interleukin-2 in the presence or absence of the anti-DR antibody at 37°C for 48 hr. Proliferation was determined by the incorporation of [^{3}H]thymidine during the last 12 hr of the culture period.

[b] Stimulation index, mean ± SEM of five separate experiments.

Effect of the Anti-DR Antibody on the Production of IL-2 in the AMLR

In order to proliferate a T-cell population must be "activated" both to produce IL-2 and to become responsive to it (26). Therefore, we also studied whether or not the anti-DR antibody inhibits the synthesis of IL-2 in the AMLR. For this purpose, we first characterized the cell that produces IL-2 in the AMLR by using monoclonal antibodies that define human T-cell subsets (28). As can be seen in Table 5, the $OKT4^+$ lymphocytes synthesized IL-2 in the AMLR whereas the $OKT8^+$ cells did not. Thus, the cells that produce IL-2 in the AMLR possess the phenotype $OKT4^+$, $OKT8^-$.

We next studied whether the anti-DR antibody inhibits the synthesis of IL-2 by the $OKT4^+$ lymphocytes in the AMLR. The results (Table 5) show that addition of 40 μg/ml or more of the anti-DR antibody strongly inhibited the production of IL-2. Thus, we concluded that the anti-DR antibody abrogated the synthesis of IL-2 in the AMLR.

Inhibitory Activity of the Anti-DR Antibody on the Synthesis of IL-2 Is Not Reversed by Interleukin-1

In order to produce IL-2 a cell population must become sensitive to Interleukin-1 (IL-1). IL-1, a product of macrophage origin, normally promotes the production of IL-2 (8, 29). Thus, the anti-DR antibody could inhibit the synthesis of IL-2 in the AMLR by either decreasing the availability of IL-1 or by rending the $OKT4^+$ IL-2 producer lymphocytes unresponsive to IL-1 stimulation. To determine which of these mechanisms was operating, we carried out experiments in which IL-1 (final dilution 1:4) was added to AMLR cultures performed in the presence or absence of the anti-DR antibody. After 48 hr of incubation at 37°C, the supernatants were collected and processed as described before. The IL-2 activity of each supernatant

TABLE 5

Effect of the Anti-DR Antibody on the Synthesis of Interleukin-2 in the AMLR

Supernatant source[a]	Dilutions of IL-2 added to the cultures 1:2	1:4
$OKT8^+$ + non-T cells	2.1 ± 0.4[b]	2.0 ± 0.1
$OKT4^+$ cultured alone	1.9 ± 0.3	1.8 ± 0.2
$OKT4^+$ + non-T cells	13.8 ± 2.7	9.1 ± 2.5
$OKT4^+$ + non-T cells + 3A1 antibody	12.5 ± 3.1	8.8 ± 1.6
$OKT4^+$ + non-T cells + 40 μg/ml anti-DR	5.1 ± 2.8	3.6 ± 2.2
$OKT4^+$ + non-T cells + 50 μg/ml anti-DR	3.7 ± 1.5	1.9 ± 1.0

[a] 5×10^6 $OKT4^+$ or $OKT8^+$ lymphocytes and 5×10^6 irradiated non-T cells were incubated in the presence or absence of the anti-DR antibody or 3A1 antibody at 37°C for 48 hr. Supernatant from each culture was collected and filtered and their IL-2 activity tested in the following system: 10^4 cells from a PHA-activated T-cell line which has been maintained in culture for 8 weeks with conditioned medium containing IL-2 were incubated with two different dilutions of the supernatants. Cultures in microtiter plates were incubated at 37°C for 2 days and the incorporation of [^{3}H]thymidine during the last 12 h of the culture period measured.

[b] cpm $\times 10^{-3}$, mean ± SD of six independent experiments.

was determined in a microassay for IL-2 activity as detailed earlier. The results depicted in Table 6, show that the addition of IL-1 to cultures performed in the absence of the anti-DR antibody significantly enhanced the production of IL-2 by the $OKT4^+$ lymphocytes. In contrast, addition of IL-1 to anti-DR-treated cultures did not restore or increase the synthesis of IL-2. Furthermore, Table 6 also shows that $OKT4^+$ lymphocytes cultured but not stimulated did not produce IL-2 even when these cells were supplemented with IL-1. These results indicated: (i) IL-1 promoted the synthesis of IL-2 by IL-1 sensitive $OKT4^+$ lymphocytes, (ii) nonactivated $OKT4^+$ cells were unresponsive to IL-1 and unable to produce IL-2, and (iii) the anti/DR antibody appeared to cause $OKT4^+$ IL-2 producer lymphocytes to become unresponsive to IL-1 stimulation. Therefore, we concluded that the anti-DR antibody most probably inhibited the synthesis of IL-2 in the AMLR by preventing $OKT4^+$ IL-2 producer lymphocytes from acquiring responsiveness to IL-1.

The possibility that the anti-DR antibody exerted its inhibitory activities on AMLR by nonspecific toxic effects on the responding cells and/or on the stimulator cells was very unlikely. In fact, the viability of the cells as determined by trypan blue dye exclusion at the end of the cultures was the same in the presence or absence of the antiserum. Furthermore, the addition of the anti-DR antibody to AMLR cultures after 72 hr of initiation of the cultures did not inhibit the proliferative response. Moreover, incubation of the responding cells with the antibody did not modify their proliferative response in AMLR. Finally, stimulator non-T cells exhibited equal levels of DNA synthesis when stimulated with Epstein–Barr virus in the presence or absence of the anti-DR antibody (data not shown), excluding nonspecific toxic effects of the monoclonal anti-DR antibody.

DISCUSSION

By the use of a monoclonal antibody reactive against the complex of both chains of HLA-DR antigens, we found that addition of the antiserum inhibited the re-

TABLE 6

Effect of Interleukin-1 on the Production of Interleukin-2 in AMLR Cultures Performed in the Presence or Absence of the Anti-DR Antibody

Supernatant source[a]	Interleukin-1 added	Dilutions of IL-2 added to the cultures: 1:2	Dilutions of IL-2 added to the cultures: 1:4
$OKT4^+$ cells cultured alone	−	1.8 ± 0.3[b]	1.9 ± 0.2
	+	1.6 ± 0.5	1.7 ± 0.3
$OKT4^+$ + non-T cells	−	11.9 ± 2.4	8.5 ± 2.1
	+	19.7 ± 3.1	17.6 ± 2.9
$OKT4^+$ + non-T cells + 40 μg/ml anti-DR antibody	−	4.8 ± 1.5	3.6 ± 1.7
	+	5.0 ± 1.2	3.3 ± 2.0

[a] Cultures established as described in footnote *a*, Table 5, performed in the presence or absence of the monoclonal anti-DR antibody were supplemented with Interleukin-1 (final dilution, 1:4) or medium. The supernatants from each culture were collected after 2 days of culture at 37°C, filtered, and their IL-2 activity tested as detailed in legend to Table 5.

[b] cpm $\times 10^{-3}$, mean ± SD of four independent experiments.

sponse in AMLR. This inhibitory activity occurred very early in the process of activation of the responding cells and was detectable 48 hr after initiation of the cultures. Furthermore, the addition of the antiserum to cultures after 72 hr of initiation of the AMLR no longer inhibited the proliferative response. When the stimulator cells were preincubated with the anti-DR antibody, it was found that they lost their capacity to induce proliferation of the responding cells and, furthermore, the absorbed serum had lost its ability to inhibit the AMLR response. In contrast, incubation of the anti-DR antibody with T cells did not modify the proliferative activity of these cells and the serum recovered after the incubation period inhibited proliferation in the AMLR. Therefore, it can be concluded that the anti-DR antibody exerts its inhibitory activity on AMLR by acting specifically on the DR antigens of the stimulator cells and by interfering with very early events of the process of activation of the responding T lymphocytes.

Continuous proliferation of T cells necessarily requires of the presence of Interleukin-2 (5–9), a growth factor which supports growth of activated but not of resting T cells (8, 9), so that to achieve a proliferative response a cell population must be "activated" both to produce IL-2 and to become responsive to it. Therefore, it was important to test whether the anti-DR antibody inhibited the proliferative response of AMLR by inhibiting the responsiveness of T cells to IL-2 or by abrogating the production of the growth factor. It was found that T cells from cultures treated with the anti-DR antibody were unresponsive to IL-2, while T cells from cultures treated with the 3A1 antibody (control) or medium proliferated under the stimulus of the growth factor. It was also found that continuous proliferation of T cells that had already acquired sensitivity to IL-2 was not inhibited by the anti-DR antibody. Therefore, we concluded that the anti-DR antibody interfered with the process by which resting T lymphocytes acquire sensitivity to IL-2. Once this has occurred, the capacity of these cells to continue proliferating under the stimulus of Il-2 was no longer inhibited by the anti-DR antibody.

Interleukin-2 was found to be produced in the AMLR by OKT4$^+$ lymphocytes, a function which was also abrogated by the addition of the anti-DR antibody to the cultures. This inhibitory activity of the anti-DR antibody was not reversed by the addition of IL-1 to the cultures. On the other hand, IL-1 added to non-anti-DR-treated cultures significantly increased the synthesis of IL-2. In addition, it was found that nonactivated OKT4$^+$ lymphocytes were unresponsive to IL-1 and unable to produce IL-2. Therefore, we interpreted these results as indicating that the anti-DR antibody most probably inhibited the synthesis of IL-2 in the AMLR by preventing OKT4$^+$ IL-2 producer lymphocytes from acquiring sensitivity to IL-1.

Taken together, these results indicate that the anti-DR antibody abrogated the proliferative response in the AMLR by two different but related mechanisms, namely, by preventing resting T lymphocytes from acquiring responsiveness to IL-2 and by inhibiting the production of this growth factor.

Since resting T lymphocytes are unresponsive to IL-2 ((9) and this study), and unable to absorb IL-2 (9), and since resting OKT4$^+$ lymphocytes do not produce IL-2 or respond to IL-1 stimulation (this study), we postulate that the HLA-DR antigens of stimulator cells:

(i) Render resting T cells sensitive to Interleukin-2, probably by inducing these cells to express receptors for IL-2 (activated T cells do absorb IL-2 (9)).

(ii) These antigens enable OKT4$^+$ IL-2 producer lymphocytes to respond to IL-1 stimulation and subsequently, Il-1 promotes the synthesis of IL-2 by IL-1 reactive OKT4$^+$ cells.

(iii) Once T cells become responsive to IL-2 and the growth factor has been produced there is no further requirement for the HLA-DR antigens. The availability of IL-2 determines continuous proliferation and growth of IL-2 sensitive T cells.

REFERENCES

1. Thomas, D. W., Yamashita, M., and Shevach, E. M., *J. Immunol.* **119,** 233, 1977.
2. Persson, U., Hammarström, L., Möller, E., Möller, G., and Smith, C. E. I. *Immunol. Rev.* **40,** 78, 1978.
3. Athman, G. B., Sachs, D. H., and Hodes, R. J., *J. Immunol.* **121,** 1981, 1978.
4. Habu, S., and Raff, M. C., *Eur. J. Immunol.* **7,** 451, 1977.
5. Morgan, D. A., Ruscetti, F. W., and Gallo, R. C., *Science* **193,** 1007, 1976.
6. Gillis, S., and Smith, K. A. *Nature (London)* **268,** 154, 1977.
7. Larsson, E. L., and Coutinho, A., *Nature (London)* **283,** 664, 1980.
8. Smith, K. A. *Immunol. Rev.* **51,** 338, 1980.
9. Palacios, R., and Möller, G., *J. Exp. Med.* **153,** 1360, 1981.
10. Opelz, G., Takasugi, M., and Terasaki, P. I., *J. Exp. Med.* **142,** 1327, 1975.
11. Palacios, R., Llorente, Alarcón-Segovia, D., Ruiz-Arguelles, A., and Diaz-Jouanen, E., *J. Clin. Invest.* **65,** 1527, 1980.
12. Gottlieb, A. B., Fu, S. M., Yu, D. T. Y., Wang, C. Y., Holper, J. P., and Kunkel, H. G., *J. Immunol.* **123,** 1479, 1979.
13. Dock, N. L., and Davey, F. R., *Clin. Immunol. Immunopathol.* **17,** 123, 1980.
14. Engleman, E. G., Charron, D. J., Bewike, C. J., and Stewart, G. J., *J. Exp. Med.* **152,** (Suppl):99, 1980.
15. Weksler, M. E., and Kozak, R. J., *J. Exp. Med.* **146,** 1833, 1977.
16. Chiorazzi, N., Fu, S. M., and Kunkel, H. G., *J. Exp. Med.* **149,** 1543, 1979.
17. Innes, J. B., Kuntz, M. M., Kim, Y. T., and Weksler, M. E., *J. Clin. Invest.* **64,** 1608, 1979.
18. Tomonari, K. J., *J. Immunol* **124,** 1111, 1980.
19. Yamashita, U., and Shevach, E. M., *J. Immunol.* **124,** 1773, 1980.
20. Emery, D. C., and Morrison, W. I. *Immunology* **40,** 229, 1980.
21. Ponzio, N. M., *Cell. Immunol.* **49,** 266, 1980.
22. Palacios, R., and Alarcón-Segovia, D., *Clin. Immunol. Immunopathol.* **18,** 362, 1981.
23. Hom, J., and Talal, N., *Fed. Proc.* **39,** 1129, 1980.
24. Engleman, E. G., Benike, C. Hoppe, R. T. *et al., J. Clin. Invest.* **66,** 149, 1980.
25. Moody, C. E., Casazza, B. A., Christensson, W. N., and Weksler, M. E., *J. Exp. Med.* **150,** 1448, 1979.
26. Palacios, R., and Möller, G., *Nature (London)* **290,** 792, 1981.
27. Lachman, L. B., Hacker, M. P., and Handschumacher, R. E., *J. Immunol.* **119,** 2019, 1977.
28. Kung, P., Goldstein, G., Reinherz, E., and Schlossman, S., *Science* **206,** 347, 1979.
29. Palacios, R., *Scand. J. Immunol.,* in press.
30. Eisenbarth, G. S., Haynes, B. F., Schroer, J. A., Shelhomer, J. H., Eisenbarth, S., Strominjer, J. L., Thomas, C. A., Mostowski, H. S., and Fanci, A. S., *Proc. Natl. Acad. Sci. USA.* **77:** 2914, 1980.

CELLULAR IMMUNOLOGY **63**, 154–163 (1981)

A General Method for Studying the Secretion of Macromolecules by Single Cells

II. A Simplified Procedure with Enhanced Sensitivity

WILLIAM L. CLEVELAND, IRENE WOOD, IAN N. JACOBS, AND BERNARD F. ERLANGER

Department of Microbiology, Cancer Center/Institute of Cancer Research, Columbia University, New York, New York 10032

Received March 27, 1981; accepted May 7, 1981

A simple, sensitive precipitin-type single-cell secretion assay is described and applied to the study of immunoglobulin-secreting cells. Evidence is presented that its efficiency is comparable to that achieved with reverse hemolytic plaque techniques. Also described is a modification of the simplified procedure which possesses substantially increased sensitivity. Enhanced sensitivity is achieved through the use of monoclonal rheumatoid factors which preferentially react with rabbit or human immunoglobulins that are incorporated into immune complexes as a result of interaction with antigen. Addition of rheumatoid factor to the agarose–cell mixture leads to additional crosslinking of immune complexes that form around active cells, thereby increasing the probability of forming a detectable precipitate. The application of this procedure to the detection of cells producing T-cell products is also discussed.

INTRODUCTION

In a recent report (1), we described a highly flexible precipitin technique for detecting the secretion of macromolecules by single cells. In this technique, cells were plated in thin layers of agarose on microscope slides. The agarose gel contained an antiserum specific for the secreted macromolecule of interest. After incubation, active cells were surrounded by clusters of precipitin particles (cluster-forming cells). The use of enzyme markers in this procedure created the possibility of detecting simultaneously the secretion of several different molecular species by a single cell, and the form of the procedure presented in our initial publication was developed with this goal in mind. However, for many applications it is necessary to detect only a single secretory product. Adoption of this more restricted goal allows the single-cell assay to assume an extremely simple and convenient form with a sensitivity equal to the earlier one. It requires no enzyme-labeled reagents and none of the special techniques for removing excess immunochemical reagents that were described initially.

This report describes the new procedure and its application to the detection of immunoglobulin (Ig)-secreting cells. Evidence is presented to document its reliability for enumerating these cells. The method, however, is a general one and should be applicable to other systems, as well. For example, we have recently used

0008-8749/81/130154-10$02.00/0

it to detect T cells releasing macromolecules reactive with an antiserum raised against an antigen-specific suppressor factor (Cleveland *et al.*, in preparation). To facilitate application of the method to systems possibly requiring higher sensitivity, we introduce a modified form of our simplified procedure that uses human monoclonal rheumatoid factors to achieve substantially increased sensitivity.

MATERIALS AND METHODS

Antisera. Rabbit antisera (lyophilized) specific for mouse IgM (Lot BD042) (RαMIgM) and mouse κ chains (free and intact) (Lots BD043, CI183, and DF057) (RαMκ) were obtained from Bionetics. These antisera were reconstituted as recommended and stored at 4°C, or else at −20°C in small aliquots. A rabbit antiserum specific for mouse IgG_{2a+2b} (RαMIgG_{2a+2b}) was the generous gift of Dr. Sherie Morrison. This antiserum was heat inactivated at 56°C for 30 min and stored at −20°C in small aliquots. The Bionetics antisera were not heat inactivated since they were found to work well without such treatment.

A polyspecific goat antiserum specific for mouse immunoglobulins (GαMIg) was obtained from the Pocono Rabbit Farm, Canadensis, Pennsylvania. Affinity-purified goat anti-mouse Ig antibodies (GαMIg-Sp) were isolated according to methods described previously (1). Several hours before use, antisera were freed of microscopically visible (darkfield) debris by centrifugation at 12,800*g* for 15 or 30 min. In some cases, where sufficiently large amounts of material were available, debris were removed by passing through a low-loss syringe filter (0.45 μm, Acrodisc, Gelman No. 4184).

Mice. CBA/J females were obtained from the Jackson Laboratory, and were used at ages ranging from 8 to 24 weeks. Balb/cCr mice were obtained from the West Seneca Laboratory.

Preparation of spleen cells. Spleen cells were harvested as described previously (1) except that RPMI 1640 + 25 m*M* Hepes was replaced by Dulbecco's phosphate-buffered saline (DPBS) (Gibco) +10% fetal calf serum (FCS) (Sterile Systems, Inc.). After removing large clumps by settling at 1*g* for 5 min, the cell suspension was freed of small debris by centrifugation at 400*g* through an FCS gradient (2). Red cells were then removed by treatment with Tris-buffered ammonium chloride (3). The cells were then washed by centrifuging two times through an FCS gradient. At this point the cells were free of debris and could be used in the secretion assay. However, the second centrifugation through FCS was usually omitted and dead cells were removed by the low-ionic-strength cotton wool technique of von Boehmer and Shortman (4).

Specifically, both layers of supernatant of the first FCS gradient were removed and the cells were resuspended at a concentration of 1–5 × 10^7 cells/ml in ice-cold low-ionic-strength medium (5% DPBS + 95% 0.308 *M* sucrose) and immediately passed through a cold 5-ml disposable syringe fitted with a 40-mesh stainless-steel screen, supporting a pledget of absorbent cotton (dry weight approximately 50 mg, but usually sized by visual estimate). The cell suspension was then centrifuged at 4°C for 10 min at 200*g* and resuspended in DPBS + 10% FCS at the desired concentration. The suspending media were filtered (Acrodisc, 0.45 μm or Nalgene, 0.45 μm) to remove debris, before adding to cells. Cell concentration and viability were determined with a hemacytometer and 0.2% nigrosine in DPBS + 1% FCS. Viability was typically 95–97%.

Single-cell level secretion assay. One milliliter of 4% Sea Plaque agarose (Marine Colloids) in DPBS was prepared in a boiling water bath and immediately diluted with 9 ml of Iscove's modified Dulbecco's medium (Gibco) (5) prewarmed to 42°C. Then 290 mg of Dextran T-70 (Pharmacia) was added to the 0.4% agarose solution and dissolved. The solution was gassed to a light orange color with 100% CO_2, quickly sterile filtered (10-ml disposable syringe + 0.45 μm Acrodisc filter), and stored in an airtight test tube at 42°C. The final mixture was prepared by combining in a test tube 10 μl of FCS (Acrodisc filtered), 10 μl of antiserum (appropriately diluted and filtered or centrifuged), 70 μl of the agarose–dextran solution above, followed by 10 μl of cell suspension (usually 0.5–2 $\times 10^7$/ml). Immediately after the cells were added, the tube was removed from the 42°C H_2O bath and gently vortexed. Aliquots were then spread on a suitable supporting surface.

The optimum dilution of the antiserum is determined empirically. In general, with high titer antisera, the number of clusters detected is not a critical function of the antiserum dilution. Previously, we found that dilutions of a high titered rabbit anti-mouse IgG_1 antiserum ranging from 1/10 to 1/100 detected the same number of clusters (1). In some cases, high dilutions of an antiserum have yielded diffuse clusters. When clusters are diffuse, it is occasionally difficult to determine if a cluster is due to a single cell or is a composite of overlapping clusters. In such cases, the more compact clusters obtained with lower dilutions provide for more accurate counts of cluster-forming cells.

The stock cell concentration should be adjusted so that the number of clusters detected is large enough to provide the desired statistical accuracy. When this concentration is substantially above 2×10^7/ml, the large number of cells per unit area of the microscope field of view makes it difficult to discern precipitin clusters. It is therefore better to keep the maximum stock cell concentration in the vicinity of 2×10^7/ml and to use larger volumes of the agarose–cell suspension that are spread over correspondingly larger areas.

The most suitable and convenient supporting surfaces were Lux tissue culture flasks (No. 5327) which have 4 × 4-mm grids on their outer bottom surfaces. The margins of the grids rise to a height of about 100 μm above the surface of the flask and adequately contain the molten agarose in a defined area while gel formation is occurring. The bottom surfaces of the flasks were precoated with 0.2% Sea Plaque agarose, prepared in distilled water, and filtered (while hot through a 0.45 μm Nalgene filter unit). Coating was done in a 35°C room; about 100 flasks were prepared at a time. About 5 ml of the 0.2% agarose was deposited on the grid surface of each flask, excess was drained off, and the flask was put aside to dry. When dry (a matter of 15 min or so), the flasks were stacked in twos, grid surface to grid surface, and could be stored for many months before use.

For the assay, 25 μl of the agarose–cell suspension was distributed by pipet over an area consisting of nine grid squares (see Fig. 1). After addition of a duplicate aliquot, the flask was immediately covered by another flask using the stacking rim to prevent drying during the gelling period. Gel formation occurred in about 1–2 min depending on room temperature. The flask was immediately placed in the incubator, grid face down on a platform which was in a plastic box in which the humidity was maintained by bubbling the incubator atmosphere (using an aquarium

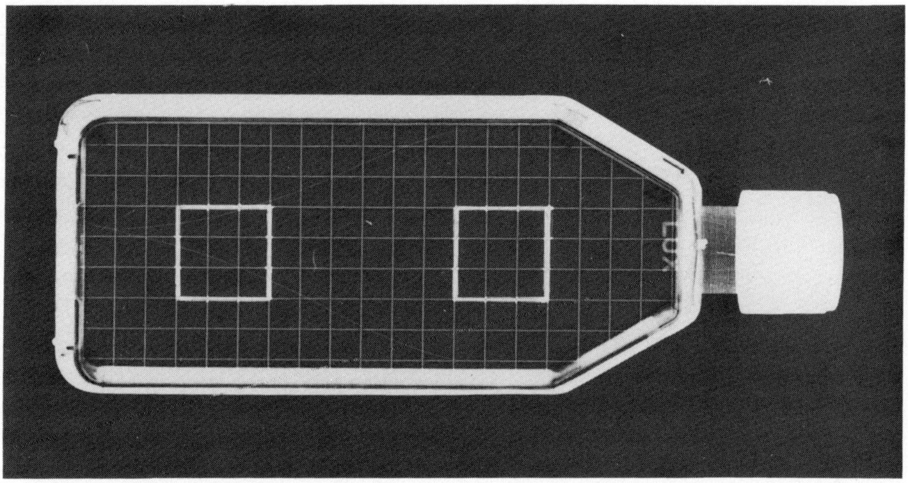

FIG. 1. Tissue culture flask used as agarose-supporting surface. Duplicate 25-μl aliquots of agarose–cell suspension were spread over areas consisting of nine squares (on this figure, areas within white squares) on the outer grid-bearing surface of the flask.

pump inside the incubator) through the water layer in the bottom of the box. The platform had been covered with wet paper toweling and the flasks were put grid face down, separated from the toweling and platform using microscope slides as spacers. For reasons of convenience, the incubation (10% CO_2, 37°C, 100% humidity) was usually carried out overnight. Although we have not carried out a systematic study, this incubation period appears to be longer than necessary for maximal detection of precipitin clusters. Previously, we found that incubation periods at 37°C of 4.3, 4.8, and 10.3 hr gave similar results, although in these early experiments, there was a subsequent incubation period at 4°C to allow precipitation to continue after the cells had stopped secreting (1).

Microscopic observation of the cells and their precipitin clusters. Precipitin clusters are best observed at 100× magnification with dark-field illumination. Typical precipitin clusters are shown in Fig. 2. These clusters have the same general appearance as those detected in the previous study (1) using immunoperoxidase staining techniques. Precipitin clusters can be observed while wet, immediately after removal from the incubator if they are kept moist by repeated additions of distilled water. It is more convenient, however, to fix the cells as follows:

Flasks are removed from the incubator, placed on a clinical rotator, and immediately covered with 4 ml of filtered DPBS (Nalgene, 0.45 μm). The rotator is set at a speed which causes visible motion of the liquid but does not cause it to run off the flasks. After 5 min, the DPBS is removed and fresh DPBS is added and agitation continued for 5 min. The DPBS is then removed and replaced by 4 ml of DPBS containing 0.5% glutaraldehyde (Taab Laboratories) and agitation is continued for 30 min. The flasks are then washed with six changes of filtered H_2O (4 ml each), 5 min each wash, and allowed to air dry at RT. When wet, flasks are handled with plastic gloves to avoid a dark-field background resulting from skin lipids. Excellent visibility of precipitin clusters results when the agarose layer is dry since cells and precipitin particles are contained in a single focal plane. Ob-

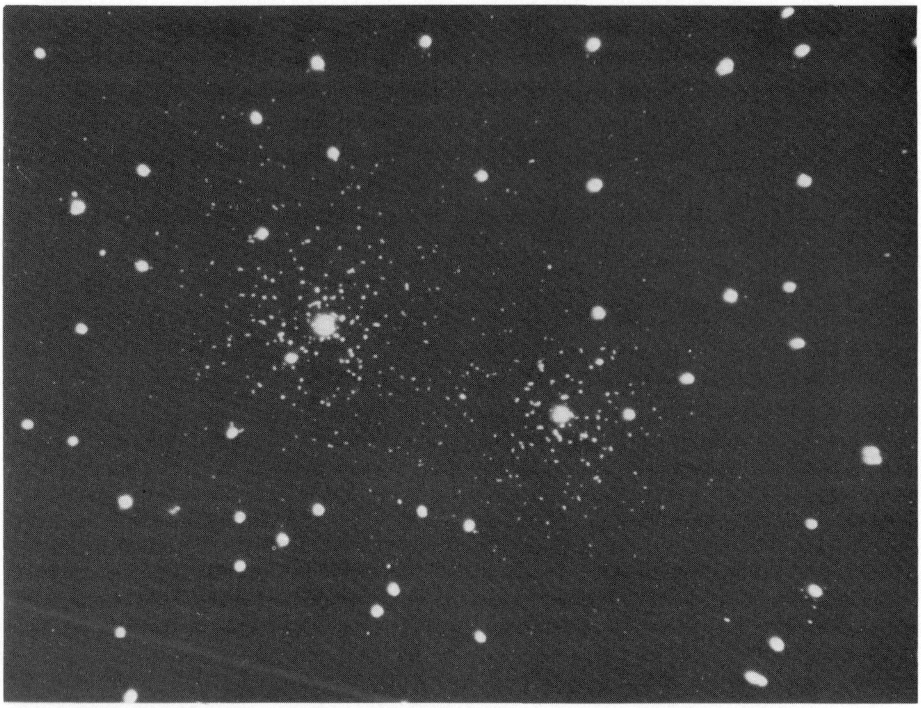

FIG. 2. Typical precipitin clusters formed by spleen cells taken from an unimmunized CBA/J mouse. A rabbit anti-mouse kappa antiserum (Lot DF057) was used at a dilution of 1/20, together with rheumatoid factor at a concentration of 25 μg/ml.

servations were made with an Olympus IMT inverted microscope with super-wide-field optics. At a magnification of 100×, a field diameter of 2.6 mm was obtained. The phase ring in the condenser for the 100× objective gave very satisfactory dark-field illumination when used with a nonphase 10× objective. Although not essential, wide-field optics are helpful in reducing observation time since precipitin clusters can easily be detected with peripheral vision while scanning rapidly. An upright microscope can be used equally as well provided it has a long working distance condenser.

Precipitin spot test. In order to evaluate antisera for use in the secretion assay and to study the sensitivity of the precipitin reaction, a precipitin spot test was employed. Essentially, the spot test is identical to the cell secretion assay, except that the aliquot of cells used to prepare the final agarose mixture is replaced by an aliquot of the same volume containing a known concentration of soluble antigen. All other details of the test were identical to the single-cell level secretion assay.

Mouse IgG_{2b} myeloma protein. The myeloma line 45.6 (derived from MPCll (6)) was the generous gift of Dr. Sherie Morrison. Ascites fluid from Balb/cCr mice injected with 45.6 cells was collected and purified on a protein A–Sepharose column (Pharmacia). The column was initially equilibrated in PBS, pH = 7.4, to avoid binding by IgG_1 (7). After washing with PBS to remove unbound material, the absorbed material was eluted with 0.2 *M* glycine–HCl, pH = 2.8, neutralized with 1 *M* K_2HPO_4, and concentrated by precipitation with 50% saturated $(NH_4)_2SO_4$

and finally dialyzed against saline. Protein concentration was calculated from the optical density at 280 nm, assuming an optical density of 1.4 for a 1 mg/ml solution.

Monoclonal rheumatoid factor. Purified monoclonal rheumatoid factor was the generous gift of Drs. Vincent Bonagura and Benvenuto Pernis. This material was isolated from serum originally supplied by Dr. H. Kunkel and referred to as "Wa" in the latter's publications (8, 9).

Other supporting surfaces. Although for the present purposes the Lux tissue culture flasks were most satisfactory, other supporting surfaces were also examined. Plastic tissue culture dishes (Nunc, 35 mm diameter) used in the conventional way suffer from a very uneven distribution of cells because of miniscus effects. These effects can be eliminated by inverting the dish and using the stacking rim on the outer bottom surface to contain the agarose layer. It accomodates about 100–300 μl of the agarose–cell mixture. However, even without miniscus effects cell distribution is not entirely uniform and the entire area occupied by the agarose must be examined and counted. The smaller, adjustable area possible with the Lux tissue culture flasks is a decided advantage.

RESULTS

Detection of Ig-Secreting Cells without Use of Immunoenzyme Techniques

To enumerate the total number of Ig-secreting cells in spleens of unimmunized CBA/J mice, two types of reagents were used: polyspecific GαMIg affinity-purified antibodies isolated with a mouse Cohn fraction II–Sepharose column and rabbit antisera specific for mouse κ-chain determinants. The latter reagent is expected to react with 95% of all mouse Ig molecules (10). The results obtained with these reagents are shown in Table 1.

As indicated, we find, with the simplified precipitin technique, that about 0.2–0.4% of spleen leukocytes are Ig-secreting cells. Using two different anti Ig reagents (RαMk (Lot CI-183) and GαMIg-Sp) and the same preparation of spleen cells (Mouse 2), essentially identical numbers of Ig-secreting cells were obtained indicating the reliability of the method. The results with GαMIg-Sp and two different preparations of spleen cells (Mice 1 and 2) are included as an example of the variations that are encountered among individual mice.

We have also used our procedure for class-specific detection of Ig-secreting cells.

TABLE 1

Detection of Total Ig-Secreting Cells

Antibody	Cluster-forming cells per 10^6 spleen leucocytes	Mouse No.
GαMIq-Sp[a]	2264	1
GαMIg-Sp[a]	3936	2
RαMk (lot CI183)[b]	3616	2
RαMk (lot DF057)[b]	3639	3

[a] Final concentration of Ab in agarose gel = 100 μg/ml.

[b] Whole antiserum at a final dilution of 1/10.

TABLE 2

Detection of Total IgM-Secreting Cells

Antibody	Cluster-forming cells per 10^6 spleen leucocytes	Mouse No.
RαMIgM (Lot BD042)[a]	1728	2
RαMk (Lot CI183)[a]	3616	2

[a] Whole antiserum at a final dilution of 1/10. Same preparation of cells used with both antisera.

Results for a RαMIgM antiserum are compared in Table 2, with those obtained with a RαMk antiserum using the same preparation of cells.

As expected the number of IgM-secreting cells is less than the total number of Ig-secreting cells. Theofilopoulos *et al.* (11), using the Molinaro and Dray reverse plaque technique (13) find 0.05–0.1% IgM-secreting cells in the spleens of unimmunized C3H/St, C57BL/6, and Balb/c mice, ranging from 1–11 months in age. Given the variations encountered among individual mice, our data are in satisfactory agreement.

Enhancement of Sensitivity with Human Monoclonal Rheumatoid Factors

The description of human monoclonal rheumatoid factors that preferentially precipitate aggregated human and rabbit immunoglobulins without apparent interaction with monomeric immunoglobulins (8,9) prompted us to use these reagents to enhance precipitation in the single-cell secretion assay. To evaluate the effect of these reagents on the antigen sensitivity of the precipitin reaction under controlled conditions, the precipitin spot test was used. The antigen–antibody system consisted of purified myeloma protein 45.6 and a rabbit antiserum specific for mouse IgG_{2a+2b}. Purified Wa rheumatoid factor was used. Results are given in Table 3.

As indicated, the presence of rheumatoid factor facilitated detection of immune

TABLE 3

Enhancement of Sensitivity with Rheumatoid Factor in Precipitin Spot Test

Antigen Conc.[a] (ng/ml)	Precipitate (with Wa)	Precipitate (without Wa)
200	+	+
100	+	+
50	+	±
25	+	−
12.5	+	−
6.25	−	−
3.125	−	−
0	−	−

Note. $R\alpha MIgG_{2a+2b}$ Antiserum dilution = 1/100. Wa concentration = 25 μg/ml.
[a] Final concentration in agarose gel of 45.6 myeloma protein.

precipitate at antigen concentrations four- to eightfold lower than the lowest concentrations yielding a detectable precipitate in the absence of rheumatoid factor. In addition the apparent "heaviness" of the precipitate in the presence of rheumatoid factor was greater at all antigen concentrations.

The ability of the Wa rheumatoid factor to enhance the antigen sensitivity of the precipitin reaction was also verified with the single-cell secretion assay. Results are shown in Table 4.

These results indicate that the rheumatoid factor Wa can also increase sensitivity in the single-cell level secretion assay. With RαMk (Lot BD043) antiserum, the number of cells detected increased dramatically by a factor of 4.6. The outer RαMk (Lot DF057) antiserum detected essentially the same number of Ig-secreting cells regardless of whether rheumatoid factor was present, suggesting that this antiserum was detecting Ig-secreting cells with high efficiency before sensitivity enhancement.

DISCUSSION

Our initial single-cell secretion assay based on the precipitin reaction (1) was designed on the assumption that the detection of the immune precipitates surrounding active cells would require highly sensitive techniques. An immunoperoxidase procedure was therefore used. Subsequently, in control experiments in which reagents not labeled with peroxidase were employed, precipitin clusters around active cells were found to be readily detectable with low-power dark-field microscopy if debris present in the agarose were removed. This could be done easily by filtration or centrifugation of the various solutions used in the assay and by removing debris from the cell suspension using the procedures already established by Shortman and co-workers (2,4).

The basic virtue of this simplified technique is that it is a "no-wash" procedure. That is, excess antibody reagent does not have to be removed, since macromolecules not incorporated into immune precipitin particles are invisible by dark-field microscopy. Elimination of the washing step removes the requirement for casting chambers (1), since uniform and critically thin layers of agarose are no longer needed. The histochemical staining steps are also eliminated, resulting in substantial savings in time and effort.

Since our initial publication, we have frequently encountered the opinion that the precipitin reaction is inherently insensitive compared with compliment fixation

TABLE 4

Enhancement of Sensitivity with Rheumatoid Factor in Single-Cell Secretion Assay

Antibody	Cluster-forming cells per 10^6 spleen leucocytes	Mouse No.
RαMk (Lot BD 043) alone[a]	260	4
RαMk (Lot BD 043) + Wa[a]	1205	4
RαMk (Lot DF 057) alone[b]	3639	3
RαMk (Lot DF 057) + Wa[b]	3844	3

[a] Whole antiserum at a final dilution of 1/50.
[b] Whole antiserum at a final dilution of 1/20.

and that a single-cell level secretion assay based on the precipitin reaction must be much less sensitive than existing reverse hemolytic plaque techniques (12, 13). In this report we apply the precipitin technique to the detection of Ig-secreting cells in spleens of unimmunized mice and compare the results with published data obtained by using a reverse hemolytic plaque technique.

Quantitation of the total number of Ig-secreting cells has been done with a rabbit antiserum specific for mouse κ chains, which are found in 95% of murine Ig molecules (10). Also, polyspecific affinity-purified antibodies eluted from a mouse Cohn fraction II column have been used. We find that Ig-secreting cells in unimmunized CBA/J mice represent 0.2–0.4% of total spleen leukocytes. Using a reverse hemolytic plaque technique (12), Steele and Cunningham have found an average of 0.57% Ig-secreting cells in CBA/H mice (14). Theofilopoulos *et al.*, using the same technique, find total Ig-secreting cells in spleens of unimmunized C3H/St, Balb/c, and C57BL/6 mice to be in the range of 0.05–0.2% of total spleen leukocytes (11). Considering the variations found among individual mice, our data are in good agreement. This indicates that the simplified precipitin technique possesses adequate sensitivity for reliably studying Ig-secreting cells.

In order to determine quantitatively the sensitivity limits of the precipitin reaction in agarose gels, we have developed a "spot test" that is identical to the single-cell secretion assay except that the cells are replaced by low levels of antigen at a known concentration. Antigen concentrations as low as 50 to 100 ng/ml were found to yield detectable immune precipitates. This is comparable to what has been found in the reverse hemolytic plaque technique. Molinaro and co-workers have reported that the antibody-coated erythrocytes used in the reverse plaque assay require antigen concentrations of the order of 100 ng/ml for hemolysis (15).

It should be emphasized that the high sensitivity we have achieved depends on the use of dark-field microscopy. Examination of the agarose layer with the unaided eye (or even bright field microscopy) as is commonly done in immunodiffusion procedures, fails to detect the precipitates that form at such low antigen concentrations. This fact is apparently the basis of the impression that procedures based on the precipitin reaction are incapable of detecting low antigen concentrations.

Although the single-cell level secretion assay appears to possess adequate sensitivity for studying Ig-secreting cells, we have explored ways to increase sensitivity, since our goal has been to develop a method that would be applicable to other cell types, such as regulatory T cells. A successful approach that preserves the "no-wash" feature of the simplified procedure described in this report is based on the existence of human monoclonal rheumatoid factors that appear to interact with aggregated IgG molecules (rabbit and human), while ignoring monomeric IgG. When rheumatoid factor was added to the agarose mixture it apparently caused additional crosslinking of the immune complexes around active cells, increasing the probability of forming detectable precipitates. Using the spot test procedure, rheumatoid factor enhanced the sensitivity 4- to 8-fold, allowing the detection of antigen at concentrations as low as 12 ng/ml. In the cell assay, use of rheumatoid factor also led to an increase in the number of active cells detected with certain antisera. For example, a RαMk (Lot BD043) antiserum, which had previously been found defective for use in the cell secretion assay, was tested with rheumatoid factor and a 4.6-fold increase in the number of cluster-forming cells detected was obtained, indicating a substantial increase in sensitivity. This antiserum is an example of antisera, which we have occasionally encountered, that possess good titer when used at high antigen concentrations but fail to be useful in the cell secretion assay where conditions of extreme antibody excess prevail. Although not proven, these antisera may be defective as a result of nonprecipitating antibodies. They apparently contain antibodies which form soluble immune complexes around cells releasing Ig, since such complexes are required for interaction with rheumatoid factor (9). Another RαMk antiserum (Lot DF057) that had been found to work well in the secretion assay failed to detect a greater number of Ig-secreting cells in the presence of rheumatoid factor, although the "heaviness" of the precipitate around cells seemed increased on the average. This suggests that this antiserum detected Ig-secreting cells with high efficiency without the additional sensitivity achieved with the use of rheumatoid factors.

The increased sensitivity obtained with rheumatoid factors should facilitate the application of the secretion assay to the study of cells releasing macromolecules in minute quantities. Of special interest are T cells which release a number of macromolecules that have important regulatory functions. Currently, very little is known about the quantitites of regulatory molecules released by individual T-cells; however, it is generally assumed that extremely minute amounts are released. If such is the case, rheumatoid factors of the type used in this study may be useful in achieving the necessary sensitivity required for single-cell level studies. Interestingly, in a recent study of T cells using the methodology described in this report, excellent clarity of detection was achieved with a rabbit anti-suppressor factor antiserum without the additional sensitivity achieved with the use of rheumatoid factors (Cleveland *et al.*, in preparation).

ACKNOWLEDGMENTS

This work was supported by a grant from the National Institutes of Health (AI-06860) and a grant from the American Cancer Society (IM-195).

REFERENCES

1. Cleveland, W. L., and Erlanger, B. F., *Cell. Immunol.* **37,** 229, 1978.
2. Shortman, K., Williams, N., and Adams, P., *J. Immunol. Methods* **1,** 273, 1972.
3. Mishell, B. B., Shiigi, S. M., Henry, C. *et al.*, *In* "Selected Methods in Cellular Immunology" (B. B. Mishell and S. M. Shiigi, Eds.), p. 23. Freeman, San Francisco, 1980.
4. von Boehmer, H., and Shortman, K., *J. Immunol. Methods* **2,** 293, 1973.
5. Iscove, N. N., and Melchers, F., *J. Exp. Med.* **147,** 923, 1978.
6. Gefter, M. L., Margulies, D. H., and Scharff, M. D., *Somat. Cell Genet.* **3,** 231, 1977.
7. Ey, P. L., Prowse, S. J., and Jenkin, C. R., *Immunochemistry* **15,** 429, 1978.
8. Kunkel, H. G., Agnello, V., Joslin, F. G., Winchester, R. J., and Kapra, J. D., *J. Exp. Med.* **137,** 331, 1973.
9. Winchester, R. J., Kunkel, H. G., and Agnello, V., *J. Exp. Med.* **134,** 286s, 1971.
10. Herzenberg, L. A., and Herzenberg, L. A., *In* "Handbook of Experimental Immunology" (D. M. Weir, Ed.), Vol. 1, 3rd ed. p. 12.4. Blackwell Scientific, Oxford, 1978.
11. Theofilopoulos, A. N., Shawler, D. L., Eisenberg, R. A., and Dixon, F. J., *J. Exp. Med.* **151,** 446, 1980.
12. Molinaro, G. A., Maron, E., and Dray, S., *Proc. Nat. Acad. Sci. USA,* **71,** 1229, 1974.
13. Gronowicz, E., Coutinho, A., and Melchers, F., *Eur. J. Immunol.* **6,** 588, 1976.
14. Steele, E. J., and Cunningham, A. J. *Nature (London)* **274,** 483, 1978.
15. Demma, F. J. Eby, W. C., Yokoyama, M. M., Siciliano, F., and Molinaro, G. A., *Immunochemistry* **15,** 213, 1978.

CELLULAR IMMUNOLOGY 63, 164–176 (1981)

The Role of Macrophages in the Acute-Phase Response: SAA Inducer Is Closely Related to Lymphocyte Activating Factor and Endogenous Pyrogen

MARCELO B. SZTEIN, STEFANIE N. VOGEL, JEAN D. SIPE,* PATRICK A. MURPHY,† STEVEN B. MIZEL,‡ JOOST J. OPPENHEIM, AND DAVID L. ROSENSTREICH§

*Laboratory of Microbiology and Immunology, National Institute of Dental Research, National Institutes of Health, Bethesda, Maryland 20205, *Arthritis and Connective Tissue Disease Section, Department of Medicine, Boston University School of Medicine, Boston, Massachusetts 02215, †Department of Microbiology, Johns Hopkins University School of Medicine, Baltimore, Maryland 21205, ‡Department of Microbiology, Cell Biology, Biochemistry, and Biophysics, Pennsylvania State University, University Park, Pennsylvania 16802, §Department of Microbiology and Immunology, Albert Einstein College of Medicine, Bronx, New York 10461*

Received March 18, 1981; accepted May 26, 1981

An increase in the concentration of the acute-phase reactant, serum amyloid A (SAA), following endotoxin treatment, is a consequence of the action of lipopolysaccharide (LPS) on macrophages to produce a monokine, the SAA inducer, which in turn, triggers SAA synthesis by hepatocytes. We have found that murine SAA inducer is closely related, if not identical, to murine lymphocyte activating factor (LAF), otherwise known as Interleukin 1 (IL 1). Furthermore, both rabbit endogenous pryrogen (EP), which is believed to be identical to LAF (IL 1), and human LAF (IL 1), induced elevated SAA concentrations in C3H/HeJ mice. Antiserum previously shown to block both pyrogenic and thymocyte proliferating activities of the species of rabbit EP exhibiting an isoelectric point of pH 7.3 (EP 7), also blocked the SAA inducing activity of EP7. Phenylglyoxal treatment of highly purified murine LAF (IL 1) abrogated both thymocyte proliferating activity and the SAA inducing activity. These studies support and extend previous reports suggesting that within 2 hr of an inflammatory stimulus, macrophages produce a monokine that acts systemically to alter body temperature, activate T cells, and induce hepatic protein synthesis of acute-phase reactants.

INTRODUCTION

Serum amyloid A (SAA)[1] is a major acute-phase reactant (1, 2) that was identified by its immunologic cross-reactivity with amyloid A fibrils that accumulate during the development of amyloidosis secondary to chronic inflammation (3, 4). Upon ultracentrifugation, SAA is isolated with the high-density lipoprotein (HDL)

[1] Abbreviations used: SAA, serum amyloid A; HDL, high-density lipoprotein; LPS, lipopolysaccharide; LAF, lymphocyte activating factor; EP, endogenous pyrogen; AA, amyloid A fibril protein; BSA, bovine serum albumin; CFA, complete Freund's adjuvant; PMA, phorbol myristic acetate; PBMNC, peripheral blood mononuclear cells; LEM, leukocyte endogenous mediator; CRP, C-reactive protein.

0008-8749/81/130164-13$02.00/0

fraction of serum (5, 6) and may account for as much as 25% of the HDL apoproteins from acute-phase serum (7).

The acute-phase SAA response of mice to endotoxin (8) begins with a latent period of 2 to 4 hr, followed by an exponential increase in SAA concentration over the subsequent 12 to 16 hr. Approximately 20 to 24 hr after LPS administration, the SAA concentration declines and returns to baseline values by 48 hr. LPS is a potent stimulus for the acute-phase SAA response in all strains of mice except for LPS nonresponder strains such as C3H/HeJ and C57BL/10ScN (1, 9). The importance of lymphoid cells in the acute-phase SAA response was demonstrated since adoptively transferred C3H/HeN bone marrow cells restored the SAA response to LPS in C3H/HeJ mice (10). Subsequent studies with lipid A-resistant mice established that during the latent period, a macrophage product called the "SAA inducer" (11) or "SAA stimulating factor" (12) arises in response to the inflammatory stimulus (LPS) and serves to initiate hepatic SAA synthesis.

During studies which demonstrated the production of SAA inducer by highly purified macrophages (11), we noted a similarity in the kinetics of SAA inducer and lymphocyte activating factor (Interleukin 1)[2] production (Fig. 1), which suggested the possibility that these two activities might be related. Lymphocyte activating factor (Interleukin 1) has recently been shown to be closely related, if not identical, to endogenous pyrogen (13, 14). At present, only one species of human LAF (IL 1) has been characterized (15); it has an isoelectric point of pI 6.8 and is pyrogenic. The rabbit appears to have two species of LAF (IL 1) which have isoelectric points of 4.6 to 4.8 (EP 5) and 7.3 (EP 7). Both species are pyrogenic (14). There are major chemical and immunological differences between these two species of rabbit LAF (IL 1) (14). Antibody raised in goats against EP 7 abrogates both the pyrogenic and the LAF (IL 1) activities, but does not affect either activity of EP 5. The mouse appears to produce only one species of LAF (IL 1) which has an isoelectric point of 5.0 to 5.4 (16).

The sequential purification of SAA inducer from LPS-stimulated, purified murine macrophage supernatants would require enormous volumes of starting material due to losses upon purification and since the *in vivo* assay for biologic activity requires larger amounts of material compared to the *in vitro* thymocyte proliferation assay for LAF (IL 1). We therefore tested partially purified preparations derived from a murine macrophage cell line and from rabbit and human macrophages for SAA inducing activity. These included partially purified specimens of mouse LAF (IL 1) derived from the $P388D_1$ cell line, both species of rabbit LAF (IL 1), and human LAF (IL 1). The findings presented in this report suggest that LAF (IL 1), EP, and the SAA inducer are closely related, if not identical moieties.

MATERIALS AND METHODS

Animals

C3H/HeJ mice were obtained from Jackson Laboratories (Bar Harbor, Maine). C3H/HeN and C57BL/10ScN mice were obtained from the Division of Research

[2] Recently, lymphocyte activating factor (LAF) has been termed Interleukin 1 (IL 1) by a number of investigators. In order to be consistent with the bulk of the literature, this material will be referred to as LAF (IL 1).

Resources (NIH, Bethesda, Md.); 5- to 8-week-old male or female mice were used. For each experiment mice were always of the same sex. New Zealand White rabbits were used for the production of anti-AA antibodies. All animals were fed and watered *ad libitum*.

Reagents

Endotoxin (LPS) was prepared from *Escherichia coli* K235 by the phenol water extraction procedure of McIntire *et al.* (17). Sterile fluid thioglycollate was obtained from the NIH Media Unit (Bethesda, Md.). RPMI 1640 tissue culture medium (RPMI) was obtained from Microbiological Associates (Walkersville, Md.) and was supplemented with penicillin (100 U/ml), streptomycin (100 μg/ml), glutamine (2 m*M*), and Hepes buffer (15 m*M*) (NIH Media Unit).

SAA Measurements

The concentration of SAA in the serum was measured by a previously described solid-phase radioimmuoassay (18). Serum was obtained from mice 18 hr following the intraperitoneal injection of 1 ml of an appropriate dilution of SAA inducer (11). C3H/HeJ or C57BL/10ScN mice were used throughout this study since these mice are genetically refractory to LPS, which was present in several preparations of SAA inducer and which is, itself, a potent stimulator of SAA (1, 9). In order to measure SAA in the serum, a 50-μl aliquot of test serum was denatured by heating at 60°C for 1 hr to unmask antigenic sites in the SAA molecule and the concentration of SAA estimated by the capacity of the denatured sample to compete with ^{125}I-AA for binding of immobilized anti-AA antibodies. The anti-AA antibodies used in this study were made by repeated immunization of New Zealand White rabbits with amyloid A fibrils (AA) denatured with 0.1 *N* NaOH or with the alkaline-denatured fibrils coupled, by the method of Avrameas and Bouteille (19), to bovine serum albumin (AA-BSA). The concentration of antigen protein was determined by the method of Spector (20) and antigens were emulsified in complete Freund's adjuvant (CFA). Rabbits were injected in alternate flanks at least weekly with 0.25 mg antigen per injection. Following a total of six injections, the rabbits were bled from the marginal ear vein and the anti-AA antibodies purified by immunoabsorption chromatography on an immobilized AA column (21). In these studies, the antibodies adsorbing to the AA column were eluted with 3 *M* ammonium thiocyanate (Fisher Scientific, Co., Fairlawn, N.J.) rather than acetic acid as previously described (21). Subsequent bleedings were obtained 5 days after booster injections with soluble AA or AA-BSA + CFA. Booster injections were administered at 2-week intervals to the rabbits. No differences were found using the AA versus the AA-BSA as the immunogen.

Materials Tested for SAA Inducer Capacity

Crude murine SAA inducer. Supernatants derived from LPS-stimulated, thioglycollate-induced, C3H/HeN macrophage cultures were prepared as previously described (11) and were used as a source of unpurified murine SAA-inducer and LAF (IL 1). Briefly, C3H/HeN mice were injected with 3 ml of thioglycollate intraperitonally and 5-6 days later the cells were collected for culture by peritoneal lavage. The cells were plated in TC-24 culture dishes (Costar, Cambridge, MA) at a final concentration of 2×10^6 cells/well. Following an adherence incubation of 2-3 hours, the cells were vigorously washed and replaced with media alone (Control) or media containing 10 μg/ml LPS for an additional 48 hours. A single pool of this LPS-stimulated culture supernatant was stored frozen at −20°C and aliquots were thawed for use as a standard (STD) in each experiment. To induce an SAA response 1 ml of a 1:4 dilution of this standard was injected intraperitoneally into C3H/HeJ mice. Even though the same standard supernatant was injected in each experiment, the resultant SAA response to this standard varied considerably from 10 to 100 μg/ml SAA at 18 hr after injection. One of the largest sources of variability in the measurement of SAA response from experiment to experiment was due to unequal denaturation of the serum samples upon heating. However, the relative concentrations of SAA for the samples within a given experiment were reproducible upon repeated assays.

LAF (IL 1) measurements. LAF (IL 1) activity was measured as the ability of a test supernatant to augment the PHA-induced proliferation of C3H/HeJ thymocytes, assessed by uptake of [^{3}H]thymidine (22). In order to compare different LAF (IL 1) preparations, each sample was serially diluted and tested for thymocyte proliferating activity. The data were then plotted on a log–log scale and the dilution that induced LAF (IL 1) activity equal to that of the standard SAA-inducer preparation was calculated. The "standard" preparation was arbitrarily assigned a value of 100 LAF (IL 1) units/ml and the activity of other samples was compared with it, as previously described (23, 24), using the formula:

$$\frac{(\text{dilution of standard resulting in cpm}_{33\%\ \text{maximum}})}{(\text{dilution of sample resulting in cpm}_{33\%\ \text{maximum}})} \times 100\ \text{units/ml} = \text{units/ml in the sample.}$$

This material (STD) was included in each experiment as a positive control for SAA induction, and as a standard for LAF (IL 1) activity.

Purified murine LAF (IL 1). The murine macrophage cell line, P388D$_1$, was incubated with 1 μg/ml phorbol myristic acetate (PMA) for 144 hr in the presence of 1% fetal calf serum. The supernatants containing LAF (IL 1) activity were partially purified by 65% ammonium sulfate precipitation, ion-exchange chromatography on DEAE cellulose, and gel filtration on Sephacryl S200 (16). The active product of this sequence was pooled and coded B-31. Some of the B-31 pool was further purified by chromatography on phenyl sepharose to give pool B-33, which had an approximate 1200-fold increase in specific LAF (IL 1) activity when compared to the starting material (23).

Human LAF (IL 1). Partially purified, human LAF (IL 1), was prepared from human mononuclear cells as previously described (25). Briefly, peripheral blood mononuclear cells were obtained following separation of whole blood by Ficoll–Hypaque gradient centrifugation. Mononuclear cells (1×10^7) were incubated in 150-cm^2 tissue culture flasks for 2–4 hr in RPMI containing 5% heat-inactivated human serum. Nonadherent cells were subsequently removed by vigoruous washing and cells were incubated for 48 hr in RPMI with or without 25 μg/ml LPS (Difco, Detroit, Mich.). The LPS-stimulated culture supernatants were concentrated and applied to a Sephacryl S-200 column. Molecular weight pools were collected and tested for LAF (IL 1) and SAA inducing capacity. Pool IV was used in these studies and includes LAF (IL 1) activity with a molecular weight ranging from 12,000 to 20,000 daltons.

Partially purified rabbit endogenous pyrogen (EP). Two species of partially purified rabbit endogenous pyrogen were prepared as previously described (26). Culture supernatants were derived from endotoxin-stimulated rabbit peritoneal exudate cells and were subjected to a sequential purification involving Sephadex gel filtration followed by isoelectric focusing. Two peaks of activity were identified by their isoelectric points of pH 4.8 and 7.3 and were designated "EP 5" and "EP 7", respectively.

Abrogation of LAF (IL 1) and SAA Inducing Activities

Two techniques were employed to abrogate SAA inducer activity. Both techniques have been previously shown to greatly reduce LAF (IL 1) activity in the thymocyte proliferation assay (14, 23). First, LAF (IL 1)-induced thymocyte proliferative activity has been shown to be completely abolished by treatment with 2% phenylglyoxal (Sigma Chemical Co., St. Louis, Mo.) for 6 hr at 25°C (23). Material treated in this manner was dialyzed back into phosphate-buffered saline, diluted, and tested for SAA inducing activity. Second, treatment of EP 7 with goat anti-EP 7 has been previously demonstrated to abrogate LAF (IL 1) activity (14). To test the effect of anti-EP 7 on SAA inducer activity, 40 μl of goat anti-rabbit EP 7 or normal goat serum was mixed with 100 μl EP 7, incubated at 37°C for 1 hr, and then incubated at 4°C overnight. The material was then centrifuged at 10,000*g* for 15 min in a Beckman Microfuge (Palo Alto, Calif.) and the supernatant diluted and tested for SAA inducing activity.

RESULTS

Correlation between Murine LAF (IL 1) Activity and SAA Inducer Activity

As can be seen in Fig. 1, the kinetics of appearance of LAF (IL 1) and that of the SAA inducer in crude endotoxin-stimulated macrophages supernatants *in vitro* are very similar, suggesting a possible relationship between the two. Therefore, C3H/HeJ mice were injected with five different LPS-stimulated murine adherent peritoneal cell supernatants or PMA-stimulated $P388D_1$ murine macrophage cell line supernatants that contained varying levels of LAF (IL 1) activity. A highly significant correlation was observed between the amount of SAA induced and the concentrations of LAF (IL 1) activity injected (Fig. 2). However, the *in vitro* LAF (IL 1) assay is significantly more sensitive than the *in vivo* assay for SAA inducer since at least 100 times more LAF (IL 1) activity is required to induce a significant SAA response *in vivo*.

In order to further test the hypothesis that LAF (IL 1) possesses SAA inducer activity, two highly purified preparations of murine LAF (IL 1) were prepared from PMA-stimulated $P388D_1$ murine macrophage cell line: B-31 (partially purified by 65% ammonium sulfate precipitation, ion-exchange chromatography on DEAE cellulose, and gel filtration on Sephacryl S200) and B-33 (B-31 further purified by chromatography on phenyl sepharose).

Initially, we compared the LAF (IL 1) activity of the SAA inducer present in our SAA inducer standard (LPS-induced C3H/HeN peritoneal adherent cells su-

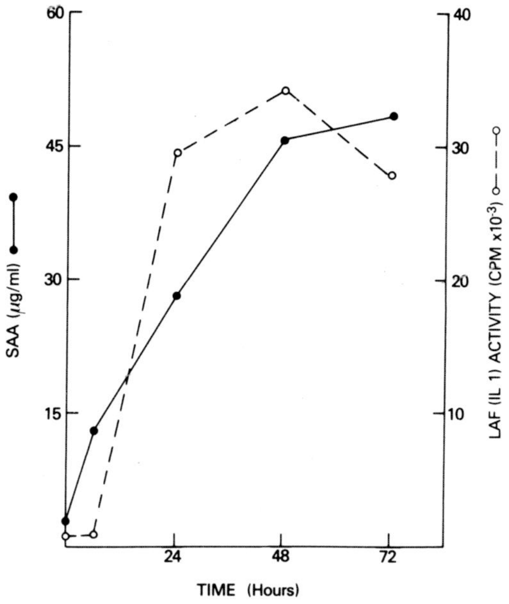

FIG. 1. Time course for the production of SAA inducer and LAF (IL 1) by LPS-stimulated macrophages. C3H/HeN macrophages were cultured as described under Materials and Methods with 10 μg/ml LPS. Culture supernatants were harvested at various times after stimulation with LPS and tested for SAA inducer and LAF (IL 1) activities. Results represent the mean responses of six individual mice per time point for SAA inducer activity and the mean of triplicate cultures for thymocyte proliferative activity.

pernatant) with that of the B-31 and B-33 preparations (Fig. 3). Based on the 33% maximum counts per minute extrapolation relative to the standard (described under Materials and Methods) we found that our SAA inducer was approximately 10 times more active than B-31 and approximately twice as active as B-33 in enhancing

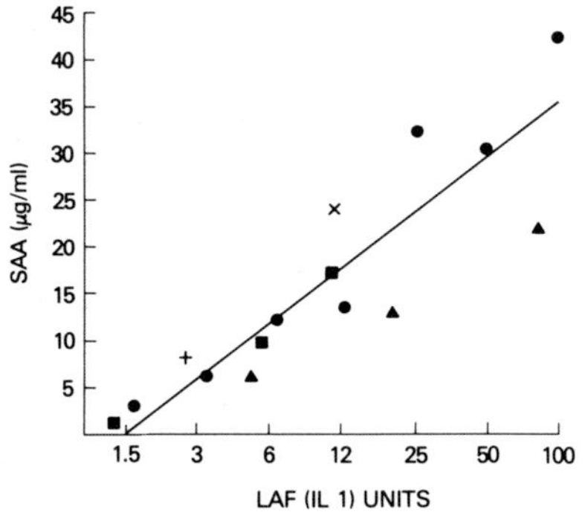

FIG. 2. Relationship between activity of injected LAF (IL 1) and SAA response. Five different preparations of murine LAF (IL 1)-containing supernatants were injected at various concentrations into C3H/HeJ mice and the SAA concentrations in serum measured 18 hr later. Each different symbol represents a distinct LAF (IL 1) preparation tested at various dilutions (five mice/dilution). Data were evaluated by a linear regression analysis ($r = 0.897$; $P < 0.005$). (+) represents the SAA response induced by pool B-31 and (x) represents the SAA response induced by pool B-33.

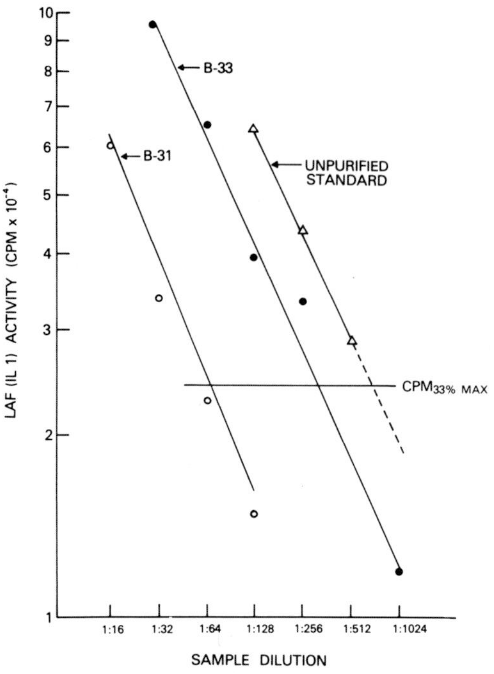

FIG. 3. Comparison of LAF (IL 1) activity in murine LAF (IL 1) samples. B-31, B-33, and unpurified murine LPS-stimulated macrophage culture supernatant standard (STD) were serially diluted and tested for thymocyte proliferating activity. Each point respresents the arithmetic mean of triplicate cultures. Based on the 33% maximum CPM extrapolation relative to the standard LAF (IL 1) preparation (described under Materials and Methods), B-31 was found to contain 10.5 units/ml and B-33 was found to contain 45.4 units/ml of LAF (IL 1) activity. The standard was arbitrarily assigned a value of 100 units/ml.

murine thymocyte proliferation. We next showed that B-31 induced a significant SAA response in the serum of C3H/HeJ mice (Fig. 4). As was observed for thymocyte proliferating activity, the unpurified standard contained more SAA inducing activity than did B-31. Pool B-33 was approximately as potent *in vivo* as our standard SAA inducer (Fig. 5A). Both of these preparations induced SAA responses consistent with the expected response based on the concentration of LAF (IL 1) injected. These points are included in Fig. 2. Furthermore, phenylglyoxal treatment, previously shown to abolish LAF (IL 1) activity (23, 27) also abrogated the SAA inducing and LAF (IL 1) activities of pool B-33 (Fig. 5A and B).

LPS-Stimulated Human Monocytes Produce LAF (IL 1) and SAA Inducer

It has been clearly demonstrated that adherent human peripheral blood mononuclear cells (PBMNC) can be stimulated by endotoxin to produce LAF (IL 1) (28). We therefore tested a partially purified preparation of human LAF (IL 1) for SAA-inducing activity. Figure 6 demonstrates that this material induced a highly significant SAA response in C3H/HeJ mice. This material also possessed thymocyte proliferating activity which was approximately nine times greater than that of our standard murine preparation (data not shown). A control supernatant

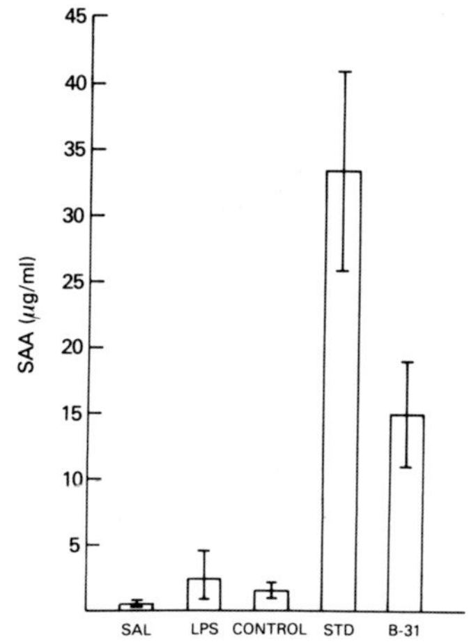

FIG. 4. SAA-inducing activity of B-31 and the standard (STD). One milliliter of a 1:4 dilution of each preparation was injected into each of 10 mice. Controls include 1 ml/mouse of pyrogen free saline, 1 μg/ml LPS, and 1:4 unstimulated macrophage supernatant (control). Results represent the arithmetic mean ± SEM of individual animals.

of unstimulated PBMNC that did not contain any LAF (IL 1) activity also did not induce an SAA response. These findings indicate that endotoxin stimulation of human monocyte cultures results not only in the production of LAF (IL 1) but also in the production of SAA inducer in the molecular weight range of 12,000 to 20,000 daltons. It is significant that the human material was able to cross a species barrier for both activities.

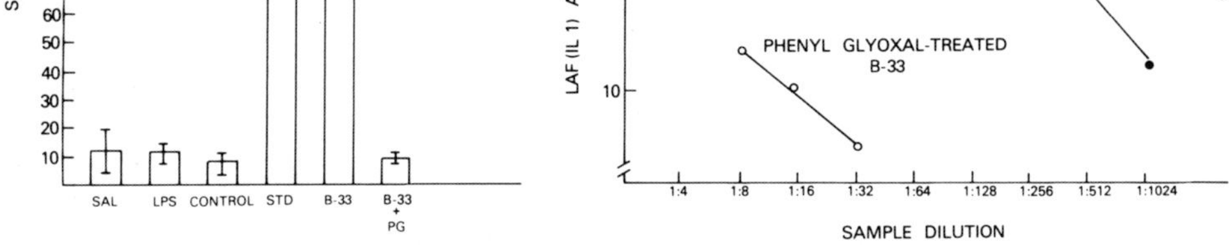

FIG. 5. Effect of phenylglyoxal treatment of B-33 on LAF (IL 1) and SAA inducer activities. B-33 (45.4 LAF (IL 1) units/ml) was treated with 2% phenylglyoxal (PG) as described under Materials and Methods. Treated and untreated B-33 were diluted 1:4 and 1 ml injected into each of six mice. Controls include 1 ml/mouse of pyrogen free saline, 1 μg/ml LPS, 1:4 unstimulated macrophage supernatant (control), and 1:4 LPS-stimulated macrophage supernatant standard (STD). Results represent the arithmetic mean ± SEM. B illutrates LAF (IL 1) activity of the treated and untreated B-33 and the murine STD supernatant. Results represent arithmetic means of triplicate cultures.

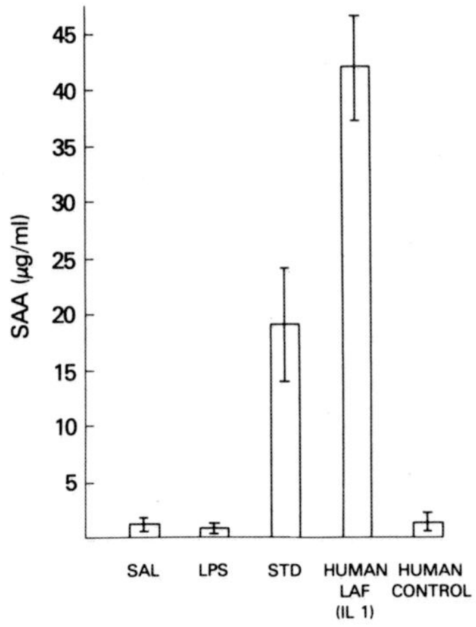

FIG. 6. Partially purified human LAF (IL 1) possesses both SAA inducer and LAF (IL 1) activities. Partially purified human LAF (IL 1) was prepared as described under Materials and Methods and was tested for SAA inducer and LAF (IL 1) activities. A 1:8 dilution of partially purified human LAF (IL 1) and a 1:4 dilution of murine supernatant standard (STD) were prepared and 1 ml was injected into each of 10 mice. Results represent the arithmetic mean ± SEM of individual animals. Controls include 1 ml/mouse of pyrogen-free saline, 1 μg/ml LPS,and a 1:4 dilution of unfractionated, unstimulated human macrophage supernatant (human control). The human LAF (IL 1) was found to contain 918 units/ml of LAF (IL 1) activity.

Rabbit Endogenous Pyrogens Induce SAA in Mice.

Recent biochemical and biological evidence strongly suggest that endogenous pyrogen (EP) and LAF (IL 1) obtained from endotoxin-stimulated, rabbit macrophages are similar, if not identical, moieties (14). Since the two highly purified murine LAF (IL 1) preparations both retained SAA inducer activity, and since a partially purified human macrophage product possessed both activities (and crossed a species barrier), we investigated whether rabbit endogenous pyrogen also possessed SAA-inducing activity in mice. It has also recently been demonstrated that LPS-stimulated rabbit peritoneal exudate cells produce two major biochemical species of endogenous pyrogen, one with an isoelectric focusing point (IEP) of pH 4.7 and the other with an IEP of pH 7.3 ("EP 5" and "EP 7", respectively) (14, 26, 29). When we tested EP 5 and EP 7 preparations, we found that both possessed SAA inducer (Fig. 7) and LAF (IL 1) activities (data not shown). Murphy *et al.* have also previously demonstrated that an antiserum made in goats against the EP 7 preparation ablated the pyrogenic activity of the EP 7 species, but not the EP 5 species (29). This same antiserum was subsequently shown by Murphy *et al.* (14, 29) to abrogate EP 7-induced, but not EP 5-induced, thymocyte proliferating activity. We therefore tested the effect of this antiserum on the SAA inducer activity of the EP 5 and EP 7 preparations. Figure 8 demonstrates that anti-EP 7 antiserum abrogated the SAA inducer activity of EP 7 but does not decrease the ability of EP 5 to induce SAA *in vivo*. Furthermore, anti- EP 7 treatment failed to alter the SAA inducer activity of our standard murine preparation. This is consistent with previous reports demonstrating that mouse LAF (IL 1) exhibits an isoelectric point of 5.0–5.4 (16).

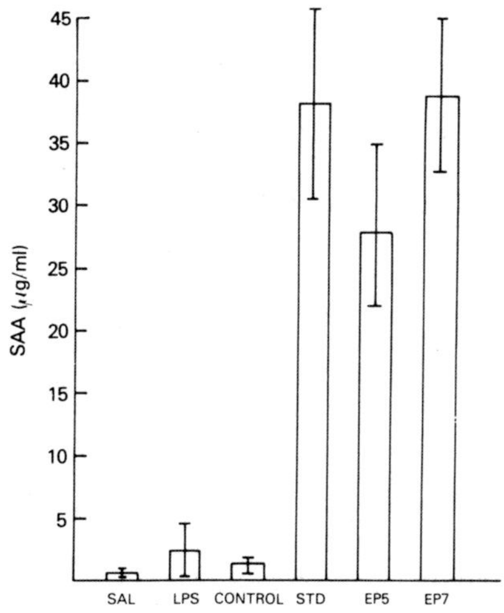

FIG. 7. Rabbit endogenous pyrogen possesses both SAA inducer and LAF (IL 1) activities. EP 5 and EP 7 preparations were tested for SAA inducer activities. One milliliter of EP 5 (diluted 1:50) or EP 7 (diluted 1:250) was injected into each of 10 animals. Controls include 1 ml/mouse of pyrogen-free saline, 1 μg/ml LPS, 1:4 unstimulated macrophage supernatant (control) and 1:4 LPS-stimulated macrophage supernatant standard (STD). EP 5 was found to contain 114.9 units/ml LAF (IL 1) activity and EP 7 was found to contain 5970 units/ml LAF (IL 1) activity.

DISCUSSION

During the past decade, a number of independent investigators have demonstrated that the *in vitro* stimulation of macrophages with endotoxin results in the production of numerous soluble factors with a broad scope of biological activities. These include thymocyte proliferation (LAF (IL 1)), fever (EP), and SAA-inducer

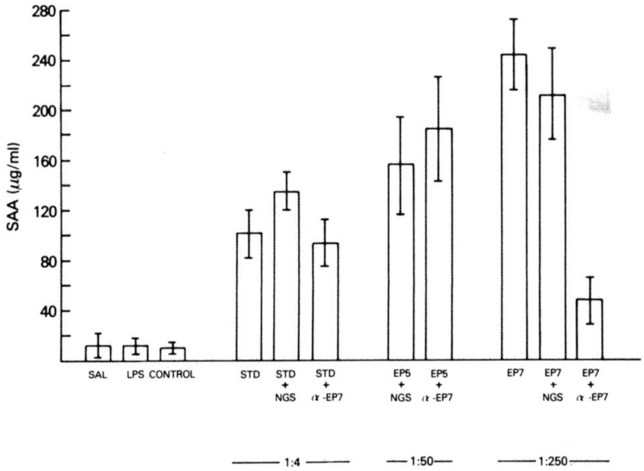

FIG. 8. Effect of anti-EP 7 on SAA inducer activity. One milliliter of the indicated dilution of untreated, normal goat serum (NGS)-treated, or anti-EP 7 (α-EP 7)-treated preparations was injected into each of 5–13 mice per point. Each point represents the arithmetic mean ± SEM of individual animals. The controls were the same as those described in Fig. 6.

activities. Recent studies by Murphy *et al.* (14) clearly demonstrated that partially purified endogenous pyrogens derived from LPS-stimulated, rabbit macrophage cultures possessed not only pyrogenic activity, but also LAF (IL 1)-induced, thymocyte proliferating activity, suggesting that the factors responsible for inducing these two very different biological effects were identical. Similarly, we observed that the production of LAF (IL 1) in LPS-stimulated murine macrophage cultures was coincidental with the production of SAA inducer, a soluble factor recently demonstrated to induce SAA synthesis by hepatocytes. In addition, we observed a direct correlation between the activity of LAF (IL 1) injected and the SAA response induced in C3H/HeJ mice. Therefore, we examined highly purified preparations of murine LAF (IL 1), two species of rabbit endogenous pyrogen, and partially purified human LAF (IL 1) for SAA-inducing activity in mice. The findings presented in this report clearly demonstrate that all of these preparations were SAA inducers. Additionally, two treatments previously demonstrated to abrogate thymocyte proliferating and/or pyrogenic activities of these preparations (23, 29) were equally effective in abrogating their SAA inducing activity. Treatment of murine LAF (IL 1) with phenyglyoxal abrogated its thymocyte proliferating activity and SAA inducing activity, and treatment of rabbit EP 7 with anti-EP 7 antibody blocked its SAA inducing activity. These findings strongly support the hypothesis that in addition to thymocyte proliferating and pyrogenic acivities, LAF (IL 1) or EP can act directly upon hepatocytes, resulting in the production of the acute-phase reactant, SAA.

Our findings support and extend earlier reports demonstrating that macrophage products can act to induce the production of "late" acute-phase reactants (30). In this regard, Sipe *et al.* (11) demonstrated that a factor produced by LPS-stimulated macrophages could induce a highly significant increase in serum SAA levels in endotoxin-unresponsive mice. This same factor was shown *in vitro* to stimulate SAA synthesis by hepatocytes (12). Kampschmidt *et al.* previously demonstrated that leukocyte endogenous mediator (LEM), obtained from rabbit peritoneal cells, could increase serum fibrinogen levels (31). It is of interest to note that recent evidence strongly supports the contention that LEM, originally thought to be produced by polymorphonuclear leukocytes, is actually endogenous pyrogen produced by contaminating macrophages (32). In addition, Kushner *et al.* (33, 34) suggested that a circulating mediator is responsible for hepatocyte C-reactive protein (CRP) synthesis after tissue injury. Based on these studies, the following model for the production of acute-phase reactant production can be proposed. Following an inflammatory stimulus, macrophages release an "early" soluble factor which, in turn, acts on the cells of the liver to produce the "late" acute-phase reactants (i.e., SAA, fibrinogen, CRP).

The fact that LAF (IL 1) and two species of EP were found in this study to induce SAA production strengthens the idea that these moieties are closely related and adds significantly to the importance of this monokine as a major immunoregulatory molecule. LAF (IL 1) has been shown to have a multiplicity of effects, including the induction of thymocyte and peripheral T-lymphocyte proliferation (35), the induction of T-cell growth factor by T lymphocytes (36), an enhancement of antibody production by B cells (37), replacement of macrophage requirement in the T-lymphocyte response to mitogens (38) and soluble antigens (39), and potentiation of mixed thymocyte reactions (40). In addition, LAF (IL 1) has been found to act on synovial cells to increase prostaglandin and collagenase production (41). The functional hallmark of endogenous pyrogen is its ability to induce fever, perhaps by acting directly on thermosensitive neurons or by inducing the endothelial cells of the hypothalamus to produce fever-inducing agents (42). Thus, this family of closely related, "early" monokine signals possesses a remarkably broad range of cellular targets. Additionally, the fact that these materials cross species barriers also suggests retention of LAF (IL 1)-like molecules as primitive immunoregulators. Specifically, in this report, both rabbit and human macrophage factors were potent SAA inducers in the mouse. Previous studies examining fever induction with endogenous pyrogen also show this capability of crossing species barriers (43). However, it must be emphasized that only when the amino acid sequence of these activities is known, will their biochemical relationship be definitively established. It is possible that LAF (IL 1), EP, and SAA inducer, as in the case of interferons (44), are polypeptides which differ considerably in their amino acid compositions, but are still able to exert similar biological activities. Alternatively, this group of molecules may be very similar polypeptides that have minor differences which enable them to interact with different target cells.

Finally, the role of SAA and other acute-phase reactants in the physiology of inflammation is currently the subject of active investigation. It has been demonstrated that late acute-phase reactants exhibit immunosuppressive activities. Benson and Aldo-Benson (45) demonstrated an inhibitory effect of SAA on T-cell-dependent antibody formation. Additionally, CRP has been shown to inhibit a number of cell-mediated immune reactions including mixed leukocyte response, sensitivity to lymphokine migration inhibition factor (MIF), and antigen-specific proliferative responses (46). If one considers the inhibitory effect of the acute-phase reactants such as those described for SAA and CRP as part of the normal process of inflammation, the following sequence of events could be proposed. The inflammatory stimulus triggers macrophages to produce a monokine that is capable of acting secondarily on a broad spectrum of cell types. Presumably, the hepatocyte products function as negative feedback regulators for systemic cell-mediated inflammatory reactions. It is paradoxical that an immunoenhancing macrophage-derived mediator appears in the circulation and, in turn, induces hepatocyte products that are immunosuppressive. Further dissection of the cellular interactions involved in the production and metabolism of acute-phase reactants will provide an understanding of disease states such as the secondary amyloidosis associated with chronic inflammation.

ACKNOWLEGMENTS

We thank Drs. S. Mergenhagen, R. Moore, and A. Weinblatt for their helpful discussions during the course of this study, Drs. A. Cohen and M. Skimmer for their review of the manuscript, and Mrs. Darleen Tenn for her secretarial help.

REFERENCES

1. McAdam, K. P. W. J., and Sipe, J. D., *J. Exp. Med.* **144,** 1121, 1976.
2. McAdam, K. P. W. J., Elin, R. J., Sipe, J. D., and Wolff, S. M., *J. Clin. Invest.* **61,** 390, 1978.
3. Isersky, C., Page, D. L., Cuatrecasas, P., DeLellis, R. A., and Glenner, G. G., *J. Immunol.* **107,** 1690. 1971.
4. Levin, M., Franklin, E. C., Frangione, B., and Pras, M., *J. Clin. Invest.* **51,** 2773, 1972.
5. Benditt, E. P., and Eriksen, N., *Proc. Nat. Acad. Sci. USA* **74,** 4025, 1977.

6. Benditt, E. P., Eriksen, N., and Hanson, R. H., *Proc. Nat. Acad. Sci. USA* **76,** 4092, 1979.
7. Bausserman, L. L., Herbert, P. N., and McAdam, K. P. W. J., *J. Exp. Med.* **152,** 641, 1980.
8. Sipe, J. D., *Brit. J. Exp. Pathol.* **59,** 305, 1978.
9. Vogel, S. N., Hansen, C. T., and Rosenstreich, D. L., *J. Immunol.* **122,** 619, 1979.
10. Rosenstreich, D. L., and McAdam, K. P. W. J., *Infect. Immunity* **23,** 181, 1979.
11. Sipe, J. D., Vogel, S. N., Ryan, J. L., McAdam, K. P. W. J., and Rosenstreich, D. L., *J. Exp. Med.* **150,** 597, 1979.
12. Selinger, M. J., McAdam, K. P. W. J., Kaplan, M. M., Sipe, J. D., Vogel, S. N., and Rosenstreich, D. L., *Nature (London)* **285,** 498, 1980.
13. Rosenwasser, L. J., Dinarello, C. A., and Rosenthal, A. S., *J. Exp. Med.* **150,** 709, 1979.
14. Murphy, P. A., Simon, P. L., and Willoughby, W. F., *J. Immunol.* **124,** 2498, 1980.
15. Lachman, L. B., Hacker, M. P., and Handschumacher, R. E., *J. Immunol.* **119,** 2019, 1977.
16. Mizel, S. B., *J. Immunol.* **122,** 2167, 1979.
17. McIntire, F. C., Sievart, H. W., Barlow, G. H., Finley, R. A., and Lee, A. Y., *Biochemistry* **6,** 2363, 1967.
18. Sipe, J. D., Ignaczak, T. F., Pollock, P. S., and Glenner, G. G., *J. Immunol.* **116,** 1151, 1976.
19. Avrameas, S., and Bouteille, M., *Exp. Cell Res.* **53,** 166, 1968.
20. Spector, T., *Anal. Biochem.* **86,** 142, 1978.
21. Linke, R. P., Sipe, J. D., Pollock, P. S., Ignaczak, T. F., and Glenner, G. G., *Proc. Nat. Acad. Sci. USA* **72,** 1473, 1975.
22. Meltzer, M. S., and Oppenheim, J. J., *J. Immunol.* **118,** 77, 1977.
23. Mizel, S. B., *Mol. Immunol.* **17,** 571, 1980.
24. Farrar, J. J., Mizel, S. B., Fuller-Bonar, J., Farrar, W. L., and Hilfiker, M. L., *J. Immunol.* **125,** 793, 1980.
25. Togawa, A., Oppenheim, J. J. and Mizel, S. B., *J. Immunol.* **122,** 2112, 1979.
26. Cebula, T. A., Hanson, D. F., Moore, D. M., and Murphy, P. A., *J. Lab. Clin. Med.* **94,** 95, 1979.
27. Glazer, A. N., DeLange, R. J., and Sigman, D. S. *In* "Laboratory Techniques in Biochemistry and Molecular Biology" (T. S. Work and E. Work, Eds.) pp. 1–56. American Elsevier, New York, 1976.
28. Gery, I., and Waksman, B. H., *J. Exp. Med.* **136,** 143, 1972.
29. Murphy, P. A., Hanson, D. F., Simon, P. L., Willoughby, W. F., and Windle, B. E., *In* "Mircrobiology, 1980" (D. Schlessinger, Ed.), pp. 158–161. American Society for Microbiology, Washington, D. C., 1980.
30. Sipe, J. D., and Rosenstreich, D. L., *In* "Cellular Functions in Immunity and Inflammation" (J. J. Oppenheim, D. L. Rosenstreich, and M. Potter, Eds.), American Elsevier/North-Holland, New York, in press, 1981.
31. Kampschmidt, R. F., Pulliam, L. A., and Upchurch, H. F., *J. Lab. Clin. Med.* **95,** 616, 1980.
32. Hanson, D. F., Murphy, P. A., and Windle, B. E. *J. Exp. Med.* **151,** 1360, 1980.
33. Kushner, I., and Feldmann, G., *J. Exp. Med.* **148,** 466, 1978.
34. Schultz, D., MacIntyre, S., and Kushner, I., *Ann. N.Y. Acad. Sci.* **349,** 387, 1980.
35. Gery, I., Gershon, R. K., and Waksman, B. H., *J. Exp. Med.* **136,** 128, 1972.
36. Shaw, J., Caplan, B., Paetkau, V., Pilarski, L. M., Delovitch, T. L. and McKenzie, I. F. C., *J. Immunol.* **124,** 2231, 1980.
37. Calderon, J., Kiely, J., Lefko, J. L., and Unanue, E. R., *J. Exp. Med.* **142,** 151, 1975.
38. Rosenstreich, D. L., Farrar, J. J., and Dougherty, S., *J. Immunol.* **116,** 131, 1976.
39. Mizel, S. B., and Ben-Zvi, A., *Cell. Immunol.* **54,** 382, 1980.
40. Oppenheim, J. J., Shneyour, A., and Kook, A. I., *J. Immunol.* **116,** 1466, 1976.
41. Mizel, S. B., Dayer, J., Krane, S. M., and Mergenhagen, S. E., *Proc. Nat. Acad. Sci. USA,* **78,** 2474, 1981.
42. Kluger, M. J., "Fever, Its Biology, Evolution, and Function" pp. 51–105. Princeton Univ. Press., Princeton, N.J., 1979
43. Bornstein, D. L., and Woods, J. W., *J. Exp. Med.* **130,** 707, 1969.
44. Weck, P., Appelson, S., May, L., and Stebbing, N., *J. Virol.,* in press, 1981.
45. Benson, M. D., and Aldo-Benson, M., *J. Immunol.* **122,** 2077, 1979.
46. Mortensen, R. F., Braun, D., and Gewurz, H., *Cell. Immunol.* **28,** 59, 1977.

CELLULAR IMMUNOLOGY **63**, 177–187 (1981)

Characterization of Suppressor T Cells Induced with the Thymus-Independent Antigen Polyvinylpyrrolidone Coupled to Syngeneic Cells[1]

VICTORIA FRASER[2] AND HELEN BRALEY-MULLEN[3]

Departments of Medicine and Microbiology, University of Missouri, Columbia, Missouri 65212

Received May 1, 1981; accepted May 28, 1981

CAF_1 mice injected iv with polyvinylpyrrolidone (PVP) coupled to syngeneic spleen cells (PVP-SC) and challenged several days later with 0.25 μg PVP produced fewer PVP-specific IgM plague-forming cells (PFC) than mice injected with Mock-SC. Both 10,000 and 360,000 MW PVP could induce unresponsiveness after coupling to SC. The unresponsiveness induced by PVP-SC was shown to be mediated, at least in part, by antigen-specific suppressor T cells (T_S). The PVP-specific T_S were I-J positive and belonged to the Lyt 1^+ 2^+ subset of T cells. The T_S precursors were sensitive to 20 mg/kg cyclophosphamide (Cy) and to antilymphocyte serum (ALS). Kinetics studies suggested that unresponsiveness induced by PVP-SC may be of two types since unresponsiveness in the intact animal appeared earlier and did not last as long as detectable T_S activity.

INTRODUCTION

Thymus-independent (TI)[4] antigens, such as Type III pneumococcal polysaccharide (S3), lipopolysaccharide (LPS), and polyvinylpyrrolidone (PVP) elicit similar antibody responses in both normal and athymic mice (1, 2). Thus TI antigens differ from thymus-dependent (TD) antigens in that they apparently do not require T helper cells (T_H) to elicit optimal antibody responses by B cells. Although TI antigens do not require T_H to induce antibody responses, there is considerable evidence which suggests that at least some TI antigens have the ability to activate T-cell subsets which are regulatory in nature such as amplifier T cells (T_A) and suppressor T cells (T_S) (3–6). However, most of the evidence that TI antigens can activate regulatory T cells is indirect. For example, elimination of T_S by treatment with antilymphocyte serum (ALS) results in enhanced antibody responses to S3 and PVP (3–6), while an appropriately timed injection of the T-cell mitogen, con-

[1] Supported by NIH Grant CA25054 and a grant from the University of Missouri Research Council.

[2] Recipient of a research scholarship from the Department of Medicine.

[3] Recipient of NIH Research Career Development Award AI00322.

[4] Abbreviations used: TI, thymus independent; S3, type III pneumococcal polysaccharide; LPS, lipopolysaccharide; PVP, polyvinylpyrrolidone; TD, thymus dependent; T_H, helper T cells; T_A, amplifier T cells, T_S, suppressor T cells; ALS, antilymphocyte serum; Con A, concanavalin A; PVP-SC, PVP-coupled spleen cells; PFC, plaque-forming cells; PVP-SRBC, PVP coupled to sheep red blood cells; Cy, cyclophosphamide; C′, complement.

0008-8749/81/130177-11$02.00/0

canavalin A (Con A) or pretreatment with low doses of these antigens results in depressed antibody responses presumably due to the activation of T_S (7–9). By contrast, there are only a few reports which have directly demonstrated that T_S activated by a TI antigen can suppress the antibody response to that antigen after transfer to normal recipients (10–13). Moreover, our laboratory has been consistently unable to demonstrate detectable T_S in the spleens of mice pretreated with widely varying doses of either S3 (9, 13) or PVP (unpublished results). Recently, however, we showed that S3-specific T_S could be induced by coupling S3 to syngeneic spleen cells (13). These studies suggested that this TI antigen activated a subset of T_S which differed in several ways from T_S which are activated by most TD antigens (13). To determine if the activation requirements and other properties of the S3-specific T_S were typical of T_S activated by other TI antigens, the studies described here were initiated in order to (i) determine if the TI antigen PVP could activate T_S which could be demonstrated after transfer to normal mice and (ii) to determine if T_S activated by PVP belonged to the same T-cell subset as the T_S activated by S3.

The method chosen to attempt to induce T_S with PVP was to couple the antigen to syngeneic spleen cells (PVP-SC) since antigen-coupled lymphoid cells have been reported to induce tolerance and/or T_S with many different types of antigens including proteins (14, 15), chemically defined haptens (16–20), polypeptide (21), and TI polysaccharide antigens (13, 22). The studies reported here indicate that PVP-SC induces a profound state of unresponsiveness in mice which is mediated in part by T_S. The T_S induced by PVP-SC were found to be different from those induced by S3-SC and also differed in some respects from T_S induced by most TD antigens. The requirements for the induction and maintenance of tolerance and T_S by PVP-SC and the characteristics of the PVP-specific T_S will be described herein.

MATERIALS AND METHODS

Mice. CAF_1 mice were obtained from the Jackson Laboratory, Bar Harbor, Maine. Female mice, 8–12 weeks old were used for all experiments.

Preparation of PVP-SC. Polyvinylpyrrolidone (PVP) with an average molecular weight of 10,000 or 360,000 was obtained from Aldrich Chemical Company, Milwaukee, Wisconsin. To prepare PVP-SC, various amounts of 10,000 or 360,000 MW PVP were added to 30×10^7 spleen cells in 6 ml 0.15 *M* NaCl. Five milliliters of 1 mg/ml chromic chloride in water was added and the cells were incubated 15 min at room temperature, centrifuged, and washed three times in 0.15 *M* NaCl. Control spleen cells (Mock-SC) were incubated with PVP, but no chromic chloride. A 0.5-ml volume of 5×10^7 PVP-SC or Mock-SC was injected into mice via the tail vein.

Antigens and immunization. The PVP used for immunization had an average molecular weight of 360,000. PVP was dissolved in phosphate-buffered saline (PBS) and injected ip at an optimal dose of 0.25 μg/mouse (6). Mice were immunized 3 or 7 days after injection of PVP-SC or immediately following the transfer of cells from tolerant mice into normal recipients. In some experiments mice were also immunized with 0.6 μg S3.

Cell transfer. Donor mice received 5×10^7 PVP-SC or Mock-SC on Day 0. At various times thereafter, spleens were removed and the spleen cells were washed and suspended in balanced salt solution (BSS). Cells were injected iv into recipient mice.

Anti-Thy 1.2 treatment of spleen cells. Spleen cells were depleted of T cells by *in vitro* treatment with anti-Thy-1.2 serum and complement as previously described (23, 24). Briefly, 10^7 spleen cells/ml were incubated on ice for 30 min with AKR anti-C_3H serum (final concentration 1:15). Agarose-absorbed guinea pig serum was added (25) and the mixture incubated for 1 hr at 37°C. Cells were washed twice with BSS and layered over fetal calf serum to remove dead cells (24) before iv transfer to normal mice. Previous studies have shown that this antiserum is specifically cytotoxic for T cells and has no effect on B cells (24).

Preparation of anti-Lyt and anti-I-J-antisera. Anti-Lyt 1.2 and anti-Lyt 2.2 sera were prepared according to the method of Shen *et al.* (26). Anti-Lyt 1.2 was prepared by immunizing C_3H/HeJ mice with C_3H.CE thymocytes and anti-Lyt 2.2 was prepared by immunizing $C_3H \times$ B62.1 F_1 mice with C^{57}Bl/6 thymocytes. The C_3H.CE and $C_3H \times$ B62.1 mice were bred in our animal facilities using breeding pairs obtained from Drs. Shen and Boyse, Sloan–Kettering Institute, New York. The other mice were obtained from Jackson Laboratories. Both antisera were cytotoxic for 85–90% of thymocytes (1:40–1:80 dilution) from appropriate Lyt 1.2- or 2.2-positive mouse strains and were not cytotoxic for Lyt 1.1 or 2.1 cells. The cytotoxic activity and specificity was comparable to that of the anti-Lyt 1.2 and 2.2 antisera marketed by Cedarlane Laboratories (Hicksville, N.Y., Mouse T-cell Function Test Kit). In addition the anti-Lyt 1.2 serum could eliminate T_H required for an *in vitro* response to SRBC but did not eliminate T_S activated by Con A or S3 whereas the anti-Lyt 2.2 serum did not affect T_H activity but did eliminate Con A- and S3-induced T_S (Braley-Mullen, unpublished results). Anti-I-J^k serum was prepared by immunizing Balb/c $\times$ B10.A(3R) F_1 mice with B10.A(5R) spleen cells and anti-I-J_b serum was prepared by immunizing B10.A(5R) mice with B10.A (3R) spleen cells. The B10.A(3R) and B10.A(5R) mice were bred in our animal facilities using breeding pairs obtained from Dr. Donald Shreffler, Washington University, St. Louis, Missouri, (B10.A(3R)) and Dr. Raymond Daynes, University of Utah, Salt Lake City (B10.A(5R)). These antisera had no detectable cytotoxic activity on spleen cells of the appropriate haplotype but they were effective in eliminating the activity of Con A- and S3-induced T_S when tested on spleen cells of the appropriate haplotype (Braley-Mullen, unpublished results).

Anti-Lyt and anti I-J treatment of spleen cells. Spleen cells of CAF_1 mice were depleted of I–J-positive cells by treatment with anti-I-J^k serum (final concentration 1.10) and agarose-absorbed guinea pig serum as a source of complement exactly as described above for treatment with anti-Thy 1.2. As a control, spleen cells were similarly treated with anti-I-J^b serum and complement. For depletion of cells with anti-Lyt antisera, spleen cells (10^7/ml) were incubated 30 min on ice with either anti-Lyt 1.2 or anti-Lyt 2.2 (final concentration 1:10). Cells were centrifuged then resuspended in a 1:12 dilution of low-toxicity rabbit complement (Cedarlane Laboratories) and incubated at 37°C for 45–60 min. Cells were washed twice and injected iv to normal CAF_1 mice. Control cells were treated with complement only.

Plaque-forming-cell (PFC) assay. The number of spleen cells producing antibody specific for PVP was determined 5 days after immunization as previously described (23, 27). Sheep red blood cells (SRBC) coated with PVP (6) were used as indicator cells. To sensitize SRBC with PVP, SRBC were washed three times in PBS and adjusted to 5%. Equal volumes of 5% SRBC and 0.05 mg/ml tannic acid in PBS were incubated at room temperature for 15 min. The PVP-SRBC were washed three times in PBS and a 5% suspension was prepared for use in the plaque assay. Results are expressed herein as PFC/spleen, but results would not differ if they were expressed as PFC/10^6 cells.

Cyclophosphamide (Cy) treatment. Cy (Mead Johnson and Co., Evansville, Ind.) was diluted in distilled water. Mice received 20 mg/kg Cy iv 2 days before injection of PVP-SC.

Antilymphocyte Serum (ALS) treatment. ALS (Microbiological Associates, Bethesda, Md., Lot 3-9510) was injected ip (0.5 ml/mouse) 2 days before injection of PVP-SC.

Experiments. Each of the experiments reported here was repeated two or three times and similar results were obtained each time.

RESULTS

Induction of Tolerance with PVP-SC

To determine whether PVP-SC could induce unresponsiveness, CAF_1 mice were given 5×10^7 PVP-SC or Mock-SC coupled with either the 10,000 or 360,000 MW PVP iv 3 days prior to immunization with 0.25 μg PVP. As seen in Table 1, the IgM response to PVP was suppressed in mice which were previously injected with either 10,000 or 360,000 MW PVP coupled to SC. Mice receiving Mock-SC (incubated with PVP in the absence of coupling agent) (lines 2 and 7 Table 1) responded similarly to mice which received no cells prior to immunization (line 1, Table 1). When PVP-SC were prepared with various amounts of PVP added per 3×10^8 spleen cells, tolerance was induced with as little as 0.05 μg 10,000 MW PVP per 3×10^8 SC, whereas a much higher amount of 360,000 MW PVP (50 μg/3×10^8 cells) was required for tolerance induction (Table 1). Unless indicated

TABLE 1

Induction of Tolerance with PVP-SC[a]

Pretreatment (μg)	Molecular weight of PVP	PVP-specific IgM PFC/spleen
None	—	11,883 ± 2062
Mock-SC (50)	10,000	14,200 ± 1965
PVP-SC (50)	10,000	3,566 ± 1893
PVP-SC (0.5)	10,000	2,800 ± 603
PVP-SC (0.05)	10,000	3,516 ± 904
PVP-SC (0.005)	10,000	9,708 ± 1626
Mock-SC (50)	360,000	10,708 ± 480
PVP-SC (50)	360,000	1,450 ± 326
PVP-SC (5)	360,000	11,566 ± 950

[a] Mice were given 5×10^7 SC coupled with different amounts of PVP. Three days later they were immunized with 0.25 μg PVP and IgM PFC were determined 5 days later. Values shown are mean PFC/Spleen ± SEM of four mice/group.

[b] The amounts of PVP refer to the amount added to 3×10^8 spleen cells. Mock-SC were treated with PVP in the absence of coupling agent.

otherwise, in all experiments shown below, spleen cells were coupled with 0.5 μg 10,000 MW PVP per 3×10^8 SC since this amount consistently induced a reproducible degree of tolerance.

Induction of Suppressor T Cells with PVP-SC

To determine if tolerance induced by PVP-SC could be transferred to normal recipients, mice were injected with PVP-SC or Mock-SC. Seven days later spleen cells from these mice were transferred to normal syngeneic recipients which were then immunized with PVP. Recipients of 10^8 or 10^7 cells from tolerant donors had much lower PFC responses compared to recipients of the same numbers of spleen cells from control mice (Table 2). The tolerant control mice which received PVP-SC and were immunized 7 days later with PVP also had lower PFC responses. In other studies (not shown) we found that as few as 2×10^6 spleen cells from tolerant donors could significantly suppress the PVP response of normal mice (about 50% suppression) whereas lower numbers of cells, i.e., 4×10^5, were not effective. In all studies described below, recipient mice received 2 to 4×10^7 tolerant cells which consistently resulted in maximal suppression of the PVP response. To determine if T cells were required for the transfer of suppression, T cells were eliminated from tolerant and control cell suspensions by treatment with anti-Thy 1.2 prior to cell transfer (Fig. 1). Mice receiving complement-treated spleen cells from tolerant donors again had PFC responses lower than those of mice receiving cells from normal donors. When the spleen cells were treated with anti-Thy 1.2 and complement, suppression was no longer observed. Anti-Thy 1 treatment of the cells from control (Mock) mice had no effect. These results indicate that PVP-SC can activate T_S. The results in Fig. 1 also show that both 10,000 and 360,000 MW PVP could activate T_S although more of the high-molecular-weight PVP (50 $\mu g/3 \times 10^8$ cells) had to be coupled to SC to induce both T_S (Fig. 1) and tolerance (Table 1).

Specificity of Suppressor Cells

To determine if the suppressor cells induced by PVP-SC were antigen specific in their action, recipients of 4×10^7 spleen cells from tolerant or control donors

TABLE 2

Effect of Tolerant Spleen Cells on the PVP Response[a]

Number of cells transferred	PVP-specific IgM PFC/spleen
10^8 PVP-SC	3,187 ± 826
10^8 Mock-SC	33,687 ± 6,119
10^7 PVP-SC	2,598 ± 652
10^7 Mock-SC	18,237 ± 1,050
No cell transfer (tolerant control)	5,587 ± 597

[a] CAF_1 mice were injected with PVP-SC or Mock-SC (0.5 μg PVP/3×10^8 SC). Seven days later spleen cells from these donor mice were transferred to normal recipients which were immunized with 0.25 μg PVP. PFC were determined 5 days later. The tolerant controls received PVP-SC and were immunized on Day 7 with the other mice. Values are mean PFC ± SEM of four mice/group.

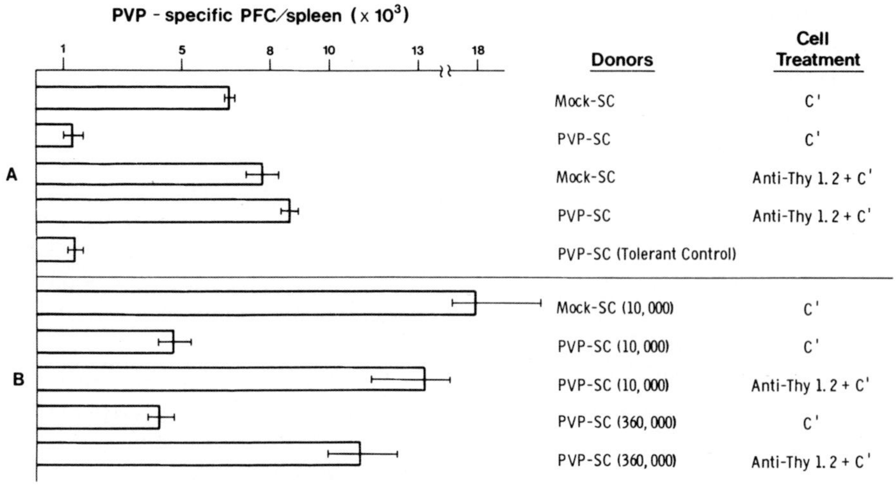

FIG. 1. Activation of suppressor T cells with PVP-SC. Donor CAF_1 mice were given 5×10^7 Mock-SC or PVP-SC iv (The PVP-SC were prepared with 10,000 MW PVP (A) or with either 10,000 or 360,000 MW PVP (B) as indicated.) Seven days later spleen cells from donor mice were treated with anti-Thy 1.2 and complement or with complement alone and transferred iv to normal CAF_1 mice (4×10^7 cells/recipient). All recipients were immunized with 0.25 μg PVP and PFC were determined 7 days later. The last group in A indicates that the donors of the suppressor cells were tolerant, i.e., these mice were given PVP-SC and immunized 7 days later with 0.25 μg PVP. Values shown are the mean PVP-specific IgM PFC/spleen of four mice/group.

were immunized simultaneously with 0.6 μg Type III pneumococcal polysaccharide (S3) and 0.25 μg PVP (both TI antigens). Mice receiving spleen cells from tolerant donors and tolerant control mice immunized with PVP-SC produced fewer PVP-specific PFC than mice receiving control spleen cells (Table 3). All groups responded similarly to S3, indicating that the suppressor cells induced by PVP-SC were antigen specific at the effector stage.

Kinetics of Tolerance and Suppressor Cell Induction.

When mice were injected with PVP-SC, tolerance was detected 3 days later (Table 1). In order to determine whether T_S could also be detected as early as 3

TABLE 3

Specificity of Tolerance Induced by PVP-SC[a]

Cells transferred	PVP IgM PFC/spleen	S3 IgM PFC/spleen
4×10^7 Mock-SC	25,700 ± 4,216	7,300 ± 1,189
4×10^7 PVP-SC	9,466 ± 940	7,633 ± 841
No cell transfer (negative control)	9,325 ± 1,311	9,900 ± 696

[a] CAF_1 cells were transferred from tolerant or control donors as previously described. Recipient mice were immunized with both 0.25 μg PVP and 0.6 μg S3. PFC were determined 5 days later. Values are mean PFC/spleen ± SEM of four mice/group.

TABLE 4

Kinetics of Tolerance and Suppressor Cell Induction[a]

Day of cell transfer	Cells transferred		
	Mock-SC	PVP-SC	None
3	25,850 ± 1,347	15,720 ± 3,927	5,633 ± 530
4	12,600 ± 1,484	7,150 ± 1,643	5,200 ± 404
7	15,350 ± 1,762	6,675 ± 614	6,400 ± 1,594
14	12,175 ± 256	4,200 ± 565	6,425 ± 432
22	15,200 ± 1,877	7,050 ± 1,317	16,933 ± 1,317

[a] CAF_1 mice were given 5×10^7 PVP-SC or Mock-SC and 4×10^7 spleen cells were transferred to normal recipients at various times thereafter. Groups designated "none" received PVP-SC and were immunized along with the spleen cell recipients at the indicated interval with 0.25 μg PVP. Values given are the mean PFC/spleen ± SEM of four mice/group determined 5 days after immunization.

days after injection of PVP-SC, CAF_1 mice were given 5×10^7 PVP-SC and their spleen cells were transferred to normal recipients 3, 4, 7, 14, or 22 days later (Table 4). Mice were maximally tolerant 3 days after the injection of PVP-SC but suppressor cells could not be detected until 4–7 days after injection of PVP-SC. On Days 7 and 14 after the injection of PVP-SC, donor mice were still tolerant and T_S activity was maximal. Surprisingly, by Day 22 mice injected with PVP-SC and challenged with PVP no longer appeared tolerant but cells from these mice could still suppress the PVP response of normal mice. These results suggest that tolerance induced by PVP-SC is of two types, i.e., tolerance mediated by T_S and a second type (? clonal inhibition) which appears earlier and does not last as long as T_S activity.

Characterization of PVP-Specific T_S

Having demonstrated that PVP-SC could induce T_S it was of interest to determine the T-cell subclass to which they belong. The following experiments were therefore designed to begin to determine the T-cell subclass of the PVP-specific T_S.

I-J Antigens

To determine if the PVP-specific T_S had surface antigens coded for by the I-J subregion of the major histocompatibility complex, spleen cells from tolerant CAF_1 ($I\text{-}J^k$) mice were treated with anti-$I\text{-}J^k$ serum (Balb/c × 3R anti-5R) and complement before transfer (see Materials and Methods). As controls other aliquots of tolerant spleen were treated with anti-$I\text{-}J^b$ and complement or with anti-Thy 1.2 and complement (Fig. 2). Recipients of untreated or anti-$I\text{-}J^b$-treated tolerant cells (groups B and D) had suppressed responses relative to those of recipients of cells from Mock-SC-injected donors (group A). Suppression was abrogated when cells were treated with either anti-Thy 1.2 (group E) or anti-$I\text{-}J^k$ (group C) and complement indicating that the T_S are I-J positive.

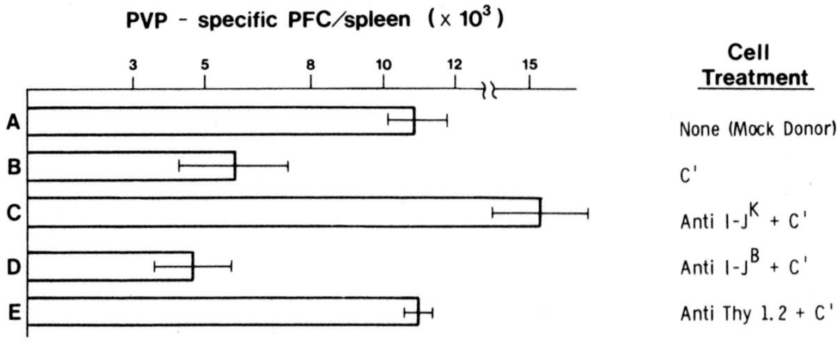

FIG. 2. Effect of anti-I-J serum on PVP-specific T_S. The experimental design is identical to that described in Fig. 1 except that spleen cells from PVP-SC tolerant CAF_1 donors were treated as indicated with complement alone or anti-I-J^k, anti-I-J^b or anti-Thy 1.2 and complement before transfer to normal recipients. Values shown are mean PVP-specific IgM PFC/spleen ± SEM of four mice/group.

Lyt Antigens

Similar experiments were done to determine the Lyt phenotype of the PVP-specific T_S. Spleen cells from tolerant mice were untreated or treated with complement alone, or were treated with anti-Thy 1.2., anti-Lyt 1.2, or anti-Lyt 2.2 and complement before transfer to normal recipients (Fig. 3). PFC responses were reduced compared to controls (group A) when tolerant cells were untreated or treated with complement alone (groups B and C). Suppression was abolished when tolerant cells were treated with anti-Thy 1.2, anti-Lyt 1.2, or anti-Lyt 2.2 (groups D, E, and G) suggesting that the T_S belong to the Lyt 1^+2^+ subclass. In order to prove that suppression was mediated by a Lyt 1^+2^+ T cell rather than a Lyt 1^+ *and* a Lyt 2^+ T cell, cells treated with anti-Lyt 1.2 were combined with cells treated with anti-Lyt 2.2 before transfer and again suppression was eliminated (group F). Thus suppression apparently is mediated by Lyt 1^+2^+ T cells and not by the interaction of Lyt 1^+2^- and Lyt 1^-2^+ T cells.

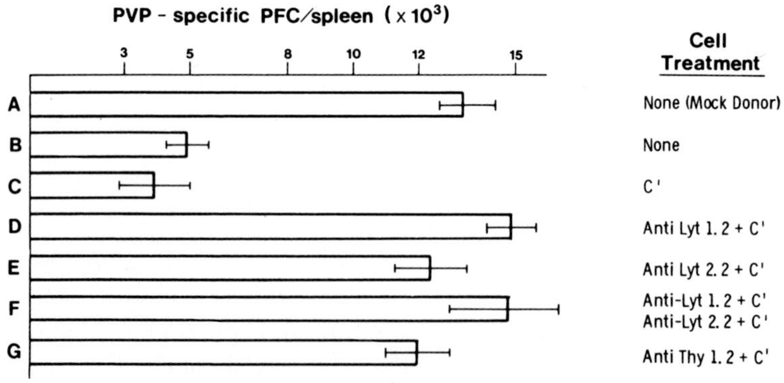

FIG. 3. Effect of anti-Lyt antisera on PVP-specific T_S. The experimental design is as described in Fig. 1. Spleen cells from tolerant CAF_1 donors were treated as indicated before transfer to normal recipients. Group F recipients received equal numbers of a cell aliquot treated with anti-Lyt 1.2 + C′ and a cell aliquot treated with anti-Lyt 2.2 + C′. Values shown are mean PVP-specific IgM PFC/spleen ± SEM of four mice/group.

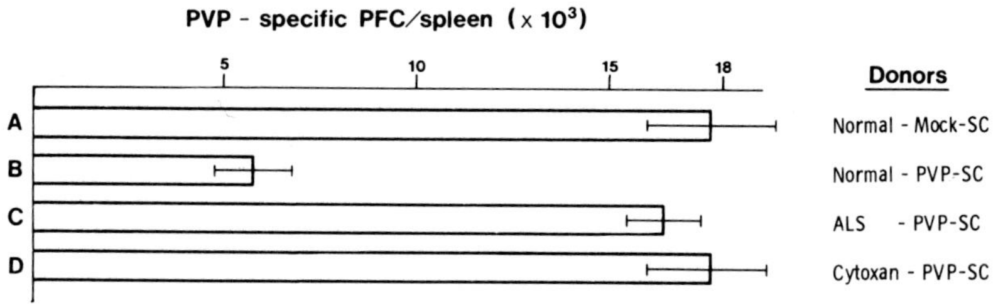

FIG. 4. Effect of ALS or cyclophosphamide (Cy) on PVP-specific T_S precursors. Groups of donor CAF_1 mice were given 0.5 ml ALS (C) or 20 mg/kg Cy (D) 2 days before injection of 5×10^7 PVP-SC. Seven days later cells from these mice or from normal mice were transferred (4×10^7 cells/recipient) to CAF_1 mice which were immunized with 0.25 μg PVP. Values shown are the mean PFC/spleen ± SEM of four mice/group.

Sensitivity to Cy and ALS

In order to determine whether the precursors of the T_S were sensitive or resistant to Cy and/or ALS, donor mice were injected with 20 mg/kg Cy or 0.5 ml ALS 2 days before injection of PVP-SC. Seven days later cells from these mice or from normal mice given PVP-SC or Mock-SC were transferred to normal recipients. As shown in Fig. 4, spleen cells from normal mice injected with PVP-SC (group B) suppressed the PVP response of recipient mice. By contrast, mice injected with Cy or ALS (groups C and D) 2 days before receiving PVP-SC did not have detectable T_S. These results indicate that the precursor of the PVP-specific T_S is sensitive to both Cy and ALS.

DISCUSSION

The iv injection of antigens coupled to syngeneic lymphoid cells often results in specific immunologic unresponsiveness which is mediated, at least in part, by antigen-specific T_S (13–22). In previous studies, we found that the TI antigen S3 coupled to syngeneic spleen cells (S3-SC) also induced tolerance in mice which was mediated by T_S (13). Because these studies suggested that the S3-specific T_S had unusual properties and activation requirements (13), the present study was undertaken in order to determine whether another TI antigen, PVP, could also activate T_S when coupled to spleen cells and if so, whether these T_S could exhibit the same properties as the T_S activated by the antigen S3.

The results presented here clearly indicate that PVP-SC can induce specific unresponsiveness in mice (Table 1). Unresponsiveness was transferrable (Table 2) and was mediated by antigen-specific T_S (Table 3 and Fig. 1). Both 10,000 and 360,000 MW PVP could induce tolerance and activate T_S when coupled to SC (Fig. 1, Table 1) although, as shown previously (10), the lower-molecular-weight antigen was somewhat more efficient in terms of the amount of antigen required (Table 1 and Figure 1).

It is of interest that both the activation requirements and cell surface properties of the T_S induced by PVP-SC were found to be markedly different from the T_S induced by S3-SC (13). For example, both the iv injection of S3-SC and an *in vitro* subculture step were required for activation of S3-specific T_S (13) whereas only a single iv injection of PVP-SC sufficed to induce PVP-specific T_S (Fig. 1). Moreover, relatively large numbers of T_S induced by PVP-SC (ca. 10^7 cells/recipient) were needed to suppress the antibody response to PVP (Table 2) whereas *only* low numbers of cells (10^5–10^6/recipient) were able to suppress the S3 response (13). As might be anticipated from the differences noted above, the T_S induced by PVP-SC also were found to belong to a different T cell subset from the T_S induced by S3-SC. Thus the PVP-specific T_S apparently arise from Cy - and ALS-sensitive precursors (Figure 4) and the T_S are I-J+ (Figure 2) and Lyt 1^+2^+ (Figure 3). By contrast, the S3-specific T_S arise from Cy-resistant, ALS-sensitive precursors, they are also I-J+ but are Lyt 1^-2^+ (H. Braley-Mullen, unpublished results). These observations therefore suggest that TI antigens coupled to lymphoid cells can activate different T-cell subsets which have the same apparent function, namely suppression of the antigen-specific primary IgM response. Similarly, multiple T_S subsets which regulate hapten-specific delayed hypersensitivity responses can be activated by hapten-coupled lymphoid cells (28, 29). Clearly, further studies are required to determine the conditions which favor activation of a particular T_S subset and to determine whether different subsets of T_S might suppress TI antibody responses by different mechanisms.

The finding that the T_S induced by PVP-SC were of the Lyt 1^+2^+ phenotype (Fig. 3) suggests that they may be similar to T_{S1} cells described by others (28). If this is the case, it is possible that these cells are not the actual effector T_S but instead they may act on or activate other T cells which then are the final effector cells for suppression of the antibody response (30, 31). However, Jandinski and Scott (32) showed that Lyt 1^+2^+ T_S induced by haptenated SC could suppress the *in vitro* antibody response of T-depleted spleen cells stimulated by a TI antigen. This observation suggests that Lyt 1^+2^+ T_S might also be capable of behaving as actual T_S effectors by directly inhibiting the responding B cell. Studies are currently in progress to determine whether the T_S induced by PVP-SC act by inducing effector T_S in the recipients (30, 31) or whether they act directly on the PVP-specific B cell.

Finally, the studies presented here indicate that PVP-SC induces two types of tolerance, only one of which is transferrable. These two types of tolerance were distinguished by kinetics studies (Table 4) and in some respects our results are similar to those reported by others (18, 33). In agreement with previous reports (18, 33) we found that tolerance in the intact animal was well established by 3 days after injection of PVP-SC whereas T_S could not be detected until 4–7 days after injection of PVP-SC (Table 4). However, tolerance in other systems has been reported to persist for long periods of time (14, 18, 20, 22) whereas T_S may only be detectable for 7–14 days (18). By contrast, we have repeatedly observed that tolerance in the intact animal is detectable for only about 14 days following the injection of PVP-SC whereas T_S are still detectable at 22 days (the latest time tested) (Table 4). At present we have no explanation for this observation although several possibilities can be suggested. As noted above, since the T_S induced by PVP-SC are Lyt 1^+2^+ (Fig. 3) they may be inducer or T_{S1} cells rather than the actual T_S effectors (28, 30, 31). If so, it is possible that the target of the T_S inducer has decayed or been exhausted in the original host so that tolerance is no longer observed. The target of the inducer T_S would, however, be present in the normal recipient since suppression occurs upon transfer. Alternatively, if T_S induced by

PVP-SC act directly on B cells to mediate suppression, the initial injection of PVP-SC might induce some changes in B cells such that with time they become resistant to suppression. Definition of the target and mechanism of action of the Lyt $1^{+}2^{+}$ T_S induced by PVP-SC should help clarify the reasons for the early loss of tolerance observed in this system.

ACKNOWLEDGMENTS

The authors thank Sue Monteer for typing this manuscript.

REFERENCES

1. Basten, A., and Howard, J. G., *Contemp. Top. Immunobiol.* **2,** 265, 1973.
2. Anderson B., and Blomgren H., *Cell. Immunol.* **2,** 411, 1971.
3. Braley-Mullen, H., *J. Immunol.* **113,** 1909, 1974.
4. Baker, P. J., Reed, N. D., Stashak, P. W., Amsbaugh, D. F., and Prescott, B., *J. Exp. Med.* **137,** 14, 1973.
5. Baker, P. J., Stashak, P. W., Amsbaugh, D. F., Prescott, B., and Barth, R. F., *J. Immunol.* **105,** 1581, 1970.
6. Lake, J. P., and Reed, N. D., *Cell. Immunol.* **21,** 264, 1976.
7. Markham, R. B., Reed, N. D., Stashak, P. W., Prescott, B., Amsbaugh, D. F., and Baker, P. J., *J. Immunol.* **118,** 952, 1977.
8. Baker, P. J., Stashak, P. W., Amsbaugh, D. F., and Prescott, B., *J. Immunol.* **112,** 2020, 1974.
9. Braley-Mullen, H., *Cell. Immunol.* **37,** 77, 1978.
10. Inaba, K., and Muramatsu, S., *Cell. Immunol.* **39,** 260, 1978.
11. Inaba, K., and Muramatsu, S., *Cell. Immunol.* **39,** 276, 1978.
12. Hammerling, G. J., Black, S. J., Segal, S., and Eichmann, K., *In* "Leukocyte Membrane Determinants Regulating Immune Reactivity" (V. R. Eijsvoogel, D. Roos, and W. P. Zeislemaker, Eds.) p. 327. Academic Press, New York, 1976.
13. Braley-Mullen, H., *J. Immunol.* **125,** 1849, 1980.
14. Sherr, D. H., Cheung, N. K., Heghinian, K. M., Benacerraf, B., and Dorf, M. E., *J. Immunol.* **122,** 1899, 1979.
15. Miller, S. D., Wetzig, R. P., Claman, H. N., *J. Exp. Med.* **149,** 758, 1979.
16. Battisto, J. R., and Bloom, B. R., *Nature (London)* **212,** 156, 1966.
17. Greene, M. I., Sugimoto, M., and Benacerraf, B., *J. Immunol.* **120,** 1604, 1978.
18. Miller, S. D., Sy, M. S., and Claman, H. N., *Eur. J. Immunol.* **7,** 165, 1977.
19. Scott, D. W., *Cell. Immunol.* **37,** 327, 1978.
20. Moody, C. E., Innes, J. B., Siskind, G. W., and Weksler, M. E., *J. Immunol.* **120,** 844, 1978.
21. Cheung, N. K., Sherr, D. H., Heghininian, K. M., Benacerraf, B., and Dorf, M. E., *J. Exp. Med.* **148,** 1539, 1978.
22. Braley-Mullen, H., *Cell. Immunol.* **52,** 132, 1980.
23. Lite, H. S., and Braley-Mullen, H., *J. Immunol.* **126,** 928, 1981.
24. Braley-Mullen, H., *Eur. J. Immunol.* **7,** 775, 1977.
25. Cohen, A., and Schlesinger, M., *Transplantation* **10,** 130, 1970.
26. Shen, F. W., Boyse, E. A., and Cantor, H., *Immunogenetics* **2,** 591, 1975.
27. Braley-Mullen, H., *J. Immunol.* **115,** 1194, 1975.
28. Germain, R. N., and Benacerraf, B., *Scand. J. Immunol.* **13,** 1, 1981.
29. Al-Adra, A. R., Pilarski, L. M., and McKenzie, I. F. C., *Immunogenetics* **10,** 521, 1980.
30. Eardley, D. D., Hugenberger, L., McVay-Boudreau, L., Shen, F. W., Gershon, R. K., and Cantor, H., *J. Exp. Med.* **147,** 1106, 1978.
31. Tada, T., *In* "Regulation of the Immune System" (E. Sercarz and L. Herzenberg, Eds.), p. 345. Academic Press, New York, 1977.
32. Jandinski, J. J., and Scott, D. W., *J. Immunol.* **123,** 2447, 1979.
33. Sherr, D. H., Heghinian, K. M., Benacerraf, B., and Dorf, M. E., *J. Immunol.* **123,** 2682, 1979.

CELLULAR IMMUNOLOGY **63**, 188–192 (1981)

SHORT COMMUNICATIONS

Adoptive Transfer of Delayed-Type Hypersensitivity to Sendai Virus

II. Different Modes of Antigen Presentation Determine *K,D*-Region or *I*-Region Restriction of T Cells Mediating Delayed-Type Hypersensitivity to Sendai Virus

H. C. J. ERTL[1,2]

Department of Microbiology, John Curtin School of Medical Research, Australian National University, Canberra, A.C.T. 2601, Australia

Received February 6, 1981; accepted May 21, 1981

Requirements for antigen presentation for *in vitro* stimulation of two subpopulations of Td lymphocytes were investigated. One subset was *K,D*-region-restricted and required infection or fusion of virus particles with stimulator cells for induction. The other subpopulation was *I*-region-restricted and required presentation of antigen by adherent cells (presumably macrophages). Presentation of antigen on Ia antigen positive stimulator cells (LPS blasts) failed to lead to stimulation of *I*-region-restricted T lymphocytes, thus suggesting that phagoctyosis and processing of antigen rather than association of viral antigens via fusion or infection was required for stimulation of these T lymphocytes.

INTRODUCTION

Murine T lymphocytes directed against viral antigens exhibit H-2 restriction (1). Cytolytic T cells (Tc) are restricted by *K*- or *D*-region gene products (1, 2), whereas most mediators (Td) of delayed-type hypersensitivity (DTH)[3] are restricted by *I*-region gene products (3, 4). However, in the case of certain viruses, Td cells also appear to be *K,D*-region-restricted (5, 6). Since these Td cells have the same Lyt phenotype (6), and H-2 fine restriction specificity as Tc cells (7), it seems likely that DTH reations can be mediated *in vivo* by antiviral Tc lymphocytes.

The intriguing aspect of these observations is that although virsuses such as lymphocytic choriomeningitis (LCM) virus which cause stimulation of *K,D*-region-restricted Tc and Td cells *in vivo* are known to infect cells which display abundant *I*-region-encoded (Ia) antigens (e.g., macrophages), this does not lead to detectable induction of *I*-region-restricted Td lymphocytes (5). This paradox has been inves-

[1] Recipient of a postdoctoral fellowship from the German Research Foundation, Grant 13-Er 9612.

[2] Present address: Harvard Medical School, Department of Pathology, 25 Shattuck Street, Boston, MA 02115.

[3] Abbreviations used: DTH, delayed-type hypersenitivity; HAU, hemagglutinating units; LCM virus, lymphocytic choriomeningitis virus; LPS, lipopolysaccharide; PBS, phosphate-buffered saline; Tc, cytolytic T cell; Td, T cell which mediates a DTH reaction; SV, Sendai virus; SV-F$^+$, fusion-positive Sendai virus, SV-F$^-$, fusion-negative Sendai virus.

0008-8749/81/130188-05$02.00/0

tigated using Sendai virus (SV), which can be used to stimulate *K,D*- and *I*-region-restricted subsets of Td cells *in vivo* (6). *In vitro* sensitization was employed to define the precise conditions for activation of these different Td-cell classes.

MATERIALS AND METHODS

Animals. Mice were bred at the John Curtin School of Medical Research in Canberra and used at the age of 8–12 weeks.

Viruses. Fusion-positive (SV-F^+) and fusion-negative (SV-F^-) Sendai viruses were prepared, titrated, inactivated, and purified as described in detail elsewhere (6).

In vitro generation of Td lymphocytes. The method described for generation of cytolytic T lymphocytes was employed (8). Briefly, 1×10^8 spleen lymphocytes of mice infected 3–8 weeks previously with SV-F^+ were restimulated *in vitro* for 5 days with 1×10^7 syngeneic stimulator cells, incubated for 2 hr with virus. P815 cells and LPS blasts were irradiated with 2000 rad before incubation with virus. Adherent cells present in spleen cell or LPS–blast preparations were removed by incubation in plastic tissue flasks at 37°C for 2 hr. Effector cells were purified over Ficoll–Isopaque gradient to remove erythrocytes and dead cells.

Adoptive transfer of DTH. Mice were inoculated with $5\text{–}10 \times 10^3$ HAU SV in 40 μl PBS into the left and 40 μl PBS into the right footpad. Three hours later, 2×10^6 effector cells, which had been depleted of adherent cells, were injected into the left footpad, the same volume of PBS was injected into the right footpad or into both footpads of control mice. Footpad thickness was measured 24 hr later. Percentage increase in footpad thickness was calculated using the formula:

$$\frac{\text{thickness of left footpad} - \text{thickness of right footpad}}{\text{thickness of right footpad}} \times 100.$$

RESULTS AND DISCUSSION

Two distinct subsets of T lymphocytes, which mediate a DTH reaction *in vivo* against SV antigens, could be activated *in vitro* by using different virus preparations (SV-F^+ vs SV-F^-, Table 1) or different methods of antigen presentation (Table 2).

SV infection of mice caused stimulation of two subpopulations of Td lymphocytes—one Lyt $1^{(-)}2^+$ and *K,D*-region-restricted, the other Lyt 1^+2^- and *IA*-region-restricted (6) which could be restimulated *in vitro* by using SV-F^+ as antigenic stimulus. SV-F^- restimulated *I*-region-restricted Td cells but failed to induce detectable levels of *K,D*-region-restricted Td effector lymphocytes (Table 1). As has been shown previously for *in vitro*-induced Td lymphocytes, both subsets of *in vitro*-stimulated effector lymphocytes responded to high concentrations of the uv-light-inactivated SV preparation upon transfer into the footpad. This virus preparation contains intact fusion-positive as well as defective fusion-negative virus particles. *K,D*-region restricted Td lymphocytes responded as well to low concentrations of infectious SV. Presumably this virus preparation can only reach the antigenic threshold for recognition by Td lymphocytes through display of newly synthesized

TABLE 1

H-2 Restriction of *in Vitro* Generated Td Lymphocytes

Virus used for induction[a]	Donor	Recipient	H-2 region shared by donor and recipient	Virus used for challenge[b]: 40 HAU inf.SV	4000 HAU uv-irradiated SV	4000 HAU cell-grown SV
				Percentage increase in footpad thickness ± SD		
SV-F$^+$	B10.AQR	CBA/H	IA,IB	4.0 ± 0.2	28.9 ± 8.0	30.4 ± 5.3
SV-F$^-$	B10.AQR	CBA/H	IA,IB	n.t.[c]	30.1 ± 5.1	n.t.
SV-F$^+$	A.TL	A.TH	K,D	34.8 ± 3.7	38.3 ± 1.1	4.3 ± 0.2
SV-F$^-$	A.TL	A.TH	K,D	n.t.	3.3 ± 3.3	n.t.
SV-F$^+$	C57Bl/6	BALB/c	—	n.t.	3.3 ± 3.3	n.t.
	—[d]	CBA/H		0.0 ± 0.0	3.3 ± 3.3	0.0 ± 0.0

[a] SV-F$^+$—1000 HAU infectious Sendai virus/10^7 stimulator cells; SV-F$^-$—4000 HAU, uv-light-inactivated, cell-grown, fusion-negative Sendai virus/10^7 stimulator cells.
[b] Virus injected into the footpad.
[c] n.t., not tested.
[d] Control mice received virus only.

antigens on the surface of infected cells. *I*-Region-restricted Td lymphocytes on the other hand responded to SV-F$^-$. This method, i.e., use of different virus preparations to elicit a DTH reaction in the foot, was employed in the next set of

TABLE 2

Requirement for Antigen Presentation for Stimulation of *K,D*- or *I*-Region-Restricted Td Lymphocytes

Conditions for restimulation	Percentage increase in footpad thickness ± SD: *K,D*-region-restricted response[a]	*I*-region-restricted response[b]
Peritoneal adherent cells, SV-F^{-c}	2.1 ± 3.1	33.3 ± 3.3
Peritoneal adherent cells, SV-F^{+d}	16.7 ± 3.3	39.9 ± 5.3
Splenocytes, SV-F^{-e}	9.8 ± 5.4	0.0 ± 0.0
Splenocytes, SV-F^{+e}	36.6 ± 5.9	4.1 ± 2.9
P815 tumor cells, SV-F^{+e}	34.3 ± 3.0	1.9 ± 2.7
LPS blasts, SV-F^{+e}	44.7 ± 1.9	0.0 ± 0.0
Control[f]	3.5 ± 3.5	0.0 ± 0.0

Note. BALB/c mice were used throughout the experiment.
[a] *K,D*-region-restricted response was elicited with 40 HAU infectious virus.
[b] *I*-region-restricted response was elicited with 4000 HAU cell-grown virus.
[c] SV-F$^-$—4000 HAU uv-light-inactivated fusion-negative virus/10^7 stimulator cells.
[d] SV-F$^+$—1000 HAU uv-light-inactivated virus/10^7 stimulator cells.
[e] Adherent cells were removed from responder cells, splenocytes, and LPS–blast preparation.
[f] Control mice received virus only.

experiments to distinguish between *K,D*- and *I*-region-restricted Td lymphocytes, restimulated *in vitro* by SV-F$^+$ or SV-F$^-$ presented by various stimulator cells (Table 2). The *K,D*-region-restricted subset could be stimulated by a variety of cell types (peritoneal adherent cells, splenocytes, tumor cells or LPS blasts), which displayed SV antigen either after infection or fusion of virus particles. The *I*-region-restricted subset could only be stimulated by SV antigens in association with plastic adherent cells (presumably macrophages) from spleen or peritoneal cavity.

These results strongly suggest that separate pathways of viral antigen presentation by stimulator cells lead to *K,D*-region restriction on one hand and *I*-region restriction on the other. Two alternative mechanisms apparently lead to viral antigen display associated with *K,D* antigens. First, the viral genome can induce synthesis of viral neoantigens which, upon insertion into the cell surface membrane *from within*, can associate with *K*- or *D*-region-encoded molecules. Second, viral proteins present in the virion envelope may, after fusion with the cell surface *from without*, become similarly associated with *K,D* molecules. In experiments presented here, there was little or no detectable functional association of SV proteins with Ia antigens by either of these pathways, at least as determined by stimulation of Td effector cells. The only demonstrable pathway to SV antigen display in association with Ia antigens in a form able to efficiently induce Td effector cells seemed to be through phagocytosis and processing by macrophages. For example, LPS blasts, which display Ia antigens, did not stimulate *I*-region-restricted Td cells after fusion with SV, though they were good stimulator cells for *K,D*-region-restricted T cells. Failure to stimulate *I*-region-restricted T cells due to lack of macrophage-secreted factors thus seems unlikely, especially as high levels of "costimulator activity" could be demonstrated in these cultures (K. J. Lafferty and H. C. J. Ertl, unpublished data).

The pathways of stimulation of different subsets of T lymphocytes described above seems biologically sensible. The antiviral protective function of *K,D*-region-restricted T cells is likely to be dependent on their ability to lyse infected tissue cells at an early stage after infection before infective virus progeny are produced (9, 10). Lysis of macrophages, which had phagocytized, processed, and displayed antigens of noninfectious virus particles, or antigens of nonobligatory intracellular parasites such as certain bacteria, would be wasteful. In the latter case, if macrophages contained living bacteria, lysis would be pointless because the bacteria could multiply after liberation from lysed macrophages.

It has been reported (11) that *I*-region-restricted T cells seem to be more important than *K,D*-region-restricted T cells in defense against bacterial infection, presumably because *I*-region-restricted cells can recruit and activate macrophages.

ACKNOWLEDGMENTS

I wish to thank Mr. R. Tha Hla for excellent technical help. My special thanks to Dr. R. V. Blanden for stimulating discussions and criticisms and revision of the manuscript.

REFERENCES

1. Zinkernagel, R. M., and Doherty, P. C., *Nature (London)* **278,** 701, 1974.
2. Schrader, J. W., and Edelman, G. M., *J. Exp. Med.* **145,** 523, 1977.

3. Nash, A. A., Pelan, J., and Wildy, P., *J. Immunol.* **126,** 1260, 1981.
4. Leung, K-N., Ada, G. L., and McKenzie, I. F. C., *J. Exp. Med.* **151,** 815, 1980.
5. Zinkernagel, R. M., *J. Exp. Med.* **144,** 776, 1976.
6. Ertl, H. C. J., *Cell. Immunol.,* **62,** 38, 1981.
7. Ertl, H. C. J., *Immunogenetics,* **12,** 579, 1981.
8. Koszinowski, U., and Simon, M., *Eur. J. Immunol.* **9,** 715, 1979.
9. Koszinowski, U., Ertl, H. C. J., Wekerle, H., and Thomssen, R., *Cold Spring Harbor Symp. Quant. Biol.* **41,** 529, 1976.
10. Jackson, D. C., Ada, G. L., and Tha Hla, R. *Aust. J. Exp. Biol.* **54,** 349, 1976.
11. Zinkernagel, R. M., Althage, A., Adler, B., Blanden, R. V., Davidson, W. F., Kees, U., Dunlop, M. B. C., and Shreffler, D. C., *J. Exp. Med.* **145,** 1353, 1977.

CELLULAR IMMUNOLOGY **63**, 193–197 (1981)

Heterogeneity of Tolerance to Xenogeneic Cells in Mice Inoculated at Birth with Rat Cells

J. CHUTNÁ, V. HOLÁŇ, AND M. HAŠEK

Institute of Molecular Genetics, Czechoslovak Academy of Sciences, 160 00 Prague 6, Czechoslovakia

Received April 7, 1981; accepted April 29, 1981

In experiments on induction of tolerance to xenogeneic cells in newborn mice with rat bone marrow cells, higher mortality was not observed even after repeated injection of cells, hence no graft-versus-host disease (GVHD) occurred. Xenogeneic skin grafts were not tolerated and showed little significant prolongation of survival. Nevertheless, complete suppression of cytotoxic antibody formation was detectable in most of the treated animals in which no graft survived longer than 12 days. At the cellular level, complete tolerance in MLC and cytotoxicity assays was also observed in the majority of animals. Thus, different detection systems seem to be a decisive criterion in detecting the tolerance state and the individual specific mechanisms of immunity may be dissociated in the split tolerance studied in the xenogeneic system in the present experiments.

INTRODUCTION

Neonatally induced transplantation tolerance is defined as a state in which the recipients inoculated at birth with lymphoid cells from the strain of the graft donor retain incompatible skin grafts which are otherwise rejected. So-defined animals, however, may display reactivity to allogeneic antigens at the cellular level (1–4) or antibody production (5–7). On the other hand, it has been described that animals which do not tolerate allogeneic skin grafts can be areactive in other tests (8–12). We investigated the latter possibility in the xenogeneic system in mice inoculated as newborns with rat cells. Using several detection systems we observed a dissociation between different specific mechanisms of immunity because animals which had rejected xenogeneic skin grafts displayed full areactivity or considerable hyporeactivity in the *in vitro* tests of immunity and also failed to develop cytotoxic antibodies in most cases. We found that tolerance to xenogeneic cells at the level of antibody formation or at the cellular level was easier to induce than was tolerance to skin grafts.

MATERIALS AND METHODS

Mice of the inbred B10.AKM strain were used as recipients. The donors of xenogeneic bone marrow cells and xenogeneic skin grafts were rats of the inbred AVN strain. Inbred C57BL10/Sn (hereafter B10) mice were used in the *in vitro* assays for the specificity of the reactivity.

0008-8749/81/130193-05$02.00/0

Tolerance was induced in B10.AKM mice by an intravenous injection of a suspension of 1×10^7 bone marrow cells in Hanks' solution within 20 hr of birth (groups A and B). A second, intraperitoneal injection of 6×10^7 bone marrow cells was given at 25 days after birth (group C). The inoculated animals were grafted with tail skin at 7–8 weeks of age using the technique described by Billingham *et al.* (13). Skin grafts were scrutinized from the seventh day after grafting.

To determine the reactivity in mixed lymphocyte culture (MLC), cells were seeded in Microtest II culture plates (No. 3040, Falcon Plastics, Oxnard, Calif.). Reactive lymph node cells (0.5×10^6) and 1×10^6 mitomycin-treated stimulating cells were incubated in 0.2 ml of RPMI 1640 medium supplemented with antibiotics (penicillin, streptomycin), glutamine, and 10% inactivated pooled human serum. Cell proliferation was determined by adding 0.5 μCi of [^{3}H]thymidine per well for the last 15 hr of a 96-hr incubation period.

For *in vitro* assays of cytotoxicity, cells were sensitized by 96 hr of incubation of 2×10^6 cells tested and 0.4×10^6 mitomycin-treated stimulating cells in 1.0 ml of RPMI 1640 medium containing antibiotics, glutamine, and 10% fetal calf serum. After sensitization, cellular cytotoxicity was determined by ^{51}Cr release from Con A blasts. Sensitized cells and 1×10^4 ^{51}Cr-labeled blasts at a ratio of 10:1 were incubated in 0.2 ml of medium, and after 4 hr the released activity was determined. Results are expressed as

$$\% \text{ cytotoxicity} = \frac{\begin{array}{c}\text{cpm after incubation with sensitized lymphocytes}\\ -\text{ cpm after incubation with control lymphocytes}\end{array}}{\text{total activity} - \text{spontaneous release}} \times 100.$$

After rejection of xenogeneic skin grafts, the presence of cytotoxic antibodies was ascertained by the ^{51}Cr release from labeled cells (14).

RESULTS

Dissociation between Different Tolerance States

B10.AKM mice did not develop a graft-versus-host disease (GVHD) when inoculated intravenously as newborns with 1×10^7 bone marrow cells from adult AVN rats (groups A and B). A further injection of 6×10^7 xenogeneic cells intraperitoneally at 25 days of life led to slight mortality only (13% of experimental animals died in group C). All groups of animals received xenogeneic skin grafts from AVN rats. The skin graft survival in group A is shown in Table 1, and the skin graft survival in groups B and C is illustrated in Fig. 1. A slight prolongation of xenogeneic skin graft survival occurred in groups A and B as compared to untreated controls. However, all xenogeneic skin grafts were rejected within 13 days in group A and within 17 days in group B. Group C animals, which were given a second injection of 6×10^7 xenogeneic cells intraperitoneally at 25 days of life after the neonatal inoculation, also showed only a slight prolongation of xenogeneic skin graft survival, with the exception of one graft which survived 39 days after grafting.

All three groups of animals were assayed for the presence of cytotoxic antibodies on Days 13 or 14 after grafting. As shown in Table 1 (group A) and Table 2

TABLE 1

Dissociation of the States of Tolerance to Xenogeneic Cells Depending on the Test System

B10.AKM mice[a]	Cytotoxicity[b]/ (% ^{51}Cr release) AVN	B10	Mixed lymphocyte culture[b] (SI)[c]	Survival time of AVN skin grafts (days)	Cytotoxic antibodies against AVN[d]
T_1	−4.6	47.3*	1.26	12	0
T_2	−1.0	−7.2	2.33*	7	0
T_3	−1.9	24.8*	0.95	10	0
T_4	−5.0	26.6*	1.03	11	0
T_5	−0.5	1.1	0.96	10	0
T_6	−3.5	22.8*	3.29*	11	64
T_7	1.1	33.3*	1.75	10	128
T_8	34.4*	47.4*	6.26*	7	0
C_1	19.9*	24.6*	4.47*	8	256
C_2	33.8*	35.6*	7.78*	8	256
C_3	5.1*	20.0*	2.04*	—	—
C_4	23.2*	30.7*	5.86*	8	256

[a] T_1–T_8 are B10.AKM mice treated at birth with 1×10^7 bone marrow cells from AVN rats. C_1–C_4 are untreated controls.

[b] Values with asterisks indicate significant reactivity ($P < 0.05$ or less).

[c] SI, stimulation index, gives the ratio of [^{3}H]thymidine incorporation in allogeneic to syngeneic cultures.

[d] Reciprocal cytotoxic antibody titers on Day 13 after grafting.

(groups B and C), cytotoxic antibody production was completely inhibited in most of the experimental mice.

Differences in Tolerance Tested by Skin Grafting and by in Vitro Assays

For the *in vitro* assays of cellular reactivity, two cervical lymph nodes were removed from mice in group A and from control mice before grafting. Lymphocytes

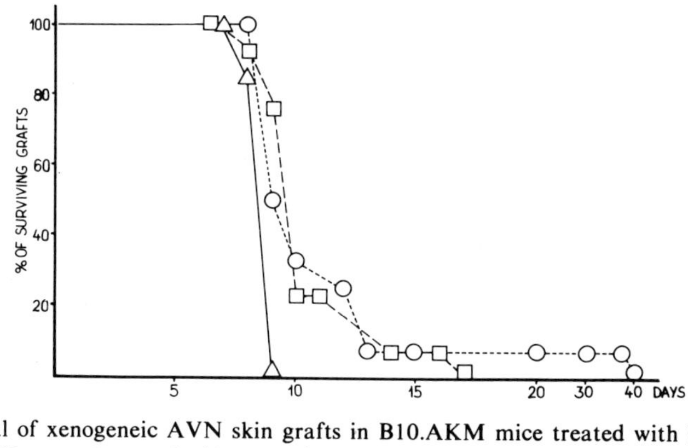

FIG. 1. Survival of xenogeneic AVN skin grafts in B10.AKM mice treated with bone marrow cells from AVN rats. Untreated controls (△ —— △), 13 mice. Group B—B10.AKM mice inoculated iv at birth with 1×10^7 bone marrow cells from AVN rats (□ - - - □), 13 mice. Group C—B10.AKM mice inoculated with 1×10^7 AVN rat bone marrow cells iv at birth and with 6×10^7 of these cells intraperitoneally at 25 days of life (○ ----- ○), 12 mice.

TABLE 2

Inhibition of Cytotoxic Antibody Formation in B10.AKM Mice Inoculated at Birth with Bone Marrow Cells from AVN Rats

Donors of serum tested[a]	Percentage ^{51}Cr release ± SE at serum dilutions[b] 1:5	1:50
Group B	8.8 ± 0.4*	8.4 ± 0.2*
Group C	8.2 ± 0.1*	8.9 ± 0.1*
Control mice	33.5 ± 8.1	12.3 ± 1.3

[a] Blood for antibody assay was collected 14 days after transplantation of xenogeneic AVN skin grafts.

[b] ^{51}Cr release during incubation of AVN cells without serum (in the presence of complement only) was 9.2 ± 0.8%. Values with asterisks indicate significant inhibition of antibody formation ($P < 0.025$ or less as compared to untreated controls).

from these animals were tested for the reactivity in the cytotoxicity and MLC assays. After an *in vitro* sensitization, cells in seven of eight neonatally treated mice were fully areactive to AVN cells in the cytotoxicity assay and two of these seven tolerant animals were also areactive to third-party B10 cells. Cells of only one of eight neonatally treated mice displayed significant reactivity to AVN cells after an *in vitro* sensitization (Table 1).

Similarly, five of eight neonatally treated mice in group A did not react in the MLC assay when stimulated with AVN cells.

Skin grafts in all these animals were rejected within 13 days and two animals with the most rapid rejection of skin grafts within 8 days also reacted at the cellular level as did untreated controls.

DISCUSSION

The present results show that tolerance detectable by xenogeneic skin grafting was not complete or that it was only short lasting under the experimental conditions used. Mice inoculated at birth with xenogeneic bone marrow cells from adult rats rejected xenogeneic skin grafts and developed no GVHD. When the treated mice were tested for the presence of humoral cytotoxic antibodies, they nevertheless differed from the controls by complete inhibition of cytotoxic antibody production in most cases. Thus, it appears that the ease with which humoral tolerance is induced as compared to the induction of tolerance to skin grafts, as has been described in various experimental models in the allogeneic relationship (9–12), is also a characteristic feature of tolerance to xenogeneic cells. Moreover, in the *in vitro* tests, i.e., cytotoxicity and MLC assays, many more animals exhibited a higher degree of tolerance at the cellular level in comparison with skin graft survival. Most of the animals were completely tolerant in these detection systems.

Similarly, Elkins *et al.* (8) observed that animals, which had rejected tolerated skin grafts after an adoptive transfer of immunity, remained areactive or were hyporeactive in another test (GVH reaction).

In our experiments, the *in vitro* tests for cellular reactivity and for cytotoxic antibodies after transplantation of xenogeneic cells showed that complete tolerance to xenogeneic antigens was achieved in most cases. However, the rejection of xenogeneic skin grafts in neonatally treated animals suggested that the mechanism responsible for the destruction of these grafts *in vivo* had been activated. Obviously cell-mediated immunity, and not cytotoxic antibodies the formation of which is inhibited in neonatally treated animals, was involved in the destruction process. However, cell populations other than those which were areactive to xenogeneic antigens in the *in vitro* tests were evidently involved in the mechanism *in vivo*.

In the *in vitro* cytotoxicity assays, two mice which did not react to the specific xenogeneic cells also displayed no reactivity to third-party B10 allogeneic antigens. This nonspecificity, even though it was observed in two animals only, might be associated with our earlier results showing that in transplantation of xenogeneic skin grafts in noninbred animals, for example, after turkey–chicken parabiosis, allogeneic skin grafts even from random donors survived (15, 16).

The results demonstrate the importance of the detection system as a criterion of immunological tolerance.

REFERENCES

1. Bansal, S. C., Hellström, I., Hellström, K. E., and Wright, P. W., *Transplantation* **16,** 610, 1973.
2. Chutná, J., Hašek, M., Sládeček, M., Viklický, V., and Bubeník, J., *Folia Biol. (Praha)* **19,** 252, 1973.
3. Wright, P. W., Bernstein, I. D., Hamilton, B., Gluckman, J. C., and Hellström, K. E., *Transplantation* **18,** 46, 1974.
4. Oppenheim, E. S., Kinsky, R., and Voisin, G. A., *Transplantation* **24,** 274, 1977.
5. Voisin, G. A., Kinsky, R. G., and Maillard, J., *Ann. Inst. Pasteur* **115,** 855, 1968.
6. Voisin, G. A., *Cell Immunol.* **2,** 670, 1971.
7. Voisin, G. A., Kinsky, R. G., and Duc, H. T., *J. Exp. Med.* **135,** 1185, 1972.
8. Elkins, W. L., Adams, J. S., Fox, D. H., Wilson, D. B., and Stuart, E. P., *Cell. Immunol.* **9,** 412, 1973.
9. Law, P. W., Appella, E., Strober, S., Wright, P. W., and Fischetti, T., *Proc. Nat. Acad. Sci. USA* **69,** 1858, 1972.
10. Wright, P. W., Law, L. W., Appella, E., and Bernstein, I. D., *Transplantation* **17,** 524, 1974.
11. Hašek, M., Chutná, J., Holáň, V., and Sládeček, M., *Nature (London)* **262,** 295, 1976.
12. Holáň, V., Hašek, M., and Chutná, J., *Transplantation* **25,** 27, 1978.
13. Billingham, R. E., Brent, L., and Medawar, P. B., *Proc. Roy. Soc. Ser. B.* **143,** 43, 1954.
14. Sanderson, A. R., *Immunology* **9,** 287, 1965.
15. Hašek, M., Hraba, T., and Hort, J., *Folia Biol. (Praha)* **6,** 1, 1960.
16. Hašek, M., and Hort, J., *In* "Mechanisms of Immunological Tolerance" (M. Hašek, A. Lengerová, and M. Vojtíšková, Eds.), pp. 143–148. Czechoslovak Academy of Sciences, Prague, 1962.

CELLULAR IMMUNOLOGY **63**, 198–202 (1981)

Fractionation of Murine Macrophage Inhibitory Factor into Two Distinct Species[1]

DANIEL BOUT, ALICE L. KÜHNER, VOLKER KLIMETZEK, HEINZ G. REMOLD[2] AND JOHN R. DAVID

Departments of Medicine, Harvard Medical School and the Robert B. Brigham Division of the Affiliated Hospitals Center, Inc., Boston, Massachusetts 02115

Received April 17, 1980; accepted April 30, 1981

Murine migration inhibitory factor (MIF) produced by concanavalin A-stimulated lymph node cells from C57BL/6 mice was fractionated by Sephadex G-100 gel filtration, density gradient electrophoresis, and isoelectrofocusing in a sucrose density gradient and assayed on *in vitro*-cultivated bone marrow macrophages from C57BL/6 mice. Two major MIF species, pH3-MIF with an isoelectric point of 3.0–4.3 and pH5-MIF with an isoelectric point of 4.6 to 5.2, were obtained. The similarity of murine MIF to guinea pig and human MIF is discussed.

INTRODUCTION

Antigenically sensitized and stimulated lymph node cells produce soluble mediators with a variety of biological functions (1, 2). In the last few years it has become apparent that several of these mediators occur in several distinct molecular species (3–6). For example, migration inhibitory factors from both guinea pigs and human can be separated into two different molecular species with different molecular weights and isoelectric points.

Previous studies have shown that murine spleen MIF[3] has an apparent molecular weight of 50,000–70,000 (7). Further studies have revealed that murine MIF produced by lymph node cells has a different elution pattern on Sephadex G-100, suggesting that species with different apparent molecular weights are originally present (7). We demonstrate here, using preparative isoelectrofocusing, that murine lymph node MIF, like guinea pig and human MIF, can be fractionated into at least two distinct species.

MATERIALS AND METHODS

Animals. Female C57BL/6 mice (Charles River Breeding Laboratories, Wilmington, Mass.) weighing 18–25 g were used in all experiments.

[1] This work was supported by a Grant-in-Aid from the American Heart Association and USPHS Grant AI-07685.

[2] To whom all correspondence should be addressed.

[3] Abbreviations used: MIF, migration inhibitory factor; MEM-PS, minimum essential medium containing 85 U penicillin and 85 μg streptomycin/100 ml; D-MEM, Dulbecco's MEM; D-PBS, Dulbecco's phosphate-buffered saline; HBSS, Hank's balanced salt solution.

0008-8749/81/130198-05$02.00/0

Production of MIF. MIF-rich and control lymphocyte supernatants were produced by incubating 2.4 × 10^7 lymph node cells/ml with and without concanavalin A (2 μg/ml) as previously described (8).

Sephadex G-100 gel filtration. The lyophilized materials (equivalent to 400 ml of starting supernatants, were filtered over Sephadex G-100 columns (2.5 × 100 cm) in phosphate-buffered saline, pH 7.4, as previously described (7). Tubes containing 2.1 ml were collected and pooled into fractions I–VIII. Pools I and II contained the exclusion volume. Pools III and IV contained molecules with the apparent molecular weight of albumin (65,000 MW). Pools V and VI indicated the position of the ovalbumin (40,000 MW) peak, and fraction VII the position of chymotrypsinogen (23,000 MW). Fractions containing molecules with an apparent molecular weight of 30,000 to 130,000 having MIF activity were pooled, concentrated to 1/100 of the original supernatant volume by vacuum dialysis, and stored at −70°C.

Sucrose density gradient electrophoresis. A Model 212 density gradient electrophoresis apparatus (Instrumentation Specialties Co., Lincoln, Nebr.) (9) with a gradient capacity of 20 ml was used for preparative electrophoresis of MIF-containing and control fractions as described before (5). The concentrated MIF-containing and control fractions (1.75 ml) from the Sephadex G-100 fractionation were applied to the column. Electrophoresis was performed in a 10–30% sucrose gradient in 0.02 *M* tris acetate buffer pH 8.6 at 5 mA for 6 hr. Two-milliliter fractions were collected and 10, 3, and 15 μl of these fractions were tested for MIF activity.

Isoelectrofocusing. A LKB Ampholine electrofocusing equipment (LKB Producter, Bromma, Sweden) with a capacity of 440 ml was employed as described (5). Pooled MIF-containing and control fractions from the electrophoretic fractionation equivalent to 100 ml of the original supernatant were fractionated. After isoelectrofocusing, the resulting 11 fractions were concentrated to 4 ml and an aliquot of 0.7 ml was reconstituted to 3.5 ml with MEM-PS; this was dialyzed extensively against MEM-PS, made to contain 15% normal guinea pig serum, and assayed for MIF activity in three dilutions (corresponding to 0.4, 0.2, and 0.1 ml of the 4 ml concentrate which represents a 14.5-, 8.75-, and 4.5-fold concentration over the original supernatants).

Assay for murine MIF. Murine MIF was assayed as previously described (7) with a modification. Bone marrow macrophages were used as indicator cells. Teflon-coated petri dishes were prepared by spraying plastic petri dishes (Falcon 3003) with Teflon aerosol (No. 6075) (Crown Industrial Products Co., Hebron, Ill.) until they were covered with a thin film. Then bone marrow cells from the femora and tibiae of three C57BL/6 mice (1.5–1.8 × 10^8 cells) were grown for 9 to 16 days at 37°C, 10% CO_2 on these petri dishes at a density of 1.3 × 10^5 cells/cm^2 in D-MEM (Microbiological Associates, Bethesda, Md) containing 15% fetal calf serum, 5% horse serum, and 20% L-cell supernatants as a source of colony-stimulating factor (10). After the cultivation period, the macrophages were removed from the incubator and allowed to sit for 10 min at 4°C. The medium was replaced with cold D-PBS containing 1 *M* EDTA, and the cultures were allowed to incubate for 15 more min at room temperature. After removing the monolayers by gently rinsing the plates with D-PBS, the cells were washed (once in D-PBS, twice in HBSS) and then resuspended in D-MEM (95% v/v) containing 15% guinea pig serum.

TABLE 1

Fractionation of Lymph Node Cell MIF on Sephadex G-100 Columns[a]

	Percentage inhibition							
Fraction:	I	II	III	IV	V	VI	VII	VIII
K_d:	0.0–0.036[b]	0.036–0.077	0.077–0.138	0.138–0.200	0.200–0.250	0.250–0.290	0.290–0.410	0.410
Expt 1[c]	13	34	46	42	55	29	26	0
Expt 2[d]	7	21	32	39	31	29	16	0
Expt 3[c]	0	31	54	33	37	37	17	ND

[a] Lyophilized lymph node cell supernatants were filtered over a Sephadex G-100 column and the effluent was pooled into the fractions I–VIII with the indicated K_d values and concentrated to 1/100 the original supernatant volume.

[b] Void volume.

[c] 400 μl/ml were tested in tissue cultures.

[d] 20 μl/ml were tested.

The cells were packed into 20-μl capillary tubes and the MIF assay was performed. The percentage of inhibition was calculated by the formula.

$$\% \text{ inhibition} = 1 - \frac{\text{average area of migration in MIF containing fraction}}{\text{average area of migration in control fraction}} \times 100.$$

An inhibition of migration of less than 20% was not considered to be significant (8).

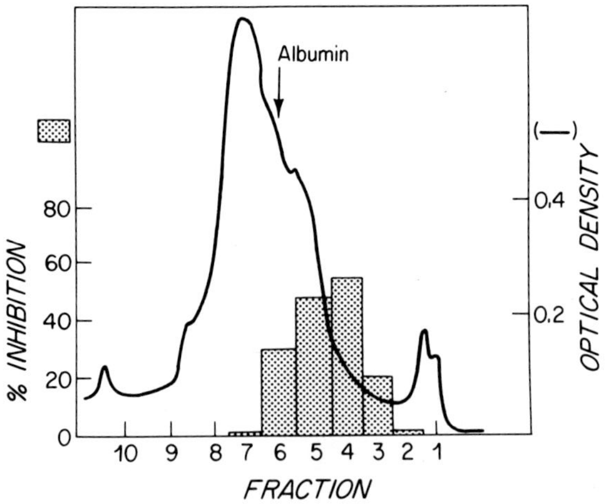

FIG. 1. Elution pattern of murine fractionated on sucrose density gradient electrophoresis in 0.02 *M* Tris acetate buffer, pH 8.6. The ordinate shows the percentage inhibition and the optical density at 280 nm of the fractions. The fraction numbers are shown on the abscissa. The origin is on the right. One hundred microliters from each 2-ml fraction was tested for MIF activity. Note that MIF activity is in the postalbumin region.

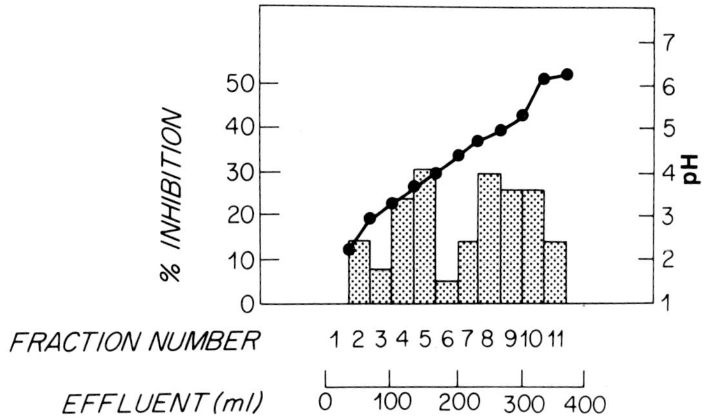

FIG. 2. Isoelectrofocusing of MIF in a pH gradient from pH 2.0–6.2. A typical experiment is shown. The pooled fractions and the elution volume are indicated on the abscissa, the pH of the fractions (solid line) and the percentage inhibition (bars) are indicated on the ordinate. The fractions were concentrated to 4 ml and dialyzed extensively against MEM-PS, and 0.7 ml were assayed for MIF activity. Note that two peaks are found, one at pH 3.5–4.0, the other between pH 4.5 and 5.5.

RESULTS AND DISCUSSION

MIF-containing and control lymphocyte supernatants from Con A-stimulated mouse lymph node cells were filtered over Sephadex G-100 columns. The MIF eluted in a broad range with molecules having an apparent molecular weight of 29,000 to over 100,000 as shown in Table 1. Peak MIF activity was found in fractions containing molecules with an apparent molecular weight of 50,000 to 70,000 (fractions III and IV). The activity in fraction II has been previously shown to be due to MIF activity by subjecting these fractions to polyacrylamide gel electrophoresis and may be based on aggregation. MIF activity from fraction II was found on polyacrylamide gel electrophoresis in the same fractions as MIF activity from fractions III and IV (Kühner and David, thesis, 1975, Harvard Medical School).

TABLE 2

Isoelectrofocusing of Mouse MIF in a pH Gradient from 1.0 to 6.2[a]

Fraction:	1	2	3	4	5	6	7	8	9	10	11
pH range:	1.0–1.2	–2.7	–3.2	–3.6	–3.9	–4.2	–4.6	–4.8	–5.1	–5.4	–6.2
Expt 1	0	0	11	20	42	36	13	30	34	33	28
Expt 2	ND[b]	14	8	24	31	5	14	30	27	26	14
Expt 3	ND	19	23	46	52	35	25	33	70	35	28
Expt 4	ND	0	13	16	39	30	20	54	15	11	ND

[a] Fractions 1 to 11 within the indicated pH range were pooled and concentrated to 4 ml. 0.25 ml of each fraction was tested for MIF activity. The numbers represent percentage of inhibition of migration. The data in fractions 6, 7, and 8 were analyzed by a one-way analysis of variance (11). It could be shown that on a 90% confidence level fractions 6 and 8 are significantly different from fraction 7, indicating the presence of two different MIF species ($P < 0.1$).

[b] ND = not done.

The fractionation pattern suggested that murine lymph node cell MIF is more heterogeneous than spleen cell MIF. To further investigate this possibility, all Sephadex fractions containing lymph node-MIF activity were pooled, concentrated, and subjected to sucrose density gradient electrophoresis and isoelectrofocusing. After preparative electrophoresis, MIF activity was recovered as a single broad peak in the postalbumin region. One out of three experiments is seen in Fig. 1. The fractions 4, 5, and 6 from the sucrose density gradient electrophoresis step were pooled and subjected to isoelectrofocussing. Figure 2 shows the results of a typical experiment. All experiments are listed in Table 2. It can be seen that two peaks of MIF activity are recovered. One peak focusses between pH 3.0 and 4.3 and the other between pH 4.6 and 5.2. The former is referred to as pH3-MIF and the latter as pH5-MIF (5). In several experiments, active fractions from Sephadex G-100 were directly subjected to isoelectrofocusing by omitting the sucrose density gradient electrophoresis step. In these experiments, the position of the peaks was identical to the peak positions of material purified on sucrose density electrophoresis (experiments not shown).

The two murine MIF species have virtually the same isoelectric points as human and guinea pig lymph node pH3-MIF and pH5-MIF. The discrepancies of the elution patterns of murine spleen cell MIF and murine lymph node MIF as indicated above suggest that pH5-MIF may be inactivated or absorbed by spleen macrophages. However, further experiments have to demonstrate that spleen cell supernatants contain only pH3-MIF activity.

In conclusion, it seems to be evident that the existence of at least two main MIF components is a common characteristic in a number of mammalian species.

REFERENCES

1. David, J. R., and David, R. A., *Progr. Allergy* **16,** 300, 1972.
2. Pick, E., *In* "Immunopharmacology" (R. Coffey and R. Spreafico, Eds.), p. 163. Plenum, New York, 1977.
3. Walker, W. M., Lee, S., and Lucas, Z. J., *J. Immunol.* **116,** 807, 1976.
4. Sorg, C., and Bloom, B. R., *J. Exp. Med.* **137,** 148, 1973.
5. Remold, H. G., and Mednis, A. D., *J. Immunol.* **118,** 2015, 1977.
6. Weiser, W. Y., Greineder, D. K., and David, J. R., *Fed. Proc. Abstr.* **38,** 1215, 1979.
7. Kühner, A. L., and David, J. R., *J. Immunol.* **116,** 140, 1976.
8. Remold, H. G., Katz, A. B., Haber, E., and David, J. R., *Cell. Immunol.* **1,** 133, 1970.
9. Brakke, M. K., Allington, R. W., and Langille, F. A., *Anal. Biochem.* **25,** 30, 1968.
10. Klimetzek, V., and Remold, H. G., *Cell. Immunol.,* **53,** 257, 1980.
11. Snedecor, G. W., and Cochran, W. G., *"Statistical Methods."* Iowa State Univ. Press, Ames, 1973.

CELLULAR IMMUNOLOGY 63, 203–209 (1981)

Migration of IgA-Bearing Lymphocytes into Salivary Glands[1]

DIANNE E. JACKSON, EDWARD T. LALLY, MARY C. NAKAMURA, AND PAUL C. MONTGOMERY

Departments of Microbiology and Pathology, Center for Oral Health Research, School of Dental Medicine, University of Pennsylvania, Philadelphia, Pennsylvania 19104

Received April 17, 1981; accepted May 20, 1981

The relative migratory properties of [^{125}I]iododeoxyuridine-labeled dividing mesenteric lymph node (MLN) and peripheral lymph node (PLN) cells were assessed in mice using the adoptive transfer system. MLN cells from virgin donors showed a greater tendency to localize in MLN, small intestine, and mammary glands (lactating recipients only) of virgin and lactating recipients. In addition, MLN cells were shown to selectively localize in the salivary (submandibular and sublingual) glands. The relative migratory properties of MLN and PLN cell populations were identical when donor cells were obtained from virgin or lactating animals. Selective depletion of IgA-bearing cells from the MLN transfer cell population abrogated the preferential localization in control mucosal tissues and salivary glands. These data show that the salivary glands can be included as an additional mucosal area populated by gut-derived IgA-bearing cells and provides direct evidence that the common mucosal immune sytstem extends to secretory tissue in the oral cavity.

INTRODUCTION

The characterization of the immune system at mucosal surfaces has included documentation on the origin of precursor cells committed to IgA synthesis. With respect to salivary glands, the origin of IgA-producing cells has not clearly been established. Antibody induction studies have provided evidence that salivary IgA responses can be triggered in the saliva of rats (1) and humans (2) following ingestion of bacterial antigens. Other studies have indicated that bronchial as well as gastrointestinal (GALT)[2] stimulation triggered IgA antibody responses in saliva and other secretions (3). Isoelectric focusing has been used to assess the IgA spectrotypes of antibodies appearing in saliva and other secretions following GALT stimulation (4). One interpretation of these data is that salivary glands are seeded with IgA precursor cells of identical clonotype potential. In addition, IgA-antibody-producing plasma cells have been found in parotid glands of mice immunized by the oral route (5). Although these studies strongly suggest that IgA precursor cells seed salivary glands following GALT stimulation, they do not rule out the possibility that direct antigen presentation to glandular tissue triggered the IgA antibody

[1] This work was supported by USPHS Grants DE-02623 and DE-05414. M.C.N. was supported by a Ford Foundation grant to Swarthmore College.

[2] Abbreviations used: GALT, gastrointestinal-associated lymphoid tissue; MLN, mesenteric lymph nodes; PLN, peripheral lymph nodes; ^{125}IUDR, [^{125}I]iododeoxyuridine; NRS, normal rabbit serum.

0008-8749/81/130203-07$02.00/0

responses. In order to directly assess the linkage of the secretoy tissue in the oral cavity to the common mucosal system by emigrating cell populations, we studied the migration of IgA-bearing cells into salivary glands.

MATERIALS AND METHODS

Animals. C57Bl/6J mice of both sexes were obtained from the Jackson Laboratory (Bar Harbor, Maine) at 6–8 weeks of age and were bred in the animal facililities of the Center for Oral Health Research.

Preparation of radiolabeled cells. Suspensions of cells from mesenteric lymph nodes (MLN) or peripheral lymph nodes (PLN; surface and deep cervical, axillary, brachial, inguinal) were prepared in ice-cold RPMI 1640 medium (pH 7.2) with 20 m*M* Hepes buffer (Grand Island Biological Co., Grand Island, N.Y.) and 10% newborn calf serum (Microbiological Associates Bioproducts, Walkersville, Md.). Pooled MLN or PLN were gently pressed through 60-mesh stainless-steel wire sieves and suspended in ice-cold medium. After large clumps were allowed to settle out, the remaining suspension was washed twice by centrifugation and viable cells were enumerated in 0.4% trypan blue. Cells were incubated for 90 min at 37°C at 5×10^7/ml in medium containing 4 μCi/ml of [^{125}I]iododeoxyuridine (^{125}IUDR, Amersham/Searle Corp., Arlington Heights, Ill.) to label those cells synthesizing DNA. The cells were then washed three times in ice-cold medium and filtered rapidly through nylon wool to yield suspensions of single, viable cells, free of unbound radiolabel (6, 7). Between 5×10^7 and 5×10^8 viable cells were transferred intravenously.

Pretreatment of cells. In some experiments, selectively depleted populations of MLN were prepared following the procedures detailed elsewhere (6, 7). Radiolabeled MLN cells were incubated with normal rabbit serum (NRS), with rabbit antisera specific for mouse $IgG_{1,2}$ (anti-γ) and IgM (anti-μ; Litton Bionetics, Kensington, Md.) or with goat antiserum to mouse IgA (anti-α; Meloy Laboratories, Inc., Springfield, Va.) plus guinea pig complement (BBL, Cockeysville, Md.) at 37°C for 45 min in Hanks' balanced salt solution (Gibco). Cells to be transferred were washed in RPMI and filtered, as above.

Antisera to mouse immunoglobulin and NRS were absorbed with mouse thymus and liver prior to use and cytotoxicity indices (anti-IgM + anti-IgG = 20; anti-IgA = 0; NRS = 0) for MLN cells determined by the trypan blue exclusion test. The specificity of the anti-IgA serum was checked by absorption with IgA myeloma XRPC-44 (IgA, κ) bound to Sepharose 2B. The XRPC-44 protein was kindly donated by Dr. M. Cancro (University of Pennsylvania Medical School). Absorption of the anti-IgA serum removed activity specific for IgA detectable by double-gel diffusion and by effects on the homing of cells.

Recovery of label. Eighteen to twenty-four hours after transfer of cells, MLN, small intestine, salivary (submandibular and sublingual) glands, and mammary tissue were removed from recipients and weighed. Care was taken to exclude PLNs from salivary and mammary gland tissue. Radioactivity was measured in an Intertechnique gamma counter (70% efficiency for ^{125}I). Recovered radioactivity is expressed as a percentage of that injected per gram of recipient tissue ± SD.

Statistical analysis. Following calculation of means and standard deviations, *P* values were determined by the unpaired, two-tailed Student's *t* test. A minimum significance level of 0.05 was used.

RESULTS

The relative migratory properties of MLN and PLN cell populations were assessed using both virgin and lactating donors. The percentage of injected label recovered from organs of virgin recipients following transfer of ^{125}IUDR-labeled MLN and PLN cells from virgin donors are shown in Table 1. As documented by the preference indices ((7) values above 1 calculated from statistically significant label recovery data indicate a greater tendency of MLN cells to migrate to the recipient organ when compared to PLN cells), MLN cells had a greater propensity to selectively localize in MLN, small intestine, and salivary (submandibular and sublingual) glands, but not mammary glands of virgin recipients. Data from similar experiments using cells from lactating donors are shown in Table 2. The findings are analogous to the results shown in Table 1 indicating that the relative migratory properties of MLN and PLN cell populations are identical whether obtained from virgin or lactating donors.

We next compared the homing patterns in lactating recipients of MLN and PLN cells obtained from virgin donors. These data are presented in Table 3. In this case the preference indices show that MLN cells had a greater tendency to home to MLN, small intestine, and salivary and mammary glands. With the exception of the differences in migration to mammary glands, the homing patterns are identical in virgin and lactating recipients.

In order to determine if the homing patterns resulted from IgA-isotype-bearing populations we studied the migratory properties of MLN cells to recipient organs

TABLE 1

Percentage of Injected Label Recovered from Organs of Virgin Recipients following Transfer of ^{125}IUDR-Labeled MLN and PLN Cells from Virgin Donors

Recipient organ (virgin)	Donor cells (virgin)	Number of recipients	Label recovered[a]	Preference index[b]	P^c
MLN	MLN	12	6.05 ± 2.10	1.65	<0.001
	PLN	16	3.67 ± 1.04		
Small intestine	MLN	13	2.18 ± 0.47	2.42	<0.001
	PLN	17	0.91 ± 0.20		
Salivary glands[d]	MLN	11	0.84 ± 0.37	1.83	<0.001
	PLN	16	0.46 ± 0.17		
Mammary glands	MLN	12	0.32 ± 0.15	1.19	N.S.[e]
	PLN	16	0.27 ± 0.24		

[a] Recovery expressed as mean % injected cpm/g tissue ± 1 SD.
[b] Preference index = % injected cpm/g in MLN recipients/% injected cpm/g in PLN recipients.
[c] Two-tailed Student's *t* test.
[d] Submandibular and sublingual glands.
[e] Not significant.

TABLE 2

Percentage of Injected Label Recovered from Organs of Virgin Recipients following Transfer of ^{125}IUDR-Labeled MLN and PLN Cells from Lactating Donors

Recipient organ (virgin)	Donor cells (lactating)[a]	Number of recipients	Label recovered	Preference index[b]	P^c
MLN	MLN	7	3.16 ± 0.57	1.61	$0.001 < P < 0.01$
	PLN	5	1.96 ± 0.33		
Small intestine	MLN	7	2.12 ± 0.31	3.59	< 0.001
	PLN	5	0.59 ± 0.14		
Salivary glands	MLN	7	1.03 ± 0.52	2.02	$0.05 < P < 0.1$[d]
	PLN	5	0.51 ± 0.22		
Mammary glands	MLN	7	0.54 ± 0.30	1.28	N.S.[e]
	PLN	5	0.42 ± 0.11		

[a] Donors 3–10 days postpartum.
[b] Preference index = % injected cpm/g in MLN recipients/% injected cpm/g in PLN recipients.
[c] Two-tailed Student's *t* test.
[d] The *P* value bordered on but was not less than the accepted level of significance.
[e] Not significant.

following selective depletion with isotype-specific antisera. Cytolysis was carried out using anti-α, anti-μ + anti-γ, or NRS and complement. The selective depletion studies were done in both virgin and lactating recipients to further assess the influence of the physiological state of the recipient on migration patterns. The results of this experiment are summarized in Table 4. These data show that the migration to small intestine, salivary glands and mammary glands (in lactating animals only) is abrogated by pretreating MLN cells with anti-α serum and complement. The

TABLE 3

Percentage of Injected Label Recovered from Organs of Lactating Recipients following Transfer of ^{125}IUDR-Labeled MLN and PLN Cells from Virgin Donors

Recipient organ (lactating)	Donor cells (virgin)	Number of recipients	Label recovered[a]	Preference index[b]	P^c
MLN	MLN	6	2.58 ± 1.13	2.21	$0.001 < P < 0.01$
	PLN	7	1.17 ± 0.32		
Small intestine	MLN	6	2.98 ± 0.89	3.35	< 0.001
	PLN	7	0.89 ± 0.23		
Salivary glands	MLN	6	1.00 ± 0.58	2.50	$0.01 < P < 0.05$
	PLN	7	0.40 ± 0.19		
Mammary glands	MLN	6	2.18 ± 0.88	2.56	$0.001 < P < 0.01$
	PLN	7	0.85 ± 0.39		

[a] Recovery expressed as mean % injected cpm/g tissue ± 1 SD.
[b] Preference index = % injected cpm/g in MLN recipients/% injected cpm/g in PLN recipients.
[c] Two-tailed Student's *t* test.

TABLE 4

Effect of Antisera, plus Complement, on Homing of ^{125}IUDR-Labeled MLN Cells to Organs of Virgin and Lactating Recipients

Recipient organ	Treatment of MLN cells (virgin)	Number of recipients	Label recovered	Percentage reduction in recovery	P^a
Virgin					
Small intestine	NRS[b]	20	1.98 ± 0.24		
	Anti-α	13	1.30 ± 0.48	34.3	< 0.001
	Anti-μ + anti-γ	12	1.97 ± 0.33		N.S.
Salivary glands	NRS	21	0.86 ± 0.32		
	Anti-α	12	0.61 ± 0.13	29.1	$0.01 < P < 0.05$
	Anti-μ + anti-γ	10	1.07 ± 0.45		N.S.
Lactating					
Small intestine	NRS	11	1.29 ± 0.16		
	Anti-α	13	0.84 ± 0.38	34.9	< 0.001
	Anti-μ + anti-γ	7	1.26 ± 0.22		N.S.
Salivary glands	NRS	10	0.36 ± 0.10		
	Anti-α	12	0.23 ± 0.06	36.1	$0.01 < P < 0.05$
	Anti-μ + anti-γ	7	0.50 ± 0.23		N.S.
Mammary glands	NRS	10	1.06 ± 0.26		
	Anti-α	12	0.68 ± 0.15	35.8	$0.001 < P < 0.01$
	Anti-μ + anti-γ	7	1.13 ± 0.31		N.S.

[a] Two-tailed Student's *t* test.
[b] Normal rabbit serum.
[c] Animals were 3–10 days postpartum.

migration is not affected with NRS or anti-μ + anti-γ serum and complement indicating that the selective localization displayed by the MLN cells is due to an IgA-bearing population.

Finally it was important to document that the abrogation of the MLN cell migration with anti-α serum was due to the specificity of the serum for IgA. In this case an aliquot of the anti-α serum was absorbed with IgA-Sepharose and the selective depletion experiment repeated. The results are summarized in Table 5. These data show that unabsorbed anti-α abrogates the MLN migration into small intestine and salivary glands, while preabsorbed sera lacking anti-α activity (as documented by agar diffusion) yield values similar to those of cells treated with NRS.

DISCUSSION

Peyer's patches are known to be enriched sources of IgA precursor cells (8) giving rise to MLN blasts which home to lactating mammary glands (5–7), lamina propria of the small intestine (9, 10), bronchus (9, 10) and urogenital tissue (10, 11). The demonstration of selective localization of IgA-bearing MLN cells in salivary glands represents an extension of these studies. The MLN and PLN homing patterns were identical when donor cells were obtained from either virgin or lactating donors suggesting that the physiological state of the donor animal has no effect on the homing ability of these lymphoid populations. Hormonal factors in

TABLE 5

Effect of Antisera, plus Complement, on Percentage Recovery of Injected ^{125}IUDR-Labeled MLN Cells from Recipient Organs

Recipient organ (virgin)	Recovery of injected label after treatment of MLN cells with: NRS	Anti-α	Anti-α/absorbed[a]	P^b
Experiment 1				
Small intestine	2.63 ± 0.19 (n = 2)	1.76 ± 0.06 (n = 3)	2.64 ± 0.25 (n = 3)	< 0.01
Salivary glands	0.58 ± 0.05 (n = 2)	0.24 ± 0.21 (n = 3)	0.58 ± 0.28 (n = 3)	$0.05 < P < 0.1$[c]
Experiment 2				
Small intestine	2.64 ± 0.38 (n = 4)	2.03 ± 0.23 (n = 4)	2.63 ± 0.40 (n = 4)	< 0.05
Salivary glands	1.14 ± 0.17 (n = 3)	0.80 ± 0.15 (n = 3)	1.28 ± 0.28 (n = 4)	< 0.05

[a] Anti-α serum absorbed with a solid-phase immunoabsorbent (XRPC-44, IgA, κ Sepharose 2B).

[b] Two-tailed Student's t test comparing the level of significance between the recovery of injected label in the anti-α- and anti-α/absorbed-treated MLN populations.

[c] The P value bordered on but was not less than the accepted level of significance.

the recipient animal have been shown to influence the emigration of IgA precursor cells to both the mammary gland (7) and urogenital tract (12). Indeed, in our studies, the migration of cell populations to mammary glands but not the other secretory sites studied (including salivary glands) depends on the physiological state of the recipient animal. Previous data have indicated that simultaneous homing to small intestine and mammary glands in lactating animals could occur (7). The present studies show that simultaneous selective homing of MLN cells can occur at these sites as well as salivary glands. In addition, the relative homing patterns of MLN and PLN cells to small intestine and salivary glands do not appear to be quantitatively diminished in the presence of active homing to lactating mammary glands (Tables 1 and 3).

As documented in earlier investigations (6, 7) our studies show that selective homing of MLN cells to salivary glands and other secretory sites was due to an IgA-bearing cell population. The mechanism responsible for selective localization of IgA precursor populations to mucosal areas remains unclear but our data and other investigations (6, 7, 9–11) show it can occur in the absence of deliberate antigen stimulation. Although the current studies do not permit us to determine if identical or different IgA-bearing subpopulations are appearing at the various secretory sites, previous evidence suggest that IgA cells of identical clonotype potential simultaneously seed distal mucosal areas following GALT immunization (4). Furthermore, recent studies suggest that intradoudenal immunization generates the dissemination of antigen-specific memory B cells to sites distant from antigen application, including lymphoid follicles associated with respiratory mucosa (13). Taken together these data document a central role for GALT in a common mucosal immune system. The secretory tissue in the oral cavity appears to be part of this common mucosal system and is linked by emigrating IgA-bearing cell populations in a manner identical to that of other distal secretory sites.

ACKNOWLEDGMENTS

We thank Doctors M. Lamm and M. McWilliams for helpful discussion on the methodology employed in these studies.

REFERENCES

1. Michalek, S. M., McGhee, J. R. Mestecky, J., Arnold, R. R., and Bozzo, L., *Science* **192,** 1238, 1976.
2. Mestecky, J., McGhee, J. R., Arnold, R. R., Michalek, S. M., Prince, S. J., and Babb, J. L., *J. Clin. Invest.* **61,** 731, 1978.
3. Montgomery, P. C., Connelly, K. M., Cohn, J., and Skandera, C. A., *In* "Secretory Immunity and Infection" (J. R. McGhee, J. Mestecky, and J. L. Babb, Eds.), p. 188. Plenum, New York, 1978.
4. Montgomery, P. C., Lemaitre-Coelho, I. M., and Vaerman, J. P., *Immunol. Commun.* **9(7),** 705, 1980.
5. Weisz-Carrington, P., Roux, M. E., McWilliams, M., Phillips-Quagliata, J. M., and Lamm, M. E., *J. Immunol.* **123,** 1705, 1979.
6. McWilliams, M., Phillips-Quagliata, J. M., and Lamm, M. E., *J. Exp. Med.* **145,** 866, 1977.
7. Roux, M. E., McWilliams, M., Phillips-Quagliata, J. M., Weisz-Carrington, P., and Lamm, M. E., *J. Exp. Med.* **146,** 311, 1977.
8. Craig, S. W., and Cebra, J. J., *J. Exp. Med.* **134,** 188, 1971.
9. Rudzik, R., Clancy R. L., Perey, D. Y. E., Day, R. P., and Bienenstock, J., *J. Immunol.* **114,** 1599, 1975.
10. McDermott, M. R., and Bienenstock, J., *J. Immunol.* **122,** 1892, 1979.
11. Bienenstock, J., McDermott, M., and Befus, D., *In* "Immunology of Breast Milk" (P. L. Ogra and D. H. Dayton, Eds.), p. 91. Raven Press, New York, 1979.
12. McDermott, M. R., Clark, D. A., and Bienenstock, J., *J. Immunol.* **124,** 2536, 1980.
13. Fuhrman, J. A., and Cebra, J. J., *J. Exp. Med.* **153,** 534, 1981.

CELLULAR IMMUNOLOGY 63, 210–215 (1981)

Lymphocyte Function in Experimental African Trypanosomiasis

IV. Immunosuppression and Suppressor Cells in the Athymic *nu/nu* Mouse[1]

JOHN M. MANSFIELD, RITA F. LEVINE, WALLA L. DEMPSEY, SAM R. WELLHAUSEN,[2] AND CARL T. HANSEN

Department of Microbiology and Immunology, School of Medicine, University of Louisville Health Sciences Center, Louisville, Kentucky 40292 and Veterinary Resources Branch, National Institutes of Health, Bethesda, Maryland 20014

Received April 30, 1981; accepted June 6, 1981

The role of T cells in the development and expression of antigen-nonspecific immunosuppression in experimental African trypanosomiasis was addressed. Nude (*nu/nu*) C57BL/6 NIH mice and their thymus-bearing (*nu/+*) littermates were infected with *Trypanosoma rhodesiense* and examined for suppression of splenic B-cell responses *in vitro* to the mitogen LPS. All animals developed splenic unresponsiveness to LPS. Further, both *nu/nu* and *nu/+* infected mice displayed suppressor cell activity in their spleen cell populations upon transfer to normal uninfected mouse spleen cell cultures. On the basis of these findings we suggest that both the generalized immunosuppression and the development of suppressor cell activity in the spleens of mice infected with *T. rhodesiense* are T-independent processes.

INTRODUCTION

The pathogenic African trypanosomes exert marked immunomodulatory effects upon their infected hosts (1). Antigen-nonspecific immunosuppression is one of the hallmarks of trypanosome infections; the cellular mechanisms underlying trypanosome-induced immunosuppression are currently being examined in detail (2–13). From most studies it is clear that African trypanosomes induce splenic suppressor cells which seem to be closely associated with the development and expression of immunosuppression. The identity and mode of action of the suppressor cells are not clear, however. Dependent upon the species of *Trypanosoma* studied, suppressor T cells (4), suppressor T cells and macrophages (3, 6, 13), or suppressor macrophages (8, 10) have been reported to arise in the spleen.

In experimental infections of mice with the human pathogen, *Trypanosoma rhodesiense*, we have described the presence of splenic suppressor cells (8–10). Although the cell affecting suppression exhibited characteristics of a macrophage, the nature of its induction as the result of infections is not yet clear. We have asked whether suppressor macrophages and immunosuppression are induced as the result

[1] This study has been supported by funds from the National Institutes of Health (Grants AI-15378 and AI-16467).

[2] Present address: Department of Immunology and Microbiology, Wayne State University School of Medicine, Detroit, Mich.

0008-8749/81/130210-06$02.00/0

of a primary stimulation of suppressor (or other) T cells by trypanosomes, or whether suppressor macrophages and immunosuppression appear independently of T-cell involvement. In the present study we report not only that the infection of athymic *nu/nu* (nude)[3] mice with *T. rhodesiense* results in a depression of splenic B cell responses but also that the suppressor macrophage is present in infected nude mouse spleen cell preparations. We suggest, therefore, that immunosuppression and splenic suppressor macrophage stimulation in experimental African trypanosomiasis are T-independent processes.

MATERIALS AND METHODS

Animals. Adult athymic *nu/nu* C57BL/6 NIH mice and thymic-bearing *nu/+* littermates were obtained from the animal procurement service of the National Institutes of Health. These animals were maintained in AAALAC-approved facilities with sterile food and bedding, acidified water, and filter bonnets for cages.

Trypanosomes and infections. Frozen stabilates of *T. rhodesiense* stock EATRO 1886 were obtained from the Walter Reed Army Institute of Research. This stock of *T. rhodesiense* was originally isolated from the blood of an African child in 1971. For the purposes of these studies, the LouTat 1.0 clone derived from this stock was used for infection of irradiated rats; when the animals exhibited parasitemia, they were exsanguinated and their blood was passed over a DEAE cellulose column as described by Lanham and Godfrey (14) in order to obtain a parasite suspension free of cellular blood elements. Infections were initiated in nude or thymus-intact mice with an ip injection of 10^6 washed, viable parasites in 0.25 ml of 0.01 *M* phosphate-buffered saline, pH 7.2, containing 50 μg/ml gentamicin.

Spleen cell cultures. At 2 and 6 weeks of infection, spleens were removed from the infected and control nude and *nu/+* mice. Spleens were aseptically teased apart in tissue culture medium (RPMI 1640 containing 5% FBS, 1 m*M* L-glutamine, and 50 μg/ml gentamicin) in order to obtain a single-cell suspension. After removal of cell clumps by sedimentation and erythrocytes by Tris–NH_4Cl lysis, the spleen cells were seeded into the wells of Microtest II plates (Falcon Plastics, Oxnard, Calif.). Each well contained 5×10^5 viable cells plus medium alone or LPS (lipopolysaccharide from *Escherichia coli* 055:B5; Calbiochem, La Jolla, Calif.) in a final volume of 200 μl. Any further additions to these cultures (see Table 2) were made in a 50-μl volume of medium. All plates were incubated at 37°C in an atmosphere of 5% CO_2 in air for 72 hr. During the terminal 18 hr of the culture period, 0.5 μCi of [^{3}H]TdR (tritiated thymidine, 20 Ci/mmol, NEN, Boston, Mass.) was added to all wells in order to assess DNA synthesis. Contents of culture wells were harvested onto glass fiber filters in a multiple-automated sample harvester, and the filters were processed for conventional liquid scintillation counting. Results are expressed as the mean counts per minute (cpm) of triplicate cultures.

RESULTS

Course of Infection

All infected animals exhibited fluctuating parasitemias throughout the infection (Fig. 1). The nude mice survived for a longer period than did the thymus-intact

[3] Abbreviations used: nude mice, athymic *nu/nu* C57BL/6 NIH mice; *nu/+*, thymus-intact mice; LPS, bacterial lipopolysaccharide; FBS, fetal bovine serum; [^{3}H]TdR, tritiated thymidine.

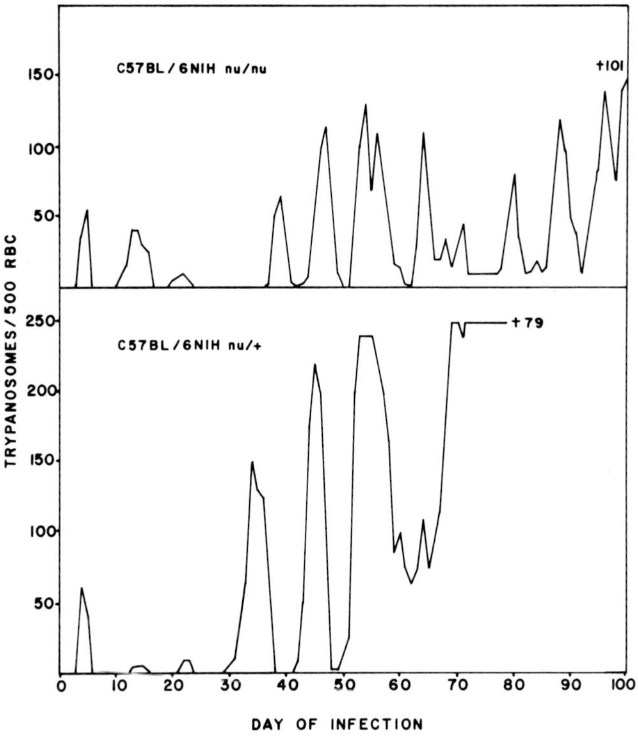

FIG. 1. Parasitemias in representative *nu/nu* and *nu/+* littermate C57BL/6 NIH mice infected with *T. rhodesiense*. Parasite numbers were enumerated daily by taking blood smears from the cut tail terminus.

littermate mice, and also exhibited less of a mean daily parasite burden. This finding is in agreement with the earlier studies of Campbell *et al.* (15) on *T. rhodesiense*-infected nude (BALB/c) mice. Splenomegaly was a common finding in all infected animals; histologically it was seen that germinal centers were markedly enlarged and that macrophages were present throughout the white and red pulp areas. As we have reported previously for other mice (7, 16), the enumeration of splenic B cells and macrophages (Ig^+ and nonspecific esterase-positive cells, respectively) revealed an increase in the proportion of these cells in infected nude and thymus-intact mice; although the proportion of T cells (Thy 1.2^+ cells) decreased in infected *nu/+* mouse spleens, T cells detectable at a low level (4%) in *nu/nu* spleens did not change in proportion. In terms of the antibody responses to the variant-specific surface antigens of the infecting clone, there was no difference in the magnitude of the *nu/nu* vs *nu/+* IgM response, but only the *nu/+* mice mounted an IgG response (Table 1).

Immunosuppression

In order to determine if infected nude mice were nonspecifically immunosuppressed, spleen cells were removed from infected mice and stimulated with LPS. All infected mice were completely depressed with respect to the blastogenic responses to LPS at 2 and 6 weeks of infection (Table 2). Thus, there was no difference between nude and thymus-intact mice with respect to a loss of B-cell stimulation

TABLE 1

Antibody Responses of Trypanosome-Infected Nude Mice to the Surface Antigen of the Initial Variant Type

Serum source[a]	Titer[b] IgM	IgG
nu/+	9	12
nu/nu	9	0

[a] Pooled sera were taken from mice which were infected for 2 weeks with clone LouTat 1.0 of *T. rhodesiense*; sera were absorbed with clone LouTat 1.6 extracts to remove antibody to common (invariant) antigens.

[b] Log_2 titers of sera were those dilutions giving a 1^+ reaction in an indirect fluorescent antibody test with *T. rhodesiense* LouTat 1.0; fluorescein-conjugated anti-mouse μ- and γ-chain-specific sera were used to determine IgM and IgG titers.

with this mitogen. Altering the dose of LPS used for stimulation (1–100 μg), the numbers of cells tested (10^5–10^6 cells), or the duration of the culture period (24–96 hr) revealed no alteration in the loss of responses in infected mice.

Suppressor Cells

A comparison of the ability of infected nude and thymus-intact mouse spleen cells to passively transfer immunosuppression to normal uninfected mouse spleen cell cultures was made. As shown in Table 2, passive transfer of infected *nu/nu* or nu/+ mouse spleen cells to the respective normal spleen cell cultures resulted in suppression of the LPS responses. Thus, a suppressor cell effect was demonstrated in spleens from both thymusintact and nude mice infected with *T. rhodesiense.*

DISCUSSION

There has been much speculation concerning the cellular events behind the immunomodulation observed in experimental and clinical African trypanosomiasis.

TABLE 2

Immunosuppression and Suppressor Cell Activity in Trypanosome-Infected Nude Mice

Responder cells[a]	Cells added[b]	cpm ($\times 10^{-3}$) Medium	LPS (20 μg/culture)
(N) *nu/nu*	—	4.2	100.1
(I) *nu/nu*	—	0.7	0.3
(N) *nu/+*	—	3.0	95.7
(I) *nu/+*	—	1.1	0.8
(N) *nu/nu*	(N) *nu/nu*	5.3	66.3
(N) *nu/nu*	(I) *nu/nu*	1.6	0.4
(N) *nu/+*	(N) *nu/+*	8.3	114.4
(N) *nu/+*	(I) *nu/+*	1.2	1.5

[a] Spleen cells (5×10^5) from nude (*nu/nu*) and thymus-intact (*nu/+*) C57BL/6 NIH littermates. N = normal (uninfected) mice; I = infected (Day 42) mice.

[b] Spleen cells (5×10^5).

Various proposals, based upon experimental studies with different *Trypanosoma* species, have been made. For example, in *T. brucei* infections of mouse it has been proposed that the primary events behind both polyclonal B-cell activation and the generalized immunosuppression are an antigen-nonspecific stimulation of helper- and suppressor-T-lymphocyte populations by the trypanosomes (4). Alternatively, polyclonal exhaustion of B- and T-cell clones by a trypanosome mitogen, coupled with generation of suppressor T cells and macrophages, has been proposed to occur (5, 6). In *T. congolense* infections of mice, it has been suggested that both suppressor T cells and suppressor macrophages are involved in immunosuppression (13).

Previously, we have demonstrated the presence of suppressor macrophages in spleens of mice infected with *T. rhodesiense* (8–10). These suppressor cells appeared within 1–3 days after infection, along with the development of spleen-associated immunosuppression, and persisted until the animals died of infection (8); if animals were drug-cured, splenic responsiveness returned as splenic suppressor cell activity declined (9). The suppressor cell was identified by several criteria (8, 10, 16): (a) adherence to plastic dishes, Sephadex G-10 and nylon wool columns; (b) nonspecific esterase staining reaction; (c) resistance to anti-Thy 1.2, anti-Lyt 2.2, and anti-Ig plus complement treatment; (d) resistance to irradiation; and, (e) sensitivity to treatment with silica particles. Although the suppressor cells exhibited these characteristics of macrophages, the nature of their induction as the result of infection was not clear. In the present study with nude mice we have asked whether the suppressor macrophages are induced by the T-dependent arm of the immune system [as with SIRS-activated macrophages (17)] or whether their appearance and activity are relatively T-independent events.

As demonstrated, both the thymus-intact and nude infected mice exhibited a loss of spleen cell responsiveness to LPS stimulation when tested at 2 and 6 weeks of infection. Thus, this demonstrates that T-cell-deficient mice infected with the African trypanosomes develop immunosuppression. In a related study with *T. brucei*-infected BALB/c nude mice, others have shown that infection does not diminish B-cell responses to LPS and that suppressor cells were not generated (2). Yet, in another study with *T. brucei*, loss of responsiveness to LPS stimulation was observed in the spleens of infected outbred ICRF nude mice (18); tests for suppressor cell activity were not made. However, in the two studies cited, a different species of *Trypanosoma* was employed and the nude mice used (BALB/c and outbred mice) were much more susceptible to infection than the *nu/nu* mice with the BL/6 background used in the present study (19). Thus, not only may different species of trypanosomes induce different types of suppressor cell populations but also the genetic background of the infected host may play a role in the development of immunosuppression.

The question of whether suppressor cells were associated with the splenic unresponsiveness to LPS in *nu/nu* and *nu/+* C57BL/6 mice was answered by cell transfer experiments. The results clearly demonstrate that suppressor cells are present in spleens at a time when these spleen cells are unresponsive to the mitogen. Thus, we demonstrate for the first time that both immunosuppression and suppressor cells arise in T-cell-deficient mice infected with *T. rhodesiense*. Although the cellular characteristics of the suppressor cell population were not elucidated in these studies because of limited supplies of nude mice with the C57BL/6 background, the suppressor cell could be removed by adherence depletion techniques from infected *nu/nu* or *nu/+* spleen cell populations (not shown) and is,presumably, a macrophage.

The studies presented here suggest that both the development of immunosuppression and the induction of suppressor cells in trypanosome-infected mice are T-independent events. However, a caveat must be introduced: namely that Thy 1.2-positive spleen cells were detected in nude mice, as others have shown (20), and that these cells may have played a role in the development both of suppression and of suppressor cells. On the other hand, these T cells were of insufficient numbers (or subclass) to induce T-dependent (IgG) antibody responses to the variant surface antigen of the infecting clone. Also, the present studies, which demonstrate an association between splenic suppressor (macrophage) cells and immunosuppression in infected nude mice, ultimately may not have relevance for the related findings in thymus-intact animals as the modes of induction and nature of the suppressor cells may be different in the presence of T cells. Another concern is the relevance of *in vitro* tests for immunocompetence in trypanosome-infected mice. Not only do infected mice (T deficient as well as thymus bearing) make sufficient protective IgM antibody responses *in vivo* to the succession of trypanosome variants arising but also make significant *in vivo* antibody responses to helper-T-cell-independent antigens (7, 15). Yet, LPS responses *in vitro* are depressed and would lead one to suspect a generalized B-cell dysfunction as the result of infection. At present, these types of paradoxical findings are unresolved.

In summary, both nude mice and their thymus-intact littermates develop B-cell unresponsiveness in spleen cell populations following infection with *T. rhodesiense*. Loss of B-cell responsiveness is correlated with the appearance of splenic suppressor cells.

REFERENCES

1. Mansfield, J. M., *Cell. Immunol.* **39,** 204, 1978.
2. Jayawardena, A. N., and Waksman, B. H., *Nature (London)* **265,** 539, 1977.
3. Eardley, D. D., and Jayawardena, A. N., *J. Immunol.* **119,** 1029, 1977.
4. Jayawardena, A. N., Waksman, B. H., and Eardley, D. D., *J. Immunol.* **121,** 622, 1978.
5. Corsini, A. C., Clayton, C., Askonas, B. A., and Ogilvie, B. M., *Clin. Exp. Immunol.* **29,** 122, 1977.
6. Askonas, B. A., Corsini, A. C., Clayton, C. E., and Ogilvie, B. M., *Immunology* **36,** 313, 1979.
7. Mansfield, J. M., and Bagasra, O., *J. Immunol.* **120,** 759, 1978.
8. Wellhausen, S. R., and Mansfield, J. M., *J. Immunol.* **122,** 818, 1979.
9. Wellhausen, S. R., and Mansfield, J. M., *J. Immunol.* **124,** 1183, 1980.
10. Wellhausen, S. R., and Mansfield, J. M., *Cell Immunol.* **54,** 414, 1980.
11. Moulton, J. E., and Coleman, J. L., *Amer. J. Vet. Res.* **38,** 573, 1977.
12. Roelants, G. E., Pearson, T. W., Tyrer, H. W., Mayor-Withey, K. S., and Lundin, L. B., *Clin. Exp. Immunol.* **37,** 457, 1979.
13. Pearson, T. W., Roelants, G. E., Pinder, M., Lundin, L. B., and Mayor-Withey, K. S., *Eur. J. Immunol.* **8,** 723, 1978.
14. Lanham, S. M., and Godfrey, D. G., *Exp. Parasitol.* **28,** 521, 1970.
15. Campbell, G. H., Esser, K. M., and Phillips, S. M., *Infect. Immunity* **20,** 714, 1978.
16. Mansfield, J. M., Wellhausen, S. R., and Bagasra, O., *In* "The Immunobiology of Parasitic Infections" (H. Friedman and W. Sodeman, Eds.). Univ. Park Press, Baltimore, 1981.
17. Tadukama, T., Kuhner, A. L., Rich, R. R., David, J. R., and Pierce, C. W., *J. Immunol.* **117,** 323, 1976.
18. Clayton, C. E., Ogilvie, B. M., and Askonas, B. A., *Parasite Immunol.* 1:39, 1979.
19. Levine, R. F., and Mansfield, J. M., *Infect. Immunity* **35,** 1981, in press.
20. Kindred, B., *Prog. Allergy* **26,** 137, 1979.

CELLULAR IMMUNOLOGY 63, 216 (1981)

ANNOUNCEMENT

Sixth Annual Premeeting Workshop on Reticuloendothelial Cell Function

October 12–13, 1981

The Reticuloendothelial Society will sponsor the Sixth Annual Premeeting Workshop on Reticuloendothelial Cell Function at Marquette University, Milwaukee, Wisconsin, on October 12–13, 1981. The workshop will be offered in two tracks covering a broad range of reticuloendothelial cell functions and is designed primarily to introduce investigators to fundamental techniques involving both macrophages and lymphocytes. An all-day session dealing with the collection, enrichment, and characterization of macrophages will be offered to a limited number of registrants on the first day. The other registrants will be given the opportunity to choose from among four or five topics in each of the sessions offered. The program will include laboratory exercises, demonstrations, and discussions allowing for hands-on experience with established laboratory procedures in an informal atmosphere encouraging free interchange of ideas and experiences among registrants and faculty. Registration will be limited.

Further information regarding the program and fees may be obtained from

Dr. Herbert B. Herscowitz
Department of Microbiology
Georgetown University Medical Center
3900 Reservoir Road, N.W.
Washington, D.C. 20007
Telephone: (202) 625-7602

CELLULAR IMMUNOLOGY 63, 217–219 (1981)

Papers to Appear in Forthcoming Issues

(Received and Accepted Dates follow Title)

MANUEL PATARROYO, PETER BIBERFELD, EVA KLEIN, AND GEORGE KLEIN. TPA Treatment Elevates the Natural Killer (NK) Sensitivity of Certain Human Lymphoid Lines. (Received 2/17/81; accepted 3/12/81).

VLADIMÍR VIKLICKÝ AND LADISLAV PAVLÍK. The Reduced Localization of i.v. Injected Lymphocytes in the Lymph Nodes, Lungs, and Small Intestine of Allogeneic Hosts Is a Consequence of Cell Destruction. (Received 12/31/80; accepted 5/5/81).

NEAL W. ROEHM, YOUNAN A. SIDKY, AND ROBERT AUERBACH. Lyt Phenotype Analysis of the Effector Cells Responsible for Evoking Lymphocyte-Induced Angiogenesis (LIA). (Received 3/25/81; accepted 5/13/81).

D. C. HOOPER AND R. A. MURGITA. Regulation of Murine T Cell Responses to Autologous Antigens by Alpha-Fetoprotein. (Received 4/27/81; accepted 5/16/81).

ROSELYNN A. DYNESIUS-TRENTHAM, DONNA ROWLAND, ELIZABETH LAROCHE, AND DAVID E. TRENTHAM. Rat Leukocyte Inhibitory Factor (LIF): Similarities to Human LIF and Generation by Cells from Rats with Collagen-Induced Arthritis. (Received 3/13/81; accepted 5/16/81).

P. HUTCHINGS AND A. COOKE. Analysis of the Cellular Interactions Involved in the Regulation of Induced Erythrocyte Autoantibodies. (Received 1/9/81; accepted 5/19/81).

S. BERRIH, J. LONDON, AND B. BONAVIDA. Murine Spleen Lymphocytes Bearing Receptors for Peanut Agglutinin. VII. Separation and Functional Characterization. (Received 2/20/81; accepted 5/27/81).

G. SEMENZATO, G. BASSO, U. FAGIOLO, A. PEZZUTTO, C. AGOSTINI, M. G. COCITO, AND G. GASPAROTTO. Active and Late Rosette Forming Cells: Immunological and Cytochemical Characterization. (Received 4/6/81; accepted 5/26/81).

MARVIN A. CUCHENS, KENNETH L. BOST, MARIE L. HOOVER, AND GERRIE A. LESLIE. Anti-IgD Enhancement of Primary Antibody Responses in Rats. (Received 4/13/81; accepted 5/29/81).

WILLIAM D. LYMAN, ANNA S. KADISH, AND CEDRIC S. RAINE. Experimental Allergic Encephalomyelitis in the Guinea Pig: Variation in Peripheral Blood Lymphocyte Responsiveness to Myelin Basic Protein during Disease Development. (Received 7/3/80; accepted 6/6/81).

MAREK ROLA-PLESZCZYNSKI. *In Vitro* Sensitization with HSV-Infected Cells Induces $T\mu$ Cells to become Cytotoxic $T\gamma$ Cells which Are Theophylline-Resistant. (Received 3/20/81; accepted 6/6/81).

L. VARESIO, H. T. HOLDEN, AND D. TARAMELLI. Suppression of Lymphokine Production: II. Macrophage-Dependent Inhibition of Production of Macrophage Activating Factor. (Received 4/8/81; accepted 6/7/81).

WULF DROEGE, MATTHIAS REDDEHASE, AND MICHAEL WOLF. Expression of Subregion and Haplotype Preference for H–2K^k Restricted Cytotoxic T Cell Responses *in Vivo* and at the Level of the Precursor Frequencies. (Received 5/5/81; accepted 6/9/81).

H. J. RADZUN, M. R. PARWARESCH, AND J. W. WITTKE. Polymorphism and Antigenic Specificity of Monocytic Acid Esterase (EC 3.1.1.6). (Received 5/29/81; accepted 6/9/81).

BERENICE KINDRED. A Comparison of H-2 Restriction of Helper Function Using T Cells from Radiation Chimeras and Nude Mice Bearing Thymus Grafts. (Received 1/21/81; accepted 6/14/81).

JOSEPH H. KORN. Modulation of Lymphocyte Mitogen Responses by Cocultured Fibroblasts. (Received 4/10/81; accepted 6/12/81).

B. L. PIKE, J. E. LAYTON, N. R. ROSE, AND G. J. V. NOSSAL. Surface Immunoglobulin Isotype, Activation and Tolerance Susceptibility of B Lymphocytes of New Zealand Black Mice. (Received 4/10/81; accepted 6/14/81).

DAVID R. WEBB AND IRENE NOWOWIEJSKI. Control of Suppressor Cell Activation via Endogenous Prostaglandin Synthesis: The Role of T Cells and Macrophages. (Received 10/6/80; accepted 6/15/81).

JOEL PICUS, RONALD N. GERMAIN, IRA J. FOX, MARK I. GREENE, BARUJ BENACERRAF, AND NORMAN L. LETVIN. Immunologic Effects of Whole Body Ultraviolet (uv) Irradiation. III. Defective Splenic Adherent Cell Function in Alloantigen Stimulated T Cell Proliferation. (Received 4/23/81; accepted 6/15/81).

R. L. DUNCAN, JR. AND W. P. MCARTHUR. Lactoferrin-Mediated Modulation of Mononuclear Cell Activities. I. Suppression of the Murine *in vitro* Primary Antibody Response. (Received 5/28/80; accepted 6/15/81).

THIERRY REME, ARNAUD DUPUY D'ANGEAC, MICHÈLE RADAL, AND BERNARD SERROU. Stimulatory Cells in the Generation of T-Cell Mediated Cytotoxicity. Potent Stimulating Activity of a Small Radioresistant Spleen Cell Population (RSCs). (Received 1/13/81; accepted 6/15/81).

JEAN-LUC TEILLAUD, CHANTAL RABOURDIN-COMBE, MARC STANISLAWSKI, CATHERINE NEAUPORT-SAUTES, AND WOLF HERMAN FRIDMAN. FcγR Expressed on T Cell Hybrids: Specificity, Behavior, and Relationship with Ia Antigens. (Received 2/24/81; accepted 6/19/81).

ADRIANA DEL REY, HUGO O. BESEDOVSKY, ERNST SORKIN, MOSÉ DA PRADA, AND STEFAN ARRENBRECHT. Immunoregulation Mediated by the Sympathetic Nervous System. II. (Received 1/12/81; accepted 6/17/81).

LEIF C. ANDERSSON, MIKKO HURME, MICHAEL A. HORTON, ELIZABETH SIMPSON, AND CARL G. GAHMBERG. Molecular Characterization of the Ly-6.2 Antigen. (Received 4/10/81; accepted 6/23/81).

EMILIA MIA SORDILLO, SUSUMU IKEHARA, ROBERT A. GOOD, AND PAUL P. TROTTA. Immunosuppression by 2′-Deoxycoformycin. Studies on the Mode of Administration. (Received 3/13/81; accepted 6/23/81).

HIDEAKI IRIBE, TOSHITAKA KOGA, KAORU ONOUE, SHOZO KOTANI, SHOICHI KUSUMOTO, AND TETSUO SHIBA. Macrophage-Stimulating Effect of the Synthetic Muramyl Dipeptide and its Adjuvant-Active and Inactive Analogs for the Production of T Cell Activating Monokines. (Received 5/28/81; accepted 6/30/81).

THIERRY HERCEND, LEE M. NADLER, JOHN M. PESANDO, ELLIS L. REINHERZ,

STUART F. SCHLOSSMAN, AND JEROME RITZ. Expression of a 26,000 Dalton Glycoprotein on Activated Human T Cells. (Received 5/22/81; accepted 7/2/81).

YONG SUNG CHOI, KEE HAK LIM, AND F. KINGSLEY SANDERS. Effect of Interferon-α on Pokeweed Mitogen-Induced Differentiation of Human Peripheral Blood B Lymphocytes. (Received 1/28/81; accepted 7/3/81).

JACQUELINE PRUNET AND JACQUES PANIJEL. *In Vitro* Recovery of Aptitude for Primary Immunization by Specifically Depleted Cell Populations: Induction by a Lipopolysaccharide. (Received 10/17/80; accepted 7/7/81).

MARK BALLOW AND ALEXANDER G. PANTSCHENKO. *In Vitro* Effects of ADA Inhibitors on Lymphocyte Mitogen Responsiveness in the Mouse. (Received 3/10/81; accepted 7/7/81).

YOUNG TAI KIM, MARC E. WEKSLER, AND GREGORY W. SISKIND. Antigen Induced *In Vitro* Inhibition of Immune Responsiveness. (Received 3/12/81; accepted 7/7/81).

RUTH NETA, S. B. SALVIN, AND MOHAMED SABAAWI. Mechanisms in the *In Vitro* Release of Lymphokines. I. Comparative Kinetics in the Release of Six Lymphokines in Inbred Strains of Mice. (Received 3/16/81; accepted 7/7/81).

SCOTT R. EVANS AND HOWARD M. JOHNSON. The Induction of At Least Two Distinct Types of Interferon in Mouse Spleen Cell Cultures by *Corynebacterium parvum*. (Received 5/8/81; accepted 7/7/81).

DOMINIQUE KAISERLIAN, MIREILLE DARDENNE, AND JEAN-FRANÇOIS BACH. Dissociated Effects of Thymectomy at Weaning on T Cell-Mediated Responses *in Vitro*. Correction by the Serum Thymic Factor, FTS, and Its Analogues. (Received 6/18/81; accepted 7/7/81).

WALLACE Y. LANGDON AND GEOFFREY R. SHELLAM. Inhibition of Antigen-Induced T Cell Proliferation by Antibodies to Endogenous AKR-MuLV. (Received 2/9/81; accepted 7/9/81).

DEBORAH WILSON AND HELEN BRALEY-MULLEN. Antigen Requirements for Priming of Type III Pneumococcal Polysaccharide-Specific IgG Memory Responses: Suppression of Memory with the T Independent Form of Antigen. (Received 6/18/81; accepted 7/11/81).

ALAN LICHTENSTEIN, RICHARD MURAHATA, MARILOU TERPENNING, JOHN CANTRELL, AND JACOB ZIGHELBOIM. Activation and Mechanism of Action of Suppressor Macrophages. (Received 5/22/81; accepted 7/11/81).

JENNIFER BAILEY, JON C. LEWIS, WILLIAM H. GROVER, DAVID HARRIS, DONALD L. EVANS, MARY J. RUEBUSH, LESLIE K. PAULUS, DONALD BURGESS, AND ARTHUR H. HALE. Surface Analysis of Early and Late MOPC-315-EL Tumor Cells. (Received 1/27/81; accepted 7/10/81).

CHARLES M. BALCH, MICHAEL R. LOKEN, PATRICIA A. DOUGHERTY, AND EDWIN W. ADES. Expression of a 16,000 m.w. Antigen on Human Suppressor T Lymphocytes. (Received 6/9/81; accepted 7/13/81).

CHARLES S. PAVIA, DANIEL P. STITES, AND ROBIN FRASER. Transplantation Antigen Expression on Murine Trophoblast Detection by Induction of Specific Alloimmunity. (Received 6/9/81; accepted 7/16/81).

M. RUCHETON, J. CARAUX, C. THIERRY, C. ESTEVE, H. VALLES, J. DUFER, A. DESPLACES, D. ZAGURY, AND B. SERROU. Human Autologous Rosettes. II. Further Characterization: Markers and Functions. (Received 7/8/81; accepted 7/20/81).

CELLULAR IMMUNOLOGY **63,** 221–227 (1981)

Analysis of the Cellular Interactions Involved in the Regulation of Induced Erythrocyte Autoantibodies

P. HUTCHINGS AND A. COOKE

Department of Immunology, Middlesex Hospital Medical School, Arthur Stanley House, 40-50 Tottenham Street, London W1P 9PG England

Received January 9, 1981; accepted May 19, 1981

When normal mice are immunised with rat red blood cells (RBC) they produce autoantibodies against their own red blood cells as well as antibodies against determinants on rat RBC non-cross-reacting with self-RBC. Spleen cells from mice primed with rat RBC specifically suppress the subsequent induction of autoantibody in normal mice. The response to non-cross-reacting determinants on rat RBC is not affected. The results presented here indicate that either T cells or a thymus have to be present in the recipient for suppression to be manifest. It may therefore be the case that suppression is in fact induced in the recipient by the primed T cells.

INTRODUCTION

Autoantibodies can be induced in normal mice by injection of antigens cross-reactive with self-determinants (1). Playfair and Marshall-Clarke demonstrated that normal mice immunised with rat RBC develop autoantibodies against their own red cells (2). The development of autoantibodies is dependent on T cells; neonatally thymectomised mice and nude mice do not make either type of response to rat RBC (2, 3).

This autoantibody response is also regulated by T cells. Spleen cells or T cells from animals rendered autoimmune following immunisation with rat RBC will suppress the subsequent induction of autoantibody on transfer to naive recipients (4–6). The suppression is antigen specific since only the autoantibody response is suppressed. The response to non-cross-reacting determinants on rat erythrocytes is not suppressed and is even enhanced in most cases (4, 5).

In order to establish whether the transferred primed spleen cells themselves directly mediate the suppression or whether they act to induce suppressor cells in the recipients, transfer experiments were performed in nude mice. The results of these experiments are described.

MATERIALS AND METHODS

Mice. CBA (Ca) mice and nu/nu CBA (Ca) mice were obtained from Dr. Colin Hetherington at the CRC, Harrow, London.

0008-8749/81/140221-07$02.00/0

Induction of red cell autoantibodies. A positive DCT was induced by injecting 2×10^8 rat RBC (obtained by cardiac puncture of Wistar rats and washed three times before use) ip four times at weekly intervals.

Direct antiglobulin (Coombs) test : DCT. Mice were bled from the retroorbital sinus and the red cells washed four times in isotonic saline before testing. A single batch of rabbit anti-mouse immunoglobulin (shown by immunoelectrophoresis to react against IgG and IgM) was stored in small aliquots at −20°C and used at a standard final solution of 1:80.

After 30 min of incubation with antiserum at room temperature agglutination was scored microscopically on a scale ranging from microscopic positive (1) to massive agglutination involving all the cells (4). Positive and negative controls were included in cell determinations. This more rapid method of assessing DCT activity has been found to correlate with a longer assay using doubling dilutions of developing antiserum to establish an endpoint.

Statistical analysis. Comparisons between groups of mice were carried out using a Mann–Whitney test.

Detection of rat agglutinins. Mice were bled from the retroorbital sinus and doubling dilutions of the heat-inactivated serum tested in microwells against freshly washed rat RBC (2%) in 1% BSA in PBS. All dilutions of the sera were in 1% BSA in PBS. Agglutination was read after 1 hr at 37°C.

Generation of antigen-specific suppressor cells and suppressor assay. Antigen-specific suppressor cells were generated as described previously (4). Briefly, mice received weekly injections of 2×10^8 rat RBC ip and spleens from these mice were used as a source of suppressor cells. Splenocytes (50×10^6) were washed three times and transferred iv from such primed mice into nu/nu mice, their littermate heterozygous controls or normal CBA (Ca) control mice. These recipients were then immunised with 2×10^8 rat RBC ip at four weekly intervals and the induced autoantibody was measured as described previously.

Preparation of T cells. T cells were purified according to the method of Mage *et al.* (7). Petri dishes 10 cm in diameter were coated with 15 ml of a 10 μg/ml solution of affinity-purified goat anti-mouse Fab at room temperature for 45 min. The antibody was recovered and the plates were washed twice with PBS and finally with PBS + 1% FCS. The plates were then stored at −20°C.

Spleen cells were prepared and the red blood cells were ammonium chloride lysed. After washing, the cells were resuspended at 10^7 cells/ml in MEM or RPMI containing Hepes, glutamine, and 5% FCS. Three millilitres of this suspension was added to each plate which was then placed on a level surface at 4°C. After 30 min, the cells were swirled gently and then left for a further 30 min. Nonadherent cells were then poured off and the plates were washed twice with cold medium (no FCS) to remove maximum nonadherent cells. Recovery was about 30%.

The goat anti-mouse Fab was a generous gift from Dr. G. G. B. Klaus (N.I.M.R), Mill Hill, London).

RESULTS

Transfer of Normal Spleen Cells into Nude Mice

When normal spleen cells or T cells are transferred into nude mice they restore the capacity to respond to rat RBC in terms of both anti-rat antibody and au-

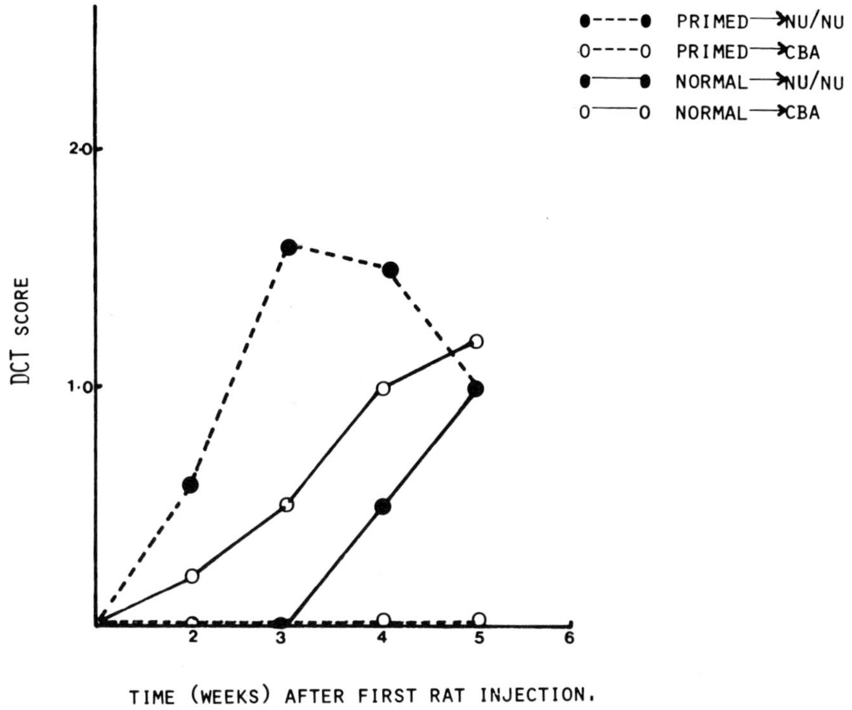

FIG. 1a. Transfer of normal or rat primed (suppressor) spleen cells into normal and nude mice: effect on the induced autoantibody response (self). Red cell autoantibody, induced by injection of rat RBC, was measured by a direct Coombs test (DCT), scored and analysed statistically as indicated under Materials and Methods. Five mice were in each group.

toantibody production. Reconstituted nude mice make antibodies to determinants on rat RBC which are detectable by serum agglutinins and autoantibodies to self-determinants detectable by DCT (Table 1, Figs. 1a and 1b).

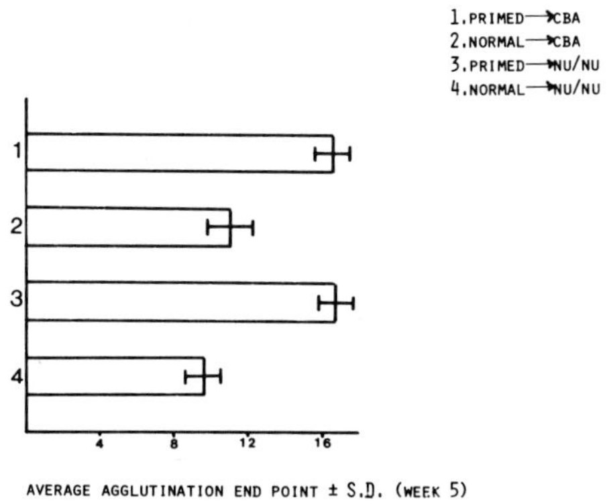

FIG. 1b. Transfer of normal or rat primed (suppressor) spleen cells into normal and nude mice: effect on serum agglutinins to rat RBC (non-self). Serum agglutinins to rat RBC were measured as described under Materials and Methods. These antibodies do not react with mouse RBC. Five mice were in each group.

TABLE 1

Restoration of Autoantibody and Rat Agglutinin Responses in CBA nu/nu Mice Reconstituted with CBA (Ca) Spleen Cells

Transferred cells	No. of DCT-positive mice	Average rate Agglutinin titre[a]
None	0/10	0
CBA (Ca) spleen	11/14	6.8 ± 1.2
CBA (Ca) "T"[b]	7/12	7.75 ± 2.5

[a] Agglutination titer is expressed as the last well giving agglutination using doubling dilutions of the test sera and starting at a dilution of 1:2.

[b] Splenic T cells were prepared as described under Materials and Methods. Recipients received 25 × 10⁶ T cells iv or 50 × 10⁶ spleen cells iv.

Transfer of Rat RBC-Primed Spleen Cells into Nude Mice

When rat RBC-primed CBA spleen cells are transferred into normal mice or heterozygous littermates of nude mice they suppress the subsequent induction of autoantibodies in the recipients (Fig. 1a). However, when such primed spleen cells are transferred into nude mice, not only do they restore the rat agglutinin response (Fig. 1b) but the autoantibody response is no longer suppressed in these mice (Table 2, Fig. 1a).

This experiment has been repeated three times and in all cases primed spleen cells transferred into normal recipients suppressed the subsequent induction of DCT but did not suppress induction in syngeneic nude recipients (at Week 4, with 14 mice in each group, $2\,\alpha = 0.01$). Indeed in two out of three experiments these responses are actually enhanced compared to the transfer of nonprimed spleen cells (Fig. 1a). Thus spleen cells which will suppress the autoantibody response in normal mice fail to do so in nude mice (Fig. 1a).

Transfer of Nude Spleen Cells to Normal Mice

Spleen cells were transferred from nude mice which had received 50×10^6 rat primed CBA spleen cells and four injections of 2×10^8 rat RBC to induce auto-

TABLE 2

Inability to Suppress an Autoantibody Response in Nude Mice[a]

Transferred spleen cells	Recipients	No. of DCT-positive mice
CBA normal	CBA	10/10
CBA normal	CBA (nu/nu)	11/14
CBA primed	CBA	2/10
CBA primed	CBA (nu/nu)	13/14
None	CBA	10/10
None	CBA (nu/nu)	0/10

[a] Recipients received 50×10^6 spleen cells iv and their first injection of 2×10^8 rat RBC ip 24 hr later.

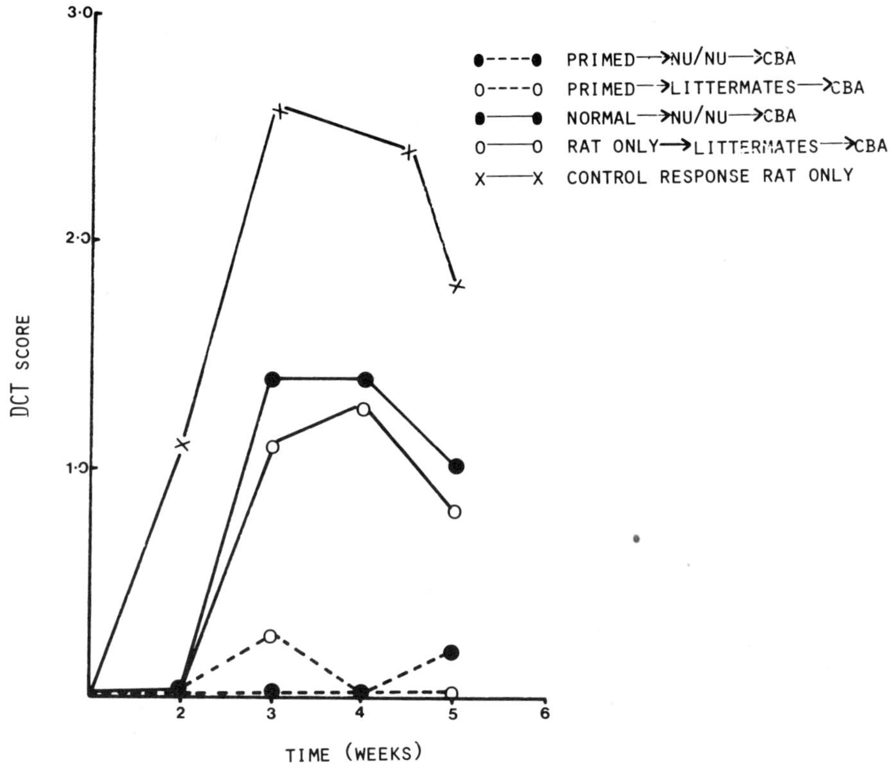

FIG. 2. The potential for suppression is parked. Rat RBC-primed CBA spleen cells do not suppress the induced autoantibody response in CBA nude mice whereas these primed spleen cells suppress the induced autoantibody response in intact mice (Fig. 1a). Nude recipients of rat RBC primed spleen cells were challenged with rat RBC and the suppressor activity of their spleen cells compared to that of spleen cells from normal littermates similarly treated. Also shown for comparison is the suppressor activity of spleen cells from nude mice reconstituted with normal CBA spleen cells and challenged with rat RBC. 5 mice in each group.

antibodies 7 weeks previously. As shown in Fig. 2 these spleen cells totally suppressed the subsequent induction of autoantibody in normal CBA recipients (Fig. 2). We have previously shown that nonreconstituted nude spleens do not mediate suppression after rat RBC priming.(3)

DISCUSSION

It has been clearly demonstrated that cells are present in the spleens of normal mice following induction of erythrocyte autoantibodies with rat erythrocytes which will suppress the subsequent induction of red cell autoantibodies following their injection into naive recipients (4–6). The data presented in this paper suggest that these "suppressor" cells are able to exert their activity when T cells or a thymus are present in the recipient mice. Cells which mediate suppression in a normal animal can enhance an autoantibody response in nude mice (See Fig. 1a). There are several possible interpretations of these results. Spleen cells from rat RBC-primed mice might induce suppressor cells in the recipient animal. Work from other investigators has shown that a subpopulation of T helper cells (T_H, Ly 1^+ Qa

1^+) is capable of inducing feedback suppressor T cells from a precursor pool of Ly 1^+ 23^+ Qa1^+ cells (8). It is possible that the suppressor cells present in the primed spleen cell preparations are, in fact, such cells with specificity for the autoantibody idiotype which on transfer will induce suppressor cells in the recipient. The deficiency of such a T_H population due to lack of production of the autoantibody idiotype could explain the observation that CBA/N mice which are defective in their ability to produce autoantibody although they respond normally to rat RBC in terms of a rat agglutinin response (9), are also defective in their ability to generate antigen-specific suppressor cells regulating autoantibody production (10). This perhaps parallels the situation described by Bottomley *et al.* (11) in which it was shown that CBA/N mice which do not make the T15 idiotype lack those T_H cells with specificity for this idiotype and fail to generate idiotype-specific suppressor T cells.

If this explanation of our data is indeed the case then our previous studies on the regulation of autoimmune states in the spontaneously autoimmune mouse strains NZB and (NZB × NZW)F_1 could give us some clue to the factors which may be involved in defective regulation.

When we examined the specific suppressor function regulating experimentally induced autoimmune states in (NZB × NZW)F_1 mice, we found that female mice, although producing an autoantibody response to rat RBC stimulation, did not appear to generate any demonstrable suppressor function (12). These animals clearly do not lack antigen-specific T_H cells involved in the production of autoantibody or the B cells producing the antoantibody. The defect in these animals must be due to a lack of inducer cells.

We have studied both nonspecific and specific suppressor function in young and old NZB mice and have shown that in both cases the spleens are capable of being stimulated to produce nonspecific suppressor cells by Con A (13) and, furthermore that old and young NZB mice can certainly generate the inducers for suppression of the antigen-specific induced autoantibodies following priming with rat RBC.

Therefore, if there is a defect in suppressor cell function in the NZB it lies not at the final effector T_S cell (Ly 23^+), nor in the inducer of suppressor population but lies in older mice in the precursor pool for inducible suppressor cells (Ly 1^+ 23^+ Qa1^+). This interpretation would be compatible with the theory proposed by Cantor *et al.* (13).

Since spleen cells have been used in these transfer experiments we cannot exclude the possibility that primed B cells themselves may contribute to the suppression seen in a normal recipient as a result of induction of an anti-idiotypic response in the recipients. There is some evidence which indicates that nude mice cannot mount an anti-idiotypic response and therefore suppression through anti-idiotype would not be seen in these animals (14). Therefore another possible explanation for the enhanced autoantibody response in nude recipients of primed spleen cells may be that this may reflect an absence of regulatory circuits in these mice.

It is interesting to note that the "suppressor" population may be successfully parked in the nude mouse spleen. The suppression seen in the second spleen transfer from the nude mouse to a normal CBA recipient was found to be equal to, if not better than, the suppression seen when primed CBA spleen cells are transferred into normal recipients. This could be the result of further challenge of committed T or B cells with antigen in the intermediate nude host (Fig. 2.).

Experiments are currently in progress to investigate the effect of transferring normal T cells back into nude recipients of primed spleen cell populations and also the possible role of B cells in mediating suppression in these experiments.

ACKNOWLEDGMENTS

We would like to thank Professor Playfair, Professor Roitt, and Dr. P. Lydyard for reading this manuscript. The work presented here was supported by grants from The Wellcome Foundation and the Medical Research Council.

REFERENCES

1. Weigle, W. O., *Clin. Exp. Immunol.* **9,** 437, 1971.
2. Playfair, J. H. L., and Marshall-Clarke, S., *Nature New Biol.* **243,** 213, 1973.
3. Cooke, A., Hutchings, P. R., and Nayak, R., *Immunology* **40,** 335, 1980.
4. Cooke, A., Hutchings, P. R., and Playfair, J. H. L., *Nature (London)* **273,** 154, 1978.
5. Naysmith, J. D., and Elson, C. J., *Abstr. Allergol. Immunopathol.* **5,** 480, 1977.
6. Gare, N. F., and Cox, K. O., *Proc. Aust. Soc. Med. Res.* **11,** 40, 1978.
7. Mage, M. G., McHugh, L. L., and Rothstein, T. L. *J. Immunol. Methods.* **15,** 47, 1977.
8. Cantor, H., and Gershon, R. K., *Fed. Proc.* **38,** 2058, 1979.
9. Marshall-Clarke, S., Cooke, A., and Hutchings, P. R., *Eur. J. Immunol.* **9,** 820, 1979.
10. Cooke, A., Hutchings, P., and Marshall-Clarke, S., *Immunology* **41,** 815, 1980.
11. Bottomley, K., Mathieson, B. J., Cosenza, H., and Mosier, D. E., *In* "B Lymphocytes in the Immune Response" (M. Cooper, D. Mosier, I. Scher, and E. Vitetta, Eds), p. 323. Elsevier/North Holland, New York.
12. Cooke, A., and Hutchings, P., *Immunology* **41,** 819, 1980.
13. Cantor, H., McVay-Boudreau, L., Hugenberger, J., Naidorf, K., Shen, F. W., and Gershon, R. K., *J. Exp. Med.* **147,** 1116, 1978.
14. Schrater, A. F., Goidl, E. A., Thorbecke, J., and Siskind, G. W., *J. Exp. Med.* **150,** 808, 1979.

CELLULAR IMMUNOLOGY **63,** 228–236 (1981)

A Comparison of H-2 Restriction of Helper Function Using T Cells from Radiation Chimeras and Nude Mice Bearing Thymus Grafts[1]

BERENICE KINDRED[2]

Institute for Immunology and Genetics, German Cancer Research Center, Im Neuenheimer Feld 280, 6900 Heidelberg, West Germany

Received January 21, 1981; accepted June 14, 1981

T cells from nude chimeras and radiation chimeras were tested for ability to cooperate with B cells of the thymus epithelium strain and B cells of the T-stem-cell strain in nude mice of appropriate strain backgrounds and also in irradiated F_1's together with bone marrow cells of the two relevant strains (i.e., A-nu ←B or A→ A × B chimera T cells were tested in A-nu and B-nu and in irradiated A × B F_1 with A bone marrow cells or B bone marrow cells). Whether the donor chimeras were antigen primed or not, all cells, when tested in nudes, provided help for the T-stem-cell type only. In contrast, in most cases, chimera T cells, tested in irradiated F_1's, provided help for bone marrow cells of both thymus and T-stem-cell strains. These data indicate the involvement of two helper cell populations and an hypothesis to explain their interaction is presented.

INTRODUCTION

H-2 restriction has been demonstrated for T cell–B cell cooperation *in vivo* (1, 2), for skin graft rejection (3), for *in vitro* killing of virus-infected cells (4), and for the transfer of delayed-type hypersensitivity (5, 6). There is extensive literature on the subject of recognition of self-histocompatibility by T cells (see *Immunological Review* **42**). The original data on cytotoxic T cells (7) support the idea that self-recognition is "learned" in the thymus but in other systems the learning was not absolute and evidence supported preference for the thymus type but not absolute committment to it (8, 9). Using radiation chimeras, similar results have been reported for helper T cells *in vivo* (10) although Tynan and McDevitt (11) found no effect of the thymus epithelium and, in nudes grafted with allogeneic or semi-allogeneic neonatal thymuses, helper cell histocompatibility recognition appeared to be genetically determined and no evidence for learning could be found (12, 13). Further, nudes with thymus grafts showed no learning by cytotoxic T cells (14).

These data have been collected in different systems and under different conditions. In studies of T cell–B cell help *in vivo* variables include the use of radiation chimeras or nude chimeras, of antigen primed or unprimed donors and of nude mice or irradiated F_1's as transfer hosts. The aim of the present work was to

[1] This work was supported by the SFB 136 of the Deutsche Forschungsgemeinschaft.

[2] Present address: Max-Planck-Institut für Biologie, Abteilung Immungenetik, Corrensstrasse 42, Tübingen, West Germany.

0008-8749/81/140228-09$02.00/0

combine these variables for a comparison to determine whether an explanation might be found for apparent contradictions and to elucidate the normal situation by use of the different available experimental systems. As summarized in Table 1, striking differences were found when chimera T cells were tested in nude mice or in irradiated F_1's. An hypothesis to explain these differences is presented.

MATERIALS AND METHODS

Mouse strains. The mouse strains used in these experiments were BALB/c (C), C57BL/6 (B6), C3H (C3), DBA/2 (D2), and CBA. These together with the BALB/c-nu and C57BL/6-nu were purchased from GL Bomholtgard, Denmark, and CBA-nu were purchased from Olac Ltd., England.

Chimeras. Nude chimeras were made by grafting a whole neonatal thymus subcutaneously in the shoulder region. Radiation chimeras were irradiated with 800 rad from a Gammatron S80F using a ^{60}Co source and a dose rate of approximately 115 rad/min. They were reconstituted with 10^7 fetal liver cells from 16- to 17-day-old donors. Nude chimeras were used after 6 weeks and radiation chimeras after 3 months. We have previously used the symbol C57 $\rightarrow$ BALB/c-nu for BALB/c-nu bearing a C57BL/6 thymus graft etc., but as, e.g., D2 $\rightarrow$ C3D2 has been widely used for C3D2 F_1 irradiated and reconstituted with D2 cells, the nude chimeras will be indicated as BALB/c-nu $\leftarrow$ C57 in order to name the strain providing the T-stem cells first in both kinds of chimera.

Cell transfer. For cell transfer, spleen and lymph node cell suspensions were passed over nylon wool columns (15) and treated with appropriate antisera and complement to remove contaminating cells, i.e., cells from BALB/c-nu $\leftarrow$ C57 chimeras were treated with BALB/c anti-C57BL/6 serum and guinea pig complement which had been absorbed with agarose and SRBC. Viable cells (5×10^6, were injected intravenously for testing in nudes. F_1 transfer recipients were irradiated with 800 rad and injected with 5×10^6 viable T cells and 5×10^6 bone marrow cells. Controls with bone marrow cells only, were made to check that there was no antibody production due to contaminating T cells or generation of T cells during the experiment. Where possible, the same pool of cells from chimeric donors was tested in both nude and irradiated recipients.

TABLE 1

Summary of Secondary Anti-SRBC Responses in Recipients of T Cells from Nude or Radiation Chimeras

	Test system			
			Irradiated F_1 (A × B)	
Chimera	A-nu	B-nu	A bone marrow	B bone marrow
A-nu $\leftarrow$ B	+	−	+ (weak)	−
A $\rightarrow$ A × B	+	−	+	+
A-nu $\leftarrow$ B Primed	+	−	+	+
A $\rightarrow$ A × B Primed	+	−	+	+

Note. Chimera T cells were injected into nudes of the T-stem-cell or thymus epithelium strains and into irradiated F_1's together with bone marrow cells from the T-stem-cell or thymus epithelium strains.

Immunization. A 0.2-ml volume of 10% SRBC solution was injected intraperitoneally on the same day as the cells. The mice were bled and boosted with the same antigen dose on Day 7 and rebled on Day 14. Antibody was assayed by hemagglutination. The number of recipients which responded and the mean positive response are shown in the tables.

RESULTS

The previous finding (12) that cells from BALB/c-nu ← C57 chimeras when transferred to BALB/c-nu and C57BL/6-nu helped only the former, i.e., the stem cell strain and not the thymus strain, was repeated using BALB/c-nu bearing CBA thymus grafts, a strain combination in which there is no hematopoietic histocompatibility difference. BALB/c-nu were grafted with neonatal CBA thymuses and after 6 weeks T-cell suspensions from these donors were transferred to BALB/c-nu and CBA-nu recipients. The anti-SRBC responses of these mice are shown in Table 2. Clearly the cells were able to reconstitute BALB/c-nu but there was no response in the CBA-nu. As in the previous experiments these BALB/c-nu recipients made only IgM antibody even after boosting. It can also be seen that with the BALB/c-CBA combination there was no primary response in nudes of the thymus donor strain. When T cells from a BALB/c-nu ← C57BL/6 or even from a BALB/c-nu ← BALB/c were transferred to C57BL/6-nu there was frequently a primary response. This was presumably an allogeneic effect and was not observed after boosting. In other experiments to be presented allogeneic effects were sometimes found in the primary response but not after boosting; similarly, Swain and Dutton (16) found no positive allogeneic effect on the secondary response. Therefore in the following presentation only secondary responses will be shown. Where antigen-primed donors were used the data presented are responses after boosting in the transfer recipient.

When cells from radiation chimeras were tested in nude recipients the results were comparable to those found using nude chimeras as donors, as shown in Table 3. Cells transferred to nude recipients permitted a response in nudes of the same strain as the fetal liver (i.e., T-stem cell) donor and not in nudes from the second

TABLE 2

$-\text{Log}_2$ Hemagglutination Titer of Anti-SRBC Antibody Produced by Nude Recipients of Antiserum and Complement-Treated T Cells from BALB/c-nu Mice Bearing Syngeneic or Allogeneic Thymus Grafts

				Primary		Secondary	
Donor	Stem cell	Thymus	Recipients	Number	Mean positive	Number	Mean positive
BALB/c-nu ← BALB/c	BALB/c	BALB/c	BALB/c-nu	7/7	6.8 ± 0.7	3/3[a]	7.7 ± 2.1
			C57BL/6-nu	7/7	6.8 ± 1.3	0/7	
BALB/c-nu ← CBA	BALB/c	CBA	BALB/c-nu	2/3	5.5 ± 2.1	1/2	4.0
			CBA-nu	0/4		0/3	
BALB/c-nu ← C57BL/6	BALB/c	C57Bl/6	BALB/c-nu	2/6	6.5 ± 0.7	5/5	6.0 ± 1.2
			C57BL/6-nu	5/6	6.6 ± 1.5	0/5	

[a] This was the only group which produced 2-mercaptoethanol-resistant antibody.

TABLE 3

$-Log_2$ Hemagglutination Titer of Secondary Anti-SRBC Antibody Produced by Nude Recipients of T Cells from Radiation Chimeras

					Whole serum		2-ME treated	
Donor	Stem cell	Thymus	T-Cell Treatment	Recipient	Number	Mean positive	Number	Mean positive
BALB/c → CB6	BALB/c	CB6	None	BALB/c-nu	7/7	8.1 ± 1.4	6/7	6.5 ± 2.9
			αC57 +C′	BALB/c-nu	3/3	7.5 ± 3.5	2/3	6.0 ± 4.2
			None	C57BL/6-nu	3/7	8.0 ± 1.0	2/7	8.0 ± 0
			αC57 +C′	C57BL/6-nu	0/3		0/3	
C57 → CB6	C57BL/6	CB6	αBALB/c +C′	BALB/c-nu	0/4		0/4	
			αC57 +C′	BALB/c-nu	0/3		0/3	
			αBALB/c +C′	C57-nu	5/5	7.8 ± 1.1	5/5	6.2 ± 0.8
			αC57 +C′	C57-nu	0/2		0/2	

parental strain of the thymus. Without antibody treatment the small number of contaminating F_1 T cells were able to restore some nudes of the second strain. Unlike nudes restored with T cells from nudes bearing allogeneic or semiallogeneic thymus grafts most of the recipients of T cells from radiation chimeras produced IgG as well as IgM antibodies.

Cells from unprimed chimeras, did however, show a difference when tested in irradiated F_1 recipients together with bone marrow cells from each parental strain (Table 4). T cells from nudes which had been grafted with an allogeneic thymus showed poor help for the stem cell strain and none for the thymus donor strain but in contrast, T cells from radiation chimeras helped B cells from both parental strains and 2-mercaptoethanol-resistant antibody was produced in the secondary response. This was not due to contamination of the bone marrow with T cells as controls which had received bone marrow cells only were always negative.

To test whether priming of the donors might result in help for both stem cell and thymus type B cells in all cases, thymus-bearing nudes and radiation chimeras were primed and then used as T-cell donors for nudes and irradiated F_1's. As shown in Table 5, priming of the chimeric donors did not affect the ability of their T cells to reconstitute nudes. There was still reconstitution only of nudes of the same H-2 haplotype as the T-cell precursors and the thymus epithelium did not appear to

TABLE 4

$-Log_2$ Hemagglutination Titer of the Secondary Anti-SRBC Antibody Response by Irradiated F_1 Mice Injected with Bone Marrow Cells from either Parental Strain and T Cells from Nude Chimeras or Radiation Chimeras

					Whole serum		2-ME treated	
Donor	Stem cell	Thymus	Irradiated recipient	Bone marrow	Number	Mean positive	Number	Mean positive
D2 → C3D2	DBA/2	C3D2	C3D2	DBA/2	5/5	9.5 ± 1.0	5/5	6.8 ± 0.45
				C3H	5/5	10.25 ± 0.5	5/5	7.0 ± 0
BALB/c-nu ← C57	BALB/c	C57BL/6	CB6	BALB/c	2/3	3.5 ± 0.7	0/2	
				C57BL/6	0/4		0/4	

TABLE 5

$-Log_2$ Hemagglutination Titer of the Secondary Anti-SRBC Antibody Response by Nude Mice Injected with T Cells from Nude or Radiation Chimeras

				Whole serum		2-ME treated	
Donor	Stem cell	Thymus	Recipient	Number	Mean positive	Number	Mean positive
BALB/c-nu ← CBA	BALB/c	CBA	BALB/c-nu	2/3	5.5 ± 2.1	0/3	
			CBA-nu	0/10		0/10	
BALB/c-nu ← BALB/c	BALB/c	BALB/c	BALB/c-nu (Expt 1)	2/3	5.0 ± 0	ND	
			BALB/c-nu (Expt 2)	3/4	7.0 ± 0	3/4	5.8 ± 2.1
			C57-nu (Expt 1)	0/4		ND	
			C57-nu (Expt 2)	0/4		0/4	
BALB/c-nu ← C57	BALB/c	C57	BALB/c-nu (Expt 1)	1/2	4.0	0/2	
			BALB/c-nu (Expt 2)	2/4	3.5 ± 0.7	0/4	
			C57-nu (Expt 1)	0/4		0/4	
			C57-nu (Expt 2)	0/5		0/5	
D2 → C3D2	DBA/2	C3D2	BALB/c-nu (Expt 1)	6/6	3.3 ± 0.5	5/6	2.9 ± 0.9
			BALB/c-nu (Expt 2)	5/5	5.8 ± 0.8	2/5	4.5 ± 0.7
			CBA-nu (Expt 1)	0/6		0/6	
			CBA-nu (Expt 2)	0/6		0/6	

Note. The donors were primed with SRBC 3 weeks before transfer.

have any influence. Further, recipients of cells from nude chimeras were unable to make IgG antibody even though IgG could be made by the donors.

When cells from primed chimeras were tested in irradiated F_1's, however, they were able to help B cells of both stem cell and thymus type whether the chimera was made by grafting a nude with an allogeneic neonatal thymus or by injecting a lethally irradiated F_1 with fetal liver from one parental strain (Table 6). Further, all recipients produced IgG antibody.

Since there was no evidence for lethal GvH reaction in these experiments, an attempt was made to test whether the cells from primed chimeras could also help bone marrow cells of both parental types in F_1 environments other than the combination of T-stem-cell and thymus strains. T cells of BALB/c-nu bearing C3H

TABLE 6

$-Log_2$ Hemagglutination Titer of the Secondary Anti-SRBC Antibody Response by Irradiated F_1 Mice Injected with Bone Marrow Cells from either Parental Strain and T Cells from Nude Chimeras or Radiation Chimeras

					Whole serum		2-ME treated	
Donor	Stem cell	Thymus	Irradiated recipient	Bone marrow	Number	Mean positive	Number	Mean positive
D2 → C3D2	DBA/2	C3D2	C3D2	C3H	7/7	10.4 ± 0.9	7/7	4.1 ± 1.35
				DBA/2	7/7	10.5 ± 1.2	7/7	5.6 ± 0.8
BALB/c-nu ← C3H	BALB/c	C3H	C3D2	BALB/c	4/4	8.0 ± 3.5	2/4	8.0 ± 0
				C3H	3/4	8.3 ± 2.1	2/4	7.0 ± 0
BALB/c-nu ← C57	BALB/c	C57BL/6	CB6	BALB/c	5/5	7.2 ± 0.8	5/5	4.8 ± 1.8
				C57BL/6	5/5	6.8 ± 1.3	4/5	5.8 ± 1.7

Note. The donors were primed with SRBC 3 weeks before transfer.

thymus grafts were able to give some help for BALB/c bone marrow cells in CB6 F_1's but not for C3H in C3B6 F_1's and there was no help for C57BL/6 bone marrow cells in either environment (Table 7).

The failure of H-2^d T cells which had differentiated in an H-2^k thymus and which could help H-2^k bone marrow cells in an H-2^d × H-2^k F_1 to help H-2^k cells in an H-2^k × H-2^b F_1 could be confirmed using radiation chimeras as T-cell donors. However, positive help for bone marrow cells of the stem cell type could not be shown as, in two experiments, all animals died of GvH effects. Why DBA/2 T cells which had differentiated in DBA/2 × C3H thymus should kill BALB/c × C57BL/6 F_1 but not C3H × C57BL/6 F_1 and why GvH effects were not seen when nude chimera donors were used is unclear.

DISCUSSION

The influence of the thymus epithelium on the restriction specificity of helper T cells from chimeras could be shown when the T cells were tested in appropriate irradiated F_1's together with parental bone marrow cells but not when the T cells were tested for ability to reconstitute nude mice even in experiments where the same cell preparation was used for both. This was the case regardless of whether the donor chimeras were made by grafting nude mice with allogeneic neonatal thymuses or by injecting irradiated F_1 with parental strain fetal liver. T-Cell dependent responses in transfer recipients were not altered by priming the chimera with antigen except when cells from nude chimeras were tested in irradiated F_1 recipients. T cells from unprimed nude gave, at best, very poor responses in irradiated F_1's while cells from primed nude chimeras were able to help bone marrow cells from both parental strains. It seems likely that this difference is merely quantitative.

A possible interpretation of these results is that two T-cell populations are involved in T-cell–B cell help. The idea of T cell–T cell synergy in helper effects has been put forward previously (17–19). Two T-cell populations are also involved in transfer of delayed-type hypersensitivity (20). Hünig and Schimpl (9) have developed the concept of specific and unspecific help, and specific and unspecific help was also demonstrated by Waldmann *et al.* (21). According to the hypothesis

TABLE 7

Secondary Anti-SRBC Responses of Mice[a] of F_1 Combinations Involving Only One of the Strains of the Chimera Donor

Donor	Stem cell	Thymus	Irradiated recipient	Bone marrow	Whole serum Number	Whole serum Mean	2-ME treated Number	2-ME treated Mean
BALB/c-nu ← C3H	BALB/c (A)	C3H (B)	CB6 (A × C)	BALB/c (A)	3/4	3.3 ± 2.5	0/4	
				C57BL/6 (C)	0/4		0/4	
			C3B6 (B × C)	C3H (B)	0/4		0/4	
				C57BL/6 (C)	0/3		0/3	
D2 → C3D2	DBA/2 (A)	C3D2 (A × B)	CB6 (A × C)	BALB/c (A)	Dead (10)			
				C57BL/6 (C)	Dead (10)			
			C3B6 (B × C)	C3H (B)	0/5			
				C57BL/6 (C)	0/5			

[a] These mice were irradiated and injected with bone marrow cells of either parental strain and chimera T cells.

presented here, not only are two populations active but also, the population which "learns" to recognize the major histocompatibility complex of the thymus epithelium cannot act alone in a nude mouse of the same strain as the thymus donor although the presence of such a population can be shown after transfer to irradiated F_1's.

I would like to suggest that the two populations are: (i) antigen-recognizing T cells (ART) which have antigen receptors coded in a similar way to B-cell immunoglobulin. For these cells the thymus provides a necessary environment for differentiation but the differentiation pathway is predetermined and the cells can only cooperate with cells having the same genetically determined H-2 haplotype. The demonstration of T-cell specificity in cells which have differentiated in the absence of a thymus (22–24) is evidence that at least some T cells do not need the thymus for the development of specificity. (ii) A larger population of T cells which are specialized for the recognition of major histocompatibility antigens. These cells (HRT) potentially have the same repertoire for recognizing major histocompatibility antigens as the ART but there is positive selection in the thymus for those which recognize the Ia antigens of the thymus epithelium. It is also necessary to postulate that negative selection occurs for ART which recognize antigens in the thymus. Tolerance to antigens of the donor thymus has been demonstrated (14, 25) and for the present argument it is not relevant whether this is brought about by thymus epithelium or thymic lymphocytes. Although the major selective force is exerted in the thymus some cells can also be selected by other elements of the cellular environment as suggested by Katz *et al.* (26) in their theory of adaptive differentiation.

In the initiation of an immune response the ART bind antigen presented by H-2-compatible macrophages (27). Both antigen-specific ART and HRT which recognize the H-2 antigens of the B cell (possibly in a particular conformation as a consequence of antigen binding) are necessary for B-cell activation to give a normal immune response.

Considering the data presented here a BALB/c-nu bearing a C57BL/6 thymus graft would have a normal repertoire of BALB/c ART, a large population of HRT which recognize C57BL/6 H-2 antigens selected by the thymus epithelium and a small population of HRT which recognize BALB/c antigens selected by the cells of the BALB/c environment. Therefore these mice are able to mount an adequate immune response in which the HRT which recognize C57BL/6 H-2 antigens play no part. After transfer of such cells to BALB/c-nu a response is possible by the same means although dilution of the already low number of BALB/c recognizing HRT cells may account for the failure to produce IgG. In a C57BL/6-nu the BALB/c ART do not cooperate with the C57BL/6 macrophages and the response does not proceed although C57BL/6 recognizing HRT are present. When cells are transferred to irradiated F_1 mice the ART can cooperate with the remaining F_1 macrophages and activate HRT of both the population which recognizes BALB/c cells and the population which recognizes C57BL/6 cells and therefore antibody production proceeds whether BALB/c or C57BL/6 bone marrow cells were injected with the T cells. This implies that ART activate HRT which in turn activate B cells. However, Tees and Schreier (28) have described reconstitution of nude mice with an antigen-specific, H-2-restricted T-helper-cell clone which permits responses similar to those found here, i.e., a good IgM response but not IgG even after boosting. Unless some HRT can develop in the absence of a thymus and are included in the Thy-1-positive cells found in nude mice, these findings must mean that ART alone can activate H-2 compatible B cells although the subsequent response is incomplete.

The failure of nude recipients of T cells from an allogeneic nude chimera to make IgG antibody suggests that HRT are necessary for the switch from IgM to IgG antibody production. Since the nude chimera donors were able to make IgG, the failure in the recipients is likely to be quantitative. However, it is also possible that the necessary cells were in organs other than the spleen and lymph nodes and were not transferred.

The experiments in which A $\rightarrow$ B chimera cells were tested in irradiated A $\times$ C and B $\times$ C mice (Table 7) are open to question as alloreactive cells were not removed from the T-cell populations. Nevertheless the data as they stand are consistent with the hypothesis presented. Thus A ART can cooperate only with syngeneic or semi allogeneic macrophages and in A $\times$ C F_1's the response begins but as the HRC include populations which can recognize A and B but not C, there is help for A bone marrow but no help for C bone marrow. In a B $\times$ C F_1, A ART cannot cooperate with the macrophages and the response is blocked at the outset.

The foregoing explanation, based on the existence of two populations of T cells, a condition which is now fairly widely accepted, seems more likely than explanations based on the existence of suppressor cells which can act in nudes but not in irradiated F_1's or on the presence in nude mice of cells which specifically prevent collaboration of H-2-incompatible cells regardless of the thymus in which the T cells have differentiated. It is also difficult to explain these data in terms of production of factors by the injected mature T cells since such factors are usually unspecific and should therefore lead to positive responses in all cases. Further, we have been able to show primary but not secondary responses in nude mice following administration of supernatants from activated T cells (29). It seems even less likely that inability of chimera T cells to restore nude mice from the thymus donor strain is due to a host versus graft reaction as allogeneic T cells can survive for a considerable time in nude mice (30) and F_1 T cells can restore parental strain nudes (31).

It should be emphasized that this is a hypothesis to explain the data presented here and must remain questionable until the two hypothetical populations of cells can be separated.

Apparent contradictions in the influence of the thymus on cytotoxic T cells have also been found. It has been shown that cytotoxic T cells from A $\rightarrow$ A $\times$ B radiation chimeras can kill virus infected cells from both strains (7) while cytotoxic T cells from nudes bearing allogeneic or semiallogeneic thymus grafts kill virus-infected cells of the host (i.e., the T stem cell) strain and not of the thymus donor strain (14). These findings are analogous to those reported here for helper cell activity and a similar situation may exist with regard to help for B cells and help for cytotoxic T cells.

Both nude mice and radiation chimeras are highly abnormal systems and comparison of the two may prove much more informative than concentration on one or the other.

ACKNOWLEGMENTS

I gratefully acknowlege the helpful discussions of Dr. Barry Skidmore and Dr. Jan Cerny and the excellent technical assistance of Miss Catherine Woodrufe.

REFERENCES

1. Kindred, B., and Shreffler, D. C., *J. Immunol.* **109,** 350, 1972.
2. Katz, D. H., Hamaoka, T., Dorf, M. E., and Benacerraf, B., *J. Exp. Med.* **137,** 1405, 1973.
3. Kindred, B., *Eur. J. Immunol.* **4,** 388, 1974.
4. Zinkernagel, R. M., and Doherty, P. C., *J. Exp. Med.* **141,** 1427, 1975.
5. Miller, J. F. A. P., Vadas, M. A., Whitelaw, A., and Gamble, J., *Proc. Nat. Acad. Sci. USA* **73,** 2486, 1976.
6. Zinkernagel, R. M., *J. Exp. Med.* **144,** 776, 1976.
7. Zinkernagel, R. M., Callahan, G. N., Althage, A., Cooper, S., Klein, P. A., and Klein, J., *J. Exp. Med.* **147,** 882, 1978.
8. Matzinger, P., and Mirkwood, G., *J. Exp. Med.* **148,** 84, 1978.
9. Hünig, T., and Schimpl, A., *Eur. J. Immunol.* **9,** 730, 1979.
10. Sprent, J., and von Boehmer, H., *J. Exp. Med.* **149,** 387, 1979.
11. Tynan, M. L., and McDevitt, H. O., *J. Immunol.* **105,** 1190, 1970.
12. Kindred, B., *Cell. Immunol.* **51,** 64, 1980.
13. Kindred, B., *In* "Proceedings of the 3rd International Workshop on Nude Mice" (N. D. Reed, Ed.), in press, 1981.
14. Zinkernagel, R. M., Althage, A., Waterfield, E., Kindred, B., Welsh, R. M., Callahan, G., and Pincetl, P., *J. Exp. Med.* **151,** 376, 1980.
15. Julius, M. H., Simpson, E., and Herzenberg, L. A., *Eur. J. Immunol.* **3,** 645, 1973.
16. Swain, S. L., and Dutton, R. W., *J. Immunol.* **119,** 1179, 1977.
17. Janeway, C. A., Jr., *J. Immunol.* **114,** 1408, 1975.
18. Muirhead, D. Y., and Cudkowicz, G., *J. Immunol.* **120,** 579, 1978.
19. Tada, T., Takemori, T., Okumura, K., Nonaka, M., and Takuhisa, T., *J. Exp. Med.* **147,** 446, 1978.
20. Strassmann, G., Eshar, Z., and Moses, E., *J. Exp. Med.* **151,** 628, 1980.
21. Waldmann, H., Lefkovits, I., and Feinstein, A., *Immunology,* **31,** 353, 1976.
22. Gillis, S., Union, N. A., Baker, P. E. and Smith, K. A., *J. Exp. Med.* **149,** 1460, 1979.
23. Ikehara, S., Hamashima, Y., and Matsuda, T., *Nature (London)* **283,** 335, 1975.
24. Wagner, H., Hardt, C., Heeg, K., Röllinghoff, M., and Pfizenmaier, K., *Nature (London),* **284,** 278, 1980.
25. Kindred, B., *Cell. Immunol.* **24,** 189, 1976.
26. Katz, D. H., Skidmore, B. J., Katz, L. R., and Bogowitz, C. A., *J. Exp. Med.* **148,** 727, 1978.
27. Erb, P., and Feldmann, M., *J. Exp. Med.* **142,** 460, 1975.
28. Tees, R., and Schreier, M., *Nature (London),* **283,** 780, 1980.
29. Kindred, B., and Bösing-Schneider, R., *Scand. J. Immunol.*, in press, 1981.
30. Kindred, B., and Loor, F., *Cell. Immunol.* **16,** 432, 1975.
31. Kindred, B., *In* "Immulogic Defects in Laboratory Animals (M. E. Gershwin and B. Merchant, Eds.), Plenum, New York, in press, 1981.

CELLULAR IMMUNOLOGY **63**, 237–248 (1981)

12-*O*-Tetradecanoylphorbol-13-acetate (TPA) Treatment Elevates the Natural Killer (NK) Sensitivity of Certain Human Lymphoid Lines

MANUEL PATARROYO, PETER BIBERFELD,* EVA KLEIN, AND GEORGE KLEIN

*Department of Tumor Biology, Karolinska Institutet, and *Department of Pathology, Karolinska Hospital, S 104 01 Stockholm, Sweden*

Received February 17, 1981; accepted March 12, 1981

The natural killer (NK) sensitivity of two Epstein–Barr virus (EBV)-carrying Burkitt lymphoma lines (Daudi and Raji) and one EBV-negative acute lymphocytic leukemia-derived T-cell line (Molt-4) increased when they were cultured for 24 hr in the presence of the phorbol ester TPA. In the EBV-carrying lines, this increase occurred independently of the entry of the cells into the viral cycle. 12-*O*-Tetradecanoylphorbol-13-acetate (TPA)-treated Daudi and Molt-4 cells cross-competed for the effectors in the NK assay as indicated by the cold-target inhibition tests. TPA-treated cells showed an increased binding of human but not of mouse lymphocytes.

INTRODUCTION

Superinfection of human Epstein–Barr virus (EBV)[1] -genome-carrying lymphoblasted lines (e.g., Raji) with the P3HR-1 strain of EBV or induction of the viral cycle with sodium butyrate increased their natural killer (NK) sensitivity (1). This increase was dependent on and coincident with the entry of a proportion of the cells into the viral cycle. The question whether elevated NK sensitivity was due to the appearance of new EBV-determined cell surface antigens had to be left open, however. It is known that EBV superinfection may change the expression of certain plasma membrane constituents, such as immunoglobulin, insulin receptors (2), and complement receptors (3). Though EBV-determined membrane antigens were shown to appear on the superinfected cells at approximately the same time, it is possible that not these but an EBV-induced change in cell membrane properties is responsible for the change in NK sensitivity (4). This was suggested by the finding that the natural killer cells did not recognize the serologically detectable EBV antigens since $F(ab')_2$ fragments of positive sera did not block the NK effect of the P3HR-1 virus-superinfected Raji cells (M. Patarroyo, E. Klein, and G. Klein, to be published).

The tumor-promoting phorbol ester TPA (12-*O*-tetradecanoylphorbol-13-ace-

[1] Abbreviations used: EBV, Epstein–Barr virus; TPA, 12-*O*-tetradecanoylphorbol-13-acetate; NK, natural killer; EA, early antigen; CFD, carboxyfluorescein diacetate; BL, Burkitt lymphoma; PBL, peripheral blood lymphocytes.

0008-8749/81/140237-12$02.00/0

tate) is a powerful modulator of the cell membrane. It increases membrane fluidity (5) and modifies the expression of differentiation properties (6). It is blastogenic for human lymphocytes (7) and can act as an inducer of the viral cycle in some EBV-carrying lymphoid lines (8).

The results reported here show that TPA treatment increases the NK sensitivity of human B- and T-lymphoblastoid lines and this increase is independent of the induction of the EBV cycle in the B lines.

MATERIALS AND METHODS

Cell lines. All cells were propagated as stationary suspension cultures in RPMI 1640 medium with 8% fetal calf serum (Grand Island Biological Co., Grand Island, N.Y.) and subcultured twice weekly. Raji and Daudi are EBV-carrying Burkitt lymphoma (BL)-derived lines (9, 10). BJAB is an EBV-negative BL line (11). BJAB/B95-8 is its *in vitro* EBV-converted subline (12). Molt-4 is an EBV-negative T-cell line, derived from an acute lymphocytic leukemia patient (13). K562 is an EBV-negative erythroleukemia line, established from a patient with chronic myeloid leukemia in blast crisis (14). Lukes is an EBV-negative B-cell lymphoma line (received from Dr. Elliot Kieff, University of Chicago, Chicago, Ill.).

TPA treatment. Lymphoid cells were suspended at a concentration of 5×10^5/ml. The tumor-promoting agent TPA (from Sigma Chemical Co., St. Louis, Mo.) was added to a final concentration of 50 ng/ml. The cells were incubated at 37°C for 24 hr, washed three times, and tested for NK sensitivity. TPA-treated cells are designated by adding the symbol T after their name.

Lymphocytes. Lymphocytes were separated from heparinized blood by the method of Böyum (15), using Ficoll (Pharmacia, Uppsala, Sweden)–Isopaque (Nyegaard & Co., Oslo, Norway).

Cytotoxic assay. ^{51}C-release tests were performed in a Falcon II microplate (Falcon Labware, Div. Becton–Dickenson, Oxnard, Calif.). Peripheral blood lymphocytes (PBL) were used as effector cells at a 100:1 effector:target ratio. Target cells (5×10^3) were added to each well in a volume of 0.1 ml, followed by 5×10^5 PBL per 0.1 ml. Finally, 0.1 ml medium was added to each well. Test combinations were set up in quadruplicate. Control wells with target cells alone were included in each experiment to determine the spontaneous and maximum release. Microplates were incubated at 37°C in a 5% CO_2 atmosphere for 4 hr. Subsequently, the plates were centrifuged at 1500 rpm for 5 min. The cell-free supernatant (0.1 ml) was removed. Specific ^{51}Cr release was determined according to the formula:

$$\frac{\text{release in test} - \text{spontaneous release}}{\text{maximal release} - \text{spontaneous release}} \times 100.$$

The microplates were placed on a Bellco (Bellco Glass, Inc., Vineland, N.J.) rocker at low speed during incubation.

Cold-target inhibition of cytotoxicity. The cytotoxic tests were performed as above, but with the addition of graded numbers of unlabeled cells, simultaneously with the target cells in 0.1 ml medium. Results were expressed as percentage inhibition.

Demonstration of EBV-associated antigens. Early antigen (EA) was stained by direct fluorescence on acetone-fixed smears, using the fluorescein isothiocyanate-conjugated IgG fraction of an EA and VCA antibody-positive BL patient serum (F-Ester) at a dilution of 1:40, as described previously (16).

Kinetic experiments. Aliquots of Daudi cells were removed from the same pool and exposed to TPA for different time intervals. All cells were harvested simultaneously, labeled with ^{51}Cr, and exposed to the same effector lymphocytes. Isotope release was measured in TPA-treated cells alone ("spontaneous release") and as target cells following effector exposure. Natural killing was calculated as mentioned above.

Enumeration of human or mouse lymphocyte-binding cells (conjugates). Human PBL and mouse lymph node lymphocytes were washed two times with plain medium and incubated in a nylon wool column at 37°C for 30 min as described (17). The nylon-wool-passed cells were washed three times and labeled with the vital dye carboxyfluorescein diacetate (CFD) as follows:

A stock solution CFD (10 mg/ml in acetone) was diluted 1:250 in BSS. Serum free lymphocytes (5×10^6) were incubated in 1 ml diluted CFD for 15 min at 37°C. Thereafter, the cells were washed three times and used as effectors for the conjugate tests.

For conjugate formation, labeled cells and targets were mixed in 1:1 ratio (0.5×10^6 each) and centrifuged for 5 min at 1500 rpm. The pelleted cells were incubated at 37°C for 15 min., resuspended by strong shaking, and counted in a Leitz Orthophan microscope with a Ploem type "Opakilluminator" system. For fluorescence, 470-nm blue excitation light, with 4-mm B-6 38 + 1.5-mm B612 + AL 470 (Schott, Mainz, West Germany) as primary filters, a 495-nm interference plate, and a K510 barrier filter was used. The cells were examined at a magnification of 312×. The percentage of conjugates was determined by counting the number of target cells that bound one or more labeled cells.

Morphology. TPA-treated and untreated Daudi cells were fixed after both overnight and 48 hr of incubation and processed for examination by transmission electron microscopy.

RESULTS

Increased NK Sensitivity after TPA Treatment

The NK sensitivity of six lymphoblastoid lines was tested after treatment with TPA (Table 1). The lines varied in their NK sensitivity prior to the treatment. In accordance with previous results, Molt-4 was highly sensitive. The EBV-negative Burkitt lymphoma line BJAB was more sensitive than its *in vitro* EBV-converted subline (BJAB/B95-8). Daudi, Raji, and Molt-4 cultured in the presence of TPA exhibited increased NK sensitivity. The effect on Daudi was particularly pronounced. The sensitivity of Lukes and BJAB did not change.

Effect of TPA on Spontaneous ^{51}Cr Release and Early Antigen (EA) Synthesis in Daudi Cells.

The spontaneous ^{51}Cr release of TPA-treated Daudi cells was similar to that of the control. TPA did not induce the EBV cycle, as judged by the frequency of EA-

TABLE 1

Effect of TPA Treatment on the Sensitivity of Lymphoid Lines to Natural Killer (NK) Cells

Cell line	TPA treatment[a]	Type of cell	EBV-DNA and EBNA	No. of experiments	Percentage specific ^{51}Cr release (mean ± SE)
Daudi	−	B[b]	+	14	12.4 ± 2.8
Daudi	+	B	+	14	25.9 ± 4.0
Raji	−	B	+	7	4.1 ± 1.1
Raji	+	B	+	7	8.5 ± 1.8
BJAB	−	B	−	5	17.4 ± 7.4
BJAB	+	B	−	5	16.0 ± 7.9
BJAB-B95-8	−	B	+	5	9.8 ± 5.6
BJAB-B95-8	+	B	+	5	9.8 ± 6.3
Lukes	−	B	−	7	10.7 ± 3.3
Lukes	+	B	−	7	9.1 ± 1.9
Molt-4	−	T[c]	−	6	31.5 ± 4.2
Molt-4	+	T	−	6	46.0 ± 6.9

[a] The cells were exposed to 50 ng TPA for 24 hours prior to the assay.
[b] B-Cell line derived from Burkitt lymphoma.
[c] T-Cell line derived from acute lymphocytic leukemia.

positive cells (Table 2). The presence of TPA in the culture medium inhibited cell proliferation but did not influence cell viability even after 4 days.

Kinetics of Change in NK Sensitivity in TPA-Treated Daudi

Daudi cells were incubated with TPA for different periods and tested for NK sensitivity, using effector cells from the same donor. NK sensitivity increased with time and peaked at 24 hr (Fig. 1).

Cold-target inhibition tests confirmed that TPA-treated Daudi (Daudi T) cells interact with NK effectors that can also damage Molt-4 or K562 cells. As shown in Fig. 2, Daudi T cells competed most effectively, when added to the homologous (anti-Daudi T) cytotoxicity system. K562 and Molt-4 could also compete, but at a lower level, whereas untreated Daudi cells competed only weakly.

TABLE 2

Spontaneous ^{51}Cr Release and Percentage of Early Antigen (EA)-Positive Cells in TPA-Treated Daudi Cells

Cell line	No. of experiments	Percentage spontaneous release (mean ± SE)	Percentage early antigen-positive cells[a]
Daudi	14	15.6 ± 1.9	1
Daudi T	14	18.0 ± 1.7	1

[a] Three hundred cells were counted.

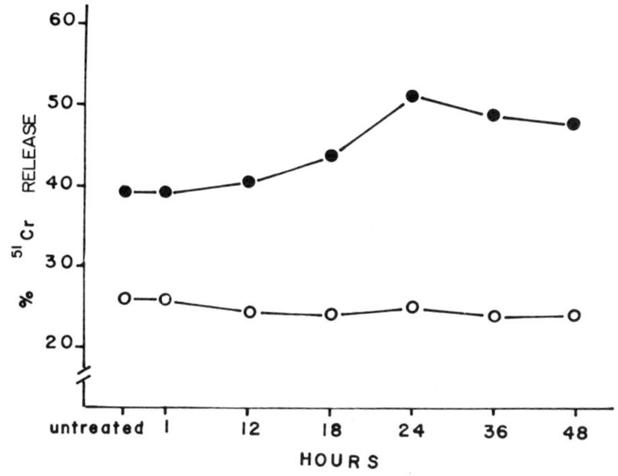

FIG. 1. NK sensitivity of Daudi cells as a function of time after TPA treatment. Aliquots of cells from the same pool were exposed to TPA for different time intervals. All cells were harvested simultaneously, and exposed to the same effector population. Percentage spontaneous release (○). Percentage of isotope release in presence of effector cells (●).

In the reciprocal experiment, Molt-4 cells were used as targets (Fig. 3). Lysis was inhibited most efficiently by Daudi T; Molt-4 competed well, while untreated Daudi and Raji did not compete. The competition experiments were repeated six times with similar results.

Conjugate Formation between TPA-Treated Daudi and Molt 4 Cells and Normal Lymphocytes

The lymphocytes were prelabeled with fluorescein and could be easily recognized within the conjugates (Figs. 4a and 4b). There was a considerable increase in the

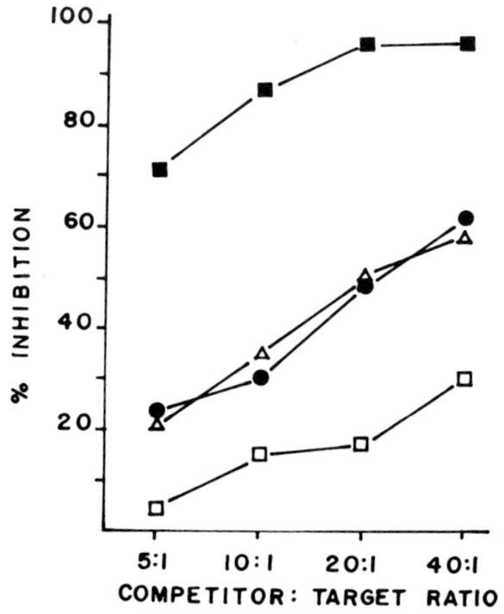

FIG. 2. Cold-target inhibition of the anti-Daudi T effect. The specific release of the uninhibited system was 48%. Competitors: Daudi T (■), Daudi (□), Molt-4 (△), and K562 (●). Measured as percentage specifice ^{51}Cr release in a 4-hr assay at a 100:1 effector:target cell ratio.

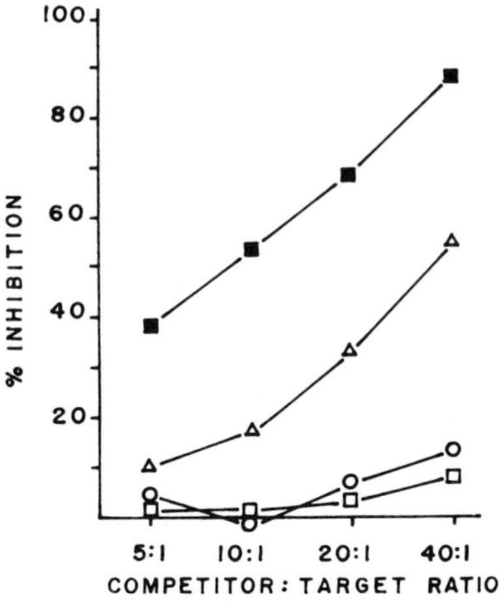

FIG. 3. Cold-target inhibition of Molt-4 lysis. The specific release of the uninhibited system was 53%. Competitors: Molt-4 (△), Daudi T (■), Daudi (□), and Raji (○). Measured as percentage specific ^{51}Cr release in a 4-hr assay at a 100:1 effector:target cell ratio.

proportion of human lymphocyte-binding Daudi and Molt-4 cells after TPA treatment (Table 3). The frequency of mouse lymphocyte-binding cells was not increased, however, which showed that the elevated conjugate formation by TPA-treated cells was not due to an increased stickiness but was specific for the interaction with human lymphocytes.

Morphological Changes Induced by TPA

The most conspicuous cytological change in Daudi cells after overnight TPA treatment was the development of surface villi (Figs. 5 and 6), an increased agglutinability of the cells and formation of cell clumps (Fig. 5b). This was evidently due to the interlacing of the villi on adjacent cells.

Apart from these marked effects of the TPA treatment, more subtle changes were also observed. There was an apparent increase in osmophilic lipid bodies, disarrangement of mitochondria, and an increase in free polyribosomes (Fig. 6b). Consistent nuclear changes were not observed.

There was no increase in cells showing cytopathic changes. Roughly the same number of mitoses were found in untreated cultures and cultures exposed to TPA for 24 hr. There was no evidence for activation of EBV synthesis.

DISCUSSION

Murine and human cell lines vary greatly in the sensitivity to natural killer (NK) cells. The reasons for this variablility are unknown, as is the membrane property that determines sensitivity to the lytic effect (19).

The panel of sensitive cells does not give any information about the nature of killing. There are certain patterns: T-cell-derived cell lines are more sensitive, as a rule, than B-cell-derived lymphoid lines. In the B-cell category, lines derived from and representative for Burkitt and other lymphomas are usually more sensitive than lymphoblastoid cell lines of normal origin, tested relatively soon after their estab-

TABLE 3

Percentage of Human and Mouse Lymphocyte-Binding Daudi and Molt-4 Cells after TPA Treatment

	Human lymphocytes[a]		Mouse lymphocytes[b]	
Cell line	No. of experiments	% of lymphocyte-binding cells (mean ± SE)	No. of experiments	% of lymphocyte-binding cells (mean)
Daudi	6	8.3 ± 1.6	2	2.0
Daudi T	6	34.2 ± 4.0	2	2.5
Molt-4	3	8.3 ± 3.0	2	3.0
Molt-4 T	3	20.0 ± 2.6	2	3.0

[a] Nylon-wool-passed blood lymphocytes.
[b] Nylon-wool-passed cells from lymph nodes.

lishment. The erythromyeloid leukemia line, K562, shows an exceptionally high NK sensitivity.

Although the presence of the EBV genome in B-cell lines is clearly not a prerequisite for NK sensitivity, EBV-related phenomena were found to play a role in modulating it. We have previously shown (1) that entry of a substantial proportion of the cells in a given, EBV-carrying line into the viral cycle (as assessed by EA synthesis), induced by superinfection with the abortively lytic P3HR-1 viral substrain, or by a chemical inducer of the viral cycle like sodium butyrate, leads to a marked increase in NK sensitivity. This association was not found on the TPA-treated lines, since the NK sensitivity of Raji and Daudi cells was elevated in the absence of induction of the viral cycle.

EBV-determined or EBV-induced membrane antigens are probably not responsible for the increased NK sensitivity in the superinfected lines. $F(ab')_2$ fragments of an antibody directed against EBV-determined membrane antigens associated with the lytic cycle failed to influence the NK sensitivity of P3HR-1 virus-superinfected Raji cells (M. Patarroyo, E. Klein, and G. Klein, to be published).

It is noteworthy that Daudi (but not Molt-4) was also agglutinated by TPA to a certain extent. TPA-treated Daudi cells showed an increased capacity to form conjugates with human, but not with mouse lymphocytes. It is conceivable that the receptors responsible for this phenomenon interact with NK cells or their precursors. Previously, activated T cells were found to bind to human but not mouse cells (18). The target structure for the latter reaction is unknown.

TPA treatment induced marked morphological changes of the Daudi cell membrane and inhibited cell proliferation. The conspicuous increase in surface villi may be correlated to the previously described TPA-induced alterations in membrane fluidity (5). Other, less pronounced cytoplasmic changes may be also induced directly by TPA or may reflect metabolic events secondary to the surface membrane changes. With regard to the increased sensitivity of TPA-treated targets to NK cells, the observed surface may have at least two important effects. One effect was the increased ability of the treated cells to form conjugates with lymphocytes. The other effect was the marked increase of the target surface area. It is possible that

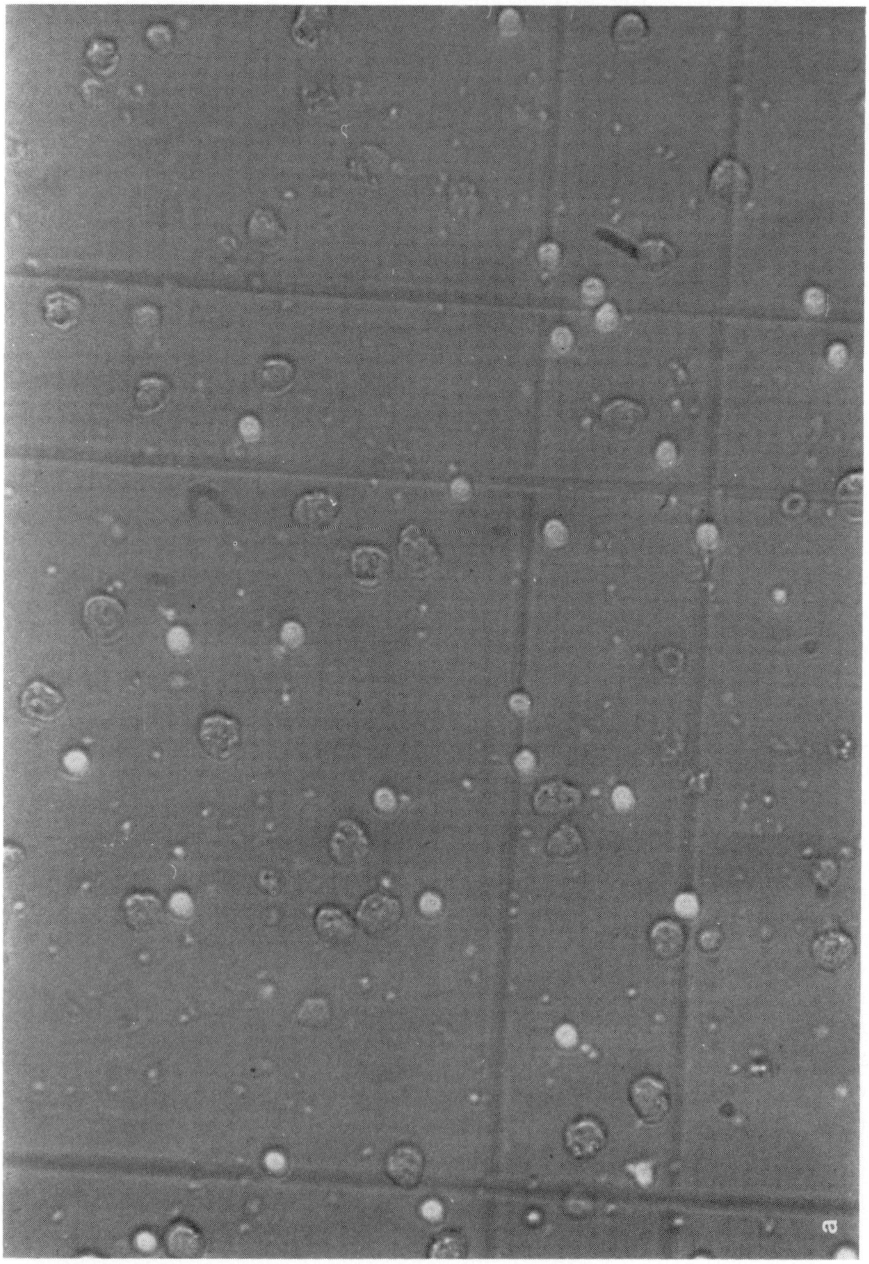
a

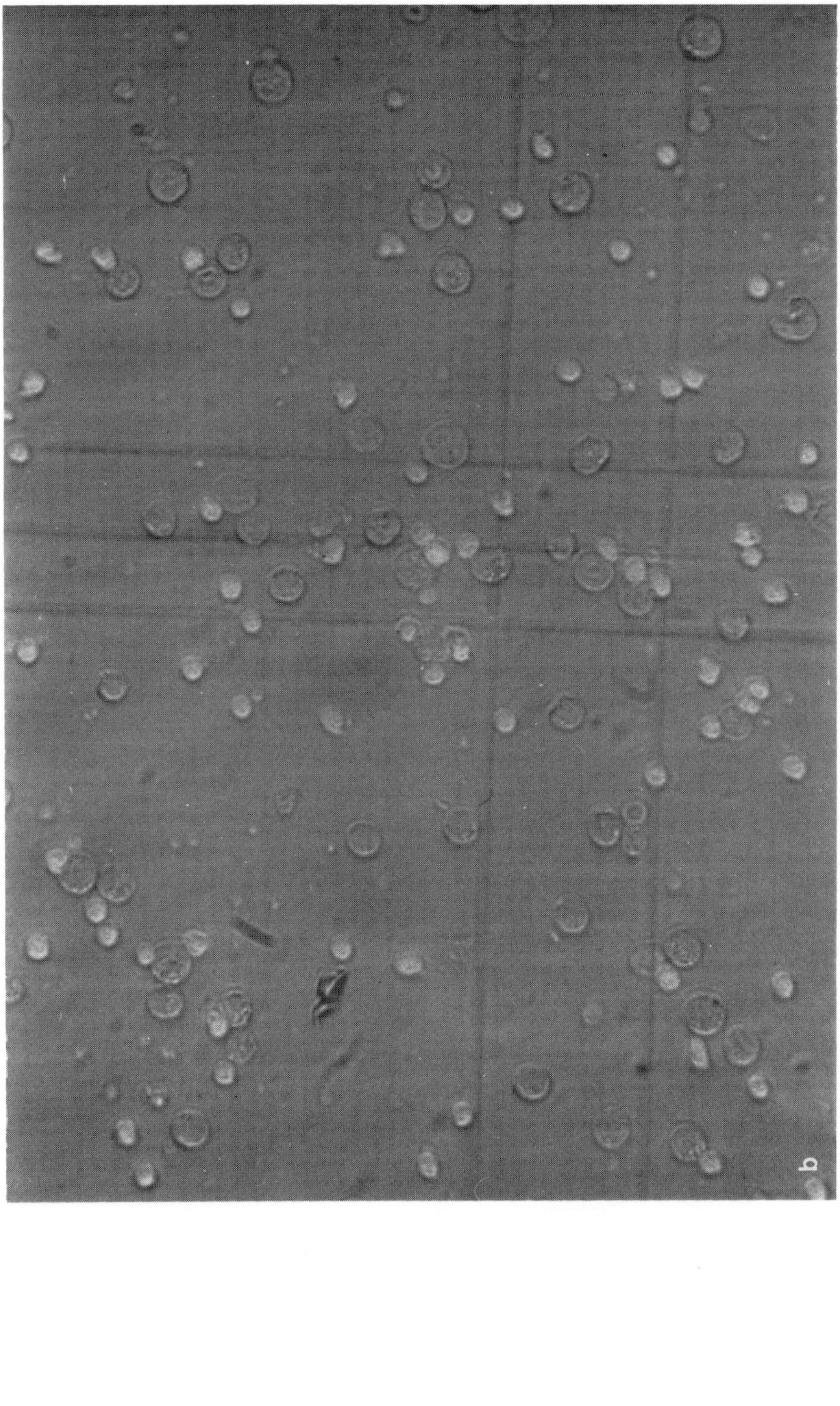

FIG. 4. Conjugates between human lymphocytes and Daudi (a) and TPA-treated Daudi (b) at a 1:1 ratio. The human lymphocytes were prelabeled with FCD (bright cells). The percentage of human lymphocyte-binding cells was 9 and 31, respectively (magnification 312×).

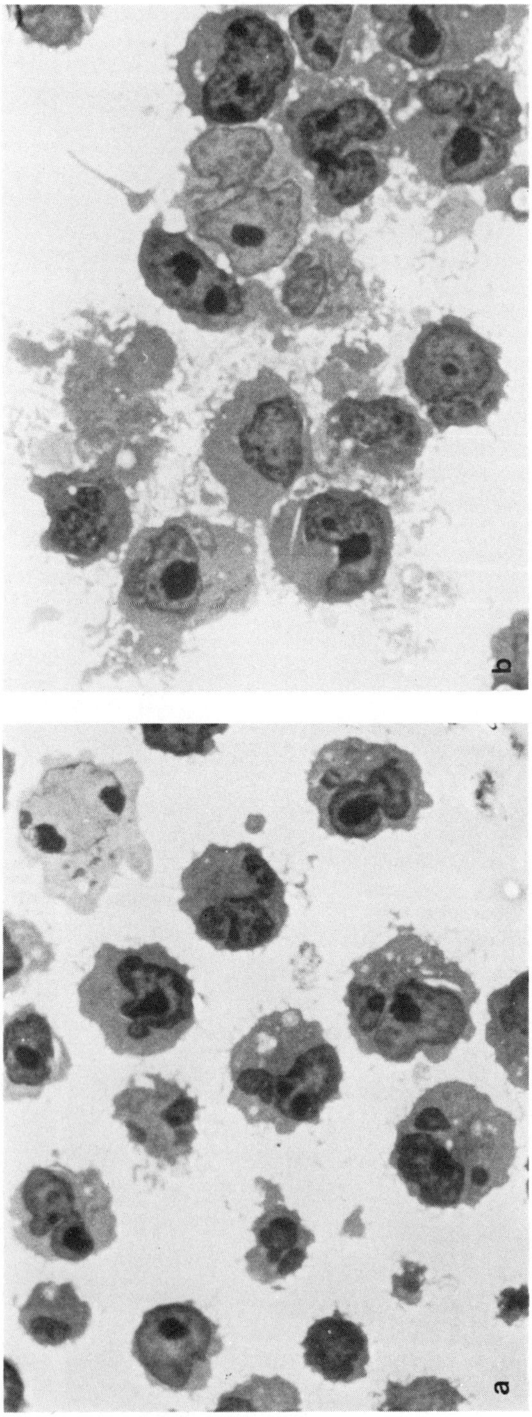

FIG. 5. Light microscopic appearance of epon-embedded and sectioned Daudi cells (a) untreated; (b) treated with TPA for approximately 20 hr. Note the veiled appearance of the TPA-treated cells (magnification ~ 1300×).

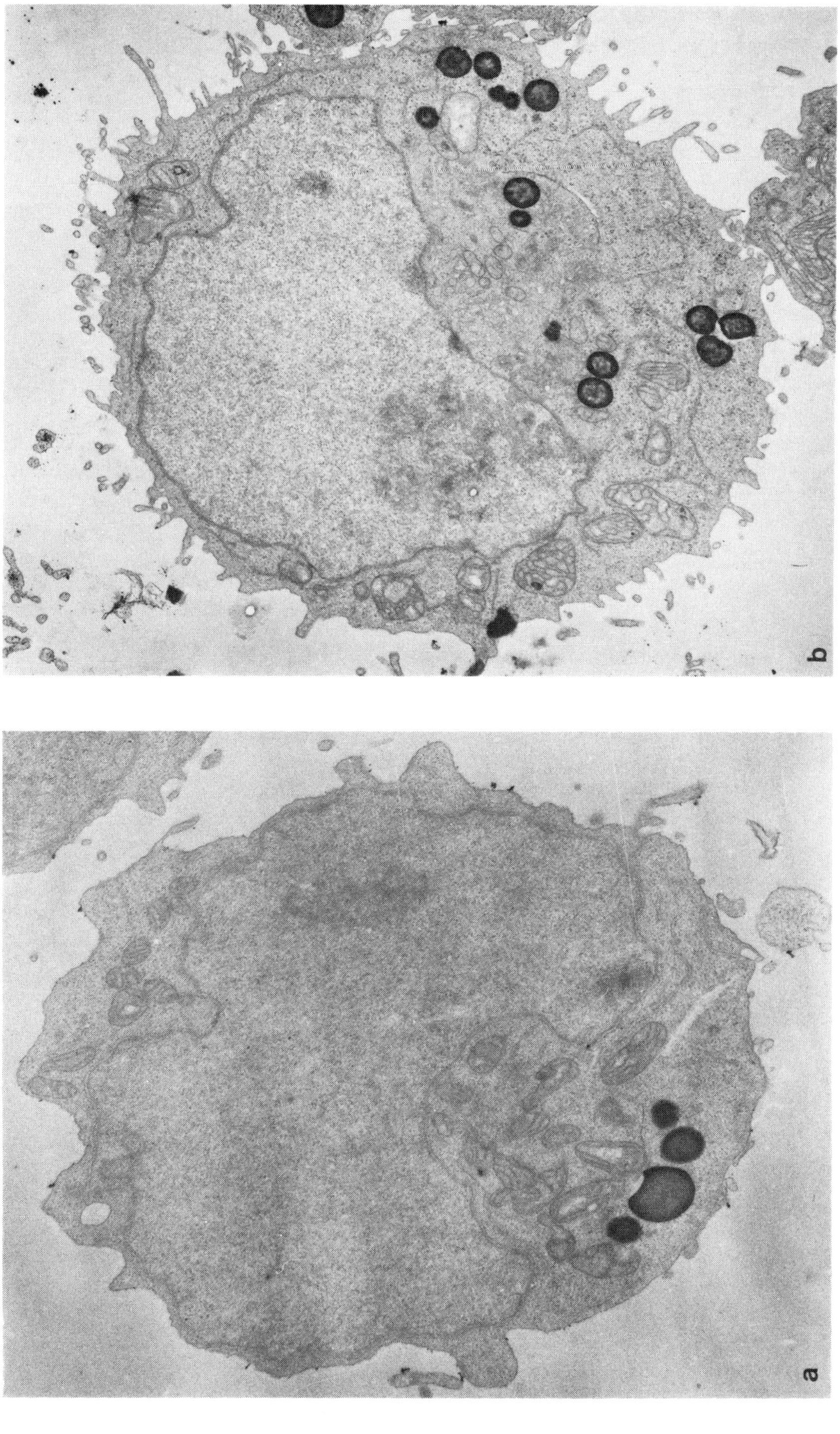

FIG. 6. Transmission electron micrograph of an (a) untreated; (b) TPA-treated Daudi cell (magnification (a) 10,500×; (b) 8000×).

the increased NK sensitivity depends on "qualitative" changes in the target membrane and/or effector target interactions. More detailed electron-microscopic studies of TPA effector–target conjugates may elucidate this question.

ACKNOWLEDGMENTS

This project has been supported by Grant 2 RO1 CA 14054-07A1 (to G. Klein) and by Grant 1 RO1 CA 23184-01A1 (to E. Klein) awarded by the National Cancer Institute, NIH, DHEW, and by the Swedish Cancer Society. We thank Dr. Måns Ullberg for helpful suggestions concerning the conjugate assay. We also thank Ms. Maria Karlsson and Mona Hedenskog for valuable technical assistance. Manuel Patarroyo is a recipient of a fellowship from the National University of Colombia.

REFERENCES

1. Blazar, B., Patarroyo, M., Klein, E., and Klein, G., *J. Exp. Med.* **151,** 614, 1980.
2. Spira, G., Åman, P., Koide, R., Lundin, G., Klein, G., and Hall, K., *J. Immunol.*, in press.
3. Jønsson, V., Klein, G., and Christensen, B. E., *Eur. J. Cancer* **16,** 533, 1980.
4. Patarroyo, M., Blazar, B., Pearson, G., Klein, E., and Klein, G., *Int. J. Cancer* **26,** 365, 1980.
5. Weinstein, B., Lee, L. Fisher, P., Mutson, A., and Yamasaki, H., *J. Supramol. Struct.* **12,** 195, 1979.
6. Tötterman, T., Nilsson, K., and Sundström, C., *Nature (London)* **288,** 176, 1980.
7. Abb, J., Dayliss, G., and Deinhardt, F., *J. Immunol.* **122,** 1639, 1979.
8. Hudewentz, J., Bornkamm, G. W., and zur Hausen, H., *Virology* **100,** 175, 1980.
9. Epstein, M. A., Achong, Y. M., Barr, Y., Zajac, B., Henle, G., and Henle, W., *J. Nat. Cancer Inst.* **37,** 547, 1966.
10. Klein, E., Klein, G., Nadkarni, J., Nadkarni, J., Wigzell, H., and Clifford, P., *Cancer Res.* **28,** 1300, 1968.
11. Menezes, J., Leibold, W., Klein, G., and Clements, G., *Biomedicine* **22,** 276, 1975.
12. Fresen, K. O., Merkt, B., Bornkamm, G. W., and zur Hausen, H., *Int. J. Cancer* **19,** 317, 1977.
13. Minowada, J., Ohnuna, T., and Moore, G. E., *J. Nat. Cancer Inst.,* **49,** 891, 1972.
14. Lozzio, C. B., and Lozzio, J., *J. Nat. Cancer Inst.* **50,** 535, 1973.
15. Böyum, A., *Scand. J. Clin. Lab. Invest.* **21,** (Suppl. 97), 77, 1968.
16. Klein, G., and Dombos, L., *Int. J. Cancer* **11,** 327, 1973.
17. Julius, M. H., Simpson, E., and Herzenberg, L. A., *Eur. J. Immunol.* **20,** 505, 1975.
18. Galili, U., Galili, N., Vánky, F., and Klein, E., *Proc. Nat. Acad. Sci. USA* **75,** 2396, 1978.
19. Klein, E., *Immunol. Today,* **1,** IV–VI, 1980.

CELLULAR IMMUNOLOGY 63, 249–258 (1981)

Murine Spleen Lymphocytes Bearing Receptors for Peanut Agglutinin

VII. Separation and Functional Characterization

S. BERRIH,* J. LONDON,[1] AND B. BONAVIDA†

*INSERM U25, Hôpital Necker, 161, rue de Sèvres, 75015 Paris, France, *Centre Chirurgical Marie Lannelongue, 133 Avenue de la Résistance, 92350 Le Plessis Robinson, France, and †Department of Microbiology and Immunology, University of Calfornia School of Medicine, Los Angeles, California 90024*

Received February 20, 1981; accepted May 27, 1981

Murine spleen lymphocytes having receptors for peanut agglutinin (PNA) were visualized by a specific rosetting technique. The number of lymphocytes forming PNA rosettes (PNA_R^+) is dependent on the PNA concentration used. T lymphocytes are the primary PNA-rosetting lymphocytes for low PNA concentration (2.5 μg/ml), while both T and B lymphocytes are involved in high PNA concentration (10 μg/ml). Functional studies show that when spleen lymphocytes are separated at a low PNA concentration, the PNA_R^+ do not respond to T mitogens and suppress antigen-specific immune responses. However, when spleen cells are separated at a high PNA concentration, the PNA_R^+ do not exhibit differential functional properties as compared to non-PNA-rosetting lymphocytes. The implication of these findings is discussed.

INTRODUCTION

The use of serological techniques for the identification of murine lymphocytes subpopulations has received considerable attention following the characterization of the Lyt series of antigens (1–3). Interest in the alloantigenic systems was enhanced by the demonstration that the expression of the Lyt 1, 2, and 3 antigens could be correlated with particular functional T-cell subpopulations (4). Recently, other surface antigens have added information to T-cell heterogeneity (5). Lectins (Con A,[2] PHA, PWM) have been used extensively as mitogens (6, 7), while other

[1] Address all correspondence to Dr. J. London, Hôpital Necker, 161 rue de Sévres, 75730 Paris Cedex 15, France.

[2] Abbreviations used: Anti-Thy 1.2 serum, serum raised against the Thy 1.2 alloantigen; Anti-Ly 6.2. serum, serum raised against the Ly 6.2 alloantigen; Con A, concanavalin A; GAMFITC, goat anti-mouse immunoglobulin coupled with fluorescein; GAMTRITC, goat anti-mouse immunoglobulin coupled with rhodamine; Ig^+, cells bearing surface immunoglobulin; Ig^-, cells without surface immunoglobulin; LPS, lipopolysaccharide of *Salmonella typhimurium*; Ly-t antigens, Alloantigens of the Ly series (1, 2, 3, . . .) present specifically on T murine lymphocytes; PFC, plaque-forming cells; PHA, phytohemagglutinin; PNA, peanut agglutinin; PNA_R^+, PNA-rosetting lymphocytes; PNA_R^-, lymphocytes which do not form PNA rosettes; PWM, pokeweed mitogen; SMIg, surface membrane immunoglobulin; SRBC, sheep red blood cells; $SRBC_N$, sheep red blood cells treated with neuraminidase; T lymphocytes, lymphocytes with the Thy 1 antigen.

0008-8749/81/140249-10$02.00/0

lectins have been used as tools for the isolation of lymphocyte subpopulations (8–11).

Peanut agglutinin (PNA), a tetrameric protein isolated from *Arachis hypogea*, has been shown to bind most of the thymocytes and some peripheral lymphocytes which are either T or "non T–non B" cells (12–14). In the thymus, peanut agglutinin binds mainly to the corticosteroid-sensitive and immunoincompetent thymocytes (12, 13). By using either the agglutination technique (12) or petri dishes covered with PNA (15) it has been possible to separate thymocytes having receptors for PNA (PNA^+) from those which do not have them (PNA^-), and study their immunological functions (15–18). In the spleen, most of the PNA^+ cells have been shown by fluorescent microscopy to bear some T lymphocyte markers (Thy-1 and Ly-6 antigens) (19), but their functional characteristics were not studied as they could not be separated directly from other lymphocytes by agglutination, PNA-covered petri dishes, or affinity chromatography techniques. The present study describes a specific rosetting technique for the detection of lymphocytes having PNA receptors. This method is more sensitive than fluorescent microscopy or flow microfluorimetry and allows for the detection of various spleen lymphocyte subpopulations possessing receptors for PNA (20). This procedure also allows for the separation of the PNA^+ and PNA^- lymphocyte subpopulations and several functional characteristics of these subpopulations have been examined.

MATERIALS AND METHODS

Animals

Female BALB/c mice were obtained from the Centre d'elevage d'Animaux de Laboratoire (CEAL, Orléans, La Source, France) and from the breeding colony of the Microbiology and Immunology Department, University of California, Los Angeles.

Cell Suspensions.

Single-cell suspensions were prepared from the various organs by teasing with tissue combs and suspending in Hanks' medium. Cells were then filtered through three layers of cotton gauze, washed three times, and centrifuged at 200*g* for 10 min at 4°C. Bone marrow cells were centrifuged on a Ficoll–Angiocontrix mixture (24 vol of 9% Ficoll, Pharmacia, Uppsala, Sweden, and 10 vol of 30% sodium ioxitalamate, Guerbet, France) for 20 min at 1800 rpm. Mononuclear cells were then washed in Hanks' medium. All suspensions were tested for viability with trypan blue and counted in Turk's medium.

Rosetting Procedure.

Mouse lymphocytes were rosetted for surface PNA receptors by modifying a procedure previously described for rosetting Ig-bearing lymphocytes (21). The procedure consisted of two steps: first, incubation of mouse lymphocytes with subagglutinating PNA concentration, and second, rosetting these lymphocytes with neuraminidase-treated sheep red blood cells ($SRBC_N$ = SRBC incubated for 30 min at 37°C with 0.04 unit of neuraminidase, *Vibrio cholerae*, Behring). One hundred microliters of cells (3×10^6 cells/ml) in Hanks' medium supplemented with 0.1% of sodium azide was incubated with 100 μl PNA (Pharma Industrie, Clichy, France), at various concentrations for 10 min at room temperature. The cells were resuspended in 0.1 ml of medium and 0.1 ml neuraminidase-treated sheep red blood cells (1.5×10^8 $SRBC_N$/ml) was added. The erythrocyte–lymphocyte mixtures were then centrifuged at 1200*g* for 5 min and gently resuspended. The percentage of PNA-rosette-forming cells was evaluated by counting 200 cells in the presence of crystal violet. Any lymphocyte binding more than three $SRBC_N$ was classified as a PNA-rosetting lymphocyte (PNA_R^+).

Separation of PNA-Rosetting and Non-PNA-rosetting cells.

Spleen cells were initially rosetted for PNA receptors as described above. PNA-rosetting cells were separated from free cells on Ficoll–Hypaque density gradient. Briefly, 4 ml of lymphocyte–$SRBC_N$ mixture was gently layered onto 4 ml of Ficoll–Hypaque ($D = 1.09$) and spun at 1200*g* for 20 min at room temperature. After centrifugation, the interface layer (nonrosetting cells) was collected and washed twice with Hanks' medium. The pellet containing the PNA-rosetting cells was lysed by osmotic shock (2 to 5 ml of distilled water was added to the pellet, shaken for 1 min) and quickly resuspended in 20 ml of Hanks' medium supplemented with 20% inactivated fetal calf serum. The white cells were then washed twice and counted with trypan blue and Turk's medium.

Fluorescence Staining.

Methods have been previously detailed (13, 14). Briefly, 3×10^6 spleen cells (in 100 μl Hanks' medium supplemented with 0.1% sodium azide and 2% bovine serum albumin) were mixed with the appropriate antibody, coupled with fluorescein, incubated for 30 min at 4°C, washed, and assessed by fluorescence microscopy using a Leitz orthoplan microscope equipped for epifluorescence (objective FL40/1.30, Oel and Eyepiece Periplan GGB × M). Surface membrane immunoglobulins (SMIg) were detected by direct immunofluorescence; 3×10^6 lymphocytes (in 100 μl) were incubated for 30 min at 4°C with 50 μl of goat anti-mouse immunoglobulin (GAMFITC, Nordic, diluted 1/10) and washed, after which 200 cells were examined by fluorescence. Thy 1.2. antigens were detected by indirect immunofluorescence; 3×10^6 lymphocytes were first incubated with either 50 μl anti-Thy 1.2 serum (diluted 1/5) or 50 μl normal AKR serum as a control for 30 min at 4°C, washed three times, and incubated with GAMFITC (diluted 1/10) for an additional 30 min and then washed, after which 200 cells were examined by fluorescence. The anti-Thy 1.2. used has been prepared by injecting AKR mice once a week for 7 weeks with 10^7 CBA thymocytes and bleeding them 1 week after the last injection. This antiserum has been tested on educated spleen cells in the presence of guinea pig complement (C) and has been shown to abrogate T-cell-mediated cytotoxicity. In the presence of guinea pig complement it has been shown to kill 42% of the adult CBA/J spleen lymphocytes and 100% of the adult CBA/J thymocytes, but none of the AKR thymocytes. In double-labeling experiments (PNA rosettes and surface antigens) cells were incubated with the appropriate antisera and then rosetted by the rosetting procedure. We have verified that the rosetting procedure does not modify the antiserum staining nor does the antiserum staining modify the percentages of rosettes. Thus PNA-rosetting cells are either Ig^+, Thy 1^+ or

Thy 1^- Ig^-. Conversely, non-PNA-rosetting cells are also Ig^+, Thy 1^+, or $Thyl^-$ Ig^-. Thus there are six different cellular subsets which are evaluated as percentages of the whole spleen population.

Functional Assays

Cultures were performed in Eagle's minimum essential medium (Gibco, Grand Island, N.Y.) supplemented with L-glutamine (1%), amino acids (1%), sodium pyruvate (1%), penicillin–streptomycin (2%), and 5% inactivated fetal calf serum.

Mitogenic Stimulation

Cultures were grown in microtest plates (Falcon Microtest II); 6×10^5 living lymphocytes (in 200 μl of medium) of each subpopulation were placed in each well. Phytohemagglutinin (Difco) and concanavalin A (Miles Yeda) were used at a concentration of 10 μg/ml. LPS (Sigma) was used at 20 μg/ml. Cultures were set up in triplicate and maintained for 48 hr at 37°C in 5% humidified CO_2-enriched atmosphere. Incorporation of [^{3}H]thymidine (CEA, Saclay, France, sp act 1 Ci/mmol) was evaluated after 20 hr of incubation.

Suppression Experiments

a. Nonspecific suppression of allogeneic cytotoxicity. Previous experiments have shown that lymphocytes incubated for 5 days in the presence of 10% fetal calf serum exhibit suppressive activity (22, 23). BALB/c cells were similarly incubated and then washed and counted. Then 2×10^6 of these cells (H-2^d) were added to a mixture of 10^7 responding cells (H-2^d) and 10^7 mitomycin-treated stimulating cells (H-2^b) in 10 ml culture medium. After 5 days, the cultures were evaluated for their cytotoxic activity against allogeneic target cells (EL-4, H-2^b).

b. Specific suppression test. The specific suppression against sheep red blood cell responses has been evaluated as previously described (24). Briefly, BALB/c mice were hyperimmunized against SRBC (2×10^5, ip) and 8 days later animals were sacrificed and spleen cells suspensions prepared. The PNA_R^+ and PNA_R^- spleen subpopulations were prepared with the PNA-rosetting technique. Spleen lymphocytes (2×10^7) or separated subpopulations were injected into BALB/c mice and at the same time immunized with sheep red blood cells (0.008 ml of SRBC at 10%/g body wt). Five days later, suppressive activity was evaluated by the plaque-forming cell assay.

RESULTS

PNA Rosetting Procedure

Lymphocytes incubated with PNA and mixed with neuraminidase-treated sheep red blood cells ($SRBC_N$) formed PNA rosettes. As shown in Table 1, the percentage of PNA-rosetting spleen lymphocytes (PNA_R^+) was highly dependent upon the PNA subagglutinating concentration. The specificity of the PNA-rosetting technique was determined by inhibition of PNA rosettes with lactose or galactose (20) and by the absence of PNA rosettes when lymphocytes were not incubated with PNA or when SRBC were not treated with neuraminidase.

TABLE 1

Phenotype of Spleen Lymphocytes

PNA concentration (μg/ml)	Percentage PNA_R^+	Thy 1^+Ig^-		Thy 1^-Ig^-		Thy 1^-Ig^+	
		PNA_R^+	PNA_R^-	PNA_R^+	PNA_R^-	PNA_R^+	PNA_R^-
0	0.6						
2.5.	13.3	12 (3)	10 (5)	4 (3)	20 (3)	2 (1)	52 (5)
5.	33.1	16 (4)	9 (4)	15 (8)	11 (1)	9 (5)	40 (5)
10.	53.9	16 (4)	13 (7)	19 (8)	9 (4)	34 (7)	9 (3)
20	75.5	16 (3)	5 (2)	18 (2)	7 (1)	45 (3)	9 (1)

Note. Results are expressed as the mean percentage of three different experiments. Numbers in parentheses represent the SEM. PNA_R^+, PNA-rosetting lymphocyte; PNA_R^-, non-PNA-rosetting lymphocyte.

The phenotype of PNA-rosetting lymphocytes was investigated using Thy 1 and Ig surface markers (Table 1). At a low PNA concentration, most of the PNA-rosetting lymphocytes were T lymphocytes while at a high PNA concentration (10 μg/ml) both T and B lymphocytes formed PNA rosettes. Surprisingly the percentage of PNA_R^+ T lymphocytes was almost independent of the PNA concentration while that of PNA_R^+ B lymphocytes was very dependent.

Separation of PNA_R^+ and PNA_R^- Spleen Cells

The separation has been performed as described under Materials and Methods. The PNA_R^- cells separated at the interface of the gradient were collected and showed a considerable enrichment (Table 2). In the pellet, the percentage of viable PNA_R^+ lymphocytes was increased considerably. The major PNA_R^+ cellular enrichment was obtained at a high PNA concentration while the major PNA_R^- subpopulation was obtained at a low PNA concentration. However, using a second separation step we were able to obtain up to 95% PNA_R^+ cells in the pellet even when

TABLE 2

Separation of Spleen Lymphocytes by the PNA-Rosetting Procedure at Various PNA Concentrations

	PNA concentration (μg/ml)			Yield of viable cells
	2.5	5	10	
	Percentage PNA_R^+ cells			
Before separation	10.4 ± 1.3	28.3 ± 2.8	50.2 ± 5.4	90
Interface	0.4 ± 0.3	2.7 ± 0.9	5.1 ± 3.3	99
First pellet fraction	71 ± 4	86 ± 6	95 ± 3	85
Second pellet fraction[a]	95 ± 3			80
Cellular yield	75.8 ± 6.7	75 ± 10	55 ± 4	

Note. PNA_R^+, lymphocytes which form PNA rosettes excluding dead cells. The results are expressed as the mean of eight different experiments ± SEM.

[a] Second pellet is obtained by centrifuging the first pellet fraction on Ficoll gradient.

TABLE 3

Mitogen Responses of PNA-Separated Subpopulations[a]

	ΔPHA (cpm)	ΔCon A (cpm)	ΔLPS (cpm)
Experiment A			
Control F	60,500 ± 1,000	125,700 ± 10,100	46,600 ± 500
Control T	58,000 ± 8,300	101,500 ± 20,000	13,500 ± 1,100
PNA_R^- cells	74,300 ± 4,200	146,500 ± 7,300	51,000 ± 5,500
PNA_R^+ cells	1,200 ± 400	9,100 ± 550	150 ± 50
Experiment B			
Control F	97,300 ± 11,800	130,000 ± 17,300	28,300 ± 9,100
Control T	76,000 ± 6,900	120,500 ± 11,500	25,500 ± 7,900
PNA_R^- cells	88,300 ± 11,900	109,000 ± 10,700	16,000 ± 4,600
PNA_R^+ cells	75,000 ± 13,700	112,600 ± 9,900	22,000 ± 5,800

Note. Experiment A, rosettes are formed at a low PNA concentration (2.5 μg/ml); Experiment B, rosettes are formed at a high PNA concentration (10 μg/ml); Control F, 6×10^5 living spleen lymphocytes passed over Ficoll gradient; Control T, 6×10^5 living spleen lymphocytes treated by the PNA-rosetting technique (but not separated) and by osmotic shock.

[a] Results are expressed as the mean Δcpm of five different experiments ± SEM.

a low PNA concentration was used. Thus, the rosetting procedure allows the separation of PNA_R^+ cells with good yield and with enrichment of both cell subpopulations.

Mitogen Responsiveness

The response to PHA, Con A, and LPS of the 6×10^5 living spleen lymphocytes separated by the rosetting technique is shown in Table 3. When PNA_R^+ and PNA_R^- were separated at low concentration (2.5 μg/ml), PNA_R^- lymphocytes responded to PHA, Con A, and LPS while PNA_R^+ lymphocytes did not respond. The two controls: spleen lymphocytes passed through Ficoll gradient (Control F) and spleen lymphocytes incubated with PNA and SRBC as described in the rosetting technique and treated by osmotic shock without any previous separation (Control T) showed similar responses to those obtained by PNA_R^- lymphocytes for PHA and Con A stimulation. For LPS stimulation, however, the response is lower in control T than in control F, but is significantly higher than the response obtained for PNA_R^+ lymphocytes. Thus, when separated at a low PNA concentration, the PNA_R^+ lymphocytes do not respond to PHA, Con A, or LPS. When separated at a high PNA concentration (10 μg/ml) both PNA_R^+ and PNA_R^- lymphocytes respond similarly to PHA, Con A, and LPS.

Nonspecific Suppression

Spleen lymphocytes incubated for 5 days in the presence of fetal calf serum are known to acquire nonspecific suppressive activity (23) which has been tested in an allogeneic cell-mediated cytotoxicity assay (24). We have investigated whether the

TABLE 4

Suppressive Activity of PNA^+-Rosetting Cells in Mixed Leukocyte Cultures[a]

Effector/target ratio	Suppressive cells added (2×10^6 cells) Total cells	PNA_R^+ cells	PNA_R^- cells	No. cells added
	Percentage cytotoxicity			
50/1	0	0	60	80
10/1	0	0	27	46
2/1	0	0	6	13

[a] Results are expressed as the percentage of suppression in comparison to initial cytotoxicity. In this experiment cells were separated at a concentration of 2.5 μg/ml.

suppressive activity of such educated lymphocytes can be preferentially found in one of the subpopulations separated by the PNA-rosetting technique. As shown in Table 4, PNA_R^+ lymphocytes function as well as unseparated cells in suppressing completely allogeneic cell-mediated cytotoxicity as suppressive cell controls do. PNA_R^- lymphocytes suppress only 40 to 50% of the lytic response regardless of what effector/target ratio is used.

Specific Suppression

Spleen lymphocytes from hyperimmune mice against SRBC are known to acquire suppressive properties when injected (iv) into mice immunized at the same time and with the same SRBC antigen (25). PNA_R^+, PNA_R^-, and unseparated spleen cells from hyperimmune mice were injected as described under Materials and Methods, and suppression was evaluated by the number of plaque-forming cells per 10^6 cells. As shown in Table 5, when cells were separated at a concentration of 2.5 μg/ml,

TABLE 5

Suppression of Sheep Red Blood Cell Responses

Injected cells from hyperimmune animals	PFC/10^6 cells
Unseparated spleen cells	151 ± 45
Supernatant of spleen cells on Ficoll gradient	145 ± 31
Rosetting mixture after osmotic shock	157 ± 75
Controls (no cells injected)	482 ± 60
A	
PNA_R^- cells	198 ± 57
PNA_R^+ cells	81 ± 10
B	
PNA_R^- cells	163 ± 9
PNA_R^+ cells	121 ± 20

Note. A, separation performed at a concentration of 2.5 μg/ml; B, at 10 μg/ml.

the unseparated spleen lymphocytes (Control N) suppressed the anti-SRBC plaque-forming cells by a factor of 3, and this suppression was not affected by passing the cells on Ficoll gradient or by osmotic shock. However, under the same conditions, PNA_R^+ and PNA_R^- behaved differently: PNA_R^- exhibited supression similar to that of controls while PNA_R^+ lymphocytes exhibited a significantly higher suppressive ability. Conversely, when separated at a high PNA concentration, both PNA_R^+ and PNA_R^- suppressed in a manner similar to that of controls.

DISCUSSION

The PNA-rosetting technique has been used in the detection and separation of spleen lymphocytes having receptors for PNA. It has been shown that the number of PNA rosetting lymphocytes is dependent on PNA concentration. At a low PNA concentration the number of PNA-rosetting lymphocytes we found in the present study correlates well with the results of previous studies (13, 14) and thereby confirms that these PNA_R^+ lymphocytes are mostly T lymphocytes. Conversely, at a high PNA concentration the percentage of PNA_R^+ is much higher than in previous findings (13, 14) and it can be seen that these PNA_R^+ cells are not only T but also B lymphocytes. The PNA-rosetting technique presented in this study is as specific as other methods used for the evaluation of lymphocytes having receptors for PNA; it is more sensitive and requires less PNA concentration. Although it was previously shown by other techniques that only spleen T lymphocytes have receptors for PNA, our present study shows that indeed some T lymphocytes have PNA receptors and form PNA rosettes at a low PNA concentration (2–5 μg/ml), but that at a higher PNA concentration (10–20 μg/ml), B lymphocytes are also able to form PNA rosettes. The present study shows that B lymphocytes have receptors for PNA but that these are fewer in number than on T cells or they have a lower affinity for PNA.

The PNA-rosetting technique was also used to separate the PNA^+ and PNA^- spleen subpopulations and study their respective immunological functions. The separation efficiency is slightly dependent on PNA concentration but in most cases a rather pure PNA^- spleen lymphocyte subpopulation and a very enriched PNA^+ subpopulation are respectively obtained. This procedure is reproducible and results in a good yield. Moreover, this method allows for the study of the functional properties of PNA_R^+ and PNA_R^- subpopulations having various phenotypes depending on the PNA concentration used. Using low PNA concentration there is a real discrepancy between the PNA_R^+ functional properties and the PNA_R^- ones. The PNA_R^+ cells do not respond to LPS stimulation, confirming that these cells do not belong to the B-cell lineage. Furthermore, they do not respond to PHA and have a very weak response to Con A stimulation, results which are in agreement with those of others (26). Conversely, the PNA_R^- lymphocytes respond to both T- and B-cell mitogens. These results suggest that the PNA-rosetting spleen lymphocytes isolated at a low PNA concentration belong to an early T subpopulation which lacks at least some of the T-cell functions. Indeed, it is known that the response to mitogen stimulation is in concordance with the stage of differentiation. Early T cells do not respond either to PHA or to Con A stimulation and their further differentiation involves a first-stage proliferation in the presence of Con A and a second-stage proliferation in the presence of both mitogens (27).

We have also investigated the suppressive activity of PNA_R^+ and PNA_R^- spleen lymphocytes in two different systems. In the first system, nonspecific suppression was induced with fetal calf sera and tested in allogeneic T-cell-mediated cytotoxicity. It was shown that the PNA_R^+ cells could completely suppress the generation of cytotoxic cells, whereas PNA_R^- cells could only suppress 40% of the response. In the second system, we have made use of specific suppression toward sheep red blood cell antigen. It was shown that both the unseparated and the PNA_R^+ subpopulations suppress only 45–60% of the response. Thus, using a low PNA concentration the PNA_R^+ spleen subpopulation does not respond to mitogen proliferation but is capable of exerting suppressive activity. To further explain these data, one could suggest that the PNA_R^+ subpopulation is heterogeneous and includes at least two subpopulations: one of them is immature and unable to proliferate in the presence of mitogen and the other one is capable of suppressive function. Using fluorescence measurements, we have shown that the number of PNA^+ T lymphocytes is almost constant from Day 17 of gestation until adult life (28). Moreover, the PNA^+ neonatal spleen T lymphocytes represent all the T lymphocytes found for that age and it is known that these T lymphocytes do not respond to mitogen but have suppressive activity (29, 30). Our results suggest that the PNA^+ spleen lymphocyte subset isolated by the rosetting technique using a low PNA concentration correlates well with an immature but suppressive T subset.

Using high doses of PNA, our present study shows that both PNA_R^+ and PNA_R^- subpopulations respond to B and T mitogens and suppress similarly the anti-sheep red blood cell response. These findings correlate well with the fact that PNA_R^+ lymphocytes obtained at a high PNA concentration contain both B and T cells.

Previous immunofluorescent studies (18) have shown that the PNA^+ spleen lymphocytes are mostly of the $PNA^+Thy\ 1.2^+Ly\ 6.2^+Ig^-$ phenotype while the PNA^- spleen T-lymphocyte subset has the phenotype $PNA^-Thy\ 1.2^+Ly\ 6.2^+Ig^-$. Thus, our present results suggest that the spleen T lymphocytes responding to T mitogens have the $PNA^-Thy\ 1.2^+Ly\ 6.2^+Ig^-$ phenotype while the suppressive spleen T-lymphocytes have the $PNA^+Thy\ 1.2^+Ly\ 6.2^+Ig^-$ phenotype.

ACKNOWLEDGMENT

We would like to thank Dr. Elie Kedar for his helpful discussions and advice.

REFERENCES

1. Boyse, E. A., Miyazawa, T., Aoli, T., and Old, L. J., *Proc. R. Soc. Lond. Ser. B* **170,** 175, 1968.
2. Boyse, E. A., Itakura, K., Stockert, E., Iritani, C. A., and Miura, M., *Transplantation* **11,** 351, 1971.
3. McKenzie, I. F. C., and Potter, T. A., *Advan. Immunol.* **27,** 179, 1979.
4. Cantor, H., and Boyse, E. A., *J. Exp. Med.* **141,** 1376, 1975.
5. Flaherty, L., Zimmerman, D., and Sullivan, K. A., *J. Immunol.* **121,** 1640, 1978.
6. Stobo, J. D., Rosenthal, A. S., and Paul, W. E., *J. Immunol.* **108,** 1, 1972.
7. Lis, H., and Sharon, N., *In* "Lectins: Their Chemistry and Application to Immunology in the Antigens" (M. Sela, Ed.), Vol. 4, p. 429. Academic Press, New York, 1977.
8. Hellström, H., Dillner, M. L., Hammarström, S., and Perlman, P., *J. Exp. Med.* **144,** 1381, 1976.
9. Swanbörg, R. M., Hellström, U., Perlman, M., Hammarström, S., and Perlman, P., *Scand. J. Immunol.* **5,** 235, 1977.

10. Boltd, D. H., and Lyons, R. D., *J. Immunol.* **123,** 808, 1979.
11. Kimura, A., Orn, A., Hölmquist, G., Wigzeel, H., and Erssön, B., *Eur. J. Immunol.* **9,** 575, 1979.
12. Reisner, Y., Linker-Israeli, M., and Sharon, N., *Cell. Immunol.* **25,** 129, 1976.
13. London, J., Berrih, S., and Bach, J. F., *J. Immunol.* **121,** 438, 1978.
14. Roelants, G. E., London, J., Mayor-Withey, K, S., and Serrano, B., *Eur. J. Immunol.* **9,** 139, 1979.
15. Berrih, S., London, J., and Bach, J. F., *Ann. Immunol.* **129,** 738, 1978.
16. Cooley, M. A., and Schmitt-Verhulst, A. M., *J. Immunol.* **123,** 2328, 1979.
17. Kruisbeek, A. M., and Astaldi, G. C. B., *J. Immunol.* **123,** 984, 1979.
18. Wagner, H., Hardt, C., Bartlett, R., Rollinghoff, M., and Pfizenmaier, K., *J. Immunol.* **125,** 2532, 1980.
19. London, J., *J. Immunol.* **125,** 1702, 1980.
20. Berrih, S., London, J., Bonavida, B., and Bach, J. F., *J. Immunol. Methods* **41,** 235, 1981.
21. Parish, C. R., Kirov, S. M., Bowern, N., and Blansden, R. V., *Eur. J. Immunol.* **4,** 808, 1974.
22. Burns, D., Marrack, P. C., Kappler, J. W., and Janeway, C. A., *J. Immunol.* **114,** 1345, 1975.
23. Hodes, R. J., and Hathcock, K. S., *J. Immunol.* **116,** 167, 1976.
24. Brunner, K. T., Mavel, J., Cerottini, J. C., and Chapuis, B., *Immunology* **14,** 181, 1968.
25. Blanchard, D., and Bach, M. A., *Clin. Exp. Immunol.* **42,** 1, 1980.
26. Reisner, Y., Ikehara, S., Hodes, M. Z., and Good, R. A., *Proc. Nat. Acad. Sci. USA* **77,** 1164, 1980.
27. Stobo, J. D., *Transplant. Rev.* **11,** 60, 1972.
28. London, J., and Horton, M., *J. Immunol.* **124,** 1803, 1980.
29. Stobo, J. D., and Paul, W. E., *Cell. Immunol.* **4,** 367, 1972.
30. Mosier, D. E., Mathieson, B. J., and Campbell, P. S., *J. Exp. Med.* **146,** 59, 1977.

CELLULAR IMMUNOLOGY 63, 259–271 (1981)

Immunosuppression by 2′-Deoxycoformycin: Studies on the Mode of Administration[1]

EMILIA MIA SORDILLO,[2] SUSUMU IKEHARA,[3] ROBERT A. GOOD AND PAUL P. TROTTA*,[4]

*Laboratories of Immunobiology and *Cell Metabolism, Memorial Sloan–Kettering Cancer Center, New York, New York 10021*

Received March 13, 1981; accepted June 23, 1981

It was previously reported that continuous infusion of 2′-deoxycoformycin (DCF), a potent inhibitor of the enzyme adenosine deaminase (ADase), produces a severe immunodeficiency of both T and B lymphocytes (A. Tedde, M. E. Balis, S. Ikehara, R. Pahwa, R. A. Good, and P. P.Trotta, *Proc. Nat Acad. Sci.* USA **77,** 4899 (1980)). In the present study the immunological and biochemical effects in C57BL/6J mice of daily single intraperitoneal injections of DCF are examined. Five days of daily injections of DCF at 0.4 mg/kg body wt/day produced both immunosuppression and lymphocytotoxicity. Parallel experiments indicated that continuous infusion of DCF at the lower dose of 0.3 mg/kg body wt/day resulted in a more potent depression of immune function and a greater lymphocytotoxicity. In particular we have observed after single injections: (i) A decrease in body weight of 4.7%, compared to 16.2% after continuous infusion; (ii) a decrease in differential lymphocyte count from 90.3% (normal) to 65.6%, compared to 31.4% after continuous infusion, and a decrease in leukocyte count (per mm^2) from 5200 (normal) to 3800, compared to 2300 after continuous infusion, while no difference in other blood parameters, including erythrocyte number, hematocrit, and hemoglobin concentration, was observed; (iii) on histological examination, a depletion of T and, to a lesser extent, B lymphocytes, and an atrophy of lymph nodes, spleen, and thymus; and (iv) significant depression in blastogenesis induced by the T-cell mitogens concanavalin A and phytohemagglutinin and, to a lesser extent, by the B-cell mitogen *Escherichia coli* lipopolysaccharide. ADase was inhibited to a high degree ranging from 84 to 94% in lymphoid organs and erythrocytes from animals receiving DCF by either mode of administration. These data provide further direct support for the importance of ADase to proper lymphocyte function, and suggest that continuous infusion may be the preferred mode of administration in clinical trials of DCF as an antileukemic agent.

[1] This research was supported by U.S. Public Health Service Grants CA-08748, CA-18856, CA-18428, CA-19267, CA-17404, AI-11843, and NS-11457, the Zelda Radow Weintraub Cancer Fund, the National Foundation March of Dimes, and U.S. Public Health Service Grant CA-14906 from the National Cancer Institute through the National Large Bowel Project.

[2] ARCS Foundation Fellow.

[3] Fellow of the J.M. Foundation.

[4] To whom all correspondence should be addressed. Recipient of American Cancer Society Faculty Research Award FRA-182.

0008-8749/81/140259-13$02.00/0

INTRODUCTION

Much evidence strongly suggests a potential use of inhibitors of the enzyme adenosine deaminase (ADase)[5] (EC 3.5.4.4) as specific immunosuppressive agents that do not affect the proliferation of nonlymphoid tissue. This application was first implied by the fact that in some patients with severe combined immunodeficiency disease (SCID) there is an associated inherited absence of ADase (1, 2). A substantial amount of *in vivo* data has supported, but not unequivocally proven, a causal relationship between the enzyme defect and this syndrome, which is characterized by selective dysfunction of both B and T cells with relatively minor impairment of nonlymphoid tissue (for reviews, see (3, 4)). Thus, for example, adenosine and 2′-deoxyadenosine, the naturally occurring substrates of ADase, can interfere with the proliferation of lymphoid cells in culture (6–8), an effect that is generally potentiated by an ADase inhibitor. It is also notable, however, that ADase inhibitors alone have not been consistently observed to inhibit lymphocyte proliferation or viability in *in vitro* test systems (5, 9–12).

Direct *in vivo* evidence for the importance of ADase to proper lymphocyte function and development was provided by the recent demonstration in our laboratory that continuous infusion into mice of 2′-deoxycoformycin (DCF), a highly specific, tight-binding inhibitor of ADase (13), could produce a specific impairment in lymphocyte function and number with no apparent toxicity to other tissues (14–16). The DCF-infused animals were characterized by atrophy of lymphoid organs, lymphopenia and a significant depression in various immune function tests, including T- and B-cell mitogen response and antibody production. These data were consistent with previous studies indicating that DCF *in vivo* is immunosuppressive in an allograft tumor test system (17) and is lymphocytotoxic to splenocytes (18). Significantly, DCF infusion did not impair the capacity of bone marrow stem cells to differentiate (16). Clinical studies have demonstrated that multiple single injections of DCF also produce a marked lymphopenia in patients with solid tumors as well as a remission in some patients with acute leukemia (19).

In contradistinction, it has been reported that multiple daily single injections of a low dose of DCF into mice are essentially without effect on the proliferative response of lymphocytes to concanavalin A (Con A) or of splenocytes in mixed lymphocyte cultures in spite of a high degree of ADase inhibition (20). In conjunction with *in vitro* experiments that failed to demonstrate an effect of ADase inhibitors alone on lymphocyte proliferation (e.g., (9)), these results suggested that inhibition of ADase does not impair the function or viability of mature T cells. In order to clarify the importance of ADase for proper immune function as well as to demonstrate unequivocally the feasibility of establishing a murine model for combined immunodeficiency, we have reexamined the immunological and enzymatic effects of multiple daily injections of DCF in C57BL/6J mice. In parallel experiments we have compared the effect of continuous infusion of a low dose of DCF on the same strain of mice under identical laboratory conditions. The data directly demonstrate that inhibition of ADase by either mode of administration is immunosuppressive and lymphocytotoxic, although continuous infusion clearly pro-

[5] Abbreviations used: ADase, adenosine deaminase; SCID, severe combined immunodeficiency disease; DCF, 2′-deoxycoformycin, (*R*)-[3-(2-deoxy-β-D-*erythro*-pentofuranosyl)-3,6,7,8-tetrahydroimidazo[4,5-*d*][1,3] diazepin-8-ol]; Con A, concanavalin A; PHA, phytohemagglutinin.

duces the more profound depression in lymphocyte function and number. These results have important implications for the clinical dose scheduling of DCF as an antileukemic agent.

MATERIALS AND METHODS

Materials

Male C57BL/6J mice aged 5–7 weeks were obtained from the Jackson Laboratory (Bar Harbor, Maine). DCF was a generous gift from the National Cancer Institute through the assistance of Dr. J. Douros. Sources for all other materials have been previously cited (14). Histological examination and hematological analysis were performed in the Departments of Pathology and Hematology, respectively, of Memorial Hospital.

Drug Administration

Single injections. Male C57BL/6J mice weighing approximately 20 g and maintained on Purina Rat Chow and tap water supplemented with terramycin were injected intraperitoneally daily for 5 days with 0.20 ml DCF dissolved in 0.9% NaCl at a concentration of 40 μg/ml. The amount of DCF injected per day was adjusted so that each animal received a dose of 0.4 mg/kg body wt/day. The DCF solution was allowed to remain at room temperature between injections to permit a direct comparison of results with those obtained following constant infusion. No significant loss of inhibitory capacity was observed after 5 days at room temperature. Control animals were injected intraperitoneally with an equal volume of 0.9% NaCl.

Constant infusions. DCF was administered by catheterization through the tail into the abdominal cavity, as previously described (21). DCF (9.2 μg/ml for a 20-g mouse) prepared as described above was infused at a constant rate of 0.3 mg/kg body wt/day for 5 days. The volume delivered per day was 0.6 ml and the concentration of DCF was varied in proportion to the weight of the animal. Control animals infused with 0.9% NaCl have previously been shown to exhibit no alterations in enzymatic or immunological properties as a consequence of the infusion process (14, 21).

Tissue Preparation

Eighteen hours after the final injection of DCF, an aliquot of blood was drawn from the retinal venous plexus for hematological analysis. Heparinized blood was drawn by heart puncture and the animals were sacrificed by cervical dislocation. Erythrocytes were obtained by centrifugation at 5000*g* for 10 min followed by three washes with phosphate-buffered saline. Lymphoid organs (spleen, lymphoid nodes, and thymus) were excised aseptically from both treated and control animals, and mononuclear cells for both ADase and mitogen stimulation studies were prepared as previously described (14). Cell viability was >90% by the trypan blue exclusion test. Organs from mice in both treated and control groups were also fixed in formalin for subsequent histological analysis.

Mitogen Response

Lymphocyte blastogenesis induced by mitogens was determined by incorporation of [^{3}H]thymidine into DNA, as previously described (14).

ADase

Mononuclear cells suspended in phosphate-buffered saline were lysed by six cycles of freezing and thawing; erythrocytes were lysed with 3 vol of 5m*M* imidazole–HCl, pH 7. ADase was determined on supernatants obtained by centrifugation at 2000*g* by conversion of [8-^{14}C]adenosine to radioactive products, as previously described (21).

Protein Determination

Protein was quantified by the method of Lowry *et al.* (22) employing bovine serum albumin as standard.

RESULTS

Weight

The administration of DCF was consistently observed to interfere with the normal weight gain characteristic of 6- to 7-week-old mice (Table 1). Control animals receiving single injections of 0.9% NaCl demonstrated a mean increase of 2.0 g over a 5-day period, representing 10.4% of total body weight. In distinction, mice receiving single injections of DCF demonstrated no significant change in weight over the same period, while mice infused with DCF demonstrated a significant ($P < .001$) decrease in mean body weight of 3.2 g, a change of 16.2%. We have previously observed that mice infused with 0.9% NaCl for the same period show no significant change in weight (14). It was also apparent from gross examination that spleen, lymph nodes, and thymus were smaller in size after administration of DCF by either method as compared to control animals. A decrease in splenic weight has also been noted after a single injection of a high dose of DCF (18).

Lymphopenia

We have compared the effect of multiple single injections and constant infusion of DCF on selected peripheral blood elements (Table 2). DCF administration by

TABLE 1

Effect of 2′-Deoxycoformycin Administration on C57BL/6J Mouse Whole-Body Weight[a]

	Weight (g)		Change	
	Day 0	Day 5	Weight (g)	Percentage
Control	19.3 ± 1.6	21.3 ± 1.4	2.0*↑	10.4↑
DCF-treated				
Injected	19.2 ± 1.5	18.3 ± 1.3	0.9 (N.S.)[b]↓	4.7↓
Infused	19.8 ± 0.8	16.6 ± 0.7	3.2**↓	16.2↓

[a] DCF was administered either by single daily intraperitoneal injections or by continuous infusion, as described under Materials and Methods. Animal weights were obtained before treatment with DCF (Day 0) and immediately prior to sacrifice (Day 5) and are expressed as the mean ± SD of determinations on five or six animals.

[b] Not significant.

* Significant at $P = 0.05$.

** Significant at $P < 0.001$.

TABLE 2

Effect of 2'-Deoxycoformycin Treatment on C57BL/6J Mouse Peripheral Blood Elements[a]

		DCF-treated	
	Normal	Single injections	Constant infusion
Erythrocytes[b]	8.2 ± 0.7	8.2 ± 0.5	8.6 ± 0.8
Leukocytes[b]	5.2 ± 1.1	3.8 ± 0.9 (26.9↓)*	2.3 ± 0.5 (55.8↓)***
Lymphocytes[b]	4.7 ± 0.9	2.5 ± 0.8 (46.8↓)**	0.7 ± 0.2 (85.1↓)***
Differential lymphocyte count (%)	90.3 ± 1.6	65.6 ± 4.9 (27.4↓)***	31.4 ± 6.7 (65.2↓)***
Non-lymphocytic leukocytes[b]	0.5 ± 0.2	1.3 ± 0.2 (160↑)***	1.6 ± 0.5 (220↑)***

[a] Data are expressed as the mean ± SD of determinations on five or six animals. Data in parentheses represent the percentage change for the mean of the measured parameter in the treated mice compared to normal controls. Heparinized blood was obtained by orbital bleeding.

[b] Expressed as number $\times 10^{-3}$ per mm^3.

* Difference between treated and normal mice is significant at $P < 0.07$.

** Difference between treated and normal mice is significant at $P < 0.005$.

*** Difference between treated and normal mice is significant at $P < 0.001$.

either method resulted in a marked lymphopenia, although the more striking effects were noted after constant infusion. The circulating lymphocyte count decreased from 4700 ± 900 in control animals to 2500 ± 800 and 700 ± 200/mm^3 after multiple single injections and constant infusion of DCF, respectively. This loss was reflected in a change in the differential lymphocyte count from a control value of 90.3 ± 1.6 to 65.6 ± 4.9% after multiple single injections and 31.4 ± 6.7% after constant infusion of DCF. In distinction, it is notable that the number of circulating nonlymphocytic leukocytes demonstrated a statistically significant increase after either mode of administration of DCF. The net effect of DCF, however, was a decrease in the leukocyte count from a control value (per mm^3) of 5200 ± 1100 to 3800 ± 900 and 2300 ± 500, representing decreases of 26.9 and 55.8% after multiple single injections and constant infusion of DCF, respectively. Thus, all animals treated with DCF were lymphopenic and leukopenic, the severity of which was dependent on the mode of administration.

In distinction, the circulating erythrocyte number was not significantly affected by either mode of administration of DCF (Table 2). Other blood parameters, including hematocrit, hemoglobin concentration, and mean corpuscular volume, were essentially unaffected by DCF injections (data not shown), similar to the lack of effect of constant infusion of DCF on these parameters that we have previously reported (14). These data support the absence of any kind of anemia in the DCF-treated animals and imply a specific cytotoxicity to lymphoid cells.

Histology

Histological evaluation provided clear evidence for a depletion of lymphoid cells and an atrophy of lymphoid organs after 5 days of single injections of DCF (Fig. 1). In the thymus a depletion of thymocytes and an atrophy of cortex and medulla were apparent (Fig. 1B). Similar effects that were substantially more marked were

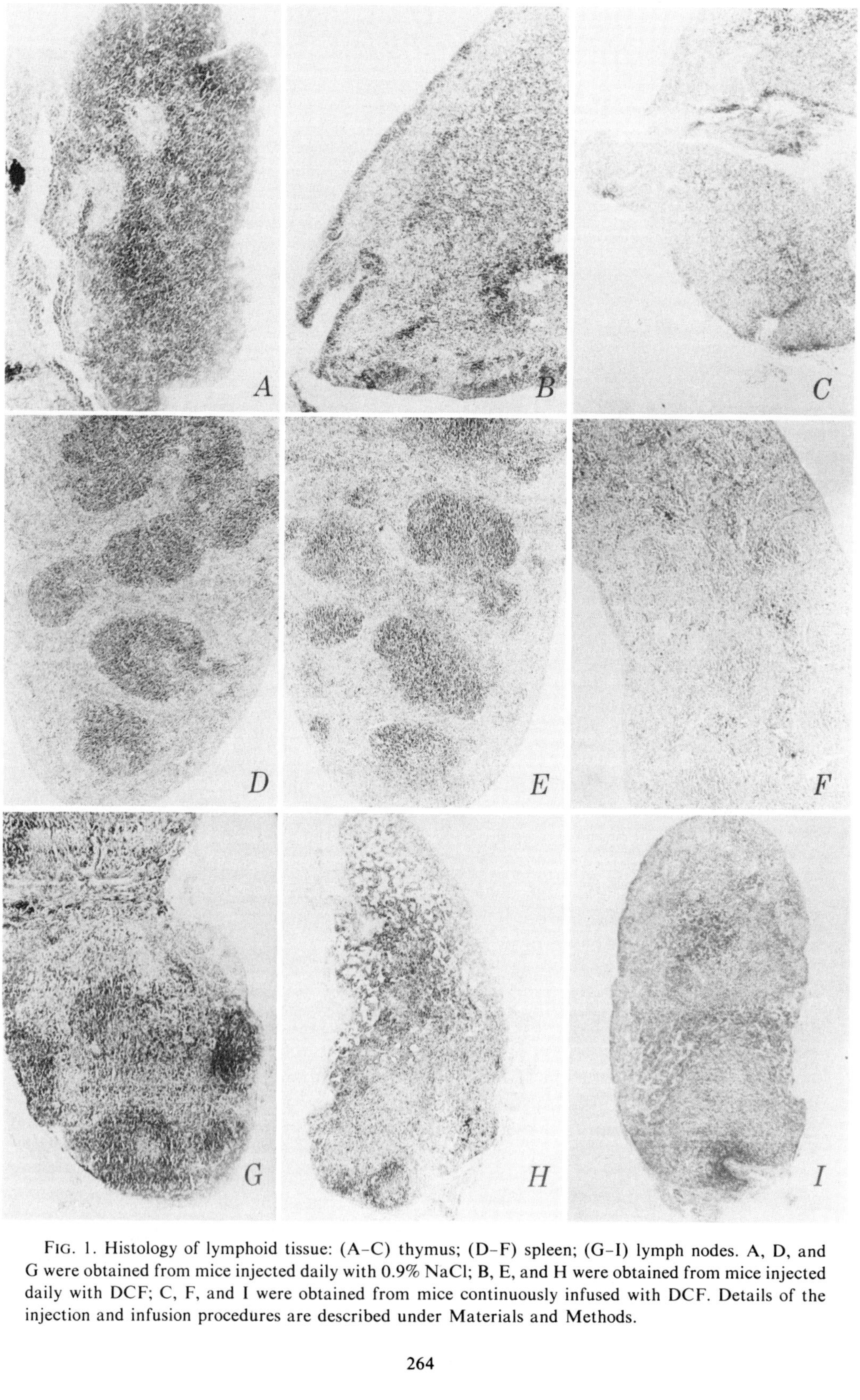

FIG. 1. Histology of lymphoid tissue: (A–C) thymus; (D–F) spleen; (G–I) lymph nodes. A, D, and G were obtained from mice injected daily with 0.9% NaCl; B, E, and H were obtained from mice injected daily with DCF; C, F, and I were obtained from mice continuously infused with DCF. Details of the injection and infusion procedures are described under Materials and Methods.

observed in the thymus after continuous infusion of DCF (Fig. 1C). In spleen (Fig. 1E) and lymph nodes (Fig. 1H) single injections of DCF produced a partial depletion of both B and T cells. The depletion of T-cell areas, however, was noticeably greater than the loss in B-cell regions, particularly in the lymph nodes. Continuous infusion of DCF resulted in an almost total ablation of both B- and T-cell areas and a virtually complete destruction of lymphoid follicles in both spleen (Fig. 1F) and lymph nodes (Fig. 1I). Thus, although morphological changes were indeed apparent in lymphoid tissue after multiple single injections of DCF, these effects were minimal in comparison to those observed after continuous infusion. In control experiments normal lymphoid architecture, characterized by dense lymphoid populations in B- and T-cell regions and abundant and normal germinal centers, was observed after either multiple injections or continuous infusion of 0.9% NaCl for a 5-day period (Figs 1A, D, and G).

Mitogen-Induced Blastogenesis

Stimulation of lymphocytes by the T-cell mitogens concanavalin A (Con A) and phytohemagglutinin (PHA) was significantly depressed by single injections of DCF in both spleen and thymus (Table 3). In all cases, however, the percentage depression was substantially greater following continuous infusion of DCF than after multiple single injections. Thus, percentage decreases in net counts per minute of [^{3}H]thymidine incorporated into DNA (background values subtracted) of 46.2 and 46.3% in PHA and Con A stimulation, respectively, of splenocytes were observed, compared to 77.8 and 88.2% decreases after constant infusion. Similarly, Con A stimulation of thymocytes and lymph node cells was depressed 12.3 and 34.2%, respectively, after single injections, compared to 68.9% and a virtually total loss of response, respectively, after constant infusion of DCF. However, DCF administered by single injections did not appear to depress PHA stimulation significantly in the lymph node cells, although it did produce a 94.5% depression when administered by constant infusion. Interestingly, the background incorporation (no mitogen present) was also significantly lowered in the thymus and spleen by constant infusion of DCF, but was essentially unaffected by multiple single injections.

Multiple single injections of DCF also depressed stimulation by the B-cell mitogen LPS, as evidenced by a reduction of 15.6% in net counts per minute in splenocytes (Table 3). This effect, however, was considerably less than the depression in the response of splenocytes to both Con A and PHA (46.3 and 46.2%, respectively). The relatively narrow standard deviations of the means from which the percentage depressions were calculated render these differences highly significant. These results suggest a greater sensitivity of T lymphocytes to ADase inhibition by multiple single injections, consistent with the histological observations cited above. In distinction, continuous infusion of DCF produced a larger depression of greater than 70% in the response to LPS, comparable to the high degree of inhibition in both Con A and PHA response, a finding that is also consistent with the histology.

When the mitogen stimulation data were expressed in terms of stimulation indices (i.e., ratio of cpm incorporated in the presence of mitogen to the background incorporated in the absence of mitogen), similar trends were observed. Thus, for example, the stimulation indices of splenocytes from animals receiving multiple

TABLE 3

Effect of 2′-Deoxycoformycin Administration on Mitogen-Induced Blastogenesis of C57BL/6J Mouse Lymphocytes[a]

	[^{3}H]Thymidine incorporation (cpm ± SD)				Stimulation index[b]		
	Background	PHA	Con A	LPS	PHA	Con A	LPS
Spleen							
Control	1063 ± 148	36,642 ± 1463	192,112 ± 17,863	34,152 ± 2532	34.5	180.7	32.1
DCF-injected	1169 ± 236	20,319 ± 2316 (46.2)*	103,698 ± 9,693 (46.3)**	29,093 ± 3156 (15.6)***	17.4 (49.6)	88.7 (50.9)	24.9 (22.4)
DCF-infused	632 ± 98 (40.5)*	8,532 ± 786 (77.8)*	23,191 ± 3,109 (88.2)*	10,343 ± 2631 (70.7)*	13.5 (60.9)	36.7 (79.7)	16.4 (48.9)
Thymus							
Control	863 ± 193	N.D.[c]	43,513 ± 1,932	N.D.	N.D.	50.4	N.D.
DCF-injected	693 ± 178 (19.7)(N.S.)[d]	N.D.	38,104 ± 2,097 (12.3)**	N.D.	N.D.	55.0	N.D.
DCF-infused	408 ± 28 (52.7)*	N.D.	13,693 ± 3,620 (68.9)*	N.D.	N.D.	33.6 (66.7)	N.D.
Lymph nodes							
Control	1262 ± 187	32,548 ± 6172	113,078 ± 4,422	24,651 ± 1020	25.8	89.6	19.5
DCF-injected	1720 ± 282	31,925 ± 334 (3.5)(N.S.)	75,297 ± 3,502 (34.2)**	23,555 ± 575 (6.6)(N.S.)	18.6 (27.9)	43.8 (51.1)	13.7 (29.7)
DCF-infused[e]	1121 ± 103 (11.2)(N.S.)	2,853 ± 402 (94.5)*	1,378 ± 461 (99.8)*	N.D.	2.6 (89.9)	1.2 (98.7)	N.D.

[a] Lymphocyte blastogenesis was determined at optimal mitogen concentrations by incorporation of [^{3}H]thymidine into DNA. cpm data represent the mean of triplicate determinations on tissues pooled from four or five animals. DCF was administered either by single daily intraperitoneal injections (DCF-injected) or by constant infusion (DCF-infused), as described under Materials and Methods. Control animals were injected daily with ca 0.2 ml of 0.9% sodium chloride. Numbers in parentheses represent the percentage depression in the net cpm incorporated (cpm in the presence of mitogen minus background), or in the stimulation index, compared to the corresponding value for the control animals. Details of each of the experimental procedures are described under Materials and Methods.

[b] [^{3}H]Thymidine incorporated into DNA in the presence of mitogen divided by the incorporation with no mitogen present.

[c] Not determined.

[d] Not significant.

[e] Lymph node cells were obtained from animals infused at a rate of 0.4 mg DCF/day/kg body wt.

* Depression significant at $P < 0.01$.

** Depression significant at $P < 0.025$.

*** Depression significant at $P < 0.05$.

TABLE 4

Effect of DCF Administration on C57BL/6J Mouse ADase Activity[a]

Tissue	Percentage inhibition[b] Infusion	Single injections
Thymus	94	90
Spleen	90	84
Lymph nodes	78	87
Erythrocytes	86	84

[a] DCF was administered by continuous infusion or as daily intraperitoneal injections, as described under Materials and Methods. Activities were determined after 5 days on cells pooled from three animals and generally agreed to within 5%.

[b] Percentage of specific activity from control tissues that was inhibited by DCF administration. ADase levels in saline-injected or saline-infused mice were similar to control values previously reported (21).

single injections of DCF were lower for both T-cell and, to a lesser extent, B-cell mitogens, although continuous infusion of DCF again produced substantially larger reductions in each case. Similarly, for lymph node cells, single injections of DCF produced decreases of 27.9 and 51.1% in stimulation indices for PHA and Con A, respectively, compared to a 90% or greater reduction after continuous infusion.

Mitogen stimulation of lymphocytes *in vitro* is generally considered to reflect, at least in part, the function of immunocompetent lymphoid cells *in vivo*. It is therefore clear that, regardless of how the mitogen stimulation data are expressed, DCF interferes with the function of both T and B cells, but to a substantially greater degree when administered by continuous infusion.

Enzyme Activity

The effect of 5 days of DCF administration on ADase in cell-free supernatants of lymphoid organs and erythrocytes is summarized in Table 4. High, but incomplete degrees of inhibition that varied from tissue to tissue were observed after both modes of administration. The percentage inhibition following either single injections or continuous infusion of DCF was similar, although small differences were noted. Thus, thymic and splenic ADase were inhibited 90 and 84%, respectively, after multiple single injections, compared to somewhat higher values of 94 and 90% after continuous infusion, whereas lymph node ADase was 87% inhibited by multiple single injections compared to 78% after continuous infusion. In control experiments, neither multiple single injections nor continuous infusion of 0.9% NaCl at the same volume employed in administration of DCF was observed to inhibit ADase specific activity in either lymphoid tissues or erythrocytes (data not shown).

DISCUSSION

Various methods of administration of DCF to mice have previously been employed to demonstrate specific immunosuppression and lymphocytotoxicity. These protocols have included: (a) a single injection of high dose of DCF (100 mg/kg body wt/day) (18); (b) multiple single injections of a low dose (ca. 1.0 mg/kg body wt/day) administered one or more times daily (17, 20, 23); and (c) continuous infusion of a low dose (14–16). The results from these various studies are not uniformly consistent. Thus, in our laboratory administration of DCF to mice by continuous infusion was found to result in striking lymphocytotoxicity, lymphopenia, and a large depression in lymphocyte response to both B- and T-cell mitogens (14). In distinction, Smyth and co-workers (18) report no lymphopenia in mice 10 days after administration of a single dose of DCF, in spite of histological evidence for severe lymphoid depletion in the spleen. According to Burridge and coworkers (20), however, daily single injections of DCF for 5 days are without effect on Con A stimulation of thymocytes or splenocyte response in a mixed lymphocyte culture assay, in spite of a high degree of ADase inhibition. Unfortunately, no histopathological examination was performed in this study. These results are also in apparent contradiction to the prolongation of skin allograft survival in animals receiving multiple single injections of DCF (17).

In the present study we have demonstrated that inhibition of ADase by daily intraperitoneal injections of a low dose of DCF (0.4 mg/kg body wt/day) into mice for a 5-day period is associated with an immunodeficiency of T and, to a lesser extent, B cells. A depression in immune function in these animals is strongly supported by (i) a marked reduction in the differential lymphocyte count and the number of circulating leucocytes; (ii) a depression in lymphocyte stimulation by the T-cell mitogens Con A and PHA and, to a lesser extent, the B-cell mitogen LPS; and (iii) hypoplasia in spleen, lymph nodes, and thymus, as evidenced by histological examination and apparent reductions in organ size. Histopathological evaluation indicated no apparent toxicity to nonlymphoid organs including those containing rapidly proliferating cells like small intestine and bone marrow. Thus, we conclude that DCF administered by multiple single injections produces a degree of ADase inhibition that is specifically lymphocytotoxic and immunosuppressive in the mouse. The fact that the affinity of DCF for other enzymes is several orders of magnitude less than for ADase (24, 25) further strengthens the conclusion that ADase is the pharmacological target for this drug.

Parallel experiments have indicated that although similar trends are observed after continuous infusion of DCF the depression of immune function is quantitatively more severe. This result is consistent with previous studies indicating that following inhibition of ADase with a single injection of DCF there is a time- and tissue-dependent recovery of activity (26, 27). In addition, it is also relevant that greater than 90% of DCF is cleared from the plasma and rapidly excreted in the urine within 2 hr after injection into mice (28). Therefore it is reasonable that continuous infusion provides a constant low level of DCF in the circulation and hence a more efficient and continuous inhibition of enzyme activity that is unattainable with multiple single injections. Although inhibition of ADase in supernatants of lymphoid tissues after 5 days of treatment was high and nearly equal after either mode of administration, the possibility of a substantial residual ADase between individual injections has not been excluded. Somewhat higher percentage inhibitions were indeed observed in both splenocytes and thymocytes after 5 days of infusion (Table 4). In addition, the possibility must also be considered that the actual inhibition of intracellular ADase *in vivo* is higher than measured in supernatants since the DCF–ADase complex may partially dissociate during tissue processing or during the assay itself (21).

The failure of Burridge and co-workers (20) to observe an impairment of either

Con A stimulation of thymocytes or of the response of splenocytes in mixed lymphocyte culture after 4- to 5-day period of single injections of DCF is not understood. These results were obtained in spite of a dose of DCF (1.0 mg/kg body wt/day) that resulted in a virtually complete inhibition (>95%) of ADase in thymus, spleen, and lymph nodes. It is notable that a different strain of mice was employed in the latter experiments (ICR Swiss mice) compared to the strain employed in the studies reported here (C57BL/6J). Thus it may be speculated that although the ADase of both strains is equally sensitive to inhibition by DCF, the biochemical target that is ultimately affected as a consequence of ADase inhibition may be different. Possible candidates that have been previously postulated include, for example, adenyl cyclase (29), *S*-adenosylhomocysteinase (30), and ribonucleoside diphosphate reductase (31). A comparison of the properties of these key enzymes in mature lymphocytes may well elucidate important details of the biochemical mechanism responsible for SCID associated with ADase deficiency.

The addition of ADase inhibitors to lymphoid cells in culture has not been consistently observed to interfere with function or viability (5, 9–12). Combined with our consistent observation of immunodeficiency in mice following DCF administration, these data suggest the importance of the interaction between lymphoid tissues and a circulating metabolite in the genesis of immunodeficiency. The trapping of deoxyadenosine by lymphoid tissue has been postulated to represent such a mechanism (32). It is pertinent, however, that Carson and co-workers (33) report that in the BALB/c mouse deoxyadenosine phosphorylating activity, the presumed "trap" for circulating deoxyadenosine, is widespread in many tissues and does not display the same lymphospecific distribution characteristic of the deoxyadenosine and deoxycytidine phosphorylating activities in man. These authors therefore suggested that the mouse is probably an inadequate model for the study of the physiological effects of ADase inhibitors, a conclusion directly disputed by the data we present. Thus, the lymphospecific trapping of deoxyadenosine and subsequent elevation of deoxy-ATP may not represent the primary biochemical mechanism for the immunosuppressive effects of DCF. The relevance of this conclusion to human immunodeficiency disease is yet to be established.

It is of special importance that single injections of DCF appear to have greater immunosuppressive activity toward T cells than B cells, as suggested by (i) a substantially greater depression in the response to the T-cell mitogens Con A and PHA compared to the B-cell mitogen LPS; and (ii) a greater depletion of T-cell regions, particularly apparent in the lymph nodes. If the mouse immunosuppressed with DCF represents an accurate animal model for human SCID, the data suggest that the primary disorder in the syndrome associated with ADase deficiency may be related to abnormalities in T-cell function, with B-cell dysfunction representing a secondary influence. The fact that a number of SCID patients demonstrate greater T-cell than B-cell abnormalities (34), as well as the ability of normal T cells to enable SCID patients' B lymphocytes to produce and secrete immunoglobulins (35), supports the existence of such clinical cases. The use of single injections of DCF may provide a means for determining the biochemical basis for the apparently greater sensitivity of T cells to ADase inhibition.

A number of clinical pharmacological studies of DCF as a selective treatment for lymphoid malignancies have been reported (19, 36–39). DCF was administered in these experiments at a relatively low dose (0–1.0 mg/kg body wt/day) as a daily injection for a period of several days. The data from these studies provide support for an application of DCF as a relatively specific antilymphocytic agent in man. Various toxicities were observed at the higher dose levels, however, and the number of patients exhibiting clinical benefit were small. The results from the animal experiments reported here suggest that constant infusion may be the preferred mode of administration for maximal lymphocytotoxicity with minimal side effects. Indeed, Benjamin and co-workers (39) have reported antileukemic activity in one of five patients treated with single injections of DCF, compared to three of six patients treated by constant infusion. These studies also indicated that the constant infusion of DCF resulted in higher and more persistent inhibition of ADase than did multiple injections. Thus, further clinical trials on the continuous infusion of DCF as a treatment for malignancies of lymphoid system appear warranted.

REFERENCES

1. Dissing, B., and Knudsen, B., *Lancet* **2,** 1316, 1972.
2. Giblett, E. R., Anderson, J. E., Cohen, B., Pollara, B., and Meuwissen, H. F., *Lancet* **2,** 1067, 1972.
3. Meuwissen, H. J., Pickering, R. J., Pollara, B., and Porter, I. H. (Eds.), "Combined Immunodeficiency Disease and Adenosine Deaminase Deficiency: A Molecular Defect." Academic Press, New York, 1975.
4. Pollara, B., Pickering, R. J., Meuwissen, H. J., and Porter, I. H. (Eds.), "Inborn Errors of Specific Immunity." Academic Press, New York, 1979.
5. Snyder, F. F., Mendelsohn, J., and Seegmiller, J. E., *J. Clin. Invest.* **58,** 65, 1978.
6. Green, H., and Chan, T. S., *Science* **182,** 836, 1973.
7. Ishii, K., and Green, H., *J. Cell Sci.* **13,** 429, 1973.
8. Fox, I. H., Keystone, E. C., Gladman, D. D., Moore, M., and Cane, D., *Immunol. Commun.* **4,** 419, 1975.
9. Ballet, J.-J., Insel, R., Merler, E., and Rosen, F., *J. Exp. Med.* **143,** 1271, 1976.
10. Carson, D. A., and Seegmiller, J. E., *J. Clin. Invest.* **57,** 274, 1976.
11. Hovi, T., Smyth, J. F. Allison, A. C., and Williams, S. C., *Clin. Exp. Immunol.* **23,** 395, 1976.
12. Hirschhorn, R., and Sela, E., *Cell. Immunol.* **32,** 350, 1977.
13. Agarwal, R. P., Spector, T., and Parks, R. E., Jr., *Biochem Pharmacol.* **26,** 359, 1967.
14. Tedde, A., Balis, M. E., Ikehara, S., Pahwa, R., Good, R. A., and Trotta, P. P., *Proc Nat. Acad. Sci. USA* **77,** 4899, 1980.
15. Trotta, P. P., Tedde, A. Balis, M. E., Ikehara, S., Pahwa, R., Sordillo, E. M., Brown, G. F., and Good, R. A., *In* "Primary Immunodeficiencies" (M. Seligmann and W. H. Hitzig, Eds.). Elsevier/North-Holland, Amsterdam, 1980.
16. Trotta, P. P., Tedde, A., Ikehara, S., Pahwa, R., Good, R. A., and Balis, M. E., *Cancer Res.,* **41,** 2189, 1981.
17. Chassin, M. M., Chirigos, M. A., Johns, D. G., and Adamson, R. H., *N. Engl. J. Med.* **296,** 1232, 1977.
18. Smyth, J. F., Young, R. C., and Young, D. M., *Cancer Chemother. Pharmacol.* **1,** 49, 1978.
19. Smyth, J. F., Chassin, M. M., Harrap, K. R., Adamson, R. H., and Johns, D. G., *Proc. Amer. Assoc. Cancer Res.* **21,** 185, 1980.
20. Burridge, P. W., Paetku, V., and Henderson, J. F., *J. Immunol.* **119,** 675, 1977.
21. Tedde, A., Balis, M. E., Schonberg, R., and Trotta, P. P., *Cancer Res.* **39,** 3044, 1979.
22. Lowry, O. H., Rosebrough, N. J., Farr, A. L., and Randall, R. J., *J. Biol. Chem.* **193,** 265, 1951.
23. Nelson, D. J., LaFon, S., and Lambe, C. U. *In* "Inborn Errors of Specific Immunity" (B. Pollara, R. J. Pickering, H. J. Meuwissen, and I. H. Porter, Eds.). Academic Press, New York, 1979.
24. Agarwal, R. P., and Parks, R. E., Jr., *Biochem. Pharmacol.* **26,** 663, 1977.
25. Henderson, J. F., Brox, L., Zombor, G., Hunting, G., and Lomax, C. A., *Biochem. Pharmacol.* **26,** 1967, 1977.
26. Agarwal, R. P., *Cancer Res.* **39,** 1425, 1979.
27. Chassin, M. M. Adamson, R. H., Zaharevitz, D. W., and Johns, D. G., *Biochem. Pharmacol.* **28,** 1894, 1970.

28. McConnell, W. R., Suling, W. J., Rice, L. S., Shannon, W. M., and Hill, D. L., *Cancer Treat. Rep.* **62,** 1153, 1978.
29. Wolberg, G., Zimmerman, T. P., Hiemstra, K., Winston, M., and Chu, L.-C., *Science* **187,** 957, 1975.
30. Hershfield, M. S., Kredich, N. M., Ownby, D. R., Ownby, H., Buckley, R., *J. Clin. Invest.* **63,** 807, 1979.
31. Cohen, A., Hirschhorn, R., Horowitz, S. D., Rubenstein, A., Polmer, S. H., Hong, R., and Martin, D. W., *Proc. Nat. Acad. Sci. USA* **75,** 472, 1978.
32. Carson, D. A., Kaye, J., Seegmiller, J. E., *Proc. Nat. Acad. Sci. USA* **74,** 5677, 1977.
33. Carson, D. A., Kaye, J., and Wasson, D. B., *J. Immunol.* **124,** 8, 1980.
34. Cooper, M. D., Faulk, W. P., Fudenberg, H. H., Good, R. A., Hitzig, W., Kunkel, H., Rosen, F. S., Seligmann, M., Soothill, J., and Wedgwood, R. J., *N. Eng. J. Med.* **288,** 966, 1973.
35. Seeger, R. C., Robins, R. A., Stevens, R. H., Klein, R. B., Waldman, D. J., Zelber, P. M., and Kessler, S. W., *Clin. Exp. Immunol.* **26,** 1, 1976.
36. Grever, M., Miser, J., Balcerzak, S., Neidhart, J., *Proc. Amer. Assoc. Cancer Res.* **21,** 335, 1980.
37. Schneider, R., Korngold, G., Vale, K., Woodcock, T., Tan, C., and Young, C., *Proc. Amer. Assoc. Cancer Res.* **21,** 185, 1980.
38. Kufe, D., Major, P., Agarwal, R., Reinherz, E., and Frei, III, E., *Proc. Amer. Assoc. Cancer Res.* **21,** 328, 1980.
39. Benjamin, R. S., Plunkett, W., Keating, M. J., Feun, L. C., Hug, V., Nelson, J. A., Bodey, G. P., and Freireich, E. J., *Proc. Amer. Assoc. Cancer Res.* **21,** 337, 1980.

CELLULAR IMMUNOLOGY 63, 272–278 (1981)

Lyt Phenotype Analysis of the Effector Cells Responsible for Evoking Lymphocyte-Induced Angiogenesis (LIA)[1]

NEAL W. ROEHM, YOUNAN A. SIDKY, AND ROBERT AUERBACH

Department of Zoology, University of Wisconsin, Madison, Wisconsin 53706

Received March 25, 1981; accepted May 13, 1981

Lymphocyte-induced angiogenesis (LIA) is a vascular response observed when allogeneic or semiallogeneic immunocompetent lymphocytes are inoculated intradermally into immunosuppressed or irradiated host mice. The reported experiments were carried out to characterize the effector cell population(s) responsible for causing LIA. Lyt 1.2, Lyt 2.2, and monoclonal Thy 1.2 antisera were used for negative selection with complement (C′) to investigate the ability of selected subsets of lymphocytes to evoke angiogenesis. Treatment of C57BL/6 spleen cells with either anti-Lyt 1.2 or anti-Thy 1.2 and C′ resulted in an almost complete abrogation of the LIA reaction. In contrast, depletion of Lyt 2+ cells, under conditions which fully abrogated their ability to generate cell-mediated cytotoxicity in allogeneic mixed leukocyte cultures, resulted only in a partial (45%) reduction in the induced vascular response. Synergistic interaction between cell preparations treated separately with either anti-Lyt 1.2 or anti-Lyt 2.2 serum was not observed. We conclude that (i) Lyt 1+2−T lymphocytes can induce a significant LIA reaction; (ii) lymphocytes resistant to negative selection with anti-Lyt-1.2 serum are incapable of inducing such a reaction; and (iii) Lyt 1+2+ cells directly or indirectly play an additional role in generating a maximal LIA response.

INTRODUCTION

The importance of angiogenesis in a variety of disease processes, as an accompaniment of tumor growth, during graft-versus-host reactions and development of delayed hypersensitivity, and as an adjunct of inflammation is well recognized. Our studies have previously demonstrated that the intracutaneous inoculation of immunocompetent lymphocytes into irradiated histoincompatible mice evokes the generation of new blood vessels, a reaction we have termed "lymphocyte-induced angiogenesis" (1). At the cell concentrations used, this characteristic neovascular response predominates, while at higher doses angiogenesis becomes obscured by erythema and induration, components of the inflammatory response extensively characterized in studies of the normal lymphocyte transfer reaction (2, 3).

That LIA[2] is a manifestation of a local graft-versus-host reaction is supported

[1] This work was supported by Grants AI 14607 and EY 3243 from the National Institutes of Health. N. W. Roehm was supported by Training Grant CA 09106, and a portion of this work was submitted in partial fulfilment of the requirements for the degree of Doctor of Philosophy in the Department of Zoology, University of Wisconsin.

[2] Abbreviations used: C′, complement; CML, cell-mediated lympholysis; HBSS, Hanks' balanced salt solution; LIA, lymphocyte-induced angiogenesis; MLC, mixed leukocyte culture; NMS, normal mouse serum.

0008-8749/81/140272-07$02.00/0

by several observations: (a) Both allogeneic and semiallogeneic leukocytes can induce angiogenesis in appropriate host animals, while such reactions are not induced by syngeneic cells or by cells from F_1 donors inoculated into parental-strain hosts (1); (b) spleen and lymph node cells as well as corticosteroid-resistant thymocytes can evoke a neovascular reaction while bone marrow cells are ineffective (1); (c) lymphocytes from athymic (nu/nu) animals cannot induce LIA (1); and (d) the major antigenic stimulus leading to LIA is associated with I-region alloantigens (4) as had previously been shown for the graft-versus-host reaction (5).

The present experiments were carried out to characterize the Lyt antigenic phenotypes of the cells which elicit angiogenesis in allogeneic recipients and to determine whether synergism between subpopulations of T cells (6–8) might play a role in the induction of vascular changes in these animals.

MATERIALS AND METHODS

Mice. Inbred Ha/ICRAu (H-2^q) mice were obtained from our own colony. C57BL/6 (H-2^b; Lyt 1.2; 2.2) and C_3H/HeSn mice were purchased from Jackson Laboratories, Bar Harbor, Maine. The B6Lyt1.1 (Lyt 1.1; 2.1) lines congenic with C57BL/6, as well as C_3H.CELyt1.2(DS) mice, were bred in our colony from breeding pairs generously provided by E. A. Boyse, Sloan–Kettering Memorial Cancer Center, New York.

Cell suspensions. Spleen cell suspensions were prepared by abrasion against a stainless-steel screen followed by disruption using a 26-gauge needle. The cell suspension was depleted of red blood cells and debris by centrifugation over Ficoll–Hypaque (9).

Preparation and use of antisera. Lyt 1.2 and Lyt 2.2 antisera were produced according to the protocols of Shen *et al.* (10, 11). The pools of antisera used in these experiments gave greater than 50% cytotoxicity against C57BL/6 thymocytes at a final antiserum concentration of 1:960 and less than 25% cytotoxicity against thymocytes of the appropriate allelic negative B6 Lyt congenic strain at a final antiserum concentration of 1:120, as determined in a single-step, complement-dependent cytotoxicity assay (12).

Rabbit serum was used as the C′ source. Sera of individual rabbits were screened for both high C′ activity and low toxicity against C57BL/6 thymocytes. The serum was used unabsorbed at a concentration which typically gave less than 10% background toxicity.

Negative selection with antiserum was conducted in two steps. Cells (20×10^6/ml) were incubated with normal mouse serum (NMS), anti-Lyt-1.2, or anti-Lyt-2.2 serum at a dilution of 1:10 for 30 min on ice. Treatment with monoclonal anti-Thy-1.2 (New England Nuclear) was conducted at a dilution of 1:1000. The cells were pelleted and resuspended in an equal volume of selected rabbit serum at a dilution of 1:9 and incubated for 30 min in a 37°C water bath. Medium 199 (Gibco) plus 2% heat-inactivated γ-globulin-free fetal calf serum (Gibco) was used as the diluent for negative selection. After treatment the cells were washed and resuspended in HBSS. Cell viability was visually assessed by trypan blue exclusion using phase microscopy.

LIA assay. Cell suspensions were adjusted to contain 10^7/ml viable cells, and 0.1 ml (10^6 cells) of this suspension was inoculated intracutaneously into irradiated allogeneic recipients (1). On the day of injection the recipient Ha/ICR mice were irradiated with 650 rad, using a cesium source at an approximate dose rate of 435 rad/min. The inoculations were made with a 26-gauge needle introduced as close to the epidermis as possible. A drop of dilute trypan blue solution was added to the cell suspension to facilitate localization of the injection sites. Each of the eight recipients used in each experiment received an injection of cells from each cell suspension. Inoculations were made along a midlateral line in the thoracolumbar portion of the trunk. Each experiment included the injection of untreated, syngeneic Ha/ICRAu spleen cells as a control.

Three days after injection the animals were killed with ether, and a midventral incision was made in the skin, which was then separated from the underlying muscles. After removing the superficial fascia, the injection sites were examined under 7× magnification and all extra vessels connected with the scar region and contrasting with the background vasculature were counted. The reader is referred to published photographs and diagrams for details of the protocols for detecting LIA (1). All injections and counts of vessels were made by one person (YAS) to assure consistency throughout the experiments, and all cell suspensions were independently coded and handled and scored blind to eliminate potential bias.

Functional correlations. In several experiments LIA assays were carried out in parallel with assays for CML and for MLC (13). In addition to confirming the previous results (13, 14) this protocol served as assurance that the serological treatment was adequate and functionally specific.

RESULTS

Before use in LIA assays, the Lyt 1.2 and Lyt 2.2 alloantisera had been extensively characterized both in terms of their ability to influence CML reactions (13, 14) and in their ability to abrogate mitogenic response to allogeneic stimulation *in vitro* (MLC) (13). Depletion of Lyt 1+ cells resulted in virtual abolishment of both the proliferative response (MLC) and the cytotoxic reaction (CML). Depletion of the Lyt 2+ population of responder lymphocytes prevented the CML reaction but left intact a substantial portion of the proliferative (MLC) response.

Our LIA studies were carried out with cell suspensions treated with anti-Lyt 1.2, anti-Lyt 2.2, or anti-Thy 1.2. The results are summarized in Fig. 1, and detailed data of individual experiments are given in Table 1. Both anti-Thy-1 treatment and anti-Lyt-1 treatment resulted in an almost complete elimination of the LIA reaction, indicating that Lyt 1+, Thy 1+ cells are essential for the vascular reaction to occur. In contrast, depletion of Lyt 2+ cells by pretreatment with anti-Lyt-2 serum reduced but by no means eliminated the angiogenesis response.

To test for possible synergism between the Lyt 1+ and Lyt 2+ cell populations, we carried out mixing experiments. Two equal aliquots from a common pool of C57BL/6 spleen cells were separately treated with anti-Lyt-1.2 and C′ or with anti-Lyt-2.2 and C′. After negative selection the aliquots were recombined, and then the viable cell concentration was adjusted to the standard 10^7 cells/ml. This procedure should maintain the relative number of cells in each operationally defined subset as they existed prior to treatment, and hence be comparable to NMS-treated cells, except for the removal of those lymphocytes bearing both Lyt 1+ and Lyt

TABLE 1

Ability of C57/BL6 Spleen Cells to Induce LIA following Pretreatment with Anti-Lyt-1, Anti-Lyt-2, or Anti-Thy-1 Sera

Experiment[a]	NMS + C′	αThy-1.2 + C′	αLyt 1.2 + C′	αLyt 2.2 + C′	Mixture[b]	Syngeneic controls
1	27.6 ± 1.0[c]	7.9 ± 0.4	4.0 ± 0.2	5.9 ± 0.3[d]	4.1 ± 0.4	0.5 ± 0.3
2	24.4 ± 2.4	4.8 ± 1.3	7.4 ± 1.3	15.2 ± 1.7	4.0 ± 0.6	0.3 ± 0.3
3	21.9 ± 1.4	3.4 ± 0.8	3.6 ± 0.6	13.8 ± 1.0	9.0 ± 1.9	0.8 ± 0.5
4	26.0 ± 2.3	5.6 ± 0.7	3.4 ± 0.3	19.4 ± 2.7	6.0 ± 0.8	2.3 ± 0.4

[a] 4 separate experiments, $n = 8$ for Experiments 1–3; $n = 7$ for Experiment 4.

[b] Reconstituted mixture of two equal aliquots of spleen cells separately treated with αLyt-1.2 + C′ or αLyt 2.2 + C′.

[c] Data presented as mean number of vessels ± SE.

[d] The Lyt 2.2 serum used in this experiment was not tested in MLC assays, and results with this particular serum may therefore not be representative.

2+ determinants. The results, shown in Table 1 and Fig. 1, indicate that mixing did not result in a significant restitution of the LIA reaction.

To be certain that our results were indeed due to Lyt-specific reactivity of the test sera, functional specificity tests of the anti-Lyt-1.2 and anti-Lyt-2.2 alloantisera were carried out using LIA assays with B6Lyt1.1 and B6Lyt2.1 mice, respectively. The results are shown in Table 2. Negative selection with anti-Lyt-1.2 + C′ under conditions which substantially reduced the LIA response evoked by C57BL/6 spleen cells did not reduce the response elicited by B6Lyt1.1 spleen cells. Similarly, negative selection with anti-Lyt-2.2 + C′ under conditions which specifically abrogated allogeneic CML responses of C57BL/6 leukocytes (data not shown; cf. (13) and (14)), did not appreciably alter the LIA response of B6Lyt2.1 spleen cells.

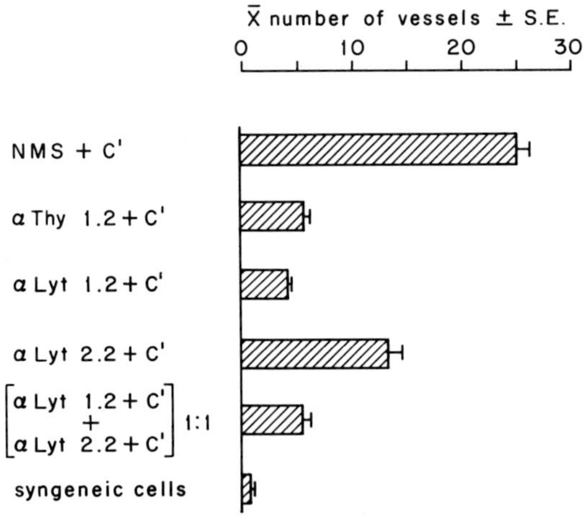

FIG. 1. Effect of negative selection with anti-Lyt 1.2, anti-Lyt 2.2, or anti-Thy 1.2 sera on C57BL/6 spleen cells, as measured by their ability to induce angiogenesis in irradiated allogeneic (Ha/ICRAu) mice: Summary of four separate experiments (Table 1).

TABLE 2

Functional Specificity of Negative Selection with Anti-Lyt 1.2 and Anti-Lyt 2.2 in LIA Assays

Experiment[a]	Donor	NMS + C′	αLyt 1.2 + C′	αLyt-2.2 + C′
1	C57BL/6	23.3 ± 3.0[b]	7.0 ± 1.1[c]	20.8 ± 2.9
	B6Lyt1.1	23.8 ± 2.3	31.0 ± 3.3	
	B6Lyt2.1	19.5 ± 2.9		15.6 ± 2.3
2	C57BL/6	36.4 ± 4.2	5.9 ± 1.1[c]	20.4 ± 2.1
	B6Lyt1.1	19.9 ± 1.5	22.0 ± 3.5	
	B6Lyt2.1	37.6 ± 2.4		19.8 ± 2.0
3	C57BL/6	26.1 ± 2.3	4.0 ± 0.5[c]	20.4 ± 2.0
	B6Lyt1.1	26.2 ± 2.6	35.4 ± 2.6	
	B6Lyt2.1	36.1 ± 2.9		36.5 ± 2.2

[a] 3 separate experiments, $n = 8$ for each value. Mean value of syngeneic controls was 3.5 ± 2.9.
[b] Data presented as number of vessels ± SE.
[c] Specific reduction in LIA.

DISCUSSION

Our experiments demonstrate that depletion of donor lymphocytes bearing either the Thy-1 or Lyt-1 surface antigens almost completely abolishes the LIA response. The correlation between the effects of anti-Thy-1 and anti-Lyt-1 treatment is consistent both with the proportion of spleen cells lysed by negative selection with these antisera and with the available cytofluorometric data which indicate that virtually all Thy 1+ cells express Lyt 1 (7, 15).

In contrast to the observations with anti-Thy-1 and anti-Lyt-1 sera, negative selection with anti-Lyt-2 serum under conditions which abrogate either the generation or expression of allogeneic cell-mediated cytotoxicity (13, 14) does not abolish the LIA reaction. We observed that depletion of Lyt 2+ effector cells had similar effects in LIA assays and in the degree of inhibition of allogeneic MLC (13), namely, the responses are partially reduced but not abolished.

The failure of Lyt 1+2− cells to exhibit enrichment proportional to the increase of cells in this subset following negative selection and readjustment of the residual viable cell concentration suggests that while this subset of T cells can elicit a significant LIA reaction, it is not the only one involved. Rather, it suggests that there may, as well, be a role for Lyt 1+,2+ cells, either directly, or through some type of helper activity. The inability to restore activity by mixing the two negatively selected subpopulations provides a more direct support for this interpretation, for clearly absent from the reconstitution mixture is the Lyt 1+,2+ subset. Other interpretations, however, are not excluded.

Similar observations have been made using the Simonsen spleen weight assay for the graft-versus-host reaction. Lyt 1+,2− cells, operationally defined by negative selection (16) or by positive selection (17), induce significant splenomegaly in allogeneic recipients, but in this instance also the response is not increased in proportion to the enrichment for cells in this subset.

The cellular immune responses which cause angiogenesis (4), induce splenomegaly in graft-versus-host reactions (5), and are seen in MLC proliferative responses (18, 19) are all related by the prominent role of I-region-associated alloantigens in stimulating these reactions. The correlations between these cellular immune responses also extend to the ability of Lyt 1+,2− T cells to elicit these responses following alloantigen recognition (15, 16, 20, 21). This preferential reactivity of Lyt 2− T cells to I-region alloantigens is further demonstrated by the observation that negative selection with anti-Lyt-2 of T cells activated in either the graft-versus-host reaction (22) or MLC (23) leads to depletion of responder cells bearing I-region-associated antigens of the stimulator haplotype.

We have recently demonstrated that LIA also results when semiallogeneic lymphocytes are transplanted intracorneally into adult normal or irradiated recipients (24). Since in this situation the limbal vasculature from which the vessels originate is at a considerable distance (1 mm) from the implanted effector cells it becomes apparent that LIA can be attributed to an effect mediated by soluble factors (lymphokines) (25). Soluble mediators have also been implicated in the *in vitro* graft-versus-host reaction, both because effector cells could induce spleen enlargement across an intervening Millipore filter barrier (26) and more directly because supernatant media obtained from allogeneically or phytohemagglutinin-stimulated splenocytes could induce significant enlargement of explanted neonatal spleen fragments (27). The identification of LIA effector cells as Lyt 1+,2− is consistent with this view for it is this subset of lymphocytes that appears responsible for the elaboration of a large number of T-cell lymphokines (25, 28).

The hypothesis that LIA results at least in part from the production and action of soluble mediators is particularly intriguing in that it permits one to consider that the neovascular reactions that are associated with a wide range of ocular diseases, with rheumatoid arthritis, with various lymphadenopathies, with a broad spectrum of autoimmune-associated pathological changes, and with inflammatory lesions in general may all have as their common feature the release of angiogenesis-promoting lymphokines following activation of a specific subset of T lymphocytes (25). By isolating and characterizing the LIA-inducing factors from activated lymphocytes it should be possible to test this hypothesis directly.

REFERENCES

1. Sidky, Y. A., and Auerbach, R., *J. Exp. Med.* **141,** 1084, 1975.
2. Streilein, J. W., and Billingham, R. E., *J. Exp. Med.* **131,** 409, 1970.
3. Brent, L., and Medawar, P. B., *Proc. Roy. Soc. Lond. Ser B.* **165,** 281, 1966.
4. Auerbach, R., and Sidky, Y. A., *J. Immunol.* **123,** 751, 1979.
5. Klein, J., and Park, J. M., *J. Exp. Med.* **137,** 1213, 1973.
6. Boyse, E. A., Miyazawa, M., and Old, L. J., *Proc. Roy. Soc. Lond. Ser. B.* **170,** 175, 1968.
7. Ledbetter, J. A., and Herzenberg, L. A., *Immunol. Rev.* **47,** 63, 1979.
8. Cantor, H., and Boyse, E. A., *Cold Spring Harbor Symp. Quant. Biol.* **41,** 23, 1976.
9. Davidson, W. F., and Parish, C. R., *J. Immunol. Methods* **7,** 291, 1975.
10. Shen, F. W., Boyse, E. A., and Cantor, H., *Immunogenetics* **2,** 591, 1975.
11. Shen, F. W., *Immunogenetics* **5,** 291, 1977.
12. Boyse, E. A., Hubbard, L., and Stockert, E., *Transplantation* **10,** 446, 1970.
13. Roehm, N., Ph.D. Dissertation, University of Wisconsin, 1980.
14. Roehm, N. W., Alter, B. J., and Bach, F. H., *J. Immunol.* **126,** 353, 1981.
15. Ledbetter, J. A., Rouse, R. V., Micklem, H. A., and Herzenberg, L. A., *J. Exp. Med.* **152,** 280, 1980.

16. Kisielow, P., Hirst, J. A., Shiky, H., Beverley, P. C. L., Hoffman, M. K., Boyse, E. A., and Oettgen, H. F., *Nature (London)* **253,** 219, 1975.
17. Mage, M., Mathieson, B., Sharrow, S., McHugh, L., and Hammerling, U., *J. Supramol. Structure* (Suppl. 4), 32, 1980.
18. Bach, F. H., Widmer, M. B., Bach, M. L., and Klein, J., *J. Exp. Med.* **136,** 1430, 1972.
19. Meo, T., Vives, G., Rijnbeek, A. M., Miggiano, V. C., Nabholz, M., and Shreffler, D. C., *Transplant. Proc.* **5,** 1339, 1973.
20. Cantor, H., and Boyse, E. A., *J. Exp. Med.* **141,** 1376, 1973.
21. Bach, F. H., and Alter, B. J., *J. Exp. Med.* **148,** 829, 1978.
22. Prud'homme, G. J., Sohn, U., and Delovitch, T. L., *J. Exp. Med.* **149,** 137, 1979.
23. Nagy, Z., Elliott, B. E., and Nabholz, M., *J. Exp. Med.* **144,** 1545, 1976.
24. Muthukkaruppan, Vr., and Auerbach, R., *Science* **205,** 1416, 1979.
25. Auerbach, R., *Lymphokines* **4,** in press, 1981.
26. Auerbach, R., and Globerson, A., *Exp. Cell Res.* **42,** 31, 1966.
27. Roehm, N., *Transplantation* **23,** 49, 1977.
28. Adelman, N. E., Ksiazek, J., Yoshida, T., and Cohen, S., *J. Immunol.* **124,** 825, 1980.

CELLULAR IMMUNOLOGY 63, 279–292 (1981)

Suppression of Lymphokine Production:

II. Macrophage-Dependent Inhibition of Production of Macrophage Activating Factor

L. VARESIO,[1] H. T. HOLDEN, AND D. TARAMELLI

Laboratory of Immunodiagnosis, National Cancer Institute, National Institutes of Health, Bethesda, Maryland 20205

Received April 8, 1981; accepted June 7, 1981

The ability of different populations of macrophages to affect the production of macrophage activating factor (MAF) by stimulated T lymphocytes was investigated. We found that activated macrophages, infiltrating MSV-induced regressing tumors or macrophages recovered from the peritoneum of mice injected with *Corynebacterium parvum*, were able to actively suppress the production of MAF. MAF production by antigen-stimulated MSV-immune or -alloimmune spleen cells and by normal spleen cells stimulated by Con A was susceptible to macrophage-dependent suppression to a similar extent. In contrast, resident macrophages or those elicited by light mineral oil or proteose-peptone did not affect MAF production. While suppressor macrophages added at the time of the lymphocyte stimulation inhibited MAF production, the same cells added 4–6 hr after stimulation were ineffective. Therefore, it seems that the macrophages suppressed the early events of lymphocyte activation leading to MAF production. Suppressor macrophages, by inhibiting MAF production, may limit the expansion of the cytotoxic activity. This regulation of macrophage functions, mediated by the effects of suppressor macrophages on T lymphocytes, could be responsible for an insufficient antitumor cytotoxic response by macrophages.

INTRODUCTION

Macrophages exert an inhibitory effect on many immune functions, including lymphoproliferative responses to antigenic or mitogenic stimulation, generation of cytotoxic T cells, and antibody production (1). Moreover, it has been shown that activated macrophages can suppress proliferation-independent functions, such as production of migration inhibitory factor (2–4), leukocyte inhibitory factor (5), lymphocyte protein synthesis (6, 7), and generation of a secondary cytotoxic response (8).

Macrophages with suppressor activity can be recovered from areas of inflammation induced either by adjuvants or by parasitic infections (9–14). In addition, suppressor macrophages have been detected in individuals bearing tumors (15–20) induced by various agents and of different histological types such as sarcomas, progressively growing or spontaneously regressing (21, 22); plasmacytomas (23, 24); spontaneous tumors (2, 15, 25); and virally (21) or chemically (26) induced neoplasms. Suppressor macrophages have usually been isolated from the peripheral blood in humans or from the spleen or peritoneal cavity of rodents. Moreover,

[1] Present address: National Cancer Institute, Biological Response Modifiers Program, Frederick Cancer Research Center, Frederick, Md. 21701.

0008-8749/81/140279-14$02.00/0

suppressor cells, with macrophage characteristics, also have been described in the infiltrates of some solid tumors (3, 4, 6, 7, 27).

The role of macrophages in tumor development is still controversial since it appears that activated macrophages have antithetical effects on the tumor–host relationship. On the one hand, as inhibitors of the antitumor immune response, macrophages could facilitate tumor growth. On the other hand, it has been shown that activated macrophages can have cytotoxic (28–30) and cytostatic (31, 32) effects on tumor cells. Therefore, *in vivo*, the balance between cytotoxic and suppressor macrophages could dictate the eventual fate of tumor growth.

Even though it is not clear how macrophages are activated *in vivo*, it has been shown *in vitro* that products of stimulated lymphocytes, e.g., macrophage activating factor (MAF),[2] can induce cytolytic macrophages (33–36). Thus, *in vivo*, MAF may be one of the intermediates involved in the physiological generation of cytotoxic macrophages. According to this hypothesis, the amount of MAF produced will correlate with the amplitude of the macrophage cytolytic activity. Therefore, in an attempt to analyze the control of the cytolytic activity of macrophages, we felt it was relevant to investigate the regulation of MAF production. Our previous studies indicated that activated macrophages could inhibit MIF production (2–4). These findings suggested that MAF production might also be sensitive to suppressor cells. However, it seemed important to directly investigate this point since the biochemical relationship among different lymphokines is not well defined, and it would be premature to generalize results based on the pattern of one lymphokine activity. In fact, MIF activity seems to be due to at least two molecular species (37) and the sensitivity to trypsin of purified lymphokines has been reported to differentiate MIF and MAF (38).

In the present paper, we report on our studies on the cellular mechanisms regulating the production of MAF. We found that activated macrophages, obtained from tumor-bearing or *Corynebacterium parvum*-injected mice, can suppress MAF production by stimulated lymphocytes. In contrast, resident macrophages, or those elicited by proteose-peptone or light mineral oil, failed to exert any suppressive activity. In comparative experiments, we noticed that macrophages with suppressor activity were also cytotoxic for tumor target cells.

MATERIALS AND METHODS

Animals

C57BL/6N mice (B6) and BALB/c mice were obtained from the Division of Research Services, National Institutes of Health, Bethesda, Maryland and AKR/J mice from the Jackson Laboratories, Bar Harbor, Maine.

Tumors and Tumor Cell Lines

Eight- to twelve-week-old B6 mice were injected intramuscularly in the right hindleg with the Moloney strain of MSV (39). Tumors appeared at 6 to 8 days

[2] Abbreviations used: MØ, macrophages; LMO-MØ, light mineral oil-induced MØ; Cp-MØ, *C. parvum*-induced MØ; p-MØ, peptone-induced MØ; T-MØ, MØ infiltrating MSV-induced regressing tumors; MAF, macrophage activating factor; ISC, immune spleen cells; NSC, normal spleen cells; MSV, murine sarcoma virus; B6, C57BL/6 mice; Con A, concanavalin A; BSS, Hanks' balanced salt solution; PEC, peritoneal exudate cells; LK, lymphokine-containing supernatants; CS, control supernatants; PBS, phosphate-buffered saline; LPS, lipopolysaccharide.

after inoculation, grew to maximal size by Day 14, and regressed by Days 21 to 25. For the current studies, tumors were removed at 13 to 14 days after injection with MSV. The following cell lines were used in these studies: RBL-5, a Rauscher virus-induced lymphoma in B6 mice, RL♂1, a radiation-induced lymphoma of BALB/c mice, and RDM-4, a spontaneous AKR/J lymphoma (40).

Media

Thc basic medium used in these studies was endotoxin-free RPMI 1640 medium (Gibco, Grand Island, N.Y.) supplemented with 100 units/ml of penicillin, 2 m*M* glutamine, 100 μg/ml of streptomycin, and 50 μg/ml of gentamicin. To harvest peritoneal exudate cells (PEC), basic medium supplemented with 10% FBS and 100 U/ml of sodium heparin (Gibco Diagnostics) was employed. For MAF production, we used basic medium supplemented with 5% FBS and 20 m*M* Hepes buffer (Gibco). For the macrophage cytotoxicity assay, the basic medium was supplemented with 10% FBS and 20 m*M* Hepes buffer. All the reagents employed were negative for endotoxin in the Limulus amoebocyte lysate assay (LAL) (M. A. Bioproducts, Walkersville, Md.). The sensitivity of the LAL assay, tested with standard preparations of endotoxin (M. A. Bioproducts), was 10^{-2} ng/ml.

In Vitro Production of Lymphokine-Containing Supernatants

(a) Mitogenic stimulation of normal spleen cells. The production of lymphokine-containing supernatants in response to concanavalin A (Con A, Calbiochem, San Diego, Calif.) was performed as previously described (41). Briefly, B6 mouse spleen cells (5×10^6 cells/ml in 1 ml) were treated for 4 hr with 2.5 μg/ml Con A or with medium. The cells were then washed three times and incubated in fresh medium for 24 hr.

(b) Secondary in vitro alloimmune response. B6 ($H\text{-}2^b$) mice were inoculated intraperitoneally (ip) with 10^7 RDM-4 ($H\text{-}2^k$) or RL♂1 ($H\text{-}2^d$) lymphoma cells. Ten days later, RDM-4 immune spleen cells (RDM-4-ISC) or RL♂1 immune spleen cells (RL♂1-ISC) (at 5×10^6/ml) were incubated with or without 5×10^5/ml AKR/J ($H\text{-}2^k$) or BALB/c ($H\text{-}2^d$) mouse spleen cells or (RL♂1), respectively, for 24 hr at 37°C in a 5% CO_2 incubator.

(c) Secondary in vitro stimulation of MSV-immune spleen cells. Lymphokine-containing supernatant was produced by *in vitro* stimulation of on MSV-immune spleen cells as previously described (4). Briefly, MSV-immune spleen cells obtained from B6 mice 14 days after inoculation with virus were depleted of macrophages by the carbonyl iron/magnet technique (MSV-ISC). MSV-ISC (5×10^6) in RPMI 1640 medium with 5% FBS were incubated with or without 5×10^5 RBL-5 tumor cells (10%) at 37°C for 24 hr.

All the supernatants, hereafter referred to as lymphokines (LK) or control supernatants (CS), were harvested after 24 hr of culture, reconstituted to 10% FCS, and stored at −80°C until use.

Cells

Tissue macrophages (T-MØ) were dissociated from Moloney murine sarcoma virus-induced regressing tumors by enzymatic treatment and purified by plastic adherence, as previously described (3). Peritoneal macrophages were obtained by collecting the plastic-adherent PEC from normal mice or injected ip 2 days earlier with 1 ml of 3% proteose-peptone (Difco Laboratories, Detroit, Mich.) (p-MØ), or 4 days earlier with 2.5 ml light mineral oil (LMO-MØ), or 7–10 days earlier with 2.1 mg of *C. parvum* (Cp-MØ) (Burroughs–Wellcome Co., Research Triangle Park, N.C.) as previously described (3, 7, 41). All adherent populations, hereafter referred to as MØ, contained >95% latex-ingesting, esterase-positive cells of the macrophage–monocyte series, as determined by differential count of Giemsa-stained smears. When required, MØ were recovered by scraping with a rubber policeman as previously detailed (3, 4).

Cell Fractionation

(a) Carbonyl Iron and Magnet. The treatment was performed according to the method described by Landolfo *et al.* (42) except for the use of a magnetic column to remove the iron and iron-ingesting cells (6). Briefly, the magnetic column was prepared by filling a 35-ml plastic syringe with 1/2 × 5/16-in. sterile magnetic bars (BEL-ART Products, Pequannock, N.J.) up to the 20-ml mark. Before use, the column was washed with 50 ml of Hanks' balanced salt solution (BSS) and equipped with a sterile stopcock and a 22-gauge needle. The iron-containing cell suspension, brought to a volume of 10 ml in basic medium containing 5% FBS, was gently added to the top of the column. After 10 min of incubation at room temperature to allow complete adherence of the iron to the magnets, the column was slowly eluted. Microscopically, no colloidal iron was evident with the eluate. After treating NSC by this technique, we recovered ≥60% of the cells, which contained 0.5–1.5% latex-ingesting cells.

(b) Antiserum and complement treatment. Cells (10^6) were centrifuged in 15-ml conical tubes (Falcon, Oxnard, Calif.) and the pellet was resuspended in 0.1 ml of PBS or IgM monoclonal anti-Thy 1.2 (Becton–Dickinson, Mountain View, Calif., 1:500 final dilution). After 30 min of incubation at room temperature, the cells were washed with 10 ml of BSS, and the pellet was resuspended in 200 μl of either PBS or 1:4 final dilution of guinea pig complement (M. A. Bioproducts, Walkersville, Md.) and incubated for 30 min at 37°C. The cells were then washed and resuspended in the appropriate medium. As measured by trypan blue dye exclusion, anti-Thy 1.2 plus complement treatment killed 35–50% NSC, > 99% thymocytes, and ≤5% T-MØ, Cp-MØ, or LMO-MØ and abrogated the mitogenic response of normal spleen cells to Con A and phytohemagglutinin. Killing by complement alone was ≤13%.

Assay of Macrophage Cytotoxicity

The ability of LK-containing supernatants to activate cytotoxic MØ (MAF activity) *in vitro* was tested as previously described (41). Briefly, 1.8 × 10^5 p-MØ were purified by adherence in 96-well microtiter plates (No. 3596 Costar, Cambridge, Mass.). After 2 hr of incubation at 37°C, the plates were vigorously and uniformly shaken on a microshaker (Cooke Laboratories, Alexandria, Va.) for 30 sec to resuspend the nonadherent cells and then washed five to six times with BSS using a semi-automatic device which flushes and aspirates 0.2 ml of medium per well each time. The monolayers were then treated overnight with dilutions of LK or CS or with medium alone. Ten ng/ml of lipopolysaccharide (LPS) (*E. coli* 0111:B4, Difco Laboratories) was added to the culture together with LK or CS during the preincubation except where otherwise noted. At the end of incubation, the supernatants were aspirated and replaced with ^{51}Cr-labeled RL♂1 target cells in 0.3 ml.

^{51}Cr-Release Assay

RL♂1 lymphoma cells (10^7) were labeled with 150 μCi of sodium ^{51}chromate (New England Nuclear, Boston, Mass.) for 45 min at 37°C, washed three times, resuspended at a final concentration of 5×10^3 cells/0.3 ml, and then added to the cultured p-MØ. After 18 hr of incubation, the plates were centrifuged for 10 min at 350*g*, 0.1 ml of supernatant was harvested, and the radioactivity counted in a scintillation counter (Biogamma, Beckmann). The percentage ^{51}Cr release was calculated from the average of triplicate samples as:

$$\frac{(\text{cpm with treated MØ} - \text{cpm with untreated MØ})}{\text{total cpm incorporated}} \times 100.$$

When direct MØ cytotoxicity was measured, the adherent MØ population was prepared in wells, as described above, and the target cells were added immediately. The percentage ^{51}Cr release was calculated from the average of triplicate samples as

$$\%\ ^{51}\text{Cr release} = \frac{(\text{cpm with MØ} - \text{cpm of target alone})}{(\text{total cpm incorporated})} \times 100.$$

"Student's *t*" test was employed to statistically evaluate the data. Percentage cytotoxicities with P values < 0.05 were considered to be significantly different.

RESULTS

Characteristics of the MAF System

The detection of a lymphokine in a culture supernatant is based on the measurement of a particular biological effect. Expression of MAF activity is known to be highly dependent on environmental factors, endotoxin contamination, and the type of assay (34, 41, 43).

Also in our MAF assay, activation of macrophages is strictly dependent on the presence of nanogram amounts of LPS (41). The LPS requirement for the detection of MAF in an endotoxin-free environment ($\leq$0.01 ng/ml by the LAL assay) is illustrated in Table 1 by the results of a representative experiment. In the absence of endotoxins, supernatants from resting or Con A-stimulated cultures failed to induce significant cytotoxicity. However, the addition of 10 ng/ml of LPS to the supernatant resulted in high levels of cytotoxicity with stimulated but not control supernatants. The cytotoxic activity in the presence of LPS was proportional to the amount of lymphokine used to activate the macrophages.

Stimuli other than Con A were tested for their ability to induce *in vitro* production of MAF by lymphocytes. ISC obtained from mice injected with MSV or allogeneic tumors were found to produce MAF upon *in vitro* incubation with the appropriate stimulator cells (Table 2). LPS-dependent MAF activity was consis-

TABLE 1

LPS Requirement for Induction of Cytotoxic Macrophages by Lymphokine

Source of lymphokine			Macrophage treatment[a]			
				Lymphokine		
Responder cell	Stimulator	LPS[b] (10 ng/ml)	Medium	1/3	1/9	1/27
NSC	Con A	−	526 ± 18[c]	523 ± 32 (−0.3)	468 ± 14 (−5.3)	478 ± 22 (−4.4)
		+	514 ± 30 (−1.2)	925 ± 68 (36.4)	886 ± 48 (31.2)	684 ± 55 (14.4)
	None	−	—	488 ± 29 (−3.5)	476 ± 34 (−4.6)	485 ± 12 (−3.8)
		+	—	482 ± 16 (−4.0)	473 ± 20 (−4.9)	479 ± 11 (−4.3)

[a] p-MØ from B6 mice were incubated for 18 hr with medium alone or dilution of lymphokine-containing supernatants, then washed and used as effector cells against RLδ1 tumor cells.

[b] LPS was added to LK or CS at a final concentration of 10 ng/ml.

[c] cpm ± SE of ^{51}Cr release from RLδ1 target cells at 36:1 A/T ratio. Total incorporation of the target cells was 1.3×10^5 cpm/10^6 cells. Percentage ^{51}Cr release is shown in parentheses.

tently generated by each type of ISC used, with titers ranging from 1/9 to 1/81. Very low levels of MAF activity were always detected in the absence of LPS (data not shown).

Kinetic studies of *in vitro* lymphocyte stimulation were performed to determine at what time MAF could be detected in the culture supernatants. The experiment in Fig. 1 shows the kinetics of MAF production by Con A-stimulated NSC. MAF was consistently detected in supernatants obtained within 4–6 hr of the initiation

TABLE 2

Induction of Cytotoxic Macrophages by Lymphokine from Different Sources

Source of lymphokine		Percentage ^{51}Cr release ± SE		
Responder cell	Stimulator cell	1/3[a]	1/9	1/27
MSV-ISC	—	2.3 ± 1.2[b]	1.7 ± 1.3	0.4 ± 1
	RBL-5	28.7 ± 1.7	11.2 ± 1.4	6.8 ± 0.9
RLδ1-ISC	—	0.5 ± 0.1	1.4 ± 0.9	2.1 ± 1.2
	RLδ1	43.3 ± 2.1	27.9 ± 1.9	3.9 ± 1.1
RDM-4-ISC	—	2.3 ± 1.7	2.1 ± 1.4	1.3 ± 1.5
	AKR/J[c]	43.6 ± 3.2	38.9 ± 2.2	24.5 ± 2.4

[a] Dilutions of the lymphokine-containing supernatant, assayed in the presence of a final concentration of 10 ng/ml of LPS, using p-MØ from B6 mice as effector cells.

[b] Percentage ^{51}Cr release ± SE from RLδ1 target cells at 36:1 A/T ratio. Total incorporation of the target cells was 1×10^5 cpm/10^6 cells.

[c] Spleen cells from AKR/J mice.

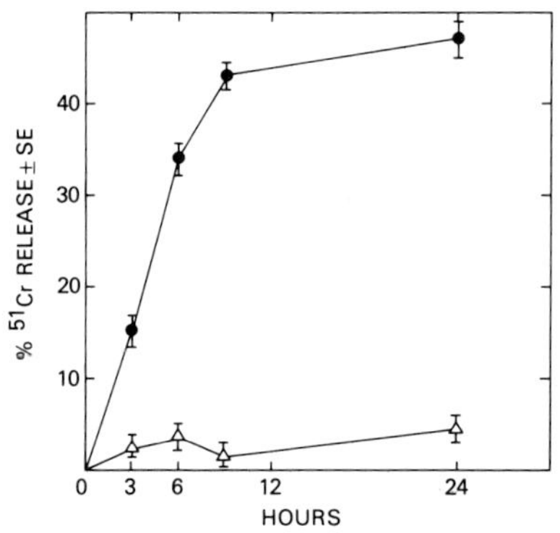

FIG. 1. Kinetics of MAF production by B6 NSC stimulated with Con A. At various times after the pulse, supernatants were harvested and tested for their ability to induce cytolytic activity by MØ. Effector cells: 1.8×10^5 B6 p-MØ activated *in vitro* by 1/3 dilution of supernatants and 10 ng/ml LPS. Target cells, ^{51}Cr-labeled RL♂1 tumor cells, A/T 36:1. ●, LK supernatant from NSC + Con A. △, CS. Horizontal bars represent the standard error from the mean of triplicate samples.

of the culture. Similar results were obtained when the kinetics of MAF production by ISC were examined (data not shown). Thus, irrespectively of the responder system used, MAF production represents a very early manifestation of lymphocyte activation.

Macrophage-Dependent Suppression of MAF Production

Experiments were performed to study the effect of various populations of macrophages on MAF production by stimulated lymphocytes. Initially, we examined macrophages obtained from MSV-induced regressing tumors and compared their activity with that of LMO-MØ. The results of a representative experiment, in which Con A-stimulated NSC were used as MAF producers, are shown in Fig. 2.

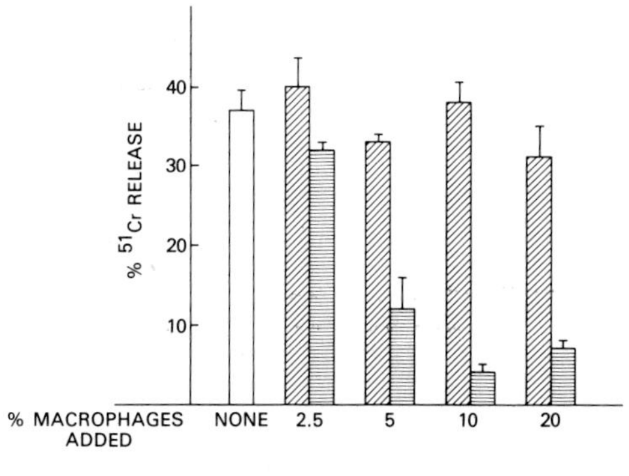

FIG. 2. Effect of T-MØ and LMO-MØ on MAF production. The above percentages of T-MØ (▤) or LMO-MØ (▨) were added to Con A-stimulated B6 NSC. The supernatants were harvested after 24 hr and tested for their ability to induce cytotoxic activity by MØ. Effector cells: 1.8×10^5 B6 p-MØ treated *in vitro* with 1/3 dilution of the supernatants and 10 ng/ml of LPS. Target cells: ^{51}Cr-labeled RL♂1 tumor cells, A/T 36:1. The open bar represents the MAF activity of Con A-stimulated NSC in the absence of MØ. Horizontal lines indicate the SE of the average of triplicate samples.

T-MØ caused a dramatic decrease of MAF activity in the supernatant when added to stimulated lymphocytes at concentrations of 5% or more. In contrast, LMO-MØ, up to a concentration of 20%, had no effect on MAF production.

To determine whether activated macrophages, from other sources, could suppress MAF production, the effect of Cp-MØ was investigated. A representative experiment, in which the activity of Cp-MØ was compared to that of p-MØ, is shown in Fig. 3. Cp-MØ significantly suppressed MAF production when added at concentrations of 5% or higher, whereas no suppressive effect was seen with p-MØ. LMO-MØ, in 3 out of 10 experiments, and p-MØ, in 2 out of 8 experiments, caused significant inhibition in MAF activity when added at 20% concentration. However, these macrophages never produced appreciable inhibition at lower concentrations, whereas the T-MØ and Cp-MØ were consistently inhibitory at 5% concentration.

To assess whether activated macrophages also could inhibit MAF produced by sensitized lymphocytes stimulated by a specific antigen, MSV-ISC triggered by RBL-5, a Rauscher virus-induced lymphoma, were used as responder cells (Table 3). T-MØ and Cp-MØ, but not LMO-MØ or resident MØ, were effective in inhibiting MAF production in response to stimulation by RBL-5. The same pattern of results was observed when the above macropahge population was tested for their suppressor activity on MAF production by alloimmune (anti-H-2^k) spleen cells stimulated by AKR/J spleen cells (data not shown). The viability of the cultures was routinely tested by trypan blue exclusion, after the supernatants were harvested. No significant differences were ever observed when the viability of lymphocytes from cultures with or without macrophages was compared.

Cytolytic Activity of Macrophage Populations

In order to correlate the ability to suppress MAF production with another parameter reflecting macrophage activation, we examined the direct cytotoxic activity of Cp-MØ, T-MØ, R-MØ, LMO-MØ, and p-MØ. Macrophages were first purified by plastic adherence and tested for cytotoxicity in an 18-hr ^{51}Cr-release assay against RL♂1 target cells. The results (Table 4) showed that Cp-MØ and T-MØ were strongly cytotoxic at as low as a 10:1 ratio, whereas R-MØ, LMO-MØ, and p-MØ did not cause any appreciable lysis even at 40:1.

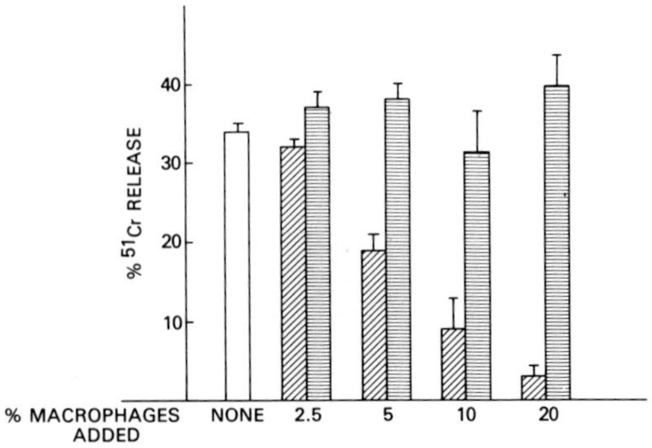

FIG. 3. Effect of Cp-MØ and p-MØ on MAF production. Different percentages of Cp-MØ (▨) or p-MØ (▤) were added to Con A-stimulated NSC. The same protocol described in the legend of Fig. 2 was used.

TABLE 3

Suppressor Activity of Macrophages from Different Sources on MAF Production by ISC

Adherent cells added to the culture[a]	Percentage ^{51}Cr release ± SE		
	1/3[b]	1/9	1/27
None	40.1 ± 2.3[c]	11.1 ± 2	3.8 ± 1.4
20% T-MØ	2.7 ± 1.4	1.9 ± 1.6	2.1 ± 2
20% *C. parvum*-MØ	4.3 ± 1.9	3.2 ± 2.1	3.0 ± 1.8
20% LMO-MØ	38.4 ± 3.2	9.3 ± 1.9	2.7 ± 0.9
20% Resident-MØ	35.3 ± 2.8	12.5 ± 0.7	7.2 ± 0.2

[a] MØ were purified by adherence and then added to cultures of RL♂1-ISC stimulated *in vitro* by BALB/c spleen cells.

[b] Dilutions of culture supernatant assayed in the presence of a final concentration of 10 ng/ml of LPS, using p-MØ from B6 mice as effector cells.

[c] Percentage ^{51}Cr release ± SE from RL♂1 target cells, at A/T 36:1 ratio. Total incorporation of the target was 1.5×10^5 cpm/10^6 cells.

Thus, among the populations tested, only those endowed with suppressor activity were also cytotoxic.

Characterization of Suppressor Cells

In all the experiments described so far, adherent cells were always used as the source of macrophages, and special care was taken to remove the loosely adherent cells. The adherent populations recovered were 90–98% positive for latex ingestion and nonspecific esterase staining. To exclude that plastic adherent T lymphocytes were involved in the suppression of MAF production, adherent cells were treated with anti-Thy 1.2 plus complement before testing for suppressor activity (Table 5). Since anti-Thy 1.2 plus complement treatment did not affect the suppressor

TABLE 4

Cytolytic Activity of B6 Macrophages Induced by Different Agents

Macrophage source[a]	Yield $\times 10^{-6}$/ mouse	Composition of PEC[b]			Percentage ^{51}Cr release ± SE		
		P	MØ	L	40:1[c]	20:1	10:1
C. parvum	9	10	70	19	35.8 ± 2	34.4 ± 2	14.9 ± 3
T-MØ	120	10	50	30	43.1 ± 1.7	35.1 ± 3	21.0 ± 1.7
Resident	2	1	77	22	−4.6 ± 1	−2.1 ± 1.7	−3.1 ± 1.9
Peptone	7	6	79	15	4.1 ± 2	3.1 ± 2.1	1.5 ± 1.4
LMO	15	8	78	12	2.1 ± 1.5	3.1 ± 1.6	3.4 ± 2.1

[a] MØ from B6 mice were elicited, harvested, and purified as described under Materials and Methods.

[b] Differential cell count was performed on Giemsa-stained smears. P = Polymorphonuclear cells, MØ = monocyte macrophage-like cells, L = lymphocyte. Values are expressed as percentage of the total cells counted.

[c] A/T ratios at which the macrophages were tested against ^{51}Cr-labeled RL♂1. Total incorporation was 1.1×10^5 cpm/10^6 target cells.

TABLE 5

Characterization of the Cells Inhibiting MAF Production

Suppressor cell	Treatment	Percentage ^{51}Cr release ± SE		
		1/3[a]	1/9	1/27
None	—	25.6 ± 2[b]	13.1 ± 0.9	9.5 ± 2.1
10% Cft[c]	—	8.6 ± 2.1	4.2 ± 2.6	0.9 ± 0.9
10% T-MØ	—	4.3 ± 1.7	1.3 ± 0.3	1.0 ± 1.0
	Anti-Thy 1.2 + C′	5.4 ± 1.8	3.2 ± 0.9	1.4 ± 1.6
	C′	4.9 ± 2.1	4.4 ± 1.4	1.9 ± 0.8
	Medium	3.4 ± 1.9	3.6 ± 2	2.4 ± 1
	Carbonyl iron magnet (I treat.)	15.4 ± 3	8.2 ± 1.3	3.0 ± 0.7
	Carbonyl iron magnet (II treat.)	22.1 ± 1.8	11.4 ± 2.3	6.2 ± 0.9

[a] Supernatants from MSV-ISC stimulated *in vitro* by RBL-5 tumor cells. They were assayed for MAF activity in the presence of LPS at a final concentration of 10 ng/ml, using p-MØ from B6 mice as effector cells.

[b] Percentage ^{51}Cr release ± SE from RLδ1 target cells, at 36:1 A/T ratio. Total incorporation was 0.9×10^5 cpm/10^6 target cells.

[c] Cft—whole population recovered by MSV-induced regressing tumor by enzymatic dissociation, before purification by plastic adherence.

activity, we concluded that contaminating T cells were not responsible or required for the suppression. In addition, repeated treatment of the cells from the tumor (Table 5) or of Cp-induced PEC (data not shown) with carbonyl iron plus magnet abrogated the suppressive activity.

Since the suppressor cell population was adherent to plastic, phagocytic, highly enriched in cells with macrophage-monocyte morphology, and Thy 1.2 negative, we attributed the suppressor activity to macrophage or macrophage-like cells.

Evidence That MØ Inhibit Early Events of MAF Production

Attempts were made to determine whether MØ could exert their inhibitory activity at any time after the stimulation of the lymphocytes. Addition of T-MØ at the beginning of the culture of alloimmune spleen cells and stimulator cells resulted in complete inhibition of MAF production (Fig. 4). However, when the same population of T-MØ was added 6 hr after the beginning of culture, no suppressor activity was observed. Titration of the supernatants (Fig. 5) confirmed the lack of suppression when MØ were added at a later time point, and showed intermediate levels of suppressor activity when the MØ were added at 4 hr. To exclude that these results could be accounted by loss of suppressor activity of T-MØ caused by the *in vitro* cultures, similar experiments were performed using different protocols. The suppressor cells were either incubated at 37 or 4°C and mixed with stimulated cultures at different times, or the responder cells were stimulated at different times and fresh suppressor cells were added at the same time in all the tubes. Irrespective of the protocol employed, the T-MØ did not exert suppressor activity when added 4 to 6 hr after the mixture of the responder cells

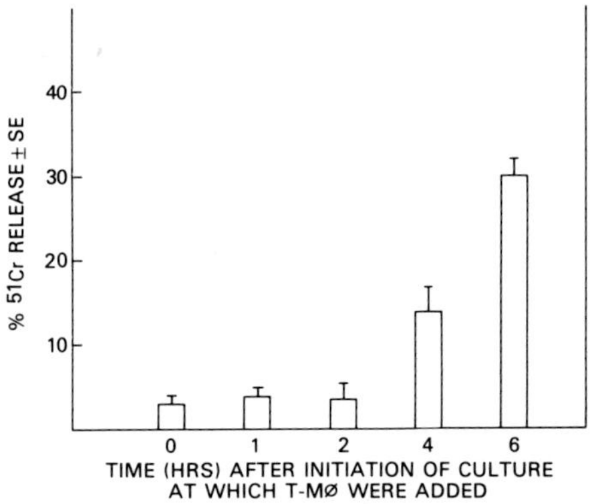

FIG. 4. Suppressive effect on MAF production of T-MØ added to ISC at different times after lymphocyte stimulation. The supernatants generated by adding 10% of T-MØ to cultures of RL♂1-ISC stimulated by BALB/c NSC, at different times after stimulation, were collected 24 hr later and tested for MAF activity. Effector cells: 1.8×10^5 B6 p-MØ treated with 1/3 dilution of supernatants and 10 ng/ml of LPS. Target cells: ^{51}Cr-labeled RL♂1 tumor cells, A/T 36:1. The MAF activity by culture stimulated in the absence of T-MØ was 35 ± 3%. The vertical lines represent the standard error of the average of three replicates.

with the stimulator. Thus, it seems that the suppressor MØ inhibit MAF production through a block of early events preceding or contemporaneous with the production of MAF.

DISCUSSION

In the present work, we showed that activated macrophages, T-MØ and Cp-MØ, can suppress *in vitro* the production of MAF by stimulated T-lymphocytes, whereas resident or elicited peritoneal macrophages did not affect MAF production. As an additional parameter of activation, we examined the cytolytic activity of macrophages and found that T-MØ and Cp-MØ were cytolytic against RL♂1 while p-MØ, R-MØ, and LMO-MØ were not, confirming previous reports (29, 30).

It is of interest to note the coexistence in the same macrophage population of

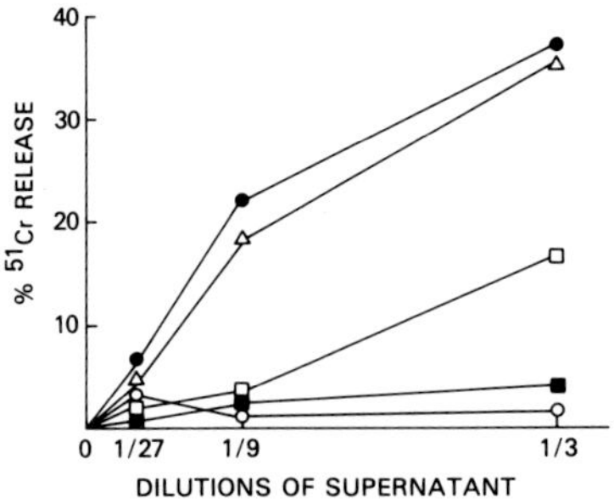

FIG. 5. Titration of the MAF activity in supernatants generated by ISC in which T-MØ were added at different times after the initiation of culture. Supernatants, generated as described in Fig. 4, by adding 10% T-MØ at Time 0 (■), Time 2 (○), Time 4 (□), Time 6 (△), or in the absence of T-MØ (●) were tested for MAF activity. Effector cells: 1.8×10^5 p-MØ from B6 mice treated with dilution of the supernatants and 10 ng/ml of LPS. Target cells: ^{51}Cr-labeled RL♂1, A/T 36:1.

both cytotoxicity and inhibitory effects on MAF production. These activities could be expected to have opposite *in vivo* effects and it seems possible that this is a reflection of regulation of MØ function by MØ. When the cytotoxic activity of a macrophage population reaches a certain threshold level, suppressor cells may be generated which can inhibit the production of MAF and thus block the further activation of recruited macrophages. In other words, the generation of cytotoxic macrophages may be regulated by a homeostatic mechanism dependent on suppressor macrophages. This regulatory process could be an important physiological control which prevents or minimizes tissue damage by activated MØ during the course of an inflammatory process. In this context, it must be considered that activated macrophages have an increased secretion of tissue-damaging substances, including collagenase, hydrolases, and peroxidases (44–46). At the tumor site, such a homeostatic regulatory mechanism could severely impair the antitumor defense activity mediated by the cytotoxic macrophages. In this case, it becomes crucial to fully understand the mechanisms by which the suppressor activity is generated in macrophages. As opposed to the MAF-dependent macrophage activation for cytotoxicity, the pathway(s) leading to the generation of suppressor macrophages is poorly understood. It has been shown that treatment of peripheral blood mononuclear cells with lymphokines activates cells capable of suppressing the mitogenic response of lympocytes (47). Moreover, we obtained evidence that peritoneal murine macrophages treated with MAF-containing supernatants become suppressive for MAF production (48). The possibility that lymphokines, maybe MAF itself, induce suppressor macrophages, together with the ability of MAF to activate cytotoxic macrophages, would provide a feedback mechanism by which the macrophages self-regulate their cytotoxic activity by finely tuning the MAF production. It remains to be determined whether the same macrophage can be at once cytotoxic and suppressive, or the two activities are sequentially acquired, or different subpopulations of macrophages have different functions. In addition, it is possible that a different pattern of signals is required to induce suppressor and cytotoxic macrophages. In fact, we observed that LPS did not stimulate macrophages to suppress lymphokine production under conditions in which it activated macrophages to become cytotoxic (49). Moreover, we observed that traces of LPS in the lymphokine preparation were absolutely required for the induction of cytotoxic MØ (41). In contrast, MAF-containing supernatants, free of detectable endotoxin contamination and without exogenously added LPS, could induce *in vitro* suppressor macrophages (48).

The failure to detect MAF in supernatants of lymphocyte cultures containing activated MØ could be explained by several possibilities other than the selective inhibition of MAF production. For example, the added MØ might have toxic effects on the MAF-producing cells. However, this seems unlikely since suppressor cells did not inhibit MAF production when added 6 hr after the beginning of the stimulation. Furthermore, there was no decrease in viability in cultures containing suppressor MØ. Another possible mechanism was that MØ absorbed or inactivated MAF after it was produced by lymphocytes and secreted into the culture medium. Again, this would have been expected to occur when the MØ were added at 6 hr. The results of these kinetic experiments also exclude the possibility that products of suppressor cells decreased the sensitivity of the responder cells used to assay MAF activity. Thus, it seems most likely that the suppressor MØ mediated their effects by interfering with some early critical processes in the stimulated lymphocytes that are required for lymphokine production and that they do not interfere with the release of the lymphokine or with its further production after it has been triggered.

It remains to be determined whether suppression of lymphokine production by activated MØ is mediated by release of suppressor factors or by direct contact with the responder lymphocytes. It has been shown that addition to the culture medium of exogenous prostaglandins inhibits MIF production by T lymphocytes (50). Although we have observed that indomethacin, a prostaglandin synthesis inhibitor, does not affect the suppressor activity of macrophages on MIF production (4), we do not have direct information on the role of prostaglandins in the suppression of MAF. The role of prostaglandins as well as of other products of macrophages, such as hydrogen peroxide, interferon, proteases, etc., in the suppressive phenomenon is under investigation.

Finally, it is interesting to note that we have found that the early proteins synthesized within the first few hours after lymphocyte stimulation are absolutely required for lymphocyte proliferation in response to Con A (51), and for the production of MIF and MAF (52). In addition, we observed that T-MØ and Cp-MØ are able to inhibit the lymphocyte protein synthesis by lymphocytes within 6 hr of mixed culture (6). It is possible, therefore, that inhibition of MAF production by activated macrophages is caused by the macrophage-mediated inhibition of macromolecular synthesis during the first few hours of lymphocyte stimulation by Con A.

ACKNOWLEDGMENTS

The authors gratefully thank Dr. R. B. Herberman and Dr. M. J. Brunda for their many suggestions during this work and for their thorough review of the manuscript.

REFERENCES

1. Oehler, J. R., Herberman, R. B., and Holden, H. T., *Pharmacol. Ther.* **2A**, 511, 1978.
2. Varesio, L., Giovarelli, M., Landolfo, S., and Forni, G., *Cancer Res.* **39,** 4983, 1979.
3. Varesio, L., Herberman, R. B., Gerson, J. M., and Holden, H. T., *Int. J. Cancer* **24,** 97, 1979.
4. Varesio, L., and Holden, H. T., *Cell. Immunol.* **56,** 16, 1980.
5. Lomnitzer, R., and Rabson, A. R., *Cell. Immunol.* **43,** 41, 1979.
6. Varesio, L., and Holden, H. T., *J. Immunol.* **125,** 1694, 1980.
7. Varesio, L., Eva, A., and Holden, H. T., *In* "Manual of Macrophage Methodology: Collection, Characterization and Function" (H. B. Herscowitz, H. T. Holden, J. A. Bellanti, and A. Ghaffar, Eds.), pp. 369–375. Dekker, New York, 1981.
8. Klimpel, G. R., and Henney, C. S., *J. Immunol.* **120,** 563, 1978.
9. Kirchner, H., Glaser, M., and Herberman, R. B., *Nature (London)* **251,** 396, 1975.
10. Baird, L. G., and Kaplan, A. M., *Cell. Immunol.* **28,** 22, 1977.
11. Pan Yung, Y., and Cudkowicz, G., *J. Immunol.* **121,** 1990, 1978.
12. Mehra, V., Mason, L. H., Fields, J. P., and Bloom, B. R., *J. Immunol.* **123,** 1813, 1979.
13. Riglar, C., and Cheers, C., *Cell Immunol.* **49,** 154, 1980.
14. Varesio, L., Landolfo, S., Giovarelli, M., and Forni, G., *Develop. Comp. Immunol.* **4,** 11, 1980.
15. Forni, G., Varesio, L., Giovarelli, M., and Cavallo, G., *In* "Tumor Associated Antigens and Their Specific Immune Response" (F. Spreafico and R. Arnon, Eds.), pp. 167. Academic Press, New York, 1979.
16. Herberman, R. B., Varesio, L., Tagliabue, A., Maca, R., Holden, H. T., White, S., Bonnard, G. D., Jerrells, T., and Dean, J. H., *In* "Immunobiology and Immunotherapy of Cancer" (W. D. Terry and Y. Yamamura, Eds.), pp. 191–203. Elsevier/North-Holland, New York, 1979.

17. Holden, H. T., Varesio, L., Taniyama, T., and Puccetti, P., *In* "Macrophages and Lymphocytes" (M. R. Escobar and H. Friedman, Eds.), Pt. B, pp. 509–520. Plenum, New York, 1979.
18. Naor, D., *Adv. Cancer Res.* **29,** 45, 1979.
19. Herberman, R. B., Holden, H. T., Djeu, J. Y., Jerrells, R. T., Varesio, L., Tagliabue, A., White, S. L., Oehler, J. R., and Dean, J. H., *In* "Macrophages and Lymphocytes" (M. R. Escobar and H. Friedman, Eds.), Pt. B, pp. 361–379. Plenum, New York, 1980.
20. Herberman, R. B., *In* "Human Suppressor Cells" (B. Serrou, Ed.). North-Holland, Amsterdam (in press).
21. Kirchner, H., Chused, T. M., Herberman, R. B., Holden, H. T., and Lavrin, D. H., *J. Exp. Med.* **139,** 1473, 1974.
22. Fernbach, B. R., Kirchner, H., and Herberman, R. B., *Cell. Immunol.* **22,** 399, 1976.
23. Kolb, J. P., Arrian, S., and Zolla-Pazner, S., *J. Immunol.* **118,** 702, 1978.
24. Kennard, J., and Zolla-Pazner, S., *J. Immunol.* **124,** 268, 1980.
25. Whitney, R. B., Kelly, B. S., and Levy, J. G., *Eur. J. Cancer* **14,** 699, 1978.
26. Pope, B. L., Whitney, R. B., Levy, J. G., and Kilburn, D. G., *J. Immunol.* **116,** 1342, 1976.
27. Gerson, J. M., Varesio, L., and Herberman, R. B., *Int. J. Cancer* **27,** 243, 1981.
28. Russell, S. W., Doe, W. F., and McIntosh, A. T., *J. Exp. Med.* **146,** 1511, 1977.
29. Puccetti, P., and Holden, H. T., *Int. J. Cancer* **23,** 123, 1979.
30. Taniyama, T., and Holden, H. T., *Int. J. Cancer* **24,** 151, 1979.
31. Kirchner, H., Holden, H. T., and Herberman, R. B., *J. Nat. Cancer Inst.* **55,** 971, 1975.
32. Holden, H. T., Haskill, J. S., Kirchner, H., and Herberman, R. B., *J. Immunol.* **117,** 440, 1976.
33. Nathan, C. F., Karnovsky, M. L., and David, J. R., *J. Exp. Med.* **133,** 1356, 1971.
34. Hibbs, J. B., Taintou, R. R., Chapman, H. A., and Weinberg, J. B., *Science* **197,** 279, 1977.
35. Ruco, L. P., and Meltzer, M. S., *J. Immunol.* **119,** 889, 1977.
36. David, J. R., and Remold, H. G., *In* "Biology of Lymphokines" (S. Cohen, E. Pick, and J. J. Oppenheim, Eds.), pp. 121–140. Academic Press, New York, 1979.
37. Remolds, H. G., and Mednis, A., *J. Immunol.* **122,** 1920, 1979.
38. Churchill, W. H., Mednis, A. D., and Remold, H. G., *Fed. Proc.* **39,** 1156, 1980.
39. Lavrin, D. H., Herberman, R. B., Nunn, M., and Soares, N., *J. Nat. Cancer Inst.* **51,** 1497, 1973.
40. Herberman, R. B., Aoki, T., Nunn, M., Lavrin, D. H., Soares, N., Gazdar, A., Holden, H., and Chang, K. S. S., *J. Nat. Cancer Inst.* **53,** 1103, 1974.
41. Taramelli, D., Holden, H. T., and Varesio, L., *J. Immunol. Methods* **37,** 225, 1980.
42. Landolfo, S., Herberman, R. B., and Holden, H. T., *J. Immunol.* **118,** 1266, 1977.
43. Weinberg, J. B., Chapman, H. A., and Hibbs, J. B., *J. Immunol.* **121,** 72, 1978.
44. Unkeless, J. C., Gordon, S., and Reich, E., *J. Exp. Med.* **139,** 834, 1974.
45. Werb, Z., and Gordon, S., *J. Exp. Med.* **142,** 346, 1975.
46. Werb, Z., and Gordon, S., *J. Exp. Med.* **142,** 361, 1975.
47. Larsson, E. L., and Blomgren, H., *Scand. J. Immunol.* **9,** 53, 1979.
48. Taramelli, D., Holden, H. T., and Varesio, L. *J. Immunol.* **126,** 2123, 1981.
49. Taramelli, D., Brunda, M. J., Holden, H. T., and Varesio, L., *Fed. Proc.* **40,** 3076, 1981.
50. Gordon, D., Bray, M. A., and Morley, J., *Nature (London)* **262,** 401, 1976.
51. Varesio, L., and Holden, H. T., *J. Immunol.* **124,** 2288, 1980.
52. Varesio, L., Holden, H. T., and Taramelli, D., *J. Immunol.* **125,** 2810, 1980.

CELLULAR IMMUNOLOGY **63,** 293–299 (1981)

Anti-IgD Enhancement of Primary Antibody Responses in Rats[1]

MARVIN A. CUCHENS, KENNETH L. BOST, MARIE L. HOOVER, AND GERRIE A. LESLIE

Department of Microbiology, University of Mississippi Medical Center, Jackson, Mississippi, 39216 and Department of Microbiology and Immunology, University of Oregon Health Sciences Center, Portland, Oregon 97201

Received April 13, 1981; accepted May 29, 1981

The role of membrane IgD in immune responses was examined by treating adult rats with anti-IgD. Anti-IgD when administered to rats in conjunction with optimal or suboptimal doses of either SRBC, a T-dependent antigen, or DNP-Ficoll, a T-independent antigen, enhanced the antibody responses. The greatest enhancement was obtained when anti-IgD was administered before the antigen. The effects of anti-IgD on antibody responses to SRBC were: (i) significant antibody responses to suboptimal antigen concentrations; (ii) greater antibody responses to optimal antigen concentrations; (iii) accelerated antibody responses; (iv) an early shift from IgM to IgG antibodies; (v) prolonged antibody responses. Similar effects on the immune response to DNP-Ficoll were observed with the exception that all antibodies were 2ME sensitive (IgM). These results suggest that an anamnestic type of immune response can be induced in anti-IgD-treated rats when given a primary antigen exposure. Injection of anti-IgD without SRBC or DNP-Ficoll induces B-cell proliferation without detectable antibody production to these antigens, indicating at least two signals are required for the enhanced antibody responses.

INTRODUCTION

The disproportionately high expression of IgD on B-cell surfaces as compared to low serum concentrations of IgD has led to the hypothesis that IgD may function primarily as a B-cell antigen receptor (1). Similarly the coexpression of IgM and IgD on most B cells suggests that these cell surface immunoglobulins may have different biological functions (2). Indirect evidence in support of this suggestion has been obtained by *in vivo* studies involving the administration of anti-δ or anti-μ sera into neonatal rats (3). Anti-μ suppressed normal B-cell ontogeny whereas anti-δ induced a proliferation of the B lymphocytes.

In addition, anti-δ given to adult rats resulted in increased numbers of $\mu^+\delta^+$ B lymphocytes and an increase in the total serum immunoglobulin (4). Elevated serum immunoglobulins have also been observed in anti-δ-injected monkeys and seem, for the most part, to represent antibodies to the multiple antigens present in the heterologous antisera employed (4–7). In order to better understand the apparent enhancing effects of anti-δ, studies in the rat with more defined antigens

[1] This investigation was supported by grants awarded by the National Cancer Institute, DHEW (7 R23 CA28046), The National Institutes of Health, DHEW (5507 RR 05386) and HD 12381 (GAL).

0008-8749/81/140293-07$02.00/0

were undertaken. The results of the studies to be reported here clearly demonstrate enhancing effects of *in vivo*-administered anti-δ sera on the antibody responses to both optimal and suboptimal doses of thymus-dependent and thymus-independent antigens.

MATERIALS AND METHODS

Animals. Three- to four-month-old, normal, female Copenhagen rats (NCI, Fort Dietrich, Md.) were used.

Antiserum. Pooled antisera from two sheep immunized with rat B-cell membrane IgD were used in these studies. The antiserum was twice precipitated with 40% saturated $(NH_4)_2SO_4$ and passed over appropriate affinity columns to ensure δ-chain specificity (4, 8). The specificity of the antiserum has been rigorously tested and previously reported (8). Normal sheep serum treated in a similar fashion was used as a control and was adjusted to an equivalent concentration of protein. Sera were dialyzed versus phosphate-buffered saline (0.01 *M* phosphate, 0.15 *M* NaCl, pH 7.4; PBS) and filter sterilized (0.45 μm Millipore filter).

Antigens. A sheep erythrocyte (SRBC; H type antigen, sheep No. 20, Colorado Serum Co., Denver, Colo.) suspension and DNP-Ficoll (DNP_{16} Ficoll), conjugated and quantitated as described elsewhere (9), were used as thymus-dependent and thymus-independent antigens, respectively. Several concentrations of each antigen, ranging from an optimal concentration which elicited the greatest antibody response when administered alone (1.0 ml of 0.1% SRBC or 100 μg DNP-Ficoll) to a suboptimal concentration of antigen which would not elicit a primary hemagglutinating antibody response (1 ml of 10^{-5}% SRBC or 0.1 μg DNP-Ficoll), were employed. Only the results obtained from rats injected with the optimal and suboptimal concentrations are reported here.

Injections. Three rats per experimental group were each injected with 1.0 ml of anti-δ antiserum 3 days before, simultaneously with, or 3 days after the injection of the antigen. All injections were given subcutaneously at three sites; two dorsal and one vental. Control rats received (i) antigen alone, (ii) antigen plus normal sheep globulin, or (iii) anti-δ alone. Bleedings were obtained from the caudal tail vein prior to the injection of antigen and at 3- to 4-day intervals over a 4-week period. Sera obtained from individual bleedings were stored at −20°C until assayed.

Assays. All serum samples were heat inactivated (56°C, 30 min) prior to assaying for hemagglutinating antibody. Hemagglutination titers of untreated and 2-mercaptoethanol (2ME) reduced (0.1 *M* 2ME; 1 hr) samples were determined using trinitrobenzene conjugated SRBC, prepared as described (10), or SRBC suspensions in microtiter assays with serial twofold dilutions of the sera. The anti-TNP activity was totally inhibitable by 0.01 *M* DNP-OH.

Spleen and lymph node cell suspensions were prepared by gently teasing the lymphoid organ apart and passing the dissociated lymphoid organ through a 60-mesh screen. Cells were treated with 0.83% NH_4Cl to lyse erythrocytes and were subsequently washed three times with PBS. Plaque-forming cells (PFC) were detected using a slide modification (11) of the Jerne hemolytic plaque assay (12). Guinea pig serum (Gibco Laboratories, Grand Island, N.Y.), diluted 1:20, was used as a source of complement.

RESULTS

In order to examine the *in vivo* effects of anti-δ interactions with membrane IgD on primary immune responses, a single injection of anti-δ was administered in conjunction with antigen. Representative data from one of three similar experiments are presented in Figs. 1 and 2. The results clearly demonstrated an enhancement of the hemagglutinating antibody responses in rats administered anti-δ in conjunction with either SRBC or DNP-Ficoll injections over those animals that received only antigen. The most significant effect of anti-δ on the antibody responses was observed in rats given a dose of antigen (suboptimal), which did not induce detectable hemagglutinating antibody in rats not given anti-δ. Increased antibody titers were also observed in rats injected with anti-δ plus optimal antigen concentrations. Statistically significant (Student's *t* analyses) increases over antigen control groups were observed in all anti-δ plus antigen-injected groups, except in rats immunized with the optimal concentration of DNP-Ficoll and injected with anti-δ simultaneously or 3 days after the immunization (Figs. 2B and C).

The most significant enhancement of the antibody responses was observed when anti-δ was administered 3 days before the antigen. Antibody titers were higher and in SRBC immunized rats were detected as early as 4 days after the antigen injection. Injections of anti-δ simultaneously with SRBC or 3 days after SRBC resulted in a lag period before significant antibody responses were detected, when compared wtih injections of anti-δ 3 days before the antigen. This was observed with both optimal and suboptimal doses of SRBC, as well as with the suboptimal dose of DNP-Ficoll.

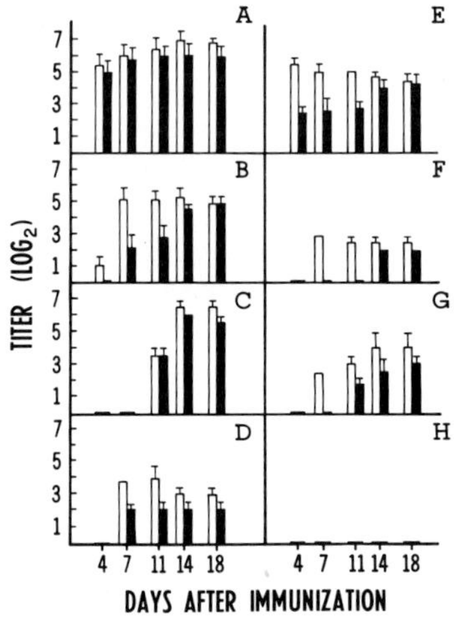

FIG. 1. Hemagglutination titers of sera from SRBC-immunized rats. Open bars represent total hemagglutinin titers; shaded bars represent hemagglutinin titers after 2ME reduction. (A–D) Rats were immunized with 1 ml of 10^{-1}% SRBC. (E–H) Rats were immunized with 1 ml of 10^{-5}% SRBC. (A and E) Anti-δ injected 3 days before the antigen. (B and F) Anti-δ injected at the same time as the antigen. (C and G) Anti-δ injected 3 days after the antigen. (D and H) No anti-δ. Three rats per experimental group were used. An arithmatic mean of reciprocal titers of individually assayed samples obtained for each time point is expressed as the log_2. Standard deviations are indicated above each bar. Preimmunization sera had no detectable agglutinating antibodies.

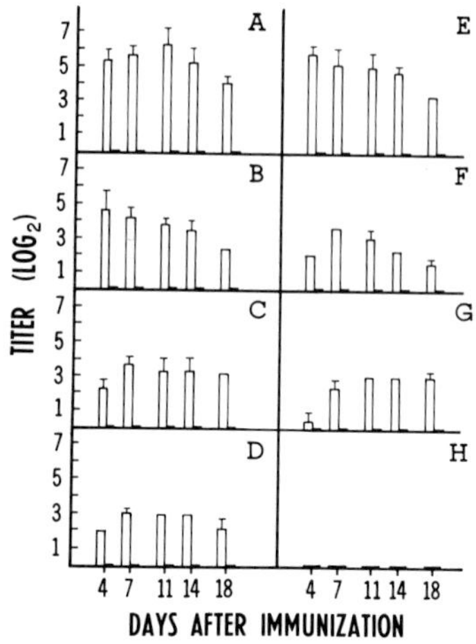

FIG. 2. Hemagglutination titers of sera from DNP-Ficoll-immunized rats. Open bars represent total hemagglutinin titers; shaded bars represent hemagglutinin titers after 2ME reduction. (A–D) Rats were immunized with 100 μg DNP-Ficoll. (E–H) Rats were immunized with 0.1 μg DNP-Ficoll. (A and E) Anti-δ injected 3 days before the antigen. (B and F) Anti-δ injected at the same time as the antigen. (C and G) Anti-δ injected 3 days after the antigen. (D and H) No anti-δ. Three rats per experimental group were used. An arithmatic mean of reciprocal titers of individually assayed samples obtained for each time point is expressed as the $\log_2$. Standard deviations are indicated above each bar. Prebleeds had no detectable agglutinating antibodies.

The hemagglutinating antibodies to SRBC and DNP-Ficoll were compared with respect to their sensitivity to 2ME reduction. No hemagglutination activity to TNP-SRBC was detected after 2ME reduction of sera obtained from the DNP-Ficoll-injected rats. Antibodies sensitive to 2ME reduction were also present early in the responses of all but two of the groups injected with SRBC. Rats receiving anti-δ before or after an optimal SRBC immunization (Figs. 1A and C) produced predominantly 2ME-resistant antibodies throughout the response. However, the hemagglutinating antibodies in serum samples obtained later in the responses of the remaining SRBC-injected groups were also resistant to 2ME reduction.

Anti-SRBC responses were more prolonged in the anti-δ-plus-antigen rats than in the control group only given antigen. Significant anti-SRBC titers were detected up to 45 days after antigen injection in anti-δ-treated rats, whereas preimmune titers were obtained by Day 30 in the antigen-only control rats. The DNP-Ficoll antibody responses were more transient than the SRBC antibody responses and no significant differences in the duration of the responses were observed between the experimental and control groups of animals.

Rats injected only with anti-δ or normal sheep globulin (no antigen) did not produce detectable hemagglutinating antibodies to either SRBC or TNP-SRBC. Additional controls included rats injected with normal sheep globulin (see Materials and Methods) or dilutions of the anti-δ (1:10 or 1:100) 3 days after optimal or suboptimal doses of SRBC or DNP-Ficoll. No hemagglutinin titers were detected in any of these groups which received a suboptimal antigen dose and no enhanced antibody responses (statistically not different from antigen control groups; Figs. 1D and 2D) were observed in any of the control groups injected with optimal antigen concentrations. These results indicate that sheep proteins were not responsible for the observed effects and the enhanced responses were dependent on the concentration of anti-δ employed. Furthermore no hemagglutinating antibodies to SRBC were detected in sera from DNP-Ficoll-immunized rats and the TNP-SRBC titers were DNP-OH inhibitable, demonstrating specificity of the responses.

To determine if the 2ME-sensitive and -resistant hemagglutinating antibodies were high-molecular-weight (19 S) or low-molecular-weight (7 S) antibodies, respectively, column chromatography was used to estimate the molecular weight of the antibodies. A pool was made of sera obtained on Day 11 from rats injected with anti-δ 3 days before immunization with optimal concentrations of SRBC or DNP-Ficoll. Each pool was chromatographed into three major fractions on a Sephadex G-200 column; a "macroglobulin" (excluded) peak, a "7 S" peak, and an "albumin" peak. Hemagglutinins in the serum pool from DNP-Ficoll-immunized rats were detected in the "macroglobulin" peak whereas antibodies in the SRBC-immunized rat serum pool were in the "7 S" peak. These data suggest that the 2ME-sensitive antibodies were probably of the IgM class and the 2ME-resistant antibodies were low-molecular-weight antibodies, likely IgG.

To address the question of whether more plasma cells were present and producing more antibody or whether more efficient antibody production from a limited number of plasma cells contributed to the enhanced antibody titers, one additional experiment was done. Rats injected with or without anti-δ 3 days before immunization with 1 ml of 0.1% SRBC were sacrified on Day 5 and spleen and popliteal lymph node cell suspensions assayed for direct plaque-forming cells. Antigen-injected controls had 150–300 PFC/10^7 lymph node cells whereas rats injected with anti-δ prior to receiving antigen had 10,500–14,000 PFC/10^7 cells. PFC were not detected in splenic cell suspensions of antigen control rats and fewer PFC were detected in the spleens than in the lymph nodes (0–250 PFC/10^7 splenocytes) of anti-δ-plus-antigen-injected rats. However, due to the subcutaneous route of immunization, a lower PFC response would be expected. Thus, the anti-δ-plus-antigen treatment clearly resulted in plasma cell expansion over the antigen-alone treatment.

DISCUSSION

The presented data clearly show that anti-δ can enhance the humoral immune responses to optimal and suboptimal doses of thymus dependent and thymus independent antigens. Collectively the data suggest that a secondary type of antibody response can be induced in rats with a primary antigenic exposure; i.e., responsiveness to a lower antigen dose, increased antibody production, earlier antibody production, a rapid shift to 2ME-resistant low-molecular-weight antibodies (in SRBC-immunized rats) and prolonged antibody production. These results therefore extend our previous observations in rats (3, 4) and are consistent, in part, with results obtained in mice (13–15).

Antigen presentation in conjunction with an anti-δ injection was necessary to induce the enhanced antibody responses since anti-δ alone did not elicit the production of hemagglutinating antibodies to either SRBC or DNP. This suggests that at least two events (signals?) are required and also argues against a polyclonal differentiation induced by anti-δ. However, the significant increases in antibody titers, as well as the increased number of antibody-producing cells (PFC to SRBC), clearly indicate a clonal expansion of the B cells responding to the antigen in anti-

δ-treated rats. Therefore possible cellular mechanisms involved in the immune enhancement should take into account the clonal expansion and differentiation of antigen-reactive B lymphocytes, as well as the two-signal concept involving anti-δ and antigen.

Several lines of evidence indicate that anti-δ induces B-cell proliferation without differentiation. Our initial report demonstrated a significant increase in the number of $\mu^+\delta^+$ lymphocytes in anti-δ-injected rats. Furthermore the hypergammaglobulinemia observed in these studies primarily was due to a specific antibody response to the heterologous serum proteins in the antiserum rather than strictly polyclonal immunoglobulin production (4). *In vitro* studies also support the contention that anti-δ interactions with membrane IgD induce proliferation without differentiation (16). In addition, the delays in antibody responses observed in rats injected with anti-δ and antigen simultaneously or with anti-δ 3 days after the antigen suggest that anti-δ-induced events may interrupt or supersede the antigen-induced events. Optimal responses were observed when anti-δ was administered before the antigen. Collectively these data suggest that proliferation induced *in vivo* by anti-δ may be an important prerequisite in the enhanced antibody responses and that an antigenic stimulus is an independent event necessary for further differentiation of the B cells involved in the enhanced antibody responses.

Although anti-δ-induced proliferation has been observed *in vivo* and appears to be an important event in the cellular responses leading to enhanced antibody production, the data does not exclude the possible activation of B lymphocytes, either concomitant with or independent of the proliferative events. A partial activation could lead to more efficient B lymphocyte responses to antigen or cellular interactions and would explain the rapid switch in antibody class, responses to suboptimal antigen doses and early antibody production. Along these lines, if interactions with mIgD are involved in triggering the differentiation of B cells into B-memory cells, as proposed by Layton *et al.* (17), then the enhanced responses may in fact be secondary responses in which anti-δ interactions with mIgD induce virgin B cells to function as B-memory cells. It should also be pointed out that Finkelman *et al.* have demonstrated an augmentation of antibody responses to optimal concentrations of antigens (TNP-Ficoll and SRBC) without demonstrable B-cell proliferation in anti-δ-treated mice (13, 14). However, responses to suboptimal doses of the antigens were not augmented, suggesting there may be significant differences in protocols or reagents used in the mouse and rat studies.

Speculatively, the antigen-induced events may bypass the requirement for T-cell help. This is in part supported by the enhancing effects of anti-δ on DNP-Ficoll (a putative T-independent antigen) responses. An attractive hypothesis proposed by Kettman *et al.* (18) which may offer a T-independent, two-signal model for enhancement involving mIgD and mIgM is that mIgD interactions (via anti-δ?) provide a proliferation signal and mIgM interactions (via antigen?) provide a differentiation signal. If this is the case one would expect B-cell proliferation to be polyclonal and differentiation to plasma cells to be antigen restricted in the studies presented here. However the T-cell independence of the high-molecular-weight, 2ME-sensitive anti-DNP antibody responses to DNP-Ficoll in rats has not been rigorously proven. Furthermore anti-δ augmentation of DNP-Ficoll responses in mice apparently requires T-cell help (13). A T-cell role in the antigen-induced signaling events would be consistent with reports proposing a two-signal model which involves a proliferative signal from antigen–membrane immunoglobulin interactions and a differentiation signal from T cell or T-cell product(s) interactions (19). The recent *in vitro* experiments by Parker have demonstrated that T-cell products are also necessary for polyclonal B-cell differentiation of anti-IgD-stimulated cultures (16). Extrapolating to the *in vivo* studies presented here, antigen-stimulated T cells (via specific T-cell factors?) may provide the second signal necessary for anti-δ-stimulated B cells to differentiate. Alternatively, stimulated B cells may produce a factor or alter the expression of surface molecules (IgD, Ia?) which in turn stimulate a T-cell subpopulation that can cooperate with the appropriate B cells. For example a quantitative increase in membrane IgD may stimulate IgD-Fc receptor-bearing T cells that would then cooperate with the IgD-bearing B cells. In this regard increases in IgG, IgA, and IgE Fc-receptor-bearing T cells in mice with IgG, IgA, and IgE myeloma, respectively, have been demonstrated (20, 21). Finkelman *et al.* have demonstrated a quantitative increase in Ia determinants expressed on B cells of anti-δ-treated mice and suggest that T cell–B cell cooperation may be enhanced through Ia interactions (13, 14). Our own data in the human support the notion that T-cell functions can be affected by anti-δ treatment of B cells (22, 23). Whether T cells and/or IgM are important in an antigen-specific second signal remains to be elucidated.

REFERENCES

1. Rowe, D. S., Hug, K., Forni, L., and Pernis, B., *J. Exp. Med.* **138,** 965, 1973.
2. Vitetta, E. S., and Uhr, J., *Science* **189,** 964, 1975.
3. Cuchens, M. A., and Leslie, G. A., *In* "Developmental Immunobiology" (J. B., Solomon and J. D. Horton, Eds.), pp. 197–204. Elsevier/North Holland, Amsterdam, 1977.
4. Cuchens, M. A., Martin, L. N., and Leslie, G. A., *J. Immunol.* **121,** 2257, 1978.
5. Pernis, B., *Immunol. Rev.* **37,** 210, 1977.
6. Martin, L. N., and Leslie, G. A., *Immunology* **37,** 253, 1979.
7. Finkelman, F. D., and Lipsky, P. E., *Immunol. Rev.* **45,** 117, 1979.
8. Golding, H., Cuchens, M. A., Leslie, G. A., and Rittenberg, M. B., *J. Immunol.* **123,** 2751, 1979.
9. Sharon, R., McMaster, P. R. B., Kask, A. M., Owens, J. D., and Paul, W. E., *J. Immunol.* **114,** 1585, 1975.
10. Rittenberg, M. B., and Pratt, K. L., *Proc. Soc. Exp. Biol. Med.* **132,** 575, 1969.
11. Mishell, R. I., and Dutton, R. W., *J. Exp. Med.* **126,** 423, 1967.
12. Jerne, N. K., and Nordin, A. A., *Science* **40,** 405, 1963.
13. Finkelman, F. D., Woods, V. L., Wilburn, S. B., Mond, J. J., Stein, K. E., Berning, A., and Scher, I., *J. Exp. Med.* **152,** 493, 1980.
14. Finkelman, F. D., Mond, J. J., Woods, V. L., Wilburn, S. B., Berning, A., Sehgal, E., and Scher, I., *Immunol. Rev.* **52,** 55, 1980.
15. Dresser, D. W., and Parkhouse, R. M. E., *Immunology* **35,** 1027, 1978.
16. Parker, D. C., *Immunol. Rev.* **52,** 115, 1980.
17. Layton, J. E., Teale, J. M., and Nossal, G. J. V., *J. Immunol.* **123,** 709, 1979.
18. Kettman, J. R., Cambier, J. C., Uhr, J. W., Ligler, F., and Vitetta, E. S., *Immunol. Rev.* **43,** 69, 1979.
19. Cohn, M., and Blomberg, B., *Scand. J. Immunol.* **4,** 1, 1975.
20. Lynch, R. G., Milburn, G. L., Hoover, R. G., Rohrer, J. W., and Deckgraefe, B. J., *Supramol. Struct. Cell. Biochem. Suppl.* **5,** 10, 1981.
21. Hoover, R. G., and Lynch, R. G., *J. Immunol.* **125,** 1280, 1980.
22. Cuchens, M. A., Burger, D., and Leslie, G. A., *In* "The Molecular Basis of Immune Cell Function" (J. G. Kaplan, Ed.), pp. 668–670. Elsevier/North Holland, Amsterdam, 1979.
23. Leslie, G. A., and Martin, L. N., *Contemp. Top. Mol. Immunol.* **7,** 1, 1978.

CELLULAR IMMUNOLOGY 63, 300–307 (1981)

Immunologic Effects of Whole-Body Ultraviolet (uv) Irradiation

III. Defective Splenic Adherent Cell Function in Alloantigen-Stimulated T-Cell Proliferation[1]

JOEL PICUS, RONALD N. GERMAIN, IRA J. FOX, MARK I. GREENE, BARUJ BENACERRAF, AND NORMAN L. LETVIN

Department of Pathology, Harvard Medical School, 25 Shattuck Street, Boston, Massachusetts 02115

Received April 23, 1981; accepted June 15, 1981

The daily exposure of a mouse to ultraviolet (uv) radiation causes a selective depletion of Ia-bearing adherent cells in that animal's spleen. This depletion manifests itself in functional deficiencies in the presentation of protein antigens and haptens to T cells. The present studies demonstrate a defect in splenic adherent cells (SAC) from uv-irradiated mice resulting in defective alloantigen presentation. We show that unfractionated splenocytes and SAC from uv-irradiated mice show decreased stimulatory activity in allogeneic MLR. We then utilize this phenomenon induced by uv radiation to characterize the stimulator cell in the M locus (Mls) determinant-driven MLR. We show that the stimulator cell in Mls determinant-driven MLR is an adherent cell and demonstrate that this stimulator cell bears Ia determinants by showing that whole spleen cells and SAC from mice treated with uv radiation are inefficient stimulators of the Mls determinant-driven MLR. The importance of the Ia determinant on the stimulator cells in Mls determinant-driven MLR is corroborated by the demonstration that a monoclonal antibody directed at this determinant fully blocks the Mls determinant-driven MLR. The significance of these studies to the problem of alloreactions *in vivo* is discussed.

INTRODUCTION

The daily exposure of a mouse to ultraviolet (uv) radiation causes a selective depletion of Ia-bearing adherent cells in that animal's spleen (1). This selective loss of Ia-bearing adherent cells manifests itself in functional deficiencies in the presentation of protein antigens and haptens to T cells in a number of experimental models. Trinitrophenyl (TNP)[2]-conjugated splenic adherent cells (SAC) prepared from normal mice efficiently prime uv-irradiated mice for a delayed-type hypersensitivity (DTH) response, but TNP-conjugated SAC prepared from uv-irradiated mice are incapable of sensitizing uv-irradiated mice for DTH reactivity (2). SAC from uv-irradiated mice are unable to reconstitute a primary *in vitro* plaque-forming

[1] Supported by Grants AI-14732 and AI-16396 and Training Grant 5T32-CA-09130-05 from the National Institutes of Health and Grant IM-277 from the American Cancer Society.

[2] Abbreviation used: DTH, delayed-type hypersensitivity; FCS, fetal calf serum; G-10, Sephadex G-10; MLR, mixed lymphocyte reactions; Mls, M locus; PFC, plaque-forming cell(s); RAMIg, rabbit anti-mouse immunoglobulin; SAC, splenic adherent cells; TNP, trinitrophenyl.

0008-8749/81/140300-08$02.00/0

cell (PFC) response to a soluble T-dependent antigen when added to adherent cell-depleted splenocytes (3). Finally, primed T cells are not efficiently activated to proliferate by antigen-pulsed or hapten-coupled SAC from mice exposed to uv radiation (4).

Ia-bearing SAC are required for the activation of T cells in settings other than protein antigen or hapten presentation. It is by no means certain that the same subpopulation of Ia-bearing SAC are required in these various interactions. The present studies were undertaken to extend the spectrum of functional deficits seen in SAC from uv-irradiated mice with the thought, in so doing, of perhaps finding a functional subset of Ia-bearing SAC not affected by this procedure.

Although we were unable to detect such an Ia-bearing SAC subpopulation, this series of experiments shows that the stimulation of T-cell proliferation by allogeneic SAC from uv-irradiated mice is inefficient. Then, using the uv-radiation-induced depletion of Ia-bearing SAC as a tool, we characterize the stimulator cell in M-locus (Mls)-determinant-driven mixed lymphocyte reactions (MLR).

MATERIALS AND METHODS

Mice. DBA/2 (H-2^d, Mls^a), C57BL/10Sn (H-2^b), B10.D2/nSn (H-2^d), B10.BR/SgSn (H-2^k), A/J (H-2^a), and C3H/HeJ (H-2^k, Mls^c) mice were purchased from the Jackson Laboratories, Bar Harbor, Maine; BALB/c (H-2^d, Mls^b) mice from Charles River Breeding Colonies, Wilmington, Massachusetts and AKR/Cum (H-2^k, Mls^a) mice from Cumberland View Farms, Clinton, Tennessee. The mice were maintained in our animal facilities and used at 2 to 9 months of age.

uv radiation source and treatment. uv radiation was delivered as previously described (3). Briefly, a bank of six FS-40 "Sun Lamp" fluorescent tubes (Westinghouse, Pittsburgh, Pa.) provided 1.2 to 1.4 J/m^2/sec measured at 20 cm. After shaving their backs, the mice were exposed 20 cm from the bank of lights for 1/2 hour daily over 7 consecutive days. Mice were used for experiments within 24 hr of the last uv radiation exposure.

Antiserum. Hybridoma supernatants from the 10.2.16 line (anti-I-A^k, Salk Institute) were used at 25% final concentration in antibody blocking studies.

Responder cells for mixed lymphocyte reactions (MLR). Spleen cells were teased to a single-cell suspension in RPMI-5% heat-inactivated FCS, washed once and passed over nylon wool columns (5). These cells were then passed over Sephadex G-10 columns as previously described (3) with 1.2×10^7 cells per milliliter of beads. The eluted cells were incubated in Tris-buffered ammonium chloride (0.83%), pH 7.65, for 4 min to lyse erythrocytes and then washed.

Stimulator cells. Whole spleen cells or splenic adherent cells (SAC) were used as stimulator cells. The SAC were prepared by a 2-hr adherence as previously described (3), but using plastic Falcon 3003 petri dishes (Becton, Dickinson Co., Oxnard, Calif.) rather than glass dishes. B cells were then removed from this population with a 30-min incubation period of the SAC on plastic dishes coated with rabbit anti-mouse Ig (RAMIg) as previously described (6). Stimulator cells were treated with 1500 R γ radiation (^{137}Cs source).

MLR assay. Cells were resuspended in RPMI 1640 (M.A. Bioproducts, Walkersville, Md.) supplemented with 2 m*M* L-glutamine, 100 units/ml penicillin, 100 μg/ml streptomycin, 10 m*M* Hepes buffer solution, 1× nonessential amino acids,

10% heat-inactivated fetal calf serum (FCS) (M.A. Bioproducts) and 5×10^{-5} *M* 2-mercaptoethanol. Responder cells (5×10^5) and decreasing numbers of irradiated stimulator cells were cultured in 0.2-ml volumes in the wells of flat-bottom microtiter plates (Linbro Scientific, Inc., Hamden, Conn.) in quadruplicate groupings. Controls were always done using syngeneic stimulator cells treated in the same manner as the allogeneic stimulators. Cultures were incubated at 37°C in a 5% CO_2–humidified air atmosphere. On the third day of culture, the wells were pulsed with 1 μCi of tritiated thymidine (New England Nuclear, Boston, Mass.), harvested 16–18 hr later onto glass fiber filter paper strips (No. 934 AH, Whitman, Inc., Clifton, N.J.) with an automated harvesting device (MASH II, M.A. Bioproducts) and processed for liquid scintillation counting. The results are expressed as the change in counts per minute ± SE. The counts per minute incorporated per well when control syngeneic stimulator cells were used was usually less than 10% of the counts per minute incorporated per well when allogeneic stimulator cells were used.

RESULTS

Spleen Cells from uv-Irradiated Mice Inefficiently Stimulate Allogeneic MLR

It has been previously shown that *in vitro* uv irradiation of a cell population abrogates its capacity to stimulate MLR (7). Since Ia-bearing SAC have been reported to act as stimulators in allogeneic MLR (8) and uv-irradiated mice have a decreased number of Ia-bearing adherent cells in their spleens (1), we predicted that splenocytes from uv-irradiated mice would show diminished stimulatory activity in allogeneic MLR. As shown in Table 1, whole spleen cells from uv-irradiated mice are poor stimulators in MLR, eliciting proliferation of allogeneic T cells with less than half the efficiency of normal spleen cells. This effect is even more pronounced when SAC made from normal spleen cells are compared as allogeneic MLR stimulators with those prepared from uv-irradiated mice. These data also demonstrate that splenocyte populations enriched for SAC show increased stimulatory activity in allogeneic MLR, confirming the earlier work of Ahmann *et al.* (8).

SAC Stimulate Mls-Determinant-Driven MLR

Gene products of the M locus stimulate strong MLR between H-2-identical strains of mice (9). We sought to characterize the stimulator cell in this Mls-driven MLR. As shown in Table 2, passage over Sephadex G-10 markedly decreases the efficiency of T-cell activation by the stimulator population in an Mls-determinant-driven MLR. SAC were more efficient, about two to five times more so, than whole spleen cells in stimulating H-2-identical, Mls-disparate T-cell populations to proliferate. Therefore, SAC can serve as potent stimulator cells in the Mls-determinant-driven MLR.

Spleen Cells from uv-Irradiated Mice Inefficiently Stimulate Mls-Determinant-Driven MLR

To determine if the stimulator population in the Mls-determinant-driven MLR requires a cell bearing Ia determinants, normal whole spleen cells and SAC or similar populations from uv-irradiated mice were compared as stimulators. As

TABLE 1

Spleen Cells from uv-Irradiated Mice Show Decreased Stimulatory Activity in MLR

Responder cell[a]	Stimulator cell	Δcpm ± SE[c] Normal	*In vivo* uv-treated
5 × 10^5 A/J	10.0 × 10^5 BALB/c WSC[b]	80,300 ± 3,450	38,800 ± 2,200
	5.0 × 10^5	74,800 ± 6,690	37,500 ± 3,600
	2.5 × 10^5	65,400 ± 8,090	21,100 ± 1,400
	4.0 × 10^5 BALB/c SAC	77,700 ± 16,000	40,100 ± 3,100
	1.3 × 10^5	58,600 ± 5,900	29,700 ± 3,300
	.44 × 10^5	25,300 ± 2,600	14,600 ± 4,700
5 × 10^5 C57BL/10	5.0 × 10^5 BALB/c WSC	71,200 ± 5,240	61,700 ± 5,000
	1.2 × 10^5	18,000 ± 2,720	11,500 ± 1,270
	.62 × 10^5	6,400 ± 2,000	2,500 ± 270
	4.0 × 10^5 BALB/c SAC	83,700 ± 1,820	38,400 ± 4,400
	1.3 × 10^5	64,400 ± 3,760	7,500 ± 2,580
	.44 × 10^5	22,100 ± 2,320	500 ± 530
	5.0 × 10^5 B10.D2 WSC	45,700 ± 4,100	29,100 ± 3,050
	2.5 × 10^5	66,200 ± 1,880	21,900 ± 2,200
	1.25 × 10^5	47,100 ± 2,030	12,000 ± 3,230
	1.33 × 10^5 B 10.D2 SAC	74,200 ± 6,430	32,000 ± 2,580
	.44 × 10^5	46,800 ± 4,910	13,400 ± 1,600
5 × 10^5 B10.D2	10.0 × 10^5 B10.BR WSC	62,400 ± 2,700	25,100 ± 600
	5.0 × 10^5	41,100 ± 2,900	21,000 ± 1,250
	2.5 × 10^5	11,700 ± 3,300	9,800 ± 2,020
	3.0 × 10^5 B10.BR SAC	83,400 ± 4,100	9,800 ± 960
	1.0 × 10^5	51,100 ± 3,540	14,200 ± 2,050
	.33 × 10^5	26,400 ± 880	1,500 ± 950

[a] Nylon wool, then G-10-passed splenocytes.

[b] Whole spleen cells.

[c] Value represents mean ± SE of [^{3}H]thymidine incorporation in culture groups in wells containing H-2-different stimulators minus the incorporation in wells containing an equal number of syngeneic stimulator cells.

shown in Table 3, stimulation by cell populations from uv-irradiated mice is often only half as efficient as stimulation by similarly prepared cells from normal mice, indicating that in the Mls-determinant-driven MLR, as in the H-2-determinant-driven MLR, the splenic adherent cell population bearing Ia determinants is needed to stimulate the proliferative response of Mls-disparate T cells.

Anti-IA Antibody Blocks Mls-Determinant-Driven MLR

Antibody blocking studies were undertaken to confirm the necessary role played by Ia surface determinants in stimulating Mls-determinant-driven MLR. If the Ia determinants on the stimulator cell are indeed necessary for the activation of Mls disparate T cells, antibodies directed against Ia determinants of the stimulator cell should alter an Mls-determinant-driven MLR. As shown in Table 4, the C3H/HeJ anti-AKR/Cum MLR, an MLR generated by the Mls difference between these two H-2^k strains, was completely blocked by a monoclonal anti-IA^k antibody. That the anti-IA antibody is not blocking T-cell proliferation by reacting with the responding T cells is demonstrated by the absence of blocking seen in a C3H/HeJ anti-DBA/2 H-2-determinant-driven MLR. While all these findings are consistent with the possibility that the monoclonal anti-IA antibody simply cross-reacts with the Mls determinants, this is unlikely given the lack of demonstrable blocking of proliferation in the BALB/c anti-DBA/2 MLR with the anti-IA^k antibody as shown in Table 4. That these MLR may be inhibited in a nonspecific manner by the binding of monoclonal antibodies to the adherent cells in the stimulator population is unlikely in view of the recent studies of Nepom *et al.* (10). They showed that while both IA and IE coded products are present on the same antigen presenting adherent cell subpopulations, the proliferative responses of primed T cells to GLPhe or GAT can be blocked independently using anti-IE or anti-IA monoclonal antibodies, respectively. Their work was done with the same hybridoma supernatant used in the present experiments.

DISCUSSION

Splenocytes from uv-irradiated mice serve as inefficient stimulators of allogeneic MLR. This observation is consistent with previous work demonstrating the im-

TABLE 2

Splenic Adherent Cells Stimulate MLR to Mls Determinants

Responding cell	Stimulator cell	Δcpm ± SE	
		Whole spleen cells	G-10-passed cells
Experiment I			
5 × 10^5 BALB/c	5.00 × 10^5 DBA/2	46,200 ± 6,100	22,200 ± 3,300
	2.50 × 10^5 DBA/2	33,300 ± 3,700	4,700 ± 310
	1.25 × 10^5 DBA/2	12,200 ± 1,000	500 ± 450
		Whole spleen cells	
Experiment II			
5 × 10^5 BALB/c	2.50 × 10^5 DBA/2	43,700 ± 2,100	
	1.25 × 10^5 DBA/2	14,800 ± 1,100	
	0.62 × 10^5 DBA/2	2,610 ± 300	
		SAC	
	1.33 × 10^5 DBA/2	30,300 ± 1,500	
	0.44 × 10^5 DBA/2	8,300 ± 1,600	
		Whole spleen cells	
5 × 10^5 C3H/HeJ	2.50 × 10^5 AKR/Cum	18,000 ± 890	
	1.25 × 10^5 AKR/Cum	7,900 ± 1,700	
	0.62 × 10^5 AKR/Cum	2,200 ± 620	
		SAC	
	1.33 × 10^5 AKR/Cum	20,600 ± 1,700	
	0.44 × 10^5 AKR/Cum	15,300 ± 1,740	

Note. See footnotes to Table 1.

TABLE 3

Spleen Cells from uv-Irradiated Mice Are Inefficient Stimulators of Mls-Determinant-Driven MLR

Responder cell	Stimulator cell	Δcpm ± SE Normal	Δcpm ± SE *In vivo* uv-treated
5 × 10^5 BALB/c	10.0 × 10^5 DBA/2 WSC	53,000 ± 5,900	42,000 ± 2,500
	5.0 × 10^5 DBA/2 WSC	64,300 ± 3,200	48,880 ± 10,900
	2.5 × 10^5 DBA/2 WSC	71,600 ± 2,700	38,400 ± 2,800
	4.0 × 10^5 DBA/2 SAC	60,800 ± 1,100	31,400 ± 9,100
	1.3 × 10^5 DBA/2 SAC	63,900 ± 5,200	41,900 ± 3,700
	0.44 × 10^5 DBA/2 SAC	30,000 ± 4,500	19,354 ± 1,500
5 × 10^5 C3H/HeJ	5.0 × 10^5 AKR/Cum WSC	18,400 ± 990	5,100 ± 520
	2.5 × 10^5 AKR/Cum WSC	18,000 ± 890	5,800 ± 620
	1.25 × 10^5 AKR/Cum WSC	7,900 ± 1,690	1,180 ± 240
	4.0 × 10^5 AKR/Cum SAC	22,000 ± 1,460	8,200 ± 290
	1.3 × 10^5 AKR/Cum SAC	20,600 ± 1,670	9,200 ± 1,420
	0.44 × 10^5 AKR/Cum SAC	15,300 ± 1,740	4,660 ± 780

Note. See footnotes to Table 1.

portance of Ia-bearing SAC in MLR. Ahmann *et al.* (8) showed that a non-T, radiation-resistant SAC expressing Ia determinants is the predominant stimulator cell in the allogeneic MLR. The functional importance of the Ia determinant on the stimulator cell population of the allogeneic MLR was made apparent by studies of Schwartz *et al.* (11) and Meo *et al.* (12) which demonstrated that anti-Ia alloantisera inhibit the stimulatory capacity of whole spleen cells in an MLR. We have confirmed these findings, demonstrating that monoclonal antibodies against IA determinants of the stimulator population block H-2-determinant-driven MLR (data not shown).

A concern in studies aimed at characterizing the antigen presenting cell in an

TABLE 4

Anti-IA Antibody Blocks MLR to Mls Determinants

Responder cell	Stimulator cell	Δcpm ± SE No antibody	Δcpm ± SE Anti-IA^k	Percentage Blocking
5 × 10^5 C3H/HeJ	10 × 10^5 AKR/Cum	40,600 ± 5,000	4,500 ± 980	89
	5 × 10^5 AKR/Cum	47,900 ± 4,100	4,900 ± 1,100	90
	2.5 × 10^5 AKR/Cum	26,400 ± 1,500	1,300 ± 410	95
	10 × 10^5 DBA/1	196,000 ± 4,900	176,100 ± 12,300	10
	5 × 10^5 DBA/1	199,000 ± 9,300	194,000 ± 8,100	1.5
	2.5 × 10^5 DBA/1	196,000 ± 9,900	167,000 ± 4,900	15
5 × 10^5 BALB/c	5 × 10^5 DBA/2	138,000 ± 3,900	102,000 ± 9,000	26
	2.5 × 10^5 DBA/2	81,900 ± 8,000	84,700 ± 4,300	0

Note. See footnotes to Table 1.

MLR is whether antigen re-presentation by the responder population to itself occurs. This is an unlikely possibility in our experiments for two reasons. The responding spleen cells were passed over nylon wool, then Sephadex G-10 columns, both procedures which deplete antigen-presenting cells from splenocyte populations. Furthermore, monoclonal antibodies directed at Ia determinants of the responder population, antibodies which block antigen presentation by adherent cells, had no effect on proliferative responses stimulated by allogeneic spleen cells in the MLR. While the responder populations thus prepared are deficient in cells which serve an accessory function in these cultures, it is unlikely that the proliferation seen upon addition of allogeneic adherent cells to these cultures merely reflects a reconstitution of this accessory function. Experiments similar to those shown in this study, done using nylon but not G-10-passed responder splenocytes, a population less rigorously depleted of adherent cells, demonstrated results identical to those reported here (data not shown). Furthermore, IA-negative SAC have been shown not to reconstitute MLR (8).

The Mls was discovered when strong MLR were observed between lymphoid cells of H-2-identical strains of mice. Characterization of the stimulator cell in the Mls-determinant-driven MLR illuminates two important issues concerning antigen presentation in that MLR: the identity of the cell type involved in antigen presentation and the nature of the H-2 restriction of cell–cell interactions in the Mls-determinant-driven MLR. Schirrmacher *et al.* (13) have shown that peripheral lymph node cells can be stimulated to proliferate by H-2-identical, Mls-disparate peritoneal macrophages. The present study carries this observation further, demonstrating that the adherent cell is the critically important cell in stimulating this type of MLR.

While T cells respond to conventional antigens in the context of self-H-2 determinants, whether an MLR driven by Mls determinants demonstrates H-2 restriction has been a controversial issue. Peck *et al.* (14) showed an I-region restriction in secondary responses to weakly stimulatory Mls^c-controlled determinants. Swain (15) lent further support to the notion of an I-region restriction in Mls-determinant presentation by showing that a monoclonal anti-IA antibody blocks the T-cell replacing factor generated in Mls-driven MLR. Yet Molnar-Kimber and Sprent (16), using negative and positive selection procedures, demonstrated that strongly stimulatory Mls^a determinants activate T cells without showing H-2 restriction. Janeway *et al.* (17) have shown that T-cell responses to Mls determinants involve the recognition of self-Ia antigens, and also have demonstrated that anti-Ia antibodies inhibit Mls-determinant-driven MLR in an H-2-specific fashion. We have confirmed these observations using a monoclonal anti-IA regent to block Mls-determinant-driven MLR. Furthermore, in showing that splenocytes from uv-irradiated mice are inefficient stimulators of Mls-determinant driven MLR, we further strengthen the observation that Mls determinants must be presented in the context of Ia to stimulate T-cell proliferation.

Since a lower concentration of Ia-bearing adherent cells is present in whole spleen cell than in SAC populations, one would expect the loss of MLR stimulatory capacity after uv irradiation of mice to be greater in splenocytes than in SAC. Yet the loss of stimulatory capacity after uv irradiation was more marked in SAC than in whole spleen populations. This suggests the possibility that a cell population, not susceptible to the effect of uv irradiation and not present in the SAC populations, may contribute to the stimulation of allogeneic or Mls-driven MLR. This phenomenon might, on the other hand, be due to an active process of suppression *in vitro* initiated by SAC from uv-irradiated mice.

These studies indicate that the capacity to present alloantigen in the living animal may be susceptible to abrogation by exposure of that animal to uv radiation. Preliminary studies indicate that mice are unable to generate an anti-minor alloantigen DTH response if both the donor cells and the recipient mice are uv irradiated. Whether this uv-radiation-induced phenomenon may be applied in blocking allograft rejection is being currently pursued in our laboratories.

ACKNOWLEDGMENTS

We wish to acknowledge the secretarial assistance of Teresa Greenberg and Harriet Yake in the preparation of this manuscript.

REFERENCES

1. Letvin, N. L., Nepom, J. T., Greene, M. I., Benacerraf, B., and Germain, R. N., *J. Immunol.* **125,** 2550, 1980.
2. Greene, M. I., Sy, M. S., Kripke, M., and Benacerraf, B., *Proc. Nat. Acad. Sci. USA* **76,** 6591, 1979.
3. Letvin, N. L., Greene, M. I., Benacerraf, B., and Germain, R. N., *Proc. Nat. Acad. Sci. USA* **77,** 2881, 1980.
4. Letvin, N. L., Fox, I. J., Greene, M. I., Benacerraf, B., and Germain, R. N., *J. Immunol.* **125,** 1402, 1980.
5. Julius, M. F., Simpson, E., and Herzenberg, L. A., *Eur. J. Immunol.* **3,** 645, 1973.
6. Weinberger, J. Z., Germain, R. N., Benacerraf, B., and Dorf, M. E., *J. Exp. Med.* **152,** 161, 1980.
7. Bach, F. H., Crillot-Courvalin, C., Kuperman, O. J., Sollinger, H. W., Hayes, C., Dondel, P. M., Alter, B. J., and Bach, M. L., *Immunol. Rev.* **35,** 76, 1977.
8. Ahmann, G. B., Nadler, P. I., Birnkrant, A., and Hodes, R. J., *J. Immunol.* **123,** 903, 1979.
9. Festenstein, H. *Transplant. Proc.* **8,** 339, 1976.
10. Nepom, J. T., Benacerraf, B., and Germain, R. N., *J. Immunol.* **127,** 31, 1981.
11. Schwartz, R. H., Fathman, C. G., and Sachs, D. H., *J. Immunol.* **116,** 919, 1976.
12. Meo, T., David, C. S., and Shreffler, D. C., *In* "The Role of Products of the Histocompatibility Gene Complex in Immune Responses" (D. H. Katz and B. Benacerraf, Eds.), p. 167. Academic Press, New York. 1976.
13. Schirrmacher, V., Pena-Martinez, J., and Festenstein, H., *Nature (London)* **255,** 155, 1975.
14. Peck, A. B., Janeway, C. A., and Wigzell, H., *Nature (London)* **266,** 840, 1977.
15. Swain, S. L. *J. Immunol.* **125,** 1224, 1980.
16. Molnar-Kimber, K., and Sprent, J., *J. Exp. Med.* **151,** 407, 1980.
17. Janeway, C. A., Lerner, E. A., Jason, J. M., and Jones, B., *Immunogenetics* **10,** 481, 1980.

CELLULAR IMMUNOLOGY **63**, 308–320 (1981)

Lactoferrin-Mediated Modulation Of Mononuclear Cell Activities

I. Suppression of the Murine *in Vitro* Primary Antibody Response[1]

R. L. DUNCAN, JR.,[2] AND W. P. MCARTHUR[3]

Department of Pathology and Center for Oral Health Research, School of Dental Medicine, University of Pennsylvania, Philadelphia, Pennsylvania 19104

Received May 28, 1980; accepted June 15, 1981

The effect of the iron-binding glycoprotein lactoferrin (LF) on the *in vitro* primary antibody response of mouse splenic cells to a T-lymphocyte-dependent antigen, sheep erythrocytes (SE), and a T-lymphocyte-independent antigen, trinitrophenolated *Brucella abortus*, was examined. Both iron-saturated and native LF (8% saturated) at 10^{-10} to 10^{-6} *M* concentrations but not transferrin (an iron-binding glycoprotein similar to LF) significantly ($P < 0.05$) decreased the number of direct (IgM) plaque-forming cells (PFC) to SE and trinitrophenol (TNP) as determined by the hemolytic plaque assay. LF was equally effective in decreasing the PFC response to TNP in T-lymphocyte-depleted splenic cell cultures. Concentrations of LF which decreased the PFC response were noncytotoxic. A 1-hr exposure of splenic cells to LF at the beginning of the 5-day culture period but not 1 hr prior to assaying for PFC, or exposure of isolated macrophage-rich but not lymphocyte-rich populations to LF prior to reconstitution resulted in a significant decrease in the anti-SE response. These data suggest that LF which is synthesized and released by polymorphonuclear leukocytes and present in inflammatory lesions may play a role in modulating the antibody response through an effect on the macrophage.

INTRODUCTION

Inflammatory lesions consist of a variety of inflammatory cell types as well as soluble inflammatory products such as lysosomal materials, lymphokines, monokines, activated complement components and immunoglobulins. Many of these agents have been shown to enhance or inhibit cellular activities. Modulation of the lymphoid cell responses by macrophages (1) and the effect of lymphocyte products on macrophages (2, 3) have been extensively documented. However, only recently has much attention been given to the potential effects of polymorphonuclear leukocytes (PMNs) on mononuclear cell functions.

PMNs are the initial inflammatory cells in a site of trauma and/or antigenic challenge as well as being the primary cellular infiltrate in chronic immunopathologic conditions such as immune-complex disease. PMNs respond to stimuli (e.g.,

[1] Supported by Grants DE 02623 and DE 03995 from the U.S. Public Health Service.

[2] Current address: Department of Dermatology, Emory University School of Medicine, Atlanta, Ga. 30322.

[3] Recipient of Research Career Development Award DE 00070 from the National Institute of Dental Research.

0008-8749/81/140308-13$02.00/0

immune complexes and bacteria) by lysosomal release with and without phagocytosis. PMN lysosomes contain numerous enzymes and other agents that have been demonstrated to mediate a variety of biological functions such as capillary permeability (4, 5), histamine release (6), tissue damage (7–9), and mononuclear cell chemotaxis (10). PMNs and PMN lysosomal products have also been reported to enhance or inhibit lymphocyte functions (11–17).

The PMN lysosomal granule constituent, lactoferrin (LF), possesses several characteristics which could implicate lactoferrin as a potential modulator of lymphocyte activities. This glycoprotein is found extracellularly at sites of inflammation, and its levels have been reported to correlate directly with the degree of inflammation in rheumatoid joints (18). Murine lymphocytes and macrophages bind lactoferrin (19), and lactoferrin has been reported to inhibit the production of granulocyte colony-stimulating factor (CFS) by macrophages (20). We have recently found that lactoferrin can also modulate lymphocyte functions (17).

The objective of this study was to define the effect(s) of lactoferrin on the primary *in vitro* humoral immune responses of murine splenic cells.

MATERIALS AND METHODS

Animals. Four-week-old B6D2F$_1$ (C57Bl/6 × DBA/2) female mice, obtained from Jackson Laboratory (Bar Harbor, Maine), were maintained in our animal facilities on Purina Mouse Chow (Ralston Purina Co., St. Louis, Mo.). Animals were 8 to 16 weeks old when used in this investigation.

Lactoferrin. Lactoferrin (Calbiochem, La Jolla, Calif.) derived from human colostrom was used throughout this investigation. The crude lactoferrin preparation (approximately 70% lactoferrin, 15% immunoglobulin, and 15% albumin) was used in the initial experiments. For subsequent experiments lactoferrin purified by passage over a Sepharose 4B conjugated with anti-human serum (AB+) was used. This immunoabsorption resulted in removal of >90% of the IgG and albumin contaminants in the lactoferrin preparation as determined by rocket electrophoresis. The protein concentrations of lactoferrin preparations were also estimated spectrophotometrically. Stock lactoferrin was maintained frozen at −20°C. Immediately before use lactoferrin was diluted in tissue culture medium and added to the cultures to final concentrations stated in the text. Human transferrin (siderophilin) was obtained from Sigma Chemical Company (St. Louis, Mo.) and was used without further purification. The transferrin in this form was essentially iron free. Immunoelectrophoresis analysis using rabbit anti-human serum detected only one precipitin band in the transferrin preparation which corresponded to the precipitin band formed with anti-transferrin.

Splenic cell cultures. The primary *in vitro* antibody response against sheep erythrocytes (SE) by dissociated mouse spleen cells was generated according to the method described previously by Mishell and Dutton (21) with the modifications described below. The medium used was RPMI 1640 (Grand Island Biologicals, Grand Island, N.Y.) supplemented with 1% 200 mM *l*-glutamine, 1% penicillin–streptomycin, 1% 1 *M* Hepes buffer (Flow Laboratories, Rockville, Md.) 5×10^{-5} *M* 2-mercaptoethanol (Eastman Kodak Co., Rochester, N.Y.), and 10% fetal calf serum (Irvine Scientific, Santa Anna, Calif.) Lactoferrin in medium was added to cultures to achieve the final concentrations described in the text. Cultures were immunized with 0.05 ml of a 0.5% suspension of washed SE (Flow Laboratories, McLean, Va.).

The primary *in vitro* antibody response against trinitrophenolated *Brucella abortus* (TNP-BA) by splenic cells was generated in 96-well microtiter dishes according to the method described by Mosier *et al.* (22) with the following modifications. RPMI 1640 (as described above) was used as the medium in this culture system. Splenic cells (10^6) in 0.2 ml medium were cultured with or without a 10^{-2} final dilution of TNP-BA (prepared as described below) for 3 days at 37°C in an atmosphere of 5% CO_2 and 5% air.

Preparation of TNP-BA. TNP-BA was prepared by haptenating formalin-fix *B. abortus* (USDA, Vet. Services Lab, Diag. Reag. Center; Ames, Iowa) at a concentration of 1.25 × 10 cells/ml with 2, 4, 6-trinitro benzenesulfonic acid (Eastman Kodak Co.). TNP (20 μg) was added to a 5-ml suspension of washed BA in borate-buffered saline solution (BBS), pH 8. After 1 hr of incubation in the dark at room temperature, the TNP-BA was washed in BBS until the supernatant no longer appeared yellow and resuspended in 5 ml of BBS. The TNP-BA suspension was pasturized (70°C for 2 hr) and stored at 4°C in 0.5-ml aliquots until used. Prior to addition of TNP-BA to our cultures, it was rewashed in sterile phosphate-buffered saline solution (PBS), pH 7.2, to remove the BBS.

Assay for antibody-producing cells. On Day 5 of the primary *in vitro* response against SE and on Day 3 of the primary *in vitro* response against TNP-BA, the number of direct plaque-forming cells in cultures was determined using the Mishell and Dutton modification of the Jerne hemolytic plaque assay (21). To test the anti-TNP response, TNP-haptenated SE were used in the assay (23).

Determination of splenic cell viability. The percentage of viable cells/culture based on the starting number of cells in each culture was determined at various intervals and at the end of the culture period. Viable cell counts from lactoferrin-containing and control cultures were made using trypan blue exclusion as the criteria for viability.

Antisera. Antisera to LF and to human AB+ serum were raised in rabbits by three subcutaneous injections of chromatographically purified LF (100 μg) or AB serum (0.5 ml in complete Freund's adjuvant over a period of 2 months. The serum was ammonium sulfate precipitated according to the method of Campbell *et al.* (24) and dialyzed against BBS. When examined by immunodiffusion, the anti-LF antiserum gave one precipitin band against commerical lactoferrin and showed no cross-reactivity with human serum. The anti-human AB serum showed numerous precipitin bands against human serum but no cross-reactivity with lactoferrin.

Insoluble immuno absorbant. Insoluble immuno absorbants were prepared by complexing the anti-LF (135 mg) and anti-human AB serum (135 mg) each to 200 mg of cyanogen bromide-activated Sepharose 4B (25). Greater than 90% of the protein was bound to the Sepharose in both of the preparations. Portions of a single preparation of LF were run through columns of the insolubilized antibodies and effluent tested in murine splenic cell primary response cultures. Absorbed solutions were monitored for removal of lactoferrin by semi-quantitative rocket electrophoresis as described elsewhere (26, 27). Results of the absorptions are illustrated in Fig. 1. The anti-lactoferrin removed the LF from the preparation while the anti-human serum did not significantly alter the quantity of LF in the preparation.

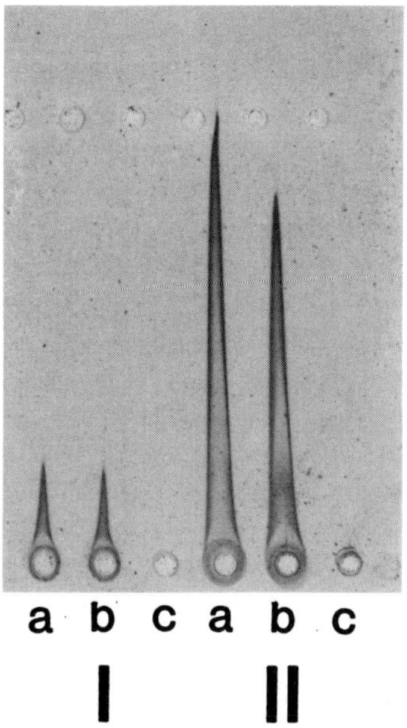

FIG. 1. Rocket immunoelectrophoresis of purified lactoferrin and lactoferrin preparations passed over immunoabsorbent columns against rabbit anti-human lactoferrin. I. Lactoferrin preparation, 0.2 mg/ml protein. II. Lactoferrin preparation, 1.0 mg/ml protein; (a) lactoferrin passed over Sepharose 4B column; (b) lactoferrin passed over anti-human AB+-serum-conjugated Sepharose 4B column; (c) lactoferrin passed over anti-human lactoferrin-conjugated Sepharose 4B column.

Lactoferrin treatment of adherent and/or nonadherent splenic cells. Splenic cells were separated into plastic adherent and nonadherent populations by repeated culturing and removal of nonadherent cells from 35-mm culture dishes. Splenic cells (10^7/dish) in RPMI 1640 + 5% FCS were incubated for 2 hr at 37°C in 5% CO_2 and 95% air. The nonadherent cells were removed by multiple gentle rinses with warm HBSS. The nonadherent cells were collected by centrifugation, readjusted to 10^7/ml, and recultured on fresh dishes for another 2 hr. The cells which did not adhere to the culture dishes after two incubation periods were removed, counted, characterized, and used as nonadherent cell sources for *in vitro* primary anti-SE immune responses. The resulting nonadherent cells morphologically appeared to be lymphocytes (>96%). Less than 1% of these cells stained positive for nonspecific esterase activity.

Adherent cells were isolated by culturing splenic cells (10^7/35 mm dish) for 2 hr as described above. The nonadherent cells were removed by rinsing with warm HBSS. The nonadherent cells were cultured in RPMI 1640 supplemented with 5% FCS for 2 days with washing of the adherent cells at 24 hr and again at 48 hr immediately before LF treatment or addition of nonadherent cells. The adherent cell population was essentially 100% nonspecific esterase positive, >95% phagocytosed latex, and >96% bound erythrocyte–antibody (IgG) complexes.

Lactoferrin (10^{-7} *M*) was added to 1-ml cultures of adherent splenic mononuclear cells in 35-mm tissue culture dishes or to 1-ml suspensions of nonadherent mononuclear cells (10^7 cells/ml) in 12 × 75-mm tissue culture tubes (Falcon Plastics, Oxnard, Calif.) Cultures were incubated for 1 hr at 37°C in RPMI 1640. Nonadherent cells were then washed three times in HBSS by centrifugation and resuspended 2×10^7/ml in tissue culture medium. Adherent cells were washed by repeated rinsing with HBSS. Warm (37°C) HBSS was added to the adherent cell cultures and again removed by suction. Lactoferrin-treated nonadherent cells (10^7) were added to lactoferrin-treated adherent cells (from 10^7 splenic cells) or to adherent cells which were not exposed to lactoferrin. Nonadherent cells not exposed to lactoferrin were also added to both lactoferrin-treated and untreated adherent cell populations. SE were added to the appropriate cultures, and the number of anti-SE synthesizing cells in the cultures after 5 days was assayed. Control cultures consisted of nonadherent cells alone plus SE and both populations without SE.

Depletion of T lymphocytes. T lymphocytes were depleted from mouse splenic cells by treatment with rabbit anti-mouse brain serum prepared by a method described by Golub (28) and kindly provided by Dr. E. Lally, Department of Pathology, University of Pennslyvania. The serum fraction was heat-inactivated (56°C for 30 min.). A 1.0-ml sample of heat-inactivated serum (56°C, 30 min.) was diluted 1:5 and absorbed with a homogenate of three livers and 0.5 ml of packed peripheral blood cells from $B6D2F_1$ splenic and thymic cells (10^7 cells/ml) in RPMI 1640. The antiserum was tested at final dilutions ranging from 1:5 to 1:1600. The rabbit anti-mouse brain serum killed, as indicated by trypan blue exclusion, 100% of the thymus cells and 26–36% splenic cells at a 1:200 dilution. These data correspond with accepted values for specific killing of T lymphocytes (28). Guinea pig serum alone at a 1:20 dilution was not cytotoxic for splenic and thymic cells. T-Lymphocyte-depleted cultures were obtained by treating mouse splenic cells with a 1:200 final dilution of rabbit anti-mouse brain (anti-Thy-1) and a 1:20 final dilution of guinea pig serum, both of which had been sterilized by passage through a 0.45-μm syringe filter (Gelman, Ann Arbor, Mich.). After incubation for 1 hr at 37°C as described above, cells were washed three times in HBSS and were resuspended to their 10^7/ml in RPMI 1640 containing 10^{-5} *M* 2-ME and 10% FCS. Control cultures were treated in an identical manner but were not subject to rabbit anti-mouse brain antiserum treatment. The effect of lactoferrin or anti-mouse brain treatment on normal mouse splenic cells was tested in primary *in vitro* anti-TNP antibody cultures as described previously.

Statistical analysis. The *t* test for paired observations was used to determine the probability of differences between experimental groups.

RESULTS

Effect of Lactoferrin on Lymphocyte Viability

Since LF has been shown to be bactericidal, its effect on mouse splenic cell viability was examined. No difference in the percentage of viable cells between cultures exposed to lactoferrin (10^{-5} *M*) and cultures without LF over a 3-day incubation period were noted (Table 1). In addition, cell viability after 5 days in the control (i.e., no SE) *in vitro* antibody synthesis cultures was the same in lactoferrin-containing cultures and cultures without lactoferrin (data not illustrated).

Effect of Lactoferrin on the in Vitro Primary Anti-SE Response

To test the effect of LF (10^{-14}–10^{-6} *M*) and TF (10^{-10}–10^{-6} *M*) on the primary antibody response, these reagents were added to mouse splenic cell cultures before

TABLE 1

Effect of Lactoferrin on Lymphocyte Viability[a]

Treatment	Percentage[b] of viable cells per hours in culture				
	0 hr	1 hr	24 hr	48 hr	72 hr
None	100	90	81	59	30
Lactoferrin[c]	100	90	79	70	40

[a] 1 ml cultures of 10^7 murine splenic cells in RPMI 1640 supplemented with 10 FCS and incubated at 37°C in an atmosphere of 5% CO_2 and 95% air.

[b] Percentage of viable cells (trypan blue excluding) in culture based on the starting number. Mean of three cultures. Standard deviation was <10%.

[c] Native lactoferrin at a concentration of 10^{-5} *M*.

the addition of SE and were left in the culture throughout the incubation period. The LF added to cultures was approximately 8% saturated with iron, and the TF was essentially iron free. LF at concentrations of 10^{-10} to 10^{-6} significantly ($P < 0.05$) decreased the number of antibody-synthesizing (plaque-forming, PFC) cells to a level of approximately 50% of the control cultures (Fig. 2). Transferrin (TF) had no significant effect on the numbers of PFC generated during the 5-day culture period at concentrations identical to LF. To determine if the effect of LF on the anti-SE response was reversible, cells were incubated with LF (10^{-6} *M*) for 1 hr,

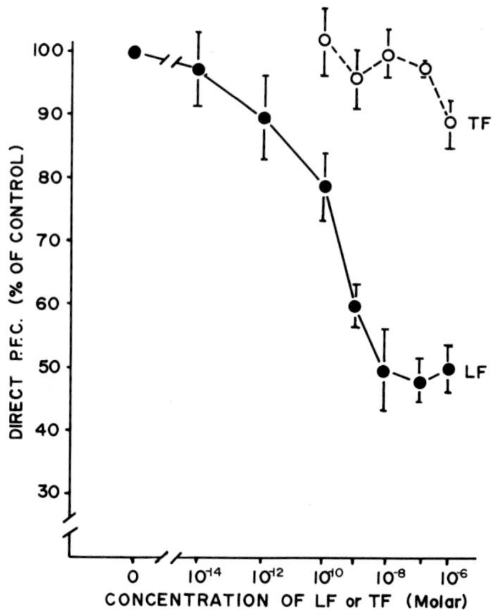

FIG. 2. The effect of various molar concentrations of lactoferrin (● —— ●) and transferrin (○ - - - ○) on the 5-day *in vitro* primary antibody response to sheep erythrocytes. The number of direct (IgM-synthesizing) plaque-forming cells (PFC) was monitored. Lactoferrin or transferrin was added to the splenic cell cultures immediately before the antigen (i.e., zero time). Results are expressed as the mean percentage of PFC in untreated cultures (i.e., 100% which represented 100 to 320 PFC/10^6 cells in culture) from three or more experiments ±SD. Lactoferrin or transferrin had no effect on the numbers of PFC per cultures detected in cultures not stimulated with antigen.

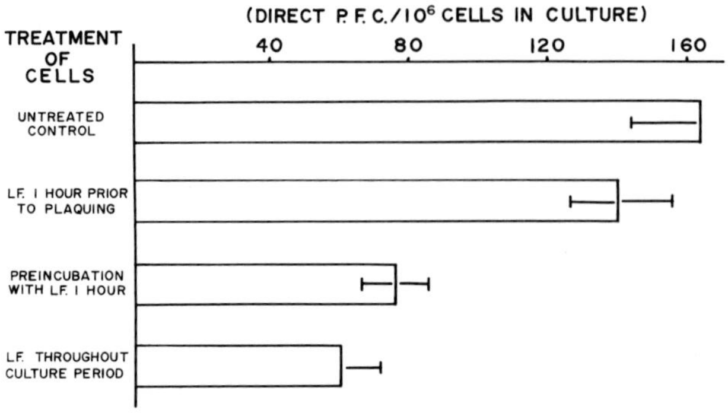

FIG. 3. The effect of various times of exposure of murine splenic cells to lactoferrin (LF, 10^{-6} *M*) on the *in vitro* primary anti-sheep erythrocyte response (5 days). Direct plaque-forming cells were monitored. Each bar represents the mean number of PFC ± SD for six identically treated cultures. The *t* tests for paired observations were used to determine the significance of the difference between LF-treated and the control cultures.

washed, and then were cultured for 5 days. Washing the splenic cells after 1 hr of incubation did not reverse the suppressive effect of 10^{-6} *M* LF (Fig. 3). Addition of LF (10^{-6} *M*) to antibody-synthesizing cultures 1 hr prior to plaquing had no effect on the number of plaque-forming cells.

Effect of Lactoferrin on the Anti-TNP Response

To test the effect of LF on a thymus-independent antibody response, the effect of LF on the antibody response to the T-lymphocyte-independent antigen TNP-BA was examined. The LF was 8% iron saturated, and the TF was iron free. LF at concentrations of 10^{-12} to 10^{-5} *M* decreased the number of anti-TNP antibody-synthesizing cells generated during a 3-day culture period as compared to control cultures or cultures containing 10^{-7} to 10^{-5} *M* TF (Fig. 4). Lactoferrin also inhibited the anti-TNP response by T-lymphocyte-depleted (anti-mouse brain "Thy 1" and complement-treated) splenic cells to the same degree that it did control splenic cells exposed to normal rabbit serum and complement (Fig. 5.).

Specificity of Lactoferrin Effect

The passage of a soluble LF solution over a column of Sepharose 4B conjugated with rabbit anti-lactoferrin Ig removed the suppressive effect of the lactoferrin preparation of the generation of anti-TNP-synthesizing cells (Table 2). Absorption of a separate portion of the same LF preparation with rabbit anti-human serum conjugated to Sepharose 4B or unconjugated Sepharose 4B alone resulted in no depletion in the ability of the preparation to inhibit the *in vitro* primary anti-TNP response. As reported earlier, rocket electrophoresis analysis of the absorbed solutions revealed that the anti-lactoferrin column removed all detectable lactoferrin (Fig. 1), while the anti-human serum column (Fig. 1) or the unconjugated Sepharose column had no significant effect on the lactoferrin concentration.

Effect of Iron Saturation of Lactoferrin

The effect of iron saturation on LF-mediated suppression of the anti-SE and anti-TNP responses was examined by comparing the effects of iron-saturated and

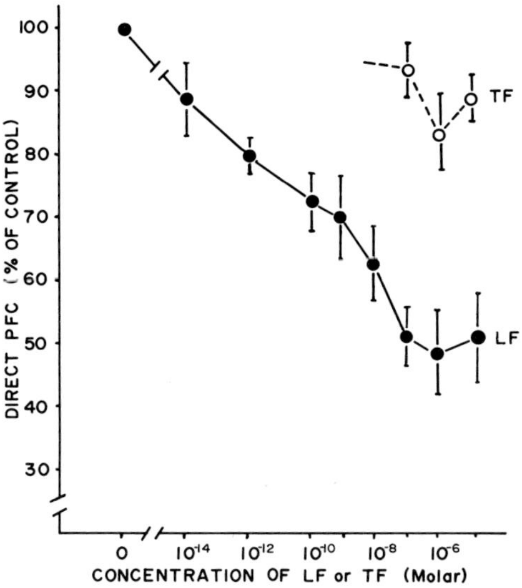

FIG. 4. The effect of various concentrations of lactoferrin (● —— ●) and transferrin (○ - - - ○) on the 3-day *in vitro* primary antibody response against TNP-*B. abortus*. The number of direct (IgM-synthesizing) plaque-forming cells (PFC) was monitored. Lactoferrin or transferrin was added to the splenic cell cultures immediately before the antigen. Results are expressed as the mean percentage of PFC detected in untreated cultures (i.e., 100% which represented 150 to 350 PFC/10^6 cells) from four or more experiments ±SD. Lactoferrin or transferrin had no effect on the numbers of PFC per culture detected in cultures which did not receive antigen.

native LF (8% saturated) in this response. The effect of iron alone added to anti-SE cultures in the form of ferric citrate to yield iron concentrations equivalent to those present with iron-saturated LF was also tested. No significant difference ($P > 0.10$) was detected between the effects of native and iron-saturated LF on the number of PFC in the anti-SE response (Fig. 6). Both native and saturated LF significantly suppressed the anti-SE response at concentrations ranging from 10^{-10} to 10^{-7} *M*. Iron alone added to cultures in the form of ferric citrate had no significant effect on the anti-SE response.

In contrast, the 1°C anti-TNP antibody-synthesizing cell response was inhibited more efficiently by the iron-saturated LF than the native LF at concentrations of 10^{-10}–10^{-7} *M* (Fig. 6). Below 10^{-7} *M* the native and iron-saturated LF inhibited the immune response to the same degree. Ferric citrate at the concentrations tested (10^{-10}–10^{-5} *M*) had no inhibitory effect.

Lactoferrin Effect on Adherent and Nonadherent Splenic Cells

In an attempt to define the splenic cell types whose role in the primary humoral immune response was suppressed by LF, splenic cells were seperated into adherent and nonadherent populations. Each population was either exposed to LF (10^{-7} *M*) or to medium alone for 1 hr, washed, repooled in various combinations, and the primary anti-SE response tested after 5 days exposure to SE. LF-treated adherent cells combined with LF-treated nonadherent cells had a decreased (>50%) number of PFC as compared to cultures of untreated combined adherent and nonadherent cells (Fig. 7). The PFC response of LF-treated adherent cells combined with untreated nonadherent cells was also decreased. No significant difference ($P > 0.05$) in the number of PFC in these cultures as compared to cultures in which both adherent and nonadherent cells were exposed to LF was seen. In contrast, the PFC response in cultures composed of LF-treated nonadherent cells and untreated adherent cells was not significantly different from the number of PFC in untreated (both populations) SE-stimulated cultures. The response of untreated nonadherent cells alone was 5% of the PFC response of the combined nonadherent and adherent cells, indicating that the adherent cells (macrophages) were effectively removed from the nonadherent cell population.

DISCUSSION

The results reported in this communication indicate that native human lactoferrin (LF), an iron-binding glycoprotein commonly found in inflammatory fluids (29) and secretions (30), can suppress the primary *in vitro* antibody response of murine splenic cells. LF specifically inhibits the *in vitro* primary antibody response to both a thymic-dependent (i.e., sheep erythrocytes) and a thymic-independent (i.e., TNP-*B. abortus*) antigen.

Although LF has reported bactericidal (31) and bacteriostatic properties (32), LF was not cytotoxic for splenic adherent cells of plasma cells. LF concentrations as low as 10^{-10} *M* significantly inhibited both *in vitro* immune responses. Within

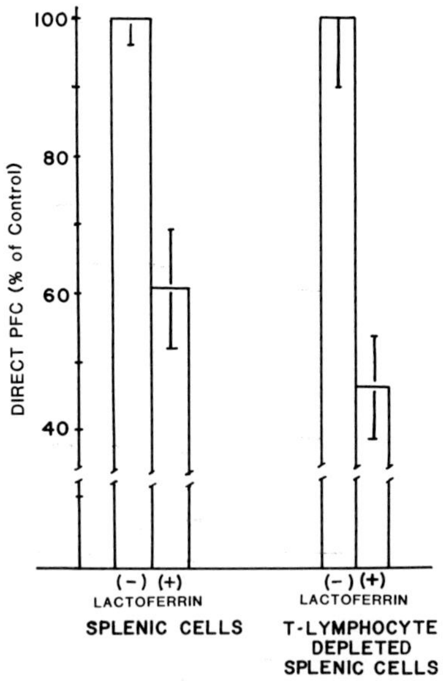

FIG. 5. The effect of lactoferrin (10^{-6} *M*) on the anti-TNP response by normal and T-lymphocyte-depleted mouse splenic cells. Splenic cells were depleted of T lymphocytes by treatment with appropriately absorbed rabbit anti-mouse brain serum and complement. Antiserum was used at a concentration which was cytotoxic for >98% thymic cells and which was cytotoxic for 30–40 splenic cells. Each bar represents the mean percentage of PFC numbers in control, untreated cultures or anti-mouse-brain and complement-treated cultures not exposed to lactoferrin. In both antiserum-treated and untreated cultures lactoferrin significantly ($P > 0.01$) reduced the numbers of PFC. No difference in the effect of lactoferrin on T lymphocytes depleted as compared to whole splenic cell cultures was noted.

TABLE 2

Effect of Specific Immunoabsorption of Lactoferrin on Its Ability To Inhibit the *in Vitro* Primary Immune Response to SE[a] and TNP[b]

Culture treatment: Lactoferrin Added (10^{-6} *M*)	Culture treatment: Absorbant Used	ANTI-SE PFC/10^6 Cells[c] Exp. #1	Exp. #2	Exp. #3	ANTI-TNP PFC/10^6 Cells[c] Exp. #1	Exp. #2	Exp. #3
−	None	87 ± 15	251 ± 25	142 ± 12	304 ± 2	200 ± 10	185 ± 6
+	None	43 ± 7[e]	115 ± 10[e]	67 ± 6[e]	142 ± 20[e]	72 ± 14[e]	102 ± 12[e]
+	Anti-LF on Sepharose 4B[d]	93 ± 12[f]	247 ± 8[f]	137 ± 18[f]	324 ± 20[f]	212 ± 28[f]	175 ± 15[f]
+	Anti-Human Serum on Sepharose 4B[d]	52 ± 8	112 ± 13	17 ± 14	136 ± 46	100 ± 8	102 ± 14

[a] Murine splenic cells cultured with or without lactoferrin (10^{-6} *M*) in the presence of SE for 5 days. The direct (IgM) anti-SE plaque-forming cell response was measured.

[b] Murine splenic cells were cultured with or without lactoferrin (10^{-6} *M*) and in the presence and absence of TNP-BA for 3 days *in vitro*. The direct (IgM) anti-TNP antibody-synthesizing cell response was measured.

[c] PFC = plaque-forming cells (i.e., anti-TNP or anti-SE antibody-synthesizing cells). Values are the means ± SD of three cultures.

[d] Aliquots of lactoferrin (10^{-5} *M*) preparation were passed through a Sepharose 4B column to which was conjugated anti-lactoferrin immunoglobulin or anti-human serum immunoglobulin.

[e] Significantly different ($P < 0.05$) from PFC numbers detected in cultures not exposed to lactoferrin and cultures exposed to the lactoferrin preparation absorbed with anti-lactoferrin.

[f] Not significantly different from PFC numbers in cultures not exposed to lactoferrin but significantly different ($P < 0.05$) from PFC numbers in cultures exposed to lactoferrin or lactoferrin absorbed with anti-human serum.

a range of 10^{-10} to 10^{-5} *M* LF the decrease in the number of antibody-synthesizing cells per culture was proportional to an increased LF concentration. In contrast, transferrin (TF), another iron-binding protein, at concentrations equal to those of LF did not significantly affect the *in vitro* immune responses studied.

The inhibiting activity was determined to be due to LF and not possible contaminants of the preparation. Absorption of the LF preparation with immobilized specific anti-LF antibody removed the inhibitory activity, while absorption with

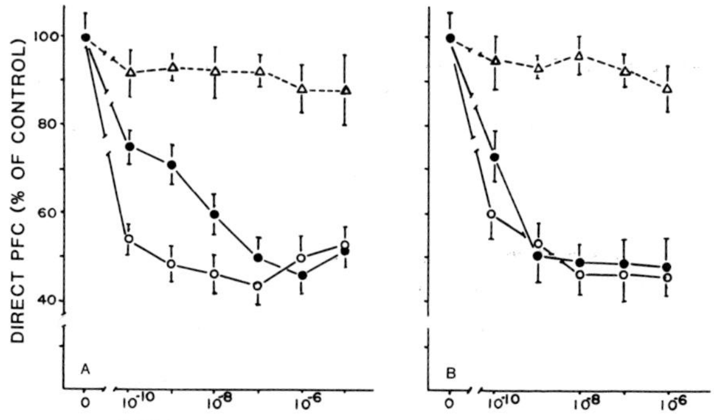

FIG. 6. Effect of ferric citrate (△ - - - △), iron-saturated lactoferrin (○ —— ○), and native lactoferrin (● —— ●) on the *in vitro* primary humoral response to TNP (A) and SE (B). The number of PFC is expressed as the mean percentage ± SD of PFC in control, untreated cultures. Each point represents data from three or more experiments. Lactoferrin or iron citrate was added before the antigen at zero time.

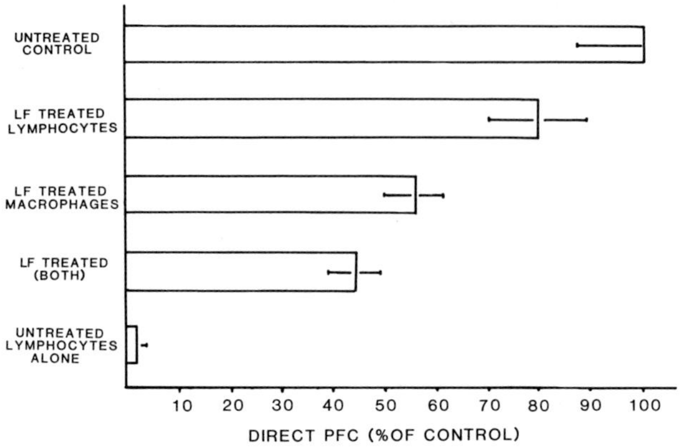

FIG. 7. Effect of exposure of adherent and/or nonadherent splenic cells to lactoferrin (LF, 10^{-7} *M*) on the 5-day *in vitro* primary anti-SE-synthesizing cell response. Separated adherent and/or nonadherent cell populations were exposed to lactoferrin for 1 hr, washed, repooled, and then cultured for 5 days with and without SE. Each bar represents the mean ± SD of the percentage of total PFC in lactoferrin-exposed cultures based on the number of PFC in SE-stimulated cultures of cells not exposed to lactoferrin.

immobilized anti-human serum antibodies did not affect the inhibitory activity of the LF preparation and did not remove significant levels of LF. In addition, human serum albumin and human γ-globulin were tested in the experimental system at concentrations greater than would be expected to possibly contaminate the LF preparations, and they had no effect (data not illustrated).

Iron-saturated LF was found to be more effective in the inhibition of CSF production by macrophages than iron-unsaturated LF (20). Similarly, we found iron-saturated LF was somewhat more effective than native lactoferrin (8% saturated) in suppression of the anti-TNP primary response. In contrast, no difference was detected in the ability of iron-saturated versus native lactoferrin in the ability to suppress the *in vitro* primary antibody response to SE. As no attempt was made to control iron availability in culture, the latter results may reflect lactoferrin's becoming iron saturated after its addition to the cultures.

That lactoferrin in the iron-saturated state was as effective if not more effective in suppressing the *in vitro* antibody response than native lactoferrin suggests that this suppression is not a direct result of lactoferrin's chelating ability. In this respect, the mechanism by which lactoferrin suppresses the *in vitro* antibody response differs from the putative mechanism by which lactoferrin imposes its bacteriostatic or bactericidal activity (31, 32).

In the initial experiments LF or TF remained in the cultures throughout the experimental period. However, inhibition of the *in vitro* immune responses was achieved by a 1-hr exposure to LF followed by washing and subsequent antigenic challenge and culturing. This relatively rapid and irreversible effect of LF could have been facilitated by cell surface receptors for LF. Such receptors have previously been demonstrated on murine lymphocytes and macrophages (19). LF did not seem to inhibit the secretion of antibodies from plasma cells since exposure of SE-primed splenic cells to LF for 1 hr before assessment of plaque-forming cells did not alter the number of antibody-synthesizing cells as compared to untreated or TF-treated controls.

The ability of LF to mediate an inhibitory effect on the splenic cells after a 1-hr exposure made possible cell separation experiments to determine which cell population(s) LF affected. The plastic-adherent splenic cells (predominately macrophages) appeared to be the cells affected by LF. Treatment of the nonadherent splenic cells (i.e., lymphocytes) with LF did not significantly alter the anti-SE response of these cells in the presence of untreated macrophages. The anti-SE response in cultures of adherent cells treated with LF and then combined with untreated nonadherent cells was significantly less than the response of the untreated control cultures. It was similar to the response of cultures in which both cell populations had been exposed to LF. The predominant cell in the adherent cell population was the macrophage, suggesting that LF may have modulated the macrophage in a way which affected its function in the initiation of the antibody response. In this connection LF has been shown to inhibit synthesis and/or secretion of another macrophage product, colony-stimulating factor (8). Since soluble macrophage products have been associated with the induction of the antibody response (33–38), it is tempting to speculate that lactoferrin may likewise inhibit the synthesis or release of such factors by a mechanism similar to that involved for CSF. Consistent with this possibility is the observation that LF suppresses the synthesis of CFS by Ia antigen positive but not by Ia antigen-negative macrophages (39), and an Ia-positive population of macrophages is required as an accessory cell in the *in vitro* primary antibody response (40). To determine if lactoferrin specifically affects Ia-positive cells and, if so, why the inhibition of the *in vitro* antibody response does not exceed 50–60%, will require further investigation.

In vivo PMNs respond to a variety of chemotactic stimuli and migrate from the peripheral blood through the capillary endothelium and into the tissue. The passing of PMN through the capillary wall is accompanied by lysosomal release into the extracellular interstitual milieu (41). Since LF is a component of the specific lysosomes, it must be released into the tissues. In addition, extracellular release of lysosomes occurs during PMN phagocytosis, endocytosis, and cell death, all of which occur in inflammatory lesions. These processes result in readily detectable levels of LF in inflammatory fluids (18). LF has been proposed as a direct indicator of PMN activity in an inflammatory lesion (18). LF inhibition of CSF *in vivo* has been presented as a potential feedback mechanism for the inhibition of leukocyte production by peripheral PMNs (20). De Sousa *et al.* (42) have hypothesized that LF may play a role in directing migration of mononuclear cells into acute inflammatory lesions and certain areas of lymphoid tissues. Once in the area, the LF under certain conditions may suppress the response of these cells to antigen. This may represent yet another regulatory mechanism in the immune response. An exaggerated example of this phenomenon may occur in those chronic inflammatory lesions which have PMNs constantly migrating into and through the area. Although the mechanism of LF suppression of the antibody response is not understood, these results do indicate another potential leukocyte-derived modulator of the immune response and may represent another potential mechanism by which an inflammatory cell affects the function(s) of another.

ACKNOWLEDGMENT

We wish to thank Lisa McDonough for her assistance in the preparation of this manuscript.

REFERENCES

1. Nelson, D. S. (Ed.), "Immunology of the Macrophage." Academic Press, New York, 1976.
2. Bloom B. R., and Bennett, B., *Science* **153,** 80, 1966.
3. David, J. R., *Proc. Nat. Acad. Sci. USA* **56,** 72, 1966.
4. Randive, N. S., and Cochrane, C. G., *J. Exp. Med.* **128,** 605, 1968.
5. Janoff, A., Shaeffer, S., Scherer, J., and Bean, M. A., *J. Exp. Med.* **122,** 841, 1965.
6. Randive, N. A., and Cochrane, C. G., *J. Immunol.* **106,** 506, 1971.
7. Cochrane, C. G., and Janoff, A., *In* "The Inflammatory Process" (B. W. Zeviefach, L. Grant, and R. T. McCloskey, Eds.), Vol. 3. Academic Press, New York, 1974.
8. Gladston, M., Janoff, A., and Davis, A. C., *Amer. Rev. Respir. Dis.* **107,** 718, 1973.
9. Kidokoro, Y., Kravis, T. C., Moser, K. M., Taylor, J. C., Crawford, I. P., *Amer. Rev. Resp. Dis.* **115,** 793, 1977.
10. Ward, P. A., Senior, R. M., and Cole, S., *Monogr. Pathol.* **19,** 188, 1978.
11. Yoshinaga, M. S., Nakamura, S., and Hayashi, H., *J. Immunol.* **115,** 533, 1975.
12. Nakamura, S., Yoshinaga, M., and Hayashi, H., *J. Immunol.* **117,** 1, 1976.
13. Visher, T. L., Bretz, U., and Baggiolini, M., *J. Exp. Med.* **144,** 863, 1976.
14. Yamaske, K., and Ziff, M., *Clin. Exp. Immunol.* **27,** 254, 1977.
15. McArthur, W. P., Taichman, N. S., Baehni, P., and Tsai, C. C., *J. Dent. Res.* **56B,** B157, 1977.
16. McArthur, W. P., Duncan, R. L., Tsai, C. C., and Taichman, N. S., *J. Periodont. Res.* **14,** 259, 1979.
17. Duncan, R. L. Jr., and McArthur, W. P., *Abstr. Amer. Soc. Microbiol.* 52, 1980.
18. Bennett, R., and Skosey, J., *Arthritis Rheum.* **20,** 84, 1977.
19. Van Snick, J. L., and Masson, P. L., *J. Exp. Med.* **144,** 1568, 1976.
20. Broxmeyer, H. E., Smithyman, A., Eger, R. R., Meyers, P. A., and De Sousa, M., *J. Exp. Med.* **148,** 1052, 1978.
21. Mishell, R. I., and Dutton, R. W., *J. Exp. Med.* **126,** 423, 1966.
22. Mosier, D. E., Scher, I., and Paul, W. E., *J. Immunol.* **117,** 1363, 1976.
23. Rittenberg, M. B., and Pratt, K. L., *Proc. Soc. Exp. Biol. Med.* **132,** 575, 1969.
24. Campbell, D. H., Garvey, J. S., Cremer, N. E., and Sussdorf, D. H., "Methods in Immunology," pp. 189–197. Benjamin, New York, 1970.
25. Cuatrecasas, P. J., *Biol. Chem.* **245,** 3059, 1970.
26. Weeke, B., *In* "A Manual of Quantitative Immunoelectrophoresis" (N. A. Axelsen, J. Kroll, and B. Weeke, Eds.) *Scand. J. Immunol.* **2,** Suppl. 1, pp. 37–46. Universitetsforlaget, Oslo, 1973.
27. Tsai, C. C., Hammond, B. F., Baehni, P., McArthur, W. P., and Taichman, N. S., *J. Periodont. Res.* **13,** 504, 1978.
28. Golub, E. S., *Cell. Immunol.* **2,** 353, 1971.
29. Bennett, R. M., and Skosey, J. L., *Arthritis Rheum.* **20,** 84, 1977.
30. Masson, P. L., Heremans, J. F., and Dive, C., *Clin. Chem. Acta* **14,** 735, 1966.
31. Arnold, R. R., Cole, M. F., and McGhee, J. R., *Science* **197,** 263, 1977.
32. Murphy, P., *In* "The Neutrophil" (S. S. Klebanoff and R. A. Clark, Eds.), p. 172. Plenum, New York, 1976.
33. Dutton, R. W., McCarthy, M., Mishell, R. I., and Raidt, D. J., *Cell. Immunol.* **1,** 196, 1970.
34. Hoffman, M., and Dutton, R. W., *Science* **172,** 1047, 1971.
35. Bach, F. H., Alter, B. J., Solliday, S., Zoschke, D. C., and Janis, M., *Cell. Immunol.* **1,** 219, 1970.
36. Nossal, G. J. V., and Schrader, J. W., *Transplant. Rev.* **23,** 138, 1975.
37. Schrader, J. W., *J. Exp. Med.* **138,** 1466, 1973.
38. Wood, D. D., and Gaul, S. L., *J. Immunol.* **113.** 925, 1974.
39. Broxmeyer, H. E., *J. Clin. Invest.* **64,** 1717, 1979.
40. Neiderhuber, J. E., Allen, P. M., and Mays, *J. Immunol.* **122,** 1342, 1979.
41. Zucker-Franklin, D., and Hirsch, J. F., *J. Exp. Med.* **120,** 569, 1964.
42. De Sousa, M., Smithyman, A., and Tan, C., *Amer. J. Pathol.* **90,** 497, 1978.

CELLULAR IMMUNOLOGY 63, 321–328 (1981)

Control of Suppressor Cell Activation via Endogenous Prostaglandin Synthesis: The Role of T Cells and Macrophages

DAVID R. WEBB AND IRENE NOWOWIEJSKI

Roche Institute of Molecular Biology, Nutley, New Jersey 07110

Received October 6, 1980; accepted June 15, 1981

Splenic macrophages were cultured in the inner chamber of a Marbrook flask and their ability to induce suppressor activity in a glass-wool-adherent T-cell population was determined. Nontreated, lipopolysaccharide-, or phytohemagglutinin-treated macrophages, all induced comparable levels of suppressor activity in glass-wool-adherent T cells. Suppression induced by untreated macrophages was reversible by the addition of a prostaglandin synthetase inhibitor. In addition, macrophages enhanced non-glass-adherent T-cell activation of glass-wool-adherent cells. The results indicate that macrophage in concert with T cells may activate T suppressor cells via a prostaglandin-dependent pathway.

INTRODUCTION

Prostaglandins[1] (or products of the prostaglandin pathway) play a role in regulating immune responses. Studies performed in this laboratory and by many other workers indicate that endogenously synthesized prostaglandins are a significant element in the fine tuning of both humoral and cell-mediated immune responses (1). At least a portion of this fine tuning involves a PG-producing monocytic cell (2) or as we have reported previously a murine suppressor T cell which is activated by PG (3, 4). We have established that glass-wool, nonadherent splenic T cells, stimulated by PHA, are capable of activating glass-adherent, splenic T suppressor cells via endogenous PG. This PG-sensitive T suppressor cell releases a low-molecular-weight suppressor which can suppress PHA-induced blastogenesis in the non-glass-adherent T cells. We have hypothesized that this represents a prostaglandin-mediated feedback loop between suppressor and responder T cells (5). Since it has been well established that macrophages also make PG in response to antigenic and mitogenic stimuli (6, 7), we were interested to know whether or not in addition to splenic T cells, splenic macrophages could activate the PG-sensitive suppressor T cell. The experiments reported in the present communication indicate that macrophages can indeed activate suppressor T cells via a PG-mediated mechanism. Furthermore, there is an apparent synergy between macrophages and mitogen-responsive T cells leading to enhanced activation of the PG-sensitive sup-

[1] Abbreviations used: NAL, nonadherent T lymphocyte; PG, prostaglandin; Mϕ, macrophage; PHA, phytohemagglutinin; LPS, lipopolysaccharide; HBSS, Hanks' balanced salt solution; [^{3}H]Tdr, [^{3}H]thymidine; iPG, immunoreactive PG; indo, indomethacin.

0008-8749/81/140321-08$02.00/0

pressor T cell when the three cell populations, the glass-wool-adherent T cell, the glass-wool-nonadherent T cell, and the macrophage, are allowed to interact.

MATERIALS AND METHODS

Mice. Male, C57Bl/6 mice, 6–10 weeks of age, were obtained from Charles River (Waltham, Mass.).

Drugs. PGE_2 was obtained from PL Biochemicals (Milwaukee, Wisc.) and dissolved in 95% ethanol. It was stored at −20°C and diluted with culture medium immediately prior to use. Control cultures received appropriately diluted 95% ethanol and medium. Indomethacin was obtained from Sigma (St. Louis, Mo.); *d,l*-6-chloro-α-methylcarbazole-2-acetic acid (Ro-20-5720) was a gift from Dr. W. E. Scott (Hoffmann–LaRoche, Nutley, N.J.). Both compounds were stored as dry powders and prepared freshly for each experiment by mixing in 95% ethanol and diluting with medium.

Mitogens. Phytohemagglutinin (PHA) was obtained from Burroughs–Wellcome (Research Triangle Park, N.C.). Bacterial lipopolysaccharide (LPS) *Escherichia coli* strain 128:B12 was obtained from Difco (Chicago, Ill.).

Cell cultures. Spleens were removed aseptically following sacrifice, and mashed, using forceps, in Hanks' balanced salt solution (HBSS). A single-cell suspension was made by repeatedly expelling the spleen cell suspension through a 20-gauge needle. Spleen cell suspensions were then washed twice in HBSS. Spleen cells were separated into nonadherent lymphocyte (NAL) and adherent T-cell (Tad) (termed GAT in previous publications) populations on glass wool columns as described previously (3, 4). Adherent monocytes, which for the sake of this discussion will be called macrophages, were prepared by incubating the spleen cell suspension on plastic petri dishes (Falcon, Oxnard, Calif.) at 37°C in RPMI 1640 + 0.25% BSA for 1 hr. The nonadherent cells were removed by repeated washings of the petri dish. The plastic-adherent cells ($M\phi$) were collected using a rubber policeman and washed two times in HBSS. Cells were cultured in RPMI 1640 containing penicillin–streptomycin but no serum supplement. In the studies measuring the effects of $M\phi$ on Tad lymphocyte activation the $M\phi$ were placed in the inner chamber of a Marbrook flask (Bellco Glass, Vineland, N.J.) and Tad lymphocytes in the outer chamber. The two chambers were separated by a dialysis membrane. After 24 hr of incubation the Tad lymphocytes were removed, washed once, placed in RPMI 1640, and assayed for suppressor activity. The assay of suppressor function was carried out as reported previously (3, 4). Briefly, NAL (5×10^5 cells/0.2 ml) and Tad lymphocytes were mixed in varying ratios in microtiter wells along with PHA (0.031 μg/well). DNA synthesis was assessed after 72 hr by the addition of [^{3}H]Tdr for 6–24 hr prior to culture termination. Cultures were harvested using an automated harvester (Bellco) and incorporation was assessed by scintillation spectroscopy. Cell cultures were done in triplicate and the values reported represent the average counts per minute ± SEM.

Measurement of PGE. PGE was measured with an antibody to PGE_2 prepared by Miles Laboratories (Kankakee, Ill.) using methods previously described (8). Since this antibody does not easily discriminate between PGA, B, and E_1 the abbreviation "iPG" referring to immunoreactive PG is used.

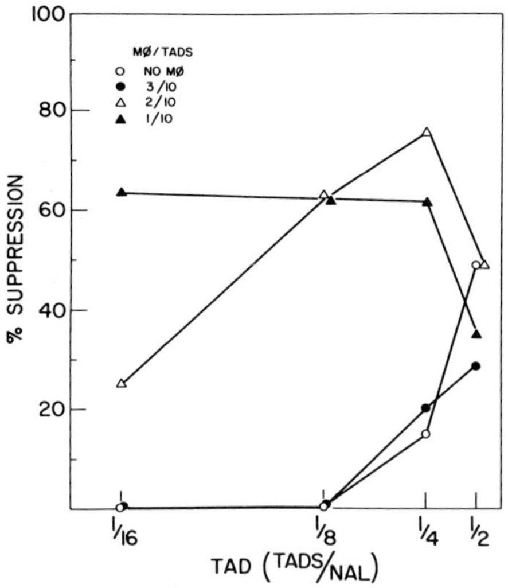

FIG. 1. Effect of various concentrations of macrophages on activation of TadS. Values above 20% suppression are significant to $P \leq 0.05$ as determined by student's t test when compared to NAL cultures not exposed to TadS. Macrophages were prepared as outlined under Materials and Methods. TadS were added to the outer chamber of Marbrook flasks with Mϕ in the inner chamber. After 24 hr the TadS were recovered, washed, and mixed with fresh NAL + PHA (0.031 μg/200 μl of culture) in varying dilutions indicated in the figure. DNA synthesis was assessed after 72 hr. The cpm in triplicate NAL cultures stimulated with PHA alone was 42,382 ± 894.

RESULTS

Effect of Mitogens on Mϕ Induction of Tad Suppressor Cells

Previous experiments carried out in our laboratory had shown that NAL, when stimulated by PHA, were able to stimulate increased suppressor activity in Tad (3, 4). Initial experiments were carried out using varying ratios of Mϕ/TadS in order to determine whether Mϕ could also activate TadS. A representative experiment is shown in Fig. 1. These data show that Mϕ/Tad ratios of 2/10–1/10 appear to result in comparably good activation of TadS whereas a Mϕ/Tad ratio of 3/10 seems to be less effective in activating TadS. It should be noted that Mϕ have not been rigorously excluded from the TadS for routine experiments. Previous studies have shown macrophage contamination to vary between 1 and 5% of TadS (3, 4). This may account for the observation that at the highest TadS concentration (1/2) there is little difference in the degree of suppression observed; that is the number of macrophages is either at or above the optimum for TadS activation. Using these data as a guideline, subsequent experiments were carried out at ratios which were in the optimal range for TadS activation. The data in Fig. 2 summarize the results of several experiments in which Mϕ treated with medium, PHA, or LPS were cultured with TadS for 24 hr in a Marbrook flask. The TadS were then mixed with NAL + PHA and assayed for DNA synthesis after 72 hr. The results show that there is very little difference in the capacity of isolated Mϕ treated with LPS or PHA to stimulate Tad suppressor activity when compared to untreated Mϕ.

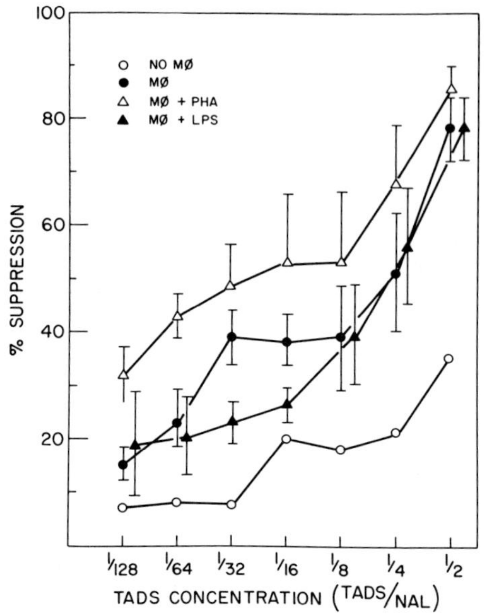

FIG. 2. Summary of the effects of PHA and LPS on macrophage activation of TadS suppressor cells. The values represent the percentage suppression ± SE of DNA synthesis in NAL cultures exposed to TadS in varying dilutions. The TadS had previously been incubated in the outer chamber of a Marbrook flask with Mϕ treated with mitogens present in the inner chamber. After 24 hr the TadS were washed and added to NAL cells as outlined under Materials and Methods. Each point represents an average of at least four separate experiments. (○) Represent Marbrook cultures in which no Mϕ were present in the inner chamber during the 24-hr preincubation period. PHA dose = 2.0 μg/ml; LPS dose = 3 μg/ml.

The Effects of Inhibitors of Prostaglandin Synthesis on Macrophage Activation of Tad Suppression

The preceding experiments show that macrophages can stimulate suppressor activity of TadS. However, it was not clear from these experiments to what degree mitogen stimulation affected the capacity of macrophages to stimulate Tad suppression. The possibility of a simple feeding effect seemed to be ruled out since the recovery of viable TadS from Marbrook flasks was the same regardless of the presence or absence of macrophages. In experiments using NAL it had been shown that PG production by NAL was necessary for NAL activation of Tad suppressor cells (4). In the representative experiment shown in Fig. 3, unstimulated macrophages were preincubated in Marbrook Chambers for 24 hr in the presence or absence of indomethacin in order to block PG synthesis. Adherent T cells were added to the outer chamber and the cultures incubated for an additional 24 hr. The TadS were collected and mixed with fresh NAL + PHA with or without Ro-20-5720 (to block NAL PG synthesis). The results show that unstimulated Mϕ make sufficient quantities of some product of the PG pathway to activate Tad suppressors. Illustrative of this point is the much greater suppression observed in TadS exposed to untreated Mϕ compared to Mϕ exposed to indomethacin. The presence or absence of a prostaglandin synthesis inhibitor during TadS incubation with NAL shows that following exposure to Mϕ, the TadS may still be influenced

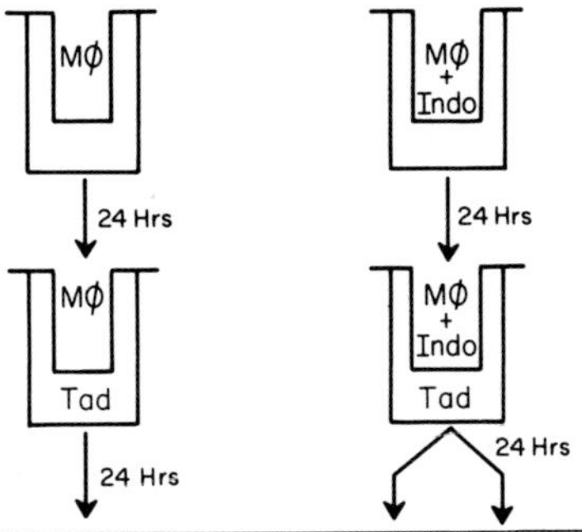

Ratio T/N[a]	% SUPPRESSION		
1/10	86 %	83 %	86 %
1/15	83 %	18 %	76 %
1/20	72 %	No Supp	47 %
	PHA[b] + NAL + Tad	PHA + NAL + Tad + 5720	PHA + NAL + Tad

FIG. 3. The effect of prostaglandin synthetase inhibitors on Mϕ activation of TadS. Splenic Mϕ and TadS were collected and prepared as described under Materials and Methods. The Mϕ were incubated at 37°C in the Marbrook chambers for 24 hr prior to the addition of TadS. The ratio of TadS to Mϕ was 10/1. Indomethacin was added at a final concentration of 1×10^{-6} *M* in the Mϕ cultures; Ro-20-5720 was added at a concentration of 1×10^{-5} *M*. [a]After 24 hr incubation in the Marbrook flasks the TadS were collected, washed, and added in varying ratios to fresh NAL cultures. [b]PHA concentration used was 0.031 μg/well.

by PG production in cultures containing NAL. These experiments show that unstimulated Mϕ may activate TadS via a PG-dependent mechanism. In the previous section data were presented showing that unstimulated Mϕ were comparable to mitogen-treated Mϕ in their capacity to activate TadS. This implies that mitogen stimulation may not significantly raise PG levels in isolated Mϕ during the 24 hr culture period. To check this we measured PG levels in Mϕ exposed to various doses of PHA. As shown in Table 1, supernatants from Mϕ cultured for 24 hr with increasing doses of PHA contain comparable amounts of iPG. This, in conjunction with the results shown in Figs. 2 and 3 suggests that perhaps Mϕ alone may not be solely responsible for the activation of TadS following mitogen stimulation.

TABLE 1

Effects of PHA Dose on iPG Levels in Macrophage Cultures[a]

Dose of PHA	iPG levels/culture (PG)
0	650 ± 25
0.125 μg/ml	615 ± 25
0.250 μg/ml	570 ± 24
0.50 μg/ml	587 ± 68

[a] 1-ml duplicate cultures of 1×10^{6} Mϕ were incubated for 24 hr. After centrifugation the supernatants were collected and 0.1 ml was assayed for "iPG" levels by radioimmunoassay. Each tube was assayed in duplicate. The data represent the mean of the two tubes/group ± SEM.

The question thus arises whether in the normal splenic milieu both Mφ and NAL act on TadS to control their suppressor activity. To test this, NAL were prepared as outlined under Materials and Methods with the additional step being to incubate these cells on plastic petri dishes to insure the removal of any remaining Mφ. Splenic macrophages and TadS were prepared as in previous experiments. The experiments were set up so that both NAL and Mφ concentrations in the inner chamber of the Marbrook flasks were optimal for TadS activation. PHA was added to the inner chamber at a concentration optimal for NAL activation of TadS. After 24 hr of incubation the TadS were removed and counted using a viable stain (trypan blue) and TadS in varying concentrations were then added to fresh NAL + PHA. DNA synthesis was assessed after 72 hr. These experiments were designed to test how Mφ might influence NAL-induced TadS suppression. The results of a typical experiment are presented in Fig. 4. These data show that NAL-induced activation of Tad suppression may be considerably augmented by the addition of Mφ.

DISCUSSION

The results of the experiments presented in this report show that exposure to Mφ may enhance the suppressor activity of TadS lymphocytes. The ability of unstimulated Mφ to enhance suppressor cell activity appears to be dependent on PG pathway synthetic activity. The splenic Mφ were isolated via an adherence technique which has been shown to induce PG synthesis (P. Dore-Duffy, personal communication). This may account for the observations that "unstimulated" Mφ can enhance the activity of TadS to an extent similar to that of Mφ stimulated by

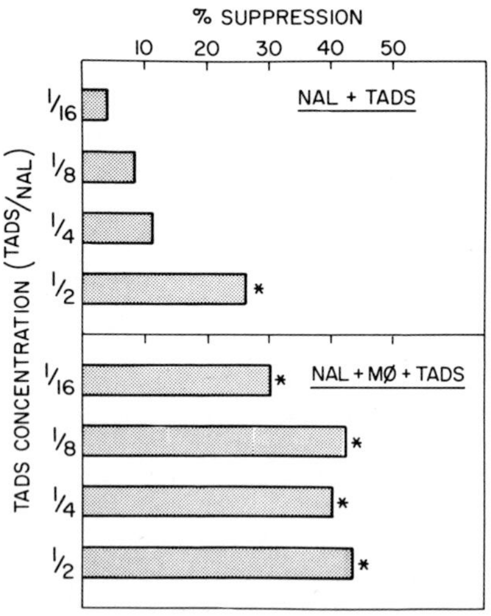

FIG. 4. Effect of Mφ and NAL on TadS suppressor cell induction. The numbers represent percentage suppression of DNA synthesis in cultures exposed to TadS as compared to cultures of NAL alone. The ratio of NAL to TadS in the Marbrook flask was 1:2 (5×10^6 NAL:1×10^7 TadS); the ratio of Mφ to TadS was 1:10. The cpm in NAL cultures stimulated with PHA was 45,543 ± 1705. (*) Represent values where suppression was significant to the $P \leq 0.05$ level as determined by Student's t test comparing cultures of NAL/TadS to NAL.

mitogens. In the normal spleen the TadS lymphocyte population is exposed to both NAL and Mϕ; thus it was of interest to know whether the NAL and Mϕ together could enhance TadS suppressor activity. The results indicate that Mϕ may enhance NAL activation of TadS. It is not clear if this effect is additive, synergistic, or some combination of these two. It is worth noting that in experiments where Mϕ were not rigorously excluded, NAL invariably activated TadS to a degree greater than is evident in the experiments shown here (3, 4).

We have previously reported that splenic macrophages alone when added to NAL do not directly suppress PHA-induced DNA synthesis (4). This result was somewhat unexpected since other workers had reported the suppressive effect of macrophages in a variety of experimental protocols (9–13). In some of these results there was a clear difference between species examined (e.g., rat and mouse (11); macrophages are suppressive in the rat and human, and yet, macrophages are required for the generation of an immune response in the mouse. Further, there are clearly differences in macrophage populations obtained from different experimental conditions such as those obtained from tumor-bearing hosts (9) or thioglycolate-induced peritoneal exudate (10) as compared to macrophages obtained from normal, untreated mice. Also, while the function of NAL in immunized mice seems largely to be as a source of helper cells (Webb & Nowowiejski, unpublished observations) exactly what cell population is being inhibited by TadS following PHA stimulation is unknown. Recent studies by Kemp *et al.* (14), Orme and Shand (15) and by ourselves may bear on this issue. Kemp *et al.* carried out a series of studies in rats and mice which suggested that indomethacin-sensitive suppression was macrophage mediated. This result is not inconsistent with the data reported by us since our data could be interpreted to argue that the macrophage is the driving force in PG-mediated suppressor effects; the TadS then becoming a target of macrophage-produced PG and representing a mechanism for amplifying or controlling the macrophage PG signal. Both Orme and Shand (15, 16) as well as ourselves (Webb & Nowowiejski, unpublished observations) have found that removal of glass-adherent T cells enhances the primary immune response to sheep erythrocytes. Furthermore, after glass-adherent T cells are removed, indomethacin no longer causes an enhancement in the number of 19 S antibody-forming cells to sheep erythrocytes. Consistent with the data of Kemp *et al.* (14), Orme and Shand (16) have found that Con A-induced suppressor cells are sensitive to PG synthesis inhibitors only if added at the same time as the Con A. Incubation of T cells and Con A for a few days gives rise to a suppressor cell population which is no longer sensitive to PG synthesis inhibitors. Coupled with the data presented in this report, it may be argued that while the macrophage is the major PG-producing cell it may have as its target not only helper T cells or B cells but a glass-adherent, thy-1-sensitive lymphocyte which can be induced by PG to act as a suppressor cell. A last comment in this regard concerns the work by Wieder & Webb (submitted for publication) in which it is shown that immunization abolishes PG-mediated suppression. We interpret these results to suggest that the PG-sensitive suppressor T-cell functions only during the early stages of a primary immune response when cells are relatively undifferentiated. Antigen or perhaps mitogen driven differentiation can cause the loss of this PG-activated suppressor function by what are likely to be immature T cells.

REFERENCES

1. Goodwin, J. S., and Webb, D. R., *Clinical Immunol. Immunopathol.* **15,** 106, 1980.
2. Goodwin, J. S., Bankhurst, A. D., and Messner, R. P., *J. Exp. Med.* **146,** 1719, 1977.
3. Webb, D. R., and Jamieson, A. T., *Cell Immunol.* **24,** 45, 1976.
4. Webb, D. R., and Nowowiejski, I., *Cell Immunol.* **41,** 72, 1978.
5. Webb, D. R., Rogers, T. J., and Nowowiejski, I., *Ann. N.Y. Acad. Sci.* **332,** 262, 1979.
6. Humes, J. L., Bonney, R. J., Pelus, L., Dahlgren, M. E., Sadowski, S. J., Kuehl, F. A., and Davies, P., *Nature (London)* **269,** 149, 1977.
7. Grimm, W., Seitz, M., Kirchner, H., and Gemsa, D., *Cell. Immunol.* **40,** 419, 1978.
8. Jaffe, B. M., and Behrman, H. R., *In* "Methods of Hormone Radioimmunoassay," p. 19. Academic Press, New York, 1974.
9. Kirchner, H., Muchmore, A. V., Chused, T. M., and Holden, H. T., *J. Immunol.* **114,** 206, 1975.
10. Fernbach, B. R., Kirchner, H., and Herberman, R. B., *Cell. Immunol.* **22,** 399, 1976.
11. Weiss, A., and Fitch, F., *J. Immunol.* **120,** 357, 1978.
12. Oehler, J., Herberman, R., Campbell, D., and Djeu, J., *Cell. Immunol.* **29,** 238, 1977.
13. Goodwin, J., Bankhurst, A., and Messner, R., *J. Exp. Med.* **146,** 1719, 1977.
14. Kemp, J., Lovie, D., Mattingly, J., Bennet, J., Higuchi, C., Pretell, J., Horowitz, M., and Gershon, R., *J. Immunopharmacol.* **2,** 471, 1980.
15. Orme, I. M., and Shand, F. L., *Int. J. Immunopharmacol.* **2,** 245, 1980.
16. Orme, I. M., and Shand, F. L., *Int. J. Immunopharmacol.* **3,** 15, 1981.

CELLULAR IMMUNOLOGY 63, 329–334 (1981)

Immunoregulation Mediated by the Sympathetic Nervous System, II

ADRIANA DEL REY,* HUGO O. BESEDOVSKY,* ERNST SORKIN,* MOSÉ DA PRADA,† AND STEFAN ARRENBRECHT‡

*Medical Department, Swiss Research Institute, CH-7270 Davos, †Pharmaceutical Research Department, F. Hoffmann–La Roche & Company, AG, CH-4002 Basel, and ‡University Hospital, CH-8000 Zürich, Switzerland

Received January 12, 1981; accepted June 17, 1981

The effect of acute immunization or continuous environmental antigenic exposure on noradrenaline (NA) content of rat lymphoid organs was studied. Immunization with sheep red blood cells resulted in a decrease in splenic NA content. In other experiments, NA levels were determined in lymphoid and nonlymphoid organs of SPF rats exposed to naturally occurring environmental antigens, as well as in germ-free animals of the same strain. Spleen, thymus, and lymph nodes in SPF rats contained about 50% less NA than germ-free animals. With the exception of the adrenals, nonlymphoid organs showed no such a difference. Taken as a whole, the present results and our previous data on immunosuppressive influences of the sympathetic innervation on lymphoid organs support the notion that the sympathetic system plays a role in immunoregulation.

INTRODUCTION

Cells involved in the immune response perform in an environment containing hormones and neurotransmitters. It has been already shown that these regulatory mediators can influence the intensity and time course of such a response (1). However, the possibility that the immune response itself can affect neuroendocrine function has only recently been considered. Experimental evidence shows in fact that the immune response can bring about phasic changes in hormone (2) and neurotransmitter (3) levels as well as in electrical activity of neurons located in the medial hypothalamus (4). On the basis of these findings, we have proposed a network of dynamic interactions between the immune and neuroendocrine systems which could operate in a regulatory fashion during ontogeny and adult life (1).

With regard to the involvement of the sympathetic nervous system, it has been previously reported that interference with its activity or administration of adrenergic agonists affects immune mechanisms (3). Thus, sympathetic denervation enhances the immune response to sheep red blood cells (SRBC) whereas α-agonist drugs exert suppressive effects. Still more impressive is the fact that phasic changes in splenic noradrenaline (NA) were detected during the immune response, which reflect changes in the sympathetic nerve activity of the spleen. These data strongly suggest a contribution of the sympathetic system to immunoregulation.

In the present work we report on further experimental evidence in support of

0008-8749/81/140329-06$02.00/0

this concept. The level of the sympathetic neurotransmitter NA in lymphoid organs of rats exposed to two different modalities of immunological stimulation is studied. In one type of experiment, animals were exposed to one acute antigenic challenge under conventional environmental conditions and NA was determined in spleen. In other experiments, NA levels of lymphoid and nonlymphoid organs of animals continuously exposed to naturally occurring environmental antigens under specific pathogen-free (SPF) conditions, were compared with those of their germ-free (GF) counterparts.

MATERIALS AND METHODS

Animals. SPF female Holtzman rats, 250–300 g were used for the immunization experiments using SRBC as antigen. Germ-free and SPF male Albino rats (Wistar origin, outbred stock) were supplied by the Institute of Biological and Medical Research, Ltd., Füllinsdorf. SPF rats were kept under barrier-maintained conditions. GF animals were grown in plastic isolators. Both SPF and GF animals were fed with identical sterilized NAFAG No. 857 DVOD pellets (121°C, 20 min), manufactured by NAFAG Nähr- und Futtermittel, AG, Gossau. Sterile autoclaved water was given *ad lib.* Extensive microbiological tests were performed by the animal supplier. In contrast to GF rats, SPF animals contained, as expected, a varied microbial flora.

Immunization. SRBC were used as antigen to immunize Holtzman rats. SRBC were washed three times with saline (0.8% NaCl) and thereafter 1 ml of a cell suspension containing 5×10^9 erythrocytes was injected intraperitoneally into rats. Controls were injected with 1 ml physiological saline solution.

Evaluation of the immune response. Plaque-forming cells (PFC) were determined according to the Jerne–Nordin technique (5) using splenic cells taken 3 days after the injection of SRBC.

Measurement of noradrenaline content of organs. For measurement of NA, animals were injected ip with pentobarbital (Nembutal, Abbott, 60 mg/kg) and killed by decapitation. Spleens from those animals which were injected with SRBC or saline (controls) were removed and weighed and each organ divided into two parts. One portion was used for evaluation of the immune response, the other was stored at −80°C until NA assay. For the GF and SPF experiments, spleen, thymus, mesentric lymph nodes, adrenals, and a portion of stomach fundus and small intestine (ileum) were removed, immediately frozen, and stored until assay.

The radiometric–enzymatic assay for measurement of femtomolar ($10^{-15}\,M$) quantities of catecholamines as described by Da Prada and Zürcher (6) was applied to quantify NA in the different organs as well as NA and adrenaline (A) in adrenals. The method consists essentially in conversion of the catecholamines into their *O*-methylated analogs by catechol-*O*-methyltransferase in the presence of *S*-adenosyl [^{3}H]methionine and thereafter extraction in the presence of sodium tetraphenylborate. This extraction, together with an improved quick chromatographic separation and the oxidation of the labeled NA derivative to vanillin, yields extremely high sensitivity and specificity.

Statistical evaluation. Student's *t* test was used to assess the significance between two means. Results are expressed as mean ± SEM.

TABLE 1

Immune Response Induced Decrease in Noradrenaline Content of Rat Spleen

	PFC per spleen	Noradrenaline (ng/g spleen)	Noradrenaline (ng/spleen)
Control ($n = 8$)	—	1371 ± 132	1372 ± 95
Immunized ($n = 8$)	293,758 ± 68,722	799 ± 57	962 ± 42
P		<0.005	<0.005

RESULTS

The Immune Response against SRBC Induces a Decrease in Spleen NA Levels

Rats were immunized with SRBC and killed 3 days later. This time was chosen because it was shown before that just prior to the peak of the immune response as measured by direct PFC, the maximum change in splenic NA levels occurs (3). In agreement with previous findings, immunized animals have 30–40% less splenic NA content when compared with the controls. This fact was observed regardless of whether the results are expressed as NA content per gram tissue or per total spleen (Table 1).

Differences in NA Levels in Lymphoid Organs of GF and SPF Animals

In order to investigate whether continuous exposure to environmental antigenic challenge can influence sympathetic nervous activity, we determined NA tissue content in lymphoid and nonlymphoid organs of SPF and GF rats.

For the assessment of the immunological status of the animals, total serum IgG was determined using the agar precipitation assay both in GF and in SPF rats. SPF rats had as expected IgG blood levels threefold higher than those of GF animals. No differences were noted in blood albumin levels. An additional control for the GF status was served by the weights of spleen and thymus, which were higher in SPF than GF rats.

We next proceeded to determine whether NA contents of lymphoid organs dif-

TABLE 2

Comparison between NA Content of Lymphoid and Nonlymphoid Organs in SPF and Germ-Free Rats

	Spleen NA		Thymus NA		Lymph node NA	Stomach Na	Intestine NA
	ng/g	ng/spleen	ng/g	ng/thymus	(ng/g)	(ng/g)	(ng/g)
Germ-free ($n = 10$)	1219.12 ± 86.37	661.8 ± 29.04	82.89 ± 8.19	27.95 ± 2.81	130.8 ± 8.6	268.80 ± 9.29	294.98 ± 9.36
SPF ($n = 10$)	608.02 ± 88.44	515.25 ± 44.40	46.84 ± 1.63	21.12 ± 0.83	74.0 ± 3.6	298.77 ± 23.15	300.03 ± 10.42
P	<0.001	<0.02	<0.001	<0.05	<0.001	n.s.	n.s.

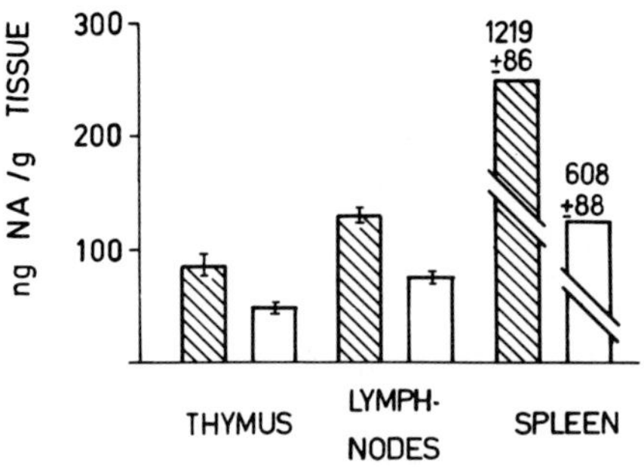

FIG. 1. Lymphoid organs of SPF rats contain less noradrenaline than those of GF animals. □, SPF; ▨, GF. Each column represents the average ± SEM.

fered by measuring NA in spleen, thymus, and lymph nodes. Stomach and intestine served as control tissues. The results shown in Table 2 and Fig. 1 indicate that lymphoid tissue of SPF animals contain about 50% less NA than GF animals. This difference can not only be accounted for by differences in organ weights as the total NA organ content was also lower in SPF rats. In contrast to the lymphoid organs, the NA contents of stomach and intestine were similar regardless of whether the rats were kept in SPF or in GF conditions. It is noteworthy that also in the acute form of immunological challenge by SRBC (Table 1), NA reduction occurred in the spleen but not in the heart (3).

Adrenal Catecholamine Content in SPF and GF Animals

In order to evaluate whether the function of the adrenal medulla also differs in SPF and GF conditions, A and NA contents of the adrenal gland were simultaneously determined. GF animals had adrenals larger than those of SPF animals and, as shown in Table 3, the total adrenal NA and A content was significantly higher in GF animals.

DISCUSSION

In the present report, it is shown that immunization with SRBC generates a decrease in NA content in the spleen of rats (Table 1). These data confirm previously reported results (3) which suggested that it is the immune response which leads to the NA decrease. This phenomenon was interpreted to be a consequence of an immunologically triggered sympathetic mechanism with immunoregulatory implications. In the conditions studied, animals were exposed to a massive antigenic challenge. While such a procedure is common to many experimental designs it

TABLE 3

Adrenal Glands of SPF Rats Contain Less Catecholamines than Those of GF Animals

	Noradrenalin (μg/adrenal)	Adrenaline (μg/adrenal)
Germ-free	4.67 ± 0.25	16.43 ± 1.02
SPF	3.33 ± 0.15	13.93 ± 0.58
P	< 0.001	<0.001

probably has similarities only with infections where acute antigenic stimulation occurs. Whether immune responses elicited by continuous exposure to environmental antigens contribute to define NA levels in lymphoid organs was studied by comparing SPF and GF animals. We chose to make this comparison as it allowed the prediction that SPF rats as a consequence of their higher immunological activity should show lower neurotransmitter levels in lymphoid organs than their GF counterparts. The experimental evidence supports this assumption in that three lymphoid organs (spleen, thymus, and lymph nodes) of SPF animals contained about half as much NA than GF animals (Fig. 1 and Table 2). We assume that it is the response to a more continuous and varied antigenic stimulation which contributes or even is the cause of the lower NA content in lymphoid tissue of SPF animals. In support of this view is the fact that differences in NA content are restricted to organs with immunologic functions.

The mechanism(s) responsible for the lowering in NA in lymphoid organs of SPF rats is unknown. It is likely that similar to the NA decrease in the spleen of SRBC-challenged animals, this decrease is *not* caused by the antigen, but is induced by the immune response itself.

Is the NA decrease to be viewed as a purely local phenomenon or is it regulated by central mechanisms? It is known that locally generated changes in tissue NA levels are rapidly counteracted by changes in tyrosine hydroxylase activity, the rate-limiting step for NA synthesis (7). Thus, unless specific inhibitors of tyrosine hydroxylase activity are released from immunologically responding cells which in turn may reduce NA synthesis, local factors are hardly the only cause of the NA decrease. The fact that the thymus, an organ with only marginal direct involvement in immune responses, also has a lower NA content in SPF animals favors the interpretation that factor(s) released locally by immunologically responding cells are not directly inhibiting the sympathetic nerve activity of lymphoid organs.

Furthermore, the fact that adrenal catecholamine content is lower in SPF than in GF animals indicates that products of activated lymphoid cells reach central structures which directly or indirectly control adrenal medulla function (Table 3). All these data and arguments together support the view that the immune response influences, probably via central mechanisms, the sympathetic nerve activity of lymphoid organs. However, our experiments can not exclude that a local mechanism also may contribute to the observed NA changes in lymphoid tissues. Thus, local NA levels could be influenced by alterations or shifts in immunologically competent cell populations which diminish NA receptors or other binding sites per cell.

The previously described evidence that sympathetic innervation and neurotransmitters exert inhibitory effects on immune mechanisms (3) implies that changes in tissue NA content can affect the performance of immunological cells. The decrease in catecholamine levels induced by immune responses is therefore likely to reflect the existence of sympathetic immunoregulatory circuits. What one likes to know now is the nature of the links between the immune system and the sympathetic nervous system and how sympathetic signals are coordinated with autoregulatory immunologic circuits.

ACKNOWLEDGMENTS

This work was supported by the Swiss National Science Foundation, Grant 3.213.77 and by F. Hoffmann-La Roche & Company, AG, Basel.

REFERENCES

1. Besedovsky, H. O., and Sorkin, E., *Clin. Exp. Immunol.* **27,** 1, 1977.
2. Besedovsky, H. O., Sorkin, E., Keller, M., and Müller, J., *Proc. Soc. Exp. Biol. Med.* **150,** 466, 1975.
3. Besedovsky, H. O., del Rey, A., Sorkin, E., Da Prada, M., and Keller, H. H., *Cell. Immunol.* **48,** 346, 1979.
4. Besedovsky, H. O., Sorkin, E., Felix, D., and Haas, H., *Eur. J. Immunol.* **7,** 325, 1977.
5. Jerne, N. K., and Nordin, A. A., *Science* **140,** 405, 1963.
6. Da Prada, M., and Zürcher, G., *Life Sci.* **19,** 1161, 1976.
7. Euler, U. S. v., *In* "Handbook of Experimental Pharmacology" (O. Eichler, A. Rarah, H. Herken, and A. D. Welch, Eds.), Vol. XXXIII, pp. 186–230. Springer-Verlag, Berlin/Heidelberg/New York, 1972.

CELLULAR IMMUNOLOGY 63, 335–348 (1981)

Stimulatory Cells in the Generation of T-Cell-Mediated Cytotoxicity: Potent Stimulating Activity of a Small Radioresistant Spleen Cell Population (RSCs)[1]

THIERRY REME,[2] ARNAUD DUPUY D'ANGEAC, MICHÈLE RADAL, AND BERNARD SERROU

Laboratorie d'Immunopharmacologie des Tumeurs, Centre Paul Lamarque, Hôpital St. Eloi, 34033 Montpellier, France

Received January 13, 1981; accepted June 15, 1981

The combined effects of irradiation followed by cultivation on a total spleen cell population in order to study the evolution of the stimulating potential in the *in vitro* generation of allogeneic cytotoxic T lymphocytes (CTLs) were tested. Results revealed that, after 3 days and up to at least 7 days of cultivating irradiated (1000 rad) spleen cells, the remaining living cells (radioresistant spleen cells or RSC) have the same potential to generate CTLs as irradiated noncultivated spleen cells. RSC can resist a 5000-rad irradiation and induce a primary cytotoxic response pattern similar to that of total spleen cells; they act in primary as well as in secondary cultures with optimal responder to RSC ratios of about 100, but are still stimulatory at MLC ratios up to 1000 or 5000. They are lysed by specific allogeneic CTLs and readily inhibit the specific lysis of H-2-identical labeled targets by CTLs. RSCs do not express unusual levels of H-2 or Ia antigens and do stimulate purified T cells. Alloantisera anti-H-2 are able to completely block the RSC-induced generation of CTL. This RSC population may prove to be a good model to study non-H-2- or H-2-associated, nonserologically detectable determinants interacting in the generation of T-cell-mediated cytotoxicity.

INTRODUCTION

The generation of cytolytic T lymphocytes (CTL) in allogeneic mixed lymphocyte cultures (MLC) is generally achieved using either lethally irradiated or mitomycin C-treated spleen cells as stimulating cells. It is generally believed that these stimulating cells, having presented the antigen during the first 24 to 48 hr of culture, are then dead or become unnecessary after 2 days (1, 2). Once triggered, a responder T-cell subpopulation differentiates into CTL and proliferates according to cooperative mechanisms now under intensive study (3–6). The resulting cytotoxic activity reaches a peak after 4–6 days according to the culture conditions (7, 8).

However, it has been suggested that proliferative T cells in mixed leukocyte reactions could bind alloantigens released by stimulating cells (9). Moreover, it is not excluded that soluble antigens can bind to macrophage determinants interacting with T cells (10–12). This raises the problem of knowing whether the presence of

[1] INSERM U 236; CNRS ERA 844.
[2] To whom reprint requests should be addressed.

0008-8749/81/140335-14$02.00/0

stimulator determinants, whatever their form, is necessary or not for the further development of cytotoxic activity.

Our experiments were designed to study the residual stimulating potential in MLC after supposed sensitization of responder populations. We report that the combined effects of irradiation and precultivation during at least 2 to 3 days of spleen cells reveal a non-T, highly radioresistant, nonadherent subpopulation (RSC) having a stimulating potential about 100 times higher than the total spleen cell population used immediately after irradiation. RSCs express relatively high levels of Ia antigens which have been shown to actively participate in stimulation.

Further characterization of these RSCs showed that their susceptibility to lysis by specific allogeneic CTLs is good compared to that of normal spleen cells, which are at most only poorly lysed (13–15), and to Con A-activated splenocytes and DBA/2 P 815 tumor cells, which are readily lysed by CTLs (16, 17). In parallel, the amount of H-2 antigens present in RSCs membranes was quantitatively evaluated and compared to that present on Con A blast cells and P 815 tumor cells.

Since this population does not express unusual levels of serologically detected alloantigens, it may prove to be a good model to study the role of non-H-2 or nonserologically detectable H-2-associated determinants in the generation of cytolytic T lymphocytes.

MATERIALS AND METHODS

Mice. H-2 haplotypes are represented in parentheses. C57Bl/6 (B6,b), DBA/2 (d), B10D2 (d), C57B1/10 (B10,b), B10A (5R) (b/a), AKR (k), mice were purchased from the Centre de Selection et Elevage des Animaux de Laboratoire (Orléans) and maintained in our animal facilities under standard conditions.

Primary MLC. B6 spleen cells (5×10^6) were placed in each of 24 flat-bottomed wells of a Linbro plate (Linbro Scientific, Hamden, Conn.) in RPMI 1640 medium (Flow Laboratories, Rockville, Md.) with antibiotics, 5×10^{-5} *M* in 2-mercaptoethanol, supplemented with 5% fetal calf serum (FCS, Flow). This medium is referred to as MLC medium. Various ratios of the different stimulator cells in the same medium were added to each flask to give a final volume of 2 ml per well. Cultures were left at 37°C for the desired period in a water-saturated atmosphere containing 5% CO2. The standard yield for a 4-day culture is usually 60–80% of the total cell input.

In view of eliciting a secondary CTL activity, primary cultures were modified as follows: B6 spleen cells (25×10^6) and 25×10^6 irradiated (1000 rad) DBA/2 spleen cells were placed in 20 ml of MLC medium in 3013 F culture flasks (Falcon, Oxnard, Calif.) and cultivated in an upright position for 12 to 14 days. Memory cells were then harvested and washed twice. The standard yield of such primary cultures is 15–20% of the total responder cell input.

Secondary MLC. Secondary MLC were established by mixing 2×10^6 viable nucleated 14-day-stimulated C57Bl/6 anti-DBA/2 memory cells with 2×10^6 viable nucleated DBA/2 spleen cells in 24 flat-bottomed linbro plate wells (Linbro Scientific). The killing assay was performed on Day 3 or 4.

RSC preparation. Spleens were excised under sterile conditions in RPMI medium and immediately irradiated at a rate of 500 rad/min in No. 2006 tubes (Falcon) placed directly on the collimator of an inverted ^{60}Co bomb. Spleens were then minced and 200×10^6 cells seeded with 30 ml of MLC medium in 3024 F flasks (Falcon). Flasks were placed in the horizontal position at 37°C in a water-saturated atmosphere containing 5% CO2 for the desired culture period (standard 3 days) then harvested by gently flushing the cells with fresh MLC medium. Adherent cells were left in the flask, and supernatant cells (RSC) were removed. The standard yield of such a preculture ranges between 1 and 5% of the total cell input. For MLC initiation with RSC, the optimal responder to stimulator cell ratio is calculated as:

Responder to stimulator total spleen cell ratio used in control experiments (i.e., 1) ÷ % of surviving RSC after irradiation and precultivation.

Target cells. P 815 (DBA/2 mastocytoma, H-2^d) was maintained as an ascites by serial transfer of 10^7 cells weekly in DBA/2 mice. P 815 was also passaged *in vitro* in tissue culture flasks (Falcon, 3024 Division of Bioquest) in a final volume of 30 ml. The culture medium was RPMI 1640 (Microbiological Associates, Bethesda, Md.) supplemented with penicillin, streptomycin, and 10% fetal calf serum. the cells were incubated at 37°C in a 5% CO_2–95% air atmosphere. EL4 (B6 thymoma, H-2^b) and RDMA (AKR lymphoma, H-2^k) were maintained *in vitro* under the same conditions as P 815.

Con A-activated spleen cells were prepared by incubating 5×10^7 viable cells in 35-mm plastic dishes in 2 ml of medium containing 2 μg of Con A (Calbiochem, San Diego, Calif.) per milliliter. After 2 days, the cells were harvested and incubated with 0.05 *M* methyl mannoside for 1–3 hr before use as targets. Lipopolysaccharide (LPS)-activated spleen cells were prepared by incubating 5×10^6 viable cells in plastic dishes in 2 ml of medium (300 I Falcon Plastics) containing 25 μg/ml of LPS (Sigma, St. Louis, Mo.). Cells were collected after 2 days and washed. Viability was greater than 90% by trypan blue exclusion. RSCs, P 815, Con A blasts, and LPS blasts were labeled by incubation for 30 min at 37°C with 200 μCi of Na_2CrO_4 (CEA, France) in RPMI 1640-supplemented medium in a 5% CO_2–95% air atmosphere.

Chromium release. The micromethod used and described extensively elsewhere (18, 19) is a modification of the assay of Brunner *et al.* (20). Briefly, 10^4 ^{51}Cr-labeled target cells in 100 μl of RPMI 1640 containing 5% fetal calf serum (assay medium) were incubated for 3 hr in U-bottomed plates (Linbro) with various ratios of effector cells in 100 μl of assay medium. Supernatants were then collected with a "Skatron" apparatus (Skatron, Sweden). Lytic units per million cells (LU/M) and per culture (LU/C) were calculated according to the number of effector cells giving a 50% chromium release compared to the spontaneous release and total release in 0.1 *N* HCl.

Experiments involving inhibition of lysis of ^{51}Cr-labeled normal P 815 cells by anti-H-2^d CTLs are performed by adding serial dilutions of unlabeled targets in 100 μl of medium to 10^4 ^{51}Cr-labeled P 815 cells in 100 μl of medium prior to the addition of 100 μl medium containing effector cells.

Nylon wool column treatment. This technique is modified from the original method by Julius *et al.* (21): nylon wool in RPMI 1640 (0.6 g) was carefully dilascerated in a large petri dish, using two 19-gauge needles, then placed in a 10-ml syringe, equilibrated with MLC medium, and covered with Blenderm tape (3M, St. Paul, Minn.) After the columns were stabilized for 40 min at 37°C in 5% CO_2

water-saturated air, up to 2×10^8 spleen cells were allowed to penetrate the column and incubation continued for another 40 min.

Nonadherent cells were harvested by elution with MLC medium and the usual yield for such a separation is 25% of the cell input.

Antisera. Alloantiserum to H-2 was prepared by multiple ip injections of 2×10^7 B10D2 spleen cells into C57B1/10 mice. B10S anti-B10S (7R) was a gift from Dr. Liabeuf at the Centre d'Immunology INSERM CNRS, Marseille. Anti-Ia^k (ATH anti-ATL) antiserum was purchased from Cedarlane and monoclonal anti-Thy 1.2 from New England Nuclear (Boston, Mass.).

Antisera and complement treatment. Cells to be tested were labeled with 200 μCi of ^{51}Cr as described for the CRT and washed twice, and aliquots of packed cells were resuspended to the desired concentration in the final dilution of antiserum to be tested. After 30 min on ice with occasional shaking, cells were washed twice, distributed in microtiter plates in 150 μl volumes, and 100 μl of either medium (spontaneous release), 0.1 *N* HCl (total release) or complement to a final dilution of 1/12 of normal rabbit complement was added. Complement was previously selected for minimal cytotoxicity and adsorbed with a mixture of normal cells. After 1 hr at 37°C, supernatants were collected as described for the CRT and counted.

Adsorption of antibodies to H-2. Serial dilutions of cells, P 815 cells, DBA/2 RSCs, DBA/2 Con A blast spleen cells, and C57Bl/6 RSCs washed three times by repeated cycles of centrifugation were distributed into microtest tubes and centrifuged (450*g*, 5 min). The supernatants were removed and the packed cells were resuspended in 60 μl of antiserum to $H\text{-}2^d$ or antiserum to $H\text{-}2D^d$ at dilutions that would lyse approximately 75% of the target cells with complement in a standard cytotoxic assay.

After 30 min on ice, during which time the tubes were periodically agitated by gentle vortex mixing, the cells were packed by centrifugation (800*g* 5 min.), and samples of the supernatant were diluted and distributed for storage at −70°C until assayed for cytotoxic antibodies.

Fc receptor determination. This technique is adapted from the method originally described by Caraux *et al.* (22). Chicken red blood cells (CRBC) were washed twice in PBS and conjugated volume to volume with a subagglutinating dilution of rabbit IgG anti-CRBC at 37°C for 30 min. After washing, complexed CRBC were adjusted to 0.5%. Cells (200,000) to be tested in 100 μl were added to 100 μl of the complex and centrifuged at 300*g* for 5 min at 4°C. Erythrocyte-antibody (EA) rosettes were then resuspended and counted immediately.

RESULTS

Kinetics of the Primary Response to RSC

We first compared the kinetics for the development of primary cytotoxic activity raised by RSC stimulation to the activity generated in MLC with irradiated DBA/2 spleen cells used immediately. RSC in this stimulation were used at the optimal MLC ratio as indicated under Material and Methods.

Figure 1 shows that the B6 CTL activity per culture for RSC primary stimulation peaks slightly later than the stimulation by irradiated spleen cells in the experimental culture conditions used. The levels of cytotoxicity in both cases are com-

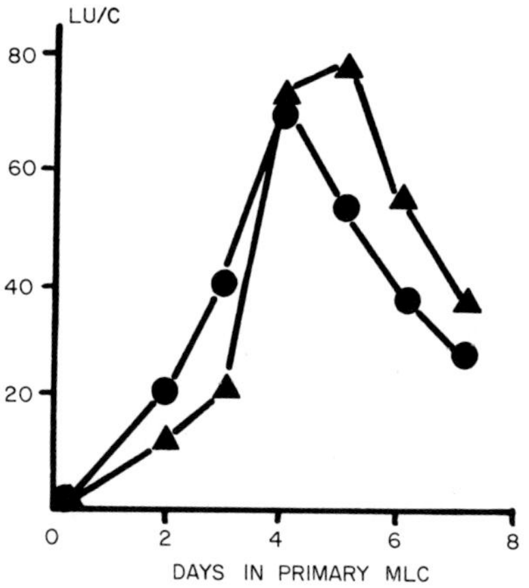

FIG. 1. Kinetics of the primary cytotoxic response of B6 spleen cells stimulated in MLC with either total DBA/2 spleen cells. (●) 1000-rad-irradiated fresh DBA/2 spleen cells at 1:1 B6) or DBA/2 RSC (▲) 1000-rad-irradiated DBA/2 spleen cells (preincubated for 3 days) at the optimal MLC ratio, 0.07:1 B6).

parable at Day 4 for irradiated total DBA/2 spleen cells and Days 4 to 5 for DBA/2 RSC.

Effects of γ-Ray Doses on RSC Expression

We analyzed the effect of increasing ^{60}Co doses on the stimulating potential of total DBA/2 spleen cells used immediately compared to RSC receiving the same dose and precultivated for 3 days. The responder to stimulator cell ratio was always 1 for DBA/2 spleen cells, but was corrected for cell death for RSC after each dose studied and 3 days of precultivation. In the experiment described in Fig. 2, this yield ranged from 1% for a 1000-rad irradiation, to 0.25% for 5000 rad and 0.1% for 10,000 rad. The first curve displayed on Fig. 2 shows that the stimulation on normal B6 spleen cells by differently irradiated DBA/2 spleen cells is maintained

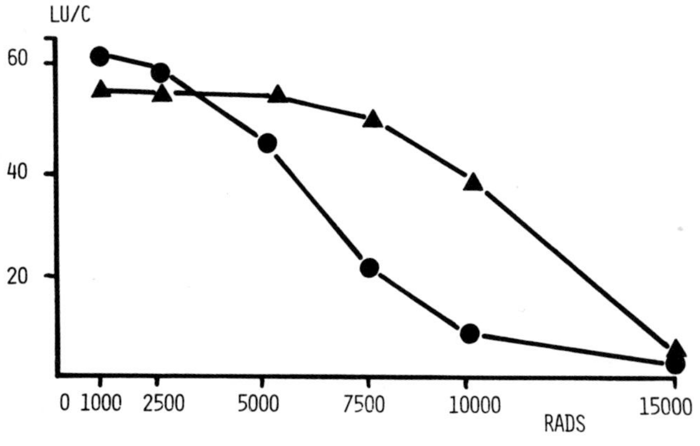

FIG. 2. Four-day primary cytotoxic response of B6 spleen cells to freshly irradiated normal DBA/2 spleen cells (▲) receiving various doses of γ rays or DBA/2 RSC (●) induced by the same doses.

at a high level even after a 7500-rad irradiation. Immediately and for a few hours following irradiation, no stimulating cells died when evaluated by trypan blue exclusion test. The second curve which represents the stimulation of normal B6 spleen cells by the DBA/2 RSCs as a function of irradiation dose shows that stimulation decreases above 5000 rad, suggesting that RSC or their precursors are highly radioresistant.

Influence of the Precultivation Period and Dose–Response Analysis of the RSC Stimulating Activity

At least 3 days are necessary to eliminate the cells committed to die after irradiation. We tested the ability of a longer period of precultivation to yield RSC: after 7 days of preculture, the viable cell yield from the 1000-rad-irradiated DBA/2 is about twofold less than the one obtained for a 3-day preculture. The upper part of Table 1 shows the stimulating potential of total spleen cells compared to RSC generated after either 3 or 7 days cultivation. There is clear evidence that RSC are still strongly active after 7 days (73 LU/C at the optimal ratio of 130 responder cells for one stimulator cell compared to 103 LU/C at the optimal MLC ratio of 60 for 3 day RSC).

The optimal concentration of cells responsible for stimulation in the stimulating population was further assessed by dilution experiments in primary as well as in secondary activations. Results of a typical experiment are displayed in the lower part of Table 1. The stimulating potential of RSC was evaluated for the optimal MLC ratio (80 responder cells for 1 stimulator cell) as well as for fourfold concentrated or diluted suspensions. For primary, as in secondary responses, maximal cytotoxic activity is obtained for the optimal MLC ratio calculated for viable cell yield. Cytolytic activity is then comparable to that obtained with freshly irradiated DBA/2 spleen cells, though slightly higher. When the concentration of RSC used in the stimulation is increased beyond optimum, there is a decrease in cytotoxic response and primary (23 versus 53 LU/C) and secondary (34 versus 49 LU/C) response.

In the same way, dilution of the optimal concentration of RSC leads to a decrease of induced cytotoxicity. This decrease is more sensitive for secondary than primary response. However, there is still a consistent cytotoxic activity induced by MLC ratios of more than 1000 responder cells per stimulating cell in primary culture, whereas the response against total spleen cells is abolished at MLC ratios greater than 100. There is a still detectable cytotoxicity induced in secondary response with a MLC ratio greater than 5000 responder cells per stimulating cell.

Surface Markers on RSC

Some of the antigenic markers have been looked at on the DBA/2 RSCs. First, labeling of RSC with chromium-51 and lysis assay of these targets by anti-Thy 1.2 plus complement leads to the conclusion that RSCs are not T cells, since they do not express detectable Thy 1.2 antigen (Table 2). A parallel experiment on thymocytes confirmed the activity of the antiserum and complement used (data not shown). Markers were studied in parallel on normal DBA/2 spleen cells.

The ability of these cells to bind anti-H-2^d alloantibodies was then used to determine whether the presence of the serologically defined cell surface antigen coded

TABLE 1

Stimulating Activity of DBA/2 RSC as a Function of Precultivation Period and MLC Ratio in Primary and Secondary 4-Day MLC

	Responder cell	Number ($\times 10^6$)	Stimulator cell	Number	MLC ratio	LU/M	LU/C
Expt 1							
Primary response	Normal B6 spleen	5	Total DBA/2 spleen	5.0×10^6	1[a]	31	118
		5	DBA/2 RSC precultured for 3 days	8.3×10^4	60[a]	43	103
		5	DBA/2 RSC precultured for 7 days	3.8×10^4	130[a]	19	73
Expt 2							
Primary response	Normal B6 spleen	5	Total DBA/2 spleen	5.0×10^6	1[a]	7	36
		5		2.5×10^5	20	3	10
		5		6.3×10^4	80	1	4
		5		1.6×10^4	320	0	0
		5	DBA/2 RSC precultured for 3 days	2.5×10^5	20	8	23
		5		6.3×10^4	80[a]	12	49
		5		1.6×10^4	320	10	10
		5		3.9×10^3	1280	2	4
		5		9.8×10^2	5120	0	0
Secondary response	B6 anti-DBA/2 spleen	2	None	—	—	0	0
		2	Total DBA/2 spleen	2.0×10^6	1[a]	20	41
		2	DBA/2 RSC precultured for 3 days	1.0×10^5	20	30	34
		2		2.5×10^4	80[a]	36	53
		2		6.3×10^3	320	16	37
		2		1.6×10^3	1280	6	6
		2		3.9×10^2	5120	1	2

[a] Optimal MLC ratio calculated as indicated under Materials and Methods.

TABLE 2

Surface Markers of DBA/2 RSC Compared to Normal DBA/2 Spleen Cells

Cell treatment	DBA/2 RSC: % chromium release, –	DBA/2 RSC: % chromium release, + complement	DBA/2 RSC: % positive cells (range)	Normal DBA/2 spleen cells: % trypan blue excluding cells, –	Normal DBA/2 spleen cells: % trypan blue excluding cells, + complement	Normal DBA/2 spleen cells: % Positive cells (range)
Normal mouse serum	0	6		5	4	
Anti-Thy 1.2 antiserum (monoclonal) diluted 1/20	0	4		4	36	
Anti-H-2D^d antiserum (B10S αB10S (7R)) diluted 1/50	11	66		3	61	
Anti-Ia^k antiserum (ATL α ATH) diluted 1/20	8	39		5	55	
Anti-Ig antiserum (FITC) diluted 1/5			7–12			46–54
Peroxydase staining			≤10 (mostly granulocytes)			≤10 (granulocytes and monocytes)
Fc Receptors detected with chicken red cells and rabbit anti-CRBc antiserum			25–70			28–41

for by the H-2 complex was different on DBA/2 RSCs compared to DBA/2 Con A blast spleen cells or P 815 cells. The RSCs were identical to P 815 and DBA/2 Con A blast spleen cells in their capacity to absorb cytotoxic antibodies from anti-H-2^d (C57B1/10 anti-B10D2) antisera (Fig. 3B). They were also equally able to absorb cytotoxic antibodies from antisera restricted to the D^d gene products (B10S anti-B10S (7R)) as P 815 and DBA/2 Con A spleen cells (Fig. 3C). These results show that DBA/2 RSCs, P 815, and DBA/2 Con A blast spleen cells have similar amounts of the serologically defined cell surface products of the H-2 complex. In addition DBA/2 RSCs, DBA/2 Con A blast spleen cells, and P 815 were equally susceptible to lysis by B10 anti-B10D2 (anti-H-2^d) antibodies (Fig. 3A) as well as B10S anti-B10S (7R) (anti-H-2D^d) antibodies (Table 2) in the presence of complement. Moreoever, DBA/2 RSC express about 40% Ia-positive cells as shown by anti-Ia^k antiserum and complement treatment, which cross-react with Ia antigens expressed in the H-2^d haplotype (23) of normal cells (Table 2). The presence of B cells and macrophages was further assessed by rabbit anti-mouse Ig membrane fluorescence and peroxidase staining. Results summarized in Table 2 show that very few surface Ig-positive (mean 10%) and peroxidase-positive cells (<1%; granulocyte contamination was less than 10%; all granulocytes were peroxidase positive) are found among RSC. Controls were, respectively, purified B spleen cells, which, under the same conditions were 80% Ig-positive cells; and plastic-petri-dish-adherent spleen cells, which were 72% peroxidase positive (mean values).

Finally DBA/2 RSCs were evaluated for receptors for Fc fragments of IgG using the rosette formation with chicken red blood cells precoated with rabbit anti-CRBC immunoglobulins. The mean of three experiments is depicted in Table 2 and shows that about one-half of DBA/2 RSCs expresses Fc receptors for IgG. However, the variability of such a result is high and the Fc receptor content ranges from 25 to 70% of cells, depending on the experiment. The EA complex was always verified on P 815 cells which express a rather constant level of 25% Fc receptors.

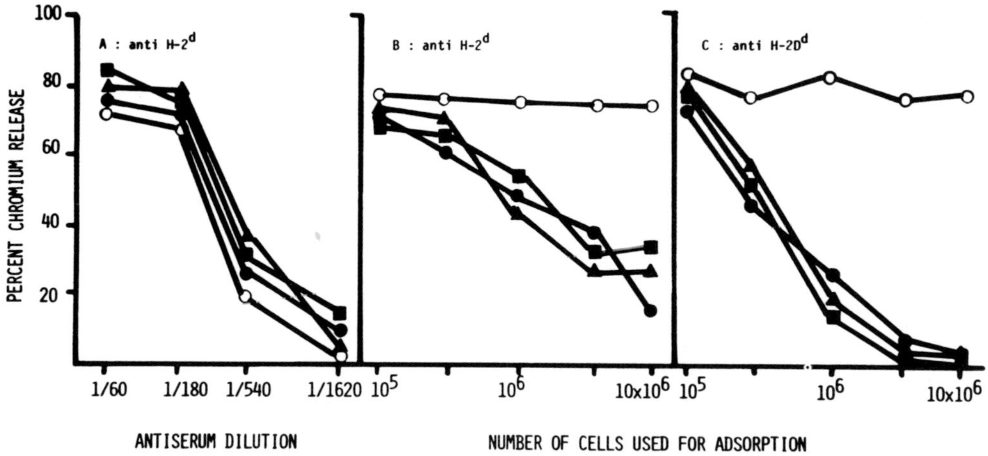

FIG. 3. (A) Detection of H-2^d products on various ^{51}Cr-labeled target by sensitivity to alloantiserum and complement. Serial dilutions of an anti-H-2^d serum (B10 anti-B10D2) and rabbit complement (1/10) were tested for their ability to lyse (●) P 815, (■) DBA/2 Con A-stimulated spleen cells, (○) DBA/2 LPS-stimulated spleen cells and (▲) DBA/2 RSCs. Lysis by normal mouse serum in the presence of complement was 6%. (B) Detection of cell surface products of the H-2^d locus on various cells by adsorption of anti-2^d serum (B10 anti-B10D2). (C) Detection of cell surface product of the H-$2D^d$ locus on various cells by adsorption of anti-H-$2D^d$ serum (B10S anti-B10S(7R) The absorbed and unabsorbed serum samples were tested on ^{51}Cr labelled P 815. The cells used for absorption were (●) P 815, (■) DBA/2 ConA activated spleen cells, (○) B6 RSCs and (▲) DBA/2 RSCs. Lysis by normal mouse serum in the presence of complement was 8%.

Cellular Requirements for RSC Expression

Several experiments have been undertaken to define the prerequisite conditions for expression of RSC-stimulating activity.

Effect of antisera directed against whole H-2 products and Ia antigens during MLC. The generation of CTL to H-$2K^d$ and D^d gene products is specifically inhibited by antisera directed against these same products (24). We therefore tested the central role of alloantigen in such a mechanism during the RSC stimulation by adding an antiserum directed against stimulating cells alloantigens to optimal numbers of RSC. Table 3 (Expt 1) shows that an anti-H-2^d serum added at the onset of MLC abolishes the cytotoxic response of normal B6 spleen cells. (84 LU/C versus 3 LU/C). In the same way, anti-Ia antiserum greatly diminishes the same response. A higher serum concentration might be necessary to completely abolish the response. A nonspecific effect of anti-H-2^d antiserum was further excluded by repeating the experiment with a third-party haplotype (H-2^k RSC from AKR mice), which only slightly decreases (30 LU/C versus 21 LU/C) the CTL generation by RSCs; this might be due to the cross-recognition of some H-2^k determinants by anti-H-2^d antiserum. Furthermore, an eventual toxicity of the antiserum used was excluded by stimulating normal AKR spleen cells with B10 RSC; CTL generation remains unchanged in the presence of B10 anti-B10D2 antiserum (59 LU/C versus 51 LU/C).

Elimination of Ia-positive RSC before MLC. As shown in Table 3 (Expt 2), pretreatment of RSC with anti-ia antiserum plus complement diminishes the ab-

TABLE 3

Cellular Requirements for DBA/2 RSC Expression

Expt	Responder cell	Stimulator cell at optimal MLC ratio	Antiserum added on Day 0 in MLC	LU/M	LU/C	Target cell
1	Normal B6 spleen	Total DBA/2 spleen	—	15	60	P 815
		DBA/2 RSC	—	24	84	P 815
			B10 anti-B10D2 1/20 final	2	3	P 815
			Anti-Ia antiserum 1/10 final	1	2	P 815
		AKR RSC	—	10	30	RDM4
			B10 anti-B10D2 1/20 final	7	21	RDM4
	Normal AKR spleen	B10 RSC	—	28	59	EL4
			B10 anti-B10D2 1/20 final	23	51	EL4
2	Normal B6 spleen	DBA/2 RSC pretreated with medium	—	36	200	P 815
		DBA/2 RSC pretreated with medium + complement 1/12	—	37	266	
		DBA/2 RSC pretrated with anti Ia antiserum 1/20	—	25	160	
		DBA/2 RSC pretreated with anti-Ia antiserum 1/20 + complement 1/12	—	24	48	
3	Normal B6 spleen	DBA/2 RSC	—	12	56	P 815
	B6 spleen cells	DBA/2 RSC	—	27	175	
	nonadherent to nylon wool column	DBA/2 spleen cells not adhering to nylon wool	—	0	0	
4	Normal B6 spleen	DBA/2 RSC generated from total spleen cells	—	28	52	P 815
		DBA/2 RSC prepared from plastic-non-adherent spleen cells	—	20	48	
		DBA/2 RSC prepared from nylon-wool-nonadherent spleen cells	No RSC generated			

solute number of lytic units but the frequency remains unchanged. Efficacy of anti-Ia treatment was assessed by DBA/2 LPS blast killing, which was always greater than 75%.

Elimination of adherent cells from responder cells or RSC before MLC. Cytotoxic activity requires accessory cell cooperation of different origins in order to develop (5, 25). Therefore, we tested the ability of the RSC induction technique to keep active "helper-like" activity in the stimulating population. For this, normal responder B6 spleen cells were purified by nylon wool column (NWC) treatment to eliminate macrophage-like helper cells (25, 26). This was further assessed by stimulating NWC-eluted responder cells by normal DBA/2 NWC-eluted stimulating cells, which repeatedly failed to generate CTLs (Expt 3, Table 3). Normal or NWC-treated responder cells (5×10^6 of each) were then stimulated *in vitro* by DBA/2 RSCs at the optimal MLC ratio.

Results depicted in Table 3 (Expt 3) show that the NWC-treated B6 cells respond two- to threefold more than untreated cells. This supports the fact that RSC are always able to activate purified T cells, the enhancement of cytolytic activity being due only to concentration of CTL precursors by NWC treatment. On the contrary, elimination of cells adherent to nylon wool completely abolishes the generation of RSC (Table 3, Expt 4). However, RSC generated from DBA/2 spleen cells incubated twice on plastic petri dishes for 30 min at 37°C (50% yield) then washed, show unchanged stimulating potential (48 LU/C versus 52 LU/C for controls).

Susceptibility to Lysis of RSCs

When red blood cells are removed by Percoll sedimentation or NH_4Cl treatment, RSCs are lysed by anti-H-2^d CTLs. Their spontaneous release is comparable to that of Con A-activated spleen cells (15–25%).

DBA/2 RSCs are lysed as well as Con A-activated spleen cells and much better than normal unstimulated DBA/2 spleen cells which are almost refractory to cytolysis (Figs. 4B and 5A). DBA/2 RSCs are less susceptible to lysis than P 815.

In order to investigate the expression of H-2 gene products on RSC membranes we used CTLs directed against only the K or D part of H-2^d. B10 A (5R) anti-DBA/2 and HTG anti-DBA/2 directed respectively against H-$2K^d$ and H-$2D^d$ were compared to C57Bl/6 anti-DBA/2 in their ability to lyse P 815, DBA/2 RSCs, and DBA/2 Con A-activated spleen cells. The results in Fig. 4 show that there are no differences between these cells whether the effector cells are directed against both K and D or selectively against only K or D.

Inhibition of lysis of P 815

DBA/2 RSCs, P 815, DBA/2 Con A-activated, and normal spleen cells were tested for their ability to inhibit lysis of ^{51}Cr-labeled P 815 by anti-H-2^d CTLs (C57Bl/6 anti-DBA/2) (Fig. 5B). Contrary to the reduced susceptibility to lysis of DBA/2 RSCs compared to P 815, these cells inhibit the lysis of ^{51}Cr-labeled P 815 almost as well as P 815 and better than DBA/2 Con A-activated, normal spleen cells. Normal DBA/2 spleen cells are poor inhibitors of P 815 lysis. As expected C57Bl/6 RSCs syngeneic to the effectors do not inhibit P 815 lysis. There

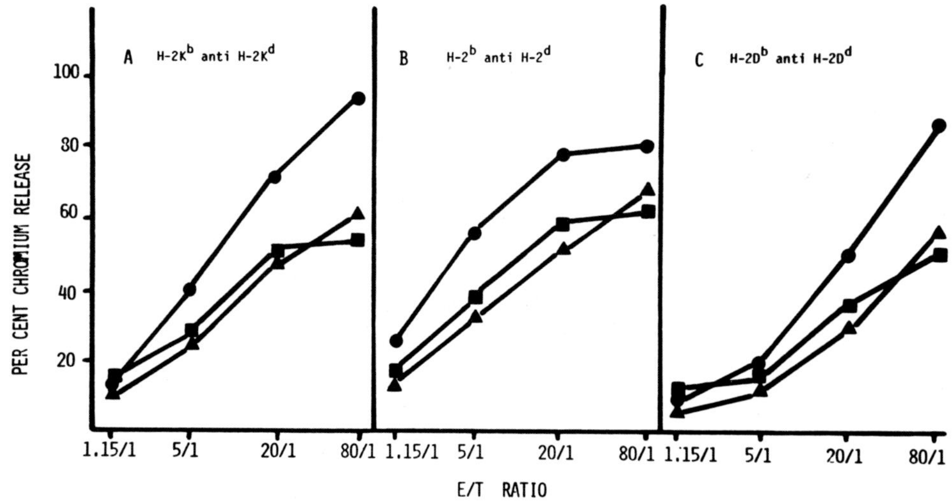

FIG. 4. Lysis of P 815, DBA/2 Con A-activated spleen cells, and DBA/2 RSCs by anti-H-$2K^d$ and anti-H-$2D^d$ CTLs. (A) Primary B10A (5R) CTLs generated by stimulation with DBA/2 spleen cells were tested on Day 4 against: (●) P 815, (■) DBA/2 Con A-activated spleen cells and (▲) DBA/2 RSCs. (B) Primary C57Bl/6 CTLs generated by stimulation with DBA/2 spleen cells were tested on Day 4 against the same target as in A. (C) Primary HTG CTLs generated by stimulation with DBA/2 spleen cells were tested on Day 4 against the same target as in A. Spontaneous release by target cells alone was, respectively, 8, 20, and 18%.

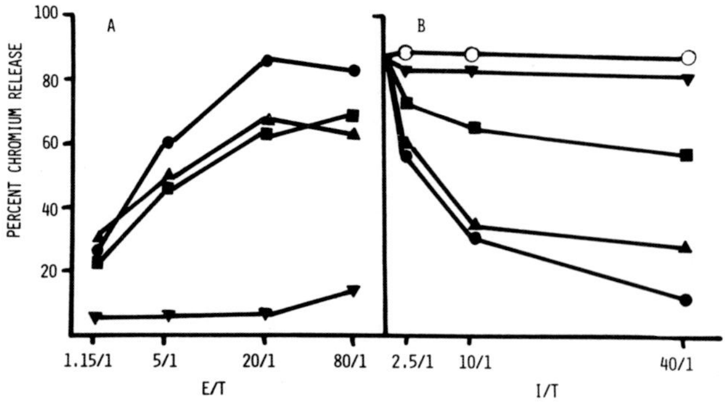

FIG. 5. (A) Lysis of different ^{51}Cr-labeled target cells by anti-H-2^d CTLs. Primary B6 CTLs generated by stimulation with DBA/2 spleen cells were tested on Day 4 against (●) P 815, (■) DBA/2 Con A-activated spleen cells, (▲) DBA/2 RSCs, and (▼) total DBA/2 spleen cells. Spontaneous release of ^{51}Cr-labeled target cells alone was 10, 25, 20, and 25%, respectively. (B) Inhibition of lysis of ^{51}Cr-labeled P 815 by various unlabeled inhibitor cells. Effector cells are the same as in Fig. 4A. The inhibitor cells are a serial dilution of: (●) P 815, (■) Con A-activated spleen cells, (▲) DBA/2 RSCs, (▼) normal spleen cells, and (○) B6 RSCs syngeneic to the effector cells as a control.

was no significant difference in the inhibition experiments if the effectors were primary or secondary *in vitro* H-2^b anti-H-2^d CTLs (data not shown).

DISCUSSION

Our experiments, designated to test residual stimulating activity in a spleen cell population undergoing culture conditions similar to those of an MLC, surprisingly revealed a small subpopulation of large, non-T, nonadherent, highly radioresistant and long-lived cells. This subpopulation is able to replace, on a per cell basis, the whole spleen cell population generally used as stimulator in MLC for induction of cell-mediated lympholysis.

Irradiation appears to be a useful mean of selection for RSCs since they are still induced after more than a 5000-rad dose; thus, RSC progenitors are fairly resistant to mitotic death in the 2500- to 5000-rad range. Freshly irradiated spleen cells stimulate even after 10,000 rad, but this is easily explained by sufficiently long antigen presentation during MLC by cells which will die within one to two post-irradiation mitoses (27). In the same way, we have shown that a 7-day precultivation still induces strong stimulating activity, suggesting that RSC are living after more than 1 week. Thus, the combined effects of irradiation and preculture seem to be the easiest and most efficient method to isolate a highly stimulating splenic population with high potential for generating allogeneic CTLs.

Analysis of membrane alloantigens of RSC did not reveal special features which could exlain their high stimulating potential; RSCs express H-2 antigen levels comparable to those of normal blastic or tumor cells, as shown by complement-dependent cytotoxicity and absorption experiments. However, alloantigens are recognized on RSCs since they are lysed much better than normal spleen cells which poorly interact with CTLs. They are as equally well lysed as Con A-activated spleen cells but interact more efficiently with anti-H-2^d CTLs than Con A blasts as shown by cold-target experiments. RSCs are more poorly lysed than P 815 but interact with the same efficiency with anti-H-2^d CTLs.

Hence RSCs are distinguished from total spleen populations by their susceptibility to lysis as well as their inhibitory activity in competition experiments, suggesting that the involvement of RSC H-2 antigen in the recognition and binding process might depend on nonserologically detectable H-2 determinants and/or interaction of H-2 determinants with non-H-2 factors.

It is of interest that 40% of RSCs are lysed by anti-Ia antiserum and complement. Moreover, anti-Ia antiserum during MLC greatly decreases the generation of CTL by RSCs. Finally, anti-Ia antiserum and complement pretreatment of RSC before MLC decreases the absolute number of lytic units generated in primary sensitization. These results reinforce the crucial role of Ia antigens in CTL generation which have been often implicated in MLC induction (10–12, 28, 29) and recently shown to actively participate in alloantigen presentation by splenic adherent cells (30).

Many attempts in murine systems to purify populations generating a cytotoxic activity in normal spleen cells (reviewed in (31, 32)) led to the conclusion that if T and B lymphocytes were equally active stimulating cells, fibroblasts and purified macrophages were far less efficient. Populations like lymphoid dendritic cells (33) or spleen adherent cells (34) have been described as possessing a very high stimulating activity in inducing by themselves the proliferation of primary mixed leukocyte reactions. However, their role in the generation of CTL specific for H-2 gene products has been poorly envisaged (35). They can act as accessory cells (36, 37) or at low cellularity as antigen presenting cells (35). Dendritic cells are low-density, glass-adherent lymphoid cells possessing particular cytomorphologic features (38) and surface markers (39) purified either by rosetting with opsonized erythrocytes (39) or by negative readherence of the low-density adherent fraction on plastic (35). RSCs are not adherent to plastic at the end of the preincubation time, nor are they, or their precursors, adherent at the beginning, since removal of adherent spleen cells on plastic does not abolish the induction of RSCs by irradiation and precultivation. It should be noted that RSCs are rather easily prepared, and that the best cytotoxic response generated by RSC is obtained when using the number of RSCs determined by the number of total spleen cells giving the best generation of CTL in our MLC conditions. That is, it seems that all stimulating RSCs available are obtained by our RSC induction method, although RSC may not be the only population with the ability to induce cytotoxicity in MLC.

Such a hyperstimulating population in the generation of CTLs is of great interest to study the modalities of antigen presentation in the initiation of cytotoxic response; however, it raises the problem of why, although antigen is present in an active form all during the development of MLC, the cytotoxic activity decreases after a peak to lead to nonlytic memory cells.

ACKNOWLEDGMENT

This work was supported by grants from INSERM and CNRS.

REFERENCES

1. Lohmann-Mathes, M. L., Koren, H. S., and Fischer, H., *Int. Arch. Allergy Appl. Immunol.*, **42**, 110, 1972.

2. Cerottini, J. C., and Brunner, K. T., *Advan. Immunol.* **18,** 67, 1974.
3. Miller, R. G., Shilling, R. M., and Phillips, R. A., *J. Immunol.* **118,** 166, 1977.
4. Okada, M., Klimpel, G. R., Kuppers, R. C., and Henney, C. S., *J. Immunol.* **122,** 2527, 1979.
5. Lutz, C. T., and Fitch, F. W., *J. Immunol.* **122,** 2598, 1979.
6. Wagner, H., Röllinghoff, M., Schawaller, R., Hardt, C., and Pfizenmaier, K., *Nature (London)* **280,** 405, 1979.
7. Wagner, H., and Feldmann, M., *Cell. Immunol.* **3,** 405, 1972.
8. Fitch, F., Engers, H. D., MacDonald, H. R., Cerottini, J. C., and Brunner, K. T., *J. Immunol.* **115,** 1688, 1975.
9. Nagy, Z., Elliot, B. E., Nabolz, M., Kramme, P. M., and Pernis, B., *J. Exp. Med.* **143,** 648, 1976.
10. Lee, K. C., Wilkinson, A., and Wong, M., *Cell. Immunol.* **48,** 79, 1979.
11. Werdelin, O., and Shevach, E. M., *J. Immunol.* **123,** 2779, 1979.
12. Lee, S. T., and Paraskevas, F., *Cell. Immunol.* **48,** 1, 1979.
13. Brunner, K. T., Mauel, J., Rudolf, H., and Chapuis, B., *Immunology* **18,** 501, 1970.
14. Holm, G., *Exp. Cell. Res.* **48,** 327, 1967.
15. Bevan, M. J., *J. Immunol.* **114,** 316, 1975.
16. Bevan, M. J., and Cohn, M. J., *Immunology* **114,** 559, 1975.
17. Wagner, H., and Kollinghoff, M., *J. Exp. Med.* **138,** 1, 1973.
18. Reme, T. X., Gomard, E., and Levy, J. P., *Cell. Immunol.* **34,** 299, 1977.
19. Reme, T. X., Dupuy D'Angeac A., Radal, M., and Serrou, B., *Ann. Immunol. (Paris)* **130C,** 827, 1979.
20. Brunner, K. T., Mauel, J., Cerottini, J. C., and Chapuis, B., *Immunology* **14,** 181, 1968.
21. Julius, M. M., Simpson, E., and Herzenberg, L. A., *Eur. J. Immunol.* **3,** 645, 1973.
22. Caraux, J., Thierry, C., and Serrou, B., *Eur. J. Immunol.* **8,** 806, 1978.
23. Klein, J., "Biology of the Mouse Histocompatibility-2 Complex," p. 451. Springer-Verlag, New York, 1975.
24. Lemonnier, F., Burakoff, S. J., Mescher, M., Dorf, M. E., and Benacerraf, B., *J. Immunol.* **120,** 1717, 1978.
25. MacDonald, H. R., Phillips, R. A., and Miller, R. G., *J. Immunol.* **111,** 575, 1973.
26. Wagner, H., Feldmann, M., Boyle, W., and Schrader, J. W., *J. Exp. Med.* **136,** 331, 1972.
27. Anderson, R. E., and Warner, N. L., *Advan. Immunol.* **24,** 215, 1976.
28. Niederhuber, J. E., *Immunol. Rev.* **40,** 1978.
29. Habu, S., Hayakawa, K., and Okulura, K., *Cell. Immunol.* **47,** 416, 1979.
30. Weinberger, O., Hermann, S. M., Mescher, M. F., Benacarraf, B., and Burakoff, S. J., *Proc. Nat. Acad. Sci. USA* **77,** 6091, 1980.
31. Engers, H. D., and MacDonald, H. R. *Contemp. Top. Immunobiol.* **5,** 145, 1976.
32. Wagner, H., and Wyss, C., *Eur. J. Immunol.* **3,** 549, 1973.
33. Steinman, R. M., and Witmer, M. D., *Proc. Nat. Acad. Sci. USA* **75,** 5132, 1978.
34. Ahmann, G. B., Nadler, P. I., Birnkrant, A., and Hodes, R. J., *J. Immunol.* **123,** 903, 1979.
35. Nussenzweig, M. C., and Steinman, R. M., *J. Exp. Med.* **151,** 1196, 1980.
36. Klinkert, W. E. F., Cabadie, J. H., O'Brien, J., Beyer, C. F., and Bowers, W. E., *Proc. Nat. Acad. Sci. USA* **77,** 5414, 1980.
37. Nussenzweig, M. C., Steinman, R. M., Gutchinov, B., and Cohn, Z. A., *J. Exp. Med.* **152,** 1070, 1980.
38. Steinman, R. M., and Cohn, Z. A., *J. Exp. Med.* **139,** 380, 1974.
39. Steinman, R. M., Kaplan, G., Witmer, M. D., and Cohn, Z. A., *J. Exp. Med.* **149,** 1, 1979.

CELLULAR IMMUNOLOGY **63**, 349–361 (1981)

FcγR Expressed on T-Cell Hybrids: Specificity, Behavior and Relationship with Ia Antigens

JEAN-LUC TEILLAUD,* CHANTAL RABOURDIN-COMBE,† MARC STANISLAWSKI,‡ CATHERINE NEAUPORT-SAUTES,†,[1] AND WOLF HERMAN FRIDMAN†

**Laboratoire d'Expérimentation Animale, Institut de Recherches sur les Maladies du Sang. Hôpital Saint-Louis, 75475 Paris Cedex 10, and †Laboratoire d'Immunologie Cellulaire and ‡Laboratoire de Chimie des Protéines, Institut de Recherches Scientifiques sur le Cancer, BP n°8.94800 Villejuif, France*

Received February 24, 1981; accepted June 19, 1981

The fine specificity of receptor for the Fc portion of IgG (FcγR) expressed on T-cell hybrids secreting soluble FcγR (sFcγR) which suppresses antibody production, was investigated. FcγR was found to bind IgG from mouse, human, and rabbit species. It reacted with mouse IgG1 and IgG2a but not IgG2b, and human IgG1 and IgG3 but not IgG4. Mouse IgG and their subclasses bound more avidly to FcγR than human and rabbit IgG. FcγR of T-cell hybrids was sensitive to pronase and resistant to trypsin. In kinetics experiments, the behavior of FcγR on the membrane of T-cell hybrids was analyzed and compared to that of I-region-coded antigens expressed on these hybrids. Upon incubation at 37°C in balanced salt solution (BSS), T-cell hybrids released FcγR into the medium. The reexpression of FcγR, after pronase cleavage or shedding, was complete within 3 hr of incubation in culture medium and required protein synthesis. I–A-coded antigens, present on these hybrids, disappeared simultaneously with FcγR upon incubation of cells at 37°C in BSS. Within 3 hr of incubation in culture medium, although the reexpression of FcγR was complete, no Ia antigens could be detected. They were reexpressed later, as tested after 19 hr of culture. During a single growth cycle, the expression of FcγR was maximal during log phase.

INTRODUCTION

Receptors for the Fc portion of IgG (FcγR)[2] have been detected on a variety of lymphoid cells involved in the immune system such as B cells (1, 2), T cells (3, 4) and K cells (5). Although they mediate different effector functions, the FcγR expressed on these different cell populations exhibit a series of common properties.

First, analysis of their fine specificity has demonstrated that FcγR are not species specific (1, 6) but IgG subclass specific (5–8). For instance, FcγR of B cells (9),

[1] To whom correspondence should be sent.

[2] Abbreviations used: BSS, balanced salt solution; E, sheep erythrocytes; EA IgG, sheep erythrocytes sensitized with rabbit IgG anti-Forssman antibodies; EA IgM, sheep erythrocytes sensitized with rabbit IgM anti-Forssman antibodies; FcεR, receptor for the Fc fragment of IgE; FcγR, receptor(s) for the Fc fragment of IgG; FCS, fetal calf serum; HAT, hypoxanthine–aminopterin–thymidine; IBF, immunoglobulin binding factor; MEM, minimum essential medium; MHC, major histocompatibility complex; PEG, polyethylene glycol; RFC, rosette-forming cells; sFcγR, soluble receptor for the Fc fragment of IgG.

0008-8749/81/140349-13$02.00/0

T cells (7), and K cells (5, 10) bind human IgG1 and IgG3 avidly whereas human IgG2 and IgG4 bind weakly or not at all. Second, FcγR expressed on these different cell types share common sensitivities to proteolytic enzymes since they have been shown to be resistant to trypsin but sensitive to pronase (11–14). Finally, on B cells (15, 16) and T cells (17, 18), blocking experiments using antisera reacting with products of the major histocompatibility complex (MHC) have suggested an association, on the cell surface, between FcγR and antigens coded by the I region of the MHC.

Beside these common characteristics, FcγR expressed on the different lymphocyte subpopulations exert different effector functions. With regard to T lymphocytes, FcγR-bearing T cells have been demonstrated to act as suppressor cells of antibody production (19, 20). In previous studies we have shown that the suppressive role of murine FcγR-positive T cells is mediated by the FcγR itself (20) which is released from T cells (12). This soluble form of FcγR, previously called immunoglobulin binding factor (IBF) (4, 12), is now named soluble FcγR (sFcγR) (21). Thus, upon incubation at 37°C in serum-free buffer, FcγR-bearing activated T cells release molecules capable of binding the Fc portion of IgG (12) and suppressing *in vitro* antibody synthesis (22). In addition, these molecules, similarly to other non-antigen-specific T-cell factors (23), have been found to bear Ia antigens (24).

Since FcγR is shed from T cells and from macrophages as well (25), the question arises of its behavior on the cell surface in long-term kinetics experiments. On human lymphocytes, it has been shown that a complete reexpression of FcγR occurred 12 hr after proteolytic cleavage (13) and that 50% of the initial level of rosette formation with sheep erythrocytes sensitized with IgG anti-Forssman antibodies (EA IgG) was observed 6 hr after modulation of FcγR by insoluble antigen-IgG antibody complexes (26). Since mouse-activated T cells die within several hours after incubation at 37°C, the demonstration that T cells themselves are able to synthesize their FcγR and the analysis of the behavior of FcγR on the membrane of T cells would thus come from studies using FcγR-positive T cell lines or hybrids. In this context, we have previously prepared FcγR-positive T cell hybrids by fusion of FcγR-bearing activated T cells with BW-5147 T-lymphoma cells (27). During the past 3 years, these hybrids have been shown to express FcγR and release suppressor sFcγR (27). Recently, we have shown, by using monoclonal antibodies and conventional antisera directed against the I-region-coded products, that these hybrids and their FcγR-positive clone derivatives, (1) express determinants coded by the I-A subregion of the MHC, (2) produce sFcγR which bears Ia determinants (28). In the present work, the behavior and the turnover rates of FcγR and Ia antigens on the surface of T-cell hybrids and their FcγR-positive clones was investigated by kinetics experiments. The fine specificity and enzyme susceptibilities of FcγR of T-cell hybrids were also analyzed.

The results indicate that FcγR of T-cell hybrids are non-species specific but IgG subclass specific, and sensitive to pronase but resistant to trypsin, thus demonstrating that they exhibit properties similar to those of FcγR expressed on normal lymphoid cells. Upon incubation of T-cell hybrids at 37°C in serum-free buffer, the disappearance of FcγR from the cell surface was found to be concomitant with that of I–A-coded antigens. Within 3 hr of incubation in culture the reexpression of FcγR was complete whereas the Ia antigens remained undetectable. The complete recovery of Ia antigens was observed later in the incubation period as shown after 19 hr of culture.

MATERIALS AND METHODS

Obtention, Culture, and Cloning of T-Cell Hybrids

T-Cell hybrids were obtained as previously described (27). Briefly, a T2D4 hybrid cell line was prepared by fusion of BW 5147 T-lymphoma cells ($H\text{-}2^k$, Thy 1.1., FcγR negative) with B10.BR alloantigen-activated T cells ($H\text{-}2^k$, Thy 1.2, 40% FcγR positive) using polyethylene glycol (PEG) (Serva, Heidelberg) as a fusion agent. After selection in HAT medium, hybrids were tested for the presence of FcγR by rosette formation with EA IgG and cultured in medium RPMI 1640 (Eurobio, France) containing 10% fetal calf serum (FCS) (Eurobio) L-glutamine, sodium pyruvate, and antibiotics. T2D4 hybrid cells were cloned by limiting dilution on feeder layers of C3H ($H\text{-}2^k$) thymocytes. FcγR-positive or -negative clones were then detected by rosette formation with EA IgG.

Enzymatic Treatment of T-Cell Hybrids

In some experiments, hybrid cells were treated with a different concentration of trypsin (Difco-Osi, France) or pronase (Calbiochem, San Diego, Calif.) in balanced salt solution (BSS) for 30 min at 37°C. Cycloheximide (Sigma, St. Louis, Mo.) was added at a final concentration of 100 μg/ml. These different treatments did not affect cell viability as determined by trypan blue exclusion.

Preparation of Whole Immunoglobulins, Immunoglobulin Subclasses, and Fragments

IgG fractions of rabbit sera were isolated by DEAE cellulose (DE 52 Whatman) chromatography in 0.02 *M* phosphate buffer, pH 7.0. IgM fractions were separated by Sephadex G-200 gel filtration in 0.1 *M* Tris–HCl buffer, 1 *M* NaCl, pH 8.0. $(Fab')_2$ fragments of rabbit IgG were prepared by treatment of IgG with 2% pepsin (Worthington Biochemicals, Freehold, N.J.) in 0.2 *M* acetate buffer at pH 4.5 at 37°C for 20 hr and isolated by Sephadex G-200 gel filtration. Human IgG pool was purified by ammonium sulfate precipitation followed by ion-exchange chromatography on a DEAE cellulose column. IgG subclasses and Fc and $(Fab')_2$ fragments were prepared as previously described (7). Briefly, monoclonal IgG subclasses were obtained from patients with multiple myeloma and purified by ammonium sulfate precipitation followed by ion-exchange chromatography on a column of DEAE cellulose (Whatman DE 52). The IgG subclass types were determined by double-diffusion analysis using monospecific anti-subclass antisera and by chemical typing. Fc and $(Fab')_2$ fragments were obtained by papain and pepsin digestion, respectively. These fragments were separated by gel filtration on a Sephadex G-150 column in 0.15 *M* Nacl, 0.01 *M* Tris–HCl buffer, pH 7.6. Human IgM pool was kindly provided by Dr. Danon (Institut de Recherches sur les Maladies du Sang. Hôpital Saint-Louis). In order to eliminate heterophilic antibodies, human and rabbit IgG, IgM, and $(Fab')_2$ fragments were absorbed on sheep erythrocytes and C3H/He mouse spleen cells for 1 hr at 37°C and 1 hr at 4°C as previously described (7, 12).

Mouse IgM pool was isolated by chromatography of mouse serum on Sephadex G-200. Mouse IgG pool was purchased from Miles Laboratories (Kankakee, Ill.). Myeloma proteins MOPC 21 (IgG1), MOPC 173 (IgG2a), and MOPC 195 (IgG2b) were purified from ascitic fluid by combined preparative electrophoresis on starch block (Veronal-HCl buffer 0.1 *M*, pH 8.6, 18 hr at 4°C) followed by gradient elution from QAE-Sephadex (0.03 to 0.25 *M* phosphate buffer pH 7.0). The MOPC 104E (IgM) and J 558 (IgA) anti-α 1 $\rightarrow$ 3 dextran proteins were affinity purified on Sepharose columns to which dextran B 1355 was covalently coupled as described by Hiramoto *et al.* (29). For preparation of Fab and Fc fragments of MOPC 21 and MOPC 173, the proteins (5–7 mg/ml) were cleaved with papain (Worthington Biochemicals), 1% w/w final, in 0.01 *M* L-cysteine, 0.001 *M* EDTA, and phosphate buffer, pH 7.0, for 2 hr at 37°C. Uncleaved material was removed by gel filtration over a column of Sephadex G-100, and the second peak, containing Fab and Fc fragments, was applied to a column of QAE-Sephadex. The fragments were separated using a gradient of 0.005 to 0.5 *M* phosphate buffer, pH 8.0.

Rosette Formation

Rosette determination (4) was carried out at 4°C using sheep erythrocytes (E) sensitized with IgG rabbit anti-Forssman antibodies (EA IgG). Briefly, rosette formation was performed by mixing 10^7 sensitized erythrocytes with 5×10^5 T-cell hybrids in 0.5 ml BSS. After centrifugation at 1000 rpm for 10 min and gentle suspension, the percentage of rosette-forming cells (RFC) was counted in the presence of trypan blue.

Inhibition of rosette formation was performed by addition of increasing quantities of immunoglobulins or their fragments to 5×10^5 hybrid cells for 30 min at 4°C in 0.5 ml of BSS before addition of EA IgG.

Immunofluorescence

Hybrid cells (3×10^5) were first incubated with 1 μg of monoclonal IgG2a anti-I-A^k antibody (10.3.6) (kindly provided by L. A. Herzenberg) for 30 min at 4°C, and after three washings in minimum essential medium (MEM) supplemented with 2% FCS, with a fluorescein-conjugated anti-mouse Ig serum (Institut Pasteur, France) at 1/40 dilution for 30 min at 4°C. Mouse myeloma protein IgG2a (UPC10) (Litton Bionetics, Kensington, Md.) at a dose of 1 μg or medium alone was used as control. All reagents were centrifuged 5 min at 10,000 rpm before use. The percentage of labeled cells was counted under a fluorescence microscope (Orthoplan, Wild Leitz, France) equipped with filters 2KP 490, K 445, TK 510, and K 515.

RESULTS

Specificity of FcγR

In all these experiments, the binding of Ig classes, subclasses, and fragments isolated from different species was determined by inhibition of rosette formation

TABLE 1

Specificity of T-Cell FcγR of T2D4 Hydrid Cells as Determined by Inhibition of EA IgG Rosettes with Ig Classes, Subclasses, and Fragments from Different Species

Mouse		Human		Rabbit	
Protein	Binding[a]	Protein	Binding[a]	Protein	Binding[a]
IgM	−	IgM	−	IgM	−
IgG	++	IgG	++	IgG	++
IgA	−			$(Fab')_2$ IgG	−
IgG1	+++	IgG1	++		
Fc IgG1	++	Fc IgG1	+		
IgG2a	+++	$(Fab')_2$IgG1	−	ND[c]	ND[c]
Fc IgG2a	++	IgG2	[b]		
Fab IgG2a	−	IgG3	++		
IgG2b	−	IgG4	−		

[a] Binding is expressed as the dose of protein required to obtain a 50% inhibition of EA IgG rosettes: +++, $<10^{-7}$ mol; ++, 1–10 $\times 10^{-7}$ mol; +, 10–50 $\times 10^{-7}$ mol; −, no inhibition at doses up to 500 $\times 10^{-7}$ mol.

[b] Since the human IgG2 preparation systematically agglutinated the sensitized sheep red blood cells, no conclusion could be drawn from these experiments.

[c] Not done.

with EA IgG of T2D4 hybrid cells or their FcγR-positive clone derivatives. The data summarized in Table 1 indicate the approximate doses of protein required to obtain a 50% inhibition.

First, IgG from either mouse, human, or rabbit species could block rosette formation. By contrast, IgM from the same species, mouse IgA, or $(Fab')_2$ fragments of rabbit IgG had no effect. An example of the inhibition exerted by various doses of mouse immunoglobulins is illustrated in Fig. 1a using the FcγR-positive cloned T-cell hybrid F3T2D4. The addition of increasing amounts of mouse IgG led to a progressive inhibition of rosette formation up to a complete blocking observed at a dose of 6×10^{-7} mol. No blocking could be obtained with mouse IgM or IgA for doses up to 5 and 13×10^{-7} mol, respectively. These results confirm the existence of receptors specific for the Fc fragment of IgG on T2D4 cells. Furthermore, they suggest that these receptors, like those expressed on other lymphoid cells of the immune system (1, 6, 7) are not species specific.

With regard to subclass specificity, Table 1 shows that FcγR of T2D4 cells could bind human IgG1 and IgG3 but not IgG4. Concerning mouse IgG subclasses, mouse IgG1 and IgG2a but not IgG2b could block rosette formation (Table 1 and Fig. 1b). The latter finding was confirmed by indirect immunofluorescence (data not shown). Therefore, these results demonstrate the subclass specificity of FcγR of T2D4 hybrid cells. In addition, the fact that Fc fragments of human IgG1 and mouse IgG1 and IgG2a inhibited rosette formation confirms the location of the cytophilic site on the Fc portion of IgG (7) (Table 1 and Fig. 1b).

Interestingly, an approximately 10-fold higher amount of human IgG subclasses (5 to 6×10^{-7} mol) as compared to mouse IgG subclasses (6 to 10×10^{-8} mol) was required to obtain a 50% inhibition of rosette formation with EA IgG. A similar

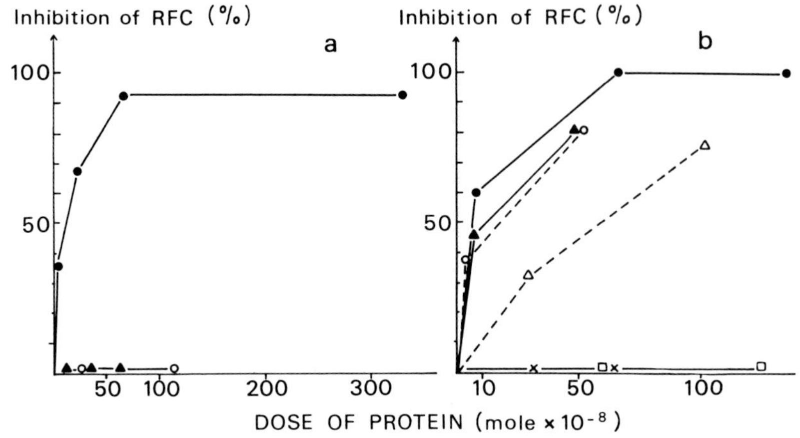

FIG. 1. Inhibitory effect of mouse immunoglobulins and their fragments on rosette formation on FcγR-positive cloned T-cell hybrids (F3T2D4), with EA IgG: (a) ● —— ●, IgG; ▲ —— ▲, IgM; ○ —— ○, IgA; (b) ● —— ●, IgG1; ○ - - - ○, Fc IgG1; ▲ —— ▲, IgG2a; △ - - - △, Fc IgG2a; □ —— □, Fab IgG2a; x —— x, IgG2b.

phenomenom was observed between Fc fragments and entire IgG from mouse and human species (Table 1 and Fig. 1b) where 3 to 10 times more Fc fragments than IgG of the same species were needed to exert an identical inhibitory effect.

Enzyme Sensitivity of FcγR

FcγR expressed on activated T cells (12), B cells (11), and K cells (14) are known to be trypsin resistant and pronase sensitive. To test if FcγR or T2D4 hybrid cells exhibit the same properties, the percentage of rosettes with EA IgG was measured before and after treatment with different concentrations of trypsin or pronase. As shown in Fig. 2 the incubation of T2D4 cells with trypsin at 0.1% for

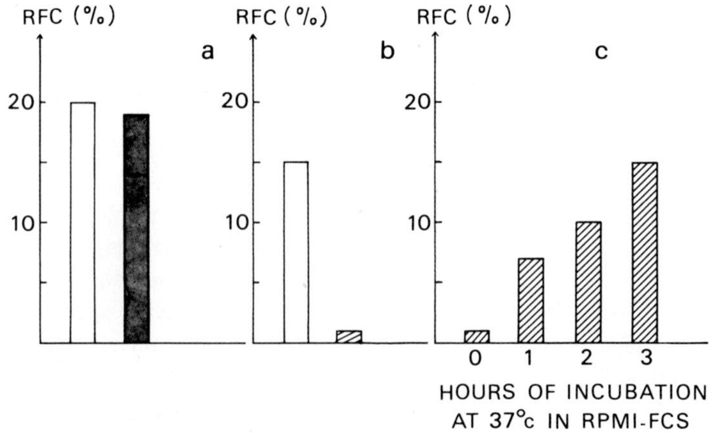

FIG. 2. Enzyme sensitivity (a and b) and kinetics of reexpression after pronase treatment (c) of FcγR of T2D4 hybrid cells: Percentage of EA IgG rosette-forming cells after incubation of T2D4 cells with: ■, trypsin (0.1%), ▨ pronase (0.05%); □, BSS.

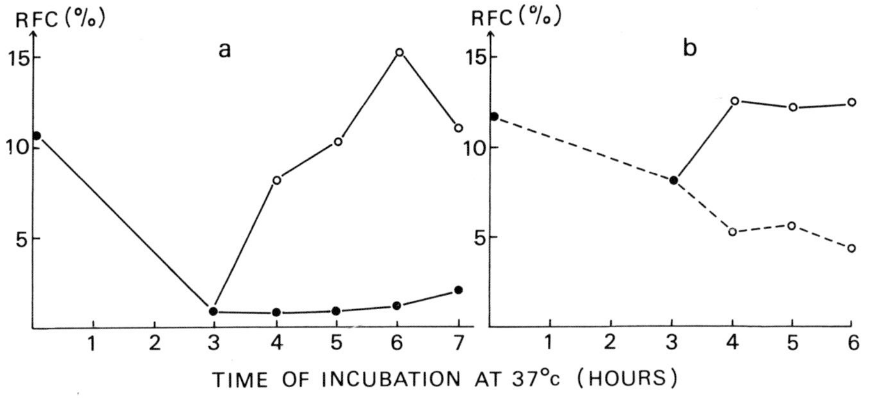

FIG. 3. Kinetics of expression of FcγR of T2D4 hybrid cells in different media as determined by rosette formation with EA IgG: (a) ● —— ●, BSS; ○ —— ○, RPMI-10% FCS; (b) ● - - - ●, BSS with cycloheximide (100 μg/ml); ○ - - - ○, RPMI-10% FCS with cycloheximide (100 μg/ml); ○ —— ○, RPMI-10% FCS.

30 min at 37°C did not modify their ability to bind IgG (Fig. 2a) whereas 0.05% pronase abolished their capacity to form rosettes with EAIgG (Fig. 2b).

Kinetics of Expression of FcγR

In a first set of experiments, the kinetics of reexpression of FcγR on the surface of T2D4 cells was investigated after its complete removal by pronase proteolysis. As shown in Fig. 2c, the incubation in RPMI–10% FCS led to the progressive ability of enzyme-treated cells to form new EA IgG rosettes. Within 3 hr, the percentage of rosette-forming cells reached the same level as before treatment (14% RFC).

In a second set of experiments, since T-cell FcγR is known to be shed from the cell surface upon incubation of T cells in serum-free BSS at 37°C, (4, 12, 27), the removal of FcγR from T-cell hybrids was induced by a 3-hr incubation period in BSS. The kinetics of its reexpression was then followed during incubation at 37°C in RPMI–10% FCS. As shown in Fig. 3a, the ability of T2D4 cells to bind EA IgG first disappeared after the 3-hr incubation period in BSS (from 12 to 0% of rosette-forming cells). Then, within a few hours of incubation in culture medium, their capacity to form new EA IgG rosettes reappeared progressively, up to a maximum level (15% RFC) reached after 3 hr.

This phenomenon was due to the reexpression of receptors specific for Fc fragments of IgG on T2D4 cells, since (i) the addition of rabbit IgG inhibited rosette formation with EA IgG and (ii) no rosettes could be formed with EA IgM or E (data not shown). However, when the cells having shed their FcγR were incubated in BSS instead of RPMI–10% FCS, no reexpression of FcγR was detectable even after a 4-hr incubation period (Fig. 3a). This result suggests that the reappearance of FcγR on T2D4 cells requires the presence of amino acids in the medium, probably for protein synthesis. To investigate this possibility, the kinetics of reexpression of FcγR was followed in the presence of a reversible inhibitor of protein synthesis, cycloheximide (100 μg/ml). As shown in Fig. 3b, when the cells were incubated

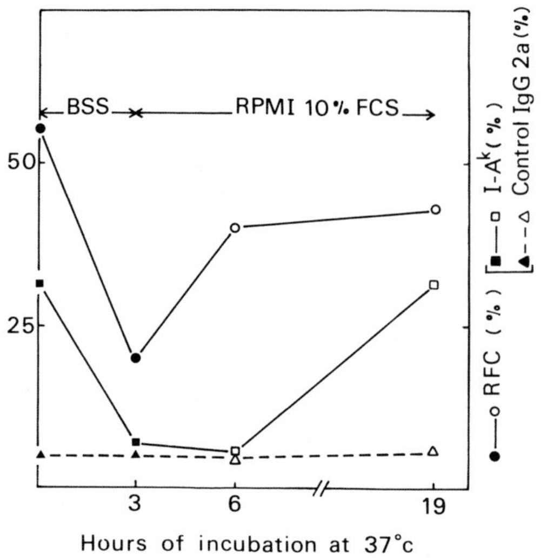

FIG. 4. Kinetics of expression of FcγR and I-A^k-coded antigens on F3T2D4 cloned hybrid cells. FcγR was detected by rosette formation with EA IgG upon incubation of F3T2D4 cells in BSS (● —— ●) and then in RPMI-10% FCS (○ —— ○); I-A^k-coded antigens were detected by indirect immunofluorescence using 1 μg of 10.3.6 monoclonal IgG2a anti-I-A^k antibody after incubation of cells in BSS (■ —— ■) and RPMI-10% FCS (□ —— □); ▲ —— ▲ and △ - - - △: binding of control IgG2a (1 μg) revealed by indirect immunofluorescence after incubation of cells in the same medium.

in the presence of cycloheximide, first for 3 hr in BSS and then for several hours in RPMI–10% FCS, no reexpression of FcγR was detectable. As previously observed with activated T cells (12), the shedding rate of FcγR in BSS containing cycloheximide was inhibited as compared to the release in BSS alone. When the cells were incubated for 3 hr in BSS with cycloheximide, washed, and then, incubated in RPMI–10% FCS in the absence of cycloheximide, the percentage of EA IgG rosettes increased within 1 hr. Therefore, these data provide evidence that the reexpression of FcγR on the surface of T2D4 cells require *de novo* protein synthesis.

Relationships between FcγR and Ia Antigens

In previous studies we have shown that T2D4 hybrid cells, as well as their FcγR-positive clone derivatives, express I–A^k-coded determinants (28). Since an association has been described between Ia antigens and T-cell FcγR (17, 18) and since the soluble form of FcγR, sFcγR, bears Ia antigens (24), the expression of Ia antigens was also evaluated and compared to that of FcγR in kinetic studies. Ia antigens were detected on a FcγR-positive cloned T cell hybrid (F3T2D4) by indirect immunofluorescence using a monoclonal IgG2a anti-I-A^k antibody at dilution avoiding its fixation through the Fc portion of the molecule. Under these conditions, 32% of F3T2D4 cells were labeled. Indeed, control IgG2a, at the same dose (1 μg), did not react with F3T2D4 cells (5% of stained cells). As shown in Fig. 4, upon a 3-hr incubation period in BSS at 37°C, while the percentage of FcγR-positive T-cell hybrids dropped from 55 to 20%, the percentage of I–A^k-positive cells decreased also from 32 to 7%. Interestingly, after incubation for 3 hr in RPMI–10% FCS, although the reexpression of FcγR on the surface of F3T2D4 cells was almost complete (40% RFC), the Ia antigens were still not detectable by immunofluorescence (6% labeled cells). Their reexpression was complete (32% of labeled cells) when tested after 19-hr incubation period in RPMI–10% FCS.

Expression of FcγR during a Single Growth Cycle

Since the expression of cell surface antigens on cell lines (30) and T-cell hybrids (31) is known to be dependent upon the cell cycle, the expression of FcγR was followed during a single growth cycle. As shown in Fig. 5, when the cells started to grow (from Days 1 to 2 after explantation), the percentage of rosettes increased from 16 to 29%. By contrast, when the cells entered into stationary phase (from Days 3 to 6 after seeding), the percentage of rosettes decreased from 29 to 14%. These modifications of FcγR expression were not due to a diminution of cell viability (Fig. 5).

DISCUSSION

In the present work, the fine specificity, enzyme sensitivity and behavior of FcγR of T-cell hybrids were investigated. With regard to their fine specificity, the results show that FcγR on mouse T-cell hybrids are non-species specific since they bind

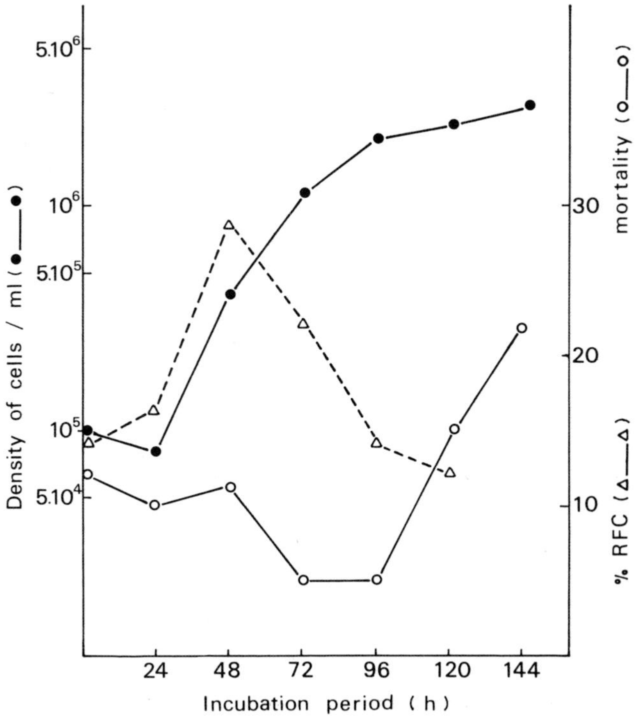

FIG. 5. Kinetics of expression of Fcγ receptors on T2D4 hybrid cells during a single growth cycle: ● —— ●, number of cells/ml; △ - - - △, percentage of rosette-forming cells with EA IgG; ○ —— ○, percentage of dead cells as determined by trypan blue test.

mouse, rabbit, and human IgG but are IgG subclass specific. Thus, using human IgG subclasses, IgG1 and IgG3, but not IgG4, were found to bind to FcγR, and using mouse IgG subclasses, IgG1 and IgG2a, but not IgG2b, exhibited affinity for FcγR. Using Fc, Fab, and $(Fab')_2$ fragments of IgG from both human and mouse origin, the cytophilic site was located on the Fc portion of the IgG molecule. On the other hand, the studies of proteolytic enzyme sensitivities indicated that FcγR are resistant to trypsin but sensitive to pronase.

These data provide evidence that T-cell hybrids bear FcγR with properties similar to those expressed on T cells (12), B cells (8), and K cells (10) which have been found to bind Fc but not $(Fab')_2$ fragments of IgG. Moreover, all these receptors have been described as non-species specific, but IgG subclass specific and trypsin resistant, but pronase sensitive (11–14). With regard to the non-species specificity of FcγR of T-cell hybrids it should be pointed out that comparison of the amount of IgG required to obtain a 50% inhibition of EA IgG rosettes revealed that FcγR bound mouse IgG more avidly than rabbit or human IgG. These data may reflect a species preference of FcγR. However, it cannot be excluded that the preparation of mouse IgG differed from those of rabbit and human IgG in the content of aggregates which have been shown to bind to FcγR more avidly than monomeric IgG (32).

Concerning IgG subclass specificity, it is clear that FcγR of T-cell hybrids, like FcγR on B cells (9), T cells (7), and K cells (5, 10) binds human IgG1 and IgG3 avidly, whereas IgG4 bind weakly or not at all. However, with regard to mouse IgG subclasses, whereas we found that FcγR of T-cell hybrids reacted with IgG1 and IgG2a, but not IgG2b, Krammer *et al.* (33) reported that mouse-activated T cells bind IgG2b but not IgG1 and IgG2a. This discrepancy could be due to the fact that different myeloma proteins have been used in both studies. Another possibility to explain these contradictory findings is that the myeloma proteins used differ in the amount of aggregates (32). Finally, our T-cell hybrids may represent a subpopulation of activated T cells binding IgG1 and IgG2a which has been selected during the fusion procedure.

Recently, two kinds of FcγR have been described on mouse macrophages (34). They can be distinguished by their specificity for mouse IgG subclasses and protease sensitivities. Interestingly the present results show that, on T-cell hybrids, each IgG subclass could completely inhibit the subsequent binding of EA IgG and that FcγR was totally insensitive to trypsin treatment. These data are compatible with the possibility that the different IgG subclasses bind to the same FcγR on T-cell hybrids as on B cells (8) and activated T cells (7).

Several reports have demonstrated that mouse-activated T cells shed their FcγR upon incubation at 37°C in serum-free buffer (4, 12). This phenomenon has been also described with human T lymphocytes (13); moreover, with human lymphocytes, an accelerated decrease in the percentage of EA IgG RFC was observed after modulation of FcγR by immune complexes (26). The present results show that within 3 hr of incubation at 37°C in serum-free BSS, FcγR disappears from the membrane of T-cell hybrids. Supernatants of these T-cell hybrids contain FcγR in a soluble form (sFcγR) which suppresses the *in vitro* antibody production (27). Following disappearance of FcγR induced by release at 37°C in BSS, or by proteolytic cleavage with pronase, incubation of cells in culture medium led to the progressive reexpression of FcγR. Its reappearance was complete within 3 hr of culture. It did not occur in the presence of protein synthesis inhibitor thus suggesting that the reexpression of FcγR is due to *de novo* protein synthesis. Therefore these results provide further evidence for the endogeneous origin of FcγR on T cells and confirm that proteins participate in the formation of its binding site (21). Interestingly, only 3 hr of incubation at 37°C was required to obtain a maximal reexpression of FcγR on T-cell hybrids. This phenomenon is extremely rapid as compared to that of human lymphocytes, where 12 hr are needed for a complete reappearance of FcγR (13). Such a discrepancy could be explained by the origin of T cells since resting peripheral blood T lymphocytes have been used in the human situation. Nevertheless, the present data support the existence in T-cell hybrids of a large amount of intracellular pool of FcγR or its precursor(s). Furthermore, together with the fact that FcγR is rapidly shed from the cell surface, these results indicate that FcγR behaves, on T-cell hybrids, rather as a passenger membrane molecule than a structural component. A similar observation has been recently made by Ishizaka and collaborators with the T-cell Fc recptor for IgE (FcεR). These authors have shown that, upon incubation at 37°C, the FcεR-positive T cells release their FcεR within 4 hr (36). Moreover, supernatants contain an IgGE binding factor which regulates the IgE response (37).

The expression of FcγR was found to be dependent not only on incubation medium but also on the cell cycle. Clearly, during the log phase, cells displayed maximum levels of FcγR, while its expression dropped during the resting phase. Interestingly, the amount of H-2 antigens on cell lines (30) and the susceptibility of T-cell hybrids to complement-dependent lysis of anti-Ia antisera (31) have also been found to be dependent on the cell cycle. However, concerning these molecules, an inverse situation was observed, since the expression or the susceptibility to complement-dependent lysis was maximal during the resting phase and minimal during the log phase.

Although the expression of FcγR was increased during the log phase, T-cell hybrids could never form 100% of EA IgG rosettes. This phenomenon cannot be explained by the fact that in some experiments uncloned T-cell hybrids were used since it was also observed using cloned FcγR-positive T-cell hybrids. In addition, among the 30 clones obtained, 95% expressed FcγR and 5% were FcγR negative as detected by rosette formation with EA IgG (28). Thus, these results are probably due to the limits of the sensitivity of the rosette technique and to the fact that the hybrid cell population contain cells at different physiological stages.

Since the T2D4-cell hybrids and their FcγR-positive clone derivatives express I-A^k-coded antigens (28), the kinetics of expression of FcγR and Ia antigens was compared in the work described here using monoclonal anti-I-A^k antibodies.

Upon incubation in BSS at 37°C both FcγR and Ia antigens disappeared from the cell membrane. This observation is compatible with the finding that, in its soluble form, FcγR bears or is associated with Ia determinants since its suppressive activity could be specifically retained and eluted from relevant anti-Ia immunoadsorbents (24). Although FcγR were reexpressed within 3 hr of incubation of T-cell hybrids in culture medium, the Ia antigens remained undetectable after this incubation period but reappeared later. This finding is compatible with the fact that the turnover rate of MHC antigens has been found to be 6 hr. In addition, these results provide evidence that FcγR and Ia antigens expressed on T-cell hybrids are in fact distinct molecular entities which may be associated on the cell surface. A similar finding has been obtained on B cells, where capping of FcγR did not lead to the redistribution of Ia antigens (38).

In conclusion, the present work shows that FcγR present on T-cell hybrids exhibit the same properties as FcγR expressed on activated T cells, thus demonstrating that T-cell hybrids represent a useful tool to study the physiological properties of FcγR and to produce large amounts of sFcγR. In addition, the work described herein demonstrate that FcγR is a molecule whose expression can be easily and rapidly modulated, thus arguing for its functionnal importance in regulation of the immune response.

ACKNOWLEDGMENTS

We wish to thank Pr. L. A. Herzenberg for the gift of monoclonal antibody (10.3.6), Mrs. J. Moncuit for expert technical assistance, and Mrs. J. Vignau for typing the manuscript. This work was supported by grants from the Institut de la Santé et de la Recherche Médicale (ATP 59-78-91, CRL 78-4-081-1) and from the Delegation Générale à la Recherche Scientifique et Technique (Contract 79-7-275).

REFERENCES

1. Basten, A., Miller, J. F. A. P., Sprent, J., and Pye, J., *J. Exp. Med.* **135,** 610, 1972.
2. Dickler, H. B., and Kunkel, H. G., *J. Exp. Med.* **136,** 191, 1972.
3. Anderson, C. L., and Grey, H. M., *J. Exp. Med.* **139,** 1175, 1974.
4. Fridman, W. H., and Golstein, P., *Cell. Immunol.* **11,** 442, 1974.
5. MacLennan, I. C. M., *Transplant. Rev.* **13,** 67, 1972.
6. Basten, A., Miller, J. F. A. P., Warner, N. L., Abraham, R., Chia, E., and Gamble, J., *J. Immunol.* **115,** 1159, 1975.
7. Klein, M., Neauport-Sautes, C., Ellerson, J. R., and Fridman, W. H., *J. Immunol.* **119,** 1077, 1977.
8. Basten, A., Warner, N. L., and Mandel, T., *J. Exp. Med.,* **135,** 627, 1972.
9. Lawrence, D. A., Weigle, W. O., and Spiegelberg, H. L., *J. Clin. Invest.* **55,** 368, 1975.
10. Wisløff, F., Michaelsen, T. E., and Frøland, S. S., *Scand. J. Immunol.* **3,** 29, 1974.
11. Dickler, H. B., *J. Exp. Med.* **140,** 508, 1974.
12. Neauport-Sautes, C., Dupuis, D., and Fridman, W. H., *Eur. J. Immunol.* **5,** 849, 1975.
13. Mingari, M. C., Moretta, L., Moretta, A., Ferrarini, M., and Preud'homme, J. L., *J. Immunol.* **121,** 767, 1978.
14. Horwitz, D. A., and Lobo, P. I., *J. Clin. Invest.* **56,** 1464, 1975.
15. Dickler, H. B., and Sachs, D. H., *J. Exp. Med.* **140,** 779, 1974.
16. Basten, A., Miller, J. F. A. P., Abraham, R., Gamble, J. and Chia, E., *Int. Arch. Allergy Appl. Immunol.* **50,** 309, 1976.
17. Dickler, H. B., Arbeit, R. D., Henkart, P. A., and Sachs, D. H., *J. Exp. Med.* **144,** 282, 1976.
18. Stout, R. D., Murphy, D. B., McDevitt, H. O., and Herzenberg, L. A., *J. Exp. Med.* **145,** 187, 1977.
19. Moretta, L., Webb, S. R., Grossi, C. E., Lydyard, P. M., and Cooper, M. D., *J. Exp. Med.* **146,** 184, 1977.
20. Fridman, W. H., Fradelizi, D., Guimezanes, A., Platter, C., and Leclerc, J. C., *Eur. J. Immunol.* **7,** 549, 1977.
21. Fridman, W. H., Rabourdin-Combe, C., Neauport-Sautes, C., and Gisler, R. H., *Immunol. Rev.,* in press, 1981.
22. Gisler, R. H., and Fridman, W. H., *J. Exp. Med.* **142,** 507, 1975.
23. Armerding, D., Sachs, D. H., and Katz, D. H., *J. Exp. Med.* **140,** 1717, 1974.
24. Rabourdin-Combe, C., Dorf, M. E., Guimezanes, A., and Fridman, W. H., *Eur. J. Immunol.* **9,** 237, 1979.
25. Lee, S. T., and Paraskevas, F., *Cell. Immunol.* **40,** 141, 1978.
26. Samarut, C., and Revillard, J. P., *Eur. J. Immunol.,* **10,** 352, 1980.
27. Neauport-Sautes, C., Rabourdin-Combe, C., and Fridman, W. H., *Nature (London)* **277,** 656, 1979.
28. Neauport-Sautes, C., Teillaud, J. L., Rabourdin-Combe, C., Fonteneau, P., and Fridman, W. H., submitted for publication.

29. Hiramoto, R., Ghanta, V. K., McGhee, J. P., Schroehenloher, R., and Hamelin, N. R., *Immunochemistry* **9,** 1251, 1972.
30. Cikes, M., *J. Nat. Cancer Inst.* **45,** 979, 1970.
31. Osborne, B. A., Goldsby, R. A., and Herzenberg, L. A., *In* "Current Topics in Microbiology and Immunology" (F. Melchers, M. Potter, and N. L. Warner, Eds.), pp. 217–220. Springer-Verlag, Berlin, 1978.
32. Heusser, C. H., Anderson, C. L., and Grey, H. M., *J. Exp. Med.* **145,** 1316, 1977.
33. Krammer, P. H., Hudson, L., and Sprent, J., *J. Exp. Med.* **142,** 1403, 1975.
34. Unkeless, J. C., *J. Exp. Med.* **145,** 931, 1977.
35. Pichler, W. J., Lum, L., and Broder, S., *J. Immunol.* **121,** 1540, 1978.
36. Yodoi, J., and Ishizaka, K. *J. Immunol.* **123,** 2004, 1979.
37. Hirashima, M., Yodoi, J., and Ishizaka, K., *J. Immunol.* **125,** 2154, 1980.
38. Dickler, H. B., Kubicek, M. T., Arbeit, R. D., and Sharrow, S. O., *J. Immunol.* **119,** 348, 1977.

CELLULAR IMMUNOLOGY 63, 362–373 (1981)

Rat Leukocyte Inhibitory Factor (LIF): Similarities to Human LIF and Generation by Cells from Rats with Collagen-Induced Arthritis[1]

ROSELYNN A. DYNESIUS-TRENTHAM, DONNA ROWLAND, ELIZABETH LAROCHE, AND DAVID E. TRENTHAM[2,3]

Department of Medicine, Harvard Medical School, and the Division of Immunology and Rheumatology, Brigham and Women's Hospital, Boston, Massachusetts 02115

Received March 13, 1981; accepted May 16, 1981

Rat lymph node cells (LNC) produce a mediator which exhibits functional and physicochemical similarities to human leukocyte inhibitory factor (LIF). Measurement of LIF can be used to quantify cellular sensitivity in rats to foreign protein antigens or to a heterologous antigen *in vitro*. Concanavalin A-induced rat LIF has a molecular weight of 100,000–60,000 daltons and retains activity after heating to 56°C for 30 min. Rat LIF is not synthesized in the presence of puromycin and appears to be a protein, since it is inactivated by treatment with chymotrypsin. Moreover, the activity of rat LIF is susceptible to the serine esterase inhibitor, diisopropylphosphofluoridate, but it is resistant to neuraminidase treatment. Finally, rat LIF preferentially inhibits the migration of rat and human polymorphonuclear leukocytes but not that of rat or guinea pig peritoneal exudate cells enriched for macrophages. Except for the more dispersed size of rat LIF, these properties are analogous to those described for human LIF. LIF activity is generated, in an antigen-specific manner, by LNC sensitized to ovalbumin or purified protein derivative of tuberculin when cultured with the antigen used for sensitization. LNC from rats rendered arthritic by prior intradermal (id) injection of native chick type II collagen in incomplete Freund's adjuvant produce LIF in response to this heterologous antigen. These studies delineate a new assay for cellular sensitivity in rats and provide additional evidence that cellular reactivity to type II collagen is present in this animal model of arthritis.

INTRODUCTION

Arthritis induced in rats (1) or mice (2) by type II collagen has histologic (1–5) and immunologic (6–8) similarities to rheumatoid arthritis (9–12). Passive transfer of the arthritis by sensitized spleen and lymph node cells (LNC)[4] but not by

[1] This work was supported by Grants AM-21490, AI-07685, and AI-07167 from the National Institutes of Health and by a grant from the New England Peabody Home Foundation.

[2] Recipient of an Arthritis Senior Investigator Award.

[3] To whom correspondence should be addressed at: The Seeley G.Mudd Bldg., 250 Longwood Ave., Boston, Mass. 02115.

[4] Abbreviations used: CFA, complete Freund's adjuvant; DFP, diisopropylphosphofluoridate; HBSS, Hanks' balanced salt solution; HIA-FCS, heat-inactivated fetal calf serum; ICFA, incomplete Freund's adjuvant; LIF, leukocyte inhibitory factor; LNC, lymph node cells; MIF, macrophage migration inhibitory factor; MLC, mixed lymphocyte culture; M199, medium 199; OVA, ovalbumin; PEC, peritoneal exudate cells; PMN, polymorphonuclear leukocytes; PPD, purified protein derivative of tuberculin; S-D, Sprague–Dawley; W–L, Wistar–Lewis.

0008-8749/81/140362-12$02.00/0

serum (3) has suggested that cellular processes may be involved in the pathogenesis of what appears to be an autoimmune disease. In attempting to establish a lymphokine assay to study cellular sensitivity to collagen in this model, we found that a technique similar to that used to detect leukocyte inhibitory factor (LIF) responses in humans (10) identified a LNC product with activities and physicochemical properties analogous to human LIF. We also show in this paper that this is a useful assay to quantify cellular sensitization in rats.

MATERIALS AND METHODS

Rats

Female Wistar, Wistar–Lewis (W–L), or Sprague–Dawley (S–D) rats (Charles River Breeding Laboratories, Wilmington, Mass.) weighing 125–175 g were used.

Histocompatibility Evaluation

This commercial colony of W–L rats had been demonstrated in 1976 to be histocompatible in our laboratory, on the basis of survival of full-thickness skin grafts and results of mixed lymphocyte cultures (MLC) (3). This strain provided the LNC for all pooled cultures described in this paper. When the genetic identity of this colony was recently questioned (13), we reevaluated the histocompatibility of this strain, by a MLC technique previously described (3), using W–L rats obtained from the breeder in October 1980. Eight MLC assays yielded a mean counts per minute (cpm) ± SEM of 1572 ± 359 for tritiated thymidine incorporated by the single W–L blood mononuclear cell cultures, 9118 ± 2987 for the two-way W–L × W–L cell cultures, 10, 061 ± 4559 for the one-way W–L × mitomycin-treated S–D stimulator cell cultures, and 24,838 ± 7231 for the W–L cells cultured for 5 days with phytohemagglutinin. We cannot ascertain when, after 1976 (3), the syngeneicity of this colony was lost.

Collagen

Pepsin-solubilized native chick type II collagen was prepared and analyzed for purity by methods previously described (1).

Sensitizations

Arthritis was induced in Wistar rats by intradermal (id) injection of approximately 300 μg of native type II collagen solubilized in 0.5 ml 0.1 *M* acetic acid at 4°C and emulsified in 0.5 ml cold incomplete Freund's adjuvant (ICFA, Difco Laboratories, Detroit, Mich.) (1). Wistar rats were sensitized to ovalbumin (OVA) and purified protein derivative of tuberculin (PPD) by id injection of 250 μg of OVA (grade V, Sigma Chemical Co., St. Louis, Mo.) solubilized in 0.5 ml 0.9% NaCl and emulsified in 0.5 ml complete Freund's adjuvant (CFA containing *Mycobacterium tuberculosis* strain H37Ra, 0.5 mg/ml, Difco Laboratories). Rats injected with an emulsion of saline and ICFA provided LNC for controls.

LIF Production

By a mitogen. Cervical, axillary, and inguinal lymph nodes, hypertrophied by the id injection of the ICFA emulsion without antigen 2–3 weeks earlier, were aseptically removed from W–L rats and teased in Hanks' balanced salt solution (HBSS, Microbiological Associates, Bethesda, Md.). The LNC were washed with HBSS and centrifuged (500*g*, 35 min at room temperature) on Ficoll–Hypaque gradients (sp grav 1.076–1.078) (6) to aid in removal of nonviable cells. The interface cells were washed twice with the tissue culture medium and then cultured in Falcon 3024 flasks (Falcon Plastics, Division of BioQuest, Oxnard, Calif.) at a concentration of 10^7 cells/ml in medium 199 (M199, Microbiological Associates), supplemented with penicillin–streptomycin (100 units and 100 μg/ml, respectively), buffered with 20 m*M* Hepes solution (Grand Island Biological Co., Grand Island, N.Y.) and made to contain 2% heat-inactivated fetal calf serum (HIA-FCS, Lot 3656, IBL Tissue Culture Products, Div. of Associated Biomedic Systems Inc., Rockville, Md.), for 48 hr at 37°C in a humidified atmosphere containing 95% air–5% CO_2 in the presence or absence of concanavalin A (Con A, Miles–Yeda Laboratory, Elkhart, Ind.), 10 μg/ml. At the onset of culture, LNC viability exceeded 95% as determined by exclusion of 0.04% trypan blue. At the end of the culture period, an equivalent quantity of Con A was added to control cell suspensions, and the supernatants were clarified by centrifugation (12,000*g*, 20 min). The supernatants were collected and dialyzed extensively against 0.9% NaCl at 4°C and finally against distilled water. They were then lyophilized and stored at −20°C.

By antigens. LNC (2×10^7) from Wistar rats injected 2–3 weeks earlier with antigen or inoculated with saline–ICFA alone were processed and cultured in Falcon 3033 tubes, as described above, in the presence or absence of OVA or PPD (kindly supplied by the National Institute of Allergy and Infectious Diseases through the Joint U.S.–Japan Tuberculosis Program), 25 μg/ml, or native particulate type II collagen, 50 μg/ml (6). All antigen assays included LNC cultured with Con A, 10 μg/ml, as a control. After addition of the antigens and Con A to the control cultures and centrifugation (1050*g*, 10 min), the supernatants were routinely dialyzed in M199, sterilized by passage through 0.45-μm Millipore filters (Millipore Corp., Bedford, Mass.), and tested for LIF activity.

Assay for LIF

LIF activity was measured by its ability to inhibit the migration of rat polymorphonuclear leukocytes (PMN) from glass capillary tubes (14). Peritoneal exudate cells (PEC), enriched for PMN, were induced in three to four normal rats by injecting 10 ml of sterile 10% aqueous proteose peptone (Difco Laboratories) intraperitoneally. Approximately 16–18 hr later, the rats were sacrificed; the peritoneal wall was aseptically opened and retracted, and the cavity was gently lavaged with 35 ml HBSS. After washing the PEC once with HBSS, the suspension was centrifuged (500*g*, 35 min at room temperature) on the Ficoll–Hypaque gradients. The pellets at the bottom of the gradient, containing PMN and erythrocytes, were resuspended in 1 ml HIA-FCS, and the latter cells were lysed by addition of 10 ml of sterile water for 22 sec. Osmolarity was reestablished by adding 40 ml of M199. The remaining cells were washed twice with M199, resuspended to 15% by volume in M199 with Hepes and pen–strep, and made to contain 10% HIA-FCS. The cells were approximately 96% viable and, typically, consisted of 94% PMN, 3% eosinophils, and 3% mononuclear cells. Twenty-microliter Drummond capillary tubes (Bolab Inc., Derry, NH) were filled with the cell suspension, sealed with paraffin wax, and gently centrifuged (250g, 5 min at room temperature) (15). As in other indirect migration inhibition assays (14–19), the capillaries were cut at the cell–fluid interface and placed on glass coverslips in Mackaness-type chambers (Frank Spada, Adaps Inc., Greenlodge St., Dedham, Mass.), two capillaries per chamber. The chambers were filled with the supernatants or fractions to be tested and sealed. Each supernatant fraction was tested in two chambers. The PMN were allowed to migrate for 16–18 hr at 37°C, and the migration patterns were drawn using a projection microscope (Nikon Optical Co., New York, NY) by a person who was unaware of the identity of the media being tested. Areas of migration were determined by planimetry, and the mean areas ± SEM were calculated for the four capillaries. The percentage of inhibition of migration was then derived by the following formula:

$$\%\ \text{migration inhibition} = 1.0 - \frac{\text{mean area of migration in the supernatants from cultures with Con A or antigens}}{\text{mean area of migration in the supernatants from unstimulated cultures}} \times 100.$$

Statistical significance for the mean areas of migration was determined by Student's t test.

Fractionation of Supernatants by Gel Filtration.

Lyophilized material, derived from Con A-stimulated and unstimulated cultures, equivalent to approximately 450 ml of culture supernatant, was resuspended in 4 ml of running buffer, 0.01 M sodium phosphate, 0.15 M NaCl, pH 7.2–7.4 (18). After clarification by centrifugation (12,000g, 20 min), the material was applied to 2.5 × 100-cm columns (Pharmacia Inc., Piscataway, N.J.) containing either Sephadex G-100 or G-200 (Pharmacia). G-100 and G-200 columns were previously calibrated with blue dextran (Pharmacia), normal rat serum, bovine chymotrypsinogen A (Sigma), and bovine pancreatic RNAase (Sigma). In addition, rabbit aldolase (Pharmacia) was used to calibrate the G-200 columns. Tritiated water (New England Nuclear, Boston, Mass.) provided an internal marker for the volume of the columns. The columns were maintained at 4°C with a flow rate of 0.4 ml/min against gravity. Fractions (2.5 ml) were collected with an LKB model 7000 UltroRac fraction collector (LKB-Produkter AB, Bromma, Sweden). Beginning in the region of the void volume and prealbumin peak and continuing through the region containing molecules of the size of RNAase, fractions were formed by pooling 5 tubes. For the G-100 columns, fractions I–III contained material eluting from the void volume to the beginning of the prealbumin peak; fractions IV–VII contained molecules of the size of prealbumin and albumin; fractions X–XIII contained molecules having the size of chymotrypsinogen, and fractions VIII–IX contained material eluting between the albumin and chymotrypsinogen peaks. These pools were subsequently dialyzed in 0.9% NaCl for 12 hr and then in distilled water for 12 hr. The retentate was lyophilized and stored at −20°C. Prior to testing, the lyophilysate was rehydrated with phosphate-buffered saline (PBS) to 1/10 of its original supernatant volume. Test aliquots of 50–100 μl were taken, to which M199, supplemented with Hepes, pen–strep, and containing 10% HIA-FCS, was added to provide a total volume of 2.0 ml. This material was passed through a Millipore filter and assayed for LIF activity as described above.

Thermostability.

To assess the thermostability of our LIF activities, G-100 fractions were tested for LIF activity prior to and after heating to 56°C for 30 min (15, 18).

Effect of Puromycin.

De novo protein synthesis was inhibited in selected antigen assays by the addition of puromycin (Calbiochem–Behring Corp., La Jolla, Calif.), 1×10^{-4} *M*, at the onset of LNC culture, followed by extensive dialysis in M199 (20–22).

Treatment with Chymotrypsin.

To study whether rat LIF is a protein, G-100 Con A-stimulated and control fractions were incubated with chymotrypsin (15, 18). Lyophilized active and control fractionated material, equivalent to 40 ml of supernatant, was dissolved in 4 ml PBS and divided into two equal aliquots. The pH was adjusted to 8.4 with 0.1 *M* NaOH. To one aliquot of active and control supernatant, 4.0 mg of water-insoluble chymotrypsin (Miles Laboratories, Kankakee, Ill.) was added. The supernatants were kept at pH 8.6 and room temperature for 18 hr with constant mixing. The remaining aliquots were incubated under the same conditions in the absence of the enzyme. After incubation, chymotrypsin was removed by centrifugation (15,000*g*, 10 min) and the supernatants were reequilibrated to pH 7.2 with 0.1 *N* HCl, made to contain 10% HIA-FCS, membrane sterilized, and tested for LIF activity.

Treatment with Neuraminidase.

For assessing the role of sialic acid residues in the biologic activity of rat LIF, we performed experiments using the glycosidase, neuraminidase (15). Lyophilized material derived from 40 ml of G-100 LIF-enriched and control fractions was dissolved in 4 ml of 0.03 *M* sodium acetate buffer, pH 5.1 and clarified, and, again, each fraction was divided into two equal aliquots. One hundred microliters of neuraminidase from *Vibrio cholerae* (sp act 500 units/ml, Grand Island Biological Co.), dissolved in 0.03 *M* Na-acetate, was added to one aliquot of active and control supernatants. One hundred microliters 0.03 *M* Na acetate was added to the other samples as a buffer control. The mixtures were incubated at 37°C for 1 hr with constant rocking. After incubation, the pH was adjusted to 7.4 with 0.1 *M* NaOH; HIA-FCS was added to a final concentration of 10%, and the supernatants were passed through a Millipore filter and assayed for LIF activity. This neuraminidase preparation was found to be active during concurrent experiments in our laboratory (23).

Treatment with a Serine Esterase Inhibitor.

Since human LIF is sensitive to serine esterase inhibitors (24,25), we subjected our rat LIF preparations to diisopropylphosphofluoridate (DFP) treatment. G-100-active and control fractions were incubated in the presence or absence of 2×10^{-4}

M DFP (Sigma) at 37°C for 45 min. They were then dialyzed extensively, first in 0.9% NaCl and then in M199 (25). Just prior to testing, the retentates were made to contain 10% HIA-FCS and filtered.

Ability of LIF to Inhibit the Migration of Other Indicator Cells.

G-100-derived LIF preparations were assayed on rat and human PMN (10), as well as rat and guinea pig macrophage-rich PEC, to determine whether rat LIF exhibited preferential inhibitory activity for PMN migration. Previously described methods were used to obtain human PMN (10) and guinea pig PEC (17). Macrophage-rich rat PEC were obtained by harvesting PEC from normal rats injected with proteose peptone 72 hr earlier and centrifuged on the Ficoll–Hypaque gradients. The interface cells were used as indicator cells in a manner identical to that followed for the PMN. The interface cells and the guinea pig PEC both contained approximately 80% macrophages by esterase staining (26) and were contaminated by less than 5% PMN.

RESULTS

Fractionation by Gel Filtration.

When crude supernatants from Con A-stimulated W–L LNC cultures were chromatographed on Sephadex G-100 in six separate experiments, LIF activity was

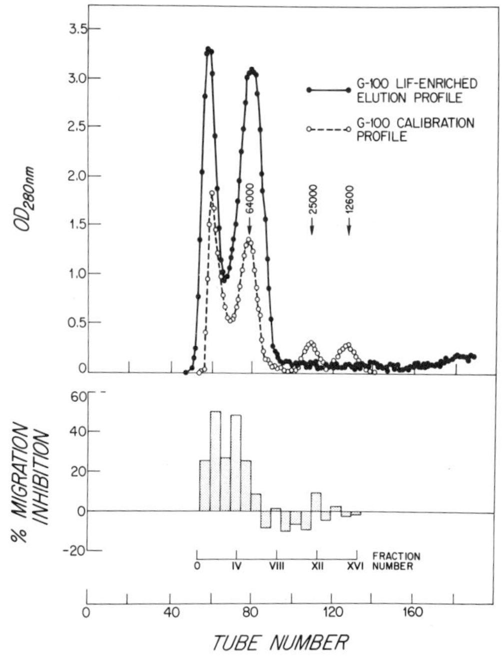

FIG. 1. Fractionation of Con A-induced rat LIF on Sephadex G-100 columns. The solid line in the upper graph depicts the elution pattern at 280 nm of a LIF-containing supernatant. The control supernatants had a similar elution pattern. The dotted line shows the locations of the markers rat serum albumin, molecular weight 63,600, bovine chymotrypsinogen A, molecular weight 25,000, and bovine pancreatic RNAase, molecular weight 12,600. In the bottom graph, the bars represent the inhibition of rat PMN migrations found in the various fractions in a representative experiment. Fractionation on Sephadex G-200 columns indicated that molecules whose size exceeded 100,000 daltons did not contain inhibitory activity.

TABLE 1

Stability of Rat LIF at 56°C for 30 min

Experiment	1	2	3	4
Unheated	29[a]	45	24	40
Heated	38	37	34	42

[a] Percentage inhibition of migration.

recovered as shown in Fig. 1. Maximal inhibition of migration was found in fractions I–V (mean % LIF ± SEM 26 ± 3, $P < 0.001$) containing molecules ranging in molecular weight from 100,000 to 60,000. Fractions VI–XVI did not contain significant activity. Passage of crude supernatants over Sephadex G-200 columns also indicated that molecules exhibiting significant inhibitory activity (mean % LIF 50 ± 4) possessed molecular weights ranging from 100,000 to 60,000.

Thermostability and Puromycin Inhibition of Synthesis.

G-100-fractionated rat LIF retained activity after heating to 56°C for 30 min (Table 1). Moreover, fractionated LIF remained active after storage in a lyophilized state for several months at −20°C. Generation of LIF by antigens required protein synthesis, since induction of activity could be blocked by addition of puromycin at the onset of culture (Table 2). Exclusion of trypan blue showed that greater than 90% of the LNC were still viable at the end of cultures conducted in the presence or absence of puromycin.

Sensitivity to Chymotrypsin but Resistance to Neuraminidase Treatment.

The activity of fractionated LIF could be destroyed by incubation with water-insoluble chymotrypsin, indicating that rat LIF is a protein (27) (Table 3). However, neuraminidase treatment did not alter its activity, suggesting that terminal sialic acid residues are not involved in the biologic activity of this lymphokine (Table 4).

Inactivation by DFP.

Identical to human LIF (24, 25), experiments with DFP and active G-100 fractions suggested that rat LIF possesses properties characteristic of an esterase (Fig.

TABLE 2

Inhibition of Antigen Production of Rat LIF by Puromycin

	Experiment		
Antigen	1	2	3
OVA			
No puromycin	52[a]	44	39
Puromycin	8	10	5
PPD			
No puromycin	48	46	54
Puromycin	5	2	18

[a] Percentage inhibition of migration.

TABLE 3

Inactivation of Rat LIF by Chymotrypsin

Experiment	Prior to incubation	After incubation	
		With chymotrypsin	Alone
1	44[a]	−24	42
2	69	−12	36

[a] Percentage inhibition of migration.

2). The conditions and concentration of DFP used in these incubations have been previously shown to inactivate serine esterases (28).

Preferential Activity for PMN Migration.

Since products of activated lymphocytes can inhibit the migration of macrophages–monocytes, as well as PMN (14), we assayed LIF-active fractions for their ability to inhibit the migration of homologous and heterologous macrophage-rich PEC and PMN. As shown in Table 5, rat LIF exhibited inhibitory activity for rat and human PMN but did not affect the migration of rat or guinea pig PEC enriched for macrophages. In additional experiments, we found that human LIF, generated in crude supernatants by the antigen, streptokinase–streptodornase (10, 14) inhibited the migration of rat PMN in the presence of 10% HIA-human AB serum or HIA-FCS (data not shown). Thus, rat LIF, like human LIF (14), appears to be a distinct mediator functionally separable from the previously described lymphokine, rat macrophage migration inhibitory factor (MIF) (29).

Induction by Antigens and a Heterologous Antigen, Type II Collagen.

Rat LNC, cultured in the presence of the antigen used for sensitization, generated LIF activity which was nondialyzable (Fig. 3). Approximately 50% of Wistar rats injected id with native type II collagen emulsified in ICFA developed macroscopic evidence of arthritis 2–3 weeks later. As shown in Fig. 4, LIF responses to type II collagen correlated with the occurrence of arthritis in these experiments (mean % LIF 29 ± 3 for 51 arthritic rats vs 9 ± 2 for 30 nonarthritic rats, $P < 0.0001$). These assays provide additional evidence that cellular sensitivity to type II collagen can be achieved in this model without the use of CFA. We observed that the induction of LIF was antigen specific, since LNC from 12 rats sensitized to collagen

TABLE 4

Resistance of Rat LIF to Neuraminidase

After incubation with	Experiment			
	1	2	3	4
Buffer	51[a]	45	41	52
Neuraminidase	52	57	62	45

[a] Percentage inhibition of migration.

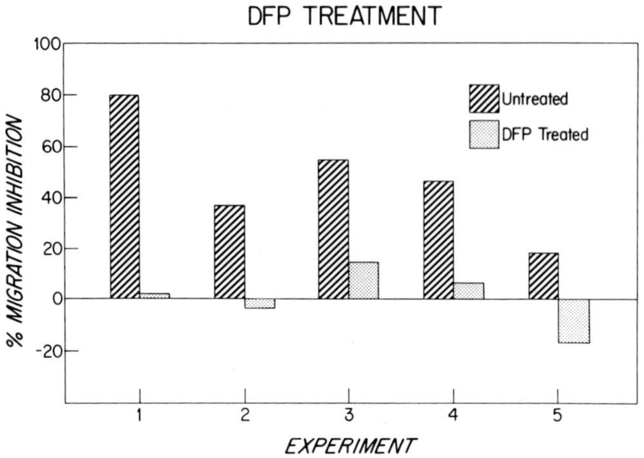

FIG. 2. Inactivation of G-100-fractionated rat LIF by prior incubation with 2×10^{-4} *M* DFP. Control fractions were incubated under identical conditions in the absence of DFP.

(mean % LIF 28 ± 3) did not produce LIF in response to OVA or PPD (mean % LIF 2 ± 2 and 4 ± 2, respectively). Likewise cells from 8 rats injected with OVA in CFA responded to OVA and PPD (mean % LIF 31 ± 4 and 34 ± 5, respectively) but failed to react to collagen (mean % LIF 3 ± 2).

DISCUSSION

In this paper, we have shown that rat LIF is a LNC product which is inducible by a mitogen as well as several antigens. Since mononuclear cells other than lymphocytes may produce or modify mediators of immune reactions, our experiments do not definitively identify this LIF as a lymphokine. Rat LIF exhibits physicochemical, enzymatic, and functional properties similar to those previously reported for human LIF (Table 6) (14, 15, 21, 24, 25). The only difference that we have

TABLE 5

Inhibitory Activity of Rat LIF for Various Indicator Cell Migrations[a]

G-100 fraction	Indicator cells[b]: Rat PMN	Human PMN	Rat PEC	Guinea pig PEC
Control (C)	64 ± 4[c]	75 ± 1	22 ± 2	18 ± 0
Active (A)	20 ± 2	31 ± 4	24 ± 2	16 ± 2
% inhibition (A/C)	70 (0.001)[d]	59 (0.001)	−8 (N.S.)	14 (N.S.)

[a] Results in a representative assay from three separate experiments using a Sephadex G-100 fraction enriched for LIF.

[b] Migration of all indicator cells occurred in the presence of 10% HIA-FCS. PMN contained less than 5% mononuclear cells. PEC consisted of approximately 80% macrophages by esterase staining and less than 5% PMN.

[c] Mean ± SEM area of migration in planimeter units from quadruplicate capillaries.

[d] *P* value by Student's *t* test. N.S., not significant.

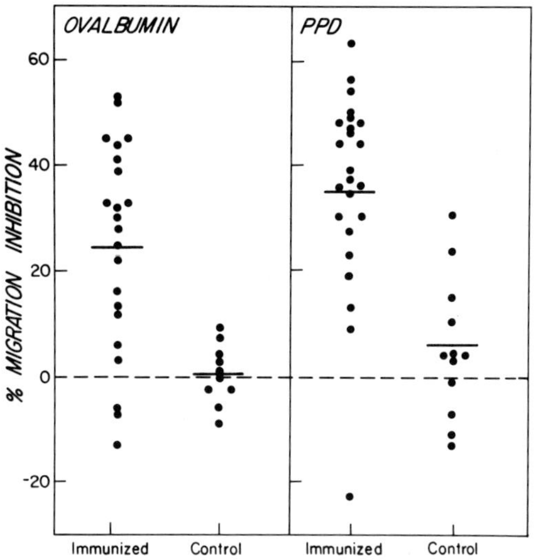

FIG. 3. LIF responses to the soluble protein antigens OVA and PPD using Wistar rat LNC sensitized by id injection of OVA emulsified in CFA 2–4 weeks earlier. Control LNC were obtained from Wistar rats injected 2–4 weeks earlier with a saline–ICFA emulsion. The mean responses to both antigens by sensitized LNC were significantly ($P < 0.0001$) greater than the corresponding responses by the non-sensitized LNC in these assays. LIF production to Con A by LNC from the immunized and control groups was similar (mean % LIF 58 ± 5 vs 62 ± 6, respectively, P not significant). Although these assays routinely included antigen addition to control cultures at the end of incubation and subsequent dialysis of the supernatants, additional experiments indicated that both of these practices had little effect on indicator cell migrations or magnitude of the LIF responses to these antigens.

found is that molecules possessing LIF activity in the rat appear to be more heterogeneous than human proteins with LIF activity (15), based on the greater molecular weight range exhibited by the rat mediator during gel filtration studies. The resemblance of rat LIF to its human counterpart is of interest, since other lymphokines, with analogous biologic activities *in vitro*, possess even greater species variability in their physicochemical behavior. Differences among guinea pig (30), human (31), murine (18), and sheep (32) MIF illustrate this point.

LNC from Wistar, as well as W–L, rats produced LIF activity in response to Con A in these experiments. However, we would caution that the characterization studies of Con A-induced rat LIF utilized pooled cultures of LNC from a W–L

TABLE 6

Comparison of the Properties of Rat and Human LIF

	Rat LIF	Human LIF
Indicator cell	PMN	PMN
Temp 56°C	Stable	Stable
Puromycin	Inhibits synthesis	Inhibits synthesis
G-100 filtration	100,000–60,000 daltons	68,000 daltons
Chymotrypsin	Sensitive	Sensitive
Neuraminidase	Resistant	Resistant
DFP	Sensitive	Sensitive
Antigen induction	Specific	Specific

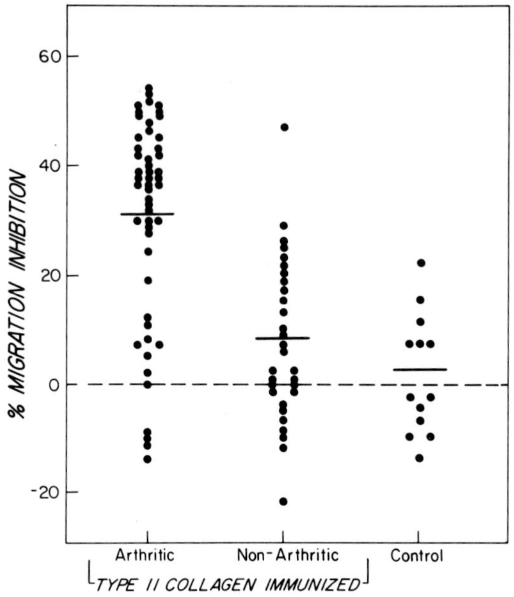

FIG. 4. Comparison of LIF responses to particulate native type II collagen by LNC from arthritic and nonarthritic Wistar rats injected 2–4 weeks earlier with the collagen emulsified in ICFA. Control LNC were obtained from Wistar rats injected 2–4 weeks earlier with a saline–ICFA emulsion. Again, LIF responses to Con A by LNC from all three groups were comparable (mean % LIF 62 ± 4 arthritic vs 55 ± 5 nonarthritic vs 62 ± 5 control, *P* not significant). The majority of these assays included addition of collagen to control cultures at the end of the incubation period. However, after determining that the presence of collagen at these concentrations does not influence indicator cell migrations, we have terminated this practice, as in our human LIF assay (10), to conserve collagen.

colony which we and others (13) have subsequently found to be nonidentical at the major histocompatibility complex. Thus, we cannot exclude, at present, the participation of alloantigenic determinants in the generation of the LIF activity which we observed after Sephadex fractionation.

The antigen-specific LIF responses to OVA, PPD, and type II collagen that we found in this study, using LNC from Wistar rats, parallels our earlier results *in vitro* using thymidine incorporation assays (6) or *in vivo* with a radiometric ear assay (8) to quantify delayed hypersensitivity in this strain of rats. Moreover, the reproducibility of our results in this paper suggests that the indirect LIF assay has utility in assessing an additional parameter of cellular sensitivity in the rat.

Previous studies have indicated that rats with type II collagen-induced arthritis manifest cellular sensitivity to this protein (6–8). There is a temporal correlation between the onset of this polyarthritis and the acquisition of cellular sensitivity to type II collagen, as measured by cellular proliferation responses *in vitro* (6, 7). In the present study, the production of LIF to type II collagen also correlated with the occurrence of arthritis in rats injected with the collagen in ICFA. This provides additional evidence for the presence of cellular sensitivity to collagen in arthritic rats. As was previously shown in guinea pigs with experimental allergic encephalomyelitis (33), our data also demonstrate that a soluble factor can be detected to a heterologous antigen which is capable of inducing an immunologically mediated (3) disease.

ACKNOWLEDGMENT

The authors wish to thank Dr. John R. David for his advice and critical review of this manuscript.

REFERENCES

1. Trentham, D. E., Townes, A. S., and Kang, A. H., *J. Exp. Med.* **146,** 857, 1977.
2. Courtenay, J. S., Dallman, M. J., Dayan, A. D., Martin, A. B., and Mosedale, B., *Nature (London)* **283,** 666, 1980.
3. Trentham, D. E., Dynesius, R. A., and David, J. R., *J. Clin. Invest.* **62,** 359, 1978.
4. Stuart, J. M., Cremer, M. A., Dixit, S. N., Kang, A. H., and Townes, A. S., *Arthritis Rheum.* **22,** 347, 1979.
5. Morgan, K., Clague, R. B., Shaw, M. J., and Holt, P. J. L, *Ann. Rheum. Dis.* **39,** 285, 1980.
6. Trentham, D. E., Townes, A. S., Kang, A. H., David, J. R., *J. Clin. Invest.* **61,** 89, 1978.
7. Stuart, J. M, Cremer M. A., Kang, A. H., and Townes, A. S., *Arthritis Rheum.* **22,** 1344, 1979.
8. Trentham, D. E., McCune, W. J., Susman, P., and David, J. R., *J. Clin. Invest.* **66,** 1109, 1980.
9. Andriopoulos, N. A., Mestecky, J., Miller, E. J., and Bradley, E. L., *Arthritis Rheum.* **19,** 613, 1976.
10. Trentham, D. E., Dynesius, R. A., Rocklin, R. E., and David, J. R., *N. Engl. J. Med.* **299,** 327, 1978.
11. Endler, A. T., Zielinski, Ch., Menzel, E. J., Smolen, J. S., Schwägerl, W., Endler, M., Eberl, R., Frank, O., and Steffen, C, *Z. Rheumatol.* **37,** 87, 1978.
12. Stuart, J. M., Postlethwaite, A. E., Townes, A. S., and Kang, A. H., *Amer. J. Med.* **69,** 13, 1980.
13. Bitter-Suermann, H., and Lewis, M. G., *Transplantation* **30,** 158, 1980.
14. Rocklin, R. E., *J. Immunol.* **112,** 1461, 1974.
15. Rocklin, R. E., *J. Immunol.* **114,** 1161, 1975.
16. David, J. R., and Schlossman, S. F., *J. Exp. Med.* **128,** 1451, 1968.
17. David, J. R., and David, R. A., *In* "*In Vitro* Methods in Cell-Mediated Immunity" (B. R. Bloom and P. R. Glade, Eds.), pp. 249–258. Academic Press, New York, 1971.
18. Kühner, A. L., and David, J. R., *J. Immunol.* **116,** 140, 1976.
19. Rocklin, R. E., Meyers, O. L., and David, J. R., *J. Immunol.* **104,** 95, 1970.
20. Trentham, D. E., Dynesius, R. A., Rocklin, R. E., and David, J. R., *Trans. Assoc. Amer. Physicians XCI* **118,** 1979.
21. Mitchell, C. C., Smith, M. G. M., Golding, P. L., Eddleston, A.L.W.F., and Williams, R., *Clin. Exp. Immunol.* **11,** 535, 1972.
22. Sharma, S. D., and Piessens, W. F., *Cell. Immunol.* **38,** 264, 1978.
23. Liu, D. Y., Petschek, K. D., Remold, H. G., and David, J. R., *J. Immunol.* **124,** 2042, 1980.
24. Bendtzen, K., *Scand. J. Immunol.* **6,** 125, 1977.
25. Rocklin, R. E., and Rosenthal, A. S., *J. Immunol.* **119,** 249, 1977.
26. Koski, I. R., Poplack, D. G., and Blaese, R. M., *In* "*In Vitro* Methods in Cell-Mediated and Tumor Immunity" (B. R. Bloom and J. R. David, Eds.), pp. 359–362. Academic Press, New York, 1976.
27. Remold, H. G., and David, J. R., *J. Immunol.* **107,** 1090, 1971.
28. Aldridge, W. N., and Reiner, E., "Enzyme Inhibitors as Substrates," p. 11. North Holland, Amsterdam, 1972.
29. Bakker, W. W., Engelhart, J. J., Mulder, I., and Hoedemaeker, P. J., *Int. Arch. Allergy Appl. Immunol.* **49,** 491, 1975.
30. Remold, H. G., and David, J. R., *In* "Proceedings of the Sixth Leukocyte Culture Conference" (M. R. Schwartz, Ed.), pp. 283–295. Academic Press, New York, 1972.
31. Rocklin, R. E., Remold, H. G., and David, J. R., *Cell. Immunol.* **5,** 436, 1972.
32. Scott, D. M., McConnell, I., Agomo, P., and Lachmann, P. J., *Immunology* **34,** 591, 1978.
33. David, J. R., and Paterson, P. Y., *J. Exp. Med.* **122,** 1161, 1965.

CELLULAR IMMUNOLOGY 63, 374–384 (1981)

Modulation of Lymphocyte Mitogen Responses by Cocultured Fibroblasts[1]

JOSEPH H. KORN[2]

Division of Rheumatology, Department of Medicine, Veterans Administration Medical Center and University of Connecticut School of Medicine, Newington, Connecticut 06111

Received April 10, 1981; accepted June 12, 1981

Immunological reactions *in vivo* occur in an environment rich in fibroblasts (FB) and other connective tissue cells. The possibility that FB might affect mononuclear cell proliferative responses to mitogens *in vitro* was examined in a microculture system. Human peripheral blood mononuclear cells (MC) were cocultured with mitomycin C-treated FB in the presence of phytohemagglutinin (PHA) or pokeweed mitogen (PWM). Cocultured FB (at a 1:100 to 1:10 FB:MC ratio) suppressed the response of MC to PHA (by as much as 35%) but did not significantly affect PWM responses. Cocultures of FB and MC were characterized by 10- to 30-fold increases in prostaglandin E_2 concentrations compared to MC or FB cultured alone. Inhibition of prostaglandin synthesis with indomethacin or mefenamic acid significantly reversed the FB-mediated suppression of lymphocyte PHA responses. Prostaglandin-dependent FB suppression of lymphocyte PHA responses was seen only when FB:MC coculture was initiated at the onset of exposure of MC to PHA. When FB were added to MC after 24 hr of culture with PHA, no effect was seen. Addition at 48 or 66 hr resulted in prostaglandin-independent enhancement of lymphocyte proliferative responses to PHA. Thus in cocultures of FB and MC, MC reactivity to PHA may be influenced in part via alterations in FB prostaglandin metabolism. The interaction between FB and MC may be important in the modulation of immune responses in inflammatory lesions.

INTRODUCTION

Immunological reactions *in vivo* occur in a milieu which includes not only leukocytes but other cellular elements such as fibroblasts (FB),[3] smooth muscle cells, and endothelial cells. The possible role of these other cell types in modulating immune processes has not been well delineated. Accumulating evidence does, however, indicate that a variety of products of FB may influence lymphocyte and monocyte function. Such products include prostaglandins, interferon, hyaluronic acid, and collagen (1–4). In addition, activation of connective tissue cells at the sites of inflammatory lesions may lead to great increases in the concentrations of these mediators. For example, we and others have shown that products of mono-

[1] This work was supported by grants from the Medical Research Service of the Veterans Administration and the University of Connecticut Research Foundation

[2] Recipient of a Veterans Administration Clinical Investigator Award.

[3] Abbreviations used: FB, fibroblasts; MC, mononuclear cells; PGE_2, prostaglandin E_2; PHA, phytohemagglutinin; PWM, pokeweed mitogen; INDO, indomethacin.

0008-8749/81/140374-11$02.00/0

nuclear cells (MC) may markedly stimulate prostaglandin synthesis by connective tissue cells (5, 6).

The present studies were undertaken to determine whether FB and FB products might alter lymphocyte reactivity to mitogens *in vitro*. A technique for MC–FB coculture was developed which would allow examination of dynamic interactions between MC and FB. This model was used to determine the effect of cocultured FB on the response of human peripheral blood MC to the mitogens phytohemagglutinin (PHA) and pokeweed mitogen (PWM). Our results suggest that in the presence of MC there were large increases in FB prostaglandin synthesis which in turn altered the lymphocyte response to mitogens. This interaction between MC and FB may have pathophysiological significance.

MATERIALS AND METHODS

Cell cultures. Human foreskin FB were obtained from collagenase digests of neonatal foreskin and maintained as described previously (5). FB were used between the 5th and 20th subpassage in culture. Human peripheral blood mononuclear cells were obtained by Ficoll–Hypaque (LSM, lymphocyte separation medium, Litton Bionetics, Kensington, Md.) flotation as described previously (5). Cells were washed twice in RPMI 1640 (Grand Island Biological Co., Grand Island, N.Y.) before use.

FB–MC cocultures. Confluent FB cultures were harvested by brief exposure to 0.25% trypsin (type III, Sigma Chemical Co., St. Louis, Mo.) with 0.02% EDTA. The cells were washed twice and resuspended at 10^5 cells/ml RPMI 1640 containing 50 μg/ml of mitomycin C (Sigma Chemical Co.). After incubation at 37°C for 30 min cells were washed twice in RPMI 1640 and resuspended at appropriate concentration in RMPI/20% AB serum.

Mitomycin-treated fibroblasts (FB_M) were dropped in 100-μl volumes into quadruplicate wells of flat-bottomed 96-well tissue culture plates (Costar, Bellco Glass, Vineland N.J.) and cultured overnight at 37°C in a 95% air/5% CO_2 humidified atmosphere. The culture medium was then removed and the FB overlayed with 50 μl of RMPI/20% AB serum followed by 50 μl of 0.32% agarose (Seaplaque agarose, Marine Colloids, Rockland, Maine) heated to 42.5°C. Control wells (to which no fibroblasts had been added) were identically treated. After allowing the agarose to harden at room temperature for 5 min, 10^5 MC in 100 μl RPMI/20% AB serum containing phytohemagglutinin (PHA) or pokeweed (PWM) were added to control and FB-containing wells.[4] Final concentrations of both PHA and PWM were 2.5 μg/ml, a previously determined optimal mitogen dose.

The culture plates were incubated at 37°C (in humidified 95% air/5% CO_2) for 72 hr. One microcurie of tritiated thymidine ([^{3}H]TdR, 6.7 Ci/mol, New England Nuclear, Boston, Mass.) was added to each well for the final 6 hr of culture. Cells were harvested onto glass fiber filters (Microbiological Associates, Kensington, Md.) using a semiautomated cell harvester (Otto Hiller Co., Madison, Wisc.). Filter discs were counted in liquid scintillation medium (Econofluor, New England Nuclear) using a Packard-Tricarb Scintillation Counter.

[4] When MC and FB are cocultured in the absence of a separating layer of agarose, there is significant FB cytotoxicity (J. H. Korn, unpublished observations).

The adequacy of mitomycin treatment was ascertained by pulsing and harvesting wells with FB_M to which no MC had been added. [^{3}H]TdR incorporation for mitomycin-treated FB ranged from 190 ± 24 to 229 ± 32 cpm at FB concentrations of 10^3 to 10^4 cells/well.

Assay for PGE_2 in lymphocyte–fibroblast cultures. PGE_2 in lymphocyte–fibroblast cultures was determined by radioimmunoassay using a commercial rabbit anti-PGE_2 antiserum (Boeringer–Mannheim, Indianapolis, Ind., Lot 0.01). The antibody to PGE_2 shows a 3.2% cross-reaction with PGE_1 and less than 0.5% with prostaglandins A_1, A_2, B_1, B_2, $F_{1\alpha}$, and $F_{2\alpha}$. Samples for assay were obtained by withdrawing 50–100 μl of media from quadruplicate culture wells; samples from the first and second and the third and fourth wells were pooled to give duplicate samples of 100–200 μl. Samples were frozen at −20°C until assayed, usually within 3 weeks.

For assay of PGE_2, 100 μl each of: test sample, tritiated PGE_2 (100–200 Ci/mmol, New England Nuclear) diluted to 30,000 cpm/ml, and antibody to PGE_2 were added to 1.5-ml polypropylene tubes (Sarstedt, Princeton, N.J.), and incubated for 1 hr at 37°C. All dilutions (of antibody, labeled PGE_2, and test sample) were made in 0.1 *M* phosphate buffer, pH 7.35, containing 0.9% NaCl, 0.2% gelatin, and 0.02% NaN_3 (assay buffer). Antibody-complexed PGE_2 was removed by overnight incubation at 4°C of the reaction mixture with 40 μl of agarose-bound goat anti-rabbit IgG beads (Miles-Yeda, Elkhardt, Ind.) followed by centrifugation at 4°C for 10 min at 1000*g*. Supernate (170 μl) was removed, added to 3.0 ml scintillation fluid (Aquasol, New England Nuclear) and counted in a Packard-Tricarb Scintillation Counter. PGE_2 concentrations were estimated from a standard curve of 0.05–5.0 ng/ml PGE_2 (Upjohn Co., Kalamazoo, Mich.) vs percentage [^{3}H]PGE_2 bound. Total binding in the absence of test sample ranged from 35 to 45%. Each test sample was assayed at two or more dilutions (in assay buffer).

RESULTS

Fibroblasts cultured with MC significantly inhibited the MC response to PHA (Fig. 1). The inhibition ranged from 16 ± 3% (SEM) ($P < 0.01$) at a FB:MC ratio of 1:100 to 35 ± 4% ($P < 0.01$) at a FB:MC ratio of 1:10. Conversely, the MC response to PWM was not significantly altered by coculture with FB, with 100, 107, and 110% of the control response at FB:MC ratios of 1:100, 1:30, and 1:10, respectively. The failure of FB to inhibit the PWM response made it unlikely that the inhibition of PHA responses was due to a nonspecific toxic effect of the FB on MC such as might occur from release of residual mitomycin C into the culture medium. There was also no mitogenic effect of the allogeneic FB on the MC cultures; MC cultured with FB in the absence of mitogen incorporated no more [^{3}H]TdR than did MC without cocultured FB (data not shown).

Role of Prostaglandins in FB–MC Interaction

We have previously shown that supernates of MC stimulate FB PGE_2 synthesis (5). Because prostaglandins of the E series are known to modulate lymphocyte responses (1, 7), we examined generation of PGE_2 in the MC–FB cocultures and the effect of inhibiting prostaglandin synthesis.

Coculture of MC with FB resulted in a marked enhancement of PGE_2 synthesis

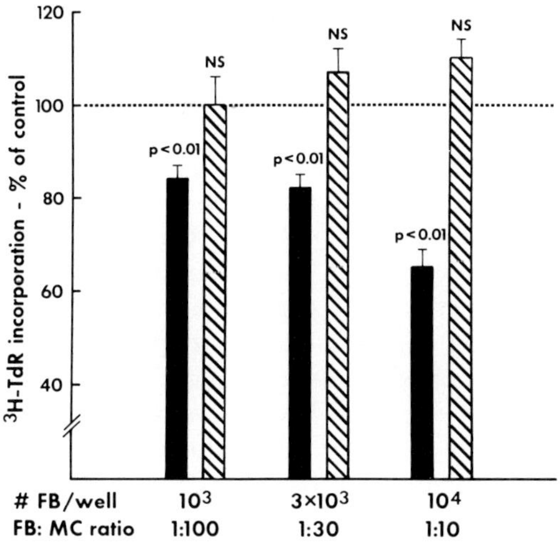

FIG. 1. Suppression of MC PHA response by cocultured FB. MC (10^5/well) were cultured with increasing concentrations of FB in the presence of PHA (solid bars) or PWM (hatched bars). Each bar represents the mean ($\pm$SEM) for nine separate experiments. [^{3}H]Thymidine incorporation is expressed as percentage of control cultures, i.e., MC cultured with mitogen in the absence of FB. Mean ($\pm$SEM) cpm for PHA-stimulated MC and PWM stimulated MC and PWM stimulated MC were 94,260 $\pm$ 8146 and 18,650 $\pm$ 3158, respectively. The *P* values were determined by a paired *t* test comparing cultures with added FB to those without added FB.

(Fig. 2). When 10^4 FB were cultured alone, the PGE_2 concentration achieved was 1.8 $\pm$ 0.5 ng/ml. In the absence of mitogen, the PGE_2 concentration in MC cultured alone was 0.5 $\pm$ 0.1 ng/ml; with PHA this increased to 0.8 $\pm$ 0.2 ng/ml. The concentration of PGE_2 in FB:MC cocultures increased from 3.2 $\pm$ 0.6 ng/ml with 10^3 FB/well to 29.3 $\pm$ 10.2 ng/ml with 10^4 FB/well. The increases in PGE_2 synthesis with MC–FB coculture were similar in cultures containing PHA and PWM.

Although supernates of MC can stimulate FB PGE_2 synthesis, it was possible that the increased PGE_2 in the cocultures was largely or partly monocyte derived. To determine whether FB products might stimulate monocyte PGE_2 synthesis, supernates of FB cultures were added to MC stimulated with PHA and the supernatant medium of these cultures, in turn, assayed for PGE_2. Furthermore, to examine the possibility that stimulatory FB products might only be released after MC-mediated stimulation of the FB, supernates of FB cultures that had been so stimulated were also examined. MC synthesis of PGE_2 increased from 2.5 $\pm$ 0.2 ng/ml to 8.6 $\pm$ 0.9 and 7.6 $\pm$ 1.8 ng/ml in the presence of 1.5 and 25% FB supernate, respectively (Table 1). "Stimulated" FB supernates increased the PGE_2 concentration in MC cultures to an even greater extent: 9.3 $\pm$ 2.1 and 28.0 $\pm$ 3.1 ng/ml at supernate concentrations of 1.5 and 25%, respectively, increases of 4- to 10-fold. In contrast, 25% MC supernates increased FB PGE_2 synthesis from 1.7 $\pm$ 0.3 to 130 $\pm$ 14 ng/ml, a 75-fold increase (not shown). Furthermore, much of the increased PGE_2 in MC cultures to which 25% FB supernate had been added can be explained by passive carry-over of PGE_2 in the FB supernate. Thus, it appears likely that most of the increased PGE_2 in MC–FB cocultures is FB derived.

To examine whether the increased PGE_2 synthesis in MC–FB cocultures was playing a role in the modulation of MC mitogen responses, cocultures were established in the presence or absence of indomethacin. Addition of indomethacin to MC cultured with PHA in the absence of FB resulted in enhanced mitogen responsiveness to 112 ± 3% of control levels. The depressed PHA responses of MC cultured with FB were restored by the addition of indomethacin (Fig. 3, upper panel). At the two lower FB concentrations, the depressed responses were reversed completely ($P < 0.05$ by paired t test). At the highest FB concentration, reversal of the FB-mediated suppressive effect was incomplete and not statistically significant. The failure of indomethacin to completely reverse the suppressive effect of 10^4 FB on MC proliferation occurred despite inhibition of PGE_2 synthesis; PGE_2 concentrations of the presence of indomethacin decreased by 97% to 0.9 ± 0.4 ng/ml. The FB-mediated suppression of MC PHA responses was similarly reversed by mefenamic acid, another inhibitor of prostaglandin synthesis (Table 2). Like indomethacin, mefenamic acid was effective only in reversing the FB suppressive effect of the two lowest FB concentrations. The effects of indomethacin and mefenamic acid in paired cultures was comparable.

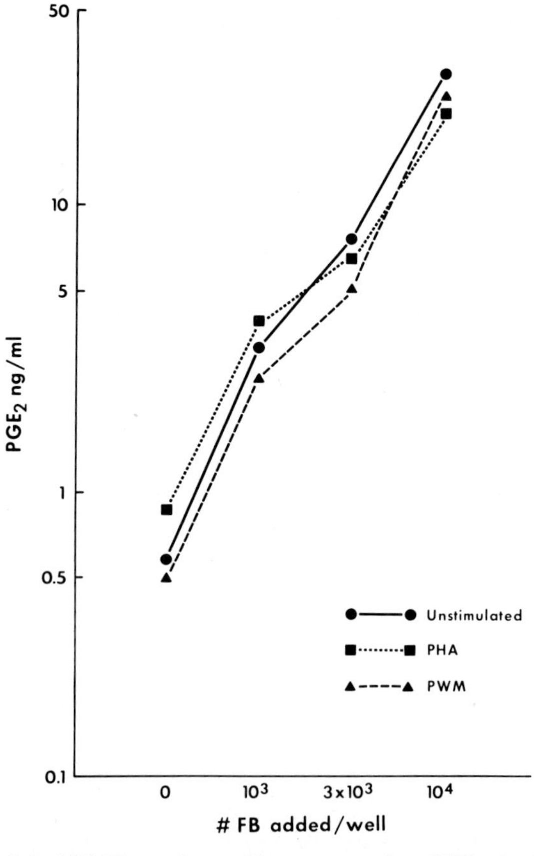

FIG. 2. PGE_2 synthesis in MC:FB cocultures. The concentration of PGe_2 in the supernatant medium of MC or MC–FB cultures was determined by radioimmunoassay. Each point represents the mean for five separate experiments. The concentration of PGE_2 in supernates of FB (10^4) cultured without MC was 1.8 ± 0.5 ng/ml (mean ± SEM, $n = 4$).

TABLE 1

Effect of Fibroblast Supernates on Mononuclear Cell PGE_2 Synthesis

Addition to MC culture[a]	PGE_2 (ng/10^5 cells)
None	2.5 ± 0.2[b]
FB Supernate[c] (%)	
1.5	8.6 ± 0.9**
25	7.6 ± 1.8*
"Stimulated" FB Supernate[d] (%)	
1.5	9.3 ± 2.1*
25	28.0 ± 3.1***

[a] 10^5 MC were cultured in quadruplicate wells of culture plates for 72 hr in the presence of 2.5 μg/ml of phytohemagglutin +/− FB supernate. At the termination of culture, the supernatant medium from adjacent wells was pooled to yield duplicate samples for PGE_2 assay.

[b] Each value represents the mean ± SEM for four experiments. *$P < 0.05$, **$P < 0.01$, and ***$P < 0.001$ compared to MC with no addition (Student's t test).

[c] FB were cultured at 3.1×10^4 cells/cm^2 in 60-mm culture dishes for 48 hr. (This cell density is equivalent to 10^4 FB/microwell.) The supernatant medium was rendered cell free by passage through a 0.45-μm filter and added in a 1.5 or 25% (v/v) final concentration to the MC cultures. The FB supernate contained 1.7 ± 0.3 ng/ml of PGE_2.

[d] "Stimulated" FB supernates were made by adding 25% MC-SN (obtained from 3-day PHA-stimulated MC cultures) to the FB cultures which were then treated as in c above. Stimulated FB supernates contained 130 ± 14 ng/ml of PGE_2.

The reversal of FB-mediated suppression by these two different inhibitors of prostaglandin synthetase (cyclooxygenase) suggested that one or more prostaglandins were indeed involved in the suppression seen. To determine whether the increased synthesis of PGE_2 observed was responsible for the suppression, exogenous PGE_2 was added to MC cultures (in the absence of FB) stimulated with PHA. PGE_2 added at final concentrations of 5 and 50 ng/ml suppressed the MC response to PHA by 12 ± 4% (mean ± SEM, $n = 4$, $P < 0.05$ by paired t test) and 20 ± 4% ($n = 4$, $P < 0.025$), respectively. Thus PGE_2, at concentrations achieved in the MC:FB cocultures, was capable of suppressing the MC response to PHA.

With PWM-stimulated cultures, addition of indomethacin had no effect on MC cultured alone. Indomethacin enhanced the response to PWM in MC – FB cocultures but this did not achieve statistical significance ($P < 0.2$).

Time Course of FB Effect on MC PHA Response

To further examine the interaction of MC and FB in the response to PHA, the duration and timing of FB–MC coculture was varied. MC cultures were initiated (0 hr) in 17 × 100-mm conical tubes (Falcon 2006) with 10^6 cells/ml in RPMI 1640/10% fetal calf serum in the presence of 2.5 μg/ml of PHA. At 0, 24, 48, and 66 hr, 100-μl aliquots were removed and added to quadruplicate wells containing either agarose alone or mitomycin-treated FB overlayed with agarose. FB for all time points were plated simultaneously (at −24hr). MC were harvested at 72 hr, 6 hr after pulsing with [^{3}H]thymidine.

When FB–MC coculture was commenced at "0" hr, there was suppression of MC responses that increased with increasing FB number (Table 3). When MC were cultured for 24 hr in the absence of FB, and added to the FB for only the final 48 hr of culture, no FB effect was seen. FB–MC cocultures initiated at 48 and 66 hr of the 72-hr culture period had an enhanced response compared to MC added to agarose alone at the same time points. This enhancing effect of FB on the MC response to PHA increased with increasing numbers of FB/well.

Cocultures of MC and FB established at different time points were also examined in the presence and absence of indomethacin (Table 3). As before (Fig. 3), indomethacin reversed the FB-mediated suppression of the PHA response when coculture was initiated at 0 hr. However, the presence of indomethacin in cocultures initiated at 24, 48, and 66 hr had no significant effect on MC responses. To determine whether the failure of FB to suppress MC PHA responses in cocultures initiated after 24 hr was associated with less stimulation of PGE_2 synthesis, PGE_2 concentrations were measured in the media of cocultures initiated at different times. Even in cocultures initiated at 24, 48, and 66 hr, PGE_2 concentrations were higher than those seen in cultures of MC added to agarose alone at the same time point (Table 4). Comparable PGE_2 concentrations were achieved when cocultures were initiated at 0 or 24 hr; these levels were approximately 10-fold greater than PGE_2

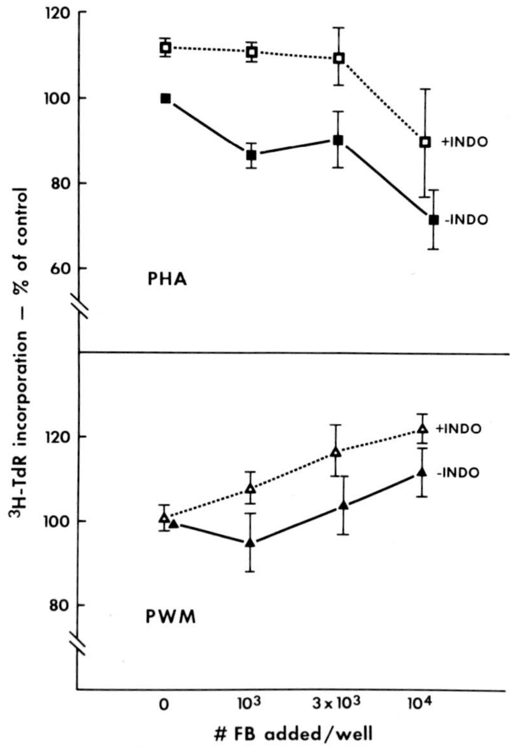

FIG. 3. FB suppression of the MC response to PHA: effect of indomethacin. The effect of FB on MC responses to PHA (top) and PWM (bottom) was examined in the presence or absence of indomethacin (±INDO). Indomethacin was added with the agarose to each well to achieve a final concentration of 1 μg/ml. All results are expressed as percentage of cultures with mitogen in the absence of added FB. Each point represents the mean of six separate experiments; vertical bars represent SEM. Statistical significance was examined by paired *t* test comparison of indomethacin-treated vs untreated cultures at each FB concentration.

TABLE 2

Effect of Mefenamic Acid on MC:FB Cocultures[a]

	No. FB/well		
	10^3	3×10^3	10^4
	[^{3}H]TdR incorporation—% of control		
MC + FB	76 ± 5	57 ± 9	42 ± 12
MC + FB + mefenamic acid	90 ± 6 [b]	79 ± 11 [c]	44 ± 8 NS[d]
MC + FB + indomethacin	105 ± 6 [c]	85 ± 10 [c]	52 ± 10 NS

[a] Mefenamic acid (1 μg/ml), indomethacin (1 μg/ml), or buffer (phosphate-buffered saline) was added at the time FB were overlayed with agarose. All results shown are mean ± SEM for five experiments.

[b] $P < 0.05$ by paired t test.

[c] $P < 0.01$.

[d] NS, not significant.

concentrations in culture of MC alone. With later addition of MC, however, there was a progressive decrease in the PGE_2 concentrations achieved by the end of the culture period.

DISCUSSION

In the present studies, coculture techniques were used to determine whether FB and FB products might alter lymphocyte reactivity *in vitro*. One approach to the study of potential FB-derived mediators might be the addition of FB-conditioned medium to MC cultures. However, many potential mediators are released in in-

TABLE 3

FB Effect on PHA Response of Human MC: Time Dependence

Time MC added[a] (hr)	No. FB/well			
	0	10^3	3×10^3	10^4
		^{3}HTdR incorporation—% of control[b]		
0	100	78 ± 8[c]	71 ± 11	54 ± 12
+INDO[d]	109 ± 11	103 ± 6	98 ± 5	82 ± 3
24	100	91 ± 7	95 ± 6	102 ± 3
+INDO	93 ± 8	93 ± 6	100 ± 5	104 ± 3
48	100	102 ± 6	117 ± 4	130 ± 9
+INDO	92 ± 3	106 ± 7	111 ± 4	132 ± 10
66	100	120 ± 6	125 ± 6	125 ± 2
+INDO	98 ± 7	111 ± 17	118 ± 9	117 ± 8

[a] MC-FB cocultures were established at different times during the course of a 72-hr PHA-stimulated culture (See text).

[b] 10^5 MC cultured over agarose with no added FB.

[c] Mean ± SEM for three experiments.

[d] Indomethacin, (1 μg/ml final concentration) was added at the time FB were overlayed with agarose.

TABLE 4

PGE_2 Synthesis in MC and MC:FB Cultures Initiated at Different Times

Time of MC addition[a]	PGE_2 (ng/ml)[b] MC	PGE_2 (ng/ml)[b] MC:FB coculture	MC vs MC:FB[c] P
0	1.5	21.5	<0.001
		$P = 0.4$	
24	2.4	18.2	<0.01
		$P < 0.05$	
48	4.3	8.5	=0.2
		$P = 0.3$	
66	3.0	4.3	=0.4

[a] Time of addition of MC to control wells (agarose alone) or wells containing 3×10^3 FB. Time "0" is time of addition of PHA to MC.

[b] PGE_2 concentration at 72 hr in MC cultures or cocultures of 10^5 MC and 3×10^3 FB. Each value represents the geometric mean concentration for five experiments.

[c] P values for comparisons shown were determined by paired t test.

creased amounts on exposure to MC products (5, 6, 8, 9). Thus stimulated or "activated" FB might have effects on immune function not discernable from study of supernates of resting FB populations. The use of coculture technique allowed examination of a dynamic interaction between cell populations that might better reflect events occurring in inflammatory lesions.

In coculture, FB suppressed the PHA response of MC. The suppression increased with increasing FB:MC ratio, was reversed with two different inhibitions of prostaglandin synthesis, indomethacin and mefenamic acid, and appeared, therefore, to be due, at least in part, to the increased prostaglandin synthesis observed in the cocultures. Although PGE_2 is the major prostaglandin metabolite produced by FB in culture, and PGE_2 was shown to suppress lymphocyte responses at concentrations achieved in the cocultures, prostaglandin compounds other than or in addition to PGE_2 may have been responsible for the suppressive effect observed.

The increased PGE_2 in the cocultures was probably FB derived but could have resulted from FB activation of monocyte PGE_2 synthesis. However, concentrations of PGE_2 achieved were comparable to those seen when FB are exposed to supernates of MC cultures (Table 1 and (5)) and far in excess of PGE_2 concentrations achieved in cultures of activated MC alone (Table 1). The increased PGE_2 concentrations present in cocultures of FB and unstimulated MC are consistent with the observation that supernates of unstimulated MC markedly stimulate FB PGE_2 synthesis (5). The conditions of MC isolation and culture thus appear to be an adequate stimulus for release into the supernatant medium of MC cytokines that stimulate FB PGE_2 synthesis. If indeed FB are the source of the increased PGE_2 in MC:FB cocultures, even greater stimulation of FB PGE_2 synthesis might be expected in the presence of mitogens; this was not, however, the case (Fig. 2). One possible explanation is the release of other factors by mitogen-activated lymphocytes or monocytes (e.g., lymphotoxin) which might, to some extent suppress FB metabolic activity in general or PGE_2 synthesis in particular. MC products that might stimulate FB PGE_2 synthesis include a 14,000–20,000 MW monocyte product probably identical with interleukin-1 (lymphocyte activating factor (LAF)) (10) and leukocyte interferon (9). To the extent that PGE_2 is an important mediator of immunological reactions, FB-derived PGE_2 is quantitatively greater and thus perhaps physiologically more important than macrophage-derived PGE_2.

PGE_2 has been shown to suppress T-cell proliferative responses with little or no effect on B-cell proliferative responses (1). The failure of FB to suppress the proliferative response of MC to PWM, a predominantly B-lymphocyte mitogen, is consistent with this previous observation. The slight enhancement of PWM responses observed when indomethacin was added to MC:FB coculture might have been due to augmentation of the T-lymphocyte component of the PWM response.

The effects of the FB on MC PHA responses were critically time dependent. When MC were added to FB after the MC had been exposed to mitogen for 24 hr, there was no FB effect; with even later addition an enhancement of MC proliferative responses was seen. Although some T-cell populations show increased proliferative responses when exposed to PGE_2 (6), the lack of an indomethacin effect on cocultures initiated at 24, 48, and 66 hr make it unlikely that prostaglandins are mediating enhanced responses in cocultures initiated at later time points.

The failure of FB to suppress MC responses when MC were added after the first 24 hr is of interest. In cocultures initiated after 24 hr, the PGE_2 concentrations achieved were lower than in cocultures initiated earlier. Even though the PGE_2 concentrations achieved were in excess of those shown to suppress T-lymphocyte responses in lymohocyte–monocyte cultures (1), suppressive PGE_2 concentrations may not have been present for long enough during the culture period to exert an effect. Another possibility is that FB might be affecting early events in mitogen activation of MC; once activated the MC may be resistant to suppressive influences. Alternatively, there may be changes in the MC population during the first 24 hr of culture that render them insensitive to suppressive influences (11, 12); only a subpopulation of T cells are suppressed by PGE_2 (7) and these may be altered during the first 24 hr of mitogen exposure. Finally, the FB effect might be mediated via activation of a short-lived suppressor cell (13, 14). T lymphocytes with receptors for IgG-Fc (T_γ) have been shown to have suppressor cell activity. PGE_2 has been shown to promote expression of receptors for the Fc-fragment of IgG on T lymphocytes without Fc-receptors or T cells with receptors for the Fc fragment of IgM (T_μ) (15). PGE_2 has also been shown to activate T suppressor cells from Fc-receptor-negative populations; furthermore the target of PGE_2 action is a short-lived suppressor cell (16).

FB interferon has also been shown to augment expression of IgG-Fc fragment receptors on lymphocytes (17). Both FB and leukocyte interferons may suppress *in vitro* lymphocyte responses by modulating or mediating suppressor cell activity (18, 19). The failure of indomethacin to reverse the FB-mediated suppression at the highest FB:MC ratios could be due to release by FB of other immunoregulatory molecules such as interferon.

The interaction of MC and connective tissue cells may be important in a variety of pathologic states including rheumatoid arthritis, scleroderma, psoriasis, and granulomatous disease (reviewed in (20)). Coculture of MC and FB presents a model system for study of these interactions. Further exploration of this model may yield information leading to a better understanding of the events occurring in flammatory lesions.

ACKNOWLEDGMENTS

The author wishes to thank E. Downie and G. Neuman for expert technical assistance, T. Testa for typing the manuscript, and Dr. N. Rothfield for helpful critical comments on the manuscript.

REFERENCES

1. Goodwin, J. S., Bankhurst, A. D., and Messner, R. P., *J. Exp. Med.* **146,** 1719, 1977.
2. Zarling, J. M., Sosman, J., Eskra, L., Borden, E. C., Horoszewicz, J. S., and Carter, W. A., *J. Immunol.* **121,** 2002, 1978.
3. Balazs, E. A., and Darzynkiewicz, Z., *In* "Biology of Fibroblasts" (E. Kulonon and J. Pikkarainen, Eds.), pp. 237–252. Academic Press, New York, 1973.
4. Sobel, J. D., and Gallin, J. I., *J. Clin. Invest.* **63,** 609, 1979.
5. Korn, J. H., Halushka, P. V., and LeRoy, E. C., *J. Clin. Invest.* **65,** 543, 1980.
6. Dayer, J. M., Robinson, D. R., and Krane, S. M., *J. Exp. Med.* **145,** 1399, 1977.
7. Stobo, J. D., Kennedy, M. S., and Goldyne, M. E., *J. Clin. Invest.* **64,** 1188, 1979.
8. Yaron, M., Yaron, I., Gurari-Rotman, D., Revel, M., Lindner, H. R., and Zor, U., *Nature (London)* **267,** 457, 1977.
9. Yaron, M., Yaron, C., Wiletzki, C., and Zor, U., *Arthritis Rheum.* **1,** 694, 1978.
10. Mizel, S. B., *In*"Biochemical Characterization of Lymphokines" (A. L. deWeck, F. Kristensen, and M. Landy, Eds.) pp. 411–415. Academic Press, New York, 1980.
11. McCombs, C. C., Michalski, J. P., and Talal, N., *J. Immunol.* **120,** 532, 1978.
12. Sohnele, P. G., and Collins-Lech, C., *Clin. Immunol. Immunopathol.* **13,** 47, 1979.
13. Bresnihan, B., and Jasin, H., *J. Clin. Invest.* **59,** 106, 1977.
14. Feighery, C., Whclan, C. A., Weir, D. G., and Greally, J. F., *Clin. Exp. Immunol.* **32,** 459, 1978.
15. Kaszubowski, P. A., and Goodwin, J. S., *Clin. Res.* **28,** 40A, 1980.
16. Fischer, A., Durandy, A., and Griscelli, C., *J. Immunol.* **126,** 1452, 1981.
17. Itoh, K., Inoue, M., Karaoka, S., and Kumagai, K., *J. Immunol.* **124,** 2589, 1980.
18. Kadish, A. S., Tansey, F. A., Yu, G. S. M., Doyle, A. T., and Bloom, B. R., *J. Exp. Med.* **151,** 637, 1980.
19. Miörner, H., Landström, L. E., Larner, E., Larsson, I., Lundgren, E., and Stannegard, Ö., *Cell. Immunol.* **35,** 15, 1978.
20. Korn, J. H., *Int. J. Dermatol.* **19,** 487, 1980.

CELLULAR IMMUNOLOGY **63**, 385–399 (1981)

Surface Immunoglobulin Isotype, Activation, and Tolerance Susceptibility of B Lymphocytes of New Zealand Black Mice

B. L. PIKE, J. E. LAYTON, N. R. ROSE,[1] AND G. J. V. NOSSAL

The Walter and Eliza Hall Institute of Medical Research, Post Office, Royal Melbourne Hospital, Melbourne, Victoria 3050, Australia

Received April 10, 1981; accepted June 14, 1981

Fluorescence-activated cell sorter (FACS) analysis of B-lymphocyte surface isotype expression, and limiting dilution B-lymphocyte cloning techniques, have been used to establish characteristics of B lymphocytes from New Zealand Black (NZB) mice which might contribute to the predisposition of this strain to autoimmune disease. The NZB mice and two other strains (BALB/c and CBA) used were either specific pathogen free (SPF) or germ free (GF). The NZB B lymphocytes differed from the normal strains in the following respects: they showed considerably higher spontaneous conversion into antibody-forming cell clones in the absence of antigen or mitogen; substantially higher cloning efficiency at optimal antigen or mitogen concentration; a slightly lower antigen concentration optimum; and an abnormally high proportion of large cells among the s-IgM$^+$, s-IgD$^-$ lymphocyte subset. All these differences argue for a heightened excitability of the NZB B cell to triggering stimuli. Although there was a small-to-moderate increase in the proportion of s-IgM$^+$, s-IgD$^-$ b cells, the differences in μ:δ ratio were less than those previously reported. Finally, only a minor and barely significant resistance to tolerance induction *in vitro* was observed. The results suggest that the heightened B-cell excitability is only one factor in the etiology of autoimmune disease.

INTRODUCTION

The New Zealand Black (NZB)[2] mouse has long been used as a model of spontaneous autoimmune disease. This inbred strain regularly develops erythrocyte autoantibodies and hemolytic anemia (1), and some animals also develop antinuclear antibodies and an immune-complex-induced glomerulonephritis closely resembling human systemic lupus erythematosus. There is little doubt that the etiology of these diseases is multifactorial, and theories incriminating abnormalities of thymic epithelium (2), macrophages (3), T lymphocytes (4), B lymphocytes (5) and hemopoietic stem cells (6) have all received some experimental support. More recently, a defect in suppressor T lymphocytes has been described (7, 8).

[1] Present address: Department of Immunology and Microbiology, Wayne State University School of Medicine, 540 E. Canfield Ave. Detroit, Mich. 48201.

[2] Abbreviations used: DNP, 2,4-dinitrophenyl; FACS, fluorescence-activated cell sorter; FCS, fetal calf serum; FITC, fluorescein isothiocyanate; FLU, fluorescein; GF, germ free; HGG, human γ-globulin; LPS, *Escherichia coli* lipopolysaccharide; NIP, 4-hydroxy-3-iodo-5-nitrophenyl; NZB, New Zealand Black; PFC, plaque-forming cell; POL, polymerized flagellin; s-IgD, surface immunoglobulin, class IgD; s-IgM, surface immunoglobulin, class IgM; SPF, specific pathogen free; SRC, sheep red blood cells; TNP, 2,4,6-trinitrophenyl; TRITC, 2,4-tetramethylrhodamine.

0008-8749/81/140385-15$02.00/0

Our interest in this subject was reawakened by several claims that one fundamental flaw in this and related mouse strains was intrinsic to the B lymphocyte itself (9–14). These studies have described a spontaneous polyclonal activation, characterized by an abnormally high proportion of spleen cells with surface IgM and a lower proportion with IgD, resembling the pattern in mice stimulated with sheep red blood cells (9, 10). Further abnormalities reported include a greatly increased spontaneous secretion of IgM (10) or of anti-dinitrophenol antibodies (11, 12). Of great interest is a claim that the B lymphocytes are inherently less sensitive to the negative signalling involved in the induction of B-lymphocyte tolerance (13, 14) and may thus partially escape physiological processes responsible for self-tolerance.

One problem in interpreting these claims is that the NZB mice used in most of these investigations produce large amounts of xenotropic virus (15), which might play a role in B-cell activation. Less well documented, but still of concern, is the possibility that some of the studies were performed with mice subject to considerable antigenic stimulation through infections and infestations. At the Walter and Eliza Hall Institute, we have received two lines of NZB mice from the original Bielschowsky stock and which we have maintained isolated from other mice and raised in specific pathogen-free or germ-free conditions for several years. Furthermore, these animals, though probably not free of retroviruses, exhibit very few C-type virus particles on electron microscopic examination (16). We considered these animals to be useful for a detailed characterization of the reported B-cell defects. Using limiting dilution microculture techniques, we have shown them to possess a higher spontaneous rate of B-cell activation and a lower B-lymphocyte activation threshold. By this approach, allowing accurate enumeration of immunocompetent B cells, we found only a marginally decreased susceptibility to induction of tolerance *in vitro* among NZB splenic B cells. Analysis of B-cell surface isotype expression using the fluorescence-activated cell sorter (FACS), revealed a small but definite increase in large s-IgM$^+$, s-IgD$^-$ B cells, of NZB compared with other strains.

MATERIALS AND METHODS

Mice. Mice from the inbred strains NZB (NZBlWehi and NZB1_2), BALB/c.An BradleyWehi, and CBA/CaHWehi were used at the ages specified in the text. In general, adult donors were aged 8 to 10 weeks and neonatal donors 3 days. (CBA × BALB/c)F_1 hybrids, and aged 4 to 6 weeks, were used as thymus donors for *in vitro* studies. All mice were maintained under germ-free (GF) or specific pathogen-free (SPF) conditions as specified until use. Germ-free mice used were from the NZBl_2 strain.

Antigens. The hapten fluorescein (FLU) was conjugated to human γ-globulin (HGG) and polymerized flagellin (POL) as previously described (17). The FLU-HGG conjugates used as tolerogens in these studies contained either approximately 4 (FLU$_4$HGG) or 8 (FLU$_8$HGG) mol of FLU per mole of HGG. The FLU-POL used to induce antibody formation *in vitro* contained 1 mol of FLU per mole of monomeric flagellin. Where specified, *Escherichia coli* lipopolysaccharide (LPS) (Batch 0111:B4, Difco, Detroit) was used to induce antibody formation *in vitro.*

Antisera. Hybridoma anti-Igh-5a (10-4.22) (18) was purified from culture supernatant by affinity chromatography using protein A–Sepharose (Pharmacia,

Uppsala, Sweden). Purified antibody was biotin conjugated (biotin-anti-δ) by incubating antibody at 1 mg/ml with succinimidyl-D-biotin (Molecular Probes, Plano, Tex.) at 100 μg/mg antibody in 0.1 *M* $NaHCO_3$ for 1 h at room temperature. The reaction mixture was separated by gel filtration on Sephadex G-25 (Pharmacia). Fluorescein-conjugated avidin (FITC-avidin) was prepared by conjugating avidin (Sigma Chemical Co., St. Louis, Mo.) with fluorescein isothiocyanate (Molecular Probes) in 0.1 *M* bicarbonate buffer, pH 9.5, for 2 hr at room temperature. The final product had an F/P ratio of 2–4. Tetramethylrhodamine isothiocyanate-conjugated polyvalent sheep anti-mouse IgG (TRITC-anti-Ig) was prepared as described previously (19).

Preparation of cell suspensions. Spleen and thymus suspensions were prepared for *in vitro* cell culture studies as previously described (20). Thymus cells were pretreated with anti-Ia^k serum and complement (21) prior to their use as "filler" cells in the culture system.

Spleen and femoral bone marrow suspensions were prepared for fluorescence studies by removal of erythrocytes (22) and damaged cells (23). Lymph node cells from pooled peripheral and mesenteric lymph nodes were prepared similarly except that erythrocyte removal was omitted. Cells were finally suspended at approximately 50×10^6/ml in a buffered, balanced salt solution (2) supplemented with 5% (v/v) fetal calf serum (BSS-FCS).

Isolation of FLU-gelatin-binding cells. Spleen cells were fractionated on FLU-gelatin-coated petri dishes as previously described (17, 21), and the isolated FLU-gelatin-binding population was treated with collagenase prior to culture.

Antibody formation in vitro. The limiting dilution microculture system used for the enumeration of the frequency of precursors of anti-FLU plaque-forming cell (PFC) clones has been previously described (20, 21). Briefly, spleen cells were cultured in limiting numbers in the presence of 2×10^6 anti-Ia- and complement-treated thymus filler cells in medium containing 0.1 μg/ml of FLU-POL (unless otherwise specified) or 20 μg/ml of LPS. After 3 days, cultures were individually assayed against FLU-conjugated sheep erythrocytes (FLU-SRC) for anti-FLU PFC clones as previously described (17, 24) and the frequency of precursors statistically determined (20). Where specified, cultures were assayed against SRC-conjugated with one of the haptens 4-hydroxy-3-iodo-5-nitrophenylacetic acid (NIP), dinitrophenyl acetic acid (DNP), or trinitrophenyl acetic acid (TNP).

Tolerance induction in vitro. The protocol for *in vitro* tolerance induction has been previously described (25, 26). Briefly, spleen cells were cultured a limiting dilution in the presence of thymus filler cells in medium containing graded concentrations of the tolerogen FLU-HGG. After 24 hr, the medium containing tolerogen was removed and replaced by fresh medium containing thymus cells and 0.1 μg/ml of the immunogen FLU-POL. The frequency of anti-FLU PFC clones was then determined 3 days later as described above.

Fluorescent labeling. Approximately 5×10^6 cells from each sample were labeled in 0.1 ml of optimal reagent concentration. In most experiments, cells were labeled with biotin-anti-δ (20 μg/ml), then FITC-avidin (40 μg/ml), then TRITC-anti-Ig (100 μg/ml) containing 5 μg/ml propidium iodide (Calbiochem, San Diego, Calif.). Cells were held with each reagent for 30 min on ice, then diluted in BSS-FCS and washed once through 1 ml FCS. After the final step, cells were washed twice.

Analysis of labeled cells. Labeled cells were analyzed by a fluorescence-activated cell sorter (FACS) (Becton-Dickenson FACS II, Mountain View, Calif.) as described by Herzenberg and Herzenberg (27). For each sample, 10^5 cells were analyzed for low-angle light scatter, green fluorescence, and red fluorescence, and the data then analyzed by computer. Dead cells were excluded by their low-angle light scatter characteristics and by their uptake of propidium iodide (28). In order to use propidium iodide as well as TRITC, the voltage for the red fluorescence detector was set so that, when cells labeled with TRITC-anti-Ig alone were analyzed, less than 0.2% were off scale (i.e., >Channel 246). When cells were labeled with 5 μg/ml propidium iodide as well, the dead cells (propidium iodide positive) could be excluded because they were off scale, without excluding TRITC-anti-Ig-labeled cells.

RESULTS

Comparison of Total s-Ig Expression on Cells of NZB and Normal Mouse Strains

SPF NZB mice were compared with two other strains maintained under similar SPF conditions, namely BALB/c and CBA, to determine the relative intensities of staining with a polyvalent, fluoresceinated anti-Ig reagent, as an approximation of total s-Ig density. Mice of various ages were studied, as previous work had reported differences as early as 2 weeks of age (29). A modified FACS II capable of correlated, three-parameter analysis, was used, permitting simultaneous study of total s-Ig or s-μ chain density, s-IgD density, and low-angle light scattering behavior, related to cell size. The percentage of s-Ig^+ cells in the total viable nucleated cell portion and in the large cells which form a shoulder to the right of the main small lymphocyte peak in the light scatter profile of the spleen was examined. No substantial, consistent differences were seen among the strains. When the fluorescence intensity profiles (not shown) were compared, the adult but not the suckling NZB spleen cells showed a slightly lower fluoresence intensity.

Pooled lymph node cells and femoral bone marrow cells were also examined and although some substantial differences between the strains were recorded at various age points, it was difficult to discern a pattern that demarcated the autoimmune strain. In addition, the fluoresence intensity profiles showed little difference between the strains.

Comparison of s-IgD Expression on B Cells of NZB and Normal Mouse Strains

Studies by Chused *et al.* (10) using FACS concluded that the reduced total s-Ig density on NZB B cells was caused by reduction of s-IgD, but not s-IgM. Using a surface radioiodination approach Cohen *et al.* (29) found a markedly increased ratio of μ/δ in NZB mice. We stained cells for IgD as well as total Ig and performed FACS analysis. It should be noted that an elevated μ/δ ratio determined following cell surface radioiodination cannot be directly compared with the ratio of s-IgM^+/s-IgD^+ cells. Therefore, although most of the results that we present are given in terms of the percentages of cells showing immunofluorescence above a given threshold, we also carefully studied the relative intensities of staining of the various cell populations following labeling with anti-δ. Nevertheless, the important methodological difference should be noted. Table 1 gives the proportion of s-Ig^+ cells which were s-IgD^+ in spleen. There is strain variation in rate of acquisition of s-IgD with

TABLE 1

The Percentage of s-Ig$^+$ Spleen Cells That Are s-IgD$^+$[a]

Age (days)	All viable cells			Large cells[b]		
	NZB	BALB/c	CBA	NZB	BALB/c	CBA
5	11.4	7.5	46.4	12.8	10.6	
7	34.3	17.7	36.2	38.2	15.9	45.1
11–12	47.5	36.6	41.0	43.2	39.8	49.4
16	41.7	41.4	69.9	51.1	46.4	72.1
50	70.6	75.8	82.5	53.4	66.2	
105	64.4	79.8	78.5	48.5	70.1	67.5

[a] As determined by above-background labeling (usually >Channel 20) in the FACS.
[b] As determined by light scattering. See Materials and Methods.

age, as the BALB/c strain shows the lowest and the CBA strain the highest percentage of s-IgD$^+$ cells among the suckling mice. In the adults, the NZB showed a slightly lower percentage of s-IgD$^+$ cells, and this was marginally more pronounced in the large cells than in the typical small lymphocytes. No consistent difference in fluorescence intensity of s-IgD$^+$ cells was observed. These differences are in the same direction as the difference in μ/δ ratio observed by Cohen *et al.* (29). In lymph node cells (Table 2), the results showed a slight but consistent lowering of the proportion of s-IgD$^+$ cells at all ages. Differences between BALB/c and NZB bone marrow cells varied with age and in adult mice, NZB cells actually had a higher proportion of IgD$^+$ cells compared to BALB/c. In three experiments (not shown), spleen cells were labeled with FITC-conjugated anti-μ (Nordic) and analyzed by the FACS. No differences were found between NZB and normal mice confirming previous reports (10).

One consistent difference which was observed between NZB and BALB/c or

TABLE 2

The Percentage of s-Ig$^+$ Cells That Are s-IgD$^+$ in Lymph Node and Bone Marrow[a]

Age (days)	NZB	BALB/c	CBA
Lymph node (all viable cells)[b]			
5	26.0	37.8	56.0
7	43.0	58.2	72.2
11–12	56.9	71.5	72.6
16	72.5	86.2	87.0
50	86.3	92.6	92.6
105	81.8	95.5	85.9
Bone marrow (small cell peak)[b]			
12	18.5	6.6	11.5
16	19.1	28.8	24.4
50	47.7	33.2	42.5

[a] As determined by above-background labeling (usually >Channel 20) in the FACS.
[b] As determined by light scattering. See Materials and Methods.

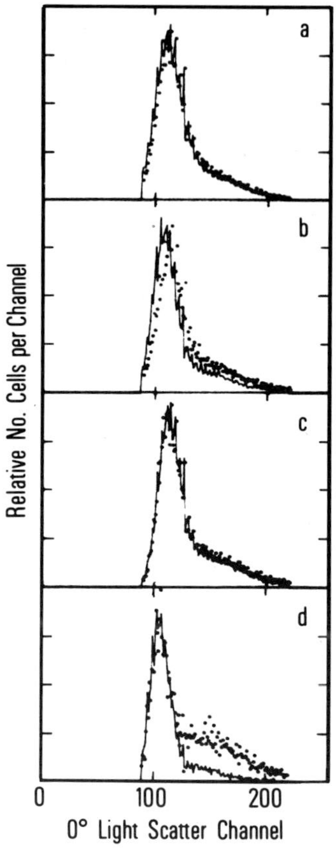

FIG. 1. Low-angle light scatter profiles of viable spleen cells from 50-day-old NZB (dotted lines) and BALB/c (solid lines) mice. (a) Total cells; (b) Ig^+ cells; (c) IgD^+ cells; (d) IgM^+IgD^- cells. Curves were normalized to the same peak height.

CBA mice was in the size distribution of s-IgM^+, s-IgD^- cells or s-IgD^+, s-IgD^- cells. Figure 1 shows a typical experiment with spleen cells from 50-day-old mice in which the total cell profiles were virtually identical, as were the total s-Ig^+ cell profiles. In contrast, the NZB mice had a much higher proportion of large s-IgM^+, s-IgD^- cells compared to the BALB/c.

Effect of Nonpathogenic Intestinal Flora on the Proportion of s-IgD^+ Cells

In an attempt to determine whether the degree of exposure to commonly encountered antigens, e.g., gut flora, affected the proportion of s-IgD^+ cells, GF and SPF mice of NZB, BALB/c, and CBA strains were compared. There were no major differences in spleen, lymph node, or bone marrow cells in either adult or suckling mice. Perhaps our SPF mice are not sufficiently different in antigen load from GF mice to cause a detectable difference.

Frequency of Anti-FLU B Cells as Judged by Induction of Antibody-Forming Clones in Vitro

NZB splenic B cells have been reported to be polyclonally activated from as early as 1 week of age (10–12, 30). To date, there has been no analysis of the

TABLE 3

Frequency of Clonable Anti-FLU B Cells in Spleen Cells from Newborn and Adult SPF Mice

Age of mice	Frequency of anti-FLU PFC precursors/10^6 spleen cells[a]		
	NZB	BALB/c	*P*
3 days	52.1 ± 7.9	42.3 ± 10.8	<0.15[b]
8–10 weeks	304 ± 20.4	98.3 ± 13.1	<0.03

[a] Spleen cells from donors were cultured at limiting dilution in the presence of thymus filler cells and 0.1 μg/ml of FLU-POL for 3 days prior to assay for anti-FLU PFC clones as described under Materials and Methods. Neonatal spleen cells from both strains were cultured at 2×10^4/culture; adult spleen cells from NZB donors were cultured at 1.5×10^3/culture and from BALB/c donors at 3×10^3/culture.

[b] *P* values obtained using the Student's *t* distribution test.

antibody response of NZB splenic B cells at the clonal level although Kincade *et al.* (30) have shown that NZB spleen contains significantly higher numbers of B-lymphocyte colony-forming cells. Using the limiting dilution analysis and a T-independent antigen (FLU-POL), we investigated the *in vitro* anti-FLU responsiveness of NZB mouse spleen cells in a limiting dilution microculture system utilizing thymus "filler" cells. After 3 days, each culture was assayed for the presence or absence of an anti-FLU PFC clone and the frequency of clonable anti-FLU precursors statistically determined by Poisson analysis (20). The incidence of anti-FLU PFC precursor cells among SPF newborn and young adult NZB splenic cells was compared with that of a normal strain, BALB/c. No significant difference was demonstrable in the frequency of precursor cells at 3 days of age but at 8 to 10 weeks the value for NZB splenic cells was significantly higher than that of BALB/c (Table 3). No difference was demonstrable within each strain between male and female donors (data not shown). No significant difference in spleen cell size was noted between the two strains.

Comparative in Vitro Triggerability

To further investigate the hyperreactivity of NZB splenic B cells, we compared thresholds for antigenic triggering of spleen cells from SPF adult NZB and BALB/c donors. Spleen cells were cultured at limiting dilution with increasing concentrations of FLU-POL for 3 days prior to assay for anti-FLU PFC clones. The results, shown in Table 4, show that 10 ng/ml of FLU-POL triggered a near-maximal response from NZB spleen cells and that 1 ng/ml yielded over half the potential number of anti-FLU PFC clones. In contrast, 100 ng/ml was optimal for BALB/c cells, and 1 ng/ml stimulated only 29% of the maximum response. All concentrations of FLU-POL stimulated significantly higher numbers of NZB splenic cells. Table 5 shows the results from a series of similar experiments where young adult GF donors were used. The behavior of GF NZB splenic cells was similar to that of SPF donors. In this case, 10 ng/ml appeared maximally to trigger cells from BALB/c donors as well. Again the frequency of anti-FLU PFC precursors was greater in the NZB strain.

TABLE 4

Comparative *in Vitro* Triggerability of NZB and BALB/c Spleen Cells from Young Adult SPF Donors

FLU-POL[a] (ng/ml)	Frequency of anti-FLU precursors/10^6 spleen cells[b]			
	NZB	P^c	BALB/c	P^c
0	46.9 ± 13.5[d]	—	4.9 ± 0.4	—
1	169 ± 11.4	0.01	34.0 ± 7.2	⩽0.05
10	303 ± 23.7	0.03	71.0 ± 21.1	⩽0.1
100	319 ± 26.7	NS	119 ± 5.9	⩽0.1
1000	185 ± 20.2	0.05	53.0 ± 6.5	⩽0.03

[a] Concentration of the T-independent immunogen FLU-POL present in the culture medium.
[b] Frequency of anti-FLU PFC clones detected after 3 days culture of limiting numbers of spleen cells in the presence of thymus filler cells and the indicated amount of FLU-POL.
[c] *P* values by Students *t* test. Value given of frequencies obtained following induction by the indicated dose and the next lowest dose, e.g., 1 ng cf 10 ng, 10 ng cf 100 ng, etc. *P* values across the table, i.e., NZB cf BALB/c were ⩽0.03 for all FLU-POL concentrations.
[d] Data derived from pools of three to four experiments; means ± SEM.

Comparative Frequency of Clones Arising Spontaneously in Vitro

Tables 4 and 5 also show the frequencies of anti-FLU PFC clones generated after 3 days in culture by spleen cells in the absence of added specific antigen. The frequency of clones generated by NZB spleen cells was found to be significantly higher than BALB/c from both GF and SPF donors. There was little difference in the frequency of clones detected between SPF and GF donors within each strain.

Response of Neonatal Spleen Cells

The response of spleen cells from newborn donors was investigated with respect to triggerability threshold and comparative frequency. The results of a single experiment (Table 6) showed spleen cells from both strains to be maximally stimulated

TABLE 5

Comparative *in Vitro* Triggerability of NZB and BALB/c Spleen Cells from Young Adult Germ-Free Donors

FLU-POL[a] (ng/ml)	Frequency of anti-FLU PFC precursors/10^6 spleen cells[b]			
	NZB	P^c	BALB/c	P
0	50.1 ± 9.8[d]	—	8.3 ± 2.7	—
1	207 ± 36.9	⩽0.05	40.4 ± 4.5	⩽0.005
10	272 ± 52.3	NS	134 ± 56.0	⩽0.15
100	251 ± 71.4	NS	76.9 ± 25.0	⩽0.15
1000	267 ± 77.5	NS	51.9 ± 14.9	⩽0.10

Note. *P* values across the table, BALB/c to NZB comparison, 0, 1, and 1000 ng/ml FLU-POL, $P \leqslant 0.05$; 10 and 100 ng/ml FLU-POL, NS (10 = 0.2; 100 = 0.15). Data derived from a pool of three to four experiments.
[a-d] As in Table 4.

TABLE 6

Comparative *in Vitro* Triggerability of NZB and BALB/c Spleen Cells from 3-Day-Old SPF Donors

FLU-POL[a] (ng/ml)	Frequency of anti-FLU PFC precursors/10^6 spleen cells[b] NZB	BALB/c
0	ND	0
1	13.0	5.4
10	25.3	25.3
100	32.4	30.2
1000	16.3	8.4

Note. Data from one experiment only.
[a,b] See footnotes *a* and *b*, Table 4.

by 100 ng/ml of FLU-POL as shown in Table 3, similar frequency values were obtained for both strains using this concentration.

Specificity of Anti-FLU Response

In order to investigate whether the higher activity detected by spleen cells from adult NZB donors was marked by an abnormal cross-reactivity pattern, cells were cultured for 3 days with FLU-POL, then assayed against SRC coupled with three other different haptens, or against unconjugated SRC. The results (Table 7) show the response to be specific for FLU with the same degree of cross-reactivity being detected from both NZB and BALB/c spleen cells.

LPS-Induced Responsiveness to Various Haptens

The possibility that the repertoire or NZB mice may be slanted toward reactivity against FLU was investigated. Limiting dilution cultures of spleen cells from young adult SPF NZB or BALB/c donors were stimulated with LPS and assayed for clones reactive against various haptens. The results (Table 8) demonstrate no bias

TABLE 7

Specificity of the Anti-FLU Response Generated by Spleen Cells Stimulated *in Vitro* by FLU-POL[a]

Indicator-SRC used in plaque revelation assay	Frequency of PFC clones/10^6 spleen cells NZB spleen	BALB/c spleen
FLU-SRC	530	179
DNP-SRC	5.3	0
TNP-SRC	47.9	13.4
NIP-SRC	22.3	6.5
SRC	5.3	0

Note. Results shown are from one experiment only.
[a] Spleen cells were cultured at limiting dilution in the presence of thymus fillers and 0.1 μg/ml of FLU-POL for 3 days prior to assay against either FLU-SRC, DNP-SRC, etc. as indicated. Spleen cell donors were 8–10 weeks old and maintained under SPF conditions until use.

TABLE 8

Frequency of Anti-Hapten PFC Clones Generated by NZB and BALB/c Spleen Cells Stimulated *in Vitro* by LPS[a]

Indicator-SRC used in plaque revelation assay	Frequency of PFC clones/10^6 spleen cells	
	NZB spleen	BALB/c spleen
FLU-SRC	732	114
DNP-SRC	732	187
TNP-SRC	588	178
NIP-SRC	448	70.9

[a] Antibody production was induced by 20 μg/ml LPS instead of FLU-POL.

toward FLU by either strain. The frequency values obtained for the NZB strain are significantly higher for all four antigens.

Frequency of Precursor Cells Among Isolated FLU-Binding Cells

The hapten–gelatin fractionation technique allows the isolation of B cells enriched for clonable anti-hapten PFC precursor cells (17, 20, 21). This technique, which tends to select B cells that have a higher avidity for the antigen (17), was used to investigate whether the elevated response of NZB mice was due to the presence of more cells possessing a higher FLU-binding capacity. Spleen cells were fractionated on FLU-gelatin dishes as previously described (17, 20, 21) and the numbers of bound cells were counted. The cells were recovered by the addition of medium containing collagenase at 37°C and cultured at a limiting dilution with either FLU-POL or LPS for 3 days. The results of two separate experiments are shown in Table 9. In both cases the enriched population from NZB spleen contained approximately twice the proportion of clonable anti-FLU PFC precursors than

TABLE 9

Frequency of Clonable Anti-FLU PFC Precursors among FLU-Gelatin-Binding Spleen Cells from NZB, BALB/c, and CBA Donors[a]

Expt	Strain of spleen donor	Frequency of anti-FLU PFC precursors/10^4 FLU-gelatin-binding cells[b]		
		FLU-POL stimulus	LPS stimulus	Binding ratio[c]
1	NZB	251	272	1
	BALB/c	128	144	0.59
2	NZB	274	277	1
	CBA	166	106	0.63

[a] Spleen cells from the various donors were fractionated on FLU-gelatin-coated petri dishes and the binding cells recovered as described under Materials and Methods.

[b] The frequency of anti-FLU PFC clones detected among recovered FLU-gelatin-binding cells following 3 days culture with either 0.1 μg/ml of FLU-POL or 20 μg/ml of LPS.

[c] The ratio of the number of cells binding to FLU-gelatin-coated petri dishes.

either control strain. Furthermore, 60 to 70% more cells bound to the dishes, so the overall yield of triggerable precursors was nearly fourfold higher in the case of NZB mice, supporting the data presented in Tables 4, 7, and 8. Both LPS and FLU-POL stimulated equivalent numbers of clones.

In another experiment, FLU-binding spleen cells from NZB donors were stimulated with FLU-POL, then assayed against either FLU-SRC or protein A-SRC (31). When assayed against FLU-SRC, 347 precursors per 10^4 enriched cells were detected and in the case of protein A-SRC the frequency was 325 per 10^4 cells.

Comparative in Vitro Tolerizability of Adult SPF Spleen Cells

The literature contains many reports that spleen cells from NZB donors exhibit a relative resistance to tolerance induction when compared to other strains. All the studies performed *in vitro* have been using "bulk" culture systems where tolerance is assayed by a reduction in the number of PFC generated at the end of the culture period. Having established by clonal analysis that there is a higher number of clonable anti-FLU B cells among splenic cells from adult NZB donors, we investigated their *in vitro* tolerizability in the belief that this provides a better insight into events at the level of the individual B cell.

We believe, but cannot formally prove, that the limiting dilution system used (20, 17) probes B-cell tolerance independently of any possible T-cell-suppressor influences. First, limiting dilution would dilute out suppressor cells, which would distribute independently of anti-FLU B cells. Second, the triggering antigen, FLU-POL, has a carrier different from that of the *in vivo* tolerogen, FLU-HGG. Third, FLU-POL is generally regarded as a "thymus-independent" trigger, though the presence of thymus filler cells in the assay leaves the possibility of *in vitro* induction of helper or suppressor cells at least as a formal possibility.

Spleen cells from adult SPF NZB or BALB/c donors were exposed *in vitro* to tolerogen for 24 hr, after which the tolerogen was removed and replaced with immunogen for a further 3 days. The pooled results of three experiments are shown in Table 10. We tested two conjugates known from previous work (24) to have considerably different properties. FLU_4HGG is an efficient tolerogen *in vitro* for immature B cells, but relatively high concentrations are required for negative signalling of mature cells (cf. Tables 10 and 11). FLU_8HGG is powerfully tolerogenic even for mature B cells, and much less still is needed to silence immature B cells (24). With the less tolerogenic conjugate, no significant differences were found between the strains. With the more powerful conjugate, the NZB cells were slightly less sensitive to tolerance induction.

Comparative Tolerizability of Neonatal Spleen Cells

The comparative tolerizability *in vitro* of spleen cells from 3-day-old donors was investigated, bearing in mind that no difference in immune reactivity between the two strains was demonstrable at this age (Tables 3 and 6). No significant resistance to tolerance could be shown in the autoimmune strain (Table 11).

DISCUSSION

This study represents a critical analysis of B-lymphocyte surface isotype expression, *in vitro* activation characteristics, and tolerance susceptibility using SPF and

TABLE 10

Comparative *in Vitro* Tolerizability of Spleen Cells from Young Adult SPF NZB and BALB/c Donors

Tolerogen present in preculture period[a]	Percentage of control response[b]	
	NZB	BALB/c
μg/ml FLU_4HGG		
250	12.5 ± 7.1	7.5 ± 3.9
100	37.6 ± 4.2	36.3 ± 11.2
10	77.8 ± 15.7	74.5 ± 21.0
1	90.4 ± 2.0	81.1 ± 13.3
μg/ml FLU_8HGG		
10	4.1 ± 2.9	1.3 ± 1.3
1	35.4 ± 4.6	16.2 ± 3.2
0.1	89.4 ± 21.1	88.4 ± 23.1

[a] Tolerogen was present for first 24 hr of culture period—the supernatant medium was then removed and replaced with fresh medium containing 0.1 μg/ml of the immunogen FLU-POL. Cultures were assayed for the presence of anti-FLU PFC clones 3 days later as described under Materials and Methods.

[b] The frequency of anti-FLU precursors/10^6 spleen cells in control groups was 158 ± 27.9 for NZB donors and 61.3 ± 9.4 for BALB/c donors. This is somewhat lower than in other tables because of nonspecific death of cells in the first (tolerogenesis) day. (Pooled results of three experiments for FLU_4HGG, four experiments for FLU_8HGG).

GF NZB mice. it was undertaken against the background of claims, largely from laboratories in the United States, using mice under considerably greater endogenous antigenic stimulation, of a number of substantial abnormalities within the B-cell compartment. The dominant conclusion from our work, on mice whose autoimmune diathesis is undoubted, is that the differences between NZB and other B lymphocytes in these "clean" mice are of rather a subtle nature and, in some cases, not as profound as previously reported.

We found three definite and three more marginal differences between NZB and the other strains. First, adult cells placed *in vitro* in the absence of any intentional stimulation other than that provided by 2-mercaptoethanol and fetal calf serum,

TABLE 11

Comparative *in Vitro* Tolerizability of Spleen Cells from SPF Neonatal NZB and BALB/c Donors

Tolerogen present in preculture period (μg/ml FLU_4HGG)[a]	Percentage of control response[b]	
	NZB	BALB/c
10	27.4 ± 5.8	27.5 ± 4.7
1	53.8 ± 11.8	58.2 ± 4.9
0.1	110 ± 24.1	78.2 ± 5.3

Note. Results shown are from a pool of four separate experiments.

[a] Concentration of the tolerogen FLU_4HGG present during the first 24 hr of the culture period.

[b] The frequency of anti-FLU precursors/10^6 spleen cells in control groups was 15.5 ± 2.6 for NZB donors and 17.2 ± 6.8 for BALB/c donors.

formed "spontaneous" PFC clones six- to nine-fold more frequently (Tables 4 and 5). Second, when optimal antigenic or mitogenic stimulation was added, the cloning efficiency of the NZB cells, in an assay for the development of PFC clones, was considerably higher (Tables 4, 5, and 7–9), a finding reminiscent of their higher efficiency in yielding agar mitogen-induced B-lymphocyte colonies (30). Third, and less impressive, when graded antigen concentrations were used to stimulate antibody formation, the NZB cells appeared to be more sensitive to triggering by low concentrations (Tables 4 and 5). These differences were apparent in young, adult, still healthy mice, but not in newborn mice (Table 6). They all suggest that the NZB B cell is more readily thrown into mitotic cycle (i.e., more easily excited) than normal B cells. The fourth finding, namely that of an excess of large cells among the s-IgM$^+$, s-IgD$^-$ B cells (Fig. 1), suggests that this lowered activation threshold is reflected in increased background stimulation *in vivo*, even in SPF and GF mice, as these cells probably represent recently activated B cells. What is not apparent from these or, we believe, other studies is whether the observed instability of the B cells is an intrinsic defect. On one hand, Gershwin *et al.* (32) have reported that athymic (nu/nu) NZB/NZW mice form the same abnormally high number of B cell clones as normal (nu/+) NZB/NZW mice, showing that thymus-derived cells as such, do not account for the elevated B-cell activation. On the other hand, B-cell mitogenesis could also be caused by excessive *in vivo* production of stimulatory cytokines, in its turn due either to intrinsic defects or excessive physiological stimulation. In that case, the higher *in vitro* cloning performance could simply mean that a cell already partially activated *in vivo* is readier to respond positively to *in vitro* signals. Whichever is the case, greater *in vivo* antigenic stimulation, such as could be caused by a heavy load of endogenous viruses or other organisms, would augment the observed effects. This seems the likely explanation for the grosser differences observed in some previous studies.

The fifth, and quite marginal, difference was in susceptibility to tolerance induction *in vitro* to FLU_8HGG (Table 10) in a system which we believe to monitor B-cell effects, but where suppressor T-cell influences have not been formally ruled out. From prior work by others, we expected quite marked resistance in NZB B cells, but in fact we found no difference using the presumed physiological targets for self-tolerance, immature B cells (Table 11); no difference using FLU_4HGG which is tolerogenic to adult cells at >100 μg/ml due to newborn cells at >1 μg/ml; and only a slight difference using the stronger tolerogen FLU_8HGG. Experiments of a design rather similar to that of some of the present ones were reported by Goldings *et al.* (14) while this work was in progress. Using *in vitro* tolerance induction followed by a bulk culture readout, they studied the tolerance susceptibility of the B cells of NZB/NZW F_1 hybrid mice, a strain less prone to hemolytic anemia but more to the lupus-like syndrome. With TNP_7HGG (unlike our data with FLU_8HGG shown in Table 10), they reported a very flat antigen concentration:tolerance induction dose:response curve, normal strains yielding approximately 60, 50, and 45% of control responses with 0.1, 1, and 10 μg/ml of tolerogen respectively. Their NZB/NZW cells gave approximately 90, 85, and 75% of control responses, respectively, using those three doses. Their differences between control and autoimmune strains were statistically significant and basically in the same direction as ours, but again not very marked. Interestingly, a more powerfully tolerogenic conjugate, $TNP_{32}HGG$, affected NZB/NZW cells as profoundly as control cells, showing that resistance to tolerogenesis was by no means absolute in their studies.

We failed to confirm differences in B-cell surface isotype expression as marked as previously reported (10, 29), though of course FACS analysis and immunochemical studies following cell surface radioiodination represent quite different methodological approaches. We did not see a reduced total s-Ig nor a markedly increased s-IgM to s-IgD ratio, as judged by FACS-generated fluorescence intensity profiles. As our sixth difference, we did see a slight reduction in the proportion of B cells carrying s-IgD, that is, a slight increase in s-IgM$^+$, s-IgD$^-$ cells (Tables 1 and 2). The differences in spleen were small and confined to adult mice. The differences in lymph node were more considerable and present also in suckling mice. For example, lymph node cells from 7-week-old NZB mice had almost twice as many s-IgM$^+$, s-IgD$^-$ cells (13.7% as the other two strains (7.4%). The s-IgM:s-IgD ratio certainly fluctuates during the life history of the B cell. S-IgM is acquired first, and s-IgG later, perhaps following nonspecific activation of preprogenitor B cells (33). Once a mature s-IgM$^+$, s-IgD$^+$ B cell is formed, it loses its s-IgD early after activation by antigen or mitogen. It is easy to see, therefore, how the ratio could vary widely, depending, *inter alia*, on variations in detailed maturational patterns and size of antigenic load.

Taken as a whole, our results lend support to the idea that an abnormally excitable B cell is one element in the complex, multifactorial web which constitutes the autoimmune diathesis of the New Zealand strains. This B-lymphocyte hyperactivity is further supported by a very recent study (34), which also casts some doubt on the idea of a generalized suppressor T-cell deficit. The subtle and indeed rather variable differences in susceptibility to tolerance induction as revealed by the literature and this study serve as a reminder that differences between various B lymphocytes in tolerizability are relative rather than absolute (24). Thus research on autoimmunity must continue to address many interacting factors—genetic, hormonal, viral—as well as all the aspects of the immunoregulatory network.

ACKNOWLEDGMENTS

We wish to thank Kim Bamford for his excellent technical assistance. The advice of Dr. F. L. Battye was invaluable in the FACS analysis studies. This work was supported by the National Health and Medical Research Council, Canberra, Australia; by Grant Number AI-03958 from the National Institute of Allergy and Infectious Diseases, U.S.A., Public Health Services; and by the generosity of a number of private donors to the Walter and Eliza Hall Institute. NRR was the recipient of a Fellowship from the Josiah Macy, Jr., Foundation.

REFERENCES

1. Howie, J. B., and Helyer, B. J., *Advan. Immunol.* **9,** 215, 1968.
2. DeVries, M. J., and Hijmans, W., *Immunology* **12,** 179, 1967.
3. McCombs, C., Hom, J., Talal, N., and Mischell, R. I., *J. Immunol.* **115,** 1695, 1975.
4. Barthold, D. R., Kysela, S., and Steinberg, A. D., *J. Immunol.* **110,** 1652, 1973.
5. DeHeer, D. H., and Edgington, T. S., *J. Immunol.* **118,** 1858, 1977.
6. Morton, J. I., and Siegel, B. V., *Proc. Nat. Acad. Sci. USA* **71,** 2162, 1974.
7. Klassen, L. W., Krakauer, R. S., and Steinberg, A. D., *J. Immunol.* **119,** 830, 1977.
8. Cantor, H., McVay-Boudreau, L., Hugenberger, J., Naidorf, K., Shen, F. W., and Gershon, R. K., *J. Exp. Med.* **147,** 1116, 1978.
9. Cohen, P. L., and Ziff, M., *J. Immunol.* **1534,** 1977.

10. Chused, T. M., Moutsopulos, H. M., Sharrow, S. O., Hansen, C. T., and Morse, H. C., *In* "Genetic Control of Autoimmune Disease" (N. Rose, P. Bigazzi, and N. L. Warner, Eds.), p. 177. Elsevier/North Holland, New York, 1978.
11. DeHeer, D. H., and Edgington, T. S., *Clin. Immunol. Immunopathol.* **15,** 472, 1980.
12. Izui, S., and Dixon, F. J., *Fed. Proc.* **37,** 1373, 1978.
13. Staples, P. J., and Talal, N., *J. Exp. Med.* **129,** 123, 1969.
14. Goldings, E. A., Cohen, P. L., McFadden, S. F., Ziff, M., and Vitetta, E. S., *J. Exp. Med.* **152,** 730, 1980.
15. Izui, S., McConahey, P. J., Theofilopoulos, A. N., and Dixon, F. J., *J. Exp. Med.* **149,** 1099, 1979.
16. Russell, P. J., Hicks, J. D., Boston, L. E., and Abbott, A., *Clin. Exp. Immunol.* **6,** 227, 1970.
17. Nossal, G. J. V., Pike, B. L., and Battye, F. L., *Eur. J. Immunol.* **8,** 151, 1978.
18. Oi, V. T., Jones, P. P., Goding, J. W., Herzenberg, L. A., and Herzenberg, L. A., *Curr. Top. Microbiol. Immunol.* **81,** 115, 1978.
19. Goding, J. W., *J. Immunol. Methods* **13,** 215, 1976.
20. Nossal, G. J. V., and Pike, B. L., *Immunology* **30,** 189, 1976.
21. Nossal, G. J. V., and Pike, B. L., *J. Immunol.* **120,** 145, 1978.
22. Shortman, K., Williams, N., and Adams, P., *J. Immunol. Methods* **1,** 273, 1972.
23. von Boehmer, H., and Shortman, K., *J. Immunol. Methods* **2,** 293, 1973.
24. Pike, B. L., Battye, F. L., and Nossal, G. J. V., *J. Immunol.* **126,** 89, 1981.
25. Nossal, G. J. V., and Pike, B. L., *J. Exp. Med.* **148,** 1161, 1978.
26. Nossal, G. J. V., Pike, P. L., Teale, J. M., Layton, J. E., Kay, T. W., and Battye, F. L., *Immunol. Rev.* **43,** 185, 1978.
27. Herzenberg, L. A., and Herzenberg, L. A., *In* "Handbook of Experimental Immunology" (D. M. Weir, Ed.), 3rd ed. Vol. 2, Chap. 22. Blackwell Scientific, Melbourne, 1978.
28. Krishnan, A., *J. Cell Biol.* **66,** 188, 1975.
29. Cohen, P., Ziff, M., and Vitetta, E. S., *J. Immunol.* **121,** 973, 1978.
30. Kincade, P. W., Lee, G., Fernandes, G., Moore, M. A. S., Williams, N., and Good, R. A., *Proc. Nat. Acad. Sci. USA* **76,** 3464, 1979.
31. Gronowicz, E., Coutinho, A., and Melchers, F., *Eur. J. Immunol.* **6,** 588, 1976.
32. Gershwin, M. E., Ohsugi, Y., Ahmed, A., Castles, J. J., Scibienski, and Ikeda, R. M., *J. Immunol.* **125,** 1189, 1980.
33. Layton, J. E., Baker, J., Bartlett, P. F., and Shortman, K., *J. Immunol.* **126,** 1227, 1981.
34. Theofilopoulos, A. N., and Dixon, F. J., *Immunol. Rev.* **55,** 179, 1981.

CELLULAR IMMUNOLOGY 63, 400–408 (1981)

Polymorphism and Antigenic Specificity of Monocytic Acid Esterase (EC 3.1.1.6)[1]

H. J. RADZUN, M. R. PARWARESCH, AND J. W. WITTKE

Department of Pathology, University of Kiel, Hospitalstrasse 42, 2300 Kiel, West Germany

Received May 29, 1981; accepted June 9, 1981

With the aim to provide a biochemical or immunological marker for human blood monocytes, their differentiational derivatives, and neoplastic variants the polymorphism of acid α-naphthyl acetate esterase was investigated. Using an isoelectric focusing technique it could be shown that the five enzyme variants of normal human blood monocytes, which do not occur in other human blood cell types, were regularly detectable in human peritoneal and alveolar macrophages. Antisera, raised against isoenzymes of monocytic acid esterase in rabbits, reacted in all cases with every five isoenzymes of blood monocytes; no cross-reactivity was observed with the isoenzymes of acid esterase obtained from purified human granulocytes, peripheral lymphocytes, B lymphocytes, and thymocytes as shown by immunoprecipitation. The results indicate that monocytic acid esterase and its variants could be regarded as a biochemical as well as immunological marker for this cell line.

INTRODUCTION

The morphological recognition of human blood monocytes in tissue, their functional and differentiational derivatives as well as their neoplastic forms, has been met with a considerable diagnostic insecurity (1, 2). Enzyme cytochemical aims like acid α-naphthyl acetate esterase reaction lack appropriate specificity due to widespread occurrence. Immunological attempts at this issue have brought about a certain advance. Heteroantisera raised against whole cells, however, necessitate extensive absorptions, yet always retaining some cross-reactivity with other tissue structures (3–8). The introduction of hybridoma technique opened new perspectives in this field (9–11). The specificity of the monoclonal antibodies, however, relies to a great extent on the specificity of the antigen used for immunization.

Recently, evidence has been provided indicating that the more or less ubiquitary acid hydrolases as detected by biochemical and cytochemical tests show a blood-cell-specific polymorphism using an isoelectric focusing technique (12, 13). This applied to acid phosphatase and acid esterase (AcE), extracted from lysosomes of purified human blood cells, rendering unambiguous recognition of the individual cell types and their neoplastic variants (14, 15).

The aim of the following study is to analyze the enzyme polymorphism of AcE from human blood monocytes and to compare it with the corresponding results

[1] This study was supported by the Deutsche Forschungsgemeinschaft SFB 111, Projects CL 3 and CN 2.

0008-8749/81/140400-09$02.00/0

from peritoneal macrophages (PM) and alveolar macrophages (AM) as functional derivatives of monocytes. In a further attempt monocytic AcE isoenzymes have been examined as to their antigenic specificity in comparison with the other blood cell types.

MATERIALS AND METHODS

(1) Separation of Blood Monocytes, PM, and AM

Fresh heparinized venous blood (40 IU/ml) from young donors was centrifuged on a Ficoll–Urografin (Pharmacia, Uppsala, Sweden; Schering, Berlin, West Germany) density gradient (D = 1077 g/ml) as described by Boyum (16). Blood monocytes were separated from the mononuclear cells of the interphase by glass adherence (17).

PM were obtained from peritoneal cavity of healthy infertile female during diagnostic pelviscopy. Cells were separated by centrifugation (400*g*, 10 min, 4°C) and washed twice.

For isolation of AM the bronchial system of fresh human lungs, ectomized due to neoplasm or bullous emphysema, were rinsed several times with RPMI 1640 (Mediapharm, Aschaffenburg, West Germany). Following centrifugation of the combined washing solutions AM were obtained from the sediment after osmotic lysis of contaminating erythrocytes.

The cell fractions were checked for viability by trypan blue exclusion test. Purity control was established on cytocentrifuge preparations (Shandon, London, England) by differential counting using Pappenheim staining and acid esterase reaction (18). Only cell populations with a purity range of over 80% were used for further analyses.

(2) Enzyme Assay and Isoelectric Focusing of AcE

AcE was extracted from the different cell populations by incubation with 1% (v/v) Triton X-100 solution (Serva, Heidelberg, West Germany) for 30 min at room temperature followed by ultracentrifugation (100,000*g*, 60 min, 4°C). The enzyme activity was measured spectrophotometrically in the 100,000*g* supernatants using α-naphthyl acetate (Sigma, Munich, West Germany) as substrate and fast blue RR (Sigma) as coupler (12).

Sixty milliunits of AcE activity in 20 μl was subjected to isoelectric focusing on 4.3% polyacrylamide thin-layer slabs using the multiphor system 2117 from LKB (Bromma, Sweden). The gels contained 13.3% (wt/v) sucrose, 1% (wt/v) Triton X-100, 0.057% (wt/v) riboflavin (Canalco, Rockville, Md.), and for establishing the pH gradient 5.0% (v/v) ampholine (pH 3.5–10.0) as well as 0.36% (v/v) pH 4.0–6.0 and pH 5.0–7.0 (LKB), respectively. As anolyte and catholyte, 1 *M* phosphoric acid and 1 *M* sodium hydroxide were used (19), respectively. After 4 hr running time at 4°C, during which the initial voltage of 200 V increased to a terminal level of 1200 V, the enzyme variants of AcE were visualized by the histochemical method (18) and the isoelectric points (p*I*) of the bands were determined by measuring the pH of aliquots of gel strips.

(3) Preparation of Antisera against Monocytic AcE

After termination of isoelectric focusing of the 100,000*g* supernatants of monocytes in 10 parallel runs on one and the same gel slab the two outer strips were separated and stained for AcE reaction. Thus, the individual bands could easily be localized in the unstained gel region.
Narrow gel segments, containing either all five isoenzymes or the most anodal band of monocytic AcE only, were cut out in eight aliquots and combined. To make sure that the desired bands were completely resolved, the remainders of the gel were controlled for AcE activity by the same staining procedure.

The gel segments, containing enzyme samples of the eight applications with a total activity of 480 mU in the case of all five isoenzymes and 370 mU in the case of the anodal band (20), were solubilized in 2 ml saline and emulsified with an equal volume of complete or incomplete Freund's adjuvant for the first and the booster injections. Rabbits were immunized subcutaneously on Days 0, 14, 21, and 28, on Day 34 the hyperimmune sera were collected. Control sera were obtained prior to immunization. All sera were heat inactivated at 56°C for 30 min and stored at −20°C.

(4) Specificity Control of the Antisera by Immunoprecipitation

Immunoprecipitation was done according to Ritchie and Smith (21). After isoelectric focusing of samples containing 60 mU of AcE activity gel strips were overlayered with antisera raised against monocytic AcE and incubated for 2 hr at room temperature in a humidified chamber. Gel strips were then extensively washed under mild shaking at room temperature for 2 days in saline. The latter were changed every 6 hr. Thereafter the gel strips were stained for AcE.

In addition to monocytes immunoprecipitation was carried out on AcE extracts of human granulocytes, peripheral lymphocytes, B lymphocytes, and thymocytes. Granulocytes and peripheral lymphocytes were gained from the bottom fraction and the nonadherent cells of the interphase after density centrifugation. B lymphocytes were isolated from tonsillar cell suspensions after excluding T lymphocytes by rosetting with 2-aminoethylisothiouronium bromide (Sigma)-treated sheep erythrocytes (22), followed by repeated centrifugation on Ficoll–Urografin (23). Thymocytes were harvested from cell suspensions of thymus glands using gradient centrifugation.

The purity rate of these cell fractions was checked by Pappenheim and AcE (18) staining of cytocentrifuge preparations. In addition rosetting with neuraminidase-treated sheep erythrocytes (24) and immunofluorescence staining of surface immunoglobulins (25) were used as immunological tests for the T- and B-cell system, respectively. For further details refer to Radzun *et al.* (12, 13).

Cell populations with a purity rate of over 80% were subjected to AcE extraction and immunoprecipitation as described above.

RESULTS

(1) Enzyme Activity and Isoelectric Focusing Pattern of AcE

The enzyme activities related to the cell count showed a characteristic distribution among the three cell lines examined. Monocytes showed a mean activity value of

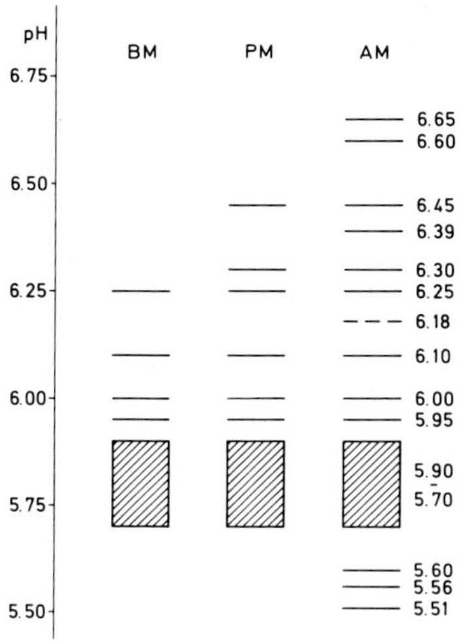

FIG. 1. Schematic presentation of isoelectric focusing patterns and p*I* values of AcE in human blood monocytes (BM), peritoneal macrophages (PM), and alveolar macrophages (AM).

39.3 ± 31.5 mU/1 × 10^7 cells ($n = 7$). The corresponding value for PM amounted to 58.4 ± 32.8 mU/1 × 10^7 cells ($n = 5$). AM regularly presented the highest enzyme content with a mean value of 342 ± 273 mU/1 × 10^7 cells ($n = 5$).

The isoelectric focusing patterns are summarized schematically in Fig. 1. Monocytes showed a broad band of high activity between pH 5.90 and 5.70, accounting for about 77% of the total AcE activity. The other enzyme variants were localized at pH 5.95, 6.00, 6.10, and 6.25, of which the bands with p*I* values of 5.95 and 6.00 were occasionally seen to be fused. PM expressed, in addition to the monocytic loci, enzyme variants at pH 6.30 and 6.45. AM presented, in addition to the bands seen in monocytes and PM, further AcE loci. These appeared in the anodal region of the gel with p*I* values of 5.51, 5.56, and 5.60 as well as in the cathodal region with p*I* values of 6.39, 6.60, and 6.65. An inconstant enzyme variant was observed at pH 6.18.

Figure 2 shows the original isoelectric focusing patterns of the described cell populations.

(2) Control of Antigen Purity and Specificity of Antisera

The remainders of the gel slabs, stained for AcE after removal of the enzyme-bearing gel portions, are shown in Figs. 3 and 4. It is evident that bands, intended for immunization, are lacking in the rest of the gel. Parallel gel strips, containing aliquots of the 100,000*g* monocytic supernatant, stained with Coomassie blue (Merck, Darmstadt, West Germany) as an unspecific protein dye, displayed no bands other than those representing the monocytic AcE variants (Fig. 5). This implicates the high purity of the enzyme fractions used for immunization.

The antiserum raised against all five monocytic isoenymes as well as the one directed against the separated anodal band immunoprecipitated all five isoenzyme loci of monocytic AcE (Fig. 6). AcE extracts, diluted up to 1:10, corresponding to 6 mU net enzyme activity, were readily precipitated by the antisera.

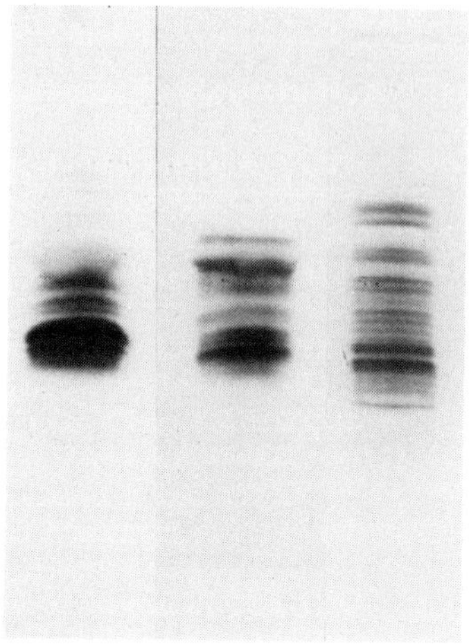

FIG. 2. Original isoelectric focusing patterns of AcE. From left to right blood monocytes, peritoneal macrophages, alveolar macrophages.

In Fig. 7 AcE isoenzymes of granulocytes, peripheral lymphocytes, B lymphocytes, and thymocytes separated by isoelectric focusing are demonstrated after incubation with the antiserum raised against AcE derived from blood monocytes. A positive immunoprecipitation was not observed in samples obtained from granulocytes, B lymphocytes, and thymocytes. An exception occurred in samples of separated total peripheral blood lymphocytes. In these strips immunoprecipitated bands of weak intensity were detectable on the typical loci of monocytic AcE isoenzymes. Since the contamination rate of total peripheral blood lymphocytes with monocytes amounted to 10–20% in these samples, it is evident that the positive immunoprecipitation is due to the monocyte admixture. In line with this finding was the net enzyme activity of peripheral lymphocyte fractions amounting to about 10.5 mU/1 $\times$ 10^7 cells and exceeding those of highly purified T and B lymphocytes by a factor of 2 (12). Preimmunization sera showed in no case a positive immunoprecipitation with the enzyme bands of the cell lines investigated (Fig. 6).

DISCUSSION

Monocytes and macrophages are characterized cytochemically by the α-naphthyl acetate esterase reaction, displaying a diffuse strong activity (26–29). Except for

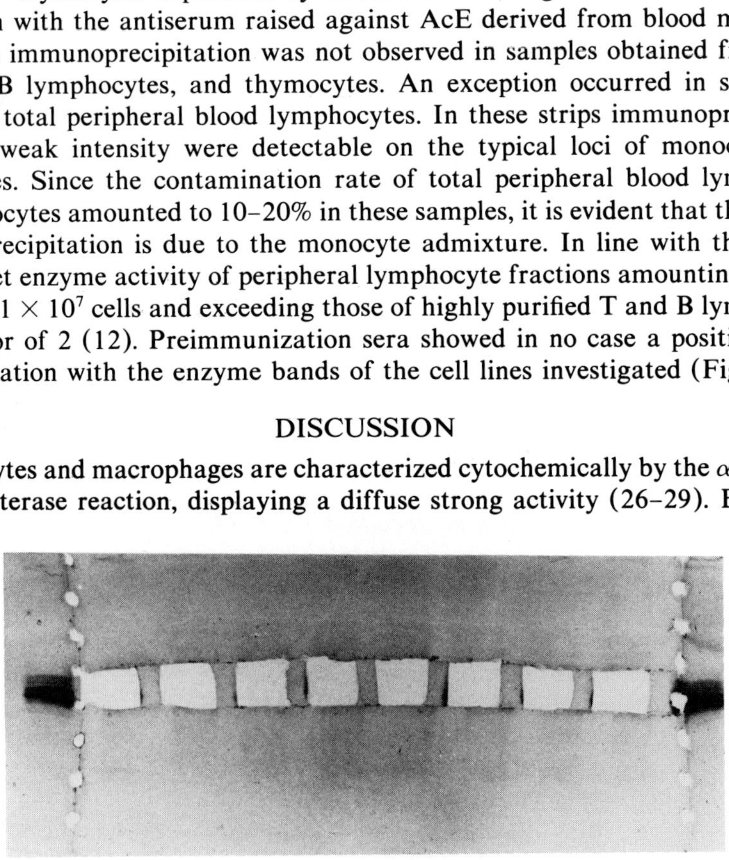

FIG. 3. Control staining for ACE after removal of all five monocytic AcE isoenzymes.

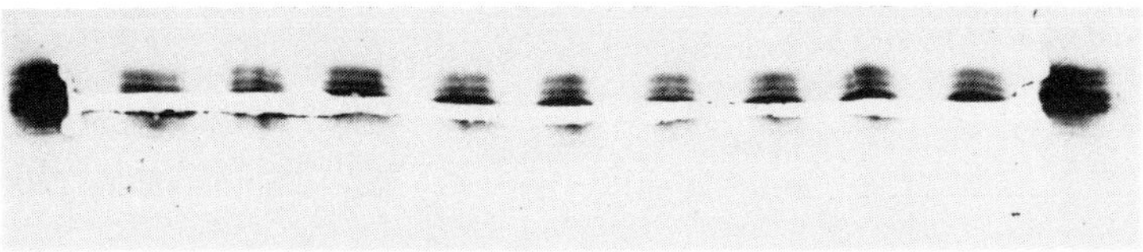

FIG. 4. Control staining for AcE after removal of the anodal band of monocytic AcE.

a certain subgroup of T lymphocytes, having a dot-like reaction product (30), no other blood cell type is provided with such a distinct AcE pattern on cytochemical tests. In a recent study using isoelectric focusing we could demonstrate that these cytochemical differences were associated with a blood-cell-specific polymorphism of AcE isoenzymes (12). Similar results could be obtained from the analysis of acid phosphatase, again showing a specific isoenzyme constellation for every blood cell type (13). In addition, it could be shown that the B-cell-specific isoenzyme pattern of acid phosphatase was detectable in four different entities of B-cell lymphoma (14); furthermore, leukemic cells displayed the patterns of the underlying normal counterpart (15). The high specificity of isoenzymes of acid hydrolases to the individual human blood cells and the unique focusing pattern of monocytic AcE initiated the present study to see whether or not monocytic AcE could be regarded as a biochemical as well as immunological marker for this blood cell type.

The results of isoelectric focusing showed that the monocytic AcE with five bands between pH 6.25 and 5.70 could regularly be recognized in the corresponding patterns of PM and AM (Figs. 1 and 2). The higher enzyme activities measured in PM and AM were at least partly due to the occurrence of new isoenzymes. These additional enzyme variants of PM and AM were not present in other blood cell types (12). It is suggestive to assume that they were induced during differentiation of blood monocytes into macrophages going along with alterations in

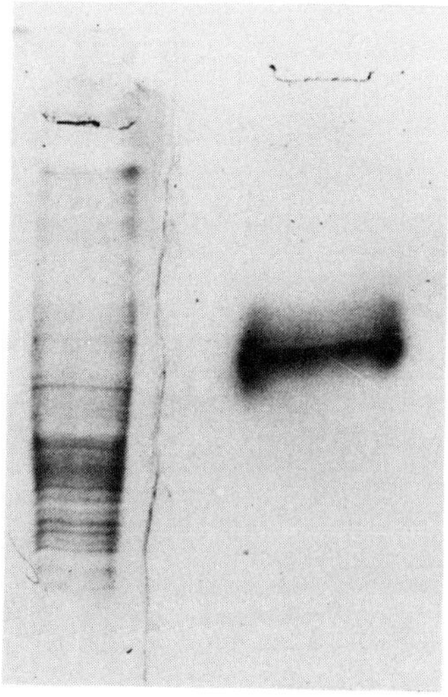

FIG. 5. Monocytic 100,000*g* supernatant, stained with Coomassie blue (left) in comparison with AcE staining (right).

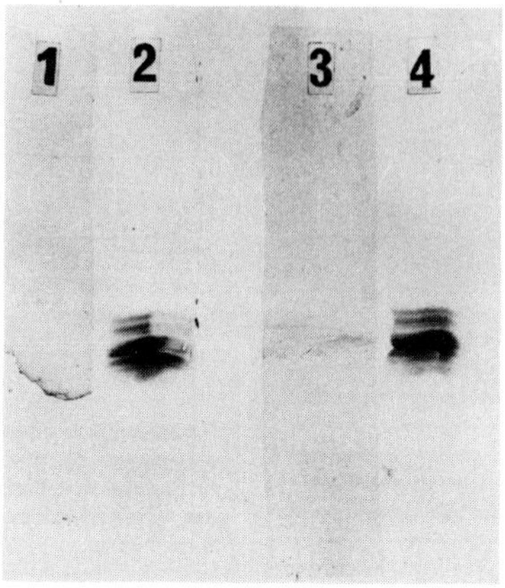

FIG. 6. Immunoprecipitation of monocytic AcE (1 and 3 = preimmunization sera; 2 = antiserum against all five monocytic AcE isoenzymes; 4 = antiserum against the anodal band of monocytic AcE).

metabolic as well as functional activities (31). A gradual transition of the monocytic AcE pattern into that of PM could already be observed during prolonged glass adherence of blood monocytes (20). It remains to be clarified, however, as to what kind of stimulation is responsible under physiological conditions for the transformation of monocytic isoenzyme pattern into that of AM.

The origin of macrophages were considered by several authors. Using the polymorphism of enzyme variants (32), the surface equipment with Fc receptors (33), and the lysosomal content for different hydrolases (34), as well as kinetic criteria (35), PM and AM were claimed to derive from blood monocytes. All these studies were performed in experimental animals. It has to be established, whether the same conclusions were applicable to the human system. Corresponding results on human are limited to a few studies (20, 36). As far as we know, this is the first report on a direct evidence for the cytogenetic relationship between blood monocytes and PM as well as AM in the human system. The results confirm our working hypothesis that cell-specific isoenzyme patterns can be applied as a reliable biochemical marker for a given cell type.

In a further attempt we examined the intra- and intercellular antigenic heterogeneity of AcE isoenzymes of monocytes as compared with those of other blood cell types. The high resolution capacity of isoelectric focusing spared us elaborative

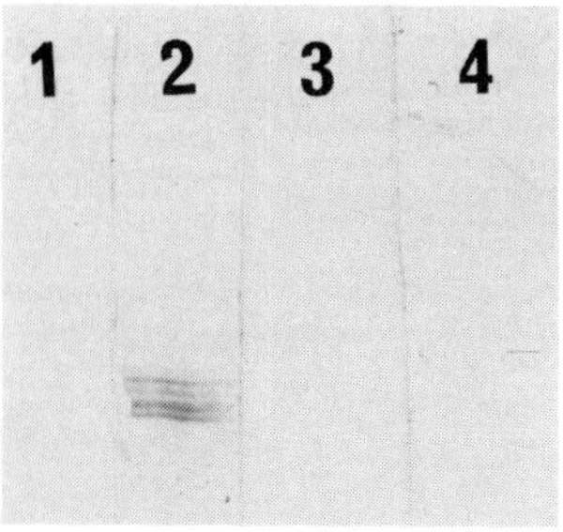

FIG. 7. Immunoprecipitation of AcE extracted from granulocytes (1), peripheral lymphocytes (2), B lymphocytes (3), and thymocytes (4).

purification procedures. As shown by unspecific protein staining hardly any protein band other than those representing the monocytic AcE loci between pH 6.25 and 5.70 were detectable in repeated runs (Fig. 5). This issue encouraged us to inject directly the homogenized gel segments containing AcE into rabbits. By this procedure we made use of the additional adjuvant properties of polyacrylamide. The obtained antisera were found to immunoprecipitate the monocytic AcE isoenzymes only (Fig. 6). The AcE variants of the other blood cell types showed no reaction with the raised antisera (Fig. 7). Thus, the AcE isoenzymes of the individual blood cell populations most probably differ in their antigenic determinants. The five AcE variants of blood monocytes on the other hand seem to be antigenetically related. Because the antiserum against the anodal complex as the major isoenzyme of monocytic AcE, which accounts for 77% of the total enzyme activity in monocytes, precipitated also the loci at pH 6.25, 6.10, 6.00, and 5.95 (Fig. 6).

There are a good number of studies on antisera specific for monocytes or macrophages (3–8). Most of these investigations, having prepared antisera against surface antigens, bear more or less the shortcoming of excessive necessary absorptions before getting the desired specificity. The antisera described in this study were revealed to be operationally specific for the monocytic AcE isoenzymes without any preceding absorption steps as far as could be tested by immunoprecipitation. The present study reveals no information as to what extent the antisera directed against monocytic AcE would react with PM and AM as functional derivatives of blood monocytes (Radzun *et al.* in preparation). It remains further to be established, whether these antisera are also appropriate to be used in immunohistochemical tests for a selective staining of monocytic AcE.

In a recent report Ugolini *et al.* (9) were successful in preparation monoclonal antibodies against human blood monocytes, characterizing a surface antigen with a molecular weight of 200,000. This and other monoclonal antibodies against blood monocytes (10, 11) displayed but a weak cross-reaction with granulocytes and T lymphocytes. Using antigens of a restricted occurrence, limited to a certain cell type, in raising monoclonal antibodies could probably reduce the time consuming screening assays and cloning procedures otherwise unavoidable in hybridoma technique. Isoenzymes of monocytic AcE seem to represent such candidates.

REFERENCES

1. Cline, M. J., and Golde, D. W., *Amer. J. Med.* **55,** 49, 1973.
2. Shaw, M. T., *Human Pathol.* **11,** 215, 1980.
3. Unanue, E. R., *Nature (London)* **218,** 36, 1968.
4. Baker, M. A., Falk, R. E., Falk, J., and Greaves, M. F., *Brit. J. Haematol.* **32,** 13, 1976.
5. Stuart, A. E., Young, G. A., and Grant, P. F., *Brit. J. Haematol.* **34,** 457, 1976.
6. Roberts, M. M., and Greaves, M. F., *Brit. J. Haematol.* **38,** 439, 1978.
7. Boltz-Nitulescu, G., and Foerster, O., *Immunology* **38,** 621, 1979.
8. Breard, J., Lazarus, H., and Schlossman, S. F., *Clin. Immunol. Immunopathol.* **16,** 438, 1980.
9. Ugolini, V., Nunez, G., Smith, R. G., Stastny, P., and Capra, J. D., *Proc. Nat. Acad. Sci. USA* **77,** 6764, 1980.
10. Breard, J., Reinherz, E. L., Kung, P. C., Goldstein, G., and Schlossman, S. F., *J. Immunol.* **124,** 1943, 1980.
11. Reinherz, E. L., Moretta, L., Roper, M., Breard, J. M., Mingari, M. C., Cooper, M. D., and Schlossman, S. F., *J. Exp. Med.* **151,** 969, 1980.
12. Radzun, H. J., Parwaresch, M. R., Kulenkampff, Ch., Staudinger, M., and Stein, H., *Blood* **55,** 891, 1980.

13. Radzun, H. J., Parwaresch, M. R., Kulenkampff, Ch., and Stein, H., *Clin. Chim. Acta* **102,** 227, 1980.
14. Schmidt, D., Radzun, H. J., Schwarze, E.-W., Stein, H., and Parwaresch, M. R., *Cancer* **46,** 2676, 1980.
15. Radzun, H. J., Parwaresch, M. R., and Feller, A. C., *Proc. Soc. Exp. Biol. Med.,* **167,** 394, 1981.
16. Boyum, A., *Scand. J. Clin. Lab. Invest.* (Suppl.) **21,** 77, 1968.
17. Bennett, W. E., and Cohn, Z. A., *J. Exp. Med.* **123,** 145, 1966.
18. Mueller, J., Brun del Re, G., Buerki, H., Keller, H. U., Hess, M. W., and Cottier, H., *Eur. J. Immunol.* **5,** 270, 1975.
19. Vesterberg, O., *Biochim. Biophys. Acta* **257,** 11, 1972.
20. Parwaresch, M. R., Radzun, H. J., and Dommes, M., *Amer. J. Pathol.* **102,** 209, 1981.
21. Ritchie, R. R., and Smith, R., *Clin. Chem.* **22,** 1982, 1976.
22. Kaplan, M. E., and Clark, C., *J. Immunol. Methods* **5,** 131, 1974.
23. Wybran, J., and Chantler, S., *Lancet* **1,** 126, 1973.
24. Weiner, M. S., Bianco, C., and Nussenzweig, V., *Blood* **42,** 939, 1973.
25. Möller, G., *J. Exp. Med.* **114,** 415, 1961.
26. Braunsteiner, H., *J. Histochem. Cytochem.* **7,** 202, 1959.
27. Leder, L. D. (Ed), "Experimentelle Medizin, Pathologie und Klinik," Vol. 23. Springer-Verlag, Heidelberg/New York, 1967.
28. Rosenszayn, L., Leibovich, M., Shoham, D., and Epstein, J., *Brit. J. Haematol.* **14,** 605, 1968.
29. Yam, L. T., Li, C. Y., and Crosby, W. H., *Amer. J. Clin. Pathol.* **55,** 283, 1971.
30. Grossi, C. E., Webb, S. R., Zicca, A., Lydyard, P. M., Moretta, L., Mingari, M. C., and Cooper, M. D., *J. Exp. Med.* **147,** 1405, 1978.
31. Hearst, J. E., Warr, G. A., and Jakob, G. J., *J. Reticuloendothel. Soc.* **27,** 443, 1980.
32. Brunstetter, M.-A., Hardie, J. A., Schiff, R., Lewis, J. P., and Cross, C. E., *Arch. Intern. Med.* **127,** 1064, 1971.
33. Kávai, M., Laczkó, J., and Csaba, B., *Immunology* **36,** 729, 1979.
34. Fishman, M., and Weinberg, D. S., *Cell. Immunol.* **45,** 437, 1979.
35. Van Furth, R., and Cohn, Z. A., *J. Exp. Med.* **128,** 415, 1968.
36. Van Furth, R., Raeburn, J. A., and Van Zwet, T. L., *Blood* **54,** 485, 1979.

CELLULAR IMMUNOLOGY **63**, 409–416 (1981)

SHORT COMMUNICATIONS

Experimental Allergic Encephalomyelitis in the Guinea Pig: Variation in Peripheral Blood Lymphocyte Responsiveness to Myelin Basic Protein during Disease Development

WILLIAM D. LYMAN, ANNA S. KADISH, AND CEDRIC S. RAINE

Departments of Pathology and Neuroscience and The Rose F. Kennedy Center for Research in Mental Retardation and Human Development, Albert Einstein College of Medicine, 1300 Morris Park Avenue, Bronx, New York 10461

Received July 3, 1980; accepted June 6, 1981

Peripheral blood lymphocytes (PBL) from guinea pigs with experimental allergic encephalomyelitis (EAE) induced by sensitization with bovine whole white matter, proliferated *in vitro* upon exposure to bovine myelin basic protein (B-MBP). The degree of the response increased with clinical severity. PBL from EAE-sensitized guinea pigs which failed to develop clinical disease did not respond to B-MBP. PBL from complete Freund's adjuvant-sensitized and nonsensitized normal guinea pigs were not responsive to B-MBP. EAE-sensitized animals displaying clinical signs of disease showed concanavalin A (Con A) responsiveness which paralleled that of B-MBP. Animals that did not develop EAE demonstrated Con A responses similar to those of control guinea pigs. Thus, in this acute autoimmune demyelinating condition, PBL responsiveness to B-MBP might provide a monitor of disease development.

INTRODUCTION

Experimental allergic encephalomyelitis (EAE) has long served as a model for studies on delayed-type hypersensitivity (1, 2) and the inflammatory demyelinating diseases (3). The role of T cells sensitized to central nervous system antigens in EAE has been well documented since the disease can be passively transferred with lymph node cells, but not serum (2) and prevented by thymectomy prior to sensitization (4, 5). Recent studies on T-cell subsets in EAE have shown that fluctuations in the percentages of early-rosetting (high-affinity) T cells occur and that these changes correlate with the clinical course of both acute and chronic EAE in Strain 13 guinea pigs (6, 7). Since numerical variation of a specific subset might not accurately reflect differences in T-cell function, the present study was initiated to assess changes in functional activity of peripheral blood lymphocytes (PBL) during the course of acute EAE.

A lymphocyte transformation test was used to measure mitogen and EAE-associated antigen-induced lymphocyte proliferation (8). These studies revealed a correlation between *in vitro* lymphocyte responses and the clinical stage of acute EAE.

MATERIALS AND METHODS

Animals. Thirty-five male Hartley guinea pigs (400–600 g) were separated into three groups: (1) EAE-sensitized; (2) complete Freund's adjuvant (CFA)-sensi-

0008-8749/81/140409-08$02.00/0

tized; and (3) nonsensitized, normal animals. All animals were checked daily for clinical signs and weighed. The initial clinical change observed in animals which developed signs of EAE was a dramatic overnight weight loss of 50–100 g.

The clinical course of acute EAE was divided into three periods: a latent period, prior to the appearance of clinical signs, lasting approximately 10–12 days post-inoculation (DPI); a disease onset phase, during which weight loss, flaccidity, incontinence, and neurological signs began to appear between 10 and 19 days after sensitization; and a severe disease phase, during which EAE animals demonstrated hindleg paraparesis and urinary and fecal incontinence which culminated in a quadriparetic, moribund state between Days 12 and 23 postsensitization.

Induction. Induction of EAE was by subcutaneous injection, in the nuchal area, of 0.5 ml of an emulsion containing 0.25 ml of a 50% (w/v) suspension of bovine white matter in saline and 0.25 ml of CFA containing 10 mg of killed *Mycobacterium tuberculosis*/ml. CFA-sensitized animals were given 0.25 ml of CFA alone from the same stock.

Cell preparation. After inoculation, animals were bled on Days 2 and 8 and during the disease onset and severe disease phases. Bleedings were by cardiac puncture into heparinized syringes. When EAE-sensitized animals became moribund, they were exsanguinated together with control animals.

Mononuclear cells were separated on a Ficoll–Hypaque gradient (Pharmacia), washed three times in Hanks' balanced salt solution containing heparin (1 unit/ml), counted, and adjusted to 2×10^6 cells/ml in RPMI 1640 (Grand Island Biological Co.) containing 15% heat-inactivated guinea pig serum (Grand Island Biological Co.) supplemented with 1% each of penicillin, streptomycin (Microbiological Associates), and glutamine. Preliminary assays were performed in which fetal bovine (Flow Laboratories), human AB (collected from volunteers), and pooled isologous guinea pig sera were used at concentrations of 5, 10, and 15% instead of the commercially prepared guinea pig serum.

Preparation of antigens. Bovine myelin basic protein (B-MBP) and as a control, the P peptide (MBPep) derived from it [lacking the guinea pig encephalitogenic tryptophan residue which had been cleaved by iodobenzoic acid (9)], were dissolved in the same medium used to suspend the cell preparation and the concentration of each protein was adjusted to two times the final concentration. Bovine IgG, cytochrome C, and histone (Sigma) were likewise dissolved in the same medium used above and the concentration of each was adjusted to two times the final concentration.

Bovine kidney and lung were finely minced, after trimming the fat and connective tissue, and then homogenized in cold 3 *M* KCl (Omnimixer-Sorval). The homogenate was stirred overnight at 4°C followed by low-speed centrifugation at 4°C to pellet large pieces of debris. Following this, the putative protein suspensions were dialyzed extensively and repeatedly against PBS. The bovine kidney extract (BKE) and bovine lung extract (BLE) were centrifuged at 4°C for 30 min at 30,000 rpm (100,000*g*) to remove all cellular debris. The protein concentration of the supernatant was determined by the Lowry–Folin method and stock solutions were adjusted to 1 mg/ml, passed through a 0.22-μm-pore-size Millipore filter and stored at −90°C in aliquots. Before each culture was established, BKE and BLE aliquots were thawed and the protein concentration was adjusted to two times the final concentration in medium.

Lymphocyte transformation assay. The cell suspension was dispensed at a concentration of 2×10^5 cells/0.1 ml/well, into 96-well flat-bottom microtiter plates (Costar). Medium alone or medium containing one of the following: 20 μg/ml concanavalin A (Con A) (Miles Laboratories); 100 μg/ml MBP, 100 μg/ml MBPep, 100 μg/ml BKE, 100 μg/ml BLE, 100 μg/ml bovine histone, 8.4 μM bovine IgG, or 8.4 μM cytochrome *C* was added (0.1 ml/well) therefore making the final concentrations: 10 μg/ml Con A, 50 μg/ml MBP, 50 μg/ml MBPep, 50 μg/ml BKE, 50 μg/ml BLE, 50 μg/ml bovine histone, 4.2 μM bovine IgG, and 4.2 μM cytochrome *C*. The cultures were then incubated for 48 hr at 37°C, 7% CO_2. Thereafter, 1.25 μCi of tritiated thymidine ([^{3}H]TdR) (Amersham) was added to each well. The cultures were allowed an additional overnight incubation and were harvested onto glass filters (Enzo Biochemicals) using a multiple cell harvester (Skatron, Flow Laboratories). Econofluor scintillation cocktail (New England Nuclear) was used and samples were counted in a Beckman liquid scintillation counter.

All cultures were prepared in triplicate and the values expressed as the mean value ± 1 SD. All values were tested at the $P < 0.05$ confidence level by Student's *t* test or paired *t* test. Before harvesting, sample cultures were tested for cell viability with trypan blue. Cell survival was invariably greater than 85%.

RESULTS

Clinical Findings

Ten of the seventeen EAE-sensitized guinea pigs developed initial clinical signs between 14 and 18 DPI. By 16 to 25 days, these EAE animals demonstrated severe disease and were moribund. The remaining 7 EAE-sensitized guinea pigs did not develop clinical signs of EAE and continued to gain weight until the end of the experiment—28 DPI. CFA and normal controls demonstrated no abnormal signs and thrived throughout the course of the experiment.

Lymphocyte Responsiveness

Con A was used to monitor T-cell proliferative responses. During the latent period, PBL from both EAE and CFA animals gave Con A responses similar to those of PBL from nonsensitized normals. By 16 DPI (the disease onset phase for EAE-sensitized guinea pigs with clinical signs of disease), their responses increased significantly above those of nonsensitized normal controls. PBL from EAE-sensitized animals demonstrated approximately 10-fold more stimulation than PBL from CFA controls (Fig. 1). PBL from EAE-sensitized guinea pigs responded to B-MBP whereas PBL from CFA-sensitized controls and normal animals showed no response. As with Con A stimulation, PBL from EAE animals began to respond to B-MBP at the beginning of the disease onset phase and their responsiveness peaked when they became moribund (Fig. 2).

While Figs. 1 and 2 illustrate the responses of PBL from representative animals to both Con A and B-MBP stimulation, Fig. 3 shows the results of all animals' PBL studied. Although the mean values of PBL responses from EAE-sensitized guinea pigs to B-MBP were less than the corresponding Con A mean values, some animals' PBL responded more to B-MBP than to Con A. The mean value of B-MBP responses at the time of disease onset was not statistically different from that

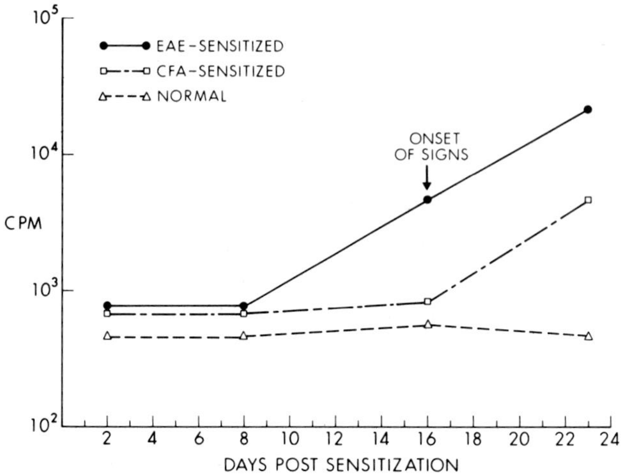

FIG. 1. Kinetics of Con A stimulation for the three groups of experimental animals. Values represent the mean for two animals in each group having the same clinical history and bled sequentially. All values have been adjusted for background stimulation (by subtraction) which ranged from 800 ± 120 to 1135 ± 280 cpm (mean ± 1 SD).

of the mean value for the latent period, even at a confidence level of $P < 0.5$ using Student's *t* test, because of the large standard deviation during the disease onset phase. Nevertheless, when values for an individual animal's PBL were compared using the paired *t* test, each animal's PBL showed a statistically significant difference between its latent and disease onset phase responses to B-MBP (Table 1). The difference between the mean values for the disease onset and severe disease phases was statistically significant at a confidence level of $P < 0.05$. Three of ten animals tested at the time of severe disease were also bled during the disease onset phase. The *in vitro* responsiveness of their PBL to B-MBP, on an individual as well

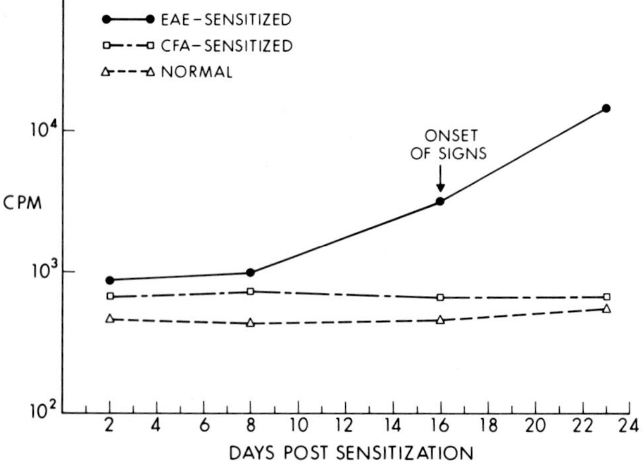

FIG. 2. Kinetics of B-MBP stimulation for the same animals as in Fig. 1.

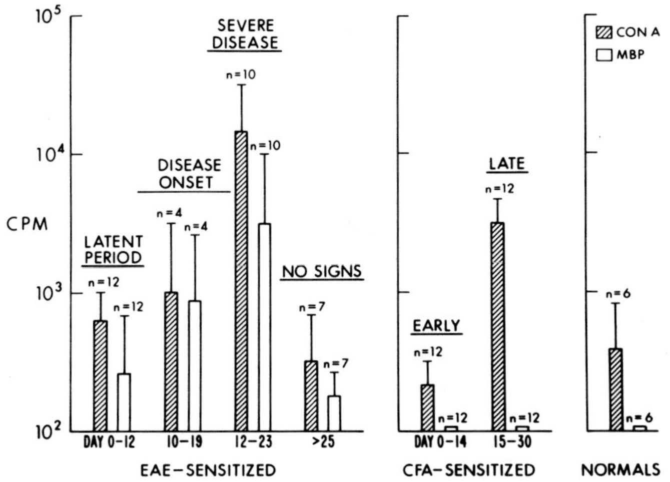

FIG. 3. Stimulation of PBL by Con A (shaded bars) and B-MBP (open bars) during different phases of acute EAE. Bars represent the means ± 1 SD of group data. Three of the four animals tested during the disease onset phase were also bled at the time of severe disease.

as a group basis, was greater during severe disease and was statistically significant at a confidence level of $P < 0.05$ (Table 1).

As shown in Fig. 3, seven animals sensitized for EAE which failed to develop clinical disease failed to demonstrate a significant PBL response to B-MBP. However, their PBL responsiveness to Con A was similar to that of normals and CFA controls.

PBL from CFA-sensitized animals showed an increasing sensitivity to Con A with time following injection but failed to respond to B-MBP. PBL from normal guinea pigs were sensitive to Con A but unresponsive to B-MBP (Fig. 3).

PBL from normal, CFA-sensitized, and EAE-sensitized animals (during all disease phases) were unresponsive *in vitro* to all control bovine antigens tested as well as to MBPep (Table 2).

Lymphocyte transformation assays utilizing sera other than commercially prepared guinea pig serum were conducted in preliminary trials and, to a limited degree, in parallel with the study presented here. None of these sera, at the concentrations used, enabled us to achieve consistent results.

TABLE 1

PBL Responses to B-MBP Days Postsensitization

Animal number	2	8	16	23
1	881 ± 127	1005 ± 65	2665 ± 189	11,358 ± 940
2	1105 ± 24	960 ± 205	4425 ± 315	9,580 ± 118
3	N.T.	N.T.	3017 ± 185	12,760 ± 408

Note. Values represent the mean ± 1 SD ($P < 0.05$) for triplicate cultures. All values have been adjusted for background stimulation (by subtraction) which ranged from 600 to 1455 cpm. Lymphocyte responses during the latent, disease onset and severe disease phases are represented here by Days 2 and 8, Day 16, and Day 23, respectively.

TABLE 2

PBL Responses to Bovine Antigens

Animal group	MBP	MBPep	IgG	Cyto C	Histone	BKE	BLE
EAE-sensitized clinically sick	5.9	1.1	0.9	0.9	1.0	1.4	1.1
EAE-sensitized clinically well	1.6	0.6	1.0	0.8	1.6	1.2	1.0
CFA-sensitized	1.0	1.3	0.9	1.2	1.2	1.1	1.4
Nonsensitized normals	1.4	1.1	1.1	0.7	0.9	1.2	0.8

Note. Values are stimulation indices (S.I.) which were calculated as the quotient of mean of triplicate cultures with antigen/mean of triplicate cultures without antigen. The S.I. shown here from EAE-sensitized sick, CFA-sensitized, and nonsensitized normals were determined at the time of the severe disease phase. S.I. of PBL from EAE -sensitized clinically well guinea pigs were determined at the time of sacrifice which was 25–29 days postinoculation. S.I. calculated from data derived from other disease phases (latent and disease onset) was equivalent to that expressed above with the exception of the MBP S.I. for EAE-sensitized sick guinea pigs which was less than the S.I. for the severe disease phase.

DISCUSSION

The present study on acute EAE in the guinea pig has confirmed the existence of an *in vitro* PBL response to B-MBP which correlated with the development of clinical signs of disease. In contrast, animals sensitized for EAE which failed to develop disease were also of interest in that they did not demonstrate an *in vitro* lymphoproliferative response to B-MBP. The elucidation of the relationship between *in vitro* lymphocyte proliferation and clinical EAE on a functional level holds much promise for investigating possible suppressor mechanisms in animals which are apparently resistant to the disease.

Using similar techniques, previous investigators have reported differing results on PBL responsiveness in EAE (10, 11). Lisak and Zweiman found that PBL from Hartley guinea pigs sensitized for EAE did not show significant proliferation *in vitro* with the addition of MBP to the culture medium (11). The disparity may have been related to the authors' use of heterologous MBP for EAE induction and homologous guinea pig MBP in the culture system, whereas in the present study, bovine white matter was used in the sensitizing emulsion and B-MBP in the cultures. Subsequently, Lisak showed greater stimulation when the same MBP was used for sensitization and for *in vitro* tests (12). While in this latter study, the responses of peritoneal exudate lymphocytes were measured rather than PBL, the use of the same MBP for sensitization and *in vitro* assays may have contributed to the enhanced stimulation.

With regard to the progressive increase in PBL responsiveness to B-MBP in EAE with increasing time and signs shown here, a temporal relationship between the development of delayed-type skin reactions to MBP and the onset of EAE has also been noted (13). Furthermore, the appearance of blast-like cells in the peripheral blood of rabbits sensitized with central nervous system tissue before the onset of clinical signs has been reported (14). Similarly, other studies have noted that the proliferative activity of lymphocytes from EAE animals and their blast transformation *in vitro* appear maximal immediately prior to the onset of clinical signs

(15–19). In contrast, it has been found here that the *in vitro* uptake of [^{3}H]TdR by PBL exposed to B-MBP and Con A increased progressively as the animals became ill and that this uptake was maximal when the animals were moribund. To demonstrate that the B-MBP responses were specific and not merely responses to heterologous bovine antigens, several antigenic preparations from bovine sources were tested. PBL exposed to bovine antigens other than B-MBP showed no increase in stimulation over background. The specificity of the response to B-MBP is further supported by the fact that PBL exposed to MBPep, a nonencephalitogenic peptide fragment, showed no proliferative activity.

While *in vitro* blast transformation and lymphocyte proliferation in response to MBP stimulation correlate temporally with clinical EAE, the role of these responses in the pathogenesis of the disease remains uncertain. It has been demonstrated that such *in vitro* responses may correlate with delayed-type hypersensitivity (20). The validity of these *in vitro* tests as measures of disease has been studied by comparing the encephalitogenicity of specific peptides from the antigenic region of guinea pig MBP with their ability to induce lymphocyte proliferation (21). While the most encephalitogenic peptides caused blast transformation and lymphocyte proliferation, it is conceivable that enzyme-induced changes in these peptides, occurring *in vivo*, may render the peptide antigenically different from that used for the *in vitro* tests.

In the present experiments, the commercially prepared guinea pig serum used enabled us to obtain optimal stimulation indices and reproducible results. In preliminary experiments, PBL from EAE-sensitized and control animals were tested using a variety of sera. None of the sera (fetal bovine, human AB, or isologous guinea pig) gave consistent results regardless of the concentration used. We feel that the disparity between our findings of peak responses at the time the guinea pigs became moribund and those of previous investigators may be explained, at least in part, by differences in culture conditions.

We are presently attempting to determine the *in vivo* function of those lymphocytes from EAE-sensitized animals which have been observed to proliferate *in vitro* in response to MBP. It is our hope that such studies may lead to a better understanding of the pathogenesis of this disease.

ACKNOWLEDGMENTS

The authors thank Drs. Celia F. Brosnan and P. Andrew Neighbour for discussion and constructive criticism, Angela Doyle for technical assistance, and Mary Palumbo for her expert secretarial help. We are indebted to Dr. Edwin H. Eylar, Department of Biochemistry, University of Toronto, Toronto, Ontario, who kindly provided us with both bovine MBP and its P peptide derivative. The data in this paper are from a thesis to be submitted in partial fulfillment of the requirements for the Degree of Doctor of Philosophy at the Sue Golding Graduate Division of Medical Sciences, Albert Einstein College of Medicine, Yeshiva University. Supported in part by USPHS Grants NS 07098, NS 08952, and NS 11920; National MS Society Grant RG 1001-C-3; and Grant IM 179 from the American Cancer Society.

REFERENCES

1. Waksman, B. H., *Int. Arch. Allergy Suppl.* **14,** 1, 1959.
2. Paterson, P. Y., *In* "Textbook of Immunopathology" (P. A. Miescher and H. J. Müller-Eberhard, Eds.), pp. 179–213. Grune & Stratton, New York, 1976.
3. Raine, C. S., *In* "Progress in Neuropathology" (H. M. Zimmerman, Ed.), Vol. 3, pp. 225–251. Grune & Stratton, New York, 1976.

4. Gonatas, N. K., and Howard, J. C., *Science* **186,** 839, 1974.
5. Ortiz-Ortiz, L., and Weigle, W. O., *J. Exp. Med.* **144,** 604, 1976.
6. Traugott, U., and Raine, C. S., *Cell. Immunol.* **34,** 146, 1977.
7. Traugott, U., Stone, S. H., and Raine, C. S., *J. Neurol. Sci.* **41,** 17, 1979.
8. Oppenheim, J. J., and Rosenstreich, D. L., *In* "*In Vitro* Methods in Cell-Mediated and Tumor Immunity" (B. R. Bloom and J. R. David, Eds.), pp. 573–585. Academic Press, New York, 1976.
9. Burnett, P. R., and Eylar, E. H., *J. Biol. Chem.* **246,** 3425, 1971.
10. Spitler, L. E., von Muller, C. M., Fudenberg, H. H., and Eylar, E. H., *J. Exp. Med.* **136,** 156, 1972.
11. Lisak, R. P., and Zweiman, B., *Cell. Immunol.* **11,** 212, 1974.
12. Lisak, R. P., Zweiman, B., and Levinson, A. I., *Int. Arch. Allergy Appl. Immunol.* **51,** 253, 1976.
13. Shaw, C. M., Alvord, E. C., Jr., Kaku, J., and Kies, M. W., *Ann. N.Y. Acad. Sci.* **122,** 318, 1965.
14. Dowling, P. C., and Cook, S. D., *Neurology* **18,** 953, 1968.
15. Dau, P. C., and Peterson, R. D. A., *Int. Arch. Allergy* **35,** 353, 1969.
16. Warnatz, H., Scheiffarth, F., and Kuntz, H., *J. Neuropathol. Exp. Neurol.* **29,** 575, 1970.
17. Fowler, I., *J. Immunol.* **108,** 903, 1972.
18. Bergstrand, H., and Källen, B., *Acta Pathol. Microbiol. Scand.* **79,** 551, 1971.
19. Shioiri-Nakano, K., Nagai, Y., Otani, S., and Tsumita, T., *Japan. J. Exp. Med.* **41,** 159, 1971.
20. Mills, J. A., *J. Immunol.* **97,** 239, 1966.
21. Jen Chou, C. H., Fritz, R. B., Chou, F. C. H., and Kibler, R. F., *J. Immunol.* **123,** 1540, 1979.

CELLULAR IMMUNOLOGY 63, 417–425 (1981)

Regulation of Murine T-Cell Responses to Autologous Antigens by α-Fetoprotein

D. C. HOOPER AND R. A. MURGITA

Department of Microbiology and Immunology, McGill University, Montreal, Quebec, Canada

Received April 27, 1981; accepted May 16, 1981

Murine α-fetoprotein (AFP), a major component of fetal and newborn sera, was shown to exert potent immunosuppressive effects on autologous mixed lymphocyte reactions (AMLR) *in vitro*. Thus, the relatively vigorous proliferative response of newborn CBA/J thymocytes reacting in mixed cultures against adult syngeneic spleen cells was almost totally abrogated by 200 and 100 μg/ml AFP over the 6-day time course studied, with significant suppression still evident in the presence of 10 μg/ml AFP. In contrast, the maximum achievable suppression of parellel allogeneic MLRs was only 40 to 60%. The newborn thymocyte anti-adult syngeneic spleen AMLR was shown to be mediated by an Lyt $1^{+}23^{-}$ T-cell subset reacting against Ia^{+} adult non-T stimulator cells. Newborn and adult AMLRs resulting from autochthonous T responder/non-T stimulator cell mixtures from individual animals were also found to be highly sensitive to AFP-mediated suppression. The fact that fetal-derived AFP could be shown to efficiently inhibit neonatal thymocyte responses to autologous antigens when tested *in vitro* in amounts 20 to 50 times lower than the levels present in fetal and newborn sera suggests a potentially important role for endogenous AFP in the regulation of autosensitization during ontogeny.

INTRODUCTION

According to traditionally held views (1, 2) natural self-tolerance is acquired early in ontogeny by the removal of potentially deliterious clones of autoreactive lymphocytes following contact with self-antigen. Although the evidence in support of clonal deletion and/or abortion is strong (3, 4) it is becoming increasingly clear that such mechanisms are not absolute since self-reactive B and T cells can be shown to exist in the normal adult (5–7). Autologous mixed lymphocyte reactions (AMLR) between autochthonous human T responder cells and non-T stimulator cells (8, 9), and murine neonatal thymocytes (10) or adult lymph node cells (11) responding to syngeneic non-T spleen cells have been regarded as *in vitro* expressions of anti-self-reactivity because they occur in the apparent absence of foreign antigen (12, 13). While the exact nature of these *in vitro* reactions is still unclear, they do seem to represent true immunological phenomena as autoactivated T lymphocytes demonstrate specific memory (14), provide a proliferative stimulus for generation of cytotoxic T cells (15), and mediate positive (16) and negative (17) regulatory influences on other immune functions. Indeed, Altman and Katz (13) suggest that autoreactive and alloreactive cell interactions may differ only in their binding affinities. Since self-recognizing lymphocytes can produce autoimmune

0008-8749/81/140417-09$02.00/0

reactions *in vivo* when normal control mechanisms are circumvented (7, 18), tolerance to certain self-antigens may depend, particularly during the perinatal period, on immunoregulatory factors capable of effectively blocking self-recognition. One such factor may be α-fetoprotein (AFP), an embryo-specific glycoprotein which has been shown to have selective capacity to suppress MHC (major histocompatibility complex) I-region-associated immune responses through direct antiproliferative effects (19, 20), or via the induction of regulatory suppressor T cells (19, 21, 22). In support of this contention we report here that murine AMLRs mediated by either neonatal or adult T cells are suppressed in a highly efficient manner by purified fetal-derived AFP in concentrations that are well below the normal endogenous serum levels in the fetus and newborn (23).

MATERIALS AND METHODS

Animals. Adult male and female CBA/J and Balb/c mice (6–8 weeks old) were purchased from the Jackson Laboratory, Bar Harbor, Maine. All the mice were bred and maintained in our own animal facility.

Antisera. Monoclonal anti-Lyt antisera were purchased from New England Nuclear, Boston, Massachusetts. The anti-Lyt 1.1 antiserum (NEI-003, Lot No. FPA-172) has a cytolytic titer (at which 50% of mouse thymocytes from Lyt 1.1 congenic strain C57BL/6 Lyt 1.1 are lysed) of 8×10^{-5}. The corresponding cytolytic titer of the anti-Lyt 2.1 (NEI-004, Lot No. FPA-066) was 1×10^{-4}. Newborn thymocytes were selectively lysed with anti-Lyt antisera in a two-step killing protocol. Thymocytes (3×10^6) were incubated with anti-Lyt 1.1 (1/1000), or anti-Lyt 2.1 (1/1000) for 30 min at 37°C. Cells were then washed by centrifugation, resuspended in rabbit serum (Low-Tox rabbit complement, Cedarlane Laboratories Ltd., London, Ontario) diluted 1/10, and incubated for an additional 45 min at 37°C. Viable lymphocytes remaining after the second-step incubation were washed thoroughly in RPMI 1640 medium and appropriately diluted for use. Adult CBA/J and Balb/c spleen stimulator cell populations were depleted of T cells by cytotoxic pretreatment with rabbit anti-mouse brain serum (24) plus rabbit complement.

Culture conditions. All autologous and allogeneic mixed lymphocyte cultures were performed in 96-well round-bottom microtiter plates (Flow Laboratories). RPMI 1640 medium (Flow Laboratories) supplemented with 0.5% fresh adult syngeneic mouse serum, plus 20 m*M* Hepes, 5×10^{-5} *M* 2-mercaptoethanol, 4 m*M* L-glutamine, 100 U/ml penicillin, and 100 μg/ml streptomycin was used throughout. Different ratios of responder and stimulator cells were used in newborn and adult autologous and allogeneic MLRs as noted in the footnotes to Table 1 and Figs. 1 and 2. α-Fetoprotein, isolated from mouse amniotic fluid as previously described (25) was added at the initiation of cultures in final concentrations ranging from 200 to 10 μg/ml with equivalent amounts of homologous mouse serum or albumin serving as protein controls. Cultures were maintained at 37°C in 95% humidified air and 5% CO_2 for various lengths of time ranging from 48 to 144 hr. Four hours prior to harvesting, the cultures were pulsed with 1.0 μCi tritiated thymidine ([^{3}H]TdR; specific antivity 56 Ci/mmol, NEN, Boston, Mass.). Cells were harvested onto glass fiber filters using a multiple sample harvestor (Skatron, Flow Laboratories) and total [^{3}H]TdR incorporation was measured in a Beckman

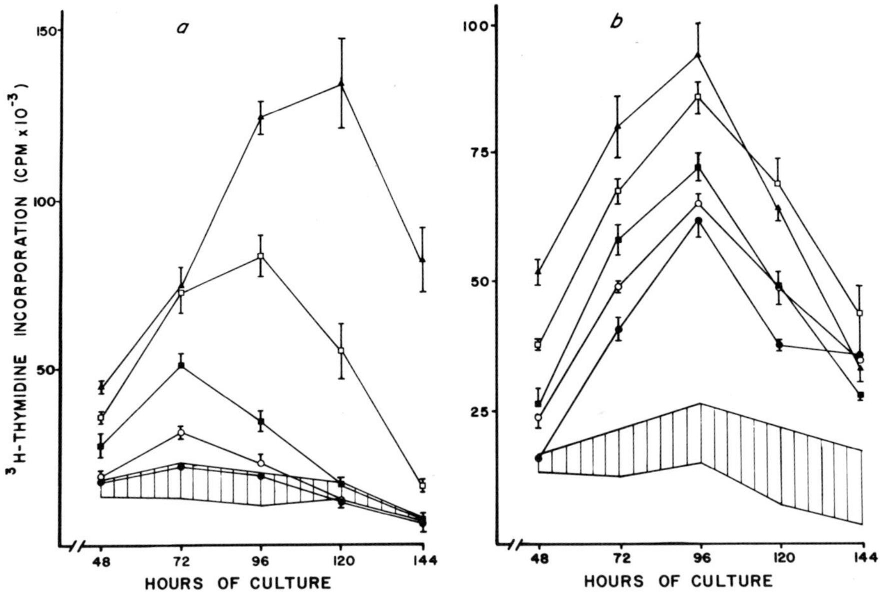

FIG. 1. Effect of AFP on newborn autologous (a) versus adult allogeneic (b) MLR. Purified fetal-derived mouse AFP was added at initiation of cultures in final concentrations of 200 μg/ml (●), 100 μg/ml (○), 50 μg/ml (■), and 10 μg/ml (□); (▲) designates cultures without added protein. For newborn AMLR (a), 2.5×10^5 thymocytes from 2-day-old CBA/J mice were cultured in quadruplicate with 2.5×10^5 spleen cells from 8-week-old CBA/J mice in RPMI 1640 medium supplemented with 0.5% fresh adult syngeneic mouse serum. Data are expressed as mean counts per minute ± SEM. Background activities for the newborn thymocytes and adult spleen cells alone were within the hatched area. For adult allogeneic MLR (b), 2.5×10^5 adult CBA/J spleen cells were cultured with 5×10^5 mitomycin C-treated Balb/c spleen stimulator cells.

8000 liquid scintillation counter (Beckman Instruments, Fullerton, Calif.). Data are expressed as mean counts per minute ±SEM of quadruplicate cultures.

RESULTS

In initial studies that are outlined in Fig. 1, we compared the effects of various concentrations of AFP on the kinetics of primary MLC (mixed lymphocyte culture) activation induced by syngeneic versus allogeneic stimuli. As shown in Fig. 1a, purified AFP produced a dose-dependent suppression of the autologous response by newborn CBA/J thymocytes reacting in mixed culture against adult syngeneic spleen cells. The unidirectional nature of this reaction was established in separate experiments by reciprocal treatments of each cell population with mitomycin C (data not shown.) Essentially complete inhibition of the neonatal AMLR was obtained by adding fetal-derived AFP in final concentrations of 200 and 100 μg/ml, with significant suppression still evident in the presence of as little as 10 μg/ml AFP. A parallel dilution analysis of AFP was performed on a representative allogeneic MLR consisting of adult CBA/J spleen cells (H-2^k, MLs^d) responding against mitomycin C-treated Balb/c spleen cells (H-2^d, MLs^b). The results presented in Fig. 1b demonstrate a clear difference in sensitivity to AFP-mediated suppression between the allogeneic MLR and the AMLR. Thus, in contrast to the

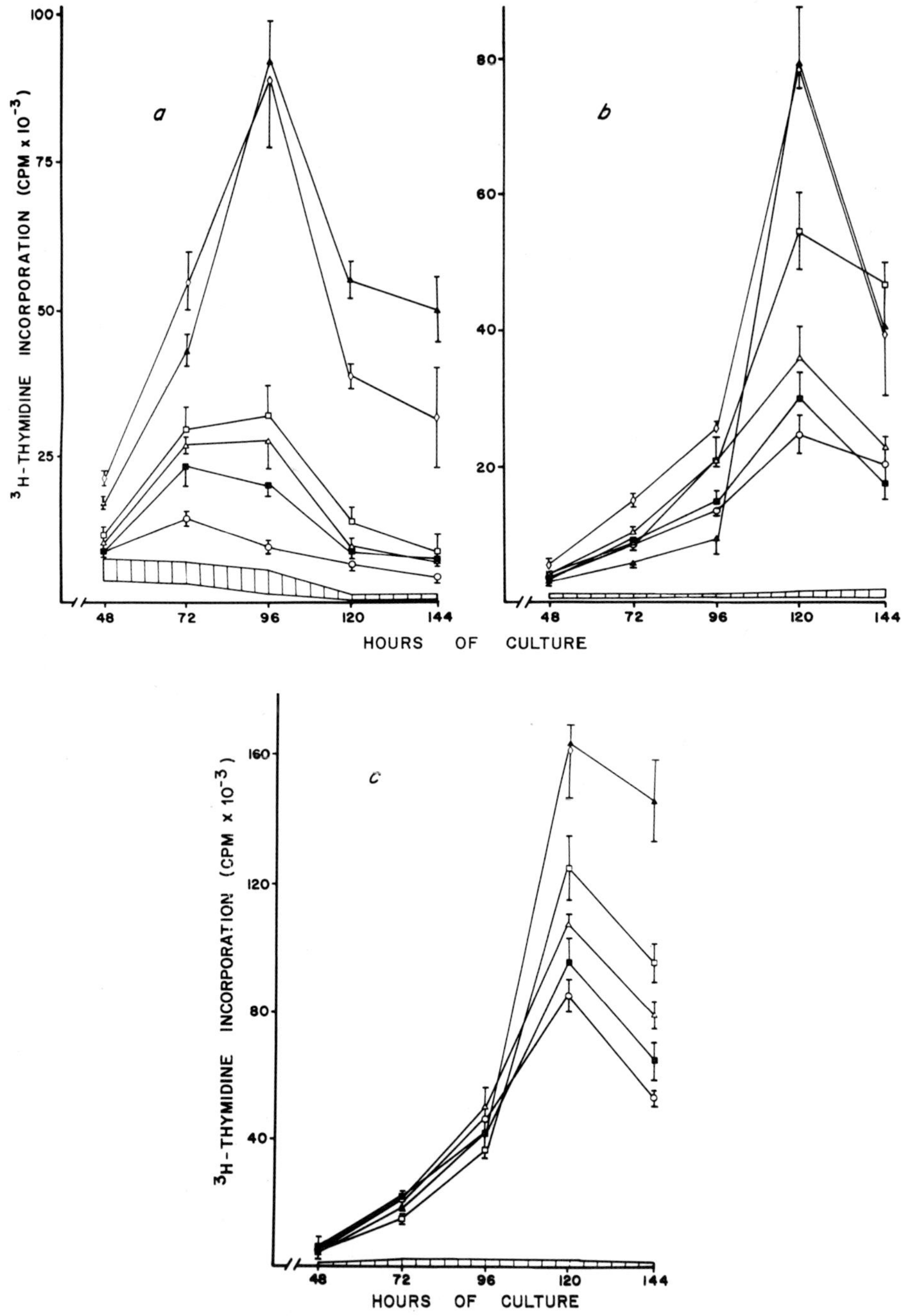

FIG. 2. Comparative effects of AFP on proliferating Lyt 1$^+$23$^-$ T cells in newborn autologous MLR (a), newborn allogeneic MLR (b), and in adult allogeneic MLR (c). All MLRs were performed in RPMI 1640 medium supplemented with 0.5% fresh adult syngeneic mouse serum. Cultures were carried out in the absence of additional protein (▲), in the presence of 100 μg/ml mouse serum albumin (◇), or in the presence of AFP in final concentrations of 100 μg/ml (○), 50 μg/ml (■), 25 μg/ml (△), and 10 μg/ml (□). Newborn autologous (a) and newborn allogeneic (b) MLRs consisted of 0.75×10^5 neonatal (1–3 days old) thymocytes responding against 2.5×10^5 T-cell-depleted spleen cells (by treatment with rabbit anti-mouse brain antiserum plus complement, Cedarlane Laboratories, Hornby, Ontario) from adult CBA/J and Balb/c mice, respectively. The adult allogeneic MLR (c) consisted of 0.75 $\times 10^5$ LYT 1$^+$23$^-$ adult CBA/J spleen T cells responding against 2.5×10^5 T-cell-depleted Balb/c spleen

complete abrogation of the AMLR by the higher concentrations of AFP (100 and 200 μg/ml), the maximum achievable suppression of the allogeneic MLR with the highest concentration of AFP tested (200 μg/ml) was only in the range of 40 to 60%. It is notable here that a very similar pattern of partial susceptibility to suppression by AFP has been observed in studies on allogeneic MLR stimulation using several congenic strain combinations differing only at the MHC or at isolated MHC I subregions (20).

The knowledge that Lyt 1^+23^- T cells account for most of the proliferative responses in adult allogeneic and in adult autologous MLRs directed against incompatible MHC I-region determinants (26) and syngeneic Ia-bearing stimulator cells (27, 28), respectively, prompted us to investigate the nature of the responder cell in the neonatal AMLR. In doing so we found that all of the autologous proliferative activity of newborn CBA/J thymocytes was removed by cytotoxic pretreatment with a heterologous antiserum specific for mouse T cells (rabbit anti-mouse brain serum) and rabbit complement (RC), and by anti-Lyt 1.1 plus RC, while treatment with anti-Thy-1.2 and RC caused partial reduction, and anti-Lyt 2.1 and RC did not affect the AMLR. Furthermore, addition of anti-Ia serum (A.TH anti-A.TL) directly to the cultures could be shown to effectively block the newborn AMLR, and cytotoxic studies suggested that this effect was at the level of the stimulator cell (data not shown). These findings, together with the recent studies by Pasternak *et al.* (27) and Lattime *et al.* (28) which similarly characterize adult murine AMLRs, imply that both the newborn and adult types of autologous MLRs involve autorecognition of MHC I-region gene products by Lyt 1^+23^- T cells.

Having established that AFP exerts its suppressive activity in autologous, as well as in allogeneic ((20) and reviewed in (29)) MLC through selective interference with I-region triggering of Lyt 1^+23^- responder T cells, we next sought to determine whether autoreactive and alloreactive T cells of the Lyt 1^+23^- subset might differ in their sensitivity to suppression by AFP. Results presented in Fig. 2 indicate that this is indeed the case. Here the degree of suppression by AFP, tested over the concentration range of 100 to 10 μg/ml, is shown to be significantly greater on isolated Lyt 1^+23^- newborn CBA/J thymocytes responding in AMLR against T-cell-depleted adult syngeneic spleen cells (Fig. 2a), than on equivalent numbers of newborn CBA/J Lyt 1^+23^- thymocytes reacting against adult Balb/c T-cell-depleted spleen (Fig. 2b), while the proliferative response of adult CBA/J Lyt 1^+23^- spleen T cells in one-way MLC against T-cell-depleted Balb/c spleen is least affected by AFP (Fig. 2c). The relative differences in sensitivity to AFP-mediated suppression between Lyt 1^+23^- T cells responding in autologous versus allogeneic MLCs were highly consistent through several repeat experiments and were independent of the relative magnitude of proliferation in the MLRs.

We next examined the effect of AFP on two other types of AMLR resulting from autochthonous lymphoid cell mixtures. The results shown in Table 1 dem-

---

cells. Balb/c spleen stimulator cells were treated with mitomycin C(50 μg/10^7 cells). Purification of spleen T cells was accomplished by affinity fractionation on mouse immunoglobulin(Ig)-rabbit-anti-mouse Ig-coated glass bead columns as previously described(22). Isolation of CBA/J Lyt 1^+23^- T cells was accomplished by negative selection with monoclonal anti-Lyt 2.1 antiserum(NEN, Boston, Mass.) plus rabbit complement using a two-step killing protocol(see Materials and Methods).

TABLE 1

Suppression of Newborn and Adult Autochthonous AMLRs by α-Fetoprotein

AMLR type	Addition to AMLR				
	0	200 μg ml^{-1} NMS[a]	200 μg ml^{-1} AFP	100 μg ml^{-1} AFP	10 μg ml^{-1} AFP
	[^{3}H]Thymidine incorporation [Δcpm[b] ±SE] (% inhibition)[c]				
Newborn → newborn[d]	5,412 ± 214	5,186 ± 500 (4)	1717 ± 347 (68)[e]	1807 ± 1377 (67)[f]	3,950 ± 497 (27)[f]
Adult → adult[g]	40,076 ± 2921	36,389 ± 9,992 (9)	965 ± 5443 (98)[e]	2388 ± 2797 (94)[e]	15,475 ± 3,405 (61)[f]

[a] Normal mouse serum.

[b] Calculated according to Ting and Ranney (34) as Δcpm = cpm of responder/stimulator mix − cpm responder alone − cpm stimulator alone.

[c] $\% \text{ inhibition} = 1 - \dfrac{\text{cpm test (protein added)}}{\text{cpm control (without added protein)}} \times 100.$

[d] 0.75×10^5 newborn CBA/J Lyt 1^+23^- thymocytes cocultured with 2.5×10^5 newborn T-cell-depleted spleen cells prepared from the same animals. Culture conditions and cell separations are as described in Figs. 1 and 2.

[e] $P < 0.001$ compared to control response without added protein.

[f] $P < 0.03$ compared to control response without added protein.

[g] 0.75×10^5 lymph node cells cocultured with 2.5×10^5 spleen cells taken from 20-week-old CBA/J female mice. Culture conditions are the same as for experiments shown in Figs. 1 and 2.

onstrate that Lyt 1^+23^- thymocytes from 1- to 3-day-old CBA/J newborns can produce a low level but still significant AMLR when cocultured with non-T spleen stimulator cells prepared from the same animals, and that this reaction is significantly suppressed by concentrations of AFP as low as 10 μg/ml. The generally weaker AMLR resulting from neonatal thymocyte/neonatal spleen cell mixtures, in comparison to the quite vigorous neonatal thymocyte/adult spleen cell autologous reactions, may be attributable not so much to a lack of stimulating antigens in the newborn spleen (11), as to the presence of an efficient neonatal suppressor cell residing within the stimulating cell population (D. C. Hooper and R. A. Murgita, in preparation). Finally, results are presented in Table 1 which indicate that the strong AMLR occurring in mixed cultures of lymph node and spleen cells from the same adult CBA/J mouse is also very effectively inhibited by purified AFP in a dose-dependent manner.

DISCUSSION

There is at present an increased awareness that autoreactive lymphoid cells exist as normal components of the immune system (30). Self-recognizing lymphocytes have already been postulated to play important roles in cell–cell communication (13), immune regulation (16, 17), and in surveillance (31). The apparent prevalence of cells with self-reactive potential makes it likely that regulatory mechanisms have evolved to control the beneficial expressions of autoimmunity in order to avert possible conversions to disease-provoking autodestructive immune processes. Indeed, several components of normal human and rodent sera, including thymic humoral factor (32, 33), hydrocortisone (34, 35), and α-globulin (36) have all been shown capable of suppressing various types of autologous immune reactions *in vitro*. In the present investigation we have evaluated the regulatory effects of AFP, one of the major protein components of fetal and newborn serum, on the proliferative response of murine neonatal thymocytes and adult lymph node T cells against autologous non-T spleen stimulator cells. Our findings clearly demonstrate that purified fetal-derived AFP can inhibit AMLRs in a highly efficient manner when tested in concentrations that are physiologically relevant with respect to the fetus and newborn. Thus, we observed close to complete suppression of AMLR throughout the time course studied when AFP was present in the cultures in amounts approximately 20 to 50 times less than the levels found in fetal and newborn serum (23). Additional experiments are now underway to determine whether AFP can similarly inhibit the functions of effector cells (i.e., suppressor and/or cytotoxic cells) generated in murine AMLRs.

As previously noted by von Boehmer and Byrd (37) the proliferative response which occurs when newborn thymocytes are cocultured with adult syngeneic non-T spleen cells may not represent a genuine anti-self-recognition event in the sense that adult spleen cells could be expressing lymphocyte activating determinants not normally present in the newborn. However, we were also able to show that AFP could exert an equally potent inhibitory effect on two other types of autologous reactions which do provide evidence for true self-reactivity, namely the proliferative responses resulting from mixtures of autochthonous T and non-T cells obtained from the lymphoid tissues of individual newborn or adult mice (Table 1). It is worthwhile stressing here that the culture medium used in these experiments was supplemented with 0.5% fresh homologous mouse serum thereby eliminating the possibility of introducing *in vitro* artifacts resulting from the use of heterologous serum additives, particularly fetal calf serum.

Our present findings are in general agreement with earlier studies showing that primary targets for AFP-mediated immunosuppression are Lyt $1^{+}23^{-}$ T cells which serve as helper cells for thymus-dependent antibody synthesis (22, 24), and for collaboration with precursors of cytotoxic T killer cells in the generation of cell-mediated lympholysis (20). However, a comparative analysis of the inhibitory effects of AFP on auto- versus alloreactive Lyt $1^{+}23^{-}$ T cells revealed a clear difference in sensitivity to suppression with autoreactive T cells being most affected. Interestingly, both hydrocortisone (34, 35) and thymic humoral factor (32, 33) have also been reported to exert a similar selective inhibitory action on autologous reactions *in vitro.* This has led Ilfeld *et al.* (35) to suggest that auto- and alloreactive T cells are generated from distinct clones of cells which respond to different regulatory mechanisms.

We would conclude, on the basis of the results presented in this communication, that AFP may be an important regulatory agent for autologous lymphocyte reactions. The relatively high circulating levels of AFP which persist throughout the perinatal period in the murine species, could very well be sufficient to help exert effective control on autosensitization. Moreover, we speculate that the preferential suppressive action by AFP on autoreactive rather than on alloreactive T cells may have teleological significance. Thus, if AFP were to have evolved a specialized regulatory function to selectively control autoreactivity during ontogeny, it would allow the developing immune system to function sufficiently to protect against infectious agents and alloaggressive maternal lymphocytes while at the same time there would be appropriate controls for potentially harmful self-recognition events.

ACKNOWLEDGMENTS

This investigation was supported by grants from the Medical Research Council of Canada (MA-6470) and the National Cancer Institute of Canada. D.C.H. is the recipient of a fellowship from the Cancer Research Society, Inc.

REFERENCES

1. Burnet, F. M., *Nature (London)* **218,** 426, 1968.
2. Lederberg, J., *Science* **129,** 1649, 1959.
3. Nossal, G. J. V., and Pike, B. L., *J. Exp. Med.* **141,** 904, (1975).
4. Robinson, J. H., and Owen, J. J. T., *Nature (London)* **271,** 758, 1978.
5. Dresser, D. W., *Nature (London)* **274,** 480, 1978.
6. Steele, E. J., and Cunningham, A. J., *Nature (London)* **274,** 483, 1978.
7. Cohen, I. R., and Wekerle, H., *J. Exp. Med.* **137,** 224, 1973.
8. Opelz, G., Kiuchi, M., Takasugi, M., and Terasaki, P. I., *J. Exp. Med.* **142,** 1327, 1975.
9. Kuntz, M. M., Innes, J. B., and Weksler, M. E., *J. Exp. Med.* **143,** 1042, 1976.
10. Howe, M. L., Goldstein, A. L., and Battisto, J. R., *Proc. Natl. Acad. Sci. USA* **67,** 613, 1970.
11. Ponzio, N. M., Finke, J. H., and Battisto, J. R., *J. Immunol.* **114,** 971, 1975.
12. Cunningham, A. J., *In* "Strategies of Immune Regulation" (E. E. Sercarz and A. J. Cunningham, Eds.), p. 27, Academic Press, New York, 1980.
13. Altman, A., and Katz, D. H., *Immunol. Rev.* **51,** 3, 1980.
14. Weksler, N. E., and Kozak, E., *J. Exp. Med.* **146,** 1833, 1977.
15. Miller, R., and Kaplan, H. S., *J. Immunol.* **121,** 2165, 1978.
16. Chiorazzi, N., Fu, S. M., and Kunkel, H. G., *J. Exp. Med.* **149,** 1543, 1979.
17. Smith, J. B., and Knowlton, R. P., *J. Immunol.* **123,** 419, 1979.

18. L'age-Stehr, J., and Diamanstein, T., *Nature (London)* **271,** 663, 1978.
19. Murgita, R. A., and Wigzell, H., *Prog. Allergy,* in press.
20. Peck, A. B., Murgita, R. A., and Wigzell, H., *J. Exp. Med.* **147,** 667, 1978.
21. Murgita, R. A., Goidl, E. A., Kontiainen, S., and Wigzell, H. *Nature (London)* **267,** 257, 1977.
22. Murgita, R. A., Goidl, E. A., Kontiainen, S., Beverley, P. C. L., and Wigzell, H., *Proc. Nat. Acad. Sci. USA* **75,** 2897, 1978.
23. Ruoslahti, E., and Seppala, M., *Advan. Cancer Res.* **29,**275, 1979.
24. Golub, E. S., *Cell. Immunol.* **2,** 353, 1971.
25. Murgita, R. A., and Tomasi, T. B., *J. Exp. Med.* **141,** 269, 1975.
26. Cantor, H., and Boyse, E. A., *J. Exp. Med.* **141,** 1376, 1975.
27. Pasternak, R. D., Bocchieri, M. H., and Smith, J. B., *Cell. Immunol.* **49,** 384, 1980.
28. Lattime, E. C., Golub, S. H., and Stutman, O., *Eur. J. Immunol.* **10,** 723, 1980.
29. Murgita, R. A., and Wigzell, H., *La Ricerca Clin. Lab.* **9,** 327, 1979.
30. Wigzell, H., *In* "Autoimmunity" (N. Talal, Ed.), p. 256. Academic Press, New York, 1977.
31. Tomonari, K., *J. Immunol.* **124,** 1111, 1980.
32. Trainin, N., Carnoud, C., and Ilfeld, D., *Nature (London)* **245,** 253, 1973.
33. Small, M. and Trainin, N., *Cell. Immunol.* **20,** 1, 1975.
34. Ying, J. P. Y., and Ranney, D. F. *Cell. Immunol.* **53,** 138, 1980.
35. Ilfeld, D. N., Krakauer, R. S., and Blaese, R. M., *J. Immunol.* **119,** 428, 1977.
36. Kolb, H., *Cell. Immunol.* **37,** 127, 1978.
37. von Boehmer, H., and Byrd, W. J., *Nature (London)* **235,** 50, 1972.

ANNOUNCEMENTS

International Symposium on Current Concepts in Human Immunology and Cancer Immunomodulation

The International Symposium will be held in Montpellier, France, on January 18–20, 1982. The major topics include: types, functions, and differentiation of human lymphocyte subpopulations; NK cells, macrophages, autologous response; immunology of the cancer patient; cancer immunomodulation (new chemically characterized specific modifiers of biologic response).

The symposium is organized by Dr. B. Serrou (Montpellier), Dr. C. Rosenfeld (Villejuif), and D.-J. Daniels (Galveston, Tex., U.S.A.). Presentations are by invitation only. Due to a limited number of places available, participation will be restricted to the first 150 registrants. The registration fee is 800 Frs, which should be mailed to Dr. B. Serrou.

For additional information contact

Dr. B. Serrou,
Laboratoire d'Immunopharmacologie
des Tumeurs, Inserm U236
Centre Paul Lamarque
B.P. 5054
34033 Montpellier Cedex, France

18th National Meeting of the Reticuloendothelial Society

Pfister Hotel, Milwaukee, Wisconsin

October 12–16, 1981

The program will begin with a workshop on "Monoclonal Antibodies to Macrophage Surface Determinants," chaired by Noel L. Warner. The symposia will deal with "Macrophage Effector Function," chaired by Zanvil A. Cohn; "Macrophage-Dependent Events of the Immune Response," chaired by Emil R. Unanue; and "Interferons and Macrophage Function," chaired by Edward A. Havell. In addition, there will be 12 targeted sessions and two poster sessions dealing with the properties and functions of macrophages and related cells.

For further information and registration forms contact:

Dr. Peter Abramoff
Biology Department
Marquette University
Milwaukee, Wisconsin 53233
Telephone: (414) 224-7355

CELLULAR IMMUNOLOGY **63**, 427–429 (1981)

Papers to Appear in Forthcoming Issues

(Received and Accepted Dates Follow Title)

VLADIMÍR VIKLICKÝ AND LADISLAV PAVLÍK. The Reduced Localization of i.v. Injected Lymphocytes in the Lymph Nodes, Lungs, and Small Intestine of Allogeneic Hosts Is a Consequence of Cell Destruction. (Received 12/31/80; accepted 5/5/81).

G. SEMENZATO, G. BASSO, U. FAGIOLO, A. PEZZUTTO, C. AGOSTINI, M. G. COCITO, AND G. GASPAROTTO. Active and Late Rosette Forming Cells: Immunological and Cytochemical Characterization. (Received 4/6/81; accepted 5/26/81).

MAREK ROLA-PLESZCZYNSKI. *In Vitro* Sensitization with HSV-Infected Cells Induces Tμ Cells to become Cytotoxic Tγ Cells which Are Theophylline-Resistant. (Received 3/20/81; accepted 6/6/81).

WULF DROEGE, MATTHIAS REDDEHASE, AND MICHAEL WOLF. Expression of Subregion and Haplotype Preference for H–2K^k Restricted Cytotoxic T Cell Responses *in Vivo* and at the Level of the Precursor Frequencies. (Received 5/5/81; accepted 6/9/81).

LEIF C. ANDERSSON, MIKKO HURME, MICHAEL A. HORTON, ELIZABETH SIMPSON, AND CARL G. GAHMBERG. Molecular Characterization of the Ly-6.2 Antigen. (Received 4/10/81; accepted 6/23/81).

HIDEAKI IRIBE, TOSHITAKA KOGA, KAORU ONOUE, SHOZO KOTANI, SHOICHI KUSUMOTO, AND TETSUO SHIBA. Macrophage-Stimulating Effect of the Synthetic Muramyl Dipeptide and its Adjuvant-Active and Inactive Analogs for the Production of T Cell Activating Monokines. (Received 5/28/81; accepted 6/30/81).

THIERRY HERCEND, LEE M. NADLER, JOHN M. PESANDO, ELLIS L. REINHERZ, STUART F. SCHLOSSMAN, AND JEROME RITZ. Expression of a 26,000 Dalton Glycoprotein on Activated Human T Cells. (Received 5/22/81; accepted 7/2/81).

YONG SUNG CHOI, KEE HAK LIM, AND F. KINGSLEY SANDERS. Effect of Interferon-α on Pokeweed Mitogen-Induced Differentiation of Human Peripheral Blood B Lymphocytes. (Received 1/28/81; accepted 7/3/81).

JACQUELINE PRUNET AND JACQUES PANIJEL. *In Vitro* Recovery of Aptitude for Primary Immunization by Specifically Depleted Cell Populations: Induction by a Lipopolysaccharide. (Received 10/17/80; accepted 7/7/81).

MARK BALLOW AND ALEXANDER G. PANTSCHENKO. *In Vitro* Effects of ADA Inhibitors on Lymphocyte Mitogen Responsiveness in the Mouse. (Received 3/10/81; accepted 7/7/81).

YOUNG TAI KIM, MARC E. WEKSLER, AND GREGORY W. SISKIND. Antigen Induced *In Vitro* Inhibition of Immune Responsiveness. (Received 3/12/81; accepted 7/7/81).

RUTH NETA, S. B. SALVIN, AND MOHAMED SABAAWI. Mechanisms in the *In Vitro* Release of Lymphokines. I. Comparative Kinetics in the Release of Six Lymphokines in Inbred Strains of Mice. (Received 3/16/81; accepted 7/7/81).

SCOTT R. EVANS AND HOWARD M. JOHNSON. The Induction of At Least Two Distinct Types of Interferon in Mouse Spleen Cell Cultures by *Corynebacterium parvum*. (Received 5/8/81; accepted 7/7/81).

DOMINIQUE KAISERLIAN, MIREILLE DARDENNE, AND JEAN-FRANÇOIS BACH. Dissociated Effects of Thymectomy at Weaning on T Cell-Mediated Responses *in Vitro*. Correction by the Serum Thymic Factor, FTS, and Its Analogues. (Received 6/18/81; accepted 7/7/81).

WALLACE Y. LANGDON AND GEOFFREY R. SHELLAM. Inhibition of Antigen-Induced T Cell Proliferation by Antibodies to Endogenous AKR-MuLV. (Received 2/9/81; accepted 7/9/81).

DEBORAH WILSON AND HELEN BRALEY-MULLEN. Antigen Requirements for Priming of Type III Pneumococcal Polysaccharide-Specific IgG Memory Responses: Suppression of Memory with the T Independent Form of Antigen. (Received 6/18/81; accepted 7/11/81).

ALAN LICHTENSTEIN, RICHARD MURAHATA, MARILOU TERPENNING, JOHN CANTRELL, AND JACOB ZIGHELBOIM. Activation and Mechanism of Action of Suppressor Macrophages. (Received 5/22/81; accepted 7/11/81).

JENNIFER BAILEY, JON C. LEWIS, WILLIAM H. GROVER, DAVID HARRIS, DONALD L. EVANS, MARY J. RUEBUSH, LESLIE K. PAULUS, DONALD BURGESS, AND ARTHUR H. HALE. Surface Analysis of Early and Late MOPC-315-EL Tumor Cells. (Received 1/27/81; accepted 7/10/81).

CHARLES M. BALCH, MICHAEL R. LOKEN, PATRICIA A. DOUGHERTY, AND EDWIN W. ADES. Expression of a 16,000 m.w. Antigen on Human Suppressor T Lymphocytes. (Received 6/9/81; accepted 7/13/81).

CHARLES S. PAVIA, DANIEL P. STITES, AND ROBIN FRASER. Transplantation Antigen Expression on Murine Trophoblast Detection by Induction of Specific Alloimmunity. (Received 6/9/81; accepted 7/16/81).

M. RUCHETON, J. CARAUX, C. THIERRY, C. ESTEVE, H. VALLES, J. DUFER, A. DESPLACES, D. ZAGURY, AND B. SERROU. Human Autologous Rosettes. II. Further Characterization: Markers and Functions. (Received 7/8/81; accepted 7/20/81).

PHILIP O. LIVINGSTON, RICHARD MICHITSCH, HIROSHI SHIKU, CARL M. PINSKY, AND HERBERT F. OETTGEN. Antibody-Dependent Cell-Mediated Cytotoxicity for Cultured Autologous Melanoma Cells. (Received 3/6/81; accepted 7/27/81).

ANTONINO CATANZARO. Suppressor Cells In Coccidioidomycosis. (Received 5/18/81; accepted 7/24/81).

JAN L. CEUPPENS, JAMES S. GOODWIN, AND ROBERT P. SEARLES. The Presence of Ia Antigen on Human Peripheral Blood T Cells and T-Cell Subsets: Analysis with Monoclonal Antibodies and the Fluorescence-Activated Cell Sorter. (Received 6/4/81; accepted 7/25/81).

WULF DROEGE. A Random Repertoire of V Genes for the T-Cell Receptors? Theoretical Implications of Recent Experimental Observations on T-Cell Specificity and Self-Restriction. (Received 5/29/81; accepted 7/25/81).

MAURO PIANTELLI, LIBERO LAURIOLA, NICOLA MAGGIANO, FRANCO O. RANELLETTI, AND PIERO MUSIANI. Role of Interleukins 1 and 2 on Human Thymocyte Mitogen Activation. (Received 5/22/81; accepted 7/27/81).

ROY H. L. PANG, Y. K. YIP, AND JAN VILČEK. Immune Interferon Induction by a Monoclonal Antibody Specific for Human T Cells. (Received 7/2/81; accepted 7/24/81).

MENACHEM SHLESINGER AND YVES BOREL. Stimulation of Prostaglandin E_2 (PGE_2) Secretion by Benzyl-penicilloyl (BPO) Carrier Conjugates in Human Peripheral Blood Lymphocytes. (Received 6/1/81; accepted 7/29/81).

DAVID S. CHI, NESTOR BLYZNAK, ARTHUR KIMURA, MICHAEL A. PALLADINO, AND G. JEANETTE THORBECKE. Cytotoxicity to Allogeneic Cells in the Chicken. II. Specific Cytotoxic T Cells and Macrophages in the Spleens of Agammaglobulinemic and Normal Alloimmune Chickens. (Received 5/22/81; accepted 7/30/81).

DAVID S. CHI AND G. JEANETTE THORBECKE. Cytotoxicity to Allogeneic Cells in the Chicken. III. Antibody-Dependent Cell-Mediated Cytotoxicity in Normal and Agammaglobulinemic Chickens. (Received 5/22/81; accepted 7/30/81).

CELLULAR IMMUNOLOGY 63, 430–431 (1981)

Author Index for Volume 63

A

Adler, William H., 28
Arrenbrecht, Stefan, 329
Auerbach, Robert, 272

B

Bahsam, Teresa Y., 118
Benacerraf, Baruj, 300
Berrih, S., 249
Besedovsky, Hugo O., 329
Biberfeld, Peter, 237
Bonavida, B., 249
Bost, Kenneth L., 293
Bout, Daniel, 198
Braley-Mullen, Helen, 177

C

Cartier, Pierre, 81
Chutná, J., 193
Cleveland, William L., 154
Cooke, A., 221
Cuchens, Marvin A., 293
Curl, G. Richard, 71

D

D'Angeac, Arnaud Dupuy, 335
Da Prada, Mosé, 329
David, John R., 198
Del Rey, Adriana, 329
Dempsey, Walla L., 210
Dinarello, Charles A., 134
Duncan, R. L., Jr., 308
Dynesius-Trentham, Roselynn A., 362

E

Erlanger, Bernard F., 154
Ertl, H. C. J., 188
Evans, Charles H., 1
Evans, Donald L., 42

F

Finkelman, Fred, 118
Fraser, Victoria, 177
Fridman, Wolf Herman, 349
Fox, Ira J., 300

G

Garreau, Florianne, 81
Germain, Ronald N., 300
Gilbert, Colleen J., 91
Good, Robert A., 259
Greene, Mark I., 300

H

Hale, Arthur H., 42
Hansen, Carl T., 210
Hašek, M., 193
Holáň, V., 193
Holden, H. T., 279
Holt, Patrick G., 57
Hooper, D. C., 417
Hoover, Marie L., 293
Hutchings, P., 221
Hutt-Fletcher, Lindsey M., 91

I

Ikehara, Susumu, 259

J

Jackson, Dianne E., 203
Jacobs, Ian N., 154

K

Kadish, Anna S., 409
Kindred, Berenice, 228
Klein, Eva, 237
Klein, George, 237
Klimetzek, Volker, 198
Korn, Joseph H., 374
Kouttab, Nicola M., 106
Kühner, Alice L., 198

L

Lally, Edward T., 203
LaRoche, Elizabeth, 362
Layton, J. E., 385
Leslie, Gerrie A., 293
Letvin, Norman L., 300
Levine, Rita F., 210
London, J., 249
Lyman, William D., 409

M

Mansfield, John M., 210
Mayrhofer, Graham, 57
McArthur, W. P., 308
McGee, Maria P., 42
Mizel, Steven B., 164
Möller, Göran, 143
Montgomery, Paul C., 203
Morgan, Edward L., 16
Murgita, R. A., 417
Murphy, Patrick A., 164

N

Nakamura, Mary C., 203
Neauport-Sautes, Catherine, 349
Neefe, John R., 71
Nordin, Albert A., 28
Nossal, G. J. V., 385
Nowowiejski, Irene, 321

O

Oppenheim, Joost J., 164

P

Palacios, Ronald, 143
Parwaresch, M. R., 400
Patarroyo, Manuel, 237
Picus, Joel, 300
Pike, B. L., 385

R

Rabourdin-Combe, Chantal, 349
Radal, Michèle, 335
Radzun, H. J., 400
Raine, Cedric S., 409
Reme, Thierry, 335

Remold, Heinz G., 198
Roehm, Neal W., 272
Rose, N. R., 385
Rosenstreich, David L., 164
Rosenwasser, Lanny J., 134
Rowland, Donna, 362

S

Saxena, Rajiv K., 28
Serrou, Bernard, 335
Sidky, Younan A., 272
Sipe, Jean D., 164
Sordillo, Emilia Mia, 259
Sorkin, Ernst, 329
Stanislawski, Marc, 349
Sztein, Marcelo B., 164

T

Taramelli, D., 279
Teillaud, Jean-Luc, 349
Thoman, Marilyn L., 16
Thuillier, Laure, 81
Trentham, David E., 362
Trotta, Paul P., 259
Toyoshima, Satoshi, 118
Twomey, Jeremiah J., 106

V

Varesio, L., 279
Vogel, Stefanie N., 164

W

Warner, Louise A., 57
Waxdal, M. J., 118
Webb, David R., 321
Weigle, William O., 16
Wellhausen, Sam R., 210
Wittke, J. W., 400
Wood, Irene, 154
Woody, James N., 71

NOTICE

The Subject Index for Volume 63 will appear in the December 1981 issue as part of a cumulative index for the year 1981.

Cellular Immunology

AN INTERNATIONAL JOURNAL

EDITOR-IN-CHIEF: H. Sherwood Lawrence

Volume 64, 1981

ACADEMIC PRESS

A Subsidiary of Harcourt Brace Jovanovich, Publishers

New York London Toronto Sydney San Francisco

MADE IN THE UNITED STATES OF AMERICA

Contents of Volume 64

Number 1, October 1981

Jacqueline Prunet and Jacques Panijel. *In Vitro* Recovery of Aptitude for Primary Immunization by Specifically Depleted Cell Populations: Induction by a Lipopolysaccharide 1

Vladimír Viklický and Ladislav Pavlík. The Reduced Localization of iv-Injected Lymphocytes into the Lymph Nodes, Lungs, and Small Intestine of Allogeneic Hosts Is a Consequence of Cell Destruction 13

Yong Sung Choi, Kee Hak Lim, and F. Kingsley Sanders. Effect of Interferon α on Pokeweed Mitogen-Induced Differentiation of Human Peripheral Blood B Lymphocytes 20

Mark Ballow and Alexander G. Pantschenko. *In Vitro* Effects of Adenosine Deaminase Inhibitors on Lymphocyte Mitogen Responsiveness in the Mouse 29

Young Tai Kim, Marc E. Weksler, and Gregory W. Siskind. Antigen-Induced *in Vitro* Inhibition of Immune Responsiveness 44

Wulf Dröge, Matthias Reddehase, and Michael Wolf. Expression of Subregion and Haplotype Preference for $H\text{-}2K^k$ Restricted Cytotoxic T-Cell Responses *in Vivo* and at the Level of the Precursor Frequencies 53

Scott R. Evans and Howard M. Johnson. The Induction of at Least Two Distinct Types of Interferon in Mouse Spleen Cell Cultures by *Corynebacterium parvum* 64

Hideaki Iribe, Toshitaka Koga, Kaoru Onoue, Shozo Kotani, Shoichi Kusumoto, and Tetsuo Shiba. Macrophage-Stimulating Effect of a Synthetic Muramyl Dipeptide and Its Adjuvant-Active and -Inactive Analogs for the Production of T-Cell Activating Monokines 73

Charles M. Balch, Michael R. Loken, Patricia A. Dougherty, and Edwin W. Ades. Expression of a 16,000 Molecular Weight Antigen on Human Suppressor T Lymphocytes 84

Dominique Kaiserlian, Mireille Dardenne, and Jean-François Bach. Dissociated Effects of Thymectomy at Weaning on T-Cell-Mediated Responses *in Vitro*: Correction by the Serum Thymic Factor, FTS, and Its Analogs 93

Wallace Y. Langdon and Geoffrey R. Shellam. Inhibition of Antigen-Induced T-Cell Proliferation by Antibodies to Endogenous AKR-MuLV 102

David Harris, Jennifer Bailey, Jon C. Lewis, William H. Grover, Marguerite Panetti, Donald L. Evans, Mary J. Ruebush, Leslie K. Paulus, Donald Burgess, and Arthur H. Hale. Surface Analysis of Early and Late MOPC-315-EL Tumor Cells 119

Philip O. Livingston, Richard Michitsch, Hiroshi Shiku, Carl M. Pinsky, and Herbert F. Oettgen. Antibody-Dependent Cell-Mediated Cytotoxicity for Cultured Autologous Melanoma Cells 131

Brigitte Grouix, Janine Charreire, Dominique Erard, Pierre Galanaud, and Jean-François Bach. Serum Thymic Factor (FTS) Restores the Ability of Adult Thymectomized Mice to be Suppressed by Hapten-Modified Self 144

Alan Lichtenstein, Richard Murahata, Marilou Terpenning, John Cantrell, and Jacob Zighelboim. Activation and Mechanism of Action of Suppressor Macrophages .. 150

Charles S. Pavia, Daniel P. Stites, and Robin Fraser. Transplantation Antigen Expression on Murine Trophoblast Detection by Induction of Specific Alloimmunity 162

Deborah Wilson and Helen Braley-Mullen. Antigen Requirements for Priming of Type III Pneumococcal Polysaccharide-Specific IgG Memory Responses: Suppression of Memory with the T-Independent Form of Antigen 177

Short Communications

Leif C. Andersson, Mikko Hurme, Michael A. Horton, Elizabeth Simpson, and Carl G. Gahmberg. Molecular Characterization of the Ly-6.2 Antigen 187

Thierry Hercend, Lee M. Nadler, John M. Pesando, Ellis L. Reinherz, Stuart F. Schlossman, and Jerome Ritz. Expression of a 26,000-Dalton Glycoprotein on Activated Human T Cells 192

Announcement 200

Papers to Appear in Forthcoming Issues 201

NUMBER 2, NOVEMBER 1, 1981

RUTH NETA, S. B. SALVIN, AND MOHAMED SABAAWI. Mechanisms in the *in Vivo* Release of Lymphokines. I. Comparative Kinetics in the Release of Six Lymphokines in Inbred Strains of Mice ... 203

MAREK ROLA-PLESZCZYNSKI. *In Vitro* Sensitization with HSV-Infected Cells Induces T_μ Cells to Become Cytotoxic T_γ Cells Which Are Theophylline Resistant ... 220

G. SEMENZATO, G. BASSO, U. FAGIOLO, A. PEZZUTTO, C. AGOSTINI, M. G. COCITO, AND G. GASPAROTTO. Active and Late Rosette-Forming Cells: Immunological and Cytochemical Characterization ... 227

ANTONINO CATANZARO. Suppressor Cells in Coccidioidomycosis ... 235

DAVID S. CHI, NESTOR BLYZNAK, ARTHUR KIMURA, MICHAEL A. PALLADINO, AND G. JEANETTE THORBECKE. Cytotoxicity to Allogeneic Cells in the Chicken. II. Specific Cytotoxic T Cells and Macrophages in the Spleens of Agammaglobulinemic and Normal Alloimmune Chickens ... 246

DAVID S. CHI AND G. JEANETTE THORBECKE. Cytotoxicity to Allogeneic Cells in the Chicken. III. Antibody-Dependent Cell-Mediated Cytotoxicity in Normal and Agammaglobulinemic Chickens ... 258

MENACHEM SHLESINGER AND YVES BOREL. Stimulation of Prostaglandin E_2 (PGE_2) Secretion by Benzylpenicilloyl (BPO) Carrier Conjugates in Human Peripheral Blood Lymphocytes 267

JAN L. CEUPPENS, JAMES S. GOODWIN, AND ROBERT P. SEARLES. The Presence of Ia Antigen on Human Peripheral Blood T Cells and T-Cell Subsets: Analysis with Monoclonal Antibodies and the Fluorescence-Activated Cell Sorter ... 277

IGAL GERY, PHILIP DAVIES, JULIA DERR, NANCY KRETT, AND JOHN A. BARRANGER. Relationship between Production and Release of Lymphocyte-Activating Factor (Interleukin 1) by Murine Macrophages. I. Effects of Various Agents ... 293

ROY H. L. PANG, Y. K. YIP, AND JAN VILČEK. Immune Interferon Induction by a Monoclonal Antibody Specific for Human T Cells ... 304

M. RUCHETON, J. CARAUX, A. REY, C. THIERRY, C. ESTEVE, H. VALLES, J. DUFER, A. DESPLACES, D. ZAGURY, AND B. SERROU. Human Autologous Rosettes. II. Further Characterization: Markers and Functions ... 312

MARCONDES LIMA AND ROSS E. ROCKLIN. Histamine Modulates *in Vitro* IgG Production by Pokeweed Mitogen-Stimulated Human Mononuclear Cells ... 324

MAURO PIANTELLI, LIBERO LAURIOLA, NICOLA MAGGIANO, FRANCO O. RANELLETTI, AND PIERO MUSIANI. Role of Interleukins 1 and 2 on Human Thymocyte Mitogen Activation 337

STEPHEN H. LEECH AND MARIAM ALI. Low-Dose Restriction in Ir-Gene Control Reflects Susceptibility to Tolerance Induction ... 350

DAVID M. GARAGIOLA, THOMAS K. HUARD, AND ALBERT F. LOBUGLIO. Comparison of Monocyte and Alveolar Macrophage Antibody-Dependent Cellular Cytotoxicity and Fc-Receptor Activity ... 359

FLORENCE M. ROLLWAGEN AND OSIAS STUTMAN. Culture-Generated Suppressor Cells: Evidence for an Adherent Cell Component ... 371

COMMENTARY

WULF DROEGE. A Random Repertoire of V Genes for T-Cell Receptors? Theoretical Implications of Recent Experimental Observations on T-Cell Specificity and Self-Restriction ... 381

ANNOUNCEMENTS ... 392

PAPERS TO APPEAR IN FORTHCOMING ISSUES ... 393

AUTHOR INDEX FOR VOLUME 64 ... 395

The Subject Index for Volume 64 will appear in the December 1981 issue as part of a cumulative index for the year 1981.

CELLULAR IMMUNOLOGY 64, 1–12 (1981)

In Vitro Recovery of Aptitude for Primary Immunization by Specifically Depleted Cell Populations: Induction by a Lipopolysaccharide[1]

JACQUELINE PRUNET AND JACQUES PANIJEL

Service de Physiopathologie de l'Immunité, Institut Pasteur, 28 rue du Dr. Roux, 75724 Paris Cedex 15, France

Received October 17, 1980; accepted July 7, 1981

After specific immunocytoadsorption by filtration through PRBC columns, the spleen cell populations of adult mice no longer respond *in vitro* to primary immunization against the homologous antigen. However, the capability to become immunized against this antigen is recovered after preculture in the presence of a lipopolysaccharide (LPS). The *in vitro*, LPS-induced restoration probably involved several B-lymphocyte subgroups, since the responses of the filtered spleen cells to LPS varied according to the experimental conditions. It is assumed that this restoration of filtered spleen cells may have been due to the sum of various responses to LPS stimulation dependent on the degree of differentiation of various B subpopulations present in the filtrates.

INTRODUCTION

Various B-lymphocyte subgroups have been characterized in mouse spleen cell populations (1–5). According to a number of data, several of these subpopulations could be implicated in the process of primary immunization by given antigens (6). These distinct subpopulations most probably consist of B lymphocytes at different stages of evolution, evolving from stem cells to antibody-producing cells (AFC) (7, 8).

In order to determine the role of relatively immature B lymphocytes in immunization, we have used the spleens of normal mice, because they contain heterogeneous populations of B lymphocytes. We have tried to deplete spleen populations of cells capable of binding a definite antigen in order to obtain uncompetent populations. If AFC could be made to reappear, one might be able to determine the type of original B lymphocyte concerned. The nature of the lymphocytes involved in immunity restoration could be inferred from the properties of the agents used in the assays.

Previous *in vivo* experiments had shown that spleen cell populations, specifically depleted in cells immunocompetent for a thymodependent antigen (pigeon red blood cell, or PRBC), by specific immunocytoadsorption (9), retained undifferentiated B lymphocytes. Furthermore, the latter were capable of acquiring, through non-

[1] This work was supported by grants from CNRS, INSERM and DGRST.

0008-8749/81/150001-12$02.00/0

specific stimulation (10, 11), an aptitude for *in vivo* primary immunization against the homologous antigen. The process probably involved T lymphocytes.

The purpose of this work was to determine, by *in vivo* experiments, which B subgroups were involved in such restoration, and whether any B-lymphocyte activating agent might help in restoring the capability of antibody production against the homologous antigen. Mouse spleen cells, rendered unresponsive toward a certain antigen (PRBC) by specific immunocytoadsorption and referred to as filtered spleen cells (FSC), were exposed to a lipopolysaccharide (LPS) to see whether LPS could stimulate such cells, since LPS is known to be a polyclonal activator (4, 12–14) and a mitogen (15–21) of B lymphocytes.

MATERIALS AND METHODS

Animals. Seven- to nine-week-old male DBA/2 and C3H/HeJ mice were obtained from CNRS (Orléans-la-Source). The former were chosen because they gave the highest response to PRBC *in vitro*, and the latter because they were genetically unresponsive to LPS (22).

Antigens. Pigeon red blood cells (PRBC) and sheep red blood cells (SRBC) were prepared as previously described (9).

Cell suspensions. The cell suspensions were prepared by teasing mouse spleens on nylon filters (mesh 125, Fyltis). The cells were suspended in Shortman buffer (23) supplemented with 10% heat-inactivated fetal calf serum (FCS, Cat. 629, Gibco). The spleens of 30 mice were pooled for each experiment.

Culture medium reagents. The following reagents were used: RPMI 1640 medium (Microbiological Associates, Bethesda, Md.) supplemented with 0.3 mg/ml of L-glutamine (grade A, Calbiochem), 2.5% sodium pyruvate (Gibco, Biocult), 10% FCS, 100 units/ml of penicillin (Specilline G, Specia) and 100 μg/ml of streptomycin (Specia). The medium was prepared just before use and bubbled with CO_2 to pH 7.2. Lipopolysaccharide (LPS) (type I, 0127-B8 *Escherichia coli*, Sigma Chemical Co.) was prepared according to the method described by Watson and Riblet (22). It was diluted to a suitable concentration just before use.

PRBC immunocompetent cell elimination. The specific immunocytoadsorption method for elimination of PRBC immunocompetent cells has already been described (9). In short, it consisted of filtering the spleen cell suspensions through PRBC sieves, at 4°C. The PRBC sieves consisted of columns prepared by hemagglutination at 4°C of PRBC by formol-treated influenza virus X21 (from Institut Pasteur) bound, through a covalent reaction, to cyanogen-activated beads of Sepharose 4B (Bromcyan, Fluka A, Buchs SG; Pharmacia Fine Chemicals AB). The virus–bead complexes were washed carefully with PBS buffer (pH 7.2, 4°C) before hemagglutination. On the day of use the PRBC columns were washed with PBS buffer in order to eliminate any unfixed PRBC. The cells suspensions to be filtered were diluted to an appropriate low density in the same medium and cooled to 4°C.

Culture conditions. Triplicate cultures of 14×10^6 nucleated cells were incubated in petri dishes (Falcon Plastics 3001 F 35 mm, Becton–Dickenson) containing 2 ml of medium, with or without PRBC (at 7×10^5), and with or without LPS (10 μg/ml), for 5 days in an atmosphere of 5% CO_2–85% N_2, with rocking.

The precultures were incubated in Falcon flasks (Falcon Plastics 3013, 25 cm^2, Becton–Dickenson). Cell suspensions, 65 to 90×10^6 in 10 ml of medium, with or without LPS (at 5 or 10 μg/ml), were incubated for 2 days in a humidified atmosphere of 10% CO_2. The cells were then harvested by washing the flasks with gentle agitation. The cells were washed three more times to eliminate unfixed LPS, then counted in order to prepare suspensions suitable for subcultures and immunizations. The subcultures were prepared similarly to the above-mentioned cultures.

Cell viability. All cell suspensions, including those from precultures and cultures, were counted before use. Viability was assessed by the trypan blue exclusion method. The cells which did not take up the dye were counted in a Malassez hemocytometer.

Preimmunized T lymphocytes. DBA/2 mice were immunized by intraperitoneal injection of PRBC (2×10^8 cells in 0.2 ml of PBS). Two days later, the spleens were removed and their cells teased, washed, and filtered in order to harvest the T lymphocytes by method of Julius *et al.* (24). The T lymphocytes were added to immunized subcultures and their controls, in amounts up to 7×10^6 per dish.

Hemolytic plaque assays. The cells were harvested by scraping the dishes with a rubber policeman and the three samples of each kind were pooled in PBS medium (1/2, v/v) for counting and plaque-forming assays. The number of plaque-forming cells (PFC) was determined by the Cunningham and Szenberg method (25). Eight samples were counted for each PFC preparation. All data were expressed as the average of eight PFC counts per 10^6 viable nucleated cells recovered from three pooled cultures.

RESULTS

I. Efficiency of PRBC Filtration at 4°C on Spleen Cell Populations of Normal Adult Mice

In vitro PRBC immunizing assays with FSC showed that the latter had lost their original ability to produce anti-PRBC antibodies (Table 1). Nevertheless, they retained part of the initial background of PRBC PFC. In contrast, FSC remained capable of high antibody production against an heterologous antigen (SRBC) (Table 1). These results confirmed previous ones obtained *in vivo* (9). Moreover, some nonspecific activation of preprogenitor B cells probably occurred during filtration, since both control and SRBC-immunized FSC cultures contained, at Day 5 (as *in vivo*) (9), more anti-SRBC PFC than analogous cultures of initial cell populations, an observation to be compared with the results observed *in vivo*, at Day 8, by Shortman *et al.* (28–29). Even though a nonspecific activation of preprogenitor B cells at Day 3 could not be demonstrated *in vitro*, by these authors, the discrepancy between their results and ours is probably due to the different timing of the *in vitro* experiments. Our cultures were incubated longer than theirs, long enough to allow filtered preprogenitor B cells to mature *in vitro*, thus giving rise to an increase in anti-SRBC PFC at Day 5. Preprogenitor B cells are considered strictly glass adherent (30). However, according to our observation, it could be possible that some of them would escape filtration (as in the experiments of Schlegel and Shortman) (30) and were responsible for this nonspecific activation of the filtered cells.

Independently, FSC exposed to a minimal efficient dose of LPS (5 or 10 μg/ml) according to Melchers *et al.* (1), showed an increase in PRBC PFC (Table 2). It should be noted that the results were evaluated at Day 5, i.e., too late to obtain

TABLE 1

Effect of PRBC Filtration on the *in Vitro* Production of Anti-PRBC-PFC or Anti-SRBC-PFC by Mouse Spleen Cells

		Average number of PFC/10^6 recovered cells on Day 5[a]												
		Anti-PRBC-PFC											Anti-SRBC-PFC	
Mouse cell	Immunizing treatment	Expt[b]:	1	2	3	4	5	6	7	8	9	10	11	12	13
Initial spleen															
DBA/2	none		32	8	26	60	17	11	1	11				41	52
	PRBC		117	93	107	257	109	103	117	191					
	SRBC													903	1422
C3H/HeJ	none										72	11	75		
	PRBC										187	210	638		
Filtered spleen															
DBA/2	none		1	4	44	0	0	7	0	4				183	209
	PRBC		4	1	41	13	8	2	7	1					
	SRBC													2147	2837
C3H/HeJ	none										0	0	14		
	PRBC										0	5	19		

Note. A high proportion of lymphocytes were retained in the PRBC columns by simple mechanical obstruction (about 40%). However, a limited number of cells were fixed through strong attachment to PRBC (27). Macrophages were also retained (about 50%).

[a] The data represent the average of eight PFC counts.

[b] Three pooled cultures were used for each experiment. The background was significant. Its increase over the original PFC (1 to 2 × 10^6 nucleated cells in the case of DBA/2 spleen cell populations) may be due to mitogenic factors of FCS (26).

an optimal response of polyclonal activation. However, this time was chosen because it was the best time to observe simultaneously a possible adjuvant effect of LPS, which was our main objective.

It should be noted that LPS-activated FSC populations contained fewer anti-PRBC PFC than the initial populations similarly activated. The difference in response of the two populations may be explained if one assumes the presence of two subgroups of PRBC-precommitted cells bearing LPS receptors. Both of them would be responsible for activation in the initial populations, but only one of them would remain in the FSC, thus explaining the diminished response of the latter to LPS. It can be deduced that, in the FSC population, the PRBC-precommitted cells belonging to the LPS subgroup were not fully mature, which permitted them to escape filtration, while the PRBC-precommitted cells belonging to the other LPS subgroup were retained in the PRBC columns, because they had previously acquired a PRBC specificity, and were more mature. This hypothesis is in agreement with the data of Vitetta *et al.* (31), who characterized two LPS subgroups: IgD^+ and IgM^+.

When LPS was used as an adjuvant for immunity and added together with PRBC to the cultures, the responses differed depending on the nature of the stimulated cultures, i.e., whether they were initial spleen cells or FSC (Table 2). A well-known synergistic effect (26) was usually observed in initial populations thus stimulated. However, no adjuvant effect was observed in FSC cultures. On the contrary, the number of anti-PRBC PFC was drastically reduced in comparison with that obtained by polyclonal activation only. Be as it may, the presence of PRBC did not influence the polyclonal production of heterologous PFC (anti-SRBC PFC) by FSC (Table 2).

The latter results encouraged us to investigate the reason for the inhibitory effect which appeared when FSC were stimulated by both LPS and PRBC, and whether it might be possible to dissociate, in time, the effects of the two types of stimulation.

II. Efficiency of LPS in Restoring the Aptitude of FSC to PRBC Immunization

Since LPS could stimulate any B lymphocytes in FSC, it seemed of interest to determine the properties acquired by the latter after LPS activation. The experiments were based on the known antitolerogenic properties of LPS (32, 33). As expected, it was found that, after a preculture with LPS, the DBA/2 FSC responded again to PRBC stimulation resulting in the production of anti-PRBC PFC (Table 3). Furthermore, the restoration did not occur if LPS was absent in the precultures, or if the period of preculture in the presence of LPS was shortened by 24 hr. Thus, the 48 hr LPS incubation period increased significantly the background anti-PRBC PFC of FSC. On the other hand, restimulation with LPS was unsuccessful. A similar result was found with normal spleen cell populations (3).

An additional observation was in favor of the idea that the restoration of the aptitude of DBA/2 FSC to anti-PRBC immunization was due to LPS: the FSC of C3H/HeJ origin (mice genetically resistant to LPS (22)), were not restored by preculture in an LPS-supplemented medium (Table 4).

A comparison between the numbers of anti-PRBC PFC found at Day 5 in immunized cultures of initial spleen cells (Table 1) and in LPS-precultured FSC

TABLE 2

Effect of LPS or PRBC Immunization on the *in Vitro* Response of DBA/2 Mouse Initial Spleen Cell Population or DBA/2 Mouse FSC

		Average number of PFC/10^6 recovered cells on Day 5[a]										
		Anti-PRBC-PFC						Anti-SRBC-PFC				
Mouse cell	Treatment Expt[b]:	1	2	3	4	5	6	7	8	9	10	11
Initial spleen	none	17	26	1	11	8	60	1	5	3	0	0
	LPS	19[c]	151	52	94	67	260	36[c]	25[c]	42[c]	65	396
	PRBC	109	107	117	191	93	257	1	27	1	4	4
	LPS + PRBC	231[c]	355	136	110	210	440	55[c]	97[c]	35[c]	144	343
Filtered spleen	none	1	4	0	0	0	7	1	29	16	—	8
	LPS	9[c]	53	29	120	20	80	41[c]	62[c]	67[c]	150	236
	PRBC	4	1	13	7	8	2	4	14	19	2	13
	LPS + PRBC	3[c]	14	3	19	4	2	18[c]	55[c]	50[c]	53	349

[a] The data represent the average of eight PFC counts.
[b] Three pooled cultures were used for each experiment.
[c] Samples cultured with 5 μg/ml of LPS. In the other LPS or LPS + PRBC cultures, 10 μg/ml of LPS was used.

TABLE 3

Recovery of Anti-PRBC response in DBA/2 Mouse FSC after a 48-hr Preculture in the Presence of LPS (10 μg/ml)

Preculture	Addition to subculture	Average number of anti-PRBC-PFC/10^6 recovered cells on Day 5[a] Expt[b]: 1	2	3	4	5	6	7
Without LPS	none	0	4	16	7	0	9	5
	LPS[c]	50	186	—	—	93	100	—
	PRBC	14	1	15	2	8	35	5
With LPS	none	18	33	14	31	55	57	—
	LPS[c]	0	11	1	21	14	9	0
	PRBC	48	260	325	62 ± 20.9[d]	83 ± 14.9[d]	128 ± 141.3[d]	175.7 ± 145.2[d]

[a] The data represent the average of eight PFC counts.
[b] Three pooled subcultures were used for each experiment, with the exception indicated in footnote [d].
[c] The subcultures were also incubated with 10 μg/ml of LPS.
[d] In this case each subculture was examined separately, and the results are expressed as the average of the three subcultures (± SE).

TABLE 4

Inability of C3H/HeJ Mouse FSC to Be Immunized by PRBC after a 48-hr Preculture in the Presence of LPS (10 μg/ml)

Preculture	Addition to subculture	Expt[b]: 1	2	3	4	5	6	7
		Average number of anti-PRBC-PFC/10^6 recovered cells on Day 5[a]						
Without LPS	none	8	0	0	0	0	0	0
	LPS[c]	3	8	15	9	0	2	14
	PRBC	3	0	0	0	0	0	0
With LPS	none	0	0	23	57	12	20	13
	PRBC	0	0	11	2	2.5 ± 3.5[d]	2.7 ± 3.1[d]	21.7 ± 19.9[d]

[a] The data represent the average of eight PFC counts.
[b] Three pooled subcultures were used for each experiment, with the exception indicated in footnote [d].
[c] The subcultures were also incubated with 10 μg/ml of LPS.
[d] In this case each subculture was examined separately, and the results are expressed as the average of the three subcultures (± SE).

(Table 3) showed that the restoration of the anti-PRBC immunization aptitude of the latter was incomplete.

For this reason, it was of interest to see whether educated T lymphocytes (ETL), added to LPS-precultured FSC, might not improve the response to PRBC immunization. We used T educated lymphocytes in preference to T normal lymphocytes, because the former, like FSC, has been in contact with PRBC antigens. As expected, the addition of educated T lymphocytes triggered a high production of anti-PRBC PFC (Table 5). It seems probable that educated T lymphocytes allowed a normal process of cooperation between B and T lymphocytes, resulting in a better anti-PRBC immunization of the LPS-precultured DBA/2 FSC.

The latter result is in favor of a complete restoration by LPS of the response to PRBC immunization. I should be noticed that the number of PRBC-precommitted B lymphocytes precultured with FSC was small and variable.

Finally, when educated T lymphocytes were added to LPS-precultured DBA/2 FSC, the latter responded to the same extent (Table 5) as initial spleen cells immunized with PRBC (Table 2).

DISCUSSION

I. Changes Observed in Mouse Spleen Cell Populations after Filtration through PRBC Columns

When spleen cell populations from adult mice are filtered through PRBC columns at 4°C (FSC), their immunological behavior is affected. The results of Table 1

TABLE 5

Effect of Educated T Lymphocytes (ETL) on the Restoration of Anti-PRBC Response in DBA/2 Mouse LPS-Precultured FSC

Mouse cell	Cultures supplemented with	Average number of anti-PRBC-PFC/10^6 recovered cells on Day 5[a] Expt[b]: 1	2	3
Initial spleen	none	75	21	1
	PRBC	462	59	134
	LPS	91	63	18
	PRBC + LPS	638	—	—
FSC	none	14	16	5
	PRBC	19	25	5
	PRBC + ETL	38	45	9
	LPS	159	120	44
	PRBC + LPS	13	—	—
LPS-precultured FSC	none	0	0	0
	PRBC	325	23	35
	PRBC + ETL	573	105	642

Note. We made sure that the control culture in the case of LPS-precultured cells did not produce any plaque whether or not supplemented with ETL. Plaque-forming cells were obtained only in such cultures stimulated with PRBC either in the absence or in the presence of ETL.

[a] The data represent the average of eight PFC counts.

[b] Three pooled subcultures were used for each experiment.

show that the FSC have lost the ability to be immunized *in vitro* against PRBC. In contrast, the response to an heterologous thymodependent antigen (SRBC) remained positive. These observations confirm previous results obtained *in vivo* by adoptive transfers (9). The lack of response does not seem to be only the result of cell blockade (34, 35) due to filtration.

On the one hand, the background anti-PRBC PFC of the initial population were not inhibited, but retained in the filtration column, since they could be found again by elution of the columns at 37°C (results not shown). On the other hand, the control cultures of FSC contained small quantities of anti-PRBC PFC. Therefore, the latter were not inhibited. They consisted either of PFC having escaped filtration, or, what seems more likely according to previous experiments (9), of PRBC-precommitted B progenitors having also escaped filtration: the latter would have evolved spontaneously to the stage of PFC during the culture time (see controls, Table 1).

In any case, the lack of responsiveness to PRBC immunization shown by FSC is not irreversible. Evidence for reversibility had already been found in previous *in vivo* experiments (10, 11), in which FSC could be made to recover the ability to be immunized against PRBC, by the simultaneous administration of some nonspecific stimulating agents (picryl chloride, muramyl dipeptide) to the animals.

These experimental results suggested several hypothesis on the nature of the process(es) involved in restoration. One of them was that the anti-PRBC PFC resulted from the proliferation of rare PRBC progenitor B cells having escaped filtration, a second hypothesis was that PRBC-precommitted cells would mature and differentiate in AFC. According to a third hypothesis, the anti-PRBC PFC could, through a quite different process, return to the state of PRBC-precommitted B lymphocytes somehow inhibited during filtration, then stimulated by nonspecific agents so that they could regain their anti-PRBC competence.

In previous *in vivo* experiments, T lymphocytes were involved in the restoration of immunity together with B lymphocytes. Therefore, the question was whether restoration could occur *in vitro* through a direct nonspecific stimulation of B lymphocytes.

II. The Effects of LPS

Since LPS selectively stimulates B lymphocytes, its action on FSC was tested. Several observations could thus be made. Different types of FSC-B precursors could be identified, depending on the assay conditions.

(1) The polyclonal activation effect. LPS induced an increase in anti-PRBC PFC, whose proportion reached roughly that of anti-SRBC PFC (heterologous antigen). This result suggests the presence, in the FSC, of PRBC-precommitted lymphocytes bearing surface IgM, in agreement with the data of Vitetta *et al.* (31).

(2) The mitogenic effect. LPS may stimulate in particular lymphocytes bearing surface IgD, inducing their blastogenesis and proliferation (31). It can thus be expected that the $PRBC^+$ clones, required for an LPS-restored PRBC immunizing aptitude of DBA/2 FSC (Table 3), originate from IgD lymphocytes. If so, attempts of restoration with cells from C3H/HeJ mice, genetically unresponsive to LPS, should be and were unsuccessful (Table 4). Nevertheless, the sole proliferation of

PRBC clones could not yield sufficient PRBC progenitors to explain the full restoration of LPS-precultured FSC, which was often observed after 48 hr. We looked, therefore, for additional effects of LPS on FSC, which might explain the process of restoration.

(3) The maturing effect. The renewed stimulation of FSC with LPS gave no result (Table 3). It is known that B lymphocytes stimulated a second time after a short interval do not respond (3). This inhibition could be due to a maturation of B lymphocytes (3, 4, 36, 37), together with a production of suppressor B lymphocytes (38).

Thus, the above-mentioned lack of response suggested that, in FSC, all lymphocytes bearing LPS receptors would be induced to mature by preculture in LPS, including the PRBC-precommitted lymphocytes.

(4) Suppressor effect, induced by filtration, on the PRBC tolerance of B lymphocytes. When LPS was added together with PRBC and as an immunization adjuvant, the FSC response was not improved; no significant change of the number of PFC was found (Table 2). Thus it appears that the effect of polyclonal activation—observed when LPS only was used—did not occur in this case; this inhibition was antigen specific: it depended on the preliminary filtration, during which spleen cells came in contact with PRBC antigens.

This unresponsiveness of FSC against PRBC presents some similarities to the "Miller–Sprent" transient tolerance effect observed both *in vivo* and *in vitro* (38–40). Howard *et al.* (41) have shown that the prestimulation of B preprogenitor cells would be responsible for this kind of tolerance. In the line of this hypothesis it could be assumed that during the filtration process some preprogenitor B cells did not bind to the columns and would be present in the filtrates. However, in the actual state of our experiments, there is no direct evidence for this.

Nevertheless, in contrast with normal spleen populations which can be stimulated *in vitro*, at 4°C, by picogram quantities (10^{-6}, 10^{-8} pg) of a thymoindependent antigen, and whose unresponsiveness is very transient and can be reversed at 37°C (42), the FSC remained unresponsive to an immediate homologous immunization.

III. Effect of Filtration through PRBC Columns on the T Lymphocytes of Mouse Spleen Cell Populations

The responses of LPS-activated FSC subcultures to PRBC immunization were improved by the addition of educated T lymphocytes (Table 5). This result suggested the absence of T helper cells in FSC. Furthermore, when the T lymphocytes were added to the subcultures, they triggered a process of immunization, with a result equivalent to that obtained with initial populations stimulated with both PRBC and LPS.

ACKNOWLEDGMENTS

We wish to thank Mr. J. Le Goff and Mrs. J. Maridat for excellent technical assistance. We also wish to thank Dr. Y. Théry Lanni for her help in the preparation of the manuscript and Mrs. L. Lecarpentier for typing the manuscript.

REFERENCES

1. Melchers, F., Von Boehmer, H., and Phillips, R. A., *Transplant. Rev.* **25,** 26, 1975.
2. Sidman, C. L., and Unanue, E. R., *J. Immunol.* **114,** 1730, 1975.

3. Gronowicz, E., and Coutinho, A., *Transplant. Rev.* **24,** 3, 1975.
4. Hämmerling, U., Chin, A. F., and Abbot, J., *Proc. Nat. Acad. Sci. USA* **73,** 2008, 1976.
5. Howard, M. C., Fidler, J. M., Baker, J., and Shortman, K., *J. Immunol.* **122,** 309, 1979.
6. Mishell, R. I., Dutton, R. W., and Raidt, D. J., *Cell. Immunol.* **1,** 175, 1970.
7. Nossal, G. J. V., Shortman, K., Howard, M., and Pike, B. L., *Immunol. Rev.* **37,** 187, 1977.
8. Rosenberg, Y. J., and Parish, C. R., *J. Immunol.* **118,** 612, 1977.
9. Prunet, J., Panijel, J., Liacopoulos, P., Birrien, J. L., and Thibon, M., *Cell. Immunol.* **16,** 192, 1975.
10. Prunet, J., Birrien, J. L., Panijel, J., and Liacopoulos, P., *Cell. Immunol.* **23,** 223, 1976.
11. Prunet, J., Birrien, J. L., Panijel, J., and Liacopoulos, P., *Cell. Immunol.* **37,** 151, 1978.
12. Melchers, F., and Andersson, J., *Transplant. Rev.* **14,** 76, 1973.
13. Quintans, J., and Lefkovits, I., *J. Immunol.* **113,** 1373, 1974.
14. Hämmerling, U., Chua, R., and Hoffman, M. K., *J. Immunol.* **120,** 750, 1978.
15. Andersson, J., Möller, G., and Sjöberg, O., *Cell. Immuno.* **4,** 381, 1972.
16. Watson, J., Trenkner, E., and Cohn, M., *J. Exp. Med.* **138,** 699, 1973.
17. Melchers, F., Braun, V., and Galanos, C., *J. Exp. Med.* **142,** 473, 1975.
18. Skidmore, B. J., Chiller, J. M., Morrison, D. C., and Weigle, W. O., *J. Immunol.* **114,** 770, 1975.
19. Rozenszajn, L. A., Michlin, H., Kalechman, Y., and Sredni, B., *Immunology* **32,** 319, 1977.
20. Hoffmann, M. K., Galanos, C., Koenig, S., and Oettgen, H. F., *J. Exp. Med.* **146,** 1640, 1977.
21. Axelrod, B. J., and Shands, J. W., Jr., *Cell. Immunol.* **42,** 61, 1979.
22. Watson, J., and Riblet, R., *J. Immunol.* **114,** 1462, 1975.
23. Shortman, K., Williams, N., and Adams, P., *J. Immunol. Methods* **1,** 273, 1972.
24. Julius, M. H., Simpson, E., and Herzenberg,L. A. *Eur. J. Immunol.* **3,** 645, 1973.
25. Cunningham, A., and Szenberg, A., *Immunology* **14,** 599, 1968.
26. Coutinho, A., and Möller, G., *Advan. Immunol.* **21,** 113, 1975.
27. Prunet, J., *In* "Joint Meeting of European Societies for Immunology Strasborg, Sept 1973."
28. Shortman, K., Howard, M. C., and Baker, J. A., *J. Immunol.* **121** 2060, 1978.
29. Shortman, K., Howard, M., Teale, J., and Baker, J., *J. Immunol.* **122,** 2465, 1979.
30. Schlegel, R. A., and Shortman, K., *J. Immunol.* **115,** 94, 1975.
31. Vitetta, E. S., Forman, J., and Kettman, J. R., *J. Exp. Med.* **143,** 1055, 1976.
32. Claman, H. N., *J. Immunol.* **91,** 833, 1963.
33. Louis, J. A., Chiller, J. M., and Weigle, W. O., *J. Exp. Med.* **138,** 1481, 1973.
34. Schrader, J. W., *Eur. J. Immunol.* **5,** 808, 1975.
35. Boyd, A. W., and Schrader, J. W., *J. Exp. Med.* **151,** 1436, 1980.
36. Hämmerling, U., and Chin, A. F., *Eur. J. Immunol.* **8,** 533, 1977.
37. Watson, J., *J. Immunol.* **118,** 1103, 1977.
38. Koenig, S., and Hoffmann, M. K., *Proc. Nat. Acad. Sci. USA* **76,** 4608, 1979.
39. Sprent, J., and Miller, J. F. A. P., *J. Exp. Med.* **138,** 143, 1973.
40. Sprent, J., and Lefkovits, I., *J. Exp. Med.* **143,** 1289, 1976.
41. Howard, M., Baker, J., Teale, J., and Shortman, K., *Scand. J. Immunol.* **11,** 327, 1980.
42. Baltz, M., and Rittenberg, M. B., *Eur. J. Immunol.* **7,** 218, 1977.

CELLULAR IMMUNOLOGY 64, 13–19 (1981)

The Reduced Localization of iv-Injected Lymphocytes into the Lymph Nodes, Lungs, and Small Intestine of Allogeneic Hosts Is a Consequence of Cell Destruction[1]

VLADIMÍR VIKLICKÝ AND LADISLAV PAVLÍK

Institute of Molecular Genetics, Institute of Nuclear Biology and Radiometry, Czechoslovak Academy of Science, 142 20 Prague 4, Czechoslovakia

Received December 31, 1980; accepted May 5, 1981

The organ localization of ^{51}-Cr-labeled lymph node cells was compared in syngeneic and allogeneic recipients. Twenty hours after transfer, a large reduction of the radioactivity in the lymph nodes, lungs, and small intestine and increased radioactivity in the kidneys were found in allogeneic recipients compared to the syngeneic controls. An audit of total radioactivity in the recipients of labeled cells revealed greater losses within the first 24 hr of transfer in allogeneic recipients. Neither splenectomy of the recipients nor transfer of syngeneic thymocytes abolished the allogeneic reduction of homing into the lymph nodes. After splenectomy, transferred cells settled increasingly in the livers and lymph nodes of syngeneic and allogeneic recipients. The results indicate that the destruction of cells is responsible for a major part of the reduced numbers of labeled cells in some organs of the allogeneic recipients.

INTRODUCTION

Selective entry into the lymphoid organs is a property of lymphocytes recirculating between blood and lymph (1). Obviously physiological processes mediated by cells surfaces of the circulating and sessile cells are involved in the selective localization, even though all factors are not yet known. It has been demonstrated that the entry of cells into the lymph nodes occurs via postcapillary venules (2, 3). It seems that the presence of a certain glycoprotein or glycoproteins on the surface of the migrating lymphocytes provides a signal of initiation of cell migration. Following recognition of these structures by endothelia of the postcapillary venules, adherence and an active movement of lymphocytes between endothelial cells to the parenchyma of the lymph nodes takes place. When adherence or active cell movement is impeded, cells stop migrating to the lymph nodes (4–7). In spite of many attempts in various laboratories, the chemical characterization of the sites responsible for lymphocyte adherence to the endothelium of the postcapillary venules is far from complete. Experiments involving the specific blocking or removal of suspected molecules on the surfaces of the circulating lymphocytes have not yielded expected results. Apparently the migration of cells from the blood into the lymph nodes can be inhibited by many agents.

[1] This investigation received financial support from the World Health Organization

0008-8749/81/150013-07$02.00/0

Localization of lymphocytes in lymph nodes is also influenced by gene products of the major histocompatibility locus between the transferred donor cells and recipient cells (8–11). In the case of some reactions *in vitro* the nature of the interactions is understood but the explanation of the *in vivo* observations is much less certain. Thus the reduced localization of lymphocytes after allogeneic cell transfer may be due not only to a failure of recognition of the lymphocytes by endothelia of the postcapillary venules but also to the recognition and subsequent excessive trapping (or elimination?) by other lymphoid and nonlymphoid organs. Therefore we have tried to elucidate the fate of cells in allogeneic recipients and to determine other factors which might be responsible for the reduced localization of transferred cells into the lymph node under these conditions. We have found that marked losses in total radioactivity occur in allogeneic recipients during the first 20 hr after cell transfer, suggesting that many cells are destroyed. The allogeneic reduction of homing remains unaltered even in splenectomized recipients.

MATERIALS AND METHODS

Mice. Inbred mouse strains were produced in the Institute's breeding colony. B10·A and C57BL/10ScSn (B10) mice represented an allogeneic combination. Recipients and donors of lymphocytes were matched for sex; recipient mice were 2–3 months old.

Splenectomy. Mice were splenectomized or sham splenectomized under pentothal anesthesia 3 days or 7 weeks before cell transfer.

^{51}Cr-labeled lymphocytes. Lymphocytes from the axillary, inguinal, and mesenteric lymph nodes were labeled by incubation at 37°C for 45 min with sodium chromate (^{51}Cr, Radiochemical Centre, Amersham, England) at a concentration of 100 μCi/1 $\times$ 10^8 cells/ml of H-MEMd (modified minimum essential culture medium). After three washes in medium, the final concentration was adjusted to 15–20 $\times$ 10^6 cells/ml. Cell viability estimated by trypan blue exclusion was never below 90%. Mice from each group were injected via the tail vein with 7–10 $\times$ 10^6 cells in 0.5 ml of the suspension, and specimens of every suspension were kept as standards.

Evaluation of cell localization. The recipients were killed 20 hr following injection and all lymph nodes (see above), spleens, lungs, livers, femurs, intestines, and kidneys were removed. Radioactivity of the organs and blood samples was measured for 1 min in a gamma counter (Nuclear Chicago). After the subtraction of the background counts, the radioactivity of individual organs (cpm) was expressed as percentage radioactivity of the injected ^{51}Cr-labeled cells. In some cases, the method of a whole-body detection of radioactivity *in vivo* (12) was used with the aim of determining the retention of radioactivity in individual allogeneic and syngeneic recipients during the first 20 hr after cell transfer. In each experiment, syngeneic and allogeneic mice were injected with labeled cells from the same pool. In this way, the variations due to working with two different suspensions could be eliminated. All experiments were repeated at least three times and only the values from one typical experiment are shown in the results, for the reasons stated above.

Irradiation. In some groups, the recipients were submitted to a whole-body exposure of γ-irradiation from a ^{60}Co source (850 rad measured in air, 14 rad/min) 24 hr prior to inoculation of lymphoid cells.

TABLE 1

Migratory Patterns of Labeled Lymph Node Cells into Organs of Syngeneic and Allogeneic Recipients (B10 donor–B10.A recipient combination)

Recipient organ	Percentage recovery[a] (mean ± SD) Syngeneic	Allogeneic	Allogeneic/syngeneic ratio × 100
Lymph nodes	10.0 ± 1.1	4.4 ± 0.3[b]	44
Spleen	23.1 ± 1.3	23.8 ± 0.8	103
Liver	18.8 ± 0.4	19.3 ± 0.6	103
Lung	2.2 ± 1.0	1.4 ± 0.4[b]	64
Bone marrow	1.1 ± 0.3	1.0 ± 0.2	91
Kidneys	1.0 ± 0.1	1.3 ± 0.2[b]	130
Small intestine	1.7 ± 0.4	1.2 ± 0.2[b]	71
Blood (0.2 ml)	0.6 ± 0.1	0.6 ± 0.1	100

[a] Groups of five mice, 20 hr after iv injection of 5 × 10^6 ^{51}Cr-labeled lymph node cells.
[b] Significant difference from the syngeneic control at the 0.01 level.

RESULTS

Fate of Transferred Cells in Allogeneic Recipients

It has been shown in a previous paper (8) that the localization of cells in the lymph nodes is considerably reduced after cell transfer to allogeneic recipients. A similar deficit of allogeneic cells occurs in the lungs and small intestine (Table 1). Increased radioactivity was noted only in the kidney of allogeneic recipients. In other organs, including peripheral blood, the values between syngeneic and allogeneic recipients did not differ. When total radioactivity in the recipients of labeled cells was measured we found that 21% of injected radioactivity was lost in syngeneic recipients and 30% was lost in allogeneic recipients during the first 24 hr (Table 2).

Effect of Splenectomy

The results are confined to cell transfers performed at 7 weeks after splenectomy (Table 3) because no essential differences were found between mice at 3 days or 7 weeks after splenectomy. Splenectomy always led to a marked increase in the

TABLE 2

Total Radioactivity in Syngeneic and Allogeneic Mice, 24 hr after Inoculation of ^{51}Cr-Labeled Lymph Node Cells

Donor/recipient relationship	Percentage of initial radioactivity[a] (mean ± SD)
Syngeneic	78.3 ± 2.8
Allogeneic	70.5 ± 2.1[b]

[a] Initial radioactivity was measured 10 min after cell transfer in groups of 10 mice.
[b] Significant difference from the syngeneic control at the 0.01 level.

TABLE 3

Effect of Splenectomy on the Migratory Patterns of Labeled Lymph Node Cells into Lymph Nodes and Livers of Syngeneic and Allogeneic Recipients

Donor/recipient relationship (strain)	Splenectomy	Percentage recovery[a] (mean ± SD) Lymph nodes	Liver
Syngeneic (B10)	−	9.2 ± 2.3	18.2 ± 3.4
	+	13.6 ± 0.9[b]	28.0 ± 3.1[b]
Allogeneic (B10.A)	−	3.6 ± 0.4[c]	20.0 ± 1.1
	+	7.6 ± 1.4[b,c]	29.7 ± 4.0[b]

[a] See footnote *a*, Table 1.
[b] Significant difference from the nonsplenectomized mice at the 0.01 level.
[c] See foonote *b* Table 1.

reentry of transferred cells into the lymph nodes. The absolute values obtained in allogeneic splenectomized recipients were not different from those observed in syngeneic, nonsplenectomized controls. However, the difference in the homing values between splenectomized syngeneic and allogeneic recipients remained. Splenectomy also led to a considerable increase in the homing of labeled cells into the liver but no difference between syngeneic and allogeneic recipients was found (Table 3).

Effect of Host Irradiation and Transfer of Thymocytes

The absolute values of homing into the lymph nodes, spleens, and livers in irradiated recipients did not substantially differ from those observed in unirradiated controls. However, it is interesting that a decrease in the ratio of syngeneic and allogeneic values was repeatedly observed. While in unirradiated recipients the

TABLE 4

Effect of Host Irradiation[a] and Transfer of Thymocytes (2 hr before Application of Labeled Cells) on Recovery of ^{51}Cr-Labeled Lymph Node Cells in Syngeneic and Allogeneic Recipients

Donor/host relationship (strain)	B10 thymocytes transfer (5×10^6/mouse)	Percentage recovery[b] (mean ± SD) Lymph nodes	Spleen	Liver
Syngeneic (B10)	−	9.5 ± 0.3	24.5 ± 2.8	17.1 ± 3.5
	+	10.5 ± 1.6	24.0 ± 3.4	20.5 ± 2.1
Allogeneic (B10.A)	−	5.7 ± 1.4[b]	23.7 ± 2.0	17.9 ± 3.3
	+	5.9 ± 0.8[b]	22.6 ± 1.8	19.7 ± 1.2

[a] 850 rad, 24 hr before application of labeled cells.
[b] See footnote *a*, Table 1.
[c] See footnote *b*, Table 1.

mean allogeneic/syngeneic ratio was around 40, this value reached 60 after irradiation. The presence of thymocytes compatible with the transferred labeled cells in the recipient's bloodstream had no effect on the homing of these cells into the lymph nodes of allogeneic recipients. The values seen in the spleens and livers also did not differ from those of irradiated controls (Table 4).

DISCUSSION

Cells transferred from various lymphoid organs selectively migrate to and settle in the recipient's tissues. The highest percentage of cells from the lymph nodes migrate to the lymph nodes. Some of the transferred cells also localize in the spleens, livers, lungs, small intestines, and some other tissues. Transfers of allogeneic cells in mice have revealed that cells from donors differing from the recipients at the H-2 haplotypes migrate to most of these organs just as do syngeneic cells. Only with localization in the lymph node was a marked difference noted (5, 8, 9). In a series of experiments on which the present report is based we have also observed the allogeneic reduction of homing into the lungs and small intestines in the majority of cases. The marked sensitivity of the level of localization in lymph nodes to various experimental treatments is thought to be associated with some special anatomical structures of the lymph nodes. In the lungs and small intestines, special categories of lymphoid tissues, such as bronchial-associated lymphoid tissue (BALT) (13) and gut-associated lymphoid tissue (GALT), have been described. In the case of the lungs, a major portion of the radioactivity is carried by cells which are trapped in the bloodstream and which leave the lungs again soon after the transfer (in the first minutes to hours). The passage of the trapped cells into the BALT structures may occur only at later intervals. The low amount of radioactivity in the blood of allogeneic recipients, which is comparable to the results obtained with the syngeneic transfer, excludes the possibility of decreased migration of cells from the blood, or conversely a rapid return to the blood (14). However, we have repeatedly observed a slight though significant increase of radioactivity in the kidneys. Since the emission from ^{51}Cr is not suitable for autoradiography, it is difficult to determine whether tissue-bound radioactivity is in intact lymphocytes or in dead lymphocytes. However, it is more likely that the ^{51}Cr released from dead cells is selectively concentrated. This explanation is supported by the finding of a greater total decrease of radioactivity in allogeneic recipients. Therefore it seems that the destruction of allogeneic cells in the recipients causes the allogeneic reduction of localization in lymph nodes, lungs, and small intestines. Because the classical immune response was practically excluded in these situations (5, 9, 10), the destruction of cells may be due either to the presence of "natural" antibodies or to another type of a rapid elimination with subsequent destruction of the cells based, for example, on a mechanism similar to the destruction of allogeneic haemopoietic grafts (15).

The adherence to the endothelium of the postcapillary venules represents the initiation of the migration of circulating cells from the blood to the lymph nodes. Recently it was demonstrated that this first step can be done even by xenogeneic lymphocytes, which, however, rapidly disappear from the lymph nodes (16). One possible explanation is an early destruction of the adhering cells incapable of migration. However, destruction need not occur only in the lymph nodes. Interactions with other cells in the circulation or in some lymphoid or nonlymphoid organs may also play an important role. For example, in a follow-up study of the fate of transferred stem cells and bone marrow Goodman (17) has shown that the presence of thymocytes is of primary importance in the final differentiation of CFU. However, in our experiments the presence of syngeneic thymocytes did not abolish the allogeneic reduction of homing. An important role in the regulation of lymphocyte recirculation is ascribed to the spleen (18, 19). In cases of inhibition of localization in the lymph nodes induced by concanavalin A binding, Freitas and de Sousa (20) found that the inhibition was due to the trapping of the recirculating cells by the spleen and that splenectomy abolished this inhibition. The allogeneic inhibition of homing to the lymph nodes in rats has been in part explained by Rolstad (10) by the elimination of allogeneic cells in the spleen. In comparing all these results it should be taken into account that transferred allogeneic cells are permanently foreign to the recipient. In contrast, after syngeneic transfer, cells treated with enzymes, hormones, or lectins may recover the altered structure of their surfaces during a relatively short time and as a result of this alteration they are redistributed according to their physiological pattern (21, 22). If some of the transferred cells are dead during allogeneic transfer, it should not be surprising that splenectomy does not lead to the abolition of inhibition of their localization. The results from experiments with splenectomized recipients pointed to one important fact, however. Lymphocytes, called "spleen-seeking" lymphocytes in the literature, which are supposed to have a specific affinity to the spleen, migrate into other lymphoid and nonlymphoid organs in the absence of the spleen. They migrate into the livers, lungs, and bone marrow, in addition to the lymph nodes. Thus, the ability of transferred cells to migrate into other organs in the absence of the spleen speaks against the notion that a limited subpopulation of lymphocytes migrates exclusively into the spleen. Redistribution of transferred cells is also supported by the fact that the total number of labeled cells in the blood decreases at a slower rate (Viklický, unpublished). The migrating cells thus have a greater opportunity to get repeatedly into contact with the endothelium of the postcapillary venules and start migrating to the lymph nodes. Thus it appears that the final site of lodging of the circulating lymphocytes is not rigidly determined and is subject to additional regulation by a number of physiological influences.

REFERENCES

1. Ford, W. L., *Prog. Allergy* **19,** 1, 1975.
2. Gowans, J. L., and Knight, E. J., *Proc. Roy. Soc. Ser. B* **159,** 257, 1964.
3. Stamper, H. B., and Woodruff, J. J., *J. Immunol.* **119,** 772, 1977.
4. Bradfield, J. W. B., and Born, G. V. R., *Cell. Immunol.* **14,** 22, 1974.
5. Viklický, V., Pěknicová, J., and Poláčková, M., *Folia Biol.* **22,** 159, 1976.
6. Viklický, V., and Dráber, P., *In* "Lymphology, Proceedings of the VIth International Congress, Prague" (P. Málek, V. Bartoš, H. Weissleder, and M. H. Witte, Eds.), pp. 261–264. Thieme, Stuttgart/Aviceum, Prague, 1978.
7. Smith, M. E., and Ford, W. L., *In* "Function and Structure of the Immune System" (W. Müller-Ruchholtz and H. K. Müller-Hermelink, Eds./, pp. 85–91. Plenum, New York, 1979.
8. Viklický, V., and Micková, M., *J. Immunogenet.* **6,** 245, 1979.
9. Degos, L., Pla, M., and Colombani, J. M., *Eur. J. Immunol.* **9,** 808, 1979.
10. Rolstad, B., *Cell. Immunol.* **45,** 389, 1979.
11. Pincott, E. E., and Bainbridge, D. R., *Eur. J. Immunol.* **10,** 250, 1980.
12. Pavlík, L., Babický, A., and Pařízek, J., *Physiol. Bohemoslov.* **18,** 502, 1969.
13. Kaltzeider, H. B., *Amer. Rev. Resp. Dis.* **113,** 347, 1976.

14. Kretchmar, A. L., and Conover, W. R., *Proc. Soc. Exp. Biol. Med.* **131,** 703, 1969.
15. Lotzová, E., *Exp. Hematol.* **5,** 215, 1977.
16. Butcher, E., Scollay, R., and Weissman, I., *In* "Function and Structure of the Immune System" (W. Müller-Ruchholtz, and H. K. Müller-Hermelink, Eds.), pp. 65–72. Plenum, New York, 1979.
17. Goodman, J. W., *Transplant. Proc.* **3,** 430, 1971.
18. Pabst, R., and Trepel, F., *Cell Tissue Kinet.* **8,** 529, 1975.
19. Pabst, R., and Trepel, F., *Cell Tissue Kinet.* **9,** 179, 1976.
20. Freitas, A. A., and de Sousa, M., *Eur. J. Immunol.* **5,** 831, 1975.
21. Woodruff, J. J., *Cell. Immunol.* **13,** 378, 1974.
22. Viklický, V., and Poláčková, M., *Folia Biol.* **26,** 396, 1980.

CELLULAR IMMUNOLOGY **64**, 20–28 (1981)

Effect of Interferon α on Pokeweed Mitogen-Induced Differentiation of Human Peripheral Blood B Lymphocytes[1]

YONG SUNG CHOI, KEE HAK LIM, AND F. KINGSLEY SANDERS

Sloan-Kettering Institute for Cancer Research, Walker Laboratory, 145 Boston Post Road, Rye, New York 10580

Received January 23, 1981; accepted July 3, 1981

The effect of human leukocyte interferon (IFN-α) on pokeweed mitogen (PWM)-triggered differentiation of human B cells has been studied *in vitro.* Graded doses of IFN-α were added to the culture of human peripheral blood monocytes, and total antibody synthesis was measured after 6 to 7 days of culture by using a highly sensitive reverse hemolytic plaque assay. The results suggest that a low dose (10^2 U/ml) enhances and a high dose (10^4 U/ml) suppresses B-cell differentiation. Its action occurred in an early stage of B-cell differentiation. Since PWM-triggered differentiation of human B cells requires T cells and monocytes in the culture, we have examined separately the effects of IFN-α on T cells and monocytes. The data indicate that enhancement was mediated by activation of monocytes and suppression was due to inhibition of helper T-cell proliferation. At a high dose, B-cell proliferation may be also directly inhibited by IFN. The implication of these findings is discussed with regard to immunoregulation during viral infection.

INTRODUCTION

Interferon (IFN)[2] has antiviral activity as well as an ability to inhibit cell multiplication (1–3). Interferon preparations are also known to influence various immune responses: enhancement of cytotoxicity by immune T cells (4, 5), natural killer cells (6), and macrophages (7) and suppression of proliferative response of lymphocytes to various mitogens as well as allogeneic cells (8–10). Agents such as lectins and synthetic polynucleotides which are known to induce IFN also modulate antibody production in the mouse (11–14).

IFN can either suppress or inhibit antibody production by mouse lymphocytes *in vitro.* Johnson and Baron (15) reported that virus-induced IFN preparation inhibited the primary plaque-forming cell (PFC) response to both thymus-dependent and -independent antigens. Braun and Levy (16) demonstrated that the number of PFC in mouse spleens increased with a low dose of IFN and decreased with a high dose. Gisler *et al.* (17) further showed that this suppressive effect of IFN

[1] This work was supported by Grants CA-08748 and CA-17404 from the National Cancer Institute. K. H. L. is recipient of a scholarship from the James S. Mountain Memorial Fund, Inc.

[2] Abbreviations used; IFN, interferon; PFC, plaque-forming cells; PWM, pokeweed mitogen; PBM, peripheral blood mononuclear cells; BSS, phosphate-buffered balanced salt solution; Ig, immunoglobulin; SRBC, sheep erythrocytes; NA-SRBC, SRBC treated with neuraminidase; RFC, rosette-forming cells; nRFC, non-rosette-forming cells; FCS, fetal calf serum; [^{3}H]Tdr, tritiated thymidine.

0008-8749/81/150020-09$02.00/0

is attributed to its direct effect on B cells but not on T cells or macrophages. These studies were all carried out with murine lymphoid cells using murine IFN. However, very little information is available on the effect of human leukocyte IFN (IFN-α) on antibody production by human peripheral blood lymphocytes. In this paper, we present a study of the effect of human leukocyte IFN preparations on antibody synthesis by human lymphocytes stimulated by pokeweed mitogen (PWM). We have also investigated the effect of IFN-α on different subpopulations of lymphocytes to determine which are the "target cells" through which the different effects of IFN-α on PFC response are mediated.

MATERIALS AND METHODS

Preparation of cells. Peripheral blood mononuclear (PBM) cells were obtained from normal adult volunteers and T cells separated by erythrocyte-rosette formation as described elsewhere (18); 20 ml of heparinized blood, diluted 1:2 in phosphate-buffered balanced salt solution (BSS), was layered over 15 ml Ficoll–Hypaque (sp grav 1.076–1.078) and spun at 400*g* for 30 min. Cells collected in the interface were harvested, washed twice with BSS, and cultured. T cells were allowed to form rosettes with neuraminidase-treated sheep red blood cells (NA-SRBC). Rosette-forming cells (RFC) and non-RFC (nRFC) were separated by centrifugation of the mixture over Ficoll–Hypaque. After spinning at 400*g* for 30 min, RFCs formed pellets on the bottom of the tube and were retrieved by lysing the attached SRBC with 0.83% ammonium chloride in 0.05 *M* Tris buffer, pH 7.2. nRFCs remaining at the interface were harvested and washed once in RPMI 1640 and subjected again to E rosetting to further deplete T cells.

Culture conditions. To determine the PFC response, 2×10^4 nRFCs were co-cultured with varying numbers of T cells with 1 μl/ml PWM for 6 days in RPMI 1640 (Gibco, Grand Island, N.Y.) supplemented with 15% decomplemented fetal calf serum (FCS) (Gibco, R0180923), 80 m*M* glutamine and 80 mg/liter gentamicin throughout the experiment unless otherwise stated. Cells were cultured in 0.1 ml medium in round-bottom Linbro tissue culture plates (No. 76-014-05, Linbro, Hamden, Conn.) at 37°C in a humidified atmosphere with 5% CO_2. Cultures were in quadruplicate and fed with 10 μl fresh medium every other day.

IFN-α. IFN-α was obtained from the Interferon Laboratories, Sloan–Kettering Institute. Two batches were employed: one (PIF) had a specific activity of 10^6 antiviral units/mg protein, and the other (PPIF) a specific activity of 1.3×10^7 U/mg protein. They were both a gift from Dr. K. Cantell and had been concentrated and partially purified to the specific activities noted above from preparation of normal human leukocytes induced with Sendai virus (25). Their activities were measured against National Institutes of Health human leukocyte IFN references standard (reagent G 029309D1-527) by measuring inhibition of vesicular stomatitis virus (VSV)-induced cytopathic effect in human FS-4 fibroblast. The interferon preparations were stored at −70°C as a lyophilized powder and reconstituted immediately before use. Only the amount needed was diluted to the desired concentrations in RPMI 1640, kept at 4°C, and used within 1 week.

Preparation of PWM-primed nRFCs. PWM-"pulse primed" nRFCs were prepared by culturing nRFCs, 1×10^6/ml in a plastic tube for 18 hr with PWM (1 μl/ml). The "primed" nRFCs were harvested, washed twice in RPMI, mixed with T cells, and cultured for PFC response.

Preparation of IFN-pretreated cells. nRFCs were adjusted to a concentration of 2×10^5/ml in culture medium in a plastic tube and the desired amount of IFN added. Cells were then incubated at 37°C for 18 hr in a humidified incubator with 5% CO_2. T cells were subjected to the same pretreatment conditions at concentration of 10^5 cells/ml.

Irradiation of cells. Cells suspended in culture medium were irradiated with a ^{137}Cs-irradiator (J. L. Shepherd and Associates, Glendale, Calif.) set to deliver the needed amounts of radiation at a rate of 2183.3 rad/min.

Assay of Ig-secreting cells. Immunoglobulin (Ig)-secreting cells were detected through the use of the reverse plaque assay of Gronowicz *et al.* (19). Staphylococcal protein A (Pharmacia Fine Chemicals, Uppsala, Sweden) was coupled to SRBC through treatment with $CrCl_3$ for 1 hr in a water bath at 30°C. Twenty microliters of 30% (v/v) protein A-coated SRBC, 25 μl of rabbit anti-human $F(ab')_2$ (0.13 mg/ml, prepared by ammonium sulfate precipitation of rabbit anti-sera), 25 μl of SRBC-absorbed guinea pig complement (1/5 diluted, BBL, Microbiological Systems, Cockeysville, Md.), and 100 μl of cultured cells were mixed with 300 μl of 0.5% agar (Bactoagar, Difco, Detroit, Mich.) in BSS supplemented with DEAE-dextran (Pharmacia, 2.25 mg/10 ml agar solution). The mixture was plated in 100 × 10-mm petri dishes (Lab-Tek Div., Miles Laboratories, Inc., Naperville, Ill.), which were incubated for 5–6 hr at 37°C in a humidified atmosphere and the number of plaques counted using a magnifier under an indirect light. Three plates were prepared for each sample of pooled cells. Samples that had concentrations higher than 2×10^5 cells/ml were diluted, while those with lower concentrations were used unadjusted. PFCs on each plate were counted and means and standard deviations were calculated.

Assay of [^{3}H]Tdr incorporation. nRFCs irradiated with 5000 rad were cocultured with T cells under the same conditions as for PFC responses. On the appropriate day, [^{3}H]Tdr (specific activity 3 Ci/mmol, Schwartz/Mann, Orangeburg, N.Y.) was added (10 μl per well at a concentration of 50 μCi/ml in RPMI 1640). After 18 hr of further incubation, the cells were collected on glass fiber filter paper (Reeveangel, Clifton, N.J.) using a multiple-automated sample harvester (Otto Hiller Co., Madison, Wisc.), and radioactivity was measured with a Mark II liquid scintillation system (Searle, Arlington Heights, Ill.) using Biofluor Scintillation Fluid (New England Nuclear, Boston, Mass.).

RESULTS

Effect of IFN on PBM

When PBM are cultured with PWM, the PFC response begins to increase approximately 2–3 days after culture and reaches a peak on approximately Days 6–7 (18). To determine at which stage of B-cell differentiation IFN exerts effect, different doses of IFN-α (10^2, 10^3, 10^4, U/ml) were added at different times to cultures containing 10^5 PBL and 1 μl/ml PWM.

As shown in Table 1, the effect of IFN on PFC response differed depending on the dose used. At 10^2 U/ml, PFC response was enhanced, but with 10^4 U/ml, the response was diminished. When IFN was added more than 3 days after PWM

TABLE 1

Effect of Different Doses of IFN and Time of Addition On PFC Response of Human PBM

Day of addition	Dose of IFN (U/ml)			
	0	10^2	10^3	10^4
0	346 ± 77	1492 ± 264	368 ± 107	109 ± 20
1		1202 ± 232	1111 ± 137	178 ± 38
2		1211 ± 380	1628 ± 340	292 ± 29
3		1028 ± 500	800 ± 272	245 ± 62
4		428 ± 378	765 ± 171	257 ± 51
5		336 ± 77	507 ± 70	257 ± 44

Note. 1×10^5 PBL were cultured with PWM (1 μl/ml) in 0.1 ml RPMI 1640 plus 15% decomplemented FCS.

introduction, enhancement was no longer observed. On the other hand, significant suppression was no longer seen when 10^4 U IFN were added more than 1 day after addition of PWM. Although the degree of enhancement at 10^2 U/ml was about the same whenever the IFN was added during the first 3 days, the most inhibition was seen when 10^4 U IFN was added simultaneously with PWM. IFN seems to exert its effect during the early stages of B-cell differentiation, and either enhances or suppresses PFC response in a dose-dependent manner.

Effect of IFN on Different Subpopulations of PBM

Because of the dose-dependent effect of IFN, experiments were performed to determine whether a particular subpopulation of PBM was affected by IFN. It is well known that B cells can differentiate into immunoglobulin-secreting cells when cocultured with T cells and monocytes in the presence of PWM.

After PBMs had been separated into two different populations, nRFC and RFC were incubated for 18 hr with either 10^2 U/ml or 10^4 U/ml. The cells were spun down to remove unbound IFN and washed once with the medium. The IFN-treated cells were then mixed with untreated nRFC or RFC and PWM was added to the culture (Table 2).

When nRFCs were treated with 10^2 U/ml of IFN, there was a 65% increase in the number of PFCs. With a high dose, however, there was no sign of significant suppression. When RFCs were treated with low doses of IFN, there was no visible effect on the PFC response. However, with 10^4 U/ml IFN, a suppression was observed. These data suggest that the enhancement seen with low doses of IFN could have been mediated through nRFCs and suppression through RFCs. This result has been consistently observed in three separate experiments.

Suppression Is Due to Inhibition of Helper T Cells by IFN

Suppression of PFC response at high doses of IFN could result from two different processes. First, it could be due to stimulation of suppressor T cells or, second, a lack of helper activity on the part of T cells because PWM-induced PFC response is T cell dependent.

TABLE 2

Effect of IFN on Different Subpopulations of Human PBM

Dose of IFN (U/ml) Cell treated with IFN:	PFC nRFC	RFC
0	202 ± 29	202 ± 29
10^2	334 ± 46	201 ± 27
10^4	164 ± 29	102 ± 19

Note. nRFC and RFC cells were treated with different doses of IFN for 18 hr, mixed with untreated RFC or nRFC, and cultured with 1 μl/ml PWM for 7 days. nRFC usually consist of 40% monocytes, 40% B cells, 18% null cells, and 2% T cells by overnight rosette assay.

Previously, we showed that PWM-"pulse-primed" B cells could differentiate into Ig-secreting cells when cocultured with unprimed T cells in the absence of added PWM (18). The magnitude of the PFC response is equivalent to the response when PWM is added directly to the culture. Using this experimental system, we have been able to demonstrate that helper T cells must proliferate in order to generate helper activity toward the PFC response. This experimental method can be used to measure the generation of helper T cells for B-cell differentiation, and thus to assess the effect of IFN on helper T cells.

When PWM-"pulse primed" B cells were cocultured with T cells in the presence of suppressing doses of IFN, 10^4 U/ml, ~90% suppression of PFC and ~40% of DNA synthesis were observed (Table 3). It is known that those T cells which proliferate on Day 2 of the culture are the helper T cells and that the ones which continue to proliferate after Day 2 exert suppressor activity (20). Since proliferation of helper T cells is relatively radioresistant and suppressor T cells are radiosensitive, RFC were irradiated (1000-rad) before culture to deplete suppressor T cells from RFC. As shown in Table 3, 1000-rad irradiation of RFC almost completely abolished DNA synthesis on Day 5 but decreased DNA synthesis on Day 2 by 50%.

TABLE 3

Effect of IFN on Generation of Autologous Reactive Helper T Cells

Culture condition	IFN (U/ml)	PFC[a]	$[^2H]Tdr$[b] Day 2	Day 5
nRFC′[c] + RFC	0	191 ± 53	3223 ± 335	19,805 ± 2927
	10^4	17 ± 1	1965 ± 168	5,226 ± 1271
nRFC′ + Irr. RFC (1000 rad)	0	204 ± 32	1419 ± 79	98 ± 25
	10^4	3 ± 2	868 ± 93	3 ± 4

[a] For PFC response, 2×10^4 nRFC′ were mixed with 10^4 irradiated or nonirradiated RFC and cultured for 6 days.

[b] nRFC′ were irradiated (5000 rad) before mixing with RFC for cell proliferation assay.

[c] nRFC′: nRFC primed with 1 μl/ml PWM for 18 hr.

TABLE 4

Effect of IFN on Adherent Cells for PFC Response

No. of adherent cells[a] (×10⁴)	PFC		
	0 U/ml	10 U/ml	10^2 U/ml
1	217 ± 4	176 ± 15	338 ± 57
2	144 ± 19	137 ± 21	311 ± 22

[a] Adherent cells were pretreated with various doses of IFN by culturing at 37°C for 16 hr, collected by gently rubbing with a rubber policeman, and washed two times with culture medium. Two different numbers of adherent cells were mixed with 10^4 RFC and 2×10^4 nRFC (depleted of adherent cells) and cultured with 1 μl/ml PWM for 6 days.

However, the helper activity for PFC response remains almost intact. DNA synthesis observed with irradiated RFC may reflect proliferation of helper T cells. When 10^4 U/ml IFN was added, both PFC response and DNA synthesis decreased even more strikingly.

Since suppressor T cells were not generated after irradiation, this result suggests that the suppression of PFC response can be attained by an inhibition effect of IFN on helper T cells. However, a possibly direct effect on B-cell proliferation itself was not excluded because IFN was present throughout the culture period in this experiment. This result merely indicates that suppressor T cells are not activated by IFN to cause the suppression of the PFC response.

Enhancement Is Due to Activation of Monocytes in nRFC

It is interesting to note that pretreatment of nRFC with low doses of IFN, 10^2 U/ml, enhanced PFC response (Table 2). A high dose of IFN, 10^4 U/ml, had little effect on nRFC. Since nRFC usually consist of 40% B cells, 40% monocytes, and 20% null cells and others, we investigated whether IFN would activate monocytes since monocytes are known to play an active role in supporting PFC response *in vitro* (18).

Monocytes were prepared from PBM by adherence to plastic petri dishes at 37°C as previously described (18) and cultured with low doses (~10 and 10^2 U/ml) of IFN for 16 hr. At the end of the culture, the cells were harvested by gently rubbing the dishes with a rubber policeman. Most (~90%) of the cells collected were identified to be monocytes by their ability to phagocytize latex beads (18). Viability of the cells was usually 80–90% by exclusion of trypan blue. Monocytes were mixed with appropriate numbers of nRFC and RFC and cultured in the presence of PWM for 6 days. As shown in Table 4, PFC response was enhanced in the culture where IFN-treated monocytes were added. When monocytes were treated with 10 U/ml IFN, PFC response was not enhanced.

DISCUSSION

Pokeweed mitogen has been widely used to induce human B-cell differentiation into plasma cells producing polyclonal antibodies. This mitogen mimics thymus-dependent antigens in that it requires helper T cells for optimal responses to be achieved (18). The continuous presence of PWM is not necessary for B-cell differentiation, since once B cells have been "pulse" stimulated for 18 hr with PWM, they can differentiate into plasma cells in its absence. However, such "pulse" stimulated B cells did not differentiate in the absence of T cells. We have shown further that autologous reactive T cells can be triggered to proliferate by HLA-DR antigens on PWM-primed B cells and that a subpopulation of these proliferating T cells can then help PWM-primed B cells to differentiate into Ig-secreting cells (20).

IFN-α preparations either enhanced or suppressed the primary PFC response of human B cells depending on dose and time of addition to the culture. A low dose (10^2 U/ml) enhanced and a high dose (10^4 U/ml) suppressed the PFC response. Its action was on an early stage of B-cell differentiation. These results are in accordance with some of the observations made with murine lymphocytes (15, 17, 21).

It was previously demonstrated that the cultures of human lymphocytes with PWM produced IFN in 3 days (26). Hence, it is possible that a small amount of IFN-γ may be produced in the cultures, affecting the PFC response measured in our study. To monitor the effect of the endogenously produced IFN, we have included the control culture without exogenous IFN-α in every experiment and added different amounts of IFN-α to study its immunoregulatory action. The enhancing and suppressive effect of the exogenous IFN-α may affect the production of IFN-γ during the culture period with PWM, resulting in potentiation of IFN effect as reported by Fleishmann *et al.* (27).

We further analyzed the two alternate effects of IFN on B-cell differentiation by examining the effects of treating T cells and nRFC separately with IFN. When nRFC were treated with IFN, PFC response was enhanced, whereas treatment of T cells suppressed the response. nRFC are usually composed of B cells, monocytes, and Ig-negative nonadherent cells. It is difficult to identify the cell type directly involved in the enhancing effect. The enriched populations still represent various cells with certain types being predominant. Hence, it is possible that the enhancing effect can result from the cellular interactions among these subpopulations.

Since monocytes are known to support human B-cell differentiation *in vitro* (18), we have investigated whether monocytes can be activated by IFN. When IFN-treated monocytes were introduced to T and B cells in the culture, PFC response was enhanced significantly. This result suggests that monocytes may play an important role in the enhancement observed when nRFC are treated with low doses of IFN. It is also possible that the enhancing activity of IFN was due to other contaminating mediators (lymphokines) although the IFN preparation used was relatively pure (1.3×10^7 U/mg protein). This problem has been raised previously in the similar observations made with the murine system (15–17, 22), and its solution awaits the eventual use of more highly purified IFN.

Suppression of the PFC response appears to be due to a direct effect of IFN on the T-cell population. As shown in Table 3, the generation of T-cell helper activity is affected. Suppression does not seem to be mediated by activation of suppressor cells because a PFC response was consistently observed with T cells among which the generation of a suppressor T-cell population was prevented by irradiation. It has been shown previously that autologous reactive T cells proliferating on Day 2 of the culture play a crucial helper role in B-cell differentiation (20). The proliferation of these helper T cells is relatively resistant either to irradiation or to mitomycin C. When T-cell proliferation was inhibited by anti-Ia, the generation of helper T cells was inhibited in parallel, the result being a suppressed PFC response. A high dose of IFN appeared to inhibit proliferation of autologous reactive T cells, affecting PFC response more extensively (Table 3).

Utilizing cell cultures where T cells, B cells, or macrophages were treated separately by IFN, Gisler *et al.* (17) have shown that suppression of antibody-producing cells results from a direct effect on B cells, probably by interfering with their proliferation. In our experiments, PFC response was suppressed when RFC were treated with IFN before mixing with B cells. It is not likely that small amounts of IFN carried over on the surface of RFC would be able to suppress B-cell proliferation. Furthermore, we have always observed enhancement of PFC response with low doses of IFN. However, when IFN was continuously present (Table 3), it is possible that a high dose of IFN would also suppress B-cell proliferation.

Johnson and Baron (15) have studied the effect of IFN on the *in vitro* PFC response of mouse spleen cells to T-cell-dependent and -independent antigens and stated that PFC response to T-cell-dependent antigens was inhibited much more easily than T-cell-independent antigens in terms of both the inhibitory dose required and the time of IFN addition after introduction of an antigen.

Since IFN produced by human leukocytes can both enhance and suppress the PFC response, it could be a part of natural immune regulatory system. One way in which it might function is as follows: In an early stage of viral infection, leukocytes might begin to produce IFN, but the concentration in the system would be low and such low concentrations of IFN in the system would enhance antibody production. However, as viral infection continues and more leukocytes begin to produce more IFN, and as the level of IFN rises, antibody synthesis will be suppressed to inhibit the lymphocytes from overproducing antibody. Recently, investigators have found that immune IFN-γ produced in response to antigenic stimulation by lymphocytes is more potent in its effect on cellular multiplication and immune responses (23, 24). Currently, there are no available data on effect of IFN-γ on the human system. Further work should be done in this area to determine if indeed IFN produced by immune lymphocytes plays a regulatory role in the human immune system.

REFERENCES

1. Stewart, W. E., II., *In* "Interferon" (I. Gresser, Ed.), Vol 1, p. 32. Academic Press, New York, 1979.
2. Stewart, W. E., Gresser, I., Tooey, M. G., Bandu, M., and Goff, S. L., *Nature (London)* **262,** 300, 1976.
3. Gresser, I., Brouty-Boye, D., Thomas, M. T., and Macieira-Coehlo, A., *Proc. Nat. Acad. Sci. USA* **66,** 1052, 1970.
4. Heron, I., Berg, K., and Cantell, K., *J. Immunol.* **117,** 1370, 1976.
5. Lindahl, P., Leary, P., and Gresser, I., *Proc. Nat. Acad. Sci. USA* **69,** 721, 1972.
6. Senik, J. P., Kolb, A. O., and Gidlund, M., *Scand. J. Immunol.* **12,** 51, 1980.
7. Huang, K. Y., Donahoe, R. M., Gordon, F. B., and Dressler, H. R., *Infect. Immunity* **4,** 581, 1971.
8. Blomgren, H., Strander, H., and Cantell, K., *Scand. J. Immunol.* **3,** 697, 1974.
9. Lindahl-Magnusson, P., Leary, P., and Gresser, I., *Nature New Biol.* **273,** 120, 1972.
10. Rozee, K. R., Lee, S. H., and Ngan, J., *Nature (London)* **245,** 16, 1973.
11. Pacheco, D., Falcoff, R., Catinot, L., Floc'h, F., Werner, G. H., and Falcoff, E., *Ann. Immunol. (Paris)* **127C,** 163, 1976.

12. Schmidtke, J. R., and Johnson, A. G., *J. Immunol.* **106,** 1191, 197.
13. Collavo, P., Finco, B., and Chieco-Bianchi, L., *Nature New Biol.* **237,** 154, 1972.
14. Johnson, H. M., Bukovic, J. A., and Smith, B. G., *Proc. Soc. Exp. Biol. Med.* **148,** 599, 1975.
15. Johnson, H. M., and Baron, S., *Cell. Immunol.* **25,** 106, 1976.
16. Braun, W., and Levy, H. B., *Proc. Soc. Exp. Biol. Med.* **141,** 769, 1972.
17. Gisler, R. H., Lindahl, P., and Gresser, I., *J. Immunol.* **113,** 438, 1974.
18. Shin, H. S., and Choi, Y. S., *Cell. Immunol.* **58,** 323, 1981.
19. Gronowicz, S., Coutino, A., and Melchers, F., *Eur. J. Immunol.* **6,** 588, 1976.
20. Shin, H. S., Wang, C. Y., and Choi, Y. S., *J. Immunol.* **126,** 2485, 1981.
21. Brodeur, B. R., and Merigan, T. C., *J. Immunol.* **114,** 403, 1975.
22. Johnson, H. M., Bennett, S. G., and Baron, S., *J. Immunol.* **114,** 403, 1975.
23. Sonnenfeld, G., Mandel, A. D., and Merigan, T. C., *Cell. Immunol.* **40,** 285, 1978.
24. Sonnelfeld, G., Mandel, A. D., and Merigan, T. C., *Cell. Immunol.* **34,** 193, 1977.
25. Cantell, K., Hirvonen, S., Mogensen, K. E., and Phyälä, L., *In* "Proceedings of a Tissue Culture Association Workshop. In Vitro: Monograph No. 3," p. 35. Tissue Culture Assoc. Rockville, Md., 1974.
26. Epstein, L. B., Kreth, H. W., and Herzenberg, L. A., *In* "Lymphocyte Recognition and Effector Mechanisms" (K. Lindahl-Kiessling and D. Osoba, Eds.), p. 169. Academic Press, New York, 1974.
27. Fleischmann, W. R., Georgiades, J. A., Osborne, L. C., and Johnson, H. M., *Infect. Immunity* **26,** 248, 1979.

CELLULAR IMMUNOLOGY **64**, 29–43 (1981)

In Vitro Effects of Adenosine Deaminase Inhibitors on Lymphocyte Mitogen Responsiveness in the Mouse

MARK BALLOW AND ALEXANDER G. PANTSCHENKO

Department of Pediatrics, University of Connecticut Health Center, School of Medicine, Farmington, Connecticut 06032

Received March 10, 1981; accepted July 7, 1981

The effects of two adenosine deaminase (ADA) enzyme inhibitors, EHNA and 2′dCF, were examined on mitogen-induced lymphocyte blastogenesis in mice. The proliferative response of spleen cells stimulated with PHA was more sensitive to the inhibitory effect of 2′dCF than was the proliferative response to Con A, 78 and 39% inhibition, respectively. The inhibitory effect increased with increasing concentrations of 2′dCF up to a concentration of 1.0 μM and then plateaued. A dose-related inhibitory effect of EHNA was observed with both PHA and Con A-induced spleen cell mitogenesis. No differences in the susceptibility to EHNA were observed for the two mitogens. EHNA had little inhibitory effect on the LPS-induced mitogenic response of spleen cells. Moreover, at low concentrations of EHNA (0.1–20 μM), an augmentation in the proliferative response to LPS was observed which was eliminated by removing T cells from the spleen cell suspension by treatment with anti-Thy 1.2 and complement. In contrast, 2′dCF produced 50% inhibition at 50 μM concentrations. The effect of these ADA inhibitors was also tested on thymocyte subpopulations separated by peanut agglutination (PNA) and cortisone treatment (CRT). The less mature cortical thymocytes (PNA^+) were more susceptible to ADA inhibition by 2′dCF and EHNA than the more mature medullary thymocytes (PNA^-, CRT). These results demonstrate that the susceptibility of thymocyte subpopulations to ADA inhibitors changes with different stages of maturation. The spleen cell studies suggest that there are two subpopulations of mitogen responsive T cells, one which is relatively sensitive and the other resistant to the inhibitory effects of 2′dCF. ADA inhibitors, especially 2′dCF, may be useful tools to better define lymphocyte subpopulations and to study lymphocyte differentiation and cellular interactions.

INTRODUCTION

The inherited deficiencies of two purine enzymes, adenosine deaminase (ADA)[1], and purine nucleoside phosphorylase (PNP), have been associated with immunodeficiency diseases (1–7). These abnormalities of purine metabolism have generated new interest in the mechanism(s) of immune dysfunction. In attempts to explain the biochemical basis of the immune dysfunction, investigators have focused primarily on ADA- and PNP-deficient patient material, i.e., their cells, tissues, plasma,

[1] Abbreviations used: ADA, adenosine deaminase enzyme; PNP, purine nucleoside phosphorlyase; EHNA, erythro-9-(2-hydroxyl-3-nonyl)adenine; 2′dCF, 2-deoxycoformycin; HSaγ, agammaglobulinemic horse serum; FCS, fetal calf serum; PHA, phytohemagglutinin P; Con A, concanavalin A; LPS, lipopolysaccharide; PNA, peanut agglutinin; PNA^+, PNA-positive cells; PNA^-, PNA-negative cells; CRT, cortisone-resistant thymocytes.

0008-8749/81/150029-15$02.00/0

and urine (2, 5, 8–12), and on *in vitro* cell culture systems (13–16). Although a number of hypotheses (12, 16–22) have been considered, probably no single mechanism but rather several mechanisms contribute to the immune abnormalities.

Two inhibitors of ADA enzyme activity, erythro-9-(2-hydroxyl-3-nonyl)adenine or EHNA and 2-deoxycoformycin (2′dCF), have been used to study the effects of impaired purine metabolism on lymphocyte function *in vitro*(17, 23–26). These inhibitors also have been used *in vivo* to enhance the antitumor activity of certain chemotherapeutic agents (27, 28) and as a selective lymphocytotoxic drug to treat certain leukemias (29, 30). More recently, both EHNA and dCF have been employed *in vivo* as immunosuppressive agents in tissue and tumor allograft transplantation systems. Lum *et al.* (31, 32) reported prolonged skin graft and pancreatic islet allograft survival in mice receiving EHNA. Chassin *et al.* (33) demonstrated impaired tumor allograft rejection in mice treated with 2′dCF. Thus, ADA inhibitors not only have potential usefulness as adjunct agents in tumor chemotherapy but also in modulating immune function.

Studies were undertaken to examine the effects of ADA inhibitors on lectin-induced spleen and thymus cell mitogenesis. This model was used to determine whether these inhibitors may have selective effects on different immune functions. The results indicate that the PHA- and Con A-responsive spleen cell subpopulations and thymocytes at different stages of maturation have different susceptibilities to the inhibitory effects of 2′dCF. These studies suggest that the therapeutic potential of 2′dCF as an immunopharmacological agent may be related to the selective lymphospecific effects of 2′dCF on certain functional lymphocyte subpopulations.

MATERIALS AND METHODS

Animals and cell preparations. Female Balb/c mice, 17–22 g, were obtained from Charles River Labs (Wilmington, Mass.) and Jackson Labs (Bar Harbor, Maine). Mice were sacrificed by cervical dislocation and the spleen and thymus were removed aseptically. Single cell suspensions were prepared by teasing the tissues with fine forceps or by pressing the tissue between frosted glass slides and passing the cell suspension through a fine mesh screen to remove the tissue debris. Red cells were removed from the spleen cell suspensions by lysis with Tris-buffered ammonium chloride. The mononuclear cell suspensions were washed three times in Hanks' balanced salt solution (HBSS), counted, and adjusted to the desired concentration in RPMI 1640 (Flow Labs, MacLean, Va) containing Hepes buffer, penicillin/streptomycin, and L-glutamine (prepared RPMI 1640 medium). Cell viability was >95% as determined by trypan blue dye exclusion.

Lymphocyte mitogen responsiveness. Spleen and thymus lymphocytes were cultured in round-bottom microtiter tissue culture plates (Linbro Scientific, Hamden, Conn.) containing 5×10^5 cells per well in a final volume of 180 μl. Cells were cultured in prepared RPMI 1640 medium supplemented in either 8% (final concentration) heat-inactivated agammaglobulinemic horse serum ($HS_a\gamma$) (Gibco, Grand Island, NY) or 8% (final concentration) heat-inactivated fetal calf serum (FCS) (Gibco, Lot No. A187520). Several concentrations of phytohemagglutinin P (PHA) (Difco Labs, Detroit, Mich.), concanavalin A (Con A) (Miles Laboratory, Elkhart, Ind.), and lipopolysaccharide (LPS) (*Escherichia coli* 055:B5, Difco Labs) were employed in each experiment to determine optimal mitogenic responses. The

ADA inhibitors, EHNA and 2′dCF, were added to the lymphocyte cultures to make final concentrations ranging from 0.1 to 50 μM. Cultures were incubated at 37°C in a humidified 5% CO_2 atmosphere for 72 hr. Three to four replicate cultures were performed in each experiment depending on the cell numbers available. Eighteen hours prior to harvest, cultures were pulsed with 1 μCi of [^{3}H]thymidine (New England Nuclear, Boston, Mass; 6.7 Ci/mmol), harvested onto glass fiber filters, and counted by liquid scintillation spectrophotometry. The [^{3}H]TdR incorporation of spleen cells stimulated by optimal concentrations of PHA and Con A ranged from 100,791 to 205,712 cpm, and 291,000 to 464,210 cpm, respectively. The incorporation of [^{3}H]TdR into Con A-stimulated thymus cells ranged from 128,567 to 208,835 cpm. Results were normalized to lectin-stimulated control cultures for each experiment to control for day to day variation and to allow for the statistical analysis of data for experiments with the same design. The results are expressed as a percentage of control cultures in which the mean counts per minute or delta value (experimental minus background) of the ADA inhibitor containing mitogen-stimulated cultures is divided by the mean counts per minute (delta value) of the mitogen-stimulated cultures without ADA inhibitors:

$$\%\ [^3\text{H}]\text{TdR incorporation of control cultures} = \frac{\text{cpm of experimental cultures with ADA inhibitors}}{\text{cpm of control cultures without inhibitors}} \times 100.$$

Peanut agglutinin separation of thymocytes. Differential agglutination and separation of thymocytes by peanut agglutinin (PNA) was done by the methods of Reisner *et al.* (35) and Betel *et al.* (36) with minor modifications. Briefly, thymocytes were suspended at 6–8 $\times 10^8$ cells/ml in HBSS and an equal volume of PNA (Vector Labs, Burlingame, Calif.) at a concentration of 1 mg/ml, and incubated at room temperature for 10 min. The suspensions were layered onto 20% $HS_a\gamma$ in HBSS. After 30 min at room temperature, the PNA^+ thymocytes settled through the $HS_a\gamma$ to the bottom, and the top PNA^- thymocytes were removed. The top fraction of PNA^- cells and the aggregated PNA^+ cells were resuspended individually in 0.25 *M* galactose (305–310 mOsm) and the cells mixed by gentle pipetting with a Pasteur pipet. Each cell preparation was washed twice in HBSS containing 0.1% bovine serum albumin and counted and the viability checked with trypan blue.

Preparation of cortisone-resistant cells (CRT). Balb/c mice (17–22 g) were injected intraperitoneally with 0.25 mg of dexamethasone sodium phosphate. Seventy-two hours later the thymus was removed aseptically and a cell suspension was prepared as described above.

Enrichment of spleen cell suspensions for B cells. Spleen cells (1 $\times 10^7$ ml) were incubated with anti-Thy 1.2 antisera at a final concentration of 1:1000 (IgM Hybridoma Monoclonal Antibody, LK-114, New England Nuclear) for 15 min at 37°C. Rabbit serum diluted 1:20 as a source for complement was added to the cell suspension and incubated at 37°C for 30 min. The cell suspensions were washed three times in prepared medium, viability was checked, and cell numbers were counted. The enrichment of B cells was determined by EAC rosetting (37) of lymphocytes which have a receptor for C3.

Reagents. Adenosine (Ad) and deoxyadenosine (dAd) were purchased from

Sigma Chemical Company (St. Louis, Mo.). EHNA was obtained from Burroughs-Wellcome Research Labs (Research Triangle Park, N.C.). The 2′dCF was generously supplied by Dr. J. D. Douros, Developmental Therapeutics Program, Chemotherapy, of the NCI. The anti-Thy 1.2 antisera (IgM monoclonal antibody) was obtained from New England Nuclear.

RESULTS

Effect of ADA Inhibitors on Spleen Lymphocyte Responses to T-Cell Mitogens

Spleen lymphocytes were cultured with PHA and Con A in the presence of different concentrations of EHNA or 2′dCF. Figure 1 shows the inhibitory effect of specified concentrations of EHNA and 2′dCF on the proliferative response of spleen lymphocytes cultured in FCS to an optimal dose of PHA (5 μg/ml). EHNA inhibited the proliferative response in a dose-dependent manner with almost complete suppression of mitogenesis at 50 *μM* (97.4%). The inhibitory effects of 2′dCF, however, plateaued between 10 and 50 *μM* at 72.5 and 76.6% inhibition, respectively.

Experiments were also performed in horse serum which is genetically deficient in ADA activity (38). The inhibition of PHA-induced spleen cell mitogenesis by EHNA and 2′dCF in cultures containing $HS_a\gamma$ was similar to the inhibitory profiles in cultures supported by FCS. The inhibitory effects of EHNA on the spleen cell response was dose related with 99% inhibition at 50 *μM*, while the inhibitory effects

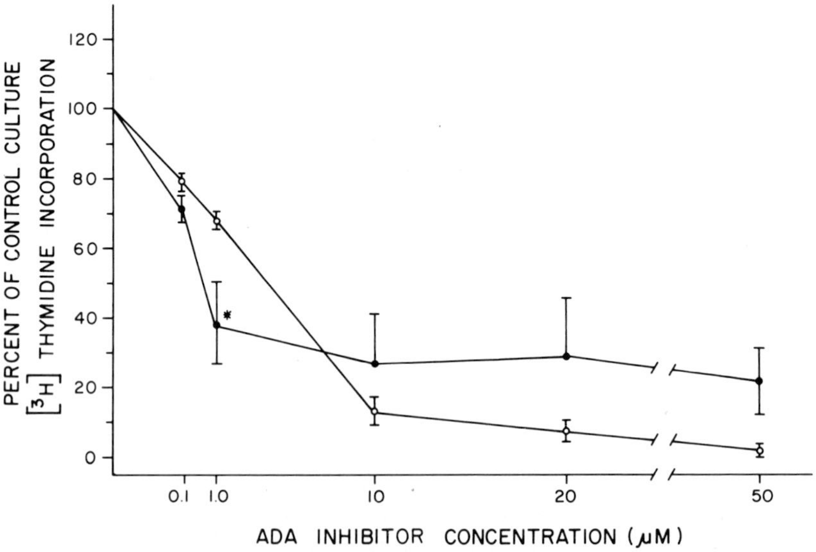

FIG. 1. Effects of ADA enzyme inhibitors on the incorporation of [^{3}H]TdR into PHA-stimulated spleen cells. Spleen cells (5 × 10^5) from Balb/c mice were cultured in FCS with optimal concentrations of PHA (5 μg) in the presence of different concentrations of EHNA (○) or 2′dCF (●). Cultures were pulsed at 48 hr with 1 μCi of [^{3}H]TdR and harvested 18 hr later. The results are expressed as the mean ±SEM percentage of control culture [^{3}H]TdR counts without inhibitor of three to four separate experiments (triplicate/quadruplicate cultures per experiment). *$P < 0.05$. Student's *t* test was used to compare the EHNA- and 2′dCF-containing culture groups.

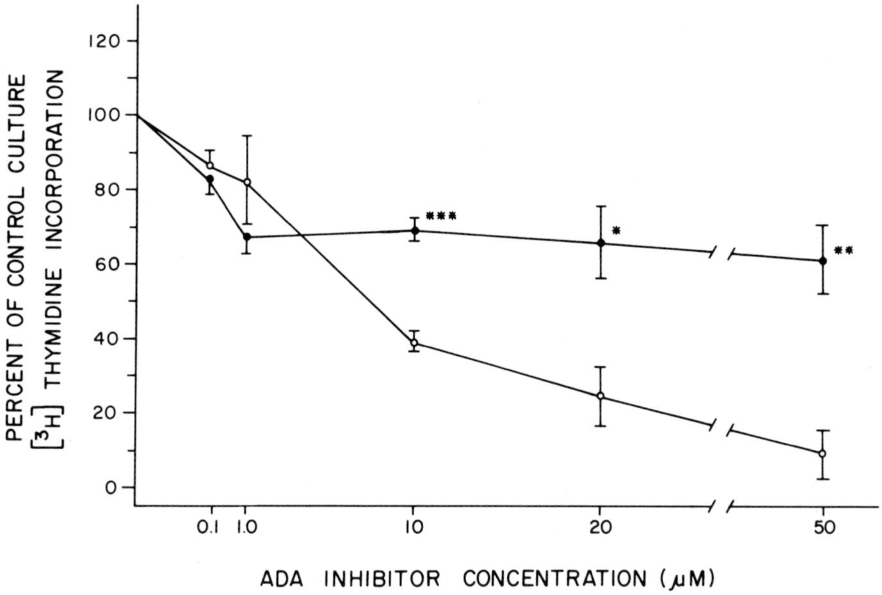

FIG. 2. Effects of ADA enzyme inhibitors on the incorporation of [^{3}H]TdR into Con A-stimulated spleen cells. Spleen cells (5×10^5) from Balb/c mice were cultured in FCS with optimal concentrations of Con A (1 μg/ml) in the presence of different concentrations of EHNA (○) or 2′dCF (●) (See Materials and Methods). The results are expressed as the mean ±SEM percentage of control culture [^{3}H]TdR counts without inhibitor of three to four separate experiments (triplicate/quadruplicate cultures per experiment). *$P < 0.05$, **$P < 0.01$, and ***$P < 0.001$. Student's *t* test was used to compare the EHNA- and 2′dCF-containing culture groups.

of 2′dCF changed very little between 10 *μM* (60% inhibition) and 50 *μM* (72% inhibition) (data not shown).

Figure 2 shows the Con A response of splenic lymphocytes in cultures containing EHNA and 2′dCF supported by FCS. There is a dose-related inhibitory effect of EHNA on the Con A response with almost complete suppression at 50 *μM* (90%). In contrast, after a progressive inhibition of the Con A response at low concentrations of 2′dCF, the inhibitory effect plateaus beyond 1 *μM* at 30.6–38.6% inhibition. Similar EHNA and 2′dCF inhibitory profiles for Con A responses were obtained when spleen lymphocytes were cultured in $HS_a\gamma$ (data not shown). The inhibitory effect of 2′dCF plateaued between 1 *μM* (37% inhibition) and 50 *μM* (40% inhibition) as observed previously with FCS.

Increasing concentrations of EHNA inhibited in a dose-related manner both the PHA and Con A mitogenic responses of spleen cells. On the other hand, although the inhibitory effects of 2′dCF on the PHA and Con A mitogenic response plateaued between 10 and 50 *μM*, the inhibitory effect at a 50 *μM* concentration of 2′dCF on the spleen cell PHA response (76.6% inhibition) was much greater than that on the Con A-induced mitogenic response (38.6% inhibition) ($P < 0.025$).

Mitogenesis of Spleen Lymphocytes to E. coli LPS

The effects of ADA inhibition on B-cell proliferation were studied using the LPS-induced mitogenic response of spleen lymphocytes. Figure 3 shows the effects

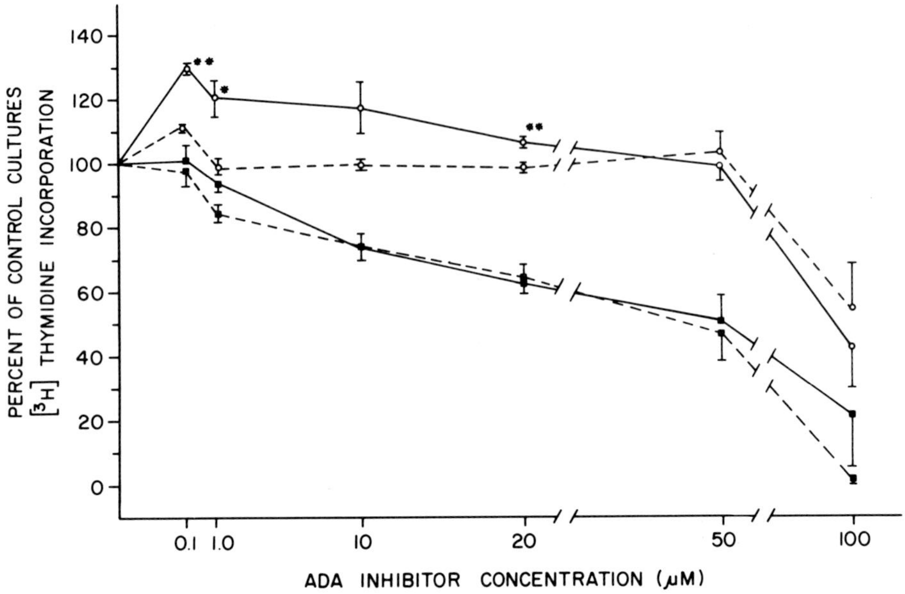

FIG. 3. Effects of ADA inhibitors on the response of spleen cells to LPS-induced mitogenesis. *E. coli* LPS-stimulated spleen lymphocytes, untreated (solid line) or treated (dashed line) with anti-Thy 1.2 antisera plus complement to remove T cells, were cultured with EHNA (○) or 2′dCF (■) for 48 hr pulsed with 1 μCi of [^{3}H]TdR for an additional 18 hr. and harvested. The results are expressed as the mean ±SEM percentage of [^{3}H]TdR counts of three separate experiments (triplicate/quadruplicate cultures per experiment). *$P < 0.05$, **$P < 0.01$. P values represent significant differences between whole spleen cell suspensions and α-Thy 1.2-treated (B-cell-enriched) spleen cells for those cultures incubated with the same ADA inhibitor.

of EHNA and 2′dCF on the response of whole spleen cells (solid lines) to LPS in cultures supported by FCS. At low concentrations (0.1 to 20 μ*M*) of EHNA, a significant augmentation in the proliferative responses to LPS were seen. At higher concentrations EHNA had little further effect on the LPS-induced mitogenic response until 100-μ*M* concentrations were used. In contrast, increasing concentrations of 2′dCF progressively inhibited the LPS response with 80% inhibition at 100 μ*M*. These findings were in marked contrast to the greater effects of EHNA on the T-cell mitogens, PHA and Con A.

Since whole spleen cells represent a mixed population of T and B lymphocytes, the augmentation in proliferative responses to LPS in the presence of EHNA could be related to modulation of T-cell function by the ADA inhibitors. T cells were removed from the spleen cell population by treatment with anti-Thy 1.2 antisera and rabbit complement. The proportion of complement (C3) bearing receptor spleen lymphocytes (EAC-rosetting cells) increased from 31.9 ± 4.9% (±1 SD) (three experiments) before treatment to 81.4 ± 8.9% (three experiments) after treatment with anti-Thy 1.2 antisera plus rabbit complement. The effects of the ADA inhibitors on the mitogenic response to LPS of this enriched B-cell spleen population is shown in Fig. 3 (dashed lines). After removal of T cells to obtain an enriched B-cell population, there was no change in the inhibitory profile of 2′dCF. However, in cultures containing EHNA, the augmentation in LPS-induced proliferation was eliminated. At high concentrations of EHNA (50 and 100 μM), the inhibitory profile was similar to whole, untreated spleen cells.

Effects of ADA Inhibitors on the Mitogenic Response of Thymocytes

Thymocytes were cultured with EHNA and 2′dCF to study their effects on the Con A response. Increasing concentrations of EHNA progressively inhibited the thymocyte Con A response (Fig. 4). In contrast, 2′dCF inhibited the thymocyte Con A response effectively at low concentrations but at higher concentrations (1 to 20 μM), the inhibitory effects plateaued. Similar drug effects of EHNA and 2′dCF on the thymocyte Con A response were obtained in cultures supported by $HS_a\gamma$ (data not shown). Thus, the inhibitory profiles of EHNA and 2′dCF for the Con A response were remarkably similar for the thymus and the spleen (Fig. 2).

The effects of these ADA inhibitors were examined on thymocyte subpopulations which were obtained by cortisone treatment (CRT) and separation by peanut agglutination (PNA). The cortisone treatment enriches for medullary thymocytes (35, 39). PNA selectively enriches for cortical thymocytes (PNA^+), while unagglutinated cells (PNA negative, PNA^-) are enriched for medullary thymocytes. The effects of EHNA on the PNA-separated thymocyte subpopulations are shown in Fig. 5. EHNA produced a dose-dependent inhibition of the mitogenic response to Con A of the unseparated thymocytes and PNA^+ thymocytes. However, at low concentrations (0.1 to 10 μM), EHNA had less of an inhibitory effect on the Con

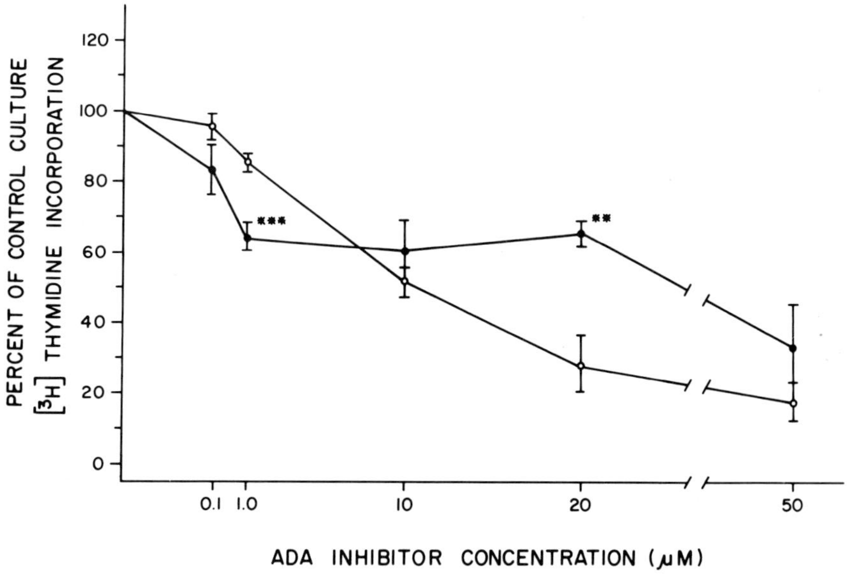

FIG. 4. Inhibitory effects of EHNA and 2′dCF on the incorporation of [^{3}H]TdR into Con A-stimulated thymus cells. Balb/c thymocytes (5×10^5) were cultured in the presence of various concentrations of EHNA (○) or 2′dCF (●) with optimal concentrations of Con A (1–2 μg/ml) in medium supported by FCS. Cultures were harvested at 72 hr after an 18-hr pulse with 1 μCi of [^{3}H]TdR. The results are expressed as the mean ±SEM percentage of control culture [^{3}H]TdR counts without ADA inhibitor of four to six separate experiments. $^{**}P < 0.01$, $^{***}P < 0.001$. Student's *t* test was used to compare the EHNA- and 2′dCF-containing culture groups.

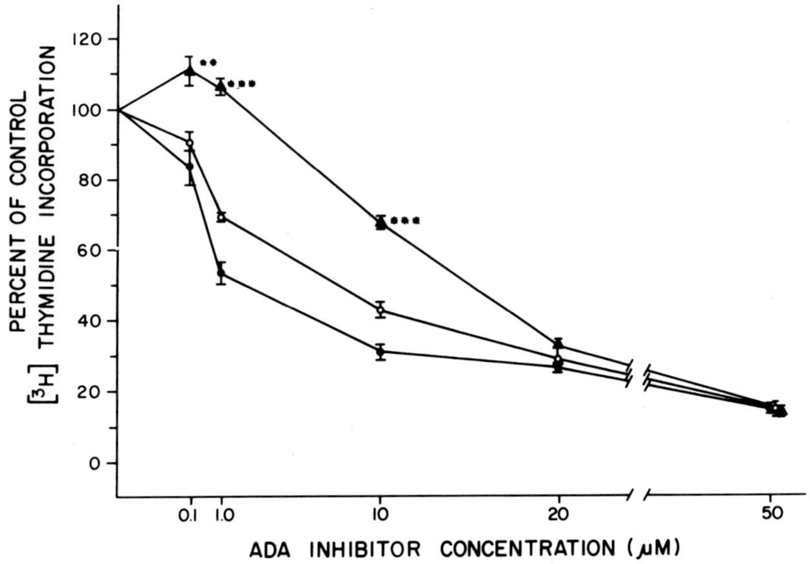

FIG. 5. Inhibitory effects of EHNA on the Con A response of peanut agglutinin (PNA)-separated thymus cells. Thymus cell suspensions (●) from Balb/c mice were separated into PNA-positive (○) and PNA-negative (▲) populations. Varying concentrations of EHNA were added to cultures with optimal concentrations of Con A for each cell subpopulation, and cultured as described previously. Each point represents the mean ±SEM of triplicate cultures. $^{**}P < 0.01$, $^{***}P < 0.001$. Student's t test was used to compare the inhibitory effects of EHNA between the PNA^- and PNA^+ cell populations and the unseparated thymus cells.

A response of the PNA^- thymocyte subpopulation. A marked difference in the inhibitory effects of 2′dCF on the Con A response of the two thymocyte subpopulations was demonstrated (Fig. 6). For the PNA^+ thymocyte subpopulation, a dose-related inhibition of the Con A response was observed. The PNA^- subpopulation and the unseparated thymocytes were markedly less susceptible to the inhibitory effects of the 2′dCF. In fact, the inhibitory effects on the PNA^- thymocyte subpopulation (Fig. 6) were minimal (20%) between a broad range of concentrations of 2′dCF (1–50 μM).

Since 2′dCF and EHNA had a different inhibitory effect on the Con A response of the PNA^+ cells compared to the PNA^- subpopulation of thymocytes, the effects of these ADA inhibitors on the Con A response of CRT were examined (Fig. 7). At low concentrations (0.1–10 μM) of EHNA, the CRT were less sensitive to the inhibitory effects of EHNA than the thymocytes from saline-treated animals. However, there was still a dose-dependent inhibitory effect at the higher concentrations of EHNA in which similar inhibitory patterns were demonstrated for the CRT and saline-treated thymocytes. In contrast, 2′dCF had essentially no inhibitory effects on the Con A-induced mitogenic response of CRT at concentrations as high as 50 μM (Fig. 7).

The inhibitory effects of EHNA and 2′dCF were also examined on the PHA response of the medullary thymocyte-enriched (PNA^- and CRT) subpopulations. The PHA responses of PNA^+ and unseparated thymocytes were poor and thus could not be studied. The inhibitory effects of EHNA and 2′dCF on the PHA response of the PNA^- and the CRT subpopulations were similar to the inhibitory patterns seen with spleen cells (data not shown).

Cell Viability in the Presence of ADA Inhibitors

Cell viability and counts at the end of the culture period (72 hr) were determined by trypan blue dye exclusion. In the presence of either EHNA or 2′dCF at concentrations between 0.1 and 20 μM, thymus cell numbers ranged from 107 to 88% of the thymocyte counts of control cultures without ADA inhibitors. Cell counts decreased slightly to 77 and 74% of control cell counts at 50 and 100 μM, respectively. At 2′dCF concentrations of between 0.1 and 100 μM spleen cell numbers ranged from 88 to 77% of control cultures. At EHNA concentrations of 0.1 and 100 μM spleen cell counts ranged from 91 to 57%, respectively. Except for the moderate cytotoxic effect of EHNA for spleen cells at high concentrations (50 and 100 μM), the marked inhibitory effects of EHNA and 2′dCF on the proliferative response do not appear to be related to a cytolytic effect.

DISCUSSION

In this study, we employed the ADA inhibitors, EHNA and 2′dCF, as probes to determine the effects of the inhibition of ADA activity on lectin-induced lymphocyte proliferation. The inhibitory effects of EHNA were different from those of 2′dCF. The inhibitory effect of EHNA on the PHA- and Con A-induced mi-

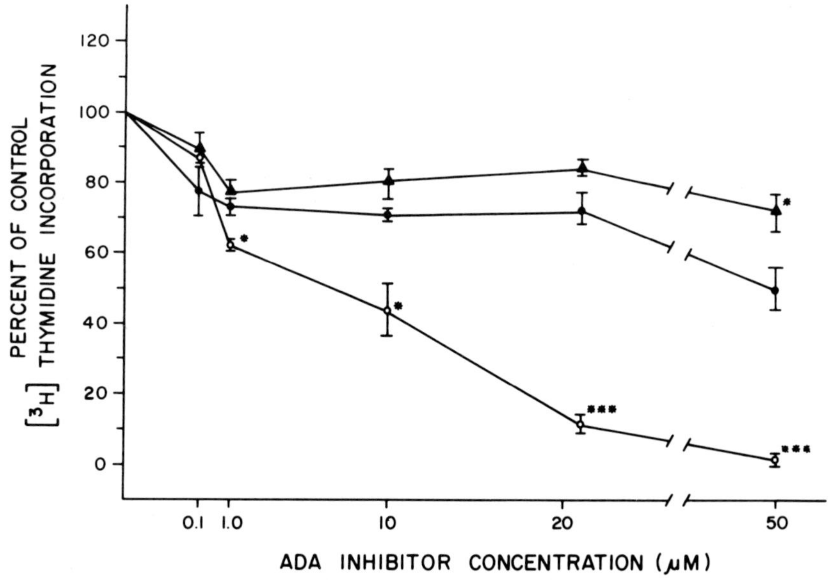

FIG. 6. Inhibitory effects of 2′dCF on the Con A response of PNA-separated thymocytes. Thymus cells (●) from Balb/c mice were separated into PNA-positive (○) and PNA-negative (▲) subpopulations (See Materials and Methods). Varying concentrations of 2′dCF were added to cultures containing optimal concentrations of Con A for each cell subpopulation. Each point represents the mean ±SEM of triplicate cultures. $*P < 0.05$, $***P < 0.001$. Student's t test was used to compare the inhibitory effects of 2′dCF between the PNA^- and PNA^+ cell populations and the unseparated thymus cells.

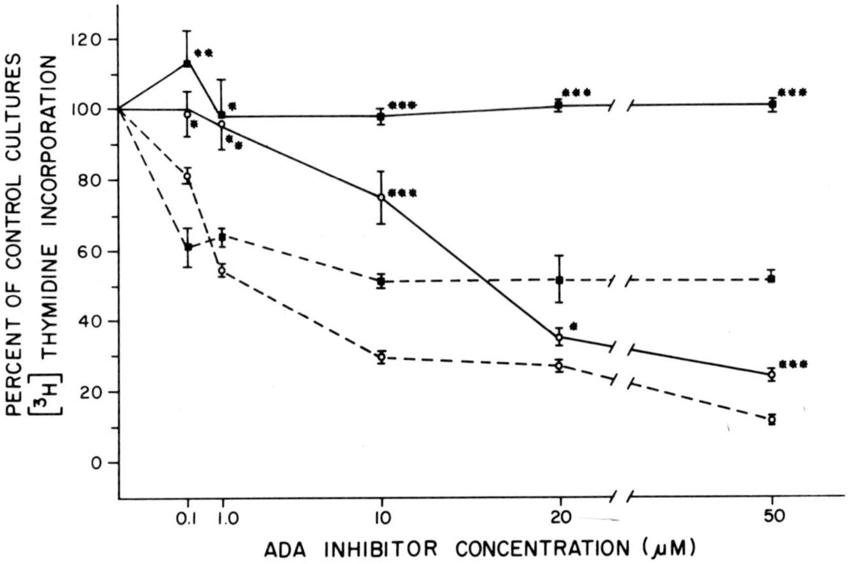

FIG. 7. Inhibitory effect of ADA inhibitors on the incorporation of [^{3}H]TdR into Con A-stimulated thymus cells from cortisone or PBS-treated mice. Balb/c mice were injected ip with either PBS (dashed lines) or 0.25 mg dexamethasone (solid line). The thymus was removed 72 hr later and cell suspensions were prepared for culture (See Materials and Methods). Thymocytes from cortisone-treated and PBS-treated mice were cultured in FCS in the presence of different concentrations of EHNA (○) or 2′dCF (■). Each point represents the mean ±SEM percentage of control culture [^{3}H]TdR counts without ADA inhibitor of quadruplicate cultures. *$P < 0.05$, **$P < 0.01$, ***$P < 0.001$. P values represent the statistical analysis of the inhibitory effects of EHNA/2′dCF between the Con A response of thymocytes from cortisone-treated vs saline-treated mice.

togenic response of spleen cells was dose related with 97 and 90% inhibition, respectively, at concentrations of 50 μM. In contrast, the inhibitory effects of 2′dCF plateaued beyond 1.0 μM concentrations to a maximum inhibition of 78% for the PHA and 39% for the Con A responses even at 50 μM concentrations of 2′dCF.

The lesser inhibitory effects of 2′dCF on the lectin-induced spleen cell mitogenesis as compared to EHNA is not due to differences in the potency of the two inhibitors. In fact, EHNA is a less potent inhibitor (K_i 1.6 × 10^{-9} M) of ADA activity than is the more tightly bound 2′dCF (K_i 2.5 × 10^{-12} M) (40). Even at the lower concentrations that were employed in our cultures (1 μM), EHNA and 2′dCF inhibit 95–99% of the ADA activity in lymphocyte extracts (17, 23). Hirschhorn and Sela (17) found that 10-fold higher concentrations of EHNA were required to inhibit the degradation of adenosine in whole cell cultures as compared to lymphocyte homogenates. However, Snyder *et al.* (26) demonstrated over 95% inhibition of ADA activity with coformycin at concentrations of 3.7 μM for PHA-stimulated and unstimulated human peripheral blood lymphocyte cultures even over a 72-hr period. Thus, the potency or the ability of 2′dCF to inhibit ADA activity in culture does not appear to account for the plateau effect and the dose-related differences between EHNA and 2′dCF. EHNA is not only a less potent inhibitor of ADA activity than 2′dCF but is also less specific. Henderson *et al.* (41) have demonstrated that EHNA inhibits other enzymes of the purine metabolic pathways, especially at high concentrations. This lack of specificity of EHNA may account, at least in part, for the differences in the inhibitory profiles between EHNA and 2′dCF on the mitogenic response of spleen and thymus lymphocytes to PHA and Con A. In addition, since we have not correlated the dose-dependent lymphocyte proliferative inhibitory effects of EHNA or 2′dCF with a dose-dependent inhibition of ADA enzyme activity, the differential inhibitory actions of these ADA inhibitors may be due to effects at sites other than that of ADA inhibition. Furthermore, in the congenital absence of ADA, the immune impairment is thought to be related to the accumulation *in vivo* of adenosine and/or deoxyadenosine and their metabolites (8, 10, 11, 16, 19–21). Therefore, our observations of the effects of ADA inhibitors, EHNA and 2′dCF, on murine lymphocyte proliferative responses may be related to both the accumulation of potential toxic nucleoside metabolites as a result of ADA inhibition, and/or a direct effect of these ADA inhibitors on lymphocyte function.

The spleen cell proliferative response to PHA was much more sensitive to the inhibitory effects of 2′dCF than the proliferative response of spleen cells to Con A. Hirschhorn and Sela (17) and Ballet *et al.* (42) have also demonstrated that the PHA-induced proliferative response of human peripheral blood lymphocytes was more sensitive to the inhibitory effects of EHNA and coformycin than the lectin-induced stimulation of lymphocytes with Con A or pokeweed mitogen. These observations suggest the existence of lectin-responding T-cell subsets which have selective susceptibilities to the ADA inhibitors. Besides being enzyme inhibitors, both 2′dCF and EHNA are also nucleoside analogs. The effects we observed on lectin-induced lymphocyte proliferation may be related to a mechanism(s) other than ADA inhibition. Further studies will be necessary to elucidate the mechanism(s) of the selective susceptibility of certain lectin responding T-cell subsets to these ADA inhibitors.

Until recently T-cell heterogeneity was studied by physical cell separation procedures, cell surface densities of isoantigenic determinants, and the response to different mitogens in culture. Using the latter approach, Stobo and Paul (43) described subsets of T lymphocytes in mouse peripheral lymphoid organs which differed in their relative responsiveness to PHA and Con A. One T-cell subpopulation had equal reactivity to both mitogens while another T-cell subpopulation responded mainly to Con A. Other differential characteristics included recirculation patterns, radiation sensitivities, and location in the peripheral lymphoid tissue (43). More importantly, Stobo and coworkers (43, 44) demonstrated that the T-cell subsets delineated by their lectin-induced proliferative response appeared to serve different immunological functions. The development of reagents and methodology for the subdivision of lymphocyte populations by cell surface antigenic determinants has led to major advancements in the separation of subsets of T and B cells by cell surface phenotype and the ability to correlate these membrane phenotypes with cell function (45). For example, Hirst *et al.* (46) using Ly antisera showed that T cells with the Ly 1+ phenotype exhibited helper function and responded primarily to Con A, while the T cells of the Ly 1,2+ phenotype responded to both PHA and Con A. In our studies, the different sensitivities to the inhibitory effects of 2′dCF of the spleen cell response to the lectins may also be related to T-cell heterogeneity. 2′dCF appears to selectively inhibit a subpopulation of T cells which responds well to both PHA and Con A, while a subpopulation of T cells which is mainly responsive to Con A appears to be resistant to the inhibitory effects of 2′dCF. These findings support the hypothesis that 2′dCF may have a selective effect on functionally different T-cell subsets.

Whereas EHNA was more inhibitory than 2′dCF for the PHA and Con A-induced mitogenic response of spleen cells, 2′dCF was a more potent inhibitor of the response of spleen cells to the B-cell mitogen, LPS. The inhibitory effects of both ADA inhibitors on the LPS-induced mitogenesis was less than their effects on the PHA-induced proliferation. These findings suggest that T and B lymphocytes exhibit a different sensitivity to the inhibitory effects of ADA blockers. Hovi *et al.* (25) investigated the effects of exogenous adenosine and coformycin on the mouse spleen cell proliferation to PHA and LPS. These investigators also noted that the PHA response was inhibited to a greater degree than the LPS response. At very low concentrations of coformycin (0.01 μM), Hovi *et al.* (25) observed enhancement of the LPS response, while higher concentrations of coformycin (1 μM) produced 53% inhibition. We also observed substantial augmentation of the LPS proliferative response in the presence of low concentrations of EHNA (0.1–20 μM) and occasionally at low concentrations of 2′dCF (0.1 μM). The mechanism for this augmentation in the LPS-induced response may be related to enhanced uptake of the [^{3}H]thymidine during pulse labeling (17), or possibly some interaction between the T and B lymphocytes in the spleen cell preparation. Accordingly, the effect of ADA inhibition on the mitogenic response of an enriched B-cell preparation (81.5% EAC-rosetting cells) to LPS was examined. Augmentation was no longer observed in the LPS response of the EHNA-containing cultures. One possible mechanism is that the T cells have a slight modulating influence on the degree of the B-cell response to LPS in whole spleen cell suspensions. In the presence of low concentrations of EHNA, these modulating T-cell influences are negated allowing a heightened B-cell response to the LPS. Removal of the T cells from the spleen cell suspension eliminated the modulating influence such that upon the addition of EHNA, little or no enhanced responses were obtained. Support for this hypothesis comes from several observations. McGhee *et al.* (47) reported that the LPS response of spleen cells in germ-free mice is two- to three fold greater than that of conventional mice. These investigators suggest that a splenic T cell regulates B-cell responses to bacterial endotoxin. Seegmiller *et al.* (48) studied the effects of adenosine and ADA inhibitors on the *in vitro* production of antibodies to sheep erythrocytes by mouse spleen cells. A marked increase in the number of plaque-forming cells was observed with adenosine alone (1 mM) or adenosine with the addition of low concentrations of EHNA (1 μM). In more recent studies, Dosch *et al.* (49) and Gelfand *et al.* (18) reported that antigen-induced T-suppressor-cell activity was abrogated by deoxyguanosine. These studies, together with our own observations suggest that certain T-cell subpopulations, e.g., suppressor cells, are susceptible to ADA inhibitors and/or deoxynucleoside accumulation.

The 2′dCF and EHNA inhibitory profiles of the thymocyte response to Con A were similar to the inhibition curves obtained with spleen lymphocytes except at high drug concentrations (50 μM). However, the thymus afforded us the opportunity to study the effects of these two ADA inhibitors at various stages of T-cell maturation. Two approaches were used to partially separate immature cortical thymocytes from more mature, medullary thymocytes: agglutination with the peanut lectin (35, 36) and cortisone treatment (35, 39). Between the two ADA inhibitors, 2′dCF appeared to discriminate the best for subpopulations of thymocytes. The Con A-induced response of PNA^+ thymocytes, enriched for cortical thymocytes, was more effectively inhibited by 2′dCF than unseparated thymocytes. The PNA^- cells, i.e., medullary thymocytes, were less susceptible to 2′dCF inhibition. These studies suggest that the more mature, differentiated medullary thymocytes are more resistant to the inhibitory effects of 2′dCF. This latter finding was corroborated using the thymocytes from cortisone-treated mice (CRT) in which the Con A response of the CRT was not inhibited by 2′dCF even at concentrations of 50 μM. The small differences in the inhibitory profile of 2′dCF between PNA^- cells and CRT probably reflects the heterogeneity of the PNA^- cells in which some PNA^- cells are steroid sensitive (50). Similarly, the more mature thymocytes (PNA^-, CRT) were less susceptible to the inhibitory effects of EHNA at low concentrations than the less differentiated (PNA^+) thymocytes. These findings are consistent with the observations of Barton *et al.* (34) that rat cortical thymocytes have substantially higher concentrations of ADA enzyme activity compared to medullary thymocytes. The studies of Ballet *et al.* (42) in which inhibition of ADA activity affected precursor T-cell maturation, and Gelfand *et al.* (18) in which the early stages of lymphocyte differentiation appear to be more susceptible to ADA inhibition and deoxyadenosine toxicity support our observations of the preferential susceptibility of the less mature, less differentiated thymocytes to the inhibitory effects of 2′dCF.

The inherited deficiencies of the purine metabolic enzymes, ADA and PNP, have clearly indicated the importance of these metabolic pathways in lymphocyte differentiation and immune function (1–26). Recently, widespread interest has been generated in the potential application of these inhibitors of ADA activity in the pharmacological modification of the immune response and in the treatment of certain lymphoid malignancies (27–33, 51–53). Our findings extend these studies and suggest that 2′dCF has a selective inhibitory effect on T cells at different stages of maturation and on functionally specific T-cell subsets. Thus, the importance of 2′dCF in the treatment of immunologically mediated disorders and certain malignancies may be related to its therapeutic potential as a selective immunological agent. In addition, 2′dCF may also be useful as a new tool in delineating lymphocyte subpopulations, and in studying lymphocyte differentiation and cellular interactions in models of the immune response.

ACKNOWLEDGMENTS

The authors wish to thank Drs. L. Cates, F. Rickles, R. Barton, and S. Schwartz for their helpful discussions, Mr. K. Sparks for his technical help, and L. Nawrocki for her secretarial assistance.

REFERENCES

1. Giblett, E. R., Anderson, J. E., Cohen, F., Pollara, B., and Meuwissen, J. H., *Lancet* **2,** 1067, 1972.
2. Hirschhorn, R., *Fed. Proc.* **36,** 2166, 1977.
3. Parkman, R., Gelfand, E. W., Rosen, F. S., Sanderson, A., and Hirschhorn, R., *N. Engl. J. Med.* **292,** 714, 1975.
4. Meuwissen, J. H., Pollara, B., and Pickering, R. J., *J. Ped.* **84,** 173, 1974.
5. Hirschhorn, R., *Prog. Immunol.* **3,** 67, 1977.
6. Stoop, J. W., Zegers, J. M., Hendrickx, G. F. M., van Keukelom, L. H. S., Staal, G. E. J., de Bree, P. K., Wadman, S. K., and Ballieus, R. E., *N. Engl. J. Med.* **296,** 651, 1977.

7. Giblett, E. R., Ammann, A. J., Sandman, R., Wara, D. W., and Diamond, L. K., *Lancet* **1,** 1010, 1975.
8. Polmar, S. H., Stern, R. C., Schwartz, A. L., Wetzler, E. M., Chase, P. A., and Hirschhorn, R., *N. Engl. J. Med.* **295,** 1337, 1976.
9. Mills, G. L., Schmalstieg, F. C., Trimmer, K. B., Goldman, A. S., and Goldblum, R. M., *Proc. Nat. Acad. Sci. USA* **73,** 2867, 1976.
10. Schmalstieg, F. C., Mills, G. C., Nelson, J. A., May, L. T., Goldman, A. S., and Goldblum, R. M., *J. Ped.* **93,** 597, 1978.
11. Donofrio, J., Coleman, M. S., and Hutton, J. J., *J. Clin. Invest.* **62,** 884, 1978.
12. Cohen, A., Gudas, L. J., Ammann, A. J., Staal, G. E. J., Martin, D. W., Jr., *J. Clin. Invest.* **61,** 1405, 1978.
13. Chen, S. H., Scott, C. R., and Swedberg, K. R., *Amer. J. Human Genet.* **27,** 46, 1975.
14. Green, H., and Chan, T., *Science* **182,** 836, 1973.
15. Chan, T. -S., *Proc. Nat. Acad. Sci. USA* **76**(2), 925, 1979.
16. Carson, D. A., Kay, J., Matsumoto, S., Seegmiller, J. E., and Thompson, L., *Proc. Nat. Acad. Sci. USA* **76,** 2430, 1979.
17. Hirschhorn, R., and Sela, E., *Cell. Immunol.* **32,** 350, 1977.
18. Gelfand, E. W., Lee, J. J., and Dosch, H.-M., *Proc. Nat. Acad. Sci. USA* **76**(4)**,** 1998, 1979.
19. Carson, D. A., Kaye, J., and Seegmiller, J. E., *Proc. Nat. Acad. Sci. USA* **74,** 5677, 1977.
20. Fox, I. H., and Kelley, W. N., *Annu. Rev. Biochem.* **47,** 655, 1978.
21. Kredich, N. M., and Hershfield, M. S., *Proc. Nat. Acad. Sci. USA* **76,** 2450, 1979.
22. Wortmann, R. L., Mitchell, B. S., Edwards, N. L., and Fox, I. H., *Proc. Nat. Acad. Sci USA* **76,** 2434, 1979.
23. Carson, D. A., and Seegmiller, J. E., *J. Clin. Invest.* **57,** 274, 1976.
24. Fox, I. H., Keystone, E. C., Gladman, D. D., Moore, M., and Cane, D., *Immunol. Commun.* **4,** 419, 1975.
25. Hovi, T., Smyth, J. F., Allison, A. C., and Williams, S. C., *Clin. Exp. Immunol.* **23,** 395, 1976.
26. Snyder, F. F., Mendelsohn, J., and Seegmiller, J. E., *J. Clin. Invest.* **58,** 654, 1977.
27. LePage, G. A., Worth, L. S., and Kimball, A. P., *Cancer Res.* **36,** 1481, 1976.
28. Cass, C. E., and Au-Yeung, T. H., *Cancer Res.* **36,** 1486, 1976.
29. Prentice, H. G., Ganeshaguru, K., Bradstock, K. F., Goldstone, A. H., Smyth, F., Wonke, B., Janossy, G., Hoffrand, A. V., *Lancet* **2,** 170, 1980.
30. Smyth, J. F., *Ciba Found. Symp.* **68,** 263, 1979.
31. Lum, C. T., Sutherland, D. E. R., Eckhardt, J., Matas, A. J., and Najarian, J. S., *Transplantation* **27,** 355, 1979.
32. Lum, C. T., Sutherland, D. E. R., and Najarian, J. S., *N. Engl. J. Med.* **296,** 819, 1977.
33. Chassin, M. M., Chirigos, M. A., Johns, D. G., and Adamson, R. G., *N. Engl. J. Med.* **296,** 1232, 1977.
34. Barton, R., Martinick, F., Hirschhorn, R., and Goldschneider, I., *J. Immunol.* **122,** 316, 1979.
35. Resiner, Y., Linker-Israeli, M., and Sharon, N., *Cell. Immunol.* **25,** 129, 1976.
36. Betel, I., Mathieson, B. J., Sharrow, S. O., and Asofsky, R., *J. Immunol.* **124,** 2209, 1980.
37. Bianco, C., Patrick, R., and Nussenzweig, U., *J. Exp. Med.* **132,** 702, 1970.
38. Ishii, K., and Green, H., *J. Cell Sci.* **13,** 429, 1973.
39. Fathman, C. G., Small, M., Herzenberg, A., and Weissman, I. L., *Cell. Immunol.* **15,** 109, 1975.
40. Agarwal, R. P., Spector, T., and Parks, R. E., *Biochem. Pharmacol.* **26,** 359, 1977.
41. Henderson, J. F., Brox, L., Zombor, G., Hunting, D., and Lomax, C. A., *Biochem. Pharmacol.* **26,** 1967, 1977.
42. Ballet, J.-J., Insel, R., Merler, E., and Rosen, F. M., *J. Exp. Med.* **143,** 1271, 1977.
43. Stobo, J. D., and Paul, W. E., *J. Immunol.* **110,** 362, 1973.
44. Stobo, J. D., Paul, W. E., and Henney, L. S., *J. Immunol.* **110,** 652, 1973.
45. Cantor, H., and Gershon, R. K., *Fed. Proc.* **38,** 2058, 1979.
46. Hirst, J. A., Beverley, P. C. L., Kisielow, P., Hoffman, M. K., and Oettgen, H. F., *J. Immunol.* **115,** 1555, 1975.
47. McGhee, J. R., Kiyono, H., Michalek, S. M., Babb, J. L., Rosenstreich, D. L., and Mergenhagen, S. E., *J. Immunol.* **124,** 1603, 1980.
48. Seegmiller, J. E., Watanabe, T., and Schreier, M. H., The effect of adenosine on lymphoid cell

proliferation and antibody formation. *In* "Ciba Foundation Symposium No. 48: Purine and Pyrimidine Metabolism," pp. 249–297. Elsevier/Excerpta Medica/North-Holland, Amsterdam, 1976.
49. Dosch, H.-M., Mansour, A., Cohen, A., Shore, A., Gelfand, E. W., *Nature (London)* **285,** 494, 1980.
50. London, J., Berrih, S., and Bach, J.-F., *J. Immunol.* **121,** 438, 1978.
51. Carson, D. A., and Kaye, J., *Ciba Found. Symp.* **68,** 115, 1979.
52. Tedde, A., Balis, M. E., Ihehara, S., Pahwa, R., Good, R. A., and Trotta, P. O., *Proc. Nat. Acad. Sci. USA* **77,** 4899, 1980.
53. Smyth, J. F., Chassin, M. M., Harrap, K. R., Adamson, R. H., and Johns, D. G., *Proc. Amer. Assoc. Cancer Res.* **20,** 47, 1979.

CELLULAR IMMUNOLOGY **64**, 44–52 (1981)

Antigen-Induced *in Vitro* Inhibition of Immune Responsiveness[1]

YOUNG TAI KIM, MARC E. WEKSLER,[2] AND GREGORY W. SISKIND

Division of Allergy and Immunology and Division of Gerontology, Department of Medicine, Cornell University Medical College, New York, New York 10021

Received March 12, 1981; accepted July 7, 1981

Addition of the dinitrophenyl derivative of the copolymer of D-glutamic acid and D-lysine (DNP-D-GL) or dinitrophenyl bovine γ-globulin (DNP-BGG) to spleen cell cultures specifically inhibited their capacity to produce an anti-DNP plaque-forming cell (PFC) response to the T-independent antigen dinitrophenylated polyacrylamide beads (DNP-PAA) or to the T-dependent antigen TNP-burro erythrocytes. The degree of unresponsiveness was dependent upon the tolerogen concentration and the duration over which the tolerogen was present in the culture. Treatment with rabbit anti-mouse brain antiserum and complement did not alter the induction of unresponsiveness suggesting a state of B-cell tolerance. Culture of spleen cells for 4 days in the absence of antigen led to the appearance of nonspecific suppressor activity which was demonstrable by its effect on the response of fresh spleen cells to antigen. Preculture in the presence of the immunogen DNP-PAA induced both nonspecific and specific suppressor activities. Induction of specific suppressor activity was not prevented by the presence of the tolerogen DNP-D-GL in the culture. The suppressor activity resided in an adherent T-cell population and did not appear to require macrophages for its induction.

INTRODUCTION

A number of workers have reported the induction of specific states of immunological unresponsiveness, *in vitro*, which appear to be comparable to classical immunologic tolerance induced *in vivo* (1–7). The dinitrophenyl (DNP) derivative of the copolymer of D-glutamic acid and D-lysine (D-GL) is known to be an excellent B-cell tolerogen (8–11). In previous studies we have obtained evidence that, in addition to inducing B-cell tolerance, DNP-D-GL also stimulates the generation of antigen-specific suppressor T cells *in vitro* (12). This was a curious finding since in elegant *in vivo* studies by other workers (10, 13, 14) no induction of suppressor activity had been observed with this apparently obligate tolerogen. In the present studies we have shown that addition of DNP-D-GL or DNP-bovine γ-globulin (DNP_{11}-BGG) to a lymphocyte culture specifically inhibits the elicitation of a primary immune response by either the T-independent antigen dinitrophenylated polyacrylamide beads (DNP-PAA) or the T-dependent antigen trinitrophenylated burro erythrocytes (TNP-BRBC). Evidence for the induction and characterization

[1] Supported in part by research grants from the National Institutes of Health, USPHS Grants AI-11694, AG-00239, AG-00842, and AG-00541.

[2] Recipient of a Research Career Development Award from the National Institutes of Health, USPHS Grant CA-32102.

0008-8749/81/150044-09$02.00/0

of antigen-specific suppressor activity during culture of spleen cells with DNP-PAA is presented.

MATERIALS AND METHODS

Animals. Eight- to twelve-week-old LAF_1 male mice were obtained from the Jackson Laboratory (Bar Harbor, Maine).

Preparation of antigens, tolerogens, and antisera. Preparation of DNP-PAA has been described previously (15). DNP-D-GL was prepared by the reaction of 500 mg D-GL (34,000 mw) dissolved in 10 ml deionized water (containing 33 mg K_2CO_3), with 280 mg of 1-fluoro-2, 4-dinitrobenzene (DNFB: Eastman Organic Chemicals Division, Eastman Kodak Co., Rochester, N.Y.) dissolved in 0.5 ml *p*-dioxane. The reaction mixture was stirred overnight at room temperature and the product was dialyzed extensively against 0.001 *M* phosphate buffer (pH 7.2). DNP derivatives of human serum albumin (HSA) and BGG were prepared by the reaction of DNFB with HSA and BGG (Miles Laboratories, Kankakee, Ill.) respectively, under alkaline conditions, essentially as described by Eisen *et al.* (16). The concentration of the derivitized protein was determined by dry weight analysis and the degree of derivitization was estimated spectrophotometrically from the absorbance at 360 nm (ϵ for DNP-lysine = 14,700). TNP derivatives of BRBC and sheep erythrocytes (SRBC) were prepared as described by Rittenberg and Pratt (17). Rabbit anti-mouse brain (RAMB) antiserum was prepared by the method of Golub (18) and was absorbed with mouse bone marrow cells and kidney powder. The absorbed antiserum was cytotoxic for over 95% of mouse thymus cells, less than 5% of bone marrow cells, and approximately 40% of spleen cells. A monoclonal anti-mouse Thy 1.2 antibody was purchased from New England Nuclear (Boston, Mass.).

Cell culture system. Spleens were removed aseptically and were teased in Hanks' balanced salt solution (Grand Island Biological Co., Grand Island, N.Y.) containing 0.35 mg/ml Na_2HCO_3 and 0.02 mg/ml sodium heparin sulfate. The cells were filtered through a thin layer of cotton gauze to remove clumps, washed once, and resuspended in an appropriate amount of RPMI 1640 medium (Microbiological Associates, Bethesda, Md.) supplemented with 10% fetal calf serum (Microbiological Associates), 0.02 *M* glutamine, 100 IU of penicillin, and 100 μg streptomycin/ml and 1.5×10^{-4} *M* 2-mercaptoethanol. In 1 ml of medium 7.0×10^6 cells were cultured in plastic petri dishes (Falcon No. 1008, Oxnard, Calif.) with 10^7 SRBC, 1 mg DNP-PAA, or 10^7 TNP-BRBC alone or together with various concentrations of DNP-D-GL or DNP-BGG for 4 days. Cultures were incubated on a rocking platform (7 cycles/min), at 37°C, in a 5% CO_2/95% air environment for 4 days. The cells were then harvested using a rubber policeman, washed once, and assayed for anti-SRBC or anti-DNP PFC.

Assay of plaque-forming cells (PFC). Anti-SRBC PFC and anti-DNP or anti-TNP PFC in the cell cultures were assayed by the Dresser and Greaves (19) slide modification of the method of Jerne *et al.* (20). The target cells used for assay of anti-SRBC PFC and anti-DNP or anti-TNP PFC were SRBC and TNP-SRBC, respectively. Data are reported as direct PFC/10^6 viable cells. Cell viability was assayed, at the termination of culture, by trypan blue exclusion.

RESULTS

Depression of the in Vitro Primary Anti-DNP PFC Response by DNP-D-GL or DNP_{11}-BGG

Addition of DNP-D-GL or DNP_{11}-BGG to lymphocyte cultures inhibited the *in vitro* primary anti-DNP PFC response to DNP-PAA or to TNP-BRBC. The suppressive effect was dependent upon the concentration of tolerogen (Fig. 1). Thus, a significant depression of the PFC response was seen at 0.5 μg/ml and a maximal depression of 70% was observed with 1.0 μg/ml DNP-BGG and of 80% with 5.0 μg/ml DNP-D-GL. The degree of depression was also affected by the time at which the tolerogen (DNP-D-GL or DNP_{11}-BGG) was added to the culture. Maximum depression occurred when the tolerogen was added at the onset of the culture (Fig. 2). The degree of depression of anti-TNP PFC decreased as the time between initiation of culture and addition of tolerogen was increased. Even when the tolerogen was added 3 days after the establishment of culture (1 day before assay), some decrease (8–40%) in the number of PFC was observed.

The addition of DNP-D-GL to spleen cell cultures did not depress the anti-SRBC PFC response (Table 1). Curiously, addition of DNP_{11}-BGG to spleen cell cultures appeared to augment the anti-SRBC PFC response (Table 1). This effect was accentuated by reducing the concentration of spleen cells in culture (Table 2). When 2.5×10^6 spleen cells were cultured, DNP_{11}-BGG increased the anti-SRBC PFC response threefold.

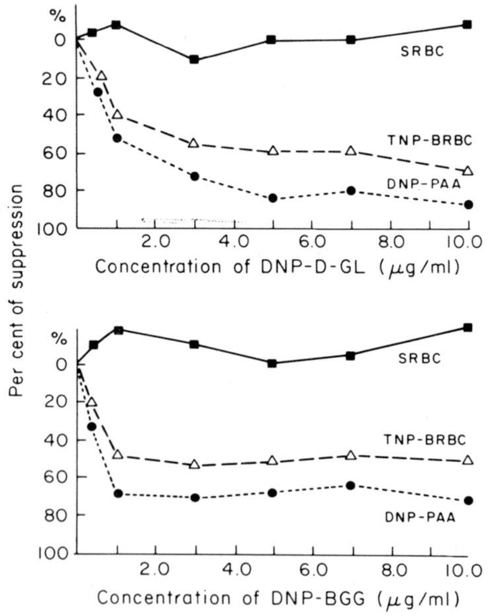

FIG. 1. Hapten-specific depression of PFC responses by various concentrations of DNP-D-GL (top) or DNP_{11}-BGG (bottom). Spleen cell cultures were incubated with the indicated tolerogen (DNP-D-GL or DNP_{11}-BGG) and immunogen (DNP-PAA, TNP-BRBC, or SRBC) for 4 days. Direct PFC were assayed by using SRBC or TNP-SRBC as target cells. The data, at each concentration of tolerogen, are expressed as the percentage of depression from the control: (1.00 − PFC with tolerogen/PFC without tolerogen) × 100. Data are the mean percentage of depression for three independent experiments.

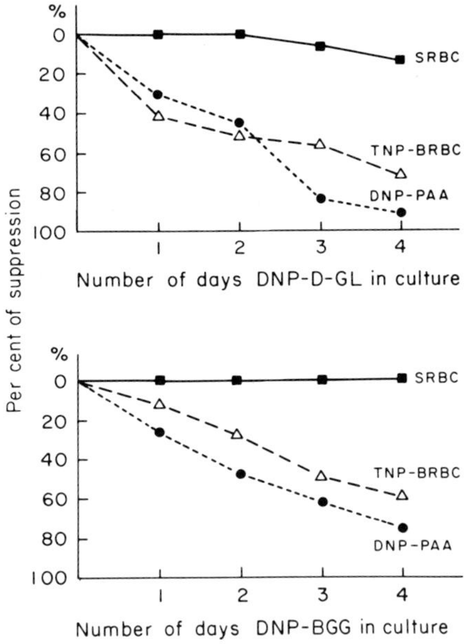

FIG. 2. Effect of varying the length of time during which 10 μg/ml tolerogen is present on the degree of depression of the PFC response. Spleen cell cultures were incubated with the indicated immunogen (DNP-PAA, TNP-BRBC, or SRBC) for 4 days. Tolerogen (DNP-D-GL, top; or DNP_{11}-BGG, bottom) was added at various times after the onset of culture and then remained in the cultures until their termination. Direct PFC were assayed, after 4 days of culture, using SRBC or TNP-SRBC as target cells. The data are expressed as the percentage of depression from the control: (1.00 − PFC with tolerogen/PFC without tolerogen) × 100. Data are the mean percentage of depression for three independent experiments.

The possibility that tolerogen, transferred with the cells into the assay mixture, caused an inhibition of plaque formation was unlikely because the degree of depression increased as the time the tolerogen was present in the culture was increased. The possibility that the results were due to transferred tolerogen was rendered still

TABLE 1

Specific Depression of the Anti-DNP PFC Response by DNP-D-GL or DNP_{11}-BGG[a]

	Immunogen		
Tolerogen	DNP-PAA (Anti-TNP PFC)	TNP-BRBC (Anti-TNP PFC)	SRBC (Anti-SRBC PFC)
None	1611 ± 342	220 ± 44	724 ± 95
DNP-D-GL	123 ± 83	85 ± 18	672 ± 151
None	1074 ± 372	200 ± 42	330 ± 54
DNP_{11}-BGG	276 ± 55	99 ± 16	457 ± 76

[a] Spleen cells were incubated with 10 μg/ml of DNP-D-GL or DNP_{11}-BGG and the optimal concentration of the indicated immunogen for four days. Data given are the mean of the direct PFC/culture after 96 hr in culture ± SD for four experiments. Target cells used in the PFC assay were SRBC or TNP-conjugated SRBC.

TABLE 2

Augmentation of the Anti-SRBC Response by DNP_{11}-BGG[a]

Number of spleen cells/ culture ($\times 10^6$)	Anti-SRBC PFC/10^6 viable cells	
	SRBC	SRBC + DNP_{11}-BGG
2.5	304 ± 100	820 ± 483
5	272 ± 9	462 ± 121
10	229 ± 18	289 ± 117

[a] The indicated number of spleen cells were incubated with SRBC alone or with SRBC and 10μg/ml DNP_{11}-BGG for 96 hr. Data given are the mean of the direct PFC/10^6 viable spleen cells after 96 hr in culture ±SD for four experiments. SRBC were used as target cells in the PFC assay.

more unlikely by the following experiment. Mixtures of cells cultured with tolerogen (DNP-D-GL or DNP-BGG) and cells cultured with immunogen (DNP-PAA) were assayed and found to give within 15% of the expected number of PFC (four experiments). Thus, the amount of tolerogen transferred with the cells into the plaque assay was insufficient to cause a significant inhibition of plaque formation.

Cellular Basis for the Depression of the Anti-DNP PFC Response by DNP-D-GL or DNP_{11}-BGG

The fact that DNP-D-GL or DNP-$_{11}$-BGG depresses the response to the T-independent antigen DNP-PAA suggests that at least one target of these tolerogens might be the B lymphocyte. It was, however, possible that suppressor T cells were involved in the induction of unresponsiveness. As expected, treatment of spleen cells with RAMB antiserum and complement markedly depressed the anti-SRBC PFC response but had no effect on the anti-DNP PFC response induced by the T-independent antigen DNP-PAA (Table 3). Treatment with RAMB antiserum and complement had no effect on the depression of the anti-DNP PFC response by DNP-D-GL or by DNP_{11}-BGG (Table 3). Thus, the depression of the immune response caused by DNP-D-GL or DNP_{11}-BGG does not require T lymphocytes for either its induction or expression.

It was of interest to determine if the suppressor cell activity was generated during culture with the immunogen DNP-PAA. Spleen cells were incubated for 4 days with DNP-PAA alone, with a mixture of DNP-PAA and DNP-D-GL, or without antigen. These cells were washed extensively to remove the antigens. These cells, which had been precultured with immunogen, a mixture of immunogen and tolerogen or nothing, were then mixed with fresh spleen cells and were cultured with DNP-PAA for 4 days. As shown in Table 4, addition of spleen cells which had been cultured in the absence of antigen or tolerogen caused a 50% depression in both the anti-DNP and the anti-SRBC responses. Addition of cells which had been cultured with DNP-PAA caused approximately a 75% depression of the anti-DNP response and a 50% depression of the anti-SRBC response. Addition of spleen cells which had been precultured with a mixture of DNP-PAA and DNP-D-GL also caused approximately a 70% depression in the anti-DNP response and a 50% depression in the anti-SRBC response. Thus, the results suggest that nonspecific suppressor

TABLE 3

Induction of Tolerance by DNP-D-GL or DNP_{11}-BGG in the Absence of T- Lymphocytes[a]

Treatment of spleen cells	Tolerogen	Immunogen: DNP-PAA (Anti-TNP PFC)	Immunogen: SRBC (Anti-SRBC PFC)
NRS	0	1674	645
RAMB	0	1803	185
NRS	DNP-D-GL	142	891
RAMB	DNP-D-GL	239	242
NRS	0	1282	677
RAMB	0	1636	232
NRS	DNP_{11}-BGG	178	1009
RAMB	DNP_{11}-BGG	302	303

[a] Spleen cells treated with NRS plus complement or with RAMB antiserum plus complement were incubated for 4 days with 10 μg of the indicated tolerogen per ml and with DNP-PAA or SRBC. Anti-SRBC or anti-TNP PFC were then assayed using SRBC or TNP-SRBC as target cells. The data given are the mean of the direct PFC/culture for four independent experiments with DNP-D-GL and two experiments with DNP-BGG.

activity appears during preculture of spleen cells in the absence of antigen. In contrast, in the presence of antigen, both nonspecific suppressor activity and antigen-specific suppressor activity are induced during preculture. The presence of the tolerogen DNP-D-GL does not prevent the induction of specific suppressor activity during the culture with DNP-PAA.

The cellular basis of the suppression induced during preculture of spleen cells was studied in mixed cell culture experiments in which precultured cells were added to fresh spleen cells and incubated with DNP-PAA. As shown in Table 5, both the antigen-specific suppression and the nonspecific suppression were completely eliminated by treating the precultured cells with a monoclonal anti-Thy 1.2 antibody

TABLE 4

Induction of Antigen-Specific and Antigen Nonspecific Suppressor Activity *in Vitro*

Precultures	Anti-TNP PFC/culture: Expt I	Expt II	Expt III	Anti-SRBC PFC/culture: Expt I	Expt II	Expt III
None	3259	1006	2160	440	372	620
Spleen cells	1540 (53)	411 (54)	1208 (44)	242 (45)	175 (53)	340 (45)
Spleen cells + DNP-PAA	460 (86)	299 (68)	280 (87)	229 (48)	206 (45)	320 (48)
Spleen cells + DNP-PAA + DNP-D-GL	131 (88)	97 (53)	285 (87)	206 (53)	193 (48)	335 (46)

[a] Spleen cells were precultured with 1 mg DNP-PAA or with 1 mg DNP-PAA and 10 μg DNP-D-GL for 4 days. The cells were then washed extensively, mixed with fresh syngeneic spleen cells, and cultured with 1 mg DNP-PAA or 10^7 SRBC for an additional 4 days. The cultures were then assayed for anti-DNP or anti-SRBC direct PFC. The results are expressed as PFC/culture present at the end of the culture period, with the percentage in parentheses.

TABLE 5

Cellular Basis of Suppressor Activity Generated during the Culture of Spleen Cells[a]

Cells added	Anti-Thy 1.2 + C treatment[b]	Anti-TNP PFC/culture
None	—	1501 ± 267
Cultured spleen cells	—	650 ± 160 (57)[c]
Cultured spleen cells	+	1437 + 166 (4)
Spleen cells cultured with DNP-PAA	—	335 ± 93 (78)
Spleen cells cultured with DNP-PAA	+	1389 ± 204 (7)

[a] 1×10^6 spleen cells which had been cultured alone or with DNP-PAA for 3 days were added to 7×10^6 fresh spleen cells and incubated with DNP-PAA for 4 additional days before assay of their anti-DNP PFC response.

[b] Where indicated, the cultured spleen cells were treated with anti-Thy 1.2 and complement before being added to the fresh spleen cells.

[c] Numbers in parentheses indicate the percentage of depression of the response of the fresh spleen cells.

and complement. Thus, the suppressor activities generated during spleen cell culture appear to reside in the T-cell population. The possibility that macrophages were involved in the suppression was investigated. Spleen cells, depleted by macrophages either by the use of carbonyl iron and a magnet or by passage through a Sephadex G-10 column, generated suppressor activity in a normal manner during preculture (Table 6). Furthermore, depleting precultured spleen cells of macrophages by use of carbonyl iron and a magnet did not eliminate the suppressor activity (Table 7).

TABLE 6

Generation of Suppressor Activity in Macrophage Depleted Spleen Cells[a]

Precultured cells added	Anti-TNP PFC/10^6		
	Expt. 1	Expt. 2	Expt. 3
None	798	1012	440
Spleen cells	295 (63)[b]	321 (68)	229 (48)
Spleen cells cultured with DNP-PAA	145 (82)	207 (80)	133 (70)
Macrophage-depleted spleen cells	308 (61)	426 (58)	222 (50)
Macrophage-depleted spleen cells cultured with DNP-PAA	156 (80)	300 (70)	176 (60)

[a] 1×10^6 macrophage depleted spleen cells by Sephadex G-10 column cultured for 3 days with or without DNP-PAA were added to 7×10^6 fresh spleen cells and incubated with DNP-PAA for 4 days before assay of their anti-DNP PFC response.

[b] Numbers in parentheses indicate the percentage of depression of the anti-DNP PFC response.

Thus, macrophages do not appear to be necessary for either the generation or expression of suppressor activity. However, preincubated spleen cells, depleted of adherent cells by passage through a Sephadex G-10 column, did not manifest suppressor activity (Table 6). Thus, the suppressor activity appears to reside in an adherent T-lymphocyte population.

DISCUSSION

The studies reported here show that the presence of DNP_{11}-BGG or DNP-D-GL in the cultures depresses the PFC response of spleen cells to both the T-dependent antigen TNP-BRBC and the T-independent antigen DNP-PAA. The inhibition is specific and the degree of inhibition depends upon the concentration of tolerogen. It is likely that the tolerant state is manifest in B cells as the response to a T-independent antigen is inhibited and the inhibition occurs in the absence of T cells. The mechanism of unresponsiveness does not appear to be that of "effector cell blockade" (7), since addition of tolerogen 1 day prior to assay (3 days after onset of culture) caused only minimum depression of the PFC response. That is, the degree of depression in the PFC response increases as the tolerogen is present for longer periods of time. In contrast, effector cell blockade is reported to occur essentially immediately upon mixing antibody-secreting cells with polyvalent antigens.

While the data in general are consistent with the view that the unresponsive state, which is observed when spleen cells are cultured with the polyvalent-soluble antigens DNP-D-GL and DNP-BGG, is primarily a B-cell tolerance; it was found that, as had been reported by previous workers (21, 22), preculture of spleen cells for 4 days, in the absence of antigen, led to the activation of nonspecific suppressor activity. This suppressor activity effected both T-dependent and T-independent immune responses *in vitro*. Of particular interest was the finding reported here that culture of spleen cells in the presence of antigen (either DNP-PAA or a mixture of DNP-PAA and DNP-D-GL) led to the appearance of antigen-specific suppressor activity, in addition to the nonspecific suppressor activity observed after preculture

TABLE 7

Effect of Removing Macrophages on the Generation of Suppressor Activity during the Culture of Spleen Cells[a]

Cells added	Treatment after preculture[b]	Anti-TNP PFC/culture
None	—	1909 ± 832
Cultured spleen cells	—	824 ± 214 (57)[c]
Cultured spleen cells	Carbonyl iron	534 ± 417 (72)
Cultured spleen cells	Sephadex G-10	1754 ± 626 (8)

[a] 1×10^6 spleen cells cultured for 3 days were added to 7×10^6 fresh spleen cells and incubated with DNP-PAA for 4 days before assay of their anti-DNP PFC response.

[b] Where indicated, cultured spleen cells were depleted of phagocytic cells by treatment with carbonyl iron and a magnet or were depleted of adherent cells by passage over Sephadex G-10 prior to their being added to fresh spleen cells.

[c] Numbers in parentheses indicate percentage of depression of the response of the fresh spleen cells.

in the absence of antigen. The specific suppressor activity was shown to reside in an adherent T-cell population and did not require the presence of macrophages for its induction. It is interesting that the appearance of the specific suppressor activity was not inhibited by the presence of the "obligate" tolerogen DNP-D-GL in the culture medium. Recent work by a number of laboratories has detected the appearance of suppressive activity, presumably having a regulatory role, during the normal immune response *in vivo*, e.g., the appearance of idiotype-specific antibody (23, 24) and specific suppressor cell activity (25).

The nonspecific augmentation of the SRBC response as a consequence of the presence of DNP_{11}-BGG in the cultures is a curious finding. The augmentation is consistent, spleen cell concentration dependent, and, under optimal conditions, of marked degree. The mechanism of this augmentation has not been determined.

REFERENCES

1. Diener, E., and Feldman, M., *Transplant. Rev.* **8,** 76, 1972.
2. Feldmann, M., *J. Exp. Med.* **135,** 735, 1972.
3. Schrader, J. W., *J. Exp. Med.* **139,** 1303, 1974.
4. Sercarz, E., and Coons, A. H., *J. Immunol.* **90,** 478, 1963.
5. Thorbecke, G. J., Siskind, G. W., and Goldberger, N., *J. Immunol.* **87,** 174, 1961.
6. Nossal, G. J. V., and Pike, B. L., *J. Exp. Med.* **141,** 904, 1975.
7. Schrader, J. W., and Nossal, G. J. V., *J. Exp. Med.* **139,** 1582, 1974.
8. Katz, D. H., Hamaoka, T., and Benacerraf, B., *J. Exp. Med.* **139,** 1404, 1972.
9. Hamaoka, T., and Katz, D. H., *J. Exp. Med.* **139,** 1404, 1974.
10. Nossal, G. J. V., Pike, B. L., and Katz, D. H., *J. Exp. Med.* **138,** 312, 1973.
11. Katz, D. H., Hamaoka, T., and Benacerraf, B., *J. Exp. Med.* **139,** 1464, 1974.
12. Kim, Y. T., Mager, T., Weksler, M. E., and Siskind, G. W., *J. Immunol.* **121,** 1315, 1978.
13. Hamaoka, T., and Katz, D. H., *J. Exp. Med.* **139,** 1446, 1974.
14. Liu, F., and Katz, D. H., *Proc. Nat. Acad. Sci. USA* **76,** 1430, 1979.
15. Inman, J. K., and Dintzis, H. M., *Biochemistry.* **8,** 4074, 1969.
16. Eisen, H. N., Belman, S., and Caster, M. E., *J. Amer. Chem. Soc.* **75,** 4583, 1953.
17. Rittenberg, M. B., and Pratt, K. L., *Proc. Soc. Exp. Biol. Med.* **132,** 575, 1969.
18. Golub, E. S., *Cell. Immunol.* **2,** 353, 1971.
19. Dresser, D. W., and Greaves, M. R., *In* Handbook of Experimental Immunology" (D. M. Weir, Ed.), p. 271. Blackwell Scientific, Oxford, 1973.
20. Jerne, N. K., Nordin, A. A., and Henry, C., *In* "Cell-Bound Antibody" B. Amos and H. Kaprowski, Eds.), p. 109 Wistar Institute Press, Philadelphia, 1963.
21. Hodes, R. J., and Hathcock, K. S., *J. Immunol.* **116,** 167, 1976.
22. Kedar, E., and Schwartzbach, M., *Cell. Immunol.* **43,** 326, 1979.
23. Goidl, E. A., Schrater, A. F., Siskind, G. W., and Thorbecke, G. J., *J. Exp. Med.* **150,** 154, 1979.
24. Kim, B. S., *J. Exp. Med.* **149,** 1371, 1979.
25. DeKruyff, R. H., Simonson, B. G., and Siskind, G. W., *J. Immunol.* **125,** 142, 1980.

CELLULAR IMMUNOLOGY **64**, 53–63 (1981)

Expression of Subregion and Haplotype Preference for H-2K^k Restricted Cytotoxic T-Cell Responses *in Vivo* and at the Level of the Precursor Frequencies

WULF DRÖGE, MATTHIAS REDDEHASE, AND MICHAEL WOLF

Institut für Immunologie und Genetik, Deutsches Krebsforschungszentrum, D-69 Heidelberg, Federal Republic of Germany

Received May 5, 1981; accepted June 9, 1981

Several strains of mice bearing the H-2K^k allele were found to generate *in vivo* strong CTL responses against TNP-haptenated syngeneic cells, while several other strains of mice were found to generate comparably weak or no responses. (C3H × DBA/2)F1 mice (H-2^k × H-2^d) and A/J mice with the recombinant haplotype H-2$^{k/d}$ generated CTL responses *in vivo* that were completely restricted toward the H-2^k haplotype or the K end of the H-2$^{k/d}$ haplotype, respectively. The CTL activity of (C3H × DBA/2)F1 and A/J mice against haptenated H-2^k targets was found to be more than 25-fold higher than the CTL activity on H-2^d targets. The CTL responses *in vitro* under macroculture conditions showed, on the other hand, only a 3- to 6-fold higher cytotoxic activity against the haptenated H-2^k targets as compared with haptenated allogeneic or H-2^d targets; and limiting dilution experiments in microcultures revealed that the CTL precursor frequencies were only 2- to 3-fold smaller for TNP-haptenated H-2^d or haptenated allogeneic targets than for haptenated H-2^k target cells. This indicated that sufficient numbers of H-2^d-restricted and allorestricted CTL precursors were actually present in these strains, but did not develop detectable cytotoxic activity *in vivo*. The exceptional property of the H-2^k haplotype is, therefore, only partly determined by a difference in the CTL precursor frequencies, and to the larger extent determined at the level of the activation of the CTL response.

INTRODUCTION

It is well established that certain genes in the major histocompatibility gene compelx (MHC)[1] regulate immune responses (1–3). These immune response genes (Ir-genes) usually determine a low responsiveness against one or a few antigens. An MHC-linked immune regulation of a different type seems to be responsible for several properties of the self-restricted cytotoxic T-lymphocyte (CTL) responses of H-2K^k-bearing mice, since the exceptional immune response pattern of these mice is observed with several apparently unrelated antigens such as haptenic, viral, and male-specific determinants (4–14). The H-2K^k allele was found to determine an exceptionally high degree of self-restriction (4) and a remarkably high restriction to products of the H-2K^k allele as compared to the corresponding D subregion (subregion preference) or to products of the other halotype in heterozygous animals

[1] Abbreviations used: CTL, cytotoxic T lymphocyte(s); CSCS, supernatant from concanavalin A-activated spleen cells; TNP, trinitrophenyl; MHC, major histocompatibility complex.

0008-8749/81/150053-11$02.00/0

(haplotype preference) (5–10). The analysis of the CTL responses against TNP-haptenated cells revealed, moreover, that mice with the H-$2K^k$ allele were able to respond against TNP-haptenated cells with a hapten density lower than that of other strains of mice (15).

The present experiments were designed to analyze the expression of the H-$2K^k$-controlled subregion and haplotype preference *in vivo* and at the level of the CTL precursor frequencies. They revealed clear-cut but surprisingly small differences between the CTL precursor frequencies with restriction for the different subregions or haplotypes under test; and they indicated that this phenomenon is expressed at least in part at the level of the activation of the CTL.

MATERIALS AND METHODS

Animals. The SJL mice were obtained from the Jackson Laboratories, Bar Harbor, Maine. The B10 congenic mouse strains B10.BR(H-2^k), B10.D2(H-2^d), B10.A(H-$2^{k/d}$), and B10.M(H-2^f) were maintained at the German Cancer Research Center and were originally derived from the Jackson Laboratories. The C3H and DBA/2 mice were obtained from Gl. Bomholtgaard, Ry, Denmark. The responder mice were usually 2 to 3 months old.

Treatment with cyclophosphamide. Cyclophosphamide (Endoxan) was obtained from ASTA, Brackwede, Germany and applied at a single dose of 3 mg per mouse 2 days before immunization.

Irradiation. Stimulator cells were irradiated with 1500 rad if not indicated otherwise using a ^{60}Co source.

Induction and assay of cytotoxic T lymphocytes. Our procedures for the induction of CTL in microcultures and macrocultures (16) and *in vivo* (17) have previously been described in detail. In brief, the *in vivo* cytotoxic responses were obtained by skin painting with trinitrochlorobenzene (usually 2×10 μl 30% in acetone on two separate spots on the abdominal skin) 2 days after treatment with cyclophosphamide. The cytotoxic activity of the pooled inguinal and axillary lymph node cells and of spleen cells were usually tested 5 days after the immunization at the attacker: target cell ratios 25:1, 5:1, and 1:1, if not indicated otherwise.

Macrocultures contained usually 1×10^7 responder cells and 1×10^7 irradiated TNP-haptenated stimulator cells in 4.5 ml culture medium and were also tested after 5 days at the attacker: target cell ratios 25:1, 5:1, and 1:1. The microcultures contained the indicated numbers of responder cells together with 3×10^5 irradiated (1500 rad) TNP-haptenated stimulator cells in the presence or absence of additional 3×10^5 irradiated (1500 rad) SJL cells and/or 0.08 ml concanavalin A-activated spleen cell supernatant (CSCS) in 8–36 parallel microcultures of 0.2 ml, for 5 days, if not indicated otherwise. These were basically the procedures of Shearer (18) and Teh *et al.* (19), respectively, with modifications. The data from cytotoxic assays were indicated as specific ^{51}Cr release or as cytotoxic activities (Nat) which were computed according to the equation:

$$\text{Nat} = -\log_e\left(1 - \frac{P}{100}\right),$$

where P = Percentage specific ^{51}Cr release. The CTL-precursor frequencies were determined from the proportion of nonresponding microcultures with a computer

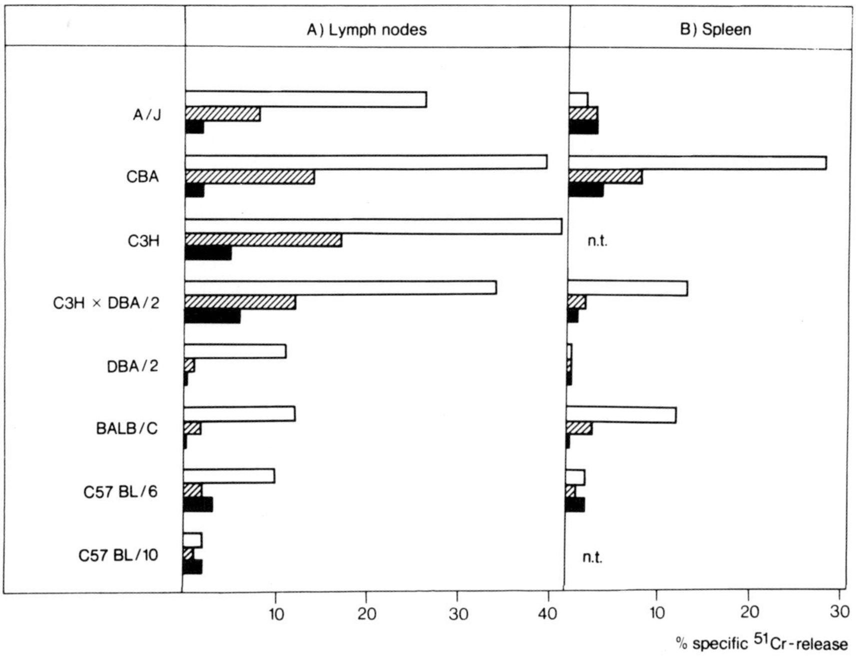

FIG. 1. Cytotoxic responses against syngeneic TNP-haptenated cells *in vivo* in different strains of mice. Mice of the indicated strains were treated with cyclophosphamide, immunized, and tested for CTL activity on TNP-haptenated syngeneic target cells as described under Materials and Methods. The data indicate the percentage specific ^{51}Cr release at the attacker:target cell ratios 25:1, □; 5:1, ▨; and 1:1, ■.

program kindly provided by Dr. R. G. Miller, or estimated from the semilogarithmic plots (Fig. 5) by the number of responder cells that showed 37% nonresponding cultures. It was previously established (20) that CSCS preparations usually provide satisfactory help for allogeneic and not MHC-compatible microculture systems, but synergize in the latter case with additional irradiated allogeneic cells. The present experiments were, therefore, either performed with a CSCS preparation that was selected to mediate equally strong CTL responses in the presence or absence of irradiated SJL cells (Figs. 5 and Table I, Expt I), or with unselected CSCS preparations in the presence of SJL cells (Table I, Expts II–V).

RESULTS

Restriction Pattern of the CTL Responses of (C3H × DBA/2)F$_1$ and AJ Mice against TNP haptenated Cells in Vivo and in Vitro

Some strains of mice all of which bear the K end of the H-2^k haplotype were found to produce strong CTL responses against TNP-haptenated syngeneic cells after treatment with cyclophosphamide and subsequent skinpainting with trinitrochlorobenzene 2 days later (Fig. 1). The analysis of the CTL response of (C3H × DBA/2)F$_1$ mice (H-2^k × H-2^d) *in vivo* revealed that this response was completely self-restricted with strong cytotoxic activity on TNP-haptenated C3D2F1 cells and no activity on the haptenated allogeneic C57BL/6 cells (Fig. 2). However, this cytotoxic response was completely restricted to the H-2^k haplotype with practically

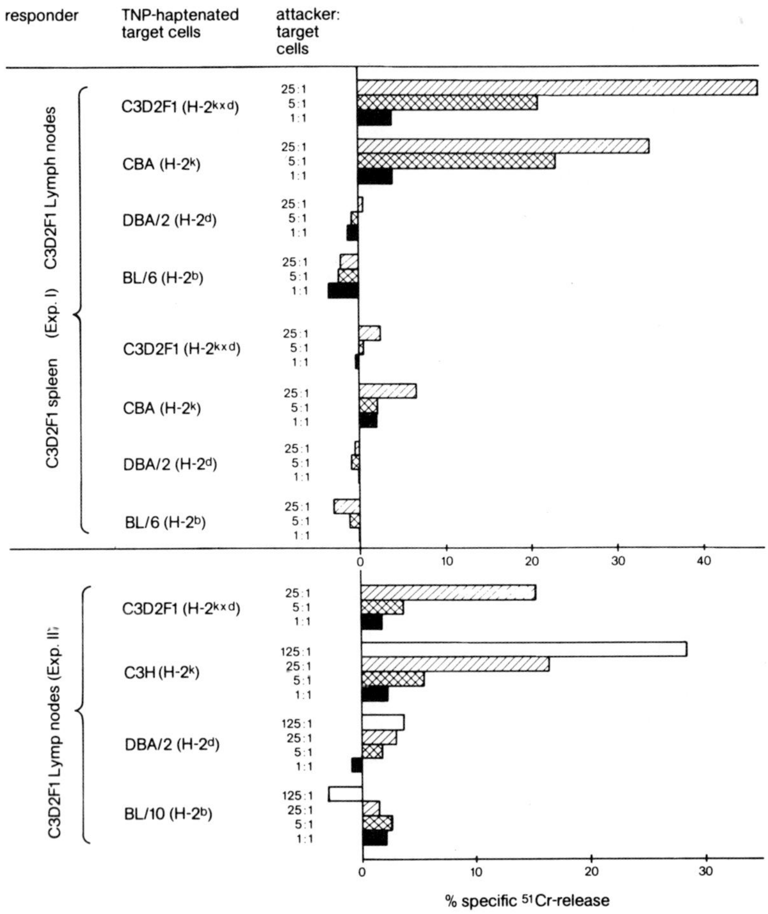

FIG. 2. Restriction pattern of the cytotoxic responses of C3H × DBA/2 F_1 mice *in vivo.* The mice in Experiment I have been treated with 2.4 mg cyclophosphamide, immunized 2 days later with 2 × 0.01 ml 30% TNCB in acetone on the abdominal skin, and tested for cytotoxic activity in spleen and lymph nodes 4 days after immunization. The mice in Experiment II received 3 mg cyclophosphamide, 6 × 0.01 ml 15% TNCB in acetone on the abdominal skin and on the four footpads, and were tested for cytotoxic activity in the lymph nodes 5 days later. Their lymphoid cells were tested on the indicated TNP-haptenated target cells and at the indicated attacker:target cell ratios.

no activity on haptenated DBA/2 cells. The comparison of the cytotoxic activities at different attacker:target cell ratios (125:1, 25:1, 5:1, and 1:1) indicated that the H-2^k-restricted response was more than 25-fold higher than the H-2^d-restricted response (Fig. 2). A series of experiments with slightly varying immunization protocols revealed that the cytotoxic activities of C3D2F1 lymph node cells against haptenated DBA/2 (H-2^d), B10.D2 (H-2^d) (data not shown) or against the allogeneic C57BL/6 or C57BL/10 (H-2^b) target cells were never clearly above background levels even if tested at the attacker:target cell ratio of 125:1. In contrast, significant levels of cytotoxicity against the haptenated H-2^k targets of the strains CBA, C3H, or B10.BR (data not shown) were usually obtained with attacker:target cell ratios of 5:1. The spleen cells showed relatively low cytotoxic activities even against H-2^k targets (Fig. 2).

The results of the *in vivo* immunization of A/J mice or B10.A mice with the recombinant haplotype H-$2^{k/d}$ were similar (Fig. 3). There was practically no activity on haptenated H-$2D^d$-bearing target cells or haptenated C57BL/10 (H-2^b) targets (Fig. 3) even if tested at the attacker:target cell ratio of 125:1. Cytotoxic activity against haptenated H-2^k-bearing targets (A/J or C3H) was, on the other hand, already demonstrable at an attacker: target cell ratios of 5:1, i.e., again at least 25-fold higher than the activity on H-2^d targets. The cytotoxic response was in this case presumably restricted to the K^k subregion of the H-2 complex with no activity toward products of the H-$2D^d$ subregion. A similar restriction pattern was also observed when A/J mice were tested on haptenated B10.BR (H-2^k) and B10.D2 (H-2^d) targets (data not shown).

Mice with B10 background were found to produce relatively weak cytotoxic responses against TNP-haptenated cells *in vivo* even if they bear the K end of the

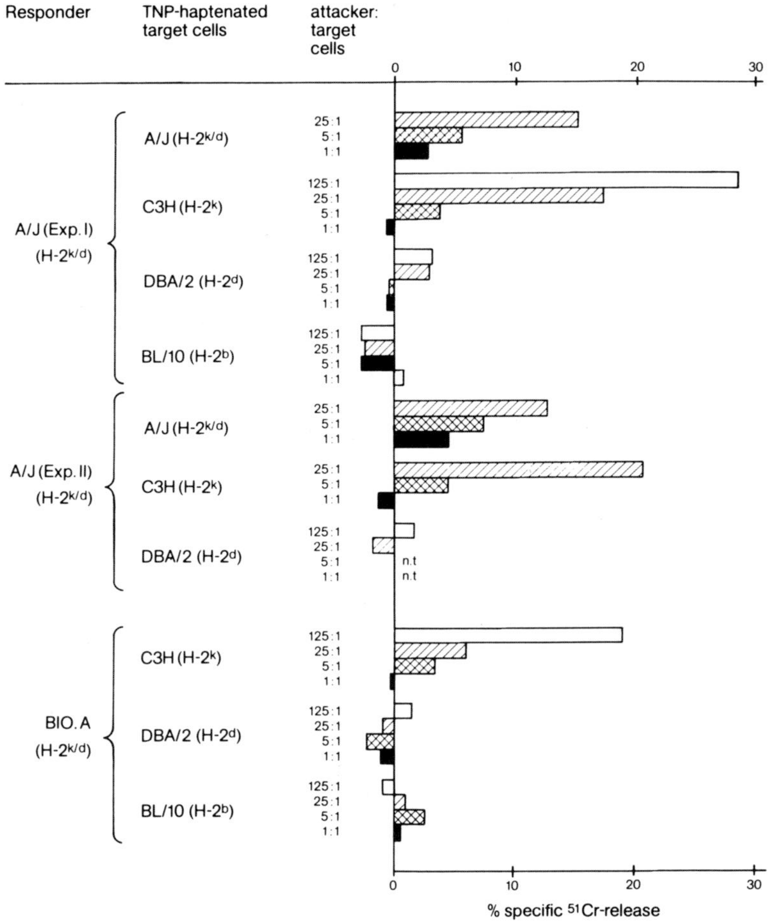

FIG. 3. Restriction pattern of the cytotoxic responses of A/J and B10.A mice *in vivo*. The B10.A mice have been treated with 2.4 mg, the A/J mice with 2.4 mg (Expt. I) or 3 mg (Expt II) of cyclophosphamide. All mice were immunized 2 days later with 6 × 0.01 ml 15% TNCB in acetone on the abdominal skin and on the four footpads; and their lymph nodes were tested for cytotoxic activity 5 days (A/J) or 4 days (B10.A) after immunization on the indicated TNP-haptenated target cells.

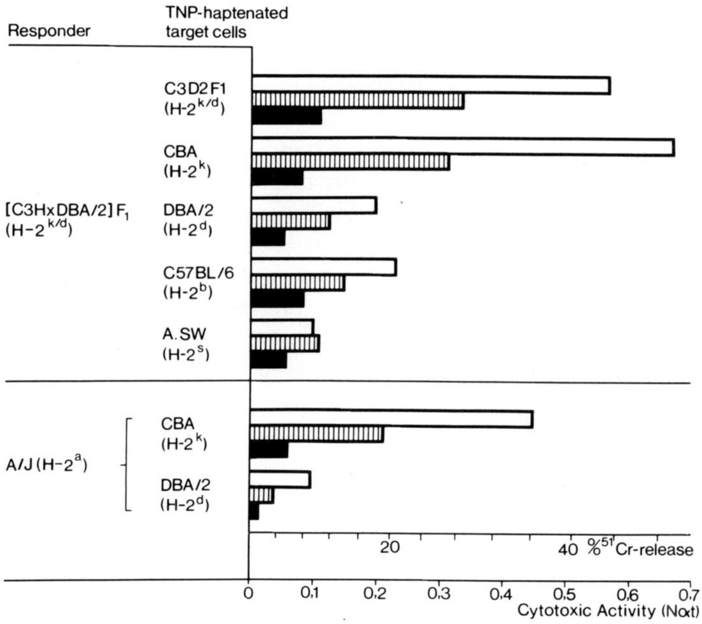

FIG. 4. Restriction pattern of the cytotoxic responses *in vitro* of (C3H × DBA/2)F_1 and A/J responder cells. Responder cells (1×10^7) were activated against TNP-haptenated syngeneic stimulator cells in macrocultures (see Materials and Method) and tested on TNP-haptenated target cells of the indicated strains at the attacker:target cell ratio 25:1, □; 5:1, ▥; and 1:1, ■.

H-2^k haplotype (P. Müller and W. Dröge, unpublished observation). The response of the B10.A mice (Fig. 3) was, therefore, weak in comparison to the A/J response; but it was again completely restricted to the H-2^k haplotype with practically no activity on the haptenated H-2^d or H-2^b target cells.

The cytotoxic responses in macrocultures *in vitro* showed also a preferential restriction for the H-2^k haplotype or H-$2K^k$ subregion; but this restriction was much less complete (Fig. 4, see also (8)). The cytotoxic activity of (C3H × DBA/2)F1 and A/J responder cells against haptenated H-2^k targets was only about three to six times higher than the cytotoxic responses on haptenated H-2^d targets (Fig. 4).

Microculture and Limiting Dilution Analysis of CTL Responses of (C3H × DBA/2)F1 and A/J Responder Cells against TNP-Haptenated Cells

The limiting dilution experiments with (C3H × DBA/2)F1 and A/J responder cells revealed in comparison to the *in vivo* experiments remarkably high CTL precursor frequencies for the haptenated H-2^d target cells and even for TNP-haptenated allogeneic targets (Fig. 5 and Table 1). The CTL precursor frequencies for the TNP-haptenated H-2^k target cells were in all experiments clearly higher but not more than three times higher than the frequencies for the H-2^d target cells. This ratio was relatively consistent in the various experiments despite the variation in the absolute precursor frequency values in different experiments and with different batches of mice (Table 1). Similar results were obtained with H-2^k and H-

2[d] target cells of different non-H-2 background, i.e., with C3H and DBA/2 targets (Expts I and II), B10.BR and B10.D2 targets (Expts III and V), and CBA versus DBA/2 targets (Expt IV). The helper component in these limiting dilution experiments was either a combination of conventional CSCS and irradiated allogeneic cells (Table 1, Expts II–V), which was previously shown to mediate optimal cytotoxic responses against MHC-compatible target cells (20), or a CSCS preparation that was selected for its ability to mediate equally strong cytotoxic responses against MHC-compatible target cells in the absence or presence of irradiated allogeneic cells (Table 1, Expt I, see also Fig. 1). The two types of helper components revealed similar results.

The treatment with cyclophosphamide (3 mg per mouse) reduces the number of nucleated cells in the peripheral lymphoid organs usually by a factor of 3–4; i.e., the cell yield from the pooled axillary and inguinal lymph nodes in Experiment I (Table 1) was 1.5×10^7 per untreated mouse and 6×10^6 per cyclophosphamide-treated mouse. On top of this, there was a roughly twofold reduction in the relative frequencies of the CTL precursor cells in the cyclophosphamide treated mice, implying a total reduction by a factor of 6–8. Nevertheless, the ratios of the CTL precursor frequencies and cytotoxic activities against the haptenated H-2^k versus H-2^d targets were not detectably affected by this drug (see Table 1); and there was clearly a substantial number of CTL precursor cells (i.e., 83 per 10^6 cells) in the cyclophosphamide-treated C3D2F1 mice, that were able to generate cytotoxic

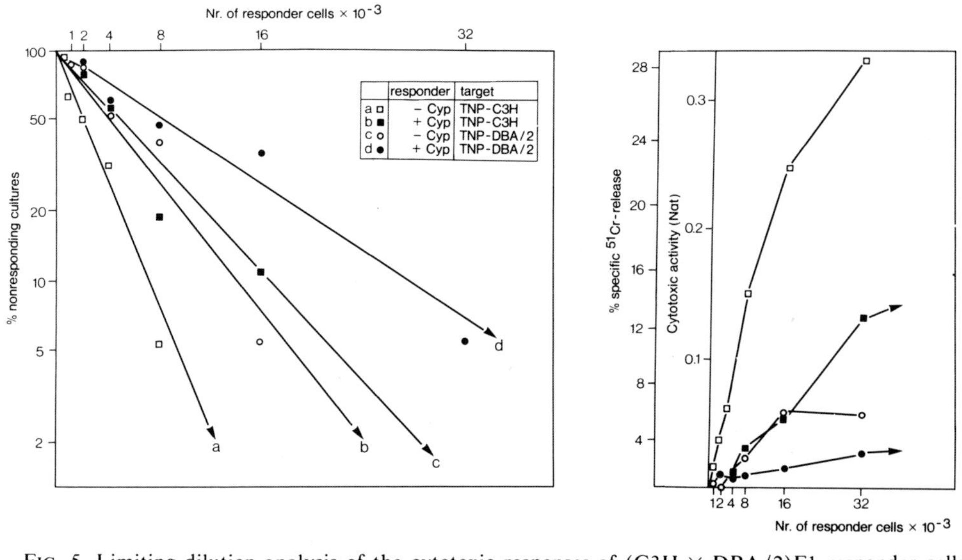

FIG. 5. Limiting dilution analysis of the cytotoxic responses of (C3H × DBA/2)F1 responder cells against TNP-haptenated cells. The indicated numbers of lymph node cells from cyclophosphamide-treated (■, ●) or untreated (□, ○) C3D2F1 mice were incubated in microcultures together with 3×10^5 TNP-haptenated irradiated (1500 rad) syngeneic cells and 0.06 ml of a CSCS preparation that was selected to mediate equally strong responses against TNP-haptenated stimulator cells in the presence or absence of additional irradiated allogeneic cells (see Materials and Methods). The cultures were then tested on TNP-C3H (□, ■) or TNP-DBA/2 (○, ●) target cells. Thirty-six parallel microcultures were tested for each point, i.e., for each target cell and each responder cell concentration. The resulting proportion of nonresponding cultures (left) and cytotoxic activities (right) are illustrated in the figures. The calculated CTL precursor frequencies from this experiment are given in Table 1, Experiment I.

TABLE 1

Expression of Haplotype and Subregion Preference *in Vitro* under Limiting Dilution Conditions

Expt	Responder	Target cell	Minimum estimate of CTL precursor frequencies (× 10^6)		Cytotoxic activity (Nat) normalized to 10^6 responder cells	
Ia	C3D2 (−CyP)	TNP-C3D2	570		12.7	
		TNP-C3H	311	Ratio 2.3	16.9	Ratio 5.5
		TNP-DBA/2	136		3.1	
		TNP-B10.M	74		3.7	
Ib	C3D2 (+CyP)	TNP-C3D2	184		2.4	
		TNP-C3H	163	Ratio 2.0	3.7	Ratio 3.6
		TNP-DBA/2	83		1.0	
II	C3D2 (−CyP)	TNP-C3D2	771		40.5	
		TNP-C3H	583	Ratio 2.9	61.7	Ratio 5.3
		TNP-DBA/2	198		11.7	
		TNP-B10.M	328		15.4	
		TNP-B1/6	174		12.8	
III	C3D2 (−CyP)	TNP-B10.BR	1300	Ratio 2.8	118	Ratio 6.2
		TNP-B10.D2	460		19	
IV	A/J (−CyP)	TNP-A/J	90		17.3	
		TNP-CBA	101	Ratio 1.7	13.5	Ratio 2.3
		TNP-DBA/2	61		5.8	
		TNP-B10.M	30		2.4	
V	A/J (−CyP)	TNP-A/J	507		47.3	
		TNP-B10.BR	701	Ratio 3.3	68.4	Ratio 2.4
		TNP-B10.D2	210		28.9	
		TNP-C57B1/6	90		8.8	

Note. Graded numbers of lymph node cells from cyclophosphamide-treated (+CyP) or untreated (−CyP) mice of the indicated responder strain were incubated in 0.2-ml microcultures together with 3 × 10^5 TNP-haptenated 1500-rad-irradiated syngeneic cells and 0.06 ml of a selected CSCS preparation (Expt I, see Fig. 5) or 0.08 ml of an unselected CSCS preparation plus 3 × 10^5 irradiated (1500 rad) SJL spleen cells (Expts II–V, see Materials and Methods). The cultures were then tested on the indicated target cells. The data are based on 36 parallel microcultures (Expts Ia and b), 22 parallel microcultures (Expts II, III, and V) or 8 parallel cultures (Expt IV). The indicated precursor frequencies were calculated from the proportion of nonresponding cultures with a computer program kindly provided by Dr. R. G. Miller. The basic mathematical procedure has been described previously (19). The cytotoxic activities (Nat) were calculated as described by Teh *et al.* (19), and divided by the number of responder cells. The cytotoxic data indicate the mean of these normalized cytotoxic activities. This calculation included only the cytotoxic data from the initial linear portions of the cytotoxic profiles (see Fig. 5) and indicates the slope of this linear function.

activity against TNP-haptenated H-2^d targets after appropriate activation (Fig. 5 and Table 1). The failure of these mice to generate cytotoxic activity against these targets *in vivo* was therefore not explained by a lack of potentially reactive CTL precursor cells but rather by inefficient activation of these cells.

The cytotoxic activities that were generated by the A/J responder cells under these microculture conditions corresponded essentially to the CTL precursor frequencies (Table 1). Responder cells from (C3H × DBA/2)F1 mice, on the other hand, showed a small but consistent discrepancy between the ratios of H-2^k versus

H-2^d restricted CTL precursor frequencies (average ratio, 2.5) and the ratios of the corresponding cytotoxic activities (average ratio 5.2) (see Table 1). These data implied that the TNP-H-2^d reactive CTL precursor cells of the C3D2F1 mice generated less cytotoxic activity per precursor than the TNP-H-2^k-reactive CTL precursor cells.

DISCUSSION

Our experiments on the CTL responses of mice against TNP-haptenated syngeneic cells *in vivo* revealed that strong cytotoxic activities were generated by a group of strains, all of which bear the K end of the H-2^k haplotype. Moreover, the activity was completely restricted toward the H-2^k haplotype if tested in (C3H × DBA/2)F1 mice (H-2^k × H-2^d), or toward the H-2K^k subregion when tested in A/J mice with the recombinant haplotype H-2$^{k/d}$. These latter observations thus demonstrated the expression of a haplotype and subregion preference in the MHC-restricted TNP-specific CTL responses *in vivo*, similar to the phenomenon that has previously been demonstrated and analyzed by Shearer *et al.* (6–8) under macroculture conditions *in vitro*. Shearer *et al.* speculated that the H-2^k allele might suppress responses with a restriction toward other H-2 subregions or haplotypes in the same animal. Our results are also basically in line with the finding of Billings *et al.* (4) that mice with the H-2K^k allele generate CTL responses against TNP-haptenated syngeneic stimulator cells with a high degree of self-H-2 restriction. These authors defined a corresponding immune response gene, Ir-X-TNP, and reported that the restrictive behavior is recessive in F1 hybrids (4), while the experiments of Shearer (8) and those herein (Figs. 2 and 4) revealed a high degree of self-restriction also present in F1 hybrids. The reason for this discrepancy is not known.

The major point of the present paper is that the haplotype and subregion preference was found to be more complete under the *in vivo* conditions than under *in vitro* conditions using densely coupled stimulator and target cells. The *in vivo* results corresponded better to the *in vitro* results with lightly coupled stimulator cells or with TNP-haptenated non-H-2 proteins on syngeneic stimulator cells (15). The *in vivo* response of (C3H × DBA/2)F1 and AJ mice against haptenated H-2^k targets was at least 25-fold higher than the activity against haptenated H-2^d targets, i.e., there was practically a complete unresponsiveness toward haptenated H-2^d targets (Figs. 2 and 3). This phenomenon was observed with target cells of different non-H-2 genetic background including B10.BR and B10.D2 target cells (data not shown).

The *in vitro* responses in macrocultures generated, on the other hand, only three- to sixfold higher lytic activity against haptenated H-2^k targets compared with H-2^d or allogeneic targets as judged from the cytotoxic activities and the number of cells needed to yield a given activity (Fig. 4). This is consistent with the substantial H-2^d-restricted cytotoxic activity that was observed in macroculture experiments by Shearer and colleagues (8). Our limiting dilution experiments revealed that these *in vitro* results reflect essentially the respective CTL precursor frequencies: There are remarkably high numbers of CTL precursor cells with a potential capability to generate cytotoxic activity against haptenated H-2^d targets; and yet the CTL precursor frequencies were consistently two- to threefold higher when tested on haptenated H-2^k targets compared to H-2^d targets or haptenated H-2-incompatible targets.

Previous studies by Burakoff *et al.* (21, 22) and Teh *et al.* (23) on the CTL responses against TNP-haptenated syngeneic cells in several strains of mice have shown that the cytotoxic activity on TNP-haptenated allogeneic target cells results from a heteroclitic cross-stimulation of allorestricted CTL which recognize the TNP determinant preferentially in association with individual foreign haplotypes. This heteroclitic cross-stimulatiion is expected to activate only a small proportion of the allorestricted CTL precursor cells. We therefore interpret our results to mean that the H-$2K^k$-bearing mice contain a very large number of TNP-specific CTL precursor cells with a restriction to foreign haplotypes and also a large number with restriction to other haplotypes or subregions of the same animal, but that the activation of the H-$2K^k$-restricted CTL is strongly favored under our conditions of immunization *in vivo*.

The question remains why the cytotoxic activity against haptenated H-2^d and haptenated allogeneic targets is efficiently activated *in vitro* especially in our microculture systems and on the other hand so inefficiently activated *in vivo*. Our experiments excluded the possibility that CTL precursor cells with potential reactivity towards haptenated H-2^d or allogeneic target cells are more sensitive than H-2^k-restricted precursor cells against the effects of cyclophosphamide and therefore not detectable *in vivo*. Our experiments showed that TNP-specific H-2^k- and H-2^d-restricted precursors are both reduced about twofold with respect to relative frequencies and about six- to eightfold in absolute numbers by these high doses of cyclophosphamide. It is, therefore, concluded that H-2^k-restricted CTL precursor cells are not exceptionally resistent against cyclophosphamide, but either less affected by suppression or more efficiently activated than H-2^d or allorestricted CTL precursor cells under the *in vivo* conditions. It was previously shown, that H-$2K^k$-restricted TNP-specific CTL precursor cells are activated by lower antigen concentrations and by stimulator cells with lower hapten density as compared to other TNP-specific CTL precursor cells (15); and activated H-2^k-restricted CTL are able to kill targets with relatively low hapten density, while CTL restricted to other haplotypes kill only target cells with relatively high hapten density (15). Moreover, H-2^k-restricted T-cell populations can recognize TNP-haptenated non-H-2 proteins on appropriate stimulator (15) or target cells (24), while T-cell populations restricted to other H-2 haplotypes recognize chemically (trinitrobenzenesulfonate) modified syngeneic stimulator and target cells but not TNP-haptenated non-H-2 proteins on syngeneic stimulator or target cells. This suggests that the exclusively H-$2K^k$-restricted *in vivo* responses in our experiments reflect a relative low concentration of antigen and/or a low hapten density on the stimulating cells in these animals. There is also the possibility that the H-2^k-restricted T-cell population contains cells which recognize TNP-haptenated non-H-2 proteins in complex with H-2^k determinants in a dual-recognition fashion, while the H-2^d-restricted T-cell population may recognize only chemically altered H-2^d determinants.

Our experiments with (C3H $\times$ DBA/2)F1 mice revealed that the H-2^k-restricted CTL precursor cells generated slightly but consistently more cytotoxic activity per precursor than the H-2^d-restricted precursor cells (Table 1). This phenomenon, however, did not apply to the A/J mice and may, therefore, result from the fact that the density of H-2K^k and H-2D^d determinants is higher on the homozygous A/J stimulator cells than on the heterozygous (C3H × DBA/2)F1 cells.

ACKNOWLEDGMENTS

The expert technical assistance of Mr. N. Franze, Mr. W. Dotterer, Mrs. C. Roesel, Mrs. W. Seyfert, and Mrs. S. Panknin is gratefully acknowledged. We also thank Dr. R. G. Miller for helpful discussions and for providing the computer program for the mathematical evaluation of the microculture assays and limiting dilution experiments.

REFERENCES

1. McDevitt, H. O., Deak, B. D., Shreffler, D. C., Klein, J., Stimpfling, J. H., and Snell, G. D., *J. Exp. Med.* **135,** 1259, 1972.
2. Benaceraff, B., and McDevitt, H. O., *Science* **175,** 273, 1972.
3. Benaceraff, B., and Germain, R. N., *Immunol. Rev.* **38,** 70, 1978.
4. Billings, P., Burakoff, S. J., Dorf, M. E., and Benaceraff, B., *J. Exp. Med.* **148,** 341, 1978.
5. Shearer, G. M., Rehn, T. G., and Garbarino, C. A., *J. Exp. Med.* **141,** 1348, 1975.
6. Schmitt-Verhulst, A.-M., and Shearer, G. M., *J. Exp. Med.* **142,** 914, 1975.
7. Schmitt-Verhulst, A.-M., and Shearer, G. M., *J. Exp. Med.* **144,** 1701, 1976.
8. Levy, R. B., and Shearer, G. M., *J. Exp. Med.* **149,** 1379, 1979.
9. Gordon, R. D., Samelson, L. E., and Simpson, E., *J. Exp. Med.* **146,** 606, 1977.
10. Haas, W., Pohlit, H., and v. Boehmer, H., *Eur. J. Immunol.* **9,** 868, 1979.
11. Zinkernagel, R. M., Althage, A., Cooper, S., Kreeb, G., Klein, C. A., Sefton, B., Flaherty, L., Stimpfling, J., Shreffler, D., and Klein, J., *J. Exp. Med.* **148,** 592, 1978.
12. Zinkernagel, R. M., Althage, A., Cooper, S., Callahan, G., and Klein, J., *J. Exp. Med.* **148,** 805, 1978.
13. Doherty, P. C., Biddison, W. E., Bennink, J. R., and Knowles, B. B., *J. Exp. Med.* **148,** 534, 1978.
14. Pfizenmaier, K., Trinschieri, G., Solter, D., and Knowles, B. B., *Nature (London)* **274,** 691, 1978.
15. Shearer, G. M., Schmitt-Verhulst, A.-M., Pettinelli, C. B., Miller, M. W., and Gilheany, P. E., *J. Exp. Med.* **149,** 1407, 1979.
16. Galli, P., and Dröge, W., *Eur. J. Immunol.* **10,** 87, 1980.
17. Dröge, W., Suessmuth, W., Franze, R., Mueller, P., Franze, N., Balcarova, J., *In* "Cell Biology and Immunology of Leukocyte Function" (M. Quastel, Ed.), p. 467. Academic Press, New York, 1979.
18. Shearer, G. M., *Eur. J. Immunol.* **4,** 527, 1974.
19. Teh, H.-S., Harley, E., Phillips, R. A., and Miller, R. G. *J. Immunol.* **118,** 1049, 1977.
20. Dröge, W., Reddehase, M., Suessmuth, W., and Wolf, M. *Behring Inst. Res. Commun.* **67,** 139, 1980.
21. Burakoff, S. J., Germain, R. N., and Benaceraff, B., *J. Exp. Med.* **144,** 1609, 1976.
22. Billings, P., Burakoff, S. J., Dorf, M. E., and Benaceraff, B. *J. Exp. Med.* **148,** 341, 1978.
23. Teh, H.-S., Phillips, A., and Miller, R. G., *J. Immunol.* **121,** 1711, 1978.
24. Hale, A. H., and McGee, M. P., *Cell. Immunol.* **58,** 147, 1981.

CELLULAR IMMUNOLOGY **64**, 64–72 (1981)

The Induction of at Least Two Distinct Types of Interferon in Mouse Spleen Cell Cultures by *Corynebacterium parvum*[1]

SCOTT R. EVANS AND HOWARD M. JOHNSON[2]

University of Texas Medical Branch, Department of Microbiology, Galveston, Texas 77550

Received May 8, 1981; accepted July 7, 1981

Stimulation of dissociated C57Bl/6 mouse spleen cells with *Corynebacterium parvum* resulted in the production of interferon (IFN) activity that was only partially neutralized by separate treatment with anti-L-cell IFN (anti-IFN-α/β) or anti-γ IFN (anti-IFN-γ) antisera. Treatment of the IFN preparation simultaneously with the two antisera resulted in complete neutralization of antiviral activity, thus *C. parvum* induced both IFN-α/β and IFN-γ in spleen cells. The total number of units of antiviral activity in untreated cultures was greater than the sum of the titers of the individual IFNs. This is consistent with the phenomenon of "potentiation", where mixtures of IFN-α/β and IFN-γ have been shown to exhibit increased antiviral activity. Kinetic studies showed that IFN-α/β activity in cultures peaked at 12 to 24 hr, while IFN-γ peaked at 48 to 72 hr. The different IFNs induced by *C. parvum* were separated by gel filtration chromatography, with IFN-α/β exhibiting a molecular weight of about 25,000 daltons and IFN-γ a molecular weight of 35,000 to 40,000 daltons. Separation of the spleen cells into plastic-adherent and nonadherent populations showed that nonadherent cells were the major producers of both IFN-α/β and IFN-γ following stimulation with *C. parvum*. Treatment of spleen cell cultures with monoclonal anti-Thy 1.2 antibody and complement greatly reduced the production of IFN-γ but had little or no effect on the production of IFN-α/β. These data suggest that T lymphocytes are the producers of IFN-γ, and that IFN-α/β is produced by a nonadherent, non-T cell. Preliminary data suggest that the IFNs may play a role in *C. parvum*-induced immunosuppression.

INTRODUCTION

The bacterial organism *Corynebacterium parvum* (*C. parvum*) has been shown to be an effective antitumor agent in both animal models and clinical trials (for review, see (1)). This organism can also modulate delayed-type hypersensitivity (2), mixed-lymphocyte reactions (3), graft-vs-host disease (3), cell-mediated cytotoxicity (4), and the humoral immune response ((5, 6) and S. R. Evans and H. M. Johnson, unpublished data). It has also been shown that *C. parvum* induces IFN in both human peripheral leukocytes (7–9) and mouse spleen cells (10, 11), although there is some disagreement regarding the type of IFN being produced by these cells. Since IFN also has immunomodulating and antitumor effects, it is possible that some of the biological activity attributed to *C. parvum* may result

[1] This investigation was supported by PHS Grant AI 16428, Awarded by the National Institute of Allergy and Infectious Diseases, DHHS. S.R.E. was supported by a James W. McLaughlin Predoctoral Fellowship.

[2] To whom correspondence should be directed.

0008-8749/81/150064-09$02.00/0

from the induction of IFN. Therefore, it is important to characterize the IFN produced in *C. parvum*-stimulated cultures. The availability of specific antisera to both mouse IFN-α/β and IFN-γ has allowed us to accurately type this IFN.

MATERIALS AND METHODS

IFN assay. IFN was assayed on mouse L-929 cells in microtiter plates as previously described (12), except that methylcellulose was used in place of carboxymethylcellulose. Briefly, L cells were seeded into microtiter plates (6×10^4 cells per well) and allowed to form confluent monolayers. The cells were then overlayed with serial dilutions of the IFN and incubated overnight at 37°C. Following removal of the IFN the cells were challenged with vesicular stomatitis virus (approximately 40 PFU per well) and overlayed with 0.5% methylcellulose. Approximately 24 hr later the cells were stained with a 1% solution of crystal violet and the number of plaques per well was determined. One unit of IFN is that amount required to reduce the number of PFU per well by 50% compared to the virus control. All samples were assayed in duplicate and the coefficients of variation averaged approximately 25%.

IFN typing experiments. Antiserum to mouse L-cell IFN (anti-IFN-α/β) was kindly supplied by Barbara Dalton and Kurt Paucker. Anti-IFN-γ antiserum was produced in our laboratory as previously described (13). For IFN neutralization experiments small aliquots of IFN (100–200 μl) were mixed with appropriate concentrations of anti-IFN-α/β, anti-IFN-γ, or both and incubated at room temperature for 60 min. For each experiment the amounts of anti-IFN-α/β and anti-IFN-γ employed were sufficient to completely neutralize the corresponding IFNs. Following incubation the residual IFN activity in each aliquot was assayed as described above. Neutralization of antiviral activity by the specific antisera was not affected by dilution of the samples during the IFN assay.

Spleen cell cultures. Spleen cells from adult female C57Bl/6 mice were maintained in RPMI 1640 medium supplemented with 10% fetal calf serum at a normal concentration of 1.5×10^7 cells per ml. Heat-killed *C. parvum*, strain CN6134, which was obtained from Burroughs Wellcome Co., Research Triangle Park, North Carolina, was added to the cultures at final concentrations of between 10 and 140 μg/ml. These concentrations resulted in maximum production of IFN activity. Supernates were routinely harvested at 24 to 48 hr after addition of *C. parvum* and were kept frozen until assayed for IFN.

Ultrogel AcA 34 gel filtration of C. parvum-induced IFN. Culture supernates containing the IFN activity were concentrated in an Amicon ultrafiltration cell, and 10 ml of this concentrated material was loaded onto an Ultrogel AcA 34 (LKB Instruments, Inc., Rockville, Md.) column (2.5 × 100 cm) and eluted with PBS at 4°C. The column had been previously standardized with markers of known molecular weight. Fractions of 2.4 ml were collected.

Plastic-adherent and nonadherent cells. Dissociated spleen cells were plated in 60-mm plastic petri dishes and incubated at 37°C for 45 min. Following incubation the nonadherent cells were removed and the plates, which contained the adherent cells, were washed twice to completely remove nonadherent cells. Fresh medium was then added back to the plates, and the cells were stimulated with *C. parvum.* The nonadherent spleen cells were transferred to another petri dish and incubated for an additional 45 min to insure complete removal of adherent cells. Following this incubation the nonadherent cells were carefully withdrawn with a pipet, centrifuged, resuspended to a concentration of 1.5×10^7 cells/ml, and stimulated with *C. parvum.*

Treatment of spleen cells with anti-Thy 1.2 antibody. Spleen cells at a concentration of 3×10^7 cells/ml were mixed with the appropriate dilution of monoclonal anti-Thy 1.2 antibody and incubated at 37°C for 30 min. Guinea pig complement (1:30 dilution) was then added, and the cells incubated for an additional 30 to 45 min. The cells were then pelleted by centrifugation, washed twice with medium, and resuspended to a concentration of 1.5×10^7 cells/ml. Control cells were incubated at 37°C for the entire time, but without adding either anti-Thy 1.2 antibody or complement. Treatment of cells with complement alone had no effect on *C. parvum*-induced IFN production.

RESULTS

Neutralization of C. parvum-Induced IFN by Specific Antisera

In order to determine the type of IFN induced in our spleen cell cultures by *C. parvum* we treated culture supernates with anti-IFN-α/β and anti-IFN-γ antisera and measured residual IFN activity after each treatment (Table 1). The antiviral activity of IFN-γ was completely neutralized by anti-IFN-γ but was not affected by treatment with anti-IFN-α/β, and the antiviral activity of IFN-α/β was blocked by anti-IFN-α/β. Although not presented in the table, others have shown that anti-IFN-γ will not cross-react with IFN-α/β ((13) and K. Paucker and B. Dalton, personal communication). The antiviral activity induced by *C. parvum* was only partially neutralized by the separate treatments with the different antisera. In order to completely block this activity, it was necessary to use the two different antisera in combination. These data suggest that there are at least two distinct types of IFN (IFN-γ and IFN-α/β) present in our spleen cell cultures. It is interesting to note that the sum of titers of the individual IFNs induced by *C. parvum* was less than the total amount of antiviral activity present in untreated cultures. This is similar to the phenomenon of "potentiation" (14), where it has been shown that IFN-γ increases, or "potentiates" the activity of IFN-α/β, or vise versa. However, it is also possible that other factors present in the *C. parvum*-induced supernates are responsible for this increased antiviral activity.

TABLE 1

Neutralization of *C. parvum*-Induced IFN by Anti-IFN-α/β and Anti-IFN-γ Antisera

Treatment	*C. parvum*-induced IFN (units)	IFN-α/β[a] (units)	IFN-γ[b] (units)
None	88	90	34
Anti-IFN-α/β	16	<3	36
Anti-IFN-γ	29	N.D.[c]	<3
Combination of antisera	<3	N.D.	<3

[a] IFN-α/β, IFN induced in mouse L cells with Newcastle disease virus (NDV).

[b] IFN-γ, IFN induced in C57Bl/6 mouse spleen cells with staphylococcal enterotoxin A (SEA).

[c] N.D., not done.

Kinetics of Production of C. parvum-Induced IFN

We next examined the kinetics of production of the two different IFNs induced by *C. parvum* (Fig. 1). Significant antiviral activity was present in spleen cell cultures by 12 hr and generally reached a maximum at 24 to 48 hr after addition of *C. parvum*. Treatment of the culture supernates with anti-IFN-γ revealed that the titer of IFN-α/β reached maximum at about 12 hr and declined thereafter. Treatment of the supernates with anti-IFN-α/β showed that production of IFN-γ did not peak until about 48 hr after addition of *C. parvum*. Treatment with a combination of the two antisera completely neutralized all antiviral activity. The kinetics of production of IFN-γ and IFN-α/β induced by *C. parvum* is similar to the kinetics of production of these IFNs individually in other systems using different inducers (12, 15, 16).

Gel Filtration Chromatography of C. parvum-Induced IFN

We next determined if the two IFNs could be separated by gel filtration chromatography. Figure 2 represents the profile of antiviral activity obtained by AcA 34 gel filtration chromatography of *C. parvum*-induced IFN. The bulk of the IFN activity was eluted in two or three major peaks in the molecular weight range of 25,000 to 40,000 daltons. To determine the type of IFN present in these peaks, we treated the column fractions with the different anti-IFN antisera (Fig. 3). Separate treatments with the two antisera produced two major peaks of activity. The first peak represents the interferon activity remaining after treatment with anti-IFNα/β. The IFN-γ in this peak has a molecular weight of about 35,000 daltons, which is similar to the molecular weight previously reported for mouse IFN-γ (12). The second peak of activity, which was obtained after treating the

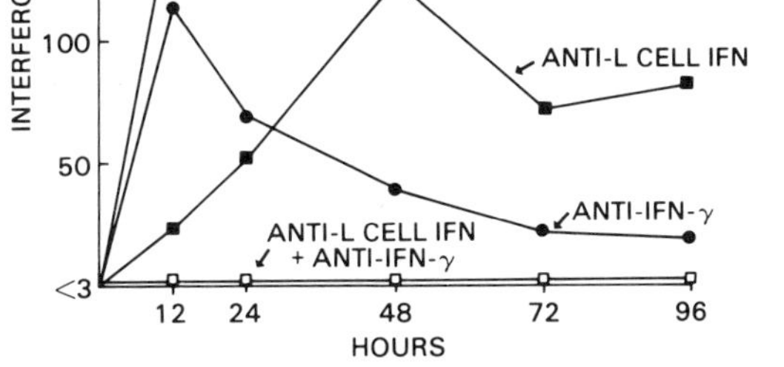

FIG. 1. Kinetics of *C. parvum*-induced IFN production. Spleen cells were cultured as described and supernates were harvested at various times following addition of *C. parvum*. (○), IFN titer before treatment with specific antisera; (●), IFN titer after treatment with anti-IFN-γ (■), IFN titer after treatment with anti-L-cell IFN (anti-IFN-α/β); (□), IFN titer after treatment with a combination of the two antisera.

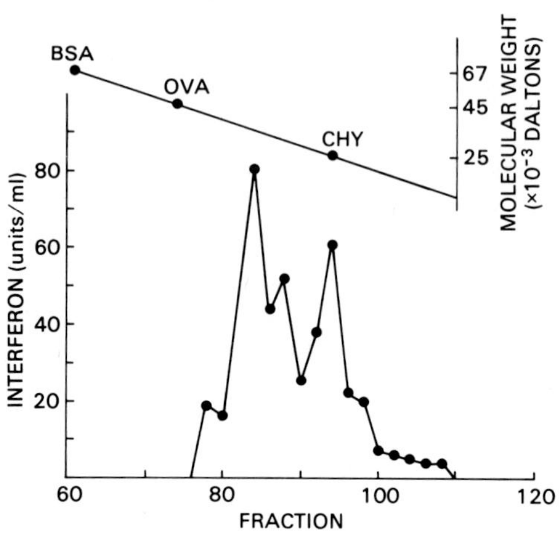

FIG. 2. AcA 34 chromatography of *C. parvum*-induced IFN. IFN activity eluted from the column was determined after pooling each two successive fractions. Molecular weight markers are bovine serum albumin (BSA), 67,000 daltons; ovalbumin (OVA), 45,000 daltons; and chymotrypsinogen (CHY), 25,000 daltons.

column fractions with anti-IFN-γ, represents the IFN-α/β induced by *C. parvum* and has a molecular weight of about 25,000 daltons. The data show that *C. parvum*-induced IFN can indeed be separated into two different IFN components by gel filtration chromatography.

C. parvum Induction of IFN in Plastic-Adherent and Nonadherent Cells

To examine the cell types involved in the production of *C. parvum*-induced IFN in mouse spleen cell cultures we first looked at the ability of plastic-adherent and nonadherent cells to produce IFN (Table 2). The data show that the nonadherent cells appear to be responsible for most of the IFN production in *C. parvum*-stimulated cultures. We next used specific anti-IFN antisera to determine the type of

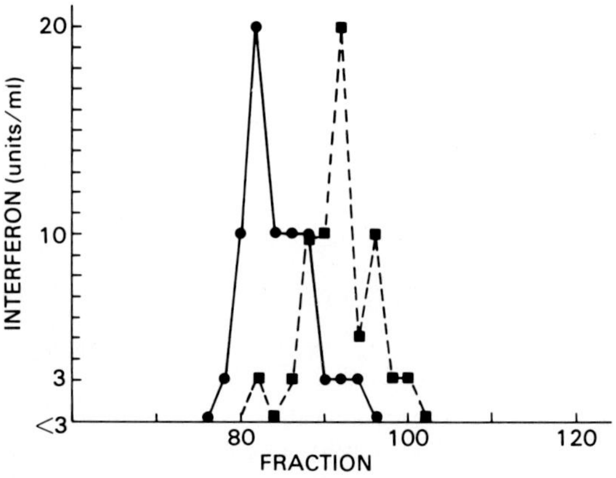

FIG. 3. Typing of IFN eluted from AcA 34 gel filtration column. IFN activity was measured in column fractions after treatment with either anti-IFN-α/β (● —— ●) or anti-IFN-γ (■ - - - ■).

TABLE 2

IFN Induction in Plastic-Adherent and Nonadherent Spleen Cells by *C. parvum*

Cell population	IFN[a] (units/ml)	Percentage antiviral activity neutralized by: Anti-IFN-α/β	Anti-IFN-γ
Unfractionated	128	77	71
Nonadherent	61	>90	41
Adherent	6	—[b]	—

[a] Antiviral activity in spleen cell culture supernates 24 hr after addition of *C. parvum*.
[b] The IFN activity in adherent cell supernates was insufficient for typing with the specific antisera.

IFN produced by the different cell populations. The IFN produced by nonadherent cells was neutralized by greater than 90% with anti-IFN-α/β, indicating that IFN-α/β was predominant. However, anti-IFN-γ treatment of this same IFN preparation resulted in a 41% reduction in antiviral activity. Since anti-IFN-γ is highly specific and does not cross-react with IFN-α/β, these results indicate that nonadherent cells also produce IFN-γ. The total neutralization obtained by the two separate antisera treatments was more than 100% because the total antiviral activity in samples that contain both IFN-α/β and IFN-γ is greater than the sum of the titers of the individual IFNs. The IFN produced by unfractionated cells was neutralized about equally by separate treatments with anti-IFN-α/β and anti-IFN-γ, and again we see greater than 100% neutralization. These data show that in this particular experiment, the unfractionated cells produced approximately equal amounts of IFN-α/β and IFN-γ, whereas the nonadherent cells produced mainly IFN-α/β, and very little IFN-γ. This difference may be due to the depletion of macrophages from the nonadherent population, as macrophages have been shown to augment the production of IFN-γ by lymphocytes (17). The amount of IFN produced by adherent cells was too low for accurate typing with the antisera. We feel that these data suggest the importance of using the two different types of anti-IFN antisera for accurate IFN typing, and for precise quantitation of the two different IFNs when present together in a single sample.

C. parvum-Induced IFN Production in Anti-Thy 1.2-Treated Cells

To further characterize the cells involved in *C. parvum*-induced IFN production, we examined the IFN produced in cultures that had been treated with anti-Thy 1.2 antibody and complement. Treated spleen cells were completely unresponsive to the mitogenic effects of phytohemagglutinin P (PHA) and staphylococcal enterotoxin A (SEA) and failed to produce IFN following stimulation with SEA, whereas untreated cells responded normally to the mitogens and produced significant amounts of IFN in response to SEA. These data suggest that treated cultures were largely depleted of functional T cells. IFN titers in treated and untreated cultures stimulated with *C. parvum* indicated that anti-Thy 1.2 treatment significantly reduced the production of *C. parvum*-induced IFN (Table 3). Typing of the IFN produced in treated and untreated cultures showed that anti-Thy 1.2 treatment nearly abolished the production of IFN-γ, but had little or no effect on the production of IFN-α/β. These data indicate that in *C. parvum*-induced spleen cell cultures, T cells play a major role in the production of IFN-γ, but have little or no role in the production of IFN-α/β.

DISCUSSION

The data presented provide strong evidence that *C. parvum* can induce at least two distinct types of IFN in the same mouse spleen cell cultures. The availability of anti-IFN-α/β antiserum that was highly specific for IFN-α/β, and anti-IFN-γ antiserum that would neutralize IFN-γ but not IFN-α/β, made it possible to accurately determine the type of IFN produced in our cultures. Treatment of IFN-γ with anti-IFN-γ antiserum completely neutralized its antiviral activity, and IFN-α/β was completely neutralized by anti-IFN-α/β. However, the antiviral activity of *C. parvum*-induced IFN was only partially neutralized by separate treatments with the different antisera, and a combination of the two antisera was necessary to completely block this IFN activity. These experiments also showed that untreated supernates contained more antiviral activity than would be expected by simply adding together the individual titers of the two IFNs. A similar increase in antiviral activity has previously been observed by mixing IFN-γ and IFN-α/β (14). We have also provided evidence for two types of IFNs in *C. parvum*-induced cultures by separating the IFNs using gel filtration chromatography. Treatment of the column fractions with the specific anti-IFN antisera showed distinct peaks of IFN-γ and IFN-α/β. Kinetic studies demonstrated that the two IFNs are produced at different rates in our cultures and these kinetics are similar to those previously reported for IFN-α/β and IFN-γ production (12, 15, 16). Examination of the cell types involved in the production of *C. parvum*-induced IFN showed that cells which did not adhere to plastic surfaces played the major role in this production, and that T cells produced the IFN-γ. The data also suggest that the plastic-adherent cells may be necessary for optimal production of IFN-γ, confirming previous observations (17).

We feel that our studies have demonstrated the importance of using antisera to more than one type of IFN in typing experiments. In samples that contain both IFN-α/β and IFN-γ the total antiviral activity is greater than the sum of the titers of the individual IFNs, and neutralization of these samples with a single antiserum could lead to an incorrect interpretation of the type of IFN present. This is especially true when one of the IFNs is present in relatively small amounts, as we demonstrated

TABLE 3

C. parvum-Induced IFN Production in Spleen Cells Treated with Anti-Thy 1.2 Antibody

	IFN activity[a] (units/ml) after treatment with:			
Anti-Thy-1.2 treatment	Untreated	Anti-IFN-α/β	Anti-IFN-γ	Anti-IFN-α/β + anti-IFN-γ
+	50	4	18	<3
−	177	97	10	<3

[a] IFN titers in cultures 24 hr after addition of *C. parvum*. Values reported are the average of triplicate cultures.

with the IFN induced by *C. parvum* in nonadherent spleen cells. Neutralization of this IFN with anti-IFN-α/β resulted in a large loss of antiviral activity (>90%), and it appeared that only one type of IFN was present in these samples. However, the use of anti-IFN-γ, which would only neutralize IFN-γ, clearly demonstrated the presence of IFN-γ even though the titer of this IFN was relatively low. Also, because of the potentiating effect in mixed IFN preparations, the different antisera are necessary to accurately quantitate each of the individual IFNs.

There are several reports in the literature concerning the IFN-inducing potential of *C. parvum*, although there has been disagreement over the exact type of IFN produced. One group reported that mouse spleen cells stimulated with *C. parvum* produced IFN-γ (10), whereas another group reported the production of IFN-α/β by macrophages from mouse spleens (11). Similar results have been obtained using human peripheral leukocytes. Two reports concluded that *C. parvum* induces IFN-γ (7, 8), while a third report suggested that IFN-α (leukocyte) is produced following stimulation with *C. parvum* (9).

Our findings should provide an explanation for the seemingly contradictory reports regarding the type of IFN induced by *C. parvum*. First, we have shown that the kinetics of production of IFN-α/β and that of IFN-γ are different, with IFN-α/β predominant early in the response and IFN-γ later in the response. Thus the ratio of the two types of IFN varies at different times after induction of the response, and this could lead to different conclusions regarding the type of IFN produced. Second, we have shown that because of the potentiating effect observed with mixtures of IFN-α/β and INF-γ, neutralization with a single antiserum might not identify each of the IFNs present. This could also be true for other techniques used for IFN typing, such as pH stability and heat sensitivity.

The role that the IFNs may have in mediating the various biological affects attributed to *C. parvum* is currently unknown. Others have shown that both IFN-α/β and IFN-γ are capable of suppressing humoral immunity (18–20), and we have preliminary evidence that these IFNs are involved in *C. parvum*-mediated suppression of the *in vitro* antibody response (S. R. Evans and H. M. Johnson, unpublished data). The specific antisera to the different IFNs should be very helpful in studying the mechanisms involved in the antitumor and immunoregulatory effects of *C. parvum*.

REFERENCES

1. Milas, L., and Scott, M. T., *Advan. Cancer Res.* **26,** 257, 1978.
2. Scott, M. T., *Cell. Immunol.* **13,** 251, 1974.
3. Scott, M. T., *Cell. Immunol.* **5,** 459, 1972.
4. Lichtenstein, A., Murahata, R., and Zighelboim, J., *Cancer Immunol. Immunother.* **8,** 39, 1980.
5. Ghaffer, A., and Sigel, M. M., *Immunology* **35,** 685, 1978.
6. Šljivić, V. S., Brown, C. A., and Watson, S. R., *Develop. Biol. Standard* **38,** 147, 1978.
7. Hirt, H. M., Schwenteck, M., Becker, H., and Kirchner, H., *Clin. Exp. Immunol.* **32,** 471, 1978.
8. Sugiyama, M., and Epstein, L. B., *Cancer Res.* **38,** 4467, 1978.
9. Vilcek, J., Sulea, I. T., Volvovitz, F., and Yip, Y. K., *In* "Biochemical Characterization of Lymphokines" (A. L. DeWeck, Ed.), pp. 323–329. Academic Press, New York, 1980.
10. Hirt, H. M., Becker, H., and Kirchner, H., *Cell. Immunol.* **38,** 168, 1978.
11. Neumann, C., Macher, E., and Sorg, C., *Immunobiology* **157,** 12, 1980.
12. Osborne, L. C., Georgiades, J. A., and Johnson, H. M., *Infect. Immunity* **23,** 80, 1979.
13. Osborne, L. C., Georgiades, J. A., and Johnson, H. M., *Cell. Immunol.* **53,** 65, 1980.

14. Fleischmann, W. R., Jr., Georgiades, J. A., Osborne, L. C., and Johnson, H. M., *Infect. Immunity* **26,** 248, 1979.
15. Cantell, K., and Paucker, K., *Virology* **21,** 11, 1963.
16. Kronenberg, L. H., and Friedmann, T., *J. Gen. Virol.* **27,** 225, 1975.
17. Epstein, L. B., *In* "Immunobiology of the Macrophage" (D. S. Nelson, Ed.), pp. 201–234. Academic Press, New York, 1976.
18. Johnson, H. M., *In* "Texas Reports on Biology and Medicine" (S. Baron and F. Dianzani, Eds.), Vol. 35, pp. 357–369, 1977.
19. Lucero, M. A., Wietzerbin, J., Stefanos, S., Billardon, C., Falcoff, E., and Fridman, W. H., *Cell. Immunol.* **54,** 58, 1980.
20. Sonnenfeld, G., Mandel, A. D., and Merigan, T. C., *Cell. Immunol.* **34,** 193, 1977.

CELLULAR IMMUNOLOGY **64**, 73–83 (1981)

Macrophage-Stimulating Effect of a Synthetic Muramyl Dipeptide and Its Adjuvant-Active and -Inactive Analogs for the Production of T-Cell Activating Monokines[1]

HIDEAKI IRIBE,* TOSHITAKA KOGA,* KAORU ONOUE,† SHOZO KOTANI,‡ SHOICHI KUSUMOTO,§ AND TETSUO SHIBA§

**Department of Biochemistry, Kyushu University School of Dentistry, Fukuoka 812, †Department of Immunobiochemistry, Kumamoto University, Medical School, Honjho, Kumamoto 860, ‡Department of Microbiology, Osaka University, Dental School, Kitaku, Osaka 530, and §Department of Chemistry, Faculty of Science, Osaka University, Toyonaka, Osaka 560, Japan*

Received May 28, 1981; accepted June 30, 1981

A synthetic muramyl dipeptide (MDP), which has the minimal adjuvant-active structure that can substitute for *Mycobacterium* in complete Freund's adjuvant, could stimulate peritoneal macrophages of the guinea pig to produce T-cell activating soluble factors. The culture supernatant of MDP-stimulated macrophages could help the proliferative response of the T-lymphocyte-enriched fraction of lymph nodes to PHA. It also helped the antigenic activation of immune T lymphocytes deprived of macrophages to produce macrophage migration inhibitory factor (MIF). Gel filtration of the culture supernatant showed that both of the helping activities were found mainly in the fraction emerging at the 53,000- to 85,000-MW range. A series of MDP analogs which are known to be adjuvant active or inactive was tested for their ability to stimulate macrophages to produce these factors. The adjuvant activity of these synthetic compounds was found to be parallel to the ability to stimulate the production of these T-cell activating monokines. Since both of these activities are highly dependent on the precise stereochemical structures of the MDP analogs, the parallelism of these activities would suggest the possibility that the immunopotentiating effect of the MDP and its analogs is related at least partially to their activity to stimulate macrophages to produce T-cell activating monokines.

INTRODUCTION

Most microorganisms and bacterial products are potent immunological adjuvants which enhance *in vivo* immune responses. A simple synthetic adjuvant, *N*-acetylmuramyl-L-alanyl-D-isoglutamine, or muramyl dipeptide (MDP),[2] has been shown to have a minimal effective structure for adjuvant activity of cell wall peptidoglycans (1–4). This MDP has been also shown to stimulate a number of macrophage

[1] Supported by grants-in-aid for scientific research from the Ministry of Education, Science and Culture and for the intractable diseases from the Ministry of Health and Welfare of Japan.

[2] Abbreviations used: MDP, muramyl dipeptide; LAF, lymphocyte activating factor; LPS, lipopolysaccharide; MIF, migration inhibitory factor; PHA, phytohemagglutinin; TAF, T-cell activating factor; FCS, fetal calf serum; HBSS Hanks' balanced salt solution; [^{3}H]TdR; tritiated thymidine; PPD, purified protein derivative.

0008-8749/81/150073-11$02.00/0

functions (5–12). Oppenheim *et al.* (11, 13) have shown that a number of stimulants including mycobacterial components and MDP could induce human and mouse mononuclear cells to produce lymphocyte activating factor (LAF), and suggested that macrophage-derived LAF activity might contribute to the nonspecific immunoenhancing effects of adjuvants. Similar LAF activity has been obtained using MDP-stimulated adherent peritoneal cells from mice injected with trehalose dimycolate (12).

Macrophages are necessary as accessory cells for the activation of lymphocytes as indicated in various experimental systems (14, 15), and their function can be replaced at least partially by culture supernatants of macrophages (16–22).

Our previous studies showed that LPS-pulse-stimulated macrophages of the guinea pig produced a soluble factor with a molecular weight of around 70,000–80,000 daltons which could help the antigenic activation of immune T lymphocytes to produce migration inhibitory factor (MIF) in the presence of a very small number of macrophages (22, 23). It was shown by subsequent studies that the same fraction of the culture supernatant of LPS-stimulated macrophages could also support the mitogen (PHA)-induced proliferation of the macrophage-depleted T lymphocytes of lymph nodes (Sakamoto and Onoue, unpublished data). This latter activity is similar to that of T-cell activating factor (TAF) reported by Rosenstreich and Mizel (14). Both of these monokines appear to have a molecular weight of above 50,000 which is significantly higher than that of LAF (presently called interleukin 1 (24)) which is 12,000–18,000 daltons (25). Although the molecular relationship among these factors is not yet clear, these monokines seem to play important roles in the process of the T-cell activation in immune responses.

In the present study, we tested a series of adjuvant-active and adjuvant-inactive MDP analogs to see if there is any relationship between the adjuvant activity and the macrophage-stimulating activity. The results showed that MDP and its adjuvant-active analogs effectively stimulated guinea pig peritoneal macrophages to produce T-cell activating monokines *in vitro*, whereas adjuvant-inactive analogs failed to do so, suggesting that the immunopotentiating effect of MDP and its analogs may be mediated at least partially through their activity to stimulate macrophages to produce these soluble factors.

MATERIALS AND METHODS

Experimental animals. Outbred Hartley guinea pigs weighing 350–400 g were used.

Immunization. Guinea pigs were immunized with complete Freund's adjuvant containing 1 mg of *Mycobacterium tuberculosis*, Aoyama B strain, by injecting intramuscularly into the back and subcutaneously into the hind footpads. After 4 weeks, the animals were sacrificed and lymph nodes were collected from popliteal, inguinal, and retroperitoneal regions.

Culture medium. Tissue culture medium 199 (Chiba-ken Serum Inst., Chiba, Japan) was supplemented with 5% heat-inactivated fetal calf serum (FCS) unless otherwise stated, 7 m*M* Hepes (*N*-2-hydroxyethyl-piperazine-*N*′-2-ethanesulfonic acid, Doujin Yakukagaku Institute, Japan), 5×10^{-5} *M* 2-mercaptoethanol, 50 units/ml of penicillin, and 50 μg/ml of streptomycin. This culture medium referred to as 199-FCS was used throughout the present studies. Hanks' balanced salt solution (HBSS) purchased from Nissui Pharmaceutical Company Ltd., Tokyo, was used for washing the cells.

Purification of T lymphocytes on a nylon wool column. The suspension of lymph node cells was prepared by teasing the lymph nodes and filtering the cells through a 200-mesh stainless-steel sieve. The purified T lymphocytes were prepared by passing the lymph node cells (LNC) through a nylon wool column to which macrophages and B lymphocytes adhered (26). The nonadherent cells from the column were further incubated in plastic dishes at 37°C for 30 min to remove residual adherent cells. About 10% of the applied cells were obtained as purified T lymphocytes, which consisted of 80 to 90% T lymphocytes (rosette-forming cells with rabbit erythrocytes), 2 to 3% B lymphocytes (EAC-rosette-forming cells) (27), and no detectable macrophages (nonspecific esterase-positive cells).

Purification of macrophages. Peritoneal exudate cells autologous to T lymphocytes were collected from the immune guinea pig 4 days after the ip injection of sterilized paraffin oil. The cells were incubated in glass dishes for 1 hr to allow adhesion to the glass wall. The adherent cells were collected by repeated siphoning with a pipet. The adherent cells were further purified by repeating the adhesion once more. More than 99% of the adherent cells thus obtained were esterase-positive cells. Viability of the cells was over 95%. These cells will be referred to as the purified macrophages.

Preparation of the culture supernatant of macrophages stimulated with MDP or its analogs. Peritoneal exudate cells were collected from normal guinea pigs 4 days after the ip injection of sterilized paraffin oil. The cells (1×10^7 cells in 5 ml of 199-FCS medium per dish) were incubated at 37°C for 60 min in plastic dishes (No. 3002, Falcon Plastics, Los Angeles, Calif.). After 1 hr, the nonadherent cells were removed and the dishes were washed three times with HBSS and refilled with fresh 199-FCS medium which contained 10% FCS and was 2ME free. To the adherent cells (about 5×10^6 cells in 5 ml/dish) were added MDP or its analogs at various concentrations and cultured for 24 hr. MDP and its analogs were synthesized as described previously (28, 29). MDP was kindly provided by Dr. Atsuro Inoue (Daiichi Pharmaceutical Co., Tokyo) or purchased from Protein Research Foundation, Osaka. The adherent cells consisted of 97% macrophages as determined by nonspecific esterase staining. The culture supernatants of adherent cells incubated without MDP or its analogs were supplemented with these compounds at the end of the culture and served as the control supernatant. These culture supernatants were dialyzed three times against HBSS and finally against tissue culture medium 199 without FCS, filtered through a Millipore membrane (pore size, 0.45 μm; Sartorius, Göttingen, West Germany) and kept frozen at −20°C until use.

PHA-induced lymphocyte proliferation in vitro. PHA (2 μg/ml) was added to purified T lymphocytes (2×10^5 cells/0.25 ml) and the mixture cultured in the presence or absence of the culture supernatant of macrophages in flat-bottomed Falcon Microtest II tissue culture plates for 72 hr. The cultures were pulsed with 0.2 μCi tritiated thymidine ([^{3}H]TdR) (5 Ci/mmol, RCC, Amarsham, England) for the final 18 hr of incubation. The cells were collected on a glass fiber filter with a Mash II harvester (Microbiological Associates, Rockville, Md.) and radioactivity was measured by liquid scintillation spectrometer (Packard Instrument Co.,

Downer's Grove, Ill.) The data are expressed as the arithmetic mean ± SE of triplicate cultures. The statistical significance of the data was evaluated with Student's *t* test.

MIF production in vitro by the immune lymphocytes. Nonpurified lymph node cells or purified T lymphocytes (1×10^7 cells/ml) from *M. tuberculosis*-immunized guinea pigs were cultured with or without antigen (PPD, 25 μg/ml) in the 199-FCS medium containing 10% FCS. The culture supernatant of MDP-stimulated macrophages or control culture supernatant was added for the test. A small number of macrophages (1×10^3 cells/ml) were added to the culture of T lymphocytes in some case. After 72 hr, the culture supernatants were collected.

Migration inhibition test. Migration inhibition test was performed by the indirect capillary method (30) as described previously (31). The mean migration area of duplicate capillaries was determined for each sample. The migration index was calculated as follows:

$$\text{Migration index} = \frac{\text{mean migration area in test supernatant}}{\text{mean migration area in control supernatant}} \times 100.$$

On the basis of the previous experiments (27), a migration index below 75% was taken as a definitely positive indication of MIF production.

Fractionation of the MDP-stimulated macrophage culture supernatant on a Sephadex G-200 column. The culture supernatant of macrophages stimulated with MDP (1 μg/ml) was concentrated and fractionated on a Sephadex G-200 column (26 × 93 cm) in 0.30 *M* NaCl–0.01 *M* Tris–HCl buffer at pH 8.0. The control culture supernatant of macrophages which was added with MDP (10 μg/ml) at the end of culture was also fractionated on it. Each fraction was dialyzed against HBSS and finally against medium 199, filtered through a Millipore membrane, and kept frozen at −20°C until use.

Heat-treatment of the F3 fraction of the macrophage culture supernatant. The F3 fraction of gel filtration was incubated in a water bath for 30 min at 85°C with mild shaking.

RESULTS

Production of T-Cell Activating Factor from Macrophages Stimulated with MDP

Peritoneal macrophages from a nonimmune guinea pig were cultured in the presence or absence of graded concentrations (0.001–10 μg/ml) of MDP. As shown in Fig. 1, the culture supernatant of nonstimulated macrophages exhibited a certain degree of T-cell activating activity which was significant compared with the 199-FCS medium alone ($P < 0.02$). A definitely enhanced production of T-cell activating factor was seen when macrophages were cultured at concentrations of MDP over 0.01 μg/ml ($P < 0.01$). The culture supernatant of MDP-stimulated macrophages alone in the absence of PHA could not induce proliferation of T lymphocytes.

MDP-stimulated macrophages were cultured in the FCS-free medium or in the medium supplemented with various concentrations of FCS. The T-cell activating activity was found even in the FCS-free medium as well as in the medium supplemented with 1–10% FCS (data not shown).

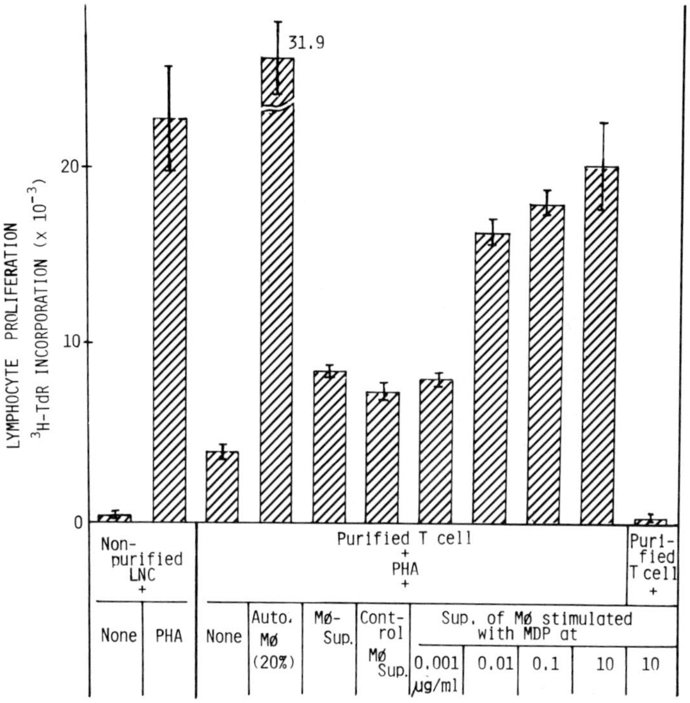

FIG. 1. T-Cell activating activity of the culture supernatant of macrophages stimulated with or without MDP. Peritoneal adherent cells from a normal guinea pig were cultured with MDP at graded concentrations or without MDP. The culture supernatant of nonstimulated macrophages to which MDP (10 μg/ml) was added at the end of culture was used as the control supernatant. These culture supernatants were thoroughly dialyzed and added at 20% (v/v) to the culture of purified T lymphocytes (2×10^5 cells/well) stimulated with PHA (2 μg/ml). The subsequent proliferative response was measured.

Production of T-Cell Activating Factor from Macrophages Stimulated with MDP Analogs

A series of synthetic analogs of MDP, the adjuvant activities of which had been determined by previous studies (4, 32), was tested for their ability to stimulate macrophages to produce T-cell activating factor. As shown in Table 1, three MDP analogs (Mur-NAc-L-Ser-D-isoGln, Mur-NAc-L-Val-D-isoGln, [L18]-Mur-NAc-L-Ala-D-isoGln) as well as MDP, all of which had been shown to be adjuvant active (4, 32), had a strong stimulating effect on macrophages to produce T-cell activating factor at the two concentrations (0.1, 10 μg/ml) tested ($P < 0.01$). Mur-NAc-L-Ala-D-Gln, which was shown to enhance antibody production when administered with antigen in saline to mice (4), but failed to induce delayed-type hypersensitivity when administered with antigen in a water-in-oil emulsion (3), enhanced the production of T-cell activating factor at 10 μg/ml ($P < 0.02$), but not at a lower concentration (0.1 μg/ml). In addition, four MDP analogs (Mur/NAc-L-Ala-L-isoGln, Mur-NAc-L-Ala-D-isoAsn, Mur-NAc-L-Ala-L-Gln, Mur-NAc-Gly-L-isoGln) which were adjuvant inactive (4) could not stimulate macrophages. Thus, a striking parallelism was found between the adjuvant activity of these compounds and their ability to stimulate macrophages to produce T-cell activating factor.

TABLE 1

T-Cell Activating Activity of Culture Supernatants of Macrophages Stimulated with MDP or Its Analogs

Stimulants	Adjuvant activity	Concentration (μg/ml)	[^{3}H]-TdR incorporation (Δ cpm $\pm$ SE)[a]
1.			
Mur-NAc-L-Ala-D-isoGln (MDP)	+	0.1	14,014 ± 1932
		10	14,579 ± 1327
Mur-NAc-L-Ala-D-Gln	±	0.1	−56 ± 731
		10	6,707 ± 1498
Mur-NAc-L-Ala-L-isoGln	−	0.1	92 ± 152
		10	117 ± 426
Mur-NAc-L-Ala-D-isoAsn	−	0.1	−71 ± 833
		10	−91 ± 545
2.			
MDP	+	0.1	7,020 ± 2316
		10	10,440 ± 2753
Mur-NAc-L-Ser-D-isoGln	+	0.1	10,545 ± 2144
		10	11,732 ± 4014
Mur-NAc-L-Val-D-isoGln	+	0.1	13,487 ± 3983
		10	10,781 ± 1617
Mur-NAc-L-Ala-L-Gln	−	0.1	970 ± 1438
		10	−772 ± 967
3.			
MDP	+	0.1	13,575 ± 2998
		10	12,953 ± 2433
[L18]-Mur-NAc-L-Ala-D-isoGln	+	0.1	8,961 ± 493
		10	11,436 ± 2494
Mur-NAc-Gly-L-isoGln	−	0.1	−401 ± 1601
		10	98 ± 1334

[a] Δ cpm = (cpm of culture added with stimulated Mϕ supp.) − (cpm of culture added with non-stimulated Mϕ supp. to which MDP or its analogs were added at the end of culture).

Effect of the Culture Supernatant of MDP-Stimulated Macrophages on the Antigenic Activation of Immune T Lymphocytes to Produce Migration Inhibitory Factor (MIF)

Our previous studies demonstrated that the culture supernatant of LPS-stimulated macrophages contains a soluble factor which helps the antigenic activation of immune T lymphocytes to produce MIF in the presence of a very small number of macrophages (27). In this report, we examined whether the same activity was also found in the culture supernatant of MDP-stimulated macrophages.

Purified T lymphocytes from the guinea pig immunized previously with *M. tuberculosis* were cultured with PPD (25 μg/ml). Autologous macrophages (0.01%) and the culture supernatant of MDP-stimulated macrophages were added to the culture as indicated in Fig. 2. A definite production of MIF was observed in the presence of the culture supernatant and a small number of macrophages (column D) but not in the absence of macrophages or the culture supernatant (columns C and E).

In one of these experiments, the FCS-free culture supernatant of MDP-stimulated macrophages which was concentrated 10-fold was used. This culture supernatant also showed definite activity. These findings clearly indicate that MDP stimulated the macrophages to produce a soluble factor which helps the antigenic activation of immune T lymphocytes to produce MIF as did LPS.

Fractionation of the Culture Supernatant of MDP-Stimulated Macrophages on Sephadex G-200

A pooled culture supernatant of MDP-stimulated macrophages was concentrated and fractionated on a Sephadex G-200 column. The elution profile of T-cell activating factor is shown in Fig. 3. Most of the activity was found in the molecular weight range of 53,000 to 85,000 daltons with a peak activity at 70,000 daltons. Another lower peak of the activity was found in the <15,000-MW fraction. The culture supernatant was divided into four fractions (F1–F4) as indicated in Fig. 3 and the helping activity of these fractions for the antigenic activation of immune T lymphocytes to produce MIF was tested. As shown in Fig. 4, F3 and F4 fractions were found to be active (columns F and G). The activity of F3 appeared to be higher than that of F4. The corresponding fractions of control culture supernatant was inactive. These findings suggest that a soluble factor which helps the antigenic activation of T lymphocytes to produce MIF coeluted with the activity to enhance the T-lymphocyte response to PHA from a Sephadex G-200 column.

Heat-Treatment of the F3 Fraction

The F3 fraction was treated at 85°C for 30 min. Both T-cell activating activity for proliferative response to PHA and activity to help the antigenic activation of

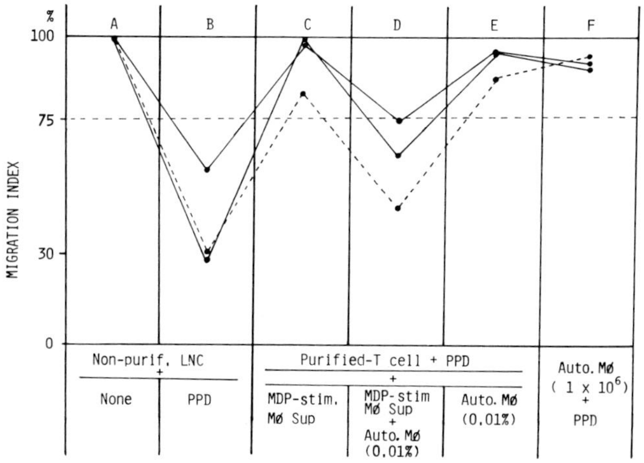

FIG. 2. Effect of the culture supernatant of MDP-stimulated macrophages on the antigenic activation of immune T lymphocytes. Purified T lymphocytes (1×10^7 cells/ml) of *M. tuberculosis*-immunized guinea pigs were cultured with PPD (25 μg/ml). The culture supernatant of MDP (1 μg/ml)-stimulated macrophages was added at 20% to the cultures (C, D). A small number of macrophages (1×10^3 cells/ml) was added to the cultures (D, E). After 72 hr of culture, the supernatants were collected and tested for MIF activity. In one of these experiments (dotted line), the FCS-free culture supernatant of MDP (1 μg/ml)-stimulated macrophages was used. This culture supernatant was concentrated to 1/10 of the original volume, dialyzed, and added to the culture at 100% concentration as calculated on the basis of the original volume.

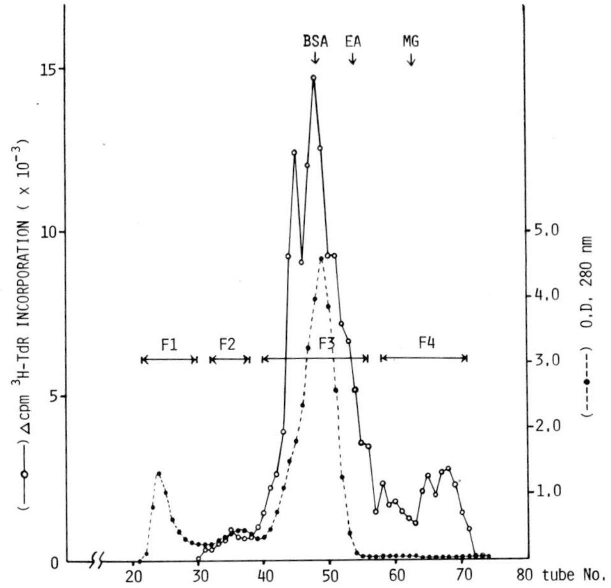

FIG. 3. Fractionation of the culture supernatant of MDP-stimulated macrophages. The culture supernatant of MDP (1 μg/ml)-stimulated macrophages containing 10% FCS (98 ml) was concentrated and fractionated on a Sephadex G-200 column (2.6 × 93 cm) in 0.3 *M* NaCl–0.01 *M* Tris–HCl buffer, pH 8.0. The elution profile (-----) was obtained by measuring the optical density at 280 nm. Each fraction of the eluate was dialyzed and added at 20% (v/v) concentration to the culture of purified T lymphocytes (2×10^5 cells/well) stimulated with PHA (2 μg/ml). T-Cell activating activity is expressed as Δ cpm which is a difference between cpm of the cultures added with the fractions and cpm of the cultures without the fraction. Arrows indicate the positions where reference proteins were eluted from the same column: BSA, bovine serum albumin; EA, egg albumin; MG, whale myoglobin.

immune T lymphocytes for MIF production were completely abolished by this treatment (data not shown).

DISCUSSION

In the present study, we showed that MDP or its adjuvant-active analogs stimulated peritoneal macrophages of guinea pigs to produce T-cell activating soluble factor which could help the proliferative response of T lymphocytes to PHA. The stimulating activity of MDP was apparent at a very low concentration (10^{-2} μg/ml). In addition, the enhanced production of the soluble factor was also seen when the MDP-stimulated macrophages were cultured in serum-free medium, excluding the possibility that the factor was derived from the fetal calf serum or macrophage components associated with it. The carry-over of MDP to the culture supernatant of MDP-stimulated macrophages tested would be negligible, since low-molecular-weight MDP was removed by exhaustive dialysis. Furthermore, control culture supernatants of macrophages to which MDP was added at the end of the culture exhibited, after dialysis, only as low activity for T-cell activation as the supernatant of macrophage culture without MDP.

Previous studies in our laboratory showed that LPS-stimulated macrophages of guinea pigs produced a heat-labile soluble factor with helping activity for the antigenic activation of immune T lymphocytes to produce MIF and the activity was found in the fraction which mostly overlapped with serum albumin by gel filtration on Sephadex G-200 (22, 23). Further studies showed that the factor worked for T lymphocyte activation in the presence of a small number of macrophages which were required for antigen presentation (27).

Our present study showed that the soluble factor(s) with similar activity was also produced by MDP-stimulated macrophages. The activity was heat labile and eluted at the molecular weight range of 53,000–85,000 daltons by gel filtration. These results strongly suggest that the same factor was produced by both stimulants, LPS and MDP. The same G-200 fraction also showed helping activity for proliferative response of T lymphocytes to PHA. Whether this factor corresponds to TAF reported by Rosenstreich and Mizel (14) is not known since they only reported that the factor was found in the >50,000-dalton fraction obtained by an Amicon filtration. Some T-cell activating activity was also found in the <15,000-dalton fraction (F4). This fraction may contain conventional LAF (interleukin 1) but no further characterization was attempted in this report.

In the present study, we tested a series of synthetic analogs of MDP, the adjuvant activities of which had been determined previously (4, 32), to investigate whether the adjuvant activities of these compounds are related to their ability to stimulate macrophages to produce T-cell activating monokines. It was shown that MDP and its adjuvant-active analogs effectively stimulated the production of the monokines, whereas adjuvant-inactive analogs did not. Since the results indicate that both the adjuvant activity and macrophage-stimulating activity are highly dependent on the

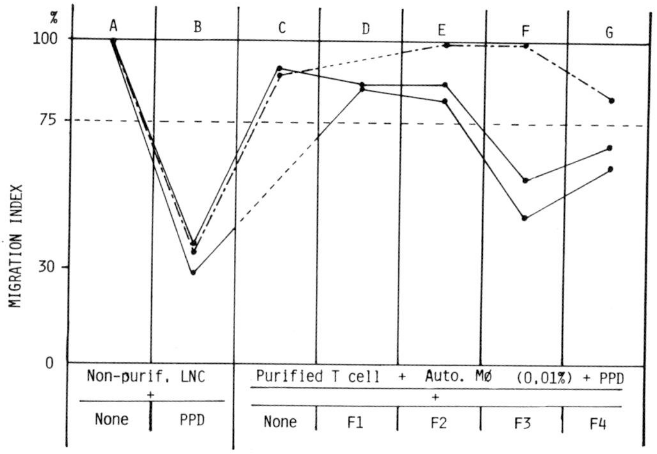

FIG. 4. Activity of the fractions of the culture supernatant of MDP-stimulated macrophages to help antigenic activation of immune T lymphocytes. The eluates from a Sephadex G-200 column of the culture supernatant of MDP (1 μg/ml)-stimulated macrophages and the control culture supernatant which was added with MDP (10 μg/ml) at the end of culture were divided into four fractions (F1, F2, F3, F4) as indicated in Fig. 3. Purified T lymphocytes (1×10^7 cells/ml) of *M. tuberculosis*-immunized guinea pigs were cultured with PPD (25 μg/ml). Each fraction was concentrated and added to the culture at 100% concentration as calculated on the basis of the original volume of the macrophage culture supernatant. A small number of macrophages (1×10^3 cells/ml) was also added to the culture. After 72 hr of the culture, the supernatants were collected and tested for MIF activity. Results (——) of two experiments with the same sample and results (- - -) of one experiment with the control culture supernatant are shown.

precise stereochemical structures of the MDP analogs, the parallelism between the two activities would suggest the possibility that the immunopotentiating effect of MDP and its analogs is mediated at least partially through their ability to stimulate macrophages to produce T-cell activating monokines. It was previously reported that MDP was effective for the production of LAF from human- and murine-adherent mononuclear cells (11, 12). Oppenheim *et al.* (11) suggested that macrophage-derived LAF activity might contribute to the nonspecific immunopotentiating effect of the adjuvant. Our results further strengthen this hypothesis.

Finally, the use of MDP as a stimulant of macrophages to obtain the soluble factor would have definite advantages over LPS since it is a small synthetic compound with a simple defined structure, has a remarkable stimulatory effect at a very low concentration, and can be separated from the factor by gel filtration.

ACKNOWLEDGMENTS

We wish to thank Dr. Shigeru Sakamoto of this department for his close collaboration and Dr. Atsuro Inoue of the Research and Development Division, Daiichi Pharmaceutical Co. Tokyo (Japan) for the supply of a synthetic muramyl dipeptide. We also thank Ms. Kyoko Higuchi for her secretarial work in preparing this manuscript.

REFERENCES

1. Ellouz, F., Adam, A., Ciorbaru, R., and Lederer, E., *Biochem. Biophys. Res. Commun.* **59,** 1317, 1974.
2. Merser, C., Sinay, P., and Adam, A., *Biochem. Biophys. Res. Commun.* **66,** 1316, 1975.
3. Kotani, S., Watanabe, Y., Kinoshita, F., Shimono, T., Morisaki, I., Shiba, T., Kusumoto, S., Tarumi, Y., and Ikenaka, K., *Biken J.* **18,** 105, 1975.
4. Chedid, L., Audibert, F., and Johnson, A., *Prog. Allergy* **25,** 63, 1978.
5. Juy, D., and Chedid, L., *Proc. Nat. Acad. Sci. USA* **72,** 415, 1975.
6. Wahl, S. M., Wahl, L. M., McCarthy, J. B., Chedid, L., and Mergenhagen, S. E., *J. Immunol.* **122,** 226, 1979.
7. Yamamoto, Y., Nagao, S., Tanaka, A., Koga, T., and Onoue, K., *Biochem. Biophys. Res. Commun.* **80,** 923, 1978.
8. Fevrier, M., Birrieu, J. L., Leclerc, C., Chedid, L., and Liacopoulos, P., *Eur. J. Immunol.* **8,** 558, 1978.
9. Tanaka, A., Nagao, S., Imai, K., and Mori, R., *Microbiol. Immunol.* **24,** 547, 1980.
10. Pabst, M. J., and Johnston, R. B., Jr., *J. Exp. Med.* **151,** 101, 1980.
11. Oppenheim, J. J., Togawa, A., Chedid, L., and Mizel, S., *Cell. Immunol.* **50,** 71, 1980.
12. Tenu, J.-P., Lederer, E., and Petit, J.-F., *Eur. J. Immunol.* **10,** 647, 1980.
13. Oppenheim, J. J., Mizel, S. B., and Meltzer, M. S., *In* "Biology of the Lymphokines" (S. Cohen, E. Pick, and J. J. Oppenheim, Eds.), pp. 291–323. Academic Press, New York, 1979.
14. Rosenstreich, D. L., and Mizel, S. B., *Immunol. Rev.* **40,** 102, 1978.
15. Persson, U., Hammarström, E., Möller, E., Möller, G., and Smith, C. I. E., *Immunol. Rev.* **40,** 78, 1978.
16. Bach. F. H., Alter, B. J., Sollidary, S., Zoschke, D. C., and Janis, M., *Cell. Immunol.* **1,** 219, 1970.
17. Dutton, R. W., McCarthy, M. M., Mishell, R. I., and Raddit, D. T., *Cell. Immunol.* **1,** 196, 1970.
18. Hoffmann, M., and Dutton, R. W., *Science* **172,** 1047, 1971.
19. Shortman, K., and Palmer, J., *Cell. Immunol.* **2,** 399, 1971.
20. Gery, I., and Waksman, B. H., *J. Exp. Med.* **136,** 143, 1972.
21. Erb, P., and Feldmann, M., *Eur. J. Immunol.* **5,** 759, 1975.
22. Ohishi, M., and Onoue, K., *Cell. Immunol.* **26,** 295, 1976.
23. Yamamoto, Y., Onoue, K., and Ohishi, M., *Cell. Immunol.* **37,** 432, 1978.
24. Aarden, L. A., Brunner, T. K., Cerottini, J.-C., Dayer, J.-M., Weck, A. L., Dinarello, C. A., Sabato, G. D., Farrar, J. J., Gery, I., Gillis, S., Handschumacher, R. E., Henney, C. S., Hoffmann, M. K., Koopman, W. J., Krane, S. M., Lachman, L. B., Lefkowits, I., Mishell, R. I., Mizel,

S. B., Oppenheim, J. J., Paetkau, V., Plate, J., Röllinghoff, M., Rosenstreich, D., Rosenthal, A. S., Rosenwasser, L. J., Schimpl, A., Shin, H. S., Simon, P. L., Smith, K. A., Wagner, H., Watson, J. D., Wecker, W., and Wood, D. D., *J. Immunol.* **123,** 2928, 1979.
25. Mizel, S. B., *J. Immunol.* **122,** 2167, 1979.
26. Julius, M. H., Simpson, E., and Herzenberg, L. A., *Eur. J. Immunol.* **3,** 645, 1973.
27. Yamamoto, Y., and Onoue, K., *J. Immunol.* **122,** 942, 1979.
28. Kusumoto, S., Tarumi, Y., Ikenaka, K., and Shiba, T., *Bull. Chem. Soc. Japan* **49,** 533, 1976.
29. Kusumoto, S., Okada, S., Yamamoto, K., and Shiba, T., *Bull. Chem. Soc. Japan* **51,** 2122, 1978.
30. David, J. R., *Proc. Nat. Acad. Sci. USA* **56,** 72, 1966.
31. Ohishi, M., and Onoue, K., *Cell. Immunol.* **18,** 220, 1975.
32. Kotani, S., Kinoshita, F., Morisaki, I., Shimono, T., Okunaga, T., Takada, H., Tsujimoto, M., Watanabe, Y., Kato, K., Shiba, T., Kusumoto, S., and Okada, S., *Biken J.* **20,** 95, 1977.

CELLULAR IMMUNOLOGY **64,** 84–92 (1981)

Expression of a 16,000 Molecular Weight Antigen on Human Suppressor T Lymphocytes[1]

CHARLES M. BALCH, MICHAEL R. LOKEN, PATRICIA A. DOUGHERTY, AND EDWIN W. ADES

Cellular Immunobiology Unit of the Tumor Institute, Departments of Microbiology and Surgery, the Comprehensive Cancer Center and the Veterans Hospital, University of Alabama Medical Center, Birmingham, Alabama, 35294; the Department of Microbiology, LaRabida Hospital University of Chicago Institute, Chicago, Illinois 50549; and the Department of Basic and Clinical Immunology and Microbiology, Medical College of South Carolina, Charleston, South Carolina 29401

Received June 9, 1981; accepted July 13, 1981

A human T-cell antigen with a molecular weight of 16,000 (p16) was expressed predominantly on suppressor T cells, while it had minimal representation on helper T cells. This p16 antigen was expressed on 37 ± 5% of ER^+ blood T cells, and was co-expressed on all suppressor T lymphocytes recognized by a monoclonal antibody (OKT8). When ER^+ T cells were fractionated on the basis of FcIgG receptor expression, p16 was detected on 62% of ER^+FcIgG^+ T cells (T_G^+ cells) and 26% of ER^+FcIgG^- cells. The $p16^+$ and $p16^-$ T cells were physically separated with a fluorescence-activated cell sorter and tested for their functional capability as inducer (helper) cells and suppressor cells in the terminal differentiation of pokeweed mitogen-stimulated B lymphocytes. Almost all of the helper cell activity was in the $p16^-$ fraction. Suppressor cell function was analyzed by adding $p16^+$ cells to a "helper cell combination" comprised of ER^+ T cells plus B cells. Results in four individuals demonstrated that the $p16^+$ cells could function as suppressor cells since they caused a 60 ± 3% decrease in plasma cell generation. In contrast, adding the $p16^-$ cells to the "helper cell combination" further increased the plasma cell response by an additional 10 ± 17%. The helper cell population could be identified in both the $FcIgG^-$ and $FcIgG^+$ populations by fractionating these cells with respect to p16 antigen expression.

INTRODUCTION

Human helper and suppressor T cells have been distinguished from each other by markers identified by xenoantisera, monoclonal antibodies, and Fc receptors for immunoglobulin (for reviews see 1–3). A precise characterization of human T-cell antigens expressed on helper and suppressor cell populations has been complicated by the diversity of reagents and *in vitro* functions that have been utilized. A comparison of antigens identified by these different reagents has been attempted by analyzing their reactivity with different culture cell lines. For example, some T antigens expressed on suppressor T cells in blood are shared by cultured HSB-2

[1] This work was supported by grants from the Medical Research Service of the Veteran's Administration and from the National Institutes of Health (CA-13148, CA-27197, CA-16673, AI-14872, and AI-00348).

0008-8749/81/150084-09$02.00/0

lymphoblastoid cells, while others are not (1, 4). A more precise approach for comparing differences among surface membrane antigens expressed on human suppressor cells is to analyze some of their molecular properties. This approach may also aid in determining the functional role of these surface molecules and their cellular interactions with other subpopulations of lymphoid cells.

In this study, we characterized the immunoregulatory function of the human lymphocyte subpopulation defined by a selectively adsorbed anti-T-cell antiserum. The results demonstrated that the antiserum recognized a 16,000 MW T-cell antigen and that this antigen is primarily expressed on suppressor T cells but not on helper T cells.

MATERIALS AND METHODS

1. Isolation of cells. Human T lymphocytes binding AET-treated sheep red blood cells were isolated from blood of seven healthy volunteers as previously described (5). Cultured human T lymphoid cells MOLT-3, MOLT-4, and HSB-2 were maintained as suspension cultures (6–8).

2. Xenoantisera and monoclonal antibodies. Anti-monkey thymocyte antiserum (AMT-188) was prepared, characterized, and adsorbed to specificity for human T cells as previously described (5, 9, 10). This reagent recognizes two distinct T-cell antigens with molecular weights of 25,000 and 16,000 (6). These antigens have different representation on human T lymphoblastoid cell lines, with a predominance of the p25 antigen on MOLT-4 cells and the p16 antigen on HSB-2 cells (6).

An aliquot of AMT was directly conjugated with fluorescein isothiocyanate (FITC) prior to adsorption for immunofluorescence studies while the remainder of unconjugated antiserum was used for immunochemical studies. The unconjugated antiserum was adsorbed to T-cell specificity in an identical manner as the FITC-conjugated serum. After adsorption with non-T-cell sources, this reagent (AMT-FITC) reacted with all ER^+ T cells from blood and thymus and was completely unreactive with sIg-bearing B cells in a double-fluorochrome assay both by visual and by quantitative immunofluorescence (5, 11). In the present studies, T-cell-specific AMT was further adsorbed four to five times with one of two cultured T lymphoblastoid cells (MOLT-3 or MOLT4) as described (5, 6). These selectively adsorbed reagents are designated as AMT/M3 and AMT/M4, respectively.

A monoclonal anti-T-cell antiserum (OKT8, Ortho Diagnostics) was used to detect a subpopulation of T cells with suppressor activity (12). Cells reactive with these monoclonal antibodies were identified by indirect immunofluorescence using a fluorochrome-conjugated goat anti-mouse IgG. This reagent was previously adsorbed with insolubilized rabbit serum to remove any antibodies cross-reacting with rabbit AMT (13).

3. Fluorescence-activated cell sorting. Preparation and staining of blood T cells for sorting experiments have been described (11). Quantitative fluorescence was performed with a FACS-II (Becton–Dickinson Co., Mountain View, Calif.). Histograms of fluorescence reactivity for a population of 10^4 cells were recorded on a pulse-height analyzer as described previously (14). Lymphocyte populations were sorted under sterile conditions based upon their relative fluorescence intensity at an approximate rate of 5000 cells/sec. Large cells (predominantly monocytes), as identified by forward angle light scattering, were excluded.

4. *Immunoprecipitation and SDS–PAGE analysis of T-cell antigens.* Surface membrane antigens reactive with AMT and AMT/M4 were coprecipitated from detergent-solubilized T-lymphocyte membranes and examined on polyacrylamide gels as described previously (6). Briefly, 1.0×10^7 cells were radiolabeled with ^{125}I by the lactoperoxidase method and then solubilized in 0.5% sodium deoxycholate. The radioiodinated cell surface proteins were isolated by coprecipitation with AMT/M4 and formalin-fixed *Staphylococcus aureus* Cowan strain 1, and then analyzed by sodium dodecyl sulfate–polyacrylamide gel electrophoresis (SDS–PAGE) in 5 to 20% gradient gels (6).

5. *Analysis of helper and suppressor T-cell function.* T-Cell regulation of cytoplasmic immunoglobulin synthesis by B cells was examined using the method of Moretta and colleagues (15, 16) with minor modifications. Cell fractions of peripheral blood mononuclear cells were obtained from healthy young adults. Assays of helper cell function were performed by combining 2.5×10^5 ER^+ T cells with 2.5×10^5 cells from a B-cell-enriched population of E-rosette-depleted T lymphocytes. The cells were suspended in a 1-ml volume of RPMI 1640, supplemented with 20% heat-inactivated fetal calf serum and gentamycin, and then cultured upright in 5-ml plastic test tubes at 37°C in 5% CO_2. After a 7-day incubation in the presence of pokeweed mitogen (PWM; 25 μg/ml culture), the cells were washed, centrifuged onto glass slides, fixed in alcohol, and then stained for cytoplasmic IgM and IgG (15, 17).

Mixing experiments were also performed to test for suppressor cell function. In this assay, a "helper cell combination" consisting of equal numbers (2.5×10^5) of T cells and enriched B cells was used to generate a standard response. Aliquots of lymphocyte fractions (2.5×10^5 cells) sorted by the FACS were then added to this T- and B-cell combination to determine whether they could suppress the number of plasma cells generated by baseline cultures of helper T cells plus B cells.

RESULTS

I. *Immunochemical Analysis of Antigens*

The molecular profile of the selectively adsorbed AMT xenoantiserum was first analyzed by SDS–PAGE gel profiles. AMT was sequentially adsorbed four times with either MOLT-3 cells (designated AMT/M3) or MOLT-4 cells (AMT/M4) and then used to isolate T-cell antigens solubilized in 0.5% deoxycholate from extracts of ER^+ blood T cells by indirect immunoprecipitation. These cell lines were chosen for this selective adsorption of AMT because MOLT-3 cells expressed both T antigens (p25 and p16) while MOLT-4 cells primarily expressed the p25 antigen (6). As expected, both anti-p25 and anti-p16 antibodies were completely removed by four or five adsorptions with MOLT-3 cells (Fig. 1A). The MOLT-4 adsorptions removed almost all (>95%) of the antibodies recognizing the p25 antigen, while the anti-p16 antibodies were not depleted at all (Fig. 1B). This selectively adsorbed reagent, AMT/M4, therefore, reacted with a detergent-soluble T-cell antigen having a molecular weight of approximately 16,000 and is designated in the remainder of this report as an anti-p16 antiserum.

II. *Distribution of p16 Antigen on Lymphoid Cell Populations*

The p16 antigen was expressed on an average of 37 ± 5% of ER^+ cells from six normal individuals as assessed by visual immunofluorescence. Its distribution

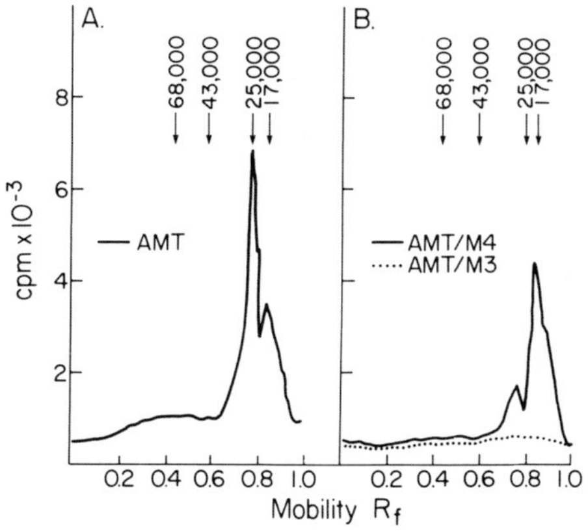

FIG. 1. SDS-PAGE analysis of ^{125}I-labeled solubilized membrane antigens from ER^+ blood T cells with a specific T-cell antiserum (AMT). (A) AMT precipitated two distinct antigen peaks on ER^+ blood T cells having molecular weights of 25,000 (p25) and 16,000 (p16). (B) Adsorption of AMT with MOLT-4 cells (AMT/M4) selectively removed antibodies recognizing the p25 antigen. Adsorption of AMT with MOLT-3 cells (MOLT-3) removed antibodies reacting with both p25 and p16 antigens.

was further examined in a subpopulation of ER^+ cells isolated by their expression of FcIgG receptors (T_G^+ cells). Anti-p16 antibody reacted with 62 ± 13% of T_G^+ cells and 26% ± 10% of T_G^- cells. None of the cells reacting with the anti-phagocyte antibody (detected by RITC-goat anti-mouse IgG) were double-labeled when counterstained with FITC-conjugated anti-p16 antiserum. A double-label immunofluorescence assay was also used to compare expression of p16 antigen with that defined by monoclonal anti-suppressor cell antisera (OKT8). Of the 20% of ER^+ T cells reactive with OKT8, virtually all of these expressed the p16 antigen. However, an additional 20 to 30% of ER^+ T lymphocytes were $p16^+$. Thus the p16 antigen has a broader representation on T cells and is distinct from that defined by the OKT8 monoclonal anti-suppressor cell antibody.

III. Helper Cell Function Studies of $p16^+$ and $p16^-$ T Cells

When ER^+ cells were stained with anti-p16 antiserum (AMT/M4) and examined by the FACS, two distinct populations of cells were discerned (Fig. 2A). The $p16^-$ cells represented approximately 60% of the ER^+ lymphocytes. A smaller population of $p16^+$ cells (representing about 40% of the ER^+ T-cell population) exhibited relatively bright fluorescent intensity. The 30% of cells having the brightest stain with anti-p16 antibody ($p16^+$) were then separated from the 30% of cells having little or no fluorescent stain ($p16^-$) (Fig. 2A). Reanalysis of these purified populations indicated that the two fractions of cells ($p16^+$ and $p16^-$) were greater than 97% pure (Fig. 2B).

The isolated T-cell fractions were then added to a B-cell-enriched lymphocyte population of ER^-sIg^+ cells. The cell mixtures were incubated in the presence of PWM for 6 days to determine which T-cell subset could function as helper T cells in the terminal differentiation of B cells. The results showed that the $p16^-$ population contained almost all of the helper cell activity as demonstrated by a 49% increase in plasma cell generation above that obtained by using unsorted ER^+ T

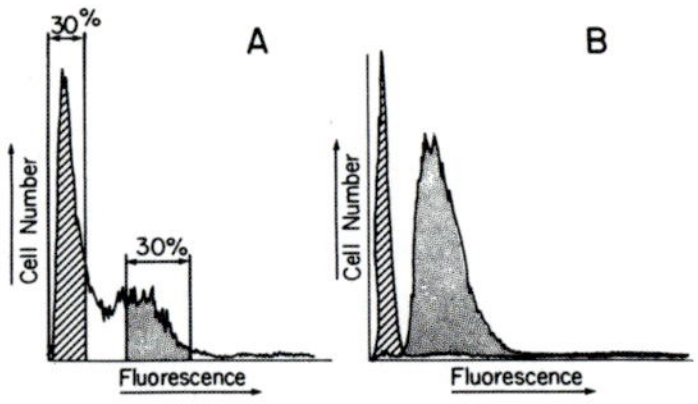

FIG. 2. Fluorescence histograms of anti-p16 antisera on ER$^+$ blood T lymphocytes analyzed with the FACS II. (A) Bimodal curve of anti-p16 reactivity. The 30% least reactive (dull cells) and the 30% most reactive (bright cells) were separated by the FACS and tested for helper and suppressor activity. (B) Histogram of bright and dull cells after FACS sorting indicating that each fraction represented a homogenous population with respect to p16 antigen expression.

cells (Table 1). In contrast, the p16$^+$ subpopulation of cells had very little helper cell function as demonstrated by a 77% decrease in plasma cell generation compared to unsorted ER$^+$ T cells.

IV. Suppressor Cell Function Studies of p16$^+$ and p16$^-$ T Cells

The above experiments demonstrated that p16$^+$ cells lacked significant helper cell activity. Mixing experiments were then performed to determine if this p16$^+$ T-cell subpopulation could actively suppress the generation of plasma cells. In four separate experiments, equal numbers of p16$^+$ and p16$^-$ cells were added to a cell mixture comprised of helper T cells (ER$^+$FcIgG$^-$sIg$^-$) and an enriched population of B lymphocytes (ER$^-$sIg$^+$). The addition of the p16$^+$ cells resulted in a 60 ± 3% decrease in plasma cell generation while the addition of p16$^-$ cells caused up to a 10 ± 17% increase in plasma cell generation compared to controls (Fig. 3).

V. FcIgG Receptor and p16 Antigen Expression

To further correlate functional activity with cell surface antigenic expression, ER$^+$ T cells were fractionated into FcIgG$^+$ cells (T_G^+) and FcIgG$^-$ cells (T_G^-). These two cell populations were then stained with FITC-conjugated anti-p16 antiserum. Expression of p16 antigen was evenly distributed among the FcIgG$^+$ and FcIgG$^-$

TABLE 1

Helper (Inducer) T-Lymphocyte Activity in p16$^+$ and p16$^-$ Blood Lymphocytes as Separated on the FACS

	No. of plasma cells (×10^3)					Mean percentage
T cells added[a]	Expt: 1[b]	2	3	4	Mean	change
Total T (ER$^+$)	50	105 (105)[c]	37 (40)[c]	90	70.5	
T Dulls (p16$^-$)	100	162	55	85	100.5	+49
T Brights (p16$^+$)	5	34	0.5	45	21.1	−77

[a] T cells added to B-cell-enriched fraction (ER$^-$, sIg$^+$) and incubated for 6 days with PWM.
[b] Separate results from four normal individuals.
[c] Total T cells stained with AMT/M4 but unsorted.

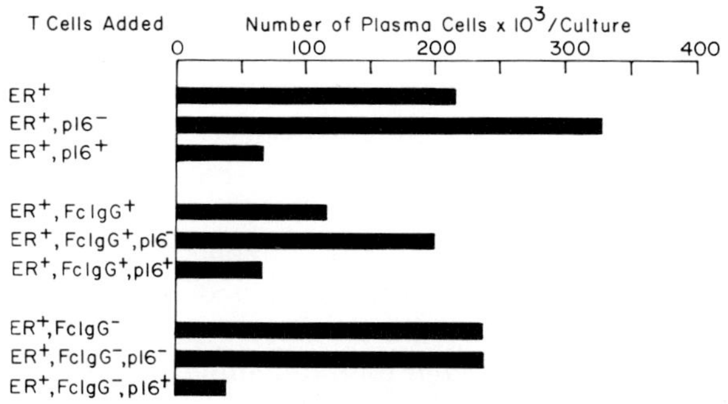

FIG. 3. Suppressor cell activity was measured for $p16^+$ and $p16^-$ T lymphocytes by adding each sorted fraction to a "helper cell combination" comprised of helper T cells (ER^+, $FcIgG^-$, sIg^-) plus B cells (ER^-, sIg^+). Cells were cultured for six days with PWM and assayed for plasma cell generation. The results in three separate experiments showed that $p16^-$ cells increased the number of plasma cells in two out of three experiments while added $p16^+$ cells suppressed the response by 60% or greater.

cells, with about 50% of the lymphocytes within each fraction reacting with anti-p16. The ER^+FcIgG^+ and ER^+FcIgG^- cell fractions were each stained with FITC-conjugated anti-p16 antiserum and then sorted with the FACS into $p16^+$ and $p16^-$ subfractions. The four fractions of cells were tested for helper cell function in pokeweed mitogen-induced B-cell differentiation. The results demonstrated that the $p16^-$ cells could function as helper cells regardless of whether they expressed FcIgG receptors or not (Fig. 4). Thus, there was no relationship with FcIgG receptor expression and p16 antigen expression with respect to immunoregulatory function in this assay.

DISCUSSION

These results demonstrate that a detergent-soluble, 16,000 MW antigen is expressed on human suppressor T lymphocytes and has minimal representation on helper T lymphocytes. The p16 antigen is a specific T-cell marker since it reacts exclusively with a proportion of thymocytes and T lymphocytes in peripheral lymphoid compartments, but it is unreactive with B lymphocytes, tumor cells, granulocytes, platelets, and monocytes (5, 6). Furthermore, it is not related to β_2-

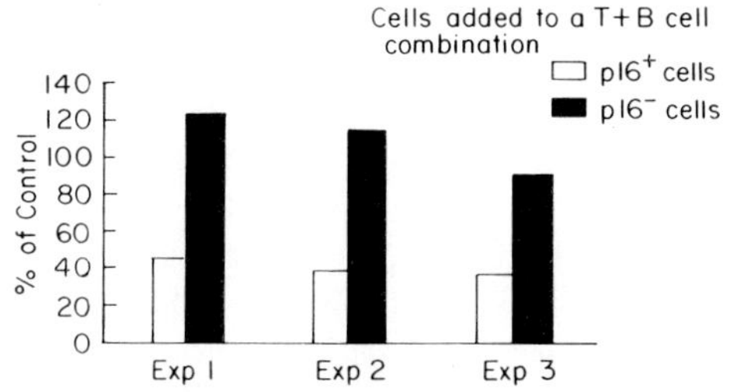

FIG. 4. Helper function associated with T-cell subfractions. ER^+ T cells were separated into two populations based upon their expression of Fc receptors. Cells were subsequently sorted on the FACS into subfractions which expressed ($p16^+$) or lacked ($p16^-$) the p16 antigen using AMT/M4 as the selecting antiserum. Within both Fc^+ and Fc^- fractions, the $p16^-$ cells could act as helper cells.

microglobulin or other histocompatibility determinants, including Ia-like antigens (10). Since monocytes can contaminate purified populations of T lymphocytes isolated by E rosetting over Ficoll–Hypaque, it is important to exclude monocyte reactivity with this anti-p16 antiserum. The evidence excluding monocyte reactivity is fourfold: (i) the anti-p16 antiserum has no specific reactivity with latex-ingesting monocytes by direct immunofluorescence (11), (ii) the anti-p16 antiserum did not react with monocytes counterstained with a monoclonal antibody (18) reacting with monocytes and granulocytes (unpublished observation), (iii) AET-treated sheep red blood cells were used in these experiments to enhance their binding avidity to ER receptors on T cells and therefore minimize monocyte contamination, and (iv) the cells selected for these experiments using the FACS were gated by size as detected by light scattering so as to exclude large- to medium-sized monocytes.

It is clear from the FACS cell separation experiments that the p16 antigen is not expressed on helper cells, but is expressed on suppressor cells. The anti-p16 binding to T cells was not nonspecifically related to FcIgG receptor binding on T_G^+ cells by multiple criteria. First, the prebleed normal rabbit IgG (FITC-conjugated and adsorbed) was incubated with lymphocytes under the same experimental conditions used for separating cells stained with the adsorbed rabbit AMT. The FACS histogram showed no fluorescence reactivity with normal rabbit IgG (11). Second, the AMT-stained lymphocytes had a smooth, continuous ring stain on their surface (5), without patching or capping that is seen on cells reacting with fluorescein-conjugated IgG aggregates (19). Third, the rabbit AMT had the same staining distribution on ER^+ T cells even after it had been ultracentrifuged for 1 hr to remove any aggregated complexes (unpublished observation). Finally, FITC conjugation of rabbit Ig has been shown by others to block its binding to Fc receptors on human lymphocytes (20, 21).

The p16 antigen is also different from the antigens identified by monoclonal antibodies generated by Ledbetter *et al.* (22). Leu-2a and Leu-2b are subunits of approximately 32,000 and 43,000 MW respectively while Leu-1 is approximately 67,000 MW. The p16 antigen is also not related to the antigens expressed on HSB-2 identified by Anderson and Metzgar (23) or by Eisenbarth *et al.* (24).

The p16 antigen is clearly distinct from the antigens detectable with a panel of monoclonal reagents (OKT3, OKT4, OKT8) developed by Reinherz and colleagues (25). This series of monoclonal antisera was unreactive with HSB-2 cells, while the AMT/M4 reagent identified the p16 antigen on the HSB-2 cell line by immunofluorescence and immunochemical assays. Nevertheless, both the OKT8 antibody and the anti-p16 antiserum appear to define overlaping subsets of T cells with suppressor cell properties. The OKT8 reacts with 20% of ER^+ T cells while anti-p16 antiserum reacts with 40–50%. A double-label immunofluorescence analysis directly comparing these antisera demonstrated that the p16 antigen is expressed on 100% of the $OKT8^+$ cells, but also has a wider distribution since it reacts with an additional 20 to 30% of ER^+ T cells.

Comparison of the p16 antigen expression on suppressor cells with T-cell antigens identified by other xenogeneic sera is more difficult, since the molecular properties of their reactive antigens have not been reported. Hirano and colleagues (4) prepared an anti-HSB-2 antiserum that recognized a subset of blood T cells that suppressed PWM-driven Ig synthesis but was unreactive with helper T cells. Both the anti-HSB-2 serum defined by Hirano and the anti-p16 reagent described in this study reacted with an average of 40% of total PBL. Evans and colleagues (26) defined a T-cell-differentiation antigen with a xenoantiserum (anti-TH_2) selectively adsorbed with T-cell-leukemic leukocytes. Just as our selectively adsorbed anti-thymoctye antisera recognized a subset of blood T cells, the anti-TH_2 reagent recognized 30% of blood T cells. The TH_2^+ population functioned as suppressor cells in the PWM-driven B-cell differentiation assay and as cytotoxic cells in a cell-mediated cytotoxicity assay (26).

The expression of p16 antigen defines a subset distinct from the T_G subpopulations of ER^+ cells bearing FcIgG receptors as defined by Moretta and colleagues (15). The present studies using both the FACS analysis of cell surface marker expression and functional studies of the sorted cells within the T_G^+ subpopulation confirmed that suppressor cell function can be defined by properties other than the FcIgG receptor. It is interesting that some $FcIgG^+$ cells could function as helper or inducer T cells. Haynes and colleagues (27) have also isolated helper cells within the T_G^+ population when the cells were further fractionated with a monoclonal antibody (3A1). It is possible that the helper cell properties in this minor population of the T_G^+ fraction were not detectable when these cells were isolated strictly on the basis of FcIgG expression, since the dominant function of this subpopulation had a negative regulatory effect. This balance of functional activity between help and suppression may be similar to that observed in the mouse (28).

It is evident that there are a multiplicity of T-cell antigens and even a multiplicity of suppressor T-cell populations. The marked diversity of antigen expression as defined by both monoclonal and heteroantisera has now reached sizeable proportions. Only by correlating molecular properties and cellular distribution of these suppressor cell antigens will direct comparisons be possible.

REFERENCES

1. Reinherz, E. L., *Cell* **19,** 821, 1980.
2. Moretta, L., Ferrarini, M., and Cooper, M. D., *Contemp. Top. Immunobiol.* **8,** 251, 1978.
3. Balch, C. M., and Ades, E. W., *J. Reticuloendothel. Soc.* **25,** 635, 1979.
4. Hirano, T., Kishimoto, T., Kuritani, T., Miuaguchi, A., Yamamura, Y., Ralph, P., and Good, R. A., *J. Immunol.* **123,** 1133, 1979.
5. Balch, C. M., Dougherty, P. A., Dagg, M. K., Diethelm, A. G., and Lawton, A. R., *Clin. Immunol. Immunopathol.* **8,** 448, 1977.
6. Ades, E. W., Bukacek, A., Zwerner, R. K., Dougherty, P., and Balch, C. M., *J. Immunol.* **121,** 613, 1978.
7. Minowada, J., Ohnuma, T., and Moore, G. E., *J. Nat. Cancer Inst.* **49,** 891, 1973.
8. Foley, G. E., Lazarus, H., Farber, S., Uzman, B. G., Boome, B. A., and McArtny, R. E., *Cancer* **18,** 522, 1965.
9. Dougherty, P. A., Ades, E. W., and Balch, C. M., *Transplantation* **26,** 434, 1978.
10. Ades, E. W., and Balch, C. M., *Advan. Exp. Med. Biol.* **114,** 593, 1979.
11. Balch, C. M., Ades, E. W., Loken, M., and Shore, S. L., *J. Immunol.* **124,** 1845, 1980.
12. Reinherz, E. L., Kung, P. C., Goldstein, G., and Schlossman, S. F., *J. Immunol.* **124,** 1301, 1980.
13. Balch, C. M., and Feldman, J. D., *J. Immunol.* **112,** 79, 1974.
14. Loken, M. R., and Herzenberg, L. A., *Ann. N.Y. Acad. Sci.* **254,** 163, 1975.
15. Moretta, L., Webb, S. R., Grossi, C. E., *et al., J. Exp. Med.* **146,** 184, 1977.
16. Moretta, L., Mingari, M. C., Moretta, A., and Cooper, M. D., *J. Immunol.* **122,** 984, 1979.
17. Kearney, J. F., and Lawton, A. R., *J. Immunol.* **115,** 671, 1975.
18. Hanjan, S. N. S., and Cooper, M. D., *Fed. Proc.* **40,** 1095, 1981.
19. Dickler, H. B., *J. Exp. Med.* **140,** 508, 1974.

20. Feorino, P. M., Shore, S. L., and Reimer, C. B., *Int. Arch. Allergy Appl. Immunol.* **53,** 222, 1977.
21. Thrasher, S. G., Bigazzi, P. E., Yoshida, T., and Cohen, S., *J. Immunol.* **114,** 762, 1975.
22. Ledbetter, J. A., Evans, R. L., Lipinsky, M., Cunningham-Rundles, C., Good, L. A., and Herzenberg, L. A., *J. Exp. Med.* **153,** 310, 1981.
23. Anderson, J. K., and Metzgar, R. S., *J. Immunol.* **120,** 262, 1978.
24. Eisenbarth, G. S., Haynes, B. F., Schroei, J. A., and Fauci, A. B., *J. Immunol.* **124,** 1237, 1980.
25. Reinherz, E. L., Kung, P. C., Goldstein, G., Levey, R. H., and Schlossman, S. F., *Proc. Nat. Acad. Sci. USA* **77,** 1588, 1980.
26. Evans, R. L., Lazarus, H., Penta, A. C., and Schlossman, S. F., *J. Immunol.* **120,** 1423, 1978.
27. Haynes, B. F., *Immunol. Rev.* **57,** 1, 1981.
28. Herzenberg, L. A., Okumura, K., and Metzler, C. M., *Transplant. Rev.* **27,** 57, 1975.

CELLULAR IMMUNOLOGY **64**, 93–101 (1981)

Dissociated Effects of Thymectomy at Weaning on T-Cell-Mediated Responses *in Vitro*: Correction by the Serum Thymic Factor, FTS, and Its Analogs

DOMINIQUE KAISERLIAN, MIREILLE DARDENNE, AND JEAN-FRANÇOIS BACH

INSERM U 25, Hôpital Necker, 161, rue de Sévres, 75015 Paris, France

Received June 18, 1981; accepted July 7, 1981

Thymectomy at weaning (3 weeks) causes a long-lasting diminution of T-cell mitogen (phytohemagglutinin, concanavalin A) responsiveness which is detectable by the first week following thymectomy and persists for at least 11 weeks. However, the capacity to produce alloreactive cytotoxic T lymphocytes (CTL) is not affected by thymectomy. Treatment with serum thymic factor or its synthetic analogs restores mitogen responsiveness and does not alter CTL production.

INTRODUCTION

Several reports have indicated that thymus-derived lymphocytes (T cells) are heterogeneous in their level of maturation (1–3), in their functional capacities (4–6), surface antigens (7, 8), and receptors (9). Distinct subpopulations of T cells have been implicated in the proliferative responses to phytomitogens and alloantigens (10) and in the cell-mediated lympholysis (CML) reaction (11). The characterization of such T-cell subsets has been essentially achieved by three approaches; study of T-cell allo- or xenoantigens, cellular cooperation experiments, and analysis of the differential effect of neonatal and adult thymectomy (Tx). Conflicting data have been reported on the effect of adult Tx on mitogen and alloantigen-induced T-cell proliferation. Whereas all T-cell functions are depressed by neonatal Tx (12, 13), only part of them are decreased after adult Tx. PHA and Con A responses as well as MLC have not been reported to be significantly decreased after adult TX, except in the study of Folch and Waksman for PHA responses in rats (14). Anderson *et al.* (11) showed a decrease in CML 2 months post-Tx, but conversely, Simpson and Cantor (15) reported a CML increase 1 month post-Tx, which they attributed to the loss of suppressor T cells following Tx. In *in vivo* studies, M. A. Bach observed a depressive effect of Tx on the generation of anti-H-2 cytotoxic T cells only when using suboptimal conditions of *in vivo* immunization.

In this work, we have analyzed the effects of Tx at weaning on the mitogen-induced T-cell response and on lymphocyte-mediated cytotoxicity (CML) after *in vitro* allogeneic sensitization, and have examined the capacity of the serum thymic

0008-8749/81/150093-09$02.00/0

factor (FTS) and of its synthetic analogs to restore the abnormalities induced by Tx.

MATERIALS AND METHODS

Mice. C57BL/6 male mice were obtained at weaning (3 weeks) from IFFA CREDO (Domaine des Oncins, 69210 L'Arbesle, France), DBA/2 male mice (5–6 weeks old) were purchased from the CSEAL (Orléans La Source, France).

Thymectomy. Thymus ablation was performed in C57BL/6 mice at weaning, under Nembutal anesthesia by suction with a Pasteur pipet, as described by Miller (16). Sham-thymectomized mice as well as normal mice were used as controls.

Treatment with FTS. Previous studies have demonstrated that FTS is rapidly degraded (a few minutes) when injected alone subcutaneously or intraperitoneally. However, its half-life is much increased (2 hr) when it is injected with a vehicle such as carboxymethyl cellulose (CMC) (17) which was used in this study. Ten nanograms of FTS was dissolved in 0.5 ml of phosphate buffer (0.02 *M*, pH 6.35) and mixed with 25 mg of CMC previously washed in the same buffer. The suspension obtained was injected sc three times a week. Control mice received 0.5 ml of CMC suspension in the same buffer.

Treatment with FTS analogs. Several structural analogs of FTS have been synthesized: [DAla^6]-FTS (<Glu–Ala–Lys–Ser–Gln–DAla–Gly–Ser–Asn), [DAsn^9]-FTS (<Glu–Ala–Lys–Ser–Gln–Gly–Gly–Ser–DAsn), and [Har^3]-FTS (<Glu–Ala–Har–Ser–Gln–Gly–Gly–Ser–Asn) showing the same biological *in vitro* activity, but half-life longer than that of the original peptide, which permits their *in vivo* utilization without CMC. Ten nanograms of the [DAla^6]-FTS, [DAsn^9]-FTS, or [Har^3]-FTS analogs was dissolved in the buffer described above for FTS and injected ip without CMC according to the same protocol. Control mice were injected with phosphate buffer alone.

Mitogen-induced proliferation. Spleen cells were homogenized in a potter homogenizer and washed in Hanks' medium. Suspensions of cells at 5×10^6 cells/ml were made in RPMI medium supplemented with 1% glutamine, 1% Hepes, 2% penicillin–streptomycin, and 10% fetal calf serum; 0.2 ml (1×10^6 cells) was added in the wells of a microplate (Falcon II Microtest). Twenty microliters of concanavalin A (Con A) at final concentrations of 1.25, 2.5, and 10 μg/ml, or phytohemagglutinin (PHA) at a final dilution of 1/200, 1/100, or 1/50 per well was then added (each concentration being tested in triplicate). Control cultures, without addition of mitogen, were included for each individual mouse. After 24 hr at 37°C in a humidified atmosphere with 5% CO_2, 1 μCi of tritiated thymidine (sp act 1 Ci/mmol) was added. Cultures were harvested after 24 hr of culture on Titer-tek filters (Flow Laboratories). Thymidine uptake was evaluated in a β counter (Delta). Results were expressed either as the change in counts per minute (=cpm in culture with mitogen − cpm in control cultures) or by the stimulation index:

$$\frac{\text{cpm in culture with mitogen}}{\text{cpm in control cultures}}$$

Statistical analysis was performed using Student's *t* test.

Cell-mediated lympholysis (CML). C57BL/6 spleen cells (2.5×10^6) were mixed with 5×10^6 DBA/2 irradiated spleen cells in 2 ml of RPMI medium supplemented with 1% L-glutamine, 1% Hepes, 2% penicillin–streptomycin, 10% fetal calf serum, and 1% 2-mercaptoethanol (5×10^{-5} *M*). After 5 days of culture at 37°C in 5% CO_2, cells were harvested and viability was assessed by the trypan blue dye exclusion test. Graded amounts of viable cells (1×10^6, 5×10^5, 2.5×10^5, and 1.25×10^5 cells) were added into the wells of a round-bottom microplate together with 10^4 P815 mastocytoma cells previously labeled with ^{51}Cr by incubating 10×10^6 P815 cells with 100 μCi of $Na_2{}^{51}CrO_4$. After a 4-hr incubation period at 37°C in 5% CO_2, the plates were spun down at 500*g* for 10 min, the supernatants collected, and specific ^{51}Cr calculated according to Cerottini and Brunner (18):

$$\% \text{ specific cytotoxicity} = \frac{\text{exp. cpm} - \text{spont. cpm}}{\text{total cpm} - \text{spont. cpm}} \times 100,$$

where spontaneous counts per minute represents the radioactivity released in supernatants of wells containing medium and target cells alone, and total counts per minute represents the radioactivity released in wells containing 10% RBS and target cells alone. The background release was less than 15% of maximal release in all experiments. In mitogen responses as well as in MLC–CML experiments, lymphocytes from individual mice were tested in all cases.

RESULTS

1. *Effect of Thymectomy at Weaning on PHA and Con A Responsiveness*

The effect of thymectomy at weaning on the proliferative response of spleen cells to PHA and Con A was tested at various intervals after surgery. Results of the kinetic studies are shown in Tables 1 and 2 and in Fig. 1. One can note that both PHA and Con A responses are depressed by thymectomy but that the decrease of PHA responsiveness in thymectomized mice is faster and more pronounced than

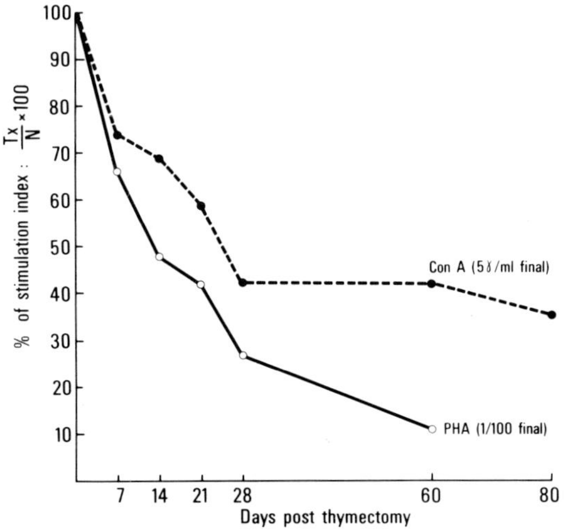

FIG. 1. Effect of thymectomy at weaning on PHA and Con A responses. The results are expressed for Tx mice as the percentage of normal response. Each point represents the value obtained for five or six mice —PHA (final dilution 1/100); – – –, Con A (final concentration 5 μg/ml).

TABLE 1

Kinetics of PHA Responsiveness after Thymectomy at Weaning

	PHA (1/100)				
	Normal mice		Thymectomized mice		
Days after TX	Exp. cpm[a] ± SE[b]	Background cpm[c] ± SE	Exp. cpm ± SE	Background cpm ± SE	P^d
7	30,981 ± 1,762	9,318 ± 995	18,933 ± 1,579	9,210 ± 456	$10^{-3} < P < 10^{-2}$
14	27,104 ± 1,750	8,913 ± 363	14,099 ± 1,072	10,364 ± 1,778	$<10^{-3}$
21	44,866 ± 3,101	10,344 ± 466	27,215 ± 6,154	12,498 ± 2,519	$=10^{-2}$
28	43,866 ± 1,496	6,931 ± 769	11,979 ± 316	7,185 ± 506	$<10^{-3}$
60	24,458 ± 1,372	1,284 ± 258	9,087 ± 1,336	4,032 ± 938	$<10^{-3}$
80	N.T.[e]	N.T.	N.T.		

[a] Experimental cpm = cpm in culture with mitogen.
[b] Standard error of the mean of five to six mice.
[c] Background cpm = cpm in control culture without mitogen.
[d] P values determined by Student's t test.
[e] N.T., not tested.

that of Con A responsiveness. Each experimental point corresponds to three distinct experiments using six mice. A twofold decrease of proliferative responses to both mitogens is already noted after 3 weeks postsurgery, and a significant diminution is even observed after 1 week. The depressive effect of thymectomy was seen at all mitogen concentrations used (1/200, 1/100, 1/50, for PHA and 2.5, 5, and 10 μg/well for Con A). Since the responsiveness to PHA and Con A of sham-thymectomized mice was identical to that of normal mice, the latter were used as controls in all the experiments.

2. *Restoration of PHA and Con A Responsiveness by FTS*

Groups of six mice which had been thymectomized at weaning were treated with FTS (+CMC) at doses of 10 ng, beginning from Day +2 after thymus ablation

TABLE 2

Kinetics of Con A (5 μg) Responsiveness after Thymectomy at Weaning

	Normal mice		Thymectomized mice		
Days after TX	Exp. cpm[a] ± SE[b]	Background cpm[c] ± SE	Exp. cpm ± SE	Background cpm ± SE	P^d
7	76,135 ± 3,873	8,614 ± 1,084	61,748 ± 4,333	9,210 ± 456	$0.01 < P < 0.02$
14	54,357 ± 1,435	8,913 ± 363	47,688 ± 6,726	11,688 ± 1,728	$=0.05$
21	141,134 ± 6,360	13,483 ± 475	82,348 ± 14,377	10,577 ± 1,816	$10^{-3} < p < 10^{-2}$
28	77,182 ± 1,546	6,931 ± 769	35,562 ± 657	7,185 ± 506	$<10^{-3}$
60	95,488 ± 7,560	6,396 ± 473	39,412 ± 804	5,525 ± 444	$<10^{-3}$
80	89,115 ± 7,840	4,640 ± 502	37,142 ± 927	5,042 ± 427	$<10^{-3}$

[a] Experimental cpm = cpm in culture with mitogen.
[b] Standard error to the mean of five to six mice.
[c] Background cpm = cpm in control culture without mitogen.
[d] P values determined by Student's t test.

until Day −2 before sacrifice. Control mice included thymectomized mice that were left untreated or received CMC alone, as well as normal mice of the same age or sham-Tx mice.

FTS treatment was continued for 1 to 2 months. Figures 2a and b present a typical experiment taken out of three comparable ones. One-month treatment induces a significant increase of mitogen responses up to 52% of the normal responses for both PHA and Con A. Two-month treatment has still a more clear-cut effect, with PHA response increasing up to 85% and Con A response to 65% of the normal response of untreated, nonthymectomized control mice. Treatment of thymectomized mice with CMC alone has no statistically significant effect.

3. *Restoration of PHA and Con A Responses by FTS Analogs*

Mice were treated with [DAsn^9]-FTS, [DAla^6]-FTS, and [Har^3]-FTS at the dose of 10 ng, three times weekly for 1 month, and tested for their PHA and Con A responses. Control mice were thymectomized (at the same age) and only received the diluent (NaCl 0.9%) or were left untreated.

The [DAsn^9]-FTS analog had no effect on PHA response and only a marginal and nonsignificant effect on Con A response. Conversely, the two other analogs showed a significant effect either on both mitogen responses for [Har^3]-FTS or on

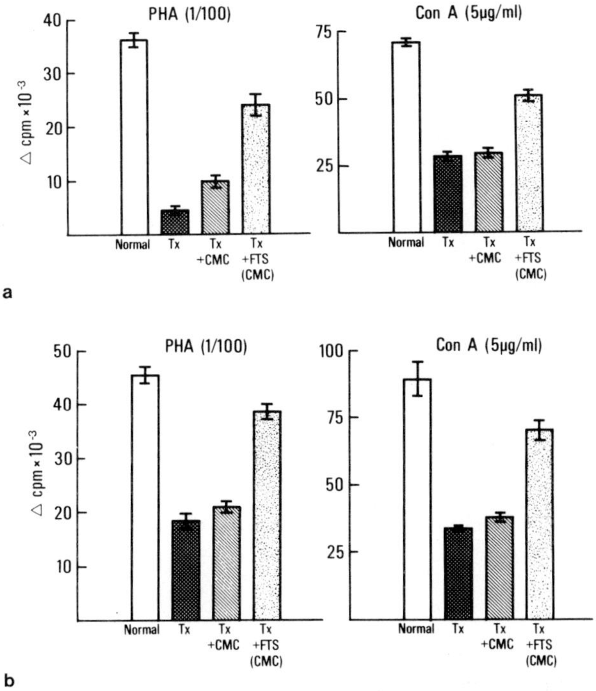

FIG. 2. Restoration of mitogen responsiveness in mice thymectomized at weaning after *in vivo* treatment with FTS. Results are expressed as Δcpm (cpm in cultures with PHA or Con A − cpm in culture without mitogen). (a) Effect of 1-month treatment with FTS; (b) effect of 2-month treatment with FTS.

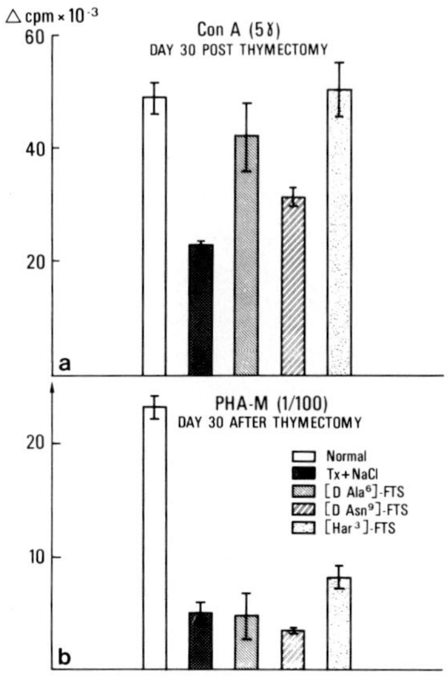

FIG. 3. Effect of FTS synthetic analogs on PHA and Con A responsiveness of mice thymectomized at weaning. Spleen cells were tested for either: Con A-induced (a) or PHA-induced (b) responses. Results are expressed as Δcpm (cpm in culture with mitogen − cpm in control culture without mitogen).

Con A response only for [DAla^6]-FTS. In the case of [Har^3]-FTS a complete restoration of Con A response was observed (Fig. 3a).

4. *Effect of Thymectomy at Weaning on CML*

Spleen cells of C57BL/6 mice were tested at various intervals after thymectomy for their capacity to generate cytotoxic T cells after *in vitro* stimulation with allogeneic DBA/2 lymphocytes. No difference was observed between normal or sham-Tx mice and thymectomized mice at any time between Days 7 and 80 after thymus ablation. Table 3 shows the results of a typical experiment (two experiments for each test) performed 28 days after surgery. Since the mice used for these CML studies are the same mice in which depressed responses to mitogens have been

TABLE 3

Effect of Thymectomy at Weaning on Cell-Mediated Lympholysis (CML)

Mice	Number of mice	Percentage cytotoxicity[a] ± SE[b]			
		100/1	50/1	25/1	12.5/1
Normal	6	70.6 ± 7	58.2 ± 6	44.4 ± 3.5	35 ± 3
Thymectomized	6	62.2 ± 5	54.5 ± 5	42.8 ± 4	30.2 ± 3

Note. Results are expressed as percentage of specific lysis at the effector/target cell ratios of 100/1, 50/1, 25/1, and 12.5/1.

[a] % specific lysis = cpm exp. − cpm spont./cpm max. − cpm spont. × 100.

[b] Standard error of the mean of six mice.

TABLE 4

Effect of Treatment with FTS or Its Synthetic Analogs on Cell-Mediated Lympholysis (CML) of Mice Thymectomized at Weaning

Mice	Percentage cytotoxicity[a] ± SE[b]			
	100/1	50/1	25/1	12.5/1
Normal	72.6 ± 7	59 ± 4	48 ± 4	40 ± 4.5
Tx	63.2 ± 5	54 ± 3.5	45 ± 3	38 ± 4.5
Tx + CMC	69 ± 4	52 ± 3	43 ± 4	36 ± 3
Tx + FTS (CMC)	64 ± 5	51 ± 4.5	44 ± 3.5	35 ± 3
[D Ala^6]-FTS	65 ± 6	50 ± 5	40 ± 4.5	33 ± 4
[D Asn^9]-FTS	62 ± 3	55 ± 4	39 ± 3.5	28 ± 5.5
[Har^3]-FTS	54 ± 4	53 ± 5.5	45 ± 4	35 ± 3.5

Note. MLC-CML after *in vitro* stimulation with DBA/2 spleen cells was tested in normal mice, Tx mice, Tx mice injected with CMC, or Tx mice treated with FTS or its analogs. The specific percentage lysis of P815 ^{51}Cr labeled mastocytoma cells was calculated at effector/target cell ratio of 100/1.

[a] % specific lysis = cpm exp. − cpm spont./cpm max. − cpm spont.

[b] Standard error of the mean of six mice.

reported above, these data indicate a dissociation between the effects of thymectomy at weaning on T-cell-mediated responses.

5. *Effect of Treatment with FTS and Its Analogs on the CML Reaction in Mice Thymectomized at Weaning*

In vitro CML reactivity of spleen cells from thymectomized mice was tested after 1 month treatment with either FTS or its analogs. The mice used for this study were again the same as those used for mitogen responses. Results shown in Table 4 indicate no modification of CTL induction in FTS-treated or in untreated thymectomized mice, compared to normal control mice. Similar negative results were obtained with FTS analogs.

DISCUSSION

The results reported here demonstrate that Tx at weaning significantly depresses the spleen cell responses to PHA and Con A. This diminution of the T-cell-specific mitogen responses which appears as early as the first week post-Tx and persists for at least 11 weeks, is more rapid and more profound for PHA than for Con A. Several groups have described the effect of Tx on mitogen responsiveness in mice and rats. Takiguchi *et al.* (12) reported a rapid and long-lasting diminution of PHA responsiveness in neonatally Tx mice which was as low as 15% of the normal response within 3 weeks after Tx. Andersson *et al.* (11) observed that spleen lymphocytes from adult Tx mice responded less efficiently to PHA between 3 and 8 weeks after surgery and then returned to control levels. A similar (although less striking) transient fall in the Con A response was noted. Folch and Waksman (14) showed that adult Tx in rats caused a significant but temporary loss of PHA responsiveness. Jacobs and Byrd reported that Tx of young adult mice (4 weeks old) caused a depression of both PHA and Con A responses between 4 and 36 weeks following surgery (19) after an initial increase of mitogen responses during the first 4 weeks post-Tx. However, the time required before this drop was detected was 3 weeks for adult Tx mice and 1 week for mice Tx at weaning. This delay can be explained by the presence of a higher number of circulating mature T lymphocytes in adult Tx mice than in mice thymectomized at weaning.

It is interesting to note that in contrast to the observations of Andersson *et al.* (11) the depression that we find subsequent to Tx at weaning is long lasting both for PHA and Con A (for at least 11 weeks after surgery). Moreover, our data indicating a more profound decrease in the PHA than in the Con A response confirm those of Folch and Waksman (14) in rats, and those of Andersson *et al.* (11) in mice.

Although previous reports have generally indicated that adult Tx has no effect (10) or only a transient one (11, 14, 20) on T-cell functions other than mitogen responses, some investigators have observed a decline in certain T-cell subsets, subsequent to Tx. Raff and Cantor (7) and Kappler *et al.* (21) have demonstrated a diminution of T helper cells within 6 weeks after adult Tx. The number of splenic Thy-1-positive cells is decreased by 5 weeks postadult Tx, and this decrease is primarily caused by the loss of those cells with a high rather than a low density of Thy-1 (22), bearing the Lyt 1, 2, and 3 antigens (8). Bash *et al.* (23) found that the transient fall in mitogen responsiveness of adult Tx rats was eliminated after the removal of a glass-wool-adherent spleen cell population of suppressor cells rather than a depletion of responding cells.

Our studies show a long-lasting effect of Tx at weaning, which is corrected by FTS treatment. One may hypothesize that this effect is due to the depletion of the pool of post-thymic precursor cells, as defined by Stutman (24). Such post-thymic cells are known in other systems to be target cells for thymic factors, in particular FTS (25). They cannot undergo further maturation in the absence of FTS.

We have observed that Tx at weaning does not affect the capacity of C57BL/6 spleen cells to generate allogeneic CTL against P815 tumor cells, and that treatment with either FTS or its analogs is without effect on CTL production by spleen cells from normal or Tx animals. Conflicting data are found in the literature concerning the effect of adult Tx on MLC-induced allogeneic killer cells using a two-way MLC. M. A. Bach described a depressive effect of adult Tx between 6 and 12 weeks postsurgery (26). Similarly, Andersson *et al.* (11) demonstrated a CML decrease 2 months post-Tx whereas Simpson and Cantor (15) reported a CML increase which they attributed to the loss of suppressor T cells after Tx. In view of M. A. Bach's (26) observation that the depressive effect of Tx on *in vivo* CTL production can only be detected under suboptimal conditions of immunization, one may suppose that, similarly, suboptimal culture conditions are needed in MLC to show a depressive effect of Tx. This interpretation would fit with the findings of Lau and Goldstein (27) showing that TP5 (a pentapeptidic fragment of thymopoietin) only increased the frequency of cytotoxic T-cell precursors when suboptimal conditions of *in vitro* stimulation were used. Thus, the differing results obtained after *in vitro* sensitization could be explained by minor differences in culture techniques.

Finally, our data and previous works indicate that the T cells involved in phytomitogen response are not yet fully mature at weaning and that Tx at weaning finally has effects on mitogen response comparable to those of adult Tx. The importance of thymic hormone secretion on the last stages of T-cell maturation is shown by the correction of Tx effects afforded by FTS or some of its analogs. These results confirm the interest of these analogs which can be used without CMC with the same efficiency as FTS injected with CMC as a vehicle. At variance with mitogen responsive cells, cytotoxic T-cell precursors are apparently already mature and long lived at weaning, at least when they are studied under optimal conditions of alloimmunization. When it is not the case (infraoptimal dose of allogeneic cells or suboptimal conditions of lymphocyte cultures), the CTL generation apparently depends upon an adult Tx-sensitive Lyt 123^{+} population (8).

ACKNOWLEDGMENTS

We are grateful for the excellent technical assistance afforded by I. Gaillard, Mrs. V. Hunbert and Mrs. E. Charveriat-Seignot. We would like to thank Dr. E. Bricas and his colleagues for the synthesis of the FTS analogs.

REFERENCES

1. Bach, J. F., Cantor, H., Roelants, G., and Stutman, O., *In "Biological Activity of Thymic Hormones"* (D. Van Bekkum, Ed.), p. 159. Kooyker Scientific Rotterdam, 1975.
2. Cantor, H., *In "Proc. 2nd Annual Lepetit Colloquium,"* p. 73. North-Holland, Amsterdam, 1971.
3. Stutman, O., Yunis, E. J., and Good, R. A., *J. Exp. Med.* **132,** 583, 1970.
4. Cantor, H., and Asofsky, R., *J. Exp. Med.* **131,** 235, 1970.
5. Cantor, H., and Asofsky, R., *J. Exp. Med.* **135,** 764, 1972.
6. Stobo, J. D., Paul, W. E., and Henney, C. S, *J. Immunol.* **110,** 65, 1973.
7. Raff, M. C., and Cantor, H. *In "Progress in Immunology"* (B. Amos, Ed.), p. 83. Academic Press, New York, 1971.
8. Cantor, H., and Boyse, E. A., *J. Exp. Med.* **141,** 1376, 1975.
9. Stout, R. D., and Herzenberg, L. A., *J. Exp. Med.* **142,** 1041, 1975.
10. Stobo, D., and Paul, W., *J. Immunol.,* **110**(2), 362, 1973.
11. Andersson, L. C., Haÿry, P., Bach, M. A. and Bach, J. F., *Nature (London)* **252,** 252, 1974.
12. Takiguchi, T., Adler, W. H., and Smith, R. T. *J. Exp. Med.* **133,** 63, 1971.
13. Trainin, N., Small, N., and Globerson, A., *J. Exp. Med.* **130,** 765, 1969.
14. Folch, H., and Waksman, B. H., *J. Immunol.* **109,** 1046, 1972.
15. Simpson, E., and Cantor, H., *Eur. J. Immunol.* **5,** 337, 1975.
16. Miller, J. F. A. P. *Brit. J. Cancer* **14,** 93, 1960.
17. Bach, J. F., Dardenne, M., Pléau, J. M., and Bach, M. A., *Ann. N.Y. Acad. Sci.* **249,** 186, 1976.
18. Cerottini, J. C., and Brunner, K. T. 1971. "*In Vitro Methods in Cell-Mediated Immunity*" p. 369, Academic Press, New York.
19. Jacobs, D. M., and Byrd, W., *Nature (London)* **255,** 153, 1975.
20. Folch, H., and Waksman, B. H., *Cell. Immunol.* **9,** 25, 1973.
21. Kappler, J., Hunter, P., Jacobs, D., and Lord, E., *J. Immunol.* **113,** 27, 1974.
22. Cantor, H., Simpson, E., Sato, V., Fathman, C. G., and Herzenberg, L. A., *Cell. Immunol.* **15,** 80, 1975.
23. Bash, J. A., Dardenne, M., Bach, J. F., and Waksmann, B. H. *Cell. Immunol.* **26,** 308, 1976.
24. Stutman, O. *Contemp. Top. Immunobiol.* **7,** 1, 1977.
25. Bach, J. F., *J. Immunopharmacol.* **1**(3), 277, 1979.
26. Bach, M. A., *J. Immunol.* **119,** 641, 1977.
27. Lau, C., and Goldstein, G., *J. Immunol.* **124,** 1861, 1980.

CELLULAR IMMUNOLOGY **64**, 102–118 (1981)

Inhibition of Antigen-Induced T-Cell Proliferation by Antibodies to Endogenous AKR-MuLV

WALLACE Y. LANGDON AND GEOFFREY R. SHELLAM

Department of Microbiology, University of Western Australia, Queen Elizabeth II Medical Centre, Nedlands, Western Australia 6009, Australia

Received February 9, 1981; accepted July 9, 1981

Lymph node cells from BALB/c mice immunized with ovalbumin or human γ-globulin were restimulated *in vitro* with these antigens and assayed for antigen-induced proliferation. The proliferative response was shown to be antigen specific and T cell dependent. A rabbit antiserum to envelope and core proteins of AKR murine leukemia virus was found to inhibit antigen-induced T-cell proliferation. The IgG fraction and $F(ab')_2$ fragments of the antiserum were also inhibitory. The inhibition occurred after the initial step of antigen–T cell interaction and viral absorption studies showed the inhibition to be specific for anti-AKR virus antibodies. A hypothesis for the mechanism of inhibition is discussed in relation to a functional role for endogenous murine leukemia virus.

INTRODUCTION

The genetic information coding for murine leukemia viruses (MuLV) is integrated into the chromosomal DNA of all mouse strains and transmitted vertically through the germ line (for reviews see (1–3)). Three distinct classes of endogenous MuLV have been isolated from inbred mice and have been classified on the basis of their host range and interference specificity. They are ecotropic MuLV—either N-, B-, or NB-tropic (4), xenotropic MuLV (5), and mink cell focus-inducing MuLV which have dualtropic host ranges (6). In recent years it has been hypothesized that the persistence of these genes through evolution indicates they may be involved in the normal cellular functions of the host (7, 8). The study of this hypothesis has involved two principle areas of investigation. First, studies demonstrating the activation of endogenous MuLV by mitogenic and allogeneic stimulation, and second, the inhibitory effects of MuLV antisera on various immunological functions. It has been found that B-cell mitogens which trigger terminal B-cell differentiation are effective inducers of xenotropic MuLV (9–15). Concanavalin A, in the presence of bromodeoxyuridine, is the only known T-cell mitogen which can induce lymphocytes to release xenotropic MuLV. However, the virus release has been shown to occur from B cells activated by factors produced by the mitogen-stimulated T cells (16). Allogeneic stimulation, both *in vivo* and *in vitro*, also induces the release of MuLV (17, 18). Both N- and B-tropic MuLV are induced (17) and their release is dependent on a viable T-cell population (18).

Studies using various MuLV antisera have shown that the antisera will suppress

0008-8749/81/150102-17$02.00/0

humoral immune responses, colony formation in the spleen, mitogenic responses, and naturally occurring lymphocyte-mediated immunity to endogenous MuLV. A rabbit antiserum to Balb-2 xenotropic virus has been shown to suppress the production of antibodies to sheep red blood cells both *in vitro* and *in vivo* in all mouse strains tested (7, 8). Pretreatment with the same antiserum suppressed colony formation in the spleen by hemopoietic stem cells (19). Rabbit antisera directed against the major envelope glycoprotein, gp70, of AKR-MuLV and Rauscher MuLV, suppressed both lipopolysaccharide and phytohemagglutinin responses of spleen cells from a number of mouse strains (20). Natural cell-mediated cytotoxicity of lymphoid cells against tumor cells containing MuLV was also blocked either by sera from normal mice naturally immune to MuLV or by homologous or heterologous hyperimmune sera to Rauscher-MuLV (21).

In this study we have examined the effect of a rabbit antiserum against endogenous ecotropic AKR-MuLV on an antigen-induced, *in vitro* proliferative response of BALB/c lymph node cells. The antiserum was found to suppress T-cell proliferation and the suppression could be removed by absorption with AKR virus.

MATERIALS AND METHODS

Mice

Inbred BALB/c mice of either sex aged 7–10 weeks were obtained from the Animal Breeding Unit of the University of Western Australia.

Antigens

Twice-crystallized ovalbumin (OVA, Schwarz/Mann, Orangeburg, N.Y.) was suspended in phosphate-buffered saline (PBS). Human γ-globulin (HGG, Commonwealth Serum Laboratories, Australia) was purified by DEAE cellulose column chromatography and heat aggregated at 63°C for 25 min before use. For immunizations the antigens were emulsified in an equal volume of complete Freund's adjuvant (Difco, Detroit, Mich.) and mice were injected subcutaneously at the base of the tail with 50 μl of the emulsion containing 100 μg of antigen.

In Vitro Culture

Inguinal and periaortic lymph nodes were removed aseptically from the antigen-primed mice 8–10 days after immunization. A single-cell suspension of lymph node cells (LNC) was obtained by mincing the lymph nodes through a stainless-steel sieve in RPMI 1640–Hepes supplemented with 5% fetal calf serum (FCS). The LNC were washed by centrifugation and resuspended in Ealge's medium enriched with Hanks' salts and amino acids (EHAA) (22), supplemented with 2% heat-inactivated FCS (56°C for 30 min) or 0.5% autologous normal mouse serum (NMS). In some experiments the LNC were enriched for T lymphocytes by passing the LNC through a nylon wool column exactly as described elsewhere (23) before resuspension in EHAA–2% FCS or EHAA–0.5% NMS. The LNC suspensions were dispensed in 0.1-ml volumes in 96-well, flat-bottom microtiter trays (Falcon, Becton–Dickenson, Oxnard, Calif.) at 4×10^5 LNC/well. OVA, HGG, or PBS were added to the LNC in a volume of 10 μl giving final concentrations of OVA or HGG of 100 and 50 μg/ml, respectively. Preliminary experiments showed these concentrations gave the optimal proliferative responses. Triplicate dilutions of antiviral antisera or control sera in 0.1 ml of EHAA–2% FCS or 0.1 ml of EHAA–2% FCS alone were added to the LNC. The control rabbit serum was a prebleed of the rabbit used to produce the anti-AKR MuLV serum. The cells were incubated at 37°C in a humidified atmosphere of 10% CO_2 in air for 4 days.

Assay for Antigen-Induced Proliferation

LNC proliferation was determined by pulsing the cultures with 0.2 μCi of [^{3}H]methylthymidine in 10 μl of RPMI 22 hr before harvesting. The cells were harvested using a Skatron automatic harvester and the dried filter disks were counted in 5 ml of scintillant using a Packard Tri-Carb-2600 liquid scintillation spectrometer. The results were expressed as mean disintegrations per minute ± standard error of the triplicate cultures. Statistical analysis of responses was determined by a two-tailed Student's *t* test.

Treatment of LNC with Anti-Thy 1.2 and Complement (C)

OVA-primed LNC were incubated at a final concentration of 8×10^6 cells/ml with either anti-Thy 1.2 antiserum (Miles-Yeda, 1:5 final dilution) or normal BALB/c serum (1:5 final dilution) for 35 min at 4°C. The LNC were washed twice in RPMI–Hepes–5% FCS and resuspended in either complement (C) (1:20 final dilution), using rabbit serum absorbed with mouse thymus and spleen cells as a source of complement, or PBS for 45 min at 37°C. The LNC were washed twice and viability was determined by trypan blue exclusion. Pretreatment with anti-Thy 1.2 and C killed 38% of the LNC. Cell numbers were adjusted so that 4×10^5 viable cells were added to each well. The cells were cultured and cellular proliferation assayed as described above. OVA-primed LNC cultured for 3 days with 100 μg/ml of OVA were also treated with anti-Thy 1.2 and C as described above. Treatment with anti-Thy 1.2 and C killed 60% of the OVA-cultured LNC. Cell numbers were adjusted so that 2×10^5 viable cells were added to each well and cultured for a further 22 hr with 100 μg/ml OVA and 0.2 μCi of [^{3}H]thymidine.

Preparation of AKR-MuLV

AKR-MuLV was purified from the supernatants of roller bottle cultures of virus-infected SC-1 cells on sucrose gradients as described previously (24). AKR virus was originally obtained from Electronucleonics Inc., Bethesda, Maryland, through the courtesy of Dr. J. Gruber, NIH (Lot Nos. 681-32-7 and 681-32-11).

Antiviral Antisera

A rabbit was immunized by multiple-site, subcutaneous injections of 500 μg of AKR-MuLV emulsified with an equal volume of complete Freund's adjuvant followed by 500 μg in incomplete Freund's adjuvant 2 weeks later. The rabbit was bled 3 weeks after the second injection and the antiserum (and all control sera) were heat-inactivated (56°C 30 min). The antiserum was absorbed twice on ice for 30 min with a 20% packed cell volume of uninfected SC-1 cells, followed by absorption with a 20% packed cell volume of spleen cells from 7-week-old BALB/c mice. Goat antiserum to AKR p30 (5S-333) was prepared by Dr. R. Wilsnack,

Huntingdon Research Center, Maryland, and made available by Dr. J. Gruber. A rabbit antiserum to influenza virus (A2 Jap strain) with a hemagglutination inhibition titer of 1920 units/ml was a gift of Dr. H. Watanabe of this department. These antisera were also absorbed on ice for 30 min with a 20% packed cell volume of spleen cells from 7-week-old BALB/c mice.

Fractionation of Rabbit Anti-AKR-MuLV Antiserum

The IgG fraction of the rabbit antiserum was prepared by column chromatography using DEAE cellulose, and was digested with pepsin to obtain $F(ab')_2$ fragments (25). The digest was applied to a Sephadex G-150 column and further separated from contaminating IgG by protein A column chromatography (Pharmacia, Uppsala, Sweden).

Characterization of the Antiviral Antiserum

(1) Immunofluorescence. Rabbit anti-AKR-MuLV antiserum was examined by indirect immunofluorescence for its ability to bind to SC-1 cells infected with AKR-MuLV, uninfected SC-1 cells, and inguinal and periaortic lymph node cells from unimmunized BALB/c mice 7–10 weeks old. Indirect immunofluorescence was carried out using a fluorescein-conjugated goat anti-rabbit IgG which was affinity-purified as described elsewhere (25).

(2) Detection of anti-OVA antibodies. The presence of antibodies to OVA in the antiviral antisera was examined by hemagglutination of sheep red blood cells tanned with OVA (SRBC-OVA). If anti-OVA antibodies were detected the antiserum was absorbed twice with a 25% packed cell volume of SRBC-OVA at room temperature for 30 min and then reexamined for anti-OVA antibodies.

(3) Antiviral titer. The antiviral titer of the rabbit anti-AKR-MuLV antiserum was determined using a radioimmune precipitation (RIP) assay as described previously (24). The RIP titer of the antiserum was calculated from the titration curve as the reciprocal dilution of antiserum that precipitated 50% of the [^{3}H]leucine-labeled AKR-MuLV.

(4) Sodium dodecyl sulfate–polyacrylamide gel electrophoresis (SDS–PAGE). Immune precipitates between Triton X-100 disrupted ^{3}H-labeled AKR-MuLV (260,000 dpm) and rabbit anti AKR-MuLV antiserum (1 μl) were prepared by a method described by Ihle *et al.* (26), and electrophoresis was carried out on 10% gels (27). Low-molecular-weight calibration proteins (Pharmacia, Uppsala) were used as molecular weight standards and the gel was sectioned into 1-mm slices using a gel slicer (Mickle Laboratory Engineering Co., England). The radioactivity of each slice was determined by liquid scintillation counting using scintillant containing 10% Permafluor III and 10% Soluene (Packard Instrument Co., Inc., Downer's Grove, Ill.) in toluene.

Absorption of Rabbit Anti-AKR-MuLV Antiserum with AKR Virus

The antiserum (0.5 ml) was absorbed with 2 mg of AKR-MuLV for 45 min at 37°C followed by 45 min at 4°C. The virus was then removed by centrifugation at 100,000*g* for 1 hr at 4°C in a Beckman SW 50.1 rotor. Antiviral antibodies in the IgG fraction were removed by absorption to detergent disrupted AKR-MuLV bound to cyanogen bromide (CNBr-activated Sepharose 4B) (Pharmacia). The virus used for absorption was disrupted for 1 hr at 4°C by the addition of 1 ml of disruption buffer (1.2 *M* KCl–0.1 *M* Tris–1% Triton X-100 and 0.03 *M* 2-mercaptoethanol) to 1 ml of virus (8 mg). The disrupted virus was dialyzed for 24 hr at 4°C against 0.1 *M* $NaHCO_3$, pH 8.3, in 0.5 *M* NaCl. Following dialysis the volume of disrupted virus was made up to 5 ml of the above buffer and added to 1 g of CNBr-activated Sepharose 4B. The mixture was reacted by vortex mixing for 1 hr at room temperature and 16 hr at 4°C. The procedure bound 92% of the disrupted virus. Any remaining unbound active groups were blocked by incubation at room temperature for 90 min with 1 *M* ethanolamine. After extensive washings, two cycles of affinity absorption were carried out using a method described by Watanabe *et al.* (28).

Estimation of Protein Concentration

IgG, $F(ab')_2$ and virus concentrations were estimated by the method of Lowry *et al.* (29).

Detection of MuLV Cell Surface Antigens

(1) Immunofluorescence. MuLV antigens on the surface of LNC were examined by indirect immunofluorescence using the rabbit anti-AKR-MuLV antiserum and fluorescein-conjugated goat IgG anti-rabbit IgG described above. LNC were obtained from BALB/c mice immunized 10 days previously with 100 μg of OVA. The LNC were nylon wool fractionated and either examined immediately for AKR-MuLV cell surface antigens or cultured for 4 days in EHAA 0.5% NMS with 100 μg/ml of OVA or 10 μl of PBS. The cultured cells were harvested and washed twice before resuspension in 0.5 ml of rabbit anti-AKR antiserum diluted 1:20 in RPMI Hepes supplemented with 3% FCS and containing 15 m*M* NaN_3. The cells were incubated on ice for 30 min, washed three times at 4°C, then resuspended in 0.5 ml (0.5 mg) of fluorescein-conjugated goat IgG anti-rabbit IgG. After a further 30 min of incubation on ice the cell suspension was layered on 3.5 ml of Ficoll–Paque (Pharmacia) and centrifuged at 1200*g* for 10 min. This removed dead cells and the viable cells at the interface were washed three times before their examination by fluorescent microscopy. At least 300 cells were counted and the cells were scored as fluorescent positive or fluorescent negative.

(2) SDS-PAGE analysis of radiolabeled cell surface antigens. LNC from BALB/c mice immunized with 100 μg of OVA 11 days previously were cultured for 4 days in EHAA 0.5% NMS with 100 μg/ml of OVA and then harvested and centrifuged through Ficoll–Paque to remove dead cells. The recovered viable cells were washed three times in PBS before radiolabeling. Lymph nodes from the same group of OVA-primed BALB/c mice were removed 15 days after immunization and the LNC were washed three times in PBS before radiolabeling. LNC from both groups were resuspended in 0.5 ml of PBS at 5×10^7 cells/ml. Lactoperoxidase-catalyzed radioiodination was performed by the method described by Kessler (30). Briefly, 0.5 mCi of $Na^{125}I$, 100 μg of lactoperoxidase (76 units/mg protein, (Sigma, St. Louis, Mo.), and 25 μl of 0.03% H_2O_2 were added to the cell suspensions. The reaction proceeded for 4 min at 25°C followed by the addition of 10 μg of lactoperoxidase and 10 μl 0.03% H_2O_2. After a further 4 min of reaction

the labeling was terminated by the addition of 10 ml of cold PBS and three washes in cold PBS. Cell lysis was performed by suspending the cells in 0.8 ml of 0.5% Nonidet P40 and incubating for 30 min at 4°C. Cell debris was removed by ultracentrifugation at 100,000*g* for 45 min at 4°C and the cell lysates were held overnight at 4°C for 12 hr after which 0.1 ml of 5X concentrated PBS was added to 0.4 ml of each lysate. Immune precipitates between solubilized cell surface antigens and rabbit anti-AKR-MuLV antiserum (10 μl) were prepared by the method described by Ihle *et al.* (26) and electrophoresis was carried out on 10% gels (27). The gels were sliced and molecular weight mobilities determined by the method described above. The radioactivity of each slice was determined using a Packard gamma scintilation spectrometer.

In all experiments to detect MuLV cell surface antigens on cultured cells, EHAA medium supplemented with 0.5% normal BALB/c serum was used instead of 2% FCS-supplemented medium. This removed the possibility of MuLV induction by FCS since it has been shown that certain batches of FCS induce xenotropic MuLV release from B lymphocytes (31).

RESULTS

Antigen Specificity and T-Cell Dependency of OVA- and HGG-Induced Proliferation

The specificity of the antigen-induced proliferation of primed LNC *in vitro* is shown in Table 1. As expected the response was antigen-specific and the difference in proliferation in the presence of the relevant compared with the irrelevant antigen was always highly significant ($P < 0.001$).

The characteristics of the cells involved in the proliferative response were examined by nylon wool column fractionation or treatment with anti-Thy 1.2 and C (Table 2). Primed LNC which were not adherent to nylon wool retained the capacity for antigen-induced proliferation and although the response was reduced, the stimulation index for both antigens was higher than with unfractionated cells due to a proportionally greater decrease in the response of the PBS controls (Table 2A). Further evidence for T-cell involvement in antigen-induced proliferative responses

TABLE 1

Antigen Specificity of Ova- and HGG-Induced LNC Proliferation *in Vitro*

Immunizing antigen	*In vitro* antigen	Mean dpm $\times 10^{-3} \pm$ SE
OVA	PBS	8.3 ± 0.7
OVA	OVA	99.6 ± 6.8
OVA	HGG	6.5 ± 0.8
HGG	PBS	9.9 ± 0.6
HGG	OVA	12.7 ± 0.4
HGG	HGG	67.3 ± 3.6

Note. BALB/c mice aged 7 weeks were injected subcutaneously at the base of the tail with 100 μg of OVA or HGG. Draining lymph nodes were removed 10 days later and LNC were cultured in EHAA–2% FCS with either 10 μl of PBS, 100 μg/ml of OVA, or 50 μg/ml of HGG. Cellular proliferation was determined by pulsing the cultures with 0.2 μCi of [^{3}H]thymidine 22 hr before harvesting.

TABLE 2

Characterization of Cells Involved in Antigen-Induced Proliferation

A. Effect of nylon wool fractionation on OVA- or HGG-induced proliferation

	Unfractionated LNC	Nylon-wool-fractionated LNC
	Mean dpm × 10^{-3} ± SE	
OVA (μg/ml)		
0	13.0 ± 0.7[a]	2.8 ± 0.6
100	106.6 ± 3.7	56.8 ± 3.4
HGG (μg/ml)		
0	7.8 ± 0.2	2.3 ± 0.2
50	78.4 ± 2.3	57.3 ± 0.5

B. Effect of anti-Thy 1.2 antiserum + complement treatment on OVA-induced proliferation

	Untreated control	Complement control	Thy 1.2 + complement
OVA (μg/ml)		Mean dpm × 10^{-3} ± SE	
(i) Before culture			
0	30.8 ± 2.7	34.9 ± 1.6	9.8 ± 0.7
100	164.2 ± 7.0	176.8 ± 4.8	20.5 ± 2.3
(ii) After 3 days in culture			
100	140.1 ± 1.3	144.8 ± 1.2	9.9 ± 0.3

Note. (A) LNC from OVA- or HGG-primed BALB/c mice were nylon wool fractionated or unfractionated then restimulated *in vitro* with 100 μg/ml of OVA, 50 μg/ml of HGG, or 10 μl of PBS in EHAA-2% FCS. (B) LNC from OVA-primed BALB/c mice were (i) pretreated with anti-Thy 1.2 + C, NMS + C, or nothing and then restimulated *in vitro* with 10 μl of PBS or 100 μg/ml OVA for 4 days; or (ii) cultured with 100 μg/ml OVA for 3 days and then treated as in (i). Cellular proliferation in (A) and (B) was determined by pulsing the cultures with 0.2 μCi of [^{3}H]thymidine 22 hr before harvesting.

is shown in Table 2B. Treatment of OVA-primed LNC with anti-Thy 1.2 antiserum and C almost totally abrogated the proliferative response whereas the C controls remained unaffected. Similar results were also obtained when the LNC were treated with anti-Thy 1.2 antiserum and C after 3 days in culture with OVA then restimulated for a further 22 hr for [^{3}H]DNA synthesis to be determined. These results demonstrated that the antigen-induced response was T cell dependent and that the proliferating cells were T cells.

Characterization of the Antiviral Serum

(1) Immunofluorescent studies of rabbit anti AKR-MuLV antiserum following the cellular absorption procedures described under Materials and Methods showed that the antiserum did not recognize uninfected SC-1 cells or normal inguinal and

periaortic LNC of BALB/c mice aged 7–10 weeks. However, SC-1 cells infected with AKR-MuLV exhibited strong membrane fluorescence.

(2) Anti-OVA antibodies were present in high titer in the rabbit anti-influenza antiserum (HA titer: 1:2048) but were not detected in the anti-leukemia virus antisera. The OVA antibodies were absorbed to a titer of zero before the rabbit anti-influenza antiserum was used in the OVA-induced proliferation assays.

(3) The rabbit anti AKR-MuLV antiserum had a RIP titer of 6280 and 42.5 μg/ml of the IgG fraction also precipitated 50% of the radiolabeled virus. Following viral absorption the titer of the antiserum was reduced to 960 and 2 cycles of affinity absorption reduced the RIP titer of the IgG fraction to zero.

(4) The SDS–PAGE profile of the viral proteins recognized by the rabbit anti-AKR-MuLV antiserum is shown in Fig. 1. The antiserum recognized viral proteins of molecular weights of approximately 71,000; 69,000; 45,000; 30,000 and 16,000.

Effect of Rabbit Anti-AKR MuLV Antiserum, -IgG and -F(ab')₂ on Antigen-Induced Proliferation

The presence of rabbit anti AKR-MuLV antiserum in the culture medium was found to have an inhibitory effect on antigen-induced proliferation whereas the prebleed control serum had no effect (Fig. 2A). OVA-induced proliferation was

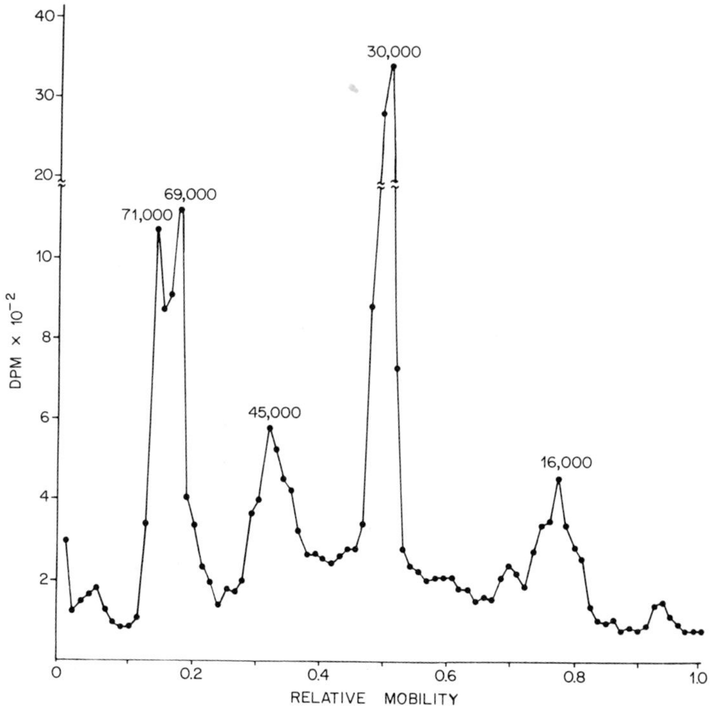

FIG. 1. SDS–PAGE analysis of antiviral specificities in rabbit anti-AKR antiserum. The immune precipitates between detergent disrupted AKR-MuLV and rabbit anti-AKR MuLV antiserum were electrophoresed on a 10% gel. The gel profile was analyzed by slicing the gel into 1-mm sections which were counted by liquid scintillation techniques described under Materials and Methods.

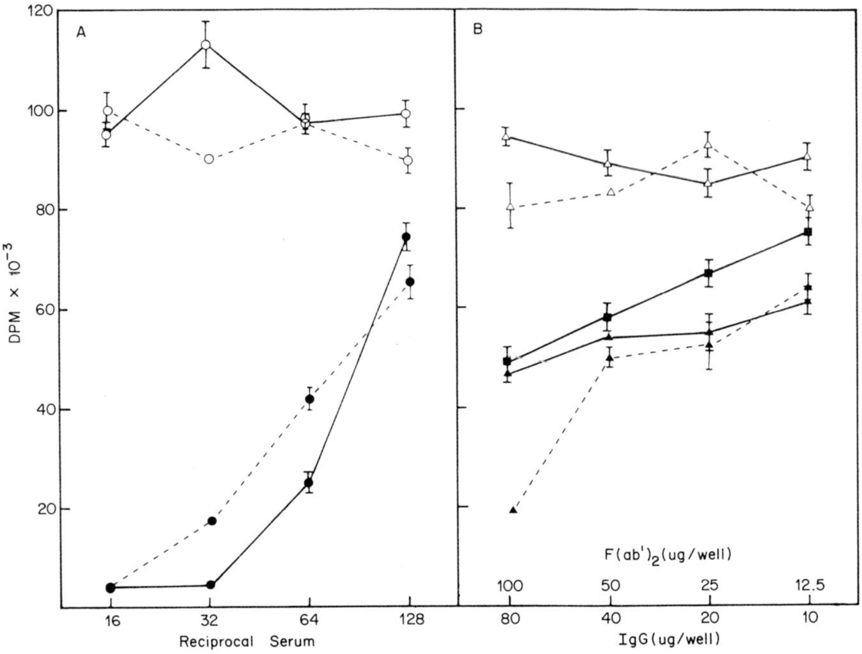

FIG. 2. Inhibition of antigen-induced proliferation by (A) rabbit anti-AKR antiserum; (B) rabbit anti-AKR IgG or $F(ab')_2$. LNC from OVA- and HGG-primed BALB/c mice were restimulated *in vitro* with 100 μg/ml OVA (——) or 50 μg/ml HGG (-----) for 4 days together with (A) triplicate dilutions of rabbit anti-AKR antiserum (●) or normal rabbit serum (○); or (B) triplicate concentrations of rabbit anti-AKR IgG (▲), $F(ab')_2$ (■) or normal rabbit IgG (△). Cellular proliferation was determined by pulsing the cultures with 0.2 μCi of [^{3}H]thymidine 22 hr before harvesting.

inhibited by 96% at dilutions of 1:16 and 1:32 ($P < 0.001$) and by 25% at a dilution of 1:128 ($P < 0.025$). Similar inhibition was observed for HGG-induced proliferation. The IgG fraction of the antiserum also inhibited proliferation; in the OVA-stimulated cultures there was 50% inhibition at 80 μg of IgG/well ($P < 0.001$) and 33% inhibition at 10 μg/well ($P < 0.02$) (Fig. 2B). Furthermore the $F(ab')_2$ fragments of the IgG antibody inhibited proliferation by 47% at 100 μg of $F(ab')_2$/well ($P < 0.005$) and 16% at 12.5 μg/well (Fig. 2B).

Inhibition of Unfractionated or T-Enriched LNC Proliferation by Rabbit Anti-AKR-MuLV Antiserum

In Fig. 3 a comparison of the effect of the antiserum on OVA-induced proliferation of unfractionated LNC and T-enriched LNC is shown. The proliferation of T-enriched LNC was inhibited more effectively than that of the unfractionated LNC. Thus at an antiserum dilution of 1:256 the unfractionated LNC were inhibited 19% whereas the T-enriched LNC were inhibited to the same extent at a dilution of 1:2048.

Comparison of the Inhibitory Effects of Other Antiviral Antisera on OVA-Induced Proliferation

The inhibitory effect of rabbit anti-AKR-MuLV antiserum on OVA-induced proliferation was compared with that of a goat antiserum to AKR-MuLV p30, and

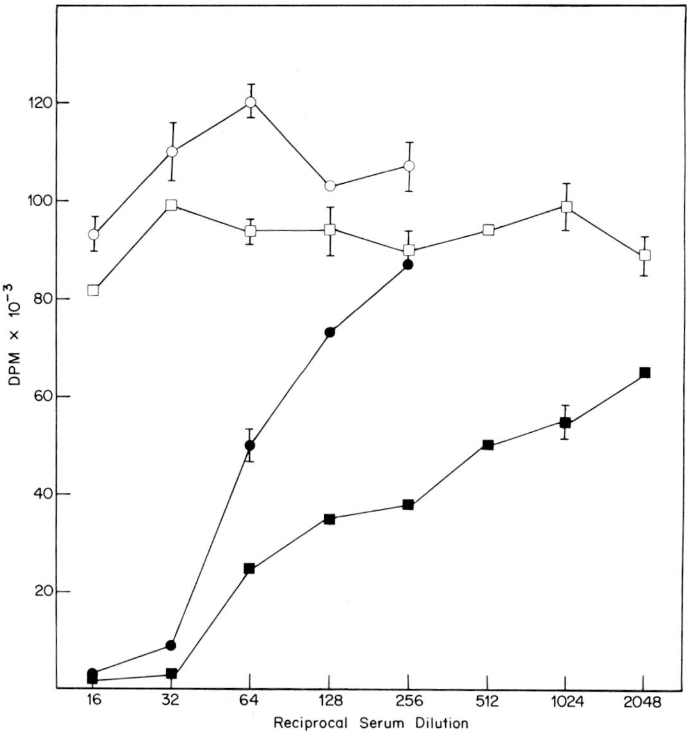

FIG. 3. Inhibitory effects of rabbit anti-AKR antiserum on OVA-induced proliferation. Comparison between unfractionated and T-enriched LNC. Unfractionated LNC + rabbit anti-AKR antiserum (●), unfractionated LNC + normal rabbit serum (○); T-enriched LNC + rabbit anti-AKR antiserum (■), T-enriched LNC + normal rabbit serum (□). LNC from OVA-primed BALB/c mice were enriched for T cells by nylon wool fractionation or unfractionated then restimulated *in vitro* with 100 μg/ml OVA together with triplicate dilutions of rabbit anti-AKR antiserum or control serum. The LNC were cultured for 4 days and cellular proliferation was determined by pulsing the cultures with 0.2 μCi of [^{3}H]thymidine 22 hr before harvesting.

a rabbit antiserum to influenza virus. As shown in Table 3 the antiserum to AKR-MuLV p30 was inhibitory at a 1:16 dilution ($P < 0.005$) although the inhibition was not as marked as that observed with the rabbit anti-AKR-MuLV antiserum ($P < 0.001$ at 1:16, 1:32, 1:64; $P < 0.005$ at 1:128). The anti-influenza antiserum did not inhibit OVA-induced proliferation. The percentage inhibition of the response in the presence of the antisera compared to that of the normal sera controls is shown in parentheses in Table 3.

Kinetics of Antibody-Mediated Inhibition

The rabbit anti-AKR-MuLV antiserum or normal rabbit prebleed serum was added in 5-μl volumes to the OVA-stimulated LNC at 0, 2, 4, 8, 12, 24, 48, or 72 hr after the addition of the antigen. Inhibition of proliferation was greatest (97%) when the anti-AKR-MuLV antiserum was added to the cultures during the first 24 hr (Fig. 4) although at 72 hr when the antiserum was added at the time of [^{3}H]thymidine pulsing, the proliferative response was still inhibited by 50%.

TABLE 3

Effects of Antiviral Antisera on Ovalbumin Induced Proliferation

Reciprocal serum dilution	Rabbit anti-AKR MuLV	Rabbit anti-influenza virus	Normal rabbit serum	Goat anti-AKR p30	Normal goat serum
			Mean dpm × 10^{-3} ± SE		
16	3.7 ± 0.3 (96)[a]	90.9 ± 2.4 (2)	92.9 ± 2.9	38.5 ± 2.4 (44)	68.2 ± 1.8
32	28.3 ± 0.3 (74)	102.8 ± 0.9 (6)	109.7 ± 5.8	54.7 ± 1.8 (26)	73.4 ± 6.0
64	50.1 ± 0.7 (56)	108.5 ± 3.5 (4)	112.7 ± 3.0	57.1 ± 0.5 (24)	74.6 ± 2.5
128	85.3 ± 2.3 (23)	109.0 ± 2.5 (1)	110.4 ± 1.8	62.9 ± 2.8 (11)	70.9 ± 3.4

Note. LNC from OVA-primed BALB/c mice were restimulated *in vitro* with 100 μg/ml OVA together with triplicate dilutions of the above sera or antisera. The LNC were cultured for 4 days and cellular proliferation determined by pulsing the cultures with 0.2 μCi of [^{3}H]thymidine 22 hr before harvesting.
[a] Percentage inhibition compared to serum controls.

Effect of Virus Absorption of Inhibitory Antibody

One cycle of absorption of the rabbit anti-AKR-MuLV antiserum with AKR virus reduced the RIP titer from 6280 to 960. The unabsorbed or virus-absorbed antisera were then titrated in the OVA-induced proliferation assay to examine their inhibitory effects. The results (Table 4) show that virus absorption reduced the capacity of the antiserum to inhibit OVA-induced proliferation. The percentage inhibition at each dilution compared to the normal serum controls is shown in parentheses in Table 4. Furthermore two cycles of affinity absorption of the IgG fraction of the antiserum with AKR virus reduced the RIP titer to zero and almost restored the proliferative response to the level of the normal IgG control. Again the percentage inhibition compared to the normal IgG control is shown in parentheses.

Detection of MuLV Cell-Surface Antigens

1. Immunofluorescence. The results of immunofluorescence studies using the rabbit anti-AKR antiserum are shown in Table 5. In these experiments efforts were made to minimize the influence of culture conditions, unrelated to the presence of the antigen, on the expression of MuLV since exposure of lymphocytes to fetal calf serum can induce the expression of xenotropic virus (31). Accordingly LNC were cultured in 0.5% autologous serum which supported the OVA-induced proliferative response but in the absence of antigen did not induce high proliferative responses or the expression of MuLV antigens (Table 5). Under these conditions it was observed that secondary *in vitro* exposure of OVA-primed LNC to OVA resulted in the number of MuLV positive cells being expanded from zero, in the primed noncultured LNC, to 45% MuLV positive. OVA-primed cells cultured for 4 days

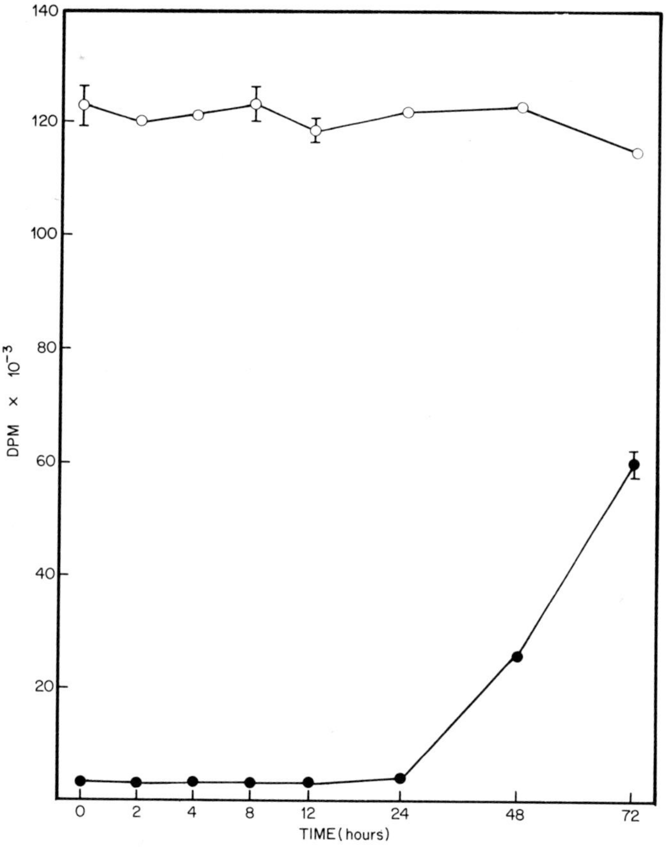

FIG. 4. Time-course addition of antiviral antisera to LNC stimulated *in vitro* with OVA. LNC from OVA-primed BALB/c mice were restimulated *in vitro* with 100 μg/ml OVA for 4 days. 5 μl of rabbit anti-AKR antiserum (●) or normal rabbit serum (○) were added in triplicate to the cultures at the above time points. Cellular proliferation was determined by pulsing the cultures with 0.2 μCi of [^{3}H]thymidine 22 hr before harvesting.

without OVA also contained MuLV-positive cells but at markedly lower numbers than the OVA cultured cells. The activation of MuLV antigens on the surface of OVA-primed cells cultured without OVA was not surprising since the culture of antigen-primed cells consistently resulted in a proliferative response higher than that observed in 4-day cultures of normal LNC from unimmunized mice (unpublished observations; Table 5). The proliferation and resultant MuLV antigen induction was most probably due to macrophage or T-cell-bound OVA present in the primed LNC population supplying a small and less than optimal amount of antigen to induce a low level of secondary *in vitro* proliferation. The culture of LNC from unimmunized BALB/c mice for 4 days with or without OVA did not evoke proliferation or induce the expression of detectable levels of MuLV cell surface antigens. The results shown in Table 5 demonstrated a positive correlation between the percentage of MuLV positive cells and the level of cellular proliferation. These observations were confirmed in three further experiments. Thus the expres-

TABLE 4

Effect of AKR Virus Absorption of Rabbit Anti-AKR Antiserum and IgG on OVA-Induced Proliferation

Reciprocal serum dilution	Rabbit anti-AKR antiserum RIP titer 6280[a]	Virus absorbed antiserum RIP titer 960	Normal rabbit serum RIP titer 0
	Mean dpm $\times 10^{-3} \pm$ SE		
16	1.3 ± 1.1 (99)[b]	25.4 ± 6.9 (73)	93.6 ± 4.5
32	8.8 ± 5.8 (92)	86.1 ± 7.3 (22)	110.6 ± 7.1
64	41.8 ± 2.5 (65)	107.4 ± 5.9 (10)	120.0 ± 2.9
128	73.6 ± 1.8 (29)	96.4 ± 1.7 (7)	103.7 ± 2.2
IgG (μg/well)	Rabbit anti-AKR RIP titer 42.5[a] μg/ml	Virus-absorbed anti-AKR IgG RIP titer 0	Normal rabbit IgG RIP titer 0
80	37.4 ± 1.4 (70)	104.5 ± 4.1 (17)	126.0 ± 7.3
40	55.7 ± 5.7 (59)	116.5 ± 4.7 (13)	134.3 ± 4.9
20	88.4 ± 0.5 (30)	121.2 ± 2.3 (4)	126.4 ± 5.6
10	104.4 ± 5.7 (20)	132.5 ± 4.2 (−2)	130.2 ± 4.1

Note. Rabbit anti-AKR antiserum and IgG were absorbed with AKR virus as described under Materials and Methods. LNC from OVA-primed Balb/c mice were restimulated *in vitro* with 100 μg/ml OVA together with triplicate dilutions of unabsorbed or virus-absorbed antiserum or IgG, or control serum or IgG for 4 days. Cellular proliferation was determined by pulsing the cultures with 0.2 μCi of [^{3}H]thymidine 22 hr before harvesting.

[a] Reciprocal serum dilution or IgG concentration that precipitated 50% of the radiolabeled AKR virus.

[b] Percentage inhibition compared to serum controls.

sion of MuLV antigens was positively correlated with the level of cellular proliferation and when the data from the four experiments were analyzed the correlation was highly significant ($r = 0.975$, $P < 0.001$).

2. *SDS–PAGE analysis of radiolabeled cell surface antigens.* The SDS–PAGE analysis of the cell surface antigens recognized by the rabbit anti-AKR-MuLV antiserum are shown in Fig. 5. The antiserum precipitated antigens from OVA-primed LNC before culture with molecular weights of approximately 72,000, 45,000, and 31,000 which are presumed to be gp70, gp45, and p30, respectively (Fig. 5A). After 4 days in culture with 100 μg/ml of OVA the expression of these three molecular weight species was augmented, and in addition the antiviral an-

TABLE 5

Detection of MuLV Cell Surface Antigens by Immunofluorescence

Lymph node cells	Days in culture	*In vitro* antigen	Percentage fluorescent-positive cells	Proliferative response (dpm ± SE)
OVA-primed	0	—	0	—
OVA-primed	4	PBS	13.8	8,832 ± 494
OVA-primed	4	OVA	45.2	155,903 ± 3422
Unprimed	4	PBS	0	1,697 ± 54
Unprimed	4	OVA	0	122 ± 2

Note. LNC from BALB/c mice immunized with 100 μg of OVA were nylon wool fractionated and examined for MuLV cell surface antigens or cultured with 10 μl of PBS or 100 μg/ml of OVA in EHAA 0.5% NMS. After 4 days in culture the cells were harvested and examined for MuLV cell surface antigens. Proliferative responses were determined in parallel cultures by pulsing the cells with 0.2 μCi of [^{3}H]thymidine 22 hr before harvesting.

tiserum detected the expression of antigens of 11,000, 15,000, and 18,000 MW which were not expressed prior to culture.

DISCUSSION

The relationship between the expression of endogenous murine leukemia viruses and cellular differentiation has been extensively studied in recent years in an attempt to find a functional role for these viruses. The data presented here suggest that there is an association between antigen-induced differentiation of T cells and their cell surface expression of the antigen of MuLVs since the antigen-specific proliferative response evoked the expression of viral antigens detected by immunofluorescence and antibodies to AKR-MuLV-inhibited proliferation. The inhibitory effect was removed by virus absorption.

The antiserum was found to more effectively inhibit OVA-induced proliferation when the LNC were enriched for T cells before *in vitro* culture. The proliferation of unfractionated LNC was inhibited with dilutions of antiserum lower than that of T-enriched LNC which required 10-fold less antibody for comparable inhibition. These results suggested that the antiserum selectively inhibited T-cell proliferation. A possible explanation for the antiserum being less inhibitory toward unfractionated LNC may be that non-T-cell proliferation was induced by fetal calf serum and was unaffected by the antiserum. The viral specificity of the inhibition by rabbit anti-AKR MuLV antiserum was shown by absorption of the antiserum and the IgG fraction with AKR-MuLV. A reduction of the antiviral RIP titer of the antiserum resulted in a similar reduction in the antiserum's inhibitory properties. Furthermore, absorption of antiviral antibodies from the IgG fraction to a RIP titer of zero removed almost all inhibition.

As a preliminary study of the mechanisms involved in the inhibition of OVA-induced T-cell proliferation, the antiserum was added to the cultures at various times. We recently demonstrated that the time required for the initial step of OVA presentation by macrophages to primed T cells was 4 hr or less and that following this initial antigen presentation the T cells will proliferate without further antigenic

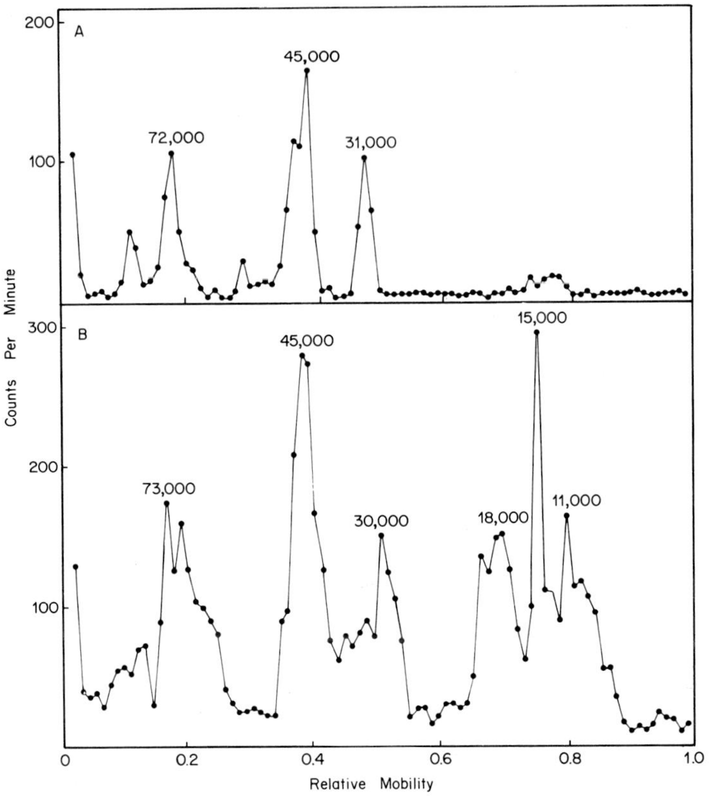

FIG. 5. SDS–PAGE analysis of radioimmune precipitates of cell surface viral antigens. ^{125}I-Labeled antigen preparations from (A) OVA-primed uncultured LNC and (B) OVA-primed LNC cultured for 4 days with 100 μg/ml OVA were reacted with rabbit anti-AKR-MuLV antiserum and the immune precipitates were electrophoresed on 10% gels. The relative mobilities of the viral antigens were determined from molecular weight standards run in a parallel gel.

stimulation (32). The results presented here show that maximum inhibition was still achieved when the antiserum was added to the LNC 24 hr after culturing with OVA. Furthermore, cellular proliferation was inhibited by 50% when the antiserum was added after 72 hr of culture. This indicated that anti-AKR antibodies do not interfere with the initial step of antigen–T cell interaction but inhibit proliferation after the antigen primed T cells are restimulated in culture.

These results suggest that T cells engaged in antigen-induced proliferative responses express MuLV antigens and that antibodies binding to these viral antigens inhibit T-cell proliferation. To investigate whether *in vitro* antigenic stimulation of OVA-primed T cells does result in the expression of MuLV cell surface antigens, OVA-primed T cells were examined before and after culture. Immunofluorescence studies showed that MuLV antigens were not detectable on OVA-primed T cells before culture whereas following 4 days in culture, with an optimal concentration of OVA, MuLV antigens were present on nearly half of the viable T cells. This result demonstrated that secondary OVA stimulation of OVA-primed T cells induced MuLV antigen expression. The MuLV antigen induction was not due to the fact that the cells were in culture since smaller numbers of MuLV-positive cells were detected in the PBS control cultures of OVA-primed T cells and no MuLV-positive cells were detected in unimmunized LNC cultures. This suggested that secondary OVA stimulation was the major inductive agent.

Furthermore there was a positive correlation between the number of cells expressing MuLV antigens and the level of T-cell proliferation. This result suggested a relationship between T-cell differentiation and MuLV antigen expression. In total these results support the observation that the inhibitory AKR-MuLV antibodies act after the initial antigen–T cell interaction. In addition, results from SDS–PAGE analysis of the MuLV cell surface antigens recognized by anti-AKR virus antibodies were consistent with the immunofluorescence studies. Secondary OVA-stimulation results in both a quantitative and qualitative activation of MuLV antigens. Before culture low levels of viral antigens of approximate molecular weights of 72,000, 45,000, and 31,000 were detected in the cell lysates from OVA-primed cells. Following culture with OVA the cells expressed higher levels of these determinants and in addition viral antigens of molecular weights of 18,000, 15,000, and 11,000 were expressed. The expression of viral antigens of equivalent molecular weights to both the envelope and core proteins of MuLV possibly suggests why the monospecific anti-AKR-p30 antiserum was less inhibitory than the polyspecific anti-AKR-MuLV antiserum. It is not yet clear which viral antigens are the target for antibody-mediated inhibition of the proliferative response. The resolution of this point using monoclonal antibodies is in progress.

Recent reports have indicated that an antiserum to a xenotropic MuLV suppresses the development of immune reponses *in vitro* (7, 8) and *in vivo* (8), and an antibody to ecotropic MuLV has been shown to inhibit mixed lymphocyte responses (R. A. Knight, personal communication). Our results indicate that an antigen-induced T-cell proliferation response can be similarly inhibited. The former observations have been taken as evidence that virus-coded cell surface structures may be ligands involved in the development of immune responses (8). This of course does not exclude the possibility that nonviral cell surface antigens are important in the regulation of the immune response; antibodies to Lyt-2 (33) and to a rat T-cell antigen (34) block T effector cells suggesting that such antigens may have functional significance (34). The function of cell surface virus-associated structures has not been resolved, but the possibility that viral antigen or the virus binding site is a mitogen-linked receptor has been raised. Thus antisera to Friend luekemia virus stimulated B-cell proliferation (35) and monoclonal antibodies to a murine T-cell lymphoma inhibited lymphoma proliferation through a mechanism attributed to the blocking of the receptor for an endogenous MuLV (36). These suppressive and stimulatory effects can be reconciled if the sera bind to different target structures or to different lymphocyte subsets (35). In addition the suppressive effects may be attributable to the inhibition of binding to mitogen-linked receptors of shed virus or gp70. Whatever the explanation evidence is accumulating in favor of a role for endogenous MuLVs in lymphocyte differentiation.

ACKNOWLEDGMENTS

The work was supported by grants from the National Health and Medical Research Council and the Kidney Foundation of Australia. The support of Professor N. F. Stanley and the advice of Dr. H. C. Morse is gratefully acknowledged. We acknowledge the contribution of Dr. R. A. Knight who provided the stimulus for this study.

REFERENCES

1. Aaronson, S. A. and Stephenson, J. R., *Biochim. Biophys. Acta* **458,** 323, 1976.
2. Levy, J. A., *Curr. Top. Microbiol. Immunol.* **79,** 111, 1978.
3. Elder, J. H., Gautsch, J. W., Jensen, F. C., and Lerner, R. A., *J. Nat. Cancer Inst.* **61,** 625, 1978.
4. Lilly, F., and Pincus, T., *Advan. Cancer Res.* **17,** 231, 1973.
5. Levy, J. A., and Pincus, T., *Science* **170,** 326, 1970.
6. Hartley, J. W., Wolford, N. K., Old, L. J., and Rowe, W. P. *Proc. Nat. Acad. Sci. USA* **74,** 789, 1977.
7. Moroni, C., and Schumann, G., *Nature (London)* **269,** 600, 1977.
8. Schumann, G., and Moroni, C., *J. Immunol.* **120,** 1913, 1978.
9. Moroni, C., and Schumann, G., *Nature (London)* **254,** 60, 1975.
10. Moroni, C., Schumann, G., Robert-Guroff, M., Suter, E. R., and Martin, D., *Proc. Nat. Acad. Sci. USA* **72,** 535, 1975.
11. Schumann, G., and Moroni, C., *J. Immunol.* **116,** 1145, 1976.
12. Moroni, C., and Schumann, G., *J. Gen. Virol.* **38,** 497, 1978.
13. Greenberger, J. S., Phillips, S. M., Stephenson, J. R., and Aaronson, S. A., *J. Immunol.* **115,** 317, 1975.
14. Phillips, S. M., Stephenson, J. R., Greenberger, J. S., Lane, P. E., and Aaronson, S. A., *J. Immunol.* **116,** 1123, 1976.
15. Phillips, S. M., Stephenson, J. R., and Aaronson, S. A., *J. Immunol.* **118,** 622, 1977.
16. Moroni, C., Matter, A., Stoye, J. P., Monckton, R. P., Delamarter, J. F., and Schumann, G., *Cell. Immunol.* **54,** 107, 1980.
17. Armstrong, M. Y. K., Ruddle, N. H., and Richards, F. F., *J. Exp. Med.* **145,** 1060, 1977.
18. Phillips, S. M., Hirsch, M. S. André-Schwartz, J., Solnick, C., Black, P., Schwartz, R. S., Merrill, J. P., and Carpenter, C. B., *Cell. Immunol.* **15,** 169, 1975.
19. Staber, F. G., Schläfli, E., and Moroni, C., *Nature (London)* **275,** 669, 1978.
20. Lee, J. C., and Ihle, J. N., *J. Immunol.* **117,** 1033, 1976.
21. Kende, M., Hill, R., Dinowitz, M., Stephenson, J. R., and Kelloff, G. J., *J. Exp. Med.* **149,** 358, 1979.
22. Peck, A. B., and Bach, F. H., *J. Immunol. Methods* **3,** 147. 1973.
23. Julius, M. H., Simpson, E., and Herzenberg, L. A., *Eur. J. Immunol.* **3,** 645, 1973.
24. Langdon, W. Y., Shellam, G. R., Morgan, G. M., and McKenzie, I. F. C., *Immunogenetics* **10,** 141, 1980.
25. Hudson, L., and Hay, F. C., "Practical Immunology." Blackwell Scientific, Oxford, 1976.
26. Ihle, J. N., Hanna, M. G., Jr., Roberson, L. E., and Kenney, F. T., *J. Exp. Med.* **139,** 1568, 1974.
27. Weber, K., and Osborn, M., *J. Biol. Chem.* **244,** 4406, 1969.
28. Watanabe, H., Pollet, M., and Mackenzie, J. S., *Aust. J. Exp. Biol. Med. Sci.* **57,** 303, 1979.
29. Lowry, O. H., Rosebrough, N. J., Farr, A. L., and Randall, R. J., *J. Biol. Chem.* **193,** 265, 1951.
30. Kessler, S. W., *J. Immunol.* **115,** 1617, 1975.
31. Monckton, R. P., and Moroni, C., *J. Gen. Virol.* **47,** 59, 1980.
32. Langdon, W. Y., Holt, P. G., and Shellam, G. R., *Immunology* **43,** 555, 1981.
33. Hollander, N., Pillemer, E., and Weissman, I. L., *J. Exp. Med.* **152,** 674, 1980.
34. Webb, M., Mason, D. W., and Williams, A. F., *Nature (London)* **282,** 841, 1979.
35. Moroni, C., Forni, L., Hunsmann, G., and Schumann, G., *Proc. Nat. Acad. Sci. USA* **77,** 1486, 1980.
36. McGrath, M. S., Pillemer, E., and Weissman, I. L. *Nature (London)* **285,** 259, 1980.

CELLULAR IMMUNOLOGY **64**, 119–130 (1981)

Surface Analysis of Early and Late MOPC-315-EL Tumor Cells[1]

DAVID HARRIS, JENNIFER BAILEY, JON C. LEWIS, WILLIAM H. GROVER, MARGUERITE PANETTI, DONALD L. EVANS, MARY J. RUEBUSH, LESLIE K. PAULUS, DONALD BURGESS, AND ARTHUR H. HALE[2]

Department of Microbiology and Immunology and the Department of Pathology, Bowman Gray School of Medicine, Wake Forest University, Winston-Salem, North Carolina 27103

Received January 27, 1981; accepted July 10, 1981

The surface properties of a tumor line which undergoes a cyclic change in reactivity with cytotoxic T lymphocytes (CTLs) have been analyzed. The findings indicate that MOPC-315-EL when transplanted into the peritoneum of a BALB/c mouse for 4–5 days (early MOPC-315-EL) becomes sensitive to lysis by anti-H-2^d CTL. After 9 to 10 days of growth in the peritoneal cavity these tumor cells (late MOPC-315-EL) become unreactive to CTLs. The amount of H-2 antigens on the surface of the cells is the same on the early and late tumor cells. By scanning electron microscopy (SEM) we have shown that the early population is a mixture of two cell types which are characterized by surface villi or surface blebs; the late cells are essentially one population which are characterized by surface villi. The net charge on the surface of the cell was evaluated by two methods: (i) rate of cell migration across an electric potential and (ii) binding by cationic ferritin to the glycocalyx. Both techniques indicated that the early cells have a higher net negative charge. The implication of this work is that surface charge may be involved in T cell–target cell interactions.

INTRODUCTION

Previously, it has been shown that the BALB/c ascites tumor, MOPC-315-EL (H-2^d), when transplanted intraperitoneally (ip) into a BALB/c mouse is reactive with T lymphocytes 3–4 days (early MOPC-315-EL) after introduction into the animal. Subsequently, after 6–7 more days (late MOPC-315-EL) of growth in the peritoneum, these tumor cells become unreactive to T cells (1). Late tumor cells (unreactive), when transplanted into a new host, rapidly (within 2–3 days) reverse their phenotype and become reactive to T cells. Reactivity was measured by the susceptibility of early and late MOPC-315-EL tumor cells to lysis by both cytotoxic T lymphocytes (CTLs)[3] specific for the H-2K and H-2D gene products (allogeneic)

[1] This work was supported by a research grant from the Forsyth Cancer Service and a grant to the Bowman Gray School of Medicine, Cancer Center Support (Core) Grant (2-P30-CA 12197-08), from the National Institutes of Health, Bethesda, Maryland, the American Cancer Society IM-224, and National Institutes of Health, CA 26084. Arthur H. Hale is a recipient of a Research Career Development Award (AI00383).

[2] To whom all correspondence should be addressed at: Department of Microbiology, Bowman Gray School of Medicine, Winston-Salem, N.C. 27103.

[3] Abbreviations used: Con A, concanavalin A; CTL, cytotoxic thymus-derived lymphocyte; HBSS, Hanks' balanced salt solution; PBS, phosphate-buffered saline (0.15 *M* NaCl, 0.01 *M* potassium phosphate, pH 7.4); RBC, red blood cell; SEM, scanning electron microscopy; TEM; transmission electron microscopy.

0008-8749/81/150119-12$02.00/0

and by CTLs in which the CTL and the target cell (MOPC-315-EL in this example) have the same H-2 products, but differ with respect to non-H-2 antigens (TNP and minor histocompatibility antigens, syngeneic) (2). Reactivity was also measured by the ability of these tumor cells to elicit specific CTL responses. Late MOPC-315-EL tumor cells were unable to elicit anti-H-2^d-, anti-TNP-, or anti-minor histocompatibility antigen-specific CTLs. In contrast, early MOPC-315-EL tumor cells were significantly more reactive with the appropriate precursor or memory T cell. The lack of reactivity of the late tumor cells with these CTLs was not the result of a diminished amount of the serologically defined H-2K or H-2D gene products as evidenced by their susceptibility to lysis by anti-H-2^d antibodies plus complement and also their relative capacity to absorb anti-H-2^d antibodies (1–3).

In a recent publication (4) we investigated the minimal molecular requirements for T-cell recognition of a MOPC-315-EL. Enucleation of MOPC-315 cells, either sensitive or resistant to reaction with T cells, did not alter the ability of the resulting cytoplasts to elicit or serve as targets for anti-H-2 or anti-Sendai viral cytotoxic T lymphocytes (CTL), despite the fact that there were no detectable differences in serologically defined H-2 or viral antigens on their surface. Likewise, when plasma membranes isolated from sensitive or resistant cells were tested for their ability to elicit anti-H-2 CTL, they retained the phenotype of the cells from which they were isolated. However, solubilized and partially purified H-2 antigens from both sensitive and resistant cells were able to elicit secondary anti-H-2 CTL when incorporated alone into liposomes. These results suggested that a cellular surface component(s) exists that was probably not an H-2K or H-2D gene product and was responsible for the reversible variation in the reactivity of the tumor cells with T cells.

In the present study we have investigated by SEM the cell surface morphology of early and late cells. In addition, we have quantitated the net charge on the surface of the early and late tumor cells. The results indicate marked differences on the cell surfaces of these tumor cells.

MATERIALS AND METHODS

Mice. Male and female mice of the following strains were used: BALB/c AnN (d,d), B10·D2 (d,d), C57BL/10 (b,b), BALB·B (b,b), DBA/2J (d,d), and C57BL/6 (b,b). These were either purchased from Cumberland View Farms (Clinton, Tenn.) or produced in our own breeding colony from breeding stock obtained from Herman Eisen (Massachusetts Institute of Technology). Letters in parentheses indicate the H-2K and H-2D alleles.

Antiserum. Anti-H-2^d serum was prepared by multiple ip injections of 2.0×10^7 B10·D2 spleen cells into B10 mice. Anti-H-2^b alloantiserum was prepared with 2.0 $\times$ 20^7 B10 spleen cells injected ip into B10·D2 mice (1).

Medium. RPMI 1640 was supplemented with 10% fetal calf serum (heat inactivated, 56°C, 45 min), 0.03% glutamine, 2-mercaptoethanol (50 μM), and penicillin and streptomycin (Flow Laboratories, Inc., McLean, Va.) (1).

Tumors. All tumors were obtained from Herman Eisen (Massachusetts Institute of Technology). MOPC-315-EL is a subline of MOPC-315 originally induced and maintained by Michael Potter. MOPC-315-EL is maintained by a weekly ip transfer of 1.0×10^7 cells collected in the course of a normal transfer. P815 (H-2^d) and

EL-4 (H-2^b) were maintained by weekly ip transfers of 1.0×10^6 ascites cells in mice of the strain of origin, DBA/2 and C57BL/6, respectively.

Production of CTLs. Anti-H-2 CTLs were elicited as previously described (1). Briefly, 4.0×10^7 viable spleen cells (responder cells) in upright 25-cm^2 flasks (Corning Glass Works, Corning, N.Y.) were incubated with 4.0×10^7 irradiated (1000 rad, X-ray, Picker) spleen cells (stimulator cells) or 1.0×10^3–1.0×10^7 irradiated (10,000 rad, X-ray, Picker) tumor cells in a total volume of 10 ml of supplemented RPMI 1640. After 5 days incubation, in an atmosphere of 6% Co_2 and 94% air, the cells were harvested and washed by centrifugation (450*g*), counted, and resuspended in supplemented RPMI 1640 at various cell concentrations for the cytotoxicity assays (below).

Cytotoxic assays. Cytotoxic cell-mediated lysis; ^{51}Cr-labeled target cells (1.0×10^4) were mixed with serial dilutions of effector spleen cells in a total volume of 200 μl of supplemented RPMI 1640. This mixture was incubated 4 to 6 hr at 37°C in an atmosphere of 6% CO_2 and 94% air. The assay was stopped by diluting with cold PBS and the amounts of radioactivity in the supernatant and pellet were determined (2). Percentage specific release (spec. rel.) was calculated as 100 (E − C/1 − C) where E is the fraction of ^{51}Cr released by antigen-stimulated effector cells and C is the fraction of ^{51}Cr released by a mock-stimulated responder population. Percentage release was calculated as 100 E/T where E is the amount of radioactivity released by target cells incubated with antigen-stimulated effector cells, and T represents the total amount of radioactivity in each assay tube (Fig. 1).

Antibody-mediated cytotoxic assays were carried out essentially as previously described (2). Percentage release was calculated as 100 (A/T) where A is the amount of radioactivity released by target cells incubated with serum in the presence of complement, and T represents the total amount of radioactivity in each assay well.

Target cells. Target cells (1.0×10^6) were labeled with 500 μCI of $Na_2{}^{51}CrO_4$ in 200 μl of 0.15 *M* NaCl for 20 min at 37°C. This suspension was then diluted 1:3 with supplemented RPMI 1640 and incubated for another 60 min at 37°C in an atmosphere of 94% air and 6% CO_2. The cells were then washed by centrifugation at 450*g* and suspended with effector cells in a total volume of 100 μl of supplemented RPMI 1640.

Absorption of antibodies. Serial dilutions of cells that had been washed three

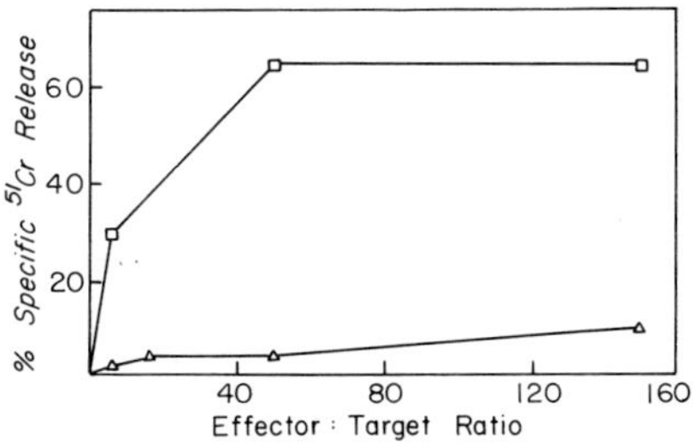

FIG. 1. BALB·B anti-BALB/c CTLs were incubated with ^{51}Cr-labeled early (□) or late (△) MOPC-315-EL tumor cells for 4 hr at 37°C. The percentage spontaneous ^{51}Cr release was 16.7 and 14.2 for the early and late tumor cells, respectively.

times by repeated cycles of centrifugation were distributed into microtest tubes (Sarstedt, Princeton, N.J.) and centrifuged (450*g*, 5 min); the supernatants were removed, and the packed cells were resuspended in 60 μl of antiserum at dilutions that would lyse approximately 80% of the target cells in a standard cytotoxic assay with complement. After 30 min on ice, during which the tubes were periodically agitated by gentle mixing, the cells were packed by centrifugation (1000*g*, 10 min) and samples of the supernatant were distributed into microtiter plates (Linbro Scientific) for storage at $-70°C$ until assayed for cytotoxic antibodies (above).

Electron microscopy. Cells which had been prepared as described above were subsequently processed for electron microscopy as previously described (5,6). Primary fixation for both SEM and TEM was carried out at room temperature for 1–3 hr in 2.5% glutaraldehyde buffered to pH 7.2 with 0.1 *M* cacodylate. All SEM samples were rinsed in the same buffer, the cells concentrated on an ultrafiltration membrane (6) (Nuclepore Corp., Pleasanton, Calif.), dehydrated through a graded ethanol series to 100%, dried from CO_2 by the critical point method, and sputter coated with gold–palladium prior to observation in a Philips SEM-501, scanning electron microscope (Philips Electronics Instruments, Mahwah, N.J.). For routine TEM the cells, fixed and rinsed as described above, were postfixed for 1 hr in cacodylate-buffered 1% OsO_4, dehydrated through ethanols to propylene oxide, and embedded as a pellet in EPON 812. Thin sections obtained with a diamond knife in a Sorvall MT-2B ultramicrotome (Dupont Instruments, Norwalk, Conn.). Prior to microscopy at 60 kV using a Philips EM-400 transmission electron microscope, the sections were double stained with aqueous lead citrate and methanolic uranyl acetate.

Cationized ferritin (Polysciences, Warrington, Pa) binding to cell surfaces was done by a modification (5) of the method described by Danon and Skutelsky (7). To accomplish this, washed cells were fixed in 1% glutaraldehyde in 0.1 *M* cacodylate buffer for 10 min, washed in three changes of the cacodylate buffer containing 0.1 *M* glycine, and then incubated in cacodylate-buffered cationized ferritin (500 μg/ml). The cells were then washed, postfixed, dehydrated, embedded, and sectioned as described above. Unstained sections were observed and photographed at 40 kV to enhance contrast. Each cell was photographed at 9000× to confirm surface characteristics (for SEM correlation) and then a series of three photomicrographs at 45,000× was taken of the cell surface. These higher magnification

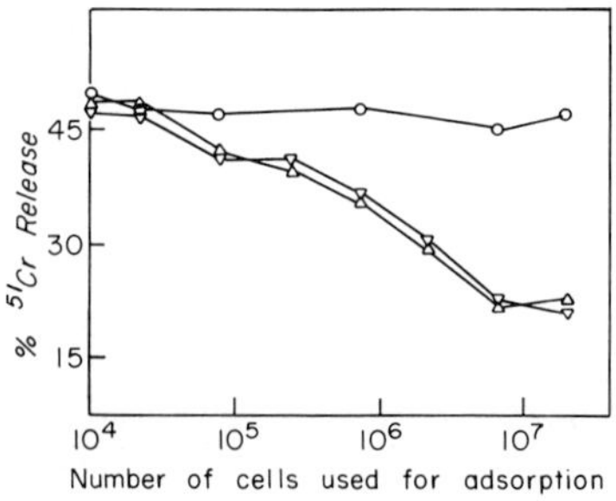

FIG. 2. Detection of surface products which result from synthesis by the H-2^d locus was done by absorption of anti-H-2^d antibodies. Serial dilutions of early (▽) and late (△) or EL-4 (H-2^b) (○) tumor cells were incubated with a 1/50 dilution of anti-H-2^d antisera at 4°C. The cells were centrifuged (1000*g*, 10 min) and the unabsorbed antibodies were tested for their ability to lyse ^{51}Cr-labeled P815 tumor cells in the presence of complement. Lysis of P815 cells with unabsorbed serum and complement was 48.2%; lysis by normal mouse serum was 17.8% in the presence of C.

micrographs were printed at an enlargement factor of 2.6 (final working magnification = 117,000), and then the number and distribution of cationized ferritin particles was determined using standard morphometric techniques.

Electrophoresis of early and late MOPC-315-EL tumor cells. Isolated cells were sedimented through three aliquots of 10 ml 0.013 *M* phosphate buffer (8,9) pH 7.4 30°C with sodium hypaque (Winthrop) addition to a density of 1.07 (w/v). The washed cells were placed in the cleansed chamber (10% NaOH in 70% ethanol, H_2O, 1% HCl, H_2O) of a microscope-monitored calibrated (10) electrophoresis apparatus (Grant Instruments; Cambridge), immersed in a constant temperature water bath, and prefocused by means of a micrometer (Mercer, England) to a constant depth to avoid electroosmotic streaming phenomena (8,9). Uncharged liposome immobility in the system confirmed that particle charge was responsible for mobility at this focus point. The mobility (μ) of a cell population was compared to that of human RBCs (1.33 ± 0.01 μsec^{-1} cm V^{-1}) using 50 V across the electrodes. The formula:

$$\mu = \frac{l}{\bar{X}(I \cdot R/q)}$$

where l = distance in cm., $\bar{X}$ = average time to cover distance 1 (sec) in to and from determinations, I = current in amperes, R = specific resistance, and q = cross-sectional area of the chamber (cm^2) was used to calculate cell mobility for 25 separate cells of a population.

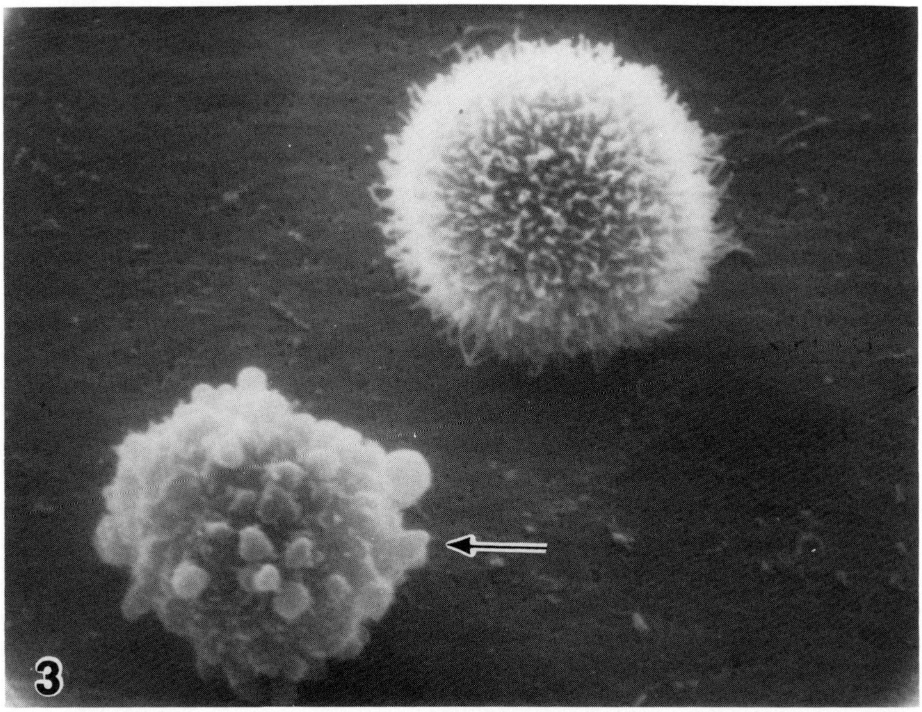

FIG. 3. Scanning electron micrograph illustrating the heterogeneity of the MOPC-315-EL cells. Shown are the two major surface morphologies found in these cells. The blebbed surface configuration (arrow) comprised 6.3% of the cells in the late and 55.9% of the early population with villus cells comprising the balance. ×5000.

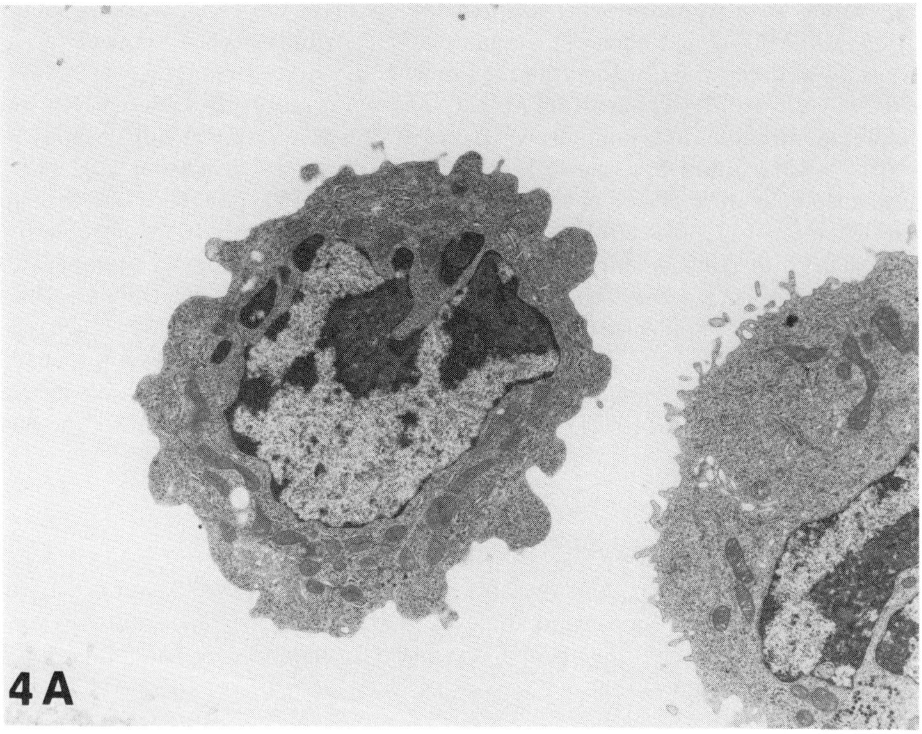
4A

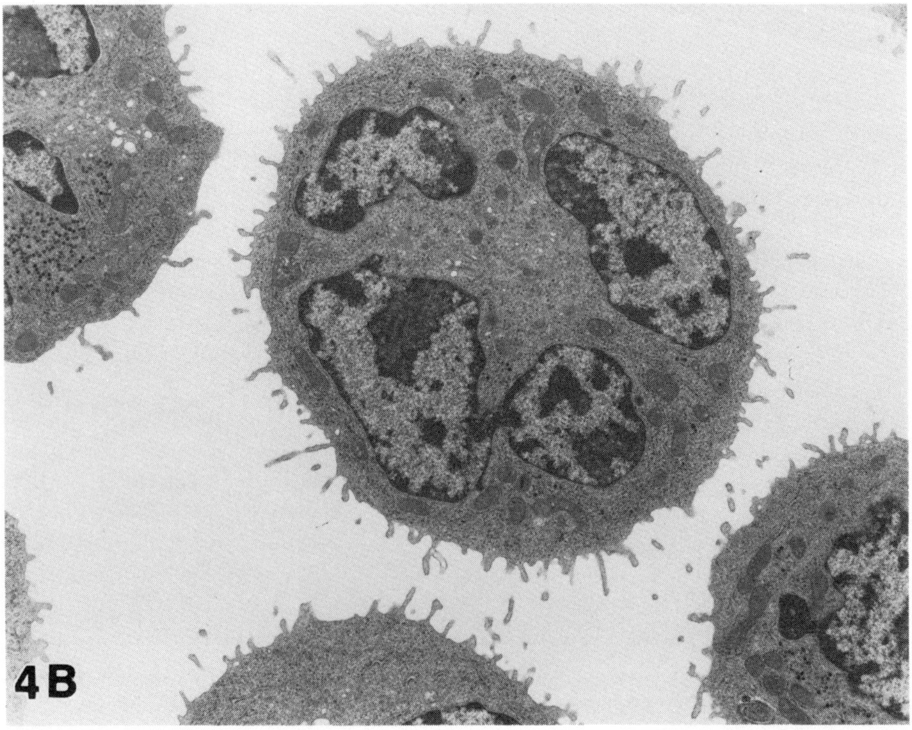
4B

RESULTS

Reactivity of Early and Late Tumor Cells with Anti-H-2^d CTLs and Antibodies

We tested the early and late tumor cells analyzed below for their susceptibility to lysis by anti-H-2^d (BALB·B anti-BALB/c) CTLs. The results indicate that late MOPC-315-EL tumor cells were not susceptible to lysis by anti-H-2^d CTLs. This confirms our previous work (1). It was important to confirm if the differences between the late and early MOPC-315-EL tumor cells were the result of differential expression of H-2 antigens (Fig. 2). Anti-H-2^d antisera clearly do not detect any differential ability of the early or late tumor cells to present H-2-specific antigens.

Surface Morphology of Early and Late MOPC-315-EL

In order to evaluate the homogeneity of the early and late populations, and to derive some information concerning their surface morphology, the cells were observed by electron microscopy. As illustrated in Figs. 3 and 4, the early population was heterogeneous with two prominent groups of cells: one displaying microvilli and the other, surface blebs. The late MOPC-315-EL population in marked contrast to this early stage was composed primarily (>80%) of cells with surface microvilli. The relative percentages of each population are summarized in Table 1. Because the early MOPC-315-EL is a mixture of cells with surface villi or blebs, this population may be composed of cells with both the early and late phenotypes.

Net Ionic Charge of Early and Late Tumor Cells

We evaluated the net charge of early and late MOPC-315-EL tumor cells in two ways: (i) binding of cationized ferritin and (ii) rate of migration across an electric potential.

As shown in Table 2 the net charge of early and late tumor cells differed when analyzed by their rate of migration across an electric potential. The early population migrated significantly ($P < 0.005$) faster than the late population. These results were confirmed by electron microscopy. When the fixed cells were treated with cationized ferritin, the molecular marker bound avidly to both the early and late tumor cells; however as shown in Fig. 5 and summarized in Table 3, differences were noted between the early and late cells. To count these particles a distinction was made of the different surface morphologies within the population (i.e., bleb and villi). Quantitation of the number of electron dense particles per unit area and the unit area not associated with cationic ferritin indicated that early and late tumor cells differed with respect to these parameters. The early MOPC-315-EL tumor cells possessing blebs had significantly greater numbers of electron dense particles than late villi cells ($P < 0.01$). In addition, the total early population binds a significantly greater number of ferritin particles (Table 3). This correlates with the average rate of migration observed for early and late tumor cells as a function

---

FIG. 4. Transmission electron micrographs of each of the major MOPC-315-EL cells types. Bleb cells (A) were characterized by irregularly contoured surface with multiple 1–2 μm diameter cytoplasmic blebs protruding from the cell surface. Villus cells (B) in marked contrast had innumerable villi with diameters in the range 500–1000 Å and ranging in length to 1.5 μm which projected from the cell surface. (A) ×7500. (B) ×7500.

TABLE 1

SEM of Early and Late MOPC-315-EL

MOPC-315-EL	Surface morphology[a]		
	Villi	Bleb	Bleb–Villus[b]
Late	92.5	6.3	2.1
Early	40.7	55.9	16.0

[a] MOPC-315-EL tumor cells were harvested 2 days (early) and 9 days (late) after transfer to BALB/c mice. The cells were fixed for SEM and different surface morphologies were enumerated. More than 200 cells were counted. The data are expressed as percentage of cells with a given surface morphology. See Figs. 3 and 4 for ultrastructural characterization of each cell type.

[b] Although not illustrated, a small percentage of cells in each experiment possessed both surface features suggestive of a transition from one morphology to the other.

of an electrical potential (Table 2). The percentage of surface not associated with cationic ferritin was greater on the late villi cells (Table 4). This suggests that the distribution of the surface molecules binding cationic ferritin may be different. No significant difference was observed between the early or late cells possessing blebs on their surfaces.

DISCUSSION

We report the cell surface analysis of MOPC-315-EL. This tumor, 3–4 days (early) after transplantation to a syngeneic host is reactive with T cells, however, after 9–12 days (late) in the host, the tumor cells become unreactive with T cells (Fig. 1). In addition, the amount of H-2 antigens on these tumor cells are identical (Fig. 2).

Early MOPC-315-EL is a heterogeneous population as indicated by SEM. The

TABLE 2

Rate of Migration across an Electric Potential[a–c]

Experiment	Cell type	Rate of migration (μ sec^{-1} cm V^{-1})
1	RBC[d]	1.31 ± 0.035
	Early MOPC-315-EL	1.15 ± 0.08
	Late MOPC-315-EL	0.92 ± 0.09
2	RBC	1.30 ± 0.02
	Early MOPC-315-EL	1.11 ± 0.02
	Late MOPC-315-EL	0.92 ± 0.05

[a] Isolated tumor cells were placed in the calibrated electrophoresis apparatus and analyzed for rate of movement across an electric potential.

[b] The data are expressed as μsec^{-1} cm V^{-1} ± the standard deviation over 100 cells for each cell type analyzed.

[c] The difference between the rate of movement between early and late tumor cells was significant at a $P < 0.005$ for both experiments.

[d] Red blood cells (RBC).

population is made up of cells with villi or blebs, or both. The late population is primarily (>80%) of the villi surface phenotype. These results could be interpreted to indicate: (i) two populations exist in which the relative proportions vary with time in the animal or (ii) the villi population differentiates into the bleb population. Evidence not given here supports the latter, since it has been shown that: (i) irradiated (hence nondividing tumor cells) early cells can become unreactive to T cells (data not shown) and (ii) since MOPC-315-EL tumor cells derived from single-cell clones display the early–late phenomenon (data not shown).

We next evaluated the differences of MOPC-315-EL tumor cells by TEM and found none (data not shown). This was not anticipated since differences in cytoskeleton organization might be expected. As a further step, however, we evaluated the net ionic surface charge on the early and late tumor cells. The results indicated a significant difference, with the early cells migrating faster across an electric potential than late cells and thus suggesting that they were more negatively charged (Table 2). The result was confirmed by TEM studies in which the association of cationic ferritin to the cell surface of early or late tumor cells was measured. In this work we confirmed the electrophoresis data by demonstrating that the total early population possessed a higher average number of binding sites for cationic ferritin compared to late tumor cells. In addition, it was clear that bleb cells had a higher negative charge than did late villi cells. These results indicated that: (i) net charge measured by cationic ferritin does correlate with surface morphology and (ii) although our TEM data correlate with the average rate of cell migration

TABLE 3

Binding of Cationized Ferritin to Early and Late MOPC-315-EL Tumor Cells[a]

Experiment	Cell type	Total cells[b]		Cell morphology[c,d] Bleb		Villi	
1	Early	48.8	($P \leq 0.01$)	57.3	($P \leq 0.1$)	31.7	($P \leq 0.1$)
	Late	37.6		58.7		36.1	
2	Early	327.9	($P \leq 0.01$)	477.2	($P \leq .2$)	195.3	($P \leq 0.1$)
	Late	228.4		394.3		219.1	

[a] Cells were incubated with cationic ferritin, fixed, and photographed at 45,000 × as described under Materials and Methods. The number and distribution of cationized ferritin were determined by counting electron dense ferritin cores. The length of cell membrane areas were calculated by the use of a digitizer, which utilized an electronic grid system and a minicomputer to calculate cell lengths.

[b] The average particles/mm was determined for all cells within the early or late population regardless of surface morphology. The *P* values in parentheses are given to indicate the degree of significance between the early and late population. The statistical analysis was a routine analysis of variance determination.

[c] The average particles/mm was determined for early and late cells of a given morphology (bleb or villi). The *P* values in parenthesis are given to indicate the significance between the early and late populations.

[d] Comparisons of early bleb with late villi or early villi with late bleb indicate that the number of particles/mm is significantly different ($P \leq 0.01$).

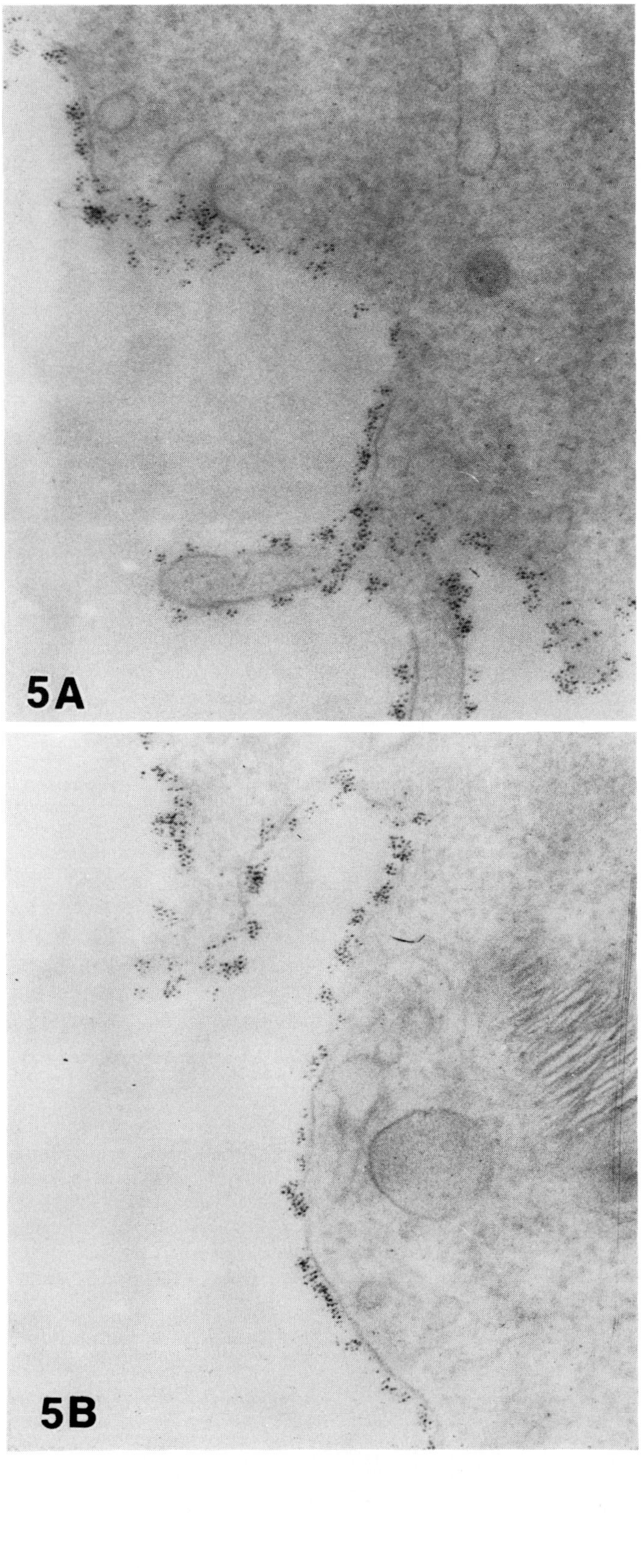
5A
5B

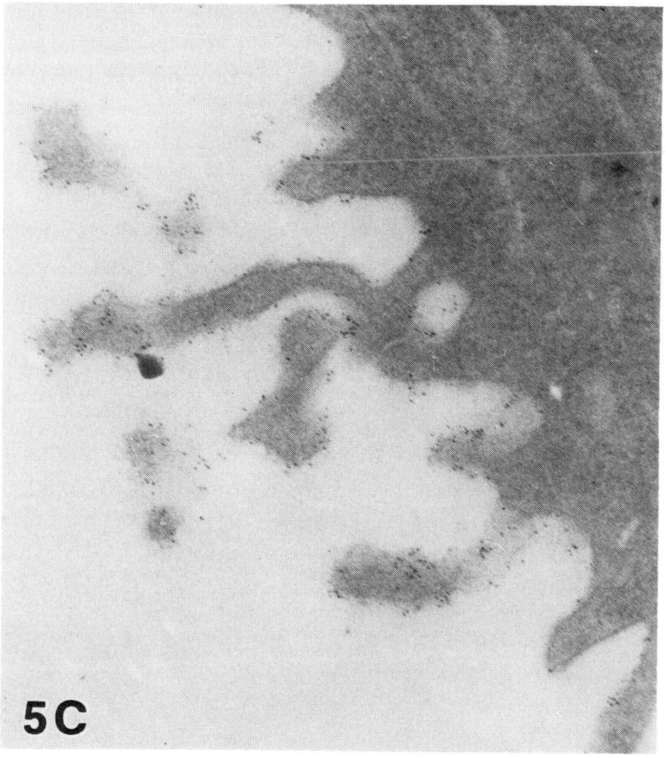

FIG. 5. Transmission electron micrographs illustrating the distribution of cationized ferritin on early villus (A) and bleb (B) cells. Particles, fairly uniformly distributed on the major surface of each cell type (arrow), tended to cluster on microvilli (MV) and over plasma membrane invaginations (PI). Late villus cells (C) bound significantly fewer particles than the early cells. (A–C) ×68,000.

TABLE 4

Distribution of Bound Cationized Ferritin[a]

Experiment	Cell type	Total cells[b]		Cell morphology[c] (% of surface with bound ferritin)			
				Bleb		Villi	
1	Early	90.7		96.6		75.6	
			($P \leq 0.01$)		($P < 0.1$)		($P < 0.1$)
	Late	72.7		85.5		70.3	
2	Early	86.2		97.2		71.7	
			($P \leq 0.01$)		($P < 0.1$)		($P < 0.1$)
	Late	73.4		87.8		71.0	

[a] Data accumulation was as described under Table 3 and Materials and Methods.

[b] The percentage surface associated with ferritin was determined by use of a digitizer in which the surface which had bound three or more ferritin molecules was considered to possess molecules capable of binding ferritin and area with two or less was considered negative. Early and late populations were analyzed without regard for surface morphology. The statistical significance between early and late cells of the homologous morphology is given in parentheses.

[c] Comparisons of early bleb with late villi or early villi with late bleb indicate that the percentage of surface bound with ferritin are significantly different ($P \leq 0.01$).

across an electric potential, it is clear that a significant percentage of the early population (villi morphology—approximately 50%) binds reduced amounts of cationic ferritin. Indeed if an arbitrary distinction is made between cells which migrate fast (>1.0 μsec^{-1} cm V^{-1}) or slow (<1.0 μsec^{-1} cm V^{-1}) across an electric potential, we observed that approximately 50% of the early population migrated more rapidly than the rest of the population. When this analysis was done on late cells only 10–15% of cells could migrate at a rate faster than 1.0 μsec^{-1} cm V^{-1}; the remaining proportion of the population migrated less than 1.0 μsec^{-1} cm V^{-1}. These data correlated closely to the percentages of cells possessing blebs or villi in the early and late populations (Table 1). The distribution of binding of cationic ferritin also correlates with cell surface morphology.

In conclusion, it is clear that the net charge between the early and late tumor cells does differ. This result is significant since it can be suggested that increased surface charge is a factor in T cell–target cell interaction, possibly by promoting a more stable interaction. Although evidence of this kind has not been described previously, it has been suggested by others that nonspecific binding forces are important for stable association between target cells and CTLs (11). This tumor model system is the first evidence of its kind to suggest that indeed nonspecific ionic interactions may be a major factor in forming a stable CTL–target cell conjugate.

REFERENCES

1. Russell, J. H., Hale, A. H., Ginns, L. C., and Eisen, H. N., *Proc. Nat. Acad. Sci. USA* **75,** 441, 1978.
2. Russell, J. H., Hale, A. H., Inbar, D., and Eisen, H. N., *Eur. J. Immunol.* **8,** 640, 1978.
3. Hale, A. H., and Paulus, L. K., *Cell. Immunol.* **46,** 337, 1979.
4. Hale, A. H., Lyles, D. S., Paulus, L. K., and Ruebush, M. J., *J. Immunol.* **124,** 2063, 1980.
5. Taylor, R. G., and Lewis, J. C., *Scanning Electron Microsc.* **3,** 775, 1979.
6. Danon, D., and Skutelsky, E., *Ann N.Y. Acad. Sci.* **275,** 47, 1976.
7. Lewis, J. C., and Roberts, M., *EMSA Bull.* **6,** 17, 1976.
8. Lerche, C., *Acta Pathol. Microbiol. Scand.* **98,** 1953.
9. Gallin, J. I., Durocher, J. R., Kaplan, A. P., *Clin. Investi.* **55,** 967, 1975.
10. Black, A. P., and Smith, A. L., *Amer. Waterworks Assoc. J.* **58,** 445, 1966.
11. Berke, G., Tzur, R., and Inbar, M., *J. Immunol.* **120,** 1378, 1978.

CELLULAR IMMUNOLOGY **64**, 131–143 (1981)

Antibody-Dependent Cell-Mediated Cytotoxicity for Cultured Autologous Melanoma Cells

PHILIP O. LIVINGSTON, RICHARD MICHITSCH, HIROSHI SHIKU,[1] CARL M. PINSKY, AND HERBERT F. OETTGEN

Memorial Sloan–Kettering Cancer Center, 1275 York Avenue, New York, New York 10021

Received March 6, 1981; accepted July 27, 1981

Sera from 33 patients with malignant melanoma were tested for antibody-dependent cell-mediated cytotoxicity (ADCC) against cultured autologous melanoma cells prelabeled with [^{3}H]proline in a 36-h assay. Effector cells (autologous or from normal donors) were obtained by Ficoll–Hypaque separation of peripheral blood. Assay sensitivity (but not specificity) was affected by the effector cells used, the optimal source of effector cells varying between different autologous serum–target cell combinations. The activity of autologous effector cells appeared to correlate inversely with the extent of disease. Sera from 18 patients gave positive direct tests. In seven cases reactivity was strong enough to permit analysis of specificity with absorption tests. Serum from one patient recognized a melanoma antigen restricted to autologous melanoma cells and three other melanoma cell lines, and not present on other melanoma cell lines or autologous tissues, nonmelanoma tumor cells, or xenogeneic cells. Sera from 5 patients detected a diverse group of widely distributed antigens, all related to fetal calf serum (FCS). Serum from the seventh patient reacted with a widely distributed antigen not related to FCS.

INTRODUCTION

While there are many clinical indications that patients with malignant melanoma respond immunologically to their tumors (1, 2) it has been exceedingly difficult to develop conclusive evidence that melanoma-specific antigens, and immune reactions to them, in fact exist. Tests of serum or lymphoid cells of one patient on melanoma cells of another (usually one or more established cell lines) form the basis of many reports in the literature. Interpretation of the results of such tests has been difficult, if not impossible, because of the unknown role of alloantigens in the reactions observed. Other studies that have been restricted to fresh melanoma cells or primary cultures raise questions related to specificity and reproducibility because the analysis is necessarily limited by the number of tests that can be performed. For these reasons we have restricted our studies of malignant melanoma to reactions between serum or lymphocytes and melanoma cells from the same patient and to melanomas that could be established in continuous culture (3–7). Using four serological assays detecting cell surface antigens, mixed hemadsorption (MHA), immune adherence (IA), C-3 mixed hemadsorption (C3-MHA), and staphylococcal protein A (PA),

[1] Present address: First Department of Internal Medicine, Nagoya University School of Medicine, Tsurumai-cho 65, Showa-Ku, Nagoya 466, Japan.

0008-8749/81/150131-13$02.00/0

TABLE 1

Influence of Effector Cell Source on the Results of ADCC Assays with Autologous Combinations of Serum and Cultured Melanoma Cells

Source of target cells and serum	Source of effector cells					
	Autologous	RG[a]	HK	RM	WB	KO
	Percentage ADCC (CMC)[b]					
BG	29 (10)	60 (22)	48 (0)	54 (15)	38 (11)	
CN	0 (11)	38 (0)	30 (31)		26 (0)	56 (12)
BD	45 (18)	45 (10)	0 (0)	0 (0)	0 (0)	28 (12)
AV	55 (63)	12 (16)	45 (38)	10 (10)	0 (10)	45 (65)

[a] Except for the autologous donors, all donors are normal individuals.
[b] CMC calculated according to the formula %CMC = (A − B)/A × 100 where A is the residual counts per minute (cpm) of target cells incubated without lymphocytes (medium control) and B the residual cpm of target cells incubated with lymphocytes.

and extensive absorption tests, we have defined three classes of cell surface antigens on melanoma cells. Class 1 antigens are restricted to autologous melanoma and not found on any other cell, Class 2 antigens are shared melanoma antigens, and Class 3 antigens are widely distributed on normal and neoplastic cells, including cells of other species. We have now applied this approach, termed autologous typing, to the study of antibody-dependent cell-mediated cytotoxicity. This report summarizes our initial experience.

METHODS

Target cells. The derivation of melanoma and other cell lines has been described (3, 8, 9–11). The cells were cultured in Eagle's minimum essential medium (MEM) supplemented with 2 mM glutamine, 1% nonessential amino acids (NEAA), 100 IU/ml penicillin and 100 μg/ml streptomycin (1% P/S), and 10% fetal calf serum (FCS). All cultures were tested frequently for mycoplasma infection. Infected cultures were discarded.

To prepare target cells (13) 70–90% confluent monolayer cultures in T-60 or T-30 plastic flasks (Falcon Plastics, Oxnard, Calif.) were washed gently three times with a total volume of 30 or 10 ml., respectively, of MEM supplemented with 15% FCS but not NEAA (i.e., without proline). Five or 2.5 ml of the same medium, containing 50 μCi/ml of [^{3}H]proline (45.7 Ci/mmol, New England Nuclear, Boston, Mass.), were added and the cultures incubated for 16–20 h at 37°C. After labelling, the cultures were washed gently three times with MEM containing 10% FCS, 2 mM glutamine, 1% NEAA (as a source of excess unlabeled proline), and 1% P/S (test medium). The cells were detached with 0.25% tryptar (Difco Laboratories, Detroit, Mich.) in Puck's saline A (Grand Island Biological Co., Grand Island, N.Y.), washed twice, and resuspended in test medium. Using a 500 μl syringe (Hamilton Co., Whittier, Calif.), 2000 cells in 10 μl were distributed into the wells of Falcon No. 3040 microcytotoxicity plates to which 0.05 ml test medium had been added.

Effector cells. Venous blood was defibrinated in sterile Erlenmeyer flasks containing 3-mm glass beads. Twenty-milliliter aliquots of defibrinated blood were diluted 1:1 with phosphate-buffered saline (PBS), underlayed with 10 ml of a Ficoll–Hypaque solution (sp grav 1.077), and centrifuged at 400*g* for 20 min at room temperature (12). The interphase was aspirated and the cells were washed in Earle's balanced salt solution containing 2.5% FCS and then incubated in T-60 plastic flasks in 5% CO_2 in air for 40 min to remove adherent cells. Unattached cells were washed twice more and diluted to 2.5×10^6 cells/ml in test medium. Greater than 90% of cells in the resulting suspensions had the morphological appearance of small lymphocytes. We refer to these cell suspensions as effector cells or peripheral blood lymphocytes with the understanding that other white blood cells present in these suspensions may contribute to the ADCC reaction.

Serum. Serum was diluted with MEM. For absorption tests, the serum dilution which gave 50% ADCC was used. Cells used for absorption were harvested from plastic tissue culture flasks with a rubber policeman and washed three times in MEM. Serum (0.15 ml) was absorbed with 0.1 ml packed cells. Various noncultured cells or cell preparations were also used for absorption. These included human A+ or AB+ red blood cells, sheep red blood cells (SRBC), horse red blood cells, boiled guinea pig kidney (GPK) antigen or bovine red blood cell extract (BBL, Cockeysville, Md.) and fetal liver and brain from 20-week fetuses (single-cell suspensions were prepared by mincing and then stored frozen in 10% human serum (HS) and 10% dimethysulfoxide (DMSO). These preparations were washed four times in MEM prior to use. Absorption was carried out on ice for 1 hr, agitating the tubes at 20-min intervals. After absorption, the mixture was centrifuged and the serum removed for testing. Absorptions that reduced reactivity to less than 50% of the unabsorbed ADCC to an actual ADCC below 20% were considered positive.

Medium supplemented with HS. For some experiments, the test medium was supplemented with 10% AB + HS instead of FCS. The target cells, fed twice weekly, were passed in HS medium at least four times over a period of 4 weeks prior to use. In these experiments, the labeling and plating of target cells and preparation of the effector cells were also performed in HS medium.

ADCC assay. One day after plating the target cells, diluted serum alone (0.01

TABLE 2

Correlation between Extent of Disease and Autologous versus Normal Donor (Allogeneic) Effector Cell Reactivity

ADCC effector cell activity[a]	No known residual disease	Measurable disease
Autologous $\gtrsim$ allogeneic	BT,[b] BD, AV, AL	
Allogeneic > autologous		AS, BG,[b] BH, BT[b] CF, CH, CN, CW
Autologous activity absent Allogeneic activity present		AD, AU, BC, BJ, CI, CV, CX, DC
Autologous and Allogeneic activity absent	AH, AQ,[b] AZ, DR, BG[b]	AN, AP, AQ,[b] AT, BW, CB, CM, CS, CV, CW

[a] Freshly drawn serum and lymphocytes were used in all tests.

[b] Patients developing measurable disease during the course of study are listed in both categories.

TABLE 3

ADCC Assays with Autologous Serum-Cultured Melanoma Cell Combinations: Summary of Results

Patient designation	Clinical stage[a]	Number of effector cell donors tested (total positive)	No. sera tested (Total positive)	Months between collection of first and last serum specimen	Maximum percentage ADCC	Class of specificity
AD	IV	10 (2)	4 (2)	3	25	
AH	III	12 (0)	10 (0)	43	0	
AL	II	10 (3)	14 (12)	40	40	
AN	IV	2 (0)	2 (0)	4	0	
AP	III→IV	11 (0)	4 (0)	5	0	
AQ	III→IV	12 (0)	12 (0)	11	0	
AS	II→IV	12 (6)	24 (18)	26	39	
AT	II→IV	9 (0)	11 (0)	13	0	
AU	III→IV	10 (3)	18 (18)	16	40	
AV	III	12 (3)	24 (24)	41	70	
AZ	II	11 (0)	10 (0)	39	0	3
BC	IV	14 (2)	10 (3)	18	25	
BD	III	14 (5)	28 (18)	44	65	2
BG	II→IV	10 (10)	26 (23)	26	78	3
BH	IV	11 (0)	12 (3)	12	25	
BT	III→IV	10 (5)	27 (9)	27	50	3
BW	III→IV	12 (0)	10 (0)	7	0	
CB	IV	8 (0)	8 (0)	4	0	
CC	IV	11 (5)	12 (3)	22	30	
CF	III→IV	11 (8)	9 (9)	7	54	3
CH	II→IV	10 (6)	30 (15)	19	76	3
CL	III→IV	11 (5)	12 (10)	14	35	
CM	IV	7 (0)	9 (0)	4	0	
CN	IV	11 (8)	12 (12)	9	67	3
CO	IV	14 (7)	5 (5)	11	38	
CS	IV	10 (0)	14 (0)	9	0	
CV	IV	11 (0)	2 (0)	2	0	
CW	IV	10 (0)	2 (0)	2	0	
CX	IV	11 (6)	4 (2)	6	25	
DC	III→IV	12 (11)	10 (5)	14	35	
DE	II→IV	5 (4)	11 (4)	12	21	
DN	IV	5 (0)	4 (0)	4	0	
DX	II	6 (0)	11 (0)	13	0	

[a] Stage of disease: II, metastases in regional skin or lymph nodes only; III, systemic metastases in skin or lymph nodes; IV, metastases in sites other than skin or lymph nodes.

ml), effector cells alone (25×10^4), both serum and effector cells, or nothing were added to the wells as previously described (13). The plates were incubated at 37°C in 5% CO_2 in air for 40 hr, inverted, dipped in PBS with 5% FCS (37°C) inverted, dipped, and inverted again. The plates were processed as described previously (13). The median of five replicates was used to calculate ADCC according to the formula $\%ADCC = (A - B)/A \times 100$, where A is the residual counts per minute of target cells incubated with lymphocytes alone, and B the residual counts per minute of target cells incubated with lymphocytes and serum. The significance of the difference between the reduction of counts per minute by lymphocytes and serum, and by lymphocytes alone, was determined by the two-sample ranks test (14). Test results are listed as 0% unless ADCC was at least 15% with a P value of less than 0.025. Sera that caused cytotoxicity in the absence of lymphocytes (a rare occurrence) were first inactivated at 56°C for 20 min. Absorption of serum, and also medium, with GPK or fetal brain sometimes resulted in a decrease of counts per minute unrelated to ADCC or complement-dependent cytotoxicity. In tests using these preparations, ADCC was calculated according to another formula: %ADCC $= (A - B)/A \times 100$, where A is the counts per minute of target cells incubated with lymphocytes and absorbed MEM, and B the counts per minute of target cells incubated with lymphocytes and absorbed serum.

RESULTS

Influence of Effector Cell Source

The degree of cytotoxicity seen in ADCC assays was profoundly affected by the source of effector cells. Lymphocytes from some normal (allogeneic) donors were consistently more reactive than those from others in tests with most autologous serum–target cell combinations. The optimal source of allogeneic effector cells for a given autologous serum–target cell combination could not be predicted, however, as shown in Table 1. While lymphocytes from several normal donors were reactive

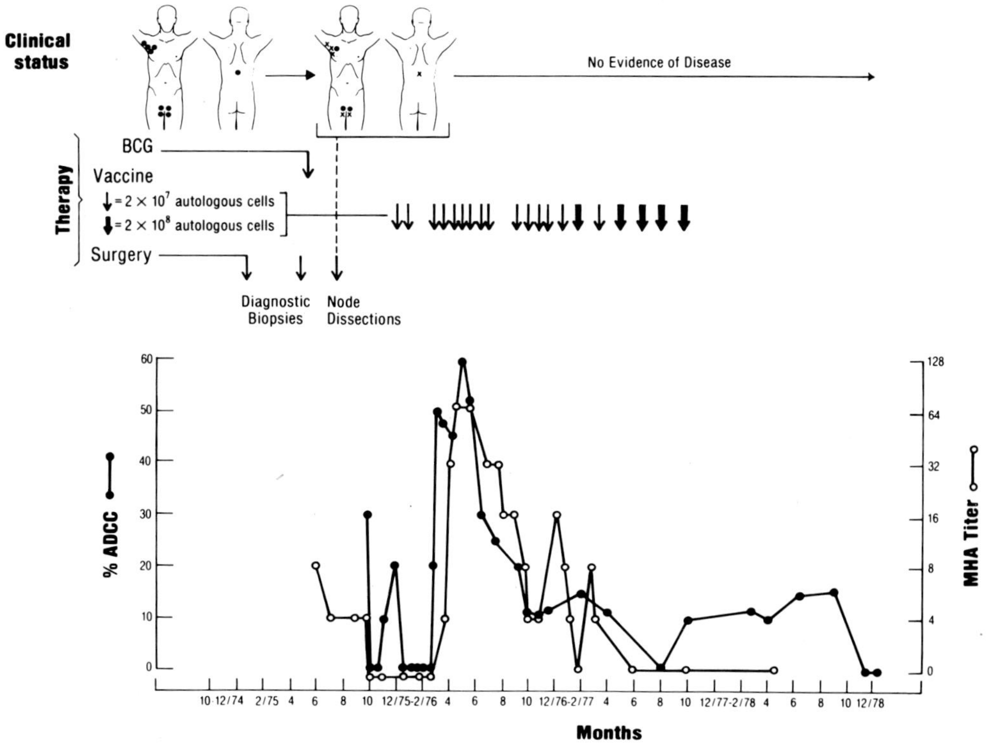

FIG. 1. Patient BD: Correlation to clinical course of serological reactivity for autologous melanoma cells (SK-MEL-37) as determined by ADCC and MHA assays.

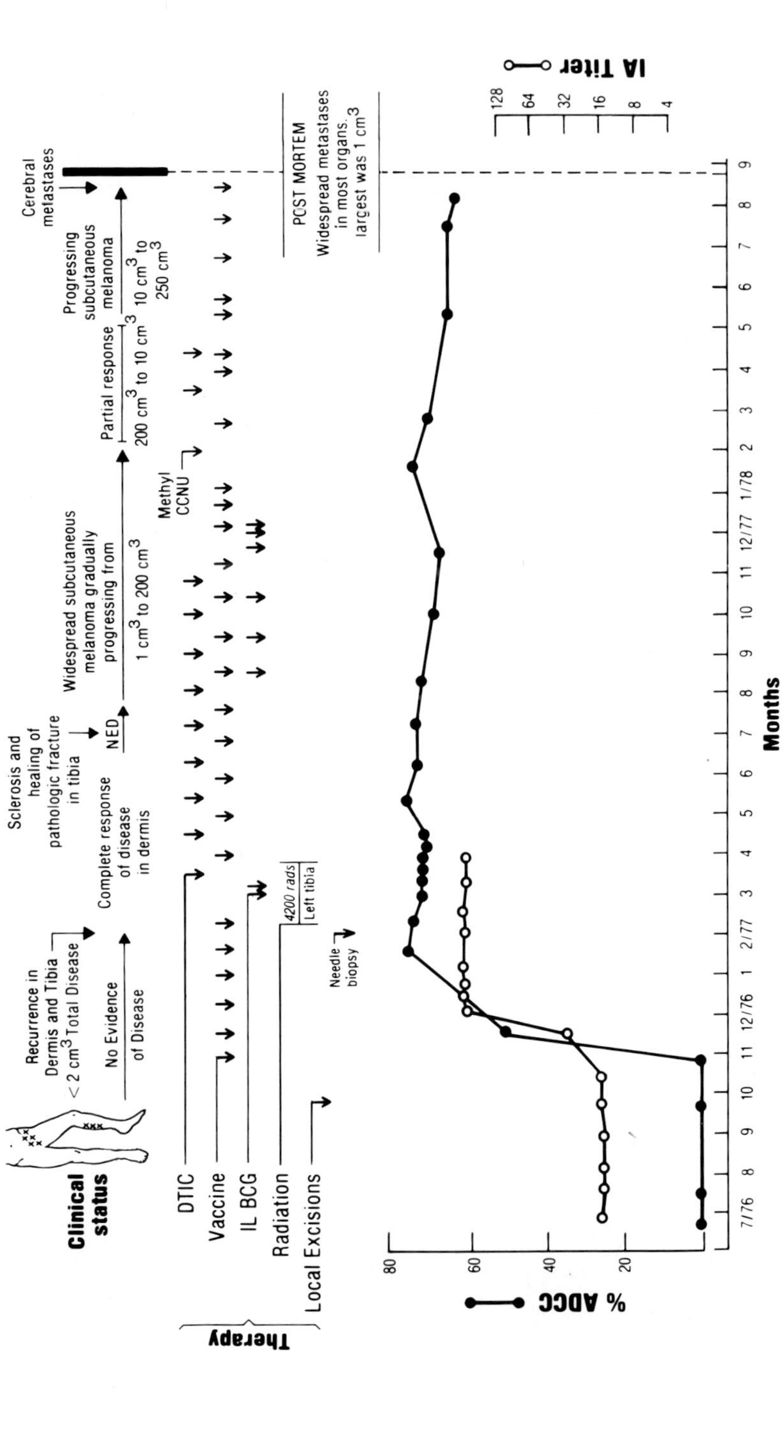

FIG. 2. Patient BG: Correlation to clinical course of serological reactivity for autologous melanoma cells (SK-MEL-40) as determined by ADCC and IA assays.

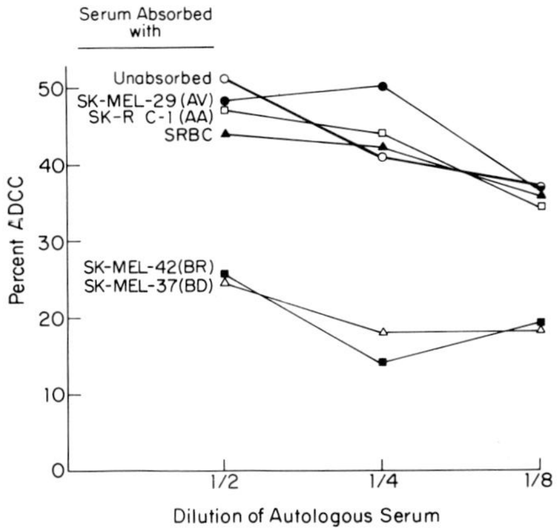

FIG. 3. Example of an individual absorption test with BD serum. Autologous melanoma and one allogeneic melanoma line (SK-MEL-42) absorbed ADCC reactivity of BD serum to autologous melanoma (SK-MEL-37). Another allogeneic melanoma line, a renal cancer line, and sheep erythrocytes did not.

in tests with BG and CN, only RG lymphocytes were strongly reactive with BD and only KO and HK lymphocytes with AV. Lymphocyte cytotoxicity (CMC) values are also shown in Table 1. A general correlation between effector cell reactivity in CMC and ADCC assays is apparent.

It appeared that when ADCC was demonstrable at all, autologous effector cells were as reactive as normal donor effector cells in patients with no detectable residual melanoma, but less reactive than normal donor effective cells or completely unreactive in patients with known metastases. In Table 2, four categories of test results are listed. In the first category, autologous effector cells were at least as reactive as normal donor effector cells. None of the four patients in this category had detectable residual melanoma at the time of the tests. In the second category, autologous effector cells were less reactive than allogeneic effector cells. All eight patients in this category had measurable metastatic melanoma. In the third category, autologous effector cells were nonreactive but allogeneic effector cells were reactive. All eight patients in this category had metastatic disease. In the fourth category, no ADCC was detected so effector cell reactivity could not be compared.

On the basis of these initial findings we screened sera for ADCC activity on autologous melanoma cells first with normal donor effector cells that had been shown to be generally reactive (i.e., RG, KO, HK). Positive sera were then tested with lymphocytes from a larger group of allogeneic donors, usually 10 or more, and with autologous lymphocytes when available. Effector cells that were most reactive in a given autologous serum–target cell combination were used for all further tests with that combination.

In the course of the specificity analysis of positive sera by absorption tests, effector cells from more than one source were frequently used. While variations in degree of cytotoxicity were common, the specificity of the reaction was not changed by changing the source of effector cells. For example, when the specificity of the BD reaction was investigated, effector cells from BD or RG (when BD was not available) were used interchangeably with the same results.

TABLE 4

Absorption of ADCC Reactivity of BD Serum Tested on Autologous Melanoma (SK-MEL 37)

Positive absorption	Negative absorption
Autologous cultured melanoma cells SK-MEL-37 (BD)	Autologous normal cells BD Fibroblasts, BD RBC, BD B cells
Allogeneic cultured melanoma cells SK-MEL-13 (AH) SK-MEL-41 (BH) SK-MEL-42 (BR)	Allogeneic cultured melanoma cells SK-MEL-26, 27, 29, 40, 47, 59, 62, 63
	Allogeneic cultured nonmelanoma cells T-24, SK-RC-1, 2, 9 SK-LC-LL, Me 180, fetal liver erythrocytes A+, AB+
	Xenogeneic cells sheep RBC

Note. Serum drawn: 3/2/76–6/8/76.

Results of Direct Tests

Table 3 summarizes the results of tests with sera from 33 patients on cultured autologous melanoma cells. Sera from 18 patients were positive; sera from 7 demonstrated sufficient reactivity (50% ADCC or more) to permit absorption analysis.

No consistent serological changes in ADCC reactivity were seen after patients were treated with DTIC, dexamethasone, intralesional Bacillus Calmette–Guerin (BCG), radiation therapy, or partial surgical excision. Similarly, there was no apparent correlation of ADCC with stage of disease or tumor mass. By contrast, ADCC appeared to be affected by vaccination with melanoma cells. In 7 of 18 patients, reactivity first appeared after vaccination with autologous (AD, BC, BG, BT, CH, CL) or allogeneic (DC, BT) cultured melanoma cells. The course of two

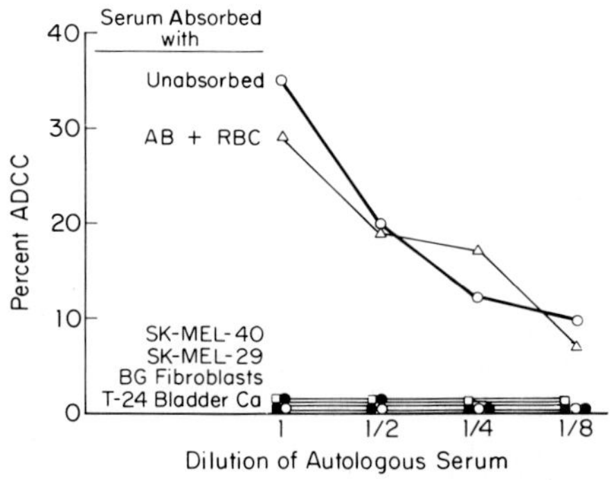

FIG. 4. Example of an individual absorption test with BG serum. Autologous melanoma and fibroblasts, and allogeneic melanoma and bladder cancer absorbed ADCC reactivity of BG serum to autologous melanoma (SK-MEL-40). Type AB+ erythrocytes did not.

TABLE 5

Absorption of ADCC Reactivity of BG Serum Tested on Autologous Melanoma (SK-MEL-40)

Positive	Negative
Autologous	Autologous
SK-MEL-40	BG RBC
BG fibroblasts	
Allogeneic	Allogeneic
SK-MEL-13, 27, 29, 37	AB + RBC
	fetal liver
T-24, Me180, SK-LC-LL and BK, SK-RC-SN, U-178-Mg	
BT, AL fibroblasts	
Xenogeneic	
sheep, beef, and horse RBC guinea pig, and kidney extract	

Note. Serum drawn: 12/18/76 and 1/18/77.

patients, shown in Figs. 1 and 2 demonstrates this point. In the case of patient BD (Fig. 1), antibodies to cultured autologous melanoma cells were detected in BD's serum before vaccination but became undetectable during the period when axillary and inguinal metastases were injected with BCG and then removed by surgery. After vaccination with cultured autologous melanoma cells, ADCC reactivity increased initially and then declined again despite continued vaccination. These changes paralleled changes in the titer of antibodies detected by the MHA reaction. In the case of patient BG (Fig. 2), the serum became reactive after vaccination and remained reactive despite progression of disease and chemotherapy with DTIC and Methyl-CCNU. Similar changes were seen in the titer of antibodies detected by IA assays.

Results of Absorption Tests

An individual absorption test with BD serum is shown in Fig. 3. The series of absorptions performed with BD sera is summarized in Table 4. The antibody defined by the ADCC reaction of BD serum with autologous melanoma cells was absorbed by autologous melanoma cells (SK-MEL-37) and also by three other melanoma cell lines (SK-MEL-13, 41, and 42) but not by any other autologous, allogeneic, or xenogeneic cells tested, normal or malignant. The antigen detected by the ADCC reaction can thus be classified as a Class 2 antigen. (These results are identical with the results of absorption analysis of the MHA reaction in this case.) In the case of patient BG (Fig. 4 and Table 5), absorption tests showed that the antigen detected by the ADCC reaction on autologous cultured melanoma cells was also present on autologous fibroblasts as well as normal and malignant allogeneic cells and xenogeneic cells. The antigen detected by ADCC in this case is therefore a Class 3 antigen. (Absorption analysis of IA reactivity of this patient's serum had the same result.) Sera from four other patients (AV, BT, CH, and CN) were analyzed in this fashion. They also detected Class 3 antigens, present not only on autologous melanoma cells but also on a variety of allogeneic cells cultured in FCS and xenogeneic cells. Absorption tests with the serum of the seventh patient (CF)

TABLE 6

Cell Surface Antigens of Melanoma Cells Defined by Absorption Analysis of ADCC Reactivity of Autologous Serum

	Result of absorption[a]						
Serum absorbed with	BD	AV	BG	BT	CH	CN	CF
Cultured autologous melanoma	+	+	+	+	+	+	+
Cultured allogeneic melanoma	+ or −	+ or −	+	+	+	+ or −	+ or −
Cultured nonmelanoma tumor cells	−	+ or −	+	+ or −	+	+ or −	+ or −
Cultured fibroblasts of B cells	−		+		+		
Fresh xenogeneic cells	−	+	+	+ or −	+ or −	+ or −	+ or −
Class of antigen	2	3	3	3	3	3	3

[a] Reactivity with autologous melanoma cells removed (+) or not removed (−) by absorption.

showed that the antigen detected by this serum in ADCC assays on autologous melanoma cells was also a Class 3 antigen, although the pattern of distribution was different from the pattern of the BG antigen. The results of the absorption analysis of these seven sera are summarized in Table 6. To define the specificity of the six Class 3 reactions further, sera were absorbed with a variety of xenogeneic cells, fetal tissues, or melanoma cells grown in FCS-free medium, or tested in 50% FCS. As shown in Table 7, five of the six sera (AV, BG, BT, CH, and CN) clearly defined antigens related to FCS which were not present on the same cells when they were cultured in the absence of FCS. In three cases (BG, BT, CH) this reactivity appeared only after vaccination with autologous melanoma cells cultured in medium supplemented with FCS. Sera from the other two patients (AV and CN) were reactive before vaccine administration, and their titers were not changed by vaccination, chemotherapy (DTIC), or progression of disease. Direct tests with autologous sera on all five of these target cells were positive when the target cells were cultured in medium containing FCS, and negative when they were cultured in FCS-free medium. The sixth patient's (CF) serological reactivity was present before the initial lymph node dissection and also persisted despite DTIC and progression of disease. It was only slightly decreased when the test was performed in 50% FCS, and was completely absorbed by some cell lines (melanoma and testicular cancer) cultured in FCS or HS, and by guinea pig kidney extract and fetal brain. The patient's serum was reactive in direct tests with autologous and some allogeneic target cells cultured in FCS-free medium supplemented with HS.

DISCUSSION

In the ADCC reaction, target cells are destroyed by lymphocytes that have Fc receptors which attach to the Fc region of target-cell-bound antibody. Antibody, therefore, determines the specificity of ADCC reactions. As was the case in our previous serological studies of malignant melanoma, our study of ADCC in malignant melanoma has been based on the use of autologous combinations of serum and cultured melanoma target cells. The strength of ADCC reactions varies when effector cells from different sources are used. We observed, as others have before, that effector cells from some normal donors were generally more reactive than effector cells from other donors. We found, however, that the optimal effector cell source could not be predicted for a given combination of serum and target cells. Several sera that were considered negative initially turned out to be positive when different effector cells were used. Autologous effector cells from patients with no known residual disease were at least as reactive as allogeneic effector cells. Autologous effector cells from patients with metastatic disease were generally less reactive or completely unreactive. On the basis of these initial findings we tested all autologous serum-target cell combinations with lymphocytes from 5 to 15 normal donors as well as autologous lymphocytes (when available) before a negative result was accepted. The reasons for these differences in effector cell activity are not clear. They are of practical importance because they increase the technical complexity of the ADCC assay as compared with other serologic assays.

Antibody to cell surface antigens of cultured autologous melanoma cells was demonstrated in sera from 18 of 33 patients. In 7 of these patients, the strength of the reaction was sufficient for analysis of specificity by absorption tests. Serum from one patient (BD) was found to recognize a shared (Class 2) melanoma antigen present in 3 of 11 allogeneic melanoma cell lines but not on any other cell type from autologous, allogeneic, or xenogeneic sources. Sera from the other 6 patients recognized Class 3 antigens present not only on autologous melanoma cells but also on a variety of normal and malignant cells including xenogeneic tissues. We have previously defined antigens of similarly broad distribution by autologous typing of melanoma (6), renal cancer (15), and astrocytomas (16) using MHA, IA, C3-MHA, and PA assays. In the present study, we have further examined the relation of these antigens to FCS by testing the same cell lines cultured in FCS-free medium supplemented with human serum as well as standard medium containing FCS. The antigen defined by sera from 1 of the 6 patients (BG) was present on all cells cultured in FCS containing medium and all xenogeneic erythrocytes tested, but not on cells cultured in FCS-free medium. This pattern is consistent with the distribution pattern of the heterologous membrane antigen described by Irie *et al.* (17). The antigens defined by the sera of 4 other patients, though clearly related to FCS, were not the same in that they were not found on all cells cultured in FCS (sera

TABLE 7

Absorption Analysis of Class III Antigens Defined by ADCC Tests with Autologous Serum–Target Cell Combinations[a]

	A+ RBC	HS cell line	FCS cell line	Beef RBC	GPK extract	Sheep RBC	Horse RBC	FCS	Fetal brain	Fetal liver
BG	−	−	+	+	+	+	+	+	−	−
CH	−	−	+	±	±	−	−	+	−	−
CN	−	−	+ or −	±	+	±	−	+	−	−
AV	−	−	+ or −	+	+	+	+	+	±	±
BT	−	−	+ or −	+	−	−	−	+	−	±
CF	−	+ or −	+ or −	±	+	±	−	±	+	±

[a] Reactivity with autologous melanoma cells cultured and tested in FCS-medium removed (+) or not removed (−) by absorption.

of patients CN, AV, and BT), or on all nonhuman mammalian cells tested (sera of patients CH, CN, and BT). In the sixth case (CF), no relation to FCS could be demonstrated for the Class 3 antigen detected by the patient's serum. For three of the six cases (BG, BT, and CH) antibodies detecting Class 3 antigens appeared after treatment with autologous melanoma cell vaccine (18). For the remaining three cases (AV, CF, and CN), the antibodies were present prior to any systemic therapy, and their titer was not affected by subsequent chemotherapy (DTIC), immunotherapy (intralesional BCG or autologous melanoma vaccine), surgery, or radiation therapy.

In comparing the seven antigens defined by ADCC assays with antigens detected on the same melanoma target cells by other serological tests, we find similar patterns of antigen distribution in five cases. In the case of patient BD (Fig. 1); absorption analysis showed reactivity to be directed against a Class 2 antigen present on the same four melanoma cell lines as the antigen detected by ADCC (5). Absorption analysis of sera from patients AV, BG, BT, and CH by PA, IA, or C3-MHA assays showed that the antibodies detected by these reactions also recognized Class 3 antigens (5, 6). In the two remaining cases (CN, CF), sera that detected Class 3 antigens in ADCC assays showed little or no reactivity in PA, C3-MHA, or IA assays.

ADCC can be used to detect antibodies to autologous melanoma cell surface antigens, and to define their specificity. Considering the technical disadvantages of the method (i.e., the more complex basic procedure as well as the difficulty to adapt it for use as a micromethod), the question arises whether it offers information other serological methods do not provide. While the endpoint of tumor cell destruction is attractive, there is no certainty that the test reflects tumor cell destruction *in vivo*. Some findings point in that direction. A rise in antibody titers against EBV-related antigens that can be measured by ADCC but not other serological assays in patients with nasopharyngeal cancer (19) or Burkitt's lymphoma (20, 21) was found to be associated with a more benign course. In our own study patient BD, the only patient whose serum recognized an antigen restricted to melanoma cells, is also one of the few patients who have remained free of disease. More patients with serologic reactivity for Class 1 or 2 antigens have to be followed, however, before the clinical significance of these antibodies measured by ADCC or other serological assays can be determined.

ACKNOWLEDGMENTS

The authors thank Ms. L. Resnick, Dr. T. Watanabe, and Ms. L. T. C. Li for their cooperation in establishing the many tissue culture lines used, and Ms. Carol McCormack for preparation of this manuscript. This work was supported by a Junior Faculty Award from the American Cancer Society, grants from the National Cancer Institute (CA-19765, CA-19267, CA-08748), and NCI Contract CB-64062.

REFERENCES

1. Clark, W. H., Jr., Mastrangelo, M. J., Ainsworth, A. M., Berd, D., Bellet, R. E., and Bernardino, E. A., *Advan. Cancer Res.* **24,** 267, 1977.
2. Hellstrom, D. E., and Hellstrom, I., *Advan. Immunol.* **18,** 209, 1974.
3. Carey, T. E., Takahashi, T., Resnick, L. A., Oettgen, H. F., and Old, L. J., *Proc. Nat. Acad. Sci. USA* **73,** 3278, 1976.

4. Shiku, H., Takahashi, T., Oettgen, H. F., and Old, L. J., *J. Exp. Med.* **144,** 873, 1976.
5. Shiku, H., Takahashi, T., Carey, J. E., Resnick, L. A., Oettgen, H. F., and Old, L. J., *In* "Biological Markers of Neoplasia: Basic and Applied Aspects" (R.W. Ruddon, Ed.), pp 73–90. Elsevier/North-Holland, 1978.
6. Shiku, H., Takahashi, T., Resnick, L. A., Oettgen, H. F., and Old, L. J., *J. Exp. Med.* **145,** 784, 1977.
7. Livingston, P. O., Shiku, H., Bean, M. A., Pinsky, C. M., Oettgen, H. F., and Old, L. J., *Int. J. Cancer* **24,** 1, 1979.
8. Fogh, J., and Trempe, G., "Human Tumor Cells in Vitro" (J. Fogh, Ed.), p. 115. Plenum, New York, 1975.
9. Blan, M. A., Pees, H., Fogh, J. E., Grabstald, H., and Oettgen, H. F., *Int. J. Cancer* **14,** 186, 1974.
10. Pollack, M. S., Heagney, S. D., Livingston, P. O., and Fogh, J., *J. Nat. Cancer Inst.*, in press, 1981.
11. Watanabe, T., and Livingston, P. O. *In* "Laboratory Manual" (W. Braun, and A. Zachery, Eds.). American Association for Histocompatibility Testing (AACHT), 1981.
12. Boyum, A., *Scand. J. Lab. Clin. Invest.* **21,** (Suppl. 97), 77, 1968.
13. Kodera, Y., and Bean, M. A., *Int. J. Cancer* **16,** 579, 1975.
14. Huntsberger, D. V., and Leaverton, P. E., "Statistical Inference in the Biomedical Sciences," pp. 138–240, Allyn and Bacon, Boston, 1970.
15. Ueda, R., Shiku, H., Pfreundschuh, M., Takahashi, T., Li, L. T. C., Whitmore, W. F., Oettgen, H. F., and Old, L. J., *J. Exp. Med.* **150,** 564, 1979.
16. Pfreundschuh, M., Shiku, H., Takahashi, T., Ueda, R., Ransohoff, J., Oettgen, H. F., and Old., L. J., *Proc. Nat. Acad. Sci. USA* **75,** 5122, 1978.
17. Irie, R. F., Irie, K., and Morton, D. L., *J. Nat. Cancer Inst.* **52,** 1051, 1974.
18. Livingston, P. O., Oettgen, H. F., and Old, L. J., *In* "Immunological Aspects of Cancer Therapeutics" (E. Mihich, Ed.). Wiley, New York, 1982.
19. Chan, S. H., Levine, P. H., De-The, G. B., Mulroney, S. E., Lavoue, M. E., Glen, S. P. P., Goh, E. H., Khor, T. H., and Connelly, R. R., *Int. J. Cancer* **23,** 181, 1979.
20. Pearson, G. R., Qualtiere, L. F., Klein, G., Norin, T., and Bal, I. S., *Int. J. Cancer* **24,** 402, 1979.
21. Granlund, D. J., Nkrumah, F., Perkins, I. V., Biggar, R. J., Levin, P. H., and Fuccillo, D. A., *Int. J. Cancer* **24,** 567, 1979.

CELLULAR IMMUNOLOGY **64,** 144–149 (1981)

Serum Thymic Factor (FTS) Restores the Ability of Adult Thymectomized Mice to be Suppressed by Hapten-Modified Self

BRIGITTE GROUIX,* JANINE CHARREIRE,† DOMINIQUE ERARD,* PIERRE GALANAUD,* AND JEAN-FRANÇOIS BACH†

**INSERM U 131, 32 rue des Carnets, 92140 Clamart, and †INSERM U 25, Hôpital Necker, 161 rue de Sèvres, 75730 Paris Cedex 15, France*

Received May 21, 1981; accepted July 8, 1981

The injection of trinitrophenyl (TNP) conjugated spleen cells (TNP-SC) into normal recipients induces a specific suppresion of the anti-TNP antibody response to the T-independent antigen TNP polyacrylamide. The T-cell dependency of this suppression is shown by two arguments. (i) Splenic T cells from TNP-SC-treated mice suppress the *in vitro* antibody response of normal mouse spleen cells. (ii) The anti-TNP response of adult thymectomized (ATX) mice is not suppressed after injection of TNP-SC. Treatment of such ATX mice with a synthetic analog of serum thymic factor (FTS) 7–9 weeks after thymectomy restores their susceptibility to TNP-SC-induced suppression.

INTRODUCTION

The injection of a hapten coupled to syngeneic lymphocytes is able to suppress the subsequent immune response to this hapten. This suppression involves suppressor T cells both in delayed-type hypersensitivity reactions (1, 2) and in antibody responses (3). Borel *et al.* (4) recently reported that the ability to induce suppression of the antibody response by guanosine-modified lymphocytes was abolished shortly after adult thymectomy (ATX).[1] Thus the presence of an intact thymus is apparently required for hapten-modified lymphocytes to induce hapten-specific suppressor T cells. Two hypotheses may be put forward to explain such a thymus dependency. Hapten-specific suppressor cells are short lived and possibly require the presence of the thymic epithelium to differentiate. Alternatively the suppressor cells could persist after ATX, but would be inactive without the influence of circulating thymic hormones. The latter interpretation was supported by previous experiments dealing with picrylsulfonic acid-induced suppressor cells of contact sensitivity to picryl chloride (5).

We report here that short-term treatment with serum thymic factor (FTS) restores the ability of ATX mice to be suppressed by trinitrophenyl-conjugated lymphocytes (TNP-SC). In addition we confirm that T cells play an essential role in

[1] Abbreviations used: ATX, adult thymectomized mice; FTS, serum thymic factor; HBSS, Hanks' balanced salt solution; SRBC, sheep red blood cells; SC, unconjugated spleen cells; TNP-PAA, trinitrophenyl-polyacrylamide beads; TNP-SC, trinitrophenyl-conjugated spleen cells.

0008-8749/81/150144-06$02.00/0

the suppressive effect of spleen cells from TNP-SC-treated mice on the anti-TNP response of normal spleen cells.

MATERIALS AND METHODS

Animals. Three- to eight-week-old male Balb/c mice and CBA mice were obtained from Charles River (France) and from the Chester Beatty Institute (London), respectively. Thymectomy (ATX) was performed at the age of 3 to 4 weeks by suction under sodium barbital anesthesia.

Antigens. DNP-Ficoll was a gift of Dr. Huchet, ICIG, Villejuif. TNP-polyacrylamide beads (TNP-PAA) were prepared as previously described (6).

Hapten-labeling of cells. Erythrocyte-free spleen cell suspensions were prepared in Hanks' balanced salt solution (HBSS) and were trinitrophenylated (TNP-SC) with 10 m*M* trinitrobenzenesulfonic acid according to Scott and Long (7). TNP-SC were washed extensively in HBSS. Control spleen cells (SC) were prepared in parallel.

Induction of tolerance. The animals received iv 10^7 of either TNP-SC or untreated SC on Days 0 and 1. In some cases an additional group was injected with saline. On Day 7 recipient mice were challenged with DNP-Ficoll (10 μg/ip) or sheep red blood cells (SRBC). The anti-TNP and anti-SRBC responses were measured respectively 4 and 5 days later by the hemolytic plaque assay (8) using TNP-SRBC (9) and SRBC as targets.

Preparation of T cells. Spleen cells obtained on Day 7 from TNP-SC or SC-injected mice were passed over nylon fiber columns as described by Julius *et al.* (10). The nylon-nonadherent cells contained less than 10% of surface immunoglobulin-bearing cells (SIg^+).

In vitro culture. Cultures were performed according to Mishell and Dutton (11) using a culture medium supplemented with 5% fetal bovine serum and 5×10^{-5} *M* 2-mercaptoethanol. Briefly normal spleen cells were stimulated with TNP-PAA and various numbers of T cells from TNP-SC or SC-treated mice were added to these cultures to a final cell concentration of 3×10^6 cells/culture. The anti-TNP response was measured 5 days later.

Treatment by FTS (serum thymic factor). A long-lived synthetic analog of FTS, (D-Ala^6) FTS synthesized by Bricas and his colleagues (12) was a gift of M. Dardenne. One nanogram of FTS was administered intraperitoneally on several occasions preceding and following TNP-SC injection (on Days −2, −1, 0, +1, +4, +5, and +6). Control groups were injected with saline according to the same protocol.

Expression of results and statistical analysis. All experimental groups included four to five mice or culture dishes and their responses were assayed individually. The results were expressed as the average number (mean ± SEM) of plaque-forming cells per 10^6 cells (PFC/10^6) obtained in different experiments. For statistical analysis the results of different experiments were compared using variance analysis, and the values of F and of the corresponding P are provided.

RESULTS

Induction of Hapten-Specific Suppressor T Cells

In all seven experiments performed, the anti-TNP response of TNP-SC-treated mice was markedly suppressed (481 ± 168 PFC/10^6) as compared to that of SC-treated mice (1 122 ± 397 PFC/10^6). This suppression was strictly specific since: (i) TNP-SC-treated mice exhibited a normal response to SRBC and (ii) the anti-TNP and anti-SRBC responses of SC-treated mice were identical to those of saline-treated animals (results not shown).

Spleen cells from TNP-SC, or SC-treated mice were added to normal mouse spleen cells which were stimulated *in vitro* by TNP-PAA (Fig. 1). At a 1:1 suppressor:responder ratio (1.5 × 10^6 T cells) cells from both groups suppressed the anti-TNP antibody response. However T cells from TNP-SC-treated mice exhibited a suppressive effect more pronounced ($F(1, 12) = 21.37$, $P < 0.001$) than that of T cells from SC-treated mice. At a 1:30 suppressor:responder ratio (10^5 T cells) only T cells from TNP-SC-treated mice could inhibit the response of normal spleen cells ($F(1, 12) = 21.37$, $P < 0.001$).

FTS Treatment Restores the Ability of ATX Mice to Be Suppressed by TNP-SC

Thymectomy was performed at 3–4 weeks of age. Seven to twenty-eight weeks later ATX and control mice received TNP-SC or SC and were immunized with DNP-Ficoll (Table 1). ATX mice exhibited a moderately and nonsignificantly decreased antibody response ($P \simeq 0.20$ by Student's paired t test). More importantly, treatment by TNP-SC did not suppress this response ($P > 0.40$) whereas it lowered the response of control mice ($P < 0.05$). Furthermore, in TNP-SC-treated mice, the response of ATX mice was significantly higher than that of control

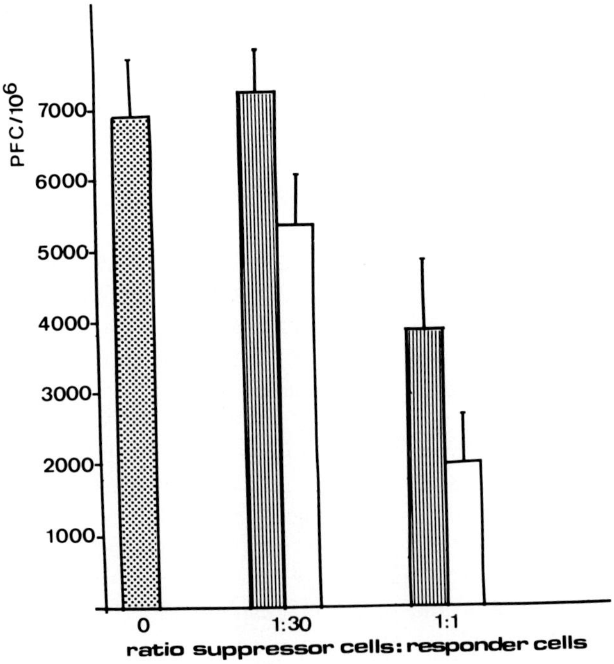

FIG. 1. Suppressor T cells induced by TNP-SC. Anti-TNP response of cultures containing normal spleen cells (dotted bars), normal spleen cells + spleen cells from SC-treated mice (dashed bars), normal spleen cells + spleen cells from TNP-SC-treated mice (open bars). Suppressor cells were used at two different concentrations. Mean ± SEM of the responses in three different experiments.

TABLE 1

ATX Prevents the Suppressive Effect of TNP-SC

Treatment with	Response of mice[a]	
	Control	ATX
SC	1283 ± 379*,**	922 ± 175*,***
TNP-SC	645 ± 145**,****	853 ± 139***,****

[a] Control and ATX mice were treated with SC or TNP-SC and immunized with DNP-Ficoll. The results are the mean (±SE) PFC responses in seven experiments (four to six mice/group). Statistical comparison (paired Student's t test):

* $P \simeq 0.20$.
** $P < 0.05$.
*** $P > 0.40$.
**** $P < 0.05$.

mice ($P < 0.05$), showing that the lack of suppression in the former group was not the artifactual consequence of a hyporesponsiveness to DNP-Ficoll in ATX mice. In three of these experiments, the anti-SRBC response was also evaluated and shown to be unmodified (results not shown) confirming the specificity of the suppression observed in the nonthymectomized group.

We then tested the effect of FTS analog on the ability of ATX mice to be suppressed by TNP-SC. Seven to nine weeks after thymectomy ATX mice received seven injections of (D-Ala^6) FTS (1 ng) or saline, starting 2 days before TNP-SC (or SC) injection. DNP Ficoll was injected on Day 7 and the anti-TNP antibody PFC level was evaluated 4 days later (Fig. 2). In control mice TNP-SC suppressed the response regardless of FTS treatment, whereas in ATX mice only FTS-treated animals were suppressed by TNP-SC injection. In these three experiments, ATX mice developed an antibody response lower than that of control mice, and FTS improved this response. Beside this positive effect in SC-treated ATX mice, FTS had a suppressive effect in TNP-SC-treated ATX mice: the absolute response of these mice was significantly lower in the FTS-treated group ($F(1, 24) = 16.03$, $P < 0.001$).

DISCUSSION

These results support the hypothesis that the suppression of the B-cell response provided by preinjection of hapten-modified spleen cells is mediated by suppressor T cells (13, 14) although results indicative of a B-cell tolerance have been produced (15). Splenic T cells from TNP-SC-treated mice suppressed the *in vitro* antibody response of normal spleen cells (13). At a 1:1 suppressor cell:responder cell ratio, cells from TNP-SC-treated mice induced a 48% mean suppression when compared to control T cells (obtained from SC-treated mice) which were able to suppress the response of normal spleen cells but to a lesser extent. Whether the latter suppression (which we found to be non-TNP-specific) was due to an imbalance between T cells and the responding B cells or developed after the injection of syngeneic SC is under investigation. When the number of T cells was decreased (down to a 1:30 suppressor:responder ratio) only spleen cells from TNP-SC-treated mice proved to

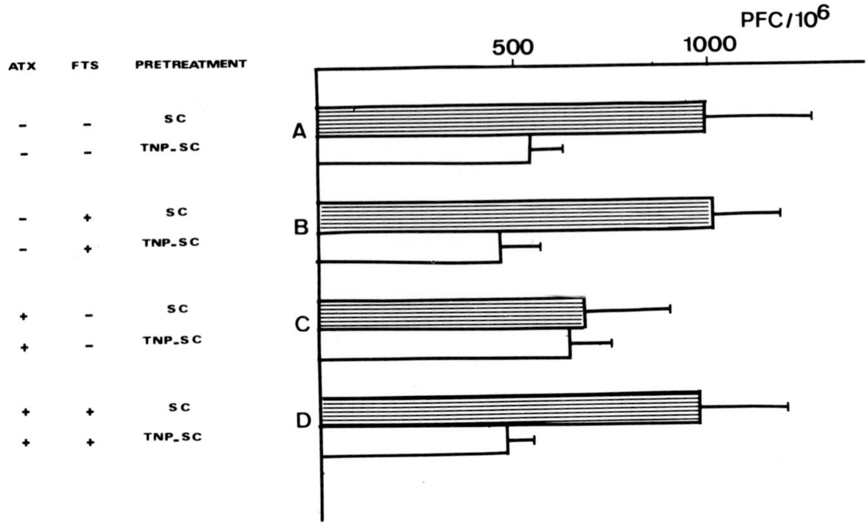

FIG. 2. FTS restores the ability of ATX mice to be suppressed. Anti-TNP response of mice injected with S. C. (dashed bars) or TNP-SC (open bars). Groups C and D were thymectomized and groups B and D received FTS. The effect of TNP-SC is statistically significant within groups A ($F(1, 24) = 22.56$, $P < 0.0001$); B ($F(1, 24) = 61.15$, $P < 0.0001$); D ($F(1, 24) = 43.39$, $P < 0.0001$); and not significant within group C ($F(1, 24) = 0.27$, $P > 0.60$). Mean ± SEM of the responses in three different experiments).

be suppressive. The T-cell dependency of the suppression induced by modified spleen cells was supported by its absence in ATX mice. Borel *et al.* also showed that suppression of the antibody response induced by guanosine-SC could not be induced 4 weeks after ATX (4).

The rapid disappearance after ATX of the susceptibility to a modified-self-induced suppression suggests that it depends upon a functionally short-lived T cell (putatively of the Lyt 1^+ 2^+ 3^+ phenotype) (16). In fact Jandinski and Scott (13) have shown that the suppressor cells induced by TNP-SC are sensitive to treatment with both anti-Lyt 1 and anti-Lyt 2 sera in the presence of complement.

In order to test whether these cells (or their precursors) require thymic hormone for their maintenance, we used a long-lived synthetic analog of FTS, (D-Ala^6) FTS (12). FTS is able to induce thymic markers (17) and restore several functions in NZB mice (18) and in ATX mice, notably the cytotoxic T-cell response (19) and contact sensitivity (20).

We show here that short-term treatment with a physiological dose of (D-Ala^6) FTS can influence the response of ATX mice and its susceptibility to suppression by modified self. FTS corrects the moderate hyporesponsiveness of ATX mice to DNP-Ficoll. In contrast when ATX mice are treated with TNP-SC, FTS lowers their antibody response. Thus FTS restores the susceptibility to suppression by modified self in ATX mice, probably by two mechanisms: a positive effect on the anti-TNP response and a potentiation of the suppressor cells induced by the injection of TNP-SC (13). These results are similar to observations made in NZB mice, which, like ATX mice, lack thymic hormone in their serum (21). In a cell transfer system using histocompatible DBA/2 mice, it was shown that NZB mice can produce suppressor cells but are deficient in a subset necessary for the expression of the suppression (22). Recent experiments have shown that, as in the present study, FTS augments the deficient susceptibility to suppressor signals observed in these mice (M. A. Bach, personal communication).

The injection of hapten-modified lymphocytes represents an efficient method to suppress the immune response to the hapten (1–3) the mechanism of which may be relevant to that of self-tolerance. We have confirmed in this work that this suppression requires the presence of a functional thymus (4) and shown that FTS can fully replace the thymic gland up to 2 months after ATX. This can have important implications for the potential use of hapten-modified self to manipulate the immune response in immunopathological situations where a thymic dysfunction is present.

ACKNOWLEDGMENT

M. Dardenne is acknowledged for the gift of (A-Ala^6) FTS.

REFERENCES

1. Miller, S. D., and Claman, H. N., *J. Immunol.* **117,** 1519, 1976.
2. Weinberger, J. Z., Germain, R. N., Ju., S. T., Greene, M. I., Benacerraf, B., and Dorf, M. E., *J. Exp. Med.* **150,** 761, 1979.
3. Scott, D. W., *Cell. Immunol.* **37,** 327, 1978.
4. Borel, Y., Kilman, L., Kurtz, S. E., and Reinisch, C. L., *J. Exp. Med.* **151,** 743, 1980.
5. Asherson, G. L., Zembala, M., Mayhew, B., and Goldstein, A., *Eur. J. Immunol.* **6,** 699, 1976.
6. Delfraissy, J. F., Galanaud, P., Dormont, J., and Wallon, C., *J. Immunol.* **118,** 630, 1977.
7. Scott, D. W., and Long, C. A., *J. Exp. Med.* **144,** 1369, 1976.
8. Jerne, N. K., and Nordin, A. A., *Science* **140,** 405, 1963.
9. Rittenberg, M. B., and Pratt, K. L., *Proc. Soc. Exp. Biol. Med.* **132,** 575, 1969.
10. Julius, M. H., Simpson, E., and Herzenberg, L. A., *Eur. J. Immunol.* **3,** 645, 1973.
11. Mishell, R. I., and Dutton, R. W., *J. Exp. Med.* **126,** 423, 1973.
12. Blanot, D., Martinez, J., Sasaki, A., Auger, G., Bricas, E., Dardenne, M., and Bach, J. F., *In* "Proceedings of the 6th American Peptide Symposium" (E. Gross and J. Meinhofer, Eds.), Pierce Chemical Company, 1979.
13. Jandinski, J. J., and Scott, D. W., *J. Immunol.* **123,** 2447, 1979.
14. Braley-Mullen, H., *Cell Immunol.* **52,** 132, 1980.
15. Ramos, T., Möller, E. and Möller, G., *Eur. J. Immunol.* **10,** 100, 1980.
16. Cantor, H., and Boyse, E. A., *J. Exp. Med.* **141,** 1376, 1975.
17. Bach, M. A., Fournier, C., and Bach, J. F., *Ann. N. Y. Acad. Sci.* **249,** 316, 1975.
18. Bach, M. A., and Niaudet, P., *J. Immunol.* **117,** 760, 1976.
19. Bach, M. A., *J. Immunol.* **119,** 641, 1977.
20. Erard, D., Charreire, J., Auffredou, M. T., Galanaud, P., and Bach, J. F., *J. Immunol.* **123,** 1573, 1979.
21. Bach, J. F., Dardenne, M., and Salomon, J. C., *Clin. Exp. Immunol.* **14,** 247, 1973.
22. Blanchard, D., and Bach, M. A., *Clin. Exp. Immunol.* **42,** 1, 1980.

CELLULAR IMMUNOLOGY **64**, 150–161 (1981)

Activation and Mechanism of Action of Suppressor Macrophages[1]

ALAN LICHTENSTEIN,[2] RICHARD MURAHATA, MARILOU TERPENNING, JOHN CANTRELL, AND JACOB ZIGHELBOIM

Division of Hematology/Oncology, Department of Medicine, Wadsworth Veteran's Administration Medical Center, Los Angeles, California 90073, Department of Microbiology and Immunology and Division of Hematology/Oncology, Department of Medicine, University of California Center for the Health Sciences, University of California School of Medicine, Los Angeles, California 90024, and Rocky Mountain Laboratories, NIAID, Hamilton, Montana, 59840.

Received May 22, 1981; accepted July 11, 1981

Intravenous administration of *Corynebacterium parvum* to alloimmunized mice activates splenic suppressor macrophages that effectively curtail primary and secondary generation of cytotoxic T lymphocytes (CTLs) *in vitro*. CTL generation was significantly inhibited in suppressed primary cultures by Day 3, the earliest time point that activity is first detected in control cultures. Suppressor macrophages had to be present during the first 24–48 hr of culture to effectively curtail the generation of CTLs. However, if suppressor macrophages were reactivated by 48-hr *in vitro* culture and then added to primary sensitizations that had been initiated 48 hr previously, they were capable of significant suppression. Suppressor cells produced a soluble factor that mediated the inhibition of CTL generation. The production or action of this factor could not be counteracted by indomethacin.

INTRODUCTION

It is apparent that macrophages play an important role in the regulation of lymphocyte activation and proliferation. They are necessary for the activation of T and B lymphocytes by antigens (1, 2), mitogens (3, 4), and allogeneic cells (5). Macrophages obtained from normal animals (6) and humans (7, 8) can also down-regulate responses of T and B lymphocytes. This suppression is greatly enhanced when macrophages are induced by various stimuli to enter an "activated state" characterized by alterations in physical properties and enzyme content (9). Thus, macrophages obtained from animals undergoing graft-versus-host disease (10), following injection of immunoadjuvants (11, 12), during infection with certain microorganisms (13) or in the course of tumor progression (14, 15) are more likely to suppress rather than amplify responses when added to lymphocyte cultures.

We have previously reported on suppressor macrophages generated by injection

[1] Supported by Grant T32 CA 09120, National Cancer Institute, Department of Health, Education and Welfare and Grant CA 12800, National Cancer Institute, National Institutes of Health, Bethesda, Md. 20014.

[2] To whom requests for reprints should be sent at: Department of Microbiology and Immunology, University of California School of Medicine, Los Angeles, Calif. 90024.

0008-8749/81/150150-12$02.00/0

of the adjuvant *Corynebacterium parvum* (16, 17). These reports indicated that suppressor macrophage activation was more effective when *C. parvum* was injected into alloimmunized mice compared to naive mice. The current study was initiated to further explore the process by which macrophages become activated to express suppressive effects and the mechanism by which they mediate these effects. The results indicate that before *C. parvum*-induced suppressor macrophages are capable of curtailing the generation of cytotoxic T lymphocytes (CTLs),[3] a final level of activation (or reactivation) must be reached *in vitro*. Furthermore, the inhibitory effects are mediated through the production and release of soluble suppressive factor(s).

MATERIALS AND METHODS

Animals. Male C57Bl/6 mice (Jackson Laboratory, Bar Harbor, Maine) were obtained at 6–8 weeks of age and were rested at least 1 week prior to beginning an experiment. Female DBA/2 mice (retired breeders) were obtained from Jackson Laboratory and used for *in vivo* passage of P815.

Tumor. The P815 mastocytoma tumor was maintained in ascites form by weekly passage in DBA/2 mice, the strain of origin.

C. parvum. Heat-killed suspensions of *C. parvum* (strain CN6134) were kindly supplied by Dr. R. Tuttle, Burroughs–Wellcome, Research Triangle Park, North Carolina. All intravenous injections were made in 0.2 ml of phosphate-buffered saline (PBS) into the lateral tail vein.

Drugs. Indomethacin was obtained from Merck, Sharp and Dohme (Division of Merck & Co., Inc., Westpoint, Pa.). The drug was dissolved in 95% ethyl alcohol and diluted with medium to the appropriate concentration. Using this preparation the final concentration of ethyl alcohol in the cultures ranged between 0.01 and 0.025%.

Immunization. C57Bl/6 mice (H-2^b) were alloimmunized by a subcutaneous injection of 2×10^7 P815 cells (H-2^d) into the right flank. The mice were divided into two groups; one received no further treatment (alloimmune controls) and the other was injected intravenously (iv) with 700 μg of *C. parvum* on the ninth day after immunization. Seven days after *C. parvum* injection (16 days postalloimmunization), mice were sacrificed, and their spleen cells assayed for the ability to suppress the primary or secondary *in vitro* generation of cytotoxic lymphocytes (CTLs).

In vitro sensitization. Naive mice (for primary sensitization) or alloimmune mice (immunized subcutaneously with 2×10^7 P815 16 days previously) were sacrificed and single cell suspensions prepared from the spleens by expression through a stainless-steel mesh. After three washes, 5×10^6 spleen cells were cultured with 5×10^5 mitomycin-c-treated P815 in 2.5 ml of minimum Eagle's medium (MEM) (Microbiological Associates, Walkersville, Md.), supplemented with 10% fetal calf serum (Reheis, Phoenix, Ariz.), L-glutamine, antibiotics and 5×10^{-5} *M* 2-mercaptoethanol. Putative suppressor spleen cells 5×10^6 from alloimmune, *C. parvum*-

[3] Abbreviations used: CTLs, cytotoxic T lymphocytes; PBS, phosphate-buffered saline; MEM, minimum Eagle's medium; ATS and C′, anti-thymocyte serum and complement; HCl, hydrochloric acid; E:T, effector–target cell ratio; LU, lytic unit; RES, reticuloendothelial system; CMC, cell-mediated cytotoxicity.

treated mice or identical numbers of alloimmune control (non-*C. parvum*-treated) spleen cells were added to responder cells at varying times of culture. In attempts to suppress primary sensitizations, putative suppressor cells were treated with rabbit anti-mouse thymocyte serum and complement (ATS and C′) prior to addition to cultures to remove any activated suppressor T cells present. In attempts to suppress secondary sensitizations, prior ATS and C′ treatment of suppressors was not performed as we have found that *C. parvum*-activated suppressor T cells are incapable of inhibiting secondary sensitizations (16). The cells were cultured at 37°C in a humidified incubator with a constant source of 5% CO_2 for 5 days at which time cells were harvested and assayed for cytotoxic activity.

Assay for cytotoxic activity. Cells were assayed for activity against ^{51}cr-labeled target cells according to the method of Brunner and Cerottini (18). Freshly obtained P815 cells were chromated and used as targets. Percentage specific release was calculated as

$$\frac{\text{percentage release experimental group} - \text{percentage background release}}{\text{percentage maximal release}} \times 100.$$

Maximal release was determined by addition of HCl to a final concentration of 1M and resulted in release of between 80 and 90% of total incorporated counts. Medium alone served to determine background release which was between 7 and 15% of total incorporated counts. The effector cells were tested at several effector-target cell ratios (E:T) and the results fitted by linear regression to a plot of log (E:T) versus percentage specific release. One lytic unit (LU) was defined as the number of effector cells to cause a specific release of 25% in primary cultures and 50% in secondary cultures.

Statistics. Percentage inhibition was determined by the formula

$$1 - \frac{\text{LU}/10^6 \text{ cells generated in experimental cultures}}{\text{LU}/10^6 \text{ cells generated in control cultures}} \times 100.$$

P-values were determined between control and experimental groups by *t*-test.

Fractionation of suppressor cells. Phagocytic cells were removed by incubation of spleen cells with carbonyl iron (Gaf, New York, N.Y.) for 30 min at 37°C followed by separation over a magnet. Recovery was between 40 and 60% of starting cell numbers. The percentage of nonspecific esterase + cells in spleens from *C. parvum*-injected mice was 20–25% compared to 3–5% in alloimmune control mice. Treatment with carbonyl iron and magnet reduced the percentage of esterase + cells to less than 1%.

T cells were removed by incubation of 10^7 cells/ml in a 1:45 dilution of absorbed rabbit anti-mouse thymocyte serum (Microbiological Associates) for 30 min at 4°C. The cells were centrifuged and incubated at the same concentration in a 1:15 dilution of agarose-absorbed guinea pig complement (Microbiological Associates) for 30 min at 37°C. This procedure killed 100% of thymocytes, less than 10% bone marrow cells, and approximately 40% of spleen cells. Furthermore, the treatment abrogated the proliferative response to phytohemagglutinin and the cytotoxic response to allogeneic target cells. The cells were washed and resuspended at the desired concentration of viable cells as determined by trypan blue exclusion.

Preparation of adherent cell monolayers. Putative suppressor cells or alloimmune control cells were cultured with or without mitomycin C-treated P815. After 48 hr nonadherent cells were removed and C57Bl/6 anti-P815 primary cultures were replated on top of the remaining adherent cell monolayers.

Generation of soluble suppressor supernatant. Putative suppressor cells were obtained from alloimmune, *C. parvum*-treated mice and control spleen cells were obtained from alloimmune control mice. The cells were cultured for 48 hr with mitomycin C-treated P815 (suppressor:P815 = 10:1). Supernatant harvested from these cultures was filtered and frozen at −70°C. The culture conditions for generating supernatant were the following: 5×10^6 spleen cells cultured with 5×10^5 mitomycin C-treated P815 in 2.5 ml of MEM, supplemented with 10% fetal calf serum, L-glutamine, antibiotics, and 5×10^{-5} M 2-mercaptoethanol.

RESULTS

Effect of Suppressor Macrophages on Kinetics of Primary CTL Generation

We investigated the effect of suppressor macrophages on the kinetics of CTL generation in primary cultures. Seven days after *C. parvum* injection (700 μg) of alloimmunized mice, animals were sacrificed and splenocyte suspensions were treated with rabbits ATS and C′ to isolate suppressor macrophages. The macrophages were then added to primary *in vitro* sensitizations. Cultures were terminated at 3, 4 or 5 days and CTL generation assayed in a chromium release assay (CRA). Figure 1 describes the kinetics of CTL generation in these cultures. At the time point when significant CTL activity is first detected in control cultures (Day 3), corresponding cocultures containing suppressor macrophages already show significantly decreased cell-mediated cytotoxicity (CMC).

Suppressor Macrophages Are Not Active when Added at 48 hr of Culture

The data presented in Fig. 1 suggested that suppressor macrophages act early during culture to prevent normal sensitization rather than aborting a response that has been normally initiated. If this is true, delaying their addition to culture might allow normal sensitization and prevent the suppressive effects on the *in vitro* response. We, thus, attempted to suppress CTL generation by adding suppressor

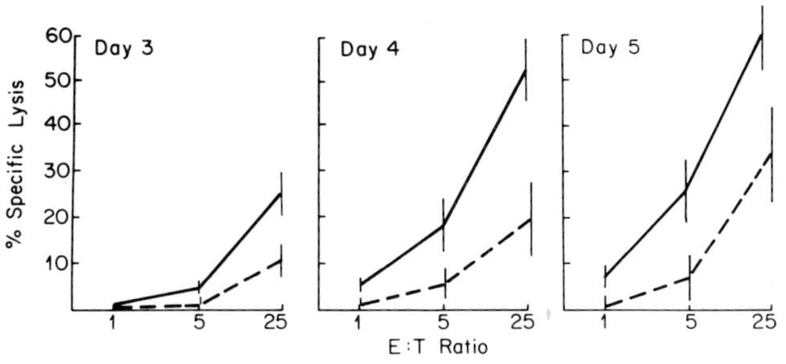

FIG. 1. Effect of suppressor macrophages on kinetics of CTL generation in primary *in vitro* sensitization. Primary sensitizations initiated with addition of control spleen cells (obtained from alloimmune control mice) or suppressor cells (from alloimmune *C. parvum*-injected mice). Control or suppressor spleen cells were ATS + C′ treated prior to addition to culture. Cultures were terminated at Days 3, 4, and 5 and cytotoxicity was assayed at several E:T ratios. Solid line, control; broken line, suppressed cultures. This experiment was performed three times with identical results.

TABLE 1

Addition of Suppressor Macrophages to Primary Control Cultures at Various Times After Initiation of Culture[a]

Macrophages added	Time added (hr)	Specific release $\bar{X} \pm SD$		
		25:1	5:1	1:1
Control, from alloimmune non-*C. parvum*-injected mice	0	73 ± 6	37 ± 8	9 ± 3
Suppressor cells, from alloimmune, *C. parvum*-injected mice	0	35 ± 6[b]	10 ± 4[b]	3 ± 2[b]
Suppressor cells	24	72 ± 7	43 ± 9	11 ± 5
	48	70 ± 8	45 ± 6	10 ± 4

[a] Suppressor or control spleen cells (obtained from C57Bl/6 mice 16 days after alloimmunization and 7 days after *C. parvum* injection) were treated with ATS and C′ and added to primary *in vitro* sensitizations at various times of culture. Responder:suppressor ratio = 1:1 in culture. The addition of control splenocytes (ATS and C′ treated) to culture at 24 and 48 hr resulted in CTL generation that was identical to that of cultures where control cells were added at time 0 and these data (at 24 and 48 hr) are not shown. Data presented as mean ± SD specific release of four separate experiments.

[b] $P < 0.05$ as compared to control.

macrophages at varying time points after initiation of culture. Table 1 indicates that suppressor macrophages are ineffective when added to primary cultures 24 or 48 hr after initiation. In other experiments, (data not shown) there was no suppression observed when culture duration was extended to 6 and 7 days ruling out the possibility that suppressor cells did not have sufficient time for interaction with responder cells to cause suppression.

Table 2 demonstrates that delaying the addition of suppressor macrophages to secondary cultures also prevents the suppression of secondary CTL generation. In

TABLE 2

Addition of Suppressor Macrophages to Secondary Cultures at Various Times after Initiation of Culture[a]

Time of addition (hr)	Percentage inhibition
0	89 ± 5
6	54 ± 8
24	20 ± 9
48	9 ± 6

[a] Suppressor spleen cells (obtained from alloimmune, *C. parvum*-injected mice) were added to secondary cultures at various times and CTL generation was assayed 5 days later. Secondary cultures initiated with spleen cells from alloimmunized C57Bl/6 mice (16 days postalloimmunization). Percentage inhibition determined as described under Materials and Methods utilizing cultures where alloimmune, non-*C. parvum*-injected spleen cells are added at Time 0 as the control. Addition of these control spleen cells to culture at 6, 24, and 48 hr resulted in CTL generation identical to that where control cells are added at Time 0 and, thus, these data are not shown. Data expressed as mean ± SD inhibition of three experiments.

these experiments, delaying the addition of regulatory cells by as little as 6 hr decreased the suppressive effect.

Effect of Suppressor Macrophages Previously Cultured for 48 hr on Primary Sensitizations when Added 48 hr after Initiation

The requirement for suppressor macrophage presence during the first 24–48 hr of culture may stem from the need to undergo reactivation *in vitro* for the suppressive effect to be expressed. The trigger for *in vitro* reactivation may be P815 cells expressing the alloantigens to which suppressor spleen cells were originally primed. By 48 hr of culture, there are few, if any, whole P815 cells remaining, and delaying the addition of suppressor cells for that length of time may prevent their *in vitro* reactivation. We, thus, attempted to activate suppressor cells by culturing them with or without P815 for 48 hr before adding them to primary cultures that had been initiated 48 hr previously. We took advantage of the adherence properties of *C. parvum*-activated suppressor macrophages to separate them after 48 hr of culture. Table 3 indicates that adherent suppressor macrophages become reactivated by 48-hr culture such that their addition to primary sensitizations initiated 48 hr previously results in significant suppression. After 48 hr of mixed lymphocyte tumor culture, cells were removed from their wells and replated on adherent suppressor cell monolayers that had been in culture for 48 hr. Table 3 shows that simply removing cultured control cells and replating them at 48 hr into new wells has no effect. Likewise, there is no effect when they are replated on cultured adherent cell monolayers derived from non-*C. parvum*-treated alloimmune control splenocytes. Significant suppression, however, occurs when they are replated on cultured adherent cell monolayers derived from *C. parvum*-treated alloimmune mice. Interestingly, suppression is comparable whether or not P815 had been present during the 48-hr incubation period of suppressor cells. Similar data were obtained when suppressor macrophages were reactivated and then added to secondary cultures that had been initiated 48 hr previously (data not shown). Thus, *C. parvum*-activated suppressor macrophages are capable of suppressing the *in vitro* generation of CTLs when added at 48 hr of culture if they have been previously reactivated *in vitro.*

Effect of Removing Suppressor Macrophages from Responder Cells after 24 and 48 hr of Culture

We investigated the effect of removing suppressor macrophages from responder cells after initiation of culture. In these experiments, adherent cells were removed from restimulated secondary cultures 24 and 48 hr after initiation. As shown in Table 4, removal of adherent cells from control cultures had no effect on the generation of secondary CTLs. Removal of adherent regulatory cells from suppressed cultures 48 hr after initiation did not restore the ability of the nonadherent population to respond. Removal of suppressor adherent cells after 24 hr of culture resulted in intermediate activity. These results suggest that once the suppressive event has taken place in cocultures containing regulatory macrophages, the ensuing inhibition of CTL generation is irreversible.

C. parvum-Activated Macrophages Produce a Soluble Suppressor Factor

Soluble products of *C. parvum*-generated suppressor macrophages significantly inhibit the generation of primary (Table 5) and secondary (Table 6) CTLs. Unfractionated and fractionated suppressor cells were cultured for 48 hr with P815 and supernatants were harvested. Soluble material from unfractionated suppressor cells significantly inhibit the primary *in vitro* generation of CTLs. Depletion of macrophages by treatment with iron and magnet prior to initiation of culture abrogated the production of active supernatant from suppressor splenocytes. Treatment of suppressor cells with ATS and C′ had little effect on the production of active supernatant.

Suppression Can Not Be Counteracted by Indomethacin

Grimm *et al.* have reported that macrophages obtained from *C. parvum*-injected animals produce significantly increased levels of prostaglandin in culture (19). Since prostaglandins are potent inhibitors of T-cell proliferative responses (7), we investigated whether they were playing a role in the observed macrophage-mediated suppression. We attempted to reverse *in vitro* suppression and the production of suppressive supernatant material by the addition of indomethacin, an inhibitor of prostaglandin synthetase. Table 7 indicates that addition of indomethacin to secondary cultures containing suppressor macrophages has no effect on the observed suppression. Control secondary cultures were modestly enhanced by the addition of indomethacin possibly due to the inhibition of endogenously produced prostaglandin in control secondary cultures. Other experiments (data not shown) also suggest that prostaglandin is not the active substance in suppressor macrophage supernatants since the addition of indomethacin (10 μg/ml) could not prevent the production of soluble suppressor material during culture.

DISCUSSION

The results of this study indicate that suppressor macrophages activated by iv injection of *C. parvum* undergo further changes *in vitro* during the first 24–28 hr of culture to express their suppressive capabilities. When the addition of fresh suppressor macrophages is delayed for 48 hr suppression is prevented. However, if suppressor macrophages are precultured for 48 hr to simulate *in vitro* conditions and then added to control cultures initiated 48 hr previously, suppression occurs. The *in vitro* activation process is not antigen specific in that suppressor cells incubated without P815 for 48 hr were capable of comparable suppression. Although nonspecific, reactivation is more than simple adherence and spreading on surfaces since suppressor macrophages isolated and enriched by adherence for 1 hr are still incapable of inhibiting CTL generation when added at 48 hr of culture. *In vitro* activation of regulatory macrophages to a fully suppressive state is dependent upon prior *in vivo* administration of *C. parvum.* Macrophages obtained from alloimmunized control mice were not suppressive after 48 hr of incubation. This suggests that *C. parvum* administration expands and/or activates a subset of macrophages programmed to exert suppressive effects. As a result of this *in vivo* process, suppressor macrophages are prepared for their regulatory function and only require a second nonspecific signal to initiate this function.

TABLE 3

Addition of Adherent Suppressor Cells at 48 hr to Control Cultures[a]

Culture	Sources of adherent monolayer	Preactivation of adherent monolayer	Percentage specific release $\bar{X}$ SD		
			25:1	5:1	1:1
(A) Primary control culture	—	—	72 ± 4	34 ± 8	8 ± 3
(B) Fresh suppressors added at Time 0	—	—	40 ± 6[b]	10 ± 4[b]	2 ± 1[b]
(C) Fresh suppressors added at 48 hr	—	—	67 ± 7	30 ± 6	11 ± 5
(D) Control replated into new empty wells at 48 hr	—	—	69 ± 5	36 ± 5	9 ± 5
(E) Control replated on monolayer at 48 hr	Alloimmune, control mice	Culture with P815 for 48 hr	74 ± 8	33 ± 7	9 ± 2
(F) Control replated on monolayer at 48 hr	Alloimmune, *C. parvum*-injected	Culture without P815 for 48 hr	39 ± 9[b]	16 ± 6[b]	2 ± 1[b]
(G) Control replated on monolayer at 48 hr	Alloimmune, *C. parvum*-injected	Culture with P815 for 48 hr	40 ± 6[b]	14 ± 6[b]	2 ± 1[b]

[a] Primary *in vitro* sensitization initiated with addition of control spleen cells (A) or suppressor spleen cells at Time 0 (B) or 48 hr (C). In addition, four groups of control cultures were removed from their wells at 48 hr and replated into empty wells (D), adherent monolayer derived from alloimmune, control mice cultured with P815 (E), monolayer derived from alloimmune, *C. parvum*-injected mice cultured without P815 (F), and identical cells cultured with P815 (G). CTL generation assayed at 5 days and expressed as mean ± SD specific release of three separate experiments.

[b] $P < 0.05$ as compared to control cultures.

TABLE 4

Irreversibility of Suppression of Secondary CTLs[a]

Spleen cells added to culture	Removal of adherent cells	Time of adherent cell removal (hr)	Percentage specific release (E:T = 1:1)	
			Expt 1	Expt 2
(A) Control	−	—	62 ± 3	60 ± 4
(B) Control	+	48	66 ± 2	55 ± 3
(C) Suppressors	−	—	17 ± 0.4	25 ± 1
(D) Suppressors	+	48	26 ± 1	32 ± 1
(E) Control	+	24	66 ± 3	64 ± 2
(F) Suppressors	+	24	38 ± 2	42 ± 2

[a] Secondary cultures (with spleen cells obtained from C57Bl/ 6 mice 16 days after alloimmunization) initiated with addition of alloimmune, control spleen cells (A, B, E) or suppressor spleen cells (C, D, F) from alloimmune, *C. parvum*-injected mice. At 24 or 48 hr of culture four groups (B, D, E, F) were removed from their wells with Pasteur pipets and replated into new wells for the remainder of culture. After 5 days, cultures were assayed for CTL generation and results expressed as percentage specific release at a 1:1 effector-to-target cell ratio.

Other studies using different suppressor cell systems have shown that CTL generation is susceptible to suppression only during the first 48 hr of culture (20–23). As suggested by Klimpel *et al.* (20), this finding may relate to the fact that this period of time corresponds to the time period (15–48 hr of culture) when maximal soluble helper factor is produced (24) and regulatory cells may exert their effects on helper T cells preventing production and/or release of these helper factors (20,

TABLE 5

Inhibition of Primary Cytotoxicity by Soluble Material Derived from *C. parvum*-Activated Macrophages[a]

Cell source of supernatant	Treatment of cells prior to generation of supernatant	Lytic units/10^6 cells	
		Expt 1	Expt 2
—	—	22	16
Alloimmune control mice	—	27	12
Alloimmune control	ATS and C′	19	12
Alloimmune control	Iron and magnet	Not tested	15
Alloimmune, *C. parvum* injected	—	7	4
Alloimmune, *C. parvum* injected	ATS and C′	1	4
Alloimmune, *C. parvum* injected	Iron and magnet	18	13

[a] Primary *in vitro* sensitization was initiated with and without addition of *in vitro*-generated supernatant at 20% concentration v/v. Supernatant generated by culturing whole or fractionated spleen cells from alloimmune control (16 days postimmunization) or alloimmune, *C. parvum*-injected mice with P815 cells for 48 hr. CTL generation assayed after 5 days of culture.

TABLE 6

Inhibition of Secondary Cytotoxicity by Soluble Material Derived from *C. parvum*-Activated Macrophages[a]

Source of supernatant	Percentage release (E:T = 5:1)
—	47 ± 3
Alloimmune control, Expt 1	54 ± 2
Alloimmune, *C. parvum*-injected, Expt 1	28 ± 2
Alloimmune control Expt 2	44 ± 4
Alloimmune, *C. parvum*-injected, Expt 2	24 ± 1

[a] Secondary *in vitro* sensitizations initiated with and without addition of *in vitro*-generated supernatant at 20% concentration v/v. Supernatant generated from two separate experiments by culturing unfractionated spleen cells from alloimmune control mice or alloimmune, *C. parvum*-injected mice with P815 for 48 hr.

25, 26). However, the data presented here indicate that, at least in some systems, significant inhibition can occur after maximal production of helper factors if regulatory cells are preactivated.

The effect of *C. parvum*-activated suppressor macrophages on the kinetics of CTL generation differs from that of conconavalin A-induced suppressor cells (27). The effect of the latter cells is predominantly expressed late in culture (27); while suppressed cultures are comparable to controls at Day 3 or 4, they are clearly decreased by Days 5 and 6 suggesting that the regulatory cells abort a response that has been normally initiated. In contrast, *C. parvum*-activated macrophages cause decreased CTL generation by Day 3, the first time point at which significant CTL generation occurs in control cultures. This suggests that *C. parvum*-activated suppressor macrophages prevent normal sensitization and might suppress CTL generation by degrading and/or eliminating stimulator cells such that normal sensitization does not occur. However, two lines of evidence argue against this concept: First, as we have previously reported (17), suppressor cells are not toxic to stimulator cells as judged by a 4-hr chromium-release assay; second, *in vitro*-reactivated suppressor cells can curtail CTL generation even when added at 48 hr of culture, presumably after normal sensitization has taken place. They, thus, appear to affect

TABLE 7

Effect of Indomethacin on Macrophage-Mediated Suppression of Secondary Cultures[a]

Suppressor cells	Indomethicin (10 μg/ml)	Percentage release (E:T = 1:1)	
		Expt 1	Expt 2
−	−	37 ± 2	32 ± 3
−	+	52 ± 2	40 ± 3
+	−	10 ± 1	4 ± 0.3
+	+	3 ± 1	4 ± 0.5

[a] Secondary *in vitro* cultures initiated with and without suppressor cells (from alloimmune *C. parvum*-injected mice). Indomethicin added at initiation of culture and CTL generation assayed 5 days later.

the proliferative ability of responder cells rather than the integrity of stimulator cells.

Previous studies of suppressor macrophages have demonstrated the production of a soluble suppressive mediator (6, 28–31). Since prostaglandins are potent inhibitors of T-cell responses (7) and they are produced in significant quantities by macrophages obtained from *C. parvum*-injected animals (19), they seemed to be likely candidates as the suppressive mediators described in this report. However, since the addition of indomethacin does not abrogate suppression in cocultures and does not prevent the production of soluble suppressive mediators, it appears that macrophage-mediated suppression and suppressor material are not related to prostaglandins. A role for prostaglandin in the observed suppression, however, is not completely ruled out by these experiments; it is possible that the increased prostaglandin production due to *C. parvum* injection has taken place *in vivo* and when activated macrophages are added to culture, the addition of indomethacin, an inhibitor of prostaglandin synthesis, would have no effect on the release and ensuing inhibitory effects of preformed prostaglandins. Experiments attempting to reverse suppression by *in vivo* administration of indomethacin to *C. parvum*-injected mice are planned to investigate this question.

The data presented in this report lead us to a tentative hypothesis as to the temporal sequence of events that take place in the generation and action of these suppressor macrophages: *In vivo* administration of *C. parvum* to alloimmunized mice causes a generalized activation of the cells of the RES. This activation process enhances the intracellular production of numerous macrophage enzymes and mediators. Within the subset of suppressor macrophages, the production of mediators that inhibit the activation and/or proliferation of lymphocytes is enhanced as well. When placed into tissue culture, as a result of a second nonspecific activation process, suppressor macrophages are stimulated to release their suppressive substances thereby preventing the generation of CTLs. If the addition of suppressor macrophages is delayed for 24–48 hr, the reactivation process does not take place, intracellular substances are not released, and CTL precursors are, thus, able to clonally expand in a normal fashion.

REFERENCES

1. Seeger, R. C., and Oppenheim, J. J., *J. Exp. Med.* **132,** 44, 1970.
2. Chused, T. M., Kassan, S. S., and Mosier, D. E., *J. Immunol.* **116,** 1579, 1976.
3. Rosenstreich, D. L., Farrar, J. J., and Dougherty, S., *J. Immunol.* **116,** 131, 1976.
4. Persson, U. C. I., Hammarstrom, L., and Smith, C., *J. Immunol.* **119,** 1138, 1977.
5. Alter, B. J., and Bach, F. H., *Cell. Immunol.* **1,** 207, 1970.
6. Baird, L. G., and Kaplan, A. M., *Cell. Immunol.* **28,** 36, 1977.
7. Goodwin, J. S., Bankhurst, A. D., and Messner, R. P., *J. Exp. Med.* **146,** 1719, 1977.
8. Knapp, W., and Baumgertner, G., *J. Immunol.* **121,** 1177, 1978.
9. Allison, A. C., *Immunol Rev.* **40,** 3, 1978.
10. Sjoberg, O., *Clin. Exp. Immunol.* **12,** 365, 1972.
11. Klimpel, G. R., and Henney, C. S., *J. Immunol.* **120,** 563, 1978.
12. Scott, M. T., *Cell. Immunol.* **5,** 269, 1972.
13. Youdim, S., *Cell. Immunol.* **45,** 377, 1979.
14. Kirchner, H., Chused, T. M., Herberman, R. B., Holden, H. T., and Lavrin, D. H., *J. Exp. Med.* **139,** 1473, 1974.
15. Pope, B. L., Whitney, R. B., Levy, J. G., and Kilburn, D. G., *J. Immunol.* **116,** 1342, 1976.
16. Murahata, R., and Zighelboim, J., *Cell Immunol.* **42,** 289, 1979.

17. Lichtenstein, A., Murahata, R., Sugasawara, R., and Zighelboim, J., *Cell. Immunol.* **58,** 257, 1981.
18. Brunner, K. T., Engers, H. D., and Cerottini, J.-C., *In* "In Vitro Methods in Cell-Mediated Immunity" (B. R. Bloom and J. R. David, Eds.), pp. 423–428. Academic Press, New York, 1976.
19. Grimm, W., Seitz, M., Kirchner, H., and Gemsa, D., *Cell. Immunol.* **40,** 419, 1978.
20. Klimpel, G. R., Okada, M., and Henney, C. S., *J. Immunol.* **123,** 350, 1979.
21. Hirano, T., and Nordin, A. A., *J. Immunol.* **117,** 2226, 1976.
22. Hodes, R. J., and Hathcock, K. S., *J. Immunol.* **116,** 167, 1975.
23. Peavy, D. L., and Pierce, C. W., *J. Exp. Med.* **140,** 356, 1974.
24. Okada, M., Klimpel, G. R., Kuppers, R. C., and Henney, C. S., *J. Immunol.* **122,** 2527, 1979.
25. Rode, H. N., Uotila, M., and Gordon J., *Eur. J. Immunol.* **8,** 213, 1978.
26. Northoff, H., Carter, C., and Oppenheim, J. J., *J. Immunol.* **25,** 823, 1980.
27. Pierce, C. W., Peavy, D. L., and Tadakuma, T., *Ann. N.Y. Acad. Sci.* **256,** 365, 1975.
28. Nelson, D. S., *Nature (London)* **246,** 306, 1973.
29. Tadakuma, T., and Pierce, C. W., *J. Immunol.* **120,** 481, 1978.
30. Metzger, Z., Hoffeld, J. T., and Oppenheim, J. J., *J. Immunol.* **124,** 983, 1980.
31. Keller, R., *Cell. Immunol.* **17,** 542, 1975.

CELLULAR IMMUNOLOGY **64,** 162–176 (1981)

Transplantation Antigen Expression on Murine Trophoblast Detection by Induction of Specific Alloimmunity[1]

CHARLES S. PAVIA,[2] DANIEL P. STITES, AND ROBIN FRASER

Departments of Laboratory Medicine, Medicine, and Obstetrics, Gynecology, and Reproductive Sciences, University of California, San Francisco, California 94143

Received June 9, 1981; accepted July 16, 1981

Cell-mediated immune responses to murine embryonic trophoblast cells were investigated using lymphocyte trophoblast cultures (LTC) and cell-mediated lympholysis (CML). Spleen cells from CBA (H-2^k) or C57BL/6 (H-2^b) mice hyperimmunized with 3.5-day-old Balb/c (H-2^d) blastocysts did not undergo DNA synthesis after *in vitro* exposure to Balb/c blastocyst outgrowths nor were cytotoxic lymphocytes (CTL) generated against H-2^d alloantigens. Splenocytes from Balb/c mice presensitized with semiallogeneic (Balb/c female × C57BL/6 male) trophoblast cells derived from 17- to 20-day placental tissue expressed a weak proliferative response in the presence of semiallogeneic placental trophoblast and produced a moderate number of CTL against H-2^b (paternal strain) alloantigens when compared to mixed lymphocyte cultures (MLC) between Balb/c responder and semiallogeneic (stimulator) spleen cells. CTL were also generated *in vitro* after splenocytes from Balb/c mice hyperimmunized with semiallogeneic spleen cells were restimulated *in vitro* with placental trophoblast cells. These studies showing that early-stage trophoblast cells fail to evoke transplantation immunity and placental trophoblast is capable of generating alloimmunity only after combined *in vivo* hyperimmunization with *in vitro* restimulation suggest that these trophoblast cells are poorly immunogenic due in part to the relatively weak functional expression of major transplantation antigens.

INTRODUCTION

The immunologic role of the mammalian placenta remains incompletely defined despite evidence for potential immunocompetence (1), hematopoietic function (2), and immunosuppressive activity (3, 4) on the part of various elements of mouse and human placenta. The principal cell type of the placenta is an intervening layer of trophoblast which functions as a physical and anatomical barrier between the developing histoincompatible fetus and the mother. Its prevention of passage of potentially harmful maternal antibody and immune lymphoid cells could provide an explanation for the survival of the fetal allograft.

Of paramount importance to any ascribed protective role of the trophoblast is whether these cells possess paternal transplantation antigens which could be targets

[1] This work was supported in part by Grant HD-03939 from the National Institutes of Health, Bethesda, Md., and by a grant from the Rockefeller Foundation.

[2] Recipient of a Lalor Foundation Postdoctoral Fellowship. Current address: Department of Immunology, Division of Communicable Diseases and Immunology, Walter Reed Army Institute of Research, Washington, D.C. 20012.

0008-8749/81/150162-15$02.00/0

for maternal immune destruction *in utero*. While transplantation antigens have been detected on certain components of pre- and postimplantation embryonic tissue (5) the exact antigenic status of the trophoblast cells themselves remains unresolved. Using serological techniques with various antisera it has been shown that paternal non-H-2 and to a lesser extent H-2 antigens are present on the trophectoderm of the murine blastocyst just prior to implantation (5–7), but H-2 antigens are usually not found on the trophoblast at later stages, either on *in vitro* blastocyst outgrowths (8) or on ectoplacental cone (EPC)[3]-derived trophoblast cells from 7½ day mouse embryos (5, 7, 9). Nonetheless, both paternal and maternal H-2 antigens are expressed on trophoblast cells derived from mid- to late gestation placental tissue (9–11). It also appears that little, if any, Ia antigens are expressed on trophoblast of various gestational stages (12) although they are present on some embryonic tissues (13).

Some data are available concerning the immunogenicity of the trophoblast. Fertilized semiallogeneic mouse ova do not provoke an allograft response when transplanted to histoincompatible recipients (14) although trophoblast development can be prevented by presensitizing with paternal strain allografts. In contrast with the 7½-day egg cylinder, EPC derived trophoblast cells survive longer and display marked proliferative activity when transplanted to allogeneic hosts hyperimmunized with paternal strain alloantigens (15). However, another study (16) has shown that 7½-day trophoblast cells are capable of eliciting second-set graft rejection after repeated transplants into allogeneic recipients. Furthermore placental allografts from 10½-day mouse embryos are usually rejected by allogeneic recipients which at the same time sensitized them to subsequent paternal strain skin allografts (17).

To further study alloantigen expression on mouse trophoblast cells we have used genetically defined pregnancies in inbred mice and examined the ability of trophoblast cells from different gestational stages to induce cellular immune responses *in vivo* and *in vitro* directed toward H-2 antigens of paternal strain origin. The results reported here with the CML assay demonstrate that trophoblast derived from the blastocyst, EPC, and placenta are poor *in vivo* immunogens while placental cells are capable of generating cytotoxic activity after combined *in vivo* priming and *in vitro* restimulation.

MATERIALS AND METHODS

Mice. Balb/c (H-2^d), C57BL/6 (H-2^b), and DBA (H-2^d) mice were obtained from Simonsen Laboratories, Gilroy, California, and CB6F_1 (Balb/c × C57BL/6)F_1 mice were bred and maintained in our colony. CBA mice (H-2^k) were purchased from Jackson Laboratory, Bar Harbor, Maine.

Embryonic material. Male mice were caged with spontaneously ovulating or superovulated 8- to 12-week-old females. The latter were first injected ip with 5 IU of pregnant mare serum (Calbiochem, La Jolla, CA) and then with 5 IU of human chorionic gonadotrophin (Ayerst, New York, N.Y.) 44–48 hr later. Successful matings were noted by the presence of vaginal plugs the following morning (Day 0 of pregnancy). Preimplantation blastocysts were recovered by flushing each

[3] Abbreviations used: EPC, ectoplacental cone; CML, cell-mediated lympholysis; CTL, cytotoxic lymphocytes; MLR, mixed lymphocyte reaction; LTC, lymphocyte trophoblast cultures; HBSS, Hanks' balanced salt solution; HEPES, *N*-2-hydroxyethylpiperazine-*N*'-2-ethanesulfonic acid.

uterine horn with Hanks' balanced salt solution (HBSS) 3½ days postcoitum. After washing twice, blastocysts were used either immediately for injection (see below) or were resuspended in RPMI 1640 medium containing 50 units of penicillin/ml, 50 μg streptomycin/ml, 2 mM L-glutamine, 5×10^{-5} M 2-mercaptoethanol, and 5% heat-inactivated fetal calf serum (culture medium) and were placed in wells (5–10 embryos/well) of tissue culture plates (Linbro, New Haven, Conn.) in a total volume of 0.2 ml. These blastocysts were incubated for 3–4 days in a humidified chamber with 95% air and 5% CO_2. During this period blastocysts shed their zona pellucida and produce extensive outgrowths of trophoblastic cells. Ectoplacental cones (EPC) were obtained on the seventh day of pregnancy by first dissecting conceptuses free from surrounding decidual tissues of the uteri and then separating the EPC from the embryonic sac. Groups of two or three cones were placed in wells of tissue plates with culture medium and were transferred to a CO_2 incubator for 2–3 days or until a monolayer of trophoblast cells had developed on each well bottom. Placentas obtained at 17–20 days of pregnancy were excised from the uteri with most of the surrounding maternal decidual cells and fetal membranes being carefully dissected away. Placentas were finely minced with forceps and were filtered through sterile gauze to remove gross material. The resulting cell suspension was washed twice in HBSS and then the cells were separated by centrifugation (500g, 20 min) through Lympholyte-M (Cedarlane Laboratories, London, Canada) density gradients. Most of the placental lymphocytes formed a distinct band at the medium–gradient interface (Wright or Giemsa stains showed 80–85% of the cells were lymphocytes) while a trophoblast-enriched fraction (70–75%) was recovered from the resulting pellet along with red blood cells (RBC). A small percentage of leukocytes (8–15%), normoblasts (6–12%), and decidual cells (3–6%) were also identified in this fraction. The placental lymphocytes were washed twice in HBSS while the enriched trophoblast cell population was washed three times following lysis of contaminating RBC with 0.83% NH_4Cl.

Immunization schedule. Embryonic material of known gestational age was obtained by timed syngeneic or allogeneic pregnancies of Balb/c or C57BL/6 primagravida. Groups of three to five age- and sex-matched mice were injected ip five times (once/week) with either freshly recovered blastocysts or three or four times over 21–28 days with EPC or placental trophoblast cells. The cell number used per injection for most experiments was 40 blastocysts, 10 EPC, or 2×10^7 placental trophoblast cells, respectively. Seven days after the last injection mice were killed and spleens removed and examined in the direct cell-mediated lympholysis (CML) assay (see below) for the development of cytotoxic lymphocytes directed against H-2 antigens syngeneic to the injected embryonic tissue or were restimulated *in vitro* and subsequently assayed for proliferation and lytic activity on ^{51}Cr-labeled tumor cells as previously described (18). In some experiments mice were preimmunized with 2×10^7 semiallogeneic splenocytes given weekly for 3–4 weeks.

Lymphocyte–trophoblast cultures (LTC) and mixed lymphocyte reaction (MLR). Mouse splenocytes were prepared as previously described (18) and resuspended in culture medium. LTC were designed using adult splenocytes from normal or immunized CBA, Balb/c, and C57BL/6 males as responders with trophoblast derived from either 3- to 4-day outgrowths of blastocysts or EPC or placental cells serving as a source of stimulator cells. LTC were established in quadruplicate in flat-bottomed tissue culture plates with each well containing 5×10^5 responder lymphocytes and each of the various trophoblast cell populations as indicated under Results.

It should be noted that unlike a conventional MLR where the lymphoid stimulator cell is usually irradiated or treated with mitomycin C to block DNA synthesis, semiallogeneic trophoblast cells used in all LTC were not inactivated prior to culture with responder lymphocytes. In preliminary experiments we found that reactivity induced by trophoblast (acting as stimulators) was nearly equivalent whether or not they were inactivated by irradiation.

Unless otherwise specified, mixed lymphocyte cultures (MLC) were designed as previously described (18) using adult splenocytes from C57BL/6 and Balb/c male mice as responder cells. Semiallogeneic stimulator spleen cells were obtained from $CB6F_1$ mice. Each well contained 5×10^5 responder lymphocytes and 5×10^5 stimulator lymphocytes in a total volume of 0.2 ml. Stimulator lymphocytes were irradiated with 2500 rad from a cesium source in order to block DNA synthesis.

LTC and MLC were incubated for 120 hr in a humidified incubator with 95% air and 5% CO_2. Then, 1 μCi of tritiated thymidine ($[^3H]$TdR), specific activity 6.7 Ci/mol, was added to each well for an additional 6 hr. Lymphocytes were assayed for DNA synthesis by harvesting onto glass fiber filter paper with a MASH II automatic sample harvester (Microbiological Associates, Bethesda, Md). Samples were counted for radioactivity in a liquid scintillation spectrometer by using toluene containing 4 g/liter PPO and 50 mg/liter POPOP as scintillation fluid. Data are expressed as mean counts per minute $[^3H]$TdR incorporation $\pm$SD.

Cytotoxic lymphocyte (CTL) experiments. Cultures for the primary and secondary *in vitro* generation of CTL were established identically and in parallel to those for LTC and MLC experiments except that each well of the microtissue culture plate contained in a volume of 0.2 ml 1×10^6 responder splenocytes from normal or immunized mice cocultivated with either outgrowths of blastocysts or EPC of various concentrations ($1-5 \times 10^5$) of freshly obtained placental cells or irradiated stimulator splenocytes. Secondary CML is defined as *in vitro* MLC where responder spleen cells are derived from mice primed *in vivo* with the corresponding embryonic tissue.

EL4 (H-2^b) and P815 (H-2^d) tumor cells maintained in tissue culture or in ascites form by weekly passage in C57BL/6 and DBA/2 mice, respectively, were employed as a source of target cells. Tumor cells were washed twice with HBSS and resuspended to 5×10^6 viable cells/ml in culture medium containing 25 m*M* Hepes buffer (test medium). Then, 200 μCi ^{51}Cr (1 mCi/ml, sodium chromate, Amersham–Searle, Arlington Heights, Ill.) was added to 5×10^6 cells and incubated for 45 min at 37°C. The cells were washed three times with test medium and resuspended at 1×10^6 cells/ml.

Cell-mediated lympholysis (CML). The CML assay was performed with a modification of the technique of Cerottini and Brunner (19). Effector cells were freshly harvested splenocytes from mice immunized ip with either blastocysts, EPC, placental cells, or 2×10^7 allogeneic splenocytes 7 days previously or from primary or secondary *in vitro* spleen cell cultures and LTC described above. Viable cells from the latter group, after a 5-day incubation period, were enumerated by trypan blue exclusion. Effector cells were diluted to various concentrations with test medium and transferred to individual wells of microculture plates (Linbro, IS-FB-96-TC) in a volume of 0.2 ml. Then, 0.020 ml (2×10^4 cells) of the ^{51}Cr-labeled target cell suspension was added to each well and the plates were incubated at 37°C in a humidified atmosphere of 5% CO_2 in air. After 4hr, the plates were centrifuged (200*g*, 10 min), 0.1 ml of supernatant was collected from each well, and radioactivity was measured in a gamma spectrometer. Spontaneous release of ^{51}Cr, which was determined by incubating target cells in medium alone, varied from 6 to 15%. The total release of ^{51}Cr was measured by adding 0.25 ml of target cells to 2.25 ml of distilled H_2O and freeze–thawing the mixture three times. Cytotoxic activity was expressed as a percentage of specific release of ^{51}Cr-labeled cells determined according to the formula:

$$\% \text{ specific release} = 100 \times \frac{\text{experimental release} - \text{spontaneous release}}{\text{total release} - \text{spontaneous release}}.$$

RESULTS

Embryonic Tissue Cultures

Except for placental cells, embryonic material from preimplantation (blastocyst) and postimplantation (EPC) stages of gestation freshly recovered from the uterine horns were maintained in culture and incubated separately for 3–4 days before exposure to spleen cells from nonimmunized or hyperimmunized mice. Blastocysts (3.5 days) placed in individual wells of microtissue culture plates escaped from their zona pellucida (hatched) usually within 24–36 hr and then adhered to and spread out along the bottom of each well. During the next 2–3 days confluent monolayer outgrowths of trophoblastic giant cells were formed along with a few centrally located overlying cells resulting from growth and differentiation of the inner cell mass. The number of blastocysts hatching and producing outgrowths ranged from 70–85%.

Cultures of EPC displayed within 3 days a rapid outgrowth consisting mostly of contiguous trophoblastic giant cells and a variable group of smaller cells. Nearly the entire surface area of each culture well was covered by this rapid expansion of trophoblast cells.

Ability of Embryonic Tissue to Induce in Vivo Sensitization to Paternal Strain Alloantigens

Spleen cells from Balb/c, C57BL/6, and CBA male mice that had been hyperimmunized with semiallogeneic trophoblast cells from various stages of pregnancy were directly assayed for the development of CTL toward the corresponding paternal strain alloantigens present on EL4 or P815 tumor cells. Table 1 shows that with each trophoblast cell type tested (3½-day blastocyst to 20-day placental cells) there was no significant increase in the amount of specific lysis by splenocytes when assayed against ^{51}Cr-labeled target cells. The percentage specific release varied from 1 to 5%. This range of cytotoxicity was considered insignificant when compared to the levels of cytotoxic activity expressed by splenocytes freshly harvested from C57BL/6 males deliberately alloimmunized with Balb/c spleen cells (39–52% spe-

TABLE 1

Effect of Preimmunization with Embryonic Tissue on Direct *in Vitro* Alloimmune Cell-Mediated Lympholysis

Source of tissue for immunization[a]	Strain (No.) of immunized mice	Percentage specific release of ^{51}Cr-labeled cells	
		200:1[b]	100:1
Balb/c blastocyst 3½ days	CBA (3)	5 (P815)	2
Balb/c blastocyst	C57BL/6 (3)	4 (P815)	2
Balb/c 17-day placental trophoblast	C57BL/6 (4)	4 (P815)	3
C57BL/6 17-day placental trophoblast	Balb/c (4)	5 (EL4)	3
Balb/c 20-day placental trophoblast	C57BL/6 (3)	3 (P815)	1
C57BL/6 20-day placental trophoblast	Balb/c (4)	4 (EL4)	2
Balb/c adult spleen	C57BL/6 (4)	52 (P815)	39
C57BL/6 adult spleen	Balb/c (4)	46 (EL4)	37

[a] All groups were given three to four weekly injections as described under Materials and Methods. To exclude possible contamination by allogeneic maternal cells all immunizations were done with semiallogeneic material possessing the relevant paternal alloantigens.

[b] Effector: target cell ratio. Data were calculated according to the formula given under Materials and Methods and are reported as mean percentage of specific release. The standard deviation was ±10% or less for each experimental group and is not shown. The tumor target cells used in the 4-hr assay are enclosed in parentheses. The data presented are representative of three or four separate experiments.

cific release) or after immunizations were made in the reciprocal direction (37–46% specific release).

Effect of in Vivo Priming Followed by in Vitro Restimulation with Trophoblast Cells on in Vitro Generation of CTL

Balb/c mice were immunized *in vivo* with semiallogeneic trophoblast cells as outlined for the experiments in Table 1. Their spleen cells were removed and sensitized *in vitro* with the corresponding trophoblast cell type and were then assayed for cytotoxic activity. For generation of CTL 1×10^6 Balb/c splenocytes were cultured with either 5–10 blastocyst outgrowths or 2 or 3 EPC outgrowth or 1×10^5 placental trophoblast cells for 5 days. Figure 1 shows that only spleen cells primed *in vivo* and *in vitro* with 17- to 20-day placental trophoblast were significantly more cytotoxic (41% mean specific release) than cultures stimulated by blastocyst or EPC outgrowths or when compared to cultures subjected to primary *in vitro* stimulation with trophoblast cells without prior *in vivo* sensitization.

In another set of experiments Balb/c males were injected 3–4 times with $CB6F_1$

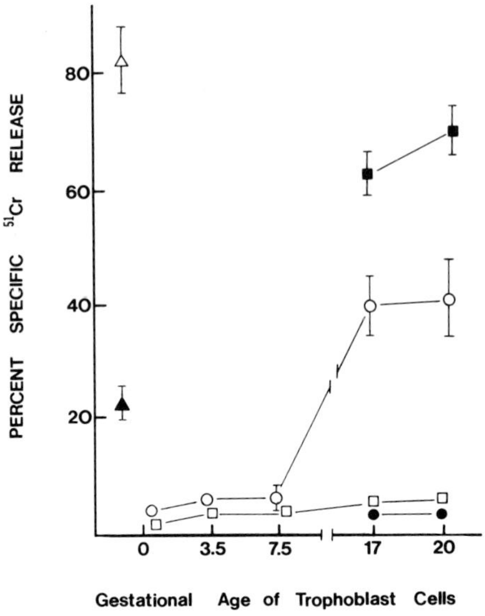

FIG. 1. *In vitro* activation of Balb/c cytotoxic lymphocytes using trophoblast cells as stimulators after prior *in vivo* immunization (secondary CML) with (Balb/c female × C57BL/6 male)F_1 embryonic tissue (○) of the indicated gestational age. After a 5-day incubation period cultures were tested for cytotoxic activity in a 4-hr assay. Values show mean percentage of specific lysis ± standard deviation of ^{51}Cr-labeled EL4 (paternal strain haplotype) target cells. Controls included Balb/c effector cells resulting from (i) primary *in vitro* sensitization by trophoblast cells (□) without prior *in vivo* immunization, (ii) unstimulated cultures containing placental cells and irradiated adult spleen cells (●). Additional cultures were established using responder spleen cells from mice immunized *in vivo* with adult semiallogeneic spleen cells and then restimulated *in vitro* with either 17- or 20-day placental trophoblast cells (■) or semiallogeneic spleen cells (△) or no cells (▲) (spontaneous background control). Day zero points (○, □) are baseline-specific cell lysis of spleen cell cultures without stimulating embryonic material.

(semiallogeneic) spleen cells. Seven days after the last injection spleen cells were removed and cocultured for 5 days with one of the following: 17- or 20-day CB6 placental trophoblast cells or adult spleen cells. Effector spleen cells from the trophoblast stimulated group displayed (Fig. 1) heightened levels of lytic activity (62–70% specific release) which was slightly less than the degree of cytotoxicity (82% mean specific release) achieved in secondary MLC (△).

Reactivity of Balb/c Spleen Cells in LTC and MLC

The data in Table 2 show that spleen cells from hyperimmunized Balb/c mice responded positively when cocultured with 17- or 20-day CB6 placental trophoblast in LTC (stimulation indices of 3.02 and 3.56) in comparison to the degree of stimulation in cultures containing responder cells which had not been previously immunized to placental trophoblast (stimulation indices of 1.08 or less). Equivalent responses (stimulation index of 4.15) were also observed in LTC-containing Balb/c lymphocytes primed *in vivo* with CB6F_1 adult spleen cells and then sensitized *in vitro* with 20-day placental trophoblast cells. These results contrast strikingly with the lack of significantly augmented DNA synthesis when trophoblast cells from 3½-day blastocysts were used for *in vivo* priming followed by *in vitro* secondary

TABLE 2

Ability of (C57BL/6♂ × Balb/c ♀) Trophoblast Cells to Stimulate Balb/c Spleen Cells to Undergo DNA Synthesis

In vivo pretreatment[a]	*In vitro* sensitization[b]	Uptake of $[^3H]TdR$ (cpm × 10^{-3} ± SD)	Stimulation index[c]
None	3½-Day blastocyst	30.7 ± 3.4[d]	1.02
3½-Day blastocyst	3½-Day blastocyst	33.5 ± 2.9	1.44
None	17-Day placental trophoblast	7.4 ± 1.1	—
17-Day placental trophoblast	17-Day placental trophoblast	22.2 ± 2.4	3.02
None	20-Day placental trophoblast	9.3 ± 0.7	1.08
20-Day placental trophoblast	20-Day placental trophoblast	25.8 ± 2.6	3.56
Adult spleen	20-Day placental trophoblast	27.6 ± 2.9	4.15
None	Adult spleen	48.7 ± 5.2	7.3
20-Day placental trophoblast	Adult spleen	56.2 ± 5.5	8.4
Adult spleen	Adult spleen	73.4 ± 6.9	11.03

[a] Mice received three to four weekly injections ip of 2×10^7 semiallogeneic trophoblast cells of the indicated gestation stage or adult spleen cells.

[b] *In vitro* secondary response of Balb/c responder spleen cells to trophoblast cells. Cultures contained 5×10^5 spleen cells stimulated by 5–10 blastocyst outgrowths, 1×10^5 placental trophoblast cells, or 5×10^5 irradiated $CB6F_1$ spleen cells and were incubated together for 5 days.

[c] Stimulation index equals counts per minute of semiallogeneically stimulated cultures after subtraction of cpm of cultures containing only blastocyst outgrowths (23,930 mean cpm) or placental trophoblast cells (2116 mean cpm) divided by cpm of unstimulated control cultures.

[d] Values are reported from stimulated cultures of six replicate experiments and represent mean cpm ± standard deviation of semiallogeneic mixtures. Background cpm of the various types of unstimulated control cultures averaged 6652 cpm for Balb/c spleen cells alone, 28,671 cpm for Balb/c spleen cells plus syngeneic blastocyst outgrowths, and 8117 cpm for Balb/c spleen cells plus syngeneic placental trophoblast cells.

stimulation. However, the maximal levels of DNA synthesis occurred in secondary MLR when responder cells were from Balb/c males immunized *in vivo* with either 20-day placental trophoblast or adult spleen cells and then subsequently restimulated *in vitro* with adult spleen cells (stimulation indices of 8.4 and 11.03, respectively).

Dose–Response Kinetics of Placental Trophoblast Cells in LTC and CML

Various numbers ($0.5–5.0 \times 10^5$) of 17- to 20-day CB6 placental trophoblast cells (stimulators) were cultured with a constant number (5×10^5) of maternal strain Balb/c spleen cells (responders) that had been hyperimmunized *in vivo* with placental trophoblast. Similar cultures were established containing CB6 placental lymphocytes (obtained from Lympholyte-M density gradients) or adult semiallogeneic spleen cells as stimulators (secondary MLR). The responses were evaluated by uptake of [^{3}H]TdR after a 5-day incubation period. Figure 2 shows that in an average of five separate experiments significant levels of DNA synthesis occurred using $0.5–2.0 \times 10^5$ trophoblast cells as stimulators (stimulation indices of 2.8 to 3.2) with Balb/c spleen cells responding optimally in the presence of 10^5 trophoblast cells. Proliferation closely paralleled the levels of DNA synthesis observed in cultures stimulated by semiallogeneic placental lymphocytes but in most experiments were approximately one-half the response achieved in secondary MLC between Balb/c and $CB6F_1$ spleen cells.

Mouse spleen cells cultured under similar conditions for LTC were tested for the ability of different concentrations of 17- to 20-day placental trophoblast to induce the formation of cytotoxic cells *in vivo* against ^{51}Cr-labeled EL4 target cells in the CML assay. Varying the Balb/c responder:trophoblast stimulator cell ratio affected the level of cytotoxicity elicited (Fig. 3). Maximal responses (41% specific release) were observed using 1×10^5 trophoblast stimulators which was considerably less than the levels of lytic activity attained in cultures stimulated by adult spleen cells (62–75% specific release) but comparable to cytotoxicity induced by placental lymphocytes. There was a gradual reduction in lytic activity when more than the optimal number (10^5) of trophoblast cells was used as stimulators.

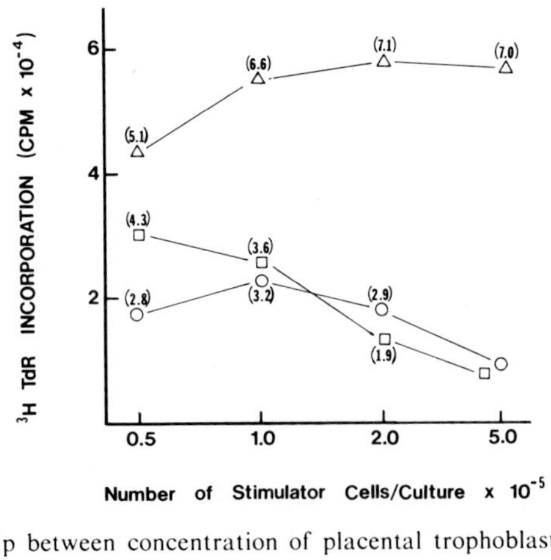

FIG. 2. The relationship between concentration of placental trophoblast cells and the proliferative response in LTC and MLC. Responder splenocytes from Balb/c males hyperimmunized *in vivo* were cultured for 5 days with each of the following stimulators: 17- to 20-day CB6 placental trophoblast cells (○), placental lymphocytes (□), or adult spleen cells (△). Values are reported as described in footnote *d*, Table 2 with each point representing mean cpm. Number enclosed in parentheses is stimulation index calculated as described in footnote *c*, Table 2. Standard deviations were ±10% or less and are not shown.

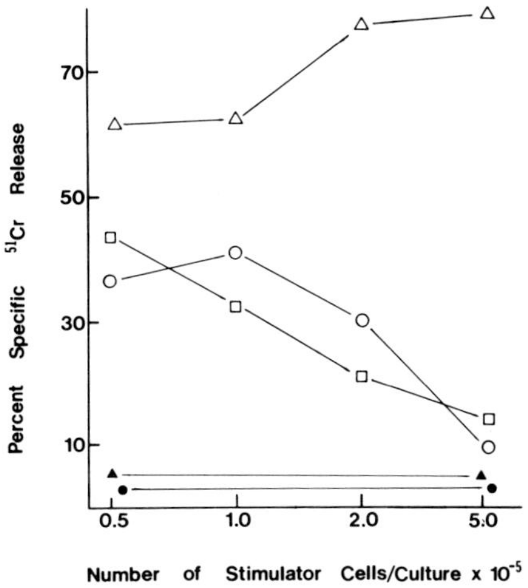

FIG. 3. Effect of concentration of placental trophoblast cells (stimulators) on the *in vitro* generation of cytotoxic lymphocytes. Balb/c responder spleen cells that were hyperimmunized *in vivo* were cultured with 17- to 20-day semiallogeneic placental trophoblast cells (○) as described in text. After 5 days of incubation individual cultures were assayed for effector cells using ^{51}Cr-labeled EL4 target cells in a 4-hr assay. Effector:target cell ratio is 25:1. Each value is reported as mean percentage specific lysis of five replicate experiments. The standard deviations were ±10% or less and are not shown. Additional cultures contained placental lymphocytes (□) or adult semiallogeneic spleen cells (△) as stimulators. Background cytotoxicity of cultures containing Balb/c spleen cells alone or placental trophoblast cells alone is represented by (▲) and (○), respectively.

Alloantigen Specificity of CTL

In certain cases (20) tumors and syngeneic fetal cells share common antigens (oncofetal) that cannot be identified on normal adult cells. To verify that trophoblast-induced, cytotoxic activity is directly attributable to alloantigenic differences between responder and trophoblast cells and not due to recognition of oncofetal antigens the following experiments were performed (Table 3). Balb/c males were hyperimmunized with semiallogeneic placental trophoblast cells. When splenocytes from these mice were cocultured with (Balb/c × Balb/c) trophoblast cells for 5 days insignificant levels of cytotoxic activity (2.2–4.8% specific release) directed against ^{51}Cr-labeled EL4 or P815 target cells were observed. In addition we found that Balb/c effector cells cytotoxic (41.1% specific release) for EL4 after sensitization with semiallogeneic placental cells expressed minimal lytic activity (7.2% specific release) when exposed to syngeneic ^{51}Cr-labeled P815 target cells. Similarly when immunizations and cultures were performed in the reciprocal direction (i.e., C57BL/6 mice immunized *in vivo* and then their spleen cells cocultured with [Balb/c male × C57BL/6 female] placental cells in LTC) significant levels of cytotoxic activity (39.4% specific release) were generated against only paternal alloantigen-bearing ^{51}Cr-labeled P815 target cells and not toward syngeneic EL4 targets.

DISCUSSION

Previous investigations (15, 17, 21–23) of the cellular immune response induced by histocompatibility antigens present on the cell surface of embryonic trophoblast

TABLE 3

Alloantigen Specificity for Generation of CTL by 17- to 20-Day Placental Trophoblast Cells

Strain of immunized mice	*In vivo* pretreatment[a]	*In vitro* sensitization[b]	Percentage specific release of ^{51}Cr-labeled cells[c]	
			EL4	P815
Balb/c	Balb/c♀ × C57BL/6♂	Balb/c × Balb/c	2.2	4.8
Balb/c	Balb/c♀ × C57BL/6♂	Balb/c♀ × C57BL/6♂	41.1	7.2
C57BL/6	C57BL/6♀ × Balb/c♂	C57BL/6 × C57BL/6	3.9	1.8
C57BL/6	C57BL/6♀ × Balb/c♂	C57BL/6♀ × Balb/c♂	2.5	39.4

[a] Balb/c or C57BL/6 mice were hyperimmunized with trophoblast obtained from 17- to 20-day placenta of the indicated mating combinations.

[b] *In vitro* secondary response of Balb/c or C57BL/6 responder spleen cells to trophoblast cells. Cultures contained 1×10^6 spleen cells stimulated by 1×10^5 placental trophoblast cells from the indicated maternal–paternal strain combinations.

[c] After 5 days of incubation cultures were tested for effector cells using ^{51}Cr-labeled EL4 or P815 target cells in a 4-hr assay. Effector:target cell ratio was 25:1. Data are reported as described in footnote *b*, Table 1, and are representative of three separate experiments.

tissue have usually relied on *in vivo* studies involving extrauterine transplantation of blastocysts, EPC, or placental cells into nonimmunized or immunized allogeneic hosts. Except for placental cells (17) murine trophoblast growth and development usually proceeds unimpeded without eliciting a detectable allograft rejection response and probably relates directly to the massive invasion and proliferation into neighboring maternal decidua and phagocytic activity on the part of these cells (24). In addition prior immunization with EPC trophoblast does not decrease the survival rate of subsequent skin grafts received by genetically dissimilar mice (15, 23). Based upon these findings and those of other studies (5–8) utilizing direct serological detection of H-2 it would seem that early mouse trophoblast is deficient in the full expression of major histocompatibility antigens or they are masked by a nonspecific coat of fibrinoid-like substance (25, 26) or bound maternal immunoglobulins (27). The data presented in our study strengthen these concepts. We have shown that cytotoxic effector cells directed against H-2 antigens of paternal origin cannot be generated after deliberately immunizing allogeneic mice with preimplantation blastocysts or EPC derived from semiallogeneic matings. These findings correlate well with previous reports of ours (18) and other investigators (28) demonstrating that lymphoid cells from multiparous allopregnant mice were not cytotoxic for paternal alloantigen-bearing ^{51}Cr-labeled tumor target cells. Similar *in vitro* cell-mediated cytotoxicity studies (29, 30) have been reported in which spleen cells from mice hyperimmunized with allogeneic adult tissue did not prevent the growth and development of trophoblast-derived components while those elements originating from the embryo itself were destroyed. Furthermore we have shown that spleen cells from nonimmunized mice cannot be stimulated *in vitro* by trophoblast cells to proliferate and undergo DNA synthesis and develop into CTL.

Unlike the trophoblast, cells derived from the inner cell mass (ICM) of the blastocyst and the embryonic sac of 7.5-day conceptuses show evidence of alloantigen expression (5, 6) of K- and D-region determinants of the major histocompatibility complex which are capable of mediating immune destruction after transfer to allogeneic recipient mice (22). However, the selective presence of transplantation antigens on these early embryonic tissues is probably low since one of these tissues (ICM) was unable to elicit reactivity in the LTC or CML assay. Alternatively our results could be attributed to the demonstrated lack of Ia antigens on early gestational tissue (12) which are known to play a major role in lymphocyte activation (31).

While alloantigen expression on early trophoblast is, at best, minimal (5–7), several investigators (32, 33) have detected xenogeneic responses using anti-trophoblast antiserum raised after immunizing rabbits with presumably pure murine trophoblastic nodules and a partially purified rat placental trophoblast preparation. In preliminary experiments we have found that peripheral blood lymphocytes isolated from guinea pigs or rabbits hyperimmunized with Balb/c blastocysts undergo significant levels of DNA synthesis after *in vitro* culture with blastocyst outgrowths. These responses are probably initiated by the expression of tissue or stage-specific (oncofetal) (20) antigens along with species-specific antigens characteristic of this particular course of embryonic development.

The central part of this study demonstrates that late gestational placental trophoblast cells are capable of inducing specific cell-mediated immunity. This production of CTL after sensitization by semiallogeneic trophoblast was found to be specific for the relevant paternal alloantigenic determinants since ^{51}Cr-labeled target cells syngeneic to the effector cell could not be readily lysed (Table 3). However it must be emphasized that the *in vitro* generation of cytotoxic effector cells as well as a significant proliferative response occurred only after *in vivo* priming was followed by *in vitro* restimulation. In addition these trophoblast-induced responses were considerably lower in comparison to MLC and CML where adult spleen cells provided the immunologic stimulus. Our data are consistent with and extend serologic studies (9, 11) which clearly demonstrate that there are detectable quantities of H-2 antigens on placental trophoblast. Although the alloantigen density appeared to be equivalent to that of adult thymocytes (11) our results suggest that the expression of these antigens on the cell surface of the trophoblast must be altered somewhat in a form not easily recognizable by adult spleen cells, or Ia antigens must be present before augmented reactivity could occur. Indeed maternal immunoglobulins directed at paternal H-2 antigens have been eluted off placental tissue (34, 35), and there is evidence that trophoblast cells become coated with fibrinoid-like mucoprotein material (25) and Ia antigen expression is confined to the liver and spleen during embryogenesis (13). Additional factors that could account for the relatively weak immunogenicity of placental trophoblast are the potent *in vitro* immunosuppressive effects exerted by specific trophoblast antigens (4), placental steroid, and protein hormones (36, 37), anti-trophoblast antibody (38), and other, as yet, unidentified trophoblast or placental (3, 4) components.

Although our results do not rigorously exclude the possible contribution by non-MHC antigen determinants present on the trophoblast in eliciting reactivity in LTC and the CML test it would appear based upon currently available evidence (19, 39, 40) on the nature of the antigens recognized by these two *in vitro* assays that, except for *M*-locus gene products, non-MHC components play, at best, a minor role in activating lymphocytes under MLR-like culture conditions. In fact Bevan (39, 40) has shown that alloimmunity resulting from non-MHC antigen differences can only occur when responder and stimulator cells simultaneously express the same H-2 antigens. Furthermore, while the strains of mice used in our study (Balb/c and C57BL/6) differ at H-2 they share identity at the *M*-locus region (41) thereby ruling out the participation of these alloantigens in the recognitive and effector phases of cellular interaction between lymphocytes and trophoblasts. Additional studies to exclude the potential role of non-H-2 antigens in evoking these reactions using congenic resistant mouse strains differing only at the H-2 region are currently in progress.

There is no convincing evidence (42, 43) for the presence of analogous histocompatibility antigens (HLA) on human placental trophoblast although their presence on stromal cells and endothelium has been noted. Nonetheless provocative data from some studies (44, 45) have demonstrated that maternal lymphocytes are capable of killing cultured trophoblast cells from their own placenta, possibly as a result of recognition of embryo-specific antigens. However, in order to achieve lysis, a 2- to 4-day incubation period was required which, in view of the comparatively short period (4 hr or less) that is needed for measuring significant cytotoxic activity in the standard CML assay, makes it difficult to interpret whether cytotoxicity was induced directly by pregnancy or resulted from *de novo* restimulation *in vitro*.

The placenta is a complex organ containing a number of cell layers, blood vessels, and circulating blood elements. Our nonenzymatic disruption of placentas and subsequent density gradient fractionation are extensions of previous separation procedures since we were able to recover a trophoblast-enriched fraction that contained only a small percentage of nontrophoblastic elements such as leukocytes, fibroblasts, and decidual cells. This was further verified in control placental cell cultures where trophoblast was found to be the predominant cell type throughout the 5-day culture period and where the trophoblast hormone progesterone can be detected (C. S. Pavia, D. P. Stites, and R. Fraser, unpublished observations). Similar findings (46) have been described for short-term cultures of rat placental cells where the trophoblast is the prevalent cell population. Although fetal leukocytes present in the enriched trophoblast preparation might be partially responsible for inducing reactivity this possibility appears highly unlikely since the volume was far too small to account for the sensitivity produced and these cells, unlike the lymphocyte fraction isolated at the gradient interface, are functionally inert based upon their inability to respond to the classical T- and B-cell mitogens concanavalin A and lipopolysaccharide (47). In addition we have found (C. S. Pavia and D. P. Stites, unpublished data) that elimination of contaminating lymphocytes by prior exposure of the enriched trophoblast population with a highly specific anti-mouse lymphocyte serum does not reduce the levels of cytotoxicity or proliferation elicited in the LTC. Therefore the reactivity that was observed in these *in vitro* reactions can be directly attributed to the placental trophoblast or components derived from it with paternal strain alloantigens providing the stimulus since semiallogeneic tissue was used to exclude possible recognition of any contaminating maternal cells.

Numerous theories have been proposed to explain the failure of rejection of the fetus by the mother (48), some of which are based upon the unique biological properties of the trophoblast. This particular tissue acts as the anatomical barrier between fetal and maternal tissues and as such represents the first line of defense against any maternal antifetal alloimmunity. Likewise the integrity of the trophoblast is dependent upon minimal interference from the maternal immune system which can be directly attributed to the lack of the complete functional expression of paternally derived transplantation antigens on the surface of the trophoblastic cells. This protective mechanism is especially attractive in light of evidence (49) showing that at least in humans, syncytiotrophoblast is continually shed from the placenta and circulates in maternal blood for the latter half of gestation and thus would normally be expected to provoke a vigorous immune response. At the same time while the trophoblast under normal physiological conditions seems to be invulnerable to immune attack it is very probable that some maternal reactivity to this tissue does arise primarily to protect the pregnant host from extensive and otherwise unchecked growth and invasion of the trophoblast as occurs in the malignant disease choriocarcinoma.

REFERENCES

1. Dancis, J., Douglas, G. W., and Fierer, J., *Amer. J. Obstet. Gynecol.* **94,** 50, 1966.
2. Dancis, J. Jansen, V., Gorstein, F., and Douglas, G., *Amer. J. Obstet. Gynecol.* **100,** 1110, 1968.
3. Pavia, C. S., and Stites, D. P., *Cell Immunol.* **58,** 202, 1981.
4. McIntyre, J. A., and Faulk, W. P., *Proc. Nat. Acad. Sci. USA* **76,** 4029, 1979.
5. Searle, R. F., Sellens, M. H., Elson, J., Jenkinson, E. J., and Billington, W. D., *J. Exp. Med.* **143,** 348, 1976.
6. Hakansson, S., and Sundqvist, K. G., *Transplantation* **19,** 479, 1975.
7. Billington, W. D., Jenkinson, E. J., Searle, R. F., and Sellens, M. F., *Transplant. Proc.* **9,** 1371, 1977.
8. Heyner, S., *Transplantation* **16,** 675, 1973.
9. Sellens, M. H., Jenkinson, E. J., and Billington, W. D., *Transplantation* **25,** 173, 1978.
10. Schlesinger, M., *J. Immunol.* **93,** 255, 1964.
11. Chatterjee-Hasrouni, S., and Lala, P., *J. Exp. Med.* **149,** 1238, 1979.
12. Jenkinson, E. J., and Searle, R. F., *J. Reprod. Immunol.* **1,** 3, 1979.
13. Delovitch, T. L., Press, J. L., and McDevitt, H. O., *J. Immunol.* **120,** 818, 1978.
14. Simmons, R. L., and Russell, P. S., *Ann. N.Y. Acad. Sci. USA* **99,** 717, 1962.
15. Simmons, R. L., and Russell, P. S., *Ann N.Y. Acad. Sci.* **129,** 35, 1966.
16. Hulka, J. F., and Mohr, K., *Science* **161,** 696, 1968.
17. Uhr, J. W., and Anderson, S. G., *Nature (London)* **194,** 1292, 1962.
18. Pavia, C. S., and Stites, D. P., *J. Immunol.* **123,** 2194, 1979.
19. Cerottini, J. C., and Brunner, K. T. *Advan. Immunol.* **18,** 67, 1974.
20. Chism, S. E., Wallis, S., Burton, R. C., and Warner, N. L., *J. Immunol.* **117,** 1870, 1976.
21. Vandeputte, M., and Sobis, H., *Transplantation* **14,** 331, 1972.
22. Pathey, H. L., and Edidin, M., *Transplantation* **15,** 211, 1973.
23. Searle, R. F., Jenkinson, E. J., and Johnson, M. H., *Nature (London)* **255,** 719, 1975.
24. Billington, W. D., *Advan. Reprod. Physiol.* **5,** 27, 1971.
25. Kirby, D. R. S., Billington, W. D., Bradbury, S., and Goldstein, D. J., *Nature (London)* **204,** 548, 1964.
26. Currie, G. A., Van Doornick, W., and Bagshawe, K. E., *Nature (London)* **219,** 191, 1968.
27. Bernard, O., Ripoche, M. A., and Bennett, D., *J. Exp. Med.* **145,** 58, 1977.
28. Hamilton, M. S., and Hellstrom, I., *Transplantation* **23,** 423, 1977.
29. Jenkinson, E. J., and Billington, W. D. *Transplantation* **18,** 286, 1974.
30. Billington, W. D., and Jenkinson, E. J., *In* "Early Development of Mammals" (M. Balls and A. E. Wild, Eds.), p. 219. Cambridge Univ. Press, Cambridge, 1975.
31. Bach, F. H., Bach, M. L., and Sondel, P. M., *Nature (London)* **259,** 273, 1976.
32. Behrman, S. J., *In* "The Biology of the Blastocyst" (R. J. Blandau, Ed.), p. 479. Univ. of Chicago Press, Chicago, 1971.
33. Beer, A. E., Billingham, R. E., and Yang, S. L., *J. Exp. Med.* **135,** 1177, 1972.
34. Faulk, W. P., Jeannet, M., Creighton, W. D., and Carbonara, A., *J. Clin. Invest.* **54,** 1011, 1974.
35. Chaouat, G., Voisin, G. A., Escalier, D., and Robert, P., *Clin. Exp. Immunol.* **35,** 13, 1979.

36. Pavia, C. S., Siiteri, P. K., Perlman, J. D., and Stites, D. P., *J. Reprod. Immunol.* **1,** 33, 1979.
37. Kaye, M. D., and Jones, W. R., *Amer. J. Obstet. Gynecol.* **109,** 1029, 1971.
38. McIntyre, M. A., and Faulk, W. P., *J. Exp., Med.* **149,** 824, 1979.
39. Bevan, M. J., *J. Exp, Med.* **142,** 1349, 1975.
40. Bevan, M. J., *Immunogenetics* **3,** 177, 1976.
41. Festenstein, H., *Transplant. Proc.* **8,** 339, 1976.
42. Faulk, W. P., and Temple, A., *Nature (London)* **262,** 399, 1976.
43. Faulk, W. P., Anderson, A. R., and Temple, A., *Transplant. Proc.* **9,** 1379, 1977.
44. Douthwaite, R. M., and Urbach, G. I., *Amer. J. Obstet. Gynecol.* **109,** 1023, 1971.
45. Taylor, P. V., and Hancock, K. W., *Immunology* **28,** 973, 1975.
46. Ferguson, F. G., and Palm, J., *J. Embryol. Exp. Morphol.* **39,** 195, 1976.
47. Pavia, C. S., and Stites, D. P., *Immunobiology* **159,** in press.
48. Stites, D. P., Pavia, C. S., Clemens, L. E., Kuhn, R. W., and Siiteri, P. K., *Arthritis Rheumat.* **22,** 1300, 1979.
49. Douglas, G. W., Thomas, L., Carr, M., Cullen, N. M., and Morris, R., *Amer. J. Obstet. Gynecol.* **78,** 960, 1959.

CELLULAR IMMUNOLOGY **64**, 177–186 (1981)

Antigen Requirements for Priming of Type III Pneumococcal Polysaccharide-Specific IgG Memory Responses: Suppression of Memory with the T-Independent Form of Antigen[1]

DEBORAH WILSON[2] AND HELEN BRALEY-MULLEN[3]

Division of Immunology–Rheumatology, Department of Medicine, University of Missouri Health Sciences Center, Columbia, Missouri 65212

Received June 18, 1981; accepted July 11, 1981

Injection of donor CAF_1 mice with doses of the thymus-independent (TI) antigen Type III pneumococcal polysaccharide (S3) which are optimally (0.6 μg) or supraoptimally (5 μg) immunogenic prior to, with, or following priming with a T-dependent (TD) form of S3 (S3-HRBC) suppressed the induction of memory in S3-specific IgG-producing B cells (B_γ). Subimmunogenic doses (0.06, 0.006, μg) of S3 had no effect on B_γ memory induction. The effect was of long duration and occurred in the apparent absence of T cells. S3 also suppressed mature S3-specific memory cell expression when given to primed donor mice prior to cell transfer or when given to recipient mice within 2 days after cell transfer and secondary TD antigen challenge. The possible mechanisms by which TI antigens suppress the induction of memory in S3-specific IgG memory cell precursors and mature memory cells are discussed.

INTRODUCTION

It is now well established that most of the so-called T-independent (TI)[4] antigens differ from T-dependent (TD) antigens in that they are unable to induce immunologic memory which is characterized by the production of increased amounts of IgG antibody following a second exposure to antigen (1–5). The general inability of TI antigens to induce memory in IgG-producing B cells (B_γ) has been suggested to be due to the fact that TI antigens generally do not activate helper T cells (T_H) (6, 7) which are often required to induce B_γ memory with TD antigens (8–11). Moreover, previous studies from this laboratory have shown that some TI antigens such as type III pneumococcal polysaccharide (S3) and polyvinylpyrrolidone (PVP) can actually interfere with the induction (12, 13) or expression (13) of B_γ memory which is induced by TD forms of these antigens. An understanding of the mechanisms by which TI antigens can actively interfere with the induction or expression

[1] Supported by NIH Grant CA25054.

[2] Recipient of an Arthritis Foundation Postdoctoral Research Fellowship.

[3] Recipient of NIH Research Career Development Award AI100322.

[4] Abbreviations used: TI, thymus independent; TD, thymus dependent; B_γ, IgG-producing B cells; T_H, helper T cells; S3, type III pneumococcal polysaccharide; PVP, polyvinyl pyrrolidone; S3-HRBC, S3 coupled to horse erythrocytes; ALS, antilymphocyte serum; PFC, plaque-forming cells; S3-SRBC, S3 coupled to sheep erythrocytes.

0008-8749/81/150177-10$02.00/0

of B_γ memory is important in furthering our understanding of the basic mechanisms by which antigen activation (or inactivation) of B cells occurs.

The present study was therefore undertaken to examine in more detail the requirements for and mechanism of suppression of S3-specific IgG memory responses by the TI antigen S3. The results indicate that the ability of S3 to suppress B_γ memory *induction* is antigen dose dependent, of long duration and can apparently occur in the absence of T cells. S3 could also suppress the *expression* of B_γ memory although the duration of this suppression was shorter and similar in some ways to that ascribed previously to B-cell receptor blockade (4, 14, 15).

MATERIALS AND METHODS

Mice. Female CAF_1 mice were obtained from the Jackson Laboratories, Bar Harbor, Maine. All mice were 8 to 12 weeks old at the time of primary immunization.

Antigens and immunizations. The preparation and immunizing properties of the S3 have been described previously (16). In some experiments mice were given various amounts of S3 ip at the same time or at various times before or after primary immunization with a TD form of S3, S3 coupled to horse erythrocytes (S3-HRBC) (17). In other experiments S3 was given ip to recipients of S3-HRBC-primed spleen cells at various times relative to cell transfer (see below) and secondary immunization with S3-HRBC. The doses of the TI form of S3 used were considered to be suboptimal (0.006 or 0.06 μg), optimal (0.6 μg), and supraoptimal (5 μg) in terms of the ability of this antigen to elicit a primary IgM response (2, 16). S3-HRBC were prepared as previously described (7, 18), and 2×10^8 S3-HRBC were given iv. The same dose of S3-HRBC was used for secondary immunization of irradiated recipient mice (see below).

ALS treatment. Some mice were given rabbit anti-mouse lymphocyte serum (ALS) (Microbiological Associates, Bethesda, Md., Lot 15070) at the time of injection of S3. ALS was given ip on Days −1 (0.3 ml), 0 (0.5 ml), and +1 (0.3 ml) relative to S3. Mice so treated were then primed 30 days later with S3-HRBC at which time the T_H eliminated by ALS should have returned to normal levels (11). This amount of ALS has been shown to cause a transient (ca. 14 days) elimination of splenic T cells and has been shown not to affect B cells (11, 19–22). Control mice received only S3 since normal rabbit serum has been shown not to affect the S3 response.

Hemolytic plaque assay. The plaque-forming cell (PFC) assay for S3 has been described in detail previously (22). Chromic chloride was used to couple S3 to sheep RBC (S3-SRBC) which were used as indicator erythrocytes (19). IgG PFC were developed with a rabbit antiserum to mouse IgG_1 and IgG_2. The number of IgG PFC were determined by subtracting the number of IgM PFC from the number of PFC developed by the antiserum to mouse IgG_1 and IgG_2. IgM and IgG background PFC to SRBC were determined and subtracted from the respective numbers of PFC to S3-SRBC. IgM background PFC were minimal (100–1000 PFC/spleen) and IgG background PFC were usually 10–20% of the S3-specific PFC. All data are expressed as PFC/spleen but the results would not differ if data were expressed as PFC/10^6 spleen cells. Each of the experiments described below was repeated two or more times with similar results.

Preparation of enriched T and B cells. In some experiments spleen cells from S3-HRBC-primed mice were separated into T- and B-cell-enriched fractions. T cells were obtained by passing spleen cells through nylon wool as described by Julius *et al.* (23). The effectiveness of this technique for enriching for T cells has previously been verified in our laboratory (6). The nylon-wool-nonadherent fraction consistently contained 20–30% of the original number of spleen cells. Anti-Thy 1.2 antiserum (AKR anti-C3H) and complement treatment of spleen cells was used to obtain B cells (11). This antiserum has been shown to be effective in eliminating T cells but to have no effect on B cells (11).

Irradiation and repopulation of mice. CAF_1 female mice were irradiated (700 rad) using the cobalt-60 source at the University of Missouri Research Reactor as previously described (17). Mice were repopulated iv within 8 hr of irradiation with 2×10^7 unfractionated spleen cells, 2×10^6 T cells, 2×10^7 B cells, or with a mixture of 2×10^6 T cells and 2×10^7 B cells. Immediately after cell transfer mice were challenged with 2×10^8 S3-HRBC. S3-specific PFC were determined 7 days later (6).

RESULTS

Suppression of IgG Memory Induction with S3

To determine the amount of the TI antigen S3 which was needed to suppress the induction of IgG memory to S3-HRBC, mice were given varying doses of S3 4 days before primary immunization with 2×10^8 S3-HRBC. Three months later spleen cells from these mice and from control mice which received only S3-HRBC were transferred to irradiated recipients and PFC were determined 7 days later

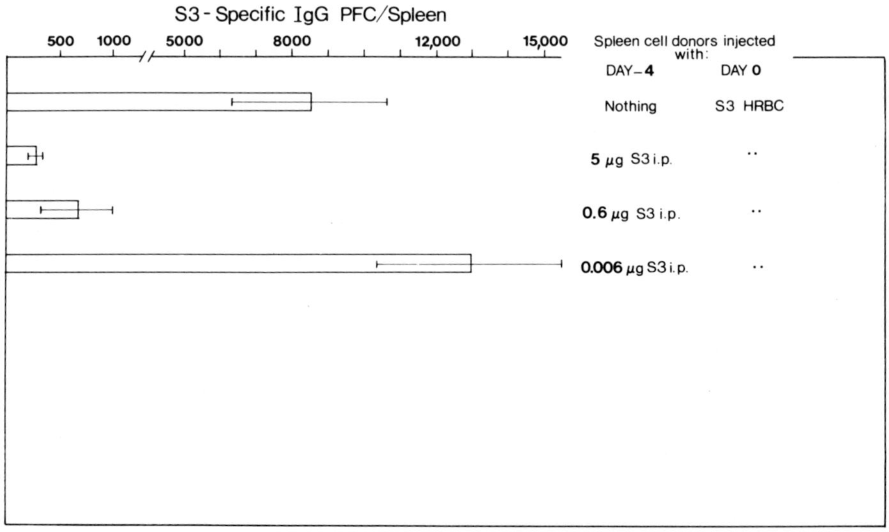

FIG. 1. Effect of dose of TI form of S3 on S3-specific memory cell induction. Spleen cell donors were injected with the indicated doses of S3 4 days prior to priming with S3-HRBC. Irradiated recipients were repopulated with 2×10^7 spleen cells from mice of each donor group and challenged with S3-HRBC. Mean S3 IgG PFC/spleen ± SEM are shown (four or five mice/group).

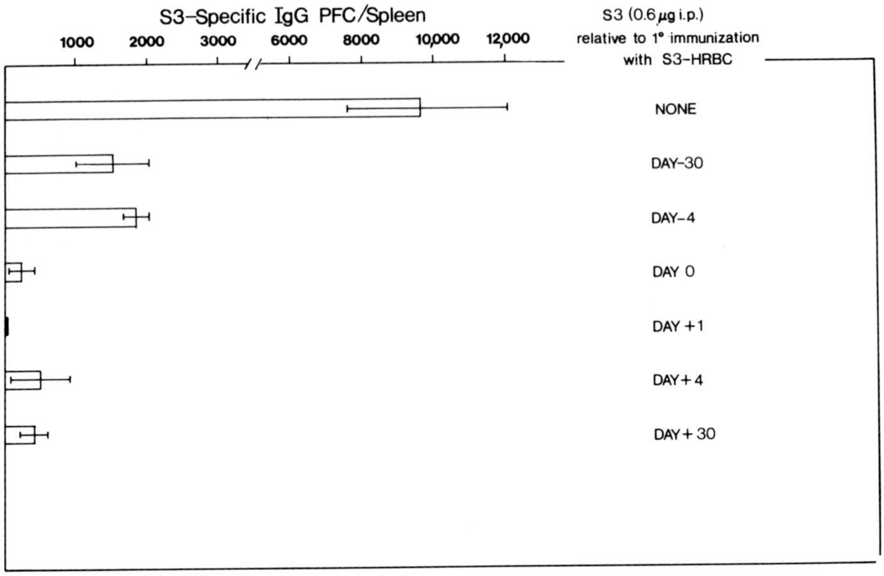

FIG. 2. Effect of timing of S3 injection relative to priming with S3-HRBC on memory cell induction. Donor mice were given 0.6 μg S3 at various times relative to primary immunization with S3-HRBC as indicated. Three months after primary immunization, 2×10^7 spleen cells from indicated donor groups were transferred to irradiated recipients which were challenged with S3-HRBC. Mean IgG PFC/spleen $\pm$ SEM are shown (four mice/group).

(Fig. 1). Low doses (0.006 μg) of S3 failed to suppress induction of the IgG memory response while both the optimally immunogenic (0.6 μg) or supraoptimal (5 μg) doses of S3 given 4 days before priming with S3-HRBC resulted in greater than 90% suppression of the S3-specific secondary IgG response. The IgM responses are not shown since they were always low (<1600 PFC/spleen) and of similar magnitude in all groups.

To determine at what time relative to primary immunization with S3-HRBC the S3 had to be given in order to suppress the induction of IgG memory, 0.6 μg S3 was given to mice at various times from 30 days before to 30 days after primary immunization with S3-HRBC (Fig. 2). Their spleen cells were transferred to irradiated recipients 3 months after priming. Suppression of the S3-specific IgG memory response occurred throughout this interval indicating that the effect of 0.6 μg S3 on B_γ memory cell precursors was long lasting and that S3 could suppress both memory cell precursors and maturing memory cells. Again the IgM PFC responses were low and not different between groups (not shown).

Suppression of B_γ-Cell Priming by Pretreatment with S3

To determine whether suppression of IgG memory induction by S3 was due to an effect on S3-specific B cells, mice were given 0.6 or 5 μg S3 on Day +4 or Day 0 relative to primary immunization with S3-HRBC. Control mice received only S3-HRBC. Two months later spleen cells from each experimental and control group were treated with anti-Thy 1.2 and complement to eliminate T cells. Irradiated recipients were reconstituted with 2×10^7 B cells from either control or experimental donors and all mice received in addition 2×10^6 nylon-wool-passed spleen cells from mice primed 2 months earlier with S3-HRBC. Unfractionated spleen cells from each experimental and control group were also transferred to irradiated recipients in order to assess the degree of suppression of memory by S3. As shown in Fig. 3, recipients of spleen cells from mice given 0.6 or 5 μg S3 either 4 days after or at the time of priming with S3-HRBC (Groups C, E, and G) again had much lower IgG responses than mice primed only with S3-HRBC (Group A). Recipients of B cells (together with S3-HRBC primed T cells) from these same mice had similarly low responses (Groups D, F, and H) compared to controls (Group B) indicating that the suppressive effect of S3 on IgG memory induction was due to suppression at the level of B cells.

Effect of ALS on S3-Induced IgG Memory Cell Precursor Tolerance

In order to determine indirectly whether S3 might also suppress the induction of memory in T cells, ALS was given to mice on Days −1, 0, and +1 relative to injection of 5 μg S3 in order to eliminate T cells (11). Other mice received S3 without ALS and control mice received no S3 or ALS. Thirty days later (when T cells eliminated by ALS should have returned to normal (11)) all mice were primed with S3-HRBC. Two months later spleen cells of mice from each donor group were pooled and transferred to irradiated recipients which were immunized with S3-HRBC (Fig. 4). Although the degree of suppression induced by S3 was

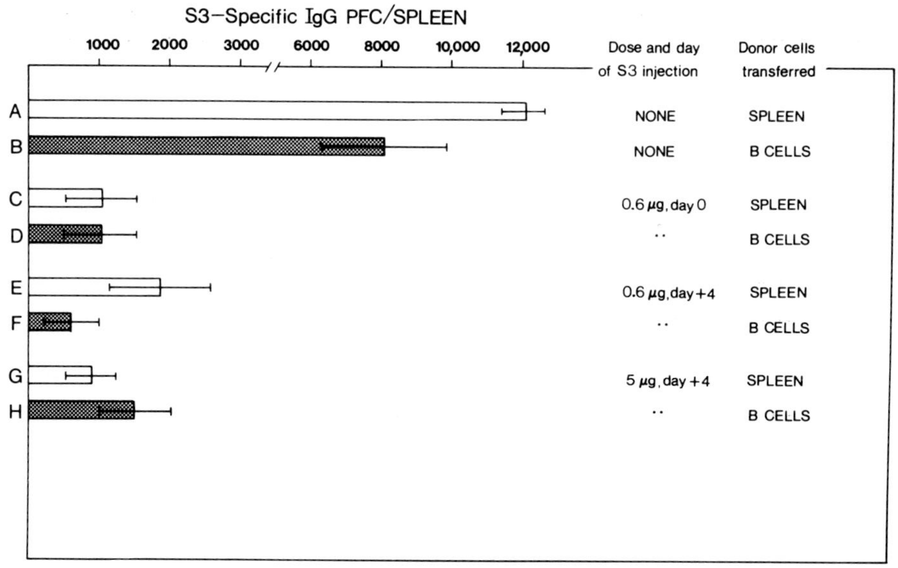

FIG. 3. S3 induces tolerance in S3-specific Bγ cells. Donor mice were given 0.6 or 5 μg S3 on Day 0 or Day +4 relative to priming with S3-HRBC. Two months later, irradiated recipients were repopulated with 2×10^7 spleen cells or 2×10^7 B cells from each donor group. B-Cell recipients also received 2×10^6 T cells from mice primed with S3-HRBC. Values shown are mean IgG PFC/spleen ± SEM (four or five mice/group). Mice repopulated with primed T cells alone produced 17 ± 13 IgG PFC/spleen.

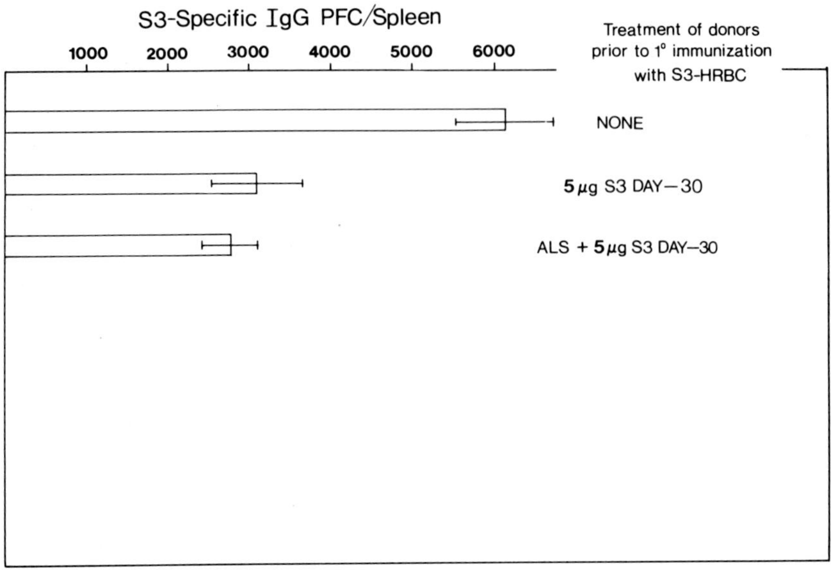

FIG. 4. Effect of ALS on S3-specific memory cell tolerance induced by S3. Thirty days prior to priming with S3-HRBC donor mice were treated with S3-HRBC or no S3. One group also received ALS on Day −1 (0.3 ml), Day 0 (0.5 ml), and Day +1 (0.3 ml) relative to S3. Donor spleen cells (2×10^7) were transferred to irradiated recipients 2 months after priming with S3-HRBC. All recipients were challenged with S3-HRBC. Values shown are mean IgG PFC/spleen ± SEM (four mice/group).

less than in previous experiments (see Fig. 2), the results suggest that T cells are not required for the suppression of B_γ memory induction by S3 since the same degree of suppression was obtained in both normal and T-cell-depleted (ALS-treated) mice.

Suppression of S3-Specific IgG Memory Cell Expression by S3

The above results indicate that S3 can suppress the induction of IgG memory responses when S3 is given before, at the same time as, or after primary immunization with S3-HRBC. The effect of S3 on mature S3-specific IgG memory cells was next determined. Mice primed 9 months previously with S3-HRBC were given 0.6 or 5 μg S3 4 days or 12 hr prior to transfer of their spleen cells to irradiated recipients which were then challenged with S3-HRBC (Fig. 5). The results indicate that the higher dose (5 μg) of S3 could suppress IgG memory cells when given either 4 days or 12 hr before cell transfer whereas the lower (0.6 μg) dose suppressed the response only when given 4 days prior to transfer. It thus appears that mature memory cells require some period of time to become inactivated by relatively low doses of antigen. It is also possible that 0.6 μg S3 given 12 hr before transfer may have acted as an immunogen since it has been shown that S3 can elicit an IgG memory response in S3-HRBC-primed mice (6). When S3-HRBC-primed spleen cells were transferred to irradiated recipients and challenged with the TD antigen, 0.6 μg S3 was capable of suppressing the S3 IgG memory response if given to the recipients on Day 0, +1, or +2 relative to secondary immunization. However, the memory cell response could not be suppressed if the S3 was given on day +3 or

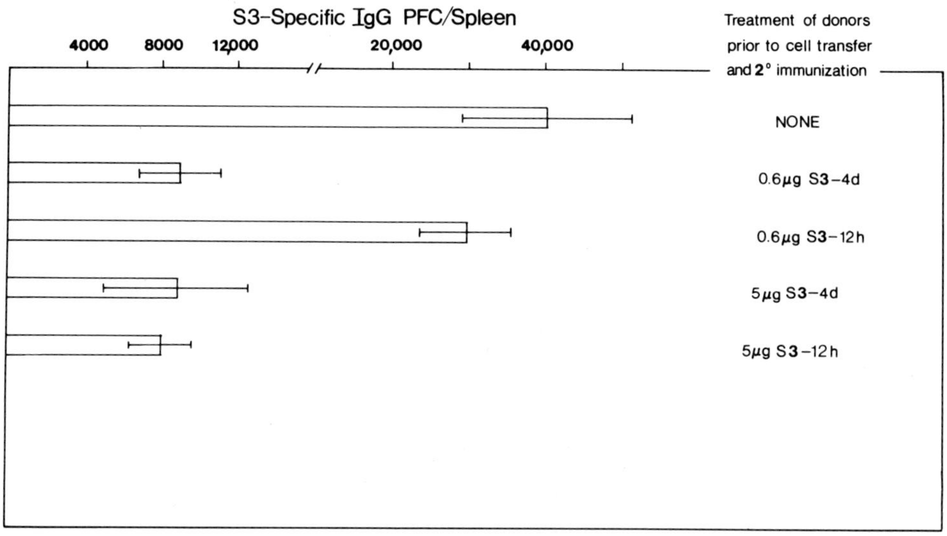

FIG. 5. Suppression of mature S3-specific memory cells by S3. All donor groups were primed with S3-HRBC. Five months later donor groups were given 0.6 or 5 μg S3 either 4 days or 12 hr prior to transfer of 2×10^7 spleen cells to irradiated recipients. All recipients were challenged with S3-HRBC. Mean IgG PFC/spleen $\pm$ SEM are shown (four mice/group).

+4 indicating that the expression of the memory response may be more resistant to suppression than is the induction of memory. These results also suggest that the suppression induced by S3 is an active process and is not due solely to blocking of B-cell receptors by S3 since suppression does not occur once the secondary response is well underway.

DISCUSSION

The results presented here confirm our previous observations that certain TI antigens such as S3 (12) and PVP (13) can interfere with the induction and expression of IgG memory in spleen cells which are induced to differentiate into IgG-producing memory cells by TD forms of these antigens. The studies described here were undertaken to extend those observations by examining in detail the antigen dose requirements, duration, and mechanism of suppression of IgG memory responses by the TI antigen S3. The results indicate that the suppression of IgG memory *induction* by S3 requires amounts of S3 (0.6 or 5 μg) (Fig. 1) which are optimal or supraoptimal in terms of the ability of S3 to induce primary IgM responses in CAF_1 mice (2, 16). By contrast, lower amounts of S3 (0.006 or 0.06 μg) (Fig. 1 and data not shown) are unable to suppress IgG memory induction although 0.006 μg of S3 can markedly suppress primary antibody response to S3-HRBC (24). Thus suppression of IgG memory induction by S3 is not due solely to its ability to suppress the primary antibody response to S3-HRBC.

When 0.6 μg of S3 was given to mice at various times before or after priming with S3-HRBC, the S3-specific IgG memory response was markedly suppressed at all times tested, from 30 days before to 30 days after S3-HRBC (Fig. 2). Thus the effect of S3 on memory cell precursors is long lasting and S3 can suppress both memory cell precursors as well as differentiating memory cells. Suppression of memory cell induction by S3 was apparently due to an effect on S3-specific B_γ cells since B cells from mice given S3 and S3-HRBC were unresponsive to secondary challenge with S3-HRBC after addition of T cells from mice primed only with S3-HRBC (Fig. 3). Moreover, elimination of T cells with ALS (11) at the time of injection of S3 did not prevent suppression of $B\gamma$ memory induction (Fig. 4) suggesting that S3 may interact directly with B cells to mediate its effect. However S3 persists *in vivo* for long periods of time (25) and residual S3 may have interacted with T cells which regenerated by 30 days after ALS treatment (11), the time of primary immunization with S3-HRBC (Fig. 4). Since T cells are absolutely required for the generation of B_γ memory with S3-HRBC (11), the question of whether residual S3 might interact with T cells which must be present at the time of priming is difficult to assess with certainty. Since TI antigens such as S3 (2, 26) and PVP (27, 28) can activate suppressor T cells (T_S), T_S activated by S3 may be at least partially responsible for the suppression of B_γ memory induction by S3. However, low doses (0.006 μg) of S3 also have been reported to activate T_S (2) yet 0.006 μg S3 did not suppress B_γ memory induction (Fig. 1). Moreover, spleen cells from mice immunized with 0.6 μg S3 did not suppress S3-specific IgG memory responses when they were cotransferred with S3-HRBC-primed spleen cells (H. Braley-Mullen, unpublished results). Thus there is presently no direct evidence that T_S play a role in this system. Since the amounts of S3 that suppress B_γ memory induction also elicit S3-specific primary IgM responses (2, 16), it is possible that antigen–antibody complexes (29), antibody (30), or autoantiidiotypic antibody (31) could suppress B_γ memory cell differentiation. Alternatively, the *in vivo* persistence of S3 (25) may induce an exhaustive differentiation of B cells to antibody-forming cells (1) or persisting antigen may bind to B-cell receptors and prevent their activation (4, 15, 32). Further studies, currently in progress, are needed to determine which of these mechanisms is responsible for the suppression of B_γ memory induction by the TI antigen S3.

The effect of S3 on mature S3-specific memory cells was also assessed in these experiments. These results indicate that both 0.6 and 5 μg S3 can suppress IgG memory responses when given to S3-HRBC primed mice 4 days before cell transfer (Fig. 5). Since low amounts (0.006 μg) of S3 are ineffective in the same situation (24), it would appear that the antigen dose requirements for suppression of mature memory cells are similar to those required for suppression of memory induction (Fig. 1). Since previous studies have shown that high-affinity (mature) B cells are more easily suppressed by DNP-S3 than are low-affinity (primary) B cells (15, 33), this observation suggests, but does not prove, that S3-specific memory cells may have a relatively low affinity for antigen as compared to B cells primed by hapten–protein conjugates such as DNP-KLH. When S3 was given to S3-HRBC-primed mice just 12 hr before cell transfer, only the 5-μg dose of S3 was able to suppress the IgG memory response (Fig. 5). This suggests that suppression by lower amounts (0.6 μg) of S3 is not due merely to blocking of B-cell receptors by antigen. Thus suppression of mature memory cells by 0.6 μg S3 could be mediated by T_S, by antibody, or by any of the other mechanisms discussed above for suppression of B_γ memory induction. By contrast, 5 μg of S3 suppressed mature memory cells within 12 hr (Fig. 5) so that high doses of S3 may directly block B-cell receptors

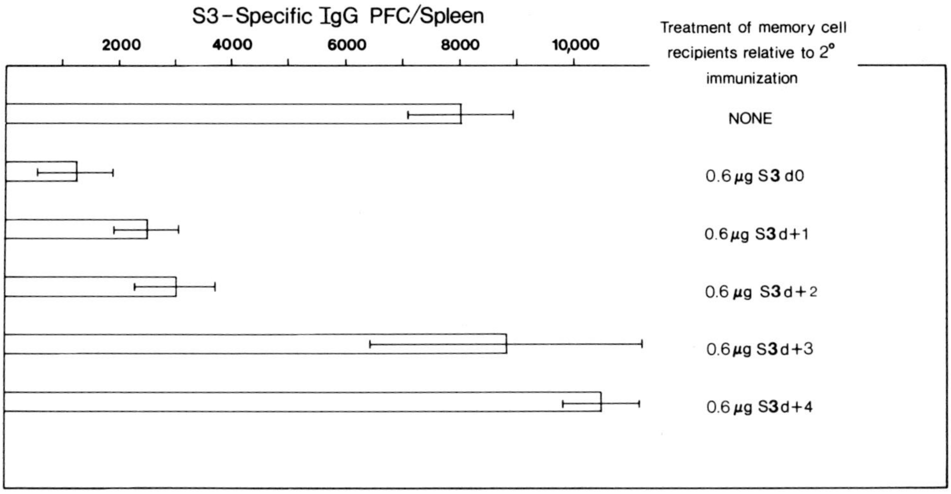

FIG. 6. Suppression of S3-specific Bγ memory cell expression by S3. Spleen cells (2×10^7) from donor mice primed with S3-HRBC were transferred to irradiated recipients. S3 (0.6 μg) was given to recipients on days indicated relative to secondary immunization with S3-HRBC. Values shown are mean IgG PFC/spleen ± SEM (four mice/group).

and prevent their activation. Indeed, blocking of B-cell receptors by DNP-S3 can prevent the expression of DNP-specific IgG memory responses (15).

S3 also suppressed IgG memory responses when given to recipients of S3-HRBC-primed speen cells at the same time as, or up to 3 days after, secondary challenge with S3-HRBC (Fig. 6). These observations are similar to those described previously for DNP-S3 (14, 15) and indicate that S3 is also an effective "blocker" of responding memory B cells. Since S3 given 3–4 days after S3-HRBC does not block the response (Fig. 6) the S3 is presumably acting on B cells which are undergoing differentiation to antibody-producing cells since typical effector cell blockade of antibody-producing cells should occur at any time up to the day of PFC assay (24).

Finally, the results presented here indicate that the TI antigen S3 is a potent tolerogen for S3-specific IgG-producing B memory cells and their precursors. Whereas TI antigens or haptens have been shown to suppress primary responses to TD forms of these antigens (24, 33, 35, 36) and often suppress or block mature memory cells ((4, 9, 13–15, 25, 33) Figs. 5 and 6), most TI antigens or haptens do not suppress B_γ memory *induction* (7, 36). The ability of S3 and PVP (13) to suppress B_γ memory induction is thus unique and suggests that these antigens may be of potential use in preventing the production of potentially harmful antibodies to determinants which could be attached to them. Indeed, hapten conjugates of PVP have recently been shown to suppress the production of hapten-specific IgE antibodies in mice (37).

ACKNOWLEDGMENTS

The authors thank Vicky Spate of the University of Missouri Research Reactor for irradiating the mice and Dianne Breedlove for typing the manuscript.

REFERENCES

1. Howard, J. G., *Transplant. Rev.* **8,** 50, 1972.
2. Baker, P. J., Stashak, P. W., Amsbaugh, D. F., and Prescott, B., *Immunology* **20,** 469, 1971.
3. Sharon, R., McMaster, P. R. B., Kask, A. M., Owens, J. D., and Paul, W. E., *J. Immunol.* **114,** 1585, 1975.
4. Lerman, S. P., Romano, T. J., Mond, J. J., Heidelberger, M., and Thorbecke, G. J., *Cell Immunol.* **15,** 321, 1975.
5. Lake, J. P., and Reed, N. D., *J. Reticuloendothel. Soc.* **20,** 307, 1976.
6. Braley-Mullen, H., *J. Immunol.* **116,** 904, 1976.
7. Braley-Mullen, H., *J. Exp. Med.* **147,** 1824, 1978.
8. Davie, J. M., and Paul, W. E., *J. Immunol.* **113,** 1438, 1974.
9. Romano, T. J., and Thorbecke, G. J., *J. Immunol.* **115,** 332, 1975.
10. Etlinger, H. M., and Chiller, J. M., *Cell. Immunol.* **33,** 297, 1977.
11. Braley-Mullen, H., *Eur. J. Immunol.* **7,** 775, 1977.
12. Braley-Mullen, H., *Immunology* **40,** 521, 1980.
13. Lite, H. S., and Braley-Mullen, H., *J. Immunol.* **126,** 928, 1981.
14. Mitchell, G. F., Humphrey, J. H., and Williamson, A. R., *Eur. J. Immunol.* **2,** 460, 1972.
15. Romano, T. J., Lerman, S. P., and Thorbecke, G. J., *Eur. J. Immunol.* **6,** 434, 1976.
16. Braley, H. C., and Freeman, M. J., *Cell. Immunol.* **2,** 73, 1971.
17. Braley-Mullen, H., and Sharp, G. C., *Cell. Immunol.* **12,** 49, 1974.
18. Baker, P. J., Stashak, P. W., and Prescott, B., *Appl. Microbiol.* **17,** 422, 1969.
19. Martin, W. J., and Miller, J. F. A. P., *J. Exp. Med.* **128,** 855, 1968.
20. Braley-Mullen, H., *J. Immunol.* **113,** 1909, 1974.
21. Janeway, C. A., *J. Immunol.* **114,** 1408, 1975.
22. Braley-Mullen, H., *J. Immunol.* **115,** 1194, 1975.
23. Julius, M. H., Simpson, E., and Herzenberg, L. A., *Eur. J. Immunol.* **3,** 645, 1973.
24. Braley-Mullen, H., *Cell. Immunol.* **37,** 77, 1978.
25. Humphrey, J. H., *Eur. J. Immunol.* **11,** 212, 1981.
26. Braley-Mullen, H., *J. Immunol.* **125,** 1849, 1980.
27. Inaba, K., Nakano, K., and Muramatsu, S., *Cell. Immunol.* **39,** 260, 1978.
28. Braley-Mullen, H., and Lite, H. S., *In* "B Lymphocytes in the Immune Response" (N. Klinman, D. Mosier, I. Scher, and E. Vitetta, Eds.), p. 401. Elsevier North-Holland, Amsterdam, 1981.
29. Tite, J. P., and Taylor, R. B., *Immunology* **38,** 225, 1979.
30. Brodeur, P. H., and Wortis, H. H., *J. Immunol.* **125,** 1499, 1980.
31. Schrater, A. F., Goidl, E. A., Thorbecke, G. J., and Siskind, G. W., *J. Exp. Med.* **150,** 138, 1979.
32. Klaus, G. G. B., and Humphrey, J. H., *Eur. J. Immunol.* **4,** 370, 1974.
33. Klaus, G. G. B., and Humphrey, J. H., *Eur. J. Immunol.* **5,** 361, 1975.
34. Schrader, J. W., and Nossal, G. J. V., *J. Exp. Med.* **139,** 1582, 1974.
35. Del Guercio, P., Poirier, M. F., and Thobie, N., *J. Immunol* **115,** 1239, 1975.
36. Merchant, B., Snippe, H., Lizzio, E. F., and Inman, J. K., *J. Exp. Med.* **147,** 1755, 1978.
37. Lee, W. Y., Sehon, A. H., and vonSpecht, B. U., *Eur. J. Immunol.* **11,** 13, 1981.

CELLULAR IMMUNOLOGY **64**, 187–191 (1981)

SHORT COMMUNICATIONS

Molecular Characterization of the Ly-6.2 Antigen[1]

LEIF C. ANDERSSON,* MIKKO HURME,† MICHAEL A. HORTON,‡,[2] ELIZABETH SIMPSON,§ AND CARL G. GAHMBERG†

**Transplantation Laboratory and †Department of Bacteriology and Immunology, University of Helsinki, Helsinki, Finland, and ‡Department of Haematology, St. Bartholomew's Hospital, London, and §Transplantation Biology Section, Clinical Research Centre, Harrow, Middlesex, United Kingdom*

Received April 10, 1981; accepted June 23, 1981

Lymphoid cells and cell lines from Ly-6.2-positive and negative mouse strains were surface labelled by the GO + NE-NaB^3H_4 technique. Immune precipitations were performed from membrane lysates with anti-Ly-6.2 alloantisera raised by immunization of (CBA/Ca × A-*Thy-1*^{a})F_1 mice with AKR/CRC lymphocytes. Sodium dodecyl sulphate–polyacrylamide gel electrophoresis analysis of the precipitates revealed that the Ly-6.2 specificity is carried by a single surface glycoprotein of 78,000 apparent molecular weight.

INTRODUCTION

The murine Ly-6 locus determines a cell surface antigen (1) for which two allelic specificities, Ly-6.1 and Ly-6.2 (2) have been defined. The Ly-6 antigen which originally was reported to constitute a selective T-cell marker (1) has been found on various cells and tissues also outside the T-lymphocyte system (3). There are apparent quantitative differences in the surface expression of the Ly-6 antigen on functional subsets of T lymphocytes and during various stages of T-cell differentiation (4–6). While only low Ly-6 activity was found on thymocytes (1, 5, 7) the activation of T killer cells coincided with an enhanced surface expression of Ly-6 antigens (4, 6).

The molecular nature of the Ly-6 antigen has not been defined. We have used anti-Ly-6.2 alloantiserum and performed immunoprecipitations from membrane lysates of surface-labelled lymphoid cell populations and cell lines of appropriate mouse strains. Here we report that the molecule carrying the Ly-6.2 specificity is

[1] This work was supported by Grant 1 RO1 CA 26294-O1A1 PBC from the National Institutes of Health, Bethesda, Md., and grants from the Academy of Finland, The Association of Finnish Life Insurance Companies, and the Finska Läkaresällskapet, Helsinki.

[2] A Wellcome Trust Senior Research Fellow in Clinical Science.

0008-8749/81/150187-05$02.00/0

a surface glycoprotein with an apparent molecular weight of 78,000 (GP78)[3] when analyzed by polyacrylamide gel electrophoresis under reducing conditions.

MATERIALS AND METHODS

Animals. Mice of the following inbred strains with indicated Ly-6 phenotypes were used: C57Bl/6 (Ly-6.2), DBA/2 (Ly-6.2), AKR (Ly-6.2), BALB/c (Ly-6.1), A (Ly-6.1), and CBA (Ly-6.1). In addition the Ly-6.2-positive thymoma cell lines, EL-4 (of C57Bl/6 origin) and BW5147 (of AKR origin), were studied.

Antisera. Anti-Ly-6.2 alloantiserum was raised by repeated immunization of (CBA/Ca × A-*Thy-1*^{a})F_1 hybrid mice with AKR/CRC lymphocytes as described (7). Anti-mouse IgG was produced in rabbits and the IgG fraction isolated by $(NH_4)_2SO_4$ precipitation and DEAE chromatography.

Purification and activation of lymphoid cells. Spleens were brought into single-cell suspensions as described and T cells enriched by passage over a nylon wool column (8). Alloactivated T cells were generated in one-way mixed lymphocyte cultures with T-cell-enriched spleen cells (2×10^6/ml) as responders and ($2–3 \times 10^6$/ml) mitomycin C-treated spleen cells as stimulators using RPMI 1640 culture medium supplemented with 5% fetal calf serum as described (9). The alloactivated T blasts were collected on Days 5–6 of culture.

Radioactive cell surface labelling. Lymphoid cells (MLC blasts, EL-4, BW5147 cells, or spleen cells (50×10^6) were washed in Dulbecco's phosphate-buffered saline (PBS) and surface labelled with ^3H using the NE-GO/NaB^3H_4 labelling technique (10). After labelling, the cells were washed and lysed at 0°C in PBS containing 1% Triton X-100, 2 m*M* phenylmethylsulphonyl fluoride and 1% ethanol. Nuclei were pelleted by centrifugation at 1000*g* for 5 min and the supernatants were recovered and used for immune precipitation.

Immune precipitations and SDS–PAGE. The labelled cell supernatants were divided into two equal aliquots and first treated with 5 μl of rabbit preimmune serum and 20 μl of packed protein A-containing staphylococci (strain Cowan I) (11) for 2 hr. All incubations were performed at 0°C. After centrifugation the supernatants were recovered and treated with either 5 μl of anti-Ly-6.2 antiserum or mouse preimmune serum for 2 hr. Then 5 μl of rabbit anti-mouse IgG (1 mg/ml) was added and the samples were further incubated for 1 hr. After addition of 20 μl of packed protein A-containing staphylococci, the incubation was continued for 30 min and the staphylococci were washed by centrifugation and the radioactive antigens eluted by boiling for 2 min in 1% sodium dodecyl sulphate. Polyacrylamide gel electrophoresis in the presence of sodium dodecyl sulphate was performed according to Laemmli (12) using an acrylamide concentration of 8% in the separating gel. ^{14}C-Labelled marker proteins were obtained from the Radiochemical Centre, Amersham. After electrophoresis the gels were fixed (13), treated for fluorography (14), and exposed at −70°C using Kodak X-Omat R film.

[3] Abbreviations used: GP78, surface glycoprotein with an apparent molecular weight of 78,000; GO, galactose oxidase; NE, neuraminidase; MLC, mixed lymphocyte culture; DEAE, diethylaminoethyl; SDS–PAGE, sodium dodecyl sulphate–polyacrylamide gel electrophoresis; PBS, Dulbecco's phosphate-buffered saline.

RESULTS

Figure 1B shows the fluorography patterns of labelled surface glycoproteins of C57Bl/6 MLC blasts activated against A spleen cells and electrophoresed on SDS–PAGE. Immune precipitations from the membrane lysates were carried out with anti-Ly-6.2 antiserum or with control preimmune serum and the precipitates run on parallel slots. The antiserum precipitated a single radioactive band with an apparent molecular weight of 78,000 (GP78) (Fig. 1C). No specific immune precipitate was obtained with the control serum (Fig. 1D). When membrane lysates from BALB/c blasts activated against A cells in MLC were performed no specific precipitation was obtained either with anti-Ly-6.2 antiserum or with control serum (Figs. 1E and F). When immune precipitation was performed from membrane lysates of surface-labelled unstimulated DBA/2 spleen T cells (the fluorography pattern shown in Fig. 1G), the 78,000 MW band was specifically obtained (Fig. 1H). Control serum did not precipitate any specific molecules (not shown). One single band was also obtained from membrane lysates of the Ly-6.2-positive T-cell leukemia line EL-4 (data not shown). The surface glycoprotein pattern of the cell line BW5147 is shown in Fig. 1I. The immune precipitation with anti-Ly-6.2 alloantiserum from the membrane lysate of this cell line (Fig. 1J) yielded two radioactive proteins, one with an apparent molecular weight of 78,000, apparently corresponding to that obtained from the MLC blasts, T cells of relevant mouse strains, and the EL4 cell line. The other had an apparent molecular weight of about 68,000 (GP68) (Fig. 1J). Neither of these bands was obtained with control sera (Fig. 1K).

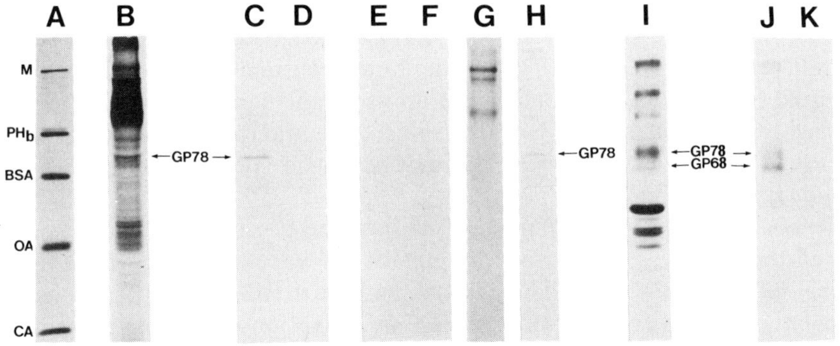

FIG. 1. Fluorography pattern of a polyacrylamide slab gel of Ly-6.2-positive T lymphoblasts and immune-precipitated Ly-6.2 antigen. (A) ^{14}C-Labelled standard proteins: M = myosin, PH_b = phosphorylase *b*, BSA = bovine serum albumin, OA = ovalbumin, CA = carbonic anhydrase; (B) pattern of C57Bl/6 (Ly-6.2) anti-A MLC blasts labelled with NaB^3H_4 after treatment with NE + GO; (C) immune precipitate obtained from ^{3}H-labelled C57Bl/6 MLC blasts with anti-Ly-6.2 antiserum. GP78 = the Ly-6.2 antigen with an apparent molecular weight of 78,000; (D) control with preimmune serum from an identical sample as in C; (E) control with anti-Ly-6.2 alloantiserum from ^{3}H-labelled BALB/c (Ly-6.1) anti-A MLC blasts; (F) control with preimmune serum from an identical sample as in E; (G) pattern of unstimulated DBA/2 spleen T cells labelled with NaB^3H_4 after treatment with NE + GO; (H) immune precipitate from ^{3}H-labelled DBA/2 spleen T cells with anti-Ly-6.2 antiserum; (I) pattern of the BW5147 cell line labelled with NaB^3H_4 after treatment with NE + GO; (J) immune precipitation from ^{3}H-labelled BW5147 cells with anti-Ly-6.2 antiserum; (K) immune precipitation with control serum from BW5147 cells.

DISCUSSION

Correlation between structure and function of lymphocyte cell membrane glycoproteins is of fundamental importance for understanding the molecular events occurring during cell activation and differentiation. The availability of highly inbred congenic mouse strains allows the production of antisera against surface molecules which express polymorphism. With the aid of such antisera, and recently also with monoclonal antibodies, a variety of surface molecules carrying differentiation antigens have been identified.

The Ly-6.2 antigen has been found on a variety of cells and also on some tissues outside the hematopoietic system. There are serological and genetic data (7, 15–17; F. Takei and M. A. Horton, submitted for publication) to indicate that the Ly-6.2 antigen might be identical, or at least closely linked to, the previously described alloantigens, DAG, Ala-1.2, and Ly-8, and a series of monoclonal antibody defined differentiation antigens, H9/25 (18), ThB (17), and Lym-6.2 (19). Whether these antigens are identical to one another or part of a tightly linked gene cluster is not at issue here, but clearly their molecular characterisation will be crucial to the solution of this question.

Here we show that the Ly-6.2 alloantiserum used in this study precipitates a surface glycoprotein of 78,000 apparent molecular weight, both on activated and resting murine lymphoid cells. It is likely that this membrane component represents the Ly-6.2 allospecificity, although immunoprecipitation of another, genetically linked, antigen with this serum cannot be excluded. The GP78 is rather weakly labelled and does not seem to comprise the major surface component of unstimulated T cells (Fig. 1G), but does increase on MLC stimulation (Fig. 1B). We and others have previously shown that blast activation of resting T lymphocytes results in the appearance of "new" surface labelled glycoproteins (13), but the Ly-6.2 antigen is, however, distinct from the "killer-T-cell specific" glycoprotein T-145 in the murine system (20) or GP130 in the human system (21). On the other hand, we reported a surface glycoprotein with an apparent molecular weight of 77,000, which was more strongly labelled after blast activation of resting lymphoid cells (13). This protein band might well correspond to the GP78 which carries the Ly-6.2 specificity.

While a single band was obtained after immune precipitation from membrane lysates of the EL-4 cell line, two distinct bands were obtained from the AKR thymoma cell line, BW5147. The reason for this is still unclear, but we assume that this might be due to variations in the glycosylation of surface proteins of the malignant cell line, which could explain the changed mobilities of the proteins on SDS–PAGE. However, the possibility that the alloantiserum used might contain contaminating antibodies to a further antigenic specificity (for example, an endogenous viral component) cannot be excluded.

REFERENCES

1. McKenzie, I. F. C., Cherry, M. and Snell, G. D., *Immunogenetics* **5,** 25, 1977.
2. Potter, T. A., McKenzie, I. F. C., Morgan, G. M., and Cherry, M., *J. Immunol.* **125,** 541, 1980.
3. Halloran, P. F., Dutton, D., Chance, H., and Cohen, Z., *Immunogenetics* **7,** 185, 1978.
4. Woody, J. N., *Nature (London)* **269,** 61, 1977.
5. McKenzie, I. F. C., and Potter, T. A., *Advan. Immunol.* **27,** 179, 1979.
6. Horton, M. A., Beverley, P. C. L., and Simpson, E., *Eur. J. Immunol.* **9,** 345, 1979.

7. Horton, M. A., Beverley, P. C. L., and Simpson, E., *Immunogenetics* **7,** 173, 1978.
8. Julius, M. H., Simpson, E., and Herzenberg, L. A., *Eur. J. Immunol.* **3,** 645, 1973.
9. Häyry, P., Andersson, L. C., Nordling, S., and Virolainen, M., *Transplant. Rev.* **12,** 91, 1972.
10. Gahmberg, C. G., and Hakomori, S.-I., *J. Biol. Chem.* **248,** 4311, 1973.
11. Andersson, L. C., Karhi, K. K., Gahmberg, C. G., and Rodt, H., *Eur. J. Immunol.* **10,** 359, 1980.
12. Laemmli, U. K., *Nature (London)* **227,** 680, 1970.
13. Gahmberg, C. G., Häyry, P., and Andersson, L. C., *J. Cell Biol.* **68,** 642, 1976.
14. Bonner, W. M., and Laskey, R. A., *Eur. J. Biochem.* **46,** 83, 1974.
15. Feeney, A. J., *Immunogenetics* **7,** 537, 1978.
16. Horton, M. A., and Sachs, J. A., *Immunogenetics* **9,** 273, 1979.
17. Eckhardt, L. A., and Herzenberg, L. A., *Immunogenetics,* **11,** 275, 1980.
18. Takei, F., Galfre, G., Alderson, T., Lennox, E. S., and Milstein, C., *Eur. J. Immunol.* **10,** 241, 1980.
19. Kimura, S., Tada, N., Nakayama, E., and Hämmerling, U., *Immunogenetics* **11,** 373, 1980.
20. Kimura, A., Wigzell, H., Holmquist, G., Ersson, B., and Carlsson, P., *J. Exp. Med.* **149,** 473, 1979.
21. Andersson, L. C., Gahmberg, C. G., Kimura, A. K., and Wigzell, H., *Proc. Nat. Acad. Sci. USA* **75,** 3455, 1978.

CELLULAR IMMUNOLOGY **64**, 192–199 (1981)

Expression of a 26,000-Dalton Glycoprotein on Activated Human T Cells[1]

THIERRY HERCEND,[2] LEE M. NADLER, JOHN M. PESANDO, ELLIS L. REINHERZ, STUART F. SCHLOSSMAN, AND JEROME RITZ

Division of Tumor Immunology, Sidney Farber Cancer Institute and Harvard Medical School, 44 Binney Street, Boston, Massachusetts 02115

Received May 22, 1981; accepted July 2, 1981

In the present study, we describe the expression of a 26,000-dalton glycoprotein on human T cells following stimulation by either mitogen or alloantigen. This glycoprotein, which is the target antigen of a monoclonal antibody designated J2, is distinct from Ia-like molecules and is not present on resting T cells. We demonstrate GP 26 expression in both major immunoregulatory subsets, i.e., T4$^+$ (inducer) and T8$^+$ (cytotoxic/suppressor) following activation and show that the GP 26-bearing cells are not directly responsible for the cytotoxicity generated in MLR. The relationship of the J2 target antigen to other glycoproteins with similar molecular weight which have been described on activated T cells is discussed.

INTRODUCTION

Cell activation has been shown to be an important aspect of the response of T cells to specific antigens or mitogens and results in the acquisition of specific functions. The characterization of antigens which appear on T cells during activation provides one method of studying the mechanisms involved in T-cell responses. In this regard, it has been previously shown that human T cells express Ia antigens following activation by a variety of stimuli. However, not all activated T cells express Ia antigens and it has been demonstrated that within the major immunoregulatory subsets, i.e., T4$^+$ (inducer) and T8$^+$ (cytotoxic/suppressor), there are subsets of cells which become Ia positive whereas others remain Ia negative (1–4). Subsequently, these phenotypic differences have been used to further separate cells within the T4$^+$ and T8$^+$ subsets, and functionally distinct subpopulations have been defined (12, 13).

In this report we examine the expression of a glycoprotein on activated T lymphocytes and describe some basic characteristics of the T cells which express this antigen. The molecular weight of this glycoprotein varies from 25,000 to 28,000 daltons depending on the conditions used to prepare it, and we designated it GP 26. In normal unstimulated peripheral blood, GP 26 does not appear to be present on lymphocytes, monocytes, granulocytes, or red cells, but is present on platelets.

[1] This work was supported by NIH Grants CA 28740, CA 19589, CA 25369, and AI 12069.

[2] To whom requests for reprints should be sent at: Sidney Farber Cancer Institute, 44 Binney St., Boston, Mass. 02115.

0008-8749/81/150192-08$02.00/0

This glycoprotein is recognized by several monoclonal antibodies recently developed as a result of immunization with leukemic cells from a patient with lymphoblastic leukemia (J. Ritz, submitted for publication). For the purpose of this study, we utilized one of these monoclonal antibodies designated J2.

MATERIALS AND METHODS

Monoclonal antibodies. The method for generation and characterization of a series of monoclonal antibodies specific for a 26,000-dalton cell surface glycoprotein is described elsewhere (19). Briefly, Balb/c mice were immunized with acute lymphoblastic leukemia cells and immune spleen cells were fused with NS-1 myeloma cells using polyethylene glycol as described by Kennett *et al.* (6). A series of monoclonal antibodies of different isotypes were found to have identical reactivity with ALL[3] cells and were found to be specific for a 26,000-dalton cell surface glycoprotein. One of these reagents, designated J2, was used in the present studies. J2 is a murine IgM antibody by standard typing reagents (Meloy Laboratories).

The specificities of other monoclonal antibodies Anti-T3, Anti-T4, Anti-T8 and I_2 (anti-Ia) have been described previously (7, 13, 18).

Isolation of lymphocytes populations. Human peripheral blood mononuclear cells were isolated from healthy volunteer donors by Ficoll-Hypaque density gradient centrifugation (Pharmacia Fine Chemicals, Piscataway, N.J.). Subsequently, lymphocytes were separated into E-rosette-positive (E+) and E-rosette-negative (E−) subpopulations by use of 5% sheep erythrocytes (Microbiological Associates, Walkerville, Md.) (4). Normal human macrophages were obtained from the E− population by adherence to plastic plates (4).

T-Cell stimulation by alloantigens, and mitogens. E+ cells were stimulated with either EB transformed B lymphoblastoid cells (mitomycin-treated Laz 388), phytohemagglutinin (4 μg/ml), or concanavalin A (12.5 μg/ml) as described (7). Culture medium was RPMI 1640 containing 20% AB human serum (American Red Cross Blood Services, Boston, Mass.), 1% sodium pyruvate (Grand Island Biological Company, Grand Island, N.Y.) and 1% nonessential amino acid mixture (Microbiological Associates). Cells were cultured in 75-cm^2 growth area tissue culture flasks (Falcon) at an initial concentration of 10^6 cells/ml. Five percent macrophages were added to the E+ cell suspensions at the initiation of the cultures.

Proliferative responses were measured by a ^{3}[H]thymidine incorporation test (4).

Cytofluorographic analysis. Cytofluorographic analysis of all cell populations were performed by indirect immunofluorescence with fluorescein-conjugated goat anti-mouse FAB IgG as described (4) on a cytofluorograph FC 200/4800A (Ortho Instruments). Background staining was obtained by substituting a 0.1-ml aliquot of 1:1000 ascites from a BALB/c mouse injected intraperitioneally with a nonspecific clone (designated J-0). Percentage of positive cells was calculated by subtracting the number of cells which were reactive with J-0 from the number reactive with specific antibody.

Plate technique for separation of T-cell subsets. A modification of the plate

[3] Abbreviations used: ALL, acute lymphoblastic leukemia; EB, Epstein–Barr; PBS, phosphate-buffered saline; PHA, phytohemagglutinin; Con A, concanavalin A; MLR, mixed lymphocyte reactions.

technique reported by Wysocki and Sato (7) was utilized to separate T-cell subsets. Briefly, plastic plates (Fisher Catalog No. 8-757-120) were coated with 10 μg of affinity-purified goat anti-mouse Ig in 10 ml of PBS and kept at 4°C overnight. The next morning plates were washed. T cells were incubated for 30 min with either anti-T4 or anti-T8 monoclonal antibodies, washed, and then 5×10^6 cells in a 3-ml volume were applied to a single goat anti-mouse Ig-coated plate. After 60 min of incubation at 4°C, supernatants were removed. In plates incubated with anti-T4-coated T cells, the nonadherent population contained less than 5% of $T4^+$ cells, similar purification was obtained with anti-T8-coated cells. Cells from these supernatants were respectively designated as $T8^+$ and $T4^+$ subsets.

Complement-mediated lysis of cultured E^+ cells. E^+ cells (20×10^6) were incubated for 1 hr at 4°C with 1 ml of antibody at the appropriate dilution. Subsequently cells were washed two times, and 0.4 ml fresh rabbit complement (1:2 dilution) added, and cells were incubated for an additional hour in a shaking water bath at 37°C. Cells were then washed once, layered on Ficoll–Hypaque, spun for 15 min at 1000*g*, washed twice more, and analyzed on the cytofluorograph.

Cell-mediated lymphocytoxicity. Cell-mediated lysis was performed in microplate assay. Laz 388 or K562 cells (5×10^6 of either) were treated with 0.2 ml sodium [^{51}Cr]chromate (292 Ci/ml) (New England Nuclear) and incubated in a 37°C shaking water bath for 90 min. Cells were washed twice and diluted to 10^5/ml. Labeled target cells (100 μl) were added to microplate wells with 100 μl of responding cells at various dilutions and incubated at 37°C for 6 hr. After incubation plates were spun for 5 min at 300*g* and 100 μl of supernatant was aspirated and counted on a gamma scintillation counter (Packard Instrument Co., Downers Grove, Ill.). Specific cytotoxicity and natural killer activity were calculated using the formula:

$$\text{Percentage specific lysis} = \frac{\text{Exp.} - \text{SR}}{\text{FT} - \text{SR}} \times 100,$$

where Exp. = mean of the observed triplicate, SR = spontaneous release, and FT = freeze–thaw.

RESULTS

Expression of GP 26 on Activated T Cells following Mitogen and Alloantigen Stimulation

The first goal of this study was to determine if GP 26 is consistantly expressed on activated T lymphocytes following various stimuli. For this purpose, E^+ cells were isolated from peripheral mononuclear cells from numerous healthy donors. T-Cell activation was induced by either mitogens (PHA and Con A) or alloantigens (Laz 388-EB virus-transformed B-cell line). Activated T cells were tested for expression of GP 26 7 days after the initiation of each culture. GP 26-bearing cells were found in 21 out of 22 experiments (Table 1). A similar percentage of GP 26-bearing cells was found following either PHA or Con A stimulation. In contrast, there were one third as many J2-reactive cells in MLR cultures. Although the mechanisms underlying this differential expression remain unclear, it is noteworthy since this was not observed with expression of Ia antigens. To the contrary, after 6 days of stimulation, MLR cultures contain greater percentages of Ia^+ cells than mitogen-activated cultures (4).

TABLE 1

Expression of GP 26 on Activated T Lymphocytes[a] 7 Days after Stimulation

Stimulation[b]	Number of cultures tested	Number GP 26-positive cells[c]	
		Mean% +	Range
PHA	12	33 ± 38	0–78
Con A	5	37 ± 21	8–52
LAZ 388[d]	5	12 ± 2	10–16

[a] Anti-T3 monoclonal antibody reacted with more than 95% of cells in each experiment.

[b] Agglutination, increased cell counts, and high [^{3}H]thymidine incorporation were used as activation criteria.

[c] Positive cells were identified by indirect immunofluorescence reactivity with J2 monoclonal antibody. 10.000 cells were analyzed on the cytofluorograph in each sample.

[d] Allogeneic EB virus-transformed cell line.

Kinetics of GP 26 Expression on PHA- and Alloantigen-Activated T Cells

Since it has been shown that the expression of membrane proteins on activated T cells varies dramatically with time (9), the observed difference between mitogen activated and alloreactive cells could have been due to differences in the time of expression of GP 26 following stimulation. Therefore, we investigated the kinetics of expression of GP 26 in both systems. E^+ cells from nine additional donors were stimulated either by PHA (6), or alloantigens (3) over a 10-day period. Each day cultures were tested for three parameters: (i) percentage of J2-positive cells; (ii) Number of viable cells/mm^3; and (iii) [^{3}H]thymidine incorporation. As shown in Fig. 1, the percentage of GP 26-positive cells found daily with each type of activation remained quite different, but the time of expression of GP 26 antigen was similar. With both mitogen and alloantigen activation, the percentage of J2-positive cells reached a peak on Days 5–6 and then decreased to Day 10. This peak correlated

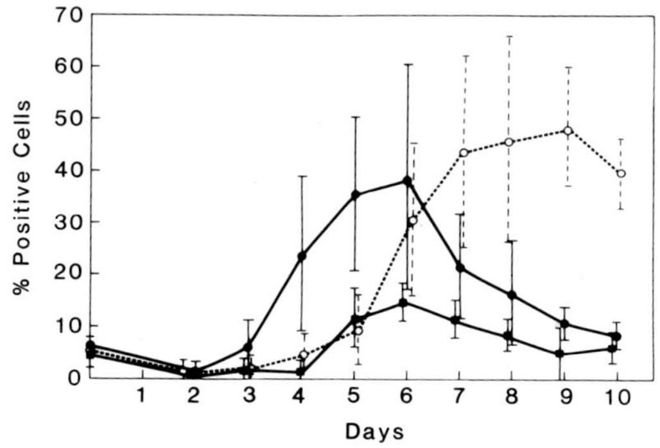

FIG. 1. Kinetics of GP26 expression on PHA-activated and alloreactive T cells. ● —— ●, Expression of GP26 on PHA-activated T cells. Each point represents the mean and SEM for six different cultures. ■ —— ■, Expression of GP26 on alloreactive T cells. Each point represents the mean and SEM for three different cultures. ○ - - - ○ = Expression of Ia-like molecules on PHA-activated T cells. Each point represents the mean and SEM for six different cultures. The small percentage of J2-reactive cells on Day 0 is due to platelets which are adherent to macrophages added at the initiation of the cultures.

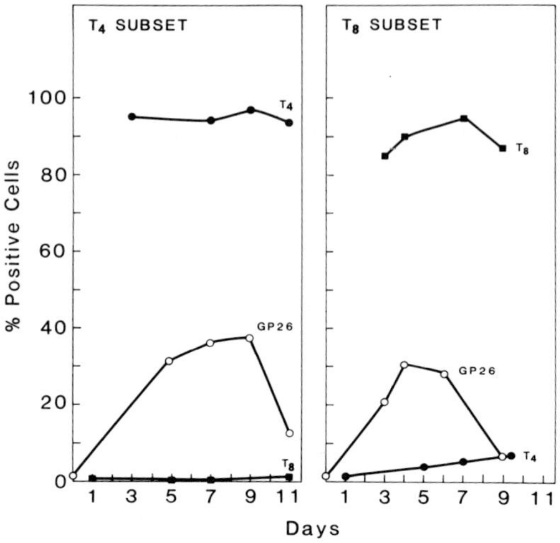

FIG. 2. Expression of GP26 in T4$^+$ (inducer) and T8$^+$ (cytotoxic/suppressor) subsets after PHA stimulation.

with the highest [^{3}H]thymidine incorporation which occurred on Days 5–6 but preceded the peak in cell counts which occured on Days 7–9. The range of expression (Table 1) and consequently the standard deviations (Table 1, Fig. 1) were very wide in PHA cultures but much tighter in MLR, which suggests strong individual variations in the response to this mitogen. In the six cultures stimulated by PHA, the expression of Ia-like molecules was also tested using the I_2 monoclonal antibody (18). As shown in Fig. 1, the pattern of expression of Ia antigen is quite different from that of GP 26.

Expression of GP 26 on both T4$^+$ (Inducer) and T8$^+$ (Cytotoxic/Suppressor) Cells following PHA Stimulation

To further characterize the GP 26-bearing cells, we separated E$^+$ cells in peripheral blood into two major functional subgroups: T4$^+$ (inducer) and T8$^+$ (cytotoxic/suppressor). Cells were separated using the plate technique described under Materials and Methods. Subsequently, T4$^+$ and T8$^+$ cells were each cultured for 10 days after PHA stimulation and expression of GP 26 in each subset was determined during this culture period. As shown in Fig. 2, similar percentages of GP 26-bearing cells were found in both cultures with the only difference being that there were 37% J2-reactive cells still present in the T4$^+$ subset on Day 9. Furthermore, these percentages were comparable to those obtained with whole E$^+$ cells (Fig. 1, Table 1). These results suggest that GP 26 expression in not strongly modified by T4–T8 cell interactions during mitogen induced T-cell activation. This was confirmed by further experiments in which PHA-activated E$^+$ cells were treated on Days 4 and 7 by either anti-T4 or anti-T8 plus rabbit complement, and subsequently analyzed on the cytofluorograph for GP 26 expression. The percentages of J2-reactive cells in the surviving populations, i.e., T4$^-$ (as T8 subset); T8$^-$ (as T4 subset), were similar to those shown in Fig. 2.

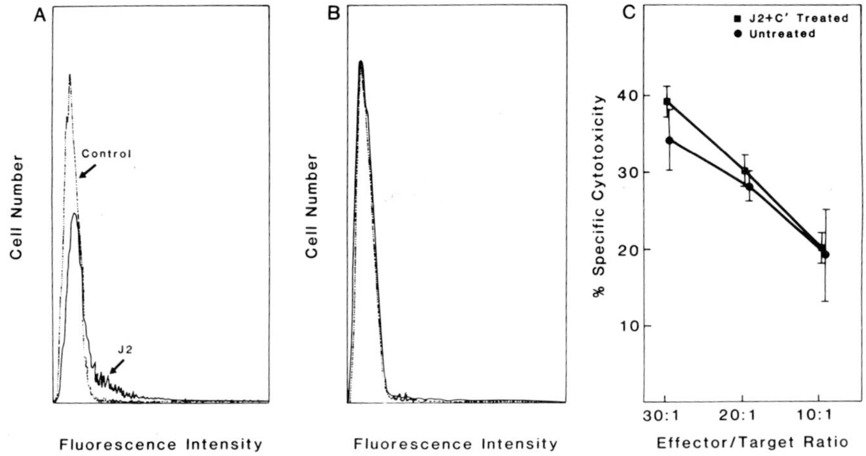

FIG. 3. Cytotoxic activity of 7-day MLR-activated T cells. Dotted line represents background fluorescence of control ascites and GM/FITC; solid line represents reactivity with J2 antibody. (A) Cytofluorograph analysis of reactivity of J2 with alloreactive T cells used in (C). (B) Cytofluorograph analysis of reactivity of J2 with alloreactive T cells following treatment by J2 plus rabbit complement, and subsequently used in (C). (C) Specific cytotoxicity of whole (●) and GP26-depleted (■) alloreactive cells against chromium labeled Laz 388 cells. Identical results were found in three different experiments.

Absence of GP 26 on Human Cytotoxic T Cells

As demonstrated above, $T8^+$ cells can express GP 26 following activation. Therefore, we studied the possibility that the cytotoxic cells generated in MLR, which have a controversial phenotype (11, 12), would be recognized by J2 antibody. E^+ cells were stimulated by the Laz 388 cell line in a one-way MLR and responding cells were assayed for cytotoxicity against chromium-labeled Laz 388 cells either directly or after treatment with J2 plus complement. As shown in Fig. 3, complement lysis removed any detectable GP 26-positive cells (B) and the surviving cells were slightly more cytotoxic (C) than the control (concentration effect). Identical results were found using K562 cells as targets (data not shown). These results indicate that activated T cells defined by a GP 26^+ phenotype are not directly responsible for specific cytotoxicity or natural killer-like activity (16).

Failure of J2 Monoclonal Antibody to Block T-Cell Responses

Finally, we investigated a possible functional role of the GP 26 molecule in a series of blocking experiments. A 1/100 dilution of J2 antibody added at the initiation of the cultures failed to block proliferation induced by either mitogens, alloantigens, or soluble antigens. This did not modify either generation of cytotoxicity in MLR or immunoglobulin secretion in a pokeweed mitogen driven system (data not shown).

DISCUSSION

The present study suggests that GP 26 is a monomorphic antigen which is present on activated T cells. Peripheral blood from more than 20 donors was examined and in all cases except one, J2-positive cells were found following stimulation; cells from the single negative donor were retested and in this subsequent examination, 15% of J2-positive cells were present on Day 4 but diminished to 2% of J2 positive on Day 7 following PHA stimulation. Thus, T cells from all donors tested thus far have been shown to express GP 26. In addition, our data demonstrate that following PHA stimulation, GP 26 is expressed earlier on activated T cells and is consequently distinct from Ia-like molecules. Although some characteristics of GP 26-bearing cells are demonstrated, the biological function of this molecule remains unknown. Kersey *et al.* (10) have recently identified a cell surface structure in leukemic cells from 77% of patients with null–ALL which has a similar molecular weight of 24,000 daltons. This protein, recognized by a monoclonal antibody designated BA-2, was thought to represent a surface marker of lymphohematopoietic progenitor cells in normal bone marrow. The reactivity of J2 with leukemic cells is very similar to that of BA-2 and it is possible that both antibodies are specific for the same surface molecule. The reactivity of BA-2 with activated T cells and platelets has not been described. In studies utilizing [^{35}S]methionine labeling techniques, Udey and Parker (14) have identified the synthesis of a family of 28,000 MW cell surface glycoprotein by Con A-activated T cells. This glycoprotein could also be similar to the target antigen identified by J2 antibody, although the kinetics of expression of GP 26 seems different since it was found on activated T cells within several hours of mitogen stimulation. In other studies (15), a 28,00 MW glycoprotein was identified 3–4 days after mitogen stimulation but the expression of this protein by activated T cells was relatively weak. Further studies will be necessary to determine the functional significance of the expression of this glycoprotein (or family of glycoproteins) in T-cell activation.

ACKNOWLEDGMENTS

We would like to thank Herb Levine and John Daley for assistance in performing these studies and Daniela Colangelli for preparing this manuscript.

REFERENCES

1. Evans, R. L., Faldetta, T. J., Humphreys, R. E., Pratt, D. M., Yunis, E. J., and Schlossman, S. F., *J. Exp. Med.* **148,** 1440, 1978.
2. Fu, S. M., Chiotazzi, Wang, C. Y., Montazeri, G., Kunkel, H. G., Ko, H. S., and Gottlieb, A. B., *J. Exp. Med.* **148,** 1423, 1978.
3. Socu-Foca, N., Sunsinmo, E., Kiernam, P., Rohowsky, C., Weiner, J., and Rubinstein, P., *Transplant. Proc.* **10,** 845, 1978.
4. Reinherz, E. L., Kung, P. C., Pesando, J. M., Ritz, J., Goldstein, G., and Schlossman, S. F., *J. Exp. Med.* **150,** 1472, 1979.
5. Reinherz, E. L., and Schlossman, S. F., *J. Immunol.* **122,** 1335–1341, 1979.
6. Kennet, R. H., Denis, R. A., Tung, A. S., and Klinman, N. R., "NIH Workshop: Lymphocyte Hybridomas." Bethesda, Md. (Springer, Berlin) pp. 77, 91, 1978.
7. Reinherz, E. L., Kung, P. C., Goldstein, G., and Schlossman, S. F., *Proc. Nat. Acad. Sci. USA* **78,** 4061, 1979.
8. Reinherz, E. L., Morimoto, C., Penta, A., and Schlossman, S. F., *J. Immunol.* **126,** 67, 1981.
9. Boto, W. O., and Humphreys, R. E., *J. Immunol.* **126,** 759, 1981.
10. Kersey, J. H., LeBien, T., Abramson, C. S., Newman, R., and Greaves, M., *J. Exp. Med.* **153,** 726, 1981.
11. Moretta, A., Mingari, M. C., Haynes, B. F., Sekaly, R. P., Moretta, L., and Fauci, A. S., *J. Exp. Med.* **153,** 213, 1981.

12. Reinherz, E. L., Hussey, R., and Schlossman, S. F., *Immunogenetics* **11,** 421, 1980.
13. Reinherz, E. L., Hussey, R., and Schlossman, S. F., *Eur. J. Immunol.* **10,** 758, 1980.
14. Udey, M. C., and Parker, C. W. *J. Immunol.* **126,** 1106, 1981.
15. Andersson, C., Gahmberg, C. G., Kimura, A. K., and Wigzell, H., *Proc. Nat. Acad. Sci. USA* **7,** 3455, 1978.
16. Seeley, J. K., Masucci, G., Poros, A., Klein, E., and Golub, S. B. *J. Immunol.* **123,** 1303, 1979.
17. Wysocki, L. J., and Sato, V. L., *Proc. Nat. Acad. Sci. USA* **75,** 2844, 1978.
18. Nadler, L. M., Stashenko, P., Hardy, R., Pesando, J. M., Yunis, E. J., and Schlossman, S. F., *Human Immunol.* **1,** 77, 1981.
19. Ritz, J., Pesando, J. M., Notis-McConarty, J., Lazarus, H., and Schlossman, S. F., *Nature (London)* **283,** 583, 1980.

CELLULAR IMMUNOLOGY **64**, 200 (1981)

ANNOUNCEMENT

Second Houston Symposium: Hybridomas and Cellular Immortality

Houston, Texas

November 5–6, 1981

The exploitation of hybridoma technologies and monoclonal antibody production is one of the most rapidly evolving areas of biological research. Because of the exponential growth of the information in this area, it is essential that investigators actively engaged in hybridoma research have frequent opportunities for personal in-depth interactions. Since this technology will find many applications outside of the domain of immunology and cell biology (for example, in expediting solutions to research problems in protein chemistry, virology, pharmacology, and indeed clinical investigations), it is thus important to disseminate current information on hybridoma approaches to a broad audience of biological scientists. This major goal of the present symposium will be promoted through a format which includes overview presentations on the background and development of specific areas, presentations of research results, and discussion of future trends. A poster session covering the same topics is scheduled to complement and expand upon the formal presentation and allow students, other investigators, and speakers to interact with each other.

The symposium will focus on three general areas: (1) the use of lymphocyte hybridomas in problems of B-cell and T-cell differentiation and function; (2) the use of monoclonal antibodies as potential reagents for cancer therapy and clinical diagnosis; and (3) the application of monoclonal antibodies and somatic cell hybrid systems which improve on the present technology.

For further information, contact

Ms. Sherry Smith
Office of Continuing Education
The University of Texas Medical School at Houston
6431 Fannin
Houston, Texas 77030
Telephone: (713) 792-5346

CELLULAR IMMUNOLOGY **64**, 201–202 (1981)

Papers to Appear in Forthcoming Issues

(Received and Accepted Dates Follow Title)

G. SEMENZATO, G. BASSO, U. FAGIOLO, A. PEZZUTTO, C. AGOSTINI, M. G. COCITO, AND G. GASPAROTTO. Active and Late Rosette Forming Cells: Immunological and Cytochemical Characterization. (Received 4/6/81; accepted 5/26/81).

MAREK ROLA-PLESZCZYNSKI. *In Vitro* Sensitization with HSV-Infected Cells Induces Tμ Cells to become Cytotoxic Tγ Cells which Are Theophylline-Resistant. (Received 3/20/81; accepted 6/6/81).

RUTH NETA, S. B. SALVIN, AND MOHAMED SABAAWI. Mechanisms in the *In Vitro* Release of Lymphokines. I. Comparative Kinetics in the Release of Six Lymphokines in Inbred Strains of Mice. (Received 3/16/81; accepted 7/7/81).

M. RUCHETON, J. CARAUX, C. THIERRY, C. ESTEVE, H. VALLES, J. DUFER, A. DESPLACES, D. ZAGURY, AND B. SERROU. Human Autologous Rosettes. II. Further Characterization: Markers and Functions. (Received 7/8/81; accepted 7/20/81).

ANTONINO CATANZARO. Suppressor Cells In Coccidioidomycosis. (Received 5/18/81; accepted 7/24/81).

JAN L. CEUPPENS, JAMES S. GOODWIN, AND ROBERT P. SEARLES. The Presence of Ia Antigen on Human Peripheral Blood T Cells and T-Cell Subsets: Analysis with Monoclonal Antibodies and the Fluorescence-Activated Cell Sorter. (Received 6/4/81; accepted 7/25/81).

WULF DROEGE. A Random Repertoire of V Genes for the T-Cell Receptors? Theoretical Implications of Recent Experimental Observations on T-Cell Specificity and Self-Restriction. (Received 5/29/81; accepted 7/25/81).

MAURO PIANTELLI, LIBERO LAURIOLA, NICOLA MAGGIANO, FRANCO O. RANELLETTI, AND PIERO MUSIANI. Role of Interleukins 1 and 2 on Human Thymocyte Mitogen Activation. (Received 5/22/81; accepted 7/27/81).

ROY H. L. PANG, Y. K. YIP, AND JAN VILČEK. Immune Interferon Induction by a Monoclonal Antibody Specific for Human T Cells. (Received 7/2/81; accepted 7/24/81).

MENACHEM SHLESINGER AND YVES BOREL. Stimulation of Prostaglandin E_2 (PGE_2) Secretion by Benzyl-penicilloyl (BPO) Carrier Conjugates in Human Peripheral Blood Lymphocytes. (Received 6/1/81; accepted 7/29/81).

DAVID S. CHI, NESTOR BLYZNAK, ARTHUR KIMURA, MICHAEL A. PALLADINO, AND G. JEANETTE THORBECKE. Cytotoxicity to Allogeneic Cells in the Chicken. II. Specific Cytotoxic T Cells and Macrophages in the Spleens of Agammaglobulinemic and Normal Alloimmune Chickens. (Received 5/22/81; accepted 7/30/81).

DAVID S. CHI AND G. JEANETTE THORBECKE. Cytotoxicity to Allogeneic Cells in the Chicken. III. Antibody-Dependent Cell-Mediated Cytotoxicity in Normal and Agammaglobulinemic Chickens. (Received 5/22/81; accepted 7/30/81).

DAVID M. GARAGIOLA, THOMAS K. HUARD, AND ALBERT F. LOBUGLIO. Comparison of Monocyte and Alveolar Macrophage Antibody-Dependent Cellular Cytotoxicity and Fc-Receptor Activity. (Received 6/12/81; accepted 8/9/81).

IGAL GERY, PHILIP DAVIES, JULIA DERR, NANCY KRETT, AND JOHN A. BARRANGER. Relationship between Production and Release of Lymphocyte Activating Factor (Interleukin 1) by Murine Macrophages. I. Effects of Various Agents. (Received 6/23/81; accepted 8/10/81).

FLORENCE M. ROLLWAGEN AND OSIAS STUTMAN. Culture Generated Suppressor Cells: Evidence for an Adherent Cell Component. (Received 2/18/81; accepted 8/19/81).

MARCONDES LIMA AND ROSS E. ROCKLIN. Histamine Modulates *in Vitro* IgG Production by Pokeweed Mitogen-Stimulated Human Mononuclear Cells. (Received 4/17/81; accepted 8/19/81).

STEPHEN H. LEECH AND MARIAM ALI. Low Dose Restriction in ir-Gene Control Reflects Susceptibility to Tolerance Induction. (Received 7/16/81; accepted 8/22/81).

REIKO M. NAKAMURA AND MONTE S. MELTZER. Macrophage Activation for Tumor Cytotoxicity: Control of Cytotoxic Activity by the Time Interval Effector and Target Cells Are Exposed to Lymphokines. (Received 7/7/81; accepted 8/30/81).

PNINA BRODT AND JULIUS GORDON. Anti-tumor Immunity in B Lymphocyte-Deprived Mice. II. *In Vitro* Studies. (Received 4/30/81; accepted 8/31/81).

HAIM OVADIA AND PHILIP Y. PATERSON. Cellular Transfer of Experimental Allergic Encephalomyelitis in Lewis Rats: Effects of Different Sensitization Regimens on *in Vitro* Reactivity of Donor Spleen Cells to Concanavalin A. (Received 7/7/81; accepted 8/31/81).

PETER C. DOHERTY AND ROBERT KORNGOLD. Effects of Cyclophosphamide and Cortisone on the Virus-Immune Response Characteristics of Thymocytes and the Early Reconstitution Profiles of P → F1 Chimeras. (Received 5/6/81; accepted 8/31/81).

CELLULAR IMMUNOLOGY **64**, 203–219 (1981)

Mechanisms in the *in Vivo* Release of Lymphokines[1]

I. Comparative Kinetics in the Release of Six Lymphokines in Inbred Strains of Mice

RUTH NETA,* S. B. SALVIN,† AND MOHAMED SABAAWI†

**Department of Microbiology, University of Notre Dame, Notre Dame, Indiana 64556, and †Department of Microbiology, School of Medicine, University of Pittsburgh, Pittsburgh, Pennsylvania 15261*

Received March 16, 1981; accepted July 7, 1981

Lymphokines were detected in the sera of 16 strains of inbred mice sensitized intravenously with cell walls of *Mycobacterium bovis* strain BCG and challenged subsequently intravenously with old tuberculin (OT). Variations occurred between the strains in the types and quantities of six lymphokines studied, namely, chemotactic factor (CF), type II interferon (IF II), lymphotoxin (LT), migration inhibitory factor (MIF), mitogenic factor (MF), and skin reactive factor (SRF). The times for maximum release of the lymphokines in the different strains were similar for MIF, IF II, SRF, and MF, but differed for CF and LT. The degree of activity of MIF and IF II generally paralleled one another in the different strains but such parallelism did not occur for the other four lymphokines. Each of the 16 strains was a high responder for at least one of the lymphokines, indicating that in sensitized mice the release or presence in the circulation of lymphokines in response to a specific antigen is a selective process. Thus, each strain may have an individual combination of lymphokines, interactions of which may determine the types of pathway utilized in an immunological response.

INTRODUCTION

Lymphokines are lymphocyte-derived soluble mediators of cellular immunity. They were originally described as products of sensitized lymphoid cells after *in vitro* stimulation with specific antigen (1, 2). Numerous investigations resulted in (a) description of various effects that these soluble mediators had on the cells of the immune and other body systems (3); (b) recognition that cells other than lymphocytes (stimulated or unstimulated), i.e., macrophages (4), fibroblasts (5), and various cell lines (6) produced soluble substances with properties similar to those of lymphokines; (c) the finding that stimulation of lymphoid cells *in vitro* with a variety of agents might result in efficient production of lymphokines (7); and (d) the accumulation of evidence that such lymphokines were important in the development of cell-mediated immunity (CMI) (8). Because of difficulties encountered in the separation and purification of various lymphokines, evidence for

[1] This work was supported by the Public Health Service, National Institute of Allergy and Infectious Diseases (Grant AI-16064) (S.B.S.) and by the American Lung Association and National Institutes of Health, IF 32CA 06519 (R.N.).

0008-8749/81/160203-17$02.00/0

their role in cell-mediated immunity has been limited to the demonstrations that lymphokine-enriched preparations can cause inflammatory responses (9), skin reactions (10), and rejection of certain tumors (11–13).

Lymphokine release was detected *in vivo* at the site of an immune response (14). However, it is still not known whether some or all of the known lymphokines are necessary for the normal functions of the immune system. Consequently, the question arises as to whether certain immunodeficiency diseases develop because one or several of the lymphokines are selectively not produced. Clinical data indicate a possible deficiency in the production of some and not other lymphokines in certain disease states (15, 16). Yet, limited information is available on similar differences in the production of inflammatory lymphokines in experimental animals (17).

In a previous report (18), evidence was presented that marked differences existed in the amounts of type II interferon (IF II)[2] and of migration inhibitory factor (MIF) released *in vivo* into the circulation of different inbred strains of mice after sensitization with cell walls of *Mycobacterium bovis* strain BCG and subsequent challenge with old tuberculin (OT). The occurrence of these variations introduced a possible means for (a) separation of the mechanisms of production of individual lymphokines and (b) studies of the role of the individual lymphokines in cell-mediated processes.

In this paper, evidence is presented that activities associated with such lymphokines as IF II, MIF, SRF (skin reactive factor), CF (chemotactic factor), MF (mitogenic factor), and LT (lymphotoxin) are not necessarily released *in vivo* in parallel to one another in time or in quantity.

MATERIALS AND METHODS

Mice. Outbred female Swiss Webster mice were purchased from Taconic Farms, Germantown, New York. Peritoneal exudate cells were harvested from these mice approximately 5 days after intraperitoneal injection of 5 ml light mineral oil. The 16 strains of inbred mice, purchased from Jackson Laboratory, Bar Harbor, Maine, were as follows: A/J, C57Bl/6J, C57Bl/10J, C57B1/10SNJ, C57L/J, Balb/cByJ, C57B1/KsJ, DBA/2J, Sec/1ReJ, CBA/CaJ, C3H/HeJ, AKR/J, RF/J, DBA/1J, SWR/J and SJL/J.

Antigens. Lyophilized BCG cell walls were prepared by and obtained through the courtesy of Dr. Edgar Ribi, Rocky Mountain Laboratory, Hamilton, Montana. The cell walls were ground in Drakeol, then emulsified in Tween 80–saline (19). Mice were sensitized by intravenous injection of 300 μg BCG cell walls in 0.2 ml, and 3 weeks later challenged intravenously with 50 mg old tuberculin (OT) in 0.2 ml, purchased from Jensen–Salsbury, Kansas City, Missouri. The mice were exsanguinated at varying intervals after challenge, and the sera removed for assay. "Zero" time refers to bleeding of sensitized, nonchallenged mice.

Purified protein derivative (PPD), obtained from either Parke, Davis & Company, Detroit, Michigan, or from the National Institutes of Health, Bethesda,

[2] Abbreviations used: BCG, *Mycobacterium bovis* strain BCG; CF, chemotactic factor; CMI, cell-mediated immunity; CW/Dr, cell walls of BCG in Drakeol–Tween 80 emulsion; IF II, type II interferon; LT, lymphotoxin; MEM, minimum essential medium; MF, mitogenic factor; MIF, migration inhibitory factor; MLR, mixed lymphocyte reaction; OT, old tuberculin; PE, peritoneal exudate; PPD, purified protein derivative of old tuberculin; SRF, skin reactive factor.

Maryland, was used for footpad testing for delayed hypersensitivity by injection of 30 μg in 0.05 ml in a hind footpad. A similar quantity of normal autologous serum was injected as a control into the other hind footpad.

Migration inhibitory factor (MIF). This lymphokine was titered by determining what dilution of experimental mouse serum resulted in an inhibition of 20% or more of the migration of peritoneal exudate cells on agar, in comparison with the effect of control serum from the same strain of inbred mice (20). The serum dilution (0.6 ml) was mixed with 2.4 ml of an agar medium containing medium 199, 0.5% Oxoid ion agar, and 100 units/ml of penicillin and 100 μg/ml of streptomycin at 45°C, all dispensed in a volume of 3 ml in a 30-ml Falcon flask. A small drop of packed peritoneal exudate cells was placed on the surface of the agar, and after incubation at 37°C for 48 hr the distance of migration was measured with the aid of a micrometer in a low-power microscope. The percentage of inhibition of migration was equal to

$$1 - \frac{\text{migration of PE cells in experimental serum}}{\text{migration of PE cells in control serum}} \times 100.$$

The reciprocal of the maximum dilution of experimental serum causing at least 20% migration inhibition was regarded as the titer of MIF activity.

Interferon. Interferon activity was determined by an assay involving the use of encephalomyocarditis (EMC) virus hemagglutination reduction yield (21). Here L-929 cells were cultured overnight in minimum essential medium (MEM) with 10% fetal calf serum in glass tissue culture tubes to form monolayers. The medium was decanted and the cells were washed twice with phosphate-buffered saline. The experimental and control sera were diluted 10-fold to obtain 10^{-2} to 10^{-6} dilutions of each serum in MEM containing 2% fetal calf serum. The tubes with the cell monolayers were inoculated in triplicate with 1 ml of each of the serum dilutions. After a 24-hr incubation period at 37°C, the medium was removed, cell monolayers were washed twice with phosphate-buffered saline, and 0.25 ml EMC virus (hemagglutination titer, 1:16,384) in a buffer containing 0.5% gelatin and 0.2% lactoalbumin hydrolysate in Hanks' solution was added to the monolayers. After 30 min incubation at 37°C, the infected cells were washed twice with PBS, fresh MEM with 2% fetal calf serum was added, and the tubes were incubated for an additional 18 hr. The virus was harvested by repeated freezing and thawing, and the titer was determined in a hemagglutination assay using human type "O" erythrocytes. The titer of interferon was expressed as a reciprocal of the serum dilution that produced a reduction of 0.5 log hemagglutination yield of EMC virus. Ten units of interferon in this assay was equivalent to 1 unit of a reference mouse interferon standard (obtained from The Antiviral Substances Program of NIAID, NIH).

Skin reactive factor. Serum (0.05 ml) from one of the inbred strains of mice was injected into a rear footpad of a normal Swiss Webster mouse; control serum was injected into one hind footpad, experimental serum, into the other hind footpad. The extent of swelling was then measured at 1/2-h intervals up to 4 hr postchallenge with the aid of a calipers-micrometer (Schnelltäster). An increase greater than 10% was considered to be indicative of a positive response. Histologic sections of appropriate footpads were made in order to determine the type of cellular infiltrate.

Tissues were fixed in 10% buffered formalin, embedded in paraffin, sectioned, and stained with hematoxylin and eosin.

Chemotactic factor. Chemotaxis was assayed by a technique involving the migration of adherent peritoneal exudate (PE) cells under agar (22). Here, one part of 5% agarose, i.e., 10 ml, was mixed with 5 parts, i.e., 50 ml, of the following medium: five milliliters medium 199 (10x), 0.5 ml 200 m*M* L-glutamine, and 100 units per 100 μg/ml penicillin–streptomycin, brought to 50 ml at 45°C with distilled water. Hepes buffer was added (1 *M*, pH 8.0) to adjust the pH to 7.2. Five milliliters of the agarose medium were added to each 60 × 15-mm tissue culture dish (#3002, Falcon Plastics, Oxnard, Calif.) and allowed to harden at room temperature before transfer to 4°C for at least an hour. With the aid of a template, a series of three wells, 2.4 mm in diameter and 2.4 mm apart, was cut into the agar and the plugs were removed with an 18-gauge needle.

Adherent peritoneal exudate cells were obtained by suspending 1×10^7 cells/ml in MEM containing 10% guinea pig serum in a petri plate for an hour at 37°C in 5% CO_2, decanting the supernatant, removing the adherent cells with a rubber policeman, then reconstituting the cells to 1×10^8/ml in a medium (Hanks' supplemented with L-glutamine) containing 1% human serum albumin. With the aid of an automatic pipet, 5μl of the cell suspension were placed in the center well, and either experimental serum or normal autologous serum placed in the outside wells. After incubation at 37°C in a CO_2 incubator for 18 hr. the cells were fixed by the addition of 3 ml absolute methanol for 30 min and stained with Wright's stain. Distances of migration were determined in a low-power microscope with the aid of an ocular micrometer cell. Results are presented as the difference in units of migration between experimental and normal autologous sera. Each unit represents 1.75 mm.

Mitogenic factor. The capacity of lymphokine-containing sera to stimulate cell replication was assessed with spleen cells from normal Swiss Webster mice. The lymphoid cells were recovered from the interphase of a Ficoll–Hypaque gradient of teased spenic cells (23). Of these cells 4×10^5 in 0.1 ml were cultured in each well of a microtiter plate containing medium RPMI 1640 with Hepes buffer, and 4% of either control serum or experimental serum. After 48 hr of incubation at 37°C in 5% CO_2, 1 μCi of tritiated thymidine was added to each well. Twenty-four hours later, the cells were harvested with a MASH II Systems Harvester (Microbiological Associates). The filter disks with the cellular material were placed in scintillation vials with 9 ml Econofluor, and the counts per minute of the samples was measured in a liquid scintillation counter. The data are reported as the stimulation index of triplicate samples, namely,

$$\frac{\text{cpm of cells in experimental serum}}{\text{cpm of cells in control serum}}.$$

Colony inhibition assay. In vitro-propagated PA III tumor cells (24) derived from the spontaneous prostate carcinomas of germ-free Lobund Wistar rats were removed from the monolayers by trypsinization in 0.25% trypsin solution. The cells were washed and counted and then suspended to a final concentration of 6×10^2/ml cells in MEM supplemented with 10% fetal calf serum. The suspension (0.45 ml) was distributed in tissue culture petri dishes (Falcon 3008). Normal control mouse sera and the assayed sera were added to make up the final concentration of 2.5% of the mouse serum. Cells in culture in triplicates were incubated for 5 or 6 days. The medium was removed and the cells were fixed in methanol and stained with 0.1% crystal violet solution. The number of cell colonies consisting of five or more cells was counted with the aid of a stereomicroscope. The data are expressed either as percentages of suppression of target cell growth (Table 1) or as percentages of cell growth in experimental serum in comparison with cell growth in control serum (Fig. 6).

RESULTS

Release of MIF

Sixteen strains of inbred mice belonging to six different H-2 haplotypes were assayed for their capacity to release MIF *in vivo*, after intravenous sensitization with 300 μg of cell walls of *M. bovis* strain BCG in Drakeol–Tween 80 emulsion (CW/Dr), intravenous challenge 3 weeks later with 50 mg old tuberculin (OT), and exsanguination 4 hr later (Table 1). This schedule was used, since maximum titers were obtained in Swiss Webster outbred mice at this time interval in previous experiments (25). The titers of MIF in the mouse sera varied from less than 4 to 256, depending on the strain. Four strains of the H-2^k haplotype and two of the H-2^q haplotype were low responders, i.e., had titers ranging from less than 4 to 16. Three strains of the H-2^b haplotype were high responders, in that their sera had MIF titers of 256; the sera of a fourth strain (C57L/J) had a titer of 16. Three of four strains of H-2^d haplotype had sera with titers of 64 to 256; the fourth strain, Balb/cByJ, varied in different experiments from less than 4 to 256 in its titer. The single strains belonging to the H-2^a (A/J) and H-2^s (SJL/J) haplotypes were high responders, with titers of 256 and 64, respectively.

The possibility was present that these differences were due to variations in the times for the release of maximum activities of MIF. Accordingly, 10 inbred strains of mice were assayed for their capacity to release MIF at times varying from 0 to 24 hr after challenge with OT. Five of the strains were high responders, i.e., A/J, C57Bl/6J, C57Bl/10SNJ, C57Bl/KsJ, and SJL/J, while five other strains were low responders, i.e., AKR, CBA/CaJ, C3H/HeJ, DBA/1J, and RF/J (Fig. 1). In all cases, maximum titers were obtained at approximately 4 hr post challenge.

Release of Type II Interferon (IF II)

The sera of 16 strains, obtained 4 hr after challenge, were also assayed for their contents of IF II after the mice had been appropriately sensitized and challenged (Table 1). The titers in the sera of these strains varied from less than 100 to more than 1,000,000. For example, the 4 strains of the H-2^k haplotype had titers of less than 100 to 21,000; the 2 strains of the H-2^q haplotype had titers of <100 and 11,500. Three of the four strains of the H-2^b haplotype had titers of about 1,000,000, while the fourth strain (C57L/J) had a titer of 14,000. Three of four H-2^d strains had titers higher than 100,000, while the fourth strain, Balb/cByJ mice, in one experiment, had a titer higher than 10,000; in another experiment, a titer of 2500, while in five other experiments the IF II titers were lower than 100. In studies on the time intervals after challenge for maximum release of IF II, the highest titers were found in the sera at 4 hr after challenge (Fig. 2).

TABLE 1

Activities of Six Different Lymphokines Released *in Vitro* into the Circulation of 16 Inbred Strains of BCG-Sensitized Mice 4 hr after Challenge with OT

Strain	H-2	MIF titer	IF II titer	SRF (% increase of swelling ± SE	CF (unit of migration ± SE)	MF (stimulation index ± SE)	LT (% cytotoxicity ± SE)
A/J	a	256	950,000	24.0 ± 0.5	0 ± 1.05	3.6 ± 0.3	84.4 ± 4.4
C57Bl/6J	b	256	500,000	13.7 ± 2.3	−7.5 ± 0.78	2.0 ± 0.4	32.4 ± 9.1
C57Bl/10J	b	256	1,300,000	25.9 ± 2.5	N.D.	N.D.	N.D.
C57Bl/10SNJ	b	256	1,100,000	17.0 ± 3.2	+1.81 ± 1.17	2.3 ± 0.64	N.D.
C57L/J	b	16	14,000	22.3 ± 2.1	N.D.	N.D.	N.D.
Balb/cByJ	d	32*	2,500*	24.3 ± 2.3	−3.12 ± 1.6	1.4 ± 0.2	15.6 ± 11.7
C57Bl/KsJ	d	256	1,300,000	30.6 ± 3.2	−4.68 ± 0.6	1.1 ± 0.32	−3.5 ± 9.2
DBA/2J	d	256	120,000	13.8 ± 0.5	0 ± 0	1.2 ± 0.37	N.D.
Sec/1ReJ	d	64	200,000	22.0 ± 2.2	N.D.	N.D.	N.D.
CBA/CaJ	k	16	19,500	13.0 ± 6.5	+3.0 ± 0.93	3.4 ± 0.7	39.1 ± 6.7
C3H/HeJ	k	4	850	<10	+0.68 ± 0.68	2.3 ± 0.5	N.D.
AKR/J	k	4	1,100	<10	0 ± 1.77	1.5 ± 0.46	48.8 ± 9.2
RF/J	k	<4	<100	N.D.	+1.5 ± 0.46	N.D.	10.0 ± 2.9
DBA/1J	q	<4	<100	16.8 ± 5.5	+4.17 ± 1.1	0.5 ± 0.21	N.D.
SWR/J	q	<4	11,500	23.8 ± 2.6	N.D.	3.6 ± 0.3	N.D.
SJL/J	s	64	260,000	31.9 ± 1.9	−1.25 ± 0.72	1.3 ± 0.2	78.8 ± 4.9

Note. See Materials and Methods for procedures for sensitization and challenge, units of migration and units of measurement. In each experiment, a pool of sera from 10 mice was used. Exclusive of strains SWR/J and C57L/J, the figures represent results from two to five experiments. * Indicates variable results, cf text. N.D., not done.

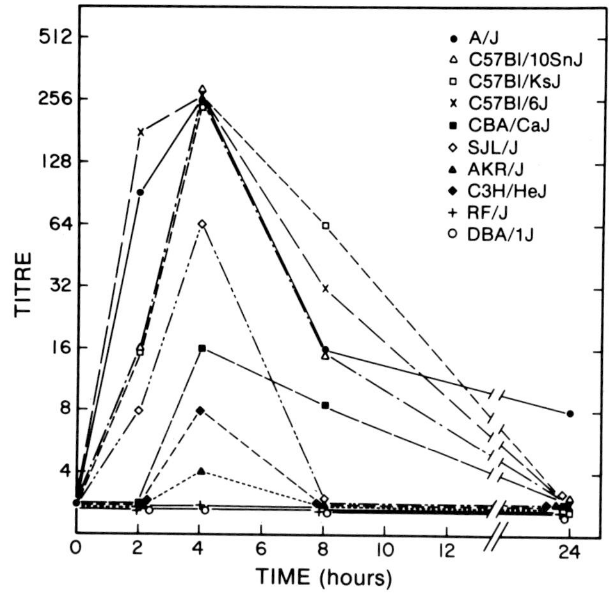

FIG. 1. Titers of MIF at different time intervals after challenge. Mice were sensitized intravenously with 300-μg cell walls of BCG in Drakeol–Tween 80 emulsion, and 3 weeks later challenged intravenously with 50 mg OT. A minimum of 10 mice was exsanguinated at varying time intervals thereafter. The titers are the reciprocal of the serum dilutions that inhibited the migration of normal peritoneal exudate cells by at least 20%.

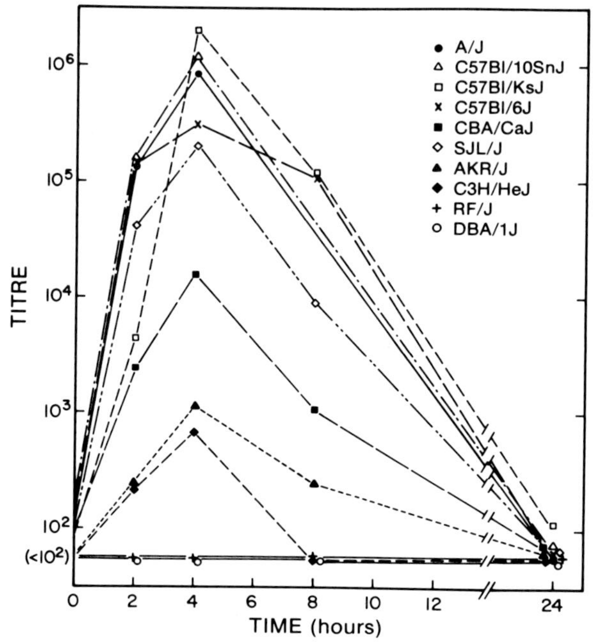

FIG. 2. Titers of IF II at different time intervals after challenge. See Fig. 1. The titers are the reciprocals of the serum dilution that produced a reduction of 0.5 log hemagglutination yield of EMC virus growth in L cells. Ten units of interferon in this assay was equivalent to 1 unit of a reference mouse interferon standard.

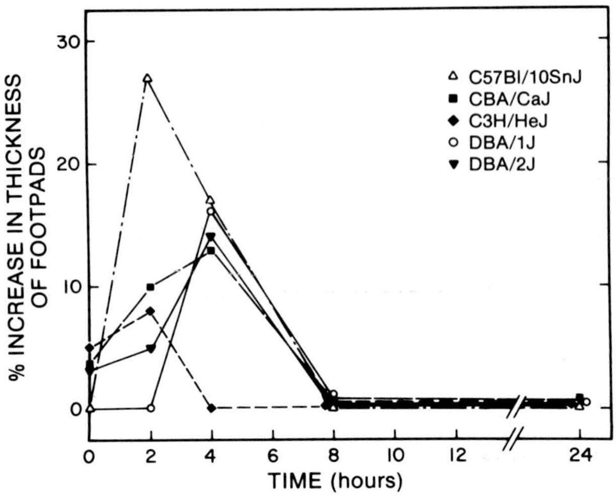

A

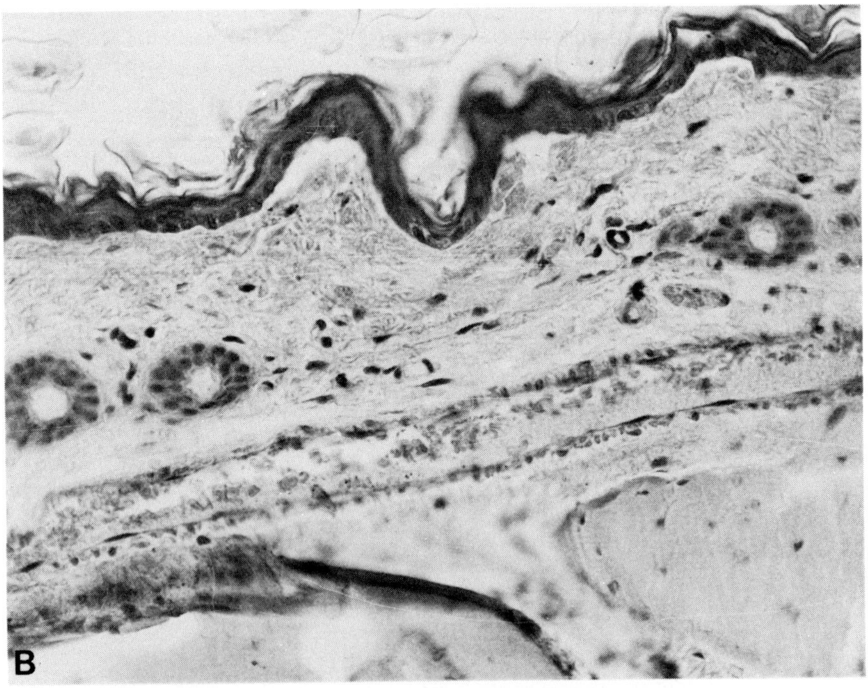

FIG. 3A. Extent of footpad swelling induced by sera obtained at different time intervals after challenge from five strains of inbred mice. See Fig. 1. The percentage increase in footpad thickness was obtained by comparing one hind footpad injected with experimental serum with the other hind footpad injected with control serum. A minimum of four mice was used for experiment.

FIG. 3B. Section of a footpad of a mouse inoculated with control serum from C57Bl/KsJ mice, and sacrificed 2½ hr later. ×750.

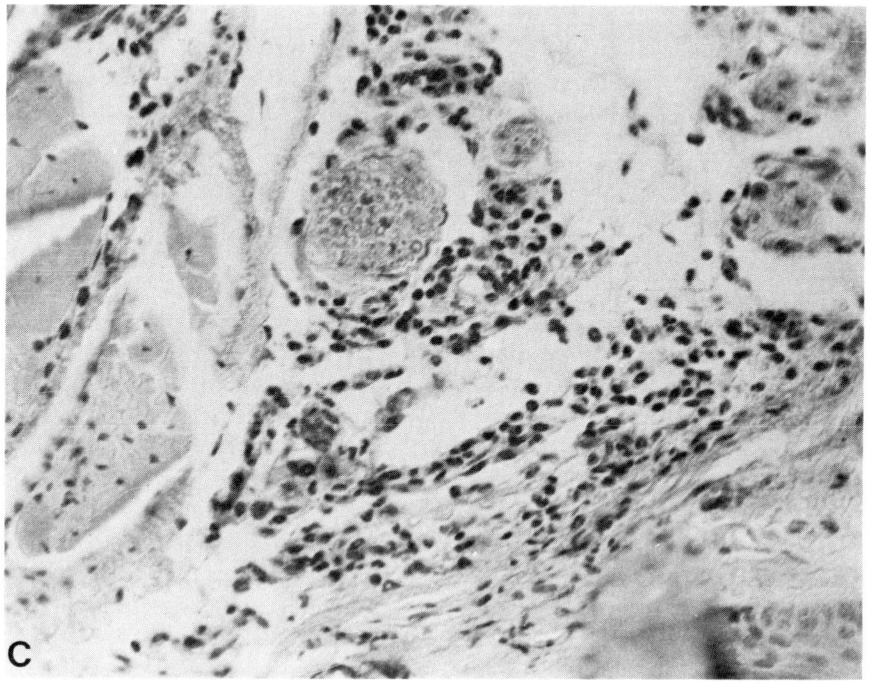

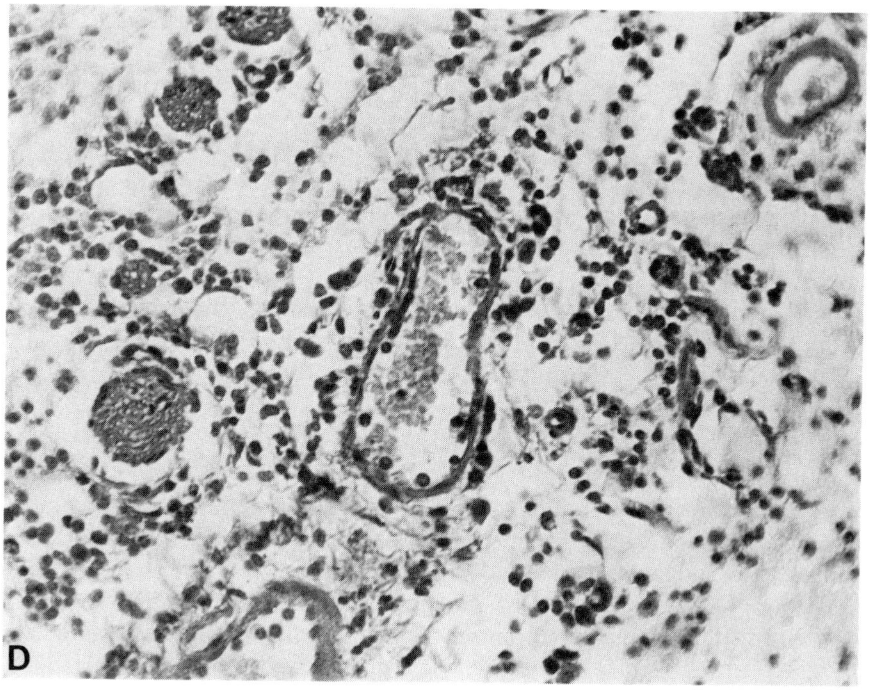

FIG. 3C. Section of a footpad of a mouse inoculated with lymphokine-containing serum of C57Bl/KsJ mice and sacrificed 2½ hr later. ×750.

FIG. 3D. Section of a footpad of a mouse actively sensitized subcutaneously with 300 μg CW/Dr, tested in the footpad 3 weeks later with 30 μg PPD, and sacrificed 24 hr later. ×750.

A striking parallelism was apparent in the different strains of mice in the quantities of IF II and MIF released *in vivo* into the circulation at varying times of exsanguination after challenge (Table 1; Figs. 1 and 2). The presence of low titers or the absence of detectable titers of IF II and MIF in the sera of AKR/J, C3H/HeJ, CBA/CaJ, RF/J, and DBA/1J strains at all times after challenge indicates the inherent inability of these strains to develop high titers of these two lymphokines under the conditions of experimentation.

Presence of Skin Reactive Factor (SRF)

Introduction of lymphokine-containing preparations intradermally results in an inflammatory reaction that resembles delayed hypersensitivity (10). What lymphokine, or lymphokines, is necessary for this reaction to develop has not been established. Because marked differences occurred in the amounts of MIF and IF II in the sera of the various strains of mice, experiments were initiated to determine whether a parallelism existed in the capacity of a given strain to release the two lymphokines and the capacity of the serum from that strain to induce an inflammatory skin response, presumably of the mononuclear or delayed type. Accordingly, outbred Swiss Webster mice were inoculated in one hind footpad with experimental serum and in the other hind footpad with control serum. Analysis of the footpad reactions by the sera of each of 15 strains of mice indicated that a correlation did not always exist between the presence of the two lymphokines in a serum and that of SRF (Table 1). Sera obtained from 13 of the 15 strains at 4 hr after OT challenge had the capacity to induce footpad reactions passively of more than 10%. Of sera from 6 strains that were low responders in the release of MIF and IF II and that were examined for skin reactivity, 2 did not induce footpad reactions passively, i.e., C3H/HeJ and AKR, and 4 did, i.e., DBA/1J, CBA/CaJ, SWR/J, and C57L/J. The maximum swelling developed with sera from bleedings at 2–4 hr post challenge (Fig. 3A). Of 2 strains that were low responders for MIF (4 or <4) and IF II (<100), *i.e.,* C3H/HeJ and DBA/1J, the sera from the C3H/HeJ mice did not induce responses at any of the times studied, while the sera from DBA/1J did induce swellings.

On histological examination, sections of the footpads of the mice which developed swelling of more than 10% had dense cellular infiltration, primarily of the mononuclear type (Figs. 3B, 3C, and 3D).

Release of Chemotactic Factor (CF)

Because of differences in the capacity of sera from low responder strains to induce skin reactions, experiments were conducted to determine the presence of chemotactic activity. At the same time, information would be obtained as to the possible parallelism in the release of MIF, IF II, SRF, and CF. Sera from the various strains obtained at different times after challenge were examined for their chemotactic activity. Unlike the patterns of activity for MIF, IF II, and SRF, maximum activity did not occur with sera obtained at a single period after challenge. Three types of patterns for chemotactic activity seemed to develop when the experimental sera were compared with normal autologous sera (Figs. 4A–C). In

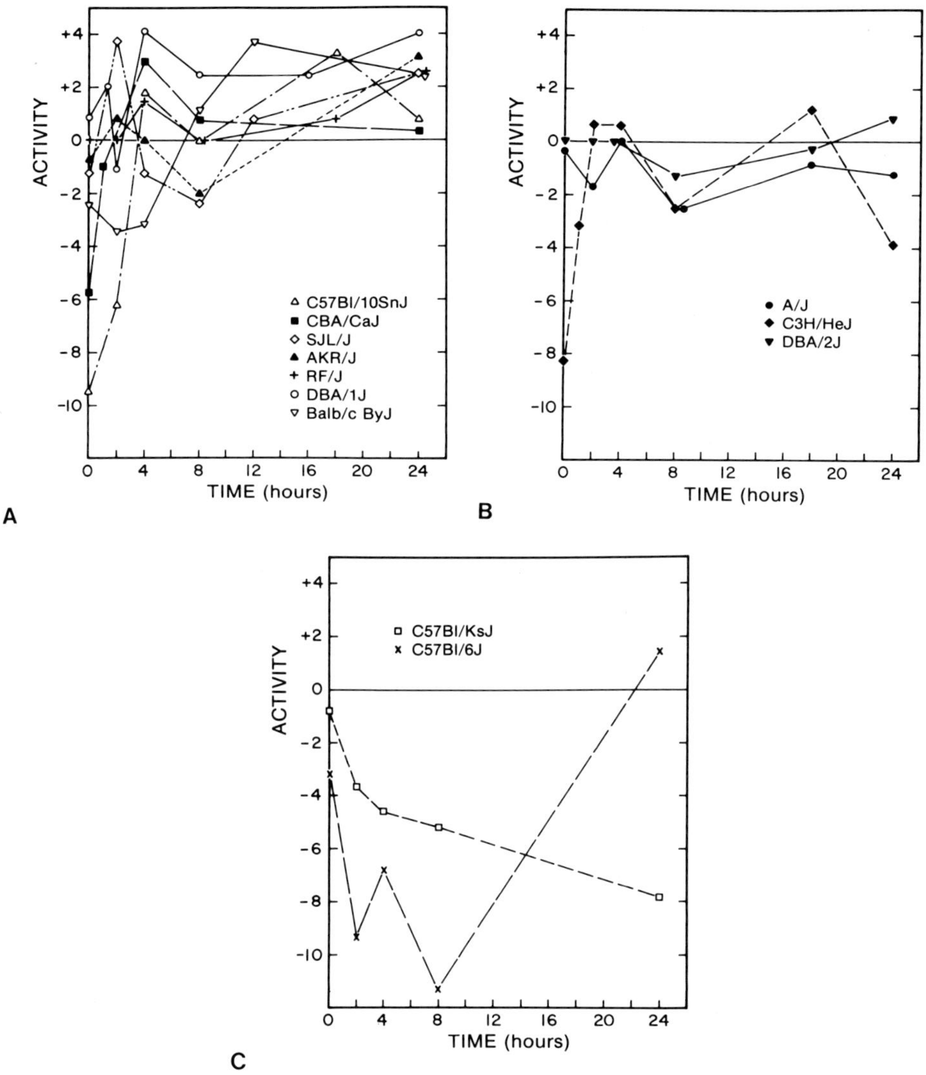

FIG. 4. (A–C) Chemotactic activity of sera obtained at different time intervals after challenge of 12 inbred strains of mice. Oil-induced peritoneal exudate macrophages were obtained from Swiss Webster mice. Numbers represent the average differences in units of cell migration between experimental and normal autologous sera. Each point represents an average of 10–12 readings. 1 unit = 1.75 mm.

addition, multiple peaks of activity appeared in some of the sera, thus indicating the possible presence of several chemotactic factors. Of sera examined from 12 strains, 7 indicated chemotactic activity at some period up to 24 hr postchallenge, namely, C57Bl/10SNJ, Balb/cByJ, AKR/J, RF/J, SJL/J, CBA/CaJ, and DBA/1J. Of the two inactive sera (AKR/J and C3H/HeJ) for induction of skin reactivity, one, AKR/J, had chemotactic activity. Also, a correlation did not exist between the capacity of a strain to release IF II and MIF into the circulation and the capacity to release CF *in vivo*. Of the low responders for MIF and IF II release, four strains had chemotactic activity, namely, AKR/J, CBA/CaJ, RF/J, and DBA/1J. Of the high responders for MIF and IF II, four strains did not have detectable quantities of CF in their sera, namely, A/J, C57Bl/KsJ, C57Bl/6J, and DBA/2J. Thus, it appears that, in a given strain, the capacity to release SRF, MIF, IF II, or CF is under separate genetic control.

Release of Mitogenic Factor (MF)

One of the characteristics of cell-mediated immunity and delayed hypersensitivity is the enhanced mitotic activity of sensitized lymphocytes in the presence of specific antigen. This increased lymphocyte replication is due in part to a mediator produced *in vitro* or *in vivo* by sensitized lymphocytes exposed to specific antigen. The question arises as to how the release of this factor (MF) *in vivo* is related to the release of other lymphokines (MIF, IF II, SRF, LT, and CF).

The degree of mitotic activity varied between the strains (Table 1) and did not correlate with the levels of MIF and IF II within a given strain. For example, C57Bl/KsJ, DBA/2J, and SJL/J, high responders in the release of MIF and IF, did not have mitogenic activity, while SWR/J and CBA/CaJ, low responders in the release of MIF and IF, had pronounced mitogenic activity.

When the sera from seven inbred strains were obtained at different times after challenge and examined for MF, the maximum activity was at 4 hr postchallenge (Fig. 5).

Release of Lymphotoxin

Another lymphokine, or group of lymphokines, associated with cell-mediated immunity and released by sensitized lymphoid cells after exposure to specific antigen, is lymphotoxin (LT), a substance inhibitory in low concentrations to cell growth and capable in high concentrations of lysis of selected cells (26). Experiments were initiated to determine what correlation existed, if any, in the release of LT with reference to other lymphokines in eight inbred strains. An analysis of sera obtained 4 hr after challenge indicated that the cytotoxic activities varied from strain to strain (Table 1, Fig. 6). A correlation did not exist with the high and low responder strains of the previously mentioned five lymphokines with regard to the degree of response and the time of maximum activity. Serum of a low responder mouse strain of MIF and IF II, such as CBA, was highly cytotoxic, in that a concentration of 1:40 caused 100% lysis of target cells (Fig. 6). On the other hand, high responder strains of MIF and IF II, such as C57Bl/6J and C57Bl/KsJ, did not show strong cytotoxicity in that a similar serum concentration reached a maximum lytic activity of only 57% at 24 hr after challenge. In addition, maximum cytotoxic activity of the sera from the various inbred strains developed at different times after challenge. For example, the sera from SJL/J mice had maximum cytotoxicity at 4 hr after challenge; sera from CBA/CaJ, A/J, and RF/J were at a maximum at 8 hr; and sera from C57Bl/6J and C57Bl/KsJ had maximum cytotoxicity at 24 hr. Therefore, LT, like CF, varies either in the kinetics of its release or in the appearance of its activity in the serum independently of the other lymphokines in the strains studied.

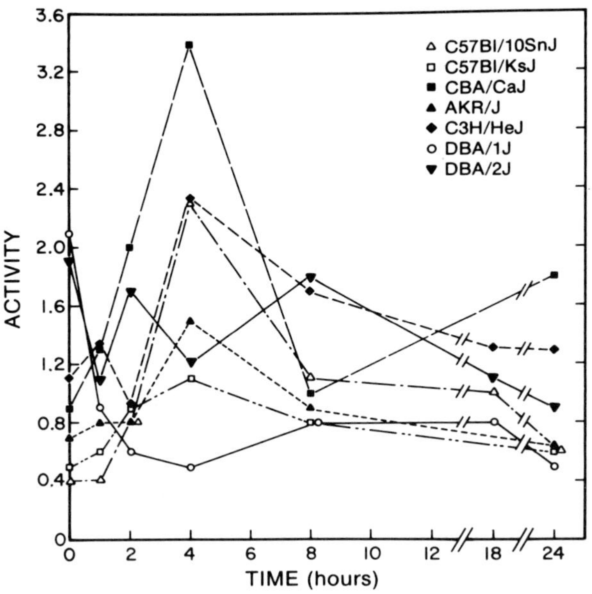

FIG. 5. Mitogenic activity of sera obtained at different time intervals after challenge of seven inbred strains of mice. Numbers represent the ratio of cpm from splenic cells cultured in experimental sera vs. the cpm of those cells cultured in normal autologous sera. The data are derived from two experiments.

DISCUSSION

Numerous reports have indicated that variations in cell-mediated immunity and in delayed hypersensitivity to microbial organisms or to purified antigens occur in different strains of inbred mice (27–29). Few studies, however, have been reported on similar variations in the production of lymphokines. Variations have been described in the release of MIF *in vitro* (30) and MIF and IF II *in vivo* (18) in different strains of inbred mice. In experiments on five strains of mice, splenic cells from two strains, namely, DBA/2 and C57Bl/6 challenged *in vitro* with either antigen or Con A, did not produce MIF (30). However, lymph node cells or peritoneal exudate cells from C57Bl/6 mice did produce MIF after challenge with Con A (31). Intravenous sensitization and challenge of the two above strains caused the release of high titers of IF II and MIF into the sera. Therefore, the capacity to release lymphokines in the spleen may be independent of the capacity to release such lymphokines in other lymphoid organs or into the circulation, possibly because of homing and sequestration of suppressor cells in the spleens (32).

The system to measure the release of lymphokines into the blood was chosen, since this release not only reflected immunologic events *in vivo* in the circulation but also occurred in parallel with the capacity of mice to develop resistance to challenge with virulent organsims (19). Mice sensitized with components of BCG in a manner that induced the capacity to release lymphokines into the circulation also had increased resistance to challenge with virulent H37Rv. In contrast, sensitization via the subcutaneous route or with components of BCG which did not induce the release of IF II and MIF *in vivo* did not produce enhanced resistance

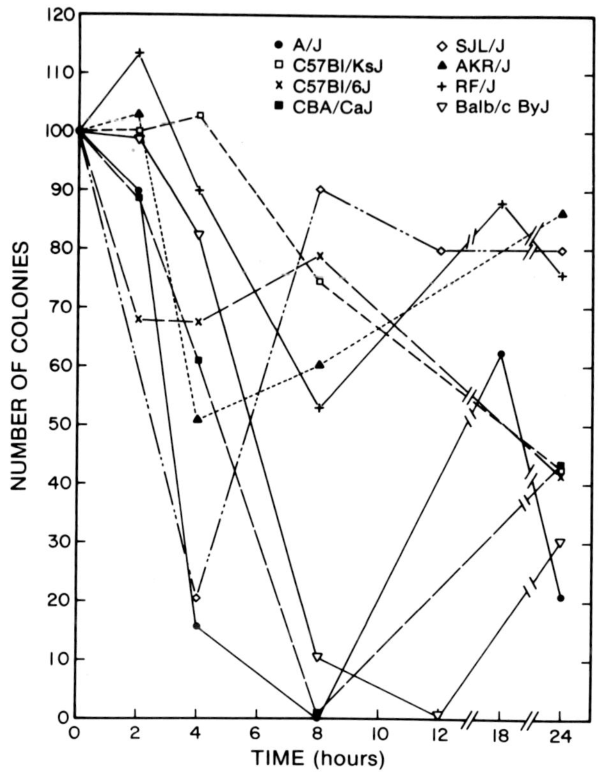

FIG. 6. Cytotoxic effect of sera from eight inbred strains obtained at different times after challenge. See Fig. 1 for conditions for obtaining the sera. Each point represents the number of colonies (percentage) of rat prostate tumor cells grown in 2.5% experimental serum, as compared with cells grown in control autologous serum. (Standard errors were less than 10%.)

to challenge with a virulent strain of *Mycobacterium tuberculosis*. Other experiments ((29), Neta and Salvin, unpublished results) also indicated that C57Bl/10SNJ and C57Bl/KsJ strains, which were high responders in the release of serum MIF and IF II, were resistant to infection with BCG or *Candida albicans*, while low responder strains, such as DBA/1 or C3H/HeJ, were highly susceptible to such infections.

In the present study of sera from 16 strains, 7 (not including Balb/cByJ, which will be discussed separately) had titers of IF II and MIF markedly lower than the titers in the sera of the other strain, i.e., titers of 16 or less for MIF, and less than 20,000 for IF II (Table 1). The maximal titers of IF II and MIF were detected in the sera of 10 strains of mice, 5 of which were low responders, when these mice were bled 4 hr after challenge (Figs. 1 and 2). The differences in the titers of MIF and IF II between mouse strains could not therefore be explained on the basis of different kinetics of their release in the blood.

Occasionally, production of some, but not all, lymphokines has been detected in a given human patient (15, 16). Yet, only few attempts have been made to observe a similar dissociation in the release of various lymphokines in experimental animals (33). The assumption has been that an appropriately sensitized animal can produce all of the known lymphokines after stimulation with specific antigen or with mitogen. The existence of strains of mice that can release different levels of IF II and MIF into their circulations provided a model to test this assumption. Therefore, other activities of lymphokines were examined in the same sera to determine possible correlation or dissociation of these lymphokines with MIF and IF II.

The activities of lymphokines in the sera of sensitized and challenged mice were determined by biological assays. However, the two lymphokines, MIF and IF II, released *in vivo* into the mouse circulation had been determined to have physicochemical properties similar to those of the *in vitro*-produced lymphokines ((34) Bout, David and Salvin, unpublished results). Rigorous definitions in terms of such physicochemical characteristics as molecular weight, electrophoretic mobility, density centrifugation, or sensitivity to specific inhibitors for other lymphokines were not included. The consideration of such characterizations would not make it possible to carry out the work in its present scope. In this regard (a) the challenge of normal mice of the same strain with OT did not result in the presence of detectable MIF, IF, SRF, MF or LT activities in the sera; (b) challenge of strains A/J, Balb/cByJ, C57Bl/KsJ, AKR/J, SJL/J, and DBA/1J previously sensitized subcutaneously with complete Freund's adjuvant did not result in the release of detectable quantities of IF or LT (R. Neta, unpublished data) despite the fact that such mice produced specific circulating antibody (35);[3] (c) heating of the sera to 56°C for 1 hr did not alter the activity of CF. Thus, involvement of the chemotactic components of complement becomes unlikely (36, 37). It may, therefore, be assumed that the presence of all the above activities is related to the function of sensitized lymphoid cells. While the absence of any given lymphokine activity in the presence of MIF and IF indicates (a) a possible selective defect in the release of such a lymphokine or (b) existence of different mechanisms regulating its presence in the circulation, the presence of these activities in the sera will require further confirmation as to their precise characteristics.

For example, the nature of SRF and CF activities in the sera of DBA/1J mice in which MIF and IF II activities were not detected requires further analysis. Similarly, further investigations will be required to determine the exact nature of the factors causing strong cytotoxicity in the sera of CBA/CaJ and Balb/cBy mice, which were low responders in the release of IF II and MIF. However, (a) lack of cytotoxic, chemotactic, or mitogenic activities in the sera of C57B1/KsJ mice, or (b) lack of mitogenic and chemotactic activities in DBA/2J or SJL/J mice, which were all high responders in the release of MIF and IF II, could not be related to the low sensitivity of the assays, since sera from DBA/1J, CBA/CaJ, and SWR/J mice were obtained under the same experimental conditions and responded in one or more of these assays.

The activities represented by MIF and IF II parallel each other in degree and in time of appearance after challenge, with the exception of Balb/cByJ (see Results). The variability in the titers of MIF in this strain may be the result of the activity of an inhibitory substance similar to that active against IF II (38). The lack of correlation in the presence of MIF vs IF observed in this strain may be explained by the existence of multiple molecular entities of these activities (39, 40), only some of which may be active in the circulation.

[3] R. Neta, S. B. Salvin, and D. C. Shreffler, *Manuscript in preparation.*

In some cases (e.g., C57Bl/KsJ and C57Bl/6J), migration of macrophages toward the experimental serum was less than that toward the autologous control serum. The possibility therefore exists that suppressor factors for chemotaxis may be induced under these conditions. Suppressor factors for chemotaxis have been reported in sera from normal and diseased humans (41, 42).

The significance of the capacity to develop high or low titers of lymphokines in the circulation with respect to the development of a variety of immunologic responses remains to be determined. For example, if lymphokines play an important role in protection, then differences in local vs systemic resistance (43) may be related to the level of responsiveness of individual lymphoid tissues. Such responsiveness would involve the release of particular lymphokines or pattern of lymphokines. The composition of the lymphokines would then determine the type of immune response.

ACKNOWLEDGMENTS

The authors thank Robert B. Propes and T. C. Schuler for their outstanding and valuable assistance in the laboratory.

REFERENCES

1. David, J. R., Al Askari, S., Lawrence, H. S., and Thomas, L., *J. Immunol.* **93,** 264, 1964.
2. Bloom, B. R., and Bennett, B., *Science* **153,** 80, 1966.
3. David, J. R., and David, R. R., *Prog. Allergy* **16,** 300, 1972.
4. Gery, I., and Waksman, B. H., *J. Exp. Med.* **136,** 143, 1972.
5. Tubergen, D. C., Feldman, J. D., Pollock, E. M., and Lerner, R. A., *J. Exp. Med.* **135,** 255, 1972.
6. Papageorgiou, P. S., Henley, W. L., and Glade, P. R., *J. Immunol.* **108,** 494, 1972.
7. Pick, E., Cohen, S., and Oppenheim, J. J., *In* "Biology of the Lymphokines" (S. Cohen, E. Pick, and J. J. Oppenheim, Eds.). Academic Press, New York, 1979.
8. Adelman, N. E., Hammond, M. E., Cohen, S., and Dvorak, H. F., *In* "Biology of the Lymphokines" (S. Cohen, E. Pick, and J. J. Oppenheim, Eds.). Academic Press, New York, 1973.
9. Andreis, M., Stastny, P., and Ziff, M., *Arthritis Rheum.* **17,** 537, 1974.
10. Bennett, B., and Bloom, B. R., *Proc. Nat. Acad. Sci. USA* **59,** 756, 1968.
11. Bernstein, I. D., Thor, D. E., Zbar, B., and Rapp, H. J., *Science* **172,** 729, 1971.
12. Papermaster, B. W., Holtermann, O. A., Rosner, D., Klein, E., and Dao, T., *Res. Commun, Chem. Pathol. Pharmacol.* **8,** 413, 1974.
13. Salvin, S. B., Youngner, J. S., Nishio, J., and Neta, R., *J. Nat. Cancer Inst.* **55,** 1233, 1975.
14. Neta, R., and Salvin, S. B., *Lymphokines* **2,** 295–308, 1981.
15. Chilgren, R. A., Meuwissen, H. G., Quie, P. G., Good, R. A., and Hong, R., *Lancet* **1,** 1286, 1969.
16. Kirkpatrick, C. H., Rich, R. R., and Bennett, J. E., *Ann. Intern, Med.* **74,** 995, 1971.
17. Boraschi, D., and Meltzer, M. S., *J. Immunol.* **125,** 777, 1980.
18. Neta, R., and Salvin, S. B., *Cell, Immunol.* **51,** 173, 1980.
19. Salvin, S. B., Ribi, E., Granger, D. L., and Youngner, J. S., *J. Immunol.* **114,** 354, 1975.
20. Salvin, S. B., and Nishio, J., *J. Immunol.* **103,** 138, 1969.
21. Jameson, P., Dixon, M. A., and Grossberg, S. E., *Proc. Soc. Exp. Biol. Med.* **155,** 173, 1977.
22. Nelson, R. D., Quie, P. G., and Simmons, R. L., *J. Immunol.* **115,** 1650, 1975.
23. Bøyum, A., *Scand. J. Clin. Lab. Invest.* **21:**Suppl. **97,** 51, 1968.
24. Pollard, M., *J. Nat. Can. Inst.* **51,** 1235, 1973.
25. Salvin, S. B., Youngner, J. S., and Lederer, W. H., *Infect. Immunity* **7,** 68, 1973.
26. Granger, G. A., Daynes, R. A., Runge, P., Jeffes, E., and Prieur, A. M., *Contemp, Top. Mol. Immunol.* **4,** 205, 1975.
27. Allen, E. M., Moore, V. L., and Stevens, J. O., *J. Immunol.* **119,** 343, 1977.
28. Cheers, C., McKenzie, I. F. C., Pavlov, H., Waid, C., and York, J., *Infect. Immunity* **19,** 763, 1978.
29. Nakamura, M. R., and Tokunaga, T., *Infect. Immunity* **22,** 657, 1978.
30. Adelman, N., Cohen, S., and Yoshida, T., *J. Immunol.* **121,** 209, 1978.

31. Kuhner, A. L., Cantor, H., and David, J. R., *J. Immunol.* **125,** 1117, 1980.
32. LaGrange, P. H., and Mackaness, G. B., *J. Exp. Med.* **148,** 235, 1978.
33. Wolstencraft, R. A., Bray, M. A., Dumonde, D. C., DeFranco, M. F., Hanson, J. M., Morley, J., and Smart, J. V., *Cell Immunol.* (Abstr.) **27,** 332, 1976.
34. Youngner, J. S., and Salvin, S. B., *J. Immunol.* **111,** 1914, 1973.
35. Neta, R., and Salvin, S. B., *Infect. Immunity,* in press, 1981.
36. Leonard, E. J., and Meltzer, M. S., *Cell Immunol.* **26,** 200, 1976.
37. Ward, P. A., Cochrane, C. G., and Müller-Eberhard, H. J., *J. Exp. Med.* **122,** 327, 1965.
38. Neta, R., *Cell Immunol.* **60,** 100, 1981.
39. Weiser, W. Y., Greineder, D. K. Remold, H. G., and David, J. R., *J. Immunol.* **125,** 1958, 1981.
40. Weiser, W. Y. Remold, H. G., and David, J. R., *Fed. Proc.* (Abstr.) **40,** 1001, 1981.
41. Berenberg, J. L., and Ward, P. A., *J. Clin. Invest.* **52,** 1200, 1973.
42. Ward, P. A., and Berenberg, J. L., *N. Engl. J. Med.* **290,** 76, 1974.
43. LaGrange, P. H., and Hurtrel, B., *Clin Exp. Immunol.* **38,** 461, 1979.

CELLULAR IMMUNOLOGY 64, 220–226 (1981)

In Vitro Sensitization with HSV-Infected Cells Induces T_μ Cells to Become Cytotoxic T_γ Cells Which Are Theophylline Resistant[1]

MAREK ROLA-PLESZCZYNSKI[2]

Division of Immunology, Department of Pediatrics, Faculté de Médecine, Université de Sherbrooke Sherbrooke, Québec J1H 5N4, Canada

Received March 20, 1981; accepted June 6, 1981

Following *in vitro* sensitization with HSV-infected cells, T_γ cells comprise most of the cytotoxic effector cell population. However, whereas freshly obtained T_γ cells exhibit theophylline sensitivity in the sheep erythrocyte rosette assay, presensitized T_γ cells are theophylline resistant. Similarly, when T cells are fractionated according to their theophylline sensitivity before the sensitization culture, theophylline-resistant T_μ cells appear as the precursors of T_γ cytotoxic effector cells, the T_μ–T_γ switch occurring with a transitory eclipse of Fc receptors, and maintenance of theophylline resistance.

INTRODUCTION

In recent years, human T cells have been shown to possess several surface markers which have permitted useful functional identification of various subpopulations. Thus studies by Moretta *et al.* (1) indicated that Fc receptors for IgM on T cells (T_μ) were associated with helper function in immunoglobulin production; on the other hand, Fc receptors for IgG on T cells (T_γ) were associated with suppressor function both in immunoglobulin production and in proliferative responses to mitogens.

Shore *et al.* (2) have reported that a proportion of T cells lost their ability to form E rosettes when pretreated with theophylline, whereas others did not, and that such a theophylline-sensitive T-cell subset contained most of the suppressive activity.

Recent studies from this laboratory have presented evidence that T_γ cells are the principal effector cells in *in vitro*-induced cytotoxicity against HSV-infected target cells (3). In this report, we present evidence that these induced effector cells develop from preexistent T_μ cells of peripheral blood, with a switch in Fc receptor affinity occurring during sensitization. In the newly generated T_γ population, theophylline sensitivity appears to be lacking, in contrast to T_γ cells freshly obtained from peripheral blood.

[1] Supported in part by a grant from the Medical Research Council of Canada (MA-6822).

[2] Scholar of the Conseil de la Recherche en Santé du Québec.

0008-8749/81/160220-07$02.00/0

MATERIALS AND METHODS

Donors. Blood donors were healthy adult volunteers with a negative history for herpes labialis or genitalis. All had antibodies against HSV-1, as measured by indirect hemagglutination (4), their titers ranging from 1:16 to 1:128.

Blood cell separation. Peripheral blood mononuclear leukocytes (PBML) were isolated from venous blood on a Ficoll–Hypaque gradient as described previously (3). These cells consisted of 70–90% lymphocytes and 10–30% monocytes, as determined by Wright–Giemsa staining and neutral red ingestion or phagocytosis of IgG-sensitized sheep erythrocytes (5).

Fractionation and identification of PBML subpopulations. Adherent and phagocytic cells were removed by incubating PBML for 2 hr at 37°C in glass petri dishes, followed by carbonyl iron treatment (6).

T cells were identified by their ability to form spontaneous E rosettes with neuraminidase-treated sheep erythrocytes.

T cells were separated from non-T cells by use of E rosetting as described by Moretta *et al.* (1). The rosetted mixture was centrifuged on a Ficoll–Hypaque gradient, and the T cell pellets were treated with distilled water for 10 sec to lyse red cells. Greater than 95% of the pelleted cells were T cells.

In order to identify a T-lymphocyte subset bearing receptors for the Fc portion of IgG (T_γ), 0.1 ml of purified T cells was mixed with a 2% suspension of ox erythrocytes coated with purified rabbit anti-ox erythrocyte IgG (7). The mixture was centrifuged to form a pellet and incubated at 37°C for 20 min. The pellet was then gently resuspended and the percentage of rosette-forming cells (T_γ) counted. Similarly, in order to identify T cells bearing receptors for the Fc portion of IgM (T_μ), purified T cells were incubated overnight in medium MEM with 20% fetal bovine serum (FBS). After incubation, 0.1 ml of T cells was added to 0.1 ml of 0.5% suspension of ox erythrocytes coated with purified rabbit anti-ox erythrocyte IgM (1). The mixture was spun into a pellet and incubated at 4°C for 45 min, followed by gentle resuspension and counting of rosetting T_μ cells.

In some experiments, purified populations of T cells were further fractionated into T_γ and T_μ subpopulations by forming T_γ rosettes with ox erythrocytes and pelleting the T_γ-enriched fraction through two successive Ficoll–Hypaque gradients. Nonpelleted cells contained approximately 70% T_μ with less than 3% T_γ cells. The pelleted fraction contained 90–95% T_μ cells. T_μ rosettes were found to be fragile for repetitive centrifugation and thus enriched fractions obtained through this method were not used routinely.

In order to identify theophylline-sensitive (Th_s) T cells, PBML were pre-treated with 5×10^{-3} *M* theophylline before rosetting with sheep erythrocytes, and the percentage of cells having lost their ability to form rosettes was called Th_s (2). In several experiments, Th_s cells (60% T_γ and 40% T non_μ, non_γ, in freshly drawn peripheral blood) were separated from theophylline-resistant (Th_r) T cells (95% $T\mu$, in freshly drawn peripheral blood) by treating purified T cells with theophylline before rosetting with sheep erythrocytes and pelleting Th_r through a Ficoll–Hypaque gradient (2).

Virus-infected cells. Cells used as sensitizing cells in the sensitization cultures or as target cells in the cytotoxicity assays consisted of the human prostatic adenoma MA-160 cell line, uninfected or infected with HSV-1 (MA-72064), kindly supplied by M. M. Vincent, Bethesda, Maryland. This cell line was originally derived from a male donor with the following HLA phenotype: HLA-A2, 28; B14, 17. Once established, however, the cell line showed no detectable HLA-A or -B antigens. All cells were grown and passaged as described (3).

Sensitization culture. In this paper, thc incubation of PBML (or fractions thereof) with uninfected or HSV-1-infected MA-160 cells in order to generate cytotoxic effector cells is referred to as sensitization.

PBML (or fractions thereof) at a cencentration of 2×10^6/ml were incubated with 5×10^5 sensitizing cells/ml in 2-ml aliquots as described previously (3). After the incubation period, PBML were removed, washed twice in Eagle's minimum essential medium and resuspended at the desired concentration in medium supplemented with 10% FBS. Viability was 85–95% by trypan blue exclusion.

Cytotoxicity assay. The ^{51}Cr-release cytotoxicity assay was performed as described previously (3). The amount of ^{51}Cr released was measured in a Nuclear Chicago gammacounter and expressed as average counts per minute (cpm) of triplicate samples. The percentage of specific ^{51}Cr release was determined as follows: (cpm of ^{51}Cr released from target cells with PBML during incubation − cpm of ^{51}Cr released from target cells alone during incubation)/(total releasable ^{51}Cr − ^{51}Cr released at zero time) × 100.

Statistical methods. Results were compared by using the two-tailed Student *t* test.

RESULTS

Theophylline Sensitivity and Fc Receptors of Presensitized Cells

We had previously found that sensitization with HSV-infected cells progressively induced the appearance of T_γ cells accompanied by a reduction in the proportion of T_μ cells (3). Since most freshly obtained T_γ cells are theophylline sensitive in the sheep erythrocyte rosette assay, we compared Fc receptor affinity and theophylline sensitivity at 3 and 6 days of incubation with HSV-infected cells. Table 1 presents our findings: whereas the T_μ subset was markedly reduced during sensitization, a similar proportion of theophylline-resistant T cells was found at initiation and at termination of sensitization.

Moreover, when the theophylline-resistant T-cell subset was characterized ac-

TABLE 1

Cell Markers of Human PBML at 0, 3, and 6 Days of Sensitization with HSV-Infected Cells

Period of sensitization (days)	Cell markers (% of PBML)[a]				
	sE-RFC	$T\gamma$	$T\mu$	Th_s	Th_r
0	74 ± 3	13 ± 2	56 ± 5	16 ± 3	60 ± 5
3	78 ± 6	23 ± 2[b]	14 ± 2[c]	6 ± 2	66 ± 6
6	82 ± 8	57 ± 3[c]	3 ± 3[c]	4 ± 2[b]	64 ± 5

[a] Mean percentage ± SEM of six separate experiments.

[b] $P < 0.05$.

[c] $P < 0.005$.

cording to its Fc receptor affinity for IgM or IgG, it was found that, whereas freshly obtained theophylline-resistant T cells are predominantly T_μ cells, most theophylline-resistant T cells express Fc receptors for IgG at the end of the sensitization period (Fig. 1; same cell population as in Table 1). Of interest was the observation that a substantial proportion of theophylline-resistant T cells exhibit neither Fc receptor at 3 days of sensitization, suggesting that the sensitization-induced switch of T_μ into T_γ theophylline-resistant cells is accompanied by a transitory eclipse of Fc receptors.

Cytotoxic Activity of Presensitized T Cells According to Their Theophylline Sensitivity

Since most cytotoxic activity of presensitized T cells had been shown to be mediated by T_γ cells (3), a first series of experiments was intended to determine theophylline sensitivity of presensitized cytotoxic effector lymphocytes. Figure 2 illustrates the observations that HSV-induced and directed cytotoxicity was found mainly in the theophylline-resistant subset of T cells. When T_γ cells were positively selected out of this latter subset, no cytotoxic activity was found in the remaining cells and all cytotoxic activity was recovered in the T_γ fraction.

Theophylline Sensitivity and Fc Receptors of Cytotoxic Precursor Cells

In a second series of experiments, we attempted to characterize the precursor cells responsible for *in vitro*-induced cytotoxic activity. Fresh E-rosetting T cells were separated into T_γ (positively selected) cells and T_μ (negatively selected) cells *before* sensitization with HSV-infected cells. Minimal cytotoxic activity was induced in the T_γ subset, whereas the T_μ-cell subset, containing approximately 20% T non_μ, non_γ cells, showed significant inducible virus-directed cytotoxicity (Fig. 3). Because of the fragility of T_μ rosettes, it was difficult to deplete adequately the T cell population of all T_μ cell, and thus the possibility remained that T non_μ, non_γ cells participated as cytotoxic precursor cells. Partial depletion in T_μ cells (T_μ < 25%, T_γ 30–40%, T non_μ, non_γ 30–40%), however, was accompanied by a marked drop (^{51}Cr release < 10%) in inducible cytotoxicity. Furthermore, when T cells

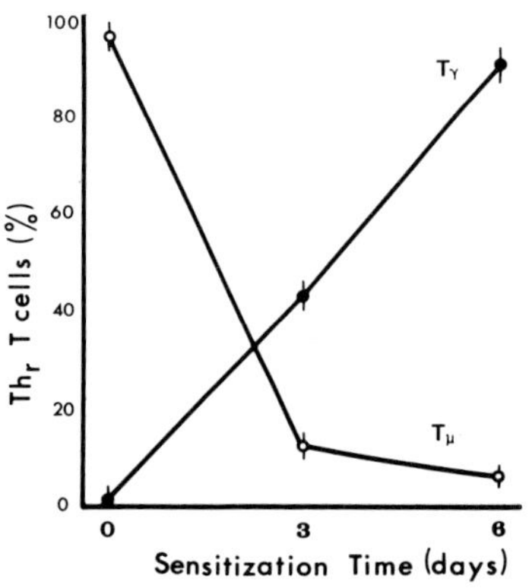

FIG. 1. Most fresh Th_r T cells were found to bear Fc receptors for IgM (T_μ). Sensitization with HSV-infected cells was accompanied by a switch of the Th_r cells to Fc IgG-receptor-bearing T_γ cells.

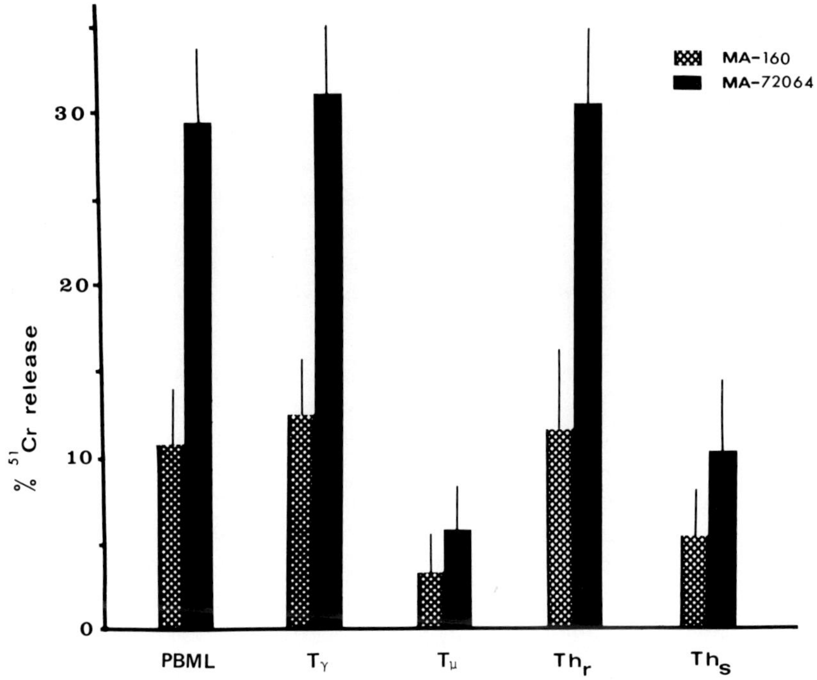

FIG. 2. Most of the HSV-directed cytotoxic activity was mediated by sensitized PBML enriched for T_γ or Th_r cells. Data represent mean ± SEM cytotoxicity of four separate experiments; after sensitization for 6 days, PBML were fractionated and reacted with either uninfected MA-160 cells or HSV-infected MA-72064 cells.

were separated into theophylline-sensitive (Th_s) and theophylline-resistant (Th_r) subsets *before* the sensitization culture, cytotoxic activity was induced principally in the Th_r subset, containing > 95% T_μ. The Th_s subpopulation, containing most T_γ and T non_μ, non_γ cells, failed to show significant inducible cytotoxicity, and positively selected T_γ cells wihin this Th_s subset were also nonreactive (data not illustrated).

It thus appears that the *in vitro*-induced cytotoxic effector cells result from the switch of the theophylline-resistant T_μ subpopulation into a theophylline-resistant T_γ subpopulation.

DISCUSSION

The present study was undertaken to further analyze the changes in effector cell population that occur during *in vitro* sensitization of human PBML with HSV-infected cells. The initial PBML population, freshly isolated from peripheral blood manifested the known predominance of T_μ and Th_r cells. At the end of the sensitization culture, however, most PBML were found to be T_γ. In contrast to fresh T_γ cells which are mainly comprised in the Th_s subset of T cells, sensitized T_γ cells were found to be Th_r. In fact, time-course kinetics showed a switch within the Th_r population from T_μ to T_γ during the sensitization culture. Such a switch from T_μ to T_γ cells has been observed in mixed leukocyte cultures and in mitogen stimulated

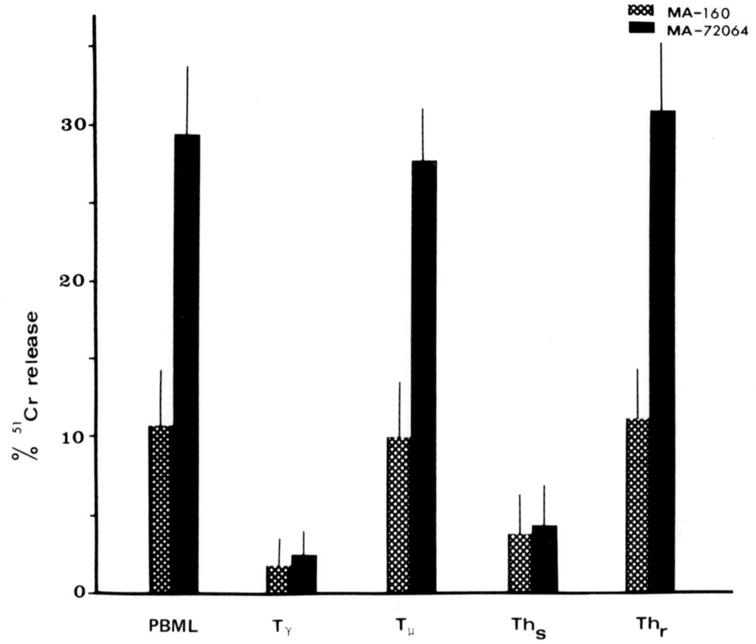

FIG. 3. When PBML were fractionated into T_γ and T_μ cells, and into Th_s and Th_r cells before sensitization, cytotoxicity was found to be mainly induced in T_μ-Th_r-enriched subsets. Data represent mean ± SEM cytotoxic activity of six separate experiments. After fractionation, PBML subsets were sensitized for 6 days and then reacted with either uninfected MA-160 cells or HSV-infected MA-72064 cells.

PBML (7). On the other hand, a reverse situation has been described by Pichler *et al.* where T_γ cells switched to T_μ cells after interaction with immune complexes (8). Our findings of theophylline resistance in this newly generated T_γ subpopulation suggest possible maturational changes within the sensitization process and reinforce the concept that the expression of FcIgG or FcIgM receptors represents different activational states of T cells.

Our previous work has suggested that T_γ cells were the principal effectors in the *in vitro*-induced cytotoxicity against HSV. The present study showed that the cytotoxic effector cell was Th_r. At that stage, it remained possible however that the cytotoxic T_γ-Th_r cell developed through expansion of the initial T_γ-Th_s subset. Additional experiments were carried out to show that separation of T cells into Th_s and Th_r *before* sensitization allowed for induction of cytotoxic effector cells only in the Th_r-T_μ subset, the Th_s-T_γ cells failing to show any significant, inducible cytotoxicity.

In summary, *in vitro*-induced cytotoxic effector T lymphocytes bear Fc receptors for IgG, develop from an initial pool of Th_r-T_μ cells, and retain the theophylline resistance of the latter.

ACKNOWLEDGMENTS

I am grateful to Mrs. Hien Lieu for excellent technical assistance, and to Miss Marie Braun for preparing the manuscript.

REFERENCES

1. Moretta, L., Webb, S. R., Grossi, C. E., Lydard, P. M., and Cooper, M. C., *J. Exp. Med.* **146,** 184, 1977.
2. Shore, A., Dosch, H.-M., and Gelfand, E. W., *Nature (London)* **274,** 586, 1978.
3. Rola-Pleszczynski, M., *J. Immunol.* **125,** 1475, 1980.
4. Fuccillo, D. A., Moder, F. L., Catalano, L. W., Vincent, M. M., Sever, J. L. *Proc. Soc. Exp. Biol. Med.* **133,** 735, 1970.
5. Rola-Pleszczynski, M., and Churchill, W. H., *J. Immunol. Methods* **20,** 255, 1978.
6. Lundgren, G., Zukoski, G. H. F., and Moller, G., *Clin. Exp. Immunol.* **3,** 817, 1968.
7. Moretta, L., A., Bacigalupo, A., Moretta, G. W., Canonnica, and Mingari, M. C. (B. Serrou and C. Rosenfeld, Eds.) Elsevier/North-Holland, Amsterdam 1980, in press.
8. Pichler, W. J., Lum, L., and Broder, S., *J. Immunol.* **121,** 1540, 1978.

CELLULAR IMMUNOLOGY **64,** 227–234 (1981)

Active and Late Rosette-Forming Cells: Immunological and Cytochemical Characterization

G. SEMENZATO, G. BASSO, U. FAGIOLO, A. PEZZUTTO, C. AGOSTINI, M. G. COCITO, AND G. GASPAROTTO

Department of Internal Medicine, 2nd Medical Clinic and Immunopathology Division, Department of Pediatrics, and 1st Medical Clinic, Padua University School of Medicine, Padua, Italy

Received April 6, 1981; accepted May 26, 1981

In order to characterize T-cell subpopulations with different affinities for sheep red blood cells, a possible correlation between active and late rosette-forming cells (RFC), expression of Fc receptors, and the presence of Ia antigens was investigated. Further analysis of their spontaneous *in vitro* DNA synthesis, and their cytochemical pattern was also performed. Most of the active T cells lacked Fc receptors and expressed Ia antigens, whereas the large majority of cells with Fc-IgG and -IgM receptors were included as late T cells, but lacked Ia determinants. Analysis of spontaneous blastogenesis showed that late RFC, but not active RFC, synthesize DNA in unstimulated cultures. Cytochemical analysis suggested that Active RFC display a more immature phenotype compared to late RFC, which have enzymatic markers present in mature T cells. Possible interpretations of these findings are discussed.

INTRODUCTION

In recent years evidence for the existence of human T-lymphocyte subpopulations responsible for certain immunoregulatory functions has been established using different approaches. These T cells have been subdivided on the basis of (i) different affinity for SRBC (1–3), (ii) presence of Fc-Ig receptors (4–5), and (iii) identification of surface antigens by means of hetero-, auto-, or alloantisera or monoclonal antibodies (6–8). The last two approaches attempted to define lymphocyte subsets with restricted *in vitro* activities (9–11), as was done in mice with the Ly system. On the other hand, different affinities for SRBC allow the identification of T-cell subclasses which may have a major clinical significance; the most reliable and promising assay appears to be the determination of active rosette-forming cells (A-RFC) which correlate better than total E Rosettes (T-RFC) with *in vivo* and *in vitro* T-cell function (12–16). In fact, both clinical (13–16) and experimental (12–17) studies demonstrate that the A-RFC represent a specific lymphocyte subpopulation which seems to be involved in certain immune defense mechanisms. However, the precise nature and function of these cells have not completely been determined so far. In particular, studies performed on isolated active and late (L-RFC) populations have been rather contradictory (18–21).

For a better characterization of T-cell subpopulations with different affinities for SRBC we have analyzed whether a correlation exists between active and late RFC and the expression of Fc-IgG or Fc-IgM receptors (T_G and T_M lymphocytes,

0008-8749/81/160227-08$02.00/0

respectively). In addition we have assayed these cell fractions for the presence of Ia antigens, for [^{3}H]thymidine incorporation in unstimulated cultures, and for their cytochemical pattern.

MATERIALS AND METHODS

Separation of active and late (or nonactive) E-rosette-forming cells. Lymphocytes from 10 normal donors between 25 and 47 years of age were isolated from peripheral blood as described by Böyum (22). Isolation of active (about 30% of T cells) and late (about 70% of T cells) E-rosette fractions by sedimentation of preformed rosettes on Ficoll/Hypaque (F/H) was assessed as follows. After removal of adherent cells from plastic petri dishes, nonadherent cells were mixed at room temperature with unsensitized SRBC (erythrocyte:lymphocyte ratio, 16:1) in round-bottom plastic tubes. The tubes were incubated at 37°C for 15 min and centrifuged at 200*g* for 5 min. Following centrifugation the pellet was immediately resuspended and layered on a F/H gradient. Two sequential centrifugations at room temperature for 20 min at 400*g* separated active E-rosette-forming cells which were recovered in the pellet after NH_4Cl lysis (>89% A-RFC; >96% E^+; <1% $SmIg^+$).

Nonactive T cells and non-T cells were carefully aspirated at the above gradient interface, washed twice, and then rerosetted by mixing with neuraminidase (Sigma, St. Louis, Mo.)-treated SRBC (erythrocyte:lymphocyte ratio, 100:1). The tubes were incubated for 15 min at 37°C, centrifuged at 200*g* for 5 min and incubated for 45 min at +4°C. After incubation the pellet was gently resuspended and rosette-forming cells were separated by two F/H gradients. Late T cells were obtained at the bottom of the second gradient and were depleted of SRBC by NH_4Cl treatment (<3% A-RFC; >95% E^+; <1% $SmIg^+$). The two populations so obtained (active E rosettes and late E rosettes) were resuspended in RPMI (Gibco Laboratories Grand Island, N.Y.) and processed as follows.

Viability of the cells in these populations was more than 98% as judged by trypan blue exclusion. Contaminating monocytes (less than 3%) were brought to light by latex ingestion and excluded from the counts.

Detection of Fc-IgG and Fc-IgM receptors. Ox RBC were washed three times in Hanks' solution and resuspended to a concentration of 2%. Equal volumes of ox RBC and purified rabbit anti-bovine erythrocyte IgG and IgM antibodies were mixed and incubated in ice for 30 min. Following incubation, cells were washed three times and resuspended to a concentration of 0.5% ox IgG (EA_G) and IgM (EA_M).

One hundred microliters of lymphocyte suspension was mixed with 100 μl of 0.5% EA_G and centrifuged at 200*g* for 5 min followed by incubation at 4°C for 20 min. The pellet was resuspended and 200 cells were counted. Each lymphocyte bearing three or more red cells was considered a rosette.

For optimal expression of Fc-IgM receptor the cells were incubated overnight in TC medium 199 supplemented with 30% FCS, penicillin (100 μg/ml), and streptomycin (100 μg/ml) at a concentration of 0.5×10^6 lymphocytes/ml at 37°C in a humidified incubator with 5% CO_2 and 95% air. At the end of the incubation the cells were washed three times in Hanks' solution and resuspended to a concentration of 2×10^6/ml. More than 96% of the cells were viable as tested by trypan blue exclusion. One hundred microliters of this suspension was mixed with 100 μl of 0.5% EA_M, centrifuged at 200*g* for 5 min, incubated at 4°C for 30 min, and resuspended very gently and rosette-forming cells were then counted.

T cells bearing Ia antigens. Ia^+ T cells were identified in T-lymphocyte-purified suspensions by indirect immunofluorescence using a mouse monoclonal anti-human Ia common-structure antibody (kindly provided by Dr. S. Ferrone). The features of this antibody (No. 513) are reported elsewhere (23). Briefly, 100 μl of T-lymphocyte suspension was mixed with 100 μl of monoclonal antibody (dilution 1:10) at room temperature for 30 min, washed three times, and incubated at 4°C for 30 min with 100 μl of rabbit anti-mouse fluorescein-conjugated IgG. After washing, determination of Ia^+ T cells was performed on 200 cells.

Spontaneous lymphocyte transformation. Spontaneous [^{3}H]thymidine incorporation was evaluated by the method partially described previously (24, 25). Briefly, triplicate cultures of 2×10^5 cells in 0.2 ml of RPMI 1640 (Gibco) containing 20% autologous serum were made in wells of V—bottom microplates. Neither fetal calf serum nor antibiotics were added. Cultures were incubated at 37°C in a CO_2 atmosphere for 5 days. DNA was quantified by incorporation of 0.5 μCi [^{3}H]thymidine (CEA IRE Sorin, sp act 26 mCi/mmol) in 20 μl of medium for the last 6 hr of culture. Cultures were harvested with a multiple-automated sample harvester (Sacrificator, Laboratories Eurobio, Paris). Counts per minute was determined in a Packard liquid scintillation counter. The results are expressed as the mean counts per minute per 10^5 lymphocytes of triplicate tubes ± SEM.

Cytochemical stains. The smears were made from the cell suspension by using a cytocentrifuge (Shandon-Elliot) at 300 rpm for 10 min. Acid phosphatase (AcP), α-naphthyl acetate esterase (ANAE) (pH 5.8), β-glucuronidase (BG), α-naphthyl acetate esterase (NAE) (pH 7.4), α-naphthyl butyrate esterase (NBE) and *N*-acetyl-β-glucuronidase (NABG) were detected and evaluated by methods and criteria previously described (26).

The results are expressed as the mean ± SEM. Student's *t* test was used to estimate the significance.

RESULTS

Figure 1 shows that the cells positive for Fc-IgG receptors are mostly present in the cell fraction with low affinity for the SRBC, while the population enriched in active E rosettes contains a very low proportion of T_M and T_G cells. The difference observed in the distribution of T_G and T_M cells in the two populations is statistically significant (T_G cells present in A-RFC- and L-RFC-enriched populations were 6.3 ± 0.6 and 30.6 ± 3.5%, respectively, $P < 0.001$; T_M cells present were 27.6 ± 2.7 and 62.0 ± 3.2%, respectively, $P < 0.001$).

Ia^+ T cells were mostly detected in the A-RFC population (Fig. 2), whereas L-RFC lacked these antigens (A-RFC: 9.2%, L-RFC: 1.7%; $P < 0.001$).

Spontaneous DNA synthesis (Table 1) appears to be restricted to the late rosette-forming cells (2.592 ± 57 cpm/2×10^5 cells). Active rosette-forming T cells, on the other hand, show a very low [^{3}H]thymidine uptake (300 ± 92 cpm/2×10^5 cells; $P < 0.001$).

Table 2 summarizes the cytochemical analysis. AcP, BG, ANAE, and NABG reactions were highly positive in both RFC populations. On the other hand, dif-

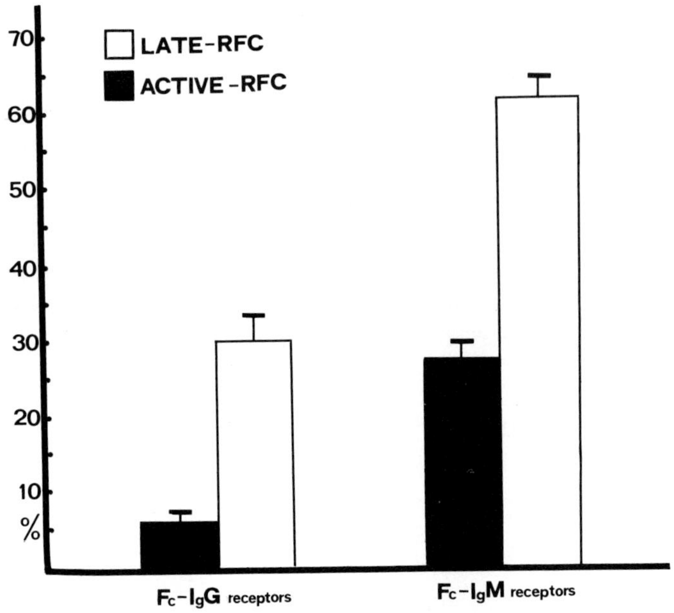

FIG. 1. Percentage of Fc-receptor-positive cells in active- and late-RFC-enriched populations. The difference in distribution of the Fc receptors between the two populations is statistically significant ($P < 0.001$).

ferences were observed in NAE and NBE reactions. These two enzymes demonstrated a high percentage of positive cells in the L-RFC-enriched population and a low percentage of positive cells in the A-RFC-enriched population (Fig. 3), and the differences were statistically significant ($P < 0.001$).

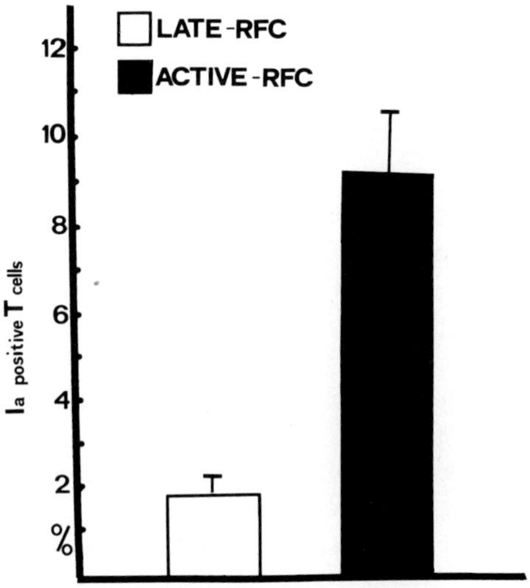

FIG. 2. Expression of Ia antigens by T cells with different affinity for SRBC (9.2 ± 1.6% vs 1.7 ± 0.4%, respectively, in A- and L-RFC populations; $P < 0.001$, Student's *t* test.)

TABLE 1

Spontaneous Blastogenesis in Active and Late RFC Populations

RFC-enriched population	No.	Spontaneous [^{3}H]thymidine incorporation (cpm/min/10^5 cells; mean ± SE)	*P*
Active	10	300 ± 92	<0.001
Late	10	2592 ± 57	

DISCUSSION

Active E-rosette-forming cells include T lymphocytes actively involved in cell-mediated immunity. In human disease states the evaluation of A-RFC has been found to be a useful tool in that A-RFC correlate more precisely than total E rosettes with patients' immunocompetence (12–16). Low levels of A-RFC have been described in patients with deficient T-cell-mediated immunity, whereas increased proportions were found in conditions associated with various antigenic stimulations (reviewed by Wybran (27)). However, the significance of A-RFC has not yet been defined. Some authors have reported that A-RFC could represent activated circulating T cells; this hypothesis is substantiated by experimental studies demonstrating that T cells activated *in vitro* are able to form A-RFC more efficiently than unstimulated cells (17, 20–28). On the other hand, it has also been hypothesized that A-RFC could be relatively immature T lymphocytes (13–29). This hypothesis is supported by the fact that A-RFC are numerous in fetal thymuses (3, 30) and A-RFC increase following incubation of lymphocytes with thymosine (31); in addition this marker is found in relatively immature T-cell leukemias (25, 29).

Our studies on active and late T-cell fractions suggest some possible conclusions. First, a correlation was observed between A-RFC and cells lacking Fc receptors, in particular T_G cells; Fc-R-positive cells were mostly present in the L-RFC population. These data confirm the results of West and co-workers (32) who observed a correlation between the presence of Fc-IgG receptors and cells with low affinity for SRBC. In addition we show that this correlation exists also for T_M cells. We can conclude that: (i) active T cells are mostly represented by $T_{\text{non G–non M}}$ cells with

TABLE 2

Cytochemical Reactions in Active and Late RFC Populations[a]

Cytochemical reaction	Active RFC	Late RFC	*P*
AcP	84.1 ± 2.3	82.0 ± 2.9	n.s.[b]
BG	89.3 ± 1.5	77.0 ± 8.0	n.s.
NABG	61.3 ± 8.5	79.7 ± 3.8	n.s.
ANAE	53.1 ± 6.8	67.1 ± 4.3	n.s.
NAE	21.4 ± 5.2	56.6 ± 3.5	<0.001
NBE	27.8 ± 3.9	79.2 ± 6.2	<0.001

[a] Percentage ± SE.

[b] n.s., not significant.

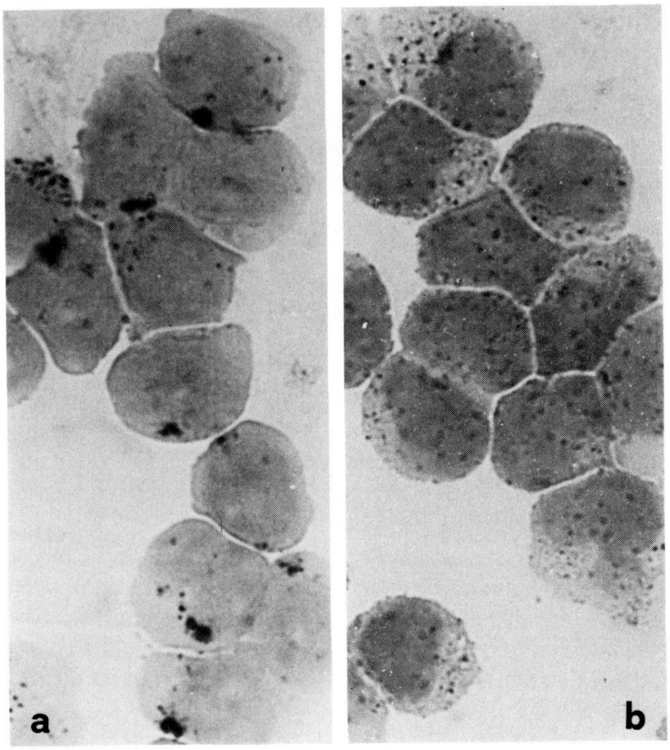

FIG. 3. Cytochemical pattern in active and late rosette-forming cells populations: (a) Dot-like positivity of NBE in L-RFC-enriched population (b) Nonspecific reaction (diffuse granularity) of NBE in A-RFC-enriched population.

few T_M cells, (ii) T_G and T_M cells are largely included in the late RFC fraction. This would imply that loss of T cells with low affinity (which easily occurs during T-lymphocyte isolation) can significantly alter the number of cells bearing Fc receptors.

To the authors' knowledge the presence of Ia antigens on T-cell subsets with different affinities for SRBC has never been investigated. Human Ia-like antigens were first recognized on B lymphocytes, on monocytes, and on the surface of non-blood cells (33–35). More recently it has been found that T cells also express these antigens (36). Two distinct types of Ia-positive T cells have been described: large blastoid, strongly positive T cells obtained following *in vitro* stimulation and a small, but definite, number of normal peripheral T lymphocytes, with a weak expression of Ia antigens, which increase after immunizations and in various pathological states (37–38). Following this interpretation the enrichment of Ia^+ cells in E-active lymphocytes could support the viewpoint that the A-RFC population includes activated T cells.

The results of spontaneous blastogenesis differ from those of a previous report (39). We have found that late RFC, and not active RFC, synthesize DNA in unstimulated cultures. On the other hand, De Bruyere *et al.* (39) stated that the majority of T lymphocytes spontaneously incorporating [^{3}H]thymidine are A-RFC. The reasons for this discrepancy are not clear. Perhaps differences in the techniques used in the two studies may account for the different results. It is noteworthy that contradictory data have also been reported on the ability of A- and L-RFC to respond to mitogenic and allogenic stimuli (18–21, 40). This may be due to the different experimental protocols used for cell isolation. It is generally agreed that spontaneous increases in DNA synthesis by lymphocytes follow a prior *in vivo* immunological stimulation (41, 42). Lack of this activity in the A-RFC-enriched population further supports the idea that we are dealing with a less mature population. Direct evidence of this interpretation is provided by cytochemical analysis.

Since we have shown that T-cell maturation is characterized by the progressive appearance of certain enzymatic reactions (26), we have come to the conclusion that, based on the enzymatic pattern, A-RFC are at an earlier stage of maturation than are L-RFC.

Whether A-RFC are activated T cells or immature T cells is yet unclear. Our results and the data available from the literature support the theory that A-RFC include both activated and immature T cells. Nevertheless, from structural, functional, and cytochemical studies we can conclude that A-RFC and L-RFC represent distinct populations of T cells.

ACKNOWLEDGMENTS

The authors thank Dr. L. Moretta for reviewing the manuscript, Dr. J. Wybran for reading the paper and for helpful discussions, and Dr. S. Ferrone for supplying the mouse monoclonal anti-human Ia antibody. We are also grateful to Miss I. Cappellotto for expert technical assistance.

REFERENCES

1. Galili, U., and Schlesinger, M., *J. Immunol.* **112,** 1028, 1975.
2. West, H. W., Sienknecht, C. W., Townes, A. S., and Herberman, R. B., *Clin. Immunol. Immunopathol.* **5,** 60, 1976.
3. Wybran, J., Carr, M. C., and Fudenberg, H. H., *J. Clin. Invest.* **51,** 2537, 1972.
4. Ferrarini, M., Moretta, L., Abrile, R., and Durante, M. L., *Eur. J. Immunol.* **5,** 70, 1975.
5. Moretta, L., Ferrarini, M., Durante, M. L., and Mingari, M. C., *Eur. J. Immunol.* **5,** 565, 1975.
6. Ferrara, G. B., Strelkauskas, A. J., Longo, A., McDowell, J., Yunis, E. J., and Schlossman, S. F., *J. Immunol.* **123,** 1272, 1979.
7. Reinherz, E. L., Kung, P. C., Goldstein, G., and Schlossman, S. F., *J. Immunol.* **123,** 1312, 1979.
8. Strelkauskas, A. J., Schauf, V., Wilson, B. S., Chess, L., and Schlossman, S. F., *J. Immunol.* **120,** 1278, 1978.
9. Evans, R. L., Lazarus, H., Penta, A. C., and Schlossman, S. F., *J. Immunol.* **120,** 1423, 1978.
10. Moretta, L., Webb, S. R., Grossi, C. E., Lydyard, P. M., and Cooper, M. D., *J. Exp. Med.* **146,** 184, 1977.
11. Reinherz, E., Kung, P. C., Goldstein, G., and Schlossman, S. F., *Proc. Nat. Acad. Sci.* **76,** 4061, 1979.
12. Felsburg, P. J., and Edelman, R., *J. Immunol.* **118,** 62, 1977.
13. Horowitz, S., Groshong, T., Albrecht, R., and Hong, R., *Clin. Immunol. Immunopathol.* **4,** 405, 1975.
14. Kerman, R. H., Smith, R., Stefani, S. S., and Ezdinli, E. Z., *Cancer Res.* **36,** 3274, 1976.
15. Semenzato, G., Pezzutto, A., Gerosa, M., Ancona, E., Amadori, G., and Gasparotto, G., *Eur. J. Cancer* **16,** 1311, 1980.
16. Wybran, J., Levin, A. S., Fudenberg, H. H., and Goldstein, A. L., *Ann. N.Y. Acad. Sci.* **249,** 300, 1975.
17. Semenzato, G., Amadori, G., Sarasin, P., and Gasparotto, G., *Immunology* **34,** 721, 1978.
18. Hokland, P., and Heron, I., *Scand. J. Immunol.* **9,** 333, 1979.
19. Tanigughi, N., Miyawaki, T., Moriya, N., Nagaoki, T., Kato, E., and Okûda, N., *J. Immunol.* **118,** 193, 1977.

20. Traycoff, R. B., Worstman, J., Myers, W. L., and Rogers, W., *Clin. Immunol. Immunopathol.* **13,** 383, 1979.
21. Yu, D. T. Y., *Clin. Immunol. Immunopathol.* **10,** 11, 1978.
22. Böyum, A., *Scand. J. Clin. Lab. Invest.* **21**(Suppl. 97), 77, 1968.
23. Molinaro, G. A., Quaranta, V., Ferrone, S., *Transplant. Proc.* **11,** 1748, 1979.
24. Semenzato, G., Amadori, G., Tosato, F., and Gasparotto, G., *Clin. Exp. Immunol.* **28,** 542, 1977.
25. Semenzato, G., Milano, A., Pezzutto, A., Basso, G., Cocito, M. G., Amadori, G., and Gasparotto, G., *Clin. Immunol. Immunopathol.* **16,** 238, 1980.
26. Basso, G., Cocito, M. G., Semenzato, G., Pezzutto, A., and Zanesco, L., *Brit. J. Haematol.* **44,** 577, 1980.
27. Wybran, J., *In* "Cell Biology and Immunology of Leukocyte Function" (M. R. Quastel, Ed.), pp. 745–753. Academic Press, New York, 1979.
28. Touraine, J. L., Hadden, J. W., Touraine, F., Hadden, E. M., Estensen, R., and Good, R. A., *J. Exp. Med.* **145,** 460, 1977.
29. Gelfand, E. W., and Chechik, B. E., *N. Engl. J. Med.* **294,** 275, 1976.
30. Han, T., Diegelman, P., Subramanian, S., and Minowada, J., *Immunology* **38,** 585, 1979.
31. Wybran, J., Levin, A. S., Fudenberg, H. H., and Goldestein, A. L., *Ann. N.Y. Acad. Sci.* **249,** 300, 1975.
32. West, W. H., Payne, S. M., Weese, J. L., and Herberman, R. B., *J. Immunol.* **119,** 548, 1977.
33. Schlossman, S. F., Chess, L., Humphreys, R. E., and Strominger, J. L., *Proc. Nat. Acad. Sci. USA* **73,** 1288, 1976.
34. Winchester, R. J., Fu, S. M., Wernet, P., Kunkel, H. G., Dupont, B., and Jersild, C., *J. Exp. Med.* **141,** 924, 1975.
35. Winchester, R. J., and Kunkel, H. G., *Advan. Immunol.* **28,** 22, 1980.
36. Fu, S. M., Chiorazzi, N., Wang, C. Y., Montazeri, G., Kunkel, H. G., Ko, H. S., and Gottlieb, A. B., *J. Exp. Med.* **148,** 1423, 1978.
37. Yu, D. T. Y., McCune, J. M., Fu, S. M., Winchester, R. J., and Kunkel, H. G., *J. Exp. Med.* **152,** 89s, 1980.
38. Yu, D. T. Y., Winchester, R. J., Fu, S. M., Gibofsky, A., Ko, H. S., and Kunkel, G. H., *J. Exp. Med.* **151,** 91, 1980.
39. De Bruyere, M., Lachapelle, J. M., and Anguita, T., *Int. Arch. Allergy Appl. Immunol.* **54,** 50, 1977.
40. Dillner-Centerlind, M. L., Hellström, U., Robertsson, E. S., Hammarström, S., and Perlmann, P., *Scand. J. Immunol.* **12,** 13, 1980.
41. MacKinney, A. A., Jr., *Blood* **26,** 36, 1965.
42. Parker, J. W., and Lukes, R. J., *In* "Proceedings of the Fourth Annual Leukocyte Culture Conference" (O. R. McIntyre, Ed.), p. 281. Meredith, New York, 1971.

CELLULAR IMMUNOLOGY **64**, 235–245 (1981)

Suppressor Cells in Coccidioidomycosis

ANTONINO CATANZARO[1]

Pulmonary Division, Department of Medicine, University of California School of Medicine, University of California Medical Center, San Diego, California 92103

Received May 18, 1981; accepted July 24, 1981

Patients with coccidioidomycosis manifest a wide variety of severity of infection. Patients with unifocal and particularly multifocal dissemination manifest a defect in host defense mechanisms. This study focuses on the *in vitro* response to PHA as an indicator of immunoregulatory mechanisms. Study subjects are divided into four groups: Group I—17, patients with active disseminated coccidioidomycosis and lesions in multiple organs; Group II—15, patients with active disseminated coccidioidomycosis and a single lesion; Group III—16, patients with active coccidioidomycosis confined to the lungs; and Group IV—18, patients in whom coccidioidomycosis is inactive. The response to PHA was heterogeneous, even within groups. When cells were cultured in the presence of indomethacin or R020-5720, Group I cells demonstrated highly significant augmentation of the response to PHA ($P < 0.002$), whereas cells from Groups II to IV were unaffected. When adherent cells were removed by passage through a nylon wool column, the effect of indomethacin could no longer be demonstrated. Direct measurement of prostaglandin production (PGE_2 and $PGF_{2\alpha}$) and thromboxane suggest that there is no difference in the quantity of these compounds produced by unstimulated or PHA-stimulated cells by Group I versus Group IV cells ($P = 0.2$–0.4). Indomethacin or R020-5720 markedly inhibit the production of these compounds. Studies of the effect of exogenous prostaglandin on PHA-stimulated cells suggest that Group I cells may be more inhibited by $PGF_{1\alpha}$ and $PGF_{2\alpha}$ compared to Group IV cells. The data demonstrate that PHA cultures of cells from Group I patients are suppressed. The suppressor cell can be removed by adherence to nylon wool and is inhibited by indomethacin or R020-5720.

INTRODUCTION

Coccidioidomycosis is an infection acquired by inhalation of airborne arthrospores of *Coccidioides immitis.* At least 50% of infected individuals experience no symptoms. The remainder may experience relatively mild symptoms which include cough, headache, and low-grade fever for 2–6 days. One to five percent experience prolonged pulmonary infection. In 1% the fungus spreads to other organs resulting in unifocal or multifocal dissemination (1). Cellular responses are believed to be of fundamental importance in containment of infection to the initial site of entry (2). Conversely, patients with unifocal or multifocal dissemination have been thought to have a defect in host defense mechanisms (1–5), presumably cell-mediated immunity. This hypothesis was developed on the basis of clinical and pathological observations and the skin test response to the antigens derived from *C.*

[1] To whom requests for reprints should be sent at: Pulmonary Division, Department of Medicine, University Hospital, 225 W. Dickinson St., San Diego, Calif. 92103.

0008-8749/81/160235-11$02.00/0

immitis [coccidioidin (CDN)]. Experimental studies tend to confirm the hypothesis (6).

Studies from this laboratory have demonstrated that patients with disseminated coccidioidomycosis have a normal number of T cells and B cells in the circulation (5). Lymphocytes from patients with severe forms of coccidioidal infection may demonstrate an altered response to phytohemagglutinin (PHA) and CDN.

The peak response to PHA is reduced in certain patients. The *in vitro* and *in vivo* response to antigens may be blunted as well (5). Similar findings appear to be a manifestation of one of several types of suppression in certain clinical settings. Indomethacin-sensitive suppressor cells have been identified in sarcoidosis and Hodgkin's disease (7); suppressor T cells in tuberculosis (8), and a soluble product of macrophages acting on a subset of T cells in certain fungal infections (9), not including coccidioidomycosis.

The present study confirms that patients with coccidioidomycosis are by no means a homogeneous group immunologically. In certain patients with widespread dissemination the response to PHA is suppressed.

METHODS

Subjects. Patients with coccidioidomycosis available at the University of California, San Diego, during the study period (21 months) were examined. Subjects were placed into four groups based on clinical characteristics: Group I, patients with active disseminated coccidioidomycosis and lesions in multiple organs (multifocal); Group II, patients with active disseminated coccidioidomycosis and a single extrapulmonary lesion (unifocal); Group III, patients with active coccidioidomycosis confined to the lungs; and Group IV, patients whose coccidioidomycosis is inactive—six recovered from lesions confined to the lungs and 11 from disseminated disease. Table 1 presents additional data on study subjects.

Preparation of cells. Peripheral venous blood was drawn into a sterile syringe containing 10 units of heparin per 1 ml of blood. Erythrocytes were removed by sedimentation at 37°C. Cells were resuspended in F10 medium (Gibco, Santa Clara, Calif.), and designated unfractionated cells. Unfractionated cells were characterized by morphology as presented in Table 2.

Removal of adherent cells. Adherent cells were removed by the following technique. Nylon wool (nylon staple, 30 denier, DuPont) was washed with Duponal, rinsed thoroughly, dried, and packed loosely in a 10-ml plastic syringe. The column was equilibrated with Hanks' balanced salt solution with 10% AB+ plasma for 30 min. Five milliliters of a cell suspension (20×10^6 unfractionated cells) was incubated for 30 min. The suspension of nonadherent cells was allowed to drain and the column washed gently with an additional 30 ml of warm Hanks' balanced salt solution with 10% AB+ plasma. Cells were characterized and counted and identified as nonadherent to nylon wool column cells (Table 2).

Mitogen, antigen, and drugs. PHA-P (Burroughs–Wellcome Research, Triangle Park, N.C.) was used. Dose–response studies were performed. The dose selected and used in these studies was 3 μg (5). This dose produced a maximal response as measured by thymidine incorporation. Indomethacin was a gift from Dr. Clement Stone (Merck, Sharp and Dohme Research Laboratories, West Point, Pa.). In-

TABLE 1

Study Subjects

		Age		Sex		Racial background		
Group	Number	Mean	SD	M	F	Caucasian	Oriental	Black
I	17	42	16	15	2	10 (3 Mexican)	—	7
II	15	44	19	11	4	11 (4 Mexican, 2 Filipino)	—	4
III	16	35	15	11	7	15 (2 Mexican, 2 Filipino)	—	1
IV	18	45	16	16	2	14 (2 Mexican, 2 Filipino)	2	2

Note. Basic data on Groups I–IV are presented. Differences in sex and race among these groups are typical of the patient population with each manifestation of coccidioidal disease.

domethacin was dissolved in F10 and used at final concentrations of 1, 10, 20, 50, and 70 μg/ml. R020-5720 (*d,l*-6-chloro-α-methylcarbazole-2-acetic acid) was a gift from Dr. W. E. Scott (Hoffman–La Roche, Inc., Nutley, N.J.). R020-5720 is an experimental drug whose only known activity is the inhibition of prostaglandin synthetase (10). R020-5720 was used at 1 μg/ml. Prostaglandin PGE_1, E_2, $F_{1\alpha}$, and $F_{2\alpha}$, were a gift from Dr. John Pike (Upjohn, Kalamazoo, Mich.).

Cell cultures. Cells were cultured in microtiter plates, 1×10^5 lymphocytes/200 μl. Tissue culture medium F10 (Gibco) was enriched with 5% AB+ plasma. Indomethacin or R020-5720 was added, then mitogen was added subsequently. Cells were incubated at 37°C in 5% carbon dioxide for 1–5 days. The cultures were pulsed with tritiated thymidine (New England Nuclear, Boston, Mass.), 4 μCi per well, 24 hr prior to harvest. Cell viability was examined in parallel cultures and was always greater than 85%. Cells were collected on a glass wool filter with a Brandel Model M24V cell harvester. Filters were placed in Bray's solution and

TABLE 2

Morphologic Characteristics of Two Study Cell Populations

	Unfractionated cells			Nonadherent cells		
Group	Lymphocytes	Monocytes	Polymorphonuclear	Lymphocytes	Monocytes	Polymorphonuclear
I	16 ± 7	4.6 ± 2	78 ± 10	41 ± 29	0.8 ± 0.7	58 ± 29
II	22 ± 14	4.0 ± 3	74 ± 15	63 ± 21	1.8 ± 2.2	34 ± 19
III	25 ± 13	5.6 ± 4	69 ± 10	68 ± 16	1.8 ± 1.8	31 ± 15
IV	27 ± 8	5.8 ± 2	67 ± 9	60 ± 11	1.7 ± 0.4	37 ± 12

Note. Morphologic characteristics of unfractionated cells did not vary significantly between groups. As expected the nonadherent cells were nearly depleted of monocytes. While the number of polymorphonuclear cells was decreased, many persisted.

β radiation was quantitated in a Searle scintillation counter. All cultures were performed in quadruplicate. The arithmetic mean of quadruplicate samples was determined and expressed as counts per minute. Samples greater than 50% from the mean were excluded from the final computation. Suppression index (SI) was calculated as follows:

$$SI = \frac{\text{cpm PHA with indomethacin} - \text{cpm PHA without indomethacin}}{\text{cpm PHA without indomethacin}} \times 100.$$

Measurement of Thromboxane (TBX_2), PGE, and $PGF_{2\alpha}$. Cell cultures were established as described above. Supernatant fluid was collected after 72 hr of culture. Frozen samples were sent to Dr. James O. Shaw, University of Texas Health Science Center, San Antonio, Texas, for analysis. TBX_2 (Upjohn) was assayed by radioimmunoassay as described previously (11). Rabbit antiserum against TBX_2-keyhole limpet hemocyanin (KLH) (Sigma, St. Louis, Mo.) was used. KLH was conjugated to TBX_2 with carbodiimide (12). Antiserum raised in rabbits was employed in the assay at a final dilution of 1:36,000.

Cross-reactivity to TBX antiserum is less than 0.1% with prostaglandins E_1, E_2, A_2, $F_{1\alpha}$, 6 keto-$F_{1\alpha}$, 13,14-dihydro15-keto-E_2, 13,14-dihydro-15-keto-$E_{2\alpha}$, and arachidonic acid.

PGE_2 and $PGF_{2\alpha}$ were also assayed by radioimmunoassay. These assays have been fully described previously (11). Cross-reactivity of the PGE_2 antiserum is 4% with PGF_2, and less than 1% with PGD_2, PGA_2, TBX_2, and arachidonic acid.

The lower limit of detectability is 400 pg/ml PGE_2, 400 pg/ml $PGF_{2\alpha}$, and 40 pg/ml TBX_2. The antiserum against $PGE_{2\alpha}$ does not distinguish between PGE_1 and PGE_2. The antiserum against $PGF_{2\alpha}$ reacts with $PGF_{1\alpha}$ 35% and PGD_2, PGA_2, PGE_2, and arachidonic acid <0.1%.

Statistics. Comparison of paired data was performed using Student's *t* test. One- or two-way analysis of variance (ANOVA) or the Wilcoxon signed ranks test was used when multiple groups were involved. Pearson's correlation coefficient was used to compare the effect of indomethacin with R020-5720 (13).

RESULTS

Effect of Indomethacin on Response to PHA

The response of unfractionated cells to PHA was examined on Days 3–5. In parallel cultures indomethacin was added prior to the addition of PHA. In Group I augmentation of the response to PHA was observed at doses of 1, 10, and 20 μg of indomethacin. The effect at 50 and 70 μg was less dramatic and less consistent. Subsequent experiments were performed at 1 μg indomethacin/ml. In Group I indomethacin augmented the response to PHA, whether the response to PHA without indomethacin was reduced or not. Furthermore, maximal differences were observed on Day 3 of the culture. In Groups II–IV cultures had identical responses to PHA whether or not indomethacin was added.

Since the indomethacin effect was maximal on Day 3, further analysis focused on the data from the response of unfractionated cells to PHA with and without indomethacin on Day 3 (Fig. 1). Group I demonstrated very significant augmentation in the response to PHA in the presence of indomethacin ($P < 0.002$). In

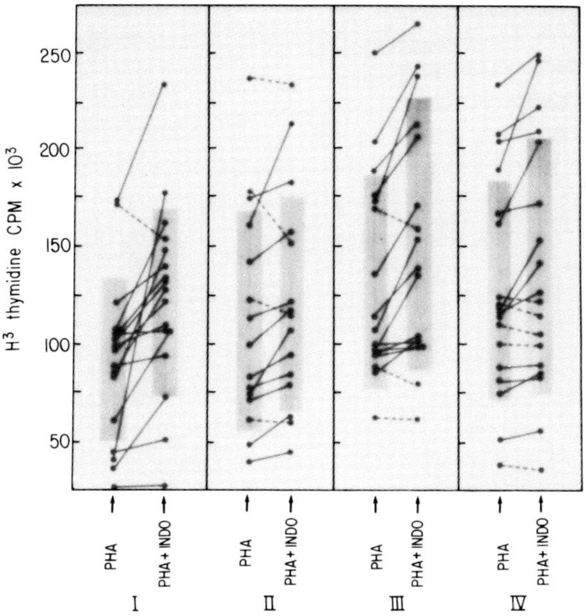

FIG. 1. The response of Group I cells to PHA was less vigorous than the response of Group II, III, or IV cells. Means ±1 SD: Group I, 66,932 ± 42,203; Group II, 88,286 ± 56,891; Group III, 109,304 ± 53,098; Group IV, 103,111 ± 56,114 ($P < 0.1$). When the cultures are performed in the presence of indomethacin there are no differences between groups.

Groups II–IV there was no difference between responses in the presence ($P = 0.32$) and responses in the absence ($P = 0.73$) of indomethacin.

In order to focus on the change in the response to PHA between cultures grown without indomethacin and with indomethacin, we calculated a suppression index according to the formula described under Methods (Fig. 2). The suppression index is plotted in Fig. 2 by groups. Group I differs from Groups II–IV dramatically ($P < 0.03$, ANOVA). The difference is primarily due to four subjects with markedly increased suppression indicies. In contrast, Groups II–IV are homogeneous and demonstrate little or no augmentation in the response to PHA in the presence of indomethacin.

Four subjects in Group I stand out as having a suppression index of greater than 100. Three of the four are low responders to PHA (less than 50,000 cpm). Eight patients in Groups II, III, and IV were also low responders, none of them had a suppression index greater than 100, in fact, the mean was only 10.

Effect of R020-5720 on Response to PHA

Since indomethacin may have actions other than its effect on prostaglandin synthesis we sought to further define the effect by the use of R020-5720. R020-5720 is a specific inhibitor of prostaglandin synthetase (10). The effects of indomethacin and R020-5720 were compared in 28 subjects whose unfractionated cells demonstrated an augmented response to PHA in the presence of indomethacin. The effects of R020-5720 and indomethacin paralleled each other closely ($r = 0.78$, $P < 0.005$, Pearson 's correlation coefficient).

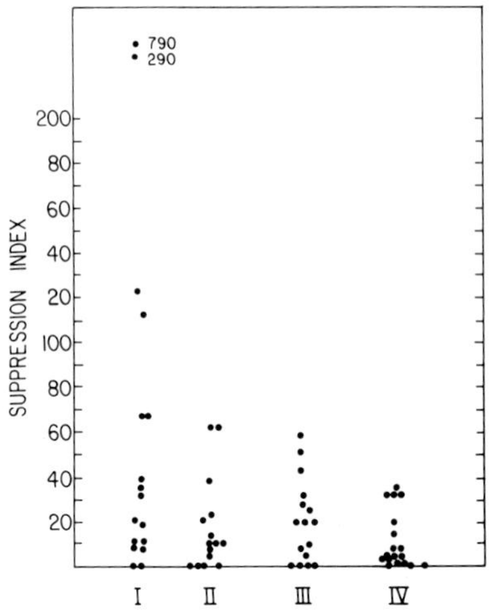

FIG. 2. The suppression index = (cpm PHA with indomethacin − cpm PHA without indomethacin)/cpm PHA without indomethacin × 100. A high suppression index is observed when suppression is abrogated by indomethacin.

Prostaglandin Production

Since the major effect of indomethacin and R020-5720, at the concentration used, is to decrease the production of prostaglandin, direct measurements were undertaken. PGE and $PGF_{1\alpha}$ have been demonstrated to inhibit lymphocyte response to PHA (14). Thromboxane is one of the more important compounds in the group (12). Unfractionated cells from patients in Group I were cultured. Cells from Group IV subjects served as controls. Endogenous release into the medium of the compounds was measured from unstimulated cells, cells stimulated with PHA, and cells stimulated with PHA in the presence of 1 μg/ml of indomethacin or 1 μg/ml of R020-5720. The data in Table 3 demonstrate that unstimulated cultures produce a small quantity of PGE_2 and $PGF_{2\alpha}$. PHA stimulation results in a significant increase in the release of PGE_1 and $PGF_{2\alpha}$. The amount of these compounds produced by PHA-stimulated cells did not differ by group (I versus IV) (PGE_2 $P = 0.4$; $PGF_{2\alpha}$, $P = 0.2$; TBX, $P = 0.2$, Wilcoxon signed rank test). Endogenous production of the compound was markedly inhibited by indomethacin or R020-5720. Thromboxane production was similar to PGE_2 and $PGF_{2\alpha}$ production, except that in one patient unstimulated cells were producing large amounts and PHA did not induce any further stimulation.

Effect of Removal of Adherent Cells

Adherent cells were removed by passage through a nylon wool column. The response of nonadherent cells to PHA, with or without indomethacin, was compared with the response of the whole unfractionated cell population in a series of patients from Groups I to IV (Table 4). The response to PHA is greater in the presence of indomethacin than in its absence. Nonadherent column passed cells from Group I patients, respond to PHA more vigorously than do unfractionated cells. In fact, their response to PHA is the same as Groups II, III, or IV, and is not further

TABLE 3

Endogenous Production of Prostaglandins E_2, $F_{2\alpha}$, and Thromboxane *in vitro*

	Unstimulated			PHA-stimulated			Increase due to PHA[a]			PHA + INDO[b]			PHA − RO20-5720[c]		
Group	PGE_2	$PGF_{2\alpha}$	TBX	PGE_2	$PGF_{2\alpha}$	TBX	PGE_2	$PGF_{2\alpha}$	TBX	PGE_2	$PGF_{2\alpha}$	TBX	PGE_2	$PGF_{2\alpha}$	TBX
I	<400[d]	954	3032	1440	2260	11,080	1040	1306	8048	<400	1019	3720	<400	831	3820
	<400	729	2779	<400	1543	6,534	—	814	3755	<400	852	3160	<400	748	3500
	546	1440	16,928	2305	2018	13,492	1754	578	-0-	<400	1396	6922	1062	1459	7848
IV	611	1044	6038	734	1642	8,368	123	598	2330	<400	936	3452	762	476	4562
	<400	458	1236	842	729	2,840	442	458	1604	<400	604	860	<400	586	1120

Note. Production of various prostaglandins by cell cultures from Groups I and IV are shown. Unstimulated cultures produce small quantities of prostaglandins. PHA stimulation results in significant increases. Group I and IV cells do not differ. Indomethacin or RO20-5720 markedly inhibit the production of these compounds.

[a] PHA-stimulated − unstimulated.

[b] Indomethacin 1 μg/ml.

[c] RO20-5720 1 μg/ml.

[d] pg/ml supernatant fluid.

TABLE 4

Response to PHA without and with Indomethacin by Unfractionated Cells versus Nonadherent Column Cells

	Unfractionated cells		Nonadherent column	
Group	PHA	PHA + indomethacin[a]	PHA	PHA + indomethacin[a]
I	77,800[b]	107,875	295,064	247,696
	79,758	90,850	92,212	62,218
	94,500	150,476	172,091	109,780
Mean	86,965	115,859	186,158	151,854
SD	9,501	25,100	83,436	82,213
II	187,380	196,249	91,360	104,966
	179,532	218,835	258,843	217,581
	81,159	128,415	100,374	94,269
Mean	183,456	181,169	150,192	138,939
SD	5,549	4,706	94,202	68,316
III	192,740	237,003	125,468	209,810
	262,475	122,806	281,192	158,914
	81,987	105,312	75,159	88,136
	118,061	123,277	98,241	111,869
Mean	163,816	147,100	145,015	157,262
SD	80,332	60,516	93,084	57,535
IV	125,158	136,624	249,680	182,688
	142,201	167,460	71,891	67,616
Mean	133,680	152,042	160,786	125,152
SD	12,051	21,804	125,716	81,368

Note. Two to four subjects in each group were studied to determine the effect of removal of adherent cells on the response to PHA in the presence of indomethacin compared with culture performed without indomethacin. Unfractionated cells from Group I subjects demonstrate a suppressed response to PHA in comparison to Groups II-IV, whereas nonadherent Group I cells respond as well to PHA as do unfractionated Group II–IV or nonadherent column cells from Groups II–IV. An effect of adding indomethacin to stimulated cultures is readily apparent in Group I unfractionated cells but this effect is removed with the removal of adherent cells.

[a] 1 μg/ml.

[b] Counts per minute.

incremented by indomethacin. This observation suggests that suppression of the response to PHA in Group I patients is mediated by an adherent cell population and that the response to indomethacin is resident in that population of cells.

Effect of Exogenous Prostaglandin on PHA-Stimulated Cultures

The response to PHA of Group I patients was augmented when the release of endogenous prostaglandins was blocked. Direct measurements indicate that excessive production of prostaglandins is not demonstrated in Group I cultures. The next question is whether Group I patients have an increased sensitivity to the inhibiting effect of prostaglandins. The effect of PGE_1, PGE_2, $PGF_{1\alpha}$ and $PGF_{2\alpha}$ on the response of cells from Group I to PHA was evaluated; cells from Group IV again served as comparisons (Table 5). PGE_1 and PGE_2 are inhibitory at the concentra-

TABLE 5

Sensitivity of PHA-Stimulated Lymphocytes to Exogenous Prostaglandins

Prostaglandin concentration (M)	Percentage inhibition[a]		P
	Group I	Group IV	
PGE_1			
2.69×10^{-6}	26 ± 37[b]	42 ± 28	0.64
2.69×10^{-5}	53 ± 55	76 ± 14	0.51
PGE_2			
2.70×10^{-6}	40 ± 6	6 ± 25	0.02
2.70×10^{-5}	46 ± 19	54 ± 26	0.75
PGF_1			
2.67 ± 10^{-6}	28 ± 4	−77 ± 119	0.15
2.67×10^{-5}	23 ± 7	−9 ± 9	0.03
PGF_2			
1.96×10^{-6}	24 ± 7	−74 ± 105	0.30
1.96×10^{-5}	25 ± 14	5 ± 8	0.13

Note. Sensitivity to inhibitory effects of prostaglandins is shown for Group I cells (three patients) in comparison with Group IV cells (three patients). At the concentrations tested all prostaglandins tested had an inhibitory effect on Group I cells. PGE_1 and PGE_2 had a similar effect on Group IV cells. $PGF_{1\alpha}$ and $PGF_{2\alpha}$ were not inhibitory on cells from Group IV; in fact, they were stimulatory. P values listed in column at right were obtained using Student's t test.

[a] Percentage inhibition = (cpm PHA-stimulated cultures without PG − cpm PHA-stimulated cultures with PG)/cpm PHA-stimulated cultures without PG × 100.

[b] Mean ± SD.

tions tested. There was no difference in the degree of inhibition of the response to Group I in comparison with Group IV cells ($P = 0.2$–0.6). $PGF_{1\alpha}$ and $PGF_{2\alpha}$ were mildly inhibitory to Group I cells and tended to stimulate Group IV cells. The difference was not significant for $PGF_{2\alpha}$ but was significant at the high concentration of $PGF_{1\alpha}$ ($P = 0.03$). These data suggest that the defect under evaluation does not reside at the lymphocyte level.

DISCUSSION

Clinical criteria were used to classify patients with various stages of infection with *C. immitis* into one of four groups. The four clinical groups are also significant from the viewpoint of host defense. Immunologic responses of cells from Group I patients differed from those of Groups II–IV in several important ways. Cells from Group I patients demonstrate a dramatic increase in their reactivity to PHA when the cells were cultured in the presence of indomethacin. This effect was particularly pronounced in four subjects in Group I. This observation suggests that the response to PHA was suppressed in Group I patients. Indomethacin at the dose used in this study causes an irreversible block in the synthesis of prostaglandins (15). Recent studies have shown that indomethacin also inhibits cyclic AMP-dependent protein kinases and endogenous phosphorylation (16). The only known action of R020-5720 is the reversible inhibition of prostaglandin synthetase (10). The effect of R020-5720 on the response to PHA correlated closely with the effects of indomethacin ($r = 0.78$). The changes induced by indomethacin and R020-5720 suggested that prostaglandins are involved in the control (or suppression) of the response to PHA in this group of patients. Direct measurements of the production of PGE_1, $PGF_{2\alpha}$, and TBX in a subset of Group I patients and controls demonstrate that these compounds are produced in small quantities in unstimulated cultures; the amounts produced are markedly increased in PHA stimulated cultures and those increases are blocked by indomethacin and R020-5720. These responses are essentially normal and there are no differences between the behavior of Group I and IV cells.

The response to PHA can be profoundly influenced by various exogenous prostaglandins. We studied the sensitivity of cells from a subset of patients to the inhibitory effect of several prostaglandins. PGE_1, PGE_2, $PGF_{1\alpha}$ and $PGF_{2\alpha}$ had similar effects on the response of Group I and control cells to PHA. These studies suggest that the defect observed in Group I cells is not at the lymphocyte level. Group I and control cell cultures do not differ in their production of prostaglandins measured or their sensitivity to exogenous prostaglandins. These findings suggest that indomethacin and R020-5720 act on a very localized intracellular site whose output makes a small contribution to the overall cell output.

Clearly, the response of cells from some patients in Group I to PHA is suppressed. Not surprisingly, the effect of indomethacin is most dramatic in low responders. When cells adherent to nylon wool were removed, the response to indomethacin could no longer be demonstrated. These findings suggest that suppression of the response to PHA observed in Group I cells is mediated by a cell which is adherent to nylon wool.

Adherent cells that cause suppression of T-cell responses have been found in several related diseases. These cells appear to be T cells in patients with tuberculosis (8), and macrophages in several widespread fungal infections (coccidioidomycosis has not been previously studied) (9). Patients with multifocal disseminated coccidioidomycosis (Group I) described in this report manifest a reduced response to PHA which appears to be based on mechanisms surprisingly similar to those of the patients with sarcoidosis and Hodgkin's disease described by Goodwin *et al.* (7).

These studies do not address the question of how circulating suppressor cells are generated. Collins and Watson injected large doses of live BCG organism intravenously in mice and found suppressor cells in the spleen (17). Druker *et al.* used BCG walls to provide a similar effect in the rat spleen (18). In both cases the suppressor cell was removed by surface adherence. Perhaps *C. immitis*, or its cell wall, has a similar effect in patients with multifocal disseminated coccidioidomycosis.

These studies fit in well with the clinical observation that patients in Group I (multifocal disseminated coccidioidomycosis) appear to have a large fungus load and are the patients with most severe immunosuppression as judged by skin testing with coccidioidal and noncoccidioidal antigen. One must consider whether the indomethacin (or R020-5720)-sensitive cell is an effector cell causing clinical impaired cell-mediated immune responses or a marker of a more fundamental defect.

ACKNOWLEDGMENTS

The dedicated technical assistance of Louis Bridgeman and Sharon Batcher is gratefully acknowledged. The author also wishes to acknowledge Jim Marsh for the statistical analysis and Barbra Malone for her invaluable assistance in the preparation of the manuscript.

REFERENCES

1. Drutz, D., and Catanzaro, A., *Amer. Rev. Respir. Dis.* **117**(3), 559 (Part 1), 1978. **117**(4), 727 (Part II), 1978.
2. Mackenzie, D. W. R. *In* "Immunological Aspects of Infectious Disease" (Dick, Ed.), pp. 21–75. Baltimore, Univ. Park Press, 1979.
3. Smith, C. E., Whiting, E. G., Baker, E. E., Rosenberger, H. G., Beard, R. R., and Saitor, M. T., *Amer. Rev. Tuberc.* **57**, 330, 1975.
4. Rea, T. H., Einstein, H., Johnson, R., and Levan, N. E., *In* "Coccidioidomycosis. Current Clinical and Diagnostic Status" (L. Ajello, Ed.), pp. 365–370. Symposia Specialists, Miami, 1977.
5. Catanzaro, A., Spitler, L. E., and Moser, K. M. *Cell. Immunol.* **15**, 360, 1975.
6. Beaman, L. V., Pappagianis, D., and Benjamini, E. *Infect. Immunity* **23**, 681, 1979.
7. Goodwin, J. S., DeHoratius, R., Israel, H., Peake, G. T., and Messner, R. P. *Intern Med.* **90**, 169, 1979.
8. Ellner, J. J. *Immunol.* **121**(6), 2573, 1978.
9. Stobo, J. D. *Immunol.* **119**(3), 918, 1977.
10. Gaut, Z. N., Baruth, H., Randall, L. O., Ashley, C., and Paulsrud, J. R. Department of Biochemical Nutrition and Department of Pharmacology, Hoffman La Roche, Inc. New Jersey. Prostaglandins. Vol 10, No. 1, 1975, page 59.
11. Shaw, J. O., Printz, M. P., Hirabayashi, K., and Henson, P. M. *J. Immunol.* **121**(5), 1939, 1978.
12. Fitzpatrick, F. A., Gorman, R. R., McGuire, J. C., Kelly, R. C., Wynalda, M. A., and Sun, F. F. *Anal. Biochem.* **82**, 1977.
13. Brown, B. W., and Hollander, M. *In* "Statistics. A Biomedical Introduction." (R. A. Bradley, J. S. Hunter, D. G. Kendall, and G. S. Watson, Eds.). Wiley, New York/London/Sydney/Toronto, 1977.
14. Smith, J. W., Steiner, A. L., and Parker, C. W. *J. Clin. Invest.* **50**, 442, 1971.
15. Bray, M. A., Gordon, D. *Brit. J. Pharmacol.* **57**, 466, 1976.
16. VanCalker, D., Muller, M., and Hamprecht, B. *Nature (London)* **276**, 341, 1978.
17. Collins, F. M., and Watson, S. R. *Infect. Immunity* **25**, 491, 1979.
18. Druker, B. J., Wepsic, H. T., Alaimo, J., and Murray, W. *J. Cancer Immunother. Immunol.* in press, 1980.

CELLULAR IMMUNOLOGY **64**, 246–257 (1981)

Cytotoxicity to Allogeneic Cells in the Chicken

II. Specific Cytotoxic T Cells and Macrophages in the Spleens of Agammaglobulinemic and Normal Alloimmune Chickens[1]

DAVID S. CHI,*[,2] NESTOR BLYZNAK, ARTHUR KIMURA,† MICHAEL A. PALLADINO,[3] AND G. JEANETTE THORBECKE

**Department of Internal Medicine, East Tennessee State University College of Medicine, Johnson City, Tennessee 37601, Department of Pathology, New York University Medical Center, 550 First Avenue, New York, New York 10016, and †Department of Immunology, University of Uppsala Biomedical Center, Uppsala, Sweden*

Received May 22, 1981; accepted July 30, 1981

Repeated intravenous injections with allogeneic RBC or spleen cells caused a rapid but brief appearance of specific cellular cytotoxic activity in both NL and Aγ chickens. The activity was much higher in Aγ than in NL chickens, of longer duration, and contained a significant cytotoxic T-cell component which could not be demonstrated in NL chickens. A large fraction of the cytotoxic T cells adhered to *Vicia villosa* and showed relatively low density on Percoll gradients. Specificity of the cytotoxic cells in Aγ alloimmune chickens appeared to be directed at antigens of the major histocompatibility locus. Plastic-adherent cells from Aγ animals showed some specific and nonspecific killer activity. The specific component was removed by treatment with rabbit anti-T-cell serum and C. Specific cytotoxic activity in Aγ spleen cells was approximately equally distributed over Fc+ and Fc− cells. No evidence for specific cytotoxicity of nonT cells was obtained with cells from Aγ alloimmune chickens.

INTRODUCTION

Positive (1) and negative (2) contributions of humoral antibody arising as a consequence of alloimmunization have increased the difficulty in predicting the relative roles of the various effector cell types in the allograft reaction.

The development of defined genetic systems in chickens and ease of neonatal bursectomy now allow a means of dissecting the importance of various effector cell compartments, influenced or obscured by the presence of sensitizing and blocking antibodies. In previous studies it was found that repeated intravenous immunization with allogeneic red blood cells induced the appearance of cytotoxic cells in the spleens of both normal and agammaglobulinemic (Aγ) chickens (3). Although the cytotoxic cells demonstrated specificity for the major histocompatibility (B locus)

[1] Supported by USPHS Grants AI-14829, CA-16247 and IR23CA30160-01.

[2] Fellow under Grant 5T32 CA-09161 awarded by the National Cancer Institute, DHEW.

[3] Present address: Memorial Sloan–Kettering Cancer Center, 1275 York Avenue, New York, N.Y. 10021.

0008-8749/81/160246-12$02.00/0

antigens of the immunizing cells, virtually all of the activity appeared with monocytes rather than with T cells, particularly in the normal alloimmune chickens. Partial inactivation of the cytotoxic effect of Aγ spleen cells by treatment with anti-T serum and C suggested the presence of a cytotoxic T-cell component in the spleen of Aγ but not in normal alloimmune birds. The cytotoxic cells in normal alloimmune spleen were nylon wool adherent and absent from spleen cells depleted of plastic-adherent cells.

Further characterization of the cytotoxic cell populations in spleens from immunized birds was of interest because (i) cytotoxic T cells in the chicken have not received much attention, although their presence has been suggested in spleens from Marek's disease virus-infected chickens (4), and (ii) cytotoxic macrophages with specificity for the immunizing cells in the absence of any antibody production suggested the presence of a T-cell-derived specific arming factor such as described by Alexander and co-workers (5, 6). This seemed of even more importance in view of our recent studies on tumor immunity to carcinogen-induced fibrosarcomas in chickens in which immune T cell–normal macrophage collaboration was found to mediate the immunity expressed in Winn tests (7).

Since both of these aspects could be studied with spleen cells from Aγ alloimmune chickens, the cytotoxic cell populations of such chickens were further examined in more detail in the present report.

MATERIALS AND METHODS

Animals and immunization. FP(B15/B21) and SC(B2/B2) chicken eggs were obtained from Hyline Poultry Farms (Dallas Center, Iowa). Line-6 chickens (EL-6, B2/B2) were obtained as chickens from the Regional Poultry Research Laboratories, East Lansing, Michigan. Hormonal bursectomy was performed on Day 11 of embryonation by injection of 3.75 mg testosterone proprionate (Biochemicals Corp., Cleveland, Ohio) (8). After hatching, these chicks received cyclophosphamide (Cytoxan, Meade Johnson, Evansville, Ind.) on Days 1 (4 mg) and 2 (3 mg), ip, and at 7 weeks of age their sera were analyzed for the presence of IgM and IgG by double diffusion in agar against a dilution of rabbit anti-chicken Ig, strongly reacting with Fab fragment of chicken IgG and readily detecting IgG in a 1:100 dilution of normal chicken serum. Animals were classified as being Aγ only if their sera failed to give any precipitin lines, meaning that they lacked both serum IgM and IgG.

Individual 3- to 5-month-old chickens were immunized, for 5–8 weeks, with weekly intravenous (iv) injections of 0.5 ml of 20% allogeneic red blood cells (RBCs) in saline. Spleen cells were removed and used as effector cell sources for cytotoxicity studies.

Spleen cell preparations. Spleens were removed and gently teased in RPMI 1630 (Associated Biomedic Systems, Buffalo, N.Y.). After filtration through gauze, all cells were washed three times, counted in Natt–Herrick stain (9), and resuspended to the desired concentration in RPMI 1640 + 2% Aγ chicken serum. For some experiments, spleen cells were γ-irradiated *in vitro* at doses indicated in Table 1 (^{137}Cs-Gammator M, Radiation Machinery Corp., Parsippany, N.J.), immediately before mixing with target cells.

Fractionation of spleen cells. Percoll dilutions for gradients were made up from 100% Percoll (density = 1.1294 g/ml) prepared by adding nine parts of straight Percoll (Pharmacia Fine Chemicals, Uppsala, Sweden) to one part of a 10× phosphate-buffered saline (PBS, Flow Laboratories, Rockville, Mass.) (10). Gradients consisted of 2 ml of 70% (1.090 g/ml), 60% (1.077 g/ml), 50% (1.067 g/ml), 40% (1.056 g/ml), and 30% (1.043 g/ml) Percoll each layered in 15-ml plastic tubes with the heavy-density solution at the bottom. Two milliliters of 2×10^7/ml spleen cells in PBS was layered onto the top of such a gradient and centrifuged at 1300 rpm (800*g*) for 15 min at 4°C. Fractions 0, 1, 2, 3, and 4 were designated to represent the interfaces between cell suspensions and 30%, 30 and 40%, 40 and 50%, 50 and 60%, 60 and 70% Percoll, respectively. While most dead cells went to Fraction 1, RBCs were pelleted at the bottom of the tube.

Vicia villosa-adherent cells were separated using *V. villosa*-coated petri dishes (11). A 0.5 mg/ml *V. villosa* stock solution was made in 0.1 *M* citrate-buffered saline (pH 5.5), and 2.5-ml aliquots of this solution were added to 100-mm-diameter tissue culture grade petri dishes (Falcon 3003, Falcon, Oxnard, Calif.). After incubation at room temperature for 45 min the solution was recovered (can be reused up to 20 times). The petri dishes were washed 3 times with PBC pH 7.4, and then incubated with RPMI 1630 + 2% Aγ serum at room temperature for 15 min to minimize nonspecific adherence of cells to the plate. Ten milliliters of 7×10^6/ml spleen cell suspension in RPMI 1630 + 5% Aγ serum was then applied to *V. villosa*-coated petri dishes and incubated at 37°C for 45 min. At the end of this incubation period, nonadherent cells were collected after gently rocking the plate, and residual nonadherent cells were removed with a wash of 10 ml RPMI 1630 + 5% Aγ serum. The adherent cells were eluted with 5 ml of *N*-acetyl-D-galactosamine (1 mg/ml in RPMI 1630) to cover the bottom of the plate. The plate was incubated at 37°C for 5 min and the eluted *V. villosa* adherent cells were gently pipetted into tubes and washed 3 times before use.

Plastic-adherent and -nonadherent cells were separated according to the procedure described previously (3). Briefly, 10 ml of 2×10^7/ml spleen cells in RPMI 1640 + 2% Aγ serum was added to a 100-mm plastic petri dish (Nunc, Vangard International, Inc., Neptune, N.J.) and incubated at 37°C in a 10% CO_2 incubator for 1 hr. Plastic-nonadherent cells were collected after three such consecutive incubations. The plates were washed three times with RPMI 1630, to remove the residual nonadherent cells, and adherent cells were detached with a rubber policeman.

EA rosettes were prepared according to the method described by deKruyff *et al.* (12). Chicken anti-sheep erythrocyte (SE) serum was incubated with 0.1 *M* 2-mercaptoethanol (ME) for 3 hr at room temperature to inactivate 19S antibodies. A washed 1% SE suspension was mixed in equal volume with a subagglutinating dilution of ME-treated chicken anti-SE antiserum. The washed sensitized SE (1%) were then mixed in equal volume with spleen cells (10^7/ml), spun at 1500 rpm for 10 min, and gently resuspended to one-half of original volume in RPMI 1630. The mixture was then layered onto a Ficoll–Hypaque gradient (density = 1.090) and centrifuged at 2000 rpm for 4.5 min. The EA-rosette-depleted cells remained in the interface. The EA-rosette-forming cells were recovered from the bottom of the tube and SE were lysed by Tris–NH_4Cl (0.1 *M*) (13).

Treatment of spleen cells (10^7/ml) with rabbit anti-T-cell serum (1:75) and guinea pig C (1:24) was for 45 min at 37°C. This antiserum was described previously (3) and kills approximately 60% of normal chicken spleen cells.

In vitro cytotoxic assay. Cell-mediated lysis with spleen cells was determined by the ^{51}Cr-release assay (14). Briefly, 5×10^8 allogeneic chicken RBCs were labeled with 250 μC/$Na_2{}^{51}CrO_4$ (sodium chromate, New England Nuclear, Boston, Mass.) for 45 min at 37°C in RPMI 1640 + 2% Aγ serum. The ^{51}Cr-labeled target RBCs were washed three times and resuspended to 10^6 cells/ml. Mixtures of 200 μl of target cells and 200 μl of killer spleen cells at various concentrations in RPMI 1640 were then added to 15 × 75-mm plastic tubes (2003, Falcon Plastics, Oxnard, Calif.). At the end of 5- or 24-hr incubation periods at 37°C, 600 μl of medium was added to each tube and the cells were spun at 1000 rpm for 10 min. Aliquots of 500 μl supernatant were counted in an autogamma counter (Model 1185, Searle Analytical Inc., New York). The percentage of ^{51}Cr release for each sample was calculated as described (14):

$$\%\ ^{51}\text{Cr release} = \frac{(\text{exp.} - \text{spont.})\ \text{release}}{(\text{max.} - \text{spont.})\ \text{release}} \times 100\,.$$

Mean spontaneous release was 2.0 ± 0.4% at 5 hr and 8.8 ± 2.4% at 24 hr of incubation ($n = 6$). Maximum release was determined by the addition of 0.5% NP40 for 5 hr at 37°C. In some experiments cold NL spleen cells or fibrosarcoma cells (CHCT-NYU 1) (15) were added to the mixture to inhibit the cytotoxic effect of alloimmune spleen cells.

Assays in microtiter plates, using 10^4 labeled target RBC, gave very similar cytotoxic indices as did the tube assay using 2×10^5 target cells, but gave more variable spontaneous release, whereas spontaneous release in the tube tests was never more than 15% of total radioactivity. Maximal release was always >90%.

A typical dose–response curve for varying effector:target ratios with Aγ spleen cells from which RBC had been removed is shown in Fig. 1. In experiments where RBC had not been removed prior to assays the higher E/T ratios frequently showed

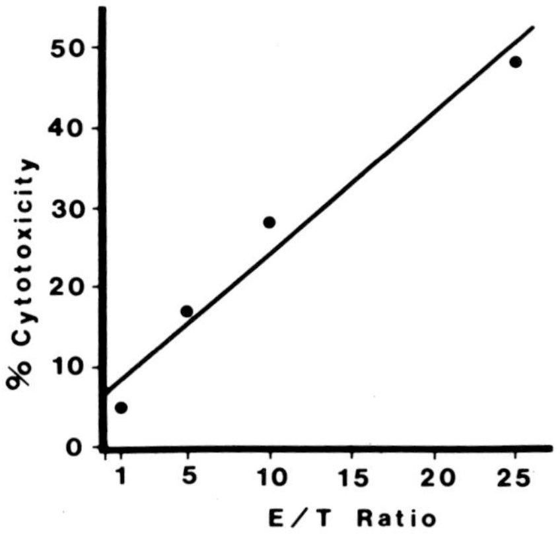

FIG. 1. Cytotoxic effect of Aγ alloimmune FP spleen cells on SC-RBC at different effector–target (E/T) ratios in the 24-hr assay. After effector cells had been passed through a Percoll gradient there was a significant correlation between E/T ratio and percentage cytotoxicity ($r = 0.984$, $P < 0.05$).

lower cytotoxicity than lower E/T ratios, apparently due to interference by RBC in the effector cells.

RESULTS

Comparison of Cytotoxic Effect in Spleen from Aγ And NL Birds on Various Days after the fourth to sixth iv Injection of Allogeneic Red Blood Cells

The results in Fig. 2 show the rapid *in vivo* development of cytotoxic activity after the last of a series of weekly iv injections of allogeneic RBC. In both FP and SC NL chickens the peak activity was seen on Day 3, whereas peak activity in Aγ chickens continued to increase until Day 5. In general, activity seen with 5 hr of incubation paralleled but was lower than that seen after 24 hr incubation. It was noted, however, that the only time at which cells from normal birds gave significant killing over background with 5 hr incubation was at 3 days after the last immunizing injection. Activities on Days 5 and 7 were both low with 5 hr, but with 24 hr of incubation some activity was seen on Day 7. Although the degree of activity of individual spleens varied, there clearly was significantly higher activity in Aγ than in normal chickens even when immunized simultaneously as was done in the experiments represented in Fig. 2. Additional experiments (not represented in the tables and figures) have consistently borne out this difference between Aγ and NL chickens. Immunization with allogeneic spleen cells induced entirely comparable cytotoxic activity to that seen after immunization with RBCs (data not shown). Although spleen cells taken 3 days after the last immunizing injection showed greater activity, some cytotoxic effect could also be detected in peripheral blood cells from Aγ alloimmune birds. These cells were obtained by low-speed (600 rpm, 12 min) centrifugation of heparinized blood. In a typical experiment peripheral blood cells caused 7% cytotoxicity as compared to 31% by spleen cells.

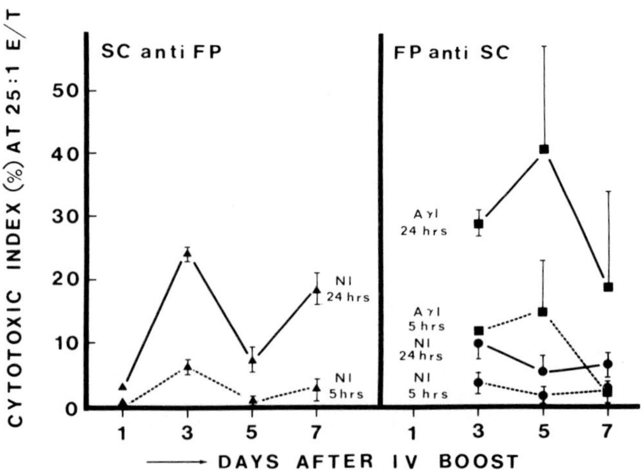

FIG. 2. Cytotoxic effect in spleen cells from normal (NI) (▲, ●) or Aγ (AγI) (■) chickens taken 1–7 days after the last of 4 to 6 weekly iv injections of 0.5 ml 20% allogeneic red blood cells (RBC). Results are given for 5 hr (---) or 24 hr (——) incubations. Vertical bars indicate standard errors (*n* = 3–5).

It is possible that the difference between the two incubation periods for Day 7 cells might be the result of the induction of a secondary response *in vitro*, during the 24 hr of incubation. In order to determine whether proliferation of cells was needed to obtain the higher level of cytotoxic activity in the 24-hr incubation period, cells from Aγ immune spleen, taken 3 days after the last immunizing injection, were irradiated prior to assay. The results in Table 1 show that even 2000-rad γ-irradiation, which is sufficient to inhibit >95% [^{3}H]TdR incorporation by chicken spleen cells (data not shown), caused only a minor decrease in the cytotoxic activity of Aγ spleen cells.

Density Distribution Of Cytolytic Cells in Aγ And NL Alloimmune Spleen

Since previous studies indicated a T-cell component in the cytotoxic effect of Aγ larger then that of NL alloimmune spleen an attempt was made to characterize these T cells of Aγ birds further. Percoll density gradient fractionation was done on spleen cells from both Aγ and NL birds, taken 3 days after the last iv injection.

The data in Table 2 show that cell fractionation by Percoll density gradients resulted in a different overall distribution for Aγ and NL spleen cells. The main difference in density distribution between the two was a reproducible tendency for spleen cells from alloimmune Aγ chickens to be skewed toward the lower density fractions. A functional significance related to these lower-density fractions ("activated" lymphoblast and macrophage) is seen by the corresponding distribution of lytic activity in these Aγ alloimmune chickens. This distribution in cell density and cytotoxic activity is different from that found in NL chickens where a larger number of cells and greater cytotoxic activity are found in the higher density fraction (1.090 g/ml).

It was noted that cells from Percoll fractions frequently had higher activity compared to unfractionated spleen cells tested at the same E/T ratio, particularly at E/T ratios of 25:1 or higher (see Table 2, Expt 1). Pooled Percoll fractions also had higher activity compared to spleen cells which had not been passed through Percoll. The main difference appeared to be in the RBC content, since all RBC were removed by the passage through Percoll. This inhibition by RBC was not noted in experiments on antibody-dependent cell-mediated cytotoxicity (16).

TABLE 1

Effect of γ-Irradiation on Cytotoxic Activity of Alloimmune Aγ FP Spleen Cells on SC-RBC

	Percentage cytotoxic activity[b] after irradiation[c] with		
E/T[a]	None	1000 rad	2000 rad
5:1	39	27	30
1:1	27	23	19

[a] E/T, effector to target ratio; 24 hr of incubation.

[b] Percentage of cytotoxic activity was expressed as described under Materials and Methods; activity on FP RBC control was <2%.

[c] Effector cells were γ-irradiated *in vitro* immediately before mixing with target cells.

TABLE 2

Cytotoxic Effect of Percoll-Fractionated Alloimmune Spleen Cells: Comparison of Aγ and Normal Chickens

Effector cells				
Animals	Spleen cell fraction[a]	Percentage of viable cells recovered[b]	Percentage cytotoxicity[c] Expt 1	Expt 2
Aγ	Unfractionated	—	18	89
	2 (1.067 g/ml)	4.5; 4.2	77	81
	3 (1.077 g/ml)	89.7; 88.5	67	87
	4 (1.090 g/ml)	5.8; 7.3	47	48
NL	Unfractionated	—	24	4
	2	8.1 ± 1.7	2	3
	3	69.2 ± 2.5	7	5
	4	22.7 ± 2.8	9	9

[a] Fractions 2, 3, and 4 were corresponding to the interfaces between 40 and 50%, 50 and 60%, and 60 and 70% Percoll solutions, respectively.

[b] Results of two separate fractionations recorded for Aγ and mean values ± SE given for three experiments with NL spleen cells.

[c] Effector to target ratio was 25:1 (Expt 1, Aγ), 15:1 (Expt 1 and 2, NL) and 5:1 (Expt 2, Aγ); activity on FP RBC control was <2%. 24-hr assay.

Enrichment of Cytolytic Cells from Alloimmune Aγ Chickens By Adherence to V. villosa Lectin

Table 3 shows results of two representative experiments in which spleen cells from which red cells were removed with a Percoll gradient were separated into cells adherent and nonadherent to *V. villosa* lectin. The fraction of spleen cells adherent to *V. villosa* was clearly larger in Aγ than in normal chicken spleen cell suspensions. Cytotoxicity tests showed that *V. villosa*-adherent cells from the Aγ alloimmune spleen cells had relatively more activity than the nonadherent cells, although activity was not significantly depleted from the nonadherent cell fraction. A major part of the cytotoxic activity of *V. villosa*-adherent cells was lost after treatment with anti-T and C, suggesting that these cells were primarily cytotoxic T cells. In contrast the adherent cells from NL alloimmune spleen had no activity even at 10:1 ratios, while the nonadherent fraction had low but significant cytotoxic activity above background. It seemed, however, that the fractionation procedure had caused a loss of total activity from the NL alloimmune spleen, since the cytotoxic activity of unfractionated spleen was higher than that of either one of the fractions.

Specificity Of Cytotoxic Adherent Spleen Cells

In previous studies it was shown that alloimmune NL spleen cells were cytotoxic only for the immunizing red cells or for red cells sharing the major histocompatibility locus antigens with the immunizing red cells. Antibody might have been formed by the alloimmune NL spleen cells and the mechanism of the target cell

TABLE 3

Adherence of Cytotoxic Cells in Alloimmune Aγ and NL Spleen[a] to *V. villosa* (V.V.) Lectin

Effector cells: Animals	Effector cells: Spleen cell fractions	Aver. percentage viable cells recovered	Percentage cytotoxicity: E/T[b]	Percentage cytotoxicity: Expt 1	Percentage cytotoxicity: Expt 2
Aγ	Unfractionated	—	10:1	ND[c]	28
			5:1	24	17
			1:1	ND	5
	V.V. nonadh.	85.7	10:1	32	39
			5:1	20	25
			1:1	6	7
	V.V. adh.	14.3	10:1	48	ND
			5:1	36	34
			1:1	9	6
	Anti-T + C-treated V.V. adh.		10:1	ND	11
			5:1	ND	6
			1:1	ND	1
NL	Unfractionated	—	50:1	16	30
			15:1	ND	24
	V.V. nonadh.	94.5	15:1	7	2
			5:1	0	0
			1:1	1	1
	V.V. adh.	5.5	10:1	1	ND
			5:1	0	0
			1:1	0	0

[a] Spleen cells were first centrifuged through a Percoll gradient, the fractions containing viable cells were pooled and used for adherence to *V. villosa* lectin-coated petri dishes. Adherent cells were removed from the dish with *N*-acetyl-D-galactosamine. In Experiment 2 plastic-adherent cells were removed prior to adherence to *V. villosa*-coated dishes.

[b] E/T, effector to target ratio; activity on allogeneic RBCs represented after subtraction of activity on syngeneic RBC.

[c] ND, not done.

killing could have been antibody-dependent cell-mediated cytotoxicity (ADCC), obtaining its specificity from the antibody. In fact, serum antibody titers of the alloimmune NL chickens were very high ($\log_2 = 14$) as determined by hemagglutination tests on sera taken after the fifth RBC injection. It was thus of interest to determine whether the adherent spleen cell component could show similar specificity in the total absence of antibody.

The results in Table 4 show that the plastic-adherent cells from alloimmune Aγ FP chicken spleen had at least as strong a cytotoxic effect on EL-6 RBC as on the immunizing SC-RBC. Since EL-6 and SC strains are both B2 in the major histocompatibility locus, and syngeneic RBC were not killed to the same extent (Expt 2) or not at all (Expt 1), the findings with nonadherent cells demonstrated an equally strong specificity as did the alloimmune NL cells studied previously. However, the plastic-adherent cells showed a high cytotoxic effect also on syngeneic RBC, which remained as the only component after treatment of these adherent cells with anti-T + C (Table 5 and footnote *c,* Table 4). The results in Table 5

TABLE 4

Specificity of Cytotoxic Effect of Plastic-Adherent and Nonadherent Spleen Cell Fractions from Aγ B2 Immune FP Chickens

			Percentage cytotoxicity[b] on		
Expt	Effector cells	E/T[a]	SC(B2)	EL-6(B2)	FP(B15/B21)
1	Unfractionated	50:1	54	ND	1
		8:1	43	ND	ND
	Plastic nonadh.	50:1	63	ND	ND
		8:1	44	ND	2
	Plastic adh.	8:1	51	ND	1
2	Unfractionated	10:1	22.5	25.0	0.8
		5:1	18.3	20.8	2.5
		1:1	10.6	12.2	1.6
	Plastic nonadh.	10:1	22.9	25.3	0
		5:1	17.7	19.1	1
		1:1	6.5	6.4	2.7
	Plastic adh.[c]	10:1	60.1	60.2	39.1
		5:1	43.3	48.5	45.7
		1:1	14.5	15.8	14.5

[a] E/T, effector to target ratio.

[b] 24-hr assay.

[c] Anti-T + C-treated plastic adherent cells gave 39.1(10:1), 47.6(5:1), and 15.6%(1:1) cytotoxicity on SC target cells. Spleen cells taken 4 (Expt 2) or 3 days after last immunizing injection of SC cells.

suggest that, after treatment with anti-T + C, plastic-adherent cells from Aγ alloimmune spleen had either nonspecific killer activity, which was as high on syngeneic as on allogeneic cells, or no activity. Thus, no evidence for a specific adherent cytotoxic component such as had previously been seen with NL alloimmune chickens was observed in Aγ chickens.

Fc-receptor-bearing cells were enumerated in NL and Aγ spleen and in their plastic-adherent and -nonadherent fractions. There were 12.5 and 10% Fc+ cells in NL and Aγ nonadherent spleen cells, whereas plastic-adherent cells contained 30 and 39%, respectively. The results in Table 6 show that cells from alloimmune Aγ spleen bearing Fc receptors had some specific cytotoxic activity, but were less active than the unfractionated cells or than cells from which the Fcγ+ cells had been depleted. The further characteristics of these cells were not determined.

Fibrosarcoma (CHCT-NYU 1) cells, derived from carcinogen-induced tumors in SC chickens, were also killed by both Aγ and NL FP alloimmune chicken spleen cells, but they were clearly less susceptible to the cytotoxic effect than SC-RBC, and they never showed >20% cytotoxicity above background. Studies of comparative inhibition of the cytotoxic effect on SC-RBC, by addition of spleen or fibrosarcoma cells, showed a greater ability of spleen cells to inhibit cytotoxicity (Fig. 3). It is thus possible that the SC fibrosarcoma cells are less susceptible to the cytotoxic effect because they express fewer of the relevant surface antigen(s). Addition of 2% normal chicken serum to the incubation medium did not affect the cytotoxic effect of Aγ alloimmune spleen cells on the allogeneic RBC either at 25:1 or at 5:1 E/T ratios. This same serum concentration caused a 50% inhibition of antibody-mediated cellular cytotoxicity (16).

TABLE 5

Effect of Treatment with Anti-T + C on Cytotoxic Effect of Nonadherent and Plastic-Adherent Alloimmune FP Spleen Cells (Aγ)

Expt	Effector cell pretreatment[a]	E/T ratio[b]	Activity on SC targets of: Untreated cells	Activity on SC targets of: Anti-T + C-treated cells	Activity on FP targets[c]
1	Unfractionated	20:1	51.8	ND	.3
		5:1	27.7	ND	.5
	Nonadherent	20:1	55.5	6.1	.3
		5:1	22.2	1.8	−.1
	Adherent	4:1	ND	2.8	2.1
2	Unfractionated	25:1	51	ND	.9
		10:1	52	ND	.5
	Nonadherent	25:1	65	19	.9
		10:1	56	26	1.4
	Adherent	4:1	ND	3.9	1.5
3	Nonadherent	10:1	8		−3
		5:1	6	ND	0
		1:1	4		1
	Adherent	5:1	24	18	25
		1:1	46	42	56

[a] Spleen cells taken 3 (Expt 3) or 5 days after last immunizing injection of SC cells.
[b] E/T, effector to target ratio.
[c] Results with control targets represent averages of results with untreated and anti-T + C-treated cells, since these results were very similar.

DISCUSSION

The cytotoxic effect of Aγ spleen cells after repeated iv immunizations was consistently higher than that of NL spleen cells. It is likely that this difference between NL and Aγ birds is due to the presence of high serum antibody titers to the allogeneic RBC in the NL alloimmune chickens. Such serum antibody can

TABLE 6

Cytotoxicity of Fc Receptor Bearing Spleen Cells from Aγ Alloimmune FP Chickens

Effector cell pretreatment	E/T[a]	Percentage cytotoxicity on: SC-RBC	Percentage cytotoxicity on: FP-RBC
Unfractionated	5:1	82	−1
	1:1	37	1
FcR-depleted[b]	5:1	97	−1
	1:1	49	1
FcR+ cells	1:1	31	−1

[a] E/T, effector to target ratio.
[b] FcR-depleted: spleen cells from which EA-rosette-forming cells were removed by Ficoll–Hypaque gradient centrifugation.

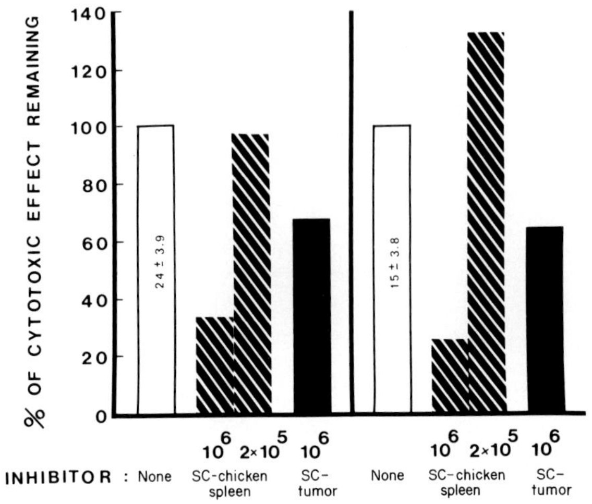

FIG. 3. Effect of cold target inhibition on cytotoxic activity of normal alloimmune spleen cells. Numbers inside open columns indicate the actual cytotoxicity indices ± standard errors (n = 3) used as 100% activity. Remaining activity in presence of inhibitors is given as percentages of these. E/T = 50:1 (left) and 25:1 (right).

probably block effective sensitization of the host (2, 17). Thus, with the method of immunization used, cytotoxic T-cell immunity may well be attained more readily in the absence of serum antibody.

The activity in Aγ alloimmune spleen cells on Day 3 after the last of a series of iv injections of allogeneic RBC is apparently due to a combination of activated T cells and monocytes, both of which are resistant to 2000-rad γ-irradiation. A few days later (Day 7), activity was lacking in the 5 hr assay but could still be detected upon 24 hr of incubation, perhaps related to the reactivation of cytotoxic cells *in vitro* as a result of the reexposure to antigen.

The presence of a cytotoxic T-cell component in the Aγ chicken spleens was clearly shown in a previous publication (3) by the lack of adherence of the cytotoxic cells to nylon wool and by their inactivation after exposure to rabbit anti-T-cell serum + C. This conclusion was reinforced in the present studies by the adherence of at least a large portion of these cytotoxic cells to *V. villosa* lectin. The cytotoxic cells in NL alloimmune spleen do not exhibit these properties and also differ with respect to Percoll fractionation by concentrating in the higher-density fractions. It seems, therefore, that most of the cytotoxic T-cell component in the Aγ spleen fractionated in lower-density Percoll fractions than did the non-T-cell component of NL alloimmune spleen.

It is possible that the low-density cytotoxic cells in Aγ spleen represented T lymphoblasts similar to those described by others in cultures of murine alloimmune cells after reexposure to the immunizing antigen *in vitro* (18, 19). Since the alloimmune spleen cells were taken relatively early after an *in vivo* challenge, such blast cells would be expected to be present. It is also known that murine T lymphoblasts are much more adherent to nylon wool and to plastic than are small T lymphocytes. It is therefore not surprising that much of the specific cytotoxic effect of Aγ chicken spleen cells in the present experiments, even that found in the adherent cell fractions, was inactivated by ATS + C. Both FcR + cells and FcR−

cells had specific cytotoxic activity in the present experiments. This is also consistent with the properties of activated T blasts from murine mixed lymphocyte cultures (20).

The majority of the cytotoxic cells in both NL and Aγ alloimmune chickens showed specificity for the immunizing RBC, cross-reacting strongly with RBC of a similar major histocompatibility locus. The specificity of killing correlated well with the high degree of inhibition which could be obtained with cold allogeneic, but not with syngeneic spleen cells. However, the plastic-adherent anti-T + C-treated cells from some of the Aγ alloimmune chickens still showed a strong cytotoxic effect on syngeneic as well as allogeneic RBC. This might be attributed to the presence of macrophages which had become activated *in vivo* in response to the recent intravenous challenge with allogeneic RBC. In no case was any antigen-specific cytotoxic effect observed in adherent cell fractions from Aγ chickens that could be attributed to cells other than T cells. Thus, the adherent cell component of Aγ chickens was primarily nonspecific and evidence for specific "arming" of macrophages by T cells from Aγ chickens was not obtained. On the other hand "arming" of effector cells by serum antibody may account for the specific cytotoxic effect of non-T cells found in NL alloimmune spleen (3).

ACKNOWLEDGMENTS

The superb technical assistance of Mr. Pedro Sanchez is gratefully acknowledged. The patience and expertise of Ms. Anita Clark have been invaluable in the preparation of this manuscript.

REFERENCES

1. Perlmann, P., and Cerottini, J. -C., *In* "The Antigens" (Michael Sela, Ed.), Vol. 5. Academic Press, New York, 1981.
2. Welsh, K. I., Batchelor, J. R., Maynard, A., and Burgos, H., *J. Exp. Med.* **150,** 465, 1979.
3. Palladino, M. A., Chi, D. S., Blyznak, N., Paolino, A. M., and Thorbecke, G. J., *Develop. Comp. Immunol.* **4,** 309, 1980.
4. Ross, L. J. N., *Nature (London)* **268,** 644, 1977.
5. Evans, R., and Alexander, P., *Nature (London)* **228,** 620, 1970.
6. Grant, C. K., Currie, G. A., and Alexander, P., *J. Exp. Med.* **135,** 150, 1972.
7. Palladino, M. A., and Thorbecke, G. J., *Cell. Immunol.* **38,** 350, 1978.
8. Palladino, M. A., Lerman, S. P., and Thorbecke, G. J., *J. Immunol.* **116,** 1673, 1976.
9. Natt, M. P., and Herrick, C. A., *Poultry Sci.* **31,** 735, 1952.
10. Kurnick, J. T., Östberg, L., Stegagno, M., Kimura, A. K., Örn, A., and Sjöberg, O., *Scand. J. Immunol.* **10,** 563, 1979.
11. Kimura, A., Wigzell, H., Holmquist, G., Ersson, B., and Carlsson, P., *J. Exp. Med.* **149,** 473, 1979.
12. DeKruyff, R. H., Ponzio, N. M., and Thorbecke, G. J., *Eur. J. Immunol.* **7,** 237, 1977.
13. Gorden, W. C., Prager, M. D., and Carroll, M. C., *Cell. Immunol.* **49,** 329, 1980.
14. Cerottini, J. C., Nordin, A. A., and Brunner, K. T., *Nature (London)* **228,** 1308, 1970.
15. Lerman, S. P., Palladino, M. A., and Thorbecke, G. J., *J. Nat. Cancer Inst.* **57,** 295, 1976.
16. Chi, D. S., and Thorbecke, G. J., *Cell. Immunol.* **64,** 258, 1981.
17. Batchelor, J. R., Welsh, K. I., and Burgos, H., *Nature (London)* **273,** 54, 1978.
18. MacDonald, H. R., Cerottini, J. C., and Brunner, K. T. *J. Exp. Med.* **140,** 1511, 1974.
19. Häyry, P., *Immunogenetics* **3,** 417, 1976.
20. Häyry, P., and Anderson, L. C., *Cell. Immunol.* **25,** 237, 1976.

CELLULAR IMMUNOLOGY **64,** 258–266 (1981)

Cytotoxicity to Allogeneic Cells in the Chicken

III. Antibody-Dependent Cell-Mediated Cytotoxicity in Normal and Agammaglobulinemic Chickens[1]

DAVID S. CHI*,[2] AND G. JEANETTE THORBECKE

**Department of Internal Medicine, East Tennessee State University College of Medicine, Johnson City, Tennessee 37601, and Department of Pathology, New York University Medical Center, 550 First Avenue, New York, New York 10016*

Received May 22, 1981; accepted July 30, 1981

Spleen cells from normal and Aγ chickens mediate antibody-dependent cellular cytotoxicity ADCC on syngeneic or allogeneic RBC. They are non-T, non-B cells with Fc receptors. They are nylon wool adherent; a proportion of them are also plastic adherent and inhibitable by trypan blue. They are resistant to 2000-rad γ-irradiation *in vitro*. Spleen cells can be armed to mediate ADCC on unsensitized target RBC by incubation with antibody.

INTRODUCTION

Antibody-dependent cellular cytotoxicity (ADCC) is mediated by a variety of cell types in human (1–4) and mouse (5, 6) lymphoid tissue which include monocytes (2, 4, 6) and lymphocytes (1, 3–5). Originally ADCC was described as a property of non-T lymphoid cells, possibly Ig bearing (5), but it was soon realized that most of the activity was associated with non-T, non-B cells (7), also called "null cells," with relatively avid Fc receptors (8). Some of these null lymphocytes may belong to the B-cell lineage (pre-B cells) (9) or to the T-cell lineage (10–14). Recently ADCC activity has been found in activated cells (15, 16).

Since bursectomized, agammaglobulinemic (Aγ) chickens lack both B and pre-B cells (17, 18), it is of interest to determine their level of ADCC activity as compared to that in normal (NL) chickens. Cytotoxicity to antibody-coated target RBC has been demonstrated using normal chicken effector cells and chicken antibody (19, 20). ADCC activity has also been described in ducks, where it was suggested to be of importance in allograft rejection (21). In studies on cytotoxic activity in alloimmune chickens a prominent non-T-cell component was found with monocyte-like properties and target specificity (22). Such monocytes with target cell specificity were not found in Aγ alloimmune chickens (23). In the present studies the serum antibody of alloimmune NL chickens was studied for its capacity

[1] This investigation was supported by Grant AI-14829 awarded by the National Institute of Allergy and Infectious Diseases and Grants CA-16247 and IR23CA30160-01 awarded by the National Cancer Institute, DHEW.

[2] Fellow under Grant 5T32 CA-09161 awarded by the National Cancer Institute, DHEW.

0008-8749/81/160258-09$02.00/0

to arm NL and Aγ chicken effector cells and to mediate ADCC. The effector cell capable of mediating ADCC was also characterized.

MATERIALS AND METHODS

Animals and antiserum. FP (B15/B21) and SC (B2/B2) chicken eggs were obtained from Hyline Poultry Farms (Dallas Center, Iowa). Line-6 chickens (EL-6, B2/B2) were obtained from the Regional Poultry Research Laboratories, East Lansing, Michigan. Hormonal bursectomy was performed on Day 11 of embryonation by injection of 3.75 mg testosterone proprionate (Biochemicals Corp., Cleveland, Ohio) (24). After hatching, these chicks received cyclophosphamide (Cytoxan, Meade Johnson, Evansville, Ind.) on Days 1 (4 mg) and 2 (3 mg), intraperitoneally, and at 7 weeks of age their sera were analyzed for the presence of IgM and IgG by double diffusion in agar against a dilution of rabbit anti-chicken Ig, strongly reacting with Fab fragment of chicken IgG and readily detecting IgG in a 1:100 dilution of normal chicken serum. Animals were classified as being Aγ only if their sera failed to give any precipitin lines, meaning that they lacked both serum IgM and IgG. Surgical thymectomy was performed on Day 1 after hatching. Animals were examined for thymic remnants at autopsy and used only if found to be free of detectable thymus.

Spleen cells from unimmunized 3- to 5-month-old chickens were removed and used as effector cell sources for ADCC. In some cases, FP chickens were immunized with five to six weekly intravenous (iv) injections of 0.5 ml of 20% SC red blood cells (RBC) in saline.

The alloantisera used were obtained by immunizing 3- to 5-month-old NL FP or SC chickens with five weekly iv injections of 0.5 ml of 20% allogeneic RBC in saline. Alloantisera were inactivated at 56°C for 30 min. In some experiments the alloantiserum was treated with 0.1 M 2-mercaptoethanol at room temperature for 3 hr prior to sensitization of target RBC (25).

Spleen cell preparations. Spleens were gently teased in RPMI 1630 (Associated Biomedic Systems, Buffalo, N.Y.). After filtration through gauze, cells were washed three times, counted in Natt–Herrick stain (26), and resuspended to the desired concentration in RPMI 1640 + 2% Aγ chicken serum. To eliminate T cells, the spleen cells were incubated with rabbit anti-chicken thymocyte serum (1:75) and guinea pig C (1:18) at 37°C for 45 min (22). The specificity of this antiserum for T cells has been tested and described previously (22, 27). For some experiments, spleen cells were γ-irradiated *in vitro* (^{137}Cs-Gammator M, Radiation Machinery Corp., Parsippany, N.J.), immediately before mixing with target cells. In some cases, spleen cells were incubated with 0.4 mg/ml trypan blue (22) at 37°C for 30 min prior to cytotoxicity testing.

Fractionation of spleen cells. Percoll dilutions for gradients were made up from "100%" Percoll prepared by adding 9 parts of straight Percoll (Pharmacia Fine Chemicals, Uppsala, Sweden) to 1 part of a 10× phosphate-buffered saline (PBS) solution (Flow Laboratories, Rockville, Md.) (23). Gradients consisted of 2 ml each of 70, 50, and 30% Percoll layered in 15-ml plastic tubes with the heavy-density solution at the bottom. Two milliliters of 2×10^7/ml spleen cells in PBS were layered onto the top of such a gradient and centrifuged at 1300 rpm (800*g*) for 15 min at 4°C. Fractions 1, 2, and 3 were designated to represent the three interfaces. While most dead cells went to Fraction 1, RBC were pelleted at the bottom of the tube. The cells from Fractions 2 and 3 were pooled and used for ADCC.

Nylon wool (NW)-nonadherent and -adherent spleen cell populations were separated on NW columns (Fenwal Laboratories, Morton Grove, Ill.) according to the method of Julius *et al.* (28) except the cells were suspended in RPMI 1640 and 2% Aγ serum.

Plastic adherent and nonadherent cells were separated according to the procedure described previously (22). Briefly, 10 ml of 2×10^7/ml spleen cells in RPMI 1640 + 2% Aγ serum were added to a 100-mm plastic petri dish (Nunc, Vanguard International, Inc., Neptune N.J.) and incubated at 37°C in a 10% CO_2 incubator for 1 hr. Plastic-nonadherent cells were collected after three such consecutive incubations. The plates were washed three times with RPMI 1640 to remove the residual nonadherent cells, and adherent cells were detached with a rubber policeman.

EA rosettes were prepared according to the method described by deKruyff *et al.* (29). Chicken anti-sheep erythrocyte (SE) serum was incubated with 0.1 *M* 2-mercaptoethanol (ME) for 3 hr at room temperature to inactivate 19S antibodies. A washed 1% SE suspension was mixed in equal volume with a subagglutinating dilution of this ME-treated chicken anti-SE antiserum. The washed sensitized SE (1%) were then mixed in equal volume with spleen cells (10^7/ml), spun at 1500 rpm for 10 min, and gently resuspended to one-half the original volume in RPMI 1640. The mixture was then layered onto a Ficoll–Hypaque gradient (density = 1.090) and centrifuged at 2000 rpm for 4.5 min. The EA-rosette-depleted cells remained in the interface. The EA-rosette-forming cells were recovered from the bottom of the tube and SE were lysed by Tris–NH_4Cl (0.1 *M*) (30). Depleted cells were retested for rosette formation and found negative. Control cells were sham depleted with uncoated SE and had not changed in their percentage of Fc+ cells upon retesting.

CMC and ADCC assays. Cell-mediated lysis with spleen cells was determined by a ^{51}Cr-release assay (31). Briefly, 5×10^8 chicken RBC were labeled with 250 μCi $Na_2{}^{51}CrO_4$ (sodium chromate, New England Nuclear, Boston Mass.) for 45 min at 37°C in RPMI 1640 + 2% Aγ serum. The ^{51}Cr-labeled target RBC were washed three times and resuspended to 10^6/ml for the CMC assay. For the ADCC assay, the ^{51}Cr-labeled target RBC were resuspended to 10^7 cells/ml and further incubated with appropriate dilutions of alloantiserum at 37°C for 30 min. Alloantiserum-treated ^{51}Cr-labeled target RBC were washed three times and resuspended to 10^6 cells/ml.

Mixtures of 200 μl of target cells and 200 μl of spleen cells at various concentrations in RPMI 1640 were then added to 15×75-mm plastic tubes (2003, Falcon Plastics, Oxnard, Calif.). At the end of 5- or 24-hr incubation periods at 37°C, 600 μl of medium was added to each tube and the cells were spun at 1000 rpm for 10 min. Aliquots of 500 μl supernatant were counted in an autogamma counter (Model 1185, Searle Analytical Inc., New York). The percentage of ^{51}Cr release for each sample was calculated as described (31):

$$\% \ ^{51}\text{Cr release} = \frac{(\text{exp.} - \text{spont.})\ \text{release}}{(\text{max.} - \text{spont.})\ \text{release}} \times 100.$$

Spontaneous release was always tested on antibody-coated as well as on uncoated RBC and the appropriate control was used in each calculation. Mean spontaneous release of antibody-coated RBC was less than 10% at 5 hr and 18.5 ± 1.7% (n = 15) at 24 hr of incubation. Mean spontaneous release of uncoated RBC was 2.0 ± 0.4% at 5 hr and 8.8 ± 2.4% at 24 hr of incubation. Maximum release was determined after incubation with 0.5% NP40 for 5 hr at 37°C, and was always >90%.

RESULTS

Demonstration of ADCC Activity in NL and Aγ Chicken Spleen

The initial results, in confirmation of those of Imir *et al.* (19), demonstrated that chicken spleen cells were able to lyse antibody-coated target cells (Table 1). When SC-RBC were incubated with either untreated or ME-treated alloantibody (FP anti-SC), washed, and exposed to allogeneic or syngeneic spleen cells from unimmunized chickens, a percentage lysis was obtained which decreased with decreasing effector to target cell (E/T) ratios. ME-treated serum was somewhat more effective in mediating this lysis than was untreated antiserum. The FP anti-SC antiserum was titrated and showed plateau activity when used up to 1:160 final dilution for incubation with target cells. If the antiserum was absorbed with target RBC prior to use, no lysis was observed. Moreover, normal chicken serum did not confer upon RBC any susceptibility to the lytic activity of normal spleen cells. Spleen cells also lysed FP-RBC which had been incubated with SC anti-FP alloantiserum (data not shown).

The results in Table 2 show that the presence of 2% normal chicken serum (NCS) during the cytotoxicity assay caused approximately 50% inhibition of cytotoxicity at the 25:1 E/T ratio, while 1% NCS was less inhibitory. Since the presence of 2% Aγ serum had no inhibitory effect, the effect of NCS was attributed

TABLE 1

Effect of Mercaptoethanol Pretreatment on the Ability of Alloantiserum to Coat RBC for ADCC

		Percentage cytotoxicity[c]								
		Expt 1			Expt 2			Expt 3		
Spleen donor[a]	Alloantiserum pretreatment[b]	E/T 25	E/T 5	E/T 1	E/T 25	E/T 5	E/T 1	E/T 25	E/T 5	E/T 1
NL Chicken	Untreated	15	9	1	10	2	0	23	18	4
	ME-Treated	29	16	8	14	5	2	30	14	5
Aγ chicken	Untreated	31	27	24	4	3	3	ND	ND	ND
	ME-Treated	47	33	33	8	2	3	ND	ND	ND

[a] Unimmunized spleen cells taken from FP chickens (Expts 1 and 2) or SC chickens (Expt 3) were used as effector cells (E).

[b] Alloantiserum at the appropriate dilution was incubated with 0.1 *M* mercaptoethanol at room temperature for 3 hr prior to use.

[c] ^{51}Cr-labeled SC-RBCs incubated for 30 min at 37°C with FP anti-SC antiserum (1:20 final dilution) were used as targets (T) in all experiments; incubation time was 24 hr.

TABLE 2

Inhibition of ADCC by NL Chicken Serum (NCS)

	Percentage cytotoxicity	
Inhibitor	E/T[a] 25	E/T 5
None	45	9
NCS 1%	33	3
NCS 2%	22	1

[a] E/T, effector to target cell ratio; incubation time was 24 hr.

to the presence of serum Ig blocking the ADCC activity. Incubation of the spleen cells with alloantiserum either at 37 or at 4°C, prior to mixing with target cells, also caused a low but significant degree (11–14%) of cytotoxicity above background at the 25:1 E/T ratio (data not shown). Thus, at least some of the antibody mediating the target cell lysis was able to adhere to the killer cells.

Characterization of Cell Type Mediating ADCC

The experiments recorded in Table 1 already showed that spleen cells from Aγ chickens were at least as capable of mediating ADCC as were spleen cells from NL chickens. This aspect was studied in more detail in experiments recorded in Table 3. The overall comparison of Aγ and NL spleen cells showed greater activity in the Aγ spleen, although the difference was statistically significant at the 25:1 E/T ratio only. This could be due to the relatively higher representation of the effector cells in the absence of the B cells, which normally represent 30% of the cells in the spleen. Neonatal thymectomy did not appear to affect the ADCC activity of spleen cells taken 13 weeks after hatching.

Further experiments were aimed at detecting a possible T-cell component in the ADCC-mediating cell population (Table 4). It was found that the entire activity in both Aγ and NL spleen was resistant to treatment with rabbit anti-T-cell serum

TABLE 3

Effect of Bursectomy (Aγ) and Thymectomy (TX) on ADCC activity of FP Spleen Cells

	Percentage cytotoxicity[a] ± SE (*n*)		
Spleen donor	E/T 25	E/T 5	E/T 1
Aγ	36 ± 6.8(7)[b]	27 ± 8.1(7)	13 ± 4.6(5)
TX[c]	35	40	ND
TX[c]	32	27	ND
NL	18 ± 2.0(6)[b]	13 ± 3.1(6)	4 ± 1.5(3)

[a] ^{51}Cr-labeled FP-RBCs incubated with mercaptoethanol-treated SC anti-FP antiserum were used as targets. Incubation time was 24 hr.

[b] $0.05 > P > 0.025$ (*t* test).

[c] TX on the day of hatching and tested at 13 weeks of age. Data shown are values for individual chickens.

TABLE 4

Non-T-Cell Nature of ADCC Effector Cell

Effector cell treatment	Spleen donor	Percentage cytotoxicity E/T[a] 25	E/T 5
Anti-T + C-treated[b]	Aγ	30	24
Control		31	27
Anti-T + C-treated	NL	21	4
Control		15	9
Nylon wool adh.	NL	15	19
Nylon wool nonadh.		1	1
Unfractionated		32	24

[a] E/T, effector to target cell ratio; incubation time was 24 hr.

[b] Effector cells were incubated with rabbit anti-thymus serum (1:75) and guinea pig C (1:18) at 37°C for 45 min.

+ C. Moreover, the ADCC activity fractionated with the NW-adherent (non-T) rather than with the NW-nonadherent spleen cells. The bulk of the ADCC activity was found to reside in FcR+ spleen cells as was also found in mammals (Table 5). The remaining activity in the FcR-depleted population in Experiment 1 could have been due to persistence of some FcR+ cells in this population, which were possibly less able to form rosettes and therefore not removed by the fractionation method used.

Since a large percentage of ADCC activity in both humans and mice is associated with monocytes, it seemed of interest to determine the ability of the ADCC-mediating cells to adhere to plastic and to be inhibited by preincubation with trypan blue (Table 6). The results suggested heterogeneity of the ADCC-mediating cells in that approximately two-thirds of the activity was in the plastic-adherent population and about the same portion of the activity was inhibited by trypan blue (Table 6, Expt 3). The ADCC fractionation by adherence was similar to the dis-

TABLE 5

Cytotoxic Effect of Fc Receptor (FcR)-Bearing Aγ Spleen Cells in ADCC

	Percentage cytotoxicity					
	Expt 1			Expt 2		
Treatment[a]	E/T[b] 25	E/T 5	E/T 1	E/T 25	E/T 5	E/T 1
Unfractionated	48	42	ND	39	14	4
FcR-depleted	10	15	ND	−3	−9	1
FcR^+ cells	ND	ND	34	ND	ND	33

[a] FcR-depleted = EA-rosette-forming cells removed by Ficoll–Hypaque gradient centrifugation.

[b] Effector to target cell ratio; incubation time was 24 hr.

TABLE 6

Effect of Fractionation, Trypan Blue Treatment and γ-Irradiation of Spleen Cells on ADCC

Expt	Spleen donor	Effector[a] treatment	Incubation time (hr)	Percentage Cytotoxicity[b] E/T 25	E/T 5	E/T 1
1	NL	Unfractionated	24	20	10	2
		Plastic-adh.		17	10	7
		Plastic nonadh.		5	3	−2
	Aγ	Unfractionated	24	34	24	16
		Plastic-adh.		48	38	30
		Plastic nonadh.		20	17	9
2	NL	Untreated	24	11	9	ND
		1000R		14	ND	ND
		2000R		13	ND	ND
3	Aγ	Untreated	5	34	18	4
		Trypan blue		15	5	ND
		Untreated	24	39	14	4
		Trypan blue		12	16	ND

[a] Effector cells were either γ-irradiated *in vitro* (Expt 2) or incubated with trypan blue (0.4 mg/ml) at 37°C for 30 min prior to test (Expt 3).

[b] ^{51}Cr-labeled SC RBCs incubated with mercaptoethanol-treated FP anti-SC antiserum were used as targets in all experiments; E/T, effector to target cell ratio.

tribution of FcR+ cells in that nonadherent cells contained approximately 10% and plastic-adherent cells 30–40% FcR+ cells. An enriched cytotoxic activity of plastic-adherent fraction was shown in Aγ, but not in NL spleen (Table 6, Expt 1). It is perhaps because B cells in NL spleen also adhere somewhat to plastic and thereby decrease the proportion of cytotoxic adherent cells. The cells mediating ADCC appeared resistant to 2000R γ-irradiation *in vitro.*

DISCUSSION

As in mammals (32), ADCC in the chicken appears to be mediated primarily by ME-resistant, and thus presumably IgG (25) antibody. This antibody is also capable of "arming" chicken lymphoid cells, primarily NW adherent cells, *in vitro.* The observation that normal, but not Aγ, chicken serum inhibits the ADCC activity is in agreement with observations in mammalian systems showing inhibition of ADCC by IgG (8, 32). Arming of chicken lymphoid cells by chicken, but not by mammalian, antibody was previously shown by Imir *et al.* (19). They also found, as was seen in the present studies, that arming of the lymphoid cells is less effective for mediation of ADCC than sensitization of the target cells.

The effector cell for ADCC is present in Aγ to at least the same extent as in NL chickens. These findings clearly exclude pre-B and B cells as ADCC contributors, and are in agreement with the normal level of ADCC found in Aγ patients (33). ADCC is unaffected by treatment with anti-T-cell serum + C and by neonatal thymectomy. The nylon wool adherence further confirms the non-T-cell nature of the effector cell. The majority of the cells appear both to be adherent to plastic and to bear Fc-receptors. The inhibitory effect of trypan blue on ADCC activity in Aγ spleen cells suggests a monocyte (macrophage) nature of a large proportion of the effector cells, as has previously been suggested for ADCC-mediating cells in mice (6) as well as for chickens (34). The ADCC component attributed to K cells in man is mediated by nonphagocytic, nonadherent "null" lymphocytes (35). It seems that, in the chicken spleen, the proportion of the non-T, non-B cells mediating ADCC, which is nonadherent to plastic and might represent the K cell in this species, is relatively small, as has also been found to be the case in mice (6, 36). The resistance of the effector cell to 2000 rad γ-irradiation is in agreement with a macrophage-like nature. Relative resistance to γ-irradiation *in vitro* was also found for K cells in mice, although *in vivo* K-cell activity declined within 1 day after 800-rad total body γ-irradiation (37).

The cytotoxic cells found in the alloimmune NL chickens share many properties with the ADCC-mediating cells described in the present studies. The cytotoxic cells in such animals are largely plastic adherent, inhibitable by trypan blue, and resistant to treatment with anti-T serum + C (22). On the basis of the present results, as well as those of Runnlund and Linna (20), it seems likely that the mechanism of specific target cell killing in these animals includes an ADCC component in which the effector cells are "armed" with antibody *in vivo*. Although, alloimmune Aγ chickens also show, in addition to nonadherent T-cell cytotoxicity, specific target cell killing by plastic-adherent cells (23), this activity is abolished by anti-T-cell serum and C. Thus, various components can be demonstrated in the specific cytotoxic response to alloantigens, which assume different proportions in the NL and Aγ chickens.

REFERENCES

1. Härafast, B., Andersson, T., and Perlmann, P., *J. Immunol.* **114,** 1820, 1975.
2. Thorsteinsson, L., Frøland, S. S., and Natvig, J. B., *Scand. J. Immunol.* **6,** 1305, 1977.
3. Pape, G. R., Troye, M., and Perlmann, P., *J. Immunol.* **118,** 1919, 1977.
4. Shaw, G. M., Levy, P. C., and LoBuglio, A. F., *Cell. Immunol.* **41,**122, 1978.
5. Pross, H. F., Tracey, D. E., Wigzell, H., and Schirmacher, V., *Scand. J. Immunol.* **3,** 769, 1974.
6. Tada, M., Hinuma, S., Abo, T., and Kumagai, K., *J. Immunol.* **124,** 1929, 1980.
7. van Oers, M. H. J., Zeijlemaker, W. P., and Schellekens, P. Th. A., *Eur. J. Immunol.* **7,** 143, 1977.
8. Gormus, B. J., Woodson, M., and Kaplan, M. E., *Clin. Exp. Immunol.* **43,** 274, 1978.
9. Brier, A. M., Chess, L., and Schlossman, S. F., *J. Clin. Invest.* **56,** 1580, 1975.
10. Evans, R. L., Chess, L., Levine, H., and Schlossman, S. F., *J. Exp. Med.* **147,** 605, 1978.
11. Caraux, J., Thierry, C., and Serrou, B., *Eur. J. Immunol.* **8,** 806, 1978.
12. Johnsen, H. E., and Madsen, M., *Scand. J. Immunol.* **9,** 429, 1979.
13. Chiao, J. W., Gee, T. S., and Good, R. A., *Immunol. Commun.* **8,** 213, 1979.
14. Balch, C. M., Ades, E. W., Loken, M. R., and Shore, S. L., *J. Immunol.* **124,** 1845, 1980.
15. Kimura, A. K., Rubin, B., and Andersson, L. C., *Scand. J. Immunol.* **6,** 787, 1977.
16. Rubin, B., and Høier-Madsen, M., *Acta Pathol. Microbiol. Scand.* **85,** 267, 1977.
17. Warner, N. L., Szenberg, A., and Burnet, F. M., *Aust. J. Exp. Biol. Med. Sci.* **40,** 373, 1962.
18. Eskola, J., and Toivanen, A., *Cell. Immunol.* **26,** 68, 1976.
19. Imir, T., Saksela, E., and Mäkelä, O., *Scand. J. Immunol.* **6,** 827, 1977.
20. Runnlund, R. D., and Linna, T. J., *Fed. Proc.* **39,** 924, 1980.
21. Bubenik, J., Perlmann, P., and Hasek, M., *Transplantation* **10,** 290, 1970.
22. Palladino, M. A., Chi, D. S., Blyznak, N., Paolino, A. M., and Thorbecke, G. J., *Develop. Comp. Immunol.* **4,** 309, 1980.
23. Chi, D. S., Blyznak, N., Kimura, A., Palladino, M. A., and Thorbecke, G. J., *Cell. Immunol.* **64,** 246, 1981.
24. Palladino, M. A., Lerman, S. P., and Thorbecke, G. J., *J. Immunol.* **116,** 1673, 1976.
25. Benedict, A. A., Brown, R. J., and Hersh, R., *Proc. Soc. Exp. Biol. Med.* **113,** 136, 1963.

26. Natt, M. P., and Herrick, C. A., *Poultry Sci.* **31,** 735, 1952.
27. Chi, D. S., Galton, J., and Thorbecke, G. J., *In* "Avian Immunology" (B. M. Freeman, Ed.), p. 103., 1981.
28. Julius, M. H., Simpson, E., and Herzenberg, L. A., *Eur. J. Immunol.* **3,** 645, 1973.
29. deKruyff, R. H., Ponzio, N. M., and Thorbecke, G. J., *Eur. J. Immunol.* **7,** 237, 1977.
30. Gordon, W. C., Prager, M. D., and Carroll, M. C., *Cell. Immunol.* **49,** 329, 1980.
31. Cerottini, J. C., Nordin, A. A., and Brunner, K. T., *Nature (London)* **228,** 1308, 1970.
32. Ziegler, H. K., and Henney, C. S., *J. Immunol.* **119,** 1010, 1977.
33. Shore, S. L., Melewicz, F. M., and Gordon, D. S., *J. Immunol.* **118,** 558, 1977.
34. Fleischer, B., *J. Immunol.* **125,** 1161, 1980.
35. Nelson, D. L., Bundy, B. M., Pitchon, H. E., Blaese, R. M., and Strober, W., *J. Immunol.* **117,** 1472, 1976.
36. Greenberg, A. H., Shen, L., Walker, L., Arnaiz-Villena, A., and Roitt, I. M., *Eur. J. Immunol.* **5,** 474, 1975.
37. Santoni, A., Herberman, R. B., and Holden, H. T., *J. Nat. Cancer Inst.* **63,** 995, 1979.

CELLULAR IMMUNOLOGY **64**, 267–276 (1981)

Stimulation of Prostaglandin E_2(PGE_2) Secretion by Benzylpenicilloyl (BPO) Carrier Conjugates in Human Peripheral Blood Lymphocytes[1]

MENACHEM SHLESINGER AND YVES BOREL[2]

Division of Pediatrics, Harvard Medical School and Department of Medicine, Children's Hospital Medical Center, 300 Longwood Avenue, Boston, Massachusetts 02115

Received June 1, 1981; accepted July 29, 1981

The conjugates of the main determinant of penicillin, benzylpenicilloyl (BPO), with various protein carriers can stimulate mononuclear cells from human peripheral blood lymphocytes (PBL) to increase PGE_2 secretion. Thus, BPO bound to either human γ-globulin (BPO-HGG), bovine γ-globulin (BPO-BGG), and keyhole limpet menocyanin (BPO-KLH) increased the PGE_2 level 8–20 times above the level produced by stimulation with the carriers alone. Since in previous studies it was shown that preincubation with BPO-HGG can suppress the thymidine uptake after subsequent stimulation with BPO-KLH, we investigated if the induction of this unresponsiveness could be caused by PGE_2. The results of this study show that: (a) although the amount of PGE_2 secreted by the stimulation of BPO-HGG was 20-fold greater than the basic level, this amount is not sufficient to suppress significantly the thymidine uptake; (b) preincubation of PBL with higher than physiological concentration of externally added PGE_2 caused significant suppression of thymidine uptake after stimulation with BPO-KLH, but the addition of physiological concentration of PGE_2 did not show the same effect; (c) preincubation with BPO-HGG had no effect on PGE_2 level after subsequent challenge with BPO-KLH; and (d) inhibitor of PGE fails to influence the suppression of BPO-KLH proliferation induced by BPO-KLH.

INTRODUCTION

The prostaglandins of the E series (PGE)[3] have been shown to play an important role as mediators in immune regulation (1, 2), particularly by suppressing many *in vitro* functions and occasionally by enhancing them (3, 4). The secretion of PGE_2 by monocytes and macrophages can be induced by various substances, including Con A and PHA (1, 5). While the whole human γ-globulin (HGG) does not stimulate PGE_2 production, some structural changes in the IgG molecule such as enzymatic cleavage by papain, and heat aggregatin of IgG will do it (2, 6). Since the binding of a hapten to HGG can also change its structure (7, 8) and create

[1] This work is supported by the American Cancer Society Grant IM-178A.

[2] To whom correspondence should be addressed.

[3] Abbreviations used: PGE, prostaglandin of the E series; PHA, phytohemagglutinin; Con A, concanavalin A; BPO, benzylpenicilloyl; KLH, keyhole limpet hemacyanin; BGG, bovine γ-globulin; BPO-HGG, conjugate of BPO with HGG; BPO-KLH, conjugate of BPO with KLH; BPO-BGG, conjugate of BPO with BGG; PBL, peripheral blood lymphocytes; S.I., stimulation index; S.D., standard deviation.

0008-8749/81/160267-10$02.00/0

an immunologically active conjugate, it was interesting to find out if this conjugate has a similar effect on PGE_2 secretion. The hapten that was chosen for this purpose was the major determinant of penicillin, benzylpenicilloyl (BPO).

In the present study we investigated if HGG bound to BPO stimulates peripheral blood lymphocytes (PBL) and monocytes to increase PGE_2 production. In addition, we determined the production of PGE_2 by PBL and monocytes after stimulation with BPO bound to other carriers, such as keyhole limpet hemocyanin (KLH) and bovine γ-globulin (BGG). The reasons were twofold. First, we found (9) that preincubation of human PBL with BPO-HGG suppressed the proliferative effect of BPO-KLH. In contrast preincubation with BPO-KLH did not (9). Second, a recent report shows (10) that PGE_2 suppresses both T- and B-cell proliferation. Thus, it was of interest to determine whether hapten carrier conjugate stimulates the release of PGE_2 by human PBL and whether this can explain the suppression of PBL proliferation.

MATERIALS AND METHODS

Human peripheral blood lymphocytes (PBL) were prepared by Ficoll–Hypaque sedimentation (11) of heparinized blood from volunteer blood donors. The cells prepared contained >95% mononuclear cells (80–85% lymphocytes and 15–20% monocytes). The viability as tested by trypan blue dye exclusion was >99%. The following assays were performed utilizing these cells.

Monocyte culture (for PGE_2 determination). The cells, prepared as above, were adjusted to 10×10^6 cells/ml, and aliquots of 0.4 ml were pipetted into wells of tissue culture trays (16 mm diameter; Linbro Chemical Co., New Haven, Conn.). Adherence of monocytes was facilitated by gentle rocking at 37°C for 45 min, after which the nonadherent cells were removed by washing vigorously three times. The resultant monolayer contained more than 90% monocytes, as evidenced by their morphological appearance, phagocytosis of latex particles, and by perioxidase staining (12). The cells were cultured in complete medium (0.5 ml/well) to which the various test substances (0.2 mg protein/ml) were added. The cultures were maintained at 37°C in a humidified atmosphere of 5% CO_2, for 24 hr, after which the supernatants were harvested and stored at −20°C. Aliquots of these supernatants were used for prostaglandin E_2 (PGE_2) determinations.

PBL culture (for PGE_2 determination). The PBL prepared as above were cultured in complete medium to which the test substances were added. Aliquots of 0.2 ml of the medium with the various substances and 4×10^5 cells (in 0.2 ml) were pipetted into microtiter tissue culture plates (Linbro Scientific, Hamden, Conn.), cultured, and prepared for PGE_2 determinations, as described above.

PBL culture for thymidine uptake (and treatment with PGE_2). The cultures were prepared in a fashion similar to that used for PGE_2 determination except that BPO-KLH and BPO-HGG (0.2 mg/ml each) were left for 2 days in culture and pulsed with [^{3}H]thymidine sp act 2 Ci/mmole, (New England Nuclear, Boston, Mass.); 18 hr later the cells were harvested and the radioactivity was measured by a scintillation counter. To measure the effect of PGE_2 on thymidine uptake, a part of the cells were treated either by the addition of PGE_2 (kindly provided by Dr. John Pike from UpJohn Co., Kalamazoo, Mich.) to the cultures, or by pretreatment with PGE_2 for 24 hr, during which the cells were cultured in a concentration of 5×10^6 cells/ml of complete medium at 37°C in a humidified atmostphere of 5% CO_2, then washed two times with HBSS, adjusted to 4×10^5 cells/ml, cultured, and tested for thymidine uptake (as above).

PREPARATION OF COMPOUNDS

Preparation of human γ-globulin (HGG). Peripheral blood from volunteer blood donors was left to clot. The serum prepared from it was dialyzed against a large volume of 0.001 *M* phosphate buffer, pH 7.4, and chromatographed on a DEAE cellulose 32 column (Whatman, Inc., Clifton, N.J.). Part of the HGG was treated the same way as described under "Preparation of other compounds," only without adding the BPO. This "sham-treated HGG" served as control to BPO-HGG (sham HGG).

Preparation of the other compounds. Keyhole limpet hemocyanin (KLH) was purchased from Sigma Chemical Company, St. Louis, Missouri. BPO was covalently bound in the penicilloyl configuration to protein carriers (KLH, BGG, & HGG) as previously described (13). Finally, all the compounds (including HGG and aggregated HGG) were dialyzed three times (1×1000) against RPMI 1640. In addition, BPO-HGG and BPO-BGG were centrifuged at 180,000*g* for 30 min. No aggregates were visible, but to exclude the possibility that small (invisible) aggregates were present, the upper parts of the centrifuged materials were taken and tested for their effect on PGE_2 secretion by PBL. All the compounds (except HGG aggregates) were passed through a Millipore filter (0.45 mm, acrodise, Germo) and added to cultures in concentration of 0.2 mg protein/ml.

Preparation of aggregated HGG. Aggregation of HGG was obtained by heating the HGG in a shaking water bath at 62°C for 20 min. The protein concentration was determined by subtracting the amount of protein found in the supernatant after aggregation of HGG from the total protein (before aggregation).

Phytohemaglutinin (PHA) (Wellcome Research Laboratories, Beckman, England) and concanavalin A (Con A) were made in appropriate stock solution of HBSS, and used within 1–2 days of preparation. Indomethacin (Merck, Sharp and Dohme, West Point, Pa.) was prepared freshly before use and added to cultures at final concentration of 5 μg/ml.

Prostaglandin determination. The concentration of PGE_2 in culture medium was measured by a radioimmunoassay using an antiserum with specificity to PGE_2 (Boehringer, Mannheim, GmbH Biochemica). The assay was done as previously described (14). Briefly, the 0.1-ml aliquot to be tested was added to 0.1 ml of antiserum and 0.1 ml of ^{3}H-labeled PGE_2 (New England Nuclear) and left 10 min at room temperature and then 2 hr in an ice bath. After this time, 1 ml of dextran–charcoal was added, followed by an additional 10 min in ice. The mixture was centrifuged, the supernatant was transferred to vials to which 10 ml of scintillation solution was added, and the radioactivity was measured in a scintillation counter. PGE_2 concentration was determined by using a standard curve of known amounts of PGE_2.

TABLE 1

PGE_2 Production by PBL

	Dose (mg/ml)	PGE_2 concentration (ng/ml)
Cells alone	—	0.27 ± 0.2
+ aggregated HGG	0.2	4.8 ± 0.92
+ BPO-HGG	0.2	7.0 ± 1.16
+ sham HGG	0.2	0.28 ± 0.15
+ BPO-KLH	0.2	6.2 ± 0.42
+ KLH	0.2	0.47 ± 0.5
+BPO-BGG	0.2	6.8 ± 1.84
+ BGG	0.2	0.83 ± 0.47

Note. PBL were cultured for 24 hr, and the supernatants were assayed for PGE_2 with radioimmunoassay. Each value represents data of three separate experiments (different blood donors). Each experiment was done in duplicate, and each value represents mean ± SD.

RESULTS

(1) PGE_2 Production by Monocytes and PBL after Stimulation with BPO Carrier Conjugate

The production of PGE_2 from either monocytes or PBL by BPO bound to HGG, BGG, and KLH is shown in Tables 1 and 2. As control Con A or aggregated HGG was also used. As can be seen, both BPO-HGG, BPO-BGG, and BPO-KLH stimulated PBL and monocytes to increase the production of PGE_2 8–20 times above that secreted by stimulation with the carriers alone. This amount similar to that produced by aggregated HGG and Con A.

Since aggregated HGG stimulates PGE_2 production, one possible explanation is that BPO–protein conjugate formed an aggregate which is responsible for the PGE_2 produced by the PBL. To rule out this possibility, PGE_2 stimulation was

TABLE 2

PGE_2 Production by Human Monocytes

	Dose (mg/ml)	PGE_2 concentration (ng/ml)
Cells alone	—	0.59 ± 0.26
+ Con A	0.005	11.2 ± 3.1
+ Aggregated HGG	0.2	5.2 ± 0.51
+ BPO-HGG	0.2	7.4 ± 1.2
+ Sham HGG	0.2	0.51 ± 0.32
+ BPO-KLH	0.2	6.9 ± 1.1
+ KLH	0.2	0.58 ± 0.49

Note. Monocytes were cultured for 24 hr, and the supernatants were assayed for PGE_2 with radioimmunoassay. Each value represents data of three separate experiments (different blood donors). Each experiment was done in duplicate and each value represents mean ± SD.

TABLE 3

PGE_2 Production after Stimulation with Hapten-Protein Carriers, before and after Ultracentrifugation[a]

	Dose (mg/ml)	PGE_2 concentration (ng/ml)
BPO-HGG before centrifugation	0.2	6.6
BPO-HGG after centrifugation	0.2	6.5
Sham-HGG	0.2	0.6
BPO-BGG before centrifugation	0.2	5.2
BPO-HGG after centrifugation	0.2	5.0
BGG	0.2	0.82

[a] BPO-HGG and BPO-BGG were centrifuged (180,000*g* for 30 min). Samples were taken both before and after centrifugation, and added to PBL culture. After 24 hr, the supernatants were assayed for PGE_2.

done before and after ultracentrifugation with the same hapten carrier conjugate. After ultracentrifugation, no visible aggregate was found. As additional control, the "sham" carriers were used.

As can be seen from Table 3, the secretion of PGE_2 was the same whether the PBL were stimulated by BPO-HGG and BPO-BGG before or after ultracentrifugation. The amount of PGE_2 was 6–11 times less when the cells were stimulated by the "sham" protein alone.

Role of PGE_2 in Thymidine Uptake of BPO-HGG- and BPO-KLH-Stimulated Cells

Since it was shown previously by our laboratory (9) that BPO-KLH increased the thymidine uptake of BPL and that this uptake can be suppressed by preincubation with BPO-HGG, we investigated the possible role of PGE_2 in these reactions. This was done by investigating: (a) the effect of preincubation with BPO-KLH or BPO-HGG on PGE_2 production, (b) the effect of incubation and preincubation with external PGE_2 on the thymidine uptake of BPO-KLH stimulated PBL.

(a) As can be seen from Table 4, preincubation with BPO-HGG did not inhibit significantly the PGE_2 secretion by BPO-KLH stimulated PBL. Similarly, preincubation with BPO-KLH did not inhibit the PGE_2 secreted by preincubation with BPO-KLH.

(b) In these experiments we tested the effect of external PGE_2 on thymidine uptake of BPO-KLH-stimulated PBL. This was done either by preincubation with PGE_2 for 24 hr or by leaving the PGE_2 together with BPO-KLH throughout the incubation period.

As can be seen from Tables 5 and 6, the addition of BPO-KLH to the culture medium increased the thymidine uptake of PBL from 1340 cpm to 8535 (S.I. = 6.37). High concentration of PGE_2 (200 mg/ml) suppressed the thymidine uptake of the stimulated cells but not of the unstimulated cells. Furthermore, it is important to note that low concentration of PGE_2 (7 ng/ml), which was the actual amount

TABLE 4

Effect of BPO-KLH on PGE_2 Secretion from Human PBL after Preincubation with BPO-KLH and BPO-HGG

Preincubation with:	PGE_2 concentration (ng/ml) after incubation with BPO-KLH
Medium alone	7.2 ± 1.3
BPO-KLH (0.2 mg/ml)	6.5 ± 1.1
BPO-HGG (0.2 mg/ml)	6.3 ± 1.0

Note. Cells were pre-incubated with various compounds for 24 hours and washed three times. The number of cells was adjusted to 4×10^5/culture, the mixture left in culture for an additional 24 hr with BPO-KLH, and the supernatants were assayed for PGE_2.

secreted by BPO/HGG stimulated PBL, had no effect on the proliferation (Last row, Table 5). This phenomenon was even more striking when the cells were preincubated with high concentration (200 mg/ml) of PGE_2.

(c) To find out the role of PGE_2 in the unresponsiveness to BPO-KLH after preincubation with BPO-HGG, cells were preincubated with BPO-HGG and indomethacin. As can be seen in Table 7 the addition of PGE_2 inhibitor (5 μg/ml indomethacin), which does inhibit the secretion of PGE_2 (result not shown) did not influence the antigen-specific inhibition of lymphocyte proliferation after preincubation with BPO-HGG (49% inhibition without indomethacin versus 35% with indomethacin). Similar results were obtained when cells were incubated for 3 days instead of 7 with BPO-KLH (50% inhibition without indomethacin versus 52% with indomethacin).

DISCUSSION

Prostaglandin of the E series (PGE) can be found in the culture medium of peripheral blood lymphocytes (PBL) undergoing various immunological reactions,

TABLE 5

The Effect of PGE_2 on Thymidine Uptake[a]

	PGE_2 concentration (ng/ml)	cpm	S. I.
Cells alone		1,340 ± 172	
+ BPO-KLH		8,535 ± 428	6.37
+ PGE	200	1,897 ± 66	
+ BPO-KLH + PGE_2	200	5,935 ± 340	3.1
+ PGE_2 (medium after preincubation with BPO-HGG)	7	2,002 ± 331	
+ BPO-KLH + PGE_2 (medium after preincubation with BPO-HGG)	7	10,010 ± 1930	5.0

[a] Cells were cultured for 48 hr, pulsed with [^{3}H]thymidine, and harvested after 18 hr. PGE_2 was present during the incubation. The results are expressed in cpm (±SD) and stimulation index (S.I.).

TABLE 6

The Effect of Preincubation with PGE_2 on Thymidine Uptake

	PGE_2 concentration (ng/ml)	cpm	S. I.
Cells alone		2,664 ± 466	
+ BPO-KLH		15,810 ± 1569	5.9
+ PGE_2	200	3,755 ± 900	
+ BPO-KLH + PGE_2	200	5,439 ± 10	1.4

[a] The cells were cultured for 24 hr both with PGE_2 and without it, washed three times, adjusted to appropriate number, and cultured with BPO-KLH (as in Table 5). The results are expressed in cpm (±SD) and stimulation index (S.I.).

and it has been suggested that it has a regulatory function in those reactions. This suggestion was made, especially since it has been shown that PGE is secreted from monocytes and macrophages (6, 15, 16) whose function in immune reactions is well documented (17, 18). It has been also shown that addition of various compounds to macrophages and monocytes stimulates increased production of PGE (6, 15, 16). The compound used, included Fc fragments, Con A, aggregated γ-globulin (2, 6), and macrophage activating factor (19), all of which may play an important role in immune reactions.

Since the binding of hapten to a carrier can change its immunological properties, it was interesting to determine whether this can also change its ability to stimulate PGE production. For this, we determined the PGE_2 secretion from PBL and monocytes from normal donors after stimulation with BPO bound to HGG, BGG, and KLH. All the donors had been previously exposed to penicillin, but no one of them was allergic to penicillin. Indeed, we were able to show that the addition of this conjugate resulted in PGE_2 secretion 8- to 25-fold above the level secreted when exposed to the carrier alone. This amount was similar to the amount produced after

TABLE 7

The Effect of Indomethacin on the Suppressive Effect of BPO-KLH

Preincubation	Subsequent incubation with	cpm	S. I.	Percentage inhibition
Medium only	Medium only	1,814 ± 221		
	BPO-KLH	1,0351 ± 510	5.7	
BPO-HGG	Medium only	1,637 ± 104		
	BPO-KLH	4,784 ± 431	2.9	49
BPO-HGG	Medium only	1,701 ± 193		
+ indomethacin	BPO-KLH	6,387 ± 340	3.75	35

Note. PBLs were incubated with either medium alone or medium with BPO-HGG for 24 hr. The medium was then replaced by medium containing BPO-KLH (with and without indomethacin 5 μg/ml), cultured for 7 days, and assayed as described above. The results are given in cpm ± SD (of triplicates) and by stimulation index (S.I.) and percentage inhibition.

stimulation with other known PGE_2 stimulators such as Con A and aggregated HGG. This secretion of PGE_2 was not due to aggregates which may have been formed when BPO was bound to the carriers since (a) no aggregate was seen after ultracentrifugation (180,000*g* for 30 min) and (b) the supernatant (even after passing through a Millipore filter) had the same effect on PGE_2 production as the uncentrifuged material.

The exact mechanism by which the hapten-carrier conjugates stimulate PGE_2 is not known, but some observations may give a possible clue to it. It has been shown (17) that the insertion of a mercuric ion between the cysteinyl sulfurs of rabbit anti-polyalanyl immunoglobulin G reduces a single inter-heavy-chain disulfide bond, and the author suggests that binding of hapten to immunoglobulin may alter the steric relation within the hinge region (changing the relation between Fab and Fc domains) and that antigen (or hapten) binding will impose structural changes in the hapten binding domain, and possibly in the whole Fab which may then propagate to the Fc (18). It is possible, therefore, that the binding of BPO to HGG changes its structure (especially at the Fc region) and enables it to stimulate PGE_2 production from monocytes. This is consistent with reports that showed clearly that while an unchanged IgG does not stimulate PGE_2 production, structurally changed IgG, such as aggregated IgG and Fc fragments, is capable of doing it (2, 6). It was also suggested that binding of antigen to specific antibody, enzymatic cleavage of IgG by papain, and heat aggregation of IgG may produce conformational changes in the molecule that would activate the cell via its Fc receptor (20).

Less is known about the structural changes caused by binding of hapten to other carriers, and it is difficult to predict whether a similar explanation can hold for PGE_2 production by BPO-KLH-stimulated monocytes. On the other hand, since all the donors were previously in contact with penicillin (although no one was allergic to it) we cannot exclude, absolutely, that the stimulatory effect was due to antigen-activated mononuclear cells, although it is unlikely to be the sole reason, since the supernatants from mononuclear cells activated by antigen, such as tetanus toxoid, caused much less PGE_2 production than does Con A (2), while both BPO-HGG and BPO-KLH had stimulatory effects similar to that of Con A.

Another goal of this communication was to investigate whether and what possible role PGE_2 plays in the thymidine uptake of BPO-KLH-stimulated mononuclear cells. In a previous study done in our laboratory, it has been shown (9) that BPO-KLH stimulated the thymidine uptake of PBL from normal blood donors. Preincubation with BPO-HGG decreased this response, while preincubation with BPO-KLH did not. Therefore, it was interesting to find out if those findings can be explained by PGE_2 production. PGE_2 can inhibit many *in vitro* assays of immune function, including macrophage inhibitory factor production (19, 21), hemolytic plaque formation (22), direct cytolysis (23), leukocyte inhibitory factor production (24), and especially mitogenesis (1, 25). Although PGE_2 may also augment T-cell reactivity (3), and may have different effects on different T-cell subpopulations, the net effect on peripheral blood lymphocytes is suppression (4). The secretion of prostaglandin from cells activated by Con A, Fc fragment, antigen–antibody complex, etc., on one hand, and its inhibitory effect on many immune reactions, on the other suggests that PGE_2 has a nonspecific regulatory function in the proliferative response of human lymphocytes to protein antigens and mitogens. The

PGE_2 produced by BPO-KLH and BPO-HGG may have the same nonspecific regulatory function. The question is whether the PGE_2 secreted by preincubation with BPO-HGG plays a role in the unresponsiveness to a subsequent incubation with BPO-KLH. For this purpose, we investigated: (a) if the amount of PGE_2 secreted is sufficient to induce that unresponsiveness (b) whether preincubation with BPO-HGG will reduce PGE_2 production to a subsequent challenge with BPO-KLH, (c) whether the PGE_2 produced *in vitro* as a result of BPO-HGG preincubation will inhibit antigen-specific T-cell proliferation, and (d) whether the addition of indomethacin will alter the effect of preincubation with BPO-HGG.

The data, thus far, indicate that the amount of PGE_2 secreted by the stimulation of BPO-HGG was 20-fold greater than the basic level. However, this concentration of PGE_2 (2×10^{-8} *M*) in the study of Goodwin *et al.* suppressed less than 26% of the proliferation of PHA-stimulated PBL (1). In addition, despite the fact that we were able to show that preincubation with a much higher concentration of PGE_2 (200 mg/ml = 5.6×10^{-7}) suppresses significantly (70%) the proliferative response to BPO-KLH, we could not find the same effect with the physiological concentration (2×10^{-8} *M*). Also, pretreatment with BPO-HGG had no effect on PGE_2 level after subsequent challenge with BPO-KLH and treatment, and pretreatment with BPO-KLH had the same effect on PGE_2 as pretreatment with BPO-HGG, but preincubation with BPO-HGG only suppressed the proliferative response to BPO-KLH. Lastly, addition of PGE_2 inhibitor does not appear to influence the suppression caused by preincubation with BPO-HGG. This suggests that the secretion of PGE_2 does not play an important role in the induction of unresponsiveness to BPO-KLH by preincubation with BPO-HGG. The mechanism of this unresponsiveness is not known. It was suggested (9) that helper T cells are made tolerant by receptor blockade. This is consistent with studies in adult thymectomized mice which have demonstrated that helper T cells are made tolerant directly by hapten isologous IgG without suppressor T cells (26). On the other hand, other investigators believe (27) that short-lived suppressor T cells are generated in carrier-determined tolerance, and this may serve as an additional (less important) mechanism of tolerance induction, in addition to the major mechanism (receptor blockade). According to these authors, these mechanisms play a role at the early stage of tolerance induction. If this is the case, it is possible that the secretion of PGE_2 after BPO-HGG stimulation plays a role in this early stage, since it was shown that the induction of some suppressor cells is PGE_2 dependent (10). The fact that this mechanism operates only very briefly and is not the main mechanism of tolerance may be responsible for the lack of correlation between PGE_2 production and tolerance induction in our experiments. This may also be consistent with our finding that preincubation with higher than physiological concentrations of PGE_2 were required for suppression of thymidine uptake of BPO-KLH-stimulated cells, since it was suggested (10), that the sensitivity to PGE_2 may clarify some of the contradictions found in the literature regarding the concentration of PGE_2 required for the suppression of the thymidine uptake of PHA-stimulated PBL.

Although the precise kinetics of PGE_2 and its effect on lymphocyte function is not clear, the data brought by many investigators suggest that PGE_2 may have an important role in modulating many immune reactions. It may be hypothesized that the secretion of PGE_2 from human monocytes stimulated by the hapten BPO bound to KLH, BGG, or HGG is important in the regulation of the immediate immune reaction, but it has probably no major role in the induction of unresponsiveness to BPO-KLH by preincubation with BPO-HGG.

ACKNOWLEDGMENT

We are grateful to Dr. Fred Rosen for his interest and suggestions during this study, and for the review of this manuscript.

REFERENCES

1. Goodwin, J. S., Bankhirst, A. D., and Messner, R. P., *J. Exp. Med.* **146,** 1719, 1977.
2. Passwell, J., Rosen, F. S., and Merler, E., *Cell. Immunol.* **52,** 395, 1980.
3. Yoneda, J., and Mundy, G. R., *J. Exp. Med.* **149,** 279, 1979.
4. Stobo, J. D., Kennedy, M. S., and Goldyne, M. E., *J. Clin. Invest.* **64,** 1188, 1979.
5. Novogrodsky, A., Rubin, A. L., and Stenzel, K. H., *J. Immunol* **122,** 1, 1979.
6. Passwell, J. H., Dayer, J. M., and Merler, E. *J. Immunol.* **123,** 115, 1979.
7. Vuk-Pavlovic, S., Isenman, D. E., Elgarish, G. A., Gafni, A., Licht, A., and Pecht, I., *Biochemistry* **18,** 1125, 1979.
8. Vuk-Pavlovic, S., Blott, Y., Glaudemans, C. P. Y., Lancet, D., and Pecht, I., *Biophys. J.* **24,** 61, 1978.
9. Geha, R. S., Fruchter, L., and Borel, Y., *J. Clin. Invest.* **65,** 1509, 1980.
10. Fischer, A. Durandy, A. and Griscelli, C., *J. Immunol* **126,** 1452, 1981.
11. Boyum, A., *Scand. J. Clin. Lab. Invest.* **21**(Suppl. 97)**,** 77, 1968.
12. Graham, R. C., Jr., and Karnovsky, M. J., *J. Histochem. Cytochem.* **14,** 291, 1966.
13. Hyslop, N. E., and Milligan, R. M. *Antimicrob. Agents Chemother.* **5,** 617, 1974.
14. Dray, F., Charbonnel, B., and Maclouf, J., *Eur. J. Clin. Invest.* **5,** 311, 1975.
15. Freidman, S. A., Remold-O'Donnell, E., and Piessens, F. W., *Cell Immunol.* **42,** 213, 1979.
16. Kurland, J. I., and Bockman, R., *J. Exp. Med* **147,** 952, 1978.
17. Unanue, E. R., *N. Engl. J. Med.* **303,** 977, 1980.
18. Resenthal, A. S., *N. Engl. J. Med.* **303,** 1153, 1980.
19. Koopman, W. J., Gillis, M. H., and David, J. R., *J. Immunol.* **110,** 1609, 1973.
20. Berman, M. A., Gillis, M. H., and David, J. R., *J. Immunol.* **110,** 1609, 1973.
21. Gordon, D., Bray, M. A., and Morley, J. *Nature (London)* **262,** 401, 1976.
22. Melman, K. L., Bourne, H. R., Weinstein, Y., Shearer, G. M., Kram, J., and Bauminger, S., *J. Clin. Invest.* **53,** 13, 1974.
23. Henney, C. R., Bourne, H. R., and Lichtenstein, L. M., *J. Immunol.* **108,** 1526, 1972.
24. Lonnitzer, R., Robson, A. R., and Noornhunt, H. J., *Clin. Exp. Immunol.* **24,** 42, 1976.
25. Smith, J. W., Steiner, A. L., and Parker, C. W., *J. Clin. Invest* **50,** 442, 1971.
26. Borel, Y., Kilham, L., Kurtz, S. E., and Reinisch, C. L., *J. Exp. Med.* **151,** 743, 1980.
27. Aldo Benson, M. A., *Eur. J. Immunol.* **9,** 214, 1979.

CELLULAR IMMUNOLOGY **64**, 277–292 (1981)

The Presence of Ia Antigen on Human Peripheral Blood T Cells and T-Cell Subsets: Analysis with Monoclonal Antibodies and the Fluorescence-Activated Cell Sorter[1]

JAN L. CEUPPENS,[2] JAMES S. GOODWIN,[3] AND ROBERT P. SEARLES

Department of Medicine, University of New Mexico School of Medicine, and Clinical Research Division, Lovelace Medical Center, Albuquerque, New Mexico 87131

Received June 4, 1981; accepted July 25, 1981

Peripheral blood T cells from normal donors, from newborns, and from patients with rheumatoid arthritis were analyzed for the presence of surface Ia antigens using monoclonal anti-Ia reagents and a fluorescence-activated cell sorter. Two out of four monoclonal anti-Ia antibodies detected Ia antigen on 2–22% (mean 7.4 ± 5.9%) of normal E rosette (+) cells. A subpopulation of E rosette (+) cells thus expresses an Ia molecule with antigenic determinants similar to the Ia on B cells. The staining is weak in comparison to the staining with anti-Ia of B cells, but could not be blocked by preincubation of the T cells with aggregated human IgG. Confirming a previous report by Yu *et al.* (D. T. Y. Yu, R. J. Winchester, S. M. Fu, A. Gibefsky, H. S. Ko, and H. G. Kunkel, *J. Exp. Med.* **151,** 91, 1980) in rheumatoid arthritis more Ia-positive T cells were detected (mean 17.4 ± 12.5%) that also express a higher number of Ia molecules on their surface. On the contrary, the number of Ia(+) T cells was decreased in cord blood. Both helper T cells [OKT4(+)] and suppressor T cells [OKT8(+)] contain a subfraction that is Ia(+), as evidenced by additive staining and two-color immunofluorescence experiments. In RA, an increase in Ia(+) cytotoxic/suppressor cells is mainly responsible for the higher proportion of Ia(+) T cells. We have previously identified a subpopulation of T cells staining with both OKT8 and OKM1, a marker thought to be specific for cells of myelomonocytic lineage. We now report that this OKT8(+) OKM1(+) overlap population is almost entirely Ia(+) and therefore could represent an activated cell type. However, Ia antigen was also detected on OKT3(+) cells after removing OKM1(+) E rosette (+) cells.

INTRODUCTION

Ia (immune-response-associated) antigens in mice are encoded for by genes in the I-locus of the H-2 complex. Human Ia or Ia-like antigens are expressed on B cells and monocytes and have also been found on a variety of tumor cells, Langerhans cells, and erythroid and myeloid precursor cells (for review see (1)). Human Ia molecules are composed of two glycopeptide chains of approximate molecular weights of 38,000 and 28,000 daltons and bear antigenic determinants encoded for

[1] This work was supported in part by Grants (AG-01245) and (AM-00793) from the National Institutes of Health.

[2] Supported by a grant from the Belgian National Fund of Scientific Research. Present address: Division of Clinical Immunology, Department of Medicine, St. Rafael Hospital, University of Louvain, Louvain, Belgium.

[3] To whom requests for reprints should be addressed.

0008-8749/81/160277-16$02.00/0

by the HLA-DR and probably HLA-D loci (1). There are several regions in mice encoding for different Ia molecules (2–4), and this may be the case in humans as well (5, 6). Stimulated human T cells (7–10) and T cells grown in tissue culture (11) express Ia antigens reacting with antisera and monoclonal antibodies raised against Ia molecules on B cells. The presence of Ia antigens on resting human T cells has been denied in some reports (10, 12) and confirmed in others (13–16). An increased proportion of Ia-positive T cells has been described after immunization (17) and in inflammatory conditions: rheumatoid arthritis (RA)[4] (17), systemic lupus erythematosus (17), and infectious mononucleosis (18, 19). The failure to detect Ia on resting human T cells can be related to the real absence of the molecules from T-cells membranes, to a low density of Ia antigens on T-cell membranes, or to a difference in antigenic specificity of Ia on T cells.

The recent development of monoclonal antibodies and of cytofluorographic analysis allows for increased specificity and sensitivity in the detection of membrane antigens. We have used these means for the detection of Ia on T cells and report here that some peripheral blood T cells do express Ia. We confirm a previous report by Yu *et al.* (17) that the number of Ia(+) T cells is increased in RA. We have analyzed which T-cell subpopulations as defined with monoclonal antibodies (reviewed in (20)) contain Ia-positive cells. E-Rosette-positive cell preparations are composed of approximately 80–90% OKT3(+) cells and 10–20% OKM1(+) cells, whose origin and function are still unclear (21, 22). E rosette (+) OKM1(+) cells do not have the classical features of monocytes. We have previously shown that these OKM1(+) cells stain with a monoclonal antibody against the E receptor (Ab 9.6), that about 10% of E rosette (+) cells express both definite T-cell markers (OKT3 and/or OKT8) and the OKM1 antigen, and that about 48% of OKM1(+) cells are also OKT8(+).[5] We now report that Ia is preferentially expressed on those T cells that also express the OKM1 antigen.

MATERIALS AND METHODS

Isolation of peripheral blood mononuclear cells and T cells. Peripheral blood mononuclear cells (PBMC) from heparinized blood of 13 healthy adult donors and 14 patients with definite active rheumatoid arthritis, were isolated on Ficoll–Hypaque (Pharmacia) density gradients (23). None of the patients took more than 7.5 mg of prednisone per day. Glass-adherent cells were removed by incubation of the cells at 37°C for 45 min on glass petri dishes in RPMI 1640 with 10% fetal calf serum (FCS). T cells were subsequently isolated by two different methods:

(a) Rosetting with AET-treated sheep red blood cells (SRBC) (24) followed by centrifugation over Ficoll–Hypaque for 30 min at 300 *g*. The pellet always contained more than 90% rosetting mononuclear cells and more than 95% (range 96–99%) of the cells reacted with a monoclonal antibody (Clone 9.6) against the E receptor (25). The nonrosetting fraction was recovered as non-T cells. The SRBC in the pellet were lysed with Tris–NH_4Cl buffer.

[4] Abbreviations used: Ab, antibody; FACS, fluorescence-activated cell sorter; FCS, fetal calf serum; ND, normal donor; NT, not tested; PBS, phosphate-buffered saline; RA, rheumatoid arthritis; PBMC, peripheral blood mononuclear cells; SRBC, sheep red blood cells.

[5] J. L. Ceuppens, J. S. Goodwin, K. Okudaira, and C. J. Froelich, Reactivity of OKM1 monoclonal antibody with a subset of the cytotoxic/suppressor T cell population. Submitted for publication.

(b) Nylon wool columns: Cells (50×10^6) were incubated on nylon wool (0.5 g nylon wool in a 10-ml syringe barrel) for 45 min at 37°C in RPMI 1640 supplemented with 10% FCS (26). The nonadherent cells were eluted with 20 ml prewarmed medium.

With both methods the number of contaminating B cells, as determined by immunofluorescence with fluorescein-conjugated anti-human IgM (Cappel Laboratories, Cochranville, Pa.) was $\leq 1\%$. Monocyte contamination [as determined by peroxidase staining and scatter on the fluorescence-activated cell sorter (FACS)] was $\leq 4\%$ (mean 1.9%).

Monoclonal antibodies and rabbit anti-Ia antiserum. Four different monoclonal anti-Ia antibodies, directed against the invariant part of the Ia molecule, were used: L243, (Becton–Dickenson, Sunnyvale, Calif.) (5); OKI1, (Ortho Pharmaceuticals, Raritan, N. J.) (10); a monoclonal antibody, Q 5/13, kindly provided by Dr. S. Ferrone (Scripps Clinic and Research Foundation, La Jolla, Calif.) (27); and 19/9 HLK (Pel-Freeze Biologicals, Rogers, Ark.). A rabbit heteroserum, produced and characterized before (15) was used for comparison on B35M cells (a human B-cell line). This rabbit antiserum was absorbed with platelets from 30 different donors and with thymocytes. Background staining was obtained with the use of mouse IgG_2 purified on Sepharose–protein A and used at a concentration of 10 μg/ml or with OKT_6, a monoclonal antibody against thymocytes and not reacting with peripheral blood T cells (20). Identical background staining was also obtained with normal mouse serum (1/200). Normal rabbit serum was used as the negative control for the rabbit anti-Ia antiserum. Monoclonal antibodies to T cells and T-cell subpopulations (21) (OKT3:pan T; OKT4:helper/inducer T cells; OKT8:cytotoxic/suppressor cells), and to cells of myelomonocytoid origin (OKM1) (21, 22) were provided by Ortho Pharmaceuticals. Biotin-conjugated monoclonal antibodies were purchased from Becton–Dickenson. Antibody Leu 2a detects the suppressor/cytotoxic subpopulation and antibody Leu 3a the helper cell population (28, 29) analogous to OKT8 and OKT4, respectively. A monoclonal antibody to the receptor for SRBC (Clone 9.6) was purchased from New England Nuclear, Boston, Massachusetts (25).

Indirect immunofluorescence analysis of T cells on FACS III. A cell pellet containing 10^6 T cells was incubated with 50 μl of an appropriate dilution of the monoclonal antibody (2.5–5 μg/ml) for 30 min on ice. The cells were washed twice in a refrigerated centrifuge with phosphate-buffered saline (PBS) containing 0.01% azide. The pellet was further incubated with 50 μl of fluorescein-conjugated goat anti-mouse IgG (Meloy, Springfield, Va.) for 30 min on ice. This second label antibody was previously absorbed with human Cohn fraction II insolubilized on Sepharose 4B. The cell pellet was washed twice, resuspended in 1 ml PBS–azide and analyzed with the FACS III (Becton–Dickenson, Mountain View, Calif.). The 488-nm line of the laser was used and electronic amplifier and gain settings were such that the majority of cells in the control sample were in fluorescence channel 1 to 20. The number of positive cells was calculated after correction for background staining. Additive staining experiments (30) were performed to determine the percentage of cells reacting with two different monoclonal antibodies. This percentage was calculated by subtracting the number of positive cells after simultaneous staining with two monoclonal antibodis from the total number of positive cells after staining with the separate antibodies. In these experiments the final concentration of monoclonal antibody was kept constant by adding 50 μl medium to these tubes with only one monoclonal antibody.

Two-color immunofluorescence. For two-color immunofluorescence we used unconjugated monoclonal antibodies and FITC-conjugated goat anti-mouse IgG, followed by biotin-conjugated monoclonal antibodies and rhodamine-conjugated avidin (Becton Dickenson) (31). Cells were incubated with the first unconjugated monoclonal antibody (e.g., Q 5/13), washed, incubated with FITC-conjugated anti-mouse IgG (Meloy), washed, incubated with the biotin-conjugated monoclonal antibody (e.g., Leu 2a), washed, and finally incubated with rhodamine-conjugated avidin and washed again. The cells were then examined fresh on a Zeiss fluorescence microscope and the number of double-staining cells was determined. In preliminary control experiments it was determined that with this method no Leu 2(+) OKT4(+) and no Leu 3(+) OKT8(+) cells were detected in normals.

Separation of T-lymphocyte subpopulations defined with monoclonal antibodies. OKT3(+) human T cells were further purified with a monoclonal antibody rosetting technique (32). Bovine red blood cells were coupled to immunoadsorbent-purified goat anti-mouse IgG (Tago, Burlingame, Calif.) with the $CrCl_3$ method (32) and resuspended at a 0.5% suspension in RPMI 1640 with 10% FCS. After incubation for 30 min with a saturating dose of monoclonal antibody OKM1, the E rosette (+) cells were washed twice with cold PBS in a refrigerated centrifuge, resuspended to a concentration of 4×10^6 cells/ml in RPMI 1640 + 10% FCS, and mixed with an equal volume of the anti-IgG-coated ox red blood cells. The mixture was centrifuged for 10 min at 200*g*, incubated for 30 min on ice, and gently resuspended. Rosetting cells were separated from nonrosetting cells by centrifugation over Ficoll–Hypaque for 30 min at 300*g*. Only the negative population was used for further staining procedures to avoid any interference from the monoclonal antibody used for cell separation. As further shown in the results section, these cell preparations contained a mean of 2.5 ± 2.7% residual contaminating OKM1(+) cells and a mean of 98 ± 1.5% OKT3(+) cells. The same method was also used to remove Ia(+) cells from T-cell preparations. The Ia(−) cells were shown in indirect immunofluorescence to contain less than 1% residual Ia(+) cells. Nonspecific rosette formation of the T cells with the treated ox red blood cells was ≤2%.

RESULTS

Reactivity of Anti-Ia with B35M Cells and Peripheral Blood Non-T Cells

The reactivities of the four monoclonal anti-Ia antibodies and the rabbit antiserum were first compared on B35M cells (a human B-cell line with high Ia density on its surface) and with human non-T cells. For these experiments the second label antibody (fluorescein-conjugated goat anti-mouse IgG) was additionally absorbed with B35M cells.

The values obtained are given in Table 1. It is clear that the monoclonal antibodies L243 and Q 5/13 have a high antibody titer and/or antibody affinity against Ia antigens. The other two monoclonal antibodies had a weak reactivity with the B35M cells. The same difference between the monoclonal anti-Ia antibodies was obtained when peripheral blood non-T cells (E-rosette-negative) were stained (data not shown).

TABLE 1

Reactivity of Four Monoclonal Antibodies and a Rabbit Heteroantiserum Against Ia with B35M Cells (Human B-Cell Line)[a]

Antibody	Antibody concentration (μg/ml)					
	40	20	10	5	2.5	1.25
L243	ND	98	96	86	77	64
OKI1	ND	64	38	10	0	ND
Q 5/13	ND	96	92	81	70	55
19/19HLK	9	9	0	0	0	0
	Antibody dilution					
	1/2.5	1/5	1/10	1/20	1/40	1/80
Rabbit anti-Ia serum	ND	99	92	87	69	50

[a] 10^6 B35M cells in 100 μl were incubated with 50 μl of different antibody dilutions. Results are expressed as percentage of positive cells (after correction for background staining) in indirect fluorescence (FACS).

Reactivity of E Rosette (+) Cells from Normal Donors with Anti-Ia

Peripheral blood T cells isolated by E rosetting with SRBC were stained with a 1/10 dilution of the different anti-Ia preparations (Table 2). Ninety-six to ninety-nine percent of these cells reacted with a monoclonal antibody against the sheep erythrocyte receptor (Ab 9.6) and a mean of 87 ± 6% reacted with OKT3. Reactivity with the monoclonal anti-Ia antibodies was as follows: 11.3 ± 5.9% of the T cells showed reactivity with Q 5/13, 7.4% ± 3.2% reacted with L243, and 3.5 ± 1.9% with OKI1; 19/9 HLK was unreactive with T cells. About the same proportion of nylon-wool-nonadherent cells stained with anti-Ia (Table 3). In those experiments where L243, Q 5/13, and OKI1 were all used on the same sample

TABLE 2

Reactivity of Peripheral Blood E Rosette (+) Cells with Monoclonal Anti-Ia[a]

Donor	L243	Q 5/13	OKI1
1	3	10	2
2	12	13	—
3	9	10	4
4	9	22	6
5	5	6	—
6	4.5	4	2
7	9	14	—
Mean ± SD	7.4 ± 3.2	11.3 ± 5.9	3.5 ± 1.9

[a] Reactivity of peripheral blood E-rosette-positive cells from seven normal donors with monoclonal anti-Ia antibodies. B-Cell contamination of E rosette cell preparations was ≤1% and the monocyte contamination was ≤4% (mean 1.9%). Results are expressed as percentage of positive cells in indirect immunofluorescence (FACS).

TABLE 3

Reactivity of Nylon-Wool-Nonadherent Cells with Monoclonal Anti-Ia Antibodies[a]

Donor	L243	Q 5/13	B-Cell contamination (anti-IgM)
1	NT	13	1
2	11	9	1
3	5	5	0.5
Mean ± SD	8.0 ± 4.2	9.0 ± 4.0	0.8 ± 0.3

[a] T cells were isolated by passage of glass nonadherent PBMC from three normal donors over nylon wool columns and stained with monoclonal anti-Ia L243, Q 5/13 and with anti-IgM. Results are expressed as percentage of positive cells in indirect immunofluorescence for anti-Ia, and direct immunofluorescence for anti-IgM.

(donors 1, 3, 4, and 6 in Table 2), it is clear that the reactivity of these reagents against T cells was Q 5/13 > L243 > OK11. L243 was, however, the strongest reagent against B-cell Ia (Table 1). For all further experiments Q 5/13 or L243 was used to determine the number of Ia(+) T cells.

No shedding nor increase of Ia antigen was observed after overnight incubation of T cells at 37°C. The number of Ia(+) cells was not different when the T cells were incubated overnight at 37°C in different batches of FCS or in autologous serum.

B-Cell contamination does not account for the Ia positivity since less than 1% of the cells reacted with anti-human IgM. Monocytes could be differentiated on the basis of their light scatter intensity. The staining with anti-Ia of T cells was much weaker than that of B cells. A typical pattern for the staining of T cells with anti-Ia is shown in Fig. 1. On this histogram the Ia(+) T-cell population forms a shoulder to the negative population. This pattern suggests a continuous transition from Ia(−) to Ia(+) cells. That some cells are stained more intensively can be seen in Fig. 2 (dot plot). All the cells are small (low light scatter) and are therefore not typical monocytes. In one experiment performed, the monoclonal antibodies L243 and Q 5/13 were shown to react with the same T-cell subpopulation, since rosetting out of cells reacting with one of the antibodies also eliminated reactivity with the other one.

Although very low final IgG concentrations of monoclonal antibodies were used (1.25–2.5 μg/ml), and a control for background staining with OKT6 or mouse IgG_2, isolated on protein A–Sepharose and used in a concentration of 10 μg/ml, was always included in the experiments, we further excluded Fc receptor binding by preincubation of the T cells in human aggregated IgG. T cells preincubated with 500 μg aggregated human IgG for 30 min on ice had the same reactivity with anti-Ia as T cells preincubated in medium with FCS (Fig. 3).

Reactivity of T Cells from Rheumatoid Arthritis (RA) Patients with Anti-Ia

We isolated E rosette positive T cells from peripheral blood of 14 patients with definite active rheumatoid arthritis. The reactivity of these T cells with monoclonal anti-Ia, in comparison to the T cells of 13 normal donors, is given in Fig. 4.

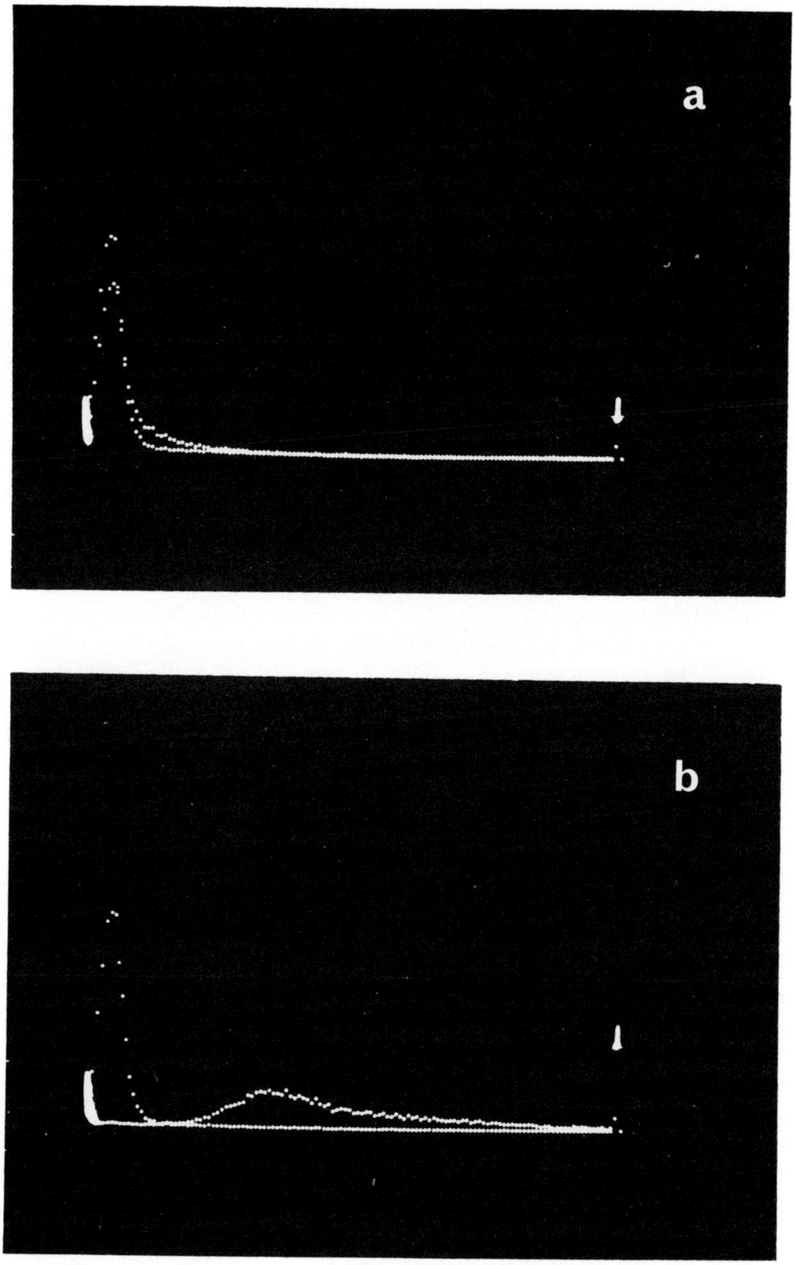

FIG. 1. (a) Typical pattern of reactivity of peripheral blood E rosette (+) cells with monoclonal anti-Ia Q 5/13. The monoclonal antibody was ultracentrifuged at 100,000*g* (20 min) just before use. The second label antibody (FITC-conjugated goat anti-mouse IgG) was diluted 1/40. The fluorescence histograms of the population stained with anti-Ia was superimposed over the histogram of the control sample incubated with mouse IgG_2 (10 μg/ml) and goat anti-mouse IgG. *x* axis = fluorescence intensity increasing from left to right, linear scale, 128 channels. *y* axis = number of cells. (b) Fluorescence histogram of the same population stained with monoclonal antibody 9.6 (anti-E receptor): 99% of the cells are positive.

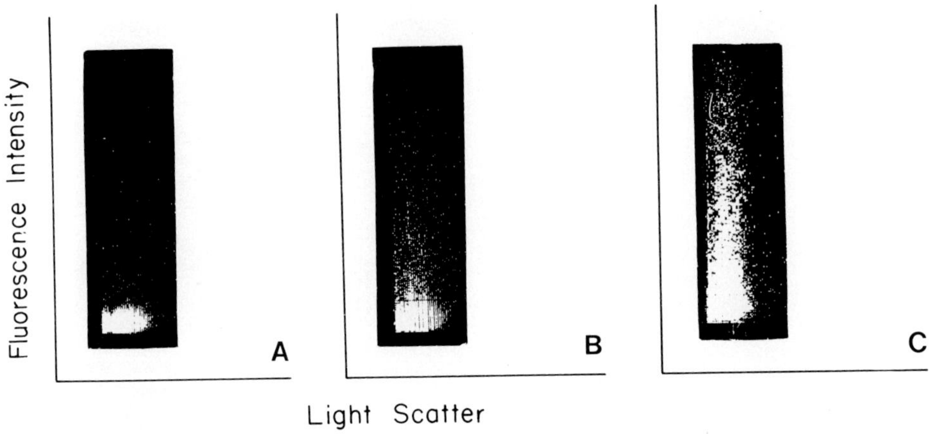

FIG. 2. Dot plot obtained on FACS after staining of: (A) E. rosette (+) cells from a normal donor with OKT6 (negative control). (B) E rosette (+) cells from a normal donor with anti-Ia (L243). (C) E rosette (+) cells from RA patient with anti-Ia (L243). The second label antibody is FITC-conjugated goat anti-mouse IgG. The ordinate represents fluorescence intensity, the abscissa light scatter (cell size).

Rheumatoid patients often had a higher proportion of Ia-positive T cells. We detected a mean of 17.4 ± 12.5% Ia(+) cells in the RA samples (range 7–51%) versus 7.4 ± 5.9% for the normal controls (range 2–22%). The difference between both is statistically significant ($P = 0.02$, Student's t test). In addition, the intensity of staining was often higher (Fig. 2), although it never reached the intensity of staining of a non-T-cell preparation.

Reactivity of Cord Blood T Cells with Anti-Ia

Cord blood T cells have a high spontaneous thymidine incorporation in culture and also have been shown to contain spontaneously activated suppressor T cells (33). For this reason one might expect a high proportion of Ia(+) T cells in cord blood. T cells were isolated from five cord blood samples and stained with the

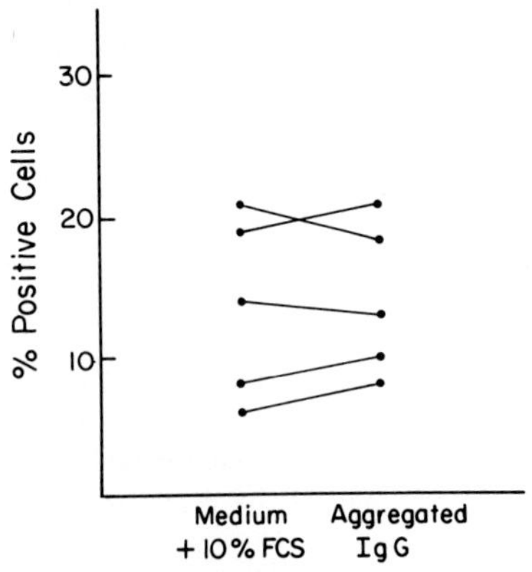

FIG. 3. Percentage of E rosette (+) cells staining with anti-Ia after preincubation of the cells in medium with 10% FCS or with aggregated human IgG for 30 min at 4°C. The second label antibody had previously been absorbed with human IgG.

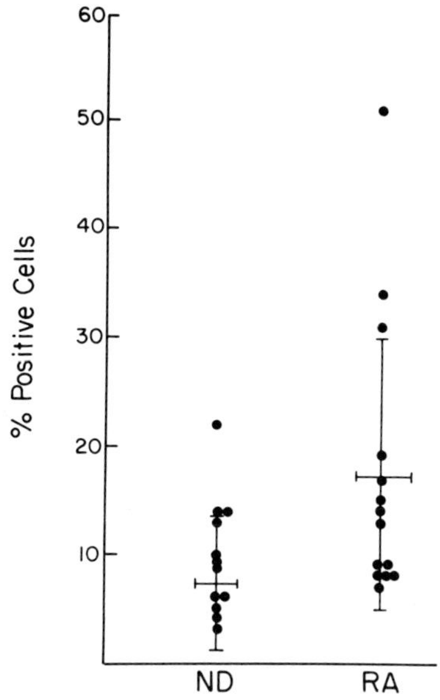

FIG. 4. Ia-positive T cells in normal donors (ND) and in patients with rheumatoid arthritis (RA). The difference between the two populations is statistically significant ($P < 0.05$ with Student's t test of nonpaired samples). When more than one sample of the same patient was obtained, only the mean of the experiments is represented.

monoclonal anti-Ia L243. Interestingly, only 2.6% (range 0–4%) of the cord blood T cells were Ia positive, which was significantly lower compared to the control values.

Presence of Ia Antigen on T-Cell Subpopulations

E rosette (+) cells from 17 rheumatoid patients and 17 normal donors were analyzed with monoclonal antibodies against T cells and T-cell subpopulations. The number of OKT8(+) cells was slightly decreased in RA, and the number of OKM1(+) cells slightly increased. However, these differences did not reach statistical significance (Table 4). The presence of Ia on these T-cell subpopulations was first analyzed with additive staining experiments (30). T cells from normals and patients with RA were incubated with anti-Ia together with either OKT3, OKT4, OKT8, or OKM1. The actual number of positive cells in these additive staining experiments was compared with the number of positive cells when stained with these antibodies separately. From these data, the number of Ia(+) cells in each subpopulation could be calculated. A representative experiment using T cells of an RA patient is shown in Table 5. The first column gives the characterization of patients' T cells, the second column the results of additive staining with anti-Ia and OKT3, OKT4, OKT8, or OKM1, the third column gives the percentage of cells reacting with both monoclonal antibodies (anti-Ia and the OK-reagent), and the fourth column gives the calculated percentages of Ia-positive cells in the OKT3(+), OKT4(+), OKT8(+), or OKM1(+) subpopulations, as explained in footnote *a*, Table 5. Additive staining experiments showed that the majority of the

TABLE 4

T-Cell Subpopulations in Normals and RA Patients[a]

	Percentage normal donors (n = 17)	Percentage RA patients (n = 17)
AB 9.6 (E rosette (+) cells)	97 ± 2	97 ± 2
OKT3	87 ± 7	81 ± 11
OKT4 (helper/inducer T cells)	54 ± 9	57 ± 14
OKT8 (suppressor/cytotoxic T cells)	34 ± 8	29 ± 9
OKM1	21 ± 6	27 ± 14

[a] E rosette (+) cells were stained with monoclonal antibodies and analyzed on a FACS III (indirect immunofluorescence). No significant differences between both populations were found.

Ia(+) cells is OKT3(+) and that both the T helper and T suppressor/cytotoxic subpopulations in normals and RA patients contain Ia(+) cells (Table 6). Relatively more OKT8 than OKT4(+) cells are Ia positive: 4.7% of the OKT4(+) cells and 6.2% of the OKT8(+) cells in the normal population are Ia positive. For the rheumatoid population 8.9% of the OKT4(+) cells and 23.3% of the OKT8(+) cells are Ia positive. These data also show that the increase in Ia(+) T cells in RA patients is more pronounced in the suppressor/cytotoxic subpopulation.

The existence of Ia(+) helper and Ia(+) suppressor cells was also confirmed with two-color immunofluorescence (Table 7). In these experiments the biotin-conjugated monoclonal antibodies Leu 2a and Leu 3a (analogous to OKT8 and OKT4, respectively) were used and the number of Ia(+) cells in each subpopulation was visually determined on a Zeiss microscope. It is again demonstrated in these ex-

TABLE 5

Ia on T-Cell Subpopulations: Additive Staining on T Cells of an RA Patient[a]

Staining with one Ab (%)	Additive staining with anti-Ia (%)	Percentage of T cells reacting with both monoclonal Ab's (%)	Ia(+) cells in each subpopulation (%)
Ab 9.6 (E receptor) (98.5)			
Ia (37)			
OKT3 (69)	OKT3 (80)	Ia(+) OKT3(+) (26)	OKT3 (38)
OKT4 (50)	OKT4 (75)	Ia(+) OKT4(+) (12)	OKT4 (24)
OKT8 (28)	OKT8 (45)	Ia(+) OKT8(+) (20)	OKT8 (71)
OKM1 (43)	OKM1 (58)	Ia(+) OKM1(+) (22)	OKM1 (51)

[a] E rosette (+) cells of an RA patient were stained with monoclonal anti-Ia (L243) and with OKT3, OKT4, OKT8, and OKM1 separately (column 1) or in additive staining experiments (column 2). The number of cells staining with both monoclonals for each subpopulation (column 3), was calculated by subtracting the percentage of cells positive when stained simultaneously with, e.g., OKT3 and anti-Ia (80%), from the sum of the percentage of positive cells obtained when the cells were stained by each reagent separately [37% (anti-Ia) + 69% (OKT3) = 106%). In column 4 these data are expressed as the percentage of Ia(+) cells in each subpopulation.

TABLE 6

Presence of Ia Antigen on T-Cell Subpopulations[a]

	Percentage of Ia(+) cells			
	Total E rosette (+) cell population	OKT3(+) cells	OKT4(+) cells	OKT8(+) cells
Normal donor				
1	7	NT	4	8
2	8	8	6	16
3	2	2	4	0
4	4	5	4	NT
5	5	4	2	4
6	4	NT	0	9
Mean ± SD	5.0 ± 2.2	4.7 ± 2.5	3.3 ± 2.1	6.2 ± 4.7
RA Patient				
1	10	13	6.5	13
2	6	5	3	NT
3	13	10	0	21
4	13.5	11	7	19
5	37	38	24	71
6	7	6	NT	9
7	8	5	6	7
Mean ± SD	13.5 ± 10.7	12.6 ± 11.6	8.9 ± 7.5	23.3 ± 24

[a] The percentage of Ia(+) cells on T-cell subpopulations was calculated from additive staining with anti-Ia (L243) and either OKT3, OKT4, or OKT8. For example, for RA patient 3, 13% of the cells were Ia(+), 84% were OKT3(+), 44% OKT4(+), and 43% OKT8(+). After additive staining, 89% stained with the combination of OKT3 and Ia, 57% with OKT4 and Ia and 47% with OKT8 and Ia. The number of cells staining for both anti-Ia and one of the OKT antibodies was then calculated by subtracting the percentage of cells positive when stained simultaneously with, e.g., OKT4 and anti-Ia, from the sum of percentage positive cells obtained when the cells were stained by each reagent separately. These numbers were then expressed as percentage of that particular subpopulation.

periments that an increase in Ia(+) cytotoxic/suppressor cells is mainly responsible for the increase in Ia(+) T cells in RA.

Ia Antigen Is Preferentially Expressed on OKM1(+) T Cells

We removed the OKM1(+) cells from E-rosette-positive cell preparations with a monoclonal antibody rosetting technique (32) and stained the remaining population with anti-Ia. Contaminating monocytes were also completely removed with this procedure. As shown in Table 8, this population is almost completely OKT3(+) [97.9 ± 1.5% OKT3(+)] and still contains Ia(+) cells, although less than the whole E rosette (+) cell preparation: Ia on whole T cells was 7.8 ± 4.1% and on OKT3(+) cells was 4.2 ± 3.0%. In rheumatoid arthritis, elimination of OKM1(+) cells also partly depleted Ia(+) cells, but still a substantial number of OKT3(+) cells was stained: 10.3 ± 8.1%. These experiments confirm that Ia antigen is detectable on OKT3(+) OKM1(−) cells. The depletion of Ia(+) cells was, however, unexpected since additive staining experiments (Table 6) had shown that >70% of the Ia(+) cells were also OKT3(+). When we enriched the E rosette (+) cell population for OKM1(+) cells by eliminating the OKT3(+) cells, there was no enrichment for

TABLE 7

Ia on T-Cell Subpopulation: Two-Color Immunofluorescence[a]

	Expt 1 (ND)[b]	Expt 2 (RA)	Expt 3 (RA)
Ia(+) cells in the E rosette (+) cells	NT[c]	7	14
Ia(+) cells in the Leu 2a (suppressor) population	8	32	23
Ia(+) cells in the Leu 3a (helper) population	4	5	11
Ia(+) cells in the M1(+) population	NT[c]	44	30

[a] Two-color immunofluorescence was performed with unconjugated monoclonal antibodies and FITC-conjugated goat anti-mouse IgG, followed by biotin-conjugated monoclonal antibodies and rhodamine-conjugated avidin. Results were read on a Zeiss fluorescence microscope.

[b] ND, normal donor.

[c] NT, not tested.

Ia(+) cells (data not shown). Since approximately 10% of E rosette (+) cells actually stain for both OKT3 and OKM1,[5] and since removal of OKM1(+) cells also eliminates this overlap population, Ia could be preferentially expressed on these double-staining cells.

In many additive staining experiments with OKM1 and anti-Ia, the maximal fluorescence intensity was higher than for OKM1 and anti-Ia separately which suggests that OKM1 and Ia are expressed on the same cell. An example of these phenomena is given in Fig. 5.

In some RA patients with high density of Ia antigens or T cells, it was possible to calculate the minimal number of OKM1(+) Ia(+) cells from additive staining results. A representative example in an RA patient with a high percentage of Ia(+) cells is given in Table 5. From the overlaps in the first column it can be calculated that at least 12% of the cells expressed both OKT3 and OKM1 (the sum of OKT3(+) and OKM1(+) cells is 112%). OKT4 and OKT8 represent nonoverlapping populations (21); OKT4 and OKM1 are also nonoverlapping.[5] Since 50% of the T cells in Table 5 are OKT4(+), the other 50% are comprised of OKT8 (28%) and OKM1 (43%). This means that 21% of the cells are OKT8(+) OKM1(+) [28% + 43% = 71% minus 50% = 21%]. These data were confirmed with additive staining experiments. From the data in the third column we can further calculate that the sum of Ia(+) OKT3(+) cells and of Ia(+) OKM1(+) cells is 48% while only 37% of the total population is Ia(+). Thus 11% of the cells are Ia(+) OKT3(+) OKM1(+) which represent >90% of the OKT3(+) OKM1(+) population. According to analogous calculations, 18% of the cells are OKT8(+) OKM1(+) Ia(+) which represent >80% of the OKT8(+) OKM1(+) population. Similar results were found in other patients with rheumatoid arthritis.

Further indirect evidence for the simultaneous expression of Ia antigen and the M1 antigen on T cells was provided by the positive correlation between the percentage of Ia(+) and OKM1(+) T cells in 23 samples from RA patients (Fig. 6).

TABLE 8

Reactivity of Purified OKT3(+) Cells with Anti-Ia[a]

	Ia(+) cells in total T-cell population	Staining of OKT3-enriched population with: OKT3	OKM1	Anti-Ia
Normal donors				
1	10	96.5	4.5	7
2	4	99	0.3	1.2
3	14	95.5	1	8
4	6	98.5	1	5
5	ND	99	7	0.5
6	5	99	1	3.5
Mean ± SD	7.8 ± 4.1	97.9 ± 1.5	2.5 ± 2.7	4.2 ± 3.0
RA patients				
1	11	99	5	9
2	10	99.5	1	3
3	34	91	4	19
Mean ± SD	18.3 ± 13.6	96.5 ± 4.8	3.3 ± 2.1	10.3 ± 8.1

[a] T cells were enriched for OKT3(+) cells by eliminating the OKM1(+) cells with the antibody rosetting technique. The nonrosetting fraction was then stained with OKT3, OKM1, and anti-Ia. The percentage of Ia(+) cells in the original total T-cell population is given for comparison. Results are expressed as percentage positive cells in indirect immunofluorescence on a FACS III. These numbers were calculated by comparing T cells stained with mouse IgG_2 and anti-mouse IgG-FITC to T cells stained wtih the monoclonal Ab and anti-mouse IgG-FITC. Ten thousand cells were counted. The limit of negativity was so that the majority of cells in the control sample (with mouse IgG) were negative. The percentage of positive cells was calculated from the absolute number of cells above this limit after correction for the positive cells in the control sample: (absolute number of positive cells − nonspecific positive cells)/(10,000 − nonspecific positive cells) × 100.

DISCUSSION

With the use of two monoclonal antibodies (L243 and Q 5/13) Ia antigen was detected on 2 to 22% of normal peripheral blood E rosette (+) cells. Both the number of Ia(+) T cells and the intensity of staining are increased in rheumatoid arthritis. These data confirm a previous report by Yu *et al.* (17). The number of Ia(+) cells reported by these authors was lower compared to our results when

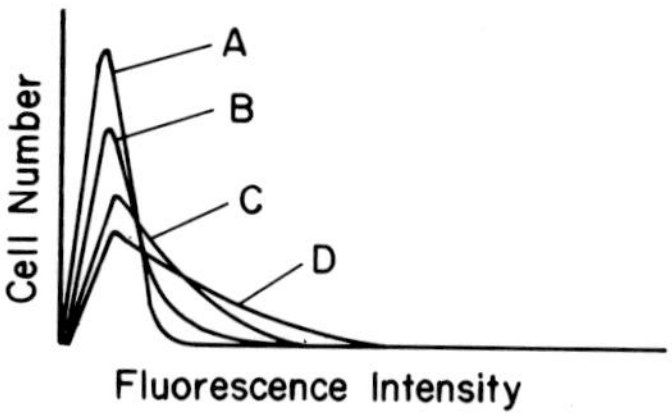

FIG. 5. Histogram representing the staining of E rosette (+) cells from an RA patient with: (A) Normal mouse serum 1/200. (B) anti-Ia L243. (C) OKM1. (D) Additive staining with OKM1 and anti-Ia. There is a population of cells in D with a higher fluorescence than in either B or C. This implies that this highly fluorescent population stains with both OKM1 and anti-Ia.

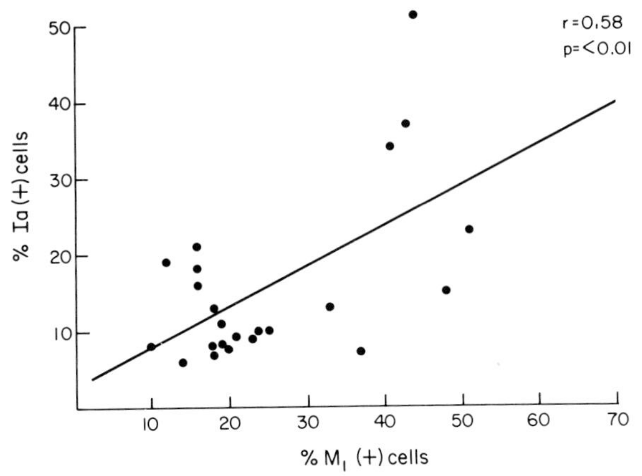

FIG. 6. Correlation between percentage OKM1(+) and percent Ia(+) E rosette (+) cells in 23 samples from 17 patients with active rheumatoid arthritis. A significant positive correlation was found between both surface antigens ($r = 0.58$, $P < 0.01$).

immunofluorescence was used, but quite similar when they used a more sensitive rosetting assay with rabbit anti-Ia and anti-rabbit IgG-coated ox red blood cells.

The Ia(+) T-cell population is not clearly separated from the Ia(−) population. There is a continuous transition from negative to positive (Fig. 1). A recent report using DR-specific antisera suggested that in fact all T cells bear Ia antigens (34). The increase of Ia(+) T cells in rheumatoid arthritis thus may represent either expansion of an Ia-positive subpopulation or an increase of Ia density on T cells in general.

It is unlikely that the binding of anti-Ia to the T cells represents Fc receptor binding since: (i) very low monoclonal IgG concentrations were used and a control with mouse IgG_2 or OKT6 was always included to correct for nonspecific staining; (ii) preincubation with aggregated IgG did not block staining with anti-Ia; and (iii) cord blood cells known to have high numbers of T_γ cells were almost completely unreactive with anti-Ia. The intensity of staining is weak in comparison to the staining of B cells with the same antibody concentrations. The lower staining intensity probably reflects a lower number of binding sites on the cell membrane. Only the two monoclonal antibodies with a high antibody titer, as determined on B35M cells, allowed for the detection of Ia antigens on T cells.

The Ia(+) T cells are not blast cells since their light scatter is not different from that of other T cells. The Ia(+) cells are not B cells since reactivity with anti-human-IgM was consistently low (<1%). Contaminating monocytes can be differentiated since they have higher scatter intensity.

We further showed that Ia(+) T cells are present in both the OKT3(+) and OKM1(+) populations and in both the OKT4(+) (helper) and OKT8(+) (suppressor/cytotoxic) subpopulations. These data were obtained with depletion, additive staining, and two-color immunofluorescence experiments. That some OKT4(+) cells (helper cells) are Ia positive is in accordance with the fact that in mice some helper T cells are Ia positive (4, 35). In humans an Ia(+) helper cell has also been demonstrated in functional *in vitro* studies (13). Reinherz *et al.* have shown that both the OKT4 and OKT8 subpopulations of mitogen-activated T cells contain

Ia(+) cells (10). The use of two high-affinity monoclonal antibodies allowed us to extend these observations to resting peripheral T cells. Reinherz *et al.* have also shown that cytotoxic cells activated in a mixed lymphocyte culture are OKT8(+) Ia(−) (36). Engleman *et al.* (37) have demonstrated that Ia(+) blasts have suppressor cell activity in an MLC. The Ia antigen thus could allow a distinction between activated suppressor cells and cytotoxic cells. Our finding that cord blood T cells are almost completely Ia(−) was therefore surprising since these cells contain activated suppressor cells (33). The possibility that Ia on these cells is blocked by circulating anti-HLA-DR antibodies has to be considered. In RA patients, the number of Ia(+) cells was increased in both the helper and suppressor/cytotoxic subpopulation, but was more prominent in the suppressor/cytotoxic population.

We have previously found that the OKM1 antigen is not restricted to cells of myelomonocytic origin, since about half of the E rosette (+) OKM1(+) cells are also OKT8 positive.[5] Very intriguing was the observation that this overlap population with both the OKM1 and the OKT8 antigen is also Ia(+). Although the significance of the OKM1 antigen on T cells is unknown, its expression together with Ia on suppressor/cytotoxic T cells would suggest that this subpopulation represents activated cells.

ACKNOWLEDGMENTS

We thank Dr. S. Ferrone (La Jolla) for providing the monoclonal anti-Ia Q 5/13, Dr. N. Warner for the use of the FACS III and helpful discussion, Dr. A. Bankhurst for providing blood samples of rheumatoid patients, Mr. J. Zawadzki for analysis of the samples on the FACS III, Ms. J. Buckelew and Ms. A. Grant for excellent technical assistance, and Ms. K. Aragon for skillfull typing of the manuscript.

REFERENCES

1. Winchester, R. J. and Kunkel, H., *Advan. Immunol.* **28,** 221, 1979.
2. Cook, R. G., Uhr, J. W., Capra, J. D., and Vitetta, E. S., *J. Immunol.* **121,** 2205, 1978.
3. Murphy, D. B., Herzenberg, L. A., Okumura, K., Herzenberg, L. A., and McDevitt, H. O., *J. Exp. Med.* **144,** 699, 1976.
4. Tada, T., Takemori, T., Okumura, K., Nonaka, M., and Tokuhisa, T., *J. Exp. Med.* **147,** 446, 1978.
5. Lampson, L. A., and Levy, R., *J. Immunol.* **125,** 293, 1980.
6. Tanigaki, N., Tosi, R., Pressman, D., and Ferrara, G. B., *Immunogenetics* **10,** 151, 1980.
7. Evans, R. L., Faldetta, T. J., Humphreys, R. E., Pratt, E. M., Yunis, E. J., and Schlossman, S. F., *J. Exp. Med.* **148,** 1440, 1978.
8. Ko, H. S., Fu, S. M., Winchester, R. J., Yu, D. T. Y., and Kunkel, H. G., *J. Exp. Med.* **150,** 246, 1979.
9. Indiveri, F., Wilson, B. S., Russo, C., Quaranta, V., Pellegrino, M. A., and Ferrone, S., *J. Immunol.* **125,** 2673, 1980.
10. Reinherz, E. L., Kung, P. C., Pesando, J. M., Ritz, J., Goldstein, G., Schlossman, S. F., *J. Exp. Med.* **150,** 1472, 1979.
11. Metzgar, R. S., Buroglio, J., Anderson, J. K., Bonnard, G. D., and Ruscetti, F. W., *J. Immunol.* **122,** 949, 1979.
12. Wilson, B. S., Indiveri, F., Pellegrino, M. A., and Ferrone, S., *Transplant. Proc.* **11,** 712, 1979.
13. Fu, S. M., Chiorazzi, N., Wang, C. Y., Montaseri, G., Kunkel, H. G., Ko, H. S., and Gottlieb, A. B., *J. Exp. Med.* **148,** 1423, 1978.
14. Schuurman, R. K. B., Gelfand, D. W., Matheson, D., Zimmerman, B., and Dosch, H. M., *J. Immunol.* **124,** 1924, 1980.
15. Kaszubowski, P. A., Goodwin, J. S., and Williams, R. C., Jr., *J. Immunol.* **124,** 1075, 1980.
16. Greaves, M. F., Verbi, W., Festenstein, H., Papasteriadis, C., Jaraguemada, D., and Hayward, A., *Eur. J. Immunol.* **9,** 356, 1979.

17. Yu, D. T. Y., Winchester, R. J., Fu, S. M., Gibefsky, A., Ko, H. S., and Kunkel, H. G., *J. Exp. Med.* **151,** 91, 1980.
18. Johnson, H. F., Madsen, M., Kristensen, T., and Kissmeyer-Nielsen, F., *Acta Pathol. Microbiol. Scand.* Sect C **86,** 307, 1978.
19. Reinherz, E. L., O'Brien, C., Rosenthal, P., and Schlossman, S. F., *J. Immunol.* **125,** 1269, 1980.
20. Reinherz, E. L., and Schlossman, S. F., *N. Engl. J. Med.* **303,** 370, 1980.
21. Reinherz, E. L., Moretta, L., Roper, M., Breard, J. M., Mingari, M. C., Cooper, M. D., and Schlossman, S. F., *J. Exp. Med.* **151,** 969, 1980.
22. Breard, J., Reinherz, E. L., Kung, P. C., Goldstein, G., and Schlossman, S. F., *J. Immunol.* **124,** 1943, 1980.
23. Boyum, A., *J. Clin. Lab. Invest.* **21** (Suppl. 97), 77, 1968.
24. Madsen, M., Johnson, H. E., Wendelboe-Hansen, P., and Christiansen, S. E., *J. Immunol. Methods* **33,** 323, 1980.
25. Kamoun, M., Martin, P. J., Hansen, J. A., Brown, M. A., Siadak, A. S., Nowinski, R. C., *J. Exp. Med.* **153,** 207, 1981.
26. Greaves, M. F., and Brown, G., *J. Immunol.* **112,** 420, 1974.
27. Quaranta, V., Pellegrino, M. A., and Ferrone, S., *J. Immunol.* **126,** 548, 1981.
28. Evans, R. L., Wall, D. W., Platsoucas, C. D., Siegal, F. P., Fikrig, S. M., Teska, C. M., and Good, R. A., *Proc. Nat. Acad. Sci. USA* **78,** 544, 1981.
29. Ledbetter, J. A., Evans, R. L., Lipinski, M., Cunningham-Rundles, C., Good, R. A., and Herzenberg, L. A., *J. Exp. Med.* **153,** 310, 1981.
30. Ledbetter, J. A., Rouse, R. B., Micklem, H. S., and Herzenberg, L. A., *J. Exp. Med.* **152,** 280, 1980.
31. Warnke, R., and Levy, R., *J. Histochem. Cytochem.* **28,** 771, 1980.
32. Stocker, J. W., Garotta, G., Hausmann, B., Tucco, M., and Ceppellini, R., *Tissue Antigens* **13,** 212, 1979.
33. Morito, T., Bankhurst, A. D., and Williams, R. C., Jr., *J. Clin. Invest.* **64,** 990, 1979.
34. Mann, D. L., and Sharrow, S. O., *J. Immunol.* **125,** 1889, 1980.
35. Swierkosz, J. E., Marrack, P., and Kappler, J. W., *J. Exp. Med.* **150,** 1293, 1979.
36. Reinherz, E. L., Hussey, R. E., and Schlossman, S. F., *Immunogenetics* **11,** 421, 1980.
37. Engleman, E., Benike, C. J., and Charron, D. J., *J. Exp. Med.* **152,** 114S, 1980.

CELLULAR IMMUNOLOGY 64, 293–303 (1981)

Relationship between Production and Release of Lymphocyte-Activating Factor (Interleukin 1) by Murine Macrophages

I. Effects of Various Agents

IGAL GERY, PHILIP DAVIES, JULIA DERR, NANCY KRETT, AND JOHN A. BARRANGER

Laboratory of Vision Research, National Eye Institute and Development and Metabolic Neurology Branch, National Institute of Neurological and Communicative Disorders and Stroke, National Institutes of Health, Bethesda, Maryland 20205, and Department of Immunology, Merck Institute for Therapeutic Research, Rahway, New Jersey 07065

Received June 23, 1981; accepted August 20, 1981

The relationship between the production and release of lymphocyte-activating factor (LAF, or interleukin 1) by cultured murine peritoneal macrophages (Mϕ) was investigated. Unstimulated Mϕ produce high levels of intracellular LAF within a few hours after culturing, but release little of this activity into their culture medium. Addition of various agents was found to increase significantly the production and release of LAF, with three different patterns: (a) Both intracellular and extracellular LAF activities were increased in response to latex beads. (b) A marked increase of intracellular LAF, with just a minimal elevation of extracellular activity, was stimulated by LPS. (c) Sharp increases in LAF release, with small increments of the intracellular activity, were induced by silica and glucocerebroside (GL_1). Silica and GL_1 damaged the cultured Mϕ, as indicated by the increased release of lactate dehydrogenase. It is significant, therefore, that silica and GL_1 increased both intracellular and extracellular LAF levels, suggesting that damage of Mϕ may stimulate total LAF production. A combination of LPS with silica or GL_1 acted synergistically on Mϕ to release very high levels of LAF, which far exceeded those released by the individual agents. The agents were also tested on Mϕ which were precultured, to deplete their LAF content. Latex, LPS, or silica increased LAF production and release by precultured Mϕ, but the levels were lower than those obtained with freshly cultured Mϕ. The results of this study thus show that the level of LAF release does not necessarily reflect the level of total LAF production by cultured Mϕ and suggest that injurious agents may promote LAF production.

INTRODUCTION

The release by macrophages (Mϕ)[1] of lymphocyte-activating factor (LAF, also designated interleukin 1, or IL 1 (1)) has been thoroughly studied (2–6). Less is known, however, about the production and accumulation of intracellular LAF and its relationship to the secreted portion of this mediator. Unanue and Kiely (7) demonstrated that murine peritoneal Mϕ produce substantial amounts of intra-

[1] Abbreviations used: FCS, fetal calf serum; GL_1, glucocerebroside; LAF, lymphocyte-activating factor; LDH, lactate dehydrogenase; LPS, lipopolysaccharide; Mϕ, macrophages; PBS, phosphate-buffered saline (Dulbecco's); PHA, phytohemagglutinin; SUP, supernatant.

0008-8749/81/160293-11$02.00/0

cellular LAF within 1–2 hr following culturing, with a sharp decline of this activity 24 hr later. These changes in intracellular LAF activity had no apparent effect on the levels of extracellular LAF (7). A basically similar pattern of LAF production was reported by Mizel and Rosenstreich (8) in monolayers of the P388D1 cell line. Stimulation of these cells with phorbol myristate acetate increased the levels of LAF in both the cell lysate and culture medium (8).

The present study was aimed at further analysis of the relationship between production and release of LAF in Mϕ cultures incubated with various agents. The agents included latex beads, lipopolysaccharide (LPS), silica particles, and glucocerebroside (GL_1, the storage sphingolipid of Gaucher's disease (9)). Silica (10) and GL_1[2] were found to be selectively injurious to Mϕ.

MATERIALS AND METHODS

Mϕ cultures. Resident peritoneal cells were collected by lavage from Swiss outbred mice (6–8 weeks of age, NIH breeding facilities), washed once and resuspended in M 199 medium (Gibco, Grand Island, NY), supplemented with 10% fetal calf serum (FCS, Gibco). The peritoneal cells were cultured in aliquots of 1 ml containing $3–4 \times 10^6$ cells in multiwell plates, 24×17 mm (Linbro, Hamden, Conn.). After incubation for 2 hr, nonadherent cells were removed by thorough washing and the adherent cells were further incubated in 1 ml of M 199 medium with 5% FCS, with or without the following agents: (a) lipopolysaccharide W from *Salmonella typhimurium* (LPS, Difco, Detroit, Mich.) (b) latex beads, 1 μm (Dow Diagnostic, Indianapolis, Ind.); (c) quartz silica particles, <5 μm (Lot A, a gift from Dr. A. C. Allison), suspended in PBS by sonication; (d) glucocerebroside (GL_1, Supelco, Bellefonte, Pa.), suspended in water by sonication and sterilized by 10,000 rad irradiation. In some experiments, the tested agents were added, in fresh medium, to Mϕ monolayers which had been preincubated for various intervals with the medium alone. Following incubation for 4 or 20 hr with the added agents, the supernatants (SUPs) were collected and centrifuged at 900 *g* for 15 min. Monolayers assayed for LAF activity were washed three times with Hanks' balanced salt solution (NIH media unit), covered with 1 ml of M 199 medium with 5% FCS and frozen at −20°C. After thawing, the cells were scraped off with a rubber policeman, sonicated and filtered (0.45 μm). Monolayers tested for enzyme activities either were treated as those assayed for LAF activity, or were washed three times with PBS, lysed with 1 ml of 0.1% Triton X-100, and scraped off with a rubber policeman.

LAF assay. The original method (11) was modified for microcultures as follows: the tested samples were diluted in RPMI 1640 medium (Gibco) with 5% FCS and added in triplicate to flat-bottomed microplates (Linbro, 8×6 mm), in aliquots of 0.1 ml. Thymocytes from CBA/N mice (6–10 weeks of age, NIH breeding facilities) were added in aliquots of 1.5×10^6 cells in 0.1 ml, shortly after being mixed with phytohemagglutinin P (PHA, Difco) at a final concentration of 0.5 μl/ml. After incubation for 66 hr the cultures were pulsed for 6 hr with [^{3}H]thymidine (New England Nuclear, Boston, Mass. 2 Ci/mmol 0.5 μCi/well)

[2] I. Gery, J. S. Zigler, R. O. Brady, and J. A. Barranger. Selective effects of glucocerebroside (Gaucher's storage material) on macrophage cultures. *J. Clin. Invest.*, in press.

and harvested by a MASH II (Microbiological Associates, Bethesda, Md.). The radioactivity in the collecting filter disks was measured by an LKB 1216 Rackbeta scintillation counter. The levels of LAF activity in the tested Mϕ preparations are expressed by two parameters: (a) the mean counts per minute values ± SEM of [^{3}H]thymidine incorporated by thymocyte cultures stimulated by a representative dilution of the tested preparation and (b) "LAF units," which were introduced to simplify the data presentation and in order to present accurately the LAF levels in preparations with exceptionally high activity, which gave a plateau at a wide range of dilutions. One LAF unit was defined as the LAF activity found in SUPs of the control Mϕ cultures to which no additions were made; the unit values in tested preparations were calculated by the dilutions needed to bring the LAF activity in these preparations to the 1 unit level. LPS potentiates the mitotic responses of thymocytes (2) and, therefore, the unit values of SUPs containing LPS were calculated by using as 1 unit the control SUP to which LPS was added after removal of cells. Agents other than LPS had no direct effect on the thymocyte responses, nor did they affect the stimulatory activity of preformed LAF.

Enzyme assays. β-*N*-Acetylglucosaminidase (hexosaminidase) was determined by the method of Pugh *et al.* (12), while β-galactosidase was assayed according to Suzuki (13). These assays were carried out in duplicate, with the means usually differing from the actual values by less than 15%. Lactate dehydrogenase (LDH) was assayed by the method of Amador *et al.* (14). Lysosomal enzyme activities are presented as nanomoles per hour per milliliter, while the level of enzyme release is expressed as the percentage of total activity (cell lysate + SUP) found in the culture SUP (15).

RESULTS

Release of Mϕ Products by Various Agents.

Monolayers of mouse Mϕ were incubated with the tested agents and the levels of LAF, hexosaminidase, and LDH released into the SUPs were measured. Table 1 summarizes the effects of representative concentrations of each of the agents; the effects of other concentrations are reported below. Different patterns of effect were observed. LPS at a wide range of concentrations stimulated moderately the release of LAF, but did not increase enzyme secretion. Latex particles, at 5×10^7/ml, did not increase the release of the enzymes, but markedly elevated LAF secretion. On the other hand, silica and GL_1 at 100 μg/ml increased markedly the release of all three tested Mϕ products. Increased release of LDH, a cytoplasmic enzyme, is indicative of cell damage (15) and thus, the elevated release of hexosaminidase and LAF by Mϕ incubated with silica or GL_1 may be attributed in part to cell injury. This notion was further studied in the following experiments in which both intracellular and extracellular activities were assayed.

LAF and Lysosomal Enzymes in SUPs and Lysates of Mϕ Cultures.

The relationship between the production and release of LAF, hexosaminidase, and β-galactosidase was investigated by measuring their levels in SUPs and lysates ("extracellular" and "intracellular" activities, respectively) of Mϕ cultured with no additive or with LPS, silica, or GL_1. The main findings, as illustrated by results

TABLE 1

Release of LAF, Hexosaminidase, and LDH by Macrophages Incubated with Various Agents[a]

Agent added (concentration)[b]	LAF activity[c]: $[^3H]$Thymidine uptake (mean cpm ± SEM)	LAF activity[c]: LAF units	Enzymes (% of total): Hexosaminidase	Enzymes (% of total): LDH
None	862 ± 228	1	26.3	26.2
LPS (20)	3,568 ± 372	3	18.2	16.1
Latex (5 × 10^7)	5,371 ± 540	16	14.3	16.8
Silica (100)	26,719 ± 522	80	51.6	73.8
GL_1 (100)	5,215 ± 575	16	48.5	56.1

[a] Cultures were harvested after 20 hr of incubation.

[b] Concentrations are expressed as beads/ml for latex, or as μg/ml for all other agents.

[c] LAF activity is presented as $[^3H]$thymidine incorporated by thymocyte cultures, incubated with the tested SUPs in a final dilution of 1:40. The definition of "LAF units" is detailed under Materials and Methods. Control thymocyte cultures, incubated with medium alone, incorporated 428 ± 55 cpm, cultures incubated with medium containing LPS (diluted 1:40) incorporated 2628 ± 372 cpm, while cultures with medium containing the other agents resembled the control cultures (incorporation range, 327–519 mean cpm).

of a typical experiment, are exhibited in Fig. 1; detailed data of another experiment are recorded in Table 2. The results show the following:

(a) high levels of intracellular LAF activity were detected in Mϕ cultured for 4 hr with no additive, followed by a sharp decline by the 20-hr interval. (Negligible levels of LAF activity were found in lysates of Mϕ before culturing, data not shown.) Little change was observed, on the other hand, in the levels of extracellular LAF of these cultures when tested after 4 or 20 hr of incubation. In contrast with the fluctuations in levels of LAF, no changes were noted in levels of the lysosomal enzymes of these unstimulated Mϕ cultures.

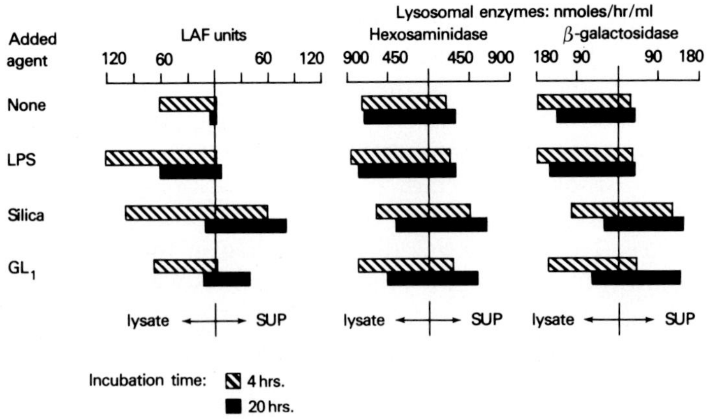

FIG. 1. Levels of LAF and lysosomal enzymes in lysates and SUPs of Mϕ cultured with various agents for 4 or 20 hr. LPS was added to a concentration of 20 μg/ml, silica, to 60 μg/ml and GL_1, to 100 μg/ml.

TABLE 2

Levels of LAF and Hexosaminidase in SUPs and Lysates of Macrophages Cultured with Various Doses of Silica and Other Agents

		LAF activity					
		Lysates		SUPs		Hexosaminidase (nmol/hr/ml)	
Agent added (μg/ml)	Incubation time (hr)	[^{3}H]Thymidine uptake (cpm ± SEM)[a]	LAF units	[^{3}H]Thymidine uptake (cpm ± SEM)[a]	LAF units	Lysates	SUPs
None	4	16,138 ± 183	20	843 ± 112	1	1543	419
	20	988 ± 148	2	537 ± 55	1	1507	490
LPS (20)	4	24,364 ± 2405	80	2,509 ± 208	3	1735	403
	20	22,877 ± 2010	40	2,287 ± 173	3	1331	520
GL_1 (60)	4	23,197 ± 2227	25	580 ± 122	1	1396	466
	20	1,435 ± 178	4	3,499 ± 507	6	1076	726
Silica (12)	4	30,265 ± 101	25	1,472 ± 240	4	1371	429
	20	2,049 ± 301	4	2,364 ± 277	5	1491	523
Silica (25)	4	30,842 ± 1995	30	7,313 ± 793	10	1352	488
	20	3,473 ± 503	6	9,145 ± 823	10	1139	606
Silica (50)	4	28,806 ± 1636	35	23,080 ± 1164	30	1287	683
	20	2,505 ± 266	6	20,749 ± 840	35	925	763
Silica (100)	4	15,436 ± 1077	20	24,831 ± 2300	30	868	1040
	20	1,376 ± 44	4	17,660 ± 1342	30	668	852

[a] Recorded values were obtained with lysates and SUPs at a final dilution of 1:40. Control thymocyte cultures incubated with medium alone incorporated 442 ± 60 cpm; cultures incubated with medium containing LPS, 1531 ± 158 cpm.

(b) Incubation of Mϕ with LPS had no significant effect on the enzyme activities, but greatly increased the levels of intracellular LAF, as manifested by very high levels at the 4-hr interval and the sustained high activity at the 20-hr interval. LPS also increased moderately the release of LAF, but the levels in the SUPs were far lower than those in the lysates.

(c) Silica particles increased markedly the release of LAF activity, with a clear dose responsiveness (Table 2). The increase in extracellular LAF levels was accompanied in all cultures by a slight to moderate increase in intracellular LAF activity, when measured after either 4 or 20 hr of incubation. High doses of silica also caused a substantial increase in release of lysosomal enzymes. Unlike LAF, however, the increased release of enzymes was accompanied by matched decrease in levels of intracellular enzymatic activity, leaving the *total* activity practically unchanged.

(d) The effects of GL_1 resembled those of silica at 20 hr of incubation, but, unlike silica, GL_1 had no effect at the 4-hr interval.

These results thus indicate that the release of LAF does not necessarily correlate with the total production of this mediator. Also, LAF differs from lysosomal enzymes in showing marked variations in its total activity in Mϕ cultures incubated with various agents; the total enzyme activities did not change in these cultures. In addition, the data show that the damaging agents, silica or GL_1, elevated the intracellular and the total LAF activity, along with increasing LAF release.

Effects of Latex on LAF Production and Release.

Unlike the asymmetrical effects of the other tested agents on LAF levels, latex beads increased to a similar extent the levels of intracellular and extracellular activity. A typical experiment is summarized in Table 3; very similar results were obtained in two other experiments. The effect of latex beads exhibited an outstanding dose responsiveness with the high activity at 10×10^7 beads/ml diminishing to a marginal effect at 1.2×10^7 beads/ml. A considerable increase in hexosaminidase release was also observed in cultures incubated with latex beads at the highest

TABLE 3

Effects of Latex Beads on Intracellular and Extracellular LAF Activities of Macrophages[a]

Latex concentration (beads/ml, $\times 10^7$)	Lysates		SUPs	
	[^{3}H]Thymidine uptake (cpm ± SEM)[b]	LAF units	[^{3}H]Thymidine uptake (cpm ± SEM)[b]	LAF units
None	4,090 ± 251	5	716 ± 144	1
10	43,639 ± 2135	60	27,706 ± 936	60
5	26,063 ± 3308	30	9,839 ± 189	10
2.5	10,820 ± 1543	10	2,208 ± 587	3
1.2	4,670 ± 504	6	1,177 ± 271	1.5

[a] Lysates and SUPs of macrophage cultures were obtained after 20 hr of incubation.

[b] The [^{3}H]thymidine uptake values recorded here were obtained with the lysates and SUPs in a final dilution of 1:40. Control thymocytes, cultured with medium alone, incorporated 343 ± 44 cpm.

concentration (10×10^7/ml). Little or no effect on enzyme release was found, however, at lower latex concentrations, which still increase LAF production and release (data not shown).

Synergy between Different Agents.

The aforementioned difference between the patterns of effect of LPS and silica or GL_1 suggested that these agents affect Mϕ by different mechanisms. This notion is supported by results showing that LPS synergizes with silica or GL_1 to induce the production and release of exceedingly high levels of LAF (Table 4). The synergy was particularly manifested by the increase in levels of released LAF, which surpassed by far the added values of activity released by each of the individual agents. Lysates of cultures incubated with the combination of LPS and silica or GL_1 contained high levels of LAF, but these were similar to the activity produced by LPS alone. Experiment II, shown in Table 4, and two other similar experiments examined the effect of combination between latex beads and silica or LPS. A moderate level of synergy was found between latex and silica, while only additivity was noted in cultures incubated with the combination of latex and LPS.

LAF Production and Release by Precultured Mϕ.

The following experiments were performed in order to evaluate the extent to which the effects of the tested agents depend on the content of preformed LAF;

TABLE 4

Synergy between Different Agents in Increasing LAF Production and Release[a]

		Lysates		SUPs	
Expt	Agent added (μg/ml or beads/ml)	[^{3}H]Thymidine uptake (cpm ± SEM)[b]	LAF units	[^{3}H]Thymidine uptake (cpm ± SEM)[b]	LAF units
I	None	701 ± 96	4	399 ± 39	1
	LPS (20)	9,175 ± 1032	80	842 ± 116	3
	Silica (60)	1,944 ± 258	16	12,983 ± 632	100
	Silica + LPS	7,611 ± 871	80	52,026 ± 132	400
	GL_1 (80)	1,976 ± 232	16	1,010 ± 144	12
	GL_1 + LPS	16,028 ± 1859	120	26,676 ± 2301	200
II	None	648 ± 91	5	239 ± 10	1
	Latex (5×10^7)	6,840 ± 554	30	1,757 ± 322	10
	LPS (20)	11,210 ± 389	60	1,100 ± 88	3
	Silica (50)	1,552 ± 169	8	6,164 ± 290	30
	Latex + LPS	11,726 ± 837	60	3,453 ± 524	16
	Latex + silica	7,453 ± 574	35	14,701 ± 726	60
	LPS + silica	12,118 ± 473	60	20,636 ± 371	100

[a] Lysates and SUPs were collected after 20 hr of incubation and used at a final dilution of 1:160 in the assays recorded here.

[b] Control thymocytes cultured with medium alone incorporated 298 ± 33 cpm in Expt I and 343 ± 44 in Expt II; control cultures with LPS incorporated 1450 ± 209 cpm in Expt I and 1190 ± 186 in Expt II.

TABLE 5

Production and Release of LAF by Precultured Macrophages

Time (hr)[a]	Added agent[b]	Lysates: [^{3}H]Thymidine uptake (cpm ± SEM)[c]	Lysates: LAF units	SUPs: [^{3}H]Thymidine uptake (cpm ± SEM)[c]	SUPs: LAF units
0–20	None	710 ± 109	0.3	2,128 ± 448	1.0
	GL_1	6,564 ± 377	3.0	17,528 ± 1657	7.0
	Silica	5,963 ± 623	4.0	37,038 ± 1342	30.0
	LPS	58,305 ± 5389	60.0	10,651 ± 1231	4.0
	Silica + LPS	61,206 ± 1281	80.0	42,484 ± 2934	200.0
24–44	None	424 ± 110	0.2	316 ± 42	0.1
	GL_1	1,491 ± 164	0.4	828 ± 131	0.4
	Silica	1,372 ± 195	0.5	11,865 ± 1211	5.0
	LPS	3,828 ± 236	3.0	3,110 ± 228	1.5
	Silica + LPS	55,882 ± 2812	50.0	51,454 ± 1497	200.0
48–68	None	634 ± 137	0.1	347 ± 52	0.1
	GL_1	1,117 ± 32	0.5	270 ± 41	0.3
	Silica	1,084 ± 239	0.5	10,404 ± 622	5.0
	LPS	12,149 ± 1294	10.0	3,803 ± 513	1.0
	Silica + LPS	30,385 ± 1181	25.0	47,225 ± 2054	200.0

[a] Time measurement started after removal of nonadherent cells.

[b] GL_1 was added to a concentration of 100 μg/ml, silica to 60 μg/ml, and LPS to 20 μg/ml.

[c] Recorded values were obtained with the lysates and SUPs diluted 1:40. Control thymocytes, cultured with medium alone, incorporated 294 ± 50 cpm; cultures with medium and LPS, 1695 ± 209 cpm.

preincubation of Mϕ was found to deplete their levels of preformed LAF. Agents were added to Mϕ cultures after 0, 24, or 48 hr of incubation with medium alone and their effects measured on levels of intracellular and extracellular LAF 20 hr later (Table 5). Mϕ precultured for 24 or 48 hr contained and released very low levels of LAF when incubated with no additive. Minimal effects on LAF levels were produced by addition of GL_1 to the precultured Mϕ. Silica particles, on the other hand, increased considerably the release of LAF by the precultured Mϕ, while substantial elevation in intracellular LAF activity was noted in these cultures when incubated with LPS. The capacity of precultured Mϕ to produce LAF was best demonstrated when the combination of LPS and silica was added; the levels of LAF activity released by these cultures resembled those of cultures stimulated at Time 0. Latex beads, tested in experiments not included here, increased both the intracellular and extracellular levels of LAF when added to precultured Mϕ.

DISCUSSION

Early studies concerning the biological characterization of LAF have not made a clear distinction between the production and release of this mediator (2–4). The studies of Unanue and Kiely (7) and Mizel and Rosenstreich (8), as well as data presented here, have demonstrated, however, that no direct relationship exists in many systems between the levels of total LAF production (intracellular and extracellular) and release (extracellular). Our results with unstimulated Mϕ cultures confirm data of Unanue and Kiely (7), namely, intracellular LAF increases sharply after 2–6 hr of incubation and declines later, with practically no change in the level of extracellular activity. LAF production and release were minimally affected in the study of Unanue and Kiely (7) by the addition of latex beads to the cultures and no other stimuli were examined by these authors. However, both intracellular and extracellular LAF levels were found by Mizel and Rosenstreich (8) to increase markedly in cultures of P388D1 cells shortly after the addition of phorbol myristate acetate. The present study extended the investigation of LAF production and release by testing the effects of various agents on the Mϕ cultures. Three patterns of effect were observed in these cultures: (a) both intracellular and extracellular levels are increased by high concentrations of latex beads; (b) intracellular activity is stimulated more than the extracellular by LPS; (c) extracellular levels are elevated more than intracellular levels by silica or GL_1 particles. These data thus indicate that determination of both intracellular and extracellular LAF levels is essential to learn about the effects of tested agents on LAF production by Mϕ.

The difference between the patterns of effect of LPS and silica or GL_1 suggests different modes of action of these agents. This notion is supported by the observation that LPS acts synergistically with silica or GL_1 to stimulate the release of high levels of LAF which exceed by far the activity released by the individual agents. Furthermore, SUPs from cultures incubated with the combinations of LPS and silica or GL_1 also showed high levels of two other activities of LAF or interleukin 1, i.e., direct mitogenic activity on thymocyte cultures (without added PHA (11)), and potentiation of antibody production by spleen cultures of nude mice (16). (Data not included. The latter assay was kindly performed by Dr. D. D. Wood, Merck Institute for Therapeutic Research.) Both assays are less sensitive than the assay for LAF potentiating activity used in the present study (11, 16). The use of combinations of agents thus provides a new procedure to obtain outstanding high yields of interleukin 1. Experiments to be reported elsewhere[2] have shown that the chromatographic profile of the high LAF activity released by the combined agents resembles the profile of activity released by LPS alone (main peak activity at about 20K daltons).

Of particular interest are the effects of silica and GL_1, two agents which have been shown in this and other studies ((10) and footnote 2) to be selectively injurious to Mϕ. A direct correlation was observed between the level of injury (i.e., LDH release) and LAF production and release and it is conceivable, therefore, that the two processes are related. It should be emphasized, however, that the injury caused by these agents did not merely cause an increased leakage of LAF from the Mϕ, since the intracellular levels of the mediator were also elevated. The increase in production and release of LAF by Mϕ cultured with silica or GL_1 could be attributed to two hypothetical mechanisms: (a) the damage itself could bring about the increased production of LAF, and/or (b) the agents may stimulate the production of LAF, concurrently with the cell injury. The hypothesis that damage may increase LAF production is supported by reports showing that LAF release is increased by various injurious agents like dimethylsulfoxide (4), colchicine (6), or carrageenan (17). Furthermore, Mϕ damage could play a role in the reported increase in both intracellular and extracellular LAF levels that follows cycloheximide treatment (7). The effect of cycloheximide has been attributed to the superinduction phenomenon (7, 18), but increased death rate was observed in Mϕ

after 12 hr or more of incubation with this drug (7). Using the hypothetical framework of Unanue and Kiely (7), one can propose that Mϕ damage by any of the different agents may either enhance the process of conversion of the inactive precursor to the active LAF, or reduce the rate of degradation of the active molecule.

The net stimulatory effect of the various agents was analyzed in experiments with precultured Mϕ (Table 5); these cells have practically no "background" LAF activity. Precultured Mϕ produced and released increased amounts of LAF after incubation with silica; data which indicate, again, that silica particles do not just release preformed LAF. GL_1, however, was only slightly active on precultured Mϕ, a finding which is under further investigation.

The data presented here demonstrate a striking difference between the patterns of production and release of LAF and other Mϕ products, like the two lysosomal enzymes. In contrast with the large fluctuations in the total LAF activity in Mϕ cultured with the various agents, very small variations were observed in the total activity of hexosaminidase or β-galactosidase in these cultures (Fig. 1 and Table 2). The unique pattern of production and release of LAF may be useful therefore for examining its presumed close relationship with other Mϕ-derived factors, namely, the endogenous pyrogen (19) and a mediator which stimulates rheumatoid synovial cells (20).

Both silica and GL_1 are accumulated in cells of the reticuloendothelial system in specific pathologic conditions, namely, silicosis (10) and Gaucher's disease (9). Little is known about the pathogenesis of these diseases, but it is tempting to speculate that Mϕ-derived mediators could play some role in stimulating reactions characteristic of these diseases, i.e., the fibrosis in silicosis (10) and the high frequency of gammopathies in Gaucher's disease (21, 22). While T- or B-lymphocyte-activating factors (5, 6, 23) may contribute toward gammopathy formation, Mϕ factors which stimulate the metabolism and growth of fibroblasts (10, 24, 25) could enhance fibrosis (10).

ACKNOWLEDGMENTS

We thank Dr. Joost J. Oppenheim for his critical comments and Mrs. Noreen Beavers and Ms. Joyce McIntyre for expert secretarial assistance with the manuscript.

REFERENCES

1. Aarden, L. A. *et al. Cell. Immunol.* **48,** 433, 1979.
2. Gery, I., and Waksman, B. H., *J. Exp. Med.* **136,** 143, 1972.
3. Unanue, E. R., Kiely, J.-M., and Calderon, J., *J. Exp. Med.* **144,** 155, 1976.
4. Blyden, G., and Handschumacher, R. E., *J. Immunol.* **118,** 1631, 1977.
5. Unanue, E. R., *Immunol. Rev.* **40,** 227, 1978.
6. Oppenheim, J. J., Mizel, S. B., and Meltzer, M. S., *In* "Biology of the Lymphokines" (S. Cohen, E. Pick, and J. J. Oppenheim, Eds.), pp. 291–323. Academic Press, New York, 1979.
7. Unanue, E. R., and Kiely, J.-M., *J. Immunol.* **119,** 925, 1977.
8. Mizel, S. B., and Rosenstreich, D. L., *J. Immunol.* **122,** 2173, 1979.
9. Brady, R. O., *In* "The Metabolic Basis of Inherited Disease" (J. B. Stansbury, J. B. Wyngaarden, and D. S. Fredrickson, Eds.), pp. 731–746. 4th ed. McGraw–Hill, New York, 1978.
10. Allison, A. C., and Morgan, D. M. L., *In* "Lysosomes in Applied Biology and Therapeutics Vol. 6" (J. T. Dingle, P. J. Jacques, and I. H. Shaw, Eds.) (Frontiers of Biology, Vol. 48), pp. 149–159. North-Holland, Amsterdam, 1979.
11. Gery, I., Gershon, R. K., and Waksman, *J. Exp. Med.* **136,** 128, 1972.
12. Pugh, D., Leaback, D. H., and Walker, P. G., *Biochem. J.* **65,** 464, 1957.

13. Suzuki, K. *In* "Methods in Enzymology" (V. Ginsburg, Ed.), Vol. 50, p. 456. Academic Press, New York, 1978.
14. Amador, E., Dorfman, L. E., and Wacker, W. E. C. *Clin. Chem.* **9,** 391, 1963.
15. Dean, R. T., Hylton, W., and Allison, A. C. *Biochim. Biophys. Acta,* **584,** 57, 1979.
16. Wood, D. D., *J. Immunol.* **123,** 2400, 1979.
17. Stamenkovic, M., Stosic-Grujicic, S., and Simic, M. M., *Period. Biol.* **81,** 171, 1979.
18. Mizel, S. B., and Mizel, D., *J. Immunol.* **126,** 834, 1981.
19. Rosenwasser, L. J., Dinarello, C. A., and Rosenthal, A. S., *J. Exp. Med.* **150,** 709, 1979.
20. Mizel, S. B., Dayer, J.-M., Krane, S. M., and Mergenhagen, S. E., *Proc. Nat. Acad. Sci.* **78,** 2474, 1981.
21. Pratt, P. W., Estren, S., and Kochwa, S., *Blood* **31,** 633, 1968.
22. Turesson, T., and Rausing, A., *Acta Med. Scand.* **197,** 507, 1975.
23. Kurland, J. I., Kincade, P. W., and Moore, M. A. S., *J. Exp. Med.* **146,** 1420, 1977.
24. Wahl, S. M., Wahl, L. M., McCarthy, J. B., Chedid, L., and Mergenhagen, S. E., *J. Immunol.* **122,** 2226, 1979.
25. DeLustro, F., Sherer, G. K., and LeRoy, E. C., *J. Reticuloendothel. Soc.* **28,** 519, 1980.

CELLULAR IMMUNOLOGY 64, 304–311 (1981)

Immune Interferon Induction by a Monoclonal Antibody Specific for Human T Cells[1]

ROY H. L. PANG[2], Y. K. YIP, AND JAN VILČEK[3]

Department of Microbiology, New York University School of Medicine, New York, New York 10016

Received July 2, 1981; accepted July 24, 1981

OKT3, a monoclonal antibody reactive with a surface antigen shared by all human T lymphocytes, was found to act as a potent interferon (IFN) inducer in cultures of human mononuclear white blood cells. Two other monoclonal antibodies reactive with T-cell subpopulations failed to induce IFN. IFN-inducing activity of OKT3 was similar to that of phytohemagglutinin (PHA). The phorbol ester, 12-*O*-tetradecanoylphorbol-13-acetate (TPA) had a strong potentiating effect on IFN production stimulated with OKT3 or PHA. IFN produced after stimulation with OKT3, like PHA-induced IFN, had properties characteristic for "immune" IFN (IFN-γ).

INTRODUCTION

Three major types of interferon (IFN) can be clearly distinguished on the basis of different physicochemical characteristics, antigenic properties, and host range (1). They have recently been termed IFN-α (leukocyte), IFN-β (fibroblast), and IFN-γ (immune) (2). Human IFN-α and IFN-β have been extensively characterized, the proteins have been purified to homogeneity and the sequence of *N*-terminal amino acids determined (3, 4). In addition, several IFN-α and IFN-β genes have been cloned and sequenced (5). On the other hand, little is known about the structure and properties of IFN-γ. The major problem has been the production of sufficient amounts of IFN-γ for purification and physicochemical analysis. Recently we have developed a procedure for human IFN-γ production based on combined stimulation of lymphocyte cultures with 12-*O*-tetradecanoylphorbol-13-acetate (TPA) and phytohemagglutinin (PHA) (6). IFN-γ produced by induction with TPA and PHA was partially purified to a specific activity of at least 10^7 units/mg protein (7).

Several years ago, Falcoff *et al.* (8) reported that IFN-γ could be induced in lymphocyte cultures by stimulation with anti-lymphocytic serum. The recent availability of monoclonal antibodies against human T lymphocytes (9) and the demonstration of potent mitogenic activity of the OKT3 antibody (10) prompted us

[1] Parts of this work were presented at the First Annual International Congress for Interferon Research, Washington, D.C., November 9–12, 1981.

[2] Present address: Genex Corporation, Rockville, Md. 20852.

[3] To whom all correspondence should be sent at: New York University School of Medicine, 550 First Ave., New York, N.Y. 10016.

0008-8749/81/160304-08$02.00/0

to analyze the IFN-γ-inducing ability of some monoclonal antibodies specific for T lymphocytes.

In this study we show that monoclonal antibody OKT3 is a potent inducer of IFN-γ, while OKT4 and OKT8 fail to induce IFN from lymphocyte cultures. Characterization of the IFN induced by OKT3 revealed that its properties are identical to those of IFN-γ induced by stimulation with TPA and PHA.

MATERIALS AND METHODS

Materials. Purified PHA-L was obtained from P-L Biochemicals, Inc. (Milwaukee, Wisc.) and TPA from Consolidated Midland Corporation (Katona, N.Y.). Monoclonal antibodies OKT3, OKT4, and OKT8 were gifts from Dr. Gideon Goldstein (Ortho Pharmaceutical Co., Raritan, N.J.). According to information provided by the manufacturer, OKT3 is reactive with 100% of peripheral T lymphocytes, OKT4 is reactive with 65% of peripheral T cells (inducer/helper T lymphocytes), and OKT8 is reactive with 35% of peripheral T cells (suppressor/cytotoxic T lymphocytes). Human IFN-α (approx. 100,000 international units/ml, 5×10^4 units/mg of protein) was the kind gift of Dr. Kari Cantell, Helsinki, Finland. Human IFN-β (800,000 units/ml, 8×10^4 units/mg of protein) was prepared by Rentschler Arzneimittel and Co., Laupheim, West Germany, and supplied by the National Cancer Institute, Bethesda, Maryland.

Preparation of human lymphocyte cultures. The preparation of lymphocyte cultures for IFN-γ production has been described in detail elsewhere (6). Briefly, lymphocyte-rich plateletpheresis residues (obtained from the New York Blood Center through the courtesy of Dr. Alan Waldman) were diluted twofold with serum-free RPMI 1640 medium. The diluted cell suspension was overlaid onto Ficoll–Hypague and centrifuged at 400*g* for 30 min at 20°C in a Beckman refrigerated centrifuge TRJ-6. After centrifugation, the cell layer at the interphase was removed, suspended in serum-free RPMI 1640 medium, and washed twice by centrifuging (400*g*) and resuspending in serum-free RPMI 1640 medium. After washing, the cell density was adjusted to a final concentration of 6×10^6 cells/ml (unless otherwise stated). The lymphocyte preparations were contaminated with up to 10% polymophonuclear neutrophils and monocytes as determined by differential staining.

In some experiments the entire cell population present in plateletpheresis residues was used for seeding cultures. Total white blood cell counts were taken by diluting unprocessed residues with 3% acetic acid. The residues were then simply diluted with serum-free RPMI 1640 to the desired final cell density and used for seeding cultures.

IFN induction and assay. The cell suspension was dispensed in 24-well plastic tissue culture plates at 1 ml per well. Monoclonal antibodies OKT3, OKT4, or OKT8, or PHA were added as indicated. For priming with IFN and for TPA pretreatment, the cell cultures were incubated with IFN-α, IFN-β, or TPA for 2 hr before addition of the inducer as indicated. Culture supernatants were generally harvested 48 to 72 hr after induction or as indicated. All incubations were at 37°C in a humidified CO_2 incubator.

For IFN assays human diploid FS-7 fibroblasts, or human GM-258 fibroblasts trisomic for chromosome 21, were used as indicator cells. FS-7 cells were challenged with encephalomyocarditis (EMC) virus, while GM-258 cells were challenged with vesicular stomatitis (VSV) virus. Both assays were based on inhibition of cytopathic effect in 96-well plates (11). The two cell/virus combinations employed gave comparable titers. A human IFN-α standard and a laboratory standard for IFN-γ were included in all assays. However, all interferon titers are reported in laboratory units without correction (6).

Neutralization of interferon by antiserum to IFN-α and IFN-β. Antiserum was prepared by immunization of rabbits with a partially purified preparation of human IFN-α as described (12). The neutralizing titer of the antiserum, measured against 10 interferon units/ml (13), was 1:64,000 against IFN-α and 1:4,000 against IFN-β. This antiserum exerted no neutralizing activity against human IFN-γ at a dilution of 1:32 or greater.

Stability of IFN at pH 2. IFN preparations were dialyzed against 0.1 *M* glycine·HCl buffer, pH 2.0, overnight at 4°C. To restore physiological pH, IFN preparations were then dialyzed against phosphate-buffered saline (PBS), pH 7.4, overnight at 4°C. As a control, the same preparations were dialyzed only against PBS. Residual IFN activity was determined after dialysis.

RESULTS

IFN Induction by Monoclonal Antibody

IFN-inducing ability of monoclonal antibodies OKT3, OKT4, and OKT8 was analyzed at concentrations of 1 to 20 ng/ml (Table 1). OKT3 reacts with a surface antigen on all T lymphocytes, while OKT4 and OKT8 react only with T helper and T suppressor lymphocytes, respectively. Culture fluids were collected for IFN assays 48 hr after the addition of monoclonal antibody since preliminary experiments showed that IFN levels after stimulation with OKT3 usually peaked by this time. Only OKT3 was found to induce IFN, with high levels of production reached after stimulation of lymphocyte cultures with 5 ng/ml of monoclonal antibody. Lymphocytes from several other donors also did not produce IFN in response to OKT4 or OKT8 while responding to OKT3. A mixture of OKT4 and OKT8 also failed to induce IFN from the lymphocyte cultures (not shown).

TABLE 1

IFN Induction by Different Doses of Monoclonal Antibodies OKT3, OKT4, and OKT8

Antibody concentration (ng/ml)	IFN yield with antibody[a]		
	OKT3	OKT4	OKT8
1	40	<40	<40
2	240	<40	<40
5	1280	<40	<40
10	1920	<40	<40
20	1280	<40	<40

[a] IFN titers (units/ml) in media collected 48 hr after addition of the monoclonal antibody to cultures of Ficoll–Hypaque-purified mononuclear cells.

Comparison of IFN Induction by OKT3 and PHA in Lymphocyte Cultures from Various Donors

IFN titers from lymphocyte cultures from individual donors stimulated with OKT3 ranged from <40 units/ml up to 20,480 units/ml (Table 2). A similar range of titers was found on stimulation with PHA. It is interesting that there was a very close correlation between IFN yields obtained with OKT3 and PHA in cultures from six different donors.

Effect of TPA on IFN Production

Effects of the phorbol ester TPA were analyzed in two types of cell cultures stimulated with OKT3 or PHA (Table 3). In general, cultures from unprocessed cells were superior in IFN production to Ficoll–Hypaque-purified mononuclear cell cultures. It is interesting that treatment with TPA alone stimulated IFN production from unprocessed plateletpheresis residue cell cultures but not from Ficoll–Hypaque-purified cell cultures. The same observation was reported earlier (6). Stimulation with OKT3 alone also produced high IFN titers from cultures of unprocessed cells whereas only a low yield was obtained after the same mode of stimulation from Ficoll–Hypaque-purified cells derived from the same plateletpheresis residue. In contrast, PHA alone did not stimulate markedly higher IFN yields from unprocessed cell cultures than from Ficoll-Hypaque-purified cultures. Cell density was also an important factor; the optimal cell concentration varied with the inducer and type of cell culture employed.

Effect of Priming on IFN Production

It is known that treatment of cultures with IFN before exposure of cells to IFN inducers often leads to enhanced IFN yields ("priming") (1). The effect of priming with IFN-α or IFN-β on IFN yields produced with OKT3 or PHA is summarized in Table 4. Although neither OKT3 nor PHA alone produced detectable IFN in this experiment, pretreatment with TPA resulted in high levels of IFN production

TABLE 2

IFN Induction with Monoclonal Antibody OKT3 or PHA in Cultures Prepared from Different Platelet Residues

Platelet residue No.	IFN yield after stimulation with[a]	
	OKT3	PHA
1	1,280	640
2	1,920	5,120
3	80	320
4	20,480	10,240
5	<40	<40
6	15,360	7,680

[a] IFN titers (units/ml) in media collected 48 or 72 hr after the addition of OKT3 (5 ng/ml) or PHA (5 μg/ml) to cultures of Ficoll–Hypaque-purified mononuclear cells. Platelet residues from six different donors were used.

TABLE 3

Effects of TPA on IFN Production Induced with OKT3 Antibody or PHA

Cell population[a]	Cell density ($\times 10^6$)[b]	IFN yield after stimulation with[c]				
		TPA	OKT3	TPA/OKT3	PHA	TPA/PHA
Ficoll–Hypaque-purified	1	<40	160	<40	40	<40
	2	<40	240	80	40	160
	3	<40	120	160	160	320
	6	<40	160	640	80	1920
Unprocessed	1	<40	960	320	160	480
	2	240	2560	2,560	240	1920
	3	480	2560	10,240	320	5120
	6	3840	320	10,240	80	5120

[a] A plateletpheresis residue from one donor was divided into two portions. Mononuclear cells were isolated from one portion by Ficoll–Hypaque centrifugation. The other portion was simply diluted in RPMI 1640 medium to the desired cell concentration before seeding cultures in 24-well plates.

[b] Indicates total number of white blood cells present at the time of seeding.

[c] Units/ml in media collected 48 hr after addition of appropriate inducer. TPA and OKT3 were used at 5 ng/ml, PHA at 5 μg/ml. In cultures first treated with TPA and then stimulated with OKT3 or PHA (TPA/OKT3 or TPA/PHA), TPA was added to cultures 2 hr before OKT3 or PHA.

with both OKT3 or PHA. Priming with IFN-α did not enhance IFN production by OKT3 and priming with IFN-β produced only moderate enhancement. In contrast, when PHA was employed as the inducer, priming of lymphocyte cultures with IFN-α or IFN-β was almost as effective as TPA treatment in enhancing IFN production. When doses below 300 units/ml of IFN-α or IFN-β were used for priming, enhancement of PHA-stimulated IFN production was less marked (not shown).

TABLE 4

Enhancement of IFN Production by Priming with IFN-α or IFN-β, or by Treatment with TPA

Priming treatment[a]	IFN yield after stimulation with[b]	
	OKT3	PHA
None	<40	<40
TPA, 5 ng/ml	7680	11,600
IFN-α, 300 units/ml	<40	10,240
IFN-α, 1000 units/ml	40	3,840
IFN-β, 300 units/ml	320	7,840
IFN-β, 1000 units/ml	320	10,240

[a] Cultures of Ficoll–Hypaque-purified cells were incubated with TPA, IFN-α, or IFN-β for 2 hr before stimulation with OKT3 or PHA.

[b] IFN titers in media collected 48 hr after induction with OKT3 (5 ng/ml) or PHA (5 μg/ml). Before assay samples were treated with an excess of anti-IFN (α + β) serum in order to neutralize all residual IFN-α or IFN-β used for priming. The efficacy of the antiserum was checked in control experimental groups run in parallel with the experiment shown in the table.

TABLE 5

Effect of Dialysis at pH 2 on the Activity of Various IFN Preparations

IFN preparation induced with[a]	IFN titer after dialysis at		Percentage inactivation at pH 2
	pH 7.4	pH 2.0	
OKT3 antibody	5,120	1,024	80
PHA	1,920	384	80
TPA/PHA	2,560	512	80
PHA (IFN-α primed)	2,560	384	85
PHA (IFN-β primed)	3,840	768	80
Control IFN-α	10,240	15,360	0
Control IFN-β	2,560	5,120	0

[a] In cultures of Ficoll–Hypaque-purified cells as described in Tables 3 and 4.

Some Properties of IFN Produced in Lymphocyte Cultures Stimulated with Monoclonal Antibody OKT3

IFN-γ can be distinguished from the other IFN species by its characteristic lability at low pH (1). In its lack of stability at pH 2 OKT3-induced IFN activity was similar to PHA-induced IFN but different from control IFN-α or IFN-β (Table 5).

IFN obtained by induction with the OKT3 antibody was also antigenically different from IFN-α or IFN-β because potent antiserum neutralizing IFN-α and IFN-β did not reduce the activity of OKT3-stimulated IFN. PHA or TPA/PHA-induced IFN was also not neutralized (Table 6). Since antiserum to human IFN-γ is not yet available, we were unable to establish whether OKT3- and PHA-induced IFN preparations are antigenically homologous.

DISCUSSION

Monoclonal antibody OKT3 against human T cells was found to act as a potent inducer of human IFN in human lymphocyte cultures. In contrast, two other mono-

TABLE 6

Effect of Antiserum to Human IFN (α + β) on the Activity of Various IFN Preparations

IFN preparation induced with[a]	IFN titer after addition of[b]	
	Control serum	Anti-IFN (α + β) serum
OKT3	192	256
PHA	128	128
TPA/PHA	128	128
Control IFN-α	128	<4
Control IFN-β	64	<4

[a] In cultures of Ficoll–Hypaque-purified cells as described in Table 3.

[b] IFN preparations were diluted to a concentration of approximately 100–200 units/ml. Control rabbit serum or anti-IFN (α + β) serum sufficient to neutralize ≥1000 units/ml of IFN-α or IFN-β was added. The mixtures were incubated for 1 hr at 37°C and residual IFN activity was determined.

clonal antibodies, OKT4 and OKT8, reacting with subpopulation of T cells showed no IFN-inducing activity. IFN-inducing activity of OKT3 is undoubtedly the result of its proven mitogenic action in T lymphocytes (10). Since OKT3 is known to react only with T lymphocytes, our results provide strong evidence that IFN is produced as a result of T-cell activation.

We reported previously that TPA and several structurally related diterpene esters act as potent stimulants of IFN production, especially when used in combination with other mitogens (6, 14). Others had reported that TPA is a potent mitogen or comitogen for lymphocytes (15, 16). More recently TPA was shown to increase the synthesis of interleukin-2 from lymphocyte cultures stimulated with plant lectins (17). It is likely that combined stimulation of lymphocyte cultures with TPA and some other mitogen may lead to enhanced production of other lymphokines as well.

It is interesting that there was a quite close correlation in the amounts of IFN produced after stimulation of lymphocyte cultures from individual donors with OKT3 and PHA. Units responding well to one inducer usually responded with good IFN production to the other mitogen as well. Units not responding to one stimulus usually also failed to respond to the other mitogen. However, in all instances IFN production could be boosted by preincubation of cells with TPA. The enhancement afforded by TPA was generally more marked in nonresponding or poorly responding units. We do not have enough data to conclude whether the magnitude of IFN response after stimulation with OKT3 or PHA remains relatively constant in the same donor on repeated blood donations or whether there are significant fluctuations due to changes in T-cell responsiveness or other variables.

One apparent difference between the IFN response to PHA and OKT3 was that only the former could be markedly enhanced by priming with IFN-α or IFN-β. Enhancement of PHA-induced IFN-γ production by priming with IFN was observed earlier (18). Fisher *et al.* (19) recently pointed out that some similarities exist in the effects of TPA and IFN on different cell functions. For instance, both TPA and IFN are known to affect cell differentiation (20, 22). The similarities also include an enhancing effect of treatment with TPA (6, 14, 23, 24) or with IFN (1, 18) on subsequent IFN production in some systems.

Cultures prepared from the entire unprocessed plateletpheresis residues generally produced higher yields of IFN than cultures of Ficoll–Hypaque-purified mononuclear cells. This finding could be due to the contributing role of accessory cells needed for optimal IFN-γ production by T lymphocytes. Accessory cells (possibly monocytes and macrophages) might be removed during Ficoll–Hypaque centrifugation. Epstein *et al.* (25) had earlier demonstrated that macrophages can augment IFN-γ production by T cells.

IFN produced after stimulation with OKT3 had the general characteristics of IFN-γ, as evidenced by its lack of stability at pH 2 and by its antigenic properties. In addition, OKT3-stimulated IFN was found to have the same apparent molecular weight (approximately 58,000) as PHA-induced IFN-γ (7) when analyzed by gel filtration on Biogel P-200 (not shown). Also similar and characteristic for IFN-γ (7) was the elution pattern of OKT3-induced IFN from concanavalin A–Sepharose columns, with the bulk of activity recovered after elution with the specific carbohydrate ligand α-methyl-D-manopyranoside (not shown).

Final evidence for the identity of OKT3- and PHA-induced IFN will have to await the availability of specific antibodies against human IFN-γ. Successful preparation of small quantities of such antibodies against mouse IFN-γ was recently reported (26). The potent IFN-γ inducing activity of OKT3 in human lymphocytes could be useful for the production of human IFN-γ and for the elucidation of its induction mechanisms.

ACKNOWLEDGMENTS

We thank Dr. Gideon Goldstein for the gift of monoclonal antibodies, Dr. Alan Waldman for the supply of plateletpheresis residues, and Dr. Douglas Testa for helpful discussions. Michele Cassano, Angel Feliciano, Dorothy Henriksen, and Leela Jashnani provided expert technical assistance. This work was supported by USPHS Grants NO1-AI-07057 and AI-12948 and Contract NO1-AI-02169, and by grants from Flow Laboratories, Inc. and Rentschler Arzneimittel GmbH & Co.

REFERENCES

1. Stewart, W. E., II, "The Interferon System." Springer-Verlag, Vienna/New York, 1979.
2. Committee on Interferon Nomenclature, *Nature (London)* **286,** 110, 1980.
3. Zoon, K. C., Smith, M. E., Bridgen, P. J., Anfinsen, C. B., Hunkapiller, M. W., and Hood, L. E., *Science* **207,** 527, 1980.
4. Knight, E., Jr., Hunkapiller, M. W., Korant, B. D., Hardy, R. W. F., and Hood, L. E., *Science* **207,** 525, 1980.
5. Taniguchi, T., Mantei, N., Schwarzstein, M., Nagata, S., Muramatsu, M., and Weissmann, C., *Nature (London)* **285,** 547, 1980.
6. Yip, Y. K., Pang, R. H. L., Oppenheim, J. D., Nachbar, M. S., Henriksen, D., Zerebeckyj-Eckhardt, I., and Vilček, J., *Infect. Immunity,* in press, 1981.
7. Yip, Y. K., Pang, R. H. L., Urban, C., and Vilček, J., *Proc. Nat. Acad. Sci. USA* **78,** 1601, 1981.
8. Falcoff, R., Oriol, R., and Iscaki, S., *Eur. J. Immunol.* **2,** 476, 1972.
9. Kung, P. C., Goldstein, G., Reinherz, E. L., and Schlossman, S., *Science* **206,** 347, 1979.
10. Van Wauwe, J. P., De Mey, J. R., and Goossens, J. G., *J. Immunol.* **124,** 2708, 1980.
11. Havell, E. A., and Vilček, J., *Antimicrob. Ag. Chemother.* **2,** 476, 1972.
12. Vilček, J., Yamazaki, S., and Havell, E. A., *Infect. Immunity* **18,** 863, 1977.
13. Havell, E. A., Berman, B., Ogburn, C., Berg, K., Paucker, K., and Vilček, J., *Proc. Nat. Acad. Sci. USA,* **72,** 2185, 1975.
14. Vilček, J., Sulea, I. T., Volvovitz, F., and Yip, Y. K., *In* "Biochemical Characterization of Lymphokines (A. L. De Weck, F. Kristensen, and M. Landy, Eds.), p. 323. Academic Press, London, 1980.
15. Mastro, A. M., and Mueller, G. C., *Exp. Cell Res.* **88,** 40, 1974.
16. Wang, J. L., McClain, D. A., and Edelman, G. M., *Proc. Nat.. Acad. Sci. USA* **72,** 1917, 1975.
17. Farrar, J. J., Mizel, S. B., Fuller-Farrar, J., Farrar, W. L., and Hilfiker, M. L., *J. Immunol.* **125,** 793, 1980.
18. Wiranowska-Stewart, M., Lin, L. S., Braude, E. A., and Stewart, W. E., II, *In* "Biochemical Characterization of Lymphokines (A. L. De Weck, F. Kristensen, and M. Landy, Eds.) p. 331. Academic Press, London, 1980.
19. Fisher, P. B., Mufson, R. A., and Weinstein, I. B., *Biochem. Biophys. Res. Commun.* **100,** 823, 1981.
20. Yamasaki, H., Fibach, E., Nudel, U., Weinstein, I. B., Rifkind, R. A., and Marks, P. A., *Proc. Nat. Acad. Sci. USA* **74,** 3451, 1977.
21. Rossi, G. B., Dolei, A., Cioe, L., Benedetto, A., Matarese, G. P., and Belardelli, F., *Proc. Nat. Acad. Sci. USA* **74,** 2036, 1977.
22. Keay, S., and Grossberg, S. E., *Proc. Nat. Acad. Sci. USA* **77,** 4099, 1980.
23. Klein, G., and Vilček, J., *J. Gen. Virol.* **46,** 111, 1980.
24. Adolph, G. R., and Swetly,, P., *J. Gen. Virol.* **51,** 61, 1980.
25. Epstein, L. B., Cline, M. J., and Merigan, T. C., *Cell. Immunol.* **2,** 602, 1971.
26. Osborne, L. C., Georgiades, J. A., and Johnson, H. M., *Cell. Immunol.* **53,** 65, 1980.

CELLULAR IMMUNOLOGY 64, 312–323 (1981)

Human Autologous Rosettes

II. Further Characterization: Markers and Functions[1]

M. RUCHETON,* J. CARAUX,* A. REY,* C. THIERRY,* C. ESTEVE,* H. VALLES,* J. DUFER,† A. DESPLACES,† D. ZAGURY,‡ AND B. SERROU*

**Laboratoire d'Immunopharmacologie des Tumeurs, INSERM U 236, ERA-CNRS No. 844, Centre Paul Lamarque, Hopital St. Eloi, B.P. 5054, 34033 Montpellier Cedex, France, †Centre Réne Huguenin, 35 rue Dailly, 92000 St. Cloud, France, and ‡Universite Pierre et Marie Curie, UER61 4 Place Jussieu (Tour 32), 75005 Paris, France*

Received July 8, 1981; accepted July 20, 1981

Purification of peripheral blood lymphocytes able to form autologous rosettes (ARFC) overnight has been obtained with satisfactory yield and enrichment, using short-term centrifugation on a Percoll cushion. Purified ARFC form E-rosettes, express human T-lymphocyte antigens, and contain cell-bearing Fc receptors for IgM but very few for IgG. They are also OKT4 positive. Morphological structure and cytochemistry (β-glucuronidase and acid phosphatase) do not suggest activation. The ARFC subset has poor antibody-dependent cell-mediated cytotoxicity and NK activity. They respond strongly to PHA and demonstrate a higher response in mixed allogeneic or autologous culture compared to non-ARFC or total PBL.

INTRODUCTION

Several functional subsets of human T lymphocytes have been characterized as a result of membrane markers—rosettes or monoclonal antibodies (2, 3). Some of these T cells are capable of binding autologous red cells in the presence of autologous serum (autorosette-forming cells: ARFC). This has been described by several authors (4). In our laboratory, approximately 26% of peripheral blood lymphocytes are ARFC. Moreover, the level of ARFC undergoes significant changes in the peripheral blood of cancer patients (6).

In recent years, several studies investigated autologous lymphocyte reactions, i.e., the T-lymphocyte blastogenesis induced by non-T lymphocytes from the same donor (7, 8). Whether this is an immune response remains to be settled. An attempt to define this phenomenon could begin by a purification of ARFC to ascertain whether they respond in autologous mixed lymphocyte culture. The present study describes such a purification of ARFC from human peripheral mononuclear cells and an investigation of their role in the autologous response. *In vitro* functions and cell markers are also studied.

MATERIALS AND METHODS

Lymphocytes, Autologous Erythrocytes, and Autologous Rosettes

Peripheral blood mononuclear cells were extracted from heparinized whole blood by the Boyum method using a Ficoll–Metrizoate cushion. This procedure and prep-

[1] This work was supported by INSERM Grants ATP 79-4-059-2, DGRST 80-70306, and Federation Nationali des Centres de Lutte contre le Cancer.

0008-8749/81/160312-12$02.00/0

aration of autologous erythrocytes and autologous rosettes have been previously described (5). Briefly, 2×10^6 lymphocytes in 200 μl of Hanks' salt solution were incubated 30 min at 4°C with 50 μl of autologous serum. This was followed by the addition of 15×10^6 autologous RBC in 50 μl after which the mixture was centrifuged for 5 min at 150*g* in a MSE Multex centrifuge and incubated for 18 hr at 4°C. The mixture of autologous lymphocytes and erythrocytes was then carefully resuspended and ARFC scored in the cold using acridine orange as a fluorescent probe of nucleated cells.

Separation of ARFC

(a) Percoll solutions. P*x* designates a solution which, in 100 ml, contains *x* ml of 1.13 g/cm^3 pure Percoll (Pharmacia), 8 ml of 10× Hanks' salt solution (HBSS, Institut Pasteur), 1.8 ml of PBS (10×, pH 7.2), 2 ml of 1 *M* Hepes buffer, pH 7.2, 2 ml of autologous serum, and 50 μl calciparin. P_{76} and P_0 refer to solution of given and verified osmolarity, 305 to 325 and 295 to 305, respectively. Small volumes (1 ml) of different densities were formed by mixing P_0 and P_{76} in different ratios: 1.00, 0.98, 0.96, 0.94, 0.92, and 0.90 (volume ratio of P_{76} to P_0).

(b) Determination of the Percoll banding density of ARFC (P_{AR}). Percoll discontinuous gradients were formed in 75 × 13-mm plastic tubes using 500 μl of each of the above-mentioned solutions. A small number of erythrocytes was layered onto the gradient and the tubes centrifuged for 10 min at 250*g*. The density of the red cells for a given donor (P_{RBC}) was defined as that of the last layer of the RBC band. The Percoll solution P_{AR} chosen to isolate autorosettes from the same subject contained 2% P_0 and 98% P_{RBC}.

(c) Separation of autorosettes. Autorosettes were formed overnight as indicated above excepted that 14×10^6 lymphocytes in 350 μl of autologous serum were placed in contact with 140×10^6 autologous RBC in a 10-ml plastic tube. The rosettes were gently resuspended at 4°C and 1.5 ml of a solution of cold Percoll P_{AR} was slowly introduced underneath this suspension. The tube was then centrifuged in a MSE Multex centrifuge for 10 min at 250*g* and 4°C. It is important that vibrations do not occur during centrifugation.

Lymphocytes recovered from the pellet or floating band were then scored for percentage ARFC and then fractions were also diluted in HBSS, warmed for 30 min at 25°C, then slightly vortexed to impede binding between red and white cells. Each pool of cells was then recentrifuged and diluted in HBSS (adjusted to 290 mOsm), and centrifuged over 1.5 ml of P_{AR} for 10 min at 500*g* in a MSE Multex centrifuge to remove free erythrocytes. Lymphocytes were harvested from the ring and washed twice. Control lymphocytes were stored in the cold. Other control lymphocytes were obtained from disruption of rosettes (25°C, 30 min) before centrifugation on P_{AR}. In this case lymphocytes were collected from the ring and washed as above.

Evaluation of Cell Surface Markers

(a) The percentage ERFC was estimated using a micromethod. Sheep red blood cells (SRBC), collected in sodium citrate solution, were washed three times in Hanks' solution and adjusted to 300×10^6 cells/ml. Of this SRBC suspension 2 μl was placed in contact with 1 μl of fetal calf serum previously absorbed on SRBC

and 1 μl of Hanks' solution containing 16.5×10^3 lymphocytes into a well of a microtest tissue culture plates (Falcon 3034) which was then centrifuged at 300*g* for 5 min and incubated overnight in the cold. Cells were resuspended by adding 20 μl of Hanks' solution. The plate was inverted for 10 min at 4°C, nucleated cells stained with 1 μl of 0.002% of acridine orange (37), and rosettes were scored. Each count was made in duplicate.

(b) Cells with Fc receptor for IgM or IgG were identified by a rosetting technique using OxRBC coated with IgM or IgG anti-ox antibody. Scores were made as for ERFC except that 5×10^3 lymphocytes in 1 μl of Hanks' solution were in contact with 1 μl of Hanks' solution containing 1% OxRBC IgG or OxRBC IgM and that incubation was for 1 hr at 4°C.

(c) The percentage of cells expressing human T-lymphocyte antigen (HTLA) was determined using a micromethod adapted from Touraine and Touraine (35). Briefly, 1 μl of Hanks' solution containing 3×10^3 lymphocytes were placed in contact with 1 μl of solution of HTLA antiserum and incubated at room temperature. Then 5 μl of Hanks' solution was added, and after 10 min at room temperature, the supernatant was aspirated and 2 μl of rabbit serum (controlled for absence of cytotoxicity) was added for 20 min at 37°C. Reaction was stopped by incubation at 4°C for 5 min, cells were then stained with trypan blue dye, washed twice, and scored for viability.

(d) Viability was estimated by trypan blue dye exclusion.

(e) Monoclonal antibodies were employed to identify lymphocyte subsets, using OKT4 for helper T lymphocytes and OKT8 for suppressor cytotoxic T lymphocytes (1–3) all of which were carried out in the same way as the HTLA test.

Cytochemistry

Slides were prepared by cytocentrifugation of rosettes followed by specific cytochemical tests for acid phosphatase (37) and β-glucuronidase (38). The intensity of the reaction was a semi-quantitative measure of these substances. Each cell was scored from 0 to 4. This score was multiplied by the number of cells with the same score. One hundred cells were evaluated for each slide. Control reactions were performed for each enzyme deleting either the substrate or the color reagent.

Ultrastructure

Cell morphology was studied by an ultrastructural cytochemical technique described by Bernard *et al.* (39). Briefly, rosette-forming cells were collected and placed in a Beam chamber using a micromanipulator. Cells were then fixed in glutaraldehyde treated with osmium tetroxide and dehydrated in alcohol baths of progressively increasing strength. The cells were embedded in Spurr's medium (4) and sections prepared using a LKB III ultramicrotome. These sections were then placed on a copper grid and stained with uranyl acetate. Preparations were examined and photographed using a Hitachi HU 11E microscope.

Mitogenic Stimulation of Lymphocytes

We used a method previously described (36). Briefly, 100 μl of the lymphocyte suspension adjusted to 1×10^6 ml was placed in the wells of a microplate (Microtest

II, Falcon) and 50 μl of the appropriate mitogen were distributed to each sample. The microplates were covered by a Blenderm (3M Co.) and placed at 37°C in a humid atmosphere for 72 hr. Sixteen hours before termination of the culture, 50 μl of tritiated methylthymidine (CEA, Saclay, France; sp act of 20 Ci/mmol) containing 0.2 μCi was added to each well. The cultures were then filtered through fiber glass (Fug, France) with the aid of a multiple-automated sample harvester (Mash 1, Otto-Hiller), dried, and then counted in a liquid scintillation counter (SL 30 Intertechnique). Mean and standard errors were calculated.

Evaluation of Natural Killer Activity and Antibody-Dependent Cell-Mediated Cytotoxicity

Natural killer (NK) activity was measured by release of radioactivity from ^{51}Cr-labeled K562 target cells as previously described (41) using different effector/target ratios.

The ADCC assay using L1210 target cells coated with rabbit anti-L1210 serum was described by Caraux *et al.* (34).

Mixed Allogeneic Culture

Lymphocytes (2×10^5) in 100 μl of medium 199 (20% AB serum + antibiotics) were introduced into the wells of a flat-bottomed microplate (Linbro 3040) then stimulated with 2×10^5 irradiated (20 Gray) lymphocytes from a different donor. After a 5-day incubation at 37°C, cells were labeled with 0.2 μCi of tritiated methylthymidine (sp act 20 Ci/mmol) incubated for 16 hr at 37°C, recovered using a Mash 1 cell harvester, and counted.

Mixed Autologous Cultures

The same method was employed except that stimulating cells were autologous non-T cells. Non-T cells were obtained by depleting total mononuclear cells from ERFC. Briefly, 750 μl of medium 199 containing 16.5×10^6 lymphocytes/ml was mixed with an equal volume of SRBC-absorbed fetal calf serum and 1500 μl of medium containing 350×10^6 SRBC/μl in a hemolyse plastic tube. The suspensions were centrifuged for 5 min at 400*g* and incubated overnight at 4°C. Cell pellets were then gently resuspended and rosettes were separated by centrifugation (300*g*, 20 min 4°C) on a Ficoll–Metrizoate (D = 1.077 g/m3) cushion. Non-T cells from the ring were recovered and washed twice in medium 199.

RESULTS

1. Separation of Autorosette-Forming Cells (ARFC)

Peripheral blood lymphocytes were allowed to form rosettes over an 18-hr incubation period in the cold, then centrifuged over a cushion of Percoll. Two different cell populations were collected—the first, in the ring above the Percoll cushion, contained few autorosette-forming cells (3 to 10%). The second, in the pellet, contained a majority of ARFC (80 to 95%).

Results concerning three experiments are presented in Table 1. About 200×10^6 lymphocytes were used in each experiment. Percentages ARFC were 23% in initial total lymphocyte population, 81% in the ARFC-rich population, and 3% in the ARFC-poor population. Cell yield after centrifugation was 49% of the total in the light density fraction and 18% in the high density fraction. In order to test the selectivity of the losses in respect to ARFC formation, we calculated the ratio of ARFC in the total population recovered after centrifugation (ARFC-rich population + ARFC-poor population). Calculated percentage was 24%, almost identical to the initial ratio (23%), which suggests no selective loss.

When 50 to 80 × 10^6 PBL instead of 200 × 10^6 PBL were fractionated on Percoll using the technique described above, percentage ARFC in the high-density fraction increased (95 versus 81%). Very high losses were encountered when fewer cells were fractionated. Normally, cell yields were between 40 and 70% of the total PBL population (11 experiments).

When thymocytes instead of PBL were fractionated in the same way, a 80% ARFC-rich fraction and a 30% ARFC-poor fraction were obtained. Cell yield was 50%.

2. *Lymphocyte Marker Studies*

Viabilities of the ARFC-rich and ARFC-poor populations after fractionation by centrifugation on Percoll were 85 and 90%, respectively, and 93% in the initial population.

The total lymphocyte population contained 66% E-rosette-forming cells (ERFC); 71% of cells expressed the human T-lymphocyte antigen (HTLA); 23% formed ARFC; 48% of these cells expressed the Fc receptor for IgM, and 20% the Fc receptor for IgG.

The ARFC-rich population (81% of ARFC) contained mostly T cells since 81% of the cells formed E rosettes and 87% expressed the HTLA. This fraction contained few lymphocytes with Fc receptor for IgG (6%) and was enriched for cells which expressed the Fc receptor for IgM (58%). After rosette dispersion and lymphocyte recuperation by Percoll centrifugation, capacity to form new autorosettes was reduced (37%). In the ARFC-poor population only 47% of the cells were T lymphocytes when evaluated by E-rosetting test and 57% by HTLA test. One-third

TABLE 1

Percoll Separation of Autorosette-Forming Cells

	Number of lymphocytes × 10^6	Percentage[a]	Percentage ARFC[b]
1 Total initial lymphocytes	198 ± 45[c]	100	23 ± 5
2 ARFC-depleted population (ring)	98 ± 13	49	3 ± 2
3 ARFC-enriched population (pellet)	35 ± 12	18	81 ± 1
4 Recovery, 2 + 3	133	67	24[d]

Note. ARFC, autorosette-forming cells.

[a] Percentage lymphocytes in each fraction following Percoll separation.

[b] Percentage ARFC in each of the fractions before centrifugation on Percoll for 1, after centrifugation for 2 and 3.

[c] Value ± SD.

[d] Calculation represents the weighted percentages of 2 and 3.

TABLE 2

Lymphocyte Subset Markers

	Viability (%)	ER (%)	HTLA (%)	ARFC[a] (%)	Second formation ARFC[b] (%)	OxRBC IgG (%)	OxRBC IgM (%)
Total lymphocytes	93 ± 3[c]	66 ± 2	71 ± 3	23 ± 5	25 ± 20	20 ± 2	48 ± 7
ARFC-depleted population	85 ± 17	47 ± 5	57 ± 3	3 ± 2	24 ± 13	33 ± 2	35 ± 15
ARFC-enriched population	90 ± 9	81 ± 8	87 ± 6	81 ± 1	37 ± 8	6 ± 1	58 ± 10

Note. ER, E rosettes; HTLA, human T lymphocyte antigen; ARFC, autorosette-forming cells; OxRBC IgG, EA rosettes with ox red blood cells coated with IgG anti-ox antibody; OxRBC IgM, EA rosettes with ox red blood cells coated with IgM anti-ox antibody.

[a] ARFC percentage obtained before and after the Percoll separation.

[b] Cells were tested for the capability to reform autorosettes after dispersion of initial rosettes.

[c] Value ± SD.

expressed Fc-receptor for IgG and 35% for IgM. Three percent of cells formed autologous rosette and 24% showed capacity to form autorosette a second time (Table 2).

Functional markers used were the monoclonal OKT4 and OKT8 antibodies. The total lymphocyte population contained approximately 45% OKT4-positive cells and 18% OKT8-positive cells. The ARFC-enriched population contained 82% OKT4-positive cells and only 22% OKT8. The ARFC-depleted population contained 7% OKT4 and 19% OKT8 (Table 3).

3. *Cytochemical and Immunocytochemical Characterization of ARFC*

(a) Cytochemistry. Table 4 shows that ARFC were slightly less rich in acid phosphatase and β-glucuronidase than cells forming E rosettes.

(b) Ultrastructure. The ARFC presented the following morphological features: a well-developed golgi apparatus with a cytoplasm rich in endoplasmic reticulum but relatively poor in lysosomes; a very irregular plasmic membrane with pro-

TABLE 3

Characterization of Lymphocyte Subsets Using Monoclonal Antibodies[a]

	OKT 4 (%)	OKT 8 (%)
Total lymphocytes	45 ± 7	18 ± 8
ARFC-depleted population	7 ± 2	19 ± 14
ARFC-enriched population	82 ± 12	22 ± 10

[a] Percentage lymphocytes identified by monoclonal antibodies OKT 4 (helper cells) and OKT 8 (suppressor and cytotoxic cells) and expressed ± SD.

TABLE 4

Cytochemistry of Acid Phosphatase and β-Glucuronidase of Lymphocytes Forming E-Rosettes and Autorosettes

	ERFC	ARFC
Acid phosphatase	158 ± 11[a]	135 ± 5
β-Glucuronidase	172 ± 11	137 ± 8

[a] Mean ± SD of reaction intensity multiplied by percentage of cells.

nounced villi—some of them observed around the lymphocytes were probably sectioned (Fig. 1).

4. *Functional Study of ARFC-Enriched and -Depleted Populations*

(a) Mitogen response. The cells of the total lymphocyte population responded to all three mitogens (PHA, PWM, and Con A used). The ARFC-rich cells showed a strong response to PHA (twice that observed for the combined population). These same cells responded in similar fashion to PWM but only demonstrated one-third the Con A response. The ARFC-poor population presented a threefold increase in PHA response, a five- to sixfold increase in PWM response and an eight- to ninefold increase to Con A (Table 5).

(b) Antibody-dependent cell-mediated cytotoxicity and NK activity. ADCC of

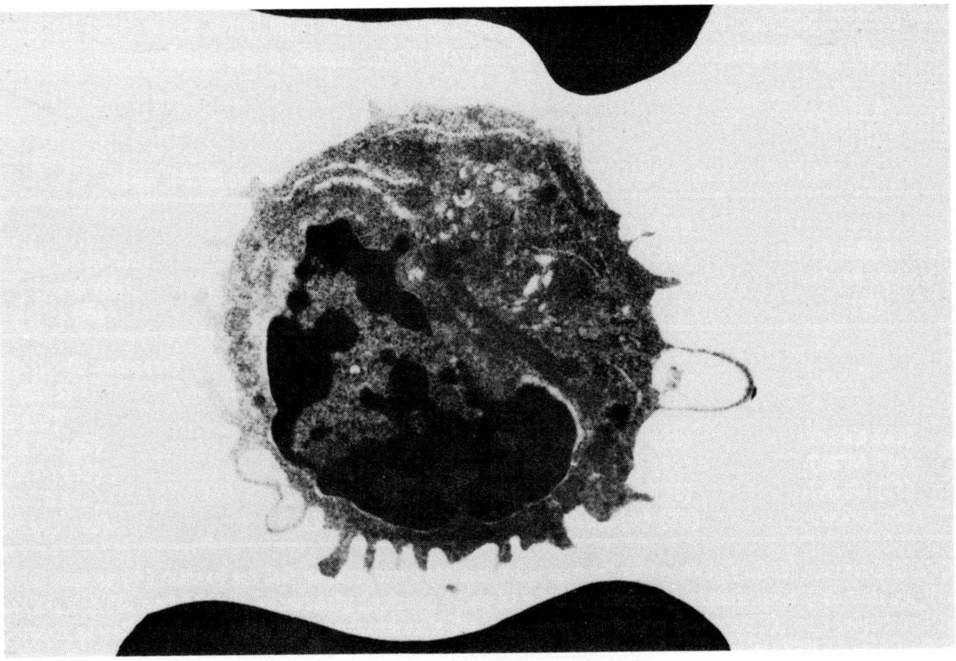

FIG. 1. Microphotography of an autologous rosette-forming cell: the print shows a well-developed Golgi, a cytoplasm rich in endoplasmic reticulum but poor in lysosomes, and pronounced villi on the membrane. ×12,500.

TABLE 5

Mitogen Response of Lymphocyte Subsets[a]

[³H]Thymidine uptake (cpm × 10³)	Spontaneous uptake	PHA (4 μg/ml)	PWM (4 μg/ml)	Con A (4 μg/ml)
Total lymphocytes	0.40 ± 0.1	45.1 ± 3.9	11.4 ± 1.2	11.4 ± 1.8
ARFC-depleted population	0.15 ± 0.1	118.1 ± 2.6	60.9 ± 3.8	93.0 ± 9.6
ARFC-enriched population	4.7 ± 1	88.1 ± 5.7	10.4 ± 0.4	4.2 ± 1

[a] Each lymphocyte subset was stimulated by mitogen for 48 hr followed by thymidine uptake over an 18-hr period; cpm are given with their corresponding SD.

the enriched population was low compared to the ADCC of the total lymphocyte pool or the ARFC-depleted population which presented an even higher response. NK activity presented approximately the same pattern. The ARFC enriched population responded weakly compared to the total or ARFC-depleted pool (Fig. 2).

(c) Mixed lymphocyte cultures. We compared results from mixed allogenic and autologous cultures of the total PBL, T-cell population and the two populations obtained after centrifugation on Percoll (Fig. 3). In the allogenic system the purified T-cell population presented a better response compared to the total cell pool. The ARFC-depleted population responded in approximately the same manner as the ERFC population. The ARFC-rich population response was approximately twice that of the ARFC poor cells (Fig. 3). However, autologous mixed culture results (Fig. 4) showed that the ARFC population presented a response fourfold stronger than that of the ARFC-poor population and the ERFC cells demonstrated activity intermediate to that of the ARFC-depleted population and enriched population which significantly exceeded all other populations.

DISCUSSION

The results presented are based on an ARFC purification technique using a new application of Percoll. These ARFC are T lymphocytes as previously shown (5)

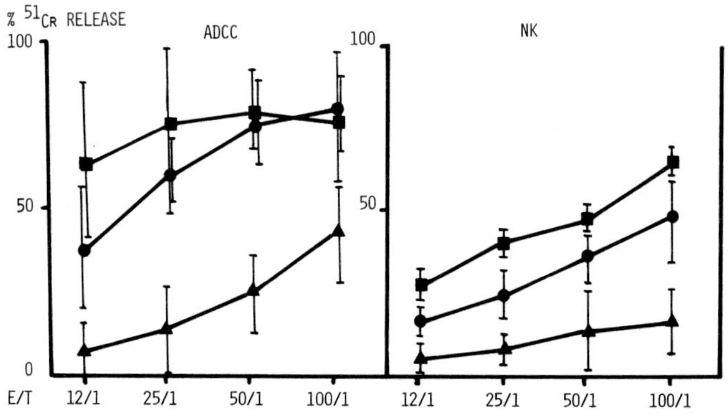

FIG. 2. Natural killer activity (NK) and antibody cell-mediated cytotoxicity (ADCC) of lymphocyte subsets. Percentage ^{51}Cr release from labeled target cell was plotted as a function of effector/vertical target cell ratio (E/T) for different effector populations Vertical bars indicate standard deviation. (●), Total mononuclear cell population:(■), ARFC-depleted population: (▲), ARFC-enriched population. For the NK test, target cells were K 562. For the ADCC test, target cells were L 1210 cells coated with heat-inactivated rabbit anti-L 1210 serum.

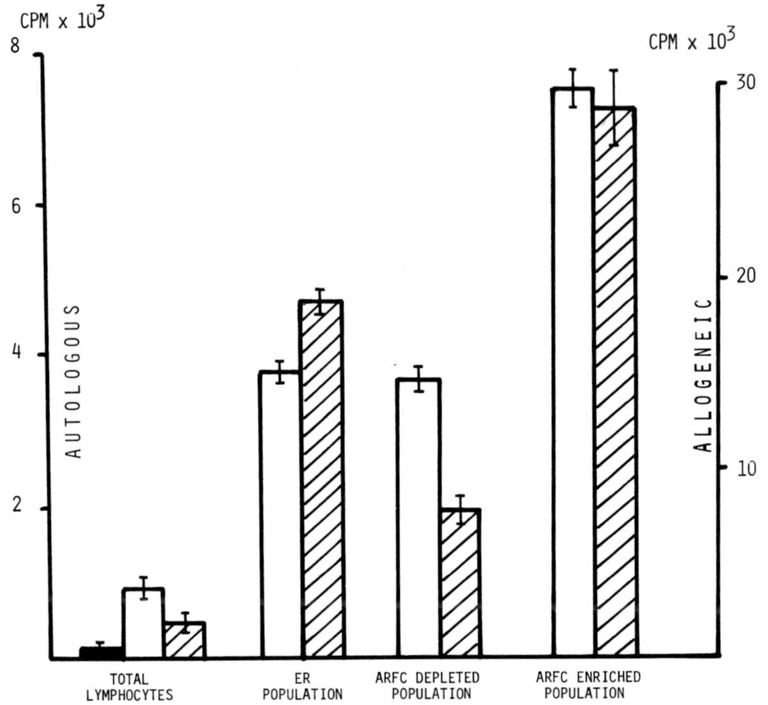

FIG. 3. [^{3}H]Thymidine uptake in allogeneic and autologous mixed lymphocyte culture. The indicated subsets were stimulated by irradiated allogeneic PBL (clear bars) or by autologous irradiated non-T cells (hatched bars) or for control by autologous irradiated PBL (dark bars). [^{3}H]Thymidine uptake into DNA was measured over a 18-hr period following 5 days incubation. Values are given with their standard deviation.

and are identified by OKT4 monoclonal antibodies, suggesting they are mostly helper cells. They possess few receptors for IgG but an increased number of IgM Fc receptors, respond well to PHA and PWM but poorly to Con A, demonstrate weak ADCC and NK activity, and respond strongly in mixed allogenic and specifically autologous lymphocyte cultures. These cells are well characterized cytochemically and always present Golgi apparatus and an endoplasmic reticulum but few lysosomes in correlation with low levels of lysosomial enzymes acid phosphatase and β-glucuronidase. Some morphological features suggest a weak or early activation. The ARFC population was found to be remarkably homogeneous, in contrast to ERFC, which may or not possess a Golgi apparatus, endoplasmic reticulum, or lysosomes (14, 33).

Several authors have reported techniques for characterizing ARFC (4, 5). The normal values reported vary widely depending on the technique. We employed here an entirely autologous sytem (5) in which lymphocytes, red cells, and serum are obtained from the donor. In our hands, the results obtained have been reproducible. The questions which can be asked are: do these cells fulfill a precise role, thereby corresponding to a specific functional subpopulation and is this erythrocyte–lymphocyte binding related to a self-recognition event as suggested by Dausset and Contu (26)? We have previously shown that ARFC levels can be altered in solid tumor patients, particularly in anticipation of patient relapse (6).

Very few authors (4, 20) have described an ARFC purification technique, probably due to the instability of the autologous rosette and to the heterogeneity of rosettes—variable number of red cells per rosette and different densities noted for both T cells (15–17) and red cells (18, 19). Moreover, these studies did not until recently (21) include cell recoveries and probably they were dealing with a completely different subpopulation.

Various separation solutions (Ficoll, Hypaque, glucose) proved unsatisfactory. We reproduced the Ficoll–Hypaque centrifugation techniques reported by Palacios *et al.* (20). This approach resulted in only 45% ARFC in the enriched fraction. This may explain the reason these authors employ a second centrifugation. Percoll is a widely used substance which is reportedly inert for lymphocytes (12, 22–25) although weakly absorbed by mastocytes (23). The technique described here yields a very rich ARFC fraction of 90% ARFC with cell yields between 40 and 70%. This was considered acceptable if attributed to a 40% loss due to rosetting and 20% due to cell washes, which was comparable to that noted by others (12). The Percoll density employed was chosen by empirical studies for each donor. The technique can be used for any donor and can be applied to different lymphocyte sources in addition to peripheral blood. However, the pellet contains lymphocytes which did not form autorosettes. The same fact has been reported for ERFC (9, 10). Several possibilities were envisaged to account for this observation: disruption of autorosettes, "trapping" of cells (10), or changes of the lymphocyte density (11). The fact that no autorosettes with one or two red blood cells were observed in the ARFC-rich population argues against the first possibility. We cannot exclude possibility of "trapped" cells but we favor the change of lymphocyte density. Indeed, less than 2% of cells are found in the pellet when fresh PBL are centrifuged on a Percoll cushion. But this percentage reaches 20% when PBL are 24 hr old. Moreover, their viability is also decreased (50–70 versus 85%) and falls to 14% 1 day after. This suggests that non-ARFC in the pellet may represent nonviable cells with a modified density (4, 12, 13).

The availability of an ARFC purification method would also facilitate the development of monoclonal antibodies against this subpopulation which in turn could be used to elucidate the role of these cells in the immune response. This is currently under investigation in our laboratory. In the present work, we confirmed, as have others (4), our previous results (5), indicating that ARFC cells are a T-cell subpopulation (forming E rosettes, HTLA positive, showing a T-cell biochemistry) and are not suppressor cell since they neither express IgG-Fc receptor nor are they OKT8 positive. Functionally, these cells exhibit weak ADCC and NK activity and respond poorly to Con A. However, Con A has been shown to induce supressor cell formation *in vitro*, which expresses IgG-Fc receptor (30). In addition, Strelkauskas *et al.* (28) showed that JRA-negative cells (i.e., cells not recognized by autoantibody which is capable of combining with suppressor cells) are stimulated by PHA, but not by Con A and ARFC have been shown to be JRA negative (personal communication). Nevertheless, part of the ARFC fraction express IgM-Fc receptors (57%) suggesting that this population may compose part of the T helper pool. If this possibility is pursued using monoclonal OKT4 antibody one notes that the majority of ARFC binds this marker. This serves to underscore the finding of Reinherz *et al.* (29) showing no strict superposition of cell populations with IgM-Fc receptor and those designated as helpers as judged by OKT4 monoclonal antibodies.

These findings suggest that ARFC are OKT4 positive and therefore helper cells but not all helper cells demonstrate IgM-Fc receptors. Only one of every two ARFC possesses this receptor. These OKT4-positive cells are primarily allogeneic mixed lymphocyte culture responders, a finding which supports the observations described by Reinherz and Schlossman (30) who also noted a preferential response in mixed autologous cultures. The present results therefore demonstrate a superposition of results from allogeneic and autologous mixed culture responses for the ARFC purified fraction. This contradicts the reports by some workers of a dissociation whereby the ARFC-enriched population responded only within an autologous context but not in allogeneic mixed lymphocyte cultures (17, 20, 31). Gupta and Damle (32) report findings similar to the present one where cells responding in one test were also capable of responding in the other.

It should also be noted that mixed culture response of the ARFC subset was significantly higher in the allogeneic setting than the autologous for the ARFC-deficient fraction. Reinherz and Schlossman (27) have shown that OKT4-positive cells respond as well as in allogeneic mixed cultures as the OKT4-negative fraction. It therefore appears that ARFC are a subpopulation of OKT4-positive cells (2, 27, 29) and the present study resulted in better separation techniques.

This preliminary analysis required the development of an ARFC purification technique, which, up to now, has been unsatisfactory according to the literature. The present finding encourage the possibility of obtaining a monoclonal antibody and a study of ARFC markers and functions. These first results permit a classification as OKT4-positive T cells, i.e. helper cells, even though they do not all exhibit IgM-Fc receptors as previously reported in the literature (24). Indeed, these ARFC are OKT8 negative, respond poorly to Con A, but strongly to PHA and PWM when compared to the complete lymphocyte population. This suggests that these helper cells may induce B cells to synthesize intracytoplasmic immunoglobulins, a possibility presently under investigation. The absence of IgGFc receptors is suggested also by the low ADCC and NK activity. These cells appear to respond to both allogeneic and autologous cells in culture. The observation that ARFC which are modified in the tumor patient can be influenced by substances such as thymic factors (42) leads one to believe that these cells are a functional subset of T lymphocytes whose role in immune balance has yet to be defined. Studies along these lines should be encouraged and could progress considerably faster as extremely precise monoclonal antibody markers become available.

REFERENCES

1. Reinherz, E. L., Kung, P. C., Goldstein, G., and Schlossman, S. F., *J. Immunol.* **123,** 1312, 1979.
2. Reinherz, E. L., Kung, P. C., Goldstein, G., and Schlossman, S. F., *Proc. Natl. Acad. Sci. USA* **76,** 4061, 1979.
3. Reinherz, E. L., Kung, P. C., Goldstein, G., Raphael, H., Levey, R. H., and Schlossman, S. F., *Proc. Natl. Acad. Sci. USA* **77,** 1588, 1980.
4. Gallinger, L. A., Pross, H. F., and Baines, M. G. *Int. J. Cancer.* **26,** 139, 1980.
5. Caraux, J., Thierry, C., Esteve, C., Flores, G., Lodise, R., and Serrou, B., *Cell. Immunol.* **45,** 36, 1979.
6. Caraux, J., Thierry, C., and Serrou, B. *J. Nat. Cancer Inst.* **63,** 593, 1979.
7. Opeltz, G., Kinchi, M., Tagasugi, M., and Terasaki, P. I., *J. Exp. Med.* **142,** 1327, 1975.
8. Kuntz, M. M., Innes, J. B., and Weksler, M. E., *J. Exp. Med.* **143,** 1042, 1976.
9. Pertoft, H., Johnssonn, A., Warmegard, B., and Seljelid, R., *J. Immunol. Methods* **33,** 221, 1980.

10. Madsen, M., Johnsen, H. E., Wendelboe, P., Hansen, and Christiansen, S. E., *J. Immunol. Methods* **33,** 323, 1980.
11. Splinter, T. A. W. Beuseker, M., and Van Beek, A., *Exp. Cell Res.* **111,** 245, 1978.
12. Gmelig-Meyling, F., and Waldmann, T. A., *J. Immunol. Methods* **33,** 1, 1980.
13. Davidson, P., *J. Immunol. Methods* **7,** 295, 1975.
14. Desplaces, A., Dufer, J., Choppin, J., Benoist, H., and Saracino, R. T., *Nouv. Rev. Fr. Hématol.* **20,** 423, 1978.
15. Gutierrez, C. Rosa R., Bernabe, Vega J., and Kreisler, M., *J. Immunol. Methods* **29,** 57, 1979.
16. Bom, W., and Wekerle, H. *Immunobiology* **156,** 243, 1979.
17. Peeters, H., *In* "Separation of Cells and Subcellular Elements," (D. Hutchins and C. M. Steel, Eds.). Pergamon Press, Oxford/New York, 1979.
18. Spooner, R. J., Percy, R. A., Rumley, A. G., *Clin. Biochem.* **12,** 289, 1979.
19. Rennie, C., Thompson, S., Parker, A., *et. al., Clin. Chim. Acta* **98,** 119, 1979.
20. Palacios, R., Llorente, L., Alarcon-Segovia, D., Ruiz-Arguelles, A., and Diaz-Jouanen, E., *J. Clin. Invest.* **65,** 1527, 1980.
21. Palacios R., Alarcon-Segovia, D., Llorente L., Ruiz-Arguelles, A., and Diaz-Jouanen, E., *Immunology* **42,** 127, 1981.
22. Saksela, E., Timonen, T., Ranki, A., *et al., Immunol. Rev.* **44,** 71, 1979.
23. Enerback, E., and Svensson, I., *J. Immunol. Methods* **39,** 135, 1980.
24. Kurnick, J. T., Ostberg, L., Stegagno, M., Kimura, A. K., Orn, A., and Sjoberg, O., *Scand. J. Immunol.* **10,** 563, 1969.
25. Segal, A. W., Fortunato, A., and Herd, T., *J. Immunol. Methods* **32,** 209, 1980.
26. Dausset, J., and Contu, L., *Human Immuno.* **1,** 5, 1980.
27. Reinherz, E. L., and Schlossman, S. F., *N. Eng. J. Med.* **14,** 370, 1980.
28. Strelkaukas, A. J., Schauf, V., Wilson, B. S., Chess, L., and Schlossman, S. F., *J. Immunol.* **120,** 1278, 1978.
29. Reinherz, E. L., Moretta, L., Roper, M., Brear, J. M., Mingari, M. C., Cooper, M. D., and Schlossman, S. F., *J. Exp. Med.* **151,** 969, 1980.
30. Reinherz, E. L., and Schlossman, S. F., *J. Immunol.* **122,** 1335, 1979.
31. Ilfeld, D. N., Krakauer, R. S., and Blaese, M. R., *J. Immunol.* **119,** 428, 1977.
32. Gupta, S., and Damle, N., *Human Lymphocyte Differentiation*, in press, 1981.
33. Nabarra, B., and Charreire, J., *Scand. J. Immunol.* **9,** 15, 1979.
34. Caraux, J., Thierry, C., and Serrou, B., *Eur. J. Immunol.* **8,** 806, 1978.
35. Touraine, J. L., and Touraine, F., *Clin. Exp. Immunol.* **16,** 503, 1974.
36. Thierry, C., and Serrou, B., *In* "La Stimulation Blastique des Lymphocytes par les Mitogènes." Séminaire INSERM 6–7 Novembre 1974 (B. Serrou, Ed.). Inserm Publ., Paris.
37. Kalland, T., *J. Immunol. Methods* **17,** 279, 1977.
38. Lorbacher, P., Yam, L. T., and Mitus, W. J., *J. Histochem. Cytochem.* **15,** 680, 1967.
39. Bernard, J., Jeannesson, P., Zagury, D., Fridman, W. H., Ternynck, T., and Avrameas, S., *Ann. Immunol. (Paris)* **1260,** 565, 1975.
40. Spurr, J., *J. Ultrastruct. Res.* **26,** 31, 1969.
41. Denis, M., Callewaert, D. M., Kaplan, J., David, F., Johnson, R. A., and Peterson, W. D., Jr., *J. Cell Biol.* **42,** 103, 1979.
42. Caraux, J., Goldstein, A., Esteve, C., and Serrou, B., *Biomedicine* **31,** 89, 1979.

CELLULAR IMMUNOLOGY **64,** 324–336 (1981)

Histamine Modulates *in Vitro* IgG Production by Pokeweed Mitogen-Stimulated Human Mononuclear Cells[1]

MARCONDES LIMA[2] AND ROSS E. ROCKLIN

Division of Allergy and Immunology, Department of Medicine, Tufts University School of Medicine, New England Medical Center Hospital, Boston, Massachusetts 02111

Received April 17, 1981; accepted August 19, 1981

The modulatory role of histamine was investigated in an *in vitro* model involving immunoglobulin production by human blood mononuclear cells. The addition of histamine *in vitro* had little effect on the spontaneous production of IgG (measured by double-antibody radioimmunoassay). However, the addition of histamine (10^{-4}–$10^{-9}M$) to mononuclear cells stimulated with an optimun concentration of pokeweed mitogen (PWM) significantly suppressed IgG production in a dose-dependent fashion from 10^{-4} to 10^{-6} M (range 55–37% suppressor, respectively). The kinetics of histamine-induced suppression was investigated by adding histamine to mononuclear cells at the time of stimulation by PWM or up to 4 days later. Histamine only significantly suppressed PWM induced IgG synthesis if added up to 72 hr after the addition of PWM.

In order to characterize the histamine-responsive suppressor cell in this system we employed a coculture technique and compared our findings to those of Con A-induced suppression. Mononuclear cells were either separated into E-rosette-positive (T-enriched) or E-rosette-negative (T-depleted) populations, irradiated, or treated with monoclonal antibodies plus complement; cells were then stimulated with histamine or Con A for 24 hr and cocultured with autologous E-rosette-negative populations that were then stimulated with PWM, and IgG production was measured. The histamine- and Con A-responsive suppressor cell was found within the T-enriched population, was radiation sensitive to 2000 and 3000 rad, respectively, and was identified by OKT8 antisera but not OKT4 antisera. Of particular interest, the addition of histamine to irradiated T cells and PWM-stimulated T-depleted populations did not result in suppression of IgG production, implying that B cells were not being inhibited directly by histamine.

The nature of the histamine receptor present on the suppressor cell was investigated. The H_1 antagonist, diphenhydramine (10^{-4} M), inhibited IgG production as effectively as histamine. The combinations of H_1 antagonist and histamine did not result in an additive effect. Cimetidine (10^{-4} M), had no effect by itself on *in vitro* IgG production and the combination of cimetidine plus histamine in equimolar concentrations did not abrogate histamine-induced inhibition of IgG production. Studies employing the H_1 and H_2 agonists (10^{-4} to 10^{-6} M), 2-pyridylethylamine and Dimaprit, respectively, resulted in an equivalent suppression of IgG production. The H_1 and H_2 agonist-responsive suppressor cell was found in the T-enriched population and was sensitive to 3000 rad. These experiments imply that the histamine-reactive cell suppressing IgG synthesis may be activated through either its H_1 or H_2 receptor.

[1] Supported by USPHS Grant AI-16312.
[2] Supported by a grant from CAPES of Brazil.

0008-8749/81/160324-13$02.00/0

INTRODUCTION

The ability of histamine to influence the inflammatory process by modulating a variety of polymorphonuclear leukocyte and lymphocyte functions is well established and its role in regulating certain immune responses, in particular, has become an area of intense investigation. Thus far, the effects of histamine on lymphocyte function have been studied in greater detail in systems that employ T-cell assays. For example, it has been shown that histamine directly inhibits cell-mediated cytolysis by sensitized T cells through a mechanism which appears to involve cyclic AMP (1, 2). On the other hand, such T-cell functions as lymphocyte proliferation to mitogens and antigens and lymphokine production are also inhibited by histamine but possibly through another mechanism (3–7). The latter involves the activation of a histamine receptor bearing suppressor T cell by histamine which then results in the production of a soluble suppressor factor (histamine-induced suppressor factor or HSF[3]). HSF may inhibit the proliferating T cells directly, or more likely, work through an indirect mechanism involving monocytes and prostaglandin synthesis (8). The histamine-induced suppressor cell, as well as the suppression of T-cell-mediated cytolysis, involves stimulation of the histamine type 2 receptor (2–7).

Regulation of B-cell responses by histamine has been less well studied. Shearer and co-workers have previously shown that plaque-forming cell numbers may be increased if murine splenic lymphocytes are first chromatographed on columns containing insolubilized histamine (9). Furthermore, histamine may suppress plaque formation *in vitro* when spleen cells are cultured in the presence of the drug (10, 11). Employing a model of tolerance involving SJL/J mouse spleen cells made unresponsive to the multichain synthetic peptide (T,G)-Pro-L, Moses *et al.* showed that prior incubation of these spleen cells with histamine abrogated the suppression (12). Little information has been accumulated thus far concerning immunoregulation of humoral responses by histamine in man. In the present study, we have investigated the effects of histamine on human IgG production *in vitro* using a double-antibody radioimmunoassay. Our results demonstrate that histamine, in a dose-dependent fashion, suppresses human IgG production generated by pokeweed mitogen (PWM) *in vitro*. Furthermore, the histamine-responsive suppressor cell is contained within the E-rosette-positive population, bears on its surface a differentiation antigen identified by $OKT8^+$ antisera, is radiation sensitive (2000 rad), and is probably activated through either its histamine type 1 or type 2 receptor.

MATERIALS AND METHODS

Reagents. Pokeweed mitogen (Grand Island Biological Co., Grand Island, N.Y.) was dissolved in 5 ml of sterile distilled water and then diluted 1:10 with medium TC-199. Concanavalin A (Miles Yeda, Elkhart, Ind.) was dissolved in TC-199 at a concentration of 1 mg/ml. H_1 (diphenhydramine) and H_2 (cimetidine) antagonists and H_1 (2-pyridylethylamine) and H_2 (dimaprit) agonists were kindly supplied by Smith, Kline, and French, Philadelphia. Monoclonal antibodies (OKT4 and OKT8) against T-cell subsets were kindly supplied by Ortho Pharmaceutical Corporation, Raritan, New Jersey.

[3] Abbreviations used: Con A, concanavalin A; HSF, histamine-induced suppressor factor; PWM, pokeweed mitogen.

Production of supernatants containing IgG by human lymphocytes. Heparinized venous blood was drawn from normal donors after obtaining informed consent. The mononuclear cells were isolated on Ficoll–Hypaque density gradients (13). Cells at the interface were harvested and washed four times with medium TC-199 containing 5% heat-inactivated fetal calf serum. The cell concentration was adjusted to 2×10^6 mononuclear cells/ml in medium TC-199 containing 10% fetal calf serum, 25 m*M* Hepes buffer, 100 units/ml penicillin, and 100 μg/ml streptomycin. Two-milliliter cultures were incubated in 12 × 75-mm plastic tubes (Falcon Plastics) at 37°C in a 5% CO_2–95% humidified air atmosphere for 7 days. At the end of the incubation period, the cell-free supernatants were harvested following centrifugation and were assayed for their content of IgG antibody.

Assay of IgG. IgG was measured by the use of a double-antibody radioimmunoassay (14). Purified IgG was obtained from Cappel Laboratories (Cochranville, Pa) and further purified by gel filtration on a Sephadex G-150 column. Goat anti-human IgG (Cappel Laboratories) was absorbed with free κ and λ light chains (Cappel Laboratories) to render them specific for γ chains. Specificities of the antiserums were confirmed by Ouchterlony double-diffusion tests. IgG was iodinated by the Chloramine-T method (15). More than 98% of the I^{125} bound to IgG was precipitable with trichloroacetic acid. IgG content in the supernatants of the cultured mononuclear cells was measured by use of a double-antibody radioimmunoassay performed in microtiter wells (Microtiter Plates, Gibco) with rabbit anti-human IgG (first antibody), I^{125}-labeled IgG, and a goat anti-rabbit IgG as the second antibody. The techniques used to define the specificity and accuracy of the tests were identical to those described for double-antibody radioimmunoassays of other immunoglobulins (16).

Preparation of T-enriched and non-T-cell populations by E-rosette formation. Human blood mononuclear cells that were isolated by Ficoll–Hypaque density gradient centrifugation were incubated with neuraminidase (*Vibrio cholera*)-treated sheep red blood cells (0.5 ml SRBC:0.5 ml mononuclear cells at 10×10^{-6} cells/ml) as previously described (17). Following a 2-hr incubation at 4°C, the rosettes were gently resuspended and overlaid on a Ficoll–Hypaque gradient (4 ml cell suspension:3 ml Ficoll–Hypaque). The cells were centrifuged (400*g*) and the E-rosette-negative or non-T cells (interface layer) and the E-rosette-positive or T-enriched cells (pellet) were recovered. The sheep red blood cells were lysed by treatment with ammonium chloride. Following the latter procedure, the T-enriched cells were washed three times in medium TC-199 and resuspended in their appropriate cell concentration. In some experiments, T-enriched cells or E-rosette-negative cells were initially cultured with histamine and/or either H_1 or H_2 antagonists or agonists alone for 24 hr. These cells were then washed twice and cocultured with autologous E-rosette-negative cells. The latter cell mixture was then stimulated with pokeweed mitogen and IgG content of the supernatant was measured. The purity of the E-rosette-positive and -negative populations was determined. The E-rosette-positive population contained 92–98% E-rosette-"positive" cells and the E-rosette-negative population was contaminated by 2–8% E-rosette-"positive" cells.

Characterization of suppressor cells by radiation and monoclonal antisera. T-Enriched cells were irradiated (cesium source) with a dose of 1000–3000 rad. These cells and nonirradiated E-rosette-positive cells were then analyzed for their ability to function as suppressor cells following a 24-hr preincubation with histamine or

Con A. The latter cells were cocultured with autologous E-rosette-negative indicator cells. E-Rosette-positive cells were also treated with OKT4 and OKT8 antisera (5 μl antibody/10^{-6} cells) for 30 min at 37°C, washed three times, and then treated with guinea pig serum as a source of complement (1:3 by volume) for 1 hr at 37°C (18). The cells were washed three times and the viability of the remaining cells was determined by trypan blue exclusion. In general, treatment of T-enriched cells with OKT4 antisera plus complement lysed approximately 40–60% of the cells while treatment with OKT8 plus complement caused the lysis of 10–20% of the cells. E-Rosette-positive cells treated with the above monoclonal antibodies were then evaluated for their ability to mediate histamine- or Con A-induced suppression of IgG production when cocultured with autologous E-rosette-negative cells stimulated with PWM.

RESULTS

Effect on IgG Production of the Direct Addition of Histamine to Mononuclear Cells

Our preliminary studies culturing human mononuclear cells for the detection of IgG *in vitro* indicated that the optimum concentration of PWM was 100 μl/ml cells and that 7 days of culture was also optimum for IgG production. Mononuclear cells from normal subjects were cultured with and without PWM and varying concentrations of histamine (10^{-4} and 10^{-9} *M*). The IgG content of the supernatants was assayed using double-antibody radioimmunoassay. The results of nine experiments are summarized in Fig. 1. PWM induced almost a mean fivefold increase in IgG production compared to the amount that was spontaneously released. In the presence of histamine, PWM-induced IgG content of supernatants was significantly reduced ($P < 0.01$) between 10^{-4} and 10^{-6} *M*. This corresponded to a 55% (10^{-4} *M*) to 37% (10^{-6} *M*) reduction in IgG production. Histamine had no significant effect upon the spontaneous production of IgG in the cultures. These ex-

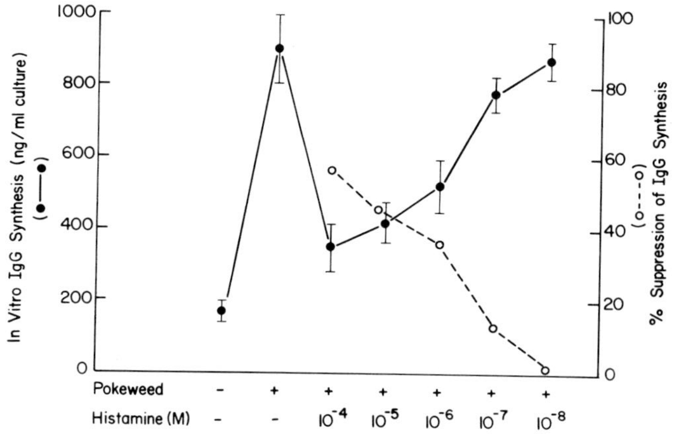

FIG. 1. Suppression of *in vitro* IgG production by the direct addition of histamine to mononuclear cells from normal subjects stimulated by PWM. Data expressed as ng/ml IgG (● —— ●) and percentage suppression of IgG (○ – – – ○). Mean (±SD) of nine experiments.

periments do not distinguish whether histamine is inhibiting synthesis and/or secretion of IgG.

The kinetics of inhibition by histamine was then examined. Mononuclear cells were cultured in the presence of pokeweed mitogen and then histamine was added at the same time or at 24-hr intervals thereafter for up to 96 hr. The results of four experiments are summarized in Fig. 2. Histamine added at time zero caused significant suppression of IgG at all three concentrations used (10^{-4} to 10^{-6} *M*). When histamine was added at 24, 48, 72, and 96 hr after the addition of PWM, there was a time-dependent reduction in the amount of suppression observed. At 10^{-4} *M*, histamine added at 72 hr after the addition of PWM still induced 20% suppression of IgG synthesis. However, with lower concentrations of histamine, suppression was not significant if the addition of the drug was delayed until 24 hr after the addition of PWM.

Characterization of the Histamine-Responsive Cell Using a Coculture Technique

In order to partially characterize the histamine-responsive suppressor cell, a coculture technique was employed in which the "suppressor" cell was preactivated with histamine (or Con A for purposes of comparison) for 24 hr, washed, and then combined with autologous E-rosette-negative cells. The putative suppressor cell populations were either divided into E-rosette-positive and E-rosette-negative cells, treated with monoclonal antibodies, or irradiated prior to their incubation with histamine or Con A.

T-Enriched or non-T cells were initially cultured in the presence of histamine (10^{-4} or 10^{-5} *M*) or Con A (5 μg/ml) for 24 hr. These cells were then washed and cocultured in a 1:1 ratio with autologous E-rosette-negative cells that were stimulated with PWM, and IgG production was measured. The results of three experiments are summarized in Fig. 3. Both the unfractionated and E-rosette-positive suppressor cell populations accounted for virtually all of the suppression due to

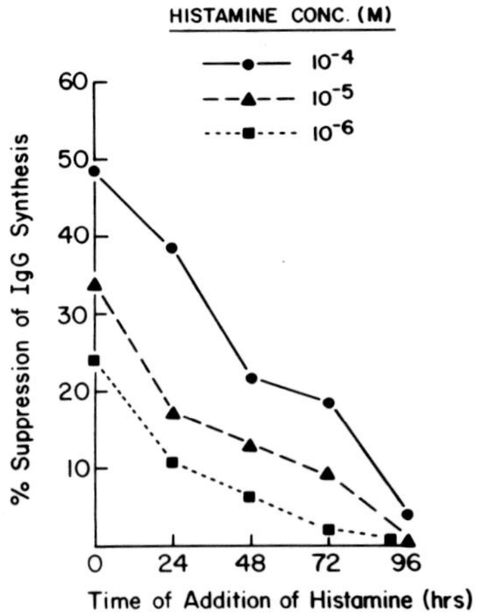

FIG. 2. Kinetic study of histamine-induced suppression of IgG production. Human mononuclear cells were stimulated with PWM and histamine was added at the same time or at 24-hr intervals thereafter. Histamine (10^{-4} *M*) suppressed IgG up to 72 hr after the addition of PWM.

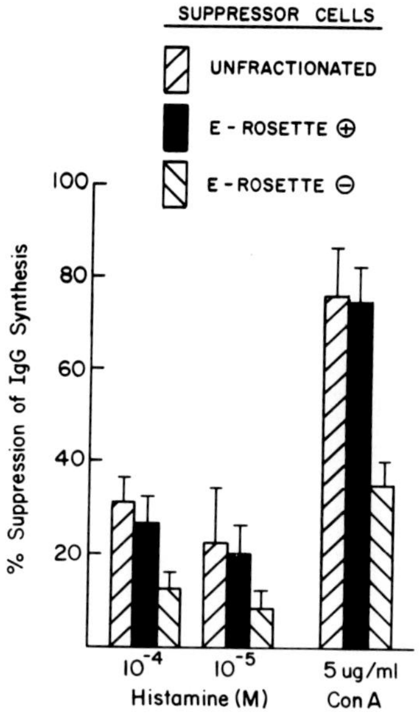

FIG. 3. Histamine- and Con A-induced suppression of IgG by T-enriched and non-T cells using a coculture technique. Unfractionated, E-rosette-positive, or E-rosette-negative populations were preincubated with histamine or Con A, washed, and cocultured with autologous E-rosette-negative populations that were then stimulated by PWM and IgG measured.

histamine. Moreover, Con A-induced suppressor activity was also present to the same degree in the unfractionated and E-rosette-positive populations. However, the E-rosette-negative populations preactivated with Con A also induced significant suppression of IgG production, albeit less than that caused by the other populations.

The E-rosette-positive population was then treated with monoclonal antibodies directed against T-cell subsets (18). A source of complement was provided (guinea pig serum) in an attempt to delete the relevant populations of helper ($OKT4^+$) and suppressor ($OKT8^+$) cells. The remaining treated cells were adjusted to the concentration of the untreated cells and incubated with histamine (10^{-4} M) or Con A (5 μg/ml) for 24 hr, washed, and recombined with autologous E-rosette-negative cells that were then stimulated with PWM. The results of four experiments are summarized in Fig. 4. Histamine-and Con A-pretreated cells both significantly suppressed PWM-induced IgG production when their incubation took place in the presence of buffer or guinea pig serum alone (37 and 75% suppression for histamine and Con A, respectively). Cells treated with OKT4 plus complement were much less able to provide help and therefore IgG synthesis per se was markedly reduced. However, both histamine and Con A were able to proportionally inhibit the amount of IgG made under these conditions compared to cells treated with buffer or guinea pig serum (i.e., the degree of suppression for histamine and Con A was similar to that described above for control cells). In contrast, cells treated with OKT8 plus complement were much less able to suppress IgG following incubation with histamine or Con A. Under these conditions both spontaneous and PWM-induced IgG production were markedly increased. OKT8-treated cells stimulated by histamine or Con A only inhibited IgG production by 9 and 20%, respectively. These

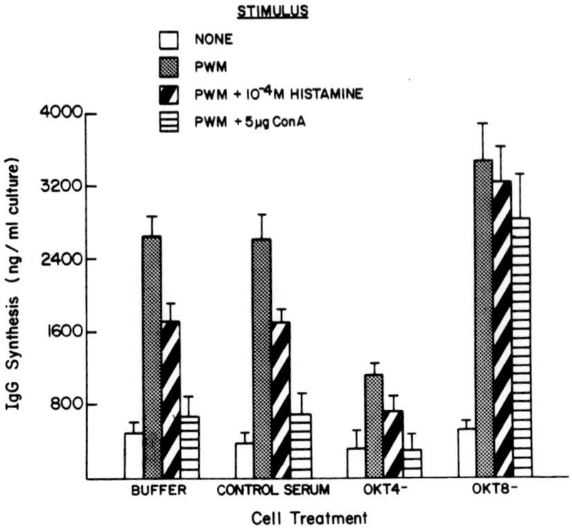

FIG. 4. Treatment of histamine- and Con A-induced suppressor cells with monoclonal antibodies directed against T-cell subsets. T-Enriched cells were incubated in buffer alone, buffer + complement, OKT4 antiserum + complement, or OKT8 antiserum + complement, washed, and then incubated with or without histamine or Con A for 24 hr. After incubation, the remaining cells ($OKT4^-$ or $OKT8^-$) were cocultured with autologous E-rosette-negative cells that were then stimulated by PWM.

levels of suppression are statistically less ($P < 0.05$) than that obtained for the control-treated cells. These results indicate that both the histamine- and Con A-responsive suppressor cells are contained within the $OKT8^+$ population. Futhermore, deletion of the $OKT4^+$ population does not appear to alter suppressor activity to any significant degree.

E-Rosette-positive cells were exposed to varying concentrations of irradiation and then stimulated with histamine (10^{-4} or 10^{-5} *M*) or Con A (5 μg/ml) for 24 hr. The latter cells were washed and recombined with autologous E-rosette-negative cells that were then stimulated with PWM. As shown in Fig. 5 (mean of four experiments), histamine-induced suppressor activity was not significantly reduced until 2000 rad was applied to the cells. In contrast, Con A-induced suppression was not significantly reduced until 3000 rad was applied. These results suggest that histamine- and Con A-induced suppressor cells have differing sensitivities to irradiation.

In related experiments, in order to determine whether B cells were responding to histamine directly, E-rosette-positive cells were radiated with 3000 rad and recombined with E-rosette-negative cells. The latter were stimulated with PWM and 10^{-4} *M* histamine was added. The results of these experiments (Table 1) documented that histamine had no direct effect on IgG production, suggesting that under these experimental conditions B cells did not demonstrate functional histamine receptors.

Nature of the Histamine Receptor

In our previous experiments, histamine-induced suppression of lymphocyte proliferation or lymphokine production was mediated through the H_2 receptor (3–7).

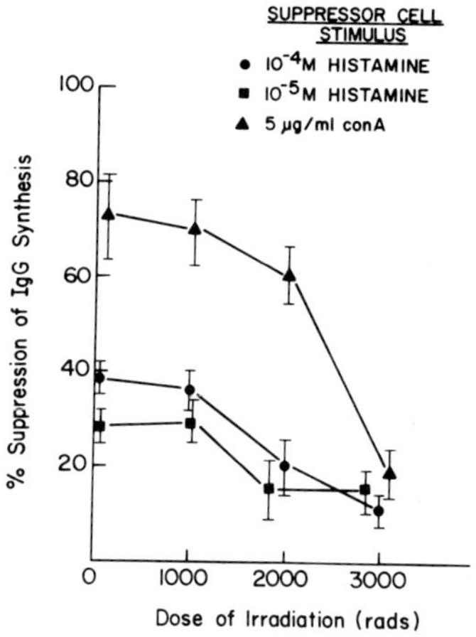

FIG. 5. Effect of irradiation on histamine and Con A-induced suppressor cells. T-Enriched cells were exposed to 1000–3000 rad and then incubated with histamine or Con A for 24 hr. and washed and coculture was carried out. Histamine-induced suppressor activity was abolished by 2000 rad, while inhibition of Con A-induced suppression activity required 3000 rad.

In the present studies we sought to describe the nature of the receptor in the histamine-induced suppression of IgG production. For these experiments, E-rosette-positive cells were cultured for 24 hr in the presence of histamine alone, or histamine plus an H_1 antagonist (diphenhydramine) or an H_2 antagonist (cimetidine), washed, and then cocultured with autologous E-rosette-negative cells. Histamine-induced suppression of IgG production was then measured. T-Enriched cells were also cultured with diphenhydramine or cimetidine alone for their effects on IgG production. Three experiments are shown in Table 2. Histamine (10^{-4} *M*) alone caused a 23–32% suppression of IgG production. Diphenhydramine alone induced suppressor activity at levels that were even greater than that for histamine. Cimetidine alone had no effect on IgG synthesis. The combination of histamine plus diphenhydramine

TABLE 1

Lack of Direct Effect of Histamine on IgG Production

Histamine (*M*)	*In vitro* IgG production (ng/ml)			
	Experiment I		Experiment II	
	Control	3000 rad	Control	3000 rad
None	4500[a]	6000	1800	2700
10^{-4}	3400 (24)[b]	7000 (−16)	1000 (44)	2500 (7)
10^{-5}	3500 (22)	7500 (−25)	1250 (30)	2800 (−4)
10^{-6}	3900 (13)	5900 (2)	1300 (27)	2800 (−4)

Note. E-Rosette-positive cells were either irradiated (3000 rad) or not irradiated, and cocultured with E-rosette-negative cells that were stimulated by PWM and to which histamine was added.

[a] ng/ml IgG in culture supernatant.

[b] Percentage suppression of IgG production in parentheses.

TABLE 2

Effect of H_1 and H_2 Antagonists on Histamine-Induced Suppression of IgG Production[a]

Drug (10^{-4} *M*)	Experiment I	Experiment II	Experiment III
None	2600	1600	2000
Histamine	2000 (23)[b]	1100 (32)	1500 (25)
Diphenhydramine	1700 (40)	900 (44)	1000 (50)
Cimetidine	2500 (4)	1500 (6)	1700 (15)
Histamine and diphenhydramine	1500 (12)[c]	900 (0)[c]	1300 (−30)[c]
Histamine and cimetidine	1900 (24)[d]	1000 (33)[d]	1400 (18)[d]

[a] E-Rosette Positive cells were incubated with histamine, diphenhydramine, cimetidine, or histamine plus the H_1 or H_2 antagonists for 24 hr. washed, and cocultured with autologous B cells that were then stimulated with PWM for 7 days.

[b] Numbers in parentheses indicate percentage suppression of IgG synthesis induced by histamine, diphenhydramine, or cimetidine compared to PWM alone.

[c] Percentage suppression of IgG synthesis calculated using PWM + diphenhydramine as the "control" value.

[d] Percentage suppression of IgG synthesis calculated using PWM + cimetidine as the "control" value.

did not result in an additive effect. However, histamine plus cimetidine did not alter the level of histamine-induced suppression.

E-Rosette-positive cells were also incubated with an H_1 agonist (2-pyridylethylamine) or an H_2 agonist (dimaprit) for 24 hr, washed, and cocultured with autologous E-rosette-negative cells that were stimulated with PWM. As shown in Fig. 6, in which four experiments are summarized, both the H_1 and H_2 agonists significantly suppressed IgG production in a dose-dependent manner. Inhibition occurred in the unfractionated population and to the same degree in the rosette-positive population. E-Rosette-negative cells preincubated with either drug failed to inhibit IgG production. Furthermore, E-rosette-positive cells initially exposed to 3000 rad and then to the drugs also failed to inhibit IgG production. The results with the agonists and antagonists suggest that both the H_1 and H_2 receptor may be involved in activation of histamine-induced suppressor cells involved with IgG regulation. These results are in contrast with histamine-induced suppression of T-cell functions.

DISCUSSION

The purpose of the present study was to evaluate the immunoregulatory effects of soluble histamine on *in vitro* IgG production by human mononuclear cells. We found that histamine, when added to cultures of mononuclear cells stimulated with PWM, inhibited IgG production in a dose-dependent manner. IgG was measured in culture supernatants using a double-antibody radioimmunoassay. Histamine had no significant effect on the spontaneous amounts of IgG produced in culture over a 7-day period. Maximum suppression (55%) was achieved with 10^{-4} *M* histamine. That the inhibitory effect of histamine on IgG production was not merely a toxic one was suggested by kinetic experiments. Histamine added at varying times after the addition of pokeweed mitogen was only effective in significantly suppressing

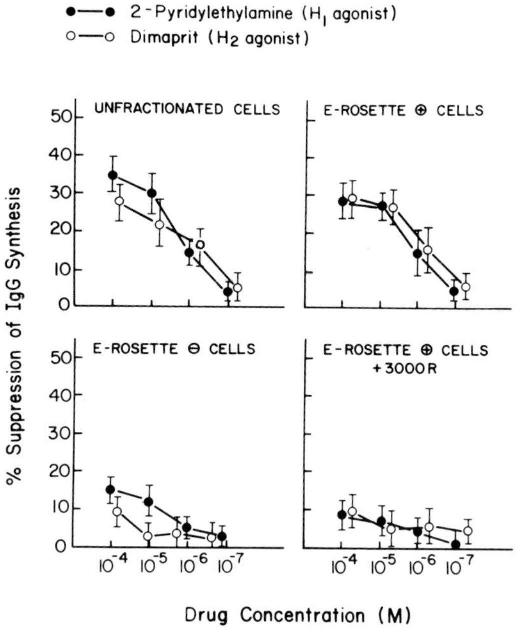

FIG. 6. Ability of H_1 and H_2 agonists to cause suppression of IgG. T-enriched cells or T-depleted cells were preincubated with 10^{-4} to 10^{-7} *M* 2-pyridylethylamine or Dimaprit for 24 hr., washed, and cocultured with PWM-stimulated autologous T-depleted cells. In some experiments, T-enriched cells were exposed to 3000 rad prior to incubation with agonists.

IgG production for the first 48–72 hr. After 72 hr, the addition of histamine did not alter IgG levels.

A variety of studies in animals has suggested that there are complex interactions between T cells, B cells, and macrophages for the regulation of antibody production (19–21). A number of *in vitro* studies have been carried out in humans as well in an attempt to analyze immunoregulation of humoral responses. Polyclonal stimulants such as PWM (22–28) and staphylococcal protein A (28, 29) as well as specific stimuli such as TNP-polyacrylamide (30) and tetanus (31) have been employed to measure *in vitro* plaque-forming cells and immunoglobulin content of culture supernatants. Immunoregulation in these studies has been analyzed using either preincubation or aging of cultures (22), concanavalin A (24, 26–28, 30, 32–34), sodium periodate (35), or tetanus antigen (31) to activate suppressor cells. Suppressor cell activity has been identified in a number of mononuclear subpopulations and these cells have been partially characterized.

For example, the suppressor cell induced by aging or preculturing mononuclear cells *in vitro* has been identified as being a T cell that requires DNA synthesis before being able to express its activity and is hydrocortisone sensitive (22). Spontaneously generated suppressor cells capable of inhibiting pokeweed-induced plaque-forming cells have been identified as being contained within both the E-rosette-positive and E-rosette-negative populations (25). The latter suppressor cells have in common, however, the presence of an Fc receptor, are radiosensitive (2000 rad), and also require DNA synthesis before expressing their activity (22–25). In addition, a radioresistant adherent cell, presumably a macrophage, has also been described as mediating this type of immunosuppression (25). Furthermore, Con A-induced suppressor cells capable of inhibiting PWM-induced plaque-forming cells or IgG synthesis *in vitro* have been characterized as being contained within the E-rosette-positive population, are lymphoblastoid, and are sensitive to mitomycin C treatment (24, 26, 28, 30, 32). A Con A-responsive cell is also present within the E-rosette-negative population having Fc receptors for IgG but lacks receptors for complement (24). Con A-reactive suppressor cells were also identified in a T-cell-depleted population which was nonadherent and complement receptor negative (24). Recently, differentiation antigens detected by monoclonal antibodies have characterized suppressor cells as being contained within the $OKT8^+$ subpopulation (36, 37).

The cell bearing a histamine receptor having immunoregulatory effects on *in vitro* IgG synthesis has also been partially characterized in the present study and can be contrasted with the above-reported suppressor cells. Using a coculture technique, we found that histamine-responsive suppressor cells were present within the E-rosette-positive population (Fig. 3). This finding was also true for the Con A-activated suppressor cell response detected in parallel. In addition, the histamine-responsive cell was radiosensitive in that its activity was abolished by exposing E-rosette-positive cells to 2000 rad. The Con A-induced suppressor cell activity was not abolished until 3000 rad had been administered. We cannot determine at this point whether the latter results imply that the histamine- and Con A-responsive suppressor cells are within different subpopulations or, if in the same cell, whether the histamine stimulus is a much weaker signal or affects fewer cells than the Con A stimulus. Of particular interest, irradiated T-enriched cells cocultured with E-rosette-negative cells to which histamine was added failed to inhibit IgG production, implying that B cells were not directly responsive to histamine. Moreover, the histamine-responsive cell bears the $OKT8^+$ antigen on its surface, since treatment of T-enriched cells with OKT8 antisera and complement abolished histamine-induced suppressor activity (Fig. 4). Consistent with previous findings, the Con A-induced suppressor cell was also found to possess the OKT8 antigen (36, 37). In contrast, treatment of E-rosette-positive cells with OKT4 antisera + complement, while significantly reducing pokeweed-driven IgG production per se, did not alter the amount of suppression of IgG compared to control-treated cells. The significance of the latter finding is discussed below.

The mechanism by which suppressor cells regulate antibody production has been analyzed to some extent in a number of studies. It appears that suppressor cells must be present early in culture with B cells that have been stimulated by whatever means. In our experiments, the histamine-induced suppression diminished significantly with time after the addition of pokeweed. One study suggested that Con A-activated suppressor cells act directly on T cells that are involved with cooperation (34). On the other hand, several studies have indicated that suppressor cell activity is expressed only after interactions between precursor suppressor cells and a suppressor cell inducer (26, 37, 38). Furthermore, Haynes and Fauci (33) have suggested that Con A-activated suppressor cells generate an autoreactive population of cells that mediate an autologous lymphocyte reaction against non-T cells that lead to suppression of B-cell function.

In the mouse system, Rich and Pierce have demonstrated that Con A-activated

T cells secrete a soluble substance (soluble immune response suppressor or SIRS) that does not act directly on T cells but rather affects macrophages in such a way that the latter cells then inhibit B-cell function (39). In man, recent studies suggest that human splenic lymphocytes activated with Con A produce a soluble factor that leads to suppression of plaque-forming cells and immunoglobulin secretion (27). While not directly addressed in the present study, we have recently obtained evidence which suggests that the histamine-induced suppressor factor (HSF) may have some direct effects on T-helper-cell function (40). In the latter experiments, human HSF has suppressed T-helper-cell function generated during a mixed lymphocyte reaction. This has lead to decreased production of IgG, IgM, and IgA plaque-forming cells. Of particular interest in the latter studies, HSF has also decreased the appearance of Ia/DR antigen expression on T cells generated during a mixed lymphocyte reaction. We have also observed that Con A- and histamine-induced suppression of lymphocyte proliferation can be blocked by the presence of indomethacin (41). The latter finding would suggest a SIRS-like effect of histamine- or Con A-induced suppressor cells such that the soluble factor thus generated alters monocyte function in a way that results in increased synthesis of prostaglandins. The latter then may be involved in the final pathway leading to suppression. It is not clear at the present time whether the same mechanism applies to histamine- or Con A-induced suppression of immunoglobulin production.

The nature of the histamine receptor present on regulatory cells activated by histamine was evaluated in the present study but the results are somewhat open to interpretation. Using H_1 and H_2 antagonists, the data could suggest that the H_1 receptor is primarily involved. For example, we noted that the H_1 antagonist (diphenhydramine) on its own was capable of suppressing IgG production to a greater extent than even histamine. When histamine and diphenhydramine were combined in equimolar concentrations, instead of obtaining increased activity due to each drug, we essentially obtained an amount of suppression equal to either drug alone (Table 1). The H_2 antagonist (cimetidine) had no effect per se on pokeweed mitogen-induced IgG production and, when combined with histamine in equimolar concentrations, essentially did not change the suppression achieved by histamine. Employing H_1 (2-pyridylethylamine) and H_2 agonists (Dimaprit) with the same coculture technique, we noted that both agonists were capable of suppressing IgG production in a dose-dependent manner (Fig. 6). In addition, the H_1 and H_2 agonist-responsive cell was present within the E-rosette-positive population and was sensitive to 3000 rad. While the interpretation of these data is still open to question, it certainly implies that the H_1 receptor, as well as the H_2 receptor, is involved in the regulation of IgG production. The finding that both H_1 and H_2 receptors may be involved in modulating IgG production is of interest and contrasts with previous studies involving the effects of histamine on T-cell function (2–7). In the latter studies the H_2 receptor was found to be predominantly involved.

In summary, we have shown that the addition of soluble histamine *in vitro* to cultures of human mononuclear cells stimulated with pokeweed mitogen suppresses IgG production by these cells. The histamine-responsive cell is most likely a T cell that is sensitive to irradiation and may be activated through both H_1 and H_2 receptors to express its regulatory function. We are currently investigating the mechanism of histamine-induced suppression and the nature of the histamine-responsive regulatory cell.

REFERENCES

1. Henney, C. S., Bourne, H. R., and Lichtenstein, L. M., *J. Immunol.* **108,** 1526, 1972.
2. Plaut, M., Lichtenstein, L. M., Gillespie, E., and Henney, C. S., *J. Immunol.* **111,** 389, 1973.
3. Rocklin, R. E., *J. Clin. Invest.* **57,** 1051, 1976.
4. Rocklin, R. E., *J. Immunol.* **118,** 1734, 1977.
5. Rocklin, R. E., Greineder, D., Littman, B. H., and Melmon, K. L., *Cell. Immunol.* **37,** 162, 1978.
6. Rocklin, R. E., Greineder, D., and Melmon, K. L., *Cell. Immunol.* **44,** 404, 1979.
7. Rocklin, R. E., Breard, J., Gupta, S., Good, R. A., and Melmon, K. L., *Cell. Immunol.* **51,** 226, 1980.
8. Beer, D. J., Rosenwasser, L. J., Dinarello, C. A., and Rocklin, R. E., *J. Allergy Clin. Immunol.* (Abstract), in press.
9. Shearer, G. M., Weinstein, Y., and Melmon, K. L., *J. Immunol.* **113,** 597, 1974.
10. Melmon, K. L., Weinstein, Y., Shearer, G. M., Bourne, H. R., and Bauminger, S., *J. Clin. Invest.* **53,** 22, 1974.
11. Weinstein, Y., and Melmon, K. L., *Immunol. Commun.* (Abstract) **5,** 401, 1976.
12. Moses, E., Weinstein, Y., Bourne, H. R., Melmon, K. L., and Shearer, G. M., *Cell. Immunol.* **11,** 57, 1974.
13. Boyum, A., *Scand. J. Clin. Lab. Invest.* **21 (Suppl. 97),** 77, 1968.
14. Miller, K. B., and Schwartz, R. S., *N. Engl. J. Med.* **301,** 803, 1979.
15. Greenwood, F. C., Hunter, W. M., Glover, J. C., *J. Biochem.* **89,** 114, 1963.
16. Waldmann, T. A., Polmar, S. H., Balestra, S. T., Jost, M. C., Bruce, R. M., and Terry, W. D., *J. Immunol.* **109,** 304, 1972.
17. Littman, B. H., David, J. R., and Rocklin, R. E., *Cell. Immunol.* **24,** 241, 1976.
18. Kung, P. C., Goldstein, G., Rheinherz, E. L., and Schlossman, S. F., *Science* **106,** 347, 1979.
19. Gershon, R. K., *Contemp. Top. Immunobiol.* **3,** 1, 1974.
20. Moller, G., *Transplant Rev.* **26,** 1975.
21. Cantor, H., and Boyse, E. A., *J. Exp. Med.* **141,** 1376, 1975.
22. Lipsky, P. E., Ginsburg, W. W., Finkelman, F. D., and Ziff, M., *J. Immunol.* **120,** 902, 1978.
23. Fauci, A. S., Pratt, K. R., and Whalen, G., *Immunology* **35,** 715, 1978.
24. Haynes, B. F., and Fauci, A. S., *J. Immunol.* **121,** 559, 1978.
25. Haynes, B. F., and Fauci, A. S., *J. Immunol.* **123,** 1289, 1979.
26. Lydyard, P. M., and Hayward, A. R., *Clin. Exp. Immunol.* **39,** 496, 1979.
27. Ilfeld, D. N., and Krakauer, R. S., *Clin. Immunol. Immunopathol.* **17,** 196, 1980.
28. Kurnick, J. T., Pandolfi, F., and Wigzell, H. *Cell. Immunol.* **54,** 373, 1980.
29. Lipsky, P. E., *J. Immunol.* **125,** 155, 1980.
30. Galanaud, P., Crevon, M. C., Delfraissy, J. F., Segond, P., Wallon, C., and Dormont, J., *Clin. Exp. Immunol.* **38,** 106, 1979.
31. Stevens, R. H., and Saxon, A., *Cell. Immunol.* **55,** 85, 1980.
32. Haynes, B. F., and Fauci, A. S., *J. Immunol.* **118,** 2281, 1977.
33. Haynes, B. F., and Fauci, A. S., *J. Immunol.* **120,** 700, 1978.
34. Nespoli, L., Moller, G., Waterfield, D., and Ekstedt, R., *J. Exp. Med.* **145,** 631, 1977.
35. Guenounou, M., and Agneray, J., *Immunology* **37,** 53, 1979.
36. Reinherz, E. L., Kung, P. C., Goldstein, G., and Schlossman, S. F., *J. Immunol.* **124,** 1301, 1980.
37. Thomas, Y., Sosman, J., Irigoyen, O., Friedman, S. M., Kung, P. C., Goldstein, G., and Chess, L., *J. Immunol.* **125,** 2402, 1980.
38. Broder, S., Poplack, D., Whang-Peng, J., Durm, M., Goldman, C., Muul, L., and Waldmann, T. A., *N. Engl. J. Med.* **298,** 66, 1978.
39. Tadakuma, T., and Pierce, C. W., *J. Immunol.* **117,** 967, 1976.
40. Garovoy, M. R., Reddish, M. S., and Rocklin, R. E., *Clin. Res.* (Abstract), in press.
41. Beer, D. J., Dinarello, C. A., Rosenwasser, L. J., and Rocklin, R. E., *In* "Immunopathology: VIIIth International Symposium" (P. A. Miescher and F. Dixon, Eds.), Schwabe Basel, in press.

CELLULAR IMMUNOLOGY **64**, 337–349 (1981)

Role of Interleukins 1 and 2 on Human Thymocyte Mitogen Activation[1]

MAURO PIANTELLI, LIBERO LAURIOLA, NICOLA MAGGIANO, FRANCO O. RANELLETTI,* AND PIERO MUSIANI

*Departments of Pathology and *Histology, Catholic University, Rome, Italy*

Received May 22, 1981; accepted July 27, 1981

Recent studies have dealt with the fundamental role of interleukins 1 and 2 (IL-1, IL-2) in promoting lectin-stimulated proliferation of peripheral T lymphocytes as well as thymocytes, both in experimental animal and in human systems. In this study we have investigated the role of IL-1 and IL-2 on the mitogen-stimulated proliferation of the total thymocyte population and of the various thymocyte subsets separable by the presence on their membrane of receptors for peanut lectin (PNA) and for the Fc portion of IgM (T_M). The present study has revealed that the mitogen responsiveness is confined to the PNA-negative T_M subset of more mature, medullary thymocytes. Only PNA-negative T_M cells are able to produce significant amounts of IL-2 under the influence of IL-1, a macrophage product. From our data it became evident that the low response to mitogen of unfractionated thymocyte suspensions can be ascribed both to deficiency of accessory cells, which produce IL-1, as well as to the high percentage of cells (PNA-positive and PNA-negative T non_M thymocytes) unresponsive to mitogen even after addition to the culture medium of optimal concentrations of IL-1 and IL-2. Moreover, PNA-negative T_M-depleted cells show the capacity to undergo mytotic cycle after prolonged culture in the presence of conditioned medium from PHA-stimulated peripheral mononuclear cells. A similar influence of differentiative type is exherted on the PNA positive T_M subset, a fraction of immature cortical thymocytes.

INTRODUCTION

Studies on T-lymphocyte activation in both experimental animals and human have demonstrated monocyte dependence for optimal initial mitogenesis (1). Such dependence has been reported for T lymphocytes stimulated with either mitogens or antigens (2–6). It has been postulated that monocytes exert their effect at least in part through the production of interleukin 1 (IL-1) (7). Moreover it has been recently demonstrated that macrophage-derived conditioned media augment both thymocyte and mature T-cell blastic responses to mitogens (8–12) and that IL-1 effectively replaces the requirement of adherent cells for T-lymphocyte mitogenesis through a facilitation of interleukin 2 (IL-2) release from a T-cell sub set (13–15).

Different lymphocyte subpopulations have been identified in the human thymus. Peanut agglutinin (PNA) binds to the majority of human thymocytes. These PNA-

[1] This work was supported by Grant 80.01537.96 from Consiglio Nazionale delle Ricerche, Progetto Finalizzato "Controllo della Crescita Neoplastica."

0008-8749/81/160337-13$02.00/0

positive (PNA^+) cells (mainly cortical thymocytes) respond very poorly to PHA and in mixed lymphocyte culture whereas the minor PNA-negative (PNA^-) subset (mainly composed by medullary thymocytes) responds to both stimuli (16). More recently we found that in both PNA^+ and PNA^- subsets there is a distinct subset bearing a receptor for the Fc portion of IgM (T_M cells) (17, 18).

The aim of this study was to verify if the widely accepted mechanism for peripheral T-cell activation is also working in human thymocyte blastogenesis. We particularly investigated the relationships between IL-1 and the production of IL-2 and the role of these subcellular factors in the blastic responses of the various thymocyte subpopulations as defined on the basis of their different expression of surface membrane receptors.

Data in this work indicate that within the human thymus only T_M cells from the PNA^- (medullary) compartment are able to produce significant amounts of IL-2, under the influence of IL-1 from macrophages, and to respond to mitogen. Moreover a minor fraction of PNA^+ thymocytes (T_M cells) shows the capacity to undergo mytotic cycle after prolonged culture in the presence of conditioned medium from PHA-stimulated peripheral mononuclear cells.

MATERIALS AND METHODS

Thymocyte preparation. Cell suspensions were prepared from fragments of human thymus obtained from children 4 months to 7 years old undergoing open heart surgery. This tissue, aseptically removed, was finely minced in Hanks' balanced salt solution (HBSS). Thymocytes were then dispersed by repeated pipetting and passage through a 200-mesh stainless-steel screen. The cells were washed three times in RPMI 1640 with 10% heat-inactivated fetal calf serum (FCS). After this procedure thymocytes were >95% viable as assessed by trypan blue dye exclusion test.

Cell affinity chromatography of PNA^+ thymocytes. Peanut agglutinin was purified from fresh unpeeled shelled peanuts using a sialic acidless fetuin–Sepharose column following the procedure described by Irlé (19). Purified PNA was used to raise rabbit anti-PNA antiserum. The IgG fraction of this antiserum was coupled to cyanogen bromide-activated Sepharose 6MB (Pharmacia Fine Chemicals, Uppsala, Sweden). Cell affinity chromatography was performed as reported by Irlé *et al.* (20). Briefly, cells (1.0×10^7 cells/ml) were incubated for 30 min at 4°C in HBSS with 20 μg/ml of purified PNA. After washing, cells were applied to an anti-PNA Sepharose column (10 ml of beads in a plastic syringe). After 20 min at 4°C, the column was washed with 60 ml of HBSS to remove unbound cells (PNA^- thymocytes). PNA-binding thymocytes were recovered by washing the column with phosphate-buffered saline containing 0.15 *M* galactose.

Detection of cells with receptors for IgG (T_G) and IgM (T_M) and separation of T_M cells. T_G and T_M were detected by rosetting thymocytes with ox erythrocytes coated with purified rabbit IgG or IgM antibody. Detailed descriptions of the procedures employed were recently reported by us (21, 22). Briefly, equal volumes of 2% ox red blood cells (OxRBC) and subagglutinating dilutions of rabbit IgM or IgG antibody against OxRBC were mixed and incubated at room temperature for 45 min. After four washings sensitized OxRBC were suspended to a final 1% concentration in medium 199 containing 15% selected FCS. Thymocytes (3.0

$\times 10^6$/ml), cultured overnight in 199–15% FCS, were mixed with equal volumes of sensitized OxRBC. After centrifugation (200*g*, 5 min) the pellets were incubated in an ice bath for 45 min. The cells were then very gently resuspended by hand-rotating the tube. Thymocytes rosetting with IgM-coated OxRBC were separated from the nonrosetting fraction on Ficoll–Hypaque density gradient (4°C, 800*g*, 20 min). The OxRBC were lysed using Tris buffer with 0.83% ammonium chloride.

Preparation of Interleukin 1 (IL-1) Containing Supernates. IL-1 was obtained following the procedure reported by Blyden and Handschumacher (23). Briefly, 20 ml of peripheral blood mononuclear cells (PBL) (3.0×10^6 cells/ml) were incubated at 37°C for 4 hr in RPMI 1640 containing 5% human AB serum in Falcon petri dishes (100 × 20 mm). At the end of incubation the supernatant fluid was discarded and the petri dishes containing the adherent cells were extensively washed and then incubated with 20 ml RPMI 1640 and 5% AB serum containing 20 μg/ml of LPS (Difco Laboratories, Detroit, Mich.). After 24 hr of incubation at 37°C in a CO_2 incubator, the culture fluid was harvested after centrifugation, extensively dialized against RPMI 1640, sterilized by Millipore filtration (Swinnex 0.45 μm) (Millipore Corporation, Bedford, Mass.). IL-1 activity was determined following the procedure described by Lachman *et al.* (24). IL-1 containing supernates demonstrated human thymocyte lectin-augmenting activity that diminished upon serial dilutions. Detectable activity was still found in most of these supernates even at 1:160 dilutions. In our culture conditions dilutions capable of sustaining maximal blastogenic responses ranged between 1:5 and 1:10. All IL-1 preparations were screened for IL-2 activity using the IL-2 quantitative microtiter assay described below and were found to be negative.

Preparation of conditioned medium (CM) containing IL-2. IL-2 containing supernates were prepared from Ficoll–Hypaque separated PBL of single donors (25). Briefly, PBL (1.0×10^6/ml) in RPMI 1640 with 3% FCS and 0.5 μg/ml PHA (Wellcome Laboratories, Beckenham, England) were incubated at 37°C for 48 hr. At the conclusion of the culture period, cells were removed by centrifugation (400*g* for 10 min). Conditioned media were also prepared from PHA (5 μg/ml)-stimulated thymocyte subsets at cell concentration ranging from 0.5 to 2.0×10^6 cells/ml under the same conditions reported above. In the experiments designed to investigate the influence of IL-1 on IL-2 production, IL-1 preparation was added to the thymocyte cultures at 1:10 final dilution.

Quantitative microtiter well assay for IL-2 activity. IL-2 activity was assayed according to the procedure described by Bonnard *et al.* (25, 26) with minor modifications. Briefly, sensitized cells from 7-day primary one-way mixed lymphocyte culture were counted, washed, and resuspended at 5.0×10^5 cells/ml in RPMI 1640 medium, containing 10% FCS and 10–25% of IL-2-containing CM. By Day 3 or 4 the cultured T cells (CTC) reached 10^6/ml and were fed by dilution with the same medium to 5.0×10^5/ml. Every 3 days thereafter, the cells were split in a similar manner. Serial 1:3 dilutions of various CM preparations were assayed for their ability to stimulate proliferation of the third passage, approximately 14-day-old, CTC (10^5) during 3 days of incubation in microtiter wells. Proliferative activity was measured by incorporation of tritiated thymidine ([^{3}H]TdR, sp act 5 Ci/mmol, Amersham, England) added during the last 4 hr of culture. As a control PHA (0.5 μg/ml) was also used in all experiments. CTC usually were only weakly stimulated by the mitogen. The proliferative responses observed represent a quantitative measure of IL-2 in a given supernate. By determining the dilutions of supernates needed to produce a similar stimulatory effect, it was possible to estimate graphically the relative IL-2 activity of various supernates. According to Bonnard *et al.* (25, 26) there was an excellent correlation between the results of the assay in microtiter plates and the ability of the various CM to promote actual T-cell growth.

Thymocyte response to mitogen. Cell response to PHA was determined as previously reported (27) with some modifications. Unfractionated thymocytes and cells from the various thymocyte subsets were suspended in RPMI 1640 medium, supplemented with 10% heat-inactivated FCS. Cultures were established in microtiter flat-bottomed plates (Microtest II; Falcon 3040) in triplicate and consisted of 0.2 ml of complete culture medium containing thymocytes at various cell concentrations (ranging from 1.0×10^5 to 6.0×10^5 cells/well). Phytohemagglutinin (1 μg) was added to each well. Cultures were incubated for various time intervals (see results) in a 5% CO_2 humidified environment; for the last 16 hr of the culture period, 0.5 μCi of [^{3}H]TdR was added to each culture well. The cultures were then harvested for scintillation spectrometry.

FITC-PNA binding assay. Thymocytes (0.1 ml, 3.0×10^6 cells) were incubated with FITC-PNA (0.1 ml, 350 μg/ml) for 20 min at room temperature.

RESULTS

Human Thymocyte Subpopulations

Virtually all lymphocytes (>98%) obtained from human thymus were T cells, as identified by the neuraminidase-treated erythrocyte rosette technique. B cells were practically absent, as assessed by enumerating surface membrane immunoglobulin-positive cells (<1%). In the unfractionated thymocyte suspensions 78.3 ± 5.3% (mean ± SD of 15 cases) of the cells were FITC-PNA$^+$.

By cell affinity chromatography using anti-PNA as ligand, about 60% of thymocytes were specifically eluted from the column in the presence of galactose while cells nonadherent to the column were about 15%. Cells specifically eluted from the column (thereafter indicated as PNA$^+$ cells) were virtually all (>98%) FITC-PNA$^+$, while the nonadherent thymocyte fraction (PNA$^-$ cells) contained about one-third of weakly FITC-PNA$^+$ cells (Table 1). In the 10 experiments in which thymocytes with receptors for IgM were isolated, T_M cells represented 25 ± 6.0% of the unfractionated cell suspensions and 24 ± 4.0% and 33 ± 3.0% of PNA$^+$

TABLE 1

Fractionation of Human Thymocytes into PNA$^+$ and PNA$^-$ Cells by Cell Affinity Chromatography[a]

Cell	Recovery (%)	Direct immune fluorescence (%) PNA$^+$	Direct immune fluorescence (%) PNA$^-$
Unfractionated thymocytes	100	80	20
Cells specifically eluted from the column	58	>98	<2
Cells nonadhering	14	28	72

[a] Representative experiment out of 15 performed.

TABLE 2

Cells with Fc-IgM Receptors (T_M) in Unfractionated, PNA^+ and PNA^- Thymocytes[a]

Cell	T_M (%)
Unfractionated thymocytes	25 ± 6
PNA^+ cells	24 ± 4
PNA^-	33 ± 3

[a] Percentage ± SD (10 experiments) relative to total cell population.

and PNA^- subsets respectively (Table 2). T_G cells were practically absent in unfractionated as well as PNA^+ and PNA^- fractions.

Response to PHA and IL-2 Production by Thymocyte Subpopulations

Results concerning the proliferative responses of the various thymocyte subsets are shown in Fig. 1. When thymocytes were cultured at a low cell concentration (0.5×10^6 cells/ml) very low blastic proliferation was observed. Nevertheless at this low cellular concentration the PNA^- medullary population and particularly T_M cells from the PNA^- subset exhibited the highest responses. For increasing cell concentrations up to 3.0×10^6/ml the level of response strongly increased. Furthermore there is no linear relationship between the [^{3}H]TdR incorporated and the

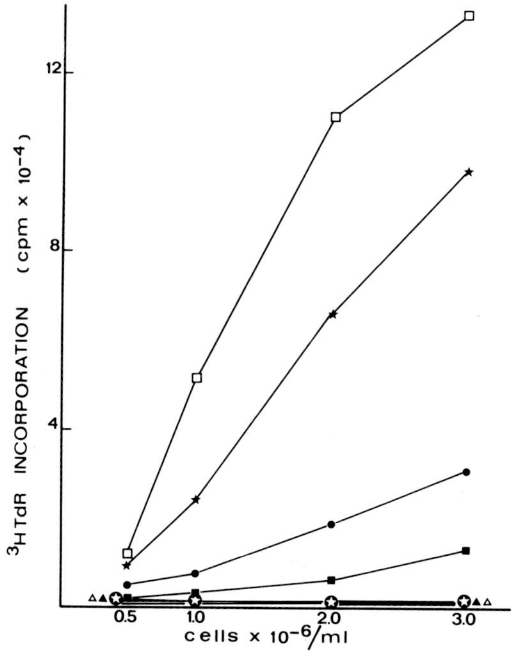

FIG. 1. Proliferative responses of unfractionated (●), PNA^- (★), PNA^- T_M (□), PNA^- T non_M (■), PNA^+ (✪), PNA^+ T_M (△), and PNA^+ T non_M (▲) thymocytes cultured for 84 hr at various cell to volume ratios in microtiter well. 1 μg of PHA was added to each well containing a final volume of 200 μl.

T-cell number in the sense that the nucleotide incorporated per cell increased for increasing cell number (Fig. 1). This cell concentration dependence of [^{3}H]TdR incorporation was present only in the PNA subset. It should be noted that the PNA^- response to PHA can be almost exclusively attributed to the minor T_M medullary component considering that PNA^-, T non_M did not show significant response at any of the cellular concentrations used. Moreover, as indicated in the same figure, both T_M and T non_M cells from PNA^+ compartment were unresponsive to mitogen. The observation that, at low cell number (0.5×10^6 cells/ml), the contact with mitogen alone was inadequate for stimulation even for the more mature thymocytes, led to the hypothesis that, as observed in laboratory animals (28), human thymocytes cultured at low cell-to-volume ratio did not show significant mitogenic responses because cell-produced factors essential for thymocyte activation were diluted out.

Because IL-2 is obligatory for, and mediates T-cell proliferation after, initial contact with lectin or antigen (29), we designed experiments to verify the capacity of the various thymocyte subsets to produce IL-2. Supernates obtained from PHA-stimulated thymocyte subsets (0.5 and 2.0×10^6 cells/ml) were assayed for their ability to stimulate proliferation of CTC from mixed lymphocyte culture. CTC proliferative responses to supernates from the various thymocyte subsets, by the quantitative microtiter well assay, are shown in Fig. 2. For comparison the activity of supernate generated from PHA-stimulated PBL (1.0×10^6 cells/ml) was also

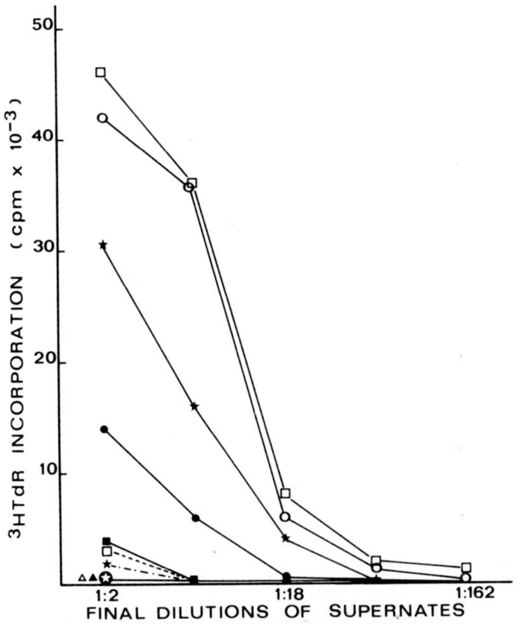

FIG. 2. CTC proliferative responses in the quantitative microtiter well assay for IL-2 activity to several supernates tested at various dilutions. Supernates were from: unfractionated (●), PNA^- (★), PNA^- T_M (□), PNA^- T non_M (■), PNA^+ (⭘), PNA^+ T_M (△), and PNA^+ T non_M (▲) thymocytes cultured at 2.0 $\times 10^6$ cells/ml (——). Values representing the effect of supernates from PBL (○) cultured at 1.0×10^6 cells/ml and from PNA^- T_M (□) and PNA^- (★) cultured at 0.5×10^6 cells/ml (- - -, -·-·-) are also indicated.

investigated. Dilutions of this PBL supernate were able to maintain T-cell growth in flasks. At a low cellular concentration (0.5×10^6 cells/ml) only supernates from $PNA^- T_M$ thymocytes contained barely detectable IL-2 activity. At cellular concentration of 2.0×10^6 cells/ml the supernates from PHA-stimulated $PNA^- T_M$ cells had levels of IL-2 activity comparable to those of PBL supernate produced at a cell concentration of 1.0×10^6 cells/ml (Fig. 2) and were also able to promote CTC growth in flasks. At this cell concentration (2.0×10^6 cells/ml) supernates from PNA^- and total thymocyte preparations showed a lesser but nonetheless evident ability to produce IL-2 while PNA^+ subset did not. As supernates from PNA^- T non_M cells did not contain significant IL-2 activity, it can be concluded that in the human thymus only $PNA^- T_M$ medullary cells are able to produce IL-2.

Effect of IL-1 and IL-2 on Thymocyte Blastogenesis

An effective replacement for the essential role of accessory cells in the initiation of mitogenic responses of T cells has been achieved by the addition of IL-1, a macrophage product. Moreover an obligatory role of IL-2, a T-cell product, in T-cell blastogenesis is widely accepted. Therefore in a series of experiments we evaluated the effects of IL-1 and IL-2 containing supernates on the mitogenic responses of the various thymocyte preparations in which accessory cells were very poorly represented (0.5% as estimated by nonspecific esterase staining). Addition of IL-1 or IL-2 strongly augmented the blastic responses of unfractionated thymocytes cultured at low cellular density (Fig. 3). A similar increase was observed in the PNA^- fraction while a more pronounced increment was found in the T_M subset from PNA^- compartment. The addition of the two interleukins did not promote nor augment the poor, if any, blastic responses of PNA^+ and of $PNA^- T_M$ depleted cells, at least in short-term culture (84 hr). It is noteworthy that the lectin re-

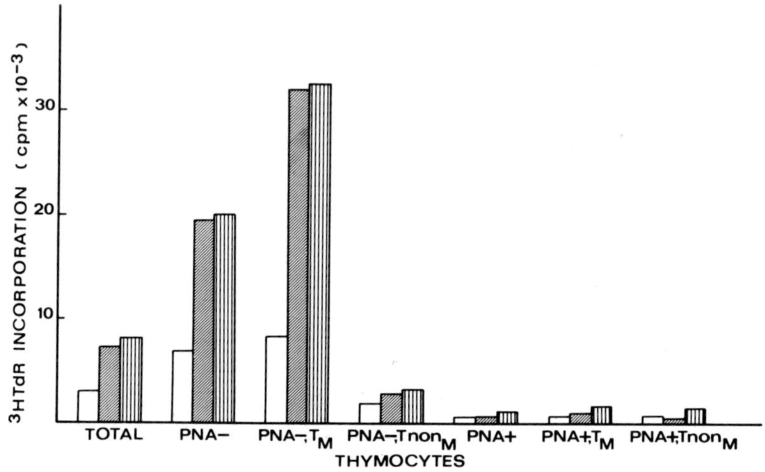

FIG. 3. Proliferative responses of the various thymocyte subsets cultured for 84 hr at 0.5×10^6 cells/ml in microtiter well (final volume 200 μl). (□) PHA (1 μg/well), (▥) PHA + IL-1 containing supernate (30 μl/well), and (▨) PHA + IL-2 containing supernate (20 μl/well). Preliminary data indicated that these conditioned media concentrations yielded optimum mitogenesis.

sponsiveness was amplified to a similar extent by IL-1 and IL-2. Furthermore, it should be noted that the IL-2-containing supernates, used in the present work, were always contaminated by IL-1; thus we were unable to assess the effect of IL-2 alone. However, the effect of IL-1-contaminated IL-2 supernates was not changed by the addition of saturating IL-1 concentrations (data not shown).

IL-1-Dependent Production of IL-2 by Thymocyte Subsets

Very recent studies (13, 14, 30) on the functional relationship of the interleukins in experimental animals have indicated that IL-1 can promote the production of IL-2 by T cells. In another series of experiments we have investigated the ability of various thymocyte subpopulations to produce IL-2 under the presence of saturating concentrations of IL-1 in the culture medium. Addition of IL-1 to thymocyte cultures at low cellular density (0.5×10^6/ml), in the presence of optimal PHA concentrations, promotes the production of IL-2 only by $PNA^- T_M$ cells (Fig. 4). As indicated in the same figure in the IL-2 microassay, the [^{3}H]TdR incorporation by CTC induced by $PNA^- T_M$ supernates was roughly one-third of that induced by the supernate from PBL. However, considering that thymocytes for the generation of supernates used in these experiments were cultures at a concentration half that of PBL (0.5 and 1.0×10^6 cells/ml, respectively), it can be concluded that $PNA^- T_M$ are good IL-2 producers.

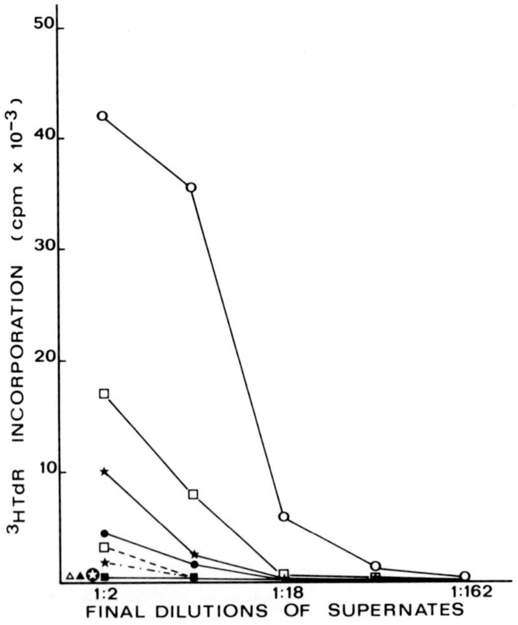

FIG. 4. IL-2 activity of supernates generated from: unfractionated (●), PNA^- (★), $PNA^- T_M$ (□), PNA^- T non_M (■), PNA^+ (✪), $PNA^+ T_M$ (△), and PNA^+ T non_M (▲) thymocytes cultured at 0.5 $\times 10^6$ cells/ml, in the presence of optimal PHA concentrations, with (——) or without (- - -) the addition of IL-1 containing medium (30 μl/well). For comparison, values representing the effect of supernate from PBL (○) cultured at 1.0×10^6 cells/ml are also indicated.

Inducibility of Blastogenesis by IL-2 in PHA-Unresponsive Thymocyte Subsets

In the light of the above reported findings it appeared interesting to investigate whether culture periods longer than 4 days in IL-2-containing medium could induce blastogenic response to PHA in otherwise unresponsive thymocyte subsets. Figure 5 shows the PHA proliferative responses of thymocyte subsets cultured at low cell-to-volume ratio (0.5×10^6/ml) for various time intervals. In culture without the addition of exogenous IL-2 the highest responses were recorded at 84 hr. Under the influence of IL-2, unfractionated and PNA^- T_M thymocytes reached the response peak at 84 hr while PNA^- and PNA^- T non_M reached maximal responses at 108 hr. Moreover the PNA^+ T_M subset, which was unable to respond in medium containing PHA alone, showed a distinct although delayed (132 hr) blastic response when exogenous IL-2 was present in the culture. Unfractionated PNA^+ and T_M depleted cells from PNA^+ never displayed detectable responses.

DISCUSSION

The experimental results described here relate to the mitogen responsiveness of thymocyte subsets defined by their PNA binding capacity and their Fc IgM receptor expression.

T_M cells are a distinct subset (~25%) of positively selected PNA^+ thymocytes, so far equated with immunoincompetent cortical cells (16, 20, 31–34) and comprising about 80% of the overall cell population. In the PNA^- thymocytes, so far equated with immunocompetent, medullary thymocytes (16, 20, 31–34), T_M represent one-third of the cells.

The proliferation of T cells in response to phytomitogens is often taken as a model for the proliferative aspect of immune response and as a proof for immunocompetence. This model appears now to be fairly complex. Among its complexities are the interactions between distinguishable types of cells and the presence of cell-produced soluble factors (interleukins) (7).

Unfractionated thymocytes exhibit mitogen responsiveness much lower than that of peripheral blood lymphocytes, which could be ascribed, at least in part, to the low amount of accessory cells in thymocyte preparations. In effect, the addition of IL-1 strongly enhances the response of thymocytes to PHA. However, the levels of thymocyte proliferation in presence of optimal IL-1 concentrations do not attain the peaks exhibited by PBL. The above data led us to hypothesize that the low mitogen responsiveness expressed by thymocytes, other than being in relation to the scarcity of accessory cells, could also be related to a low responsiveness of these lymphocytes on the whole or to the presence of subsets incapable of response to mitogens.

We have then analyzed the mitogen response exhibited by the thymocyte subsets under the influence of PHA alone or with the addition of IL-1 or IL-2 in order to obtain more detailed insights into the blastogenic properties of these various populations. In the presence of PHA alone, only PNA^- T_M cells show a significant response while the PNA^+, PNA^+ T_M, and PNA^+ T non_M subsets are practically devoid of response capacity. Moreover, PNA^- T non_M shows a very poor response. From these data it can be inferred that the capacity to mount a good blastogenic response is confined to the PNA^- subset of thymocytes. However, this capacity is not a property of the PNA^- cells on the whole: the increased peak response obtained

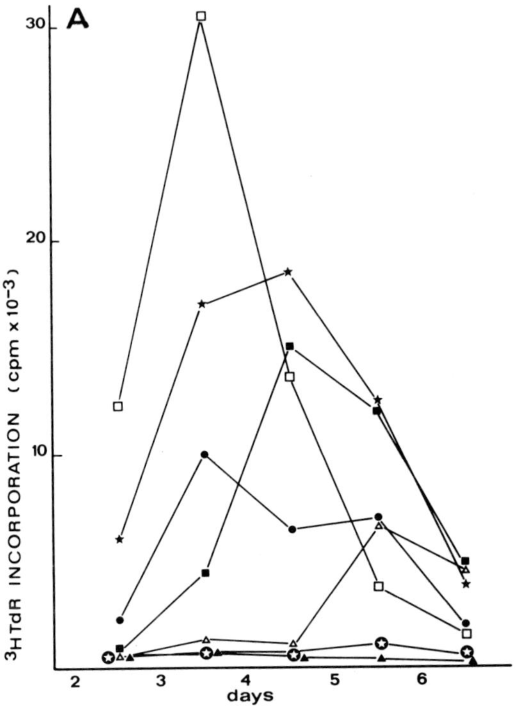
A
30
20
10
3HTdR INCORPORATION (cpm x 10-3)
2
3
4
5
6
days

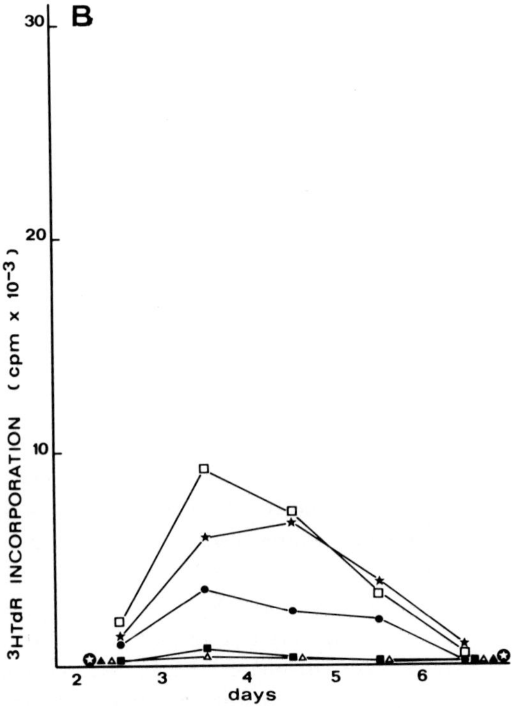
B
30
20
10
3HTdR INCORPORATION (cpm x 10-3)
2
3
4
5
6
days

by depleting PNA^- thymocytes of T non_M cells suggests that human thymocytes capable of mounting a blastic response to PHA reside in the PNA^- T_M population of medullary thymocytes. A first remark could be afforded at this point considering that separative procedures may influence the response capacity of the various thymocyte fractions by depletion or enrichment of accessory cells. The addition of exogenous IL-1 to the culture medium may overcome such a potential artifact by offering a saturating concentration of IL-1 to any culture. Experimental results of blastic proliferation of thymocyte fractions under the above culture conditions show a substantial increase in mitogen responsiveness, after Il-1 addition, in total PNA^- and in PNA^- T_M but not in PNA^- T non_M nor in all PNA^+ subsets. These data reinforce the impression that the possibility of responding to PHA stimulation is mainly confined to cells in PNA^- T_M subpopulations and suggest that their inherent blastic capacity is ordinarily masked by the scarcity of macrophages and/or their products.

The role of IL-1 in the production of IL-2 by some lymphocyte subsets and the obligatory role of IL-2 on blastogenesis are presently, at least in the laboratory animal system, widely accepted (13, 14). The dependency of IL-2 production on IL-1 presence in culture becomes evident from the results of those experiments by which we attempted to investigate the amount of IL-2 released in culture medium by thymocyte subsets under low cell densities, with or without addition of IL-1 to the culture. Having determined that LPS did not cause the release of detectable IL-2, accordingly with previous observations (13), we could be confident that our IL-1 preparation was free of any contaminating IL-2. The addition of IL-1 substantially enhanced IL-2 production by PNA^- subsets. The results of these experiments, together with the above-mentioned results on the beneficial effect of IL-1 addition on [^{3}H]TdR incorporation by PNA^- subsets, reinforce the assumption that mitogen responses are ultimately influenced, in this experimental model, by the amount of IL-1 present in the medium. Accordingly, it is noteworthy that the addition of IL-2 to culture medium does not raise the response above the levels attained when IL-1 is added to the culture medium. This may be the proof that macrophage product availability is the limiting factor in initiating thymocyte mitogen stimulation by influencing endogenous IL-2 production. However, the greater than expected increase of thymocyte [^{3}H]TdR incorporation attained by augmenting cell concentration cannot be exclusively explained by an increased IL-1 level which is dependent upon higher accessory cell concentrations. In fact one could suppose that in these experimental conditions a higher number of IL-2 producing cells per volume is present resulting in optimal IL-2 levels. Comparing Fig. 1 with Fig. 3, we can note that cells from PNA^- cultured at 0.5×10^6/ml in the presence of exogenous IL-1 were capable of a blastogenic response one-fourth as great as that exhibited by 2.0×10^6 PNA^- cells/ml (cultured without exogenous IL-1), in which a fourfold number of putative IL-2-producing cells should be present. In consequence, the prominent role of IL-1 in promoting the inherent blastic capacity of human thymocytes is firmly substantiated.

FIG. 5. Time-dependent proliferative responses to PHA (1 μg/well) of the various thymocyte subsets cultured at 0.5×10^6 cells/ml in microtiter well (final volume 200 μl) in the presence (A) or absence (B) of IL-2 containing medium (20 μl/well). Unfractionated (●), PNA^- (★), PNA^- T_M (□), PNA^- T non_M (■), PNA^+ (○), PNA^+ T_M (△), and PNA^+ T non_M (▲) thymocytes.

At this point, considering unresponsive thymocyte subsets, one could suspect that these thymocytes are incapable of a response to mitogen due to the absence of cells producing IL-2, in presence of either endogenous or exogenous IL-1. However, exogenous IL-2, at concentrations capable of saturating the requirement in other systems (CTC), was unable to sustain an increase of [^{3}H]TdR incorporation in otherwise unresponsive subsets. These data imply various possibilities to explain the mitogen unresponsiveness of these subsets. They may lack the capacity to be triggered by the lectin, may lack receptors for IL-2, or may be unable to proliferate after absorption of IL-2; whatever the mechanism, a double signal cannot switch them to proliferative events.

Recently it was reported that, in the presence of various conditioned media, immature thymocytes from experimental animals can be induced *in vitro* to differentiate into functional T cells (20, 32, 35–38). In light of these findings we therefore investigated whether exogenous IL-2 could influence the blastic responses of thymocyte subsets in culture for more than 4 days. IL-2 was able to promote a blastic response in two subpopulations otherwise unable to mount a significant proliferative response (PNA$^-$ T non$_M$ and PNA$^+$ T$_M$). One possible explanation of the delayed [^{3}H]TdR peak incorporation by PNA$^-$ T non$_M$ could reside in our previous observation (18) that the majority of PNA$^-$ thymocytes have the capacity to acquire with time in culture the Fc receptor for IgM, a marker considered a step in the differentiation and in the maturation of thymocytes to peripheral T lymphocytes. Under the influence of IL-2, in the PNA$^+$ compartment only T$_M$ cells showed a detectable mitogen proliferation. Cells with IgM Fc receptor represent about 25% of PNA$^+$ thymocytes and, unlike PNA$^-$ cells, do not increase significantly *in vitro* (18). These findings indicate that only a minor fraction of PNA$^+$ cells are the target for IL-2-containing supernate enabling these cortical thymocytes to mount a detectable blastic response. These results are in agreement with very recent reports on laboratory animal systems where a minor subpopulation of PNA$^+$ thymocytes could be induced under the influence of IL-2-containing supernates to proliferate in response to mitogen (38) and to differentiate into cytotoxic T lymphocytes (37).

REFERENCES

1. Rosenstreich, D. L., and Mizel, S. B. *Immunol. Rev.* **40,** 102, 1978.
2. Rosenstreich, D. L., Farrar, J. J., and Dougherty, S., *J. Immunol.* **116,** 131, 1976.
3. Arala-Chaves, M. P., Hope, L., Korn, J. H., and Fudemberg, H., *Eur. J. Immunol.* **8,** 77, 1978.
4. Maizel, A. L., Mehta, S., and Ford, R. J., *J. Reticuloendothel. Soc.* **28,** 357, 1980.
5. Twomey, J. J., Sharkey, O., Brown, J. A., Laugher, A. H., and Jordan, P. H., *J. Immunol.* **104,** 845, 1970.
6. Waldron, J. A., Horn, R. G., and Rosenthal, A. S., *J. Immunol.* **111,** 58, 1973.
7. Mizel, S. B., and Farrar, J. F., *Cell. Immunol.* **48,** 433, 1979.
8. Gery, I., and Waksman, B. H., *J. Exp. Med.* **136,** 143, 1972.
9. Shaw, J., Monticone, V., and Paetkau, V., *J. Immunol.* **120,** 1967, 1978.
10. Larson, E. L., Iscove, N. N., and Coutinho, A., *Nature (London)* **283,** 664, 1980.
11. Togawa, A., Oppenheim, J. J., and Mizel, S. B., *J. Immunol.* **122,** 2112, 1979.
12. Mizel, S. B., and Ben-Zvi, A., *Cell. Immunol.* **54,** 382, 1980.
13. Smith, K. A., Lachman, L. B., Oppenheim, J. J., and Favata, M. F., *J. Exp. Med.* **151,** 1551, 1980.
14. Shaw, J., Caplan, B., Paetkau, V., Pilarski, L. M., Delovitch, T. L., and McKenzie, I. F., *J. Immunol.* **124,** 2231, 1980.
15. Maizel, A. L., Mehta, S. R., Ford, R. J., and Lachman, L. B., *J. Exp. Med.* **153,** 470, 1981.

16. Reisner, Y., Biniaminov, M., Rosenthal, E., Sharon, N., and Ramot, B., *Proc. Nat. Acad. Sci. USA* **76,** 447, 1979.
17. Musiani, P., Lauriola, L., Carbone, A., Piantelli, M., and Dina, M. A., *In* "Thymus, Thymic Hormones and T Lymphocytes" (F. Aiuti and H. Wigzell, Eds.), Proceedings of the Serona Symposia, Vol. 38, p. 89. Academic Press, New York/London, 1980.
18. Musiani, P., Lauriola, L., Carbone, A., Maggiano, N., and Piantelli, M., *Thymus* **2,** 225, 1981.
19. Irlé, C., *J. Immunol. Methods* **17,** 117, 1977.
20. Irlé, C., Piguet, P. F., and Vasalli, P., *J. Exp. Med.* **148,** 32, 1978.
21. Piantelli, M., Lauriola, L., Carbone, A., Evoli, A., Tonali, P., and Musiani, P., *Clin. Exp. Immunol.* **36,** 85, 1979.
22. Carbone, A., Piantelli, M., Musiani, P., Pozzuoli, R., and Lauriola, L., *J. Immunol. Methods* **29,** 245, 1979.
23. Blyden, G., and Handschumacher, R. E., *J. Immunol.* **118,** 1631, 1977.
24. Lachman, L. B., Hacker, M. P., and Handschumacher, R. E., *J. Immunol.* **119,** 2019, 1977.
25. Bonnard, G. D., Yasaka, K., and Maca, R. D., *Cell. Immunol.* **51,** 390, 1980.
26. Bonnard, G. D., Schendel, D. J., West, W. H., Alvarez, J. M., Maca, R. D., Yasaka, K., Fine, R. L., Herberman, R. B., De Landazuri, M. O., and Morgan, D. A., "Human Lymphocyte Differentiation: Its Application to Cancer," pp. 319–326. North-Holland, Amsterdam, 1978.
27. Lauriola, L., Piantelli, M., Carbone, A., Dina, M. A., Scoppetta, C., and Musiani, P., *Clin. Exp. Immunol.* **37,** 502, 1979.
28. Paetkau, V., Mills, G., Gerhart, S., and Monticone, V., *J. Immunol.* **117,** 1320, 1976.
29. Smith, K. A., Gillis, S., and Baker, P. E., *In* "The Molecular Basis of Immune Cell Functions" (J. G. Kaplan, Ed.), p. 223. Elsevier/North-Holland, Amsterdam, 1979.
30. Farrar, J. J., Mizel, S. B., Fuller-Bonar, J., Farrar, W. L., and Hilfiker, M. L., *J. Immunol.* **125,** 793, 1980.
31. Reisner, Y., Linker-Israeli, M., and Sharon, N., *Cell. Immunol.* **25,** 129, 1976.
32. Kruisbeek, A. M., and Astaldi, G. C. B., *J. Immunol.* **123,** 904, 1979.
33. London, J., Berrih, S., and Bach, J. F., *J. Immunol.* **121,** 438, 1978.
34. Roelants, G. E., London, J., Mayor-Witney, K. S., and Sarrano, B., *Eur. J. Immunol.* **9,** 139, 1979.
35. Beller, D. I., and Unanue, E. R., *J. Immunol.* **118,** 1780, 1977.
36. Di Sabato, G., Moraes, E. K., and Altin, M., *Cell. Immunol.* **44,** 252, 1979.
37. Wagner, H., Hardt, C., Bartlett, R., Röllinghoff, M., and Pfizenmaier, K., *J. Immunol.* **125,** 2532, 1980.
38. Draàber, P., and Kisielow, P., *Eur. J. Immunol.* **11,** 1, 1981.

CELLULAR IMMUNOLOGY **64,** 350–358 (1981)

Low-Dose Restriction in Ir-Gene Control Reflects Susceptibility to Tolerance Induction

STEPHEN H. LEECH[1] AND MARIAM ALI

Department of Medicine, Louisiana State University Medical Center, New Orleans, Louisiana 70112

Received July 16, 1981; accepted August 22, 1981

Low-dose restriction has been demonstrated in the Ir-gene-controlled response to a variety of antigens. With regard to the murine antibody response to low (1 μg) doses of DNP-BGG in $Al(OH)_3$: strains A, CBA, and SJL are responders; DBA/1, C57BL/6, and BALB/c are nonresponders. In at least the last two strains, that nonresponsive state results from induction of tolerance. Although genetic factors play a role in determining susceptibility to induction of that tolerant state by the antigen in low doses, the type of adjuvant used with it is of fundamental importance. Thus, BALB/c mice, which are resistant to tolerance induction by ultracentrifuged BGG, are readily tolerized by administration of DNP-BGG in $Al(OH)_3$ or as an alum precipitate with DPT.

INTRODUCTION

A puzzling feature of certain Ir-gene-controlled responses is that the control is highly dose dependent. This restriction has been reported for high doses of a few antigens, and for low (limiting) doses of many other antigens. High-dose restriction occurs in the murine antibody responses to the native antigen, sperm whale myoglobin (1), and to the synthetic antigen, (T,G)-Pro—L (2). Low-dose restriction has been demonstrated with a variety of native antigens administered to mice, guinea pigs, and rats (3).

At least three different hypotheses have been proposed to explain these restrictions, the first two being based on *a priori* arguments. Jormalainen *et al.* (2) assumed that optimal doses of antigen provide equal stimulation and suppression in all strains. They proposed that, after immunization with a higher than optimal dose, the suppression is more pronounced in the low responder strain. McDevitt (4) assumed that, for each of the multiplicity of determinants on a native antigen, there is a different threshold of response. He proposed that at high doses, the response threshold is exceeded for sufficient determinants to stimulate antibody production. As the dose decreases, the number of determinants to which the response threshold is exceeded falls below that necessary for genetically deficient mice to produce antibody. No experimental evidence, however, has been reported to support either of these hypotheses.

In contrast with the first two hypotheses, the third is supported by experimental

[1] Recipient of a Young Investigator's Award (USPHS R23 CA 25668-03) from the National Cancer Institute.

0008-8749/81/160350-09$02.00/0

results. Reese (5) demonstrated that inbred Wright strain 2 guinea pigs, which are genetically nonresponsive to low doses (1 μg) of DNP-GPA, also fail to respond to a higher dose (100 μg) of this conjugate when it is administered in monomeric form. His interpretation of those results was that doses of antigen low enough to identify nonresponder strains also were sufficiently free of contaminating polymers of the antigen to be immunogenic. There is, however, an alternative interpretation of his results; the inability of an animal to respond to monomeric antigen may be the result, not of a genetic defect in responsiveness, but rather of a tolerant state induced by the antigen in that form. Such an interpretation is supported by the fact that salt fractionation, the method used by Reese to render his antigen monomeric, is also known to make an antigen tolerogenic (6).

A new hypothesis can therefore be formulated to explain the phenomenon of low-dose restriction. This states that the genetically determined inability of an animal to respond immunologically to low doses of an antigen is the result of its susceptibility to the induction of tolerance by the antigen in such doses. Such a hypothesis was suggested by the fact that many different antigens in low doses (10 mg/kg body wt) induce tolerance in mice, rabbits, and guinea pigs (7).

The present study was undertaken to test this new hypothesis. For two reasons, the native antigen BGG was used in mice. First, low doses of BGG induce tolerance in this species (7). Second, the genetic control of both tolerance (8) and immunity (9–11) to this antigen have been investigated extensively in the mouse. This report shows that the type of injection protocol used previously to identify nonresponders to low doses of BGG actually induces tolerance. Although genetic factors may be involved in determining susceptibility to the induction of such tolerance, two types of adjuvant are here shown to be critical for its induction.

MATERIALS AND METHODS

Animals. Female mice, 2–3 months old, of inbred strains A, CBA, SJL, C57BL/6, BALB/c and DBA/1 were purchased from The Jackson Laboratory, Bar Harbor, Maine. They were entered into experiments in groups of six. Male and female New Zealand white rabbits, 8–10 weeks old and weighing between 1.3 and 1.8 kg each, were purchased from Lee's Rabbitry, Theodore, Alabama. All animals were maintained on Purina Laboratory Chow and tap water, with 12 hr of artificial light per 24 hr.

Antigens. BGG was purchased from the Sigma Chemical Company, St. Louis, Missouri, and dinitrophenylated by the method of Eisen (12). Coupling ratios (hapten:protein) were estimated on the basis of a molar extinction coefficient of DNP of 1.74×10^2 M^{-1} cm^{-1} at 360 nm.

Mouse immunoglobulin (MIg) was prepared from sera obtained by tail bleeding. It was precipitated with 45% saturated ammonium sulfate and purified by anion-exchange chromatography using DEAE-cellulose.

Injections. Two preparations of DNP_{11}-BGG were used to immunize mice ip. In the first, $Al(OH)_3$ gel was used as an adjuvant in a ratio of 1000:1 weight for weight. The second involved alum precipitation by the method of Proom (13) and suspension in DTP (Lederle Laboratories, Pearl River N.Y.).

Radioimmune assay. Anti-BGG antibody was measured individually in each serum by a coprecipitation method as described previously (14). For that method, anti-MIg sera were raised in rabbits and purified by adsorption on Sepharose beads, to which BGG had been coupled by the method of Axen *et al.* (15). BGG was purified by G-200 column chromatography, and labeled with ^{125}I by the chloramine-T method (16). The fraction of antigen bound was determined by subtracting the counts per minute (cpm). Thus

$$\text{fraction bound} = \frac{\text{observed cpm} - \text{anti-MIg cpm}}{\text{TCA-precipitable cpm}}.$$

Because there is a direct linear relationship between antigen-binding capacity (ABC) and the fraction bound up to the 0.6 limit (14) used in all the assays in this communication, then:

$$\text{ABC} = \text{fraction bound} \times \text{dilution factor}.$$

The result represents the moles of BGG bound in a solution of stated molarity by 1 ml of antiserum, and is shown as the mean ABC ± SEM for each group of mice. These data were computed with a programmable desk-top calculator (Hewlett–Packard 9815A) and analyzed statistically by Student's *t* test.

RESULTS

Initially, the anti-BGG antibody response was compared among six inbred strains of mice to low (1 μg) doses of DNP-BGG in $Al(OH)_3$. That is the standard injection protocol that has been used in all previous reports of genetic control of BGG responsiveness (9–11). Whereas those reports were based largely on measurements of antibody responses to the hapten DNP previously conjugated with BGG, this experiment differed in that antibody responses to the carrier BGG were measured

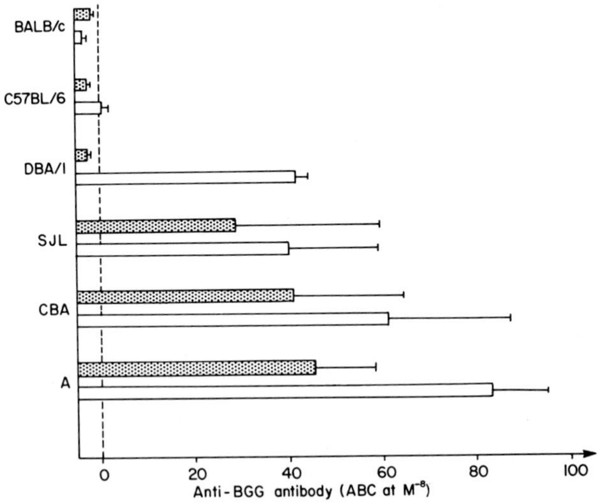

FIG. 1. Antibody responsiveness to low doses of BGG in six inbred strains of mice. Mice were injected with DNP-BGG 1 μg ip monthly with 1% $Al(OH)_3$. They were bled from the tail at monthly intervals, and the anti-BGG antibody concentration was measured in individual sera. The mean ABC values after two injections are represented by stippled data bars, and after three injections by open bars. SEM values are represented as (——|).

directly. The results illustrated in Fig. 1 demonstrate a pattern of BGG responsiveness after two injections. On one hand, strains A, CBA, and SJL produced significant concentrations of antibody; on the other hand, strains DBA/1, C57BL/6, and BALB/c produced little if any antibody. The strains are therefore referred to in this communication as "responders" and "nonresponders," respectively. Although responses of SJL mice appeared to be of intermediate magnitude, they differed significantly from those of noresponders ($P < 0.02$) but not from those of responders ($P < 0.2$). The differences in response between responders and nonresponders became more pronounced after three injections except in the previously nonresponsive DBA/1 mice, which appeared to have become responders.

The nonresponsiveness of C57BL/6 and BALB/c mice could be caused by a variety of mechanisms including an Ir-gene defect, active suppression, or induction of tolerance. In preparation for testing for the last possibility, a form and dose of the antigen was sought that would be immunogenic, even in nonresponders. Mice were injected ip with DPT and alum-precipitated DNP-BGG in either low or high doses (Table 1). Although there was no antibody response to low doses in any of the six strains tested, high doses stimulated good responses in all strains except DBA/1. As that strain had also responded erratically in the previous experiment, it was excluded from all subsequent experiments. Because alum- precipitated DNP-BGG (100 μg + DPT) was capable of circumventing nonresponsiveness in BALB/c and C57BL/6 mice, it was used in the following tests for tolerance.

The first test for tolerance was in mice injected with the standard protocol (9–11). Mice of five inbred strains were injected with low doses of DNP-BGG in $Al(OH)_3$. The serum anti-BGG antibody concentration was then measured before and after challenge with the antigen in a dose and form known to be immunogenic. The results, shown in Table 2, again showed that three low doses of the antigen in $Al(OH)_3$ had, by Day 90, stimulated production of anti-BGG antibody in the responder strains A, CBA, and SJL, but not in the nonresponder strains C57BL/6 and BALB/c. After immunogenic challenge, anti-BGG antibody concentrations rose in all three responder strains but remained undetectable in both nonresponder strains.

The demonstration that unresponsiveness had been induced in BALB/c mice was surprising as that strain had been reported previously to be genetically resistant

TABLE 1

Comparison of the Anti-BGG Antibody Responses to Low (1 μg) with High (100 μg) Doses of DNP-BGG plus DTP

Mouse strain	Anti-BGG antibody (ABC, M^{-8})[a] Low dose	High dose
A	−4.0 ± 0.4	91.9 ± 7.8
CBA	−4.4 ± 0.4	106.5 ± 8.0
SJL	−3.0 ± 1.0	108.5 ± 9.9
C57BL/6	−1.5 ± 3.5	115.7 ± 2.7
BALB/c	−4.7 ± 0.6	110.7 ± 4.4

[a] Mice were bled from the tail 2 months after receiving either high or low doses of alum-precipitated conjugate plus DTP.

TABLE 2

The Effect on BGG Responsiveness of Repeated Low Doses of DNP-BGG in $Al(OH)_3$

Mouse strain	Anti-BGG antibody (ABC, M^{-8})[a]	
	Day 90	Day 150
A	75.4 ± 12.3	93.1 ± 8.3[b]
CBA	45.5 ± 25.6	84.8 ± 19.3[b]
SJL	40.2 ± 23.1	71.4 ± 29.1
C57BL/6	−2.5 ± 0.5	0.2 ± 1.3
BALB/c	−2.5 ± 0.5	−3.0 ± 0.7

[a] Mice received three monthly 1-μg injections of DNP-BGG in $Al(OH)_3$ ip. On Day 90, they were bled from the tail and challenged with an immunogenic dose (100 μg) of alum-precipitated DNP-BGG + DTP ip. They were rebled 2 months later on Day 150.

[b] $P < 0.05$ (two-tailed t test).

to tolerance induction by BGG (8). As the BGG used in those reports was administered in high (2-mg) doses after ultracentrifugation, the next experiment was designed to test susceptibility to tolerance induction by low (1-μg) doses of ultracentrifuged BGG in BALB/c mice, and in other strains. The serum anti-BGG antibody concentration on Day 90 after three low doses of ultracentrifuged BGG demonstrated wide variability among the strains tested (Table 3). The rise in serum antibody concentration after immunogenic challenge was significant in all strains except C57BL/6. BALB/c mice are therefore resistant to tolerance induction by ultracentrifuged BGG not only in high doses (8), but also in low doses.

It appeared paradoxical that BALB/c mice, although resistant to tolerance induction by ultracentrifuged BGG in low doses, could be rendered unresponsive by the same doses administered with an "adjuvant" (Table 2). An adjuvant is classically a substance that augments immunogenicity and not tolerogenicity. In order to determine whether other adjuvants would have a similar effect, DNP-BGG was alum-precipitated and injected with DPT. After three low doses of the antigen with

TABLE 3

The Effect on BGG-Responsiveness of Repeated Low Doses of Ultracentrifuged BGG

Mouse strain	Anti-BGG antibody (ABC, M^{-8})[a]	
	Day 90	Day 150
A	9.0 ± 9.1	64.1 ± 13.5[b]
CBA	0.5 ± 1.4	39.4 ± 18.9[c]
SJL	86.2 ± 24.4	94.8 ± 23.7[c]
C57BL/6	1.2 ± 0.3	1.5 ± 0.7
BALB/c	21.9 ± 13.4	50.5 ± 17.6[c]

[a] Mice were bled on Day 90 after 3 monthly low (1 μg) doses of ultracentrifuged BGG. They were then challenged with a high (100 μg) dose of alum-precipitated BGG + DPT. Anti-BGG antibody concentrations in the serum were measured after repeat tail-bleeding 60 days later on Day 150.

[b] $P < 0.01$.

[c] $P < 0.05$.

TABLE 4

The Effect of BGG Responsiveness of Repeated Low Doses of Alum-Precipitated DNP-BGG with DPT

Mouse strain	Anti-BGG antibody (ABC, M^{-8})[a]	
	Day 90	Day 150
A	−2.9 ± 0.5	62.3 ± 29.2[b]
CBA	−2.4 ± 0.2	117.7 ± 5.4[c]
SJL	−0.6 ± 0.7	119.2 ± 8.8[c]
C57BL/6	−1.5 ± 0.6	7.5 ± 9.8
BALB/c	−1.6 ± 1.1	0.3 ± 2.7

[a] Mice were bled from the tail on Days 90 and 150. Day 90 was after three monthly low (1 μg) doses of the alum-precipitated conjugate DPT. They were immediately challenged with a high (100 μg) dose of that conjugate + DPT. The antibody response was measured 60 days thereafter at Day 150.
[b] $P < 0.05$.
[c] $P < 0.0001$.

that adjuvant, no anti-BGG antibody could be found on Day 90 in the serum of any of the strains examined (Table 4). After immunogenic challenge, there was a significant rise in antibody concentration in all three responder strains, but not in either of the nonresponder strains.

DISCUSSION

Strain differences in the murine antibody response to DNP-BGG have previously been demonstrated to depend on both the dose of that antigen and the adjuvant injected with it (9–11). In order to duplicate the standard immunization regimen used in all previous reports of BGG responsiveness (9–11), 1 μg DNP-BGG in $Al(OH)_3$ was used in the first experiment reported here. Whereas those reports were based largely on measurements of antibody responses to the hapten DNP, this experiment differs in that antibody responses to the carrier BGG were measured directly. The pattern of BGG responsiveness demonstrated by this direct method is almost identical to that demonstrated indirectly in previous reports (9–11), sum-

TABLE 5

Strain Differences in Antibody Responsiveness to Low (1 μg) Doses of DNP-BGG + $Al(OH)_3$ as Determined by Four Independent Groups of Investigators

Mouse strain	Vaz and Levine (9)	Freed *et al.* (10)	Newton and Warner (11)	This study
A	R[a]	R	R	R
SJL	R	nt[b]	R	R
CBA	R	R	N[c]	R
C57BL/6	N	nt	N	N
BALB/c	nt	N	N	N

[a] *R*, responsive.
[b] nt, not tested.
[c] N, nonresponsive.

marized in Table 5. That demonstrates that the only discrepancy was in Newton and Warner's demonstration of nonresponsiveness in CBA mice (11). They ascribed that to differences in molar coupling ratios of hapten to carrier. Thus, for example, their conjugate was DNP_{56}-BGG, whereas that used by Vaz and Levine was DNP_{42}-BGG (9). They postulated that the extra DNP groups on their BGG masked its determinants so that it was no longer recognizable to strains of mice such as CBA. That hypothesis is still tenable as the DNP used in the experiments reported here had a much lower molar coupling ratio (11:1).

In one of the previous reports of BGG responsiveness (9), a similarity in the magnitude of the response to both the carrier and to the hapten was reported in only two strains—one responder and one nonresponder. That phenomenon is confirmed and extended in this report to include four more strains. When considered in the light of two established facts about hapten-carrier relationships, that phenomenon is consistent with the hypothesis that the relevant Ir-gene(s) is (are) expressed in T cells (17). First, although the final phase of the anti-hapten antibody response to a conjugate is a function of B cells, it cannot occur until there has been a response to the carrier (18). Second, this carrier effect is mediated exclusively by T cells (19).

The most important finding in these experiments is that the type of injection protocol previously reported to identify nonresponders to BGG (9–11) actually induces tolerance. Pretreatment with repeated low doses of DNP-BGG suppresses the subsequent response to challenge with the conjugate in a dose and form that would otherwise circumvent nonresponsiveness. With regard to the dosage used for pretreatment, this finding is consistent with the new hypothesis of low dose restriction, which states that the genetically determined inability of an animal to respond immunologically to low doses of an antigen is the result of its susceptibility to the induction of tolerance by the antigen in such doses. These experiments indicate, however, that an environmental factor other than low dosage is important in the induction of tolerance. This factor is the type of adjuvant used. Its importance can be appreciated by first considering those genetic factors that may make an animal susceptible to the induction of tolerance by BGG.

The fact that such genetic factors are involved is suggested by the observation that the H-2 haplotype of the strains rendered tolerant here was the same (b and d) as that of strains previously reported to be nonresponsive (9–11). Moreover, the concept that susceptibility to tolerance induction is the basis for genetically determined nonresponsiveness is not without precedent, having been reported previously for other antigens and strains (20–22). Finally, and most relevant to ultracentrifuged BGG, murine susceptibility to tolerance induction by the antigen in that form has been reported to have a genetic basis, ascribed to allelic genes at the *Tol-l* locus (8). One of those genes (*Tol-l*^{a}) renders strains such as DBA/2 (8) and probably C57BL/6 (23) susceptible to tolerance, and is dominant to the other gene (*Tol-l*^{b}), which renders BALB/c mice resistant. The results with ultracentrifuged BGG (Table 3) are consistent with the presence of such alleles; tolerance was complete in C57BL/6 and partial in BALB/c mice. In contrast, the tolerant state induced in BALB/c mice by BGG in forms other than ultracentrifuged (Tables 2 and 4) appears at variance with the report that *Tol-l*^{b} confers resistance to tolerance (8). If there is a genetic basis for that tolerant state, other genes must be considered. Dual genes designated *Ir-l-BGG*, for example, may determine the effect on the immune system of low doses of BGG with $Al(OH)_3$; expression of the primary, immune response gene is modified by the secondary, suppressor gene (10). Activation of the latter gene by BGG in either of the forms used for pretreatment could thus explain how tolerance was induced.

Although both adjuvants used for those pretreatments have been used classically to augment immune responses, increasing numbers of reports indicate that they may have the opposite effect. $Al(OH)_3$, for example, suppresses the IgE response to low doses (1 μg) of penicilloylated BGG in guinea pigs if the conjugate is administered weekly (24). It has a similar effect on the murine IgE and IgG responses, the "adjuvant-generated suppression" being more marked with complete Freund's adjuvant (25). Furthermore, alum precipitation of the conjugate used for hapten priming suppresses the subsequent circumvention of BGG tolerance (14). Finally, pertussigen, the component of the *Pertussis* in DTP that is usually considered to be an immunostimulant, suppresses IgG and IgM responses (26) and various expressions of delayed hypersensitivity (27) if administered before the antigen.

Adjuvants therefore possess, in addition to their immunostimulant qualities, the capacity to suppress under appropriate conditions various types of immune response. Furthermore, both those properties may be so powerful that they override the genetic determinants of an immune response. For example, on one hand, both $Al(OH)_3$ and DTP helped low doses of BGG overcome the inherited resistance of BALB/c mice to BGG-tolerance induction. In contrast, complete Freund's adjuvant enables the same low dose of BGG to overcome the genetically determined nonresponsiveness of other strains of mice (11). The new hypothesis of low-dose restriction must therefore be modified to include some specification of the type of adjuvant used.

ACKNOWLEDGMENTS

We wish to thank our secretary, Mrs. Shari Clement. The editorial assistance of Miss Virginia Howard was much appreciated, as were critical comments and suggestions from colleagues too numerous to be named.

REFERENCES

1. Young, C. R., Ebringer, A., and Archer, J. R., *Immunology* **34,** 571, 1978.
2. Jormalainen, S., Mozes, E., and Sela, M., *J. Exp. Med.* **141,** 1057, 1975.
3. Benacerraf, B., and Katz, D. H. *Advan. Cancer Res.* **21,** 121, 1975.
4. McDevitt, H. O., *Hosp. Pract.* **8,** 61, 1973.
5. Reese, R. T., *Cell Immunol.* **33,** 245, 1977.
6. Golub, E. S., and Weigle, W. O., *J. Immunol.* **102,** 389, 1969.
7. Dresser, D. W., and Mitchison, N. A., *Advan. Immunol.* **8,** 129, 1968.
8. Lukic, M. L., Wortis, H. H., and Leskowitz, S., *Cell. Immunol.* **15,** 457, 1973.
9. Vaz, N. M., and Levine, B. B., *Science* **168,** 852, 1970.
10. Freed, H. H., Deak, B. D., and McDevitt, H. O., *J. Immunol.* **117,** 1514, 1976.
11. Newton, R. C., and Warner, C. M., *Immunogenetics* **4,** 449, 1977.
12. Eisen, H. N., *Methods Med. Res.* **10,** 94, 1964.
13. Proom, H., *J. Pathol. Bacteriol.* **55,** 419, 1943.
14. Leech, S. H., and Mitchison, N. A., *Eur. J. Immunol.* **6,** 810, 1976.
15. Axen, R., Porath, J., and Ernback, S., *Nature (London)* **214,** 1302, 1967.
16. Hunter, W. M., and Greenwood, F. C., *Nature (London)* **194,** 495, 1962.
17. Benacerraf, B., and McDevitt, H. O., *Science* **175,** 273, 1972.

18. Mitchison, N. A., *Symp. Int. Soc. Cell Biol.* **7,** 29, 1968.
19. Raff, M. C., *Nature (London)* **226,** 1257, 1970.
20. Hardy, D., and Rowley, D., *Immunology* **14,** 401, 1968.
21. Gershon, R. K., Maurer, P. H., and Merryman, C. F., *Proc. Nat. Acad. Sci. (USA)* **70,** 250, 1973.
22. Debré, P., Kapp, J. A., and Benacerraf, B., *J. Exp. Med.* **142,** 1436, 1975.
23. Das, S., DiPadua, D., and Leskowitz, S., *Proc. Soc. Exp. Biol. Med.* **144,** 373, 1973.
24. Geczy, A. F., deWeck, A. L., Geczy, C. L., and Toffler, O., *J. Allergy Clin. Immunol.* **62,** 261, 1978.
25. Chiorazzi, N., Tung, A. S., and Katz, D. H., *J. Immunol.* **122,** 1495, 1979.
26. Asakawa, S., *Japan. J. Med. Sci. Biol.* **22,** 23, 1969.
27. Ochiai, T., Okumura, K., Tada, T., and Iwasa, S., *Int. Arch. Allergy Appl. Immunol.* **43,** 196, 1972.

CELLULAR IMMUNOLOGY **64**, 359–370 (1981)

Comparison of Monocyte and Alveolar Macrophage Antibody-Dependent Cellular Cytotoxicity and Fc-Receptor Activity[1]

DAVID M. GARAGIOLA, THOMAS K. HUARD, AND ALBERT F. LOBUGLIO

Simpson Memorial Institute, University of Michigan, Ann Arbor, Michigan 48109

Received June 12, 1981; accepted August 9, 1981

The cytotoxic potential of rabbit peripheral blood monocytes and alveolar macrophages in antibody-dependent cellular cytotoxicity (ADCC) toward both erythrocyte (RBC_{OX}) and tumor cell (CEM T-lymphoblast) targets was examined. ADCC was measured in a 4-hr ^{51}Cr-release assay. Alveolar macrophages were more efficient at killing the tumor cell targets (optimally sensitized with rabbit antisera) than monocytes at similar effector cell/target cell (E/T) ratios. Tumor cell targets sensitized with seven different antisera (anti-CEM) were lysed by alveolar macrophages but not by the monocytes. In marked contrast, the monocytes were more effective at lysing the sensitized erythrocyte target cells. The degree of cytolysis of RBC_{OX} and CEM was dependent on the E/T ratio and the degree of sensitization of these target cells. It was demonstrated that the effector cell selectivity in ADCC was directly related to their ability or inability to bind the sensitized target cells as determined by Fc-receptor rosette formation. The transition from monocyte to macrophage may, therefore, have resulted in an alteration in the criteria necessary for Fc-receptor binding to antibody-sensitized target cells and subsequent ADCC.

INTRODUCTION

Peripheral blood monocytes are the circulating precursors of the tissue-bound macrophages. Both cell populations are directly involved in antigen processing and clearance, and play an active role in the regulation of the immune response. The cells are derived from pluripotent stem cells generated in the bone marrow (1, 2). Although monocytes and macrophages may have unique functional characteristics, they share certain membrane receptors including the receptor for C3b (3, 4) and for the Fc portion of IgG (5–8). Both cell populations have been shown to be capable of binding soluble immune complexes and antibody-sensitized erythrocytes (EA[2]) (6–9), and have been shown to effectively lyse EA in antibody-dependent cellular cytotoxicity (ADCC) ((10–13); as reviewed in (14–16)). More recently,

[1] This work was supported in part by National Cancer Institute Grant Ca 25641-02 and National Institutes of Health Grant AI 17139-01.

[2] Abbreviations used: ADCC, antibody-dependent cellular cytotoxicity; CEM, human CEM T-cell lymphoblasts; E/T, effector to target ratio; FCS, fetal calf serum; HBSS, Hanks' balanced salt solution; PBS, phosphate-buffered saline; RBC_{OX}, ox red blood cells; SBSS, Seligmann's balanced salt solution; SRBC, sheep red blood cells; NZW, New Zealand White rabbits; SPA, Staph.-protein A; EA, antibody-sensitized erythrocytes; TA, antibody-sensitized tumor cells.

0008-8749/81/160359-12$02.00/0

human monocytes have been shown to be capable of killing sensitized tumor cells in ADCC (17, 20), as well.

In this investigation, we have examined the cytotoxic potential of rabbit peripheral blood monocytes and alveolar macrophages in ADCC toward both erythrocyte and tumor cell targets. The alveolar macrophages were clearly more efficient at killing the sensitized tumor cells, while the monocytes were more effective at lysing erythrocytes. This effector cell selectivity was directly related to Fc-receptor-mediated binding of the target cells and was dependent on the degree of sensitization of the target cells. The differentiation from monocyte to macrophage may, therefore, be accompanied by changes in criteria required for Fc-receptor-mediated binding and lysis of antibody-sensitized targets.

MATERIALS AND METHODS

Animals

Normal healthy female 5-kg New Zealand White (NZW) rabbits (Langshaw Distributors, Haslett, Mich.) were used as a source of both monocytes and alveolar macrophages. Rabbits were maintained in the animal care facility of Simpson Memorial Research Institute. Food and water were available *ad libitum*. No antibiotics or other drugs were administered.

Effector Cells

Monocytes. Rabbit monocytes were isolated from the peripheral blood of a single rabbit for each experiment. The blood was collected by venipuncture of the central ear artery into 5% EDTA (0.3 ml/10 ml blood). Mononuclear cells were isolated by Ficoll–Hypaque density gradient centrifugation (19). Briefly, the blood was diluted 1:2 in Seligmann's balanced salt solution (SBSS), then centrifuged at 1150*g* for 25 min through Ficoll–Hypaque. The mononuclear cells were collected, washed twice, and resuspended in SBSS. Monocytes were then isolated from the mononuclear cell suspension as described by Shaw *et al.* (20). Briefly, 50×10^6 mononuclear cells (1 ml) were added to 100-mm tissue culture plates (Corning No. 25020) containing 10 ml of Hanks' balanced salt solution (HBSS) supplemented with 13% autologous serum. After incubation for 90 min at 37°C in a humidified atmosphere of 5% CO_2 in air, the adherent cell monolayer was washed vigorously five times with complete medium consisting of RPMI 1640, 10% heat-inactivated fetal calf serum (FCS), 100 U/ml penicillin, and 100 μg/ml streptomycin. After washing, the adherent cells were incubated for 2 min in 5 ml of cold 0.2% EDTA in physiological saline containing 0.1% bovine serum albumin. The adherent cells were harvested by gentle scraping with a rubber policeman, washed twice in complete medium, and adjusted to the appropriate concentrations (as indicated in the text). Cell viability was determined by trypan blue dye exclusion. The adherent cell suspension was characterized by morphology (Wright stain), phagocytosis of opsinized zymosan (21) and staining for the nonspecific esterase (22) and found to be ≥95% monocytes by these three criteria. Cell viability was ≥95%.

Macrophages. Rabbit alveolar macrophages were obtained by pulmonary lavage (23). Briefly, rabbits were sacrificed and the lungs dissected free. The lungs were filled with 50 ml of HBSS and massaged gently and the cell suspensions aspirated.

This procedure was repeated an additional three times. The cell suspensions were combined, washed twice in complete medium, and adjusted to the appropriate concentrations (as indicated in the text). Viability and purity were assessed as for the monocytes. The alveolar macrophages were ≥95% viable and ≥95% pure by all three criteria.

Target Cells

Erythrocytes. Fresh ox erythrocytes (RBC_{OX}) (Colorado Serum Company Laboratories, Denver, Colo.) were washed three times in HBSS and radiolabeled by incubating 250×10^6 cells with 30 μCi of $Na_2{}^{51}CrO_4$ (New England Nuclear, Boston, Mass.) for 60 min at 37°C. The RBC_{OX} were then washed two times with HBSS and sensitized by incubating 50×10^6 targets with 50 μl of varying dilutions of rabbit anti-sheep red blood cell (SRBC) antisera (Cordis Corp., Miami, FL) for 45 min and 37°C with gentle agitation every 15 min. The cell concentration was adjusted to 2×10^6/ml for use in all ADCC experiments. Radiolabeled RBC_{OX} incubated with phosphate-buffered saline (PBS) were used as control (nonsensitized) target cells.

Tumor cells. A human T-cell lymphoblast cell line (CEM, ref. (24)) was radiolabeled by incubation of 10×10^6 cells in 0.3 ml of a Tris–phosphate buffer (25) containing 100 μCi of $Na_2{}^{51}CrO_4$ for 90 min at 37°C with gentle agitation every 15 min. The CEM were subsequently washed twice in complete medium and sensitized by incubation of 2.5×10^6 CEM with 50 μl of varying dilutions of rabbit anti-CEM antisera for 45 min at 37°C with gentle agitation every 15 min. The cells were washed two times in complete medium and adjusted to 2×10^5/ml for use in all ADCC experiments. Radiolabeled CEM incubated with PBS were used as control (nonsensitized) target cells.

Antisera

Rabbit anti-SRBC antiserum (7 S IgG; Cordis Corporation, Miami, Fla.) was used at dilutions of 1:2, 1:8, 1:32, and 1:128 (in PBS) to sensitize the RBC_{OX} targets. RBC_{OX} (instead of SRBC) were used as target cells and sensitized with anti-SRBC antisera to avoid the hemagglutination that occurred from the sensitization of SRBC with homologous antisera [even at dilutions (1:128) which would not mediate ADCC].

Anti-CEM T-lymphoblast antisera was raised in rabbits as previously described (20). The antisera was used undiluted, or at dilutions of 1:8, 1:32 and 1:128 in PBS to sensitize CEM target cells. All antisera were heat inactivated at 56°C for 30 min prior to use for sensitizing the target cells.

Antibody-Dependent Cellular Cytotoxicity (ADCC)

The ability of rabbit monocytes and alveolar macrophages to lyse antibody-sensitized target cells was determined by a 4-hr ^{51}Cr-release assay (20). Briefly, 0.1 ml of the effector cells (at various concentrations as indicated in the text) was mixed with 0.1 ml of the antibody-sensitized RBC_{OX} (2×10^6/ml) or CEM (2×10^5/ml) target cells in 0.3-ml flat-bottom well tissue culture plates (Costar, Cambridge, Mass.). The plates were centrifuged for 3 min at 50*g* to initiate cell–

cell contact. Plates were incubated at 37°C for 4 hr in a humidified atmosphere of 5% CO_2 in air. After 4 hr, 100 μl of supernatant was aspirated from each well to determine the amount of ^{51}Cr released. Percentage cytotoxicity was calculated by the formula

$$\% \text{ ADCC} = (A - B)/(C - B) \times 100,$$

where (A) = mean counts per minute in supernatants from wells (triplicate) containing both effector and target cells; (B) = mean counts per minute in supernatants from wells containing target cells alone (spontaneous release); and (C) = mean counts per minute of the total number of target cells added to each well. Spontaneous release from RBC_{OX} was ≤6% and from CEM targets ranged from 6 to 15%.

Determination of Target Cell Binding

Effector cell binding of RBC_{OX} was determined by modification of the EA (antibody-sensitized erythrocyte) rosette formation assay (26) as previously described (27). To determine the binding of RBC_{OX}, 100 μl of purified effector cells (10×10^6/ml) was mixed with an equal volume of the antibody-sensitized target cells (250×10^6/ml) and sedimented by centrifugation at 100*g* for 3 min. The cell pellet was incubated at an ambient temperature for 15 min and the cells were resuspended in their own supernatant. One drop of cell suspension was mixed with one drop of 0.1% toluidine blue and examined microscopically. Effector cells binding 0, 1–4, or ≥5 sensitized RBC_{OX} were enumerated. Duplicate slides were examined and 200 cells were counted on each slide.

To determine the effector cell binding of sensitized CEM tumor cell targets, 100 μl of purified monocytes or alveolar macrophages (1.0×10^5/ml) was mixed with an equal volume of the antibody-sensitized target cells (2.5×10^6/ml) and sedimented as described above. After incubation for 15 min the cells were resuspended and the cell suspension was stained for the nonspecific esterase to differentiate the effector cells from the CEM T-lymphoblast targets. The cell suspension was examined microscopically and effector cells binding 0, 1–4, or ≥5 sensitized CEM tumor cells were enumerated.

Quantitation of Target Cell-Bound IgG

The amount of antibody (IgG) on the target cell surface was quantitated using ^{125}I-radiolabeled protein A (SPA) from *Staphylococcus aureus* (Cowan I) as previously described (28).

RESULTS

Monocyte and Macrophage ADCC of Erythrocyte Targets

We compared monocyte and macrophage ADCC to RBC_{OX} targets using (a) varying numbers of effector cells, and (b) target cells sensitized with varying dilutions of antisera. As seen in Fig. 1, monocyte ADCC to RBC_{OX} was significantly higher than macrophage ADCC across a wide range of effector cell concentrations ($P < 0.05$ by t test). Increasing the number of monocytes produced increasing

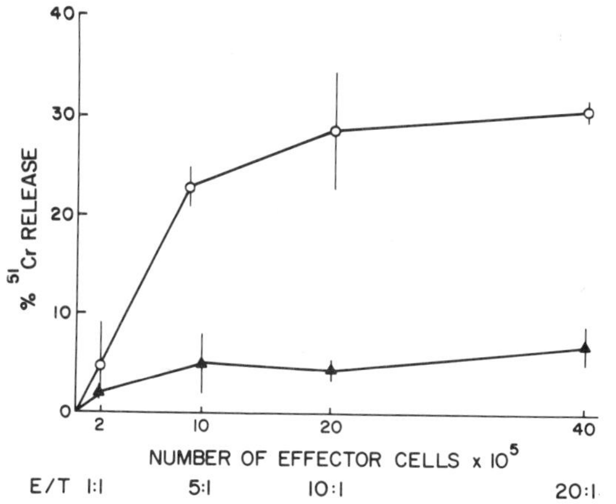

FIG. 1. The effect of varying numbers of monocytes (○) and alveolar macrophages (▲), on ADCC to RBC_{OX} targets. Effector cells were incubated with 2×10^5 RBC_{OX} sensitized with rabbit anti-SRBC antisera diluted 1:2 in PBS. The data are presented as the mean percentage ^{51}Cr release ± SD of triplicate values from at least three experiments. Total cpm/2×10^5 targets was 1800 ± 200; spontaneous release was ≤6%.

ADCC up to an effector cell number that was equivalent to an effector/target cell ratio (E/T) of 10:1. Increasing the number of macrophages, however, failed to elevate the small amount of ADCC against the same target cells.

To examine the effect of varying the amount of antibody on the target cell surface, RBC_{OX} were sensitized with varying dilutions of the rabbit anti-SRBC antisera (1:2 to 1:128) (Fig. 2). These antisera dilutions produced a range of molecules of IgG/target cell of 60,000 to 15,000 as determined by the ^{125}I-SPA assay. Monocyte ADCC exceeded that of the macrophages at all levels of antibody sensitization of the target cells examined. The degree of monocyte ADCC to RBC_{OX}

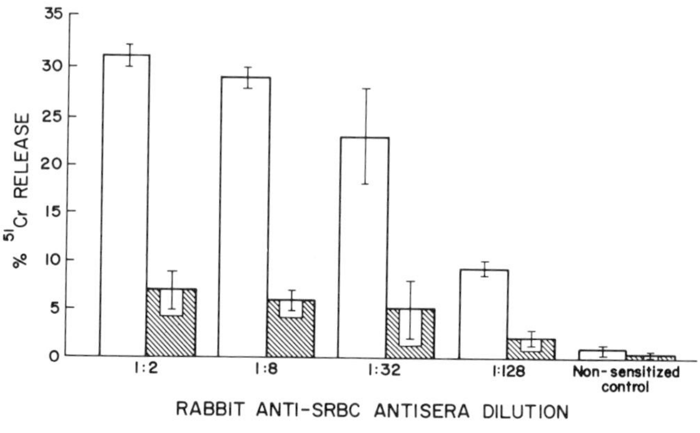

FIG. 2. The effect of varying the degree of target cell sensitization on monocyte (□) and alveolar macrophage (▨) ADCC to RBC_{OX} targets. Effector cells were incubated with 2×10^5 target cells at a 20:1 E/T ratio. The data are presented as the mean percentage ^{51}Cr release ± SD of triplicate values from at least three experiments. Total cpm/2×10^5 targets was 1800 ± 200; spontaneous release was ≤6%.

was dependent upon the degree of antibody sensitization. Neither effector cell produced significant lysis of the nonsensitized target cells at any E/T ratio examined.

Monocyte and Macrophage ADCC of Tumor Cell Targets

In the same experiments, monocytes and macrophages were examined for their ability to carry out ADCC to antibody-sensitized tumor cells. As seen in Fig. 3, increasing numbers of macrophages produced progressively increasing degrees of ADCC while monocytes failed to produce significant ADCC at any of these effector cell numbers. This is in marked contrast to the target cell preferences exhibited for RBC_{OX}, where monocytes were more effective at ADCC. As shown in Fig. 4, using dilutions of sensitizing antisera to yield varying levels of IgG/target cell from 400,000 to 25,000 (by ^{125}I-SPA assay) revealed that the degree of ADCC by macrophages was dependent on the amount of antibody on the target cell surface. Monocytes failed to carry out ADCC at any antibody concentration tested. Nonsensitized tumor cells were not lysed by either effector cell population.

We also examined six other rabbit antisera to these target cells for their ability to mediate ADCC by monocytes and macrophages. As seen in Table 1, monocytes produced little or no ADCC with these antibody-sensitized tumor cells while the macrophages produced varying degrees of ADCC depending on the antisera used.

Monocyte and Macrophage Ability to Bind Antibody-Sensitized Target Cells

In order to determine whether the differences in effector cell ADCC might be related to initial Fc-receptor binding or to a postbinding event, we examined the ability of monocytes and macrophages to bind these antibody-sensitized target cells. Figure 5 illustrates typical rosettes formed between effector cells and antibody-sensitized RBC_{OX} (5a) or tumor cells (5b). As seen in Table 2, monocytes were

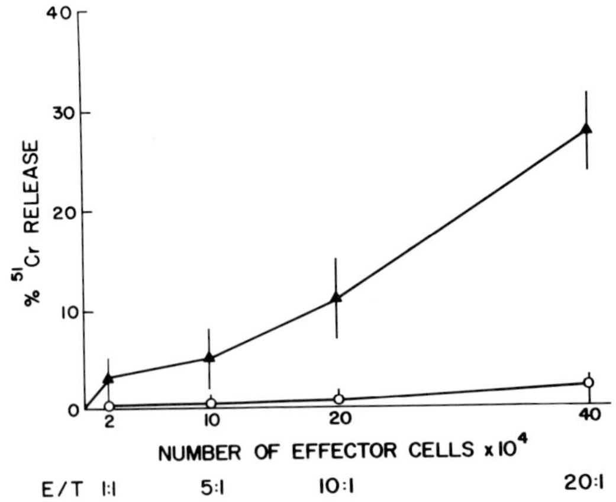

FIG. 3. The effect of varying numbers of monocytes (○) and alveolar macrophages (▲), on ADCC to CEM T-lymphoblast targets. Effector cells were incubated with 2×10^4 CEM sensitized with undiluted anti-CEM antisera. The data are presented as the mean percentage ^{51}Cr release ± SD of triplicate values from at least three experiments. Total cpm/2×10^4 targets was 12,000 ± 2000; spontaneous release ranged from 6 to 15%.

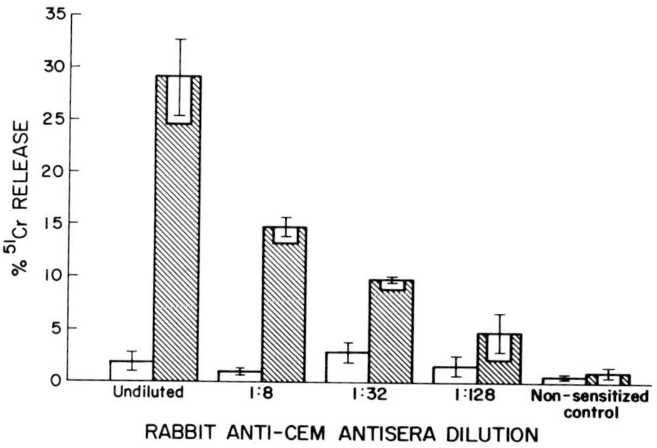

FIG. 4. The effect of varying the degree of target cell sensitization on monocyte (□) and alveolar macrophage (▨) ADCC to CEM T-lymphoblast targets. Effector cells were incubated with 2×10^4 target cells at a 20:1 E/T ratio. Data are presented as a mean percentage ^{51}Cr release ± SD of triplicate values from at least three experiments. Total cpm/2×10^4 targets was 12,000 ± 2000; spontaneous release ranged from 6 to 15%.

able to bind antibody-sensitized RBC_{OX} while over 80% of these cells failed to bind the antibody-sensitized tumor cells. Conversely, few macrophages were able to bind antibody-sensitized RBC_{OX} but a majority were able to bind antibody-sensitized tumor cells. Thus, the differences seen in terms of lysis of target cells correlated well with the ability of the effector cells to recognize and bind the antibody-sensitized targets. In the absence of antibody, little or no target cell binding was seen with either effector cell population.

DISCUSSION

The membrane Fc-receptors of monocytes and macrophages have been shown to be capable of binding soluble immune complexes, aggregated IgG, and antibody-

TABLE 1

Monocyte and Alveolar Macrophage ADCC to CEM Tumor Cells

		Percentage ADCC[a]					
Cell source	E/T[b]	1[c]	2	3	4	5	6
Alveolar macrophage	20:1	9	52	35	27	22	16
	10:1	9	54	24	17	12	9
	5:1	4	37	12	9	6	4
	1:1	0	10	2	2	1	1
Monocyte	20:1	0	7	1	5	6	1
	10:1	0	3	0	3	3	1
	5:1	0	1	0	1	1	1
	1:1	0	0	0	0	0	0

[a] Percentage ADCC = mean percentage ADCC from triplicate samples.
[b] E/T, effector cell:target cell ratio.
[c] 1–6 refer to six different rabbit anti-CEM T-Lymphoblast antisera preparations.

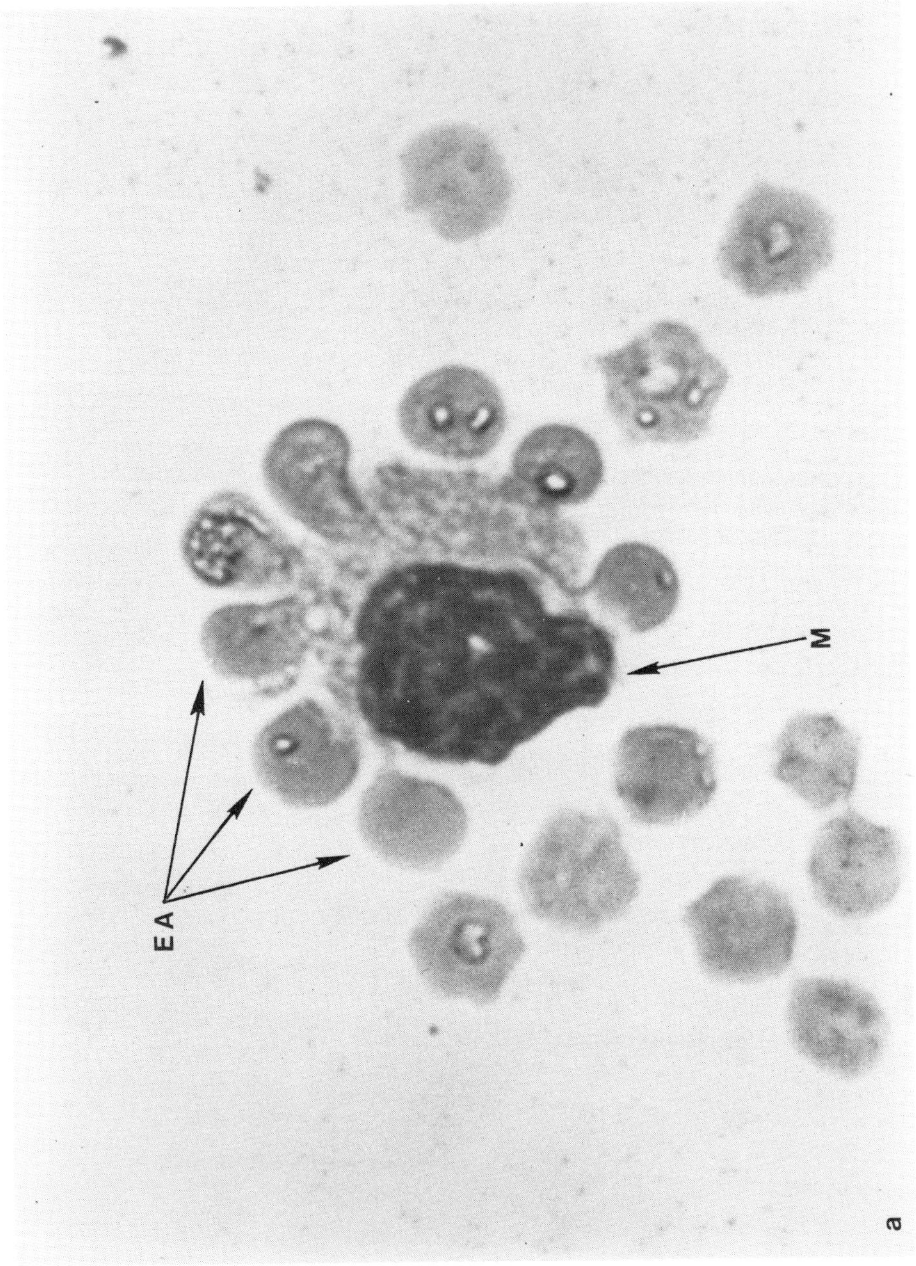
M
EA
a

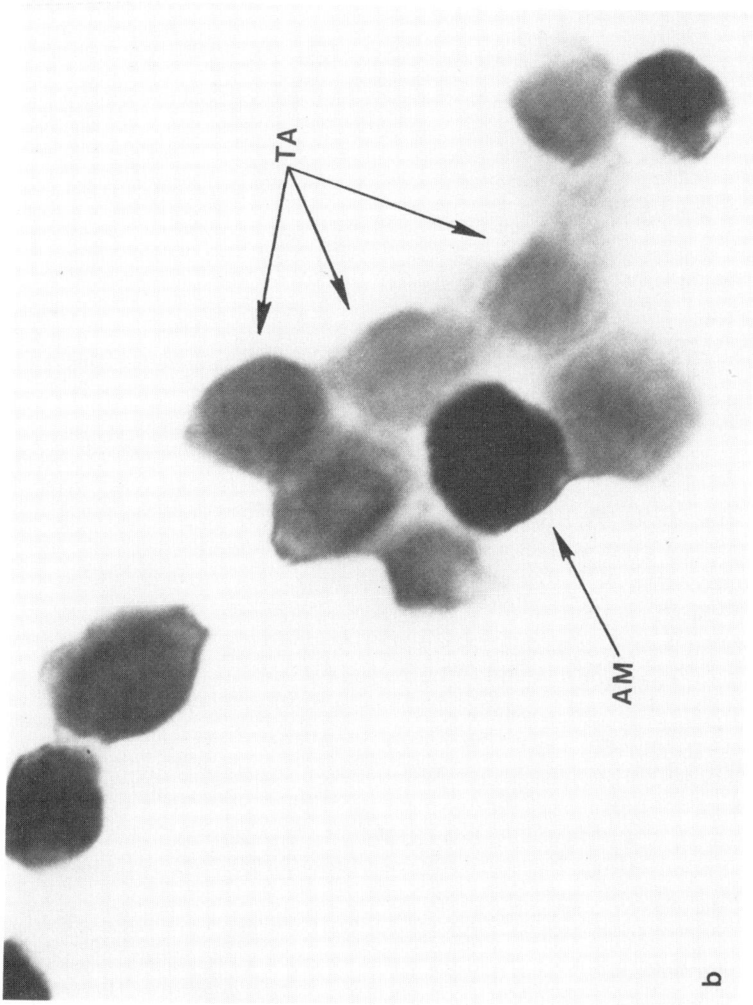

FIG. 5. Monocyte and alveolar macrophage rosette formation with sensitized target cells. (a) A monocyte (M) binding RBC_{OX} (EA) sensitized with a 1:2 dilution of anti-SRBC antisera. (b) An alveolar macrophage (AM) (stained for the nonspecific esterase) binding CEM T lymphoblasts (TA) sensitized with undiluted anti-CEM antisera.

TABLE 2

Target Cell Binding by Rabbit Monocytes and Alveolar Macrophages

Target cell[a]	Percentage monocytes binding varying numbers of target cells[b]		
	0	1–4	≥5
EA	15 ± 3	45 ± 5	40 ± 9
E	96 ± 3	4 ± 2	0 ± 0
TA	83 ± 4	16 ± 4	1 ± 1
T	98 ± 2	2 ± 2	0 ± 0
	Percentage of alveolar macrophages binding varying numbers of target cells		
	0	1–4	≥5
EA	74 ± 5	22 ± 3	4 ± 3
E	97 ± 3	3 ± 3	0 ± 0
TA	6 ± 2	23 ± 3	71 ± 5
T	92 ± 4	7 ± 3	1 ± 1

[a] E indicates control RBC_{OX}; EA indicates RBC_{OX} sensitized with a 1:2 dilution of rabbit anti-SRBC antisera; T indicates control CEM tumor cells; TA indicates CEM tumor cells sensitized with undiluted rabbit anti-CEM antisera.

[b] Percentage expressed as the mean ± 1 SD of ≥three experiments.

coated target cells (6–9). By this Fc-receptor:antibody interaction, these effector cells are also capable of postbinding cytolysis of sensitized target cells in ADCC (10–16). The expression of Fc-receptor activity may vary with different cell populations. For example, Rhodes (29) has presented evidence that guinea pig peritoneal macrophage subpopulations may vary in avidity of their Fc-receptor for immune complexes. Hunninghake and Fauci (18) attempted to compare the ADCC capacity of guinea pig alveolar, spleen, and blood mononuclear phagocytes toward sensitized chicken red blood cells and Chang liver cells. They noted that alveolar macrophages had a cytotoxic capacity against antibody-coated chicken red blood cells greater than that of blood monocytes or splenic macrophages. They were unable to demonstrate significant ADCC to tumor cells by any of these monocyte–macrophage cell populations. No studies were done to examine Fc-receptor binding of the target cell preparations.

In this study, we were interested in comparing the ability of rabbit blood monocytes and alveolar macrophages from the same animal with regard to their ability to bind and lyse two different target cells coated with rabbit antibody. In this way, we hoped to gain some insight into potential changes in Fc-receptor-mediated cell functions during the transition from monocytes to tissues macrophages. The results were surprising in that RBC_{OX} coated with adequate rabbit IgG to mediate strong monocyte binding and subsequent target cell lysis were not readily recognized or lysed by alveolar macrophages. Conversely, CEM tumor cells heavily sensitized by rabbit IgG were bound and lysed by alveolar macrophages while serving as poor target cells for binding and lysis by blood monocytes. Clearly, the criteria used by these two cell populations for membrane Fc-receptor interaction with antibody displayed on a target cell surface had undergone significant modification in the maturation process from monocyte to tissue macrophage. Recent studies in our laboratory suggest, however, that monocyte Fc-receptor interaction with antibody-coated tumor cells can occur following *in vivo* activation of monocytes with mycobacteria and their active adjuvant component muramyl dipeptide (38–40).

There have been other examples of effector cells which differ in their criteria for membrane Fc-receptor interaction with antibody displayed on target cell surfaces. Human Fc-receptor-positive lymphocytes (K cells) and monocytes appear to have membrane Fc-receptors with similar specificities for the IgG_1 and IgG_3 subclasses of immunoglobulin (30–33). However, these lymphocytes are unable to bind and lyse human red cells coated with certain human antisera (anti-D) while monocytes from the same donor bind and lyse these target cells well (34). Alteration of the distribution of antibody on these red cells (clustering) allows lymphocytes to bind and lyse red cell targets when sensitized with the same anti-D antisera (28, 34). These studies suggest that antibody distribution represents a criteria for lymphocyte Fc-receptor interaction with at least some types of antibody-sensitized target cells not shared by the monocyte. In addition, binding of soluble IgG oligomers appears to be similar by human granulocytes, lymphocytes, and monocytes (35). Despite this, ADCC of CEM tumor cells by Fc-receptor-positive human granulocytes has been found to require 100 times the concentration of rabbit antibody on the tumor cell surface than required for either lymphocyte or monocyte ADCC (36). Differences in ability to recognize and lyse antibody-coated target cells by the same cell populations from different species have been reported (37). We have also reported that human monocytes are quite effective at recognition and lysis of the same rabbit antibody-coated CEM target cells (20) that failed to elicit ADCC by rabbit monocytes in this study. Thus, it would appear that different effector cell populations or similar populations of effector cells from different species differ in their criteria for interaction with IgG displayed on target cell surfaces.

The current study extends these observations by indicating that criteria for Fc-receptor interaction with antibody-sensitized target cells can differ dramatically at different stages of differentiation in the monocyte/macrophage cell lineage. These differences may be related to alteration in Fc-receptor requirements for antibody density, distribution, subclass, or other as yet undetermined factors which alter the Fc-receptor interaction with the Fc portion of IgG displayed on cell surfaces. Further, this study indicates that the variation seen in the sensitivity of certain target cells to ADCC by unique effector cell populations can be explained at least in part by variation in Fc-receptor binding of target cells rather than postbinding events.

ACKNOWLEDGMENTS

The authors wish to thank Ms. Maxine Solvay and Ms. Pam Graham for their technical assistance, and Ms. Helen Ilc and Ms. Jerrie CeBulkey for their assistance in the preparation of this manuscript for publication.

REFERENCES

1. van Furth, R., and Cohn, Z. A., *J. Exp. Med.* **128,** 415, 1968.
2. van Furth, R., Raeburn, J. A., and van Zwet, T. C., *Blood* **54,** 485, 1979.

3. Huber, H., Polley, M. J., Lensott, W. D., Fudenberg, H. H., and Müller-Eberhard, H. J., *Science* **162,** 1281, 1968.
4. Lay, W. H., and Nussenzweig, V., *J. Exp. Med.* **128,** 991, 1968.
5. Howard, J. G., and Benacerraf, B., *Brit. J. Exp. Pathol.* **47,** 193, 1966.
6. LoBuglio, A. F., Cotran, R. S., and Jandl, J. H., *Science* **158,** 1582, 1967.
7. Arend, W. P., and Mannik, M., *J. Exp. Med.* **136,** 514, 1972.
8. Arend, W. P., and Mannik, M., *J. Immunol.* **110,** 1455, 1973.
9. Daughaday, C. C., and Douglas, S. D., *J. Reticuloendothel. Soc.* **19,** 37, 1976.
10. Holm, G., *Int. Arch. Allergy* **43,** 671, 1972.
11. Walker, W. S., and Demus, A., *J. Immunol.* **114,** 765, 1975.
12. Shaw, G. M., Levy, P. C., and LoBuglio, A. F., *Blood* **50,** 177, 1977.
13. Shaw, G. M., Levy, P. C., and LoBuglio, A. F., *Cell. Immunol.* **41,** 122, 1978.
14. MacLennan, I. C. M., *In* "Clinical Tumor Immunology" (J. Wybran and M. J. Staquet, Eds.), p. 47. Pergamon, Oxford, 1976.
15. Perlman, P., *In* "Clinical Immunobiology" (F. H. Bach and R. A. Good, Eds.), Vol. 3, p. 107. Academic Press, New York, 1976.
16. Henney, C. S., *In* "Mechanisms of Tumor Immunity (S. Cohen and R. T. McCluskey, Eds.), p. 55. Wiley, New York, 1977.
17. Shaw, G. M., Levy, P. C., and LoBuglio, A. F., *J. Immunol.* **121,** 573, 1978.
18. Hunninghake, G. W., and Fauci, A. S., *Cell. Immunol.* **26,** 98, 1976.
19. Bøyum, A., *Scand. J. Immunol.* **5,** 9, 1976.
20. Shaw, G. M., Levy, P. C., and LoBuglio, A. F., *J. Clin. Invest.* **62,** 1172, 1978.
21. Webb, L. S., Keble, B. B., Jr., and Johnson, R. B., Jr., *Infect. Immunity* **9,** 1051, 1974.
22. Tucker, S. B., Pierre, R. V., and Jordan, R. E., *J. Immunol. Methods* **14,** 267, 1977.
23. Myrvik, Q. N., Leake, E. S., and Fariss, B., *J. Immunol.* **86,** 128, 1961.
24. Foley, G. E., Lazarus, H., Farber, S., *et al.*, *Cancer* **18,** 522, 1965.
25. Brunner, K. T., Engers, H. D., and Cerottini, J. C., *In* "*In Vitro* Methods in Cell-Mediated and Tumor Immunity" (B. R. Bloom and J. R. David, Eds.), p. 423. Academic Press, New York, 1976.
26. Frøland, S. S., and Wisløff, F., *In* "*In Vitro* Methods in Cell-Mediated and Tumor Immunity" (B. R. Bloom and J. R. David, Eds.), p. 137. Academic Press, New York, 1976.
27. Shaw, G. M., Levy, P. C., and LoBuglio, A. F., *Clin. Exp. Immunol.* **36,** 496, 1979.
28. Shaw, G. M., Aminoff, D., Balcerzak, S. P., and LoBuglio, A. F., *J. Immunol.* **125,** 501, 1980.
29. Rhodes, J., *J. Immunol.* **114,** 976, 1975.
30. Wisløff, F., Michaelsen, T. E., and Frøland, S. S., *Scand. J. Immunol.* **3,** 29, 1974.
31. Holm, G., Engwall, E., Hammarström, S., and Natvig, J. B., *Scand. J. Immunol.* **3,** 173, 1974.
32. Urbaniak, S. J., *Brit. J. Hematol.* **42,** 315, 1979.
33. Walker, W. S., *J. Immunol.* **119,** 367, 1977.
34. Shaw, G. M., Levy, P. C., and LoBuglio, A. F., *Blood* **52,** 696, 1978.
35. Alexander, E. L., Titus, J. A., and Segal, D. M., *J. Immunol.* **123,** 295, 1979.
36. Levy, P. C., Shaw, G. M., and LoBuglio, A. F., *J. Immunol.* **123,** 594, 1979.
37. Zighelboim, J., and Gale, R. P., *J. Immunol.* **113,** 1145, 1974.
38. Garagiola, D. M., Huard, T. K., and LoBuglio, A. F., *Fed. Proc.* **39,** 933, 1980.
39. Garagiola, D. M., LoBuglio, A. F., and Huard, T. K., *Clin. Res.* **28,** 733A, 1980.
40. Huard, T. K., Garagiola, D. M., and LoBuglio, A. F., *Clin. Res.* **29,** 369A, 1981.

CELLULAR IMMUNOLOGY **64**, 371–380 (1981)

Culture-Generated Suppressor Cells: Evidence for an Adherent Cell Component[1]

FLORENCE M. ROLLWAGEN[2] AND OSIAS STUTMAN[3]

Cellular Immunobiology Section, Memorial Sloan–Kettering Cancer Center, New York, New York 10021

Received February 18, 1981; accepted August 19, 1981

Cells which suppress mixed lymphocyte reaction (MLR) and cytotoxic T-lymphocyte (CTL) generation can be demonstrated after culture for 3 to 5 days in the absence of added antigen. Such precultured suppressors are resistant to the cytotoxic effects of commercial rabbit anti-mouse brain serum, congenic anti-Thy-1.2 serum, and monoclonal anti-Thy-1.2 reagent. In addition, these cells, which adhere to both nylon wool and Sephadex G-10, ingest carbonyl iron. These properties suggest that precultured suppressors may not be thymus-processed. Precultured suppressor cells, when irradiated, are able to suppress only the MLR, and not the generation of allo-CTL. This finding, taken with our previously published work on the differential ontogeny of cells which suppress the MLR or CTL generation in culture, suggests that at least two kinds of suppressors are generated. One suppressor acts on CTL generation, is radiosensitive, and develops late in ontogeny; the other suppressor acts on proliferative cells in the MLR, is radioresistant, and develops early in ontogeny. Both kinds of suppressors, however, are adherent to nylon wool and Sephadex G-10, ingest carbonyl iron, and are resistant to anti-T-cell sera.

INTRODUCTION

It has been shown in several laboratories that culture of mouse spleen cells without added antigen permits the detection of cells which can suppress T-cell functions. Such suppressive effects have been described for antibody responses to T-dependent (1–3) as well as T-independent antigens (1, 3) using mixed lymphocyte reactions (MLR)[4] and cell-mediated lympholysis (CML) assays (2, 4–8) or proliferative responses to mitogens (7, 8). These suppressor cells have been described as Thy-1^+, using a variety of anti-T-cell sera (1, 3, 4, 7, 9) and Lyt-1^+, 2, 3^- Ia^-, using highly specific antisera to those surface antigens (1). None of these studies

[1] This work was supported by Grants CA-08748 and 17818 from the National Cancer Institute, U. S. Department of Health and Human Services.

[2] Present address: Laboratory of Microbial Immunity, National Institute of Allergy and Infectious Diseases, National Institutes of Health, Bethesda, Md. 20205.

[3] To whom correspondence and requests for reprints should be addressed.

[4] Abbreviations used: MLR/MLC, mixed lymphocyte reaction/culture; CML/CTL, cell-mediated lympholysis/cytotoxic T lymphocyte; RAMB, rabbit anti-mouse brain; CM/TM/LM, culture/test/lysis medium; B6, C57BL/6; D2, DBA/2; HBSS + FCS, Hanks' balanced salt solution + 5% fetal calf serum; P, precultured; CFe, carbonyl iron; Mls, minor lymphocyte stimulating.

0008-8749/81/160371-10$02.00/0

has used monoclonal anti-T-cell reagents (1–9). Although there is no formal proof, it is assumed that one type of suppressor cell is generated nonspecifically in culture and is the same in all of these assay systems (1–8).

Hodes and Hathcock (4) as well as Nadler and Hodes (5) have done extensive work on characterizing culture-generated suppressor cells. Using MLR and CML assay systems, they found a precultured suppressor cell which is adherent to nylon wool and sensitive to rabbit anti-mouse brain (RAMB) serum. However, since this xenogeneic serum has been reported to react with antigens other than Thy-1 (10, 11), the results obtained do not necessarily prove that precultured suppressor cells are of thymic origin.

In the present work, highly specific, congenic, or hybridoma-derived anti-Thy-1 sera were used to examine the characteristics of culture-generated suppressor cells in more detail. The results reported here and elsewhere (12, 13) indicate that different subpopulations of cells may be involved in mediating the suppressive effects observed on the expression of MLR and CML activity by the precultured (P) cells, and that such culture-generated suppressors may not express T-cell markers.

MATERIALS AND METHODS

Mice. C57BL/6J (B6) and DBA/2J (D2) mice were obtained from the Jackson Laboratory, Bar Harbor, Maine, maintained on standard laboratory chow and water *ad libitum*, and used at approximately 2 to 6 months of age.

Cell cultures. Cells were cultured in complete medium (CM) consisting of Eagle's complete minimum essential medium (MEM) supplemented with 15% fetal calf serum (FCS), 100 U/ml penicillin, 100 mg/ml streptomycin, 1% MEM nonessential amino acids mix, and 2 m*M* L-glutamine. All media and sera were obtained from Grand Island Biological Company Grand Island, New York. Batches of sera were screened for both high plating efficiency and low background mitogenicity for mouse lymphocytes. Tumor cell lines were passed three times weekly and were diluted (1:1) the day before use in the ^{51}Cr-release assay. The following cell lines, which were obtained from Drs. P. Ralph and J. Tung of the Sloan–Kettering Institute, were used: EL-4, a B6 benzpyrene-induced T-cell leukemia; P815, a methylcholanthrene-induced D2 mastocytoma; and SL-8, a spontaneous T-cell lymphoma of AKR origin.

Preparation of P cells. P cells were prepared by a modification (12, 13) of the method of Hodes and Hathcock (4). B6 spleen cells were pressed gently through a sterile 60-mesh screen into warm Hanks' balanced salt solution + 5% heat-inactivated FCS (HBSS + FCS); clumps were dispersed by passage through a 26-gauge needle. The cells were centrifuged (200*g* for 10 min) at room temperature and the pellet was resuspended in 1 ml HBSS + FCS and then treated for 15 sec with 8 ml Tris–NH_4Cl lysis medium (LM) consisting of 1 part 2.1% Tris + 9 parts 0.8% NH_4Cl. The added LM was diluted 10-fold with HBSS + FCS, the cells were centrifuged again and adjusted to 2×10^6/ml in test medium (TM),[5] and the medium was supplemented with 2-mercaptoethanol to a final concentration of 5

[5] Composition same as CM except that 10% heat-inactivated FCS was substituted for 15% FCS.

$\times 10^{-5}$ *M* and plated in 160-mm diameter petri dishes (35–40 ml/plate). Four days later, the nonadherent and loosely adherent cell populations were harvested by gentle pipetting and are referred to as P cells.

MLC. The MLC test was performed in Falcon 3040 microtiter plates (Falcon Labware, Division of Becton–Dickenson, Co., Oxnard, Calif.) in a total volume of 0.2 ml, according to the method of Peck and Bach (14). A constant number (2×10^5) of irradiated D2 (allogeneic) or B6 (syngeneic) spleen cells was incubated with varying numbers of either normal or P cells, or a mixture of the two, as responders. After 5 days of incubation, (37°C, 5% CO_2 in air), 0.2 μCi of [^{3}H]thymidine (New England Nuclear, Boston, Mass.) was added (sp act 2 Ci/mmol). Eight hours later, the cells were harvested on glass filter paper disks (Reeve Angel, Whatman, Inc., Clifton, N.J.) using a Skatron harvester. The disks were dried overnight, and counted in a Packard scintillation counter, using POPOP as fluor.

Generation of cytotoxic lymphocytes. Generation of CTL was carried out in a total volume of 6 ml TM using a modification of the method of Burton *et al.* (15). Twelve million irradiated D2 spleen cells were incubated in 17 × 100-mm test tubes with an equal number of B6 spleen cells plus P cells at a 1:10 or 1:2 ratio. The tubes were incubated for 5 days, after which the desired number of viable cells was used in the ^{51}Cr-release assay.

^{51}Cr-release assay of CTL estimation. The ^{51}Cr-release assay was performed according to a modification of the method of Brunner *et al.* (16). Nonadherent target cells were incubated for 30 min at 37°C with 100 μCi of ^{51}Cr (as $Na^{51}CrO_4$) (New England Nuclear). Radioactively labeled targets (2×10^3) were plated in 50 μl in wells of Cooke round-bottom microtiter plates (Cooke Engineering Co., Alexandria, Va.). Effector cells at the appropriate concentration and ratio were added in 100 μl TM. After 4 hr of incubation at 37°C, the plates were centrifuged at 200*g* for 10 min and 100 μl supernatant was removed and counted in a Beckman well-type gamma counter. Spontaneous release of isotype was measured by incubating the labeled target cells in 100 μl of medium alone. Maximum release was determined by freezing and thawing target cells three times in 100 μl medium. Percentage cytotoxicity was calculated by the formula

$$\% C = \frac{\text{cpm exp} - \text{cpm spont}}{\text{cpm max} - \text{cpm spont}} \times 100.$$

Antisera. Congenic anti-Thy-1.2 serum was the kind gift of Dr. F.-W. Shen. It was prepared by the method of Scheid *et al.* (17) in which (A/Thy-1.1 × AKR/H-2^b)F_1 mice were immunized with the A strain spontaneous leukemia cell line ASL.1. For mass cytolysis, the antiserum was used at 1:50 dilution which is fourfold greater than that required for 100% lysis of a comparable number of thymocytes. Noncytotoxic rabbit complement was used at a 1:13 dilution.

Monoclonal anti-Thy-1.2 was kindly provided by Dr. U. Hammerling. This reagent was produced by fusing the MOPC-21 myeloma cell line X-63-Ag-8 with (A/Thy-1.1 × AKR/H-2^b)F_1 anti-ASL.1 IgM producing cells, according to the method of Kohler and Milstein (18). Dr. Hammerling has titered this reagent on BALB/c thymocytes to a 50% endpoint of 1:1,000,000. It was used at 1:50 as described above. We believe that prozone effects due to the high concentration of antibody were avoided since effectiveness controls were performed and reduced the counts per minute of 2 × 10^5 spleen cells in the MLR from 60,000 to 1600 cpm, as shown in footnote *b* to Table 1.

Rabbit anti-BALB/c mouse brain was obtained from Litton Bionetics, Kensington, Maryland. This antiserum was produced according to the method of Golub (19), as modified by Hodes *et al.* (20). It was heat-inactivated at 56°C for 30 min, and adsorbed with mouse red blood cells, which inactivates complement proteins in the serum and removes nonspecific cytolytic antibody. It has been shown that this immunization method produces an antiserum which has specificity for thymocytes as well as for other determinants found in brain tissue (10, 11). For mass cytolysis, the antiserum was used at a 1:40 dilution. Guinea pig complement was supplied by Litton to be used with the antiserum; it was used at a 1:4 dilution, as described by Hodes and Hathcock (4).

Cells to be treated with antibody and complement were centrifuged at 200*g* for 10 min and brought up in 1 ml of diluted antibody, as described by Shen *et al.* (21). Cells were incubated (4°C) with diluted antibody for 30 min, washed once, and resuspended in 1 ml diluted complement. The cell suspension was incubated at 37°C for 45 min after which the cells were washed three times and adjusted to the desired concentration before addition to normal cells.

Cell separation procedures. Nylon wool (Leukopac) was soaked in 0.9% NaCl for 2 hr at 37°C. The soaked fibers were washed for 2 days in double-distilled water, which was changed three times daily, and dried overnight at 37°C. The nylon wool (1.2 g) was packed into 12 ml of a 20-ml plastic syringe, and the entire package was autoclaved. The column was saturated with HBSS + FCS and allowed to equilibrate for 1 hr at 37°C before use. The medium was allowed to flow out to the top of the nylon wool; then 2 × 10^8 cells in 1 ml were layered on the top of column and washed in with 2 ml warm HBSS + FCS. The column was incubated for 45 min at 37°C in 5% CO_2 in air. Nonadherent cells were collected by elution with warm HBSS + FCS. Adherent cells were obtained by transferring the nylon wool to a petri dish containing HBSS + FCS and teasing the fibers apart with sterile forceps, winding the nylon wool around the forceps to expel the fluid. The collected cells were centrifuged at 200*g* for 10 min. Approximately 30 to 40% of the original population was recovered in the nylon-column-adherent and -nonadherent fractions.

Sephadex G-10 beads were swollen in normal saline, and the slurry was sterilized by autoclaving at 100°C for 40 min. The slurry was poured into a sterile 5-ml syringe until the beads reached the 4-ml mark. The beads were washed with 10 ml HBSS + FCS and 5 × 10^6 cells were layered on and then washed through the column by gravity with the addition of another 10 ml HBSS + FCS. Nonadherent cells were collected in a sterile test tube; the adherent cells remained on the column. Approximately 35% of the original cells were recovered in the nonadherent fraction.

Carbonyl iron (CFe) (GAF Corp., New York) was incubated with HBSS + 10% FCS (200 mg/10 ml) for 60 min at 37°C, according to the method of Sanderson *et al.* (22). The cells were allowed to phagocytose the CFe by incubating 5 × 10^7 cells with 100 mg CFe in 1 ml TM for 30 min at 37°C. Cells which had phagocytosed the CFe were removed from the suspension by holding a magnet at the bottom of the tube and decanting the supernatant. The nonphagocytic cells were decanted twice. About 75% of the original population of P cells treated with CFe was recovered in the nonphagocytic population.

RESULTS

Effects of Treatment of P Cells with Antisera Specific for T Cells

The proliferative and cytotoxic responses of normal cells, as well as the modification of these responses by untreated P cells (P_{untr}) or antibody and complement-treated P cells (P_{Ab+C}), are summarized in Table 1. Experiment 1 of Table 1 shows that untreated P cells suppressed the proliferative response of normal cells by about 60% (60,618 vs 24,830 cpm). Treatment of P cells with congenic anti-Thy-1.2 serum + C did not abrogate their ability to suppress this response (60,618 vs 19,221 cpm). The capacity of normal cells to generate alloreactive cytotoxic cells was similarly suppressed by P_{untr} or P_{Ab+C} cells (98% cytotoxicity vs 26 and 36% cytotoxicity at an effector:target of 10:1), respectively. Experiments 2 and 3 of Table 1 also show that neither monoclonal anti-Thy-1.2 nor commercial RAMB serum eliminated the suppressive activity of P cells. Indeed, P cells treated with the latter antiserum appeared to be even more suppressive; this could be attributed to the enrichment of suppressors as a result of the elimination of other cells lysed by treatment with Ab + C. Once again, it should be noted that treatment with Ab

TABLE 1

Effect of Various Anti-T-Cell Sera upon the Ability of Precultured Cells to Suppress Proliferation in the MLR

Expt	Cells tested[a]	Source of antibody[b]	[^{3}H]Thymidine uptake[c] Syn	Allo	Percentage cytotoxicity[d] 10:1	5:1 (Effector:target)	1:1
1	Normal B6	—	2170	60,618	98	77	65
	P_{untr} + B6	—	4933	24,830	26	13	9
	P_{Ab+C} + B6	Congenic	5642	19,221	36	21	14
2	Normal B6	—	395	42,178	88	78	56
	P_{untr} + B6	—	2743	27,730	62	43	24
	P_{Ab+C} + B6	Hybridoma	3967	15,292	58	39	21
3	Normal B6	—	678	45,453	98	78	56
	P_{untr} + B6	—	2973	17,966	35	21	11
	P_{Ab+C} + B6	RAMB	2689	2,766	18	12	6

[a] *Proliferation assay*. Normal B6 spleen cells (2×10^5/well) were incubated with an equal number of irradiated B6 spleen cells (Syn) or D2 spleen cells (Allo). Precultured cells, either untreated (P_{untr}) or treated with anti-T-cell serum + C (P_{Ab+C}) were added at a ratio of 1:2 to normal B6 cells (1×10^5 P + 2×10^5 B6). *Cytotoxicity assay*: 12×10^6 normal B6 cells incubated for 5 days with 12×10^6 irradiated D2 cells, then assayed in a 4-hr ^{51}Cr-release assay against P815. Precultured cells, either untreated or treated with anti-T-cell serum and complement, were added at a ratio of 1:2 (6×10^6) to normal B6 cells and irradiated D2 cells at the beginning of the sensitization period.

[b] In all experiments, anti-T-cell serum and complement abrogated the proliferative response of 2×10^5 normal B6 cells to 2×10^4 irradiated D2 cells (Expt 1: 1572 cpm; Expt 2: 7760 cpm; Expt 3: 40 cpm). Complement alone affected neither the precultured cells' ability to suppress nor the normal cells' ability to proliferate or to generate CTL (data not shown).

[c] Eight-hour pulse of [^{3}H]thymidine (2 Ci/mmol). Counts represent mean of six replicates per experiment. SEM <10% for all groups.

[d] Four-hour ^{51}Cr-release assay against P815. SEM (n = 4) <5% for all groups.

+ C completely eliminated the ability of normal cells to proliferate in the MLR, whereas treatment with complement alone was without effect. In addition, treatment with monoclonal anti-Thy-1.2 completely eliminated the cytotoxicity of *in vitro*-generated CTL; treatment of P cells with anti-Lyt-1.2 or Lyt-2.2 + C also did not eliminate the observed suppression (data not shown).

These findings attest to the fact that the antisera employed, though not effective in eliminating the suppression induced by P cells, were able to remove the activity of T cells involved in the expression of MLR and CTL reactions.

Adherence Properties of P Cells

The data of Table 2 (Experiment 1) show the MLR and allo-CTL expressed by normal cells, as well as P unseparated cells (P_{unsep}), nylon-adherent (P_{adh}), and

TABLE 2

Adherence Properties of Cells Which Suppress Proliferation and the Generation of Allo-CTL

Expt	Line	Method of separation	Cells tested[a]	[^{3}H]Thymidine uptake[b] Syn	Allo	Percentage Cytotoxicity[c] 10:1	5:1	1:1
						(Effector:target)		
1	1	Nylon wool	Normal B6	705	42,017	100	90	65
	2		Precultured B6	2139	8,447	8	5	2
	3		P_{nonadh}[a]	3287	67,765	95	87	50
	4		P_{adh}	1762	3,359	ND[d]	ND	ND
	5		P_{unsep} + B6	4377	26,484	60	55	18
	6		P_{nonadh} + B6	7515	60,612	95	80	40
	7		P_{adh} + B6	3556	10,459	10	8	2
2	8	Sephadex G-10	Normal B6	798	18,662	100	65	40
	9		Precultured B6	ND	ND	10	8	5
	10		P_{nonadh}	800	23,913	ND	ND	ND
	11		P_{unsep} + B6	2576	5,614	42	21	9
	12		P_{nonadh} + B6	3567	24,650	85	65	43
3	13	CFe + magnet	Normal B6	706	27,586	79	57	38
	14		Precultured B6	1900	3,637	ND	ND	ND
	15		P_{CFe}	3162	32,752	64	46	37
	16		P_{unsep} + B6	2127	8,781	42	23	14
	17		P_{CFe} + B6	4245	44,020	93	80	49

[a] Normal B6 spleen cells (2×10^5/well) were incubated with an equal number of irradiated B6 spleen cells (Syn) or D2 spleen cells (Allo). Precultured cells, either unseparated (P_{unsep}) or treated with various separation procedures (nylon wool, Sephadex G-10, or carbonyl iron [CFe] + magnet) were added at a ratio of 1:2 to normal B6 cells. In the case of nylon wool separation, both nonadherent (P_{nonadh}) and adherent (P_{adh}) were tested. Only the nonadherent fraction could be tested after Sephadex G-10 separation or carbonyl iron fractionation.

[b] Eight-hour pulse of [^{3}H]thymidine (2 Ci/mmol). Counts represent mean of six replicates per experiment. SEM <10% for all groups.

[c] Percentage cytotoxicity calculated as under *Materials and Methods* for effector:target ratios ranging from 1:1 through 10:1. Results of a 4-hr ^{51}Cr-release assay against P815 are shown. SEM (n = 4) <5%.

[d] Not determined.

nylon-nonadherent (P_{nonadh}) P cells. Note that nylon-nonadherent P cells were just as reactive (or more so) in the MLR as normal cells (compare lines 1 and 3). Any increase in the response of nylon-nonadherent P cells above that of normal cells is probably due to enrichment. When unfractionated P cells were mixed with normal fresh responders, the suppressive effect (line 5) was demonstrable once more for both proliferation and the generation of allo-CTL. The nylon-nonadherent fraction was not suppressive when mixed with normal cells (line 6). The nylon-wool-adherent subpopulation of P cells, however, was not only nonreactive (line 4) but highly suppressive for both MLC and CML (line 7); in fact, the suppressive activity was greater than that of the unseparated population. This experiment clearly shows that the proliferative reactivity of T cells is not lost during the preculture phase; rather, it is masked by the generation of suppressor cells, a finding which is in agreement with the work of Hodes and Hathcock (4). Since it can be seen from the nylon column experiments that nonadherent P cells are themselves capable of reacting in the MLC, it follows that the unseparated population must consist of a mixture of suppressor cells and some other potentially reactive cell population. Thus, when the anti-Thy-1.2 serum eliminated the responsive potential of these "nylon-nonadherent" P cells, the resulting population consisted only of suppressors. This could explain the increased suppression observed after treatment with various anti-T-cell sera (Table 1). Nylon-nonadherent P cells were also nonsuppressive in the generation of allo-CTL (line 6).

Since it was apparent that the suppressive effects of P cells were resistance to anti-T-cell sera and adherence to nylon, we investigated other non-T-cell properties of the precultured population. Cells which had been precultured and then passed over a column of Sephadex G-10 beads were depleted of suppressive activity and restored to normal proliferative capacity (line 10). The data in Table 2, Experiment 2, show that cells which suppress the MLR and the generation of allo-CTL are adherent to Sephadex G-10 since the suppressive activity (line 11) is removed after G-10 passage (line 12). Furthermore, the column-passed cells were restored to full proliferative capacity (line 10). The data of Table 2, Experiment 3, show that the removal of phagocytic cells from the precultured population by means of CFe also restored their ability to proliferate in response to alloantigen (compare lines 13 and 15). P cells treated with CFe and magnet were also ineffective in suppressing the proliferative response of normal cells (compare line 16 with line 17). Similar results were found in the cytotoxicity assay where the CFe and magnet treatment of the P population completely removed the suppressive effect of these cells and almost restored the reactivity of the P population. All of the above findings show that suppressor cells generated in culture may be removed by procedures which remove adherent cells. Although it was not possible to test the Sephadex G-10-adherent cells (as in the nylon column adherence tests) it may be assumed that the Sephadex G-10-adherent cells are also suppressive. In addition, suppressor cells also belong to the subpopulation which ingests CFe (i.e., are phagocytic).

Effect of Radiation of P Cells

It is accepted that lymphoid cells are sensitive to radiation *in vivo* or *in vitro*, whereas macrophages are resistant (23, 24). P cells which were irradiated with 1000 rad (600 rad/min) *in vitro* after the preculture period, and then added directly

TABLE 3

Effect of Radiation upon the Ability of Precultured Cells to Suppress T-Cell Responses

Line	Cells tested[a]	[^{3}H]Thymidine uptake[b] Syn	Allo	Percentage Cytotoxicity[c] 10:1	5:1 (Effector:target)	1:1
1	Normal B6	767	16,076	95	62	18
2	P_{untr} + B6	1496	1,969	14	9	5
3	P_{irr} + B6	1306	5,114	65	48	17
4	Normal $B6_{irr}$	62	49	ND[d]	ND	ND

[a] Precultured cells, either untreated (P_{untr}) or irradiated with 1000 rad (P_{irr}), were added at a ratio of 1:2 to normal B6. Line 4: normal B6 irradiated with 1000 rad as an effectiveness control.

[b] See Table 1, footnote *a*, for details of method. Eight-hour pulse of [^{3}H]thymidine. Counts represent mean of six replicated per experiment. SEM <10% for all groups.

[c] See Table 1, footnote *a*, for details of experiment. Four-hour ^{51}Cr-release assay against P815. SEM (n = 4) <5% for all groups.

[d] Not done.

to MLC and sensitization cultures, were able to suppress the MLC but were unable to suppress the generation of cytotoxicity (Table 3). A dose of 1000 rad completely eliminates proliferation of normal cells in the MLC (line 4); irradiated P cells (lines 3) were just as suppressive as the untreated P cells in the MLC. These data suggest that the suppression seen in the MLC is not due to the nonspecific effects of blasts in the culture.

When irradiated P cells were tested for their effects on the generation of cytotoxicity, however, a different result was found (Table 3); irradiation almost completely abrogated the suppressive effects of P cells on the generation of cytotoxicity. These data suggest that there may be two populations of suppressors generated by *in vitro* culture: one which suppresses MLC reactivity, and another which suppresses the generation of cytotoxic cells directed toward alloantigens.

DISCUSSION

The results presented here are at variance with the majority of published work concerning the cellular nature of P cells. In almost all reported studies, the suppressive activity of P cells was shown to be sensitive to treatment with various anti-T-cell sera (1, 3, 4, 7, 9). Although this suggests that such suppressors are thymus-processed, it is known that the rabbit antiserum used by some laboratories (4) may contain anti-stem cell activity (10, 11) or other viral specificities,[6] or may be specific for only a subgroup of T cells (3). The mouse AKR anti-C3H antiserum used for Thy-1 studies has been shown to contain specificity against other Ly (25, 26) or the newly described minor lymphocyte-stimulating (Mls)-linked determinant, LyM-1 (27, 28). Since Mls-linked determinants may be borne on some peritoneal exudate macrophages (29), it follows that abrogation of the suppressive effect by use of this antiserum may not necessarily be interpreted to mean that T cells are the effectors. These antiviral contaminants are quite dependent upon the prepa-

[6] W. Davidson, personal communication.

ration of antigen and, as such, are difficult to compare with the specific antisera used here. We attempted to parallel other published experiments using highly specific anti-Thy-1.2 monoclonal or congenic antisera instead of such AKR anti-C3H serum because of the potential batch-dependent contaminations described above. It can be seen in Table 1 that the suppressor cells described in this report are not eliminated by conventional anti-T-cell reagents. In addition, other data (not shown) indicate that the suppressive effects of P cells are not eliminated by their treatment with anti-Lyt-1.2 or anti-Lyt-2.2 + C. Although the monoclonal anti-Thy-1 reagent used in this study has been reported to be less effective in mass cytolysis than congenic or allogeneic anti-Thy-1 serum,[7] the controls for effectiveness described under Materials and Methods, as well as in footnote *b* to Table 1, would suggest in this case that most, if not all, proliferative capacity of normal cells had been removed by treatment with this reagent. However, it cannot be excluded that the suppressor cells described here may bear small amounts of Thy-1 antigen and thus may escape the cytotoxic effects of the monoclonal reagent and congenic anti-Thy-1 serum used in this report. We are unable to explain why we cannot repeat the findings that P spleen cells are sensitive to the cytotoxic effects of anti-T-cell sera + C (1–4, 7–9). It is possible that the anti-T-cell sera used in other laboratories contained contaminants which were effective against non-T cells; however, it is significant that one other laboratory, using AKR anti-C3H serum, was unable to eliminate suppression by P cells (8). We suggest that the antiserum used by these workers contained only anti-T-cell activity and, as such, would not eliminate non-T suppressors. This finding supports the notion that several kinds of suppressor cells are generated *in vitro*, perhaps in response to serum or other environmental antigens, and these cells are of different lineages. The apparent paradox that P suppressors are recovered as nonadherent cells from plastic dishes, and subsequently removed by adherence columns, has not escaped us. Plastic-adherent P cells, recovered from the petri dish using a rubber policeman, were found to be highly suppressive in both MLR and CTL generation. These cells represented less than 25% of the plastic-nonadherent cells, however, and it was impractical to use them in the analyses described in this report.

Although suppressor cells generated *in vitro* have been described as thymus-processed (1, 3, 4, 7, 9), this report and one other (8) suggest that some suppressors may not belong to the T-cell pool. Adherent, radioresistant cells have been isolated from tumor-bearing mice (30), BCG-infected mice (31), or mice undergoing a graft-vs-host reaction (32) and have been shown to be suppressive in *in vitro* assays. The results presented in Table 2 suggest that for suppression of CTL generation, at least a round of cell division (which may mean a differentiation step) must precede the expression of suppressor activity. The results presented in this report suggest that some regulatory functions of immune responses may reside in a compartment of the immune system with adherent cell characteristics.

ACKNOWLEDGMENTS

The authors wish to thank Drs. W. Davidson and B. Mathieson for in-depth discussion of the antiserum specificities, and Drs. P. Baker and J. Oppenheim for assistance with the text. We wish to thank Drs. U. Hammerling and F.-W. Shen for the generous gifts of monoclonal reagent and antisera. Thanks also to Ms. O. Childers, V. Shaw, and the NIAID Editorial Office for assistance with the manuscript.

[7] B. Mathieson, personal communication.

REFERENCES

1. Parish, C. R., *Immunology* **33,** 597, 1977.
2. Janeway, C. A. Jr., Sharrow, S. O., and Simpson, E., *Nature (London)* **253,** 544, 1975.
3. Burns, F. D., Marrack, P. C., Kappler, J. W., and Janeway, C. A., Jr., *J. Immunol.* **114,** 1345, 1975.
4. Hodes, R. J., and Hathcock, K. S., *J. Immunol.* **116,** 167, 1976.
5. Nadler, L. M., and Hodes, R., *J. Immunol.* **118,** 1886, 1977.
6. Ferguson, R. M., Anderson, S. M., and Simmons, R. L., *Transplant. Proc.* **9,** 919, 1977.
7. Ferguson, R. M., Anderson, S. M., and Simmons, R. L., *Transplantation* **26,** 331, 1978.
8. Anaclerio, A., Moras, M. L., Honorati, C., Ruggeri, A., Conti, G., and Spreafico, F., *Transplantation* **27,** 329, 1979.
9. Kedar, E., Schwartzback, M., Unger, E., and Lupu, T., *Transplantation* **26,** 63, 1973.
10. Monette, F. C., Eichacker, P. Q., Garver, R. I., Byrt, W., and Gilio, M. J., *Exp. Hematol.* **6,** 299, 1978.
11. Golub, E. S., *J. Exp. Med.* **136,** 369, 1972.
12. Rollwagen, F. M., and Stutman, O., *Fed. Proc.* **38,** 2075, 1978.
13. Rollwagen, F. M., and Stutman, O., *J. Exp. Med.* **150,** 1359, 1979.
14. Peck, A. B., and Bach, F. H., *J. Immunol. Methods* **3,** 147, 1973.
15. Burton, R., Thompson, J., and Warner, N. L., *J. Immunol. Methods* **8,** 135, 1975.
16. Brunner, K. T., Mauel, J., Cerottini, J.-C., and Chapuis, B., *Immunology* **14,** 181, 1968.
17. Scheid, M., Boyse, E. A., Carswell, E. A., and Old, L. J., *J. Exp. Med.* **135,** 938, 1972.
18. Kohler, G., and Milstein, C., *Nature (London)* **256,** 469, 1975.
19. Golub, E. S., *Cell. Immunol.* **2,** 353, 1971.
20. Hodes, R. J., Handwerger, B., and Terry, W., *J. Exp. Med.* **140,** 1646, 1974.
21. Shen, F.-W., Boyse, E. A., and Cantor, H., *Immunogenetics* **2,** 591, 1975.
22. Sanderson, C. J., Clark, I. A., and Taylor, G. A., *Nature (London)* **253,** 376, 1975.
23. Schmidtke, J. R., and Dixon, F. J., *J. Immunol.* **108,** 1624, 1972.
24. Perkins, E. H., Nettesheim, P., and Morita, T., *J. Reticuloendothel. Soc.* **3,** 71, 1966.
25. Davidson, W. F., Betel, I., Sharrow, S. O., and Mathieson, B. J., *J. Supramol. Struct.* (Suppl. 3), **625,** 1976 (Abstract).
26. Frelinger, J. A., and Murphy, D. B., *Immunogenetics* **3,** 481, 1976.
27. Tonkonogy, S. L., and Winn, H. J., *Immunogenetics* **5,** 57, 1977.
28. Tonkonogy, S. L., and Winn, H. J., *J. Immunol.* **116,** 835, 1976.
29. Schirrmacher, V., Pena-Martinez, P., and Festenstein, H., *Nature (London)* **255,** 155, 1975.
30. Kirchner, H., Muchmore, A. V., Chused, T. M., Holden, H. T., and Herberman, R. B., *J. Immunol.* **114,** 206, 1975.
31. Klimpel, G. R., and Henney, C. S., *J. Immunol.* **120,** 563, 1978.
32. Shand, F. L., *Transplant. Proc.* **9,** 227, 1977.

CELLULAR IMMUNOLOGY 64, 381–391 (1981)

COMMENTARY

A Random Repertoire of V Genes for T-Cell Receptors? Theoretical Implications of Recent Experimental Observations on T-Cell Specificity and Self-Restriction

WULF DROEGE

Institut für Immunologie und Genetik, Deutsches Krebsforschungszentrum, D-69 Heidelberg, West Germany

Received May 29, 1981; accepted July 25, 1981

Several theoretical implications of recent experimental observations on T-cell specificity and self-restriction are described. Recent experiments suggest strongly that the preferential restriction for the self-major-histocompatibility antigens (MHA) results from selection during the somatic development of the T cells. Under the simple assumption that this selection for self-restriction and the generation of self-tolerance are two independent and counterproductive stochastic selection processes, it is shown that these processes ultimately select for intermediate affinities for self-antigens. This assumption implies also that the T-cell repertoire may be described (and precursor frequencies may be calculated) by a simple probability function of the affinity for self-antigens. The available experimental data also suggest strongly that T cells recognize conventional antigens (i.e., non-MHA) in association with MHA by one receptor with two binding sites. This implies that the induction of self-tolerance spares typically self-restricted cells with relatively high affinity for self-MHA if they have low affinity for conventional self-antiens, and spares cells with relatively high affinity for conventional self-antigens, if the second binding site has low affinity for self-MHA. Cells in this latter group are expected to recognize *foreign MHA* on allogeneic cells *in complex with nonpolymorphic conventional self-antigens*. Self-restricted T cells and alloreactive T cells are thus predicted to be members of one continuous spectrum of cells. The established fact that helper T cells and cytotoxic T cells are mainly restricted to I-region and K- or D-region determinants, respectively, implies that the selection for self-MHA restriction commits inherently the selected young T lineage cells to helper *or* cytotoxic function depending on the type of selecting MHA. There are basically two major alternatives: (1) The recognition of I- and K- or D-region products is based on two different V gene pools; or (2) the products of all MHC-subregions are recognized by receptors which are derived by selection from one common and essentially random pool of V genes. The latter case would imply inevitably that the MHA play an active role in the selection process, and that I- and K- or D-region determinants cause the selecting cells to deliver different inductive signals to the selected T cells. With respect to this requirement for antigen recognition plus a second signal (possibly an interleukin), the selection for MHC restriction is similar and possibly identical to the process which initiates the early proliferative events during the activation of the effector T cells, and is possibly identical to the generation of T-cell memory.

I. INTRODUCTION

It is the main function of the thymus-derived (T) lymphocytes to communicate with other cells: helper cells, for example, regulate the activity of other immuno-

0008-8749/81/160381-11$02.00/0

logically relevant cells, and cytotoxic T lymphocytes kill virus-infected cells or other unwanted cells in the organism. It therefore makes sense that T lymphocytes recognize antigens usually on cell surfaces and not in solution (1, 2). The cytotoxic and the regulatory T lymphocytes distinguish their respective groups of target cells from each other and from soluble antigens through special cell surface markers, namely the major histocompatibility antigens (MHA).[1] Cytotoxic T lymphocytes (CTL) recognize conventional antigens[2] (i.e., non-MHA) mainly in association with cell surface molecules that are encoded in the K or D region of the major histocompatibility gene complex (MHC), while helper cells (and cells mediating delayed hypersensitivity) recognize conventional antigens mainly in association with I-region-controlled cell surface molecules (1–6). This phenomenon is called MHC restriction. The tissue distribution of these MHC-encoded cell surface markers is correlated with the respective target cells of the T cells: I-region determinants are present on certain immunologically relevant cells (7), and K- or D-region determinants are present on practically all cells of the organism (8).

This paper describes theoretical conclusions which are derived from the available experimental data on MHC restriction. The experimental observations are compatible with the simple and attractive concept that the binding sites which recognize the MHC-encoded cell surface determinants as well as the binding sites for the conventional (= non-MHC-encoded) antigens are derived from a random repertoire of V genes.

II. BASIC EXPERIMENTAL OBSERVATIONS

Two sets of experimental observations and conclusions are the basis for our theoretical considerations.

(i) MHA are highly polymorphic; and recent experiments suggest that the ability of the T-cell population to recognize the "correct" allelic variant of MHA in their environment is "learned" by *selection during the ontogenetic development* rather than determined by the genetic program of the T cells (2, 9–17). The observation that cells of different MHC haplotypes interact in parent $\rightarrow F_1$ radiation chimeras, where lymphocytes of both parental types mature in an F_1 hybrid environment (9, 10), indicated that the recognition of the "self-MHA" is not mediated by a like–like interaction (dimerization) as proposed earlier (18, 19), nor by a combination of genes which code for complementary surface structures, but rather by selection of complementary receptors; and the observation that $A \times B \rightarrow A$ radiation chimeras generate T-cell responses with a restriction to MHA from parent A but not parent B (2, 11, 17) indicated that T cells as a population recognize preferentially allelic variants of MHA which they have experienced in their environment during maturation. These experiments suggested furthermore that the preference for self-MHA exists not only at the level of the activated effector T-cell but already at the level of the precursor T cells, i.e., before deliberate immunization. This latter conclusion is important for the following considerations; but it is conceded that this

[1] Abbreviations used: CTL, cytotoxic T lymphocytes; MHA, major histocompatibility antigens (encoded in the MHC); MHC, major histocompatibility gene complex.

[2] Definitions: "Conventional antigens" or "CA" are antigens that are not encoded in the MHC; The term "T-cell repertoire" is defined as the qualitative and quantitative composition of the T-cell pool at a given time. This term refers essentially to the different T-cell functions and specificities, but also to the relative frequency of T cells with a given function and specificity.

point is not generally accepted. The uncertainty is based on the possibility that most or all experimental techniques that have been used to generate unresponsiveness toward the foreign haplotype under test might have affected also the responses against conventional antigens in association with MHA of that haplotype. Therefore, it is not rigorously excluded that the population of precursor T cells before intentional immunization may recognize conventional antigens equally well or even better in association with foreign MHA, and that the self-restrictedness of T-cell responses (2) results from selection during the experimental immunization (see (20, 21)).

(ii) There is circumstantial evidence that T cells recognize conventional antigens and MHA normally by *two binding sites on one complex antigen receptor.* That MHC restriction is based either upon the recognition of newly formed neoantigenic determinants which are formed by the interaction of conventional antigen and MHA ("altered self model"), or upon the recognition of unmodified determinants on both types of antigens ("dual recognition") was pointed out many years ago (see (17)). The recognition of both types of antigens by two separate sets of receptors, however, seems unlikely at present: A T-cell hybridoma line that was derived by fusion with T cells of two different specificities was found to be induced into interleukin 2 production by conventional $antigen_1$ in association with MHA_1 and by conventional $antigen_2$ together with MHA_2 but not by conventional $antigen_1$ in association with MHA_2 or by conventional $antigen_2$ together with MHA_1 (Marrack and Kappler, communicated at the UCLA Conference, February 1981, Salt Lake City); and it is also argued that in the case of two independent receptors, the receptor against self-MHA would always be occupied by this ligand; one would not expect to observe MHC restriction (see (22)). A true altered self-model, on the other hand, is also unlikely if our previous assumption (i) on the selection of self-MHC-restriction is correct. Whenever a T cell recognizes a foreign and previously inexperienced conventional antigen together with self-MHA, this new self-MHA/CA complex must have something in common with the MHA determinants in the selecting environment before the encounter of this new conventional antigen. This implies always a "twist of dual recognition" (22). This leaves us essentially with the concept of a single T-cell receptor with two binding sites as illustrated in Fig. 3 (AR = antigen receptor). The two binding sites could be formed by one or more polypeptide chains and could be encoded in one or more distinct gene loci. However, even if "dual recognition" by two binding sites is likely to be the normal recognition mode, it is not excluded that the two binding sites are parts of one big cavity with several interaction points and without a well-defined and constant borderline between the two binding sites. Such a cavity may occasionally accommodate foreign MHA or chemically modified MHA molecules also in an "altered-self-mode." The widely observed cross-reactivity between allogeneic cells and virus-infected or haptenated syngeneic cells (e.g., (23, 24)) may partly reflect such an abnormal recognition in the "altered-self-mode."

III. THE T-CELL REPERTOIRE AS A PROBABILITY FUNCTION OF THE AFFINITY TO SELF-ANTIGENS; THE SELECTION FOR INTERMEDIATE AFFINITIES

If self-MHA-restriction is expressed at the level of the T-cell-precursor population, and if this restriction results indeed from selection, then this selection must ultimately favor intermediate affinity for self-antigens. This conclusion was already contained in the theory of Janeway *et al.* (20) and results simply from the expectation that cells with low affinity for self-MHA are selected against while cells with high affinity are eliminated by the induction of self-tolerance.

The mechanistic details for the selection of MHA restriction (positive selection) and for the generation of self-tolerance (negative selection) are unknown; but it seems reasonable to consider both as two independent stochastic processes. The selection for self-MHA-restriction seems to occur largely (11) although not exclusively (25, 26) in the thymus; but for the following conclusions it does not matter whether the two processes occur in parallel or at different times or even at different anatomical sites. The probability that a cell will experience one or the other selective process must be a function of its affinity to antigens in the selecting environment. Since the available evidence favors a model of a single receptor with two binding sites (see the previous paragraph), it is likely that both selection processes depend on the affinity for complex antigens in the selecting environment, i.e., for self-MHA in complex with conventional self-antigens. But positive selection on the basis of affinity for self-MHA only would be sufficient for the generation of self-MHC-restriction and would lead to similar results (27, 28).

The mature T-cell repertoire can then be described and calculated as a probability function of the affinity to self-antigens: $P_m = f(A_{self})$. And the effect of the two stochastic selection processes is described by the probability function: $P_m = P_o \cdot P^+ \cdot (1 - P^-)$, which indicates that the frequency of a given receptor in the mature repertoire P_m is derived from its relative frequency in the original (i.e., germ line) repertoire P_o by multiplication with the corresponding probability for positive selection P^+ and by subtraction of the probability for tolerance induction P^-. Figure 1 illustrates the effect of these two counterproductive selection processes under the possible but not obligatory assumption that both processes operate with the same affinity function: $P^+ = P^- = f(A_{self})$. Future experimentation may allow us to test these equations and will show eventually whether the great variation in the frequencies of individual specificities or idiotypic variants depends mainly on the corresponding affinity to self-antigens or results from a nonrandom nature of the germ line repertoire of V genes.

The generation of the T-cell repertoire resembles according to these conditions a heteroclitic immune response: most of the selected cells are expected to have only intermediate affinity toward the selecting antigen but high affinity toward one or the other foreign antigen, against which they will eventually defend the organism. It is predicted, on the other hand, that only very few T cells in the mature repertoire are available to react with conventional antigens which do not cross-react with previously experienced conventional antigens. This seems to apply to certain tumor antigens (see e.g., (29, 30)), the male-specific antigen (31), minor histocompatibility antigens (25), and certain viruses (see e.g. (32)), which were found to activate detectable cytotoxic T-cell responses only after secondary immunization.

IV. THE CONCEPT OF ONE RECEPTOR WITH TWO BINDING SITES AND ITS THEORETICAL IMPLICATIONS

The experimental observations which argue for a single T-cell receptor with two binding sites have been discussed in section II, part ii. The following considerations will show that this receptor model provides a simple explanation for the appearance

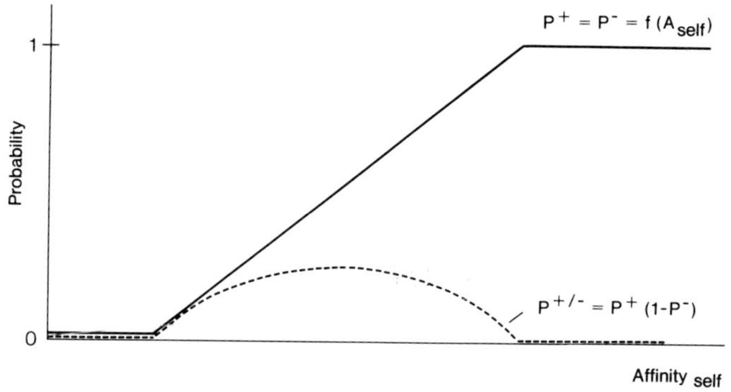

FIG. 1. Selection for T cells with intermediate affinities for self-antigens by two independent stochastic processes (schematic illustration). Available experimental evidence favors the notion that a preferential restriction for self-MHA exists already at the precursor T-cell level before intentional immunization, and that this restriction results from selection during the ontogenetic development of the T-cell repertoire. This selection must involve binding to MHA determinants on selecting cells in the environment, and must operate according to the affinity for binding to the MHA together with or without conventional antigens on the selecting cells. The probability of selection is low in the case of low-affinity values for the self-antigens, high for high-affinity values, and probably intermediate for intermediate affinities as schematically illustrated by the solid line. The process of self-tolerance induction is a negative selection process; and the probability for tolerance induction as a function of the affinity for self-antigens must be similar to the probability profile of the positive selection. For the purpose of this schematic illustration, we assumed that both probability functions are identical (solid line). The probability for a given cell to be positively selected without being rendered tolerant is then indicated by the dashed line. Cells with high affinity may be induced by 100%, but completely eliminated from the mature repertoire by a 100% probability of tolerance induction. Cells with low affinity are not positively selected in the first place. Cells with a certain intermediate affinity, however, may be positively selected with 50% probability, and 50% of these cells will be eliminated by tolerance induction. This leaves a finite probability value of 25% for this intermediate affinity.

of alloreactive T lymphocytes and for the variable degree of self-restrictedness that was found with different antigens.

In a one receptor model with two binding sites, conventional antigens and MHA determinants are expected to contribute *approximately* additively to the total binding energy and, therefore, in a multiplicative way to the total binding affinity of the receptor, irrespective of what proportion each determinant contributes to the binding and irrespective of whether the receptor uses one or more distinct V regions: $A_{CA/MHA} = A_{CA} \cdot A_{MHA}$. Self-tolerance induction is therefore expected to operate in an MHC-restricted fashion and to spare receptors with high affinity to self-MHA, if the affinity toward conventional self-antigens is low, and to spare also receptors with high affinity to conventional self-antigens if the affinity to self-MHA is low. This is illustrated by the diagonal lines in Fig. 2B (lower right). The two-dimensional distribution profile in this figure contains all T cells, i.e., all possible combinations of affinities to the best fitting self-MHA (ordinate) and to the best fitting conventional self-antigen (abscissa). All combinations with a given total affinity $A_{CA/MHA}$ to self-antigens (i.e., a given constant product of $A_{CA} \cdot A_{MHA}$) fall on a straight line in this logarithmic plot for the affinities. The two diagonal lines in Fig. 2B correspond to the affinity thresholds in Fig. 1 for 0% selection (i.e., 0% T-lineage induction) and 100% selection (i.e., 100% tolerance induction), respectively.

The essential conclusion from these considerations is that the mature T-cell

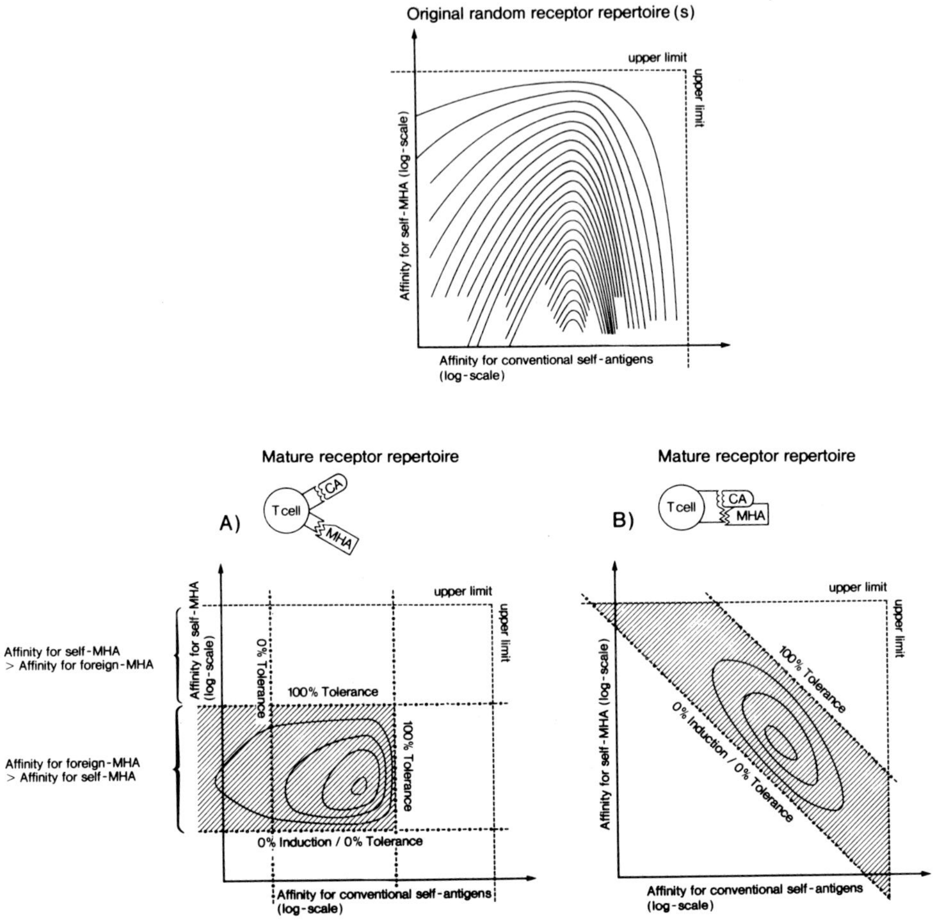

FIG. 2. Selection of the T-cell repertoire according to two theoretical models. (Top) Expected frequency distribution (frequency contour lines) of cells with a random repertoire of receptors according to their affinity to self-MHA (ordinate) or their affinity to conventional self-antigens (abscissa). More detailed explanations are given in the text. (A) Mature repertoire according to the two receptor model. The T cells are plotted again in a two-dimensional distribution profile as in FIG. 2 (top). Cells with high affinity to self-MHA or high affinity to conventional self-antigens are expected to be deleted by the process of self-tolerance induction, and cells with low affinity to self-MHA are not represented as they are not driven into proliferation or functional maturation by these antigens. Self-tolerance induction operates independently on both types of receptors according to this theoretical model. (B) Mature receptor repertoire according to the one receptor model. The cells are plotted again in a two-dimensional frequency distribution according to their affinity toward self-MHA (ordinate) and conventional self-antigens (abscissa). Cells on a given diagonal line (dotted lines) are expected to have the same total affinity to complex self-antigens in the logarithmic plots for the affinities (see text). According to this model the generation of self-tolerance involves both binding sites and is therefore an MHC-restricted process. Cells with high affinity to conventional self-antigens in complex with self-MHA are deleted by the process of self-tolerance induction (upper right corner), while cells with low affinity (lower left corner) are not represented in the mature repertoire as they are not positively selected into T-cell function.

repertoire (shaded area in Fig. 2B) must be located on a narrow diagonal band in this two-dimensional distribution plot and contains self-restricted and alloreactive groups of cells in the two ends of this continuous spectrum of cells: The cells with relatively high affinity to self-MHA in one binding site and low affinity to conventional self-antigens in the other binding site are expected to generate self-restricted responses to foreign antigens. On the other hand, there are cells which have by chance high affinity for one or the other foreign MHA alleles and which are expected to have *low but finite affinity for the self-MHA* on the selecting cells because of the considerable cross-reactivity (33) between different allelic variants of MHA. Cells with these properties appear at the other (i.e. lower) end of the mature T-cell repertoire (see Fig. 2B); and the cells at this end of the repertoire have according to Fig. 2B a second (conventional) binding site with intermediate or high affinity to conventional self-antigens. As these conventional self-antigens include nonpolymorphic structures which are also present on allogeneic cells, this model predicts that alloreactivity involves both binding sites.

The mature repertoire is, thus, expected to contain "self-restricted" cells which recognize self-MHA with higher affinity than allogeneic MHA, and "allo-restricted" cells which recognize allogeneic MHA with higher affinity than self-MHA. The self-restrictedness of an immune response will be determined by the ratio of these two types of cells in the responding T-cell population; and this is predicted to be different for different conventional antigens. Self-restrictedness is expected to be the lower, the more the antigen cross-reacts with conventional self-antigens.

These considerations do not exclude that *environmental pathogens* participate also in the shaping of the repertoire: The two selection processes are likely to be driven by all antigens that persist for a period of time in sufficient quantities in the organism; and this would include mainly self-antigens and to a lesser extent environmental antigens.

The shaded area in the two-dimensional distribution profile of Fig. 2A (lower left) illustrates in comparison the expected distribution of the T-cell repertoire according to the theory of Janeway *et al.* (20, 21). This theory assumes that the T cells have two independent sets of receptors, i.e., one which recognizes conventional antigen and one for the recognition of MHA. The affinity to conventional self-antigens is in this case expected to be always low as a result of self-tolerance induction. The induction of self-tolerance of syngeneic MHA, on the other hand, is assumed to eliminate selectively cells with high affinity to self-MHA, irrespective of their conventional specificity; and the theory assumes that stimulation by self-MHA expands clones of cells with *intermediate* affinity for these antigens. The theory states that *all* anti-MHA receptors have intermediate affinity for self-MHA but by chance high affinity for MHA of one or the other allogeneic haplotype; and it states that the alloreactivity is based upon recognition by this anti-MHA receptor only and does not involve the second receptor for conventional antigens. This implies that essentially every individual T cell is alloreactive and allorestricted, but nevertheless able to react against a conventional antigen in association with self-MHA (20, 21).

The available experimental data favor a one receptor model and therefore in principle a distribution according to Fig. 2B; but they provide no information about the threshold, where the affinity for self-MHA exceeds the affinity for the best fitting foreign MHA. There are no data to exclude the extreme possibility that in fact the *majority* of T cells have higher affinity for one of the many foreign haplotypes as also predicted by the theory of Janeway *et al.* (20, 21). The widely observed cross-reactivity between allogeneic cells and virus-infected or haptenated syngeneic cells (23, 24) suggests at least a considerable degree of overlap between the cells that become engaged in self-restricted responses and those which react toward allogeneic cells.

V. A RANDOM REPERTOIRE OF V GENES WOULD LEAD TO A HIGH PROPORTION OF ALLOREACTIVE CELLS IN THE MATURE T-CELL REPERTOIRE

The two-dimensional frequency distribution for a random repertoire of receptors is schematically illustrated by the frequency contour lines in Fig. 2 (top). One expects for a random repertoire that the frequency of receptors with low affinity for self-MHA will be high and that the frequency will decrease for receptors with increasing affinity to self-MHA; and one would also expect a finite upper limit for this affinity. The many conventional self-antigens, on the other hand, express in comparison with the MHA more antigenic determinants; and the majority of receptors in the random repertoire is therefore expected to bind with intermediate affinity to one of the many conventional self-antigens, while receptors with very low or very high affinity to the best fitting self-antigen are expected to be rare. This implies in principle a bell-shaped distribution profile along the affinity axis for conventional antigens (Fig. 2, top); but one also expects an upper limit for this affinity. If such a distribution profile is subjected to the selection processes according to the affinity toward self-antigens as described before, it will lead indeed to a very high frequency of alloreactive cells and to relatively small frequencies of self-restricted cells as indicated by the frequency contour lines in Fig. 2B (lower right, solid lines). This consideration gives indeed support to the notion of Matzinger and Bevan (34) that it is mainly the *multiplicity* of the conventional nonpolymorphic *self-antigens* which is responsible for the overrepresentation of alloreactive cells. This overrepresentation has been a major theoretical puzzle for many years (35–46).

VI. THE CONCEPT OF A RANDOM REPERTOIRE OF V GENES AND ITS THEORETICAL IMPLICATIONS WITH RESPECT TO THE POSITIVE SELECTION; HELPER T CELLS AS ANTIGEN PRESENTING AND SELECTING CELLS FOR CYTOTOXIC T LYMPHOCYTES?

It is well established that helper T cells are mainly restricted to I-region products and cytotoxic T lymphocytes to K- or D-region products of the MHC (see Introduction). If a selection process links the induction toward T-cell function to the preferential recognition of a given allelic variant of MHA (see paragraph II), then it links obviously the helper function mainly to a variant of I and the cytotoxic function to a variant of K- or D-region products. There are two fundamentally different explanations for this phenomenon. One explanation is based upon the assumption that there are two different V gene pools with preferential specificity for I-region and K- or D-region products, and that the expression of these V gene pools is mechanistically linked to the commitment toward helper and cytotoxic function, respectively. The other explanation is based upon the assumption that one random repertoire of V genes is used by all T cells to recognize products of all MHC subregions. In this latter case one has to postulate an active role of the I- and K- or D-region determinants during the positive selection process in order to ensure (i) that the positive selection by MHA of different subregions (i.e., I versus

K/D) determines different functional pathways (i.e., help versus cytotoxicity), and (ii) to ensure also that MHA and not other cell surface antigens are used as restriction elements. A random repertoire of receptors would not recognize the MHA as special antigens; and the special role of the MHA has to be determined therefore by the MHA themselves and not by the anti-MHA receptors. (These points have been excellently discussed by Cohn and Epstein (22).)

The resulting prediction that the selection for MHC-restriction involves different inductive signals for I-region products and K- or D-region products is reminiscent of the recent experimental observations that the activation of helper T cells and cytotoxic T cells depends on different soluble mediators. The helper T cells require antigen plus the macrophage product interleukin 1, while CTL require antigen plus the helper-T-cell product interleukin 2 (47). It is conceivable that these or similar soluble mediators determine also the selection and functional commitment of these two sets of T cells (see Fig. 3); and it is conceivable that the selection for MHC restriction and the initial events in the antigen-driven activation of effector T cells are identical processes. This would imply, however, that CTL precursor cells must bind to K- or D-region determinants on helper T cells in order to receive optimal help (see Fig. 3). This is a testable possibility and is indeed reminiscent of the model of Lafferty *et al.* (48). *In vitro* studies have indicated that cell to cell contact

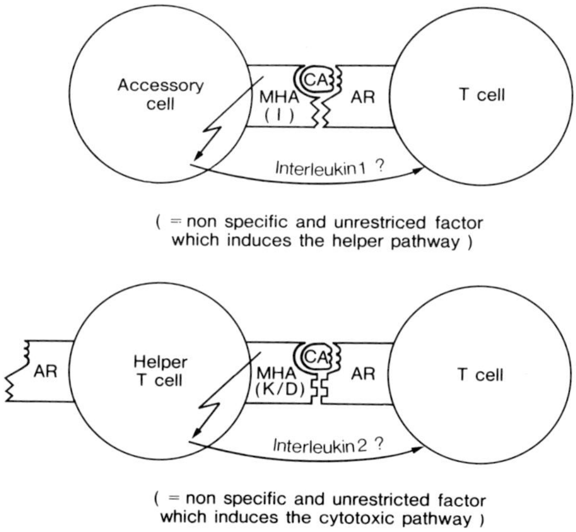

FIG. 3. A model for the selection toward MHA-restriction from a random repertoire of V genes. This model accounts for the experimental observations 1. that the restriction of T cells to a given MHC subregion is linked to a corresponding functional pathway, and 2. that at least the recognition of a given allelic variant of MHC determinants is mediated by selection (see paragraph II). The model explains by a single process on the basis of a random repertoire of V genes the commitment to a given *functional pathway*, to a given *MHC subregion*, and to a given *allelic variant*. The concept of a random repertoire implies inevitably that the MHC determinants are able to transmit signals in order to ensure that not all cell surface antigens are used as restriction elements (see text). It is also inevitable that the signal which is mediated by the K- or D-region determinants is different from the signal that is mediated by the I-region determinants. Interleukin 1 and interleukin 2 are ideal candidates for such signal transmitters since they are nonspecific and unrestricted, but selective with respect to the helper function on the one hand and to the cytotoxic function on the other hand. This model leads to the interesting prediction that the physiological interaction between helper cells and cytotoxic T-cell precursors involves the recognition of MHA determinants on helper T cells by the antigen receptors of the CTL precursor cells.

between helper T cell and cytotoxic T-cell precursor is not required for the cytotoxic response to occur (49), but this may reflect an unphysiological situation. Other investigators have claimed that the interaction between helper cells and cytotoxic T-cell precursors requires the recognition of I-region determinants on the CTL precursor cells by the I-region-restricted helper cell receptors (50). A specific interaction in this direction has not been generally confirmed and seems incompatible with the general failure to demonstrate substantial amounts of I-region determinants on CTL precursor cells. If there is recognition in this direction, this could well add to the stability of the two-cell complex without excluding the requirement for a specific recognition in the opposite direction involving the K/D-restricted receptor of the CTL precursor cell.

VII. THE NATURE OF "T-CELL MEMORY"

Selection for self-MHA-restriction implies that *almost all mature T cells are "memory cells"* in the sense, that they are derived from progenitor cells the receptors of which have already interacted with specific antigen. How is this compatible with the experimentally observed differences between primary and secondary T-cell responses, such as different requirements for DNA synthesis (51) or possible differences in the Ly phenotype of the responding cells (52, 53)? The nature of "T-cell memory" is certainly not completely understood, but the observed differences may simply reflect an amplification of the specific helper cells or a different ratio of recently activated versus resting cells in the responding cell population, rather than a qualitative difference between "memory cells" and "unprimed" T cells. The expansion of T-cell clones by self-antigens is possibly a stochastic process with relatively low frequency; and only a few cells will be at a given time in a recently activated state. There are no experimental data to exclude that selection for MHC restriction is equivalent to the generation of T-cell memory.

VIII. CONCLUDING REMARKS

The present paper describes some theoretical principles which allow us to explain the development of MHC restriction and alloreactivity from an originally random repertoire of T-cell receptors. They provide a coherent explanation for a broad and complex set of experimental observations. It is hoped that these theoretical principles will serve as a useful guideline for further experimentation.

REFERENCES

1. Reviewed in: Möller, G., Ed., Conditions for T cell activation. *Immunol. Rev.* **35,** 1977.
2. Reviewed in: Möller, G., Ed. Acquisition of the T cell repertoire. *Immunol. Rev.* **42,** 1978.
3. Kindred, B., and Shreffler, D. C., *J. Immunol.* **109,** 940, 1972.
4. Reviewed in: Katz, D. H., "Lymphocyte Differentiation, Recognition, and Regulation." Academic Press, New York, 1977.
5. Zinkernagel, R. M., and Doherty, P. C., *Contemp. Top. Immunobiol.* **7,** 179, 1977.
6. Vadas, M. A., Miller, J. F. A. P., Whitelaw, A., and Gamble, J. R. *Immunogenetics* **4,** 137, 1977.
7. Hämmerling, G. J., *Transplant. Rev.* **30,** 64, 1976.
8. Klein, J., *In* "Biology of the Mouse Histocompatibility-2 Complex." Springer-Verlag, Heidelberg, 1975.
9. Von Boehmer, H., Hudson, L., and Sprent, J., *J. Exp. Med.* **142,** 989, 1975.
10. Von Boehmer, H., and Sprent, J., *Transplant. Rev.* **29,** 3, 1976.

11. Zinkernagel, R. M., Callahan, G. N., Althage, A., Cooper, S., Klein, P. A., and Klein, J., *J. Exp. Med.* **147,** 882, 1978.
12. Bevan, M. J., *Nature (London)* **269,** 417, 1977.
13. Bevan, M. J., and Fink, P. J., *Immunol. Rev.* **42,** 3, 1978.
14. Katz, D. H., *Cold Spring Harbor Symp. Quant. Biol.* **41,** 611, 1977.
15. Sprent, J., *Immunol. Rev.* **42,** 108, 1978.
16. Waldmann, H., *Immunol. Rev.* **42,** 202, 1978.
17. Zinkernagel, R. M., *Immunol. Rev.* **42,** 224, 1978.
18. Katz, D. H., and Benacerraf, B., *Transplant. Rev.* **22,** 175, 1975.
19. Katz, D. H., Hamaoka, T., Dorf, M. E., and Benacerraf, B., *J. Exp. Med.* **137,** 1405, 1973.
20. Janeway, C. A., Wigzell, H., and Binz, H., *Scand. J. Immunol.* **5,** 993, 1976.
21. Janeway, C. A., Jones, B., Binz, H., Frischknecht, H., and Wigzell, H., *Scand. J. Immunol.* **12,** 83, 1980.
22. Cohn, M., and Epstein, R., *Cell. Immunol.* **39,** 125, 1978.
23. Finberg, R., Burakoff, S. J., Cantor, H., and Benacerraf, B., *Proc. Nat. Acad. Sci. USA* **75,** 5145, 1978.
24. Levy, R. B., Gilheany, P. E., and Shearer, G. M., *J. Exp. Med.* **152,** 405, 1980.
25. Hünig, T., and Bevan, M. J., *J. Exp. Med.* **152,** 688, 1980.
26. Katz, D. H., Katz, L. R., Bogowitz, C. A., and Bargatze, R. F., *J. Immunol.* **124,** 1750, 1980.
27. Dröge, W., *Immunobiology* **156,** 2, 1979.
28. Dröge, W. *Cell. Immunol.* **57,** 251, 1981.
29. Takei, F., Levy, J. G., and Kilburn, D. G., *J. Immunol.* **116,** 288, 1976.
30. Schirrmacher, V., Bosslet, K., Shantz, G., Clauer, K., and Hübsch, D., *Int. J. Cancer* **23,** 245, 1979.
31. Gordon, R. D., Simpson, E., and Samuelson, L. E., *J. Exp. Med.* **142,** 1108, 1975.
32. Zweerink, H. J., Askonas, B. A., Millican, D., Courtneidge, S. A., and Skehel, J. J., *Eur. J. Immunol.* **7,** 630, 1977.
33. Teh, H. -S., Phillips, R. A., and Miller, R. G., *J. Immunol.* **120,** 425, 1978.
34. Matzinger, P., and Bevan, M., *Cell. Immunol.* **29,** 1, 1977.
35. Simonsen, M., *Cold Spring Harbor Symp. Quant. Biol.* **32,** 517, 1962.
36. Simonsen, M., *Transplant. Rev.* **3,** 22, 1970.
37. Burnet, F. M., *Nature (London)* **218,** 426, 1968.
38. Jerne, N., *Eur. J. Immunol.* **1,** 1, 1971.
39. Szenberg, A., and Warner, N. L., *Brit. J. Exp. Pathol.* **43,** 123, 1962.
40. Bach, F. H., Bock, H., Graupner, K., Day, E., and Klostermann, H., *Proc. Nat. Acad. Sci. USA* **62,** 377, 1969.
41. Wilson, and Nowell, P. C., *J. Exp. Med.* **133,** 442, 1971.
42. Wilson, D. B., Howard, J. C., and Nowell, P. C., *Transplant. Rev.* **12,** 3, 1972.
43. Fischer-Lindahl, K., and Wilson, D. B., *J. Exp. Med.* **145,** 508, 1977.
44. Teh, H. -S., Harley, E., Phillips, R. A., and Miller, R. G., *J. Immunol.* **118,** 1049, 1977.
45. Binz, H., and Wigzell, H., *J. Exp. Med.* **142,** 1218, 1976.
46. Rajewsky, K., and Eichmann, K., *Contemp. Top. Immunobiol.* **7,** 69, 1977.
47. Reviewed in: Möller, G., Ed. T cell stimulating growth factors. *Immunol. Rev.* **51,** 1980.
48. Lafferty, K. J., Andrus, L., and Prowse, S. J., *Immunol. Rev.* **51,** 279, 1980.
49. Wagner, H., Hardt, C., Heeg, K., Pfizenmaier, K., Solbach, W., Bartlett, R., Stockinger, H., and Röllinghoff, M., *Immunol. Rev.* **51,** 215, 1980.
50. Zinkernagel, R. M., Callahan, G. N., Althage, A., Cooper, S., Streilein, J. W., and Klein, J., *J. Exp. Med.* **147,** 897, 1978.
51. Cerottini, J. C., Engers, H. D., MacDonald, H. R., and Brunner, K. T., *J. Exp. Med.* **140,** 703, 1974.
52. Burakoff, S. J., Finberg, R., Glimcher, L., Lemonnier, F., Benacerraf, B., and Cantor, H., *J. Exp. Med.* **148,** 1414, 1978.
53. Koszinowski, U. H., and Simon, M. M., *Eur. J. Immunol.* **9,** 715, 1979.

CELLULAR IMMUNOLOGY **64**, 392 (1981)

ANNOUNCEMENTS

Eighth International Convocation on Immunology

June 14–17, 1982

The Ernest Witebsky Center for Immunology, State University of New York at Buffalo, announces the Eighth International Convocation on Immunology to be held June 14–17, 1982, at the Buffalo Marriott Inn, Amherst, New York. The theme of the program, "Regulation of the Immune Response," will include presentation of papers by distinguished scientists internationally recognized as experts on the topics: Systemic Immunoregulatory Mechanisms; Mucosal Immunoregulatory Mechanisms; Immune Regulation to Exogenous Antigens; and Implications in Clinical Disease States. Further information may be obtained by contacting:

Dr. James F. Mohn, Director
The Ernest Witebsky Center for Immunology
Room 210, Sherman Hall
State University of New York
Buffalo, New York 14214
Telephone: (716) 831-2848

First International Congress of Neuroimmunology

Stresa, Lake Maggiore, Italy

September 27–October 1, 1982

ORGANIZERS

Federico Spreafico, M.D.
Mario Negri Pharmacological Research Institute
Via Eritrea, 62
20157 Milano, Italy

Peter O. Behan, M.D.
Institute of Neurological Sciences
Southern General Hospital
1345 Govan Road
Glasgow G51 47F, Scotland

CELLULAR IMMUNOLOGY **64**, 393–394 (1981)

Papers to Appear in Forthcoming Issues

(Received and Accepted Dates Follow Title)

REIKO M. NAKAMURA AND MONTE S. MELTZER. Macrophage Activation for Tumor Cytotoxicity: Control of Cytotoxic Activity by the Time Interval Effector and Target Cells Are Exposed to Lymphokines. (Received 7/7/81; accepted 8/30/81).

PNINA BRODT AND JULIUS GORDON. Anti-tumor Immunity in B Lymphocyte-Deprived Mice. II. *In Vitro* Studies. (Received 4/30/81; accepted 8/31/81).

HAIM OVADIA AND PHILIP Y. PATERSON. Cellular Transfer of Experimental Allergic Encephalomyelitis in Lewis Rats: Effects of Different Sensitization Regimens on *in Vitro* Reactivity of Donor Spleen Cells to Concanavalin A. (Received 7/7/81; accepted 8/31/81).

PETER C. DOHERTY AND ROBERT KORNGOLD. Effects of Cyclophosphamide and Cortisone on the Virus-Immune Response Characteristics of Thymocytes and the Early Reconstitution Profiles of P → F1 Chimeras. (Received 5/6/81; accepted 8/31/81).

SOO RAY WANG, JYH HSIUNG HUANG, AND SHARON WANG. *In Vitro* Glucocorticoid Inhibition of Steroid-Treated Residual Circulatory Human Lymphocytes. (Received 6/24/81; accepted 9/9/81).

MAREK ROLA-PLESZCZYNSKI AND HIEN LIEU. Concomitant Induction of Cytotoxic and Suppressor Cells. Modulation by Theophylline. (Received 4/13/81; accepted 9/9/81).

MOHAN L. SOPORI, JAMES M. SHEIL, THOMAS L. ROSZMAN, AND WILLIAM H. BROOKS. T Lymphocyte Heterogeneity in Rat: Role of Adherent T-Cell Subpopulation in the Regulation of Cytotoxic T-Cell Response to Alloantigens. (Received 8/13/81; accepted 9/12/81).

JUNMING LE, SUSUMU IKEHARA, RAJENDRA PAHWA, PAMELA BURTON, ABRAHAM WHITE, AND ROBERT A. GOOD. *In Vitro* Effects of Prealbumin on T Cell Dependent Immune Responses of the Mouse. (Received 2/12/81; accepted 9/12/81).

RAJIV K. SAXENA, QUEEN B. SAXENA, AND WILLIAM H. ADLER. Modulation of Natural Cytotoxicity by Alloantibodies. V. The Mechanism of a Selective Augmenting Effect of Anti H-2 Antisera on the Natural Killer Activity of Mouse Spleen Cells. (Received 12/29/80; accepted 9/12/81).

STEPHANIE L. JAMES, MARGARET LABINE, AND ALAN SHER. Mechanisms of Protective Immunity Against *Schistosoma Mansoni* Infection in Mice Vaccinated with Irradiated Cercariae. I. Analysis of Antibody and T Lymphocyte Responses in Mouse Strains Developing Differing Levels of Immunity. (Received 7/15/81; accepted 9/15/81).

R. B. NARAYANAN, JILL CURTIS, AND JOHN L. TURK. Release of Soluble Factors from Lymph Nodes Containing Mycobacterial Granulomas and Their Effect on Fibroblast Function *in Vitro*. (Received 8/4/81; accepted 9/15/81).

MYRON R. SZEWCZUK, RITA J. CAMPBELL, AND JAMES W. SMITH. Evidence for Histamine-Induced Auto-Anti-Idiotypic Antibody Immunoregulation *in Vivo*. (Received 6/18/81; accepted 9/23/81).

PAWEŁ KISIELOW AND PETER DRÁBER. Expression of T-Cell Differentiation Antigens on Activated Thymocytes. (Received 7/1/81; accepted 9/23/81).

MICHAEL I. LUSTER, GARY A. BOORMAN, JACK H. DEAN, LELA D. LAWSON, RALPH E. WILSON, LLOYD D. LAUER, ROBERT W. LUEBKE, JOHN RADER, AND LUCILLA CAMPBELL. Increased Resistance to Listeria Monocytogenes following Subchronic Cyclophosphamide Exposure: Relationship to Altered Bone Marrow Function. (Received 6/23/81; accepted 9/24/81).

DANIELA SANTOLI, MARY KAY FRANCIS, AND MASSIMO TRUCCO. Phenotypic and Functional Characterization of Allospecific and Nonspecific (NK- and K-Like) Cytotoxic T Lymphocytes Generated in Human Mixed Lymphocyte Cultures from Noncytotoxic Precursors. (Received 6/25/81; accepted 9/23/81).

IRENE R. KATZ, JUDITH CHAPMAN-ALEXANDER, ETHEL B. JACOBSON, STEPHEN P. LERMAN, AND G. JEANETTE THORBECKE. Growth of SJL/J-Derived Transplantable Reticulum Cell Sarcoma as Related to Its Ability to Induce T-Cell Proliferation in the Host. III. Studies on Thymectomized and Congenitally Athymic SJL Mice. (Received 7/24/81; accepted 9/25/81).

YEHUDITH AZAR, PAULA EIDELSZTEIN, EITAN YEFENOF, EVELYNE CHRIQUI, AVIVA KATZ-GROSS, ELI KEDAR, AND SHLOMO ZALMAN BEN-SASSON. Antigen Specific Murine T Cell Lymphomas: Functional Heterogenicity. (Received 7/28/81; accepted 9/25/81).

VÉRONIQUE DUPREZ, PATRICE DEBRE, AND JEAN-PAUL LEVY. Genetic Control of Sensitivity to Moloney Leukemia Virus in Mice. V. Role of H-2-Linked Genes in the Control of Anti-FMR Cytolytic T Lymphocytes. (Received 6/17/81; accepted 9/29/81).

JEAN-PIERRE B. KOLB, ANNA SENIK, AND MONIQUE CASTAGNA. *In Vitro* Stimulation of Mouse NK Cell Activity by Phorbol Esters: A Pathway Different from Interferon-Induced Activation. (Received 7/15/81; accepted 9/30/81).

DAVID S. MATHESON, BRIDGET GREEN, AND Y. H. TAN. Human Interferons α and β Inhibit T Cell Dependent and Stimulate T Cell Independent Mitogenesis and Natural Cytotoxicity: Relationship to Chromosome. (Received 2/25/81; accepted 10/3/81).

MAUREEN H. BOCCHIERI, JEFFREY A. WOLOS, AND J. BRUCE SMITH. Primary and Secondary Autologous Mixed Lymphocyte Interactions in Mice Occur via Antigens Encoded by Genes in the I Region of the Major Histocompatibility Complex. (Received 7/29/81; accepted 10/5/81).

CELLULAR IMMUNOLOGY 64, 395–396 (1981)

Author Index for Volume 64

A

Ades, Edwin W., 84
Agostini, C., 227
Ali, Mariam, 350
Andersson, Leif C., 187

B

Bach, Jean-François, 93, 144
Bailey, Jennifer, 119
Balch, Charles M., 84
Ballow, Mark, 29
Barranger, John A., 293
Basso, G., 227
Blyznak, Nestor, 246
Borel, Yves, 267
Braley-Mullen, Helen, 177
Burgess, Donald, 119

C

Cantrell, John, 150
Caraux, J., 312
Catanzaro, Antonino, 235
Ceuppens, Jan L, 277
Charreire, Janine, 144
Chi, David S., 246, 258
Choi, Yong Sung, 20
Cocito, M. G., 227

D

Dardenne, Mireille, 93
Davies, Philip, 293
Derr, Julia, 293
Desplaces, A., 312
Dougherty, Patricia A., 84
Droege, Wulf, 381
Dröge, Wulf, 53
Dufer, J., 312

E

Erard, Dominique, 144
Esteve, C., 312
Evans, Scott R., 64
Evans, Donald L., 119

F

Fagiolo, U., 227
Fraser, Robin, 162

G

Gahmberg, Carl G., 187
Galanaud, Pierre, 144
Garagiola, David M., 359
Gasparotto, G., 227
Gery, Igal, 293
Goodwin, James S., 277
Grouix, Brigitte, 144
Grover, William H., 119

H

Hale, Arthur H., 119
Harris, David, 119
Hercend, Thierry, 192
Horton, Michael A., 187
Huard, Thomas K., 359
Hurme, Mikko, 187

I

Iribe, Hideaki, 73

J

Johnson, Howard M., 64

K

Kaiserlian, Dominique, 93
Kim, Young Tai, 44
Kimura, Arthur, 246
Koga, Toshitaka, 73
Kotani, Shozo, 73
Krett, Nancy, 293
Kusumoto, Shoichi, 73

L

Langdon, Wallace Y., 102
Lauriola, Libero, 337
Leech, Stephen H., 350
Lewis, Jon C., 119
Lichtenstein, Alan, 150
Lim, Kee Hak, 20
Lima, Marcondes, 324
Livingston, Philip O., 131
LoBuglio, Albert F., 359
Loken, Michael R., 84

M

Maggiano, Nicola, 337
Michitsch, Richard, 131
Murahata, Richard, 150
Musiani, Piero, 337

N

Nadler, Lee M., 192
Neta, Ruth, 203

O

Oettgen, Herbert F., 131
Onoue, Kaoru, 73

P

Palladino, Michael A., 246
Panetti, Marguerite, 119
Pang, Roy H. L., 304
Panijel, Jacques, 1
Pantschenko, Alexander G., 29
Paulus, Leslie K., 119
Pavia, Charles S., 162
Pavlík, Ladislav, 13
Pesando, John M., 192
Pezzutto, A., 227
Piantelli, Mauro, 337
Pinsky, Carl M., 131
Prunet, Jacqueline, 1

R

Ranelletti, Franco O., 337
Reddehase, Matthias, 53
Reinherz, Ellis L, 192
Rey, A., 312
Ritz, Jerome, 192

Rocklin, Ross E., 324
Rola-Pleszczynski, Marek, 220
Rollwagen, Florence M., 371
Rucheton, M., 312
Ruebush, Mary J., 119

S

Sabaawi, Mohamed, 203
Salvin, S. B., 203
Sanders, F. Kingsley, 20
Schlossman, Stuart F., 192
Searles, Robert P., 277
Semenzato, G., 227
Serrou, B., 312
Shellam, Geoffrey R., 102
Shiba, Tetsuo, 73
Shiku, Hiroshi, 131
Shlesinger, Menachem, 267
Simpson, Elizabeth, 187
Siskind, Gregory W., 44
Stites, Daniel P., 162
Stutman, Osias, 371

T

Terpenning, Marilou, 150
Thierry, C., 312
Thorbecke, G. Jeanette, 246, 258

V

Valles, H., 312
Viklický, Vladimír, 13
Vilček, Jan, 304

W

Weksler, Marc E., 44
Wilson, Deborah, 177
Wolf, Michael, 53

Y

Yip, Y. K., 304

Z

Zagury, D., 312
Zighelboim, Jacob, 150

NOTICE

The Subject Index for Volume 64 will appear in the December 1981 issue as part of a cumulative index for the year 1981.

Statement of ownership, management and circulation required by the Act of October 23, 1962, Section 4369, Title 39, United States Code: of

CELLULAR IMMUNOLOGY

Published monthly (semimonthly in January, March, May, July, September, and November) by Academic Press, Inc., 111 Fifth Avenue, New York, N. Y. 10003. Number of issues published annually: 18. Editor: H. S. Lawrence, New York University Medical Center, 550 First Avenue, New York, N. Y. 10016.
Owned by Academic Press, Inc., 111 Fifth Avenue, New York, N. Y. 10003.
Known bondholders, mortgagees, and other security holders owning or holding 1 percent or more of total amount of bonds, mortgages, and other securities: None.
Paragraphs 2 and 3 include, in cases where the stockholder or security holder appears upon the books of the company as trustee or in any other fiduciary relation, the name of the person or corporation for whom such trustee is acting, also the statements in the two paragraphs show the affiant's full knowledge and belief as to the circumstances and conditions under which stockholders and security holders who do not appear upon the books of the company as trustees, hold stock and securities in a capacity other than that of a bona fide owner. Names and addresses of individuals who are stockholders of a corporation which itself is a stockholder or holder of bonds, mortgages or other securities of the publishing corporation have been included in paragraphs 2 and 3 when the interests of such individuals are equivalent to 1 percent or more of the total amount of the stock or securities of the publishing corporation.
Total no. copies printed: average no. copies each issue during preceding 12 months: 2068; single issue nearest to filing date: 2042. Paid circulation (a) to term subscribers by mail, carrier delivery or by other means: average no. copies each issue during preceding 12 months: 1487, single issue nearest to filing date: 1528. (b) Sales through agents, news dealers, or otherwise: average no. copies each issue during preceding 12 months: 0; single issue nearest to filing date: 0. Free distribution by mail, carrier delivery, or by other means: average no. copies each issue during preceding 12 months: 67; single issue nearest to filing date: 67. Total no. of copies distributed: average no. copies each issue during preceding 12 months: 1554; single issue nearest to filing date: 1595.

(Signed) Roselle Coviello, Senior Vice President

Cellular Immunology

AN INTERNATIONAL JOURNAL

EDITOR-IN-CHIEF: H. Sherwood Lawrence

Volume 65, 1981

ACADEMIC PRESS

A Subsidiary of Harcourt Brace Jovanovich, Publishers

New York London Toronto Sydney San Francisco

MADE IN THE UNITED STATES OF AMERICA

Contents of Volume 65

NUMBER 1, NOVEMBER 15, 1981

JUNMING LE, SUSUMU IKEHARA, RAJENDRA PAHWA, PAMELA BURTON, ABRAHAM WHITE, AND ROBERT A. GOOD. *In Vitro* Effects of Prealbumin on T-Cell-Dependent Immune Responses of the Mouse 1

MAREK ROLA-PLESZCZYNSKI AND HIEN LIEU. Concomitant Induction of Cytotoxic and Suppressor Cells: Modulation by Theophylline 13

PNINA BRODT AND JULIUS GORDON. Antitumor Immunity in B-Lymphocyte-Deprived Mice. II. *In Vitro* Studies 20

PETER C. DOHERTY AND ROBERT KORNGOLD. Effects of Cyclophosphamide and Cortisone on the Virus-Immune Response Characteristics of Thymocytes and the Early Reconstitution Profiles of P → F1 Chimeras 33

SOO RAY WANG, JYH HSIUNG HUANG, AND SHARON WANG. *In Vitro* Glucocorticoid Inhibition of Steroid-Treated Residual Circulatory Human Lymphocytes 43

REIKO M. NAKAMURA AND MONTE S. MELTZER. Macrophage Activation for Tumor Cytotoxicity: Control of Cytotoxic Activity by the Time Interval Effector and Target Cells Are Exposed to Lymphokines 52

HAIM OVADIA AND PHILIP Y. PATERSON. Cellular Transfer of Experimental Allergic Encephalomyelitis in Lewis Rats: Effects of Different Sensitization Regimens on *in Vitro* Reactivity of Donor Spleen Cells to Concanavalin A 66

STEPHANIE L. JAMES, MARGARET LABINE, AND ALAN SHER. Mechanisms of Protective Immunity against *Schistosoma mansoni* Infection in Mice Vaccinated with Irradiated Cercariae. I. Analysis of Antibody and T-Lymphocyte Responses in Mouse Strains Developing Differing Levels of Immunity 75

IRENE R. KATZ, JUDITH CHAPMAN-ALEXANDER, ETHEL B. JACOBSON, STEPHEN P. LERMAN, AND G. JEANETTE THORBECKE. Growth of SJL/J-Derived Transplantable Reticulum Cell Sarcoma as Related to Its Ability to Induce T-Cell Proliferation in the Host. III. Studies on Thymectomized and Congenitally Athymic SJL Mice 84

R. B. NARAYANAN, JILL CURTIS, AND JOHN L. TURK. Release of Soluble Factors from Lymph Nodes Containing Mycobacterial Granulomas and Their Effect on Fibroblast Function *in Vitro* 93

MOHAN L. SOPORI, JAMES M. SHEIL, THOMAS L. ROSZMAN, AND WILLIAM H. BROOKS. T-Lymphocyte Heterogeneity in Rat: Role of Adherent T-Cell Subpopulation in the Regulation of Cytotoxic T-Cell Response to Alloantigens 103

RAJIV K. SAXENA, QUEEN B. SAXENA, AND WILLIAM H. ADLER. Modulation of Natural Cytotoxicity by Alloantibodies. V. The Mechanism of a Selective Augmenting Effect of Anti-H-2 Antisera on the Natural Killer Activity of Mouse Spleen Cells 115

MICHAEL I. LUSTER, GARY A. BOORMAN, JACK H. DEAN, LELA D. LAWSON, RALPH E. WILSON, LLOYD D. LAUER, ROBERT W. LUEBKE, JOHN RADER, AND LUCILLA CAMPBELL. Increased Resistance to Listeria Monocytogenes following Subchronic Cyclophosphamide Exposure: Relationship to Altered Bone Marrow Function 131

MAUREEN H. BOCCHIERI, JEFFREY A. WOLOS, AND J. BRUCE SMITH. Primary and Secondary Autologous Mixed-Lymphocyte Interactions in Mice Occur via Antigens Encoded by Genes in the I Region of the Major Histocompatibility Complex 142

MYRON R. SZEWCZUK, RITA J. CAMPBELL, AND JAMES W. SMITH. Evidence for Histamine-Induced Auto-Anti-idiotypic Antibody Immunoregulation *in Vivo* 152

KEITH A. KROLICK AND ELI E. SERCARZ. Changing Behavior of Surface Immunoglobulin on Mouse B Lymphocytes during Immune Development. I. LPS-Induced Changes in the Lateral Mobility of B Lymphocyte Surface Immunoglobulins on Two Populations Which Express Different Surface Immunoglobulin Phenotypes 166

KEITH A. KROLICK AND ELI E. SERCARZ. Changing Behavior of Surface Immunoglobulin on Mouse B Lymphocytes during Immune Development. II. Surface Immunoglobulin Modulation Clearly Distinguishes Two Stages of B-Cell Maturation in the Neonate 175

PAWEŁ KISIELOW AND PETR DRÁBER. Expression of T-Cell Differentiation Antigens on Activated Thymocytes 180

SHORT COMMUNICATIONS
YEHUDITH AZAR, PAULA EIDELSZTEIN, EITAN YEFENOF, EVELYNE CHRIQUI, AVIVA KATZ-GROSS, ELI KEDAR, AND SHLOMO ZALMAN BEN-SASSON. Antigen-Specific Murine T-Cell Lymphomas: Functional Heterogenicity 194
STEVEN P. BALK AND MATTHEW F. MESCHER. Cytolytic T Lymphocyte Mediated Chromium-51 Release Versus Spontaneous Release from Blast and Spleen Cell Targets at Low Temperatures 201

ANNOUNCEMENT 206

PAPERS TO APPEAR IN FORTHCOMING ISSUES 207

NUMBER 2, DECEMBER 1981

JOHN L. STERNICK, ELIZABETH M. ALLEN, LINDA M. RIPANI, DENIS J. SCHRIER, AND VERNON L. MOORE. BCG-Induced Granulomatous Pulmonary Inflammation and Splenomegaly in Mice: A T-Cell-Dependent Response 211
GEORGE C. TSOKOS AND JAMES E. BALOW. Suppressor Cells Generated from Human Peripheral Mononuclear Cells by Stimulation with Pokeweed Mitogen 221
DANIELA SANTOLI, MARY KAY FRANCIS, AND MASSIMO TRUCCO. Phenotypic and Functional Characterization of Allospecific and Nonspecific (NK- and K-like) Cytotoxic T Lymphocytes Generated in Human Mixed-Lymphocyte Cultures from Noncytotoxic Precursors 230
JEENAN TSENG. IgA Allotype Suppression in Mice: A Cellular Implication for the IgA Preponderance in the Gut 247
JEAN-PIERRE B. KOLB, ANNA SENIK, AND MONIQUE CASTAGNA. *In Vitro* Stimulation of Mouse NK Cell Activity by Phorbol Esters: A Pathway Different from Interferon-Induced Activation 258
BRIAN A. POLLOK AND EDDIE W. LAMON. Murine T Cells That Lyse Antibody-Sensitized Target Cells. IV. Analysis of Thy 1 and Lyt Surface Antigen Expression among Thymic K Cells 272
BARBARA E. T. BUSBY AND BOB S. ROBERSON. Phytohemagglutinin-Induced Enhancement and IgG Subclass Restriction of the Immune Response to Type III Pneumococcal Polysaccharide 280
SUSUMU KAWAGUCHI. Ontogenical Studies on Kinetics of Lipopolysaccharide-Induced Response to Bromelain-Treated Mouse Erythrocytes in Mouse Spleen Cells. I. Differences from the Response of Total IgM-Secreting Cells 293
PIERRE ÅMAN, GUNNEL LUNDIN, KERSTIN HALL, AND GEORGE KLEIN. Insulin Receptors on Human Lymphoid Lines of B-Cell Origin 307
VÉRONIQUE DUPREZ, PATRICE DEBRE, AND JEAN-PAUL LEVY. Genetic Control of Sensitivity to Moloney Leukemia Virus in Mice. V. Role of H-2-Linked Genes in the Control of Anti-FMR Cytolytic T Lymphocytes 317
FRANCIS V. CHISARI AND LINDA K. CURTISS. Modulation of Peripheral Blood Mononuclear Cell Cyclic Adenosine Monophosphate Levels by Human Very Low Density Lipoprotein 325
MICHAEL G. GOODMAN AND WILLIAM O. WEIGLE. Nonspecific Activation of Murine Lymphocytes. VIII. Effects of D-Penicillamine 337
GEORGE CARAYANNIOTIS AND PHILIP F. HALLORAN. The Regulation of Immune Responses to Multiple Non-H-2 Antigens on Tumor Cells. I. Differential Responses of BALB/c F_1 Hybrids to the P815 Mastocytoma *in Vivo* 352

SHORT COMMUNICATIONS
DAVID S. MATHESON, BRIDGET GREEN, AND Y. H. TAN. Human Interferons α and β Inhibit T-Cell-Dependent and Stimulate T-Cell-Independent Mitogenesis and Natural Cytotoxicity: Relationship to Chromosome 21 366
BYUNG S. KIM. Tumor-Specific Immunity Induced by Somatic Hybrids. III. Persistence of Adoptively Transferred Immunity Specific for TEPC-15 Plasmacytoma in Normal BALB/c Mice 373
HAIM OVADIA AND PHILIP Y. PATERSON. Enhanced Proliferation, Survival, and Yield of Cultured Myelin Basic Protein (MBP)-Reactive Lewis Rat Lymph Node Cells Following Dual Activation with Concanavalin A and MBP 380

PAPERS TO APPEAR IN FORTHCOMING ISSUES 386

AUTHOR INDEX FOR VOLUME 65 390

CUMULATIVE SUBJECT INDEX FOR VOLUMES 57–65 391

CELLULAR IMMUNOLOGY 65, 1–12 (1981)

In Vitro Effects of Prealbumin on T-Cell-Dependent Immune Responses of the Mouse

JUNMING LE,[1] SUSUMU IKEHARA, RAJENDRA PAHWA, PAMELA BURTON,* ABRAHAM WHITE,*[,2] AND ROBERT A. GOOD

*Memorial Sloan–Kettering Cancer Center, New York, New York 10021, and *Institute of Biological Sciences, Syntex Research, Palo Alto, California 94304*

Received February 12, 1981; accepted September 12, 1981

The immunological activities of human prealbumin preparation were investigated *in vitro*. Prealbumin was effective at inducing precursors in nylon wool-nonadherent spleen cells of *nu/nu* mice to express Thy-1 antigens. At 100–250 μg/ml a four- to sixfold enhancement of cytotoxic index was observed. In the presence of prealbumin, mitogenic responses of spleen cells from normal C57Bl/6J mice to phytohemagglutinin (PHA) or concanavalin A (Con A) but not lipopolysaccharide (LPS) were increased. The most significant effect of prealbumin at the optimal concentration (250 μg/ml) on PHA-induced proliferation of spleen cells was found in mice 12 months of age. An *in vitro* plaque-forming cell (PFC) assay showed prealbumin to exert a stimulating effect on PFC formation in spleen cells from normal C57Bl/6J mice at different ages. No such activity was exhibited by human serum albumin preparation. In comparison with prealbumin, synthetic facteur thymique serique (FTS) was tested in mitogenic responses and the PFC assay. FTS showed no influence on responses of mouse spleen cells to PHA, Con A, or LPS. At concentrations of 100–200 μg/ml, however, FTS enhanced PFC formation from normal spleen cells. The findings indicate that it is unlikely that FTS is responsible for the activities of the prealbumin preparation.

INTRODUCTION

During the past decade several thymic hormones have been discovered, among which thymosin Fr. 5 and α_1 (1, 2), thymopoietin (3), thymic humoral factor (THF) (4), and facteur thymique serique (FTS) (5) have received much attention, and a number of investigations are presently being carried out.

Recently Burton *et al.* (6) found two putative thymic hormone fractions with molecular weights ca. 1000 and 50,000–60,000 daltons in normal human serum by using an azathioprine-sensitive spleen cell rosette assay, which had been developed in Bach's laboratory to monitor the isolation of FTS (7). The high-molecular-weight fraction was composed chiefly of albumin and a small amount of prealbumin (6, 8). Prealbumin was reported to behave like a thymic hormone. Repeated injections of prealbumin preparations resulted in an increase in the number of azathioprine-sensitive E-rosette-forming cells (E-RFC) in adult thymecto-

[1] Visiting Investigator from Shanghai Institute of Materia Medica, Chinese Academy of Sciences, Shanghai, China: To whom reprint requests should be addressed.

[2] Deceased.

0008-8749/81/170001-12$02.00/0

tomized mice. Such treatment also enhanced the ability of neonatally thymectomized mice to reject allogeneic skin grafts, and increased the number of direct plaque-forming cells (PFC) in spleen cell preparations from neonatally thymectomized mice (8). In a recent report, however, Dardenne *et al.* presented a series of observations suggesting that the biological activity found in the high-molecular-weight fraction of normal human serum is due to FTS bound to a carrier molecule that may be pre-albumin (9).

The objective of the present study was to explore *in vitro* activities of prealbumin in the following assays: (i) Thy-1 antigen induction; (ii) mitogenic responses; and (iii) hemolytic plaque-forming cell (PFC) assay. The activities of synthetic FTS were compared with those of prealbumin. The results indicated that the prealbumin preparation was effective in inducing Thy-1-positive cells in a nylon wool-nonadherent spleen cell preparation from *nu/nu* mice, and enhancing the number of PFC and mitogenic responses to PHA and Con A in spleen cells from both young and aged mice. It seems to us from the observations presented that the activities of the prealbumin preparation were different from those of FTS.

MATERIALS AND METHODS

Animals. Inbred C57Bl/6J mice at different ages were purchased from The Jackson Laboratory, Bar Harbor, Maine. NIH Swiss *nu/nu* mice at 8 weeks of age were obtained from the Animal Facility of Sloan–Kettering Institute for Cancer Research.

Reagents. Human serum prealbumin preparation used in the study was fraction 3 (Lot No. SR 270258), which was isolated from Cohn fraction IV-1 of pooled human plasma. The method of preparation and physicochemical properties of the fraction have been detailed in previous publications (6, 8). Purified human serum albumin (HSA) (Lot No. 288911) contained in prealbumin fraction 3 was prepared in Syntex Research. Since there is not, as yet, an appropriate inactivated prealbumin preparation available, HSA was used as control for prealbumin although to some extent it might not be ideal. Synthetic FTS (Lot No. 1080502-A) was obtained from Boehringer–Mannheim Biochemicals. RPMI 1640 medium (Grand Island Biological Co. (Gibco), Grand Island, N.Y.), Eagle's minimum essential medium (MEM; Gibco) fetal calf serum (FCS; Microbiological Associates, Bethesda, Md.), anti-Thy-1.2 serum (Litton Bionetics, Bethesda, Md.), rabbit complement (Gibco) guinea pig complement (Gibco), [^{3}H]thymidine (New England Nuclear, Boston, Mass.), phytohemagglutinin P (PHA; Difco Laboratories, Detroit, Mich.), concanavalin A (Con A; Calbiochem, San Diego, Calif.), lipolysaccharide B from *Escherichia coli* 0127:B8 (LPS; Difco), and 2-mercaptoethanol (2-ME; Sigma, St. Louis, Mo.) were obtained from the manufacturers indicated.

Cell separation. The mice were sacrificed by decapitation. Spleens were removed aseptically and minced. The spleen cells were gently passed through a fine-mesh stainless-steel sieve into phosphate-buffered saline (PBS), and washed twice with PBS at 4°C. Cell viability was more than 90% as estimated by trypan blue exclusion. To test the induction of Thy-1-positive cells, spleen cells from *nu/nu* mice were separated on a nylon wool column (FT-242, Fenwall Laboratories, Morton Grove, Ill.), essentially as described by Julius *et al.* (10).

Induction of Thy-1-positive cells. An assay modified from that originally developed by Twomey *et al.* (11) was used for the induction of Thy-1 antigen. The nylon wool-nonadherent cells from *nu/nu* mice were incubated in Tris–NH_4Cl solution for 5 min at 37°C to deplete erythrocytes, then washed three times with PBS. The cells thus obtained were incubated with or without prealbumin or HSA in RPMI 1640 medium for 90 min at 37°C, and then washed once with PBS. The cells (2.5×10^5) were incubated with 50 μl of a 1:20 dilution of anti-Thy-1.2 serum for 30 min at 4°C. After one washing the cells were resuspended in 100 μl of a 1:20 dilution of rabbit complement and incubated for a further 30 min at 37°C. The viability of the cells was determined by exclusion of trypan blue dye. The counts were converted to a cytotoxic index by the formula

$$\text{cytotoxic index} = \frac{\%\text{viable cells (C alone)} - \%\text{viable cells (Ab + C)}}{\%\text{viable cells (C alone)}} \times 100,$$

where C represented complement and Ab, antibody.

Mitogenic responses. Mitogenic responses were determined by measuring the incorporation of [^{3}H]thymidine into DNA. Triplicate cultures of spleen cells from C57Bl/6J mice at different ages were set up in wells of flat-bottom microtiter plates (Falcon 3040 Micro Test II, B-D, Oxnard, Calif.). Each well contained 1×10^6 lymphoid cells in 0.2 ml of RPMI 1640 medium supplemented with 5% FCS, penicillin (100 μ/ml), streptomycin (100 μg/ml), and 4 m*M* L-glutamine. The cells were incubated in the presence of mitogens at optimal concentrations, i.e., PHA (25 μg/ml), Con A (2.5 μg/ml), or LPS (25 μg/ml), for 72 hr at 37°C in a humidified atmosphere of 5% CO_2 in air. Various concentrations of prealbumin, HSA, or FTS were added at the beginning of the culture. [^{3}H]Thymidine (1 μCi in 10 μl) was added 4 hr before harvest. The ^{3}H counts incorporated into trichloroacetic acid-insoluble material were measured by a liquid scintillation counter. The results were expressed as a stimulation index, which was defined as counts per minute with mitogen divided by counts per minute without mitogen.

Plaque-forming cell assay. Cultures were set up in duplicate in Linbro tissue culture multiwell plates (Flow Lab., Hamden, Conn.). Each well contained 5×10^6 lymphoid cells and 5×10^6 washed sheep red blood cells (SRBC) in 2.2 ml of RPMI 1640 medium supplemented with 10% FCS, penicillin (100 μ/ml), streptomycin (100 μg/ml), and 5×10^{-5} *M* 2-ME. The cells were incubated in the absence or presence of various concentrations of prealbumin, HSA, or FTS at 37°C in a humidified atmosphere of 5% CO_2 in air. Five days later, direct PFC assay was performed. The cells of the same group were pooled and washed twice in MEM, and 100 μl (5×10^5 lymphoid cells) of the cell suspension in MEM was mixed with 50 μl of 10% washed SRBC and 0.4 ml of 0.5% agarose in MEM at 45°C. The mixtures in triplicate were poured immediately into small petri dishes (Falcon 3001, B-D). Then each plate was covered with 0.4 ml of a 1:10 dilution of guinea pig complement absorbed with SRBC. The dishes were incubated for 16 hr at 37°C in a humid chamber before counting plaques. The results were expressed as PFC/10^6 lymphoid cells.

Each experiment in the present study was repeated at least three times and representative results were presented.

TABLE 1

Induction of Thy-1-Positive Cells by Human Prealbumin Fraction

Inducer	Dose (μg/ml)	Cytotoxic index (%) Expt I	Expt II	Expt III
None	—	3	4	5
Human serum albumin (HSA)	25	5	5	ND
	50	3	ND	ND
	100	5	7	7
	500	11	8	9
Human prealbumin	10	ND	ND	6
	25	10	ND	12
	50	16	11	15
	100	12	17	19
	250	21	15	22
	500	22	20	23
	1000	25	ND	20

Note. Nylon wool-nonadherent spleen cells from *nu/nu* mice were incubated with factors for 90 min.

RESULTS

Induction of Thy-1-Positive Cells in Spleen Cells of nu/nu Mice by Prealbumin Preparations

The capacity of prealbumin and HSA preparations at various concentrations ranging from 10 to 1000 μg/ml to induce Thy-1-positive cells in *nu/nu* spleen cells was examined. As shown in Table 1, after incubation for 90 min with prealbumin, the percentages of Thy-1-bearing cells in nylon wool-nonadherent spleen cells of *nu/nu* mice were remarkably increased. At concentrations of prealbumin preparation of 100–250 μg/ml, a four- to sixfold enhancement of the cytotoxic index was observed, whereas HSA, as a control for prealbumin, exhibited a rather poor effect. It could, therefore, be suggested that under the influence of prealbumin a population of T-cell precursors matured and expressed the Thy-1 antigen at their surfaces.

Effect of Prealbumin on Mitogenic Responses of Spleen Cells from Normal Mice at Different Ages

To test the effect of prealbumin on the functions of T and B lymphocytes, mitogenic responses of spleen cells to PHA, Con A, and LPS in the presence of prealbumin or HSA preparations were analyzed. The result showed that while HSA displayed no activity, prealbumin preparations markedly enhanced mitogenic responses to PHA and Con A of spleen cells from both young (3 months old) and aged (18 months old) C57Bl/6J mice (Tables 2 and 3). At 125 and 250 μg/ml, a two- to threefold augmentation of the stimulation index was constantly observed. By contrast, no effect on the mitogenic response to LPS was found at any concentration tested. A higher concentration (500 μg/ml) of prealbumin resulted in a poor response, perhaps due to a cytotoxic effect on the spleen cells.

TABLE 2

Effect of Prealbumin Fraction on the Mitogenic Responses of Young (3 Months) C57Bl/6J Mouse Spleen Cells

Factor	Dose (μg/ml)	Concentration of mitogens: Background	PHA (25 μg/ml)	Con A (2.5 μg/ml)	LPS (25 μg/ml)	Stimulation index: PHA	Con A	LPS
		cpm × 10^{-3} (mean ± SD)						
None	—	1.1 ± 0.1	108.6 ± 7.7	156.9 ± 18.9	54.2 ± 4.3	99.9	144.4	49.9
HSA	125	1.2 ± 0.5	98.7 ± 4.6	172.1 ± 17.0	58.3 ± 2.9	82.0	143.1	48.5
	250	1.2 ± 0.1	107.0 ± 15.3	163.4 ± 15.0	49.8 ± 4.0	92.7	141.7	43.2
	500	0.9 ± 0.1	105.4 ± 15.0	149.6 ± 18.0	56.3 ± 2.1	117.4	166.6	62.7
Prealbumin	32	1.1 ± 0.1	98.7 ± 6.3	149.6 ± 15.1	50.4 ± 2.1	93.9	142.2	47.9
	63	1.2 ± 0.1	152.9 ± 17.9	190.7 ± 18.0	45.6 ± 4.9	131.6	164.1	39.3
	125	1.1 ± 0.1	218.8 ± 19.0	309.7 ± 16.1	56.4 ± 3.9	200.2	283.3	51.6
	250	1.0 ± 0.1	266.5 ± 14.1	321.2 ± 10.8	32.7 ± 4.3	275.3	331.8	33.8
	500	0.6 ± 0.1	4.3 ± 1.0	19.5 ± 2.6	5.5 ± 1.3	6.8	30.6	8.7

TABLE 3

Effect of Prealbumin Fraction on the Mitogenic Responses of Aged (18 Months) C57Bl/6J Mouse Spleen Cells

Factor	Dose (μg/ml)	Concentration of mitogens				Stimulation index		
		Background	PHA (25 μg/ml)	Con A (2.5 μg/ml)	LPS (25 μg/ml)	PHA	Con A	LPS
		cpm $\times 10^{-3}$ (mean $\pm$ SD)						
None	—	2.9 ± 0.4	15.2 ± 0.7	67.3 ± 9.5	29.3 ± 1.7	5.2	23.2	10.1
HSA	125	2.4 ± 0.3	14.2 ± 1.5	60.9 ± 3.2	30.1 ± 2.3	5.9	25.4	12.5
	250	3.6 ± 0.4	16.3 ± 0.9	70.3 ± 4.6	38.1 ± 1.0	4.4	19.0	10.3
	500	5.6 ± 0.6	39.4 ± 1.5	89.0 ± 5.0	39.6 ± 1.9	8.6	19.3	8.6
Prealbumin	32	3.4 ± 0.9	18.2 ± 2.7	83.4 ± 1.8	23.9 ± 3.0	5.4	24.5	7.0
	63	4.5 ± 0.1	49.0 ± 3.7	95.5 ± 6.1	30.7 ± 1.1	10.9	21.2	6.8
	125	4.0 ± 0.8	52.6 ± 2.2	102.6 ± 17.3	31.6 ± 3.0	13.2	25.7	7.9
	250	3.0 ± 0.9	65.3 ± 1.3	209.4 ± 13.6	36.9 ± 4.2	21.8	69.8	12.3
	500	0.9 ± 0.1	3.0 ± 0.7	8.2 ± 1.4	3.6 ± 0.9	3.3	9.1	4.0

In a further experiment, the effect of the prealbumin preparation at the optimal concentration (250 μg/ml) on the mitogenic responses of spleen cells from mice at different ages was examined. The results shown in Table 4 indicated that the most significant enhancement of PHA-induced proliferation of spleen cells was found in mice at the age of 12 months. It was shown that the prealbumin preparation enhanced the response of spleen cells to T-cell mitogens but not to B-cell mitogens, and it was most effective in enhancing the response to PHA of spleen cells from mice 12 months of age.

Since prealbumin might be a carrier of FTS (9), it seemed important to test the activity of FTS in this regard. Thus, the effects of synthetic FTS on the mitogenic responses of aged mouse spleen cells were investigated. No effect on responses to PHA, Con A, and LPS could be observed either when FTS was present at various concentrations ranging from 6.3 to 200 μg/ml during the 3 days of culture, or when the spleen cells were preincubated with FTS for 3 hr at 37°C in RPMI 1640 plus 5% FCS (Table 5).

Effect of Prealbumin on the Number of Spleen PFC from Young and Aged Mice

As indicated in Table 6, prealbumin was found to be active in increasing the number of spleen PFC from both young (3 months old) and aged (12 months old) C57Bl/6J mice. A significant enhancement of plaque formation was noted at 100 μg/ml of the prealbumin preparation. Only a few PFC were observed at a high concentration (500 μg/ml) of prealbumin. The result was compatible with findings in the study of mitogenic responses that an optimum concentration was found and higher concentrations were inhibitory. Once again, HSA showed no activity at any concentration tested. In comparison with prealbumin, the effect of synthetic FTS on spleen cells from young mice was determined in the same assay. Table 7 shows that the stimulating effect on PFC was observed only at the concentration of at least 100 μg/ml of FTS. At 0.1 μg/ml, however, FTS suppressed PFC formation, perhaps due to the induction of suppressor cells (12).

DISCUSSION

In the long list of putative thymic hormone or hormone-like factors that have been isolated from the thymus or serum, prealbumin appeared as a newcomer. Previous investigations on the biological activities of serum proteins have concluded that prealbumin should be included among the thymic hormone-like factors (8), although the exact relationship between prealbumin and the thymus still remains to be elucidated. Obviously, it is important to analyze the activities of prealbumin and to compare them with those of other factors, especially FTS, because of the possibility that prealbumin might act as a carrier of FTS (9).

The induction of Thy-1-negative cells into Thy-1-positive cells has been considered a common characteristic of thymic hormones and hormone-like factors. Two assays are available for study, i.e., an azathioprine-sensitive rosette assay and a cytotoxicity test of cells, such as bone marrow or spleen cells before and after *in vitro* treatment with such factors. Like FTS, prealbumin showed high activity in inducing azathioprine-sensitive E-RFC from adult thymectomized mice as was reported previously (6, 8). The present study using a cytotoxicity test showed that the prealbumin preparation exerted a notable induction of Thy-1-positive cells in

TABLE 4

Effect of Prealbumin Fraction on Mitogen-Induced Proliferation of Lymphocytes from C57Bl/6J Mice at Different Ages

Age (months)	Dose (μg/ml)	Background	Concentration of mitogens: PHA (25 μg/ml)	Con A (2.5 μg/ml)	LPS (25 μg/ml)	Stimulation index: PHA	Con A	LPS	Enhancement rate: PHA	Con A	LPS
		cpm $\times 10^{-3}$ (Mean ± SD)									
1	0	0.5 ± 0.1	26.8 ± 4.1	40.7 ± 1.3	—	53.6	81.4	—	—	—	—
	250	0.5 ± 0.1	33.0 ± 1.0	124.0 ± 8.6	—	66.0	248.0	—	1.2	3.8	—
2	0	1.0 ± 0.1	51.7 ± 1.5	110.4 ± 14.0	—	51.7	110.4	—	—	—	—
	250	0.9 ± 0.1	91.9 ± 3.0	249.3 ± 13.0	—	102.1	277.0	—	2.0	2.5	—
3	0	1.1 ± 0.1	108.6 ± 7.6	156.9 ± 18.9	54.2 ± 4.3	98.7	142.6	49.3	—	—	—
	250	1.0 ± 0.1	266.5 ± 14.0	321.2 ± 10.0	32.7 ± 4.3	266.0	321.2	32.7	2.7	2.3	0.7
12	0	2.0 ± 0.4	29.5 ± 1.0	163.2 ± 15.3	64.3 ± 4.3	14.8	81.6	32.2	—	—	—
	250	1.6 ± 0.2	253.6 ± 14.9	286.4 ± 18.6	43.6 ± 3.8	158.5	179.0	27.3	10.7	2.2	0.8
18	0	2.9 ± 0.4	15.2 ± 0.7	67.3 ± 9.5	29.3 ± 1.7	5.2	23.2	10.1	—	—	—
	250	3.0 ± 0.9	65.3 ± 1.3	209.4 ± 13.6	36.9 ± 4.2	21.8	69.8	12.3	4.2	3.0	1.2
24	0	1.3 ± 0.3	2.0 ± 0.2	27.7 ± 5.2	—	1.5	21.3	—	—	—	—
	250	1.2 ± 0.1	5.4 ± 0.7	58.2 ± 2.0	—	4.5	48.5	—	3.0	2.3	—

TABLE 5

Effect of Synthetic FTS on the Mitogenic Responses of Aged C57Bl/6J Mouse Spleen Cells

Age (months)	Factor	Dose (μg/ml)	Background	Concentration of mitogens: PHA (25 μg/ml)	Concentration of mitogens: Con A (2.5 μg/ml)	Concentration of mitogens: LPS (25 μg/ml)	Stimulation index: PHA	Stimulation index: Con A	Stimulation index: LPS
			cpm $\times 10^{-3}$ (mean ± SD)						
14	None	—	2.6 ± 0.1	34.4 ± 3.1	132.5 ± 10.3	53.6 ± 4.2	13.2	51.0	20.6
	FTS (present during entire culture)	6.3	3.0 ± 0.2	40.5 ± 5.2	129.6 ± 18.2	41.8 ± 6.3	13.5	43.2	13.9
		12.5	3.2 ± 0.4	38.6 ± 4.2	136.5 ± 20.1	49.6 ± 5.1	12.1	42.7	15.5
		25	2.9 ± 0.2	42.8 ± 4.3	153.6 ± 14.9	52.0 ± 7.9	14.8	53.0	17.9
		50	4.2 ± 0.4	48.8 ± 3.2	148.2 ± 18.6	54.6 ± 5.1	11.6	35.3	13.0
		100	3.5 ± 0.2	43.5 ± 2.1	151.7 ± 10.9	59.8 ± 4.1	12.4	43.3	17.1
		200	4.3 ± 0.3	50.3 ± 3.9	167.2 ± 12.1	56.3 ± 5.0	11.7	38.9	13.1
	FTS (preincubation)	—	2.1 ± 0.3	36.3 ± 4.2	136.4 ± 19.3	44.3 ± 5.3	17.3	65.0	21.1
		6.3	2.5 ± 0.3	37.4 ± 4.6	125.6 ± 13.8	48.6 ± 6.3	15.0	50.2	19.4
		12.5	2.4 ± 0.3	30.0 ± 1.3	118.6 ± 13.6	49.6 ± 5.3	12.5	49.4	20.7
		25	2.9 ± 0.4	47.6 ± 5.2	153.9 ± 18.6	54.3 ± 4.9	16.4	53.1	18.7
		50	2.4 ± 0.3	32.8 ± 3.5	127.4 ± 21.4	39.8 ± 5.6	13.7	53.1	16.6
		100	2.3 ± 0.1	35.6 ± 4.1	129.5 ± 10.3	53.6 ± 4.8	15.5	56.3	23.3
		200	2.3 ± 0.2	37.6 ± 4.5	156.4 ± 20.3	50.4 ± 6.2	16.3	68.0	21.9

TABLE 6

Effect of Prealbumin Fraction on Spleen Plaque-Forming Cells of Young and Aged C57Bl/6J Mouse

		PFC/10^6 cells (mean ± SD)	
Factor	Dose (μg/ml)	Young mouse (3 months)	Aged mouse (12 months)
None	—	155 ± 12	91 ± 3
HSA	25	131 ± 9	49 ± 6
	50	132 ± 7	75 ± 1
	100	113 ± 13	55 ± 1
	200	95 ± 8	58 ± 2
	500	91 ± 10	41 ± 5
Prealbumin	25	200 ± 8	107 ± 1
	50	241 ± 22	115 ± 8
	100	312 ± 21	165 ± 9
	200	259 ± 23	97 ± 9
	500	3 ± 1	5 ± 1

a nylon wool-nonadherent spleen cell preparation from nude mice. Similarly, Bach *et al.* (13) reported that FTS at a lower concentration induced Thy-1-positive cells in normal mouse spleen cells fractionated by the Komuro–Boyse method (14).

In the *in vitro* PFC assay, the prealbumin preparation at an optimal concentration of 100 μg/ml was shown to enhance the number of direct PFC in a spleen cell preparation (Table 6). FTS was reported to be inactive at concentrations of 10^{-7} to 10^{-5} μg/ml in the PFC assay using "B" mice (12). At much higher concentrations, however, an enhancing effect of FTS could be observed in normal mouse spleen cells. As shown in Table 7, a dose of at least 100 μg/ml was necessary for FTS to exhibit a significant stimulating effect on development of PFC. On a molar basis, the effective concentration of prealbumin should be considered to be much lower than that of FTS because of the molecular weight difference between FTS (867 daltons) and prealbumin (52,000 daltons). Therefore, it seems unlikely that

TABLE 7

Effect of Synthetic FTS on Spleen Plaque-Forming Cells of Young (3 Months) C57Bl/6J Mouse

Factor	Dose (μg/ml)	PFC/10^6 cells (Mean ± SD)
None	—	76 ± 4
FTS	0.01	62 ± 3
	0.1	35 ± 1
	1	72 ± 2
	5	79 ± 6
	10	78 ± 4
	25	63 ± 6
	50	87 ± 8
	100	177 ± 10
	200	211 ± 14

the activity of the prealbumin preparation shown herein could be attributed to FTS, unless FTS presumptively bound to prealbumin is much more active than free FTS, or each prealbumin molecule binds an enormous number of FTS molecules. These possibilities might be analyzed directly in subsequent studies.

Moreover, a clearly different influence on mitogenic responses was noted between the prealbumin preparation and synthetic FTS, the biological activities of which had been determined to be identical with those of natural FTS (12, 15). The prealbumin preparation at concentrations of 125–250 μg/ml significantly enhanced the responses of normal spleen cells to PHA or Con A, and the most remarkable effect on the responses to PHA appeared in the spleen cells from mice 12 months of age. On the other hand, in agreement with the result reported by Bach *et al.* (12), neither the constant presence of FTS nor preincubation of cells with FTS for a 3-hr period could augment these mitogenic responses. The only possible explanation for the inactivity of FTS in the mitogenic response assay comes from the finding that substances of high molecular weight contained in fetal calf serum inhibit activity of FTS by binding the latter molecule (13, 16). However, the binding did not seem to be critical in the present study, since as mentioned above, synthetic FTS at a concentration of 100 μg/ml showed activity in enhancing the development of PFC in the cultures containing even 10% fetal calf serum.

Therefore, it seems unlikely that FTS is responsible for the activity of prealbumin observed in the present study. These findings and interpretations are in accord with recent unpublished observations by Burton *et al.* that after intraperitoneal injection of 1 μg of synthetic FTS absorbed to CM-cellulose, the enhancement of rosette activity was noted only in the 1000-dalton fraction, but not in a 60,000-dalton fraction from the serum of adult thymectomized mice that contains prealbumin. Further, Burton *et al.* observed that treatment with the enzyme pyrrolidone carboxyl peptidase inactivated synthetic FTS, but caused no loss in activity of prealbumin in the *in vitro* rosette assay (unpublished observations).

Nevertheless, since the prealbumin preparation used in the present study is not pure, the possibility that the activities described herein originate from other active molecules carried by prealbumin or contaminants of the prealbumin preparation still exists. Further experiments should be carried out using a highly purified prealbumin preparation to prove that prealbumin itself is a biologically active protein in the blood which possesses capacity to induce Thy-1 antigenicity on T-cell precursors and to enhance certain functions which are normally T-cell dependent. Also, it would be of interest to prepare prealbumin from thymectomized or aged donors instead of the commercial Cohn fraction to see if such preparations were active in the assays used here. Results in either direction would be valuable in clarifying the exact relationship between prealbumin and the thymus.

ACKNOWLEDGMENTS

This work was aided by grants from the World Health Organization; USPHS Research Grants CA-08748, CA-19267, CA-17404, AI-11843, NS-11457, and AG-00541 from the National Institutes of Health; the Judith Harris Selig Memorial Fund; and the Zelda R. Weintraub Cancer Fund.

REFERENCES

1. Hooper, J. A., McDaniel, M. C., Thurman, G. B., Cohen, G. H., Schulof, R. S., and Goldstein, A. L., *Ann. N.Y. Acad. Sci.* **249,** 125, 1975.

2. Goldstein, A. L., Low, T. L. K., McAdoo, M., McClure, J., Thurman, G. B., Rossio, J. L., Lai, C. Y., Chang, D., Wang, S. S., Harvey, C., Ramel, A. H., and Meienhofer, J., *Proc. Nat. Acad. Sci. USA* **74,** 725, 1977.
3. Goldstein, G., *Ann. N.Y. Acad. Sci.* **249,** 177, 1975.
4. Trainin, N., Small, M., Zipori, D., Umiel, T., Kook, A. I., and Rotter, V., *In* "Biological Activity of Thymic Hormones" (D. W. van Bekkum, Eds.), pp. 117–144. Kooyker Scientific, Rotterdam, 1975.
5. Bach, J. F., Dardenne, M., Pleau, J. M., and Rosa, J., *Nature (London)* **266,** 55, 1977.
6. Burton, P., Iden, S., Mitchell, K., and White, A., *Proc. Nat. Acad. Sci. USA,* **75,** 823, 1978.
7. Dardenne, M., and Bach, J. F., *In* "Biological Activity of Thymic Hormones" (D. W. van Bekkum, Eds.), pp. 235–243. Kooyker Scientific, Rotterdam, 1975.
8. White, A., and Burton, P., *Ann. N.Y. Acad. Sci.* **332,** 1, 1979.
9. Dardenne, M., Pleau, J. M., and Bach, J. F., *Eur. J. Immunol* **10,** 83, 1980.
10. Julius, M. H., Simpson, E., and Herzenberg, L. A., *Eur. J. Immunol.* **3,** 645, 1973.
11. Twomey, J. J., Goldstein, G., Lewis, V. M., Bealmear, P. M., and Good, R. A., *Proc. Nat. Acad. Sci. USA* **74,** 2541, 1977.
12. Bach, J. F., Bach, M. A., Charreire, J., Dardenne, M., and Pleau, J. M., *Ann. N.Y. Acad. Sci.* **332,** 23, 1979.
13. Bach, M. A., Fournier, C., and Bach, J. F., *Ann. N.Y. Acad. Sci.* **249,** 316, 1975.
14. Komuro, K., and Boyse, E. A., *Lancet* **1,** 740, 1973.
15. Pleau, J. M., Dardenne, M., Blouquit, Y., and Bach, J. F., *J. Biol. Chem.* **252,** 8045, 1977.
16. Bach, J. F., and Dardenne, M., *Immunology* **25,** 353, 1973.

CELLULAR IMMUNOLOGY **65**, 13–19 (1981)

Concomitant Induction of Cytotoxic and Suppressor Cells: Modulation by Theophylline[1]

MAREK ROLA-PLESZCZYNSKI[2] AND HIEN LIEU

Division of Immunology, Department of Pediatrics, Faculté de Médecine, Université de Sherbrooke, Sherbrooke, Québec J1H 5N4, Canada

Received April 13, 1981; accepted September 9, 1981

Previous studies in man have shown that T cells with suppressor activity were mainly found among a subset bearing Fc receptors for IgG (T_γ). Recently, we found that virus-induced cytotoxic effector cells were also found predominantly among T_γ cells. In the present studies, we present evidence that similar, possibly overlapping T-cell populations can mediate both suppressor and cytotoxic activities when sensitized *in vitro* with virus-infected cells. In fact, both activities are found within the positively selected T_γ subset, but not in the T_γ-depleted population; both activities are abolished by irradiation but not by treatment with mitomycin C; a 1-hr exposition to theophylline at the onset of sensitization enhances both cytotoxic and suppressor activities. The data suggest that development of antiviral cell-mediated immune responses *in vivo* may also be accompanied by a concurrent induction of nonspecific suppressor cells. Such suppressor activity may play a role in the depressed cellular immune responsiveness which is associated with several systemic virus infections.

INTRODUCTION

Human peripheral blood mononuclear leukocytes (PBML) have been induced through *in vitro* sensitization to become cytotoxic against the sensitizing cells. Such inducer target cells have consisted of allogeneic leukocytes (1), tumor cells (2), or virus-infected cells (3). More recently, we have developed a model of *in vitro*-induced cytotoxic effector PBML directed against herpes simplex virus (HSV)-infected cells (4). These effector cells are predominantly found among the T_γ subset, and are generated from theophylline-resistant T_μ cells, while maintaining the theophylline resistance of the latter.

Parallel experiments attempting to induce immunoregulatory cells with suppressor activity on cytotoxic effector cells were hampered by the cytotoxic potential of the suppressor cells themselves. It thus became apparent that overlapping subsets of PBML were potentially responsible for both activities. Recent use of monoclonal antibodies directed at antigens of specific T-cell subsets confirmed the notion that similar antigens revealed a "cytotoxic-suppressor" T cell, in both mice (5) and men (6).

The aim of the present work was to verify whether cytotoxic and suppressor

[1] This research was supported by a grant (MA-6822) from the Medical Research Council of Canada.
[2] Research Scholar of the Conseil de la Recherche en Santé du Québec.

0008-8749/81/170013-07$02.00/0

activity could be generated concomitantly during sensitization with HSV-infected cells. Moreover the effect of short or prolonged exposure of PBML to the phosphodiesterase inhibitor theophylline was analyzed.

MATERIALS AND METHODS

Donors. Blood donors were healthy adult volunteers with a negative history for herpes labialis or genitalis. All had antibodies against HSV-1, as measured by indirect hemagglutination (7), their titers ranging from 1:16 to 1:128.

Blood cell separation. Peripheral blood mononuclear leukocytes (PBML) were isolated from venous blood on a Hypaque–Ficoll gradient as described previously (4). These cells consisted of 70–90% lymphocytes and 10–30% monocytes, as determined by Wright–Giemsa staining and neutral red ingestion or phagocytosis of IgG-sensitized sheep erythrocytes (sE) (8).

Fractionation and identification of PBML subpopulations. Adherent and phagocytic cells were removed by incubating PBML for 2 hr at 37°C in glass petri dishes, followed by carbonyl iron treatment. T cells were identified by their ability to form spontaneous rosettes with neuraminidase-treated sE.

PBML forming spontaneous rosettes (RFC) with sE were separated from non-sE-RFC by use of neuraminidase-treated sE as described by Moretta *et al.* (9). The rosetted mixture was centrifuged on a Ficoll–Hypaque gradient, and the sE-RFC (T cells) pellet treated with distilled water for 10 sec to lyse sE. Greater than 95% of the pelleted cells were sE-RFC.

In order to identify a T-lymphocyte subset bearing receptors for the Fc portion (FcR) of IgG (T_γ), 0.1 ml of purified (sE-RFC) T cells was mixed with a 2% suspension of ox erythrocytes (oE) coated with purified rabbit anti-oE IgG. The mixture was centrifuged to form a pellet and incubated at 37°C for 20 min. The pellet was then gently resuspended and the percentage of rosette-forming cells (T_γ) counted. Similarly, in order to identify T cells bearing receptors for the Fc portion of IgM (T_μ), purified T (sE-RFC) cells were incubated overnight in medium MEM with 20% fetal bovine serum (FBS). After incubation, 0.1 ml of T cells was added to 0.1 ml of 0.5% suspension of oE coated with purified rabbit anti-oE IgM. The mixture was spun into a pellet and incubated at 4°C for 45 min, followed by gentle resuspension and counting of rosetting T_μ cells.

In some experiments, purified populations of T (sE-RFC) cells were further fractionated into T_γ and T_μ subpopulations by rosetting T cells with oEIgG and pelleting the T_γ-enriched fraction through two successive Ficoll–Hypaque gradients. Nonpelleted cells contained approximately 70% T_μ with less than 3% T_γ cells. The pelleted fraction contained 90–95% T_γ cells. T_μ rosettes obtained by reacting T cells with oEIgM were found to be fragile and thus enriched fractions obtained through this method were not used routinely.

In order to identify theophylline-sensitive (Th_s) T cells, PBML were pretreated with 3 m*M* theophylline before rosetting with sE, and the percentage of cells having lost their ability to form rosettes was called Th_s (10, 11). In several experiments, Th_s cells (60% T_γ and 40% T non_μ non_γ, in freshly drawn peripheral blood) were separated from theophylline-resistant (Th_r) T cells (95% T_μ in freshly drawn peripheral blood) by treating purified T cells with theophylline before rosetting with sE and pelleting Th_r sE-RFC through a Ficoll–Hypaque gradient.

Virus-infected cells. Cells used as sensitizing cells in the sensitization cultures or as target cells in the cytotoxicity assays consisted of the human prostatic adenoma MA-160 cell line, uninfected, or infected with HSV-1 (MA-72064), kindly supplied by M. M. Vincent, Bethesda, Maryland. This cell line was originally derived from a male donor with the following HLA phenotype: HLA-A2, 28; B14, 17. Once established, however, the cell line showed no detectable HLA-A or -B antigens. All cells were grown and passaged as described (4).

Sensitization culture. In this paper, the incubation of PBML (or fractions thereof) with uninfected or HSV-1-infected MA-160 cells in order to generate cytotoxic effector cells is referred to as sensitization.

PBML (or fractions thereof) at a concentration of 2×10^6/ml were incubated with 5×10^5 sensitizing cells/ml in 2-ml aliquots as described previously (4). After the incubation period, PBML were removed, washed twice in EMEM, and resuspended at the desired concentration in EMEM supplemented with 10% FBS. Viability was 85–95% by trypan blue exclusion.

Suppressor cell assay. Blastogenesis of fresh PBML cultured in the presence of mitogens was measured by the uptake of [^{3}H]thymidine. Mitogens included concanavalin A (Con A, Pharmacia Fine Chemicals, Piscataway, N.J.) phytohemagglutinin (PHA, Wellcome Laboratories, Research Triangle Park, N.C.), and pokeweed mitogen (PWM, Gibco, Grand Island, N.Y.) at final concentrations of 10 μg/ml, 0.1%, and 0.02%, respectively. Potential suppressor cell activity was assayed by adding 1×10^6 presensitized autologous PBML to 2×10^6 fresh PBML cultures (12). The former were treated after sensitization with either mitomycin C (mit C, Sigma, St. Louis, Mo.), 30 μg/ml for 30 min, or 2000 rad from a cobalt source before being added to the cocultures.

Cytotoxicity assay. The ^{51}Cr-release cytotoxicity assay was performed as described previously (4). The amount of ^{51}Cr released was measured in a Nuclear Chicago gamma counter and expressed as average counts per minute (cpm) of triplicate samples. The percentage of specific ^{51}Cr release was determined as follows: (cpm of ^{51}Cr released from target cells with PBML during incubation − cpm of ^{51}Cr released from target cells alone during incubation)/(total releasable ^{51}Cr − ^{51}Cr released at zero time) $\times$ 100.

Treatment with theophylline. In order to assess the effect of the drug theophylline on the induction of virus-directed cytotoxicity or suppressor activity, cultures were supplemented with 1 m*M* theophylline for 1 hr, washed, and reconstituted to the original conditions for subsequent culture. Alternatively, theophylline was added to the cultures and left throughout the sensitization phase. In preliminary experiments, 1 m*M* final concentration of theophylline was found to be optimal for our studies.

Statistical methods. Results were compared by using Student's two-tailed *t* test.

RESULTS

To determine if suppressor cells were generated during the sensitization culture leading to the induction of cytotoxic cells, PBML were sensitized with HSV-infected cells for 3 days, recovered, washed, and treated either with mitomycin C or irradiation. The newly induced cytotoxic activity was measured in the 5-hr microcytotoxicity assay, whereas the induction of suppressor cells was determined by coculture of sensitized PBML with autologous fresh PBML in the presence of mitogens. In addition, the effect of short or prolonged exposure to theophylline during sensitization was evaluated in regard to the induction of cytotoxic and suppressor cells.

Fresh PBML exhibited very little cytotoxic activity. Presensitization with HSV-infected cells for 3 days, although not of optimal duration, was used in order to permit the observation of enhanced cytotoxicity. Figure 1 illustrates the significant cytotoxic activity induced through sensitization. When PBML were preexposed for 1 hr to theophylline, an enhanced cytotoxic activity was seen ($P < 0.01$). Contact with theophylline throughout sensitization abolished cytotoxicity. Treatment with mit C at the end of sensitization did not affect the cytotoxic response. Irradiation with 2000 rad, however, had a strong inhibitory effect on cytotoxicity, bringing it to the nonsignificant level of fresh PBML. Pretreatment with theophylline had no effect on irradiated cells.

When presensitized mit C-treated PBML were cocultured with autologous PBML in the presence of Con A, a significant suppressor activity was observed ($P < 0.01$, Fig. 2). This was further enhanced by a 1-hr pretreatment with theophylline ($P < 0.05$) but abolished by contact with theophylline throughout sensitization. Sensitized and irradiated PBML showed no suppressor activity. A similar pattern of response was seen with PHA (Fig. 2). In contrast, suppressor cell activity of sensitized PBML was not evident in the presence of PWM, except when PBML had been pretreated for 1-hr with theophylline before sensitization (Fig. 2). Again, irradiated PBML failed to manifest any such suppressor activity.

In order to investigate whether the concomitant cytotoxic and suppressor activities originated from the same PBML subpopulation, PBML were fractionated into

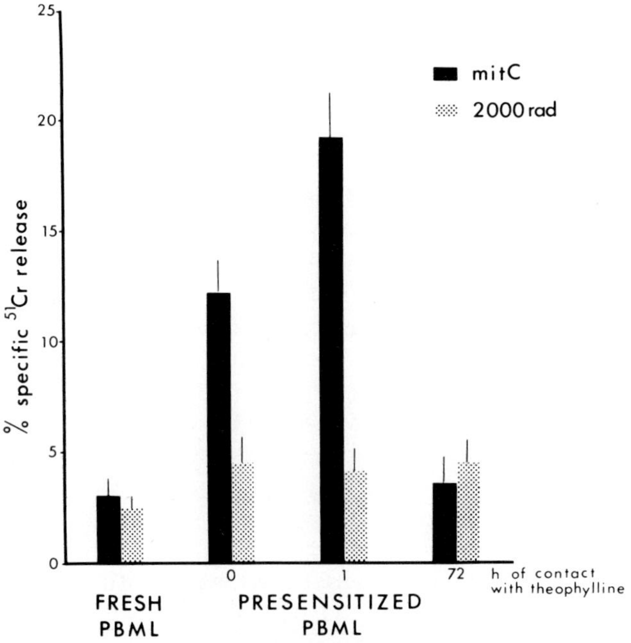

FIG. 1. Cytotoxic activity of fresh or presensitized PBML following either mitomycin C treatment or irradiation. A short preincubation (1 hr) with theophylline enhanced cytotoxicity whereas prolonged exposure throughout sensitization abolished it. Irradiated PBML showed no cytotoxicity.

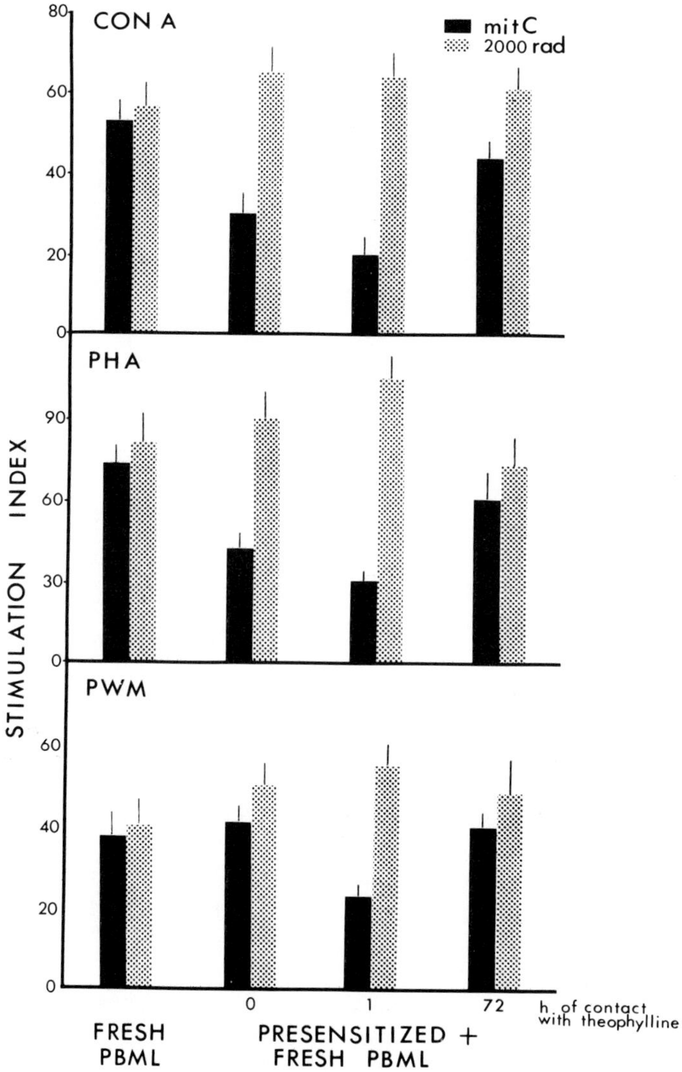

FIG. 2. Suppressor cell activity induced during sensitization of PBML with HSV-infected cells. Enhancement of suppressor activity by 1 hr of pretreatment with theophylline. Abolition of irradiation and prolonged contact with theophylline.

T_γ and T_μ enriched subsets after sensitization with HSV-infected cells in the absence of theophylline, or after a 1-hr pulse with the drug. Table 1 shows that mit C-treated T_γ cells manifested more cytotoxic activity and greater suppression of blastogenesis than unseparated PBML. A 1-hr contact with theophylline enhanced both activities in this subset as it did with unfractionated PBML. T_μ cells showed neither activity. Irradiation abolished both cytotoxic and suppressor cell activites of T_γ as well as of unseparated PBML.

DISCUSSION

The present data demonstrate that mixed cultures of human PBML and virus-infected cells can generate concomitantly cytotoxic cells and suppressor cells. We

TABLE 1

Concomitant Cytotoxic and Suppressor Activity of T-Cell Subsets Sensitized with HSV-Infected Cells. Effects of a 1-hr Pulse with Theophylline at the Onset of Sensitization

Effector cell population		Theophylline[a]	Cytotoxicity[b]	Blastogenesis[c]
MitC-treated	PBML	−	12 ± 1	32 ± 3
		+	19 ± 2	20 ± 2
	T_γ	−	18 ± 2	14 ± 2
		+	25 ± 2	10 ± 1
	T_μ	−	4 ± 1	48 ± 4
		+	4 ± 2	45 ± 5
Irradiated	PBML	−	5 ± 1	65 ± 5
		+	4 ± 1	63 ± 6
	T_γ	−	6 ± 2	55 ± 5
		+	6 ± 2	58 ± 4
	T_μ	−	2 ± 1	61 ± 6
		+	4 ± 1	62 ± 5

[a] One-hour contact with 1 m*M* theophylline at the onset of the sensitization culture.
[b] % ^{51}Cr release (±SE) from MA-72064 target cells.
[c] Stimulation index of cocultures of fresh and presensitized lymphocyte populations with Con A.

have previously shown that such *in vitro*-induced cytotoxic cells are found principally in the T-cell fraction, more precisely among T_γ cells, although some cytotoxic activity was also induced among non-E-rosetting cells (4). Suppressor cells generated in human lymphocyte cultures stimulated with soluble antigen, Con A, or allogeneic leukocytes have also generally been shown to be T cells (13–16), and more specifically T_γ cells (17). Our findings are consistent with these studies since suppressor activity was present predominantly in the T_γ-cell fraction of virus-sensitized PBML.

Manifestation of suppressor cell activity was not dependent on proliferative capacity of suppressor cells since complete blocking of DNA synthesis by mit C did not affect it. This is in agreement with some observers (13, 16, 18), but not with others (19, 20). In contrast, irradiation abrogated suppressor activity as well as cytotoxicity, suggesting that the more profound metabolic effect of this treatment affected cellular functions essential for these activities. Suppressor T cells have previously been found to be radio-sensitive (21), in contrast to helper T_μ cells which were radioresistant.

Generation of virus-directed cytotoxic activity also induced suppressor cells which appeared to lack specificity, since they inhibited proliferative responses of autologous fresh PBML to the mitogens Con A and PHA. Interestingly, however, no suppression of responses to PWM was observed unless sensitized cells were pretreated for 1 hr with theophylline. Preferential activity directed at the predominantly T-cell mitogens may be operative in this situation, but additional studies would be required to further analyze this aspect. Con A-induced suppressor T cells do not exhibit specificity and have been shown to inhibit lymphocyte proliferation in response to mitogens or antigens (13–15). Suppressors induced by antigens have been shown to exhibit some degree of antigenic specificity (16, 21, 22).

Several lines of evidence suggest that cells effecting antiviral cytotoxicity and those suppressing Con A-stimulated lymphocyte cultures may belong to overlapping, if not identical PBML subpopulations: (a) both activities are found within the positively selected T_γ subset of PBML, whereas T_γ-depleted, negatively selected T_μ cells mediated neither activity; (b) both activities were abolished by irradiation, but not by treatment with mit C; (c) a short, one-hour exposition to theophylline enhanced both cytotoxic and suppressor activities, whereas prolonged exposition to the drug throughout sensitization depressed both activities.

Such an exposure-dependent effect of theophylline on cytotoxic cell induction has been consistently observed (23). Transient increase in intracellular cAMP levels by a 1-hr exposure to theophylline may be responsible for the enhancing effect, whereas prolonged exposure and persistently elevated cAMP levels would have the opposite effect. Theophylline-sensitive cells in the E-rosette assay (T_γ) may not necessarily be "sensitive" in more functional assays such as cytotoxicity or proliferation.

The concomitant induction of cytotoxic effector cells directed at virus-infected target cells and suppressor cells may be of clinical importance. It may play a role as modulator of immune responses. It may also be responsible for the depression of cellular immune functions associated with acute virus infection or immunization with live viruses (24, 25).

REFERENCES

1. Hayry, P., and Defendi, V., *Science* **168,** 133, 1970.
2. Zarling, J. M., Raich, P. C., McKeough, M., and Bach, F. H., *Nature (London)* **262,** 691, 1976.
3. Santoli, D., Trinchieri, G., and Lief, F. S., *J. Immunol.* **121,** 526, 1978.
4. Rola-Pleszczynski, M., *J. Immunol.* **125,** 1475, 1980.
5. Cantor, H., and Boyse, E. A., *J. Exp. Med.* **141,** 1390, 1975.
6. Reinherz, E. L., Kung, P. C., Goldstein, G., and Schlossman, S. F., *J. Immunol.* **121,** 1301, 1980.
7. Fuccillo, D. A., Moder, F. L., Catalano, L. W., Vincent, M. M., and Sever, J. L., *Proc. Soc. Exp. Biol. Med.* **133,** 735, 1970.
8. Rola-Pleszczynski, M., and Churchill, W. H., *J. Immunol. Methods* **20,** 255, 1978.
9. Moretta, L., Ferrarini, M., Mingari, M. C., Moretta, A., and Webb, S. R., *J. Immunol.* **117,** 2171, 1976.
10. Shore, A., Dosch, H.-M., and Gelfand, E. W., *Nature (London)* **274,** 586, 1978.
11. Rola-Pleszczynski, M., *Cell. Immunol.* **63,** 000, 1981.
12. Rola-Pleszczynski, M., and Blanchard, R., *Int. Arch. Allergy Appl. Immunol.* **64,** 361, 1981.
13. Fineman, S. M., Mudawwar, F. B., and Geha, R. S., *Cell. Immunol.* **45,** 120, 1979.
14. Reinherz, E. L., and Schlossman, J. F., *J. Immunol.* **122,** 1335, 1979.
15. Roff, H. F., Cochrum, K. C., and Stobo, J. D., *J. Immunol.* **121,** 2311, 1978.
16. Rinehart, J. J., *Cell. Immunol.* **56,** 142, 1980.
17. Moretta, L., Webb, S. R., Grossi, C. E., Lydyard, P. M., and Cooper, M. D., *J. Exp. Med.* **146,** 184, 1977.
18. Hayes, B. F., and Fauci, A. S., *J. Immunol.* **120,** 700, 1978.
19. Shou, L., Schwartz, S. A., and Good, R. A., *J. Exp. Med.* **143,** 1100, 1976.
20. Hollgren, H. M., and Uanis, E. J., *Immunology* **118,** 2004, 1977.
21. McMichael, A. J., and Sasazukis, T., *J. Exp. Med.* **146,** 368, 1977.
22. Borkowsky, W., and Balentine, F. T., *J. Immunol.* **122,** 1867, 1979.
23. M. Rola-Pleszcynski and H. Lieu, *Immunopharmacol.,* in press.
24. Brody, J. A., McAlister, R., *Amer. Rev. Resp. Dis.* **90,** 607, 1964.
25. Kantzler, G. B., Lauteria, S. F., Cusumano, C. L., Lee, J. D., Ganguly, R., and Waldman, R. H., *Infect. Immunity* **10,** 996, 1974.

CELLULAR IMMUNOLOGY 65, 20–32 (1981)

Antitumor Immunity in B-Lymphocyte-Deprived Mice

II. *In Vitro* Studies[1]

PNINA BRODT AND JULIUS GORDON[2]

Department of Surgery, Division of Surgical Research, McGill University, Donner Building, 740 Docteur Penfield Avenue, Montreal, Quebec H3A 1A4, Canada

Received April 30, 1981; accepted August 31, 1981

In a previous publication, we reported that B-lymphocyte-deprived mice possess a heightened *in vivo* resistance to a methycholanthrene-induced syngeneic fibrosarcoma. The present *in vitro* study has disclosed that spleens of such mice possess a significantly higher cytotoxic activity against the same tumor compared to normal rabbit globulin-injected control animals, and that this increase cannot be accounted for by the mere elimination of B lymphocytes. The cell mediating this response was found to be a natural-killer-like cell on the basis of its organ distribution, its full activation without immunization, its target specificity shown directly and by cold target inhibition experiments, and by its surface markers. It is suggested that this increased activity, which does not appear to decline with age, may be responsible for the heightened *in vivo* antitumor resistance of T mice.

INTRODUCTION

In a previous communication, we reported that mice, selectively depleted of B lymphocytes by the continuous administration of rabbit anti-mouse IgM serum from birth, have a heightened resistance to both the growth and metastasis of a syngeneic, transplantable, methylcholanthrene (MCA)-induced sarcoma (1). This observation was later extended to include a heightened resistance to the transplantation of other chemically induced tumors, as well as an increased resistance to the induction of primary tumors by MCA (P. Brodt and J. Gordon, submitted for publication). The present *in vitro* study of cell-mediated cytotoxicity in B-lymphocyte-deprived mice was consequently undertaken. The results to be described indicate that spleens of the immunosuppressed mice have a heightened natural-killer (NK)-like activity directed at both the MCA-induced sarcoma originally studied and other unrelated tumor targets. Although the NK cell has been extensively studied and well characterized, firm evidence for its relevance to host resistance to neoplasia *in vivo* is still lacking. We believe that our results serve to reaffirm that the NK cell may indeed provide an efficient line of defense against tumor growth and metastasis.

[1] This work was supported by a grant from the National Cancer Institute of Canada.

[2] Medical Research Council of Canada Career Investigator.

0008-8749/81/170020-13$02.00/0

MATERIALS AND METHODS

Animals. C57BL/6 and (C57BL/6xC3H)F1 mice used throughout this investigation were purchased from BioBreeding Laboratories, Ottawa, Ontario.

Anti-IgM-mediated suppression. The procedure for the production of rabbit anti-IgM serum and suppression of neonatal animals has been previously described (2). Briefly, serum pools from 50 to 90 rabbits immunized with IgM derived from the Balb/c plasmacytoma MOPC 104-E were precipitated twice with ammonium sulfate, and the final product obtained at 33% saturation was dialyzed, centrifuged at 100,000*g*, and frozen in small aliquots. A normal rabbit serum pool (NRG) purchased from Pel-Freez Biologicals, Inc. (Rogers, Ark.) was processed in an identical manner. Before use, antibodies to mouse red cells were removed from both preparations by absorption with rat and mouse erythrocytes fixed with 0.5% gluteraldehyde. For suppression of neonatal mice, 5–10 mg of the serum preparation in a volume of 0.05–0.1 ml was injected within the first 2 days of life and three times a week thereafter for the duration of the experiment.

Mice treated with anti-IgM from birth by the above procedure have been shown to be deprived of B lymphocytes and of B-lymphocyte functions. Analyses carried out on mice up to the age of 20 weeks or longer included tests for surface Ig-bearing cells by radioautography (3, 4) and by the fluorescence-activated cell sorter (P. de Baetselier and J. Gordon, unpublished observations), for serum IgM by immune diffusion and by a radioimmunoassay (K. Abikar and J. Gordon, in preparation), and for the production of specific antibody by immunization with sheep erythrocytes (K. Abikar and J. Gordon, in preparation). Other tests carried out on mice up to 31 weeks of age included activation of cells *in vitro* with LPS and immunization with a variety of antigens (2). Mice used throughout these studies were defined as B-cell deprived based on the above criteria. Some of these mice possessed a variable, low level of serum IgG, which probably represents secretion from long-lived cells and does not bear on the immunocompetence of these animals (K. Abikar and J. Gordon, in preparation).

The immunosuppressed status of the mice was routinely confirmed at 5 to 6 weeks of age by assay of serum IgM and by the detection of an excess of circulating rabbit anti-IgM antibodies. Throughout this study, mice treated with anti-IgM in this manner will be referred to as suppressed, anti-IgM-treated, or B-cell deprived, interchangeably.

Mice treated from birth with NRG were normally used as controls. They are referred to as NRG-treated or controls. In some experiments, nontreated mice were also employed and they are referred to as normal mice.

Tumors. Sarcomas MCA-2, MCA-3, and T-10 were induced in our laboratory in B6C3F1 mice by the injection of 3-methylcholanthrene following the procedure of Klein *et al.* (5).

B-16, a spontaneous C57BL/6J metastasizing melanoma, was obtained courtesy of Dr. Gilles Lamoureux (Institut Armand Frappier, Laval, Quebec). It was maintained as a solid tumor in C57BL/6 females and was grown as an adherent monolayer in culture.

C3H/HeJ, a spontaneous mammary adenocarcinoma, was a kind gift of Dr. R. Kerbell (Department of Pathology, Queen's University, Kingston, Ontario). It arose in an 18-month-old female retired breeder and was maintained in tissue culture as an adherent monolayer.

P815-X2, a methylcholanthrene-induced mastocytoma of DBA/2 origin, was a kind gift from Dr. Robert Phillips of the Ontario Cancer Institute. The tumor was maintained in the ascites form in DBA/2 males and in suspension cultures *in vitro*.

YAC-1, a Moloney leukemia virus (MLV)-induced lymphoma of A/Sn origin, was a kind gift of Dr. G. Dorval (Royal Victoria Hospital, Montreal, Quebec). Tumor cells were maintained *in vitro* in suspension cultures.

All tumors were cultured in RPMI 1640 containing 1% Hepes buffer (1 *M* solution), 0.001% gentamicin sulfate and 10% FCS. Those which grew as adherent monolayers were trypsinized for each passage using a 0.25% solution of trypsin in MD medium (6).

Cytotoxic assays. Adherent tumors used as target cells were labeled with ^{125}IUdR (7). Cultured tumor cells (5×10^5) in RPMI medium containing 20% FCS were seeded in 60 × 15-mm tissue culture dishes 1 day before the assay. On the day of the assay, 2 μci/ml ^{125}IUdR and 10% FUdR 10^{-4} *M* were added to the cells and incubation was continued for 4 hours. The cells were then trypsinized, washed three times, and seeded at a concentration of 5×10^3/well in 0.1 ml medium into 96-well flat-bottom microplates (Falcon Microtest II tissue culture plates). Lymphocytes in 0.1 ml medium were added to the target cells in varying effector:target cell (E:T) ratios in quadruplicate. Mixtures were incubated at 37°C in a humid 5% CO_2 incubator on a rocker platform. Rocking was carried out for 16 hr at 7 cycles/min. It was then stopped and incubation continued for 2 more hr. Aliquots (0.05 ml) of the supernatants were then collected and ^{125}I was counted in a gamma counter model LKB. Specific release was calculated as

$$\frac{^{125}\text{I released into the supernatant} - \text{spontaneous release}}{\text{Maximum release} - \text{spontaneous release}}.$$

Spontaneous release was calculated from wells containing target cells and medium only. It normally ranged from 10 to 20% of the maximum release. Addition of nonlabeled (cold) target cells to the wells did not alter the level of spontaneous release. Maximum release was determined by treating target cells with 0.1% SDS.

Tumor cells grown in suspension culture (YAC-1) were labeled with ^{51}Cr by incubating 5×10^6 cells in 0.2 ml of 100 μci/ml $Na_2{}^{51}CrO_4$ solution in saline for 1 hr, followed by three washes. Labeled (1×10^4) target cells were mixed with different numbers of effector cells in a total volume of 0.2 ml in microtiter plates. Incubation was carried out for 4–5 hr with rocking (7 cycles/min). Each effector–target cell combination was assayed in triplicate, and the cytotoxic activity was expressed either as percentage specific release or in lytic units, defined as the number of effector cells required to yield a specific release of 20%.

Fractionation of effector cells. The effector cells assayed were from bone marrow (two femurs) or spleen, from which erythrocytes have been eliminated by treatment with ACK (0.155 *M* NH_4Cl, 0.1 m*M* Na_2 EDTA, 0.01 *M* $KHCO_3$) (8).

T lymphocytes were removed by treatment with a rabbit anti-mouse T-cell serum (Litton Bionetics, Kensington, Md.) and Cedarlane Laboratories (Toronto, Ontario) and rabbit complement (Lowtox complement, Cedarlane Laboratories), absorbed, where stated with an equal volume of packed spleen cells.

Spleen cells (50×10^6) were incubated in a 1:10 dilution of antiserum for 45 min at room temperature. Cells were washed once before treatment with a 10-fold diluted complement, for 30 min at 37°C. Nontreated cells, or cells incubated with complement only served as controls. Removal of T cells was confirmed by lack of activation of the surviving lymphocytes with concanavalin A.

Spleen cells were fractionated by passage over nylon wool columns according to the procedure of Julius *et al.* (9).

Phagocytic cells were removed by agitating spleen cells with carbonyl iron at 37°C for 35 min; the carbon-laden cells were removed with a magnet (10). Depletion of phagocytic cells was ascertained by testing the ability of the remaining cells to ingest latex particles.

Fc receptor-bearing cells were isolated on SRBC anti-SRBC monolayers by the method of Kedar *et al.* (11). Tissue culture dishes were first coated with poly(L-lysine), then SRBC, followed by a hyperimmune anti-SRBC serum, gift of Dr. R. Murgita, Department of Microbiology and Immunology, McGill University, Montreal, Quebec; twenty million spleen cells were added to each 5 cm dish, incubated at 37°C for 30 min with and 30 min without rocking (5 cycles/min). After removal of nonadherent cells, adherent cells were dislodged by a further incubation in the presence of 36 μg/ml protein A.

A *cold target inhibition* assay was carried out according to a modification of the one described by Koren *et al.* (12). To assay inhibition of labeled target cell lysis by tumors growing in suspension, several concentrations of the latter in 0.05 ml RPMI-FCS were seeded into microtiter wells. To each well, 8×10^5 spleen cells in 0.05 ml medium were added and the mixtures were incubated at 37°C for 30 min. To study inhibition by adherent tumor cells, they were seeded into the wells and incubated at 37°C for either 4 or 18 hr prior to the addition of spleen cells, to allow the regeneration of surface antigens after trypsinization (13). Adherent or nonadherent cells were then incubated with effector spleen cells for 30 min. This incubation was followed in both assays by the addition to each well of 0.1 ml RPMI-FCS containing 10^4 Cr-labeled target cells. The incubation was then continued for 5 additional hr and the specific release determined as previously described. Percentage inhibition was calculated as

$$\frac{\text{Specific release without inhibitor-specific release in the presence of inhibitor}}{\text{Specific release without inhibitor}}.$$

Only cold target cells which gave a dose-dependent inhibition of isotope release were considered to have specifically competed for the killer cells (14).

RESULTS

In the initial *in vitro* experiments, the cytotoxicity of spleen cells from T-10 tumor-bearing normal and suppressed mice against T-10 was compared. These experiments disclosed that the increased *in vivo* resistance of the suppressed mice to this tumor was paralleled by an increased cytotoxicity *in vitro*. However, these experiments have also demonstrated that suppressed mice which had not been injected with the tumor also displayed a heightened cytotoxicity against T-10 (Fig. 1), as well as against two other unrelated tumors of parental origin (Table 1). These results raised the possibility that the cells responsible for the increased ac-

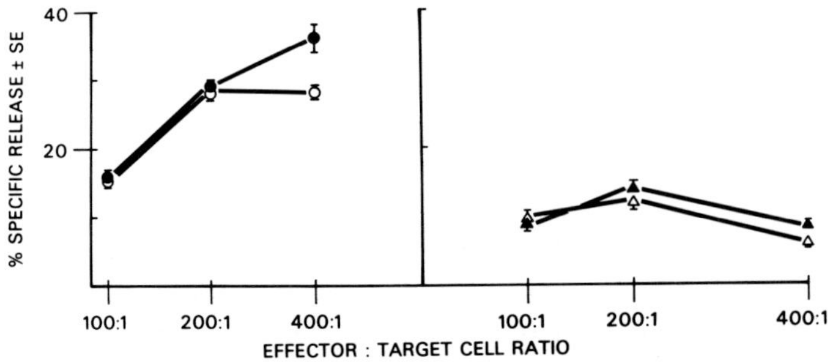

FIG. 1. The effect of injection of tumor T-10 on spleen cell cytotoxicity. Six- to eight-week-old suppressed and normal males were injected sc with 1 × 10^6 T-10 cells. Their spleens were assayed for cytotoxicity 9 days later, together with cells from mice which had not been injected with tumor. The target cells were labeled with ^{125}IUdR; for details of the assay see text. The left diagram shows the reactivity of anti-IgM-suppressed mice injected with T-10 (●) or uninjected (○). The right diagram represents normal mice injected with T-10 (▲) or uninjected (△).

tivity in the spleen of suppressed mice may share characteristics with NK cells. This suggestion was reinforced by the distribution of cytotoxic activity, i.e., its presence in the spleen and its absence from lymph nodes (data not shown) and by its insensitivity to an anti-T-cell serum. As can be seen in Table 2, treatment of spleen cells of anti-IgM-injected mice with anti-T-cell serum and complement, which eliminated 70–85% of the cells, did not reduce but enriched cytotoxic activity 1.6- to 3.6-fold. Based on these observations, further analyses were carried out with cells of unimmunized mice using YAC-1, a lymphoma of A/Sn origin, widely employed as a target for NK cells.

Spleen cells from 7- to 10-week-old anti-IgM- and NRG-treated mice were assayed for their ability to lyse ^{51}Cr-labeled YAC-1 cells. The results from 11 experiments shown in Fig. 2 demonstrate that target cell lysis by splenocytes from the immunosuppressed mice was higher than that by splenocytes of NRG-treated

TABLE 1

Cytotoxicity of Spleen Cells to B-16 Melanoma and C3H/HeJ Adenocarcinoma following Injection of the Tumor T-10[a]

Mice	Percentage specific cytotoxicity on target cells: B-16	C3H/HeJ
Anti-IgM-treated, injected with T-10[b]	15	20
Normal, injected with T-10	3	0
Noninjected controls	1	0
Maximum release	16,580 ± 144 (cpm)	14,356 ± 44
Spontaneous release	3,184 ± 90 (cpm)	6,711 ± 114

[a] Results are expressed as percentage specific release of ^{125}IUDR after an 18-hr incubation period of effector and target cells at a ratio of 250:1. SE was 0.3–5% of the mean.

[b] The assays were carried out 9 and 10 days after the sc injection of 1 × 10^6 T-10 cells.

TABLE 2

The Effect of Elimination of T Cells on the Cytotoxic Activity of Spleen Cells from Suppressed Mice

Experiment	Percentage specific release of ^{125}IUDR[a]: Nontreated spleen cells	Percentage specific release of ^{125}IUDR[a]: Spleen cells treated with anti-T-cell serum and complement	Maximum release, spontaneous release (cpm ± SE)
1	8	22	5,721 ± 22 377 ± 24
2A	23	34	7,422 ± 467
2B	20	32	1,580 ± 66
3	28	100	14,462 ± 902 7,394 ± 265
4	15	55	16,580 ± 144 3,184 ± 90

[a] Effector and target cells mixed in a ratio of 200:1 were incubated for 18–20 hr. except in Experiment 3, where the reaction was allowed to proceed for 42 hr. The target cells used in Experiments 1–3 were T-10 tumor cells; in Experiment 4, the B-16 melanoma was substituted.

controls. An increase was also observed in the cytolytic activity in the bone marrow of B-lymphocyte-deprived mice (results not shown). For quantitative analysis of the results, the cytotoxicity of spleen cells measured at four killer to target cell ratios was computed as a single parameter k according to the procedure of Pross *et al.* (15).[3] The k values thus calculated from data of 10 separate experiments

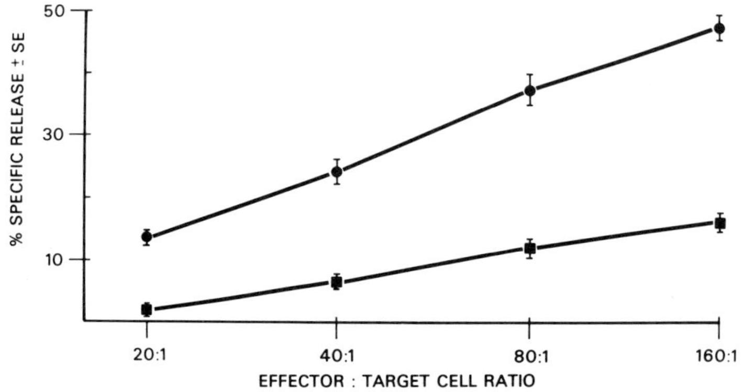

FIG. 2. Cytotoxicity of spleen cells from anti-IgM- and NRG-treated mice assayed on ^{51}Cr-labeled YAC-1 target cells. 2×10^5–1.6×10^6 spleen cells from either anti-IgM- or NRG-treated mice were incubated for 5 hr at 37°C in microtiter wells with 1×10^4 ^{51}Cr-labeled YAC-1 cells. The isotope released into the supernatants was then counted. Results are expressed as a mean ± SE of 11 experiments in which mice ranged in age from 7 to 10 weeks. Spleens from anti-IgM-treated mice (●); spleens from NRG-treated mice (■).

[3] This analysis was used rather than the conventional one which is based on measurement of lytic units because the dose–response curves obtained for the two experimental groups were not parallel.

were three to eight times higher for the anti-IgM-treated, compared to that of the NRG-injected group, with a mean ratio of *k* of 4.8. Accordingly, the increase in cytotoxic activity in the spleens of anti-IgM-treated mice was far greater than could be accounted for by an approximately twofold enrichment of the killer cells due to the elimination of B lymphocytes. Thus, our initial interpretation of the results obtained with the T-10 tumor target was confirmed using the YAC-1 assay. Reciprocal cold target inhibition assays also suggested that the effector cell against the two targets may be one and the same. As shown in Fig. 3 using effector cells from suppressed mice, nonlabeled T-10 cells could inhibit the lysis of ^{51}Cr-labeled YAC-1, and nonlabeled-YAC-1 could inhibit the lysis of ^{125}IUdR-labeled T-10. Similarly, two additional MCA-induced tumors, which like T-10 grew less well in anti-IgM-treated mice, could also compete with YAC-1 target cells (Fig. 4). It is to be noted that the NK-insensitive tumors P815-X2 and EL-4 (not shown) did not compete with the YAC-1 target cells, indicating that the target specificity of the effector cells from the suppressed mice is similar to that of NK cells from normal animals.

The aim of an additional control experiment was to rule out the participation of serum factors in the lytic reaction observed. Such factors could be of murine origin, or present in the serum but originating from the rabbit anti-IgM or NRG injected. As shown in Table 3, addition of serum either from NRG or from anti-IgM-injected mice, or the rabbit anti-mouse IgM preparation had no influence on the cytotoxic assay.

In subsequent experiments, additional characteristics of the lytic reaction and of the effector cells as seen in anti-IgM-treated mice and in the conventional NK reaction were compared.

Spleen cells of suppressed and NRG-treated mice were passed through columns of nylon wool: 75–85% of the cells of the former and 40–50% of the latter were recovered in the nonadherent fraction. Whereas such depletion of B lymphocytes

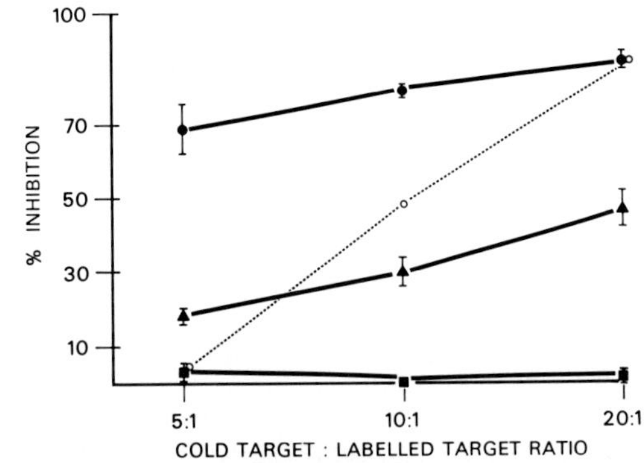

FIG. 3. Cold target inhibition assay. Results of two series of reciprocal cold target inhibition experiments are shown. The heavy, uninterrupted lines illustrate experiments using ^{51}Cr-labeled YAC-1 cells as target and unlabeled YAC-1 (●), T-10 (▲), and P815-X2 (■) tumor cells as inhibitors. The effector cells used were from 10- to 15-week-old anti-IgM-treated mice; the ratio of effector to target cell was 80:1, with a mean specific ^{51}Cr release in the absence of competing targets of 38%. The mean and SE of three experiments are shown. The interrupted line refers to a competition experiment using ^{125}IUdR-labeled T-10 cells as target. The effector-to-target ratio used was 200:1, yielding a specific release of 21%. The competing unlabeled tumor shown is YAC-1 (O --- O).

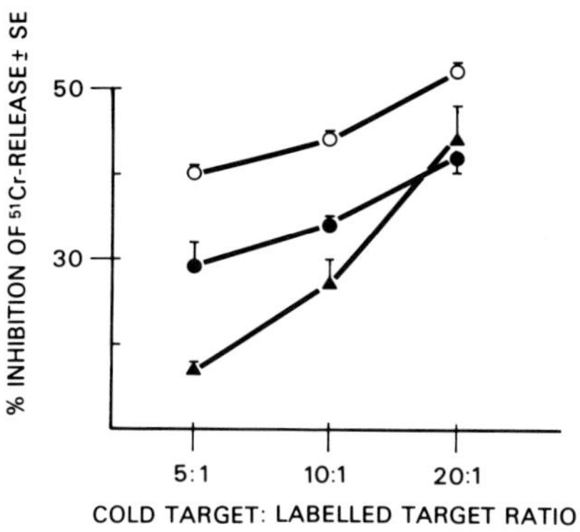

FIG. 4. Cold target inhibition assay. Unlabeled tumor cells used as inhibitors were seeded in microtiter wells in triplicates in concentrations of 20, 10, and 5 $\times 10^4$. They were incubated for 30 min with 8 $\times 10^5$ spleen cells, followed by the addition of 10^4 ^{51}Cr-labeled YAC-1 target cells, and were incubated for a further 5 hr. The results obtained are expressed as percentage inhibition of ^{51}Cr release at different ratios of cold to radiolabeled target cell. The following tumors were used as competitors: MCA-2 (○), MCA-3 (●), and T-10 (▲).

increased the anti-YAC-1 reactivity of the control cell suspension, it failed to elevate this activity to the level given by the splenocytes of suppressed animals, which in turn was not enriched by passage through nylon wool (Fig. 5).

The removal of phagocytic cells by treatment with carbonyl iron, which resulted in a loss of 20–25% of the spleen cells with elimination of 90% of the phagocytic activity, as tested by carbonyl iron uptake, resulted in a 20–30% loss of cytotoxicity from the suppressed spleen preparation (Table 4).

On the basis of the forgoing results, an attempt was made to enrich the killer cell population by a two-step fractionation procedure aimed at the selective removal of nylon-wool-adherent and Thy-1-positive cells. Spleen cells from suppressed mice

TABLE 3

The Effect of Serum from Anti-IgM and NRG Treated Mice on the Lysis of ^{51}Cr-Labeled YAC by Spleen Cells

Source of spleen cells	Nil	Mouse serum added[b] serum dilution: No. 1 10^{-2}	No. 1 10^{-3}	No. 2 10^{-2}	No. 2 10^{-3}	No. 3 10^{-2}	No. 3 10^{-3}	No. 4 10^{-1}	No. 4 10^{-2}	Rabbit anti-mouse IgM 10^{-2}	Rabbit anti-mouse IgM 10^{-3}
NRG-treated mice	10[a]	9	10	13	12	12	11			12	11
Anti-IgM-treated mice	47							45	47		

[a] Results are expressed as percentage specific release of ^{51}Cr after a 4-hr incubation period of effector and target cells at a ratio of 80:1, in the presence or absence of the test sera, in the dilutions indicated.

[b] Sera 1, 2, and 3 were collected from three anti-IgM-treated mice. Preparation No. 4 was a pool of sera from two NRG-treated mice. The rabbit anti-mouse IgM preparation shown in the last column was the one used routinely to suppress mice.

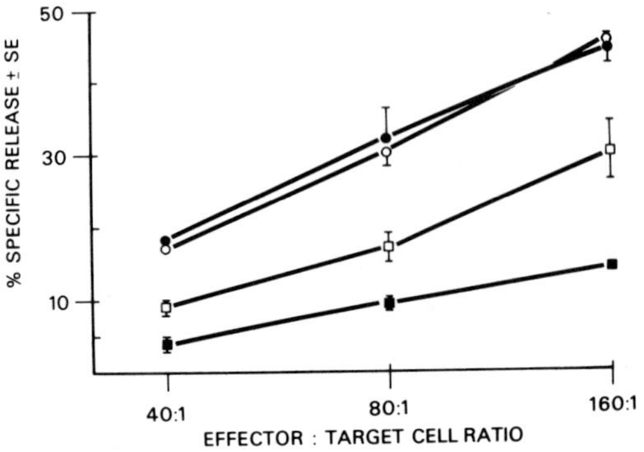

FIG. 5. Cytotoxicity of nylon wool-fractionated spleen cells. Results are expressed as the mean ± SE from two experiments carried out with cells of 9- and 12-week-old mice. Splenocytes from anti-IgM treated mice: (●) non-fractionated; (○) nylon wool passed. Splenocytes of NRG-treated mice: (■) nonfractionated; (□) nylon wool passed.

were passed through a nylon wool column and the nonadherent fraction was treated with anti-T-cell serum and complement. The combined procedure resulted in the elimination of 90–95% of the viable cells present in the original suspension. The lytic activity of the remaining 5–10% is illustrated in Fig. 6. It demonstrates a marked, fourfold enrichment of the killer cells in this fraction as compared to non-adherent spleen cells treated with complement only. Smears prepared of the killer cell-enriched preparation revealed a preponderance of small lymphocytes and some, mostly immature, granulocytes.

DISCUSSION

The present investigation was prompted by our previous observation that anti-IgM-injected mice have a heightened resistance to the chemically-induced synge-

TABLE 4

The Effect of the Removal of Phagocytic Cells on the Ability of Spleen Cells from Anti-IgM-Treated Mice to Lyse T-10 Cells

Experiment	Percentage specific release of ^{125}IUDR[a]: Nontreated cells	Percentage specific release of ^{125}IUDR[a]: Cells treated with carbonyl iron and magnet	Maximum release, spontaneous release (cpm ± SE)
1	12	8	14,954 ± 80 1,900 ± 142
2[b]	23	17	80,600 ± 7,000 10,973 ± 564
3	54	44	11,646 ± 458 4,233 ± 22

[a] The assay was carried out at a killer to target cell ratio of 200:1, the incubation was for 18 hr. except for Experiment 3, where it was prolonged to 24 hr. SE was 2–8% of the mean.

[b] Mice were injected sc with 10^6 T-10 cells 9 days prior to assay. Other animals in the study were not injected with the tumor.

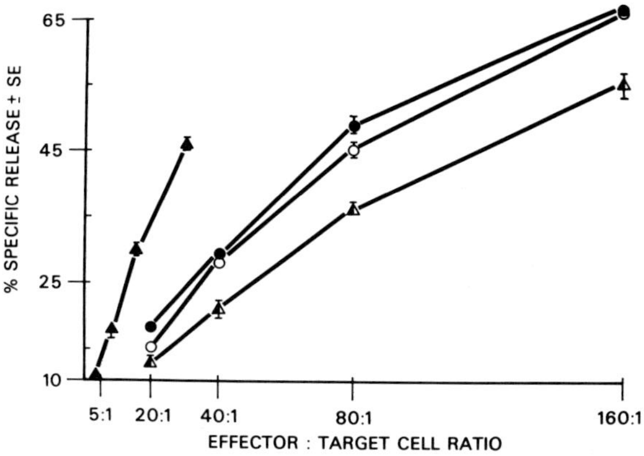

FIG. 6. Enrichment of cytotoxic cells from the spleen of anti-IgM-treated mice. These results were obtained with a pool of spleen cells from 5- to 9-week-old anti-IgM-treated mice. (○) nonfractionated cells; (●) nylon-wool-passed cells; (△) nylon-wool-passed cells treated with rabbit complement; (▲) nylon-wool-passed cells treated with rabbit anti-T-cell; serum and complement.

neic sarcoma T-10 (1), and was undertaken to elucidate the cellular basis of this increased resistance.

The initial *in vivo* experiments carried out with ^{125}IUdR-labeled T-10 cells showed that spleen cells of suppressed tumor-bearing mice displayed a consistently and significantly higher lytic activity than cells from control, NRG-treated tumor-bearing animals. Subsequent experiments revealed that this cytotoxic activity lacked target specificity and furthermore, that it was detectable at equally high levels in suppressed mice, regardless whether they had been previously injected with the tumor. These results, as well as those indicating that the cytolytic activity was not mediated by T cells, suggested common features between these and NK-mediated reactions. Using the NK sensitive YAC-1 lymphoma as a target confirmed this hypothesis. Thus spleen, bone marrow, but not lymph node cells from the suppressed mice displayed a heightened reactivity against YAC-1 cells, and cold target inhibition assays demonstrated that the same effector cells were likely to be active against the two targets. Using the NK-insensitive targets, EL-4 lymphoma and P-815 mastocytoma maintained the analogy further, as spleen cells from suppressed mice also failed to kill these targets. Subsequent fractionation experiments lent further support to this interpretation.

Thus there is general agreement that NK activity is not mediated by Ig-bearing B lymphocytes (10, 16), nor by cells expressing high levels of Thy-1 antigens, such as cells which would be eliminated by a single treatment with anti-T cell antibodies (16–19). Furthermore, NK cells do not take up iron particles (17), nor are they thought to have readily detectable high avidity receptors for Fc (20). Morphologically they have been shown to resemble small lymphocytes (20, 21). In parallel with these observations, the cytolytic anti-YAC-1 activity of spleen cells of suppressed mice, which are devoid of B lymphocytes was not modified by passage through nylon wool, it was enriched by treatment with anti-T cell serum and complement, and it was only partially reduced by the removal of phagocytic cells and Fc-receptor-bearing lymphocytes (results not shown). In a highly enriched population of killer cells representing 5–10% of the original spleen cell population, the preponderant cell identified, besides some immature granulocytes, was a small lymphocyte.

Accordingly, in terms of all the parameters examined, the effector cells present in the spleen of the anti-IgM-treated mice could not be distinguished qualitatively from the cells present in normal spleens which mediate NK functions. Quantitatively, the total cytotoxic activity in the spleen was higher in the suppressed animals despite the lower cellularity of their spleen, and the increase was considerably greater than could be accounted for by mere removal of B lymphocytes. Furthermore, NK activity was also higher in the bone marrow of suppressed mice, where the cellularity in suppressed and in control animals was comparable.

Our initial observation was that anti-IgM-treated mice displayed a heightened resistance to T-10 *in vivo*. The results described in the present communication have shown an augmented NK activity in the spleen of suppressed mice directed against the same tumor *in vitro*. The very same experiments which assigned the increased *in vitro* responsiveness to NK, failed to identify an increase in any other immune parameter in suppressed mice. Accordingly, the most plausible interpretation of the overall results is that the augmented NK reactivity may be responsible for the heightened anti-tumor resistance of suppressed mice *in vivo*.[4]

An alternative to the above interpretation is that the anti-IgM preparation injected may be directly involved and thus be responsible for the observed augmented lysis of tumor cells. Indeed, Hansson *et al.* (23) and Durdik and his collaborators (24) have shown that some rabbit sera may contain natural antibodies which react preferentially with NK-sensitive target cells via an ADCC-like mechanism. However, several lines of evidence would suggest that this is not the case in the present investigation. Thus whereas the putative natural antibodies reactive to NK-sensitive targets should be present in the NRG, as well as in the anti-IgM preparations, heightened reactivity was not observed in any of our experiments carried out with NRG-injected mice *in vivo* or *in vitro*. Furthermore, the anti-IgM preparations used failed to show cytotoxic activity in a ^{51}Cr-release assay against the T-10 fibrosarcoma, or against the YAC-1 tumor with or without the addition of normal spleen cells. Similarly, sera from tumor-bearing or tumor-free suppressed mice which contained circulating rabbit globulins were also without activity *in vitro* or *in vivo* upon injection into tumor-bearing control mice following different dose and time schedules (P. Brodt and J. Gordon, unpublished observations). Finally, our interpretation is greatly reinforced by the demonstration that in addition to resistance to tumor, other *in vivo* manifestations of natural resistance are also significantly augmented in anti-IgM-treated mice, activities which would be difficult to attribute to natural antibodies in the rabbit serum. Among these augmented natural resistance mechanisms are the early resistance to *L. monocytogenes*, to *T. musculi* and hybrid resistance to parental bone marrow and tumor (25). The latter have been shown to be closely associated to NK reactivity against tumors (26).

Although the reason why treatment with anti-IgM results in augmentation of NK activity is presently not clear, several possibilities may be envisaged. It is

[4] In a previous study, Gidlund *et al.* (22) failed to detect a considerable increase of NK activity in anti-IgM-treated mice. Although we cannot at present offer a satisfactory explanation for this discrepancy, NK activity has previously been shown to be greatly dependent on factors such as strain of origin and environmental conditions. A difference in the protocol of immunosuppression, as well as the assay systems used, may also account for this discrepancy.

conceivable that treatment may effect NK levels indirectly. Thus possible subclinical viral infections in the immunosuppressed mice could activate NK via interferon production. This alternative is however unlikely as interferon levels are not elevated in anti-IgM-treated mice (experiments performed in collaboration with Dr. R. B. Stewart, Queen's University, Kingston, Ontario). Furthermore, whereas interferon-activated NK cells were reported in the past to loose their characteristic target selectivity (19), splenocytes from suppressed mice did not kill target cells normally insensitive to NK.

Anti-IgM antibodies have been shown to activate B lymphocytes (27–29), and the experiments described cannot formally rule out a similar direct activation of NK cells by antibody. This explanation is however also unlikely as such activation of B lymphocytes involves fully differentiated cells presumably via their membrane-bound Ig (30), which has not been detected up-to-date on NK cells.

It is possible that anti-IgM by blocking B cell differentiation may shunt a common precursor to an alternative differentiation pathway. Such a mechanism might be plausible based on the observation that nude mice deprived of T cells show a similar increase in NK activity (31). This view would identify the common precursor as a pre-T pre-B pre-NK lymphocyte. A weakness of this interpretation is that no increase in T cell or T cell reactivity was detected in B lymphocyte-deprived mice (2). An alternative explanation advanced for the increase in NK activity in athymic mice has been the elimination of a T cell which might regulate NK levels (32). However, this view would not explain the increase in NK in anti-IgM-treated mice unless one were to postulate the existence of regulatory B cells, as well as T cells for NK activity. Alternatively, an increase in NK in anti-IgM-treated or B mice may be a reflection of a homeostatic regulation, providing a compensation for the removal of an important immune pathway.

The experiments described have clearly established that there is an increase in the level of cytolytic activity in the spleen of B lymphocyte-deprived mice, and by all the criteria examined, this activity is indistinguishable from that mediated by NK cells. Indirect evidence suggests that this activity may indeed be involved in the protection of anti-IgM-treated mice against tumor growth *in vivo*. Elucidation of the mechanisms responsible for the increase of natural host resistance in anti-IgM-treated mice requires further experimentation.

ACKNOWLEDGMENTS

We wish to thank Els Schotman and Brian Doyle for their excellent technical assistance and Brenda Bewick for typing this manuscript. We are grateful to Dr. H. Pross of Queen's University, Kingston, Ontario for analyzing our data by his method described in reference 15. Dr. Pross is supported by a grant from the Ontario Cancer Treatment and Research Foundation.

REFERENCES

1. Brodt, P., and Gordon, J., *J. Immunol.* **121,** 359, 1978.
2. Gordon, J., *J. Immunol. Methods* **25,** 227, 1979.
3. Osmond, D. G., and Gordon, J., *Cell. Immunol.* **42,** 188, 1979.
4. Osmond, D. G., and Gordon, J., *In* "Experimental Hematology Today 1979" (S. J. Baum and G. D. Ledney, Eds.), pp. 129–138. Springer-Verlag, New York, 1979.
5. Klein, G., Sjögren, O., Klein, E., and Hellström, K. E., *Cancer Res.* **20,** 1561, 1960.
6. Ruddle, N. H. *In* "In Vitro Methods of Cell-Mediated Immunity" (B. R. Bloom and P. R. Glade, Eds.), pp. 401–407. Academic Press, New York, 1971.

7. Ting, C.-C., Bushar, G. S., Rodrigues, D., and Herberman, R. B., *J. Immunol.* **115,** 1351, 1975.
8. Ting, C.-C., Rodrigues, D., Bushar, G. S., and Herberman, R. B., *J. Immunol.* **116,** 236, 1976.
9. Julius, M. H., Simpson, E., and Herzenberg, L. A., *Eur. J. Immunol.* **3,** 645, 1973.
10. Kiessling, R., Klein, E., Pross, H., and Wigzell, H., *Eur. J. Immunol.* **5,** 117, 1975.
11. Kedar, E., Ortiz de Landazuri, M., and Bonavida, B., *J. Immunol.* **112,** 1231, 1974.
12. Koren, H. S., and Williams, M. S., *J. Immunol.* **121,** 1956, 1978.
13. Roder, J. C., Kiessling, R., Biberfield, P., and Andersson, B., *J. Immunol.* **121,** 2509, 1978.
14. Herberman, R. B., Nunn, M. E., and Holden, H. T., *In* "In Vitro Methods of Cell-Mediated and Tumor Immunity" (B. R. Bloom and J. R. David, Eds.), pp. 489–495. Academic Press, New York, 1976.
15. Pross, H. F., Baines, M. G., Rubin, P., Shragge, P., and Patterson, M. S., *J. Clin. Immunol.* **1,** 51, 1981.
16. Kiessling, R., Petranyi, G., Karre, K., Jondal, M., Tracey, D., and Wigzell, H., *J. Exp. Med.* **143,** 772, 1976.
17. Herberman, R. B., Nunn, M. E., Holden, H. T., and Larvin, D. H., *Int. J. Cancer* **16,** 230, 1975.
18. Shellam, G. R., *Int. J. Cancer* **19,** 225, 1977.
19. Herberman, R. B., Djeu, J. Y., Kay, H. D., Ortaldo, J. R., Riccardi, C., Bonnard, G. D., Holden, H. T., Fagnani, R., Santoni, A., and Puccetti, P., *Immunol. Rev.* **44,** 43, 1979.
20. Kiessling, R., and Wigzell, H., *Immunol. Rev.* **44,** 165, 1979.
21. Roder, J. C., and Kiessling, R., *Scand. J. Immunol.* **8,** 135, 1978.
22. Gidlund, M., Ojo, E., Orn, A., Wigzell, H., and Murgita, R. A., *Scand. J. Immunol.* **9,** 167, 1979.
23. Hansson, M., Kärre, K., Kiessling, R., Roder, J., Andersson, B., and Häyry, P., *J. Immunol.* **123,** 765, 1979.
24. Durdik, J. M., Beck, B. N., Clark, E. A., and Henney, C. S., *J. Immunol.* **125,** 683, 1980.
25. Brodt, P., Kongshavn, P., Vargas, F., and Gordon, J., *J. Reticuloendothel. Soc.,* in press, 1981.
26. Kiessling, R., Hochman, P. S., Haller, O., Shearer, G. M., Wigzell, H., and Duckowicz, G., *Eur. J. Immunol.* **7,** 655, 1977.
27. Parker, D. C., *Nature (London)* **258,** 361, 1975.
28. Weiner, H. L., Moorehead, J. W., and Claman, H., *J. Immunol.* **116,** 1656, 1976.
29. Sieckmann, D. G., Asofsky, R., Mosier, D. E., Zitron, I. M., and Paul, W. E., *J. Exp. Med.* **147,** 814, 1978.
30. Sieckmann, D. G., Scher, I., Asofsky, R., Mosier, D. E., and Paul, W. E., *J. Exp. Med.* **148,** 1628, 1978.
31. Warner, N. L., Woodruff, M. E., and Burton, R. C., *Int. J. Cancer* **20,** 146, 1977.
32. Herberman, R. B., and Holden, H. T., *Advan. Cancer Res.* **27,** 305, 1978.

CELLULAR IMMUNOLOGY **65**, 33–42 (1981)

Effects of Cyclophosphamide and Cortisone on the Virus-Immune Response Characteristics of Thymocytes and the Early Reconstitution Profiles of P → F1 Chimeras

PETER C. DOHERTY AND ROBERT KORNGOLD

The Wistar Institute of Anatomy and Biology, 36th Street at Spruce, Philadelphia, Pennsylvania 19104

Received May 6, 1981; accepted August 31, 1981

Thymocytes from normal adult mice that have been treated 1 or 2 days previously with a low dose of cyclophosphamide (30 or 40 mg/kg), hydrocortisone acetate (2.5 mg), or hydrocortisone succinate (5.0 mg) show an enhanced potential to generate vaccinia-immune cytotoxic T lymphocytes (CTL) when stimulated for 6 days in irradiated, virus-infected recipients. However, the capacity of thymocytes (though not of spleen cells) to develop such CTL activity is lost within 8 days of treatment with the depot drug, hydrocortisone acetate. In contrast, thymocytes from mice treated 8 days previously with hydrocortisone succinate show response patterns equivalent to those found for normal adults, with the increased response characteristic of recent corticosteroid treatment being recalled by giving a second dose 2 days prior to sampling. "Cortisone resistance" is thus both a function of the form of drug given, and the time of sampling. A large dose of cyclophosphamide (150 mg/kg) completely eliminates thymocyte responder potential within 2 days of treatment. This protocol, and the administration of 2.5 mg of hydrocortisone acetate (but not hydrocortisone succinate), serves to remove the radiation-resistant host cells which initially (14 days after bone marrow reconstitution) dominate the CTL response patterns of adoptively transferred thymocytes from P1 → (P1 × P2)F1 bone marrow chimeras. A smaller dose of cyclophosphamide (100 mg/kg) delays the emergence of the radiation-resistant host component in both thymus and lymph node, and skews the emerging CTL activity toward the donor.

INTRODUCTION

It has been known for some time that many of the cells that initially populate the thymus of an irradiated mouse reconstituted with bone marrow are of host rather than donor origin (1–4). Recent exeriments have shown that these host cells may, on adoptive transfer into irradiated, vaccinia-infected recipients, generate a strong, virus-specific, cytotoxic T-lymphocyte (CTL) response (5, 6). The host-derived component dominates the response profile at 2 weeks after irradiation and reconstitution but, within another 2 weeks, only thymocytes of donor origin are found.

Some drugs, such as cortisone and cyclophosphamide (Cy), are also known to have profound effects on the thymus (reviewed in (6–8)). We thus asked how such treatments might influence virus-immune CTL precursor function in thymus of normal mice. Similar protocols were then used to treat (P1 × P2)F1 chimera re-

0008-8749/81/170033-10$02.00/0

TABLE 1

The Influence of a Single Dose of 30 or 150 mg/kg of Cyclophosphamide Given 24 hr Previously on the Capacity of Spleen and Thymus Cells to Respond to Vaccinia Virus

					Percentage specific ^{51}Cr release					
					L cells (K^kD^d)		KHTGSV (K^dD^b)		K5RSV (K^bD^d)	
Cell population	Dose of Cy (mg/kg)	Group	No. of cells transferred ($\times 10^6$)	E:T ratio	Vacc.	*N*	Vacc.	*N*	Vacc.	*N*
C3H (K^kD^k) thymus	Nil	A	20	15	59	1	6	0	13	16
	Nil	B	10	15	36	1	0	0	2	3
	30	C	20	15	66	1	0	0	0	0
	30	D	10	15	62	3	2	1	2	4
	150	E	20	15	18	5	—	—	—	—
	150	F	10	15	6	5	3	2	1	0
C3H spleen	Nil	G	40	15	47	1	5	0	1	1
	30	H	40	15	76	0	0	0	2	1
	150	I	40	15	11	10	0	0	0	0
CB6F1 ($K^d \times D^d \times K^b \times D^b$)F1 thymus	Nil	J	20	30	3	9	7	8	11	0
	Nil	K	10	15	1	3	5	0	10	0
	30	L	20	30	3	4	23	0	26	0
	30	M	10	15	2	2	13	0	1	0
	150	N	20	15	1	4	4	4	0	0
	150	O	10	15	0	1	2	5	2	0

TABLE 2

Response Patterns for Cells from Mice Pretreated with Different Doses of Cyclophosphamide

					Percentage specific ^{51}Cr release			
					L cells (K^kD^k)		MC57G (K^bD^b)	
Expt[a]	Cell population	Dose of Cy (mg/kg)	Group	No. of cells transferred ($\times 10^6$)	Vacc.	*N*	Vacc.	*N*
1	C3H H-$2K^kD^k$							
	Thymus	0	A	20	6	1	0	0
		40	B	20	50	2	1	0
		60	C	20	16	1	1	0
	Spleen	0	D	50	22	1	1	0
		40	E	50	44	0	1	0
		60	F	50	55	1	0	0
2	B10.A(2R) H-$2K^kD^b$							
	Thymus	0	G	30	11	0	6	0
		40	H	30	62	1	14	0
		60	I	30	9	1	5	0
		80	J	30	14	3	6	0
	Spleen	0	K	40	61	1	10	0
		40	L	40	70	3	13	0
		60	M	40	79	6	14	0
		80	N	40	55	1	11	0
Unirradiated controls								
Expt 1	B6(K^bD^b)				4	4	37	2
Expt 2	(CBA × B6)F1, ($K^kD^k \times K^bD^b$)				77	1	55	0

[a] The C3H mice were 14 weeks and the B10.A(2R) mice 17 weeks at time of treatment. The lymphocytes were stimulated with virus by adoptive transfer into lethally irradiated, syngeneic recipients, as described under Materials and Methods.

cipients prior to irradiation and reconstitution with parental bone marrow, to determine the effects on the irradiated (P1 × P2)F1 host component.

MATERIALS AND METHODS

The procedures and reagents (with the exception of the drugs) used in these experiments were all described in detail in the previous paper (5). A brief account is given again here.

Mice. The AKR/J, B10.A, and (C57BL/6J × BALB/c)F1 (CB6F1) mice were purchased from the Jackson Laboratories, Bar Harbor, Maine. The C3H mice were from the Institute for Cancer Research, Fox Chase, Pennsylvania, while the B10.A(4R) and (C57BL6/J × C3H)F1 (B6C3F1) mice were supplied via the Division of Cancer Treatment at the National Cancer Institute.

Drugs. Adult (10–14 weeks) mice were injected intramuscularly (im) with 2.5

TABLE 3

The Influence of a Single Dose of 2.5 mg of Cortisone Acetate on the Responder Characteristics of Thymocytes

				Adoptive transfer, No. of cells			Percentage specific ^{51}Cr release			
							L cells		MC57G	
Expt	Mice	Group	Day treated	Donors	($\times 10^6$)	E:T ratio	Vacc.	*N*	Vacc.	*N*
1	C3H H-2K^{k}D^k (12 week)	A	Nil	5	20	30	35	0	2	1
		B	Nil		10	30	9	0	1	1
		C	Nil		5	30	16	0	0	1
		D	Nil		2.5	30	0	0	1	1
		E	−2	10	10	30	62	1	1	1
		F	−2		5	30	29	0	1	2
		G	−2		2.5	30	9	0	1	1
2	B6 K^{b}D^b (14 week)	H	Nil[a]	2	40	15	1	1	33	0
		I	−3	5	4	15	0	0	35	0
		J	−10	5	2	15	3	3	5	3
		K	−24	2	50	15	5	5	21	6
3	B10.A(4R) K^{b}D^b (12 week)	L	Nil	2	20	15	17	0	10	4
		M	−2	3	8	15	30	3	12	10
		N	−8	3	10	15	1	1	1	7
Spleen populations from expt 3		O	Nil	2	40	30	23	0	6	0
		P	−2	3	40	30	21	1	6	1
		Q	−8	3	40	30	35	3	11	14

[a] Groups I, J, and K were tested at three separate time points, the value given for H is a mean of the controls for those days. All cell populations were stimulated with virus for 6 days in irradiated, virus-infected recipients, as described under Materials and Methods.

mg of cortisone acetate (United Research Laboratories, Philadelphia, Pa.), subcutaneously (sc) with 5.0 mg of cortisone succinate ("Solu-Cortef," Upjohn, Kalamazoo, Mich.), or intraperitoneally (ip) with different doses of cyclophosphamide ("Cytoxan," Mead Johnson, Evansville, Ind.).

Radiation chimeras. The chimeras were prepared by lethally irradiating (1000 rad from a ^{137}Cs source) 12- to 14-week-old mice 24 hr prior to reconstitution with 1.0×10^7 anti-Thy1 + guinea pig complement-treated bone marrow cells. Lymphoid organs from these mice were antigenically typed (5) with monoclonal antibodies to Thy1.1 (New England Nuclear, Boston, Mass.), Thy1.2 (JiJ, from Dr. J. Sprent), and serum antibodies specific for H-2^b and H-2^k. These results are not presented here, but are in accord with the findings for treatment of adoptively stimulated effector populations shown in Table 7.

Stimulation of T cells, the cytotoxic assay, and limitations of the system. Lymphoid populations from drug-treated and chimeric mice were injected into irradiated (850 rad, −24 hr), vaccinia-infected (5×10^6 PFU) recipients, and cell populations from these mice were tested for CTL activity 6 days later. The CTL assays were incubated for 7–8 hr at 38°C, and results are expressed as percentage specific ^{51}Cr release. Wherever possible populations were assayed at ratios of 30:1 and 15:1. However, the recovery of lymphocytes from irradiated mice given thymocytes and virus was often so poor that only one effector:target (E:T) ratio could be tested. The results given throughout are for the highest E:T ratio available, as this shows the effects most clearly. The limitations of this approach are that it is obviously not highly quantitative and can only be considered to show trends. This constraint was imposed by the lack of experimental material, especially in the studies with chimeras. A number of the experiments were repeated several times in order to compensate for this defect.

RESULTS

The initial series of experiments concentrated on determining the effects of cyclophosphamide and corticosteroid treatment protocols on the virus-immune CTL response profiles of thymocytes from normal, adult mice.

Cyclophosphamide

Administration of a low dose of Cy (30 to 40 mg/kg) on the day preceding the removal of organs for adoptive transfer caused a slight degree of enhancement of CTL activity for both thymus (groups A to D, J to M, Table 1; groups A and B, G and H, Table 2) and spleen (groups G and H, P and Q, Table 1; groups D and E, Table 2). However, increasing the dose to 150 mg/kg led to an almost total obliteration of vaccinia-specific responder potential (groups A, B, E, and F; G and I; J, K, N, and O, Table 1). An intermediate dose of Cy (60 or 80 mg/kg) seemed to largely eliminate evidence of CTL precursor function for thymus (groups B and C, H to J, Table 2), but not for spleen (groups D to F, K to M, Table 2).

Cortisone Acetate

Intramuscular (im) injection of 2.5 mg of the depot drug hydrocortisone acetate (CA) caused an enhancement, on a cell for cell basis, of CTL activity for thymocytes

TABLE 4

Effect of a Single Dose of Cortisone Succinate on the Responder Characteristics of Thymocytes from Normal, Adult Mice[a]

	Mice				Cortisone treatment			Percentage specific ^{51}Cr release					
								L cells(kk)		MC57G(bb)		KD2SV(dd)	
Expt	Strain	H-2KD	Age (weeks)	Group	5.0 mg sc	Day	E:T ratio	Vacc.	*N*	Vacc.	*N*	Vacc.	*N*
1	C3H	kk	25	A	−	−2	30	37	6	11	2	0	1
				B	+	−2	30	54	7	11	6	8	2
				C	−	−8	15	36	2	8	6	2	1
				D	+	−8	30	32	6	17	14	21	9
1	C3H	kk	41	E	−	−2	30	11	4	10	5	4	3
				F	+	−2	30	41	4	9	4	4	3
				G	−	−8	15	14	1	7	6	4	5
				H	+	−8	15	16	11	18	8	18	11
1	B10.A(2R)	kb		I	−	−2	30	22	2	5	1	1	0
				J	+	−2	30	70	6	16	2	3	2
2				K	−	−8	15	7	0	0	0	0	0
				L	+	−8	30	21	0	2	1	3	2
1	B10.A(2R)	kb	50	M	−	−2	30	11	2	9	1	2	5
				N	+	−2	30	33	3	8	0	3	0
2				O	−	−8	30	14	6	12	1	0	0
				P	+	−8	30	10	0	7	2	1	0
Untreated control spleen													
B6(bb)													
Expt 1							30	4	4	56	0	5	4
Expt 2							30	9	7	55	3	6	3
BALB/c(dd)													
Expt 1							30	3	3	3	1	28	3
Expt 2							30	3	4	4	5	55	4

[a] Syngeneic mice that had been irradiated (850 rad, −24 hr) were injected iv with 2.0×10^7 thymocytes followed, 3 hr later, with 4×10^6 PFU of vaccinia virus. The spleens from these mice were assayed for CTL activity 6 days later. Comparable recipients were also injected with 4.0×10^7 spleen cells from cortisone-treated or normal mice; all responded, and the cortisone treatment did not obviously modify the level of virus-immune CTL activity.

TABLE 5

Thymocyte Response Patterns from Mice Given Sequential Treatments with 5.0 mg of Cortisone Succinate[a]

Expt	Mice: Strain	Mice: H-2KD	Age (weeks)	Group	Day treated: −2	Day treated: −8	E:T ratio	Percentage specific ^{51}Cr release: L cells(kk) Vacc.	L cells(kk) *N*	MC57G(bb) Vacc.	MC57G(bb) *N*
1	B10.A	kd	14	A	−	−	30	30	9	2	1
				B	−	+	30	8	5	4	3
				C	+	+	15	41	2	2	7
				D	+	−	30	49	10	4	6
2	B10.A(2R)	kb	12	E	−	−	30	24	7	12	0
				F	−	+	30	6	2	1	0
				G	+	+	15	30	3	11	2
	B10.A	kb	12	H	−	−	15	17	3	3	0
				I	+	−	15	33	5	3	5
				J	+	+	15	29	5	12	9

[a] The results given are for spleen cells from irradiated recipients given virus and thymocytes 6 days previously.

from mice treated 2 or 3 days previously (groups A to G, H and I, L and M, Table 3). Within another 6 days, however, the residual thymocytes seemed to have completely lost the capacity to respond (groups H and J, L and N, Table 3). Comparable effects were not observed for the spleen (groups O to Q, Table 3).

Cortisone Succinate

Thymocytes stimulated 2 days after treatment with the short-acting cortisone succinate also showed evidence of increased CTL precursor activity (Groups A and B, E and F, I and J, M and N, Table 4). This had returned to background levels within 8 days of administering the drug (groups C and D, G and H, K and L, O and P, Table 4). The enhanced response could be recalled by giving such mice a second dose of cortisone succinate 2 days prior to cell transfer (groups C, G, and J, Table 5).

Effect of Drug Pretreatment on the Early Reconstitution of P → F1 Chimeras

Two treatment protocols (2.5 mg of cortisone acetate, 150 mg/kg of cyclophosphamide) which caused complete elimination of CTL precursors from the thymus of normal, adult mice also prevented the emergence, when given prior to irradiation, of the host component which dominated the early response profile for thymocytes from P → F1 radiation chimeras (5). Few cells were recovered from the thymuses of such chimeras, and no CTL activity was observed (groups A to F, G and I, Table 6). However, the viability of these drug-treated chimeras was poor, and time points later than 21 days were not examined.

We thus tested a further set of chimeras that were treated with 100 mg/kg of

TABLE 6

CTL Activity for Thymocytes from k → (k × b)F1 Chimeras Treated with Cyclophosphamide and Cortisone 2 Days prior to Irradiation (1000 rad) and Reconstitution with Anti-Thy1-Treated Bone Marrow

				Adoptive transfer		Percentage specific ^{51}Cr release			
						L cells		MC57G	
Chimera	Group	Day	Drug[a]	No. of donors	No. of cells ($\times 10^6$)	Vacc.	*N*	Vacc.	*N*
C3H →	A	14	Nil	4	175	16	0	37	1
(B6C3)F1	B	14	Cy	4	0.3	No cells recovered			
	C	14	CA	4	0.1	No cells recovered			
	D	21	Nil	4	140	47	0	30	0
	E	21	Cy	4	16	0	0	0	0
	F	21	CA	4	14	3	0	0	0
AKR/J →	G	14	Nil	3	219	31	7	24	2
(B6C3)F1	H	14	Cy	3	98	10	5	9	3
	I	14	CA	3	0.7	No cells recovered			
	J	14	CS	3	172	18	3	46	0
	K	21	Nil	3	102	31	6	31	4
	L	21	Cy	3	112	24	6	17	6
	M	21	CS	3	169	20	14	30	6
	N	28	Nil	3	125	14	1	18	0
	O	28	Cy	3	148	16	0	18	0
	P	28	CS	4	239	13	0	25	0

[a] The mice were given 2.5 mg of cortisone acetate (CA) im, 5.0 mg of cortisone succinate (CS) sc, or cyclophosphamide (Cy) ip. The C3H → (B6C3)F1 mice were given 150 mg/kg of Cy, the AKR/J → (B6C3)F1 were given 100 mg/kg. All cell populations were stimulated with virus for 6 days in 850-rad (B6C3)F1 recipients and spleen cells from the recipients were assayed at an effector:target ratio of 30:1.

Cy before irradiation and bone marrow reconstitution. This protocol delayed the appearance of the irradiated host component (groups G and H, Table 6), and also skewed the later-emerging thymocyte response pattern toward the donor (Groups K and L, Table 6; Table 7). However, the host-derived CTL precursors were not completely eliminated from the Cy-treated mice. A similar effect was seen for the lymph node, with the responders being predominantly (though not totally) of donor bone marrow (Thy1.1) origin by 28 days after reconstitution (groups N and O, Table 7). Pretreatment with a single dose of cortisone succinate had no demonstrable effect on either lymph node or thymus in the chimeras (groups G and J, Table 6; K and M, N and P, Table 6; Table 7).

DISCUSSION

The apparent increase in CTL precursor frequency for thymocytes from mice given a low dose of Cy could reflect the removal of a suppressor population (9, 10). However, cell-mixture experiments aimed at examining this point have not

TABLE 7

Analysis of Effector Populations from AKR → (B6C3)F1 Chimeras Sampled at 21 and 28 Days after Bone Marrow Reconstitution

				Percentage specific ^{51}Cr release from vaccinia targets by effectors derived from			
				Thymus		Lymph node	
Group[a]	Day	Drug	Antiserum treatment	L cells	MC57G	L cells	MC57G
K	21	Nil	Thy1.1	38	33	38	36
			Thy1.2	15	14	1	2
L	21	Cy	Thy1.1	19	27	Not tested, too few cells	
			Thy1.2	32	31		
M	21	CS	Thy1.1	27	30	25	25
			Thy1.2	18	28	0	0
N	28	Nil	Thy1.1	9	11	38	40
			Thy1.2	18	19	19	21
O	28	Cy	Thy1.1	4	0	21	12
			Thy1.2	20	9	40	31
P	28	CS	Thy1.1	2	14	27	17
			Thy1.2	15	28	28	26

[a] The groups are the same as those shown in Table 6. Effector populations were treated with antibody and complement at 6 days after adoptive transfer and priming with virus. The effector:target ratio (30:1) was calculated for cells viable following treatment. Lysis of normal target cells by the lymph node populations was always less than 3%.

given clear evidence of suppression to date (6). Elimination of suppressors may also be invoked to explain the augmentation of responsiveness soon after treatment with both cortisone acetate and cortisone succinate. It is equally probable, however, that the effect is simply due to concentration of the relevant precursors which cannot, in all experiments, be demonstrated in the thymus (6).

Our data may be variously interpreted to support or refute the idea that the "cortisone-resistant" thymocytes are a long-lived population which does not leave the thymus (8). This concept is tenable for mice treated with 5.0 mg of hydrocortisone succinate: the increase in CTL precursor frequency is transient, but can be recalled by giving a second dose of the drug 5 or 6 days later. Alternatively, a single dose of the depot drug hydrocortisone acetate leads to a total depletion of thymocyte responder potential. The "cortisone-resistant" status of thymocytes is thus determined by both the form of the drug and the time of sampling. We do not know whether the "resistant" thymocyte population in mice given cortisone acetate has died, or emigrated from the thymus, in mice sampled 7 or more days after treatment.

The same spectrum of cortisone resistance and susceptiblity is reflected in the capacity of T-cell precursors to survive exposure to 1000 rad. Pretreatment with cortisone acetate (or 150 mg/kg of Cy) eliminates the radiation-resistant host cells, while cortisone succinate has no effect. Perhaps the fact that combined drug and irradiation protocols are often found to be useful in clinical transplant programs (11) reflects that a more complete removal of host T cells is achieved by such procedures, thus minimizing possible host-versus-graft disease.

The poor viability of the P1 → (P1 × P2)F1 chimera recipients given cortisone acetate, or the maximum dose of Cy, could reflect that the few surviving T cells of irradiated host origin are important in controlling infection before lymphocytes of donor origin differentiate to the stage where they can assume this function. Alternatively, residual T cells may play a physiological role in stimulating hematopoiesis or thymopoiesis (12–14). The thymus can eventually be reconstituted in the Cy (150 mg/kg)-treated mice, as some surviving (P1 × P2)F1 → P1 chimeras made in this way showed virus-immune response patterns which were restricted to P1 when tested at 8 weeks after irradiation (R. Korngold and P. C. Doherty, submitted for publication).

ACKNOWLEDGMENTS

This research was supported by Grant AI-15412 from the National Institutes of Health and Grant CA-10815 from the National Cancer Institute. We thank Ms. Pauline Angerman and Kathy Fienstein for capable technical assistance.

REFERENCES

1. Micklem, H. S., Ford, C. E., Evans, E. P., and Gray, J., *Proc. Roy. Soc. Ser. B* **165,** 78, 1966.
2. Kadisch, J. L., and Basch, R. S., *J. Immunol.* **114,** 452, 1975.
3. Kadisch, J. L., and Basch, R. S., *Cell. Immunol.* **30,** 12, 1977.
4. Sharrow, S. O., Mathieson, B. J., and Singer, A., *J. Immunol.* **126,** 1327, 1981.
5. Korngold, R., Bennink, J. R., and Doherty, P. C., *J. Immunol.* **127,** 124, 1981.
6. Doherty, P. C., Korngold, R., Schwartz, D. H., and Bennink, J. R., *Immunol. Rev.* **58,** 37, 1981.
7. Stutman, O., *Contemp. Top. Immunobiol.* **7,** 1, 1977.
8. Stutman, O., *Immunol. Rev.* **42,** 138, 1978.
9. Gershon, R. K., *Contemp. Top. Immunobiol.* **3,** 1, 1975.
10. Rollinghoff, M., Starzinski-Powitz, A., Pfizenmaier, K., and Wagner, H., *J. Exp. Med.* **145,** 455, 1977.
11. Chabner, B. A., *In* "Biology of Bone Marrow Transplantation" (R. P. Gale and C. F. Fox, Eds.), ICN-UCLA Symposia on Molecular and Cellular Biology, Vol. 17, pp. 137–143. Academic Press, New York, 1980.
12. Schrader, J. W., Arnold, B., and Clark-Lewis, I., *Nature (London)* **283,** 197, 1980.
13. Goodman, J. W., and Shinpack, S. G., *In* "Biology of Bone Marrow Transplantation" (R. P. Gale and C. F. Fox, Eds.), ICN-UCLA Symposia on Molecular and Cellular Biology, Vol. 17, pp. 461–476. Academic Press, New York, 1980.
14. Schrader, J. W., and Clark-Lewis, I., *J. Immunol.* **126,** 1101, 1981.

CELLULAR IMMUNOLOGY **65**, 43–51 (1981)

In Vitro Glucocorticoid Inhibition of Steroid-Treated Residual Circulatory Human Lymphocytes[1]

SOO RAY WANG, JYH HSIUNG HUANG, AND SHARON WANG

Section of Allergy and Immunology, Chang Gung Memorial Hospital, Taipei 105, Taiwan

Received June 24, 1981; accepted September 9, 1981

Various doses of glucocorticoids given *in vivo* caused a similar degree of maximal lymphopenia. The sensitivities of mitogen-induced proliferation to the suppressive effects of glucocorticoid added *in vitro* were studied in residual lymphocytes obtained after steroid injection. Methylprednisolone (MP) administered intravenously depleted circulatory lymphocytes and reduced markedly the proliferative responses of residual cells to mitogens (phytohemagglutinin and concanavalin A) 4 to 8 hr after the injection. The addition of MP *in vitro* to the residual cells further inhibited the cell proliferation. The degrees of proliferation inhibition induced by *in vitro* MP were compared in cells obtained at various intervals after MP injection. At each specific mitogen concentration, lymphocytes obtained at various intervals were inhibited to a similar degree by MP in the cultures. There was no evidence that cells obtained at the period of maximal lymphopenia, 4 to 8 hr after MP injection, were more resistant to the inhibition of glucocorticoid added *in vitro*. Hence, the residual lymphocytes were not "steroid-resistant" in the sense of proliferative responses to T-cell mitogens. These results indicate the mechanism of lymphocyte sequestration is unrelated to the suppressive effects of glucocorticoid on cell proliferation.

INTRODUCTION

Glucocorticoid injection causes transient lymphopenia in humans (1–5). Although both T and B lymphocytes are depleted from the circulation, there is a proportionately greater depletion of circulatory T lymphocytes (1, 6, 7). The residual T lymphocytes following *in vivo* glucocorticoid treatment show a decrease of *in vitro* proliferative responses to T-cell mitogens, i.e., phytohemagglutinin (PHA) and concanavalin A (Con A) (2, 3). Thus, a functionally defined T-cell subpopulation is selectively depleted from the circulation.

Various studies of glucocorticoids *in vivo* have all shown the effects of profound but transient lymphopenia with maximum at 4 to 6 hr after administration. The glucocorticoids administered included (a) 60 mg of prednisone orally (1), (b) 100 or 400 mg of hydrocortisone intravenously (iv) (2), (c) 1 mg/kg body wt of methylprednisolone (iv) (3), (d) 1 g of methylprednisolone (iv) (4), (e) 1 g of prednisolone (iv) (5). Particularly notable is the finding that the degree of maximal lymphopenia is essentially the same in each regimen with a decrease in lymphocyte counts in the range between 50 and 70%. In some instances, the residual lympho-

[1] Supported by Chang Gung Research Grant MRP 030.

0008-8749/81/170043-09$02.00/0

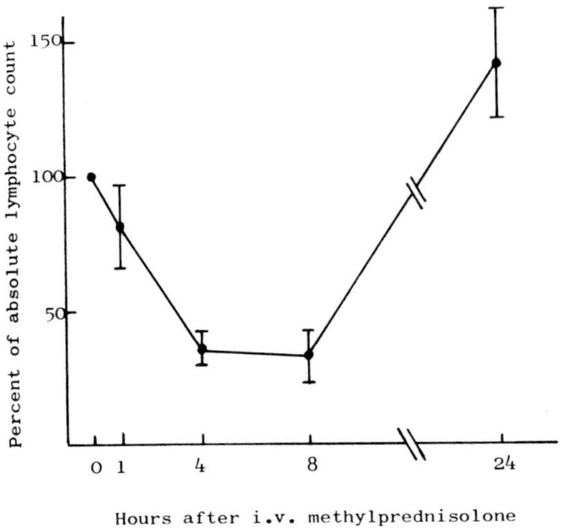

FIG. 1. Relative circulating lymphocyte counts after MP administration. Mean levels (±SEM) for the various time intervals after injection of MP are shown.

cytes were termed "steroid-resistant lymphocytes." Their sensitivity of mitogen-induced proliferation to *in vitro* glucocorticoid inhibition was studied, showing that the residual lymphocytes were not steroid resistant.

MATERIALS AND METHODS

Subjects. Five normal healthy volunteers (age 21 to 40) taking no medications for at least 5 days were selected for this study. Informed consent was obtained from all subjects.

For *in vivo* experiments, methylprednisolone sodium succinate (MP) (Solu-Medrol; kindly supplied by Upjohn Co., Kalamazoo, Mich.), 1 mg/kg body wt, was injected intravenously at 9 AM. Blood samples were taken immediately before and at 1, 4, 8 and 24 hr after injection. The blood samples taken before the injections served as the controls for each subject.

Lymphocyte culture. Lymphocytes were separated and cultured by methods described previously (3). Briefly, lymphocytes were separated on a Ficoll–Hypaque density gradient, washed twice, and suspended in culture medium. Cell suspensions thus prepared were 85–90% lymphocytes, 10–15% monocytes (identified by nonspecific esterase stain), and occasional granulocytes. The final culture medium contained RPMI 1640 supplemented with L-glutamine (2 m*M*), penicillin G (100 u/ml), streptomycin (100 μg/ml), and 10% (v/v) heat-inactivated fetal calf serum (all from Grand Island Biological Co., Grand Island, N.Y.). The cells were cultured in quadruplicate in conical-bottomed microtiter plates (Flow Lab, Linbro Scientific Co.) for a total of 72 hr in the presence of either 1 and 3 μg/ml of phytohemagglutinin (PHA) (Lot HA-16, Burroughs–Wellcome Research, Triangle Park, N.C.) or 3 and 9 μg/ml of concanavalin A (Con A) (Lot 901261, Calbiochem-Behring Corp., La Jolla, Calif.). Their proliferative responses were measured by [^{3}H]thymidine incorporation in a terminal 4-hr pulse. For *in vitro* glucocorticoid studies, cells were cultured in the absence of and in the presence of MP (10^{-6}, 10^{-5}, and 10^{-4} *M*), as well as with the mitogen.

TABLE 1

In Vitro Suppressive Effects of MP on the Proliferative Responses of Human Lymphocytes Obtained after MP Injection

Mitogen	Concentration of MP in cultures (M)	Hours after MP injection				
		0	1	4	8	24
PHA, 1 μg/ml	0	42,267 ± 19,871[a]	32,243 ± 7,824 ($P < 0.05$)[b]	22,908 ± 7,583 ($P < 0.05$)	21,656 ± 8,167	48,450 ± 15,808
	10^{-6}	32,714 ± 5,459	24,752 ± 5,677	14,486 ± 4,792 ($P < 0.02$)	9,963 ± 3,037	36,692 ± 8,563
	10^{-5}	25,341 ± 4,337	17,701 ± 4,669	10,826 ± 3,584 ($P < 0.02$)	6,822 ± 2,265 ($P < 0.01$)	32,697 ± 9,399
	10^{-4}	8,263 ± 1,586	6,267 ± 1,935	2,312 ± 658 ($P < 0.01$)	2,048 ± 656 ($P < 0.01$)	13,651 ± 5,532
PHA, 3 μg/ml	0	61,388 ± 22,330	49,230 ± 15,330	26,363 ± 9,841 ($P < 0.01$)	18,276 ± 7,127 ($P < 0.05$)	44,260 ± 17,603
	10^{-6}	49,541 ± 17,341	34,434 ± 7,202	24,380 ± 9,207	13,983 ± 4,337	41,568 ± 18,951
	10^{-5}	42,378 ± 19,657	24,065 ± 5,841	18,207 ± 6,999	7,877 ± 2,620	31,321 ± 10,690
	10^{-4}	15,044 ± 3,393	9,042 ± 2,171	5,614 ± 2,673 ($P < 0.01$)	2,075 ± 790 ($P < 0.02$)	14,657 ± 4,074
Con A, 3 μg/ml	0	7,083 ± 1,140	5,477 ± 843	2,136 ± 691 ($P < 0.01$)	1,179 ± 292 ($P < 0.01$)	8,607 ± 2,867
	10^{-6}	1,701 ± 295	1,613 ± 328	611 ± 270 ($P < 0.01$)	212 ± 38 ($P < 0.01$)	2,676 ± 1,047
	10^{-5}	1,108 ± 154	672 ± 70 ($P < 0.05$)	437 ± 144 ($P < 0.01$)	239 ± 51 ($P < 0.01$)	1,914 ± 839
	10^{-4}	459 ± 104	270 ± 46	239 ± 91	210 ± 59 ($P < 0.05$)	759 ± 278
Con A, 9 μg/ml	0	35,999 ± 6,251	25,259 ± 4,465 ($P < 0.02$)	11,094 ± 3,628	3,703 ± 1,131	20,869 ± 8,001
	10^{-6}	14,618 ± 4,219	10,315 ± 2,145	2,534 ± 954 ($P < 0.05$)	1,021 ± 509 ($P < 0.05$)	13,204 ± 5,022
	10^{-5}	8,333 ± 1,647	4,081 ± 955 ($P < 0.05$)	1,294 ± 668 ($P < 0.01$)	513 ± 208 ($P < 0.01$)	11,387 ± 5,685
	10^{-4}	2,590 ± 753	1,648 ± 463	395 ± 143 ($P < 0.05$)	265 ± 55 ($P < 0.05$)	3,848 ± 2,210

[a] cpm ± SEM.

[b] Paired *t* test comparing the cpm with that of lymphocytes obtained prior to MP injection.

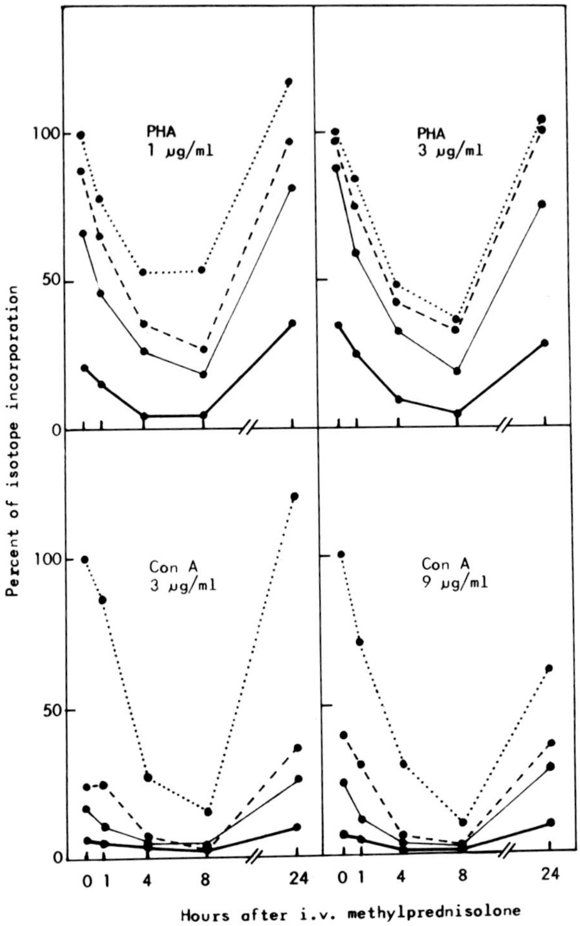

FIG. 2. Proliferative responses of lymphocytes obtained immediately before, and 1, 4, 8, and 24 hr following MP injection. The cells were incubated without (···) and with MP 10^{-6} *M* (– – –), 10^{-5} *M* (——), and 10^{-4} *M* (**——**) for the total culture period.

Statistical analysis. Statistical analyses of the lymphocyte proliferative responses were made with Student's *t* test for paired specimens.

RESULTS

Effects of in Vivo MP on Circulatory Lymphocytes

Lymphocytes were depleted from circulation after MP injection and reached the lowest level (one-third of zero-hour level) at 4 to 8 hr (Fig. 1). There was a rebound effect on circulatory lymphocyte count at 24 hr.

Effects of in Vivo MP on Mitogen-Induced Lymphocyte Proliferation

Lymphocytes obtained immediately before and 1, 4, 8 and 24 hr after MP injection were incubated with either PHA or Con A. Suboptimal and optimal doses

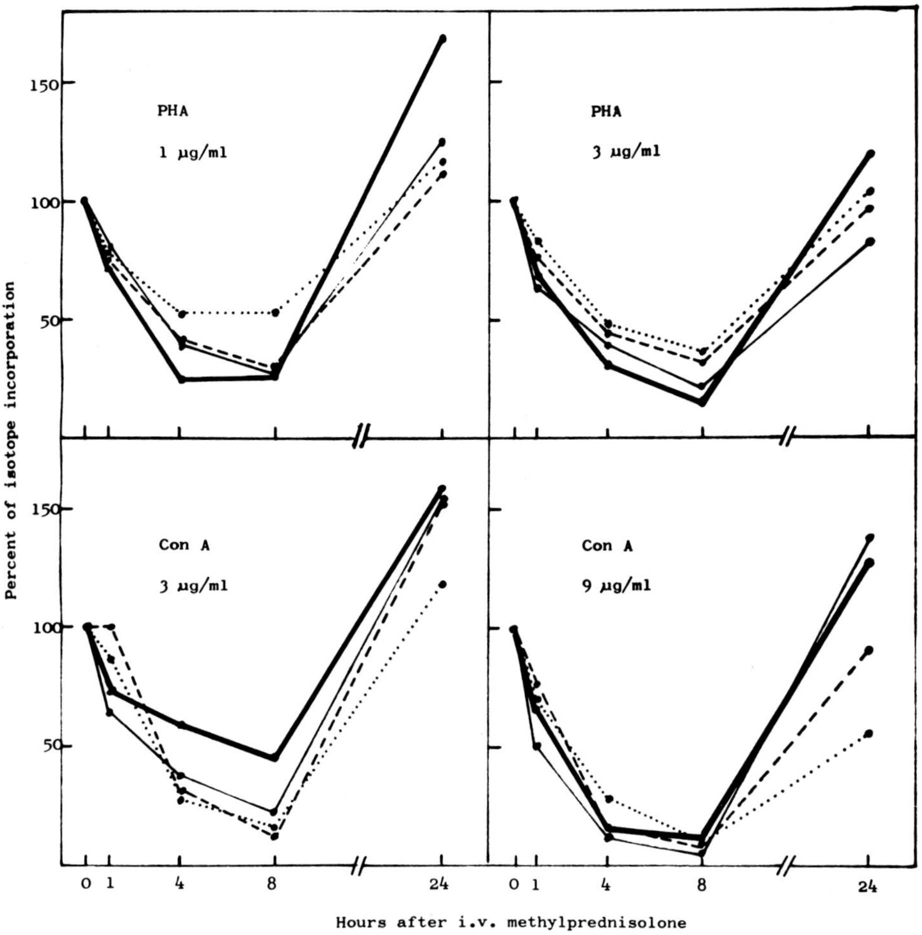

FIG. 3. Reconstructed from Fig. 2 by using the proliferative responses of zero time lymphocytes to represent 100%. The cells were incubated without (···) and with MP 10^{-6} *M* (– – –), (10^{-5} *M* (——), and 10^{-4} *M* (**——**) for the total culture period.

of PHA (1 and 3 µg/ml, respectively) and Con A (3 and 9 µg/ml, respectively) were used as mitogens in the cultures. The results are shown in Table 1. The cell proliferation decreased with time after MP injection, reached the lowest level at 4–8 hr, and returned to normal level or above at 24 hr (Fig. 2, dotted line).

Effects of in Vitro MP on Mitogen-Induced Lymphocyte Proliferation Obtained after MP Injection

Lymphocytes obtained before and at various periods after MP injection were incubated without and with 10^{-6}, 10^{-5}, and 10^{-4} *M* of MP *in vitro*. The proliferative responses of cells are shown in Table 1 and Fig. 2. The cell proliferations were lowest at 4 and 8 hr. The addition of MP *in vitro* further depressed the cell proliferations.

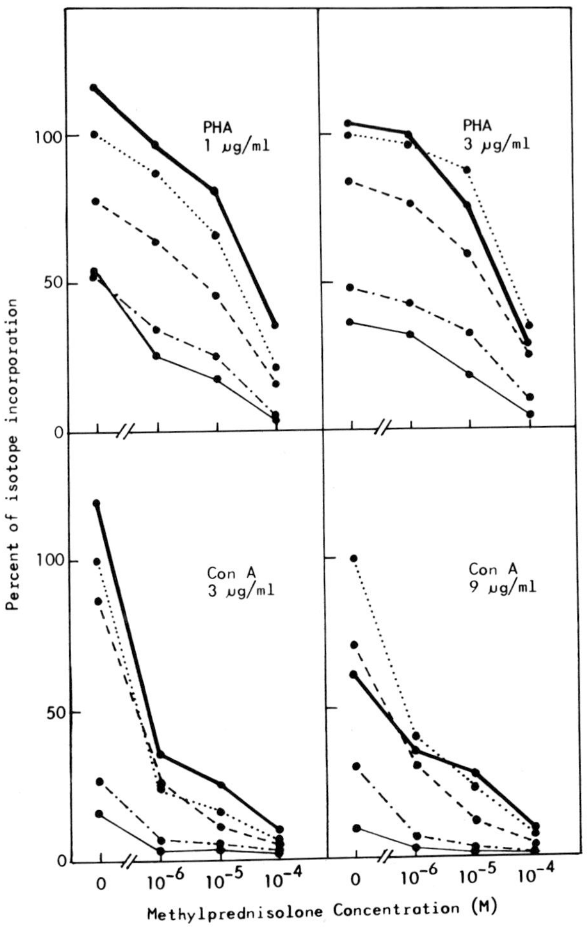

FIG. 4. Suppressive effects of MP *in vitro* on the proliferative responses of lymphocytes. The cells were obtained immediately before (· · ·), and 1 hr (– – –), 4 hr (– · –), 8 hr (——), and 24 hr (**——**) after MP injection.

Figure 3 is reconstructed from Fig. 2 by using the proliferative responses of zero time lymphocytes to represent 100%. The responses of cells in the presence of various concentrations of MP in cultures are compared. These responses showed that the lymphocytes obtained at 4 and 8 hr were not more resistant to increasing concentrations of MP *in vitro*. The relative proliferative responses of each cell population in the presence of MP from 0 to 10^{-4} *M* were not significantly different from that of zero time population, except for the cells obtained at 4 hr in the presence of 1 μg/ml PHA and 10^{-4} *M* MP, which cells appeared to be more sensitive ($P < 0.05$), rather than more resistant to *in vitro* MP suppression.

Lymphocyte proliferation decreased progressively in the presence of increasing concentrations of MP (Table 1 and Fig. 4).

Figure 5 is reconstructed from Fig. 4 by using the proliferative responses of cells in the absence of *in vitro* MP to represent 100%. At each specific MP concentration in the culture, the proliferation of cells obtained at various time intervals after MP

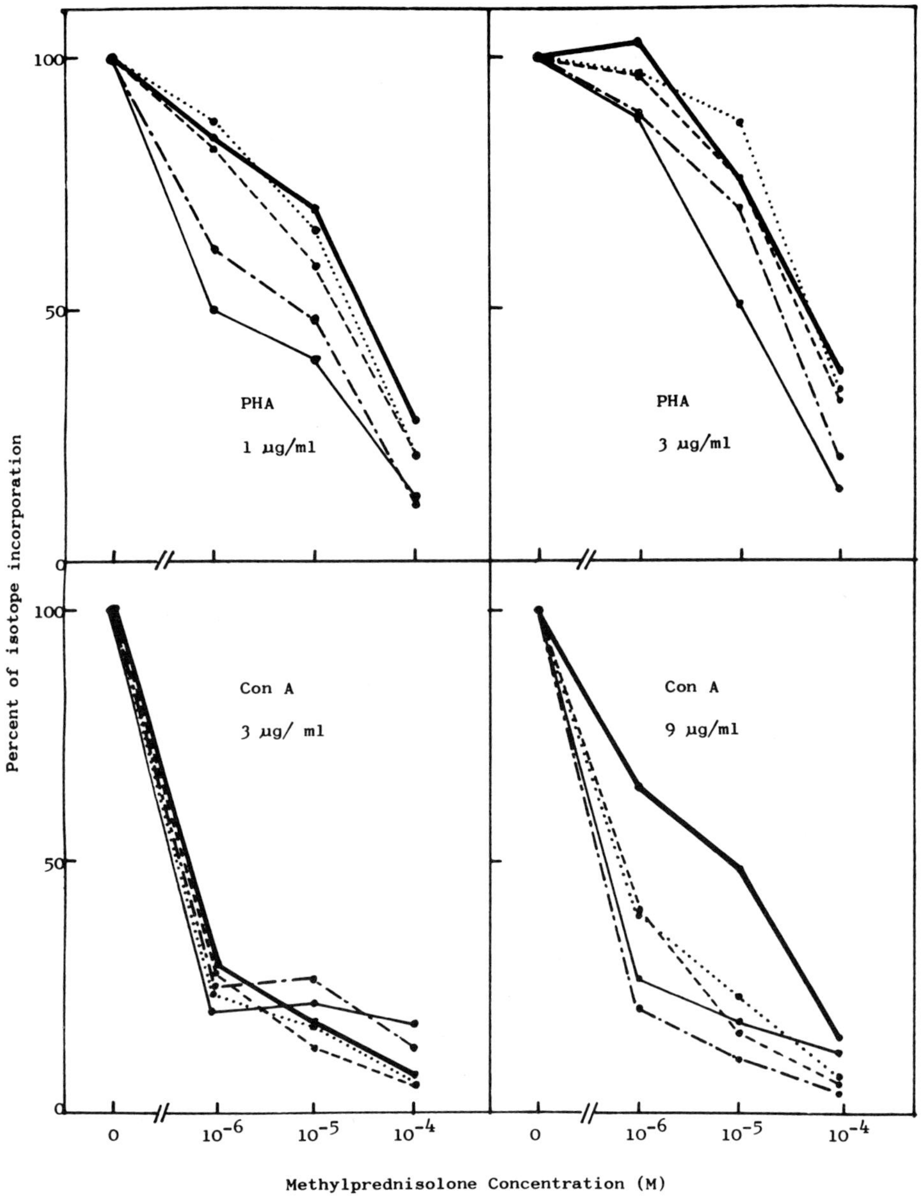

FIG. 5. Reconstructed from Fig. 4 by using the proliferative responses of cells in the absence of *in vitro* MP to represent 100%. The cells were obtained immediately before (· · ·), and 1 hr (– – –), 4 hr (– · · –), 8 hr (——), and 24 hr (**——**) after MP injection.

injection were compared and showed that the lymphocytes obtained at 4 and 8 hr were not more resistant to *in vitro* MP suppression ($P > 0.05$ in all comparisons). Instead, they appeared to be more sensitive to suppression by *in vitro* MP addition, although not to a statistically significant degree. In cultures with 9 μg/ml Con A the cells obtained at 24 hr were significantly ($P < 0.02$) more resistant to suppression by 10^{-5} *M* MP.

Responsiveness of Lymphocytes to Mitogens at a Pharmacological Concentration of MP

Figure 5 shows that at a pharmacological concentration of MP, 10^{-6} *M*, lymphocyte proliferations in response to PHA and Con A stimulations were suppressed. Cell proliferation was depressed more in Con A than in PHA cultures regardless of the timing of the cell sampling. These differences became less apparent at a higher MP concentration of 10^{-4} *M*.

DISCUSSION

Glucocorticoids cause transient depletion of circulatory human T lymphocytes much more than of B lymphocytes (1, 6, 7). Glucocorticoids do not cause cell death or lysis of normal human lymphocytes (7–9). The lymphodepletive effects of the steroid were explained by redistribution of circulatory lymphocytes (7, 10). The pool of lymphocytes which were recirculated was sequestered in the bone marrow (1, 2, 11).

Indeed, in the guinea pig, a steroid-resistant species similar to the human (9, 12), there was a dramatic increase in the bone marrow of both proportions and absolute numbers of T and B lymphocytes (13). Also, there was a marked increase in responses of bone marrow lymphocytes to mitogen stimulation during the period of maximal circulatory lymphocytopenia caused by the administration of glucocorticoids (13). Hence, the effector lymphocytes capable of responding to mitogen stimulation were sequestered in bone marrow and the remaining effector lymphocytes in the circulation decreased in number making them less responsive to mitogen stimulation.

Despite the great range of glucocorticoid doses given *in vivo* in various experiments (1–5), the degree of maximal lymphocytopenia is essentially the same, with a decrease in counts of from 50 to 75%. The residual lymphocytes were frequently termed "steroid-resistant" in the sense of resistance to the lymphodepletive effects of glucocorticoids. However, their sensitivity to glucocorticoid suppression has not been determined.

In present experiments, in comparison with the proliferative responses of lymphocytes obtained prior to MP injection, the cells obtained 4 and 8 hr after MP injection had the lowest responses to either PHA or Con A stimulation at either optimal or suboptimal doses (Table 1). The addition of MP to these *in vitro* cultures further suppressed the proliferative responses relative to MP concentration (Fig. 2). However, when the degrees of suppressibility of cells by *in vitro* MP addition were compared (Fig. 3), each concentration of MP exerted similar effects of relative suppression on the cells from either before or 1, 4, 8, or 24 hr after MP injection. These results indicate the residual lymphocytes responded to *in vitro* MP in a fashion similar to that of the original cells obtained prior to MP injection.

Looking from another aspect, as shown in Fig. 4, the cells obtained 4 and 8 hr after MP injection responded much less to mitogen stimulation. The addition of MP *in vitro* further suppressed the proliferative responses to mitogens of these cells. When comparing the degrees of suppressibility of cells by *in vitro* MP addition (Fig. 5), cells obtained at different times after MP injection responded to MP suppression in a similar fashion. These results indicated that the residual lymphocytes had a responsiveness to *in vitro* Mp suppression similar to that of the original cells. Thus although the effector cells in the residual lymphocytes were fewer in number than the original ones, they were suppressed by *in vitro* MP to a degree similar to that of the cells prior to MP injection. The residual lymphocytes were not at all more resistant to MP suppression. Hence, they were not steroid resistant in the sense of mitogen-induced proliferation. Most of the effector cells were sequestered in the marrow (13). The residual circulatory effector cells were qualitatively similar to the sequestered cells and responded to mitogen in a fashion similar to that of the original effector cells.

Despite the fact that equivalent anti-inflammatory doses of different glucocorticoid preparations caused almost identical suppression of the number of circulating lymphocytes, they had a differential effect on mitogen-induced cell proliferation (14). Hydrocortisone and prednisone given *in vivo* caused only a slight suppression of PHA-induced lymphocyte proliferation. This suppression could be reversed at supraoptimal concentrations of PHA in the cultures. On the contrary, dexamethasone administered *in vivo* caused a marked suppression of PHA responses, which was not reversed by supraoptimal PHA stimulation. These results, as well as our data presented, suggest the mechanism of lymphocyte sequestration is unrelated to the suppressive effects of glucocorticoid on cell proliferation.

REFERENCES

1. Yu, D. T. Y., Clements, P. J., Paulus, H. E., Pater, J. B., Levy, J., and Barnett, E. V., *J. Clin. Invest.* **53,** 565, 1974.
2. Fauci, A. S., and Dale, D. C., *J. Clin. Invest.* **53,** 240, 1974.
3. Wang, S. R., and Zweiman, B., *Immunopharmacology* **2,** 95, 1980.
4. Webel, M. L., Ritts, R. E., Jr., Taswell, H. F., Donadio, J. V. Jr., and Woods, J. E., *J. Lab. Clin. Med.* **83,** 383, 1974.
5. Coburg, A. J., Gray, S. H., Katz, F. H., Penn, I., Halgrimson, C., and Starzl, T. E., *Surg. Gynecol. Obstet.* **131,** 933, 1970.
6. Parrillo, J. E., and Fauci, A. S., *Annu. Rev. Pharmacol. Toxicol.* **19,** 179, 1979.
7. Fauci, A. S., Dale, D. C., and Balow, J. E., *Ann. Intern. Med.* **84,** 304, 1976.
8. Claman, H. N., Moorhead, J. W., and Benner, W. H., *J. Lab. Clin. Med.* **78,** 499, 1971.
9. Caron, G. A., *In* "Proceedings, 3rd Annual Leukocyte Culture Conference" (W. O. Rieke, Ed.), pp. 287–305. Appleton–Century–Crofts, New York, 1969.
10. Fauci, A. S., *Transplant. Proc.* **7,** 37, 1975.
11. Fauci, A. S., and Dale, D. C., *Blood* **46,** 235, 1975.
12. Claman, H. N., *J. Allergy Clin. Immunol.* **55,** 145, 1975.
13. Fauci, A. S., *Immunology* **28,** 669, 1975.
14. Fauci, A. S., *Clin. Exp. Immunol.* **24,** 54, 1976.

CELLULAR IMMUNOLOGY **65**, 52–65 (1981)

Macrophage Activation for Tumor Cytotoxicity: Control of Cytotoxic Activity by the Time Interval Effector and Target Cells Are Exposed to Lymphokines

REIKO M. NAKAMURA AND MONTE S. MELTZER

Immunopathology Section, Laboratory of Immunobiology, Division of Cancer Biology and Diagnosis, National Cancer Institute, National Institutes of Health, Bethesda, Maryland 20205

Received July 7, 1981; accepted August 30, 1981

Macrophages continuously exposed to lymphokines (LK) and target cells throughout a 48-hr cytotoxicity assay exhibit 3-fold more tumoricidal activity than do cells optimally treated with LK before addition of tumor cells. Increased cytotoxic activity induced by continuous LK treatment was not due to direct toxic effects of LK on tumor target cells or to alterations in target cell susceptibility to cytopathic effects of LK-activated macrophages. Moreover, sensitivities of responsive macrophages to LK activation signals and time courses for onset and loss of tumoricidal activity during continuous exposure or LK pulse were identical. Analysis of macrophage or LK dose responses and time courses for development of cytotoxicity each suggest that differences in tumoricidal activity between macrophages continuously exposed or pulsed with LK were quantitative: the number of cytotoxic events was increased 2.7 ± 0.2-fold (mean ± SEM for 11 experiments) during continuous LK treatment. Optimal levels of macrophage tumoricidal activity then occur only if effector cells, target cells and activation stimuli are simultaneously present for a defined time interval: tumor cells need not be present during the initial 2 to 3 hr of culture; LK can be removed after 8 hr with little or no loss of cytotoxic activity. However, removal of LK *or* target cells during the critical 4- to 8-hr interval decreased levels of cytotoxicity 3-fold. Thus, nonspecific effector function by LK-activated macrophages in controlled by both the physicochemical nature of the LK mediator and the time interval effector and target cells are exposed to LK.

INTRODUCTION

Activated macrophages, cells with nonspecific tumoricidal and microbicidal activities, can be recovered from animals with certain chronic infections for months after inoculation (1, 2). Yet regulatory mechanisms for induction and control of macrophage activation are operative for only a relatively brief interval, several hours. For example, accumulation of lymphocytes able to release lymphokines (LK)[1] and mononuclear phagocytes best able to respond to LK occurs within 6 hr after initiation of the inflammatory reaction (3, 4). Activation of these LK-re-

[1] Abbreviations used: LK, lymphokine-rich supernatants from antigen- or mitogen-stimulated spleen cell cultures; LPS, bacterial endotoxic lipopolysaccharides; BCG, *Mycobacterium bovis*, strain BCG; PPD, purified protein derivative of tuberculin; Con A, concanavalin A; PEC, peritoneal exudate cells; [^{3}H]TdR, tritiated thymidine; SDS, sodium dodecyl sulfate; FBS, fetal bovine serum; DMEM, Dulbecco's modified Eagle's minimum essential medium.

0008-8749/81/170052-14$02.00/0

sponsive macrophages is evident after 2 to 3 hr and reaches maximal levels by 4 to 8 hr. After this maximum, nonspecific effector activities of LK-activated macrophages are gradually lost with time. By 24 hr, these once activated cells remain viable, but have lost tumoricidal and microbicidal capacities and do not regain these activities with continued LK exposure (5–7). Populations of activated macrophages that develop during a chronic infection persist only because of continued presence of initiating antigens and constant replacement of both LK signals and responsive mononuclear phagocytes.

Development of nonspecific effector function by activated macrophages occurs after a series of reactions, each of which requires the simultaneous presence of a responsive mononuclear phagocyte intermediate and an effective LK activation signal (8, 9). The physicochemical nature of the LK stimulus and the state of maturation and/or differentiation for the responsive macrophage may change with each stage in the activation sequence. The requirement for a reaction cascade, similar to that for blood coagulation or complement-mediated hemolysis, forms the basis of control mechanisms for regulation of macrophage effector function. We present evidence in this report that the time interval effector and target cells are exposed to LK constitutes another element in regulation of macrophage activation. Under optimal conditions, tumoricidal activity by macrophages continuously exposed to LK during the cytotoxic reaction was threefold higher than that by macrophages pulsed with LK before addition of tumor cells.

MATERIALS AND METHODS

Animals. C3H/HeN mice were obtained from the Division of Research Services, National Institutes of Health. C3H/HeJ and P/J mice were purchased from the Jackson Laboratory, Bar Harbor, Maine. All animals were routinely screened and found to be negative for bacterial pathogens and for subclinical viral infections through the serodiagnostic services of Microbiological Associates, Bethesda, Maryland.

Lymphokine Supernatants. Mice were immunized intradermally with viable BCG (Phipps substrain, TMC 1029, Trudeau Mycobacterial Collection, Saranac Lake, N.Y.) (4). Animals were sacrificed 3 to 6 weeks after BCG immunization. Spleens were aseptically removed and passed through No. 50 mesh stainless-steel sieves into tissue culture medium (RPMI 1640 with antibiotics, Gibco, Grand Island, N.Y.). Single-cell suspensions, obtained by serial aspirations through 19- and 23-gauge needles, were treated with NH_4Cl lysis buffer to remove red blood cells. Spleen cells were centrifuged at 250*g* for 10 min at 4°C and resuspended to a concentration of 5×10^6 viable cells/ml in medium with 5% heat-inactivated fetal bovine serum (FBS, Sterile Systems, Inc., Logan, Utah). FBS contained <0.01 ng/ml LPS by the Limulus amoebocyte lysate assay. Twenty milliliters of spleen cell suspension with 50 to 100 μg/ml purified protein derivative of tuberculin (PPD, Connaught Medical Research Laboratories, Toronto, Canada) were incubated in 75-cm^2 plastic tissue culture flasks (No. 3023, Falcon Plastics, Oxnard, Calif.) for 48 to 60 hr at 37°C. Supernatant fluids from replicate cultures were pooled, centrifuged at 450*g* for 15 min at 4°C, and divided into aliquots. Aliquots were stored at 4°C until used. Suspensions of spleen cells from untreated mice cultured with 5 μg/ml concanavalin A (Con A) (Pharmacia Fine Chemicals, Uppsala, Sweden) for 48 hr were also used as a LK source. Con A was adsorbed by 10 mg/ml Sephadex G-10 (Pharmacia Fine Chemicals) before storage (10).

Peritoneal cells. Peritoneal exudate cells (PEC) from mice treated 4 to 7 days previously with 3 ml sterile 1.2% sodium caseinate (Difco Laboratories, Inc., Detroit, Mich.) in saline were collected after intraperitoneal injection of 8 ml Dulbecco's modified Eagle's medium (DMEM, Gibco) (11). This medium contained 2 g/liter $NaHCO_3$, 10% FBS, and 50 μg/ml gentimicin (Microbiological Associates). Peritoneal fluid was withdrawn through the abdominal wall with a 19-gauge needle. Fluid was collected from groups of mice and centrifuged in polypropylene tubes (No. 2074, Falcon Plastics) at 250*g* for 10 min at 4°C. A sample was taken for differential and total cell counts. Differential counts were made on Wright-stained (Diff-Quik, Harleco, Gibbstown, N.J.) cell smears prepared by cytocentrifugation (Cytospin centrifuge, Shandon Southern Instruments, Camberley, England).

Macrophages were exposed to dilutions of LK supernatants as adherent PEC monolayers (2). PEC suspensions from casein-treated mice (8×10^5 macrophages/0.5 ml) were added to 16-mm culture wells (Cluster[24], Costar, Cambridge, Mass.) and incubated for 1 to 2 hr at 37°C in 5% CO_2 in moist air. Nonadherent PEC were removed by repeated washing with cold medium and adherent PEC monolayers were incubated for various times with LK.

Macrophage-induced tumor cytotoxicity. Fibrosarcoma 1023 was induced in a C3H/HeNicr male mouse with pellets of 1% 3-methylcholanthrene in paraffin (4). Target cell lines were established from enzyme-digested tumor fragments and were maintained in culture with DMEM and 10% FBS. For the cytotoxicity assay, prelabeled tumor cells were obtained from trypsin-digested monolayers (3 to 5 $\times 10^6$ viable cells/75-cm^2 culture flask in 20 ml DMEM with 5% FBS and 0.25 μCi/ml [^{3}H]TdR ([*methyl*-^{3}H]thymidine, sp act 2.0 Ci/mmol, New England Nuclear, Boston, Mass.) for 18 to 24 hr), washed, and added to culture wells (4×10^4 target cells/well) containing adherent PEC monolayers. Labeled tumor cell monolayers digested with 0.5% sodium dodecyl sulfate (SDS) in water were used to estimate total incorporated counts. Cytotoxicity was estimated by measuring release of incorporated [^{3}H]TdR from prelabeled tumor cells in triplicate cultures and expressed as a percentage of SDS total counts. Culture wells were examined daily by phase microscopy to confirm results obtained by [^{3}H]TdR release.

RESULTS

Macrophages continuously exposed to LK throughout the 48-hr cytotoxicity assay exhibit higher levels of tumoricidal activity than do cells treated with LK prior to addition of tumor target cells (Fig. 1). In both instances, however, LK dose responses were similar: maximal but different cytotoxic levels were reached by the 1/16 dilution in each case; both remained at plateau thereafter. Tumoricidal activity at the plateau by macrophages treated with LK continuously was about threefold higher than that by LK-pulsed cells. Tumor cells cultured in LK dilutions without macrophages for 48 hr released no more nuclear label (<5%) than cells cultured in medium. Moreover, tumor cells exposed to LK for 6 hr before addition to LK-activated macrophages were not more susceptible to macrophage-induced cytotoxicity at any LK concentration during either continuous exposure or LK

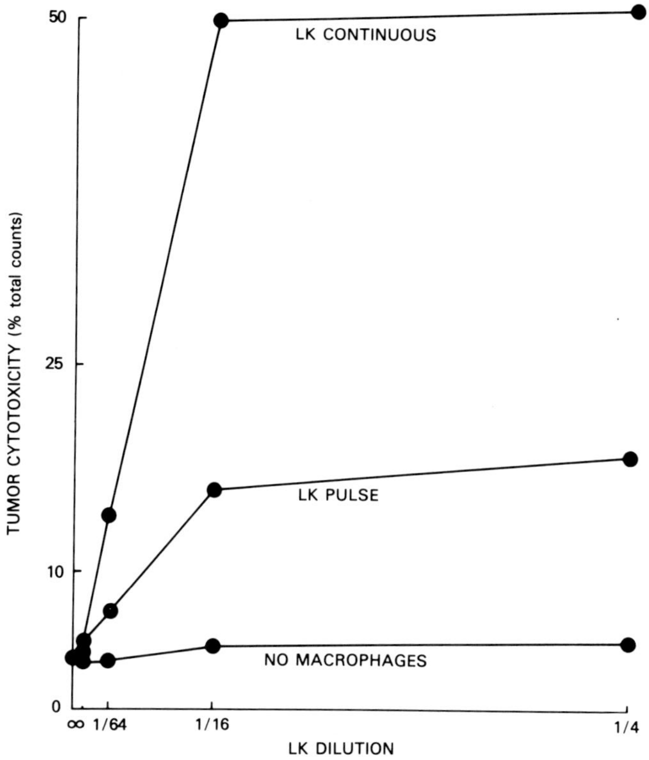

FIG. 1. Tumor cytotoxicity by macrophages continuously exposed or pulsed with LK. Adherent PEC from casein-injected mice were cultured in LK dilutions for 5 hr. Certain cultures were washed with medium. Tumor cells prelabeled with [^{3}H]TdR were added to washed (LK PULSE) and unwashed (LK CONTINUOUS) monolayers. Cytotoxicity was estimated by measurement of radiolabel release in triplicate cultures at 48 hr and expressed as a percentage of SDS total counts. Release of [^{3}H]TdR from tumor cells incubated with LK alone through 48 hr is designated by the line, NO MACROPHAGES.

pulse than cells exposed to medium (Fig. 2). It should also be noted that manipulations associated with washing LK-treated macrophages did not contribute to the differences in cytotoxicity (Fig. 3). Macrophages continuously exposed to LK were significantly more cytotoxic to tumor target cells than macrophages pulsed with LK for 5 hr. No differences in tumoricidal activity were observed between cells continuously incubated in LK and cells incubated in LK for 5 hr, washed, and treated with new LK at the same dilution for the remainder of the 48 hr assay (dashed line, Fig. 3).

These data suggest that the threefold difference in tumoricidal activity between macrophages continuously exposed or pulsed with LK was not due to changes in sensitivities of macrophages to LK activation signals or of target cells to the cytotoxic effects of LK-activated macrophages. This conclusion was supported by analysis of macrophage dose responses at given LK concentrations (Fig. 4). Different numbers of macrophages were continuously exposed or pulsed with 1/9 or 1/27 dilution of LK. With all treatments, macrophage tumoricidal activity was directly and linearly related to cell number. At each macrophage concentration,

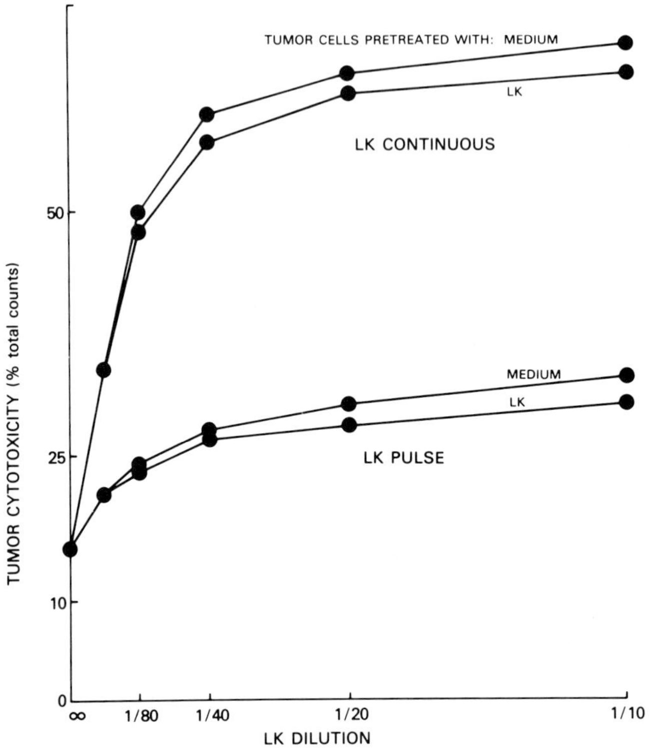

FIG. 2. Tumor cytotoxicity by macrophages continuously exposed or pulsed with LK: effect of LK pretreatment on target cell susceptibility. Adherent PEC from casein-injected mice were cultured in LK dilutions for 5 hr. Certain cultures were washed with medium. Tumor cells prelabeled with [^{3}H]TdR were treated with 1/10 LK or medium for 6 hr before addition to LK-activated macrophages, then added to washed (LK PULSE) and unwashed (LK CONTINUOUS) monolayers. Cytotoxicity was estimated by measurement of radiolabel release in triplicate cultures at 48 hr and expressed as a percentage of SDS total counts.

however, cells continuously exposed to LK were about threefold more cytotoxic than equal numbers of LK-pulsed macrophages. Cell dose–response curves for continuous LK exposure or LK pulse were superimposable after multiplication by a constant factor. This factor represents the relative difference in cytotoxic activity induced by the two types of LK treatment (4). At 1/9 dilution of LK, this factor was 2.8; at 1/27 the factor was 2.6. For 11 separate experiments, over a broad range of LK dilutions, the factor was 2.7 ± 0.2 (mean ± SEM). Thus, differences in cytotoxic levels induced by continuous LK exposure or LK pulse were not due to qualitative changes in macrophage killing mechanisms but rather to a threefold quantitative increase in killing events. Whether this reflects a threefold increase in killer cells within the macrophage population or a threefold increase in killer events per cell is not known.

The quantitative increase in cytotoxicity induced by continuous LK exposure was also evident with macrophage populations that are poorly responsive or unresponsive to an LK pulse for any length of time. For example, macrophages recovered from inflammatory exudates induced by sterile peritoneal irritants are 10- to 20-fold

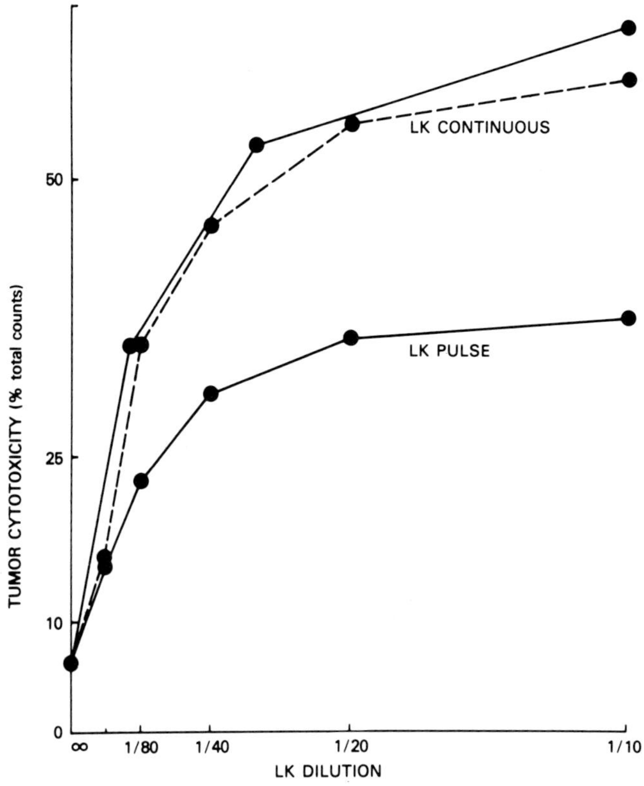

FIG. 3. Tumor cytotoxicity by macrophages continuously exposed or pulsed with LK: effect of washing on tumoricidal activity of macrophages continuously exposed to LK. Adherent PEC from casein-injected mice were cultured in LK dilutions for 5 hr. Certain cultures were washed with medium; LK were added back to some cultures at the same dilution (dashed lines). Tumor cells prelabeled with [^{3}H]TdR were added to washed (LK PULSE) and unwashed (LK CONTINUOUS) monolayers. Cytotoxicity was estimated by measurement of radiolabel release in triplicate cultures at 48 hr and expressed as a percentage of SDS total counts.

more responsive to LK activation than an equal number of resident peritoneal macrophages (4). Resident peritoneal macrophages continuously exposed to LK throughout the cytotoxicity assay, however, showed significant cytotoxic activity (Fig. 5). Similarly, macrophages from C3H/HeJ or P/J mice, strains with different genetic defects in development of macrophage tumoricidal activity, fail to develop cytotoxic activity after an LK pulse over a wide range of experimental conditions (12). Yet cells from both of these genetically unresponsive mouse strains develop significant levels of tumoricidal activity during continuous LK exposure (Fig. 6).

Macrophage activation for tumor cytotoxicity can potentially be affected by changes in either the activation signals or in the mononuclear phagocyte subpopulations capable of response. It is possible that differences in macrophage tumoricidal activity induced by continuous LK exposure or by LK pulse reflect responses to different activation signals. We examined this possibility by analysis of macrophage cytotoxic responses induced by fractions of LK separated by Sephadex G-100 chromatography (Fig. 7). Activity for induction of macrophage tumoricidal

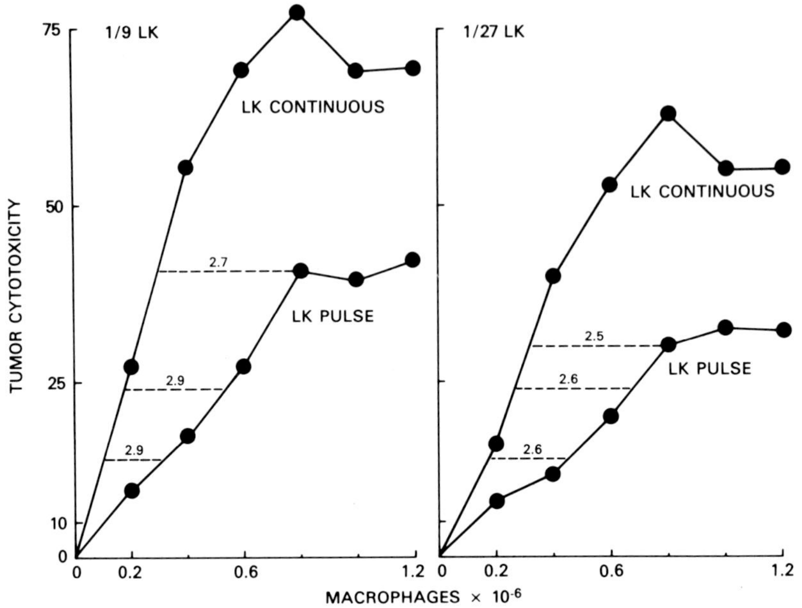

FIG. 4. Tumor cytotoxicity by macrophages continuously exposed or pulsed with LK: effect of macrophage concentration. Varying numbers of PEC from casein-injected mice with 0.2 to 1.2 × 10^6 macrophages/culture were incubated for 1 to 2 hr. Nonadherent cells were washed away and adherent PEC were cultured in LK dilutions for 5 hr. Certain cultures were washed with medium. Tumor cells prelabeled with [^{3}H]TdR were added to washed (LK PULSE) and unwashed (LK CONTINUOUS) monolayers. Cytotoxicity was estimated by measurement of radiolabel release in triplicate cultures at 48 hr and expressed as a percentage of SDS total counts. Macrophage dose–response curves for cells continuously exposed or pulsed with LK were superimposable after multiplication by a constant factor (shown above dashed lines); this factor represents the relative difference in cytotoxic activity for each population at a given concentration of LK.

activity in LK derived from antigen (PPD-stimulated BCG immune cells) stimulated spleen cell cultures eluted as a single peak in the 50,000 MW region (10). The areas of activity for both continuous LK exposure or LK pulse were comparable for each of the two different LK preparations. In each case, however, macrophage cytotoxic activity induced by active fractions was increased two- to threefold after continuous LK exposure. Thus, at this level of analysis, LK signals active during continuous LK exposure and LK pulse were similar.

Optimal levels of macrophage tumoricidal activity at any concentration of LK develop after 4–8 hr of treatment; cells cultured in LK beyond 8 hr progressively lose cytotoxic activity and return to background levels by 24 hr (5). Loss of cytotoxic activity is not due to LK depletion or macrophage death (6, 13). The time courses for development of cytotoxicity by cells continuously exposed or pulsed with LK were similar (Fig. 8). As previously reported, little or no cytotoxicity was detected with macrophages pulsed with LK for 2 hr (5, 6, 13). Optimal levels of tumor cytotoxicity were evident by 4 to 8 hr of LK pulse or continuous treatment; tumoricidal activity decreased thereafter in both instances. At each time point, however, macrophages continuously exposed to LK developed higher levels of cytotoxicity than an equal number of LK-pulsed cells. It is important to note that little

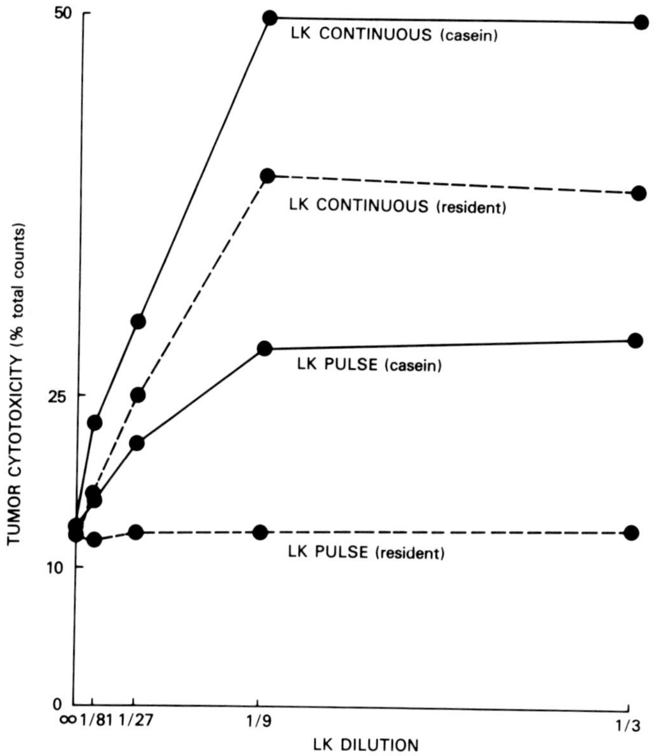

FIG. 5. Tumor cytotoxicity by macrophages continuously exposed or pulsed with LK: tumoricidal activity of inflammatory and resident macrophages. Adherent PC from untreated (resident macrophages) and casein-injected mice were cultured in LK dilutions for 5 hr. Certain cultures were washed with medium. Tumor cells prelabeled with [^{3}H]TdR were added to washed (LK PULSE) and unwashed (LK CONTINUOUS) monolayers. Cytotoxicity was estimated by measurement of radiolabel release in triplicate cultures.

or no difference in the increase of cytotoxic activity by macrophages continuously exposed to LK was observed whether tumor target cells were added at time 0 or 4 hr later. Addition of target target cells after 8 hr, however, considerably reduced cytotoxic activity.

The preceding results clearly show that macrophages continuously exposed to LK kill tumor cells threefold better than LK-pulsed cells. This increase in cytotoxicity was not due to: (a) changes in sensitivity of macrophages to LK activation signals, (b) changes in sensitivity of LK-treated targets to the cytopathic effects of activated macrophages, or (c) changes in the time course for onset and loss of macrophage tumoricidal activity. Results presented in Fig. 9 suggest that by whatever mechanism, the determinant interactions of LK, macrophages, and target cells for amplification of cytotoxicity occur relatively early. Macrophages and tumor cells were exposed to LK together for various times. After LK treatment, cultures were washed free of LK. Replicate macrophage cultures without tumor cells were pulsed with LK for identical times. Target cells were added to the LK-pulsed macrophages; medium was added to LK-treated macrophages and tumor cell cul-

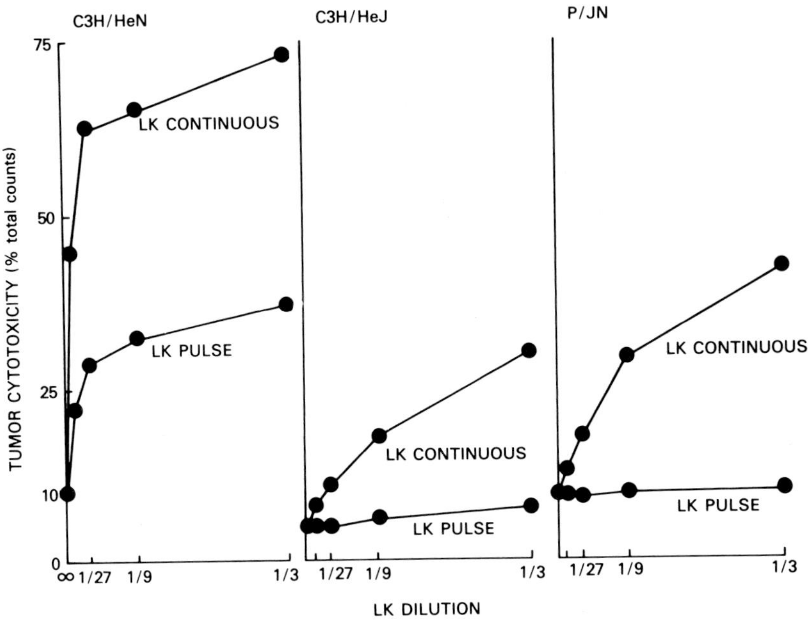

FIG. 6. Tumor cytotoxicity by macrophages continuously exposed or pulsed with LK: tumoricidal activity of macrophages from C3H/HeN, C3H/HeJ, and P/J mice. Adherent PEC from casein-injected C3H/HeN, C3H/HeJ, or P/J mice were cultured in LK dilutions for 5 hr. Certain cultures were washed with medium. Tumor cells prelabeled with [^{3}H]TdR were added to washed (LK PULSE) and unwashed (LK CONTINUOUS) monolayers. Cytotoxicity was estimated by measurement of radiolabel release in triplicate cultures at 48 hr and expressed as a percentage of SDS total counts.

tures. Release of [3H]TdR was measured at 48 hr. It should be emphasized at the outset that release of [^{3}H]TdR from labeled target cells during the initial 24 hr of this assay is negligible (14). After 2 hr of incubation, cytotoxic activities of macrophages treated with LK in the presence or absence of tumor cells were comparable and low. By 4 to 8 hr, however, macrophages exposed to LK in the presence of tumor cells and LK then removed by washing, were two- to threefold more cytotoxic than macrophages pulsed with LK alone for an identical time (target cells added after the LK pulse). Thus, the full effect of continuous exposure to LK was achieved within 4 to 8 hr. Amplifying interactions of LK, macrophages, and target cells were essentially complete during this early time and LK could be removed with no loss of effect.

These results suggest a critical period for optimal development of macrophage tumoricidal activity. Macrophages, LK, and target cells all must be present during this critical interval for maximal cytotoxicity. Tumor cell targets need not be present during the initial 2 to 3 hr of this interaction and LK can be removed after 8 hr with little or no decrease in cytotoxic activity. For maximal tumoricidal activity, however, target cell, effector cell, and activation stimulus must be simultaneously present during the 4- to 8-hr period. This period could represent either increased levels of macrophage activation induced by tumor cells (tumor cells provide additional activation stimuli that amplify LK-derived signals) or a critical effector period during which the target cells themselves must be present. That macrophages

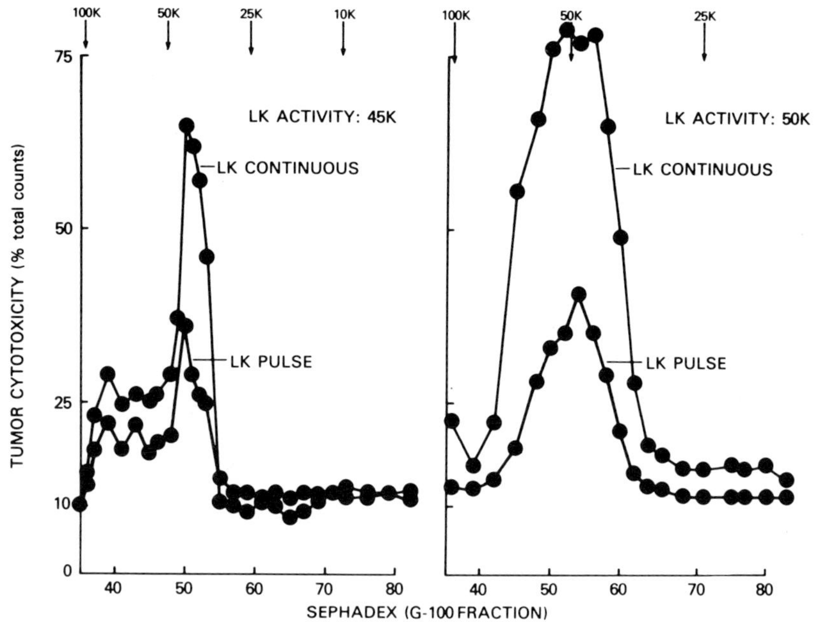

FIG. 7. Tumor cytotoxicity by macrophages continuously exposed or pulsed with LK: characterization of the LK activity by Sephadex G-100 gel chromatography. Adherent PEC from casein-injected mice were cultured in 1/20 (left diagram or 1/15 right diagram) dilutions of LK fractions eluted from Sephadex G-100 for 5 hr as previously described (10). Certain cultures were washed with medium. Tumor cells prelabeled with [^{3}H]TdR were added to washed (LK PULSE) and unwashed (LK CONTINUOUS) monolayers. Cytotoxicity was estimated by measurement of radiolabel release in triplicate cultures at 48 hr and expressed as a percentage of SDS total counts.

pulsed with LK in the presence of unlabeled (cold) target cells were no more cytotoxic than macrophages pulsed with LK alone (without cold target cells) (Fig. 10) suggests the second alternative is more likely.

DISCUSSION

Optimal levels of macrophage tumoricidal activity develop only if effector cell, target cell, and activation stimulus are simultaneously present during a critical time interval. Interactions that occur during this interval provide a regulatory mechanism for control of macrophage effector function. Macrophages activated by exposure to certain factors in LK supernatants require 2 to 3 hr for initial development of cytotoxic activity Maximal cytotoxic levels occur 4 to 8 hr after LK treatment. Cytotoxicity decreases with time thereafter and returns to baseline by 24 hr (5, 6). For optimal levels of macrophage tumoricidal activity, tumor cells need not be present during the initial 2 to 3 hr of culture; LK can be removed after 8 hr with little or no loss of cytotoxic activity (when macrophages are exposed to LK in the presence of target cells). However, removal of LK *or* target cells during the critical 4 to 8 hr interval decreased macrophage cytotoxic activity two- to threefold.

The precise nature of molecular or cellular events that occur during this critical interval are not yet known. Interactions of macrophages, LK, and target cells to amplify cytotoxic responses did not represent: (a) direct effects of LK on either

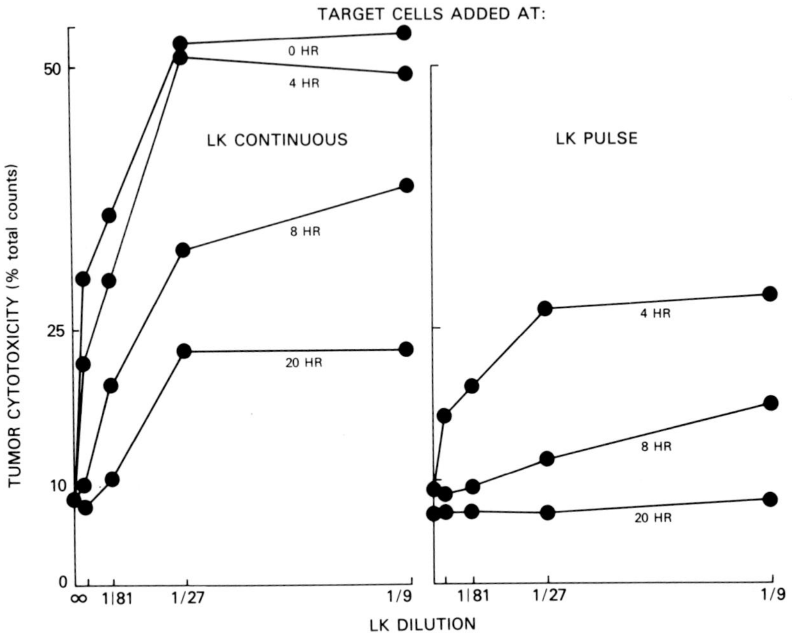

FIG. 8. Tumor cytotoxicity by macrophages continuously exposed or pulsed with LK: effect of incubation time in LK. Adherent PEC from casein-injected mice were cultured in LK dilutions for various times. Certain cultures were washed with medium. Tumor cells prelabeled with [^{3}H]TdR were added to washed (LK PULSE) and unwashed (LK CONTINUOUS) monolayers. Cytotoxicity was estimated by measurement of radiolabel release in triplicate cultures at 48 hr and expressed as a percentage of SDS total counts.

tumor cell viability or susceptibility of target cells to cytopathic effects of activated macrophages, (b) alterations in sensitivity of responsive macrophages to LK activation signals or induction of cell responsiveness to new, qualitatively different LK stimuli, or (c) changes in the time course for acquisition and loss of macrophage tumoricidal activity. Analysis of macrophage or LK dose responses and time courses for tumor cytotoxicity each suggests that differences in cytotoxic activity between macrophages treated with an LK pulse or continuously exposed to LK were quantitative: the number of cytotoxic events (cytotoxic cells or cytotoxic molecules per cell) within a given macrophage population was increased threefold by continuous LK exposure.

A model can be constructed from observations in this report and from previous analysis of LK-induced macrophage activation to account for this threefold increase. Macrophages respond to certain factors in LK supernatants to become activated tumoricidal effector cells. The tumoricidal activity of activated macrophages, however, is a short-lived cell function. With time, the number of cytotoxic cells decrease. This decrease is not due to LK depletion or macrophage cell death (6, 13). Current evidence suggests that the decrease in number of cytotoxic cells with time is irreversible and most likely secondary to mononuclear phagocyte maturation and/or differentiation. The capacity of macrophages to respond to LK for development of tumoricidal activity is also a short-lived cell function. With time, the number of LK-responsive cells within the macrophage population decreases

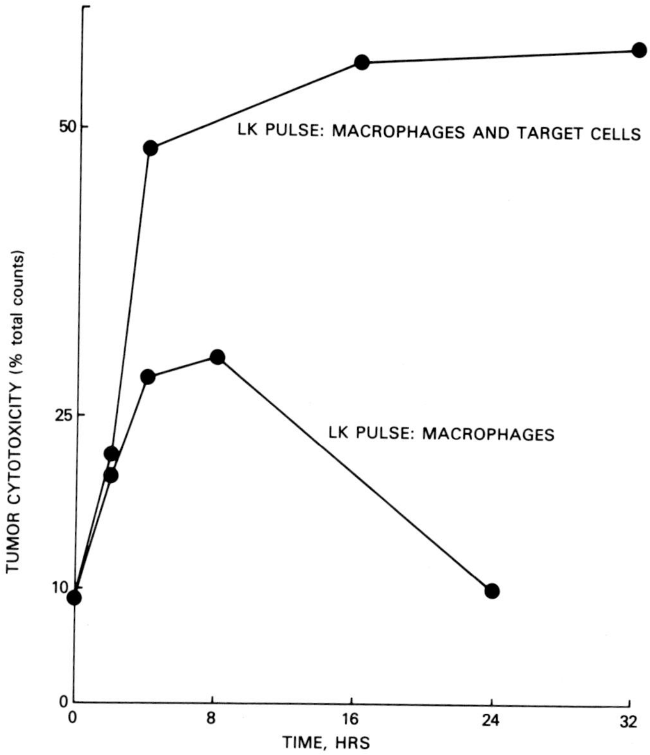

FIG. 9. Tumor cytotoxicity by macrophages treated with LK in the presence and absence of target cells. Adherent PEC from casein-injected mice were cultured in 1/10 LK with or without [^{3}H]TdR-labeled target cells for various times. After these time intervals, LK was removed from all cultures by washing with medium. Labeled target cells were added to the LK-pulsed macrophages; medium was added to LK-treated macrophages and tumor cell cultures. Cytotoxicity was estimated by measurement of radiolabel release in triplicate cultures at 48 hr and expressed as a percentage of SDS total counts.

with a coincident increase in the number of cells unable to develop cytotoxic activity (13). The decrease in numbers of LK-responsive cells with time is also irreversible and occurs at the same rate (about 5% loss of total activity per hour) in medium or in LK (5, 9). This loss too may represent macrophage maturation and/or differentiation.

Schematically, the preceding chain of events can be represented by

$$\begin{array}{l} A \xrightarrow{LK} B \rightarrow C. \\ \downarrow \\ D \end{array}$$

A represents macrophages able to respond to LK to become B, the activated tumoricidal effector cell. C and D represent noncytotoxic, LK-unresponsive macrophages (C, the decay product of B; D, the decay product of A). C and D may be identical cells. The threefold difference in cytotoxic activity between macrophages pulsed with LK and cells exposed to LK continuously during the critical 4- to 8-hr interval may reflect changes in the conversion of A (LK-responsive cells) to B

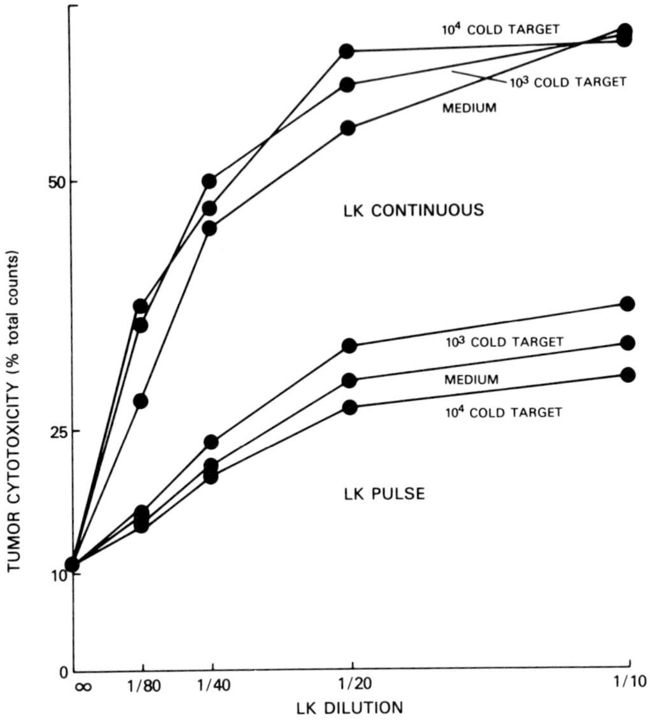

FIG. 10. Tumor cytotoxicity by macrophages continuously exposed or pulsed with LK: effect of cold target cells on macrophage tumoricidal activity. Adherent PEC from casein-injected mice were cultured in LK dilutions for 5 hr with and without 1 or 10×10^3 unlabled target cells. Certain cultures were washed with medium. Tumor cells prelabeled with $[^3H]$TdR were added to washed (LK PULSE) and unwashed (LK CONTINUOUS) monolayers. Cytotoxicity was estimated by measurement of radiolabel release in triplicate cultures at 48 hr and expressed as a percentage of SDS total counts.

(tumoricidal macrophages). If this reaction were reversible ($A^{LK}B$), then continued presence of LK would drive the reaction towards B. In the absence of LK, and LK-responsive A formed by the reverse reaction from B could only decay to the inactive D. Thus, continued presence of LK would substantially increase the numbers of B from a given macrophage population. Increased numbers of tumoricidal B would, in turn, increase cytotoxicity. The model proposed here is consistent with the two- to threefold quantitative increase in numbers of cytotoxic cells observed in this report.

Characterization of regulatory mechanisms for macrophage activation remains incomplete. Macrophage effector function is controlled through interactions of a diverse group of endogenous mediators that includes prostaglandins (15, 16), granulocyte–macrophage colony-stimulating factors (17, 18), interferon (15), and other factors in LK supernatants (5, 10). We have shown that LK supernatants have at least two functionally different mediators: macrophages exposed to one stimulus (priming signal) enter into a receptive state in which they are not yet active but can respond to a second stimulus (trigger signal) for full expression of effector function (11). These mediators, LK priming and trigger signals, form the basis of a regulatory system that sets the threshold and determines the onset of macrophage effector responses. In addition to onset, LK mediators also determine the quality of macrophage effector reactions. For example, macrophage activation for certain tumoricidal and microbicidal pathways are regulated by entirely different LK mediators (19).

The observations described in this report now suggest that the period of time macrophages are exposed to LK during an effector response also regulates macrophage activation. A similar conclusion was suggested by the work of Nogueira and Cohn for induction of macrophage microbicidal activity against *Trypanosoma cruzi* (20). Macrophages pretreated with LK supernatants for 24 hr were activated for secretion of plasminogen activator; these cells also displayed a transient period of trypanocidal activity. However, complete destruction of the intracellular parasite occurred only with continuous presence and daily renewal of active LK. Thus, control of certain tumoricidal and microbicidal properties of LK-activated macrophages is mediated by both the physicochemical nature of the LK mediator and the time interval effector and target cells are exposed to LK.

REFERENCES

1. Hibbs, J. B., Jr., Lambert, L. H., Jr., and Remington, J. S., *Nature New Biol.* **235,** 48, 1972.
2. Cleveland, R. P., Meltzer, M. S., and Zbar, B., *J. Nat. Cancer Inst.* **52,** 1887, 1974.
3. Rosenstreich, D. L., Blake, J. T., and Rosenthal, A. S., *J. Exp. Med.* **134,** 1170, 1971.
4. Ruco, L. P., and Meltzer, M. S., *J. Immunol.* **120,** 1054, 1978.
5. Ruco, L. P., and Meltzer, M. S., *J. Immunol.* **119,** 889, 1977.
6. Meltzer, M. S., Ruco, L. P., and Leonard, E. J., *Advan. Exp. Med. Biol.* **121,** 381, 1980.
7. Nacy, C. A., and Meltzer, M. S., *J. Immunol.* **123,** 2544, 1979.
8. Ruco, L. P., and Meltzer, M. S., *J. Immunol.* **121,** 2035, 1978.
9. Meltzer, M. S., *Lymphokines* **3,** 319, 1981.
10. Leonard, E. J., Ruco, L. P., and Meltzer, M. S., *Cell. Immunol.* **41,** 347, 1978.
11. Meltzer, M. S., *J. Immunol.,* **127,** 179, 1981.
12. Meltzer, M. S., Ruco, L. P., Boraschi, D., Männel, D. N., and Edelstein, M. C., *In* "Genetic Control of Nonspecific Resistance to Infection and Malignancy" (E. Skamene, P. A. L. Kongshavn, and M. Landy, Eds.). Academic Press, New York, 1980.
13. Meltzer, M. S., Ruco, L. P., Boraschi, D., and Nacy, C. A., *J. Reticuloendothel. Soc.* **26,** 403, 1979.
14. Meltzer, M. S., Tucker, R. W., Sanford, K. K., and Leonard, E. J., *J. Nat. Cancer Inst.* **54,** 1177, 1975.
15. Schultz, R. M., Pavlidis, N., Stylos, W. A., and Chirigos, M. A., *Science,* **202,** 320, 1978.
16. Taffet, S. M., and Russell, S. W., *J. Immunol.* **126,** 424, 1981.
17. Handman, E., and Burgess, A. W., *J. Immunol.* **122,** 1134, 1979.
18. Moore, R. N., Oppenheim, J. J., Farrar, J. J., Carter, C. S., Waheed, A., and Shadduck, R. K., *J. Immunol.* **125,** 1302, 1980.
19. Nacy, C. A., Leonard, E. J., and Meltzer, M. S., *J. Immunol.* **126,** 204, 1981.
20. Nogueria, N., and Cohn, Z. A., *J. Exp. Med.* **148,** 288, 1978.

CELLULAR IMMUNOLOGY 65, 66–74 (1981)

Cellular Transfer of Experimental Allergic Encephalomyelitis in Lewis Rats: Effects of Different Sensitization Regimens on *in Vitro* Reactivity of Donor Spleen Cells to Concanavalin A[1]

HAIM OVADIA[2] AND PHILIP Y. PATERSON

Department of Microbiology–Immunology, Medical and Dental Schools, Northwestern University, Chicago, Illinois 60611

Received July 7, 1981; accepted August 31, 1981

Splenocytes from Lewis rats sensitized to guinea pig spinal cord (GPSC) and complete Freund's adjuvant (CFA) or to myelin basic protein (MBP)-CFA plus pertussis vaccine were less effective than spleen cells from MBP-CFA sensitized donors in transferring EAE to syngeneic recipients following culture with concanavalin A (Con A). Moreover, splenocytes from rats sensitized to GPSC-CFA plus pertussis vaccine showed no EAE transfer activity following culture with Con A. Diminished EAE transfer activity occurred in parallel with decreased proliferative responses of primed splenocytes to Con A. These effects were due, at least in part, to the use of pertussis vaccine and to Con A activation of a suppressive adherent cell subpopulation in sensitized donor spleens. Proliferative responses and EAE transfer activity were restored upon removal of plastic-adherent cells from splenocytes of rats sensitized to MBP-CFA plus pertussis vaccine prior to Con A activation of the non adherent lymphoid cells. Deletion of plastic-adherent cells from splenocytes of donors sensitized to GPSC-CFA plus pertussis vaccine prior to activation with Con A, however, had no effect on proliferative responses or EAE transfer activity. Furthermore, EAE transfer activity of Con A-activated splenocytes from MBP-CFA-sensitized donors was lost when such cells were cultured with splenocytes from donors sensitized to GPSC-CFA plus pertussis vaccine.

INTRODUCTION

Experimental allergic encephalomyelitis (EAE)[3] can be transferred to outbred Wistar rats or isohistogeneic Lewis rats by means of lymph node cells (LNC) from donor rats sensitized to central nervous system (CNS) antigens emulsified in complete Freund's adjuvant (CFA) (1–3). Pertussis vaccine, when used to sensitize donor rats to neural antigen in conjunction with CFA, or injected into syngeneic recipients, results in an accelerated and much more severe form of actively induced as well as transferred disease (4, 5). Despite the relative ease and reproducibility

[1] This work was supported in part by USPHS Research Grant NS 06262.

[2] Present address: Department of Neurology, Hadassah Medical School, Jerusalem, Israel.

[3] Abbreviations used: BCG, Bacillus Calmette–Guérin; CFA, complete Freund's adjuvant; CNS, central nervous system, Con A, concanavalin A; EAE, experimental allergic encephalomyelitis; EAN, experimental allergic neuritis; FBS, fetal bovine serum; GPSC, guinea pig spinal cord; Hepes, *N*-2-hydroxyethylpiperazine-*N'*-2-ethanesulfonic acid; HBSS, Hanks' balanced salt solution; IFA, incomplete Freund's adjuvant; LNC, lymph node cells; MBP, myelin basic protein; 2-ME, 2-mercaptoethanol; PBS, phosphate-buffered saline; [^{3}H]TdR, tritiated thymidine.

0008-8749/81/170066-09$02.00/0

of transfer of EAE with LNC, successful transfer of the disease has rarely been accomplished using splenocytes of otherwise competent LNC donors (3).

Recently, Panitch and McFarlin (6) and Richert *et al.* (7) have reported that splenocytes of sensitized Lewis rats exhibit markedly augmented EAE transfer activity when the primed donor cells were activated by *in vitro* culture with either concanavalin A (Con A) or neural antigen. In these studies, the donor rats were sensitized to myelin basic protein (MBP), an important encephalitogenic antigen of myelin comprising a fair percentage of whole CNS tissue (wet weight), in combination with CFA. To the best of our knowledge, studies of EAE transfer activity of *in vitro*-activated splenocytes have not included donor rats subjected to other sensitization regimens, specifically those including whole CNS tissue and/or pertussis vaccine. Since whole CNS tissue, despite its relatively small content of MBP, is more encephalitogenic than purified MBP, and because of the striking EAE adjuvanticity of pertussis vaccine, we anticipated that even greater Con A augmentation of EAE transfer activity would be observed with Con A-cultured splenocytes from donors sensitized to GPSC-CFA with or without pertussis vaccine or donors sensitized to MBP-CFA plus pertussis vaccine.

Much to our surprise, transfer activity of splenocytes from donors subjected to the foregoing sensitization regimens was completely inhibited or markedly diminished. While diminished splenocyte transfer activity could be clearly traced to sensitization with spinal cord-CFA, as opposed to MBP-CFA, the major factor in inhibition of transfer activity was pertussis vaccine. Abrogated or diminished transfer activity occurred in association with reduced proliferative responses of Con A-activated splenocytes. These effects have been shown to be due, to a large degree, to the emergence of an adherent cell subpopulation in spleens of donor rats sensitized to pertussis vaccine which has striking suppressor properties when activated by Con A.

MATERIALS AND METHODS

Animals. Male Lewis rats, 8–12 weeks old (M.A. Bioproducts, Bethesda, Md.) were used as donors and recipients. The rats were kept in plastic cages and given water and food pellets *ad libitum.*

Antigens. Guinea pig spinal cords (GPSC) (Pel-Freeze, Rogers, Ark.) were obtained frozen and the meninges were discarded before use. Guinea pig myelin basic protein (GPMBP) was prepared in our laboratory following the procedure of Swanborg *et al.* (8), and was assayed for homogeneity by means of polyacrylamide disc electrophoresis carried out under acid conditions.

Sensitization of animals. Rats were injected with a 33% homogenate of GPSC emulsified in an equal volume of CFA containing 4 mg/ml Bacillus Calmette–Guérin (BCG) (obtained from Drs. Eva Leake and Quentin Myrvik, Wake Forest University, Winston-Salem, N.C.) as previously described (9). The rats were injected with 0.1 ml of the emulsion in each hind footpad. GPMBP was suspended in phosphate-buffered saline (PBS) and emulsified in an equal volume of CFA. A total of 50 μg of this antigen was injected via both hind footpads. Concentrated pertussis vaccine was purchased from Michigan State Laboratory, East Lansing, and contained 200×10^9 *Bordetella pertussis* organisms per milliliter. When used as a supplemental EAE adjuvant, 0.1 ml was injected into the dorsum of both hind footpads immediately after inoculation of neuroantigen-CFA.

In vitro activation of spleen cells and cell transfer. Spleens were removed aseptically and expressed through a stainless-steel screen (120 mesh), washed three times in Hanks' balanced salt solution (HBSS), and finally suspended in RPMI 1640 (Gibco) supplemented with 2 m*M* glutamine, streptomycin (100 μg/ml), penicillin (100 U/ml), 25 m*M* Hepes buffer, 5×10^{-5} *M* 2-mercaptoethanol (2-ME), and 5% heat-activated and mycoplasma-free fetal bovine serum (FBS) (Gibco). Nonadherent spleen cells were obtained by using the plastic adherence method. Cells (10×10^6/ml) were seeded onto plastic petri dishes (Falcon, tissue culture grade) and incubated at 37°C in a CO_2 incubator for 2 hr. Unfractionated, as well as nonadherent spleen cells, were transferred to tissue culture flasks (Corning, 75 cm^2) at a concentration of 2×10^6 cells/ml and incubated at 37°C in a humidified environment with 5% CO_2 for 72 hr. Either Con A, 1 μg/ml (Miles Yeda, Rehovot, Israel), or GPMBP, 10 μg/ml, was added to the cultures. Following incubation, the cells were pooled and washed twice with HBSS. Viability was determined by trypan blue exclusion and aliquots of $20–50 \times 10^6$ cells were injected into syngeneic Lewis recipient rats via the lateral tail vein.

Irradiation of cells. Spleen cells from normal Lewis rats were suspended at a concentration of 1×10^7/ml and exposed to 2000 rad (Gammacell 40, cesium-137, Atomic Energy, Canada).

Mitogenic response of splenocytes. Blast transformation and DNA synthesis were assessed by counting blast cells in a hemocytometer and by quantitation of [methyl-^{3}H]thymidine ([^{3}H]TdR) uptake by cultured cells, respectively. Following 72 hr of culture, aliquots of activated cells, 2×10^5/0.2 ml, were placed in flat-bottom microplates (Linbro, Flow Lab). The cells were pulsed with 1 μCi/well of [^{3}H]TdR, 2 Ci/m*M* (RPI, Elk Grove Village, Ill.) for 6 hr after which the cells were collected by means of a cell harvester. The glass fiber filters were dried and then counted in a Packard Tri-Carb scintillation counter.

Clinical and histopathological determination of EAE. Actively sensitized rats and animals injected with splenocytes were checked daily for clinical neurologic signs. Clinical status was scored as follows: no clinical signs, 0; loss of tail tonicity, 0.5; ataxia, 1; early paralysis of hind legs, 2; complete paralysis of both hind legs, 3. Recipients of activated spleen cells were sacrificed 12 days after cell transfer. The brains and spinal cords were fixed in 10% formaldehyde, cut into blocks, embedded in paraffin, and sectioned for routine hemotoxylin and eosin staining as described previously (10). Sections of the brain at the level of the thalamus, mesencephalon, and cerebellum-pons, as well as longitudinal sections of the entire spinal cord were examined for perivascular cellular infiltrates. CNS lesions were scored as follows: 1–10 discrete lesions, 1; 11–30 lesions, 2; and greater than 30 lesions, 3.

RESULTS

The results of several experiments depicting EAE transfer activity of primed splenocytes secured from Lewis rats subjected to different types of sensitization regimens and activated *in vitro* with Con A are summarized in Table 1. In confirmation of results reported by Panitch and McFarlin (6), splenocytes from donors

TABLE 1

Effect of Sensitization Regimen upon Augmentation of EAE Transfer Activity of Primed Spleen Cells following *in Vitro* Activation with Con A

Donor sensitization		Adherent cells present	Occurrence of EAE in cell recipients[a]	
Neuroantigen CFA	Pertussis vaccine		Clinical signs	CNS lesions
MBP	0	+	3/3	3/3
Spinal cord	0	+	3/6	4/6
MBP	+	+	0/14	5/14
Spinal cord	+	+	0/8	0/8
MBP	+	0	4/11	8/11
Spinal cord	+	0	0/8	0/8

[a] 20–50 × 10^6 activated spleen cells were injected iv. Clinical signs within the different groups were of the same severity.

sensitized to MBP-CFA and activated by Con A transferred both clinical and histopathological evidence of EAE to all recipients. Splenocytes from donors sensitized to spinal cord-CFA exhibited a comparative diminution in transfer activity, viz, only a proportion of recipients developed evidence of disease. Most striking was the reduced transfer activity of splenocytes derived from donors sensitized to MBP-CFA plus pertussis vaccine, and total inhibition of such activity by splenocytes of donors sensitized to spinal cord-CFA plus pertussis vaccine. In contrast, when plastic-adherent cells were deleted prior to Con A activation, reexpression of some EAE transfer activity was observed with cells from donors sensitized to MBP-CFA plus pertussis vaccine. Following deletion of plastic-adherent cells from splenocyte suspensions derived from donors sensitized to spinal cord-CFA plus pertussis vaccine, however, reexpression of transfer activity was not demonstrable.

The results of a number of experiments relating EAE transfer activity to *in vitro* proliferative responses of splenocytes, viz, [^{3}H]TdR incorporation, appearance of blast cells, and final yield of viable cultured lymphoid cells, are summarized in Table 2. Four conclusions can be drawn. First, proliferative responses *per se* were not associated with transfer activity unless the splenocytes were derived from donors sensitized to MBP-CFA (compare lines 1 and 2 of Table 2). Second, a slight reduction in proliferative responses and transfer activity was observed with splenocytes from donors sensitized to spinal cord-CFA (line 3, Table 2). Third, there was a profound decrease in proliferative responses and transfer activity with splenocytes secured from donors sensitized to MBP-CFA plus pertussis vaccine. Furthermore, deletion of plastic-adherent cells from such splenocyte suspensions resulted in a clear-cut increase in proliferative responses which occurred in parallel with reexpression of some EAE transfer activity (lines 4 and 5, Table 2). Fourth, a comparable degree of reduction of proliferative responses in parallel with complete loss of transfer activity was observed with splenocytes from donors sensitized to spinal cord-CFA plus pertussis vaccine. In addition, deletion of adherent cells did not result in appreciable increases in proliferative reponsiveness and no evidence of EAE transfer activity was detected (lines 6 and 7, Table 2). In sharp contrast,

TABLE 2

Proliferative Responses and EAE Transfer Activity of Primed Spleen Cells following *in Vitro* Activation with Con A

Donor sensitization	Status of cultured spleen cells	Spleen cell responses: [^{3}H]Tdr (mean cpm ± SD)	% blasts	Final cell count[a] ($\times 10^6$)	EAE-transfer activity[b]
NIL	Unfractionated	58650 ± 3519	32	24	0
MBP-CFA	Unfractionated	66851 ± 5284	34	28	++
GPSC-CFA	Unfractionated	32060 ± 1955	20	16	+
MBP-CFA and pertussis vaccine	Unfractionated	1189 ± 128	2	6	±
	Plastic-adherent cells deleted	11247 ± 482	12	16	+
GPSC-CFA pertussis vaccine	Unfractionated	1769 ± 270	2	4	0
	Plastic adherent cells deleted	5280 ± 550	4	6	0
	Activated with MBP	788 ± 123	2	4	++

[a] Initial cell count was 80 × 10^6 viable cells/flask.

[b] The symbols represent relative activity *in vivo* as expressed by the incidence of both clinical signs and CNS lesions.

splenocytes from donors sensitized to spinal cord-CFA plus pertussis vaccine, even when plastic-adherent cells were not deleted, exhibited transfer activity following *in vitro* activation with MBP, which was unaccompanied by any parallel significant proliferative responsiveness (line 8, Table 2). This dissociation of splenocyte proliferative responsiveness and EAE transfer activity reinforced that already noted with Con A-activated splenocytes from nonsensitized donors (line 1, Table 2).

The results of experiments in which splenocytes from rats sensitized to GPSC-CFA plus pertussis vaccine were tested directly for their capacity to suppress the EAE transfer activity of other splenocytes are shown in Fig. 1. In order to better

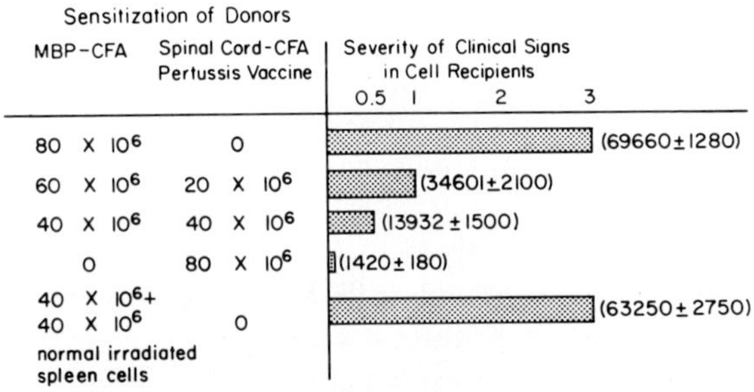

FIG. 1. *In vivo* primed splenocytes obtained from rats sensitized with MBP-CFA were admixed with variable numbers of primed splenocytes secured from rats sensitized with spinal cord-CFA plus pertussis vaccine. Either type of splenocyte suspension or mixtures of both types of splenocytes were incubated for 3 days in the presence of Con A followed by intravenous injection of 3–6 × 10^7 cells into syngeneic recipient rats. Values in brackets next to each bar represent [^{3}H]TdR uptake by cultured cells (mean cpm ± SD).

illustrate suppressor effects in these experiments, we used primed spleen cells from rats sensitized 12 days earlier with MBP-CFA. Upon activation *in vitro* with Con A, these cells were able to transfer severe clinical signs, i.e., complete paralysis of hindlegs, using as few as 20×10^6 cells. When admixed with equal numbers of Con A-activated spleen cells from animals sensitized with spinal cord-CFA and pertussis vaccine, the yield of viable cells, the rate of thymidine uptake, and the EAE transfer activity of clinical signs were all markedly suppressed. To exclude the possibility that this merely reflected cell dilution, primed splenocytes taken from rats sensitized to MBP-CFA were admixed with an equal number of irradiated normal spleen cells and then activated with Con A. No inhibitory effects on either cell proliferation or EAE transfer activity were observed. It would appear from these experiments (Fig. 1) that not only are spleen cells from rats sensitized with spinal cord-CFA and pertussis vaccine themselves refractory to Con A (Tables 1 and 2), but that they can exert an inhibitory effect on the capacity of otherwise competent splenocytes to respond to Con A *in vitro.*

DISCUSSION

In the studies here described, we have shown that the degree of expression of EAE transfer activity of primed Lewis rat splenocytes following *in vitro* activation with Con A is related to the type of neural antigen and the type of immunologic adjuvant used to sensitize splenocyte donors. Splenocytes from rats sensitized to MBP-CFA and activated by Con A exhibit augmented EAE transfer activity (Table 1), as originally reported by Panitch and McFarlin (6). In contrast, Con A-activated splenocytes from rats sensitized to GPSC-CFA or MBP-CFA plus pertussis vaccine showed diminished EAE transfer activity, and Con A-activated spleen cells from rats sensitized to GPSC-CFA plus pertussis vaccine were devoid of such transfer activity (Table 1). On balance, the data indicate that sensitization regimens known to be progressively more effective for induction of EAE (i.e., MBP-CFA < spinal cord-CFA < MBP-CFA plus pertussis vaccine < spinal cord-CFA plus pertussis vaccine (3, 11) exhibit this same progression in terms of their capacity to decrease or abolish EAE transfer activity of otherwise competent Con A-activated splenocytes.

Use of pertussis vaccine as a supplementary EAE adjuvant appeared more important than use of spinal cord with respect to suppression of EAE transfer activity (Table 1). Diminished or abolished transfer activity was observed to occur in concert with decreased proliferative responses of splenocytes during their period of *in vitro* culture with Con A (Table 2). However, as already noted, proliferation per se, as measured by [^{3}H]TdR uptake, was not a prerequisite for expression of EAE transfer activity (compare lines 1 vs 2 vs 8, Table 2). Proliferation of splenocytes was observed without demonstrable EAE transfer activity and transfer of EAE was accomplished without concomitant proliferation (Table 2).

Exactly how different types of neural antigens and EAE adjuvants, especially pertussis vaccine, exert opposing influences on the autoreactive immune responses of rats, guinea pigs and other species of animals remains undefined and a matter which only future studies can clarify. There is no dearth of examples of such opposing effects with respect to EAE. In terms of encephalitogenic activity for rats, whole guinea-pig or rat nervous tissue is superior to purified MBP, especially when used for sensitization in combination with incomplete Freund's adjuvant (IFA) (3, 12, 13). Guinea pig or rat MBP, on the other hand, particularly when emulsified in IFA, has a profound EAE inhibitory activity unmatched by whole nervous tissue (14). Most immunologic adjuvants can be shown to have immunosuppressive activity under appropriate experimental conditions (15). This is true for many of the adjuvants which have been found to potentiate induction of EAE. For example, CFA is essential for induction of EAE in guinea pigs sensitized to MBP or whole guinea pig nervous tissue and superior to IFA for induction of severe EAE in rats (12, 13). Yet a single injection of CFA prior to challenge with neural antigen-CFA results in suppression of the disease (16). Pertussis vaccine has a striking potentiating influence on development of EAE in rats and mice when employed as a supplemental adjuvant in concert with sensitization to neural antigen-CFA (4, 17). In the guinea pig, however, pertussis vaccine has no comparable EAE potentiating influence and, depending on the number of *B. pertussis* microorganisms injected, may exert EAE inhibitory activity (9). In Lewis rats sensitized to sciatic nerve-CFA, use of pertussis vaccine as a supplemental adjuvant not only had no augmenting influence on the development of experimental allergic neuritis (EAN), but abolished expression of this neuroautoimmune disease of the peripheral nervous system while simultaneously augmenting development of EAE in the same sensitized host (18). Occurrence of EAE rather than EAN in such animals presumably occurred due to CNS and peripheral nerve tissues sharing a common MBP antigen, designated as P1. Pertussis vaccine also has been reported to augment or suppress production of anti-MBP antibodies in Lewis rats sensitized to this purified encephalitogenic protein emulsified in CFA, depending on the number of *B. pertussis* bacterial cells injected per rat (19).

The mechanism responsible for diminished EAE transfer activity, at least in splenocytes secured from rats sensitized with MBP-CFA plus pertussis vaccine, appears to be a subpopulation of plastic-adherent cells. Direct support for this thesis was provided by our finding of increased proliferative responses in concert with reexpression of EAE transfer activity when splenocyte suspensions were depleted of plastic-adherent cells prior to activation by Con A (Tables 1 and 2). We presume that the adherent cells in question are macrophages, but hasten to add that their precise characterization is a matter of considerable complexity and is the subject of ongoing studies. Macrophages with potential suppressor activity normally exist in rat spleens (20). There is evidence that Con A may cause such macrophages, if present in excessive numbers, to exert an inhibitory effect on nonmacrophage effector cells (21).

While our studies were being completed, Panitch and Ciccone (22) reported that deletion of macrophages from splenocyte suspensions from MBP-CFA-sensitized donor rats prior to Con A activation resulted in loss of augmented EAE transfer activity and proliferative responsiveness to this mitogen. In their work, the macrophages were deleted by plastic adherence combined with passage of cells over Sephadex G-10. Addition of 2-ME to the medium in which the macrophage-depleted splenocytes were cultured resulted in return of augmented EAE transfer activity, indicating that 2-ME can substitute for macrophages as a prerequisite for augmented activity of EAE effector cells. We are keenly aware that our use of plastic adherence as a means for removing adherent cells/macrophages is not as effective as the use of Sephadex G-10 (23) or carbonyl iron (24). Practically speaking, it is nigh impossible to remove all macrophages from a given suspension of heterogenous lymphoid cells, irrespective of what method(s) is employed (25). In our studies, it should be noted, the exact number of macrophages remaining in the splenocyte suspensions following plastic adherence is not an important issue, since our culture medium routinely contained 2-ME.

There are at least two different interpretations of our observation that deletion of plastic-adherent cells from splenocyte suspensions from donors sensitized to GPSC-CFA plus pertussis vaccine did not result in reexpression of proliferative responses to Con A and return of EAE transfer activity (Table 2). First of all, the obviously more intensive suppressor effects of this sensitization regimen may have influenced nonadherent EAE effector cells to such a degree that, even before *in vitro* culture and Con A activation, removal of adherent cells made little difference in the overall outcome. Second, a nonadherent splenocyte subpopulation may have been transformed into nonspecific suppressor cells as a result of *in vitro* stimulation by Con A. Occurrence of such Con A-induced suppressor lymphocytes has been reported in studies with human and murine lymphoid cells, using relatively high concentrations of Con A (26, 27). This thesis is supported by the finding that EAE transfer activity of MBP-CFA-sensitized donor splenocytes was abolished when such cells were cocultured with Con A-refractory splenocytes plus the mitogen (Fig. 1).

At the very least, our studies underline the potential role of the spleen in modulating development of EAE in actively sensitized rats, and provide a clearer explanation for observations reported from this and other laboratories. Many years ago, prior to the present era of suppressor cell activities, we reported that the removal of the spleen before sensitization of Wistar rats with spinal cord-CFA markedly increased the capacity of sensitized donor LNC to transfer EAE to allogeneic Wistar recipient rats (28). At the time we believed that removal of the spleen eliminated nonspecific trapping of circulating EAE effector lymphoid cells, thereby allowing such cells to "home to" and become more numerous in draining lymph nodes. While we, as well as other investigators (5, 29), have observed no appreciable influence of the spleen on development of EAE in Lewis rats or on LNC transfer of the disease to syngeneic recipients, detailed experiments involving different types of sensitization regimens were not carried out. More recently, the EAE inhibitory effects of dietary unsaturated fatty acids in Lewis rats have been found to be mediated exclusively by the spleen (30). Finally, splenocytes secured from Lewis rats at the time of maximum expression of clinical signs of EAE, or a few days thereafter, have been reported to transfer an EAE suppressive effect in syngeneic recipients subsequently challenged with neural antigen-CFA (31).

ACKNOWLEDGMENTS

The authors wish to acknowledge the invaluable assistance of Mrs. C. Clark and Mrs. C. Walker for all tissue preparation and staining procedures. Ms. Amy Carbone offered many fruitful suggestions during the course of this work, and provided superb help with manuscript preparation.

REFERENCES

1. Paterson, P. Y., *J. Exp. Med.* **111,** 119, 1960.
2. Paterson, P. Y., *Advan. Immunol.* **5,** 131, 1966.

3. Paterson, P. Y., *In* "Textbook of Immunopathology," (P. A. Miescher and H. J. Muller-Eberhard, Eds.), 2nd Ed., p. 179. Grune & Stratton, New York, 1976.
4. Levine, S., and Wenk, E. J., *Amer. J. Pathol.* **47,** 61, 1965.
5. Levine, S., and Wenk, E. J., *Amer. J. Pathol.* **50,** 465, 1967.
6. Panitch, H. S., and McFarlin, D. E., *J. Immunol.* **119,** 1134, 1977.
7. Richert, J. R., Driscoll, B. F., Kies, M. W., and Alvord, E. C., Jr., *J. Immunol.* **122,** 494, 1979.
8. Swanborg, R. H., Swierkosz, J. E., and Saieg, R. G., *J. Immunol.* **112,** 594, 1974.
9. Paterson, P. Y., *J. Reticulendothel. Soc.* **14,** 426, 1973.
10. Paterson, P. Y., Richardson, W. P., and Drobish, D. G., *Cell Immunol.* **16,** 48, 1975.
11. Hoffman, P. M., Gaston, D. D., and Spitler, L. E., *Clin. Immunol. Immunopathol.* **1,** 364, 1973.
12. Bell, J., and Paterson, P. Y., *Science* **131,** 1448, 1960.
13. Paterson, P. Y., and Bell, J., *J. Immunol.* **89,** 72, 1962.
14. Swanborg, R. H., *Clin. Exp. Immunol.* **26,** 597, 1976.
15. Allison, A. C., *In* "Immunopotentiation," Ciba Foundation Symposium 18, p. 73. Elsevier, New York, 1973.
16. Lisak, R. P., and Zweiman, B., *Cell. Immunol.* **14,** 242, 1974.
17. Bernard, C. C. A., and Carnegie, P. R., *J. Immunol.* **114,** 1537, 1975.
18. Ballon-Landa, G. R., Paterson, P. Y., and Dal Canto, M. C., *Clin. Immunol. Immunopathol.* **10,** 148, 1978.
19. Pitts, O. M., Varitek, V. A., and Day, E. D., *J. Immunol.* **115,** 1114, 1975.
20. Oehler, J. R., Herberman, R. B., Campbell, D. A., Jr., and Djeu, J. Y., *Cell. Immunol.* **29,** 238, 1977.
21. Parkhouse, R. M. E., and Dutton, R. W., *J. Immunol.* **97,** 663, 1966.
22. Panitch, H. S., and Ciccone, C., *Cell Immunol.* **60,** 24, 1981.
23. Ly, I. A., and Mishell, R. I., *J. Immunol. Methods* **5,** 239, 1974.
24. Levine, S., *Science* **123,** 185, 1956.
25. Larsson, E. L., Coutinho, A., and Martinez, A., *Immunol. Rev.* **51,** 61, 1980.
26. Shou, L., Schwartz, S. A., and Good, R. A., *J. Exp. Med.* **143,** 1100, 1976.
27. Rich, R. R., and Rich, S. S., *J. Immunol.* **114,** 1112, 1975.
28. Paterson, P. Y., and Didakow, N. C., *Proc. Soc. Exp. Biol. Med.* **108,** 768, 1961.
29. Swierkosz, J. E., and Swanborg, R. H., *J. Immunol.* **119,** 1501, 1977.
30. Mertin, J., and Stackpoole, A., *Clin. Exp. Immunol.* **36,** 449, 1979.
31. Adda, D. H., Beraud, E., and Depieds, R., *Eur. J. Immunol.* **7,** 620, 1977.

CELLULAR IMMUNOLOGY **65**, 75–83 (1981)

Mechanisms of Protective Immunity against *Schistosoma mansoni* Infection in Mice Vaccinated with Irradiated Cercariae

I. Analysis of Antibody and T-Lymphocyte Responses in Mouse Strains Developing Differing Levels of Immunity[1]

STEPHANIE L. JAMES,[2] MARGARET LABINE, AND ALAN SHER

Department of Medicine, Harvard Medical School, Brigham and Women's Hospital, Boston, Massachusetts 02115, and the Laboratory of Parasitic Diseases, National Institute of Allergy and Infectious Diseases, National Institutes of Health, Bethesda, Maryland 20205

Received July 15, 1981; accepted September 15, 1981

The kinetics of cellular and humoral responses directed against schistosomula were examined in mice of three inbred strains which demonstrate differences in the degree of resistance induced by immunization with irradiated cercariae. T-Cell reactivity was observed during the first 4 weeks after vaccination but declined to control levels thereafter. Anti-schistosomulum antibody was first detected 2 weeks after vaccination, peaked by 6 weeks, and persisted as late as 15 weeks. In sera obtained at 6 weeks, antibody activity was detected in affinity chromatography-purified fractions containing IgM, IgA, IgG_1, IgG_{2a}, and IgG_3 immunoglobulins. In general, the cellular and humoral responses observed in C57Bl/6J mice, which consistently developed a high level of immunity after vaccination, were not significantly different from those observed in C3H/HeJ or CBA/J mice, which achieved only low to moderate levels of immunity. Thus, although antibody production appears to correlate more closely than T lymphocyte responsiveness with the typical long-term resistance pattern observed in this model, the absence of striking differences in parasite-specific antibody levels between mice of these different strains suggests that additional mechanisms may be involved in the development of immunity after vaccination.

INTRODUCTION

Partial or complete protective immunity has been shown to develop in laboratory animals during chronic *Schistosoma mansoni* infection (reviewed in Ref. (1)). However, this immunity to challenge infection is manifested in the presence of surviving adult worms from the initial exposure. Under these conditions, termed "concomitant immunity" by Smithers and Terry (2), egg-related immunopathologic responses proceed, thus complicating the analysis of protective mechanisms. Vaccination of experimental animals with cercariae that have been attenuated by high-

[1] This work was supported by Grants from the National Institute of Allergy and Infectious Diseases (National Institutes of Health), the Edna McConnell Clark Foundation, the Rockefeller Foundation, and the UNDP/World Bank/WHO Special Programme for Research and Training in Tropical Diseases.

[2] Address correspondence and reprint requests to: Dr. Stephanie L. James, National Institutes of Health, NIAID, LPD, Building 5, Room 112, Bethesda, Md. 20205.

0008-8749/81/170075-09$02.00/0

dose irradiation has also been shown to result in partial immunity (3–7). In the mouse, this immunity develops within 2 weeks after vaccination and persists as long as 15 weeks (7). The life span of attenuated cercariae is short, with the majority of the organisms apparently dying in the skin, so that patent infection does not result (8, 9). The use of this model therefore allows the study of immune responses to the infective form of the parasite, in the absence of severe disease.

In the current study, we examined the development of humoral and cell-mediated responsiveness specifically directed toward schistosomula, the putative target of resistance mechanisms in vaccinated mice (9). These analyses were conducted in mice of three inbred strains, C57Bl/6, CBA, and C3H/He, chosen on the basis of differences in the level of protection induced by exposure to attenuated cercariae (10).

MATERIALS AND METHODS

Animals and Immunization

Six- to seven-week-old female mice of the C57Bl/6J, CBA/J, and C3H/HeJ strains were procured from Jackson Laboratories (Bar Harbor, Maine). C57Bl/6J mice have consistently been shown, in many laboratories including our own, to develop a high level of resistance following vaccination, while CBA/J and C3H/HeJ mice develop moderate or low levels of protection [(10), Lewis, F., personal communication]. *Schistosoma mansoni* (Puerto Rican strain) was maintained in our laboratory by passage through *Biophalaria glabrata* snails and outbred CF1 mice.

Cercariae were collected after shedding infected snails for 2 hr under light and were attenuated by a modification of the method of Minard *et al.* (7), receiving ≧30 krad of gamma irradiation (5 krad/min) from a ^{60}Co source. Mice were immunized by percutaneous infection on the abdomen (11) with 500 irradiated cercariae. Age-matched control animals were maintained for each experiment.

Preparation of Schistosomula

For analysis of cell-mediated responses, skin-stage schistosomula were obtained by allowing fresh cercariae to penetrate an isolated preparation of rat skin *in vitro*, in a modification of the method of Stirewalt *et al.* (12). For measurement of antibody levels, schistosomula were prepared either by skin penetration or by mechanical transformation (13). Equivalent results were obtained with parasites prepared by either method.

Assay of T Lymphocyte Reactivity With Schistosomula

Sensitization of T lymphocytes against skin-stage schistosomula as a result of vaccination was analyzed by the criteria of lymphokine production and T-cell proliferation. When previously studied in natural infections, these responses were shown to be T-cell-dependent functions as determined by nylon wool fractionation and depletion with anti-Thy-1 antiserum plus complement (14, 15). Lymphoid cells were obtained from the spleens (SP)[3] or pooled axillary, cervical, mesenteric, and inguinal lymph nodes (LN) of two or more similarly treated mice.

[3] Abbreviations used: LN, lymph node; SI, stimulation index; SP, spleen.

(a) Lymphokine production. Twenty million SP cells were incubated with 2000 living schistosomula for 24 hr at 37°C in 2 ml of RPMI 1640 with 150 units of penicillin and 150 μg of streptomycin/ml (Microbiological Associates, Walkersville, Md.). Supernatant fluids were collected and stored at −70°C. Lymphokine activity present in these fluids was quantitated by measurement of their ability to stimulate the migration of eosinophils and mononuclear cells to the far side of a 3-μm pore-sized polycarbonate membrane (Uni-pore, Bio-Rad Laboratories, Richmond, Calif.) in blind-well chemotaxis chambers, as described previously (14). Migrating cells were obtained by proteose peptone elicitation of a peritoneal exudate in *S. mansoni*-infected CBA mice. Results are presented as the mean stimulation index (SI) ± standard error of the mean (SEM) for three separate assays of the same test fluid. The SI in each assay was determined as the number of cells responding to the test fluid, divided by the number of cells responding to a control fluid obtained from the same SP cells cultured in the absence of larvae.

(b) Proliferation assay. LN cells (4×10^5) and living schistosomula (400) were cultured together in the wells of flat-bottomed microtiter plates for 2 days at 37°C in 0.2 ml of RPMI 1640 suplemented with 5% heat-activated (56°C/45 min) normal human A^+ serum and 3% penicillin–streptomycin (150 units or μg/ml, respectively). At the end of the second day, 0.5 μCi of [^{3}H]thymidine (New England Nuclear, Boston, Mass.) was added to each well and incubation was continued overnight. Contents of the wells were harvested (MASH II, Microbiological Associates) and counts incorporated into water-insoluble material were quantitated in a beta scintillation counter. These conditions were established as optimal for this assay in a previous study (15). Data are presented as the mean tritium counts per minute for triplicate samples.

For both assays, a mitogen control (2.5 μg/ml conconavalin A) (Miles Laboratories, Elkhart, Ind.) was included as an indication of the viability of the cell populations. In the proliferation assay, the response of LN cells toward soluble worm antigenic preparation at a concentration of 25 μg/ml was also avaluated. This antigen was prepared by homogenization of adult male and female *S. mansoni*, followed by extraction of the soluble components as previously described (15). These concentrations of mitogen and antigen have been determined to elicit optimal response by cells from mice with chronic *S. mansoni* infections (14, 15).

Assays for Anti-Larval Antibodies

Blood from a minimum of three vaccinated or age-matched control mice was collected from the tail veins and pooled. Sera were heat-inactivated (56°C, 30 min) and stored at −20°C. In one set of experiments, 1 ml of pooled sera from C57Bl/6J or C3H/HeJ mice vaccinated 6 weeks earlier was separated on protein A–Sepharose according to the method of Ey *et al.* (16). Four fractions were collected and analyzed by immunodiffusion against monospecific antisera: pH 8.0 (IgM and IgA), pH 5.5 (IgG_1), pH 4.5 (IgG_{2a} and IgG_3), and pH 3.5 (IgG_{2b}). Each fraction was dialyzed against phosphate-buffered saline, pH 7.4, and concentrated to the original volume of the sera.

Test sera were evaluated for the presence of antibodies which react with the surface of skin-stage schistosomula by the technique of indirect immunofluorescence (17). Larvae were incubated with doubling dilutions of sera in minimum essential medium (MEM, Microbiological Associates) with 10% normal heat-inactivated rabbit serum for 60 min at 37°C, washed three times, and subsequently incubated for 30 min at 23°C with a 1:20 dilution of fluorescein-conjugated polyvalent rabbit anti-mouse immunoglobulin (heavy and light chains) or monospecific rabbit anti-mouse IgM (Cappel Laboratories, Cochranville, Pa.). Larvae were then washed twice in buffered saline and either examined immediately or incubated for 30 min at room temperature with Karnovsky's 1% paraformaldehyde–3% glutaraldehyde fixative (18) at a concentration of 1:1, v/v. Fixed larvae were held at 4°C in 0.1 *M* cacodylate buffer for subsequent reading on a Leitz Ortholux fluorescence microscope at 125× magnification. The degree of fluorescence associated with each schistosomulum was quantitated as negative, + (weak fluorescence) to ++++ (strong fluorescence). The larval fluorescent antibody (FA) titer was taken as that dilution at which more than half of the 10 larvae counted had a fluorescence of + or higher, with serum from age-matched uninfected animals at the same dilution serving as the negative control.

Alternatively, antibody reactivity to schistosomula was quantitated (19) by assaying the fluorescence emission of a 143-μm^2 area of each parasite with a Leitz MPV photometer and was calculated as the mean fluorescence in relative units of a minimum of six measurements performed on different parasites.

Assay of Immunity to Challenge Infection

Groups of eight C57Bl/6J mice that had been immunized either 1 ½ or 6 weeks previously with 500 irradiated cercariae were challenged percutaneously on the abdomen with 200 fresh *S. mansoni* cercariae (11). Age-matched control animals were similarly infected. Six weeks after challenge infection, adult worms were perfused from the hepatic portal system (11), and the differences in mean worm burden between immunized and control animals were compared by the two-tailed Student *t* test.

RESULTS

Protective Immunity in Mice of Different Strains

As shown in Table 1, mice of the C57Bl/6J, CBA/J, and C3H/HeJ strains all developed significant levels of immunity to challenge infection after vaccination with irradiated cercariae ($P < 0.01$). This immunity was apparent as early as 1½ weeks after vaccination in C57Bl/6J mice. However, by 4 weeks after immunization, C57Bl/6J mice achieved higher levels of resistance (as determined by the percent reduction of worm burden) than mice of either of the other two strains. These observations confirmed the differences in immunity among mouse strains reported previously (10).

T-Cell Reactivity toward Schistosomula

As shown in Fig. 1, in all three strains a peak of lymphokine production, measured by enhancement of eosinophil (upper panels) and mononuclear cell (lower panels) migration, was observed 2 weeks after immunization. At this time, at least a threefold stimulation was observed in all cases. Reactivity waned with increasing time after immunization and was down to background levels at Weeks 9 and 15. The

TABLE 1

Protective Immunity in Vaccinated C57Bl/6J, CBA/J, and C3H/H3J Mice

Expt No.	Mouse strain	Weeks after vaccination[a]	Worm burden[b] Control	Worm burden[b] Vaccinated	Percentage reduction[c]	P value[d]
1	C57Bl/6J	4	68 ± 5	22 ± 4	67	<0.001
	C3H/HeJ	4	66 ± 5	43 ± 3	35	<0.001
2	CBA/J	6	65 ± 6	38 ± 4	44	<0.01
3	C57Bl/6J	6	97 ± 5	32 ± 4	67	<0.001
4	C57Bl/6J	1½	126 ± 7	74 ± 8	41	<0.001

[a] Mice were challenged percutaneously with 200 cercariae 1½–6 weeks after vaccination with 500 irradiated cercariae.

[b] The figures given represent the mean worm burden ± SEM.

[c] Percentage reduction of worm burden was calculated as [1 − (the number of schistosomes recovered from the vaccinated mice divided by the number of worms recovered from the control mice)] × 100.

[d] The level of significance was determined by the two-tailed Student t test.

patterns of lymphokine production by SP cells from the poorly protected strains were approximately equivalent to those shown by the respective, simultaneously immunized, C57Bl/6J mice. Cells from the normal age-matched control groups yielded SI values ranging from 0.6 to 1.4.

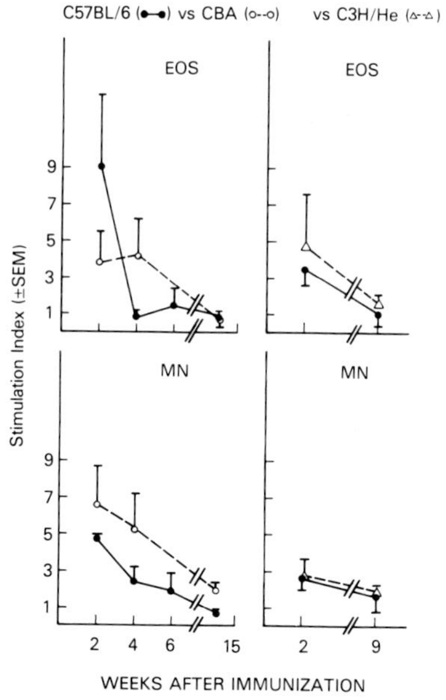

FIG. 1. Lymphokine production by spleen cells from immunized mice in response to *in vitro* exposure to living schistosomula. The reactivity of cells obtained from C57Bl/6J mice at various times after immunization was compared to that of CBA/J or C3H/HeJ mice in two experiments. Lymphokine activity was measured by the ability of culture supernatant fluids to stimulate the migration of eosinophils (upper panels) or mononuclear cells (lower panels). Spleen cells from normal mice yielded SI values ranging from 0.6 to 1.4.

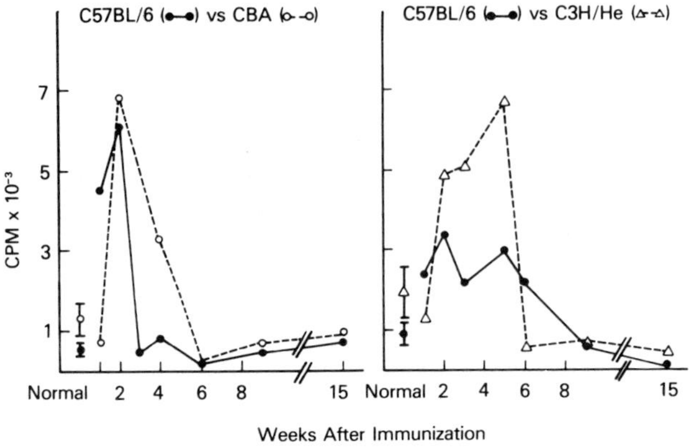

FIG. 2. Proliferation of lymph node cells from immunized mice in response to *in vitro* culture with schistosomula. The reactivity of cells from C57Bl/6J mice at various times after immunization was compared to that of CBA/J or C3H/HeJ mice in two experiments.

Figure 2 shows the development of proliferative response to living schistosomula by LN cells from the same groups of mice. Again, an early reactivity was observed (1–4 weeks after immunization) which gradually waned. At some later time points in both experiments, thymidine uptake by LN cells from vaccinated mice in response to schistosomula was actually lower than that by cells from normal age-matched control mice under the same conditions. However, no evidence for suppression of concanavalin A responsiveness in vaccinated mice was observed. As was the case with lymphokine production, vaccinated mice of the poorly protected CBA/J and C3H/HeJ strains responded as well or better than C57Bl/6J mice to *in vitro* exposure to schistosomula.

Anti-Schistosomulum Antibodies

Analyses of the time course of antibody production in C57Bl/6J and C3H/HeJ mice were run in parallel, using sera from the same animals whose T-cell responses were assayed above. As seen in Fig. 3, antilarval antibodies (titer > 1:20) were first detectable by 2 weeks and peaked at 6 weeks after immunization in both strains

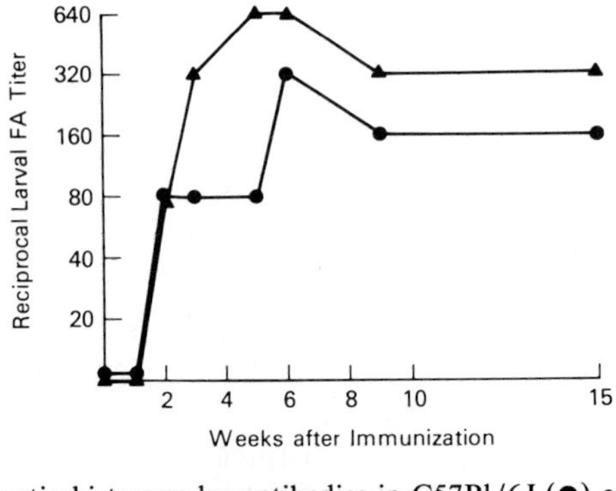

FIG. 3. Development of antischistosomular antibodies in C57Bl/6J (●) or C3H/HeJ (▲) mice after immunization, as measured by indirect immunofluorescence.

of mice. Significant levels of antibody were still present when measured as late as 15 weeks after vaccination. Interestingly, in this experiment, titers of antilarval antibodies appeared to be somewhat lower in the more resistant C57Bl/6J mice. Sera from age-matched control animals were consistently negative, while sera from mice with a chronic (12–16 weeks) natural infection had titers in excess of 1:10,000 and consistently gave more intense larval staining patterns than did sera from vaccinated mice even when employed at high dilution.

A second set of immune serum pools, obtained at 6 weeks after vaccination, were analyzed for the isotypes of their antischistosomulum antibodies. As shown in Fig. 4, the C57Bl/6J and C3H/HeJ total serum pools produced similar reaction curves with schistosomula when assayed with fluorescein-conjugated anti-IgM (left panel) or with a polyvalent anti-immunoglobulin serum which was shown by Ouchterlony analyses to react with mouse IgG and IgA but not IgM (right panel). When the sera were fractionated on protein A–Sepharose and tested for their reactivity with schistosomula using the anti-Ig fluorescein conjugate, significant antibody activity was detectable in the IgA, IgG_1, and IgG_{2a} plus IgG_3 fractions (Fig. 5). Only marginal activity was detected in the IgG_{2b} fraction. No striking differences were observed in the reactivity of Protein A fractions from vaccinated C57Bl/6J or C3H/HeJ mice.

DISCUSSION

Cell proliferation and lymphokine production directed against living schistosomula have been shown to be T-cell-dependent responses (14, 15). T-cell reactivity after vaccination, as measured by these criteria, was similar in the three different strains of mice. Significant antilarval activity was observed early after vaccination and gradually waned to background levels with time (Figs. 1 and 2). It should be noted that the pattern of reactivity in C57Bl/6J mice varied somewhat between the two experiments, exhibiting an early peak at 2 weeks in one case and a broader peak between 2 and 4 weeks in the other. This discrepancy is probably due to the fact that immunization is carried out with living organisms which may not behave

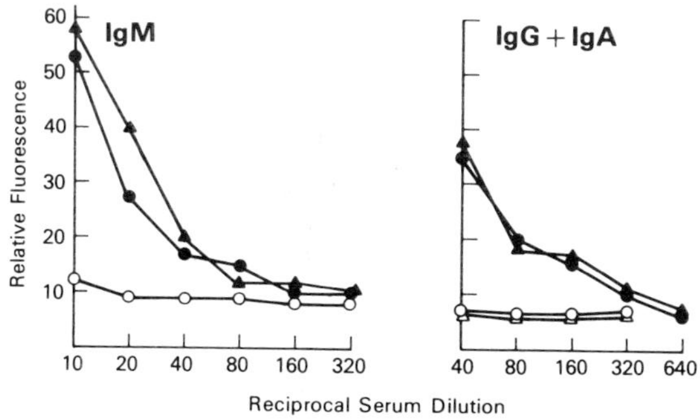

FIG. 4. Titration of IgM (left panel) and IgG plus IgA (right panel) antischistosomulum antibodies in serum from vaccinated mice by quantitative immunofluorescence. The serum pools analyzed were from C57Bl/6J (●) or C3H/HeJ (▲) mice vaccinated 6 weeks earlier with 500 irradiated cercariae or from age-matched control C57Bl/6J (○) or C3H/HeJ (△) animals. The values on the ordinate refer to the mean fluorescence per schistosomulum in relative units.

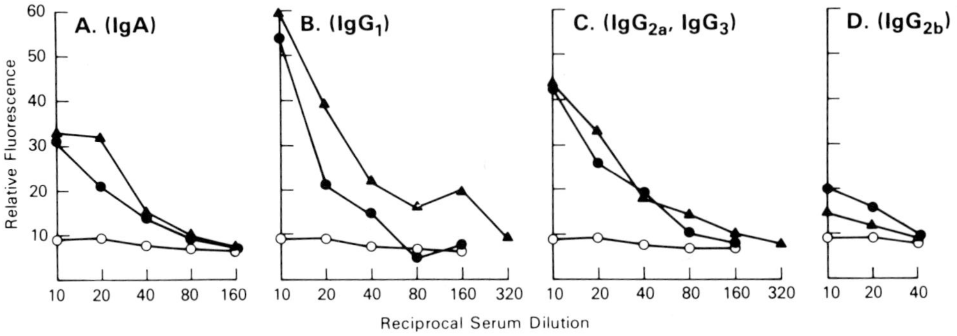

FIG. 5. Titration by quantitative immunofluorescence of anti-schistosomulum antibody activity in protein A–Sepharose fractions of immune sera. The four fractions analyzed (A, B, C, D) were shown by immunodiffusion to contain only the immunoglobulins listed and were free of detectable contamination with other isotypes. The starting serum samples were obtained from C57Bl/6J (●) or C3H/HeJ (▲) mice vaccinated 6 weeks previously or from age-matched control C57Bl/6J mice (○).

identically in terms of survival or migration pattern in every experiment due to initial differences in larval vigor after irradiation.

Antibodies toward schistosomula were first observed in the serum of vaccinated mice after 1–2 weeks (Fig. 3). Titers in both C57Bl/6 and C3H/HeJ mice peaked after 6 weeks and persisted as late as 15 weeks after vaccination. The differences observed in the time course of humoral and cellular reactivity are puzzling. It has been shown that highly irradiated cercariae do not mature into adult worms residing in the hepatic portal system (9), and it is assumed that the majority of the irradiated larvae die shortly after penetrating the skin of the host. The pattern of cellular responsiveness observed in this study seems to support this theory since sensitization declines with time after vaccination, whereas in mice with ongoing *S. mansoni* infection, cell prolifertion, and lymphokine production in response to schistosomula continue for at least 20 weeks (14, 15). However, significant levels of antibody were found in the sera of vaccinated mice as late as the last time point tested (15 weeks), implying a state of continued sensitization, which is consistent with the long-term immunity observed in this model (7), and suggesting that antibody may play a role in the resistance seen at later times after vaccination.

Antibody titers in the more resistant C57Bl/6J strain were the same as, if not lower than, those in the C3H/HeJ mice (Figs. 3 and 4). Similarly, no correlation was evident in the antibody activities of the different immunoglobulin classes and subclasses (Fig. 5). Our failure to observe differences in the antibodies produced by C57Bl/6J and C3H/HeJ mice does not rule out the possibility that antibody is involved in immunity. However, if a difference in the humoral reactivity of the two strains explains the different levels of immunity that they develop, this difference must lie in the antigenic specificity or affinity of the antibodies produced by these animals or alternatively in the levels of parasite-specific IgE, which were not examined here.

Thus, it appears from the present study that T-cell reactivity toward schistosomula develops earlier after vaccination and is subsequently relaced by humoral reactivity. During both of these phases of immune response, resistance to challenge infection is evident (Table 1). The lack of any genetically determined differences in the parameters of immunity examined here strongly suggests that additional, possibly nonspecific, mechanisms must be involved in resistance to challenge infection after vaccination.

ACKNOWLEDGMENTS

We thank Drs. Fred Lewis and M. A. Stirewalt of the Biomedical Research Institute, Rockville, Maryland, for supplying the cercariae used in the latter part of this study.

REFERENCES

1. Smithers, S. R., and Terry, R. J., *Advan. Parasitol.* **14,** 399, 1976.
2. Smithers, S. R., and Terry, R. J., *Ann. N.Y. Acad. Sci.* **160,** 826, 1969.
3. Villela, J. B., Gromberg, H. J., and Gould, S. E., *Science* **134,** 1073, 1961.
4. Radke, M. G., and Sadun, E. H., *Exp. Parasitol.* **13,** 134, 1963.
5. Hsu, S. Y. L., Hsu, H. F., and Osborne, J. W., *Proc. Soc. Exp. Biol. Med.* **131,** 1146, 1969.
6. Taylor, M. G., James, E. R., Nelson, G. S., Bickle, Q., Dunne, D. W., and Webbe, G., *J. Helminthol.* **50,** 1, 1976.
7. Minard, P., Dean, D. A., Jacobson, R. H., Vannier, W. E., and Murrell, K. D., *Amer. J. Trop. Med. Hyg.* **27,** 76, 1978.
8. Murrell, K. D., Stirewalt, M. A., and Lewis, F. A., *Exp. Parasitol.* **48,** 265, 1979.
9. Miller, K. L., and Smithers, J. R., *Exp. Parasitol.* **50,** 212, 1980.
10. Murrell, K. D., Clark, S., Dean, D. A., and Vannier, W. E., *J. Parasitol.* **65,** 829, 1979.
11. Smithers, S. R., and Terry, R. J., *Parasitology* **55,** 695, 1965.
12. Stirewalt, M. A., Minnick, D. R., and Fregeau, W. A., *Trans. Roy. Soc. Trop. Med. Hyg.* **60,** 352, 1966.
13. Gazzinelli, G., Olveira, C. C., Figueirredo, E. A., Pereira, L. H., Coelho, P. M. Z., and Pellegrino, J., *Exp. Parasitol.* **34,** 181, 1973.
14. James, S. L., and Sher, A., *J. Immunol.* **124,** 1837, 1980.
15. James, S. L., *Parasitology,* **83,** 147, 1981.
16. Ey, P. L., Prowse, S. J., and Jenkin, C. R., *Immunochemistry* **15,** 429, 1978.
17. Goldring, O. L., Sher, A., Smithers, S. R., and McLaren, D. J., *Trans. Roy. Soc. Med. Hyg.* **71,** 144, 1977.
18. Karnovsky, M. J., *J. Cell Biol.* **27,** 137A, 1965.
19. Samuelson, J. C., Sher, A., and Caulfield, J. P., *J. Immunol.* **124,** 2055, 1980.

CELLULAR IMMUNOLOGY **65**, 84–92 (1981)

Growth of SJL/J-Derived Transplantable Reticulum Cell Sarcoma as Related to Its Ability to Induce T-Cell Proliferation in the Host

III. Studies on Thymectomized and Congenitally Athymic SJL Mice[1]

IRENE R. KATZ, JUDITH CHAPMAN-ALEXANDER, ETHEL B. JACOBSON,* STEPHEN P. LERMAN,† AND G. JEANETTE THORBECKE

*Department of Pathology, New York University School of Medicine, New York 10016; *Merck, Sharpe & Dohme Research Laboratories, Rahway, New Jersey 07065; and †Department of Immunology and Microbiology, Wayne State University Medical Center, Detroit, Michigan 48201*

Received July 24, 1981; accepted September 25, 1981

When SJL mice are irradiated and reconstituted with syngeneic bone marrow (XBM) they support growth of transplantable reticulum cell sarcoma to approximately 60% of that in normal mice. The ability to support RCS growth gradually improves with time after irradiation and reaches 90% of normal by 8–12 weeks. However, if the mice are thymectomized 4 weeks prior to treatment (Tx-XBM) they initially show 50% which increases to only 65% of growth in normal mice after 12 weeks. The ability of lymphoid cells from these mice to proliferate *in vitro* in response to irradiated RCS cells is normal 4 weeks after treatment in XBM, but remains <10% of normal in Tx-XBM mice. Nude mice of SJL background also show greatly diminished RCS growth. It is concluded that T cells promote RCS growth *in vivo* possibly via their tendency to proliferate upon exposure to RCS.

INTRODUCTION

It has been shown that Ly1 T cells from normal SJL mice proliferate in mixed cell cultures with γ-irradiated syngeneic lymphoma (RCS) cells (1). This response is genetically determined primarily by the I region of the *H-2* complex, and appears strongly correlated with the ability of mice to support growth of the lymphoma *in vivo* (2). Other studies showed a lack of growth of transplantable RCS in irradiated syngeneic mice and the stimulation of RCS growth by normal lymphoid cells in such irradiated animals (3). These data were interpreted as demonstrating a positive effect on lymphoma growth of host–tumor cell interaction, possibly involving both T cells and other lymphoid cells which could be deleted by treatment with carbonyl iron (3). SJL mice treated with anti-μ from birth on, and as a result lacking in normal B-cell development, support RCS growth to approximately 60% of normal (4).

The present studies were undertaken to evaluate the role of thymus-derived cells in promotion of tumor growth. The relative effects of irradiation and thymectomy of the host in its ability to support RCS growth and the effect of the combination of these two treatments were studied in more detail. We also included a study of the ability of transplantable RCS to grow in congenitally athymic mice backcrossed

[1] This work was supported by Grant CA14462 from the National Cancer Institute, U.S.P.H.S.

0008-8749/81/170084-09$02.00/0

to the SJL strain. It will be demonstrated that mice depleted of T cells, able to give proliferative responses to RCS, show an impaired ability to support growth of transplantable RCS.

MATERIALS AND METHODS

Mice and tumors. SJL/J mice were purchased from the Jackson Laboratory (Bar Harbor, Maine). RCS-5 and RCS-X lymphoma lines originated from two different spontaneous RCS (5, 6). Both tumor lines have been maintained by serial intravenous passage of approximately 10^7 tumor-infiltrated lymph node (LN) cells into syngeneic recipients, at weekly intervals.

"Purified" RCS cells were prepared by treatment with rabbit anti-mouse brain (RAMB) (1:120) for 30 min at 4°C, followed by guinea pig C (1:24) for 45 min at 37°C. SJL and (SJL × C57BL/6)F_1 nude mice were bred at the Merck Institute, Rahway, New Jersey. The backcross generation of these mice is indicated in the table.

Thymectomy. Adult thymectomy (ATx) was performed on SJL mice at 6 weeks of age using the technique of Miller (7). A small incision was made into the sternum of mice anesthetized with Nembutal (0.4 mg of sodium pentobarbital per gram of body weight, Abbot Laboratories, North Chicago, Ill.). The thymus was immediately removed by suction and the incision closed with wound clips. Some control mice were sham-thymectomized. Absence of thymus was verified at autopsy.

Total-body irradiation and bone marrow reconstitution. Four weeks following thymectomy, ATx and control mice received 640 R γ-irradiation, using a ^{137}C source (Isomedix, Parsippany, N.J.). The mice were reconstituted by intravenous injection of 10^7 syngeneic bone marrow cells on the same day. Treatment with the available anti-Thy-1.2 sera and monoclonal antibodies did not result in complete removal of T cells from SJL lymphoid tissues and was therefore not applied to the bone marrow cells. Anti-RAMB is more effective, but might also affect stem cells. Thus untreated bone marrow was used in these experiments. Daily subcutaneous injections of 1 mg gentamycin (Schering Corp., Bloomfield, N.J.) were given during the next 2 weeks.

Cell cultures. Lymphocyte cultures from single-cell suspensions of mesenteric, brachial, and axillary lymph nodes (LN) from adult, thymectomized, γ-irradiated, and BM-reconstituted SJL (ATx-XBM) and γ-irradiated and BM-reconstituted SJL controls (XBM) were set up in flat-bottom Linbro tissue culture plates (No. 76-003-05, Linbro Chemical Co., Hamden Conn.) in RPMI 1640 (Associated Biomedic Systems, Buffalo, N.Y.) with 10% fetal calf serum (Grand Island Biological Co., Grand Island, N.Y.) and 5×10^{-5} *M* 2-mercaptoethanol (Eastman Kodak Co., Rochester, N.Y.). Responder cells were used at 2×10^5 cells/well (10^6 cells/ml), whereas γ-irradiated (6000 R) RCS stimulator cells (γ-RCS) were used at 5×10^4 cells/well. Mitomycin-treated BALB/c (M.BALB/c) spleen cells were used as allogeneic stimulators at 2×10^5 cells/well. The cells were treated prior to use with 25 μg mitomycin for 45 min at 37°C (5×10^6 cells/ml). Concanavalin A (Con A, 5 μg/ml; Miles-Yeda, Miles Laboratories Inc., Elkhart, Ind.) and phytohemagglutinin (PHA-P, 5 μg/ml; Difco Laboratories, Detroit, Mich.) were used as mitogens to measure lymphocyte reactivity. Thymidine incorporation into cell DNA was measured in five replicate cultures. [^{3}H]Thymidine (1 μCi, 0.36 Ci/

mmol; Schwartz/Mann Div., Becton, Dickinson & Co., Orangeburg, N.J.) was added to each well on Day 3 of culture. On Day 4, the cultures were collected on glass fiber filter disks (H. Reeve Angel & Co., Inc., Clifton, N.J.) with an automated cell harvester. Radioactivity was measured in a Packard Tri-Carb scintillation counter (Packard Instrument Co., Inc., Downers Grove, Ill.), using Scintiverse (Fisher Scientific Co., Pittsburgh, Pa.) liquid scintillator cocktail. Proliferative responses to RCS and mitomycin-treated BALB/c spleen cells were expressed as increases in counts per minute over the counts per minute in control cells cultured in the absence of stimulation. Responses of LN cells from ATx-XBM and XBM mice were expressed as percentages of the response obtained with SJL/J LN cells, cultured at the same time and stimulated with same γ-RCS and M.BALB/c spleen cells.

Growth of transplantable RCS in ATx XBM and XBM SJL/J mice. At varying intervals following γ-irradiation and bone marrow reconstitution (see tables) different groups of ATx-XBM and XBM mice were injected iv with 10^7 viable RCS cells in order to study the ability of the mice to support tumor growth. The mice were killed 7 days following injection of RCS. The lymphoma growth was measured by weighing pooled mesenteric, brachial, and axillary LN and calculating their weight as percentage of body weight. Growth of RCS in spleen was also measured as percentage of body weight. The data were expressed as tumor growth in normal SJL controls. In some experiments, RCS cells were treated with rabbit anti-mouse brain + guinea pig C (8) or anti-Thy 1.2 + rabbit C (9) prior to injection.

Growth of transplantable RCS in athymic mice. In order to examine the role of T cells in the ability of the host to support transplantable tumor growth, 10^7 RCS cells were injected iv into SJL nude mice. In an additional experiment, two groups of ATx mice, which were not exposed to γ-irradiation, were also injected iv at 4 and 16 weeks after TX with viable 10^7 RCS tumor cells. All injected mice were killed on Day 7 following injection, and the lymphoma growth was measured as described above.

RESULTS

Growth-Promoting Effect of Bone Marrow on RCS

In previous studies (3) the growth-promoting effect of lymph node, bone marrow, and thymus on RCS in irradiated syngeneic mice was analyzed. It seemed of interest to compare an immediate effect of bone marrow injection on tumor growth with the growth potential of RCS in long-term bone marrow-reconstituted mice. Table 1 shows that RAMB + C-treated RCS did not grow well in lymph node (LN) and spleen of irradiated mice: 56 and 31% of the growth in unirradiated controls, respectively. Bone marrow cells, injected 2 days prior to the tumor cells, enhanced this growth by approximately 20% in both LN and spleen. Part of this enhancement was due to the increased spleen weight caused by bone marrow alone. Thus, the growth-promoting effect of bone marrow was significant though moderate and similar to that described previously (3). In view of the fact that untreated bone marrow was used in these experiments, this early effect may have been due to contaminating T cells.

TABLE 1

Effect of Bone Marrow on RCS Growth in γ-Irradiated Mice

Treatment of recipient[a]			Organ weight[b]				
Day −2		Day 0					
640 R	BM cells	RCS	LN × 100/BW	% of control	Spl × 100/BW	% of control	n
+	+	+	2.72 ± 0.25	77.3	1.75 ± 0.12	54.8	4
+	−	+	1.96 ± 0.20	55.7	0.99 ± 0.09	30.9	5
+	+	−	0.45 ± 0.05	12.9	0.63 ± 0.01	19.6	4
+	−	−	0.43 ± 0.05	12.3	0.23 ± 0.04	7.2	5
−	−	+	3.52 ± 0.20	100	3.20 ± 0.24	100	5
−	−	−	0.50 ± 0.02	14.2	0.65 ± 0.07	20.3	3

[a] γ-Irradiation (640 R) and bone marrow reconstitution with 10^7 cells iv.
[b] Determined 6 days after injection of anti-BAT + C-treated 10^7 RCS-X cells iv.

Growth of RCS in Thymectomized and Normal γ-Irradiated and Bone Marrow-Reconstituted Mice and in Nude Mice

The recovery of the ability of XBM and ATx-XBM mice to support RCS growth was next investigated. The XBM mice were examined, using two different γ-irradiation doses. The higher dose resulted in lower growth in the lymph nodes, particularly during the first 2 weeks after γ-irradiation. Thereafter, RCS-X grew to approximately the same extent in 640-R and 750-R XBM mice (Table 2).

Growth of the two lymphoma lines, RCS-X and RCS-5, was also compared using one dose of irradiation. No large differences were noted in the support of tumor growth of the two RCS cell lines studied, although in the case of RCS-X, tumor growth reached almost 100% of control at 12 weeks after γ-irradiation, while the recovery for support of RCS-5 appeared somewhat slower and not as complete. In all experiments reported in Tables 2 and 3 RCS growth in experimental mice was expressed as percentage of growth in 8-week-old normal mice. In a few experiments age-matched controls were also included (data not shown). Six-month-old controls showed slightly higher growth in spleen and slightly less growth in lymph nodes than 2-month-old controls, but the differences were not large enough to influence the results significantly. Tumor cells depleted of T cells always showed growth comparable to that of untreated tumor cells in control mice.

Adult Tx-XBM mice (Table 3), studied simultaneously with XBM mice (Table 2), supported tumor growth equally well in the case of RCS-5 and only slightly less well in the case of RCS-X at 2 weeks after irradiation. Recovery of tumor growth support began to lag behind that of XBM mice as time progressed, and at 12 weeks after irradiation growth in these mice was only 55–65% that in controls. Treatment of tumor cells with RAMB + C prior to injection did not significantly affect the ability of ATx-XBM mice to support tumor growth at 12 weeks after irradiation. In some experiments (not shown) the survival of these mice after injection of RAMB + C-treated RCS was compared with that of controls. They showed 100% mortality between Days 9 and 10, whereas control mice died between Days 7 and 8 after RCS injection. Thus, the reduced growth allowed only slightly

TABLE 2

Growth of RCS in γ-Irradiated and Bone Marrow-Reconstituted Adult SJL/J Mice

Expt	γ-Irradiation	Time after γ-Irradiation (weeks)	Organ/body weight ratio as percentage of control			
			RCS-X[a]		RCS-5[a]	
			LN	Spl. (n)	LN	Spl. (n)
1	750 R + BM[b]	1	38.3 ± 3.8	58.6 ± 3.9 (3)		
		2	45.6 ± 1.3	70.3 ± 4.3 (3)		
		3	77.6 ± 1.6	71.6 ± 4.6 (3)		
2	640 R + BM	1	53.6 ± 3.3	66.6 ± 3.8 (3)	57.6 ± 5.6	50.8 ± 6.8 (5)
		2	59.2 ± 2.7	77.5 ± 2.8 (4)	46.0 ± 4.4	61.0 ± 2.3 (4)
		3	79.5 ± 3.8	81.5 ± 1.6 (4)	61.0 ± 1.3	61.0 ± 2.3 (4)
		4	81.7 ± 7.1	71.2 ± 8.0 (4)	65.5 ± 3.8	70.5 ± 2.0 (8)
		5			61.7 ± 2.0	71.0 ± 7.1 (4)
		6	70.6 ± 12.8	72.1 ± 1.5 (3)	76.6 ± 11.8	68.0 ± 2.3 (3)
		12	92.2 ± 4.4	98.7 ± 4.0 (4)	65.8 ± 1.6[c]	83.4 ± 3.6 (5)
		13			65.3 ± 0.8	83.7 ± 6.1 (5)
		20			93.3 ± 14.8	79.3 ± 12.4 (3)

[a] Mice were injected intravenously with 10^7 RCS-X or RCS-5 tumor-infiltrated lymphoid cells and their organ weights were determined 7 days later.
[b] On day of irradiation mice were reconstituted intravenously with 10^7 syngeneic bone marrow cells.
[c] In this experiment RCS-5 tumor cells were treated with RAMB + C prior to injection.

TABLE 3

Growth of RCS in Thymectomized[a], γ-Irradiated (640 R), and Bone Marrow-Reconstituted Adult SJL/J Mice

Time After γ-Irradiation (weeks)	Organ/body weight ratio as percentage of control			
	RCS-X[b]		RCS-5[b]	
	LN	Spl. (n)	Ln	Spl. (n)
2	41.1 ± 6.1	58.6 ± 2.8 (4)	47.6 ± 2.8	69.8 ± 9.5 (5)
4	53.5 ± 6.6	63.5 ± 4.1 (5)		
6	35.4 ± 3.0	50.6 ± 2.0 (5)		
9			44.0 ± 2.6	63.6 ± 2.0 (3)
12	54.4 ± 6.4	53.7 ± 4.9 (4)		
12[c]	61.9 ± 5.8	65.9 ± 10.2 (4)	60.0 ± 3.7	64.3 ± 6.8 (5)

[a] Mice were thymectomized at about 6 weeks of age. Following a 4-week recovery period the animals were irradiated and injected intravenously with 10^7 syngeneic bone marrow cells on the day of irradiation.

[b] As in Table 1, mice were injected intravenously with 10^7 RCS-X or RCS-5 tumor-infiltrated lymphoid cells and their organ weights were determined 7 days later. These experiments were performed simultaneously with Expt 2, Table 1.

[c] In this experiment RCS-X tumor cells were treated with anti-Thy 1.2 + C and RCS-5 tumor cells were treated with anti-BAT + C prior to injection.

longer survival in the ATx mice. In one additional experiment serial transplants of T-depleted RCS cells were performed in ATx-XBM mice and the growth on each transfer was compared with that in control mice. After two serial transplantations growth in the lymph node and spleen of ATx-XBM mice was still high (52.4 ± 5.1 and 79.6 ± 6.0%, respectively), while a reduction was seen after the third transplant (23.0 ± 7.8 and 50.0 ± 5.7%). This diminished growth potential might have been due to a progressive loss of contaminating host cells persisting after anti-Thy 1.2 + C treatment.

In order to further evaluate the role of T or other accessory cells in enabling the host to support tumor growth, SJL nude mice as well as their littermate controls were examined for their ability to support RCS growth. *nu/nu* mice were shown to support tumor growth only to about 50% of their littermate controls in spleen and to a somewhat variable but lower percentage in LN (Table 4). Growth of RCS in controls depended greatly on the numbers of backcrosses into SJL (see footnote, Table 4). After 19 backcrosses *nu/nu* SJL mice were difficult to rear, and *nu/nu* F_1 mice (SJL × C57BL/6) were used instead. This F_1 hybrid was chosen because normal mice of this cross support RCS growth reasonably well, and in the present experiment showed 63 and 85% of SJL control growth in lymph nodes and spleens, respectively (not shown).

Tumor growth was also examined in adult thymectomized unirradiated mice. Four weeks after thymectomy these mice could fully support tumor growth, but by 16 weeks they showed a slight reduction in this ability (Table 4).

Proliferative Responses to γ-RCS in Vitro

Proliferative responses of LN cells from ATx-XBM mice were examined at different intervals after irradiation and compared to responses of LN cells from

TABLE 4

Growth of Transplantable RCS in SJL/J Backcrossed Nude Mice

Expt	Mice	*n*	Organ/body weight ratio as percentage of control[a] Spl.	LN
	nu/nu mice			
1	SJL, 5th backcross	5	60.2 ± 7.5	44.2 ± 8.5
2	SJL, 7th backcross	3	54.4 ± 5.8	18.0 ± 4.7
3	SJL × C57BL/6[b]	3	45.8 ± 4.7	45.5 ± 6.3
	Adult thymectomized mice			
4	SJL (4 weeks after TX)	6	112.9 ± 1.7	101.6 ± 2.8
	SJL (16 weeks after TX)	4	82.7 ± 8.8	82.8 ± 5.2

[a] Data are given as means ± SE. Growth indices for spleen and LN as percentage of BW were, respectively: in 8 littermate controls, 1.70 and 1.37 (Expt 1); in 6 littermate controls, 4.25 and 3.91 (Expt 2); in 9 littermate controls, 2.36 and 2.31 (Expt 3); in 10 SJL/J controls, 4.13 and 3.15 (Expt 4).

[b] SJL 19th backcross × C57BL/6 16th backcross.

XBM mice. Responses to various stimuli were examined simultaneously (Table 5). All responses were abolished 1–3 weeks after irradiation and bone marrow reconstitution. By 4 weeks the response to Con A had completely recovered in XBM mice, but responses to γ-RCS, PHA, and allogeneic spleen were still below normal at 6 weeks. ATx-XBM mice showed a slower recovery of the response to Con A and essentially no recovery of the other three responses, even as late as 3 months after irradiation. Thus, the response to γ-RCS remained <10% of that of control mice throughout the observation period.

Additional experiments were performed to determine proliferative responses of (SJL × C57BL/6)F_1 nude mice. The proliferative response of *nu/nu* LN cells to γ-RCS was 2.3% of that seen in LN cells from littermate controls. The response to Con A in spleen cells from the *nu/nu* mice was 0.8% that of the control spleen.

DISCUSSION

The present results show that SJL lymphomas do not grow well in the absence of normal T-cell function. Although growth in XBM mice after irradiation is initially as low as in ATx-XBM mice, recovery to near normal growth occurs over the ensuing 2–3 months in XBM but not in thymectomized mice. Moreover, nude syngeneic mice show much less RCS growth than littermate controls.

Previous studies in this laboratory have established that irradiated RCS cells, which do not grow but induce strong proliferative responses *in vivo* (6), cause only slight increases in spleen and lymph node weights of recipients 7 days after intravenous injection, amounting to 25 and 22% of spleen and lymph node weights in mice receiving unirradiated RCS. This is only about 10 and 7% more than the weight ratios of uninjected SJL mice. Thus, the lack of proliferative responses *in vivo*, while probably contributing to the reduction in lymphoid organ weights after RCS injection in T-deficient mice, cannot account for all of the 40–60% reduction.

TABLE 5

Proliferative Responses of Host T Cells at Different Intervals after Thymectomy, γ-Irradiation, and Bone Marrow Reconstitution[a]

Interval after γ-Irradiation	Responses to	Δcpm as percentage of control response[b] XBM (n)	ATx-XBM (n)
1–3 weeks	PHA	0 (3)	ND
	M/BALB/c Spl.[c]	7.7 ± 6.2 (3)	ND
	γ-RCS	1.3 ± 1.3 (3)	ND
4 weeks	PHA	19.0 ± 6.8 (5)	0.4 ± 0.4 (4)
	Con A	109.4 ± 19.6 (5)	22.5 ± 10.4 (4)
	M.BALB/c Spl.	26.7 ± 11.8 (5)	1.8 ± 1.8 (4)
	γ-RCS	59.0 ± 11.2 (6)	5.3 ± 3.1 (4)
6 weeks	PHA	84.8 ± 12.5 (5)	1.5 ± 1.0 (4)
	Con A	104.4 ± 22.4 (5)	126.5 ± 54.9 (4)
	M.BALB/c Spl.	18.3 ± 4.7 (7)	18.0 ± 8.3 (4)
	γ-RCS	50.7 ± 12.6 (7)	9.8 ± 9.1 (4)
9–13 weeks	PHA	95.3 ± 4.3 (3)	12.1 ± 5.5 (7)
	Con A	99.0 ± 33.8 (3)	111.1 ± 27.9 (7)
	M.BALB/c Spl.	100.0 ± 15.0 (2)	10.6 ± 2.2 (5)
	γ-RCS	96.0 ± 5.7 (3)	9.7 ± 3.1 (7)

[a] Thymectomy at 6 weeks of age; at 10 weeks of age mice were exposed to 640 R total-body irradiation, followed by intravenous reconstitution with 10^7 syngeneic bone marrow cells.

[b] Δcpm of average SJL control response was as follows: PHA—13,719 in 9 experiments; Con A—16,150 in 6 experiments; M.BALB/c Spl.—21,297 in 9 experiments; RCS—24,539 in 10 experiments.

[c] Stimulator BALB/c spleen cells were treated with mitomycin C, 25 μg/ml, for 45 min at 37°C.

Recent studies by Hayama *et al.* (10) have shown that mixtures of lymph node and RCS cells secrete significant amounts of interleukin 2 into culture supernatants. This lymphokine was recently shown to promote B-cell (11) as well as T-cell (12–14) proliferation. RCS lymphomas have been identified as belonging to the B-cell lineage (15). It is thus possible that RCS growth is influenced by lyumphokine release *in vivo*, but further studies are needed to determine the mechanism of RCS growth promotion by T cells.

Although SJL/J mice are known to be deficient in NK cell activity (16), ATx and *nu/nu* SLJ mice have higher NK cell activity than normal (Cudkowicz, SUNY, Buffalo, personal communication). Previous studies have shown, however, that RCS is insensitive to NK activity and, in fact, induces immune interferon (18) and NK activity (17) in lymphoid tissue of the host. Thus, increased NK activity in thymectomized or athymic mice is not likely to be the cause of the decreased RCS growth in such mice.

While the recent results show a T-cell dependence of tumor growth, they also demonstrate a significant degree of RCS growth in the apparent absence of T cells *in vivo*, particularly in the spleen. In previous studies it has been shown that the ability of lymph node cells to give proliferative responses to RCS *in vitro* is markedly reduced 8 weeks after adult thymectomy (19), whereas the present studies show that tumor growth is still 80% of that in control mice as late as 16 weeks after adult TX. Similarly, neither ATx-XBM nor *nu/nu* mice show any T-cell responsiveness to γ-RCS *in vitro*. However, both groups demonstrate highly significant RCS growth, even after injection of RAMB + C-treated RCS, resulting in death of the host with only a few days delay as compared to control mice. It cannot be excluded that T-cell induction from precursor cells occurs *in vivo* under the influence of the interaction with RCS cells. T-Cell function induced in pre-T cells, in ATx-XBM and nude mice, has been described by various authors (14, 20). It is also possible that the remaining growth of RCS in athymic mice is totally T independent. In previous studies the growth promotion of RCS obtained with normal lymph node cells in irradiated mice was found to be due primarily to a cell type that could be depleted with carbonyl iron but not by anti-Thy 1 and C. However, it is quite likely that cell interaction between RCS and more than one host cell type is needed to support maximal RCS growth.

REFERENCES

1. Lerman, S. P., Chapman-Alexander, J., Umetsu, D., and Thorbecke, G. J., *Cell. Immunol.* **43,** 209, 1979.
2. Katz, I. R., Lerman, S. P., Ponzio, N. M., Shreffler, D. C., and Thorbecke, G. J., *J. Exp. Med.* **151,** 347, 1980.
3. Lerman, S. P., Carswell, E. A., Chapman, J., and Thorbecke, G. J., *Cell. Immunol.* **23,** 53, 1976.
4. Katz, I. R., Asofsky, R., and Thorbecke, G. J., *J. Immunol.* **125,** 1355, 1980.
5. Carswell, E. A., Wanebo, H. J., Old, L. W., and Boyse, E. A., *J. Nat. Cancer Inst.* **44,** 1281, 1970.
6. Ponzio, N. M., Lerman, S. P., Chapman, J., and Thorbecke, G. J., *Cell. Immunol.* **32,** 10, 1977.
7. Miller, J. A. F. P., *Brit. J. Cancer* **14,** 93, 1960.
8. Golub, E. S., *J. Exp. Med.* **136,** 369, 1972.
9. Hammerling, U., Chin, A. F., Abbit, J., and Sheid, M. P., *J. Immunol.* **115,** 1425, 1975.
10. Hayama, T., Umetsu, D., Chapman-Alexander, J., and Thorbecke, G. J., *Fed. Proc.* **39,** 458, 1980.
11. Parker, D. C., and Parkash, S., *In* "B Lymphocytes in the Immune Response" (Klinman, Mosier, Scher, and Vitetta, Eds.), pp. 193–199. Elsevier/North-Holland, Amsterdam, 1981.
12. Gillis, S., Ferm, M. M., Ou, W., and Smith, K. A., *J. Immunol.* **120,** 2027, 1978.
13. Watson, J., Gillis, S., Marbrook, J., Mochizuki, D., and Smith, K. A., *J. Exp. Med.* **150,** 849, 1979.
14. Gillis, S., Union, M. A., Baker, P. E., and Smith, K. A., *J. Exp. Med.* **149,** 1460, 1979.
15. Scheid, M. P., Chapman, J. M., Hayama, T., Katz, I. R., *et al., In* "B Lymphocytes in the Immune Response" (Klinman, Mosier, Scher, and Vitetta, Eds.), pp. 475–482. Elsevier/North-Holland, Amsterdam, 1981.
16. Herberman, R. B., and Holden, H. T., *In* "Advances in Cancer Research" (G. Klein and S. Weinhouse, Eds.), Vol. 27, pp. 305. Academic Press, New York, 1977.
17. Fitzgerald, K. L., and Ponzio, N. M., *Cell. Immunol.* **43,** 185, 1979.
18. Ponzio, N. M., Fitzgerald, K. L., Vilcek, J., and Thorbecke, G. J., *Ann. N.Y. Acad. Sci.* **350,** 157, 1980.
19. Ponzio, N. M., Chapman-Alexander, J., and Thorbecke, G. J., *Cell. Immunol.* **41,** 157, 1978.
20. Ropke, C., *Scand. J. Immunol.* **13,** 255, 1981.

CELLULAR IMMUNOLOGY **65**, 93–102 (1981)

Release of Soluble Factors from Lymph Nodes Containing Mycobacterial Granulomas and Their Effect on Fibroblast Function *in Vitro*

R. B. NARAYANAN, JILL CURTIS, AND JOHN L. TURK

Department of Pathology, Royal College of Surgeons of England, London, WC2A 3PN, England

Received August 4, 1981; accepted September 15, 1981

A study has been made of the action of culture supernatants from guinea pig lymph nodes containing mycobacterial granulomas on protein and DNA synthesis of homologous fibroblast cultures. Supernatants from both the Bacillus Calmette–Guerin (BCG) and *Mycobacterium leprae* granulomas release soluble nondialysable factors *in vitro* which stimulate [^{14}C]proline and [^{14}C]leucine incorporation by fibroblasts and depress their [^{3}H]thymidine uptake. These supernatants did not show any detectable migratory inhibitory activity *in vitro*. On the other hand, supernatants from sensitized lymphocytes incubated with purified protein derivative (positive migratory inhibitory activity) had no effect on fibroblast function. Thus, the effect of granuloma supernatants is unlikely to be due to lymphokines. However, supernatants from dinitrofluorobenzene-sensitized lymph nodes also showed a stimulation of [^{14}C]proline incorporation into total protein synthesised by fibroblasts and depressed the [^{3}H]thymidine uptake. Furthermore, supernatants from live BCG organisms in culture on addition to fibroblasts enhanced their [^{3}H]thymidine uptake *in vitro*. It would appear therefore that fibroblast activation in lymph nodes containing mycobacterial granulomas could result from the release of soluble factors of lymphocyte origin rather than from cells of the mononuclear phagocyte system. These factors appear to be independent of classical lymphokines that act on macrophages *in vitro*. An additional factor may be derived from the mycobacteria themselves.

INTRODUCTION

Epithelioid cell granulomas are prevalent in diseases such as tuberculosis, tuberculoid leprosy, schistosomiasis, and sarcoidosis (1, 3, 4). Many of these granulomatous reactions resolve with fibrosis which leads to functional disabilities, particularly in the lung and in the liver (3, 12). Very little is known about the mechanisms by which fibroblast activation occurs in the granuloma (3, 7). We have previously reported that live Bacillus Calmette–Guerin (BCG) vaccine induced an epithelioid cell granuloma in guinea pig lymph nodes which resolves by fibrosis. In contrast, the granulomas which develop following the injection of cobalt-irradiated armadillo-derived *Mycobacterium leprae* were not associated with epithelioid cell formation or fibrosis (8). These granulomas were quantitated by the measurement of lymph node weights and the assessment of collagen synthesis on the lymph node explants cultured *in vitro* supported the histological and ultrastructural findings. The cells of the mononuclear phagocyte series in an epithelioid cell granuloma were nonadherent to glass surface. In contrast, *M. leprae*-induced

0008-8749/81/170093-10$02.00/0

granulomas contained these cells which were adherent. In both the granulomas, the majority of the infiltrating cells were esterase positive and showed the presence of fibronectin. However, most of these infiltrating cells in the granulomas did not carry receptors for the Fc component of IgG or the C3 component of complement and did not exhibit peroxidase activity (9). We further suggested that the granulomas induced by live BCG and Co-irradiated *M. leprae* in lymph nodes appear to form a good model for the study of granulomas of tuberculoid and lepromatous leprosy, respectively. In this communication, using the above model, we have investigated the release of soluble factors from these two types of granulomas and their effect on protein synthesis and division of fibroblasts grown *in vitro*, and compared this with a similar function produced by lymph nodes involved in specific T-lymphocyte proliferation without granuloma development. In this way we hoped to analyse the relative contributions of immunologically activated lymphocytes and cells of the mononuclear phagocyte system to changes in fibroblast function.

MATERIALS AND METHODS

Materials

Lipopolysaccharide was from *Escherichia coli* (Difco Laboratories).

Streptomycin–penicillin, fungizone, and L-glutamine were obtained from Flow Laboratories; foetal calf serum (Flow Laboratories), RPMI 1640 (Gibco Laboratories) Eagle's MEM (Wellcome Laboratories) U.K.); trypsin 2.5% solution, in Hanks' balanced salt solution without magnesium, calcium and phenol red (Flow Laboratories); purified protein derivative (PPD) (Central Veterinary Research Laboratory, Weybridge, U.K.); trichloroacetic acid (TCA) (Hopkins and Williams); L-ascorbic acid, L-glycine (Sigma Chemical Co. L-[U-^{14}C]proline, 283 mCi/mmol; L-[U-^{14}C]leucine, 339 mCi/mmol; and [*methyl*-^{3}H]thymidine, 2 Ci/mmol (Radiochemical Co.) 1,4-bis(2-(4-methyloxazolyl))benzene (POPOP) (Sigma Chemical Co.); 2,5-diphenyloxazole (PPO) (Hopkins and Williams); Triton X-100 (BDH Chemicals); 75-cm^2 tissue culture flasks; plastic leighton tubes (Nunc Laboratories); NaOH (BDH Chemicals); dinitrofluorobenzene (DNFB) (Sigma Chemical Co.).

Culture medium. To 100 ml of RPMI, 8 m*M* L-glutamine, 250 μg fungizone, and 10,000 IU/10,000 μg streptomycin–penicillin were added and supplemented with 10% heat-inactivated foetal calf serum (FCS). The heat inactivation of FCS was carried out at 56°C in a water bath for 30 min.

Assay medium. To 100 ml of RPMI, 65 mg L-glycine, 100 mg L-ascorbic acid, 8 m*M* L-glutamine, 250 μg fungizone, and 10,000 IU/10,000 μg streptomycin–penicillin were added.

Triton X-100 scintillant. POPOP, 1.5 g, and 15 g PPO were dissolved in 5 litres of toluene. Two litres of this solution was mixed with 1 litre of Triton X-100 and used as the scintillation mixture.

Animals. Outbred Hartley strain of guinea pigs of either sex weighing 300–350 g were obtained from A. Tuck and Sons Limited. They were fed on RGP pelleted diet and supplemented with cabbage.

Mycobacteria. Live BCG of the Pasteur strain and cobalt-irradiated armadillo-derived *M. leprae* (Batch AB40) were kindly provided by Dr. R. J. W. Rees,

National Institute for Medical Research, Mill Hill, London. Mycobacteria were obtained as a suspension in saline and counted, as previously reported (9).

Preparation of Various Supernatants

1. Supernatants from lymph node granulomas. Immunization: The mycobacteria were suspended in saline before use. Organisms, 1×10^7, of live BCG or 1×10^9 organisms of *M. leprae* were injected intradermally into each ear in a batch of 15 animals. Twenty-five microliters of 10% DNFB in acetone–olive oil (1:1 ratio) was dropped onto each ear of a separate batch of guinea pigs.

The postauricular lymph nodes draining the ear were removed at 2 weeks from the animals injected with BCG, at 5 weeks from the animals receiving *M. leprae*, and at 4 days from DNFB-sensitized animals and weighed. Two grams wet weight of lymph nodes was cut into small pieces and cultured in 100 ml of RPMI containing antibiotics in 75-cm^2 flasks, for 24 hr at 37°C in an atmosphere of 5% CO_2 in air. The culture supernatants from these sources were collected.

2. Supernatants from sensitized lymphocytes. A batch of 25 animals was used. Each animal was injected with 0.1 ml of an emulsion of Freund's complete adjuvant in saline into each footpad. Four weeks later, the lymph nodes draining the feet were removed, and a single-cell suspension was prepared at a concentration of 10^7 viable lymphocytes/ml. This was then divided into two equal fractions. The first fraction (P) was incubated with 25 μg/ml PPD at 37°C for 24 hr in an atmosphere of 5% CO_2 in air. The second fraction was reconstituted with the same concentration of PPD after 24 hr of incubation (R). The supernatants from P and R were collected.

3. Supernatants from peritoneal exudate macrophages. A batch of 10 animals were injected each with 20 ml of sterile paraffin oil, intraperitoneally. Five days later, the peritoneal exudate cells were collected, pooled, and plated at a concentration of 4×10^7 cells in a 75-cm^2 culture flask and allowed to adhere for 2 hr at 37°C in an atmosphere of 5% CO_2 in air. The nonadherent cells were washed off. The adherent cells were incubated in 10 ml of RPMI containing antibiotics for 24 hr at 37°C in an atmosphere of 5% CO_2 in air. The supernatant from this source was collected and termed *macrophage supernatant.* After the supernatants had been collected, 10 ml of fresh RPMI was added to each flask and the cells were frozen and thawed three times. The supernatant from this source was termed *freeze–thawed macrophage supernatant.* In a separate set of experiments, the adherent cells were incubated with 2×10^7 live BCG organisms for 24 hr at 37°C in an atmosphere of 5% CO_2 in air, and the supernatant from this source was collected.

4. Supernatants from mycobacteria. Live BCG organisms, 2×10^8, 2×10^{10} cobalt-irradiated BCG organisms or 2×10^{10} cobalt-irradiated *M. leprae* organisms were incubated in 100 ml of RPMI at 37°C for 24 hr in an atmosphere of 5% CO_2 in air. The supernatants from these sources were collected.

Processing of Supernatants

All the supernatants were centrifuged at 400*g* for 15 min and concentrated to five times their original volume using a Millipore concentration kit (Catalogue No. PTGC 11K 00, obtained from Millipore Corp.). They were dialysed against fresh RPMI for 24 hr at 4°C and stored at −20°C. The supernatants were passed through a Millipore filter (0.22 μm) before use. The supernatants derived from lymph node granulomas, DNFB-sensitized lymph nodes, and the sensitized lymphocytes were assayed for the activity of migration inhibition factor (MIF) on oil induced peritoneal exudate cells from normal animals (5).

Fibroblast Cultures

Guinea pig flanks were shaved free of hair using a scalpel blade. A portion of skin was removed under sterile conditions and cut into 4-mm^2 pieces. Four or five pieces were incubated in a 75-cm^2 falcon flask in 1 ml of culture medium at 37°C in an atmosphere of 5% CO_2 in air. After a day or two, 10 ml of culture medium was added to each flask. A week later, the cells started migrating out from the explants. These cells were maintained in continuous culture in an atmosphere of 5% CO_2 in air with a change of culture medium every 3 days. They were trypsinised with 0.25% trypsin in medium, *only once*, and used as *primary cultures* in all the experiments carried out in this study.

[^{14}C]Proline Incorporation by Fibroblasts

Fibroblast cultures were grown from an initial concentration of 3 to 7×10^4 cells/leighton tube for about 7 days. At this time they became 90–95% confluent. Such cultures were used for the incorporation studies.

Assay Procedure

Control cultures (three replicates each experiment)—1 ml of assay medium. Test cultures (three replicates each experiment)—0.75 ml of supernatant +0.25 ml of assay medium.

Both sets of cultures were incubated in the presence of 0.25 μCi of L-[U-^{14}C]proline at 37°C for 24 hr in an atmosphere of 5% CO_2 in air. The cell layer was washed with PBS, lysed with Triton X-100 solution (0.5%), and the proteins were precipitated with 10% TCA at 4°C for 30 min. The precipitates were centrifuged at 400*g* for 15 min and the pellet was subsequently washed twice with PBS. The pellet was then dissolved in 200 μl of 0.1 *N* NaOH at room temperature. One milliliter of PBS and 10 ml of Triton X-100 scintillant were added to each tube and the whole mixture was transferred into scintillation vials and counted in a Packard scintillation counter, Model 2405. The supernatants which showed a stimulation of [^{14}C]proline incorporation were further analysed for collagen synthesis by the method using collagenase (10).

[^{3}H]Thymidine Uptake by Fibroblasts

Assay procedure. Cells, 3 to 7×10^4, were plated per tube and allowed to adhere for 24–48 hr at 37°C in an atmosphere of 5% CO_2 in air, and so only *nonconfluent* cultures were used. At this stage the cells were dividing and incorporated tritiated thymidine.

Control cultures (three replicates for each experiment)—1 ml of RPMI containing antibiotics + 9% heat-inactivated fetal calf serum (final concentration).

Test cultures (three replicates for each experiment)—0.75 ml of supernatant

+ 0.25 ml of RPMI containing antibiotics + 9% heat-inactivated fetal calf serum (final concentration).

Both sets of cultures were incubated at 37°C for 24 hr in an atmosphere of 5% CO_2 in air. Later, the supernatants were discarded and the cell layer was washed with medium. One milliliter of fresh RPMI containing antibiotics and 1 μCi of (*methyl*-^{3}H)thymidine were added to each tube. The tubes were incubated at 37°C for 2 hr in an atmosphere of 5% CO_2 in air. The cell layer was washed with PBS and lysed with 0.5% Triton X-100 solution and DNA was precipitated with 10% TCA at 4°C for 30 min. Further processing was carried out as described for [^{14}C]proline experiments.

[^{14}C]Leucine Incorporation by Fibroblasts

Cultures of fibroblasts were grown from an initial concentration of 3 to 7 × 10^4 cells/tube for about 7 days. At this time they became 90–95% confluent. Such cultures were used for the incorporation studies.

Assay Procedure

Control cultures (three replicates)—1 ml of RPMI containing antibiotics.

Test cultures (three replicates)—0.75 ml of supernatant + 0.25 ml of RPMI containing antibiotics.

Both the sets of cultures were incubated in the presence of 0.25 μCi of L-[U-^{14}C]leucine at 37°C for 24 hr in an atmosphere of 5% CO_2 in air. Further processing was carried out, as described for [^{14}C]proline experiments.

Statistical Tests

The results were analysed using Student's *t* test for paired data (2).

RESULTS

Fibroblast Cultures

The cells migrating out of the skin were identified on the basis of their morphology as fibroblast-like cells, spindle shaped, forming characteristic monolayers and initially dividing at a high rate.

Assessment of MIF Activity in the Supernatants

Table 1 summarizes the MIF activity in the various supernatants examined *in vitro*. Supernatants from BCG and *M. leprae* lymph node granulomas showed no detectable MIF activity, but the supernatant P from sensitized lymphocytes incubated with PPD had MIF activity. Furthermore, out of the two batches of supernatants from DNFB-sensitized lymph nodes tested for MIF, one of them showed a very high inhibitory activity.

Effect of Supernatants from Lymph Node Granulomas and Lymphokine on [^{14}C]Proline and [^{3}H]Thymidine Incorporation by Fibroblasts

The addition of supernatants from both the BCG and *M. leprae* granulomas to fibroblasts stimulated [^{14}C]proline incorporation into total protein and depressed

TABLE 1

Assessment of MIF Activity in the Supernatants and Their Effect on the Activity of Guinea Pig Skin Fibroblasts, *in Vitro*

Culture supernatans from	Percentage migration of inhibition	Batch No.	[^{14}C]Proline incorporation (cpm) Test–control paired	[^{14}C]Proline incorporation (cpm) T/C (mean)	[^{3}H]Thymidine uptake (cpm) Test–control paired	[^{3}H]Thymidine uptake (cpm) T/C (mean)
1. BCG lymph node granulomas	No inhibition	I	1212 ± 209 (4)	2.6 (4)	−6,298 ± 2,920 (4)	0.5 (4)
	No inhibition	II	2283 ± 364 (4)	2.93 (4)	−10,813 ± 2,511 (4)	0.28 (4)
2. *M. leprae* lymph node granulomas	No inhibition	I	3049 ± 2301 (4)	2.0 (4)	−22,581 ± 5,979 (4)	0.15 (4)
	No inhibition	II	2248 ± 651 (4)	2.2 (4)	−9,722 ± 2,790 (4)	0.56 (4)
3. DNFB-sensitized lymph nodes	70	I				
		Expt 1	+ 1457	1.3	−4,452	0.36
		Expt 2	+ 1126	1.1	−10,617	0.73
	No inhibition	II				
		Expt 1	+ 5003	4.1	−4,718	0.90
		Expt 2	+ 9319	2.9	−5,330	0.62
4. Sensitized lymphocytes incubated with PPD	30	I	−1238 ± 990 (4)	0.8 (4)	+2,596 ± 1,773 (4)	1.2 (4)

Note. Inhibition of 20% and above was considered positive. Number in the parentheses indicates the number of experiments. Each experiment was carried out on a different batch of cultures.

[^{3}H]thymidine uptake (Table 1). The supernatants from BCG granulomas produced a more consistent stimulation of [^{14}C]proline incorporation in comparison with the supernatants derived from *M. leprae* granulomas. However, neither supernatant affected the synthesis of collagen by fibroblasts (data not shown). It is interesting that the addition of supernatants from DNFB-sensitized lymph nodes also resulted in an increased incorporation of [^{14}C]proline into total protein and depressed uptake of [^{3}H]thymidine (Table 1). The lymphokine, however, had no significant effect on [^{14}C]proline or [^{3}H]thymidine uptake by fibroblasts.

Effect of Supernatants from Lymph Node Granulomas on [^{14}C]Leucine Incorporation by Fibroblasts

It is evident that in two out of three experiments the addition of the supernatants from BCG and *M. leprae* lymph node granulomas stimulated [^{14}C]leucine incorporation by fibroblasts. The degree of stimulation observed in these experiments was similar to that in the [^{14}C]proline incorporation studies (Table 2).

Effect of Supernatants from Macrophages and Mycobacteria on [^{14}C]Proline and [^{3}H]Thymidine Incorporation by Fibroblasts

Supernatants from macrophages, freeze–thawed macrophages and macrophages incubated with BCG had no effect on fibroblast function. On the other hand, supernatants prepared from live BCG organisms on addition to fibroblasts stimulated the uptake of [^{3}H]thymidine, but had no effect on [^{14}C]proline incorporation (Table 3). However, the supernatants from Co-irradiated BCG and Co-irradiated *M. leprae* did not affect the [^{14}C]proline or the [^{3}H]thymidine incorporation by fibroblasts.

Effect of Mycobacteria and the Cell Wall Components on Fibroblast Activity in Vitro

The incubation of fibroblasts directly with live BCG, Co-irradiated *M. leprae*, and LPS had no effect on [^{14}C]proline incorporation or [^{3}H]thymidine uptake.

TABLE 2

Effect of Supernatants from BCG and *M leprae* Lymph Node Granulomas on [^{14}C]Leucine Incorporation by Fibroblasts

Culture supernatants from	Expt No.	Control (cpm)	Test (cpm)
1. BCG lymph node granulomas	1	20,042	19,736
	2	10,352	23,074
	3	7,379	20,288
2. *M. leprae* lymph node granulomas	1	20,042	21,342
	2	10,352	26,762
	3	7,379	25,324

Note. Each experiment was carried out on a different batch of fibroblast cultures. Each value (cpm) is a mean of triplicate culture tubes.

TABLE 3

Effect of Culture Supernatants from Different Types of Macrophages and Different Mycobacteria on the Activity of Guinea Pig Skin Fibroblasts *in Vitro*

	Counts per minute	
Material tested on fibroblasts	[^{14}C]Proline incorporation into total protein	[^{3}H]Thymidine uptake
I. Culture supernatants from different types of macrophages		
(a) Freeze and thawed macrophages	374 ± 157 (4)	3524 ± 5180 (5)
(b) Macrophages	223 ± 149 (9)	1869 ± 6735 (5)
(c) Macrophages incubated with live BCG (Pasteur)	313 ± 352 (9)	196 ± 5973 (5)
II. Culture supernatants from mycobacteria		
(a) Live BCG Pasteur	73 ± 340 (9)	5780 ± 1109 (6)**
(b) Co-irradiated BCG Pasteur	765 ± 1621 (3)	3083 ± 1094 (4)
(c) Co-irradiated *M. leprae*	−930 ± 464 (3)	−6420 ± 2916 (3)
III. Direct incubation with various bacterial components		
(a) Live BCG (Pasteur) 2×10^6 organisms/ml	146 ± 86 (3)	−675 ± 2450 (4)
(b) Co-irradiated *M. leprae* 2×10^9 organisms/ml	1377 ± 621 (4)	817 ± 5188 (3)
(c) LPS, 125 μg/ml	369 ± 88 (3)	485 ± 1847 (4)
(d) Cord factor, 150 μg/ml	−1328 ± 487 (4)*	898 ± 4316 (3)

Note. Number in the parentheses indicates the number of experiments done. Each experiment was carried out on a separate batch of cultures.

* $P = 0.05$.

** $P < 0.01$.

However, the addition of cord factor showed a marginal depression of [^{14}C]proline incorporation into total protein, but had no effect on the [^{3}H]thymidine uptake.

DISCUSSION

There are several advantages of using draining lymph nodes for the study of granuloma formation and its relationship to *in vitro* fibroblast activity. As the infiltrating cell population comprises a high proportion of the lymph node volume, biochemical experiments can be carried out on these lymph nodes. Such experiments can be of two types (a) those studying the properties of intact granulomas by culturing lymph node explants *in vitro* (9), (b) those studying the release of factors from granulomas and their effect on *in vitro* fibroblast function. DNFB produces an increase in lymph node weight at 4 days mainly as a result of T-lymphocyte proliferation. This therefore acts as a good model to compare the relative contributions of immunological mechanisms with the contribution of cells of the mononuclear phagocyte system to the granuloma.

The study of lymph node granulomas may be important in understanding two main aspects of mycobacterial induced granulomas. First, the properties of the granuloma characterizing hypersensitivity reactions, namely "the epithelioid cell granuloma" and, second, the relationship of this granuloma to subsequent fibroblast activation and collagen deposition. We have previously shown that live BCG (Pasteur) induces an epithelioid cell granuloma at 2 weeks in the post auricular lymph nodes and that this granuloma resolves by fibrosis. By contrast, Co-irradiated *M. leprae*, where there is little evidence of epithelioid cell formation, was associated with much less fibrosis (8, 9). So, the question arises why the BCG granuloma resolves by fibrosis. The present study has shown that both the BCG and *M. leprae*-induced granulomas in lymph nodes release nondialysable soluble factor *in vitro* which enhanced total protein synthesis by fibroblasts and depressed their [^{3}H]thymidine uptake (Tables 1 and 2). Furthermore, the activity of these supernatants was not affected by repeated freeze–thawing. The effect of these supernatants is unlikely to be due to lymphokines because, (a) these supernatants did not show any detectable MIF activity *in vitro*, (b) supernatants from sensitized lymphocytes having MIF activity did not affect the fibroblast function. As a comparison, similar supernatants from DNFB-sensitized lymph nodes stimulated protein synthesis by fibroblasts and depressed the [^{3}H]thymidine uptake. Furthermore, one of the batches of DNFB-sensitized lymph node supernatant showed a high migration inhibitory activity. Thus, the involvement of lymphokines cannot be ruled out. This discrepancy could be explained by the way these supernatants are prepared. In previous published experiments, lymphokines have been shown to stimulate collagen synthesis by fibroblasts. In one case, the source of lymphokine was human peripheral blood mononuclear cells stimulated with phytohaemagglutinin and this was assayed on a human fibroblast cell line in culture (6). In another, lymphokine was derived from peritoneal exudate cells of DNP-ovalbumin-sensitized guinea pigs and the activity was assayed on *5–10 times passaged nonconfluent* guinea pig skin fibroblasts (13). Thus, the difference in nature of lymphokine and the stage and type of fibroblast cultures used could be the reason why we were unable to detect any effect of lymphokine on fibroblast function. Similar studies in mice infected with *Schistasoma mansoni* have been reported where the supernatants from the liver granulomas released factors which stimulated the fibroblast [^{3}H]thymidine incorporation and thus increasing its proliferation *in vitro* (14).

The supernatants from various types of macrophages or direct incubation of various mycobacteria or the cell wall components did not alter fibroblast function. However, it is interesting that the supernatant from live BCG (Pasteur) organisms stimulated fibroblast division *in vitro* and had no effect on protein synthesis, but the supernatants from Co-irradiated BCG or Co-irradiated *M. leprae* organisms did not affect the fibroblast function. So, the type of mycobacteria causing the granuloma could be an important additional factor in fibroblast activation, and the subsequent fibrosis and resolution of the lesion. Similar studies in the alteration of fibroblast function have been reported where the addition of a sonic extract of *Capnocytophaga sputigena* to human fibroblasts resulted in an inhibition of cell proliferation (11).

In summary, it would appear that factor(s) are released from lymph nodes containing BCG or *M. leprae* granulomas that increase protein synthesis and decrease DNA synthesis in fibroblasts cultured *in vitro.* A similar activity is released from DNFB-sensitized lymph nodes, indicating that this is likely to be derived from activated T lymphocytes rather than from cells of the mononuclear phagocyte system. However, dissociation from migration inhibitory activity suggests that these activities are not a function of classical lymphokines.

ACKNOWLEDGMENTS

This work was supported by LEPRA. We thank Dr. R. J. W. Rees and Dr. P. Badenoch-Jones for helpful discussions during this work. Cord factor from *Mycobacterium tuberculosis* (Peuroi's strain) was a gift from Dr. E. Lederer, Institut de Chimie des Substances Naturelles, CNRS, Gif Sur Yvette, France. The technical assistance of Mr. P. Papasava is gratefully acknowledged.

REFERENCES

1. Allison, A. C., Clark, I. A., and Davies, P., *Ann. Rheum. Dis.* **36** (Suppl.), 1977.
2. Bailey, N. T. J., "Statistical Methods in Biology," p. 43. English Univ. Press, London, 1975.
3. Boros, D. L., *Prog. Allergy.* **24,** 183, 1978.
4. Epstein, W. L., *Pathobiol. Ann.* **7,** 1, 1977.
5. George, M., and Vaughan, J. H., *Proc. Soc. Exp. Biol. Med.* **111,** 514, 1962.
6. Johnson, R. L., and Ziff, M., *J. Clin. Invest.* **58,** 240, 1976.
7. Kang, A. H., *J. Lab. Clin. Med.* **92,** 1, 1978.
8. Narayanan, R. B., Badenoch-Jones, P., and Turk, J. L., *J. Pathol.,* **134,** 253, 1981.
9. Narayanan, R. B., Badenoch-Jones, P., Curtis, J., and Turk, J. L., *J. Pathol.,* in press, 1981.
10. Peterofsky, B., and Diegelmann, R., *Biochemistry* **10,** 988, 1971.
11. Stevens, R. H., Sela, M. N., Shapiro, J., and Hammond, B. F., *Infect. Immun.* **27,** 271, 1980.
12. Tamayo, R. P., *Amu. J. Pathol.* **92,** 509, 1978.
13. Wahl, S. M., Wahl, L. M., and McCarthy, J. B., *J. Immunol.* **121,** 942, 1978.
14. Wyler, D. J., Wahl, S. M., and Wahl, L. M., *Science* **202,** 438, 1978.

CELLULAR IMMUNOLOGY **65,** 103–114 (1981)

T-Lymphocyte Heterogeneity in Rat: Role of Adherent T-Cell Subpopulation in the Regulation of Cytotoxic T-Cell Response to Alloantigens[1]

MOHAN L. SOPORI, JAMES M. SHEIL, THOMAS L. ROSZMAN, AND WILLIAM H. BROOKS

Department of Pathology, Albert B. Chandler Medical Center, University of Kentucky, Lexington, Kentucky 40536

Received August 13, 1981; accepted September 12, 1981

Based on the property of adherence to glass bead columns, we have separated two populations of spleen cells from alloantigen-primed rats that interact synergistically in generation of secondary *in vitro* CML response. Further analysis of these populations reveals that the adherent cell fraction contains a radioresistant (2500 rad) T helper population (Th1) that enhances the CTL response to alloantigens, a macrophage-type suppressor cell (Mϕs), and a radio-sensitive suppressor component of yet undetermined nature. The nonadherent cell fraction contains precursors of CTLs and a helper T cell (Th2) that helps in the generation of a T-dependent antibody response to SRBC.

INTRODUCTION

Thymus-derived (T) lymphocytes are important for the regulation and expression of many immunological functions (1–3). Murine T cells can be classified on the basis of the expression of cell surface antigens encoded by Ly and Qa-1 loci and on biological function into helper (Th), suppressor (Ts), and cytotoxic T cells [CTL (4–9)]. In rats, such a series of T-cell differentiation antigenic markers are not available and rat T-cell subsets and their functional interactions have remained largely unknown. Lack of a well-characterized rat T-cell-specific antiserum has further hindered progress in this area. Williams *et al.* (10) described a monoclonal xenogeneic antibody designated W3/25 that is represented on a subpopulation of thymocytes. Subsequently, White *et al.* (11) demonstrated that W3/25+ T cells functioned as helper T cells in an anti-heptane plaque-forming cell response and mediated graft-vs-host reactivity. However, since the antibody is noncytotoxic and represents only a subset of T cells, its use in many situations is limited.

In this paper, we have investigated the *in vitro* response of rat splenic T cells to different specific and nonspecific stimuli. Removal of an adherent population of cells resulted in either decreased or increased T-cell responsiveness dependent on the stimulus. The adherent cell population was shown to contain macrophage-type suppressor cells that inhibit mitogen reactivity and the mixed lymphocyte reaction

[1] This investigation is supported by Grant 1M-248 from the American Cancer Society and NIH grants CA-23891 and NS-17423.

0008-8749/81/170103-12$02.00/0

(MLR) as well as helper T cells for the secondary cell-mediated lympholysis (CML) response. The nonadherent cell population contained cytotoxic T-cell (CTL) precursors for the secondary CML response and helper T cells for the T-dependent antibody response.

MATERIALS AND METHODS

Animals. Inbred strains of rats 8–20 weeks of age were employed in these studies. F344 rats were purchased from Harlan–Sprague–Dawley, while LEW and NBR were obtained from the Microbiological Associates and the Mammalian Genetics Animal Production Section, NCI, respectively. BDIX rats, originally obtained from NIH, were bred at the University of Kentucky Medical Center Animal facility.

Glass bead column fractionation of spleen cells. Spleen cell suspensions were fractionated on glass bead columns by the method of Shortman *et al.* (12) as modified by Elliott and Roszman (13). Briefly, 30-ml plastic syringes are plugged with siliconized glass wool and subsequently filled with siliconized glass beads (Class IV, Type 203, Cataphote Corp.). The glass bead columns were washed first with bicarbonate-free RPMI 1640 followed by the same medium containing 60% (v/v) fetal calf serum (FCS). Spleen cells were suspended in RPMI 1640 containing 50% FCS and loaded on the column. The column was incubated at 37°C for 10 min. The glass bead nonadherent cell fraction (GBNA) was eluted with prewarmed (37°C) RPMI 1640 containing 25% FCS. The column was then washed with 3 vol of the medium and the adherent cell fraction (GBA) was eluted with 0.02 *M* EDTA in isotonic salt solution (12). Both cell fractions were washed three times with the medium before their use. The cell recovery from glass bead columns ranged from 40 to 60% in the GBNA cell fraction and 5–10% in the GBA cell fraction.

Peritoneal exudate cells (PEC). Peritoneal exudate cells were obtained by injecting 10 ml RPMI 1640 into the rat peritoneal cavity. The medium containing PEC was withdrawn and cells were sedimented and washed twice. The percentage of macrophages as determined by nonspecific esterase staining (14) ranged from 70 to 95% in this fraction.

Purification of GBA macrophages by adherence to plastic dishes. The GBA cell fraction eluted from glass bead columns was cultured on plastic dishes as described by Calderon *et al.* (15) to further enrich for macrophages. Briefly, GBA cells (1×10^7/ml) suspended in complete medium containing 10% FCS were layered in 35×10-mm plastic dishes (Falcon 3001) and incubated at 37°C in 95% air–5% CO_2 atmosphere. After 24 hr, the dishes were rinsed with medium and the adherent cells were scraped off the plastic dishes in the presence of 0.02 *M* EDTA in PBS. The cells (>80% macrophages by esterase staining) were washed twice with complete medium before use.

In vivo alloantigen priming. F344 rats were primed by a single intraperitoneal injection of 5×10^7 γ-irradiated (2500 rad) BDIX spleen cells suspended in 1 ml of PBS. Two weeks after the inoculation, spleens were removed and cell suspensions were prepared. For comparison, spleen cell suspensions were also prepared from unimmunized animals (unprimed).

MLR. For the mixed lymphocyte reaction (MLR), 5×10^5 F344 spleen cells were stimulated with 5×10^5 γ-irradiated BDIX cells or with 5×10^5 γ-irradiated F344 cells (syngeneic control), in 0.2 ml of complete medium (RPMI 1640 containing 50 μM 2-mercaptoethanol, vitamins, nonessential amino acids, glutamine, penicillin, and streptomycin) supplemented with 10% pooled heat-inactivated human serum in microtiter plates (Linbro 76-002-05). The plates were incubated in a 95% air–5% CO_2 atmosphere at 37°C. On the fourth day of culture, 1 μCi of [^{3}H]Tdr was added and 6 hr later the plates were harvested on a Mash-II harvester (M. A. Bioproducts). Results are expressed as counts per minute of [^{3}H]Tdr incorporated.

Cell-mediated lympholysis (CML). For the CML response, 1.5×10^7 responding F344 cells were cultured together with 1.5×10^7 γ-irradiated (2500 rad) BDIX-stimulating cells in 5 ml complete medium containing 10% heat-inactivated human serum in six-well cluster plates (Costar 3506). However, when comparisons are made between CML and the plaque-forming cell (PFC) response, the CML conditions were slightly different and are discussed under PFC response in this section. The cultures were incubated at 37°C in 5% CO_2. After 5 days (unless mentioned otherwise), the cultures were assayed for cytotoxicity on ^{51}Cr-labeled targets according to the procedure described previously (6). Briefly, 1×10^4 ^{51}Cr-labeled target cells were incubated with appropriate numbers of viable effector cells in 0.2 ml of RPMI 1640 containing 10% heat-inactivated FCS in microtiter wells (Linbro IS-MRC-96-TC). Radioactivity released into the supernatant is recovered with the Skatron Titer-Tek supernatant collecting system (Flow Laboratories). Spontaneous release (SR) represents counts per minute released by 1×10^4 ^{51}Cr-labeled target cells alone and the maximum release (MR) is the amount of radioactivity released by 1×10^4 detergent-lysed target cells. Results are expressed as percentage cytotoxicity calculated as

$$\frac{\text{cpm experimental release} - \text{cpm SR}}{\text{cpm MR} - \text{cpm SR}} \times 100.$$

CML target cells. ^{51}Cr-labeled cloned astrocytoma cell lines RG2 (derived from F344) and P521 (derived from BDIX) were used as the target cells in the CML assay.

Mitogen responses. In 0.2 ml of complete medium containing 10% human serum, 0.5×10^6 cells were cultured with appropriate concentrations of concanavalin A (Con A) or phytohemagglutinin (PHA) in microtiter wells and incubated at 37° for 3 days in 95% air–5% CO_2 atmosphere. The cells were labeled with [^{3}H]Tdr and harvested as described for the MLR.

PFC responses. The anti-sheep red blood cell (SRBC) PFC response was determined essentially according to the method of Mishel and Dutton (17). Briefly, 1×10^7 spleen cells were cultured together with 2×10^7 SRBC in complete medium containing 10% pooled heat-inactivated human serum (pretested for PFC responses) in multiwell tissue culture plates (Linbro 76-033-05). The cultures were fed with 100 μl of nutrient cocktail (17) every day except on the third day of culture when the cells were centrifuged and resuspended in fresh medium. The number of PFC in the cultures was determined on the sixth day by the Cunningham–Szenberg technique (18).

Anti-T-cell serum. NBR anti-LEW thymocyte serum (19) was raised and absorbed on F344 red blood cells. After absorption, the antiserum lysed F344 thymocytes (>98%), lymph nodes (55%), and spleen cells (35–40%). There was no detectable cytotoxicity against F344 macrophages obtained from peritoneal exu-

TABLE 1

Generation of *in Vitro* CTL Response from F344 Spleen Cells to BDIX

Responding cells	E/T	Percentage CML ± SD	
		RG2	P521
Experiment 1			
F344 (normal)	45	3.8 ± 1.7	5.6 ± 3.7
F344 (primed)	5	4.5 ± 2.8	23.1 ± 1.0
	15	4.1 ± 3.3	44.6 ± 4.5
	45	2.7 ± 1.9	56.8 ± 5.2
Experiment 2			
F344 (primed) + NRS + C	15	5.5 ± 2.0	38.7 ± 0.3
F344 (primed) + anti-T + C	15	—	6.9 ± 1.8

Note. F344 animals were injected ip, either with 5×10^7 γ-irradiated BDIX spleen cells in PBS (primed) or with an equal volume of PBS alone (normal). After 15 days, spleen cell suspensions were made and cultured together with BDIX cells as described under Materials and Methods. The cultures were harvested on Day 5. In Experiment 2, prior to CML assay, the effector cells were treated either with NRS + C or with anti-T serum + C and assayed for cytotoxicity on ^{51}Cr-labeled or P521 targets at indicated effector to target (E/T) ratios. The cell numbers were not corrected for loss due to antiserum treatment.

dates and bone marrow cells, nor against antibody-producing B cells. Detailed description of the antiserum will be published elsewhere.

Anti-T-cell antiserum treatment. Approximately 1×10^7 cells were suspended in 1 ml RPMI 1640 containing 5% heat-inactivated FCS, together with 0.1 ml of anti-T-cell serum and 0.05 ml of guinea pig complement. After 1 hr of incubation at 37°C the cells were washed three times and the cell viability was determined by trypan blue dye exclusion. In some experiments cells were preincubated with the antiserum for 30 min at 37°C before the addition of guinea pig complement. No significant differences in percentage cell lysis were observed between the two procedures.

RESULTS

Cytotoxic T-Cell Response of Spleen Cells from Normal (Unprimed) and in Vivo Alloantigen-Primed Rats

The data presented in Table 1 (Expt. 1) demonstrate that F344 spleen cells obtained from unprimed animals did not give a significant primary *in vitro* CML response against BDIX cells. However, 2 weeks after *in vivo* priming with BDIX cells a strong secondary *in vitro* CML response was obtained. The cytotoxic response was specific, being directed to the target cells bearing the stimulating alloantigens (P521) and not toward the targets bearing F344 alloantigens (RG2). Moreover, the CML response was mediated by T cells, because the treatment of the effector cells with anti-T serum + C abrogates the cytotoxic response (Expt. 2).

Are Suppressor Cells Responsible for the Inability of Unprimed Spleen Cells to Respond to Primary in Vitro Allosensitization?

It has been previously reported that "natural" splenic suppressor cells inhibit *in vitro* T-cell responses (20–24). The suppressive influence of these cells on T-cell responses to mitogens and in MLR is alleviated by the removal of adherent cell populations (22, 25, 26). In order to ascertain if an adherent cell population contributed to our failure to obtain an *in vitro* primary CML response, spleen cells from unprimed F344 were passed over glass bead columns to obtain the glass bead-nonadherent (GBNA) and -adherent cells (GBA). As seen in Fig. 1, GBNA cells exhibited significantly higher responsiveness to the T-cell mitogens Con A and PHA. The GBA cells did not respond to these mitogens, but were capable of suppressing the mitogenic response of the GBNA cells. This suppression was not the result of cell crowding, because cultures containing 7.5×10^5 GBNA cells responded as well as did cultures containing 5×10^5 cells (data not shown). The cultures containing GBNA plus 2.5×10^5 GBA cells exhibited responses significantly lower than those of the cultures containing unfractionated cells. This may reflect a lower proportion of adherent suppressor cells in the unfractionated spleen cell population.

Removal of the adherent cells also enhanced the MLR response, but not the CML response to BDIX cells (Table 2). Therefore, normal rat spleens contain adherent cells that inhibit a number of *in vitro* correlates of cell-mediated immunity, i.e., Con A, PHA, and MLR responses. However, the inability of rat spleen cells to give a primary *in vitro* CML response cannot be solely attributed to the presence of these adherent cells.

Nature of the Inhibitory Cell in the GBA Fraction of Unprimed Spleen Cells

Others have demonstrated that the adherent suppressor cells present in rat spleen cell preparations have characteristics best associated with macrophages (23–24). However, the phenomenon of adherence is not only observed with macrophages;

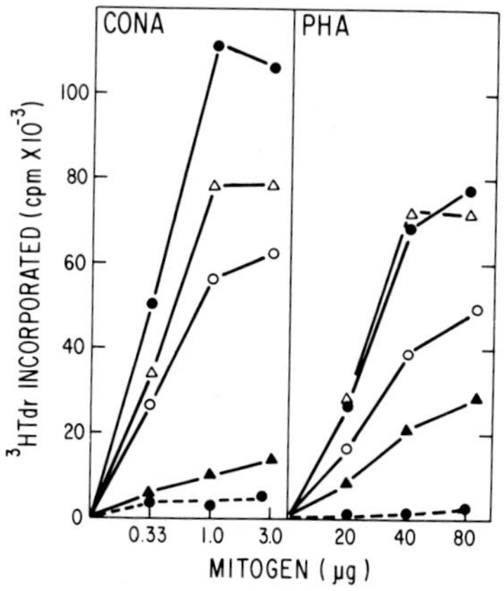

FIG. 1. Effect of addition of GBA on the Con A and PHA response of normal F344 spleen cell fractions. Unfractionated (○ —— ○), GBNA (● —— ●), GBA (● - - - ●), GBNA + 5×10^4 GBA (△ —— △), GBNA + 2.5×10^5 GBA (▲ —— ▲).

TABLE 2

Effect of Adherent Cells on the MLR and CML Response of Normal F344 Spleen Cells Fractionated on Glass Bead Columns

Responding cell fraction	Adherent cells	MLR (cpm [^{3}H]Tdr)	Percentage CML ± SD
1. Unfractionated	—	4308 ± 109 (1072 ± 236)[a]	2.9 ± 1.3
2. GBNA	—	7308 ± 526 (896 ± 85)	4.8 ± 2.5
3. GBA	—	1713 ± 652 (1275 ± 377)	2.9 ± 2.0
4. GBNA	GBA	4932 ± 425 (1562 ± 367)	6.3 ± 3.3
5. GBNA	GBA treated with anti-T serum + C	3993 ± 257 (1993 ± 476)	0.8 ± 1.2
6. GBNA	GBA-Mϕ treated with anti-T serum + C[b]	1973 ± 198 (1327 ± 77)	−1.6 ± 1.4

Note. MLR and CML cultures were set up between responding F344 spleen cell fractions and γ-irradiated BDIX cells as described under Materials and Methods. Wherever indicated, 2.5×10^5 and 6×10^6 GBA cells were added to the MLR and the CML cultures, respectively. In those cultures where GBA cells were pretreated with anti-T serum + C, the cell numbers were not corrected for cell loss due to the antiserum treatment. CML was assayed on ^{51}Cr-labeled P521 targets at E/T of 50:1.

[a] Numbers in parentheses indicate the values for syngeneic controls.

[b] GBA cells were enriched for macrophages in plastic dishes. The cells were scraped and treated with anti-T serum + C.

some T-cell subsets are also adherent (9, 27). It was necessary to determine if the suppression to mitogens and MLR is mediated by T cells present in the GBA cell fraction. The GBA cell fraction was treated with anti-T-cell serum and complement (C) prior to their addition to GBNA cell cultures. Table 2 (line 5) shows that GBA cells capable of inhibiting the MLR response of GBNA cells were resistant to treatment with anti-T serum + C. This suggests that the GBA cells capable of suppressing MLR response do not belong to the T-cell class and may represent macrophage suppressor cells (Mϕs). This is further strengthened by the finding that GBA macrophages purified by adherence to plastic surfaces and treated with anti-T serum + C are also capable of suppressing the MLR response (Table 2, line 6). Similar results (data not given) were also seen with responses to Con A and PHA.

T-Cell Responses with Alloantigen-Primed Spleen Cells

We have demonstrated that spleen cells obtained from *in vivo* alloantigen-primed animals respond well in the secondary CML response (Table 1). To determine if this response can be improved by removing the adherent cells, spleen cells from F344 primed *in vivo* with BDIX spleen cells were fractionated on glass bead columns. As seen in Fig. 2, the secondary *in vitro* CML response of spleen cells

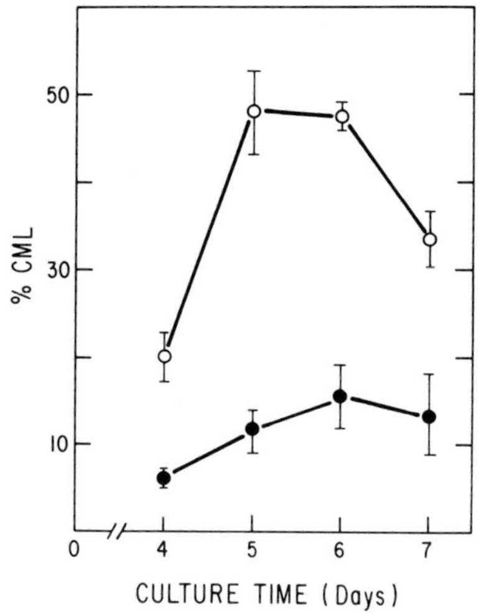

FIG. 2. Secondary *in vitro* CML response of unfractionated (○——○) and GBNA (●——●) from F344 primed with BDIX spleen cells. ^{51}Cr-Labeled P521 cells were used as targets at an effector to target (E/T) ratio of 40:1.

decreases significantly after removal of adherent cells. This decrease in the cytotoxic response was not due to a change in the kinetics of the CML response, since maximal levels of cytotoxicity were obtained on the same day in both the unfractionated and the GBNA cell cultures. These data suggest some degree of cooperativity between GBNA and GBA cells from primed spleens in eliciting the secondary CTL response.

Experiments were done to investigate if mitogen reactivity and the MLR of spleen cells from *in vivo* alloantigen-primed animals exhibited similar effects. Results presented in Table 3 indicate that these responses are not significantly altered after removal of adherent cells.

Synergistic Interaction between GBA and GBNA Cells in the Secondary CML Response

To test if the decrease in the CML response observed after the removal of adherent cells from BDIX-primed F344 spleen cells could be reconstituted, various

TABLE 3

Mitogen and MLR Response of F344 Spleen Cells Primed *in Vivo* with BDIX Cells

	[^{3}H]Tdr incorporated (cpm)				
	Mitogen			MLR[a]	
Responding cells fraction	Control (medium)	Con A (1 μg)	PHA (50 μg)	Control	Experimental
1. Unfractionated	1612 ± 209	100,516 ± 2612	43,891 ± 5160	1216 ± 43	12,467 ± 973
2. GBNA	991 ± 187	110,631 ± 7515	53,316 ± 5308	1076 ± 255	16,860 ± 1003
3. GBA	1993 ± 392	5,826 ± 172	4,110 ± 495	1593 ± 202	2,451 ± 125

[a] For MLR response the cells were either stimulated with γ-irradiated F344 spleen cells (syngeneic control) or with BDIX cells (experimental), under conditions described under Materials and Methods.

numbers of GBA cells were added to a constant number of GBNA cells. The results in Fig. 3 show that the decrease in CML response of GBNA cells can be restored by addition of GBA cells. Furthermore, the GBA cells themselves do not manifest any detectable CML response under these conditions. These results suggest that GBA cells play essentially a helper role in enhancing the CML response and do not contain any significant numbers of CTL precursors.

Nature of GBA Cells that Cooperate with GBNA Cells in the CML Response

Macrophages play a crucial role in the *in vitro* activation of lymphocytes induced by a variety of different stimuli (24, 25, 28–31). It is conceivable, therefore, that GBA cells obtained from *in vivo*-primed spleens contain macrophages that help the CML response to alloantigens. However, peritoneal exudate cells (PEC), obtained from either primed or unprimed animals, strongly inhibit the CML response (Fig. 4, D and E). Second, as seen in Fig. 4 (G), helper cells in the GBA cell fraction are sensitive to treatment with anti-T serum + C, indicating that the helper cell present in the GBA cell fraction belongs to the T-cell class. This helper T cell is designated as Th1.

Figure 5 shows that the CML-enhancing activity of Th1 is resistant to γ-irradiation (2500 rad). Thus, the functional activity of the Th1 cell is independent of a proliferative response. Addition of γ-irradiated GBA cells to GBNA cells, in fact resulted in a better CML response than addition of nonirradiated GBA cells. These data suggest that there may be a radiosensitive suppressor cell present in the adherent cell fraction.

Presence of a Second Helper T Cell (Th2) in the GBNA Fraction

In many instances the helper cells activated in the CML response have been shown to respond strongly in MLR (5, 30). As demonstrated previously, the MLR

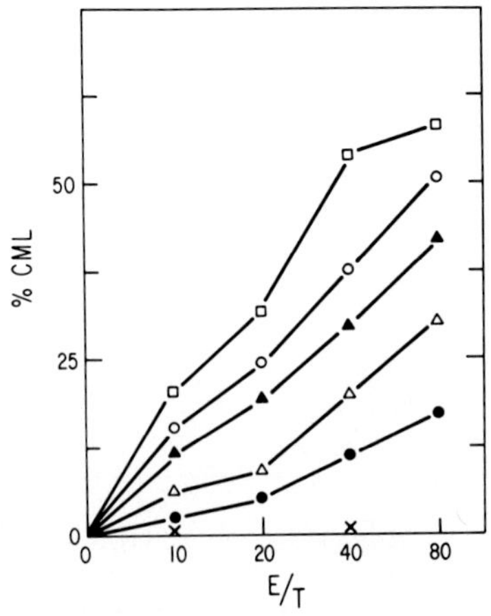

FIG. 3. Secondary *in vitro* CML response of F344 spleen cells primed with BDIX. Effect of addition of GBA cells to GBNA cells. Unfractionated (○——○), GBNA (●——●), GBNA + 2 × 10⁶ GBA (△——△), GBNA + 4 × 10⁶ GBA (▲——▲), GBNA + 6 × 10⁶ GBA (□——□), 6 × 10⁶ GBA cells alone (X——X).

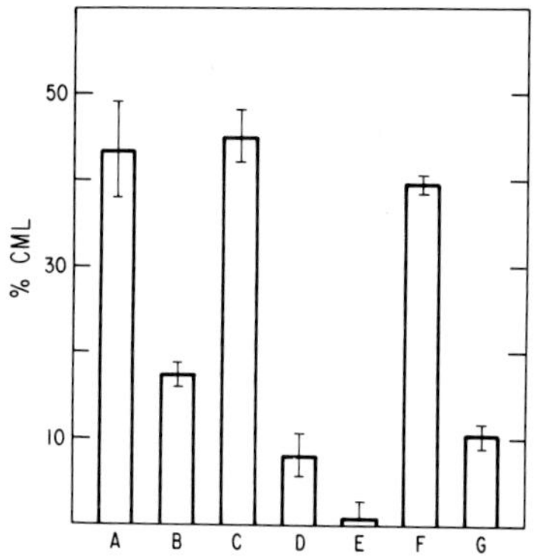

FIG. 4. Effect of PEC and anti-T serum-treated GBA cells on the secondary *in vitro* CML response of GBNA. (A) Unfractionated, (B) GBNA, (C) GBNA + 5 × 10^6 GBA, (D) GBNA + 2.5 × 10^5 PEC, (E) GBNA + 1 × 10^6 PEC, (F) GBNA + 5 × 10^6 GBA treated with NRS + C, (G) GBNA + 5 × 10^6 GBA treated with anti-T serum + C. Responding cells were F344 spleen cells primed with BDIX. The E/T ratio was 50:1. Cell numbers were not corrected for loss due to anti serum treatment.

response under our experimental conditions is mainly localized to the GBNA cell fraction of both normal and BDIX-primed spleen cells. Since we have yet no way of separating CTL precursors from the tentative helper T cells in the GBNA cell fraction, we investigated if the GBNA cell fraction obtained from F344 animals primed *in vivo* with BDIX could produce antibodies to a T-cell-dependent antigen like SRBC. The results presented in Table 4 show that GBNA cells were capable of making PFC against SRBC. Thus, the GBNA fraction contains both B cells and helper T cells. The PFC response against SRBC was completely abrogated when GBNA cells were pretreated with anti-T serum + C, suggesting that a T-cell

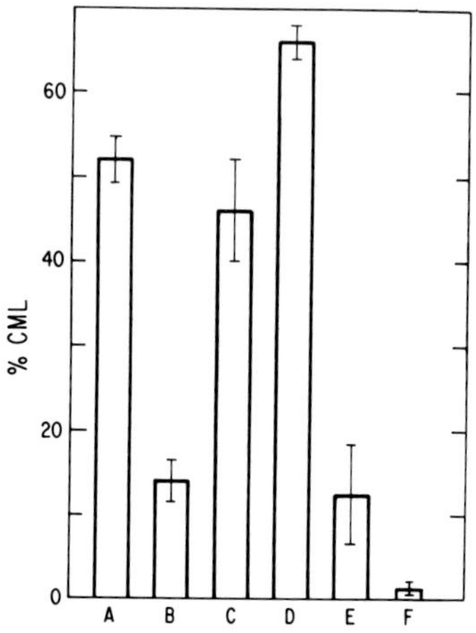

FIG. 5. Effect on anti-T serum treatment and γ irradiation on the "helper" function of GBA cells in the secondary *in vitro* CML response. (A) Unfractionated, (B) GBNA, (C) GBNA + 5 × 10^6 GBA, (D) GBNA + 5 × 10^6 γ-irradiated (2500 rad) GBA, (E) GBNA + 5 × 10^6 anti-T serum + C-treated GBA, (F) GBNA + 5 × 10^6 anti-T serum + C-treated and γ-irradiated GBA. Other conditions same as in Fig. 4.

TABLE 4

Differential Effect of Adherent Cells on the PFC and the CML Response of Primed F344 Spleen Cells Separated on Glass Bead Columns

Responding cells	Cell fraction added	PFC/1 × 10^6 cells	Percentage CML ± SD
1. Unfractionated	—	572	38.0 ± 1.3
2. GBNA	—	1284	14.5 ± 0.9
3. GBNA	GBA	729	30.6 ± 2.1
4. GBA	—	32	—
5. GBNA treated with anti-T serum + C	—	50	—
6. GBNA treated with anti-T serum + C	GBA	12	—
7. GBNA treated with anti-T serum + C	GBNA	834	7.6 ± 2.6
8. GBNA[a]	—	203	9.8 ± 3.5

Note. Responding cells (1 × 10^7) obtained from F344 rats (primed *in vivo* with BDIX cells) were cultured with SRBC (PFC) or γ-irradiated BDIX cells (CML) under conditions described under Materials and Methods. Wherever indicated, GBA or GBNA cells were added to the cultures at a concentration of 1 × 10^6/culture.

[a] Cultures contained 1 × 10^6 GBNA responding cells to serve as a control for the data on line 7.

present in the GBNA cell fraction is needed to obtain an anti-SRBC PFC response. Addition of 1 × 10^6 untreated GBNA cells (as a source of T cells) to 1 × 10^7 GBNA cells treated with anti-T serum + C (T-depleted) partially restored the PFC response of the latter. Interestingly, 1 × 10^6 GBA cells were not capable of providing helper activity for the PFC response of T-cell-depleted GBNA cells. These data suggest the presence of a nonadherent T-cell in the GBNA cell fraction that acts as a helper T cell for the T-dependent antibody response. This helper T cell has been designated as Th2.

DISCUSSION

The immune response is regulated to a large extent by the action of helper and suppressor cells (8). In the murine system, delineation of immunoregulatory pathways has relied heavily on the use of antibodies directed against cell surface differentiation markers such as Ly and Qa-1 antigens (4–7). In the rat, it is the lack of such antisera and well-characterized *in vitro* systems for studying cell-mediated immune responses that has hampered similar studies.

Previous reports indicate the presence of macrophage-like adherent cells present in rat spleens which inhibit many *in vitro* correlates of cell-mediated immunity (20–23). The results herein confirm that removal of a splenic adherent cell results in increased T-cell mitogenic activity and MLR. Furthermore, we have demonstrated that the addition of GBA cells to GBNA cells inhibits these responses. The GBA cells capable of inhibiting these responses are not T cells. This was an important point to ascertain in view of the fact that T cells with adherent properties have been reported in murine systems (9, 27). The suppressor activity is localized in the GBA cell fraction and appears to be a macrophage suppressor cell (Mϕs). Contrary to some reports (22), removal of adherent cells does not improve a primary *in vitro* CML response of rat spleen cells. Under our experimental conditions, *in vivo* priming with alloantigens appears obligatory for obtaining an *in vitro* CML response in rat spleen cell preparations in a reproducible manner. Surprisingly, removal of GBA cells from *in vivo* allo-primed spleen cells significantly reduces the *in vitro* CML response. Conversely, addition of GBA cells to GBNA cells restores the CML response. Our studies further indicate that the cell(s) involved in augmentation of the CML response is of the T-cell lineage. Thus, the results favor the notion that two distinct T cells characterized by properties of adherence to glass bead columns interact synergistically in the generation of the *in vitro* CML response.

It could be argued that the GBA cells that enhance the CML response are actually CTL precursors. This assumption seems unlikely for two reasons: First, the GBA cells themselves exhibit no CTL response when stimulated with sensitizing alloantigen; second, the enhancing activity of the GBA cells is resistant to γ-irradiation (2500 rad). Therefore, the GBA T cells that are involved in stimulating the CML response appear to be helper T cells (Th1) whose activity is independent of their proliferative response. Some helper T cells in mice have also been reported to be radioresistant (32, 33). Furthermore, Agarossi *et al.* (27), based on properties of nylon wool adherence and radiosensitivity of some mouse splenic T-cell subsets, have arrived at similar conclusions.

A surprising finding was a lack of strict correlation between MLR and CML responses in rat spleen cells. For example, GBNA cells from primed animals give a good MLR response, but a relatively poor CML response. This, however, does not imply that CTLs do not contribute to MLR response, but may suggest that GBNA T cells that contribute strongly to MLR response may be distinct from CTL precursors. This interpretation is also supported by experiments in mice, where use of the "three cell protocols" and Ly antisera (5, 34) indicates that the major contributors to the MLR response are the T helper cells that respond to H-2I-region stimulation. Experiments described in this paper suggest that helper-T-cell activity for the T-dependent antibody response to SRBC is indeed present in the MLR reacting population (GBNA cells) and not in the GBA cell fraction. This nonadherent helper T cell has been designated as Th2. The adherent helper T cell (Th1) appears specific for CML response while Th2 helps the antibody response. However, the role of Th2 in CML response (if any) remains to be investigated. The presence of two types of helper T cells has also been reported in the murine system (9, 27, 35, 36).

The helper activity of the GBA cells in the CML response is markedly improved after irradiation, suggesting the presence of a radiosensitive suppressor cell(s). It would appear unlikely that the cell is a macrophage because macrophages are radioresistant (37, 38). However, it is possible that the radiosensitive suppressor cell is a T-cell subset. While we have no direct proof, this possibility is supported by the known radiosensitivity of some T suppressor cells (39, 40).

ACKNOWLEDGMENTS

We wish to thank Drs. Fritz Bach and Heinz Kunz for their helpful discussions and reading of the manuscript. We would also like to thank Ms. Karen Metot for excellent technical assistance.

REFERENCES

1. Cantor, H., Simpson, E., Sato, V., Fathman, G., and Herzenberg, L. A., *Cell. Immunol.* **15,** 180, 1975.

2. Gershon, R. K., *Contemp. Top. Immunobiol.* **3,** 1, 1974.
3. Cantor, H., *Cell. Immunol.* **3,** 461, 1972.
4. Cantor, H., and Boyse, E. A., *J. Exp. Med.* **141,** 1376, 1975.
5. Cantor, H., and Boyse, E. A., *J. Exp. Med.* **141,** 1390, 1975.
6. Jandinski, J., Cantor, H., Tadakuma, T., Peavy, D. L., and Pierce, C. W., *J. Exp. Med.* **143,** 1382, 1976.
7. Stanton, T. H., Calkins, C. E., Jandinski, J., Schendel, D. J., Stutman, O., and Boyse, E. A., *J. Exp. Med.* **148,** 963, 1978.
8. Eardley, D. D., Hugenberger, J., McVay-Boudreau, L., Shen, F. W., Gershon, R. K., and Cantor, H., *J. Exp. Med.* **148,** 106, 1978.
9. Tada, T., Takemori, T., Okumura, K., Nonaka, M., and Tokuhisa, T., *J. Exp. Med.* **147,** 446, 1978.
10. Williams, A. F., Giovanni, G., and Milstein, C., *Cell* **12,** 663, 1977.
11. White, R. A. H., Mason, D. W., Williams, A. F., Galfre, A., and Milstein, C., *J. Exp. Med.* **147,** 664, 1978.
12. Shortman, K., Williams, N., Jackson, H., Russell, P., Byst, P., and Diener, E., *J. Cell Biol.* **48,** 566, 1971.
13. Elliott, L. H., and Roszman, T. L., *Cell. Immunol.* **40,** 46, 1978.
14. Yam, L. T., Li, C. Y., and Crosby, W. H., *Amer. J. Clin. Pathol.* **55,** 283, 1971.
15. Calderon, J., Williams, R. T., and Unanue, E. R., *Proc. Nat. Acad. Sci. USA* **17,** 4273, 1974.
16. Sopori, M., Bernstein, A., and Bach, F. H., *J. Exp. Med.* **148,** 1523, 1978.
17. Mishell, R. I., and Dutton, R. W., *J. Exp. Med.* **126,** 423, 1967.
18. Cunningham, A. J., and Szenberg, A., *Immunology* **14,** 599, 1968.
19. Lubaroff, D. M., Rasmussen, G. T., and Hunt, H. D., *Transplant. Proc.* **11,** 1642, 1979.
20. Folch, H., and Waksman, B. H., *J. Immunol.* **113,** 140, 1974.
21. Raff, H. V., and Hinrichs, D. H., *Cell Immunol.* **29,** 109, 1977.
22. Oehler, J. R., Herberman, R. B., Campbell, D. A., Jr., and Djeu, J. Y., *Cell. Immunol.* **29,** 238, 1977.
23. Weiss, A., and Fitch, F. W., *J. Immunol.* **120,** 357, 1978.
24. Mattingly, J. A., Eardley, D. D., Kemp, J. D., and Gershon, R. K., *J. Immunol.* **122,** 787, 1979.
25. Bernstein, I. D., and Wright, P. W., *Transplantation* **21,** 173, 1976.
26. Folch, H., and Waksman, B. H., *J. Immunol.* **113,** 127, 1974.
27. Agarossi, G., Mancini, C., and Doria, G., *J. Immunol.* **126,** 955, 1981.
28. Mosier, D. E., *Science* **158,** 1573, 1967.
29. Seeger, R. C., and Oppenheim, J. J., *J. Exp. Med.* **132,** 44, 1970.
30. Alter, B. J., and Bach, F. H., *Cell. Immunol.* **1,** 207, 1970.
31. Waldron, J. A., Jr., Horn, R. G., and Rosenthal, A. S., *J. Immunol.* **112,** 746, 1974.
32. Dutton, R. W., *J. Exp. Med.* **138,** 1496, 1973.
33. Wagner, H., *J. Exp. Med.* **138,** 1379, 1973.
34. Bach, F. H., Bach, M. L., and Sondel, P. M., *Nature (London)* **259,** 273, 1976.
35. Marrack, P., and Kappler, J. W., *J. Immunol.* **116,** 1373, 1976.
36. Swierkosz, J. E., Marrack, P., and Kappler, J. W., *J. Exp. Med.* **150,** 1293, 1979.
37. Rosentreich, D. L., Farrar, J. J., Dougherty, S., *J. Immunol.* **116,** 131, 1976.
38. Rosentreich, D. L., and Mizel, S. B., *Immunol. Rev.* **40,** 136, 1978.
39. Kapp, J. A., Pierce, C. W., Schlossman, S., and Benacerraf, B., *J. Exp. Med.* **140,** 648, 1974.
40. Holan, V., Hasek, M., and Chutna, J., *Transplant. Bull.* **29,** 91, 1978.

CELLULAR IMMUNOLOGY **65,** 115–130 (1981)

Modulation of Natural Cytotoxicity by Alloantibodies

V. The Mechanism of a Selective Augmenting Effect of Anti-H-2 Antisera on the Natural Killer Activity of Mouse Spleen Cells

RAJIV K. SAXENA, QUEEN B. SAXENA, AND WILLIAM H. ADLER

Clinical Immunology Section, Gerontology Research Center, NIA, National Institutes of Health, Baltimore, Maryland 21224

Received December 29, 1980; accepted September 12, 1981

Treatment of mouse spleen cells with specific anti-H-2 antisera augments their natural killer (NK) activity against K562 cells but not against YAC target tumor cells. The same population of natural killer cells was found to lyse K562 as well as YAC target cells, since (a) depletion of YAC reactive NK cells by absorption on YAC monolayers resulted in a concomitant depletion of anti-K562 NK activity of mouse spleen cells, and (b) both K562 and YAC cells could inhibit their own as well as each others lysis in a cross-competition assay. Anti-H-2 antiserum could not induce anti-K562 NK activity in spleen cells previously depleted of NK cells by absorption on YAC monolayers, indicating that alloantiserum does not act by recruiting otherwise nonreactive cells to become cytotoxic toward K562 target cells. In a target-binding assay, K562 binding of NK cells (T-cell-, B-cell-, and macrophage-depleted spleen cells) increased five- to eightfold in the presence of anti-H-2 antiserum whereas YAC cells binding of NK cells was not increased. H-2 antigens per se did not appear to be involved in the alloantisera effect since anti-NK antiserum directed against a non-H-2 antigen selectively expressed on NK cells, showed a similar selective NK enhancing effect. Protein A, a reagent which binds to the Fc region of immunoglobulin molecules, completely blocked the alloantiserum induced augmentation of anti-K562 NK activity, but did not alter basal NK activity. Moreover, the $F(ab)_2$ fraction of alloantibodies failed to enhance anti-K562 cytotoxic activity of mouse spleen cells, indicating a crucial role for the Fc portion of the alloantibodies attached to the NK cells, in NK augmentation. Utilization of several target cell lines with or without membrane Fc receptors (FcR) revealed that alloantiserum enhanced the lysis of only FcR^+ target cells. It is proposed that alloantibody-coated NK cells, as a result of a secondary interaction between attached alloantibody and Fc receptors on target cells, interact more readily with the target cells and thereby cause a higher level of lytic activity.

INTRODUCTION

Spleen cells derived from normal unimmunized mice can lyse a variety of tumor cell lines *in vitro* (1–5). Cells responsible for this activity have been termed natural killer (NK)[1] cells and appear to fall in a category different from conventional T cells, B cells, or macrophages (2, 4, 6). Recently it has been of great interest to understand the nature of the interactions between NK effector and target cells.

[1] Abbreviations used: FcR, receptors for the Fc region of IgG; FDA, fluorescein diacetate; FITC, fluorescein isothiocyanate; NK, natural killer; TBA, target-binding assay; YMA, spleen cells obtained after absorption on YAC monolayers.

0008-8749/81/170115-16/$02.00/0

Evidence reported so far seems to indicate that there is no significant heterogeneity within the NK cell category and different NK-susceptible tumor cells may share certain common target structures recognized by NK cells. Some such target structures have recently been isolated from a NK-susceptible tumor cell line, which (a) inhibit the binding of effector cells with susceptible tumor target cells and (b) are absent from NK-resistant target cells (7). An hypothesis of common target membrane structures leaves many gaps in the understanding of natural killer phenomenon. Susceptibility to NK cells is not an all-or-none phenomenon and different target cells with a spectrum of susceptibilities have been described. Whether these differences arise due to quantitative differences in expression of a common target structure(s) or other factors may also play a role in defining the susceptibility of a given target cell, is not clear.

Previous work from our laboratory has shown that the lysis of the human leukemia cell line K562 by mouse NK cells can be significantly enhanced by treating the effector cells with specific anti-H-2 antiserum (8, 9). Though other agents like interferon, interferon inducers, and mitogens are also known to enhance the NK activity of mouse spleen cells, the effect of anti-H-2 antiserum differs from these agents in that the augmented NK activity target cells (K562 and some human lymphoblastoid cell lines) and not against others (YAC, L1210, P815 murine cell lines, and the WFu/G1 rat cell line) (8, 10). NK activation by interferon and mitogens was nonspecifically observed regardless of the target cells used (10, 11).

The aim of the present investigation was to understand the mechanism of selective modulation of NK activity by alloantiserum. On the basis of the evidence obtained, it is proposed that the higher anti-K562 NK activity of alloantiserum-treated mouse spleen cells is due to an increased affinity of these cells in their interaction with K562 cells, which in turn results from a secondary interaction of Fc portions of the attached alloantibodies with Fc receptors on K562 target cells.

MATERIALS AND METHODS

Animals. Five-week-old female C57BL/6J or DBA/2 mice were obtained from the Jackson Laboratories, Bar Harbor, Maine and were maintained in our animal colony until 6 to 16 weeks of age.

Chemicals and antisera. Protein A from *Staphylococcus aureaus* and protein A–Sepharose for affinity chromatography were purchased from Pharmacia Fine Chemicals, Piscataway, New Jersey. Poly-L-lysine, MW 50,000, and pepsin were obtained from Sigma Chemical Company, St. Louis, Missouri. Culture media were supplied by the NIH media unit and fetal calf serum (FCS) was obtained from GIBCO, Grand Island, New York. Low-tox rabbit complement was a product of Cedarlane Laboratories Ltd. and was purchased from Accurate Chemical and Scientific Corporation, Hicksville, New York. FITC-conjugated rabbit antisera specific to $F(ab)_2$ or Fc regions of mouse IgG were products of Cappel Laboratories, Cochranville, Pennsylvania. Hybridoma HO13-4 producing monoclonal anti-thy-1 IgM antibody was obtained from the Salk Institute and its culture supernatants were used as a source of anti-thy-1 antibodies. Anti-H-2^b alloantiserum was raised in CBA (H-2^k) or DBA (H-2^d) mice by repeated intraperitoneal injections of spleen cells derived from C57BL/6 mice (H-2^b). Anti-H-2^d antiserum was raised by immunization of C57BL/6 mice with DBA/2 spleen cells. Anti-NK-1 antiserum

(C3H × Balb/C vs CE antiserum) was kindly provided by Dr. Fung-Win Shen of the Memorial Sloan–Kettering Cancer Center, New York.

Target cells. K562 and MOLT-4 (human leukemia cell lines), P815 (DBA/2 mastocytoma), YAC (A/SN lymphoma) and EL-4 (C57BL/6 lymphoma) cell lines were originally obtained from NCI, NIH (courtesy of Drs. H. T. Holden and R. B. Herberman), and were maintained in our laboratory as suspension cultures in tissue culture medium RPMI 1640 + 10% FCS. Three human lymphoblastoid cell lines V280, J180 and B180 were initiated in our laboratory by spontaneous *in vitro* transformation of normal human peripheral blood leukocytes (courtesy of Dr. Jim Nagel and Mr. Joe Chrest).

Absorption of spleen cells on YAC monolayers. Monolayers of YAC tumor cells were prepared using a modification of previously described procedure (12, 13). Two milliliters of a poly-L-lysine solution (50 μg/ml) in phosphate-buffered saline (PBS) was aliquoted to plastic petri dishes (60 × 15 mm, Falcon Labware) and kept at room temperature for 1 hr. The petri dishes were then rinsed repeatedly with fresh PBS prior to the addition of 2 ml of YAC tumor cells (40×10^6/ml) in PBS. The plates were incubated at room temperature for 45 min. Nonattached YAC cells were poured off and the petri dishes were gently rinsed three times by dipping in PBS. Two milliliters of mouse spleen cells (20×10^6/ml in RPMI + 10% FCS) was slowly added to the YAC monolayer and the dishes were incubated at 37°C for 45 min. At the end of this period nonadherent spleen cells were gently poured off. Recovery of spleen leukocytes after this procedure was 25 to 30% and contamination of the nonadherent spleen cells by YAC cells (monitored on the basis of cell size) was 2 to 4%.

Target-binding assay. The target-binding assay (TBA) was performed essentially as described by Roder *et al.* (14). Spleen cell preparations were subjected to a water lysis step to remove erythrocytes, passed through nylon wool columns by the method of Julius *et al.* (15), and then treated with anti-thy-1 monoclonal antibodies and complement as previously described (6). Effector lymphocytes were labeled with fluorescein diacetate (FDA) by incubating at 4°C for 5 min, with 25 μg/ml of an FDA solution in phosphate-buffered saline followed by two washings. FDA-labeled lymphocytes (0.1 ml, 10^6/ml) were mixed with equal number of target cells (K562 or YAC) in a 0.2-ml total volume of RPMI + 10% FCS containing a 1/200 dilution of anti-H-2^b antiserum where required. Mixtures of spleen lymphocytes and target cells were centrifuged at 200*g* for 5 min and then incubated initially for 5 min at room temperature and later for 30 to 60 min at 4°C. After the incubation period, the supernatant from each tube was discarded and the pellet gently resuspended in 20 μl fresh medium by repeated aspirations with 10-μl Eppendorf pipet. The cell suspensions were placed on a glass slide and examined with fluorescent microscopy (Leitz, Rockleigh, N.J.). At least 300 lymphocytes were counted and the number bound to tumor cells were recorded. Fortuitous associations between tumor cells and lymphocytes were tested by gently tapping the cover slip. Results of the TBA are expressed as the total number of lymphocytes observed, the number of lymphocytes bound to tumor cells and the bound lymphocytes as a percentage of the total.

^{51}Cr release assay. Target cells were labeled with ^{51}Cr by incubating 2×10^6 target cells in 150 μl Tris-buffered saline (pH 7.4) with 200 μl of radioactive sodium chromate (^{51}Cr, 1 mCi/ml) at 37°C for 30 min. Labeled cells were washed twice

and suspended in RPMI 1640 with 10% FCS at a density of 1×10^5 cells/ml. Required numbers of effector spleen cells along with 10^4 ^{51}Cr-labeled target cells were placed in wells of a 96-well round-bottom microtiter plate (Falcon Products, Oxnard, Calif.). The total incubation medium volume (RPMI 1640 + 10% FCS) in each well was 0.2 ml which contained the required concentrations of unlabeled competitor cells or alloantisera. Plates were centrifuged at 400*g* for 3 min and incubated at 37°C for 4 hr. After incubation, 0.1 ml of supernatant was removed from each well without disturbing the cells and the radioactivity level was determined in a nuclear Chicago gamma counter. Base line release of ^{51}Cr was studied by incubating target cells in medium alone and was always less than 15% for any target cell. Estimation of the maximum release of ^{51}Cr was determined by suspending 10^4 labeled target cells in 2 ml of water. After an incubation period of 4 hr at 37°C, the radioactivity of 1 ml of supernatant was determined. Percentage specific lysis of target cells was calculated by the following formula.

Percentage lysis

$$= \frac{\text{cpm in supernatants of the test well} - \text{cpm of base line release}}{\text{cpm released by water} - \text{cpm of base line release}} \times 100.$$

Preparation of $F(ab)_2$ fragment of alloantibodies from anti-H-2 antiserum. Two milliliters of mouse anti-H-2^b or anti-H-2^d antisera was used as source material. To obtain the IgG fraction alloantisera were passed through a protein A–Sepharose CL-43 (Pharmacia) column as described by Ey *et al.* (16). The column was composed of 1.5 g of protein A–Sepharose equilibrated in 1.5 *M* phosphate-buffered saline (PBS) at a pH of 8.4. After passage of the antisera through the column at pH 8.4, the IgG which remained attached to the protein A–Sepharose column was eluted with a 0.1 *M*, sodium citrate/citric acid buffer, pH 3. About 10 mg of pure IgG could be obtained in this manner. The IgG was dialyzed and equilibrated against a 0.1 *M* sodium acetate buffer, pH 4.5. Pepsin (Sigma) was added after equilibration at a concentration of 1 mg/8 mg IgG in a 10-ml volume. The mixture was incubated at 37°C with constant stirring for 6 hr. After digestion the mixture was dialyzed against 0.15 *M* PBS, pH 8.4, and reapplied to the protein A–Sepharose column equilibrated with the same buffer. The fall-through peak was designated as the $F(ab)_2$ fragment. The IgG and $F(ab)_2$ fractions were lyophilized, reconstituted in water, and dialyzed against 0.15 *M* PBS, pH 7.3, prior to testing in the NK experiments.

Detection of Fc receptors on target cell lines. Presence of Fc receptors on various target cell lines was tested by staining with fluoresceinated and heat-aggregated human IgG. Preparation of the staining reagent and the procedure for visualization of Fc receptors has been previously described (17).

RESULTS

NK Activity of Mouse Spleen Cells after Absorption on YAC Monolayers

Treatment of mouse spleen cells with specific anti-H-2 antisera results in an enhanced NK activity against the K562 human leukemia cell line but not against YAC murine lymphoma cells (8–10). In order to determine if the NK cell population responsible for the lysis of these two different target cells are the same, the

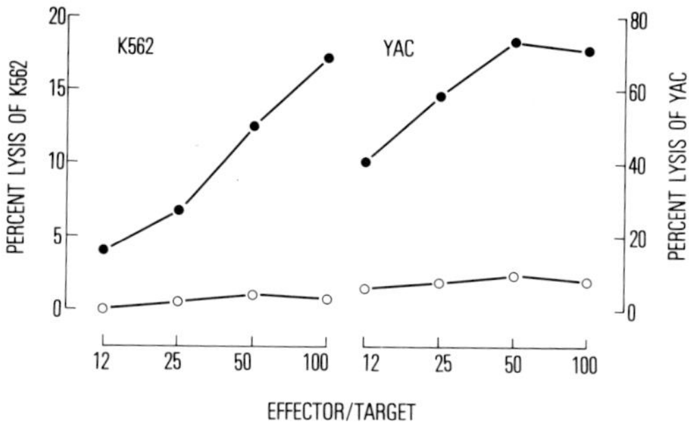

FIG. 1. NK activity of mouse spleen cells before and after absorption on a monolayer of YAC tumor cells. Spleen cells pooled from four C57BL/6J mice were absorbed on a monolayer of YAC tumor cells prepared and carried out as described in the text. NK activity of control (●) and absorbed (○) spleen cells was studied against YAC and K562 tumor target cells at different E:T ratios in a 4-hr ^{51}Cr release assay. Each value of lysis is a mean of four replicate observations.

following experiments were performed. Mouse spleen cells were absorbed on monolayers of YAC tumor cells to remove any cells which can attach to YAC cells, and the NK activity of the resulting nonadherent cell population was tested against both K562 and YAC target cells. The results of a representative experiment showing the dose–response curves for the NK activity of control and YAC monolayer absorbed spleen cells (YMA cells) against the two target cells are given in Fig. 1. These results indicated that YMA cells lost their NK activity against both the K562 and YAC targets. An important consideration in the evaluation of the validity of these results is the level of contamination of YMA cells by YAC cells acquired during the process of the spleen cell incubation on YAC monolayers. Contaminating YAC cells can competitively inhibit the lysis of YAC or K562 cells causing an apparent loss of NK activity. It was found that YAC contamination of YMA cells ranged between 2 and 4% and as described later in this paper, at this level of concentration YAC cells can cause significant inhibition of both anti-K562 and anti-YAC NK activity of mouse spleen cells. However, the decrease in NK activity of the adsorbed YMA cells was of a greater magnitude than could result from a 2 to 4% YAC contamination. For example in Fig. 1, lysis of K562 by YMA cells at a E:T ratio of 100:1 is about 6% of the lytic level induced by control spleen cells. This decrease if due only to the presence of contaminating YAC cells, would require at least a level of 25% contaminating YAC cells in the YMA cells (data derived from Fig. 2). However, in order to establish whether or not the low NK activity in YMA cells was partially due to contaminating YAC cells, the YMA cells were treated with an anti-YAC reactive antiserum + C to remove any contaminating YAC cells. After treatment the NK activity of YAC-depleted YMA cells was tested. An anti-H-2^d antiserum was used as a YAC-reactive antiserum.[2] Results in Fig. 2 show that the NK activity of anti-H-2^d + C-treated YMA cells remained low indicating that the presence of any contaminating YAC cells did not contribute to the loss of NK activity in YMA cells. Therefore, the results of the adsorption experiments appear valid and suggest that the NK cells which can lyse

[2] YAC cells have a H-2^a haplotype in which the K end is similar to the H-2^k and the D end is similar to the H-2^d haplotype. An anti-H-2^d antiserum therefore will react with YAC cells.

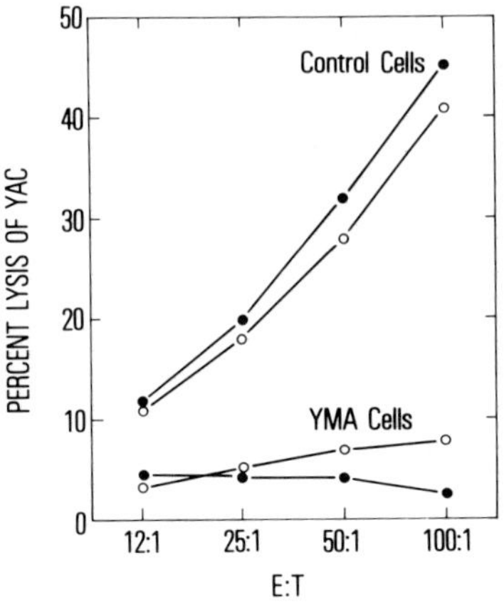

FIG. 2. Effect of anti-H-2^d antiserum + C treatment on the NK activity of normal and YMA C57BL/6 spleen cells. Normal or YMA spleen cells (10^7/ml) were incubated with 1:10 dilution of anti-H-2^d antiserum for 30 min at 4°C. Cells were washed twice and then incubated at 37°C for 45 min with 1:10 dilution of rabbit complement. Control cells were treated with complement alone. In parallel incubations, this anti-H-2^d + C treatment could completely lyse a pure YAC cell preparation (10^6/ml). Anti-H-2^d + C (○) or C alone (●)-treated normal and YMA spleen cells were tested for NK activity in a 4-hr ^{51}Cr release assay using YAC cells as target, at different E:T ratios.

K562 or YAC cells are the same population since the depletion of one type on a YAC monolayer results in a concomitant depletion of the other.

Inhibition of NK Activity of Mouse Spleen Cells by K562 and YAC Tumor Cells

Since the previous experiments showed that anti-K562 reactive NK cells could be depleted by absorption on YAC monolayers, we further tested the possibility that YAC and K562 share determinants recognized by NK cells. To test for this possibility cold competition experiments were performed in which anti-K562 and anti-YAC spleen cell NK activity was studied in presence of variable concentrations of unlabeled K562 and YAC cells. Results of three experiments are shown in Fig. 3. In all experiments the NK activity of mouse spleen cells against K562 and YAC cells could be inhibited by adding either of the two unlabeled cells. Another finding in these experiments was that on a cell-to-cell basis unlabeled YAC cells were a more effective inhibitor than K562 cells in preventing the lysis of either K562 or YAC cells. For example, in the presence of 3% unlabeled YAC cells in the effector spleen cell population, the lysis of K562 and YAC target cells was inhibited by 55 and 72%, respectively, whereas, the same concentration of unlabeled K562 cells resulted in only a 38 and 26% inhibition of K562 and YAC lysis, respectively (these are the mean values of the levels of inhibition found in the three experiments given in Fig. 3). These results suggest that the same NK cell population can lyse both target cells, though the affinity of NK cells may be greater for YAC cells than for K562 cells.

Lack of Induction of Anti-K562 Cytotoxicity in YMA Cells by Anti-H-2 Antiserum

Previous experiments in our laboratory had shown that an alloantiserum with specificity against spleen NK effector cells can lead to an augmentation of NK anti

K562 lytic activity. It was of interest to determine the mechanism of action of this enhancing effect of the alloantisera. It was thought that the effect could be a result of an enhanced interaction of effectors and targets or alternatively, alloantiserum may recruit otherwise nonreactive cells to become cytotoxic for K562 target cells. To test this possibility, in view of the results of the above experiments, the effect of anti-H-2^b antiserum on the anti-K562 NK activity of C57BL/6 spleen cells which had been absorbed on a YAC monolayer (YMA cells) was studied. Results of three experiments are shown in Table 1. In each experiment, the addition of anti-H-2^b antiserum in the assay medium stimulted the lysis of K562 cells by the control nonabsorbed C57BL/6 spleen cells but the alloantisera had no effect when YMA cells were used as effectors. These results indicate that the population of mouse spleen cells responsible for the alloantiserum mediated augmentation of NK activity against K562 cells, is lost as a result of absorption on YAC monolayers, and that antisera augmentation of NK activity is not a result of an induction of activation of non-NK population.

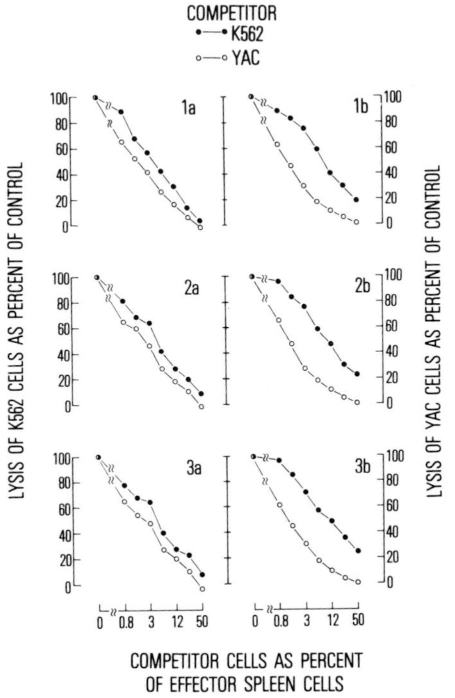

FIG. 3. Inhibition of NK activity of mouse spleen cells against ^{51}Cr-labeled K562 and YAC target cells, by unlabeled K562 and YAC cells. In each experiment NK activities of C57BL/6J mouse spleen cells were studied against ^{51}Cr-labeled K562 and YAC cells at a E:T ratio of 100:1. Different concentrations of unlabeled K562 or YAC cells were also added to the cytotoxicity assay medium. Control values of percentage target lysis obtained in the absence of any added unlabeled tumor cells, were taken as 100 and the lysis values obtained in the presence of unlabeled tumor cells were expressed as percentage of control. Actual control lysis values were: 53.1 ± 0.9 (Expt 1), 57.7 ± 1.1 (Expt 2) and 49.4 ± 1.4 (Expt 3) for YAC target cells, and 6.6 ± 0.4 (Expt 1), 9.8 ± 0.5 (Expt 2), and 7.3 ± 0.5 (Expt 3) for K562 target cells.

TABLE 1

Effect of Anti-H-2^b Antiserum on NK Activity of Normal C57BL/6J Mouse Spleen Cells and on Spleen Cells Absorbed on YAC Monolayers[a]

Expt. No.	Effector spleen cells	Percentage lysis of K562 cells: Control	Percentage lysis of K562 cells: +Anti-H-2 antiserum[b]
1	Normal	6.4 ± 0.7	12.3 ± 0.5
	Absorbed	0.3 ± 0.3	0.4 ± 0.1
2	Normal	9.5 ± 0.1	17.3 ± 0.2
	Absorbed	0.9 ± 0.3	0.9 ± 0.2
3	Normal	6.6 ± 0.2	13.6 ± 0.5
	Absorbed	0.1 ± 0.2	0.2 ± 0.4

[a] Spleen cells were pooled from three C57BL/6J mice and a portion was absorbed on a monolayer of YAC tumor cells as described in the text. NK activity of control or absorbed spleen cells was studied in a 4-hr ^{51}Cr release assay at an E:T ratio of 100:1.

[b] Anti-H-2^b antiserum (CBA anti-C57BL/6J) was added to the cytotoxicity assay medium at 1/200 final dilution.

The Effect of Anti-H-2 Antiserum on the Binding of NK-Enriched Spleen Lymphocytes with K562 and YAC Tumor Cells in a Target-Binding Assay

The effects of anti-H-2 antiserum on the NK effector–target interactions were studied using a target-binding assay. In order to minimize any possible interference by cell types other than NK cells, spleen cell preparations were subjected to (a) water lysis to remove erythrocytes (b) passage through a nylon wool column to remove B cells and other adherent cells, and (c) treatment with monoclonal anti-thy-1 antibody and complement to deplete T cells. Recovery of lymphocytes after these fractionation/purification steps ranged from 3 to 8% in various experiments. To determine the percentage of lymphocytes bound to tumor cells the NK cell-enriched lymphocyte preparations were labeled with fluorescein diacetate (FDA) and were incubated with K562 or YAC tumor cells at an E:T of 1:1. Results of three experiments are given in Table 2. In control incubations, K562 cells were observed to be associated with 1.7 to 2.5% of the lymphocytes. In the presence of a 1/200 dilution of anti-H-2^b antiserum however, the percentage of bound lymphocytes increased by five- to eightfold in different experiments. In contrast to the effect of anti-H-2^b antiserum on lymphocyte K562 binding, binding of NK cells with YAC cells was not enhanced by anti-H-2^b antiserum (Table 2).

Effect of Anti-NK-1 Antiserum on NK Activity of Mouse Spleen Cells

To determine if the increased binding of alloantibody-coated spleen lymphocytes with K562 cells was a consequence of a specific masking or engaging of H-2 antigens on the effector cells, or a nonspecific result of bound antibody molecules on the NK cell membrane, we tested the effect of an anti-NK-1 antiserum. Anti-NK-1 antiserum reacts with a non-H-2 antigen, NK-1, which is expressed selectively on NK cells of C57BL/6J mice. Preparation and properties of this antiserum have been reported previously (18). Treatment with anti-NK-1 antiserum would effec-

TABLE 2

Effect of Anti-H-2^b Antiserum on the Binding of NK-enriched C57BL/6J Spleen Cells with K562 or YAC Tumor Cells[a]

Expt. No.	Antiserum added[b]	Binding of effector cells with K562			Binding of effector cells with YAC		
		Total	Bound	%	Total	Bound	%
1	None	321	7	2.18	331	20	6.04
	Anti-H-2^b	312	42	13.46	325	15	4.62
2	None	352	6	1.70	345	19	5.51
	Anti-H-2^b	346	44	12.71	325	16	4.92
3	None	322	8	2.48	366	17	4.64
	Anti-H-2^b	402	51	12.69	321	16	5.00

[a] In each experiment, C57BL/6J spleen cells were depleted of erythrocytes by water lysis, passed through nylon wool column and finally treated with anti-thy-1 antibody and complement. Resulting NK-enriched spleen lymphocytes were used in target-binding assays as described under Materials and Methods.

[b] Where ever indicated, a 1/200 dilution of anti-H-2^b antiserum was included in the incubation medium for target-binding assay.

tively coat NK cells with antibody molecules leaving H-2 antigens unengaged. Results of a representative experiment are given in Fig. 4 and demonstrate that anti-NK-1 antiserum significantly enhanced the NK activity of the spleen cells against K562 targets but not against YAC targets. The enhancing effect of anti-NK-1 antiserum was therefore similar to the effect of anti-H-2 antiserum in inducing a selective modulation of NK activity. Therefore, antibody molecules bound to effector NK lymphocytes can cause the augmentation of anti-K562 cytolytic activity and there is no necessity of specifically involving H-2 antigens.

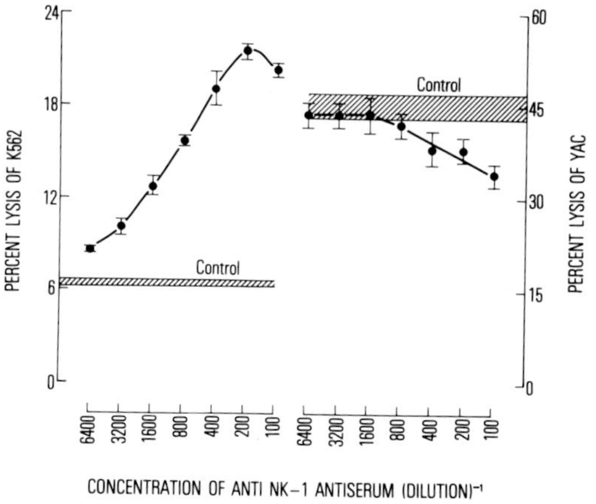

FIG. 4. Dose–response curve for the effect of anti-NK-1 antiserum on the NK activity of mouse spleen cells against K562 and YAC target cells. NK activity of spleen cells pooled from three C57BL/6J mice was studied against K562 and YAC target cells in a 4-hr ^{51}Cr release assay in the presence of various concentrations of anti-NK-1 antiserum. E:T ratio was 100:1 in each case. Each value of lysis is a mean of three replicate ± SD.

The Role of the Fc Portion of Bound Alloantibodies in Augmenting the Anti-K562 NK Activity of Mouse Spleen Cells

K562 cells are known to have Fc receptors for Ig molecules (19) and the improved interaction between antibody-coated NK cells and K562 target cells could be a result of the interaction of the Fc portion of bound antibody molecules with the Fc receptors on K562 cells. To test this possibility, the effect of protein A on alloantiserum-induced anti-K562 NK activity was studied. For this purpose, C57BL/6J spleen cells were pretreated with suboptimal concentrations of anti-H-2^b antiserum and washed. The NK activity of control and alloantiserum-treated spleen cells was then determined against K562 target cells in the presence of different concentrations of protein A. Data obtained from three experiments are given in Table 3. In each experiment, anti-K562 NK activity of control spleen cells was not significantly altered by protein A. However, protein A inhibited the augmented anti-K562 lysis by anti-H-2^b antiserum-treated spleen cells. Since protein A binds the Fc region of immunoglobulins, the results indicate a central role for the Fc portion of bound alloantibodies on NK cells in the phenomenon of augmentation of anti-K562 NK activity by alloantiserum-treated mouse spleen cells.

In order to confirm the role of the Fc region of alloantibody in the NK augmentation phenomenon, we prepared the $F(ab)_2$ fractions from anti-H-2 antisera and tested their effect on the anti-K562 NK activity of mouse spleen cells. Anti-H-2^b (DBA/2 anti-C57BL/6) and anti-H-2^d (C57BL/6 anti-DBA/2) antisera were used as starting material for the preparation of $F(ab)_2$. EL-4 (H-2^b) or P815 (H-2^d) tumor cells were used for testing the binding ability of $F(ab)_2$ fractions with the cell membrane associated alloantigens. Results in Fig. 5 indicate that anti-H-2^b antiserum-treated EL-4 cells could be stained using either an anti-$F(ab)_2$ or anti-Fc reactive FITC-tagged rabbit antiserum. EL-4 cells reacted with the $F(ab)_2$

TABLE 3

Effect of Protein A on the Anti-H-2 Alloantiserum-Augmented NK Activity of Mouse Spleen Cells against K562 Cells

Treatment to effector spleen cells[a]	Concentration of protein A (μg/ml)	Percentage K562 lysis[b]		
		Expt. 1	Expt. 2	Expt. 3
None	0.0	7.0 ± 0.1	9.2 ± 0.2	6.7 ± 0.5
	25.0	7.2 ± 0.2	9.4 ± 0.9	5.8 ± 0.5
	50.0	6.7 ± 0.7	8.7 ± 0.7	5.7 ± 0.5
	100.0	6.3 ± 0.6	8.9 ± 0.3	5.8 ± 0.2
Anti-H-2^b antiserum	0.0	13.7 ± 0.4	15.8 ± 0.5	19.8 ± 0.7
	25.0	9.4 ± 0.4	11.4 ± 0.7	7.7 ± 0.6
	50.0	8.6 ± 1.0	10.8 ± 0.2	7.1 ± 0.6
	100.0	6.4 ± 0.8	10.1 ± 0.9	6.2 ± 0.8

[a] In each experiment, C57BL/6J mouse spleen cells (10×10^6/ml in RPMI + 10% FCS) were treated with 1:500 dilution of anti-H-2^b antiserum for 30 min in ice and then washed twice with fresh medium.

[b] NK activity of control or anti-H-2^b antiserum-treated cells were tested against K562 target cells in a 4-hr ^{51}Cr release assay in the presence of different concentrations of protein A. Each value of percentage lysis is a mean of four replicate observations ±SD.

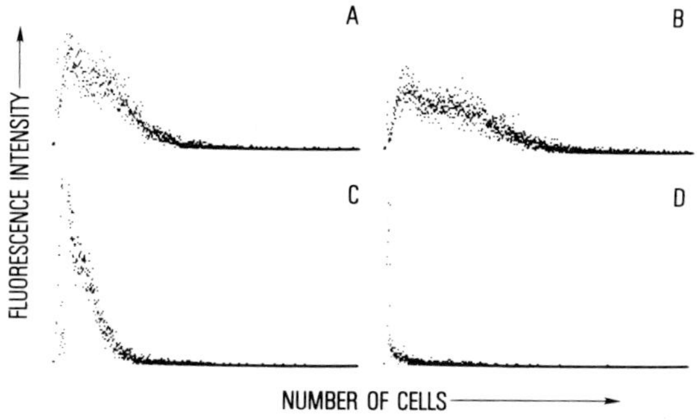

FIG. 5. Binding of anti-H-2^b alloantibodies and its $F(ab)_2$ fragment to EL-4 tumor cells. EL-4 tumor cells 10^7/ml were treated with 1:20 dilution of an anti-H-2^b antiserum or 200 μg/ml $F(ab)_2$ fraction derived from anti-H-2^b antiserum, for 30 min at 4°C. After two washings each cell preparation was incubated with FITC-tagged rabbit antisera directed against $F(ab)_2$ or Fc regions of mouse IgG. Cells were washed three times with PBS and suspended at 0.5×10^6/ml concentration in PBS. These cell suspensions were analyzed for spectrum of fluorescein-stained cells on a fluorescein-activated cell sorter (Ortho). EL-4 cells treated with (A) anti-H-2^b antiserum followed by rabbit antimouse $F(ab)_2$ antiserum–FITC, (B) anti-H-2^b antiserum followed by rabbit anti-mouse Fc antiserum–FITC, (C) $F(ab)_2$ fragment from anti-H-2^b antiserum followed by rabbit anti-mouse $F(ab)_2$ antiserum–FITC, and (D) $F(ab)_2$ fragment from anti-H-2^b antiserum followed by rabbit anti-mouse Fc antiserum–FITC. Each staining pattern represents 10 to 11×10^3 cells.

fraction of anti-H-2^b antibodies could also be stained with FITC-tagged rabbit anti-mouse $F(ab)_2$ antiserum indicating that the $F(ab)_2$ fragment could bind alloantigens on the EL-4 cells. EL-4 cells treated with anti-H-2^b $F(ab)_2$ fraction, could not be stained with FITC-tagged rabbit anti-mouse Fc antiserum, indicating that intact IgG was not a significant contaminant of our $F(ab)_2$ preparation. The purity and binding capacity of the $F(ab)_2$ fractions isolated from an anti-H-2^d antiserum could also be shown by using P815 tumor cells (results not shown).

Results in Fig. 6 indicate that alloantiserum or the IgG alloantibody could augment the anti-K562 NK activity of mouse spleen cells but $F(ab)_2$ fragments derived from these alloantibodies were ineffective in this respect. Therefore, the augmentation of NK activity is not due to changes induced in NK cells by an Fc-deficient alloantibody because the intact Fc regions of bound alloantibody are necessary for this phenomenon.

Correlation of Alloantiserum NK Augmentation with the Presence of an Fc Receptor on Target Cells

From the results presented so far, it appears that the interaction of alloantibody attached to NK cells, with the Fc receptor on target cell may be crucial for the NK augmentation phenomenon. Since YAC cells do not express Fc receptors this may explain its lack of increased susceptibility to lysis by alloantibody-coated NK cells. This hypothesis was tested by using several Fc receptor negative or positive target cell lines. The presence of an Fc receptor on target cell lines was tested by staining the cells with a heat-aggregated IgG–FITC reagent (17). More than 90% of K562 cells and 40 to 60% of human lymphoblastoid cells could be stained with heat-aggregated IgG–FITC, whereas this reagent failed to detect a significant expression of Fc receptors on the YAC, MOLT-4, and EL-4 cell lines. Results in

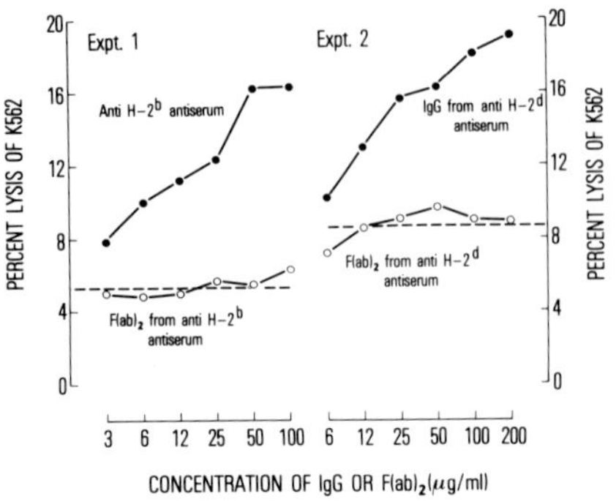

FIG. 6. Effect of anti-H-2 antiserum or IgG and $F(ab)_2$ fragment derived from anti-H-2 antisera, on the anti-K562 NK activity of mouse spleen cells. Spleen cells derived from C57BL/6 (Expt 1) or DBA/2 (Expt 2) were tested for NK activity against K562 target cells, at E:T ratio of 100:1, in a 4-hr (Expt 1) or 20-hr (Expt 2) ^{51}Cr release assay. Anti-H-2^b antiserum (IgG concentration, 5 mg/ml) as a source of intact anti-H-2^b alloantibodies, was used in Expt 1, whereas IgG alloantibodies isolated from anti-H-2^d antiserum were used in Expt 2. Different given concentrations of IgG or $F(ab)_2$ were added to the cytotoxocity medium and were present throughout the incubation period. Dotted lines (- - -) represent the control lysis of target cells.

Table 4 show that NK augmentation by alloantiserum could only be obtained on Fc receptor-positive target cell lines indicating that the augmentation of lysis by antibody-coated NK cells can only proceed when the target cells have membrane Fc receptors.

DISCUSSION

We have previously reported that the treatment of mouse spleen cells with specific anti-H-2 antisera resulted in an increased NK activity against the K562 human leukemia cell line (8). The presence of T cells, B cells, or macrophages in the treated population was not necessary for this effect and the alloantibodies appear to exert their effect directly by binding to the NK cells (8, 9). Alloantisera directed against single or multiple determinants in the K, D, or I regions of the H-2 complex were also effective in stimulating anti-K562 NK activity of mouse spleen cells which indicated that no particular H-2 subregion was more effective in this regard (9). The comparison of the NK augmenting effect of alloantisera with other augmenting agents like interferon, interferon inducers, and some mitogens revealed many mechanistic differences (10). The most intriguing characteristic of the effect of anti-H-2 antisera was that the augmented NK activity could only be demonstrated against certain target cell lines whereas all other activating agents could nonspecifically augment the NK activity against any target cell line.

Since anti-H-2 antisera treatment enhances anti-K562 NK activity of mouse spleen cells without influencing their anti-YAC NK activity, the possibility of two separate subsets of NK cells having differential susceptibility to aloantiserum was considered. Absorption of spleen cells on YAC monolayers, however, depleted both anti-YAC as well as anti-K562 NK activity. The depletion of NK cells from spleen cells by absorption on YAC cells is unlikely to be nonspecific since anti-YAC NK activity of mouse spleen cells could not be depleted by absorption on monolayers of mouse thymocytes, sheep erythrocytes, and NK-resistant L1210 tumor cells (21

TABLE 4

Effect of Treatment with Anti-H-2^b Antiserum on the NK Activity of C57BL/6J Mouse Spleen Cells against Several Human and Mouse Lymphoid Cell Lines[a]

Target cells	Type and origin	Expression of Fc receptors[b]	Expt. No.	Percentage target lysis by C57BL/6 spleen cells[c]: Control	+Anti-H-2^b antiserum
K562	Human leukemia	Yes	1	4.9 ± 0.2	20.1 ± 1.2[d]
			2	5.6 ± 0.8	24.6 ± 0.6[e]
			3	4.1 ± 0.1	17.6 ± 0.5[e]
V280	Human lymphoblastoid	Yes	1	16.9 ± 2.4	36.6 ± 1.2[d]
			2	22.0 ± 1.4	39.1 ± 2.4[e]
J180	Human lymphoblastoid	Yes	1	7.5 ± 1.1	17.7 ± 0.3[d]
			2	9.7 ± 0.4	19.5 ± 0.8[e]
B180	Human lymphoblastoid	Yes	1	14.9 ± 1.1	26.0 ± 2.1[d]
			2	18.1 ± 1.2	32.7 ± 0.4[e]
MOLT-4	Human leukemia	No	1	14.9 ± 2.4	10.8 ± 3.5[d]
			2	15.7 ± 0.9	11.9 ± 1.0[e]
EL-4	C57BL/6 lymphoma	No	1	1.6 ± 0.6	1.8 ± 0.2[e]
			2	2.2 ± 1.0	2.6 ± 0.5[e]
YAC	A/SN lymphoma	No	1	49.1 ± 1.0	32.3 ± 0.5[d]
			2	48.1 ± 2.8	35.1 ± 1.2[e]

[a] NK activity of C57BL/6 spleen cells was tested against various human and mouse lymphoid cell lines, in a 4-hr ^{51}Cr release assay at an E:T ratio of 100:1.

[b] Presence of receptors for Fc region of IgG on the target cells was studied by the binding of FITC–heat-aggregated IgG complex to the cell membranes.

[c] Each value of target lysis is a mean of three replicates ±SD.

[d] Anti-H-2^b antiserum was present at a 1:200 dilution in the assay medium.

[e] Effector cells were pretreated with anti-H-2^b antiserum by incubating 10^7 spleen cells/ml with 1:100 dilution of alloantiserum for 30 min in ice, followed by three washings with fresh medium.

and our unpublished data). Results of our absorption experiments suggested that the K562-reactive NK cells could also react with YAC cells. Evidence in the literature has indicated that NK cells may recognize a limited number of target structures which may be shared by susceptible cell lines (7, 22, 23). In view of that evidence and our experimental results, it appears likely that K562 and YAC cells share some surface determinants which are recognized by the same population of NK cells. This proposition was further supported by the experiments in which both K562 and YAC cells could competitively inhibit their own as well as each other's lysis by mouse spleen cells. However, it is interesting to note that when compared to K562 cells, YAC cells were cell for cell, more efficient inhibitors not only of anti-YAC NK activity but also of anti-K562 NK activity. NK cells responsible for both anti-YAC and anti-K562 activities, may therefore have a comparatively higher affinity for YAC cells than for K562 cells.

Treatment with anti-H-2 alloantisera would result in coating of spleen lymphocytes with alloantibodies and the presence of these antibodies on the cell membrane of NK cells may influence the quality of the NK cell–target interaction. Since alloantibody-coated NK cells have higher lytic activity selectively against K562 cells, alloantibodies may in some way increase the affinity of NK cells toward K562 target cells. Results obtained in target binding assays indicated a five to eight-fold increase in the percentage of non-B–non-T lymphocytes bound to K562 tumor cells in the presence of anti-H-2 antiserum, whereas a similar increase could not be demonstrated by using YAC target cells. Increased association of K562 target cells and NK cells may be the reason for high anti-K562 NK activity of alloantiserum-treated effector cells. Previous results and those presented in this paper showed that K562 but not YAC cells express Fc receptors on their cell surface (19, 20). Therefore, an increased association of alloantibody-coated NK cells with K562 cells could result from the interaction of the Fc portion of the coating alloantibody and the Fc receptors on the target cells. If the interaction of Fc receptors on K562 cells is responsible for the higher binding and enhanced lytic activity of alloantiserum-treated NK cells, the following predictions could be made and experimentally verified: (a) Any antiserum capable of coating NK cells should enhance anti-K562 NK activity and it should not be necessary to use a specific anti-H-2 antiserum. This point was verified by using an anti-NK-1 antiserum which reacts with an antigen present only on NK cells but not on T or B cells. Anti-NK-1 antiserum, like anti-H-2 antiserum, selectively enhanced the anti-K562 NK activity but had no similar effect on anti-YAC NK activity. (b) If interaction between antisera-coated NK cells and the Fc receptor of the target cells is crucial, the augmentation of anti-K562 NK activity should be blocked by an agent which can interfere with this interaction. Protein A, a reagent which binds the Fc portion of Ig and prevents its interaction with a cell-associated Fc receptor (24), was used to test this point. Though the basal level of anti-K562 NK activity of mouse spleen cells was not altered by protein A, the alloantiserum-induced augmentation of lytic activity was abrogated in the presence of protein A. Moreover, The $F(ab)_2$ fraction of alloantibodies failed to augment the anti-K562 cytotoxicity of mouse spleen cells even though it could bind membrane associated H-2 antigens. These experiments clearly established the important role of the Fc region of NK-cell bound antibody in bringing about the augmentation of cytotoxicity. (c) The presence of Fc receptors on target cells must constitute a necessary condition in order to get enhanced target lysis by alloantibody-coated NK cells. This was indeed found to be true and alloantibody treatment of mouse spleen cells enhanced their cytotoxicity against cell lines having an Fc receptor but not against cell lines without Fc receptors. Whether the presence of an Fc receptor constitutes a sufficient condition in this regard is not clear from our experiments. Our previous work has shown that alloantiserum did not augment the lysis of P815 and LI210 target cells by mouse spleen cells, even though both these cell lines express Fc receptors (8). However, it should be noted that both P815 and LI210 cell lines are not significantly susceptable to lysis by normal mouse spleen cells and this insensitivity to lysis by NK cells may be the reason for the lack of an alloantiserum effect.

The explanation we have proposed as the mechanism of selective enhancement of murine spleen cell NK activity by alloantiserum resembles the antibody-dependent cell-mediated cytotoxicity (ADCC) since in both phenomena an antibody bridge is formed between the target and effector cells. In ADCC, antibody binds to target cells and interacts with killer cells through an Fc receptor whereas the polarity of the antibody is reversed in the phenomenon of alloantiserum-induced augmentation of NK activity. It is possible that in both ADCC and "reverse ADCC" the role of an antibody bridge is to facilitate the interaction between effector amd target cells. This proposition would, however, require vigorous experimental verification.

In a recent paper, Brunda *et al.* (25) have confirmed several of our earlier observations regarding the enhancing effect of alloantiserum on the NK activity of normal or nude mouse spleen cells (8, 9), but did not favor the ADCC-like mechanism to explain the selective NK augmenting effect of alloantibodies. These authors have founded their conclusion on the following results: (a) anti-MOLT (a Fc receptor negative cell line) NK activity of mouse spleen cells could be augmented by alloantibodies and (b) protein A failed to block the NK augmenting effect of alloantibodies. We have obtained opposing results on both points. Reasons for this discrepancy in results using the MOLT-4 cell line are not clear. It is possible that the differences in the sublines of MOLT-4 may have contributed to this discrepancy, though this point would require additional investigation. In our experiments protein A could block the enhanced anti-K562 NK activity of mouse spleen cells *pretreated* with *suboptimal* concentrations of anti-H-2 antiserum. This protocol was used to minimize the concentrations of irrelevant IgG in the cytotoxicity assay medium, which would otherwise compete for binding with protein A. If alloantiserum is directly added to the assay medium, the resulting high concentration of IgG may lower the effective concentration of protein A below the levels which would completely block the Fc regions of effector cell bound alloantibodies. Total reduction of alloantiserum NK augmentation by protein A may not be able to be observed under these conditions. Since Brunda *et al.* have not presented either the experimental design or the data regarding their protein A experiments, it is difficult to ascertain the validity of their conclusion regarding ineffectiveness of protein A in blocking the alloantiserum effect. Finally, it is interesting to note that in the study of Brunda *et al.* (25), only IgG but not IgM-type alloantibodies could augment the NK activity; a result which would be predicted by the reverse ADCC hypothesis.

ACKNOWLEDGMENTS

We wish to thank Ms. Eleanor Wielechowski for her secretarial assistance and Ms. Charlotte Adler for preparing the illustrations. We also wish to thank Mr. Joe Chrest for helping in obtaining data given in Fig. 5.

REFERENCES

1. Herberman, R. B., Nunn, M. E., and Lavrin, D. H., *Int. J. Cancer* **16,** 216, 1975.
2. Herberman, R. B., Nunn, M. E., Holden, H. T., and Lavrin, D. H., *Int. J. Cancer* **16,** 230, 1975.
3. Kiessling, R., Klein, E., and Wigzell, H., *Eur. J. Immunol.* **5,** 112, 1975.
4. Kiessling, R., Klein, E., Pross, H., and Wigzell, H., *Eur. J. Immunol.* **5,** 117, 1975.
5. Nunn, M. E., Herberman, R. B., and Holden, H. T., *Int. J. Cancer* **20,** 381, 1977.
6. Saxena, R. K., Adler, W. H., and Nordin, A. A., *Immunol. Commun.* **9,** 371, 1980.
7. Roder, J. C., Rosen, A., Fanyo, E. M., and Troy, F. A., *Proc. Nat. Acad. Sci. USA* **76,** 1405, 1979.
8. Saxena, R. K., and Adler, W. H., *J. Immunol.* **123,** 846, 1979.
9. Saxena, R. K., Saxena, Q. B., and Adler, W. H., *Cell. Immunol.* **56,** 89, 1980.
10. Saxena, R. K., Adler, W. H., and Nordin, A. A., *Cell. Immunol.* **63,** 28, 1981.
11. Senik, A., Gresser, I., Maury, C., Gidlund, M., Orn, A., and Wigzell, H., *Cell. Immunol.* **44,** 186, 1979.

12. Kedar, E., Oritz de Landazuri, M., Bonavida, B., and Fahey, J. L., *J. Immunol. Methods* **5,** 97, 1974.
13. Stulting, R. D., and Berke, G., *J. Exp. Med.* **137,** 932, 1974.
14. Roder, J. C., Kiessling, R., Biberfeld, P., and Andersson, B., *J. Immunol.* **121,** 2509, 1978.
15. Julius, M. H., Simpson, E., and Herzenberg, L. A., *Eur. J. Immunol.* **3,** 645, 1973.
16. Ey, P. L., Prowse, S. J., and Jenkin, C. R., *Immunochemistry* **15,** 429, 1978.
17. Dickler, H. B., *J. Exp. Med.* **140,** 508, 1974.
18. Glimcher, L., Shen, F. W., and Cantor, H., *J. Exp. Med.* **145,** 1, 1977.
19. Huber, C. H., Sundstrom, C., Nilsson, K., and Wigzell, H., *Clin. Exp. Immunol.* **25,** 367, 1976.
20. de Landazuri, M. O., Silva, A., Alvarez, J., and Herberman, R., *J. Immunol.* **123,** 252, 1979.
21. Kumar, V., Leuvano, E., and Bennett, M., *J. Exp. Med.* **150,** 531, 1979.
22. Kiessling, R., and Wigzell, H., *Immunol. Rev.* **44,** 165, 1979.
23. Henney, C.S., Tracey, D. E., Durdik, J. M., and Klimpel, G., *Amer. J. Pathol.* **93,** 459, 1978.
24. Rosenblatt, J., Zeltzer, P. M., Portaro, J., and Seeger, R. C., *J. Immunol.* **118,** 981, 1977.
25. Brunda, M. J., Herberman, R. B., and Holden, H. T., *Int. J. Cancer* **27,** 205, 1981.

CELLULAR IMMUNOLOGY **65**, 131–141 (1981)

Increased Resistance to Listeria Monocytogenes following Subchronic Cyclophosphamide Exposure: Relationship to Altered Bone Marrow Function[1]

MICHAEL I. LUSTER,* GARY A. BOORMAN,† JACK H. DEAN,† LELA D. LAWSON,* RALPH E. WILSON,† LLOYD D. LAUER,† ROBERT W. LUEBKE,* JOHN RADER,† AND LUCILLA CAMPBELL†

**Laboratory of Environmental Chemistry and †National Toxicology Program, National Institute of Environmental Health Sciences, Research Triangle Park, North Carolina 27709*

Received June 23, 1981; accepted September 24, 1981

Mice administered multiple doses of cyclophosphamide demonstrated a marked resistance to infection with the bacterium, *Listeria monocytogenes*. In contrast, acute exposure rendered mice more susceptible to infection than untreated controls. Resistance to infection with *Listeria*, a facultative intracellular organism, is thought to be dependent upon normal antimicrobial activity early after infection and subsequently through generation of primed T cells. Examination of various macrophage and immune functions, however, failed to demonstrate a significant difference between the two cyclophosphamide-treated groups although both groups were immunosuppressed when compared to untreated controls. Adoptive transfer studies into X-irradiated recipients revealed that repopulation with bone marrow cells from subchronic but not acute cyclophosphamide-treated mice, restored resistance. Furthermore, the numbers of granulocyte/macrophage progenitor cells in the bone marrow were elevated in subchronically treated mice but not acute or unexposed controls. These data suggest the selection of a granulocyte/macrophage progenitor cell possessing a high degree of antilisterial activity following subchronic cyclophosphamide treatment. The effects induced by this exposure regimen are probably related to the enrichment of this cell population resulting from the cell cycle stage specific activity of the drug.

INTRODUCTION

Increased resistance to infection by *Listeria monocytogenes*, a facultative intracellular microorganism, occurs in nude mice through a T-cell-independent accessory mechanism (1) and C57B1 mice through an autosomal, dominant non-H-2-linked gene (2). Increased resistance also occurs extragenically in mice which have been starved (3), splenectomized (4), pretreated with kinins (5), or treated with macrophage activators (6, 7). On the other hand, decreased resistance to *Listeria* infection occurs in mice following treatment with various immunotoxicants such as X irradiation (8), cytoreductive drugs including some alkylating agents, folic acid antagonists, antimitotic agents, and purine analogs (9), or macrophage toxins such

[1] NTP No. 81-21.

0008-8749/81/170131-11/$02.00/0

as carrageenen (8). Early studies established that resistance to *Listeria* is dependent upon mononuclear phagocytes activated by non-T-cell mechanisms early in the infectious phase (1–2 days) and by specific cell-mediated immunity of the delayed hypersensitivity type later in the infection (10). However, recent studies have implied that increased or decreased resistance to *Listeria* may be more complicated than previously suggested and are not only affected by genetic factors (2) but also by aging (11), suppressor T cells (12), precommitted T cells (i.e., Lyt 1,2,3) (13), and bone marrow cells (14).

This report describes the differential affects resulting from acute and subchronic cyclophosphamide (CY) exposure on *Listeria* resistance and the relationship of this phenomenon to bone marrow functions. The effects of varying the dosage regimen on macrophage functions, immune tests and natural killer (NK) cell activity were also examined to determine whether this could account for the differential effects on host susceptibility.

MATERIALS AND METHODS

Animals and dosing regimens. Specific pathogen-free female $B_6C_3F_1$ (C57B1/6N × C_3H) mice weighing 18–22 g were obtained through NIH production contracts (Charles River, Portage, Mich.) C57B1/6 mice were obtained from Jackson Laboratories (Bar Harbor, Maine). The mice were 6–8 weeks of age, housed 10 per cage and allowed free access to food and water. CY was obtained from Mead Johnson and Company (Evansville, Ind.) and dissolved in sterile saline immediately prior to use. Mice were injected interperitoneally (ip) with either a single dose (acute) of CY (180 mg/kg) or multiple doses (subchronic) consisting of 36 mg/kg per day for 5 consecutive days (total of 180 mg/kg) in 0.1 ml of saline. Control mice received saline. Animals were used 3 days following the last injection in various immunological, bone marrow, and host susceptibility assays.

Listeria susceptibility assays. The bacterium, *L. monocytogenes* (Strain L242/73 type 4B) from a naturally infected mouse was used from the same frozen stock throughout the study. Organisms were grown overnight at 37°C in Trypticase soy broth. The number of bacteria in the broth, taken in a logarithmic phase culture, were quantitated turbidimetrically in a Beckman DB-G spectrophotometer at 540 nm and dilutions of the stock prepared in Hank's balanced salt solution (HBSS). The number of viable bacteria in all dilutions used for animal inoculations were confirmed by conventional pour plate count procedures in Trypticase soy agar. In survival studies, groups of 10 mice received 0.5 ml of a selected dilution intravenously (iv), and were then monitored daily for 14 days or until death. Preliminary experiments had indicated that iv administration of about 1×10^6 viable organisms resulted in an LD_{20} within 14 days. Bacterial enumeration in spleens were conducted on groups of five mice following a nonlethal iv infection (2×10^4 organisms) as described previously (9). Bacterial counts were determined with an automated Artek counter (Model 880, Artek Corp., Farmingdale, N.Y.). The data on bacterial enumeration in the spleens are expressed as geometric means of viable counts based upon logarithmic scale.

Cell preparations. Spleen cells were aseptically prepared as described previously (15). T-Cell enrichment was accomplished by passage of cells through columns containing glass wool followed by nylon wool as described by Trizio and Cudkowicz (16). Over 90% of the nucleated cells from the column passage stained with anti-Thy 1.2 (FITC-conjugated anti-mouse brain (C3H) antiserum; Litton Bionetics, Kensington, Md.). Macrophages were obtained from noninduced (resident) peritoneal cells through adherence to microexudate flasks according to the method of Mantovani *et al.* (17). All cell preparations contained greater than 95% viable cells as determined by trypan blue exclusion with over 95% stainable for nonspecific esterase.

Adoptive transfer of listerial production. Recipient mice received 600 rad of total body irradiation at 40 rad/min using a Philips MG301 Model X-ray machine. Twenty-four hours later recipients were injected iv with either spleen cells, T-enriched spleen cells, adherent resident peritoneal cells, or bone marrow cells from either normal, acute, or subchronic CY-exposed mice. Mice received 4×10^4 *Listeria* organisms 3 days after cell transfer and mortality was determined over a 14-day period. In other experiments, bacterial enumeration was performed in spleens of irradiated mice reconstituted with bone marrow cells and challenged 5 days later with 2×10^4 viable *Listeria.*

Hematology and determination of splenic lymphocyte populations. Hematological profiles included erythrocyte counts, leukocyte counts, and differential. Splenic B and T cells were quantitated by the presence of surface immunoglobulins (SIg^+) or Thy 1.2 antigen, respectively, by direct immunofluorescence employing monospecific antisera. The antisera utilized were FITC-conjugated goat anti-mouse polyvalent Ig (Microbiological Associates, Bethesda, Md.) absorbed with a 2% mixture of equal parts mouse liver powder and agarose and rabbit anti-mouse brain Thy 1.2 (C_3H). Both antisera were used at a final dilution of 1:20 and a total of 200 nucleated cells were counted from each preparation using a Leitz fluorescent microscope (Model 20EB).

Immunological tests. Delayed hypersensitivity responses to the T-dependent antigen, keyhole lymphet hemocyamin (KLH) were determined by a radiometric ear assay (18) based upon the original assay described by Lefford (19). Briefly, mice were sensitized by two subcutaneous injections of 0.1 mg KLH (Pacific Biomarine, Venice, Calif.) emulsified in incomplete Freund's adjuvant 9 days apart and challenge intradermally with 0.03 mg of KLH in the pinna of the left ear. The right ear served as a control and was injected with saline. Twenty-four hours following challenge 6-mm ear plugs were taken, solubilized, and prepared for scintillation counting. The data are expressed as an index:

$$\text{DHR index} = \frac{\text{cpm sensitive ear}}{\text{cpm control ear}}.$$

In other mice antibody responses to SRBCs were determined by Cunningham's modification of the Jerne plaque assay 4 days following iv immunization with 0.2 ml of a 5% solution of washed SRBCs (20).

Macrophage (MØ) function assays. The microculture growth inhibition assay (GIA) for murine macrophage (i.e., cytostasis) activation was performed with pooled plastic adherent resident peritoneal cells using MBL-(2) leukemia target cells. The details of this procedure have been described (21). The percentage inhibition of target cell proliferation was calculated by

$$\% \text{ growth inhibition} = 1 - \frac{\text{cpm MBL(2)} + \text{M}\phi \text{ from treated mice}}{\text{cpm MBL(2)} + \text{M}\phi \text{ from control mice}} \times 100.$$

For the phagocytosis assay, SRBCs were radiolabeled with $Na^{51}CrO_4$ (New England Nuclear, Boston, Mass.) and opsonized with anti-SRBC IgG (Cordis Laboratories, Miami, Fla.). Treated SRBCs were incubated with peritoneal cells in a 16-mm-well-diameter cluster dish (No. 3524, Costar Plastic, Inc., Cambridge, Mass.) as described by Snyderman *et al.* (22). The data are expressed as mean counts per minute of triplicate cultures as well as percentage change relative to the control group.

Natural killer cell activity. Natural killer (NK) cell activity was determined in spleens of mice using YAC-1 and RL♂-1 tumor cells as described by Herberman and Holden (23). The percentage cytolysis was determined by

$$\% \text{ cytolysis} = 1 - \frac{\text{CPME-SR}}{\text{CPMT-SR}} \times 100,$$

where CPME-SR is counts per minute in the experimental minus spontaneous release and CPMT-SR is counts per minute in total cells added (total release) minus spontaneous release.

Bone marrow parameters. Marrow cells were aseptically collected from femurs and dispersed and the number of nucleated cell numbers determined with a Coulter Counter. Bone marrow granulocyte–macrophage progenitor cells (CFU-GM) were assayed using a method described by Bradley and Metcalf (24). Briefly, nucleated marrow cells were added to culture media (10^5 cells/ml) containing 1.5% (w/v) methyl cellulose and 10% mouse lung-conditioned medium. One-milliliter aliquots of the cell suspension were placed in 35-mm petri dishes and allowed to incubate for 7 days at 37° in 7.5% CO_2 in air and the number of colonies per plate was determined using a stereomicroscope (Wild, Heerbrugg, Switzerland). Pleuripotent bone marrow progenitor cells, were quantitated by determining the number of colony-forming units in spleen (CFU-S) as described by Till and McCulloch (25). This was accomplished by iv injection of 5×10^4 nucleated bone marrow cells into 12-week-old irradiated (800 rad) $B_6C_3F_1$ recipients.

Statistical analysis. The Mann–Whitney *U* test or χ^2 test was employed to assess the significance of treatment effects.

RESULTS

Susceptibility of Mice to Listeria Following CY Exposure

Groups of 10 mice administered acute or subchronic doses of CY were given various concentrations of *L. monocytogenes* and survival was monitored daily over a 14-day period (Fig. 1). Administration of approximately 4×10^6 *Listeria* resulted in an LD_{50} in untreated $B_6C_3F_1$ mice. A similar dose of *Listeria* given to mice pretreated with a single administration of CY (180 mg/kg) resulted in 100% mortality, while 100% survival occurred in mice exposed to CY subchronically (36 mg/kg body wt daily for 5 days). Approximately 7×10^7 viable organisms were required to produce an LD_{50} in mice following subchronic CY exposure as compared to less than 5×10^5 in mice that had received a single exposure. The time to death between control and CY-treated groups were similar in all experiments (data not shown).

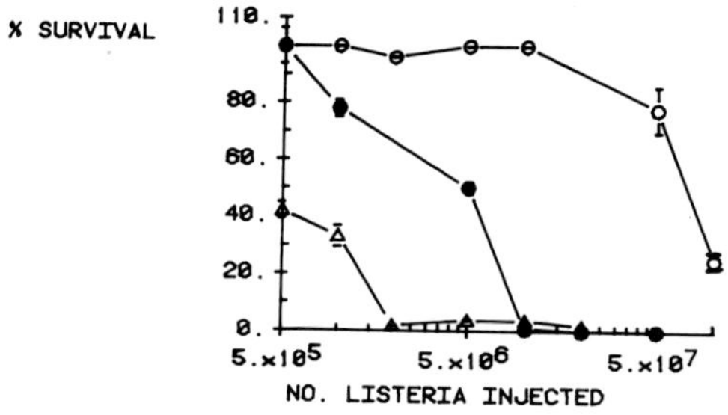

FIG. 1. Survival of mice infected with *L. monocytogenes* following saline (●), subchronic cyclophosphamide (○), or acute cyclophosphamide (△) exposure. Each value represents mean triplicate values of 10 mice per group ± SEM.

Organ Uptake of Listeria in CY-Treated Mice

Control and CY-treated mice were administered a nonlethal dose of *Listeria* (2×10^4) and the number of organisms in the spleen was determined over a 7-day period (Fig. 2). The number of bacteria in spleens of mice given a single injection of CY were similar to control values at 24 hr postinfection. However, after 24 hr a progressive bacterial growth occurred in the acutely exposed group eventually resulting in death. In contrast to acute exposure, subchronically treated mice revealed a persistent decrease in the number of organisms in the spleen when compared to controls which was comparable to survival data.

Peripheral Blood Values, Immune Parameters, and NK Activity

As summarized in Table 1, although CY treatment affected peripheral blood values, most immune parameters and NK activity, there were no marked differences between the two CY treatment groups to account for the difference in listerial resistance. Both acute and subchronic CY treatment-induced leukopenia although

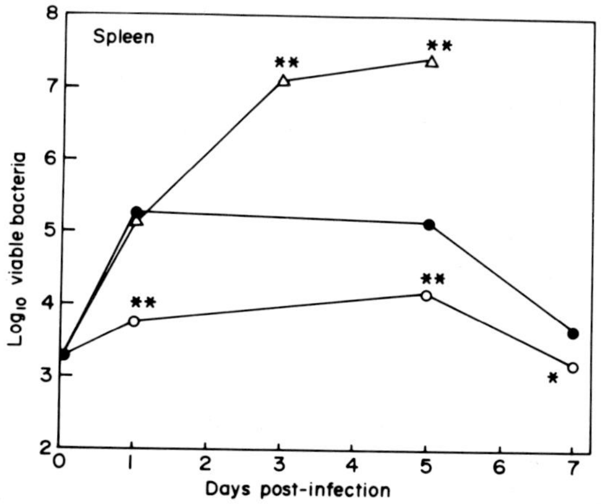

FIG. 2. Growth curve of *L. monocytogenes* in spleens of normal mice (●), acute CY-treated mice (△), and subchronic CY-treated mice (○). Each point represents a mean of five mice. Different from control values at $P < 0.01$ (**) and $P < 0.05$ (*) by Student's t test.

TABLE 1

The Effects of Varying CY Exposure Regimen on Peripheral Blood Values, Immmune Parameters and Natural Killer Cell (NK) Activity

Parameter	Treatment[a]		
	None	Acute	Subchronic
Peripheral blood			
WBC ($10^3/mm^3$)	7.4 ± 0.4	2.3 ± 0.2[b]	1.7 ± 0.2[b]
Lymphocytes (%)	82 ± 3	81 ± 2	87 ± 3
Monocytes (%)	1.5 ± 0.2	1.5 ± 0.2	2.0 ± 0.3
Spleen cell subpopulation[c]			
% SIg positive	41	23[b]	15[b]
% Thy-1,2 positive	37	15[b]	15[b]
Effector function			
DHR index[d]	2.9 ± 0.2	1.2 ± 0.1[b]	1.3 ± 0.1[b]
SRBC PFC/10^6 cells[e]	1348 ± 151	133 ± 17[b]	170 ± 40[b]
SRBC PFC/spleen ($\times 10^{-3}$)	246 ± 30	49 ± 5[b]	53 ± 7[b]
Macrophage function			
Phagocytosis of ^{51}Cr-SRBCs (cpm)	1387 ± 97	1073 ± 87	1365 ± 79
Cytostasis of MBL-2 tumor cells (cpm × 10^3)	85.4 ± 9.7	81.6 ± 11.8	81.6 ± 7.7
NK activity			
% Cytolysis with[f]			
YAC-1 tumor target	33.6	17.5[b]	9.4[b]
RL♂-1 tumor target	21.2	8.5[b]	0.5[b]

[a] All values represent mean ± SE of an average of eight mice. Separate animals were used for effector function tests since these assays required prior *in vivo* sensitization.

[b] Statistically different from untreated mice at $P < 0.05$.

[c] Represents percent positive cells stained with FITC-conjugated antiserum against mouse Igs or mouse Thy 1.2.

[d] DHRs were determined by administering 1 μCi/g body wt of [^{3}H]TdR (ip) into KLH sensitized mice 3 days following CY treatment followed 24 hr later by a challenge injection of KLH into the pinna of the left ear. The right ear was injected with saline and served as a control. The index was obtained by dividing cpm of the challenged ear by cpm of the control ear.

[e] Immunizations were performed 1 day after CY treatment by iv injection of 0.2 ml of a 5% solution of washed SRBCs 4 days prior to sacrifice.

[f] YAC-1 and RL♂-1 tumor cells were used at 100:1 effector to target cell ratios in a 4-hr ^{51}Cr release assay.

this was not selective to any particular white cell population. The percentages of B and T lymphocytes as determined by the presence of SIg^+ and Thy 1.2^+ surface markers, respectively, were likewise decreased following either CY treatment, indicating an absolute as well as relative decrease in cells possessing these markers compared to controls. Effector cell function was also equally and markedly depressed following either CY exposure. Suppression of cell mediated immunity was evidenced in CY-exposed mice by a reduced ability to mount delayed hypersensitivity responses to KLH in sensitized mice with both treatment groups showing almost total anergy. Humoral immune responses appeared also to be severely impaired in both treatment groups as evidenced by a 90% reduction in antibody placque-forming-cell numbers following immunization with sheep red blood cells.

Macrophage function was evaluated following CY exposure by quantitating *in vitro* phagocytosis using antibody coated, ^{51}Cr-radiolabeled SRBCs and cytostasis of MBL-2 leukemia target cells as measured in a growth inhibition assay. Phagocytic activity of adherent resident peritoneal cells from mice exposed to either CY exposure regimen was similar to control values. Similarly the ability of adherent peritoneal cells to inhibit the growth of MBL-2 leukemia target cells was not affected by CY treatment.

Natural killer cell activity was depressed by well over 50% in both CY treatment groups compared to control values. However, again there was no significant difference between the two treatment groups to suggest the dichotomy in listerial resistance.

Bone Marrow Functions

To evaluate whether acute and subchronic CY exposure had differential affects on myelotoxicity the bone marrow cellularity, hematopoietic stem cell growth (CFU-S) and *in vitro* colony growth of granulocyte–macrophage progenitor cells (CFU-GM) were examined (Table 2). A marked bone marrow hypocellularity occurred following acute CY exposure and to a much lesser extent in subchronically exposed mice. The numbers of CFU-S were increased almost two-fold in both treated groups. Opposing effects were seen in the two CY treatment groups with respect to the number of CFU-GM progenitors which were markedly increased following subchronic treatment but similar to control values in acute exposed mice.

Adoptive Transfer Studies

Adoptive cell transfer studies were conducted in an attempt to determine the cell type(s) responsible for the increased resistance to *Listeria* in mice subchronically exposed to CY (Table 3). In these experiments, spleen cells, T-cell-enriched spleen cells, adherent peritoneal cells, or bone marrow cells from normal or treated mice were transferred into X-irradiated recipients and subsequently challenged with *Listeria*. Approximately 4×10^4 organisms resulted in 60% mortality in irradiated, nonreconstituted controls. Mice repopulated with spleen cells or T-cell-enriched spleen cells from subchronically treated animals were as susceptible to *Listeria* as irradiated mice that had received either saline or spleen cells from untreated mice. On the other hand, some protection may have been afforded following adoptive

TABLE 2

Bone Marrow Cellularity and CFU Production following CY Administration[a]

Treatment	Nucleated cells/femur ($\times 10^{-6}$)	CFU-S/ 5×10^4 cells	CFU-GM/femur ($\times 10^{-8}$)
None	24.0 ± 1.6	8.3 ± 0.5	186 ± 20
Subchronic	19.9 ± 0.9[b]	13.5 ± 0.7[b]	258 ± 18[b]
Acute	7.9 ± 0.5[c]	15.2 ± 0.6[b]	176 ± 34

[a] Values represent mean ± SE of eight animals per group.
[b] Significantly different from controls at $P < 0.05$.
[c] Significantly different from controls at $P < 0.01$.

TABLE 3

Survival following *Listeria monocytogenes* Challenge in Irradiated Mice Repopulated with Cells from CY-Treated Mice[a]

Prior treatment of cell donors	Cell type transferred	Mortality/ No. tested	Percentage survival
None	None	13/21	38
None	Whole spleen cells	9/19	53
Subchronic CY	Whole spleen cells	12/19	37
Acute CY	Whole spleen cells	9/17	47
None	Bone marrow cells	0/10	100[b]
Subchronic CY	Bone marrow cells	0/10	100[b]
Acute CY	Bone marrow cells	8/10	20
Subchronic CY	T-Cell enriched spleens	5/10	50
Subchronic CY	Adherent cells	3/10	70

[a] Recipients received 600 rad on Day 0 and on Day 1 were injected iv with either saline, spleen cells (10^8), nylon wool-passed spleen cells (T-enriched; 5×10^7), adherent RPCs (2×10^7), or bone marrow cells (2.5×10^7) from control or CY-treated mice. On Day 4 all mice received 4×10^4 viable *Listeria*. This dose or organisms was not lethal (0 of 20) in untreated, nonirradiated control mice over a 14-day period.

[b] Significantly different from control values at $P < 0.05$ by χ^2 analysis.

transfer of adherent peritoneal cells (not significant) while marked protection ($P < 0.05$) against *Listeria* infection occurred in irradiated mice following transfer of bone marrow cells from either control mice or subchronically CY-exposed mice, but not bone marrow cells from mice that were administered a single dose of CY.

Table 4 depicts the growth of *Listeria* in spleens of irradiated mice reconstituted with bone marrow cells from normal or CY-treated mice. The differences between control and CY-treated mice were consistent with the earlier survival data. Mice repopulated with bone marrow cells obtained from subchronically exposed mice showed a significant decrease ($P < 0.05$) in the number of bacteria per spleen compared to mice reconstituted with bone marrow cells from normal or acute CY-exposed mice.

TABLE 4

Enumeration of *Listeria* in Spleens of Irradiated Mice Reconstituted with Bone Marrow Cells from CY-Treated Mice[a]

Repopulated	Treatment of cell donors	*Listeria*/spleen[b]
Yes	None	2.1×10^5
Yes	Subchronic CY	3.5×10^4[c]
Yes	Acute CY	6.0×10^5
No	—	$>10^8$[c]

[a] Twenty-four hours following irradiation, mice intravenously received 2.5×10^7 bone marrow cells, followed 5 days later with 2.0×10^4 *Listeria*. Five days following bacterial challenge, mice were sacrificed and organisms/spleen determined.

[b] Each value represents a mean of at least eight mice.

[c] Significantly different from control values at $P < 0.05$.

DISCUSSION

Studies initiated by Mackaness (10) demonstrated that resistance to *Listeria* infection during the first several days is dependent upon normal antimicrobial activity primarily through phagocytosis and killing by macrophages. Subsequently, resistance is dependent upon the induction of immunity through generation of primed T cells which activates the macrophage system resulting in increased microbicidal capacity. Consistent with this hypothesis, treatment of mice with substances which are toxic to macrophages or T lymphocytes will render animals more susceptible to infection (8, 9, 26). Conversely, immunopotentiators such as BCG or *Corynebacterium parvum* renders animals more resistant to infection (6, 7).

The present studies clearly demonstrate that subchronic CY exposure renders mice resistant to *Listeria* infection. On the other hand, acute CY exposure increases susceptibility to Listeria infection when compared to untreated controls and is consistent with earlier studies by Tripathy and Mackaness who also employed acute exposure (9). *Listeria* growth curves in spleens of mice following acute CY exposure indicate that rapid bacteria growth did not occur until several days following *Listeria* challenge. This is consistent with the view that CY preferentially affects lymphoid rather than myeloid cells (27) since Day 1 postinfection counts reflect nonspecific antimicrobial activity and Day 5 specific immunity. CY is a potent polyfunctional alkylating agent which exerts its cytotoxic action by crosslinking double-stranded DNA (28). The alkylating agent acts at the premitotic resting phase (G_2) as well as the DNA-synthetic phase and is extremely toxic to precursors of the erythroid and lymphoid but less so for the myeloid series (27, 29). In addition to affecting lymphoid precursor cells, CY may effect lymphoid cells at more advanced stages of differentiation including committed lymphocytes (30). CY-induced immunotoxicity has been reported to result in a spectrum of immune dysfunction ranging from a simple depletion of lymphocytes (30) to a functional impairment of the remaining lymphocytes (31).

In these respects, both acute and subchronic CY-treated mice resulted in lymphoid depletion, suppressed effector cell functions and intact macrophage functions which is consistent with the above-described published reports. Since this immunological profile occurred as a result of acute CY treatment as well as subchronic exposure, it would appear that the enhanced resistance in the latter group is not a result of alterations in established mechanisms of *Listeria* resistance. Recently, Kaufman *et al.* (13) demonstrated that the Lyt $1,2,3^+$ T cell and not the more mature Lyt 1 or Ly 2,3 populations may be involved in protection against *Listeria* infection as well as delayed-type hypersensitivity to listerial antigens. CY has been shown to have selective effects on T-cell subclasses, having been reported, under certain dosage regimens to spare Lyt $1^-,2,3^+$-bearing lymphocytes (32). However, lymphocytotoxicity testing employing Lyt-specific antisera did not show this to be the case since both subchronic and acute CY exposure caused a similar effect on Lyt cell populations (unpublished data). Both exposure regimens also depressed natural killer cell activity indicating a lack of relationship with altered *Listeria* susceptibility.

The two cyclophosphamide exposure regimens induced differential effects on bone marrow function. Marked hypocellularity occurred following acute CY exposure and to a lesser extent following subchronic exposure. In contrast to cellularity, the number of CFU-S were enhanced in both subchronic and particularly acutely exposed mice, while the number of CFU-GM were markedly elevated following subchronic exposure. Earlier studies have demonstrated that treatment with cell cycle stage-specific (CCSS) drugs, like CY, has a selective cytoreductive action on the bone marrow (27). Following administration of these agents is an initial decrease in the number of CFU-S and CFU-GM followed later by increases in both primary and secondary hemopoietic organs (33, 34). The mechanisms responsible for this "repletion/depletion" phenomenon following treatment with CCSS agents are not clearly defined but vary depending upon the degree of cell kill, available space in secondary hemopoietic organs, and dosage regimens (35). In this respect, Buhles and Shifrine (36) reported that CFU-GM production in the bone marrow decreases immediately following an acute CY dose (250 mg/kg) which persists for days returning to normal levels by Day 4. In contrast, when two doses of CY were administered (250 mg/kg followed by 100 mg/kg 3 days later), while bone marrow hypocellularity also occurred, there was a 20-fold greater than normal proportion of CFU-GM in the bone marrow.

In order to determine whether the differential affects on bone marrow functions induced by the two CY dosage regimens were related to listerial resistance, adoptive cell transfer studies were undertaken. Although survival data of this type should be interpreted with caution, it appears reasonable to assume that transfer of bone marrow cells from either normal or subchronically treated mice into irradiated recipients resulted in the ability of these animals to resist infection while transfer of bone marrow cells from acutely exposed mice failed to restore resistance. These data then support the theory that granulocyte–macrophage progenitor cells from the bone marrow can confer resistance against *Listeria* infection. This was further supported when spleens of irradiated mice repopulated with bone marrow cells from subchronically exposed mice were found to contain less bacterial organisms than spleens of irradiated mice repopulated with bone marrow cells from acute treated or control animals. Previous studies have shown that normal *Listeria* resistance can be restored in irradiated mice by bone marrow cell repopulation but not by transfer of peripheral lymphocytes or macrophages (14). Bennett and Baker (37) reported that mice treated with 300 mg/kg CY also demonstrated increased resistance to *Listeria* infection. They assumed this phenomenon was due to increased macrophage activation since treatment of the mice with silica abrogated the phenomenon.

Previous studies in which treatment with macrophage activators increased resistance to *Listeria* infection demonstrated the protective role of nonspecifically activated macrophages in this infection (6, 7). The data in the present study would suggest that a granulocyte–macrophage precursor cell in the bone marrow, which coincidentally is activated or selectively increased by subchronic CY treatment, is also capable of conferring resistance against *Listeria* infection although macrophage activation or immunoenhancement does not occur. The origin and function of this cell does not coincide with natural killer cells which possess antitumor activity. That a preexisting mechanism of enhanced resistance may occur in nature in response to bacterial infection is suggested by the fact that nude mice maintained under germ-free conditions are more resistant to *Listeria* infection than their normal littermates although they lack mature T cells and do not possess an activated macrophage population (38). Macrophage activation occurs in nude mice held under conventional housing (1). In any case, it would appear that accessory mechanisms, either in a quiescent or minimally active state, exist in normal mice that play a role in naturally minimizing bacterial growth early in infection until normal T-cell immunity has developed.

ACKNOWLEDGMENT

The authors are grateful to S. Wilkins for preparing the manuscript.

REFERENCES

1. Newborg, M. F. and North, R. J., *J. Immunol.* **124,** 571, 1980.
2. Sadarangani, C., Skamene, E., and Kongshaven, P. A. L., *Infect. Immun.* **28,** 381, 1980.
3. Wing, J. E., and Young, J. B., *Infect. Immun.* **28,** 771, 1980.
4. Skamene, E., Chayasirisobkon, W., and Konshaen, P. A. L., *Immunology* **34,** 901, 1978.
5. Fauve, R. M., and Hevin, M. B., *Ann. Immunol.* **130C,** 743, 1979.
6. Bennedsen, J., Riisgaard, S., Rhodes, J. M., and Larsen, S. O., *Acta Pathol. Microbiol. Scand. Sect. C* **85,** 246, 1977.
7. Yoshikai, Y., Miake, S., Matsumoto, T., Nomoto, K., and Takeya, K., *Immunology* **40,** 295, 1980.
8. Tatsukawa, K., Mitsuyama, M., Takeya, K., and Nomoto, K., *J. Gen. Microbiol.* **115,** 161, 1979.
9. Tripathy, S. P., and Mackaness, G. B., *J. Exp. Med.* **131,** 1, 1969.
10. Mackaness, G. B., *J. Exp. Med.* **116,** 381, 1962.
11. Matsumoto, T., Miake, M., Mitsuyama, K., and Nomoto, K., *J. Clin. Lab. Immunol.* **2,** 55, 1979.
12. Poirot, M. K., and Myers, R. L., *Immunology* **40,** 117, 1980.
13. Kaufmann, S. H. E., Simon, M. M., and Hahn, H., *J. Exp. Med.* **150,** 1033, 1979.
14. Campbell, P. A., Martens, B. L., Cooper, H. R., and McClatchy, J. K., *J. Immunol.* **112,** 1407, 1974.
15. Luster, M. I., Boorman, G. A., Dean, J. H., Harris, M. W., Luebke, R. W. Padarathsingh, M. L., and Moore, J. A., *Int. J. Immunopharmacol.* **2,** 301, 1980.
16. Trizio, D., and Cudkowicz, G., *J. Immunol.* **113,** 1093, 1974.
17. Mantovani, A., Jerrells, T. R., Dean, J. H., and Herberman, R. B., *Int. J. Cancer* **23,** 18, 1978.
18. Luster, M. I., Boorman, G. A., Dean, J. H., Luebke, R. W., and Lawson, L. D., *J. Reticuloendo. Soc.* **28,** 561, 1980.
19. Lefford, M. J., *Int. Arch. Allergy Appl. Immunol.* **47,** 570, 1974.
20. Cunningham, A. J., *Nature (London)* **207,** 1106, 1965.
21. Dean, J. H., Padarathsingh, M. L., and Keep, L., *Cancer Treat. Rep.* **66,** 1807, 1978.
22. Snyderman, R., Rike, M. C., Fischer, D. G., and Koren, H. S., *J. Immunol.* **119,** 2060, 1977.
23. Herberman, R. B., and Holden, H. T., *Advan. Cancer Res.* **27,** 305, 1978.
24. Bradley, J. R., and Metcalf, D., *Aust. J. Exp. Biol. Med. Soc.* **44,** 287, 1966.
25. Till, J. E., and McCulloch, E. A., *Radiat. Res.* **14,** 213, 1961.
26. Hahn, H., *Infect. Immun.* **10,** 1105, 1974.
27. Bruce, W. R., Meeker, B. E., and Valeriote, F.H., *J. Nat. Cancer Inst.* **37,** 233, 1966.
28. Palme, G., and Liss, E., *Animicrob. Ag. Cheoher* **5,** 718, 1966.
29. Rhodes, J. M., Bennedsen, J., Larsen, S. A., Riisgaard, J., and Sparck, J. V., *Infect. Immun.* **23,** 24, 1979.
30. Stockman, G. D., Hein, L. R., South, M. A., and Trentin, J. T., *J. Immunol.* **110,** 227, 1973.
31. Dean, j. H., Padarathsingh, M. L., Jerrells, F. R., Keep, L., and Northing, J. H., *Drug. Chem. Tox.* **2,** 133, 1979.
32. Turk, J. L., and Poulter, L. W., *Clin. Exp. Immunol.* **10,** 296, 1972.
33. McNeil, T. A., *Immunology* **18,** 61, 1970.
34. Quesenberry, P. J., Morley, M., Miller, K., Howard, D., and Stohlman, F., *Blood* **41,** 391, 1973.
35. Uyeki, E. M., Pazdernik, T. L., and Ashkar, A. E., *J. Pharmacol. Exp. Ther.* **198,** 246, 1976.
36. Buhles, W. C., and Shifrine, M., *J. Reticuloendothel. Soc.* **21,** 285, 1977.
37. Bennett, M., and Baker, E. E., *Cell. Immunol.* **33,** 203, 1977.
38. Meltzer, M. S., *Cell. Immunol.* **22,** 176, 1976.

CELLULAR IMMUNOLOGY **65**, 142–151 (1981)

Primary and Secondary Autologous Mixed-Lymphocyte Interactions in Mice Occur via Antigens Encoded by Genes in the I Region of the Major Histocompatibility Complex

MAUREEN H. BOCCHIERI, JEFFREY A. WOLOS, AND J. BRUCE SMITH[1]

Institute for Cancer Research, Fox Chase Cancer Center, Philadelphia, Pennsylvania 19111

Received July 29, 1981; accepted October 5, 1981

The antigens stimulating the autologous mixed-lymphocyte reactions (AMLR) were studied in experiments employing specific blocking antisera and through panels of secondary stimulating cells differing in the MHC. Antisera directed to the entire I region, I-A, I-EC, or $A_\epsilon E_\alpha$ were all effective in blocking the primary AMLR. A principal role for those determinants encoded in I-A was indicated by secondary stimulation experiments. In secondary cultures, I-EC encoded determinants generated weaker responses in the absence of I-A homology.

INTRODUCTION

The autologous mixed-lymphocyte reaction (AMLR) measures the *in vitro* proliferative response of T cells to autologous or syngeneic non-T cells. AMLR responses occur in healthy humans (1, 2) guinea pigs (3), and mice (4). They are deficient in autoimmune mouse strains (4, 5) and in humans with lymphoproliferative and autoimmune disease (2, 6, 7).

The responder T cells in mice bear the Ly 1^+ phenotype (8). The responder population in humans falls within the subset of T cells which respond to the mitogen concanavalin A and are distinct from alloreactive T cells (9). Both suppressor (10, 11) and amplifier (12, 13) functions have been found to be properties of T cells recoverable from AMLR cultures. Cell surface antigens encoded by genes within the I region of the major histocompatibility complex (MHC) have been implicated in the stimulation of allogeneic lymphocytes (14) and in the response of syngeneic T cells to reticulum cell sarcoma cells of SJL mice (15). A significant immunoregulatory role of Ir genes has been well documented (16).

Recent reports suggest a role of Ia antigens in the AMLR recognition event in mice (17, 18) and humans (19). We have, therefore, undertaken a more detailed examination of the role of Ia antigens in the AMLR in mice. Antibody blocking studies and secondary stimulations suggest that AMLR occur via recognition of antigens encoded by the I-A and/or I-EC subregions of the MHC.

[1] To whom reprint requests and correspondence should be addressed. Current address: Thomas Jefferson University Medical College, 1015 Walnut Street, Room 613, Philadelphia, Pa. 19107.

0008-8749/81/170142-10/$02.00/0

MATERIALS AND METHODS

Mice. C58/J mice were purchased from Jackson Laboratories (Bar Harbor, Maine). All other strains were bred and maintained in the Laboratory Animal Facility of the Institute for Cancer Research. A·TL mice and mice of the B10 congenic stains used were gifts from Doctors Peter Doherty, Peter Wettstein, and Barbara Knowles of the Wistar Institute, Philadelphia, Pennsylvania.

Cell cultures. Spleen cell cultures for AMLR and for mixed-lymphocyte reactions (MLR) were prepared in RPMI 1640 containing 10% fetal calf serum (Rehatuin), 5×10^{-5} *M* 2-ME, 5 m*M* Hepes, and 100 units/ml penicillin and 100 μg/ml streptomycin as reported previously (4, 8). In brief, the responders were nylon wool nonadherent T cells and the stimulators were mitomycin C-treated (25 $\mu g/10^7$ cells for 30 min at 37°C) whole spleen cells. All primary cultures were set up in triplicate at an 8:3 responder-to-stimulator cell ratio and incubated at 37°C in 5% CO_2 for 4 days (MLR) or 5 days (AMLR).

For the secondary stimulation experiments, replicate cultures of 5×10^6 nylon wool nonretained T cells and 5×10^6 mitomycin C-treated syngeneic spleen cells in flat-bottom tissue culture plates (Linbro, Hamden, Conn.) were incubated at 37°C in 5% CO_2 for 9 or 10 days. At the end of this culture period, replicate wells were pooled, and viable cells were restimulated with spleen cells from a variety of mouse strains. The number of responding and stimulating cells in these cultures are indicated in the tables. Triplicate cultures were reincubated for 2 days, at which time 0.5 μCi/well ^{125}I-Udr (New England Nuclear, Boston, Mass.) was added. All cultures were harvested 4 hr later and isotope incorporation was measured in a gamma spectrometer. All results are given as the mean net increase over background, in counts per minute, of stimulated cultures (Δcpm) ± standard deviation and analyzed for statistical significance by the Mann–Whitney test.

In some experiments, populations of cells responding to syngeneic stimulation were enriched by fractionation on a discontinuous Percoll gradient (9, 20). Briefly, replicate cultures were pooled on Day 4 and resuspended in 2 ml of 100% Percoll (made up of 9 parts Percoll, 1 part 10× hanks balanced salt solution). Two milliliters of 70% Percoll, 3 ml of 60% Percoll, 3 ml of 50% Percoll, and 2 ml of 40% Percoll were gently layered over the cell suspension. The gradient was centrifuged at 1000*g* for 10 min at room temperature and the cells at each interface were removed by pipetting, washed, and counted. These populations were reincubated until Day 9 or 10. At this time, they were washed, counted and restimulated according to the preceding protocol.

Antisera. Broad spectrum anti-Ia^k (A·TH and anti-A·TL) was purchased from Cedarlane Laboratories (Accurate Chemical and Scientific Corporation, Hicksville, N.Y.). This antiserum was diluted in culture medium and added to the cell cultures at the final concentrations and times indicated in the tables, or used at 1% concentration to pretreat responder or stimulator cell populations for 1 hr at room temperature. Pretreated cells were washed and adjusted to the appropriate cell concentrations before culture.

Monoclonal anti-I-A (anti-Ia^k, specificity 2) was purchased from Becton–Dickinson, Mountain View, California. Monoclonal anti-I-A (anti-Ia^k, specificity 17), originally made in the Herzenberg laboratory, was supplied by Doctor Bondada Subbarao of the Institute for Cancer Research. Anti-I-EC (anti-I-E^k, I-C^d S^d G^d), an alloantiserum prepared by immunizing (B10X HTI)F_1 with B10 A (3R) lymph nodes and spleen, and monoclonal Y 17 (anti-I-AE of the k haplotype), were the gifts of Drs. Donal Murphy and Charles A. Janeway, Jr., and Mr. Ethan A. Lerner, Yale University. All antisera were added to the cell cultures at the final concentrations shown in the tables. Normal mouse serum (NMS) was a pool prepared from animals at the Institute for Cancer Research and was syngeneic to the responding cell population.

RESULTS

Placement of the AMLR stimulatory antigens within H-2. Cells from BALB/c primary AMLR cultures were restimulated with spleen cells from various H-2 identical or nonidentical mouse strains. The response on Day 2 is presented in Table 1. As expected, restimulation with BALB/c produced a substantial secondary response. A similar response was observed to DBA/2, an H-2 identical strain. Only a low level response was seen toward BALB.B, a strain genetically identical to BALB/c except at H-2, and to C3H and C57BL/6, two genetically dissimilar strains.

Table 2 shows the response of Percoll fractions of BALB/c AMLR cultures to a number of mouse strains. Fraction 1, the cells at the 40/50 interface, was the most responsive to restimulation on Day 10. This fraction contained approximately 14% of the cells placed on the gradient and was composed primarily of large cells (blasts). Fraction 2, the 50/60 interface, was comprised of a mixture of small and large cells and had a weaker secondary response. Fraction 3, containing all small cells, was completely unresponsive. In this experiment, neither BALB.B nor BALB.K, two strains identical to BALB/c except at H-2, were able to elicit a secondary response. In addition, B10 A, which shares the D end of H-2 with BALB/c, failed to cause a secondary response.

I Region association of AMLR stimulatory antigens. AMLR cultures from B10·A mice were separated on discontinuous Percoll gradients and the cells in the large cell fraction were restimulated by B10 congenic and allogeneic strains (Table 3). Strain B10·A(4R), sharing I-A and the K end of H-2 with B10·A, induced a secondary response similar to that observed with B10·A, the primary stimulator. Congenic strain B10·HTT sharing I-E with B10·A, failed to stimulate a secondary response. B10·S(9R) stimulator cells, sharing JEC in the I region, and allogeneic

TABLE 1

BALB/c AMLR Secondary Stimulation[a]

Restimulating cells[b]	Δcpm, Day 2
BALB/c (d)	15,799 ± 1814
DBA/2 (d)	19,451 ± 1105
BALB.B (b)	3,508 ± 46
C3H (k)	3,674 ± 255
C57BL/6(b)	3,525 ± 378

[a] Responders + stimulators at a concentration of 1.5×10^5:3×10^5 per well.

[b] H-2 haplotype is indicated in parentheses.

TABLE 2

BALB/c AMLR Secondary Stimulation[a]—Percoll Fractions[b]

Restimulating cells[c]	Responders (Δcpm ± SD) Fraction 1 (40/50) (blast cells)	Fraction 2 (50/60) (mixed)	Fraction 3 (60/70) (small cells)
BALB/c (d)	31,878 ± 793	7599 ± 678	10 ± 36
BALB.B (b)	9,034 ± 2590	3155 ± 574	212 ± 75
BALB.K (k)	6,958 ± 986	2491 ± 469	273 ± 106
B10·A (k/d)	9,007 ± 1109	2007 ± 263	128 ± 34
C57BL/6 (b)	8,162 ± 465	3104 ± 92	139 ± 13

[a] Responders + stimulators at a concentration of 1.5×10^5:3×10^5 per well.
[b] Fractionation of responder cells on step gradients of Percoll is described in the text.
[c] H-2 haplotype is indicated in parentheses.

strain BALB/c cells, which share the I-C region with B10·A, elicited between one-third and one-half of the autologous reaction.

Table 4 presents the results of another panel of secondary stimulators. The primary AMLR in this experiment was done with C58 mice. Secondary stimulators sharing the entire I region, A·TL, or only I-A, B10·A(4R), produced proliferation similar to autologous cells. Homology at I-EC, B10·HTT, or I-JE, B10·S(9R), again gave lower proliferation. C57BL/6 and SJL, which were totally disparate from C58 in the I region, did not stimulate a response.

Blocking of primary AMLR with I region antibodies. The results of preincubating, in the absence of complement, either the responder or the stimulator population with 1% A·TH anti-A·TL are shown in Table 5. Pretreatment of the responding population in the C58 primary AMLR slightly enhanced the proliferation, although the increase observed was not statistically significant. The C58 response to the MHC identical but Mls locus disparate C3H stimulator (C58 is Mls^b, C3H

TABLE 3

B10·A Secondary Stimulation[a]—Percoll Fraction 1[b]

Restimulating cells	MHC[c] K	I-A	I-B	I-J	I-E	I-C	D	Δcpm ± SD
B10·A	k	k	k	k	k	d	d	15,974 ± 1826
B10·A(4R)	k	k	b	b	b	b	b	14,919 ± 3679
B10·HTT	s	s	s	s	k	k	d	1,826 ± 1311
B10·S(9R)	s	s	?	k	k	d	d	5,796 ± 1306
BALB/c	d	d	d	d	d	d	d	7,487 ± 1064

[a] Responders + stimulators at a concentration of 7.5×10^4:2.5×10^5 per well. Pulsed and harvested on Day 2.
[b] See text for details.
[c] Major histocompatibility complex. Shared regions are underlined.

TABLE 4

C58 Secondary Stimulation[a]—Percoll Fraction2[b]

Restimulating cells	MHC[c]							Δcpm ± SD
		I						
	K	A	B	J	E	C	D	
C58	$\underline{k}$	$\underline{k}$	$\underline{k}$	$\underline{k}$	$\underline{k}$	$\underline{k}$	$\underline{k}$	20,912 ± 874
A·TL	s	$\underline{k}$	$\underline{k}$	$\underline{k}$	$\underline{k}$	$\underline{k}$	d	17,649 ± 662
B10·A(4R)	$\underline{k}$	$\underline{k}$	b	b	b	b	b	16,380 ± 892
B10·HTT	s	s	s	s	$\underline{k}$	$\underline{k}$	d	10,634 ± 356
B10·S(9R)	s	s	?	$\underline{k}$	$\underline{k}$	d	d	7,368 ± 442
C57BL/6	b	b	b	b	b	b	b	4,655 ± 225
SJL	s	s	s	s	s	s	s	3,933 ± 709

[a] Responders + stimulators at a concentration of 1.2×10^5:3×10^5 per well. Pulsed and harvested on Day 2.

[b] See text for details.

[c] Major histocompatibilty complex. Shared regions are underlined.

is Mls[c]) was unaffected by this pretreatment. As a control, no effect was seen when C58 responders to an allogeneic MHC (C57BL/6) were pretreated.

When the stimulating populations, however, were pretreated with A·TH anti-A·TL (anti-Ia[k]) both the C58 AMLR and the C58 response to C3H were signif-

TABLE 5

Pretreatment of Responder or Stimulator Cells with 1% A·TH anti-A·TL

Responder	Stimulator	Cell Treated	Δcpm ± SD	Percentage blocking or stimulation[a]
C58	C58	Neither	8,357 ± 4464	—
C58	C58	Responder	13,853 ± 3869	+66
C58	C_3H	Neither	12,722 ± 5945	—
C58	C_3H	Responder	13,275 ± 4947	+4
C57BL/6	C57BL/6	Neither	15,546 ± 3952	—
C57BL/6	C57BL/6	Responder	22,636 ± 6114	+45*
C58	C57BL/6	Neither	82,799 ± 2490	—
C58	C57BL/6	Responder	90,484 ± 8548	+9
C58	C58	Neither	32,008 ± 7883	—
C58	C58	Stimulator	13,965 ± 4388	56*
C58	C_3H	Neither	69,470 ± 2733	—
C58	C_3H	Stimulator	10,738 ± 7185	85*
C57BL/6	C57BL/6	Neither	15,546 ± 3952	—
C57BL/6	C57BL/6	Stimulator	14,367 ± 4443	8
C58	C57BL/6	Neither	113,438 ± 2537	—
C58	C57BL/6	Stimulator	103,877 ± 6130	8*

[a] Asterisks indicate statistically significant blocking ($P \leq 0.05$ by Mann–Whitney test).

icantly reduced. The blocking of the response to C3H is not an unexpected result as recent studies by Janeway *et al.* (21) suggest that this Mls proliferative response may be I-A restricted. There was no effect on the AMLR when either the responding or stimulating cells of the H-2^b haplotype (C57BL/6) were pretreated with A·TH anti-A·TL.

The results of the addition of monoclonal antibodies to AMLR and MLR cultures are shown in Table 6. Anti-Ia^k, specificity 2, which is directed to the private specificity of the I-A subregion of the H-2^k haplotype (22) specifically blocks the C58 AMLR by 64% and the C58 response to BALB.K (which is also haplotype k throughout the MHC and Mls identical) by 65%. Neither the BALB/c AMLR (H-2^d haplotype) nor the C58 MLR response to BALB/c are decreased by this antibody. Monoclonal anti-Ia^k, recognizing public specificity 17 in I-A, also blocks the C58 AMLR. The monoclonal antibody Y-17 which recognizes the $A_\epsilon E_\alpha$ determinant (23), termed anti-I-AE in Table 6, likewise blocked this proliferative response. The addition of anti-I-EC subregion alloantibody was also found to block the C58 AMLR significantly as shown in Table 7. In C58 mice, this antibody recognizes specificity 7 of I-E. Total blocking of the primary C58 AMLR can be

TABLE 6

Effect of Monoclonal Antibody in AMLR and MLR Cultures

Responder	Stimulator	Antibody	Δcpm ± SD	Percentage blocking or stimulation[a]
C58	C58	None	23,784 ± 3339	—
		IA(2) 1:250	8,675 ± 3195	64*
		IA(2) 1:500	20,853 ± 6111	12
		NMS 1:250	32,743 ± 1364	+38*
BALB/c	BALB/c	None	18,449 ± 7745	—
		IA(2) 1:250	19,640 ± 3510	+6
		IA(2) 1:500	17,483 ± 8765	+9
		NMS 1:250	34,234 ± 4318	+86*
C58	BALB/c	None	101,633 ± 6665	—
		IA(2) 1:250	132,079 ± 6658	+29*
		IA(2) 1:500	104,387 ± 6236	+3
C58	BALB.K	None	63,170 ± 3094	—
		IA(2) 1:250	22,227 ± 5049	65*
		IA(2) 1:500	25,415 ± 525	60*
		NMS 1:250	62,218 ± 7253	2
C58	C58	None	19,048 ± 7676	—
		IA(17) 1:25	10,349 ± 2851	46*
		IA(17) 1:50	11,665 ± 2336	39*
		NMS 1:200	43,373 ± 2117	+127*
C58	C58	None	19,048 ± 7676	—
		I-AE 1:100	10,333 ± 464	46*
		I-AE 1:500	19,658 ± 1979	+3

[a] Percentage blocking or stimulation compared to control without antiserum. Differences which are statistically significant ($P \leq 0.05$) are marked by asterisks.

TABLE 7

Blocking of C58 AMLR by I Sub Region-Specific Antisera

Serum		Δcpm ± SD	Percentage blocking[a]
NMS	1:200	43,373 ± 2117	—
Anti-I-EC	1:100	6,798 ± 2728	84
Anti-I-EC	1:200	11,388 ± 6329	74

[a] Compared to NMS.

achieved by combining anti-I-A (specificity 2) and anti-I-EC or anti-I-A and anti-I-AE as shown in Table 8.

DISCUSSION

The importance of the I region of the MHC in cooperative cellular functions has been well established. Immune response (Ir) genes control responses to numerous foreign antigens (16) and the I region associated (Ia) cell surface antigens play a role in the collaborative actions between T cells, B cells, and macrophages (24, 25) and stimulate allogeneic T cells in a conventional MLR (14). In secondary stimulations and blocking experiments we have confirmed the preliminary reports of ourselves and others (15, 17–19) on the Ia requirement for the activation of T cells in the AMLR. Similar observations have been made for DR (Ia-like) antigens in the human AMLR (26). In the experiments in which AMLR-primed B10·A responder cells were used, only B10·A itself and B10·A(4R), which shares all of the I-A subregion antigenic determinants (specificities 1, 2, 3, 15, 17, 18, and 19), stimulated a strong secondary response. B10·A(4R) shares no known common determinants at I-E or I-C with B10·A, pointing to the primary importance of the I-A subregion in this functional role. A weaker role for the I-EC region as stimulator is indicated by the secondary responses of B10·A to B10·S(9R) and BALB/c.

These conclusions are supported by the use of specific blocking antisera in C58 AMLR. A·TH anti-A·TL which recognizes the entire k haplotype I region was a strong inhibitor of the AMLR when the stimulator, but not the responder cell population, was pretreated. The specificity of this reagent was demonstrated by appropriate blocking of only k haplotype stimulators. Similarly, specific blocking

TABLE 8

Combined Antibody Blocking of C58 AMLR

Antibody added	Δcpm ± SD	Percentage blocking
None	19,241 ± 3308	—
Anti-I-A 1:75	5,007 ± 2645	74
Anti-I-EC 1:200	16,506 ± 1079	14
Anti-I-A/E 1:50	4,412 ± 2149	77
Anti-I-A 1:75 + anti-I-EC 1:200	2,944 ± 2862	85
Anti-I-A 1:75 + anti-I-A/E 1:50	−4,487 ± 1440	100

of k haplotype AMLR and MLR reactions was observed with monoclonal antibodies to the I-A subregion k haplotype specific determinant, Ia-2. This anti-I-A failed to block the BALB/c AMLR (d haplotype) demonstrating its specificity. Strong blocking of the primary C58 AMLR was also observed with an anti-I-E region antiserum. Lattime *et al.* (18) also observed blocking of the primary CBA/J AMLR with anti-Ia, anti-I-A, anti-I-EC, and anti-I-A/I-E directed alloantisera. These reagents and our anti-I-A (specificity 17), anti-I-EC, and anti-I-AE are not k haplotype specific and may effect all cell interactions bearing the appropriate Ia specificities. The additive blocking by anti-I-EC and anti-I-A or anti-I-AE and anti-I-A seen in Table 8 suggests that two sites, I-A and the I-A/I-E combinatorial molecule $A_{\epsilon}E_{\alpha}$ are stimulatory in the primary AMLR. The experiment performed cannot determine if these sites are on the same or different cell populations.

The experiments shown in Tables 1 and 2 clearly place the stimulating antigens in the MHC and the panel of secondary stimulators shown in Table 4 confirms a primary role for the I-A subregion. A role for the I-EC subregion encoded determinants in the stimulation of the AMLR is again indicated. The relative importance of this second stimulating locus may vary with the strain combinations employed. B10·HTT, for example, was poorer than B10·S(9R) as a restimulating strain in the experiment involving B10·A responders (Table 3). When C58 was employed as the responder, however, B10·HTT stimulated even better than B10·S (9R). The stimulation observed with B10·HTT and B10·S (9R) (Tables 3 and 4) could also be due to their expression of $A^s_{\epsilon}E^k_{\alpha}$ which may cross react with $A^k_{\epsilon}E^k_{\alpha}$. These have been shown to be structurally very similar (27). No evidence for a necessary homology at other loci considered for possible AMLC stimulatory activity was found. We examined secondary response of T cells from primary C58 AMLR cultures to a variety of congenic strains (B10·A, 2R, AQR, 4R, 5R, 3R, 18R, 6R, B10, and B10·HTT, all obtained from Dr. Donal Murphy, Yale University). While mice having homology in the I region gave the best restimulation (data not shown), there was significant restimulation by spleen cells from mice not exhibiting I region homology. Since all of these mice are Mls^b, we cannot entirely rule out the participation of this locus in the AMLR. In other experiments, there was no correlation between the proliferative response of C58 (Table 4) and the Mls of stimulatory cells (C58, Mls^b; A-TL, Mls^c; C57BL/6, Mls^b; SJL, Mls^c).

The anti-I-EC alloantiserum employed here also precipitates the AE product controlled by two genes as described by Jones *et al.* (28) and Cook *et al.* (29). The A_{ϵ} chain, the β chain of the polypeptide, is controlled by the A subregion while the E_{α}, the α chain which carries the Ia.7 allospecificity is encoded in EC(29). Direct evidence favoring the role of $A_{\epsilon}E_{\alpha}$ in the primary AMLR was obtained with blocking by monoclonal Y17 (anti-I-AE) which has been shown by Lerner *et al.* (23) to be directed to this combined product. The secondary response experiments, however, do not indicate a fundamental stimulatory role for $A_{\epsilon}E_{\alpha}$. B10·A itself does have surface $A_{\epsilon}E_{\alpha}$, but the best stimulating strain, B10·A(4R), does not express surface $A_{\epsilon}E_{\alpha}$ whereas the poorest stimulator, B10·HTT, does. These results could indicate that requirements for stimulation in the primary and secondary AMLR are different. In the primary AMLR, perhaps recognition of the entire I region is required and, therefore, blocking of any subregion would impair the proliferative reaction. This accounts for the greater than 50% blocking found with each of the antibodies used. Monoclonal antibodies to single determinants are effective since it is known that several Ia specificities may be carried on a single molecule (30) and it is reasonable to assume that reaction with one determinant of a multispecific molecule might impair its stimulator functions.

The stimulatory requirements of the secondary AMLR are viewed as being fulfilled by homology at I-A. In the absence of I-A homology, other I region encoded determinants generate a weaker proliferative response by AMLR primed cells as demonstrated in the experiment employing B·10 congenic mice.

The apparently greater importance of the I-EC subregion implied by the strong blocking, compared with the weak secondary stimulation experiment results may also be the result of associative blocking by anti-I-EC as it is an alloantiserum. Both I-A and I-E subregion molecules are expressed on the same cells (31). Studies on the surface localization of I region determinants with A·TH and anti-A·TL (32, 33) have shown them to be distributed over the cell surface in microclusters but tell nothing about their spatial relationship. Steric interference is, therefore, feasible. This particular antiserum has also been found to cross-react with I-A (D. Murphy, personal communication). If, in fact, it is blocking both stimulatory sites for the AMLR, its strong blocking effect is not surprising.

The experiments presented in this paper do not address the problem of whether the AMLR represents a response to Ia only or whether FCS components serve as antigens in the system. We have done (Unpublished) AMLRs in 0.5% syngeneic normal mouse serum (NMS) and found that AMLR stimulation indices are the same as in parallel cultures done in FCS. In these experiments even the cell separations were done in NMS so there was no exposure to FCS antigens. We have also found that after primary cultures in FCS, secondary cultures in FCS or NMS showed similar proliferative responses.

Further evidence of a difference between the AMLR and an Ia-restricted specific antigen response system can be found in the recent report of Sprent *et al.* (34). Using some of the same reagents (anti-I-A^k specificity 2 and Y-17) they were unable to block an antigen-specific helper response when the antibodies were employed independently. When used together, however, they did block the response. In contrast, we found that either monoclonal antibody was capable of blocking an AMLR, and in combination the effect was additive.

We conclude from our experiments that AMLR reactions are restricted within the MHC by surface antigens encoded by genes in the I region. That is, AMLR represents either a reaction to I region encoded antigens, or an I region restricted recognition of an as yet unidentified determinant. Furthermore, there may be an I subregion difference in the stimulatory requirements of the primary and secondary reactions. In view of recent results from other laboratories (35, 36), the different functional characteristics of T cells recoverable from AMLC cultures may be associated with stimulation through different I subregions.

ACKNOWLEDGMENTS

We are indebted to Drs. Donal Murphy and Charles A. Janeway, Jr. and Mr. Ethan A. Lerner of Yale University for their thoughtful review and helpful suggestions. We would also like to thank Drs. Peter Brodeur, Bondada Subbarao, and Mel Bosma from the Institute for Cancer Research for their helpful review and comments. This work was supported by USPHS Grant AI 15876, NIH Grants CA 06927 and RR 05539, American Cancer Society Grant IM 251-A, NIH Training Grant CA 09035, and by an appropriation from the commonwealth of Pennsylvania.

REFERENCES

1. Opelz, G., Kiuchi, M., Takasugi, M., and Terasaki, P. I., *J. Exp. Med.* **142,** 1327, 1975.
2. Kuntz, M. M., Innes, J. B., and Weksler, M. E., *J. Exp. Med.* **143,** 1042, 1976.
3. Yamashita, U., and Shevach, E. M., *J. Immunol.* **124,** 1773, 1980.
4. Smith, J. B., and Pasternak, R. D., *J. Immunol.* **121,** 1889, 1978.
5. Horn, J. T., and Talal, N., *Fed. Proc.* **39,** 1129 (Abstract), 1980.
6. Sakane, T., Steinberg, A. D., and Green, I., *Proc. Nat. Acad. Sci. USA* **75,** 3464, 1978.
7. Smith, J. B., Knowlton, R. P., and Koons, L. S., *J. Nat. Cancer Inst.* **58,** 579, 1977.
8. Pasternak, R. D., Bocchieri, M. H., and Smith, J. B., *J. Immunol.* **49,** 384, 1980.
9. Smith, J. B., and Knowlton, R. P., *Clin. Immunol. Immunopathol.* **20,** 31, 1981.
10. Smith, J. B., and Knowlton, R. P., *J. Immunol.* **123,** 419, 1979.
11. Wolos, J. A., Smith, J. B., and Pasternak, R. D., *Fed. Proc.* **39,** 695 (Abstract), 1980.
12. Wolos, J. A., and Smith, J. B., *J. Immunol.* **127,** 711, 1981.
13. Yu, D. T. Y., Chiorazzi, N., and Kunkel, H. G., *Cell. Immunol.* **50,** 305, 1980.
14. Meo, T., David, C.S., Nabholz, M., Miggiano, V., and Shreffler, D.C., *Transplant. Proc.* **5,** 1507, 1973.
15. Ponzio, N. M., *Cell Immunol.* **49,** 266, 1980.
16. Benacerraf, B., and Germain, R., *Immunol. Rev.* **38,** 70, 1978.
17. Bocchieri, M. H., and Smith, J. B., *"Fourth International Congress of Immunology, Paris"* (Abstract 14.3.08), 1980.
18. Lattime, E. C., Golub, S. H., and Stutman, O., *Eur. J. Immunol.* **10,** 723, 1980.
19. Gottleib, A. B., Fu, S. M., Yu, D. T. Y., Wang, C. Y., Halper, J. P., and Kunkel, H. G., *J. Immunol.* **123,** 1497, 1979.
20. Gutierrez, C., Bernabe, R. R., Vega, J., and Kreisler, M., *J. Immunol. Methods* **29,** 57, 1979.
21. Janeway, C. A., Jr., Lerner, E. A., Jason, J. M., and Jones, B., *Immunogenetics* **10,** 481, 1980.
22. David, C.S., *Transplant. Rev.* **30,** 299, 1976.
23. Lerner, E. A., Matis, L. A., Janeway, C. A., Jr., Jones, P. P., Schwartz, R. H., and Murphy, D. B., *J. Exp. Med.* **152,** 1085, 1980.
24. Shevach, E. M., and Rosenthal, A. S., *J. Exp. Med.* **138,** 1213, 1973.
25. Katz, D. H., Greaves, M., Dorf, M. E., Dimuzio, H., and Benacerraf, B., *J. Exp. Med.* **141,** 263, 1975.
26. Raff, H. V., Picker, L. J., and Stobo, J. D., *J. Exp. Med.* **152,** 581, 1980.
27. McMillan, M., Frelinger, J. A., Jones, P. P., Murphy, D. B., McDevitt, H. O., and Hood, L., *J. Exp. Med.* **153,** 936, 1981.
28. Jones, P. P., Murphy, D. B., and McDevitt, H. O., *J. Exp. Med.* **148,** 925, 1978.
29. Cook, R. G., Vitetta, E. S., Uhr, J. W., and Capra, J. D., *J. Exp. Med.* **149,** 981, 1979.
30. Cullen, S. E., David, C. S., Cone, J. L., and Sachs, D. H., *J. Immunol.* **116,** 549, 1976.
31. Vitetta, E. S., and Cook, R. G., *J. Immunol.* **122,** 2122, 1979.
32. Unanue, E. R., Dorf, M. E., David, C. S., and Benacerraf, B., *Proc. Nat. Acad. Sci. USA* **71,** 5014, 1974.
33. Abbas, A. K., Dorf, M. E., Karnovsky, M. J., and Unanue, E. R., *J. Immunol.* **116,** 371, 1976.
34. Sprent, J., Lerner, E. A., Bruce, J., and Symington, F. W., *J. Exp. Med.* **154,** 188, 1981.
35. Kim, Y. T., Schwartz, A., Moody, C., Siskind, G. W., and Weksler, M. E., *J. Immunol.* **125,** 1724, 1980.
36. Sprent, J., *J. Exp. Med.* **152,** 996, 1980.

CELLULAR IMMUNOLOGY 65, 152–165 (1981)

Evidence for Histamine-Induced Auto-Anti-idiotypic Antibody Immunoregulation *in Vivo*[1]

MYRON R. SZEWCZUK,[2] RITA J. CAMPBELL, AND JAMES W. SMITH

The Host Resistance Programme, Department of Pathology, McMaster University Health Sciences Center, Hamilton, Ontario L8N 3Z5, Canada

Received June 18, 1981; accepted September 23, 1981

The *in vivo* effects of histamine injection in LAF_1 male mice on the immune reactivity to trinitrophenylated bovine γ-globulin was studied using plaque-forming cell (PFC) responses and their avidity distributions. Splenic anti-trinitrophenyl (anti-TNP) PFC responses of mice treated with histamine (5×10^{-6} mol or 1 mg, intravenously) were significantly reduced in number and restricted in heterogeneity and characterized by a preferential loss of high-avidity IgG PFCs. The reduced PFC response in histamine-treated mice was dose and time dependent. No evidence of suppressor cell activity in the spleens from histamine-treated mice was demonstrable. Only histamine-treated mice produced a significantly high percentage of anti-idiotype-blocked, hapten-augmentable IgG PFCs, suggesting the presence of auto-anti-idiotypic activity. Immune sera taken from histamine-treated mice caused an inhibition of anti-TNP PFC *in vitro*. This PFC-inhibiting factor in immune sera of histamine-treated mice was an antibody of the IgG_1 and IgG_{2a} class, lacked anti-TNP antibody activity, but reacted with anti-TNP antibody of LAF_1 origin. Passive hemagglutination study of this sera showed anti-(anti-TNP $F(ab')_2$-IgG) titer. Thus, the results of this study suggest that histamine in combination with antigen induces auto-anti-idiotypic antibody which, in turn, is involved in the normal regulation of the immune response to trinitrophenylated bovine γ-globulin *in vivo*.

INTRODUCTION

A regulatory role for histamine has been proposed by its inhibitory effects of lymphocyte responses *in vitro*. For example, histamine caused an inhibition of cytolytic cell activity (1), antigen-induced lymphocyte proliferation and production of migration inhibitory factor (2, 3), cutaneous delayed hypersensitivity (3), lymphocyte proliferation induced by phytohemagglutination and concanavalin A (4), and formation of antibody-forming cells (5, 6). In other models, histamine abrogated antigen-induced tolerance (7), and removal of cells by histamine-coated columns restored immune responsiveness of spleen cells from tolerized animals (8). Removal of histamine-binding cells also increased the relative number of antibody-forming cells in the spleen of sheep red cell-immune (9, 10) and nonimmune animals

[1] This work was supported in part by a grant-in-aid of research from the Banting Research Foundation and MRC of Canada, MA-7347.

[2] Gerontology Research Council of Ontario Scholar; formerly a Medical Research Council of Canada Scholar. Present address: Department of Microbiology and Immunology, Queen's University, Kingston, Ontario K7L 3N6, Canada.

0008-8749/81/170152-14$02.00/0

(9), as well as in the primary immune reponse induced *in vitro* by thymic-dependent antigen but not thymic-independent antigen (11).

The appearance of histamine-binding sites on lymphocytes has led to the concept that generation of detectable histamine sites may be a marker of the differentiated state of both T and B lymphocytes (12–14). In the human model, both T and B cells were shown to contain histamine-binding sites, while precursor cells did not (12, 13). In the animal model, B lymphocytes were found to have no functional histamine receptors while as T lymphocytes "mature" in immunological function from thymocytes to splenic T cells, the response to histamine increases (14). These results suggest that the appearance of histamine receptors may play an important part in the control of immunologic response.

Recently, Rocklin (15) reported that T lymphocytes (16) exposed to histamine at a 10^{-3} M concentration *in vitro* elaborate a soluble factor which suppresses antigen-induced production of migration inhibitory factor and proliferation by sensitized lymphocytes. Specifically this histamine-induced suppressor factor (HSF)[3] was generated *in vitro* by culturing normal or immune lymphocytes with histamine, and after 24 hr of culture at 37°C, the cell-free supernatant was assayed for the inhibitory activity of HSF. Other than the less well documented observations of Fallah *et al.* (6) that an *in vivo*-induced mast cell degranulation led to a reduced formation of antibody-forming cells, relatively little is known as to what type of cells histamine reacts to and what they do *in vivo*.

In the present study, we find that the splenic anti-TNP plaque-forming cell (PFC) response to trinitrophenylated bovine γ-globulin (TNP-BGG) of mice treated with histamine was significantly reduced in number with a preferential loss of high-avidity IgG PFCs. This reduced PFC response was dose and time dependent. No evidence of suppressor cell activity in the spleens from histamine-treated mice was demonstrable. However, only histamine-treated mice produced a significantly high percentage of anti-idiotype-blocked, hapten-augmentable IgG PFCs, suggesting the presence of auto-anti-idiotypic antibody. These results are consistent with the view that antigen–histamine induces an auto-anti-idiotypic antibody which, in turn, is involved in the normal regulation of the immune response to antigen *in vivo*.

MATERIALS AND METHODS

Animals. LAF_1 (C57J × A/HeJ) male mice at 6–8 weeks of age were used in all experiments. Mice were obtained from the Jackson Laboratories (Bar Harbor, Maine).

Antigens and haptens. The 2,4,6-trinitrophenyl (TNP) derivative of bovine γ-globulin (BGG; Miles Laboratories, Inc., Miles Research Products, Kankakee, Ill.) was prepared by the reaction of 2,4,6-trinitrobenzenesulfonic acid ($TNBSO_3$; Sigma Chemical Co., St. Louis, Mo.) with the protein under alkaline conditions essentially as described by Eisen *et al.* (17). Conjugated protein was purified by extensive dialysis and the concentrations were determined by dry-weight analysis. It had approximately 36 TNP groups per molecule of protein based upon its absorbance

[3] Abreviations used: BGG, bovine γ-globulin; CFA, complete Freund's adjuvant; TNP, 2,4,6-trinitrophenyl group; TNP-BGG, trinitrophenylated group; TNP-BGG, trinitrophenylated bovine γ-globulin; EACA, ϵ-amino-*n*-caproic acid; $TNBSO_4$, 2,4,6-trinitrobenzenesulfonic acid; PFC, plaque-forming cell(s); SRBC, sheep red blood cells, Hepes, *N*-2-hydroxyethylpiperazine-*N*′-2-ethanesulfonic acid; HSF, histamine-induced suppressor factor.

at 346 nm (ϵ for TNP-glycine was taken as 15,400). TNP-ϵ-amino-*n*-caproic acid (TNP-EACA) was prepared by the reaction of $TNBSO_3$ with ϵ-amino-*n*-caproic acid under alkaline conditions, and was purified by repeated crystallization from hot water as described previously (18).

Immunization. Mice were immunized by an intraperitoneal injection of 500 μg TNP-BGG emulsified in complete Freund's adjuvant (CFA) (containing 1.5 mg/ml *Mycobacterium butyricum*) in a final volume of 0.2 ml. Animals were sacrificed by cervical dislocation and their splenic PFCs were assayed 14 days after antigen injection.

Assay of number and avidity of anti-TNP plaque-forming cells (PFC). Cells to be assayed were obtained from spleens. Tissues were gently teased in a 1× Hanks' balanced salt solution, pH 7.2, containing 0.02 mg/ml of sodium heparin sulfate and 25 m*M* Hepes buffer (*N*-2-hydroxyethylpiperazine-*N*′-2-ethanesulfonic acid, Sigma). The cells were passed through a thin layer of gauze, washed once, and resuspended in Hanks' medium for assay.

Anti-TNP PFC were determined by the method of Jerne *et al.* (19) as modified for a slide assay by Dresser and Greaves (20). Washed sheep red blood cells (SRBC) were conjugated by the Rittenberg and Pratt method (21) with 2,4,6-trinitrobenzene sulfonic acid (Sigma). Fifty-microliter aliquots of immune cell suspensions were assayed for PFC. The slides were incubated for 1 hr at 37°C. Diluted (1:30) freshly frozen guinea pig serum, absorbed with SRBC, was added as a source of complement and the slides were incubated for 45 min. Rabbit anti-mouse IgG and rabbit anti-mouse IgA were used at a predetermined optimal dilution (1:300), to develop indirect IgG and IgA plaques, respectively. The IgA-developing serum was prepared in rabbits by using pure mouse myeloma MOPC 315 (IgAλ2). The antiserum was depleted to anti-light chain activity by passage through a pure mouse IgG–Sepharose 4B immunoadsorbent column. The IgG-developing serum was prepared in rabbits by using purified mouse IgG (Miles, Lot 51). The antisera showed only a single line against normal mouse sera and pure IgG on Ouchterlony analysis. Pure mouse IgA or IgG when added to the PFC assay inhibited the development of only IgA or IgG PFCs, respectively, when the respective developing serum was added. Prior to developing indirect plaques, goat anti-μ was used to inhibit >95% IgM plaques during the first incubation period. The anti-μ antiserum was prepared in goats by using pure mouse MOPC 104E (IgMλ1) (Bionetics, Lot AJ110). It was passaged through a pure mouse IgG–Sepharose 4B immunoadsorbent column to remove anti-light chain activity.

The avidity distribution of the anti-TNP PFC was assayed by the inhibition of plaque formation using various concentrations of TNP-EACA essentially according to the method of Andersson (22) as validated by other studies (23, 24). Plaque formation around high-affinity antibody-secreting cells is inhibited by low concentrations of hapten, while high concentrations of hapten are necessary to inhibit plaque formation around low-affinity antibody-secreting cells. Concentrations of TNP-EACA ranging from 1×10^{-9} to 1×10^{-5} *M* in half-log increments, were used.

Shannon heterogeneity index. The heterogeneity index is derived from Shannon's formula (25),

$$H = -\sum_{k=1}^{n} p_k \log p_k ,$$

where n is the number of states ranging from 1, 2, . . . , k, . . . , n which have respective probabilities of $p_1, p_2, \ldots p_k, \ldots p_n$. The maximal information content (maximum heterogeneity) of a system is represented by the equidistribution of information bits along all of the arbitrarily set states. The minimal information content (minimum heterogeneity) would require all bits of information to be contained in a single subpopulation.

In vitro assay for anti-idiotypic antibody (anti-anti-TNP) in immune sera. Primary Day 14 anti-TNP spleen cells from LAF_1 mice are used as indicator cells in this assay, since no appreciable hapten-augmentable PFC are seen. These cells from pooled spleens from individual donors are washed once and resuspended at $3\text{–}5 \times 10^6$ cells/ml. One-milliliter aliquots are incubated with various dilutions of pooled antisera (potentially containing anti-anti-TNP antibody), for 5 min at 4°C. The cells are centrifuged (1000 rpm, 10 min, 4°C) and, after one wash, are resuspended to the original concentration. Fifty microliters is assayed, in duplicate, for anti-TNP PFC. If the antisera contain anti-anti-TNP antibody, a decrease in the number of PFCs will be expected. This suppressive effect can be reversed by the addition of free hapten (1×10^{-9} to 1×10^{-7} *M* TNP-EACA) to the agarose and the complement solution as described previously (26, 27). The PFC inhibitory activity (anti-idiotype-blocked PFC) in the antisera was removed by passage through an anti-TNP-Sepharose 4B immunoadsorbent column. The anti-TNP antiserum that is conjugated on immunoadsorbent was prepared by immunizing LAF_1 mice with 500 μg TNP-BGG in CFA and collecting sera 14 days later. Details of this assay are described elsewhere (26).

RESULTS

Dose-dependent effect of histamine on the ability of mice to produce an anti-TNP PFC response. Groups of mice received a single dose of various amounts of histamine in normal saline, intravenously. Control mice received normal saline. One day later all animals were immunized with 500 μg TNP-BGG in CFA, intraperitoneally. Splenic anti-TNP per 10^8 nucleated cells was assayed 2 weeks after immunization. The results are shown in Fig. 1. Mice that received 0.01 mg of histamine intravenously gave a normal IgG and IgA anti-TNP PFC response, while the IgM PFCs were 27% suppressed relative to control. In contrast, mice that received a 0.1-mg or greater dose of histamine produced a progressively reduced (20–85%) number of PFCs in the three isotypes studied. The dose (1 mg) of histamine which gave a 50–60% reduction in the number of anti-TNP PFCs was subsequently used in all other experiments.

In vivo effect of histamine on the ability of mice to produce a heterogeneous anti-TNP PFC response. The effect of histamine on the ability of mice to produce a heterogeneous immune response with respect to antibody affinity was studied. Mice that received 1 mg histamine intravenously and 24 hr later were immunized with TNP-BGG in CFA showed a significant reduction in the number of IgM, IgG, and IgA anti-TNP PFCs in the spleen as compared to controls (Table 1). The distribution of IgG PFCs with regard to avidity was determined by hapten inhibition of plaque formation and is illustrated in Fig. 2. Control mice that did not receive histamine produced a highly heterogeneous PFC response with regard to antibody affinity and were of high-avidity PFC. In contrast, mice that received

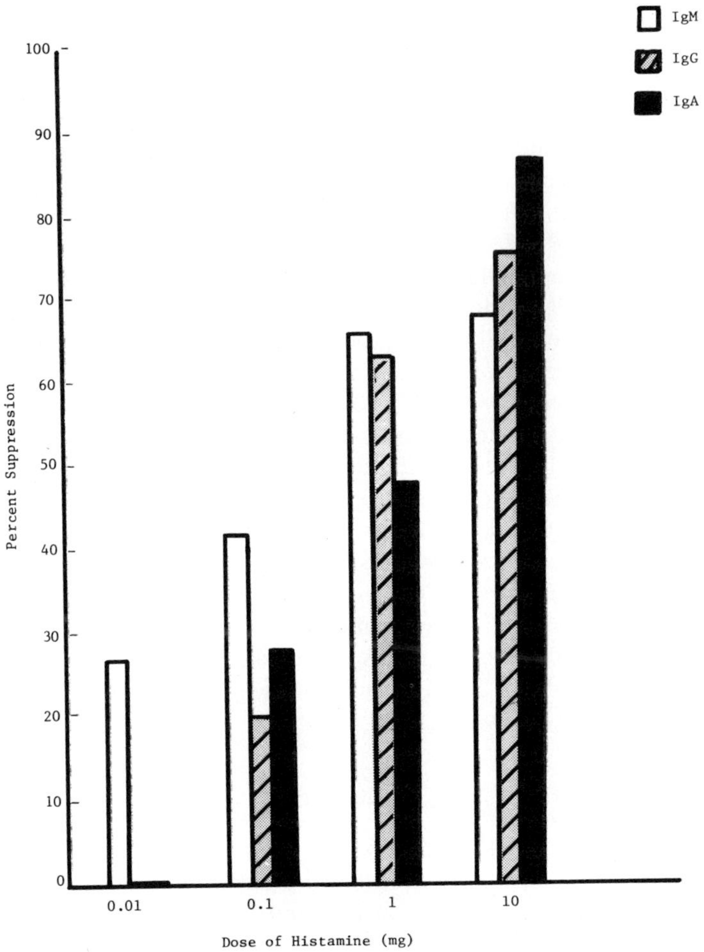

FIG. 1. Dose-dependent effect of histamine on the ability of mice to produce an anti-TNP PFC response. Groups of LAF_1 mice received a single dose of 0 or 0.01 to 10 mg histamine, intravenously. Control mice received normal saline. One day later all animals were immunized with 500 μg TNP-BGG in CFA, intraperitoneally. Splenic anti-TNP PFC per 10^8 nucleated cells were assayed 2 weeks after immunization. The PFC responses are calculated as geometric means of five individual spleens. The ordinate represents the percentage suppression of the response of groups of animals treated with the indicated dose of histamine relative to controls. The data illustrated are from one representative experiment out of three independent experiments.

1 mg histamine produced a restriction in heterogeneity characterized by a loss of high-avidity PFC subpopulations. The distribution of affinity illustrated may be quantitated using the Shannon heterogeneity index (25), thereby permitting a simple, statistical evaluation of the data. This index is expressed as a $\log_2$ term and increases with increasing heterogeneity of the PFC distribution. Thus, the heterogeneity indices calculated from these data showed a significant decrease in heterogeneity of splenic IgG PFCs in histamine-treated mice (Table 1). Thus, histamine injection into animals 24 hr prior to immunization resulted in a statistically significant decrease in the number of PFCs with a loss of high-avidity IgG PFC subpopulations.

TABLE 1

In Vivo Effect of Histamine on the Ability of Mice to Produce a Heterogeneous Anti-TNP PFC Response to TNP-BGG in LAF_1 Mice[a]

		Splenic anti-TNP PFC/10^8 cells						
Drug treatment	No. of mice	IgM PFC		IgG PFC		IgA PFC		Heterogeneity index[b] (IgG PFC)
None	4	2970		2102		3102		2.62 ± 0.27
Histamine	6	1487	50% ($P < 0.05$)	1003	52% ($P < 0.05$)	1568	49% ($P < 0.005$)	1.55 ± 0.68 ($P < 0.05$)
None	9	9123		4349		3406		2.24 ± 0.32
Histamine	9	3515	61% ($P < 0.01$)	2353	46% ($P < 0.02$)	1983	42% (N.S.)	1.73 ± 0.20 ($P < 0.02$)

[a] Male LAF_1 mice received a single dose of 1 mg histamine intravenously. Control mice received normal saline. One day later all animals were immunized with 500 μg TNP-BGG in CFA, intraperitoneally. Splenic anti-TNP-PFC per 10^8 nucleated cells were assayed 2 weeks after immunization. Data presented are the geometric means of four to nine animals from two independent experiments for each group. The *t* test is employed to evaluate the significance of differences on natural log-transformed data.

[b] The Shannon heterogeneity index (25) was used to describe the degree of heterogeneity of affinity of the indirect IgG anti-TNP PFC population of spleens from four to nine mice. The values presented are the means ± SD from two independent experiments. The larger the index, the greater the heterogeneity. The *t* test was employed to evaluate the statistical significance in the heterogeneity indices as compared with the control group.

Kinetics of suppression of the anti-TNP PFC response in mice with histamine administration. Mice were either immunized with TNP-BGG in CFA and 1 day later injected with 1 mg histamine intravenously, or injected with histamine and various days later immunized. The results are shown in Table 2. Mice that received histamine 1 to 7 days prior to immunization produced a reduced PFC response and restricted heterogeneity characterized by a preferential loss of high-avidity IgG PFC. In contrast, mice that were either immunized prior to histamine injection or simultaneously immunized and injected with histamine did not show any effect of suppressed PFC responses. Furthermore, histamine injection into animals 14 days prior to immunization resulted in no reduction in PFCs. Thus, the effect of histamine is time dependent and is active in the 1- to 7-day period prior to antigen immunization.

Lack of evidence for increased suppressor cell activity in spleen of histamine-treated mice. The possibility that the suppressed state induced in histamine-treated mice was mediated by suppressor cells was evaluated by use of cell transfer procedures in which normal mice are injected with spleen cells from either histamine-treated mice or normal mice. The results are illustrated in Fig. 3. It is clear that the cell transfer did not demonstrate any increased suppressor activity in the spleen of histamine-treated mice.

Effect of histamine on the appearance of anti-idiotype-blocked hapten-augmentable IgG, anti-TNP PFC during the normal immune response to TNP-BGG. Studies (27) have shown that auto-anti-idiotypic antibody produced during the

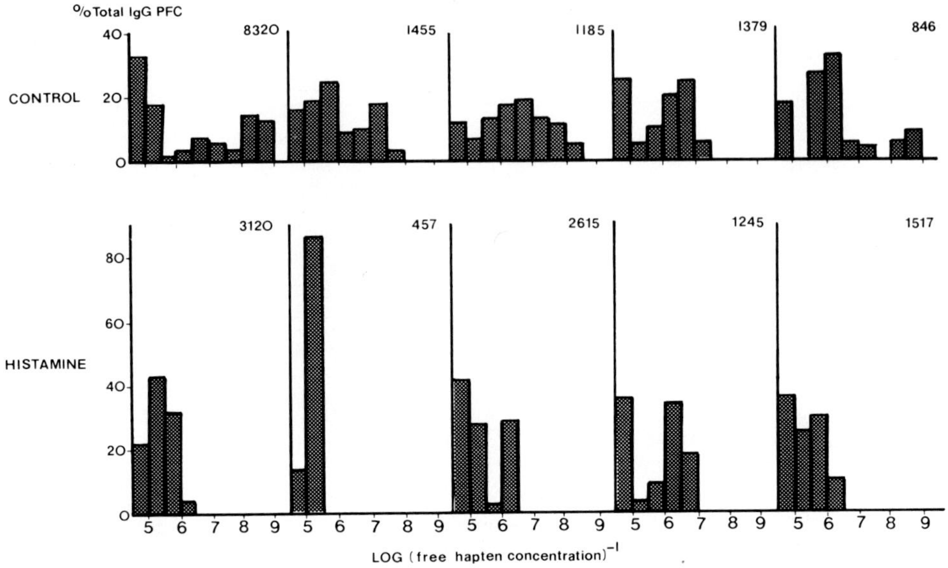

FIG. 2. Affinity distribution of the primary IgG PFC response in the spleen of LAF_1 male mice treated with histamine. Each histogram illustrates the distribution of indirect IgG anti-TNP PFC with respect to affinity in the spleen from mice 14 days after immunization with 500 μg TNP-BGG in CFA, intraperitoneally. In the first (upper) and second rows are data on the splenic PFC responses of control and histamine-treated mice, respectively. In each case, data from five individual animals from two or three independent experiments are presented. The abscissa represents the log of the inverse of the free hapten concentration used in the plaque inhibition assay. The ordinate represents the percentage of the total population of PFC present in each subpopulation. Affinity increases to the right. The number of indirect IgG PFC per 10^8 nucleated cells is indicated in the right upper corner of each histogram.

course of the primary immune response in young adult mice of certain strains is responsible for the decline in the number of PFC, the disappearance of high-affinity PFC, and the occurrence of hapten-augmentable PFC (anti-idiotype blocked). Since histamine-treated mice exhibited a decline in the number of PFC and a loss of high-affinity PFC with no suppressor cell activity it was of particular interest to investigate the appearance of auto-anti-idiotypic activity in these mice. The results are shown in Table 3. Histamine-treated mice in the 1- to 7-day period prior to immunization produced a significantly high percentage of hapten-augmentable IgG PFC responses as compared with the control mice which did not receive the drug. These data are consistent with the hypothesis that auto-anti-idiotypic activity, produced during the course of the immune response in histamine-treated animals, may be, in part, responsible for the decline in the number of PFCs and a preferential loss of high-avidity PFCs.

Anti-idiotypic antibody activity in immune sera from histamine-treated mice. Other studies (26) describe an assay for anti-idiotypic antibody that makes use of the ability of such antibody in the immune sera to inhibit plaque formation by idiotype-producing cells. This inhibition is reversible by hapten, TNP-ϵ-amino-*n*-caproic acid (EACA). Results in Table 4 show that pools of immune sera from mice treated with histamine 1 or 2 days prior to immunization and 14 days previously immunized with TNP-BGG in CFA caused a hapten-reversible block of

TABLE 2

Kinetics of Suppression of Anti-TNP PFC Response after Histamine Administration *in Vivo*[a]

Time between histamine injection and immunization (days)	Drug treatment (No. of mice)	Splenic anti-TNP PFC/10^8 cells		
		IgM PFC	IgG PFC	IgA PFC
−1	None (10)	1682	1011	433
	Histamine (10)	2221 0%	1534 0%	692 0%
0	None (10)	3541	1932	1460
	Histamine (10)	3758 0%	1737 10%	1211 17%
1	None (15)	7433	3321	4005
	Histamine (15)	2684 64%	1515 54%	2254 44%
2	None (10)	3107	1741	1712
	Histamine (10)	2364 24%	1068 39%	1347 21%
7	None (8)	6038	3752	3470
	Histamine (9)	4011 34%	2088 44%	2296 34%
14	None (19)	2101	1234	764
	Histamine (18)	2526 0%	1892 0%	980 0%

[a] Mice were either immunized with 500 μg TNP-BGG in CFA and 1 day later injected with 1 mg histamine, intravenously (−Day 1), or injected with histamine and various days later immunized (Days 0 to 14) as indicated in the first column. Splenic anti-TNP PFC per 10^8 nucleated cells were assayed 2 weeks after immunization. The data presented are the geometric means of individual spleens from 8 to 19 animals from two to four independent experiments in each group.

plaque formation by spleen cells from TNP-BGG immune mice. In contrast, immune sera from mice immunized with only TNP-BGG or from mice immunized on or one day before histamine treatment failed to inhibit the PFC response. Also, nonimmune sera from mice treated with histamine 1 or 2 days before collection of sera failed to inhibit the PFC response.

Specific absorption studies have indicated that this PFC-inhibiting factor in immune sera of histamine-treated mice is an antibody of the IgG_1 and IgG_{2a} class (Table 5), lacks anti-TNP antibody activity, but reacts with anti-TNP antibody of LAF_1 origin (Table 4). Passive hemagglutination studies on these sera showed the anti-(anti-TNP $F(ab')_2$-IgG) titer (Table 4). These findings support the view that histamine in combination with antigen induces auto-anti-idiotypic antibody which, in turn, deregulates the anti-TNP PFC responses to TNP-BGG *in vivo*.

DISCUSSION

There is little information on the effects of histamine on the immune response *in vivo*. It is unclear as to what types of cells histamine and other vasoactive amines react and what they do, in an *in vivo* situation. We have thus studied the effects of histamine on the immune response of LAF_1 male mice to a highly T-dependent antigen, TNP-BGG. Splenic IgM, IgG, and IgA anti-TNP-PFC responses of mice treated with 1 mg histamine intravenously 1 to 7 days prior to immunization are

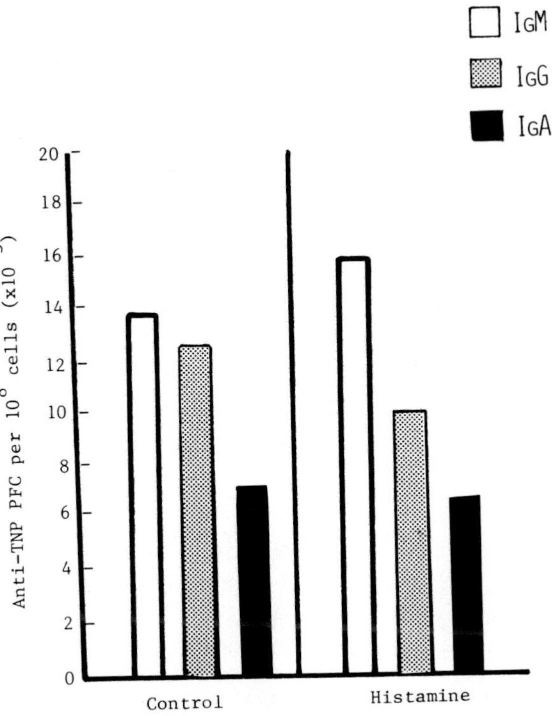

FIG. 3. Failure to demonstrate increased suppressor cell activity in spleen of histamine-treated mice. LAF_1 male mice were injected with 0 or 1 mg histamine in normal saline, intravenously. One day later spleen cells from either histamine-treated mice or control mice were injected intravenously into normal recipients of the same strain. Each recipient received the equivalent of a spleen from a histamine-treated or control donor. Recipients were immunized with 500 μg TNP-BGG in CFA 1 hr after cell transfer and splenic anti-TNP PFC per 10^8 nucleated cells were determined 14 days later. The data illustrated are from one representative experiment out of two independent experiments. The data are expressed as geometric means of PFC assays on groups of five mice.

significantly reduced in number with a preferential loss of high-avidity IgG PFCs. Fallah *et al.* (6) have demonstrated that histamine and serotonin added to lymphocytes *in vitro* caused a 46 to 72% reduction of direct (IgM) antibody-forming cells and that the effect of these mediators was active in the 0 to 24 hr after antigen immunization. However, it is unclear from these results whether histamine or serotonin contributed to the reduced PFC response to antigen. We find that histamine is the active agent for the observed reduced PFC response and restricted heterogeneity of affinity of mice given the drug, intravenously (Table 1 and Fig. 2). This is consistent with other reported data using *in vitro* T-cell function assays (16). Serotonin, nevertheless, was shown in preliminary studies (data not shown) not to be an active agent in causing diminution of immune responses to antigen. Serotonin was shown to be a potent inducer of tachyphylaxis for its role in the regulation of delayed-type hypersensitivity reactions (DTH) (28).

In studies using histamine-coated columns suppressor cells have been implicated as having histamine receptors. Specifically, removal of cells by histamine-coated columns restored immune responsiveness of spleen cells from tolerized animals (8). Removal of histamine-binding cells also increased the relative number of antibody-

TABLE 3

Effect of Histamine on the Appearance of Anti-idiotype-Blocked Hapten-Augmentable, Anti-TNP PFCs during the Normal Immune Response to TNP-BGG[a]

Time between drug injection and immunization (days)	Drug treatment (No. of mice)	TNP-EACA	Splenic anti-TNP PFC/10^8 cells		
			IgG PFC	% hapten-augmentable PFC[b]	
−1	None (10)	−	1001		
		+	1121	12	
	Histamine (10)	−	1534		
		+	1749	14	N.S.
0	None (10)	−	1932		
		+	2067	7	
	Histamine (9)	−	1737		
		+	2137	23	N.S.
1	None (9)	−	3321		
		+	3886	17	
	Histamine (9)	−	1515		
		+	3394	124	$P < 0.001$
2	None (10)	−	1741		
		+	1863	7	
	Histamine (7)	−	1068		
		+	2488	115	$P < 0.001$
7	None (14)	−	3752		
		+	4277	14	
	Histamine (13)	−	2088		
		+	3132	50	$P < 0.01$
14	None (7)	−	1234		
		+	1394	13	
	Histamine (18)	−	1892		
		+	2554	35	N.S.

[a] Mice were either immunized with 500 μg TNP-BGG in CFA and 1 day later injected with 1 mg histamine intravenously (−Day 1) or injected with histamine and various days later immunized (Days 0 to 14) as indicated in the first column. Splenic anti-TNP PFC per 10^8 nucleated cells were assayed 2 weeks after immunization. The data presented are the geometric means of individual spleens from 7 to 18 animals from two to four independent experiments in each group.

[b] Percentage augmentation of PFCs by optimal hapten concentration (1×10^{-9} to 1×10^{-7} *M* TNP-EACA) is calculated as: 100 × (PFCs in the presence of hapten − PFCs in absence of hapten)/PFC in absence of hapten. The *t* test was used to evaluate the statistical significance of differences on natural log-transformed data as compared with respective controls.

forming cells in the spleen of sheep red blood cell-immune animals (9, 10), as well as in the primary immune response induced *in vitro* by thymic-dependent antigen but not thymic-independent antigens (11). The possibility that our reduced PFC responses in histamine-treated mice was mediated by suppressor cell activity was evaluated by use of cell transfer studies. Normal mice were injected with spleen

TABLE 4

Anti-idiotypic Antibody Activity in Immune Sera from Histamine-Treated Mice[a]

Serum source[b]	Dilution	Anti-TNP titer (reciprocal)	Anti-(anti-TNP $F(ab')_2$-IgG) titer (reciprocal)	Absorption of sera	Percentage of control response		
					IgM PFC	IgG PFC	IgA PFC
NMS	1:10	<2	<2	–	100	100	100
Immune	1:10	160	<2	–	95	95	94
Day 1 histamine NMS	1:10	<2	<2	–	95	89	112
Day 2 histamine NMS	1:10	<2	<2	–	112	101	120
–Day 1 histamine immune	1:10	160	<2	–	100	97	124
Day 0 histamine immune	1:10	80	<2	–	96	98	148
Day 1 histamine immune	1:10	80	4	–	**61**	**48**	121
Day 2 histamine immune	1:10	160	4	–	**60**	**68**	126
Day 2 histamine immune	1:4	40	16	TNP-BGG	**51**	**43**	107
Day 2 histamine immune	1:4	20	<2	Anti-TNP	99	93	107

[a] Immune spleen cells were obtained from individual LAF_1 male mice that had been immunized intraperitoneally with 500 μg TNP-BGG in CFA 2 weeks before assay. The control values [PFCs determined in the presence of normal mouse serum (NMS)] ranged from 2963 IgM, 2259 IgG, and 1074 IgA anti-TNP PFCs per 10^8 nucleated spleen cells. Immune cells at 3–5 × 10^7 cells/ml were incubated with immune sera or NMS at a 1:4 or 1:10 final dilution for 5 min at 4°c. The cells were washed once, resuspended to the original volume, and plated. The inhibition of plaque formation was completely reversible by addition of hapten. The data illustrated are from one representative experiment out of seven independent experiments. Anti-TNP and anti-(anti-TNP $F(ab')_2$-IgG) titers were determined by passive hemagglutination.

[b] The NMS pool was obtained from 10 LAF_1 male mice at 6–8 weeks of age. The Day 1 or 2 NMS pool was obtained from groups of 5–10 mice 1 or 2 days previously injected with 1 mg histamine, intravenously. Pools of immune sera were obtained from groups of 5–10 mice which had been either immunized with 500 μg TNP-BGG in CFA ip and 1 day later injected with 1 mg histamine intravenously (–Day 1) or injected with histamine and immunized later at various indicated days (Days 0–2) before collection of sera 14 days after immunization. For absorption studies, aliquot samples of the original pool of immune sera were passaged through either TNP-BGG or anti-TNP antibody–Sepharose 4B column.

TABLE 5

Characterization of the Anti-idiotypic Antibody in Immune Sera from Histamine-Treated Mice[a]

Serum source[b]	Absorption of serum	Elution from immunoadsorbent[c]	Percentage of control response: IgM PFC	IgG PFC	IgA PFC
NMS (1:10	–	–	100	100	100
Immune (1:10)	–	–	95	95	94
Day 1 histamine immune (1:10)	–	–	**61**	**48**	121
Day 1 histamine immune (1:10)	Anti-MGG	–	104	98	105
	Anti-IgM	+	110	103	86
	Anti-IgA	+	91	86	112
	Anti-IgG_1	+	**63**	**71**	**47**
	Anti-IgG_{2a}	+	**70**	**77**	**34**
	Anti-IgG_{2b}	+	89	80	109
	Anti-IgG_3	+	85	106	86

[a] Immune spleen cells were obtained from individual LAF_1 male mice that had been immunized intraperitoneally with 500 μg TNP-BGG in CFA 2 weeks before assay. The control values [PFCs determined in the presence of normal mouse serum (NMS)] ranged from IgM, IgG, and IgA anti-TNP PFCs per 10^8 nucleated spleen cells. Immune cells at 3–5 × 10^7 cells/ml were incubated with immune sera or NMS at 1:10 final dilution for 5 min at 4°C. The cells were washed once, resuspended to the original volume, and plated. The inhibition of plaque formation was completely reversible by addition of hapten. The data illustrated are from one representative experiment out of three independent experiments.

[b] The NMS pool was obtained from 10 LAF_1 male mice at 6–8 weeks of age. Pools of immune sera were obtained from groups of 5–10 mice which had been either immunized with 500 μg TNP-BGG in CFA ip or injected with histamine and immunized 1 day later before collection of sera 14 days after immunization. For absorption studies, aliquot samples of the original pool of immune sera were passaged through either an anti-mouse Ig (specific for μ, γ, α heavy chains) antiserum conjugated to Sepharose 4B immunoadsorbent or individual columns containing antisera specific for heavy chains of IgM, IgA, IgG_1, IgG_{2a}, IgG_{2b}, or IgG_3.

[c] After passage of immune sera through immunoadsorbent columns, the columns were extensively washed with buffer, pH 8.0, and then eluted with acetate buffer, pH 4.0. The eluted fractions were tested for PFC-inhibiting activity.

cells from either histamine-treated mice or normal mice. The capacity of spleen cells from histamine-treated mice to suppress the immune response to antigen challenge in normal mice did not show any demonstrable evidence for increased suppressor cell activity. Preliminary studies (Szewczuk, unpublished observations) have indicated that when treated with histamine 2 weeks prior to removal of the spleen, mice generate a population of suppressor cells as evidenced by mixed cell transfer procedures using lethally irradiated recipients. These findings emphasize that the outcome of histamine exposure is determined by a complexity of events, the exact nature of which is presently unknown.

Recently, Rocklin (15) reported that T lymphocytes (16) exposed to histamine (10^{-3} *M* concentration) *in vitro* elaborate a soluble factor (23,000–40,000 MW) which suppresses antigen-induced production of migration inhibitory factor and proliferation by sensitized lymphocytes. These results suggested that the release of histamine at the sites of immediate hypersensitivity reactions, possibly by generating histamine-induced suppressor factor by lymphocytes, may play a regulatory role in the subsequent development of cellular-immune reactions at the same site. It should be noteworthy that in all these studies, HSF was generated *in vitro* by culturing normal or immune lymphocytes with histamine, and after 24 hr of culture at 37°C, the cell-free supernatant was assayed for the inhibitory activity of HSF. Whether HSF exists in an *in vivo* situation is unclear.

Auto-anti-idiotypic antibodies have been shown to be responsible for a decline in the number of PFCs, a reduction in the heterogeneity of avidity of PFCs, and the occurrence of hapten-augmentable PFCs (anti-idiotype-blocked) (27). We, therefore, investigated the effect of histamine on the appearance of anti-idiotype-blocked, hapten-augmentable anti-TNP PFCs. Histamine-treated mice produced a significantly high percentage (124%) of hapten-augmentable IgG PFC responses as compared with the control mice (17%) which did not receive the drug (Table 3). This effect was also found to be time dependent, that is, mice treated with histamine 2 weeks prior to immunization did not produce a significant percentage (35%) of hapten-augmentable PFCs. Furthermore, pools of immune sera from mice treated with histamine 1 or 2 days prior to immunization and 14 days previously immunized with TNP-BGG in CFA caused a hapten-reversible block of plaque formation by spleen cells from TNP-BGG immune mice. Nonimmune sera from histamine-treated mice failed to inhibit the PFC response. Specific adsorption studies have indicated that this PFC-inhibiting factor in immune sera of histamine-treated mice is an antibody of the IgG_1 and IgG_{2a} class, lacks anti-TNP antibody activity, but reacts with anti-TNP antibody of LAF_1 origin. Passive hemagglutination studies on these sera showed the anti-(anti-TNP $F(ab')_2$-IgG) titer. These findings suggest that histamine in combination with antigen induces an auto-anti-idiotypic antibody which, in turn, deregulates the anti-TNP-PFC response to TNP-BGG *in vivo*. Whether histamine induces auto-anti-idiotypic antibody in deregulating immune responses to allergic antigens such as pollen, ragweed, etc., remains to be determined.

It should be noted that it is unclear as to the relationship between histamine-induced suppressor factor as shown by Rocklin and co-workers (15, 16) and our histamine-induced auto-anti-idiotypic antibody, other than the fact that the former is induced *in vitro* and the latter is induced *in vivo* by histamine. The role of HSF may be in suppression of established responses and not in suppression of primary immune responses. The exact nature of these events *in vivo* remains unclear. Furthermore, anti-idiotypic antibodies have been shown to induce the activation of suppressor T cells (29) which suppress hapten-specific delayed-type hypersensitivity reactions in mice (30). In humans, recent results by Rocklin *et al.* (31) indicated that antigen-specific suppressor cells, probably bearing histamine receptors, are generated during desensitization to ragweed allergy. Whether auto-anti-idiotypic antibody regulation occurs in patients with allergies and chronic inflammation remains unclear.

REFERENCES

1. Plaut, M., Lichtenstein, L. M., and Henney, C. S., *J. Clin. Invest.* **55,** 856, 1975.
2. Rocklin, R. E., Greineder, D., Littman, B. H., and Melmon, K. L., *Cell. Immunol.* **37,** 162, 1978.

3. Rocklin, R. E., *J. Clin. Invest.* **57,** 1051, 1976.
4. Wang, S. R., and Zweiman, B., *Cell. Immunol.* **36,** 28, 1978.
5. Melmon, K. L., Bourne, H. R., Weinstein, Y., Shearer, G. M., Kram, J., and Rauminger, S., *J. Clin. Invest.* **53,** 13, 1974.
6. Fallah, H. A., Maillard, J. L., and Voisin, G. A., *Ann. Immunol. (Inst. Pasteur) C* **125,** 669, 1975.
7. Mozes, E., Weinstein, Y., Bourne, H. R., Melmon, K. L., and Shearer, G. M., *Cell. Immunol.* **11,** 57, 1974.
8. Segal, S., Weinstein, Y., Melmon, K. L., and McDevitt, H. O., *Fed. Proc.* **33,** 723, 1974.
9. Shearer, G. M., Melmon, K. L., Weinstein, Y., and Sela, M., *J. Exp. Med.* **135,** 1302, 1972.
10. Shearer, G. M., Weinstein, Y., and Melmon, K. L., *J. Immunol.* **113,** 597, 1974.
11. Brodeur, B. R., Weinstein, Y., Melmon, K. L., and Merigan, T. C., *Cell. Immunol.* **29,** 363, 1977.
12. Ballet, J. J., and Merler, E., *Cell. Immunol.* **24,** 250, 1976.
13. Saxon, A., Morledge, V. D., and Bonavida, B., *Clin. Exp. Immunol.* **28,** 394, 1977.
14. Roszkowski, W., Plaut, M. L., and Lichenstein, L. M., *Science* **195,** 683, 1977.
15. Rocklin, R. E., *J. Immunol.* **118,** 1734, 1977.
16. Rocklin, R. E., Greineder, D. K., and Melmon, K. L., *Cell. Immunol.* **44,** 404, 1979.
17. Eisen, H. N., Belman, S., and Carsten, M. E., *J. Amer. Chem. Soc.* **75,** 4583, 1953.
18. Werblin, T. P., Kim, Y. T., Quagliata, F., and Siskind, G. W., *Immunology* **24,** 477, 1973.
19. Jerne, N. K., Nordin, A. A., and Hendry, C., *In* "Cell Bound Antibody" (B. Amox and H. Koprowski, Eds.). Wistar Inst. Press, Philadelphia.
20. Dresser, D. W., and Greaves, M. R., *In* "Handbook of Experimental Immunology" (D. M. Weir, Ed.). Blackwell Scientific Publ., Oxford.
21. Rittenberg, M. B., and Pratt, K. L., *Proc. Soc. Exp. Biol. Med.* **132,** 575, 1969.
22. Andersson, B., *J. Exp. Med.* **132,** 77, 1970.
23. DeLisi, C., and Goldstein, B., *Immunochemistry* **11,** 661, 1974.
24. Goidl, E. A., Birnbaum, G., and Siskind, G. W., *J. Immunol. Methods* **8,** 47, 1975.
25. Brillouin, L., "Science and Information Theory," Academic Press, New York.
26. Goidl, E. A., Schrater, A. F., Siskind, G. W., and Thorbecke, G. J., *J. Exp. Med.* **150,** 154, 1979.
27. Schrater, A. L., Goidl, E. A., Thorbecke, G. J. and Siskind, G. W., *J. Exp. Med.* **150,** 138, 1979.
28. Schwartz, A., Askenase, P. Q., and Gershon, R. K., *J. Immunol.* **118,** 159, 1977.
29. Sy, M.-S., Bach, A. B., Dohi, Y., Nisonoff, A., Benacerraf, B., and Greene, M. I., *J. Exp. Med.* **150,** 1216, 1979.
30. Yamamoto, H., Nonaka, M., and Katz, D. H., *J. Exp. Med.* **150,** 818, 1979.
31. Rocklin, R. E., Sheffer, A. L., Greineder, D. K., and Melmon, K. L., *N. Engl. J. Med.* **302,** 1213, 1980.

CELLULAR IMMUNOLOGY **65**, 166–174 (1981)

Changing Behavior of Surface Immunoglobulin on Mouse B Lymphocytes during Immune Development

I. LPS-Induced Changes in the Lateral Mobility of B Lymphocyte Surface Immunoglobulins on Two Populations Which Express Different Surface Immunoglobulin Phenotypes

KEITH A. KROLICK[1] AND ELI E. SERCARZ

Department of Microbiology, University of California, Los Angeles, California 90024

Received August 14, 1981; accepted October 6, 1981

The redistribution of surface membrane immunoglobulin molecules (sIg) was studied in two functionally distinct populations of mouse splenic B lymphocytes, namely, those bearing membrane IgM(IgG^-) and those bearing IgG. Brief exposure to mitogenic doses of bacterial lipopolysaccharide (LPS) produced direct but differential effects on the subsequent ability of specific antibodies to induce this redistribution on each cell type. Studied as a function of temperature, antibody-induced redistribution of sIgM on cells previously exposed to LPS was observed to occur at temperatures lower than the temperatures required for similar sIgM redistribution on lymphocytes not exposed to LPS. In contrast, mitogen-treated $sIgG^+$ cells demonstrated an opposite and long-lasting effect (at least 40 hr), requiring higher temperatures to allow sIgG movement comparable to that seen on untreated sIgG-bearing lymphocytes. Thus, we conclude that LPS interacts with *both* IgM^+(IgG^-) and IgG^+ lymphocytes, but that such interactions produced different membrane effects on each B-cell subset. This membrane change can therefore be useful as a quasi-functional differentiation marker. Furthermore, differences in sensitivity to cellular activation by LPS seen between sIgM-bearing ($sIgG^-$) and sIgG-bearing B cells may be a reflection of such direct, although different, membrane effects.

INTRODUCTION

In recent years, the mouse B lymphocyte has been successfully exploited as a model of cellular differentiation. For example, the time course of the ontogenic appearance of certain membrane antigens is becoming very precisely catalogued (1–8). Functional correlations with the appearance of such membrane molecules, however, are often difficult to make. A major stumbling block in these efforts is the lack of an understanding of the molecular mechanisms underlying the transduction of signals via surface molecules to the cytoplasmic machinery receiving the signals. For this reason, we have become concerned not only with which membrane molecules are present on the B cell at a given time in cellular development, but also with certain properties of the membrane with which the activities of such molecules may be influenced.

[1] Correspondence should be sent to: K. A. Krolick, Department of Microbiology, University of Texas, Southwestern Texas Medical School, Dallas, Tex. 75235.

0008-8749/81/170166-09$02.00/0

In a previous study (9) we have shown that anti-Ig-induced redistribution of surface immunoglobulin (sIg) monitored as a function of temperature can clearly distinguish between $sIgM^+IgG^-$ B cells and $sIgG^+$ B cells. It was suggested that the differences in sIg movement which were observed reflected an important, albeit complex, set of characteristics dependent on the differentiation state of a B cell.

The present report extends the original observations by describing dramatic differences between these two B-cell subsets ($sIgM^+IgG^-$ vs $sIgG^+$) when temperature-dependent receptor modulation is studied following short-term exposure to mitogenic doses of lipopolysaccharide (LPS). The accompanying paper then describes changes in temperature-dependent receptor behavior on developing B cells obtained from mice very early in life.

MATERIAL AND METHODS

Lipopolysaccharide treatment. Spleen cells from CBA/J mice, 2–4 months old, were suspended at 5×10^6 cells/ml in RPMI 1640 (Gibco, Santa Clara, Calif.) buffered with 20 m*M* Hepes[2] (Calbiochem, San Diego, Calif.) and aliquoted as 10- to 12-ml volumes in 24-ml culture flasks (Scientific Products, Irvine, Calif.). *Escherichia coli* 0124:B8 lipopolysaccharide (LPS) purchased from Difco (Detroit, Mich.) was used at a dose of 50 μg/ml throughout this study. Incubations with LPS were performed at 37°C for 15 min, 24 hr, or 40 hr. At the end of the culture period, the cells were washed three times in RPMI 1640 at room temperature and resuspended at 5×10^7 cells/ml for surface immunoglobulin (sIg) mobility analysis.

Other mitogens employed in this study were the T-cell activator concanavalin A (Con A) purchased from Calbiochem, and the B-cell mitogen purified protein derivative (PPD), purchased from Connaught Laboratories Ltd., Ontario, Canada. Con A was used at a concentration of 3 μg/ml and PPD at 50 μg/ml.

Immunoglobulin receptor modulation. The fluoresceinated IgG fractions of goat antisera against mouse IgM and mouse IgG2 were purchased from Meloy Laboratories, Springfield, Virginia, and were spun at high speed before use in these studies (10,000*g*, 60 min). Results described below did not vary with the actual sample of antibody employed. FITC-anti-Ig (5–10 μg) was added to 0.1-ml aliquots of a 5×10^7/ml suspension, each preequilibrated to a particular water bath temperature. Incubation for either 5 or 15 min followed. At the end of the incubation period, 0.9 ml of cold 4% paraformaldehyde was added to each tube and the cells placed at ice-bath temperature for at least 30 min. Each sample was then washed three times with 1.0 ml of cold 0.01 *M* phosphate-buffered saline (PBS), pH 7.0, in a Fisher centrifuge (1000*g*, 1 min) and resuspended in PBS for microscopic examination.

Cells binding fluorescent anti-Ig were observed with a Leitz Ortholux fluorescence microscope equipped with a Ploem-type epi-illumination system, two BG-38 filters (red suppression), a 475-nm cutoff filter (uv removal), and two KP490 interference filters. Immunoglobulin positive cells were scored as capped if fluorescence was restricted to *less* than half the cell surface, patched if an irregular pattern of binding existed on *more* than half the cell surface, or described as diffusely

[2] Abbreviations used: Con A, concanavalin A; FITC, fluorescein isothiocyanate; LPS, Lipopolysaccharide; PBS, phosphate-buffered saline; PPD, purified protein derivative of tuberculin; sIg, cell surface immunoglobulin; Hepes, *N*-2-hydroxyethylpiperazine-*N*′-2-ethanesulfonic acid.

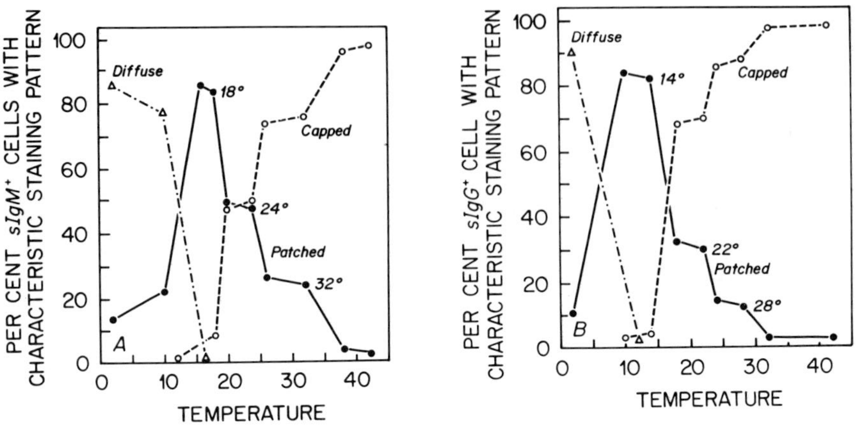

FIG. 1. Hypothetical summary of previous anti-Ig receptor movement studies (9). The extent of splenocyte receptor movement was determined after 15-min exposures of 10^7 cells to 50 μg/ml FITC-GAMIgM (A) or FITC-GAMIgG (B). Incubations were performed at various temperatures (2–40°C) and terminated by addition of a 10× volume of 4% paraformaldehyde. IgM or IgG positive cells (100–200) were scored as diffuse, patched, or capped as described under Materials and Methods. Curves are accurate to within ±1°C as judged from 13 individual experiments.

bound if surface staining appeared smooth, with no irregularities. Cells were scanned until 100–200 immunoglobulin positive cells were scored in each sample: frequencies of capped, patched, or diffuse cells were expressed as percentage of the total number of lymphocytes bearing membrane immunoglobulin and plotted vs the temperature of incubation with FITC-anti-Ig.

RESULTS

Cells Bearing sIgM(sIgG⁻) Demonstrate Different Temperature-Dependent Antibody-Induced Redistribution of Surface Immunoglobulin Than Cells Bearing sIgG

It was shown (9) that the apparent rate of antibody induced redistribution (i.e., patching and capping) of surface-bound immunoglobulin (sIg) observed on mouse B lymphocytes was highly temperature sensitive. Figure 1A is an example of an experiment (representative of 13 individual experiments) which demonstrated the temperature sensitivity of anti-IgM-induced redistribution of sIgM receptors into patches and caps. Each data point was obtained from a cell sample incubated with FITC-GAMIgM for 15 min at a given temperature, fixed, and then scored for diffuse, patched, or capped staining patterns. Therefore, each data point represents an apparent average *rate* at which the sIgM moved laterally through the membranes of the observed cells. A distinct increase or decrease of values in such a curve represents a significant change in the rate of this lateral movement. Temperatures at which such rate changes were observed were not dependent on antibody concentration. Figure 1B shows a similar experiment, focused on the temperature-dependent behavior of membrane immunoglobulin on the more mature $sIgG^+$ lymphocyte population. As can be seen, compared to anti-IgG-induced redistribution of sIgG receptors into patches and caps, sIgM required higher temperatures to attain a similar extent of lateral movement. Thus, sIg modulation on $sIgM^+sIgG^-$

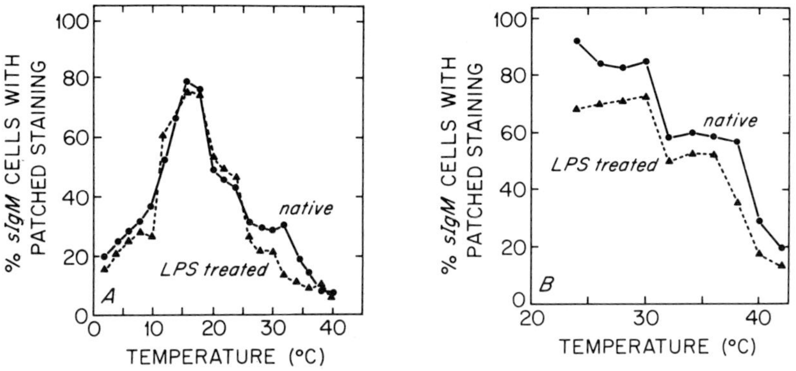

FIG. 2. Effect of short-term exposure of sIgM-bearing cells to LPS. Spleen cells were prepared as described under Materials and Methods and incubated with (▲ - - - ▲) or without (● —— ●) 50 μg/ml LPS for 15 min at 37°C. Following washing, the splenocytes were incubated with 50 μg/ml FITC-GAMIgM at the indicated temperatures for 15 (A) or 5 min (B). The cells were fixed in 4% paraformaldehyde and upon microscopic examination, 100–200 IgM positive cells were scored as diffuse, patched, or capped. For visual clarity, only the rise and fall of the numbers of patched cells is shown which corresponds to the loss of diffuse cells and increased numbers of capped cells, respectively.

B cells can be distinguished from $sIgG^+$ cells by studying such modulation as a function of temperature. The relationship between such membrane differences and the distinct functional differences observed between these two lymphocyte populations is totally unclear.

Differential Response to LPS by $sIgG^+$ and $sIgM^+$ B Cells

a. Short-term exposure to LPS. There have been various reports indicating a predominance of secreted IgM over IgG in response to LPS (10–13). Thus, in view of the clear differences in receptor behavior expressed by $sIgM^+$ vs $sIgG^+$ lymphocytes, we were led to ask if the temperature-dependent lateral mobility of their receptors would be differentially affected by exposure to mitogenic doses of LPS. Figure 2 indicates that after a 15-min exposure of spleen cells to 50 μg/ml LPS at 37°C, the sIgM-bearing cells showed a slight, but consistent enhancement of receptor movement examined at temperatures above 24°C. This temperature shift in the curve of sIgM receptor mobility was accurate to within ±1°C as judged in three individual experiments. However, the same short-term exposure of B cells to LPS dramatically shifted the curve representing the redistribution of sIgG toward higher temperatures, implying that the sIg on this B-cell subset had restricted lateral mobility compared to untreated controls (Fig. 3). These changes in temperature-dependent sIg receptor mobility, induced by LPS, were probably not dependent on a process requiring active metabolism, since similar LPS treatment performed at room temperature (20–22°C) generated effects on sIgM- and sIgG-bearing cells identical to those outlined in this report. In addition, mitogenic doses of concanavalin A or the purified protein derivative of tuberculin demonstrated no effect on temperature-dependent movement of either sIgM or sIgG (data not shown).

b. Long-term exposure to LPS. Since distinct differences were observed between B cells expressing sIgM($sIgG^-$) and those expressing sIgG with regard to the effects of short-term exposure of LPS on lateral mobility of sIg, the behavior of sIgM and

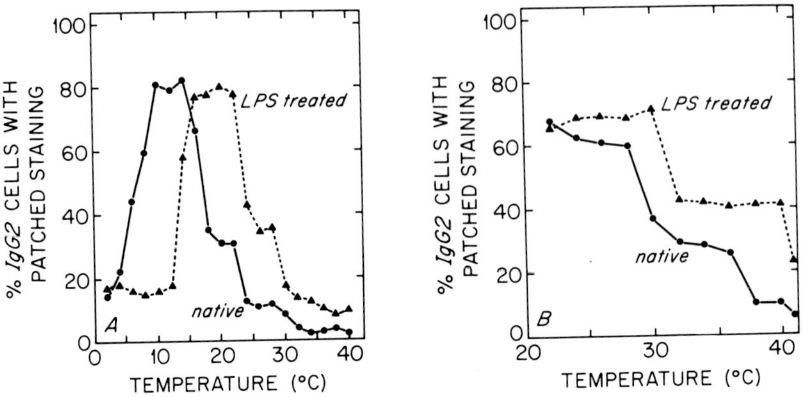

FIG. 3. Identical to legend of Fig. 2, except that spleen cells were stained for sIgG-bearing cells.

sIgG was examined on the same population of cells during different stages after *in vitro* stimulation by LPS. Figure 4 shows the temperature-dependent behavior of sIgM on cells exposed to LPS for 24 and 40 hr. Cells cultured without mitogen for either 24 or 40 hr demonstrated anti-Ig-induced receptor mobility and cell morphology similar to newly excised, uncultured spleen cells. However, in cells cultured with LPS for 24 hr, the slightly enhanced temperature-dependent receptor mobility on sIgM-bearing cells seen at 15 min (Fig. 2) was more pronounced, although after 1 day there was still no change in the overall morphology of the sIgM positive lymphocytes. In contrast, by 40 hr, about 40% of the total nucleated spleen cell population was present in the form of blasts, virtually all of which stained for sIgM. In addition, not only were all the blasts sIgM positive, but nearly all of the sIgM-positive lymphocytes were in a blast state (95%). Furthermore, by 40 hr a shift toward higher temperatures was observed in the curve representing sIgM receptor redistribution (Fig. 4). Note that the percentage of patched cells in Figs.

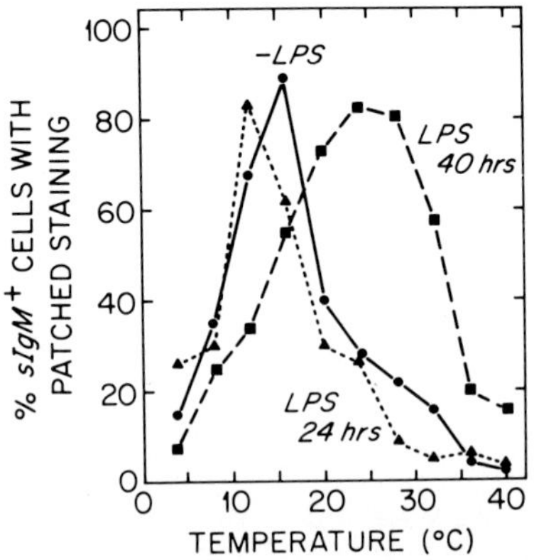

FIG. 4. Effect of 24-hr (▲ - - - ▲) or 40 hr (■ —— ■) exposure of sIgM-bearing cells to 50 μg/ml LPS at 37°C. LPS control (● —— ●) is representative of cells cultured for 24 or 40 hr without LPS. Upon harvesting cultures, the cells were examined for temperature-dependent receptor mobility induced by FITC-GAMIgM as described in Fig. 2. Note that examinations of receptor distribution were performed at 4°C increments, instead of the usual 2°C increments. For this reason, visualization of discrete discontinuities in the curves is not possible.

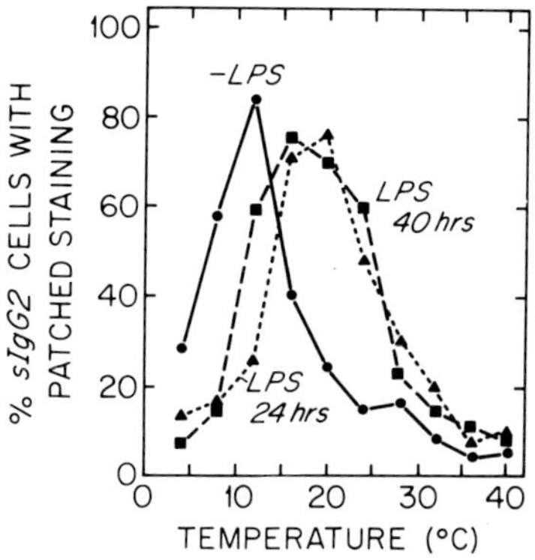

FIG. 5. Identical to legend to Fig. 4, except that spleen cells were stained for sIgG-bearing cells.

4 and 5 was determined at 4°C intervals instead of every 2°C as seen in previous curves. With the wider intervals, only trends in temperature-dependent receptor behavior are seen and fine resolution of the characteristic slope changes is lost.

LPS-stimulated cultures (40 hr) examined for sIgG lateral mobility (Fig. 5), demonstrated completely different behavior. Although the same frequency of blasts was present, none stained for sIgG. This implied that, at least by 40 hr, no $sIgG^+$ lymphocytes showed morphological signs of stimulation by LPS. Indeed, even the behavior of sIgG was little changed from the initial state of retarded mobility which was observable as early as 15 min into the LPS incubation period, suggesting that no apparent membrane changes were taking place.

Internalization of Receptors by Blasts

In addition to observing retarded movement of sIg into patches on LPS-stimulated, blast-transformed $sIgM^+$ B cells (the rising left side of the patching curve), a changed significance could be attributed to the declining right side of the curve. Unlike the previous curves, in which the decrease in the numbers of patched cells corresponded with the increase in numbers of capped cells, the sIgM-bearing blasts showed no cap formation. Instead, there was an enhanced efficiency of internalization of anti-IgM from a patched state on the cell surface, directly into the cytoplasm. The few capped cells present were included in the small, non-blast-transformed population (5%) which stained for sIgM. sIgM-bearing cells cultured without LPS rarely demonstrated any internalization during the 15-min exposure to anti-IgM, even at higher temperatures.

DISCUSSION

Ever since subpopulations of B lymphocytes have been identified, continual study and discussion has been focused on the functional and physical differences between B cells expressing membrane IgM (with no IgG) and the apparently more mature B cells expressing membrane IgG. One such distinction between these two B-cell subsets which we have previously reported (9) is that the anti-Ig induced redistribution of the surface Ig on each cell type is characteristically different if studied as a function of temperature. Another functional difference between the $sIgM^+IgG^-$ cell and the $sIgG^+$ cell is the sensitivity of each cell to stimulation by LPS. Thus,

TABLE 1

Differences between $sIgM^+(sIgG^-)$ and $sIgG^+$ Lymphocytes Stimulated for 40 hr with Lipopolysaccharide

	$sIgM^+(sIgG^-)$	$sIgG^+$
Morphology	95% blasts	All small to medium
Fate of sIg exposed to anti-Ig	Patching and internalization (no capping)	Patching and capping
Relative rate of sIg movement	Retarded	Retarded
Percentage of spleen cells stained	35–40	4–7

it has been noted that the predominance of IgM over IgG secretory responses by B cells may reflect the initially predominant, if not exclusive, proliferation of $sIgM^+IgG^-$ B cells (10–14). Therefore, in an attempt to further characterize the response of these two B-cell subpopulations to LPS with respect to their differentiation state, we have examined the ability of either anti-IgM or anti-IgG to modulate the sIg on each type of B cell during a 2-day exposure to the mitogen.

The observations made in this study allow a three-way correlation involving the influence of LPS on sIg mobility, the sIg phenotype of the cell, and its sensitivity to LPS. As depicted here, the central feature of this system is the state of differentiation of the B cell, as manifested by its sIg phenotype.

With regard to sIg mobility following LPS exposure, two conclusions are clear. First, within 15 min there is a direct effect of LPS on the membranes of *both* $sIgG^+$ and $sIgM^+IgG^-$ B cells as demonstrated by altered temperature-dependent sIg mobility on each cell type. Second, LPS has direct and *opposite* effects on the anti-Ig induced lateral movement of sIg through the membranes of each cell type; membrane IgM shows slightly enhanced mobility, while membrane IgG shows very retarded lateral movement. We would like to suggest that these very rapid LPS-induced effects will ultimately be related to the presence or absence of proliferative and secretory activities which will follow.

After 40 hr of incubation with LPS, the $sIgM^+IgG^-$ cells demonstrate characteristic changes in sIg behavior and cell morphology which further distinguish them from the $sIgG^+$ cells (Table 1). Clearly, more than 90% of IgM-bearing cells are in a blast stage, demonstrating that a majority of virgin B cells are activated by LPS, although we do not know what portion of these cells will go on to divide or secrete IgM. The previously enhanced temperature-dependent receptor mobility of the small sIgM positive cell is now highly retarded in the sIgM-bearing blast. In fact, the rate of lateral movement of sIgM receptors in the blast is now quite similar to the retarded rate of LPS-perturbed sIgG movement in the resting small lymphocyte. However, the fates of the two classes of surface molecules are distinctly different. Except for the retarded rate of sIgG receptor movement on the IgG^+ unactivated small lymphocyte, the pattern of surface redistribution into molecular patches or aggregates, and finally into polar caps is identical to untreated cells. In contrast, sIgM–anti-IgM aggregates on blast-transformed cells are internalized, with no observable capped stage. Therefore, the rates of receptor movement on $sIgM^+(sIgG^-)$ vs sIgG-bearing cells are quite similar (retarded) after exposure to LPS for 40 hr, but it is apparent that the receptor-membrane associations of the two populations must be quite different.

The molecular basis for such observations is certainly unclear. However, we favor a mechanism which involves a direct lipophilic interaction between LPS and the bilayer of the cells exposed. Evidence suggesting such an interaction occurs includes: (1) The lipid A moiety of LPS is required for polyclonal B cell stimulation (15, 16); (2) studies using synthetic glycolipid and lipoprotein mitogens have shown that the biochemical character of the lipid moiety, such as fatty acid chain length and number of fatty acids per molecule, can determine the quality of subsequent stimulation (17, 18); (3) none of the effects on sIg behavior described for LPS are observed after short exposures to mitogenic doses of nonlipophillic mitogens such as concanavalin A, a T-cell activator which also binds to B cells, or the purified protein derivative of tuberculin, a B-cell activator (this study). This implies that simple binding of *any* mitogen is insufficient as an explanation for the changes observed in lymphocyte receptor behavior; (4) a previous study suggested that anti-Ig-induced movement of sIg observed as a function of temperature reflects the composition and resulting fluid nature of the membrane bilayer of the cells expressing the sIg. Therefore, we propose that the link between the different effects of LPS on sIg movement on the surface of $sIgM^+IgG^-$ vs $sIgG^+$ B cells, and the apparent difference in the stimulatory effects of LPS between each of these B-cell subsets may reside in the quality of such lipophillic interactions. Thus, differentiation of a B cell from $sIgM^+IgG^-$ to $sIgG^+$ would include among other things, a change in the nature of the lipid bilayer which can be monitored by measuring the temperature-dependent behavior of molecules which reside in that bilayer. In addition, all cells in the treated cell cultures were probably physically affected by such LPS–membrane interactions, although only effects on B cells were determined in these studies. It would certainly be of interest to determine if other membrane molecules on B cells (e.g., products of the major histocompatibility complex) or membrane molecules or functional activities of non-B cells, or even nonlymphocytes are affected by lipophilic molecules such as LPS.

In conclusion, direct and opposite LPS-induced changes were observed in the ability of anti-Ig to cause the redistribution of sIgM on the surface of one population of B lymphocytes, and the sIgG on another. We suggest that this difference reflects some differentiation event(s) which occurs in the B-cell lineage as cells mature from a $sIgM^+sIgG^-$ phenotype to a IgG^+ phenotype.

ACKNOWLEDGMENTS

This work was supported in part by NIH Grant AI-11183. Keith A. Krolick was a predoctoral trainee of USPHS Training Grant AI-00431. We thank B. J. Wisnieski for valuable discussion.

REFERENCES

1. Vitetta, E. S., Cambier, J. Forman, J., Kettman, J. R., Yuan, D., and Uhr, J. W., *Cold Spring Harbor Symp. Quant. Biol.* **41,** 185, 1976.
2. Cooper, M. D., Kearney, J. F., Lawton, A. R., Abney, E. R., Parkhouse, M. E., Preud'homme, J. L., and Seligmann, M., *Ann. Immunol. (Paris)* **127,** 573, 1976.
3. Pernis, B., Forni, L., and Luzzati, A. L., *Cold Spring Harbor Symp. Quant. Biol.* **41,** 175, 1976.
4. Huber, B., Gershon, R. K., and Cantor, H., *J. Exp. Med.* **145,** 10, 1977.
5. Subbarao, B., Mosier, D. E., Ahmed, A., Mond, J. J., Scher, I., and Paul, W. E., *J. Exp. Med.* **149,** 495, 1979.
6. Hammerling, U., Chin A. F., and Abbott, J., *Proc. Nat. Acad. Sci. USA* **73,** 2008, 1976.
7. Elson, J. Jenkinson, E. J., and Billingham, W. D., *Nature (London)* **255,** 412, 1975.

8. Scribner, D. J., Weiner, H. L., and Moorhead, J. W., *J. Immunol.* **121,** 377, 1978.
9. Krolick, K. A., Wisnieski, B. J., and Sercarz, E. E., *Proc. Nat. Acad. Sci. USA* **74,** 4595, 1977.
10. Andersson, J., Moller, G., and Sjoberg, O., *Cell. Immunol.* **4,** 381, 1972.
11. Melchers, F., and Andersson, J., *Transplant Rev.* **14,** 76, 1973.
12. Melchers, F., and Andersson, J., *Eur. J. Immunol.* **4,** 181, 1974.
13. Gronowicz, E. S., Doss, C., Assisi, F., Vitetta, E. S., Coffman, R. L., and Strober, S., *J. Immunol.* **123,** 2049, 1979.
14. Gronowicz, E. S., Doss, C., and Schroder, J., *J. Immunol.* **123,** 2049, 1979.
15. Chiller, J. M., Skidmore, B. J. Morrison, D. C., and Weigle, W. O., *Proc. Nat. Acad. Sci. USA* **70,** 2129, 1973.
16. Andersson, J., Melchers, F., Galanos, C., and Luderitz, O., *J. Exp. Med.* **137,** 943, 1973.
17. Behling, U. H., Campbell, B., Chang, C., Rumpf, C., and Nowotny, A., *J. Immunol.* **117,** 847, 1976.
18. Heatly, R. V., and Stark, J. M., *Immunology* **29,** 143, 1975.

CELLULAR IMMUNOLOGY 65, 175–179 (1981)

Changing Behavior of Surface Immunoglobulin on Mouse B Lymphocytes during Immune Development

II. Surface Immunoglobulin Modulation Clearly Distinguishes Two Stages of B-Cell Maturation in the Neonate

KEITH A. KROLICK[1] AND ELI E. SERCARZ

Department of Microbiology, University of California, Los Angeles, California 90024

Received August 14, 1981; accepted October 6, 1981

Antibody-induced modulation of cell surface IgM was used as a probe to explore membrane-related differences between fetal and adult mouse B lymphocytes. Receptor modulation was studied as a function of temperature in B cells obtained from mice of various ages. Plots of the rate of anti-IgM induced movement of receptors with temperature showed discontinuities (changes in slope) at different characteristic temperatures for each cell. In this way, radical differences between the receptor behavior of fetal B cells and adult B cells were evident. Moreover, temperature-dependent rates of internalization of receptor–ligand complexes also were found to clearly distinguish two stages of B lymphocyte maturation in the mouse.

INTRODUCTION

The state of maturity or differentiation of B cells obtained from mice of various ages has been described using a number of criteria. For example, the comparative densities of cell surface IgM and IgD are relatively consistent indicators of the maturity of a B cell (1–3). In addition, the expression of other membrane molecules is often useful for determining the differentiation state of a B cell (4–8). The ability of a B cell to respond to certain mitogens or antigens many times offers functional correlations with the phenotypic expression of lymphocyte-specific surface molecules (9–11).

We report here that when studied as a function of temperature, anti-immunoglobulin induced movement of cell surface IgM can also be used to distinguish at least two distinct stages of B-cell maturation.

MATERIALS AND METHODS

Animals. Mouse lymphocytes of fetal origin were obtained from timed-pregnancy CBA/J females (Jackson Laboratories, Bar Harbor, Maine). CBA/J males and females from Jackson Laboratories were mated to obtain neonatal animals. CBA/J mice over the age of 4 weeks were all obtained from Jackson Labs.

[1] Correspondence should be sent to: K. A. Krolick, Department of Microbiology, University of Texas, Southwestern Texas Medical School, Dallas, Tex. 75235.

0008-8749/81/170175-05$02.00/0

Immunoglobulin receptor modulation. The fluoresceinated IgG fraction of goat antiserum against mouse IgM (FITC-GAMIgM) was purchased from Meloy Laboratories, Springfield, Virginia. Its binding specificity was described elsewhere (12). Lymphocyte suspensions at 5×10^7 cells/ml in RPMI 1640 (Gibco, Santa Clara, Calif.) were incubated with the supernatant of a high-speed centrifugation (10,000*g*, 60 min) of FITC-GAMIgM at various final anti-IgM concentrations for either 5 or 15 min at a particular water-bath temperature. At the end of the incubation period, 0.9 ml of cold 4% paraformaldehyde was added to each sample. Each sample was then washed three times before microscopic examination.

Cells binding fluorescent anti-IgM were observed with a Leitz Ortholux fluorescence microscope. Surface IgM positive cells were scored as capped if fluorescence was restricted to *less* than half the cell surface, patched if an irregular pattern of binding existed on *more* than half the cell surface, or described as diffusely bound if surface staining appeared smooth, with no irregularities. Samples were scanned until 100–200 IgM positive cells were counted. Frequencies of capped, patched, or diffuse cells were expressed as percentage of the total number of stained lymphocytes and plotted versus temperature.

RESULTS AND DISCUSSION

In a previous report (12), we demonstrated that the rate of anti-immunoglobulin-induced patching and capping of cell surface immunoglobulin (sIg) increased when measured as a function of increasing temperature. However, at distinct temperatures, discontinuities were observed in plots of increasing rate of receptor movement vs temperature. For sIgM lateral movement, 13 experiments demonstrated such discontinuities consistently at 18, 24, 32, and 38°C.

Receptor modulation discontinuities occur at higher temperature in neonatal B cells. In the present report, temperature-dependent sIgM mobility was exploited to explore membrane-related differences between mouse B cells obtained from 18-day fetal liver and spleen vs those obtained from adult spleen. First, we compared fetal and adult cell membranes by examining the characteristic temperatures at which discontinuities arise in the receptor modulation curves (Fig. 1). It was observed that these temperatures were 18, 24, 32, and 38°C for the adult B cell, and 21, 30, 36, and >42°C[2] for fetal cells. Examination of mice at various ages (Table 1) revealed that the fetal character of B-lymphocyte membrane receptor mobility was lost by 1 week of age. This was reflected by the observed shift of discontinuities on curves of temperature-dependent receptor mobility to temperatures characteristic of a 3- to 5-month-old adult. It is of interest to note that during this period of development (birth to 2 weeks) that a significant decrease in the ratio of surface IgM:IgD occurs (1–3). The relationship of the IgM:IgD ratio with various membrane properties or the functional capabilities of a B cell may be of great importance, but is certainly not understood.

Efficiency of receptor modulation. Another index of receptor behavior which differed when fetal B cells were compared to adult B cells was the kinetics at which "patched" cells were converted to the capped state. At temperatures above 30°C (Fig. 1B), receptor modulation is more efficient (rapid) on fetal cells than on cells

[2] The expected fourth-rate change did not occur before temperatures were reached which affected viability. Therefore, the last and highest temperature will be described simply as >42°C.

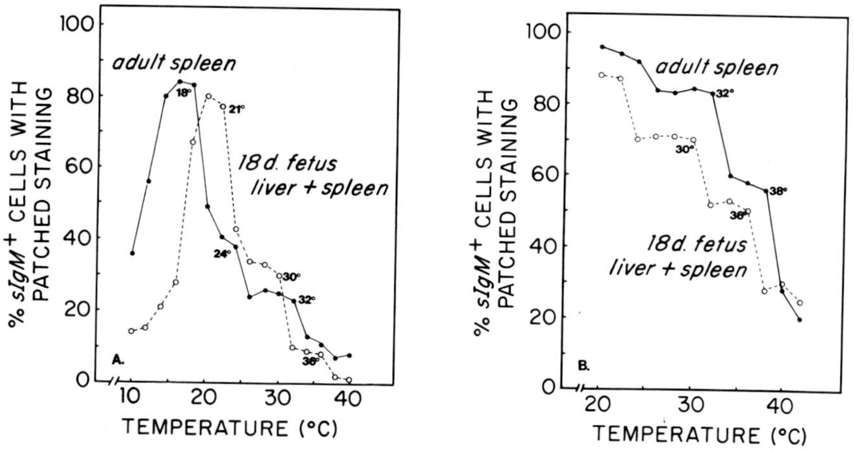

FIG. 1. Cell surface IgM on adult vs fetal B cells shows changing rates of anti-Ig-induced movement at different temperatures. Extent of B-cell receptor movement was observed at various temperatures (10–42°C) during 15- (A) or 5-min (B) exposures of 10^7 cells to 50 μg/ml of a fluorescein-labeled IgG fraction of goat antiserum against mouse IgM (FITC-GAMIgM). Lymphocytes were obtained from either CBA/J 18-day fetal liver and spleen (○ - - - ○) or from adult spleen (● —— ●). Incubations were terminated by addition of a 10× volume of cold 4% paraformaldehyde. sIgM positive cells (100–200) were scored as diffuse (smooth ring of binding), patched (irregular pattern of binding found on *more* than half the cell surface), or capped (binding restricted to *less* than half the cell surface). Although only the frequency of "patched" cells is expressed here, the rising (left) sides of these curves also represent the loss of cells showing diffuse staining. Similarly, the falling (right) sides of the patching curves represent "patched" cells proceeding to another state of receptor redistribution, "capped" for example.

of adult origin, even though the corresponding discontinuities in the curve of receptor movement occurs at higher temperatures for the fetal cells (Table 1). This is a very important point because it indicates that something much more complex is being studied than simple diffusion rates of protein through lipid. Indeed, energy-generating enzymes as well as cytoskeletal filamentous structures are major com-

TABLE 1

Changing Temperature-Dependent sIgM Behavior during Immune Development[a]

B-Cell source	No. of experiments	t_1 [b] (°C)	t_2 (°C)	t_3 (°C)	t_4 [c] (°C)	Percentage GAMIgM$^+$
18-Day fetus	3	21	30	36	>42	1
2-Day newborn	2	22	30	34	>42	10
7-Day-old	2	<20	24	32	38	16
12-Day-old	2	<20	24	32	38	26
17-Day-old	2	<20	24	32	38	39
3-Month-old	14	18	24	32	38	40
7-Month-old	3	18	24	32	38	38

[a] t_{1-4} refer to the four temperatures at which discontinuities are observed in plots of anti-IgM induced sIgM movement vs temperature.

[b] t_1 for 7, 12, and 17-day-old mice were obtained exclusively from 5-min sIgM modulation studies which include observations at temperatures from 20 to 42°C. t_1 was not detectable in this temperature range.

[c] Determination of t_4 for the 18-day fetus and 2-day neonate was not possible due to the onset of cell lysis at temperatures above 43°C.

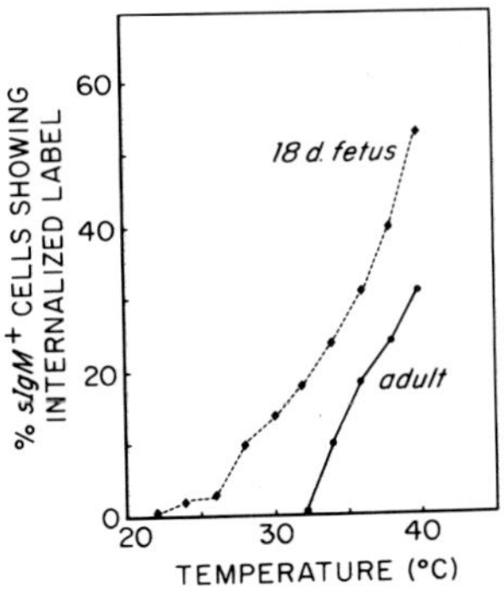

FIG. 2. Frequencies of sIgM positive cells showing internalized label at various temperatures (20–40°C) during a 15-min incubation with 50 μg/ml FITC-GAMIgM as described in Fig. 1. Lymphocytes were obtained from adult spleen (● —— ●) or fetal liver and spleen (♦ - - - ♦).

ponents of the receptor-modulating machinery (13, 14), and surely influence receptor behavior throughout the development of a cell. Thus, we should emphasize that the temperature-dependent membrane properties studied here seem to determine when receptor movement accelerates as a function of temperature, while values relating to the extent of receptor movement at a given temperature (e.g., degree of capping) will depend on the quality of associations with cytoplasmic components driving the modulation process.

Receptor–ligand internalization. A third noteworthy consideration was that the proportion of cells which demonstrated receptor–ligand internalization (via pinocytosis) started to increase at much lower temperatures in cells of fetal origin than in cells of the adult (Fig. 2). Thus, there was a full 10°C spread between the temperature at which receptor internalization was observed for B cells of fetal origin versus those of adult origin. As temperature was increased, internalization of receptor–ligand complexes could first be noted within the adult cells at 34°C. The changing rate of the appearance of new adult cells displaying internalization as temperature was further increased remained the same as for the fetal cells (in which such internalization was first observed at 24°C). Because of the parallel slopes, when physiological temperature was reached, the frequency of fetal cells showing internalization remained nearly twice that of adult cells. During a 15-min incubation at 37°C, the ratio of cells that exhibited external caps to those with internal staining was 4:1 for the adult and 1:1 for the fetus.

One further point should be made concerning experiments designed to test the dose dependence of anti-IgM-induced receptor modulation. An independent study (15) has already shown differences in the characteristic receptor modulation of each of these B-cell populations. In the present study, between 5 and 500 μg/ml FITC-GAMIgM induced temperature-dependent receptor mobility with discontinuities at the same characteristic temperatures as our standard 50 μg/ml (data not shown). Thus, there was no indication that differences in receptor density were responsible for fetal vs adult lymphocyte receptor behavior. However, the amount of labeled, internalized IgM and the frequency of cells showing internalization, did increase with increased anti-IgM concentration for both fetal and adult cells.

In conclusion, we would like to suggest a model of changing membrane bilayer properties early in life, reflected by temperature-dependent receptor mobility. We have previously suggested that one property which may influence temperature-dependent receptor movement is the composition, and therefore the fluid nature of the lipid bilayer (12). Changes in membrane fluidity may play an important regulatory role throughout development. For instance, irreversible modulation of surface receptors has previously been suggested as a possible mechanism for the establishment of tolerance to self-antigens in the neonatal period (16, 17). We contend that a crucial element in B-lymphocyte activation (or tolerance induction) is a membrane of appropriate consistency to facilitate and support the proper contacts between receptors for antigen and the next component of the activation mechanism of the B lymphocyte. Furthermore, such membrane properties, detectable by examining sIg^+ modulation as a function of temperature, are apparently intimately related to the state of maturation of a B lymphocyte.

ACKNOWLEDGMENTS

This work was supported in part by NIH Grant AI-11183. Keith A. Krolick was a predoctoral trainee of USPHS Training Grant AI-00431.

REFERENCES

1. Vitetta, E. S., Cambier, J., Forman, J., Kettman, J. R., Yuan, D., and Uhr, J. W., *Cold Spring Harbor Sym. Quant. Biol.* **41,** 185, 1976.
2. Cooper, M. D., Kearney, J. F., Lawton, A. R., Abney, E. R., Parkhouse, M. E., Preud'homme, J. L., and Seligmann, M., *Ann. Immunol. (Paris)* **127,** 573, 1976.
3. Pernis, B., Forni, L., and Luzzati, A. L., *Cold Spring Harbor Symp. Quant. Biol.* **41,** 175, 1976.
4. Huber, B., Gershon, R. K., and Cantor, H., *J. Exp. Med.* **145,** 10, 1977.
5. Subbarao, B., Mosier, D. E., Ahmed, A., Mond, J. J., Scher, I., and Paul, W. E., *J. Exp. Med.* **149,** 495, 1979.
6. Hammerling, U., Chin, A. F., and Abbott, J., *Proc. Nat. Acad. Sci. USA* **73,** 2008, 1976.
7. Elson, J., Jenkinson, E. J., and Billingham, W. D., *Nature (London)* **255,** 412, 1975.
8. Scribner, D. J., Weiner, H. L., and Moorhead, J. W., *J. Immunol.* **121,** 377, 1978.
9. Mosier, D. E., Goldings, E. A., and Bottomly, K., *In* "B Lymphocytes in the Immune Response" (M. Cooper, D. E. Mosier, I. Scher, and E. S. Vitetta, Eds.), pp. 91–95, 1979.
10. Ahmed, A., and Scher, I., *In* "B Lymphocytes in the Immune Response" (M. Cooper, D. E. Mosier, I. Scher, and E. S. Vitetta, Eds.), pp. 91–95, 1979.
11. Huber, B. T., Gathings, W. E., and Cooper, M. D., *In* "B Lymphocytes in the Immune Response" (M. Cooper, D. E. Mosier, I. Scher, and E. S. Vitetta, Eds.), pp. 125–130, 1979.
12. Krolick, D. A., Wisnieski, B. J., and Sercarz, E. E., *Proc. Nat. Acad. Sci. USA* **74,** 4595, 1977.
13. Unanue, E. R., Karnovsky, M. J., and Engers, M. D., *J. Exp. Med.* **137,** 675, 1973.
14. Schreiner, G. F., Fujiwara, K., Pollard, T. D., and Unanue, E. R., *J. Exp. Med.* **145,** 1393, 1977.
15. Gathings, W. E., *J. Exp. Med.* **142,** 1052, 1975.
16. Raff, M. C., *Cold Spring Harbor Symp. Quant. Biol.* **41,** 159, 1976.
17. Bruyns, C., Urbain-Vansanten, G., Planard, C., deVos-Cloetens, C., and Urbain, J., *Proc. Nat. Acad. Sci. USA* **73,** 2462, 1976.

CELLULAR IMMUNOLOGY 65, 180–193 (1981)

Expression of T-Cell Differentiation Antigens on Activated Thymocytes[1]

PAWEŁ KISIELOW AND PETR DRÁBER

Ludwik Hirszfeld Institute of Immunology and Experimental Therapy of the Polish Academy of Sciences, Wrocław, and Institute of Molecular Genetics of the Czechoslovak Academy of Sciences, Prague, Czechoslavakia

Received July 1, 1981; accepted September 23, 1981

The expression of Thy1, TL, Lyt1, and Lyt2 antigens on resting and proliferating thymocytes activated by concanavalin A in the presence of interleukin 2 has been studied by conventional complement-dependent cytotoxicity assay. The predominant population of resting thymocytes has a $TL^+Lyt1^+Lyt2^+$ phenotype while the predominant population of proliferating thymocytes has a TL − $Lyt1^+Lyt2^+$ phenotype. Using several separation procedures such as agglutination by peanut lectin, BSA density gradient centrifugation, and pretreatment with high dilutions of anti-H-2 serum it was impossible to obtain a 100% pure population of $TL^+Lyt1^+Lyt2^+$ cells, suggesting that the population of resting immature thymocytes contains small subpopulations of phenotypically differentiated cells. The population of proliferating thymocytes is also phenotypically heterogenous and contains cells bearing all phenotypes that were described for different stages of T-cell differentiation, including $TL^+Lyt1^+Lyt2^-$ and $TL^+Lyt1^-Lyt2^+$ with the following approximate frequency: $TL^+Lyt1^+Lyt2^+$—27%, $TL^+Lyt1^+Lyt2^-$—8%, $TL^+Lyt1^-Lyt2^+$—4%, $TL^-Lyt1^+Lyt2^+$—45%, $TL^-Lyt1^+Lyt2^-$—13%, $TL^-Lyt1^-Lyt2^+$—3%.

INTRODUCTION

Most of the present knowledge about the surface antigenic structure of thymocytes derives from studies on whole populations of thymic cells, the bulk of which consists of resting, cortical, so called "immature thymocytes." Much less information is available about the surface antigenic properties of activated thymocytes because, before the recent demonstrations (1–4) that in the presence of various conditioned media immature thymocytes can be induced to proliferate, such studies were difficult to perform. The need for such studies, among other reasons, stems from the fact that the ultimate elucidation of precursor–progeny relationships between distinct subpopulations of thymocytes and T cells, identified by their different surface antigenic phenotypes (5–8), is crucially dependent on the ability to monitor the complete sequence of surface antigenic changes accompanying the activation of thymocytes and their transition from one phenotype to another.

As a preliminary step toward such studies we have compared the expression of TL, Thy1, Lyt1, and Lyt2 antigens on normal and activated thymocytes following

[1] This study was supported by the Polish Academy of Sciences, Grant 10.5.

0008-8749/81/170180-14$02.00/0

stimulation with concanavalin A (Con A) in the presence of conditioned media containing interluekin 2 (IL2).

Our analysis of cell surface phenotypes was performed with the conventional, complement (C)-dependent cytotoxicity assay which is recently giving way to modern and more sensitive methods such as flow microfluorometry (8). However, it is our belief that studies using traditional methods are still of value, especially for functional analysis of separated subpopulations, where elimination of cells in the presence of C plays an important role and cannot be substituted by other methods.

MATERIALS AND METHODS

Mice. Six- to eight-week-old female or male mice of the BALB/c, C57BL/6 (B6), and Lyt and TL congenic (B6/Lyt1.1, B6/Lyt2.1, and B6/TL$^+$) strains used in these experiments were derived from the breeders obtained from Dr. E. A. Boyse, Memorial Sloan–Kettering Cancer Center, New York, and have been bred at the Institute of Immunology and Experimental Therapy since 1975.

Antisera. The anti-H-2, -Thy1, -TL, -Lyt1, and -Lyt2 sera (see Table 1) were prepared and characterized as described elsewhere (9, 10).

Preparation of thymocytes. Thymuses were removed with special care to exclude parathymic lymph nodes. Cell suspensions were prepared by gently pressing the thymuses through a 60-mesh nylon screen into RPMI 1640 without supplements. After two washes the cells were resuspended in phosphate-buffered saline (PBS) or in Hanks' balanced salt solution containing 2.5% fetal calf serum (HBSS–FCS). Viability of cells was always greater than 95%.

Fractionation of thymocytes. Suspensions of thymocytes were fractionated either by peanut agglutinin (PNA, Boehringer-Mannheim) by the method of Reisener *et al.* (11) or by density gradient centrifugation on bovine serum albumine (BSA, Path-O-Cyte 5, Lot 37, Miles, Kankakee, Ill.) as described by Konda *et al.* (12). One-milliliter volumes of 35, 30, 27, and 24% BSA diluted in RPMI 1640 were layered successively into 5-ml cellulose acetate tubes. Cells (10^8) suspended in 10%

TABLE 1

Antisera

Immunization	Specificity detected on thymocytes	Contaminating antibody
B10 anti-B10.D2 spleen cells	H-2^d	—
(A-Thy1.1 × AKR)F_1 anti-ASL1 leukemia	Thy1.2	—
(B6 × A-TL$^-$)F_1 anti-ASL1 leukemia	TL1,2,3;Qa-1	—
(B6 × BALB/c)F_1 anti-B6-Lty1.1 thymocytes	Lyt1.1	Anti-Ly10[a] (not cytotoxic)
C3H anti-C3H.CE-Lyt1.2:Ds[b] thymocytes	Lyt1.2	Anti-NK[c]
(C3H × B6-Lyt2.1)F_1 anti-B6 thymocytes	Lyt2.2	—

[a] New cell surface alloantigen having wide tissue distribution, coded by locus closely linked to Lyt1^a (Kimura *et al.*, *Immunogenetics* **10,** 363, 1980; Kisielow *et al.*, *Arch. Immunol. Ther. Exp.* **28,** 209, 1980).

[b] Derived stock.

[c] Anti-natural killer specificity (Glimcher *et al.*, *J. Exp. Med.* **145,** 1, 1977).

BSA were layered on top of the gradient. The gradients were centrifuged for 30 min (1800*g*, 4°C), and individual bands were aspirated with a Pasteur pipet. The cells were then washed three times in HBSS–FCS or in culture medium. The interface between 10 and 24% BSA was designated as fraction A, that between 24 and 27% as fraction B, that between 27 and 30% as fraction C, and that between 30 and 35% as fraction D. Fractions A + B and C + D were sometimes pooled and when indicated, used as one fraction. In some experiments, to obtain a pure population of immature (PNA^+, high density) thymocytes, both methods were applied sequentially.

Cytotoxicity test. A one-step or two-step procedure was used with similar results. HBSS–FCS was used as a diluent for all reagents. The one-step procedure involved mixing equal volumes of (a) cell suspension (5×10^6/ml), (b) antiserum, and (c) complement (C, selected, nontoxic rabbit serum, diluted 1/10) and incubating for 45 min at 37°C. In the two-step procedure, 5–10 $\times 10^5$ cells were first incubated in 0.1 ml of antiserum (diluted 1/10–1/20) for 30 min at 4°C, then washed twice, resuspended in the same volume of C diluted 1/25, and incubated for 40 min at 37°C. The percentage of dead cells was determined in the presence of trypan blue by double-blind reading of coded samples. Two to three hundred cells were counted for eaach estimate. The percentage of dead cells in C controls never exceeded 10%.

Elimination of thymocytes with a relatively high membrane concentration of H-2 antigens. Washed and pelleted thymocytes from high-density (C + D) fractions of the BSA gradient were suspended in serial dilutions of anti-H-2 serum (from 1/100 to 1/400) to a final concentration of 10^7 cells/ml and incubated for 30 min at 4°C. The cells were then washed once, resuspended in the same volume of C, diluted 1/25, and incubated for 40 min at 37°C. Dead cells were removed by centrifugation through a layer of 35% BSA. Viable cells (viability more than 95%) were recovered from the interface above the BSA layer, washed three times, and resuspended in the culture medium.

Preparation of conditioned media containing IL2. Conditioned medium promoting Con A-induced mitogenesis of immature thymocytes was prepared according to Irlé *et al.* (4) as previously described (9). BALB/c lymph node cells (10^7/ml) were cultured in complete medium containing Con A (4 μ/ml, Pharmacia Fine Chemicals Inc. Uppsala) for 24 hr, and the supernate was harvested, sterilized by filtration, and stored at −20°C. Con A was removed from the supernate with Sephadex G-50 (Pharmacia) according to Tadakuma *et al.* (13).

Stimulation of thymocytes with Con A and IL2. Cells were cultured for 3 days (5% CO_2, 37°C) with an optimal mitogenic dose of Con A (4 μg/ml) at 10^6 cells/ml in RPMI 1640 supplemented with 10% FCS (56°C, 30 min), 2 mM glutamine, 5 mM Hepes, 5×10^{-5} M 2-mercaptoethanol, streptomycin (100 μg/ml), and penicillin (100 units/ml). Cultures of separated immature (PNA^+, high density) thymocytes were additionally supplemented with 25% conditioned medium containing IL2.

C-Dependent cytotoxicity assay on proliferating thymocytes (9). Equal numbers of washed viable cells from Con A-activated cultures (5×10^4 to 10×10^4 in 0.1 ml) were seeded in quadruplicate into round-bottomed wells of Titertek microplates (Flow Laboratories, Irvine, Scotland) prefilled with 0.1 ml of optimal dilutions of different antisera and incubated for 30 min at 4°C. The cells were then washed twice with 0.2 ml of HBSS–FCS by spinning the plate (5 min at 1200 rpm) and removing the supernate by water pump suction. After washing, the cells were resuspended in 0.2 ml of C, diluted 1/25, and incubated for 40 min at 37°C. Then the cells were incubated for 10 hr in the culture medium containing [^{14}C-]thymidine (Radiochemical Centre, Amersham, 0.1 μCi/well = 3.7 kBq/well). Inhibition of thymidine incorporation by antiserum and C (as compared to normal mouse serum (NMS + C)) treated control is taken as a measure of the proportion of proliferating cells expressing the relevant antigen. At the end of 10 hr incubation cells were collected onto glass fiber filters with a multiple cell harvester and radioactivity was determined in a liquid scintillation counter.

RESULTS

Proportions of Cells Susceptible to T-Cell-Specific Antisera and C in Populations of Normal, Nonseparated Thymocytes and in BSA Gradient-Separated Fractions

Table 2 shows the results of cytotoxicity tests obtained with optimal dilutions of various antisera used alone or in combinations on nonseparated and BSA gradient-separated fractions of normal thymocytes from mice of the BALB/c strain. The relative proportions of different fractions and their spontaneous incorporation of [^{14}C]thymidine, indicating the proportions of spontaneously proliferating cells in each fraction, are also shown. Each antiserum, except anti-TL, lysed more than 90% of nonseparated as well as high-density (C and D) fractions of thymocytes, but small and reproducible differences were clearly detectable. The Thy1.2 antiserum lysed more cells than the Lyt1.2 antiserum and the Lyt1.2 antiserum lysed more cells than the Lyt2.2 antiserum. The same was true for cells from low-density (A and B) fractions although the number of cells sensitive to various individual antisera was smaller and the differences between them greater. This suggests a higher degree of heterogeneity among low-density fractions which is in agreement with earlier observations by other authors (12). However, the additive effect of the mixture of Lyt and TL antisera which is most clearly noted when tested on low-density fractions, suggested that in addition to the major cell population bearing the TL$^+$Lyt1$^+$Lyt2$^+$ phenotype, there were small populations of cells expressing only one or two of the above-mentioned antigens in different combinations. The higher proportion of thymocytes lysed by the mixtures of Lyt1.2 plus Lyt2.2, or Lyt1.2 plus TL, or Lyt2.2 plus TL antisera than by each of these antisera separately suggests that there are cells with Lyt1$^+$Lyt2$^-$ and Lyt1$^-$Lyt2$^+$ phenotypes some of which also bear TL antigen, i.e., TL$^+$Lyt1$^+$Lyt2$^-$ and TL$^+$Lyt1$^-$Lyt2$^+$. Thus, the above-mentioned results from direct conventional cytotoxicity assay confirm our previous findings concerning the phenotypic heterogeneity of TL$^+$ thymocytes (7, 9).

Cytotoxic Activity and Specificity of the Antisera on Proliferating Thymocytes

The activity and specificity of the antisera on proliferating thymocytes was tested on cells derived from Con A-stimulated cultures of nonseparated thymocytes of BALB/c and B6 congenic strains, differing in TL and Lyt antigens. Table 3 and Fig. 1 show the results. The proportions of Con A-activated thymocytes lysed by optimal concentrations of individual antisera are similar to those observed for low-

TABLE 2

Proportions of Cells Susceptible to T-Cell-Specific Antisera and C in Whole Populations of Normal BALB/c Thymocytes and in BSA Gradient-Separated Fractions

Thymocytes	Frequency (%)	cpm[b] ($\times 10^3$)	Percentage of cells lysed by optimal dilution of antiserum + C[a]						
			Anti-Thy1.2 (1/40)	Anti-TL (1/20)	Anti-Lyt1.2 (1/10–1/20)	Anti-Lyt2.2 (1/10–1/20)	Anti-Lyt1.2 + Lyt2.2 (1/20–1/40)	Anti-Lyt1.2 + TL (1/20–1/40)	Anti-Lyt2.2 + TL (1/20–1/40)
BSA fractions									
A	3–6	1.5	93 (92–94)	39 (30–47)	81 (80–82)	48 (46–51)	90 (86–92)	89 (87–90)	60 (54–64)
B	15–25	0.7	99 (98–99)	50 (46–53)	93 (91–94)	72 (70–75)	96 (95–96)	96 (94–98)	80 (77–82)
C	40–50	0.1	100 (99–100)	75 (72–80)	96 (94–98)	92 (90–95)	98 (97–99)	98 (98)	92 (90–94)
D	20–35	0.06	100 (99–100)	80 (75–85)	96 (95–98)	93 (92–95)	98 (98–99)	97 (96–99)	95 (94–95)
Nonseparated			98 (96–99)	78 (72–80)	94 (90–96)	90 (88–93)			

[a] Results are the means of three or more experiments, with extreme values in parentheses. C controls did not exceed 10%.

[b] Spontaneous incorporation of [^{14}C]thymidine at Day 3 of culture of 10^5 cells.

density fractions (see Table 2, fractions A and B), known to be enriched for the so-called "mature thymocytes" (14), i.e., able to respond to Con A without an external supply of IL2 (9, 15). However, the presence of TL-bearing cells in the proliferating population, as shown by the inhibitory effect of the anti-TL serum, suggested that not only mature but also immature thymocytes were stimulated by Con A, probably as a result of endogenous production of IL2 by mature thymocytes. The reactions of antisera were specific since only cells from congenic mice of "appropriate" phenotypes were inhibited. Lack of inhibition of proliferating cortisone-resistant thymocytes (known to be depleted of TL^+ cells (16)) by anti-TL serum provides additional evidence for the specificity of this antiserum for immature, cortical thymocytes. We repeatedly observed that activated thymocytes of A (data not shown) and B6/TL^+ strains of mice were lysed in much higher proportions than thymocytes from BALB/c mice. This may be explained not only by differences in expression of TL specificities (B6/TL^+ and A mice are of the TL1,2,3,$^+$Qa1$^+$ phenotype while BALB/c mice are TL2Qa1$^-$) but also by the reaction of anti-Qa1 antibody, which as shown by specific inhibition of activated B6/TL^+ lymph node cells (last row in Table 3), contaminates anti-TL serum (17). The activity of the antisera against Con-A activated thymocytes from BALB/c mice is shown in detail in Fig. 1. All antisera, except anti-Lyt1.2, display a much lower titer on activated thymocytes than on the whole population of normal thymocytes. In contrast, the titer of the anti-Lyt1.2 serum is the same on all targets.

Lyt and TL Phenotypes of Activated, Immature Thymocytes of BALB/c Mice

The detection of TL^+ cells among proliferating thymocytes prompted us to investigate in detail the surface antigenic phenotype of immature (PNA^+, high density) thymocytes, activated by Con A in the presence of IL2. Table 4 shows the results of three independent experiments. The phenotypic heterogeneity of activated immature thymocytes is reflected by the differences in susceptibility of proliferating cells to the cytotoxic effects of different antisera when used separately or in combinations. Treatment of proliferating cells with antisera without C had no effect (data not shown). The percentages of inhibition of proliferating cells by individual antisera or by their combinations are roughly comparable with the percentages of susceptible cells present in low-density fractions of the BSA gradient (see Table 2) and suggest similar patterns of expression of Lyt and TL antigens. Since each Lyt antiserum lyses more than 76% of the proliferating cells and about 40% of the cells are eliminated by TL antiserum and C, it follows that the predominant phenotype of proliferating cells is $Lyt1^+Lyt2^+$ and that some of these cells bear TL antigen (about 27%) and some do not (about 45%). The existence of cells with the $Lyt1^+Lyt2^-$ phenotype is suggested by the fact that a higher proportion of cells is lysed by the Lyt1.2 antiserum plus C than by Lyt2.2 antiserum plus C. On the other hand, the higher proportion of cells lysed by the mixture of Lyt1.2 plus Lyt2.2 antiserum than by each antiserum alone suggests the existence of cells with the $Lyt1^-Lyt2^+$ phenotype. The existence of small subpopulations of cells with $TL^+Lyt1^+Lyt2^-$ and $TL^+Lyt1^-Lyt2^+$ phenotypes is inferred from the fact that more cells were lysed by the anti-Lyt plus TL combinations than by anti-Lyt and anti-TL sera alone.

Additional strong evidence for the existence of TL^+ thymocytes with differen-

TABLE 3

Cytotoxic Activity and Specificity of the Lyt1.1, Lyt1.2, Lyt2.2, and TL Antisera on Proliferating (Con A activated) Thymocytes

		Strain of mice and T-cell antigen phenotype							
		BABL/c Lyt1.2;Lyt2.2 TL2;Qa1$^-$		B6/TL Lyt1.2;Lyt2.2 TL1,2,3;Qa1$^+$		B6/Lyt1.1 Lyt1.1;Lyt2.2 TL$^-$;Qa1$^-$		B6/Lyt2.1 Lyt1.2;Lyt2.1 Tl$^-$;Qa1$^-$	
Çells[a]	Antiserum + C	cpm ± SD[b]	% Inhib.	cpm ± SD	% Inhib.	cpm ± SD	% Inhib.	cpm ± SD	% Inhib.
Thymocytes (nonseparated)	C alone	5201 ± 253		2295 ± 65		2761 ± 40		1730 ± 199	
	Lyt1.1	5359 ± 54	0	2238 ± 134	0	266 ± 21	90	1599 ± 87	2
	Lyt1.2	675 ± 120	87	432 ± 29	79	2635 ± 184	1	364 ± 99	84
	Lyt2.2	1540 ± 43	71	1299 ± 25	40	1250 ± 100	53	1606 ± 122	1
	TL	3560 ± 289	34	711 ± 4	66	2687 ± 17	0	1554 ± 43	4
Cortison-resistant thymocytes	NMS	2097 ± 267		ND		ND		ND	
	TL	2101 ± 80	0	ND		ND		ND	
Lymph node cells	NMS	3352 ± 107		4288 ± 113		ND		4888 ± 361	
	TL	3403 ± 247	0	1320 ± 5	69	ND		4908 ± 203	0

[a] Con A-activated cells assayed on Day 3 of culture (see Materials and Methods).
[b] Uptake of [^{14}C]thymidine by Con A-activated blasts surviving the treatment with antiserum + C. The numbers of viable cells were not equalized.

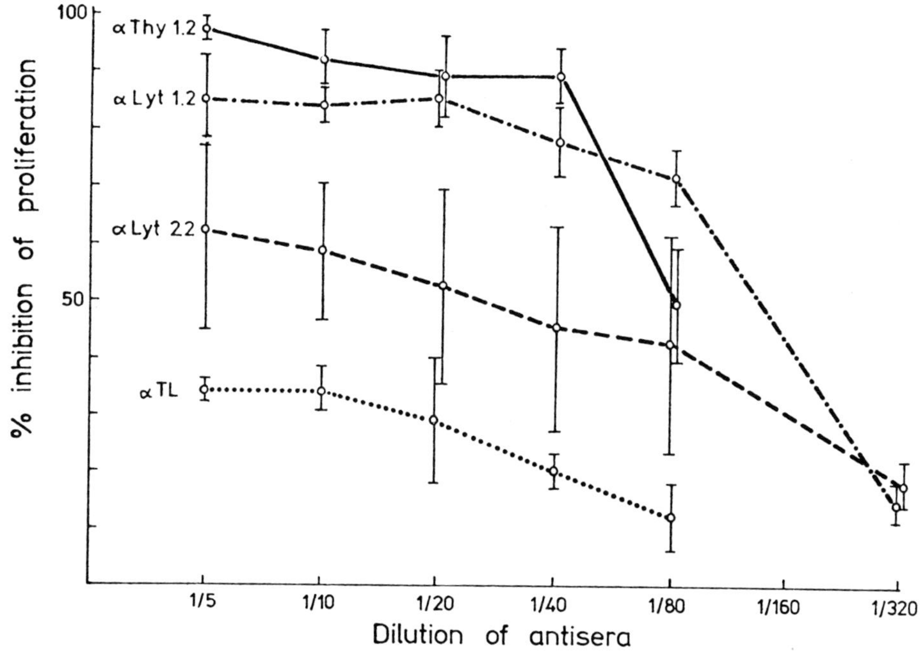

FIG. 1. Cytotoxic activity of T-cell-specific antisera on proliferating (Con A activated) BALB/c thymocytes. Cytotoxic titers of the antisera on normal, nonactivated thymocytes are as follows: anti-Thy1.2, 1/1280; anti-TL-1/2560; anti-Lyt1.2, 1/80; anti-Lyt2.2, 1/640. Vertical bars indicate the range of variation between different, individual experiments.

tiated expression of Lyt antigens is provided by the results of the experiment described below (Table 5). Nonseparated thymocytes were pretreated with the Lyt2.2 antiserum and C to eliminate Lyt2-bearing cells and the mixture of dead and surviving cells was separated on a BSA density gradient. After separation (all dead cells are found in a bottom fraction) the populations of living cells recovered from A and B (low density) fractions and C and D (high density) fractions were stimulated by Con A and the surface phenotype of proliferating cells was analyzed 3 days later. As shown in Table 5 population of proliferating cells is depleted of cells susceptible to the Lyt2.2 antiserum but not of cells susceptible to Lyt1.2 and TL antisera. Because of the lack of a sufficient quantity of Lyt1.2 antiserum, similar experiments eliminating Lyt1.2-bearing cells from the responding population were not possible.

Does Activation of Immature Thymocytes Cause Qualitative Changes in the Expression of TL and Lyt Antigens?

The experiments described so far have shown that proliferating immature thymocytes are phenotypically heterogenous and contain cells with different patterns of expression of TL and Lyt antigens. An important question remains: whether the heterogeneity of phenotypes observed among proliferating cells results from the activation of cells with "preexisting" phenotypes or whether cells with new surface

TABLE 4

Expression of TL2, Lyt1.2, and Lyt2.2 Antigens on Proliferating BALB/c Immature (PNA^+ High Density) Thymocytes Activated by Con A in the Presence of IL2

Pretreatment (antiserum + C)[a]	Uptake of [^{14}C]thymidine by activated cells surviving treatment with antiserum + C[b]						
	Expt 1		Expt 2		Expt 3		Mean % positive cells[d]
	cpm ± SD	% Inhib.[c]	cpm ± SD	% Inhib.[c]	cpm ± SD	% Inhib.[c]	
NMS	3461 ± 40		2888 ± 48		6685 ± 350		
TL	2135 ± 102	39	1765 ± 18	41	4311 ± 309	37	39
Lyt1.2	149 ± 31	98	293 ± 4	95	1180 ± 94	85	93
Lyt2.2	856 ± 52	77	617 ± 20	83	1796 ± 112	76	79
Lyt1.2 + Lyt2.2	91 ± 12	100 (standard)	150 ± 35	100	269 ± 36	100	100
Lyt1.2 + TL	134 ± 23	98	220 ± 31	97	513 ± 35	96	97
Lyt2.2 + TL	403 ± 43	90	417 ± 42	90	1414 ± 55	82	87

Antigenic phenotype implied by data	Frequency[e] (%)
$TL^+Lyt1^+Lyt2^+$	27
$TL^+Lyt1^+Lyt2^-$	8
$TL^+Lyt1^-Lyt2^+$	4
$TL^-Lyt1^+Lyt2^+$	45
$TL^-Lyt1^+Lyt2^-$	13
$TL^-Lyt1^-Lyt2^+$	3

[a] After treatment with antisera + C, the numbers of remaining viable cells were not equalized.
[b] See Materials and Methods.
[c] Percentage positive cells.
[d] Mean of three experiments.
[e] Calculated as described in Draber and Kisielow (9, Table 3).

TABLE 5

Surface Phenotype of Con A-Activated BALB/c Thymocytes, Induced from the Population Surviving Pretreatment with the Lyt2.2 Antiserum and C

		Treatment of Con A-activated thymocytes with antiserum + C						
			Lyt1.2 (1/20)		Lyt2.2 (1/20)		TL (1/20)	
Pretreatment[a]	BSA fractions	NMS (1/20) cpm + SD[b]	cpm ± SD	% Inhib.	cpm ± SD	% Inhib.	cpm ± SD	% Inhib.
Lyt2.2 + C (56°C)	A + B	2549 ± 302	734 ± 221	71	1164 ± 245	54	1697 ± 156	34
Lyt2.2 + C		2352 ± 110	963 ± 33	59	2330 ± 90	1	1035 ± 190	56
Lyt2.2 + C (56°C)	C + D	1997 ± 26	288 ± 26	86	393± 77	80	923 ± 198	54
Lyt2.2 + C		1557 ± 234	324 ± 27	79	1130 ± 92	27	628 ± 169	60

[a] Cells were pretreated with Lyt2.2 antiserum and C (control suspensions were treated with antiserum and heat inactivated C (56°C, 10 min)) and then separated on a BSA gradient before stimulation with Con A.

[b] Uptake of [^{14}C]thymidine by Con A-activated blasts surviving the treatment with antiserum + C. The numbers of remaining viable cells were not equalized. Cells from C + D fractions were stimulated with Con A + IL2.

TABLE 6

Surface Antigenic Phenotype of Resting and Proliferating Immature (High Density) BALB/c Thymocytes Surviving Pretreatment with High Dilutions of H-2^d antiserum and C

Pretreatment[a]	Culture conditions	Treatment with antisera + C[b]	Expt 1: cpm ± SD[c]	Expt 1: % Inhib.	Expt 1: % Lysis in starting population[d]	Expt 2: cpm ± SD	Expt 2: % Inhib.	Expt 2: % Lysis in starting population
None	Con A	—	275 ± 70					
	Con A + IL2	—	17,478 ± 1046					
H-2^d + C	Con A	—	12 ± 6					
	Con A + IL2	—	266 ± 33					
	Con A + IL2	NMS	232 ± 18			282 ± 11		
	Con A + IL2	Thy1.2	19 ± 5	92	100	7 ± 8	98	100
	Con A + IL2	TL	134 ± 20	42	92	232 ± 26	18	90
	Con A + IL2	Lyt1.2	73 ± 4	69	99	51 ± 6	82	98
	Con A + IL2	Lyt2.2	94 ± 26	59	97	177 ± 15	37	97
	Con A + IL2	Lyt1.2 + Lyt2.2	24 ± 8	90	99	26 ± 3	91	98
	Con A + IL2	Lyt1.2 + TL	59 ± 9	75	99	42 ± 7	85	98
	Con A + IL2	Lyt2.2 + TL	71 ± 7	69	98	131 ± 1	54	98

[a] In Expt 1, 20% and in Expt 2, 60% of the thymocytes were lysed with 1/300 and 1/150 dilutions of H-2 antiserum + C, respectively.
[b] Viable cells surviving the treatment were not equalized.
[c] Uptake of [^{14}C]thymidine by proliferating cells.
[d] Cells surviving pretreatment with H-2 antiserum + C, before activation with Con A.

phenotypes are also generated as a result of stimulation of $TL^+Lyt1^+Lyt2^+$ cells which constitute the predominant fraction of resting immature thymocytes. In the light of the generally accepted view that cells expressing the differentiated Lyt phenotype belong to medullary, mature populations of thymocytes (6) expressing a high content of H-2 antigens (15) we have attempted to obtain pure populations of $TL^+Lyt1^+Lyt2^+$ cells by pretreatment of high-density thymocytes with various dilutions of anti-H-2 serum plus C, which eliminated 20–60% of the cells. The results shown in Table 6 demonstrate that: (a) in the population of cells surviving pretreatment with anti-H-2 serum and C, the proportions of cells lysed by the TL, Lyt1.2, and Lyt2.2 antisera and C are increased in comparison with untreated, high-density thymocytes (see Table 2, fractions C and D) but in contrast to anti-Thy1.2 serum, which lysed 100% of the cells, a few cells resistant to Lyt1.2, Lyt2.2, and TL antisera always remain; (b) the IL2-dependent response of surviving cells is almost completely but never totally suppressed (about 250 cpm as compared with 17,000 cpm in positive controls and about 10 cpm in negative controls); (c) the proliferating cells, induced from such anti-H-2 purified populations are phenotypically heterogenous as shown by the different degrees of inhibition obtained with different antisera used alone or in combinations. Thus, because we have failed to obtain a 100% pure population of $TL^+Lyt1^+Lyt2^+$ cells, the experiment is inconclusive: a few proliferating cells responding to Con A plus IL2 which are phenotypically as heterogenous as those activated from nontreated population (see Table 4) may be derived from a differentiated population of cells contaminating the population of $TL^+Lyt1^+Lyt2^+$ cells but the alternative possibility cannot be excluded.

DISCUSSION

In the present study we analysed the expression of T-cell differentiation antigens on proliferating thymocytes, activated by Con A, by testing their susceptibility to the cytotoxic activity of the Thy1, TL, Lyt1, and Lyt2 antisera. The results confirm and extend our earlier observations concerning the phenotypic heterogeneity of immature thymocytes (7, 9), by providing additional evidence for the existence of TL^+ thymocytes with restricted expression of Lyt antigens. The data presented here indicate that the population of proliferating thymocytes, whether induced by stimulation of nonseparated populations of cells with Con A alone, or by stimulation of purified populations of immature thymocytes with Con A plus IL2, is phenotypically heterogenous and contains cells bearing all phenotypes that were described for different stages of T-cell differentiation, including $TL^+Lyt1^+Lyt2^-$ and $TL^+Lyt1^-Lyt2^+$ (7, 9).

It is interesting to note that when compared with a normal population of thymocytes, the proliferating thymocytes are more resistant to cytotoxic treatment with Thy1, TL, and Lyt2 antisera but not with Lyt1 antisera, which probably results from quantitative changes in the expression of those antigens. From comparative absorption studies it is known that $Lyt1^+$ T cells in different tissues carry similar amounts of the Lyt1 antigen (18) while the expression of Thy1, TL, and Lyt2 antigens is very much decreased or absent in peripheral tissue (19). Thus the higher resistance of proliferating thymocytes to Thy1, Lyt2, and TL antisera, but not to Lyt1 antisera, may reflect a general rule of behavior of those antigens during differentiation of T cells.

The limitations for the interpretation of cytotoxicity experiments in which a heterogenous population of cells is incubated with antisera to a specific membrane antigen and C were extensively discussed by Konda *et al.* (12) in their studies on membrane antigenic patterns of nonactivated subpopulations of thymocytes. It is clear that the same reservations apply to the studies reported here, especially with regard to the nature and significance of the differences in proportions of susceptible cells lysed by various antisera and C. Obviously, the final proof of the real existence of thymocytes with the phenotypes implied by our data and the answer to the question concerning the qualitative-versus-quantitative basis of the differences observed will have to await studies with cloned populations of thymocytes. However, irrespective of the results of such future studies, the presently detectable differences in susceptibility to different combinations of antisera of heterogenous populations of cells can be fruitfully used for functional analysis of the immunological potential of the population studied.

The important question which remains to be answered concerns the origin of the proliferating cells with different phenotypes. Although the possibility that some of the proliferating cells with differentiated phenotypes may be the progeny of $TL^+Lyt1^+Lyt2^+$ thymocytes cannot be excluded, we were unable to obtain supportive evidence. The results presented here and elsewhere (9) demonstrated that almost complete inhibition of the IL2-dependent proliferative response of immature thymocytes is obtained by pretreatment with high dilutions of H-2 antiserum, which eliminated phenotypically heterogenous populations of immature thymocytes with a relatively high membrane content of H-2 antigens. This indicates that the bulk of immature thymocytes with the typical phenotype of immature thymocytes, i.e., low expression of H-2 antigens, $TL^+Lyt1^+Lyt2^+$ cannot be activated to proliferation. However, inability to obtain a 100% pure population of $TL^+Lyt1^+Lyt2^+$ thymocytes, on the one hand, and the lack of total inhibition of IL2-dependent proliferation, on the other hand, preclude any definitive answers. Again the inevitable conclusion seems to be that the solution to problems concerned with the developmental potential of cells with a given specific phenotype will have to await the results of studies with cloned thymocytes. For now, our results indicate that despite some recent reports suggesting that immature thymocytes become immunologically reactive in the presence of IL2 (4, 20), the functional potential of the great majority of $TL^+Lyt1^+Lyt2^+$ cells remains unknown.

REFERENCES

1. Di Sabato, G., Chen, D. M., and Erickson, J. W., *Cell. Immunol.* **17,** 495, 1975.
2. Paetkau, V., Mills, G., Gerhart, and Monticone, V., *J. Immunol.* **117,** 1320, 1976.
3. Beller, D. I., and Unanue, E. R., *J. Immunol.* **118,** 1780, 1977.
4. Irlé, C., Piquet, P. F., and Vassalli, P., *J. Exp. Med.* **148,** 32, 1978.
5. Kisielow, P., Hirst, J. A., Shiku, H., Beverley, P. C. L., Hoffman, M., Boyse, E. A., and Oettgen, H. F., *Nature (London)* **253,** 219, 1975.
6. Cantor, H., and Boyse, E. A., *Immunol. Rev.* **33,** 105, 1977.
7. Kisielow, P., Dráber, P., and Wysocka, M., *Eur. J. Immunol.* **9,** 1023, 1979.
8. Mathieson, B., Sharrow, S. O., Campbell, P. S., and Asofsky, R., *Nature (London)* **277,** 478, 1979.
9. Dráber, P., and Kisielow, P., *Eur. J. Immunol.* **11,** 1, 1981.
10. Kisielow, P., Szkudlarek, J., and Wysocka, M., *Arch. Immunol. Ther. Exp.* **26,** 99, 1979.

11. Reisener, Y., Linker-Israeli, M., and Sharon, N., *Cell. Immunol.* **25,** 129, 1976.
12. Konda, S., Stockert, E., and Smith, R. T., *Cell. Immunol.* **7,** 275, 1973.
13. Tadakuma, T., Kühner, A. L., Rich, R. R., David, J. R., and Pierce, C. W., *J. Immunol.* **117,** 323, 1976.
14. Konda, S., Nakao, Y., and Smith, R. T., *J. Exp. Med.* **136,** 1461, 1972.
15. Shortman, K., von Boehmer, H., Lipp, J., and Hopper, K., *Transplant. Rev.* **25,** 163, 1975.
16. Old, L. J., Boyse, E. A., and Stockert, E., *J. Nat. Cancer Inst.* **31,** 977, 1963.
17. Stanton, T. H., and Boyse, E. A., *Immunogenetics* **3,** 525, 1976.
18. Boyse, E. A., Miyazawa, M., Aoki, T., and Old, L. J., *Proc. Roy. Soc. Bio. Ser. B* **170,** 175, 1968.
19. McKenzie, I. F. C., and Potter, T., *Advan. Immunol.* **27,** 179, 1979.
20. Wagner, H., Hardt, C., Bartlett, R., Röllinghoff, M., and Pfizenmaier, K., *J. Immunol.* **125,** 2532, 1980.

CELLULAR IMMUNOLOGY 65, 194–200 (1981)

SHORT COMMUNICATIONS

Antigen-Specific Murine T-Cell Lymphomas: Functional Heterogenicity[1]

YEHUDITH AZAR, PAULA EIDELSZTEIN, EITAN YEFENOF,[2] EVELYNE CHRIQUI, AVIVA KATZ-GROSS, ELI KEDAR, AND SHLOMO ZALMAN BEN-SASSON

The Lautenberg Center for General and Tumor Immunology, The Hebrew University–Hadassah Medical School, P.O. Box 1172, Jerusalem 91010, Israel

Received July 28, 1981; accepted September 25, 1981

Two ovalbumin (OVA)-specific helper lymphomas (designated ROT/6.1 and ROT/6.2) were established by transformation of enriched, OVA-immune T cells with the radiation leukemia virus (RadLV). Shortly after establishment these lymphomas provided carrier (OVA)-specific help for anti-hapten antibody response. However, 5 months later ROT/6.1 lost its OVA specificity and could augment anti-hapten antibody response in the presence of an unrelated carrier. ROT/6.2 retained its antigen-specific helper function over 10 months of repeated passaging. This OVA-specific helper line inhibited anti-hapten antibody response when given together with an unrelated carrier. Cloning of ROT/6.2 by limiting dilution revealed that only 3 of 10 clones tested had OVA-specific helper activity. None of the clones could induce antigen-specific DTH reaction. The interrelationship between the functional heterogenicity, specificity, and stability of the helper lines is discussed.

INTRODUCTION

Several approaches to obtaining large numbers of immune T lymphocytes committed to a given antigen have been undertaken in recent years. Continuous antigenic stimulation *in vitro* resulted in enrichment and expansion of T cells with specific activity toward the stimulating antigen (1). T cells recognizing unrelated antigens could be eliminated by absorption onto antigen-pulsed macrophage monolayers, prior to stimulation by the selecting antigen (2). Recently, Sredni *et al.* (3) cloned antigen-primed T cells which could be maintained in cultures containing T-cell growth factor (TCGF). However, these monospecific colonies are totally dependent on periodic stimulation with exogenous antigen or growth factor, cannot propagate *in vivo,* and may alter their properties upon maintenance *in vitro* (4).

Using the hybridoma technique, several groups reported the successful establishment of antigen-specific suppressor (5, 6) and helper (7) T-cell hybridomas. Since somatic cell hybrids are genetically unstable due to the extra genetic load of the unrelated fuser (8), hybridoma lines tend to lose their antigen-specific func-

[1] This work was supported by the Leukemia Research Foundation, Inc., Chicago; Concern Foundation, Los Angeles; Dr. and Mrs. Wilbur Schwarts, Los Angeles; Mr. and Mrs. Stewart Resnick, Beverly Hills, Calif.

[2] Recipient of fellowship from the Israel Cancer Research Fund.

0008-8749/81/170194-07$02.00/0

tion (9). In a recent publication Finn *et al.* (10) described another method for the establishment of functional, antigen-specific murine T-cell lymphomas by transformation with the radiation leukemia virus (RadLV). By employing this technique we established several antigen-specific T-cells lines capable of providing the carrier-specific help required for primary and secondary anti-hapten antibody responses (11). Such immortalized cell lines can be easily grown *in vivo* or *in vitro* and may remain antigen specific and functionally active for prolonged periods.

In the present study, one of the helper T-cell lymphomas was cloned and the function and antigenic specificity of several expanded colonies were compared with those of the original lymphoma.

MATERIALS AND METHODS

Animals. C57BL/6 mice aged 6–8 weeks at the start of the experiments were used.

Immunization. Dinitrophenylated keyhole limpet hemocyanin (DNP-KLH) was emulsified in complete Freund's adjuvant (CFA) containing 1 mg/ml killed *Mycobacterium tuberculosis* (H37Ka) (Difco Laboratories, Detroit, Mich.). Mice were immunized in each of the four footpads with 50 mg DNP-KLH in 0.1 ml emulsion.

Antigen-specific lymphoma lines. The ovalbumin (OVA)-specific ROT/6.1 and ROT/6.2 cell lines were characterized earlier (11). Briefly, enriched populations of OVA-primed T lymphocytes from male C57BL/6 donors were obtained as described elsewhere (2). The cells were infected *in vitro* with RadLV and inoculated intrathymically into irradiated female C57BL/6 recipients. Lymphatic leukemias that arose in some mice were characterized as donor types by chromosome analysis and maintained in tissue culture or by serial transplantations in syngeneic mice. Using the plaque-forming cell (PFC) assay (12), ROT/6.1 and ROT/6.2 were found to provide OVA-specific help in a cooperative anti-DNP antibody response (11).

Cloning of ROT/6.2. Tumor cells that had been cultivated for 6 weeks were cloned by the limiting dilution technique (12, 13) as follows: cells were resuspended in RPMI 1640 supplemented with 10% FCS, 5×10^{-5} *M* 2-mercaptoethanol, 10 m*M* Hepes buffer, 1% nonessential amino acid solution (×100, Gibco), 1% m*M* Hepes buffer, 1% nonessential amino acid solution (×100, Gibco), 1 m*M* glutamine, and 1% combined antibiotic solution (×100, Gibco); and seeded at 0.5 cell per well, in 20 μl, into Microtest tissue culture plates (Histoplate, No. 236-72, Costar, Cambridge, Mass.). Plates were wrapped with aluminum foil and incubated in a well-humidified atmosphere of 7% CO_2 in air at 37°C. Growing clones were passed on Days 5–10 into either 96-well U-shaped microtitration plates (No. 1482, Nunclon-Delta, Nunc, Roskilde, Denmark) or 24-well tissue culture Cluster plates (No. 3524, Costar) in 0.2- and 1.0-ml volumes, respectively. Thereafter clones were propagated first in 25-cm² and subsequently in 75-cm² culture flasks (Nunc or Falcon) in 10 or 50 ml complete RPMI 1640 medium. Flasks were incubated either in an upright position or horizontally and cultures were maintained at $0.2–1 \times 10^6$ cells/ml by splitting and feeding with fresh medium every 3 days.

Assessment of helper activity. Irradiated (1000 rads) lymphoma cells (10^7) were injected intraperitoneally together with 50 mg of either DNP-OVA, DNP-human γ-globulin (DNP-HGG), or dinitrophenylated derivative of copolymer L-glutamic (60%)/L-lysine (40%) (DNP-GL) into normal mice or into mice preimmunized with DNP-KLH 45–60 days earlier. Control mice were injected with cells or antigen alone. DNP-specific PFC in the spleen were determined 7 days following inoculation according to Jerne *et al.* (12). Sheep red blood cells coupled with 2,4,6-trinitrobenzenesulfonic acid (TNP-SRBC) served as indicator cells and normal guinea pig serum was used as a source of complement for both direct and indirect PFC. Purified rabbit anti-mouse Ig was employed as the developing antibody for the indirect plaques.

DTH activity. Enriched populations of OVA-specific T lymphocytes or lymphoma cells (5×10^6/ml) were incubated at 37°C for 3 hr together with splenocytes (1.5×10^6/ml) from mineral oil-injected mice (as a source of antigen presenting cells) and 100 μg/ml OVA in culture medium. Control cells were incubated without antigen. Subsequently, the cells were spun down and resuspended in Hanks' balanced salt solution. Control and experimental cells (10^7) were injected in a volume of 0.05 ml into the left and right hind footpads of four to six mice, respectively. Footpad swelling was determined 24 hr later with an engineer's micrometer (Mitutoyo, Japan).

RESULTS

Five months after establishment, ROT/6.2 retained its OVA-specific helper activity since it could strongly increase the anti-DNP-PFC frequency when injected together with DNP-OVA into DNP-KLH-primed C57BL/6 mice (Table 1). At that time, ROT/6.1, which initially was also an OVA-specific helper line (11), became a carrier-independent helper, as it increased the IgM and IgG anti-DNP-PFC response when inoculated together with either DNP-OVA or DNP-HGG. Inoculation of ROT/6.1 alone did not stimulate anti-DNP antibody synthesis. Interestingly, the OVA-specific ROT/6.2 helper line inhibited the stimulation of the DNP-specific B cells when injected into primed animals together with an un-

TABLE 1

Helper Activity of Antigen-Specific Lymphomas after 5 Months of Weekly Passages *in Vivo*

Injection	PFC/10^6 spleen cells[a]		Net helper activity/10^6 spleen cells[b]	
	IgM	IgG	IgM	IgG
DNP-OVA	7 ± 1	36 ± 1	—	—
DNP-HGG	96 ± 4	506 ± 7	—	—
ROT/6.2 + DNP-OVA	79 ± 3	213 ± 6	72	178
ROT/6.2 + DNP-HGG	43 ± 1	41 ± 1	−53	−465
ROT/6.1	25 ± 1	3 ± 1	—	—
ROT/6.1 + DNP-OVA	135 ± 1	291 ± 11	128	256
ROT/6.1 + DNP-HGG	115 ± 6	632 ± 36	19	126

[a] Mean ± SEM.

[b] PFC in animals injected with tumor cells and antigen minus PFC in animals injected with antigen alone.

TABLE 2

Helper Activity of ROT/6.2 Derived Clones

	PFC/10^6 spleen cells[a]	
Injection	IgM	IgG
DNP-OVA	12 ± 1	0
DNP-OVA + clone 36	18 ± 2	0
DNP-OVA + clone 39	84 ± 1	46 ± 4
DNP-OVA + clone 41	176 ± 16	155 ± 27
DNP-OVA + clone 44	18 ± 1	0
DNP-OVA + clone 46	26 ± 2	4 ± 1
DNP-OVA + clone 49	36 ± 2	0
DNP-OVA + clone 55	36 ± 3	0
DNP-OVA + clone 57	32 ± 2	0
DNP-OVA + clone 62	70 ± 3	22 ± 3
DNP-OVA + clone 64	23 ± 1	0

[a] Mean ± SEM.

related carrier (Table 1) (55% inhibition of direct plaques and 92% inhibition of indirect plaques).

The alteration in the functional specificity indicated that the original ROT/6.1 lymphoma may not have been a homogenous "monoclonal" tumor but rather a mixture of cells with different functions and/or specificities. Therefore, we decided to clone the stable, antigen-specific ROT/6.2 lymphoma in order to examine its functional homogenicity. Cloning efficiency in the Terasaki plates was about 40% and 30 clones thus obtained were further propagated. Twenty additional clones were also established in round-bottom plates (one cell per well on 0.1 ml) with about 25% efficiency. Attempts to clone the tumor cells in the presence of irradiated syngeneic spleen cells or TCGF did not improve cloning efficiency. Out of 10 clones that were screened for helper activity, only 3 (Nos. 39, 41, and 62) could increase the frequency of IgG anti-DNP-PFC when injected together with DNP-OVA into unprimed animals (Table 2). The helper activity varied considerably among the individual positive clones. Clones 39 and 41 were also tested for carrier specificity. As shown in Table 3, an increase in the anti-DNP-PFC was induced by these clones only when injected together with DNP-OVA but not with DNP-GL. As with the parental ROT/6.2 line, both clones inhibited PFC generation when inoculated with DNP coupled to an unrelated carrier (DNP-GL). The helper-negative clone 64 did not elevate the PFC frequency toward DNP-OVA, nor was it inhibitory when injected together with DNP-GL.

Enriched populations of OVA-specific T lymphocytes, from which the ROT/6.2 tumor was derived, were capable of inducing antigen-specific DTH reaction in recipient naive mice after sensitization with OVA *in vitro* (Table 4). However, neither ROT/6.2 nor 10 of its descendant clones could give a DTH reaction under the same experimental conditions.

DISCUSSION

The method of Finn *et al.* (10) for establishment of functional, antigen-specific T lymphomas by transformation with RadLV provides a powerful tool for T-cell

TABLE 3

Carrier Specificity of the *in Vivo* Help Induced by Clones of ROT/6.2

Injection	PFC/10^6 spleen cells[a]		Net helper activity/ 10^6 spleen cells[b]	
	IgM	IgG	IgM	IgG
DNP-OVA	2 ± 1	4 ± 1	—	—
DNP-GL	6 ± 1	39 ± 1	—	—
DNP-OVA + clone 39	5 ± 1	27 ± 1	3	23
DNP-GL + clone 39	3 ± 1	19 ± 1	−3	−20
DNP-OVA + clone 41	4 ± 1	37 ± 1	2	33
DNP-GL + clone 41	6 ± 1	20 ± 1	0	−19
DNP-OVA + clone 64	1 ± 1	3 ± 1	−1	−1
DNP-GL + clone 64	5 ± 1	28 ± 4	−1	−11

[a] Mean ± SEM.
[b] PFC in animals injected with tumor cells and antigen minus PFC in animals injected with antigen alone.

research. In a previous publication (11) we described several OVA-specific helper cell lines immortalized by RadLV. These lymphomas arose after 3–5 months latency in female C57BL/6 recipients inoculated with OVA-selected lymphocytes of male donors that had been infected with RadLV *in vitro*. The established tumors could

TABLE 4

DTH Activity of OVA-Specific Enriched T Lymphocytes and RadLV Immortalized Lymphoma Cells

Cells injected	Footpad swelling (mm)		
	Control cells[a]	Antigen-triggered cells[b]	Significance[c]
OVA-enriched lymphocytes	1.88 ± 0.04[d]	2.54 ± 0.09	$P < 0.005$
ROT/6.2	2.03 ± 0.06	2.09 ± 0.07	N.S.[e]
Clone			
36	1.95 ± 0.05	2.15 ± 0.05	N.S.
39	2.07 ± 0.04	2.12 ± 0.05	N.S.
41	2.33 ± 0.06	2.23 ± 0.10	N.S.
44	2.10 ± 0.10	2.10 ± 0.05	N.S.
46	2.30 ± 0.05	2.15 ± 0.05	N.S.
49	2.40 ± 0.10	2.20 ± 0.05	N.S.
55	2.15 ± 0.05	2.20 ± 0.05	N.S.
57	2.10 ± 0.05	2.10 ± 0.05	N.S.
62	2.05 ± 0.05	2.15 ± 0.05	N.S.
64	2.07 ± 0.06	2.13 ± 0.04	N.S.

[a] Cells + splenocytes.
[b] Cells + splenocytes + 100 μg/ml OVA.
[c] Determined by a Student *t* test.
[d] Mean ± SEM.
[e] Not significant.

provide carrier (OVA)-specific help for anti-DNP antibody responses in unprimed, nonirradiated mice.

Virally induced murine leukemias are considered to stem from a single progenitor cell that has been transformed by the leukemogenic virus (15, 16). However, the monoclonality of the OVA-specific-T-cell lines was questioned as one helper tumor (ROT/6.1) had a heterogeneous Lyt phenotype (11). Furthermore, 5 months after establishment ROT/6.1 lost its antigenic specificity since it induced anti-DNP-PFC in hapten-primed animals when injected together with either DNP-OVA or DNP-HGG.

To further investigate the clonal nature of the antigen-specific lymphomas, the stable, carrier-specific ROT/6.2 helper line was cloned and 50 independent clones could be expanded. Out of 10 clones that have been tested, 7 were helper negative and the remaining 3 showed helper activity of varied intensity. The carrier specificity was ascertained in 2 clones, which could provide help when injected together with DNP-OVA but not with DNP-GL. The fact that only a minority of the ROT/6.2-derived clones were helper positive suggests that this lymphoma is heterogeneous but with an overall expression of carrier-specific helper activity. The functional heterogenicity may result from simultaneous progression of several OVA-preselected lymphocytes into autonomous lymphoma cells, or may be due to functional diversity generated among monoclonally derived lymphoma cells.

The alteration in the antigenic specificity of ROT/6.1 can be, thus, attributed to a heterogeneous T-cell lymphoma population, selected against the carrier-specific helper cells during prolonged passaging. Although there is evidence suggesting that virally induced marine leukemias are monoclonal (15, 16), however, the differentiation and progression of lymphomas arising in animals inoculated with *in vitro*, RadLV-infected cells might be different and it is possible that several cells can independently progress into autonomous lymphoma cells. This hypothesis received support from our observation of two primary lymphomas (devoid of helper activity) that developed in female mice inoculated with RadLV-treated male cells, having a mixture of both male and female cells (unpublished results), suggesting thus a heterogeneous origin.

Enriched populations of OVA-specific lymphocytes could mediate both antigen-specific help and DTH reaction ((11), Azar, Y., and Ben-Sasson, S. Z., to be published). However, ROT/6.2 as well as 10 of its descendant clones were DTH negative. The inability of 3 antigen-specific helper clones (Nos. 39, 41, 62) to induce a DTH reaction indicates that these functions are not necessarily interrelated. Recently it had been reported that helper T-cell clones could also induce antigen-specific DTH (17). The fact that some cloned T cells can mediate both help and DTH does not exclude the possibility that others might be monofunctional. It is also possible that RadLV transformation impairs a potential DTH activity originally residing in helper T cells. Since only a small number of clones have been screened so far, we cannot conclude whether a DTH function can be preserved in RadLV immortalized T lymphomas. Nevertheless, our data demonstrate that helper T-cell clones do not necessarily possess a concomitant DTH reactivity as well.

Unexpectedly, we observed that the carrier-specific ROT/6.2 line and the clones derived thereof inhibited antibody responses induced by unrelated carriers (HGG and GL). The nonspecific ROT/6.2 line as well as the helper-negative clones did not inhibit the background antibody response toward either HGG or GL. A similar pattern of enhanced antibody response toward DNP-OVA and an inhibitory effect with DNP-GL were also observed with enriched populations of OVA-specific T cells (Y. Azar, and S. Z. Ben-Sasson, to be published). It seems, thus, that large numbers of antigen-committed T cells may partially suppress the immune response toward an unrelated antigen. The implication of this observation on regulation of the immune response and its relationship with the phenomenon of "antigenic competition" is now being studied in our laboratory.

REFERENCES

1. Julius, M. H., and Augustin, A. A., *Eur. J. Immunol.* **9,** 671, 1979.
2. Ben-Sasson, S. Z., and Kagan, J., *J. Immunol. Methods* **42,** 291, 1981.
3. Sredni, B., Tse, H. Y., and Schwartz, R. H., *Nature (London)* **283,** 581, 1980.
4. Schreier, M. H., Iscov, N. N., Tees, R., Aarden, L., and Von Boehmer, H., *Immunol. Rev.* **51,** 315, 1980.
5. Taniguchi, M., and Miller, J. F. A. P., *J. Exp. Med.* **148,** 373, 1978.
6. Kontainen, S., Simpson, E., Bohrer, E., Beverly, P. C. K., Herzenberg, L. A., Fitzpatric, W. C., Vogt, P., Torano, A., McKenzie, I. F. C., and Feldman, M., *Nature (London)* **274,** 477, 1978.
7. Eshhar, Z., Apte, R. N., Lowy, T., Ben-Neriah, Y., Givol, D., and Mozes, E., *Nature (London)* **286,** 270, 1980.
8. Kingertz, N. R., and Savage, R. E., "Cell Hybrids." Academic Press, New York, 1976.
9. Goding, J. W., *J. Immunol. Methods* **39,** 285, 1980.
10. Finn, O. J., Boniver, J., and Kaplan, H. S., *Proc. Nat. Acad. Sci. USA* **76,** 4033, 1979.
11. Yefenof, E., Azar, Y., Eidelsztein, P., and Ben-Sasson, S. Z., *J. Immunol.*, in press.
12. Jerne, N. K., Henry, C., Nordin, A. A., Fujii, H., Koros, A. M. C., and Letokovits, I., *Transplant. Rev.* **18,** 130, 1974.
13. Bach, F. H., Inouye, H., Hank, J. A., and Alter, B. J., *Nature (London)* **281,** 307, 1979.
14. Rosenberg, S. A., Spiess, P. J., and Schwartz, S., *Cell. Immunol.* **54,** 293, 1980.
15. Steffen, D., and Weinberg, R. A., *Cell* **15,** 1003, 1978.
16. Canaani, E., and Aaronson, S. Z., *Proc. Nat. Acad. Sci. USA* **76,** 1677, 1979.
17. Bianchi, A. T. J., Hooijkaas, H., Benner, K., Tees, R., Nordin, A. A., and Schreier, M. H., *Nature (London)* **290,** 62, 1981.

CELLULAR IMMUNOLOGY 65, 201–205 (1981)

Cytolytic T Lymphocyte Mediated Chromium-51 Release Versus Spontaneous Release from Blast and Spleen Cell Targets at Low Temperatures[1]

STEVEN P. BALK AND MATTHEW F. MESCHER

Department of Pathology, Harvard Medical School, 25 Shattuck Street, Boston, Massachusetts 02115

Received July 28, 1981; accepted October 7, 1981

The rate of spontaneous ^{51}Cr release from spleen cell and LPS blast target cells is strongly temperature dependent. Between 32 and 37°C the rate of spontaneous release increases dramatically with temperature. Cytolytic T-lymphocyte-mediated lysis of these target cells is also temperature dependent, but lysis does not increase greatly above 32°C. The ratio of specific ^{51}Cr release to spontaneous release can be significantly improved by doing ^{51}Cr-release assays at temperatures below 37°C.

INTRODUCTION

A wide variety of normal and transformed cells can serve as targets for specifc cytolytic T lymphocytes (CTL). Tumor cells of lymphoid origin are commonly used for several reasons. Large numbers of homogeneous cells in suspension can easily be prepared, especially when the cells are adapted to grow in ascites. They accumulate significant amounts of ^{51}Cr after short incubations and are readily lysed by specific CTL. Moreover, their rate of spontaneous ^{51}Cr release is usually quite low.

Mitogen-induced blast cells or, less frequently, normal spleen cells are also used as targets when killing is being compared on several different strains of mice or when a tumor from the strain of interest is not available. A major problem in using these cells is their high rate of spontaneous ^{51}Cr release, often 40% or greater. It is difficult to determine the amount of specifc lysis accurately with such high background (1). This high rate of spontaneous release can obscure small differences in killing during 4-hr ^{51}Cr-release assays and prohibits the use of longer assays which can be necessary in weak killing systems.

We have found that the rate of spontaneous release from ^{51}Cr-labeled spleen cells and LPS blasts is very temperature dependent between about 32 and 37°C. CTL-mediated lysis is also temperature dependent, as has been shown with several tumor cell targets (1–6). However, CTL-mediated lysis of spleen cells or LPS blast target cells does not increase greatly above 32°C. Carrying out ^{51}Cr-release assays

[1] This work was supported by National Institutes of Health Grant CA-14732.

0008-8749/81/170201-05$02.00/0

at temperatures between 29 and 32°C thus allows accurate assessment of specific release from these target cells.

MATERIALS AND METHODS

Target cell preparation. LPS[2] blasts were generated as described (7) from BALB/c spleen cells (Jackson Laboratories, Bar Harbor, Maine). LPS blasts cultured from one spleen and BALB/c spleen cells from one spleen were washed in RHS medium (see below) and suspended in 1 ml RHS. $Na^{51}CrO_4$ (0.3 ml, 1 mCi/ml, New England Nuclear, Boston, Mass.) was added to each and the cells were incubated at 37°C with frequent mixing for 90 min. The cells were washed once in RHS and centrifuged on a Ficoll–Paque (Pharmacia Fine Chemicals, Piscataway, N.J.) gradient. Cells at the interface and those in the Ficoll–Paque were collected, washed three times with RHS and counted. P815, a mastocytoma of DBA/2 origin, was maintained by passage in (BALB/c × DBA/2)F1 mice (Cumberland Farms, Clinton, Tenn.) or (AKR × DBA/2)F1 mice (Jackson Laboratories). Cells, 1×10^7, in 0.5 ml RHS plus 0.15 ml $Na^{51}CrO_4$ were incubated for 60 min at 37°C, washed four times in RHS and counted. P815 contained about 2500 cpm per 1×10^4 cells while LPS blasts had about 1200 cpm and spleen cells about 300 cpm per 10^4 cells.

Allogeneic CTL generation. C57BL/6 mice (Jackson) were immunized with 1×10^7 P815 ip at least 1 month prior to use. CTL were generated *in vitro* in RPMI 1640 (GIBCO, Grand Island, N.Y.) supplemented with 10 m*M* Hepes, pH 7.4, and 0.2% glucose (Sigma Chemical Co., St. Louis, Mo.), 5×10^{-5} *M* 2-mercaptoethanol (Bio-Rad, Richmond, Calif.), 2 m*M* glutamine, 50 u/ml penicillin, 50 μg/ml streptomycin, and 2% fetal calf serum (GIBCO). Primed spleen cells, 5×10^7, were mixed with 2×10^7 irradiated BALB/c spleen cells in 20 ml in Corning 25-cm² tissue culture flasks (Corning Glass, Corning, N.Y.). Flasks were incubated upright at 37°C in 5% CO_2 for 4 to 6 days. The cells were then washed three times in RHS medium and counted.

^{51}Cr release assay. Assays were done in RPMI 1640 without sodium bicarbonate and supplemented with NaCl, $MgCl_2$, and $CaCl_2$ to give final concentrations of 127, 1.8, and 1.3 m*M*, respectively, 10 m*M* Hepes, pH 7.4, 10% calf serum (GIBCO), 50 u/ml penicillin, and 50 μg/ml streptomycin (RHS medium). Stock solutions were made containing 3×10^4 targets/0.3 ml and CTL at various effector-to-target ratios. Aliquots (0.3 ml) were added to 12 × 75-m*M* round-bottom plastic tubes (Sarstedt, Princeton, N.J.). Cells were then shifted to various temperatures and the cells were allowed to settle on the bottom of the tubes. After 3.5 hr, 1.2 ml of cold phosphate-buffered saline was added, tubes were vortexed, and centrifuged and 1.0 ml of the supernatant was removed. Both the 1.0 ml of supernatant and the tubes containing the pellets and remaining 0.5 ml of supernatant were counted with the machine background automatically subtracted (Packard Model 5375, Packard Inst. Co., Downers Grove, Ill.). The percentage total release is calculated as 150 × counts per minute in 1.0 ml supernatant/total counts per minute (supernatant and pellet). The percentage spontaneous release is just the percentage total release in the absence of CTL.

[2] Abbreviations used: LPS, lipopolysaccharide; Hepes, *N*-2-hydroxyethyl-piperazine-*N'*-2-ethanesulfonic acid: RHS, RPMI 1640/Hepes/calf serum medium; CTL, cytolytic T lymphocyte.

RESULTS

Temperature dependence of spontaneous release. Figure 1 shows the effect of temperature on spontaneous release for P815 cells, LPS blasts, and spleen cells after a 3.5-hr incubation. The spontaneous release for P815 increased gradually from 22 to 37°C. With spleen cells and LPS blasts, however, there was a dramatic increase in spontaneous release with increasing temperature. The rate of increase was not constant and there appears to be an inflection point between 29 and 32°C. This increase between 29 and 32°C has been observed consistently using cells from several strains of mice (data not shown).

Temperature dependence of allogeneic CTL mediated lysis. ^{51}Cr-release assays were done at a series of temperatures to determine the temperature dependence for killing of spleen cell and blast targets. Specific ^{51}Cr-release can be calculated as just the percentage total release minus the percentage spontaneous release or this can be multiplied by 100/(100 − percentage spontaneous release) to correct for loss of ^{51}Cr associated with viable cells. The former, percentage total − percentage spontaneous, is an underestimate of the actual amount of killing. Multiplying this by 100/(100 − percentage spontaneous release) yields an overestimate, especially when the spontaneous release is high (1). Specific release was therefore calculated and plotted in both ways.

Lysis of P815 target cells was found to increase continuously from 22 to 37°C (Fig. 2A). The 100/(100 − percentage spontaneous release) correction is significant for the spleen cell and LPS blast target cells. Without this correction, lysis of spleen cell targets (Fig. 2B) plateaus at 29°C while lysis of LPS blasts (Fig. 2C) plateaus at 32°C. With the correction there is some increase at temperatures above 29–32°C. Results at lower effector-to-target ratios, utilizing the 100/(100 − percentage spontaneous release) correction, are shown in Fig. 3. With LPS blast targets, most of the increase in specific release is seen in going from 22 to 32°C (Fig. 3A). The increase from 32 to 37°C reflects, at least in part, the 100/(100 − percentage

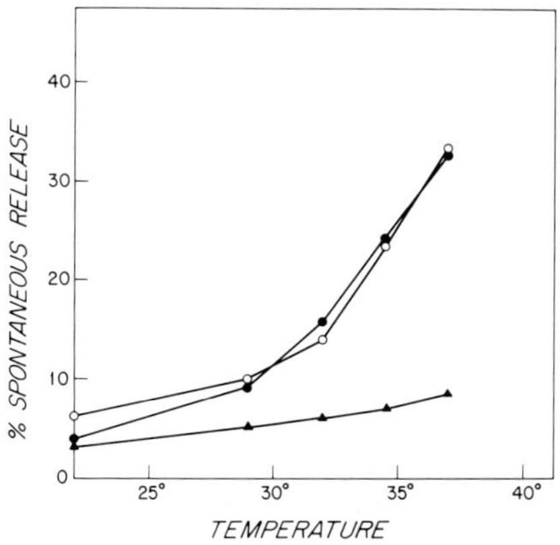

FIG. 1. Temperature dependence of spontaneous release. P815, BALB/c LPS blasts, and BALB/c spleen cells were prepared and ^{51}Cr labeled at 37°C (see Materials and Methods). Target cells, 3×10^4, in 0.3 ml of RHS medium were incubated at ambient (22°C) temperature or in water baths at 29, 32, 34.5, or 37°C. Temperatures varied less than 0.5°C from those indicated. The percentage spontaneous release was determined after 3.5 hr of incubation at the indicated temperatures (see Materials and Methods). Each point is the average of four samples. ●, Spleen cells; ○, blasts, ▲, P815.

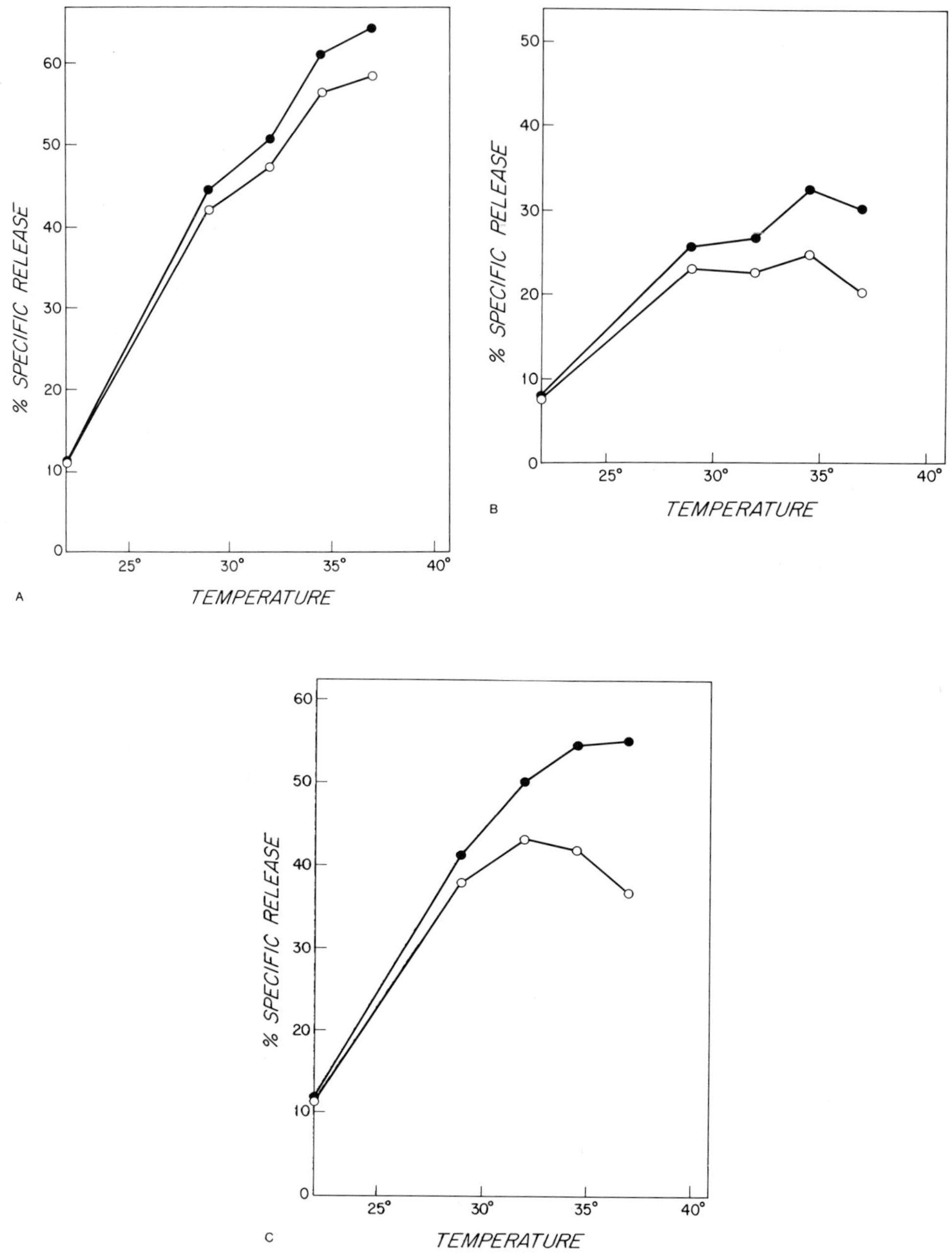

FIG. 2. Temperature dependence of CTL-mediated lysis. Target cells were the same as in Fig. 1. CTL were from B6 mice primed *in vivo* with P815 and restimulated *in vitro* with BALB/c spleen cells (see Materials and Methods). CTL and targets were mixed to give 3×10^4 targets/0.3 ml and an effector-to-target ratio of 7.6:1 and incubated for 3.5 hr at varying temperatures. The percentage spontaneous release at each temperature for this experiment is shown in Fig. 1. Specific release is calculated either as percentage total release − percentage spontaneous release, ○; or as 100 × (percentage total release − percentage spontaneous release)/(100 − percentage spontaneous release), ●. Points shown are the average of duplicate samples. A, P815 targets; B, spleen cell targets; C, blast targets.

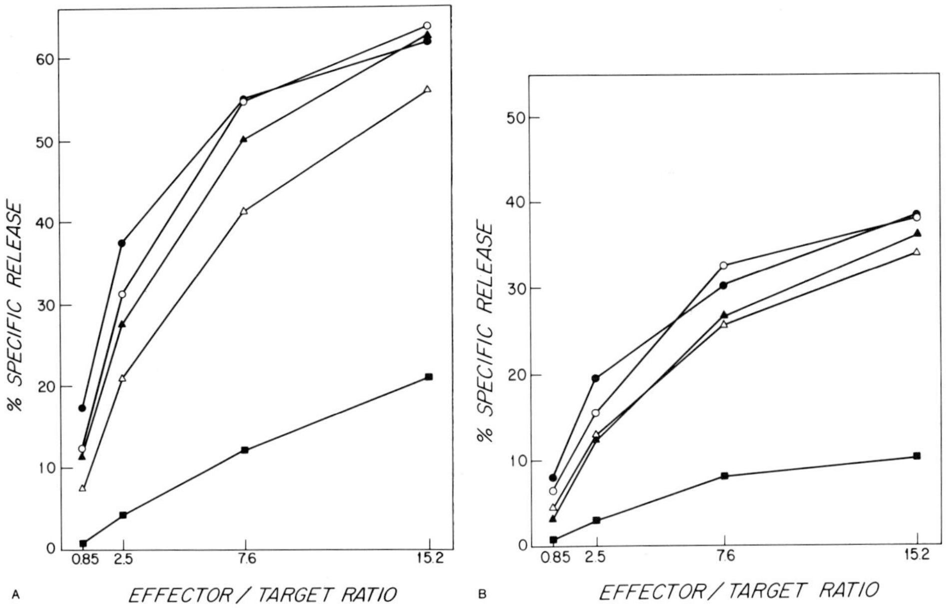

FIG. 3. Temperature dependence of CTL mediated lysis. This assay is the same as that shown in Fig. 2 except results with effector-to-target ratios of 0.85:1, 2.5:1, and 15.2:1 are shown. Specific release is calculated as 100 × (percentage total − percentage spontaneous)/(100 − percentage spontaneous): ●, 37°C; ○, 34.5°C; ▲, 32°C; △, 29°C; ■, 22°C. A, Blast targets; B, spleen cell targets.

spontaneous release) correction. The actual increase in killing above 32°C is therefore small relative to the more than twofold increase in spontaneous release (Fig. 1). With spleen cell targets (Fig. 3B), lysis at 29°C is equivalent to that at 32°C.

DISCUSSION

The rate of spontaneous release from ^{51}Cr-labeled spleen cells and LPS blasts increased dramatically at temperatures above 32°C. CTL-mediated lysis of these target cells was also temperature dependent, but the major increase in specific lysis was seen in going from 22 to 29°C (spleen cells) or 32°C (LPS blasts). The extent of increase in specific lysis achieved at 37°C was difficult to evaluate due to the higher spontaneous release, but this increase was clearly small relative to the two- to threefold increase in spontaneous release. Performing ^{51}Cr-release assays with spleen cell and LPS blast target cells at 29 and 32°C, respectively, therefore improves dramatically the ratio of specific release to spontaneous release. This makes it possible to obtain reliable quantitative data using these target cells. It may similarly be useful to use a lower temperature with other target cells which yield a high spontaneous release at 37°C.

REFERENCES

1. Martz, E., *Contemp. Top. Immunobiol.* **7,** 301, 1977.
2. Henney, C. S., *Contemp. Top. Immunobiol.* **7,** 245, 1977.
3. Berke, G., *Prog. Allergy* **27,** 69, 1980.
4. Berke, G., Sullivan, K. A., and Amos, B., *J. Exp. Med.* **136,** 1594, 1972.
5. Martz, E., and Benacerraf, B., *Cell. Immunol.* **20,** 81, 1975.
6. Berke, G., and Sullivan, K. A., *Transplant. Proc.* **5,** 421, 1973.
7. Billings, P., Burakoff, S., Dorf, M., and Benacerraf, B., *J. Exp. Med.* **146,** 623, 1977.

CELLULAR IMMUNOLOGY **65**, 206 (1981)

ANNOUNCEMENT

Fifth International Lectin Meeting, Bern, Switzerland

May 31–June 5, 1982

The Fifth International Lectin Meeting will take place in Bern, Switzerland, May 31–June 5, 1982.

Main topics of the meeting will be:

1. Detection of cancer markers
2. Biological function of lectins
3. Lectins as specific tools

The meeting will be held at the new Universitäts-Kinderspital (Babies and Childrens Hospital), Bern.

A proceedings volume is being prepared in the series "Lectins, Biology, Biochemistry, Clinical Biochemistry" (W.de Gruyter) and speakers must be prepared to hand in their manuscripts at the meeting.

Abstracts for the Abstract booklet should be typed double spaced on 2 pages A4 (21 × 29 cm) with good margins. It will be reproduced directly. Abstracts must be submitted to INTERLEC 5, The Protein Laboratory, Copenhagen, by April 1, 1982.

There will be a meeting fee of SFr 175 for all participants; students, half rate.

Organizers:

T. C. Bøg-Hansen
The Protein Laboratory
University of Copenhagen
Sigurdsgade 34
DK-2200 Copenhagen N, Denmark

G. A. Spengler
Institute for Clinical Protein Research
University of Bern
Tiefenauspital
CH-3004 Bern, Switzerland

CELLULAR IMMUNOLOGY 65, 207–210 (1981)

Papers to Appear in Forthcoming Issues

(Received and Accepted Dates Follow Title)

DANIEL SANTOLI, MARY KAY FRANCIS, AND MASSIMO TRUCCO. Phenotypic and Functional Characterization of Allospecific and Nonspecific (NK- and K-Like) Cytotoxic T Lymphocytes Generated in Human Mixed Lymphocyte Cultures from Noncytotoxic Precursors. (Received 6/25/81; accepted 9/23/81).

VÉRONIQUE DUPREZ, PATRICE DEBRE, AND JEAN-PAUL LEVY. Genetic Control of Sensitivity to Maloney Leukemia Virus in Mice. V. Role of H-2-Linked Genes in the Control of Anti-FMR Cytolytic T Lymphocytes. (Received 6/17/81; accepted 9/29/81).

JEAN-PIERRE B. KOLB, ANNA SENIK, AND MONIQUE CASTAGNA. *In Vitro* Stimulation of Mouse NK Cell Activity by Phorbol Esters: A Pathway Different from Interferon-Induced Activation. (Received 7/15/81; accepted 9/30/81).

DAVID S. MATHESON, BRIDGET GREEN, AND Y. H. TAN. Human Interferons α and β Inhibit T Cell Dependent and Stimulate T Cell Independent Mitogenesis and Natural Cytotoxicity: Relationship to Chromosome. (Received 2/25/81; accepted 10/3/81).

BARBARA E. T. BUSBY AND BOB S. ROBERSON. Phytohemagglutinin-Induced Enhancement and IgG Subclass Restriction of the Immune Response to Type III Pneumococcal Polysaccharide. (Received 7/15/81; accepted 10/6/81).

BYUNG S. KIM. Tumor-Specific Immunity Induced by Somatic Hybrids. III. Persistence of Adoptively Transferred Immunity Specific for TEPC-15 Plasmacytoma in Normal BALB/c Mice. (Received 8/14/81; accepted 10/7/81).

HAIM OVADIA AND PHILIP Y. PATERSON. Enhanced Proliferation, Survival and Yield of Cultured Myelin Basic Protein (MBP)-Reactive Lewis Rat Lymph Node Cells following Dual Activation with Concanavalin A and MBP. (Received 8/26/81; accepted 10/7/81).

JEENAN TSENG. IgA Allotype Suppression in Mice: A Cellular Implication for the IgA Preponderance in the Gut. (Received 7/10/81; accepted 10/7/81).

PIERRE ÅMAN, GUNNEL LUNDIN, KERSTIN HALL, AND GEORGE KLEIN. Insulin Receptors on Human Lymphoid Lines of B-Cell Origin. (Received 8/26/81; accepted 10/7/81).

BRIAN A. POLLOK AND EDDIE W. LAMON. Murine T Cells That Lyse Antibody-Sensitized Target Cells. IV. Analysis of Thy 1 and Lyt Surface Antigen Expression Among Thymic K Cells. (Received 6/2/81; accepted 10/8/81).

CHOU-CHIK TING, DENNIS RODRIGUES, RICHARD NORDAN, AND JIN-XIN HONG. Studies of the Mechanisms for the Induction of *in Vivo* Tumor Immunity. VI. Induction of Specific and Nonspecific Cell-Mediated Immunity in Tumor Bearing Hosts and Its Correlation with Transplantation Tumor Immunity. (Received 3/12/81; accepted 10/13/81).

Francis V. Chisari and Linda K. Curtiss. Modulation of Peripheral Blood Mononuclear Cell Cyclic Adenosine Monophosphate Levels by Human Very Low Density Lipoprotein. (Received 7/21/81; accepted 10/13/81).

John L. Sternick, Elizabeth M. Allen, Linda M. Ripani, Denis J. Schrier, and Vernon L. Moore. BCG-Induced Granulomatous Pulmonary Inflammation and Splenomegaly in Mice. A T Cell-Dependent Response. (Received 1/23/81; accepted 10/14/81).

Ronald Palacios and Ulf Andersson. Autologous Mixed Lymphocyte Reaction in Human Cord Blood Lymphocytes. Decreased Generation of Helper and Cytotoxic T Cell Functions and Increased Proliferative Response and Induction of Suppressor T Cells. (Received 7/17/81; accepted 10/18/81).

Susumu Kawaguchi. Ontogenical Studies on Kinetics of Lipopolysaccharide-Induced Response to Bromelain-Treated Mouse Erythrocytes in Mouse Spleen Cells. I. Differences from the Response of Total IgM-Secreting Cells. (Received 7/20/81; accepted 10/18/81).

George Carayanniotis and Philip F. Halloran. The Regulation of Immune Responses to Multiple Non H-2 Antigens on Tumor Cells. I. Differential Responses of BALB/c F_1 Hybrids to the P815 Mastocytoma *in Vivo*. (Received 9/1/81; accepted 10/14/81).

Yasuhiro Koga, Kazuto Taniguchi, Chiharu Kubo, and Kikuo Nomoto. Peritoneal Adherent Cells Inhibit the Generation of Cytotoxic T Lymphocytes with Prostaglandin-Mediated System. (Received 8/10/81; accepted 10/18/81).

George C. Tsokos and James E. Balow. Suppressor Cells Generated from Human Peripheral Mononuclear Cells by Stimulation with Pokeweed Mitogen. (Received 5/7/81; accepted 10/18/81).

Claude Auriault, Monique Capron, and André Capron. Activation of Rat and Human Eosinophils by Soluble Factor(s) Released by *Schistosoma mansoni* Schistosomula. (Received 5/26/81; accepted 10/18/81).

Burton Zweiman, Anne R. Moskovitz, Robert P. Lisak, and L. Douglas Wilkerson. An Approach for the Separation of Mononuclear Inflammatory Cells from Central Nervous System Tissue. (Received 9/15/81; accepted 10/20/81).

J. Kettman, A. Soederberg, and I. Lefkovits. Heterogeneity of B Cell Clones: Immunoglobulin-Secreting Subsets. (Received 6/22/81; accepted 10/20/81).

Klaus Bendtzen. Induction of Antigen-Specific Lymphocyte Unresponsiveness *in Vitro*: Possible Role of Divalent Cations and Defective Function of Human T Cell Activating Factor (TAF). (Received 9/8/81; accepted 10/21/81).

Masroor A. Baig and Aftab A. Ansari. Studies of Mouse Immunoglobulin Allotypes by Reverse Plaque Assay: Detection of Spleen Cells Secreting Immunoglobulins with Specific Allotype in C57BL/6J Mice (Received 9/28/81; accepted 10/23/81).

Robert K. Shockley and Raphael Kleinman. Bacteria-Immune System Interactions. III. Isolation of a *Bacillus globigii* Cell Wall Component Involved in Binding to Human Lymphocytes. (Received 9/15/81; accepted 10/25/81).

Michael G. Goodman and William O. Weigle. Nonspecific Activation of Murine Lymphocytes. VIII. Effects of *D*-Penicillamine. (Received 7/21/81; accepted 10/25/81).

EUGENIA HAWRYLKO. Tumor Bearer T Cells Suppress BCG-Potentiated Antitumor Responses. I. Requirements for Their Effect. (Received 8/21/81; accepted 10/27/81).

EUGENIA HAWRYLKO, CAROL ANN MELE, AND OSIAS STUTMAN. Tumor Bearer T Cells Suppress BCG-Potentiated Antitumor Responses. II. Characteristics of the Efferent Phase Suppressor. (Received 8/21/81; accepted 10/27/81).

THELMA A. KOPPI AND W. J. HALLIDAY. Further Characterization of the Cells Involved in Leukocyte Adherence Inhibition with Murine Tumor Extracts. (Received 8/26/81; accepted 10/27/81).

RICHARD F. MORTENSEN. Inhibition of the Polyclonal Antibody Plaque Forming Cell Response of Human B-Lymphocytes by C-Reactive Protein (CRP) and CRP-Complexes. (Received 8/6/81; accepted 10/29/81).

NOAH ISAKOV, MICHAEL FELDMAN, AND SHRAGA SEGAL. Acute Infection of Mice with Lactic Dehydrogenase Virus (LDV) Impairs the Antigen-Presenting Capacity of Their Macrophages. (Received 8/26/81; accepted 10/29/81).

CHRISTOPHER J. FROELICH, ANNA S. TAI, ARTHUR D. BANKHURST, AND NOEL L. WARNER. Human E-Rosette Positive Cells Which Bind Monomeric IgG Mediate Natural Cytotoxicity. (Received 7/21/81; accepted 10/31/81).

C. Y. LAU, E. Y. WANG, AND G. GOLDSTEIN. Studies of Thymopoietin Pentapeptide (TP5) on Experimental Tumors. I. TP5 Relieves Immunosuppression in Tumor Bearing Mice. (Received 6/23/81; accepted 10/31/81).

AH-KAU NG, YU-HUI ZHANG, CARLO RUSSO, AND SOLDANO FERRONE. Immunochemical and Functional Analysis of Ia-like Antigens on Human Monocyte-Macrophages with Monoclonal Antibodies. (Received 7/16/81; accepted 10/31/81).

MICHIO OHTA, IZUMI NAKASHIMA, AND NOBUO KATO. Adjuvant Action of Bacterial Lipopolysaccharide in Induction of Delayed Type Hypersensitivity to Protein Antigens. I. Action of the O3 Antigen of Klebsiella Extracted from Culture Fluid (Received 8/13/81; accepted 10/31/81).

HEINZ G. REMOLD AND ALMA D. MEDNIS. The Effect of Tunicamycin on the Molecular Heterogeneity of Guinea Pig Migration Inhibitory Factor. (Received 10/21/81; accepted 11/3/81).

JEAN-LUC TEILLAUD, CÉCILE GOUJET-ZALC, MARC FONTAINE, COLETTE BRAUN, AND GUY MAHOUY. Involvement of Human Membrane-Associated Complement Components in the Rosette Formation between Marmoset Red Blood Cells and Human Leukocytes. (Received 7/15/81; accepted 10/28/81).

JIUAN J. LIU, MARIANGELA SEGRE, AND DIEGO SEGRE. Changes in Suppressor, Helper, and B-Cell Functions in Aging Mice. (Received 10/5/81; accepted 10/28/81).

MICHAEL L. MISFELDT AND EDGAR E. HANNA. Suppressor T-Cell Hybridomas That Exhibit Various Capacities to Negatively Regulate PFC Responses in a T-Cell Dependent Mouse Model. (Received 6/2/81; accepted 11/3/81).

ROBERTA H. MEYERS-ELLIOTT AND HUMPHREY L. SUMNER. Experimental Uveitis Induced by Products of Activated Lymphocytes: Intraocular Effects of Rhodopsin-Induced Lymphokines. (Received 7/13/81; accepted 11/3/81).

TETSUFUMI INOUE AND LOUISE T. ADLER. Selective Suppressive Effects of Antiallotype Antibodies on Spleen Cells of Adult Rabbits. I. (Received 8/13/81; accepted 11/3/81).

TETSUFUMI INOUE, LOUISE T. ADLER, AKIO YAMADA, AND FRANK L. ADLER. Comparative Suppressive Effects of Antiallotype Antibodies on Spleen Cells of Immature and Adult Rabbits. II. (Received 8/13/81; accepted 11/4/81).

MARTINE PAPIERNIK AND LILIANE LAROCHE. Thymic Medullary Lymphocytes. I. Lymphokines Produced by Thymic Medullary Lymphocytes as a Second Signal for Intrathymic Stem Cell Homing. (Received 6/15/81; accepted 11/5/81).

RONALD L. WHISLER, KATHY BAKENHASTER, AND E. MITCHEL OPREMCAK. Autologous Mechanisms Generating Natural Killer Activity within Human Peripheral Lymphocytes Depleted of NK Target Binding Cells. (Received 9/17/81; accepted 11/11/81).

DOMINIQUE KAISERLIAN AND MIREILLE DARDENNE. Studies on the Mechanisms of the Inhibitory Effects of FTS on Murine Allograft Immunity. (Received 10/6/81; accepted 11/11/81).

JONATHAN W. UHR. Effect of Toxin–Antibody Conjugates on Tumor Cells.

MATTHEW D. SCHARFF. Somatic Cell Genetics of Immunoglobulin Production.

GREGORY W. SISKIND, A. FAYE SCHRATER, G. JEANETTE THORBECKE, MARC E. WEKSLER, AND EDMOND A. GOIDL. The Role of Auto-anti-idiotype Antibody in the Regulation of the Immune Response. (Received 11/8/80).

CELLULAR IMMUNOLOGY **65**, 211–220 (1981)

BCG-Induced Granulomatous Pulmonary Inflammation and Splenomegaly in Mice: A T-Cell-Dependent Response[1]

JOHN L. STERNICK,[2] ELIZABETH M. ALLEN, LINDA M. RIPANI, DENIS J. SCHRIER,[3] AND VERNON L. MOORE[4]

Research Service, Wood Veterans Administration Medical Center, Milwaukee, Wisconsin 53193, Departments of Medicine and Pathology, The Medical College of Wisconsin, Milwaukee, Wisconsin 53201, Department of Biology, Marquette University, Milwaukee, Wisconsin 53233

Received January 23, 1981; accepted October 14, 1981

When C57BL/6 mice were injected iv with BCG in an oil-in-saline emulsion, they developed intense pulmonary granulomatous inflammation (PGI) and splenomegaly as well as chemotactic activity for macrophages and angiotensin-converting enzyme (ACE) in their lung fluids. PGI, splenomegaly, and levels of chemotactic activity and ACE were markedly reduced in T-cell-deficient "B" mice. The capacity to develop PGI was fully restored and splenomegaly was partially restored in "B" mice by the provision of syngeneic thymocytes, spleen cells, or purified T cells. These results indicate that the full expression of BCG-induced PGI is dependent upon thymus-derived cells and is associated with high levels of chemotactic activity for macrophages and ACE in the lung lavage fluid. Although BCG-induced splenomegaly appears to be T cell dependent, it did not reach its full magnitude in reconstituted "B" mice.

INTRODUCTION

Granulomatous inflammation and splenomegaly are common manifestations of several infectious and noninfectious diseases. In many cases, pulmonary granulomatous inflammation (PGI)[5] is thought to be of immune etiology and most likely mediated by delayed hypersensitivity (DH) (1). However, sound evidence for this

[1] This work was supported by Grant HL-22301 from the National Heart, Lung and Blood Institute and by the Veterans Administration.

[2] This study partially fulfills the requirements for a Ph.D. in the Department of Biology, Marquette University. Present address: Memorial Sloan–Kettering Cancer Center, 1275 York Avenue, New York, N.Y. During the course of this study, J.L.S. was supported by funds from a Marquette University Teaching Fellowship.

[3] Present address: Department of Pathology, University of Michigan School of Medicine, Ann Arbor, Mich. 48109.

[4] Address correspondence and reprint requests to: Vernon L. Moore, Ph.D., Research Service/151, Veterans Administration Medical Center, Wood, Wisc. 53193.

[5] Abbreviations used: PGI, pulmonary granulomatous inflammation; DH, delayed hypersensitivity; BCG, bacillus Calmette–Guérin strain of *Mycobacterium bovis; Igh*, genetic region of the mouse that controls the production of immunoglobulin heavy chains; B6, C57BL/6 mice; ACE, angiotensin converting enzyme; C, complement; PHA, phytohemagglutinin; Con A, concanavalin A; LPS, lipopolysaccharide; SRBC, sheep erythrocytes; LDCF, lymphocyte-derived chemotactic factor; Tx, thymectomized; Ir, lethally irradiated; iv, intravenous.

0008-8749/81/180211-10$02.00/0

supposition is available only in murine schistosomiasis (1–4). Schistosomal egg-induced PGI is immunospecific, can be adoptively transferred with immune cells but not with immune serum (2), is suppressed with anti-lymphocyte serum (3), and is markedly reduced in thymus-deprived mice (4).

The prime example of PGI is tuberculosis. Although this inflammatory response is thought to be mediated by lymphocytes resulting in DH, formal proof is lacking. Myrvik *et al.* (5) have shown that the intravenous (iv) injection of killed bacillus Calmette–Guérin (BCG) into rabbits results in intense PGI. This inflammatory response is immunospecific and associated with a positive migration inhibitory test using inflammatory cells from the lung, a test which is believed to be an *in vitro* correlate of local DH in the lung (6, 7). Furthermore, several lymphokines have been demonstrated in inflamed lungs from these animals (reviewed in (8)). It is therefore likely that this inflammatory response in the lung is a manifestation of DH. Another means of studying the immunology of BCG-induced PGI is in mice where inbred strains are available for adoptive transfer studies, and it is possible to produce animals which are specifically deficient in T lymphocytes.

The iv injection of killed BCG results in the development of PGI and splenomegaly only in certain strains of mice (9) and is influenced by genes linked to the immunoglobulin heavy chain allotype (*Igh*) (10). The current study shows that normally high responder C57BL/6 (B6) mice that were deficient in T lymphocytes were unable to fully develop BCG-induced PGI and splenomegaly. In addition, T-deficient mice had reduced levels of chemotactic activity for macrophages and angiotensin-converting enzyme (ACE) in their lung fluids. The capacity to develop PGI could be fully restored by the provision of lymphocytes, spleen cells, or T cells from normal syngeneic animals, whereas BCG-induced splenomegaly was only partially restored by this procedure.

MATERIALS AND METHODS

Mice. Female B6 mice were obtained from the Jackson Laboratory, Bar Harbor, Maine. They were maintained in the Animal Facilities of Marquette University and Wood VA Medical Center and fed Purina Chow and water *ad libitum.* These facilities are fully accredited by the American Association for the Accreditation of Laboratory Animal Care. The mice were used when they were 8–12 weeks of age.

Production of PGI and splenomegaly. A killed, lyophilized BCG strain of *Mycobacterium bovis* was provided by Dr. Q. N. Myrvik, The Bowman Gray School of Medicine, Winston-Salem, North Carolina. An oil-in-saline emulsion of BCG was prepared as follows: Lyophilized BCG was ground for 15 min with a pestle and mortar in oil (Marcol 52, Humble Oil Co.) to a final stock concentration of 15 mg/ml. The mixture was frozen at −20°C until required. When needed, the BCG–oil mixture was thawed and sonicated for 30 min before mixing the BCG in oil with saline to a concentration of 300 μg/0.2 ml of oil and saline (9, 11). Mice were injected in the tail vein with 300 μg of BCG and assessed for PGI and splenomegaly 28–33 days later. Pulmonary inflammation and splenomegaly were quantified by expressing organ indices as previously described (9) and as expressed below:

$$\text{organ index} = \frac{\text{organ weight/body weight test animal}}{\text{organ weight/body weight normal syngeneic animal}}.$$

In addition, routine histologies were done on lungs and spleen. In brief, whole lung and spleen were preserved in 10% buffered formalin, the specimens were embedded in paraffin, serially sectioned, and stained with hematoxylin and eosin for evaluation.

Production of T-cell-deficient "B" mice. This procedure was performed as described by Mitchell *et al.* (12). Adult, 8- to 12-week-old B6 mice were thymectomized, lethally irradiated 7–10 days later with 800 R of total body irradiation from a General Electric Maxitron 300 X-ray unit. Twenty-four hours later, these animals were injected with 10×10^6 bone marrow cells which were treated *in vitro* with anti-Thy-1 serum + complement (C). Anti-Thy-1 (anti-Thy-1.2) serum was produced by injecting C3H thymocytes into AKR mice as described by Reif and Allen (13). The cytotoxic titer of this material against B6 thymocytes was 1:32 (50% killing). Reconstituted mice were also thymectomized, irradiated and, in addition to bone marrow, received either 20×10^6 thymus cells, 135×10^6 spleen cells, or 60×10^6 spleen T cells intraperitoneally. The thymus and spleen cells were collected by placing these organs in nylon mesh containers and pressing the organs with sterile plungers to release their cellular contents into a Petri dish containing RPMI 1640, 10% AB^+ serum, 1% glutamine, 25 mM Hepes, and Geramycin (50 μg/ml media). Splenic T cells were obtained by passing whole spleen cells (400×10^6 cells) over 1.2 g of nylon wool in a 20-ml column, incubating the spleen cells in the nylon wool for 45 min at 37°C, and washing the column gently with 40 ml of warm (37°C) media; T cells were eluted from the column. The cells were counted and tested for viability by trypan blue exclusion. Ten to fifteen days later the animals were injected iv with BCG.

To test whether these techniques had selectively depleted T lymphocytes, spleen cells from normal, "B", and "reconstituted B" mice were stimulated *in vitro* from either PHA or Con A (T-cell mitogens) and with LPS (a B-cell mitogen). These procedures have been described previously (14). In summary, spleen cells from either normal, "B", or "reconstituted B" mice were stimulated *in vitro* with PHA (10 μg/ml), Con A (1 μg/ml), or LPS (25 μg/ml), pulsed 3 days later with [^{3}H]thymidine and harvested on a MASH machine 5 hr after pulse. Data are expressed as net stimulation (cpm of cells with mitogen minus cpm of cells without mitogen). The animals were also assessed for their ability to develop DH to sheep erythrocytes (SRBC), a reaction known to be dependent upon Thy-1$^+$, Lyt-1$^+$ lymphocytes (15). DH was tested by immunizing the mice iv with 5×10^5/0.2 ml of SRBC and challenging 5 days later in the left hind footpad with 1×10^8 SRBC in 0.05 ml. The right hind footpad received sterile physiological saline. The respective footpad thicknesses were read 24 hr postchallenge with a spring-loaded micrometer (Dyer Co., Inc., Lancaster, Pa.). Footpad increments due to inflammation were measured in millimeters.

Evaluation of chemotactic activity in lung lavage fluid. Mice were killed and their lungs lavaged *in situ* with Hank's balanced salt solution (Difco, Detroit, Mich.). Approximately 1 ml of lung lavage was obtained from each mouse by cannulation in the trachea with a syringe attached to PE-60 polyethylene tubing (Clay-Adams, Parsippany, N.J.). The lavage was centrifuged at 450 g for 10 min and the supernatant stored at −20°C until used. Indicator cells for chemotaxis were normal B6 peritoneal macrophages obtained by peritoneal lavage with Hank's balanced salt solution. These cells were washed and suspended at a concentration of 2.3×10^6/ml in Gey's solution containing 2% bovine serum albumin. The positive control for chemotaxis was lymphocyte-derived chemotactic factor (LDCF) prepared as described by Boumsell and Meltzer (16). Chemotaxis was performed in blind-well lucite chambers (Neuroprobe Corp., Bethesda, Md.) using one 5-μm filter (Nucleopore, Pleasanton, Calif.) by incubation at 37°C for 90 min. Data are expressed as the mean number of cells migrating through the filter per oil immersion field.

Assay for ACE in lung lavage fluid. This was performed using a fluorometric method described by Friedland and Silverstein (17). The method employs hippuryl-L-histidyl-L-leucine as a substrate and a standard curve was prepared using known quantities of L-histidyl-L-leucine. Units of activity are presented as nanomoles of L-histidyl-L-leucine formed per minute per milliliter of lung lavage.

RESULTS

Depletion of T cells in "B" mice. Data in Fig. 1 demonstrate that normal mice responded to PHA, Con A, and LPS, while "B" mice were significantly depressed in their responses to PHA and Con A and enhanced in their response to LPS.

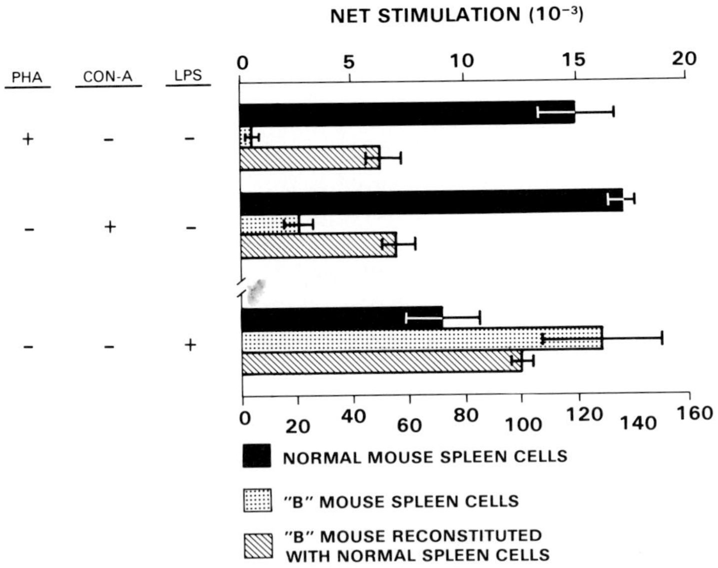

FIG. 1. Effect of thymectomy, irradiation and bone marrow reconstitution on mitogen-induced proliferation of spleen cells. "B" and "reconstituted B" mice were produced as described under Materials and Methods. Normal mice spleen cells were used as controls. Spleen cells were stimulated with optimal concentrations of PHA, Con A, and LPS. Value represents geometric mean and SE of at least five mice in each experiment. P values were obtained by using unpaired Student's t test. For PHA, $P \ll 0.001$ for differences between normal and "B" mice, and $P \ll 0.001$ for differences between "B" mice and reconstituted animals. For Con A and the same comparisons, the values are $P \ll 0.001$ and $P \ll 0.001$, respectively. For LPS and the same comparisons, the values are $P < 0.05$ and $P > 0.20$.

These data strongly suggest that the "B" mice were markedly deficient in T cells. The increase in LPS response in "B" mice was probably due to the greater proportion of B cells in the spleen. "B" mice reconstituted with normal spleen cells showed partial restoration of the normal response to these specific mitogens. Data in Fig. 2 indicate that, whereas normal B6 and "reconstituted B" mice developed potent DH to SRBC, "B" B6 mice were markedly suppressed in this response. Collectively, these experiments indicate that our technique of producing "B" mice resulted in a marked reduction of T lymphocytes in these animals and that reconstituted animals had significant T-cell function.

Reduction of PGI and splenomegaly in T-cell-deficient mice and reconstitution with thymocytes, spleen cells or T cells. First, it is apparent that an iv injection of BCG resulted in a dramatic increase in lung and spleen weights in B6 mice when examined 28–33 days later (Fig. 3, Group 2). This procedure also caused the development of intense granulomatous inflammation in these organs (9) (Fig. 4). Mice that were thymectomized (Tx), lethally irradiated (Ir), and reconstituted with anti-Thy-1 and C-treated syngeneic bone marrow demonstrated a marked diminution in organ weights (Group 3), although the magnitude of the response was increased compared to normal mice (Group 1). "B" mice restored with thymocytes, spleen cells or splenic T cells recovered their ability to develop intense chronic granulomatous inflammation in the lungs and spleen (Groups 4–6), although "reconstituted B" mice did not develop as much splenomegaly quantitatively as normal mice given BCG. These results also suggest that BCG-induced splenomegaly is T cell dependent, although the capacity to develop enlarged spleens could only be partially reconstituted in "B" mice with either syngeneic thymocytes, spleen cells or splenic T cells.

Histology of the lungs. Figure 4 depicts the histopathology of lungs from various groups of BCG-injected mice and is in agreement with the quantitative data presented in Fig. 3. B6 mice injected with BCG developed intense PGI, and the inflammation was markedly reduced in "B" B6 mice injected with BCG. Histo-

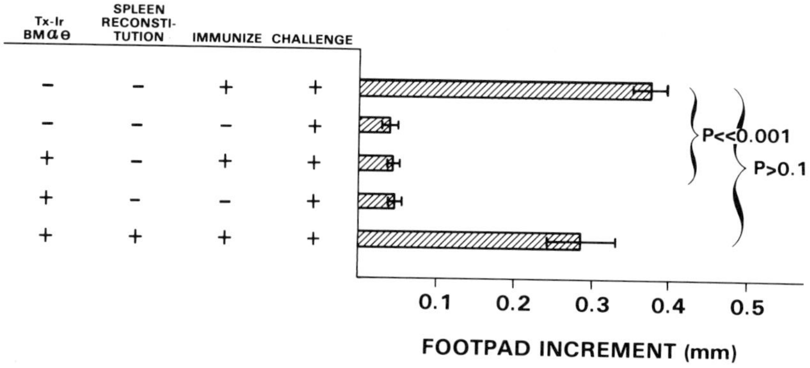

FIG. 2. Delayed hypersensitivity response to SRBC in normal, "B" mice, and spleen cell "reconstituted B" mice. Normal, "B", and "reconstituted B" mice were tested for DH to SRBC, as described under Materials and Methods. The values are represented as means and SE of at least five animals. *P* values were obtained by using unpaired Student's *t* test. Tx = thymectomy; Ir = irradiated; Bm$\alpha\theta$ = reconstituted with anti-Thy-1 + C-treated syngeneic bone marrow; spleen reconstitution = whole spleen cells injected intraperitoneally.

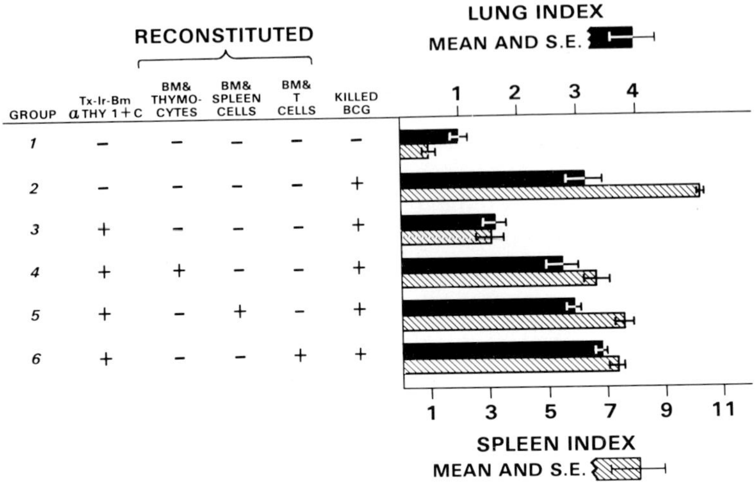

FIG. 3. Effect of BCG on normal, "B", and "reconstituted B" mice. Normal, "B", and "reconstituted B" mice were injected iv with BCG as described under Materials and Methods. Values of the lung and spleen are expressed in mean and SE of at least five mice. *P* values were obtained by unpaired Student's *t* test. For the lung, when the different groups were compared, the following *P* values were found: Groups 1 and 2, $P < 0.001$; Groups 2 and 3, $P < 0.005$; Groups 2 and 4, $P > 0.4$; Groups 2 and 5, $P > 0.4$; Groups 2 and 6, $P > 0.5$; Groups 3 and 4, $P < 0.02$; Groups 3 and 5, $P < 0.01$; and Groups 3 and 6, $P < 0.001$. For the spleen the *P* values for the comparisons were as follows: Groups 1 and 2, $P < 0.001$; Groups 2 and 3, $P < 0.001$; Groups 2 and 4, $P < 0.001$; Groups 2 and 5, $P < 0.001$; Groups 2 and 6, $P < 0.001$; Groups 3 and 4, $P < 0.001$; Groups 3 and 5, $P < 0.001$; and Groups 3 and 6, $P < 0.001$. T = nylon wool-purified spleen T cells; BCG = bacillus Calmette–Guúerin.

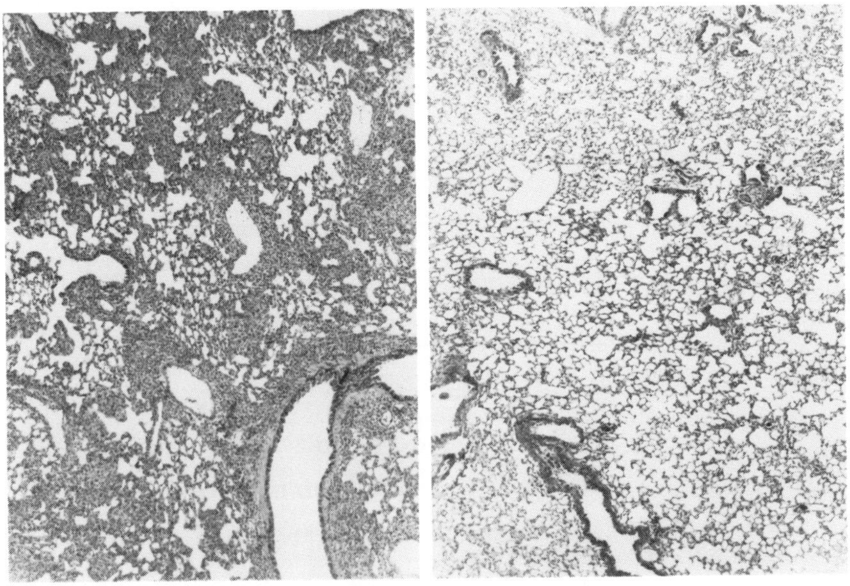

FIG. 4. Histological evidence of the effect of BCG on the lungs of BCG-injected B6 and "B" B6 mice. The mice were injected iv with BCG and 28 to 33 days postinjection were killed and their lungs evaluated for PGI. Left, BCG-injected B6 mouse; right, BCG-injected T-cell-deficient B6 mouse. (H&E × 40.)

TABLE 1

Chemotactic Activity in Lung Fluids of Normal and T-Cell-Deficient C57BL/6 Mice with BCG-Induced Granulomatous Inflammation

Experiment	Source of lung fluid	Compartment		Chemotactic activity[a]
		Upper	Lower	
1	Normal	Cells	LF[b]	2.3 ± 0.34
2	BCG-injected[c]	Cells	Medium	0.3 ± 0.1
3		Cells	LDCF[d]	16.7 ± 1.1
4		Cells	LF	11.1 ± 3.5
5		Cells, LF	Medium	0.3 ± 0.1
6		Cells, LF	LF	0.6 ± 0.21
7	T-Deficient[e] BCG-injected	Cells	LF	2.4 ± 0.55

[a] Mean ± SE of number of cells per oil immersion field.
[b] Lung fluid.
[c] Injected 28 days previously with 300 μg of killed BCG in an oil-insaline emulsion.
[d] Lymphocyte-derived chemotactic factor.
[e] Adult thymectomy, 800 R total body irradiation, reconstitution with anti-Thy-1.2 + C-treated syngenic bone marrow cells.

pathologies of BCG-injected "B" B6 mice reconstituted with syngeneic thymocytes were similar to those of BCG-injected B6 mice (not shown).

Chemotactic activity for macrophages in lung lavage fluids of T-deficient B6 mice with BCG-induced granulomatous inflammation. As shown in Table 1, lung fluids from BCG-injected B6 mice had almost as much chemotactic activity for macrophages as the positive control (experiments 3 and 4), LDCF, and approximately five-fold greater activity than lung fluid from T-deficient BCG-injected B6 mice (experiments 4 and 7). The chemotactic activity was not due to chemokinesis (experiment 5) and required a concentration gradient (experiment 6). These data show that T cells are necessary for the development of potent chemotactic activity in lung lavage from BCG-injected B6 mice.

ACE activity in lung lavage fluids of T-deficient and T-sufficient B6 mice with BCG-induced granulomatous inflammation. In another study,[6] we showed that ACE activity was increased in the lung lavage fluids of high responder C57BL/6 mice injected with BCG. The results in Table 2 indicate that this activity was markedly reduced in T-deficient B6 mice injected with BCG. These data also suggest that T cells are necessary for the production of ACE in BCG-induced granulomatous inflammation.

DISCUSSION

The purpose of the present study was to evaluate the role of T lymphocytes in the development of BCG-induced granulomatous inflammation in mice. This was accomplished by the production of T-deficient mice by thymectomy, irradiation

[6] Schrier, D. J., Ripani, L. M., Katzenstein, A.-L., and Moore, V. L. The role of angiotension-converting enzyme (ACE) in BCG-induced granulomatous inflammation. Increased ACE levels in lung lavage and suppression of inflammation with Captopril. Accepted for publication.

TABLE 2

Angiotensin-Converting Enzyme Activity in Lung Fluid of Normal and T-Cell-Deficient C57BL/6 Mice with BCG-Induced Granulomatous Inflammation

Source of lung fluid	ACE units[a]
Normal	0.02 ± 0.01
BCG-injected	29.04 ± 3.30
T-deficient,[b] BCG-injected	16.40 ± 3.10

[a] Expressed as nmol of His–Leu released per min from hippuryl-L-histidyl-L-leucine.

[b] Adult thymectomy, 800 R total body irradiation, reconstitution with anti-Thy-1.2 + C-treated syngeneic bone marrow cells.

and replenishment with syngeneic bone marrow that was treated with anti-Thy-1.2 serum and complement. First, we showed that this procedure produced mice that were T cell deficient as assessed by the reactivity of their spleen cells to T-cell mitogens and by their inability to develop DH to SRBC. Second, T-deficient mice were quantitatively depressed in their capacity to develop BCG-induced PGI and splenomegaly. This reduced response could be largely restored by reconstitution with a source of T lymphocyte and even with "purified" T cells. Lastly, T-deficient animals had reduced levels of chemotactic activity for macrophages and ACE in their lung lavage fluid.

Since the pulmonary lesions produced by killed BCG are similar to those described in several human diseases (e.g., sarcoidosis, hypersensitivity pneumonitis), we have been studying their genetics, pathogenesis, and regulation (10). Development of the inflammatory response is influenced by genes linked to the immunoglobulin heavy chain complex (*Igh*) and by other, as yet undefined, genes (10). Low-responder CBA mice develop suppressor T cells early after BCG inoculation that control the inflammatory response (18). In addition, high-responder C57BL/6 mice develop suppressor macrophages 3–4 weeks after exposure to BCG that may modulate the inflammatory response (19, 20). The present study clearly demonstrates that full development of the inflammatory response in both the lungs and spleen is dependent upon T lymphocytes. Thus, T cells are necessary both for the development of pulmonary inflammation and are involved in its regulation. Although not yet defined, different subpopulations of T cells are probably involved in these activities. In murine schistosomiasis, Lyt-1 cells are probably involved as effector cells in the induction and maintenance of pulmonary lesions and other subsets of Lyt-1 and Lyt-2 suppressor cells modulate this response (21, 22).

Although T-deficient mice, reconstituted with a source of T cells, fully recovered their ability to develop pulmonary inflammation, similarly treated animals only partially reacquired the capacity to develop splenomegaly. The reason for this incomplete restitution is not known, but it was not dependent upon the number of cells used in reconstitution since T-deficient mice given 165×10^6 normal spleen cells did not develop larger spleens than animals receiving either 135×10^6 or 100×10^6 cells. It was also apparent that T-deficient mice developed inflamed lungs and enlarged spleens following exposure to BCG, albeit of smaller magnitude. This was also reflected by increased ACE in lung fluids of these animals. The most likely explanations for this observation are low numbers of T cells in the animals, foreign body inflammation (i.e., nonimmunologic), or production of lymphokines by B lymphocytes (23–25).

The studies on chemotactic activity for macrophages and ACE in lung fluid are worthy of further comments. Although additional studies will be required, the current study suggests that T cells are necessary for the production of chemotactic activity and ACE. T-cell-dependent chemotactic activity for macrophages may be an important component for the accumulation of macrophages in BCG-induced granulomatous inflammation. In addition, ACE may be involved in the inflammatory process and may be synthesized by epithelioid macrophages (26). Schrier *et al.*[6] demonstrated that ACE activity in lung fluid correlated well with the intensity of the pulmonary inflammatory response and, moreover, that BCG-induced inflammation was impaired by the administration of Captopril, a specific inhibitor of ACE activity. The mechanism of putative ACE involvement is not known at this time.

In summary, collective data on BCG-induced pulmonary inflammation in rabbits and mice indicate that it is mediated by T lymphocytes. T cells are probably involved in the production of inflammatory mediators such as chemotactic factor as well as ACE. ACE may also be involved in the inflammatory response. Further studies on the genetics and regulation of this inflammatory response should enhance our understanding of pulmonary inflammation and will also be applicable to studies of human lung disease associated with granulomatous inflammation.

ACKNOWLEDGMENTS

The authors appreciate the typing and editorial assistance of Catherine A. Walther and Sharon T. Olechek, and the preparation of the illustrations by Ms. Carole Russell-Hilmer.

REFERENCES

1. Warren, K. S., *In* "Seventh International Conference on Sarcoidosis and other Granulomatous Disorders" (L. E. Siltzbach, Ed.), *Ann. NY Acad. Sci.* **278,** 7, 1976.
2. Warren, K. S., Domingo, E. O., and Cowan, R. B. T., *Amer. J. Pathol.* **51,** 735, 1967.
3. Domingo, E. O., and Warren, K. S., *Amer. J. Pathol.* **52,** 613, 1968.
4. Domingo, E. O., and Warren, K. S., *Amer. J. Pathol.* **51,** 757, 1967.
5. Myrvik, Q. N., Leake, E. S., and Fariss, B., *J. Immunol.* **86,** 128, 1961.
6. Moore, V. L., Myrvik, Q. N., Leake, E. S., *Infect. Immun.* **7,** 743, 1973.
7. Galindo, B., and Myrvik, Q. N., *J. Immunol.* **105,** 227, 1970.
8. Moore, V. L., and Myrvik, Q. N., *J. Reticuloendothel. Soc.* **12,** 131, 1977.
9. Allen, E. M., Moore, V. L., and Stevens, J. O., *J. Immunol.* **119,** 343, 1977.
10. Moore, V. L., Schrier, D. J., Sternick, J. L., and Allen, E. M., *In* "Basic and Clinical Aspects of Granulomatous Inflammation" (D. Boros, and T. Yoshida, Eds.), p. 201. Elsevier North-Holland, Amsterdam, 1980.
11. Barclay, W. R., Anacker, R., Brehmer, W., and Ribi, E., *J. Bacteriol.* **94,** 1736, 1967.
12. Mitchell, G. F., Grumet, F. C., and McDevitt, H. O., *J. Exp. Med.* **135,** 126, 1972.
13. Reif, A. E., and Allen, J. M. V., *Nature (London)* **200,** 1332, 1963.
14. Allen, E. M., and Moore, V. L., *J. Reticuloendothel. Soc.* **26,** 349, 1979.
15. Hahn, H. Kaufman, S. H. E., Miller, T. E., and Mackaness, G. B., *Immunology* **36,** 691, 1979.
16. Boumsell, L., and Meltzer, M. S., *J. Immunol.* **115,** 1746, 1975.

17. Friedland, J., and Silverstein, E., *Amer. J. Clin. Pathol.* **66,** 416, 1976.
18. Moore, V. L., Mondloch, V. M., Pedersen, G. M., Schrier, D. J., and Allen, E. M., *J. Immunol.* **127,** 339, 1981.
19. Schrier, D. J., Allen, E. M., and Moore, V. L., *Cell Immunol.* **56,** 347, 1980.
20. Allen, E. M., Sternick, J. L., Schrier, D. J., and Moore, V. L., *Cell. Immunol.* **58,** 61, 1981.
21. Chensue, S. W., Boros, D. L., and David, C. S., *J. Exp. Med.* **151,** 1398, 1980.
22. Chensue, S. W., Wellhausen, S. R., and Boros, D. L., *J. Immunol.* **127,** 363, 1981.
23. Amsden, A. F., Boros, D. L., and Wood, A. T., *Infect. Immun.* **27,** 75, 1980.
24. Sugane, K., Kasahara, T., and Shioiri-Nakano, K., *Japan J. Exp. Med.* **45,** 19, 1975.
25. Jenssen, H. L., Eckert, R., Werner, H., Kohler, H., Pasternak, G., and Friemel, H., *Oncology* **34,** 159, 1977.
26. Silverstein, E., Pertschuk, L. P., and Friedland, J., *Proc. Nat. Acad. Sci. USA* **76,** 6646, 1979.

CELLULAR IMMUNOLOGY **65**, 221–229 (1981)

Suppressor Cells Generated from Human Peripheral Mononuclear Cells by Stimulation with Pokeweed Mitogen

GEORGE C. TSOKOS AND JAMES E. BALOW

Arthritis and Rheumatism Branch, National Institute of Arthritis Metabolism and Digestive Diseases, National Institutes of Health, Bethesda, Maryland 20205

Received May 7, 1981; accepted October 18, 1981

Stimulation of human mononuclear cells (MNC) with pokeweed mitogen (PWM) led to the generation of lymphocytes which, when added to secondary cultures of normal MNC, were able to suppress the appearance of PWM-induced plaque-forming cells. Suppression was effective in reducing the response of both autologous and allogeneic plaque-forming cells. In contrast to concanavalin A, which induces the generation of suppressor cells within 2 days, PWM-induced suppressor activity was induced only after culture for 6 days. Suppressive activity was also present in mitogen-induced supernatants, indicating that suppression may be mediated through a soluble factor. Induction of PWM-induced suppressor cells was abrogated by monocyte depletion. Mature PWM-induced suppressor cells for plaque-forming cells were radiosensitive. The initial MNC cultures containing active suppressor cells were refractory to restimulation with PWM in terms of subsequent plaque-forming cells. These studies suggest either that PWM directly activates suppressor cells or that polyclonal B-cell activation is normally accompanied by the sequential appearance of suppressor cells which modulate the immune response.

INTRODUCTION

Suppressor cells participate in the expression of the immune response (1). They have been described to participate in either a specific or nonspecific way. Specific suppressor cells are induced by stimulation with a certain antigen. Nonspecific suppressor cells have usually been generated by stimulation of human mononuclear cells (MNC) with concanavalin A (Con A) (2–7) or phytohemagglutinin (PHA) (8, 9), and by mixed lymphocyte reaction (11, 12), autologous lymphocyte reaction, (13), fetal calf serum (FCS) (14, 15), and lipopolysaccharide in the presence of FCS (16).

Pokeweed mitogen (PWM) is a widely used stimulus for polyclonal activation of immunoglobulin synthesis and for lymphocyte proliferation, both of which are T cell dependent (17, 18). In the present series of experiments we show that stimulation of human MNC with PWM for 6 days in the presence of human serum also induces the generation of cells which are able to suppress the normal PWM-induced plaque-forming cell (PFC) response.

MATERIAL AND METHODS

Mononuclear cell isolation. Peripheral venous blood was drawn aseptically into syringes containing 10 units of heparin per milliliter of blood. The blood was diluted

0008-8749/81/180221-09$02.00/0

1:2 with phosphate-buffered saline (PBS, NIH, Media Unit). Forty-milliliter aliquots of the mixture were layered over 10 ml of Ficoll-Paque (Pharmacia, Piscataway, N.J.) in 50-ml plastic conical tubes. The tubes were centrifuged at room temperature at 400 g for 30 min and the mononuclear cell interface was carefully pipetted off. The MNC were washed once with PBS and once with medium, counted, and resuspended in RPMI 1640 (Gibco Laboratories, Grand Island, N.Y.) at the desired concentration. Cell viability was checked by the use of 0.2% trypan blue (Gibco).

Reverse hemolytic plaque assay. Immunoglobulin secreting cells were identified by the use of a previously described reverse hemolytic plaque assay, slightly modified in our laboratory (18, 19). SeaPlaque agarose (FMC Corp., Rockland, Maine) was dissolved (0.8%) in RPMI 1640 containing 2 m*M* Hepes (*N*-2-hydroxyethylpiperazine-*N*-2-ethanesulfonic acid) buffer (Microbiological Associates, Waltersville, Md.) by heating to boiling and then left to equilibrate at 42°C in a water bath. Agarose (0.85 ml) was mixed with 0.05 ml of staphylococcus protein A coupled to sheep red blood cells (SRBC) and 0.1 ml of MNC to be tested. The mixture was vortexed, poured into 15 × 16-mm petri dishes (Falcon, Oxnard, Calif.) prelayered with 1.2% SeaKem agarose (FMC Corp.) in PBS, and swirled slightly. The gel was allowed to solidify at room temperature for 10 min and then 1 ml of the developing antiserum (IgG fraction of rabbit antihuman polyvalent; Cappel Laboratories, Cochranville, Pa.) was added. The petri dishes were incubated in a humidified atmosphere containing 5% CO_2 at 37°C for 2 hr. Then the serum was pipetted off and replaced with 1 ml of 10% guinea pig complement in veronal-buffered saline containing 0.5% gelatin (NIH, Media Unit) and further incubated for 1 hr. The petri dishes were kept at 4°C until counting. The PFC were counted with the help of a dissecting microscope, although they could be easily visualized by naked eye, and expressed as PFC per 1×10^6 MNC.

Coupling of staphylococcal protein A to SRBC (18). SRBC were washed three times with normal saline before use. One milliliter of packed SRBC was suspended in 9.9 ml of saline in 50-ml plastic conical tubes to which were added 1 ml (0.5 mg/ml) of staphylococcal protein A (Pharmacia) and 0.1 of chromic chloride at 6.6 mg/ml (Mallinckrodt, Paris, Ky.) in saline. This preparation was incubated for 1 hr at 30°C in a water bath, washed three times with saline and the red blood cell pellet was finally resuspended in RPMI 1640 at a hematocrit of 25%. The coupled SRBC were kept at 4°C and used within 1 week.

In vitro lymphocyte culture technique. The cultures were carried out in 24-well flat-bottomed plates (Costar, Cambridge, Mass.). Two milliliters of MNC suspension (0.5×10^6/ml) in RPMI 1640 containing 50 μg/ml of streptomycin and 50 units/ml of penicillin (NIH Media Unit) and 10% heat-inactivated fetal calf serum (Gibco) were put in each well. PWM (Gibco) was added at the desired concentration. Each experimental point was carried out with two or more replicates. The plates were incubated at 37°C for 6 days (or as indicated) in a humidified atmosphere containing 5% CO_2. On day 6 the cells were harvested, washed two times, and resuspended at the desired concentration in RPMI 1640 containing 10% FCS.

Elimination of adherent cells by Sephadex G-10 fractionation. Beads of Sephadex G-10 (Pharmacia) were left to swell in normal saline for 2–3 days; the slurry was aliquoted in 50-ml tubes and autoclaved at 120°C for 30 min. The aliquots were stored at 4°C until use. Five milliliters of the slurry was poured into a 12-ml syringe and washed with 25 ml of medium RPMI 1640 containing 20% FCS. The column was incubated at 37°C for 15 min and then 30–60 × 10^6 MNC in 2 ml of medium were mixed with the slurry stirred with a 1-ml pipette. The column was then incubated for 15 more min at 37°C. The nonadherent cells were eluted with 25 ml of medium containing 10% FCS and washed with plain medium twice before use in subsequent assays. This procedure depleted the percentage of monocytes from 27 ± 2.2% before passage through the column to 2 ± 0.5% in the eluted cell fraction. The percentage of monocytes was estimated by staining for nonspecific α-naphthyl acetate esterase as previously described (20).

Generation of suppressor cells. Mononuclear cells at a concentration 2–3 × 10^6/ml were cultured in RPMI 1640 containing 5% heat-inactivated human male serum. To these final cultures were added (a) media alone (control), (b) Con A at a concentration of 10 μg/ml (Sigma, St. Louis, Mo.), or (c) PWM at a final concentration of 1% of the standard stock dilution. Cultures were carried out at 37°C in a humidified atmosphere containing 5% CO_2. The duration of the culture was 2 or 6 days as indicated. At the end of the culture the cells were harvested and washed once with medium and thrice with medium containing 3 mM of α-methyl-mannoside (Sigma). Irradiated cells were given 2000 rad from a cesium source (1800 rad/min). The preincubated cells were added into fresh cultures at a responder/preincubated cell ratio of 1/1.

Preparation of mitogen-stimulated supernatants. When supernatants were to be collected, 4 × 10^6 MNC were cultured in round-bottom tubes containing 2 ml of medium (5% human serum) and either 1% PWM or 10 μg/ml Con A. The cells were spun down smoothly after 2 days, the supernatant was collected, and the cells were resuspended in 2 ml of fresh medium containing the same concentration of human serum and mitogens as before. The supernatants were collected again on Day 6. The supernatants were kept at −20°C until used.

Statistics. Results are expressed as arithmetic means ± 1 standard error of the mean (SEM). The Student t test was used to compare differences between means.

RESULTS

Suppression of PWM-induced response by Con A and PWM-stimulated cells. Normal MNC were stimulated with Con A or PWM in the presence of human serum for 6 days and then added in to fresh autologous MNC at a cell ratio of 1:1. The PWM-induced PFC response was tested after 6 days. The cumulative results from five such experiments are shown in Fig. 1. PWM-prestimulated cells suppressed the normal PFC response at an amount comparable to that of Con A-prestimulated cells. Cells cultured for 6 days in the presence of human serum without any mitogen did not affect the PFC response. As shown in Fig. 1, the PWM-induced PFC responses of cells precultured with PWM, Con A, or medium (assayed on Day 12 after mitogen stimulation) were minimal.

Although normal cells precultured with PWM for 6 days significantly suppress the PWM-induced PFC response of fresh autologous cells, normal MNC precultured with PWM for 2 days fail to suppress the PFC response of fresh autologous cells. Cumulative results from five experiments are shown in Fig. 2. Con A cells prestimulated for 2 days significantly suppressed the normal PFC response as expected (2–7). These experiments led us to the conclusion that PWM stimulation

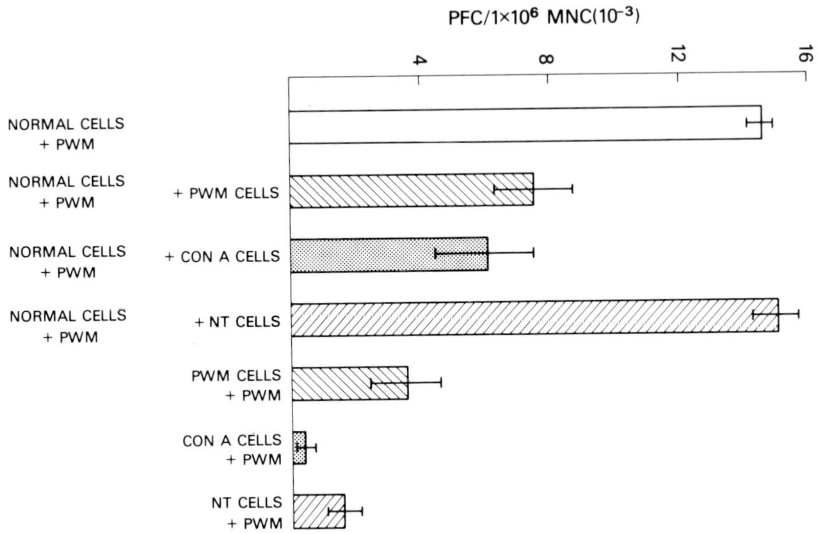

FIG. 1. Normal MNC were preincubated for 6 days with PWM, Con A, or medium and then added into a culture of normal autologous MNC with PWM. The responding:preincubated cell ratio was 1:1. The cells were assayed on Day 6. Results from five experiments (mean ± SEM) are depicted.

of normal human MNC induces the generation of suppressor cells but the time kinetics are different from those of the Con A-induced suppressor cells. The peak of the PWM induced PFC of normal human MNC is on Days 6–7 (unpublished experiments) and it seems that this is paralleled by the generation of suppressor cells which have the capacity to inhibit the response of fresh cells to the same mitogenic stimulus.

PWM-induced suppressor activity is mediated through a soluble factor. It is

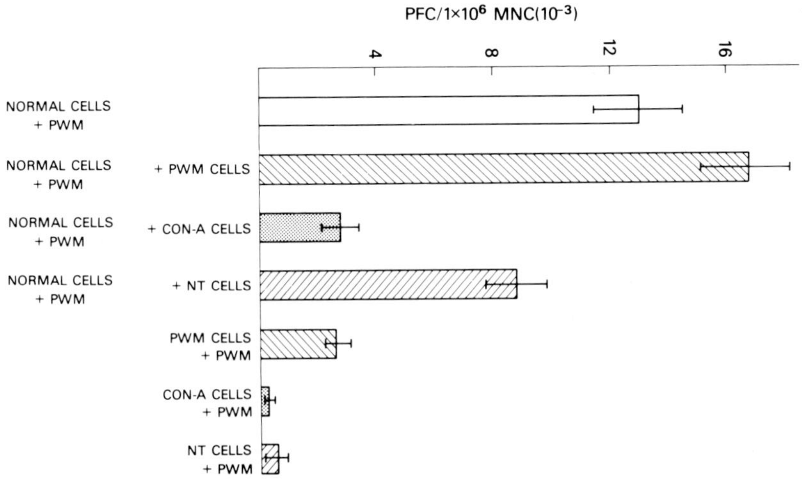

FIG. 2. Normal MNC were preincubated with PWM, Con A, or medium for 2 days and then added into autologous MNC plus PWM, at a cell ratio 1:1. The cells were assayed on Day 6. Results from five experiments are depicted (mean ± SEM).

known that Con A-induced suppressor activity is mediated through a soluble factor (21). We asked if PWM induced suppressor activity is also mediated by a soluble factor. Normal MNC (2×10^6/ml) were cultured with PWM, Con A, or medium in the presence of human serum; the culture supernatants were collected on Days 2 and 6. These were added into the culture of fresh autologous cells at a concentration 50% of the final media. The results from four experiments are shown in Fig. 3. As expected, both supernatants (Days 2 and 6) from Con A-stimulated cells profoundly suppressed the normal PFC response. However, only the supernatant harvested on Day 6 from PWM-stimulated cells suppressed the subsequent PFC response; in contrast, the Day 2 supernatant failed to do so. These results are in accordance with those obtained when the whole cells rather than supernatants were used (Figs. 1 and 2), but it is unclear whether PWM-induced cellular suppression depends on the elaboration of soluble factors.

Comparison of PWM-induced suppressor cells on autologous and allogeneic normal PFC responses. The experiments presented above were performed with autologous combinations of suppressor and responder cells. We next examined whether PWM-precultured cells also express suppressor activity on allogeneic responder cells. Cells treated for 6 days with PWM, Con A, or medium were added to fresh cultures of autologous or allogeneic cells with PWM for 6 days. Results from three experiments are presented in Fig. 4. PWM- or Con A-stimulated cells suppressed the subsequent PWM-induced PFC response of both autologous and allogeneic responder cells. However, the observed suppression in the allogeneic system was less profound and the experimental variance higher than that observed in the autologous system.

PWM-induced suppressor cells are radiation sensitive. It is recognized that

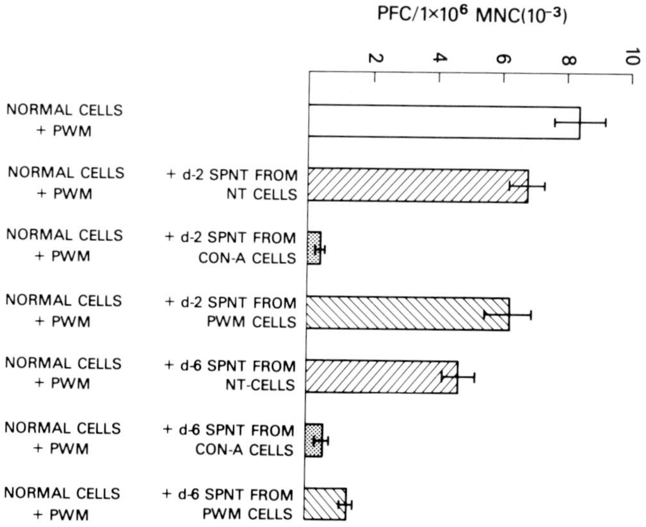

FIG. 3. Normal MNC were incubated for 2 or 6 days with PWM, Con A, or medium at a concentration of 2×10^6 MNC/ml. The supernatants were collected and added into cultures of MNC (plus PWM restimulation) at a concentration 50% of the final media. The cells were assayed on Day 6. Results from four experiments (mean ± SEM) are depicted. Two more experiments were conducted in the presence of α-methyl-mannoside and similar results were obtained.

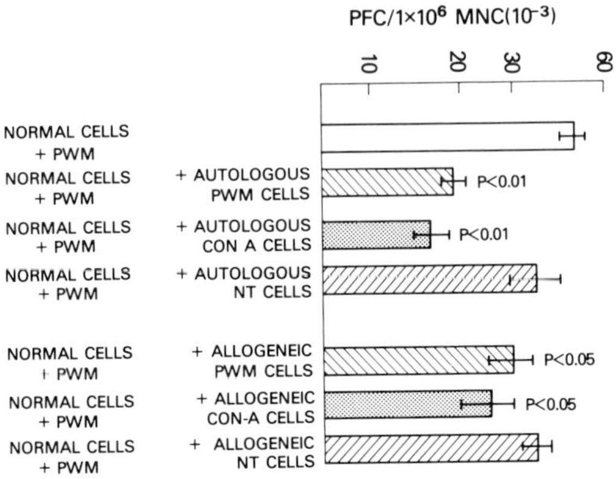

FIG. 4. Normal MNC were preincubated with PWM, Con A, or medium for 6 days and then added into a culture of autologous or allogeneic MNC plus PWM (cell ratio 1:1). The cells were tested on Day 6. Results from three experiments (mean ± SEM) were presented. The *P* values refer to differences from the response of normal cells cultured with PWM.

suppressor cells are variably sensitive to irradiation, suggesting the possibility that suppressor cells for different cell-mediated immune responses may be heterogeneous. Con A-induced suppressor cells' activity on PFC and mixed lymphocyte reaction responses are abrogated by irradiation, while that on cell-mediated lympholysis is not ((7), unpublished observations). The experiments presented in Fig. 5 show clearly that PWM-induced suppressor cells of the PFC response are sensitive to irradiation (2000 rad).

Monocytes are necessary for the induction of suppressor cells by PWM. It has been shown previously that PWM stimulates T cells which are responsible for the expressed suppressor activity (22). We wanted to test if monocytes played a role

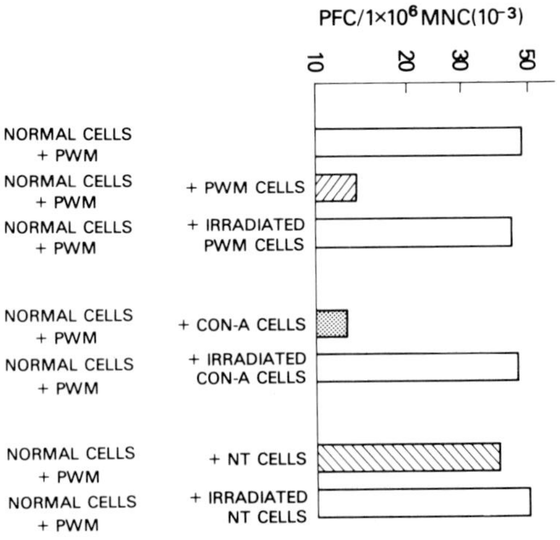

FIG. 5. Effect of irradiation (2000 rad) on the PWM-induced suppressor cell activity. MNC were preincubated with PWM for 6 days, irradiated or not and then added to a culture of autologous MNC plus PWM at a cell ratio 1:1. Cells were harvested on Day 6. Results from two experiments are presented (mean ± SEM).

in the induction of the suppressor cells by PWM. Whole mononuclear cells were passed through Sephadex G-10 columns, stimulated with PWM for 6 days and then added to fresh autologous cells subsequently stimulated with PWM. The PFC response was tested after 6 days. The results from two experiments are presented in Fig. 6 and show that PWM stimulation of monocyte-depleted cells failed to generate normal suppressor cell activity as measured by PFC responses. We concluded that the PWM-induced suppressor cell activity is monocyte dependent.

DISCUSSION

The experiments presented in this communication clearly show that stimulation of human peripheral MNC with PWM induces the generation of cells which are able directly and/or by production of a soluble factor to mediate suppression of mitogen-induced PFC response.

We first compared the kinetics of the generation of suppressor cells and factors by PWM to those generated in response to Con A. Our experiments confirm that suboptimal doses of Con A stimulate the generation of suppressor cells and suppressor supernatants within the first 48 hr of culture (2–7, 21). PWM was able to cause the appearance of similar suppressor activities but with a time course somewhat different from that of Con A. PWM stimulation for 6, but not 2, days led to the appearance of well-defined suppressor activity as measured by inhibition of normal mitogen-induced PFC responses. Similar kinetics were found for the appearance of suppressor activity in the supernatants of PWM-stimulated cells.

The present experiments examined the appearance of PWM-induced suppressor activity for B lymphocyte responses only. Hofman *et al.* (23) have previously reported that 2-day PWM-stimulated human MNC or their supernatants were able to suppress the generation of cell-mediated cytotoxic responses to allogeneic cell lines. These results suggest that different suppressor systems or a different balance

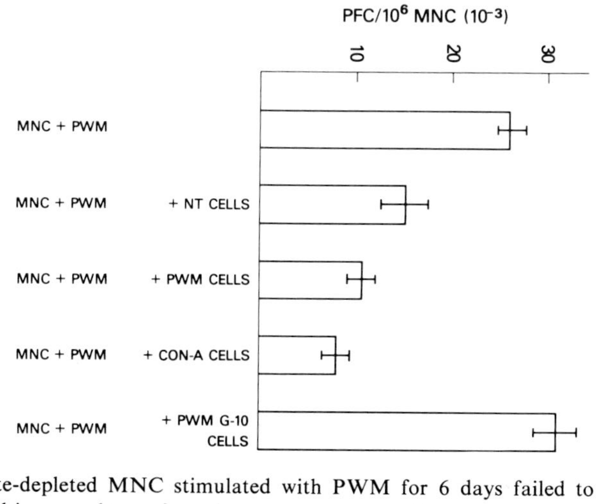

FIG. 6. Monocyte-depleted MNC stimulated with PWM for 6 days failed to express suppressive activity when added into a culture of autologous MNC plus PWM at a cell ratio 1:1 (last column). In contrast, PWM- and Con A-prestimulated whole MNC were able to significantly suppress the PWM-induced PFC response. Cells were tested on Day 6. Results from two experiments (mean ± SEM) are presented.

of helper and suppressor activities induced by PWM may be expressed in different assay systems. Indeed, Miyawaki *et al.* (24), studying the generation of suppressor supernatants by stimulation of cord T cells with PWM, reported that stimulation of adult T cells with PWM for 24 hr only led to the generation of predominantly helper rather than suppressor factors.

From our experiments it is not clear which cells are responsible for the PWM-induced suppression of PFC. However, it was shown that monocytes were necessary for the generation of suppressor activity. This adherent cell dependence is in accord with the previous studies of PWM-induced suppression (23). In contrast, Con A induces suppressor cell activity regardless of the presence or absence of adherent cells (25). Both PWM- and Con A-induced suppressor cells were found to be radiosensitive which also suggests, but does not prove, that other nonmonocytic lymphoid cells are necessary for the generation of suppressor activity.

The assay to measure suppressor activity in the present study was the PWM-induced PFC response of normal MNC. This B-cell-mediated function has a characteristic time course, i.e., the PFC response reaches a peak between the fifth and seventh days of culture and subsequently declines. It is unclear whether or not the decline of PFC responses is the result of an active regulatory event or a nonspecific exhaustion of B cells and/or trophic factors. Assuming active suppression is involved, it is also unclear whether PWM directly stimulates suppressor activity which appears in parallel to the maturation of effector (PFC) cells or whether suppressor activity is a sequentially induced regulatory mechanism as a normal consequence of effector lymphocyte activation. The observation in the present study that PWM does not induce suppressor cells during the first 2 days of culture can be interpreted to indicate that suppressor cells (i) are not directly activated by PWM, (ii) require an intermediary activation of other effector cells, or (iii) require a longer time for functional maturation than do Con A-induced suppressor cells.

The mitogen-induced suppressor activity studied in the present experiments inhibited immunoglobulin secretion by B lymphocytes during its early phases. It is unknown whether established B-cell responses are also modulated by the same types of suppressor activities or whether activity is only capable of impeding the inductive phases of immunoglobulin secretion. However, certain of the present experiments (Fig. 1) show that PWM-stimulated MNC are relatively refractory to restimulation with PWM; i.e., these cells produce poor secondary PFC responses. It is possible that this or a similar suppressor phenomenon explains the impaired PWM-induced PFC response of the spontaneously activated B cells usually seen in patients with SLE (26–28). The possibility that the appearance of suppressor activity is the normal consequence of the activation of a variety of subsets of effector lyphocytes warrants further study. Much additional work is needed to understand the mechanisms of induction of suppressor cell activity as well as the biologic events occurring during immune inhibition by cell-dependent and soluble regulatory factors.

ACKNOWLEDGMENT

The assistance of Mrs. Lena Mans in the typing of this manuscript is greatly appreciated.

REFERENCES

1. Waldmann, T. A., and Broder, S., *Prog. Clin. Immunol.* **3,** 155, 1977.
2. Dutton, R. W., *J. Exp. Med.* **136,** 1445, 1972.

3. Rich, R. R., and Pierce, C. W., *J. Exp. Med.* **137,** 649, 1973.
4. Redelman, D., Scott, C. B., Sheppard, H. W., Jr., and Sell, S., *J. Exp. Med.* **143,** 919, 1976.
5. Shou, L. S., Schwartz, A., and Good, R. A., *J. Exp. Med.* **143,** 1100, 1976.
6. Haynes, B. F., and Fauci, A. S., *J. Immunol.* **118,** 2281, 1977.
7. Peavy, D. L., and Pierce, C. W., *J. Exp. Med.* **140,** 356, 1974.
8. Kurnick, J. T., Bell, C., and Grey, H. M., *Scand. J. Immunol.* **5,** 771, 1976.
9. Lobo, P. I., and Spencer, C. E., *J. Clin. Invest.* **63,** 1157, 1979.
10. McMichael, A. J., and Sasazuki, T., *J. Exp. Med.* **146,** 368, 1977.
11. Hodes, R. J., Nadler, L. M., and Hathcock, K. S., *J. Immunol.* **119,** 961, 1977.
12. Arnesen, E., and Thorsby, E., *Acta Pathol. Microbiol. Scand. Sect. C.* **88,** 103, 1980.
13. Innes, J. B, Kuntz, M. M., Kim, Y. T., and Weksler, M. E. *J. Clin. Invest.* **64,** 1608, 1979.
14. Burns, F. D., Marrack, P. C., Kappler, J. W., and Janeway, C. A., Jr., *J. Immunol.* **114,** 134, 1975.
15. Maca, R. D., Bonnard, G. D., and Herberman, R. B., *J. Immunol.* **123,** 246, 1979.
16. Miller, R. A., Gartner, S., and Kaplan, H. S., *Cell. Immunol.* **55,** 210, 1980.
17. Keightley, R. G., Cooper, M. D., and Lawton, A. R., *J. Immunol.* **117,** 1538, 1976.
18. Janossy, G., and Greaves, M., *Transplant. Rev.* **24,** 177, 1975.
19. Ginsburg, W. W., Finkelman, F. D., and Lipsky, P. E., *J. Immunol.* **120,** 33, 1978.
20. Yam, L. T., Li, C. Y., and Crosby, W. H., *Amer. J. Clin. Pathol.* **55,** 283, 1971.
21. Tadakuma, T., Kuhner, A. L., Rich, R. R., David, J. R., and Pierce, C. W., *J. Immunol.* **117,** 323, 1976.
22. Magaoki, T., Moriya, N., Miyawaki, T., Keki, H., Kubo, M., Yokoi, T., Okuda, N., and Taniguchi, N., *J. Immunol.* **125,** 1563, 1980.
23. Hofman, F., Spina, C. A., Rand, N., and Fahey, J. L. *Cell. Immunol.* **55,** 20, 1980.
24. Miyawaki, T., Moriya, N., Nagaoki, T., Kubo, M., Yokoi, T., and Taniguchi, N., *J. Immunol.* **126,** 282, 1981.
25. Fineman, S. M., Mudawwar, F. B., and Geha, R. S., *Cell. Immunol.* **45,** 120, 1979.
26. Ginsburg, W. W., Finkelman, F. D., and Lipsky, P. E., *Clin. Exp. Immunol.* **35,** 76, 1979.
27. Fauci, A. S., Steinberg, A. D., Haynes, B. F., and Whalen, G., *J. Immunol.* **121,** 1473, 1978.

CELLULAR IMMUNOLOGY 65, 230–246 (1981)

Phenotypic and Functional Characterization of Allospecific and Nonspecific (NK- and K-like) Cytotoxic T Lymphocytes Generated in Human Mixed-Lymphocyte Cultures from Noncytotoxic Precursors[1]

DANIELA SANTOLI, MARY KAY FRANCIS, AND MASSIMO TRUCCO

The Wistar Institute of Anatomy and Biology, 36th Street at Spruce, Philadelphia, Pennsylvania 19104

Received June 25, 1981; accepted September 23, 1981

Highly efficient cytotoxic cells able to lyse unsensitized, antibody-coated, and relevant targets were generated *de novo* following sensitization in allogeneic human mixed lymphocyte cultures (MLC) of noncytotoxic IgG-Fc receptor (FcR)-negative T lymphocytes. The MLC-induced killers maintained the surface markers of T cells, as demonstrated by their reactivity with two monoclonal anti-T-cell antibodies. None of them reacted with a monoclonal antibody specific for myelomonocytic cells and up to 30% expressed DR antigens. The nonspecific (NK- and K-like) effector cells had lower affinity for sheep erythrocytes than the allospecific killers and appeared to have low-affinity FcR as compared to freshly isolated NK and K cells. Unlike fresh NK cells, the MLC-induced NK-like cells were not sensitive to trypsin treatment. However, both fresh NK and MLC-induced NK-like cells were sensitive to interferon treatment and were completely inactivated after preincubation with unlabeled K562 cells at 37°C for 4 hr. The latter observation suggests the possible use of this system to deplete NK-like effects from the MLC-generated killers and to discriminate between nonspecific and allospecific cytotoxic T lymphocytes.

INTRODUCTION

Spontaneous and antibody-dependent cell-mediated cytotoxicities (SLMC and ADCC)[2] are mediated, in humans, by two functionally distinct cell populations defined as natural killer (NK) and killer (K) cells, respectively. These cells are surface immunoglobulin (SIg)- and C3b receptor-negative, but bear receptors for the Fc fragment of IgG immunoglobulins (FcR) (1–4). Several studies have been performed to define whether or not NK and K cells belong to the T-cell lineage.

[1] This work was supported in part by NIH Grants NS 11036 and AI 17636, ACS Grant IN-143, and by the National Multiple Sclerosis Society.

[2] Abbreviations used: MLC, mixed-lymphocyte cultures; FcR, receptors for the Fc fragment of IgG; E-RFC, E-rosette-forming cells; SLMC, spontaneous cell-mediated cytotoxicity; ADCC, antibody-dependent cell-mediated cytotoxicity; CML, cell-mediated lympholysis; C, complement; NK;, natural killer cells; K, killer cells; IFN, interferon, SIg, surface immunoglobulin; SE, sheep erythrocytes; PBL, peripheral blood lymphocytes; FBS, fetal bovine serum; CTL, cytotoxic T lymphocytes; EA7S, IgG-sensitized erythrocytes; OE, ox erythrocytes; PHA, phytohemagglutinin; FS, fetal skin fibroblasts; LU, lytic units.

0008-8749/81/180230-17$02.00/0

After the separation of cells that form rosettes (E-RFC) with sheep erythrocytes (SE) from those that do not (non-E-RFC), about 50% of both activities can be found in both lymphocyte fractions, indicating that a proportion of NK and K cells have receptors for SE (1). The FcR-positive cells responsible for NK and K cytotoxic activities in the E-RFC fraction are known as Tγ and have been recently shown to be nonreactive with monoclonal antibody OKT3, which is specific for a common human T-cell antigen (5). In other studies NK and K cells were shown to be reactive with monoclonal antibody OKM1, which recognizes monocytes, granulocytes, and a small proportion of lymphocytes (6). Thus, it is not clear whether NK and K cells represent T cells, cells of the myelomonocytic lineage or a third cell type.

The NK- and K-cell cytotoxic activities gradually disappear when peripheral blood lymphocytes (PBL) are cultured *in vitro*. If, however, lymphocytes are activated during the culture period, they maintain or gain cytotoxicity. Various conditions, such as the presence of interferon (IFN) (7, 8), fetal bovine serum (FBS) (9–11), or mitogens (12), as well as coculture with certain tumor cell lines (13, 14), EBV-transformed autologous and allogeneic cell lines (15, 16), or allogeneic cells in standard mixed-lymphocyte cultures (MLC) (17–19) can trigger such cytotoxicity. In human MLC, not only are cytotoxic T lymphocytes (CTL) generated, which specifically destroy target cells carrying the sensitizing alloantigens, but also nonspecific cytotoxic cells which can mediate NK- and K-like cytotoxicity (20, 21). Seeley and Golub (19) have designated as "anomalous killing" the seemingly nonspecific cytotoxicity raised during MLC against several cultured cell lines. Because of this anomalous killing, it has been difficult so far to evaluate allospecific cytotoxicity. Moreover, although both the anomalous killing and the ADCC-like activity induced in MLC seem to be a property of activated T lymphocytes (22–25), the nature of these cells in relation to NK and K cells present in fresh blood is still controversial. The present studies were designed to analyze and compare the surface and functional properties of all killer-cell types that can be generated in human MLC in order to (1) differentiate allospecific from nonspecific effector cells, and (2) investigate the differences between the MLC-induced NK and K cells and those that occur spontaneously. In most of the experiments the analysis was restricted to cytotoxic T cells by using a highly purified FcR-negative E-RFC fraction, lacking SLMC and ADCC activities when freshly isolated (1, 3), as the source of responder–effector cells.

MATERIALS AND METHODS

Monoclonal antibodies and antisera. Monoclonal IgG2a antibodies, OKT3 and OKM1, were kindly provided by Dr. Stephen Ip (Ortho Diagnostics, Westwood, Mass.). OKT3 recognizes T cells (5); OKM1 reacts with myelomonocytic cells and a small proportion of lymphocytes (6). B36.1 is a monoclonal IgG2a antibody that reacts with the same population recognized by OKT3 in the peripheral blood, but recognizes a different determinant on the surface of T cells. B33.1 is a monoclonal IgG2b antibody with reactivity for the constant part of the DR antigens. B13.4 is a monoclonal IgM antibody that reacts with monocytes and differentiated myeloid cells (metamyelocytes and neutrophilic granulocytes).[3] B36.1, B33.1, and B13.4 were kindly provided by Drs. G. Trinchieri and B. Perussia (The Wistar Institute). Fluorescein-labeled goat F(ab′)$_2$ anti-mouse IgG (heavy and light chain) (Cappel, Cochranville, Penn.) was used as a second reagent in indirect immunofluorescence assays with the monoclonal antibodies. Fluorescein-labeled goat F(ab′)$_2$ anti-human F(ab′)$_2$ (Cappel) was used for detection of SIg-positive cells. Fluorescent cells were observed either under the microscope or using a fluorescence-activated cell sorter (Ortho Cytofluorograf 50H; Ortho Instruments, Westwood, Mass.). Rabbit IgG anti-SE was obtained from Cordis Laboratories (Miami, Fla.). For sensitization of P815y cells, IgG from a rabbit hyperimmunized with P815y cells was used.

EA7S rosette assay. The EA7S rosetting assay was performed by incubating lymphocytes with ox erythrocytes (OE) sensitized with rabbit IgG anti-OE, as described previously (1).

Lymphocyte separation. PBL were obtained by centrifugation of heparinized venous blood on a Ficoll–Hypaque (Pharmacia, Uppsala, Sweden) gradient (26). PBL were mixed with neuraminidase-treated SE, as previously described (1). Following separation of the E-RFC from the non-E-RFC on a Ficoll–Hypaque gradient, the E-RFC were rosetted and separated a second time in order to improve purification. After lysis of the SE with hypotonic medium, the E-RFC fraction was depleted of FcR-positive cells by adherence to rabbit IgG-sensitized SE monolayers prepared according to Kedar *et al.* (27). The adherence was repeated twice in order to obtain a pure FcR-negative E-RFC preparation.

Mixed lymphocyte cultures. One-way autologous and allogeneic MLC were set up in RPMI 1640 medium supplemented with 20% heat-inactivated human AB serum. FcR-negative E-RFC (10^6/ml) were used as responders and γ irradiated (4500 rad) non-E-RFC (0.5×10^6/ml) were used as stimulators. The MLC were incubated in tissue culture flasks at 37°C for 6 days in a humidified 5% CO_2 incubator.

Cytotoxic assays. Cytotoxic assays were performed on Day 0 immediately after separation of PBL fractions, and again after 6 days of sensitization in MLC. ADCC and SLMC assays have been described in detail previously (1–3, 7, 28).

Target cells in ADCC were the murine mastocytoma P815y, sensitized with anti-P815y rabbit antibodies; target cells in SLMC were the NK-sensitive human erythroleukemia line K562, which lacks HLA-A, B, C, and DR antigens (29). These cell lines were maintained and grown in our laboratory in RPMI medium supplemented with 10% FBS. Specific CTL activity was measured in the cell-mediated lympholysis (CML) assay on Day 6 against phytohemagglutinin (PHA) (Burroughs Wellcome Co., Greenville, N.C.) - induced blasts autologous to the stimulator cells. PHA (0.1 ml) was added to PBL (10^7 in 10 ml RPMI medium supplemented with 10% heat-inactivated FBS) 3 days before the cytotoxic assay. In the CML assay, lysis of PHA blasts autologous to the responder–effector cells was also measured. All cytotoxic assays were performed in round-bottom microtiter plates by incubating various dilutions of effector cells with ^{51}Cr-labeled target cells (K562 and

[3] B. Perussia, D. Lebman, S. H. Ip, G. Rovera, and G. Trinchieri. Terminal differentiation surface antigens of myelomonocytic cells are expressed on human promyleocytic leukemia cells (HL60) treated with chemical inducers, submitted for publication.

antibody-coated P815y at 10,000/well and PHA blasts at 20,000/well) for 4 hr at 37°C. When fetal skin fibroblasts (FS) were used as targets, cultures were incubated for 8 hr, and the cytotoxicity assay was performed as previously described (7). Plates were then centrifuged at 200*g* for 5 min; 100 μl of the supernatants was harvested, and the counts per minute were determined in a Packard gamma counter. All the experimental and control values were the mean of at least three replicates. Results are expressed as lytic units (LU) (1–3). Unless otherwise stated, one LU is defined as the number of effector lymphocytes that kill 50% of the target cells in the test time.

In experiments of complement (C)-dependent lysis, the effector cells (12×10^6) were treated with 1 ml of appropriate dilutions of OKT3 or B36.1 monoclonal antibodies for 1 hr at 4°C. Cells were centrifuged and the pellet resuspended in 1 ml rabbit serum for 90 min at 37°C. Control preparations were cells untreated or treated with either C or antibodies alone. After treatment, the effector cells were washed three times and resuspended in RPMI with 10% FBS at the original volume. Viability was checked by the Erythrosin B (1% in PBS) exclusion test. In some experiments the cytotoxic assays were performed on monolayers of immobolized (EA7S) immune complexes (30). Competition and inactivation assays were performed using K562 cells as unlabeled (cold) targets (31). In some cases effector cells and/or FS fibroblast targets were incubated with 500 antiviral units of an IFNα preparation (obtained by infection of human lymphocytes with Newcastle disease virus) for 18 hr at 37°C before being used in cytotoxic assays, as reported elsewhere (7).

Enzymatic treatment. The effector cells (10^7/ml) were incubated at 37°C for 30 min in serum-free medium containing either trypsin (type XI, Sigma Chemical Co., St. Louis, Mo.) or pronase (B grade, Calbiochem, San Diego, Calif.) at a concentration of 1 mg/ml (30). The cells were then washed in cold RPMI-FBS and used in cytotoxic assays. Cell recovery after trypsin treatment ranged from 65 to 80%; viability was over 95%.

RESULTS

Generation of cytotoxicity during MLC. Kinetics studies were performed to determine the time course of cytotoxic effects against various targets following stimulation of noncytotoxic precursors (FcR-negative E-RFC) in allogeneic MLC. Figure 1 illustrates a representative experiment. NK- and K-like activities were detectable on Day 3 after the onset of the MLC and reached peak levels on Days 5 through 7, declining thereafter. The kinetics of lysis for allogeneic PHA blasts and autologous blasts was similar; in both cases, peak levels occurred on Days 5 or 6. Though lysis of PHA blasts autologous to the responder–effector cells was often significant, it was always lower than specific allogeneic lysis.

All the studies reported below were performed on Day 6 after the onset of the MLC. Results concerning the generation of specific CTL and nonspecific (NK- and K-like) cytotoxic cells from inactive precursors are depicted in Fig. 2. Immediately after purification (Day 0), FcR-negative E-RFC were completely inactive against both K562 and antibody-sensitized P815y cells. However, after stimulation in MLC (Day 6), they became highly cytotoxic against the same targets. The same cells cultured in the absence of stimulator cells remained noncytotoxic. Cytotoxicity

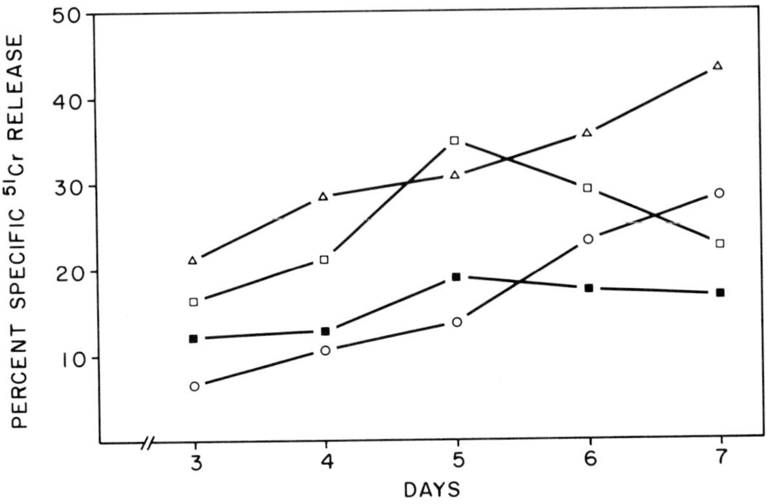

FIG. 1. Kinetics of cytotoxicity generated during MLC. Allogeneic MLC were set up using FcR-negative E-RFC as responders and γ-irradiated non-E-RFC as stimulators. The effector cells were harvested daily from Days 3 through 7 after the onset of the MLC, washed twice, and tested for cytotoxic activity in a 4-hr assay against ^{51}Cr-labeled K562 (○), antibody-sensitized P815y (△), and PHA blasts allogeneic (□) or autologous (■) to the responder cells in order to test SLMC, ADCC, and CML, respectively. Results of cytotoxicity at the effector-to-target ratio of 50:1 are shown.

was also generated in autologous MLC in which FcR-negative E-RFC were cultured with autologous γ-irradiated non-E-RFC. However, these effector cells were severalfold less efficient than the ones generated after allosensitization (Fig. 2). The non-E-RFC had high ADCC and SLMC activity when freshly isolated, but only slight activity after irradiation, and none at all after 6 days of culture (Fig. 2) with or without prior irradiation (data not shown). These data indicate that during MLC, NK-, and K-like effector cells are newly generated from inactive precursors contained in the responder FcR-negative E-RFC population and are not derived from stimulator cells that might still be active after irradiation. This is further supported by the results of the experiment depicted in Fig. 3, in which lymphoid cell lines that stimulate efficiently in MLC but lack cytotoxic capability were γ irradiated and used as stimulators. High levels of NK- and K-like activities could be generated from FcR-negative E-RFC following stimulation with irradiated allogeneic non-E-RFC or Raji B-cell line. Both FcR-negative E-RFC and Raji cells lacked cytotoxic activity when used fresh, as well as when used 6 days after the onset of the MLC.

Characterization of MLC-induced killer cells. In some experiments, two parallel sets of MLC were set up in which unfractionated PBL (MLC1) or FcR-negative E-RFC (MLC2) were used as responders. On Day 6 the cultures were harvested and fractionated into E-RFC and non-E-RFC populations. The E-rosetting technique was repeated twice in both fractions in order to improve purification. The populations obtained were tested for reactivity with two anti-T cell monoclonal antibodies (OKT3 and B36.1) and for cytotoxic capability in SLMC, ADCC, and CML assays. As shown in Table 1 and Fig. 4, two cell populations could be separated from the MLC1: the E-RFC, which were close to 100% OKT3-positive and

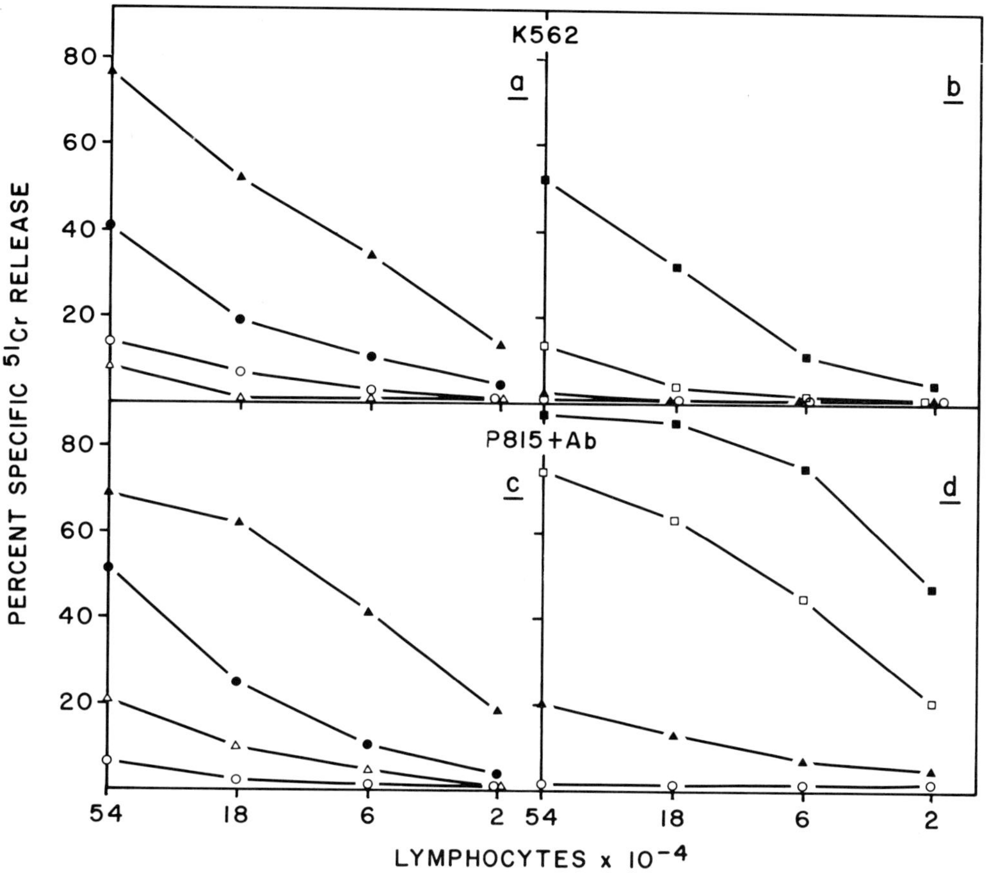

FIG. 2. Generation of NK- and K-like cells in MLC from noncytotoxic precursors. Four-hour cytotoxic assays were performed against ^{51}Cr-labeled K562 (a and b) and antibody-sensitized P815y (c and d) cells to test SLMC and ADCC, respectively. The effector cells from donor A on Day 0 (a and c) were: freshly purified E-RFC (●), FcR-negative E-RFC (○), non-E-RFC (▲), and γ-irradiated non-E-RFC (△). MLC were set up on Day 0 using FcR-negative E-RFC as responders, and non-E-RFC as stimulators. The effector cells on Day 6 after the onset of the MLC (b and d) were: cells from donor A stimulated with irradiated cells from donor B in allogeneic MLC (■), autologous MLC (□), FcR-negative E-RFC of donor A cultured alone (○), and the non-E-RFC of donor A cultured alone (▲).

able to mediate CML, and the non-E-RFC, which had a low percentage of OKT3-reactive cells and could not mediate lysis of autologous and allogeneic blasts. Both fractions mediated NK- and K-like activities. In contrast, when FcR-negative E-RFC were used as responders (MLC2), most of the cells formed rosettes with SE and were 100% OKT3-positive (Table 1); only 1–5% of the cells were recovered in the non-E-RFC fraction and the large majority of them reacted with OKT3 and formed rosettes with SE (Table 1). This indicated that most of the lymphocytes obained in MLC from a pure T-cell population maintained the surface markers of T cells. When a sufficient number of non-E-RFC was obtained from the MLC2, both E-RFC and non-E-RFC fractions were tested for cytotoxicity. Similar to what was seen in the MLC1, the non-E-RFC could only mediate NK- and K-like activities (Fig. 4).

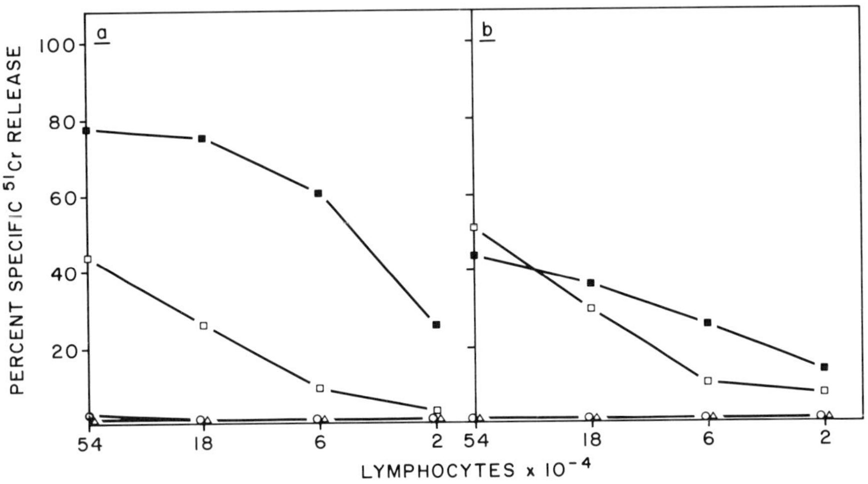

FIG. 3. Derivation of MLC-generated cytotoxic cells from the responder population. Two parallel sets of MLC were set up using the same FcR-negative E-RFC population of donor A as responder, and either allogeneic non-E-RFC or the Raji B-cell line, as stimulator. Six days after the onset of the MLC, 4-hr cytotoxic assays were performed against ^{51}Cr-labeled K562 (a), and antibody-sensitized P815y (b) cells. The effector cells were: cells from donor A stimulated with non-E-RFC of donor B (□), cells from donor A stimulated with Raji (■), responder cells cultured alone (○), and Raji cells (△).

The T-cell nature of the NK- and K-like cells generated upon allosensitization of a pure FcR-negative E-RFC population was also demonstrated by the fact that treatment of the effector cells with anti-T-cell monoclonal antibodies (OKT3 or

TABLE 1

Surface Markers of PBL and MLC Fractions

Day	Lymphocyte fraction	Percentage						
		Recovery	E-RFC	OKT3[a]	EA7S-RFC	SIg[b]	B13.4[c]	B33.1[d]
0	PBL[e]		66[f]	72	11	7	18	18
	FcR-negative E-RFC		75	98	<1	<1	<1	1
6	MLC1[g]							
	Unfractionated	100	78	78	5.6	<1	2	40
	E-RFC	67[h]	91	99	<1		<1	24
	Non-E-RFC	18	20	36	4			99
	MLC2[i]							
	Unfractionated	100	96	94	1	<1	<1	30
	E-RFC	75	95	100	3		<1	28
	Non-E-RFC	1	63	82	11		<1	18

[a] Anti-T cell monoclonal antibody.
[b] Surface immunoglobulin-positive cells.
[c] Monoclonal antibody reactive with monocytes and granulocytes.
[d] Monoclonal antibody reactive with DR antigens.
[e] Freshly separated lymphocytes from the donor used as responder of the MLC.
[f] Number of positive cells.
[g] Unfractionated PBL used as responder of the allogeneic MLC.
[h] Number of cells recovered after rosetting with SE and gradient separation.
[i] FcR-negative E-RFC used as responder of the allogeneic MLC.

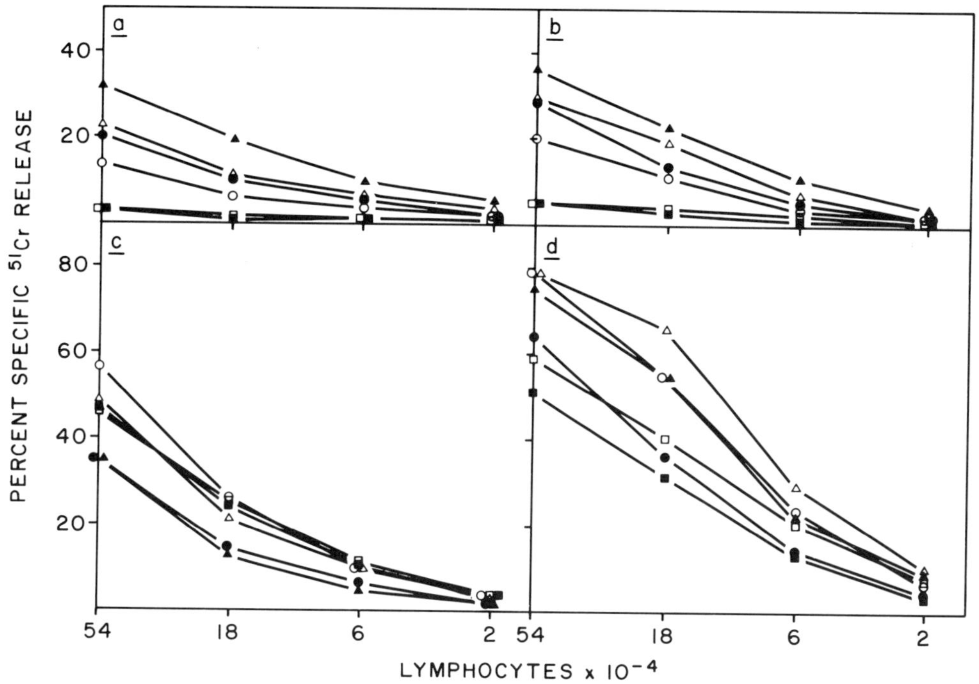

FIG. 4. Separation of different subpopulations of effector cells responsible for CML, NK- and K-like cytotoxic activities after allosensitization in MLC. Two parallel sets of MLC were set up in which unfractionated PBL (MLC1) and FcR-negative E-RFC (MLC2) were used as responders. Six days after the onset of the MLC, the cultures were harvested and separated into E-RFC and non-E-RFC populations. Four-hour cytotoxic assays against autologous (a) and allogeneic (b) blasts, K562 (c) and sensitized P815y (d) cells were performed using as effector cells: unfractionated MLC1 cells (○), MLC1, E-RFC (△), MLC1, non-E-RFC (□), unfractionated MLC2 cells (●), MLC2, E-RFC (▲), and MLC2, non-E-RFC (■).

B36.1) and with complement (C) severely affected their viability (90–95% of the cells were lysed) and reduced both cytotoxic activities (Figs. 5a and d). Treatment of the effector cells with antibodies alone at the concentrations used in these experiments affected neither viability nor cytotoxicity. The C used in these assays reduced the viability of the cells by 10–20%; such cells were about threefold less cytotoxic than the untreated or antibody-treated ones (Figs. 5a and d). Table 2 shows the surface markers present on the effector cells harvested from the same MLC represented in Fig. 5. The MLC-induced killers which derived from a pure T-responder population maintained T-cell characteristics; as described above, the majority of the cells was recovered in the E-rosetting fraction, and both E-RFC and non-E-RFC were OKT3 and B36.1 positive. The percentages of E-RFC detectable in the two fractions were consistently lower than the percentages of the cells reactive with monoclonal anti-T-cell antibodies, probably due to difficulties in rerosetting. Table 2 also shows that cells expressing DR antigens (B33.1 positive) were not present in the population used as responder at the onset of the MLC, and that almost none of the allosensitized lymphocytes expressed FcR.

In some experiments purified E-RFC and non-E-RFC obtained from fresh PBL were used as effectors after treatment with OKT3 or B36.1 and C in order to

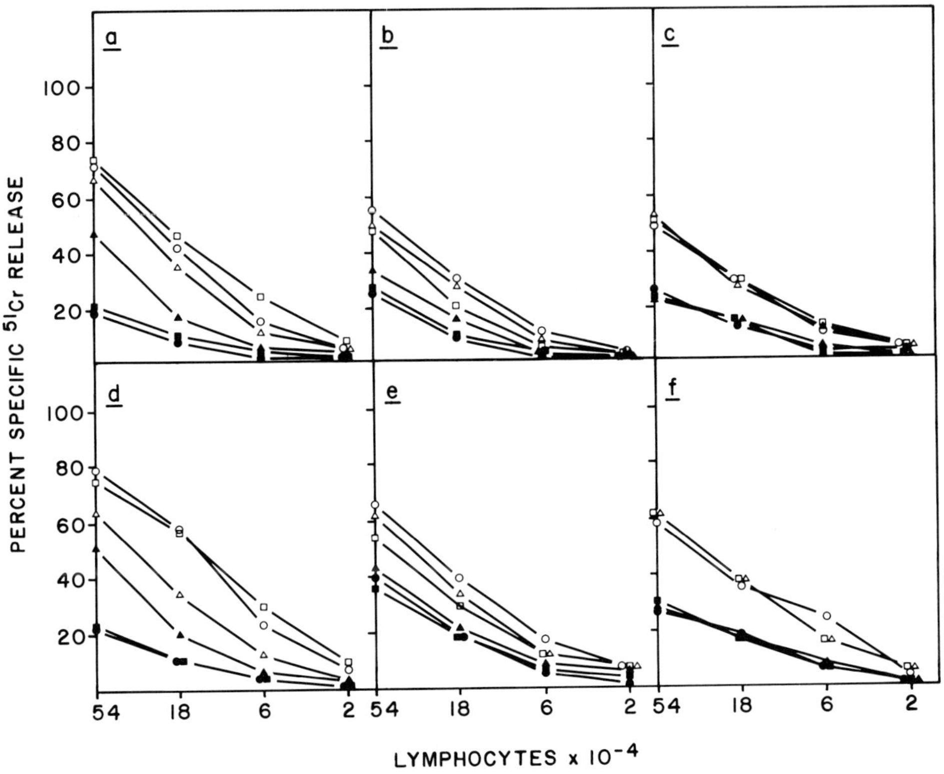

FIG. 5. Effects of monoclonal anti-T cell antibodies and C on lysis of K562 and antibody-sensitized P815y cells mediated by MLC-generated killer cells (a and d), and by E-RFC (b and e) and non-E-RFC (c and f) populations obtained from fresh PBL. The effector cells were added to the targets after incubation with medium (△), treatment with C (▲), OKT3 (○), OKT3 and C (●), B36.1 (□), and B36.1 and C (■) (see Materials and Methods).

compare them with MLC-activated killers. In the non-E-RFC fraction, about 70% of the cells remained viable after treatment with C alone, and with either one of the antibodies and C. SLMC and ADCC were decreased to the same extent after treatment with antibody and C or with C alone (Figs. 5c and f). In contrast, the viability of the E-RFC population was not affected by treatment with C, and only 15% of the cells remained viable after treatment with antibody and C. The latter cells displayed the same efficiency in both SLMC and ADCC as the C-treated ones (Figs. 5b and e), demonstrating that most or all of the cells recovered after treatment with antibody and C had cytotoxic capability. Preliminary analysis using a fluorescence-activated cell sorter indicates that the cytotoxic cells recovered after lysis of fresh E-RFC with OKT3 or B36.1 and C are OKT3-negative and largely (≥50%) OKMI positive (data not shown).

In those experiments where two different types of MLC (MLC1 and MLC2) were set up, the surface markers present on the MLC-induced cytotoxic cells and on their precursors (PBL and FcR-negative E-RFC) were analyzed and compared. As shown in Table 1, allosensitized lymphocytes derived from both MLC lacked SIg and did not react with the monoclonal antibody B13.4 which is specific for

TABLE 2

Surface Markers of PBL and MLC Fractions

		Percentage					
Day	Lymphocyte fraction	Recovery	E-RFC	OKT3[a]	B36.1[b]	B33.1[c]	EA7S-RFC
0	PBL[d]		53[e]	50	51	30	10
	FcR-negative E-RFC		88	97	97	<1	<1
6	MLC[f]						
	Unfractionated	100	96	98	92		1.4
	E-RFC	68.2[g]	88	99	99		<1
	Non-E-RFC	3.2	49	72	74		2.8

[a] Anti-T cell monoclonal antibody.
[b] Anti-T cell monoclonal antibody.
[c] Anti-DR antigen monoclonal antibody.
[d] Freshly separated lymphocytes from the donor used as responder of the MLC.
[e] Number of positive cells.
[f] Allogeneic MLC with FcR-negative E-RFC as responder.
[g] Number of cells recovered after rosetting with SE and separation on Ficoll–Hypaque gradients.

monocytes and granulocytes. On Day 0, the PBL and the FcR-negative E-RFC, which were used as responders for MLC1 and MLC2, were 18 and 1% positive, respectively, for the monoclonal anti-DR antibody B33.1. Following allosensitization, the number of cells expressing DR antigens increased in both MLC1 and MLC2, and 25% of the cells in the E-RFC fraction were DR positive.

IgG-Fc receptors on MLC-induced killer cells. Fresh NK and K cells are FcR positive, whereas we were unable to detect FcR on the MLC-generated killers using the EA7S rosetting technique (Tables 1 and 2). When fresh lymphocytes were depleted of FcR-positive cells on EA7S monolayers, both SLMC and ADCC activities of fresh lymphocytes are abolished. In contrast, passage of the MLC on such monolayers did not affect or only slightly affected their ability to mediate specific and nonspecific lysis (Table 3). Cytotoxicity assays were also performed directly in microplates containing E or EA7S monolayers to which first the effector cells at various concentrations and then the target cells were added. Fresh NK and K cells were greatly inhibited, as shown by others (30), whereas the MLC-induced killers were inhibited to a significantly lower extent (Table 4). Lysis of PHA blasts by MLC-activated CTL was not affected.

Enzymatic treatment. Unlike fresh NK cells, the MLC-induced NK-like cells were not sensitive to trypsin treatment (Table 5). The ADCC activity of fresh K and MLC-induced K-like cells was not affected by this enzyme. In contrast, cytotoxicity against autologous and allogeneic blasts was greatly enhanced. In some experiments the effector cells were treated with various concentrations (0.01–2 mg/ml) of pronase, which depletes both K and NK cell functions of fresh PBL preparations (30). This enzyme at any concentration abolished the ADCC and SLMC activities of both fresh and MLC-induced killers, as well as CTL activity of allosensitized activated lymphocytes (data not shown).

Effects of exogenous IFN. Treatment of fresh NK cells and of MLC-generated

TABLE 3

Cell-Mediated Cytotoxicity after Depletion of FcR-Positive Cells

Target	Effector	Number	Unfractionated	FcR-negative cells[a]	Inhibition (%)
K562	PBL[b]	4	560.5 ± 661.8[c]	36.7 ± 45.6	93.6 ± 1.3
	MLC[d]	4	198.0 ± 127.0	189.0 ± 154.0	12.0 ± 23.9
P815 + Ab	PBL	6	1519.8 ± 1148.9	142.3 ± 169.6	90.4 ± 5.1
	MLC	4	1712.0 ± 2860.9	1525.0 ± 2651.3	24.4 ± 19.1
Autologous blasts	MLC	4	129.0 ± 86.3	91.7 ± 42.8	18.4 ± 28.2
Allogeneic blasts	MLC	4	240.7 ± 162.0	207.2 ± 160.5	15.5 ± 10.3

[a] Depletion of FcR-positive cells on EA7S monolayers.
[b] Freshly separated PBL.
[c] Lytic units/10^8 lymphocytes. Mean ± SD.
[d] Cells harvested 6 days after the onset of allogeneic MLC (FcR-negative E-RFC were used as responders).

NK-like T cells with IFNα (500 antiviral units, 18 hr, 37°C) resulted in an enhancement of cytotoxic efficiency in both cases, as measured in an 8-hr assay against ^{51}Cr-labeled human FS fibroblasts (Table 6). Likewise, IFN treatment of FS cells protected them from lysis by both fresh and MLC-generated NK-like cells. Both effects of IFN were, however, more evident when fresh PBL were used as effectors (Table 6).

Cold-target inactivation assays. When the effectors were added to a mixture of unlabeled and ^{51}Cr-labeled K562 cells (cold and labeled targets were mixed at 2:1 to 8:1 ratios), lysis of ^{51}Cr-labeled target by both fresh NK and MLC-generated NK-like cells was reduced in a dose-dependent manner. Figure 6 shows the levels of decrease of cytotoxicity observed when the effectors were added to unlabeled and ^{51}Cr-labeled K562 cells mixed at the 2.5 ratio. In other experiments the effector

TABLE 4

Cell-Mediated Cytotoxicity in the Presence of EA7S Immune Complexes

Target	Effector	Number	E monolayers[a]	EA7S monolayers[b]	Inhibition (%)
K562	PBL[c]	8	596.7 ± 639.9[d]	327.2 ± 398.8	54.0 ± 15.4
	MLC[e]	4	118.7 ± 83.9	92.0 ± 52.3	20.2 ± 12.3
P815 + Ab	PBL	4	213.2 ± 66.9	58.2 ± 27.1	72.7 ± 9.3
	MLC	4	296.2 ± 147.7	175.2 ± 94.2	41.6 ± 8.7
Autologous blasts	MLC	3	86.3 ± 72.0	69.7 ± 46.8	10.2 ± 17.7
Allogeneic blasts	MLC	3	100.7 ± 71.7	111.7 ± 106.0	−2.4 ± 29.0

[a] Cytotoxicity performed in wells containing E monolayers.
[b] Cytotoxicity performed in wells containing EA7S monolayers.
[c] Freshly separated PBL.
[d] Lytic units/10^8 lymphocytes. Mean ± SD.
[e] Cells harvested 6 days after the onset of allogeneic MLC (FcR-negative E-RFC were used as responders).

TABLE 5

Effects of Trypsin Treatment on the Effector Cells

Target	Effector	Untreated	Trypsin-treated[a]	Cytotoxic activity[b] (%)
K562	PBL[c] (8)	1838.9 ± 2218.1[d]	88.7 ± 96.1	6.3 ± 4.3
	MLC[e] (5)	172.3 ± 111.3	133.3 ± 107.1	70.8 ± 23.6
P815 + Ab	PBL (7)	4165.0 ± 4026.2	3861.6 ± 4218.1	84.4 ± 19.5
	MLC (3)	2323.0 ± 2610.4	2334.3 ± 3035.4	102.6 ± 32.0
Autologous blasts	MLC (4)	150.0 ± 204.4	941.0 ± 1148.1	1288.0 ± 1999.5
Allogeneic blasts	MLC (5)	66.4 ± 34.0	331.4 ± 424.9	421.6 ± 326.6

[a] 1 mg/ml/10^7 cells.
[b] Data are given as mean percentage ± SD of cytotoxicity mediated by trypsin-treated effector cells as compared to cytotoxicity of untreated effector cells.
[c] Freshly separated PBL. Numbers in parentheses represent the number of samples tested.
[d] Lytic units/10^8 cells. Mean ± SD.
[e] Cells harvested 6 days after the onset of allogeneic MLC (FcR-negative E-RFC were used as responders).

cells were preincubated with cold K562 cells at 37°C for 4 hr before the addition of ^{51}Cr-labeled K562 cells. Fresh NK cells become inactivated after interaction with cold target cells in the absence of IFN induction (31). The present results showed that MLC-generated killers were also inactivated after a 4-hr incubation with unlabeled K562 cells (Fig. 6).

DISCUSSION

In addition to specific CTL, other types of cytotoxic cells that are able to mediate ADCC- and SLMC-like activities are generated in MLC following *in vitro* allosensitization of human lymphocytes (20, 21). So far, it has been difficult to dis-

TABLE 6

Effects of Exogenous Interferon on Effector and Target Cells

Experiment	Effector	Untreated FS target[a]	IFN-treated FS target[b]	IFN-treated effector cells[b] against untreated FS target	IFN-treated effector and target cells[b]
a	PBL[c]	<10[d]	<10	263	57
b	PBL	35	<10	140	45
c	PBL	41	<10	181	<10
d	PBL	76	<10	131	17
e	MLC[e]	297	106	555	243
f	MLC	384	86	1000	196
g	MLC	114	188	185	243
h	MLC	80	71	166	71

[a] Human Fs.
[b] IFNα, 500 anti-viral units/ml, 18 hr, 37°C.
[c] Freshly separated PBL from the donor used as responder of the MLC.
[d] Lytic units/10^8 cells; 8-hr assay.
[e] Cells harvested 6 days after the onset of allogeneic MLC (FcR-negative E-RFC were used as responders).

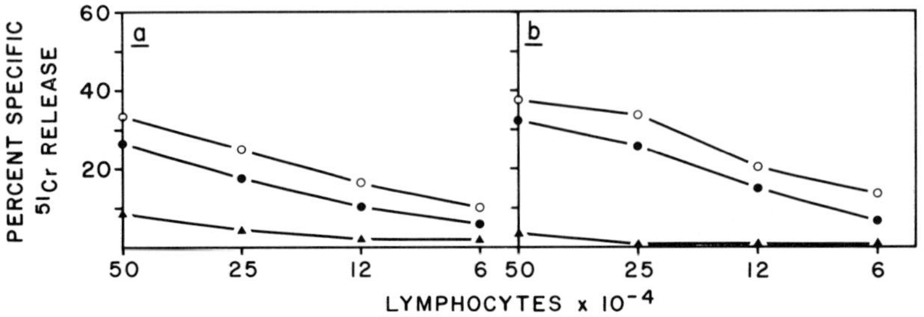

FIG. 6. Inactivation of MLC-generated NK-like cells (a), and of fresh NK cells (b) by cold K562 target. Various dilutions of effector cells were incubated either alone or in the presence of unlabeled K562 cells before being tested in a 4-hr assay against ^{51}Cr-labeled K562 cells (2×10^4/well). Part of the effector cells was preincubated for 4 hr at 37°C without target cells before adding either ^{51}Cr-labeled K562 cells alone (○) or a mixture of unlabeled and labeled K562 cells at a ratio of 2.5 (●). Another portion of the effectors were preincubated with unlabeled K562 cells (5×10^4/well) for 4 hr at 37°C before adding ^{51}Cr-labeled K562 (▲).

criminate between nonspecific effector cells and specific CTL generated in MLC, especially because both types of effectors appear to be T cells in nature (22–25). Moreover, there are conflicting reports concerning the relationship of the MLC-induced NK- and K-like cells to freshly isolated NK and K cells in terms of surface markers and mechanism of lysis. In the present study we have used various experimental approaches to analyze the functional behavior and the surface markers of allosensitized human lymphocytes in order to differentiate between nonspecific killers and specific CTL, and between *in vitro*-activated NK- and K-like cells and spontaneously occurring NK and K cells. In order to restrict the analysis to cytotoxic T cells, we used a highly purified FcR-negative E-RFC population as responder in the MLC. Such cells, which lack ADCC and SLMC activities when freshly isolated (1, 3), appeared to contain the precursors of highly cytotoxic effector cells able to mediate lysis of a large spectrum of targets, including NK-sensitive, antibody-coated, and relevant target cells. Kinetics studies showed that both specific and nonspecific effector cells were generated as early as 3 days after allostimulation in MLC. The peak of NK- and K-like activities was observed on Days 5 through 7; specific CTL activity generally peaked on Day 5 or 6, though the rate of cytotoxicity remained relatively constant on Days 4 through 7. Lysis of PHA-blasts autologous to the responder–effector cells was variable and often significant. The kinetics of lysis of these targets was very similar to that observed against allogeneic blasts, suggesting that the same lymphocyte population is responsible for autologous and allospecific killing. Other investigators have also observed that "anomalous killing" can be generated from FcR-negative and NK-negative precursors (23–25). In contrast, Shaw *et al.* (22) failed to detect ADCC after removal of FCR-positive T cells from the responder population before allosensitization. Our data indicate that both the anti-K562 and the ADCC-like activities induced upon allosensitization of FcR-negative T-cell precursors are properties of T lymphocytes in a certain stage of activation, and are not due to surviving NK and K cells but are newly generated *in vitro*, concomitantly with specific CML. The possibility that such cells might have derived from stimulator non-E-RFC with remaining activity after irradiation seems unlikely because: (1) NK and K cell functions of freshly separated PBL were abrogated after irradiation and culture of the non-E-RFC in the absence of stimulation (Fig. 2), and (2) cytotoxic cells could be generated from MLC when B-cell lines, which lack cytotoxic capability, were used as stimulators (Fig. 3). However, it is likely that the generation of effector cells with NK- and K-like activities depends on soluble factors, as is the case for specific CTL (32, 33). This is suggested by the data of Masucci *et al.* (25) who showed that NK-negative T cells cultured with K562 could not exert anti-K562 activity unless the supernatant from MLC was added to the culture.

Recent studies have indicated that two distinct types of cytotoxic cells exist within allostimulated cultures; one able to mediate nonspecific effects, and one able to lyse specific target cells (34, 35). In one study (34), treatment of MLC effector cells with monoclonal anti-T-cell antibodies (OKT3 and OKT8) and C was shown to ablate specific cytotoxicity without affecting lysis of the NK-sensitive K562 cell line. In another report (35) generation of CTL activity but not of NK- and K-like activities could be prevented by treatment of allostimulated cells with 5-bromodeoxyuridine and light. Because these studies were performed using an heterogeneous PBL population as responder of the MLC, the relative contributions of CTL and nonspecific cells to the lysis could not be completely evaluated. In order to differentiate between any type of effector cells which can be derived from a PBL population already endowed with cytotoxic capability, and those which are newly generated from purified noncytotoxic precursors, we set up parallel sets of MLC using either unfractionated PBL (MLC) or FcR-negative E-RFC (MLC2) from the same donor as responder. On Day 6, the two MLC were separated into E-RFC and non-E-RFC fractions and tested for SLMC, ADCC, and CML activities and for surface markers using monoclonal antibodies reactive with T cells (OKT3 and B36.1), monocytes and granulocytes (B13.4), and DR antigens (B33.1). When FcR-negative T cells were used as responders (MLC2), most of the cells derived from the MLC formed rosettes with SE, as only 1 to 5% of the cultures could be recovered in the non-E-RFC fraction. In contrast, when unfractionated PBL were used as responders (MLC1), the non-E-RFC represented 20% of the cultures. In both sets of MLC specific lysis was restricted to the E-RFC population (Fig. 4). Lysis of autologous blasts was always found associated with lysis of allogeneic blasts and was mediated only by cells obtained in the E-RFC fraction (Fig. 4). Such cells were 100% reactive with OKT3 (Table 1). This, together with our kinetics studies and the results of others (36, 37), suggests that the auto killing is probably mediated by cells with characteristics similar to those of the CTL responsible for specific allogeneic lysis. In contrast to the allospecific lysis and to the auto killing which were mediated only by effector cells with high affinity for SE, nonspecific cytotoxic effects induced in MLC from either an heterogeneous PBL population or from a purified T-cell fraction appeared to be mediated by two distinct populations of effector cells that differ in E-rosetting ability. However, the NK- and K-like activities generated from FcR-negative T lymphocytes (MLC2) were mediated by cells bearing T-cell markers, as (1) all of the E-RFC and the non-E-RFC recovered reacted with monoclonal anti-T-cell antibodies OKT3 and B36.1 (Tables 1 and 2), and (2) both SLMC- and ADCC-like activities were greatly reduced following treatment of the MLC2 with OKT3 and C (Fig. 5). In contrast, when PBL were used as responders (MLC1), a portion of the nonspecific lysis induced was most likely mediated by effectors lacking T-cell markers, as the non-E-RFC population was largely OKT3-negative (Table 1). This would explain why

Zarling and Kung (34), using PBL as responders, failed to observe a decrease of anti-K562 activity following treatment of the MLC killers with OKT3 and C: it is conceivable that the NK-like effector cells with low affinity for SE were not affected by that treatment. Whether the nonspecific killer cells recovered in the non-E-RFC fraction of the MLC1 represent preexisting OKT3-negative NK or K cells that have retained cytotoxicity during allosensitization or whether they are generated *de novo* remains to be determined.

The experiments performed on fresh PBL have shown that, in contrast to what occurred in the case of allosensitized FcR-negative T cells, treatment of freshly isolated E-RFC with OKT3 and C did not eliminate the population of cells that mediates NK and K cell functions (Fig. 5). In cell sorting analysis, such a population was largely positive for the monoclonal antibody OKM1 which reacts with monocytes, granulocytes, and a small proportion of lymphocytes. The same analysis is now being applied to the MLC effectors generated from allosensitized FcR-negative E-RFC to determine whether or not the cells responsible for the residual NK- and K-like effects obtained after OKT3 (or B36.1) and C treatment also react with OKM1. If so, such results would be in line with those of Zarling and Kung (34) who observed that the NK-like effectors derived from allosensitized PBL were sensitive to treatment with OKM1 and C, and suggested that fresh NK cells and MLC-activated NK-like cells are similar. From our analysis with the available monoclonal antibodies thus far, we only know that none of the MLC-induced killers (either generated from PBL or from T cells) reacted with a monoclonal antibody specific for myelomonocytic cells (B13.4) and that 30 to 40% of the killers expressed DR antigens as measured by reactivity with B33.1.

There have been conflicting reports concerning the presence of FcR on MLC-induced NK- and K-like cells (22, 23, 38, 39), although it is generally agreed that allospecific CTL lack detectable FcR (22, 39). Using the EA7S rosette assay, we found that almost none of the MLC-generated killer cells had FcR. It is unlikely that FcR were blocked by the IgG in human serum as only 1% of the cells were Ig positive (Tables 1 and 2). The fact that Moretta *et al.* (39) were able to detect FcR using this assay may be attributed to the presence of FBS in their MLC since FBS alone can induce both cytotoxic activity and FcR on FcR-negative cells (11). Because it seemed unlikely that cells lacking FcR could lyse antibody-coated target cells we used more sensitive techniques in an effort to detect FcR. Cytotoxicity after depletion of FcR-positive cells on EA7S monolayers was not reduced (Table 3). However, when the cytotoxic assays were performed in the presence of EA7S immune complexes (Table 4), ADCC-like activity was reduced by 40%, indicating that FcR are present on MLC-generated K-like effector cells, but are not detectable probably because of their low affinity. The slight reduction in NK-like activity obtained in this way may reflect the fact that the cytotoxic activity of NK cells is always less easily inhibited than that of K cells by immune complexes. That cells responsible for anomalous killing have lower affinity FcR as compared to fresh NK cells has also been suggested by other investigators (23).

To further characterize the NK- and K-like effector cells generated in MLC in relation to spontaneously occuring SLMC and ADCC effector cells, we compared their sensitivity to proteolytic enzymes and to IFN, as well as their interaction with NK-sensitive targets. The fact that trypsin abrogated the cytotoxic activity of fresh but not of MLC-induced NK cells (Table 5), suggests that the membrane components involved in the lysis by fresh NK cells differ from those of activated NK-like cells. In contrast, pronase abrogated specific and nonspecific activity of MLC-generated killers in addition to depleting NK and K functions of fresh lymphocytes. Results of IFN treatment of effectors and fibroblast targets (Table 6) showed that the effects with both fresh PBL and MLC-induced killer cells were similar though more noticeable when fresh PBL were used. The MLC-generated NK-like cells were able to lyse the FS fibroblasts much more efficiently than fresh NK cells, which may be the result of prior activation in MLC by endogenous IFNγ, or of an additive effect of CTL and NK-like cells. The latter possibility could also explain why IFN-treated fibroblasts were not protected by NK-like cells as efficiently as fresh NK cells, considering the specificity of the protective effect of IFN against NK cells and not against CTL (40). Finally, the observation that MLC-generated T cells, like fresh NK cells, could be inactivated by interaction with cold K562 cells in the absence of IFN induction (Fig. 6), suggests the possible use of this system to deplete nonspecific NK-like effects from the MLC-generated killers and to discriminate between NK-like and allospecific killing in the CTL population.

In summary, we have shown that: (1) The nonspecific killer cells generated in human MLC from unfractionated PBL or from FcR-negative T cells differ from specific CTL in their affinity for SE. (2) *De novo* generation of all the effector cell types (nonspecific and allospecific) can be demonstrated only through the use of a highly purified FcR-negative noncytotoxic T-cell fraction rather than an heterogeneous PBL population as responder in MLC. Furthermore, these newly generated effectors can be shown to maintain T-cell markers. (3) Finally, the MLC-induced NK- and K-like cells are similar to, but not identical with, freshly isolated NK and K cells.

ACKNOWLEDGMENTS

We are grateful to Dr. Stephen Ip (Ortho Diagnostics, Westwood, Mass.) for providing us with OKT3 and OKM1 monoclonal antibodies and to Drs. Giorgio Trinchieri and Bice Perussia (The Wistar Institute) who provided us with monoclonal antibodies B36.1, B33.1, and B13.4. We thank Ms. Marina Hoffman for editorial assistance.

REFERENCES

1. Santoli, D., Trinchieri, G., Moretta, L., Zmijewski, C. M., and Koprowski, H., *Clin. Exp. Immunol.* **33,** 309, 1978.
2. Trinchieri, G., Santoli, D., and Koprowski, H., *J. Immunol.* **120,** 1849, 1978.
3. Santoli, D., Trinchieri, G., and Lief, F. S., *J. Immunol.* **121,** 526, 1978.
4. West, W. H., Cannon, G. B., Kay, H. D., Bonnard, G. D., and Herberman, R. B., *J. Immunol.* **118,** 361, 1977.
5. Reinherz, E. L., Moretta, L., Roper, M., Breard, J. M., Mingari, M. C., and Schlossman, S. F., *J. Exp. Med.* **151,** 969, 1980.
6. Kay, H. D., and Horwitz, D. A., *J. Clin. Invest.* **66,** 847, 1980.
7. Trinchieri, G., and Santoli, D., *J. Exp. Med.* **147,** 1314, 1978.
8. Santoli, D., and Koprowski, H., *Immunol. Rev.* **44,** 125, 1979.
9. Zielske, J. V., and Golub, S. H., *Cancer Res.* **36,** 3842, 1976.
10. Ortaldo, J. R., Bonnard, G. D., and Herberman, R. B., *J. Immunol.* **119,** 1351, 1977.
11. Ortaldo, J. R., Kay, H. D., and Bonnard, G. D., *In* "Regulatory Mechanisms of Lymphocyte Activation: Proceedings of the Eleventh Leukocyte Culture Conference" (D. O. Lucas, Ed.), pp. 542–543. Academic Press, New York, 1977.
12. Stejskal, V., Holm, G., and Perlman, P., *Cell. Immunol.* **8,** 71, 1973.

13. Martin Chandon, M. R., Vanky, F., Carnaud, C., and Klein, E., *Int. J. Cancer* **15,** 342, 1975.
14. Treves, A. J., Feldman, M., and Kaplan, H. S., *J. Immunol.* **119,** 955, 1977.
15. Svedmyr, E., Wigzell, H., and Jondal, M., *J. Immunol.* **3,** 499, 1974.
16. Jondal, M., and Targan, S., *J. Exp. Med.* **147,** 1621, 1978.
17. Ortaldo, J. R., and Bonnard, G. D., *Fed. Proc.* **36,** 1325, 1977.
18. Poros, A., and Klein, E., *Cell. Immunol.* **46,** 57, 1979.
19. Seeley, J. K., and Golub, S. H., *J. Immunol.* **120,** 1415, 1978.
20. Miggiano, V. C., Bernocco, D., Lightbody, J., Trinchieri, G., and Ceppellini, R., *Trans. Proc.* **IV,** 231, 1972.
21. Poros, A., and Klein, E., *Cell Immunol.* **41,** 240, 1978.
22. Shaw, S., Pichler, W. J., and Nelson, D. L., *J. Immunol.* **122,** 599, 1979.
23. Seeley, J. K., Masucci, G., Poros, A., Klein, E., and Golub, S. H., *J. Immunol.* **123,** 1303, 1979.
24. Masucci, M. G., Klein, E., and Argov, S., *J. Immunol.* **124,** 2458, 1980.
25. Masucci, G., Poros, A., Seeley, J. K., and Klein, E., *Cell. Immunol.* **52,** 247, 1980.
26. Boyum, A., *Scand. J. Clin. Lab. Invest.* **21**(Suppl. 97)**,** 1, 1968.
27. Kedar, E., De Landazuri, M., and Bonavida, B., *J. Immunol.* **112,** 1231, 1974.
28. Santoli, D., Trinchieri, G., Zmijewski, C. M., and Koprowski, H., *J. Immunol.* **117,** 765, 1976.
29. Drew, S. I., Terasaki, P. I., Billing, R. J., Bergh, O. J., Minowada, J., and Klein, E., *Blood* **49,** 715, 1977.
30. Perussia, B., Trinchieri, G., and Cerottini, J.-C., *J. Immunol.* **123,** 681, 1979.
31. Perussia, B., and Trinchieri, G., *J. Immunol.* **126,** 754, 1981.
32. Uotila, M., Rode, H., and Gordon, J., *Eur. J. Immunol.* **8,** 133, 1978.
33. Symington, F. W., and Teh, H. S., *Scand. J. Immunol.* **12,** 1, 1980.
34. Zarling, J. M., and Kung, P. C., *Nature (London)* **288,** 394, 1980.
35. Callewaert, D. M., Lightbody, J. J., Kaplan, J., Jaroszewski, J., Peterson, W. D., Jr., and Rosenberg, J. C., *J. Immunol.* **121,** 81, 1978.
36. Royston, I., Smith, R. W., Buele, D. N., Huang, E. S., and Pagano, J. S., *Nature (London)* **251,** 745, 1974.
37. Zarling, J. M., Back, F. H., and Kung, P. C., *J. Immunol.* **126,** 375, 1981.
38. Evans, R. L., Chess, L., Levine, H., and Schlossman, S. F., *J. Exp. Med.* **147,** 605, 1978.
39. Moretta, A., Mingari, M. C., Haynes, B. F., Sekaly, R. P., Moretta, L., and Fauci, A. S., *J. Exp. Med.* **153,** 213, 1981.
40. Trinchieri, G., Perussia, B., and Santoli, D., *In* "Natural Cell-Mediated Immunity Against Tumors" (R. B. Herberman, Ed.), pp. 655–670. Academic Press, New York, 1980.

CELLULAR IMMUNOLOGY **65**, 247–257 (1981)

IgA Allotype Suppression in Mice: A Cellular Implication for the IgA Preponderance in the Gut

JEENAN TSENG

Department of Experimental Pathology, Division of Pathology, Walter Reed Army Institute of Research, Washington, D.C. 20012

Received July 10, 1981; accepted October 7, 1981

Paternal IgA allotype suppressions were induced in (A/HeJ × SJL/J)F_1, (BALB/cJ × CB-20)F_1, and (BALB/cJ × SJL/J)F_1 mice by perinatal exposure of the neonates to antibody against paternal IgA allotype (Ig-2b). All the Ig-2b allotype suppressions were temporary and were prominently seen at the age of 4–10 weeks. These transient Ig-2b allotype suppressions were manifested by a suppression of Ig-2b allotype in the serum and a suppression of Ig-2b allotype-producing cells in the gut lamina propria. During the suppression, no replacement of the Ig-2b allotype by IgM and IgG plasma cells was seen in the gut lamina propria. The transient IgA allotype suppression was primarily due to a depletion of IgA allotype precursors in Peyer's patches; suppressor T cells were not actively involved. These results suggest that IgA preponderance in the gut is due to the migration of the patch IgA precursors and their accumulation and maturation in the gut lamina propria.

INTRODUCTION

When neonatal animals are exposed to an antibody against one of their immunoglobulin (Ig)[1] allotypes, the production of that allotype will be suppressed in later life. This phenomenon has been termed allotype suppression (1). Allotype suppressions have been demonstrated for Ig isotypes including IgG and IgM of the rabbit (1–5) and IgG1 (Ig-4) and IgG2a (Ig-1) of the mouse (6); IgA allotype suppression, however, has not been described. Two extreme types of allotype suppressions, short and long term, have been found. The former are due to a temporary depletion of precursors for allotype-producing cells (5–9). The latter are mediated by allotype-specific T cells which may directly or indirectly suppress the allotype precursors and/or allotype producing cells (10, 11). The best examples of these two types are the short-term suppressions of the paternal and maternal IgG1 and IgG2a allotypes and the chronic suppression of paternal IgG2a allotype (Ig-1b) in (SJL♂ × BALB/c♀)F_1 mice (6, 7, 10, 11). Although chronic Ig-1b suppression in adult mice is difficult to achieve by the induction with anti-Ig-1b antibody, it can be induced in Ig allotype congenic mice transferred with sensitized T cells from Ig-1b-immunized mice (12, 13). Thus far, these chronic Ig-1b allotype suppressions are the most convincing demonstration for the presence of Ig class-specific T cells which regulate the production of an isotype.

[1] Abbreviations used: Ig, immunoglobulin; PP, Peyer's patches.

0008-8749/81/180247-11$02.00/0

The intestinal lamina propria is characterized by the presence of a vast number of IgA plasma cells which predominate over those of other Ig isotypes (14). The mechanism of this IgA preponderance is still unknown. Because of the facts that Peyer's patches (PP) are the enriched sources for the precursors of the IgA plasma cells and, possibly, T cells of the gut lamina propria (15–17) and that IgA expression is T-cell dependent (16–18), the IgA preponderance in the gut could be ascribed to the migration, accumulation, and maturation of PP IgA precursors and/or to the predominant presence of IgA class-specific T cells in gut tissues. A simple way to study these possibilities is to induce IgA allotype suppression in mice. A short-term IgA allotype suppression would favor the former possibility and a chronic suppression would favor the latter.

This report describes neonatally induced IgA allotype suppression in three strains of mice heterozygous in Ig allotype genes. The IgA allotype suppressions induced are all transient and are primarily due to a depletion of IgA allotype precursors in PP; T cells, on the other hand, are not involved at all. During the suppression, no repopulation of the suppressed allotype by IgM and IgG plasma cells was seen in the gut lamina propria. These results suggest that the IgA preponderance in the gut is due to the migration of PP IgA precursors and their accumulation and maturation in the gut lamina propria rather than to the predominant presence of IgA-specific T cells in the gut lymphoid tissues.

MATERIALS AND METHODS

Mice. A/HeJ, BALB/cJ, C57BL/6J, and SJL/J mice were purchased from Jackson Laboratories, Bar Harbor, Maine. CB-20 mice were from the colony maintained in Johns Hopkins University, Baltimore, Maryland.

Antisera. Anti-IgA sera were raised in sheep and rabbits, respectively, against MOPC-315 IgA myeloma protein and mixed IgA proteins of MOPC-320 myeloma and of C57BL/6J serum and gut secretions. The serum IgA was prepared by placing serum on a lentil lectin–Sepharose 4B column and eluting with 0.01 *M* α-methyl-D-mannoside. This IgA was then further purified by DE-52 column chromatography. The gut IgA was prepared by Sephadex G-50 gel filtration of the gut washings followed by DE-52 column chromatography. These IgA proteins each showed a single precipitation arc corresponding to IgA against goat anti-mouse serum on immunoelectrophoresis and no precipitin lines against anti-μ and anti-γ by Ouchterlony analysis. Anti-IgM and anti-IgG sera were produced in rabbits, respectively, against CBPC-112 myeloma IgM and IgG subclasses from CB-20 mouse serum. Anti-IgG2a serum was also produced in rabbits against UPC-10 myeloma IgG2a (Litton Bionetics, Kensington, Md.). The CBPC-112 IgM and MOPC-320 IgA proteins were isolated by ammonium sulfate precipitation, which was followed by DE-52 chromatography and affinity adsorption on Protein A–Sepharose columns (19). The CB-20 IgG subclasses were prepared by absorbing serum on a Protein A–Sepharose 4B column at pH 8.0 and eluting it with 0.01 *M* citrate buffer (pH 3.0) (19). Anti-α, anti-μ, anti-γ, and anti-γ2a sera were then made by absorbing the antisera with appropriate Ig myeloma proteins conjugated to Sepharose 4B beads (20).

Anti-Ig-1b and anti-Ig-2b allotype sera were raised in A/HeJ mice, respectively, against C57BL/6J IgG2 and C57BL/6J serum and gut IgA (or against MOPC-

320 myeloma IgA) as described by Lieberman and Humphrey (21). The antisera were absorbed with BALB/cJ serum Igs and gut IgA before use.

Fluorescent antibody staining. Fluorescein isothiocyanate I and tetramethylrhodamine isothiocyanate (mixed isomers) were purchased from Research Organics, Inc., Cleveland, Ohio. Conjugation of the fluorescein and rhodamine dyes to IgG molecules of the antibodies was performed as described by Wood *et al.* (22) and by Cebra and Goldstein (23).

Four random segments of the small intestine from each mouse were frozen sectioned transversely at 2–4 μm thickness. Usually, 15–20 consecutive sections were placed close to each other on a microscopic slide and fixed with 95% alcohol (5 min). The sections were doubly stained with anti-Ig-2b and anti-α with contrasting fluorescent color. The stained sections were examined under a Leitz or Zeiss fluorescent microscope and the positively stained cells were scored by counting the nucleus of the stained cells. Doubly stained cells of Ig-2b and IgA were scored as Ig-2b-positive cells and the percentages were calculated using IgA-positive cells as standard.

Isolated lymphoid cells were stained by capping the surface Igs at room temperature in cell suspension. This was followed by the cytoplasmic staining of Igs on cytocentrifuge smears (10^5 cells/spot) with contrasting fluorescent antibody reagents.

Preparation of lymphoid cell suspensions. Lymphoid cells were isolated from tissues at room temperature. Cells from PP and spleen were dispersed by gently rubbing the lymphoid tissues against a stainless-steel screen (400 meshes/cm^2) in Hanks' balanced salt solution (HBSS) containing 5% fetal bovine serum. Cells were then washed three times by centrifugation (400*g*, 10 min) with the same HBSS medium.

Lymphoid cells from gut lamina propria were isolated as described previously (24). This was performed by inactivating the cementing materials with 1 m*M* dithiothreitol (Sigma Chemical Co., St. Louis, Mo.), stripping the gut epithelium with 0.05% ethylenediaminetetraacetate disodium in HBSS without Mg^{2+} and Ca^{2+}, and digesting the lamina propria with 10 units/ml of collagenase CLSPA (Worthington Biochemical Corporation, Freehold, N.J.).

T cells were isolated by the nylon wool method (25). B-cell-enriched preparations were prepared by killing the T cells with the monoclonal anti-Thy 1.2 hybridoma antibody (Line HO-13-4-9; Salk Institute, San Diego, Calif.) plus guinea pig complement (26). Generally, T-cell preparations contained less than 5% Ig-bearing cells and B-cell preparations contained 74–81% Ig-bearing cells.

Cell culture. Lymphoid cells were cultured in RPMI 1640 medium supplemented with 10% fetal bovine serum (GIBCO), 2 m*M* glutamine, 5×10^{-5} *M* 2-mercaptoethanol, 20 μg/ml gentamicin, and 100 units/ml mycostatin. Two milliliters of cell suspensions (10^6 cells/ml) were distributed to each well of a 24-well culture plate (Costar, Cambridge, Mass.). Cells were incubated at 37°C in a humidified incubator under 5% CO_2 and 95% air. T cells were added to B cells at different proportions and cultured with pokeweed mitogen (10 μg/ml). Four days later, cells were harvested and cytocentrifuge smears were made and doubly stained with fluorescent antibodies. Mixed anti-α and anti-Ig-2b were used to stain IgA-containing cells. When staining for IgG2a-containing cells, the cells were first stained with anti-Ig-1b and then with anti-γ2a of contrasting fluorescent color.

Radioimmunoassay. Total IgA and Ig-2b allotype in the serum were quantitated by radioprecipitation inhibition assay described by Spring *et al.* (27). MOPC-320 IgA labeled with ^{125}I by the chloramine-T method (28) was used as the radioactive antigen. Rabbit anti-α and A/HeJ anti-Ig-2b antisera were used as first antibody reagents. Prequantitated MOPC-320 IgA was used to construct the standard curve. Serum samples were used as inhibitors. Goat anti-rabbit IgG and rabbit anti-γ sera were used as the second antibody to precipitate the immune complexes.

RESULTS

Suppression of IgA allotype plasma cells in the gut lamina propria. It has been found that allotype suppressions can be induced in F_1 animals either by maternal transfer of anti-allotype antibodies to the fetuses or by injection of the anti-allotype sera into the neonates (1–6). The IgA allotype suppressions in this study were performed by both methods. The suppression in (A/HeJ × SJL/J)F_1 was induced by mating SJL/J (Ig-2b allotype) males to A/HeJ females producing anti-C57BL/6J IgA (Ig-2b allotype) antibody. The suppressions in (BALB/cJ × SJL/J)F_1 and (BALB/cJ × CB-20)F_1 mice were achieved by daily intraperitoneal injection of the neonates with anti-Ig-2b serum during the first week of life (50 μl/mouse in the first 3 days and 100 μl/mouse thereafter). The mice were weaned at the age of 4 weeks. When the IgA plasma cells in the gut lamina propria were enumerated, all the suppressed mice showed a complete paternal IgA allotype suppression by the age of 4–6 weeks (Table 1). However, these mice gradually recovered from the suppression and the number of their paternal Ig-2b allotype-producing cells became normal by the age of 8–10 weeks.

It has been found in Ig-1b allotype suppression that some of the (SJL♂ × BALB/cJ♀)F_1 mice can develop chronic allotype suppression approximately half a year after their recovery from temporary Ig-1b allotype suppression (29). To see if this would happen in Ig-2b allotype suppression, (A/HeJ × SJL/J)F_1 and (BALB/cJ × SJL/J)F_1 mice were examined for IgA allotype suppression at age of 20–40 weeks after their neonatal injectionof anti-Ig-2b sera. None of these F_1 mice showed suppression during this period (Table 1).

TABLE 1

Suppression of Paternal IgA Allotype-Producing Cells in the Gut Lamina Propria

Matings[a] (♀ × ♂)	F_1 mice[b]	Percentage Ig-2b-containing cells relative to total IgA-containing cells at age (weeks)[c]									
		4	6	8	10	13	20	24	28	32	40
A/HeJ × SJL/J	Normal	72	68	70	ND[d]	67	70	72	68	65	75
	Suppressed	5	43	70	ND	70	72	65	74	68	73
BALB/cJ × CB-20	Normal	53	50	48	52	49	ND	ND	ND	ND	ND
	Suppressed	4	5	28	52	50	ND	ND	ND	ND	ND
BALB/cJ × SJL/J	Normal	66	68	67	63	64	68	74	70	68	70
	Suppressed	2	3	30	68	63	70	68	70	72	73

[a] Allotypes of SJL/J, CB-20, A/HeJ, and BALB/cJ are $IgCH^b$, $IgCH^b$, $IgCH^e$, and $IgCH^a$, respectively.

[b] (A/HeJ × SJL/J)F_1 were suppressed by maternal transfer of anti-Ig-2b antibody. (BALB/cJ × CB-20)F_1 and (BALB/cJ × SJL/J)F_1 were suppressed by intraperitoneal injection of anti-Ig-2b in the first week of life.

[c] Average of three mice; four random segments of small intestine from each mouse.

[d] ND, not done.

Repopulation of suppressed IgA allotype by IgM and IgG plasma cells in the gut lamina propria. To investigate if the suppression of Ig-2b plasma cells in the gut lamina propria could be compensated by a repopulation of IgM and IgG plasma cells, the gut sections from some of the 4 to 5-week-old suppressed (BALB/cJ × SJL/J)F_1 and (A/HeJ × SJL/J)F_1 mice were stained for IgM- and IgG-containing cells. The gut sections from both suppressed and normal mice showed essentially the same numbers of IgM- and IgG-containing cells (0.05 vs 0.04% and 0.01 vs 0.02% relative to total IgA plasma cells, respectively). This indicated that no replacement of Ig-2b by IgM and/or IgG plasma cells occurs in the gut lamina propria during the suppression.

Prominent neutrophil staining in the gut lamina propria. It should be noted that when the sections were stained with our fluorescent antibody reagents, nonspecific uptake of the fluorescent antibodies by neutrophils was seen more frequently in the suppressed mice than in normal controls. This is particularly prominent in the suppressed mice of 4–5 weeks old.

IgA allotype suppression in the serum. The concentration of Ig-2b and total IgA in the sera of the allotype suppressed and normal mice was quantitated. The results are shown in Table 2. Usually, the suppressed mice maintained a remarkably low level of Ig-2b allotype from ages 4 to 10 weeks. Interestingly, the suppression in the serum lasted 2–4 weeks longer than cellular suppression in the gut lamina propria (Table 1). When total IgA was determined, the suppressed mice at the ages of 4–10 weeks showed consistently lower concentration than did the normal mice. This reduction of serum IgA indicated a limited suppression of maternal IgA allotype.

Lymphoid cells and granulocytes in PP and in the gut lamina propria. PP are the major sources for IgA plasma cells and T cells of the gut lamina propria (15–17). To determine if the Ig-2b allotype suppression was due to a depletion of B cells, IgA precursors, and T cells in PP and the gut lamina propria, these cells in the suppressed (BALB/cJ × SJL/J)F_1 mice (5 weeks old) were enumerated. The results are summarized in Table 3. The suppressed mice showed essentially the same numbers of T cells, B cells, IgM-bearing and IgG-bearing cells as those of normal mice in either PP or the lamina propria. However, the number of IgA-bearing cells in PP was significantly less ($P < 0.001$) in the suppressed than in the normal mice. In addition, the number of IgA-containing cells in the lamina propria of the suppressed mice was significantly reduced ($P < 0.01$) although the number of IgA-bearing cells in the suppressed and the normal mice was approximately the same. These results suggested that the Ig-2b allotype suppression is mainly due to a development arrest of allotype precursors in PP and the gut lamina propria.

As mentioned previously, nonspecific staining of neutrophils in the gut lamina propria was seen more frequently in the suppressed than in the normal mice. Isolated granulocytes from PP and the gut lamina propria were identified by Giemsa stain. As also shown in Table 3, the suppressed mice possessed a significantly larger number ($P < 0.01$) of neutrophils than did the normal mice in both PP and the gut lamina propria.

Function of the T cells in the gut in in vitro Ig expressions. Although the Ig-2b allotype suppressions in this study are transient, it is possible that the suppressions might be mediated by T cells which are functionally short lived. To study this possibility, T cells from PP and the gut lamina propria of the suppressed

TABLE 2

IgA Concentrations in the Serum of Ig-2b Allotype-Suppressed Mice[a]

Matings (♀ × ♂)	F_1 mice	IgA	IgA concentration (μg/ml) at age (weeks)									
			4	6	8	10	13	20	24	28	32	40
A/HeJ × SJL/J	Normal	Ig-2b	400	900	1200	ND	1200	1400	1200	1600	1400	1600
	Normal	Total IgA	800	2000	2400	ND	2400	2600	2400	2800	2600	2800
	Suppressed	Ig-2b	<10	10	100	ND	1200	1600	1400	1400	1600	1600
	Suppressed	Total IgA	200	700	900	ND	2400	2400	2600	2400	2800	2800
BALB/cJ × CB-20	Normal	Ig-2b	200	400	500	400	400	ND	ND	ND	ND	ND
	Normal	Total IgA	400	1000	1000	900	1000	ND	ND	ND	ND	ND
	Suppressed	Ig-2b	<10	<10	40	200	400	ND	ND	ND	ND	ND
	Suppressed	Total IgA	100	300	600	800	1000	ND	ND	ND	ND	ND
BALB/cJ × SJL/J	Normal	Ig-2b	300	1000	1000	1200	1200	1600	1400	1600	1600	1600
	Normal	Total IgA	600	2000	2400	2400	2400	2800	2600	2800	3000	2800
	Suppressed	Ig-2b	<10	<10	20	400	1200	1400	1600	1600	1600	1600
	Suppressed	Total IgA	100	400	800	1600	2400	2600	2600	2800	2800	3000

[a] Same mice as in Table 1.

TABLE 3

Lymphoid Cells and Granulocytes in Peyer's Patches and the Gut Lamina Propria of Ig-2b Allotype-Suppressed (BALB/cJ × SJL/J)F_1 Mice[a]

Cells	Percentages (mean ± SD)			
	Peyer's patches		Lamina propria	
	Normal mice	Suppressed mice	Normal mice	Suppressed mice
T cells[b]	35.2 ± 5.4	36.0 ± 6.2	60.4 ± 4.8	57.3 ± 2.5
Ig-bearing cells[c]	55.1 ± 3.2	52.4 ± 3.3	18.1 ± 4.6	19.2 ± 5.1
IgA bearing	(7.2 ± 1.2)[d]	(3.4 ± 0.5)	(4.4 ± 1.2)	(5.2 ± 2.1)
IgM bearing	(80.4 ± 4.2)	(83.1 ± 6.1)	(92.3 ± 8.5)	(94.0 ± 9.2)
IgG bearing	(7.3 ± 1.3)	(6.4 ± 1.1)	(0.02 ± 0.01)	(0.03 ± 0.02)
IgA-containing cells	0.0	0.0	6.2 ± 1.8	3.6 ± 1.3
Ig-2a-containing cells[e]	ND	ND	2.4 ± 0.2	3.1 ± 0.2
Neutrophils	0.02 ± 0.01	1.5 ± 0.4	2.6 ± 0.4	4.8 ± 0.9
Eosinophils	0.0	0.2 ± 0.1	5.4 ± 1.3	5.7 ± 1.6
Basophils	0.0	0.0	0.2 ± 0.1	0.3 ± 0.1

[a] Five weeks old; six normal and six suppressed.
[b] Determined by cytotoxic test using hybridoma anti-Thy 1.2 (Line HO-13-4-9) (26).
[c] Ig-bearing and IgA-bearing cells were identified by capping with rhodamine-conjugated anti-IgG and peptic Fab of anti-α, respectively.
[d] Percentages in parentheses are percentages relative to total Ig-bearing cells.
[e] Percentages were calculated by subtracting Ig-2b containing cells from total IgA containing cells.

(BALB/cJ × SJL/J)F_1 (5 weeks old), as well as their normal litter mates, were cocultured with B cells from PP and spleen of normal F_1 mice (7–10 weeks old) and stimulated with pokeweed mitogen. The reason for using pokeweed mitogen was based on our recent finding that pokeweed mitogen is a better inducer than bacterial lipopolysaccharide for IgA and IgG expressions in mouse lymphocyte cultures (Tseng, manuscript in preparation). The expressions of IgA, Ig-2b allotype, IgG2a, and Ig-1b allotype were then compared to determine isotype and allotype specificities for T cells. The results of these coculture experiments are shown in Figs. 1 and 2. When T cells of the gut lamina propria were used (Fig. 1), both suppressed and normal mice showed essentially the same IgA and IgG2a expression curves in either the PP or the spleen B cell cultures. When SJL/J allotypes (Ig-2b and Ig-1b) were identified for these IgA- and IgG2a-containing cells, both the suppressed and the normal mice showed similar proportions at every T-cell concentration from 0 to 80%. Similarly, when T cells of PP were titrated against B cells of either PP or spleen (Fig. 2), no significant differences were seen between both groups of the mice in the expressions of IgA, IgG2a, and their allotypes. These results clearly indicated that T cells of the gut lymphoid tissues are not involved in the Ig-2b allotype suppressions.

DISCUSSION

The present study was initiated by a dual purpose: (a) to describe IgA allotype suppression and (b) to gain information about IgA preponderance in the gut from the experiments of IgA allotype suppression. Since allotype suppressed animals provide nonsuppressed allotype as an internal reference, IgA allotype suppression

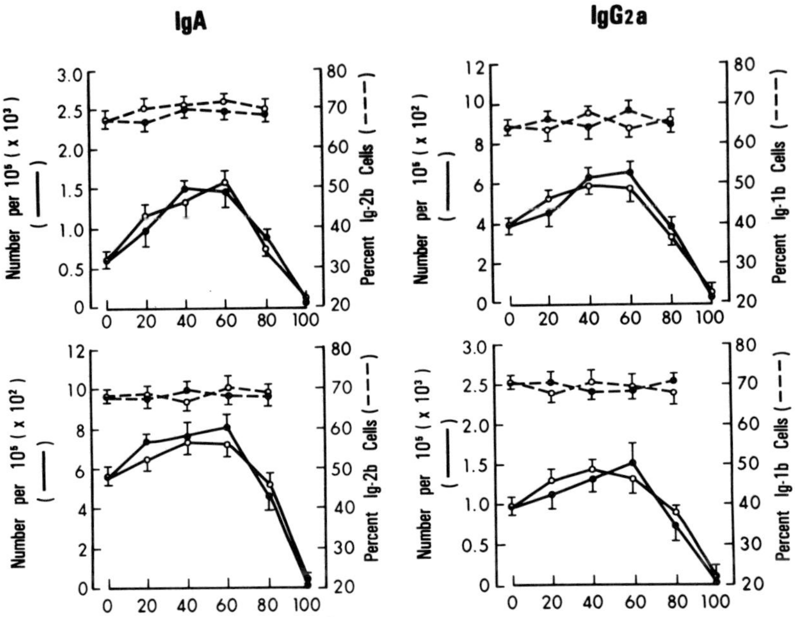

FIG. 1. Expressions of IgA and IgG2a under pokeweed mitogen stimulation by Peyer's patch (top panel) and spleen (bottom panel) B cells cocultured with different proportions of T cells from gut lamina propria of normal and IgA allotype-suppressed mice. Abscissas represent % T cells in cultures. Lines with solid circles (●) and opened circle (○) represent normal and allotype-suppressed mice, respectively. Solid lines represent total IgA or IgG2a while dashed lines represent Ig-2b- or Ig-1b-containing cells in cultures.

is a better means than IgA isotype suppression for studying the latter purpose. The results show that IgA allotype suppression can be induced in mice. The suppression is manifested by a temporary suppression of IgA allotype plasma cells in the gut lamina propria as well as of IgA allotype in the serum. The suppression is mainly due to the depletion of IgA allotype precursors in PP; T cells, however, are not involved at all. During the suppression no repopulation of the suppressed allotype by IgM and IgG plasma cells occurs in the gut lamina propria. These results suggest that the IgA preponderance in the gut is due to the migration of PP IgA precursors and their accumulation and maturation in the gut lamina propria rather than to the predominant presence of T cells specific for IgA expression in the gut.

IgA plasma cells in the gut lamina propria are mainly derived from IgA-bearing precursors in PP where the precursors first interact with antigens (15, 16). Under normal physiological conditions, although the precise migration route of the PP IgA precursors is unknown, it is generally accepted, based on lymphatic circulation, that the IgA precursors migrate from PP to mesenteric lymph nodes, enter the circulation via the thoracic duct, and eventually arrive in the gut lamina propria where they become resident plasma cells. A few of the IgA precursors may differentiate into plasma cells or plasmablasts during the migration (17, 30, 31); however, the majority remain as small lymphocytes (their characteristics are unknown) even after arrival in the gut lamina propria (32). After a second interaction

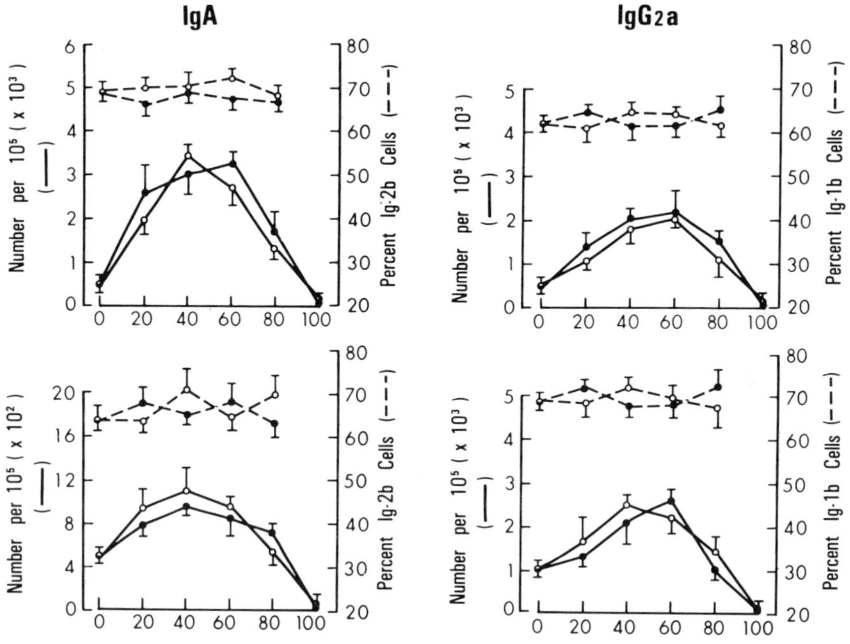

FIG. 2. Expression of IgA and IgG2a under pokeweed mitogen stimulation by Peyer's patch (top panel) and spleen (bottom panel) B cells cocultured with different proportions of T cells from Peyer's patches of normal and IgA allotype-suppressed mice. Representation of lines and circles are the same as in Fig. 1.

with antigens, these small lymphocytes divide and mature into plasma cells *in situ* (32). Our finding of the depletion of IgA precursors in PP that results in a disappearance of IgA allotype plasma cells in the gut lamina propria is compatible with the migration scheme.

It has been demonstrated that IgA expression is T-cell dependent (16–18). Although our findings suggest that IgA class-specific T cells are not involved in the mechanism of IgA preponderance in the gut, we do not exclude the role of T cells in the differentiation of IgA precursors into plasma cells. The differentiation of IgA precursors into plasma cells could be helped by the T cells which are not Ig class specific, i.e., these T cells can function equally well in the differentiation of precursors into IgM or IgG plasma cells. Although this suggestion will be at variance to those claims of the presence of IgE- and IgA-specific T cells (18, 33), accumulating results in our laboratory obtained from titration of T cells against B cells of various lymphoid tissues including the gut lamina propria support this idea. Furthermore, the demonstration of IgE-specific T cells seems to be associated with alum which was used as adjuvant in the induction and could possibly be involved in the stimulation of B cells. The IgA-specific T cells were demonstrated in lymphocyte cultures stimulated with supramitogenic dose of concanavalin A, under which condition expression of Ig isotypes could be suppressed to various degrees (18). Although these results were used as the evidence for the presence of Ig class-specific T cells, they could also be equally well interpreted as the evidences that B cells and/or Ig-secreting cells have different sensitivities to the function of same T cells in the differentiation of B cells into Ig-producing cells and/or in the secretion of Ig molecules from producing cells (18, 33, 34).

The chronic Ig-1b allotype suppression in (SJL♂ × BALB/c♀)F_1 and (SJL♂ × SJA♀)F_1 mice induced neonatally is definitely mediated by allotype-specific T cells (6, 7, 10, 11); however, the mechanism for the induction of these suppressor T cells seems to be very complicated and mysterious. This can be found in the observations that follow. The suppressor T cells can be induced not only by anti-Ig-1b antibody but also by anti-allotype antibodies against IgM and IgD of b allotype (35). The induction of the suppressor T cells can be prevented by the injection of neonates with splenic B cells and/or nonlymphoid cells from adult normal, syngenic F_1 mice of b allotype (35). Also, some of the adult (SJL♂ × BALB/c♀)F_1 mice recovered from transient Ig-1b allotype suppression can develop a chronic Ig-1b allotype suppression in later life (29). Furthermore, chronic allotype suppression has been found only for Ig-1b allotype, Ig-1a, Ig-4a, and Ig-4b allotypes have not been so chronically suppressed in these F_1 mice (6, 7, 35).

It has been suggested that chronic Ig-1b allotype suppression is probably due to the expression of SJL or the combination of SJL and BALB/c mouse genes in the (SJL♂ × BALB/c♀)F_1 mice (6). Although we have used (A/HeJ × SJL/J)F_1 and (BALB/cJ × SJL/J)F_1 mice in our studies, we could only induce transient IgA allotype suppressions in these mice. The inability of our mice to develop chronic IgA allotype suppression is apparently not due to the inactive expression of the SJL mouse genes in these mice because SJL mouse IgA (Ig-2b) in the serum and the producing cells in the gut lamina are substantially more than those in the (BALB/cJ × CB-20) mice (Tables 1 and 2). This hyperproduction of IgA is a characteristic expression of the SJL genetic abnormalities (36). Nevertheless, the transient IgA allotype suppressions described in this report are similar to Ig-4a and Ig-4b allotype suppressions in (SJL♂ × BALB/c♀)F_1 mice (6). These Ig-4 allotype suppressions are also temporary and the recoveries are autonomous, unlike the chronic Ig-1b allotype suppression (6).

The limited suppression of the maternal IgA allotype (nonsuppressed) and 2–4 weeks delayed recovery of the paternal IgA allotype (supressed) in the serum are unexpected findings in the present study. The mechanism of these limited suppressions is not clear; it could be operated by a similar or two different mechanisms. These suppressions do not appear to be due to the presence of antibodies in the anti-Ig-2b allotype sera against the common allotype determinants on parental IgA molecules and/or on the secretory components because the anti-Ig-2b sera have been absorbed with serum Igs and gut IgA of BALB/cJ mice, and the limited suppression and the delayed recovery are consistently seen in all the three strains of mice used. Because T cells are apparently not involved in our transient IgA allotype suppression and neutrophils are prominently seen in gut tissues of Ig-2b-suppressed mice, it is assumed that these auxillary suppressions are the episode of the inflammatory reaction occurring in the gut caused by the anti-Ig-2b antibody.

ACKNOWLEDGMENTS

I heartily appreciate the support by Professors John Cebra and David Levy, the constructive criticisms of Drs. David Haynes, June Whaun, Robert Reid, James Moe, and Akio Takeuchi, and the patient secretary work of Ms. Paulette E. R. Dantley. Part of this work was performed while the author was a postdoctoral trainee (T32 AI07057) supported by National Institute of Allergy and Infectious Diseases at Johns Hopkins University.

REFERENCES

1. Dray, S., *Nature (London)* **195,** 677, 1962.
2. Vice, J. L., Gilman-Sachs, A., Hunt, W. L., and Dray, S., *J. Immunol.* **104,** 550, 1970.
3. Gilman-Sachs, A., Eskinazi, D. P., and Dray, S., *J. Immunol.* **110,** 1369, 1977.
4. Dubiski, S., *Nature (London)* **214,** 1365, 1967.
5. Mage, R., *Transplant. Rev.* **27,** 84, 1975.
6. Herzenberg, L. A., and Herzenberg, L. A., *Contemp. Top. Immunobiol.* **3,** 41, 1973.
7. Herzenberg, L. A., Jones, P. P., and Herzenberg, L. A., *Ann. Inst. Pasteur Paris* **125C,** 71, 1974.
8. Lummus, Z., Cebra, J. J., and Mage, R., *J. Immunol.* **99,** 737, 1967.
9. Harrison, M. R., and Mage, R., *J. Exp. Med.* **138,** 764, 1973.
10. Herzenberg, L. A., Okumura, K., Cantor, H., Sato, V. L., Shen, F. W., Boyse, E. A., and Herzenberg, L. A., *J. Exp. Med.* **144,** 330, 1976.
11. Jacobson, E. B., *J. Exp. Med.* **148,** 607, 1978.
12. Bosma, M. J., and Bosma, G. L., *Nature (London)* **259,** 313, 1976.
13. Snodgrass, H. R., Wilson, D. B., and Bosma, M. J., *J. Exp. Med.* **154,** 480, 1981.
14. Crabbé, P. A., Carbonara, A. O., and Heremans, J. L., *Lab. Invest.* **14,** 235, 1965.
15. Craig, S. W., and Cebra, J. J., *J. Exp. Med.* **134,** 188, 1971.
16. Cebra, J. J., Gearhart, P., Kamat, R., Robertson, R., and Tseng, J., *Cold Spring Harbor Symp. Quant. Biol.* **41,** 201, 1977.
17. Guy-Grand, D., Griscelli, C., and Vassalli, P., *Eur. J. Immunol.* **4,** 435, 1974.
18. Elson, C. O., Heck, J. A., and Strober, W., *J. Exp. Med.* **149,** 632, 1979.
19. Ey, P. L., Prowse, S. J., and Jenkin, C. R., *Immunochemistry* **15,** 429, 1978.
20. Axen, R., Porath, J., and Ernback, S., *Nature (London)* **214,** 1302, 1967.
21. Lieberman, R., and Humphrey, W., *Proc. Nat. Acad. Sci. USA* **68,** 2510, 1971.
22. Wood, B. T., Thompson, S. H., and Goldstein, G., *J. Immunol.* **95,** 225, 1965.
23. Cebra, J. J., and Goldstein, G., *J. Immunol.* **95,** 230, 1965.
24. Cebra, J. J., Gearhart, P., Robertson, S., and Tseng, J., *Trans. Biochem. Soc. (London)* **5,** 1565, 1977.
25. Julius, M. H., Simpson, E., and Herzenberg, L. A., *Eur. J. Immunol.* **3,** 645, 1973.
26. Marshak-Rothstein, A., Fink, P., Gridley, T., Raulet, D. H., Bevan, M. J., and Gefter, M. L., *J. Immunol.* **122,** 2491, 1979.
27. Spring, S. B., Nisonoff, A., and Dray, S., *J. Immunol.* **105,** 653, 1970.
28. Greenwood, F. C., Hunter, W. M., and Glover, J. S., *Biochem. J.* **89,** 114, 1963.
29. Jacobson, E. B., and Herzenberg, L. A., *J. Exp. Med.* **135,** 1151, 1972.
30. Pierce, N. F., and Gowans, J. L., *J. Exp. Med.* **142,** 1550, 1975.
31. McWilliams, M., Phillip-Qualiata, J., and Lamm, M. E., *J. Immunol.* **115,** 54, 1975.
32. Husband, A. J., and Gowans, J. L., *J. Exp. Med.* **148,** 1146, 1978.
33. Kishimoto, T., and Ishizaka, K., *J. Immunol.* **111,** 720, 1973.
34. Ishizaka, K., and Adachi, T., *J. Immunol.* **117,** 40, 1976.
35. Black, S., and Herzenberg, L. A., *J. Exp. Med.* **150,** 174, 1979.
36. Wanebo, H. J., Gallmeir, W. W., Boyse, E. A., and Old, L. J., *Science* **154,** 901, 1966.

CELLULAR IMMUNOLOGY **65**, 258–271 (1981)

In Vitro Stimulation of Mouse NK Cell Activity by Phorbol Esters: A Pathway Different from Interferon-Induced Activation

JEAN-PIERRE B. KOLB,* ANNA SENIK,* AND MONIQUE CASTAGNA†

*Laboratories of *Cellular Immunology and †Cellular Dynamics, Institut de Recherches Scientifiques sur le Cancer, B.P. No. 8, 94802 Villejuif Cedex, France*

Received July 15, 1981; accepted September 30, 1981

Tumor promoters of the phorbol diester type were tested *in vitro* for their effect on mouse natural killer (NK) activity. The 12-*O*-tetradecanoyl-phorbol-13-acetate (TPA) significantly increased the spontaneous cytotoxicity of spleen cells preincubated with this reagent, with a maximal effect at 10–20 ng/ml. Higher concentrations of the weak tumor promoter phorbol-12,13-dibenzoate (PDB) were required to display the same NK-enhancing property, while the inactive tumor promoter 4-αphorboldidecanoate was ineffective at any concentration. TPA-responding spleen cells displayed the same characteristics as classical NK cells: they were present in nude mice, did not adhere to nylon wool, bore the Thy-1 antigen, and displayed the same target cell specificity as interferon-activated NK cells. A major difference with the interferon-induced NK activation resides in the fact that the TPA-inducible increase in lytic activity does not require RNA and protein synthesis. Our results suggest two different NK activation pathways for IFN and phorbol esters.

INTRODUCTION

Understanding of the physiological mechanisms for regulation of the natural killer activity has recently progressed with the discovery of the enhancing effects of interferons on murine and human natural killer (NK) cells (1–3). Beside this "positive" signal provided by molecules of interferons of both α or γ type (4), inhibitory effects, such as the ones exerted by prostaglandins (5), leading to a marked decrease of the NK activity, have been described.

In the present work we asked the question whether tumor promoters of the phorbol ester type, such as 12-*O*-tetradecanoyl-phorbol-13-acetate (TPA) could affect NK activity. The choice of this reagent was prompted by three different experimental findings. First TPA has been shown to enhance interferon production under certain conditions (6). Second, it is well established that TPA can influence the terminal differentiation of specialized cells, including those of the immune system. For instance TPA increases the LAF production (lymphocyte-activating factor) by macrophages (7), enhances the tumoricidal capacity of macrophages (8) and, on the contrary, inhibits the antibody secretion by B cells (9). Third, phorbol esters cause physicochemical alterations of the cell membranes (10), such as altered transport of ions and metabolites (11, 12), enhanced phospholipid metabolism (13), and modified membrane-bound enzyme activities (14, 15).

Our experiments show that *in vitro* pretreatment of mouse spleen cells with TPA

0008-8749/81/180258-14$02.00/0

results in a significant NK cell stimulation. Phorbol esters less active as tumor promoters than TPA, such as phorboldibenzoate (PDB) or inactive such as 4-α-phorboldidecanoate (4-α-PDD) were found to display an enhancing capacity of NK cells proportional to their tumor-promoting action.

The mechanism of this stimulation differs markedly from that involved in the enhancement of NK activity by interferon since the former requires no RNA and protein synthesis. It is suggested that TPA enhances the intrinsic cytotoxic potential of individual NK cells, presumably by direct cell membrane modification.

MATERIALS AND METHODS

Mice. Two-month-old BALB/c mice and athymic nude BALB/c and C57BL/6 mice were obtained from the breeding colonies of the IRSC.

Target cells.

Cells	Characteristics	Type of growth
YAC-1	Moloney virus-induced lymphoma in A/Sn mouse	Cell culture
YAC-222	A subline of YAC-1 cells, originally provided by Dr. K. T. Brünner	Ascitic form
L1210	Methylcholanthrene-induced lymphoma in DBA-2 mouse	Cell culture
K562	Human myeloid leukemia	Cell culture
MOLT-4	Human T-cell lymphoma	Cell culture

Cell cultures were grown in suspension in RPMI 1640 medium (Eurobio) containing 10% fetal calf serum (Eurobio), 100 IU/ml penicillin, and 100 μg/ml streptomycin.

Phorbol esters. 12-*O*-Tetradecanoyl-phorbol-13-acetate (TPA) phorbol-12,13-dibenzoate (PDB), and 4-α-phorbol-12,13-didecanoate (4-α-PDD) were purchased from P. Borchert, Eden Prairie, Minnesota. Stock solutions were made 0.02% in DMSO and stored in the dark at $-20°$C. Dilutions were made up in acetone before use and 5 μl of the reagents was added to 1 ml of cell suspensions.

Interferon. Semipurified viral IFNα mouse interferon was the gift of Dr. I. Gresser. Its specific activity was 2.8×10^6 reference units/mg of protein.

Assay for interferon. Supernatants from spleen cells incubated with the phorbol esters were tested by Dr. D. Brouty-Boyé (Laboratoire d'Oncologie Virale, Villejuif) for the presence of interferon, by a sensitive cytopathogenic inhibition test on mouse L or 10 T 1/2 cells, with vesicular stomatitis virus as challenge (16). In one case, the supernatant was concentrated by precipitation with saturated ammonium sulfate and the 0–50 and 50–70% fractions were tested for the presence of interferon in the same way.

In vitro treatment of spleen cells with phorbol esters or interferon. Spleen cells (2×10^7 ml) suspended in 1 ml culture medium (RPMI 1640 supplemented with 10% fetal calf serum, 100 units/ml of penicillin, and 100 μg/ml streptomycin) were incubated for 3 hr, at 37°C with 5 μl of phorbol esters at graded concentrations, or with the same volume of acetone in the controls. Cells were washed twice with the culture medium and tested for cytotoxicity. The same procedure was used for *in vitro* stimulation by interferon.

Cytotoxicity test. YAC-1 target cells (10^7) were suspended in 1 ml serum-free medium and labeled with 150 μCi of $Na_2{}^{51}CrO_4$ (specific activity, 166 mCi/mg; 614 GBq/mg; C.E.A., Saclay, France), for 1 hr at 37°C. They were then washed twice and adjusted to a concentration of 2×10^6/ml in culture medium. ^{51}Cr-labeled target cells (0.1 ml) were mixed with 0.1 ml of spleen cells in each well of 6-mm flat-bottomed Falcon TC 3040 microtest plates at an effector:target cell ratio varying from 100:1 to 12:1. Cultures were set up in triplicate, and incubated for 4 hr at 37°C in a humidified atmosphere containing 5% CO_2 in air. At the end of the incubation period 100 μl of the supernates was transferred into tubes and counted in multichannel gamma spectrometer (Multigamma-LKB). The percentage of specific ^{51}Cr release was determined according to the formula $(E - S)/(T - S) \times 100$, where E is the ^{51}Cr release in the presence of the effector spleen cells, S the spontaneous ^{51}Cr release, and T the total release in presence of 2 N HCl.

Spleen cell fractionation procedures. Removal of macrophages from a whole spleen cell population was performed according to the technique of Ly and Mishell (17) by filtration through a column of Sephadex G-10.

Removal of adherent and B cells was performed according to the technique of Julius *et al.* (18) by filtration through nylon wool columns.

Removal of Thy-1-positive cells was achieved using an anti-Thy-1.2 monoclonal antibody secreted by the hybridoma clone F7D5 purchased from Olac (Bicester, Oxon, England); 20×10^6 nude C57BL/6 spleen cells were pelleted and resuspended in antibody-containing medium (final dilution, 1:1000) for 30 min at 0°C. After washing, the cells were resuspended in 2 ml of selected "low tox" rabbit serum as a source of complement (at 1:15 final dilution) and were incubated for 45 min at 37°C.

Inhibitors of DNA, RNA, and protein synthesis. Various inhibitors were tested for their possible action on the TPA-induced activation of natural killer cells. Cytosine arabinoside (Ara-C), actinomycin D, and cycloheximide (Sigma, St. Louis, Mo.) which are inhibitors of DNA, RNA, and protein synthesis, respectively, were added to the cell suspensions 30 min before the addition of TPA and left during the incubation period with the phorbol ester. The cells were then washed twice to remove TPA, then resuspended in fresh culture medium containing the respective inhibitors. We had shown in a previous paper (19) that under these conditions the spontaneous NK activity was unaffected by the presence of these inhibitors during the ^{51}Cr release test at the concentrations of 50 μg/ml cycloheximide and 25 μg/ml actinomycin D used in our tests. Spontaneous release of ^{51}Cr from labeled YAC-1 cells was also found to be unchanged in the presence of inhibitors. RNA and protein synthesis were monitored by measuring the amount of [^{3}H] uridine and [^{3}H]leucine incorporation, respectively. Briefly, aliquots of the spleen cell suspensions, containing 1×10^6 cells, were placed in the wells of a flat-bottomed Falcon microtest II plate and 1 μCi of either isotope was added: [^{3}H]Uridine ([5,6-^{3}H]uridine, specific activity, 38.3 Ci/mmol) was purchased from New England Nuclear, Boston, Massachusetts, and [^{3}H]leucine (L[-4,5-^{3}H]leucine, specific activity, 146 Ci/mmol) was purchased from the Radiochemical Center, Amersham, England. After the appropriate time, the cells were disrupted and the fraction insoluble in 10% trichloroacetic acid was collected on glass-fiber filters using a multiple automated sample harvester (Mash II, Microbiological Associates, Bethesda, Md.), and counted in a liquid scintillation counter (1216, Rackbeta, LKB).

Target binding-cell assay (TBCA). TBCA was performed according to the technique of Roder *et al.* (20). Briefly, 10^8 spleen cells from C57BL/6 *nu/nu* mice were treated with distilled water for 8 sec to remove erythrocytes, then filtered through a column of 0.6 g of nylon wool. The nonadherent cells were recovered, incubated for 15 min with TPA at 15 ng/ml, then washed. Part of the cell suspension was tested for NK activity in a 4-hr ^{51} Cr release test and the remaining cells were labeled with fluorescein isothiocyanate (FITC). FITC-labeled cells (2×10^5) were mixed with 2×10^6 YAC-1 cells in 0.2 ml medium, centrifuged at 200*g* for 5 min at room temperature, then resuspended by gentle agitation. The percentage of fluorescent lymphoid cells binding to YAC-1 tumor cells was assessed by uv microscopic examination using a Leitz Orthoplan fluorescence microscope.

RESULTS

Effects of Various Phorbol Diesters on Spontaneous Mouse Spleen Cell Cytotoxicity

Spleen cells from normal or athymic nude BALB/c mice were incubated *in vitro* with increasing concentrations of TPA, PDB, or 4-α-PDD, washed extensively and tested for cytotoxicity against NK-sensitive YAC-1 target cells. A representative experiment, depicted in Fig. 1, indicates that TPA and PDB treatments resulted in a marked increase in the lytic capacity of the effector cells. Acetone, at the concentration used to dissolve the phorbol esters (0.5%), had no effect on NK activity and was nontoxic. The ability of TPA to stimulate spleen cell cytotoxicity was seen with as little as 5–10 ng/ml, while PDB stimulating effect was observed with at least 100 ng/ml. In contrast, 4-α-PDD was not stimulatory at any concentration tested up to 1000 ng/ml. Thus, the increase in spleen cell cytotoxicity against YAC-1 target cells by phorbol esters appears to be in correlation with their potency of tumor promotion: PDB known to be a less active tumor promoter than TPA was stimulatory at 10 times the optimal stimulatory concentration of TPA, whereas 4-α-PDD, an analog of PDB that is inactive as a tumor promoter, failed to enhance spleen cell cytotoxicity.

Figure 2 summarizes the general pattern of the dose–response curve established from 11 different experiments and points to the fact that the TPA effect was reproducible at low concentrations (10–20 ng/ml) whereas activation performed with a 100 ng/ml TPA concentration was not consistently reproducible. Moreover, in some experiments inhibition of spontaneous killing was observed when TPA was used at as much as 100–1000 ng/ml.

Kinetics of the Enhancing Effect of TPA

TPA (10 ng/ml) was added to *nu/nu* spleen cell suspensions at different times after the beginning of a 3-hr incubation period. The effector cells were washed twice to remove TPA, then tested for cytotoxicity. In Table 1, it can be seen that a 10-min contact with TPA was nearly sufficient for completing the full expression

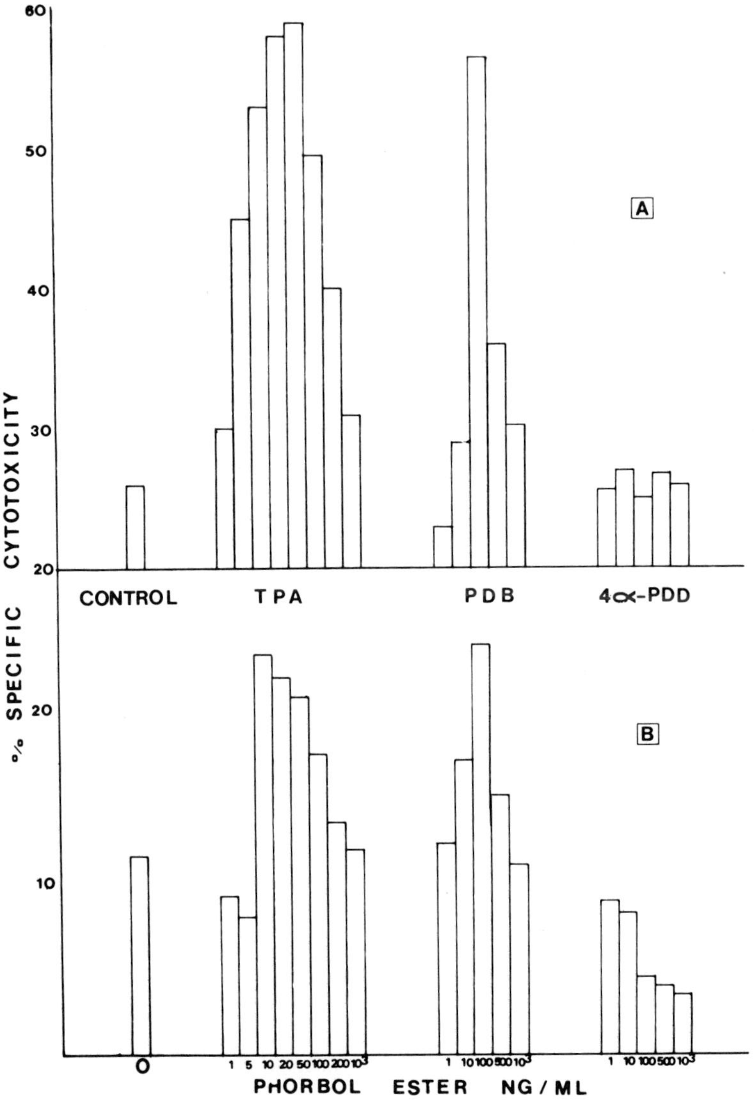

FIG. 1. Differential effects of TPA, PDB, and 4-α-PDD on the spontaneous killing activity of spleen cells from BALB/c nude mice (A) and normal BALB/c (B). Spleen cells were incubated with graded doses of the phorbol esters for 3 hr at 37°C, washed and tested in a 4-hr ^{51}Cr release test on 10^4 YAC-1 target cells at an attacker:target cell ratio of 100:1.

of TPA-enhanced cytotoxicity. Extending the time of contact with TPA up to 180 min resulted in only a slightly higher degree of stimulation.

TPA-Activated Cytotoxic Cells Display the Same Target Specificity as IFN-Activated NK Cells

The ability of TPA-treated spleen cells to lyse various tumor cells was tested simultaneously with that of INF-treated spleen cells. As shown in Table 2, TPA-

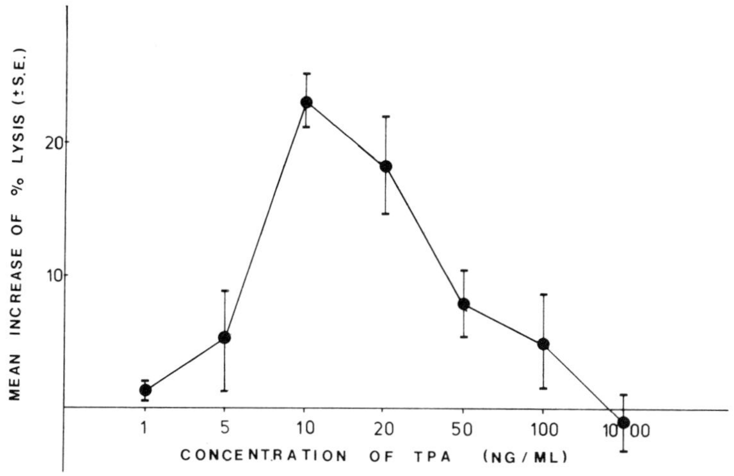

FIG. 2. Dose–effect relationship of the TPA-induced increase of spontaneous mouse spleen cell cytotoxicity. The mean increase of cytotoxicity against YAC-1 target cells (as measured by the augmentation of the percent of specific lysis displayed by TPA-treated splenocytes from $C_{57}Bl/6$ nude mice, minus the percentage of specific lysis of the control splenocytes, ±SE) has been plotted on the ordinate, and the concentration of TPA on the abscissa.

or IFN-enhanced cytotoxicity was evident on YAC-1, K562, and MOLT-4 tumor cells which are known to be NK-sensitive target cells (although the xenogeneic K562 and MOLT-4 tumor cells were lysed to a lesser extent than mouse YAC-1 cells). The degree of lysis shown by TPA and IFN-activated effector cells were the same for each tumor cell tested. In contrast, L 1210 and YAC-222 tumor cells, which display poor susceptibility to NK lysis, remained fully resistant to the cytotoxic action of both kinds of effector cells. These data indicate that TPA-stimulated cytotoxic cells behave exactly as interferon-activated NK cells in regard to their ability to discriminate among the different target cells used in this study.

TABLE 1

Kinetics of the Enhancing Effect of TPA on Spleen Cell Cytotoxicity[a]

Duration of TPA application (10 ng/ml) (min)	Attacker:target cell ratio 100:1	50:1
180	55.7[b]	34.4
120	47.8	31.7
60	36.0	23.4
30	38.3	30.0
10	41.4	28.2
Control (180-min incubation without TPA)	19.3	14.2

[a] Spleen cells from nude C57BL/6 mice were used in this experiment. TPA was applied on spleen cell suspensions at successive times of a total 180 min-preincubation period. Cells were then washed and tested for cytotoxicity on YAC-1 target cells.

[b] The results are expressed as percentage specific lysis. SE did not exceed ±5%.

TABLE 2

Cytolytic Cells Induced by TPA Manifest the Same Target Specificity as Interferon-Activated NK Cells

Preincubation with[a]	Target cells	Percentage specific lysis[b]
Medium	L1210	3.7
INFα		2.2
TPA		3.2
Medium	YAC-222	0.7
IFNα		3.4
TPA		0.8
Medium	YAC-1	20.1
IFNα		39.7
TPA		37.4
Medium	K562	9.7
IFNα		17.0
TPA		16.7
Medium	MOLT-4	13.1
IFNα		20.6
TPA		19.3

[a] C57BL/6 *nu/nu* spleen cells were pretreated for 3 hr with 2×10^3 units of interferon/ml or 10 ng/ml TPA, washed and tested for cytotoxicity.

[b] Attacker:cell ratio was 100:1. SE did not exceed ±3%.

Cytotoxic Cells Stimulated by TPA Display the Same Surface Characteristics as NK Cells

(i) Elimination of the macrophages and B cells. Filtration of nude mice spleen cells through a Sephadex G-10 column (which removes macrophages) or through a nylon wool column (which eliminates macrophages and B cells) left the whole NK basal activity in the nonadherent cell population, as well as the ability of effector cells to respond to active phorbol ester (Table 3). In contrast, the adherent cells were almost devoid of NK activity and could not be stimulated by the phorbol esters.

(ii) Elimination of Thy-1⁺ cells. As TPA activation was obtained with spleen cells from athymic nude mice, a role for mature T cells in the induced cytotoxicity could also be ruled out. Since it is now established that mouse NK cells possess a low density of Thy-1 antigen on their cell membrane (21), we tested the effect of a potent monoclonal anti-Thy-1.2 antibody and complement on the interferon and TPA-enhanced cytotoxic responses. As shown in Table 4 spleen cells from nude C57BL/6 mice became, after such a treatment, unable to display any spontaneous killing and failed to show any increased cytotoxicity after interferon and TPA treatments. Taken together, these data show that TPA-responsive cytotoxic cells, in terms of cell-surface characteristics, belong to the same pool of NK cells responsible for the spontaneous NK activity and for the interferon-enhanced spleen cell cytotoxicity.

TABLE 3

TPA or PB Only Stimulate Nylon Wool or Sephadex G-10 Nonadherent Spleen Cells

Effector cells	Preincubation with[a]	Attacker:target cell ratio[b] 100:1	50:1
Experiment 1 (nude BALB/c)			
Whole spleen cells	Medium	10.1[c]	8.9
	TPA	19.5	18.1
	PDB	20.0	19.2
Nylon wool nonadherent spleen cells	Medium	16.7	12.8
	TPA	42.1	38.4
	PDB	47.5	39.1
Nylon wool adherent spleen cells	Medium	5.0	1.9
	TPA	2.1	5.5
Experiment 2 (nude C57BL/6)			
Whole spleen cells	Medium	54.5	
	TPA	75.5	
Sephadex G-10 nonadherent cells	Medium	55.3	
	TPA	92.2	

[a] TPA used at 10 ng/ml and PDB at 100 ng/ml for 2-hr preincubation period.
[b] Target cells were YAC-1 cells.
[c] Results are expressed as percentage specific lysis. SE did not exceed ±3%.

Mechanism for in Vitro Activation of NK Cells by TPA

(i) Interferon is not produced at detectable levels during TPA activation. TPA has been reported to potentiate the synthesis of IFN_γ interferon (6) which in turn can activate NK cells (4). The question then arose of the possible involvement of interferon in our system. However, no interferon could be detected in supernatants of cells incubated with TPA when using a sensitive cytopathogenic inhibition test (16), even after ammonium sulfate precipitation and 50-fold concentration of the supernatants (data not shown).

(ii) TPA-inducible NK cells do not require cell division nor RNA and protein synthesis. The rapidity of NK activation by TPA made unlikely the involvement of cell division in this process. This was confirmed by treating the effector cells with Ara-C for 30 min before the addition of TPA and throughout the whole test. As seen in Table 5 this treatment did not affect the TPA-induced NK activity.

It is known from our previous studies that newly synthesized RNA and proteins are required for *in vitro* activation of mouse NK cells by interferon (19). Yet, when cycloheximide or actinomycin D were added to spleen cells during the preincubation with TPA, and during the ^{51}Cr release test itself, at doses inhibiting more than 90% of the incorporations of [^{3}H]leucine and [^{3}H]uridine, respectively, the TPA-enhancing effect on NK cells remained unchanged (Table 5). Our results also indicate that the inhibition of protein and RNA synthesis did not affect the cytotoxicity level of already committed NK cells, nor the spontaneous ^{51}Cr release from target cells. Since new protein and RNA synthesis are required for IFN-induced NK cytotoxicity (see Table 5) but not for TPA-induced NK cytotoxicity,

TABLE 4

Effect of a Monoclonal Anti-Thy-1.2 Antibody + Complement Treatment on the Cytotoxic Responses Induced by Interferon and TPA in *nu/nu* C57BL/6 Spleen Cells[a]

Spleen cell treatment	Stimulation with	Attacker:target cell ratio 100:1	50:1
None	—	23.0[b]	17.7
	IFNα	33.9	27.8
	TPA	33.1	22.7
Monoclonal anti-Thy-1.2 Antibody + rabbit Complement	—	4.7	4.1
	IFNα	7.4	5.4
	TPA	3.7	2.0
Monoclonal anti-Thy-1.2 Antibody alone	—	19.8	15.0
	IFNα	30.6	25.4
	TPA	29.9	19.8
Rabbit complement alone	—	20.8	16.7
	IFNα	31.2	26.3
	TPA	32.1	27.4

[a] Spleen cells were pretreated with IFNα (2×10^3 units/ml) or TPA (10 ng/ml) for 3 hr, washed twice, and tested for cytotoxicity against YAC-1 targets.

[b] Results are expressed as percentage specific lysis. SE did not exceed ±4%.

TABLE 5

Comparison between the Effects of Inhibitors of Proteins, RNA, and DNA Synthesis on Interferon and TPA-Induced Increase in NK Activity[a]

Metabolic inhibitors	Stimulation with	Percentage specific lysis	[^{3}H]Leucine incorporation (cpm/10^6 cells)	[^{3}H]Uridine incorporation (cpm/10^6 cells)
None	—	17.2	3.365	101,511
	IFNα	36.5	3.850	116,000
	TPA	30.2	6.569	268,817
Cycloheximide (50 μg/ml)	—	19.3	359	—
	IFNα	18.4	410	—
	TPA	29.0	508	—
Actinomycin D (25 μg/ml)	—	19.1	—	7.707
	IFNα	19.7	—	7.754
	TPA	30.7	—	7.815
Ara-C (10 μg/ml)	—	18.9	—	—
	IFNα	32.4	—	—
	TPA	31.9	—	—

[a] C57BL/6 *nu/nu* spleen cells were pretreated for 3 hr with either 2×10^3 units/ml of IFNα or 10 ng/ml TPA. Metabolic inhibitors were present during the pretreatment period and also during the cytotoxicity assay. Percentage specific lysis was determined at a 100:1 attacker:target cell ratio. Spontaneous release from radiolabeled YAC-1 targets was 16.8% in medium alone, 17.2% in presence of actinomycin D, 15.6% in presence of cycloheximide, and 16.5% in presence of Ara-C.

we conclude that the activation pathways involved in these two processes are different.

(iii) TPA does not alter the number of target binding cells. Previous studies from Roder *et al.* (20) have shown that the percentage of target-binding cells (TBC) in the nonadherent fraction of a spleen cell population correlates with the degree of NK lysis. We therefore determined whether the TPA-induced NK activity was associated with any change in the number of TBC.

We found that the percentage of TBC in nonadherent *nu/nu* spleen cells (recovered from a nylon wool column) was the same, whether the effector cells had been previously treated with TPA or not (Table 6). This result argues against a recruitment of new NK cells by TPA, but rather favors the possibility that the promoter enhances the cytolytic capacity of precommitted NK cells at the single cell level.

(iv) Pretreatment of YAC-1 target cells with TPA. The possibility remained that TPA molecules shed from the membrane of effector cells during the chromium release test would affect the spontaneous ^{51}Cr release from these cells. However, as shown in Table 7, incubation of YAC-1 tumor cells with graded doses of TPA, followed by extensive washing, did not affect the spontaneous ^{51}Cr release from these cells. Moreover susceptibility to NK lysis remained unchanged when target cells were pretreated with up to 100 ng/ml TPA. Yet increasing the concentration of TPA up to 200 ng/ml was followed by a significant inhibition of NK activity, which indicates that TPA-induced modifications of YAC-1 cells can occur at high doses of this reagent, modifying target cell susceptibility to lysis.

DISCUSSION

In the present study it is shown that *in vitro* pretreatment of mouse spleen cells with the phorbol esters TPA and PDB results in a pronounced enhancement of NK activity. This effect was dose dependent: the peak of the induced response was obtained with 10–20 ng/ml TPA (a potent tumor promoter) and with 100–200 ng/ml PDB (a weak tumor promoter). In contrast, phorbol ester 4-α-PDD (inactive as a tumor promoter), failed to enhance NK activity. Thus, there was a positive

TABLE 6

Effect of TPA Treatment on the Percentage of Target-Binding Cells (TBC)

Attacker cells (nude C57BL/6 spleen cells)	Pretreatment with TPA (10 ng/ml)[a]	Percentage TBC	Percentage specific lysis[b]
Whole spleen cells	No	Not done	8.5
	Yes	Not done	22.8
Nylon wool nonadherent spleen cells	No	23.2	19.5
	Yes	27.4	30.6

[a] Incubation of cells with TPA for 150 min.

[b] Attacker:target cell ratio was 40:1. SE did not exceed ±3%.

TABLE 7

Target Cell Susceptibility to NK Lysis after Pretreatment with TPA

Concentration of TPA[a] (ng/ml)	Percentage ^{51}Cr spontaneous release[b]	Percentage specific lysis[c]
0	10.3	54.3
10	11.4	51.3
20	10.4	52.5
100	10.8	58.2
200	11.8	38.2 ($P < 0.01$)[d]

[a] YAC-1 target cells were pretreated for 90 min with graded doses of TPA, washed, labeled with ^{51}Cr, and mixed with C57BL/6 nude spleen cells at an attacker:target cell ratio of 100:1.

[b] Defined as (cpm spontaneous release/cpm maximum release) × 100.

[c] SE did not exceed ±3.5%.

[d] The different groups were compared using the variance analysis test.

correlation between the enhancing properties of the phorbol esters on the NK system and their tumor-promoting activity.

Recently, several authors have reported an inhibitory effect of TPA upon the NK activity in rat (22), mouse (23), and man (24). The reason for this discrepancy is not quite clear, but several points deserve comment. In Keller's experiments with the rat system, TPA was present during the ^{51}Cr release test and thus an effect on the target cell could not be excluded; in fact, as shown in Table 7, pretreatment of the YAC-1 target cells with TPA resulted, at relatively high concentrations, in a decreased susceptibility of this target to the NK lysis. In addition, Seaman *et al.* (24), in a human system, found that pretreatments of both the effector or the target cells with TPA led to an inhibition of the NK lysis, but that the inhibition was even greater when TPA was present during the ^{51}Cr release test.

In our hands pretreatment of the attacker cells with 10–20 ng/ml TPA, very reproducibly resulted in a marked increase of the NK lysis, and these concentrations are similar to those used by Goldfarb *et al.* (23); it should be stressed, however, that in our experiments, for high concentrations of TPA, either stimulation or inhibition of NK lysis were observed. It is of value to note that, whatever the resulting effect on NK cells, either stimulatory or inhibitory, this effect parallels the tumor-promoting capacity of the phorbol ester used.

It should also be emphasized that such opposite effects of TPA are already known, as in the case of the conflicting data obtained by different groups reporting either a decrease (22) or an increase (8, 25) of the tumoricidal capacity of TPA-treated macrophages. In fact, Schultz *et al.* (26) have clearly shown that slight modifications of the experimental conditions in the treatment of macrophages with TPA will result either in a stimulation or an inhibition of their control of neoplastic cell growth.

The role of the macrophages is, we believe, crucial since Seaman *et al.* (24) have clearly pointed out that the TPA-induced inhibition of the NK activity of human peripheral blood cells was greatly reduced and even sometimes replaced by a stimulating effect when adherent cells were removed, suggesting a suppressive role of the monocytes. The importance of the regulatory role of macrophages in the control of the NK activity has already been suggested in other systems where contradictory results have been reported, as in the case of the pyran copolymer and adriamycin (27). In our experiments, whether macrophages be present or not, we always observed a stimulatory effect on the NK cells. Yet, as evidenced in Table 3, removal of adherent cells by Sephadex G-10 filtration resulted in a much greater stimulation of the NK activity by TPA.

Experiments of reconstitution of adherent cell-depleted splenocytes with macrophages treated with TPA, or not, are now in progress to elucidate a possible suppressive role of the macrophages. Finally, we should add that our mice are bred in conditions free of specific pathogens, which might have some implications upon the physiological status of their macrophages.

The cytotoxic cells responding to TPA could not be distinguished by classical spleen cell fractionation procedures from the pool of cells involved in the spontaneous natural killing or the interferon-inducible activity: they were found in nude mice, they were nonadherent to nylon wool or Sephadex G-10, and displayed the same target specificity as interferon-stimulated NK cells. Besides, they were found to be Thy-1 positive, which is in accordance with the results of Herberman *et al.* (21) showing the expression of low Thy-1 antigen density on mouse NK cells.

Like interferon, TPA seems to act directly on NK cells, since spleen cell fractionation procedures performed before the addition of TPA still allowed the cytotoxic NK response. It rapidly triggers the NK cytolytic mechanism, a 10-min contact between spleen cells and TPA being sufficient to reach a significant enhancement. Furthermore, TPA activates NK lysis to the same extent as interferon does.

The possibility that TPA might recruit new NK effector cells or modify the affinity of their receptors, as described for the epidermal growth factor (28) was investigated using the target binding-cell assay of Roder *et al.* (20). However, after treatment of spleen cells with TPA, no modification in the percentage of cells rosetting with the YAC-1 cells could be detected, as compared with the control. This suggests that the observed increase of the lytic capacity occurs on a per cell basis.

The mechanism of TPA-induced activation of NK cells is still to be elucidated. Insertion of TPA molecules into the lipid bilayer of the cell membrane is followed by marked changes in the membrane fluidity (29, 30) and in ion transports (11). Besides, TPA is known to alter some membrane bound activities such as the Na^+,K^+- and Ca^{2+}, Mg^{2+}-ATPases (14) and to increase the release of plasminogen activator (15). Since an enzymatic activity of the serine esterase type has been postulated in the lytic mechanism of NK cells (31), TPA-induced activation of NK cells might originate from such modulations of membrane-bound enzymes.

Another alternative could be that TPA enhances the release of lysosomal enzymes (32), since such a stimulus-secretion mechanism is known to play a role in the NK lytic system (33).

Whatever the mechanism involved in TPA-induced enhancement of NK lysis, a striking difference exists between the activation pathways triggered by interferon and TPA: while interferon-induced activation of NK cells is dependent on both new RNA and protein synthesis (19, 34, 35) TPA-induced activation does not require such synthesis. In the case of interferon-induced increase of reactivity, the need for synthesis of new RNA and proteins suggests either a differentiation of fully active NK cells from pre-NK cells inactive or with a low efficiency, or a further enhancement of the lytic capacity of NK cells already endowed with a cytotoxic ability, as already discussed by Djeu *et al.* (35) and Senik *et al.* (19).

On the other hand, in view of the accumulated data concerning the TPA-induced alterations of cell membrane properties, we favor the hypothesis that TPA acts on NK cells via modifications of the cell surface, possibly coupled to intracellular processes. Our results emphasize that TPA action on the NK system is not simple, since tumor target cells as well as effector cytotoxic cells are simultaneously affected, in opposite manners, and since other parameters, like macrophages, can modify the TPA-induced behavior of NK cells (24). Nevertheless these results provide clear evidence that NK cell activation can proceed by different pathways when interferon and TPA are used as stimulating agents. They corroborate the finding that interferon-independent activations of NK activity can occur, as reported by Brunda *et al.* (36), using alloantibodies or lectins as stimulatory reagents. It is noteworthy that NK activation by TPA and by these other reagents was achieved without need for RNA and protein synthesis, suggesting a mechanism centered on cell membrane modifications.

REFERENCES

1. Gidlund, M., Örn, A., Wigzell, H., Senik, A., and Gresser, I., *Nature (London)* **273,** 759, 1978.
2. Djeu, J. Y., Heinbaugh, J. A., Holden, H. T., and Herberman, R. B., *J. Immunol.* **122,** 175, 1979.
3. Trinchieri, G., and Santoli, D., *J. Exp. Med.* **147,** 1314, 1978.
4. Senik, A., Stefanos, S., Kolb, J. P., Lucero, M., and Falcoff, E., *Ann. Immunol. (Paris)* **131C,** 349, 1980.
5. Droller, M. J., Perlmann, P., and Schneider, M. U., *Cell, Immunol.* **39,** 154, 1978.
6. Vilcek, J., Sulea, I. T., Volvovitz, F., and Yip, Y. K., *In* "Biochemical Characterization of Lymphokines" (A. L. Weck, F. Kristensen, and M. Landy, Eds.), p. 323. Academic Press, New York, 1980.
7. Mizel, S. B., Rosenstreich, D. L., and Oppenheim, J. J., *Cell. Immunol.* **40,** 230, 1978.
8. Laskin, D. L., Kessler, F. K., Banks, W. L., Weinstein, I. B., and Carchman, R. A., *AACR Abstracts* 107, 1980.
9. Castagna, M., Yagello, M., Rabourdin-Combe, C., and Fridman, W. H., *Cancer Lett.* **8,** 365, 1980.
10. Wenner, C. E., Hackney, J., Kimelberg, H. K., and Mayhew, E., *Cancer Res.* **34,** 1731, 1974.
11. Moroney, J., Smith, A., Tomei, L. D., and Wenner, C. E., *J. Cell. Physiol.* **95,** 287, 1978.
12. Driedger, P. E., and Blumberg, P. M., *Cancer Res.* **37,** 3257, 1977.
13. Rohrschneider, L. R., and Boutwell, R. K., *Cancer Res.* **33,** 1945, 1973.
14. Bos, C. J., and Emmelot, P. B., *Chem–Biol. Interact.* **8,** 249, 1974.
15. Wigler, M., and Weinstein, I. B., *Nature (London)* **259,** 232, 1976.
16. Gresser, I., Fontaine-Brouty Boyé, D., Bourali, C., and Thomas, M. T., *Proc. Soc. Exp. Biol. Med.* **130,** 236, 1969.
17. Ly, I. A., and Mishell, R. I., *J. Immunol. Methods* **5,** 239, 1974.
18. Julius, M. H., Simpson, E., and Herzenberg, L. A., *Eur. J. Immunol.* **3,** 645, 1973.
19. Senik, A., Kolb, J. P., Örn, A., and Gidlund, M., *Scand J. Immunol.* **12,** 51, 1980.
20. Roder, J. C., and Kiessling, R., *Scand. J. Immunol.* **8,** 135, 1978.
21. Herberman, R. B., Nunn, M. E., and Holden, H. T., *J. Immunol.* **121,** 304, 1978.
22. Keller, R., *Nature (London)* **282,** 279, 1979.
23. Goldfarb, R. H., and Herberman, R. B., *J. Immunol.* **126,** 2129, 1981.
24. Seaman, W. E., Gindhardt, T. D., Blackman, M. A., Dalal, B., Talal, N., and Werb, Z., *J. Clin. Invest.* **67,** 1324, 1981.
25. Grim, W., Barlin, E., Lesser, H. G., Kramer, W., and Gemsa, D., *Clin. Immunol. Immunopathol.* **17,** 617, 1980.

26. Schultz, R. M., Chirigos, M. A., and Olkowski, Z. L., *Cell. Immunol.* **54,** 98, 1980.
27. Santoni, A., Ricardi, C., Barlozzari, T., and Herberman, R. B., *In* "Natural-Cell Mediated Immunity against Tumors" (R. B., Herberman, Ed.), p. 753. Academic Press, New York, 1980.
28. Lee, L. S., and Weinstein, I. B., *Science* **202,** 313, 1978.
29. Sivak, A., Ray, F., and Van Douven, L., *Cancer Res.* **29,** 624, 1969.
30. Castagna, M., Rochette-Egly, C., Rosenfeld, C., and Mishal, Z., *FEBS Lett.* **100,** 62, 1979.
31. Roder, J. C. Kiessling, R., Biberfeld, P., and Andersson, B., *J. Immunol.* **121,** 2509, 1978.
32. Pfeiffer, C. J., and Cho, C. H., *Cancer Lett.* **10,** 51, 1980.
33. Roder, J. C., Argov, S., Klein, M., Petterson, C., Kiessling, R., Andersson, K., and Hansson, M., *Immunology* **40,** 107, 1980.
34. Ortaldo, J. R., Phillips, W., Wasserman, K., and Herberman, R. B., *J. Immunol.* **125,** 1839, 1980.
35. Djeu, J. Y., Stocks, N., Varesio, L., Holden, H. T., and Herberman, R. B., *Cell. Immunol.* **58,** 49, 1981.
36. Brunda, M. J. Herberman, R. B., and Holden, H. T., *In* "Natural Cell Mediated Immunity against Tumors" (R. B. Herberman, Ed.), p. 525. Academic Press, New York, 1980.

CELLULAR IMMUNOLOGY **65,** 272–279 (1981)

Murine T Cells That Lyse Antibody-Sensitized Target Cells

IV. Analysis of Thy 1 and Lyt Surface Antigen Expression among Thymic K Cells[1]

BRIAN A. POLLOK[2] AND EDDIE W. LAMON

Veterans Administration Hospital, Departments of Surgery and Microbiology, University of Alabama in Birmingham, Birmingham, Alabama 35294

Received June 2, 1981; accepted October 8, 1981

BALB/c murine thymocytes were progressively depleted of Thy 1.2-bearing cells using a monoclonal anti-Thy 1.2 IgM plus guinea pig complement. Surviving thymocytes were assayed for antibody-dependent cellular cytotoxicity (ADCC) at a constant effector-to-target cell ratio. Dramatic increases in ADCC activity within the surviving thymocyte population occur when increasing concentrations of anti-Thy 1.2 antibody are used during the depletion step, with maximal activity attained when 95% of all thymocytes are removed by the antibody and complement treatment. At anti-Thy 1.2 concentrations above this level, a concurrent loss in ADCC activity and Thy 1-positive cells among the surviving thymocyte pool is observed. This immunocompetent thymocyte subpopulation which can mediate ADCC expresses Thy 1 surface antigen at a level characteristic of mature T cells (a 10-fold lower density relative to cortical thymocytes) and also possesses a Lyt antigen phenotype of Lyt $1^{+}2,3^{+}$.

INTRODUCTION

The characterization of murine lymphoid cells capable of mediating antibody-dependent cellular cytotoxicity (ADCC) has demonstrated that killer (K) cell activity is not a property unique to any one cellular subpopulation (1). T lymphocytes (2–5), B lymphocytes (6), null (non-T, non-B) lymphocytes (7, 8), and macrophages (9, 10) have all been reported to possess ADCC activity, with this heterogeneity being reflective of the various experimental systems that are employed. Expression of functional Fc receptors is the marker common to these effector cell types and is prerequisite for capacity to act as K cells (1).

The ability of murine splenic T lymphocytes to function as K cells has been shown by ourselves and an independent group (4, 11) through the use of a monoclonal anti-Thy 1.2 IgM as a probe for this T-cell marker. Advantages in substituting the monoclonal IgM for conventional anti-Thy 1.2 sera include a higher complement fixing titer (1000-fold stronger) and elimination of nonspecific

[1] Supported by NCI Grant CA 17273-06 and V.A. Research Grant 5132-04. E. W. Lamon is a 1980/1981 Faculty Scholar of the Josiah Macy, Jr., Foundation, New York, N.Y.

[2] To whom correspondence should be addressed at: 224 Tumor Institute, University Station, University of Alabama in Birmingham, Birmingham, Alabama 35294.

0008-8749/81/180272-08$02.00/0

inhibition of effector cells by antigen–antibody complexes via Fc receptor blockade (4).

This monospecific reagent was in turn used to examine the nature of Thy 1 surface antigen expression among ADCC-active cells within the thymus. While it has been established that cortisone-resistant, medullary-localized thymocytes are capable of mediating ADCC at levels equal to splenic effector cells (12, 13), it is not known whether these thymus-localized K cells possess markers common to mature T cells. Herein we report on the relative level of Thy 1.2 antigen expression among thymic ADCC effector cells and, in addition, define their Lyt antigen phenotype.

MATERIALS AND METHODS

Mice. Six- to twelve-week-old BALB/c mice were used as a source of thymocytes.

Antisera. Adult C57B1/6 mice were injected three times at weekly intervals with 0.2 ml of a 50% suspension of bovine erythrocytes (ORBC). These animals were bled 5 days after the last inoculation and serum was heat-inactivated and stored at −20°C before use. Pooled anti-ORBC sera had an endpoint hemolytic titer of 1:2000 vs ORBC using fresh guinea pig serum as a complement source.

Media. RPMI 1640 (Flow Laboratories) containing 10% heat-inactivated fetal calf serum and 100 μg/ml gentamycin was used for all dilutions and incubations.

Preparation of thymocytes. Thymi were dissected out under aseptic conditions and pressed through fine nylon mesh into cold media. The cells were mixed with a Pasteur pipet and passed over a fine nylon mesh filter. Thymocytes were washed twice in cold media and resuspended at a 10^7 cells/ml concentration.

Depletion of thymocyte subpopulations by complement-dependent lysis. Monoclonal anti-Thy 1.2 IgM in the form of tissue culture supernatant (14) (kindly provided by G. Hämmerling, Heidelberg) was added at appropriate dilutions to the thymocyte suspension and the mixture held on ice for 10 min. A 1:30 dilution of guinea pig serum was then added as a complement source and the cells incubated for 45 min at 37°C. After washing, the viability of the anti-Thy 1.2-treated thymocytes was determined by trypan blue exclusion.

Anti-Thy 1.2-treated thymocyte preparations to be used for Lyt antigen studies were cleared of dead thymocytes by Ficoll–Hypaque density gradient centrifugation. Cellular viability of the interface fraction was >92%. Monoclonal anti-Lyt 1.2 and anti-Lyt 2.2 antibodies (AKR × BALB/c hybridoma, Cedarlane Laboratories) were used at a 1:50 dilution for cellular depletion (as before). After incubation at 37°C, the mixture was washed twice in serumless media, trypsin-digested for 30 min at 37°C to remove immune complexes and cellular debris, diluted with an equal volume of 20% serum-enriched media, filtered through a fine nylon mesh, and washed once with complete media before use.

Anti-Thy 1.2-treated thymocytes to be assayed directly for ADCC activity were digested with trypsin and washed as described.

Cytotoxicity assay. ORBC were labeled with ^{51}Cr ($Na^{51}CrO_4$, New England Nuclear; 250 μCi/1.5 × 10^7 cells) by incubation at 37°C for 2 hr. The cells were washed twice and sensitized with a 1:1000 dilution of the anti-ORBC sera for 1 hr at room temperature. The target cells were washed again and aliquoted at 10^4 cells/tube in triplicate together with effector cells to give an effector:target ratio of 8:1 (total volume, 0.3 ml). Controls consisted of effector cells mixed with non-sensitized target cells and sensitized target cells without effector cells present. The tubes were incubated at 37°C in 5% CO_2 for 4 hr. At the end of incubation, the cells were pelleted by centrifugation and the pellets and supernatants assayed for ^{51}Cr content in a well-type gamma counter. The maximum releasable counts were determined by adding 1 ml of distilled water to tubes containing sensitized target cells. Percentage of specific lysis was calculated using the formula:

$$\% \text{ lysis} = \frac{\% \, ^{51}\text{Cr release (experimental)} - \% \, ^{51}\text{Cr release (spontaneous)}}{\% \, ^{51}\text{Cr release (maximum)} - \% \, ^{51}\text{Cr release (spontaneous)}} \times 100.$$

Surface immunofluorescent staining. Lyt cell surface antigens were detected by first staining with monoclonal rat anti-Lyt 1 and anti-Lyt 2 antibodies (Becton–Dickinson) followed by a fluorescein-conjugated mouse anti-rat Ig antibody. Expression of Thy 1.2 was examined using the monoclonal anti-Thy 1.2 IgM (diluted 1:10) and a rhodamine-conjugated goat anti-mouse IgM antibody. The fluorochrome-tagged reagents did not stain murine thymocytes in the absence of the primary antibody and all staining was performed at 4°C in media containing 0.1% sodium azide (15).

RESULTS

Relative density of Thy 1.2 expressed on ADCC-active thymocytes. Progressive depletion of thymocytes with monoclonal anti-Thy 1.2 IgM plus complement

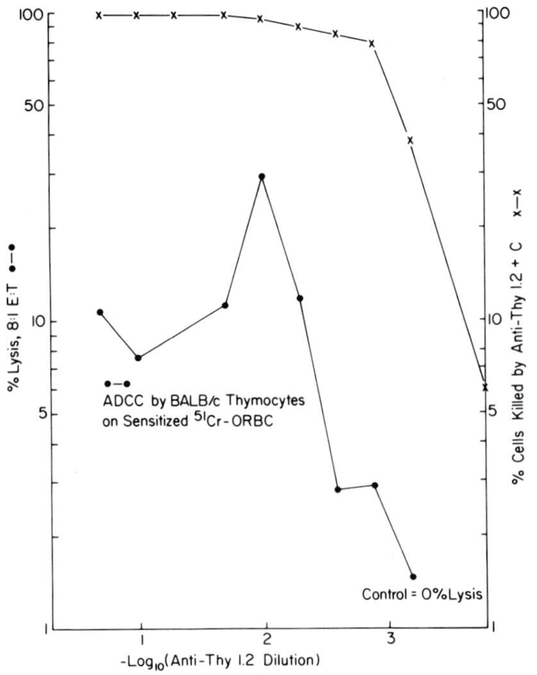

FIG. 1. Treatment of BALB/c thymocytes with dilutions of monoclonal anti-Thy 1.2 IgM. Upper curve represents percentage of thymocytes destroyed while lower curve reflects ADCC activity of surviving thymocytes at respective antibody concentrations. All treated thymocyte cultures were reconstituted to an 8:1, E:T ratio prior to assaying for cytotoxicity.

TABLE 1

Thy 1 Expression and ADCC Activity among Thymocytes after Complement-dependent Depletion with Monoclonal Anti-Thy 1.2 IgM and after Appropriate Control Procedures

Treatment of thymocytes	Percentage Thy 1.2[+ a]	Percentage specific target cell lysis[b]
1:100 anti-θ + C′	96	30 ± 4.6
1:100 anti-θ − C′	98	0.2 ± 1.0
C′ alone	98	0.4 ± 1.5
1:100 Anti-θ + C′; 1:10 anti-θ + C′	16.3	6.1 ± 2.1
1:100 Anti-θ + C′; 1:10 anti-θ − C′	96	28 ± 4.8
1:100 Anti-θ + C′; C′ alone	96	27 ± 4.2

[a] Surviving thymocytes isolated by Ficoll–Hypaque density gradient centrifugation.
[b] All values for ADCC activity in this paper represent the mean ± SE for triplicate samples. E:T = 8:1.

(measured by trypan blue exclusion and ^{51}Cr release) demonstrates the two-component nature of Thy 1 expression among thymocytes (Fig. 1, upper curve). Removal of high Thy 1-bearing thymocytes occurs rapidly at the beginning of the anti-Thy 1.2 titration, until approximately 85% of all thymocytes are depleted (1:1600 anti-Thy 1.2). The remaining proportion of thymocytes continue to be depleted with increasing concentrations of antibody, but at a much slower rate.

ADCC activity within the surviving thymocyte fraction after anti-Thy 1.2 treatment is shown to rise parallel with increased Thy 1^+ cell depletion (Fig. 1, lower curve). Removal of thymocytes expressing high relative levels of Thy 1 is necessary for cytotoxic activity to be detected among thymocytes and the most efficient ADCC effectors are among the lowest 5% of thymocytes for Thy 1 expression. Peak ADCC activity for thymocyte effectors (30% lysis) is attained when approximately 95% of all thymocytes have been killed with a 1:100 dilution of anti-Thy 1.2 plus complement. The level of ADCC activity for this thymocyte subpopulation is comparable to that found for splenic effector cells using an identical assay system (11).

Treatment of thymocytes with complement alone gave no enhancement of ADCC activity or depletion of Thy 1-bearing cells (Table 1).

Concentrations of anti-Thy 1.2 IgM above a 1:100 dilution continued to give

TABLE 2

ADCC Activity of Thymocytes after Saline Perfusion

Thymocyte treatment	Percentage specific target cell lysis
No perfusion; anti-θ + C′[a]	58 ± 5.1
No perfusion; anti-θ − C′	1 ± 0.3
No perfusion; C′ alone	0.2 ± 0.9
Perfusion; anti-θ + C′	73 ± 8.1
Perfusion; anti-θ − C′	2 ± 0.7
Perfusion; C′ alone	0 ± 1.1

[a] 1:100 Anti-Thy 1.2.

TABLE 3

Lyt Expression on Maximally Active Thymic K Cells[a]

Monoclonal antibody	Percentage low Thy 1 thymocytes stained
Anti-Lyt 1	78 (56% Lyt 1^+)
Anti-Lyt 2	23 (1% Lyt 2^+)
Anti-Lyt 1 + anti-Lyt 2	79 (22% Lyt 1^+2^+)

[a] 1:100 Anti-Thy 1.2 + C′ treated.

increased removal of thymocytes (2% increase in overall thymocyte depletion, 50% increase in relative depletion). Using a 1:10 dilution of the anti-Thy 1.2 reagent in the presence of complement, ADCC activity declined by over threefold (to 7.5% lysis) compared to the 1:100 anti-Thy 1.2 sample. Accompanying this loss in ADCC activity is a decrease in Thy 1^+ cells among the surviving thymocytes as detected by immunofluorescence (Table 1). The proportion of cells expressing Thy 1 at 1:10 anti-Thy 1.2 is one-fifth of that found at 1:100 anti-Thy 1.2 and the cytotoxic activity within the former sample is 17% of that which is detected for the 1:100 anti-Thy 1.2-treated cells. The correlation between Thy 1 expression and ADCC activity among thymocytes treated at anti-Thy 1.2 concentrations above 1:100 is also confirmed over a range of anti-Thy 1.2 dilutions (1:20 and 1:50; unpublished observations).

Nonspecific inhibition of ADCC by high concentrations of anti-Thy 1.2 IgM was not a factor in these experiments, as demonstrated in Table 1. When thymocytes are treated with 1:100 anti-Thy 1.2 plus complement and the viable population subsequently treated with 1:10 anti-Thy 1.2 minus complement, no diminution of ADCC activity occurs as compared to the control (1:100 anti-Thy 1.2 + C treated). The decline in ADCC activity observed for the 1:10 anti-Thy 1.2 sample is also not attributable to nonspecific inhibition caused by a second incubation in the presence of complement (Table 1).

Since the data indicates that thymic ADCC effectors constitute only a small proportion of the total thymocyte population, we were concerned that peripheral blood cells were contaminating the thymocyte sample and were responsible for the ADCC observed post-anti-Thy 1.2 treatment. In order to test this possibility, mice were perfused with 5 ml of normal saline via the left ventricle prior to thymic extraction, with drainage of blood occurring through a severed left axillary vein. ADCC activity among 1:100 anti-Thy 1.2-treated thymocytes is independent of circulatory perfusion (Table 2), evidencing that the ADCC-active cells detected after antibody-plus-complement treatment are not derived from blood cell contaminants, but are truly thymus localized.

Lyt antigen profile of ADCC-active thymocytes. Thymocytes were treated with a 1:100 dilution of anti-Thy 1.2 with complement to obtain the surviving thymocyte fraction possessing maximal ADCC activity. These cells were stained for expression of Lyt 1 and Lyt 2 antigens (Table 3). Low Thy 1-bearing thymocytes were found to be a heterogeneous population for Lyt-marker expression, with 22% of cells possessing an Lyt 1^+2^+ phenotype.

TABLE 4

Monoclonal Anti-Lyt Antibody Treatment of Thymic K Cells in the Presence and Absence of Complement

Treatment of thymocytes	Percentage specific target cell lysis
Anti-θ[a] − C′	4.8 ± 0.7
Anti-θ + C′	31.0 ± 3.2
C′ alone	1.0 ± 1.2
Anti-θ + C′; anti-Lyt 1 + C′	4.2 ± 1.1
Anti-θ + C′; anti-Lyt 2 + C′	5.1 ± 1.4
Anti-θ + C′; anti-Lyt 1 and anti-Lyt 2 + C′	4.4 ± 1.5
Anti-θ + C′; anti-Lyt 1 − C′	30.5 ± 4.6
Anti-θ + C′; anti-Lyt 2 − C′	29.0 ± 5.7
Anti-θ + C′; C′ alone	27.9 ± 3.6

[a] 1:100 Anti-Thy 1.2.

Depletion of the ADCC-active thymocyte pool with monoclonal anti-Lyt 1 or monoclonal anti-Lyt 2 antibody plus complement was used to determine the pattern of Lyt antigen expression on thymocytes capable of mediating ADCC. Cells depleted with anti-Lyt 1, anti-Lyt 2, or a mixture of the two antibodies showed markedly diminished ADCC potential to an equal degree (Table 4). The loss of cytotoxic activity was not due to nonspecific inhibition of ADCC by the anti-Lyt monoclonals or by complement (Table 4). The data supports the conclusion that ADCC-active thymocytes exhibit an Lyt antigen phenotype of $1^+2,3^+$.

DISCUSSION

The existence of a subpopulation of murine thymocytes capable of mediating ADCC was confirmed by implementing a cell separation procedure which takes advantage of the differential expression of Thy 1.2 surface antigen on the majority of thymocytes as compared to the small proportion of thymocytes possessing K-cell activity. Depletion of 85–95% of the total thymocyte pool with anti-Thy 1.2 plus complement lead to greatly enhanced ADCC activity among the surviving thymocytes (at equal effector:target cell ratios). The observation that continued thymocyte depletion above a 97% level caused a decrease in ADCC activity clearly demonstrates that the majority of ADCC-active thymocytes do indeed express Thy 1 surface antigen, albeit at a very low density relative to the total thymocyte population (among the lowest 5%).

Upon initial observation of Fig. 1, it appears that while a very striking decline in ADCC activity occurs at anti-Thy 1.2 concentrations above a 1:100 dilution, the level of thymocyte depletion changes very little (2%). It is important to recognize though that the upper curve in Fig. 1 represents the percentage of total thymocytes depleted by the monoclonal reagent and complement. When it is considered that the 2% change in overall thymocyte removal actually translates into a twofold increase in thymocyte depletion and an 80% loss of Thy 1^+ cells when the anti-Thy 1.2 concentration is increased from 1:100 to 1:10, it becomes clear that the degree of Thy 1^+ thymocyte depletion is significant enough to account for the dramatic drop in ADCC activity observed.

The T-cell nature of these thymus-localized K cells is also evidenced by their manifestation of Lyt antigens. Ablation of cytotoxicity in the maximally active thymocyte sample was achieved to an equal degree using either anti-Lyt 1 or anti-Lyt 2 or the monoclonal reagents in tandem. In addition, immunofluorescence studies reveal that Lyt 1^+2^+ thymocytes exist in this cell fraction, a result consistent with the assignment of K-cell activity among low Thy 1-bearing thymocytes to the Lyt $1^+2,3^+$ subset.

The finding that these thymic K cells express Thy 1 at depressed levels relative to the bulk of thymocytes is predictable based on the knowledge that: (1) mature peripheral T cells express much less Thy 1 than do the majority (95%) of thymocytes (16); and (2) that cortisone-resistant, medullary thymocytes (ADCC-active thymocytes are harbored in this fraction) also have a lower amount of Thy 1 on their surface than the major cortical thymocyte subpopulation (17). Mathieson *et al.* have recently shown that cortisone-resistant, medullary thymocytes have a restricted expression of Lyt antigens and are either Lyt 1^+ or Lyt $1^+2,3^+$ (18, 19). All of these reports are compatible with our results demonstrating that thymic K cells express a low relative density of Thy 1 and can react with monoclonal antibodies specific for both Lyt 1 and Lyt 2 antigens.

Similarities in Lyt phenotype between cortisone-resistant, ADCC-active thymocytes and the thymus migrant population (20) suggest that thymic K cells are in the terminal stages of T-cell differentiation and are soon to be exported into the peripheral immune system. Since Thy 1^+ cells possessing ADCC potential are present in the murine spleen, it is probable that the ADCC-active thymocytes characterized here are the cellular precursors for those peripheral K cells expressing mature T-cell markers. The fact that Thy 1-positive ADCC effector cells can be detected in both secondary lymphoid tissues and in the T-cell hematopoeitic region provides strong evidence that thymus-derived lymphocytes can participate in antibody-dependent cellular cytotoxicity.

ACKNOWLEDGMENTS

We thank Dr. John Kearney for providing the immunofluorescence reagents, Barbara Williams for technical advice, and Angie Campbell for preparation of this manuscript.

REFERENCES

1. Pearson, G. R., *Curr. Top. Microbiol. Immunol.* **80,** 65, 1978.
2. Gelfand, E. W., Resch, K., and Prester, M., *Eur. J. Immunol.* **2,** 419, 1972.
3. Lamon, E. W., Whitten, H. D., Skurzak, H., Andersson, B., and Lidin, B., *J. Immunol.* **115,** 1288, 1975.
4. Mattes, M. J., Sharrow, S., Herberman, R., and Holden, H., *J. Immunol.* **123,** 2851, 1979.
5. Kimura, A. K., Rubin, B., and Andersson, L., *Scand. J. Immunol.* **6,** 787, 1977.
6. Lamon, E. W., Skurzak, H., Andersson, B., Whitten, H., and Klein, E., *J. Immunol.* **114,** 1171, 1975.
7. Greenberg, A., Shen, L., Walker, L., Arnaiz-Villena, A., and Roitt, I.M., *Eur. J. Immunol.* **5,** 474, 1976.
8. Wisløff, F., Frøland, S., and Michaelson, T. E., *Int. Arch. Allergy* **47,** 139, 1974.
9. Nathan, C., Brukner, L., Kaplan, G., Unkless, J., and Cohn, Z., *J. Exp. Med.* **152,** 183, 1980.
10. Ojo, E., and Wigzell, H., *Scand. J. Immunol.* **7,** 297, 1978.

11. Lamon, E. W., Pollok, B. A., Walia, A. S., Fuson, E. W., and Williams, B., *Immunology*, **43,** 643, 1981.
12. Lamon, E. W., Shaw, M., Goodson, S., Lidin, B., Walia, A. S., and Fuson, E. W., *J. Exp. Med.* **145,** 302, 1977.
13. Lamon, E. W., Williams, B., Fuson, E., Whitten, H., and Walia, A. S., *J. Immunol.* **120,** 244, 1978.
14. Hämmerling, G. J., Lemke, H., Hämmerling, V., Hölman, C., Wallich, R., and Rajewsky, K., *Curr. Top. Microbiol. Immunol.* **81,** 100, 1978.
15. Kearney, J. F., Cooper, M., and Lawton, A., *J. Immunol.* **117,** 1567, 1976.
16. Cantor, H., and Weissman, I., *Prog. Allergy* **20,** 1, 1976.
17. Potter, T., Hogarth, P., and McKenzie, I., *Eur. J. Immunol.* **10,** 899, 1980.
18. Mathieson, B. J., Sharrow, S., Campbell, P., and Asofsky, R., *Nature (London)* **277,** 478, 1979.
19. Mathieson, B. J., Sharrow, S., Rosenberg, Y., and Hämmerling, U., *Nature (London)* **289,** 179, 1981.
20. Scollay, R., Kochen, J., Butcher, E., and Weissman, I., *Nature (London)* **276,** 79, 1978.

CELLULAR IMMUNOLOGY **65,** 280–292 (1981)

Phytohemagglutinin-Induced Enhancement and IgG Subclass Restriction of the Immune Response to Type III Pneumococcal Polysaccharide[1,2]

BARBARA E. T. BUSBY AND BOB S. ROBERSON

Department of Microbiology, University of Maryland, College Park, Maryland 20742

Received July 15, 1981; accepted October 6, 1981

The splenic plaque-forming-cell (PFC) response of mice to immunization with pneumococcal capsular polysaccharide (SSS-III), coupled with T-cell activation by phytohemagglutinin (PHA), is characterized by enhanced numbers of IgG-producing cells, largely restricted to the IgG2a and IgG2b subclasses. In contrast, immunization with SSS-III alone results in low numbers of IgG-producing cells, fairly evenly distributed among the subclasses IgG1, IgG2a, IgG2b, and IgG3. The enhanced IgG response and a concomitantly enhanced IgM response are T-cell dependent and occur only if PHA is given 2 days after SSS-III immunization. The absence of immunologic memory to SSS-III in mice previously immunized and treated with PHA implies that enhanced IgG production results from the activation of amplifier T cells and not the helper T cells which are required for memory.

INTRODUCTION

The immune response to type III pneumococcal polysaccharide (SSS-III) does not require helper T cells and the antibody produced is restricted mainly to the IgM class (1–6). Immunologic memory to this antigen normally cannot be demonstrated; however, a substantial IgG response and immune memory to SSS-III can be elicited if T cells are experimentally activated. Thus, mice undergoing allogeneic stimulation at the time of SSS-III immunization produce substantial primary IgG responses (7). Rabbits primed with type III pneumococci display striking secondary anti-SSS-III responses when challenged with SSS-III conjugated to bovine gamma globulin (BGG), but only if helper T cells have been activated by an intervening immunization with BGG (8). Similarly, mice primed with SSS-III conjugated to horse or sheep erythrocytes and challenged with either the T-dependent (SSS-III-RBC) or T-independent (SSS-III) form of the antigen produce SSS-III-specific IgG secondary responses (9–11). We reported previously that non-specific activation of murine T cells by the mitogen phytohemagglutinin (PHA), given at 24 and 48 hr after immunization with SSS-III, produced a significant T cell-dependent enhancement of the primary non-IgM PFC response to SSS-III

[1] A preliminary report of this work was presented at the annual meeting of the American Association of Immunologists, March, 1979. Abstract No. 3744, *Fed. Proc.* **38,** 938, 1979.

[2] Computer time was supplied in full by the University of Maryland Computer Science Center.

0008-8749/81/180280-13$02.00/0

accompanied by a corresponding increase in SSS-III-specific serum IgG titers (12). In the present study we have identified the non-IgM PFC as IgG PFC.

In a series of papers on subclass restriction of murine antibodies, Davie and coworkers (13–16) have provided evidence that IgG antibodies to T-independent carbohydrate antigens or hapten–carbohydrate conjugates are predominantly, but not exclusively, of the IgG3 subclass; whereas IgG responses to T-independent antigens which are also polyclonal stimulators produce about equal proportions of IgG2 and IgG3. T-dependent antigens, on the other hand, elicit antibodies which are predominantly IgG1, with smaller amounts of IgG2 and IgG3. Since immune memory normally can be demonstrated after priming with T-dependent but not T-independent antigens (17, 18), there may be a relationship between memory potential and the subclass of IgG produced during the primary response (19). Consequently, we examined the subclasses of IgG produced when mice were immunized with SSS-III alone and those produced by SSS-III-immunized mice when T cells were nonspecifically activated by PHA. We found that mice immunized with SSS-III alone produced IgG antibody which was evenly distributed among the subclasses IgG1, IgG2a, IgG2b, and IgG3. In contrast, PHA treatment resulted in a dramatic increase in SSS-III-specific PFC of the IgG2a and IgG2b subclasses, with much smaller increases in IgG1 and IgG3 PFC; yet priming for memory to SSS-III did not occur.

MATERIALS AND METHODS

Animals

Male and female BALB/c mice were obtained from Flow Laboratories, Springfield, Virginia. Female athymic (nu/nu) mice partially inbred on a BALB/c background and their thymus-bearing (nu/+) littermates were the generous gift of Dr. Bruce Merchant (Bureau of Biologics, Food and Drug Administration, Bethesda, Md.), who obtained them from Sprague–Dawley, Madison, Wisconsin. All mice employed in these studies were between 8 and 16 weeks of age. Mice were housed in the Department of Microbiology animal facility of the University of Maryland and were allowed food and water *ad libitum*. Nude mice were housed apart from other animals and were maintained on sterilized mouse diet and acidified tap water. Guinea pigs from a colony maintained at the University of Maryland were used as a source of complement (C′).

Antigen and Immunization

The preparation and immunologic properties of the SSS-III used in these studies have been described (12). The optimally immunogenic dose of 0.5 μg SSS-III was administered intraperitoneally in 0.5 ml of sterile normal saline. In each experiment, mice of one sex only were employed. Both male and female BALB/c mice respond equally well to SSS-III (unpublished observation).

Phytohemagglutinin (PHA)

Unless otherwise indicated, phytohemagglutinin (PHA-P, Difco Laboratories, Detroit, Michigan), at a dosage of 10 μg/g average mouse weight, was administered intravenously in 0.25 ml of sterile saline at 24 and 48 hr following SSS-III immunization. This dosage and injection schedule was shown previously to produce the maximum number of IgG PFC specific for SSS-III (12) and is referred to in the text as "SSS-III + PHA." Lot number 654996 was employed in the study to determine the effect of time of administration of PHA on enhancement of the IgM PFC response to SSS-III. In one experiment, enhancement of IgM and IgG PFC by several lots of PHA, as noted, were compared in a hemolytic plaque assay. Lot 636117 was used for all other experiments. In addition, this lot was tested for possible bacterial lipopolysaccharide contamination by the method of Jacobs and Morrison (20), and was found to be negative.

Antisera to Mouse Immunoglobulins

The preparation of the rabbit anti-mouse immunoglobulin (RAM) employed has been described (12). Immunoabsorbed, monospecific rabbit anti-mouse IgG(7S) and rabbit anti-mouse IgG1, IgG2a, IgG2b, and IgG3 were purchased from Litton Bionetics, Kensington, Maryland.

Hemolytic Plaque Assay

The localized hemolysis-in-gel procedure of Jerne *et al.* (21) as modified by Baker *et al.* (22), was used to detect spleen cells producing SSS-III-specific antibody. Sheep red blood cells (SRBC) were sensitized with SSS-III by the chromium chloride coupling procedure as described (12). After incubation of an appropriate number of spleen cells and 0.15 ml of sensitized SRBC in 0.3 ml of a 0.7% agarose matrix for 60 min at 37°C, direct PFC were developed with diluted guinea pig serum (C′, 1:10 dilution in veronal saline) for an additional 90 min at 37°C. Indirect plus direct PFC (total PFC) were similarly developed on a duplicate set of slides with C′ plus a 1:100 dilution of RAM or rabbit anti-mouse IgG(7S) or rabbit anti-mouse IgG subclass-specific antisera as indicated. For purposes of discussion, direct PFC are considered to be IgM PFC; total PFC as developed by RAM are considered to be IgM plus non-IgM PFC. However, additional PFC developed by anti-IgG(7S) are considered to be IgG PFC and those developed by antisera to the IgG subclasses IgG1, IgG2a, IgG2b, or IgG3 are considered to be specific for each antiserum used. Thus, by subtraction of direct PFC from total PFC, the quantity of PFC specifically producing IgG or an IgG subclass was determined.

Statistics

Statistical analysis of the data was by the Student–Newman–Keuls multiple range analysis of variance (23). Small vertical bars on all graphs represent the standard error of the geometric means (SEM).

RESULTS

Effect of PHA on the PFC Response to SSS-III

Groups of mice were immunized on Day 0 with 0.5 μg SSS-III alone or with SSS-III on Day 0 followed by 10 μg/g PHA on Days 1 and 2. Direct and total splenic PFC were assayed on Days 3, 4, and 5 following SSS-III immunization. As illustrated in Fig. 1, the peak PFC response of mice injected with SSS-III alone

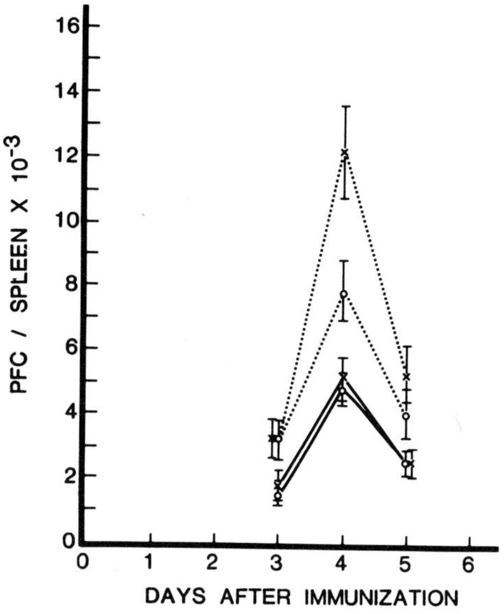

FIG. 1. Effect of PHA on the PFC response to an optimally immunogenic dose of SSS-III. Points represent the geometric means ± SEM of the direct (○——○) and total (×——×) PFC of 10 mice per day injected with SSS-III alone or the direct (○ - - - ○) and total (× - - - ×) PFC of 15 mice per day injected with SSS-III + PHA. Total PFC were developed with RAM + C′.

occurred on Day 4 and consisted almost entirely of IgM PFC (direct PFC); non-IgM PFC (total minus direct) constituted less than 15% of the total. After PHA treatment, however, non-IgM PFC comprised 36% of the total PFC on Day 4 ($P < 0.001$) and 23% of the total PFC on Day 5 ($P < 0.05$). A significant increase ($P < 0.001$) in the number of nucleated cells per spleen was also observed (data not shown). To confirm that the significant increase in non-IgM PFC was due to an increase in absolute numbers of IgG PFC, the remainder of the experiments reported here were performed employing anti-IgG(7S) + C′ to develop total PFC.

An unexpected aspect of the immune response to SSS-III as influenced by PHA was the significant enhancement of the IgM PFC response ($P < 0.05$ on all days tested). These results differed from the previously reported suppression of the IgM PFC response on Days 4 and 5 when PHA was similarly administered (12). Since a possible explanation for the discrepancy in results lay in the fact that different lots of PHA were employed in the two sets of experiments, it was decided to study other lots of PHA for their ability to augment both the IgM and IgG PFC responses to SSS-III on Day 4. The results presented in Table 1 indicate that each lot of PHA tested produced significant enhancement of both the IgM and IgG PFC responses to SSS-III when compared with the responses of mice receiving no PHA. The relative activities of each lot, however, were varied. IgM PFC responses were increased from 2.3 to 4.4 times normal. IgG PFC responses ranged from 22.5 to 65.6% of the total response as compared with the normal response of 11.4 to 12.8%. The data suggest that individual lots of PHA may preferentially increase either the IgM or the IgG responses. Those producing IgM responses under 300% of normal showed the largest increases in IgG (lots 636117, 607352, and 654996);

TABLE 1

Comparison of the Activities of Different Lots of Phytohemagglutinin in the Enhancement of the IgM and IgG PFC Responses to SSS-III

Treatment group (number of mice/group)	Mean log direct PFC/spleen ± SEM[a] (geometric mean)	IgM PFC (% of normal response)	Mean log total PFC/spleen ± SEM[b] (geometric mean)	IgG PFC/spleen (indirect PFC)[c]	IgG PFC (% of total PFC)
SSS-III only (4)	3.8828 ± 0.1645 (7,635)	100	3.9424 ± 0.1694 (8,758)	1,123	12.8
SSS-III + PHA Lot					
636117 (4)	4.2569 ± 0.1284 (18,068)	237	4.5485 ± 0.1567 (35,359)	17,291	48.9
607352 (2)	4.3552 ± 0.0564 (22,657)	297	4.7349 ± 0.0240 (54,313)	31,656	58.3
550408 (2)	4.5277 ± 0.0405 (33,705)	441	4.6384 ± 0.1484 (43,491)	9,786	22.5
596886 (3)	4.4728 ± 0.0203 (29,703)	389	4.6947 ± 0.0436 (49,511)	19,808	40.0
SSS-III only (5)	4.2024 ± 0.0471 (15,937)	100	4.2550 ± 0.0349 (17,989)	2,052	11.4
SSS-III + PHA Lot					
654996 (5)	4.6740 ± 0.0329 (47,206)	296	5.1368 ± 0.0183 (137,030)	89,824	65.6

[a] All spleens assayed on Day 4 following SSS-III immunization.
[b] Total PFC developed with anti-IgG(7S) + C′.
[c] IgG PFC obtained by subtraction of direct PFC from total PFC.

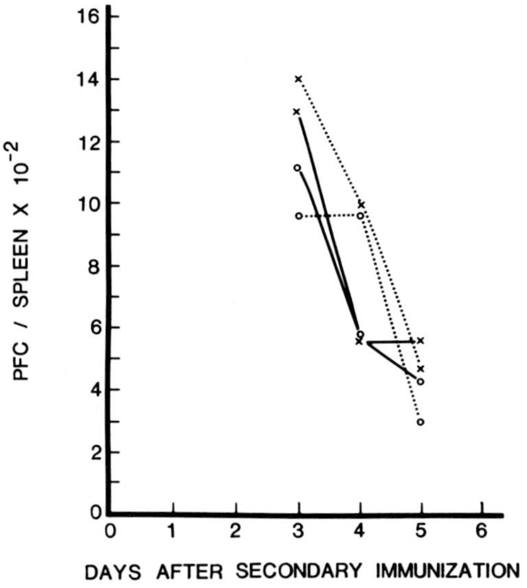

FIG. 2. Response of mice primed with SSS-III or SSS-III + PHA to a secondary challenge with SSS-III 8 months later. Points represent the geometric means of the direct (○——○) and total (×——×) PFC responses of five SSS-III-primed mice or the geometric means of the direct (○- - -○) and total (×- - -×) PFC responses of five SSS-III + PHA-primed mice per day. Error bars are omitted for clarity.

whereas those which produced the largest IgM increases showed smaller increases in IgG (lots 550408 and 596886).

The PFC Response to SSS-III of Mice Primed with SSS-III or SSS-III + PHA 8 Months Previously

To determine if the PHA-induced enhancement of SSS-III-specific IgG synthesis signals the induction of memory to this antigen, the response of mice to a second injection of SSS-III, 8 months after priming with SSS-III or SSS-III + PHA was studied. The results are presented in Fig. 2. The complete absence of a secondary response to SSS-III was evidenced by the fact that the number of PFC produced by each group of mice on all days tested was only 10% of peak numbers of PFC produced after a primary injection (Fig. 1). Qualitatively, it appeared that the peak of the response occurred on Day 3 or earlier. Although there was a suggestion on Day 3 of a greater IgG PFC response in mice previously given SSS-III + PHA, as compared to those primed with SSS-III alone, statistical analysis of the data revealed no significant differences in values for direct or total PFC for either group of mice on any day tested.

Effect of Time of PHA Administration on the IgM PFC Response

The maximum enhancement of the SSS-III-specific IgG PFC response is obtained when PHA is given twice, i.e., on Days 1 and 2 following SSS-III immunization (12). Therefore we sought to determine whether time of administration of PHA would also have an effect on enhancement of the IgM response. The results

TABLE 2

Effect of Time of Administration of PHA on the Direct PFC Response to SSS-III

Group	SSS-III (0.5 μg) on Day 0	PHA (10 μg/g) on Day	Mean log direct PFC/spleen ± SEM[a] (geometric mean)
A (4)[b]	+	None	3.8861 ± 0.0314 (7,693)
B (5)	+	0	3.6946 ± 0.0672[c] (4,950)
C (4)	+	1	3.7085 ± 0.0875[c] (5,111)
D (5)	+	2	4.0524 ± 0.0455[d,e] (11,282)
E (3)	+	1 + 2	4.2192 ± 0.0192[d,e] (16,565)
F (6)	+	2 + 3	4.2041 ± 0.0281[d,e] (15,999)

[a] Splenic PFC assayed on Day 4.
[b] Number of mice per group is given in parentheses.
[c] $P < 0.05$ compared to group A.
[d] $P < 0.01$ compared to group A.
[e] Differences between groups D, E, and F not significant.

are presented in Table 2. Groups of mice were immunized with an optimally immunogenic dose of SSS-III and at various intervals thereafter PHA was administered. PHA given at the time of immunization with SSS-III or 1 day later produced a significant inhibition of the direct PFC response. However, PHA given in one dose (Day 2) or in two doses (Days 1 and 2 or 2 and 3) produced significant enhancement of the direct PFC response. The enhancement produced by PHA given once (Day 2) was equivalent to that produced if PHA was given twice.

Effect of PHA on the Athymic BALB/c Nude Mouse Response to SSS-III

To determine if the PHA-induced augmentation of SSS-III-specific IgM and IgG PFC in BALB/c mice is the result of the activation of T cells or of a different cell population, the PFC responses of athymic nude (nu/nu) mice and nude mice reconstituted with T cells from their thymus-bearing littermates were studied. The protocol for this experiment is illustrated in Table 3 and the results are shown in Fig. 3. The IgM and IgG PFC responses of nu/nu mice to SSS-III alone (group C) were equivalent to those of their thymus-bearing littermates (group A). Modification of the response to SSS-III by PHA administration, however, resulted in a significant enhancement of both the IgM PFC response ($P < 0.01$) and the IgG response ($P < 0.001$) in nu/+ (group B) but not in nu/nu (group D) mice. A significant increase ($P < 0.01$) in the total number of nucleated spleen cells, as well as a threefold increase in average spleen weight was observed in nu/+ (group B) mice receiving SSS-III + PHA compared to nu/+ (group A) mice receiving SSS-III alone (Table 3). In contrast, no significant increase in either spleen weight or nucleated cell number was observed in nu/nu (group D) mice receiving SSS-III + PHA compared to nu/nu (group C) mice receiving SSS-III alone.

TABLE 3

Effect of PHA on Spleen Weights and Nucleated Cell Numbers in SSS-III-Immunized nu/+, nu/nu, and T Cell-Reconstituted nu/nu Mice[a]

Treatment group	Mouse type[b]	nu/+ spleen cells (5×10^7) iv Day −1	SSS-III (0.5 μg) ip Day 0	Saline (0.25 ml) iv Days 1 + 2	PHA (10 μg/g) iv Days 1 + 2	Mean spleen weight (mg)	Mean cells/spleen $\times 10^8$
A (6)[c]	nu/+	—	+	+	—	91	1.45
B (6)	nu/+	—	+	—	+	296	2.39[d]
C (4)	nu/nu	—	+	+	—	123	1.28
D (5)	nu/nu	—	+	—	+	136	1.87
E (6)	nu/nu	+	+	+	—	163	1.74
F (6)	nu/nu	+	+	—	+	182	2.26

[a] PFC responses of groups A to F are illustrated in Fig. 3.
[b] nu/+ mice were the heterozygous littermates of the nu/nu mice bred on a BALB/c background.
[c] Number of mice per group.
[d] $P < 0.01$ compared to group A.

Because PHA stimulates only mature T cells in the thymus or peripheral lymphoid organs (24, 25), nu/nu mice were reconstituted with nu/+ spleen cells rather than with nu/+ thymus cells to provide these mice with a suitable population of mature T cells. Reconstitution of mice with spleen cells also provided them with a significantly larger population of B cells capable of responding to SSS-III (unpublished observation). A comparison of the PFC responses of spleen cell-reconstituted nu/nu mice to SSS-III alone (group E) and SSS-III + PHA (group F), respectively, showed no significant difference. Spleen weights and nucleated cell

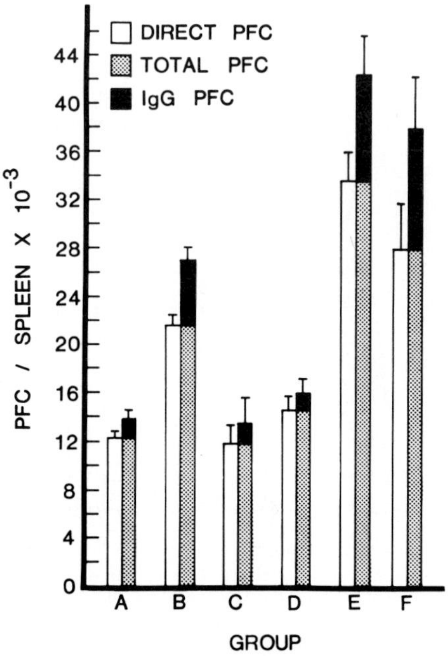

FIG. 3. Effect of PHA on the PFC responses of nu/+, nu/nu, and T cell-reconstituted nu/nu mice to SSS-III. Splenic PFC were assayed on Day 4. Total PFC were developed with anti-IgG(7S) + C′. Treatment groups A to F are described in Table 3.

numbers were also equivalent. It appears that a mild graft-vs-host (GVH) reaction may have occurred in both groups E and F which, in effect, masked any effect PHA may have had on T cells. The occurrence of a GVH reaction was not surprising, since the nude gene had only recently been introduced into the BALB/c mice at the time of this experiment and these mice were not, as yet, sufficiently inbred to be truly syngeneic.

Effect of PHA on the IgG Subclass-Specific PFC Response to SSS-III

To identify the IgG subclass or subclasses predominant in the PFC response to SSS-III and SSS-III + PHA, IgG subclass-specific antisera were employed to develop indirect PFC on Day 4 after SSS-III immunization. The results of two separate experiments are shown in Figs. 4A and B. In both experiments, the peak IgG PFC responses of mice immunized with SSS-III alone were distributed fairly evenly among the IgG1, IgG2a, IgG2b, and IgG3 subclasses. Definite IgG3 PFC responses were observed. A most surprising result of PHA modification of the PFC response to SSS-III was the observation that the PHA-induced increase in IgG PFC was due almost entirely to a dramatic increase in PFC of the IgG2a and IgG2b subclasses. In experiment A, IgG2a was increased 15.4-fold and IgG2b 6-fold, with smaller increases in IgG1 and IgG3 of 1.6-fold and 2.3-fold, respectively. The results of experiment B differ somewhat in the PFC values obtained. However, the major PHA-induced increases in IgG2a (5.4-fold) and IgG2b PFC (11.1-fold) are again very apparent compared with the smaller increases in PFC of the IgG1 and IgG3 subclasses (2.8-fold and 3.0-fold, respectively).

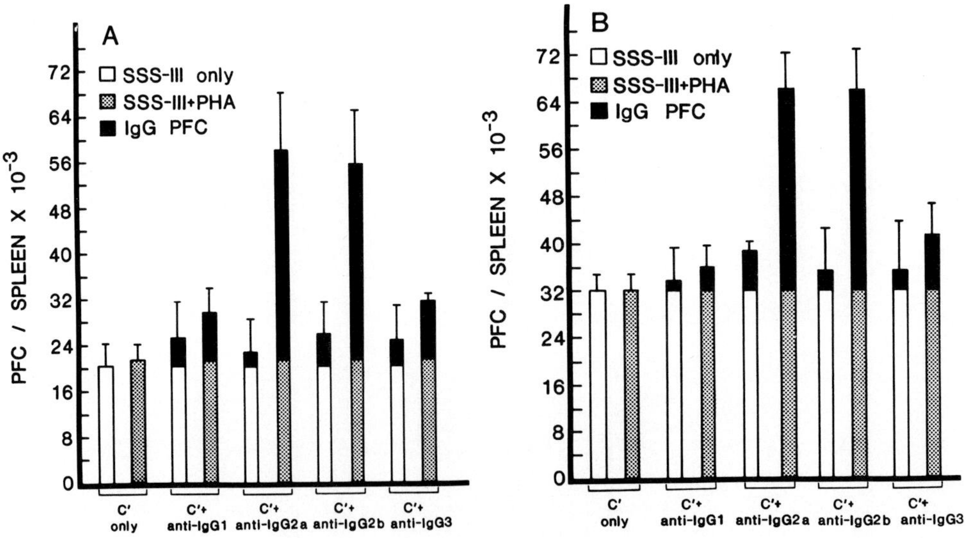

FIG. 4. The IgG subclass distribution of the PFC response of mice immunized with SSS-III or SSS-III + PHA. Splenic PFC were assayed on Day 4. Direct PFC were developed with complement only. Total PFCs for each IgG subclass were developed with complement and the specific IgG subclass antiserum, as indicated on the figure. The numbers of mice in each group are (A) 3 and 5 or (B) 5 and 5 for immunizations with SSS-III and SSS-III + PHA, respectively.

DISCUSSION

Administration of the T-cell mitogen PHA, on Days 1 and 2 following SSS-III immunization, resulted in significant T-dependent enhancement of both the IgM and IgG PFC responses to SSS-III. However, activation of T cells and primary IgG production alone did not result in priming of $B\mu$ and $B\gamma$ precursors for memory since very few IgM and IgG PFC were produced on secondary challenge with SSS-III or SSS-III + PHA up to 8 months later. Priming of SSS-III-specific memory B cells has been shown to require helper T cells (10, 11) and the IgG responses of mice to many T-dependent antigens have been reported to consist mainly of the IgG1 subclass (14, 26, 27). Therefore we sought to determine whether the subclass of IgG produced in response to immunization with SSS-III + PHA was indicative of activation of helper T cells by PHA. The IgG PFC response to immunization with SSS-III alone was distributed fairly evenly among the subclasses IgG1, IgG2a, IgG2b, and IgG3. However, the significant PHA-induced enhancement of the IgG response to SSS-III was due to a dramatic increase in PFC of the IgG2a and IgG2b subclasses, with much smaller increases in IgG1 and IgG3. It appears, therefore, that PHA treatment subsequent to SSS-III immunization does not activate SSS-III-specific helper T cells since priming for memory does not occur and the IgG1 subclass is not predominant in the response.

In our study of the effect of time of administration of PHA relative to SSS-III immunization we found that PHA, if given only on Day 2 after SSS-III immunization, induced a 2.1-fold increase in the peak numbers of IgM PFC observed. If PHA was given twice (i.e., on Days 1 and 2 or 2 and 3) there was no significant increase in the degree of enhancement obtained. The requirements for induction of these enhanced IgM PFC, therefore, were slightly different than for IgG PFC in that administration of PHA on both Days 1 and 2 was required for maximum production of the latter (12). If PHA was given at the time of SSS-III immunization or 1 day later, a small but significant inhibition (30–40%) of the IgM response occurred. These findings are strikingly similar to those of Markham and co-workers (29, 31) who found a marked suppression of the IgM PFC response when concanavalin A (Con A) was given at the time of SSS-III immunization and enhancement of this response when given 2 days after immunization. The suppression and enhancement of the response were attributed to the activation of suppressor and amplifier T cells, respectively. IgG PFC responses were not studied. PHA-induced enhancement of both the IgM and IgG responses were T-cell dependent since they occurred in euthymic mice but not their athymic nude littermates (Fig. 3) and were accompanied by a threefold increase in spleen weight and a significant increase in the total number of nucleated spleen cells (Table 3). This splenomegaly did not occur in nude mice, indicating that PHA was not directly mitogenic for B cells. Like Con A, therefore, PHA stimulates suppressive activity when given early in the response to SSS-III but enhances amplifier T cell (T_A) activity when given later in the response.

T_A cells have been shown to be a distinctly different subpopulation of T cells than helper T cells (T_H) by several criteria, including differences in their time of activation after SSS-III immunization (29), susceptibility to inactivation by hydrocortisone (30), and susceptibility to treatment with anti-lymphocyte serum (ALS) at the time of SSS-III immunization (28). Although we have not directly ruled out the possibility that PHA-induced enhancement of both IgM and IgG PFC is due to nonspecific activation of T_H by the mitogen, it is considered unlikely for the following reasons: [1] T_H increase the IgM and IgG antibody responses to SSS-III only when the mice are immunized twice with a T-dependent form of the antigen (e.g., SSS-III-RBC) in addition to pretreatment with a subimmunogenic dose of the RBC carrier (7). The primary antibody response to SSS-III-RBC is almost entirely IgM; whereas secondary challenge with SSS-III-RBC or SSS-III alone results in a substantial IgG memory response but a depressed IgM response (7, 9). PHA, in contrast, elicited enhanced IgM and IgG responses after one injection of SSS-III, i.e., no PHA "pretreatment" or second injection of either SSS-III or PHA was required. Secondary challenge with SSS-III alone or SSS-III + PHA produced a marked suppression of both IgM and IgG PFC production. [2] T_H must be activated either prior to or at the time of SSS-III immunization in order for enhanced secondary IgG responses to occur (7); PHA treatment at the time of or 1 day after SSS-III immunization suppressed both the primary IgM and IgG responses presumably due to enhanced suppressor T cell (T_S) activity. [3] T-dependent enhancement of both the IgM and IgG PFC responses to SSS-III occurred if PHA was given 2 days after SSS-III immunization, i.e., at the time when T_A activity is normally expressed (29). Similar enhanced IgM and IgG antibody responses to SSS-III occur when ALS is administered at the time of immunization with SSS-III (4, 7). This treatment is thought to inactivate T_S and allow expression of T_A activity. Like SSS-III + PHA treatment, SSS-III + ALS treatment results in enhanced primary IgM and IgG responses but depressed secondary responses. [4] Nonspecific activation of T cells by the administration of allogeneic cells at the time of SSS-III immunization also results in enhanced primary and depressed secondary IgM and IgG responses to SSS-III (7). Thus, "nonspecific" activation of T cells does not necessarily imply activation of T_H cells capable of priming SSS-III-specific $B\mu$ and $B\gamma$ precursors for memory (10). [5] PHA treatment of SSS-III-immunized mice did not result in an increase in PFC specific for SRBC (our unpublished results), indicating a lack of nonspecific activation of T_H cells. For these reasons, we believe that PHA-induced stimulation of amplifier T cell activity, not helper T cell activity, results in the observed enhancement of the primary IgM and IgG PFC responses to SSS-III.

The data with regard to the IgG subclasses in mice immunized with SSS-III were surprising. Although Perlmutter *et al.* (13) reported that several bacterial carbohydrates elicit, in mice, IgG responses largely restricted to the IgG3 subclass, we found that SSS-III elicited specific IgG antibody in which all subclasses were equally distributed. Although a definite IgG3 response was demonstrated, this subclass was not predominant. Barthold *et al.* also detected IgG1 and IgG2 subclasses in response to SSS-III although IgG3 was not evaluated in that study (4). Several observations make it unlikely that this subclass distribution arises from a polyclonal activation of B cells by SSS-III. First, Rosenberg and Chiller (26) were unable to demonstrate a polyclonal increase in total immunoglobulin-forming cells after immunization with 0.5 μg SSS-III although a specific antibody response was obtained. Second, the dose of SSS-III required for mitogenicity is 1000-fold greater than the immunogenic dose (33). Third, in our hands, the background numbers of SRBC-specific PFC in SSS-III-immunized mice were never more than 2 per 10^6 nucleated spleen cells, indicating a lack of nonspecifically stimulated PFC or polyclonal response. Furthermore, athymic nude mice gave normal IgG responses to SSS-III, indicating that functional T cells were not necessary for the response. Therefore, SSS-III most likely stimulates proliferation of SSS-III-specific IgG-bearing B cells by virtue of an idiotype receptor for SSS-III, without a requirement for any type of IgG subclass restriction.

Activation of T_A cells by PHA, on the other hand, resulted in a substantial IgG PFC response to SSS-III which was largely restricted to the subclasses IgG2a and IgG2b with little increase in either IgG1 or IgG3. Since PHA was not directly mitogenic for B cells, this finding implies that T_A cells, activated by the mitogen, preferentially stimulated the proliferation and/or differentiation of B cells bearing IgG2a or IgG2b but not those bearing IgG1 and IgG3. Alternatively, PHA-activated T_A cells preferentially caused a "shift" from IgM to IgG2a or IgG2b synthesis rather than from IgM to IgG1 or IgM to IgG3. IgG1 production is highly thymus dependent (32) and it is the major IgG subclass formed in response to helper T cell-dependent antigens. Restriction of amplifier T-cell activity to only IgM, IgG2a, and IgG2b antibody responses could have important bearing on both the observed absence of a memory response to SSS-III and on regulation of the normal antibody response to this antigen.

REFERENCES

1. Howard, J. G., Christie, G. H., Courtenay, B. M., Leuchars, E., and Davies, A. J. S., *Cell. Immunol.* **2,** 614, 1971.
2. Davies, A. J. S., Carter, R. L., Leuchars, E., Wallis, V., and Dietrick, F. M., *Immunology* **19,** 945, 1970.
3. Humphrey, J. H., Parrott, D. M. V., and East, J., *Immunology* **7,** 419, 1964.
4. Barthold, D. R., Prescott, B., Stashak, P. W., Amsbaugh, D. F., and Baker, P. J., *J. Immunol.* **112,** 1042, 1974.
5. Baker, P. J., Barth, R. F., Stashak, P. W., and Amsbaugh, D. F., *J. Immunol.* **104,** 1313, 1970.
6. Braley, H. C., and Freeman, M. J., *Cell. Immunol.* **2,** 73, 1971.
7. Braley-Mullen, H., *J. Immunol.* **113,** 1909, 1974.
8. Paul, W. E., Katz, D. H., and Benacerraf, B., *J. Immunol.* **107,** 685, 1971.
9. Braley-Mullen, H., *J. Immunol.* **115,** 1194, 1975.
10. Braley-Mullen, H., *J. Immunol.* **116,** 904, 1976.
11. Braley-Mullen, H., *Eur. J. Immunol.* **7,** 775, 1977.
12. Vogel, S. N., and Roberson, B. S., *Infect. Immun.* **22,** 901, 1978.
13. Perlmutter, R. M., Hansburg, D., Briles, D. E., Nicolotti, R. A., and Davie, J. M., *J. Immunol.* **121,** 566, 1978.
14. Slack, J., Der-Balian, G. P., Nahm, M., and Davie, J. M., *J. Exp. Med.* **151,** 853, 1980.
15. Der-Balian, G. P., Slack, J., Clevinger, B., Bazin, H., and Davie, J. M., *J. Exp. Med.* **152,** 209, 1980.
16. Perlmutter, R. M., Nahm, M., Stein, K. E., Slack, J., Zitron, I., Paul, W. E., and Davie, J. M., *J. Exp. Med.* **149,** 993, 1979.
17. Coffman, R. L., and Cohn, M., *J. Immunol.* **118,** 1806, 1977.
18. Braley-Mullen, H., *J. Exp. Med.* **147,** 1824, 1978.
19. Abney, E. R., Copper, M. D., Kearney, J. F., Lawton, A. R., and Parkhouse, R. M. E., *J. Immunol.* **120,** 2041, 1978.
20. Jacobs, D. M., and Morrison, D. C., *J. Immunol.* **118,** 21, 1977.
21. Jerne, N. H., Nordin, A. A., and Henry, C., *In* "Cell-bound Antibodies" (B. Amos and H. Koprowski, Eds.), pp. 109–125. Wistar Inst. Press, Philadelphia, 1963.
22. Baker, P. J., Stashak, P. W., and Prescott, B., *Appl. Microbiol.* **17,** 422, 1969.
23. Sokal, R. R., and Rohlf, F. J. (Eds.), "Biometry," p. 239. Freeman, San Francisco, 1969.
24. Stobo, J. D., and Paul, W. E., *Cell. Immunol.* **4,** 367, 1972.

25. Stobo, J. D., and Paul, W. E., *J. Immunol.* **110,** 362, 1973.
26. Rosenberg, Y. J., and Chiller, J. M., *J. Exp. Med.* **150,** 517, 1979.
27. Augustin, A. A., and Coutinho, A., *J. Exp. Med.* **151,** 587, 1980.
28. Baker, P. J., and Prescott, B., *In* "Immunology of Bacterial Polysaccharides" (B. Rudbach and P. Baker, Eds.), pp. 67–104. Elsevier/North-Holland, Amsterdam, 1979.
29. Markham, R. B., Reed, N. D., Stashak, P. W., Prescott, B., Amsbaugh, D. F., and Baker, P. J., *J. Immunol.* **119,** 1163, 1977.
30. Markham, R. B., Stashak, P. W., Prescott, B., Amsbaugh, D. F., and Baker, P. J., *J. Immunol.* **121,** 829, 1978.
31. Markham, R. B., Stashak, P. W., Prescott, B., Amsbaugh, D. F., and Baker, P. J., *J. Immunol.* **118,** 952, 1977.
32. Bankhurst, A. D., Lambert, P. H., and Miescher, P. A., *Proc. Soc. Exp. Biol. Med.* **148,** 501, 1975.
33. Coutinho, A., and Möller, G., *Eur. J. Immunol.* **3,** 609, 1973.

CELLULAR IMMUNOLOGY **65**, 293–306 (1981)

Ontogenical Studies on Kinetics of Lipopolysaccharide-Induced Response to Bromelain-Treated Mouse Erythrocytes in Mouse Spleen Cells

I. Differences from the Response of Total IgM-Secreting Cells

SUSUMU KAWAGUCHI

Department of Microbiology and Immunology, Shimane Medical University, Izumo 693, Japan

Received July 20, 1981; accepted October 18, 1981

The administration of lipopolysaccharides (LPS) to mouse spleen cells, either *in vivo* or *in vitro*, induced IgM-secreting cells, in which direct plaque-forming cells (PFC) against bromelain-treated mouse erythrocytes (BrMRBC), sheep erythrocytes (SRBC), horse erythrocytes (HRBC), and rat erythrocytes (RRBC) were included. The frequencies of anti-BrMRBC PFC in total IgM-PFC rose rapidly 1 day after LPS activation, and then decreased, while those of anti-SRBC PFC, anti-HRBC PFC, and anti-RRBC PFC remained fairly constant during the LPS activation. The peculiar kinetics of anti-BrMRBC PFC response was also observed in cultures of spleen cells from nu/nu mice, thereby indicating that T cells do not play a role in the kinetics. During ontogeny, the frequencies of anti-BrMRBC PFC increased, while those of anti-SRBC PFC, anti-HRBC PFC, and anti-RRBC PFC remained unchanged. The increase of frequencies of anti-BrMRBC PFC was also observed in nu/nu mice, thereby indicating that such is also T independent.

INTRODUCTION

Bacterial lipopolysaccharides (LPS) differentiate B cells polyclonally to IgM-secreting cells (1). In the LPS-induced IgM-secreting cells of mice, antibody-forming cells against bromelain-treated mouse erythrocytes (BrMRBC) have been detected in considerably high numbers (2–10). Mouse anti-BrMRBC antibodies induced by LPS react with some self-components in the mouse (5); thus, the anti-BrMRBC plaque-forming cells (PFC) can be regarded as autoreactive antibody-forming cells, and the B cells which differentiate to anti-BrMRBC PFC by LPS activation as autoreactive B cells. Studies on the anti-BrMRBC PFC response induced by LPS should provide details as to the survival of autoreactive B cells and their differentiation to autoreactive antibody-forming cells, and contribute to elucidation of the mechanism of self-tolerance and autoimmunity.

LPS can activate a certain subpopulation of B cells directly without antigens and T cells, regardless of variable region specificities (11). The precontact of an antigen may expand or reduce the clones of B cells specific to the antigen. Moreover, the presence of an antigen with or without T cells at the polyclonal activation by LPS can affect the differentiation of LPS-reactive B cells to antibody-forming cells,

0008-8749/81/180293-14$02.00/0

specifically, so as to increase or decrease PFC specific to the antigen (12). Therefore, the LPS-induced PFC response to self-antigens, such as BrMRBC, may be modified and differ from the PFC reponse to non-self-antigens.

In the present work, the kinetics of anti-BrMRBC PFC responses in the spleens of mice of different ages were analyzed both *in vivo* and *in vitro*, and findings compared to those in case of total IgM-secreting cells. The kinetic patterns of anti-BrMRBC PFC responses after LPS activation differed from those in the case of total IgM-PFC response, and the frequencies of anti-BrMRBC PFC in total IgM-PFC increased during ontogeny. These observations are discussed with regard to the modification of anti-BrMRBC PFC response by self-antigens.

MATERIALS AND METHODS

Animals. C3H/HeSlc and BALB/cCrSlc mice were originally obtained from Shizuoka Agricultural Cooperative Association for Laboratory Animals (Shizuoka), and bred in our animal care facilities. Female nu/nu and nu/+ BALB/c mice (2 and 6 weeks old) were purchased from Matsumura Yakuhin Kenkyusho (Hiroshima).

Lipopolysaccharides. LPS from *Escherichia coli* strain 0111:B4, extracted by the Westphal method (Difco, Detroit, Mich.), were used.

Erythrocytes. Sheep blood and horse blood in Alsever's solution were purchased commercially. The blood of rats and mice were collected into Alsever's solution by vein puncture. Erythrocytes of sheep (SRBC), horse (HRBC) and rat (RRBC) were washed three times just before use. Bromelain-treated mouse erythrocytes (BrMRBC) were prepared according to the technique of Cunningham (3). Briefly, mouse erythrocytes were incubated as a 50% suspension with bromelain (Sigma Chemicals, St. Louis, Mo.) at a final concentration of 10 mg/ml in phosphate-buffered saline for 30 min at 37°C, and washed three times.

LPS activation in vivo. LPS were dissolved in saline and given intraperitoneally in a dose of 10 μg (2-week-old mice) or 50 μg (8-week-old mice).

LPS activation in vitro. Spleen cells were cultured in 24-well trays (No. 1483, NUNC, Roskilde) with a cell concentration of 1 or 2×10^6 cells/ml in 1 ml medium containing LPS (5 μg/ml). The culture medium consisted of RPMI 1640 (Nissui, Tokyo), supplemented with L-glutamine (2 mM), 2-mercaptoethanol (5×10^{-5} M), Hepes (10 mM), kanamycin (100 μg/ml), and fetal calf serum (10%), lot No. 95532 (Microbiological Associates, Bethesda, Md.). In cultures of 10^6 spleen cells in 1 ml medium, thymocytes obtained from 10-day-old syngeneic mice were added at a final concentration of 8×10^6 cells/ml. This addition improved the efficiency of the cultures and increased the developed IgM-secreting cells, nonspecifically, as growth-supporting feeder cells (13). The thymocytes (8×10^6 cells/culture) alone developed no more than 10^3 IgM-secreting cells/culture during 4 days of LPS activation *in vitro*.

Assay for plaque-forming cells (PFC). Total IgM-secreting cells and direct PFC specific to BrMRBC, SRBC, HRBC, or RRBC were detected by the slide modification (14) of the Jerne and Nordin hemolytic plaque assay. The assay for IgM-PFC depends on the use of SRBC coated with protein A (Pharmacia Fine Chemicals, Uppsala, Sweden) and rabbit antiserum against mouse IgM (μ) (Medical and Biological Laboratories, Nagoya) by the methods of Gronowicz *et al.* (15).

Guinea pig complement was used in assays of IgM-PFC, anti-SRBC PFC, and anti-HRBC PFC and rabbit complement in assays of anti-BrMRBC PFC and anti-RRBC PFC (7). These complements were obtained by bleeding the respective animals and harvesting their sera. The frequencies of PFC to BrMRBC, SRBC, HRBC, and RRBC were calculated as percentages to the total IgM-PFC.

RESULTS

Kinetics of Polyclonal PFC Response in Vivo

LPS were given intraperitoneally to four groups of mice, 2-week-old C3H/He, 8-week-old C3H/He, 2-week-old BALB/c, and 8-week-old BALB/c mice. After various times, total IgM-secreting PFC and anti-BrMRBC PFC in the spleens of these mice were enumerated (Fig. 1). In all of the four groups of mice, the kinetic patterns of anti-BrMRBC PFC response differed from those seen in the case of total IgM-PFC response. The frequencies of anti-BrMRBC PFC increased rapidly by 4 to 24 times during 1 day after LPS injection, and thereafter decreased to the background frequencies. This indicates that the appearance and/or continuance of anti-BrMRBC antibody-forming cells are regulated in a different manner from those of most IgM-secreting cells with other specificities.

Figure 1 also shows that the frequencies of anti-BrMRBC PFC vary with the ages of mice. In both of the strains, 2-week-old mice have less frequencies of anti-BrMRBC PFC than do 8-week-old mice, at any day after LPS injection. This means that the frequencies of LPS-reactive B cells specific to BrMRBC in total LPS-reactive B cells are probably less in younger mice and/or the LPS-induced development of anti-BrMRBC PFC are more specifically suppressed in younger mice.

IgM-PFC induced by LPS include antibody-forming cells against a variety of heterologous erythrocytes besides anti-BrMRBC PFC (7). To determine whether PFC response to heterologous erythrocytes occur in parallel with total IgM-PFC response, LPS were injected into 8-week-old BALB/c mice. At Days 0, 1, and 3 after LPS injection, IgM-PFC and specific PFC to BrMRBC, SRBC, HRBC, and RRBC in their spleens were enumerated. The frequencies of specific PFC, except for anti-BrMRBC PFC, were fairly constant during LPS activation (Fig. 2).

To assess whether frequencies of PFC to heterologous erythrocytes vary during ontogeny, LPS were injected into 2 and 8-week-old BALB/c mice. At Day 3 after LPS injection, IgM-PFC and PFC specific to BrMRBC, SRBC, HRBC, or RRBC in their spleens were enumerated. As shown in Fig. 3, the frequencies of specific PFC to heterologous erythrocytes were much the same between 2 and 8-week-old mice.

Kinetics of Polyclonal PFC Response in Vitro

The above experiments *in vivo* revealed that the kinetic patterns of anti-BrMRBC PFC in LPS-induced polyclonal activation differ from those of total IgM-PFC, and that the frequencies of anti-BrMRBC PFC in total IgM-PFC increase during ontogeny. These phenomena may be limited to experiments *in vivo*; for instance, self-antigens reactive with anti-BrMRBC antibodies detected in plasma (17) or in the gastrointestinal tract (5) may play a role even during LPS activation.

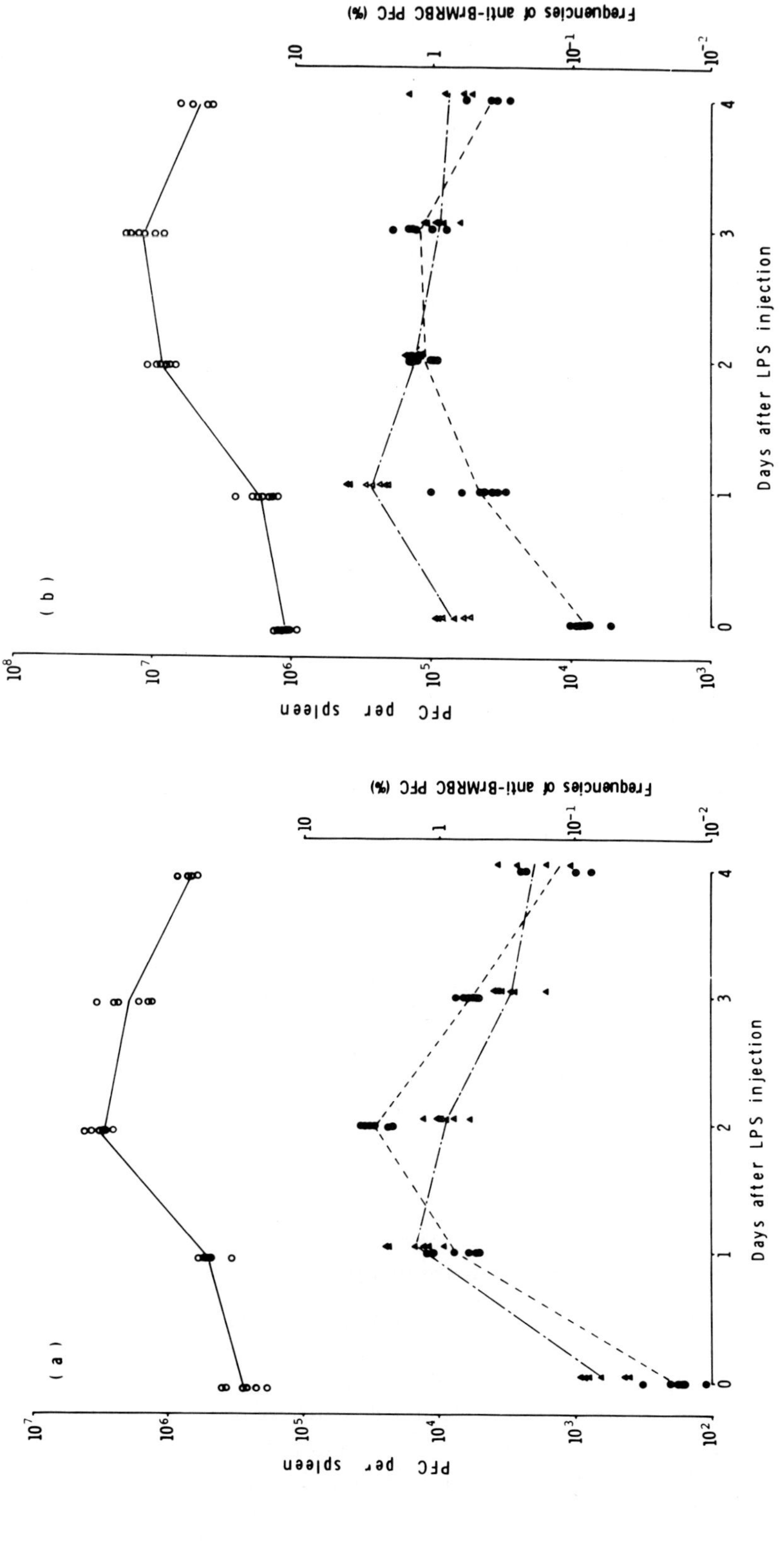
(a)
(b)
PFC per spleen
Frequencies of anti-BrMRBC PFC (%)
Days after LPS injection

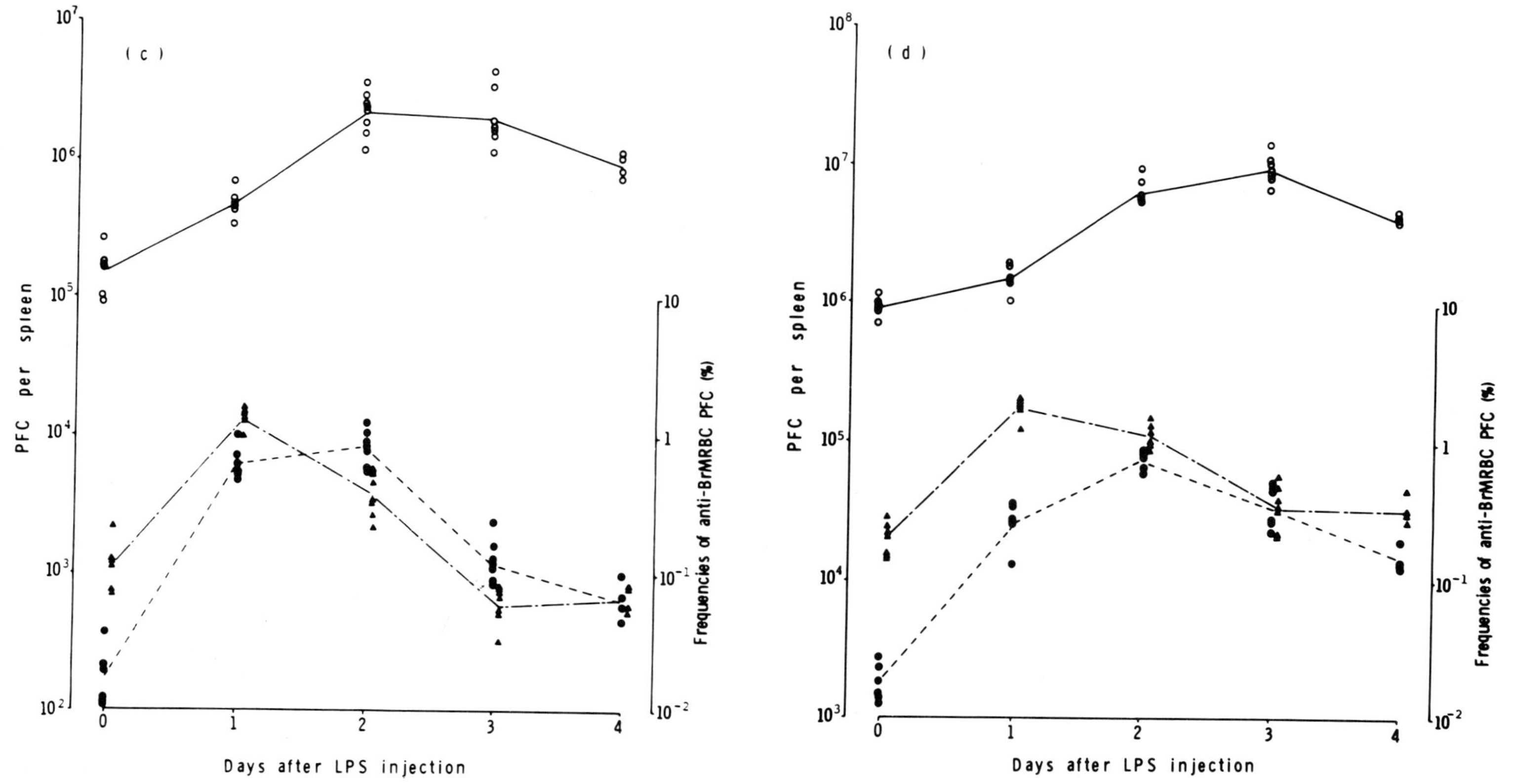

FIG. 1. Kinetics of PFC response induced by the intraperitoneal injection of 10 μg LPS to (a) 2-week-old C3H/He mice and (b) 2-week-old BALB/c mice, or 50 μg LPS in (c) 8-week-old C3H/He mice and (d) 8-week-old BALB/c mice. ——, IgM-PFC; – – –, anti-BrMRBC PFC; —·—, frequencies of anti-BrMRBC PFC in total IgM-PFC.

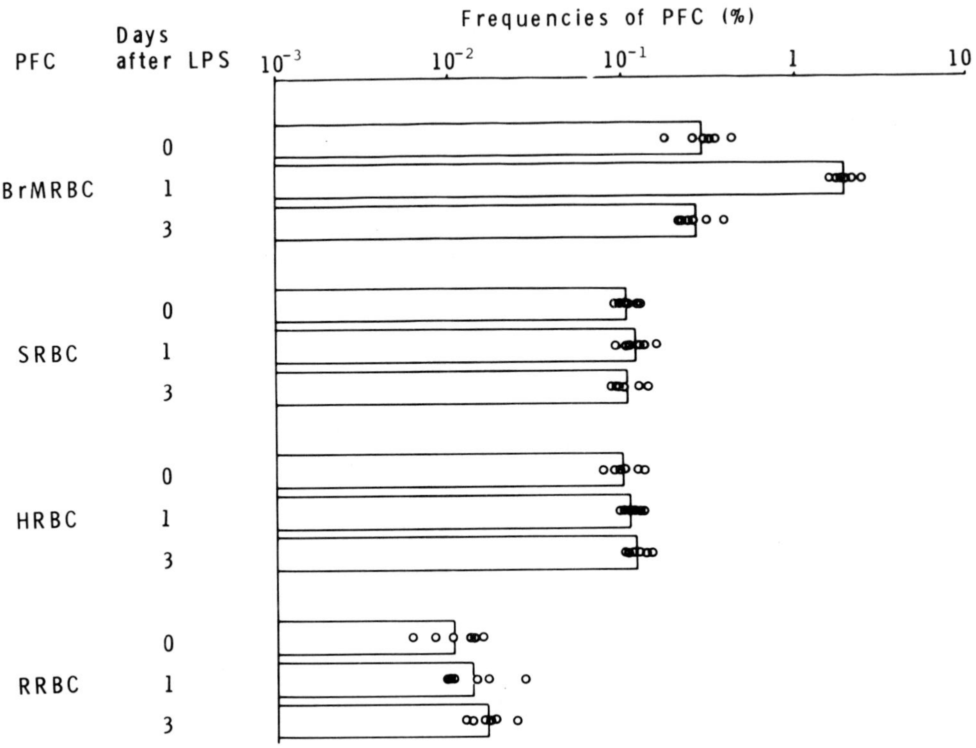

FIG. 2. Frequencies of anti-BrMRBC PFC, anti-SRBC PFC, anti-HRBC PFC, and anti-RRBC PFC in spleens of 8-week-old BALB/c mice at Days 0, 1, and 3 after the injection of 50 μg LPS. Each circle represents the individual value. The length of columns refer to the geometric mean.

Thus, in *in vitro* experiments, spleen cells from 2-week-old C3H/He, 8-week-old C3H/He, 2-week-old BALB/c, and 8-week-old BALB/c mice were cultured in the presence of LPS (5 μg/ml) and feeder syngeneic thymocytes. On various days after culture, IgM-PFC and anti-BrMRBC PFC were enumerated (Fig. 4). In all of the four groups of cultures, the frequencies of anti-BrMRBC PFC increased by 3 to 12 times during a 1-day culture, and thereafter decreased to the former frequencies (at Day 0). In both strains of mice, the frequencies of anti-BrMRBC PFC in total IgM-PFC were less in younger mice (2-week-old) than older mice (8-week-old), on any day of culture. These observations *in vitro* paralleled those *in vivo* (Fig. 1), and indicate that the peculiar behavior of anti-BrMRBC PFC induced by LPS is due to the nature of the spleen cell population itself.

In the above experiments *in vitro*, T cells were included not only in the spleen cells but also in the feeder cells. As T cells may affect the anti-BrMRBC PFC response specifically, spleen cells from 2-week-old nu/nu , 6-week-old nu/nu, 2-week-old nu/+, and 6-week-old nu/+ BALB/c mice were cultured with or without feeder BALB/c thymocytes in the presence of LPS. As shown in Fig. 5, feeder thymocytes markedly influenced the numbers of IgM-PFC and anti-BrMRBC PFC, in cultures of both nu/nu and nu/+ spleen cells. However, the frequencies of anti-BrMRBC PFC were little influenced, in any group of mice. These findings indicate that feeder T cells may not to any great extent modify anti-BrMRBC PFC spe-

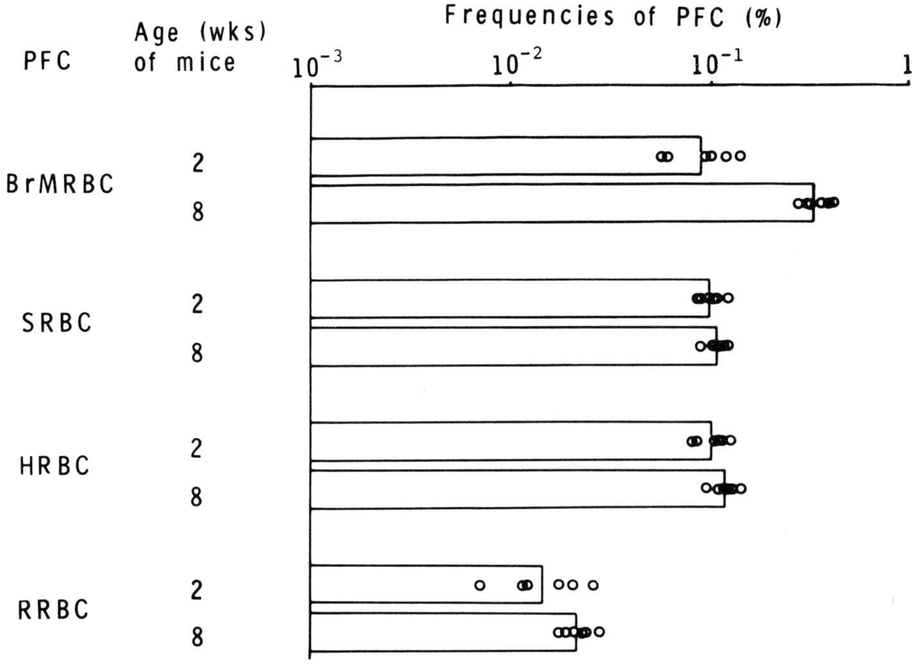

FIG. 3. Frequencies of anti-BrMRBC PFC, anti-SRBC PFC, anti-HRBC PFC, and anti-RRBC PFC in spleens of 2 and 8-week-old BALB/c mice at Day 3 after the injection of LPS. Each circle represents the individual value. The length of columns refer to the geometric mean.

cifically, even though the total number of IgM-secreting cells is increased. The frequencies of anti-BrMRBC PFC in nu/nu mice were the highest at Day 1 and thereafter decreased, coincident with findings in the nu/+ mice. This indicates that the kinetics of anti-BrMRBC PFC response is not influenced specifically by T cells, and that the peculiar kinetics is not due to T cells. The ontogenical development of frequencies of anti-BrMRBC PFC in total IgM-PFC was also observed in nu/nu mice, and the frequencies of anti-BrMRBC PFC were much the same in nu/nu mice. These findings indicate that the increase of frequencies of background and LPS-induced anti-BrMRBC PFC during ontogeny are influenced little by the T cells.

DISCUSSION

The kinetic patterns of anti-BrMRBC PFC response induced polyclonally by LPS *in vivo* or *in vitro* were analyzed by calculating and comparing relative frequencies of anti-BrMRBC PFC in total IgM-secreting PFC. The numbers of total IgM-PFC, as well as anti-BrMRBC PFC, per spleen or spleen cell *in vivo*, or per cultured cell *in vitro* varied not only with the day of PFC assay after LPS activation of the age of the mouse, but also with the dose of LPS and the number of cultured cells. Therefore, the characteristics of anti-BrMRBC PFC response are difficult to assess when looking at the intact numbers of anti-BrMRBC PFC. Nevertheless, the findings in a previous report (12) plus the present observations demonstrate that the frequencies of antibody-forming cells to some heterologous erythrocyte

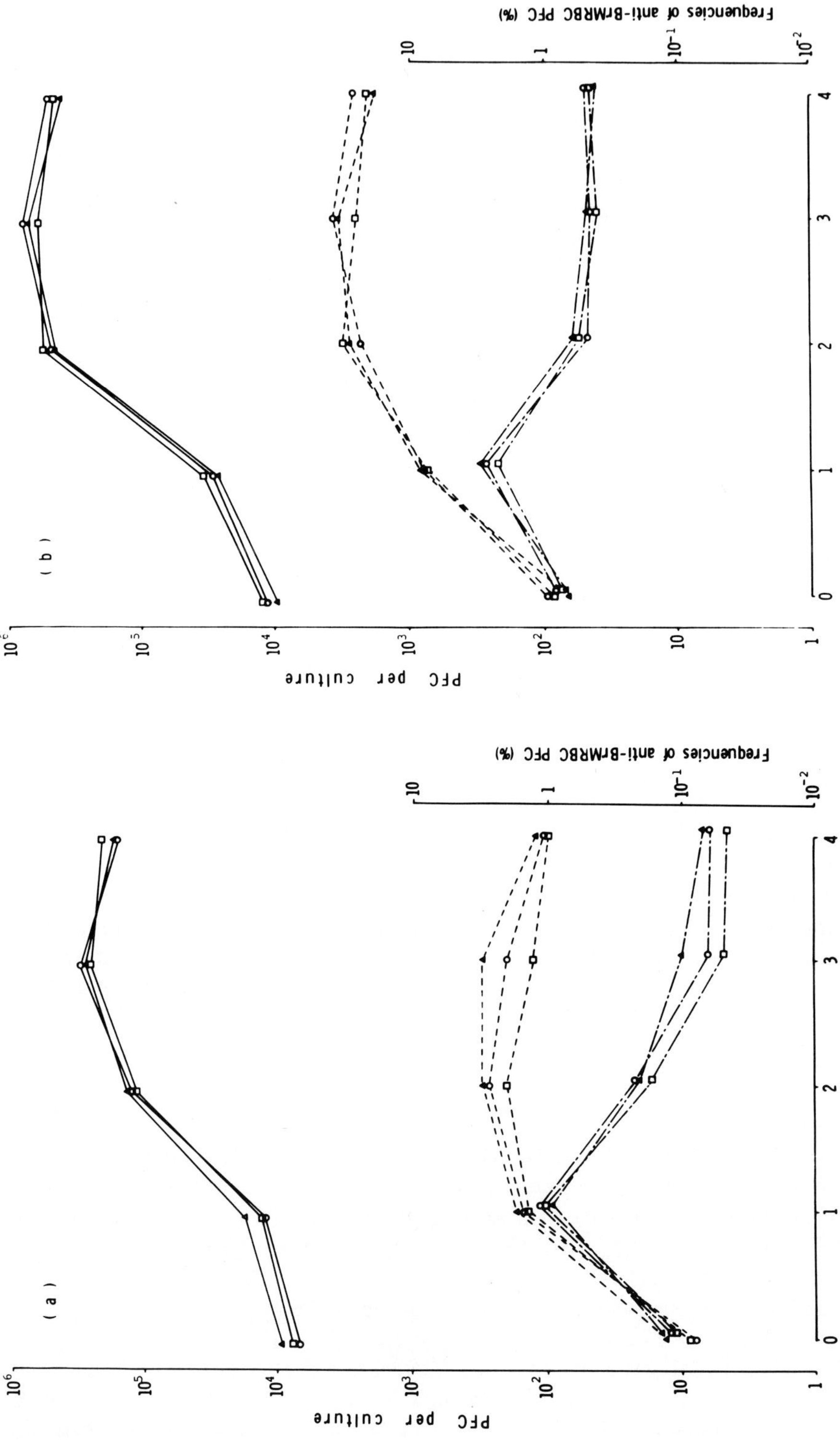

(a)
(b)
PFC per culture
1
10
10^2
10^3
10^4
10^5
10^6
Frequencies of anti-BrMRBC PFC (%)
10^{-2}
10^{-1}
1
10
Days in culture
0
1
2
3
4

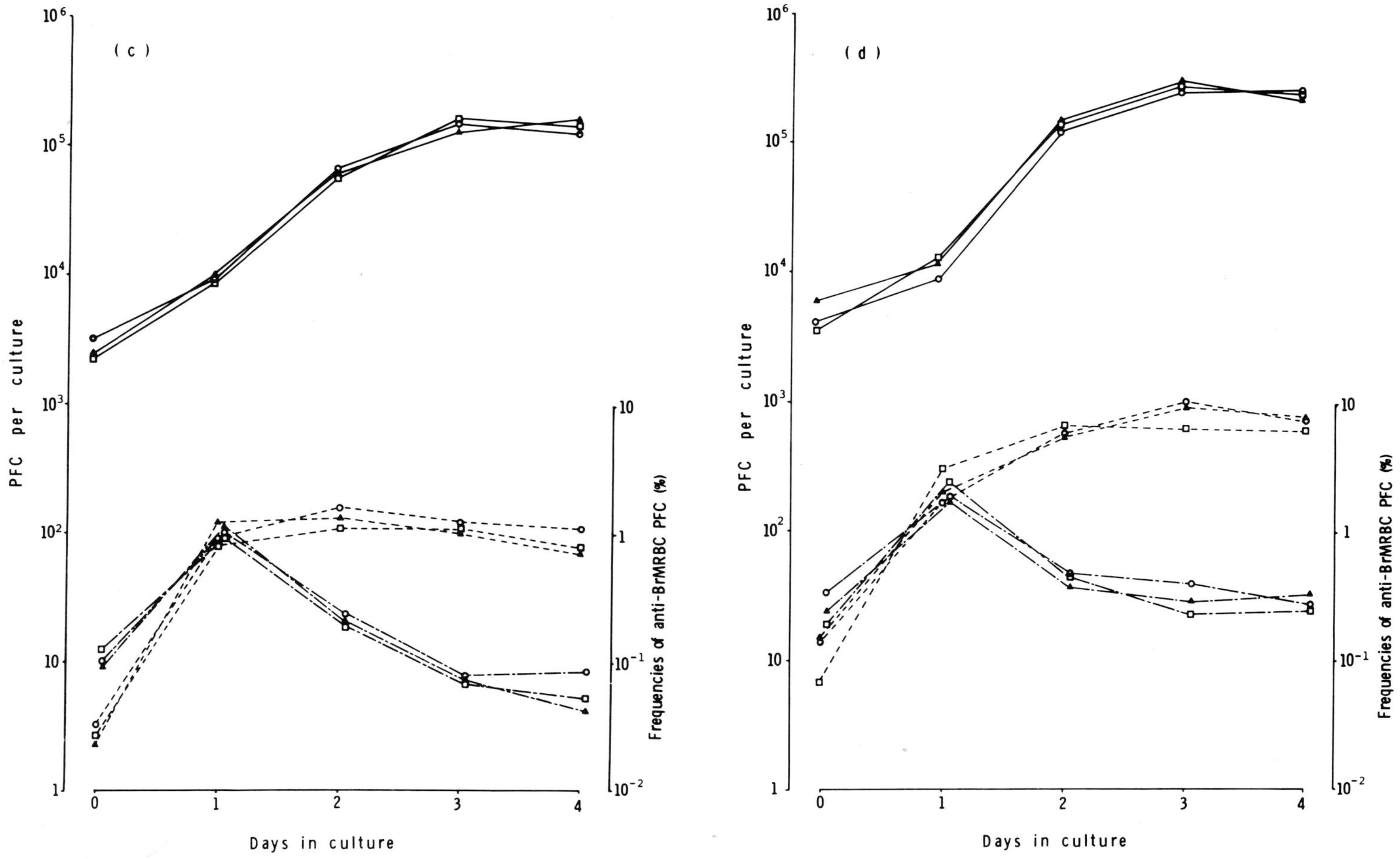

FIG. 4. Kinetics of PFC response induced by the administration of 5 μg LPS in cultures of three individual samples of spleen cells from (a) 2-week-old C3H/He mice, (b) 8-week-old C3H/He mice, (c) 2-week-old BALB/c mice, and (d) 8-week-old BALB/c mice. ——, IgM-PFC; – – –, anti-BrMRBC PFC; — · —, frequencies of anti-BrMRBC PFC in total IgM-PFC.

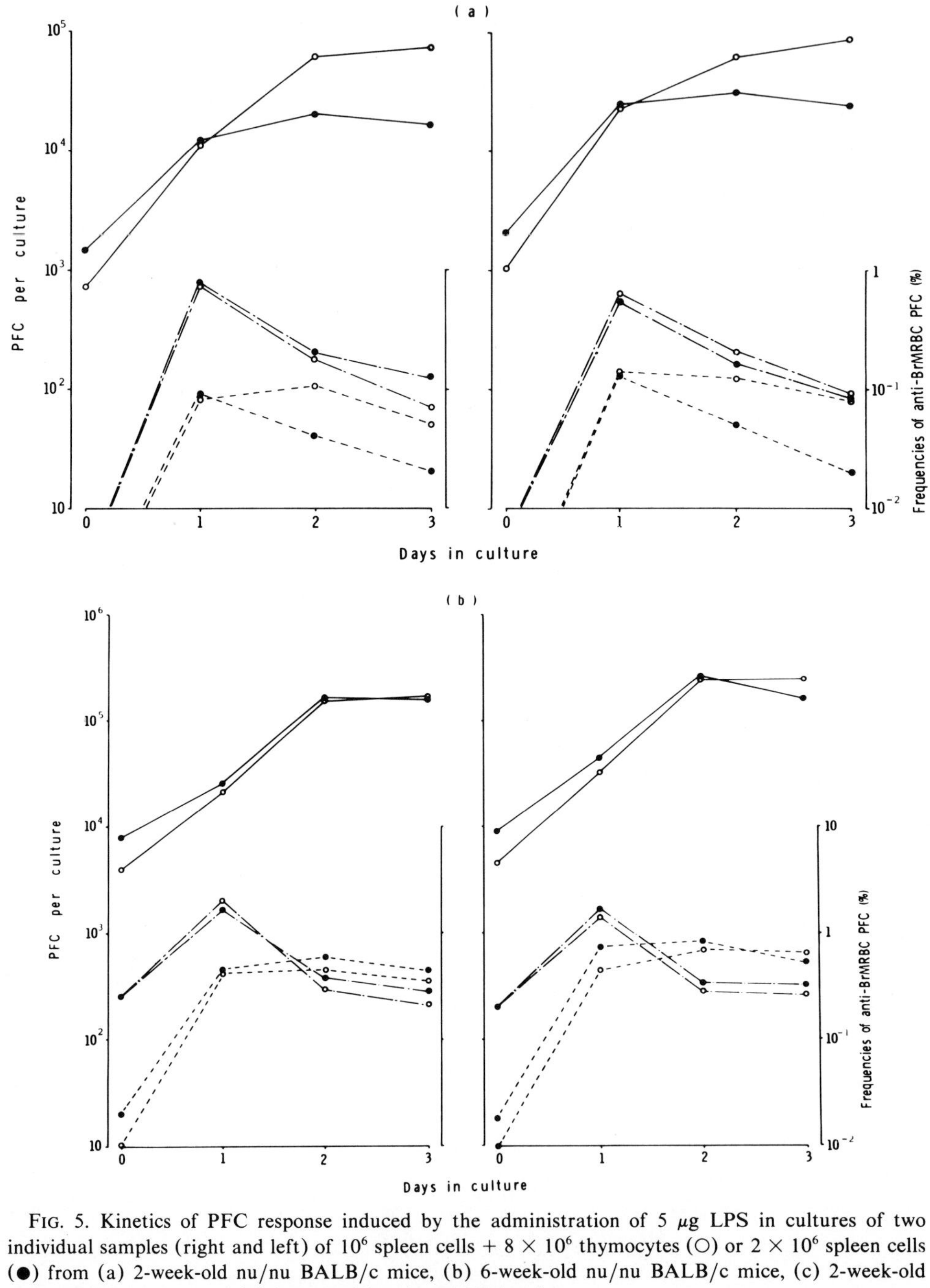

FIG. 5. Kinetics of PFC response induced by the administration of 5 μg LPS in cultures of two individual samples (right and left) of 10^6 spleen cells + 8 × 10^6 thymocytes (○) or 2 × 10^6 spleen cells (●) from (a) 2-week-old nu/nu BALB/c mice, (b) 6-week-old nu/nu BALB/c mice, (c) 2-week-old nu/+ BALB/c mice, and (d) 6-week-old nu/+ BALB/c mice.

antigens in total IgM-PFC scarcely vary with the day of PFC assay, the age of the mouse, the dose of LPS, the presence or absence of T cells, or the numbers of cultured cells. The parallelism of total IgM-PFC response with specific PFC response to heterologous erythrocyte antigens indicates that most of the IgM-PFC

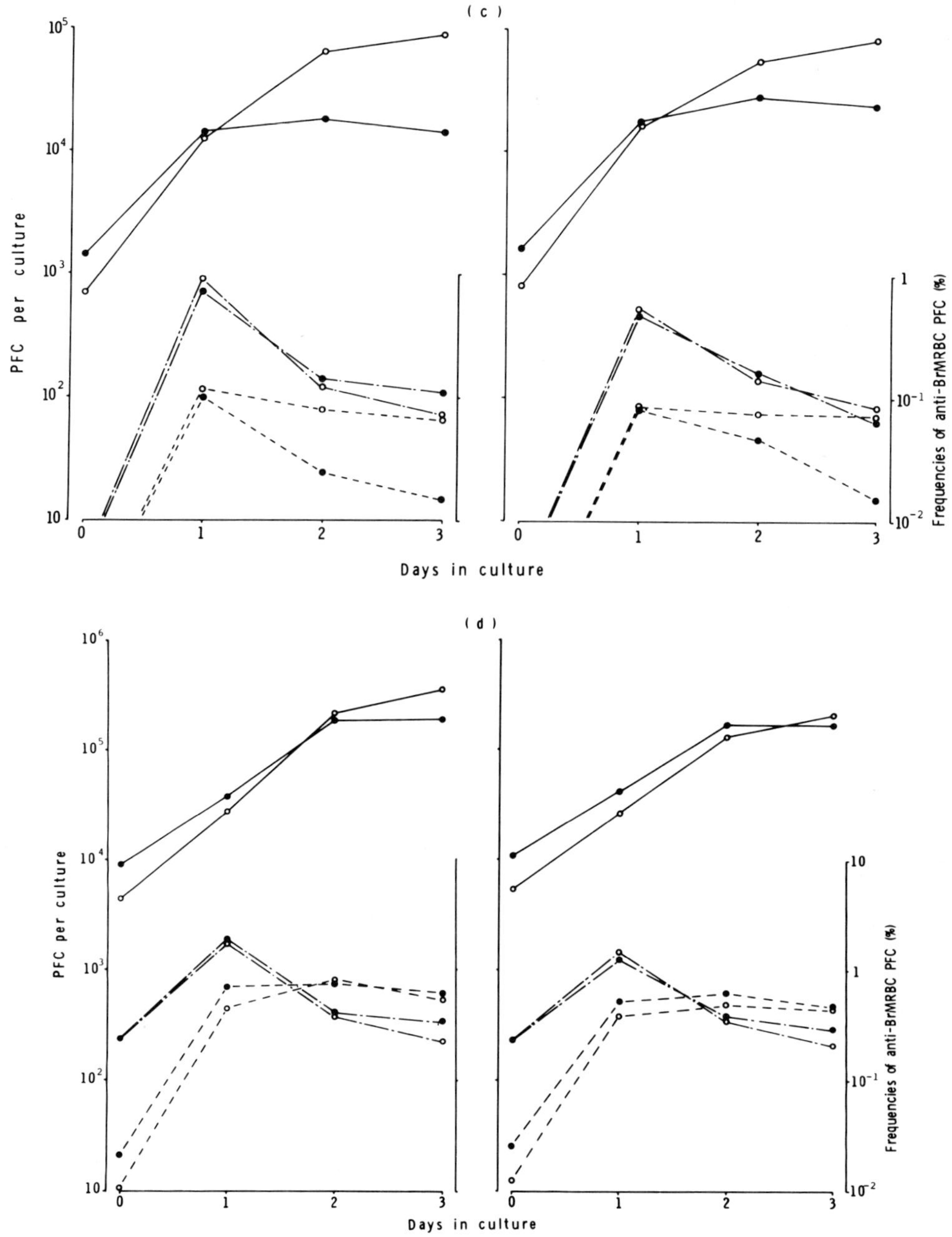

FIG. 5—*Continued.*

are induced without effects of antigens and specific T cells, as well as PFC specific to heterologous erythrocyte antigens, at the time of LPS activation. Thus, the frequencies of anti-BrMRBC PFC in total IgM-PFC may serve as a representative index for investigations on the modification of LPS-induced PFC response by self-antigens.

The kinetic patterns of anti-BrMRBC PFC response induced by LPS differ from those of total IgM-PFC response, both *in vivo* and *in vitro*; at the early phase (1 day after LPS activation) the frequencies of anti-BrMRBC PFC increased and thereafter decreased. If LPS have antigenic determinants common to BrMRBC, such may affect the anti-BrMRBC PFC response specifically. As to the PFC response to antigenic determinants on LPS, Coutinho *et al.* (16) reported that the PFC response reached its peak later than the polyclonal PFC response to other antigens, and occurred with lower doses of LPS. However, the anti-BrMRBC PFC response in our study declined sooner than the total IgM-PFC response. When lowering the dose of LPS, the frequencies of anti-BrMRBC PFC in total IgM-PFC were not elevated (data not shown). Moreover, Fujiwara and Akiyama (10) reported that the presence of LPS in the PFC assay did not inhibit the appearance of anti-BrMRBC PFC in the spleen cells of LPS-injected mice. These findings suggest that the antigenic determinants on LPS participate little in the anti-BrMRBC PFC response.

With regard to the mechanisms involved some possibilities are: (i) The B cells population which responds to LPS and differentiates to IgM-secreting cells consists of two subsets. One is a population which can differentiate to IgM-secreting cells during 1 or 2 days after LPS activation, and thereafter disappear rapidly. The other is a population which can differentiate gradually during 2 or 3 days after LPS activation. The former may contain relatively higher frequencies of anti-BrMRBC B cells than the later from which most of IgM-PFC are produced. For that matter, it has been reported that different subsets of B cells are activated by different PBAs (LPS, PPD or dextran sulfate) (18), and kinetic patterns of PFC response by LPS are different between mature and immature B cells (19, 20). However, there have been no reports on B cells which differentiate to IgM-secreting cells and disappear so rapidly as did the anti-BrMRBC B cells in this experiments. (ii) As self-antigens cross-reactive with BrMRBC may be present in the mouse body (5), anti-BrMRBC B cells may have precontact with specific antigens. This precontact with an antigen may limit the differentiation and proliferation of the specific B cells while it expands or reduces the B cell clones specific to the antigen. Thus, the kinetic patterns of anti-BrMRBC PFC which develop mostly from presensitized LPS-reactive B cells may differ from those of total IgM-PFC which develop mostly from "virgin" LPS-reactive B cells. (iii) Specific suppressive forces may act on anti-BrMRBC PFC or anti-BrMRBC B cells at the late phase of LPS activation (2–4 days after activation). Suppressor T cells reportedly suppress the development of anti-BrMRBC PFC (3, 9). This experiment, however, showed that the peculiar kinetics of anti-BrMRBC PFC response occurred even in the absence of T cells (Fig. 5). Thus, T cells probably do not play an important role in the suppression. As another suppressive force, self-antigens cross-reactive with BrMRBC may act directly on anti-BrMRBC B cells or antibody-secreting cells to inactivate them; as shown previously (12), heterologous erythrocyte antigens added even 1 day after LPS activation reduced specifically the frequencies of PFC to the antigen.

This present study has confirmed that the frequencies of LPS-reactive B cells specific to BrMRBC in total LPS-reactive B cells increase during ontogeny, as suggested by others (5, 10). As one explanation for the ontogenical change of the B-cell repertoire, Klinman *et al.* (21) and Cooper *et al.* (22) proposed and supported the idea that clonal diversity is generated by a programmed expression of genetic information in a sequential pattern during ontogeny. For the ontogenical development of frequencies of anti-BrMRBC LPS-reactive B cells in total LPS-reactive B cells, the action of self-antigens cross-reactive with BrMRBC may be also responsible. Regarding the role of self-antigens, two opposing explanations are possible. (i) Self-antigens cross-reactive with BrMRBC may serve as a positive stimuli for the anti-BrMRBC B cells. Cunningham and Steele (5) observed the increase of antigens reactive with anti-BrMRBC antibodies in the mouse body, thereby suggesting that LPS-reactive B cells to BrMRBC expand in contact with self-antigens cross-reactive with BrMRBC. There is, however, no definite report as to the clonal expansion of LPS-reactive B cells to an antigen by presensitization with the antigen (18). With regard to another positive action of antigens in LPS activation, Bretscher (7) observed that the magnitude of the IgM response to a variety of antigens in LPS-injected mice is approximately proportional to the magnitude of the background response in untreated mice, and assumed that all the IgM-secreting cells induced by LPS were due to the cooperation of LPS with antigens. However, the positive action of antigens at LPS activation was detectable only in the presence of T cells (12), while the increase of frequencies of anti-BrMRBC PFC during ontogeny occurred even in nu/nu mice defecting T cells (Fig. 5), thereby indicating that the increase cannot be ascribed to the positive action of antigens cross-reactive to BrMRBC present at LPS activation. (ii) Self-antigens may act to reduce the frequencies of LPS-reactive B cells to BrMRBC. It has been reported that LPS-reactive B cells to an antigen can be inactivated by inducing tolerance to the antigen (22–25), though opposing results have also been reported (26). If the tolerance to self-antigens cross-reactive to BrMRBC do reduce the frequencies of LPS-reactive B cells to BrMRBC, anti-BrMRBC B cells in the younger mice must be more exposed to the antigens.

ACKNOWLEDGMENTS

I thank Drs. S. Morikawa and T. Harada (Department of Pathology, Shimane Medical University) for pertinent discussion and use of facilities, Kenji Kishi for technical assistance, and M. Ohara for comments on the manuscript.

REFERENCES

1. Andersson, J., Sjöberg, O., and Möller, G., *Eur. J. Immunol.* **2,** 349, 1972.
2. Cunningham, A. J., *Nature (London)* **252,** 749, 1974.
3. Cunningham, A. J., *Nature (London)* **254,** 143, 1975.
4. Steele, E. J., and Cunningham, A. J., *Nature (London)* **274,** 483, 1978.
5. Cunningham, A. J., and Steele, E. J., *In* "B Lymphocytes in the Immune Response" (M. Cooper, D. E. Mosier, I. Scher, and E. S. Vitetta, Eds.), pp. 187–201. Elsevier/North-Holland, Amsterdam, 1979.
6. Pages, J., and Bussard, A. E., *Nature (London)* **257,** 316, 1975.
7. Bretscher, P. A., *Eur. J. Immunol.* **8,** 534, 1978.
8. Marshall-Clarke, S., Coole, A., and Hutchings, P. R., *Eur. J. Immunol.* **9,** 820, 1979.
9. Meredith, P. J., Kristie, J. A., and Walford, R. L., *J. Immunol.* **123,** 87, 1979.
10. Fujiwara, M., and Akiyama, Y., *Cell. Immunol.* **55,** 366, 1980.
11. Coutinho, A., and Möller, G., *Advan. Immunol.* **21,** 113, 1975.
12. Kawaguchi, S., *Cell. Immunol.* **55,** 456, 1980.
13. Andersson, J., Coutinho, A., Lernhardt, W., and Melchers, F., *Cell* **10,** 27, 1977.
14. Mishell, R. I., and Dutton, R. W., *J. Exp. Med.* **126,** 423, 1967.
15. Gronowicz, E., Coutinho, A., and Melchers, F., *Eur. J. Immunol.* **6,** 588, 1976.

16. Coutinho, A., Gronowicz, E., Bullock, W. W., and Möller, G., *J. Exp. Med.* **139,** 74, 1974.
17. Linder, E., and Edgington, T. S., *J. Immunol.* **110,** 53, 1973.
18. Gronowicz, E., and Coutinho, A., *Transplant. Rev.* **24,** 3, 1975.
19. Melchers, F., *Eur. J. Immunol.* **7,** 476, 1977.
20. Phillips, R. A., and Melchers, F., *J. Immunol.* **122,** 1473, 1979.
21. Klinman, N. R., and Press, J. L., *Transplant. Rev.* **24,** 41, 1975.
22. Cooper, M. D., Kubagawa, H., Vogler, L. B., Levitt, D., and Lawton, A. R., *In* "B Lymphocytes in the Immune Response" (M. D. Cooper, D. E. Mosier, I. Scher, and E. S. Vitetta, Eds.), pp. 181–186. Elsevier/North-Holland, Amsterdam, 1979.
23. Fiddler, J. M., *J. Immunol.* **121,** 245, 1978.
24. Nossal, G. J. V., Pike, B. L., Teale, J. M., Layton, J. E., Kay, T. W., and Battye, F. L., *Immunol. Rev.* **43,** 185, 1979.
25. Parks, D. E., and Weigle, W. O., *J. Immunol.* **124,** 1230, 1980.
26. Möller, G., Gronowicz, E., Persson, U., Coutinho, A., Möller, E., Hammarström, L., and Smith, C. I. E., *J. Exp. Med.* **143,** 1429, 1976.

CELLULAR IMMUNOLOGY 65, 307–316 (1981)

Insulin Receptors on Human Lymphoid Lines of B-Cell Origin

PIERRE ÅMAN,* GUNNEL LUNDIN,† KERSTIN HALL,† AND GEORGE KLEIN*

*Department of Tumor Biology, Karolinska Institute, and †Department of Endocrinology, Karolinska Hospital, S-104 01 Stockholm, Sweden

Received August 26, 1981; accepted October 7, 1981

Human lymphoid lines derived from normal or neoplastic B cells were assayed for insulin binding. ^{125}I-Labeled insulin was allowed to bind to cells. Bound radioactivity which was inhibited with unlabeled insulin was regarded as specific binding. Among 46 lines tested, 43 bound more insulin than normal peripheral B lymphocytes. The majority of the lines resembled activated lymphocytes, with regard to their insulin binding. More mature cells represented by EBV-transformed lines of normal origin, bound more insulin than the less differentiated Burkitt lymphoma lines. However, even the latter bound significantly more insulin than peripheral blood lymphocytes.

INTRODUCTION

The surface marker expression of B lymphocytes undergoes characteristic changes during differentiation. The early differentiation steps that occur prior to activation generate B lymphocytes that carry surface immunoglobulins, mainly of the IgM and IgD classes (1). Activation results in proliferation, Ig secretion, or both (2). Mature B lymphocytes of the peripheral blood, lymph nodes, and spleen do not differentiate until they are stimulated by antigen or mitogen. They respond only in the presence of certain associated cells.

Insulin receptors provide an interesting marker that undergoes characteristic changes during activation. Gavin *et al.* (3) reported that they were present on circulating human lymphocytes. This turned out to be an artifact, however, due to the presence of contaminating insulin-binding monocytes (4). Krug *et al.* (5) showed that *in vitro* activation of human peripheral lymphocytes induced the expression of insulin receptors. Helderman *et al.* (6–8) found that allografting and other types of antigenic stimulation *in vivo* induced insulin binding to T- and B-enriched lymphocyte populations derived from blood and the spleen of rats. Similar findings were made in mice and humans. The authors concluded that insulin receptors represent an universal marker of activated lymphocytes.

Established human lymphoid lines appear to be arrested at different levels of development. Burkitt's lymphoma (BL) lines express membrane Ig, as a rule, mostly of the IgM class and sometimes IgG. They do not express IgD, however, and have no or only very little secretory activity (9, 10). Together with the morphological evidence this suggests that BL cells represent a differentiation stage prior to IgD expression. The EBV-transformed lymphoblastoid cell lines (LCL) of normal origin represent a polyclonal mixture of different types in newly established lines, most

0008-8749/81/180307-10$02.00/0

cells have a blast-like morphology, secrete Ig and express membrane Ig of different classes.

The aim of the present study was to examine the insulin binding to BL and LCL lines, as a further attempt to define their position in the B-cell differentiation scheme.

The LCL group included polyclonal lines derived from normal adults (NAD lines and BL7) and, in addition, three monoclonal lines isolated from a tumor-infiltrating lymphocyte population (Dakiki Arosros lines) and four cloned lines from an ataxia telangiectasia patient, selected for clonability in agarose (ATA-E95-STO lines). We have also examined four spontaneously emerging lines, derived from the peripheral blood of infectious mononucleosis patients (SPIM lines). The tumor-derived cells included, in addition, both EBV carrying EBV-negative BL-lines, a Swedish B-cell lymphosarcoma line (U698), two myeloma lines (U-266, Simpsson), and fresh blood samples from eight patients with chronic lymphocytic leukemia (CLL). Normal peripheral blood B lymphocytes were included as negative controls.

MATERIALS AND METHODS

The cell lines (Table 1) were cultured in RPMI 1640 supplemented with 8% fetal calf serum (Gibco), 100 U penicillin and 100 μg of streptomycin/ml in a 5% CO_2 atmosphere at 37°C. The cells were fed every 3 days by resuspending them

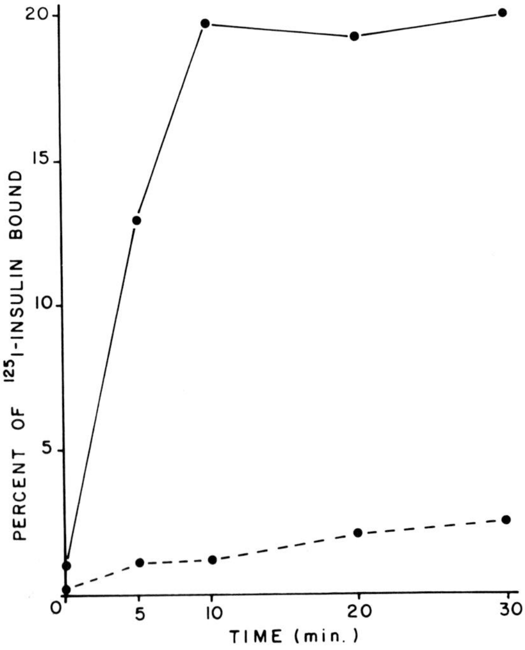

FIG. 1. Cells (12 × 10^6) were incubated at 37°C for 0 to 30 min with 0.25 ng ^{125}I-labeled insulin. Cells were separated from free hormone and the bound activity was counted. The solid line shows % total binding and the dotted line shows the binding in the presence of 10,000 ng nonlabeled hormone, regarded as nonspecific binding.

in fresh medium at a density of 0.2–0.4 × 10^6/ml. For experiments, the cells were harvested 2 days after feeding by centrifugation for 5 minutes at 400*g*. The cells were washed twice in 1.2 m*M* $CaCl_2$, 138 m*M* NaCl, 5.4 m*M* KCl 8.1 m*M* $MgSO_4$, 0.5 m*M* KH_2PO_4, 0.3 m*M* Na_2HPO_4, pH 6.9. Viability was checked by trypan blue staining before resuspending in the assay buffer: 50 m*M* Hepes, 50 m*M* Tris, 10 m*M* $MgCl_2$, 2 m*M* EDTA, 10 m*M* dextrose, 10 m*M* $CaCl_2$, 50 m*M* NaCl, 5 m*M* KCl, and 0.1% bovine serum albumin at pH 7.8. Only samples with more than 90% viable cells were used.

B-lymphocyte preparation. Mononuclear cells were prepared from peripheral blood by Ficoll–Isopaque gradient centrifugation (11), washed three times and incubated on a nylon wool column in medium for 30 min at 37°C. Nonadherent cells were eluted with medium and the adherent B-cell fraction was eluted with fetal calf serum (12). Sheep red blood cell-rosetting cells (13) were eliminated by a second Ficoll–Isopaque centrifugation and macrophages removed by adherence to the surface of plastic culture bottles.

Insulin receptor assay. The insulin receptor assay was modified from Gambhir *et al.* (14). Twelve million cells were incubated at 37°C with 0.25 ng of ^{125}I-labeled porcine insulin in absence or presence of excess (10,000 ng) insulin, in a total volume of 500 μl. Triplicates were collected from each sample and the cells were separated from free insulin by centrifugation through a layer of dinonylphtalate-

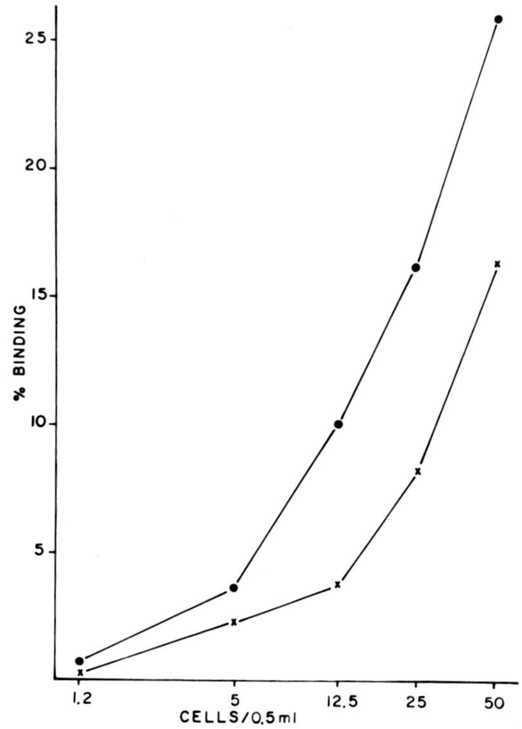

FIG. 2. Different numbers of U 698 cells (1.2–50 × 10^6/500 ml) were incubated with labeled insulin for 20 min at 37°C in the presence × or absence ● of 10,000 ng nonlabeled hormone. The cells were separated from the supernatant and the radioactivity of the pellet was counted.

TABLE 1

Insulin Binding to the Lymphoid Lines

Cell lines	EBV carrying status	Time in culture (years)	Reference	Number of experiments	Mean percentage specific binding	Standard deviation
BL-lines						
Daudi	+	12	(24)	3	3.6	1.2
Raji	+	15	(25)	3	1.5	0.6
Jijoye	+	13	(26)	3	2.0	2.2
A. K. Caren	+	1	[a]	2	0.3	
Sulubu	+	8	(27)	3	12.4	1.7
Akuba	+	8	(27)	5	5.7	3.0
Naliaka	+	8	(27)	4	3.4	3.9
Silfere	+	11	(28)	4	5.8	1.2
Salim Mwalim	+		[b]	2	9.4	
Namalwa	+	4	(27)	4	6.9	1.4
Seraphine	+	8	(27)	3	7.7	1.9
Rael	+	8	(27)	3	1.1	0.1
Lukes	−		[c]	2	8.4	
BJAB	−	8	(29)	2	2.1	
Ramos	−		(30)	3	2.4	0.9
EBV-converted, originally EBV-negative BL lines						
BJAB 28 v B	+			1	0.5	
BJAB 28 v P	+			1	0.7	
E 95 B-Ramos	+	4	(31)	1	11.3	
E 95 C-Ramos	+	4	(31)	1	7.9	
E 95 D-Ramos	+	4	(31)	1	11.2	
E 95 E-Ramos	+	4	(31)	2	6.0	
IIWA Ramos cl 10	+	4	(32)	3	2.4	1.3
AW Ramos cl 2	+	4	(32)	3	6.4	2.1
EHRA-Ramos	+	4	(31)	12	20.0	6.3
EHRB-Ramos	+	4	(31)	1	9.0	
Ramos/HRIK	+	4	(32)	4	4.4	1.4
LCL lines from normal adults, not cloned						
NAD 5	+	1		1	20.0	
NAD 7	+	1		4	14.0	2.6
NAD 8	+	1		3	10.0	1.9
NAD 12	+	1		4	17.4	6.7
NAD 13	+	1		10	24.0	9.4
B17	+			3	10.4	1.7
Cloned LCL lines						
Dakiki Arosros cl 1	+	1	(33)	7	27.1	10.4
Dakiki Arosros cl 2	+	1	(33)	4	18.5	10.8
Dakiki Arosros cl 3	+	1	(33)	3	26.0	6.2
AT-A-95-STO cl 7-III Pl.	+	1	[d]	4	26.3	8.8
AT-A-95-STO cl 7-III Ma.	+	1	[d]	3	25.1	4.8
AT-A-95-STO cl 2-III Ep.	+	1	[d]	3	24.8	1.4
AT-A-95-STO cl 2-III Po.	+	1	[d]	2	29.1	
Spontaneous lines from IM blood (not cloned)						
SPIM 160	+	1	[d]	2	3.8	
SPIM 168	+	1	[d]	2	7.5	
SPIM 169				1	8.6	
SPIM 171	+	1	[d]	3	8.5	2.0
Histiocytic lymphoma						
U 698	−		(34)	10	12.8	6.8
Myeloma						
U-266	−		(35)	2	21.1	
Simpsson	−			4	5.5	2.8
Normal peripheral blood lymphocytes						
1	−				0.5	
2	−				0.6	
3	−				0.0	
4	−				0.5	
Blood samples from CLL patients	−	−		8	0.3	0.3

[a] A. Karande, personal communication.
[b] J. Nadkarni, personal communication.
[c] E. Kieff, personal communication.
[d] I. Ernberg, personal communication.

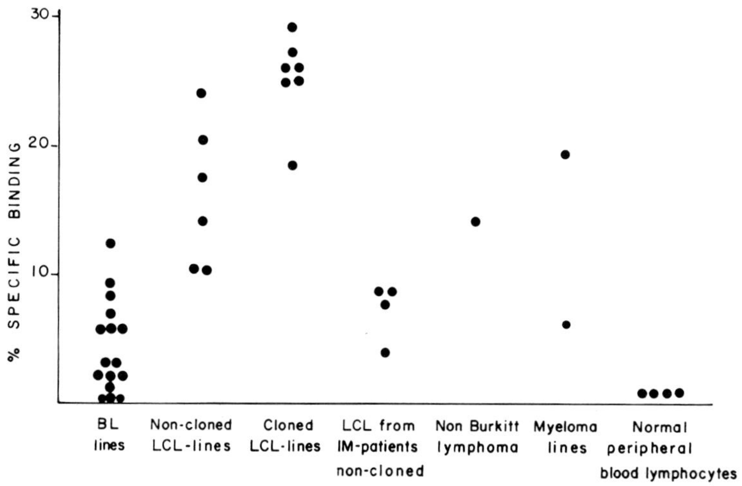

FIG. 3. The insulin binding of different groups of lines is shown in comparison with the binding of normal peripheral blood B lymphocytes.

dibutyryl phtalate, 2:3. This oil ratio was found to permit complete passage of the cells, without letting the nonbound insulin to pass. The pellets were counted in a gamma counter. Specific binding was calculated as the total binding minus binding in presence of excess insulin. Degradation was measured by incubating iodine-labeled insulin with cells as described above and rebinding the free insulin in the supernatant to placenta membranes as described by Takano *et al.* (15) or by TCA precipitation of the insulin in the supernatant: 100 μl of supernatant was added to 500 μl of 12% TCA and incubated for 10 to 20 min on ice. The precipitate was pelleted at 2000*g* for 10 min and washed with 500 μl 12% TCA. The precipitable counts indicated the nondegraded insulin while the counts remaining in the supernatants represented degraded insulin (16).

RESULTS

In order to determine the time required by the binding–dissociation reaction to reach equilibrium NAD, 13 cells were incubated with labeled insulin for time periods between 0 and 30 min at 37°C (Fig. 1). Binding reached the plateau level

TABLE 2

Correlation between Binding Lines and Degradation

Cell lines	Total binding (%)	Specific binding (%)	TCA-precipitated counts in supernatant (%)
Ramos	11.7	4.1	68
Raji	8.8	3.6	59
Daudi	12.3	5.2	68
Ramos EHR-A	38.3	26.6	42
U 698	21.4	18.2	73
Seraphine	20.3	6.5	74

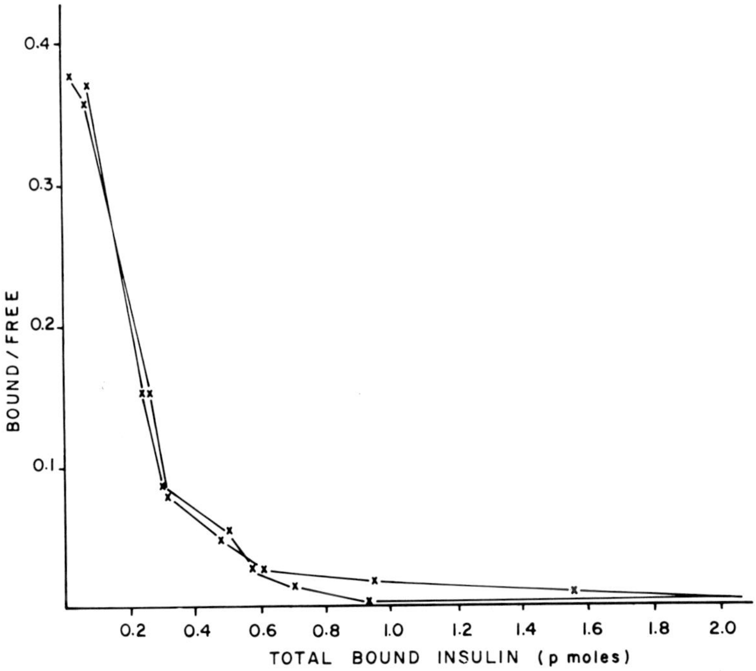

FIG. 4. Scatchard plots on a typical cell line (AT-A-E-95-STO cl 2-III Po.). The cells were incubated at 37°C for 20 min with 0.25 ng labeled insulin and different amounts of the unlabeled hormone (0–10,000 ng). Two experiments are shown.

after 10 min. The equilibrium was stable for at least 30 min. Similar results were obtained with other high- and low-binding lines. To optimize the cell/insulin ratio for the assay, different numbers of cells were incubated with 0.25 ng labeled insulin in the presence or absence of excess insulin (Fig. 2). The optimal cell number was 12 × 10;26 cells/0.25 ng insulin in 500 μl. Cell numbers exceeding 25 × 10^6 gave high nonspecific counts probably due to droplets of the incubation buffer caught between cells during separation. In all subsequent experiments, 12 × 10^6 cells/500 μl were incubated for 20 min at 37°C.

Table 1 shows the binding capacity of all lines. B lymphocytes from the peripheral blood of healthy donors showed no or very low binding, in agreement with earlier reports (4). The same result was obtained with blood samples from chronic lymphocytic leukemia cases. In contrast, all cell lines except A. K. Caren and the converted BJAB lines bound significant amounts of the hormone. Figure 3 shows the distribution of the binding in the different groups. BL-derived lines bound less than 10% except for the Sulubu line that bound 12.4%. In contrast, the EBV-transformed LCL lines bound between 10 and 29%. Surprisingly, four spontaneously established cell lines, derived from the peripheral blood of patients in the acute phase of infectious mononucleosis showed a much lower binding (between 3.8 and 8.6%), than the *in vitro* infected lines. The lymphosarcoma line U698 bound 12.8% and the IgE-producing myeloma lines 266 BL, 21.1% and Simpsson, 5.5%.

The greatest variation in specific binding between different experiments was

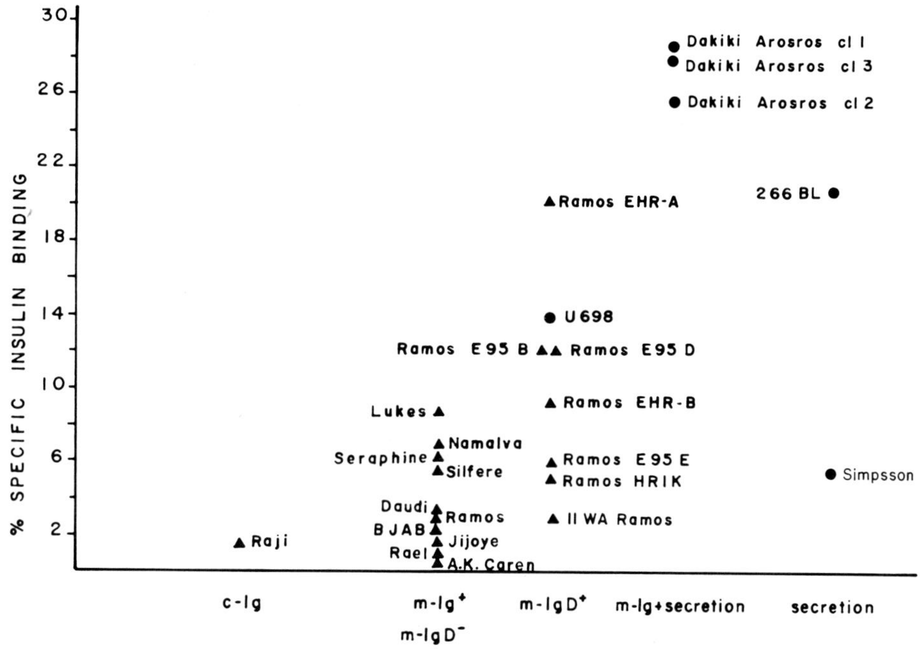

FIG. 5. Insulin binding of cell lines with different types of Ig expression. A hypothetical sequence of Ig expression during B-cell differentiation is arranged on the abscissa. Only cell lines with known Ig expression are shown. ▲, BL lines; ●, other lines.

found with the high-binding lines; the low-binding lines were more stable (Table 1). The degradation of insulin was independent of the binding, since there was no correlation between high- and low-binding lines and degradation (Table 2). Moreover, bacitracin inhibition of degradation (16) had no or only very little effect on the specific binding.

For the further study of the binding profile, 13 lines were incubated with labeled insulin and increasing amounts of nonlabeled insulin. A typical Scatchard plot (17) is shown in Fig. 4. The variation in specific binding between different lines could in all lines, except EHR-A Ramos be attributed to a variation in amount of binding sites.

DISCUSSION

The binding was stable between 10 to 30 min and could be blocked by competition with the unlabeled hormone. There was no correlation between binding capacity and degradation of insulin. The cell-free supernatant also degraded insulin, indicating that this was due to proteolytic enzymes released by the cells rather than to a receptor-dependent degradation. These results are in agreement with data published by others (16). All lines except three (A. K. Caren and converted BJAB) bound significantly more insulin than normal peripheral lymphocytes. Different groups of lines bound different amounts of insulin.

Variations in the specific binding of the same line on different occasions was probably due to changes in growth conditions, serum batches, and medium. We

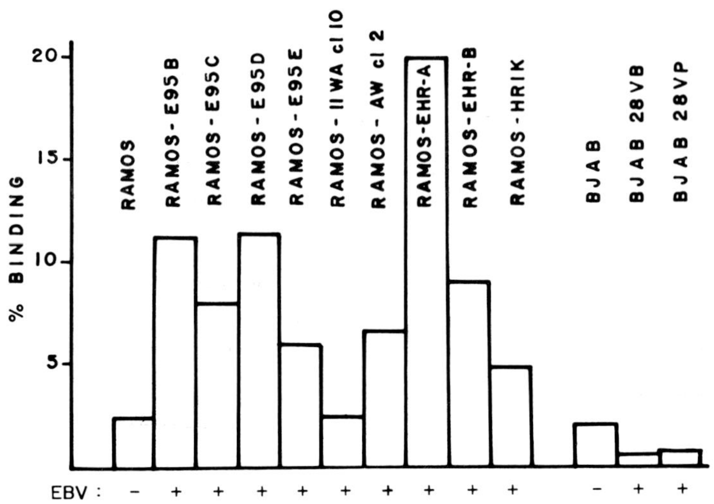

FIG. 6. Insulin binding of the two EBV-negative BL lines, Ramos and BJAB, and their EBV-converted sublines.

have observed that the binding decreased when the viability was lower or when the cells were overgrown. The largest variations were seen with the high-binding lines whereas low-binding lines showed more consistent results.

Since insulin binding was proposed as a marker of activated lymphocytes, correlated with the degree of blast transformation rather than with proliferation (5), we expected that the high- but not the low-differentiated lines would bind insulin. However, the low-differentiated IgD-negative lines bound significantly more insulin than normal peripheral blood lymphocytes, although less than the more differentiated LCL. The relationship between insulin binding and some differentiation markers is shown in Fig. 5. Only cell lines with known Ig expression are included.

The *in vitro* EBV-transformed LCLs showed the highest insulin binding. These cells resemble blasts, secrete Ig, but do not yet correspond to plasma cells; they still express surface Ig. The myeloma line represented the presumably most mature (9) cell type; however, it bound less insulin than the LCLs. This fits with the fact that the insulin binding of pokeweed mitogen stimulated cultures decreases after 4 days when Ig secretion starts and end-stage differentiation to plasma cells takes place (5).

All IgD-carrying lines tested showed high insulin binding. Since the majority of the Ig-positive cells in peripheral blood express IgD but do not bind insulin, our data indicate that the stage of differentiation as judged by Ig expression is not directly linked to the expression of insulin receptors. Insulin is one of the major metabolic hormones and it is more likely that the expression of insulin receptors is associated with different patterns of metabolic activity of cells at different stages of development. Since mitogen-activated lymphocytes express insulin receptors and EBV has been compared with B-cell mitogens (18), it was especially interesting to study the binding after EBV transformation. The EBV-transformed LCLs bound large amounts of the hormone, as discussed above.

The effect of EBV as such was most critically examined in the EBV-negative BL lines Ramos and BJAB and their *in vitro* EBV-converted sublines (Fig. 6).

EBV conversion was previously shown to reduce the serum dependence of Ramos and BJAB lines and to alter a number of surface properties (19–22). Our results show a clear difference between the two groups of lines. In the Ramos line, EBV conversion induced a higher insulin binding in eight cases of nine and this was accompanied by the expression of IgD (23). The BJAB line showed a lower binding after infection, however, indicating that the viral genome as such is not sufficient to increase insulin binding. It is noteworthy that the EBV-converted BJAB-lines showed no switch to IgD positivity either.

Spontaneously established, IM-derived lines bound less insulin than the *in vitro* EBV-transformed lines derived from normal adults or others. These differences in binding between the *in vivo* and *in vitro* infected lines could be explaind in two ways. The lines may be influenced by factors related to *in vitro* transformation that do not occur *in vivo*. Alternatively, the IM-lines may reflect a selection process *in vivo* that leads to a different cell population, compared to *in vitro* transformation.

Peripheral blood lymphocytes from CLL cases bound no or very little insulin. This is in contrast to the high binding to acute lymphatic leukemia lymphocytes reported by Krug *et al.* (5).

Further studies will have to show whether there is a regular difference between different types of lymphoid malignancies.

ACKNOWLEDGMENTS

This investigation was supported by Grant 3 R01 CA 14054-06S1, awarded by the National Cancer Institute, DHEW; the Swedish Cancer Society, and Medicinska Forskningsrådet Grant 4224.

REFERENCES

1. Gathings, W. E., Lawton, A. R., and Cooper, A. D., *Eur. J. Immunol.* **7,** 804, 1977.
2. Gronowicz, E., Coutinhou, A., and Melchers, F., *Eur. J. Immunol.* **6,** 588, 1976.
3. Gavin, J. R., Roth, J., Jen, P., and Freychet, P., *Proc. Nat. Acad. Sci. USA* **69,** 747, 1972.
4. Schwartz, R. H., Bianco, A. R., Handwerger, B. S., and Kahn, C. R., *Proc. Nat. Acad. Sci. USA* **72,** 474, 1975.
5. Krug, U., Krug, F., and Cuatrecasas, P., *Proc. Nat. Acad. Sci. USA* **69,** 2604, 1972.
6. Helderman, J. H., and Strom, T. B., *J. Clin. Invest.* **59,** 338, 1977.
7. Helderman, J. H., Reynolds, T. C., and Strom, T. B., *Eur. J. Immunol.* **8,** 589, 1978.
8. Helderman, J. H., and Strom, T. B., *Nature (London)* **274,** 62, 1978.
9. Nilsson, K., and Pontén, J., *Int. J. Cancer* **15,** 321, 1975.
10. Nilsson, K., *In* "INSERM Symposium No. 8" (B. Serrou, Ed.). Elsevier/North-Holland, Amsterdam, 1978.
11. Böyum, A., *Scand. J. Clin. Lab. Invest.* **21,** 77, 1968.
12. Julius, H. M., Simpson, E., and Herzenberg, L. A., *Eur. J. Immunol.* **3,** 645, 1973.
13. Jondal, M., Holm, G., and Wigzell, H., *J. Exp. Med.* **136,** 207, 1972.
14. Gambhir, K. K., Archer, J. A., and Bradley, G. J., *Diabetes* **27,** 701, 1978.
15. Takano, K., Hall, K., Fryklund, L., Holmgren, A., Sievertsson, H., and Uthne, K., *Acta Endocrinol. Copenhagen* **80,** 14, 1975.
16. Sonne, S., and Gliemann, J., *J. Biol. Chem.* **255,** 7449, 1980.
17. Scatchard, G., *Ann. N.Y. Acad. Sci.* **51,** 660, 1949.
18. Bird, G. H., and Britton, S., *Immunol. Rev.* **45,** 41, 1979.
19. Steinitz, M., and Klein, G., *Virology* **70,** 570, 1976.
20. Steinitz, M., and Klein, G., *Eur. J. Cancer* **13,** 1269, 1977.
21. Yefenof, E., Klein, G., Ben-Bassat, H., and Lundin, L., *Exp. Cell Res.* **108,** 185, 1977.
22. Steinitz, M., and Klein, G., *Proc. Nat. Acad. Sci. USA* **72,** 3518, 1975.
23. Spira, G., Åman, P., Koide, N., Lundin, G., Klein, G., and Hall, K., *J. Immunol.* **126,** 12, 1981.

24. Klein, E., Klein, G., Nadkarni, J. S., Nadkarni, J. J., Wigzell, H., and Clifford, P., *Cancer Res.* **28,** 1300, 1968.
25. Pulvertaft, R. J. V., *J. Clin. Pathol.* **18,** 261, 1965.
26. Hinuma, A. Y., and Grace, G. T., *Proc. Soc. Exp. Biol.* **124,** 107, 1967.
27. Klein, G., Dombos, L., and Gothoskar, B., *Int. J. Cancer* **10,** 44, 1972.
28. Nadkarni, J. S., Nadkarni, J. J., Clifford, P., Manolov, G., Fenyö, E. M., and Klein, E., *Cancer* **23,** 64, 1969.
29. Klein, G., Sugden, B., Leibold, W., and Menezes, J., *Intervirology* **3,** 232, 1974.
30. Klein, G., Giovanella, B., Westman, A., Stehlin, J., and Mumford, D., *Intervirology* **5,** 319, 1975.
31. Klein, G., Zeuthen, P., Terasaki, P., Billing, R., Honig, R., Jondal, M., Westman, A., and Clements, G., *Int. J. Cancer* **18,** 639, 1976.
32. Fresen, K. O., and zur Hausen, H., *Int. J. Cancer* **17,** 161, 1976.
33. Steinitz, M., and Klein, G., *J. Immunol.* **125,** 194, 1980.
34. Nilsson, K., and Sundström, C., *Int. J. Cancer* **13,** 808, 1974.
35. Nilsson, K., Benvich, H., Johansson, G. S., and Pontén, J., *Clin. Exp. Immunol.* **7,** 477, 1970.

CELLULAR IMMUNOLOGY 65, 317–324 (1981)

Genetic Control of Sensitivity to Moloney Leukemia Virus in Mice V. Role of H-2-Linked Genes in the Control of Anti-FMR Cytolytic T Lymphocytes[1]

VÉRONIQUE DUPREZ, PATRICE DEBRE, AND JEAN-PAUL LEVY

Laboratoire Immunologie et Virologie des Tumeurs, INSERM U 152, Hôpital Cochin, Paris 14e, France

Received June 17, 1981; accepted September 29, 1981

Three H-2-linked genes, *Rmv1*, *Rmv2*, and *Rmv3* control the resistance of mice against Moloney virus (MLV)-induced leukemias. It has been shown previously that they function as immune response (Ir) genes regulating the level of antivirus antibodies. In the present experiments, the cell-mediated anti-tumor response has been studied in a series of inbred strains selected for their resistance or sensitivity to the MLV-induced disease. We failed to detect any relationship between resistance and sensitivity and the ability to produce cytolytic T lymphocytes (CTL) directed against the virus-induced FMR cell surface antigen. Furthermore, the role of each *Rmv* gene has been studied separately using congenic pairs of mice differing at only one of these loci: we failed to evidence any influence of these genes in the cell-mediated antitumor reactions as measured by the ability to lyse syngeneic FMR(+) target cells. Nevertheless a gene mapping in the D region of the MHC but probably different from *Rmv3* controls the response of a subset of anti-FMR CTL restricted by the $H\text{-}2K^k$ antigens, with higher response in $H\text{-}2D^d$ than in $H\text{-}2D^b$ animals. This observation confirms the existence of H-2D region associated Ir genes regulating the CTL-mediated antitumor immune responses by choosing the subset of responder CTL, and suggests that a fourth H-2-linked gene plays some role in the genetic control of the anti-FMR immune response.

INTRODUCTION

Moloney virus (MLV)[2]-induced leukemias being controlled by several genes (1) including three H-2 linked (2), the question arose of their control through the level of antivirus or antitumor immune responses. We have shown previously that the three H-2-linked genes, *Rmv1*, mapping in the IA regions, *Rmv2*, mapping in IC, S, or G regions, and *Rmv3* mapping in the D region of the MHC, behave as immune response (Ir) genes regulating the level of antivirus antibodies (3). We failed, however, to detect any relationship between these genes and the production of antitumor antibodies (3). Here, we report experiments performed to study their possible role on the antitumor response mediated by cytolytic T lymphocytes (CTL)

[1] This work was supported by Grants DGRST 79.7.04.94 and INSERM ATP 79.026.2.

[2] Abbreviations used: CRT, chromium release test; CTL, cytolytic T lymphocytes; FCS, fetal calf serum; FMR, Friend, Moloney, Rauscher, or Graffi cell surface antigens; LPS, Lipopolysaccharide; LU, lytic unit; MLV, Moloney leukemia virus; MSV, murine sarcoma virus (Moloney strains); *Rmv1*, *Rmv2*, *Rmv3*, genes for resistance to Moloney leukemia virus.

0008-8749/81/180317-08$02.00/0

specific for a virus-induced cell surface antigen probably identical to the serologically defined FMR antigen (4). We failed to establish any correlation between this response and resistance or susceptibility to the leukemia. Nevertheless, a genetic control of a subset of anti-FMR CTL, restricted by $H\text{-}2K^k$ antigens, has been observed illustrating the role of H-2D region associated Ir genes in the regulation of CTL-mediated reactions.

MATERIALS AND METHODS

Mice. BALB/c, C57B1/6(B6), C57B1/10(B10), B10.S, B10.M, B10.A, B10.A(2R), B10.A(4R), B10.A(5R) mice were obtained from our own colonies.

Virus and cells. The Moloney leukemia virus (MLV) was maintained *in vivo* by passage in newborn BALB/c mice as a cell-free supernatant of leukemic organs. The murine sarcoma virus (MSV) was maintained similarly in newborn (B6xBALB/c) mice by passage of acellular tumor extracts.

Two MLV-induced lymphomas, MBL2(B6) and LSTRA (BALB/c), were maintained by intraperitoneal passage of 10^6 cells in adult syngeneic mice. They express the virus induced FMR antigen (5) at their surface, as shown by serology and CTL-mediated reactions (4). MLV-infected blast cells were obtained from 1- to 2-month-old mice inoculated at birth with 0.1 ml of MLV at a 1/100 dilution. Spleen cells of these mice were stimulated *in vitro* with LPS (25 μg/ml, Difco) for 48 hr. These cells which express the FMR antigen at their surface were used as stimulating cells in culture or as target cells in the chromium release test, as previously described (6).

Generation of secondary anti-FMR CTL. Cultures were established as detailed elsewhere (4), 8×10^6 spleen cells taken from mice which had rejected M-MSV tumor 1–3 months earlier, being set up in culture with 5×10^5 lymphoma cells (irradiated 10,000 rad) or infected blast cells (irradiated 2000 rad). Each culture was established in a final volume of 2 ml RPMI 1640 medium supplemented with 10% FCS, penicillin, streptomycin, 5×10^{-5} *M* 2-mercaptoethanol, 2 m*M* glutamine, 1% nonessential amino acid (Gibco), 1 m*M* sodium pyruvate.

Cell-mediated cytotoxicity assay. The cytolytic activity of lymphocytes recovered from mixed cultures was measured in a short-term (4 hr) ^{51}Cr release test (CRT) as previously described (4, 6), various numbers of viable lymphocyte being mixed with 10^4 ^{51}Cr-labeled target cells in a final volume of 0.2 ml in microtiters plates. Cytolytic activity was expressed as LU/10^6 cells or percentage specific chromium released as previously described (6). All experiments in which the spontaneous release was upper than 25% were discarded.

RESULTS

Anti-FMR CTL Responses of Viremic Mice

The first series of experiments was performed in two strains of mice selected for their high resistance (B6) or high sensitivity (BALB/c) to MLV infection (1, 2). Adult mice inoculated with infectious virus were tested, at various periods after inoculation, for their cytolytic response against syngeneic FMR(+) lymphoma cells. It appeared at first that B6 produced anti-FMR CTL more frequently and at a higher level than BALB/c mice. Nevertheless, nonviremic animals, whatever the strain, were able to develop a potent cytolytic response, whereas the cytolytic activity was rapidly abolished in BALB/c mice when they become viremic, as illustrated for example in Table 1. These results were regularly confirmed in various strains of mice. Moreover, when viremia occurred in B6 mice, following various experimental procedures, their CTL production was also abrogated (not shown). The difference observed between BALB/c and B6 mice was therefore probably due to the inhibition of the response by viruses or viral antigens rather than to different abilities to mount a response. Such an inhibition of CTL responses by circulating C-type viruses has been previously illustrated in another system (7). Since, in addition, different levels of antigenic stimulations, resulting from variable levels of virus replication in the different strains, might also influence the results, we conclude that the genetic control of anti-FMR responses must be studied in nonviremic animals only.

Anti-FMR CTL Responses of Nonviremic Mice

The best way to compare the levels of anti-FMR CTL responses in nonviremic animals would have been to test the primary response of mice inoculated with inactivated virus, as it has been done in the study of the antibody responses (3). This approach, however, was not possible due to the weakness of CTL responses in such animals. Secondary responses *in vitro* of spleen cells, primed *in vivo* by MSV inoculation, were therefore studied, such animals being nonviremic as assessed by MLV p30 radioimmunoassay (results not shown). The results illustrated in Table 2 show that both B10.S (very resistant) and B10.M mice (highly sensitive) produced good levels of anti-FMR CTL. Similar results were found with several other resistant and sensitive lines (not shown). Moreover, Table 3 illustrates a typical example of experiments comparing B10 (highly resistant), B10.A (4R) (highly sensitive), B10.A (sensitive), and B10.A (2R) (resistant) mice. These strains were selected because they allow to study separately the effects of the three H-2-linked genes *Rmv1, Rmv2, Rmv3*, which control *in vivo* the MLV resistance (2). It was clear from these results that mice of all four strains produced a strong anti-

TABLE 1

SECONDARY CYTOLYTIC ACTIVITIES AND VIREMIAS OF B6 OR BALB/c MICE INOCULATED WITH MLV

Weeks after MLV inoculation[a]	B6		BALB/c	
	$LU/10^6$ [b]	Viremia[c]	$LU/10^6$ [b]	Viremia[c]
1	0	—	0	—
2	4.2	—	3.1	—
3	7	—	1.2	1200
5	5.6	—	0	4530
7	4.3	—	0	8050
9	2.1	—	0	11180

[a] Three-week-old mice were inoculated by intraperitoneal route with 0.1 ml of 1/200 diluted MLV.
[b] Lytic units 33%, cytolytic activity on MBL2(B6) and LSTRA(BALB/c) targets.
[c] Circulating MLV p30 expressed in ng/ml, control mice always had less than 100 mg/ml.

TABLE 2

CYTOLYTIC ACTIVITY OF SECONDARY ANTI-FMR CTL IN MLV RESISTANT (B10.S) AND SENSITIVE (B10.M) STRAINS

Effector cells	Stimulator cells[a]	Percentage specific chromium release from[b]: B10.S blasts[a] FMR(+)	B10.S blasts[a] Normal	B10.M blasts[a] FMR(+)	B10.M blasts[a] Normal
B10.S	FMR(+)B10.S				
anti-MSV	100:1[c]	60.6	<2	<2	<2
	30:1	54.9	<2	<2	<2
	10:1	49.1	<2	<2	<2
	Normal B10.S				
	100:1	<2	<2	<2	<2
B10.M	FMR(+)B10.M				
anti-MSV	100:1	<2	<2	50.1	<2
	30:1	<2	<2	42.8	<2
	10:1	<2	<2	36.3	<2
	Normal B10.M				
	100:1	<2	<2	<2	<2

[a] Normal or MLV infected and FMR(+) LPS blasts (see Materials and Methods).
[b] Spontaneous chromium release of the four target cells measured at the different L:T ratios varied from 15.7 to 23.6%.
[c] Effector-to-target cell ratio.

FMR CTL mediated response, which appeared a little stronger in the three resistant strains B10.S, B10 and B10.A (2R). Repeated experiments in the six inbred strains used in Tables 2 and 3 failed, however, to confirm this difference. They suggested that the differences were mainly due to variations from one experiment to the other in the sensitivity of the different target cells used. The use of various doses of stimulating and responder cells failed to reveal more differences between these

TABLE 3

Rmv1, Rmv2, AND *Rmv3* GENES DO NOT INFLUENCE THE SECONDARY ANTI-FMR CTL RESPONSE

Effector cell[a]	Resistance of sensibility to MLV	Alleles at *Rmv1*	Alleles at *Rmv2*	Alleles at *Rmv3*	Percentage specific chromium release[b] 100:1	30:1	10:1
B10	R	r[c]	s	r	69.5	62.7	54.5
B10.A(4R)	S	s	s	r	41.8	42.4	23.6
B10.A(2R)	R	s	r	r	67.3	45.1	28
B10.A	S	s	r	s	45.5	39	30

[a] Secondary anti-MSV CTL stimulated *in vitro* with syngeneic MLV-infected blast cells.
[b] Cytolytic activity tested against MLV-infected cells syngeneic to the effector cells. The spontaneous chromium release of the four target cells were measured at the different L:T ratios using normal lymphocytes. They varied from 18.2 to 24.9%.
[c] r, Resistant allele; s, sensitive allele.

lines. Controls including uninfected syngeneic blast cells as stimulators and the same or allogeneic MLV-infected blast as target cells confirmed in all cases the specificity of the reactions and their H-2 restriction. The T nature of the effector cells was also controlled by anti-Thy-1.2 and complement treatment (not shown).

Comparison of K and D Restricted Anti-FMR CTL Responses in Mice Differing at Rmv1, Rmv2, or Rmv3 Locus

The results reported above suggested an absence of relationship between MLV resistance or sensitivity and the ability to mount a CTL-mediated immune response. They do not exclude however that *Rmv* genes could play a role by triggering different CTL subsets restricted by K or D products of the H-2 complex, since it has been shown previously that the anti-FMR CTL response restricted by H-$2K^b$ can be specifically controlled by an H-2D region associated Ir gene (8). As shown in Table 4 which illustrates the results of four different experiments the role of *Rmv* loci could be tested only on anti-FMR CTL restricted by H-$2D^b$ or by H-$2K^k$ antigens. The results show that B10 and B10.A (4R) CTL lysed equally well target cells compatible only at the D^b region of the MHC. These results suggested that *Rmv1* did not control D^b restricted reactions. Similarly the comparison of the response of B10.A(4R) and B10.A(2R) mice showed that the *Rmv2* gene was of no effect on D^b or K^k restricted anti-FMR responses. On the contrary, a difference was found between the responses of B10.A and B10.A(2R) mice, which differ at the *Rmv3* locus. When tested against MLV-infected B10.A target cells, B10.A CTL were clearly more efficient than B10.A(2R) CTL. This result was confirmed in repeated experiments as illustrated in Fig. 1. The higher activity of B10.A anti-FMR CTL was not due to the addition of the activities of two subgroups of CTL respectively restricted by H-$2K^k$ and H-$2D^d$ antigens. In fact, it has been found previously (8) and confirmed here, that H-$2D^d$ never functions as restricting antigen in association with FMR, so that B10.A, as well as other H-$2D^d$ CTL, are not able to lyse target cells compatible only at the D^d region. We concluded therefore that a gene, mapping in the D region of the MHC, controls the level of anti-FMR CTL-mediated responses restricted by H-$2K^k$ antigens. This gene is however, probably different from *Rmv3* since B10.A(2R) mice are low responders and B10.A mice high responders at this new locus, while B10.A(2R) mice are resistant and B10.A mice sensitive at the *Rmv3* locus.

DISCUSSION

The complex genetic system which controls the MLV-induced disease includes H-2-linked and non-H-2 genes (1, 2). The mapping of *Rmv1, Rmv2* and *Rmv3* in the major histocompatibility complex (2) suggests a possible action of these genes at the level of antivirus or antitumor immune responses. A previous paper of our group has shown all three of these genes are involved in the control of antivirus antibody responses and can be considered as Ir genes (3). By contrast, in the present experiments, no relationship was found between resistance or susceptibility to MLV and the ability to develop a CTL-mediated antitumor reaction. Moreover, when studied separately in congenic pairs of mice differing only at one of the *Rmv* loci, none of the *Rmv* genes appeared to control the cell-mediated antitumor response measured as a whole. Some control of a CTL subset directed against the FMR

TABLE 4

K OR D RESTRICTED ANTI-MSV CTL RESPONSE IN STRAINS WITH DIFFERENCES ONLY OF *Rmv1*, *Rmv2*, OR *Rmv3*

Expt	Effector cell[a]	H-2 (K/D)	*Rmv1*	*Rmv2*	*Rmv3*	H-2 shared by effector and target cell	Origin of FMR target cell[b]	Percentage specific chromium release[c]		
								100:1	30:1	10:1
A	B10	$K^b D^b$	r	s	r	D^b	B10 A (4R)	44.8	31.9	30.9
	B10 A (4R)	$K^k D^b$	s	s	r	D^b	B6	55.2	41.8	28.7
B	B10 A (4R)	$K^k D^b$	s	s	r	D^b	B6	31	11.3	4.2
	B10 A (2R)	$K^k D^b$	s	r	r	D^b	B6	23.2	10.9	2.2
C	B10 A (4R)	$K^k D^b$	s	s	r	K^k	B10 A	34.3	22.1	18.6
	B10 A (2R)	$K^k D^b$	s	r	r	K^k	B10 A	30.2	20.3	15.6
D	B10 A (2R)	$K^k D^b$	s	r	r	K^k	B10 A	21.3	10.7	1.9
	B10 A	$K^k D^d$	s	r	s	$K^k D^d$	B10 A	50.5	25	13

[a] Secondary anti-MSV CTL stimulated *in vitro* with syngeneic MLV-infected cells.

[b] MLV-infected LPS blast.

[c] The spontaneous chromium releases of the target cells used varied from 14.3 to 24.8%.

+ H-2K^k association was detected in *Rmv3* different mice, but the gene involved was probably different from *Rmv3*, B10.A mice being high responders for the anti-FMR + H-2K^k response while bearing an allele for sensitivity at the *Rmv3* locus (2). This absence of a relationship between cell-mediated antitumor response and resistance or susceptibility to the disease, was perhaps not so surprising since: (a) the relationship existing among *Rmv1, Rmv2,* and *Rmv3*, and the level of antivirus antibody synthesis was not detected when antitumor cell antibodies were examined (3); (b) other groups studying immune responses in other tumor systems failed to detect any influence on the level of cell-mediated response of the genes which control the disease *in vivo* (9, 10). However, contradictory results have been also reported (11). It has been suggested that kinetics of CTL production, rather than the final levels of CTL response might be determinant in tumor rejection, antitumor CTL being an emergency system acting at the early beginning of the antitumor reaction (10, 11, 12). No experiments have been done here to test this possibility. It must be noted that the sensitivity of the method available to quantify CTL responses are perhaps not sufficient to evidence small differences which might be determinant *in vivo.*

The study of primary CTL-mediated anti-FMR response could perhaps better detect genetic differences which are no more detectable in secondary reactions. For technical reasons this approach was not possible as mentioned above. From preliminary results obtained in various lines of mice the possibility to detect a genetic control at the level of the primary response appears, however, unlikely. It must be noted for example that primary anti-FMR responses *in vitro* are obtained as well in BALB/c (very sensitive) and B6 mice (very resistant) (13).

The genetic control of the generation of the subset of H-2K^k restricted anti-FMR CTL which was observed in these experiments is apparently not related to resistance or sensitivity *in vivo*, B10.A(2R) mice being low responders at this locus but re-

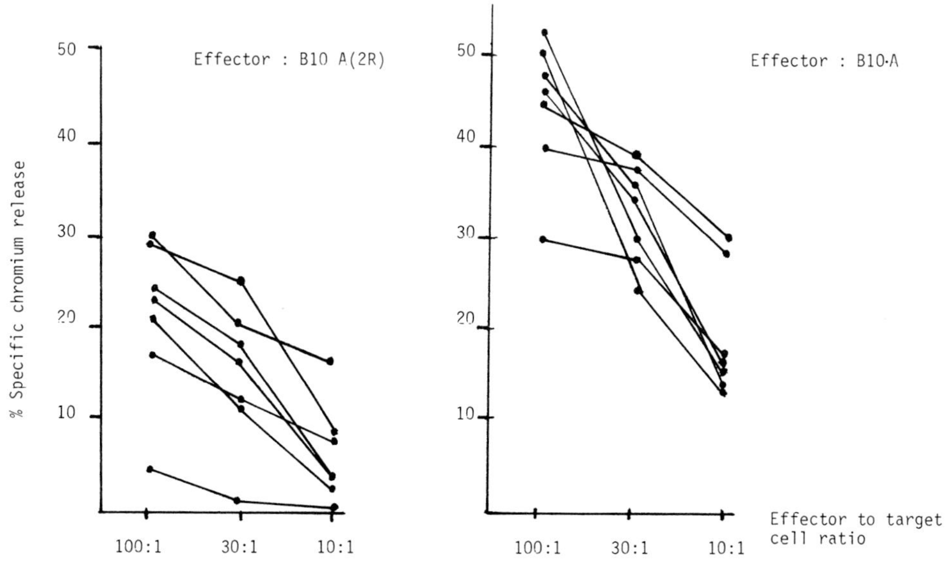

FIG. 1. Secondary anti-MSV CTL restricted to K^k in B10 A(2R) and B10.A mice tested on B10.A-infected cells.†

sistant to the disease, and the reverse being observed in B10.A mice. This is understandable since B10.A(2R) mice which produce a relatively low anti-FMR + K^k-CTL response produce simultaneously H-2D^b-restricted anti-FMR CTL. Their resistance to the disease is therefore dependent on the additional effects of these two CTL subsets. The genetic control of the subset of H-2K^k-restricted anti-FMR CTL provides, however, a new example of Ir genes associated to the H-2D region and controlling a subset of anti-FMR CTL (8) or CTL directed against nononcogenic viruses (14, 15). While other explanations are not excluded, it seems possible that an immunodominance phenomenon might explain these observations as suggested previously (14). Recent experiments in B10.A(5R) mice and their F_1 hybrid have shown that the D^b restricted anti-FMR response is dominant over the K^b restricted reaction (8). This dominance was associated with a detectable primary anti-FMR H-2D^b restricted reaction and a high level of secondary response, whereas K^b restricted reactions are never detectable in primary responses and remain weak even in secondary reactions (8). This confirmed the idea that H-2 molecules are the product of Ir genes mapping in the D (and possibly K) regions of the MHC and controlling antivirus CTL responses by directing the subset of responder CTL (8). The control of K^k restricted anti-FMR CTL responses by a D region associated Ir gene further illustrates this conclusion. In this case, however, the effect on the whole anti-FMR response was not so clear probably because K^k restricted CTL function as well as D^b restricted CTL while in the previous example K^b was associated with low responses. This shows that a hierarchy of H-2 restrictions exists in the anti-FMR response which could be related to a hierarchy in the levels of anti-FMR responses. The D^b restriction appears associated to high responses like K^d or K^k restriction, while K^b is associated with lower responses and D^d to an absence of reactivity, which in other words signify that H-2D^b, H-2K^d, and H-2K^k are high responder genes, H-2K^b a low responder, and H-2D^d a nonresponder gene.

REFERENCES

1. Gisselbrecht, S., Pozo, F., Debré, P., Hurot, M. A., Lacombe, M. J., and Lévy, J. P., *Int. J. Cancer* **21,** 626, 1978.
2. Debré, P., Gisselbrecht, S., Pozo, F., and Lévy, J. P., *J. Immunol.* **123,** 1806, 1979.
3. Debré, P., Boyer, B., Gisselbrecht, S., Bismuth, A., and Lévy, J. P. *Eur. J. Immunol.* **10,** 914, 1980.
4. Gomard, E., Lévy, J. P., Plata, F., Hénin, Y., Duprez, V., Bismuth, A., and Reme, T., *Eur. J. Immunol.* **8,** 228, 1978.
5. Old, L. J., Boyse, E. A., and Stockert, E., *Nature (London)* **201,** 777, 1964.
6. Duprez, V., Hénin, Y., and Lévy, J. P., *J. Immunol. Methods* **37,** 249, 1980.
7. Plater, C., Debré, P., and Leclerc, J. C., *Eur. J. Immunol.* **11,** 39, 1981.
8. Gomard, E., Hénin, Y., Colombani, M. J., and Lévy, J. P., *J. Exp. Med.* **151,** 1468, 1980.
9. Chesebro, B., and Wehrly, K., *J. Exp. Med.* **143,** 85, 1976.
10. Chesebro, B., and Wehrly, K., *J. Immunol.* **120,** 1081, 1978.
11. Meruelo, D., Deak, B., and McDevitt, H. O., *J. Exp. Med.* **146,** 1367, 1977.
12. Britt, W. J., and Chesebro, B., *J. Exp. Med.* **152,** 1795, 1980.
13. Gomard, E., Wybier-Franqui, J., and Lévy, J. P., *J. Immunol.* **126,** 891, 1981.
14. Zinkernagel, R. M., Althage, A., Cooper, S., Kreeb, G., Klein, P. A., Sefton, B., Flaherty, L., Strimpfling, J., Sheffler, D., and Klein, J., *J. Exp. Med.* **148,** 592, 1978.
15. Doherty, P. C., Bidisson, W. E., Bennink, J. R., and Knowles, B. B., *J. Exp. Med.* **148,** 534, 1978.

CELLULAR IMMUNOLOGY **65**, 325–336 (1981)

Modulation of Peripheral Blood Mononuclear Cell Cyclic Adenosine Monophosphate Levels by Human Very Low Density Lipoprotein[1]

FRANCIS V. CHISARI AND LINDA K. CURTISS

Departments of Clinical Research and Molecular Immunology, Research Institute of Scripps Clinic, La Jolla, California 92037

Received July 21, 1981; accepted October 13, 1981

Normal human plasma very low density lipoprotein (VLDL) can inhibit mitogen-induced lymphocyte DNA synthesis. Since early events in lymphocyte activation (e.g., cyclic nucleotide metabolism) are thought to influence the magnitude of later events (e.g., [^{3}H]thymidine uptake) we designed the current studies to compare the effects of VLDL on these two cellular processes. Two separate effects of VLDL on peripheral blood mononuclear cell (PBM) cyclic adenosine monophosphate (AMP) metabolism were observed at VLDL concentrations which inhibit phytohemagglutinin (PHA)-induced [^{3}H]thymidine uptake. VLDL suppressed the early, transient increase in PBM cyclic AMP which occurs within minutes of the addition of mitogen. VLDL exposure also stimulated a delayed (greater than 24 hr) and spontaneous increase in PBM cyclic AMP levels which corresponded temporally with progressive cellular refractoriness to mitogen stimulation. If mitogen-induced lymphoproliferation is influenced by early changes in cyclic nucleotide metabolism, as claimed by some investigators, then perhaps the ability of VLDL to modulate intracellular cyclic AMP levels may explain some of the antiproliferative properties of this bioregulatory lipoprotein.

INTRODUCTION

Normal human plasma lipoproteins, especially those of the very low, low- and intermediate-density classes, modulate a variety of immunologic phenomena (1–11). Lymphocyte activation (1–3), proliferation (4, 5), and receptor expression (6, 7) are down-regulated by these density classes. Additionally, immunoglobulin synthesis (8), cytolytic (9), helper, and suppressor T-cell function (8) are also variably modulated by the lipoproteins as are tumor cytolysis by activated macrophages (10), and the uncontrolled proliferation of human B lymphocytes infected by the Epstein Barr virus (11).

The molecular basis for the immunoregulatory activities of the plasma lipoproteins is not well understood. Since many of the immunologic processes which are modulated by lipoproteins depend on new membrane synthesis (12), calcium transport (13), phospholipid turnover (14), and may be influenced by cyclic nucleotide

[1] This is publication number 2399 from the Research Institute of Scripps Clinic, La Jolla, Calif. These studies were supported by Grants AI 13393, CA 28166, and AI 24241, and RCDA AI 00174 from the National Institutes of Health.

0008-8749/81/180325-12$02.00/0

metabolism (15), it is likely that one or more of these basic cellular events may be influenced by the bioregulatory lipoproteins. In this regard, several investigators have demonstrated that low-density lipoprotein can regulate cholesterol (16), protein and DNA synthesis (2), adenylate cyclase activity (17), cyclic guanosyl monophosphate synthesis (18), calcium ion accumulation (19), magnesium adenosine triphosphatase activity (20), and monophosphatidylinositol turnover (21).

Direct examination of the mechanism(s) responsible for the immunoregulatory activity of human serum very low density lipoprotein (VLDL)[2] has not been reported. In an earlier report, it was established that VLDL-induced inhibition of [^{3}H]thymidine uptake was limited to relatively early prereplicative events of mitogen-stimulated DNA synthesis, since no inhibition was observed if VLDL was added to the cell cultures 12 hr after phytohemagglutinin stimulation (2). Because of our continuing interest in VLDL as a bioregulatory agent and cyclic adenosine monophosphate (cyclic AMP) as a second messenger, we performed experiments to determine whether VLDL-induced alterations in lymphocyte function were accompanied by early changes in intracellular cyclic AMP. The results of these experiments are reported herein.

MATERIALS AND METHODS

Lipoprotein isolation. VLDL was isolated from fresh, fasting human plasma by preparative ultracentrifugation as described (2). Seventy milliliters of plasma (density: 1.006 g/cm^3) was layered under 23 ml of buffer consisting of 0.15 *M* NaCl, 0.05 m*M* EDTA, pH 7.2, and centrifuged at 214,000*g* for 18 hr at 10°C in a type 45-Ti rotor (Beckman Instruments, Irvine, Calif.). The opaque layer occupying the topmost 15–20 ml of the tube was washed twice by recentrifugation as described above. This material has been shown (2) to consist of a single broad absorbance peak with a mean molecular weight of approximately 10×10^6 daltons when subjected to molecular exclusion chromatography on Bio-Gel A-50 m (Bio-Rad Laboratories, Richmond, Calif.). Purity of resultant preparations was assessed by lipoprotein electrophoresis, immunoelectrophoresis vs anti-whole human serum, agargel diffusion vs specific anti-lipoprotein antisera and by determination of triglyceride/protein and triglyceride/cholesterol ratios as previously described (2). Analysis of this material revealed pre-beta electrophoretic mobility, triglyceride/protein ratio of 4.7, and triglyceride/cholesterol ratio of 3.8 compatible with pure VLDL (2). Enzymatic analysis of triglycerides were performed by the method of Bucolo and David (22) with reagents purchased from Calbiochem-Behring (La Jolla, Calif.). Cholesterol was determined according to a modification of the method of Abell *et al.* (23). Protein was determined by the method of Markwell *et al.* with BSA standards (24).

Peripheral blood mononuclear cell isolation. PBM were isolated from heparinized venous blood from a panel of healthy donors by sedimentation onto a barrier of Ficoll–Hypaque (density: 1.077 g/ml) according to the method of Boyum (25) as previously described (26). The cells collected at the interface were suspended in complete media consisting of RPMI 1640 supplemented with penicillin (100

[2] Abbreviations used: VLDL, very low density lipoprotein; AMP, adenosine monophosphate; GMP, guanosine monophosphate; PBM, peripheral blood mononuclear cell; PHA, phytohemagglutinin.

units/ml), streptomycin (50 μg/ml) L-glutamine (2 mM) and 10% heat-inactivated calf serum (Grand Island Biological Co., Grand Island, N.Y.). The cells were washed five times at 1000 rpm for 10 min to remove contaminating platelets. Platelet contamination was reduced to a level of less than one platelet per three PBM before the preparations were considered acceptable for utilization. Absolute yield of mononuclear cells was greater than 75% with greater than 95% purity and viability and consisted of 85 to 90% lymphocytes and 10–15% monocytes determined by the peroxidase reaction (27).

Cyclic nucleotide levels. Appropriate concentrations of PHA obtained from several manufacturers (see Results) and buffer control were added to sterile 12 × 75-mm culture tubes containing 1-ml suspensions of PBM at a concentration of 2 × 10^6 cells per milliliter in complete media. At varying times thereafter the cells were harvested and assayed for cyclic adenosine monophosphate (cAMP) and cyclic guanosine monophosphate (cGMP), using radioimmunoassay kits purchased from Schwartz/Mann, Division of Becton–Dickinson and Company (Orangeburg, N.Y.). Briefly, reactions were terminated by the addition of 2 ml of ice-cold RPMI. The cell suspensions were washed three times in RPMI 1640, centrifuged at 3000 rpm, and the supernatants discarded. The cell pellets were then subjected to three cycles of alternate freezing and thawing; 750 μl of freshly prepared 0.05 M sodium acetate buffer, pH 6.2, was added, and the lysates were boiled for 5 min to inactivate phosphodiesterase. The suspensions were then frozen at −70°C until assayed. Before assay the suspensions were sonicated for 30 sec in an ice-water slurry in a Heat Systems sonicator (Plainview, N.Y.) at a setting of 4. This was followed by centrifugation to remove residual precipitate and the clear supernate was transferred to a clean tube for assay of cyclic AMP and cyclic GMP by radioimmunoassay according to the manufacturer's instructions. Results were expressed as picomoles of cyclic AMP or cyclic GMP per 1 × 10^7 cells and were derived from a standard curve run internally within each assay with control reagents provided by the manufacturer.

DNA synthesis. The DNA synthetic capacity of mitogen-stimulated PBM was routinely assessed in a microculture system with flat-bottom sterile tissue-culture plates (Microtest II, Falcon Plastics, Oxnard, Calif.). Test samples (VLDL and buffer control) were added in 50-μl volumes and sterilized by ultraviolet light. Cells were adjusted to 5 × 10^5/ml in complete media and 0.20 ml was added to each well. The plates were incubated at 37°C in a humidified atmosphere containing 5% CO_2 in air. After a 24-hr incubation with VLDL or buffer control, PHA from a variety of commercial sources was added in varying concentrations and the cultures were incubated for an additional 48 hr. At that time 0.5 μCi of [^{3}H]thymidine (2.0 Ci per mmol, New England Nuclear, Boston, Mass.) was added. Cells were harvested 18 hr later with a multiple automated sample harvester (MASH 2, Microbiological Associates, Washington, D.C.) with saline washes. The dried filters were counted for ^{3}H beta emission in 3.0 ml of toluene containing Omnifluor (New England Nuclear). In selected experiments the concentrations of PBM, lipoproteins, and PHA as well as the incubation times and exposure conditions were varied as indicated under Results. All experiments were performed in triplicate and were expressed as counts per minute per culture as percentage of control derived from (cpm test cultures ÷ cpm control culture) × 100, or as percentage inhibition derived from 1 − (cpm test cultures ÷ cpm control cultures) × 100 where appropriate.

Effect of VLDL on the binding of ^{125}I-PHA on PBM. A highly purified preparation of PHA (leukoagglutinin) was purchased from Pharmacia Fine Chemicals (Piscataway, N.J.), and radiolabeled with ^{125}I according to the method of Hunter and Greenwood (28) as previously described (29). After exhaustive dialysis against 0.01 *M* phosphate, 0.15 *M* NaCl, pH 7.2 (PBS), the radiolabeled PHA was chromatographed on Bio-Gel A-l.5 m (Bio-Rad), and the major included peak of radioactivity was collected and concentrated to the original volume. The mitogenic potential of this material was assessed in the microculture system described above and was found to be equivalent to native leukoagglutinin. Portions of this material were mixed with an excess of cold leukoagglutinin and several dilutions of the mixture were prepared in PBS, 0.1% BSA, 0.01% sodium azide, pH 7.2. Fifty microliters of each dilution was added to 1.0% BSA-coated microtiter wells containing 100 μl of either buffer or PBM. The PBM were suspended in RPMI 1640 containing 0.1% BSA and 0.01% sodium azide, pH 7.2, at 1×10^6 per milliliter and had been previously incubated with either PBS or VLDL for 24 hr at 37°C. Incubation continued for 1 hr and was terminated by harvesting onto glass filters presoaked with 0.1% BSA, 0.01% sodium azide, and PBS followed by extensive washing with the same medium. Filters were dried and counted for gamma emission in a Model 1195 automatic gamma counter (Searle Analytical, Inc., San Diego, Calif.). The radioactivity recovered by the cell-free wells was subtracted from that recovered from the wells containing cells and the moles of PHA bound was calculated from the net counts bound and the specific activity of the radioligand (30).

Cell viability studies. The effect of VLDL on PBM viability was assessed by trypan blue exclusion and cell counts in a hemocytometer at varying intervals after exposure to VLDL and addition of PHA.

RESULTS

Effect of PHA on PBM Cyclic Nucleotide Levels and [^3H]Thymidine Uptake

We evaluated the influence of several concentrations of PHA obtained from various manufacturers on cyclic nucleotide metabolism and [^{3}H]thymidine uptake in order to permit selection of optimal conditions for subsequent studies. Because relatively large numbers of cells are required for assays of cyclic nucleotide levels, PBM were cultivated in 12 × 75-mm sterile culture tubes at a concentration of 2.0×10^6 per milliliter when cyclic AMP and GMP levels were to be determined. Since the culture volume (1 ml) and the total cell input (2×10^6) in this system are, respectively, 4 and 20 times greater than those used in our standard microwell culture system for measurement of [^{3}H]thymidine uptake, we evaluated the effects of 4 and 20 times the standard amount of PHA on PBM cyclic nucleotide levels.

Both concentrations of PHA induced an early, transient rise in PBM cyclic AMP. Considerable variation in the magnitude, kinetics, and optimal PHA dose was observed stressing the importance of prescreening each lot of mitogen before use. Significant and reproducible observations revealed that the peak of the response occurred very soon after the addition of PHA and that the kinetics and magnitude of the response varied with the concentration, the source of the mitogen (Fig. 1), and the PBM donor (data not shown). It is notable that cyclic GMP levels remained undetectable under all experimental conditions employed in this study presumably

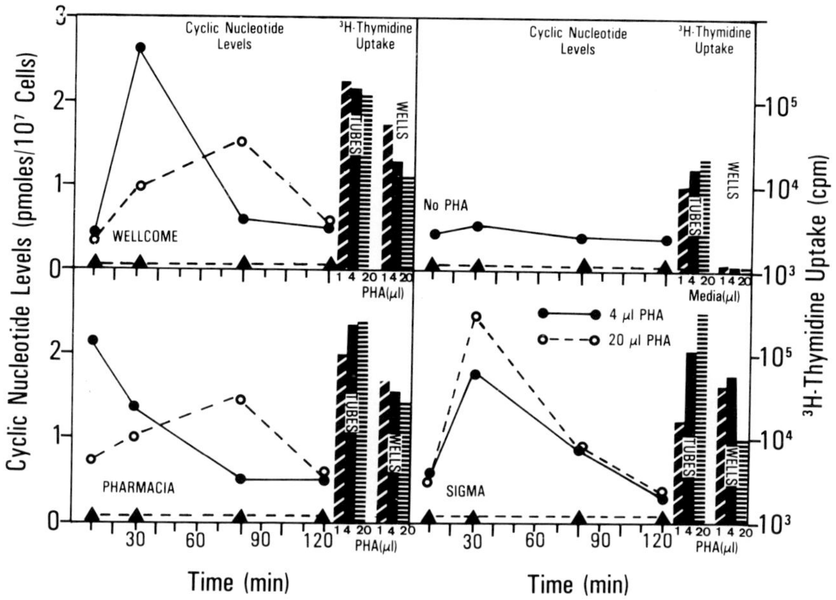

FIG. 1. Effect of PHA on PBM cyclic nucleotide levels and [^{3}H]thymidine uptake. Cyclic AMP levels were measured at the times indicated after the addition of either 4 μl (● —— ●) or 20 μl (○ - - - ○) of PHA (stock concentration = 1 mg/ml) to 1 ml cultures of PBM at 2.0×10^6 ml in 12×75-mm sterile tissue culture tubes. Cyclic GMP levels (▲ - - - ▲) were measured after the addition of 4 μl of PHA and were undetectable. [^{3}H]Thymidine uptake measured 72 hr after addition of 1, 4, or 20 μl of PHA or buffer to PBM, cultured either as described for cyclic nucleotides (tubes), and pulsed with 2.0 μCi of [^{3}H]thymidine or in microtiter wells containing 250 μl of PBM at 0.5×10^6/ml and pulsed with 0.5 μCi of [^{3}H]thymidine

on the basis of insufficient cell input. For this reason cyclic GMP determinations were not performed in subsequent experiments.

DNA synthesis (measured as [^{3}H]thymidine uptake) is also a consequence of PHA stimulation but this response is delayed and reaches a peak between 72 and 96 hr after the addition of PHA (30). Our standard conditions for the assessment of [^{3}H]thymidine uptake require relatively few PBM (1×10^5) and small volumes (250 μl) thereby permitting the use of microtiter wells as culture vessels (1, 2, 30). To determine whether our standard microwell culture conditions for [^{3}H]thymidine uptake were comparable to the tube culture conditions used in cyclic nucleotide studies, we performed [^{3}H]thymidine uptake experiments under both conditions and compared the results with the cyclic nucleotide response (Fig. 1). PHA concentrations were varied in both culture systems to: (a) validate our selection of 1 μl of PHA per 250-μl culture as a standard concentration for the microwell system; and (b) evaluate the effects of the higher PHA doses used in the cyclic nucleotide studies relative to their effects on [^{3}H]thymidine uptake. It can be seen (Fig. 1) that the [^{3}H]thymidine response to PHA is dose dependent and also varies with the source of the PHA, the culture volume, and the total cell input. Under microwell conditions 1 μl of PHA (4 μl/ml final concentration) is indeed optimal for PHA. In contrast, 1 μl of PHA is generally suboptimal under tube culture conditions while 4 μl appears optimal.

PHA obtained from Wellcome (London, England) was selected for use in all subsequent experiments. Cyclic nucleotide experiments carried out in the tube culture system received 4 μl of PHA per 1 ml of cell suspension (2×10^6 cells). Cultures were harvested precisely 30 min after the addition of PHA for cell donors prescreened to produce an optimal response at that time. These same donors were used for 72-hr [^{3}H]thymidine uptake experiments using the microtiter method and 1 μl of PHA per 250-μl culture well (1×10^5 cells) yielding a final concentration of 4 μl per milliliter. This was identical on a volume basis to that used in the cyclic nucleotide studies.

Effect of VLDL on Cyclic AMP and [^{3}H]Thymidine Uptake

It was demonstrated in a previous publication that the suppressive activity of VLDL for mitogen-stimulated [^{3}H]thymidine uptake was not immediately reversible (2). When VLDL was added to PBM cell cultures 1 to 24 hr before mitogen and removed before the addition of mitogen, [^{3}H]thymidine uptake was still inhibited. Therefore, in all of the following experiments, the PBM were incubated at 37°C with either VLDL (320 μg/ml) or lipoprotein buffer at a cell concentration of 5 to 7×10^6/ml in complete medium. After 24 hr, the non-cell-associated VLDL was removed by washing and the cell concentration adjusted to 2×10^6/ml for assay of cyclic AMP or 5×10^5/ml for assay of [^{3}H]thymidine uptake before the addition of PHA.

VLDL markedly inhibited the rise in cyclic AMP and [^{3}H]thymidine uptake measured 30 min and 72 hr, respectively, after the addition of PHA (Table 1). A concentration of VLDL (320 μg protein/ml) which completely abrogated the PHA-stimulated rise in PBM cyclic AMP at 30 min, had a similar effect on [^{3}H]thymidine uptake at 72 hr. Occasionally, [^{3}H]thymidine uptake was unaffected while cyclic AMP levels were markedly inhibited at this VLDL concentration. This phenomenon seemed to be related to PBM donor and appeared to reflect greater sensitivity of the cyclic AMP response to inhibition by VLDL in these instances. It is noteworthy that twofold-lower concentrations of VLDL were uniformly noninhibitory to both responses. The relatively high VLDL concentration (320 μg VLDL/ml/6.8×10^6 cells) needed for the expression of these activities compared with previously published concentrations (12 μg VLDL/ml/5×10^5 cells), probably reflects the increased PBM concentration employed in the current studies.

TABLE 1

Effect of VLDL on Cyclic AMP Levels and [^{3}H]Thymidine Uptake in PHA-Stimulated PBM[a]

VLDL	PHA	Cyclic AMP[b] (pmol/10^7 cells)	[^{3}H]Thymidine uptake[c] (cpm/10^5 cells)
−	−	1.5	365
−	+	6.8	72,873
+	−	0.8	297
+	+	0.6	230

[a] 24-hr preincubation of VLDL (320 μg protein/ml) and cells (6.8×10^6/ml) followed by three washes before the addition of PHA.

[b] Measured 30 min after the addition of 4 μl PHA to 1 ml cultures containing 2×10^6 cells.

[c] Measured 72 hr after the addition of 1 μl PHA to 250-μl cultures containing 1×10^5 cells.

To evaluate the effect of VLDL on PHA-induced cyclic AMP further, we delineated the time course of the effect of VLDL on PBM cyclic AMP. It can be seen in Fig. 2 that PHA-stimulated PBM displayed a marked but transient increase in intracellular cyclic AMP levels which peaked 30 min after exposure to mitogen. In contrast, VLDL markedly reduced this PHA-induced transient increase of intracellular cyclic AMP. It should also be noted that VLDL exposure similarly reduced the basal levels of cyclic AMP in unstimulated cells.

Recovery of PBM from VLDL Exposure

We next investigated the long-term reversibility of PBM suppression by VLDL. In these studies, the PBM were again cultured with VLDL at high cell concentrations for 24 hr. The VLDL was then removed by washing, and the cells were placed into culture as described for assay of cyclic AMP and [^{3}H]thymidine uptake. At daily intervals thereafter, the cells were stimulated with PHA, and examined after 30 min for cyclic AMP content and after 72 hr for [^{3}H]thymidine uptake.

At no time during the next 3 days were the PBM able to recover from VLDL suppression of [^{3}H]thymidine uptake (Fig. 3). While control PBM became somewhat less responsive to the mitogenic effects of PHA as a function of time, the VLDL-exposed PBM displayed a marked reduction in [^{3}H]thymidine uptake with increasing time after termination of the initial 24-hr exposure to VLDL.

When the intracellular cyclic AMP level of these same PBM was measured 30 min after the addition of PHA, the expected suppression of the transient increase in cyclic AMP was observed during the first 24 hr after the removal of VLDL. Control cells responded to PHA with typical increases in cyclic AMP, while VLDL-

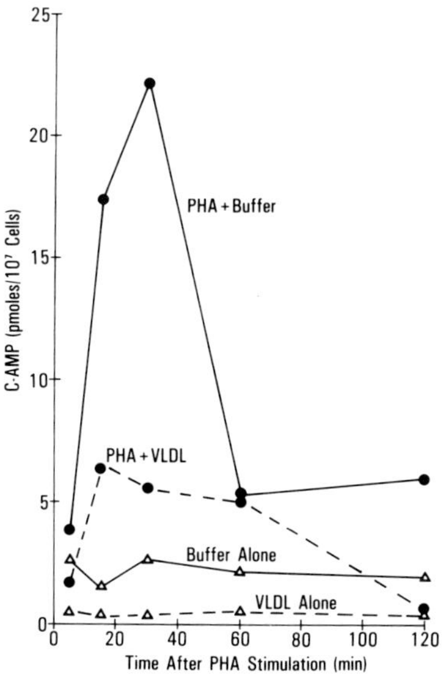

FIG. 2. Effect of VLDL on the kinetics of PHA-stimulated PBM cyclic AMP accumulation. PBM (5×10^6/ml) were incubated with 320 μg/ml of VLDL or an equivalent volume of buffer for 24 hr. The cells were washed three times, adjusted to 2×10^6/ml, and PHA or buffer was (4 μl/ml) added. At the times indicated, the cells were harvested and assayed for cyclic AMP as described.

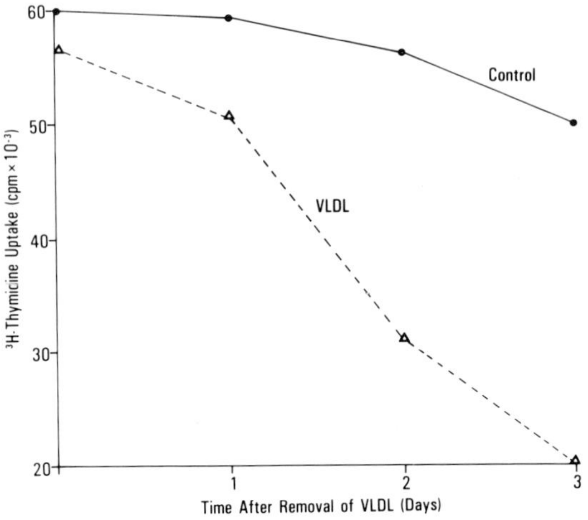

FIG. 3. Delayed effect of VLDL on PHA-stimulated PBM [^{3}H]thymidine uptake. PBM (5×10^6/ml) were incubated for 24 hr with VLDL at 320 μg protein/ml or with buffer. The cells were washed three times, adjusted to 2×10^6/ml and incubation continued. At the times indicated, the cells were adjusted to 5×10^5/ml placed into microtiter wells, stimulated with 1 μl PHA, and labeled with [^{3}H]thymidine 72 hr later. They were harvested at 96 hr.

exposed cells did not. However, after 2 days the response changed. Neither control nor VLDL-exposed PBM responded to PHA stimulation. Control PBM contained only basal levels of cyclic AMP 30 min after PHA stimulation, while VLDL-exposed PBM demonstrated a progressive increase in cyclic AMP (Fig. 4). This increase appeared to be both independent of PHA and refractory to further elevation by PHA since similar increases were noted in VLDL-exposed PBM in the presence or absence of PHA. Thus, VLDL had two effects on cyclic AMP levels.

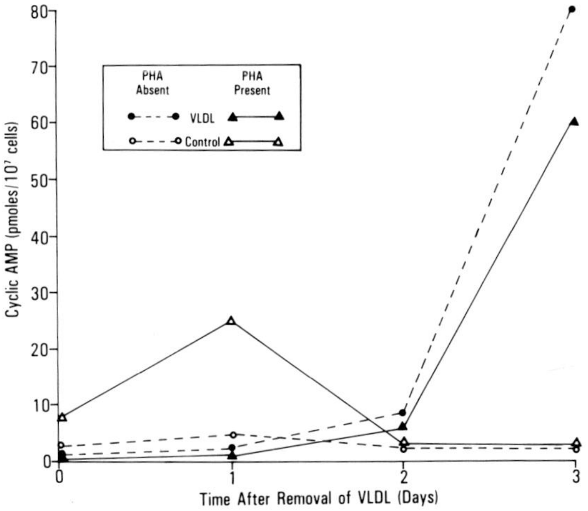

FIG. 4. Delayed effect of VLDL on spontaneous and PHA-stimulated PBM cyclic AMP levels. Experimental design as in Fig. 3 except the cells were kept at 2×10^6/ml and 4 μl/ml PHA or buffer control added at the times indicated. The cells were harvested for cyclic AMP determinations 30 min after mitogen stimulation.

Namely, an early reduction in the normal PHA-induced increase in intracellular cyclic AMP, which occurred in the absence of recovery or within 24 hr of recovery from VLDL exposure; and a delayed spontaneous increase in cyclic AMP levels which occurred after 24 hr of recovery and was independent of mitogen.

The observed effects of VLDL on [^{3}H]thymidine uptake and cyclic AMP levels could be due to either increased cell mortality or to a reduced ability of the PBM to bind PHA. To rule out these possibilities, we assessed cell viability and the number of ^{125}I-PHA receptors per lymphocyte at each harvest interval. No changes in these parameters were observed when compared with control cultures (Fig. 5).

DISCUSSION

Studies from numerous laboratories indicate that cyclic nucleotides may play an important role in the induction and expression of various aspects of the immune response. Among these, lymphocyte activation has been studied in great detail. Several investigators have found that biphasic changes in cyclic AMP occur during a normal immune response (31) and that exogenously stimulated orthodirectional changes in cyclic AMP levels are followed by enhanced responses while counter-directional changes are inhibitory (32). Furthermore, Parker and colleagues (33) have demonstrated that small, transient increases in cyclic AMP are followed by increased DNA synthesis whereas marked and sustained elevations in intracellular cyclic AMP are accompanied by a decrease in the lectin response. Ishizuka *et al.* (34) have demonstrated similar findings in studies of the murine humoral immune response to sheep red blood cells. Likewise, Plescia *et al.* have demonstrated that

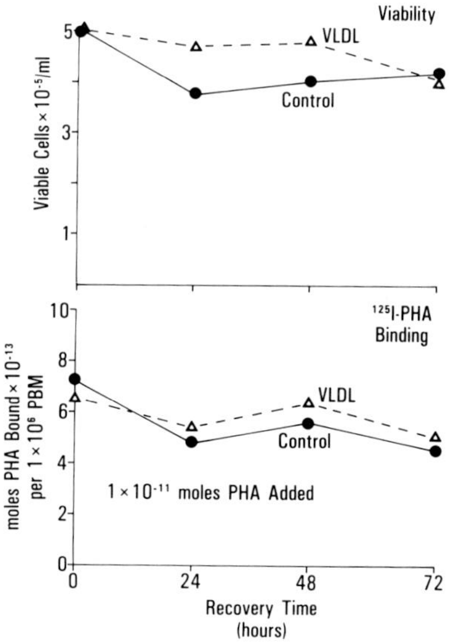

FIG. 5. Delayed effect of VLDL on PBM viability (upper panel) and binding of ^{125}I-PHA (lower panel). Experimental design as in Fig. 3 except the number of viable cells was determined by trypan blue exclusion (upper panel) and ^{125}I-PHA binding was assessed as described under Materials and Methods. Binding results are expressed as the maximum moles of ^{125}I-PHA bound per 10^6 PBM. Identical binding curves were observed for control and VLDL-exposed cells at each interval tested and reached plateau values at a ^{125}I-PHA molar input of 1×10^{-11}.

increased levels of cyclic AMP are associated with suppression of the primary immune response to sheep red blood cells in mice (32). Although still somewhat controversial, it appears that factors which influence the magnitude, the direction, and the timing of changes in intracellular cyclic AMP levels may profoundly influence various manifestations of lymphocyte function.

Human plasma lipoproteins, likewise, modulate a wide assortment of lymphocyte functions (1–7). By virtue of their well-known and previously described interactions with ligand-specific receptor systems on a variety of mammalian cell surfaces, it is conceivable that some of their biological effects might be mediated by influences on plasma membrane enzyme systems. Indeed, evidence for an alteration of membrane function by lipoproteins has been reported by Shore and Shore (20) who observed that human serum VLDL and low-density lipoprotein can specifically activate human erythrocyte membrane magnesium-ATPase. More recently, Pairault *et al.* (17) have described the activation of human and rat adipocyte plasma membrane adenyl cyclase activity by human serum low-density lipoprotein and VLDL at concentrations very comparable to those used in the current study. Harmony and associates (18) have demonstrated modest increases in cyclic guanosine monophosphate in PBM following mitogen activation and modulation of these changes by human serum lipoproteins. In contrast to our findings, these investigators found no changes in PBM cyclic AMP levels at mitogenic concentrations of PHA. The discrepancy between the two laboratories is probably related to differences in methodology. Hui and Harmony (18) used PBM at 5×10^7 per milliliter while we used 2×10^6 per milliliter. At our relatively low cell concentration cyclic GMP levels were probably below the detection limit of our assay. At their relatively high cell concentration mitogenic concentrations of PHA per cell would require very high PHA levels when expressed on a per milliliter basis as is traditional practice.

The present data indicate that VLDL inhibition of the DNA synthetic response of PBM to mitogen is a complex process which is accompanied by a dual effect on cyclic AMP metabolism. As reported by others (33), we confirmed the slight, transient increase in cyclic AMP following stimulation by PHA. Immunoregulatory concentrations of VLDL abrogate this effect. If this small, transient increase in cyclic AMP is indeed a necessary prerequisite for mitogen-induced DNA synthesis, one might predict that elimination of the cyclic AMP response might be followed by a concomitant reduction in DNA synthesis. It is also possible that the inability of PBM to recover from the DNA-synthetic inhibitory effects of VLDL may be related to the long-term effects of VLDL on cyclic AMP metabolism. VLDL-pulsed PBM display a progressive and significant spontaneous increase in intracellular cyclic AMP without the need for additional mitogen stimulation. Simultaneously, there developed a progressive, pronounced, and severe decrease in the ability of these VLDL-exposed PBM to respond to a mitogenic stimulus by increasing their uptake of [^{3}H]thymidine. This is in keeping with the observations that marked and sustained increases in intracellular cyclic AMP levels are associated with notable decreases in the lectin response (33, 35, 36).

These observations lend support to the hypothesis that plasma lipoprotein–target cell membrane interactions can lead to the generation of membrane signals which are translated via the cyclic nucleotide system into messages which are delivered throughout the interior of the cell. Thus, ligand–receptor interactions limited to the cell surface, as well as those which lead to internalization, may be mechanisms whereby lipoproteins regulate somatic cell function. The mechanism responsible for the early effect of VLDL on the transient increase in cyclic AMP levels following PHA is not entirely clear and the current studies do not shed any light on the molecular biology of this phenomenon. Hui *et al.* (19) have shown that low-density lipoproteins inhibit PHA-enhanced calcium accumulation by human PBM. Since MacManus and Whitfield (37) have shown that calcium is an effective intracellular cyclic AMP phosphodiesterase inhibitor it is conceivable that a VLDL-mediated reduction in available intracellular calcium might lead to enhanced activity of cyclic AMP phosphodiesterase with a concomitant reduction in the mitogen-induced cyclic AMP as reported herein. The mechanism responsible for the late effect of VLDL that is manifest as a sustained increase in intracellular cyclic AMP is similarly unknown. However, the time course as well as the net effect (arrested DNA synthesis) are compatible with the induction of prostaglandin synthesis and this possibility should be explored.

We conclude that VLDL can exert at least two separate effects on PBM cyclic AMP metabolism, and that both are associated with marked suppression of lymphocyte activation. Whether the remaining immunoregulatory properties of VLDL are actually due to their effects on lymphocyte cyclic AMP levels must await future studies which unequivocally demonstrate a causal linkage between lymphocyte function and cyclic nucleotide metabolism since this issue is currently somewhat controversial (38).

ACKNOWLEDGMENTS

The excellent technical assistance of M. Molden, K. Schwartz, and S. Chen, and secretarial services of L. Eddy are gratefully acknowledged.

REFERENCES

1. Curtiss, L. K., and Edgington, T. S., *J. Immunol.* **116,** 1452, 1976.
2. Chisari, F. V., *J. Immunol.* **119**(6), 2129, 1977.
3. Hui, D. Y., and Harmony, J. A. K., *J. Supramol. Struct.* **10,** Suppl. 3, 264, 1979 (Abstract).
4. Waddell, C. C., Taunton, O. D., and Twomey, J. J., *J. Clin. Invest.* **58,** 950, 1976.
5. Morse, J. H., Witte, L. D., and Goodman, D. S., *J. Exp. Med.* **146,** 1791, 1976.
6. Chisari, F. V., and Edgington, T. S., *J. Exp. Med.* **142,** 1092, 1975.
7. Ho, Y. K., Brown, M. S., Bilheimer, D. W., and Goldstein, J. L., *J. Clin. Invest.* **58,** 1465, 1976.
8. Curtiss, L. K., and Edgington, T. S., *J. Clin. Invest.* **63,** 193, 1979.
9. Edgington, T. S., Henney, C. S., and Curtiss, L. K., *In* "Regulatory Mechanisms in Lymphocyte Activation: Proceedings of the Eleventh Leukocyte Culture Conference" (D. O. Lucas, Ed.), p. 736. Academic Press, New York, 1977.
10. Chapman, H. H., and Hibbs, J. B., *Science* **197,** 282, 1977.
11. Chisari, F. V., Curtiss, L. K., and Jensen, F. C., *Fed. Proc.* **39,** 1197, 1980.
12. Chen, H. W., Heiniger, H. J., and Kandutsch, A. A., *Proc. Nat. Acad. Sci. USA* **72,** 1950, 1975.
13. Whitney, R. B., and Sutherland, R. M., *Cell. Immunol.* **5,** 137, 1972.
14. Fisher, D. B., and Mueller, G. C., *Proc. Nat. Acad. Sci. USA* **60,** 1396, 1968.
15. Parker, C. W., Smith, J. W., and Stenier, A. L., *Int. Arch. Allergy* **41,** 40, 1971.
16. Ho, Y. K., Faust, J. R., Bilheimer, D. W., Brown, M. S., and Goldstein, J. L., *J. Exp. Med.* **145,** 1531, 1977.
17. Pairault, J., Levilliers, J., and Chapman, M. J., *Nature (London)* **269,** 607, 1977.
18. Hui, D. Y., and Harmony, J. A. K., *J. Biol. Chem.,* in press, 1981.
19. Hui, D. Y., Berebitsky, G. L., and Harmony, J. A. K., *J. Biol. Chem.* **254,** 4666, 1979.
20. Shore, V., and Shore, B., *Biochem. Biophys. Res. Commun.* **65,** 1250, 1975.
21. Harmony, J. A. K., and Hui, D. Y., *Cancer Res.,* in press, 1981.

22. Bucolo, G., and David, H., *Clin. Chem.* **19,** 476, 1973.
23. Abell, L. L., Levy, B. B., Brodie, B. B., and Kendall, F. E., *In* "Standard Methods of Clinical Chemistry" (D. Seligson, Ed.), Vol. 2, p. 26. Academic Press, New York, 1958.
24. Markwell, M. A. K., Haas, S. M., Bicker, C. L., and Tolbert, N. E., *Anal. Biochem.* **87,** 206, 1978.
25. Boyum, A., *Scand. J. Clin. Lab. Invest. Suppl.* **21,** 97, 1968.
26. Chisari, F. V., Routenberg, J. A., and Edgington, T. S., *J. Clin. Invest.* **57,** 1227, 1976.
27. Kaplow, L. S., *Blood* **26,** 215, 1965.
28. Hunter, W. M., and Greenwood, F. C., *Nature (London)* **194,** 495, 1962.
29. Chisari, F. V., Gerin, J. L., and Edgington, T. S., *J. Immunol.* **113,** 543, 1974.
30. Chisari, F. V., *J. Immunol.* **121,** 1279, 1978.
31. Teh, H., and Verner, P., *Nature (London)* **250,** 505, 1974.
32. Plescia, O. J., Yamamoto, I., and Shimamura, T., *Proc. Nat. Acad. Sci. USA* **72,** 888, 1975.
33. Smith, J. W., Steiner, A. L., Newberry, W. M., and Parker, C. W., *J. Clin. Invest.* **50,** 432, 1971.
34. Ishizuka, M., Gafni, M., and Braun, W., *Proc. Soc. Exp. Biol. Med.* **134,** 963, 1970.
35. Hirschhorn, R., Grossman, J., and Weissman, G., *Proc. Soc. Exp. Biol. Med.* **133,** 1361, 1970.
36. Watson, J., Epstein, R., and Cohn, M., *Nature (London)* **246,** 405, 1973.
37. MacManus, J. P., and Whitfield, J. G., *Exp. Cell Res.* **69,** 281, 1971.
38. Hadden, J. W., Hadden, E. M., Haddox, M. K., and Goldberg, N. D., *Proc. Nat. Acad. Sci. USA* **69,** 3024, 1972.

CELLULAR IMMUNOLOGY **65**, 337–351 (1981)

Nonspecific Activation of Murine Lymphocytes

VIII. Effects of D-Penicillamine[1]

MICHAEL G. GOODMAN[2] AND WILLIAM O. WEIGLE

Department of Immunopathology, Scripps Clinic and Research Foundation, La Jolla, California 92037

Received July 21, 1981; accepted October 25, 1981

The effects of D-penicillamine on proliferation and polyclonal activation of lymphocytes were studied in cultures of spleen cells from a variety of murine strains. Inclusion in serum-free or serum-containing medium of optimal concentrations of D-penicillamine resulted in the uptake of tritiated thymidine in a dose-dependent fashion, with both lower and higher doses causing less marked effects. The kinetic peak of these responses was found to occur at Day 2 of culture. Experiments examining the responsiveness of B-cell-enriched and T-cell-enriched populations demonstrated that D-penicillamine, like 2-mercaptoethanol, stimulates both types of cell. The magnitude of the response remained unchanged in populations depleted of adherent cells. In correlation with previous results seen for 2-ME, D-penicillamine was mitogenically active both in reduced and oxidized forms. The oxidized form failed to enhance the response to LPS, in contrast to the marked effect of the reduced form. Additionally, D-penicillamine failed to evoke a mitogenic response from B cells of CBA/N mice, a strain characterized by a deficit in the function of a particular set of mature B cells. Young mice from autoimmune strains responded to D-penicillamine as well as normal mice did. No relationship could be observed between responsiveness to D-penicillamine and the H-2 phenotype of the cell donor, and in A/J mice hyporesponsiveness was shown to be a function of their background rather than H-2. D-Penicillamine was found to function as a polyclonal B-cell activator, and to significantly enhance the primary humoral immune response to sheep erythrocytes *in vitro*. These immunomodulatory effects of D-penicillamine are discussed in relation to possible pathogenetic mechanisms of its spectrum of autoimmune side effects.

INTRODUCTION

The use of D-penicillamine in the treatment of rheumatoid arthritis has become increasingly accepted since its use was extended to this disease by Dresner and Trombly (1) and by Griffin *et al.* (2). It currently constitutes one of the small number of effective therapeutic modalities for the treatment of rheumatoid arthritis

[1] This is publication No. 2305 from the Department of Immunopathology, Scripps Clinic and Research Foundation, La Jolla, Calif. This work was supported in part by United States Public Health Service Grant AI07007, American Cancer Society Grant IM-42I, and Biomedical Research Support Grant RRO-5514.

[2] Recipient of United States Public Health Service Grant AI15284 and United States Public Health Service Research Career Development Award AI00374.

0008-8749/81/180337-15$02.00/0

(RA).[3] Its efficacy has been established by a number of clinical trials (3–6) and its use in the treatment of RA has been sanctioned by the FDA.

The mechanism of action by which D-penicillamine ameliorates this disease is unclear. One suggestion well supported by experimental evidence is that this agent acts in an immunosuppressive capacity to diminish the immune responsiveness of patients with rheumatoid arthritis. Thus, penicillamine has been noted to depress levels of circulating rheumatoid factor and frequently also of immunoglobulin as well as immune complexes (7, 8). Several studies have demonstrated that D-penicillamine depresses the primary humoral immune response of experimental animals *in vivo* (9, 10) and diminishes mitogenic activation of human peripheral blood lymphocytes *in vitro* (11). Recently, Lipsky and Ziff (12) have demonstrated *in vitro* suppression of the primary humoral immune response of human PBL mediated by a selective suppression of the helper T-cell arm of this response.

Clinical use of D-penicillamine, however, is limited by its high rate of complication. Among these are the group of so-called "autoimmune" side effects which include myasthenia gravis, thyroiditis, polymyositis and dermatomyositis, autoimmune hemolytic anemia, thrombotic thrombocytopenic purpura, and a drug-induced lupus-like syndrome, among others. Case reports of undesirable immune-mediated side effects of penicillamine therapy suggest that the drug, rather than being solely immunosuppressive, may possess a variety of immunoregulatory properties, i.e., it may have immunopotentiating or activating effects as well. The report of Tobin and Altman (13) concerning the enhancement of the humoral immune response *in vivo* by D-penicillamine in rabbits supports such a concept. In previous studies we have explored the immunopotentiating and *de novo*-activating properties of 2-mercaptoethanol, a low MW hydroxy-thiol compound. Our observations that several other functional groups are active when present on thiol compounds led us to probe the effects of D-penicillamine (β-mercaptovaline) with respect to lymphocyte activation. Results of the current communication indicate that in normal mice, mitogenicity, polyclonal B-cell activation, and adjuvanticity are properties of this compound.

MATERIALS AND METHODS

Mice. C3H/St, $B6D2F_1$, B10, B10.A, and Balb/c mice, 8–12 weeks of age, were obtained from the mouse breeding facility at Scripps Clinic and Research Foundation, La Jolla, California. CBA/CaJ, A/J, C57B1/6J and SJL mice, 8–12 weeks of age, were purchased from the Jackson Laboratory, Bar Harbor, Maine. A breeding nucleus of CBA/N mice was provided by the animal production section, National Institutes of Health, Bethesda, Maryland. NZW, NZB, and $BxWF_1$ female mice, 8–12 weeks of age, were obtained from the Jackson Laboratory. All mice were maintained on Wayne Lab-Blox F6 pellets (Allied Mills, Inc., Chicago, Ill.) and chlorinated water acidified with HCl to a pH of 3.0.

Culture reagents. Constituents of the serum-free culture medium employed in these studies have been described elsewhere (14). For serum-containing medium, supportive FCS was substituted for 5% of the volume of RPMI 1640, and Hepes

[3] Abbreviations used: αTG, αthioglycerol; Ig, immunoglobulin; LPS, bacterial lipopolysaccharide; 2-ME, 2-mercaptoethanol; RA, rheumatoid arthritis, SRBC, sheep red blood cells; TNP, 2,4,6-trinitrophenyl.

buffer was omitted. *Escherichia coli* 055:B5 LPS, prepared by the Boivin procedure, was purchased from the Difco Laboratories, Detroit, Michigan. D-Penicillamine was purchased from the Sigma Chemical Company, St. Louis, Missouri, and from the Aldrich Chemical Company, Milwaukee, Wisconsin. D-Penicillamine disulfide was purchased from the Aldrich Chemical Company. LPS and D-penicillamine were diluted in phosphate-buffered saline and sterilized by filtration. Further dilution in complete medium was used for microcultures. D-Penicillamine was made up fresh from powder for each experiment.

Cell preparation. Spleen cell suspensions were prepared as described previously (14). Spleen cells enriched for T lymphocytes were prepared by passage through nylon wool (NW) columns, as described previously (15). B-Cell-enriched populations were prepared by treating 10^8 spleen cells with a 1:1000 dilution of monoclonal anti-Thy 1.2 (New England Nuclear, Boston, Mass.) for 30 min at 4°C. Treated cells were then centrifuged at 280*g* for 10 min, the antibodies removed, and the cells resuspended in a 1:6 dilution of C3H RBC-absorbed guinea pig complement at 37°C for 45 min. Cells were then washed and cultured as above. Adherent cells were depleted by passage over columns of Sephadex G-10 as described by Ly and Mishell (16). This procedure reduced the percentage of esterase-positive cells from 7% in unseparated spleen cells to approximately 0.1% in non-adherent populations.

Lymphocyte cultures. Murine spleen cells were cultured in microculture plates (No. 3042, Falcon Plastics, Oxnard, Calif.) at a cell density of 5×10^6 viable cells/ml in a volume of 0.1 ml (17). Microcultures were incubated at 37°C in a humidified atmosphere of 10% CO_2 in air. Cultures were fed daily with 8 μl of nutritional cocktail (18).

Measurement of DNA synthesis. During the final 24 hr of culture, cells were radiolabeled with 1.0 μCi of [^{3}H]TdR/culture (5 Ci/m*M*, Amersham Radiochemicals, Amersham, England). The microcultures were harvested with a Brandel cell harvester, Model M24V (Biological Research and Development Laboratories, Rockville, Md.) onto glass fiber filter strips (Reeve Angel, Clifton, N.J.). Filter disks were transferred to plastic scintillation vials (Kimball Products, Owens-Illinois, Toledo, Ohio) covered with liquid scintillation cocktail (Scintiverse, Fisher Scientific Co., Fairlawn, N.J.) and counted in a Beckman LS-230 liquid scintillation counter.

Assay of plaque-forming cells (PFC). For polyclonal activation, 10×10^6 spleen cells/ml were incubated in a 1.0-ml volume of 5% FCS-containing medium. PFC to TNP were assayed after 2 days of culture (19) using a modification of the hemolytic plaque assay of Jerne and Nordin (20). For the primary humoral response to SRBC, 10×10^6 murine spleen cells were cultured in 1 ml of 5% FCS containing medium for 4 days in the presence of 2×10^6 SRBC/culture.

RESULTS

Dose dependency of the DNA-synthetic response to D-penicillamine. The ability of D-penicillamine to activate DNA synthesis was investigated in cultures of spleen cells from C3H/St mice. Spleen cells were incubated in serum-free medium in the presence of variable concentrations of D-penicillamine. Resultant activation was measured by determination of [^{3}H]TdR uptake during the final 24 hr of a 2-day culture period. The results shown in Fig. 1 indicate that this thiol compound does indeed promote the uptake of tritiated thymidine in a dose-dependent manner. Lower concentrations were suboptimal while higher concentrations appeared to be inhibitory. Peak responsiveness appeared to be between 10^{-3} and 10^{-2} *M* D-penicillamine. Peak responsiveness varied somewhat from experiment to experiment but appeared to be highly consistent within individual experiments.

Kinetic profile of the response to D-penicillamine. The time at which the maximal D-penicillamine mitogenic effect occurred was assessed in C3H/St mice. Spleen cells were cultured either in the presence or absence of 10^{-3} *M* D-penicillamine under serum-free culture conditions. Subsequently, one set of cultures was harvested daily after a 24-hr pulse of [^{3}H]TdR. Maximal [^{3}H]TdR uptake was noted to occur at Day 2 and declined thereafter (Fig. 2).

Response of separately cultured B-enriched and T-enriched lymphocytes to D-penicillamine. C3H/St spleen cell populations enriched for B cells by treatment with monoclonal anti-Thy 1.2 plus guinea pig complement, or for T cells by passage over NW columns as described, were cultured under conditions utilizing medium containing 5% FCS. Serum was used in these experiments because of the inability of separated T cells to proliferate in the absence of serum (28). The results of such experiments (Fig. 3) demonstrate that T lymphocytes and B lymphocytes can proliferate in response to D-penicillamine. In some of the experiments, the response by B cells was greater than that exhibited by T cells, and in no case was the reverse observed. B-Cell-enriched cultures failed to respond to the T-cell mitogen concanavalin A, and T-cell cultures gave only 8% of the unseparated cell response to LPS.

Ability of D-penicillamine to activate nonadherent spleen cells. In order to gain

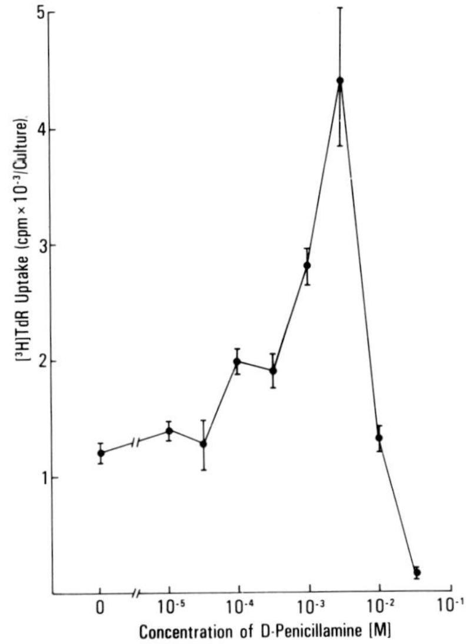

FIG. 1. Dose–response profile for D-penicillamine in serum-free culture. 5×10^5 viable C3H/St spleen cells were cultured for 2 days in 0.1 ml of serum-free medium in the presence of various concentrations of D-penicillamine. Cells were pulsed with 1.0 μCi of [^{3}H]TdR for the final 24 hr of culture. Results are expressed as the arithmetic mean of five replicate cultures ± the SE.

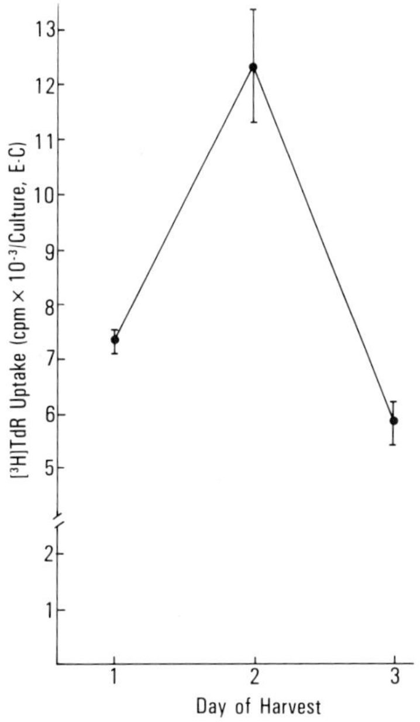

FIG. 2. Kinetic profile of the response to D-penicillamine. 5×10^5 viable C3H/St spleen cells were cultured in 0.1 ml of serum-free medium in the presence or absence of 10^{-3} *M* D-penicillamine. On each day, one set of parallel cultures was harvested after a 24-hr pulse of 1.0 μCi of [^{3}H]TdR. Results are expressed as the arithmetic mean of five replicate cultures containing D-penicillamine minus that of five replicate control cultures ± the SE. Control values were 6630 ± 510, 2310 ± 190, and 1540 ± 180 on Days 1, 2, and 3, respectively.

insight into the role played by adherent cells in the response to D-penicillamine, experiments were designed to determine whether the proliferative response to this thiol compound is mediated through such cells or is independent of them. C57B1/6J spleen cells were passed over Sephadex G-10 columns and the effluent cells used as the source of nonadherent cells. Content of esterase-positive cells was greatly diminished in this population (see Materials and Methods). The results of these experiments demonstrate that nonadherent cells respond to D-penicillamine to the same degree as do unseparated cells (Fig. 4).

Effects of reduced and oxidized D-penicillamine on murine spleen cells. Previous work has indicated that 2-ME, in addition to having mitogenic effects, is able to enhance the *in vitro* response of murine spleen cells to mitogens (15, 21, 22). In preliminary experiments, it was learned that D-penicillamine could similarly enhance the mitogenic response to bacterial LPS. Therefore, experiments were designed to investigate the requirement for free sulfhydryl groups both in D-penicillamine-mediated mitogenesis and in its LPS-enhancing effects. C3H/St spleen cells were incubated in the presence of incremental concentrations of either reduced or oxidized D-penicillamine under serum-free culture conditions (Fig. 5). Under these circumstances, both compounds were found to have mitogenic effects. The magnitude of the responses was generally equivalent, although lower doses of the disulfide were more effective than the equivalent doses of the thiol, resulting in a slight shift of the dose–response curve to the left for the disulfide. When these same

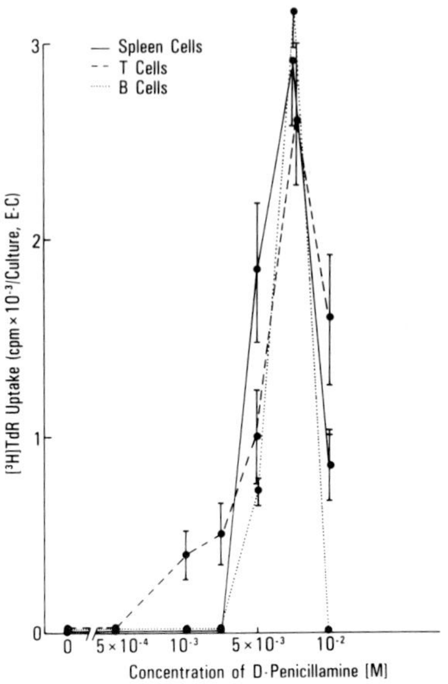

FIG. 3. Response of B-enriched and T-enriched lymphocyte cultures to D-penicillamine. 5×10^5 viable C3H/St B-enriched, T-enriched, or unseparated splenic lymphocytes were cultured in 0.1 ml of 5% FCS-containing medium for 2 days in the presence of various concentrations of D-penicillamine. Cells were pulsed with 1.0 μCi of [^{3}H]TdR for the final 24 hr of culture. Results are expressed as the arithmetic mean of five replicate cultures containing D-penicillamine minus control cultures ± the SE. Control values were 1920 ± 220, 1530 ± 250, and 880 ± 120 for unseparated, B, and T cells, respectively.

two compounds were evaluated for their ability to enhance the mitogenic response to LPS, it was found that only reduced D-penicillamine was capable of enhancing this response (Fig. 6). This effect occurred at the same dosage range as the optimal concentration for mitogenesis by D-penicillamine. Nonetheless, it is unlikely that this effect can be accounted for by a simple additivity of mitogenic responses, since the magnitude of the increased LPS response was considerably greater than that of the mitogenic response within the same experiment and since the disulfide was ineffective.

Effect of D-penicillamine in mice with an X-linked B-cell defect. Characterization of the immune deficit of the CBA/N mouse has been carried out by a number of investigators. Amsbaugh *et al.* (23) first described an X-linked defect in the CBA/N response to thymus-independent antigens. These animals have subsequently been reported to contain a diminished number of Ig-bearing cells in their spleens (24), to mount subnormal responses to thymus-dependent antigens (25), and to possess cell surface Ig and microdensities and organ distributions which suggest a deficit of mature B lymphocyte (26). Moreover, work characterizing the nature of the B-cell subset responsive to 2-ME demonstrated that the subpopulation of B cells responding to 2-ME was a mature set which was functionally absent in the CBA/N mouse (15). Therefore, it was of interest to assess the reactivity of cultures of CBA/N B cells to D-penicillamine. B cells were prepared as described under Materials and Methods. A direct comparison of the responsiveness of B lymphocytes derived from this strain with those from the histocompatible CBA/CaJ strain (Fig. 7) indicates that in contrast to the CBA/CaJ response (generally

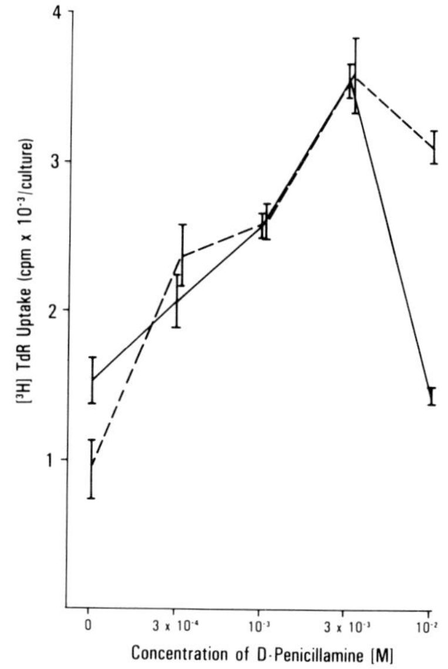

FIG. 4. Ability of D-penicillamine to activate unseparated and G-10 passed spleen cells. 5×10^5 viable C57BL/6J spleen cells, either unseparated (——) or passed over column of Sephadex G-10 (- - -) were cultured for 2 days in 0.1 ml of serum-free medium in the presence of various concentrations of D-penicillamine. Cultures were pulsed with 1.0 μCi of [^{3}H]TdR for the final 24 hr of culture. Results are expressed as the arithmetic mean of five replicate cultures ± the SE.

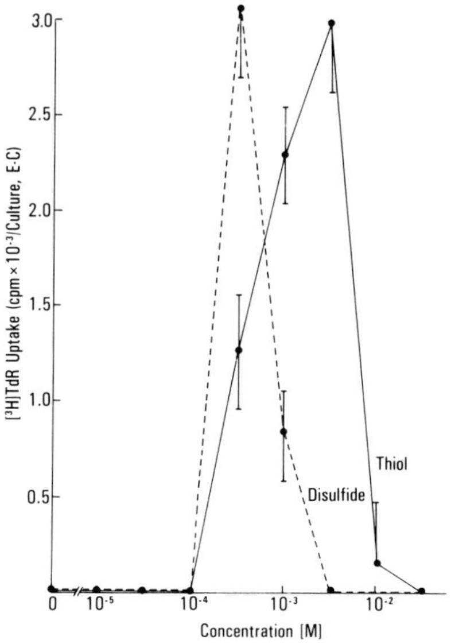

FIG. 5. Effects of reduced and oxidized D-penicillamine on murine spleen cells. 5×10^5 viable C3H/St spleen cells were cultured for 2 days in 0.1 ml of serum-free medium in the presence of various concentrations of either the thiol or the disulfide form of D-penicillamine. Cultures were pulsed with 1.0 μCi of [^{3}H]TdR for the final 24 hr of culture. Results are expressed as the arithmetic mean of five replicate cultures containing D-penicillamine minus control cultures ± the SE. Control uptake was 1310 ± 230 cpm.

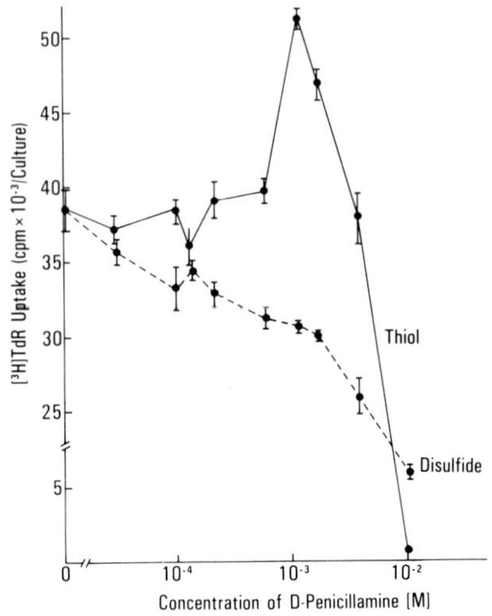

FIG. 6. Ability of reduced and oxidized D-penicillamine to enhance the mitogenic response to LPS. 5×10^5 viable C3H/St spleen cells were cultured for 2 days in 0.1 ml of serum-free medium together with 100 μg/ml LPS in the presence of various concentrations of either the thiol or disulfide form of D-penicillamine. Cells were pulsed with 1.0 μCi of [^{3}H]TdR for the final 24 hr of culture. Results are expressed as the arithmetic mean of five replicate cultures ± the SE.

of similar magnitude to that of the C3H/St), B cells from the CBA/N mouse were unresponsive to D-penicillamine.

Ability of D-penicillamine to induce polyclonal B-cell activation. Since mitogenicity and polyclonal B-cell activation are frequently very closely linked, the ability of D-penicillamine to promote polyclonal immunoglobulin secretion was evaluated. Adherent cell-depleted spleen cells (10^7) were cultured in 5% FCS-containing medium in the presence of incremental concentrations of D-penicillamine. This agent was found to be a weak polyclonal B-cell activator, significant responses being detectable only on SRBC conjugated with TNP rather than on SRBC alone (Fig. 8). Peak responsiveness again was within the range seen for peak mitogenicity.

Ability of D-penicillamine to activate spleen cells from normal and autoimmune mouse strains. In order to examine the effect of autoimmune predisposition on responsiveness to D-penicillamine, spleen cells from female C3H/St, CBA/CaJ, NZW, NZB, and NZB × NZWF$_1$ mice (8–12 weeks of age) were cultured in the presence or absence of 10^{-3} *M* D-penicillamine. The results of these experiments (Fig. 9) indicate that there is no major quantitative difference in the stimulated response to this thiol compound although background thymidine uptake varied considerably. Thus, a predisposition to develop autoimmune disease did not appear to correlate with increased susceptibility of spleen cells to activation by D-penicillamine.

Ability of D-penicillamine to activate spleen cells from mice of different H-2 phenotypes. Studies were undertaken to screen for a relationship between H-2 phenotype and degree of responsiveness to D-penicillamine. Spleen cells from a variety of murine strains were cultured with a range of concentrations of this thiol compound. Peak responsiveness occurred in the range of 3–6 × 10^{-3} *M*. Although H-2^k and H-2^d mice responded to D-penicillamine, A/J mice (a natural k/d re-

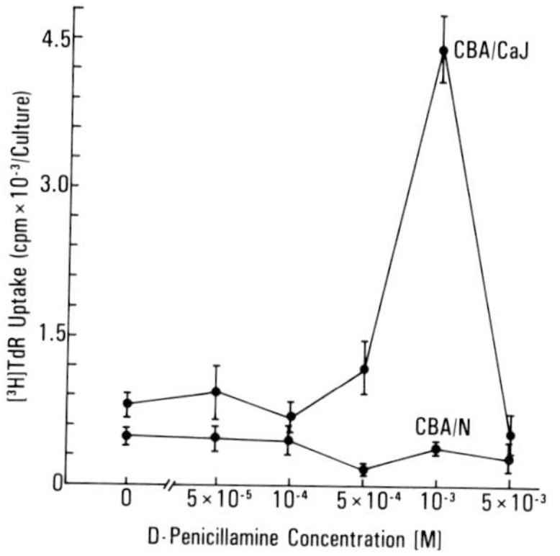

FIG. 7. The effect of D-penicillamine in mice with an X-linked B-cell defect. 5×10^5 viable CBA/CaJ or CBA/N splenic B lymphocytes were cultured for 2 days in 0.1 ml of serum-free medium in the presence of various concentrations of D-penicillamine. Cultures were pulsed with 1.0 μCi of [^{3}H]TdR for the final 24 hr of culture. Results are expressed as the arithmetic mean of five replicate cultures ± the SE.

combinant) responded poorly or not at all (Fig. 10). No other obvious relationship could be observed. In other experiments, the inability of A/J mice to respond to D-penicillamine was dissected using B10 and B10.A mice (Fig. 11). The data indicate that hyporesponsiveness is a property of the A/J genetic background and is not exclusively linked to its H-2 phenotype.

Effect of D-penicillamine on the primary humoral response to SRBC in vitro. Work by Click *et al.* (27) established that the primary humoral immune response to SRBC was augmented when cultures were supplemented with 2-ME. The effect of D-penicillamine on the primary humoral response to SRBC was therefore evaluated in order to determine whether this thiol compound similarly could enhance the response to specific antigen. The data presented in Fig. 12 indicate that addition of D-penicillamine to culture results in an enhanced response to SRBC. This effect

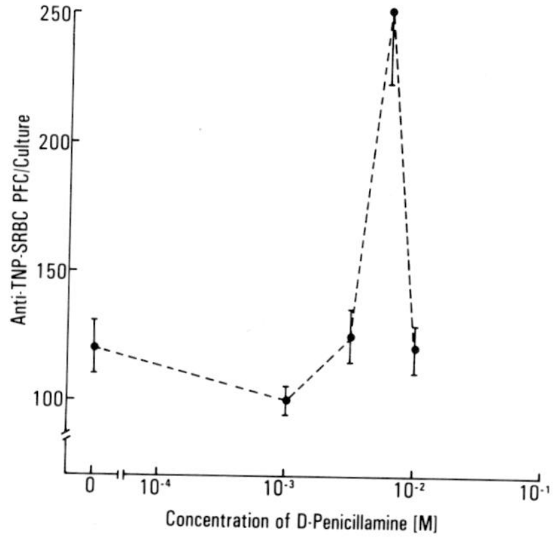

FIG. 8. Ability of D-penicillamine to induce polyclonal B-cell activation. 10×10^6 viable C3H/St nonadherent spleen cells were cultured for 2 days in 1.0 ml of 5% FCS-containing medium in the presence of incremental concentrations of D-penicillamine. Results are expressed as the arithmetic mean of triplicate cultures ± the SE.

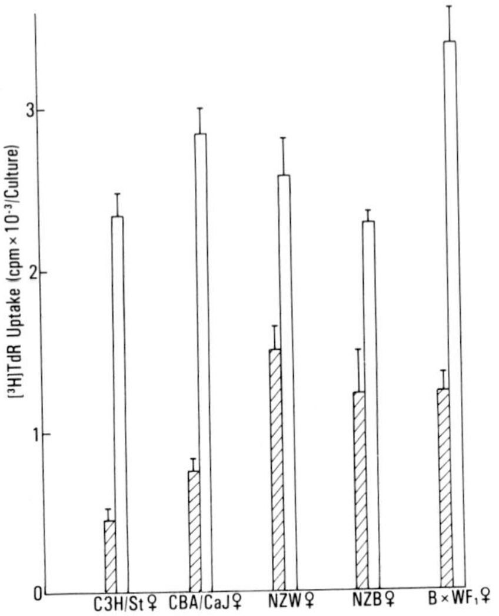

FIG. 9. Ability of D-penicillamine to activate spleen cells from normal and autoimmune mouse strains. 5×10^5 viable spleen cells from female C3H/St, CBA/CaJ, NZW, NZB, or NZB × WF_1 mice were cultured for 2 days in 0.1 ml of serum-free medium in the presence of 10^{-3} *M* D-penicillamine. Cells were pulsed with 1.0 μCi of [^{3}H]TdR for the final 24 hr of culture. Results are expressed as the arithmetic mean of five replicate cultures ± the SE. Hatched bars represent unstimulated cultures, open bars represent stimulated cultures.

was dose-dependent but occurred at lower concentrations than were required for mitogenicity or for polyclonal activation.

DISCUSSION

The effectiveness of D-penicillamine for treatment of rheumatoid arthritis has been validated by a number of clinical trials and is responsible for its increasing clinical usage. This thiol compound has been thought to function primarily as an immunosuppressor, based on *in vivo* (7–10) and *in vitro* (11, 12) studies. The data presented in the current communication, however, are more compatible with the thesis that D-penicillamine is a modulator of the immune response, capable of both enhancing and initiating immune activation as well as suppressing it.

Previous studies exploring the effects of 2-mercaptoethanol (2-ME) in the murine system *in vitro* demonstrated that certain sulfhydryl compounds induce a state of activation in resting splenic lymphocytes. Such activation involves T as well as B lymphocytes (28, 29) with the latter population of cells being induced to secrete polyclonal immunoglobulin. Igarashi *et al.* (30) further showed that 2-ME is responsible for the induction of polyclonal cytotoxicity in T cells. In addition, 2-ME has been shown to have immunopotentiating activity in a diversity of systems (31–34). Therefore, the possibility that similar effects might be mediated by D-penicillamine was examined experimentally.

Addition of D-penicillamine to cultures of murine spleen cells was found to result in a consistent increase in uptake of [^{3}H]TdR. This phenomenon occurred in a dose-related fashion, such that suboptimal doses elicited lesser responses, and supraoptimal doses caused suppression below background, similar to that seen by

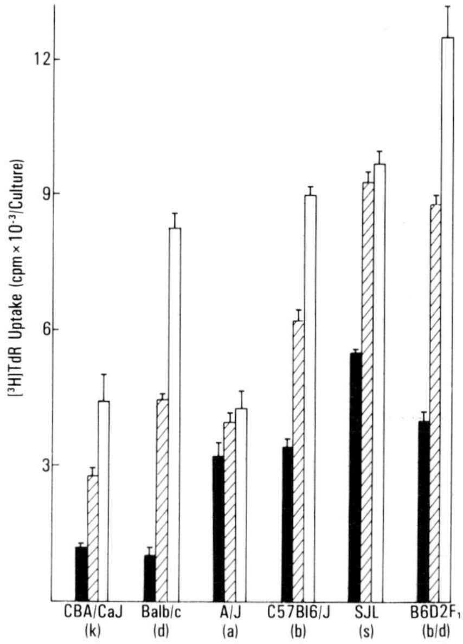

FIG. 10. Effect of D-penicillamine on mice of different H-2 phenotypes. 5×10^5 viable spleen cells from CBA/CaJ, Balb/c, A/J C57BL/6J, SJL, or B6D2F$_1$ mice were cultured for 2 days in 0.1 ml of serum-free medium in the presence of medium only (solid bars), 3×10^{-3} *M* D-penicillamine (hatched bars), or 6×10^{-3} *M* D-penicillamine (open bars). Cells were pulsed with 1.0 μCi of [^{3}H]TdR for the final 24 hr of culture. Results are expressed as the arithmetic mean of five replicate cultures ± the SE.

other investigators. The observation of increased [^{3}H]TdR uptake by spleen cells incubated with D-penicillamine contrasts with observations by some other investigators (35), but this discrepancy is in all likelihood explained by differences in the culture system and dose range employed. When cells were cultured in serum-containing medium, induction of significant stimulation by D-penicillamine was found to require a minimum of twofold higher concentrations of the drug, probably as a consequence of mixed disulfide formation.

The data presented indicate that both B- and T-lymphocyte populations repond to D-penicillamine. A similar capacity to activate both B and T lymphocytes has been reported for 2-ME and αTG (22, 28), although in those cases B cells have been found to be more responsive than have T cells. Macrophages do not appear to play a critical role in the activation of lymphocytes by D-penicillamine. Depletion of macrophages from spleen cells does not result in a concomitant decrease in the uptake of [^{3}H]TdR; on the contrary, stimulation of the G-10 nonadherent cell population is nearly equivalent to that seen in unseparated cells.

Both the oxidized and reduced forms of D-penicillamine induce mitogenesis in spleen cell populations to approximately the same degree, while only the reduced form enhances the mitogenic response to LPS, in parallel with data obtained for reduced and oxidized 2-ME (37). Supraoptimal D-penicillamine (as well as 2-ME) inhibits the underlying LPS response. These data suggest that the free sulfhydryl group is critical to the mitogen-enhancing effect of D-penicillamine, since the disulfide fails to demonstrate this effect. Similarly, Kendall and Hutchins (35) found that D-penicillamine enhanced the responses to concanavalin A or allogeneic cells,

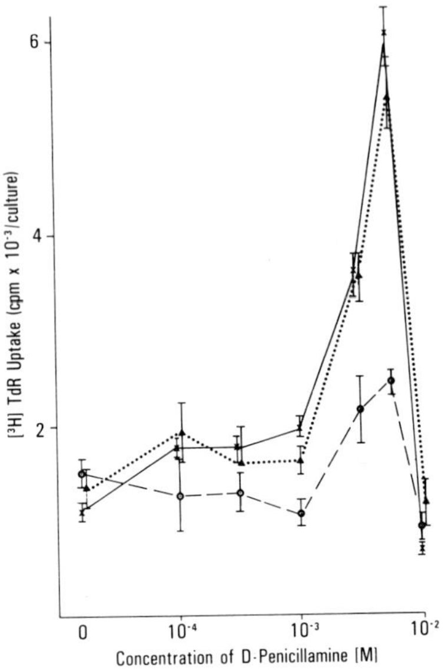

FIG. 11. Effect of D-penicillamine in A/J, B10, and B10.A mice. 5×10^5 viable spleen cells from A/J (○ – – – ○), B10 (▲ · · · ▲) or B10.A (x —— x) mice were cultured for 2 days in 0.1 ml of serum-free medium in the presence of various concentrations of D-penicillamine. Cultures were pulsed with 1.0 μCi of [^{3}H]TdR for the final 24 hr of culture. Results are expressed as the arithmetic mean of five replicate cultures ± the SE.

and that higher doses of the drug were suppressive. In contrast, a free sulfhydryl group does not appear to be mandatory for mitogenicity. Thus, one might speculate that the mitogenic effects of D-penicillamine and its disulfide occur at an intracellular site where the redox equilibrium favors the reduced form; the LPS-enhancing effect may be mediated via a membrane site where such reduction would not occur (otherwise one would expect enhancement from the disulfide as well). The effectiveness of the disulfide at concentrations approximately 1 log lower than the sulfhydryl may be due to the fact that the disulfide can pass through the membrane without its sulfur atoms reacting as thiol groups (i.e., they are protected), and that each disulfide molecule can be reduced to liberate two thiol molecules.

Previous work investigating the ability of CBA/N mice to respond to 2-ME demonstrated that the mature B-cell subset activated by 2-ME in normal strains is functionally silent in CBA/N mice (14). Similarly, the inability of B cells from this strain to respond to D-penicillamine implicates the function of a mature subpopulation of B cells in the generation of this response.

Polyclonal B-cell activation induced by D-penicillamine was found to be associated with cellular proliferation. The magnitude of the polyclonal response, however, was consistently lower than that of LPS, suggesting that if this immunostimulatory effect of D-penicillamine is responsible for the spectrum of autoimmune side effects observed in clinical situations, it must occur as a result of a very favorable microenvironment (perhaps genetically determined) or of alteration of D-penicillamine to a more highly stimulatory form (perhaps also genetically determined).

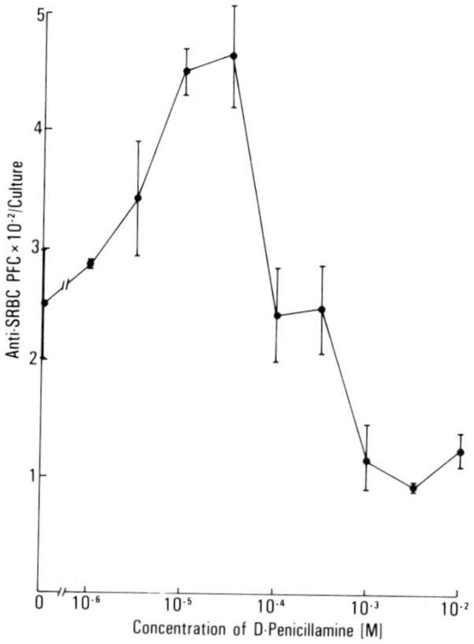

FIG. 12. Effect of D-penicillamine on the primary humoral response to SRBC *in vitro*. 10×10^6 viable C3H/St spleen cells were cultured for 4 days in 1.0 ml of 5% FCS-containing medium together with 2×10^6 SRBC in the presence of various concentrations of D-penicillamine. Anti-SRBC PFC/culture are presented as the arithmetic mean of triplicate cultures ± the SE.

The troublesome autoimmune side effects observed in patients treated with D-penicillamine are not limited in their occurrence to patients being treated for rheumatoid arthritis. Therefore, it was of interest to assess the responsiveness of lymphoid cells from both the normal and autoimmune murine models to D-penicillamine. The results indicate that cells from both normal and autoimmune strains (NZBxW, NZB) were responsive to this thiol compound, but that rather than being exaggerated in autoimmune strains, responses were generally of the same order of magnitude.

When a variety of murine strains was examined with respect to their capacity to respond mitogenically to D-penicillamine, no hyperresponder group was identified. A/J mice (H-2^a) were consistently hyporesponsive or unresponsive to this thiol compound. This strain is a natural k/d recombinant; however, spleen cells from C3H and CBA mice (H-2^k), Balb/c mice (H-2^d), and B10.A mice (H-2^a) responded well to D-penicillamine. Thus, any genetic proclivity toward hypo- or hyperresponsiveness does not appear to be a function simply of H-2 phenotype.

The observed effects of D-penicillamine are not likely to be attributable to endotoxin comtamination since (i) oxidized and reduced preparations gave very different results, (ii) T cells are responsive to D-penicillamine, and (iii) the endotoxin-responsive strains CBA/N and A/J both failed to respond to D-penicillamine.

Enhancement and suppression of the response of murine spleen cells to concanavalin A or in mixed lymphocyte cultures by D-penicillamine has been described by Kendall and Hutchins (35). Binderup *et al.* have described similar modulation of the Con A response by rat macrophages preincubated with this thiol (36). In the current report, augmentation of the primary humoral immune response to SRBC occurred at a dose of D-penicillamine lower than the other effects observed, perhaps indicative of a separate mechanism. Again, supraoptimal doses suppressed basal response to SRBC. The observation of immunopotentiating effects attributable to D-penicillamine raises this as a possible alternate mechanism whereby this compound induces the clinical spectrum of autoimmunity observed. Whether *de novo* activation or immunopotentiation is the relevant mechanism is at present unresolved.

While it is possible that the high concentrations of D-penicillamine used *in vitro* cannot be achieved *in vivo*, it is also possible that high local concentrations occur in special, localized anatomical sites. These could vary from the gut-associated lymphoid tissue to lymph nodes or to the cell surface of lymphocytes or other cells in their immediate microenvironment; the compound could then be presented in the form of a mixed disulfide at the surface of a presenting cell. Genetic control of such factors is not an unlikely possibility. An understanding of the immunomodulatory effects of D-penicillamine, together with the molecular requisites for stimulation (37) may ultimately lead to the formulation of an agent which is therapeutically effective and lacks immunostimulatory activity.

ACKNOWLEDGMENTS

The authors wish to express their appreciation to Mrs. Terry Else and Miss Anne Zumbrun for superb technical assistance, and to Ms. Janet Kuhns and Mrs. Barbara Marchand for excellent secretarial work in the preparation of the manuscript.

REFERENCES

1. Dresner, E., and Trombly, P., *Clin. Res.* **8,** 16, 1960.
2. Griffin, S. W., Ulloa, A., Henry, M., Johnston, M. L., and Holley, H. L., *Clin. Res.* **8,** 87, 1960.
3. Multicentre Trial Group, *Lancet* **1,** 275, 1973.
4. Dixon, A. St. J., Davies, J., Dormandy, T. L., Hamilton, E. B. D., Holt, P. J. L., Mason, R. M., Thompson, M., Weber, J. C. P., and Zutshi, D. W., *Ann. Rheum. Dis.* **34,** 416, 1975.
5. Tsang, I., Patterson, C. A., Stein, H. B., Robinson, H. S., and Ford, D. K., *Arthritis Rheum.* **20,** 666, 1977.
6. Shiokawa, Y., Horiuchi, Y., Honma, M., Kagiyama, T., Okada, T., and Ozuma T., *Arthritis Rheum.* **20,** 1464, 1977.
7. Goldberg, L. S., and Barnett, E. V., *Arch. Int. Med.,* **125,** 145, 1970.
8. Jaffe, I. A., *Ann. N.Y. Acad. Sci.* **256,** 330, 1975.
9. Hubner, K. F., and Gingozian, N., *Proc. Soc. Exp. Biol. Med.* **118,** 561, 1965.
10. Hunneyball, I. M., Stewart, G. A., and Stanworth, D. R., *Immunology* **34,** 1053, 1978.
11. Lipsky, P. E., and Ziff, M., *J. Immunol.* **120,** 1006, 1978.
12. Lipsky, P. E., and Ziff, M., *J. Clin. Invest.* **65,** 1069, 1980.
13. Tobin, M. S., and Altman, K., *Proc. Soc. Exp. Biol. Med.* **115,** 225, 1964.
14. Goodman, M. G., Fidler, J. M., and Weigle, W. O., *J. Immunol.* **121,** 1905, 1978.
15. Julius, M., Simpson, E., and Herzenberg, L. A., *Eur. J. Immunol.* **3,** 645, 1973.
16. Ly, I. A., and Mishell, R. I., *J. Immunol. Methods* **5,** 239, 1974.
17. Goodman, M. G., and Weigle, W. O., *J. Immunol.* **122,** 1433, 1979.
18. Mishell, R. I., and Dutton, R. W., *J. Exp. Med.* **126,** 423, 1967.
19. Coutinho, A., Gronowicz, E., Bullock, W. W., and Möller, G., *J. Exp. Med.* **139,** 74, 1974.
20. Jerne, N. K., and Nordin, A. A., *Science* **140,** 405, 1963.
21. Broome, J. D., and Jeng, M. W., *J. Exp. Med.* **138,** 574, 1973.
22. Noelle, R. J., and Lawrence, D. A., *Cell. Immunol.* **50,** 416, 1980.
23. Amsbaugh, D. F., Hansen, C. T., Prescott, B., Stashak, P. W., Asofsky, R., and Baker, P. J., *J. Exp. Med.* **139,** 1499, 1974.

24. Scher, I., Sharrow, S. O., and Paul, W. E., *J. Exp. Med.* **144,** 507, 1976.
25. Janeway, C. A., Jr., and Barthold, D. R., *J. Immunol.* **115,** 898, 1975.
26. Finkelman, F. D., Smith, A. H., Scher, I., and Paul, W. E., *J. Exp. Med.* **142,** 1316, 1975.
27. Click, R. E., Benck, L., and Alter, B. J., *Cell. Immunol.* **3,** 156, 1972.
28. Goodman, M. G., and Weigle, W. O., *J. Exp. Med.* **145,** 473, 1977.
29. Lemke, H., and Opitz, H. G., *J. Immunol.* **117,** 388, 1976.
30. Igarashi, T., Kada, M. O., Kishimoto, T., and Yamamura, Y., *J. Immunol.* **118,** 1697, 1977.
31. Heber-Katz, E., and Click, R. E., *Cell. Immunol.* **5,** 410, 1972.
32. Bevan, M. J., Epstein, R., and Cohn, M. *J. Exp. Med.* **139,** 1025, 1974.
33. Engers, H. D., MacDonald, H. R., Cerottini, J.-C., and Brunner, K. T., *Eur. J. Immunol.* **5,** 223, 1975.
34. Metcalf, D., Nossal, G. J. V., Warner, N. L., Miller, J. F. A. P., Mendel, T. E., Layton, J. E., and Gutman, G. G., *J. Exp. Med.* **142,** 1534, 1975.
35. Kendall, P. A., and Hutchins, D., *Immunology* **35,** 189, 1978.
36. Binderup, L., Bramm, E., and Arrigoni-Martelli, E., *Scand. J. Immunol.* **7,** 259, 1978.
37. Goodman, M. G., and Weigle, W. O., *J. Immunol.* **126,** 20, 1981.

CELLULAR IMMUNOLOGY **65**, 352–365 (1981)

The Regulation of Immune Responses to Multiple Non-H-2 Antigens on Tumor Cells

I. Differential Responses of BALB/c F_1 Hybrids to the P815 Mastocytoma *in Vivo*[1]

GEORGE CARAYANNIOTIS AND PHILIP F. HALLORAN[2]

The Harold Tanenbaum Department of Research, Mount Sinai Hospital and the Institute of Immunology, University of Toronto, Toronto, Canada

Received September 1, 1981; accepted October 14, 1981

Factors influencing host resistance to the growth of a tumor bearing many mismatched minor histocompatibility antigens (MiHA) were studied. BALB/c (H-2^d) and several of its F_1 hybrids were injected intraperitoneally with DBA/2 (H-2^d) P815 tumor cells. Compared to BALB/c, which was moderately susceptible, F_1 hybrids of BALB/c with CBA, AKR, C3H.OH, and B10 H-2-congenic strains were highly susceptible, whereas hybrids of BALB/c with A, A.SW, and BALB.B strains were quite resistant. Susceptibility was observed only with the intraperitoneally injected tumor, since both BALB/c and (CBA × BALB/c)F_1 were resistant to the same tumor injected subcutaneously, and survival times of DBA/2 skin grafts did not differ between susceptible and resistant strains. Susceptibility was in part a function of the number of MiHA incompatibilities between tumor and host although the specific loci involved could not be identified. For example, susceptible (CBA × BALB/c)F_1 hybrids probably shared certain MiHA with DBA/2 which BALB/c lacked, and which therefore subtracted from the net antigenic strength of the tumor in the hybrid, compared to its strength in BALB/c. This interpretation was supported by *in vitro* studies which confirmed that the susceptible hybrids shared more MiHA with DBA/2, than did the resistant hybrids. Resistance was at least partially regulated by the host H-2 genotype, as shown by the observation that (BALB/c × BALB.B)F_1 (H-$2^{d/b}$) mice were significantly more resistant than BALB/c. Segregation studies of the resistant (BALB/c × A)F_1 hybrids, indicated that in addition to H-2, a non-H-2 gene in the A background was operating to confer resistance. Thus the factors influencing susceptibility to the MiHA-incompatible tumor were: (i) site of injection; (ii) the combined strength of the disparate MiHA; (iii) the host H-2 genotype; and (iv) at least one host non-H-2 gene conferring increased responsiveness.

INTRODUCTION

The progressive elucidation of the major histocompatibility complex (MHC)[3] antigens has led to the clinical and experimental transplantation of nonsyngeneic

[1] Supported by Grant MA5739 from the Medical Research Council of Canada and by the Mount Sinai Institute.

[2] Address for correspondence: Suite 435, Mount Sinai Hospital, 600 University Ave., Toronto M5G 1X5, Canada.

[3] Abbreviations used: CTL, cytotoxic T lymphocytes; Hepes, *N*-2-hydroxyethylpiperazine-*N*′-2-ethanesulfonic acid; ip, intraperitoneal; L.N., lymph node; MHC, major histocompatibility complex; MiHA, minor histocompatibility antigens; MST, median survival time; PEC, peritoneal exudate cells; PHA, phytohemagglutinin; sc, subcutaneous.

0008-8749/81/180352-14$02.00/0

MHC-identical grafts that present the recipient with a large array of minor histocompatibility antigens (MiHA). The strength of the response to such antigens can vary remarkably, for example, in clinical transplantation many recipients of HLA-identical kidneys from sibling donors show no rejection whereas about 10–15% will have uncontrollable rejection despite maximal immunosuppression (1). Furthermore, both rejection and lethal graft-versus-host reaction after bone marrow graft exchange between MHC-identical individuals can be frequently observed (2). Although basic studies have established that parameters such as preimmunization, donor–recipient allelic combination, graft size, and recipient sex can influence the strength of the anti-MiHA response (3, 4), the factors that regulate the immunogenicity of multiple MiHA remain largely unknown.

Considerable progress has been made in the last decade in understanding the importance of the MHC in regulating the response to single MiHA. Host immune response (Ir) genes located in the H-2 complex had been demonstrated first in the response against H-Y (5–7) and later against H-4 and H-7 (8, 9). Donor H-2K or H-2D genes expressed on the graft, on the other hand, were shown to regulate the rejectability of H-Y-incompatible (10, 11) or H-7-incompatible skin grafts (12). Recent evidence suggests that high immunogenicity of single MiHA can be determined by genes associated with a particular donor H-2 haplotype and mapping in the H-2K and/or H-2D regions (13). However, due to the high polymorphism of the H-2 genes and the large number of MiHA described—at least 40 (4)—as well as the kind of the graft employed, overall effects of donor or host H-2 genes on the response to multiple MiHA are difficult to analyze.

In the present study, we found that the growth of the DBA/2 mastocytoma P815 (H-2^d) varied considerably in H-2^d strains and their F_1 hybrids. This observation provided a system in which survival differences could be used to study the effect of host genetic and other factors on the anti-MiHA response. We therefore sought to determine (a) whether such differences could be explained by the extent of MiHA incompatibility between the recipient and DBA/2, (b) whether host H-2 or non-H-2 Ir-like genes could be shown to influence the response against multiple MiHA, and (c) whether the site of inoculation of the tumor affected the response. The results show that all these factors contribute measurably and sometimes dramatically to the strength of the anti-MiHA response.

MATERIALS AND METHODS

Mice. BALB/cJ, DBA/2J, CBA/J, AKR/J, C3H.OH, A.SW/Sn, C57BL/10J (abbreviated hereafter into B10), B10.A/SgSn, B10.BR/SgSn, and B10.D2/nSn strains were purchased from the Jackson Laboratory, Bar Harbor, Maine. BALB.B and BALB.K breeding animals were a gift from Dr. F. Lilly (Albert Einstein College of Medicine, New York). With the exception of (BALB/c × A)F_1 hybrids which were purchased from the Jackson Laboratory, all F_1 hybrids and backcross mice were bred in the animal facility at the Mount Sinai Hospital. The H-2 haplotypes as well as the principal known MiHA alleles of the strains tested (14) are shown in Table 1.

Tumor cells. The P815 mastocytoma (15) was kindly provided by Dr. R. G. Miller (Ontario Cancer Institute) and was maintained in female DBA/2 syngeneic mice in ascites form by weekly passage. To avoid possible antigenic variability

TABLE 1

H-2 Haplotype and Principal Known MiHA Alleles of Strains Used[a]

Strain	H-1	H-2	H-3	H-7	H-8	H-12	H-13
DBA/2	a	d	b	a	b	a	b
BALB/c	b	d	·	b	c	a	·
A	·	a	·	b	·	·	a
CBA	a	k	·	·	·	·	a
C3H.OH	a	o^2	b	b	·	a	·
AKR	·	k	·	·	·	·	a
B10	c	b	a	a	a	a	a

Note. A · in H-1 means "not a or c," in all other loci it means "not a or b."
[a] The strongest or best defined loci at which DBA/2 carries a known allele.

resulting from repeated passage in syngeneic hosts, we kept a single batch of P815 cells frozen at −70°C in α-minimal essential medium (Media preparation service, University of Toronto) containing 10% dimethyl sulfoxide, 20% heat-inactivated (56°C, 30 min) fetal bovine serum (Flow Laboratories, Rockville, Md., Lot No. 29101038), and 10 m*M* Hepes buffer, at a concentration of 3×10^6 cells/ml. No loss of viability or change in rate of growth in syngeneic hosts was observed after 12 months of storage.

Immunizations. Small aliquots of P815 were thawed at 37°C, and the cells washed three times with phosphate-buffered saline (PBS). Mice were inoculated intraperitoneally (ip) or subcutaneously (sc) in the right flank with tumor cells suspended in 0.3–0.5 ml of PBS. Deaths were tabulated daily.

Cytotoxic T cells. For generation of cytotoxic T cells (CTL) against MiHA a method described first by Bevan (16) was followed. BALB/c mice were primed ip with 10^7 female DBA/2 spleen and mesenteric lymph node (L.N.) cells in 0.5 ml PBS. After 16 days the primed BALB/c spleen cells were boosted for 5 days *in vitro* with an equal number of irradiated female DBA/2 spleen and mesenteric L.N. cells (2000 rad at 88 rad/min from a radioactive cesium (^{137}Cs) source). Incubations were performed in tissue culture flasks containing 8×10^7 responder and 8×10^7 stimulator cells in a total volume of 40 ml, in α-minimal essential medium supplemented with 5×10^{-5} *M* 2-mercaptoethanol, 10% fetal bovine serum, and 10 m*M* Hepes buffer. The cultures were kept for 5 days at 37°C in a humidified incubator containing 5% CO_2 in air.

Mitogen stimulation and ^{51}Cr labeling. Mesenteric L.N. cells were washed three times and suspended in medium at 10^6 cells/ml. Phytohemagglutinin (PHA) was added at 1 μg/ml and the cultures were kept for 3 days at 37°C. The blasts were then washed, and labeled with 0.1 mCi of $Na_2{}^{51}CrO_4$ (Amersham Corp., Arlington Heights, Ill.) in a volume of 0.2 ml for 60 min at 37°C. Before use, they were washed five times, counted in a hemocytometer and adjusted to 1×10^5 cells/ml.

Cytotoxic assay. At the end of the 5-day culture period, the responder cells were harvested and washed once. Serial dilutions of cytotoxic cells, 0.1 ml, along with 0.1 ml of labeled targets (1×10^4 cells) were placed into the wells of v-bottom microtiter trays (Qualicum Scientific Ltd., Ottawa, Ontario) in triplicate. The trays were then spun at 60*g* for 3 min. After a 4-hr incubation at 37°C the trays were spun again at 600*g* for 5 min and 0.1 ml of supernatant was removed from each well and counted in a Beckman gamma 300 counter. The percentage specific release was calculated as

$$\frac{\text{experimental release (cpm)} - \text{spontaneous release (cpm)}}{\text{total (cpm)} - \text{spontaneous release (cpm)}}.$$

H-2 typing. (BALB/c × A)F_1 × BALB/c backcross mice were typed for H-$2K^k$ determinants in a complement-dependent microcytotoxicity assay by using a (B10.D2 × SJL)F_1 anti-B10.A antiserum obtained from Dr. John Ray, National Institute of Allergy and Infectious Diseases, National Institutes of Health, Bethesda, Maryland. Rabbit serum (Buxted Rabbit Co., Surrey, England) was used as a source of complement.

Skin grafting technique. Donor abdominal skin was cut into squares (1 cm^2) and transplanted to the dorsum of the recipient (anesthetized with chloral hydrate). Grafts were carefully fitted and the edges were sealed with collodion. The wound was covered with sterile sofra-tulle and protected with plaster-of-paris casts until the sixth day, when the casts were removed. The viable grafts were then checked daily until rejection.

Assessment of P815 content in peritoneal exudate cell (PEC) populations. Anti-Ly-6.2 antiserum was raised in (CBA × BALB/c)F_1 mice, following four weekly ip injections with DBA/2 spleen and lymph node cells. The mice were bled 4 days after the last challenge. Rabbit complement was extensively absorbed with P815 cells before use. Antiserum and complement were used at one-third final dilution in a complement-dependent microcytotoxicity assay. Under the conditions of the test 95–100% of P815 (positive control) and 0–5% of BALB/c lymph node cells (negative control) were killed.

Statistical analysis. Differences in mortality distributions between groups of mice were tested for significance by the nonparametric, rank-sum Wilcoxon test for unpaired data (17). Gehan's ranking test (18) was applied when both samples under comparison contained "censored" observations, i.e., survival values that were at least as large as the observation period. A multistage, Mantel–Haenszel χ^2 test was used in the backcross segregation analysis.

RESULTS

Differential susceptibility of BALB/c F_1 hybrids to P815. The initial observations were made when BALB/c, (BALB/c × A)F_1 and (CBA × BALB/c)F_1 mice were injected ip with P815 tumor cells. It was observed that (CBA × BALB/c)F_1 hybrids exhibited a high, BALB/c an intermediate and (BALB/c × A)F_1 a low susceptibility to P815 (data not shown). To explore this observation further, we challenged BALB/c and hybrids of BALB/c by A, A.SW, CBA, B10.BR, C3H.OH, or AKR strains with 10^6 P815 cells ip (Fig. 1). In comparison to the mortality of BALB/c control mice, which succumbed gradually to the tumor within a period of 40 days, the mortality distribution of BALB/c hybrids revealed two patterns. First, hybrids with A background, i.e., (BALB/c × A)F_1 and (A.SW × BALB/c)F_1, demonstrated a highly significant resistance to P815. Second, hybrids between BALB/c and CBA, C3H.OH, B10.BR, and AKR strains appeared significantly more susceptible to P815 than BALB/c. This pattern was observed consistently in

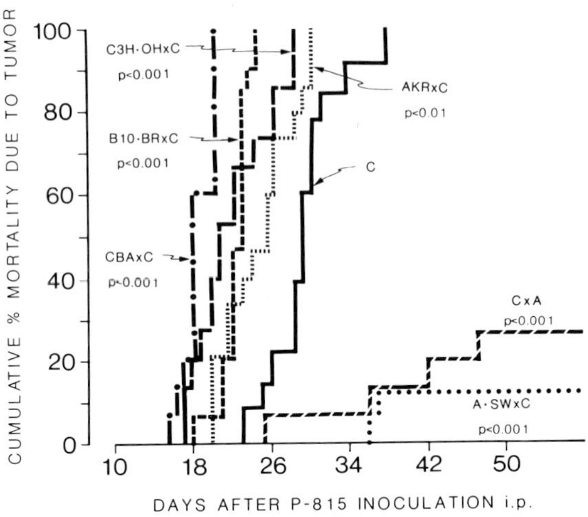

FIG. 1. Differential susceptibility of BALB/c (abbreviated into C) F_1 hybrids, after ip challenge with 10^6 P815 cells. Fifteen mice per group were tested. Significance probability p values were obtained by the nonparametric Wilcoxon rank-sum test. Comparisons were made in regard to BALB/c.

four experiments (Table 2), where the susceptibility of (BALB/c × A)F_1 (high responder) was compared to that of BALB/c (control) and (CBA × BALB/c)F_1 (low responder). The median survival time (MST) of (BALB/c × A)F_1 mice was usually prolonged when compared to that of BALB/c controls. On the other hand (CBA × BALB/c)F_1 mice exhibited a marked susceptibility with almost 80% of the mice succumbing by Day 20. Life expectancy estimates based on these data indicate that following ip inoculation with 10^6 P815 cells on Day 0, the expected proportion of survivors beyond Day 30 would be 84% for (BALB/c × A)F_1, 24% for BALB/c, and virtually 0% for (CBA × BALB/c)F_1.

The role of particular known MiHA allelic differences in resistance. An expla-

TABLE 2

Susceptibility of BALB/c and BALB/c F_1 Hybrids to 10^6 P815 Cells Administered ip

Expt no.	(BALB/c × A)F_1 S/T[a]	MST[b]	p[c]	BALB/c S/T	MST	(CBA × BALB/c)F_1 S/T	MST	p
1	11/15	>90	<0.01	0/13	30	—	—	—
2	4/15	42	NS[d]	1/15	30	0/15	14	<0.001
3	13/16	>90	<0.001	0/16	26	0/16	20	<0.001
4	8/11	>90	<0.01	1/11	23	0/10	19	NS

[a] S/T, Survivors/total; Survivors: mice that lived longer than 90 days. Six- to twelve-week-old female mice were used in all the experiments.

[b] MST, Median survival time (days).

[c] p values were obtained by the Wilcoxon rank-sum test. Comparisons were made in regard to BALB/c.

[d] Not significant.

nation for the P815 growth was sought by examining the particular allelic disparities between the various strains and DBA/2 from Table 2. All BALB/c F_1 hybrids tested were compatible at H-12 and incompatible at H-8 and H-13 loci with DBA/2. Comparison between the non-BALB/c parents of susceptible hybrids show that CBA, C3H.OH, and B10 share the same allele with DBA/2 at the H-1, H-3, and H-7 loci correspondingly, but AKR differs from DBA/2 at all these loci. Thus, it appears unlikely that compatibility at any of these loci can account for susceptibility. In addition, female susceptibility was not significantly different from that in male hosts (not shown) indicating that H-Y expression (P815 was induced in a male mouse) is unlikely to play an important role. These observations suggest that no simple explanation for susceptibility or resistance can be derived from the existing knowledge of the MiHA alleles.

Effect of low tumor dose or subcutaneous challenge on susceptibility. The effects of 10^4 and 10^6 P815 cells on susceptibility were compared after ip challenge. (CBA × BALB/c)F_1 mice appeared quite susceptible even when challenged with 10^4 P815 cells (Table 3). Their MST was doubled (44 days) when compared to that of a 100-fold larger dose (22 days), yet they remained susceptible. BALB/c showed significant overall resistance to the lower dose and increased MST (>90 days) which was similar to that of (BALB/c × A)F_1.

Subcutaneous challenge with 10^6 P815 led to high resistance in all groups (Table 3). By comparison to the ip effects of the same dose, resistance increased from 6 to 100% in BALB/c and from 0 to 87.5% in (CBA × BALB/c)F_1 mice. Under the same conditions, all syngeneic DBA/2 hosts died within 21–24 days after challenge, indicating that the tumor was capable of rapid growth in the subcutaneous site.

TABLE 3

Effect of Low Tumor Dose or sc Challenge on Susceptibility

Strain	Route of challenge	Tumor dose[a]	Survivors/total[b]	MST	p[c]
(BALB/c × A)F_1	ip	10^6	11/16	>90	<0.001
BALB/c	ip	10^6	1/16	27	—
(CBA × BALB/c)F_1	ip	10^6	0/16	22	<0.001
DBA/2	ip	10^6	0/8	15	<0.001
(BALB/c × A)F_1	ip	10^4	8/8	>90	NS[d]
BALB/c	ip	10^4	6/8	>90	—
(CBA × BALB/c)F_1	ip	10^4	2/8	44	NS
(BALB/c × A)F_1	sc	10^6	8/8	>90	NS
BALB/c	sc	10^6	8/8	>90	—
(CBA × BALB/c)F_1	sc	10^6	7/8	>90	NS
DBA/2	sc	10^6	0/8	23	<0.001

[a] P815 cells suspended in 0.3 ml PBS were injected ip or sc in the right flank.
[b] Survivors observed over a period of 90 days. Six- to twelve-week-old female mice were used.
[c] Comparisons were made in regard to BALB/c.
[d] Not significant.

Skin graft survival in susceptible and resistant hybrids. Resistant (BALB/c $\times$ A)F_1, moderately susceptible BALB/c, and highly susceptible (B10.BR $\times$ BALB/c)F_1 recipients all rejected DBA/2 skin grafts with equal vigor. In 10 (BALB/c $\times$ A)F_1 recipients the MST of the graft was 17 days; in 9 BALB/c recipients the MST was 16 days; in 9 (B10.BR $\times$ BALB/c)F_1 recipients the MST was 17 days. Thus the ability of these hosts to reject DBA/2 skin grafts did not correlate with their resistance to ip inocula of P815.

Kinetics of tumor growth. Seven to nine days following the ip inoculation of 10^6 P815, all BALB/c hybrid hosts, as well as BALB/c became distended reflecting a proliferative phase of the tumor which was similar in various host environments. By Day 15, distension had subsided in resistant hybrids such as (BALB/c $\times$ A)F_1, but there was no regression in BALB/c and the susceptible hybrids. To assess tumor growth quantitatively, (BALB/c $\times$ A)F_1, BALB/c, and (CBA $\times$ BALB/c)F_1 mice were inoculated ip with 10^6 P815 cells and at various times thereafter three mice per strain were killed and the number of nucleated PEC counted. The results obtained (Fig. 2a) correlated well with the morphologic appearance at various time intervals. Following peak on Day 8, PEC decreased rapidly in (BALB/c $\times$ A)F_1 mice reaching almost normal levels by Day 22. In contrast the number of PEC in BALB/c and (CBA $\times$ BALB/c)F_1 mice peaked on Day 8, decreased slightly but remained high throughout the observation period. Treatment of PEC populations with anti-Ly-6.2 serum and complement, which detects cells of DBA/2 origin, revealed a dramatic decrease (from 90–100 to 0–3%) in P815 content in (BALB/c $\times$ A)F_1 PEC between Days 11 and 15 after challenge (Fig. 2b). Ap-

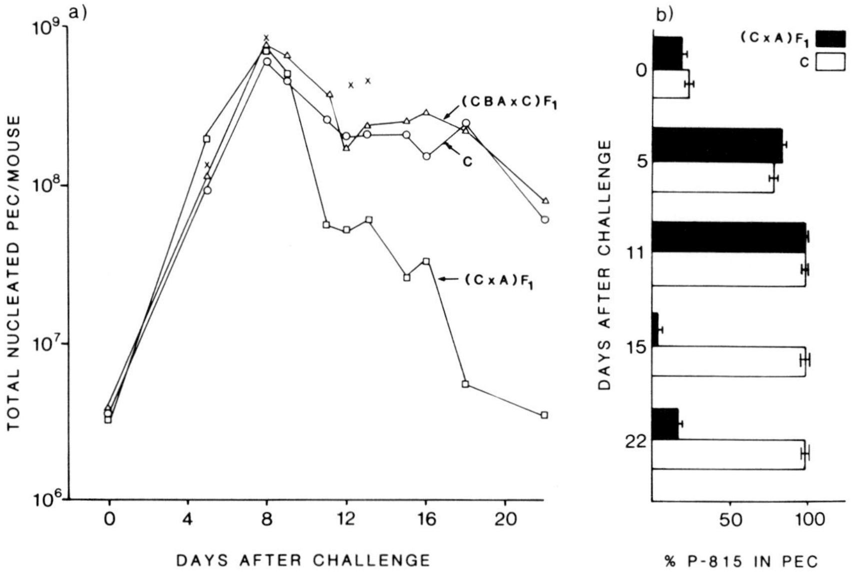

FIG. 2. (a) PEC counts from BALB/c (abbreviated into C) (CBA $\times$ C)F_1 and (C $\times$ A)F_1 mice on various days after ip challenge with 10^6 P815 cells. Counts are based on pooled PEC from three mice per strain on each of the days shown. $\times$ symbols stand for PEC numbers from syngeneic DBA/2 hosts challenged ip with the same tumor dose on Day 0. (b) Percentage content of P815 in PEC population from (C $\times$ A)F_1 and C mice assessed by anti-Ly-6.2 plus complement treatment (see Materials and Methods).

proximately 30% of Day 15 PEC from (BALB/c × A)F_1 were small lymphocytes and the remaining 70% were macrophages and granulocytes. No decrease in P815 content (90–100%) was observed in BALB/c.

Compatibility in MiHA between hybrid recipients and DBA/2 and its relative role in susceptibility. The genes which conferred susceptibility on the low responder hybrids were presumably dominant genes derived from the genome of the non-BALB/c parent. Such genes could be (i) MiHA that the non BALB/c parent shares with DBA/2 but which are not expressed in BALB/c. These antigens could subtract from the antigenicity of the tumor in the F_1 hybrids, as compared to its antigenicity in BALB/c; (ii) immune response genes carried by the non-BALB/c parent coding for dominant nonresponsiveness. We distinguished between these possibilities by examining the lysis of target PHA blasts from various hybrids by BALB/c anti-DBA/2 CTL. We reasoned that the extent of lysis of the hybrid targets should indicate the relative extent of non-BALB/c MiHA shared between each hybrid and DBA/2. As shown in Fig. 3a, (CBA × BALB/c)F_1, (AKR × BALB/c)F_1, (C3H.OH × BALB/c)F_1 and (B10.BR × BALB/c)F_1 targets were lysed very well in contrast to (BALB/c × A)F_1 and (A.SW × BALB/c)F_1 targets, thus suggesting that the highly susceptible hybrids share a considerable number of MiHA with DBA/2 (and very likely with P815). Similarly, when the ability of cold hybrid PHA blasts to inhibit lysis of labelled DBA/2 targets by BALB/c anti-DBA/2 CTL was examined (Fig. 3b), analogous results were obtained, particularly at the inhibitor target ratio of 30:1. Blasts from the highly susceptible hybrids inhibited better than blasts from the resistant (BALB/c × A)F_1 or (A.SW × BALB/c)F_1 hybrids.

The above results support the concept that susceptibility in this system may be attributed directly to the degree of MiHA sharing between recipient hybrid and

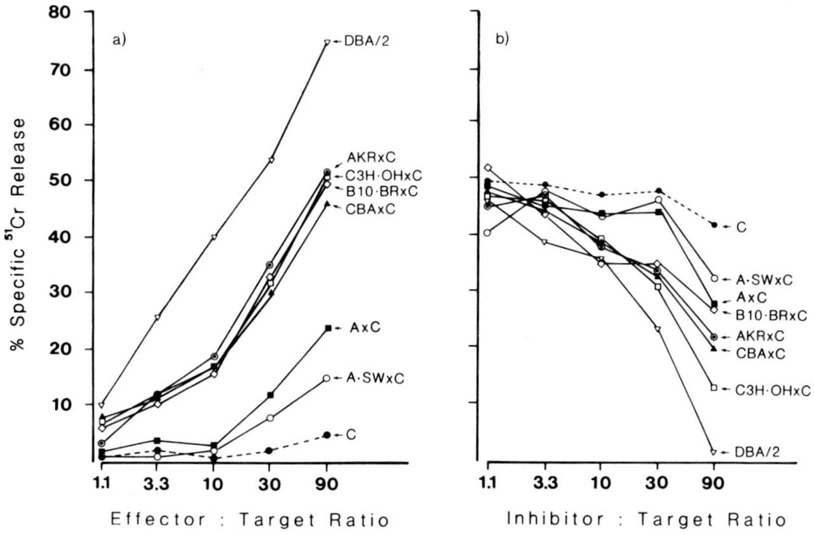

FIG. 3. (a) Lysis of BALB/c (abbreviated into C), DBA/2 and F_1 hybrid PHA blasts by BALB/c anti-DBA/2 cytotoxic T cells (see Materials and Methods). (b) Inhibition of lysis of ^{51}Cr-labeled DBA/2 PHA blasts by cold BALB/c (C), DBA/2, and F_1 hybrid targets, using BALB/c anti DBA/2 cytotoxic T cells as effector cells. The effector:labeled target ratio was 150:1

P815. However, this argument does not account for two observations: (i) the uniform resistance of all hybrid hosts to sc inocula of P815 and to DBA/2 skin grafts; and (ii) the higher resistance of (BALB/c × A)F_1 and (A.SW × BALB/c)F_1 compared to that of BALB/c after ip challenge. Indeed blasts from these strains both inhibited and were lysed slightly better than BALB/c blasts, indicating that A and A.SW do share MiHA with DBA/2 that must subtract from the total MiHA which such recipients recognize as foreign on the tumor. Therefore, it appears that immune response genes in A or A.SW genomes both offset the influencc of the shared MiHA between A and DBA/2, and further increase resistance above that of BALB/c.

Effect of BALB/c genes and H-2 genotype on susceptibility. Since the genotype of three out of four highly susceptible hybrids tested in Fig. 1 was H-$2^{k/d}$ the question was raised as to whether certain H-2 genotypes conferred increased susceptibility or resistance, independent of the particular non-H-2 tumor–host incompatibility. We tested this hypothesis by comparing survival of various F_1 hybrids, using BALB/c or B10 H-2 congenic strains. The survival data after ip challenge with 10^6 P815 are shown in Table 4.

All BALB/c hybrids with B10 background were quite susceptible to P815. H-2 effects were seen in only one experiment in which (B10.BR × BALB/c)F_1 (H-$2^{k/d}$) mice were significantly more susceptible than (B10.D2 × BALB/c)F_1 controls. Comparison of the pooled data from these experiments demonstrated a trend in survival, with (B10 × BALB/c)F_1 (H-$2^{b/d}$) more resistant than (B10.D2 × BALB/c)F_1 (H-$2^{d/d}$) controls. However, performance of statistics on this type of pooled data is not reliable.

The large difference in mortality between (B10.A × BALB/c)F_1 (H-$2^{a/d}$) (Table 4) and (BALB/c × A)F_1 (H-$2^{d/a}$) (Fig. 1 and Table 2) could be due to susceptibility

TABLE 4

Effect of BALB/c Genes and H-2 Genotype on Susceptibility to 10^6 P815 Cells

Strain	H-2 genotype	Survivors/ total	MST: Individual experiments	MST: Pooled
(B10.D2 × BALB/c)F_1	d/d	0/25	25, 28, 30	29
(B10.A × BALB/c)F_1	a/d	0/33	25, 27, 25, 35	28
(B10.BR × BALB/c)F_1	k/d	2/44	20,[a] 23, 25, 24	23
(B10 × BALB/c)F_1	b/d	2/28	33, 25, 29, 60	33
(B10.BR × B10.D2)F_1	k/d	15/15	>100	
(B10 × B10.D2)F_1	b/d	15/15	>100	
B10.D2	d	7/7	>100	
BALB/c	d	0/16	26	
BALB/c	d	1/11	23	
BALB.B	b	12/12	>100	
BALB.K	k	14/14	>100	
(BALB/c × BALB.K)F_1	d/k	7/17	>100, 19[b]	
(BALB/c × BALB.B)F_1	d/b	20/24	>100, >100	

[a] Significantly shorter MST ($p < 0.001$) than (B10.D2 × BALB/c)F_1 controls.
[b] Not significant difference from BALB/c controls.

factors (e.g., MiHA shared with DBA/2) in the B10 background or resistance factors (e.g., Ir-like genes) in the A background. Nonetheless, these data clearly indicate that the presence of the H-$2^{a/d}$ genotype alone cannot confer increased resistance to P815 growth. Conversely, the extreme resistance of B10.D2, (B10.A × B10.D2)F_1, and (B10.BR × B10.D2)F_1 to P815 (Table 4) demonstrates that the presence of the H-$2^{k/d}$ genotype alone is not a sufficient requirement for increased susceptibility. Instead, the presence of BALB/c genes appears to be a necessary precondition for the expression of susceptibility in this system.

In F_1 mice with BALB/c background alone, H-2 effects on resistance were easily detected (Table 4). Thus, (BALB/c × BALB.B)F_1 (H-$2^{d/b}$) were significantly more resistant than BALB/c, whereas (BALB/c × BALB.K)F_1 (H-$2^{d/k}$) mice demonstrated a trend for increased resistance.

The above data suggest that in BALB/c F_1 hybrids: (i) H-2 genes have a significant effect on responsiveness, the detection and magnitude of which depends on the non-H-2 tumor–host disparities, and (ii) background BALB/c genes facilitate susceptibility to P815, presumably by reducing the MiHA incompatibilities to a critical minimum number.

Backcross segregation analysis. In order to determine the number and H-2 linkage of genes involved in resistance of (BALB/c × A)F_1 hybrids, we examined the survival of (BALB/c × A)F_1 × BALB/c backcross mice after an ip challenge with 10^6 P815 cells. A total of 40 mice were tested and survival was followed over a period of 50 days. Statistical analysis was performed on the data from Days 30, 40, and 50. The results (Table 5) best fit the hypothesis of two independent dominant genes coding for resistance with either of them being sufficient for this purpose. The hypothesis of one dominant gene was not accepted on all days tested; the hypothesis of two dominant genes required simultaneously for resistance was rejected on all days tested. The data also favor the hypothesis of one of the two genes being H-2 linked, since H-$2^{a/d}$ mice were significantly more resistant (Days 40 and 50) than H-$2^{d/d}$ mice. This experiment thus supports the concept that a non-H-2 gene and one or more H-2-linked genes operate in a dominant fashion to confer resistance to P815 growth.

DISCUSSION

The observation that transplanted tumors can often kill H-2-compatible hosts despite the existence of multiple incompatible MiHA dates to the early studies of histocompatibility (19, 20) and has generally been attributed to weakness of MiHA and to tumor virulence. That such explanations are incomplete is illustrated by the present studies, in which susceptibility to an H-2^d tumor differed markedly in various H-2^d hosts, and was dependent upon the site of tumor inoculation. These susceptibility differences provide an experimental system in which the factors regulating the immunogenicity of multiple MiHA can be explored. Such factors are of interest because multiple MiHA incompatibilities occur almost invariably in clinical transplantation, and because MiHA can be viewed as models for other types of membrane antigens (e.g., viral, tumor specific).

Some of the strain differences in tumor susceptibility reported here may reflect the number of MiHA disparities between the host and DBA/2. One example of this is the difference between B10.D2, which was highly resistant, and BALB/c

TABLE 5

Backcross Segregation Analysis of (BALB/c × A) × BALB/c Mice

Ho: resistance is conferred by	Day	No. of resistant mice[a] Expected	Observed	No. of mice tested	χ^2		p
One dominant gene	30	21.6	31	40	4.84	<0.05	Ho accep
	40	18.0	21	40	1.05	NS	
	50	13.4	19	40	2.16	NS	
Two dominant genes either of which is sufficient	30	27.6	31	40	0.73	NS	Ho accep
	40	24.4	21	40	0.26	NS	
	50	19.3	19	40	0.00	NS	
Two dominant genes both of which are necessary	30	15.6	31	40	12.04	<0.005	Ho rejec
	40	11.6	21	40	6.87	<0.01	
	50	7.5	19	40	9.60	<0.005	
Gene(s) that are not linked to H-2	30	a/d	21	25	1.57	<0.100	
		d/d	10	15			
	40	a/d	17	25			
		d/d	4	15	6.04	<0.025	Ho rejec
	50	a/d	15	25			
		d/d	4	15	4.61	<0.05	

[a] The numbers of expected resistant mice were corrected for incomplete penetrance, since total mortality estimates show 16, 23, and 37% of (BALB/c × A)F_1 controls susceptible, and 24, 13, and 4% of BALB/c controls resistant on Days 30, 40, and 50 correspondingly.

which was moderately susceptible. Estimates from skin graft survival indicate that B10.D2 differs from DBA/2 at 28–44 MiHA loci (21), whereas BALB/c and DBA/2 (tested in the direction DBA/2 anti-BALB/c) differ at only 12 loci (22). Another example is the increased susceptibility of certain BALB/c hybrids, such as (CBA × BALB/c)F_1, compared to the moderately susceptible BALB/c. The non-BALB/c parent (e.g., CBA) expresses some MiHA which are absent in BALB/c but present in DBA/2, and thus the hybrid will be responsive to fewer DBA/2 antigens than will BALB/c. This concept was supported by the in vitro studies of cells from such hybrids, which were strongly lysed by BALB/c anti-DBA/2 cytotoxic T cells, and gave significant inhibition as cold targets, demonstrating that many antigens which are expressed in DBA/2 but absent in BALB/c are expressed in the hybrids such as (CBA × BALB)F_1. The number of MiHA probably influences the degree of resistance by affecting the number of precursors which can respond to P815. In addition to the number of MiHA, the strength and additive or synergistic effects of certain combinations of disparities (4, 23, 24) might account for differences in host susceptibility.

The observation that certain hybrids were more resistant than BALB/c to P815 cannot be accounted for by numbers of MiHA, and is probably due to immune response (Ir) genes in these hybrids. In the case of (BALB.B × BALB/c)F_1, such genes are presumably coded by the H-2^b haplotype. In the case of (BALB/c × A)F_1, one of the two segregating genes conferring resistance was H-2 linked. In addition, the results in the B10 congenic mice showed a trend toward an influence of H-2, with the H-$2^{k/d}$ hosts being more susceptible, and the H-$2^{b/d}$ hosts being more resistant, than the H-$2^{d/d}$ animals. Thus the H-2 genotype is a significant factor in host resistance to P815 growth. However, it should be noted that the direction of the H-2 effect may not be the same in each background: the (BALB.K × BALB/c)F_1 animals (H-$2^{d/k}$) were more resistant than their H-$2^{d/d}$ counterparts, whereas the (B10.BR × BALB/c)F_1 animals (also H-$2^{k/d}$) appeared more susceptible than their H-$2^{d/d}$ counterparts. The increased susceptibility of the (B10.BR × BALB/c)F_1 animals suggests that the H-2^k haplotype may have dominant nonresponder Ir gene effects on certain MiHA disparities, as has been reported in other systems (25).

The H-2 haplotype-mediated effects, like those of Ir genes in general, could be both on antigen presentation by host cells and on the generation, during ontogeny, of T-cell clones capable of recognizing MiHA in association with the products of that haplotype. For example, in H-$2^{b/d}$ hosts, one set of precursors would see MiHA on host antigen-presenting cells in association with H-2^b or with hybrid specificities generated by trans-complementation between H-2^b and H-2^d. Considering that such effects of host H-2 haplotype have usually been described for single, simple antigens, the detection of significant host H-2 influences on the response to a plethora of MiHA is somewhat surprising. One might have expected the different Ir effects on each separate determinant to obscure one another. However, Graff believes that when many MiHA are incompatible only the strongest two or three are actually recognized (4). H-2 effects on the immunogenicity of these determinants could thus produce a measurable difference in net responsiveness. Moreover, the H-2^b haplotype determines high responsiveness to many MiHA determinants tested (7, 8, 13), suggesting that certain MHC haplotypes may produce generally higher net responses when confronted with multiple MiHA.

The segregation of resistance in the (BALB/c × A) × BALB/c backcross mice revealed the existence of a non-H-2 gene conferring resistance in a dominant fashion. The observation that (B10.A × BALB/c)F_1 (H-$2^{a/d}$) is susceptible while (BALB/c × A)F_1, (H-$2^{d/a}$), resistant, is also compatible with the existence of at least one such gene. (We have unpublished evidence that (A × BALB/c)F_1 animals behave identically to (BALB/c × A)F_1, indicating that the H-$2^{a/d}$ and H-$2^{d/a}$ genotypes do not differ in their susceptibility.) This resistance gene could be a non-H-2 Ir-like gene governing high responsiveness to one or more MiHA. Several such non-H-2 Ir-like genes have been described in other systems involving cell membrane or chemical antigens (26–29). Of interest is the observation that a non-H-2, Ir-like gene in the A background governs the response to a serologically defined DBA/2 antigen, Ly-6.2, that is expressed on P815 (30). Whether the A background gene governing responsiveness to the DBA/2 MiHA on P815 is the same as that which governs responsiveness to Ly-6.2 is a question which deserves further study.

The dichotomy between the effects of ip and sc challenge on susceptibility reflects differences in host responsiveness rather than in inherent tumor growth rate at these sites, since sc administered P815 grew rapidly in DBA/2 controls. It is possible, however, that retarded tumor growth in the subcutaneous site could facilitate recognition or effector function. The site of P815 inoculation has recently been shown to affect immune responses to BALB/c mice in studies of Streilein et al

(31), in which intraocularly administered tumor induced unresponsiveness, whereas sc tumor induced responsiveness to DBA/2 MiHA. In the present study, immune responses to ip and sc tumor could qualitatively differ in the induction and/or in the effector phase. In the induction phase, differences could exist in antigen presentation by host cells, which may be important in recognition of MiHA on tumor cells (32). In the effector phase, delayed type hypersensitivity, which attacks the microvasculature through endothelial cell damage (33), and coagulation (34), could be much more effective against the solid vascularized sc tumor than against the ip ascites tumor.

Finally, it is necessary to consider how the characteristics of the P815 tumor might be contributing to the present findings. First, antigenic modulation of P815, which has been reported to occur during its growth in BALB/c hosts (35), could differ in the various hybrids, and contribute to the observed differences in survival. Second, host resistance is mostly due to the anti-MiHA immune response, but small effects due to tumor-specific immunity are difficult to exclude. Third, P815 is known to have immunosuppressive effects on the host, inducing suppressor cells in allogeneic and syngeneic hosts (36, 37) and inhibiting the immune response to unrelated antigens (38). Thus the tumor unlike a skin graft, may amplify differences in host responsiveness: low responders may experience enhanced tumor-induced immunosuppression, that would lead to complete unresponsiveness. This may explain why $(B10.BR \times BALB/c)F_1$ hybrids rapidly reject DBA/2 skin but succumb to P815.

ACKNOWLEDGMENTS

We wish to thank Drs. R. G. Miller and T. Delovitch for useful discussion, and Mrs. Fay Rabinovitch for typing the manuscript.

REFERENCES

1. Opelz, G., *In* "Manual of Renal Transplantation" (S. N. Chatterjee, Ed.), pp. 27–34. Springer-Verlag, New York, 1979.
2. Van Rood, J. J., van Leeuwen, A., Goulmy, E., Termijtelen, A., Bradley, B. A., Brand, A., and Eernisse, J. G., *Transplant. Proc.* **10,** 47, 1978.
3. Hildemann, W. H., *Transplant. Rev.* **3,** 5, 1970.
4. Graff, R. J., and Bailey, D. W., *Transplant. Rev.* **15,** 26, 1973.
5. Stimpfling, J. H., and Reichert, A. E., *Transplantation* **12,** 527, 1971.
6. Bailey, D. W., and Hoste, J., *Transplantation* **11,** 404, 1971.
7. Gasser, D. L., and Silvers, W. K., *J. Immunol.* **106,** 875, 1971.
8. Wettstein, P. J., and Haughton, G., *Immunogenetics* **4,** 65, 1977.
9. Wettstein, P. J., and Haughton, G., *Immunogenetics* **5,** 85, 1977.
10. Wachtel, S. S., Gasser, D. L., and Silvers, W. K., *Science* **181,** 862, 1973.
11. Kralova, J., and Demant, P., *Immunogenetics* **3,** 583, 1976.
12. Wettstein, P. J., Haughton, G., and Frelinger, J. A., *J. Exp. Med.* **146,** 1346, 1977.
13. Wettstein, P. J., and Frelinger, J. A., *Immunogenetics* **10,** 211, 1980.
14. Staats, J., *Cancer Res.* **32,** 1609, 1972.
15. Dunn, T. B., and Potter, M., *J. Nat. Cancer Inst.* **18,** 587, 1957.
16. Bevan, M. J., *J. Exp. Med.* **142,** 1349, 1975.
17. Snedecor, G. W., and Cochran, W. G., "Statistical Methods," pp. 130–131. Iowa State Univ. Press, Ames, 1967.
18. Gehan, E. A., *Biometrika* **52,** 203, 1965.
19. Snell, G. D., Russel, E., Fekete, E., and Smith, P., *J. Nat. Cancer Inst.* **14,** 485, 1953.
20. Gorer, P. A., *J. Pathol. Bacteriol.* **44,** 691, 1937.

21. Brambilla, G., Cavanna, M., Parodi, S., and Baldini, L., *Experientia* **26,** 1140, 1970.
22. Prehn, R. T., and Main, J. M., *J. Nat. Cancer Inst.* **20,** 207, 1958.
23. Bailey, D. W., *Transplantation* **11,** 419, 1971.
24. Johnson, L. L., Bailey, D. W., and Mobraaten, L. E., *Immunogenetics* **11,** 363, 1980.
25. Zinkernagel, R. M., Althage, A., Cooper, S., Kreeb, G., Klein, P. A., Sefton, B., Flaherty, L., Stimpfling, J., Schreffler, D., and Klein, J., *J. Exp. Med.* **148,** 592, 1978.
26. Gasser, D. L., *J. Immunol.* **103,** 66, 1969.
27. Mozes, E., McDevitt, H. O., Jaton, J. C., and Sela, M., *J. Exp. Med.* **130,** 1263, 1969.
28. Zaleski, M., and Klein, J., *J. Immunol.* **113,** 1170, 1974.
29. Blomberg, B., Geckeler, W. R., and Weigert, M., *Science* **177,** 178, 1972.
30. Potter, T. A., McKenzie, I. F. C., Morgan G. M., and Cherry, M. *J. Immunol.* **125,** 541, 1980.
31. Streilein, J. W., Niederkorn, J. Y., and Shadduck, J. A., *J. Exp. Med.* **152,** 1121, 1980.
32. Forni, G., Giovarelli, M., Negro-Ponzi, A., and Landolfo, S., *Immunogenetics* **9,** 199, 1979.
33. Dvorak, A. M., Mihm, M. C. Jr., and Dvorak, H. F., *Lab. Invest.* **34,** 170, 1976.
34. Colvin, R. B., and Dvorak, H. F., *J. Immunol.* **114,** 377, 1975.
35. Wolf, J. E., Faanes, R. B., and Choi, Y. S., *J. Nat. Cancer Inst.* **58,** 1407, 1977.
36. Argyris, B. F., *Cancer Res.* **37,** 3390, 1977.
37. Takei, F., Levy, J. G., and Kilburn, D. G., *J. Immunol.* **118,** 412, 1977.
38. Kamo, I., Patel, C., and Friedman, H., *J. Natl. Cancer Inst.* **56,** 333, 1976.

CELLULAR IMMUNOLOGY **65**, 366–372 (1981)

SHORT COMMUNICATIONS

Human Interferons α and β Inhibit T-Cell-Dependent and Stimulate T-Cell-Independent Mitogenesis and Natural Cytotoxicity: Relationship to Chromosome 21

DAVID S. MATHESON, BRIDGET GREEN, AND Y. H. TAN

Divisions of Paediatrics and Medical Biochemistry, Faculty of Medicine, University of Calgary, Calgary, Canada

Received February 25, 1981; accepted October 3, 1981

The effects of purified human interferons IFN-α and IFN-β on immunocompetent cells were compared. Both types of IFN inhibited blast transformation to the T-cell-dependent mitogens phytohemagglutinin, concanavalin A and pokeweed mitogen with IFN-α being more potent than IFN-β. B-Cell mitogensis induced by *Staphylococcus* Cowan I was enhanced by both IFN preparations with IFN-β being more potent than IFN-α. Both types of IFN enhanced natural killer cell activity with differences in the dose–response curves. The expression of the IFN-induced modulation of the mitogenic responses was shown to be associated with human chromosome 21. No such association could be demonstrated for the effect of IFN on natural killer cell activity.

INTRODUCTION

Although interferon (IFN) inhibits most responses of immunocompetent cells such as mitogenesis, graft-vs-host reactions, delayed hypersensitivity, and antibody formation, some functions such as natural killer cell activity and in certain circumstances, antibody production, can be enhanced by IFN (1–8). This implies that IFN could play a role in the regulation of immunocompetent cells. In this regard, we studied the effects of human IFN-α and IFN-β on the mitogenic response of peripheral blood mononuclear cells. Our investigation shows that human IFN enhanced B-cell-dependent mitogenesis and inhibited T-cell-dependent mitogenesis. Both effects are related to the number of human chromosome 21 indicating the genetic control of these effects is the same as previously reported for the antiviral and cell growth inhibitory actions of human IFN.

MATERIALS AND METHODS

Human IFN. Human IFN-α was produced from human buffy coats after the method of Kauppinen *et al.* (9). Human IFN-β was produced from normal human fibroblast cultures by the superinduction procedures of Ho *et al.* (10–13). Human IFN-α was partially purified by the method of Cantell (9), while IFN-β was purified by an immunosorbent column (14). The specific activity of the IFN-α was 1×10^7 units/mg of protein and 5×10^7 units/mg protein for human IFN-β. The activity of IFN was determined by a semi-micro antiviral assay as previously described (12).

0008-8749/81/180366-07$02.00/0

Mitogens. Phytohemagglutinin (PHA, 1:100 dilution), concanavalin A (Con A, 1 mg/ml), and pokeweed mitogen (PWM, 0.5 mg/ml) were obtained from Canlab, Pharmacia, and Grand Island Biologicals, respectively. *Staphylococcas* Cowan Strain I (STA, approximately 10^8 bacteria/ml) was obtained from Calbiochem and washed three times in phosphate-buffered saline.

Cells. Peripheral blood mononuclear (PBM) cells used in these studies were obtained by sedimenting heparinized blood from normal humans as well as from humans with trisomy chromosome 21 on Ficoll–Hypaque. The target cell used in determining natural killer cell activity was the human myelogenous leukemia cell line K-562 which was maintained in continuous culture in RPMI 1640 growth medium (GIBCO, Missisauga, Canada) plus 10% fetal calf serum (15).

Mitogenesis. PBM cells were blast transformed with the appropriate T-cell-dependent (PHA, Con A, and PWM) or the B-cell-dependent mitogens (STA) (16–19). T-Cell mitogenesis was carried out by incubating 5×10^4 PBM cells in 200 μl of RPMI 1640 growth medium containing 10% human AB serum (Red Cross, Canada) with 20 μl of the given concentrations of mitogen for 3 days at 37°C in 5% CO_2. B-Cell mitogenesis was carried out by incubating 2×10^5 PBM cells in 200 μl of RPMI 1640 growth medium containing 10% fetal calf serum (Flow, Rockville, Md.) with 20 μl of STA for 3 days at 37°C in 5% CO_2.

Natural killer assay. Natural killer (NK) cell activity was assayed using the chromium-51 release method with K-562 cells as the labeled targets. The effector-to-target cell ratios used in these experiments was 30:1, 10:1, 3:1, and 1:1. The total volume of the cellular mixture was 200 μl of RPMI 1640 containing 5% fetal calf serum. The cultures were incubated for 18 hr at 37°C in 5% CO_2. The amount of cytolytic activity was calculated as

$$\%\ \text{lysis} = \frac{\text{cpm in target cell test} - \text{cpm in target cell control}}{\text{cpm in 100\% lysis target cells} - \text{cpm in target cell control}}.$$

Total (100%) lysis of target cells was obtained by treatment with 5% sodium dodecyl sulfate. Target cell control was defined as the amount of spontaneous release in the absence of effector cells. One lytic unit (LU) was defined as the number of effector cells required to achieve 40% lysis.

IFN effects. To determine the effect of human IFN on mitogenesis or NK activity, 2×10^6 PBM cells were preincubated in RPMI 1640 growth medium with varying amounts of human IFN for 2 hr at 37°C.

RESULTS

Enhancement of B-cell-dependent mitogenesis by human IFN. Both human IFN-α and IFN-β inhibited PHA and PWM stimulation of PBM cells. Human IFN-α was more inhibitory than IFN-β (Fig. 1). On the other hand, both human IFN-α and IFN-β enhanced STA stimulation of PBM cells with the β type being more effective than the α type. These results were reproduced in six separate experiments each of which demonstrated comparable findings. Variations between experiments masked these comparisons when averages were calculated but within each experiment, IFN-α was consistently more potent at inhibiting T-cell mitogenesis and IFN-β was more potent at enhancing B-cell mitogenesis. Comparisons based upon units of antiviral activity is somewhat fallacious as the relative activities (antiviral

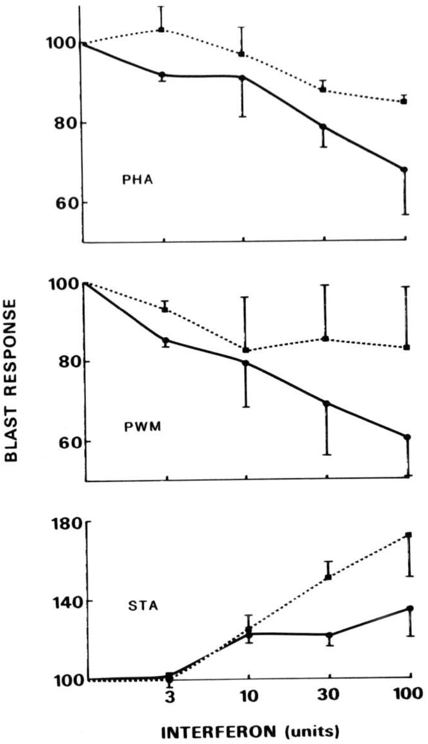

FIG. 1. Dose–response curve for mitogenesis; varying amounts (units) of IFN were incubated with 2 $\times 10^6$ cells for 30 min at 37°C prior to mitogenesis. Upper panel, PHA; middle panel, PWM; lower panel, STA.——, IFN-α; - - -, IFN-β. Each point is the average of the triplicate samples. Ordinate value (blast response) is (cpm in the presence of IFN/cpm in absence of IFN) $\times$ 100.

or immunoregulatory) per milligram of protein may vary for each type. Suffice to say, the dose–response curves based upon the antiviral units, which is still the most commonly used measure of IFN, do differ.

Both human IFN-α and IFN-β enhanced the NK activity of PBM cell preparations (Fig. 2). The IFN-α appeared to be more effective than IFN-β in the concentration range tested. Approximately equal enhancement of NK activity is achieved at about 300 units. Alternately the NK results can be expressed as lytic units. Using this technique, the IFN-α is more potent at stimulating NK activity than is the IFN-β (Table 1). These findings were reproduced in four of five experiments, the one exception failing to demonstrate any difference between IFN-α and IFN-β although both preparations enhanced the NK activity above baseline. Interexperimental variation masked the significance when the results are averaged, but there is consistency of the findings within each experiment.

Chromosome 21 enhancement of B-cell dependent mitogenesis. Experiments on the effect of IFN on cellular mitogenesis were performed to compare the response of PBM cells from normal (D-21) donors and Down's Syndrome (T-21) donors (Table 2). The enhancing effect of IFN and STA-induced mitogenesis was more pronounced in PBM cells obtained from trisomy 21 than normal donors. This greater enhancement of B-cell-dependent mitogenesis in the trisomic PBM cells

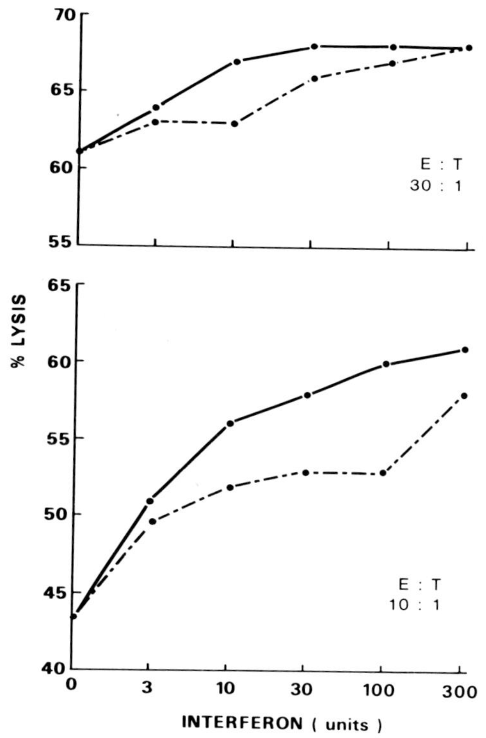

FIG. 2. Dose-response curve for NK activity; varying amounts (units) of IFN are incubated with effector cells for 2 hr at 37°C prior to their addition to an NK assay. Each point is average of three samples. Ordinate value is the percentage lysis of target cells at the concentration of IFN shown. Upper panel, 30:1 effector:target cell ratio; lower panel 10:1 effector:target cell ratio.——, IFN-α; - - -, IFN-β.

is statistically significant. Similarly Con A-induced T-cell mitogenesis in D-21 and T-21 cells was also compared, giving similar results with respect to a correlation to chromosome 21 dosage. An extensive comparison of the chromosome 21 gene dosage effect on the NK activity failed to demonstrate any statistically significant difference perhaps due to the wide range of enhancements detected (9 to 84% for the Down's patients and 6 to 95% for normals).

TABLE 1

Effect of IFN-α or IFN-β on NK Activity (lytic units/10^7 PBM)

Units	IFN-α	IFN-β
300	357	238
100	357	217
30	333	200
10	227	185
3	192	175
0	142	

TABLE 2

Effect of Human IFN-β on Mitogenesis and NK Cell Activity of PBM Cultures

	Percentage inhibition by IFN of Con A-induced cellular DNA synthesis		Percentage enhancement by IFN of STA-induced cellular DNA synthesis		Percentage enhancement by IFN of NK activity	
	T-21 cells	D-21 cells	T-21 cells	D-21 cells	T-21 cells	D-21 cells
Percentage difference ± SD.	−45 ± 26	−11 ± 9	+21 ± 12	+9 ± 7	+26 ± 23	+26 ± 18
Number	14	4	11	8	26	12
Statistical significance	$P = 0.02$		$P = 0.02$		Not significant	

Note. IFN-β was added to PBM cells of disomic or trisomic 21 donors and the change in mitogenesis or natural killer activity was assessed. The change in response is recorded as percentage inhibition (−) or enhancement (+) compared to the value without IFN. IFN 50 units/2 × 10^6 PBM. The NK result is expressed as a percentage lysis at 30:1 effector–target ratio.

DISCUSSION

No attempt was made to isolate subpopulations of T and B cells for this study. Instead specific mitogens were used to stimulate the respective T and B cells present in the PBM cell preparations (16–19). It is evident that partially purified preparations of human IFN-α and IFN-β have similar effects on T-cell and B-cell-dependent mitogenesis and NK activity of PBM cultures. However, the dose–response curves of the cellular response to each type of IFN are different. This observation is not surprising since the two IFNs are in fact different polypeptides (20–22).

Mitogenesis as described herein is a stimulation of cellular DNA synthesis which is measured by an increase in [^{3}H]thymidine incorporation into DNA. It is possible that the various effects of IFN on mitogenesis of PBM cells could be attributed to differences in [^{3}H]thymidine transport and pool size of DNA precursors. However, previous experiments have shown that IFN does not have a significant effect on soluble thymidine pools (23). Thus, our results suggest that human IFN inhibits T-cell-dependent mitogenesis and enhances B-cell-dependent mitogenesis (Fig. 1 and Table 2).

Previously it was thought that IFN only inhibited cell division and cellular DNA synthesis (23–25). This had led some investigators to attribute the cell multiplication inhibitory effect of IFN as a mechanism of its antitumor effect. The present observation that IFN can also enhance cellular DNA synthesis should caution one against this hypothesis. There are other mechanisms to be considered, for example the enhancement of NK cell activity (26).

An interesting question is how IFN can enhance cellular DNA synthesis in one case and inhibit it in another (Fig. 1). Although both PWM and STA are polyclonal B-cell mitogens, PWM is T-cell dependent whereas STA is T-cell independent (16–19). The fact the IFN decreased the proliferative response to PWM likely reflects the inhibitory activity of IFN on the T-cell-dependent phase of the assay. Alternatively, one could argue that IFN is always inhibitory and that a normally present inhibitory effect on STA mitogenesis is inhibited by IFN thus allowing an increased response. We are unaware of any evidence to support the latter interpretation, however. We favor the interpretation that IFN influences different subpopulations of cells differently. It is unlikely that the enhancement of B-cell mitogenesis by IFN is due to the IFN preparation because by itself the preparation does not induce DNA synthesis in PBM cells.

Since a chromosome 21 gene(s) is known to control the antiviral and cell multiplicatory action as well as its inhibitory effect on PHA blastogenesis (23–25, 27–30), a demonstration that the enhancing effect on B-cell mitogenesis is also controlled by chromosome 21 would strengthen the hypothesis that this effect is an IFN mediated one. A comparison of this enhancement effect was made in PBM cells disomic and trisomic for chromosome 21 and a statistically significant correlation was found (Table 2). Further, a comparison of inhibition of Con A-induced T-cell mitogenesis was made as a control for the chromosome 21 correlation (Table 2). This experiment showed a statistically significant correlation between chromosome 21 and the inhibitory effect of IFN-β.

Similar experiments were also performed with NK cell activity and chromosome 21 dosage but no association was found. The NK activity of trisomic 21 PBM was not further enhanced by human IFN in comparison to normal PBM cultures. It is possible that the gene product of chromosome 21 is not synthesized in the short-term NK assay (compared to the longer mitogenesis assays), or that the assay variance is too great to detect significance or that NK enhancement by IFN does not depend on chromosome 21.

Although IFN has been shown to enhance natural cytotoxicity and to inhibit or enhance antibody synthesis, cellular DNA synthesis has generally been inhibited. This report provides the first observation that cellular DNA synthesis can be enhanced or inhibited by IFN depending on the mitogenic stimulus. This lends support to the hypothesis that IFN is a regulator of immunocompetent cells (31) and that such regulation could be mediated by an enhancing or inhibitory effect depending upon the target.

ACKNOWLEDGMENTS

This work is supported by the Alberta Children's Hospital Foundation, Provincial Cancer Hospital's Board of Alberta and MRC of Canada. Dr. David S. Matheson is a Fellow of the Alberta Kidney Foundation and Y. H. Tan is an NCI of Canada Scholar.

REFERENCES

1. Gresser, I., and Bourali, C. J., *J. Nat. Cancer Inst.* **45,** 365, 1970.
2. Chester, T. J., Paucker, K., and Merigan, T. C., *Nature (London)* **246,** 92, 1973.
3. Gisler, R. H., Lindahl, P., and Gresser, I., *J. Immunol.* **113,** 438, 1974.
4. Brodeur, B. R., and Merigan, T. C., *J. Immunol.* **114,** 1323, 1975.
5. Heron, I., Berg, K., and Cantell, K., *J. Immunol.* **117,** 1370, 1976.
6. Parker, M. A., Mandel, A. D., and Sonnenfeld, G., *Fed. Proc.* **39,** 1161 (4704A), 1980.
7. Santoli, D., and Koprowski, H., *Immunol. Rev.* **44,** 125, 1979.
8. Herberman, R. T., and Holden H. T., *Advan. Cancer Res.* **27,** 305, 1978.
9. Kauppinen, H. L., Myllyla, G., and Cantell, K., *In* Proceedings, Meeting on Interferon, Lake Placid, N.Y. 1977.
10. Ho, M., Armstrong, J. A., Ke, Y. H., and Tan, Y. H., U.S. Patent 3773924, 1973.
11. Tan, Y. H., Armstrong, J. A., Ke, Y. H., and Ho, M., *Proc. Nat. Acad. Sci. USA* **67,** 464, 1970.
12. Tan, Y. H., and Berthold, W., *J. Gen. Virol.* **34,** 401, 1977.

13. Berthold, W., Tan, C., and Tan, Y. H., *J. Biol. Chem.* **253,** 5206, 1978.
14. Okamura, H., Berthold, W., Hood, L., Hunkapiller, M., Inoue, M., Smith-Johannsen, H., and Tan, Y. H., *Biochemistry* **19,** 3831, 1980.
15. Lozzio, C. B., and Lozzio, B. B., *Blood* **45,** 321, 1975.
16. Schuurman, R. K. B., Gelfand, E. W., and Dosch, H.-M., *J. Immunol.* **125,** 820, 1980.
17. Dosch, H.-M., Schuurman, R. K. B., and Gelfand, E. W., *J. Immunol.* **125,** 827, 1980.
18. Pryjma, J., Munoz, J., Galbraith, R. M., Fudenberg, H. H., and Virella, G., *J. Immunol.* **124,** 656, 1980.
19. Sierianni, M. C., Pandoff, F., Aiuti, F., and Wigzell, H., *Clin. Exp. Immunol.* **36,** 107, 1979.
20. Knight, E., Hunkapiler, M. W., Korent, B. D., Hardy, R. W. F., and Hood, L. E., *Science* **207,** 525, 1980.
21. Zoon, K. C., Smith, M. E., Bridgen, P. J., Anfinsen, C. B., Hunkapiler, M. W., and Hood, L. E., *Science* **207,** 527, 1980.
22. Tan, Y. H. *In* Methods in Enzymology (S. Pestka, Ed.). Academic Press, New York, in press, 1981.
23. Cupples, C. G., and Tan, Y. H., *Nature (London)* **137,** 317, 1977.
24. Tan, Y. H., *Nature (London)* **253,** 280, 1975.
25. Tan, Y. H., *Nature (London)* **260,** 141, 1976.
26. Marx, J. L., *Science* **210,** 624, 1980.
27. Chany, C., Vignol, M., Couillin, P., Cong, N. V., Boue, J. and Boue, A. *Proc. Nat. Acad. Sci. USA* **72,** 3129, 1975.
28. Epstein, L. B., and Epstein, C. J., *J. Infect. Dis.* **133,** A56, 1976.
29. Tan, Y. H., Tischfield, J., and Ruddle, F. H., *J. Exp. Med.* **137,** 317, 1973.
30. Epstein, L. B., and Epstein, C. J., *Cell. Immunol.* **51,** 303, 1980.
31. Kadish, A. S., Tansey, F. A., Yu, G. S. M., Doyle, A. T., and Bloom, B. R., *J. Exp. Med.* **151,** 637, 1980.

CELLULAR IMMUNOLOGY **65**, 373–379 (1981)

Tumor-Specific Immunity Induced by Somatic Hybrids

III. Persistence of Adoptively Transferred Immunity Specific for TEPC-15 Plasmacytoma in Normal BALB/c Mice[1]

BYUNG S. KIM

Department of Microbiology–Immunology and the Cancer Center, The Medical and Dental Schools, Northwestern University, Chicago, Illinois 60611

Received August 14, 1981; accepted October 7, 1981

Immunity against TEPC-15 tumor cells was induced in BALB/c mice by injecting semi-allogeneic hybrid cells derived from fusion of TEPC-15 tumor cells with LM(TK^-) cells of the C3H origin. Adoptive transfer of spleen cells from the immune mice into normal BALB/c recipients rendered them free from tumors following tumor challenge; the recipients were most significantly protected from the tumor when tumor cells were injected 7–14 days after the adoptive transfer of immune cells. Such immunity following adoptive transfer appeared to persist in the recipients for at least 60 days. Moreover, the tumor-specific immunity was consecutively transferrable (more than nine passages) into normal BALB/c recipients by serially passing spleen cells from the recipients every 14 days, without further stimulation with the hybrid cells or inactivated TEPC-15 tumor cells. Such consecutive transfer of the immune spleen cells induced splenomegaly in the recipients: a two- to five-fold increase over normal spleen cell recipients. The ability of spleen cells to transfer immunity, but not splenomegaly, was abrogated by treatment with mitomycin C. These results suggest that proliferation of donor cells is necessary to transfer immunity, and that splenomegaly alone does not manifest such immunity in the recipients.

INTRODUCTION

The development and function of tumor-specific immunity appear to be influenced by a number of host factors such as circulating tumor antigens (1, 2), antibody-mediated blocking factors (3, 4), and suppressor T cells (5–7). In order to study the mechanisms of maintenance and amplification of tumor-specific immunity, mitomycin C-treated or irradiated tumor cells are often used to induce tumor-specific immunity without developing tumors in the host. However, such tumor cells are generally less immunogenic than untreated, viable tumor cells (8). Recently, attempts have been made to use various hybrid cells for active immunization against the parent tumors (9–13).

To increase immunogenicity of tumor-associated antigens, we have previously employed semiallogeneic hybrid clones derived from the TEPC-15 plasmacytoma cells of BALB/c and LM(TK^-) cells of C3H origin (12, 13). A strong tumor-specific immunity against TEPC-15 could be induced in BALB/c mice by immunizing with the hybrid cells. In addition, adoptive transfer of spleen cells from

[1] This work was supported in part by grants from the National Cancer Institute (CA 14145) and American Cancer Society (IN-123).

0008-8749/81/180373-07$02.00/0

the immune mice resulted in regression of established tumors in the recipient mice, demonstrating the potential therapeutic value of such semiallogeneic hybrids.

In this study, we present evidence that tumor-specific immunity induced by hybrids persists in the recipients following adoptive transfer of spleen cells and can be consecutively transferred into normal syngeneic mice for many passages without restimulation with tumor antigens. This phenomenon may reflect an important host mechanism of maintenance and amplification of tumor-specific immunity, and may provide a valuable model system for further studies.

MATERIALS AND METHODS

Mice. An inbred strain of BALB/c mice was obtained from Cumberland View Farms, Clinton, Tennessee. Six- to eight-week-old mice were used unless otherwise indicated.

Tumor and hybrid cells. Plasmacytoma lines, TEPC-15, HOPC-8, and McPC-603, were obtained from Dr. Michael Potter, National Institutes of Health. The tumors were passed in BALB/c mice as ascites. TEPC-15 plasmacytoma cells were isolated from ascites tumors of BALB/c mice by means of repeated centrifugations as previously described (14).

The LM(TK^-) Cl 1D cell line, a subline of mouse L cells derived from the C3H strain of mice (15), was maintained in Dulbecco's modified Eagle's medium (DMEM) containing 30 μM 5-bromodeoxyuridine and 5% fetal calf serum.

Hybrid clones (LTC-1 and LTC-2) were derived by fusion of LM(TK^-) and TEPC-15 plasmacytoma cells as described previously (12). The hybrid cells exhibited both H-2^k and H-2^d antigens of both parental haplotypes (12).

Adoptive transfer. Strong tumor-specific immunity was induced in BALB/c mice by multiple injections (weekly for 3 weeks) with 1×10^6 immunogenic hybrid cells (LTC-1 and LTC-2) as previously described (12, 13). Seven to fourteen days after the last injection, spleen cells from immune mice were injected either iv into normal adult BALB/c mice or ip into BALB/c neonates. After 14 days, pretreated mice were challenged ip with 1×10^4 TEPC-15 tumor cells. As a control, spleen cells from normal BALB/c mice were injected into a separate group of normal mice.

RESULTS

Effect on tumor rejection of the time interval between adoptive transfer of immune cells and tumor challenge. Tumor-specific immunity induced by injection of BALB/c mice with immunogenic hybrid clones (LTC-1 and LTC-2) could be adoptively transferred into normal BALB/c recipients (13). In order to increase the effectiveness of immunity transfer, the optimal time period between introduction of cells and challenge with tumor cells was determined (Fig. 1). Spleen cells from immune mice were injected iv into four different groups of normal mice. After 2 hr or 3, 7, or 14 days, each group of mice was injected ip with 1×10^4 TEPC-15 tumor cells. The most effective protection from the tumor was obtained in the mice that received immune cells 7–14 days before challenge with the tumor cells; none of the 10 mice in the group developed tumors during a 100-day test period. However, mice that received immune cells 3 days before tumor challenge were less protected (5/10), and the mice challenged with tumor cells 2 hr after the adoptive transfer were not protected significantly, compared to control mice which had been injected with normal BALB/c spleen cells.

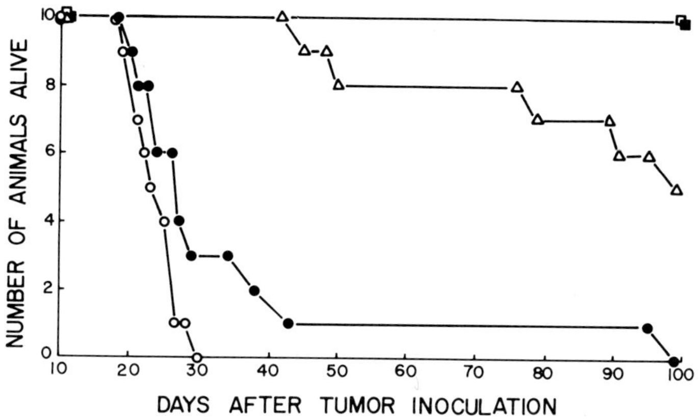

FIG. 1. Effect of time interval between adoptive transfer of immune cells and challenge with tumor cells on the survival time of recipients. Spleen cells (2×10^7 nucleated cells) from immune mice were injected iv into four different groups of normal BALB/c mice (10 mice per group). Each group of mice was challenged after 2 hr (●), or 3 (△), 7 (□) or 14 (■) days ip with 1×10^4 TEPC-15 tumor cells, and the survival of the recipient mice was scored. As a control (○), BALB/c mice that received 2×10^7 normal syngeneic spleen cells 14 days prior to the tumor challenge were used.

Consecutive transfer of tumor-specific immunity into naive syngeneic recipients. Mice that have received immune cells 1 to 2 weeks before tumor challenge acquire better protection than those that have received immune cells 3 days before (Fig. 1). To examine the possibility that an amplification of tumor-specific immune cells is necessary before tumor challenge, spleen cells (2×10^7) from immune mice were serially transferred into normal BALB/c mice. Eight recipient mice were used for each passage; five mice were challenged with 1×10^4 TEPC-15 tumor cells 14 days after the immune cell transfer, and the other three mice were sacrificed to obtain spleen cells for further passage. The spleen cells from these recipients were then transferred into another set of eight normal BALB/c mice. Normal spleen cells were similarly transferred and used as controls. The protective immunity against the TEPC-15 tumor was consecutively transferrable into normal mice for more than nine passages without restimulation either by the plasmacytoma or by hybrid cells containing the parent tumor-specific antigens (Fig. 2). The splenic cells responsible for continuous transfer of the protective immunity against TEPC-15 tumor cells were designated immunity-transfer cells (or ITC).

It was very interesting to note that the spleens of immune cell recipients were significantly enlarged compared to those of mice that received normal spleen cells. The average size of spleens from three recipient mice at each passage (14 days) was determined by wet weight: the spleens from ITC recipients weighed 179 ± 16, 197 ± 27, 347 ± 28, and 354 ± 49 mg at the second, third, fifth, and ninth passage, respectively (see Fig. 2). In contrast, spleens from mice that received normal spleen cells only weighed 100–130 mg. No other organs of the recipients (including lymph nodes and the liver) were significantly enlarged during this time period.

Ability of immune spleen cells to protect the recipients against delayed tumor challenge. The persistence of the capacity to protect the recipients was tested by delaying the inoculation of the tumor cells. Either normal or immune spleen cells at the second passage were transferred into 3-day-old normal neonates and 6-week-

TABLE 1

Persistence of the Ability of Immune Spleen Cells to Protect the Recipients from Delayed Tumor Challenge

Days after tumor inoculation	No. of surviving recipients			
	Neonates[a]		Adults[b]	
	Mock	ITC	Mock	ITC
0	8	8	10	10
20	6	7	10	10
25	1	4	3	10
30	0	4	0	10
60	0	4	0	7

[a] Three-day-old neonates were ip injected with either mock or ITC (3×10^6 cells/mouse) at the second passage; 45 days later, 1×10^4 TEPC-15 tumor cells were ip inoculated and the survival of mice from the tumor was monitored.

[b] Six-week-old adult mice were iv injected with either 2×10^7 mock or ITC; 40 days later, 1×10^4 TEPC-15 tumor cells were ip injected into the recipients and the survival from the tumor was scored.

old young adults. Forty to forty-five days later, those recipients were challenged with TEPC-15 tumor cells to determine the adoptively transferred protection against the tumor (Table 1). The immune cell recipients displayed a marked protection from the tumor, even when the tumor challenge was displayed for several weeks. These results indicate that the cells carrying immunity function for a prolonged time period in the recipients.

Requirement of donor cell proliferation for immunity transfer. In an attempt to determine whether donor cell proliferation is necessary in transferring immunity

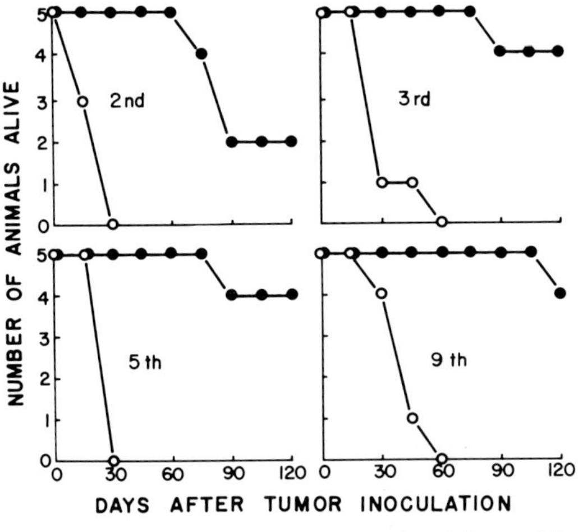

FIG. 2. Consecutive transfer of tumor immunity into normal recipients without restimulation. Spleen cells (2×10^7) from either normal mice (○) or mice that were immunized against LTC-1 hybrid cells (●) were consecutively transferred into normal BALB/c mice every 14 days. The recipients were challenged with 1×10^4 TEPC-15 tumor cells at the second, third, fifth, and ninth passage to determine the transfer of immunity against the tumor.

against TEPC-15 tumor cells, the ITC at the fifth passage were treated with mitomycin C and transferred into normal BALB/c recipients. The effect of mitomycin-treated ITC was then compared with that of untreated ITC with respect to the ability to transfer the tumor-protecting immunity (Fig. 3). Treatment of ITC with mitomycin C resulted in complete abrogation of tumor-protecting immunity in the recipients; they developed tumors at the same rate as did normal spleen cell recipients. However, treatment of ITC with mitomycin did not alter their capacity to transfer splenomegaly. Therefore, proliferation of ITC appears to be necessary to confer immunity in the recipients; splenomegaly alone is not sufficient for the development of tumor immunity.

Specificity of the transferred immunity. The specificity of consecutively transferred immunity was examined by challenging the recipients with other plasmacytomas such as HOPC-8 and McPC-603 (Table 2). The BALB/c mice which had adoptively received 2×10^6 at the third passage were challenged with TEPC-15, HOPC-8, or McPC-603 tumor cells (1×10^4 cells per mouse). The survival of these ITC recipients was then compared with that of mice injected with mock transfer cells at the same passage number. However, the ITC recipients were not significantly protected against HOPC-8 and McPC-603 plasmacytomas as compared to the mock cell (normal spleen cell) recipients, although complete protection against the TEPC-15 tumors was seen in the recipients. These results indicate that the transferred immunity is specific for the TEPC-15 tumor cells, which were one parent of the original stimulant hybrids.

DISCUSSION

We have presented evidence that tumor-specific immunity against TEPC-15 plasmacytoma induced by injection with immunogenic hybrids can be consecutively transferred into normal syngeneic mice. Although this immunity transfer accom-

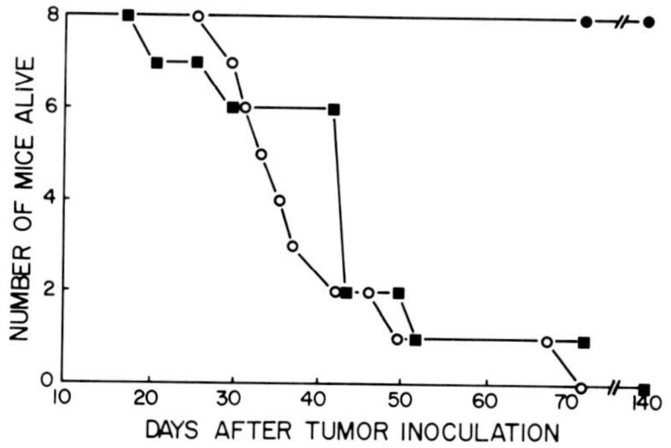

FIG. 3. Inability of mitomycin C-treated ITC to transfer immunity. Spleen cells from mice following five consecutive transfers of immune cells were treated with mitomycin C (100 μg/ml/1 $\times 10^7$ cells) for 45 min at 37°C under 7% CO_2. The treated cells (2×10^7) were then washed three times with BSS and injected into each recipient (■). An aliquot of cells was handled similarly except for the treatment with mitomycin C and used for a positive control (●). Spleen cells (2×10^7) from a mouse following five passages of normal BALB/c cells were used (○) as a negative control. After 14 days, the recipients were either challenged with 1×10^4 TEPC-15 tumor cells (five mice per group) or sacrificed for determination of spleen weights (three per group). Spleen weights of the recipient mice were: 458 ± 72 mg for the positive control group (●), 520 ± 25 mg for the recipients of mitomycin-treated cells (■), and 138 ± 11 mg for the negative control mice (○).

TABLE 2

Specificity of the Protection Mediated by Immune Transfer Cells following Adoptive Transfer

Days after tumor challenge	Percentage survivors after challenge with					
	TEPC-15		HOPC-8		McPC-603	
	Normal	Immune	Normal	Immune	Normal	Immune
20	60	100	72	100	100	100
25	0	100	16	14	50	80
30	0	100	0	0	0	0
150	0	100	0	0	0	0

Note. Normal BALB/c mice were injected with either 2×10^6 ITC or 2×10^6 mock transfer cells at the third passage. Fourteen days later, these recipients were challenged with TEPC-15, McPC-603, or HOPC-8 plasmacytoma cells: 1×10^4 tumor cells per mouse were used to challenge the recipients (7–10 mice per group).

panies splenomegaly, the splenomegaly alone was not sufficient to transfer the immunity. Since only 2×10^6 ITC (approximately 1/100 of the spleen) are sufficient for transferring immunity, either proliferation of ITC in the recipients or recruitment of specific host cells by the ITC may occur. The incubation period (7–14 days) required for maximal protection after adoptive transfer (Fig. 1) may reflect the time period necessary for amplification and/or recruitment of the immune cells. Abrogation of ITC function by treatment with mitomycin C (Fig. 3) supports the idea that proliferation of ITC may be necessary to provide adequate protection of the recipients against the tumor challenge.

The relationship between immunity transfer and splenomegaly is not yet clear. However, it is conceivable that induction of splenomegaly in the recipients may be triggered by a secondary immunological mechanism. For example, allogeneic antigens on the hybrids may influence immune response against tumor cells (17, 18). Alternatively, a nonpathogenic virus such as lactate dehydrogenase-enhancing virus (19) may be involved in immunity transfer accompanying splenomegaly.

ITC did not display a significant level of direct cytotoxicity in a preliminary experiment. Therefore, ITC may include specific helper T or initiator cells which assist induction of specific cytotoxic cells in the recipients as described in other systems (20, 21). Perhaps this helper function requires intact cells and/or cell proliferation, since mitomycin treatment eliminates the ability of ITC to transfer immunity. Alternatively, ITC may represent a memory cell population of cytotoxic T cells.

It is not yet clear whether immunogenic hybrid cells are unique in developing ITC. However, induction of ITC with inactivated parent tumor cells has not been successful. The weakly immunogenic nature of the tumor cells (13) may result in the induction of a low level of ITC. Alternatively, a distinct population of cell types may be stimulated by the hybrid cells due to the rearrangement of tumor-associated antigens resulting from cell fusion. The transfer of immunity by ITC may apply a mechanism similar to that of infectious immunological tolerance by suppressor T cells (22, 23).

Our preliminary results have suggested that the cell type responsible for consecutive transfer of immunity appears to be the nylon wool adherent, Thy 1.2^- cell population, although the initial adoptive transfer (first passage) of hybrid-induced immunity seemed to depend on the presence of a cytotoxic T-cell population (13). Because ITC are derived from spleens that are significantly enlarged, and thus may represent a cell population different from conventional cytotoxic T cells, more elaborate investigations defining cell types of ITC are currently being performed in our laboratory.

ACKNOWLEDGMENTS

I thank Ms. Benita Benewicz and Ms. Susan Hubchak for their excellent technical assistance.

REFERENCES

1. Carrie, G. A., and Basham, C., *Brit. J. Cancer* **26,** 427, 1972.
2. Alexander, P., *Cancer Res.* **34,** 2077, 1974.
3. Hellström, I., and Hellström, K. E., *Int. J. Cancer* **4,** 587, 1969.
4. Baldwin, R. W., Price, M. R., and Robbins, R. A., *Nature New Biol.* **238,** 185, 1972.
5. Treves, A. J., Carnaud, C., Trainin, N., Feldman, M., and Cohn, I. R., *Eur. J. Immunol.* **4,** 722, 1974.
6. Fujomoto, S., Greene, M. I., and Sehon, A., *J. Immunol.* **116,** 791, 1976.
7. Berendt, M., and North, R. J., *J. Exp. Med.* **151,** 69, 1980.
8. Herberman, R. B., *Biochim. Biophys. Acta* **473,** 93, 1977.
9. Jami, J., and Ritz, E., *Proc. Nat. Acad. Sci. USA* **72,** 2130, 1975.
10. Liang, W., and Cohen, E. P., *J. Immunol.* **116,** 623, 1976.
11. Watkins, J. F., and Chen, L., *Nature (London)* **223,** 1018, 1969.
12. Kim, B. S., Liang, W., and Cohen, E. P., *J. Immunol.* **123,** 733, 1979.
13. Kim, B. S., *J. Immunol.* **123,** 739, 1979.
14. Kim, B. S., Rowley, D. A., and Mallat, L., *Cell. Immunol.* **41,** 286, 1978.
15. Kit, S., Dubbs, D. R., Piekarski, L. J., and Hsu, T. C., *Exp. Cell Res.* **31,** 297, 1963.
16. Hirschberg, H., Skore, H., and Thorsby, E., *J. Immunol. Methods* **16,** 131, 1977.
17. Katz, D. H., Ellman, L., Paul, W. E., Green, I., and Benacerraf, B., *Cancer Res.* **32,** 133, 1972.
18. Invernizzi, G., and Parmiani, G., *Nature (London)* **254,** 713, 1975.
19. Riley, V., *In* Methods in Cancer Research (H. Busch, Ed.), Vol. IV, p. 493. Academic Press, New York, 1968.
20. Cohen, I. R., and Livnat, S., *Transplant. Rev.* **29,** 24, 1976.
21. Fujiwara, H., Hamaoka, T., Shearer, G. M., Yamamoto, H., and Terry, W. D., *J. Immunol.* **124,** 863, 1980.
22. Gershon, R. K., and Kondo, K., *Immunology* **21,** 903, 1971.
23. Sy, M.-S., Dietz, M. H., Germain, R. N., Benacerraf, B., and Greene, M. I., *J. Exp. Med.* **151,** 1183, 1980.

CELLULAR IMMUNOLOGY **65**, 380–385 (1981)

Enhanced Proliferation, Survival, and Yield of Cultured Myelin Basic Protein (MBP)-Reactive Lewis Rat Lymph Node Cells Following Dual Activation with Concanavalin A and MBP

HAIM OVADIA, AND PHILIP Y. PATERSON

Department of Microbiology–Immunology, The Medical and Dental Schools, Northwestern University, Chicago, Illinois 60611

Received August 26, 1981; accepted October 7, 1981

Lymph node cells (LNC) from Lewis rats sensitized 7 days previously to myelin basic protein (MBP) exhibit greatly increased survival and undergo much greater proliferation when cultured in the presence of both concanavalin A (Con A) and MBP. Dual activation, in contrast to culture with either the mitogen or the neural antigen, results in a substantially greater yield of lymphoblasts with the capacity to transfer experimental allergic encephalomyelitis (EAE) to normal syngeneic recipients. Dual activation provides a practical advantage over other methods reported to date for securing larger numbers of functional MBP-reactive lymphoid cells for immunologic studies.

INTRODUCTION

Experimental allergic encephalomyelitis (EAE) is a prototypic autoimmune disease of the central nervous system (CNS) induced in Lewis rats and other species of animals by sensitization with whole CNS tissue, purified myelin fractions, or isolated myelin basic protein (MBP) combined with an appropriate immunologic adjuvant (1–3). EAE, manifested by clinical neurologic signs and characteristic lesions of the disease, can be transferred to syngeneic recipients, providing relatively large numbers of sufficiently sensitized donor lymph node cells (LNC) are used (1–6). Transfer of the disease with sensitized splenocytes is much less effective (7); transfer with peritoneal exudate cells (PEC) is rarely successful (2, 8). Several groups of workers have recently reported augmented EAE transfer activity following *in vitro* culture of primed LNC, splenocytes, or PEC with concanavalin A (Con A) *or* MBP (8–16). In only a few of these reports (8, 13, 16) have authors made any mention of the relatively low degree of survival, proliferation, and final yield (i.e., 16 to 44%) of initially cultured lymphoid cells. This issue immediately caught our attention as we began our own studies of *in vitro* activated lymphoid cells (17). We have addressed this issue and report here that dual stimulation of primed LNC from Lewis rats using *both* Con A and MBP results in synergistic activation with augmented cell survival/proliferation, and a surprisingly large increase in the final yield of lymphoblasts capable of transferring EAE to normal Lewis rats. From the standpoint of practicality, dual stimulation provides several advantages, not the

0008-8749/81/180380-06$02.00/0

least of which is a convenient means for generating much larger numbers of functionally competent MBP-reactive cells for studies of EAE.

MATERIALS AND METHODS

Animals and sensitization. Male Lewis rats, 8–12 weeks old (M. A. Bioproducts, Bethesda, Md.) were used as donors and recipients. The animals were kept in plastic cages and given water and food *ad libitum*. Guinea pig myelin basic protein (GPMBP), prepared in our laboratory following the procedure of Swanborg *et al.*, was suspended in phosphate-buffered saline (PBS) and emulsified in an equal volume of Freund's complete adjuvant (CFA) as described elsewhere (17, 18). A total of 50 μg MBP was injected into the hind footpads of prospective LNC donors.

In vitro activation of cells and cell transfer. For most experiments, draining lymph nodes (inguinal, periaortic, and popliteal) were removed 7 days after sensitization and processed into a single-cell suspension. The cells were washed in Hanks' balanced salt solution (HBSS) and resuspended in RPMI 1640 medium containing 5% fetal bovine serum, glutamine (2 m*M*), penicillin (100 U/ml), streptomycin (100 μg/ml), 2-mercaptoethanol (5×10^{-5} *M*), and Hepes buffer (25 m*M*). Cells were cultured in tissue culture flasks (75 cm^2, Corning) at a concentration of 2×10^6/ml and incubated for 72 hr at 37°C in a humidified environment with 5% CO_2. Con A (Miles–Yeda, Rehovot, Israel, 1 μg/ml) or GPMBP (10 μg/ml) or a combination of *both* mitogen and neural antigen were added to the cell cultures. At the end of incubation the cells were harvested, washed in HBSS, and counted. Viability was assessed by trypan blue exclusion. Proliferation of cultured LNC was assessed by hemacytometer counts of lymphoblasts (easily identified by their size and morphologic features) and by measuring incorporation of tritiated thymidine ([^{3}H]TdR). Aliquots of 2×10^5 *in vitro*-activated LNC were cultured in flat-bottom microplates (Linbro, Flow Lab, 96 wells/plate) and counted in a Packard Tri-Carb scintillation counter. Activated LNC were transferred into normal Lewis rat recipients via the lateral tail vein.

Clinical and histological determination of EAE. Rats were observed daily for appearance of characteristic clinical neurologic signs, which were scored as follows: loss of tail tonicity, 0.5; hindlimb weakness, 1; partial paralysis of one or both hindlegs, 2; and complete paralysis of both hindlegs, 3. All recipients were sacrificed 12 days after cell transfer. The brains and spinal cords were fixed in 10% formaldehyde, processed, and sectioned for routine hematoxylin–eosin staining as described previously (19). Stained sections of the brain at the level of the thalamus, mesencephalon, and cerebellum–pons, as well as longitudinal sections of the entire spinal cord, were examined for perivascular infiltrates. Histopathology was scored as follows: 1–10 lesions, 1; 11–30 lesions, 2; and greater than 30 lesions, 3.

RESULTS AND DISCUSSION

The results of three experiments assessing proliferative activity, survival/final yield, and EAE transfer activity of primed LNC cultured either alone or with Con A and/or GPMBP are set out in Table 1. By itself, Con A (line 2) augmented proliferative activity of LNC 14- to 16-fold over that of lymphoid cells cultured alone (line 1) and yielded a 2-fold increase in final viable cell counts. Transfer of EAE to syngeneic recipients was not augmented using either type of cultured cells,

TABLE 1

Proliferative Responses, Survival, and EAE-Transfer Activity of Primed Lewis Rat LNC Cultured with Con-A and/or MBP[a]

Primed donor LNC cultured with	Proliferative responses[b]		Final viable cell count ($\times 10^6$)	Occurrence of EAE in recipients[c]	
	% Blasts	$[^3H]$TdR uptake		Clinical signs	Lesions
Nil	4 ± 2	3,683 ± 178	15	0/2	0/2
Con A	65 ± 7.2	54,833 ± 3200	29	0/4	0/4
GPMBP	29 ± 3.7	7,371 ± 384	16	4/4 (0.75)	4/4 (1.0)
Con A plus GPMBP	87 ± 2.3	65,718 ± 1980	48	10/10 (2.0)	10/10 (2.0)
Con A plus GPMBP[d]	73 ± 5.0	57,721 ± 2800	42	0/4	0/4
Con A plus lyzozyme	88 ± 3.3	51,528 ± 2500	48	0/4	0/4

[a] Except as indicated, LNC collected from primed Lewis rats 7 days after sensitization with GPMBP-CFA, and 80 $\times$ 10^6 dissociated cells incubated in culture flasks with Con A (1 μg/ml), GPMBP (10 μg/ml), and/or lysozyme (10 μg/ml) for 72 hr under conditions described under Materials and Methods.

[b] As determined at end of incubation period by counting blast cells in hemacytometer and recording $[^3H]$TdR uptake, in counts per minute.

[c] Recipients were injected intravenously with 40 $\times$ 10^6 incubated LNC per animal. Severity of clinical signs and lesions indicated by mean scores in parentheses, with 3.0 being maximum.

[d] LNC collected 4 days after sensitization of donors.

however, in agreement with observations reported by others (9, 12, 15). LNC cultured with MBP only (line 3), despite much less evident proliferative activity and little improvement in final yield of viable cells, nevertheless showed some increase in EAE transfer activity, again in agreement with reported results of other laboratories (12, 15, 16). That is, all four recipients developed some evidence of clinical signs of EAE following injection of 40 $\times$ 10^6 cells, and all were subsequently found to have moderate histopathologic evidence of the disease. In contrast, LNC cultured with *both* Con A and GPMBP (line 4) displayed markedly greater (19- to 20-fold) proliferative activity and better (3-fold) survival/final yield over control cell cultures (line 1). Better proliferation and especially cell survival/yield (approximately 2-fold) was also observed compared to cells stimulated with Con A only (line 2). More importantly, these dual-activated LNC showed enhanced proliferation (3- to 9-fold) and cell survival (3-fold) compared to cells cultured with GPMBP only, and exhibited near maximum EAE transfer activity. All 10 recipients receiving 40 $\times$ 10^6 dual-activated cells developed moderate to very severe paralytic signs of the disease and showed moderately intense, disseminated lesions within their brains and spinal cords. In contrast, primed LNC collected from donors 4 days after sensitization (line 5) had no evident EAE transfer activity following similar *in vitro* dual stimulation, despite exhibiting proliferative responses and survival/yields comparable to those of 7-day cells (line 4). Finally primed 7-day LNC cultured with Con A and lysozme, a nonencephalitogenic, basic protein, of molecular weight close to that of MBP, showed high levels of proliferation and survival/yield but were devoid of EAE transfer activity.

Data from three experiments bearing on the minimal number of dual-activated LNC required to transfer EAE are summarized in Table 2. Activated LNC (40 $\times 10^6$) transferred moderately severe clinical signs and histopathologic changes of EAE, whereas 20 and 10 $\times 10^6$ LNC transferred progressively less severe forms of disease, as judged by day of onset, duration and severity of clinical signs, and severity of lesions. No EAE transfer activity was observed with the lower number of LNC transferred, viz., 5 $\times 10^6$ cells.

We wondered whether small numbers of reactive cells ordinarily not identifiable in peripheral lymphoid tissues remote from the site of sensitization might be induced to proliferate and brought up to threshold level of recognition following dual activation. Previous experiments in our laboratory had shown that as many as 600 $\times 10^6$ such LNC have little, if any, capacity to transfer EAE to normal Lewis rats. To this end, cervical, subpectoral, and peritracheal lymph nodes were removed from rats sensitized 7 days earlier via the hindleg footpads. The size of such lymph nodes did not differ appreciably from those of normal rats, suggesting that their remote anatomical location had precluded appreciable amounts of the sensitizing inoculum reaching them and inducing an inflammatory response. Nonetheless, cells from these lymph nodes showed demonstrable EAE transfer activity following *in vitro* culture with Con A and MBP. For example, each of four recipients receiving 80 $\times 10^6$ cultured LNC developed mild clinical signs of EAE and moderately severe histopathologic changes of the disease (mean scores of 0.75 and 2.0, respectively). Two of four recipients receiving 40 $\times 10^6$ activated LNC exhibited essentially the same degree of intensity of EAE.

Our findings indicate that by culturing primed LNC from Lewis rats with *both* Con A and the specific neural antigen, proliferation and survival of lymphoid cells is markedly enhanced and the final number of viable effector cells transferring EAE after three days of dual activation is greatly augmented. The Con A/MBP dual activation system allows *in vitro* expansion of EAE effector cells retrieved from lymph nodes of donors 7 days following sensitization, an appreciably earlier time than that used and found effective by other workers, e.g., Holda *et al.* (16).

TABLE 2

EAE Transfer Activity of Varying Numbers of Primed LNC following Dual Activation *in Vitro* with Con A and MBP

Number of dual activated donor LNC injected IV[a] ($\times 10^6$)	Mean day onset of signs[b]	Occurrence of EAE in recipients: Clinical signs[c]	Occurrence of EAE in recipients: Lesions[c]
40	5.6 (4.1)	10/10 (2.0)	10/10 (2.0)
20	5.8 (4.0)	8/8 (1.2)	8/8 (1.0)
10	6.6 (2.3)	3/3 (0.5)	3/3 (1.0)
5	—	0/3	0/3

[a] Primed donor LNC cultured and activated with Con A plus GPMBP as described under Materials and Methods and per Table 1.

[b] Mean day of first appearance of signs, with mean days of duration in parentheses.

[c] Proportion of LNC recipients developing signs or lesions, with mean score of each indicated in parentheses.

Following dual activation, effector cells with the capacity to transfer typical EAE have been secured from nonenlarged lymph nodes remote from those draining the sites of sensitization and presumably containing very few primed lymphoid cells. The minimum number of dual-activated LNC required for transfer of EAE in Lewis rats (Table 2) is not as low as that reported by Richert *et al.* (15), who used LNC collected 11 days after sensitization of donors and which were cultured with MBP. To be sure that the time of collection of LNC in relation to donor sensitization, i.e., 7 versus 11 days, was not a crucial factor, we performed one experiment with 11-day primed LNC and showed that limiting numbers of such cells following *in vitro* culture with Con A plus MBP gave as good, if not better, transfer of full-blown, severe EAE as that reported by Richert *et al.* (15). For example, 20×10^6 primed 11-day LNC after dual activation induced clinical paralytic signs of EAE in each of four recipients which was accompanied by near maximum (mean 2.25) histopathologic changes of the disease; Richert *et al.* (15) found that 20×10^6 primed LNC following culture with MBP transferred EAE to 10 of 13 recipient rats. In this same experiment we also noted that dual activation of 11-day LNC gave results comparable to those observed with 7-day LNC (Table 1) with respect to increased survival and yield of cultured lymphoid cells. We also showed that 11-day primed LNC, like 7-day LNC, were devoid of EAE transfer after culture with only Con A.

What *is* different about the dual activation system, and the major point we want to stress, is the considerable increase in the resulting pool of functionally active EAE effector cells which can be obtained. Based on continued experience with the dual activation system, we can now anticipate yields of LNC of up to 90% or even better, in contrast to 60% (Table 1, line 4) observed in earlier experiments. As can be appreciated, there are immediate practical advantages which accrue. One can enjoy a significant reduction in the number of donor rats allocated for EAE cell transfer experiments. In addition, large numbers of functional effector cells can be generated with relative ease for various *in vitro* or *in vivo* studies.

The precise cellular mechanism(s) and cell–cell interactions that account for the effects of dual activation are obvious points of interest which ongoing studies will hopefully clarify. Our principal line of thinking at present is that Con A stimulates a subset of LNC to secrete factors, e.g., T-cell growth factor (20, 21), which, as long as specific antigen is present, enhance proliferation of a second subset of LNC, viz., MBP-reactive effector cells. Results of preliminary experiments substituting T-cell growth factor for Con A in our dual activation system are consistent with this thesis. We are reasonably confident that more definitive studies, now underway, will settle this important point.

ACKNOWLEDGMENTS

Work described here in part is supported by USPHS NIH Research Grant NS 06262. The authors wish to especially thank Ms. Amy Carbone for many fruitful discussions of these studies and her excellent help in preparation of this manuscript. Mrs. Carrie Clark and Mrs. Cecelia Walker provided essential help with the histologic studies. Mrs. Geane Kraus and Ms. Carol Fountain faithfully generated the final typescript.

Dr. H. Ovadia's present address is Dept. of Neurology, Hadassah Medical School, Jerusalem, Israel.

REFERENCES

1. Paterson, P. Y., *Advan. Immunol.* **5,** 131, 1966.
2. Paterson, P. Y., *In* "Textbook of Immunopathology" (P. A. Miescher and H. J. Muller-Eberhard, Eds.), 2nd ed., p. 179. Grune & Stratton, New York, 1976.
3. Paterson, P. Y., *In* "Immunological Diseases" (M. Samter, N. Alexander, B. Rose, W. B. Sherman, D. W. Talmage, and J. H. Vaughn, eds.), 3rd ed., p. 1400. Little, Brown, Boston, 1978.
4. Paterson, P. Y., *J. Exp. Med.* **111,** 119, 1960.
5. Stone, S. H., *Science* **134,** 619, 1961.
6. Bernard, C. C. A., Leydon, J., and Mackay, I. R., *Eur. J. Immunol.* **6,** 654, 1976.
7. Fujinami, R. S., and Paterson, P. Y., *J. Clin. Lab. Immunol.* **6,** 75, 1981.
8. Driscoll, B. F., Kies, M. W., and Alvord, E. C., Jr., *Science* **203,** 547, 1979.
9. Panitch, H. S., and McFarlin, D. E., *J. Immunol.* **119,** 1134, 1977.
10. Panitch, H. S., *Cell. Immunol.* **56,** 163, 1980.
11. Panitch, H. S., and Ciccone, C., *Cell. Immunol.* **60,** 24, 1981.
12. Driscoll, B. F., Kies, M. W., and Alvord, Jr., E. C., *J. Immunol.* **125,** 1817, 1980.
13. Richert, J. R., Driscoll, B. F., Kies, M. W., and Alvord, E. C., Jr., *J. Immunol.* **122,** 494, 1979.
14. Richert, J. R., Driscoll, B. F., Kies, M. W., and Alvord, Jr., E. C., *Cell. Immunol.* **59,** 42, 1981.
15. Richert, J. R., Kies, M. W., and Alvord, E. C., Jr., *J. Neuroimmunol.* **1,** 195, 1981.
16. Holda, J. H., Welch, A. M., and Swanborg, R. H., *Eur. J. Immunol.* **10,** 657, 1980.
17. Ovadia, H., and Paterson, P. Y., *Cell Immunol.* **64,** 66, 1981.
18. Paterson, P. Y., *J. Reticulendoth. Soc.* **14,** 426, 1973.
19. Paterson, P. Y., Richardson, W. P., and Drobish, D. G., *Cell. Immunol.* **16,** 48, 1975.
20. Baker, P. E., Gillis, S., Ferm, M. M., and Smith, K. A., *J. Immunol.* **121,** 2168, 1978.
21. Larsson, E-L., Coutinho, A., and Martinez-A, C., *Immunol. Rev.* **51,** 61, 1980.

Papers to Appear in Forthcoming Issues

(Received and Accepted Dates Follow Title)

CHOU-CHIK TING, DENNIS RODRIGUES, RICHARD NORDAN, AND JIN-XIN HONG. Studies of the Mechanisms for the Induction of *in Vivo* Tumor Immunity. VI. Induction of Specific and Nonspecific Cell-Mediated Immunity in Tumor Bearing Hosts and Its Correlation with Transplantation Tumor Immunity. (Received 3/12/81; accepted 10/13/81).

RONALD PALACIOS AND ULF ANDERSSON. Autologous Mixed Lymphocyte Reaction in Human Cord Blood Lymphocytes. Decreased Generation of Helper and Cytotoxic T Cell Functions and Increased Proliferative Response and Induction of Suppressor T Cells. (Received 7/17/81; accepted 10/18/81).

YASUHIRO KOGA, KAZUTO TANIGUCHI, CHIHARU KUBO, AND KIKUO NOMOTO. Peritoneal Adherent Cells Inhibit the Generation of Cytotoxic T Lymphocytes with Prostaglandin-Mediated System. (Received 8/10/81; accepted 10/18/81).

CLAUDE AURIAULT, MONIQUE CAPRON, AND ANDRÉ CAPRON. Activation of Rat and Human Eosinophils by Soluble Factor(s) Released by *Schistosoma mansoni* Schistosomula. (Received 5/26/81; accepted 10/18/81).

BURTON ZWEIMAN, ANNE R. MOSKOVITZ, ROBERT P. LISAK, AND L. DOUGLAS WILKERSON. An Approach for the Separation of Mononuclear Inflammatory Cells from Central Nervous System Tissue. (Received 9/15/81; accepted 10/20/81).

J. KETTMAN, A. SOEDERBERG, AND I. LEFKOVITS. Heterogeneity of B Cell Clones: Immunoglobulin-Secreting Subsets. (Received 6/22/81; accepted 10/20/81).

KLAUS BENDTZEN. Induction of Antigen-Specific Lymphocyte Unresponsiveness *in Vitro*: Possible Role of Divalent Cations and Defective Function of Human T Cell Activating Factor (TAF). (Received 9/8/81; accepted 10/21/81).

MASROOR A. BAIG AND AFTAB A. ANSARI. Studies of Mouse Immunoglobulin Allotypes by Reverse Plaque Assay: Detection of Spleen Cells Secreting Immunoglobulins with Specific Allotype in C57BL/6J Mice (Received 9/28/81; accepted 10/23/81).

ROBERT K. SHOCKLEY AND RAPHAEL KLEINMAN. Bacteria-Immune System Interactions. III. Isolation of a *Bacillus globigii* Cell Wall Component Involved in Binding to Human Lymphocytes. (Received 9/15/81; accepted 10/25/81).

EUGENIA HAWRYLKO. Tumor Bearer T Cells Suppress BCG-Potentiated Antitumor Responses. I. Requirements for Their Effect. (Received 8/21/81; accepted 10/27/81).

EUGENIA HAWRYLKO, CAROL ANN MELE, AND OSIAS STUTMAN. Tumor Bearer T Cells Suppress BCG-Potentiated Antitumor Responses. II. Characteristics of the Efferent Phase Suppressor. (Received 8/21/81; accepted 10/27/81).

THELMA A. KOPPI AND W. J. HALLIDAY. Further Characterization of the Cells Involved in Leukocyte Adherence Inhibition with Murine Tumor Extracts. (Received 8/26/81; accepted 10/27/81).

RICHARD F. MORTENSEN. Inhibition of the Polyclonal Antibody Plaque Forming Cell Response of Human B-Lymphocytes by C-Reactive Protein (CRP) and CRP-Complexes. (Received 8/6/81; accepted 10/29/81).

NOAH ISAKOV, MICHAEL FELDMAN, AND SHRAGA SEGAL. Acute Infection of Mice with Lactic Dehydrogenase Virus (LDV) Impairs the Antigen-Presenting Capacity of Their Macrophages. (Received 8/26/81; accepted 10/29/81).

CHRISTOPHER J. FROELICH, ANNA S. TAI, ARTHUR D. BANKHURST, AND NOEL L. WARNER. Human E-Rosette Positive Cells Which Bind Monomeric IgG Mediate Natural Cytotoxicity. (Received 7/21/81; accepted 10/31/81).

C. Y. LAU, E. Y. WANG, AND G. GOLDSTEIN. Studies of Thymopoietin Pentapeptide (TP5) on Experimental Tumors. I. TP5 Relieves Immunosuppression in Tumor Bearing Mice. (Received 6/23/81; accepted 10/31/81).

AH-KAU NG, YU-HUI ZHANG, CARLO RUSSO, AND SOLDANO FERRONE. Immunochemical and Functional Analysis of Ia-like Antigens on Human Monocyte-Macrophages with Monoclonal Antibodies. (Received 7/16/81; accepted 10/31/81).

MICHIO OHTA, IZUMI NAKASHIMA, AND NOBUO KATO. Adjuvant Action of Bacterial Lipopolysaccharide in Induction of Delayed Type Hypersensitivity to Protein Antigens. I. Action of the O3 Antigen of Klebsiella Extracted from Culture Fluid (Received 8/13/81; accepted 10/31/81).

HEINZ G. REMOLD AND ALMA D. MEDNIS. The Effect of Tunicamycin on the Molecular Heterogeneity of Guinea Pig Migration Inhibitory Factor. (Received 10/21/81; accepted 11/3/81).

JEAN-LUC TEILLAUD, CÉCILE GOUJET-ZALC, MARC FONTAINE, COLETTE BRAUN, AND GUY MAHOUY. Involvement of Human Membrane-Associated Complement Components in the Rosette Formation between Marmoset Red Blood Cells and Human Leukocytes. (Received 7/15/81; accepted 10/28/81).

JIUAN J. LIU, MARIANGELA SEGRE, AND DIEGO SEGRE. Changes in Suppressor, Helper, and B-Cell Functions in Aging Mice. (Received 10/5/81; accepted 10/28/81).

MICHAEL L. MISFELDT AND EDGAR E. HANNA. Suppressor T-Cell Hybridomas That Exhibit Various Capacities to Negatively Regulate PFC Responses in a T-Cell Dependent Mouse Model. (Received 6/2/81; accepted 11/3/81).

ROBERTA H. MEYERS-ELLIOTT AND HUMPHREY L. SUMNER. Experimental Uveitis Induced by Products of Activated Lymphocytes: Intraocular Effects of Rhodopsin-Induced Lymphokines. (Received 7/13/81; accepted 11/3/81).

TETSUFUMI INOUE AND LOUISE T. ADLER. Selective Suppressive Effects of Antiallotype Antibodies on Spleen Cells of Adult Rabbits. I. (Received 8/13/81; accepted 11/3/81).

TETSUFUMI INOUE, LOUISE T. ADLER, AKIO YAMADA, AND FRANK L. ADLER. Comparative Suppressive Effects of Antiallotype Antibodies on Spleen Cells of Immature and Adult Rabbits. II. (Received 8/13/81; accepted 11/4/81).

MARTINE PAPIERNIK AND LILIANE LAROCHE. Thymic Medullary Lymphocytes.

I. Lymphokines Produced by Thymic Medullary Lymphocytes as a Second Signal for Intrathymic Stem Cell Homing. (Received 6/15/81; accepted 11/5/81).

RONALD L. WHISLER, KATHY BAKENHASTER, AND E. MITCHEL OPREMCAK. Autologous Mechanisms Generating Natural Killer Activity within Human Peripheral Lymphocytes Depleted of NK Target Binding Cells. (Received 9/17/81; accepted 11/11/81).

DOMINIQUE KAISERLIAN AND MIREILLE DARDENNE. Studies on the Mechanisms of the Inhibitory Effects of FTS on Murine Allograft Immunity. (Received 10/6/81; accepted 11/11/81).

JONATHAN W. UHR. Effect of Toxin–Antibody Conjugates on Tumor Cells.

MATTHEW D. SCHARFF. Somatic Cell Genetics of Immunoglobulin Production.

GREGORY W. SISKIND, A. FAYE SCHRATER, G. JEANETTE THORBECKE, MARC E. WEKSLER, AND EDMOND A. GOIDL. The Role of Auto-anti-idiotype Antibody in the Regulation of the Immune Response. (Received 11/8/80).

YONA KEISARI. Macrophage-Mediated Cytolysis of Erythrocytes in the Guinea Pig: II. Role of Oxidative Burst Products in Macrophage Cytotoxicity Activated by Lectins and Phorbol Ester Derivatives. (Received 6/16/81; accepted 11/21/81).

THOMAS J. ROGERS, LISA CAMPBELL, KENNETH CALHOUN, IRENE NOWOWIEJSKI, AND DAVID R. WEBB. Suppression of B-Cell and T-Cell Responses by the Prostaglandin-Induced T-Cell-Derived Suppressor (PITS). I. Analysis of the $PITS_\beta$ Factor. (Received 8/3/81; accepted 11/21/81).

M. MARGARET KEMENY AND PAUL H. SUGARBAKER. Adoptive Transfer of Cells Sensitized *in Vitro* into Mice in a Skin Allograft Assay. (Received 10/15/81; accepted 11/21/81).

JANET K. YAMAMOTO, WILLIAM L. FARRAR, AND HOWARD M. JOHNSON. Interleukin 2 Regulation of Mitogen Induction of Immune Interferon (IFNγ) in Spleen Cells and Thymocytes. (Received 9/16/81; accepted 11/21/81).

BERTIE F. ARGYRIS. Nature of Neonatal Splenic Suppressor Cells in the Mouse. (Received 10/2/81; accepted 11/21/81).

WERNER ROSENAU AND GERTRUDE BURKE. Lymphotoxin-Induced Changes in Target-Cell Plasma-Membrane Protein: Enhancement of Synthesis and Content. (Received 10/6/81; accepted 11/21/81).

ASTRID FAGRAEUS, ANNEKA EHRNST, EVA KLEIN, MANUEL PATARROYO, AND GIDEON GOLDSTEIN. Characterization of Blood Mononuclear Cells Reacting with K 562 Cells after Yellow Fever Vaccination. (Received 10/30/81; accepted 11/21/81).

JOSEPHINE H. COX AND W. L. FORD. The Migration of Lymphocytes across Specialized Vascular Endothelium. IV. Prednisolone Acts at Several Points on the Recirculation Pathways of Lymphocytes. (Received 11/4/81; accepted 11/23/81).

SHARYN M. WALKER AND WILLIAM O. WEIGLE. Effect of Bacterial Lipopolysaccharide on the *in Vitro* Secondary Antibody Response in Mice. II. Abrogation of the Suppressive Capacity of Endotoxin. (Received 9/28/81; accepted 11/30/81).

REGINALD M. GORCZYNSKI AND SUSANNAH MACRAE. Analysis of Subpopulations of Glass-Adherent Mouse Skin Cells Controlling Resistance/Susceptibility to Infection with *Leishmania tropica* and Correlation with the Development of Independent Proliferative Signals to Lyt-1^+/Lyt-2^+ T Lymphocytes. (Received 6/17/81; accepted 11/30/81).

NICKOLAOS D. TSAKALOS, THEOHARIS C. THEOHARIDES, SANDRA KRAEUTER KOPS, JOHN M. DWYER, AND PHILIP W. ASKENASE. Dialyzable Leukocyte Extract Induces Mast Cell Secretion. (Received 6/19/81; accepted 11/30/81).

MATTHEW R. DUNCAN, JOHN R. SADLIK, AND JOHN W. HADDEN. Glucocorticoid Modulation of Lymphokine-Induced Macrophage Proliferation. (Received 10/7/81; accepted 12/1/81).

L. E. WALLACE, A. B. RICKINSON, M. ROWE, D. J. MOSS, D. J. ALLEN, AND M. A. EPSTEIN. Stimulation of Human Lymphocytes with Irradiated Cells of the Autologous Epstein–Barr Virus-Transformed Cell Line. I. Virus-Specific and Nonspecific Components of the Cytotoxic Response. (Received 9/29/81; accepted 12/2/81).

D. J. ALLEN, A. B. RICKINSON, L. E. WALLACE, M. ROWE, D. J. MOSS, AND M. A. EPSTEIN. Stimulation of Human Lymphocytes with Irradiated Cells of the Autologous Epstein–Barr Virus-Transformed Cell Line. II. Cytotoxic Response to Repeated Stimulation. (Received 9/29/81; accepted 12/2/81).

JUDITH A. OWEN, MICHELE ALLOUCHE, AND PETER C. DOHERTY. Limiting Dilution Analysis of the Specificity of Influenza-Immune Cytotoxic T Cells. (Received 11/3/81; accepted 12/3/81).

PATRICIO ESQUIVEL, MARIANELA MENA, AND HUGO FOLCH. Suppression of Autoimmune Thyroiditis by Phytohemagglutinin. (Received 9/8/81; accepted 12/4/81).

RONALD B. HERBERMAN, JOHN R. ORTALDO, ALBERTO MANTOVANI, DONNA S. HOBBS, HSIANG-FU KUNG, AND SIDNEY PESTKA. Effect of Human Recombinant Interferon on Cytotoxic Activity of Natural Killer (NK) Cells and Monocytes. (Received 9/16/81; accepted 12/5/81).

J. KONOWALCHUK, J. I. SPEIRS, AND L. PERELMUTTER. Immunoglobulin Properties of Epstein–Barr Virus-Transformed Human Umbilical Cord and Adult Peripheral Blood Lymphocytes. (Received 10/7/81; accepted 12/5/81).

SEYMOUR I. SCHLAGER. Relationship between Cell-Mediated and Humoral Immune Attack on Tumor Cells. II. The Role of Cellular Lipid Metabolism and Cell Surface Charge in the Outcome of Immune Attack. (Received 8/18/81; accepted 12/5/81).

JANET H. RANSOM, JOHN O. RUNDELL, JEFFREY A. HEINBAUGH, AND CHARLES H. EVANS. Biological and Physicochemical Characterization of Keyhole Limpet Hemocyanin-Induced Guinea Pig Lymphotoxin. (Received 8/24/81; accepted 12/5/81).

MORTON J. COWAN, MARK FRAGA, JULIA ANDREW, NATASHA LAMÉRIS-MARTIN, AND ARTHUR J. AMMANN. Purine Salvage Pathway Enzyme Activities in Human T, B and Null Lymphocyte Populations. (Received 9/25/81; accepted 12/5/81).

RANDALL W. BARTON. The Binding of *Maclura pomifera* Lectin to Cells of the T Lymphocyte Lineage in the Rat. (Received 8/25/81; accepted 12/6/81).

Author Index for Volume 65

A

Adler, William H., 115
Åman, Pierre, 307
Allen, Elizabeth M., 211
Azar, Yehudith, 194

B

Balk, Steven P., 201
Balow, James E., 221
Ben-Sasson, Shilomo Zalman, 194
Bocchieri, Maureen H., 142
Boorman, Gary A., 131
Brodt, Pnina, 20
Brooks, William H., 103
Burton, Pamela, 1
Busby, Barbara E. T., 280

C

Campbell, Lucilla, 131
Campbell, Rita J., 152
Carayanniotis, George, 352
Castagna, Monique, 258
Chapman-Alexander, Judith, 84
Chisari, Francis V., 325
Chriqui, Evelyne, 194
Curtis, Jill, 93
Curtiss, Linda K., 325

D

Dean, Jack H., 131
Debre, Patrice, 317
Doherty, Peter C., 33
Dráber, Petr, 180
Duprez, Véronique, 317

E

Eidelsztein, Paula, 194

F

Francis, Mary Kay, 230

G

Good, Robert A., 1
Goodman, Michael G., 337
Gordon, Julius, 20
Green, Bridget, 366

H

Hall, Kerstin, 307
Halloran, Philip F., 352
Huang, Jyh Hsiung, 43

I

Ikehara, Susumu, 1

J

Jacobson, Ethel B., 84
James, Stephanie L., 75

K

Katz, Irene R., 84
Katz-Gross, Aviva, 194
Kawaguchi, Susumu, 293
Kedar, Eli, 194
Kim, Byung S., 373
Kisielow, Paweł, 180
Klein, George, 307
Kolb, Jean-Pierre B., 258
Korngold, Robert, 33
Krolick, Keith A., 166, 175

L

Labine, Margaret, 75
Lamon, Eddie W., 272
Lauer, Lloyd D., 131
Lawson, Lela D., 131
Le, Junming, 1
Lerman, Stephen P., 84
Levy, Jean-Paul, 317
Lieu, Hien, 13
Luebke, Robert W., 131
Lundin, Gunnel, 307
Luster, Michael I., 131

M

Matheson, David S., 366
Meltzer, Monte S., 52
Mescher, Matthew F., 201
Moore, Vernon L., 211

N

Nakamura, Reiko M., 52
Narayanan, R. B., 93

O

Ovadia, Haim, 66, 380

P

Pahwa, Rajendra, 1
Paterson, Philip Y., 66, 380
Pollok, Brian A., 272

R

Rader, John, 131
Ripani, Linda M., 211
Roberson, Bob S., 280
Rola-Pleszczynski, Marek, 13
Roszman, Thomas L., 103

S

Santoli, Daniela, 230
Saxena, Queen B., 115
Saxena, Rajiv K., 115
Schrier, Denis J., 211
Senik, Anna, 258
Sercarz, Eli E., 166, 175
Sheil, James M., 103
Sher, Alan, 75
Smith, J. Bruce, 142
Smith, James W., 152
Sopori, Mohan L., 103
Sternick, John L., 211
Szewczuk, Myron R., 152

T

Tan, Y. H., 366
Thorbecke, G. Jeanette, 84
Trucco, Massimo, 230
Tseng, Jeenan, 247
Tsokos, George C., 221
Turk, John L., 93

W

Wang, Sharon, 43
Wang, Soo Ray, 43
Weigle, William O., 337
White, Abraham, 1
Wilson, Ralph E., 131
Wolos, Jeffrey A., 142

Y

Yefenof, Eitan, 194

CELLULAR IMMUNOLOGY **65,** 391–435 (1981)

Cumulative Subject Index[1]

Volumes 57–65

A

Abortion
induction by anti-trophoblast serum (rat), **62,** 271
Accessory cells
Ia-positive macrophages for induction of tumor-specific cytotoxic T cells *in vitro* (mouse), **62,** 425
interactions with mouse T cells in concanavalin A-induced proliferation, species restriction (mouse species and strains, guinea pig), **57,** 28
major histocompatibility complex-compatible nude splenocyte in cytotoxic T-cell generation (mouse), **62,** 385
Acetylesterase
polymorphism in monocytes, comparison with that of peritoneal and alveolar macrophages (human), **63,** 400
Acid esterase, *see* Acetylesterase
Adenosine
induction of Fcγ receptors on theophylline-resistant T cells (human), **57,** 455
Adenosine deaminase
deficiency, prevention of T-cell growth factor production by immunocompetent thymocytes and splenic T cells (rat), **63,** 81
2′-deoxycoformycin inhibition in lymphoid organs and erythrocytes (mouse), **63,** 259
Adenosine deaminase inhibitors
effects on thymocyte and splenocyte response to various mitogens (mouse), **64,** 29
Adenylate cyclase
macrophage, activation by stimulants of oxidative burst and by arachidonic acid, two mechanisms (guinea pig), **61,** 90
Adherent cells
requirement in
interleukin 2 production by activated T cells (human), **63,** 71
pokeweed mitogen-induced suppression of natural killer activity in mixed lymphocyte culture (human), **58,** 356
splenocytes
from *Bacillus Calmette–Guerin*-injected B6 mouse, production of suppressor factor *in vitro*, **58,** 61
as effector cells in antibody-dependent cell-mediated cytotoxicity in agammaglobulinemia (chicken), **64,** 258
suppressor cells generated in culture, assay with anti-Thy-1.2 serum (mouse), **64,** 371
from tumor-bearing mouse, suppression of mixed lymphocyte culture responses, **60,** 109
from uv-irradiated mouse, Ia-bearing cell depletion, **63,** 300
suppressor activity in coccidiodomycosis (human), **64,** 235
T cells
DNP-polyacrylamide bead-induced suppressor activity (mouse), **64,** 44
to histamine conjugated albumin, suppression of IgG response to sheep erythrocytes (BALB/c mouse), **59,** 171
role in regulation of cytotoxic T-cell responses to alloantigens (rat), **65,** 103
Adjuvant activity
of muramyl dipeptide and its analogs in monokine production stimulation by peritoneal macrophages (guinea pig), **64,** 73
polyclonal lymphocyte activators, promotion of antigen retention at site of injection and in lymph node (mouse), **57,** 477
role in tolerance induction by low doses of bovine γ globulin (mouse), **64,** 350
Advances in Immunology
Meeting in honor of Sir Peter Medawar at Royal Society (London, July 18, 1980, England), **62,** 233–310
Agammaglobulinemia
antibody-dependent cell-mediated cytotoxicity (chicken), **64,** 258

[1] Boldface numbers indicate appropriate volume; lightface numbers indicate pagination.

specific cytotoxic T cells and macrophages in spleen (chicken), **64,** 246
Aging
autologous proliferative response increase in peripheral blood lymphocytes (human), **60,** 212
B-cell and T-cell reactivity changes in Fc fragment-mediated polyclonal antibody response (mouse), **63,** 16
cytotoxic response decline due to decrease of functional T-cell number (mouse), **60,** 470
effect on null cell compartment in spleen (mouse), **63,** 106
terminal deoxynucleotidyl transferase activity decline in thymus and bone marrow (human, mouse), **58,** 39
Alloantibodies
splenocyte cytotoxicity activation by anti-H-2 antiserum (mouse), **63,** 28
Alloantigens
BL/6, cell-mediated immune response to, effect of hyperimmunization (mouse), **57,** 114
cytotoxic T-cell response to
induction in bone marrow cells *in vitro* (mouse), **61,** 154
regulation by Ia^+ cells (mouse), **62,** 82
role of adherent T-cell subpopulation (rat), **65,** 103
expression on bone marrow-derived and peritoneal macrophages, serological analysis (mouse), **59,** 151
Allogeneic effect
enhancement of cytotoxicity induction in mixed lymphocyte culture by splenocytes as third-party cells (mouse), **59,** 61
Allograft
heart, survival after priming with
parenchymal cells and passenger leukocytes from kidney (rat), **57,** 92
splenocyte populations (rat), **57,** 85
Alloimmunity
induction by transplantation antigen expressed on trophoblasts (mouse), **64,** 162
Alloimmunization
with tumor cells, challenge dose effects on direct and lectin-dependent cell-mediated cytotoxicity induction (mouse), **61,** 253
Alloreactivity
of T cells, theoretical considerations and probability model, **57,** 251
Allotype suppression
for IgA, cellular implication for IgA preponderance in gut (mouse), **65,** 247
Angiogenesis
lymphocyte-induced, Lyt phenotype analysis of effector cells (mouse), **63,** 272
Animals
annelids (*Glycera Sp-C*), **59,** 161
chicken, **64,** 246, 258
echinoderms
Asterias rubens, **57,** 136
Pisaster gigantus, **59,** 161
guinea pig, **57,** 28; **58,** 175, 238; **59,** 301; **60,** 220, 354, 367; **61,** 90, 134, 165; **62,** 28, 172; **63,** 1, 409; **64,** 73; **65,** 93
hamster, **57,** 209; **58,** 372
human, **57,** 1, 145, 307, 400, 440, 455, 529; **58,** 10, 39, 97, 134, 246, 269, 323, 356, 366, 415, 426, 464; **59,** 17, 26, 75, 82, 187, 205, 256, 268, 345, 392, 435; **60,** 43, 144, 191, 212, 240, 298, 324, 393, 403, 415, 440, 480, 489; **61,** 11, 213, 231, 265, 273, 332, 453; **62,** 140, 220, 277, 301, 367, 406; **63,** 71, 91, 134, 143, 164, 237, 362, 374, 400; **64,** 20, 84, 131, 220, 227, 235, 267, 277, 304, 312, 324, 337; **65,** 13, 43, 115, 221, 230, 307, 325, 366
invertebrates, **58,** 333
marmosets, **57,** 408
mollusks
Megathura crenulata, **59,** 161; **60,** 240
mouse, **57,** 13, 20, 28, 51, 62, 73, 99, 114, 124, 183, 219, 229, 237, 265, 293, 316, 327, 339, 348, 361, 370, 377, 389, 427, 468, 477, 495, 505, 517; **58,** 1, 9, 39, 49, 61, 72, 85, 107, 124, 134, 147, 156, 165, 188, 202, 209, 225, 257, 277, 286, 293, 302, 333, 345, 385, 398, 458; **59,** 1, 10, 54, 61, 97, 115, 127, 138, 171, 181, 219, 233, 246, 276, 289, 319, 330, 355, 378, 392, 411, 419, 429, 448; **60,** 1, 11, 34, 50, 64, 77, 91, 100, 109, 119, 136, 144, 155, 203, 228, 234, 251, 287, 308, 314, 335, 347, 376, 386, 426, 453, 470; **61,** 22, 32, 40, 52, 62, 78, 104, 114, 124, 134, 141, 154, 176, 190, 200, 220, 245, 253, 280, 292, 300, 319, 343, 365, 375, 386, 397, 404, 416, 448; **62,** 1, 8, 38, 60, 74, 82, 93, 101, 110, 119, 132, 149, 164, 186, 196, 205, 247, 251, 264, 287, 313, 324, 334, 341, 350, 377, 385, 396, 412, 425, 436, 448; **63,** 16, 28, 42, 106, 118, 134, 164, 177, 188, 193, 198, 203, 210, 221, 228, 249, 259, 272, 279, 300, 308, 321, 335, 349, 385, 417; **64,** 1, 13, 29, 44, 53, 64, 93, 102, 119, 144, 150, 162, 177, 187, 203, 293, 350, 371; **65,** 1, 20, 33, 52, 75, 84, 115, 131, 142, 152, 166, 175, 180, 194, 201, 247, 258, 272, 280, 293, 317, 337, 352, 373
pig, **57,** 175; **58,** 134
rabbit, **58,** 134, 436, 448; **60,** 498; **61,** 307; **62,** 60; **63,** 164; **64,** 359
rat, **57,** 42, 85, 92, 155, 281, 486, 524; **58,** 29, 312; **59,** 42, 289, 367; **60,** 24, 168, 181, 261, 274, 480; **61,** 1; **62,** 15, 50, 156, 271, 293; **63,** 57, 81, 221, 293, 329, 362; **65,** 66, 103, 380

Antibodies
active enhancement of allografted tumor, synergy *in vitro* and *in vivo* with suppressor cells (mouse), **58,** 107
affinity in plasmacytoma-bearing mouse, evidence for abnormality in B-cell differentiation, **62,** 149
anti-H-2, selective augmenting effect on murine splenocyte natural killer activity toward K562 cells, **65,** 115
anti-hapten, production suppression by conjugates of haptens and isologous gamma globulins (mouse), **58,** 385
anti-interferon, lack of effect on natural killer activity of peripheral blood lymphocytes (human), **62,** 220
anti-tetanus, spontaneous and mitogen-reactive production by B cells, inhibition after repetitive immunization with tetanus toxoid (human), **59,** 82
anti-TNP, effect on cell-mediated cytotoxicity against syngeneic tumors (mouse), **59,** 330
autoantibodies, *see* Autoantibodies
capping induction in T-lymphoma cells, enhancement by increase of cAMP intracellular level (mouse), **61,** 397
to DNP-Ascaris conjugates, production correlation with delayed hypersensitivity (rat), **58,** 312
to endogenous AKR-murine leukemia virus, inhibition of antigen-induced T-cell proliferation (mouse), **64,** 102
heterologous anti-μ, induction of Fc-dependent isotype suppression (mouse), **62,** 1
heterophile, formation *in vitro* by tonsilar lymphocytes, allogeneic stimulation (human), **58,** 246
to HLA-DR
ability to block herpes simplex virus antigen-induced lymphocyte proliferation (human), **61,** 11
effects of Fc-receptor-mediated functions of peripheral blood lymphocytes (human), **59,** 187
to IgM
B-cell suppression induction (C3H/St mouse), **61,** 404
proliferation response induction in B-cell subpopulations, macrophage requirement (mouse), **62,** 324
to L cells, in study of cytochalasin B effect on calcium uptake by L cells, **61,** 62
to β_2-microglobulin, effects on different Fc-receptor-mediated functions of peripheral blood lymphocytes (human), **59,** 187
monoclonal
to Ia antigen, T-cell subpopulation analysis from peripheral blood (human), **64,** 277
OKT3 specific to human T cells, interferon γ induction in peripheral blood lymphocytes (human), **64,** 304
Q5/13, recognition of HLA-DR antigen on mitogenic factor released by pokeweed mitogen-stimulated T cells (human), **62,** 406
production
antigen-specific enhancing factors in serum (mouse), **60,** 64, 77
from peripheral blood lymphocytes using tetanus toxoid as antigen, radioimmunoassay (human), **75,** 201
secretory IgA, synergism with IgG in promoting antibody-dependent cell-mediated cytotoxicity in neutrophils, monocytes, and lymphocytes (human), **59,** 75
Antibody-dependent cell-mediated cytotoxicity
in agammaglobulinemia, splenocyte subpopulation as effector cells (chicken), **64,** 258
killer cell fraction of thymocytes
obtained by isokinetic density centrifugation (mouse), **57,** 517
Thy 1 and Lyt antigen expression on (mouse), **65,** 272
peripheral blood lymphocytes enriched for subpopulations isolated from natural killer–tumor cell conjugates (human), **58,** 415
peripheral blood lymphocytes, monocytes, and neutrophils, promotion by secretory IgA antibodies synergising with IgG (human), **59,** 75
peritoneal macrophages activated by thioglycollate and *Bacillus Calmette-Guerin* (mouse), **57,** 51
sera from patients with malignant melanoma against autologous melanoma cells, role of effector cells, **64,** 119
splenocytes, inhibition by antiserum raised in rabbit against mouse brain (mouse), **59,** 419
tumor cell killing more efficient in macrophages than in monocytes (rabbit), **64,** 359
Antibody response
antigen-specific in B cells, synergy between soluble sheep erythrocyte antigen and pokeweed mitogen (human), **60,** 415
by B hybridoma line, direct regulation by concanavalin A-induced suppressor cells (mouse), **61,** 300
to DNP, depression by DNP-bovine γ-globulin in splenocytes culture (mouse), **64,** 44
to equine erythrocytes in peripheral blood lymphocytes, effect of human leukocyte interferon (human), **58,** 464
Fc fragment-mediated polyclonal, in assay of B-cell, T-cell, and macrophage reactivity in aging (mouse), **63,** 16
persistent IgE formation, participation of long-lived radioresistant antibody-forming splenocytes (mouse), **58,** 188

to pokeweed mitogen
by B cells, human interferon α effect (human), **64,** 20
in tonsillar lymphocytes, enhancement by soluble sheep erythrocyte antigens (human), **61,** 265
in schistosomiasis
to circarial and egg immunogens by B cells from various lymphoid organs (mouse), **59,** 233, 246
to schistosomula in mouse strains after vaccination, **65,** 75
to sheep erythrocytes
in vitro, inhibition by sodium periodate, reversal by borohydride and hydroxylamine (mouse splenocytes), **59,** 10
in vivo, enhancement by anti-IgD antiserum (rat), **63,** 293
to synthetic antigens, induction *in vitro* in splenocytes and lymph node cells (guinea pig), **60,** 354
to T-cell-dependent and -independent antigens by splenocytes, suppression by lactoferrin (mouse), **63,** 308
to T-dependent antigens, impairment in C3H/HeJ strain (mouse), **59,** 1
to trinitrophenyl-lipopolysaccharide, T- and B-cell function in marmoset species (*Saguinus fuscicollis, S. oedipus oedipus*), **57,** 408
Antigens
for antibody-dependent cell-mediated cytotoxicity effector cells, recognition on thymocytes, splenocytes, and neural cell line (mouse), **59,** 419
associative recognition in antigen-specific immune regulation (review), **61,** 425
bacterial, proliferative responses of cord blood lymphocytes to (human neonates), **57,** 307
from bacteriophage T2, tolerogenic and immunogenic activity amplification by binding to rabbit lymphocytes, **58,** 436, 448
cell surface
in bone marrow cell populations separated by density gradient electrophoresis (human), **59,** 345
in cleavage embryo, comparison with teratocarcinomas (mouse), **62,** 247
effects of interferon type I and type II on expression on thymocytes (mouse), **57,** 427
expression changes in thymocytes during leukemogenesis (AKR mouse), **59,** 355
lack of abnormalities in expression on lymphocytes in dystrophic mice, **59,** 138
in thymocytes maturated *in vitro*, comparison with peripheral T-cell phenotype (mouse), **57,** 237
comparative study of splenic natural killer cells and prothymocytes, distinction (mouse), **62,** 164
cross-reactivity in F-9 tumor cells and testicular cells in suppressor cell stimulation (F-9 tumor-bearing mouse), **62,** 341
different regions in human fibrinopeptide B, guinea pig T-cell response to, **58,** 238
Epstein–Barr virus
induction of cytotoxic T-cell polyclonal activation (human), **63,** 91
nuclear, inhibition of leukocyte migration (human), **58,** 269
Fraction la of bovine serum albumin, suppression of IgG immune response to intact antigen, effect of conjugation with gamma globulin (mouse), **59,** 392
H-2 (murine histocompatibility)
differential effect on T cells in graft-versus-host and host-versus-graft reactions after allogeneic splenocyte transplantation, **57,** 389
expression decrease following acute measles virus infection (neuroblastoma cell line), **59,** 319
H-2K and H-2D on anti-hapten cytotoxic T cells, role in TNP recognition, **58,** 147
H-$2K^k$ glycoprotein incorporated into lipid vesicles, molecular requirements for cytotoxic T-cell response to, **61,** 365
incorporated into phospholipid vesicles, specific interaction with allogeneic cytotoxic T cells, **63,** 42
incorporated into subcellular fractions, inability to elicit primary anti-H-2 cytotoxic T cells, **58,** 277
interpretation using allospecific T-cell assay (review), **62,** 258
as target for T-cell subsets synergizing in graft-versus-host reaction, **59,** 115
on thymocyte surface, effects of type I and type II murine interferons, **57,** 420
Hh (Hemopoietic histocompatibility)
determinants recognized on lymph node cells and bone marrow cells grafted into irradiated mice (NZB strain and hybrids), **59,** 378
histocompatibility
antigenic differences from tumor-associated fetal antigens (rat), **60,** 274
interactions with tumor-associated fetal antigens (rat), **60,** 261
HLA (human histocompatibility)
on lymphoblastoid B-cell line, connection with susceptibility to cytotoxic T cells (human), **59,** 435
role in clinical kidney transplantation (human), **62,** 277

HLA-DR
in monocyte–macrophage presentation of herpes simplex virus antigen to T cells (human), **61,** 11
recognition on mitogenic factor released by pokeweed mitogen-stimulated T cells by monoclonal antibodies Q5/13 (human), **62,** 406
in T-cell activation in mixed lymphocyte culture (human), **63,** 143
human monocyte–macrophage system, recognition by rabbit antisera, **59,** 392
H-Y
male-specific, causes of T-cell unresponsiveness to (mouse), **62,** 251
recognition by cytotoxic T cells in presence of helper T cells (mouse), **60,** 347
Ia
in active and late rosette-forming T cells (human), **64,** 227
-bearing Langerhans cells, effects of uv and drugs (murine epidermis), **60,** 50
-bearing macrophages, as accessory cells for induction of tumor-specific cytotoxic T cells (mouse), **62,** 425
-bearing T-cell suppressor factor induced during pregnancy (mouse), **62,** 186
expression on subset of Peyer's patch T cells (mouse), **57,** 420
Ia^k, enhancement of anti-H-2 cytotoxic T cell elicitation by $H\text{-}2K^k$ glycoprotein (mouse), **61,** 365
recognition by T cells in response to concanavalin A, role of accessory splenocytes (mouse), **57,** 28
on splenocytes regulating cytotoxic T-cell response to alloantigens and TNP-modified self-antigens (mouse), **62,** 82
stimulation of autologous mixed lymphocyte interactions (mouse), **65,** 142
on T-cell hybrids, relationship with Fc receptors for IgG (mouse), **63,** 349
on T-cell subpopulations from peripheral blood, coexpression with OKM1 antigen (human), **64,** 277
I-EC-encoded, stimulation of secondary autologous mixed lymphocyte interactions (mouse), **65,** 142
induction *in vivo* of enhancing factors for antibody production (mouse), **60,** 64, 77
Ly, in peanut agglutinin-binding and nonbinding thymocytes localized in peripheral lymphoid system (mouse), **60,** 228
Ly-1 on splenic T cells initiating tumor rejection (mouse), **60,** 34
Ly-2 on suppressor T-cell population induced by histamine (mouse), **62,** 396
Ly-6.2 from lymphoid cells, molecular characterization (mouse), **64,** 187
Lyt
phenotype analysis of splenocytes responsible for angiogenesis induction (mouse), **63,** 272
phenotypic differences in two T-cell subsets induced during Sendai virus infection (mouse), **62,** 38
on thymic killer cells (mouse), **65,** 272
on thymocytes in presence of interleukin 2, concanavalin A effects (mouse), **65,** 180
Lyt-1 in radioresistant peanut aggulinin-binding T cells (mouse), **62,** 74
Lyt-1,2, on helper T cells, connection with migration inhibitory factor production (mouse), **59,** 448
Lyt-2,2, on suppressor T cells, connection with migration stimulatory factor production (mouse), **59,** 448
macrophage-bound ovalbumin, effects on educated T-cell helper activity (mouse), **61,** 104
mode of presentation for induction of T-cell subpopulations mediating delayed hypersensitivity to Sendai virus (mouse), **63,** 188
mononuclear phagocyte-associated, lymphokine-induced expression in macrophage cell line U937 (human), **62,** 140
murine differentiation 1, absence on splenocytes (CBA/N mouse), **60,** 386
murine leukemia virus, increased expression in thymocytes during leukemogenesis (AKR mouse), **59,** 355
myeloma cell-related, lymphocyte sensitization *in vitro* to (human), **60,** 489
naturally occurring environmental, effect on noradrenaline in lymphoid organs of specific pathogen-free or germ-free rats, **63,** 329
non-H-2 on mastocytoma P815 cells, differential responses of BALB/c F_1 hybrids *in vivo* to (mouse), **65,** 352
nude mouse pretreatment followed with T-cell administration, induction of antigen-specific suppressor cells in splenocytes, **61,** 245
OKM1, on T-cell subpopulations from peripheral blood, coexpression with Ia antigen (human), **64,** 277
OKT4, on autorosette-forming T-cell subpopulation from peripheral blood (human), **64,** 312
OKT8, on suppressor cells activated by histamine in peripheral blood lymphocytes (human), **64,** 324
to ovalbumin-primed lymph node cells, presentation by macrophage-enriched cells from Peyer's patch after preincubation with collagenase (mouse), **62,** 110

16p T-cell, expression on suppressor T cells, but not on helper T cells (human), **64,** 84
Qa-4 and Qa-5 on T-cell subpopulation, postnatal appearance and organ distribution (mouse), **57,** 265
self-related, helper T-cell specific response to (unprimed mouse), **57,** 316
sheep erythrocytes, *see* Scheep erythrocytes
specific cell-bound in lymph node cells haptenized *in vivo*, inhibition of sensitized T-cell migration (mouse), **57,** 361
synthetic, antibody response induction in splenocytes and lymph node cells (guinea pig), **60,** 354
T-dependent, low antibody response to (C3H/HeJ mouse), **59,** 1
theta, induction *in vivo* by prostaglandin E_2 synthetic analog in splenocytes (thymectomized mouse), **62,** 8
Thy-1
on killer cells from thymocyte subpopulation (mouse), **57,** 517; **65,** 272
prealbumin-induced expression on splenocytes in culture (mouse), **65,** 1
on splenic T cells initiating tumor rejection (mouse), **60,** 34
on splenocytes lacking Fc receptors and highly active in mixed lymphocyte reaction (nude *nu/nu* mouse), **57,** 339
T-independent
ontogeny of B-cell heterogenous antibody response to (mouse), **60,** 234
polyvinylpyrrolidone, coupled with syngeneic splenocytes, suppressor T-cell induction (mouse), **63,** 177
suppression of B-cell memory induction (mouse), **64,** 177
TL, expression on thymocytes in presence of interleukin 2, concanavalin 2 effects (mouse), **65,** 180
transplantation, expression on trophoblasts, detection by specific alloimmunity induction (mouse), **64,** 162
tumor-associated fetal
antigenic differences from histocompatibility antigens (rat), **60,** 274
interactions with histocompatibility antigens (rat), **60,** 261
suppression of mitogen- and tumor-cell-induced splenocyte stimulation (rat), **57,** 155
Antiserum
anti-activated T-cell, inhibition of lytic phase of murine T-cell-mediated alloimmune cytotoxicity, **59,** 289
anti-H-2, activation of splenocyte cytotoxicity, comparison with interferon and mitogen action (mouse), **63,** 28
anti-IgD, enhancement of primary antibody response (rat), **63,** 293
anti-lymphocyte
pretreatment simultaneously with parental strain lymphocytes, effects on graft-versus-host reaction in F_1 hybrid rat, **57,** 524
specific unresponsiveness induction to skin allograft, synergy with procarbazine hydrochloride (mouse), **62,** 254
anti-μ, neonatal administration, B-cell suppression induction (C3H/St mouse), **61,** 404
anti-Thy-1.2, analysis of suppressor cells generated in mixed lymphocyte culture (mouse), **64,** 371
anti-trophoblast, abortifacient activity (rat), **62,** 271
against human peritoneal macrophages, detection of monocyte-macrophage-associated antigen system, **59,** 392
against lymphokine-activated human macrophage cell line, detection of monocyte-macrophage-associated antigen system, **59,** 392
against mouse brain
inhibition of mouse splenocyte antibody-dependent cell-mediated cytotoxicity, **59,** 419
T-cell-specific mitogenic properties (rabbit), **62,** 60
Apolar fluorescent probe
monitoring ionophore- and lectin-induced lymphocyte activation (human, mouse, porcine, rabbit), **58,** 134
Arachidonic acid
analogs, inhibition of eosinophil chemotactic factor release from human neutrophils and rat mast cells, **60,** 480
macrophage cAMP elevation, role of prostaglandins (guinea pig), **61,** 90
oxidized by lipoxidase, inhibition of splenocyte mitogenic stimulation, role of cyclic nucleotide level changes (mouse), **58,** 85
Arthritis
collagen-induced in rat, leukocyte inhibitory factor production by lymph node cells from, **63,** 362
ATPase
Na^+,K^+-activated, role in lithium ion effect on concanavalin A-induced lymphocyte stimulation (hamster), **58,** 372
Autoantibodies
anti-idiotypic, immunoregulation *in vivo* by histamine (mouse), **65,** 152
natural cytotoxic against thymocytes, T-cell suppression in spontaneously hypertensive rat, **60,** 181
suppression by splenocytes from mouse primed with rat erythrocytes, role of thymus (mouse), **63,** 221
Autoimmune disease
spontaneous in NZB mice

heightened excitability of B cells to triggering stimuli, **63,** 385
high capacity of lymphocytes to induce graft-versus-host reaction in allogeneic irradiated adult mouse, **58,** 124
Axial organ cells
tritiated thymidine incorporation, effect of various mitogens *in vitro* (starfish), **57,** 136

B

Background plaque-forming cells
maturation *in vitro* from splenocytes in absence of T cells, macrophages, and serum factors (mouse), **57,** 13
Bacteria
Bacillus Calmette–Guerin
killed, induction of
interferon type II release (mouse), **60,** 100
pulmonary granulomatous inflammation and splenomegaly, role of T cells (mouse), **65,** 211
suppressor factor production by adherent splenocytes from injected B6 mouse, **58,** 61
viable
peritoneal macrophage activation (mouse), **57,** 51; **60,** 91
synergistic effect with muramyl dipeptide in natural killer activity increase (mouse), **62,** 101
T-cell-independent activation of peritoneal macrophages in sarcoma-180-bearing mouse, **57,** 293
Bacillus subtilis
binding to B and T cells from peripheral blood, role of monosaccharides (human), **58,** 19
Brucella melitensis
binding chiefly to B cells from peripheral blood, role of monosaccharides (human), **58,** 19
Corynebacterium parvum
-activated peritoneal macrophages, inhibition of macrophage-activating factor production by splenocytes (mouse), **63,** 279
induction of interferons in splenocyte culture (mouse), **64,** 64
intravenously injected, induction of splenic suppressor T cells and macrophages in alloimmunized mouse, **58,** 257
splenic suppressor macrophage activation (mouse), **64,** 150
vaccine-elicited peritoneal macrophages that mediate interferon-independent inhibition of herpes simplex virus (mouse), **58,** 72
Corynebacterium xerosis
binding to B and T cells from peripheral blood, role of monosaccharides (human), **58,** 19
Escherichia coli
binding to B and T cells from peripheral blood, role of monosaccharides (human), **58,** 19
Klebsiella pneumoniae
antibiotic-killed, proliferative response of cord blood lymphocytes to (human neonates), **57,** 307
Listeria monocytogenes
differential effects of acute and subchronic cyclophosphamide treatment on mouse resistance to, **65,** 131
infection of tumor-bearing mouse, T-cell-independent macrophage activation by viable *Bacillus Calmette–Guerin*, **57,** 293
Pseudomonas aeruginosa
antibiotic-killed, proliferative response of cord blood lymphocytes to (human neonates), **57,** 307
Staphylococcus albus
binding chiefly to B cells from peripheral blood, role of monosaccharides (human), **58,** 19
Staphylococcus aureus
antibiotic-killed, proliferative response of cord blood lymphocytes to (human neonates), **57,** 307
binding chiefly to B cells from peripheral blood, role of monosaccharides (human), **58,** 19
formalin-treated, induction of plaque-forming cell response in allogeneic mixed lymphocyte culture (human), **59,** 256
protein A, interferon II induction and natural killer activity augmentation in peripheral blood lymphocytes (human), **57,** 1
Bactericidal activity
peritoneal macrophages, T-cell-independent stimulation by *Bacillus Calmette–Guerin* in tumor-bearing mouse, **57,** 293
Bacteriophages
T2, antigen bound to rabbit lymphocytes, enhancement of tolerogenic and immunogenic activities, **58,** 436, 448
B cells
aging-induced defects in Fc fragment-mediated polyclonal antibody response (mouse), **63,** 16
antigen-specific response induction, synergy between soluble antigen and pokeweed mitogen (human), **60,** 415
anti-tetanus antibody synthesis, inhibition by repetitive immunization with tetanus toxoid (human), **59,** 82
-deprived mice, increase of anti-tumor cell-mediated cytotoxicity, role of natural killer cells, **65,** 20
heightened excitability to triggering stimuli in

NZB mice in comparison with other strains, **63,** 385
helper-cell-dependent increase in antibody production induced by specific and nonspecific T-cell stimulators (BALB/c mouse), **61,** 416
inactivation by antigen-specific suppressor cells induced by nude mouse pretreatment with antigen and T cells, **61,** 245
insulin-binding, comparison with lymphoid cell lines of B-cell origin (human), **65,** 307
interaction with T cells in mitogenic response to staphylococcal Protein A (rabbit), **61,** 307
lipopolysaccharide-induced response *in vitro*
in filtered splenocyte populations (mouse), **64,** 1
lack of changes in zinc deficiency (mouse), **60,** 203
requirement for cell interaction removed by dextran sulfate (mouse), **61,** 176
suppression in experimental African trypanosomiasis (athymic mouse), **63,** 210
maturational defect in plasmacytoma-bearing mouse, antibody affinity study, **62,** 149
mature virgin, tolerance induction by DNP-polysaccharide conjugate, receptor–ligand interactions (mouse), **62,** 196
memory, *see* Memory cells
ontogeny, heterogenous antibody response to T-independent antigen (mouse), **60,** 234
Peyer's patch, *see* Peyer's patches
plaque-forming cell response, *see* Plaque-forming cell response
pokeweed mitogen-induced response
IgG production, suppression by histamine and its analogs (human), **64,** 324
immunoglobulin synthesis, inhibition by suppressor T cells activated by lymphoblastoid cell lines (human), **60,** 191
interferon α effect on differentiation (human), **64,** 20
monocyte role in differentiation (human), **58,** 323
proliferation and differentiation, dissimilar dose–response relations (human), **61,** 332
stimulation by T-cell-released mitogenic factor (human), **62,** 406
responses to circarial and egg immunogens in schistosomiasis (mouse), **59,** 233, 246
splenic
autologous rosette formation and mitogenesis induction by lymphoid cell line supernatants (mouse), **60,** 1
differentiation suppression *in vitro* by protease inhibitor (mouse), **60,** 155
influenza A virus-induced homotypic and heterotypic immunity (mouse), **60,** 119
subpopulations
antigen-binding, successive changes in Ig classes expressed during primary immune response (mouse), **62,** 377
C3 receptor-bearing, lack in immune defective CBA/N mouse, **61,** 386
complement receptor negative and positive, differential macrophage requirement for proliferative response to anti-IgM antibodies (mouse), **62,** 324
stimulated by carrageenan mostly nonoverlapping with those stimulated with lipopolysaccharide and dextran sulfate (mouse), **57,** 348
from thoracic duct, receptors for influenza A virus strains Cam (H1N1) and Japan (2N2) (rat), **57,** 486
unresponsive to lipopolysaccharide, cross-stimulation by fluorescein-conjugated lipopolysaccharide (mouse), **61,** 292
suppression by neonatal administration of anti-μ antiserum (C3H/St mouse), **61,** 404
surface IgM properties during immune development
lipopolysaccharide-induced changes in lateral mobility on two subpopulations (mouse), **65,** 166
temperature effects on anti-IgM-induced movements in fetal and adult murine cells, **65,** 175
tolerization by injection of hapten conjugates of isologous gamma globulins (mouse), **58,** 385
from two marmoset species, antibody response to TNP-lipopolysaccharide (*Saguinus fuscicollis, S. oedipus oedipus*), **57,** 408
ubiquitin-induced differentiation from splenic null cells, lack of steroid sensitivity (mouse), **63,** 106
uptake of calcium and thymidine, effect of ionophore A23187 and concanavalin A (human, mouse, porcine, rabbit), **58,** 134
Benzylpenicilloyl carrier conjugates
stimulation of prostaglandin E_2 secretion by peripheral blood lymphocytes (human), **64,** 267
Blastogenesis, *see* DNA synthesis
Blood transfusion
allograft tolerance induction (mouse), **62,** 254
Bone marrow
age-associated decline of terminal deoxynucleotidyl transferase activity (human, mouse), **58,** 39
cell culture, interferon production by macrophages from (mouse), **57,** 495
-derived factors, role in engraftment of alloge-

neic marrow and chimerism enduring (mouse), **57,** 219
granulocyte/macrophage progenitor cell increase after subchronic treatment with cyclophosphamide (mouse), **65,** 131
T-cell precursors, transient tolerant stage study using human IgG as antigen (DDD and C57BL/6 mice), **57,** 377
Bone marrow cells
alloantigen-induced cytotoxic T-cell response *in vitro* (mouse), **61,** 154
differentiation in different host environments, effect on allospecific T-cell receptors (mouse), **62,** 350
populations separated by density gradient electrophoresis, morphology, surface markers, and functional tests (human), **59,** 345
prostaglandin E_2, production and effect on proliferation (mouse), **60,** 335
syngeneic or allogeneic intravenously inoculated, clearance from lung and liver by natural killer cells (mouse), **60,** 136
transplantation into irradiated mouse
allogeneic engraftment and chimerism, role of bone-marrow-derived factors (C57BL/6 strain), **57,** 219
immunogenetics of graft rejection (NZB strain and hybrids), **59,** 378
Bovine γ globulin
low-dose restriction in Ir-gene-controlled response to, connection with tolerance induction (mouse), **64,** 350
retention at site of injection and in lymph node promoted by polyclonal lymphocyte activators (mouse), **57,** 477
Bovine serum albumin
IgE immune response to, suppression by free and conjugated to gamma globulin fragments (mouse), **59,** 392
low-zone tolerance to, persistence control by T cells induced in neonates and operating in adults (mouse), **62,** 436
Brain
absorption of inhibitory activity of rabbit anti-mouse brain antiserum on antibody-dependent cell-mediated cytotoxicity (mouse), **59,** 419
Bromelain
enhancement of autologous erythrocyte rosette-forming cells among peripheral blood lymphocytes (porcine), **57,** 175
Bromelain-treated murine erythrocytes
lipopolysaccharide-induced splenocyte response to, ontogenic study (mouse), **65,** 293
Bromodeoxyuridine
and light treatment of guinea pig T cells, use in assay of antigenic regions in human fibrinopeptide B, **58,** 238

C

Calcium ion
-dependent step in programming of T-cell-mediated cytolysis, inhibition by manganese (mouse), **61,** 78
effect on suppressor factor production in mixed lymphocyte culture (mouse), **61,** 353
macrophage cAMP elevation, interactions with arachidonic acid and oxidative burst stimulants (guinea pig), **61,** 90
requirement for early events in lectin-stimulated lymphocyte activation (mouse), **59,** 276
uptake
by B and T cells, effect of ionophore A23187 and concanavalin A (human, mouse, porcine, rabbit), **58,** 134
complement-dependent in antibody-treated L cells, cytochalasin B effect (mouse), **61,** 62
by human serum-permeabilized Ehrlich ascites tumor cells, **61,** 213
Candida albicans
increased susceptibility to infection in alloxan-treated and genetically diabetic mice, cell-mediated immunity assay, **62,** 205
Capping
antibody- and concanavalin A-induced in T-lymphoma cells, enhancement by increase of cAMP intracellular level (mouse), **61,** 397
inhibition by sulfhydryl reagents in lymph node cells, immunofluorescence assay (mouse), **57,** 73
Carrageenan
prevention of guinea pig lymphokine effect on macrophage-mediated tumor cell cytostasis (mouse), **61,** 134
stimulation of splenic B-cell subpopulation, comparison with lipopolysaccharide and dextran sulfate effects (mouse), **57,** 348
reversible inhibition of splenocyte natural killer activity *in vivo* by suppressor cell activation (mouse), **61,** 200
Casein
chemokinetic response of peripheral blood lymphocytes to, effect of culturing (human), **60,** 43
Cations
monovalent, ability to replace potassium during lymphocyte stimulation (hamster), **57,** 209
Cell culture
fibroblasts
coculture with peripheral blood lymphocytes, effect on mitogenic response (human), **63,** 374

protein synthesis stimulation and DNA synthesis depression by soluble factor released by lymph nodes containing mycobacterial granulomas (guinea pig), **65,** 93
interferon production by bone marrow-derived macrophages (mouse), **57,** 495
lymph nodes containing mycobacterial granulomas, soluble factors in supernatant that modulate fibroblast function *in vitro* (guinea pig), **65,** 93
monolayer of thyroid epithelial cells, DNA synthesis stimulation in syngeneic lymphocytes (mouse), **62,** 313

Cell hybrids
semiallogeneic, using plasmacytoma cells, tumor-specific immunity induction (mouse), **65,** 373

Cell lines, *see also* Tumor cells
B hybridoma, antibody production regulation by concanavalin A-induced suppressor cells (mouse), **61,** 300
hematopoietic, sensitivity to natural killing, correlation with ability to induce interferon production by human lymphocytes, **62,** 367
K562 (human leukemia), Fc role in anti-H-2 antibody-induced increase of sensitivity toward natural killer activity of murine splenocytes, **65,** 115
L (mouse fibroblasts), antibody-treated, cytochalasin B effect on complement-dependent calcium uptake, **61,** 62
lymphoblastoid B-cell
inhibition of pokeweed mitogen-induced immunoglobulin synthesis by normal B cells (human), **60,** 191
insulin binding (human), **65,** 307
killing by human cytotoxic T-cell line, **59,** 435
lymphoid
killing by Epstein–Barr virus-induced cytotoxic lymphocytes from immune donor (human), **63,** 91
Ly-6.2 antigen, molecular characterization (mouse), **64,** 187
natural killer sensitivity, elevation by 12-*O*-tetradecanoylphorbol-13-acetate, effect of Epstein–Barr virus superinfection (human), **63,** 237
supernatant effects on autologous rosette formation and mitogenesis in murine B cells (human, mouse), **60,** 1
macrophage U937, lymphokine-induced antigen expression (human), **62,** 140
mastocytoma P815, *see* Mastocytoma P815
myeloma MOPC-315-EL, *see* Myeloma
neural, absorption of inhibitory activity of rabbit anti-mouse antiserum on antibody-dependent cell-mediated cytotoxicity (mouse), **59,** 419
neuroblastoma (N_2-A), H-2 antigen expression decrease after acute measles virus infection (mouse), **59,** 319
ovalbumin-specific helper T-cell lymphomas (ROT), functional heterogeneity after cloning (mouse), **65,** 194
plasmacytoma, (TEPC-15), persistence of adoptively transferred immunity specific for (mouse), **65,** 373
T-lymphoma, cyclic AMP role in antibody- and concanavalin A-induced capping (mouse), **61,** 397
Vero (African green monkey kidney), inhibition of herpes simplex virus replication and [^{3}H]leucine uptake by murine peritoneal macrophages, **58,** 72

Cell-mediated cytotoxicity
anti-tumor and anti-TNP-self, opposite effects of intravenous administration of TNP-conjugated tumor cells on (mouse), **59,** 181
anti-tumor, heightened in B-cell-deprived mice, role of natural killer cells, **65,** 20
direct and lectin-dependent, selective induction with allogeneic tumor cells and inhibition by cyclophosphamide (mouse), **61,** 253
lectin-dependent
antiautologous, in prekiller splenocytes (mouse), **60,** 11
supported by insolubilized concanavalin A (mouse), **59,** 411
methabolic inhibitor and drug effects on tumor cell sensitivity to (mouse), **58,** 398
natural, lymphotoxin role in tumor cell colony formation inhibition (guinea pig), **63,** 1
peripheral blood lymphocytes, suppression *in vitro* by monocytes from patients with malignant melanoma, **57,** 529
splenocytes and peritoneal lymphocytes against allogeneic tumor, diminishing after hyperimmunization (mouse), **57,** 114
in response to primary skin grafts, diminishing by hyperimmunization (mouse), **57,** 99
against syngeneic tumors, characterization of splenocytes involved in (mouse), **59,** 330

Cell-mediated immunity
in alloxan-treated and genetically diabetic mice with increased susceptibility to *Candida albicans* infection, *in vitro* and *in vivo* parameters, **62,** 205
effect of delayed hypersensitivity skin reaction, *in vitro* parameters (guinea pig), **62,** 28
effects of dietary essential fatty acids of ω-6 family and prostaglandins (rat), **62,** 293
to fluorescein isothiocyanate-modified syngeneic splenocytes, H-2-linked genetic control (mouse), **59,** 97
inhibition by ectoplacental cone and placental trophoblasts (mouse), **58,** 202

Cellular secretion
intact apparatus required for natural killer activity of peripheral blood lymphocytes, assay with monensin (human), **58,** 85
Charge
net on surface of early and late MOPC-315-EL tumor cells (mouse), **64,** 119
Chemokinetics
peripheral blood lymphocytes in response to casein and fMet-Leu-Phe, effect of culturing (human), **60,** 43
Chemotactic factor
release *in vivo* in 16 inbred strains (mouse), **64,** 203
Chemotaxis
peripheral blood lymphocytes to C5a, effect of culturing (human), **60,** 43
Chimeras
bone marrow
allogeneic, role of bone marrow-derived factors (mouse), **57,** 219
radiation-resistant host component emergence in thymus and lymph node, effects of cyclophosphamide and cortisone (mouse), **65,** 33
nude and radiation, helper function comparison of T cells from (mouse), **63,** 228
tetraparental aggregation, natural killer activity suppression in splenocytes (mouse), **57,** 229
Chromatography
on IgM and IgG insolubilized columns, comparison of spleen-derived immunosuppressive peptide and immunoglobulin-binding factor (mouse), **58,** 209
Chromium-51
release from blast and splenocyte targets, spontaneous and cytolytic T-cell-mediated at low temperature (mouse), **65,** 201
Chromosome 21
association with interferon α and β effects on peripheral blood lymphocyte mitogenic response (human), **65,** 366
Cloning
ovalbumin-specific helper T-cell lymphomas, functional heterogeneity (mouse), **65,** 194
Coccidiodomycosis
peripheral blood lymphocytes from patients with, heterogenous response to phytohemagglutinin, **64,** 235
Colchicine
inhibition of antiautologous lectin-dependent cell-mediated cytotoxicity in prekiller splenocytes (mouse), **60,** 11
Collagenase
effect on Peyer's patch cells, macrophage immunological function induction (mouse), **62,** 110
Collagenous tissue
acellular of hind foot, lack of immunosuppressive agent effects on retained antigen release (immune mouse), **57,** 505
Collagen type II
-induced arthritis, connection with lymph node cell ability to produce leukocyte inhibitory factor (rat), **63,** 362
Colony-forming units
in bone marrow cell populations separated by density gradient electrophoresis (human), **59,** 345
Complements
binding by B-cell subpopulations (mouse), **62,** 324
C5a, chemotactic response of peripheral blood lymphocytes to, effect of culturing (human), **60,** 43
human serum, permeabilization of Ehrlich ascites tumor cells to inorganic cations, **61,** 213
role in cytochalasin B-induced stimulation of calcium uptake by antibody-treated L cells (mouse), **61,** 62
Concanavalin A
adjuvant action, promotion of antigen-retention at site of injection and in lymph node (mouse), **57,** 477
antiautologous cell-mediated cytotoxicity induction in prekiller splenocytes (mouse), **60,** 11
capping induction in T-lymphoma cells, enhancement by increase of cyclic AMP intracellular level (mouse), **61,** 397
effect on
[^{3}H]thymidine incorporation into axial organ cells *in vitro* (starfish), **57,** 136
T-cell differentiation antigen expression on thymocytes in presence of interleukin 2 (mouse), **65,** 180
high concentration effects on DNA synthesis and cyclic AMP level in whole lymph node cells and purified T cells (rat), **58,** 29
-induced DNA synthesis and suppressor T-cell generation, inhibition by histamine (mouse), **60,** 426
-induced interleukin 2 production by splenocytes, enhancement by phorbol myristic acetate (mouse), **58,** 156
-induced mitogen response, effects of adenosine deaminase inhibitors in splenocytes and thymocytes (mouse), **64,** 29
-induced suppressor cells
autologous rosette-forming T cells as precursors (human), **61,** 273
direct action on immunoglobulin production by B hybridoma line (mouse), **61,** 300
effect on IgG synthesis *in vitro* by fresh peripheral blood lymphocytes (human), **58,** 356
insolubilized by coupling to Sepharose beads,

support of lectin-dependent cell-mediated cytotoxicity (mouse), **59,** 411
lymphocyte stimulation, modulation by lithium ion at level of Na,K-ATPase (hamster), **58,** 372
lymphokine production induction in splenocytes and thymocytes (mouse), **59,** 448
in presence of myelin basic protein, dual activation of experimental allergic encephalomyelitis transfer by lymph node cells (rat), **65,** 380
splenocyte activation in adoptive transfer of allergic encephalomyelitis
effect of donor sensitization (rat), **65,** 66
requirement for macrophages (rat), **60,** 24
-stimulated splenocytes, supernatant effect on cytotoxic T-cell generation by H-2-containing plasma membranes (mouse), **58,** 277
T-cell stimulation
inhibition by zinc deficiency *in vitro* (mouse), **60,** 203
role of Ia studied by using allogeneic, syngeneic, and xenogeneic splenic accessory cells (mouse), **57,** 28
Cortisone
effects on virus-immune response of thymocytes and early reconstitution profiles of P → F1 chimeras (mouse), **65,** 33
Culturing
peripheral blood lymphocytes, effect on locomotion responses to casein, C5a, and fMet-Leu-Phe (human), **60,** 43
Cyclic AMP(adenosine 3′:5′-monophosphate)
15-hydroperoxyarachidonic acid-induced modulation in splenocytes, relation to mitogenic response inhibition (mouse), **58,** 85
increase in T-lymphoma cells, enhancement of antibody- and concanavalin A-induced capping (mouse), **61,** 397
in macrophages, increase by stimulants of oxidative burst and by arachidonic acid, two mechanisms (guinea pig), **61,** 90
in peripheral blood lymphocytes, modulation by human very low density lipoprotein (human), **65,** 325
response to prostaglandin E_2, loss in lymphocytes after preincubation (human), **60,** 298
in whole lymph node cells and purified T cells, effect of high concanavalin A concentration (rat), **58,** 29
Cyclic GMP (guanosine 3′:5′-monophosphate)
15-hydroperoxyarachidonic acid-induced modulation in splenocytes, relation to mitogenic response inhibition (mouse), **58,** 85
Cyclic nucleotides
role in lithium ion effect on phytohemagglutinin-induced lymphocyte stimulation (hamster), **58,** 372
Cyclophosphamide
differential effects of acute and subchronic treatment on resistance to *Lysteria monocytogenes*, role of bone marrow function (mouse), **65,** 131
effects on virus-immune response of thymocytes and early reconstitution profiles of P → F1 chimeras (mouse), **65,** 33
prevention of antibody-mediated tolerance (mouse), **58,** 302
selective inhibition of direct and lectin-dependent cell-mediated cytotoxicity (mouse), **61,** 253
Cyclosporin A
T-cell function suppression in autologous mixed lymphocyte culture (human), **61,** 453
Cytochalasin
-sensitive processes, requirement for early events in lectin-stimulated lymphocyte activation (mouse), **59,** 276
Cytochalasin B
effect on complement-dependent calcium uptake in antibody-treated L cells (mouse), **61,** 62
effect on suppressor factor produced in mixed lymphocyte culture (mouse), **61,** 353
Cytochemistry
enzymatic markers on active and late rosette-forming T cells (human), **64,** 227
Cytolysis
macrophage-mediated of erythrocytes, activation by oxidative burst stimulators (guinea pig), **62,** 172
polyclonal T-cell-mediated, specific cooperative induction by keyhole limpet hemocyanin or invertebrate hemolymph (mouse), **58,** 333
sensitized T-cell-mediated, manganese inhibition of calcium-dependent step in programming for (mouse), **61,** 78
Cytotoxicity
antibody–complement-mediated, metabolic inhibitor and drug effects on tumor cells sensitivity to (mouse), **58,** 398
antibody-dependent cell-mediated, *see* Antibody-dependent cell-mediated cytotoxicity
cell-mediated, *see* Cell-mediated cytotoxicity
cross-reactive of peripheral blood lymphocytes sensitized *in vitro* by myeloma cell lines (human), **60,** 489
freshly isolated peripheral blood monocytes toward tumor cells, ^{51}Cr release assay (human), **58,** 426
high specific against lymphoblastoid B-cell line and low spontaneous in permanent T-cell line (human), **59,** 435
for lymphoid cell lines, induction in lymphocytes from immune donor by Epstein–Barr virus *in vitro* (human), **63,** 91

natural autoantibodies against thymocytes in spontaneously hypertensive rat, **60,** 168
neonatal tolerance to xenogeneic cells in mice inoculated with rat bone marrow cells, **63,** 193
nonspecific lymphocyte-mediated, induction by immobilized IgG aggregates (human), **60,** 403
spontaneous non-antigen-dependent of invertebrate mononuclear cells toward normal and malignant vertebrate targets, inhibition by mono- and disaccharides, **59,** 161
Cytotoxic T cells
in agammaglobulinemic and normal alloimmune chicken spleen, **64,** 246
alloantigen-induced in bone marrow cells (mouse), **61,** 154
to alloantigens or TNP-modified self-antigens, regulation by Ia^+ suppressor cells (mouse), **62,** 82
alloimmune, lytic phase inhibition by antiactivated T-cell antiserum (mouse), **59,** 289
anti-H-2
eliciting by H-2-containing plasma membranes only in presence of supernatants from concanavalin A-stimulated splenocytes (mouse), **58,** 277
molecular requirement for elicitation by H-$2K^k$ glycoprotein incorporated into lipid vesicles (mouse), **61,** 365
anti-TNP, H-2 haplotype specificity of molecular requirements for TNP recognition by (mouse), **58,** 147
conjugate formation with target cells, inhibition by H-2 antigen incorporated into phospholipid vesicles (mouse), **63,** 42
development after neonatal inoculation of F_1 hybrid splenocytes (mouse), **57,** 183
effects on chromium-51 release from blast and splenocyte targets at low temperature (mouse), **65,** 201
generation in mixed lymphocyte culture, *see also* Mixed lymphocyte culture
allospecific and nonspecific, phenotypic and functional characterization (human), **65,** 230
concanavalin A-induced, inhibition by histamine (mouse), **60,** 426
effect of allogeneic third-party cells (mouse), **59,** 61
lack of thymectomy effect at weaning (mouse), **64,** 93
stimulation by radioresistant splenocyte population (mouse), **63,** 335
suppression by adherent cells in absence of antigen (mouse), **64,** 371
to syngeneic Friend virus-induced leukemia, requirement for exogenous peritoneal macrophages (mouse), **59,** 127
herpes simplex virus-induced, activation by theophylline (human), **65,** 13
H-$2K^k$-restricted responses *in vivo* and at level of precursor frequencies (mouse), **64,** 53
to H-Y-H-$2D^b$, requirement of helper T cells specific to H-Y-2-I-A^b (mouse), **60,** 347
inhibition by suppressor T cells derived from early postnatal spleen (mouse), **58,** 345
myeloma MOPC-315-EL resistance to, changes during
growth in mouse peritoneum after transfer (normal mouse), **64,** 119; (nude mouse), **62,** 119
growth *in vitro*, **62,** 119
polyclonal activation by Epstein–Barr virus antigen (human), **63,** 91
responses to
alloantigens, role of adherent T-cell subpopulation (rat), **65,** 103
Moloney murine leukemia virus infection, role of H-2-linked genes in control of (mouse), **65,** 317
schistosomula in mouse strains after vaccination, **65,** 75
vaccinia virus, decrease by prior virus priming in syngeneic environment (mouse), **61,** 220
against syngeneic tumors, subpopulation analysis (mouse), **59,** 330
theophylline-resistant, induction by herpes simplex virus-infected cells (human), **64,** 220
against TNP-haptenated syngeneic cells in microculture, nude splenocyte as accessory cells (mouse), **62,** 385
tumor-specific, Ia-positive macrophage requirement for induction *in vitro* (mouse), **62,** 425
unresponsiveness to H-Y antigen, H-2 restriction (mouse), **62,** 251
vaccinia virus-induced in thymus, effects of cyclophosphamide and cortisone (mouse), **65,** 33

D

Delayed foot pad reaction
to sheep erythrocytes, thymectomy effect on effector and suppressor T cells (mouse), **61,** 190
Delayed hypersensitivity
to H-2-associated antigens
differential T-cell responsiveness in graft-versus-host and host-versus-graft reactions (mouse), **57,** 389
generation of two T-cell subsets synergizing in graft-versus-host reaction (mouse), **59,** 115
induced by DNP-Ascaris conjugate, correlation with antibody production (rat), **58,** 312

induction by T cells developed in culture of splenocytes from mice expressing humoral immunity, **57,** 468
insulin-specific, induction by insulin coupled to syngeneic lymphoid cells (mouse), **60,** 314
-like reactions induced by same class of splenic T cells in response to fibrasarcoma H-7 (mouse), **60,** 34
to Sendai virus, adoptive transfer
antigen requirements on T cells (mouse), **63,** 188
induction of two T-cell subsets (mouse), **62,** 38
to sheep erythrocytes, suppression by soluble factor produced by adherent splenocytes from *Bacillus Calmette–Guerin*-injected B6 mouse, **58,** 61
skin reaction, effect on cell-mediated immunity *in vitro* parameters, role of serum (guinea pig), **62,** 28
T-cell requirement for desensitization (mouse), **60,** 308
tuberculin-type, inhibition by antibody administration during sensitization, cellular mechanism of (mouse), **58,** 302
weak response to H-Y antigen, correlation with H-2 graft rejection (mouse), **62,** 251
Density gradient centrifugation
effector cells in natural cell-mediated cytotoxicity (human), **61,** 231
2′-Deoxycoformycin
effect on splenocyte and thymocyte responses to various mitogens (mouse), **64,** 29
intraperitoneal injections, immunological and biochemical effects (mouse), **63,** 259
Desensitization
nonspecific, requirement of T cells (mouse), **60,** 308
Dextran B1355S
immune response to, individual variation in idiotype expression in BALB/c mouse, **58,** 286
Dextran sulfate
B-cell stimulation
comparison with carrageenan (mouse), **57,** 348
interaction with lipopolysaccharide (mouse), **61,** 176
low response of splenocytes from mouse with crosslinked B-cell defect to, **61,** 375
Diabetes
alloxan-induced and genetic, increased susceptibility to *Candida albicans* infection, cell-mediated immunity assay (mouse), **62,** 205
Dinitrophenyl (DNP)
antibody response induction in splenocyte culture, depression by DNP-bovine γ-globulin (mouse), **64,** 44
Disaccharides
inhibition of spontaneous cytotoxicity of invertebrate mononuclear cells toward normal and malignant vertebrate targets, **59,** 161
DNA synthesis
in active and late rosette-forming T cells (human), **64,** 227
concanavalin A-induced in splenocytes, inhibition by histamine (mouse), **60,** 426
in fibroblasts, inhibition by soluble factors released by lymph nodes containing mycobacterial granulomas (guinea pig), **65,** 93
induction in mouse B cells by supernatant from human and mouse lymphoid cell lines, **60,** 1
lectin-activated in splenocytes, role of Ca, Mg, and cytochalasin-sensitive processes (mouse), **59,** 276
mitogen-induced in lymphocytes
increase after delayed hypersensitivity skin reaction (guinea pig), **62,** 28
T-cell-dependent macrophage-mediated suppression (rat), **63,** 57
stimulation in T cells by syngeneic thyroid epithelial cells (mouse), **62,** 313
in whole lymph node cells and purified T cells, effect of high concanavalin A concentration (rat), **58,** 29
zinc deficiency effects on B and T cells *in vitro*, (mouse), **60,** 203
DNP–Ascaris
immunization with, delayed hypersensitivity, lymphotoxin and antibody production assay (rat), **58,** 302
DNP–bovine γ-globulin
depression of antibody response to DNP in splenocyte culture (mouse), **64,** 44
DNP-polyacrylamide beads
suppressor activity induction in splenocytes (mouse), **64,** 44
DNP–polysaccharide
tolerance induction in mature virgin B cells, role of IgM receptor (mouse), **62,** 196
Drugs
effects on antibody-complement and cell-mediated killing of tumor cells, lack of correlation with effects on macromolecular synthesis (P815 murine mastocytoma), **58,** 398

E

EDTA (ethylene diaminetetraacetate)
inhibition of concanavalin A-induced mitogenesis in T cells, reversion by zinc *in vitro* (mouse), **60,** 203
Electron microscopy
early events in cell-mediated hyperacute rejec-

tion of skin graft, vascular endothelium changes (mouse), **59,** 219
scanning
human lymphotoxin-induced changes in L-929 cell surface (mouse), **60,** 144
surface analysis of early and late MOPC-315-EL tumor cells (mouse), **64,** 119
Electrophoresis
density gradient, bone marrow cell separation on basis of their surface charge (human), **59,** 345
Embryo
cleavage, cell surface antigen comparison with teratocarcinoma (mouse), **62,** 247
Endocytosis, *see* Pinocytosis
Endogenous AKR-murine leukemia virus
antigen expression on lymph node cells (mouse), **64,** 102
Endogenous pyrogen, *see also* Leukocytic pyrogen
rabbit, close relation to human and rabbit interleukin-1 and murine serum amyloid A inducer, **63,** 164
Endotoxin
contaminating in immunological research, **58,** 216
Eosinophil chemotactic factor
release from human neutrophils and rat mast cells, inhibition by arachidonic acid analogs, **60,** 480
Epstein–Barr virus
-determined nuclear antigen, inhibition of leukocyte migration (human), **58,** 269
induction of cytotoxicity for lymphoid cell lines in lymphocytes from immune donor (human), **63,** 91
lymphoid cell line superinfection, effect on natural killer sensitivity elevation by 12-*O*-tetradecanoyl-phorbol-13-acetate (human), **63,** 237
Erythrocytes
antibody-sensitized, lysis by killer cells from normal thymus, ^{51}Cr release assay (mouse), **57,** 517
macrophage-mediated cytolysis, activation by oxidative burst stimulators (guinea pig), **62,** 172
nonspecific lymphocyte-mediated cytolysis, induction by immobilized IgG aggregates (human), **60,** 403
rat, autoantibody and antibody induction in immunized mouse, **63,** 221
sheep, *see* Sheep erythrocytes
Erythro-9-(2-hydroxyl-3-nonyl)adenine
effect on splenocyte and thymocyte responses to various mitogens (mouse), **64,** 29
Experimental African trypanosomiasis
immunosuppression and suppressor cell activity in *Trypanosoma rhodesiense*-infected athymic mice, **63,** 210
Experimental allergic encephalomyelitis
adoptive transfer
lymph node cell immunocompetence after donor treatment with myelin basic protein (guinea pig), **60,** 220
macrophage requirement for splenocyte activation *in vitro* (rat), **60,** 24
peripheral blood lymphocyte responsiveness to myelin basic protein during disease development (guinea pig), **63,** 409
suppression by antiserum against prostaglandin E_1 (rat), **62,** 293
transfer by
lymph node cells, dual activation with concanavalin A and myelin basic protein (rat), **65,** 380
myelin basic protein-sensitized splenocytes after *in vitro* activation by specific antigen (rat), **59,** 42
splenocytes, effects of donor sensitization regiments (rat), **65,** 66
supernatant from lymph node cells,
independence from conventional Ig (rat), **62,** 50
xenogeneic restriction (rat), **62,** 50

F

Fatty acids
essential of ω-6 family, regulation of cell-mediated immune response (rat), **62,** 293
Fc receptors
in active and late rosette-forming T cells (human), **64,** 227
on allospecific and nonspecific cytotoxic T cells generated in mixed lymphocyte culture (human), **65,** 230
on autorosette-forming T cells from peripheral blood (human), **64,** 312
on bone marrow-derived and peritoneal macrophages, serological analysis (mouse), **59,** 151
for IgA, specificity on neutrophils and monocytes (human), **60,** 324
for IgG
on antibody-forming splenocytes from immunized mouse, **61,** 124
induction on theophylline-resistant T cells by adenosine and impromidine (human), **57,** 455
on T-cell hybrids, specificity, behavior, and relationship with Ia antigens (mouse), **63,** 349
-mediated binding of sensitized target cells,

more active in macrophage than in monocytes (rabbit), **64,** 359
-mediated functions of peripheral blood lymphocytes, effects of anti-HLA-RD and anti-β_2-microglobulin antibodies (human), **59,** 187
-negative Thy-1-bearing splenocytes, high activity in mixed lymphocyte reaction (nude *nu/nu* mouse), **57,** 339
on target cells, interaction with anti-H-2 antibodies causing sensitivity increase toward murine splenocyte natural killer activity, **65,** 115

α-Fetoprotein
suppression of autologous mixed lymphocyte reaction (mouse), **63,** 417

Fetus
as allograft, immunoprotective requirements (rat), **62,** 271

Fibrinopeptide B
human, antigenic regions involved in guinea pig T-cell response, **58,** 238

Fibroblasts
cocultured with peripheral blood lymphocytes, mitogenic response modulation (human), **63,** 374
L-929 cell line, human lymphotoxin effects on plasma membrane lipids (mouse), **60,** 144

Fibronectin
competition for common binding site with macrophage surface component, effect on response to migration inhibitory factor (guinea pig), **58,** 175

Fluorescein
-conjugated lipopolysaccharide, cross-stimulation of B cells unresponsive to antigen itself (mouse), **61,** 292

Fluorescein isothiocyanate
-modified splenocytes, H-2-linked genetic control of splenocyte cytotoxic response to (mouse), **59,** 97

Fluorescence-activated cell sorter analysis
B-cell surface isotype expression in NZB mice, comparison with other strains, **63,** 385
Ia antigen presence on peripheral blood T-cell subpopulations (human), **64,** 277

fMet-Leu-Phe
chemokinetic response of peripheral blood lymphocytes to, effect of culturing (human), **60,** 43

G

Galactose oxidase
alloantigen-independent activation of memory cells (human), **59,** 26

Gamma globulins
conjugates with Fraction 1a of bovine serum albumin, suppression of IgG immune response to intact antigen (mouse), **59,** 392
isologous, conjugates with haptens, induction of B-cell tolerization (mouse), **58,** 385

Genes
H-2K^k allele in mice, cytotoxic T-cell responses *in vivo*, **64,** 53
H-2 restriction, *see* H-2 restriction
Ir
immune response regulation to *Leishmania enrietti* infection (guinea pig), **60,** 367
low-dose restriction in control of response to bovine γ globulin, connection with tolerance induction (mouse), **64,** 350
major histocompatibility complex
alloactivated regulatory T-cell homology with mixed lymphocyte reaction responder (human), **60,** 393
in allospecific receptor alteration during T-cell differentiation from bone marrow cells (mouse), **62,** 350
control of cytotoxic splenocyte response to syngeneic cells modified with fluorescein isothiocyanate (mouse), **59,** 97
in control of immune response to murine leukemia viruses (mouse), **65,** 317
effect on immune response to poly(Tyr-Glu-Ala-Gly)$_n$ (mouse), **62,** 132
K end, in allogeneic kidney and sarcoma survival (mouse), **62,** 287
non-H-2, effect on immune response to poly(Tyr-Glu-Ala-Gly)$_n$ (mouse), **62,** 132
V, random repertoire for T-cell receptors, role in T-cell specificity and self-restriction, theoretical conclusions, **64,** 381

Genotype
correlation between control of T-cell mitogenic response and susceptibility to experimental autoimmune thyroiditis (rat), **62,** 156
influence on mitogenic response to sequential polymer by splenocytes (mouse), **61,** 114

Glucocerebroside
effects on interleukin 1 production and release by macrophages (mouse), **64,** 293

Glucocorticoids
mitogenic response inhibition in residual circular lymphocytes obtained after glucocorticoid injection (human), **65,** 43
receptors on thymocytes, effect of thymosin Fraction 5 (mouse), **60,** 376
thymocyte resistance to, effect of thymosin Fraction 5 (mouse), **60,** 376

β-Glucuronidase
release from macrophages in response to *Schistosoma mansoni* schistosomula, effect of nonspecific IgG (rat), **62,** 15

Grafting, *see* Transplantation

Graft-versus-host disease
maternally acquired, immunology of maternal–fetal relationship (rat), **62,** 271
Graft-versus-host reaction
abnormally high induced by NZB splenocytes and lymph node cells in allogeneic irradiated adult mouse, **58,** 124
after allogeneic transplantation of lymphocytes
generation of antihost-directed T-cell subpopulations (mouse), **59,** 115
T-cell response to H-2-subregion-coded antigens, delayed hypersensitivity assay (mouse), **57,** 389
effects of pretreatment with parental strain lymphocytes and anti-lymphocyte serum (F_1 hybrid rat), **57,** 524
of lymphocytes from mice genetically selected for high or low responsiveness to phytohemagglutinin, **62,** 448
Gut
IgA preponderance, allotype suppression (mouse), **65,** 247

H

Haplotype
preference for H-2K^k-restricted cytotoxic T-cell responses *in vivo* (mouse), **64,** 53
Haptens
conjugates with isologous gamma globulins, suppression of anti-hapten IgE antibody production by B-cell tolerization (mouse), **58,** 385
Heart
allograft survival, effect of priming with
parenchymal cells and passenger leukocytes from kidney (rat), **57,** 92
splenocyte populations (rat), **57,** 85
Helper factor
antigen-specific in serum, antibody production enhancement *in vivo* (mouse), **60,** 64, 77
in supernatant from alloantigen-activated mixed lymphocyte culture, augmentation of tumor-specific immuninity induction *in vitro* (mouse), **58,** 225
Helper T cells
activity induction
in fetal thymocytes, requirement of more mature T-cell effector (human), **59,** 17
by pokeweed mitogen, role of monocytes (human), **58,** 323
by specific and nonspecific T-cell activators, effects on antibody production by B cells (BALB/c mouse), **61,** 416
adherent radioresistant, enhancement of cytotoxic T-cell responses to alloantigens (rat), **65,** 103
in antibody-producing system, allogeneic restriction of (human), **57,** 201
antigen-specific activity in ovalbumin-specific helper lymphomas and their clones (mouse), **65,** 194
concanavalin A-induced migration inhibitory factor production (mouse spleen, thymus), **59,** 448
educated to synthetic polypeptide, effects of antigen-pulsed macrophages (mouse), **61,** 104
functional heterogeneity in B-cell activation (BALB/c mouse), **61,** 416
lack of expression of 16p antigen (human), **64,** 84
from radiation chimeras and nude mice bearing thymus grafts, H-2 restriction comparison, **63,** 228
requirement for accessory function of nude splenocytes in cytotoxic T-cell generation (mouse), **62,** 385
requirement of H-Y antigen recognition by cytotoxic T cells (mouse), **60,** 347
splenic, specific for antigens closely related to self, role in tumor immunology (unprimed mouse), **57,** 316
Hemolymph
collection procedure effect on keyhole limpet hemocyanin reactivity in preparations (*Megathura crenulata*), **60,** 240
invertebrate, induction of cytolytic T cells in splenocytes from primed mouse, **58,** 333
Hemopoietic chimerism
negative influence on antibody-forming capacities *in vitro* (*Saguinus fuscicollis, S. oedipus oedipus*), **57,** 408
Herpes simplex virus
concomitant induction of cytotoxic and suppressor cells, enhancement by theophylline (human), **65,** 13
-infected cells, induction of theophylline-resistant cytotoxic T cells (human), **64,** 220
lymphocyte proliferation induction, blockage by monoclonal anti-HLA-DR antibodies (human), **61,** 11
replication inhibition by murine *Corynebacterium parvum*-elicited peritoneal macrophages, interferon-independent mechanism (Vero cells), **58,** 72
Histamine
and its analogs, suppression of pokeweed mitogen-induced IgG production by suppressor cell activation in peripheral blood lymphocytes (human), **64,** 324
-induced suppressor cells
effect on IgG synthesis *in vitro* by fresh peripheral blood lymphocytes (human), **58,** 366

inhibition of lymphocyte response to mitogens (human), **59,** 268; (mouse), **62,** 396
inhibition of concanavalin A-induced DNA synthesis and suppressor T-cell generation (mouse), **60,** 426
reduction of splenic plaque-forming cell response to trinitrophenylated bovine γ-globulin *in vivo* (mouse), **65,** 152
Histocompatibility
in clinical kidney transplantation (human), **62,** 277
Histoplasmosis
disseminated, suppressor splenocyte populations (mouse), **60,** 287
Homing
lymph node cells in allogeneic recipients, reduced localization in lymph nodes, lungs, and small intestine (mouse), **64,** 13
Horseradish peroxidase
pinocytosis assay in T cells during differentiation in mixed lymphocyte culture (mouse), **59,** 429
Host-versus-graft reaction
after allogeneic splenocyte transplantation, T-cell response to H-2-subregion-coded antigens, delayed hypersensitivity assay (mouse), **57,** 389
to H-Y antigen, correlation with T-cell responsiveness (mouse), **62,** 251
H-2 restriction
in allopregnancy-induced T-cell suppressor factor (mouse), **62,** 186
differences in two T-cell subsets induced during Sendai virus infection (mouse), **62,** 38
haplotype H-2K^k preference for *in vivo* cytotoxic T-cell responses (mouse), **64,** 53
I region-restricted T-cell subpopulation mediating delayed hypersensitivity to Sendai virus (mouse), **63,** 188
K,D region-restricted T-cell subpopulation mediating delayed hypersensitivity to Sendai virus (mouse), **63,** 188
on self-related antigen recognition by helper T cells (unprimed mouse), **57,** 316
self-restriction in T cells, role of random repertoire of V genes, theoretical conclusions, **64,** 381
on T-cell ability to induce immune response to Ehrlich ascites tumor in T-cell-deficiency (mouse), **62,** 93
on T-cell cytotoxic response to vaccinia virus (mouse), **61,** 220
of T-cell helper function in nude and radiation chimeras (mouse), **63,** 228
on T-cell responsibility to H-Y antigen (mouse), **62,** 251
Human serum albumin
oral–parenteral immunization with, induction of IgG auto-idiotypic plasma cells in mucosal tissues (rabbit), **60,** 498
retention in lymphoid follicles and connective tissue, effect of immunosuppressive agents in immune mouse, **57,** 505
Humoral immunity
splenocyte culture *in vitro*, development of T-cell population mediating delayed hypersensitivity in normal mouse, **57,** 468
Hybrids
F_1 rat, graft-versus-host reaction after pretreatment with parental strain lymphocytes and anti-lymphocyte serum, **57,** 524
Hydrogen peroxide
production by peritoneal macrophages, effects of nonphagocytic stimuli (guinea pig), **59,** 301
15-Hydroperoxyarachidonic acid
inhibition of splenocyte mitogenic stimulation, role of cyclic nucleotide level changes (mouse), **58,** 85
Hydroxylamine
reversal of sodium periodate-induced inhibition of splenocyte antibody response *in vitro* (mouse), **59,** 10
Hyperacute rejection
cell-mediated to skin grafts, ultrastructural changes of vascular endothelium (mouse), **59,** 219
Hyperimmunization
diminishing of splenocyte and peritoneal lymphocyte cytotoxicity against allogeneic tumor (mouse), **57,** 114
prior to skin grafting, diminishing of cellular cytotoxicity (mouse), **57,** 99
Hypertension
spontaneous, production of natural cytotoxic autoantibodies against thymocytes (rat), **60,** 181

I

Ibuprofen
differential effect of pyrogenicity and lymphocyte-activating activity of human leukocytic pyrogen, **63,** 134
Idiotype
expression by B cells from various strains of GAT-immunized mouse, **61,** 280
individual variation in expression studied on BALB/c mouse immunized with dextran B1355S, **58,** 286
network in antigen-specific immune regulation (review), **61,** 425
Immune responses
autologous anti-idiotype in mucosal tissues after

oral–parenteral immunization with human serum albumin (rabbit), **60,** 498
background, connection with tumor immunology, assay of helper T cells specific for antigen related to self (unprimed mouse), **57,** 316
cell-mediated anti-tumor to Moloney murine leukemia virus infection, genetic control (mouse), **65,** 317
to dextran B1355S, individual variation in idiotype expression in immunized BALB/c mouse, **58,** 286
to Ehrlich ascites tumor, role of T cells (mouse), **62,** 82
to GAT *in vitro* and *in vivo* by splenocytes from various strains (mouse), **61,** 280
to *Leishmania enrietti* infection, role of macrophage heterogeneity and Ir-gene control (guinea pig), **60,** 367
neonatal, suppression by lipopolysaccharides (mouse), **58,** 458
to poly(Tyr-Glu-Ala-Gly)$_n$, effects of H-2 and non-H-2 genes (mouse), **62,** 132
primary *in vitro*, induction by lymphocyte-bound antigen from bacteriophage T2 (rabbit), **58,** 436, 448
primary *in vivo* by antigen-binding B cells, successive changes in Ig class expression (mouse), **62,** 377
secondary IgM and IgG to TNP-KLH, avidity profiles (CBA, CBA/N, and F_1 hybrid mice), **61,** 448
to sheep erythrocyte antigen, Fc receptors on IgG antibody-forming splenocytes (mouse), **61,** 124
T-cell-dependent, stimulation by prealbumin in splenocyte culture (mouse), **65,** 1
to trinitrophenylated γ-globulin, role of histamine-induced auto-anti-idiotypic antibodies *in vivo* (mouse), **65,** 152
to type III pneumococcal polysaccharide, phytohemagglutinin-induced enhancement and IgG subclass restriction of (mouse), **65,** 280
Immune system
antigen-specific regulation via associative recognition versus idiotype network (review), **61,** 425
mucosal, IgA-bearing mesentheric and peripheral lymph node cell migration into salivary gland (mouse), **63,** 203
Immunity
influenza A virus-induced homotypic and heterotypic, role of T and B cells (mouse), **60,** 119
tumor-specific, *see* Tumor-specific immunity
Immunization
with lysozyme-lipopolysaccharide complex, induction of immune response to lysozyme in tolerant mouse, **58,** 293
oral–parenteral with human serum albumin, induction of IgG auto-idiotypic plasma cells in mucosal lymphoid tissues (rabbit), **60,** 498
repetitive with tetanus toxoid, inhibition of antigen-specific lymphoblastoid B-cell induction (human), **59,** 82
with sheep erythrocytes, noradrenaline decrease in lymphoid organs (rat), **63,** 329
against smallpox, royal experiment in England (1721-1722), **61,** 437
with syngeneic Friend virus-induced leukemia, specific T-cell-mediated cytotoxic response *in vivo* (mouse), **59,** 127
Immunoadsorbent column
migration inhibitory factor recovery from, biological activity (guinea pig), **61,** 165
Immunodeficiency
crosslinked at B-cell level
correction by transfer of C3 receptor-bearing B cells (CBA/N mouse), **61,** 386
low splenocyte responses to lipopolysaccharide, PPD, and dextran sulfate (CBA/N mouse), **61,** 375
secondary IgM and IgG responses to TNP-KLH, avidity profiles (CBA, CBA/N, and F_1 hybrid mice), **61,** 448
Immunofluorescence
capping of lymph node cells, inhibition by sulfhydryl reagents (mouse), **57,** 73
Ia-bearing Langerhans cells in epidermis, effects of uv and drugs (mouse), **60,** 50
monensin-induced changes in secretory apparatus of natural killer cells (human), **58,** 97
tumor-associated fetal antigens, interactions with histocompatibility antigens (rat), **60,** 261
Immunogenicity
isolated splenocyte populations, *in vivo* quantitation using priming prior to heart transplantation (rat), **57,** 85
keyhole limpet hemocyanin from different preparations, skin test (human), **60,** 240
Immunogens
cercarial-derived in schistosomiasis, cellular response induction (mouse), **59,** 233
egg-derived in schistosomiasis, cellular response induction (mouse), **59,** 246
Immunoglobin-binding factor
comparison with spleen-derived immunosuppressive peptide, biological activity and chromatography (mouse), **58,** 209
Immunoglobulin receptors
for IgE on alveolar and peritoneal macrophages, rosette formation assay (rat), **59,** 106
for IgM

role in tolerance induction in mature virgin B cells (mouse), **62,** 196
in splenocytes, shedding following temperature shift (rat), **60,** 168
for IgM and IgG, density decrease on B-cell membranes induced by neonatal administration of anti-μ antiserum (C3H/St mouse), **61,** 404
Immunoglobulins
-antigen complexes in serum after sheep erythrocyte injection, enhancement of antibody production (mouse), **60,** 77
conventional, lack of effect on experimental allergic encephalomyelitis transfer activity of lymph node cell supernatant (rat), **62,** 50
Fc fragments
-mediated polyclonal antibody response in assay of lymphocyte reactivity changes with aging (mouse), **63,** 16
requirement for anti-μ antibody-induced suppression (mouse), **62,** 1
IgA
allotype suppression, cellular implication for IgA preponderance in gut (mouse), **65,** 247
receptor specificity on neutrophils and monocytes (human), **60,** 324
IgD membrane, role in primary antibody response (rat), **63,** 293
IgE
anti-hapten response, suppression by conjugates of haptens and isologous gamma globulins (mouse), **58,** 385
production following immunization with DNA-Ascaris conjugates, effect of adjuvants (rat), **58,** 312
response to bovine serum albumin, suppression by free and conjugated to gamma globulin fragments of antigen (mouse), **59,** 392
IgG
anti-tetanus, spontaneous and mitogen-reactive production inhibition by repetitive immunization with tetanus toxoid (human), **59,** 82
human, tolerance induction in T-cell precursors in bone marrow of DDD and C57BL/6 mice, **57,** 377
immobilized aggregates, induction of nonspecific lymphocyte-mediated cytotoxicity (human), **60,** 403
inhibition by histamine- or concanavalin A-induced suppressor cells (human), **58,** 366
nonspecific, effect of peptides and aggregates on macrophage cytotoxicity against *Schistosoma mansoni* schistosomula (rat), **62,** 15
pokeweed mitogen-induced production by B cells, suppression by histamine and its analogs (human), **64,** 324
production following immunization with DNA-Ascaris conjugates, effect of adjuvants (rat), **58,** 312
secretion induced in splenocytes and thymocytes activated by lymphocyte-stimulating factor (mouse), **63,** 118
secondary response to TNP–KLH, avidity profile (CBA, CBA/N, and F_1 hybrid mice), **61,** 448
subclass restriction of immune response to type III pneumococcal polysaccharide, induction by phytohemagglutinin (mouse), **65,** 280
IgM
production in secondary response to TNP–KLH, avidity profile (CBA, CBA/N, and F_1 hybrid mice), **61,** 448
temperature-dependent movements on B-cell surface during immune development, effects of
anti-IgM antibodies (mouse), **65,** 166
lipopolysaccharide (mouse), **65,** 166
lipopolysaccharide-induced synthesis in peripheral blood lymphocytes only after incubation for 20 hr (human), **57,** 400
polyclonal or isotype-restricted production *in vivo*, helper-cell-dependent increase by T-cell stimulators (BALB/c mouse), **61,** 416
secretion by single cells, method for detection, **63,** 154
surface classes, successive changes in expression by antigen-binding B-cells during primary immune response (mouse), **62,** 377
synthesis by B cells
induced by circarial and egg immunogen in schistosomiasis (mouse), **59,** 233, 246
pokeweed mitogen-induced, inhibition by suppressor T cells activated by lymphoblastoid cell lines (human), **60,** 191
Immunoprecipitation
sequential, antigenic differences between tumor-associated fetal antigens and histocompatibility antigens (rat), **60,** 274
Immunoregulation
in disseminated histoplasmosis, splenocyte population characterization (mouse), **60,** 287
role of noradrenaline (rat), **63,** 329
Immunosuppression
2′-deoxycoformycin-induced, effect of mode of administration (mouse), **63,** 259
in experimental African trypanosomiasis (athymic mouse), **63,** 210
α-fetoprotein-induced of autologous mixed lymphocyte reaction (mouse), **63,** 417
IgE response to bovine serum albumin by its free or conjugated to gamma globulin fragments (mouse), **59,** 392

IgG response to sheep erythrocytes, role of suppressor T cells adherent to histamine conjugated albumin (BALB/c mouse), **59,** 171
in vitro capacity of spleen-derived immunosuppressive peptide and immunoglobulin-binding factor (mouse), **58,** 209
maternal–paternal lymphocyte interactions by trophoblast ectoplacental cone or placental tissue (mouse), **58,** 202
T-cell-mediated of splenocyte and lymph node cell mitogenic response in lymphadenopathy (MRL mouse), **61,** 40
tumor-associated fetal antigen effect on mitogen- and tumor-cell-induced splenocyte stimulation (rat), **57,** 155
Immunosuppressive agents
effect on antigen retained in lymphoid follicles and collagenous tissue of immune mouse, **57,** 505
Impromidine
induction of Fcγ receptors on theophylline-resistant T cells (human), **57,** 455
Indomethacin
potentiation of prostaglandin-mediated reduction of activated macrophage tumoricidal activity (mouse), **60,** 91
prevention loss of cyclic AMP response to prostaglandin E_2 in lymphocytes after preincubation (human), **60,** 298
reversion of suppressor splenocyte activity from tumor-bearing mouse, **60,** 109
Influenza A viruses
homotypic and heterotypic T- and B-cell immunity induced by infection with (mouse), **60,** 119
radioiodinated strains Cam (H1N1) and Japan (H2N2), binding by T- and B-cell populations from thoracic duct (rat), **57,** 486
Insulin
binding by human lymphoid lines of B-cell origin, **65,** 307
coupled to syngeneic lymphoid cells, induction of cell-mediated immunity and tolerance to insulin (mouse), **60,** 314
Interferon
Corynebacterium parvum-induced in splenocytes, distinction of α, β, and γ types (mouse), **64,** 64
Interferon α (human leukocyte)
and β, inhibition of T-cell-dependent mitogenesis, stimulation of T-cell-independent mitogenesis and natural killer activity, **65,** 366
effect on
allospecific and nonspecific cytotoxic T cells generated in mixed lymphocyte culture, **65,** 230
plaque-forming cell response of peripheral blood lymphocytes to equine erythrocytes, **58,** 464
pokeweed mitogen-induced differentiation of peripheral blood lymphocytes, **64,** 20
Interferon type I (murine)
effect on surface antigen expression on thymocytes, **57,** 427
production *in vitro* by bone marrow-derived macrophages, **57,** 495
Interferon type II (human)
OKT3 monoclonal antibody-induced in peripheral blood lymphocytes, **64,** 304
induction in peripheral blood lymphocytes by *Staphylococcus* protein A, **57,** 1
production by natural killer cells, effect of hematopoietic cell lines, **62,** 367
production by peripheral blood lymphocytes, lack of correlation with natural killer activity, **62,** 220
Interferon type II (murine)
effect on surface antigen expression on thymocytes, **57,** 427
release *in vivo* in 16 inbred strains, **64,** 203
splenocyte natural killer activity stimulation
comparison with anti-H-2 antiserum and mitogen action, **63,** 28
metabolic requirements for, **58,** 49
pathway different from phorbol ester-induced activation, **65,** 258
titer decrease in serum of sensitized and low-responder strains, **60,** 100
Interleukin 1, *see also* Lymphocyte-activating factor
effect on mature medullary thymocytes, stimulation of interleukin 2 production and mitogenic response (human), **64,** 337
effect on T-cell subpopulation in mixed lymphocyte culture, interleukin 2 production stimulation (human), **63,** 143
production and release by macrophages, effects of various agents (mouse), **64,** 293
Interleukin-2, *see also* T-cell growth factor
comparison with lymphocyte-stimulating factor produced by lymphocytes activated by pokeweed mitogen-derived mitogen Pa-2 (mouse), **63,** 118
interleukin 1-induced production by mature medullary thymocytes (human), **64,** 337
production by
activated T cells, absolute requirement for adherent cells (human), **63,** 71
concanavalin A-activated splenocytes, enhancement by phorbol myristic acetate (mouse), **58,** 156
requirement for T-cell differentiation antigen

expression on resting and proliferating thymocytes (mouse), **65,** 180
resting T-cell sensitivity to, induction by HLA-DR antigen in mixed lymphocyte culture (human), **63,** 143
T-cell proliferation and cytotoxicity induction in mixed lymphocyte culture, inhibition by cyclosporin A (human), **61,** 453
Ionophore A23187
effect on calcium and thymidine uptake by B and T cells (human, mouse, porcine, rabbit), **58,** 134
Irradiation
mitogenic response recovery after reconstitution, in peanut agglutinin-binding and nonbinding T cells (mouse), **62,** 74
Isoelectrofocusing
migration inhibitory factor fractionation into two species (mouse), **63,** 198
Isogeneic lymphocyte interactions
type 2 presence and type 1 absence in CBA/N mouse, **60,** 386
Isokinetic density centrifugation
thymocyte fraction with killer cell activity (mouse), **57,** 517
Isotype suppression
anti-μ antibody-induced, Fc dependence (mouse), **62,** 1

K

Keyhole limpet hemocyanin
induction of cytolytic T cells in splenocytes from primed mouse, **58,** 333
reactivity in preparations, effect of hemolymph collection procedure (*Megathura crenulata*), **60,** 240
Kidney
allogeneic transplant survival in certain strain combinations (mouse), **62,** 287
parenchymal cells and passenger leukocytes, effect of priming time and doses on heart allograft survival (rat), **57,** 92
transplantation, histocompatibility assay (human), **62,** 277
Killer cells (K cells)
nonspecific cytotoxic T cells generated in mixed lymphocyte culture (human), **65,** 230
in peripheral blood lymphocytes enriched for subpopulations isolated from natural killer–tumor cell conjugates (human), **58,** 415
in thymocyte subpopulation possessing Thy-1 antigens (mouse), **57,** 517
Killing, *see* Cytotoxicity

L

Lactoferrin
suppression of splenocyte primary antibody response (mouse), **63,** 308
Langerhans cells
Ia-bearing, effect of uv and drugs (murine epidermis), **60,** 50
Lectins
-dependent cell-mediated cytotoxicity, *see* Cell-mediated cytotoxicity
DNA and protein synthesis stimulation in splenocytes, role of Ca, Mg, and cytochalasin-sensitive processes (mouse), **59,** 276
lymph node cell stimulation, mechanism of lithium ion effects (hamster), **58,** 372
mitogenic and nonmitogenic, effect on interaction between human peripheral blood T cells and monocytes, **57,** 145
oxidative burst induction in peritoneal macrophages (guinea pig), **59,** 301
proliferative response of cord blood lymphocytes to (human neonates), **57,** 307
Leishmania enrietti
immune response to infection with, role of macrophage heterogeneity and Ir-gene control (guinea pig), **60,** 367
Leucine
tritiated, uptake inhibition by murine *Corynebacterium parvum*-elicited peritoneal macrophages (herpes simplex virus-infected Vero cells), **58,** 72
Leukemia
development in AKR mouse, thymocyte differentiation pattern, **59,** 355
Leukocyte inhibitory factor
bacterium-induced production by peripheral blood lymphocytes, lack of clear-cut correlation with bacterial binding by B and T cells (human), **58,** 19
generation by lymph node cells from rats with collagen-induced arthritis, comparison with human factor, **63,** 362
Leukocytes
dialyzable extract, antigen-specific activity of transfer factor (human), **62,** 301
migration inhibition by Epstein–Barr virus-determined nuclear antigen (human), **58,** 269
passenger in kidney, immunogenicity quantitation by primed heart rejection assay (rat), **57,** 92
Leukocytic pyrogen, *see also* Endogenous pyrogen
produced by stimulated macrophages, enhancement of phytohemagglutinin-induced murine thymocyte proliferation (human), **63,** 134
Lipid synthesis
hormone- and drug-induced changes, correlation with tumor cell susceptibility to antibody–complement killing (P815 murine mastocytoma), **58,** 398
human lymphotoxin-induced in fibroblast plasma membranes (mouse L-929 cells), **60,** 144

Lipopolysaccharides
activation of suppressor cells in spleen of newborn mice, **58,** 458
adjuvant action, promotion of antigen retention at site of injection and in lymph node (mouse), **57,** 477
B-cell stimulation
comparison with carrageenan (mouse), **57,** 348
requirement of cell interaction eliminated by dextran sulfate (mouse), **61,** 176
effect of interleukin 1 production and release by macrophages (mouse), **64,** 293
effect on [^{3}H]thymidine incorporation into axial organ cells *in vitro* (starfish), **57,** 136
filtered splenocyte mitogenic response to (mouse), **64,** 1
fluorescein-conjugated, cross-stimulation of B cells unresponsive to antigen itself (mouse), **61,** 292
histamine-induced inhibition of lymphocyte response to (mouse), **62,** 396
-induced mitogen response, effects of adenosine deaminnase inhibitors in splenocytes and thymocytes (mouse), **64,** 29
-induced splenocyte response to bromelain-treated mouse erythrocytes, ontogenic study *in vitro* and *in vivo* (mouse), **65,** 293
low response of splenocytes from mouse with crosslinked B-cell defect to, **61,** 375
peripheral blood lymphocyte response induction only after incubation for 20 hr (human), **57,** 400
splenocyte activation, inhibition by 15-hydroperoxyarachidonic acid (mouse), **58,** 85
synergistic effect with muramyl dipeptide in natural killer activity increase (mouse), **62,** 101
Liposomes
H-2 antigens incorporated in
induction of cytotoxic T cells only after addition of supernatants from concanavalin A-stimulated splenocytes (mouse), **58,** 277
specific interaction with allogeneic cytotoxic T cells (mouse), **63,** 42
muramyl dipeptide encapsulated in, activation *in vitro* of alveolar macrophage tumoricidity (rat), **57,** 42
Lithium ion
effect on mitogen-induced lymphocyte stimulation in presence and absence of potassium (hamster), **57,** 209
modulation of lectin-induced lymphocyte stimulation, multiple mechanisms of (hamster), **58,** 372
Locomotion, *see* Chemotaxis, Chemokinetics
Lung
Bacillus Calmette–Guerin-induced chronic granulomatous inflammation, suppression by soluble factor produced by adherent splenocytes *in vitro* (B6 mouse), **58,** 61
reduced localization of transfered lymph node cells in allogeneic host caused by cell destruction (mouse), **64,** 13
Lymphadenopathy
T-cell-mediated suppression of splenocyte and lymph node cell mitogenic response (MRL mouse), **61,** 40
Lymph node cells
antibody response *in vitro* to synthetic antigens (guinea pig), **60,** 354
antigen-induced T-cell-mediated proliferation, inhibition by antibodies to endogenous AKR-murine leukemia virus (mouse), **64,** 102
capping, inhibition of sulfhydryl reagents (mouse), **57,** 73
concanavalin A-stimulated, migration inhibitory factor production (mouse), **63,** 198
DNA synthesis and cyclic AMP level, effect of high concentration of concanavalin A (rat), **58,** 29
experimental allergic encephalomyelitis transfer
dual activation with concanavalin A and myelin basic protein (rat), **65,** 380
immunocompetence after donor treatment with myelin basic protein (guinea pig), **60,** 220
by supernatant, independence from conventional Ig (rat), **62,** 50
grafts, growth in irradiated mice, immunogenetics (NZB strain and hybrids), **59,** 378
haptenized *in vivo* as source of specific antigen, inhibition of sensitized T-cell migration (mouse), **57,** 361
lithium ion effects on lectin stimulation, multiple mechanisms of (hamster), **58,** 372
mitogenic response stimulation by muramyl dipeptide (mouse), **59,** 195
from NZB autoimmune mouse, abnormally high capacity to induce graft-versus-host reaction in allogeneic adult irradiated mouse, **58,** 124
organ localization after transfer to syngeneic and allogeneic recipients, destruction in allogeneic hosts (mouse), **64,** 13
proliferative response to reticulum cell sarcoma *in vitro* (mouse), **65,** 84
prostaglandin E_2, production and effect on proliferation (mouse), **60,** 335
from rats with collagen-induced arthritis, leukocyte inhibitory factor generation, **63,** 362
responses to circarial and egg immunogens in schistosomiasis (mouse), **59,** 233, 246
T-cell-mediated suppression of mitogenic response in lymphadenopathy (MRL mouse), **61,** 40

Lymph nodes
cells, *see* Lymph node cells
injected antigen retention, promotion by polyclonal lymphocyte activators (mouse), **57,** 477
mesentheric, superiority over peripheral as intermediate site for differentiation of IgA plasma cells from Peyer's patch precursors (mouse), **61,** 141
with mycobacterial granulomas, release of soluble factors effecting fibroblast function *in vitro* (guinea pig), **65,** 93
popliteal, localization of peanut agglutinin-negative thymocytes injected into syngeneic recipients (mouse), **60,** 228
release of retained antigen caused by cortisone acetate, azathioprine, and X rays, but not by cyclophosphamide in immune mouse, **57,** 505
Lymphocyte-activating factor, *see also* Interleukin-1
human and rabbit, close relation to murine serum amyloid A inducer and rabbit pyrogen, **63,** 164
human leukocytic pyrogen activity, ibuprofen-unsensitive in murine thymocyte culture, **63,** 134
produced by splenocytes and thymocytes activated by pokeweed mitogen-derived mitogen Pa-2, comparison with interleukin-2 (mouse), **63,** 118
Lymphocytes
allogeneic
stimulation *in vitro* of plaque-forming cell production by tonsilar lymphocytes (human), **58,** 246
transplantation, generation of specific anti-host-directed T effector cells, delayed hypersensitivity assay (mouse), **59,** 115
autologous erythrocyte rosette-forming cells in thymus, lymph nodes, tonsil, spleen, and peripheral blood (porcine), **57,** 175
binding of bacteriophage T2 antigen *in vitro*
cell types involved and absence of genetic restriction (rabbit), **58,** 448
tolerogenic and immunogenic activity enhancement (rabbit), **58,** 436
cord blood, proliferative response to plant mitogens, antibiotic-killed staphylococcus, and gram-negative bacteria (human neonates), **57,** 307
IgA-bearing from mesentheric lymph node and peripheral lymph node, migration into salivary gland (mouse), **63,** 203
immunologic function and cell surface antigen expression in dystrophic mice, lack of abnormalities, **59,** 138
membrane component capping, inhibition by sulfhydryl reagents (mouse), **57,** 73
from milk, immunological properties (rat), **62,** 271
mixed culture, *see* Mixed lymphocyte culture
parental strain, pretreatment simultaneously with anti-lymphocyte serum, effect on graft-versus-host reaction in F_1 hybrid rat, **57,** 524
peripheral blood, *see* Peripheral blood lymphocytes
peritoneal
colony-inhibitory activity for syngeneic tumor cells, role of lymphotoxin (guinea pig), **63,** 1
cytotoxicity against allogeneic tumor, diminishing by hyperimmunization (mouse), **57,** 114
natural killer activity augmentation by muramyl dipeptide and its analogs (mouse), **62,** 101
stimulation by mitogens, effect of potassium replacement by monovalent cations (hamster), **57,** 209
thoracic duct, T and B cell differentiation on basis of receptors for influenza A virus strain Cam (H1N1) (rat), **57,** 486
tonsillar
plaque-forming cell production against sheep and bovine erythrocytes, stimulation by allogeneic cells *in vitro* (human), **58,** 246
pokeweed mitogen-induced antibody response, enhancement by soluble sheep erythrocyte antigens (human), **61,** 265
various origin, T-cell-dependent macrophage-mediated suppression of mitogen-induced blastogenesis (rat), **63,** 57
Lymphocyte-stimulating factor, *see* Lymphocyte-activating factor
Lymphoid organs
noradrenaline decrease by immunological stimulation (rat), **63,** 329
T cells bearing Qa-4 and Qa-5 surface antigens, postnatal appearance and distribution in (mouse), **57,** 265
Lymphokines
antigen expression induction in macrophage cell line U937 (human), **62,** 140
guinea pig, protective effect on B16 melanoma growth in mouse, **61,** 134
inhibition of normal T-cell migration *in vitro* (mouse), **57,** 361
production *in vivo* in alloxan-treated and genetically diabetic mice with increased susceptibility to *Candida albicans*, **62,** 205
release *in vivo* in 16 inbred strains, variation in type and activity (mouse), **64,** 203

time interval effector and target cells are exposed to, effect on macrophage tumoricidity (mouse), **65,** 52
Lymphotoxin
high-molecular-weight, produced by secondarily stimulated immune splenocytes, stabilization and functional studies (mouse), **61,** 22
produced by peritoneal leukocytes, role in natural cell-mediated cytotoxicity (guinea pig), **63,** 1
production by splenocytes following immunization with DNA-Ascaris conjugates and different adjuvants (rat), **58,** 312
release *in vivo* in 16 inbred strains (mouse), **64,** 203
α-Lymphotoxin
human, effects on fibroblast plasma membrane lipids (mouse L-929 cells), **60,** 144
Lysozyme
immune response to, induction in tolerant mouse by immunization with lysozyme–lipopolysaccharide complex, **58,** 293
Lysozyme–lipopolysaccharide complex
immunization with, induction of immune response to lysozyme in tolerant mouse, **58,** 293

M

Macrophage-activating factor
comparison with purified migration inhibitory factor (guinea pig), **61,** 165
inactivation by D-mannose treatment of macrophages (rabbit), **61,** 319
production by stimulated splenocytes, inhibition by activated macrophages (mouse), **63,** 279
Macrophages
as accessory cells in Fc fragment-mediated polyclonal antibody response of splenocytes, lack of changes with aging (mouse), **63,** 16
alveolar
acetylesterase polymorphism, comparison with that of monocytes (human), **63,** 400
comparison with monocytes in antibody-dependent cell-mediated cytotoxicity and Fc-receptor activity (rabbit), **64,** 359
receptors for IgE, detection using rosette formation assay (rat), **59,** 106
tumoricidal properties, *in vitro* activation by muramyl dipeptide encapsulated in liposomes (rat), **57,** 42
antigen-stimulated, production of leukocytic pyrogen with lymphocyte-activating factor activity (human), **63,** 134
bone marrow, effects of two species from migration inhibitory factor (mouse), **63,** 198
bone marrow-derived *in vitro*
interferon production (mouse), **57,** 495
serological analysis of surface alloantigens and Fc receptors (mouse), **59,** 151
colony-inhibitory activity for syngeneic tumor cells, role of lymphotoxin (guinea pig), **63,** 1
-enriched Peyer's patch cells, antigen presentation after preincubation with collagenase (mouse), **62,** 110
herpes simplex virus-induced proliferation, blockage by anti-HLA-DR antibodies (human), **61,** 11
lipopolysaccharide-stimulated, production of serum amyloid A inducer closely related to lymphocyte activating factor and endogenous pyrogen (mouse), **63,** 164
peritoneal
acetylesterase polymorphism, comparison with that of monocytes (human), **63,** 400
activation for tumoricidity, effect of time interval effector and target cells are exposed to lymphokines (mouse), **65,** 52
adenylate cyclase activation by stimulants of oxidative burst and by arachidonic acid, (guinea pig), **61,** 90
antibody-dependent cell-mediated cytotoxicity, stimulation by thioglycollate and *Bacillus Calmette–Guerin* (mouse), **57,** 51
antigen-induced migration inhibition, reduction after delayed hypersensitivity skin test (guinea pig), **62,** 28
from *Corynebacterium parvum*-infected mouse
inhibition of macrophage-activating factor production by stimulated splenocytes (mouse), **63,** 279
interferon-independent inhibition of herpes simplex virus (mouse), **58,** 72
cytostasis of melanoma B16 cells, stimulation by guinea pig lymphokine (mouse), **61,** 134
cytotoxicity against *Schistosoma mansoni* schistosomula, role of nonspecific IgG (rat), **62,** 15
effects of migration inhibitory factor and macrophage activation factor (guinea pig), **61,** 165
erythrocyte cytolysis, activation by oxidative burst stimulators (guinea pig), **62,** 172
hydrogen peroxide production, effects of nonphagocytic stimuli (guinea pig), **59,** 301
induction of primary cell-mediated cytotoxic response *in vitro* to syngeneic Friend virus-induced leukemia (mouse), **59,** 127
interleukin 1 production and release, effects of various agents (mouse), **64,** 293
D-mannose as surface receptor component for macrophage-activating factor (mouse), **61,** 319

monokine production stimulation by muramyl dipeptide and its adjuvant-active analogs (guinea pig), **64,** 73
normal and *Bacillus Calmette–Guerin*-activated, prostaglandin effects on tumoricidal activity (mouse), **60,** 91
platelet-activating factor release during phagocytosis (rat), **57,** 281
serological analysis of surface alloantigens and Fc receptors (mouse), **59,** 151
specific antigen recognition by rabbit antisera (human), **59,** 392
subpopulations, role in immune response to *Leishmania enrietti* infection (guinea pig), **60,** 367
superoxide anion production, effects of nonphagocytic stimuli (guinea pig), **59,** 301
T-cell-independent activation by viable *Bacillus Calmette–Guerin* in sarcoma-180-bearing mouse, **57,** 293
surface component related to fibronectin, augmentation of response to migration inhibitory factor, **58,** 175
T-cell-dependent suppression of mitogen-induced blastogenesis (rat), **63,** 57
requirement for
B-cell subset responses to anti-IgM antibodies (mouse), **62,** 324
splenocyte activation *in vitro* in adoptive transfer of experimental allergic encephalomyelitis (rat), **60,** 24
splenic
antigen-pulsed, effects on educated T-cell helper activity (mouse), **61,** 104
cytotoxic in agammaglobulinemic and normal alloimmune chickens, **64,** 246
Ia-positive, accessory function for induction of tumor-specific cytotoxic T cells *in vitro* (mouse), **62,** 425
role in lactoferrin-mediated suppression of primary antibody response (mouse), **63,** 308
specific antigen recognition by rabbit antisera (human), **59,** 392
splenic suppressor
activation by *Corynebacterium parvum* and mechanism of action (mouse), **58,** 257; **64,** 150
in experimental African trypanosomiasis (athymic mouse), **63,** 210
induction in glass-wool-adherent T cells, role of prostaglandin synthesis (mouse), **63,** 321
variable occurrence in normal and tumor-inoculated rats, **59,** 367
Magnesium ion
effect on suppressor factor production in mixed lymphocyte culture (mouse), **61,** 353
requirement for early events in lectin-stimulated lymphocyte activation (mouse), **59,** 276
Manganese ion
inhibition of calcium-dependent step in programming of T-cell-mediated cytolysis (mouse), **61,** 78
D-Mannose
as component of macrophage surface receptor for macrophage-activating factor (mouse), **61,** 319
Mast cells
eosinophil chemotactic factor release, inhibition by arachidonic acid analogs (rat), **60,** 480
Mastocytoma P815
-allosensitized splenocytes, inhibition of tumor cell growth *in vitro* (mouse), **57,** 62
-bearing mouse, splenocyte cytotoxicity induction by tumor cells *in vitro,* **59,** 330
differential responses of BALB/c F_1 hybrids *in vivo* to (mouse), **65,** 352
manganese and calcium effects on T-cell-mediated cytolysis (mouse), **61,** 78
sensitivity to humoral and cellular immune attack, effects of metabolic inhibitors and drugs (mouse), **58,** 398
Mathematical model
polyclonal mitogenesis induced in peripheral blood lymphocytes by pokeweed mitogen, two division cycles (human), **57,** 440
Measles virus
acute infection causing selective decrease in H-2 antigen expression (mouse neuroblastoma cell line), **59,** 319
Melanoma
B16
growth in mouse, protection by guinea pig lymphokine, **61,** 134
murine macrophage-mediated cytostasis, stimulation by guinea pig lymphokine, **61,** 134
malignant
monocyte-mediated suppression of lymphocyte cytotoxic activity *in vitro* (human), **57,** 529
sera tested for antibody-dependent cell-mediated cytotoxicity for cultured autologous melanoma cells (human), **64,** 119
Memory cells
alloimmune, alloantigen-independent activation by neuraminidase, galactose oxidase, and sodium periodate (human), **59,** 26
depletion by irradiation, lack of effect on persistent IgE anti-hapten antibody response (mouse), **58,** 188
suppression by T-independent antigen (mouse), **64,** 177
TNP-specific, induction and differentiation in

presence of trinitrophenyl-lipopolysaccharide (mouse), **57,** 327
Metabolic inhibitors
effects on antibody-complement and cell-mediated killing of tumor cells, lack of correlation with effects on macromolecular synthesis (P815 murine mastocytoma), **58,** 398
Methylprednisolone
inhibition of mitogenic response of residual peripheral blood lymphocytes obtained after that glucocorticoid injection (human), **65,** 43
Migration
IgA-bearing lymphocytes into salivary gland (mouse), **63,** 203
leukocytes
effect of leukocyte dialyzable extract (human), **62,** 301
inhibition by Epstein–Barr virus-determined nuclear antigen (human), **58,** 269
peanut agglutinin-negative and -positive thymocytes injected into syngeneic recipients (mouse), **60,** 228
sensitized T cells *in vitro*, inhibition by specific antigen (mouse), **57,** 361
prevention by specific suppressor cells, **57,** 370
Migration inhibitory factor
concanavalin A-induced production by splenic and thymic helper cells (mouse), **59,** 448
macrophage response to, augmentation by substance released upon incubation with hypotonic buffer (guinea pig), **58,** 175
produced by concanavalin A-stimulated lymph node cells, fractionation into two species (mouse), **63,** 198
recovered from immunoadsorbent column, similarity with macrophage-activating factor (guinea pig), **61,** 165
release *in vivo* in 16 inbred strains (mouse), **64,** 203
Migration stimulatory factor
concanavalin A-induced production by splenic and thymic suppressor cells (mouse), **59,** 448
Milk
lymphocytes, immunological properties (rat), **62,** 271
Mitogenic activity
anti-mouse brain serum, T-cell specificity (rabbit), **62,** 60
induction in serum by delayed hypersensitivity skin reaction (guinea pig), **62,** 28
Mitogenic factor
released by pokeweed mitogen-stimulated T cells, expression of HLA-DR antigens (human), **62,** 406
release *in vivo* in 16 inbred strains (mouse), **64,** 203
Mitogenic response, *see also* Proliferation
adenosine deaminase inhibitor effects on thymocytes and splenocytes (mouse), **64,** 29
axial organ cells to various mitogens *in vitro* (starfish), **57,** 136
B cells
to carrageenan, lipopolysaccharide, and dextran sulfate (mouse), **57,** 348
concanavalin A-induced, lack of changes by zinc deficiency *in vitro* (mouse), **60,** 203
to lipopolysaccharide, inhibition by 2′-deoxycoformycin (mouse), **63,** 259
to supernatant from human and mouse lymphoid cell lines (mouse), **60,** 1
cord blood lymphocytes to antibiotic-killed bacteria and plant lectins (human neonates), **57,** 307
lymph node cells, T-cell-mediated suppression (MRL mouse), **61,** 40
mature medullary thymocytes to phytohemagglutinin, stimulation by interleukin 1 (human), **64,** 337
peripheral blood lymphocytes
lipopolysaccharide-induced only after incubation (human), **57,** 400
to phytohemagglutinin, suppression by cocultured fibroblasts (human), **63,** 374
to pokeweed mitogen, lack of cocultured fibroblast effect on (human), **63,** 374
splenocytes
inhibition by 2′-deoxycoformycin (mouse), **63,** 259
inhibition by muramyl dipeptide (mouse), **59,** 195
lectin-induced, role of Ca, Mg, and cytochalasin-sensitive processes (mouse), **59,** 276
to poly(Tyr-Glu-Ala-Gly), effects of genotype (mouse), **61,** 114
to staphylococcal Protein A, interaction between B and T cells (rabbit), **61,** 307
T-cell-mediated inhibition by histamine (mouse), **62,** 396
T-cell-mediated suppression (MRL mouse), **61,** 40
T cells
concanavalin A-induced, inhibition by zinc deficiency *in vitro* (mouse), **60,** 203
to concanavalin A and phytohemagglutinin, inhibition by 2′-deoxycoformycin (mouse), **63,** 259
-dependent, inhibition by human interferons α and β, association with chromosome 21 (human) **65,** 366
-independent, stimulation by human interfer-

ons α and β, association with chromosome 21 (human), **65,** 366
to ionophore A23187 and concanavalin A, different mechanism of (human, mouse, porcine, rabbit), **58,** 134
to lectins or antigens, inhibition by prostaglandins (mouse), **61,** 52
to phytohemagglutinin, genetic control in connection with thyroiditis susceptibility (rat), **62,** 156
recovery after lethal irradiation and reconstitution, earlier in peanut agglutinin-negative than in positive subpopulation (mouse), **62,** 74
to staphylococcal Protein A, interaction with B cells (rabbit), **61,** 307
to T-cell mitogens, inhibition by thymectomy at weaning, restoration by serum thymic factor (mouse), **64,** 93
to thyroglobulin in experimental autoimmune thyroiditis (mouse), **61,** 32
to various mitogens, muramyl dipeptide-induced stimulation in lymph node cells and inhibition in splenocytes (mouse), **59,** 195
Mitogens, *see also specific mitogens*
lymphocyte stimulation, ability of monovalent cations to replace potassium (hamster), **57,** 209
splenocyte cytotoxicity activation, comparison with anti-H-2 antiserum and interferon action (mouse), **63,** 28
-stimulated splenocytes, suppression by tumor-associated fetal antigens (rat), **57,** 155
Mixed lymphocyte culture
allogeneic
plaque-forming cell response to formalin-treated *Staphylococcus aureus* (human), **59,** 256
uv-induced depletion of adherent splenocytes needed for T-cell proliferation (mouse), **63,** 300
alloimmune memory cell activation by mitogenic oxidizing agents (human), **59,** 26
antigen-induced heterogenous suppressor cells, cell lineage and target assay (mouse), **58,** 1
autologous
age and sex effects on reactions (human), **60,** 212
defective isogeneic lymphocyte interaction (CBA/N mouse), **60,** 386
HLA-DR antigen-induced T-cell sensitivity to interleukin 2 and growth factor production (human), **63,** 143
primary and secondary reactions, role of antigens encoded by I region of H-2 complex (mouse), **65,** 142
T-cell activation, suppression by cyclosporin A (human), **61,** 453
autorosette-forming T-cell high activity in (human), **64,** 312
cellular immunity suppression by cytotoxic splenocytes via stimulator cell lysis (mouse), **57,** 124
concanavalin A-induced DNA synthesis and suppressor T-cell activation, inhibition by histamine (mouse), **60,** 426
cytotoxic T-cell generation, *see also* Cytotoxic T cells
decline with aging, functional cell number decrease (mouse), **60,** 470
with high killing activity against lymphoblastoid cell line and lack of spontaneous cytotoxicity (human), **59,** 435
pinocytosis during differentiation into effector cells (mouse), **59,** 429
response to autologous antigen, α-fetoprotein immunosuppression (mouse), **63,** 417
stimulation by F-9 cells and by syngeneic testicular cells (F-9 tumor-bearing mouse), **62,** 334, 341
suppression by adherent splenocytes from tumor-bearing mouse, **60,** 109
DNA synthesis reduction in splenocytes in presence of ectoplacental cone or placental trophoblasts (mouse), **58,** 202
natural killer activity suppression by factor released from pokeweed mitogen-activated peripheral blood lymphocytes (human), **58,** 356
neonatal tolerance to xenogeneic cells in mice inoculated with rat bone marrow cells, **63,** 193
one-way reaction highest in splenocytes lacking Fc receptors and bearing Thy-1 surface antigen (nude *nu/nu* mouse), **57,** 339
primary cell-mediated cytotoxic response to syngeneic Friend virus-induced leukemia, requirement of macrophages (mouse), **59,** 127
proliferative response inhibition
by alloactivated regulatory T cells (human), **60,** 393
by suppressor factor from tumor-allosensitized splenocytes (mouse), **57,** 62
suppressor cell generation, evidence for adherent cell component (mouse), **64,** 371
suppressor factor production, effect of divalent cations and cytochalasin B (mouse), **61,** 353
Moloney murine leukemia virus
genetic control of sensitivity to (mouse), **65,** 317
Monensin
inhibition of natural killer activity in peripheral blood lymphocytes by cellular secretion block (human), **58,** 97

Monocytes
acetylesterase polymorphism, comparison with that of peritoneal and alveolar macrophages (human), **63,** 400
antibody-dependent cell-mediated cytotoxicity, promotion by secretory IgA antibodies synergizing with IgG (human), **59,** 75
binding to T cells, effect of mitogenic and nonmitogenic lectins (human peripheral blood), **57,** 145
herpes simplex virus-induced proliferation, blockage by anti-HLA-DR antibodies (human), **61,** 11
peripheral blood
comparison with macrophages in antibody-dependent cell-mediated cytotoxicity and Fc-receptor activity (rabbit), **64,** 359
freshly isolated, tumoricidal activity (human), **58,** 426
specific antigen recognition by rabbit sera (human), **59,** 392
receptors for IgA, specificity assay by rosette formation (human), **60,** 324
role in pokeweed mitogen-induced differentiation of peripheral blood lymphocytes, plaque-forming cell response assay (human), **58,** 323
suppression *in vitro* of lymphocyte cytotoxic activity for melanoma cells (patients with malignant melanoma), **57,** 529
Monokines
pyrogenic activity *in vivo* and lymphocyte-activating factor activity *in vitro*, **63,** 134
relationship among murine serum amyloid A inducer, rabbit endogenous pyrogen and human and rabbit interleukin-1, **63,** 164
T-cell activating, production by macrophages, stimulation by muramyl dipeptide and its adjuvant-active analogs (guinea pig), **64,** 73
Mononuclear cells
invertebrate, spontaneous non-antigen-dependent cytotoxicity toward vertebrate targets, inhibition by mono- and disaccharides, **59,** 161
Mononuclear phagocytes
antigen expression in lymphokine-activated macrophage cell line U937 (human), **62,** 140
Monosaccharides
inhibition of spontaneous cytotoxicity of invertebrate mononuclear cells toward normal and malignant vertebrate targets, **59,** 161
role in bacterial binding to B and T cells (human), **58,** 19
Muramyl dipeptide
and its adjuvant-active analogs, macrophage-stimulating effects for monokine production (guinea pig), **64,** 73
and its analogs, natural killer activity augmentation in splenocytes and peritoneal cells (mouse), **62,** 101
encapsulated in liposomes, activation *in vitro* of alveolar macrophage tumoricidal properties (rat), **57,** 42
opposite effects on responses to mitogens by lymph node cells and splenocytes (mouse), **59,** 195
Muscular dystrophy
lack of abnormalities in immunologic function and cell surface antigen expression of lymphocytes (mouse), **59,** 138
Myelin basic protein
peripheral blood lymphocyte proliferation induction during experimental allergic encephalomyelitis development (guinea pig), **63,** 409
in presence of concanavalin A, dual activation of experimental allergic encephalomyelitis transfer by lymph node cells (rat), **65,** 380
splenocyte activation in adoptive transfer of allergic encephalomyelitis, requirement of macrophages (rat), **59,** 42; **60,** 24
Myeloma
human lines, sensitization of peripheral blood lymphocytes *in vitro*, **60,** 489
MOPC-315-EL
reactivity with cytotoxic T cells, decrease during growth in culture and in nude mouse, **62,** 119
surface properties early and late after transfer (mouse), **64,** 119

N

Natural killer activity
augmentation by muramyl dipeptide and its analogs in splenocytes and peritoneal cells (mouse), **62,** 101
of cytotoxic T cells generated in mixed lymphocyte culture (human), **65,** 230
defective in *beige* mutants, nonadherent effector splenocyte analysis *in vitro* (mouse), **61,** 343
effector cell fractionation by density gradient centrifugation and characterization (human), **61,** 231
increased in B-cell-deprived mice, role in antitumor cell-mediated cytotoxicity, **65,** 20
peripheral blood lymphocytes
augmentation by *Staphylococcus* protein A (human), **57,** 1
enriched for subpopulations isolated from natural killer–tumor cell conjugates (human), **58,** 415
toward hematopoietic cells, augmentation by interferon (human), **62,** 367

inhibition by monensin (human), **58,** 97
lack of correlation with interferon production *in vitro* (human), **62,** 220
lymphoid cell line sensitivity to, elevation by 12-*O*-tetradecanoylphorbol-13-acetate (human), **63,** 237
suppression by pokeweed mitogen-induced factor (human), **58,** 356
splenocytes
activation by anti-H-2 antiserum, interferon, and mitogens, distinct mechanisms of (mouse), **63,** 28
induction by helper factor supernatants derived from alloantigen-activated lymphocytes (mouse), **58,** 225
infiltrating transplanted chemically induced sarcoma, cytolytic activity *in vitro* (rat), **61,** 1
metabolic requirements for augmentation by interferon (mouse), **58,** 49
toward K562 cells, augmentation by anti-H-2 antibodies, role of Fc receptors (mouse), **65,** 115
reversible inhibition by carrageenan, role of adherent suppressor cells (mouse), **61,** 200
subpopulation distinct from prothymocytes (mouse), **62,** 164
suppression by subpopulations of thymocytes (mouse), **58,** 9
suppression in tetraparental aggregation chimeras (mouse), **57,** 229
stimulation by
human interferons α and β, lack of association with chromosome 21 (human), **65,** 366
phorbol esters, pathway different from interferon-induced activation (mouse), **65,** 258
against syngeneic or allogeneic normal bone marrow cells *in vivo* (mouse), **60,** 136
Negative selection
lymphocytes depleted of T cells specific for male H-Y antigen, lack of response to H-Y-H-2D^b (mouse), **60,** 347
Neonates
immune responses to antibiotic-killed bacteria and plant lectins (human), **57,** 307
null cell compartment in spleen, accumulation of ubiquitin-uninducible cells (mouse), **63,** 106
Neuraminidase
alloantigen-independent activation of memory cells (human), **59,** 26
Neutrophils
antibody-dependent cell-mediated cytotoxicity promotion by secretory IgA antibodies synergizing with IgG (human), **59,** 75
eosinophil chemotactic factor release, inhibition by arachidonic acid analogs (human), **60,** 480
receptors for IgA, specificity assay by rosette formation (human), **60,** 324
Noradrenaline
in lymphoid organs, decrease by immunological stimulation (rat), **63,** 329
Null cells
ubiquitin-induced T- and B-cell differentiation, changes in neonatal and aging mouse spleen, **63,** 106

O

Old tuberculin (OT)
challenging of low-responder strains, induction of inhibitor of interferon type II activity in serum (mouse), **60,** 100
Ontogeny
B-cells
heterogenous antibody response to T-independent antigen (mouse), **60,** 234
surface IgM movement changes (mouse), **65,** 166, 175
lipopolysaccharide-induced response of splenocyte *in vitro* and *in vivo* to bromelain-treated murine erythrocytes (mouse), **65,** 293
Oxidative burst
release of superoxide anions and hydrogen peroxide by peritoneal macrophages, induction by nonphagocytic stimuli (guinea pig), **59,** 301
stimulated by various reagents
activation of macrophage-mediated erythrocyte cytolysis (guinea pig), **62,** 172
increase of macrophage cyclic AMP level, role of calcium (guinea pig), **61,** 90

P

Peanut agglutinin
-negative T cells, higher resistance in comparison with positive subset (mouse), **62,** 74
receptor-bearing splenocytes, separation by specific rosetting technique (mouse), **63,** 249
receptor-bearing thymocytes, migration pattern in syngeneic recipients (mouse), **60,** 228
D-Penicillamine
nonspecific activation of splenocytes (mouse), **65,** 337
Peripheral blood lymphocytes
antibody-dependent cell-mediated cytotoxicity, promotion by secretory IgA antibodies synergizing with IgG (human), **59,** 75
antibody-producing system *in vitro*, role of inhibitory T cells in masking allogeneic help (human), **57,** 201
autologous proliferative response, effect of age and sex (human), **60,** 212
binding of bacteria and bacterium-induced leukocyte-inhibitory factor production, lack of

clear-cut correlation in B and T cells (human), **58,** 19
in coccidiodomycosis, suppressor activity of adherent cells (human), **64,** 235
concanavalin A-induced suppressor cells, autologous rosette-forming T cells as precursors (human), **61,** 273
cyclic AMP
metabolism during phytohemagglutinin-induced activation, effect of very low density lipoprotein (human), **65,** 325
response to prostaglandin E_2, loss after preincubation (human), **60,** 298
2′-deoxycoformycin-induced decrease of differential count (mouse), **63,** 259
DNA synthesis after activation
increase following delayed hypersensitivity skin reaction (guinea pig), **62,** 28
inhibition by histamine-induced suppressor cells (human), **59,** 268
as effector cells in antibody-dependent cell-mediated cytotoxicity of sera from patients with malignant melanoma, **64,** 119
enriched for subpopulations isolated from natural killer–tumor cell conjugates, natural killing activity and K cells (human), **58,** 415
Fcγ receptor induction on theophylline-resistant T-cell subpopulation by adenosine and impromidine (human), **57,** 455
Fc-receptor-mediated functions, effects of anti-HLA-RD and anti-β_2-microglobulin antibodies (human), **59,** 187
fractionation by density gradient centrifugation, natural killer activity and rosette formation assay (human), **61,** 231
herpes simplex virus-induced
cytotoxic and suppressor cells, activation by theophylline (human), **65,** 13
proliferation, blockage by anti-HLA-DR antibodies (human), **61,** 11
from high and low responder to hemagglutinin, graft-versus-host reaction (mouse), **62,** 448
histamine suppression of pokeweed mitogen-induced IgG production (human), **64,** 324
from immune donor, Epstein–Barr virus-induced blastogenesis and cytotoxicity for lymphoid cell lines (human), **63,** 91
interferon II production, induction by protein A from *Staphylococcus aureus* (human), **57,** 1
interferon γ production, induction by OKT3 antibodies (human), **64,** 304
locomotion response to casein, C5a, and fMet-Leu-Phe, effect of culturing (human), **60,** 43
mitogenic response
to lipopolysaccharide only after incubation for 20 hr (human), **57,** 400
modulation by cocultured fibroblasts (human), **63,** 374
natural killer activity, *see* Natural killer activity
nonspecific cytolysis of erythrocytes, induction by immobilized IgG aggregates (human), **60,** 403
plaque-forming cell response to equine erythrocytes, effect of human leukocyte interferon (human), **58,** 464
pokeweed mitogen-activated
differentiation of helper T cells and active B cells, effect of monocytes (human), **58,** 323
differentiation, interferon α effect (human), **64,** 20
enhanced secretion of IgM and IgG in coculture with fetal fetal thymocytes (human), **59,** 17
proliferation and differentiation, dose–response dissimilar relations (human), **61,** 332
proliferation, two division cycles, mathematical model (human), **57,** 440
release of factor suppressing natural killer activity in mixed lymphocyte culture (human), **58,** 356
suppressor cells for plaque-forming cells (human), **65,** 221
prostaglandin E_2 secretion, stimulation by benzylpenicilloyl carrier conjugates (human), **64,** 267
prostaglandin-independent suppression, induction by mobile mediator without cell contact (human), **60,** 440
residual obtained after methylprednisolone injection mitogenic response inhibition *in vitro* by same glucocorticoid (human), **65,** 43
responsiveness to myelin basic protein during experimental allergic encephalomyelitis development (guinea pig), **63,** 409
rosette formation with autologous erythrocytes, stimulation by bromelain (porcine), **57,** 175
sensitization *in vitro* to myeloma cell-related antigen (human), **60,** 489
Permeabilization
Ehrlich ascites tumor cells to inorganic cations by human serum, **61,** 213
Peyer's patches
B-cell differentiation pattern in secretory system after intravenous injection (mouse), **61,** 141
cell types and Ia antigen expression (mouse), **57,** 420
localization of peanut agglutinin-negative thymocytes injected into syngeneic recipients (mouse), **60,** 228
macrophage-enriched cells, antigen presentation after preincubation with collagenase (mouse), **62,** 110
Phagocytosis
connection with platelet-activating factor release

by peritoneal macrophages (rat), **57,** 281

Phorbol esters

natural killer activity stimulation, pathway different from interferon-induced activation (mouse), **65,** 258

Phorbol myristic acetate

enhancement of interleukin 2 production by concanavalin A-activated splenocytes (mouse), **58,** 156

oxidative burst stimulation in peritoneal macrophages (guinea pig), **59,** 301

Phytohemagglutinin

-activated lymphocytes, cyclic AMP metabolism modulation by very low density lipoprotein (human), **65,** 325

effect on immune response to type III pneumococcal polysaccharide, enhancement and IgG subclass restriction (mouse), **65,** 280

high and low responsiveness to, connection with graft-versus-host reactivity of lymphocytes (genetically selected mice), **62,** 448

-induced mitogenic response

effects of adenosine deaminase inhibitors in splenocytes and thymocytes (mouse), **64,** 29

inhibition by histamine-induced suppressor cells (human), **59,** 268; (mouse), **62,** 396

inhibition in lymphocytes cocultured with fibroblasts (human), **63,** 374

interleukin 1 stimulation in mature medullary thymocytes (human), **64,** 337

modulation by lithium ion at level of cyclic nucleotide metabolism (hamster), **58,** 372

suppressed in lymphocytes of some patients with coccidiodomycosis, **64,** 235

Pinocytosis

in T cells during differentiation into cytotoxic effector cells, mixed lymphocyte culture (mouse), **59,** 429

Placenta

trophoblasts, suppression of cell-mediated immunity by (mouse), **58,** 202

Plaque-forming cell response

to bromelain-treated mutine erythrocytes, lipopolysaccharide-induced in splenocytes, ontogenic study (mouse), **65,** 293

to circarial and egg immunogens in schistosomiasis by B and T cells from various lymphoid organs (mouse), **59,** 233, 246

early, Fc receptors for IgG on splenocytes from immunized mouse, **61,** 124

to equine erythrocyte by peripheral blood lymphocytes, effect of human leukocyte interferon (human), **58,** 464

to formalin-treated *Staphylococcus aureus* by allogeneic mixed lymphocyte culture (human), **59,** 256

GAT-specific by B cells from various strains (mouse), **61,** 280

to pokeweed mitogen by peripheral blood lymphocytes

inhibition by suppressor cells induced by same mitogen (human), **65,** 221

role of monocytes (human), **58,** 323

to sheep and bovine erythrocytes, stimulation by allogeneic cells *in vitro* (human tonsilar lymphocytes), **58,** 246

sheep erythrocyte-specific by B cells, synergy between soluble sheep erythrocyte antigen and pokeweed mitogen (human), **60,** 415

to synthetic antigens by splenocytes and lymph node cells (guinea pig), **60,** 354

to T-independent antigen in maturating neonatal B cells (mouse), **60,** 234

to TNP

–γ-globulin, regulation *in vivo* by histamine (mouse), **65,** 152

–lipopolysaccharide, by B cells from two marmoset species (*Saguinus fuscicollis, S. oedipus oedipus*), **57,** 408

streptococcal pyrogenic exotoxin-induced deregulation of (mouse), **57,** 20

to type III pneumococcal polysaccaride by splenocytes, phytohemagglutinin-induced enhancement and IgG subclass restriction (mouse), **65,** 280

Plasma cells

IgA-containing, differentiation from Peyer's patch precursor cells in secretory immune system (mouse), **61,** 141

IgG auto-idiotypic, induction in mucosal tissues by oral-parenteral immunization with human serum albumin (rabbit), **60,** 498

pokeweed mitogen-induced formation from B cells, dose–response relations dissimilar to proliferation induction (human), **61,** 332

Plasmacytoma

-bearing mouse, B-cell maturational defect, antibody affinity study, **62,** 149

Plasma membranes

H-2-containing, effect of suprenatant from concanavalin A-stimulated splenocytes on cytotoxic T-cell induction (mouse), **58,** 277

human lymphotoxin-induced lipid synthesis (mouse L-929 cells), **60,** 144

Platelet-activating factor

release by peritoneal macrophages during phagocytosis (rat), **57,** 281

Platelets

aggregation by platelet-activating factor released by peritoneal macrophages during phagocytosis (rat), **57,** 281

Pneumococcal polysaccharide type III

immune response to, phytohemagglutinin-induced enhancement and IgG subclass restriction (mouse), **65,** 280

Pokeweed mitogen
-derived mitogen Pa-2, induction of lymphocyte-stimulating factor production by splenocytes and thymocytes (mouse), **63,** 118
-driven coculture between fetal thymocytes and adult peripheral blood lymphocytes, enhanced secretion of IgG and IgM (human), **59,** 17
effect on [^{3}H]thymidine incorporation into axial organ cells *in vitro* (starfish), **57,** 136
-induced response
antibody production by tonsillar lymphocytes, enhancement by soluble sheep erythrocyte antigens (human), **61,** 265
IgG anti-tetanus, inhibition by repetitive immunization with tetanus toxoid (human), **59,** 82
immunoglobulin synthesis in B cells, inhibition by lymphoblastoid cell lines (human), **60,** 191
peripheral blood lymphocyte activation
differentiation of B cells and helper T cells, role of monocytes (human), **58,** 323
interferon γ effect on differentiation (human), **64,** 20
proliferation and differentiation, dissimilar dose–response relations (human), **61,** 332
release of factor suppressing natural killer activity in mixed lymphocyte culture (human), **58,** 356
suppressor activity in cells and supernatant (human), **65,** 221
two preprogrammed division cycles, mathematical model (human), **57,** 440
-stimulated T cells, release of mitogenic factor expressing HLA-DR antigens (human), **62,** 406
synergy with soluble antigen in B-cell activation (human), **60,** 415
Polienoic acids
inhibition of eosinophil chemotactic factor release from human neutrophils and rat mast cells, **60,** 480
Poliynoic acids
inhibition of eosinophil chemotactic factor release from human neutrophils and rat mast cells, **60,** 480
Polyclonal lymphocyte activators
adjuvant action, promotion of antigen retention at site of injection and in lymph node (mouse), **57,** 477
Polyclonal mitogenesis
pokeweed mitogen-induced in peripheral blood lymphocytes, two division cycles, mathematical model (human), **57,** 440
Polymers
poly(Tyr-Glu-Ala-Gly)$_n$
mitogenic properties, effects on splenocytes from different genotypes (mouse), **61,** 114
role of H-2 and non-H-2 genes in immune response to (mouse), **62,** 132
poly(Glu^{60}Ala^{30}Tyr^{10}) (GAT) coupled to sheep erythrocytes, specific antibody response induction in splenocytes from various strains (mouse), **61,** 280
Polysaccharides
capsular of *Klebsiella pneumoniae*, adjuvant action, promotion of antigen retention at site of injection and in lymph node (mouse), **57,** 477
Polyvinylpyrrolidone
coupled to syngeneic splenocytes, suppressor T-cell induction (mouse), **63,** 177
Potassium ion
replacement by monovalent cations during mitogen-induced lymphocyte stimulation (hamster), **57,** 209
Prealbumin
comparison with serum thymic factor in effects on T-cell-dependent immune responses *in vitro* (mouse), **65,** 1
Pregnancy
allopregnancy-induced T-cell suppressor factor, H-2 restricted and bearing Ia determinants (mouse), **62,** 186
Primed heart rejection assay
immunogenicity of
parenchymal cells and passenger leukocytes from kidney (rat), **57,** 92
splenocyte populations (rat), **57,** 85
Probability model
for somatic development of T-cell repertoire, **57,** 251
Procarbazine hydrochloride
specific unresponsiveness induction to skin allograft, synergy with antilymphocyte serum (mouse), **62,** 254
Proliferation, *see also* Mitogenic response
pokeweed mitogen-induced in peripheral blood lymphocytes, two division cycles (human), **57,** 420
T cells
concanavalin A-induced, control by cell surface thiol-reactive sites (mouse), **60,** 453
lectin- or antigen-activated, inhibition by prostaglandins, mechanism of (mouse), **61,** 52
thyroglobulin-induced in experimental autoimmune thyroiditis (mouse), **61,** 32
uncoupling from differentiation in pokeweed mitogen-stimulated lymphocytes (human), **61,** 332

Prostaglandin E_1
induction of nonadherent T suppressor cells in splenocyte culture (mouse), **59,** 54
Prostaglandin E_2
content increase in coculture of fibroblasts and lymphocytes, role in mitogenic response modulation (human), **63,** 374
cyclic AMP level changes in lymphocytes, effect of preincubation (human), **60,** 298
response to and production of, by thymocytes, splenocytes, bone marrow, and lymph node cells (mouse), **60,** 335
secretion by peripheral blood lymphocytes, stimulation by benzylpenicilloyl carrier conjugates (human), **64,** 267
synthetic analog, theta antigen induction *in vivo* in splenocytes (thymectomized mouse), **62,** 8
Prostaglandins
-independent peripheral blood lymphocyte suppression without cell contact (human), **60,** 440
opposite effects on antitumor activity of normal and *Bacillus Calmette–Guerin*-activated macrophages (mouse), **60,** 91
role in cell-mediated immunity regulation by essential fatty acids of ω-6 family (rat), **62,** 293
role in macrophage adenylate cyclase stimulation by arachidonic acid (guinea pig), **61,** 90
synthesis in macrophages, role in suppressor activity induction in T cells (mouse), **63,** 321
T-cell proliferation inhibition, role of T-cell growth factor (mouse), **61,** 52
Proteases
inhibition by Trasylol, suppression of B-cell differentiation *in vitro* (mouse), **60,** 155
Protein synthesis
in fibroblasts, stimulation by soluble factors released by lymph nodes containing mycobacterial granulomas (guinea pig), **65,** 93
lectin-activated in splenocytes, role of Ca, Mg, and cytochalasin-sensitive processes (mouse), **59,** 276
requirements for *in vitro* interferon-induced augmentation of splenocyte natural killer activity (mouse), **58,** 49
Prothymocytes
distinction from natural killer splenocytes, antigenic analysis (mouse), **62,** 164
Psoralens
skin depletion of Ia-bearing Langerhans cells (mouse), **60,** 50
Pulmonary granuloma
induced by *Schistosoma japonicum* egg injection, kinetics and mechanism (mouse), **60,** 251
Pulmonary granulomatous inflammation
T-cell-dependent response to *Bacillus Calmette–Guerin* (mouse), **65,** 211
Purified protein derivative of tuberculin (PPD)
low response of splenocytes from mouse with crosslinked B-cell defect to, **61,** 375
Pyrogenicity
of human leukocytic pyrogen, ibuprofen-sensitive *in vivo*, **63,** 134

R

Radiation leukemia virus
-induced transformation of ovalbumin-immune T cells, helper T-cell lymphoma production (mouse), **65,** 194
Receptors
for alloantigen C, alteration according to host environments during T-cell differentiation from bone marrow cells (mouse), **62,** 350
for bacteria, role of monosaccharides in B and T cells (human), **58,** 19
complement in B-cell subpopulations, role in macrophage requirement for response to anti-IgM antibodies (mouse), **62,** 324
for complement C3, as surface marker for functionally different B-cell subpopulation (CBA/N mouse), **61,** 386
for Fc fragments of immunoglobulins, *see* Fc receptors
for glucocorticoids on thymocytes, effect of thymosin Fraction 5 (mouse), **60,** 376
for histamine on peripheral blood lymphocytes (human), **59,** 268
for immunoglobulins, *see* Immunoglobulin receptors
for influenza A virus strains Cam (H1N1) and Japan (H2N2) on T and B cells from thoracic duct (rat), **57,** 486
for macrophage-activating factor on macrophage surface, D-mannose as component of (rabbit), **61,** 319
Resistance
to glucocorticoids in thymocytes, effect of thymosin Fraction 5 (mouse), **60,** 376
Rheumatoid factor
monoclonal, use for enhanced sensitivity of macromolecular secretion study by single cells, **63,** 154
RNA synthesis
requirement for *in vitro* interferon-induced augmentation of splenocyte natural killer activity (mouse), **58,** 49
Rosette formation
active and late by T-cell subpopulations (human), **64,** 227
in analysis of cell surface alloantigens and receptors on bone marrow-derived and peritoneal macrophages (mouse), **59,** 151

autologous
by B cells, induction by supernatants from lymphoid cell lines (mouse), **60,** 1
by lymphocyte different origin (porcine), **57,** 175
by T-cell subpopulation from peripheral blood (human), **64,** 312
with bacteria by B and T cells, modification by monosaccharides (human), **58,** 19
in bone marrow cell populations separated by density gradient electrophoresis (human), **59,** 345
with IgA-sensitized bovine erythrocytes by neutrophils and monocytes, inhibition by IgA preparations (human), **60,** 324
with IgE-coated bovine erythrocytes by alveolar and peritoneal macrophages (rat), **59,** 106
lymphocytes fractionated by density gradient centrifugation (human), **61,** 231
in response to anti-IgM antibodies by B-cell subpopulations, differential macrophage requirement for (mouse), **62,** 324
with sheep erythrocytes, active early by T-cell subset, connection with other immunologic functions (human), **59,** 205
specific technique for separation of splenocytes bearing receptors for peanut agglutinin (mouse), **63,** 249
Rubidium
uptake by human serum-permeabilized Ehrlich ascites tumor cells, **61,** 213

S

Salivary gland
IgA-bearing lymphocyte migration into (mouse), **63,** 203
Schistosoma japonicum
eggs subcutaneously injected, pulmonary granuloma formation (mouse), **60,** 251
Schistosoma mansoni
circarial and egg immunogens, cellular responses induction in various lymphoid organs (mouse), **59,** 233, 246
humoral and cell-mediated immune response in mice vaccinated with irradiated circariae of, **65,** 75
schistosomula, interaction with macrophages, role of nonspecific IgG (rat), **62,** 15
Sendai virus
delayed sensitivity adoptive transfer
antigen requirements on T cells (mouse), **63,** 188
induction of two T-cell subsets (mouse), **62,** 38
Serum
antigen-specific enhancing factors for antibody production (mouse), **60,** 64, 77
complements, permeabilization of Ehrlich ascites tumor cells to inorganic cations (human), **61,** 213
inhibitor of interferon type II activity in sensitized and low-responder strains (mouse), **60,** 100
lymphokine identification and activities in 16 strains (mouse), **64,** 203
-mediated inhibition of mixed lymphocyte culture proliferation in neonatally induced tolerance (mouse), **57,** 183
mitogenic activity induction by delayed hypersensitivity skin reaction (guinea pig), **62,** 28
from patients with malignant melanoma, antibody-dependent cell-mediated cytotoxicity against cultured autologous melanoma cells, **64,** 119
tumor necrosis factor-positive, induction of thymocyte maturation *in vitro* (mouse), **57,** 237
Serum amyloid A inducer
from lipopolysaccharide-stimulated macrophages, close relation to lymphocyte-activating factor and endogenous pyrogen (mouse), **63,** 164
Serum thymic factor
comparison with prealbumin in effects on T-cell-dependent immune responses (mouse), **65,** 1
restoration of adult thymectomized mouse ability to be suppressed by TNP-conjugated splenocytes, **64,** 144
restoration of T-cell mitogenic response inhibited by thymectomy at weaning (mouse), **64,** 93
Sex
effect on autologous proliferative response in peripheral blood lymphocytes (human), **60,** 212
Sheep erythrocytes
binding by B-cell population, effect on surface Ig expression during primary *in vivo* immune response (mouse), **62,** 377
delayed footpad reaction induction in mouse, effect of thymectomy, **61,** 190
primary antibody response to, anti-IgD enhancement of (rat), **63,** 293
soluble antigens
enhancement of human tonsillar lympohocyte antibody response to pokeweed mitogen, **61,** 265
injection to induce antigen-specific immunosuppression (BALB/c mouse), **59,** 171
synergy with pokeweed mitogen in B-cell activation (human), **60,** 415
Silica
effects on interleukin 1 production and release by macrophages (mouse), **64,** 293

Skin
allograft
rejection decrease by suppressor factor from tumor-allosensitized splenocytes (mouse), **57,** 62
specific unresponsiveness to, effect of antilymphocyte serum and procarbazine hydrochloride (mouse), **62,** 254
survival, immunosuppression by essential fatty acids (rat), **62,** 293
graft rejection
effect of hyperimmunization (mouse), **57,** 99
vascular endothelium changes (mouse), **59,** 219
reactivity to keyhole limpet hemocyanin (human), **60,** 240
Skin reactive factor
release *in vivo* in 16 inbred strains (mouse), **64,** 203
Small intestine
reduced localization of transfered lymph node cells in allogeneic host, cell destruction (mouse), **64,** 13
Smallpox
inoculation against, royal experiment in England (1721-1722), **61,** 437
Sodium borohydride
prevention of memory cell activation by mitogenic oxidizing agents (human), **59,** 26
reversal of sodium periodate-induced inhibition of splenocyte antibody response *in vitro* (mouse), **59,** 10
Sodium periodate
alloantigen-independent activation of memory cells (human), **59,** 26
inhibition of splenocyte antibody response *in vitro*, reversal by sodium borohydride and hydroxylamine (mouse), **59,** 10
Spleen
Bacillus Calmette–Guerin-induced chronic granulomatous inflammation, suppression by soluble factor produced by adherent splenocytes *in vitro* (B6 mouse), **58,** 61
cells, *see* Splenocytes
early postnatal, suppressor T cells inhibiting cytotoxic T-cell responses (mouse), **58,** 345
influenza A virus-induced homotypic and heterotypic T- and B-cell immunity (mouse), **60,** 119
neonatal
soluble suppressor factor production in culture (mouse), **62,** 412
suppressor cell activation by lipopolysaccharides (mouse), **58,** 458
tolerance induction to histoincompatible cells (mouse), **57,** 183
null cell compartment, age-dependent differences (mouse), **63,** 106
responses to circarial and egg immunogenes in schistosomiasis (mouse), **59,** 233, 246
suppressor cells, concanavalin A-induced migration stimulatory factor production (mouse), **59,** 448
suppressor macrophages, variable occurrence in normal and tumor-inoculated rats, **59,** 367
suppressor T cells and suppressor macrophages, induction by *Corynebacterium parvum* intravenous injection into alloimmunized mouse, **58,** 257
Spleen-derived immunosuppressive peptide
comparison with immunoglobin-binding factor, biological activity and chomatography (mouse), **58,** 209
Splenectomy
abrogation of cell-mediated immunity suppression by essential fatty acids (rat), **62,** 293
lack of effect on
antibody-mediated tolerance (mouse), **58,** 302
reduced lymphocyte homing in allogenic recipients (mouse), **64,** 13
Splenocytes
as accessory cells in murine T-cell response to concanavalin A, genus restriction (mouse species and strains, guinea pig), **57,** 28
adherent, *see* Adherent cells
adoptive transfer of tumor-specific immunity induced by somatic hybrids (mouse), **65,** 373
in agammaglobulinemia, cytotoxicity (chicken), **64,** 246, 258
aging-induced changes in Fc fragment-mediated polyclonal antibody response (mouse), **63,** 16
allogeneic, transplantation into lethally irradiated mouse, delayed hypersensitivity assay of responsiveness to H-2-subregion-coded antigens, **57,** 389
angiogenesis induction, role of Lyt phenotype (mouse), **63,** 272
antibody-dependent cell-mediated cytotoxicity, inhibition by antiserum against mouse brain (mouse), **59,** 419
antibody formation and unresponsiveness induction by lymphocyte-bound antigen from bacteriophage T2 (rabbit), **58,** 436, 448
antibody-forming, expression of receptors for Fc portion of IgG (mouse), **61,** 124
antibody response *in vitro* to synthetic antigenes (guinea pig), **60,** 354
anti-H-2 cytotoxic T cell elicitation by partially purified H-2 antigen (mouse), **61,** 365
from autoimmune NZB mouse, abnormally high capacity to induce graft-versus-host reaction in allogeneic irradiated adult mouse, **58,** 124
B cells, *see* B cells
concanavalin A-activated

interleukin 2 production enhancement by phorbol myristic acetate (mouse), **58,** 156
lymphotoxin production *in vitro* (mouse), **61,** 22
macrophage-activating factor production inhibition by activated macrophages (mouse), **63,** 279
supernatant, cytotoxic T-cell generation by H-2-containing plasma membranes in presence of (mouse), **58,** 277
suppression of B hybridoma antibody response (mouse), **61,** 300
Corynebacterium parvum-induced interferons, characterization (mouse), **64,** 64
coupled to insulin with carbodiimide, induction of cell-mediated immunity and tolerance to insulin (mouse), **60,** 314
cytotoxicity
activation by anti-H-2 antisera, interferon, and mitogens (mouse), **63,** 28
aging effect on affinity for target cells and cell number in mixed lymphocyte culture (mouse), **60,** 470
to alloantigens and to TNP-modified self-antigens, enhancement by pretreatment with anti-Ia plus complement (mouse), **62,** 82
against allogeneic tumor, diminishing by hyperimmunization (mouse), **57,** 114
induction by keyhole limpet hemocyanin or invertebrate hemolymph (primed mouse), **58,** 333
to syngeneic cells modified with fluorescein isothiocyanate, H-2-linked control (mouse), **59,** 97
against syngeneic tumors, cell-size analysis, sedimentation profile (mouse), **59,** 330
experimental allergic encephalomyelitis transfer
macrophage requirement for activation by concanavalin A and myelin basic protein (rat), **60,** 24
from myelin basic protein-sensitized animal after *in vitro* activation by specific antigen (rat), **59,** 42
and reactivity to concanavalin A, effects of donor sensitization (rat), **65,** 66
filtered, lipopolysaccharide-induced mitogenic response (mouse), **64,** 1
GAT idiotype expression by GAT-specific B cells from various strains (mouse), **61,** 280
15-hydroperoxyarachidonic acid-induced inhibition of mitogenic response and changes in cyclic nucleotide levels (mouse), **58,** 85
immunogenicity assay *in vivo*, effect of priming time and doses on heart allograft survival (rat), **57,** 85
lactoferrin suppression of primary antibody response to T-cell-dependent and -independent antigens (mouse), **63,** 308
lectin-activated DNA and protein synthesis, role of Ca, Mg, and cytochalasin-sensitive processes (mouse), **59,** 276
lectin-dependent cell-mediated cytotoxicity, supporting by insolubilized concanavalin A (mouse), **59,** 411
lipopolysaccharide-treated
cellular interaction requirement for mitogenesis, dextran sulfate effect (mouse), **61,** 176
impairment of immune response to erythrocyte antigens *in vitro* (newborn mouse), **58,** 458
proliferation and immunoglobulin synthesis (human), **57,** 400
lymphocyte-stimulating factor production induced by pokeweed mitogen-derived mitogen Pa-2 (mouse), **63,** 118
macrophages, *see* Macrophages
maturation *in vitro* into background plaque-forming cells in absence of T cells, macrophages, and serum factors (mouse), **57,** 13
mitogenic response, *see* Mitogenic response
mixed lymphocyte reaction, *see* Mixed lymphocyte culture
from mouse with crosslinked B-cell defect, low responses to lipopolysaccharide, purified protein derivative of tuberculin, and dextran sulfate, **61,** 375
from mouse expressing humoral immunity, development of T-cell population mediating delayed hypersensitivity in normal mouse, **57,** 468
from mouse primed with rat erythrocytes, suppression of autoantibody induction in normal mouse, role of thymus, **63,** 221
murine differentiation antigen 1 absence in CBA/N mouse, **60,** 386
natural killer cells, *see* Natural killer activity
nonadherent
low natural killer response *in vitro* in *beige* mutants (mouse), **61,** 343
Thy and Ly markers on cells rejecting tumor (mouse immune to syngeneic fibrosarcoma H-7), **60,** 34
nonspecific activation by D-pecillamine (mouse), **65,** 337
nude, as accessory cells in cytotoxic T-cell generation against TNP-haptenated syngeneic cells (mouse), **62,** 385
plaque-forming cell response, *see* Plaque-forming cell response
preculture with DNA-polyacrylamide beads, antigen-specific suppressor activity induction (mouse), **64,** 44
prekiller, antiautologous lectin-dependent cell-mediated cytotoxicity (mouse), **60,** 11

prostaglandin E_2, production and effect on proliferation (mouse), **60,** 335
radioresistant long-lived, participation in persistent IgE anti-hapten antibody response (mouse), **58,** 188
receptors for IgM, shedding following temperature shift (rat), **60,** 168
sodium periodate-induced inhibition of antibody response to sheep erythrocytes, reversal by sodium borohydride and hydroxylamine (mouse), **59,** 10
stimulated by mitogens and tumor cells, suppression by tumor-associated fetal antigens (rat), **57,** 155
subpopulations
differing in mitogenic responsiveness susceptibility to adenosine deaminase inhibitors (mouse), **64,** 29
lacking Fc receptors and bearing Thy-1 surface antigen, highest response in mixed lymphocyte reaction (nude *nu/nu* mouse), **57,** 339
peanut agglutinin receptor-bearing, separation by specific rosetting technique (mouse), **63,** 249
radioresistant, stimulation of cytotoxic T-cell induction in mixed lymphocyte culture (mouse), **63,** 335
suppressor in disseminated histoplasmosis (mouse), **60,** 287
Thy 1,1- and Thy 1,2-positive, mitogenic responsiveness to rabbit anti-mouse brain serum (mouse), **62,** 60
syngeneic coupled with polyvinylpyrrolidone, suppressor T-cell induction (mouse), **63,** 177
T cells, *see* T cells
theta antigen induction *in vivo* by prostaglandin E_2 synthetic analog (thymectomized mouse), **62,** 8
as third-party cells, allogeneic effect on cytotoxicity induction in mixed lymphocyte culture (mouse), **59,** 61
TNP-conjugated, immunosuppression in adult mice, effects of thymectomy and serum thymic factor, **64,** 144
tumor-allosensitized, suppressor factor effect on *in vitro* tumor cell proliferation and *in vivo* skin allograft survival (mouse), **57,** 62
unresponsiveness *in vitro* induced by nude mouse pretreatment with antigen and T cells, **61,** 245
zinc deficiency effects on mitogenesis in T and B cells *in vitro* (mouse), **60,** 203
Splenomegaly
T-cell-dependent response to *Bacillus Calmette–Guerin* (mouse), **65,** 211
Staphylococcal Protein A
interferon II induction and natural killer activity augmentation in peripheral blood lymphocytes (human), **57,** 1
splenocyte stimulation, interactions between B and T cells (rabbit), **61,** 307
Stimulator cells
EL-4 tumor, lysis by cytotoxic splenocytes causing suppression of cellular immunity in mixed lymphocyte culture (mouse), **57,** 124
Streptococcal pyrogenic exotoxin
deregulation of anti-TNP plaque-forming cell response in T-cell subpopulation (mouse), **57,** 20
Sulfhydryl reagents
inhibition of lymph node cell capping (mouse), **57,** 73
Superoxide anions
production by peritoneal macrophages, effects of nonphagocytic stimuli (guinea pig), **59,** 301
Suppressor cells
adherent splenocytes in tumor-bearing mouse, inhibition of mixed lymphocyte culture responses, **60,** 109
antigen-specific induced in splenocytes by nude mouse pretreatment with antigen and T cells, **61,** 245
blocking of sensitized T-cell response in migration inhibition test (mouse), **57,** 370
in coccidiomycosis, adherent indomethacin-inhibited subpopulation of peripheral blood lymphocytes (human), **64,** 235
concanavalin A-induced
autologous rosette-forming T cells as precursors (human), **61,** 273
direct action on immunoglobulin production by B hybridoma line (mouse), **61,** 300
migration stimulatory factor production (mouse spleen, thymus), **59,** 448
in mixed lymphocyte culture, inhibition by histamine (mouse), **60,** 426
generated in splenocyte culture, assay with anti-Thy-1.2 serum (mouse), **64,** 371
herpes simplex virus-induced, activation by theophylline (human), **65,** 13
heterogenous antigen-induced in mixed lymphocyte culture, cell lineage and target assay (mouse), **58,** 1
histamine-induced, inhibition of
IgG synthesis *in vitro* by fresh lymphocytes (human), **58,** 366
lymphocyte response to mitogens (human), **59,** 268
induced by lymphoblastoid cell lines, inhibition of pokeweed mitogen-induced immunoglobulin synthesis by B cells (human), **60,** 191
induction by F-9 tumor cell injection, stimulation in mixed lymphocyte culture by F-9

cells and testicular cells (mouse), **62,** 334, 341
involvement in active enhancement of allografted tumors, synergy with enhancing antibodies *in vitro* and *in vivo* (mouse), **58,** 107
lipopolysaccharide-induced activation in spleen of newborn mice, **58,** 458
monocytes from patients with malignant melanoma, effect on lymphocyte cytoxicity for cultured autologous melanoma cells (human), **57,** 529
for natural killer activity, adherent non-T Ia-negative, carrageenan-induced *in vivo* (mouse), **61,** 200
pokeweed mitogen-induced in peripheral blood lymphocytes, plaque-forming cell response inhibition (human), **65,** 221
possible role in prevention of mitogenic response to lipopolysaccharide from fresh peripheral blood lymphocytes (human), **57,** 400
prostaglandin E_1-induced activity of nonadherent T cells in splenocyte culture (mouse), **59,** 54
rat erythrocyte-induced in mouse, autoantibody suppression after transfer to normal mouse, role of thymus, **63,** 221
role in T-cell unresponsiveness to H-Y antigen (mouse), **62,** 251
splenic macrophages
activated by *Corynebacterium parvum*, soluble suppressive factor production (mouse), **64,** 150
in experimental African trypanosomiasis (athymic mouse), **63,** 210
variable occurrence in normal and tumor-inoculated rats, **59,** 367
splenic T cells and macrophages, induction by intravenous injection of *Corynebacterium parvum* into alloimmunized mouse, **58,** 257
splenocyte populations
in disseminated histoplasmosis (mouse), **60,** 287
stimulator cell lysis in mixed lymphocyte culture (mouse), **57,** 124
Suppressor factor
allopregnancy-induced in T cells, H-2 restriction and Ia antigen expression (mouse), **62,** 186
antigen-specific, blocking of sensitized T-cell response in migration inhibition test (mouse), **57,** 370
labile low-molecular-weight, release by peripheral blood lymphocytes (human), **60,** 440
production by adherent splenocytes from *Bacillus Calmette–Guerin*-injected B6 mouse, diminishing of chronic inflammation in lung and spleen, **58,** 61
soluble, produced by
activated splenic macrophage suppressors, inhibition of cytotoxic T-cell generation (mouse), **64,** 150
neonatal murine splenocytes, characterization, **62,** 412
from tumor-allosensitized splenocytes, effect on *in vitro* tumor cell proliferation and *in vivo* skin allograft survival (mouse), **57,** 62
Suppressor T cells
in allograft tolerance (mouse), **62,** 254
from early postnatal spleen, inhibition of cytotoxic T-cell responses (mouse), **58,** 345
histamine-activated, inhibition of
pokeweed mitogen-induced IgG production by peripheral blood lymphocytes (human), **64,** 324
splenocyte mitogenic response (mouse), **62,** 396
induction in mixed lymphocyte culture from F-9 tumor-bearing mice, **62,** 334, 341
induction by thymus-independent antigen polyvinylpyrrolidone coupled to syngeneic splenocytes (mouse), **63,** 177
inhibition of cytolytic T-cell activity directed against autochthonous tumor cells (mouse), **58,** 165
in lymphadenopathy, inhibition of splenocyte and lymph node cell mitogenic response (MRL mouse), **61,** 40
macrophage-induced activity in glass-wool-adherent population (mouse), **63,** 321
macrophage-mediated suppression of mitogen-induced blastogenesis (rat), **63,** 57
neonatally induced, maintenance of low-zone tolerance to bovine serum albumin (mouse), **62,** 436
16p antigen expression (human), **64,** 84
Surface markers, *see* Antigens

T

T-cell growth factor, *see also* Interleukin-2
production by immunocompetent thymocytes and splenic T cells, prevention by adenosine deaminase inhibition (rat), **63,** 81
role in prostaglandin-induced inhibition of T-cell proliferation (mouse), **61,** 52
T-cell hybrids
Fc receptors for IgG, specificity, behavior, and relationship with Ia antigens (mouse), **63,** 349
T cells
activated
interleukin 2 production, requirement for adherent cells (human), **63,** 71
by lymphoblastoid cell lines, suppression of pokeweed mitogen-induced immunoglobulin synthesis by B cells (human), **60,** 191

by macrophage-produced monokines, effects of muramyl dipeptide and its analogs (guinea pig), **63,** 73
adherent, *see* Adherent cells
aging-induced defects in Fc fragment-mediated polyclonal antibody response (mouse), **63,** 16
alloactivated regulatory (T_R), mixed lymphocyte reaction modulation (human), **60,** 393
alloantigen-stimulated proliferation, uv-induced depletion of adherent splenocyte function for (mouse), **63,** 300
allopregnancy-induced suppressor factor, H-2 restricted and hearing Ia determinants (mouse), **62,** 186
allospecific
interpretation of major histocompatibility complex (review), **62,** 258
receptor alteration after differentiation from bone marrow cells in semiallogeneic environment (mouse), **62,** 350
autologous rosette-forming, role in concanavalin A-induced suppressor cell function (human), **61,** 273
autoreactivity, DNA synthesis stimulation by syngeneic thyroid epithelial cells (mouse), **62,** 313
binding to monocytes, effect of mitogenic and nonmitogenic lectins (human peripheral blood), **57,** 145
bone marrow
populations separated by density gradient electrophoresis (human), **59,** 345
precursor tolerance against human IgG, transient stage in DDD and C57BL/6 mice, **57,** 377
concanavalin A-stimulated
mitogenesis inhibition by zinc deficiency *in vitro* (mouse), **60,** 203
role of Ia antigen, genus restriction in interaction with splenic accessory cells (mouse), **57,** 28
cytolytic activity
against autochronous tumors, inhibition by suppressor cells from thymus (mouse), **58,** 165
induction *in vitro* by keyhole limpet hemocyanin or invertebrate hemolymph (mouse), **58,** 333
inhibition by antiactivated T cell antiserum (mouse), **59,** 289
against neuroblastoma cell line, decrease after acute measles infection (mouse), **59,** 319
cytotoxic, *see* Cytotoxic T cells
-dependent immune responses to killed *Bacillus Calmette–Guerin* injection (mouse), **65,** 211
DNA synthesis stimulation by syngeneic epithelial thyroid cells in monolayer culture (mouse), **62,** 313
effector
and amplifier activities generated by allogeneic transplantation of lymphocytes, role of T_1 and T_2 cells (mouse), **59,** 115
development after allogeneic splenocyte transplantation, responses to H-2 antigens (mouse), **57,** 389
mature, requirement for helper activity of fetal thymocytes in pokeweed mitogen-driven coculture (human), **59,** 17
and suppressor activities for delayed footpad reaction to sheep erythrocytes (mouse), **61,** 190
function in *in vitro* antibody formation, lack of differences between two marmoset species *(Saguinus fuscicollis, S. oedipus oedipus)*, **57,** 408
generated in mixed lymphocyte culture, *see* Mixed lymphocyte culture
H-2-dependent restriction in ability to induce immune response to Ehrlich ascites tumor in T-cell-deficiency (mouse), **62,** 93
helper, *see* Helper T cells
inactivation by antigen-specific suppressor cells induced by nude mouse pretreatment with antigen and T cells, **61,** 245
lymph node
concanavalin A effects on DNA synthesis and cyclic AMP level (rat), **58,** 29
ovalbumin-stimulated, inhibition by antibodies to endogenous AKR-murine leukemia virus (mouse), **64,** 102
macromolecule secretion by single cells, method for detection, **63,** 154
mediating delayed hypersensitivity, development in splenocyte culture from mice expressing humoral immunity, **57,** 468
migration inhibition *in vitro* by lymphokines (mouse), **57,** 361
mitogenic response, *see* Mitogenic response
monocyte–macrophage presentation of herpes simplex virus antigen to, role of HLA-DR determinants (human), **61,** 11
nonadherent, suppressor activity induction in splenocyte culture by prostaglandin E_1 (mouse), **59,** 54
ontogeny in mouse
population bearing Qa-4 and Qa-5 surface antigens, postnatal appearance and organ distribution, **57,** 265
thymocyte maturation induced *in vitro* by tumor necrosis factor-positive serum, **57,** 237
opposite effects of intravenous administration of TNP-conjugated tumor cells on development of antitumor and anti-TNP-self cytotoxicity (mouse), **59,** 181

in Peyer's patches, Ia antigen expression (mouse), **57,** 420
plaque-forming cell response to circarial and egg immunogens in schistosomiasis (mouse), **59,** 233, 246
pokeweed mitogen-stimulated
proliferation, dose–response relations dissimilar to B-cell differentiation (human), **61,** 332
release of mitogenic factor expressing HLA-DR antigens (human), **62,** 406
prealbumin-induced Thy-1 antigen expression and mitogenic response stimulation (mouse), **65,** 1
proliferative response, *see* Mitogenic response
reactive to tumor-associated antigens, induction stimulation by helper factor supernatant *in vitro* (mouse), **58,** 225
requirement for nonspecific suppression of delayed hypersensitivity (mouse), **60,** 308
-resembling splenocytes with Thy and Ly markers, rejection of fibrosarcoma H-7 (mouse), **60,** 34
response to different antigenic regions in human fibrinopeptide B (guinea pig), **58,** 238
role in induction of enhancing factor for antibody production (mouse), **60,** 64, 77
self-restriction and specificity, role of random repertoire of V genes, theoretical conclusions, **64,** 381
sensitized
calcium-dependent step in lysis programming, inhibition by manganese (mouse), **61,** 78
migration inhibition *in vitro* by specific antigen (mouse), **57,** 361, 370
somatic development of repertoire, theoretical considerations and probability model, **57,** 251
splenic
inability to produce T-cell growth factor in adenosine deaminase deficiency conditions (rat), **63,** 81
influenza A virus-induced homotypic and heterotypic immunity (mouse), **60,** 119
lectin-dependent cell-mediated cytotoxicity, support by insolubilized concanavalin A (mouse), **59,** 411
suppressor activity induction by intravenous injection of *Corynebacterium parvum* into alloimmunized mouse, **58,** 257
from TNP-splenocyte-treated mice, suppression of *in vitro* antibody response of normal splenocytes, **64,** 144
subpopulations
active and late rosette-forming, immunological and cytochemical characterization (human), **64,** 227
autologous rosette-forming, markers and function (human peripheral blood), **64,** 312
bearing H-2-type receptors and Ly 2 membrane antigen, histamine-induced suppressors of lymphocyte response to mitogen (mouse), **62,** 396
defined by "active" rosette formation, immunologic functions (human), **59,** 205
with different susceptibility to 2′-deoxycoformycin inhibitory effect on mitogenic response (mouse), **64,** 29
differing in H-2 restriction and Lyt-phenotype, induction during Sendai virus infection (mouse), **62,** 38
generating streptococcal pyrogenic exotoxin-induced deregulation of anti-TNP plaque-forming cell response (mouse), **57,** 20
glass-wool-adherent, suppressor activity induction by macrophages, (mouse), **63,** 321
Ia antigen expression on cells with OKM1 antigen (human, peripheral blood), **64,** 277
Lyt and Thy synergism in angiogenesis induction (mouse), **63,** 272
mediating delayed hypersensitivity to Sendai virus, *K*, *D* region and *I* region restriction (mouse), **63,** 188
$p16^+$ and $p16^-$ separation, functional differences (human), **64,** 84
peanut agglutinin binding and nonbinding, mitogenic response recovery after irradiation and reconstitution (mouse), **62,** 74
receptors for influenza A virus strains Cam (H1N1) and Japan (H2N2) (rat thoracic duct), **57,** 486
Thy 1,1- and Thy 1,2-positive, mitogenic responsiveness to rabbit anti-mouse brain serum (mouse spleen), **62,** 60
$T\mu$, conversion to $T\gamma$ after *in vitro* sensitization with herpes simplex virus-infected cells (human), **64,** 220
suppression by natural cytotoxic autoantibodies against thymocytes in spontaneously hypertensive rat, **60,** 181
suppressor, *see* Suppressor T cells
suppressor factor production in mixed lymphocyte culture, effects on divalent cations and cytochalasin B (mouse), **61,** 353
theophylline-resistant in peripheral blood, induction of $Fc\gamma$ receptors by adenosine and impromidine (human), **57,** 455
thiol-reactive sites, role in proliferation control (mouse), **60,** 453
ubiquitin-induced differentiation from splenic null cells, steroid sensitivity (mouse), **63,** 106
uptake of calcium and thymidine, effect of ionophore A23187 and concanavalin A (human, mouse, porcine, rabbit), **58,** 134

Temperature effects
on chromium-51 release from blast and splenocyte targets in presence or absence of cytotoxic T cells (mouse), **65,** 201
shift from 4 to 37°, shedding of receptors for IgM in splenocytes (rat), **60,** 168
on surface IgM movements in B cells during maturation (mouse), **65,** 166, 175
Terminal deoxynucleotidyl transferase
age-associated decline in thymus and bone marrow (human, mouse), **58,** 39
Testes
cell cross-reactivity with tumor F-9 cells, suppressor stimulation in mixed lymphocyte culture from F-9 tumor-bearing mice, **62,** 341
Tetanus toxoid
repetitive immunization with, inhibition of antigen-specific lymphoblastoid B-cell induction (human), **59,** 82
as specific antigen in antibody-producing system *in vitro* (human), **57,** 201
12-*O*-Tetradecanoylphorbol-13-acetate
elevation of natural killer sensitivity of lymphoid cell lines (human), **63,** 237
natural killer activity stimulation, pathway different from interferon-induced activation (mouse), **65,** 247
potentiation of interferon γ production induced in peripheral blood lymphocytes by OKT3 antibodies (human), **64,** 304
Theophylline
enhancement of herpes simplex virus-induced cytotoxic and suppressor cell activities (human), **65,** 13
resistance in cytotoxic T cells induced by herpes simplex virus-infected cells (human), **64,** 220
resistance in T cells, connection with ability to Fc γ receptor activation by adenosine and impromidine (human), **57,** 455
Thioglycollate broth
stimulation of peritoneal macrophages in antibody-dependent cell-mediated cytotoxicity (mouse), **57,** 51
Thiol groups
T-cell surface-associated, role in proliferation control (mouse), **60,** 453
Thymectomy
in adult mice, serum thymic factor restoration effect on ability to be suppressed by TNP-conjugated splenocytes, **64,** 144
effect on effector and suppressor T cells for delayed footpad reaction to sheep erythrocytes (mouse), **61,** 190
effect on reticulum cell sarcoma growth in SJL mice, **65,** 84
prostaglandin E_2 analog treatment *in vivo*, theta antigen induction in splenocytes (mouse), **62,** 8
protection from virus-induced T-cell lymphoma development (mouse), **58,** 165
at weaning, dissociated effects on T-cell-mediated responses *in vitro*, correction by serum thymic factor (mouse), **64,** 93
Thymocytes
differentiation during leukemogenesis, cell surface and murine leukemia virus antigens (AKR mouse), **59,** 355
fetal, helper function in pokeweed mitogen-driven coculture with peripheral blood lymphocytes, requirement of more mature T-cell effector (human), **59,** 17
glucocorticoid resistance and glucocorticoid receptors, thymosin Fraction 5 effects (mouse), **60,** 376
helper, concanavalin A-induced migration inhibitory factor production (mouse), **59,** 448
immunocompetent, inability to produce T-cell growth factor in adenosine deaminase deficiency conditions (rat), **63,** 81
injected into syngeneic recipients, migration pattern differences of peanut agglutinin-negative and -positive cells (mouse), **60,** 228
isokinetic density centrifugation, killer cell activity in more rapidly sedimenting fraction (mouse), **57,** 517
killer cells, Thy 1 and Lyt surface antigen expression (mouse), **65,** 272
lymphocyte-stimulating factor production induced by pokeweed mitogen-derived mitogen Pa-2 (mouse), **63,** 118
maturation *in vitro*, induction by tumor necrosis factor-positive serum (mouse), **57,** 237
prostaglandin E_2, production and effect on proliferation (mouse), **60,** 335
subpopulations
interleukin 1-induced stimulation of interleukin 2 production and of mitogenic response in mature medullary cells (human), **64,** 337
mitogenic responsiveness susceptibility to adenosine deaminase inhibitors during maturation (mouse), **64,** 29
radioresistant fast sedimenting, suppression *in vitro* of natural killer activity of splenocytes (mouse), **58,** 9
suppressor cells, concanavalin A-induced migration stimulatory factor production (mouse), **59,** 448
surface antigen expression, effects of type I and type II interferons (mouse), **57,** 427
T-cell differentiation antigens, concanavalin A effects on expression in presence of interleukin 2 (mouse), **65,** 180
vaccinia virus-induced immune response, effects

of cyclophosphamide and cortisone (mouse), **65,** 33
Thymosin
Fraction 5, effect on glucocorticoid resistance and glucocorticoid receptors in thymocytes (mouse), **60,** 376
Thymus
age-associated decline of terminal deoxynucleotidyl transferase activity (human, mouse), **58,** 39
role in H-2 restriction of T-cell helper function (mouse nude and radiation chimeras), **63,** 228
role in regulation of rat erythrocyte-induced autoantibodies in moouse, **63,** 221
Thyroglobulin
T-cell proliferation induction in experimental autoimmune thyroiditis (mouse), **61,** 32
Thyroid gland
epithelial cells, DNA synthesis stimulation in syngeneic lymphocytes (mouse), **62,** 313
Thyroiditis
experimental autoimmune
genetic control of susceptibility to, correlation with T-cell mitogenic responsiveness (rat), **62,** 156
T-cell proliferative response to mouse thyroglobulin (mouse), **61,** 32
TNP (2,4,6-trinitrophenyl)
-conjugated splenocytes, immunosuppression in adult mice, effects of thymectomy and serum thymic factor, **64,** 144
-conjugated tumor cells, suppression of antitumor response and enhancement of anti-TNP-self response mediated by T cells (mouse), **59,** 181
plaque-forming cell response to, streptococcal pyrogenic exotoxin-induced deregulation in T-cell subpopulation (mouse), **57,** 20
recognition by anti-TNP cytotoxic T cells, H-2 haplotype specificity of molecular requirement for (mouse), **58,** 147
TNP–bovine γ-globulin
splenic plaque-forming cell response to, regulation *in vivo* by histamine (mouse), **65,** 152
TNP–Ficoll
induction of plaque-forming cell response in B cells, ontogeny (mouse), **60,** 234
TNP–keyhole limpet hemocyanin (TNP–KLH)
secondary IgM and IgG responses to (CBA, CBA/N, and F_1 hybrid mice), **61,** 448
TNP–lipopolysaccharide
effect on antibody formation and plaque-forming cell production by peripheral blood lymphocytes from marmosets (*Saguinus fuscicollis, S. oedipus oedipus*), **57,** 408
TNP-specific B memory cell induction and differentiation (mouse), **57,** 327
Tolerance
antibody-mediated, prevention by cyclophosphamide, lack of sensitivity to splenectomy, transfer to normal mouse, **58,** 302
B-cell, induction by injection of hapten conjugates of isologous gamma globulins (mouse), **58,** 385
against human IgG of T-cell precursors in bone marrow, transient stage in DDD and C57BL/6 mice, **57,** 377
induction *in vitro*
by lymphocyte-bound antigen from bacteriophage T2 (rabbit), **58,** 436, 448
in mature virgin B cells by DNP–polysaccharide conjugate, role of IgM receptor (mouse), **62,** 196
to low doses of bovine γ globulin, adjuvant effects on induction in nonresponder strains (mouse), **64,** 350
neonatal
induction to histoincompatible cells, early events (mouse), **57,** 183
low-zone to bovine serum albumin, maintenance by suppressor T cells (mouse), **62,** 436
to lysozyme, effect of immunization with lysozyme–lipopolysaccharide complex (mouse), **58,** 293
to xenogeneic cells in mice inoculated with rat bone marrow cells, heterogeneity at cellular level and to skin graft, **63,** 193
Transfer factor
antigen-specific activity in dialyzable leukocyte extract (human), **62,** 301
Transferrin
effect on primary antibody response by splenocytes (mouse), **63,** 308
Transplantation
allogeneic bone marrow, role of bone marrow-derived factors in survival (mouse), **57,** 219
allogeneic splenocyte into lethally irradiated mouse, responses to H-2-subregion-coded antigens in graft-versus-host and host-versus-graft reactions, **57,** 389
immunological aspects, Symposium in honor of Sir Peter Medawar at Royal Society (London, July 18, 1980, England), **62,** 233–310
lymph node cells and bone marrow cells, immunogenetic differences in responses to (irradiated NZB and hybrid mice), **59,** 378
kidney, survival in certain strain combinations (mouse), **62,** 287
sarcoma, survival in certain strain combinations (mouse), **62,** 287
skin allograft
specific unresponsiveness to, effects of antilymphocyte serum and procarbazine hydrochloride (mouse), **62,** 254

survival, immunosuppression by essential fatty acids (rat), **62,** 293
skin graft rejection
effect of hyperimmunization (mouse), **57,** 99
vascular endothelium ultrastructural changes (mouse), **59,** 219
xenogeneic skin graft, neonatal tolerance in mice inoculated with rat bone marrow cells, **63,** 193
Trasylol
selective suppression of B-cell differentiation in splenocyte culture (mouse), **60,** 155
Triacinolone
skin depletion of Ia-bearing Langerhans cells (mouse), **60,** 50
Trophoblasts
autoantigenic status during pregnancy (rat), **62,** 271
effects on mixed-lymphocyte reaction and cell-mediated lympholysis (mouse), **58,** 202
transplantation antigen expression, detection by specific alloimmunity induction (mouse), **64,** 162
Trypanosoma rhodesiense
-infected athymic mice, immunosuppression and suppressor cell induction, **63,** 210
Tumor cells, *see also* Cell lines
allogeneic, selective induction of direct and lectin-dependent cell-mediated cytotoxicity (mouse), **61,** 253
antibody-sensitized, Fc-receptor-mediated binding and killing by rabbit macrophages and monocytes, **64,** 359
benzo[*a*]pyrene-transformed fibroblasts, colony inhibition by peritoneal leukocytes, lymphotoxin role (guinea pig), **63,** 1
conjugates with natural killer cells, peripheral blood lymphocyte subpopulation isolation from (human), **58,** 415
Ehrlich ascites
immune response to, genetic constrains in induction (mouse), **62,** 93
permeabilization by human serum complement, **61,** 213
Gross virus-induced lymphoma, inoculation effects on splenic suppressor macrophage occurrence (rat), **59,** 367
lysis by
cytotoxic murine T cells, inhibition by rat antiactivated T-cell antiserum, **59,** 289
freshly isolated peripheral blood monocytes, ^{51}Cr release assay (human), **58,** 426
macromolecular synthesis, effects of metabolic inhibitors and drugs (P815 murine mastocytoma), **58,** 398
mastocytoma P815, *see* Mastocytoma P815
melanoma, *see* Melanoma
membranes, topography of tumor-associated fetal antigens and histocompatibility antigens (rat), **60,** 261
myeloma, *see* Myeloma
nullipotential F-9 injected in mouse, T-cell suppressor cell induction in mixed lymphocyte culture **62,** 334, 341
proliferation *in vitro*, inhibition by suppressor factor from tumor-allosensitized splenocytes (mouse), **57,** 62
-stimulated splenocytes, suppression by tumor-associated fetal antigens (rat), **57,** 155
TNP-conjugated, intravenous inoculation-induced suppression of antitumor response and enhancement of anti-TNP-self response mediated by T cells (mouse), **59,** 181
Tumoricidity
of alveolar macrophages, activation *in vitro* by muramyl dipeptide encapsulated in liposomes (rat), **57,** 42
natural killer splenocytes from transplanted chemically induced sarcoma, activity *in vitro* (rat), **61,** 1
peritoneal macrophages, effect of time interval effector and target cells are exposed to lymphokines (mouse), **65,** 52
Tumor necrosis factor
-positive serum, induction of thymocyte maturation *in vitro* (mouse), **57,** 237
Tumor promoters
natural killer activity stimulation, pathway different from interferon-induced activation (mouse), **65,** 247
Tumors
allogeneic EL-4, cellular immune response to, effect of hyperimmunization (mouse), **57,** 114
allografted, suppressor cell involvement in active enhancement of (mouse), **58,** 107
mastocytoma P815, *see* Mastocytoma P815
melanoma, *see* Melanoma
methylcholanthrene-induced fibrosarcoma
MCA-1425, MCA-1460, induction of adherent suppressor cells in spleen (mouse), **60,** 109
syngeneic (H-1, H-7, H-8), suppression by nonadherent splenocytes from immunized mouse, **60,** 34
mycobacterial granulomas in lymph nodes, soluble factor release in culture that mudulates fibroblast function *in vitro* (guinea pig), **65,** 93
myeloma, *see* Myeloma
sarcoma-180-bearing mouse, T-cell-independent activation of macrophages by viable *Bacillus Calmette–Guerin*, **57,** 293
syngeneic Friend virus-induced leukemia (FBL-3), primary cell-mediated cytotoxic re-

sponse induction *in vivo* and *in vitro* (mouse), **59,** 127
teratocarcinoma, antigen comparison with cleavage embryo (mouse), **62,** 247
transplantable reticulum cell sarcoma, growth in thymectomized and congenitally athymic SJL mice, **65,** 84
transplanted chemically induced sarcoma
graft survival in certain strain combinations (mouse), **62,** 287
infiltrating host splenocytes with natural killer activity (rat), **61,** 1
virus-induced lymphoma, development prevention by thymectomy in young age (mouse), **58,** 165
Tumor-specific immunity
induced by somatic hybrids, persistence after adoptive transfer in normal mouse, **65,** 373
induction *in vitro*, augmentation by helper factor supernatants (mouse), **58,** 225

U

Ubiquitin
null cell differentiation induction into B and T cells (mouse spleen), **63,** 106
Ultraviolet (uv)
effect on Ia-bearing Langerhans cells in epidermis (mouse), **60,** 50
whole body irradiation, defective adherent splenocyte function (mouse), **63,** 300
Uterus
as graft site, immunology of maternal–fetal relationship (rat), **62,** 271

V

Vaccination
with irradiated circariae of *Schistosoma mansoni*, effect on immunity development in mouse strains, **65,** 75
Vaccinia virus
immune response induction in thymocytes, effects of cyclophosphamide and cortisone (mouse), **65,** 33
T cell response to, H-2 restriction (mouse), **61,** 220
Velocity sedimentation
thymocytes, radioresistant fast sedimenting fraction that suppressed natural killer activity of splenocytes (mouse), **58,** 9
Very-low-density lipoprotein
effect on cyclic AMP level in peripheral blood lymphocytes (human), **65,** 325

X

X rays
B memory cell depletion by exposure of antigen-primed mouse to lethal dose of, lack of effect on persistent antibody formation, **58,** 188

Z

Zinc
EDTA-induced deficiency *in vitro*, DNA synthesis inhibition only in T cells but not in B cells (mouse), **60,** 203